THE CODE OF CANON LAW

A TEXT AND COMMENTARY

COMMISSIONED BY
THE CANON LAW SOCIETY OF AMERICA

Edited by
JAMES A. CORIDEN
THOMAS J. GREEN
DONALD E. HEINTSCHEL

PAULIST PRESS
New York / Mahwah

Acknowledgments

Parts of Ladislas Orsy's commentary on canons 7 and 23 and his notes on the literary forms of the Code originally appeared in *Studia Canonica* 11 (1983) and are reprinted by permission. Material from James Provost's article "Structuring the Community" that appeared in *Chicago Studies* is reprinted by permission. Selections from *Sources of Renewal: The Implementation of Vatican II* by Cardinal Karol Wojtyla (Pope John Paul II), translated by P.S. Falla, © 1979 by Libreria Editrice Vaticana, Vatican City, © 1980 in English translation by William Collins Sons & Co. Ltd. and Harper & Row, Pubishers, Inc., are reprinted by permission of Harper & Row. Excerpts from the English translation of *Documents on the Liturgy, 1963–1979; Conciliar, Papal, and Curial Texts* ©

1982 by the International Commission on English in the Liturgy, Inc. are reprinted by permission of ICEL. All rights reserved. *Code of Canon Law, Latin-English Edition,* copyright 1983 by the Canon Law Society of America, is reprinted by permission of the CLSA. Excerpts from *Vatican II: The Conciliar and Post-Conciliar Documents,* edited by Austin Flannery, O.P., copyright 1975, is used by permission of Costello Publishing Co., Inc. Northport, N.Y. 11768. Excerpts from *The Documents of Vatican II,* edited by Walter M. Abbott, S.J. and Joseph Gallagher, are reprinted with permission of America Press, Inc., 106 West 56 Street, New York, N.Y. 10019. Copyright 1966. All rights reserved. All Scripture quotations are taken from the *New American Bible.*

NIHIL OBSTAT:
Rev. Msgr. Donald B. Zimmermann, J.C.D.
Censor Librorum

IMPRIMATUR:
Most Rev. Peter L. Gerety, D.D.
Archbishop of Newark

January 18, 1985

The *nihil obstat* and *imprimatur* are official declarations that a book or pamphlet is free of doctrinal or moral error. No implication is contained therein that those who have granted the *nihil obstat* and *imprimatur* agree with the contents, opinions or statements expressed.

Jacket/cover design: Tim McKeen

Library of Congress
Catalog Card Number: 84-62582

ISBN: 0-8091-0345-1

Published by Paulist Press
997 Macarthur Boulevard
Mahwah, N.J. 07430

Printed and bound in the United States of America

CONTENTS

BOOK II
THE PEOPLE OF GOD (cc. 204-746)

James H. Provost

PART I
THE CHRISTIAN FAITHFUL (cc. 204-329)

Paul L. Golden, C.M.

John E. Lynch, C.S.P.

Thomas J. Green

Ellsworth Kneal

James H. Provost

PART II
THE HIERARCHICAL CONSTITUTION OF THE CHURCH (cc. 330-572)

Thomas J. Green

James H. Provost

John A. Alesandro

Thomas Richstatter, O.F.M.

PART III
SACRED PLACES AND TIMES (cc. 1205-1253)

BOOK V
THE TEMPORAL GOODS OF THE CHURCH (cc. 1254-1310)

John J. Myers

BOOK VI
SANCTIONS IN THE CHURCH (cc. 1311-1399)

Thomas J. Green

PART I
OFFENSES AND PENALTIES IN GENERAL (cc. 1311-1363)

PART II
THE CONTENTIOUS TRIAL (cc. 1501-1670)

SECTION I
THE ORDINARY CONTENTIOUS TRIAL (cc. 1501-1655)

Thomas J. Green

PART IV
PENAL PROCEDURE (cc. 1717-1731) 1023

THE CODE OF CANON LAW: A TEXT AND COMMENTARY

Thomas J. Green

James F. Parizek

January 25, 1983, was a singular day in the history of Latin Catholicism. Another milestone in the implementation of the Second Vatican Council was set in place. On that same date—the Feast of the Conversion of Saint Paul—in 1959, Pope John XXIII had revealed the pastoral plan of *aggiornamento* for his pontificate. His vision included not only an ecumenical council but also a revised Code of Canon Law to govern the post-conciliar Church. Twenty-four years were to pass before Pope John Paul II was able to promulgate the revision. Since November 27, 1983, the date on which the revised Code went into effect, this body of law has been the most significant part of "canon law" of the Latin Catholic Church.

The present work is a commentary on that revised Code of Canon Law. It was written and edited by members of the Canon Law Society of America. Like the revised Code itself, it was a long time coming to birth, but the lapse of time and the research undertaken did much to shape and enrich it, for in the intervening years canon law itself and its role in the life of the Church were the subject of much writing and debate.

The revision process was formally inaugurated on November 20, 1965. On that occasion, Pope Paul VI, in an address to the Pontifical Commission for the Revision of the Code, proposed two goals which set the course for the task ahead. First, the Holy Father noted that the revision was to be a "reformation" of canon law, not merely a reworking of the 1917 codification. Second, the decrees and acts of the Second Vatican Council were to supply the parameters of the legislative renewal, since their doctrinal richness had done so much to shape the pastoral life of the Church. Pope Paul VI summed up his mandate to the Commission as follows:

> Now, however, with changing conditions . . . for life seems to evolve more rapidly . . . Canon Law must be prudently reformed; specifically, it must be accommodated to a new way of thinking proper to the second ecumenical council of the Vatican, in which pastoral care and the new needs of the People of God are met. . . .

Paralleling the activity of the Pontifical Commission, the Canon Law Society of America established a Task Force chaired by Father Thomas J. Green of the Catholic University of America. Subcommittees were established under the umbrella of the Task Force whose responsibility it was to prepare critiques of the drafts, or schemata, as they were published. A summary of these reflections and findings was submitted to the National Conference of Catholic Bishops (NCCB) of the United States, so that they might be incorporated in the official Conference report to the Pontifical Commission.

The research by the members of the Canon Law Society of America's Task Force over the years was a basic resource for the authors of this commentary. In many instances some of the same persons worked on both projects in the areas of their competence.

The idea for a commentary was first broached and defined at the forty-first (1979) annual meeting of the Canon Law Society. An editorial board was chosen and individual commentators were selected and assigned their tasks.

It is important to know the mandate underlying a work of this kind; the specific intent identified there defines the focus of this commentary. To quote the Task Force report:

> The audience for such a commentary should be the literate Catholic leadership personnel of our country. This includes but is not restricted to our canonical peers, i.e., chancery officials, tribunal personnel, teachers in seminaries; it also encompasses bishops, parish clergy, other parish leadership personnel (e.g., DRE's) and seminarians. The commentary should also be easily intelligible to professionals in other disciplines, e.g., theology. . . . Such a commentary is not geared for a specialized canonical audience interested in probing in depth the various significant theological-legal-historical questions raised by the new law. . . .

> The major thrust of such a commentary is to provide a working manual for persons in various pastoral responsibilities. It is to be based upon the best canonical scholarship but is to be written in such a way as to be easily intelligible to the literate Catholic professional.

> It should offer a clear introduction to the *schema* being addressed, an explanation of the significant changes in the law from the Code, a clarification of the theological-legal-pastoral reasons for such a change and some bibliographical references to assist the reader interested in pursuing certain issues further. Such a commentary should clearly indicate the various legal-pastoral options provided by the new law since what is left unsaid in the law may be as significant if not more significant than those matters that are dealt with in clearly defined prescriptions. The focus of the work is to be preeminently expository, contrary

to the critical-evaluative style characterizing the various Task Force enterprises.

This it was that this commission was initiated. From the start the intent was to draft a commentary that was pastoral in character, one which would assist others in becoming knowledgeable interpreters of the law. The authors have tried to situate canon law in its theological-pastoral context, realizing that it is a discipline founded in theology which avoids juridical positivism and historicism.

A word about the commentary itself. It is the first complete commentary in English. It is not selective, that is, it treats every canon in the revised Code.

From the beginning, the editors assured the contributors that they were independent as long as their commentary reflected the mandate of the Canon Law Society. They were urged to follow the strictest scientific criteria in preparing their studies, while at the same time writing in a style and language accessible to the audience envisaged for the commentary. It was to be the editors' responsibility to achieve a certain overall unity. At times this has necessitated adding or subtracting from the copy or making adjustments in style or content. Throughout the writing and rewriting the contributors were most cooperative. Although this commentary is the product of a joint effort by many people, the authors are nevertheless finally responsible for their own work.

The structure of the commentary is that of the Code. This is important, since it says much about the revision itself and is illustrative of the frame of reference in which the law was cast. The structure is a context for understanding and interpreting the law. An introduction is inserted at the beginning of each new section, which serves as a bridge situating a particular commentary in the overall plan. While the importance of this may not be immediately apparent, it is a central element in the unity and integrity of the revised Code and is therefore an important criterion in understanding the law.

Each section by a particular author is followed by a bibliography. While these notes are not exhaustive, they do identify the most important and useful publications. Sources in English are emphasized, although on occasion an author may cite a foreign language source.

Any book is as valuable and as useful as the apparatus provided to assist the reader. Since the revised Code has many antecedents in the Code of 1917, tables of corresponding canons have been supplied. This should enable the student to trace the historical roots of the current text, besides serving as a means for discovering prior interpretation of a canon. In their own way, these tables serve the same purpose and are as important as the footnotes of the previous Code.

The editors have made a serious effort to stan-dardize abbreviations. In a work of this size, with the amount of bibliographical material contained, uniformity and consistency were imperative. The list of abbreviations will assist the reader in decoding any particular citation.

A word about the index. The page format of the commentary is such that it was difficult to decide upon a method that would satisfy all readers. After reviewing a variety of systems, the editors chose to organize the index according to canon numbers, except in those instances where thematic material is dealt with in some detail.

A word about the canons themselves. The Latin text is the only official version of the Code. It will remain the final arbiter of the meaning of the law until such time as the Pontifical Commission to Interpret the Code should rule otherwise. From the beginning, however, the editors were convinced that the commentary should contain a translation of the Code that was intelligible and accurately reflected the substance of the law. With the promulgation of the revised Code, it became possible, using norms issued by the Vatican Secretariat of State, to prepare an authorized vernacular translation. Episcopal conferences were designated as the agencies to grant approval. The translation used in this commentary is that approved in October 1983 by the Executive Committee of the National Conference of Catholic Bishops of the United States. Many members of the Canon Law Society, as well as the Committee on Canonical Affairs of the NCCB, worked over four years to prepare this translation. It reflects the style and language of United States jurists.

This was achieved by following certain principles and policies adopted by the Canon Law Society of America:

1. The Latin text is and will remain the only official version of the Code. This was affirmed by the Vatican Secretariat of State in January 1983. The English translation does not replace or replicate the Latin. Indeed, the Latin must be consulted for clarification of meaning and complete accuracy.

2. The English ought to be as accurate and faithful to the Latin original as reasonably possible. Although to translate is in some sense to interpret, the meaning of the Latin has been conveyed carefully, making every effort to avoid distortions.

3. Terms have been used with consistency throughout the Code unless there are good canonical reasons to vary the translation in different context. For example, *munus* is used for several meanings in Latin and consequently must be rendered by "function," "office," "duty," or "responsibility" depending on the context. *Proc-*

urator means "proxy" in the law on marriage but is rendered "procurator" in procedural law.

4. The canons should be intelligible to educated readers. The English, therefore, must be readable. An imitation of the style and structure of Latin impedes intelligibility in English. All terms, even technical ones, are either translated or left in Latin because of their familiar usage in church practice; others are selected as understandable from their secular usage.

5. The language in the translation is sexually inclusive wherever that is consonant with the law being expressed. Exclusive masculine or feminine word forms are not used unless absolutely required by the text. In some instances it has been necessary to render in the plural what appears in Latin in the singular or to change to the passive voice, but this has been done only where it does not affect the meaning of the canon.

6. Subjunctive verb forms are normally rendered by straightforward imperative or obligatory language rather than by shade of exhortation or recommendation (e.g., "is to appoint" rather than "should appoint"), unless another meaning is clear from the context.

7. Rather than following the Latin style for capitalization of nouns, capitalization has been minimized in keeping with current American usage and retained only in reference to God, Christ, Eucharist, Roman Pontiff, the Church universal, Catholic Church, etc.

This Preface would not be complete without a word of appreciaton to the many persons who have worked with the editors over the past four or five years to complete the work of publishing this commentary on the revised Code of Canon Law.

To our numerous authors, whose names will become known to readers as they peruse this book, the editors are deeply grateful. At times their work was difficult and trying. Acceptance and use of their reflections by those seeking to understand and appreciate the law and use it to solve pastoral problems will be among their rewards. The closing words of the text of the Code of Canon Law best sum up the role of law in the Church: ". . . having before one's eyes the salvation of souls, which is always the supreme law of the Church."

Father James Provost, the Executive Coordinator of the Canon Law Society of America, and the members of his staff have given many hours to the translation, index, and other facets of this commentary. The editors are most appreciative.

To Father Kevin Lynch, C.S.P., publisher of Paulist Press; to Mr. Donald Brophy, managing editor; and to Miss Maria Maggi, production editor, who was so often tried as she shepherded this text from manuscript to publication, go the editors' heartfelt thanks. We are grateful, too, to Mrs. Mary Brintle, who prepared the index, an indispensable tool for the use of any book.

It is our hope that this commentary will become an instrument to enrich the faith, that it will give shape to the order of the post-conciliar Church, and that it will always serve as a reminder of the dream of *aggiornamento* of Pope John XXIII.

We have said that the promulgation of the revised Code of Canon Law by Pope John Paul II on January 25, 1983, marked a milestone in the history of canon law for the Latin Church. This commentary is a milestone as well for the Canon Law Society of America. Over the years the society has done much to help bring about an *aggiornamento* in the science and study of canon law. May this commentary be fitting evidence that the members of the Canon Law Society of America are *fautores legis,* dedicated to the Church and to its ministry of truth, justice, and equity for the whole People of God.

ABBREVIATIONS

These abbreviations are found in the text of the commentary, the footnotes and the bibliographies. Where there is an English translation available of a source in another language, the translation is indicated at the end of the reference.

AA	Vatican II, decree *Apostolicam actuositatem, AAS* 58 (1966), 837–864; Abbott, 489–521
AAS	*Acta Apostolicae Sedis,* Rome 1909–
AC	*L'Année Canonique,* Paris 1952–
AcDocVat	*Acta et Documenta Concilio Oecumenico Vaticano II apparando,* Series I, (Anteprae-paratoria), vols. I–IV, Indices. Vatican City, 1960–1961; Series II (Praeparatoria), vols. I–III. Vatican City State, 1964–1969
AcSynVat	*Acta Synodalia Sacrosancti Concilii Oecumenici Vaticani II,* vols. I–IV, Indices. Vatican City, 1970–
AER	*American Ecclesiastical Review,* vols. I–XXXII, Philadelphia, 1889–1905; from 1905: *The Ecclesiastical Review,* Philadelphia, 1905–1943; from 1944 to 1974: The *American Ecclesiastical Review,* Washington, D.C.
AG	Vatican II, decree *Ad Gentes, AAS* 58 (1966), 947–990; Abbott, 584–630
AkK	*Archiv für katholisches Kirchenrecht* (Innsbruck, 1957–), Mainz, 1862–
apconst	apostolic constitution
APN	*American Procedural Norms,* July 1, 1970: L. Wrenn, *Annulments,* 3rd ed. (Toledo: CLSA, 1978), 115–119; *Jurist* 30 (1970), 363–368
Apol	*Apollinaris, Commentarium iuris canonici,* Rome, 1928–
ASS	*Acta Sanctae Sedis,* Rome, 1865–1908
B.A.C.	Biblioteca de Autores Cristianos
BCL	Bishops' Committee on the Liturgy
BCLN	*Bishops' Committee on the Liturgy Newsletter*
c.	canon
CanLawStud	Catholic University of America, *Canon Law Studies*
cc.	canons
CD	Vatican II, decree *Christus Dominus, AAS* 58 (1966), 673–696; Abbott, 396–429
CIC	1917 Code of Canon Law (*Codex Iuris Canonici*)
CICFontes	P. Gasparri and I. Seredi, eds. *Codicis Iuris Canonici Fontes,* vols. I–IX (Romae, 1923–1939)
CLD	*Canon Law Digest,* ed. by T. Bouscaren and J. O'Connor. Vols. 1–6, Milwaukee-New York: The Bruce Publishing Co., 1934–1969. Vols. 7–9 and supplements, Chicago: Canon Law Digest, 1975–
CLSA	Canon Law Society of America

CLSAP	*Canon Law Society of America Proceedings*
CLS-GBIN	*Canon Law Society of Great Britain and Ireland Newsletter*
CM	Paul VI, *motu proprio Causas matrimoniales,* March 28, 1971, *AAS* 63 (1971), 441–446; L. Wrenn, *Annulments,* 3rd ed. (Toledo: CLSA, 1978), 120–123
COD	*Conciliorum Oecumenicorum Decreta,* ed. by G. Alberigo et al., editio tertia (Bologna: Istituto per le Scienze Religiose, 1973)
CodCom	Pontifical Commission for the Authentic Interpretation of the Canons of the Code of Canon Law
ComCICRec	Pontifical Commission for the Revision of the Code of Canon Law (Pontificia Commissio Codicis Iuris Canonici Recognocendo)
Comm	*Communicationes,* Vatican City, 1979–
ComRelMiss	*Commentarium pro Religiosis et Missionariis,* Rome, 1920–
Con	*Concilium, International Journal of Theology,* 1965–
Con Lif	*Consecrated Life,* Chicago, Ill. (Institute on Religious Life), 1976–
CorpusIC	*Corpus Iuris Canonici,* ed. by E. Friedberg, parts I–II, Graz: 1955 and 1959
CR	*Clergy Review,* London, 1931–
CS	*Chicago Studies,* Mundelein, Ill., 1961
CT	John Paul II, apostolic exhortation *Catechesi Tradendae,* October 16, 1979, *AAS* 71 (1979), 1277–1340; *Catechesis in our Time,* Washington: USCC, 1979 (pub. no. 654)
CTSA	Catholic Theological Society of America
CTSAP	*Catholic Theological Society of America Proceedings*
DDC	*Dictionnaire de Droit Canonique,* tom. I–VII, Paris, 1935–1955
decl	declaration
decr	decree
DH	Vatican II, decree *Dignitatis Humanae, AAS* 58 (1966), 929–941; Abbott, 675–696
"Directives"	Sacred Congregation for the Clergy, Directive Norms for the Cooperation of the Local Churches among Themselves and Especially for a Better Distribution of Clergy in the World, March 25, 1980, *AAS* 72 (1980), 343f; English translation, Washington: USCC (pub. no. 710)
Directory	Sacred Congregation for Bishops, *Directorium de Pastorali Ministerio Episcoporum,* February 22, 1973; *Directory on the Pastoral Ministry of Bishops,* Washington: USCC, 1974 (pub. no. V591)
DOL	*Documents on the Liturgy 1963–1979, Conciliar, Papal and Curial Texts,* Collegeville, Minn.: Liturgical Press, 1982
DV	Vatican II, dogmatic constitution *Dei Verbum, AAS* 58 (1966), 817–830; Abbott, 111–128
ED	Secretariat for Promoting Christian Unity, *Ecumenical Directory,* part I, May 14, 1967, *AAS* 59 (1967), 564–592; *CLD* 6, 716–734
EI	*Enchiridion indulgentiarum,* June 29, 1968, *AAS* 60 (1968), 413–419; *CLD* 7, 675–681
EIC	*Ephemerides Iuris Canonici,* Rome, 1945–

EM	Paul VI, *motu proprio De Episcoporum Muneribus*, June 15, 1966, *AAS* 58 (1966): 467–472; *CLD* 6, 394–400
Emendations	*Emendations in the Liturgical Books Following upon the New Code of Canon Law*, Washington: ICEL, 1984
EN	Paul VI, apostolic exhortation *Evangelii Nuntiandi*, December 8, 1975, *AAS* 68 (1976), 5–76; *Evangelization in the Modern World*, Washington: USCC, 1975 (pub. no. VI–129)
Ench	H. Denzinger & A. Schönmetzer, *Enchiridion symbolorum, definitionum et declarationum de rebus fidei et morum*, 35th ed. New York, 1974
ency	encyclical
EP	Sacred Congregation for the Doctrine of the Faith, decree *De Ecclesiae pastorum vigilantia circa libros*, March 19, 1975, *AAS* 67 (1975), 281–284; *Censorship of Books*, Washington: USCC, 1975 (pub. no. V408)
ES	Paul VI, *motu proprio Ecclesiae sanctae*, August 6, 1966, *AAS* 58 (1966), 757–787; *Norms for Implementation of Four Council Decrees*, Washington: USCC, 1966 (pub. no. VI–54)
ET	Paul VI, apostolic exhortation *Evangelica Testificatio*, June 29, 1971, *AAS* 63 (1971), 497–526; *On the Renewal of Religious Life according to the Teachings of the Second Vatican Council*, Washington: USCC, 1971 (pub. no. VI–99)
EUNSA	Ediciones Universidad de Navarra, S.A.
"Explanatory Note"	*Nota explicativa praevia*, *AAS* 57 (1965): 72–75; Prefatory Note of Explanation regarding *Lumen Gentium*, III–Abbot, 98–101
GCD	Sacred Congregation for the Clergy, *Directorium Catechisticum Generale*, April 11, 1971, *AAS* 64 (1972), 97–176; *General Catechetical Directory*, Washington: USCC, 1971 (pub. no. V173)
GE	Vatican II, declaration *Gravissimum Educationis*, *AAS* 58 (1966), 728–739; Abbott, 637–651
GS	Vatican II, pastoral constitution *Gaudium et Spes*, *AAS* 58 (1966), 1025–1115; Abbott, 199–308
Guidelines	Bishops' Committee on the Permanent Diaconate, *Permanent Deacons in the United States: Guidelines on their Formation and Ministry*. Washington: USCC, 1971 (pub. no. V 174)
HPR	*Homiletic Monthly and Catechist*, New York, 1901–1917; *Homiletic and Pastoral Review*, New York, 1917–
HV	Paul VI, encyclical *Humanae Vitae*, July 29, 1968, *AAS* 60 (1968), 489–496; *On the Regulation of Birth*, Washington: USCC, 1968 (pub. no. VI–80)
IC	*Ius Canonicum*, Pamplona, 1961–
ICEL	International Commission on English in the Liturgy
ID	Paul VI, apostolic constitution *Indulgentiarum doctrina*, January 1, 1967, *AAS* 59 (1967), 5–24; *On Indulgences*, Washington: USCC, 1967 (pub. no. VI–56)
IGIC	Sacred Congregation for Divine Worship, *Introduction to the Rite of Christian Initiation*. Washington: USCC, 1977 (pub. no. 7–11)
IGMR	Sacred Congregation for Divine Worship, *Ordo missae editio typica altera* (Typis Polyglottis Vaticanis, 1975); *General Instruction of the Roman Missal;* trans. ICEL. Washington: USCC, 1975 (pub. no. 898)

IM	Vatican II, decree *Inter Mirifica, AAS* 56 (1964), 145–153; Abbott, 319–331
instr	instruction
IO	Sacred Congregation of Rites, instruction *Inter Oecumenici,* September 26, 1964, *AAS* 56 (1964), 877–900; *CLD* 6, 73–99
IP	*Ius Pontificium,* Rome, 1920–1921, 1941–
J	*The Jurist,* Washington, 1940–
LC	Paul VI, apostolic constitution *Laudis Canticum,* November 1, 1970, *AAS* 63 (1971), 527–535; *The Pope Speaks* 16 (1971), 129–131
LEF	Pontificia Commissio Codici Iuris Canonici Recognoscendo, *Lex Ecclesiae Fundamentalis,* April 24, 1980. Libreria Editrice Vaticana, 1980
LG	Vatican II, dogmatic constitution *Lumen Gentium, AAS* 57 (1965), 5–75; Abbott, 14–101
littcirc	circular letter
ME	*Il Monitore Ecclesiastico,* Rome, 1876–1948; *Monitor Ecclesiasticus,* Rome, 1948–
mp	*motu proprio*
MQ	Paul VI *motu proprio Ministeria Quaedam,* August 15, 1972, *AAS* 64 (1972), 529–534; *Laying Down Certain Norms regarding the Sacred Order of the Diaconate and by which the Discipline of the First Tonsure, Minor Orders and Subdiaconate in the Latin Church Is Reformed,* Washington: USCC, 1972 (pub. no. VI–115)
MR	Sacred Congregation for Bishops and Sacred Congregation for Religious and Secular Institutes, decree *Mutuae Relationes,* May 14, 1978, *AAS* 70 (1978), 473–506; *Directives for the Mutual Relations between Bishops and Religious in the Church,* Washington: USCC, 1978 (pub. no. V 591)
N	*Notitiae,* Vatican City, 1965–
NCCB	National Conference of Catholic Bishops
NCDD	National Conference of Diocesan Directors of Religious Education
NCE	*New Catholic Encyclopedia,* New York, 1967–
NCWC	National Catholic Welfare Conference
NFPC	National Federation of Priests' Councils
Norms	Bishops' Committee on Priestly Formation, *Norms for Priestly Formation: A Compendium of Official Documents on Training of Candidates for the Priesthood,* Washington: USCC, 1982 (pub. no. 838)
Nu	*Nuntia,* Vatican City, 1975–
OAKR	*Oesterreichesches Archiv für Kirchenrecht,* Vienna, 1950–
OE	Vatican II, decree *Orientalium Ecclesiarum, AAS* 57 (1965), 76–89; Abbott, 373–386
OEx	Sacred Congregation for Divine Worship, *Ordo Exsequiarum,* August 15, 1969, Typis Polyglottis Vaticanis, 1969; *Rite of Funerals,* BCL-USCC, New York: Catholic Book, 1971
OssRomEng	*L'Osservatore Romano,* English edition
OT	Vatican II, decree *Optatam Totius, AAS* 58 (1966), 713–727; Abbott, 437–457
P	*Periodica de re morali canonica liturgica,* Rome, 1905–

Pastoral Care	*Pastoral Care of the Sick: Rites of Anointing and Viaticum,* Collegeville, Minn.: Liturgical Press, 1983
PC	Vatican II, decree *Perfectae Caritatis, AAS* 58 (1966), 702–712; Abbott, 466–482
PF	Pius XII, *motu proprio Primo feliciter,* March 12, 1948, *AAS* 40 (1948), 283–286
PL	J. P. Migne, *Patrologiae cursus completus,* Series Latina. 221 vols. Paris, 1844–1855
PM	Paul VI, *motu proprio Pastorale Munus,* November 30, 1963, *AAS* 56 (1964), 5–12; *CLD* 6, 370–378
PO	Vatican II, decree *Presbyterorum Ordinis, AAS* 58 (1966), 991–1024; Abbott, 532–576
PPF	*Program for Priestly Formation,* third edition, NCCB, November 30, 1981
RAnointing	Sacred Congregation for Divine Worship, *Ordo unctionis infirmorum,* December 7, 1972, Typis Polyglottis Vaticanis, 1972; *Rite of Anointing, DOL,* 410, pp. 1054–1061
Ratio	Sacred Congregation for Catholic Education, *Ratio Fundamentalis Institutionis Sacerdotalis,* Jan. 6, 1970, *AAS* 62 (1970), 321–384; *Basic Plan for Priestly Formation,* Washington: USCC, 1970
RBaptC	Sacred Congregation for Divine Worship, *Ordo Baptismi Parvulorum,* May 15, 1969, Typis Polyglottis Vaticanis, 1969 (editio typica, altera, 1973); *Rite for Baptism of Children, DOL,* 295, pp. 725–731
RC	Sacred Congregation for Religious and Secular Institutes, instruction *Renovationis Causam,* January 6, 1969, *AAS* 61 (1969), 103–120; *On the Renewal of Religious Formation,* Washington: USCC, 1969 (pub. no. V 109)
RCIA	Sacred Congregation for Divine Worship, *Ordo initiationis christianae adultorum,* January 6, 1972, Typis Polyglottis Vaticanis, 1972; *Rite for Christian Initiation of Adults, DOL,* 301, pp. 736–761
RConf	Sacred Congregation for Divine Worship, *Ordo confirmationis,* August 22, 1971, Typis Polyglottis Vaticanis, 1971; *Rite of Confirmation, DOL,* 305, pp. 771–776
RDC	*Revue de Droit Canonique,* Strasbourg, 1951–
RE	Paul VI, apostolic constitution *Regimini Ecclesiae universae,* August 15, 1967, *AAS* 59 (1967), 885–928; *On the Roman Curia,* Washington: USCC, 1967 (pub. no. VI–70)
REDC	*Revista Espanola de Derecho Canonico,* Salamanca 1951–
Rel	Pontificia Commissio Codici Iuris Canonici Recognoscendo, *Relatio complectens synthesim animadversionum ab Em. mis. atque Exc. mis. Patribus Commissionis ad ultimum schema Codicis Iuris Canonici Exhibitarum, cum responsionibus a Secretaria et Consultoribus datis.* Typis Polyglottis Vaticanis, 1981
RfR	*Review for Religious,* Topeka, Kans. 1942–1967; St. Louis, Mo. 1968–
RI	*Regula Iuris*
ROils	Sacred Congregation for Divine Worship, *Ordo benedicendi oleum catechumenorum et infirmorum et conficiendi chrisma,* December 3, 1970, Typis Polyglottis Vaticanis, 1971; *DOL,* 459, pp. 1190–1191
RPen	Sacred Congregation for Divine Worship, *Ordo Paenitentiae,* December 2, 1973, Typis Polyglottis Vaticanis, 1974; *Rite of Penance,* Washington: USCC, 1975 (pub. no. V398)
RR	W. Schumacher, ed., *Roman Replies,* Washington: CLSA, 1981–

SacM	*Sacramentum Mundi, An Encyclopedia of Theology,* 6 vols. New York: Herder & Herder, 1968–1970
SapC	John Paul II, apostolic constitution *Sapientia Christiana,* April 15, 1979, *AAS* 71 (1979), 469–499; *On Ecclesiastical Universities and Faculties,* Washington: USCC, 1979 (pub. no. 623)
SC	Vatican II, constitution *Sacrosanctum Concilium, AAS* 66 (1964), 97–134; Abbott, 137–178
SCB	Sacred Congregation for Bishops
SCC	Sacred Congregation for the Clergy
SCCE	Sacred Congregation for Catholic Education
SCConc	Sacred Congregation of the Council
SCConsist	Sacred Consistorial Congregation
SCDF	Sacred Congregation for the Doctrine of the Faith
SCDW	Sacred Congregation for Divine Worship
SCOC	Sacred Congregation for the Oriental Churches
SCOf	Sacred Congregation of the Holy Office (former title of the Sacred Congregation for the Doctrine of the Faith)
SCProp	Sacred Congregation for the Evangelization of Nations/Sacred Congregation for the Propagation of the Faith
SCR	Sacred Congregation for Religious
SCRIS	Sacred Congregation for Religious and Secular Institutes
SCRit	Sacred Congregation of Rites
SCSacr	Sacred Congregation for the Discipline of the Sacraments
SCSDW	Sacred Congregation for Sacraments and Divine Worship
SCSU	Sacred Congregation of Seminaries and Universities (former title of the Sacred Congregation for Catholic Education)
SPCU	Secretariat for Promoting Christian Unity
SRRDec	*Sacrae Romanae Rotae Decisiones,* Rome, 1909–
Stud Can	*Studia Canonica,* Ottawa, 1969–
TS	*Theological Studies,* Baltimore, 1939–
UR	Vatican II, decree *Unitatis Redintegratio, AAS* 57 (1965), 90–107; Abbott, 341–366
USCC	United States Catholic Conference
Variationes	Sacred Congregation for Sacraments and Divine Worship, decree *Promulgato Codice Iuris Canonici,* September 12, 1983, *Notitiae* 20 (1983)
VC	*Vita Consacrata* (formerly *Vita Religiosa*), Rome, 1964–
VR	*Vita Religiosa,* Madrid, 1944–
Vorgrimler	H. Vorgrimler, ed., *Commentary on the Documents of Vatican II,* 5 vols., New York, 1966–1969
W	*Worship,* Collegeville, Minn. 1926–

TO OUR VENERABLE BROTHERS,
CARDINALS, ARCHBISHOPS,
BISHOPS, PRIESTS, DEACONS
AND TO THE OTHER MEMBERS OF THE
PEOPLE OF GOD,
JOHN PAUL, BISHOP,
SERVANT OF THE SERVANTS OF GOD
AS A PERPETUAL RECORD.

During the course of the centuries the Catholic Church has been accustomed to reform and renew the laws of canonical discipline so that in constant fidelity to its divine founder, they may be better adapted to the saving mission entrusted to it. Prompted by this same purpose and fulfilling at last the expectations of the whole Catholic world, I order today, January 25, 1983, the promulgation of the revised Code of Canon Law. In so doing, my thoughts go back to the same day of the year 1959 when my predecessor of happy memory, John XXIII, announced for the first time his decision to reform the existing *corpus* of canonical legislation which had been promulgated on the feast of Pentecost in the year 1917.

Such a decision to reform the Code was taken together with two other decisions of which the Pontiff spoke on that same day: the intention to hold a synod of the Diocese of Rome and to convoke an ecumenical council. Of these two events, the first was not closely connected with the reform of the Code; but the second, the council, is of supreme importance in regard to the present matter and is closely connected with it.

If we ask why John XXIII considered it necessary to reform the existing Code, the answer can perhaps be found in the Code itself which was promulgated in the year 1917. But there exists also another answer and it is the decisive one: namely, that the reform of the Code of Canon Law appeared to be definitely desired and requested by the same council which devoted such great attention to the Church.

As is obvious, when the revision of the Code was first announced the council was an event of the future. Moreover, the acts of its magisterium and especially its doctrine on the Church would be decided in the years 1962–1965; however, it is clear to everyone that John XXIII's intuition was very true, and with good reason it must be said that his decision was for the long-term good of the Church.

Therefore the new Code which is promulgated today necessarily required the previous work of the council. Although it was announced together with the ecumenical council, nevertheless it follows it chronologically because the work undertaken in its preparation, which had to be based upon the council, could not begin until after the latter's completion.

Turning our minds today to the beginning of this long journey, to that January 25, 1959 and to John XXIII himself who initiated the revision of the Code, I must recognize that this Code derives from one and the same intention, the renewal of Christian living. From such an intention, in fact, the entire work of the council drew its norms and its direction.

If we now pass on to consider the nature of the work which preceded the promulgation of the Code and also the manner in which it was carried out, especially during the pontificates of Paul VI and John Paul I, and from then until the present day, it must be clearly pointed out that this work was brought to completion in an outstandingly *collegial* spirit. This applies not only in regard to the material drafting of the work, but also to the very substance of the laws enacted.

This note of collegiality eminently characterizes and distinguishes the process of developing the present Code; it corresponds perfectly with the teaching and the character of the Second Vatican Council. Therefore not only because of its content but also because of its very origin, the Code manifests the spirit of this council in whose documents the Church, the universal "sacrament of salvation" (dogmatic constitution on the Church *Lumen gentium*, nn. 1, 9, 48), is presented as the people of God and its hierarchical constitution appears based on the college of bishops united with its head.

For this reason, therefore, the bishops individually and as episcopates were invited to collaborate in the preparation of the new Code so that by means of such a long process, by as collegial a method as possible, juridical formulae would gradually mature which would later serve for the use of the entire Church. *Experts* chosen from all over the world also took part in all these phases of the work, specialists in theology, history and especially canon law.

To one and all of them I wish to express today my sentiments of deep gratitude.

In the first place there come before my eyes the

figures of the deceased cardinals who presided over the preparatory commission: Cardinal Pietro Ciriaci who began the work, and Cardinal Pericle Felici who, for many years, guided the course of the work almost to its end. I think then of the secretaries of the same commission: Monsignor Giacomo Violardo, later cardinal, and Father Raimondo Bidagor, S.J., both of whom in carrying out this task poured out the treasures of their doctrine and wisdom. Together with them I recall the cardinals, archbishops, bishops and all those who were members of that commission, as well as the consultors of the individual study groups engaged during these years in such a difficult work, and whom God in the meantime has called to their eternal reward. I pray to God for all of them.

I am pleased to remember also the living, beginning with the present pro-president of the commission, our venerable brother Archbishop Rosalio Castillo Lara. For a very long time he has done excellent work in a task of such great responsibility. I pass then to our beloved son, Monsignor William Onclin, whose devotion and diligence have greatly contributed to the happy outcome of the work. I finally mention all the others in the commission itself, whether as cardinal members or as officials, consultors and collaborators in the various study groups, or in other offices who have given their appreciated contribution to the drafting and the completion of such a weighty and complex work.

Therefore, in promulgating the Code today, I am fully aware that this act is an expression of pontifical authority and therefore is invested with a *primatial character.* But I am also aware that this Code in its objective content reflects the *collegial solicitude* of all my brothers in the episcopate for the Church. Indeed, by a certain analogy with the council, it should be considered as the fruit of a *collegial collaboration* because of the united efforts on the part of specialized persons and institutions throughout the whole Church.

A second question arises concerning the very nature of the Code of Canon Law. To reply adequately to this question one must mentally recall the distant patrimony of law contained in the books of the Old and New Testament from which is derived the whole juridical-legislative tradition of the Church, as from its first source.

Christ the Lord, indeed, did not in the least wish to destroy the very rich heritage of the law and the prophets which was gradually formed from the history and experience of the people of God in the Old Testament, but he brought it to completion (cf. Mt. 5:17) such that in a new and higher way it became part of the heritage of the New Testament. There-

fore, although in expounding the paschal mystery St. Paul teaches that justification is not obtained by the works of the law but by means of faith (cf. Rom. 3:28; Gal. 2:16), he does not thereby exclude the binding force of the Decalogue (cf. Rom. 13:28; Gal. 5:13–25, 6:2), nor does he deny the importance of discipline in the Church of God (cf. I Cor. 5 and 6). Thus the writings of the New Testament enable us to understand even better the importance of discipline and make us see better how it is more closely connected with the saving character of the evangelical message itself.

This being so, it appears sufficiently clear that the Code is in no way intended as a substitute for faith, grace, charisms, and especially charity in the life of the Church and of the faithful. On the contrary, its purpose is rather to create such an order in the ecclesial society that, while assigning the primacy to love, grace and charisms, it at the same time renders their organic development easier in the life of both the ecclesial society and the individual persons who belong to it.

As the Church's principal legislative document founded on the juridical-legislative heritage of revelation and tradition, the Code is to be regarded as an indispensable instrument to ensure order both in individual and social life, and also in the Church's own activity. Therefore, besides containing the fundamental elements of the hierarchical and organic structure of the Church as willed by her divine founder or as based upon apostolic, or in any case most ancient, tradition, and besides the fundamental principles which govern the exercise of the threefold office entrusted to the Church itself, the Code must also lay down certain rules and norms of behavior.

The instrument which the Code is fully corresponds to the nature of the Church, especially as it is proposed by the teaching of the Second Vatican Council in general and in a particular way by its ecclesiological teaching. Indeed, in a certain sense this new Code could be understood as a great effort to translate this same conciliar doctrine and ecclesiology into *canonical* language. If, however, it is impossible to translate perfectly into *canonical* language the conciliar image of the Church, nevertheless the Code must always be referred to this image as the primary pattern whose outline the Code ought to express insofar as it can by its very nature.

From this, certain fundamental criteria are derived which should govern the entire new Code within the limits of its specific matter and of the language appropriate to that material.

It could indeed be said that from this there is derived that note of complementarity which the Code presents in relation to the teaching of the Second Vatican Council, in particular with reference to the two constitutions, the dogmatic constitution *Lumen gentium* and the pastoral constitution *Gaudium et spes.*

Hence it follows that what constitutes the substantial *newness* of the Second Vatican Council, in line with the legislative tradition of the Church, especially in regard to ecclesiology, constitutes likewise the *newness* of the new Code.

Among the elements which characterize the true and genuine image of the Church we should emphasize especially the following: the doctrine in which the Church is presented as the people of God (cf. dogmatic constitution *Lumen gentium,* chapter 2) and hierarchical authority as service (cf. ibid., chapter 3); the doctrine in which the Church is seen as a *communion* and which therefore determines the relations which are to exist between the particular churches and the universal Church, and between collegiality and the primacy; likewise the doctrine according to which all the members of the people of God, in the way suited to each of them, participate in the threefold priestly, prophetic and kingly office of Christ, to which doctrine is also linked that which concerns the duties and rights of the faithful and particularly of the laity; and finally, the Church's commitment to ecumenism.

If, therefore, the Second Vatican Council has drawn both new and old from the treasury of tradition, and the new consists precisely in the elements which I have enumerated, then it is clear that the Code should also reflect the same note of fidelity in newness and of newness in fidelity, and conform itself to this in its own subject matter and in its own particular manner of expression.

The new Code of Canon Law appears at a moment when the bishops of the whole Church not only are asking for its promulgation, but are crying out for it insistently and almost with impatience.

As a matter of fact, the Code of Canon Law is extremely necessary for the Church. Since the Church is organized as a social and visible structure, it must also have norms: in order that its hierarchical and organic structure be visible; in order that the exercise of the functions divinely entrusted to it, especially that of sacred power and of the administration of the sacraments, may be adequately organized; in order that the mutual relations of the faithful may be regulated according to justice based upon charity, with the rights of individuals guaranteed and well-defined; in order, finally, that common initiatives undertaken to live a Christian life ever more perfectly may be sustained, strengthened and fostered by canonical norms.

Finally, by their very nature canonical laws are to be observed. The greatest care has therefore been taken to ensure that in the lengthy preparation of the Code the wording of the norms should be accurate, and that they should be based on a solid juridical, canonical and theological foundation.

After all these considerations it is naturally to be hoped that the new canonical legislation will prove to be an efficacious means in order that the Church may progress in conformity with the spirit of the Second Vatican Council and may every day be ever more suited to carry out its office of salvation in this world.

With a confident spirit I am pleased to entrust these considerations of mine to all as I promulgate this fundamental body of ecclesiastical laws for the Latin Church.

May God grant that joy and peace with justice and obedience obtain favor for this Code, and that what has been ordered by the head be observed by the body.

Trusting therefore in the help of divine grace, sustained by the authority of the blessed apostles Peter and Paul, with certain knowledge, in response to the wishes of the bishops of the whole world who have collaborated with me in a collegial spirit, and with the supreme authority with which I am vested, by means of this Constitution, to be valid forever in the future, I promulgate the present Code as it has been set in order and revised. I command that for the future it is to have the force of law for the whole Latin Church, and I entrust it to the watchful care of all those concerned in order that it may be observed. So that all may more easily be informed and have a thorough knowledge of these norms before they have juridical binding force, I declare and order that they will have the force of law beginning from the first day of Advent in this year 1983, and this notwithstanding any contrary ordinances, constitutions, privileges (even worthy of special or individual mention), or customs.

I therefore exhort all the faithful to observe the proposed legislation with a sincere spirit and good will in the hope that there may flower again in the Church a renewed discipline and that consequently the salvation of souls may be rendered ever more easy under the protection of the Blessed Virgin Mary, Mother of the Church.

Given at Rome, January 25, 1983, from the Vatican Palace, the fifth year of my pontificate.

IOANNES PAULUS PP. II

John A. Alesandro

The Code of Canon Law: A Text and Commentary is a collaborative effort on the part of members of the Canon Law Society of America to explain the 1983 Code in a way that would assist pastoral ministers in fulfilling their responsibilities. Some readers who refer to this work may have very little academic background in canon law; others who have studied canon law may not be familiar in detail with the revision process. It was felt, therefore, that this General Introduction should clarify some basic concepts that would be helpful in grasping the broad context within which the 1983 Code of Canon Law was promulgated.

This General Introduction treats the following points:

- *Historical Background* – a brief synopsis of the role of ecclesiastical law in the Church, touching on several critical periods—the early Christian community, the Carolingian Reform, the Middle Ages, the Tridentine reform, and the 1917 Code of Canon Law;

- *The Process of Revision* – the development of the final text from the announcement of the revision of the 1917 Code by John XXIII to its promulgation by John Paul II: Vatican Council II and the Code, the principles of its revision, and the process of actually drafting the law;

- *The Structure of the 1983 Code* – an analysis of the content of the Code itself, starting with its underlying ecclesiological perspective and its distinctively juridic character (considerably different from the common law tradition) and proceeding to highlight some significant points in each of the seven Books;

- *Concluding Reflections* – the importance of a "new way of thinking" if the Code is to be an effective means of pastoral reform in the Church.

Historical Background

The Early Christian Community

Church law appears early in the life of the Christian community. Examples of it can be found even in the New Testament. Despite his vociferous denunciation of the "old law," St. Paul presents a rather striking figure of an early Christian legislator. In writing to his converts, he does not restrict himself to exhortations but sets down lengthy lists of moral and disciplinary directives to be observed by believers who are called to "put on Christ." In 1 Corinthians 7:12–16, he has no hesitation whatsoever in interpreting Christ's teaching about marriage and, on his own authority, solving the practical case of the convert whose pagan spouse refuses to continue married life. This "Pauline privilege," as it was later called, was developed over the centuries and is still found in the revised Code (cc. 1143–1150).

Chapter 15 of the Acts of the Apostles offers another interesting look at the early community's use of law. The "Council of Jerusalem," as it is sometimes called, settled some thorny issues raised by St. Paul concerning his Gentile converts and, in so doing, amended the accepted ritual practices of the early Church. This authoritative decision succeeded in opening up the proclamation of the gospel to all the nations, thus averting the early threat to restrict the Christian community to nothing more than a small Jewish sect.

The church legislators of the first few centuries made determinations that were fairly specific and localized. They continued to offer concrete solutions to individual problems as they arose. Their responses, however, were clearly based on a sense of authority, a quality already exemplified by the prefatory phrase of the decision of the disciples in Jerusalem: "It seems good to us and to the Holy Spirit to lay no further burden on you" (Acts 15:28). Many early canonical decisions emanated from regional and provincial councils such as the Synod of Elvira (300). Others can be found in documents such as the *Didache, Didascalia,* and *Traditio Apostolica.*

After the Edict of Constantine (313), however, the Church entered another stage of development. Suddenly free to evolve openly, it quickly underwent a major expansion, calling for more complex social structures that in turn required law to provide identity, coordination, and regulation. Extensive conversions created a need for widely applicable norms to protect and foster church unity. The Council of Nicaea (325), recognized as the first of the Church's twenty-one ecumenical councils, was convoked precisely to meet such concerns. It treated doctrinal matters such as the articulation of the Nicene Creed, recited in the liturgy even today. It also addressed, however, many points of pastoral practice and church discipline: procedures for the election of bishops, the organization of dioceses into provinces, rules concerning the patriarchate system, norms on clergy, and regulations affecting the sacraments and other liturgical matters. Some of the decrees of Nicaea and later councils, which succinctly stated certain fundamental ecclesial norms, were called "canons," the Greek word for "rule," or "measure." These canons preserved and enforced the traditional discipline that had developed and sought to accommodate the Church's pastoral practice to the new challenges of their time. Eventually, church law came to be known as "canon law."

Other sources of law in the early Church were also revered and preserved. Regional councils considered not merely local matters but also questions of wider interest and application. Various rulings by the Fathers of the Church, such as those of St. Basil in the East and St. Ambrose and St. Augustine in the West, were compiled as guides for future generations. By the end of the fourth century, the successor of St. Peter in Rome was being asked by individual bishops to settle questions about matters such as the sacraments. Many of these responses to local situations, later called decretals, were gradually accepted as normative for the entire Church. They too were collected and saved for future reference by writers such as Dionysius Exiguus (ca. 500). Finally, it should be recalled that canon law and Roman civil law were at times intermingled. Many imperial constitutions, particularly under Emperor Justinian, dealt with ecclesiastical matters, and bishops were often called upon to serve as arbiters of disputes or in other secular capacities. Some of the early church laws on subjects such as marriage can be found in the Roman law collection entitled *Corpus Iuris Civilis*.

The Carolingian Reform

The massive migration of tribes from the north and east toward and across the borders of the waning Roman Empire sealed its final disintegration. These disparate clans, with their foreign languages and laws, planted the seed of today's European nations. Initially, however, their new practices ushered in hundreds of years of societal fragmentation. There was no longer a single Roman culture. It disappeared almost overnight—and with it the system of Roman law. The Church survived by converting these immigrants and adapting itself to their unique tribal cultures, including their customs and laws. During this time, although many documents were lost, some important ones were preserved, particularly in the manuscript collections carefully maintained in various monasteries.

During this period, feudalism reigned supreme and with it the reliance on purely local, even isolated, legal determinations. An example of this phenomenon is the development of the *penitentials* in Ireland. These books were based on the local monastic experience, in which the abbot served as spiritual and secular father of the entire community. They included rules for confessors that varied widely from the ancient discipline. Two notable points

were the practice of private penance and permission for remarriage after divorce in certain circumstances. These books were welcomed as guides in England and, later, on the Continent, where they were brought by Irish and English missionaries. Eventually, these local norms were evaluated by other communities and compared to different texts. Some found their way into general practice. Other norms were rejected as incompatible with overall church doctrine and order.

Apart from the laws developed by local councils and bishops, there occurred during this period an interesting phenomenon that significantly affected the history of canon law. During the ninth century, there was a concerted effort to renew society and centralize Western civilization. It is usually called the Carolingian Reform after its initiator, Charlemagne, who was crowned Roman Emperor by the pope on the feast of Christmas in the year 800. Its intention was to stabilize the structures of Christendom, and one of its chief tools was reliance on church law. The second generation of Carolingian scholars, attempting to salvage the deceased Charlemagne's noble goal, turned to the authority of canon law to bring about reform and unity. Since texts were scattered and some irretrievably lost, one group of scholars, situated probably in northern France, drafted various canonical texts that set forth the ancient discipline. These laws, authored some time between 847 and 852, are often referred to as the *Pseudo-Isidorian,* or *False, Decretals* since the collection was attributed to one Isidore Mercator and many of the ingenious texts were masked as decretals of the early popes. (There were actually four such compositions: the *Hispana of Autun,* the *Capitula of Angilramnus,* the *False Capitularies,* and the *False Decretals.*) These documents supplemented and interpreted the existing body of ecclesiastical law in order to defend the clergy and church possessions against the designs of feudal lords. Although it is fairly certain that the Church of Rome had nothing to do with these fabrications, one of the chief strategies of the texts was to emphasize the powers, prerogatives, and supremacy of the pope (in accord with the Carolingian ideal of the empire united under ecclesiastically approved authority). This form of "creative" legislation, like the Carolingian experiment itself, proved unsuccessful. The fact that the texts were clever forgeries, however, remained undiscovered for seven centuries. In the meantime, they actually proved quite useful in helping the Church to coordinate its canonical legislation and to preserve the spirit, if not the letter, of the ancient discipline.

The Middle Ages

After the Carolingian period, Western civilization, which had been somewhat static, experienced an intellectual revival. Manuscripts containing many of the Church's laws were uncovered, and scholars began in earnest to formulate collections of such texts. These works, completed by figures such as Hincmar of Rheims and Burchard of Worms, were little more than lists of writings grouped under very general categories that lacked any real system or coordination. They served, however, to highlight the haphazard method of preserving church discipline. Discrepancies, variant readings, and even outright contradictions appeared side by side in the collections. They provided the raw material, as it were, for ecclesial renewal and canonical revision but without any effective system of organization. One of the most important of these compilers was Ivo of Chartres, who was acutely aware of the need for systematization and tried in the preface to his collection to resolve discrepancies and contradictions.

During the intellectual renaissance of the eleventh century, there occurred in the Church one of its most far-reaching reforms, initiated by Hildebrand, Gregory VII (1073–1085). The Christendom inherited by Gregory from previous centuries was ultimately disadvantageous to the Church. It was a caricature of the noble dream—one faith, one people—and it was doomed. Harmony and unity had degenerated into a power struggle with the princes. Gregory and his successors sought to move the Church in a new direction by disentangling it from secular control. They used canon law to assist them in defining the Church and in reinforcing its unique rules and independent norms. The lay investiture controversy involving Gregory and Henry IV was much more than a matter of honor and precedence. It resulted eventually in the determination that the spiritual order was truly the proper domain of the Church, a domain that could be neither ignored nor controlled by secular authorities.

To achieve his goal Gregory arranged for all the known archives of Italy to be searched for texts treating topics such as papal supremacy, the freedom of the Church, and clerical celibacy. The discovery of the texts, however, was insufficient. A system of law was required to put some order into this ancient canonical heritage. Some of Gregory's faithful followers, such as Anselm of Lucca, attempted, with varying degrees of success, to produce such collections. This crucial task was eventually accomplished in the next century by the unparalleled canonical treatise of Gratian, a Camaldolese monk teaching at the University of Bologna. In or about 1141, he produced his *Concordia Discordantium Canonum* (*The Harmony of Discordant Canons*), which represents the first successful attempt to provide a comprehensive synthesis of the Church's laws. He employed the dialectical method used in theological questions by his contemporary, Peter Lombard, and by later Scholastics such as Thomas Aquinas. As suggested by its title, "concordance" and "harmony" among the canons was

its purpose. Gratian did not simply juxtapose texts in the style of his predecessors but analyzed them and offered solutions to their sometimes obvious discrepancies. His work summarized and commented on the first millennium of church law and served as a starting point for the second millennium.

With the *Decretum Gratiani* (*Gratian's Decree,* as it became known) canon law became a *science* in the classical sense. Decretists commented on Gratian's work and decretalists on the decretals of the popes. The latter multiplied as popes, such as Alexander III (1159–1181), at one time a student of Gratian, and Innocent III (1198–1216), took up the challenge to offer authoritative solutions to practical cases submitted to them. Conciliar legislation also grew as general councils were held at the Lateran in 1179 and 1215. Within a century of Gratian, new decretals were so numerous and their collections so confusing that Gregory IX commissioned Raymond of Pennafort to organize them into a new collection. This work, entitled *Liber extra* (the book "outside of" Gratian's *Decretum*), was issued in 1234. It contained over two thousand papal and conciliar decrees, systematically arranged into five general categories. It was soon followed by the *Liber sextus* of Boniface VIII ("the sixth book" after Gregory's five), published in 1298. In 1317 John XXII issued the *Constitutiones Clementinae* containing the constitutions of his predecessor, especially those promulgated at the ecumenical Council of Vienne (1311). Finally, in 1500, John Chapuis, a scholarly canonist, edited the above works and joined to them two smaller extant collections of papal decretals (*extravagantes*) in a massive work, soon called the *Corpus Iuris Canonici.* This remained the foundational "body" of canon law until the promulgation of the 1917 Code.

The Tridentine Reform

A half-century after Chapuis's edition, the long-delayed Council of Trent began (1545–1563). It represented the Church's doctrinal and disciplinary response to Luther, Zwingli, Calvin, and the other leaders of the Reformation. This "council of the counter-reformation" not only clarified dogmatic concerns but issued many practical disciplinary norms as well. Trent's decrees brought a certain much-needed definition to the Church's position on various issues, highlighting apparently irreconcilable differences between the Church of Rome and the Reformers. At the same time, however, it brought about in one stroke a revision of law that affected almost every aspect of church life. This use of law to assist in the reform of the Church was possible only because of the highly centralized legislative structure of the sixteenth-century Church (the implicit goal of the Gregorian reformers five hundred years earlier).

The papacy attempted to restrict the multiplication of canonical interpretations by prohibiting the publication of commentaries on the legislation of Trent without Rome's approval. Instead, the Congregation of the Council was established in 1564 to offer authoritative interpretations of the Tridentine decrees, which remained the guiding juridic force in the Church for the next three hundred years. Nevertheless, legislative activity did not cease. In fact, this particular ecclesiastical period saw the development of a complex system of central government, including the formation of many Roman dicasteries—both administrative and judicial—whose decisions and decrees governed the universal Church.

The 1917 Code of Canon Law

Any process of centralization requires the issuance of universal laws in order to maintain harmony and promote unity. By the time of Vatican I (1869–1870), the Church's legislative activity, even without an intervening ecumenical council, had resulted in considerable confusion. Under the leadership of Pius IX, the Council approved constitutions on faith and revelation and on papal infallibility before it was suddenly and permanently interrupted by the triumphant entrance of Vittorio Emmanuele into Rome. Among its abandoned agenda items was the much-needed reform of canon law. Despite significant historical attempts to coordinate the Church's laws, there had never been an authoritative or official codification of all its universal legislation. Even the edition of the *Corpus Iuris Canonici* approved by Gregory XIII (1582) included both official and private collections.

Decades after the close of Vatican I, Pius X set out to accomplish this unfinished task. On March 19, 1904, he announced the establishment of a commission of cardinals to gather into one authoritative collection all of the laws of the Latin Church. This monumental task, modeled on the civil law codes of nineteenth-century continental Europe, took thirteen years to complete. Much of the work was accomplished almost single-handedly in the first ten years by Pietro Gasparri, the general secretary of the commission, although the process of law-drafting involved, at least in theory, a rather sophisticated method of scientific critique and pastoral consultation with bishops and religious superiors throughout the world. The resulting *Codex Iuris Canonici* was promulgated by Pius X's successor, Benedict XV, on Pentecost Sunday, May 27, 1917, and went into effect the following Pentecost Sunday, May 19, 1918.

The Code of Canon Law abrogated, or repealed, all other extant universal canonical legislation; as such, its 2414 canons represented the most radical revision of law the Church had ever effected, surpassing even the monumental contribution of the *Decretum Gratiani* eight centuries earlier. The canons were divided into five books: *General Norms, Persons, Things, Procedures,* and *Penalties*. While the Code presented an abstract and distilled version of the Church's juridic system, a book of principles rather than cases and details, it was rooted in the Church's lengthy and complex legal history. Its critical apparatus contained over twenty-five thousand citations of former texts. At the moment of its promulgation, the Code was the most centralized and clearest system of universal legislation the Church had ever known.

In the *motu proprio* establishing the Pontifical Commission for the Interpretation of the Code of Canon Law (*Cum iuris canonici*), Benedict XV sought to preserve this clarity by exhorting the Roman Congregations to refrain from issuing "general decrees" (new laws) and to limit themselves to the publication of "instructions" (explanations and interpretations). He even spoke of a special council (*consilium*) that would incorporate any necessary general decrees into the Code of Canon Law. It seemed as though the Code would remain an up-to-date authoritative collection of all of the Latin Church's universal legislation. In fact, only a few canons were modified and, before long, human nature took its course. Law has always been an evolving science and art. It keeps pace (at times breathlessly) with the changing life and practices of its community. It was inevitable that the Church's legal system would once again grow complicated, confusing, and unwieldy—as had occurred so many times in the past. Within a relatively short period of time, the "interpretations" clarifying (and sometimes practically changing) various canons amounted to a printed volume larger than the Code itself. Additional legislation was unavoidable. A classic example is the 1936 Instruction of the Congregation for the Sacraments, *Provida mater Ecclesia,* which concretized and supplemented the Code's norms on matrimonial annulment procedures.

The Church's first authoritative Code achieved a great deal of clarity and precluded the massive confusion of former times, but eventually a thorough revision of the canons became a necessity.

This needed renewal was not simply one of legal technique; changing theological insights and pastoral values called for a comprehensive reform of the Church's legal structures. In this situation John XXIII inaugurated another stage in the evolution of canon law, linked (as so often in the past) to a movement of ecclesial reform centered in an ecumenical council. On January 25, 1959, at the Basilica of St. Paul outside the Walls, he announced that he intended to convoke the Second Council of the Vatican and to establish a Pontifical Commission to revise the Code of Canon Law.

The Process of Revision

Vatican Council II and the Code

When John XXIII announced his intention to convoke the Second Vatican Council and revise the

Code of Canon Law, not many at the time could imagine the extent of the undertaking. Some saw the Council as simply a completion of the unfinished business of Vatican I and the revision of the Code as some sort of legal housekeeping, two projects that could be pursued simultaneously and dispatched expeditiously. As it turned out, however, it would have been impossible to revise the Code prior to or concomitantly with the Council.

Probably more than any of the twenty other ecumenical councils, Vatican II required a whole set of laws for its proper implementation. This was the direct result of John XXIII's decision to convoke a "pastoral" council. The pastoral emphasis of the deliberations and decrees directly affected church discipline and ecclesial activity. It was therefore fortuitous that the beginnings of the revision process were systematically delayed. John XXIII waited to appoint the first members of the Pontifical Commission for the Revision of the Code of Canon Law until March 28, 1963, shortly before his death and well after the completion of the Council's first session. Meeting in November of that same year under the presidency of Cardinal Pietro Ciriaci (1963–1966), the Commission itself wisely chose to suspend its activity until the completion of Vatican II. By that time, the second session of the Council was well under way, and it was quite clear that the college of bishops in union with the bishop of Rome had firmly grasped the reins of the conciliar agenda and were not about to settle for the drafts of the original planning group. The Commission would have been foolish to begin any revision without awaiting the documents expressing the Council's pastoral teaching. Thus, although seventy consultors were appointed in April 1964 to assist the cardinals of the Commission, this important task was not formally inaugurated until November 20, 1965, a few days prior to the conclusion of the Council.

At that plenary session inaugurating the work of the Commission, Paul VI stressed the close relationship of the revision to the Council in these words:

Now, however, with changing conditions—for life seems to evolve more rapidly—canon law must be prudently reformed; specifically, it must be accommodated to a new way of thinking proper to the Second Ecumenical Council of the Vatican, in which pastoral care and new needs of the people of God are met (*Comm* 1 [1969] 41).

Paul VI was in many ways the "father" of the revision—although it was left to a successor (as happened with Pius X) to promulgate the final version of the revised Code. Paul VI spoke at great length and on many diverse occasions about the interrelationship of church law and discipline, the life of faith, and the role of the magisterium. Both he and John Paul II linked the revision of church law and

the conciliar teaching in various statements: "formulate in concrete terms the deliberations of Vatican Council II" (1964); "accommodate canon law to the new way of thinking of Vatican Council II" (1965, 1973); "express more clearly the doctrinal and disciplinary thrust of the Council" (1970); "form an instrument to implement the directives of the Council and to realize the fruits desired by it" (1979); "bring the Church's legislation into harmony with the broadened understanding of the Church as found in the Vatican Council" (1981).

The process of revision was not simply a reformulation and refinement of canonical principles but a redrafting and reform of ecclesial structures and norms. Thus, the close connection between legal reform and Vatican II is a very important factor to bear in mind when studying the Code. It means that the canons, many of which repeat or summarize the Council's texts, must be interpreted in light of its teaching; they cannot properly be isolated from their historical sources. On the occasion of the formal presentation of the newly promulgated Code, John Paul II emphasized this factor by encouraging an "exegetical and critical comparison" of the conciliar texts and their respective canons (2/3/83).

Post-conciliar interim legislation was an important source for the revision of the Code. Many of the canons incorporate *verbatim,* or at least substantially, the norms implementing various pastoral directives of the Council—for example, the dispensing power of the diocesan bishop in *De episcoporum muneribus,* the revision of the law concerning entrance into religious life in *Renovationis causam,* the regulations concerning ecumenical marriages in *Matrimonia mixta,* the procedures governing marriage annulment cases in *Causas matrimoniales,* and the many disciplinary norms contained in the renewed liturgical *ordines.* Such documents, however, were disparate and affected only certain sectors of the law. Incorporating post-conciliar legislation is only one way in which the Code depends on the Council. The explicit decision to link the two is nowhere more evident than in the approval given by the first Synod of Bishops to ten principles to guide the revision of the Code of Canon Law.

The Principles of Revision

By January 1966 the consultors of the Commission had been organized into ten study groups to review different sections of the law. At the same time, conferences of bishops throughout the world were asked to nominate additional consultors and to offer suggestions to the Commission for its initial work. The next year an important development occurred. In April 1967 a central committee of consultors, under the direction of Cardinal Pericle Felici, the second President of the Commission (1966–1982), set out to develop several fundamental principles to guide the task of revision. These principles were presented to the Synod of Bishops, which approved them with a few reservations after a five-day discussion of the revision process (9/30/67–10/4/67).

One of the main purposes of the ten principles was to guarantee harmony between the Church's revised law and the conciliar documents. Throughout the revision process, the principles regulated the task of translating the pastoral decisions of the Council into the juridic content of the canons. The introduction to the principles states that "the 1917 Code of Canon Law has the function of serving as a guide, while Vatican II presents the general plan of the new Code of Canon Law." The following represents a concise summary of each of the ten principles of revision:

1. While unique in its evangelical and pastoral purpose, the Code must retain its juridic quality because of the Church's fundamentally social nature. The principal and essential object of canon law is to determine and safeguard the rights and obligations of each individual person with respect to the rights and obligations of others and of the community as a whole.

2. The Code should improve harmony between the external and internal fora, reducing conflict between them to a minimum, especially in regard to the sacraments and ecclesiastical penalties.

3. Pastoral care should be the hallmark of the Code. The Code should be neither simply a hortatory document nor on the other hand an overly preceptive one. Laws should be marked by a spirit of charity, temperance, humaneness, and moderation. The Code should be reluctant to establish laws that render juridic acts null and void or impose ecclesiastical penalties—unless the matter is of grave importance and such norms are necessary for the public good and church discipline. Norms should not be too rigid; they should leave a reasonable amount of discretionary authority in the hands of the Church's pastoral leaders.

4. The office of bishop should be presented in a positive way in accord with the conciliar teaching, particularly as found in *Christus Dominus* 8. Bishops should have the faculty of dispensing from general laws of the Church except in cases explicitly reserved to the Apostolic See.

5. The principle of subsidiarity should be more broadly and completely applied to church legislation in order to strengthen the bond between those exercising authority and those subject to authority. While canon law must remain a unified system for the universal Church, greater weight should be given to particular legislation, even at the national and regional levels, so that the unique characteristics of individual churches will become apparent. Procedural law should be uniform throughout the universal Church but can be given a more general and universal form, leaving to regional authorities the faculty to enact rules to be observed in their respective tribunals.

6. The pope and the diocesan bishops are totally empowered to fulfill their responsibilities for the service of their respective communities. The use of power in the Church should not, however, become arbitrary. The rights of all the Christian faithful should be acknowledged and protected. While individual Christians fulfill varied roles in the Church, all possess the same fundamental rights by reason of the radical equality arising from their personal human dignity and their common baptism. Rights and duties should be clarified by the canons of the Code.

7. Subjective rights should be safeguarded and fostered by legal recourses to remedy the violation of such rights. This goal should especially be pursued in the area of administrative recourse. There is a need to establish administrative tribunals of various degrees and kinds, to determine which actions can be brought before such tribunals, and to clarify the rules of administrative procedure.

8. Territory should be retained in the Code as the usual determinant of ecclesiastical jurisdiction. The pastoral purpose of a diocese and the good of the entire Church require definite territorial divisions. Nonetheless, serious circumstances may justify non-territorial jurisdictional entities for specialized pastoral care, e.g., by reason of a community's liturgical rite or common ethnic origin.

9. Ecclesiastical penalties should be kept to a minimum and their remission limited to the external forum. In general, most penalties should be *ferendae sententiae,* i.e., requiring an authoritative decision for imposition. Automatic penalties (*latae sententiae*) should be reduced to the smallest possible number and restricted to the most serious of matters.

10. The Code should be completely restructured. Its systematic framework should reflect the mind and spirit of the conciliar decrees. This order and arrangement should not be determined a priori but only after the revision of the individual parts of the Code has progressed sufficiently.

These principles were a helpful tool for those drafting the revised law. The final version of the canons illustrates the effectiveness of the principles in inculcating the spirit and directives of the Council into the Code's juridic framework. Many of the principles had a direct influence on the revision and most, although not all, were substantially implemented. (The most notable exceptions are the directives concerning subsidiarity in the judicial process and the establishment of administrative tribunals.)

The ten principles, however, are more than a historical curiosity of the process of revision. They are useful even today in understanding the theory behind certain legal changes; relating the canons to the conciliar decrees through the principles helps in interpreting the Church's universal norms faithfully and applying them properly to the concrete pastoral situation.

The Process of Law-Drafting

Although the cardinal members of the Commission had met in plenary session only twice (the suspension of Commission activity in 1963 and the formal inauguration of its work in 1965), the special groups of consultors, consisting of bishops, priests, religious, and lay persons, were very active in preparing drafts for their respective areas of the Code. These initial drafts, or schemata, were submitted for evaluation to the conferences of bishops throughout the world, the Union of Superiors General of religious and secular institutes, the agencies of the Roman Curia, and pontifical universities and faculties. These groups in turn consulted with their own advisors (canon lawyers, theologians, pastoral leaders) before returning their critiques and suggestions to the Commission. In the United States, the National Conference of Catholic Bishops relied heavily on the Canon Law Society of America, which maintained an ongoing Task Force on the Revision of the Code, to analyze and appraise the various drafts as they appeared.

The draft on administrative tribunals was circulated for consultation in 1972, followed the next year by the draft of the law on penalties. The proposed canons on the sacraments were received for comment in 1975. All the remaining drafts were distributed in 1977—the drafts on procedural law and the norms on religious early in the year and in November the final five sections: general norms, the people of God, the Church's teaching office, sacred times and places and divine worship, and temporalities. By the end of 1978 all of the official consultative bodies had completed their review of the initial schemata and returned their written comments to the Commission's staff.

The results of this worldwide consultation were submitted to small working groups of consultants to be assimilated and to serve as the basis for revision of the original drafts. The amended second drafts were then coordinated, the canons were placed in sequential order, and a one-volume version was produced for the cardinal members of the Commission on June 29, 1980. At the same time, the membership of the Commission was expanded and the cardinals were instructed to evaluate the new document in writing prior to a final plenary session. At this point, the pope was requested by some bishops to authorize a second round of worldwide consultation on the latest draft, which had so far been reserved solely to the members of the Commission. The subject was raised at the assembly of the Synod of Bishops in Rome in October 1980. Others, including the staff of the Commission, spoke against additional consultation as being both cumbersome and counterproductive. John Paul II addressed the concern for further consultation by appointing fifteen new members to the Commission as representatives of conferences of bishops throughout the world, bringing the Commission membership to seventy-four. The members from the United States were Cardinal John Krol, who was active in the Commission from the early days of the project; Cardinal John Cody, who was appointed in 1980; and Archbishop Joseph Bernardin, who, as chairman of the Canonical Affairs Committee of the National Conference of Catholic Bishops, was nominated by the Conference in 1981 and shortly thereafter appointed by the pope.

The written comments of the members of the Commission were carefully summarized by the staff in Rome and formulated into a comprehensive written report (*Relatio*) dated July 16, 1981. The 1980 draft of the proposed Code together with the proposals found in the *Relatio* formed the documentary basis for the final plenary session of the Commission. An important inclusion in the *Relatio* was a group of thirty-eight canons taken from the most recent version of the *Lex Ecclesiae Fundamentalis* (1980). This work, meant to provide a "fundamental law" or "constitution" for the entire Church (not just the Latin rite), had undergone numerous revisions and had been the subject of much controversy from the beginning of the project. In May 1981 the independent Commission responsible for its drafting (distinct from the Latin Rite Code Commission) submitted an approved draft for consideration by the pope. By July, however, it was clear that the document would not be promulgated; consequently, approximately half of its canons, which were appropriate to the Latin Code (particularly those concerning the rights and duties of Christians), were inserted into the material to be considered by the members of the Latin Rite Code Commission at their final plenary session.

The Commission's plenary session was held in Rome, October 20–28, 1981. Cardinal Felici presided at the meetings, one of which was attended personally by John Paul II. Forty-one agenda items were considered. Six were submitted at the outset by the Commission's staff: the exercise of ecclesiastical jurisdiction by lay persons (cf. c. 129, §2; mandatory review of all affirmative sentences of matrimonial nullity (cf. c. 1682); hierarchical confirmation of the dismissal of a religious (cf. c. 700); remarriage of widowed permanent deacons (cf. c. 1087); Freemasonry and automatic excommunication (cf. c. 1374); and the mandatory or optional character of administrative tribunals (cf. cc. 1732–1739).

The remaining items were placed on the agenda by individual members of the Commission by submitting a petition with the signatures of ten members. These items dealt with topics such as seminary formation, the personal prelature, secular institutes, the confessional, matrimonial consent, financial assessments, the confidentiality of tribunal records, and ecumenism. At the end of the plenary session, the Commission members voted unanimously to present the amended version of the canons to the pope for promulgation as soon as possible. The formal presentation of this work to John Paul II occurred at a special audience for the members of the Commission on October 29, 1981.

For one year, John Paul II personally studied the proposed Code with the help of a small group of canonists. During this period, Cardinal Felici, who had presided for so many years over the work of the Commission, died and was succeeded by Archbishop Rosalio Castillo Lara, the secretary of the Commission for several years, who was then named its Pro-President. The pope made several changes in the final text before announcing in December 1982 that he would promulgate the Code the next month. Despite the many years of preparation, review, and revision—and the almost endless delays—the announcement surprised many in Rome who had been expecting even a longer delay. John Paul II promulgated the revised Code of Canon Law for the Latin Church on the Feast of the Conversion of St. Paul, January 25, 1983, twenty-four years to the day after John XXIII's announcement of the project of revision. The *vacatio legis,* the period during which the obligation of the law is temporarily suspended, was set at ten months to permit a reasonable amount of time for church officials to prepare for the changes that the Code would require. On November 27, 1983, the First Sunday of Advent, the first Code of Canon Law, promulgated sixty-six years earlier, ceased to bind and the second Code of Canon Law went into effect.

The Structure of the 1983 Code

Few would be tempted to pick up the Code of Canon Law and read it from the first canon to the last, and yet an overall glance at the Code can be most enlightening. One is struck immediately by the fact that the canons touch either directly or indirectly on almost every facet of church life from its

hierarchical structure to personal spirituality, from internal governance to the mission of justice and peace. While the Code might seem lengthy at first, the number of canons pales in comparison to the subjects treated. (Actually, there are only 1752 canons in comparison to the 2414 canons of the 1917 Code.) Some canons are concerned with details, even small points; but, generally, the canons tend to express principles rather than complex directives.

The economy of words is a warning sign to the reader. The words are carefully chosen; they are placed in certain contexts for a purpose. Their meaning may be more subtle than it appears at first, and the implementation of the norms may allow for a considerable degree of discretion. In other words, the interpretation of canon law is a necessary science and an indispensable art. Many of the initial canons present rules for interpretation (e.g., cc. 16–22); canon 27 contains the remarkable, though traditional, advice that "custom is the best interpreter of laws."

The interpretation of the law must rely on many tools: the history of the Church, the canonical tradition, the theological underpinnings of the norms, the textual background of the conciliar decrees and of the canons themselves, the applicability of the pastoral directives to the concrete situation, and even analogies in the law. What has been presumed in the drafting of law must be unearthed in order to concretize rather succinct principles and apply them responsibly and accurately. Among the general presumptions underlying the Code, two examples might be of particular interest: the law's ecclesiological perspective and its juridic character.

The Code and Ecclesiology

The Code differs quite markedly from its 1917 predecessor in this area. All ecclesiastical laws reflect an ecclesiological perspective. It is clear enough that, just as the 1917 Code was the juridic expression of Vatican Council I, so also the 1983 Code reflects Vatican Council II. This itself represents a significant shift, particularly in the content of the canons; but, the transition is even deeper than one might suspect. In Paul VI's phrase, the present Code attempts to offer a "new way of thinking" (*novus habitus mentis*)—not merely a new way of perceiving or reading laws—but a new method of law itself, a new framework in which the Church's juridic system is seen as completely unique.

The 1917 Code was content to be an integrated legal system similar to any other. In this regard, it presumed that the Church was a *societas perfecta* in the classic sense, a "complete society" likened in almost all aspects to the State and differentiated from it solely by reason of its proper supernatural purpose. At the time, this theory suited the Church's stance in the world, which involved a growing separation from and independence of secular society, but, in its own way, it tied the ecclesiastical legal system to the secular model. Though the Church was a supernatural society and the State a natural one, their legal systems were looked upon as parallel and comparable, thus placing them on the same plane and, in a way, on an equal footing. Civil and canonical jurists spoke the same language though they might be interested in different subjects. This is a consistent scholastic (or some might say "classicist") position in which universal principles flowing from the genus, "society," are applied in equal measure to two species, Church and State. Vatican Council II rejected this equation and parallelism. It spoke of the Church as a unique people whose juridic or social system must also be unique. This crucial insight profoundly affects the structure and content of the revised Code and stands as one of its most important presuppositions.

John Paul II singled out this "newness" (*novitas*) of the Code in the apostolic constitution of promulgation, *Sacrae disciplinae leges,* describing the task of the Code as the translation into canonical terms of the ecclesiological doctrine of the Vatican Council. Just as the Council offered a new insight into the meaning of the Church so also the Code is imbued with a similar new vision. The pope then identified the principal elements that serve as the foundation for the Code: the teaching about the Church as the people of God and the role of service that hierarchical authority must fulfill; the reality of the Church as a communion and the essential relationship between the universal Church and the particular churches and between collegiality and primacy; the participation of all the Christian faithful in the threefold office of Christ as priest, prophet, and king and the rights and duties that flow from this dignity; and the duty to pursue ecumenical unity.

This close theological connection between the Council's teaching on the Church and canon law was again stressed in the pope's remarks on the occasion of the official presentation of the Code on February 3, 1983:

Law is not conceived as a foreign body, nor as a now useless superstructure, nor as a residue of presumed temporal claims. Law is innate to the life of the Church, to which it is, in fact, extremely useful: it is a means, a help, and is also—in sensitive questions of justice—a protection (*Comm* 15 [1983] 14).

In his response on the same occasion, Archbishop Rosalio Castillo Lara, the Pro-President of the Commission, spoke of a deeper theological inspiration in the Code, underlining its "peculiar nature" and its close dependence on Vatican II:

Not a few canons, especially in the matter of the sacraments or ecclesiology, offer theological syntheses of notable precision, and some, when the subject matter permits it, reproduce almost literally the very formulations of the Second Vatican Council (*Comm* 15 [1983] 32).

This basic shift in the revised Code appears at the outset in its systematic arrangement. Book II is entitled "The People of God" in accord with the second chapter of *Lumen Gentium* on which it depends. The image is meant to portray the Church principally as a mystery, a *sacramentum,* a people gathered together in baptism, faith, and Eucharist. The Code is concerned of course with the external forum of the sacramental communion (*koinonia*) that makes up the Church. It therefore addresses the fundamental rights and responsibilities of all the people of God as well as their diverse functions. This conciliar vision influences the structure not only of Book II but of the entire Code.

The principal criterion of unity is found in the common duty and right of all of the members of the Church to fulfill the *triplex munus Christi,* i.e., the priestly, prophetic, and royal office of Christ. The first section of Book II emphasizes the equality of Christians by treating at the outset the rights and responsibilities of all Christians, then the rights and duties of lay persons, and lastly the rights and functions of sacred ministers. This order was purposely chosen by the Code Commission to underscore the dignity and equality of all, especially the laity. The threefold *munus* to be fulfilled by every Christian is succinctly described in canon 204, §1:

The Christian faithful are those who, inasmuch as they have been incorporated in Christ through baptism, have been constituted as the people of God; for this reason, since they have become sharers in Christ's priestly, prophetic and royal office in their own manner, they are called to exercise the mission which God has entrusted to the Church to fulfill in the world, in accord with the condition proper to each one.

This threefold *munus* influences the structure of the remainder of the Code. Book III treats the office of teaching. Book IV deals with the office of sanctifying. The office of governance is treated in different Books of the Code: Book I's title on the power of governance (*potestas regiminis*), Book II's description of the Church's hierarchical structure, Book V on temporal goods and Books VI and VII on ecclesiastical sanctions and procedures. This arrangement is a far cry from the classical division of the 1917 Code into five books: general norms, persons, things, procedures, and penalties. The former Code's systematic framework, based primarily on secular legal theory, has been replaced by a system grounded in a distinctly theological perspective.

This ecclesiological shift should not be misinterpreted. It does not at all dismiss the traditional view of the Church as hierarchical. In fact, it relies heavily on the notion of the people of God as a "hierarchical communion," the phrase so carefully explained in *Lumen Gentium*'s *nota explicativa praevia* n. 2:

> It is significantly stated that *hierarchical* communion is required with the head of the Church and its members. *Communion* is an idea which was held in high honor by the ancient Church (as it is even today, especially in the East). It is understood, however, not of a certain vague feeling, but of an *organic reality* which demands a juridical form, and is simultaneously animated by charity. Hence the Commission by practically unanimous consent decreed that it must be written: "in *hierarchical* communion."

This concept is clear even in the description of *christifideles* in canon 204 (quoted above), which includes the phrase "in accord with the condition proper to each one." The notion of a "juridic condition," a phrase used throughout the Code, should be carefully studied. It is a more flexible concept than "ecclesiastical office" or "ecclesiastical state." It implies that each person has a certain position or proper place in the Church with appropriate rights and duties, a sort of "standing," or "station in life," in the community.

The ecclesiological shift occurs in understanding the basis of this hierarchical communion, i.e., sacramentality. Christians are initially commissioned to carry out the work of the Lord not by jurisdictional delegation but by their baptism and confirmation. This perspective reinforces the radical equality of all members of the Church and enhances especially the role of the laity. Lay persons are sacramentally called to participate actively in the fulfillment of the Church's mission. The Christian faithful, once initiated, receive special ecclesial roles from other sacraments. Clerics are endowed with unique rights and obligations by the sacrament of orders, and married persons are given a special call to build up the body of Christ in the sacrament of marriage. Juridically, the Church is still pictured as hierarchical and its leadership clerical. The interrelationships, however, are not seen as primarily monarchical, as though each were commissioned to fulfill his or her function in the Church by a series of delegations from the pope on downward. Instead, rights and responsibilities are considered proper to individuals based on their sacramental gifts.

A good example of this approach can be seen in the norms concerning the diocesan bishop. He is not described as a quasi-delegate of the Holy See but as the sacramental head of the particular church, the portion of the people of God "in which the one, holy, catholic and apostolic Church of Christ is truly present and operative" (c. 369). The bishop's power is defined in canon 381 as "ordinary, proper and immediate." It is presumed to exist whenever he is called upon to fulfill the episcopal responsibility of pastoral care, and its exercise is restricted only when explicitly stated, an approach to the role of bishop as pastor that is faithful to *Lumen Gentium* 27.

In this sense, hierarchical authority is seen principally in terms of service rather than power. The conciliar word *sollicitudo* is all-pervasive in the canons as a description of the bishop's office. He must have concern and solicitude for the community gathered around him, for those who are estranged from the community, for non-Catholics, for the missions, and in particular for his presbyterate. He is charged to carry out his threefold Christian office, his *sollicitudo,* not merely in an extrinsic way but by his own personal life. The Church is sanctified not only through the administration of the sacraments but by the bishop's personal holiness; the Church is taught by a bishop who learns; the Church is governed by one who serves the rest.

The norms on the diocesan bishop represent only one example among many of the effect of the Council's ecclesiological perspective on the Code. This fundamental presupposition therefore must be integrated into any proper interpretation of the canons. The interpretation must be truly theological and historical if the Code is to promote a "new way of thinking." Even when texts of the 1917 Code are retained verbatim or in slightly amended form, they may not be interpreted in precisely the same way in which they were sixty years ago. Now they must be reexamined, related to the other canons, placed in context, and studied in the light of the Council as well as the canonical tradition. In short, they must be subject to an interpretation based on a renewed ecclesiology. As Paul VI instructed the officials of the Sacred Roman Rota on February 4, 1977:

> The revision of the new Code of Canon Law cannot consist solely in the correction of the former one, by arranging the contents in proper order, by adding what it seems appropriate to add, and omitting whatever no longer applies. Rather, after the celebration of the Second Vatican Council, the new Code must prove to be an instrument most finely adapted to the life of the Church.

The Code's Juridic Character

Even apart from the use of Latin, the canons are written in a special "language," a unique *sermo canonisticus.* As readers of the law seek to interpret the canons properly, they must be well versed in this "language." The above section has already highlighted one foundation of the language, its theological (ecclesiological) basis. Those learned in civil law, for example, cannot simply peruse the canons quickly and expect to interpret them accurately—even though the juridic vocabulary might seem familiar to them. They must bring to their "translation" of the canons a theological base along with their knowledge of legal history. (Throughout this section the term "civil law" is used generically to refer to secular law as distinct from ecclesiastical law rather than as a technical reference to the specific type of law found in continental Europe.)

Throughout the centuries, ecclesiastical law and civil law have been closely connected and, at times, intimately dependent on each other. The intermingling of religious and secular laws is striking in both the *Corpus Iuris Civilis* and the *Corpus Iuris Canonici*. More recently, the nineteenth-century civil codes of Europe exercised considerable influence on the structure and content of the 1917 Code of Canon Law, an influence continued in good measure in the 1983 Code. Canon law has had its own impact on civil law. This can be seen in both the legal systems of continental Europe and the common law tradition. Much of today's civil law on marriage reflects both canon law and the ancient Roman law since for many centuries the only courts to deal with marriage questions were ecclesiastical tribunals.

Because of the historical interrelationship of ecclesiastical and civil law, one might easily yield to the temptation to equate civil and canonical concepts. Similarities, however, often conceal significant differences. The Code's concept of a *juridic person* (cc. 113–123) reflects both its own canonical heritage and modern civil law theory; and yet, though analogous, an *ecclesiastical juridic person* cannot, in actuality, simply be equated with a *civil corporation*. It would also be a mistake to identify the notion of *ownership* in some civil systems with the canonical concept of *dominium*. Translating the Code's Latin into the vernacular may be only the first of several "translations" required by the uniqueness of its juridic character. Besides its theological foundations, the Code possesses its own special legal style.

One obvious characteristic is the Code's brevity. It touches on nearly every structure of the Roman Catholic Church in fewer than two thousand canons, many of which contain not statutes or laws but exhortative or theological statements more properly classified as "a-juridic." Civil legal systems, on the other hand, are more extensive and complex than canon law since they must regulate a broader range of human affairs, requiring, for example, many different types of jurisdiction, procedures for the settlement of various conflicts, and an extremely active criminal justice apparatus.

The Code's comparative brevity, however, results not only from its unique subject matter but from its tendency to remain, in many cases, on the level of principle rather than to offer detailed regulations. To achieve church order, the Code frequently relies on the exercise of discretion by ecclesiastical administrators in applying the law to concrete situations. The administrator is called upon to humanize and accommodate the legislator's canonical principles, set them in their proper context, apply them equitably, and dispense from them whenever pastorally necessary. Civil law also expresses general principles to which administrators must be sensitive, but their discretionary application of such principles is more often circumscribed by an ever-expanding complexus of statutory legislation, administrative procedure, and case law.

The uniqueness of the Code's juridic character and its difference from civil law systems may seem a rather theoretical point, of interest mainly to specialists in comparative law. The differences as well as the similarities, however, can have a profound effect on individuals in the Church—authorities as well as those subject to authority. Since civil law is such a pervasive element of social life, it inevitably exercises a dominant influence on a person's view of law itself. One is tempted to equate all law with one's concept of law in civil society. This univocal approach to law can mislead one who is seeking to interpret the Code accurately. The following reflections on the legal system in the United States and the Code's juridic approach may serve to illustrate this point. Although canon law has elements in common with the American legal system, it also has a different emphasis and approach.

a. The United States inherited an English tradition sometimes generically labeled "the common law system." In its own unique manner it then developed this tradition into the legal system in existence today. It consists of many different forms of law: *constitutional law,* through which extremely basic and general legal principles are applied to new situations; *common law,* the sum of traditional principles used by judges to settle controversies based on the legal wisdom of custom and the community's sense of justice and equity; *statutory law,* by which legislators at every level of government regulate matters within their jurisdiction; *judicial precedents,* which bind equal or lower courts of the same jurisdiction, thus offering a practical interpretation of constitutional, common, statutory and administrative law. *Administrative law* is a specific area of law through which the many rules and regulations of public administrators are reviewed and ordered.

While the canonical system has different kinds of law, these are not so clearly defined nor do all of them play an extensive role in church order. There are canons that are similar to *constitutional law,* such as the Code's general norms (cf. cc. 1–203), the articulation of human and ecclesial rights (cf. cc. 204–223), and the description of the Church's hierarchical structure (cf. cc. 330–572). On the other hand, the concept of a *Fundamental Law of the Church (Lex Ecclesiae Fundamentalis)* has, at least temporarily, been rejected. The canonical system includes forms of "unwritten" law that are somewhat similar to the notion of *common law.* The principles of natural law and canonical custom *(consuetudo)* are certainly operative in church governance. It is interesting, however, that customary law does not remain for long in the form of interpretations and applications by learned authors or of decisions given in individual cases by ecclesiastical judges or administrators. When such principles become "customary," they are often adopted into canonical legislation. A case in point is canon 1095, which articulates customary principles of rotal jurisprudence concerning the effect of psychological disorders on matrimonial consent.

Since canon law relies heavily on written *statutes* to express its system, it is even more surprising that this latest codification can limit its treatment of church structures to a relatively small number of canons. These statutes are in no way comparable to the finely detailed norms found in civil legislation. They are often very succinct statements that the ecclesiastical administrator must concretize and apply equitably in the individual case.

In the *administrative* area, curial departments on the universal level issue many types of rules and regulations that are not, strictly speaking, laws. Similarly, a diocesan bishop and his curia may set down policies and procedures in the form of general decrees, and the conference of bishops may at times issue guidelines or even legislative decrees.

b. In the United States, the three governmental functions—legislative, executive (administrative), and judicial—are carried out by separate authorities. Their relationship with each other is described as "a balance of powers." The system of checks and balances succeeds because of a complicated and flexible tension that exists among the three. Law is based on the consent of the governed. Governmental actions must never grow independent of the people. The balance of powers prevents any branch from deviating very far from this basic characteristic. While one or the other branch of government may attain a certain ascendancy at different times in history, their basic relationship is one of distinct equals. It is significant that the performance of the chief executive of the United States is often rated not only on administrative skill but on the ability to obtain the support of the congressional legislators and on the effectiveness in appointing competent judicial personnel at the federal level.

The Church's governmental system is vastly different from the notion of a balance of powers. In fact, the three functions are situated in the same office. Not only the pope but every diocesan bishop is legislator, administrator, and judge (cf. cc. 135, 331, 391). Unlike the American system, ecclesiastical law does not arise from the will of the governed—nor does the Church's juridic structure rely on a system of checks and balances to maintain its

effectiveness. The Church's inspiration for lawmaking is ultimately the gospel as it is expressed in an ongoing tradition. In a sense, the Church seeks to "discover" its law in its own theological foundations by reexamining them in the light of historical development. The Code promotes this system through a hierarchical structure that is more vertical than horizontal. Ultimately, the highest judge, the pope, is also the highest legislator and administrator. The decision to delete administrative tribunals from the final draft of the Code underscores this juridic approach. Since the regulation of the exercise of power in the Church is based principally on the hierarchical relationship of ecclesiastical authorities to each other, recourse is pursued *within* the line of administrative authority and not outside it in a court of law.

c. Courts in the United States are, at least in theory, the most powerful of the three forms of governance. Some go so far as to label the system one of "judicial supremacy." In the area of interpretation, the courts are often called upon to "give the last word," at least in regard to a specific concrete situation. They are active in translating principles into practical norms that will be effective in the modern world. To most, their activity is nothing short of "creating new law." They keep the law relevant and safeguard its flexibility. The force of precedent *(stare decisis),* though limited to the circumstances of a particular case, is an important legal tool that controls the manner in which laws are applied and interpreted.

Ecclesiastical tribunals, at least in our present day, do not have a comparable effect on church life. They treat—almost exclusively—cases of matrimonial nullity, an important but very specialized segment of church governance. As such, their judicial impact on daily Christian living is restricted. They do not settle conflicts of rights about every aspect of church activity. Such matters are treated administratively (cf. c. 1400). The tribunal, even in matrimonial cases, does not have a precedent-setting system. The sentence of a judge in a particular case is nothing more than a weighty opinion of an expert who has sought to interpret and apply ecclesiastical, divine positive, and natural law. In the practical order, such "expert" advice functions somewhat similarly to the *stare decisis* process of American courts since judges often study and quote earlier sentences of their colleagues, especially those issued by the judges of the Roman Rota. Nonetheless, such judgments do not set a legal precedent that *must* be followed. Thus, tribunals do not create "new law" as American courts do. If their interpretation of principles becomes traditional enough, such principles obtain a legal status through the action of the legislator rather than through juridically binding judicial sentences. In other words, written law is found principally in a code, not in a case. If anything, the Church has a system of legislative supremacy—or perhaps more precisely, a system of legislative-administrative supremacy. Judicial review is not a major component of the canonical system.

d. The common law system is marked by certain obvious characteristics. It is sometimes overly complicated, even confusing, and yet its complexity gives rise to considerable versatility—causing some to depict the law as "a seamless web." It is fluid and constantly shifting, and yet it is efficiently flexible. Usually, laws are quite relevant and up to date. Inevitably, some laws become obsolete, but such conflicts are kept to a minimum and the courts make an effort to see that no law is applied inequitably. General principles are greatly revered but are limited in number. They are adopted only after a hard-fought testing in the administrative and judicial fora. Such principles are the basis for statements of public policy which themselves ground specific statutes. Statutes, on the other hand, abound and are amended frequently. Moreover, legislation is often detailed, even ornate, in order to anticipate as many contingencies as possible. It is a very active legal system, consisting of a complex, though manageable, succession of extant law and jurisprudence.

The Church's system has different juridic characteristics. Laws more easily go out of date. They fall into desuetude. Though "on the books," they are never applied. Eventually, as in this codification, the legislator addresses this discrepancy and removes them from the Code.

Lawmaking is not frequent in the Church, at least at the universal level. The system is revised on a continuing basis—not, however, to the extent that law is constantly amended in secular society. An overall revision is rather rare, although the complexity of today's world may increase the need to clarify the Church's extant laws more often.

Canon law tries to be clear and simple. It emphasizes written principles. It is not so dynamic a system as the common law tradition. Though its formulations are less complex, they are also less flexible. Since canons express principles, they are not so easily or so often changed. It should be obvious that such laws need the proper exercise of discretion by those in authority in order to be interpreted and applied to actual situations in a way that achieves their ultimate purpose.

e. Although most Americans are somewhat removed from the inner workings of their legal system, they inevitably inherit from it certain attitudes toward law. They generally perceive law as something practical. For the most part, it works. Although they realize that law is very complicated, they believe that it should make sense. If it does not make sense, it should be changed as soon as possible. Most Americans consider law to be supreme.

No one should be above the law. There should be few exceptions; all citizens should be treated equally by the law. Laws should be written in such a way that their application is predictable. Thus, they should be marked by reasonableness and should cover many details. This view of law can sometimes cause people to interpret individual laws too literally. If the law addresses many contingencies, what need is there for "interpretations" of its meaning or special exceptions? Administrators should not easily or often grant exemptions from the law. If this occurs, the law is defective. Legislators can solve some such problems, administrators others, but the final word belongs to the judge. When all other remedies fail, the individual who deserves an exemption goes to court.

This attitude toward law cherishes general principles—only, however, after they have proven their worth. It is not easy to introduce new general principles or to change those that have been in force for many years. Thus, a constitutional amendment is a rarity; it is a last resort, to be approved only if almost everyone admits its necessity.

Most Americans think of law as something very empirical. It arises from concrete situations and life experience. It is not overly abstract. Principles emerge slowly and some are never even written down in a final form. The law is eminently adaptable to changing customs and mores. Many persons—legislators, administrators, and especially judges—keep it alive and growing every day.

The Code's juridic style must be carefully studied by those who apply it and those who are affected by it, especially if their attitude toward law in general has been created by the experience of a somewhat different legal system. The canons are marked by a certain abstractness—even artificiality. In a way, all forms of law are artificial, but canon law seems, by its conciseness, to highlight this characteristic. In the concrete, therefore, it often admits of varying interpretations and applications. An exclusively literal reading can be especially risky in canon law. Proper interpretation may sometimes be rather complex, and yet, the involved administrator, not the independent judge, is required to make that interpretation and apply it.

Canon law may very well allow many exceptions. Those in authority are permitted to "dispense" from the law, i.e., "relax" it in an individual case (cc. 85–93). Such dispensations can, if circumstances call for it, be rather extensive (cf. the broad dispensing authority of the diocesan bishop in c. 87).

In general, the Code tends to be theoretical and abstract rather than empirical. It is founded on the experience of faith and relies on revealed teaching, but it tends to express the norms that are needed for Church order in a formalistic manner. This style must be clearly understood if the law is to serve as a source of both stability and growth. Concise principles can seem rather stark and unyielding unless one is sensitive to their role in ecclesiastical governance and the obligation of the administrator to interpret and apply them properly.

A proper attitude toward canon law is not an easy task for those who find themselves with one foot in the world of civil law and the other in the world of canon law. Somehow, aware of the similarities and differences of both juridic "languages," they must have the talent and patience to walk a fine line between lawlessness and rigidity if they expect the Code to be an effective element of pastoral life. In short, they must become juridically learned in their ecclesial field and fully responsible in the exercise of administrative discretion.

The Council's ecclesiology and the specific juridic character of the Code are two important foundations on which to build a proper interpretation of the law. They exemplify the need for intellectual caution and acumen when studying the canons and implementing them on the local scene. Many other factors must be taken into account as well. One of these factors is the legal context. The canons must be examined not only from the perspective of their textual composition but also from the viewpoint of their position in the Code. It may be helpful therefore to provide the reader with an overview of the entire Code and to highlight certain canonical institutes and even individual canons.

An Overview of the Code

The Code is composed of 1752 canons divided into seven Books: "General Norms"; "The People of God"; "The Teaching Office of the Church"; "The Office of Sanctifying in the Church"; "The Temporal Goods of the Church"; "Sanctions in the Church"; and "Processes." The only official version of the Code is the Latin text published in the *Acta Apostolicae Sedis* (Vol. 75, 1/25/83, and its appendix of corrections, 9/22/83). Unlike the 1917 Code, however, the newly promulgated Code has been translated into modern languages with the authorization of the Apostolic See—although such authorized translations are not considered the official text. The promulgated version contains the apostolic constitution of promulgation, *Sacrae disciplinae leges,* a preface containing a short history of canon law and the steps of revision, the canons themselves, and a table of contents. Later editions of the Code will certainly contain an index and a critical apparatus with a list of *fontes,* or sources, pertinent to each canon.

Book I: "General Norms" ("De Normis Generalibus"). The First Book (cc. 1–203) treats the juridic principles and institutes common to all the canons of the Code. It is divided into eleven titles, which offer definitions and general rules about ecclesiastical laws, custom, general decrees and instructions,

statutes, prescription, and the computation of time. Several titles lay the foundation for the exercise of governance in the Church: title IV on individual administrative acts such as dispensations; title VI on physical and juridic persons; title VII on juridic acts; title VIII on the power of governance; and title IX on ecclesiastical offices.

Many of the norms in this Book are technical but very important for the proper interpretation of later canons. Most of this section relies on canonical tradition. The following are a few points that may be of general interest.

Canons 1–6 are introductory rules explaining the limits and applicability of the canons. Canon 6 is especially important since it clarifies the abrogating function of the Code. One should note that, unlike the 1917 Code, it does not abrogate particular laws if they are not contrary to the Code even though they may touch on matters that are substantially (*ex integro*) regulated by universal law.

Canon 11 indicates that only those who have been baptized or received into the Catholic Church are bound by ecclesiastical laws, an ecumenical alteration of the former Code which theoretically bound all baptized persons, even non-Catholics, unless they were explicitly exempted in a particular canon.

Canon 87 is an important canon since it states the principle that the diocesan bishop has the right to dispense from all universal disciplinary laws unless such a dispensation is explicitly reserved to the Apostolic See. The canon, pastoral in its wording, improves the text of *De episcoporum muneribus,* from which it is taken. The canon is significant since it recognizes that this dispensing power is not delegated but is part of the bishop's pastoral office.

Canons 113–123 contain the norms concerning juridic persons, material treated in the 1917 Code in Book II, *"De Personis."* Although canon 113 uses the term "moral person" in regard to the Catholic Church and the Apostolic See, the Code generally abandons this term and replaces it with the term "juridic person."

Canon 127 has clarified the former Code concerning the necessity of consultation for the validity and liceity of juridic acts. Since the Code contains many canons requiring the consent or advice of consultative bodies, this general norm represents an important reference.

Canon 129, §2 affirms very simply that lay persons are able to participate in the exercise of the power of governance. This wording, however, is the result of a rather lengthy debate about the relationship of the sacrament of orders and the power of governance. It is an example of a canonical expression that recognizes the practice of the community yet leaves the underlying theological and legal question open to reflection and development. In fact, certain canons recognize such lay participation in governance (e.g., c. 494 on the diocesan finance officer and c. 1421 on the lay associate judge in a collegiate tribunal).

Canon 134 clarifies the meaning of the term "diocesan bishop" as distinct from the "local ordinary." The former title refers solely to the bishop who heads the diocese and not to auxiliaries or vicars. "Local ordinary" is a broader term that includes both the diocesan bishop and his vicars.

Book II: "The People of God" ("De Populo Dei"). The Second Book (cc. 204–746) is the largest in the Code. It is divided into three major parts: "The Christian Faithful" (cc. 204–329); "The Hierarchical Constitution of the Church" (cc. 330–572); and "Institutes of Consecrated Life and Societies of Apostolic Life" (cc. 573–746). The Book is not only named after the conciliar image of the Church; it also seeks to remain faithful to the vision of *Lumen Gentium* by emphasizing at the beginning all the persons who make up the Church and the roles they are called upon to play by their sacramental incorporation into Christ.

One point to note throughout the Book is its emphasis on institutes and functions rather than on authority figures. While personal authority still is an important part of church life, the canons describe such authority more in terms of structures than persons. Thus, title VIII of the former Code was termed "Episcopal Power and Those Who Participate in It"; its parallel section in the revised Code, entitled *Particular Churches* and Their Groupings," treats the notion of the particular church (structure) prior to the chapter on bishops (authority). Other examples are found in the shift from the chapter entitled "Pastors" to one called "*Parishes,* Pastors and Parochial Vicars" and the change of the part entitled "Religious" to one entitled "*Institutes* of Consecrated Life." Treating structures first might seem impersonal. It is actually a subtle recognition of the need to stress first the equality of all the Christian faithful and then to highlight the differences in their rights and duties as arising from the offices that they fulfill in the Church rather than from the power that is bestowed upon them.

The first part of Book II is concerned with the role of all Christians in the Church. It begins by describing "christifideles" (c. 204) and articulating the rights and responsibilities common to all members of the Church. It then treats the unique vocation of lay persons. It concludes with norms regarding clerics, those who have received the order of deacon, presbyter, or bishop.

This part highlights the equality of all members and places the role of authority in the perspective of service. The list of fundamental Christian rights and responsibilities at the outset sets the tone, summarized nicely in the first canon of title I:

In virtue of their rebirth in Christ there exists among all the Christian faithful a true equality

with regard to dignity and the activity whereby all cooperate in the building up of the Body of Christ in accord with each one's own condition and function (c. 208).

The canons proceed to list a set of rights and responsibilities arising from one's human dignity and rebirth in baptism. This approach is truly a novel one, unparalleled in the 1917 Code, and deserving of careful study. The articulation of human and ecclesial rights holds many implications for the future life of the Church. It should be noted that the Code Commission explicitly arranged the first part of Book II according to this framework so that the fundamental equality of all the faithful and the special vocation of the laity would be properly highlighted.

The canons on the laity (cc. 224–231), though few in number, are a step forward in regard to this shift in ecclesiological perspective insofar as they clearly recognize the role of the laity in terms of deputation by baptism and confirmation. In this regard, the limitation to men of liturgical installation in the ministries of lector and acolyte (c. 230, §1) is a curiosity. The ministries do not require the reception of the sacrament of orders; the canon itself states that women may fulfill many liturgical functions, including that of lector, by temporary deputation; and the Code has scrupulously removed from the canons nearly every other distinction between men and women apart from eligibility for orders.

The section on clerics includes norms on seminaries (seen primarily as places of comprehensive clergy formation rather than as simply educational institutions as was the case in the 1917 Code), rules on incardination, the rights and obligations of clerics (including permanent deacons), and the manner in which the clerical state is lost. This part of the Book ends with norms on personal prelatures and associations of the faithful, an attempt to make real the right of association and assembly expressed generically in canon 215.

The second part of Book II treats the hierarchical constitution of the Church. It is divided into two sections: "Supreme Church Authority"; "Particular Churches and Their Groupings." In the first section, the canons on the Roman Pontiff and the college of bishops are doctrinal in nature and should be studied in connection with the Vatican Council's decrees. The synod of bishops is treated immediately after these initial canons, underscoring its importance as a universal consultative group whose purpose is to maintain a close unity between the pope and the bishops of the world. The section concludes with norms on cardinals, two brief canons on the Roman Curia (governed by particular law such as *Regimini Ecclesiae Universae*), and papal legates.

The second section of part II treats the particular

church, defined in accord with the Council as "a portion of the people of God which is entrusted for pastoral care to a bishop with the cooperation of the presbyterate" (c. 369). The most practical of the groupings of such particular churches is the conference of bishops (cc. 447–459). Despite some restrictions on its legislative activity, this canonical institute represents a marked change from the 1917 Code and offers a concrete expression of episcopal collegiality and subsidiarity. It is another structure that will have long-lasting and far-reaching effects in the Church.

Of interest to most pastoral ministers are the canons concerning the diocese and the parish (cc. 460–572). This treatment stresses the manner in which the diocesan bishop collaborates with the people of God—with his diocesan synod in legislative matters, with his vicars and the others in the diocesan curia in administrative and judicial matters, with his presbyterate and all the people of God in pastoral matters. Pastoral action is seen as a cooperative effort, particularly in the norms on the role of consultative bodies in the Church: at the diocesan level, the presbyteral council, the finance council, the college of consultors, and the pastoral council; at the parish level, the pastoral and finance councils. The canons on the parish confirm a number of recent pastoral developments: team pastorates; the involvement of deacons, religious, and laity in pastoral care of a parish; the possibility of limited terms for pastors; increased liturgical roles for lay persons; consultation of clergy and laity regarding personnel assignments; and pastoral care as the primary norm for the parish priest. One should note especially the duties of the parish priest, beautifully described in canons 528–529—texts taken substantially from the documents of Vatican II (cf. *CD* 30).

The last part of Book II concerns institutes of consecrated life and societies of apostolic life. This topic had originally been included under the heading of "associations of the faithful" to highlight the voluntary nature of those who gather together to follow the evangelical counsels. The promulgated version, however, treats the topic separately in order to emphasize the uniqueness of this state in the Church. There are several points of interest in this section. Institutes of consecrated life may be either religious institutes or secular institutes. The members of both kinds of institutes are consecrated to follow Christ by the profession of the evangelical counsels through public vows or other sacred bonds. Members of secular institutes, however, live "in the world and of the world" (c. 713, §2) and do not necessarily live in community. Societies of apostolic life are akin to institutes of consecrated life, but the members do not make public religious vows. The most important developments in this field are the more expansive implementation of the principle of subsidiarity, the relegation of many de-

cisions to the proper law of the institute, and the encouragement of institutes to be distinctive in their manner of following the gospel. This approach contrasts starkly with that of the 1917 Code which was meticulously detailed in its norms for religious and thereby encouraged not the uniqueness of individual institutes but their uniformity. In general, the definitions and basic norms contained in this section are very faithful to the conciliar directives of *Perfectae Caritatis, Lumen Gentium,* and *Christus Dominus.* The Code relies principally on the renewal of the constitutions and statutes of the individual institutes, in accord with universal law, to shape the future of religious institutes, secular institutes, and societies of apostolic life.

Book III: "The Teaching Office of the Church" ("De Ecclesiae Munere Docendi"). The Third Book (cc. 747–833) deals with various facets of the Church's teaching mission, a responsibility incumbent upon all its members by their sacramental configuration to Christ the Prophet. It includes canons on the ministry of the word (preaching and catechesis), missionary activity, the structures of education such as Catholic schools and universities, and the use of the mass media of television, radio, and printed publications.

Title I begins with six canons succinctly stating the theological presuppositions concerning the relationship of the ministry of the word to baptism, confirmation, and orders. Canon 759 states both the call of the laity to be witnesses of the good news and their participation in the ministry of the word with bishops and presbyters. The sacramental leitmotif is continued in chapter I on preaching. Bishops, priests, and deacons have the right by ordination to preach throughout the world unless the exercise of this ministry is restricted by particular law or the diocesan bishop (cc. 763–764). While the homily is reserved to bishops, priests, and deacons (c. 767), lay persons are permitted to preach in a church or oratory in accord with guidelines to be issued by the conference of bishops (c. 766). Chapter II on catechetical formation again stresses the common responsibility (*sollicitudo catechesis*) of all members of the Church, in particular bishops, priests, religious, parents, and catechists (cc. 773, 774, 776, 780).

Evangelization is described as a "fundamental duty of the people of God" for which all of the Christian faithful have responsibility (c. 781). The role of lay missionaries and the importance of missionary catechists are emphasized in order to bring the proclamation of the gospel, liturgical celebrations, and the works of charity to those who have only recently heard the good news (c. 785).

The section on Catholic education emphasizes the rights of parents and reinforces the responsibility of the bishop in all matters affecting the teaching of the faith. Added to the chapter on schools are two new chapters on Catholic universities and other institutes of higher learning and ecclesiastical universities and faculties. The norms seek to relate more closely the magisterial responsibility of bishops and the teaching of the theological sciences at the university level. These canons were the subject of much debate during the revision process. The need to protect academic integrity and freedom motivated the introduction of several amendments into the texts, especially clauses protecting personnel procedures found in university statutes (c. 810). Canon 812 states that teachers of the theological disciplines should have a mandate ("mandatum") from competent ecclesiastical authority. This norm is conducive to the structure of universities in Europe but may be difficult to implement in the United States where it is estimated that fifty percent of all Catholic institutes of higher learning are situated. This canon exemplifies the Code's method of stating a principle very briefly and leaving its specific implementation to the local area. Many questions are left unanswered, requiring study and decision in individual dioceses and at the level of the conference of bishops.

The rules on censorship are similar to those already in effect at the time of the Code's promulgation. Canon 830 suggests the possibility of a collaborative effort on the part of the conference of bishops to make available competent consultants or even a national commission of experts to assist the diocesan bishop in evaluating works for which ecclesiastical approval is sought.

In general, Book III combines the old with the new. It depends significantly on the conciliar decrees, and yet it draws many of its texts from the canonical tradition. At times, this results more in a juxtaposition of canons than in their integration, but the intent of the legislation is clearly to harmonize the norms. This desired harmony should be kept in mind when interpreting and applying the canons.

Book IV: "The Office of Sanctifying in the Church" ("De Ecclesiae Munere Sanctificandi"). The Fourth Book, consisting of canons 834–1253, is divided into three parts: "The Sacraments"; "Other Acts of Divine Worship"; and "Sacred Times and Places." Six general introductory canons concern the role of all of the people of God, configured to Christ the High Priest, in the Church's ministry of sanctification. Part I begins with some general canons on the sacraments, including an important ecumenical canon that specifies the conditions under which the sacraments of penance, Eucharist, and anointing of the sick may be shared with baptized non-Catholics (c. 844). It then treats in separate titles each of the seven sacraments: baptism, confirmation, Eucharist, penance, anointing of the sick, orders, and marriage.

Most of the norms in this part of the Code are already familiar to pastoral ministers since, with some exceptions, they have been in effect for several years. After the Vatican Council, the liturgy was gradually renewed by the issuance of new *ordines,* or liturgical rites, for the sacraments. Many of the rules found in these *ordines* are collected in this part of Book IV. One development that is fully supported by the canons is the close connection between the celebration of the sacraments and catechetical preparation. Several canons on the individual sacraments stress the teaching role of the parish priest and the parents and the cooperation of catechists in this task. It is within this context that the right to the sacraments, firmly defended in canon 843, must be understood:

§1. The sacred ministers cannot refuse the sacraments to those who ask for them at appropriate times, are properly disposed and are not prohibited by law from receiving them.

§2. Pastors of souls and the rest of the Christian faithful, according to their ecclesial function, have the duty to see that those who seek the sacraments are prepared to receive them by the necessary evangelization and catechetical formation, taking into account the norms published by the competent authority.

This is a more pastoral approach than that of the 1917 Code which was concerned principally with conditions for validity and liceity. It is also more person-oriented since it recognizes among all the Christian faithful varying but complementary responsibilities to be fulfilled prior to reception of the sacraments.

In regard to the first six sacraments, pastoral ministers may find the following norms of particular interest: the need for a founded hope (*spes fundata*) that the infant to be baptized will be educated in the Catholic faith (c. 868, §1, 2°); the age of confirmation to be determined by the conference of bishops if it is other than the age of discretion (c. 891); the preparation of children for First Communion, which alludes to the prior celebration of penance (c. 914); the right to receive Communion during a Eucharistic liturgy more than once on the same day (c. 917); the limitation of general absolution to exceptional cases (c. 961); the extension of diocesan faculties to hear confessions worldwide unless explicitly restricted (c. 967); and the "proper bishop" of the candidate for orders (c. 1016). The above are just a few examples of the many canons concerning the sacraments that should be carefully studied by pastoral ministers and others involved in catechetical formation. It will be especially important to compare the norms to the regulations in the *ordines* to determine whether any of the latter have been abrogated or amended.

The final title of this first part of Book IV concerns marriage. More than any of the other titles, these canons (cc. 1055–1165) involve a number of changes since the renewed *ordo* of marriage did not contain disciplinary norms—as did the other *ordines*. The revision represents a valuable development marked by a personalist dimension and a pastoral attitude, based closely on the teaching of *Gaudium et Spes* 48–52. One of the most important sections is the first chapter on pastoral care and preparation for marriage. Canon 1063, for example, stresses the responsibility of the entire ecclesial community not merely for the immediate preparation of the engaged couple but also for remote catechesis about marriage and for the support of married couples in their vocation. This pastoral approach to the sacrament, which differs significantly from that of the 1917 Code, is based on a renewed description of the nature of marriage as a "matrimonial covenant" involving a "partnership of the whole of life" (c. 1055). The canons also incorporate the jurisprudence developed by the Roman Rota—recognizing that due discretion of judgment and capacity to assume the essential obligations of marriage are indispensable prerequisites for valid marital consent (c. 1095). This title contains many other important norms including a simplification of canonical impediments, the introduction of fraud as a ground of nullity, and the exemption from canonical form of those who have abandoned the Catholic faith by a formal act. Given the lack of theological development regarding marriage and the contemporary crisis of the institution, the revised canons wisely provide a renewed pastoral approach and yet leave some of the theological questions open to further investigation and discussion.

The second part of Book IV treats other acts of worship: "The Sacramentals," "The Liturgy of the Hours," "Ecclesiastical Funeral Rites," and "The Veneration of the Saints, Sacred Images and Relics." Canon 1183 introduces the possibility of Catholic burial rites for catechumens, children not yet baptized, and baptized members of a non-Catholic ecclesial community whose minister is unavailable.

The final part of Book IV on sacred times and places includes norms on dedications and blessings, churches, oratories, private chapels, shrines, altars, cemeteries, and the celebration of feast days and days of penance. Earlier drafts of the Code had limited holy days of obligation in the universal law to Christmas and one Marian feast to be chosen by the conference of bishops; the conference could also add other holy days appropriate to its region. The promulgated version returns to the traditional list of ten holy days but grants the conference the right to eliminate holy days or transfer them to a particular Sunday (c. 1246). The conference is also granted the faculty to replace the obligation of fast and abstinence found in universal law with some other form of penance such as works of charity (c. 1253).

Book V: "The Temporal Goods of the Church" (*"De Bonis Ecclesiae Temporalibus"*). The Fifth Book (cc. 1254–1310) is the shortest Book of the Code. It includes norms on the acquisition and administration of goods; on contracts, in particular the alienation of ecclesiastical property; and on pious wills and foundations. The Book begins with a clear statement concerning the threefold purpose of temporalities in the Church: the regulation of divine worship, the support of the clergy and other ministers, and the pursuit of the works of the apostolate and of charity, particularly toward those in need (c. 1254). This is an area in which canon law and civil law intertwine, a fact recognized in canon 1290; it is also a section of the Code that requires careful "translation" and accommodation in places such as the United States. The initial statement of purpose for ecclesiastical temporalities helps to clarify the uniqueness of the Church, which is unlike other non-profit corporations. Even the fundamental notion of ownership needs interpretation since it is a Roman law concept quite distinct from the concept of divisible ownership found in the common law system. It is important for civil attorneys to consult with canon lawyers in this field so that a practical harmony will exist. Title IV on pious wills and foundations, for example, should be carefully studied by any civil attorney called upon to draw up a last will and testament leaving monies to an ecclesiastical institution with religious conditions to be fulfilled by the legatee.

Canon 1263 is a new canon that recognizes the right of the diocesan bishop to impose a moderate and proportionate assessment on public juridic persons (e.g., parishes) in order to support the ordinary expenses of diocesan administration. Canon 1262, however, maintains the principle that the free will offerings of the faithful are the principal source of funding for the Church. This approach is familiar to Americans but may be innovative in many areas of the world in which benefices, a system that is gradually being eliminated in the Church, have been the main source of support for clergy (c. 1272). Another important canonical concept that requires careful study and interpretation is the alienation of "stable patrimony" (c. 1291), a traditional concept that is not so easily applicable to contemporary economic systems.

Such canons must be carefully studied by ecclesiastical administrators who accept a fiduciary responsibility for the goods of the Church and are called by the norms to accountability. The various references to consultation, budgeting, financial reporting, and canonical requirements for juridic acts are all methods of promoting responsible stewardship at every level of church administration.

Book VI: "Sanctions in the Church" (*"De Sanctionibus in Ecclesia"*). The Sixth Book (cc. 1311–1399) considerably shortens the comparable section of the 1917 Code. The first part of the book offers general rules about ecclesiastical penalties: penalties in general; their purpose in the Church; who can incur a penalty and under what conditions; the different kinds of penalties (e.g., excommunication, interdict, suspension); how penalties are incurred and how they cease. The second part of the book considers specific ecclesiastical offenses and the penalties attached to them.

In general, penalties are treated as rather rare occurrences. The one hundred and one canons of the 1917 Code specifying individual offenses and their penalties have been reduced in the revised Code to thirty-six canons. Automatic penalties (*latae sententiae*) have been drastically reduced in accord with conciliar directives. Thus, in the 1917 Code there were thirty-seven different ways in which one might automatically (ipso facto) be excommunicated, while the revised Code lists only seven serious offenses to which a *latae sententiae* excommunication is attached. Most penalties must be specifically imposed by an ecclesiastical authority (*ferendae sententiae*).

Penalties are intended to help Christians to appreciate the disparity between their attitudes and actions and the values of the gospel proclaimed by the Church. In this sense, penalties are meant to be tools of the external forum to bring about personal repentance and reconciliation with the community. It is important therefore for pastoral ministers to be familiar with the norms in this Book, and in particular with the changes from the 1917 Code, in order to counsel others properly. Confessors should especially be attentive to canon 1357 regarding the remission of certain censures in the internal sacramental forum under certain conditions—an exception to the general rule that the remission of penalties is restricted to the external forum. It is also important to be aware of those penalties that are reserved to the Apostolic See.

Book VII: "Processes" ("De Processibus"). The last Book of the Code (cc. 1400–1752) treats various judicial and administrative procedures in five parts: "Trials in General"; "The Contentious Trial"; "Certain Special Procedures"; "Penal Procedure"; and "On the Manner of Procedure in Administrative Recourse and the Removal and Transfer of Pastors." These canons, rather technical in nature, have not been substantially changed from the norms of the former Code although innovations have been introduced, including several helpful to matrimonial tribunals.

There was quite a difference of opinion about the best method of revising this Book of the Code. Some felt that procedures, especially judicial procedures, are universally applicable and should rarely be tampered with. Unless timeworn principles are shown to be faulty, the universal process set down in 1917 should be as "true" today as it was then; it is based on human nature—which does not change. Others disagreed with this classicist viewpoint. They felt that the new needs of the people of God extended to procedures as much as to any other area of law. This difference of opinion about procedural theory was reflected in the fifth principle of revision approved by the Synod of Bishops:

In regard to procedural law, grave doubts have arisen as to whether or not decentralization (as it is called) in this matter should be admitted to a greater extent than is now practiced—that is, so that decentralization would extend to autonomy of the regional and national tribunals. Indeed, everyone knows that the arrangement of tribunals, their ranks, their manner of procedure, the proofs admitted by them to establish truth, and the like, can be greatly influenced in individual nations and regions by the procedural rules of the various places. . . . It is certainly clear that for the administration of justice, one must preserve at different steps a certain amount of unified organization; the lack of such organization and unity might give occasion or offer an excuse for uncertainty of judgment, or give rise to fraud and many other disagreeable consequences, or finally cause the matter to be brought to the attention of the Apostolic See.

The implementation of the principle involved a compromise: the procedural law in the Code was to be broadened and given a more general and universal form while regional authorities were to be empowered to enact local norms.

The Code retains the traditional approach to procedural law by presenting the contentious case as the general norm. The first two parts of Book VII describe a judicial system in which two parties enter into an action against each other. It is a system in which the parties "join issues" (*contestatio litis*) before a judge who, after evidence is elicited, resolves the dispute through a sentence. This general process is contained in the first two hundred and seventy-one canons of the Book (cc. 1400–1670). Cases concerning matrimonial nullity are governed by the general rules for contentious cases (c. 1691) and by twenty-one special canons (cc. 1671–1691).

This approach to procedure sometimes causes problems since most ecclesiastical tribunals are utilized almost exclusively for matrimonial cases in which the parties may not be in conflict at all about the alleged nullity. Often, a diocesan tribunal is not called upon to settle a dispute about rights but to conduct an information-gathering exercise about the existence or absence at the time of the marriage of all the elements required for validity. Some had hoped to see the revised canons reflect the centrality of the matrimonial procedure in the Church's judicial activity rather than treat it as a species of the ordinary contentious process.

Given the decision to retain the traditional contentious format, however, the revised Code has introduced several norms that will prove helpful to tribunals throughout the world. Some of these norms retain innovations found in the *American*

Procedural Norms, the particular procedural law for the United States abrogated by the promulgation of the Code. Canon 1673 recognizes as a ground of competence for marriage cases the domicile of the petitioner when both parties reside within the jurisdiction of the same conference of bishops. Canon 1425 authorizes the conference to permit the use of a single judge in first instance in dioceses in which collegiate tribunals are not practical. Canon 1598 recognizes the need for judges to exercise discretion in regard to the publication of the acts, provided that the right of defense on the part of both parties is scrupulously protected. This norm, important for the protection of confidentiality in tribunal matters, is the direct result of interventions in the revision process by representatives of the American hierarchy.

With the abrogation of the *American Procedural Norms,* the appellate procedure for annulment cases in the United States was significantly altered. Particular law had permitted the *administrative* finalization of a declaration of nullity by the general secretary of the National Conference of Catholic Bishops, who was empowered to dispense the defender of the bond from the obligation to appeal an affirmative decision of first instance. The Code now requires a *judicial* finalization of the case, namely, the review of the affirmative sentence of nullity of first instance by a college of three judges and a defender of the bond. If, after reviewing the case, the appellate college judges that the sentence should be confirmed, it issues a decree that definitively completes the case. If the case is not confirmed by the review panel, it must be reexamined in a second trial on the appellate level. This procedure, drawn from the post-conciliar legislation found in *Causas matrimoniales,* revises considerably the requirement of the 1917 Code that a full second trial be held on the appellate level for all annulment cases.

One of the suggested procedural innovations missing from the Code is the institute of administrative tribunals. The members of the Code Commission voted at their final plenary session (10/81) to introduce such tribunals into the Church's legal system as an option that conferences of bishops could consider for their own areas rather than as an institute that would be mandatory for all conferences. This recommendation was responding to the seventh principle of revision, which called for administrative tribunals to be established in the Church in order to promote the protection of subjective rights. The notion of administrative tribunals, however, was entirely deleted from the Code prior to its promulgation.

Although administrative tribunals are not an option at this time, the Code contains other forms of redress for those whose rights are violated by administrative actions. Canons 1732–1739 specify a procedure of hierarchical recourse against individual administrative acts. In practice, such recourse is realistic when it concerns decisions made by authorities subject to the diocesan bishop, since the review is local. When such recourse, however, reaches the level of the dicasteries of the Apostolic See, the process can be rather cumbersome and at times ineffective. Canon 1733 helps the situation somewhat by encouraging the establishment of diocesan offices or commissions to facilitate equitable solutions to conflicts arising from administrative decisions, a concept similar to the due process system approved by the National Conference of Catholic Bishops in 1969 and operative in many dioceses in the United States. Such offices, however, are limited to voluntary settlements (cc. 1713–1716); they cannot issue definitive administrative or judicial determinations or settle matters in a manner contrary to the will of one or all of the parties in conflict.

The final canons of the Code (cc. 1740–1752) outline the administrative procedure for removing or transferring a pastor. (The penal process is governed by cc. 1717–1731.) Canon 1741 clarifies the grounds for such an administrative action in a manner more suited to the contemporary Church than that found in the former Code. In addition, the norms specify more precisely the administrative steps to be followed in order to safeguard the rights of both pastor and diocesan bishop. The process includes consultation by the bishop with two pastors selected by him from a special group established for this purpose by the presbyteral council. Although this last section deals with a procedure that is rarely used, it does reaffirm, as so much of the Code does, the nature of church administration as a work of service and justice committed to the spirit of equity and to "the salvation of souls, which is always the supreme law of the Church" (c. 1752).

Concluding Reflections

This General Introduction has considered several issues pertinent to a proper understanding of the 1983 Code: a short synopsis of the history of church law emphasizing certain significant periods; the post-conciliar process by which the Code was revised; the Code's fundamental ecclesiological orientation; the uniqueness of its juridic character, particularly for those influenced by the common law tradition; and an overview of the various parts of the Code highlighting some of its new elements. This presentation has had the limited goal of motivating the reader to study church law carefully and to incorporate it properly into ecclesial practice. The law, after all, is not meant to be a text for academic rumination but an effective instrument to guide the life of the people of God. The Code is so deeply rooted in the decrees of Vatican II that its practical intent should be obvious—the promotion of pastoral renewal and reform.

The Church's first authoritative codification was promulgated seventeen years after the turn of the century. It implemented the current view of the Church and its mission, particularly in the light of Vatican Council I and developments during the ensuing decades. The Church's second authoritative codification has been promulgated seventeen years before the same century draws to a close. It too hopes to implement a contemporary understanding of the Church and its mission, expressed so carefully in Vatican Council II and subsequent teaching. As law has done from the beginning, the Code tries to articulate the order and discipline that the Church needs at this time in salvation history. The message of the Code is clear: the Church needs continued renewal and reform. How can a code of laws hope to assist the Church to achieve such a noble goal?

Like other periods of church reform, the post-Vatican II Church requires laws to stabilize long-term shifts of practice and discipline. The Code seeks to achieve this goal by clarifying rights and duties. Clarity is needed in order to dispel the confusion that has arisen prior to and after the Council. It was difficult even for trained pastoral ministers to keep track of the Church's regulations during the quarter-century preceding the promulgation. The Code collects into a single volume all of the juridic changes that have occurred as part of the Church's effort at self-renewal. In doing so, it integrates them into the overall canonical tradition. The laws, so clarified, are not so vague and perplexing as before.

The Code does not reproduce all of the Church's legal history. It distills past decrees into a fairly simple system. Many pastoral ministers may have to admit that they have not even read all of the conciliar decrees much less studied, synthesized, and appropriated them. At least in regard to matters of juridic import, the Code provides a synthesis that should spark more intensive study of as well as fidelity to the foundations of the conciliar reform. This synthesis is not buried in a textual labyrinth. It is available in the vernacular not only to pastoral ministers but to all the people of God. One of the simplest means of promoting rights in the Church is to give to those endowed with such rights a book which articulates them.

Principles or norms that are clear, fairly simple, and readily available for consultation and guidance are the classic requirements of any institutional reform. The Code contributes a great deal to the fulfillment of these needs. It is a contribution that is necessarily temporary. History is not likely to alter its inexorable course. Church practice will continue to evolve and, with it, canon law. The Code will require ongoing interpretation, amendment and, eventually, abrogation. Its clarity will be dulled, its simplicity marred, and the resultant complexity will make it more difficult for those who are not canonists to be knowledgeable about extant law. Nonetheless, for the moment, the revised Code will

accomplish its important task and spur on the process of renewal.

Principally, the revised law serves to strengthen and solidify present-day ecclesial structures and trends. When certain innovations are stabilized, they cease to be thought of as experimental and begin to have a long-term effect. This steadying function provides a new stimulus to make the structures work, highlights the important values involved, deepens the motivation of the participants, and provides accountability systems for the long haul. The following are a few examples of the beneficial developments to be found in the revised Code:

a. the reliance on the image of the Church as the people of God, whose members are sacramentally commissioned to carry out the threefold mission of Christ as priest, prophet, and king;

b. the recognition of the fundamental equality of individual Christians and the rights and responsibilities that flow from baptism and confirmation;

c. the enhanced role of lay persons in the Church;

d. the shift from an emphasis on persons endowed with authority to juridically recognized functions of service;

e. the promotion of the value of subsidiarity in the hierarchical communion and an acceptance of the resultant structural pluralism;

f. the stress on the particular church as a "portion of the people of God" (*portio populi Dei*) and the importance of the diocesan bishop and particular law;

g. the implementation of structures of consultation at all levels of the Church;

h. the promotion of accountability in regard to temporalities;

i. the priority given to pastoral care and the introduction of greater flexibility into canonical institutes in order to facilitate the realization of the Church's fundamental mission (e.g., in parish structures, parish personnel, the celebration of the sacraments, the revision of ecclesiastical penalties).

Some may find this role of law hard to accept. For them law is cold and unyielding, impersonal and static, ultimately devoid of love and the Spirit. It cannot achieve reform; if anything, it thwarts reform, impedes growth, and retards progress. This raises an attitudinal (and ultimately theological) problem whose impact on the success of the revised Code is crucial. Even with its inevitable gaps and flaws, the Code is a sound pastoral document that *can* achieve its purpose. Whether it *does,* however, depends on its reception by the people of God, particularly by pastoral ministers. Receptivity to the Code depends on the individual's attitude toward the role of law in the Church. This has already been mentioned in some detail in the treatment of the influence of a common law mentality on the interpretation and application of canon law. The question of attitude is a very profound issue with a pervasive impact on the whole canonical system.

There are many attitudes in the contemporary Church that may distort the law and nullify its ecclesial effect. There are those who are ignorant of, or consciously dismiss, history. They are like little children playing with shells on the beach, unaware that behind them stretches the vast sea of knowledge that has cast their playthings before them. There are those who fail to grasp the theological underpinnings of church law. Their uninformed application of the law identifies them as the voluntarists of our present day, all too ready to exercise power but bored by the tedium of understanding. There are neo-juridicists who have welcomed the promulgation of the Code as if it would restore some long-forgotten, idyllic, and, in the end, imaginary time of uniformity and regimentation. They do not appreciate the implications of the legal system found in the Code. Finally, there are antinomians, so foolishly imprisoned by the very culture they hope to evangelize. They reject all that is "institutional" as alien to the gospel, blithely unconcerned that they are part of the historical pendulum of reaction against authority and perplexed by the need to live out the faith in a "visible" Church.

If these attitudes predominate, the Code will not achieve its true purpose of strengthening conciliar aims, solidifying desirable ecclesial structures, and promoting the rights and responsibilities of all in the Church. A new attitude toward law is needed, Paul VI's "new way of thinking." This element of the revision process cannot be achieved by the Code Commission, by consultation, or by theological or canonical experts. It can be achieved only by persons of faith who receive the law, assimilate it, apply it, and obey it.

The Code does not masquerade as the means of salvation. Salvation remains always and only the gift of God. Nonetheless, the law does represent for the people of God part of the contemporary way of "putting on Christ," the Church's vision of itself at this moment in its history. It defines and regulates the structures of church order and discipline, its decisions about itself, and its organization. Canon law is a symbol of the Church's unwillingness to abandon the weighty implications of Christ's incarnation or to relegate God's action to the purely spiritual realm. For those who accept the Code into their lives in an authentic manner, it provides an identifiable ground of commonality with the other members of the Church, underlines the basis of their identity as the people of God, and articulates legitimate expectations. In other words, the Code does not itself continue the conciliar reform—it simply offers an opportunity and a means to achieve that end. How well the opportunity is utilized depends on the people of God and the working of the Holy Spirit. If this commentary on the Code assists some members of the Church in this task, the cherished goal of its authors will be happily achieved.

When the elders in Jerusalem acceded to many of the norms proposed by St. Paul for his Gentile converts, they felt that they had made a good determination, a practical decision that was faithful to Jesus and therefore imbued with the Holy Spirit. This decision was communicated to the Christians at Antioch, accepted by them and faithfully implemented. Later on, when the long-term effect of the norms had been achieved and the Church had expanded throughout the Mediterranean, the original rules were hardly alluded to; some in fact were abandoned in favor of newer regulations. While law remains, individual laws have a life that is ephemeral at best. The promulgation of the 1983 Code is really not so different from that ancient letter to the Antiochians. Those who come to understand the canons and implement them properly might very well join with the elders of the Jerusalem community in saying: "Today, this way of putting on Christ, this way of being Church, seems good to us and to the Holy Spirit."

BOOK I
GENERAL NORMS

[cc. 1–203]

Book I of the Code lays the foundations on which our legal system rests. At first sight, the structure does not appear very cohesive; it seems to be composed of disparate elements. There is, however, a certain unity behind those two hundred three canons, which are divided into eleven titles. This unity can be best found and grasped by searching out the questions to which, ultimately, the canons respond. Those questions were clearly in the minds of the drafters, although they are not mentioned in the legal text or context. Yet, the true clue to the understanding of the canons is there in those very real, but unspoken, questions.

The Christian Church is spread far and wide. The Code comes from the head of the Catholic Church, the Bishop of Rome. The first query comes quite naturally: just how far does the binding force of the Code extend? The answers are found in the six introductory canons (cc. 1–6). These canons also give precise instructions for handling the transition from the former Code to the revised one.

The next questions should be about the norms themselves: how can they be recognized as authentic? How should they be interpreted? The first five titles (cc. 7–95) give the answers. They speak of laws and customs; of general decrees and instructions, in view of the common good; and of single administrative acts, in view of some particular good. As a quasi-appendix, some canons are added on statutes and bylaws, of interest mainly to corporations and associations.

Then comes a momentous question: who are those entitled to act within the legal system of the Church? Thus, canons 96–123 define and describe the physical and juridic persons who have rights and duties in the community. This is a central title in the Code.

Once it is known who those persons are, questions about their actions must be raised. Clearly, not every action of theirs has a special standing and brings about a legal effect. The question "What is a juridic act?" must, therefore, be settled. The answer comes in a few terse rules (cc. 124–128).

Further, many legal acts in the Church originate in the executive power. Thus, these questions arise: how can the authentic acts of this power be recognized? How should executive power function in proper balance and harmony with the other branches of power? Some, though not all, of the answers are found in canons 129–144 of Book I.

The power of governance leads to another issue, that of the ecclesiastical offices in which all powers are vested. Hence, more questions develop: what is an ecclesiastical office? How does it function? Cer-tainly this is a foundational issue. General answers are given in canons 145–196, and particular ones will be given in other Books in connection with a specific office.

Finally, two other issues enter. They do not follow quite logically from what preceded them, but they, too, are of general interest in law. The first one regards prescription: how can rights be acquired and lost through the passage of time? The practical rules given in canons 197–199 extend to all rights, not only to rights concerning property. The other issue concerns the reckoning of the passage of time (cc. 200–203): how should years, months, and days be computed in canon law? Legal time is not necessarily the same as that indicated by calendars and clocks.

The scope of Book I ("General Norms") in the revised Code is more far-reaching than it was in the former Code; there it was virtually restricted to the issues of laws, customs, and a few types of executive acts. The revised approach is significantly better than the former one was. While the substance of legal concepts has not changed much, there are innovations. Title III ("General Decrees and Instructions") is new, while title IV ("Individual Administrative Acts") is a combination of old and new. The persons, physical or juridic, are much better defined now than they were in the former law, and so are juridic acts. The rules concerning the power to govern (jurisdiction, in the older terminology) have been revised; they are conveyed through a more theological vocabulary. The duty to serve by those who preside could, perhaps, have found a better legal expression. When all is considered, the doctrine of ecclesiastical offices has been significantly updated, as have the norms on prescription and the computation of time.

The spirit that penetrates the whole Code is forcefully displayed in this first Book. It is clear that the modern Church intends to live by statutory laws and does not really want to give any serious role to customs. This, of course, raises the issue of how Catholic people can ever express their *sensus fidelium* in the practical life of the Church, if they are steadily impeded in expressing themselves in customs.

The importance of executive offices has been enhanced; their capacity to issue general decrees and instructions has been enlarged. This is a new quasi-legislative power. It is likely to lead to a greater control and centralization in the interpretation and implementation of general laws. There is a new potential for the increase of uniformity in the Church.

On the other hand, the bishops will play a larger

role in administering the universal laws. Their dispensing power is greatly enlarged. This may well lead to more exceptions regarding the uniform norms.

It is not easy to handle the power to govern in purely legal terms. The evangelical mandate is too complex for the law. The Lord gave the power of the keys to Peter and the other apostles, but he enjoined them, as well, to be the servants of the people. Law tends to put all the emphasis on the first task and remain silent about the second. The revised Code shows little progress in solving this problem.

Book I does not say anything about the need for the reception of the laws. There is no doubt, however, that the law will not become a vital force in the community unless it is received by people. A validating ratification of the laws is not being advocated here, rather only a statement of the absolute need for the intelligent appropriation of the norms. To receive the law well, the community must understand the value the law intends to uphold; then the faithful must reach for it freely, moved by internal conviction. Christian people cannot act according to their innate dignity unless they act with intelligence and freedom.

It was said of old: custom is the best interpreter of laws. This maxim can also be put into more concrete terms: there is no better interpreter of the laws than the people of God, freely dedicated and well-informed.

CANONS AND COMMENTARY

The Code Is for the Latin Church

Canon 1 — The canons of this Code affect only the Latin Church.

The universal Catholic Church consists of particular churches in communion with each other and with the Church of Rome. Each particular church is governed (apart from rare exceptions) by a bishop. The universal Church is governed by the Bishop of Rome. As the diocesan bishop is the principle of unity for a portion of the people of God, so the Bishop of Rome is the principle of unity for the entire people of God. The universal Church is divided into the eastern and the western branches, distinguishable mainly by the different rites they follow in their liturgical celebrations and by their separate administrative structures.

Each of the eastern churches has its own hierarchy, presided over by a patriarch, or a major archbishop, or a metropolitan. The Latin Church is ruled by the Bishop of Rome in his quality as "Patriarch of the West"—a rarely used title.

The present Code applies to the Latin Church alone, as did the Code of 1917. Although each eastern church has its own theological and legal traditions, a unified code for all of them is under preparation, intended to become their common law. This preparation is being carried out under the authority of the pope, as the head of the universal Church.

Liturgical Laws Have Their Own Autonomy

Canon 2 — For the most part the Code does not define the rites which are to be observed in celebrating liturgical actions. For this reason current liturgical norms retain their force unless a given liturgical norm is contrary to the canons of the Code.

The scope of the Code of Canon Law is circumscribed, even in the Latin Church. Thus, it does not apply to the field of *liturgy*, which retains its own autonomy. Should there be, however, a clear and irreconcilable conflict between the existing liturgical norms and the Code, the Code must prevail.

The sharp distinction between canon law and liturgical norms follows from the natural difference between the external structures of the Church and its intimate life of worship. Each needs to be ordered and regulated but in different ways. The main purpose of the canons is to build, to support, and to safeguard the necessary societal structures. The aim of liturgical norms is to help the community to recall God's mighty deeds and to experience his presence through the celebration of the mysteries. In this difference of intent there is an important clue regarding the interpretation of each set of norms.

There should be stability in the external order; hence, exceptions from structural and disciplinary laws should not be easily granted. There should be flexibility in worship according to the spiritual needs of the people; hence, adaptations should be more easily forthcoming.

The Code Leaves Concordats Intact

Canon 3 — **The canons of the Code neither abrogate nor derogate from the pacts entered upon by the Apostolic See with nations or other political societies. They therefore continue in force as presently, notwithstanding any prescriptions of this Code to the contrary.**

In this canon the limits of the scope of the Code are further defined. It regulates the internal life of the Latin Church; it does not apply to international legal relations. The activities of the Church among the family of nations and its participation in international organizations are subject to the general norms of international law. Since the Holy See is an international juridic person, it has the capacity to conclude agreements with other such persons, i.e., all sovereign states and international associations and organizations formed by them. An agreement between the Holy See and a sovereign state is known as a concordat.

The rule of the canon is simple and absolute: the Code does not reach out into the field of international law. Should there ever be a conflict between the canons and the pacts, the pacts must stand.

Vested Rights and Privileges Are Untouched

Canon 4 — **Acquired rights as well as privileges granted up to this time by the Apostolic See to physical or juridic persons remain unimpaired provided they are presently in use and have not been revoked, unless they are expressly revoked by the canons of this Code.**

Even within the legal life of the Latin Church, the scope of the Code is restricted. It leaves intact all rights "acquired" by physical or juridic persons, and all privileges received by them.

Acquired right, known also as vested right, is a technical concept in canon law. It is a right obtained through some form of "acquisition." The term is taken from Roman law, in which it meant primarily the acquisition of the ownership of a thing. In canon law its sense is broadened. Acquired right means all rights obtained through a completed legal transaction, either between individual persons (e.g., through a contract of sale) or between an individual and some public authority (e.g., through accepting an appointment to an office). Acquired right has a close analogy to the *ius in re* ("right attached to a thing") of the Romans, although it is broader. Note that the acquisition must be completed; no acquired right results from an incomplete transaction, e.g., from a contract of sale on credit.

Privilege is a specific right or a particular freedom arising from the gratuitous concession of the legislator or of someone who has the necessary executive power. It is always a favor. Even if it had been requested by the recipient, it is not the result of contractual transaction. The new right or freedom arises on the strength of the grant alone.

Chapter IV of title IV in Book I (cc. 76–84) contains detailed norms for the granting, the use, and the cessation of privileges. The present canon simply states that privileges existing at the time of the promulgation of this Code will continue.

Transition: Customs Preserved or Suppressed

Canon 5 — **§1. Presently existing universal or particular customs contrary to the prescriptions of these canons which are reprobated by the very canons of this Code are entirely suppressed, nor are they permitted to revive in the future. Other customs are also considered suppressed unless the Code expressly provides otherwise or unless they are centenary or immemorial, in which case they can be tolerated if in the judgment of the ordinary they cannot be removed due to circumstances of place and persons.**

§2. Presently existing universal or particular customs which are apart from the law (*praeter ius*) are preserved.

The legislator still continues to define the scope of the Code. The issue is now the applicability of the canons to a field where at the time of their promulgation, custom reigned—a rare situation in our modern Church. (Detailed rules for the development and recognition of future customs are given in title II of Book I [cc. 23–28]; here canon 5 gives the norms for the continuation of customs existing at the time of the coming into force of the Code.)

Paragraph one distinguishes two main types of custom: one *against* the law, in conflict with it; the other *existing side by side with* the law, not in conflict with it. If a custom is against the law, a further distinction is made: it is either explicitly disapproved, or it is not.

If a custom is against the law and disapproved, it must be abandoned forthwith, and must not be reintroduced, ever.

If a custom is against the law but not disapproved, it must still be discontinued, except in two cases: (1) when the Code itself allows it; (2) when it is "centenary or immemorial," and by the judgment of the ordinary it is prudent to tolerate it.

Paragraph two directs that all customs, universal or particular, existing side by side with the law should be retained and observed.

Transition: Laws Preserved or Suppressed

Canon 6 — §1. When this Code goes into effect, the following are abrogated:
1° the Code of Canon Law promulgated in 1917;
2° other universal or particular laws contrary to the prescriptions of this Code, unless particular laws are otherwise expressly provided for;
3° any universal or particular penal laws whatsoever issued by the Apostolic See, unless they are contained in this Code;
4° other universal disciplinary laws dealing with a matter which is regulated *ex integro* by this Code.
§2. The canons of this Code insofar as they refer to the old law are to be assessed also in accord with canonical tradition.

The promulgation of the Code signifies a new beginning in the legal life of the Latin Church. The former laws must cede their place to new and revised ones. In paragraph one we have the norms for this transition.
The following laws are terminated:

• all laws contained in the Code of 1917—this clearly includes also the termination of the validity of all disciplinary documents that were promulgated exclusively for the implementation of the same Code;

• all universal penal laws; also particular laws that are found to be in clear conflict with the norms of the present Code—unless there is a specific provision in this Code itself for the retaining of some particular laws;

• all universal and particular penal laws—provided they were enacted by the Holy See itself, unless any of them is explicitly enacted in this Code again;

• all universal disciplinary laws in force before the promulgation of this Code—provided their subject matter has been entirely revised by this legislation.

By implication the following laws remain and continue to bind;

• all universal and particular laws not contrary to the Code;

• all particular norms contrary to the Code, provided the Code itself grants them exception.

Paragraph two provides a general principle of interpretation. Whenever a norm has its roots in earlier tradition, the meaning of the norm should be construed with the help of that tradition. In other terms, the neglect of history may well lead to a false construction; often enough to a rigid and inflexible one as well.

In Summary

The Extent of the Binding Force of the Code

The Code binds the Latin branch of the Catholic Church only (c. 1).
The following fields or objects remain as a rule outside of the binding force of the Code, even within the Latin Church:

• liturgy (c. 2);

• conventions and pacts concluded by the Holy See (c. 3);

• acquired rights (c.4);

• privileges granted by the Holy See (c. 4);

• customs, universal or particular, not in conflict with the Code (c. 5).

Exceptions may exist, but they must be proved.

The Norms Regulating the Transition
from the 1917 Code to the 1983 Code

As regards customs, universal or particular (c. 5):

• if they are in conflict with the Code and explicitly disapproved, they are terminated forthwith, and must not be reintroduced;

• if they are in conflict with the Code but not disapproved, *and* centenary or immemorial, *and* judged by the ordinary as difficult to remove, they may be tolerated;

• if they are not in conflict but merely "outside" of the law, they should continue.

The statutory laws that are terminated by this Code (c. 6):

• the Code of 1917 in its entirety, including subsequent derivative legislation;

• all universal laws in conflict with the Code;

• all particular laws in conflict, unless excepted by the Code itself;

• all universal and particular laws of penal character, unless incorporated into the Code itself;

• all universal disciplinary laws not in conflict, but obsolete since their subject matter underwent total reorganization.

Other laws (all universal and particular laws) that retain their binding force are those:

- not contained in the Code of 1917;

- not in conflict with any of the canons;

- not of penal character;

- not about some matter that underwent a total reorganization by the Code.

TITLE I
ECCLESIASTICAL LAWS
[cc. 7–22]

Law Comes into Existence: Promulgation

Canon 7 — A law comes into existence when it is promulgated.

The application of particular norms mostly depends on the general understanding of the meaning of the *law*.

Promulgation is no more than one stage in the life span of the law.

Here an organic understanding of the law is presented, with a description of the various stages in its development.

The question "What is law?" has occupied the minds of philosophers ever since Socrates pondered the issue, and throughout the centuries it has provoked so many divergent answers.

As yet, no firm consensus has emerged—but there is no need to despair. It is possible to reach a good understanding of what law is, provided it is realized from the first moment of the search that the conclusion will flow from the premises, that is, the answer given at the end will depend on how the question is raised in the beginning. Indeed, there is a great variety of definitions because the issues can be raised in many different ways. There is no need to examine them all. Let attention be focused on just two radically different ways of initiating the inquiry.

(a) The question "What is law?" can be raised in the abstract world of essences, and there alone. "What is law?"—that is, "What is the very essence of a binding norm given to a community, irrespective of the issue whether the community lives by it?" That is how Aquinas raised the question, and he reached his answer accordingly:

law is ordinance of reason
    [a norm inspired by reason having for its purpose to create order]
from the one who is in charge of the community for the sake of the common good

promulgated (cf. *Summa Theologiae* Iᵃ–IIᵃᵉ, 90A).

This definition holds in the abstract world of essences. That is, it holds in a world that abstracts from any historical reality, in which no question is raised about the actual use of the norm by the community.

(b) The question "What is law?" can be raised within the context of the existing order, in the order of *esse*. "What is law?"—that is, "What is the normative element in the mind and heart of people which actually, *actu,* moves them to act?" Then the question concerns a norm which has a working efficacy in the existential world. The answer is that the norm is the law, accepted and acted upon by a community of intelligent and free persons.

Thus, law is an analogous concept. Each definition of it is valid, but each in its own realm only. Those who assume, probably more subconsciously than reflectively, that law is a univocal concept will continue to search for its one and exclusive meaning. Those who know that the human mind is able to construe an abstract world (non-existent but having great logical coherence) and that the same mind is able to know the real world (existent but often not so coherent) will find no difficulty in admitting that the term "law" can have two different meanings, each being valid in its own world. Thus, the point of departure of the inquirer determines the outcome of his or her search.

These reflections are not idle flights of fancy. Stress on the first type of understanding has led, often enough, to the making of laws which were intellectually attractive but unsuitable for a given community, and to the neglect of the community's role in understanding the laws and implementing them. Canon law, in particular, has suffered and is still suffering from this essentialist approach.

For a more comprehensive and balanced understanding of what law is, let us describe the "life of the law" in the midst of a community. Every law has its own preordained stages of life:

- at one point it is conceived,

- at another it is born,

- then it lives,

- until it dies or fades away.

These stages of life are not mere metaphors.

The law is *conceived* in a human mind. When the legislator perceives a value suitable and desirable for the community, and when he or she is satisfied that the community has the strength to reach out for that value and appropriate it, then, in reality, the legislator is conceiving a new law, that is, a new norm of action to be followed by the community.

The law is *born* into this world when it is promulgated, that is, when a formal mandate is given by the legislator to the community to pursue the value embedded in the new norm.

The definition of Aquinas covers the life of the law up to this point. For him, once the "ordinance of reason" is promulgated, it is law. The essence of law is there, in the norm held up for implementation.

Yet, no matter how good that norm is, it has little life at that point in the existing world, in the order of *esse. To live,* the norm must become a vital force in the community, informing the minds and hearts of the people, directing their operations. They must come to the appreciation of the value the law intends to promote. Then they must freely decide to act on the norm proposed and thus implement the law. When this happens there is a new fact: the norm is a force moving the group; it has been received by the community.

The law received is clearly different from the law which has been promulgated only. The meaning proclaimed by the legislator has been re-created by the community and has become an effective force in its life.

Finally, human laws are mortal, as people are. Once they have fulfilled their purpose, they should *die.* If they linger on, they are a burden, and they drain the community of its strength.

That is the span of life of a law.

As described here, the law is a norm of action in the existing world, adopted and used by a community of free and intelligent persons in order to build well-balanced social structures. Such orderly structures are needed by everyone to grow peacefully in grace and wisdom. Note the specific marks: a norm *adopted* and *used;* both are in the order of *esse,* beyond the stage of promulgation. This description went one step further than Aquinas.

The way that law is conceived determines also how it is interpreted. If the concept includes the whole extent of the life of the law, its interpretation must develop with it—from the law's birth to its demise. It follows that responsible interpretation must be more than the declaration of a meaning which was there, clear and certain, *in se certa,* at the time of its promulgation.

The Norms for Promulgation

Canon 8 — **§1. Universal ecclesiastical laws are promulgated by being published in the official commentary *Acta Apostolicae Sedis* unless another form of promulgation is prescribed for individual cases. These laws become effective only after three months have elapsed from the date of that issue of** the *Acta,* **unless they have binding force immediately from the very nature of the matter they treat or unless the law itself specifically and expressly suspends its force for a shorter or longer period.**

§2. Particular laws are promulgated in a manner determined by the legislator, and they begin to bind one month from the date of promulgation, unless another time period is determined in the law itself.

The canon speaks for itself, and little explanation is needed. The time which elapses between the promulgation of the law and its coming into force is called *vacation* of the law.

In recent times, there has been an increasing trend to promulgate the laws independently from their publication in the *Acta Apostolicae Sedis,* although the *Acta* remains the source for their official text. Latin remains the official language of the laws. As a rule, the Holy See does not approve "authentic" translations; hence, every translation should be handled with caution.

Laws Are for the Future

Canon 9 — **Laws deal with the future and not the past, unless specific provision be made in the laws concerning the past.**

A law is a norm of action; it focuses on future actions. Therefore, no law can be retroactive. But a law can be termed retroactive in the sense that it directs an action to be performed in the future concerning an event in the past. For instance, a law may change the rules for concluding a valid contract; at the same time, it may direct that contracts invalidly concluded in the past should be deemed valid. Such a law is called retroactive.

Retroactive laws are often used to rectify the state of a person (e.g., a child is deemed legitimate) or a property transaction (the sale is validated); but, they have no place in the field of penal, or criminal, law. It would be unjust to charge someone on the basis of a law which did not exist or had no binding force at the time of the action.

In general, the right policy is to use retroactivity sparingly—and mostly to grant a favor or to redress an unjust situation not provided for previously by the law.

Invalidating and Incapacitating Laws

Canon 10 — **Only those laws which expressly state that an act is null or that a person is incapable of acting are to be considered to be invalidating or incapacitating.**

This canon contains a foundational rule which affects every part of the legal system in America. The rule is that no act should be regarded as null and void (i.e., non-existent in the world of law), and no person should be taken as disqualified (i.e., unable to act in the world of law), unless it can be shown beyond any shadow of a doubt that the legislator intended such extreme consequences. A mere prohibition to act is not enough to make a legal transaction invalid, or a person utterly disqualified. In canon law an action can be both illegal and legally effective at the same time; a doctrine alien to the Anglo-American common law. That is, canon law distinguishes between "absolute" and "relative" illegality; the former cancels out all effects, the other does not.

An invalidating law reaches directly *the act itself,* no matter who performs it. For example, for the alienation of ecclesiastical property of certain value the authorization of the Holy See is necessary. If such authorization is missing, the contract of sale is invalid—no matter who signed it.

An incapacitating law reaches directly *the person* who performs the act. For example, persons under the prescribed age are disqualified from contracting marriage, hence, such a person could not marry anybody.

The invalidating or incapacitating character of a norm should never be presumed; it should be proved from the very text of the law. It must be there "expressly." The term *expressly,* however, allows a variety of expressions, such as the act is *invalid, ineffective, null and void,* etc., or the person is *disqualified, unable to perform the act,* etc. No matter what the words are, they must clearly convey the same meaning: the legislator intends to invalidate the act or to incapacitate the person.

The law, however, need not always use negative terms to induce invalidity or incapacity. Often it simply states positively the essential requirements for the act to be valid or the qualifications for the person to be able to act. One should see especially canons 124–128 concerning juridic acts. Such positive norms are not invalidating or incapacitating laws in the literal sense, yet if not obeyed their impact is exactly the same. Of course they too must *expressly* state what are the essential conditions for the validity of the act or the capacity of the person. For example, for the canonical form of marriage the presence of a qualified minister and of two witnesses is necessary; it follows that if any of them is missing, the marriage covenant is null and void. Similarly, the law prescribes that a newly appointed bishop must take canonical possession of his see before he can exercise his power to govern; it follows that before this is done he has no capacity to appoint pastors.

Persons Bound by the Laws

Canon 11 — Merely ecclesiastical laws bind those baptized in the Catholic Church or received into it and who enjoy the sufficient use of reason and, unless the law expressly provides otherwise, have completed seven years of age.

"Merely ecclesiastical laws" are human laws enacted by an ecclesiastical legislator. They must be distinguished from ecclesiastical laws which are also articulations of divine laws. Thus many norms for the celebration of the Eucharist are mere ecclesiastical laws; that the Church should celebrate the Eucharist is a divine law.

To be "baptized in the Catholic Church" means to receive baptism with the intention of being incorporated into the same Church with all the rights and duties that such membership includes (see c. 96). In the case of an adult, the person who receives baptism must have this intention; in the case of infants, the parents or those who stand in their place must have it. Mostly such an intention is clearly indicated, but sometimes it must be conjectured from the circumstances. A firm rule is that the intention of the one who receives the sacrament or of his or her sponsor prevails over the religion of the minister who gives it. Thus a child of Catholic parents who intend to educate him or her as Catholic is baptized in the Catholic Church even if the sacrament was given by a non-Catholic minister, and vice versa.

To be "received into it [the Catholic Church]" means the acceptance of full ecclesiastical communion by those who were baptized but not in the Catholic Church.

At this point a serious theological and canonical problem should be mentioned. There are persons who have been baptized in the Catholic Church, but they have never really believed in it. They have never left the Catholic communion, because they have never accepted it. Indeed, the world in the East and in the West abounds in persons who have received baptism in the Catholic Church but, for no fault of theirs, have never come to believe in the Christian mysteries—certainly not in the mystery of the Church. Yet, such persons may ask for the sacraments, especially for marriage, or they may wish to act as if they were members of the Church. While Catholic theology is quite firm today in saying that no grown-up persons can be fully Christian unless they have freely surrendered to God through an act of faith, canon law has not been able to work out satisfactory practical norms regarding the situation (rights and duties) of such baptized unbelievers.

Non-Catholic Christians, that is those who were baptized in, and belong to, a church or ecclesial community not in communion with the Church of Rome, are not bound by Catholic ecclesiastical laws. The Code of 1917 seemed to affirm the opposite (*all* baptized were bound), although even then some commentators doubted that baptism alone was enough upon which the Roman Catholic Church could ground a claim to full jurisdiction.

For the future, there is no doubt: the laws of the Catholic Church do not bind them.

"Sufficient use of reason" means the necessary degree of intelligence to understand the law and the freedom to implement it. "Seven years" must be completed to generate the presumption of such capacity.

To apply this norm wisely, a cautionary note is necessary. The Scholastic theologians, under the leadership of Aquinas, assumed that a child comes to the "use of reason" instantaneously and that, from the moment of this enlightenment, he or she is able to appropriate and observe laws and precepts. But modern psychology sees a human person as being in the process of dynamically developing from an early age well into adulthood. Hence, no precise moment can be detected when a child "receives" the use of reason and begins to make judgments and decisions. If this is so, the age of seven is arbitrary. Children should be taken for what they are—creatures gradually growing in knowledge and responsibility. This is their natural condition; no positive law can change it. Implicitly, canon law itself recognizes this process when it admits that although a young person may have the use of reason in the legal sense, he or she can neither be held liable for criminal actions nor be regarded as having the discretion to conclude a contract.

Universal Laws and Particular Laws

Canon 12 — §1. **All persons for whom universal laws were passed are bound by them everywhere.**

§2. However, all persons who are actually present in a certain territory are exempted from the universal laws which do not have force in that territory.

§3. With due regard for the prescription of can. 13, laws established for a particular territory bind those for whom they were passed when these persons have a domicile or a quasi-domicile there and are likewise actually present in the territory.

"Universal laws" are those which have been enacted by those who have legislative power for the entire Church, such as an ecumenical council or the pope, and they are intended primarily for the common good of the universal community. Universal laws need not bind every single member; they can be specifically addressed to particular groups but always in view of the universal good.

Paragraph one answers the question "Who are bound by universal laws?"—all those for whom they were made. For example, the canons defining the rights and duties of the bishops are universal laws enacted for the bishops; hence, they bind every bishop, but no one else.

Paragraph two answers the question about the legal situation of those who ordinarily are bound by a universal law but happen to be in a territory that has been exempted from the binding force of that law. As long as they are within the limits of the exempt territory, they too are not bound. In practice, the question may come up in connection with holy days of obligation, or norms for fasting and abstinence. In other terms, a favor enjoyed in a territory should be shared by all those who pass through it.

Paragraph three answers the question "Who are bound by laws made for a particular territory?" The people bound by them are those for whom they were made; and those who have a legal tie to the territory, such as a domicile or quasi-domicile; *and* those who are present in the territory. All three conditions must be verified together to induce an obligation to obey those laws. In other terms, a burden carried in a territory should be imposed neither on those who do not belong to it nor on those who belong to it but happen to be away.

For the definitions of domicile and quasi-domicile one should see canons 100–107.

Travelers and Transients

Canon 13 — §1. **Particular laws are not presumed to be personal but territorial, unless it is otherwise evident.**

§2. Travelers:
1° are not bound by the particular laws of their own territory as long as they are absent from it unless their violation would cause harm in their own territory or unless the laws are personal ones;

2° are not bound by the laws of the territory in which they are present with the exception of those laws which provide for public order, which determine the formalities of legal actions, or which deal with immovable goods situated in that territory.

§3. Transients (*vagi*) are bound by both universal laws and the particular laws which are in force in the place where they are present.

"Particular laws" are laws made for a "portion of the people of God." Their direct purpose is to serve the common good of a particular group—in harmony, of course, with the good of the universal Church. The legislator can be either a universal one (ecumenical council, pope) or a particular one (synod, diocesan bishop).

The "portion of the people of God" can be determined either through a territory to which the people belong or where they are (diocese), or through some personal qualities which make them the members of a special group (religious, military). The canon law distinguishes territorial laws from personal laws.

"Territorial" laws reach the subjects indirectly through a territory and may bind them as long as they retain some relationship with that territory; "personal" laws reach the persons directly and bind them wherever they go.

Paragraph one directs that particular laws should be "presumed" to be territorial, not personal.

A form of the term *presumption* (presumed) occurs here for the first time. Since its application reaches far and wide in canon law, it should be explained. It is usually defined as "a probable conjecture about an uncertain matter" (cf. c. 1584)—not a correct definition, in spite of its presence in the Code. A more precise and truthful description of it is that presumption is a procedural tool through which the operation of the law is simplified and expedited.

Presumption is the favor of the law attached either conditionally or absolutely to a situation, a stance, or a proposition that has a legal effect; the law regards it as if it represented the true state of things. A distinction, however, is to be made.

Rebuttable, or conditioned, presumption, traditionally known as *praesumptio iuris,* allows proofs to the contrary. If they are produced and valid, the presumption is reversed, and the newly found truth is honored. The favor of the law is temporary and contingent.

Non-rebuttable, or absolute, presumption, traditionally known as *praesumptio iuris et de iure,* does not allow proofs to the contrary. A plea to present the truth cannot be admitted—the presumption must not be reversed, no matter what the true state of things may be. The favor of the law is permanent and unconditioned.

Examples can be taken from the field of marriage law. Once the exchange of promises has taken place in due canonical form, the law presumes that there is a valid marriage (cf. c. 1101, §1). Proofs to the contrary are admitted, however, as the suits filed for declarations of nullity testify. Then, if the evidence so warrants, a sentence for nullity, *constat de nullitate,* is pronounced. If, however, one of the spouses has died, the law protects the marriage to the point that it allows no direct action against its validity; it enforces a presumption, irrespective of the truth (cf. c. 1675, §1, first clause).

Presumptions exist in all legal systems. Particularly good illustrations can be found in Anglo-American common law. If a person is charged with a crime, he or she must be presumed innocent until proven guilty. The trial is nothing else than an opportunity for the prosecution to rebut the presumption. If proofs are produced to the contrary, the presumption is reversed and the accused is pronounced guilty.

No one, however, should suffer double jeopardy, says another time-honored rule of common law. Hence, once a person has been found not guilty of a crime, he or she cannot be tried for the same misdeed again—even if new proofs come to light. For the sake of the common good, the law now favors the sentence of not guilty and admits no proofs to the contrary. Clearly, such a stance has nothing to do either with truth or probability; it is a legal device to uphold one value against another. In this case, the value of averting endless trials is upheld against the value of punishing every single misdeed.

With the concept of presumption clarified, paragraph one can easily be understood: it directs all concerned in any kind of legal proceedings to handle a particular law as if it had been intended for a territory, leaving room for proofs to the contrary. In this rule there is also a manifestation of the organizational preference of the Church: in general territorial divisions (dioceses) are favored over personal ones (personal prelatures).

Paragraph two refers to a frequent situation in our mobile society: persons belonging to one territory find themselves in another territory to which they have no legal relationship, either domicile or quasi-domicile (see cc. 100–107 for definition). The canonical term for them is "peregrini," perhaps best translated as "strangers" or "travelers."

Two questions may arise concerning their rights and duties outside of their "home territory":

1°– Are they bound by the particular laws of the place where they belong? The answer is that they are not bound unless the non-observance or the transgression of those laws causes damage within their home territory.

2°– Are they bound by the laws of the territory where they are strangers? The answer is that they are not bound unless those laws concern public order or determine the formalities of a legal act or refer to real property situated in the "host" territory.

"Public order" is not easily defined. It is a concept taken from civil law. But the purpose of the law is clear enough: strangers should not cause breach of peace through their non-observance of local laws. Common sense is likely to be a better guide in this matter than any definition. The "formalities" required for a legal transaction often vary from one civil jurisdiction to another. Since the Code canonizes civil law in contractual and similar matters, the norm may have frequent application. Particular care should be exercised to observe such formalities in the case of agreement concerning *real property.*

Paragraph three deals with the case of those who have no legal bond, domicile, or quasi-domicile in any territory; they are called *vagi,* which is difficult to render into English: "transients" is an acceptable translation. The rule about the laws applicable to them is quite simple: since they belong nowhere, they are subject to all laws, general and particular, of the place where they happen to be.

Doubt of Law/Doubt of Fact

Canon 14 — When there is a doubt of law, laws do not bind even if they be nullifying and disqualifying ones. When there is a doubt of fact, however, ordinaries can dispense from them. In the latter case, if it is a question of a reserved dispensation, the ordinaries can dispense so long as the dispensation is usually granted by the authority to whom it is reserved.

The question the canon answers is this: what is the right course of action if doubt emerges either concerning the meaning of a law or regarding the true state of some fact?

"Doubt" means that the cognitional process which normally should conclude with a firm judgment has been arrested. The causes of this incompleteness can be manifold. A doubt may originate outside of the person who must judge: he or she could not get enough information to arrive at a firm conclusion. A doubt may originate also in the person who is called to judge: he or she has the material information but cannot understand it. In the former case, there is an *objective doubt;* in the latter case, a *subjective doubt.* The canon speaks of objective doubt, arising in the mind either because something is amiss in the text of a law or some evidence is unobtainable to clarify the true state of a fact.

There is also the distinction between a "doubt of law" and a "doubt of fact."

There is a doubt of law when the text is so obscure that its meaning on some substantial point cannot be determined. Now, a norm of action cannot be doubtful because no one would know what to do. Hence, a doubt of law is no law at all—as our ancients used to say.

There is a doubt of fact when for lack of sufficient information the true state of some facts cannot be known. It cannot be said, however, that a doubtful fact is no fact; hence, the law makes some provisions for handling such an uncertainty.

In doubt of fact, the ordinary may give a dispensation if a dispensation is warranted, even if ordinarily it could be granted only by a higher authority. A qualification is added, however: the relevant authority must be in the habit of granting the dispensation.

The rule concerning doubt applies to all laws, including those of invalidating or incapacitating character. This should be clear already on the basis of canon 10 alone; there it is stated that no act should be taken for invalid, and no person for incapacitated, unless the law expressly says so. Expressly means also clearly—without any shadow of doubt.

Ignorance of Law/Ignorance of Fact

Canon 15 — §1. Ignorance or error concerning invalidating or incapacitating laws does not hinder

their effectiveness unless it is expressly determined otherwise.
§2. Ignorance or error about a law, a penalty, a fact concerning oneself, or a notorious fact concerning another is not presumed; it is presumed about a fact concerning another which is not notorious until the contrary is proven.

Ignorance means the absence of *data* in the process of knowing to the point that no judgment can be reached.
Error means some deficiency in the process of knowing to the point that a false judgment is reached.

Paragraph one responds to the question: what is the effect of invalidating or incapacitating laws if the person or persons involved in the situation is (are) *not* aware of the laws' existence or of their content? In other terms, can the effect of a juridical act depend on the state of mind of those involved?

The answer is that the laws operate independently from the state of mind of the persons. The reason for this rule is the need to uphold and protect legal stability and security. If the operation of the said laws ordinarily depended on the knowledge or beliefs of the persons involved, there would be no end to uncertainties and litigations. The whole community would suffer.

Paragraph two is really a procedural norm about the operation of certain presumptions; it is a directive addressed to judges and to those in executive offices.

They are entitled to presume that

(a) everyone subject to the law knows the law and any penalty that may have been attached to it;

(b) everyone knows the legally relevant facts concerning oneself;

(c) everyone knows those facts about another which are of common knowledge in the community.

They are not entitled to presume that someone knows about facts concerning another if those facts cannot be proved to be of common knowledge in the community.

Book VII of the Code, "Processes," contains many particular applications of this norm.

Interpretation: Authentic and Judicial

Canon 16 — §1. Laws are authentically interpreted by the legislator and by the one to whom the legislator has granted the power to interpret them authentically.
§2. An authentic interpretation communicated in the form of a law has the same force as the law it-

self and must be promulgated. Furthermore, if such an interpretation merely declares what was certain in the words of the law in themselves, it has retroactive force; if it restricts or extends the law or if it explains a doubtful law, it is not retroactive.

§3. However, an interpretation contained in a judicial decision or an administrative act in a particular matter does not have the force of law and binds only the persons and affects only those matters for which it was given.

The canon distinguishes two radically different types of interpretation: authentic and non-authentic.

Paragraph one determines the source of authentic interpretation: it is the legislator or any person or agency commissioned by the legislator to give it. Interpretation from any other source is non-authentic.

Paragraph two further defines authentic interpretation: it has the same authority as the law itself. It completes the law; it becomes an integral part of it.

It follows that all the usual norms for legislation come into operation: authentic interpretation must be promulgated according to canon 8. An interpretation which did not follow the proper route of promulgation, even if it comes from the legislator, cannot be authentic.

The act of promulgation, however, does not make the interpretation retroactive. *Retroactivity* depends on the nature of the original text that was in need of clarification.

If the text was such that its meaning was clear for reasonably competent persons, then the authentic interpretation does no more than to repeat and confirm what was originally there—presumably for the sake of those who were in ignorance, in error, or without the required competency to understand the law. Such an interpretation is retroactive because it adds no new cognitional element to the law.

If the text was such that it generated *doubt* in reasonably competent persons, then the law was really null and void (cf. c. 14). The authentic interpretation, then, by dispelling the doubt, establishes a new law. Consequently, it has to be handled as original legislation. It can regard the future only, not the past (cf. c. 9).

It may happen, also that the authentic interpretation goes beyond the ordinary meaning of the terms of the law, *restricting or expanding* it in an unusual way. Such an interpretation is also new legislation. The ordinary meaning is cancelled out; a new meaning is introduced. Such interpretation, too, must be handled as new legislation; it can regard the future only, not the past.

Authentic interpretation is, and should remain, a rare event in the legal life of the Church. Ordinarily, the legal life of the community develops through interpretations that are not authentic in a technical

sense, but which, in so many ways, let the law unfold.

In paragraph three, we find a principle that sets the legal system of the Church apart from classical Roman law, as well as from Anglo-American common law. It has even made the law of the Code, right from 1917, different from canon law as it existed before. The text says that ecclesiastical courts or administrative agencies are empowered to interpret the law for a particular case only; their decisions do not create precedents to be followed, no matter how high the judicial forum or how powerful the administrative agency is.

Classical Roman law developed principally through the activity of the praetors who were moving from precedent to precedent, balancing the concrete needs of the community against abstract norms, and, thus, building a coherent system of laws. Common law evolved mainly through the decisions of the judges balancing the wisdom of the past, contained in precedents, with the demands of the present, revealed through a new case. The traditional collection of canonical norms, the *Corpus iuris canonici,* was a distillation of ancient customs, conciliar decrees, decretal letters of the popes, curial decisions, and judicial decisions. Legal systems built on customs have the disadvantage of being untidy and likely to generate uncertainty; yet, they have the advantage of being close to real-life situations and of being adaptable to new demands. When the emphasis shifts from customs to statutes, the orderliness and clarity of the legal system increase, but it is at the expense of its closeness to the concrete world where persons live and die.

The presently valid canon law is statutory to the highest degree. It sides with those continental systems that have their origin in, and take their inspiration from, Justinian's collections. In 1917, with the promulgation of the former Code, the Church laid new foundations for canon law. Yet, the knowledge that the Church used a different system for most of its history can help us to understand the relative value of the present one.

The text of the paragraph is clear in itself: the binding force of judicial and administrative decisions extends only to the parties involved (a reference to personal rights and duties) and to the things over which the dispute arose (a reference to real property rights, *ius in re*). Custom, which is the best interpreter of the law, (cf. c. 27), has already gone beyond the letter of this text. The decisions of the Sacred Roman Rota and the acts of the executive offices of the Holy See are regularly published with the clear intention that they should serve as guidance for lower courts and agencies operating mainly in dioceses. They are received with respect and enjoy significant authority.

The fact stands, however, that due to the principle stated in this paragraph, the role of the courts in the legal system of the Church is weak. Apart from matrimonial jurisprudence, they contribute little to the ongoing development of its legal life. Executive offices are probably in a stronger position because nearly all legal issues, except those of matrimony, are handled by them. They play an increasingly leading role in the legal life of the Church.

Interpretation: Some General Principles

Canon 17 — **Ecclesiastical laws are to be understood in accord with the proper meaning of the words considered in their text and context. If the meaning remains doubtful and obscure, recourse is to be taken to parallel passages, if such exist, to the purpose and the circumstances of the law, and to the mind of the legislator.**

Ecclesiastical laws are human laws enacted by the ecclesiastical legislator. This canon gives direction for their interpretation.

The starting point for the construction of their meaning is in finding the ordinary signification of the words—both according to common speech and legal usage. Legal science, like any other science, developed a vocabulary for itself; often the true meaning of a term cannot be grasped without being thoroughly familiar with the technicalities of highly specialized language.

But no word stands alone; they all appear in a context, and their fuller meaning can be grasped only in that broader framework. The context can be strictly legal, determining a right-and-duty situation. The context can also represent a variety of other disciplines—such as theology, philosophy, empirical sciences, history, and so forth. In each case the specific context must be taken into account and the canon interpreted in accordance with the methodology and content of the *contextual discipline.* To give an example: a canon in a theological context should be explained with the help of theology, not vice versa.

Such an approach gives a significant flexibility to the canons: as various disciplines evolve, so does the interpretation of canons related to them. Thus, the canon stating that psychological causes may interfere with the capacity to accept marital obligations must be reinterpreted continually according to sound advances in the science of psychology.

Doubtful meanings and obscurities may remain even after the analysis of the text and its context. Such doubts must be minor ones, however, since substantial doubts would cancel out the law altogether (cf. c. 14).

An effort should be made to clear up the doubts and obscurities. This can be done by recurring to analogies; if the law gives precise directions for not identical but similar situations, a clue for interpretation can be taken from there.

The purpose of the law, the circumstances in which it was enacted, and the mind of the legislator behind it—they all can contribute to its understanding. Nonetheless, such references to external factors not present in the text and context of the law must be invoked cautiously. The presumption is that the legislator said what was meant; hence, the meaning of the text should not be changed on the bases of factors which are not expressed in the law itself.

The interpretation of the law is a subtle art; it cannot be done well without proper training in law, its history, and in a number of relevant sciences.

Laws To Be Interpreted Strictly

Canon 18 — **Laws which establish a penalty or restrict the free exercise of rights or which contain an exception to the law are subject to a strict interpretation.**

Human words used to express a legal concept hardly ever have the clarity and precision of mathematical terms. They have a certain elasticity. Their meaning can be broadened or narrowed, without taking away their original significance. Analogously, just how many shades of color can truly be called red!

In this universal linguistic phenomenon, we have the potential source for two types of interpretation of laws: broad and strict. Each interpretation retains the core meaning—but in one case it is stretched out, and in the other case it is compressed.

Broad interpretation represents the *maximum* that the term *can* honestly carry; *strict interpretation* represents the *minimum* that the term *must* honestly include. Both speak the truth, in spite of the difference, because the original meaning of the term is not destroyed.

The variations *inside* the meaning of a term should not be confused with artificially extending or restricting it beyond what it is ordinarily used for. If that happens, a different concept is really substituted for the original one—and a totally new meaning is introduced into the law that does not naturally follow from the words used. Such an extraordinary extension or restriction can be done only by the legislator, in the form of authentic interpretation. It ought to be promulgated, and it cannot be retroactive (cf. c. 16).

Canon 18 directs that three types of laws should be strictly interpreted, that is, the application of such laws should be restricted to the honest minimum their terms must cover:

(a) laws which "establish a penalty"—the legislator wants neither to impose a sanction on more persons nor to impose heavier penalties on anyone than what is absolutely necessary to protect the peace of the community (see, e.g., Book VI, title II, cc. 1313–1320);

(b) laws which "restrict the free exercise of rights"—the clause refers mainly to fundamental rights and freedoms, as are the right to life, the freedom of speech, the right to good reputation, and similar ones (see especially the rights enumerated in Book II, title I, cc. 208–223);

(c) laws which "contain an exception to the law"—this expression probably refers to laws published after the Code. Practical cases will not be frequent.

To balance the doctrine of this canon, the opposite principle, too, should be recalled: favorable laws are of broad interpretation. Benefits granted by law should be extended to as many, and to as great an extent, as the honest interpretation of the terms allows.

The operating presumption behind such norms is that the legislator is gracious and merciful and slow to anger (cf. Jl 2:13).

Lacuna:
There Is No Law when There Should Be One

Canon 19 — **Unless it is a penal matter, if an express prescription of universal or particular law or a custom is lacking in some particular matter, the case is to be decided in light of laws passed in similar circumstances, the general principles of law observed with canonical equity, the jurisprudence and praxis of the Roman Curia, and the common and constant opinion of learned persons.**

This canon gives direction as to what to do in case of a so-called lacuna: an obvious gap in the legal system.

Lacuna in the proper sense occurs when there is a right that must be supported, or an injustice that cries for redress, or a freedom that needs protection, and there is no appropriate provision in the legal system. Then those with judicial or executive power are entitled to step in, declare that a lacuna indeed exists, and take action to remedy the situation. Since they fill the gap on the direction of the law itself, their decree, sentence, or decision has full legal standing in canon law, notwithstanding that no norm can be quoted to support it.

Lacuna therefore has an objective foundation in the legal system. Only persons with judicial or executive power can declare its presence and take appropriate action. Not even they, however, are entitled to extend the doctrine of lacuna into the field of penal law.

The rest of the canon is addressed to those who must take action to fill the gap. In doing so they must recur to the following sources and resources:

• analogous cases and norms in the whole legal system;

• the general principles of law—mainly as they are expressed in the Code—but also as they have been known in canonical traditions;

• the doctrine of equity, *epieikeia* or *oikonomia* (see Notes following the commentary on c. 28);

• the jurisprudence of the Roman Curia, that is, the decisions of the courts of the Holy See and the decisions of its offices;

• the praxis of the Roman Curia—such praxis overlaps with jurisprudence—but it includes also general policies followed in transacting business, and to know it, some experience and familiarity with the Curia are necessary;

• common and constant opinion of learned persons.

To this last point, the opinion of the learned persons, an important qualification should be added: the provision that each of them took a fresh look at the issue, examined it critically, and reached a conclusion after proper reflection. Unfortunately the canonical literature of the past is filled with one author following the "authority" of another, without ever submitting the issues to fresh and rigorous scrutiny. The result is that a "myth of authorities" has been built up and invoked too much. In canon law, no less than in any other branch of science, an opinion is as good as the reasons supporting it.

Impact of New Legislation on Existing Norms

Canon 20 — **A later law abrogates a former law or derogates from it if it expressly states so, if it is directly contrary to it, or if it entirely re-orders the subject matter of the former law; but a universal law in no way derogates from a particular or special law unless the law itself expressly provides otherwise.**

The Church is a living body within an evolving world. In its internal life, as in its relationship to the rest of the human family, new needs arise continually. They demand new responses, often in the form of legislation. As new norms are made, the question arises of how to insert them into the existing body of laws without destroying their cohesion and harmony.

The spirit of canon 20 favors legal stability. It lists the cases in which a later law cancels out a former. Implicitly it says that cancellation, partial or total, should not be presumed; it should be proved that cancellation was the intention of the legislators. Such evidence is provided in three cases:

(a) the later law explicitly says that the former law is cancelled either entirely or partially;

(b) the later law is "directly contrary," that is, diametrically opposed, to the former—they cannot, together, be a guide for the community;

(c) the subject matter of the later law is the same as that of the former one, but the later gives a wholly new structure, so that the two edifices, former and later, cannot coexist in any way.

Yet, exceptions exist: particular or special laws and righs are not cancelled out or modified by a subsequent general law, unless, of course, the general law states so in unmistakable terms.

Conflict between Old and New: The Aim Is Conciliation

Canon 21 — In a case of doubt the revocation of a pre-existent law is not presumed, but later laws are to be related to earlier ones and, insofar as it is possible, harmonized with them.

In spite of the theoretically clear rules in canon 20 concerning a conflict between the former law and the later law, in practice doubts can still arise as to which of the two laws, former or later, should prevail.

Canon 21 gives a cautious answer.

It directs that the revocation of the existing law should not be presumed, but neither should it be upheld at all cost. Rather, a reconciliation of the earlier and the later should be attempted—a judicial attitude well known to common lawyers. In this process of building harmony, the earlier law should weigh heavily, but not to the point of cancelling out the later. Thus, the interpretation becomes a balancing act between the need for stability through the preservation of laws and the need for progress through subsequent laws responding to new needs.

Civil Laws Received into Corpus of Canon Law

Canon 22 — Civil laws to which the law of the Church defers should be observed in canon law with the same effects, insofar as they are not contrary to divine law and unless it is provided otherwise in canon law.

Most of the time canon law and civil law operate side by side, independently of each other; thus, there are many cases in which the same person, physical or juridic, is the subject of two distinct sets of rights and duties, one in canon law, another in civil law. If conflict arises, experts must find the best solution they can.

In some cases, however, canon law incorporates the norms of civil law into its own system, that is, making them equivalent to ecclesiastical norms. This is more than a mere recognition of civil law; it is civil law made into canon law. In fact, traditionally it is called the "canonization" of civil law. Thus in matter of contracts the law of every country is canonized and binds not only the citizens but even ecclesiastical juridic persons dealing with each other.

Canon 22 says in substance that when civil law is canonized, it is fully integrated into the canonical system; it binds all persons in the Church, and produces the same effect in the canonical forum as in the civil one. Thus, a contract is valid or invalid in civil law, and the same is true in canon law.

The two restrictions mentioned in the canon are virtually self-evident:

(1) if the effect of civil law is against divine law, it remains ineffective in canon law, e.g., a contract to perform an abortion even if valid civilly is null and void canonically;

(2) if canon law makes an explicit reservation on some point, it must prevail over civil law, e.g., the laws for prescription are canonized, but canon law requires possession in good faith for the law to take effect—even if civil law is satisfied with bad faith, no ownership will result in canon law if the possessor was of bad faith.

TITLE II
CUSTOM
[cc. 23–28]

The Legislator Gives Legal Force to Customs

Canon 23 — Only that custom introduced by the community of the faithful and approved by the legislator has the force of law, according to the following canons.

Customary laws are norms of action no less than statutory laws, but they do not arise from a legislative act; they are the fruit of the accumulated wisdom of the community.

In the beginning of its history, the Christian community shaped its social structures and created the necessary balances between the requirements of the common good and the needs of persons mainly through customs. As the Church developed, legislation began to play an increasing role, especially through conciliar decrees; yet, customs remained an integral and substantial part of the legal system until the promulgation of the first Code in 1917.

At that date, the foundational principles of the Church's legal system were changed radically. The Code became the near-exclusive source of law, and customs were left no significant role. Ancient customs were mostly eliminated, and the conditions for new ones were made so stringent that, in the practical order, they could not develop.

The Code of 1983 follows the attitude of its predecessor. It incorporates the classical doctrine on custom into the canons—but without giving much effective scope to it—despite the fact that it relaxes somewhat the requirements for the emergence of new ones.

Canon 23 distinguishes a custom approved by the legislator from a usage which lacks such approval. Only the approved custom has the force of law; the approval makes it equivalent to statutory legislation. Before approval, the usage has no authority. It does not follow, however, that it should be treated as non-existent. Rather, it should be respected and upheld as one of the ways of creating laws in the community. Such respect is due to it right from its beginning. The community should be aware that good customs can enrich its life; hence, it should not be reluctant, with due discretion, to initiate new usages.

A warning should be sounded as well. To endow long-standing practices with the force of law is not always healthy, especially when they are devotional exercises. The spontaneous generosity of the community can be spoiled or even destroyed by transforming its voluntary observances into laws and then distorting their deepest meaning through endless casuistry concerning the extent and gravity of the artificially created legal obligation.

The approval of the legislator can be granted explicitly by a legislative act, or it can be given implicitly by tacit respect for a custom. The following three canons explain the norms for approval.

No Custom against Divine Law;
No Custom against Sound Reason

Canon 24 — **§1. No custom which is contrary to divine law can obtain the force of law.**

§2. Unless it be a reasonable one, no custom which is contrary to or apart from canon law (*praeter ius*) can obtain the force of law; however, a custom which is expressly reprobated in law is not a reasonable one.

Paragraph one states that neither the community nor its legislator has the power to introduce and approve a custom which would be against the law of God. The issue of what divine law is, however, must be carefully handled. Too many times in the history of theology human opinions have been upgraded and proposed as "divine law." It should be kept in mind that unless the legislator has spoken with full apostolic authority on a given norm and determined that it was divine law, there exists no more than fallible human knowledge of the origin and nature of the law in question.

In paragraph two the key word is "reasonable." The norm laid down for the future is that the legislator will not grant approval, explicitly or implicitly, to any custom which is not reasonable. No

precise definition of reasonable follows in the text, but a practical direction is given: whatever is reprobated by the legislator is unreasonable; hence, it cannot ever become a custom having "the force of law." Thus, positive disapproval, voiced by the legislator, becomes the criterion of what is against reason.

A Community Building a Custom
Must Intend to Bind Itself

Canon 25 — **No custom obtains the force of law unless it has been observed with the intention of introducing a law by a community capable at least of receiving law.**

A practice which is neither against the law of God nor against the norms of reason may emerge as binding custom provided it fulfills a number of conditions.

The community in which the practice originates must be capable of receiving a law, that is, it must be large enough to have laws made for it. The universal Church is certainly so. A diocese is certainly such. The problem arises with smaller units in which there is no legislative authority, e.g., a parish community. Can such a small unit have its own custom? An affirmative answer can be given on the following principle: every group in the Church for which a law can be enacted by a universal or particular legislator must be able to develop a custom. Since a law for a parish could be enacted by the bishop or by the pope, the parish can develop a practice to which the legislator can grant the force of law. The same is true of units held together by personal laws, e.g., a religious community.

If the group is so small, or is so dispersed and undefinable, that no law could be made for it, it cannot develop a custom. For instance, no universal law could be made for "people young at heart," or for a "district in the parish"; one is too undefinable by law, the other is too small. They cannot, therefore, be the agents for the development of a custom.

The requirement that *the community must have the intention to introduce a law* is difficult to interpret. It is far from clear who in the community should have it, in what way—implicitly or explicitly—and for how long. The answer is probably in saying that no detailed examination of the state of mind of the community is required, or indeed necessary. If a reasonable person is able, at the end of the required period, to conclude that the community has come to a point in developing the custom where its recognition by the legislator is a sound legislative act for the sake of the common good, the presence of the required intention throughout the process should be assumed. In the practical order, such an approach is certainly satisfactory, and none other is feasible.

Norms for Handling Customs against the Law and beyond the Law

Canon 26 — Unless it has been specifically approved by the competent legislator, a custom contrary to the current canon law or one which is apart from canon law (*praeter ius*) obtains the force of law only when it has been legitimately observed for thirty continuous and complete years; only a centenary or immemorial custom can prevail over a canon which contains a clause forbidding future customs.

The practice must endure for a certain length of time before the legislator can grant it the force of law:

• thirty years are necessary if the practice does not interfere with any of the existing legal norms and simply creates a new right-and-duty situation;

• thirty years are necessary if the practice interferes with one or more norms and destroys some right-and-duty situation, provided there is no previous prohibition against such a practice;

• a long time, described as "centenary or immemorial" observance is necessary if the practice has been forbidden although not reproved.

Note the distinction between prohibited and reprobated practice: the former has the potential (remote as it may be) for obtaining recognition; the latter does not.

The required term of years, however, can be dispensed with. The legislator can grant force of law to a custom before it reaches "maturity" as well as refuse it after the required period is fulfilled.

In other terms, the community is the one who provides the material for a new norm; the legislator is the one who gives it binding force.

Role of Custom in Interpreting Laws

Canon 27 — Custom is the best interpreter of laws.

This canon prompts this question: how can the interpretation of the laws produced by custom be the best when it is neither authentic, nor judicial, nor even scholarly? The answer is that in such interpretation there is a value that cannot be found anywhere else. The law has stood the test of the real, that is, in its implementation it has been shaped and reshaped by the action and reaction of living forces in the community. No matter how perfect a general, abstract, and impersonal norm may

be, when it encounters particular, concrete, and personal situations in the community, it is "reformed" by them. As had been seen above (cf. c. 7), the law ought to become a vital force that shapes the community. Now, the opposite is found to be true: vital forces in the community ought to shape the law. It is dialectics of a sort, leading to a synthesis.

Interpretation by custom is more manifest in action than in notional articulation. It is the best because it goes beyond the authentic, beyond the judicial, and beyond the doctrinal.

In a one-line sentence, the Code points to the decisive role the community has in the interpretation of the laws. All that the community is, all that it has, must come into play in creating "the best" or "a best" interpretation through intelligent and free operations.

Vatican Council II is not irrelevant here. In the *Constitution on the Church,* it gives the place of honor to the people of God. This is very different from the treatment accorded to the same people by the first Code. The former rule that custom is the best interpreter of the law acquired a new meaning from the recently achieved self-understanding of the Church.

If the *sensus fidelium* plays an important part in finding and determining the elements of the Church's authentic traditions, the same *sensus fidelium* should play a significant part in shaping the Church's legal system and in interpreting its laws. This instinct of the faithful should not be distrusted; it should rather be encouraged.

Interplay between Laws and Customs

Canon 28 — With due regard for the prescription of can. 5, a custom, whether it is contrary to or apart from the law (*praeter legem*), is revoked by a contrary custom or law; however, unless it makes express mention of centenary or immemorial customs, a law does not revoke them, nor does a universal law revoke particular customs.

As human laws have their span of life, so do human customs. Hence, the question: how can a custom cease to exist, that is, lose its binding force?

If the custom is an ordinary one that is less than "centenary or immemorial," a newly recognized custom to the contrary or a newly enacted law to the contrary cancels it out.

If the custom is "centenary or immemorial," it may continue even if a law to the contrary has been enacted, unless the new law has explicitly mandated the termination of such a long-standing custom.

A special interplay takes place between a general law and a particular custom: the particular custom prevails unless the law explicitly mandates its termination.

Notes

Literary Forms in the Code

The Code carries the message of the legislator to those for whom the law was made. To understand the meaning of the message correctly, the subjects should know that they do not have in hand a document with an even tone and tenor throughout. Rather, they have a collection of small literary pieces widely differing from each other in nature. To catch the meaning of each, the nature of each must be determined. The literary form of a given text is part of the meaning of that text.

If an analogy is needed, there is a good one from the field of biblical sciences. We know that the Bible is not a uniform literary product from the beginning to the end, but rather a collection of many pieces—each having its own literary form. To find the correct meaning of each one, one must start with determining its nature. Mutatis mutandis, one must take a similar approach in interpreting the Code, since it contains several differing types of utterances by the legislator.

In the Code one can find the following literary forms.

There are *statements of belief,* virtually amounting to a profession of faith. Usually, such statements are there to introduce practical dispositions, e.g., about the government of the Church, or the administration of the sacraments. In those statements, the Church remembers God's mighty deeds, the *gesta Dei.* A good argument could be made for not putting such anamneses into a book of law, but once it has happened, they must be taken for what they are: *articulations of belief.* They must *not* be interpreted as laws are; they are not subject to juridical methodology. To find their meaning, the interpreter must leave the world of law and enter into the world of dogma. Christian doctrine is not proper subject matter for disciplinary legislation, and one should not assume that the legislator wanted to make it so. Therefore, even if a point of doctrine appears in the Church's book of laws, it has not become a law. It should be interpreted from theological sources and with theological methodology.

There are theological statements that do not represent any article of faith, but are *historically conditioned opinions of a theological school.* As such, they have no right to demand universal assent.

While it could be argued that such opinions should not be in a book of laws, the laws that flow from them are not necessarily out of place. Often enough, the need for an ordered and peaceful life in the community postulates a practical norm for action long before there is a theoretical consensus among theologians. Then, the legislator may well feel compelled to use one of the accepted theological opinions as the point of departure. Such opin-

ions, however, have no standing before the courts, and the laws flowing from them can be interpreted more broadly than the seemingly "canonized" opinion would allow.

There are canons that touch on *issues of morality.* Their wording may lead an interpreter to conclude that the intrinsic quality of an act, its levity or gravity, has been determined by the legislator. Yet the levity or gravity of an act, or its morality, is a matter of doctrine, too. Hence, before such a statement can be interpreted correctly, it must be restored to its natural environment, which is the field of moral theology. This may be a complex task. It may lead, in some cases, to uncertain results, but nothing is wrong with that. It is not the business of the law to give final answers on disputed ethical issues.

Some canons are *exhortations* pure and simple. They express what the legislator desires, but they do not create right-and-duty situations. An interpreter who does not grasp the literary form of such pieces will change their character and transform them into binding obligations.

There are canons with a *metaphysical content.* They offer the insights of philosophers to solve canonical problems. In interpreting such canons, the unbroken tradition of the ecumenical councils should be kept in mind: the Church has never committed itself to any school of philosophy. Hence, the interpreter is on secure ground in assuming that the legislator uses the metaphysical principles and categories as useful tools in handling and solving some canonical problems without really vouching for their ultimate correctness.

There are canons that contain *scientific statements,* e.g., from the field of psychology or psychiatry. They should be interpreted according to scientific criteria, taking into account the evolutionary nature of these sciences. In other terms, if a canon speaks of the effect of mental diseases, it should be interpreted according to the latest advances in medicine and not according to the state of information of the legislator at the time of the promulgation of the law.

The true legislative pieces are the canons that deal with *right-and-duty* situations. To interpret them, the sources and resources of law must be brought into play. Some of these canons are directly concerned with establishing certain structures and keeping them intact; some others are primarily norms of action imposed on all or some members of the community. The difference between norms for structures and norms for action is more nominal than real because, even in the case of structures, the law is concerned with actions that will either create or support them.

This list of seven literary forms should not be taken as exhaustive. Besides, even in the same category there can be nuances; the weight of one canon can be greater than that of another, e.g., a canon introducing a new chapter or a new topic in the Code can contain an important clue for the interpretation of all other canons in the same group.

The application of the doctrine of literary forms to the laws of the Church is new. It is, however, a sound doctrine, well tested elsewhere. Wisely used, it can throw new light on the canons.

To recognize and to distinguish every literary form in the Code is important because the nature of the text determines the method of interpretation. The meaning of theological texts changes and develops as theological reflection progresses. The meaning of norms of action can remain unchanged and stable for a long time.

The Balancing Role of Epieikeia

A systematic study of the science and art of interpretation of laws would be incomplete and structurally unbalanced without giving its due place to Aristotle's *epieikeia*. There are few legal institutions as clear and simple in their conception as that one, yet there are hardly any over which so many layers of theories and explanations have accumulated. The intention here is to do no more than restate the philosopher's proposition in its original form; its soundness will be enough to prove its enduring validity.

Aristotle introduces the idea of *epieikeia* in the context of his reflections on the virtue of justice in the *Nicomachean Ethics (NE)*. *To epieikes*, often translated misleadingly as "to do equity," is really an act of justice. Its scope is to bring a corrective into the application of law whenever it is so warranted. In other terms, the very nature of every law is such that, in some cases, it may grant imperfect justice only, or no justice at all. Then *epieikeia* must enter. "The reason is that all law is universal, but about some things it is not possible to make a universal statement which shall be correct" (*NE* 1137[b] 12–14). "For when the thing is indefinite, the rule also is indefinite . . ." (28–29).

There is the empirically minded philosopher, the faithful observer of nature—in this case of the nature of the norms serving a political body. He sees that real life is more complex than any set of rules which the human mind can conceive. Hence, an ad hoc corrective is necessary. It must originate in the same source as the laws, that is, in the virtue of justice.

Aristotle's *epieikeia* is not equivalent to the *equitable law* of the Romans, which was a new, flexible legal system distinct from that of the old, rigid civil law; a flexible system still may need the corrective of *epieikeia*. But his theory comes close to the practice of the English chancellor who used to grant "equity" when the literal observance of the law led to injustice.

Traditionally, canon law acknowledged the right to use *epieikeia*, even if the explanations of it varied greatly. To conceive it again in its original simplicity may enhance its scope. To confine it to extreme cases only—such as filling the gap in the case of a *lacuna legis* (there is no law *and* there should be one)—would be to restrict it too much, virtually making it useless.

In Aristotle's mind, *epieikeia* is an integral and indispensable component of every legal system, no matter what system. It goes hand in hand with statutory law. Justice for all can be achieved only through the subtle and judicious dialectics of imposing the law in most cases and letting *epieikeia* prevail in some cases.

Legal positivism, which holds many modern civil systems in captivity, of course cannot accept the idea of *epieikeia*, since it would make the validity of a decision depend on the virtue of justice. Such prejudice, however, should not operate in the field of canon law. It *should* not, but there have been periods in the history of canon law when *epieikeia* has been forgotten, in the sense that it played no serious role. For such neglect there was a penalty, flowing directly from the nature of things. As the application of *epieikeia* receded, legalism raised its ugly head.

Legalism is a sickness in the system; it places greater value on the observance of formalities than on the granting of true justice. When it is rampant, it erodes the strength of laws from the inside, and it brings them into bad repute on the outside. The best prevention against such disease is the faithful application of the laws in general and the vigorous invocation of Aristotle's *epieikeia* in particular.

Authentic Equity

Equity has been used, and at times abused, ever since the magistrates and the lawyers began to invoke it on a larger scale in the third century B.C. It has more than proved its value by bringing both new life into an aging system of law and flexibility into rigid structures. No doubt, however, it has also been invoked many times to justify illegitimate excursions into otherwise forbidden territory. All that is possible must be done to open the door to authentic equity, while keeping it closed to illegalities.

As many times, history is the best teacher. There is no doubt that equity brought powerful transformations into both the Roman and English systems of laws. The fruit of its influence has been excellent; therefore, in these systems one must be able to find an authentic expression of it.

Before doing so, however, it must be stated clearly that equity is not the same as *epieikeia*. The latter is part of the virtue of justice. With its attention to particular cases, it balances out the generality of legal norms. *Nomos* (law) and *epieikeia* are in the same category, so to say. It is not so with law and equity, as shall be seen.

Neither is equity to be equated with *oikonomia*,

which will be described later in this study. The latter is a hidden power in the Church, undefinable, that comes into play in rare and insoluble cases, through the ministry of the *oikonomoi, the bishops.* There is nothing hidden about equity, and it may well come into play quite frequently. Attention, however, must now be returned to Roman law.

The origins of Roman law are in the norms of the Twelve Tables, composed in the sixth century before Christ. They gave birth and development to a strict system of laws interpreted with literal exactness. Eventually, the shortcomings of such structures began to work to the disadvantage of the citizens whom they were supposed to help and protect. Moreover, the system proved insufficient to handle the needs of many non-citizens who either came to Rome or over whom the power of Rome was extended.

To provide for the needs of strangers and aliens, in 242 B.C. a special magistrate was appointed, the *praetor peregrinus.* Since he did not administer justice for the citizens, he was not bound by their laws. He was free to appeal to the ideals of natural justice, to the demands of human nature, to the image of a good head of the family, to the ways of a reasonable person, and to administer justice accordingly. Gradually, the praetors, succeeding each other, developed a new system of laws that depended not on the Twelve Tables anymore but on the ethical ideas of the Roman people.

There equity is found at work. The *praetor peregrinus* found the existing legal system all too narrow to accommodate the demands of life. Hence, he went out of the field of law, entered into the field of ethical principles, and with their help construed new legal norms. Equity in Rome meant to invoke higher principles than the law could provide, and with the help of those principles to give a balanced solution to legal problems. Thus, harmony between moral and legal values was reestablished.

The enterprise was so successful that, eventually, the equitable system of laws superseded all civil laws, and was applied to all, aliens and citizens alike.

The history of the entry of equity into the legal system of England was not all that different. There, too, the common law of the king, from the late Middle Ages onward, proved insufficient to bring remedy to naturally unjust situations that found shelter behind the rigid rules of common law. The chancellor, who was the keeper of the conscience of the king and had enough power at his disposal to intervene, began to distribute justice in his own way. Since, during the formative years of equity, the chancellors were always bishops, they distributed justice according to the principles of Christian morality. The common law continued to operate through the king's courts; but, if natural justice was defeated through its application, there was recourse to the chancellor's court. In reaching a sentence,

he, like the praetor, took his inspiration from outside the field of law, invoked a higher principle, and gave justice accordingly.

The pattern of development in England was not really different from the pattern that evolved in Rome. In both cases, the shortcomings of the legal system were recognized, and, through the agency of an official person, a correction was brought into the law out of the field of morality, based on the needs of human nature or on the dictates of Christian conscience.

Now it is easier to understand how authentic equity arose and developed in history. Here is the pattern.

There is a legal system, but it is not able to protect an important value or to give redress when injustice has been inflicted. Then, the value is upheld on ethical or religious grounds, and the law is sentenced (so to say) to pay respect to that value and accommodate itself to that value. Authentic equity, therefore, comes into play when the law is unable to uphold a value important for the community. The community then turns to another (non-legal) system of ideas to justify a departure from the legal system. It lets the value prosper intact, and it brings the law into the service of that value.

No legal system is perfect, not even canon law. Ecclesiastical laws are human creations; consequently, they too may prove themselves unable to protect some value in the Christian community or to provide remedy for an injustice suffered. In that case, in canon law too, there must be recourse to authentic equity. Whoever is in charge of the issue, whoever it is who must give speedy justice, that person is entitled to invoke higher principles of morality and state that the law must cease to operate, and, through necessary accommodations, must become a servant of the value that must be safeguarded.

Thus, there is no magic in equity. There is no fuzziness either. The life of human communities is regulated by various norms—legal, philosophical, religious. Each group of norms has its own built-in limits. When, in the concrete life, a case arises that cannot be justly resolved by law, it is right that the community should turn to philosophy or religion and let them prevail over the positive law. When this happens, there is authentic equity.

The Meaning of Oikonomia

In recent times theologians and canonists of the Latin Church have expressed an increased interest in *oikonomia, economy* in somewhat poor English transliteration, of the Orthodox Church. It seems to belong to the science of jurisprudence; it can solve seemingly insoluble issues. Yet it appears also to be a device that is invoked from somewhere other than the realm of law, since it is more powerful than the law can ever be. Be that as it may, it is certainly used in the Orthodox, especially the Greek Orthodox Churches—and there is a desire to introduce it into our Latin jurisprudence—if at all possible. After all, the Latin Church, too, has insoluble cases.

There are many explanations of *oikonomia* in Western literature: few of them are faithful to the Eastern original; many of them are projections of the Western legal mind. Here, the intention is to do no more than discard some misconceptions and point out the direction where the right understanding can be found. Of course, in light of the Latin rite, this is not done without some trepidation.

Oikonomia is not an Eastern version of some Latin legal institution that is there to temper the severity of the laws, such as dispensation, *sanatio in radice,* canonical equity, and others. *Oikonomia* is not part of the legal system of the Orthodox Church, although its application has legal effects.

Oikonomia is not equivalent to the *epieikeia* of Aristotle; it is not even akin to the equity of the Romans. Its origins are neither in any philosophical theory nor in some pragmatic wisdom. A good way of progressing toward the understanding of the Orthodox mind that created or discovered *oikonomia* is to think of the origins of the Christian community.

It emerged as a community turned toward a transcendental person: Christ, the Risen One. He held them all together; they were at His service. This orientation was so strong in the group that for a long time its members did not feel the need for any elaborate legal system; in fact, a really elaborate legal system developed in the West only—due perhaps just as much to the general culture of the Middle Ages as to the needs of the Church.

The early communities believed that the Spirit of Christ held them together; in their need they had to turn to Him. Now, what happens in the case of *oikonomia* is that the bishop, the *oikonomos* of the house of God, turns to the Risen One and brings the insoluble situation before Him. Through an *analogia fidei,* he searches and seeks how the Lord in His power would heal a wound, would redress an injustice, would bring peace where it is needed. Then, because the Church has the power to "bind and loose," the *oikonomos* himself (never less than a bishop, or a synod of bishops) brings redemption into the situation in which everything seemed to be amiss.

Thus, *oikonomia* is indeed more than the law can offer. It cannot be, ever, summed up in a legal maxim—nor can a precise description be given as to how it operates. It is rooted in the power of Christ, which is present in the community, and which never, absolutely, can adequately be defined by laws. This power cannot be invoked by anyone else than a sacramentally ordained bishop, or possibly by a synod of bishops. The bishop is the trustee of the forgiving and healing strength of Christ in the Church. Thus, *oikonomia* is not arbitrary, in the sense that anyone at any time can demand it.

Clearly, there is nothing like this in the Latin Church. Yet it would be difficult to refute the theological judgment of the Orthodox Church in upholding the practice of *oikonomia,* without ever wanting to define it. The Latin mind is easily repelled by such vagueness; it senses danger in the lack of precision. The Eastern mind is attracted by the mystery and senses the healing strength of it.

May the ecumenical movement progress to the point where Latins can be enriched by the great traditions of sister Churches.

d'Entreve, A.P. *Natural Law: An Introduction to Legal Philosophy.* London: Hutchinson, 1970. An excellent historical introduction to the theories of natural law.

Finnis, J. *Natural Law and Natural Rights.* Oxford: Clarendon, 1980. A modern approach to the theory of natural law.

Friedrich, C. *The Philosophy of Law in Historical Perspective.* 2nd ed. Chicago: University of Chicago Press, 1963. A clear and concise historical survey.

Nicholas, B. *An Introduction to Roman Law.* Oxford: Clarendon, 1961. The best "first book" on Roman law in English; it has many references to common law.

Orsy, L. *"The Canons on Ecclesiastical Law Revisited."* J 37 (1967): 112–159. A commentary on the canons of the old Code; most of it remains valid, since the changes are not extensive.

———. *"The Interpreter and His Art."* J 40 (1980): 27–56. An effort to apply modern hermeneutics to the canons.

Stein, P. and Shand, J. *Legal Values in Western Society.* Edinburgh: Edinburgh University Press, 1974. A comparative study about ancient and modern Western legal systems.

Walker, D.M. *The Oxford Companion to Law.* Oxford: Clarendon, 1980. An intelligently conceived and composed concise encyclopedia in the Oxford tradition; it has an international and historical dimension.

The matter treated here is appropriately included in the general norms of Book I, which regulate the disciplinary action of church legislation. As contrasted with doctrinal principles, disciplinary laws explain and urge the spiritual good of the faithful. Such laws are the prescriptions referring to the reception of the sacraments, the observance of feast days and days of penance, and the celebration of the sacrament of matrimony, e.g., the juridic form and impediments.

The basic concepts of both general decrees and instructions were expressed by Pope Benedict XV in his *motu proprio* issued on September 15, 1917, in which he said,

The ordinary function of the Sacred Congregations as regards general decrees of this kind will be to see that the prescriptions of the Code are faithfully observed, and if necessary, to issue Instructions that will bring out in clearer light the precepts of the Code and make them more effec-

tive. These documents shall be drawn up in such a way as not only to be but to serve as explanations and complements, as it were, of the canons, which should, therefore, very suitably form part of the text of the documents.[1]

Stressed in the revised Code is the administrative or executive function as a most practical way of promoting the fulfillment of the law.

Administrative, as distinguished from legislative and judicial, power is concerned with the actual execution of the law, or its fulfillment. All three forms, however, are jurisdictional in nature. The chief function of the executor is to promote, facilitate, or even urge the observance of the law.

---

[1]Benedict XV, *mp Cum Iuris Canonici, AAS* 9 (1917), 483f. Also found in the preliminary documents of *CIC.* English translation in *CLD* 1, 55–56. Decrees and instructions, however, are not specifically treated in the Code of 1917.

CANONS AND COMMENTARY

TITLE III
GENERAL DECREES AND INSTRUCTIONS
[cc. 29–34]

General Decrees:
Nature/Identification with Laws

Canon 29 — General decrees, by which common prescriptions are issued by a competent legislator for a community capable of receiving a law, are laws properly speaking and are governed by the prescriptions of the canons on laws.

The author of a general decree is the competent legislator, i.e., one who has the power to enact laws for a specified group of subjects. The community capable of receiving a general decree must also be capable of receiving a law. Such a community would be, for example, the entire body of the faithful or those of a definite region, e.g., a diocese or an

entire nation. Although it is debated whether a parish is such a community, a very limited group—such as a few families—is not a community capable of receiving a law; rather, such a group receives a particular decree or precept. General decrees are, in the true sense, laws, and they are therefore regulated by the general principles of law specified in canons 7–22.

The Roman Pontiff is a lawgiver whose community consists of the entire Christian world. The diocesan bishop enjoys true legislative power over the members of his diocese. The legislative power of particular, such as regional, councils affects the faithful of a particular region. Conferences of bishops charged with the pastoral concerns of an entire nation may issue general decrees according to conditions expressed in canon 455. The legislative power of religious institutes is determined by their own constitutions, subject to the approval of the Holy See. Directives for the application of decrees are found in the text itself, reminding the recipient that related points of the law are to be observed.

Limits on Exercise of Executive Power

Canon 30 — **Persons who possess only executive power are not able to issue the general decree mentioned in can. 29, unless in particular cases such power has expressly been granted to them by a competent legislator in accord with the norm of law and the conditions stated in the act of the grant have been observed.**

One possessing executive power is a functionary who is ultimately dependent on the legislator. The executor carries out or puts into effect the general decree according to the particular law or mandate authorizing the administrative action. According to their role as close collaborators with the Sovereign Pontiff in the governing of the Church,[2] the various congregations, offices, etc., of the Roman Curia may issue general decrees. Their dependence on the Roman Pontiff is usually stated in the document or the instrument itself. Such dependence is stated by mentioning the fact of previous consultation with or the explicit approval or even mandate of the Supreme Pontiff.

Within the last few years, a number of general decrees have been issued, such as *Dum canonicarum legum*[3] issued by the Sacred Congregation for Religious and Secular Institutes dealing with the subjects of confession, illness, and the profession of religious. Likewise, the Sacred Congregation for the Oriental Churches has decreed that marriages between Catholics and baptized non-Catholic Orientals are valid as long as a sacred minister is present[4] in conformity with the regulations of that particular church.

Purpose/Issuance of General Executory Decrees

Canon 31 — **§1. General executory decrees determine more precisely the methods to be observed in applying the law or themselves urge the observance of laws. Persons who possess executive power are able to issue such decrees within the limits of their competency.**

The canon defines general executory decrees, which are not technically laws but which presuppose laws which need to be applied and interpreted in practice. Such executory decrees may be issued by persons possessing executive authority, such as vicars (cc. 475–481). However, they may function only within the limits of their competency, which is

subordinate to the competency of those enjoying properly legislative authority, such as diocesan bishops.

Promulgation of General Executory Decrees

§2. The prescriptions of can. 8 should be observed concerning the promulgation of the decrees mentioned in §1 and concerning the period of time to elapse before they become effective.

The promulgation of a general executory decree follows the rule mentioned in canon 8, that is, the general decree, because of its affinity to or even identity with, a law,[5] is officially enacted when it is made known to those obliged to obey it. It takes effect when the period suspending the obligation until a definite date established by the legislator, or the *vacatio legis,* has elapsed—as explained in canon 8.

Subjects of General Executory Decrees

Canon 32 — **General executory decrees oblige those who are bound by the laws whose methods of application such decrees determine or whose observance they urge.**

The intimate relationship between the law and its supporting instrument, the general executory decree, explains the obligatory compliance of the passive subject of the law to its instrument.

Relation of Decrees to Laws

Canon 33 — **§1. General executory decrees, even if they are published in directories or in documents having some other title, do not derogate from laws, and the prescriptions of such decrees which are contrary to laws lack all force.**

General executory decrees are not always published under a uniform title. The conceptual content, or the tenor, of the executory decree may reveal its nature rather than the title itself. *Directories* contain guidelines for the application of accepted principles, and in content include both the ways of carrying out the law as well as pointing out its urgency.[6] Such executive instruments neither derogate from (partially change) nor abrogate (repeal) the law whose meaning they are intended to urge. In a conflict between any provisions mentioned in, e.g., a directory and the text of the law, the latter prevails.

[2]*AAS* 55 (1963), 793; *CLD* 6, 313.
[3]SCRIS, decr *Dum canonicarum legum,* Dec. 8, 1970, *AAS* 63 (1971), 318; *CLD* 7, 531–533.
[4]SCOC, decr *Crescens matrimoniorum,* Feb. 22, 1967, *AAS* 59 (1967) 165; *CLD* 6, 605–606.

[5]See c. 29.
[6]SCDW, *Directory for Masses with Children,* Nov. 1, 1973, *AAS* 66 (1974), 30; *CLD* 7, 497–516.

Cessation of General Executory Decrees

§2. Such decrees cease to have force through explicit or implicit revocation by competent authority as well as through cessation of the law for whose execution they were given, but they do not cease to have force with the termination of the authority of the one issuing them unless the contrary has been expressly provided.

General executory decrees cease either directly, i.e., by express revocation, or indirectly, by the repeal of the law for whose execution they were issued. Applicable here is the principle *accessorium sequitur principale.* The instruction is by reason of its very existence intended to promote the observance of the law. With the cessation of the latter, the former loses its reason for existence.

Since the law, too, is *de se* permanent in intent, the continued existence of its instrument is usually either necessary or very useful to its effectiveness. If, however, the decree has been sufficiently effective as to have achieved its purpose, it may be revoked—especially if its intent was to curb certain excesses which have been corrected.

Rules on Instructions

Canon 34 — §1. Instructions which clarify the prescriptions of laws and elaborate on and determine an approach to be followed in implementing them, are given for the use of those persons whose concern it is to see that the laws are implemented and oblige such persons in the execution of the laws. Persons who possess executive power legitimately issue such instructions within the limits of their competency.

§2. Regulations found in instructions do not derogate from laws, and if any of them cannot be reconciled with the prescriptions of laws, they lack all force.

§3. Instructions cease to have force not only through their explicit or implicit revocation by the competent authority who issued them or by the same authority's superior but also through the cessation of the law for whose clarification or implementation they were given.

Pope Benedict XV, in his *motu proprio Cum iuris canonici,* issued on September 15, 1917, declared that one of the ordinary functions of the sacred congregations was to issue instructions, whereby the canons of the Code were to be more fully explained and effectively carried out. Clarity of exposition was to be the characteristic of these instructions, considered to be the *complements* of the canons. Instructions call attention to the specific laws that they are intended to clarify and explain.

Within recent years, several important instructions have been issued by the Holy See.[7]

Since by their very nature instructions are intended to make the existing law as clear as possible in order to insure its observance, textual conflicts between the law and the instruction should be resolved in favor of the law; but, if the two are irreconcilable, the instruction loses its force. The *derogation* of a law means a *partial* change in the law, a modification or an amendment thereof. It is opposed to *abrogation,* or the repeal, of a law as well as to the substitution of a new law to replace it, namely, *obrogation.* The repeal or modification of a law commensurably affects its supporting instrument, namely, an instruction.

TITLE IV
INDIVIDUAL ADMINISTRATIVE ACTS
[cc. 35–93]

This title, dealing with the regulations governing individual administrative acts that are directed more immediately toward the efficacious fulfillment of the law, was not found as such in the 1917 Code. However, many of the canons contained here were found under the heading of rescripts (*CIC* 36–62). The revised Code now extends the basic canons on rescripts to all individual administrative acts, decrees and precepts—species of such acts.

CHAPTER I
COMMON NORMS
[cc. 35–47]

Author of Administrative Act

Canon 35 — With due regard for can. 76, §1, an individual administrative act, be it a decree, a precept or a rescript, can be issued by one who possesses executive power within the limits of that person's competency.

A *decree* may be taken in a broad or in a strict sense. In a broad sense, it is an ordinance issued by public authority, bearing a relation to the public good. It may be issued by one having legislative, administrative, or judicial power; however, it does not include a judicial sentence. In a strict sense—as it is

---

[7]For example, see SCRIS, instr *Renovationis causam,* Jan. 6, 1969, *AAS* 6 (1969), 103f.; *CLD* 7, 489–509 (renewal of religious formation); SCSacr, instr *Immensae caritatis,* Jan. 29, 1973, *AAS* 65 (1973), 264f.; *CLD* 8, 477–485 (easier access to Holy Communion); SCDF, instr and procedure *Ut notum est,* Dec. 6, 1973; *CLD* 8, 1177–1184 (privilege of the faith cases); SCSacr, instr *Sacramentalem indolem,* May 15, 1974; *CLD* 8, 815–818 (lay person as official witness to marriage). It is to be noted that the substance of this instruction has been epitomized in c. 1112.

to be understood here—it is an ordinance by one having public power or the power of jurisdiction, and acting in an administrative capacity by promoting compliance with the law. A *precept* is an order issued to individuals, rather than to the community as a whole, obliging them as a law. A *rescript,* as will be seen, is, generally speaking, the official response to a petition or to a communication calling for an answer. A singular or particular act may be directed toward an individual or to a juridic person, e.g., a religious community. The extent and the limits of the administrative function will be determined by the authority appointing the executor and by the canons pertinent to the case. Canon 76, §1, to which reference is made, mentions the immunity that privileges enjoy from decrees considered in this chapter.

Interpretation of Administrative Act

Canon 36 — §1. An administrative act is to be understood in accord with the proper meaning of the words and the common usage of speech. In a doubtful situation administrative acts are subject to a broad interpretation except for the following administrative acts which are subject to a strict interpretation: those dealing with lawsuits, those threatening or inflicting penalties, those which restrict the rights of a person, those which injure the acquired rights of others, or those which benefit private individuals and are contrary to the law.

§2. An administrative act must not be extended to cases other than those actually expressed in it.

Since administrative acts are closely related to the observance of the law by way of a precept or rescript, the text of these official documents must be clearly understood; if they are not, they must be explained according to the criteria of interpretation as explained in canons 16–19.[8] The proper meaning of a word is opposed to the incorrect, alien, or simply the wrong meaning. The proper sense of an expression is not exclusively restricted to the native or original acceptance of the word, but it may include one that has been accepted by common usage either in law or jurisprudence or established by the style of the Roman Curia.[9]

The general rule of interpretation is that favorable provisions are to be interpreted broadly, thus including more beneficiaries, as it were, while unfavorable or odious expressions are to be restricted in their application. According to the classification given in this canon, it is quite possible that a broad interpretation of an administrative act would be to the advantage of some and to the disadvantage of others. The number of those who might suffer from such a broad interpretation, then, should prevent unfavorable reactions. A restrictive interpretation must be used in the following situations involving a doubt:

(a) those dealing with lawsuits—since in litigation, one of the parties might suffer from the decision issued, e.g., where parish boundaries are called into dispute. Such decisions may be onerous to the losers. Likewise a broad interpretation of procedural rules might infringe on the administration of justice;

(b) those concerning the threat or infliction of penalties—since the culpability and consequently the prescribed penalty imposed on one convicted of an offense must be established with certainty, both the warning or threat of punishment as well as the infliction thereof must be interpreted strictly. A broad interpretation might result in a miscarriage of justice, which indeed would be odious to the accused, or conceivably, to the good of the faithful;

(c) those that restrict the rights of a person—some privileges, granted in favor of particular persons, whether individual or juridic, might work to the disadvantage of others, as in the case of a privileged chapel that might adversely affect the parochial ministry of a neighboring church;

(d) those that injure the vested rights of a person. A *vested right* is based on two necessary conditions: (1) that some form of law exist by which the specific right in question can be acquired; and (2) that a juridic act has been placed by which the right has been actually acquired. It is called in law, a *ius quaesitum* or *acquisitum,*[10] a right that has been fully acquired. Possession of property by just claim is one of the most familiar examples of an acquired right. The term acquired, of itself, might imply complete and inalienable ownership. The principle is founded in the nonretroactivity of law. A rightful possession cannot be extinguished by the mere enactment of a later law. The expression, acquired, or vested, right, more commonly and properly understood is a right that is acquired by a third party. A third party can suffer prejudice or a disadvantage by the change of a former law or administrative act in regard to rights which he or she had already possessed, because whenever a lawful right is tak-

---

[8]The same principles governing the interpretation and the suppletion of law—and expressed in cc. 16–19— are applicable to the interpretation of administrative acts. *CIC* 49 and 50 deal with the interpretation of rescripts. The interpretation of an administrative act by way of analogy is not permissible, in accord with *R.I.* 74 in VI, namely, "That which is freely given to one person ought not to be made a precedent by another," or "Quod alicui gratiose conceditur, trahi non debet ab aliis in exemplum."

[9]For an explanation of the *stylus curiae,* cf. A.G. Cicognani, *Canon Law,* 2nd rev. ed. (Philadelphia: Dolphin Press, 1935) 105–109 (no. 5).

[10]Cf. commentary on c. 4.

en away from someone, three persons are involved: namely, the legislator or the competent authority; the one who profits by a change in the law or the termination of the administrative act; and thirdly, the one who suffers by such changes or to whom the change is in some way odious or detrimental. For example, some bishops had received from the Sacred Congregation for the Clergy the special faculty to appoint a pastor for a period of six years. The faculty, as is obvious, looks to future pastors, i.e., to those appointed after the reception of this special faculty, which may not be applied to pastors already in office before the indult was granted. These pastors held their positions by virtue of an acquired right, which may not be extinguished by subsequent legislation or administrative acts. Although a particular administrative act is not, of itself, a law, the principle of the analogy of law may be applied;

(e) dispensations, so often expressed through the medium of executive acts, "wound the law" for the benefit of individuals; hence, there exists the need of their being interpreted strictly. Other classes of executive acts, however, may enjoy the favor of a broad interpretation, thus increasing the number of their beneficiaries.

Written Form of Administrative Act

Canon 37 — An administrative act which deals with the external forum is to be set forth in writing; likewise, if the administrative act is issued in commissorial form, its act of execution is to be in writing.

An administrative act very frequently refers to the external forum touching directly or indirectly the good of the faithful. Its proof can be more easily established by committing it to writing—thus it is recorded and may be used when needed. What is written remains; sounds and words can be forgotten, and may be challenged. A written record, however, is not necessary for validity. Rescripts from the Sacred Penitentiary, however, are not affected by the prescription of this canon, since they refer to the internal forum or the forum of conscience.[11]

Limitations on Administrative Act

Canon 38 — Even in the case of a rescript given at the initiative of its issuer (motu proprio), an administrative act lacks effect insofar as it injures the acquired right of another or is contrary to a law or an approved custom, unless the competent authority expressly adds to it a derogating clause.

Certain limitations are imposed on administrative acts that conflict with already existing laws, customs, or acquired rights. The competent authority, however, may add a clause that will modify or affect to a degree such conflicting ordinances or rights. This intended modification, however, must be clearly expressed by an appropriate clause. The term *motu proprio*[12] applies to papal instruments issued on the initiative or the will of the Roman Pontiff himself—and not prompted by any formal petition. Diocesan interests may also prompt a bishop to issue ordinances on his own initiative and within the sphere of his competence, but the term *motu proprio* is reserved to papal acts of this nature. If no qualifying expressions are found in the document—thus indicating no derogation of existing laws, customs, or acquired rights—these are left intact. Other articles contained in the text, however, will retain their force.

Conditions Affecting Validity

Canon 39 — Conditions attached to an administrative act are considered to affect its validity only when they are expressed by the particles *if* (si), *unless* (nisi), or *provided that* (dummodo).

In addition to the particles *si, nisi,* and *dummodo* affecting the validity of the administrative act, others may be found that would have the same effect—if such were clear from the text and context. Such an expression as, *in the act of sacramental confession only,* makes it abundantly clear that the validity of the administrative act depends on its use in the confessional.

Invalid Anticipation of Administrative Act

Canon 40 — The executor of an administrative act who executes it before receiving the letter and verifying its authenticity and accuracy functions invalidly, unless previous notice of the letter had

---

[11]The internal forum, or the forum of conscience, as distinguished from the external forum, looks to the good of the individual, while the latter is concerned with the public good or the good of the faithful in general.

[12]Papal documents issued by the Sovereign Pontiff of his own accord or on his own initiative are given by way of decree. Even though issued in this way it does not follow that no petition preceded it, but the term *motu proprio* signifies that he makes it his own. Among the several decrees issued *motu proprio* in more recent years are those of Pope Paul VI, such as *Ecclesiae sanctae*, which contains provisional norms to be observed for the fulfillment of the decrees of Vatican II until the promulgation of the 1983 Code of Canon Law. The Roman Pontiff uses the term *decernimus*, indicating that this document has the force of a decree. For the text of this important decree, cf. *AAS* 58 (1966), 757f.; *CLD* 6, 264–298. Other *motu proprio* decrees of the same Supreme Pontiff are, e.g., the new regulation of the Pontifical Council for the Laity, *AAS* 68 (1976), 696f.; *CLD* 8, 194–199 and the Definitive Regulation for the Pontifical Commission for Justice and Peace, *AAS* 68 (1976), 700f.; *CLD* 8, 198–204. Other examples of *motu proprio* decrees are found *passim* in the *AAS* and *CLD*.

been given to the executor by the authority who issued the act.

This provision determines the *time* when the executor of an administrative act may execute the act. The person may not anticipate official notification by way of a presumption, but rather must have previously received the letter containing instructions concerning the administrative act. Moreover, the executor must have recognized its authenticity and integrity. If, however, in an urgent situation, the executor has been notified on reliable authority, e.g., by a functionary of the Roman Curia, by telephone, or by telegram, the administrative act may be executed. Such anticipated information, however, should include whatever essential directives may be necessary to the act of execution. The executor must have certainty of notification, then, before proceeding to act.

Limitations on Activity of Executor

Canon 41 — The executor of an administrative act whose competency is limited to executing it cannot refuse to execute it unless it is manifestly apparent that the act is null, that it cannot be upheld due to another serious cause, or that the conditions attached to the administrative act itself have not been fulfilled. Nevertheless, if the execution of the administrative act appears inopportune due to circumstances of person or place, the executor should delay its execution; in all these cases the executor should immediately inform the authority who issued the act.

A *necessary* executor of an administrative act, whose function is simply to carry out the directive of the competent authority, lacks the option granted to a *voluntary* executor, to whose discretion is left the execution of the administrative act. While the *necessary* executor cannot refuse, he or she can, however, follow his or her conscientious judgment. The administrative act might be null because of the invalidating elements of either *obreptio,* the statement of a *falsehood* as a *sole* motive for requesting a favor, or *subreptio,* the *suppression* of the truth or the true reasons motivating a request.

The conditions attached to the act are usually expressed quite clearly by such qualifying particles as *si, nisi,* and *dummodo* (respectively, if, unless, and provided that) that indicate those conditions that must be fulfilled for the validity of the execution of the administrative act. The execution of the act is also to be deferred when circumstances, e.g., the publicly known mischievous behavior of the beneficiary of a papal favor, obviously unknown to the authority issuing the administrative mandate, prudently suggest the delay of any action on the part of the executor.

Invalid Execution of Administrative Act

Canon 42 — The executor of an administrative act must proceed in accord with the norm of the mandate; the execution is invalid unless the essential conditions attached in the letter have been fulfilled and unless the executor has substantially observed the procedural formalities.

This canon contains the very basic rules of executing an administrative act. The essential conditions will be introduced usually by such significant particles as "if," "unless," "provided that," etc., as already mentioned. Procedural guidelines and directive norms are formalities to be followed and will be expressed or implied in the text of the mandate. For example, a delegate of the Holy See is appointed to examine personally the conditions in a religious house or in a seminary. The mandate specifies a personal interview with each member of the community or student body. Such a directive, under pain of the invalidity of the executive act, cannot be complied with by a general exhortation to the entire community as a substitute for individual interviews. Moreover, other procedural formalities, such as prescribed reports, must be fulfilled.

Substitution of Executor

Canon 43 — The executor of an administrative act can with prudent judgment substitute another as executor unless such substitution has been forbidden or the executor has been chosen for personal qualifications, or the person of the substitute has been predetermined; however, in these cases the executor may entrust preparatory acts to another.

The "personal qualifications" mentioned in this canon may specify, e.g., a cleric in ecclesiastical dignity, or a superior, or one especially informed concerning the circumstances involved in the executive act.

The "preparatory acts" referred to herein could include gathering the necessary documents or hearing testimony relative to the case.

Succession in Office of Executor

Canon 44 — Unless the executor was chosen on account of personal qualifications, an administrative act can also be implemented by the executor's successor in office.

The general rule here prevails, namely, that "he who succeeds to the right of another ought to use the same right."[13] Again, the unauthorized substitu-

---

[13]*R.I.* 46, in VI: "Is, qui in ius succedit alterius, eo iure, quo ille, uti debebit." "The dignity and the office, which are of themselves perpetual, are more to be considered in this matter than the person." Cicognani, 765.

tion of another for a person chosen because of particular qualities ("electa industria personae") invalidates the executive act. Such an exclusive choice, however, must be clear from the document containing the appointment. A *doubt* in this matter would justify the assumption that a substitute is not excluded. The norm of executive substitution will be, generally, the relative importance of the matter involved.

Remedy for Error of Executor

Canon 45 — If in some way the executor erred in the execution of an administrative act, the executor may implement the same act again.

An error in the discharge of an executive act could be substantial or merely accidental, in which latter case there should be no need to repeat the act.[14]

Continuity of Executive Powers

Canon 46 — Unless it is expressly provided otherwise in law, an administrative act does not cease with the termination of the authority of the one issuing it.

The death or resignation of the authority issuing an administrative act does not normally interfere with its continuing execution. The general principle favors the continuity of executive activity even though the person issuing the act in question has left office for one reason or another. Counter-provisions that would impede or suspend the execution of an administrative act must be expressed so as to leave no room for doubt, e.g., cessation of privilege granted at the good pleasure of someone in authority when that authority figure leaves office (c. 81). This same principle would apply to one chosen as an executor of a given administrative act because of personal qualifications to such a degree that all others would be excluded. Even in such an extraordinary case, if the process of executing a given administrative act had already begun, its executor might complete it. The legal axiom often used, "res iam non est integra,"[15] would be applicable. In other words, the task of executing the given administrative act had already begun by the placing of one of the acts necessary for its completion.

Revocation of Administrative Act

Canon 47 — The revocation of an administrative act by means of another administrative act of a competent authority takes effect only from the moment at which the latter act has legitimately been made known to the person for whom it has been given.

The authority competent to revoke an administrative act may be the person granting the executive power or that person's successor or superior. The notification that the power has been revoked should be made by an official declaration to the executor, before which the revocatory act is ineffectual.

CHAPTER II
INDIVIDUAL DECREES AND PRECEPTS
[cc. 48–58]

The species of administrative acts to be studied in this chapter, namely, individual decrees and precepts, are regulated by the general norms considered in the preceding chapter. Canons 48–52; 57; and 58, §1 were not expressly mentioned in the Code of 1917, although the substantial content of the canons mentioned is not entirely new.

Individual Decree: Concept/Species

Canon 48 — An individual decree is an administrative act issued by a competent executive authority in which a decision is given or a provision is made in a particular case in accord with the norms of law; such decisions or provisions of their nature do not presuppose that a petition has been made by someone.

Canon 48 supplies a definition of an individual decree, states the twofold species of the same and distinguishes it from a rescript. The individual decree is distinguished from the general decree explained in canons 29–33. It is focused on a particular case that may involve one or more persons. A decision[16] is an authoritative act resolving a dispute or a situation that has caused disagreement between two or more parties. A provision[17] refers to the employment of authoritative measures to remedy a situation calling for adjustment or regularization. The provision in question is not restricted to that of filling a vacant ecclesiastical office, as out-

---

[14]A major or nullifying error would concern the identity of the person or the very matter involved. The principle mentioned in c. 66 may be applied here.

[15]"Res iam non est integra" is used in reference to a series of juridic acts, and it means, in the present instance, that the initial executive act had not been placed, thus leaving, as it were, the whole issue juridically "untouched."

[16]A decision is an administrative act resolving a particular controversy or dispute. While a decision is generally issued by way of judicial action, here it is considered as an individual administrative act. The competence to make such executive decisions may derive from the law itself, as indicated, e.g., in c. 134, or it may be granted on an ad hoc basis by the competent authority.

[17]A provision is a particular administrative act that calls for adjustment or regularization in order to remedy a particular situation. While the act of a superior filling a vacant office is not excluded from this canon, its sense includes a broader area, applying to cases calling for remedial or regulatory action. Such action does not imply, of itself, any culpability on the part of the persons involved in a situation. Etymologically, *provision* means a foreseeing of a situation and as a result, a meeting of the needs in question.

lined in canons 146–183. While the canon mentions a particular case, it does not of necessity imply that serious disciplinary problems are involved; rather, the situation may call for an ad hoc provisional remedy. The executive action must be performed according to the norms regulating it, whether the norms are derived from the Code or from any particular instructions issued by competent authorities. A rescript is understood as an administrative act requested from competent executive authority in writing, by which—of its very nature—a privilege, a dispensation, or another favor is granted.[18]

Individual Precept: Notion

Canon 49 — An individual precept is a decree directly and legitimately enjoining a determined person or persons to do or to omit something, especially concerning the urging of the observance of a law.

In order to insist on the observance of the law, an injunction—by way of a positive command or prohibitive order—may be issued by a competent executive authority. Such an injunction implies a remissness in obedience to the law on the part of an individual or a number of specified persons. The need for injunctive action is apparent when a group of parochial dissidents obstruct the installation of a pastor to whom they are opposed or when a group of religious, disobeying the repeated directives of the Holy See, refuse to comply with the decrees concerning common life. Individuals may occasion an executive precept as, e.g., when a priest arbitrarily introduces innovations into the Eucharistic liturgy or insists on taking a public stand on doctrinal and moral questions at variance with the official teaching of the Church. Briefly these and other abuses call for remedial and at times, unfortunately, penal action on the part of competent authorities.

Information and Consultation before Decree

Canon 50 — Before issuing an individual decree an authority should seek out the necessary information and proofs, and also hear those whose rights can be injured, insofar as this is possible.

This canon, newly formulated in the Code, prescribes that especially in matters relating in any way to justice, the prudent administrator must be as thoroughly informed as possible. All parties involved in a controversial issue are entitled to a fair and impartial hearing, in order that the objective truth may appear. Fact-finding is a necessary prerequisite to the issuance of a disciplinary decree; the required information can be obtained by way of testimony, dialogue, or discussion that may follow the submission of facts considered necessary or helpful to determine whether a decree or precept is advisable.[19] Such diligent investigation seeks to discover the pertinent facts not only before a disciplinary decree is issued but also before a judgment is made regarding the qualifications of a person proposed for appointment to an office. The failure to cooperate in any necessary inquiry, whether it precedes a decree or precept involving justice or the appointment of a qualified candidate for office, may render any such administrative actions more difficult to execute. Every possible means to avoid the miscarriage of justice must be employed.

Written Form of Decree/Decision

Canon 51 — A decree should be issued in writing, giving, in the case of a decision, the reasons which prompted it, at least in a summary fashion.

A decision is a judgment both that follows deliberation and precedes the decree or precept. A written statement of such a judgment is the ordinary method of communicating the matter to the parties concerned. Strictly speaking, only *decisions* are to be put in writing. Several reasons prompt this provision, e.g., the written document containing the text of the decision will reveal any lapses of logical reasoning, or any arbitrary impression of the authority issuing the document as well as give the opportunity for one's defense in case recourse is to be made to a higher authority. Since the motives alleged as influencing the decision may well be challenged, they, above all, must be expressed clearly in writing. Otherwise, serious difficulties might arise in the administration of justice in a particular case. Canons 37 and 54, §2 contain similarly appropriate provisions—the former prescribes the written record of administrative acts relating to the external forum, and, if issued in commissary form, the execution of such an act; the latter points out that a decree can be enforced if it has been issued in writing.

Limited Application of Individual Decree

Canon 52 — An individual decree has force only in respect to the matters it decides and only on be-

---

[18]See c. 59 for the notion of a rescript. From the definition therein, the distinction between a rescript and a decree and decision is clear.

[19]This rule applies to the successful operation of any prudent government or administration, e.g., in the selection of a qualified candidate for office or for the removal of an incumbent therefrom. Established information on the candidate for or the removal from a particular office must be obtained. All who might be adversely affected by an individual decree as well as any third party should have a voice in any inquiry preceding such administrative action. The present canon ends with the phrase, "insofar as this is possible," thus excluding the extremes of a mere casual effort to ascertain the facts of the case and an interminable and frustrating investigation. Experienced administrators are usually acquainted with the basic investigative procedures.

half of the persons for whom it was given; it obliges these persons everywhere, unless it is otherwise evident.

The scope of an individual decree or precept is limited to the persons mentioned therein as well as to the subject matter involved. Like a shadow, the terms of an individual decree follow the recipient everywhere. The personal nature of the individual decree or precept, acquired from the circumstances of the case, indicates its transcendence of both territory and community. An injunction—especially of a disciplinary nature—imposed by the competent ordinary must be observed by a cleric, even outside the territory in which he resides. Such a measure relates not only to the good of the individual, but also in some cases to the good of the faithful. The intemperate religious activities of anyone, cleric or lay person, would justify the restraining intervention of the competent superior. The extraterritorial consequences of unrestrained religious excesses may, for example, transcend diocesan or regional limits; this would explain why the injunction, like a shadow, must follow the offending zealots. The special terms of a particular decree, however, due to special circumstances, may limit the effectiveness of the decree to a restricted area.

Conflicting Decrees

Canon 53 — If decrees are contrary to one another, a special decree prevails over a general decree in those matters which are specifically expressed; if they are equally special or general, the later decree modifies the prior one to the extent that the later is contrary to the prior.

The conflict of decrees is resolved principally by invoking the rules of law, which are, however, founded on established jurisprudence—much of which is derived from Roman Law. Thus, Rule 34 in VI, "The specific derogates from the general." Applying this rule to the present, it may be concluded that a particular or singular decree prevails over a general decree. The present canon further specifies by adding "in those matters which are specifically expressed."[20]

Individual Decree: Operative Force

Canon 54 — §1. An individual decree whose applicaton is entrusted to an executor takes effect

[20]*R.I.* 34 in VI: "Generi per speciem derogatur." For the jurisdictional background of this rule of law, see Cicognani, 733. Rules of Law, *Regulae Iuris (R.I.)* are brief legal axioms. They propose norms either of the interpretation or the application of a law, or they express principles of the natural law. Some of these rules are authentic, since they have been inserted in the text of the law by the lawgiver. Such rules are not always applied easily, and their relevancy must be recognized in each particular case.

from the moment of its execution; otherwise, from the moment it is made known to the person through the authority of its issuer.

A particular decree committed to the agency of an executor takes effect at the moment when the destined recipient is informed of its issuance by the competent authority. It will include any particular instructions necessary to insure compliance with its terms. In virtue of their respective offices, diocesan ordinaries as well as major superiors of clerical institutes and clerical societies of pontifical right—all of whom enjoy ordinary executive power[21]— communicate to their subjects matters issued in their interest by the Holy See. The nature and circumstances surrounding each case will determine whether it is to be issued through or without the ministry of an executor.

Individual Decree: Enforcement

§2. For an individual decree to be enforced it must be communicated by means of a legitimate document in accord with the norm of law.

The enforcement of a decree demands that its provisions be expressed in legally acceptable terms, thereby supplying sufficient proof of its genuineness. The Code does not specify the formulary details necessary to prove the authenticity of the decree; it simply states that it must be drawn up according to the norms of law, "ad normam iuris." Documentary forms usually include such identifying marks as the official letterhead, the signature of a competent authority, the seal of office, etc.[22] Other documentary features established by acceptable practice may be found in the executory decree. It seems that the minimum requirements would consist in the statement of the order involved and the genuine signature of the authority competent to issue it, supported by confirmatory circumstances.

Substitute Form of Communication of Decree

Canon 55 — With due regard for the prescription of cann. 37 and 51, when a most serious reason prevents the handing over of the written text of a decree, the decree is considered to have been communicated if it is read before a notary or two witnesses to the person for whom it is destined and all present sign an instrument stating this was done.

Canon 37 states that administrative acts referring to the external forum are to be put in writing, as are their acts of execution when these are expedited in

[21]Communications from the Holy See directed to individuals— and executed by ordinaries and others—may contain favors such as dispensations, as well as admonitions or other precepts.
[22]Documentary forms issued by the sacred congregations follow a traditional form, observed often by diocesan curias.

commissary form. Canon 51 provides that a decree containing a decision should be issued in writing —giving at least in summary fashion the motives prompting the decision. Neither prescription conflicts with the tenor of this canon, which implies that it has been committed to writing since it is to be read to the destined recipient.

What would constitute "a most serious reason" (i.e., "gravissima ratio") for the employment of the substitute form of communication mentioned in this canon? If the text of the decree were made public, its content might reach a community hostile to the Church or to particular members thereof. Again, if the text of the decree were divulged to a possibly prejudiced or unfriendly press, it might be so distorted as to result in a serious misunderstanding of the nature and purpose of the decree. The reading of the decree follows the completion of the file on the case. The alternate provision of reading the decree—witnessed, notarized, and signed—should usually obviate most of the dangers associated with a less circumspect form of publication.

Presumptive Communication of Decree

Canon 56 — A decree is considered to have been communicated when the person for whom it was destined was properly summoned to receive or hear it, even if the person without a just cause, did not appear or refused to sign it.

The accepted manner of citing a person in conformity with canonical norms is by way of the ordinary postal service. To insure the reception of this citation, however, registered mail will frequently be advisable. The purpose of the citation may be achieved by telephone or telegraph, although these, strictly speaking, are not necessary to contact the person for whom the decree is destined. Once it has been sufficiently proved that the destined recipient has been notified and that failure to comply with the citation has been established, the legal presumption of contumacy, or contempt, exists. Deliberate failure to answer the citation might be attributed to the recipient's suspicion that the decree is unfavorable.

Presumptive Negative Response of Authority

The forum of justice within the Catholic Church is so constituted as to include the interests of all the faithful. Those who feel themselves aggrieved by an administrative act may submit their statement of complaint against what they consider an inadequate administration of justice—if not a direct violation thereof.

Canon 57 — §1. As often as the law requires a decree to be issued or if an interested party legitimately presents either a petition or a recourse to obtain a decree, the competent authority should provide for the matter within three months from the receipt of the petition or recourse unless another time period is prescribed by law.

One who considers himself or herself unfairly treated may have immediate recourse to the competent authority, who should carefully assess all aspects of the act that has been issued. The competent authority may reject the recourse as being unreasonable or may modify the terms of the administrative act or may even revoke it. The recourse must be reasonable and according to the norms of law, i.e., *resting on solid grounds* and neither arbitrary nor founded on such arbitrary motives as whim or caprice. If the administrator simply refuses to reconsider the alleged unfair or unjust decree, the supposed victim of such an unfavorable response may address the grievance to the immediate superior of the one issuing the decree. This is known as a hierarchical recourse. Such is the recourse submitted to the Holy See against a decree of dismissal from a religious institute. This paragraph also mentions the presenting of a petition to the competent superior, such as that made for exclaustration or the alienation of ecclesiastical property. The three-month period mentioned is not intended to terminate the obligation but to prevent any delay by the superior. The aforesaid period is to be reckoned according to canon 202, §2, i.e., the months are to be computed as stated on the calendar.

§2. When this period of time has passed, if the decree has not yet been given, the response is presumed to be negative regarding the presentation of a further recourse.

The three-month silence of the superior is construed as meaning that the recourse or petition has been rejected. This is a presumption of law that may be overthrown by contrary facts. The three-month silence may be due to culpable neglect to provide an answer. The aggrieved person, or the petitioner, may repeat his or her demand for recourse or repeat his or her petition before the same authority who has presumably denied it, or proceed to a hierarchical recourse or petition.

§3. A presumed negative response does not exempt the competent authority from the obligation of issuing the decree and even making reparation for damages possibly incurred in accord with the norm of can. 128.

The delay of the superior in meeting the obligation to answer is not an excuse from issuing the desired decree, and the virtue of justice calls for any reparation of damages due the petitioner because of administrative negligence.

Cessation of Individual Decree/Precept

Canon 58 — §1. An individual decree ceases to have force through its legitimate revocation by competent authority and also through the cessation of the law for whose execution it has been given.

A particular or singular decree is directed toward individual persons, whether physical or juridic. The present canon considers such decrees as ceasing through the external action of the competent authority. This can occur directly by revocation or indirectly by the repeal of the law itself, thus making the decree unnecessary—as well as by changed conditions that bring about the gradual collapse of the law sustaining the decree. A disciplinary decree imposed by way of an injunction will lose its force if the recipient thereof has fully complied with its terms.

§2. An individual precept which has not been imposed through a legitimate document ceases with the termination of the authority of the one issuing it.

Unless issued by means of a legitimate document, a singular precept would cease to have effect at the termination of the office of the competent authority who issued it. The specific requirements for the legitimacy of a document are explained in canon 54, §2. If such a precept were not committed to writing in a legally acceptable form, its genuineness could be challenged. If the precept were issued merely by word of mouth, the effect would cease with the termination of the office of the authority who had given it. If, for example, a penal precept contained a reprehension or an admonition, it should be expressed in writing and signed by the competent official. This would be sufficient to establish the legality of the document. The lack of documentary proof can always occasion a challenge to the legality of the action in question.

CHAPTER III
RESCRIPTS
[cc. 59–75]

Etymologically, a rescript means a written answer, being derived from the Latin verb, *rescribere,* i.e., to reply in writing. The practice of issuing rescripts is traced back to the Roman Empire, when the emperor, being an expert in the law, answered inquiries addressed to him by magistrates and sometimes even by private citizens. The particular rescript would reveal its affinity to the law. Rescripts were also used in the early history of Christianity, and Pope St. Siricius (384–399) wrote the earliest rescript that has survived. Other rescripts of this same Roman Pontiff are also recorded.

The multiplication of benefices, litigations, and consultations occasioned the proliferation of rescripts. The institute of rescripts reached its perfection in what are known as the *Regulae Cancelleriae,*[23] which were papal regulations for conducting the business of the Roman Curia. The Code of 1917 distilled and expressed in an orderly fashion the rules governing rescripts, which had been developing over the centuries. The revised Code, while retaining substantially the old discipline, has emphasized the administrative dimensions of the rescript. As already noted, many of the rules governing rescripts under the former Code are applicable now to all administrative acts.

The form of a rescript is considered from both the external and internal viewpoints. The external form is expressed according to the traditional structural formalities employed in official ecclesiastical communications. They include such features as the compositional style of the Roman Curia, traditional expressions, the signature of the authority issuing the rescript, and the seal of the office from which it originates. The internal form is composed of the petition, the motives prompting it, and the response proceeding from the competent authority. The authenticity of the rescript will be established from an examination of such features as the date and place of its issuance, the style of the document, and the signature of the authority giving the response.

Rescripts are granted directly to the petitioner in what is known as the *forma gratiosa,* or favorable form, or they may be committed to the petitioner through an intermediary or executor, in *forma commissoria.* The executor may have no choice but to execute the rescript according to the terms contained in it, i.e., in commissary form that is *necessary, in forma commissoria necessaria.* If the execution of the rescript is left to the discretionary power of the executor, it is issued *in forma commissoria voluntaria.* These classifications appear in the canons on administrative acts. In practice, rescripts from the Holy See are often left for execution to the discretion and conscience of the ordinary.

Notion of Rescript

Canon 59 — §1. A rescript is an administrative act issued in writing by competent executive authority by which through its very nature a privilege, dispensation, or other favor is granted in response to someone's request.

This canon is not found in the Code of 1917, in which the notion of administrative acts was not specifically treated. An administrative act, emanating as it does from one vested with administrative power or authority, is of its nature directed to the

[23] On the Rules of the Chancellery, see Cicognani, 322–324.

good of the Church by effectively contributing to the execution of or the fulfillment of its laws. Executive competence has as its source the law of the Church, especially as indicated in canon 134, §1, i.e, regarding vicars general, episcopal vicars, major superiors of clerical religious institutes of pontifical right, and those of clerical institutes of apostolic life of pontifical right. The executive competence of bishops, however, derives from the divine institution of the episcopal order as exercised especially by those governing a diocese.[24]

A privilege, as will be treated in chapter IV, is a favor granted to certain persons—whether physical or juridic—by the legislator or by an executive authority.[25] A dispensation is the relaxation of a merely ecclesiastical law in a particular case. Dispensations are examined under chapter V.[26] Other favors of many different classifications may be granted through the instrument of rescripts.

Among other permissions or favors, one might note, e.g., permission to alienate ecclesiastical goods—the value of which requires the permission of the Holy See, canon 1292, §2; permission for a leave of absence, canon 665, §1; permission for exclaustration, canon 686, §1, etc.

In addition to those enjoying executive power by virtue of their office, others may issue rescripts by way of delegation.

§2. The prescriptions established for rescripts also apply to the verbal granting of a permission or of favors, unless it is otherwise evident.

Favors granted orally, or *vivae vocis oraculo,* follow the regulations governing rescripts. Canon 74 further provides for the use of such a favor in the internal forum, yet its concession must be proven in the external forum if such is required.

Recipient of Rescript

*Canon 60 — **Any rescript whatsoever can be requested by all who are not expressly forbidden to do so.***

The present Code mentions no one in particular who is forbidden to request a rescript. Only positive proof would establish one's inability to make such a request. Canons 2265, §2; 2275, §3°; and 2283 of the 1917 Code referred to the ineligibility of those under excommunication, personal interdict, or suspension to obtain positions of dignity, offices, ecclesiastical pensions, or any other ecclesiastical position. No such statement of disability is found in the revised Code.

[24]Cf. cc. 131, §§1–2; 375 and 391.
[25]C. 76, §1.
[26]Cc. 85–93.

Rescript for Third Party

*Canon 61 — **Unless it is otherwise evident, a rescript can be requested on behalf of another person, even without that person's consent, and it takes effect before the person's acceptance, with due regard for contrary clauses.***

Favors for clerics or for members of the laity, such as ecclesiastical honors or other tokens of appreciation of special services rendered may be requested of the Holy See by the ordinary, without the knowledge of the recipients. The validity of the rescript does not depend upon the consent of the favored recipient, who is not bound, generally, to accept a favor. Contrary clauses in the rescript, however, may limit such freedom. A *sanatio in radice* may be granted without the knowledge of one or even of both parties, according to canon 1164. Canon 37 of the former Code contained substantially the provision expressed in canon 61.

Effects of Rescript

*Canon 62 — **A rescript for which no executor is given takes effect from the moment when the letter is issued; other rescripts take effect from the moment of execution.***

Rescripts issued without an executor take effect at the moment when the letter of response is written, while those demanding executive action produce their effects at the time when the executor discharges his or her duties. The *moment* when the document is signed is generally unknown, and any effects following from the rescript will be retroactive to the date appended to the document.

Impediments to Validity of Rescript

The basic condition on which a petition is granted is its truthfulness. This fundamental principle was also elaborated in canons 42 and 45 of the 1917 Code.

*Canon 63 — **§1. Subreption, or the concealment of the truth, invalidates a rescript if those things which must be expressed in the request for validity according to the law, style, and canonical practice were not expressed; this does not apply to a rescript of favor which was given** motu proprio.*

Subreptio, or the suppression of the truth—even if done in good faith—is an obstacle to the grant sought in a rescript, since it fails to express that which ought to be expressed in the petition. Moreover, the petition should be drawn up according to the style and practice required by canon law. While a rigid style is not demanded, certain basic formalities are required, such as a clear exposition of the facts of the case and the motives prompting the petition, with the identifying qualities of the petitioner, etc.[27] In the petition for a dispensation from the irregularities described in canon 1041, 4°, i.e., the crimes of voluntary homicide or abortion, the number of such crimes must be mentioned in the petition.[28] The omission of non-essential details of the case would not nullify the rescript. A rescript that is granted *motu proprio,* or from the spontaneous concession of the Roman Pontiff, would not be subject to the above requirements. It is unlikely, however, that the Supreme Pontiff would grant a petition laboring under such defects.

§2. Obreption, or statements of falsehood, likewise invalidates a rescript if not even one proposed motivating reason is true.

The expression of a falsehood, *obreptio,* nullifies the rescript, if no other motive is true, i.e., if the petition is founded on a falsehood or several falsehoods, as the case may be.

§3. For rescripts which have no executor the motivating reason must be true at the time when the rescript is issued; for other rescripts, at the time of execution.

If a rescript is issued without an executor, the motives sustaining the petition must be true at the time of the grant. If it is committed to the care of an executor, the reasons must be true at the time of the act of execution.

Recourse among Roman Dicasteries

Canon 64 — With due regard for the authority of the Sacred Penitentiary in the internal forum, a favor which has been denied by one dicastery of the Roman Curia cannot be validly granted by another dicastery or by another competent authority below the Roman Pontiff without the consent of the dicastery before which the matter was initiated.

The competence of the Sacred Penitentiary "comprises all things which concern the internal forum, including the non-sacramental forum. Wherefore this Tribunal grants favors, absolutions, dispensations, commutations, sanations and condonations for the internal forum."[29] The principle governing recourse from one Roman dicastery to another may be expressed in the rule of law as follows: "When anything is forbidden a person by one way, he [or she] ought not be allowed it by anoth-

er."[30] The supreme position of the Roman Pontiff obviously explains his freedom from the above rule. In addition, the refusal made by the lower authority need not be mentioned to the Supreme Pontiff. In such an omission, however, a certain procedural impropriety might be admitted.

Conflicts among Ordinaries on Granting Favors

Canon 65, with some restrictions, extends to ordinaries the provisions of the preceding canon. The basic principle applicable is that whereby jurisdictional coordination should exist between those enjoying a certain cumulative authority, a conflict in the matter of granting favors should be avoided. The notion of *ordinary* is explained in canon 134. Foreseeable conflicts, then, should be resolved according to the rules stated in this canon. Canon 44 of the former Code enunciated the same principles.

Canon 65 — **§1. With due regard for the prescriptions of §§2 and 3, no one should petition for a favor from another ordinary which has been denied by one's own ordinary unless mention of the denial has been made. Even after such mention has been made, the second ordinary should not grant the favor unless he has obtained the reasons for the denial from the prior ordinary.**

One may have two ordinaries by reason of domicile and quasi-domicile. The ordinary of such a person, by reason of domicile, may have refused a dispensation from the form of marriage. May the petitioner then ask for the same favor from the ordinary of the quasi-domicile? This cannot be done without first mentioning the refusal of the first ordinary. The second ordinary, i.e., of the petitioner's quasi-domicile, may not grant the dispensation requested before consulting the first and learning the reasons for the refusal. This prescription, however, does not bind under pain of the invalidity of the favor granted.

§2. A favor which has been denied by a vicar general or by an episcopal vicar cannot be granted validly by another vicar of the same bishop even if the reasons for the denial have been obtained from the vicar who denied it.

The denial of a favor by one vicar precludes recourse to another, even to the vicar general. One may, however, renew the petition to the same vicar who had denied it.

§3. A favor which has been denied by a vicar general or by an episcopal vicar and later procured from the diocesan bishop without mentioning this

---

[27]Rescripts of favor contain grants freely given; those of justice refer to such matters as judicial controversies.
[28]C. 1049, §2.
[29]*RE* 112, *CLD* 6, 352.

[30]*R.I.* 84 in VI: "Quum quid una via prohibetur alicui, ad id alia non non debet admitti."

denial is invalid. But a favor which has been denied by the diocesan bishop cannot be procured validly from his vicar general or episcopal vicar without the consent of the bishop, even if mention of the denial has been made.

The diocesan bishop may reverse the denial of a favor issued by any one of his vicars—but for the validity of such an act, he must be informed of the reasons for such a denial. While the vicar general shares the executive government of the whole diocese with the diocesan bishop, this power is limited to definite spheres in the case of the episcopal vicars. In the present instance, however, the higher authority of the bishop prevails. The bishop may also reconsider his own denial and grant the favor heretofore refused.

Non-Essential Errors in Rescript

Canon 66 — A rescript does not become invalid due to an error in the name of the person to whom it is given or from whom it is issued or an error in the name of the place where the person is staying or the matter being treated provided that there is no doubt concerning the identity of the person or the matter in question in the judgment of the ordinary.

It can happen that a rescript sometimes contains an error, either in the name of the person to whom it is granted, or in the name of the domicile or residence of that person, or in the subject matter of the rescript itself. Insofar as an error of this kind may be considered as *merely material,* the rescript remains valid if—after due consideration of the text and context of the rescript—the ordinary concludes that there is no reasonable doubt either about the identity of its recipient or about the subject matter. In addition to these substantial features of a rescript, the instrument should bear the signature of the authority issuing it and the seal of the office from which it proceeds.

The ordinary who decides on the authenticity of the rescript is either the local ordinary or the major superior—in the case either of clerical religious institutes of pontifical right or clerical societies of apostolic life of pontifical right.

Conflicting Rescripts

Canon 67 — §1. If it happens that two contradictory rescripts are procured concerning one and the same thing the special rescript prevails over the general one in those matters which are specifically expressed.

§2. If they are equally special or general in character, the first one issued prevails over the one issued later, unless express mention of the prior one is made in the second one or unless the person who

had procured the prior rescript had not used it out of deceit or notable negligence.

§3. When there is doubt about whether a rescript is valid or not, recourse should be had to the one issuing it.

Conflicts arising from textual divergencies in rescripts are to be resolved according to the norms presented in this canon. Paragraphs one and two repeat *verbatim* the text of canon 48, §§1 and 2 of the 1917 Code. Canon 67, §3, without limiting its focus to a doubt about the priority of rescripts issued on the same day (*CIC* 49, §3), simply leaves the solution of any doubt to the judgment of the authority who issued the rescript. Unresolved textual conflicts could foster confusion and have certain unfortunate consequences.

In paragraph one, the rescripts—one general and one particular—refer to the same object; the text, however, leads to different conclusions. The special rescript prevails over the general in those matters that are specifically expressed. The principle of preference is the norm of jurisprudence according to which the particular prevails over the general. A principle of Roman Law expresses it this way: "Throughout the law, the species takes from the genus, and that is most particularly regarded, which refers to the species."[31] Other features of the rescripts which are not in conflict with one another remain unaffected. Canon 53, referring to the conflict that may arise between general and particular decrees, enunciates the principles that are applied to contradictions found in rescripts as examined in this canon. Authors do not hesitate to attribute such documentary inconsistencies to the accumulation of work in the Roman Curia. The grantor may also be presumed to have issued the second rescript inadvertently.

According to paragraph two, priority of issuance determines the preference of one general rescript over another or of one particular rescript over another. This applies to rescripts granted either with or without an executor. Two provisos are added to this principle of priority, namely, "The one who is prior in time is the stronger in right."[32] Priority of time gives the greater claim to a right granted by a rescript. Since the day and not the hour is indicated in the rescript, the exact moment of issuance is dis-

---

[31]*R.I.* 34 in VI: "Generi per speciem derogatur." Cf. Cicognani, 733.

[32]*R.I.* 54 in VI: "Qui prior est tempore potior est iure." Cicognani elaborates on this point in reference to the present application. "If there is a question of rescripts granted *in forma commissoria necessaria,* since at the time that such a rescript is granted, it gives the beneficiary a certain *ius ad rem* (i.e., a right to the favor granted in the rescript) that is a quasi-right to obtain the favor from the executor, it should not be thought that the grantor takes away this right by issuing a later rescript. Hence the priority of such rescripts dates from the day on which they were granted" (734). *CIC* 48, §2 mentions also the principle of priority.

regarded. If priority of time involving an hour, or even less, could be proved, the recipient of such a rescript might enjoy any benefits accruing therefrom. If, in the second rescript, express mention has been made of the first, it seems that the competent authority issuing it was aware of the differences and intended that the second should prevail. The second proviso mentions both culpable intent and notable negligence, either of which would act to the disadvantage of the party receiving the prior rescript. If the second grantee acted on the grant issued in the rescript and was already enjoying a favor, that person would also have an acquired right. In the case, then, of the first petitioner's not having made use of a rescript through fraud or notable negligence, the legal axiom should be invoked: "Fraud and deceit should prove an advantage to no one."[33] Notable negligence would be sanctioned by the principle: "One delays to his own detriment."[34] Indifference or the simple refusal to avail oneself of the benefits of a rescript may result in its forfeiture. Fraud or simple negligence should be proved sufficiently to the grantor or to the executor of the rescript.

In accord with paragraph three, one who issues a rescript is presumably qualified to judge concerning its validity.

Presentation of Rescript to Ordinary

Canon 68 — **A rescript of the Apostolic See in which no executor is given must be presented to the ordinary of the person who obtained it only when such action is ordered by the rescript itself, or when it deals with public affairs, or when it is necessary to prove that the attached conditions have been satisfied.**

The provision of this canon repeats that of canon 51 of the former Code. It applies only to rescripts not calling for an executor. The presentation of such a rescript to the ordinary of the petitioner is not necessary for the validity of the favor granted—unless this has been expressly prescribed.

Since public matters will usually refer to the good of the faithful, either directly or indirectly, it is understandable that the ordinary should be made aware of such a grant. Canons 381–402 contain certain provisions, governing the office of the diocesan bishop, from which it will be quite clear why he should have a particular interest in and concern with the public affairs of his diocese. One should also consult canons 335–349 of the 1917 Code. Examples usually mentioned by commentators refer to privileges granted to individual churches, whether

exclusively spiritual—such as indulgences—or titles of honor given to individuals. Today, however, the practice of the Holy See is to confer such favors through the local ordinary. The "attached conditions" might involve questions such as the reputation of the recipient in the Catholic community or that person's fidelity to his or her religious obligations.

Presentation of Rescript to Beneficiary

Canon 69 — **When no definite time is set for its presentation, a rescript can be presented to its executor at any time whatsoever, provided fraud and deceit are absent.**

This canon repeats the norm of canon 51 of the former Code and applies to rescripts both of favor and of justice which demand execution. Circumstances possibly giving rise to the suspicion of fraud or deceit in the execution of the rescript might include the quality of the person to whom the rescript is directed, the nature of the object, or even the relative remoteness of the place where the recipient lives. It was possible, especially in former times, that a papal appointment might be maliciously prevented from reaching its destination; however, the highly efficient means of communication of the present day will help to prevent fraudulent interference or delay. To determine whether the rescript maliciously delayed became invalid, one would generally depend on an examination of the text of the rescript and the circumstances surrounding its issuance.

Discretion of Executor

Canon 70 — **If the granting of a rescript is entrusted to an executor, the favor can be granted or denied in accord with the executor's prudent judgment and conscience.**

Rescripts committed to the prudent judgment of a voluntary executor depend for their fulfillment on his or her conscientious decision. Motives prompting the withholding of a grant may often depend on detailed information not found in the petition but gathered from collateral sources. Perhaps the petitioner has proved to be unworthy of the favor requested, which, if granted, might cause not only wonderment but—occasionally—even offense to the faithful. Moreover, a more exact examination of the text of the petition might reveal the taint of either obreption, or falsehood, or subreption, or a suppression of the truth. The executor, however, following his or her conscience, will not arbitrarily deny the favor intended by a higher authority. Canon 54, §2 of the former Code contained the same prescription.

---

[33]"Fraus et dolus alicui patrocinari non debent." *Decretalium liber* 1, 3, c. 16.

[34]*R.I.* 25 in VI: "Mora sua cuilibet est nociva."

Use of Rescript

Canon 71 — No one is bound to use a rescript granted for one's own advantage alone, unless one is otherwise bound to do so by a canonical obligation.

Canon 69 of the 1917 Code applied this same general principle specifically to privileges. While a priest, enjoying the privilege of a private chapel, by way of rescript is not obliged to use it, circumstances might call for its use in order to fulfill his Mass obligations. No one should be affected adversely by the non-use of a concession granted another.

Prorogation of Rescript

Canon 72 — Rescripts granted by the Apostolic See which have expired can be extended once by a diocesan bishop for a just reason, but not beyond three months.

This explicit faculty of prorogation was not given in the Code of 1917. The just reason prompting such an extension of time for the use of apostolic rescripts will involve a spiritual benefit for the recipients. This extension may be granted only once ("semel"). This canon does not distinguish among the various kinds of rescripts. If an act of delegated jurisdiction to be used exclusively in the internal forum is placed inadvertently after the time of delegation had expired, such an act would be valid by virtue of canon 142, §2.

Effect of Contrary Laws on Rescript

Canon 73 — No rescripts are revoked by a contrary law unless it is provided otherwise in the law itself.

This principle of non-revocation restricts any contrary legal provision to an explicit mention of such in the text of the law itself. The revocation implied in a law enacted by a superior or of the authority issuing the rescript would also repeal the rescript according to canon 60, §2 of the 1917 Code. In this case, too, however, explicit mention of the revocatory intent of such a law must be indicated.

Oral Favor

Canon 74 — Although a person can use in the internal forum a favor granted only orally, the person is bound to prove it for the external forum whenever this is legitimately requested.

Canon 79 of the former Code, referring to privileges—which are usually expressed in writing, i.e., by rescripts—mentioned also those granted orally, i.e., *vivae vocis oraculo.* In addition to favors granted by the Roman Pontiff, others may be granted by competent authorities of the Roman Curia. While valid, favors granted by word of mouth may create some problems concerning their proof in particular cases.

The internal forum looks to the conscience of the individual; and so, per se, a favor orally granted will not require external proof. The favor may be used without restriction in either the sacramental or non-sacramental internal forum and even in the *external* forum as long as its concession is not challenged. The legitimate demand for proof of such an orally granted favor will be satisfied by the written and notarized or authenticated statement of a qualified witness. Quite obviously, such proof would not be considered if it involved matter relating only to the internal sacramental forum.

Other Canons on Privileges

Canon 75 — If a rescript contains a privilege or a dispensation, the prescriptions of the following canons are likewise to be observed.

Since specific provisions regarding privileges and dispensations are made in the following canons (cc. 76–93), they will supplement, when required, the norms found in the present chapter governing rescripts. This canon repeats the prescription mentioned in canon 62 of the 1917 Code.

CHAPTER IV
PRIVILEGES
[cc. 76–84]

Etymologically, a privilege is a private law granted to an individual or to a juridic person, thus creating an individual or a personal right. It is granted by a particular act not of the legislator, but usually of a competent executor. It is considered here as an administrative act. The notion of a privilege has evolved since its use under Roman Law—when it sometimes had an unfavorable connotation.[35] From the time of Gratian, however, a privilege acquired a more positive meaning and more properly was considered as a favorable private law, i.e., *lex favorabilis privata.* A privilege, then, may be defined as a particular right, granted, not through necessity, but by the benevolent intent of the legislator and—according to the discipline of the revised Code—through an administrative act. The conclusion from the definition in this canon is that a privilege in the proper juridic sense is granted only by particular

---

[35]Cicognani, 778.

acts. A favor (*gratia*) that is *contrary* to the law, or that may not be contrary to the law, yet is not contained in it (*praeter legem*)—beside the law, as it were—which modifies it or complements it, is an objective right and a norm proper to a person, whether individual or juridic. Of itself it is perpetual according to canon 78, §1 and so may be called a private favorable *law*. A privilege cannot be acquired, as formerly, through prescription, according to which subjective rights are acquired and by which objective norms are not established. Privileges are no longer obtainable through communication. Those obtained by way of administrative acts, usually through rescripts, follow the norms proper to those privileges.

Notion of Privilege

Canon 76 — §1. A privilege or a favor granted to certain persons, whether physical or juridical, by means of a special act can be granted by the legislator as well as by an executive authority to whom the legislator has granted this power.
§2. Centenary or immemorial possession induces a presumption that a privilege has been granted.

Paragraph one contains the generic notion of a privilege, namely, that it is a favor or a benefit that is granted either to individuals or to juridic persons as defined in canons 113–115, i.e., aggregations of persons or things. The competent authority granting the privilege is the legislator or one to whom the legislator has granted this power as executor. The ultimate source of privileges, however, is the legislator, or the master of the law (*dominus legis*).

Like the former Code (*CIC* 63, §2), paragraph two mentions two cases in which the actual possession of a privilege—in the absence of ordinary proof—may be sustained by a presumption of legal grant. This presumption rests on actual possession lasting for one hundred years or from time immemorial. The centenary possession (i.e., for 100 years) may, in some cases, be proved by documents. The immemorial possession of a privilege, however, presumptively rests on the memory of persons unable to recall the details of its concession. The presumption in both cases is called one of law, a *praesumptio iuris,* and it is rebuttable only by compelling evidence to the contrary. The possessor is not obliged to defend the exercise of the privilege unless challenged to do so.

Interpretation of Privileges

Canon 77 — A privilege is to be interpreted in accord with the norm of can. 36, §1, but that interpretation is always to be used so that the beneficiaries of a privilege actually obtain some favor.

The same norms of interpretation of which canon 36, §1 makes mention apply to administrative acts, the texts of which may occasionally call for clarification. This canon is further explained in the commentary thereon. Here, however, it is sufficient to say that where the concession of a privilege in some way inconveniences a third party, i.e., one who is unfavorably affected by the privilege, its text is to be interpreted strictly. A broad interpretation could be to the detriment of many. Lawsuits, penal action—whether of the threat or the actual infliction of sanctions—the restriction of personal rights, the infringement of vested rights, and the derogation of the common law in favor of privileged persons are all subject to a restrictive interpretation because a broad interpretation in such cases might involve a violation of justice. Privileges not adversely affecting others, however, are to be interpreted broadly since there is nothing offensive or detrimental to those not enjoying the privilege. It is important that the interpretation of a privilege not be so strict as to exclude the favor intended by the grantor.

Duration of Privilege

Canon 78 — §1. A privilege is presumed to be perpetual unless the contrary is proved.

The exception to the principle of the presumptive perpetuity of a privilege is to be proved principally from the tenor of the authoritative act granting it. The sustaining principle of perpetuity is enunciated in the rule of law stating that "it is fitting that the favor granted by the superior be permanent."[36]

§2. A personal privilege, namely one which follows the person, ceases with the person's death.

A personal privilege is, as it were, attached to the person himself or herself. It is non-transferable, e.g., to relatives, friends, heirs, or to anyone else. The extension of personal privileges to others is to be determined by the text of the document of concession. It ceases with the death of the person *intrinsically,* i.e., the subject of the favor no longer exists. The grantor could, on personal authority, also revoke the privilege and thus it would cease *extrinsically,* from an action external to the recipient.

§3. A real privilege ceases with the complete destruction of the thing or place; but a local privilege revives if the place is restored within fifty years.

Since real privileges may be attached to a thing or a place, their non-existence would automatically bring about the cessation of any privileges attached

---

[36] *R.I.* 16 in VI: "Decet concessum a principe beneficium esse mansurum."

to them. Thus, the destruction of religious articles, such as rosaries or crucifixes, to which special privileges were attached by way of indulgences would thereby effect the loss of such privileges. The complete destruction of a basilica brings about the cessation of any privileges attached to it, but its restoration would cause the revival of the same privileges. Rebuilding operations, begun within fifty years, but not yet completed, would revive the privileges.[37]

Cessation of Privilege

Canon 79 — **A privilege ceases through its revocation by competent authority in accord with the norm of can. 47, with due regard for the prescription of can. 81.**

The cessation of a privilege is governed by the principles mentioned in canons 46 and 47, which expressly treat of administrative acts.[38] The termination of the authority of the one granting a privilege does not automatically effect the cessation of the same. The beneficiary must be duly notified of the termination of the privilege before such an act takes effect.[39]

Renunciation of Privilege

Canon 80 — **§1. No privilege ceases through renunciation unless the renunciation has been accepted by the competent authority.**

§2. Any physical person can renounce a privilege granted on behalf of that person alone.

§3. Individual persons cannot renounce a privilege which has been granted to some juridic person or has been granted by reason of the dignity of a place or thing; nor is a juridic person competent to renounce a privilege granted to it if its renunciation prejudices the Church or others.

The renunciation of a privilege is not a unilateral act, but in order to take effect it must be accepted by the competent authority, who may accept it or, for a just reason, refuse to do so (§1).

Since privileges granted to an individual or a physical person usually benefit the individual exclusively, the renunciation of such a privilege would normally not prove to be an inconvenience to others and no social disadvantage would thereby follow (§2).

In contrast to the preceding paragraph, a private individual who is a member of any aggregate of per-

sons to which a privilege has been granted may not renounce a privilege granted to the community. The privilege has been granted to the corporate entity as such and its disposal is not at the sole discretion even of the superior (§3).

A privilege granted to a juridic person such as a religious community, often relates to the pastoral ministry and implicitly involves the good of the faithful. Such a benefit may not be curtailed because of the possible advantage that might come to the juridic person seeking the termination of such a privilege.

Cessation of Authority of Author of Privilege

Canon 81 — **A privilege is not terminated with the termination of the authority of the one issuing it unless it has been granted with the provision *ad beneplacitum nostrum* or some equivalent terminology.**

An ecclesiastical authority may counteract the general principle according to which a privilege does not cease with the termination of the authority granting it. Clauses such as "ad beneplacitum nostrum," i.e., "at our pleasure," or other equivalent expressions may qualify the grant. The rationale of such a personal proviso will appear from the text of the concession. Death, resignation, transfer, or removal from office would not effect the cessation of a privilege granted by the competent authority. The nature of a privilege supposes a degree of permanence, which, in particular cases, may be subject to the limits imposed by the grantor. These norms affect privileges granted not only by the Holy See, but also by the diocesan bishop within the limits of his competence.

Loss of Privilege by Non-Use/Contrary Use

Canon 82 — **A privilege which is not a burden on others does not cease through non-usage or through contrary usage; but if it is to the disadvantage of others, it is lost through legitimate prescription.**

The non-use of a privilege may be verified in the case of a priest, who, by virtue of a privilege, may use a portable altar for the celebration of Mass. He finds that it is more convenient for him to celebrate Mass in a nearby church. By using this option, he does not thereby lose the privilege of the portable altar. Another priest may be freed, by privilege, from reading the *Roman Breviary* while on missionary journeys. He prefers, however, when possible, to read the liturgical hours, thus performing an act to which he is not obliged by virtue of his privilege. In such circumstances he acts *contrary* to his privilege. It is to be noted that in neither case is the non-use of, or the use contrary to, a privilege harmful to

---

[37]A. Vermeersch and J. Creusen, *Epitome Iuris Canonici,* ed. 6a (Mechliniae-Romae: H. Dessain, 1937), nn. 185–186, 162.

[38]*CIC* 72–77.

[39]Privileges do not cease by the enactment of contrary laws but by the express revocatory act of the competent authority.

others; therefore there is no reason to consider that such a privilege has ceased—accordingly it may be used in the future by the grantee. The use of some privileges, however, may prove burdensome to others and may be forfeited or legally cease if the norms of liberative prescription are applicable.[40]

Cessation of Privilege

Canon 83 — §1. A privilege ceases through the lapse of the period of time or after the completion of the number of cases for which it was granted, with due regard for the provision of can. 142, §2.

§2. A privilege also ceases if in the course of time circumstances change to such a degree that the privilege becomes harmful or its use illicit in the judgment of the competent authority.

Privileged faculties relating to the sacred ministry, for example, may be granted for a limited time or extended to a definite number of cases (§1). The text of the grant of the privilege will indicate the length of time, e.g., for ten years or the number of cases, e.g., ten or more. Such a privilege ends after the period of ten years has expired or the number of cases has been completed. Canon 142, §2, however, provides that an act of delegated power, which is exercised in the *internal forum exclusively* and which has been inadvertently placed, is valid, even though the time limit for the exercise of such a faculty has expired.

During the passage of time, circumstances may change to such an extent that a privilege, once beneficial, may become harmful or even unlawful to use. Either the Holy See or the local ordinary is competent to judge the harm involved in the use of such a privilege. The dominating motive will be a spiritual one, relating in some way to the good of the faithful. A priest, for example, enjoying the privilege of a private chapel might cause scandal by his mischievous conduct and thus occasion the cancellation of his privileges.

Abuse of Privilege

Canon 84 — Whoever abuses the power given by privilege deserves to be deprived of it; therefore, the ordinary, after having admonished the grantee in vain, may deprive the one who seriously abuses it of a privilege which he himself had granted; if, however, the privilege was granted by the Apostolic See, the ordinary is bound to notify the Apostolic See.

An abuse means the excessive or improper use of a thing, and the abuse of a privilege often merits its

forfeiture.[41] A privilege is not automatically terminated by its abuse—which in some cases may be remedied so as to avoid the drastic action of official deprivation. The abuse of a privilege usually applies to a personal one; if it is granted by the local ordinary, it may cease only after the offender has been duly admonished. The case of one abusing an apostolic privilege must be reported by the ordinary to the Holy See. The privilege of a private chapel would be abused by its gradual conversion into one to which the local community had free access, thus competing with the services of the local parish church. By the same token, such a chapel might be used for purposes wholly alien to its nature, e.g., for purely secular social events.

CHAPTER V
DISPENSATIONS
[cc. 85–93]

A dispensation is an act of administrative power issued by the executor. The former legislation restricted the power of dispensation to the legislator, who, however, delegated such acts of jurisdiction to others. The present power to dispense mentioned in canon 85 differs from canon 80 of the 1917 Code, which restricted such power to the legislator, to the legislator's successor, or to those delegated to exercise such jurisdiction. The limits of the executor's competence are determined by the law and by any detailed directives peculiar to an individual case, whenever such are given.

The laws of the early Church were relatively few in number and their observance was strongly insisted upon, thus leaving little room for any relaxation from their obligations. In 313 the Roman Synod recognized the bishops who had been ordained by the Donatists. In 385, St. Siricius allowed certain Spanish clerics who had been unlawfully ordained to exercise their orders. These, as well as numerous matrimonial dispensations, were granted *post factum,* i.e., after the illegal acts of ordination or of matrimony had been performed. Later some provincial synods granted such dispensations, and certainly, from the fourth century on, the Roman Pontiffs exercised the power of dispensation—reserving many such relaxations, however, to themselves, especially those considered more difficult to grant.

In 794, Emperor Charlemagne informed Bishops Angilram of Metz and Hildebold of Cologne that the Roman Pontiff had granted him the indult to retain them in his own household—thus dispensing them from the law of residence, whereby they would be obliged to live in their own dioceses.[42]

[40]T.L. Bouscaren and A.C. Ellis, *Canon Law: A Text and Commentary,* 2nd ed. (Milwaukee: Bruce Publishing Co., 1957), 39–40 on prescription.

[41]J.F. Kelliher, *Loss of Privileges, CanLawStud* 398 (Washington, D.C.: Catholic University of America, 1964), 106.
[42]Cicognani, 829.

Notion/Author of Dispensation

Canon 85 — A dispensation, or the relaxation of a merely ecclesiastical law in a particular case, can be granted by those who enjoy executive power, within the limits of their competence, as well as by those to whom the power of dispensing has been given explicitly or implicitly either by the law itself or by lawful delegation.

The distinction between a law of divine and human origin is the first criterion to be observed in the matter of dispensations. This is emphasized by the term "merely ecclesiastical." The indirect power of the Supreme Pontiff regarding the divine law has already been explained. The dispensing power is limited to particular cases, thus excluding any general action that would include the entire Christian community. Those enjoying this competence have executive power as distinguished from legislative and judicial power. Their function is to carry out the provision—either directly or indirectly—made by a legislator. The limits of executive power are indicated either in the text of the law itself or in the letters of delegation. The power of the executor in dispensing from matrimonial impediments—enjoyed by bishops, pastors, other priests and deacons—is limited by the conditions expressed, for example, in canons 1078 through 1080 (*CIC* 1043–1045). The competence to dispense in these cases is explicitly granted by the law. The implicit power to dispense might be granted, e.g., by a bishop or ordinary, to a priest assigned to resolve a complicated marriage case involving the possibility of existing impediments. Canons 1196 and 1197 also provide for the dispensation from the obligations of private vows. Canon 1245 allows pastors and superiors of religious institutes and societies of apostolic life of pontifical right to dispense their parishioners or subjects from the obligations attached to holy days of obligation and to days of penance. Such dispensations, however, although granted by the law itself, are subject to the conditions therein expressed. Legitimate delegation means that the power of jurisdiction—as exemplified by an act of dispensation—is committed by a competent authority to a person who does not enjoy such power by his or her own right but by virtue of the power of the superior who, as it were, shares it with him or her in particular instances. Some powers of dispensation enjoyed by the diocesan bishop or by local ordinaries may be delegated to the priests of the diocese and specifically mentioned in a list of such faculties, e.g., the power to dispense from the publication of the banns of marriage wherever they are in force when there is a just pastoral reason. The power to dispense from certain obligations is also granted to some religious confessors—likewise for the spiritual good of the faithful. Such dispensations are granted in the internal forum, often in the sacramental forum exclusively.

Non-Dispensable Laws

Canon 86 — Laws, to the extent that they define that which essentially constitutes juridical institutes or acts, are not subject to dispensation.

The reason why the essential elements of both juridic institutes and juridic acts lie beyond the competence of any dispensing authority is that the absence of any one essential element would render either the institute or the act juridically or lawfully non-existent. A juridic institute is a state, a condition, an establishment created by law—divine or human—from which arise specific rights with correlative obligations. A juridic act is one productive of rights and obligations. Marriage and the consecrated life contain essential elements from which no dispensation can be granted. One cannot be dispensed from the obligation to grant his or her prospective spouse the right to acts naturally productive of offspring. A novice, prior to religious profession, could not be dispensed from including all three vows in the prospective religious profession. In these examples, the juridic institutes of both marriage and the religious state would be nonexistent because of the elimination of constitutive or essential elements. Likewise, a juridic act such as the mutual consent necessary for a bilateral contract, such as marriage, must be the product of sufficient deliberation and free will—from which a dispensation is inconceivable.

Dispensation from Universal Law

Canon 87 — §1. As often as he judges that a dispensation will contribute to the spiritual good of the faithful, the diocesan bishop can dispense from both universal and particular disciplinary laws established for his territory or for his subjects by the supreme authority of the Church. He cannot dispense, however, from procedural or penal laws or from those laws whose dispensation is especially reserved to the Apostolic See or to another authority.

§2. If recourse to the Holy See is difficult and, at the same time, there is danger of grave harm in delay, any ordinary can dispense from the above-mentioned disciplinary laws, even if the dispensation is reserved to the Holy See, provided that the matter concerns a dispensation which the Holy See is wont to grant under the same circumstances with due regard for the prescription of can. 291.

The broad power of dispensing enjoyed by diocesan bishops makes unnecessary the many petitions formerly made directly to the Holy See (§1). The diocesan bishop may exercise the dispensing powers mentioned, when, in his judgment, it would promote the spiritual good of the faithful. Disciplinary laws refer to the areas of conduct affecting the good of the faithful—such as attendance at Mass on days of obligation, observance of fast and abstinence, reception of the sacraments, and the observance of marriage laws, e.g., on impediments and canonical form. The range of the diocesan bishop's dispensing power extends not only to the disciplinary laws obliging all the faithful but also to any particular laws issued by the Holy See for his particular territory or for his subjects. Exceptions to this power, however, are procedural and penal laws and those which the Apostolic See has reserved to itself for dispensation. Since laws concerning procedure are established for the defense of rights and do not directly concern the good of the faithful, they are not included in the dispensing powers of the diocesan bishop. Since penal laws are established for the protection of the more important rights of the faithful, they too are excluded from the bishop's power to dispense. Other reserved dispensations are those from celibacy, which the Roman Pontiff alone may grant (c. 291), and from the age required for ordination to the priesthood or the permanent diaconate—if the candidate for either order lacked more than a year of the prescribed age (c. 1031, §§1, 2, 4). In addition to the aforementioned exceptions, only the Roman Pontiff may dispense from the non-consummated bond of marriage (c. 1698, §2) as well as from the natural bond in favor of the faith.

Two conditions are necessary for an exceptional dispensation from such reserved disciplinary laws: (1) that recourse to the Holy See is difficult and (2) that at the same time there is grave danger of harm while awaiting the dispensation from the Holy See (§2). The ordinary means of communication with the Holy See is by mail. The use of telephone or telegraph is not considered ordinary means and in some cases might prove to be less secure. While the papal nuncio or delegate might possess faculties to dispense—exceeding those of the diocesan bishop—and might be approached, there is no solid reason why recourse should be made to either, and the present canon makes no such recommendation. Recourse to the Holy See is prudently judged to be difficult, not impossible. The rationale of all the canons relating to dispensations—as is true for many other canons—is the good of the faithful prudently estimated.

The grave or serious harm which is to be avoided by a dispensation may be either spiritual or material—which bears some relationship to the spiritual. The laws from which a dispensation is sought are disciplinary or those referring to the good of the faithful and their pursuit of perfection in their state of life. The present canon speaks of a dispensation from disciplinary laws—and specifically from laws reserved to the Holy See. Given the conditions mentioned in this canon, *any* competent ordinary may dispense—namely, the diocesan bishop, the vicar general, and the episcopal vicars within the limits of their jurisdiction. The customary practice of the Holy See in dispensing in the same type of case is the norm to be followed in the problem confronting the ordinary.

The following cases exemplify the principles explained previously. In a diocese sorely in need of priests, a young candidate, highly qualified for the ministry, has completed the required curriculum of studies at the age of twenty-three and one-half years—one and one-half years before the prescribed age for priestly ordination, i.e., twenty-five years. Since the young candidate in question requires a dispensation reserved to the Holy See because he is more than a year younger than the prescribed age, the ordinary manner of meeting a pastoral problem arising from such a need calls for a petition to the Holy See for a dispensation as prescribed in canon 1031, §§1 and 4. The candidate's bishop, prudently assessing the grave spiritual inconvenience that would result from a delay of the ordination, might, in good conscience, apply the provision of canon 87, §2.

The serious danger of material loss to a church or to a diocese or to a religious community, thus indirectly affecting the spiritual welfare of these groups, would justify the proper ordinary in applying the same provision of canon 87, §2—by dispensing from the obligation of petitioning the Holy See for an act of alienation exceeding the value beyond which such a petition is prescribed in canon 1292, §2.

Dispensation from Infra-Universal Law

Canon 88 — **The local ordinary can dispense from diocesan laws and, as often as he judges that a dispensation will contribute to the good of the faithful, from laws passed by a plenary or provincial council or by the conference of bishops.**

When in the judgment of the local ordinary the good of the faithful recommends it, he may dispense not only from the laws of his own diocese but also from those of the provincial or plenary council or of the conference of bishops of the nation to which he belongs. He judges the reasonableness of the dispensation according to the proportionate gravity of the law and the validity of the motives alleged for a dispensation.

Dispensations by Pastors, Priests, Deacons

Canon 89 — **The pastor and other presbyters or deacons cannot dispense from a universal or particular law unless this power has been expressly granted to them.**

Canon 1079 refers to the dispensing power of bishops, pastors, other priests, and deacons regarding matrimonial impediments when one or both parties are in danger of death; canon 1080 extends the same power to the case of a wedding for which all preparations have been made but which has been prevented by the existence of an impediment. In this case, the above-mentioned clerics may dispense from any impediment, except that arising from the order of priesthood. Pastors may also dispense their parishioners and visitors in the parish from private vows in virtue of canon 1196 and from the obligation to observe feast days and days of penance according to canon 1245. Superiors of clerical religious institutes and of clerical societies of apostolic life of pontifical right may likewise exercise the same dispensing power toward their subjects as well as toward those resident in their houses, according to the same canons.

Other delegated faculties to dispense may be found in particular lists of diocesan faculties or in the special grants made to missionaries or religious.

Reason for Dispensation

Canon 90 — §1. A dispensation from an ecclesiastical law may not be granted without a just and reasonable cause and without taking into consideration the circumstances of the case and the gravity of the law from which the dispensation is to be given; otherwise the dispensation is illicit and, unless it is given by the legislator himself or his superior, it is also invalid.

For its validity, a dispensation from an ecclesiastical law demands a reason proportionate to its gravity (§1). Thus a dispensation from a diriment impediment to marriage requires a more serious reason than a dispensation from the publication of the banns where they are still in force. A dispensation from a single day of penance requires a less serious reason than one extending over the entire Lenten season.

The so-called canonical reasons for granting dispensations from matrimonial impediments are commonly known to those engaged in the pastoral ministry.[43] Other motives for dispensations of less consequence are likewise familiar to the priest and deacon. A dispensation granted for inadequate reasons would nullify the act, unless it were granted by the legislator or the legislator's superior. The hope that an unbaptized person will become a Catholic must be solidly founded on positive arguments in order to justify a dispensation from the impediment of disparity of worship. To be merely well-disposed toward the Catholic Church is not a sufficient reason to grant such a dispensation.

§2. When there is a doubt about the sufficiency of the cause, a dispensation is granted validly and licitly.

[43]Well-known reasons for dispensing from the matrimonial impediment of disparity of worship are such as the danger of the parties living in concubinage, or the high probability if not the certainty that the parties will contract a civil union, or the exceptional merits of the party or parties.

The nature of the doubt must be examined. It must be a positive doubt, resting on solid reasons—and not a mere negative doubt for which no positive reason can be adduced; otherwise, the dispensation would be null. The legislator, in approaching this matter, is lenient rather than severe.

Subjects of Dispensing Power

Canon 91 — One who possesses the power of dispensing can exercise it, even though he is outside his own territory, for his subjects, though they are absent from his territory, and also, unless the contrary is expressly established, for travelers actually present in his territory, as well as on his own behalf.

This canon, which as such was not found in the Code of 1917, mentions the legal recipients of a dispensation or its *passive* subjects. The power to dispense as provided is both personal and territorial. Either the residence or actual presence of a person within the diocesan or parochial territory qualifies him or her to receive a dispensation—presuming that the other requisites of the law are verified. If both the pastor and a parishioner are outside their parish boundaries, the former may dispense the latter, if need be. The same is to be said regarding the bishop and a member of his diocese—even though both happen to be, at the time, in another diocese. One who has no fixed residence (*vagus*) may be dispensed by the ordinary or the pastor of the territory in which he or she is actually present. The last phrase, "as well as on his own behalf," does not distinguish between the permanent residence of the one dispensing and his presence outside his own territory. Since the text of the law does not distinguish, no gratuitous distinction is to be added.

Interpretation of Dispensing Power

Canon 92 — A strict interpretation must be given not only to a dispensation according to can. 36, §1, but also to the very power of dispensing granted for a particular case.

The present canon, referring to the norms governing the restrictive interpretation of singular administrative acts, includes dispensations. If, for example, the faculty of dispensing is limited to a definite time, say three years, it must be computed according to the calendar. A bishop or a pastor may dispense his own subjects outside their respective territory—but not others who are not members of the diocese or parish concerned.

Cessation of Dispensation

Canon 93 — A dispensation which has successive applications ceases in the same ways as a privilege

and also because of the certain and complete cessation of the motivating cause.

Once the dispensation has been granted, it does not cease between the time when it is granted and when it takes effect. For the cessation of privileges, one should see the explanation of canons 78 through 84. A dispensation from fasting and abstinence might be granted for the whole season of Lent, and consequently it would not be limited or restricted during that time. A priest or a deacon might be dispensed from the reading of the canonical hours over a given period of time, e.g., until he had recovered from an eye ailment. The complete cessation of a motivating cause would be verified by the full recovery of a person who had been dispensed from his or her obligation to fast and abstain because of bodily weakness or some other justifying motive.

TITLE V
STATUTES AND RULES OF ORDER
[cc. 94–95]

Statutes: Notion/Binding Force/Regulations

Canon 94 — §1. Statutes in the proper sense are ordinances which are established in aggregates of persons or of things according to the norm of law and by which their purpose, constitution, government and operation are defined.

Statutes, according to this canon, have their own particular and proper meaning (§1). A statute is a species of ordinance—which is an authoritative rule, or a public injunction, imposing the obligation of obedience on the members of a community to which it is directed. Clearly, it bears an analogy to law. According to the norms of law, statutes are applicable to aggregates both of persons and of things, *universitates personarum et rerum.*[44] Both are called juridic persons because, as regards rights and duties, there is a similarity or an analogy between them and physical or individual persons. The statutes enacted for such persons or corporate entities or bodies determine their purpose, organic structure, government, and an appropriate program of their activities. The National Conference of Catholic Bishops, for example, is a juridic person, composed of the bishops of the United States. It is a corporate body, distinct from the individual bishops who are its members.[45] Institutes of perfection, likewise, duly established according to the prescriptions of canon law, are juridic persons in the true sense. The particular scope or purpose of such corporate bodies, or juridic persons, will both motivate and influence their activities.[46]

§2. The statutes of an aggregate of persons bind only its legitimate members; the statutes of an aggregate of things bind only those who govern it.

The legitimacy of the membership is determined by the particular regulations of the organization —which must be in conformity to the pertinent prescriptions of canon law. Bona fide members, therefore, are bound by the statutes of the corporate body, which they have freely accepted. It is obvious that juridic persons consisting of material things, such as accumulated funds (*universitates rerum*), cannot moderate or control their own activities, e.g., the distribution of revenues derived from their investment. Benefits derived from such sources are administered by such agents as trustees or directors, who are stewards—not owners—of such funds or property. In the discharge of their duties, these directors or administrators are obliged to follow the statutes governing their official actions.

§3. Those prescriptions of statutes which were issued and promulgated in virtue of legislative power are governed by the prescriptions of the canons on laws.

If either of the above-mentioned juridic persons is regulated by statutes emanating from legislative power in the strict sense, its legal structure must conform to canonical principles. The general chapters of some religious institutes enjoy true legislative power; their authoritative prescriptions, whether called statutes or decrees, are regulated by the principles of law as enunciated in canons 7 through 22.

Notion of Orders

Canon 95 — §1. Rules of order (*ordines*) are rules or norms to be observed in assemblies of persons, whether the assemblies were convoked by ecclesiastical authority or called together freely by the Christian faithful or are other kinds of celebrations. These rules define the constitution, government and procedures of the assembly.
§2. In assemblies or celebrations the rules of order oblige all those who participate.

While the term *orders* has a plurality of meanings, it is specifically understood here as indicating regulations whose purpose is to promote the methodical, systematic, and efficient procedural operations during the sessions of various types of assemblies—such as synods, chapters, conventions,

---

[44]Cc. 113–123 state the concept and the principles governing the operations of juridic persons.
[45]Cc. 447–459 outline the structure of the conferences of bishops; C. 451 mentions the power of the conferences to enact statutes and c. 455 their power to issue general decrees.

[46]C. 631 describes the nature and function of general chapters of religious institutes.

etc. (§1). These regulations apply not only to assemblies convoked by church authorities but also to any group of the faithful assembled by mutual agreement. Such prescriptions affect matters touching the organizational structure of the group convened as well as its government and program of action, which will be conducive to realizing the purpose for which the institution was established.

The Order for the Celebration of the Synod of Bishops, drawn up by the Secretariate of State and approved by Pope Paul VI on December 8, 1969,[47]

[47]*AAS* 59 (1967), 61f.; *CLD* 6, 400–411.

may serve as a general model for other assemblies. It determines the personnel, their functions, and other significant details. In any of the assemblies referred to here, the basic parliamentary rules governing the discussion, deliberation, and promotion of the programs considered are to be observed.

Special regulations govern the participation of observers admitted to the sessions, such as those admitted to the sessions of Vatican II.[48]

[48]Regarding the role of observers at Vatican Council II, see *AAS* 54 (1962), 609; *CLD* 5, 252–253.

BIBLIOGRAPHY

Abbo, J.A., and Hannan, J.D. *The Sacred Canons.* 2 vols., 2nd rev. ed. St. Louis: B. Herder Book Co., 1960.

Bouscaren, T.L., and Ellis, A.C. *Canon Law: A Text and Commentary.* 2nd ed. Milwaukee: Bruce Publishing Co., 1957.

Cappello, F.M. *Summa Iuris Canonici.* Vol. I, ed. 5a. Romae: Apud Aedes Universitatis Gregorianae, 1951.

Cicognani, A.G. *Canon Law.* 2nd rev. ed. Authorized English version by Joseph M. O'Hara and Francis J. Brennan. Philadelphia: Dolphin Press, 1935 (cited as Cicognani).

Code of Canon Law Latin-English Edition. Translation prepared under the auspices of the Canon Law Society of America. Washington: CLSA, 1983.

Codice di Diritto Canonico. Testo ufficiale e versione italiana. Romae: Unione Editori Cattolici Italiani, 1983.

Conte a Coronata, M. *Institutiones Iuris Canonici.* Ed. 4a. Romae: Marietti, 1949.

Della Rocca, F. *Manual of Canon Law.* Translated by Anselm Thatcher. Milwaukee: Bruce Publishing Co., 1959.

Gerhardt, B.C. *Interpretation of Rescripts.* CanLawStud 398. Washington, D.C.: Catholic University of America, 1959.

Green, T.J. *A Manual for Bishops: Rights and Responsibilities of Diocesan Bishops in the Revised Code of Canon Law.* NCCB. Washington, D.C.: USCC, 1983.

Kelliher, J.F. *Loss of Privileges.* CanLawStud 364, Washington, D.C.: Catholic University of America, 1964.

Kubik. S. *Invalidity of Dispensations according to Canon 84, §1.* CanLawStud 340. Washington, D.C.: Catholic University of America, 1953.

Morrisey, F.G. *Canonical Significance of Papal and Curial Documents.* CLSA, n.d.

Regatillo, E.F. *Institutiones Iuris Canonici.* Santander: Sal Terrae, 1956.

Vermeersch, A., and Creusen, J. *Epitome Iuris Canonici.* Ed. 6a. Mechliniae-Romae: H. Dessain, 1937.

Wernz, F.X., and Vidal, P. *Ius Canonicum.* Tomus I, *Normae Generales.* Romae: Apud Aedes Universitatis Gregorianae, 1938.

Woywod, S., and Smith, C. *Practical Commentary on the Code of Canon Law.* Rev. ed. New York: J. Wagner, Inc., 1952.

Zalba, M. *Theologiae Moralis Compendium.* Madrid: Biblioteca de Autores Cristianos, 1958.

TITLE VI
PHYSICAL AND JURIDIC PERSONS
[cc. 96–123]

The Notion of "Person"

What is a "person"? The answer seems almost self-evident. Yet a more exact definition of this central concept has occupied philosophers from Aristotle to B.F. Skinner. Whatever the starting point, one is conscious at once of several levels of personhood. Consider an infant, an adolescent, a citizen, a baptized human being. Each in his or her own way is a person, but each in a quite different matrix and relationship. The infant is in a sense the basic person, with potentialities only later to be realized. The adolescent has a self-intuition and self-perception, as well as ownership and moral responsibility. The relationship to a country through citizenship and "civil personality" with all their rights—in, for example, the nation of Switzerland—may be acquired upon application. One can advance at almost any stage indeed to the ultimate realization of personality—in the community of the shared life of Christ—through baptism.

The Code also considers persons at several levels. At this point, presenting "laws about laws," chapter I addresses itself to laws about simply physical persons—and their various relationships to each other and to the community: the relationship to age, to place of residence ("domicile"), physically to one another through descent or marriage, and to a given Roman Catholic "rite."

A second chapter, after the one dealing with the laws specifying these physical persons, will take essentially the same basic notion (i.e., a person as a subject of rights and obligations) and apply it by a mutual, civilized agreement—a "fiction of law"—to certain *groups* either of persons or of mere physical things. These synthetic, recognized persons are called in the Code "juridic persons." (This is the term used almost exclusively, except in the very first canon of chapter II, for what used to be called "moral persons." The notion is the same.) First, the physical person is treated.

CANONS AND COMMENTARY

CHAPTER I
THE CANONICAL CONDITION OF
PHYSICAL PERSONS
[cc. 96–112]

Personality through Baptism

Canon 96 — **By baptism one is incorporated into the Church of Christ and is constituted a person in it with duties and rights which are proper to Christians, in keeping with their condition, to the extent that they are in ecclesiastical communion and unless a legitimately issued sanction stands in the way.**

Implicit through all of the Code of Canon Law is the recognition that the physical person is open to a further, vastly higher dignity. The key word, which runs like a theme through the Code, is "Christifideles." This term "Christifideles" is at the heart of the Code. The opening canon (c. 204) of Book II of the Code, "The People of God," will describe the fashion in which this ultimate personhood is to be achieved—through baptism.

By implication, and only that, the materials of Book I are now concerned only with persons as such—their ages, relationships, etc.—without reference to their place in the larger Christian community. A human person is a minor, or related within the fourth degree of consanguinity, whether that person is a Christian or not: these are matters of definition and governance.[1]

The 1983 Code has introduced, however—in a change made at the very last moment—a significant note. This chapter originally began with "age," and

---

[1] It will be recalled that c. 11 generally excludes from Roman Catholic ecclesiastical legislation all those who are members of the Christian communities disjoined from the Roman Catholic one. It also obviously excludes in matters of ecclesiastical legislation those who are not *baptized* at all.

adulthood. It stated nothing about religious affiliation. By implication, this was secondary. The chapter rested indeed under the important legal umbrella of canon 11. (One should consult this and other canon references mentioned in this paragraph.) The laws concerning physical persons—as now equated with all "merely ecclesiastical laws"—therefore apply only to those "baptized in the Catholic Church or received into it." ALL human persons, however, reach an age, and choose a residence, and have ancestors—and may be forced (as in c. 125). What has baptism to do with these things? This is another way of asking, "Where do 'merely ecclesiastical laws' stop, applicable only to the 'Catholic baptized,' and where does 'natural law,' applicable to all human persons, begin?" Without answering this question, the protective cover of canon 11 was given dramatic reinforcement by the last-minute transplant of the present canon 96—verbatim from its previous setting at the beginning of *Book II* of the Code—to its place here in Book I. The change makes the point clear: the canons on persons apply to those who have the personality of baptism *and* are thereby incorporated into "the Church of Christ." Lest there be any uncertainty of Catholic identity here, that Church of Christ is spelled out in a wholly new later canon that reinforces the language of being "fully in communion with the Catholic Church." The touchstones are defined: the hierarchy of bishops; the profession of faith; the sacraments; and ecclesiastical governance. (See cc. 204, §2; 205.)

Personality in the Church

The language of this opening canon therefore suggests the dual effect of baptism: it incorporates a human being into the Church of Christ, and it bestows a personhood upon him or her. The two are correlative. A person is classically understood—and so defined in this canon—as a subject of rights and duties. Incorporation into the larger community then fixes these rights and duties—exhaustively spelled out in the 1983 Code—within the individual physical person. The portal is baptism—and since the Church is the visible communion reflected in the language of canons 204 and 205, the external sacramental act of affiliation must also be a visible, perceptible one, i.e., baptism of water. Put negatively, the status of person within the Church is not in the least acquired by birth, status, mere familiarity, or even enthusiastic presence. Something further has to be undertaken. Baptism is the sole, divinely instituted means. There is no specification of kind or rite or minister; neither is there even a question of freedom, where freedom is not required—as in an infant under the patronage or his or her parents.

Those rights and duties, described as proper to each Christian in his or her own condition of life, are the object of systematic and moral theology; they are only partially encapsulated within some sections of this Code. It is not the province of law to attempt to spell out all such rights and duties. It sets at best certain general limits and directions. What is emphasized is that they are the accompaniment of this new personhood of the baptized human being, now in the Christian worshiping community.

Obstacles

The law suggests a positive qualification of and a negative barrier to incorporation into the Church of Christ. "Ecclesiastical communion" is the positive touchstone of continued eligibility for this personhood. In turn, defining *that* affiliation in the external world is less than easy—but it is nonetheless very important. It is at the center of eligibility for the task of *episcopus,* i.e., bishop, to a particular church—even beyond being chosen for the task by the Supreme Pontiff; hierarchical communion is mentioned in canon 375, §2. It implies the three fidelities referred to earlier: the profession of faith; the sacraments; and ecclesiastical governance. Departure from this communion—newly recognized in the Code in certain areas as "by a positive act"—awaits more precise definition. The reality, however, is clear enough. Personality within the Church is realizable in its fullness only in communion with the full body.

Could one, however, *lose* one's personality in this context? One cannot be *un*-baptized, or *de*-baptized; yet one can be unfaithful to the implications of communion—or in a formed conscience reject them. The presence of both rights and duties does remain, however.

One could, however, be quite legitimately restricted—*by that same larger community*—in enjoying the benefits of ecclesial personality, if there be reason for the restriction, i.e., a penalty, or "sanction." The community *can* inhibit the exercise of a right within itself. It is precisely this denial of the use of certain ecclesial rights (some would argue that it is a denial of the rights themselves) that constitutes the penal legislation of the Church. Those subject to a certain denial are in no sense whatever "out of the Church." Penal law is too precise for that. The exact terms are spelled out in Book VI. The rights and duties of Christian personhood, however, may be drastically withdrawn—for an adequate reason.

Relationship to Age

Canon 97 — §1. A person who has completed the eighteenth year of age is an adult; below this age, a person is a minor.

This paragraph outlines the parameters of law that refer to the *age* of persons: those who have completed their eighteenth year are in the age of "majority"; those below are "minors." Several usages of law here are contrary to, or outside of, American terminology. The word "adult," for example, is not used in the Latin text—despite the implications of the *Rite of Christian Initiation of Adults.* The age of majority is also now reduced, in contrast to former legislation, to eighteen years.[2] The cultural implications of this are evident; in many instances, relevant civil legislation reflects a realization of a measurably earlier maturation. (The implications of being still a "minor" will be spelled out in c. 98, §2.) Further, the phrase "completed the eighteenth year of age" is utterly foreign to English usage. It should be understood as corresponding to what would be called an "eighteenth birthday." Contrary to English-American custom, however, the eighteenth year—in law—is "completed" when the full day of the anniversary is completed rather than just begun.[3]

§2. Before the completion of the seventh year a minor is called an infant and is held to be incompetent (*non sui compos*); with the completion of the seventh year one is presumed to have the use of reason.

Infancy, arbitrarily in law but in accordance with an ancient usage, is extended to the age of seven (completed) years. Beyond this, the subject is "presumed" to be "*sui compos,*" that is, to have the use of reason.

Both concepts—of presumption and of the use of reason—require explanation. A presumption is a position in law that will yield, in particular cases and in the presence of adequate proofs, to the contrary. (The canon's term "censetur"— "is held to be"—is parallel to the legal notion of "presumption.") This particular presumption is of pivotal importance with regard to subjection to divine or ecclesiastical law. The landmark canon, i.e., canon 11, holds that this age of seven years marks the threshold of *public* accountability within the church community. Prior to this, in matters of ecclesiastical law, the child is considered simply not ready to address himself or herself to religious responsibility and observance—in terms of positive law. (The precocious genius would obviously be obligated to the basic demands of divine law. His or her conformity to ecclesiastical requirements, however, would only be a personal option.)

The "use of reason" has far deeper significance. The matter becomes of supreme importance in the determination of certain obviously adult commitments—notably marriage. The traditional expression of the concept seems to imply a cognitive capacity (or incapacity); the jurisprudential approach in the Church's courts suggests an additional dimension of executive capacity or incapacity—the inability *to carry out* what may be clearly understood cognitively.[4] Cognitive disability, in a very general fashion, is found in the psychotic disorders. Executive or behavioral incapacities are found in the various clusters of symptoms called "personality disorders"—a varied but specifically psychopathological incapacity to achieve adequate social function, maintain human relationships and accept responsibility. The *presumption* is that the minor, and the adult, are *sui compos.* As a presumption, this can yield to the demonstration of contrary evidence (drawn from both behavior and professional evaluation). This is precisely the drift, to anticipate, of canon 99: if one is devoid of "the use of reason" (in this extended sense), that person is legally equated with an infant in terms of responsibility and dependency, whatever his or her physical age. It should be noted that the lack of "use of reason" suggests a diminished responsibility before the community only when this "lack" is of truly grave and truly pathological proportions and is relatively fixed. Neither transient rage nor inebriation wholly acquits one of responsibility; by the same token neither invokes the charge of "insanity" or "emotional illness." Finally, the older concerns with fixing for legal purposes the presumed onset of puberty are now dropped in law completely.[5]

Canon 98 — §1. An adult person enjoys the full use of his or her rights.

A person has a spectrum of inherent rights. With the achievement of the presumed maturity of the age of majority, he or she is then entitled to a discretionary use of these rights. This exercise of rights is in contrast to that of minors. (See cc. 98, §2; 105, §1.)

§2. A minor person remains subject to the authority of parents or guardians in the exercise of his or her rights, with the exception of those areas in which minors by divine law or canon law are exempt from their power; with reference to the designation of guardians and their authority, the prescriptions of the civil law are to be followed unless canon law determines otherwise or unless the diocesan bishop in certain cases for a just cause has decided to provide otherwise through the designation of some other guardian.

---

[2]*CIC* 91.
[3]See c. 203, §2 for the specification of this.

[4]In this conjunction, cf. c. 1095 for the canonical expression of this massive topic. L. Wrenn, *Annulments,* 3rd ed. (Toledo: CLSA, 1978) offers a concise view of the jurisprudence of this topic. The *Diagnostic & Statistical Manual* of the American Psychiatric Association offers a lucid description of the clinical entities. The case which opened the floodgates was (among others) one from Chicago, MUZZILLO vs. FRANK, *coram de Jorio,* 12–20–67, S.R.R. 8262.
[5]Cf. *CIC* 88, §3.

As far as the exercise of their rights is concerned, minors remain under the dominion of their parents or guardians. Such a norm is based on the natural lack of judgment or capacity that is anticipated in minors in varying degree as well as the necessity—gradually diminishing—of submitting such judgment to the supervision of guardians whether they be natural, or appointed. This does not imply a basic *lack* of personality within the community or of its attendant rights; rather, this speaks to the subjection of the exercise of these rights to the discretion of either the parents or those who may stand *in loco parentis*. (A later norm—canon 105—will describe the minor, past the age of infancy but short of majority, who will have left the parental home and de facto more or less has assumed his or her own responsibility, and perhaps even marriage. Such a newly and precariously responsible person is designated as "emancipated," and comes out from under the decision-making of his or her parents.)

Two figures stand *in loco parentis*. One is the *tutor*, of whom the subject is a "ward," usually so civilly appointed, and normally designated in the case of a fully competent minor (whose parents, for example, may have been found inadequate). The other is the *curator*, or guardian, of a subject who is *not* competent, regardless of his or her age. Such incompetency is associated with mental illness, or deprivation, and the subject's age extends not only through minority but also through adulthood. The minor person, prior to departure and emancipation, remains subject to the parent or "tutor"—in decreasing intensity as the age of majority approaches. There are exceptions. Divine law makes the minor always fully (if subjectively) responsible as soon as he or she recognizes approaching demands. Ecclesiastical norms offer the minor the opportunity to do many things—even in advance of the age of majority—for example, to acquire a domicile,[6] to seek baptism,[7] to seek entrance into an institute of consecrated life,[8] to select a church of burial[9] (although this is somewhat attenuated when compared with earlier legislation), and even in certain cases to act as a petitioner or respondent in an ecclesiastical court.[10]

The formalities for the appointment of a guardian (*tutor*) are to be adapted from relevant civil law.

[6]C. 105, §1.
[7]C. 852, §1.
[8]C. 643, §1, 1°.
[9]C. 1177, §2—although this is somewhat attenuated when compared with earlier legislation, which did not extend the choice of site of burial to those making the funeral arrangements.
[10]C. 1478, §2. It should be noted however, that c. 863, for baptism, confuses the issue. It states that "adults, at least those who have completed fourteen years of age" should be baptized by the bishop, where possible. This seems to be a failure in uniformity in editing of the law rather than a deliberate attempt to formulate special legislation for catechumens between the ages of fourteen and eighteen. It would seem that a catechumen of this age may licitly be baptized by his or her proper pastor or other guide in his or her instruction.

This is one of many instances in which the church law "canonizes" the civil legislation and makes it its own. Exceptions are possible if the church community itself has other needs. These are to be understood, however, in areas that affect ecclesiastical relationships only, i.e., either where special provisions for exceptional circumstances appear in canon law itself or where the bishop may deem appointment of a differing—or another—ecclesiastical guardian to be necessary. There is no bar toward appointment of a dual guardianship as long as this qualification (an ecclesiastical guardian *distinct from* the civil one) is observed. In practice, this is found most frequently in the appointment of the *curator* of an "insane" person—for the purpose of defense in the canonical trial that is to determine the validity of the subject's marriage. Because of the person's mental illness, he or she is approached in law as incapable, and in status, as an infant.

Canon 99 — Whoever habitually lacks the use of reason is held to be incompetent (*non sui compos*) and is equated with infants.

One who habitually lacks "the use of reason" is in law seen as an infant, and therefore by this itself is subject to the supervision of a *curator*.[11] The qualification "habitually" is the operative one. One is implicitly *not* considered as habitually deprived of the use of reason—or absolved from responsibility on a permanent basis—who may be drugged, impelled by overwhelming but transient emotional forces, or even, conceivably, asleep.

Relationship to Place

Canon 100 — A person is called a resident (*incola*) in the place where one has a domicile; a temporary resident (*advena*) in the place where one has a quasi-domicile; a traveler (*peregrinus*) when outside the place of domicile or quasi-domicile which is still retained; and a transient (*vagus*) if one has neither domicile nor quasi-domicile anywhere.

Certain terms are made clear in law with respect to the relationship of a physical person to a place. The "resident" is in his or her place of dwelling. The "temporary resident" ("*advena*") is in his or her quasi-domicile. The "traveler" is away from either. The "transient" has no permanent address at all. The basis for this concern in law for the legal description of the resident, the temporary resident, the traveler, and the transient is in an ancient and central concept: law is territorial rather than personal. This was explored in the commentary on canon 13. It is in this present section, dealing with the rights of persons, that the *exact* relationship of the person to his or her territory is addressed.

[11]Cc. 1478 and 1479, in conjunction with c. 99.

Canon 101 — §1. The place of origin of a child, even of a neophyte, is that in which the parents had a domicile, or in its absence a quasi-domicile, at the time the child was born or, if the parents did not have the same domicile or quasi-domicile, that of the mother.

The sigificance of the "place of origin"—i.e., the place of domicile or quasi-domicile of the *parents* at the time of the child's birth or of his or her Christian initiation—has been diminished by the mobility of contemporary society. In the past the "place of origin" was presumed to remain stable—particularly for baptism[12], for inquiry from a religious institute[13], or for the reassurance sought by an ordaining bishop.[14] The law indeed presumes baptism at the place of domicile or quasi-domicile of the parents.[15] This will be the *continued* place of residence of the baptized person only if the parents have not subsequently moved. Finally, older concerns with the technical "place of origin" of the illegitimate or the posthumous child are simply dropped from the contemporary law.[16] (The selection in the law of the domicile of the mother in the case of separated parents is neither chauvinism nor a reflection upon certain current matriarchal subcultures. It is simply historical: ancient Roman and Jewish maternal households were considered the more stable.)

§2. In the case of a child of transients, the place of origin is the place of birth; in the case of an abandoned child, it is the place in which the child was found.

If a father and mother *later* acquire a domicile or quasi-domicile, having earlier been without one (as "*vagi*"), the "place of origin" of the baptized person does not become that of the newly acquired domicile of the parents, but remains that of actual birth.

Domicile

Canon 102 — §1. Domicile is acquired by residence within the territory of a certain parish or at least of a diocese, which either is joined with the intention of remaining there permanently unless called away, or has been protracted for five complete years.

The concept of domicile is basically one of *intention,* as related to a *place,* and specifically as a residence. It is acquired by the *intent* of permanent residence, in a diocese or parish, and is held to have been demonstrated by actual residence within the place for five years. While this is an obviously criti-

cal concept in civil law, the concern here is solely ecclesial; hence, a domicile may be in a general fashion "diocesan," if there is no single fixed residence within the diocese (vicariates and prefectures apostolic also qualify in this regard), or alternatively it may be "parochial," with residence within the confines of a specific parish territory. The former is found if one moves about regularly and frequently within the diocese—with the intention of remaining within it. Intent determines, but must be conjoined with actual physical presence—however brief that presence might be. Even protracted absences at a later time do not dissolve the relationship to the place. A prospective candidate for ordination for a diocese may therefore go to that diocese to "establish a domicile," simply by traveling to it, *with the intention* of making it his permanent residence; he may then depart immediately for theological studies. Good order obviously requires that this inner intention be outwardly ascertainable, preferably through some formal and documented declaration of it—although it can be deduced from other associated actions: acquiring a house, moving possessions into it, etc.

The perpetuity of the necessary intention is qualified by realism: "unless [the person is] called away." Somewhere there is a point of honesty between casualness and commitment. The basic intent must be toward permanent residence, presumably upon the premise that conditions will remain substantially unchanged. The reason for being "called away" must be something proportionately serious to the original commitment. The casual drifter who recognizes that he or she may be "called away" by whim or climate is dishonest in proclaiming a "domicile" in this sense. Domicile, however, does not preclude the possibility of a genuine change of mind, with the coming of more grave and demanding circumstances in the future. A merely *conditional* domicile, whatever the quality of the condition ("I'm going to stay here forever, *if* I find a job") is almost contradictory: at the very least, it suspends the commitment until the condition is or is not realized. The possibility of multiple domiciles, on the other hand, is quite real; a person could divide time between two permanent domiciles (the summer home in the North and the winter one in the South—both permanent). The subject here genuinely has a dual domicile. (Lastly, a legalistic but possible reflection holds that if a residence is on a diocesan line, the *front* door determines the proper domicile!)[17]

Quasi-Domicile

§2. Quasi-domicile is acquired by residence within the territory of a certain parish or at least of

[12]*CIC* 378.
[13]*CIC* 544, §2.
[14]*CIC* 956.
[15]Cf. in this regard c. 851, §2.
[16]See *CIC* 90, §2.

[17]J. Abbo and J. Hannan, *The Sacred Canons,* rev. ed., 2 vols. (St. Louis: B. Herder Book Co., 1957), I:33.

a diocese which either is joined with the intention of remaining there at least three months, unless called away, or has in fact been protracted for three months.

"Quasi-domicile" provides for the intent of the party who may or may not have another permanent domicile, yet has the intention of genuinely remaining within another given place—but only temporarily. The intent is firm. The duration is brief. This also gives the incumbent, during that short period, a true relationship to the community there. The actual time of this intended stay is fixed, arbitrarily, at a minimum of three months (earlier legislation had fixed it at six). A student at a university has the intent—and the hope—of remaining for three months, and perhaps for four years: he or she has both a domicile at home and a quasi-domicile at school. (If still a minor, as will be seen in canon 105, §1, the student is by law considered as retaining the fixed domicile or quasi-domicile of parent or guardian; he or she nonetheless acquires a personal quasi-domicile on the campus as well. As in the case of domicile, the actual residence supplies the time-component to the commitment. By holding on for three months, the student establishes a quasi-domicile and his or her academic prospects.)

Diocesan versus Parochial Domicile

§3. A domicile or quasi-domicile within the territory of a parish is called parochial; in the territory of a diocese, even though not in a particular parish, it is called diocesan.

The distinction between *diocesan* and *parochial* domicile is adverted to earlier in the commentary on paragraph one: the former is a generalized, area-wide residence; the latter is a particular, localized one.

Religious

Canon 103 — Members of religious institutes and societies of apostolic life acquire a domicile in the place of the house to which they are attached; they acquire a quasi-domicile in the house where they are living according to the norm of can. 102, §2.

Members of both institutes of consecrated life and societies of apostolic life in a sense remand to their superiors or directors their self-determination. They are to an extent in the position of having their domicile determined not by themselves but by another. Canon law recognizes this position and determines that the domicile of the religious becomes that of the place chosen for him or her as the house of stable religious life (cc. 608 and 665). There again may be a dual/transient domicile if the candi-

date—while still attached to his or her religious house—is assigned temporarily to another place, e.g., a university for study. If the conditions, i.e., at least three months' intent or residence, of canon 102, §2 are fulfilled, a quasi-domicile is also acquired by the member.

Spouses, the Divorced

Canon 104 — Spouses may have a common domicile or quasi-domicile; either can have a proper domicile or quasi-domicile by reason of a legitimate separation or some other just cause.

The "common" domicile or quasi-domicile of spouses is a new disposition of law. It reflects new advertence to familiar roles—without determining them. In earlier church law,[18] the wife always had a "necessary" domicile (see the following canon for an analogy), one in which she had no choice: her husband's. The present legislation retreats completely from such a directive; it simply states that the two have a common domicile—and then recognizes the fact that they may be separated for a "legitimate" reason or otherwise kept apart. In either case, each can acquire his or her own distinct domicile or quasi-domicile. The legitimacy of the separation—in the external judgment of the church community—is described in canons 1152, 1153, and 1692–1696. Adultery, gross mistreatment, physical danger, as well as factual breakdown of the relationship, and divorce are all considered. The approbation of the ordinary is required in cases in which it is possible. Varying diocesan statutes and traditions will govern the actual implementation of this canon.

Minors

Canon 105 — §1. A minor necessarily keeps the domicile or quasi-domicile of the one to whose power he or she is subject. After passing beyond infancy one can also acquire a quasi-domicile of one's own; and one who has been legally emancipated according to the norm of civil law can also acquire a domicile of his or her own.

"Necessary," or "involuntary," domiciles are determined in a mandatory fashion for minors. The law also settles an older and arcane matter of dispute. This principle applies also to the "quasi-domicile" of the parent or guardian—a residence not mentioned in earlier law.[19] The present norm fixes either one as the necessary domicile of the minor child. With dependency on parents decreasing and personal independence increasing, the minor can later acquire an authentic quasi-domicile (e.g., at a

---

[18] See *CIC* 93, §1.
[19] Ibid.

distant place of education). With emancipation (determined according to civil norms), he or she can then acquire a true domicile. It is assumed that the civil legislation pertinent here is that of the place in which the newly emancipated minor wishes to establish the domicile (rather than the residence of the parents). Parallel principles of law do not require a minor to be bound *only* by the legislation of the place where the parents have their own domicile.

§2. Whoever has been legally placed under the guardianship or care of another, for some reason other than minority, has the domicile or quasi-domicile of the guardian or curator.

One other class of persons remains to be considered with regard to their involuntary, or necessary, domiciles: those placed under a *tutor* or a *curator* for safekeeping—because of their youth or mental illness, respectively. These subjects will have their domiciles determined, as do the religious of canon 103, by those in whose care they have been placed; in the present case the domicile becomes, however, that of the actual guardian, not the actual place of the subject.

Loss of Domicile

Canon 106 — **Domicile and quasi-domicile are lost by departure from the place with the intention of not returning, with due regard for the prescription of can. 105.**

Departure, coupled with the intent of not returning to a place, brings about the loss of domicile and quasi-domicile. Again, the conjunction of intent and action must be noted. Both must be simultaneously present—departure and the intention of not returning. (This will usually be the correlative of the establishment of an alternative domicile or quasi-domicile elsewhere: "I intend to move permanently from here to there.") The intention of non-return need be merely reasonable and prudent—and not absolute: it corresponds to the same provision—an unforeseen and seriously demanding future—that was present in making the first commitment. As has been seen in the case of the necessary domicile of canon 105, the subject simply has no control over the matter or discretion in it: the *tutor* or *curator* determines the matter.

Parish and Domicile

Canon 107 — **§1. Each person acquires a proper pastor and ordinary through both domicile and quasi-domicile.**

The proper pastor and ordinary of an individual is determined by his or her domicile or quasi-domicile. This canon has direct implications for parish "membership." The canonical mission to offer "the care of soul" to an individual comes as the product of his or her place of *residence*—rather than from some other more subjective attraction of the individual to a particular pastor or liturgist. In the American scene—with its even daily mobility—the tendency is toward more personal parishes rather than territorial ones; the basic intent remains nonetheless an allocation fixed by choice of residence, not by a free option.

§2. The proper pastor or ordinary of a transient is the pastor or ordinary of the place in which the transient is actually staying.

The domicile-less, rootless transient, by contrast with all of the above, finds his or her pastor and his or her parish not where the transient wishes, but wherever he or she actually is. It is assumed that the stay is brief, and that the intentions of the transient are to move on.

§3. The proper pastor of one who has only a diocesan domicile or quasi-domicile is the pastor of the place in which such a person is actually staying.

The same disposition falls upon the one who does have the intention of a continued residence within a dicocese—but no fixed base within it: this person also finds his or her spiritual care and parish wherever he or she is within the diocesan territory.

Relationship to Persons

Consanguinity

Canon 108 — **§1. Consanguinity is calculated through lines and degrees.**

The English vocabulary for the expression of blood relationship (and also of marriage) is deficient. Other languages have a whole glossary accurately describing each of many possible conjunctions. The system in use in ecclesiastical law reduces this problem by substituting an excellent and graphic description for a verbal one. "Lines" refer to generations, either "direct," as father to son, or "collateral," referring to brothers—each with his own respective and parallel lines of progeny. A "degree" represents one generation. The basis of the law is the practical one of ultimate fear of too close and too protracted intermarriages. Genetically, such unions tend to emphasize dominant—and even recessive—traits. These may be good—and the product brilliant; they may be bad—and the product tragic. The law here determines a descriptive vocabulary of relationships. It applies principally for use in marriage—in canon 1091, §2, it permits the marriages of those who are related in no closer than and including the fourth degree, or grade, of consanguinity. (In all cases, "legitimacy" or lack of it is irrelevant: it is the physical, generational relationship that is determinant.)

§2. In the direct line, there are as many degrees as there are generations or persons, not counting the common ancestor.

The direct line is completed according to the number of generations or persons involved (obviously excepting the ancestor). A great-grandmother is related to her descendant in the third degree, or third grade, of the direct line. There are three persons involved, excluding the root.

§3. In the collateral line, there are as many degrees as there are persons in both lines together, not counting the common ancestor.

The collateral, or oblique, or parallel, line (by its various names) reintroduces into law a recovered concept: computation according to a much broader and older system. This is now different from that of the 1917 Code—and simpler.[20] Relationship in the collateral lines is determined merely by the total number of generations or persons—again excepting the common ancestor or root. The marriage law inhibits marriages "in the fourth degree"—however they be realized (c. 1091, §2). This normally would be between first cousins—four persons and four generations are involved, ignoring the common ancestor. Theoretically, the line of forbiddance could be of unequal length—an uncle therefore could not marry his grandniece short of proper dispensation; he could, however, freely make his way to the altar for a union with his *great*-grandniece.

It is urgently suggested that a uniform system of representing these complex relationships, particularly of successive marriages, be adopted. A useful system follows several rules: the male is always represented by a square, the woman by a circle; a horizontal line indicates a marriage; a vertical line, and a second square *for the same man,* represent a second marriage for him. This allows graphic presentation of the most tangled sequences of unions. A simple case of previous bond would therefore look like this:

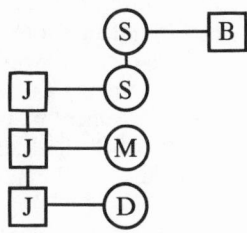

Joseph now wishes to marry Dorothy. Joseph's second wife, Mary, has died; his first wife, Sue, is still living, but had been previously and validly married

to Bernard. (Bernard was still living at the time of the attempted marriage of Sue and Joseph.) As it stands, it would seem that Joseph's first marriage is therefore invalid by reason of Sue's previous existing bond with Bernard.

Affinity

Canon 109 — **§1. Affinity arises from a valid marriage, even if not consummated, and exists between a man and the blood relatives of the woman and between the woman and blood relatives of the man.**

The concept of relationship gained through marriage, or "affinity," is difficult to grasp as it is realized in canon law, because it goes contrary to an underlying assumption of symmetry. One would expect that through marriage the relatives of one party become related to the relatives of the other. They do not. *Only* the party who marries becomes related to the relatives of the one whom he or she marries. A man's relatives do not become related to his new wife's relatives (or "in-laws," to use the English term) or vice versa. Stated another way, relatives do not become related to relatives.

Two critically important points should be borne in mind. In church law, the relationship of affinity arises only in "a valid marriage." This "valid" marriage seems certainly to refer only to a valid sacramental union between two baptized Roman Catholics[21] or to a union in which one party is baptized in the Roman Catholic Church. The *ecclesiastical* bond of affinity does not arise between unbaptized or non-Roman Catholic persons. They are outside the Church's jurisdiction, and their relationship is governed by the appropriate civil law. This had long been uncertain; the dispute was responded to at least in part in an answer of the Holy Office dated January 31, 1957.[22] Secondly, and obviously but frequently unstated, the relationship of affinity remains even after the death of the one through whom the link of affinity was formed. For Roman Catholics, one still may not marry, for example, one's (deceased) husband's son by a former wife. The enduring relationship of affinity impedes it.

§2. It is so calculated that those who are blood relatives of the man are related in the same line and degree by affinity to the woman, and vice versa.

The computation of the *degree* of affinity attained through marriage is simple: it is as though the spouses were a single person. The subject therefore acquires relationship to the blood relatives of the other party in the same number of degrees or

[20]*CIC* 96.

[21]C. 11, in conjunction with c. 1061, §1.
[22]*CLD* 4, 89; *AAS* 49–77.

grades, and in the direct or collateral line, as the spouse himself or herself. According to canon 1092 marriages are now impeded only in the *direct* line of relationship through affinity.

Adoption

Canon 110 — Children who have been adopted according to the norm of civil law are considered as being the children of the person or persons who have adopted them.

Adopted children are usually not at all, or occasionally not wholly, related to the parents adopting them. What relationship, if any, then arises between them and their parents? Could a father marry his own (adopted) daughter? Genetically, there would seem to be no bar; socially, it would speak of incest. Society expresses through its norms the governance of this relationship. Church law adopts the civil law pertinent to the area and states that adopted children are held to be the equivalent of natural children of an adopting couple in those instances in which adoption has been duly formalized according to the civil law. This last term has not as yet been clarified. In a federal republic, when there exists some jealousy of states' rights, it would be urged that the prevailing *local* regulation, as long as it is recognized by the higher federal law as constitutional, would obtain. Church law makes provision here also for the single parent: the canon applies to a single adopting parent, as well as to a couple.

Relationship to Rite

The rich and at times bewildering panoply of distinct "rites," or "churches," within the Roman Catholic Church, has already been adverted to in the very first canon of church law. Canon 111, §1 introduces a subtlety of language that conceals an intensity of feeling. The two major branches of rite are described in canon 1 as the Latin "Church" and—while not mentioned—its antonym, the Oriental, or Eastern, "Church." This term has long been offensive to some members of this ancient tradition, who correctly hold that there is but one Roman Catholic "Church," to which neither the Latin nor the Eastern mode has a distinct claim. The language of the present canon graciously heals this: the reference in paragraph two is to a "Ritual Church *sui iuris*"—with focus therefore both upon autonomy and upon variation in rituals of worship and antecedent cultures and languages.

Given this rich and fruitful autonomy, the question of how one is ascribed to an individual "rite" and its varying disciplines and subdisciplines, particularly in areas where members of the various groups live side by side and intermarry, becomes one of central importance. A "Latin Catholic" and a "Ukranian Byzantine Oriental Catholic" who wish to marry each other in a small Pennsylvania community containing only one Roman Catholic church are necessarily confined in their choice to that ritual style of worship. Their children are baptized there. Are the children then members of the "Ritual Church *sui iuris*" of *one* of the parents—or both—or of the group of which the church and its baptismal ceremony are a part? Canon 111 approaches that question.

Choice at Baptism: Parents

Canon 111 — §1. A child of parents who belong to the Latin Church is ascribed to it by reception of baptism, or, if one or the other parent does not belong to the Latin Church and both parents agree in choosing that the child be baptized in the Latin Church, the child is ascribed to it by reception of baptism; but, if the agreement is lacking, the child is ascribed to the Ritual Church to which the father belongs.

Three alternatives are suggested. They offer an increasing availability of option and free choice. Least choice is left in the case of the baptism of a child of two Latin-affiliated parents: the child ipso facto—or more accurately, *ipso Baptismo*—becomes ascribed to their same Latin "Church." It cannot be sufficiently emphasized that this wholly new canon simply does not mention the "rite" of the ceremony itself. It would presumably have been Latin. Where that was not available to parents, it might have been, for example, in the Oriental Byzantine Ukranian discipline. The ceremony would in *neither* case have dictated the affiliation of the child. The child follows the (Latin) rite of the (Latin) parents. The nature of the ceremony had no effect.

More significantly, however, this section of the canon does not indicate the intent of the parents as being the determinant of their child's rite. Suppose the two Latin parents had taken their child to the local Ruthenian parish, *with the intent* of affiliating the child with this different fashion of worship? The intent in this case remains irrelevant. It is stated in the law that the child of Latin parents becomes affiliated to the Latin Church of these Latin parents.

Intent becomes relevant in another and different situation, however. In cases in which the parents are of differing rites, one being Latin and the other Oriental, and there is agreement between the couple that the child be baptized in the Latin Church, the child is ascribed, by law, to the Latin rite of the Latin parent.

The alternative to this, however, is not mentioned by the Code. If this amiable interritual couple were to agree mutually that their child is to be ascribed to the rite of the *Oriental*-affiliated parent, could this be carried out? The language of the canon does not say that it cannot—neither does it say that the only option available to the disparate couple is the choice of the Latin alternative. Unlike the earlier example of the *two* Latins approaching an Oriental community, the case here implies an Oriental who (with the Latin spouse's concurrence) seeks to bring the child into the Oriental spouse's own "Ritual Church *sui iuris.*" The choice is as equally available to this Oriental as it is to the Latin.

In instances in which there is no agreement at all, however, an arbitrary solution is imposed by the law. Following an ancient tradition, whose basis this commentary will not in the least attempt to defend at this point, the religious affiliation of the child is placed with that of the male parent, no matter what his own ritual identity might be—Latin or Oriental. It should again be noted, however, that no choice is available here. The wish of a father to select a ritual discipline different both from his own and from his wife's cannot be implemented, e.g., a Latin father and a Maronite mother requesting Melchite affiliation for their child.

Choice at Baptism: Adults

§2. Anyone to be baptized who has completed the fourteenth year of age can freely choose to be baptized in the Latin Church or in another Ritual Church *sui iuris*, and in this case the person belongs to that Church which is chosen.

An adult has free choice of his or her ritual affiliation when presenting himself or herself for baptism. This at first sight seems self-evident. Historically the antecedents were quite different, however. It was generally expected that the catechumen would present himself or herself for baptism in the rite to which his or her own religious affiliation corresponded—a Protestant would come, for example, to the Latin rite, a Greek Orthodox to the Roman Catholic Oriental Byzantine Greek discipline. No such limitation is expressed in the 1983 law. Choice furthermore is made available to those who are not yet even adults (in the sense of c. 97). The threshold of free ritual choice for the convert is placed at the age of fourteen. He or she becomes affiliated with the "Ritual Church *sui iuris*" which is selected at the time of his or her conversion.

Change of Rite

Canon 112 — §1. After the reception of baptism, the following are enrolled in another Ritual Church *sui iuris*:

1° one who has obtained permission from the Apostolic See;

2° a spouse who declares at the time of marriage or during marriage that he or she is transferring to the Ritual Church *sui iuris* of the other spouse; but

when the marriage has ended, that person can freely return to the Latin Church;

3° children of those in nn. 1 and 2 under fourteen complete years of age; and similarly children of a Catholic party in a mixed marriage who legitimately transferred to another Ritual Church. But, when such persons reach fourteen complete years of age, they may return to the Latin Church.

After baptism a change of ritual ascription may come about through three paths. The first and self-evident one is through an explicit allowance and rescript from the Holy See—specifically from the Sacred Congregation for the Oriental Churches in the case of an Eastern Rite Roman Catholic becoming a Latin (1°). The former allowance of such a transfer through the apostolic delegation no longer holds, although the latter may, as is customary, transmit the request, and add a *votum,* coupled with those of the respective ordinaries *a quo* and *ad quem.*

In interritual marriages, the allowances to Latin spouses are now very broad, in comparison to older dispositions of law.[23] Consequently another avenue for a change of ritual ascription has evolved. Either spouse now may, at the beginning of marriage or during it, transfer to the rite of the other spouse simply by a declaration to that effect (and may rescind the commitment, with the death of the other spouse) (2°). The law makes no mention of the form in which this declaration is either made or registered. One suspects that such a change of rite at one's own initiative might best be recorded at the chancery and in the baptismal registers of the parish—but in a specialized form analogous to that of professions of faith. In addition, no statement is made about reversion to a former rite *during* a marriage. It would not seem allowed by the language of the present legislation. Finally the election of change of rite at the very beginning of a marital union might entail some question regarding the proper sacramental form for a marriage, i.e., shall it be that of the groom or the bride? Former responses suggested the Latin ceremonial in any case;[24] the implication was that the change of rite became effective only after the union was actually effected. In an uncertain case, this principle can probably be appealed to within the present law as well, but obviously with its now broader allowance of choice to either or both spouses.

The third path through which a change of ritual can be achieved involves the children of those cited in numbers one and two who change their ritual ascription. These children are also brought along, at the wish of their parents, to the parent's (or parents') new rite, if they have not yet reached their fourteenth (completed) year of age; beyond this,

23 E.g., *CIC* 98, §4. For Orientals cf. *Cleri sanctitati,* c. 8.
24 *CLD* 2, 49; *AAS* 32–212.

they may at their discretion elect to return to the original rite (3°). Again, some official recording of this fact should be made available for future verification.

§2. The custom, however prolonged, of receiving the sacraments according to the rite of another Ritual Church *sui iuris*, does not carry with it enrollment in that Church.

The final statement with regard to the sensitive matter of ritual loyalty has a positive (if restrictive) thrust: protracted sacramental reception in an alien rite does *not* bring about ascription to that rite. This was a clear principle of previous law. It is an objective guideline that is much eroded by the newer and broader allowances just discussed. It might be easier then to enumerate finally what *does* effect a change of rite: apostolic permission; a choice of either spouse at or during a marital union; a choice of return to one's original rite after one's marriage has ended; a decision upon the part of parents at the time of the baptism of their children; and a grown child's return to his or her earlier mode of worship. Apparently it is *only* upon one's own initiative, in a single adult state, that a change is inhibited by law.

CHAPTER II
JURIDIC PERSONS
[cc. 113–123]

If the aphorism "Sacramenta propter homines" has validity, so must the insight, "leges propter homines." But generally the *homines* who are the object of the law's support and protection are individual physical persons. Society is so constituted that some advances could never be achieved individually. Groups must band together for common purposes. To achieve their ends (and transcend the life span of individual members), these groups, aggregates, "*universitates*," are treated by the law as though they, too, were physical persons. "By a fiction of law" these aggregates of persons (or of things administered by persons) are treated as possessing some of the rights of physical human persons—notably those of the acquisition, possession, and transmission of property, as well as a kind of self-determination that is lodged in various members or organs of the body. In past law, these aggregates were called "moral persons";[25] a new terminology speaks of "juridic persons" (emphasizing the favor of law or "fiction" of law which they enjoy), and they are seen as subjects in church law of those rights and obligations that are in accord with the character of the group or aggregate.[26]

Juridic Persons in the Church

Canon 113 — §1. The Catholic Church and the Apostolic See have the nature of a moral person by divine law itself.

"The Catholic Church" has already been identified as the larger community of the baptized in which the "*Christifidelis*" achieves the higher personality of what comes with that baptism (cf. the earlier reflections upon c. 96). Throughout the Code, the Church makes several claims that are appropriate to a physical person but are made by a group of persons as a single entity. The rights to proclaim the gospel and to own places of worship are examples of this. The canon now at the very outset of this chapter that will deal with juridic persons asserts that by divine institution both the Catholic Church and the Apostolic See—they are mentioned separately—enjoy such juridic personality. The use of the otherwise discarded term "moral person" seems to confirm this. (As an aside, it should be noted that this first paragraph of canon 113 was inserted only in the last weeks of the twenty years of preparation of the 1983 Code.) The intent of this late addition seems to offer an affirmation of what was already stated in the second paragraph and to emphasize that the entire body of the Church as such—not to mention the corporate structure of the Holy See—is also such a juridic entity.

§2. Besides physical persons, there are also in the Church juridic persons, that is, subjects in canon law of obligations and rights which correspond to their nature.

These "juridic persons" are found also below and within the entire church body itself—sub-"persons" who are defined in paragraph two as subjects in canon law of obligations and rights that are in accord with their particular character or function. The function of this canon is simply to establish at the outset a basic foundation: within the intricate structure of church law, aggregates, or groups, or assemblies ("*universitates*"), of people—or even of objects—will be considered as truly possessing rights normally associated only with physical persons.

The Establishment of Juridic Persons

Canon 114 — §1. Juridic persons are constituted either by prescription of law or by special concession of the competent authority given through a decree; they are aggregates of persons or of things ordered towards a purpose congruent with the mis-

---

[25]*CIC* 99.
[26]C. 113. The reader is referred to what well may be the seminal article addressing itself to this complex topic as found in the

1983 Code: F. Coccopalmerio, *"De Persona Iuridica Iuxta Schema Codicis Novi, P* 70/3 (1981): 369–400.

sion of the Church and which transcends the purpose of the individuals that make them up.

It is to be expected that the juridic existence of these aggregates of persons or things comes into being through some specific initiative either of the law itself, or of a "competent authority." The former is self-evident; the law speaks in detail of the establishment of churches, religious institutes, seminaries, etc. Outside of these areas, the ecclesiastical authority can form true juridic persons within the Church, and it can offer them recognized status as possessors of rights and duties. Which "authority"? A most useful norm for insight into this directive can be found in the lengthy and virtually parallel treatment of this subject in the title of the Code entitled "Associations of the Christian Faithful" (cc. 298–329). Canon 312 speaks of three competent ecclesiastical authorities: the Apostolic See for juridic persons which have worldwide dispersion and activity; national conferences for juridic persons within a nation; and individual bishops for juridic persons formed within their own diocesan jurisdictions. Where the law itself does not determine a founding and supervising authority, canon 312 can be appealed to as a guiding norm.

Several safeguards are required for such a significant institution of law. The charter of foundation must be granted by the competent authority by a decree. (Canon 312, §2 adds the obvious note that for validity in an association of the faithful constituting a diocesan juridic person, that decree must be in writing, against an oral charter and the massive conflicts that could offer.) Such a decree, again drawing upon the more detailed treatment of these later canons, must address itself to such matters as officers, ownership of property, the makeup of the constitutions and statutes of the juridic person, rules for governance and for the adjudication of disputes, and norms for possible dissolution of the entity. A juridic person, in church law, lastly, shall possess a quality that springs from its origins and its setting: it shall be one which is ordered toward the achieving of the mission of the Church, and therefore transcending any individual's aim or betterment.

§2. The purposes spoken of in §1 are understood as those which pertain to works of piety, of the apostolate or of charity, whether spiritual or temporal.

These larger ends of a juridic person are immediately described: works of piety, of the apostolate, and of charity, whether spiritual or temporal. This threefold presentation has roots deep within the life of the worshiping community. The earlier views of juridic persons saw precisely these three, in terms respectively of personal sanctification and holiness, the proclamation of the gospel and the enhance-

ment of public worship, and the works of spiritual and temporal charities.[27] They found their setting respectively in institutes of the consecrated or apostolic life, the teaching and worshiping organs of the people of God, and "The Office of Sanctifying in the Church" (Book IV of the 1983 Code). Preceding law therefore spoke of the associations of the faithful as being, respectively and exclusively, third orders, confraternities, and pious unions.

§3. The competent ecclesiastical authority is not to confer juridic personality except upon those aggregates of persons or things which pursue a truly useful purpose and, all things considered, have resources which are foreseen to be sufficient to achieve their designated end.

It is the duty of the competent ecclesiastical authority to scrutinize the goals and the resources of a proposed juridic person before establishing it in law—to verify that its goal is one that is "useful" (to the purposes and needs of the people of God)—and, so far as can be determined, that it has the means to achieve that end. Drawing from parallel instances in law, it is clear that this envisages at best a prudential judgment against the future. It would not prohibit a projection of possible future resources as the moral person develops, and acting in the present upon that projection into the future.

A note should be added that in the American setting, with its constitutional and fruitful prohibition of an established religion or of legislation prohibiting the free exercise of religion, the ecclesiastical establishment of a juridic person does not in the least assure its possession of rights before the civil polity. Juridic persons within the Church are therefore encouraged, where appropriate, to seek such civil standing also through civil incorporation, or other appropriate steps effective in the civil arena. American constitutional law is filled with picturesque cases in which these relationships are equitably and wisely adjudicated to clarify and protect the rights both of the larger civil community and of the Church.

Kinds of Juridic Persons

Canon 115 — §1. Juridic persons within the Church are aggregates either of persons or of things.

The fiction of *personality*—of self-determination and rights of possession—can be attributed both to aggregates, or collections, of persons, or, as in the classical case of civil incorporation, to aggregates of things. This repeats the intent of canon 114, §1.

[27]See *CIC* title IX, 700–725 in general and 685 specifically in its view of "lay associations."

§2. An aggregate of persons, which cannot be constituted unless it consists of at least three persons, is collegial if its members determine its action through participation in making its decisions, whether by equal right or not, according to the norm of law and its own statutes; otherwise it is non-collegial.

In the first instance, associations of *persons* will obviously consist of more than one physical person. To provide for even the most primitive level of decision-making and voting, juridic associations of physical persons must consist of at least three—to allow for the obvious voting majority. Aggregates of physical persons can be viewed *either* as a community in which the body itself contributes to the ultimate decision-making process and has an effective franchise, e.g., the council of an institute of consecrated life or a chapter meeting, either of which can make effective decisions by a vote (and these are called "collegial" aggregates of persons) *or* perhaps as a community in which authority and decision-making, according to its own norms and constitutions, may be confined to only certain of the members or even to non-members who are its superiors, e.g., a diocese (and these are called "non-collegial" aggregates of persons). A very rough political model of the distinction might be found in that between a pure democracy and a monarchy, where the emphasis is upon the entire nation in both cases, and both are aggregates of physical, personal subjects. Determination, however, comes collegially in the first, and only in an authoritative and stratified and non-collegial fashion in the second.

§3. An aggregate of things or an autonomous foundation consists of goods or things, whether spiritual or material, and is directed by one or several physical persons or a college according to the norm of law and its statutes.

An aggregate of *things,* rather than of persons, to which the rights and duties of personality will be attributed by a fiction of law—and also called "an autonomous foundation"—is necessarily directed *by* a physical person or persons. These are to be selected by processes outlined in the statutes of establishment or incorporation. They act individually or collegially as the directing personality of the collection of inanimate goods.

Public and Private Juridic Persons

Canon 116 — §1. Public juridic persons are aggregates of persons or things which are so constituted by the competent ecclesiastical authority that, within the limits set for them in the name of the Church, they fulfill a proper function entrusted to them in view of the common good, in accord with

the prescripts of law; other juridic persons are private.

Juridic persons are considered as "public" or as "private." Those which are public act officially in behalf of the competent ecclesiastical authority by whom they are constituted, and in a larger sense in behalf of the entire Church, although always of course within their own limits of competency. Those aggregates of persons or things which are not so empowered by the authority remain only private. The word public in this sense means having the authority of a larger governing body—representing the nation or structure as a whole—the *res publica,* or again public, as in the sense of a public notary, as official witness for the government. The quality of public charter has no implication of notoriety, or lack of it, or above all of the "secret societies" of a much earlier American experience. On the contrary, the emphasis is upon a specific grant of authority to the body to act in its limited area, and for the common and public good—"in the name of" the Church and with the *full faith and credit* of the empowering Church behind its actions. It is this conscious commission to the juridic person to act "in the name of" the larger Church and for it, which constitutes a "public juridic person" before the rest of the community.

§2. Public juridic persons are given this personality either through the law itself or by a special decree of the competent authority expressly granting it; private juridic persons are given this personality only through a special decree of the competent authority expressly granting this personality.

The stature of public juridic person is conferred either expressly, in the law itself, or by the decree of establishment of the competent ecclesiastical authority—which should always *expressly* indicate the status of the new entity. The line between mere praise or commendation of a juridic person, and establishment of it as expressly public and representative of the empowering authority, can be thin indeed. Good order requires that in matters of such moment there should be no uncertainty of status; hence, there exists the requirement in law that the state of the new entity be clearly indicated. Conversely, the law requires equally express indication of the level of those juridic persons which remain merely private. This is particularly significant in public associations of the faithful in the Church.[28]

Canon 117 — No aggregate of persons or things, intending to obtain juridic personality, can achieve it unless its statutes have been approved by the competent authority.

---

[28]See for this cc. 299–301 and their attendant commentaries.

No body seeking juridic personality, whether it be of a community of persons or an aggregate of things, may pursue its functions until its statutes have been approved by the competent authority. For the identity of the competent authority, one should see the commentary on canon 312.

Canon 118 — They alone represent a public juridic person and act in its name who are acknowledged to have this competence either by universal or particular law or by its own statutes; they represent a private juridic person who have been given this competency by statute.

Both public and private juridic entitites must be represented by physical persons on whom the task of governance and decision rests. It is they who act in the name of the entities and are its voice and mind. They are designated either by the universal or particular law itself (e.g., in certain public juridic entities the major superior speaks for an institute of consecrated life),[29] or, in both public and private ones, the officers may be designated by the internal statutes of governance of the body (e.g., the Worthy Navigator of the Knights of Columbus).

Voting in Juridic Bodies

Canon 119 — With regard to collegial acts, unless provision is made otherwise by law or statutes:
1° if it is a question of elections, that action has the force of law which, when a majority of those who must be convoked are present, receives the approval of an absolute majority of those who are present; after two indecisive ballots, the choice is between the two candidates who have obtained the greater number of the votes, or, if there are several (with the same numbers), upon the two who are senior in age; after a third ballot, if the tie remains, the one who is the senior in age is considered elected;

In the collegial actions of aggregates of physical persons, there are certain precise regulations for the election of *persons* (as opposed to votes upon *actions*). Canon 119 states that (presuming there are no contrary indications in law or in the statutes of the group) a choice among persons has the force of law when it has been approved by an absolute majority of those who are present—who in turn must represent a majority of those who are to be convoked for the election as a quorum. If no absolute majority has been reached after two ballots, the candidacy should be reduced to those two who received the greater number of votes cast, or in the event of a tie, to the two oldest candidates (in terms of physical age). If there is still a tie vote on the

third ballot, the one who is senior in physical age is considered elected. This represents a change in the election rules of a past period.[30] Formerly, two votes seeking an absolute majority were to be cast, and the third ballot was determined simply by a "relative" majority—i.e., the candidate with the greatest number of votes, regardless of their number. In a large slate—of two dozen candidates and perhaps votes—the choice *might* have been settled upon by a mere three votes in favor of the winning candidate—which represented the largest number—and almost complete lack of consensus. The changed procedure could surface two candidates who still did not have a large constituency in absolute terms (although relatively the two largest); the prescribed third ballot now insures at least that *all* members each give personal consideration to only the two candidates surviving. Additionally, contemporary legislation settles the breaking of a tie upon a quality in the candidates themselves, rather than in the discretionary (and second) vote of the presiding officer. Impersonality of choice, and the presumed wisdom of age, are gained, at the loss of the opportunity for evaluation and weighing, formerly placed in the one, tie-breaking officer.

2° if it is a question of other matters, that action will have the force of law which, when a majority of those who must be convoked are present, receives the approval of an absolute majority of those who are present; if after two ballots it is a tie vote, the presiding officer can break the tie by his or her vote;

In other transactions of the body requiring a vote, the same quorum is required, of a greater part (even by as little as one person) of those who are to be convoked, and the same absolute majority. There is, however, no limit stated as to the number of ballots, and no reduction to votes upon selected leading alternatives; voting might presumably continue until an absolute majority is actually achieved. This would have the virtue of requiring a measure of consensus; it would have the danger of producing almost certain deadlock. The qualifying clarification of number two is ambiguous. The presiding officer may use his or her vote to break a *tie,* "if [this is the condition] after two ballots." It is not stated that these two tie votes *must* represent half the body (they could also represent a tie between two options with each a very small relative majority of the votes—each with 6 in a body of 50); neither is it stated that this tie must occur on the *third* ballot—or merely on *any* successive tied ballot. A clue to the intent of the lawgiver is found in advertence to the preceding law of the 1917 Code.[31] There the

---

[29]See. c. 620.

[30]Cf. *CIC* 101, §1, 1°.
[31]Ibid.

language is virtually identical but adds the evident prescription that if after two ineffective votes there is no absolute majority, the alternative that has won a *relative* majority in a third vote is considered chosen; if there is a tie here, *then* the presiding officer breaks it, etc. The intent and mechanism and parallel would seem to indicate the option of decision resting upon *any* third ballot, further clarified only in the event of a tie—even among a small number of votes.

3° what touches all as individuals must be approved by all.

One of the seminal phrases in law, from the Justinian *Digest* and out of the Rules of Law of 1298, was the charter of individual protection—and some would say, collegial decision-making: "what touches all, as individuals, should be approved by all."[32] This might be translated as holding that all who are affected should have a voice in a decision; some would hold that all should have a vote; canonists largely hold that what truly "touches all" now requires a unanimous vote of the constituency.[33] Except in the rarest cases, the Code does not indicate which actions are of this quality: canon 174, §1, requiring a unanimous vote to allow a decision by a chosen committee, is an example. The intent of the rule is to safeguard individual rights—which are intrinsically inherent in each member of the college—against destruction or alteration by a majority. A crude example would be the decision of a cloistered group to separate and establish a new and distant foundation. A disputed example would be a majority vote to induce a significant change in the spirituality and aims of a religious community toward renewal; the ancient rule might be interpreted to require unanimity in all these cases. The rule is stated in the Code, verbatim, without clarification, and without indication as to precisely where it should be applied. It is the *foundation* for a requirement of unanimous votes rather than a guide as to where *in concreto* such votes may be demanded in the actions of juridic persons. If required, it follows that for the legitimacy of the election, all affected members must have been effectively summoned to the vote (cf. c. 166).

Extinguishment of Juridic Persons

Canon 120 — §1. A juridic person is of its nature perpetual; nevertheless it is extinguished if it is legitimately suppressed by a competent authority or

---

[32]Reg. 29, *R.I. in VI°.*

[33]Cf. in this regard S. Sipos, *Enchiridion Iuris Canonici* (Romae: Herder, 1960), 79, and his citation of Vermeersch, Michiels, Wernz, Ojetto, and Maroto. It should be noted, however, that the 1983 law substitutes the word "approbari" for the older word—presumably demanding unanimity—"probari." The subtle difference may suggest evaluation more than acceptance.

has ceased activity for a hundred years; a private juridic person is furthermore extinguished if the association is dissolved according to the norm of its statutes, or if, in the judgment of the competent authority, the foundation itself has ceased to exist according to the norm of its statutes.

A juridic personality is itself independent of the physical personalities (or the material goods) which constitute it; it can endure beyond the existence of either of these; in its nature it may continue indefinitely. It may be terminated, however, by a positive action of the authority which established it. It has already been noted that examples of identification of this establishing authority are found in canon 312—the Apostolic See, a national conference or a diocesan bishop. Unless there be a statutory provision to the contrary, the establishing authority, or the successors or superiors thereof, have the power also of dissolution of a juridic entity. The act of suppression should obviously be in writing, and the decree should clarify the authority acting, the antecedents of the juridic person, the motivations for the present action, and the disposition of its assets (a matter governed by c. 123, below). By a negative circumstance a juridic personality can also cease to exist—established in law as a de facto failure to function for a hundred years. This means a continuous century. Prior to this period, a juridic person could resume its function without a new decree of establishment by the competent authority; the norm envisages a declaration of non-existence only after this prolonged and specified dormancy. Prior, briefer, transient periods of inactivity do not qualify for the action.

A specifically "private" juridic person (as defined indirectly by c. 116 and clarified in cc. 289–301 and their accompanying commentary) can also cease to exist through the operation of its own norms. These may indicate the circumstances when dissolution automatically occurs—for example, through a lapse of time, reduction to a stated minimum of members or assets, intrusion of an external circumstance (division of a diocese or conjunction of a diocese or parish), or diversion of a goal. Supervision of this and evaluation of it is named in this same canon: by a kind of declaratory judgment, the competent authority can declare that, "according to the norm of its statutes," the juridic person has now ceased to exist.

§2. If even one member of a collegial juridic person survives, and the aggregate of persons has not ceased to exist according to its statutes, the exercise of all of the rights of the aggregate devolves upon that one member.

The establishment of a juridic person consisting of an aggregate of physical persons, whether collegial or non-collegial in its decision-making, requires—as has been noted—a minimum of three persons; this is for decision processes. If there be only one, it is simply a physical person; if only two, it is open to constant impasse. Nothing prevents, however, an erosion of the membership and assets, until in fact only one physical person survives. A juridic person is of its nature indefinite and perpetual in existence; it follows that all of the rights of the entity (assuming that its own statutes have not thereby decreed its dissolution) then fall upon that one physical person. This includes voting rights, property rights, even the right to admit new members. The specific legislation of the Code on associations of the faithful would, however, prevent the survivor's rewriting the statutes and the constitutions; in public juridic persons, such steps require consultation with and the superintendence of the establishing ecclesiastical authority.[34]

Conjunction of Juridic Persons

Canon 121 — If aggregates, whether of persons or of things, which are public juridic persons, are so joined that out of all of them one aggregate is constituted, itself enjoying juridic personality, this new juridic person obtains the goods and patrimonial rights proper to the prior ones, and it also takes upon itself the obligations with which they have been burdened; however, the intention of the founders and donors and acquired rights must be respected, particularly as regards the allocation of goods and the fulfillment of obligations.

Previous law had not addressed itself to the question of a confederation or conjunction of juridic personalities. Contemporary law does so in this Book of the Code, "General Norms," and in the norms for associations of the faithful found in Book II, "The People of God." The thrust of canon 121 is not toward the extinction or suppression of a juridic personality, but rather its incorporation—by a kind of juridic symbiosis—into a newly emerging yet equal personality, with its own rights and obligations, but also a distinct and new entity. The federation acquires the assets, the rights, and the patrimony proper to the antecedent juridic persons—and also all their accompanying obligations and liabilities. Two evident qualifications are found in this norm: first, to protect the sacrosanct intention of testators with regard to property which has been conveyed by last will and testament to the juridic personality,[35] and second, to protect the "acquired rights" of others, achieved through the juridic personality in question, and realized, for instance, in contractual obligations. Subsequent amalgamation or conglomeration cannot undo these commitments.

[34]Cf. cc. 314 and 319, §1 regarding administration of the assets of the sole surviving juridic person.
[35]See cc. 1300 and 1301, §3 for the tenacious concern in ecclesiastical law for the protection of inheritances and bequests.

Division of Juridic Persons

Canon 122 — If an aggregate which has public juridic personality is so to be divided so that a part of it is united to another public juridic person, or that a distinct public juridic person is established from the separated part, it is the obligation of the ecclesiastical authority which is competent to make the division, having observed before all else the intention of founders and donors, acquired rights, and approved statutes, to see to it personally or through an executor:
1° that things held in common which are capable of division, both goods and patrimonial rights as well as the debts and other obligations, are divided among the juridic persons concerned with due proportion based on equity and justice, taking into account all the circumstances and the needs of each;
2° that the use and usufruct of those common goods which are not susceptible to division accrue to each juridic person, and that the obligations proper to them fall upon each, to be determined in like manner with proper regard for due proportion based on equity and justice.

The realignment of the personalities or assets of a public juridic entity can come about through several fashions: division, in which one entity begets two new and independent juridic persons; reapportionment, in which part of the substance of one is assigned to another, both continuing to exist; and dismemberment, in which the components of one (or of several) are severed from the parent body or bodies, and either extinguished, or themselves formed into a new juridic person. Where these actions occur, the norm requires that the "ecclesiastical authority which is competent"—usually the establishing one—supervise the transaction, either personally or through an executor. The competent authority is required in all events to verify respect for the two fixed commitments described in the immediately preceding commentary, bequests through last will and testaments, and acquired rights. The same authority is directed to see that the constitutions and statutory dispositions of the juridic personalities are observed.

A fertile source of human controversy, whenever a transfer of assets is involved, is greed and the general possessions of the previous holders. The common goods to be allocated in a realignment are foreseen to be of two classes: those that can be easily reapportioned and divided, e.g., a sum of money, and those that are not subject to easy division, e.g., rights and privileges of precedence or a specific ecclesiastical privilege—such as establishing a third order. The supervising competent authority is to verify that in the first area, the patrimony of the parent body—its rights, its credits, and indeed its obligations—are divided and conveyed to the new entity, "with due proportion ex aequo et bono."

That norm asks for wisdom; it relies ultimately upon the standard of English common law, "the reasonable judgment of prudent men." It suggests that the settlement make acknowledgment of the circumstances and necessities that surround the realigned entities. The law asks secondly that in those matters in which division is not possible—but award must be made—"the use and usufruct" of the indivisible asset be itself so far as possible allocated "ex aequo et bono" among the new entity or entitites, with the same sense of proportion and equity. In the division of a diocese, for example, these challenges to sensitivity and equity can be extensive.

Extinction of Juridic Persons

Canon 123 — Upon the extinction of a public juridic person, the allocation of its goods, patrimonial rights and obligations, is ruled by law and by statutes; if these give no indication, they go to the juridic person immediately superior, with due regard for the will of the founders or donors and for acquired rights; upon the extinction of a private juridic person the allocation of its goods and obligations is regulated by its own statutes.

Contrary to the amalgamation or the division of a juridic entity (cc. 121–122), concern must be expressed last for the assets and "patrimonial rights" of a juridic person that becomes extinct (through dissolution by law or suppression at the initiative of the competent authority). In the case of a public juridic personality, this disposition is to be regulated by the universal law (if applicable) or by its own statutes. Where, however, these have failed to provide for this need, and since it has been noted that the division of property is so often a source of contention, the common law intrudes, and specifically states here that the assets (and obligations) pass to the immediate superior of the entity in question. This is a new provision in law. It has yet to be tested in ecclesial litigation or arbitration; it provides a useful norm whose outlines will have to be filled in with future experience. Provision for review of such actions is imperative; suppression might always be a temptation—where the assets would be useful to a beleagured immediate superior. Finally, in the case of the demise of a private juridic person, the norm offers no direction beyond reference to the statutes of the entity. If these in turn offer no guidance—*lex silet*. Equity would support a decision as already enunciated in the Code—"ex aequo et bono"—by the competent original establishing authority or the successor thereof.

BIBLIOGRAPHY

Sources

Acta Apostolicae Sedis, Commentarium Officiale. Romae, 1909–1929; in Civitate Vaticana, 1929–

Acta et Documenta Concilio Oecumenico Vaticano II Apparando, Series I. (Antepraeparatoria.) 4 vols. Romae: Typis Polyglottis Vaticanis, 1960–1961.

Acta et Documenta Concilio Oecumenico Vaticano II Apparando, Series II. (Praeparatoria.) 3 vols. Romae: Typis Polyglottis Vaticanis, 1964–1969.

Acta Synodalia Sacrosancti Concilii Oecumenici Vaticani II. Romae: Typis Polyglottis Vaticanis, 1970–1978.

Bouscaren, T.L., and O'Connor, J.I., eds. *Canon Law Digest.* 9 vols. Milwaukee and New York: The Bruce Publishing Co., 1934–1967 and Mundelein: Chicago Province, S.J., 1983.

Codex Iuris Canonici Pii X Pontificis Maximi iusse digestus, Benedicti Papae XV auctoritate promolgatus. Romae: Typis Polyglottis Vaticanis, 1963.

Communicationes, Commentarium Pontificiae Commissionis Codici Iuris Canonici Recognosendo. Romae: 1969– . Schema, *People of God,* 12 (1980), 48–129 *et passim.*

Flannery, A., O.P., ed. *Vatican Council II: The Conciliar and Post Conciliar Documents.* Northport, N.Y.: Costello Publishing Co., 1975.

Hite, J.; Sesto, G.; and Ward, D. *Readings, Cases, Materials in Canon Law.* Collegeville: The Liturgical Press, 1979.

Reference Works

Abbo, J., and Hannan, J. *The Sacred Canons.* Rev. ed. 2 vols. St. Louis: B. Herder Book Co., 1957.

Beste, U., O.S.B. *Introductio in Codicem.* Ed. 5a. Neapoli: M. D'Auria, Pontificius Editor, 1961.

Blat, O.P. *Commentarium Textus Codicis Iuris Canonici.* 5 vols. Romae: Collegio 'Angelico,' 1921.

Bouscaren, T. L.; Ellis, A.; and Korth, F. *Canon Law: A Text and Commentary.* 4th ed. Milwaukee: The Bruce Publishing Co. 1966.

Conte a Coronata, M. *Institutiones Iuris Canonici.* Ed. 4a. 3 vols. Torino: A. Marietti Officina Libraria, 1950.

New Catholic Encyclopedia. W. McDonald, editor-in-chief. 15 vols. New York: McGraw-Hill, 1967.

Sipos, S. *Enchiridion Iuris Canonici.* Romae: Herder, 1960.

Wernz, F., and Vidal, P. *Ius Canonicum.* 7 vols. Romae: Universitatis Gregorianae, 1928–1952.

Articles

Alesandro, J.A. "The Revision of Church Law: Conflict and Reconciliation." *J* 40 (1980): 1, 1–26.

Green, T.J. "The Revision of Canon Law: Theological Implications." *TS* 40 (Dec. 1979): 4, 593–679.

Kelly, H.A. "Consanguinity, Incest, and the Dictates of Law." *J* 26 (Apr. 1966): 2, 181–193.

LaDue, W.J. "A Written Constitution for the Church?" *J* 32 (1972): 1, 1–13.

Provost, J.H. "The Working Together of Consultative Bodies—Great Expectations?" *J* 40 (1980): 2, 257–281.

Ryan, R.R. "The Residential Bishop as the Author of Dispensations . . ." *J* 38 (1978): 3/4, 268–279.

The last five titles of Book I, apart from the fact that they present norms applicable throughout the law of the Church, are only somewhat loosely related among themselves, although there is a logic to their order. Juridic acts, whether of physical or of juridic persons, are actions intended to affect the social or communitarian order of the Church; prominent among them in the legal order is the multifaceted exercise of the power of governance, whether this be in the form of legislation, executive action, or judicial decision. For the most part, moreover, the governance of the Church is exercised through established organs of action known as ecclesiastical offices, such as the office of diocesan bishop or of pastor, or that of finance officer or of religious superior. Book I concludes with seven canons grouped under two titles. Prescription concerns the acquisition or the loss of rights or the freedom from obligations through adverse possession in good faith. Since lapse of time, attaining a certain age, seniority, and the like play such an important role throughout both civil and canon law, the legal manner of computing time, while simple enough, is often of significant moment and requires consistent usage.

The commentary on the eighty canons of titles VII–XI frequently notes that, except for a few very important changes, their substance is not significantly modified from the parallel canons of the former Code. The title on juridic acts, for example, is new as a distinct title, but its provisions are, for the most part, found unchanged in the previous legislation. While the substance of the titles on governance and ecclesiastical offices is found in the former Code, their transfer from the law on clergy to the general norms is most important; lay persons share in the governance of the Church and, by the mandate of the Second Vatican Council, hold ecclesiastical offices in the technical and proper sense. Although the title on prescription was positioned in the 1917 Code under the rubric of ecclesiastical property, it has a much wider application and thus belongs among the general norms of canon law. Finally, the norms on the computation of time, which appeared in Book I of the previous Code, are more appropriately located in the same Book in the 1983 Code.

What is new, however, throughout these five titles is the significant, at times remarkable, simplification of the canons, the result of sixty-five years of experience with them. Despite the fact that eleven canons or parts of canons are entirely new, this section of the revised law treats the same subject matter in twenty fewer canons. These canons do not extensively employ the conciliar language as do much of the other Books of the revised law, and this is undoubtedly due to the fact that the First Book as a whole provides the basic tools and principles for the interpretation and application of the entire law, which were refined during the millennial tradition of canon law and not addressed by the recent Council except in the cases of ecclesiastical office and of the suppression of benefices. This substantive, but simplified, identity between the former Code and the new canons encourages the continued use of the standard commentaries on general norms, ordinary and delegated power, and ecclesiastical offices, provided, of course, the amendments introduced by the present law are carefully noted. The commentary calls attention to such changes and to their import.

TITLE VII
JURIDIC ACTS
[cc. 124–128]

While title VII is new in the Code, its subject matter is found in canons 103–105; 1680, §1; and 1681 of the 1917 Code, which did not speak of juridic acts as such. The substance of the former Code is repeated in the present title with some modifications which are noted in the commentary on the individual canons. A simple definition of a juridic act is that offered by O. Robleda, "an externally manifested act of the will by which a certain juridical effect is intended."[1] Some examples of what is intended by the expression, juridic act, which is a legal concept of the civil law tradition of continental Europe, will help to illustrate the definition. Among the many juridic acts found in canon law are conferral of office and removal from office; alienation of ecclesiastical assets and any other kind of contract; imposition or declaration of sanctions; sentences, appeals, and the numerous other acts of church tribunals; admission to, profession in, and separation from institutes of consecrated life and societies of apostolic life; erection and suppression of parishes; matrimony and ordination.

Of the five canons of title VII, the first identifies the canonical requirements for the validity of a juridic act and states a presumption of the law itself. The second, third, and fourth canons address certain circumstances which may or may not affect the validity of a juridic act. The final canon concerns the damage that an external act of any kind may inflict on other persons. In canons 124–126 and 128 the person in question can be either a physical or a juridic person.

Canon 124 — §1. For the validity of a juridic act it is required that it be placed by a person capable of placing it, and that it include those elements which essentially constitute it as well as the formalities and requisites imposed by law for the validity of the act.

§2. A juridic act correctly placed with respect to its external elements is presumed to be valid.

Without defining what a juridic act is this canon first determines in a generic way three elements that are necessary for the valid placing of any juridic act: the person acting, the intrinsic nature of the act itself, and any extrinsic formalities or circumstances which the law may require for validity. Then it establishes the presumption of validity.[2] The first paragraph, whose mirror image is found in 1680, §1 of the 1917 Code, identifies two factors that are always required for the validity of any juridic act, namely, that the physical or juridic person be capable in law of placing the act and that the essential elements required by the nature of the act be present. Certain juridic acts must, in addition, both be placed in a prescribed form and have specified concomitant circumstances for validity.

The capacity of the person is here understood broadly to mean that, in addition to the ability of placing a human act, the person must possess the radical capacity that is required by law and have the right to act.[3] The canon law, for example, will determine that the person acting must be ordained or possess a particular office or a faculty or be free of certain impediments or be of a certain age. A diocesan bishop may have the radical capacity to place a certain juridic act, e.g., grant a dispensation, but may not have the right to act if the matter has already been acted upon by the Holy See.

With respect to the presence of all the elements essential to a specific act, it can be said here only that it must consist of all the components that its nature and the canonical doctrine or tradition require for this kind of act. For example, a contract is of its very nature a juridic act involving at least two parties and an exchange of rights, and its object must be possible. If an action consists only of a promise by one person to another, it is not a contract; it does not create a right that is capable of judicial vindication.

The law frequently establishes formalities that must be observed in order for a juridic act to have its effect in the social order of the Church. Marital consent, for example, may in fact exist, but matrimony may not in fact result because of failure to observe the canonically required form for the valid expression of that consent,[4] or the signature of the one acting may be required for the validity of the act itself.[5] The law, moreover, will frequently prescribe the existence of elements extrinsic to the act itself or the manner of placing it, e.g., the prior consent of a certain consultative body or the advice of certain individuals.[6]

The second paragraph establishes the presumption of the law itself, i.e., a juridic act is presumed

---

[1] O. Robleda, "*De Conceptu Actus Iuridici,*" *P* 51 (1962) 413–446. Trans. by M. Hughes in "A New Title in the Code: Juridical Acts," *Stud Can* 14 (1980), 391–403. For an extensive treatment of the subject, cf. G. Michiels, *Principia Generalia de Personis, editio altera,* Desclée, 1955, 565–680.

[2] Cf. *Comm.* 6 (1974), 101–103.
[3] *Rel,* 35–36.
[4] Cf. c. 1108.
[5] Cf. c. 474.
[6] Cf. c. 127 below.

valid if its observable elements have been correctly placed. This presumption extends neither to the capacity of the one acting nor to the existence of all the essential constitutive elements of the act. The burden of proof, therefore, rests with the person who alleges invalidity, e.g., of a marriage. If the ability of the person acting or the constitutive elements are credibly denied, the person who acted must prove their existence.

Canon 125 — §1. An act placed because of extrinsic force brought to bear upon a person, which the person was not in any way able to resist, is considered not to have been placed.

§2. An act placed because of grave fear, which has been unjustly inflicted, or because of fraud is valid unless the law makes some other provision; but such an act can be rescinded by the decision of a judge, either at the instance of an injured party, or that party's successors in law, or ex officio.

This and the two following canons address circumstances or factors affecting the person who places a juridic act: irresistible force; grave fear or fraud; ignorance or error; consent or counsel with regard to the act before it is placed. The first paragraph addresses physical force or coercion. While otherwise identical with canon 103, §1 of the former Code, it is more clearly and more strongly worded by expressly requiring that the physical violence could not in any way whatsoever ("nequaquam") be resisted and thus the act placed was not a human act. It was non-existent.

The second paragraph, which is substantially identical with canon 103, §2 of the 1917 Code touches upon two other circumstances that may affect a juridic act but not deprive it of its human character. Grave fear is presumed to be the internal response of a person to the credible threat of serious evil inflicted by another human being. This threat must be unjustly made. Such a threat can, of course, be justly made. Certain superiors can, for example, threaten ecclesiastical penalties in order to compel someone to perform obligatory juridic acts,[7] or a person can justly threaten action in an ecclesiastical tribunal to vindicate a right, e.g., fulfillment of a contract.[8]

Fraud is the deliberate concealment of facts or the deliberate assertion of what is untrue precisely in order to persuade someone to act in a certain manner; the act must be the result of the fraud. In the case of either grave fear or fraud, the act placed is valid but rescindable.

The law does at times establish that certain acts are invalid if placed as a consequence of grave fear or fraud.[9] It should be noted that fraud may cause the substantive error, which is the burden of the following canon.

Paragraph two concludes that a juridic act motivated by fear or fraud as described above is rescindable through an ecclesiastical tribunal, and the judicial action can be brought by any person who alleges fear or fraud or by the person's successors, e.g., in an office such as a pastor or one's heirs. Ex officio the promoter of justice[10] can bring a rescissory action—as can other ecclesiastical superiors of physical or juridic persons.

Canon 126 — An act placed because of ignorance or error concerning an element which constitutes its substance or which amounts to a condition *sine qua non* is invalid; otherwise it is valid, unless the law makes some other provision. However, an act placed out of ignorance or error can be the occasion for a rescissory action in accord with the norm of law.

This canon, like its predecessor (*CIC* 104), addresses the cognitive aspect of a human act, i.e., knowing what one is doing. Ignorance is the absence of knowledge, whereas error, which commonly results from ignorance, is a positive judgment that is objectively false. Ignorance or error about the essential elements of a juridic act, such as what marriage is or which rights are being transferred by a contract, of its nature invalidates the act—which must always be an informed action. Both ignorance and error, however, can also concern matters that are accidental to the substance of the act in question. An error about the date when drawing up a document, for example, will not concern the indispensable elements of the act that the document contains.

An accidental or incidental aspect of the act, on the other hand, can in fact be the explicit object of the juridic act because this incidental quality or aspect of the object becomes part of the substance of the juridic act by the stipulation of the person acting. For example, a pastor could agree to purchase certain liturgical furnishings precisely because they were designed and constructed by a certain artist and had been used in a famous church. If the furnishings do not in fact possess these adventitious qualities, the pastor's error, which may or may not have been caused by fraud, is reductively substantive because it amounts to a condition of purchase *"sine qua non."*[11]

Less serious degrees of ignorance or error may provide occasion for rescissory action through a ju-

[7]Cf. c. 1319, §1.
[8]Cf. cc. 221, §1; 1400.

[9]Cf. cc. 172, §1, 1°; 188; 643, §1, 4°; 656, 4°; 735, §2; 1098; 1103; 1191, §3; 1200, §2.
[10]Cf. c. 1430.
[11]Cf. c. 1097, §2.

dicial procedure in which the gravity of the matter can be adjudicated. Canon 104 of the former Code limited this to contracts.

Canon 127 — **§1. When the law determines that in order to place certain acts a superior requires the consent or counsel of a college or group of persons, the college or group must be convoked according to the norm of can. 166, unless particular or proper law provides otherwise when counsel only is to be sought; however, for such acts to be valid it is required that the consent of an absolute majority of those present be obtained or that the counsel of all who are present be sought.**

§2. When the law determines that a superior in order to place certain acts requires the consent or the counsel of certain persons as individuals:

1° if consent is required, the action of the superior is invalid if the superior does not seek the consent of those persons or acts contrary to the opinion of the persons or person;

2° if counsel is required, the action of the superior is invalid if the superior does not listen to those persons; although in no way obliged to accede to their recommendation, even if it be unanimous, nevertheless the superior should not act contrary to it, especially when there is a consensus, unless there be a reason which, in the superior's judgment, is overriding.

§3. All whose consent or counsel is required are obliged to offer their opinion sincerely and, if the seriousness of the matter requires it, to observe secrecy sedulously, and this obligation can be insisted upon by the superior.

This canon substantially repeats canon 105 of the 1917 Code but in an improved order—and with greater clarity and precision. It is of special importance throughout the Code itself and for the correct interpretation of particular and proper law. Inasmuch as the revised Code, following the directives of the Second Vatican Council, greatly amplifies the scope and frequency of consultation in the governance of the Church, the norms presented here require attentive study because so many juridic acts depend upon them for their validity.

Consultation, as an often indispensable factor in ecclesial governance, constitutes a very significant means of participation in the exercise of the role of governance on the part of the Christian faithful, and the quality and effectiveness of church administration substantially depend on its proper use. The law here provides the indispensable requirements for such consultative activity. This canon is applicable whenever the law of the Church, whether universal or particular or proper, requires the counsel or consent of groups of persons or of individuals before a decision is reached. The first paragraph attends to consultation with designated groups of persons; the second looks to consultation with individuals as such.

When a superior, e.g., a bishop, a pastor, a religious superior, is required to obtain the consent or the advice of a group of persons, e.g., the college of diocesan consultors, the presbyteral council, the finance council, the religious provincial council, the members must be called together and the norm of their convocation is found in canon 166, which deals with a canonical election. This citation of the entirety of canon 166 causes some difficulties. It seems at least probable that the intention of the legislator was to cite canon 166 only with respect to the manner in which the members of the consultative group are to be notified or summoned and not with respect to the inadvertent oversight of even one member's opening the way to rescission of the consequent juridic act. Since there is, however, question here of validity, certainty is needed and care must be taken that the list of the membership of a consultative body be carefully maintained and updated so that no one is even inadvertently overlooked.

The possible exception to convoking a meeting of the consultative body in the case of seeking only the advice of the members—but not their consent—must be expressly permitted in particular or proper law, i.e., in statutes, bylaws, directories, and the like. If, for example, the statutes of the presbyteral council permit the bishop to gather the opinions of its members regarding the adjustment of parochial boundaries[12] by telephone or mail, this kind of consultation is legitimate; otherwise, he must bring the issue to a meeting of the council.

If it is extraordinarily difficult or costly to bring a large consultative body together, e.g., because of great distances or because of the urgency of the issue, it seems probable that the requirements of this paragraph are substantially fulfilled by a telephone conference call—especially among groupings of members—provided all are informed of the call, are heard by the superior, and can hear and discuss the opinions of the others.

Can the superior in question be considered to be a member of the consultative body in such a way that the action that results from the consultation can be understood as a collegial act or at least in such a way that the superior can break a tie when consent is required? The response must be negative. The superior cannot give advice to himself or herself and cannot be said to consent to the action that he or she has presented with the recommendation that the group consent to it. If, for example, a bishop wishes to alienate ecclesiastical property whose value exceeds the amount specified by the conference of bishops,[13] he cannot validly do so if the col-

---

[12]Cf. c. 515, §2.
[13]Cf. c. 1292, §1.

lege of diocesan consultors is equally divided between consent and dissent; he cannot himself supply the required consent by breaking the tie. There is a widespread misunderstanding in institutes of consecrated life in this matter, inasmuch as it is commonly stated that the superior and the council act together as a collegial body. At least in the universal law, except in the case of the dismissal of a member,[14] there is no instance in which the council itself makes decisions and takes actions. The proper law of such an institute may, however, determine some cases, apart from those found in the universal law, in which a council can act with the superior in a fully collegial manner.

If the law, whether universal or particular or proper, requires that the superior obtain the consent of a group of persons in order to place a certain act, the consent once given does not obligate the superior to place the act. He or she may subsequently decide not to act or to delay acting.

The second paragraph of the canon addresses a different kind of consultative process. At times the law requires the advice or even the consent of individuals who do not form a consultative body as such. The bishop, for example, is required to listen to the opinion of the vicar forane or dean with respect to the appointment of a pastor in the vicariate or deanery[15] and must obtain the consent of any persons having a legitimate interest in certain kinds of alienation.[16] A religious house cannot be legitimately established without the prior written consent of the diocesan bishop.[17] In such cases the superior acts invalidly without the advice or consent required.

It seems probable that the second part of canon 127, §2, 2°, concerning not acting contrary to the recommendation if there is a consensus, is misplaced and is applicable to the first paragraph as well. There does not appear to have been any intention to amend the prior law in this respect,[18] and the first draft of this canon did not do so.[19]

Since the third paragraph recognizes an obligation on the part of those to be consulted to state their opinions in a forthright way, it implicitly acknowledges their right to be fully informed about the matter in question so that they can form mature judgments. Failure on the part of the consulting superior to present all the relevant substantive facts can readily vitiate the advice or consent of the consultors in such a way that they can be said not to have been consulted at all. The superior, however, can insist upon secrecy even to the extent of administering an oath[20] or by penal precept.[21]

[14]Cf. c. 699, §1.
[15]Cf. c. 524.
[16]Cf. c. 1292, §1.
[17]Cf. c. 609, §1.
[18]Cf. *Comm* 6 (1974), 103, 4°.
[19]Cf. 1977 schema, c. 116.
[20]Cf. *CIC* 105, 2°.
[21]Cf. c. 1319.

Canon 128 — **Anyone who unlawfully inflicts damage upon someone by a juridic act, or indeed by any other act placed with malice or culpability, is obliged to compensate for the damage inflicted.**

This canon addresses one possible consequence of a juridic act, i.e., damage to another person. If someone's juridic act unlawfully[22] causes harm to another physical or juridic person, the physical or juridic person who acted is obliged to compensate for the resulting damage, e.g., to reputation. It is to be noted, however, that the canon correctly requires that the damage be "unlawfully" caused. Some acts can cause lawful and unavoidable harm to another person. The removal of a pastor or the dismissal of a religious, for example, may cause serious damage to the priest or religious—but it is lawful, however regrettable, if the one so affected has been fully provided the due process required by canon law; this person must be presumed to accept freely the foreseen consequences when refusing to resign or to correct the behavior which occasions the act of the superior.

The extension of the right to compensation for injury caused by any act fraudulently or otherwise culpably placed is a canonical statement of the natural obligation to make restitution for one's unjust actions.

Anyone who has been unlawfully damaged by another's juridic act—even one lawfully placed—or by any fraudulent or otherwise culpable act of another, has the right to demand adequate compensation, even through canonical recourse.[23] The canon does not, however, extend the right to compensation for accidental or unintended damage from another's non-juridic act, although equity and charity may require it.

TITLE VIII
THE POWER OF GOVERNANCE
[cc. 129–144]

Like titles VI and VII the subject matter of this title and of title IX appeared in Book II of the 1917 Code ("Persons") and has been transferred to Book I of the revised Code because the material is applicable throughout the law and not exclusively concerned with clergy. These titles are thus more properly seen as general norms.

It may be asked why this title bears the rubric, "The Power of Governance" ("De Potestate Regiminis"), and not the heading, The Office of Governance (*De Munere Regendi*), thus harmonizing with the title of Book III, "The Teaching Office of the Church," and that of Book IV, "The Office of Sanctifying in the Church." The Second Vatican Council repeatedly employed the biblical three

[22]Cf. *Comm* 6 (1974), 103, 5°.
[23]Cf. c. 221, §1.

roles or functions of Christ in presenting its teaching on the nature of the Church and in organizing the substance of its decrees. The Code, too, is significantly organized according to the three *munera.*

The distinction, however, between function, or role, of governance (*munus gubernandi*) and power of governance (*potestas gubernandi*) was the subject of extensive debate during Vatican II itself and was addressed by the Theological Commission in a "Prefatory Note of Explanation" to guide the council fathers in their understanding of *Lumen Gentium,* chapter III, "The Hierarchical Structure of the Church," prior to their final vote. This document was published as an appendix to the *Constitution on the Church* and is found in all editions of *Lumen Gentium.*

Munus is there understood as an inherent function of bishops deriving from their consecration itself. Without further specification, however, except in the case of the Roman Pontiff, this function cannot be actualized apart from an ecumenical council. A further canonical or juridical determination is required—the canonical mission referred to in *Lumen Gentium* 24. Thus, by canonical mission from the Supreme Pontiff, this inherent *munus gubernandi* becomes power ready for action (*potestas ad actum expedita*). Because this title deals with such specification of governance, the rubric is power of governance.

This title establishes the general juridical norms concerning the power of governance in the Church. While it includes legislative and judicial power among its first seven canons—an innovation since the former Code—it leaves the details of the exercise of these powers to other parts of the Code and thereafter deals only with the executive power of governance. The remainder of the Code, to be sure, also addresses the executive power of governance and its exercise in considerable detail.

The general treatment of the subject of this title was found in Book II, part I, section I ("Clergy in General"), title V ("Ordinary and Delegated Power") of the earlier Code, (*CIC* 196–210). Because the power of jurisdiction or of governance presupposed ordination in every case—a question not resolved in this Code—the matter was treated under the rubric of clergy. The revised Code attributes cooperation in the exercise of the power of governance, without actual possession of such power, to lay persons in certain circumstances.

Apart from the important change in the law introduced by canon 129 and the clarification in canon 130 of the meaning of the power of governance for the internal forum only, the remainder of the title does not substantially differ from the parallel canons in the 1917 Code (*CIC* 196–209), absorbing one canon (*CIC* 202) into canon 130 and omitting another (*CIC* 210). The canons of the previous Code are simplified and clarified wherever possible and are presented in somewhat different

order. Except for the reference to jurisdiction in the first canon, to indicate that this is the kind of power being addressed and organized, this classical term is not employed elsewhere in this title.

Canon 129 — **§1. In accord with the prescriptions of law, those who have received sacred orders are capable of the power of governance, which exists in the Church by divine institution and is also called the power of jurisdiction.**

§2. Lay members of the Christian faithful can cooperate in the exercise of this power in accord with the norm of law.

Only those who have been ordained are capable of possessing the power of governance in the Church—which may be received in a variety of ways. This reflects canon 118 of the 1917 Code. The canon, however, extends to lay persons a role of cooperation in the exercise of the power of governance for individual causes provided it has been granted by the Holy See. As is evident from canon 1421, §2, concerning the appointment of lay persons as judges in tribunals, this commission need not be granted only on a case-by-case basis. It is clear, however, that no authority below the level of the Holy See can permit such cooperation in the exercise of jurisdiction by persons who have not been ordained.

The distinction between possessing the power of governance and merely sharing in its exercise is new, and it is not at all clear what it means to cooperate in the exercise of a power that a person cannot hold. In the case of a judicial sentence in which the two clerical judges are divided, the lay judge casts the decisive and binding vote.

Canon 130 — **The power of governance is normally exercised in the external forum, but sometimes it is exercised in the internal forum only, but in such a way that the effects which its exercise normally has in the external forum are not acknowledged in this forum except as is established by law in certain instances.**

This canon clarifies the classic distinction between the power of governance exercised for the external forum or for the internal forum only. In itself the power of governance is directed toward and exercised in the external forum—the external order of society—and this is the normal ambience of its exercise in the Church. In some cases, however, its exercise may be restricted to affecting only one or a few persons and is not made known to others or is not recorded. This distinction is made—but not clarified—in canon 196 of the former Code, whose references to the forum of conscience and the sacramental and extra-sacramental forum, i.e., in sacramental confession or apart from it, are omitted. A few examples of the exercise of this power only in the internal forum may be helpful: dispensation of certain occult impediments to marriage in special circumstances;[24] secret marriages;[25] remission of reserved censures in certain cases.[26]

Canon 131 — §1. The ordinary power of governance is that which is joined to a certain office by the law itself; delegated power is that which is granted to a person, but not by means of an office.

§2. The ordinary power of governance can be either proper or vicarious.

§3. The burden of proving delegation rests with the person who claims to have been delegated.

This canon substantially repeats canons 197 and 200, §2 of the 1917 Code. The addition of the last phrase in paragraph one, which does not appear in canon 197, §1 of the earlier Code, is helpful in highlighting the distinction of the sources of the power of governance. The distinction between ordinary and delegated power is of practical importance in at least two respects. The ability to delegate or further subdelegate power of governance depends on its source. Furthermore, ordinary power, since it pertains to an office by reason of a law, cannot be restricted or removed by the person conferring such an office without amendment of the law itself. For example, a bishop cannot restrict or withdraw executive power belonging to the office of a pastor by reason of the universal law of the Church; he can, of course, establish policies and guidelines for its exercise for the good of the diocese.

The distinction between the power of governance which is proper to someone and that which is vicarious is classic and refers to the dependent relationship or lack thereof to someone else on the part of an officeholder in the Church. Certain officials possess authority that they exercise in their own names by reason of the office that they hold and this is called proper authority, or power; other officeholders, however, possess authority that they exercise in someone else's name and this, though ordinary power, is called vicarious. For example, the diocesan bishop has ordinary power to govern his diocese, and this is proper to him. A vicar general, however, or an episcopal vicar possesses ordinary power, but it is vicarious. While a vicar general or an episcopal vicar cannot have his power curtailed if it derives from the universal law, he must exercise it within any policies that the diocesan bishop has established for the exercise of his own power of governance. Religious institutes will make provision in their own law for a vicar general or vicar provincial.

If a person asserts that he or she has been delegated, the burden of proof of such delegation rests

with the one making the claim; it is not the role of others to disprove it. While this may seem self-evident, the third paragraph serves to remind the person delegating another that the mandate or charge about the purpose and extent of the delegation must be clear, and it must be in a form, e.g., written, such that the delegate can prove delegation to others. Thus, there exist the requirements that the grant of habitual faculties for hearing confessions be made in written form[27] and that the general delegation to assist at marriages be made in writing for validity.[28] The same ought to be done in the case of a canonical visitor other than one designated by law.

Canon 132 — §1. Habitual faculties are governed by the prescriptions for delegated power.

§2. However, unless otherwise expressly provided in the grant of faculties or unless an ordinary was chosen for his personal qualifications, a habitual faculty granted to an ordinary is not withdrawn when that ordinary's authority ceases, even though he has started to execute the faculty, but it transfers to any ordinary who succeeds him in governance.

In the 1917 Code habitual faculties were assimilated to privileges and were governed by the norms of privileges aside from the law (*praeter legem*).[29] This continued to be the case in the 1977 draft of Book I of the revised Code. They are, however, properly treated under the rubric of habitually delegated power of governance because they are directed, when they exist, to the governance of the Church and are not primarily favors granted to a person.

A faculty is a grant by a higher authority enabling a subordinate to act in a way that the recipient would not otherwise be empowered or authorized to act. Habitual faculties are not limited to a brief period of time or to a certain number of cases. The most common examples of habitual faculties granted in the past by the Holy See were the quinquennial faculties for dioceses and the decennial faculties for mission territories. Since Vatican II numerous habitual faculties have been granted to ecclesiastical superiors, e.g., *Pastorale Munus* (1963), *De Episcoporum Muneribus* (1966) and "Faculties of Superiors General" (1964, 1966), most of which have been incorporated into the Code or are no longer needed.

The second paragraph establishes the presumption of the law itself that habitual faculties are granted to an ordinary in view of the office he holds and not for purely personal reasons. Therefore, they pertain to his successors in office. This presumption, of course, yields to contrary proof. The

---

[24]Cc. 1079, §3; 1080, §1.
[25]Cc. 1130–1133.
[26]C. 1357.

[27]C. 973.
[28]C. 1111, §2.
[29]*CIC* 66, §1.

reference to the situation in which the predecessor has already begun to make use of the faculty in question means that the fact that he had begun to exercise the faculty, provided the action had not yet been carried into effect, neither constrains the successor to complete it nor prevents him from doing so. He is free to suspend the action, may decide not to complete it, or may carry through with it.[30] Because habitual faculties are presumed to pertain to an office, they are analogous to the ordinary power of governance and are shared by the vicar general and by the episcopal vicars.[31]

Canon 133 — §1. **A delegate who exceeds the limits of the mandate with respect to matters or to persons acts invalidly.**

§2. **A delegate who acts in delegated matters in a manner other than that determined in the mandate is not considered to have exceeded the limits of the mandate unless the manner of acting was prescribed for validity by the one delegating.**

The first paragraph of this canon repeats verbatim the provision of canon 203, §1 of the former Code. The second paragraph, while substantially the same as canon 203, §2 of the 1917 Code, is more clearly stated in the revised law. The formalities of a delegation may include such things as acting in the presence of witnesses or recording actions in writing, acting in a certain place or on a certain day. While the delegate is obliged to observe such formalities, failure to do so does not invalidate the action taken unless the instrument of delegation expressly states that these formalities are necessary for validity.

Canon 134 — §1. **By the title of ordinary in the law are understood, in addition to the Roman Pontiff, diocesan bishops and others who, even if only on an interim basis, have been placed over a particular church or over a community which is equivalent to it according to the norm of can. 368, as well as those who possess ordinary general executive power in said churches and communities, namely vicars general and episcopal vicars; and likewise for their own members the major superiors of clerical religious institutes of pontifical right and of clerical societies of apostolic life of pontifical right, who possess at least ordinary executive power.**

§2. **By the title of local ordinary are understood all those mentioned in §1, except superiors of religious institutes and societies of apostolic life.**

§3. **Whatever things in the canons in the realm of executive power which are attributed by name to**

the diocesan bishop are understood to pertain only to the diocesan bishop and to others equivalent to him in can. 381, §2, excluding the vicar general and the episcopal vicar unless they have received a special mandate.

The first two paragraphs substantially repeat canon 198 of the earlier Code but add a provision for non-territorial particular churches and for episcopal vicars. Since there are no clerical and exempt institutes in the revised Code, the major superiors of any clerical religious institute of pontifical right and of any clerical society of apostolic life of pontifical right are called ordinaries. Lay institutes, inasmuch as their superiors cannot possess ecclesiastical power of governance, are not said to have ordinaries. The third paragraph is new and finds no specific parallel in the 1917 Code, although it frequently noted that the vicar general or the administrator of a diocese required a special mandate in various matters. The addition of this paragraph forestalls the need for such frequent repetition throughout the Code. Canon 87, for example, in the very wording of its two paragraphs reflects the distinction.

Canon 135 — §1. **The power of governance is distinguished as legislative, executive and judicial.**

§2. **Legislative power is to be exercised in the manner prescribed by law, and that legislative power in the Church possessed by a legislator below the highest authority cannot be validly delegated, unless otherwise explicitly provided for in the law; a law which is contrary to a higher law cannot be validly enacted by a lower level legislator.**

§3. **Judicial power, which is possessed by judges or judicial colleges, is to be exercised in the manner prescribed by law and cannot be delegated, except to carry out acts which are preparatory to a decree or a decision.**

§4. **In regard to the exercise of executive power, the prescriptions of the following canons are to be observed.**

This canon is new, although legislative and judicial powers are attributed to the bishop in canon 335 of the earlier Code. The addition of executive power, implicit in the former Code, is logical in order to identify in a general way the power of decision which is neither legislative nor judicial. The prohibition of the delegation of legislative authority prevents a bishop or a general chapter, for example, from granting this power to any other individual or body. The delegation of judicial power, if it can be called judicial, is done by the appointment, for example, of auditors and *relators.*[32]

The fourth paragraph has the effect of providing a subtitle for the remaining canons of title VIII. Ev-

---

[30]A. Vermeersch and Creusen, *Epitome Iuris Canonici,* 7th ed. (Rome: Dessain, 1949), vol. I, 169 (cited as Vermeersch-Creusen).

[31]Cf. c. 479, §3.

[32]Cf. *CIC* 1572, §1.

erything said hereafter applies to executive authority alone.

Canon 136 — **A person can exercise executive power over his subjects, even though he himself is outside his own territory and even when they are outside his territory, unless the contrary is certain from the nature of the case or from the prescription of the law; he can also exercise this power over travelers actually present in his territory, provided it is a matter of granting favors or of enforcing either universal laws or particular laws by which they are bound according to the norm of can. 13, §2, n. 2.**

This canon parallels canon 201 of the 1917 Code, but it has been significantly simplified by omitting any reference to judicial power or to the exercise of executive power in one's own behalf.[33]

Canon 137 — **§1. Ordinary executive power can be delegated both for a single act and for all cases, unless the law expressly provides otherwise.**

§2. Executive power delegated by the Apostolic See can be subdelegated, whether for a single act or for all cases, unless the delegation was granted in view of the special qualifications of the delegate or unless subdelegation was expressly prohibited.

§3. If executive power delegated by another authority having ordinary power was delegated for all cases, it can be subdelegated only for individual cases; if, however, it was delegated for a single act or for determined acts it cannot be subdelegated except by the expressed grant of the one delegating.

§4. No subdelegated power can be again subdelegated, unless this has been expressly granted by the one delegating.

This canon reorganizes the provisions of canon 199 of the former Code in a clearer manner but does not introduce any change in the classic principles of delegation and subdelegation.

Canon 138 — **Ordinary executive power as well as power delegated for all cases is to be broadly interpreted; any other is to be strictly interpreted; however, a person who has received delegated power is understood to have also been granted whatever is necessary to exercise that power.**

This canon concerns itself with ordinary or delegated power in cases in which its meaning or extent is in some doubt. If there is no doubt, there is no room for broad or strict interpretation. This is taken practically verbatim from canon 200, §1 of the 1917 Code. The distinction between and the application of broad and strict interpretation are presented in canon 18.

[33]Cf. c. 967.

Canon 139 — **§1. Unless other provision is made in the law, the fact that a person approaches a competent authority, even one which is higher, does not suspend the executive power of another competent authority, whether this be ordinary or delegated.**

§2. Nevertheless, a lower authority should not become involved in cases which have been submitted to a higher authority, except for a grave and urgent reason, in which case the lower authority should immediately notify the higher concerning the matter.

This canon essentially repeats canon 204 of the earlier Code. The situation envisaged is the case in which two or more persons are competent to act, e.g., to grant a dispensation. The fact that someone approaches one of them does not prevent another from acting validly by granting the dispensation, and this remains the case even if the first person approached is the higher authority. Good order, however, in the Church as in any society requires that matters already submitted to higher authority should not, except in cases of urgency, e.g., an approaching deadline for action, be acted upon by subordinate authority. In this case the subordinate authority properly acts and must immediately notify the higher authority about this action and the reasons for intervening.

Canon 140 — **§1. When several persons have been delegated *in solidum* to transact the same business, the one who first undertakes to deal with it excludes the others from acting, unless thereafter that person is impeded or does not wish to proceed further in treating the matter.**

§2. When several persons have been delegated to transact some business collegially, all must proceed according to the norm of can. 119, unless in their mandate some other provision has been made.

§3. Executive power delegated to several persons is presumed to have been delegated to them *in solidum*.

This canon substantially repeats canon 205 of the 1917 Code but reorders the three paragraphs. An obligation to act is said to be *in solidum* when it rests on two or more persons equally, but it can be fulfilled by any one of them, in such a way, however, that if one fails or refuses or is unable to act the others continue to be obligated. The canon speaks of two or more persons delegated "*in solidum*" to conduct some kind of business, e.g., to negotiate for and to purchase a piece of real estate. If one has begun the transaction, the others are barred from acting unless the first is unable or unwilling to complete it.

A collegial act is one placed by all the delegates together, with their decision being arrived at by an absolute majority vote. When there is doubt whether cumulative delegation has been made *in solidum* or collegially, it is presumed by the law itself to have been made *in solidum* because this is less burdensome for the delegates inasmuch as one can act alone without inconveniencing the others.

Canon 141 — **If several persons have been successively delegated, that person should transact the business whose mandate is prior to the others and has not later been revoked.**

This repeats its predecessor (*CIC* 206) in a somewhat simpler, more direct style.

Canon 142 — **§1. Delegated power ceases by fulfillment of the mandate, by the lapse of the time or by the completion of the number of cases for which it was granted, by cessation of the final cause of the delegation, by the revocation of the one delegating directly communicated to the delegate, as well as by the resignation of the delegate made known to and accepted by the one delegating; it does not cease, however, by the expiration of the authority of the one delegating, unless this is clear from clauses appended to the grant.**
§2. An act of delegated power, however, which is exercised only for the internal forum and which is placed inadvertently after the lapse of the time of the grant, is valid.

This canon substantially repeats canon 207 of the former Code in a somewhat less qualified way. The final cause of the delegation is said to have ceased when the intended effect of the delegation can no longer be achieved. For example, if the person in whose favor the delegation was made dies before it can be exercised, the final cause which motivated the delegation no longer exists. This would also be the case if a bishop or religious superior were delegated by the Holy See to grant a favor to someone, e.g., a dispensation, after the bishop or superior has made a prudent assessment of its suitability in a particular case (*pro suo arbitrio et conscientia*), if the petitioner declines the favor or has withdrawn the petition for it, the final cause or motive has ceased and the delegated power thereby ceases. Were the petitioner later to reiterate the petition, a new grant would be necessary.

The second paragraph differs somewhat from its predecessor in that a second circumstance in which the act is valid, i.e., exceeding the number of cases for which the delegation was granted, is omitted.

Canon 143 — **§1. Ordinary power ceases by the loss of the office to which it is connected.**
§2. Unless the law provides otherwise, ordinary power is suspended in the event that a privation of or removal from office is legitimately appealed or recourse taken.

This canon substantially repeats canon 208 of the former Code but omits the superfluous statement that ordinary power does not cease when the person who conferred the office vacates his office. Removal from office is treated in canons 192–195 and privation of office is the subject of canon 196. Although the words appeal and recourse are sometimes used interchangeably, appeal is more properly a remedy against a judicial sentence, while recourse is a remedy against an administrative action.[34]

Canon 144 — **§1. In factual or legal common error, and also in positive and probable doubt about law or about fact, the Church supplies executive power of governance both for the external and for the internal forum.**
§2. This same norm applies to the faculties mentioned in cann. 882, 883, 966 and 1111, §1.

This canon substantially repeats canon 209 of the 1917 Code and canonizes what has become the received understanding of common error. If a person lacking the required executive power of governance places an act that—without it—is invalid, the Church, by way of this canon, supplies it in two cases: common error and positive and probable doubt. The purpose of the canon is to protect the people against invalid juridic acts and not to provide the power of governance to persons not possessing it either by office or by delegation.

Error is not ignorance, although ignorance is usually the cause of error which is an objectively false judgment. In the first case the erroneous judgment is that the person acting has the power to do so validly. Error is called de facto common when it is actually prevalent within an identifiable community or group. It is said to be de iure common when a person has placed a public act—other than the act itself that requires the executive power of governance—that inevitably leads even well-informed people to judge that the person has the power to act validly; the error is present and operative in its cause even before anyone is actually led to an erroneous judgment.[35]

The most understandable and perhaps most useful example of common error, although by no means the only one, has been the faculty, called the jurisdiction in canon 872 of the earlier Code, to hear confessions. If a priest who has no faculty to hear confessions announces to people assembled for

---

[34]Cf. cc. 1747, §3; 1752.

[35]This commentator holds that the translation "error about fact or about law" is misleading and even incorrect. He contends that in the Latin text the phrase "de facto aut de iure" qualifies the adjective "communi" and is not the object of "errore." Later in the paragraph the similar, but not identical, phrase, "sive iuris sive facti" is the object of "dubio." The addition of the former phrase to this paragraph, the only difference from *CIC* 209, simply canonizes what had become the received canonical opinion. For a discussion of this matter, cf. T. L. Bouscaren, A. Ellis, and F. Korth, *Canon Law,* 4th rev. ed. (Milwaukee: The Bruce Publishing Co., 1963), 143–145.

Mass that he will hear confessions before and after the liturgy, that announcement in itself creates error that is de iure common, even though no one has yet approached him for confession. The same is true if he merely goes to the confessional or the reconciliation room and sits in the confessor's chair. Error that is only de iure common becomes de facto common when it prevails in the community. It must be stressed, however, that it is the public act and not the actual exercise of the faculty that creates error that is de iure common.

The other circumstance in which the Church supplies executive power of governance when it is lacking is in positive and probable doubt—whether this doubt be about the meaning of the law or about the fact of having such power of governance. Doubt of law and doubt of fact are treated in canon 14. Doubt, i.e., a suspension of judgment, is said to be positive when there exist reasons favoring a judgment and not merely the lack of reasons sufficient to make the judgment without prudent fear of error. Doubt is said to be probable when the reasons for the judgment are serious and have a suasive effect. In the case of positive and probable doubt, the judgment that one has executive power of governance for a certain act is itself probable—as is the judgment that one does not have the needed power. This canon establishes the principle that the executive power probably possessed is sufficient to act lawfully and that in the event it becomes certain that the required power was not present, the Church supplied it by this canon. In this way the probable judgment becomes juridically certain.

The second paragraph of this canon is new and expressly extends what is said in the first paragraph about executive power of governance to three specific faculties that are no longer included under the power of governance or jurisdiction. They concern the ministers of confirmation and penance and the person assisting at a marriage. The question about the minister of confirmation is new in the Code, whereas, as was noted above, it was always applicable to the minister of penance. The person assisting at a marriage is no longer seen as exercising jurisdiction. The applicability of the principle of this canon to marriage had been debated, and this paragraph has settled the matter.

In concluding title VIII it may be noted that the revised Code offers no parallel to canon 210 of the 1917 Code, the delegation of the power of an order to someone who has not received that order. The debates surrounding this concept have become historical.

TITLE IX
ECCLESIASTICAL OFFICES
[cc. 145–196]

Apart from the very important change in the definition of ecclesiastical office, as explained in the commentary on canon 145, title IX substantially—although usually more simply and clearly—incorporates the parallel title of the former Code (*CIC* 145–195). Because of this change of definition, as explained below, this title now appears in Book I, "General Norms." The specific norms governing the acquisition and loss of ecclesiastical office remain for the most part unchanged.

Canon 145 — §1. **An ecclesiastical office is any function constituted in a stable manner by divine or ecclesiastical law to be exercised for a spiritual purpose.**
§2. The obligations and the rights proper to individual ecclesiastical offices are defined either in the law by which the office is constituted or in the decree of a competent authority by which it is at the same time constituted and conferred.

Canon 145 functions as an introduction to the entire title, redefining ecclesiastical office in conformity with the decision of Vatican II and establishing the general principle that the obligations and rights of specific offices in the Church are to be found in the law or the decree that creates them. The purpose of the fifty-two canons of title IX is to establish the general norms applicable to all church offices.

Paragraph one, while paralleling canon 145, §1 of the 1917 Code, differs from it in a substantive and important way. The corresponding canon described ecclesiastical office in a broad sense as any function that is legitimately exercised in the Church for a spiritual purpose; in the strict sense, however, it was described as a function established in a stable manner by divine or ecclesiastical law—carrying with it some participation or sharing in ecclesiastical power, whether of orders or of jurisdiction. The following paragraph (*CIC* 145, §2) then stated that office as used in the law was to be understood in the strict sense, unless the broad sense was clearly intended by the context in which the expression was employed.

Vatican II, in *Presbyterorum Ordinis* 20, had decided that in the future, office in the Church was to be understood as "any function (*munus*) conferred in a stable manner for a spiritual purpose." This reflected both the statement in *Lumen Gentium* 33 that lay persons might be deputed by the hierarchy for certain roles (*munera*) to be carried out for a spiritual purpose and the exhortation of *Lumen Gentium* 37 that bishops commit offices to lay people for the service of the Church.

In conformity with this conciliar action the revised law suppresses the distinction between office in the broad sense and office in the strict sense, combining elements of each in a single definition and, more importantly, suppressing the assertion that office requires some participation in the ecclesiastical power of orders or of jurisdiction. In the 1917 Code only a cleric could hold an office in the strict sense; now a lay person can receive an ecclesiastical office in the only sense recognized by the law. This conciliar change in the notion of ecclesiastical office required that the title concerning church offices be transferred from Book II, part I of the 1917 Code ("Clergy") to Book I of the revised Code ("General Norms").

The definition presented in paragraph one speaks of offices constituted by divine law and those constituted by ecclesiastical law. Law is used in an analogous sense when speaking about a divine law. The office of the successor of Peter and that of a bishop charged with a particular church are of divine law; the Church did not create them, although church law does define them and further specify them. The office of vicar general or of chancellor in a diocese or of a religious superior is established by ecclesiastical law.

Paragraph two is not found in the former Code and its first part is clear. Examples abound in the Code: the offices of the diocesan bishop, of the chancellor, of the episcopal vicars, of pastors, and of religious superiors. Particular law will establish and describe many other church offices, such as director of charities, superintendent of schools, councillors of religious superiors, and director of religious education. The second part of the paragraph may not be altogether clear, and the difficulty may arise from the qualification that the office must at the same time be conferred upon someone. It is necessary to call attention to the distinction made earlier between a general decree (c. 29) and an individual decree (c. 48). The former is a legislative juridic act and is properly called a law, whereas the latter is an executive juridic act that hands down a decision, such as a decree of removal of a pastor (c. 1744, §2), or makes some provision in an individual case.

The second part of this paragraph deals with an individual decree that makes a special provision in an individual case. It has the effect, in the context of this canon, of creating an office in the proper sense by an executive, not a legislative, action, such as the appointment of an administrative assistant for urban affairs—a position that has a detailed job description that includes obligations and rights and, therefore, is conferred in a stable manner, but it may never have another incumbent. A canonical visitor, sometimes called a visitator, is an example of an office constituted by a competent authority and at the same time conferred on the person named. It is not intended to be a permanent position.

It should be pointed out that the obligations and the rights inherent in an office are ordinary and not delegated.

CHAPTER I
PROVISION OF ECCLESIASTICAL OFFICE
[cc. 146–183]

As has already been noted, title IX addresses two moments in holding ecclesiastical office: its acquisition and its loss. This chapter of thirty-eight canons, distributed over an untitled introductory section (cc. 146–156) and four articles, establishes general norms for the conferral of any office and then deals with the provision of an office in the Church, which is effected by free conferral (c. 157), presentation (cc. 158–163), election (cc. 164–179), and postulation (cc. 180–183). The subject matter of five of the canons found in this untitled introductory section was treated under the heading of free conferral in the earlier Code, but the canons more properly belong here because they are applicable to any form of conferral of office.

Canon 146 — **An ecclesiastical office cannot be validly acquired without canonical provision.**

This canon repeats canon 147, §1 of the 1917 Code verbatim and introduces the canonical requirements for the valid acquisition of an ecclesiastical office, which are the burden of the following canons. The next paragraph (*CIC* 147, §2), which is suppressed as unnecessary, defined canonical provision as the grant of an office by a competent ecclesiastical authority according to canonical norms.

Canon 147 — **Provision of an ecclesiastical office occurs by the free conferral of a competent ecclesiastical authority, or by installation by the same authority if presentation preceded it, or by confirmation or admission granted by the same authority if election or postulation preceded it, or, finally, by simple election and acceptance by the one elected if the election does not require confirmation.**

This canon, which substantially repeats canon 148, §1 of the former Code, provides a summary introduction of the ways in which acquisition of an office can occur, the details of which constitute the subject matter of the four articles of this chapter. Paraphrasing the canon in another way may make it more readily understood. An office is acquired by appointment, which may entail prior presentation of a candidate, or by election, which may require subsequent confirmation by a higher authority, or by the substitute for election known as postulation.

Free conferral is by far the most common way in which offices are acquired in the Church. Diocesan bishops are freely appointed by the Roman Pontiff unless a collegiate body has the right to elect someone, in which case the Supreme Pontiff confirms the nominee (c. 377, §1). The Holy See has asked those heads of state who have traditionally had the right to present candidates for diocesan bishop to relinquish that right and most, if not all, have by now done so. This was asked for by *Christus Dominus* 20. Pastors are freely selected by the diocesan bishop, unless prior presentation or even election is required (c. 523), and superiors of religious and secular institutes and of societies of apostolic life, apart from the highest moderators, are usually appointed, although election is also common.

Installation, or investiture, refers to a case in which an individual or a body of persons, e.g., a cathedral chapter, has the right to present a candidate or several candidates to the authority who will then install the nominee or one of them in the office in question.

Confirmation of a prior election may be required before the person chosen by the electoral body acquires an office, and thus confirmation actually confers the office. In religious institutes and in societies of apostolic life, if superiors—other than the highest moderator—are elected, they always require confirmation. In other cases, however, simple election and acceptance by the one elected confer the office, as in the case of the Roman Pontiff and of superiors general.

Finally, admission of postulation involves the case in which an electoral body wishes to choose someone who is barred from the office in question by an impediment. The electoral body cannot elect the ineligible person, but it may petition, i.e., postulate, him or her from a higher authority, in which case the office is acquired by the dispensation of the impediment and the admission of the postulate.

Canon 148 — That authority which is competent to establish, modify and suppress offices is also competent to make provision for them unless the law establishes otherwise.

This canon is new in the Code and makes explicit a legal presumption that has always existed. Anyone claiming to have a right of presentation, nomination, or election bears the burden of proof against the superior who can establish, modify, or suppress an ecclesiastical office.

Canon 149 — §1. In order to be promoted to an ecclesiastical office, a person must be in the communion of the Church as well as suitable, namely endowed with those qualities which are required for the office in question by universal or particular law or by the law of the foundation.

§2. Provision of an ecclesiastical office made in favor of a person who lacks the required qualities is invalid only if the qualities are expressly required for the validity of the provision by universal or particular law or the law of the foundation; otherwise the provision is valid, but it can be rescinded by the

decree of the competent authority or by the sentence of an administrative tribunal.

§3. Simoniacal provision of an office is invalid by the law itself.

The three paragraphs of this canon are taken from the 1917 Code (*CIC* 149, 153, and 729 respectively) in a substantially simplified form. The universal law commonly establishes specific personal qualifications for ecclesiastical offices, such as age, ordination, academic degrees, and experience.[36] The particular law of a diocese or region or the proper law of an institute of consecrated life or of a society of apostolic life will regularly do the same, as do the statutes of a juridic person,[37] which are the law of their foundation.

The effect of the first two paragraphs is to establish that the appointment or election of a person who lacks the required qualifications is valid unless the law in question expressly states that this or that quality is required for the validity of the conferral of the office.[38] The second paragraph, however, provides for the subsequent removal of an unqualified incumbent.

The third paragraph establishes the absolute invalidity of a simoniacal conferral of an ecclesiastical office.[39] Simony, so named from the account of Simon the Magician's attempt to buy the power of the apostles to convey the Spirit through the imposition of hands,[40] is usually defined in moral theology as the deliberate will to buy or sell a spiritual reality or the temporal thing, e.g., benefice, joined to that spiritual reality or power for a temporal price. It is a form of bribery. Simoniacal provision of ecclesiastical offices plagued the Church throughout the feudal period and even beyond when such offices were attached to benefices and the ecclesiastical courts were also secular powers. The conferral of an office is simoniacal even if simony were perpetrated by a third party and unknown to the recipient of the office.

Canon 150 — An office entailing the full care of souls, for whose fulfillment the exercise of the priestly order is required, cannot be validly conferred upon someone who has not yet received priestly ordination.

This canon parallels canon 154 of the earlier Code but it introduces a distinction by speaking of the care of souls, i.e., the pastoral ministry that is full or total, thus implicitly recognizing a care of souls that is partial.[41] Bishops for their dioceses and

---

[36] Cf. cc. 478, §1; 521, §1; 623; 1420, §4.
[37] Cf. cc. 117–118.
[38] Cf. c. 10 for a similar statement.
[39] In addition to *CIC* 729, cf. *CIC* 1446; 1465, §2.
[40] Acts 8:18–24.
[41] Cf. c. 564.

pastors for their parishes have the full care of souls, while others may share in that responsibility. The qualifying clause inserted after the expression, "the full care of souls," must be understood as a descriptive statement of fact and not as an implication that there can exist a full care of souls for which ordination is not required. The celebrations of the Eucharist, of penance, and of the anointing of the sick are essential elements of pastoral care that can be called complete.

Canon 151 — **The provision of an office entailing the care of souls is not to be deferred without serious cause.**

This is parallel to, but less specific than, its predecessor (*CIC* 155). The former canon comprehended any ecclesiastical office regardless of whether the care of souls was attached to it.

Canon 152 — **Two or more incompatible offices, that is, offices which cannot be fulfilled at the same time by the same person may not be conferred upon one person.**

This canon conflates the first two paragraphs of canon 156 of the 1917 Code. Offices will be evidently incompatible by their very nature or declared such by the law itself. The office of pastor, for example, in one diocese is by its nature incompatible with that of pastor in another, distant diocese, but this is not necessarily true of two parishes in the same diocese.[42] On the other hand, the law itself declares the office of treasurer and that of a major superior to be incompatible (c. 636, §1).

Canon 153 — **§1. The provision of an office which is by law not vacant is by that very fact invalid, and a subsequent vacancy does not validate the provision.**
§2. But if it is a question of an office which by law is conferred for a determined period of time the provision can be made within six months before the expiration of this time, and it takes effect on the day of the vacancy of the office.
§3. A promise of an office, no matter by whom it is made, has no juridic effect.

This substantially repeats canon 150 of the former Code, but its second paragraph is new and reflects the common modern practice of appointing or electing someone to an office early in order to provide the person with the opportunity to prepare for the position. It must be noted, however, that this is permitted only in the case of an office that has a term and that the actual election or even the official appointment cannot be made more than six

months before the office will become vacant. In those cases in which existing contractual obligations and other considerations seem to indicate the need for a definite appointment or even an election more than six months early, a dispensation will be needed from the Holy See.[43] In the case of free conferral of an office the authority who will confer it when it becomes vacant is free to indicate who will be appointed. Even if this indication is tantamount to a promise, it has no juridic effect, i.e., it gives no ground for the vindication of a right to the office because the third paragraph of this canon precludes any juridic effect.

Canon 154 — **An office which is vacant by law but perhaps still held by someone illegitimately can be conferred provided that it is duly declared that the possession is illegitimate and provided that this declaration is mentioned in the document of conferral.**

This canon repeats canon 151 of the earlier Code virtually verbatim, omitting a redundant phrase. This declaration and mention of the illegitimate possession of the office is necessary for the valid conferral of the office on someone else in accord with canon 39.

Canon 155 — **A person who confers an office, while supplying for someone who is negligent or impeded, thereby acquires no power over the person upon whom the office was conferred, and the juridic situation of that person is determined just as though the provision had been made according to the ordinary norm of law.**

This substantially repeats canon 158 of the 1917 Code. It refers to a certain extraordinary situation in which an authority, who does not have jurisdiction over a juridic person, e.g., a diocese, is required by law to intervene in order to provide a temporary superior for it until the normal procedure of provision can be followed.[44] Or the law may designate someone who has the right to confer an office on a permanent basis when the individual or group —who should appoint or elect—refuses or is unable to do so.

Canon 156 — **The provision of any office whatsoever is to be made in writing.**

This repeats canon 159 of the former Code verbatim. It was found in the earlier law under the rubric of free conferral of offices and its meaning was self-evident. Applied to elections, especially to elections

---

[42]Cf. c. 526, §1.

[43]Cf. *Roman Replies, 1983*, W. A. Schumacher, ed., (Washington, D.C.: CLSA), 20–21.
[44]Cf. cc. 421, §2; 425, §3.

that require no subsequent confirmation, it would seem that the official recording of the election would meet the requirements of *scripto consignetur,* i.e., to authenticate in writing. In any event the written provision or authentication does not affect validity.

ARTICLE 1: FREE CONFERRAL
[c. 157]

The 1917 Code devoted eight canons to the corresponding article found there, only one of which is included in substance in the present article. Of the others, because they were actually applicable to any means of providing someone for an ecclesiastical office, one (*CIC* 157) has been suppressed and the remaining canons have been incorporated, at least in substance, in canons 149–152 and 155–156, as has been noted in the appropriate places.

Canon 157 — Unless otherwise explicitly determined by law, it is within the competence of the diocesan bishop to provide for ecclesiastical offices in his own particular church by free conferral.

This canon repeats canon 152 of the former Code and establishes a general rule for diocesan ecclesiastical offices to which there may be exceptions. By restricting the right of free conferral, i.e., without limitation by the rights of other persons, to the diocesan bishop, the vicar general is excluded, as was the case in the previous Code, as are episcopal vicars, unless they have received a special mandate from the diocesan bishop. It should be noted that even when the diocesan bishop is required to consult other individuals or bodies regarding the conferral of certain offices, his action is still said to be free.

ARTICLE 2: PRESENTATION
[cc. 158–163]

The subject matter of this article was treated in the earlier Code in Book III, part V, title XXV ("Benefices and Other Non-Collegial Ecclesiastical Institutes"), chapter IV ("The Right of Patronage") (*CIC* 1448–1471). The principal privilege of patrons was the right to present suitable priests for installation in churches or other benefices. The former Code rendered any new right of patronage invalid[45] and severely restricted the passing of the right to anyone except by inheritance.[46] With the revised Code, the right of patronage as such disappears from canon law, although the right of presentation remains in certain cases.

Canon 158 — §1. Presentation for an ecclesiastical office must be made by the person who has the right of presentation to the authority whose right it is to install someone in the office in question, and furthermore this presentation must be made within three months from the receipt of notice of the vacancy of the office, unless something else has been legitimately established.

§2. If the right of presentation belongs to a certain college or group of persons, the person to be presented is to be designated according to the prescriptions of cann. 165-179.

The first paragraph substantially repeats canon 1457 of the 1917 Code in a greatly simplified way, reducing the period of time within which the presentation must be made from four months to three months; the second paragraph substantially repeats canon 1460, §1 of the previous law.

Canon 159 — No one may be presented who is unwilling; hence a person proposed for presentation who has been asked about his or her willingness can be presented unless the person has declined it within eight days of available time.

This canon is new, although in canon 1468 of the earlier Code a person already presented was free to decline installation.

Canon 160 — §1. A person who enjoys the right of presentation can present one or even several candidates either at one time or successively.

§2. No one can present himself or herself; a college or group of persons, however, can present one of its own members.

The first paragraph substantially treats the same matter as canon 1460, §4 of the 1917 Code, and paragraph two repeats in its first clause the first part of canon 1461 of the previous law. The remainder of the paragraph is new.

Canon 161 — §1. Unless otherwise determined by law, a person who has presented someone found to be unsuitable can present someone else only once more and within a month.

§2. If the person presented declines or dies before the installation, the person having the right of presentation can again exercise such right within a month of the receipt of notice of the refusal or death.

The first paragraph is drawn from canon 1465, §1 of the earlier Code, and the second paragraph substantially repeats canon 1468 of the former law.

Canon 162 — A person who has not made a presentation within the available time according to the norm of cann. 158, §1 and 161 or who has twice presented someone who has been found unsuitable loses the right of presentation for that instance; and

---

[45]*CIC* 1450, §1.
[46]*CIC* 1453, §2; 1470, §1, 3°.

the authority whose right it is to install is competent to provide freely for the vacant office, with the consent, however, of the candidate's own ordinary.

This canon is drawn from canons 1458, §1 and 1465, §1 of the 1917 Code.

Canon 163 — The authority which is competent according to law to install someone who has been presented is to install the person who has been legitimately presented, whom he or she found suitable and who accepted the office; but if several have been legitimately presented who are found to be suitable, the authority must install one of them.

This canon is essentially a conflation of canon 1466, §§1 and 3 of the former Code.

ARTICLE 3: ELECTION
[cc. 164–179]

Canon 164 — Unless the law has provided otherwise, the prescriptions of the following canons are to be observed in canonical elections.

Election here refers to the election of an individual to an office, not to the election of members to the electoral body itself. Thus, the election of the members of the electoral college, e.g., a chapter in a religious institute, need not and usually does not conform to the canons of this article. The statutes of the organization in question must, however, establish how the electoral body itself comes into existence.

The clause, "unless the law has provided otherwise," is very important and worthy of note. The law that may make other provisions for elections is particular or proper law; it is not the universal law that is about to provide its own norms. Particular law usually contains specific rules that are not contrary to the canonical norms but that go beyond this law (*praeter legem*), e.g., the number of ballots that may be needed to reach the number of votes required to elect.

This canon substantially repeats canon 160 of the earlier Code, omitting its reference to the papal election, the subject of a particular law.

Canon 165 — Unless the law or the legitimate statutes of a college or group provide otherwise, if a college or group of persons has the right of election to office the election is not to be deferred beyond three months of available time from receipt of the notice of vacancy of the office; if this period of time has elapsed without action, the ecclesiastical authority having the right to confirm the election or provide for the office successively is to make provision freely for the vacant office.

As a rule, institutes of consecrated life and societies of apostolic life provide in their proper law for an interval of longer duration than three months to prepare for an election in the case of an unanticipated vacancy in the office of the highest moderator, and there is no external ecclesiastical authority who must confirm such elections or who has the right to appoint when the chapter fails to act. Apart from these institutes, the Code identifies relatively few occasions for canonical elections.[47]

Canon 166 — §1. The presiding officer of the college or group shall convoke all the members of the college or group; and the notice of convocation, when it must be communicated to each member personally, is valid if it is directed to the place of domicile or quasi-domicile or actual residence.

§2. If one of those to be convoked is overlooked and is therefore absent, the election is valid; however, upon the instance of such a one and after proof of the oversight and absence, the election, even if it has been confirmed, must be rescinded by the competent authority, provided that it has been juridically established that recourse was made within at least three days of receipt of the notice of the election.

§3. But if more than one-third of the electors were overlooked, the election is invalid by the law itself, unless all those overlooked were in fact present.

This canon substantially repeats the first four paragraphs of canon 162 of the 1917 Code, omitting the fifth as already provided for by canon 153, §1. A brief example may clarify what is meant by this canon. If a see is vacant due to the death of its bishop, the college of consultors, according to canon 421, §1, must elect an administrator of the diocese. Since the college of consultors is a permanently constituted body, the notice of the vacancy of the see has to be communicated to each member individually and the date and place of the election have to be determined by the presiding officer according to canon 502, §2. If one or more of the consultors are overlooked, whether deliberately or not, the circumstances of the second paragraph are realized, and that consultor or those consultors have the right to appeal to the competent authority—in this case the metropolitan or the senior suffragan —and, if the complaint is proved and has been made within three days of having learned of the election of the administrator, he must rescind the election and appoint an administrator according to canon 421, §2.

Canon 167 — §1. Once the convocation has been legitimately made, those present on the day and in

[47]Cf. cc. 317, §1; 352; 413, §2; 421, §1; 452; 509, §1.

the place designated in the convocation have the right to vote; the faculty of voting by mail or by proxy is excluded, unless the statutes legitimately provide otherwise.

§2. If one of the electors is present in the house in which the election takes place but cannot be present for the election because of ill health, his or her written ballot is to be obtained by the tellers.

The first paragraph repeats canon 163 of the former Code almost verbatim, while the second substantially repeats canon 168 of the previous law. The second paragraph should be understood in a rather broad sense. If, for example, the electoral body has convened in a church or a school and the place where the ailing elector is to be found is in proximity, he or she should be considered to be in the place where the election is being held. The issue here is that obtaining the ballot of this elector should not unduly delay the election.

Canon 168 — **Even if a person has the right to vote in his or her own name by more than one title, such a person can cast only one ballot.**

This repeats canon 164 of the earlier Code verbatim. The general rule is clear: one elector, one vote. The prohibition, however, against any member of the electoral body casting more than one vote does not prohibit—in cases in which the governing statutes permit it—a member to cast his or her own ballot and another as proxy for an absent elector, because the second ballot is in the name of another. It is at least probable, moreover, provided the governing statutes permit it, that a member may cast more than one vote by reason of the office which he or she holds, because the office held is a single title.[48] Such cases will be very rare.

Canon 169 — **In order that the election be valid, no one can be permitted to vote who is not a member of the college or group.**

This canon addresses the same matter as canon 165 of the 1917 Code but in a decisively different manner. In the previous law it was recognized that someone who was not a member of the electoral body might possess a privilege by law or custom to cast a vote in the election. This could be an ecclesiastical or even a civil authority. This is categorically excluded by the present canon. It should be noted that not only the ballot of the outsider is invalid, but also the election itself is fatally flawed. This canon does not, however, prohibit persons being present at the session in which the balloting takes place, e.g., staff members of the episcopal conference during the election of the officers.

Canon 170 — **An election whose freedom was in fact impaired in any way whatever is invalid by the law itself.**

This canon treats the same matter as canon 166 of the earlier Code, but again it does so in a significantly different way. In the former law an election was invalid by the law itself if lay persons intruded into an ecclesiastical election in any way that contravened its freedom. In the present Code, as has already been noted, the distinction between clerics and laity is no longer relevant with respect to ecclesiastical office. The present canon, however, goes beyond this by stating that any intrusion from whatever source that effectively hinders or impedes the freedom of the body renders any election null by the law itself. It is possible to intimidate an electoral organ; therefore, canon 1375 establishes a facultative, indeterminate sanction or penalty for anyone who impedes the freedom of a canonical election.

Canon 171 — **§1. Those persons are ineligible to vote:**

1° who are incapable of placing a human act;

2° who lack active voice;

3° who have been excommunicated either by a judicial sentence or by a decree in virtue of which the penalty has been inflicted or declared;

4° who have notoriously defected from the communion of the Church.

§2. If one of the above has been admitted, the vote is null but the election is valid, unless it is clear that by subtracting the vote the person elected did not receive the required number of votes.

This canon substantially repeats canon 167 of the 1917 Code, omitting the reference in paragraph one to age and the deliberate admission of an excommunicated elector in paragraph two. Active voice is the right to vote, while passive voice is the eligibility to be elected. Privation of active and passive voice, listed among the vindictive penalties of canon 2291, 11° of the earlier Code and required as a penalty for certain offenses, does not appear among the penalties of the revised Code. A religious, however, who has been exclaustrated lacks active and passive voice for the duration of the exclaustration according to canon 687.

The penalty of excommunication automatically (*latae sententiae*) incurred[49] is usually not known to others or at least to many people; for this reason, this canon specifies that only an excommunication inflicted by a competent tribunal or ecclesiastical superior or which, having been automatically incurred by the violation of the law in question, has

48Cf. Vermeersch-Creusen, 254.

49Cf. c. 1314.

been declared by a competent authority to have been incurred renders a person ineligible to vote.

A notorious act is more than a public act. The latter may not in fact be known by many people. In order to be notorious an act must be known by many people to have taken place and must have occurred in circumstances that are unambiguous and forestall any other explanation of it. While the revised Code does not continue the distinction of delicts as notorious in law or notorious in fact, in the present canon the defection must be in fact notorious. Ecclesiastical communion is defined in canon 205.

The second paragraph states that, in order to nullify an election, the invalid vote of the person described in the first paragraph must have been the vote necessary to achieve the required number of votes for election. For example, if election in a given instance requires an absolute majority, i.e., one more than half the total number of votes, and the person elected received exactly this required number of votes, the invalid ballot—even if in fact cast in favor of another person—invalidates the election itself. This is the case because reasonable certainty is needed when persons are elected to ecclesiastical offices without the necessity of being able to identify the ineligible voter's ballot in order to determine whether it was the decisive vote or not. Were an election to be in fact null because of the ineligibility of the person casting the decisive vote it would probably come to light only some time later, after the ballots had long since been destroyed.

Canon 172 — §1. For a vote to be valid it must be:

1° free; therefore, a vote is invalid if one has been coerced directly or indirectly by grave fear or by fraud to vote for a certain person or different persons disjunctively;

2° secret, certain, absolute, determinate.

§2. Conditions appended to a vote prior to the election are to be considered as not having been appended.

This canon repeats canon 169 of the earlier Code verbatim. Canon 170 treats the freedom of the election itself; this canon addresses the freedom of the individual electors in choosing for whom to vote. Canon 125, §2 establishes the general principle of the law that a juridic act placed because of grave fear or fraud is valid unless, for a specific kind of juridic act, the law provides otherwise. Here the law provides that a vote in an election is invalid if it is motivated by grave fear or fraud.

Canonists have been divided on one important point in this matter, and the retention of the wording of its predecessor (*CIC* 169) does not resolve the issue—itself more of a theoretical nature than of practical consequence. Is a vote substantially moti-

vated by some extrinsic factor other than fear of a threatened evil or by fraud still said to be free? If electors, motivated by loyalty or obedience, vote for someone in an election in which the votes are secret because their superior has indicated that they ought to vote this way, is the vote free? It is not certain that it is free, although there is neither grave fear nor fraud operative, and thus its validity is only probable. Given the lack of consensus about this, such votes, in the event that they were decisive in the election of someone, render the election itself probably invalid.

A secret vote refers to the act of voting itself. If an elector, however imprudently or even illegitimately, states beforehand for whom he or she intends to vote or afterward reveals the name of the person for whom he or she voted, the elector's vote is valid. If an elector is unable to write a name on the ballot and asks someone to write it for him or her, the vote is still secret and therefore valid.

A vote is said to be certain when the elector indicates without ambiguity the person for whom he or she is voting. For example, if two or more persons having the same surname are eligible for election and an elector does not distinguish between them by indicating the given name or in some other certain way, the vote is invalid and cannot be counted.

Finally, a vote is absolute when it is expressed without any condition. If an elector includes on the ballot itself a condition, e.g., that the person elected will reside in a certain place, that vote is invalid.

The second paragraph refers not to a condition written on the ballot itself but to conditions that an elector has set down prior to the election itself and presumably has expressed to others, especially to those who might be elected. Conditions such as these are to be disregarded and do not invalidate the vote or the election and do not bind the person elected.

It is worthy of note that the revised Code omits the provision of canon 170 of the previous law that one cannot validly vote for oneself. Since voting in a canonical election must be by secret, written ballot, only in the event of a unanimous vote or of a total number of votes only a few votes short of a unanimous election, in which case electors could compare the way they voted with each other, would it be realistically possible to determine that this had actually occurred. An election, moreover, effected by the exact minimum number of votes would be objectively invalid if an elector had voted for himself or herself under the former law, but this could not have become public unless the elector later, perhaps much later, revealed the fact. In order to enhance the needed certainty of ecclesiastical elections the law suppresses this provision, and collegiate bodies or institutes will want to weigh whether such a provision in particular law ought to be suppressed. Perhaps retaining a prohibition against voting for oneself that would not nullify the vote itself is a provision to consider.

Canon 173 — **§1. Before the election begins at least two tellers are to be designated from the membership of the college or group.**

§2. The tellers are to gather the ballots, determine in the presence of the presiding officer that the number of ballots is the same as the number of electors, read the ballots themselves and announce clearly how many votes each person has received.

§3. If the number of ballots exceeds the number of electors the vote is invalid.

§4. The secretary is to record accurately all the acts of the election and carefully preserve them in the file of the college, after signing them along with at least the presiding officer and the tellers.

This canon treats of the manner in which the election is to be carried out, which is the subject of canon 171 of the 1917 Code. This canon, however, greatly simplifies the formalities of a canonical election, e.g., it omits the oath of secrecy on the part of the presiding officer and the tellers, voting in order of precedence, and incinerating the ballots. Particular law can, of course, further specify the manner in which an election is to be conducted.

Canon 174 — **§1. Unless the law or the statutes provide otherwise, an election can also be effected by compromise, provided that the electors unanimously and in writing consent to transfer to a qualified individual or to several qualified individuals, from within the membership or from outside it, the right to elect for that instance; such person or persons elect in the name of all in virtue of the faculty they have received.**

§2. In the case of a college or group composed only of clerics, the persons commissioned must themselves be ordained; otherwise the election is invalid.

§3. The persons commissioned must observe the prescriptions of law concerning elections and, for the validity of the election, they must fulfill whatever conditions have been attached to the compromise agreement which are not contrary to law; conditions contrary to the law, however, are to be considered as not having been attached.

This canon, corresponding to canon 172 of the former Code, but in a somewhat simpler form, introduces the concept of election by compromise or arbitration. If the motivation in considering compromise is a deadlocked election, canon 119, 1° indicates how the tie is to be resolved and particular law may determine this further. If, however, the electoral body is experiencing serious discord in a given election, perhaps resulting in serious difficulties afterward, it might wish to resort to compromise, sometimes called arbitration. If this is decided

upon by a unanimous, written vote, this canon is to be observed.

Canon 175 — **The compromise is terminated and the right to elect reverts to the electors authorizing the compromise:**

1° by revocation by the college or group, before the persons commissioned have begun to act;

2° if a condition attached to the compromise agreement has not been fulfilled;

3° if the election has been completed but is invalid.

This substantially repeats canon 173 of the earlier Code, enumerating the three circumstances in which the mandate of the compromisers or arbitrators ceases and the right to elect reverts to the electoral body. Although the electors must have decided by unanimous vote to place an election in the hands of arbitrators, the recall of the mandate requires only a majority vote. If, however, the compromisers have begun to act, e.g., have met to prepare for the vote, the electoral body cannot revoke the faculty granted to them. Just as an election by the full body can be invalid for a variety of reasons, that of the compromisers can be null and void. If that occurs they cannot remedy the defect and repeat their own balloting but require a new mandate by unanimous consent of the electors.

Canon 176 — **Unless the law or the statutes provide otherwise, the person who has received the required number of votes according to the norm of can. 119, n.1 is to be considered elected, and this is to be announced by the presiding officer of the college or the group.**

This substantially repeats canon 174 of the previous law. Canon 119, 1°, requires an absolute majority for an election. The particular or proper law may require a higher number of votes.

Canon 177 — **§1. The election is to be communicated forthwith to the person elected, who must, within eight days of available time after having been notified, inform the college or the presiding officer of the group whether or not he or she accepts the election; otherwise the election has no effect.**

§2. A person elected who does not accept loses any right deriving from the election and does not regain any such right by a subsequent acceptance; such a person however, can be elected again; the college or group must proceed to a new election within a month of notification of the non-acceptance.

This canon substantially repeats canons 175 and 176, §1 of the 1917 Code. Here the two become paragraphs of a single canon. The second paragraph presumes that the person elected does not accept or refuse the election immediately, either because he or she is not present or because the one elected wishes to consider at some length whether to accept or not. In the meantime the electoral body may have adjourned.

Canon 178 — **The person elected who has accepted the election immediately acquires the office in full right if the election does not require confirmation; otherwise the person acquires only the right to the office.**

This canon substantially repeats its predecessor (*CIC* 176, §2). It should be noted, however, that canon 153, §2 permits provision of office as early as six months prior to the date of vacancy and therefore already permits the practice of electing someone who does not enter upon the office immediately. In this case he or she acquires a right to the office when it becomes vacant, and the electoral body cannot choose someone else in the meantime. If such an election and acceptance require confirmation by a higher authority, the one elected acquires a right to the office, *ius ad rem.* Once confirmed the one elected acquires the office itself either immediately or on the specified date.

Canon 179 — **§1. If the election requires confirmation the person elected must personally or through someone else request confirmation by the competent authority within eight days of available time from the day of acceptance of the election; otherwise the person elected is deprived of any right unless it is proved that the person has been constrained from petitioning confirmation by a just impediment.**
§2. The competent authority cannot deny confirmation if the person elected is qualified according to the norm of can. 149, §1 and the election was conducted in accord with the law.
§3. The confirmation must be given in writing.
§4. Before being informed of confirmation the person may not become involved in the administration of the office, whether this be in matters spiritual or temporal, and any acts placed by such a person are invalid.
§5. Once notified of confirmation the person elected acquires the office in full right, unless the law provides otherwise.

This canon repeats canons 176, §3 and 177 of the 1917 Code in a canon composed of five paragraphs. It is the person elected, not the presiding officer of the electoral body as in postulation, who is to seek his or her confirmation from the competent higher authority, because the one elected, unlike the person postulated, has thereby acquired a right to the office. The canon stipulates what would otherwise have been implicit, i.e., the one elected can request

confirmation through someone else. The authority who is requested to confirm an election cannot withhold it if the person elected possesses the qualifications prescribed by universal or particular law or in the statutes of the office in question. Thus, his or her judgment that someone else was better qualified, even if this is objectively true, does not permit refusal of confirmation. Once the person elected has been notified of confirmation, he or she acquires the office itself either immediately or on the specified date of vacancy of the office.

The prohibition against becoming involved in the office in question does not necessarily prohibit the person elected from assisting the incumbent by way of familiarizing himself or herself with the demands of the office. What is prohibited is any interference with the actions of the actual officeholder.

ARTICLE 4: POSTULATION
[cc. 180–183]

Canon 180 — **§1. If a canonical impediment, which can be and usually is dispensed, prevents the election of the person whom the electors believe to be more qualified and whom they prefer, they can vote to postulate such a person from the competent authority, unless something else is provided by the law.**
§2. Those commissioned to elect in virtue of a compromise cannot postulate anyone unless this was expressed in their document of compromise.

This repeats canon 179 of the former Code verbatim, omitting the unnecessary final clause of the first paragraph. What is meant by postulation is explained in the commentary on canon 147. Only an impediment of purely ecclesiastical origin, such as age, not an impediment of the natural law, such as absence of the use of reason, can be dispensed. Whether or not a competent authority, such as the Holy See, is accustomed to dispense from a given impediment is known only by reported practice and from the commentaries and may require consultation with an expert. Compromise is the subject of the preceding article.

Particular law may contain requirements that go beyond the present canons, such as a prohibition against postulating someone who is ineligible for election because of certain specified impediments.

Canon 181 — **§1. At least two-thirds of the votes are required for postulation to have any effect.**
§2. A vote for postulation must be expressed by the words, "I postulate," or the equivalent; the formula, "I elect or I postulate," or the equivalent, is valid for an election if an impediment does not exist, otherwise for a postulation.

This canon substantially repeats canon 180 of the earlier Code but it simplifies its first paragraph by always requiring a two-thirds majority of the votes. The reason for requiring a precise formula of words in the second paragraph is the need for those voting to be aware of the existence of an impediment, e.g., the fact that the person has already served in an office for the maximum number of years, and for them to deliberately request that this impediment be dispensed. The formula that elects and postulates is used if the existence of an impediment is doubtful.

Canon 182 — **§1. A postulation must be sent within eight days of available time by the presiding officer to the competent authority to whom confirmation of the election belongs, who is authorized to grant the dispensation from the impediment, or lacking the faculty to do so, request the dispensation from a higher authority to; if confirmation is not required, the postulation must be sent to the competent authority so that the dispensation may be granted.**

§2. If the postulation has not been sent within the prescribed time, it is by that very fact invalid and the college or group is deprived for that instance of the right to elect or postulate, unless it is demonstrated that the presiding officer had been constrained from forwarding the postulation by a just impediment, or had failed to send it at the opportune time out of fraud or negligence.

§3. The one postulated acquires no right from the postulation; the competent authority is not obliged to admit it.

§4. The electors cannot revoke a postulation already sent to a competent authority unless this authority consents to it.

This canon substantially repeats canon 181 of the 1917 Code, but simplifies its first paragraph and slightly expands its second for the sake of greater clarity. The present first paragraph looks to the two distinct kinds of election, one that requires confirmation by a higher authority and one that does not require confirmation in order to take effect.[50] If the election does require confirmation, the postulate is always sent to the superior who can confirm it—regardless of whether that person can dispense from the impediment or not. If, on the other hand, the election does not need confirmation, the postulation is sent directly to the authority who can dispense.

The second paragraph considers the case in which the postulate has not in fact been forwarded to the competent authority within the prescribed period of time. If the electoral body is responsible for this delay, there is a disability imposed by the law itself by reason of which it is deprived—for this election only—of the right to elect or to postulate anyone. In that case the higher competent authority would have to decide how the office in question is

to be filled this time. If, however, the cause of the delay is the presiding officer, who is supposed to act on behalf of the electoral body, the disability is not incurred, but the reasons for the failure to transmit the postulate must be explained to the higher authority.

Canon 183 — **§1. If the postulation has not been admitted by the competent authority the right of electing reverts to the college or group.**

§2. But if the postulation has been admitted, this is to be made known to the one postulated, who is obliged to respond according to the norm of can. 177, §1.

§3. The person who accepts the postulation which has been admitted immediately acquires the office in full right.

This canon substantially repeats canon 182 of the former Code. The higher superior is not obligated to admit or receive the postulation favorably; this is the reason the person postulated acquires no right to the office by the action of the electoral body. In the previous law (*CIC* 182, §1), if the electoral body had knowingly postulated someone who had an impediment that could not be or customarily was not dispensed, the electors lost the right to elect someone to an office for that instance and it belonged to the higher superior to provide an incumbent for the office. This was a rather harsh approach to a matter that would virtually always involve some degree of ambiguity and uncertainty. This canon simply states that, if the higher authority does not admit the postulation for whatever reason, the right to elect reverts immediately to the electoral body.

Once the postulation has been accepted and the impediment to election has been thereby dispensed, the procedure becomes that of a direct election: notification to the one elected, who must accept or decline, as outlined in canon 177, §1.

CHAPTER II
LOSS OF ECCLESIASTICAL OFFICE
[cc. 184–196]

It can be said in general that a person loses an office in one of two ways: by his or her initiative (resignation) or by the initiative of a competent authority (transfer, removal, or privation). Resignation is effective in one of two ways, depending on the nature of the office and the law: by simple notification communicated to the competent authority or only after its acceptance by that authority.

The 1917 Code did not divide the chapter on loss of office into articles, but it dealt successively with loss of office by resignation (*CIC* 184–191), by privation (*CIC* 192), and by transfer (*CIC* 193–194). Although it introduced the subject of loss of office by noting that an ecclesiastical office is lost in one of five ways: resignation; privation; removal; transfer; or lapse of a predetermined period of time, it did not sharply distinguish these differing processes in the subsequent canons. The revised Code speaks of six ways in which an ecclesiastical office can be lost: expiration of a term; reaching a certain age; resignation; transfer; removal; or privation, although it does not address the first two in distinct articles. It introduces four articles into the chapter, dealing successively with resignation, (cc. 187–189), transfer (cc. 190–191), removal (cc. 192–195), and privation (c. 196). The chapter begins with three untitled canons, two of which are applicable to more than one manner of loss of office.

Canon 184 — **§1. Ecclesiastical office is lost by the lapse of a predetermined time, by reaching the age determined by the law, by resignation, by transfer, by removal and by privation.**

§2. An ecclesiastical office is not lost by the expiration in any way of the authority of the one who conferred it, unless the law provides otherwise.

§3. The loss of an office once it has taken effect, is to be made known as soon as possible to all who enjoy any right with respect to the provision of the office.

The first two paragraphs of this canon are substantially derived from canon 183 of the earlier Code, adding age in the first paragraph and eliminating the reference to an office conferred at the good pleasure of the one conferring it from the second. The third paragraph derives from canon 191, §2 of the former law, which concerned loss of office only by resignation.

Loss of office at a specified age is new in the Code,[51] although the designation of a certain age is more properly the establishment of a cause for either resignation or removal if the resignation is not forthcoming. When a see becomes vacant, a vicar general or an episcopal vicar, who is not a bishop, loses his office. Persons who would enjoy some right with respect to filling a vacant office would be an electoral body or a consultative body or someone who enjoys the right of presentation.

Canon 185 — **The title of emeritus can be conferred upon the person who loses an office by reason of age or by a resignation which has been accepted.**

Canon 186 — **Loss of office by lapse of the determined time or by reaching a certain age takes effect only from the moment when it has been communicated in writing by the competent authority.**

These two canons are new and reflect the experience of the Church in recent years with respect to

terms of office and retirement at a certain age. The explicit reference to one who has lost an office by reason of age or one whose resignation has been accepted—these could be, but need not be, the same case—*being capable* of receiving the title of emeritus does not seem to disallow the title in other cases, unless it would be wholly inappropriate. It might be noted, however, that the removal of a pastor who refuses to submit his resignation at the age of seventy-five would entail a process that commences with a paternal effort to persuade him to resign.[52]

ARTICLE 1: RESIGNATION
[cc. 187–189]

Canon 187 — **Any person of sound mind can resign an ecclesiastical office for a just cause.**

This repeats canon 184 of the 1917 Code—with an important omission. That canon asserted the fundamental right to resign an ecclesiastical office for a just cause, but it added a qualification to the effect that there might exist a special prohibition against resignation in particular law. By omitting this qualifying clause, canon 187 simply asserts the right to resign from any office in the Church, thereby abrogating any provision in particular law prohibiting this.

Canon 188 — **A resignation submitted out of grave fear, which has been unjustly inflicted, or because of fraud, substantial error or simony is invalid by the law itself.**

This repeats canon 185 of the former Code verbatim. In order that a resignation be fully free it cannot be the result of unjustly inflicted grave fear, substantial error, or fraud. Grave fear is caused by the threat of serious evil, the threat being made to bring about the resignation. The grave fear, however, could also be caused by a justified threat of a serious evil, as in the case of threatening removal from office for a justifying cause if the person does not resign. Substantial error is a mistaken judgment that is not of minor importance and is truly a cause of the consequent resignation. This would be the case in which the officeholder judged that he or she had caused serious injury to someone when this was not objectively correct. Fraud is deceit perpetrated by someone else in a deliberate effort to cause the resignation. Just as simony invalidates the conferral of an office,[53] so it invalidates resignation from office.

It should be noted that a resignation must be for a just cause, i.e., a cause that is proportionate to the importance of the office held. Resignation because

[51]Cf. cc. 401, §1; 411; 538, §3.

[52]C. 1742, §1.
[53]C. 149, §3.

of anger or some other unworthy cause is not justified.

Canon 189 — §1. **To be valid a resignation, whether it requires acceptance or not, must be submitted to the authority who is responsible for the provision of the office, and this is to be done in writing or orally in the presence of two witnesses.**

§2. The authority is not to accept a resignation which is not based on a just and proportionate cause.

§3. A resignation which requires acceptance lacks all effect if it is not accepted within three months; one which does not require acceptance takes effect when it has been communicated by the one resigning in accord with the norm of law.

§4. A resignation can be withdrawn by the one resigning as long as it has not yet become effective; once it has become effective it cannot be withdrawn, but a person who has resigned can obtain the office by some other title.

This canon treats the subject matter of four canons of the earlier Code (*CIC* 186; 187; 189; 191, §1) but reorganizes and simplifies it and introduces some changes. The first paragraph substantially repeats two canons (*CIC* 186, 187) in a simplified and clearer form. The second paragraph substantially repeats part of a third canon (*CIC* 189, §1). In the former law it was not clear whether the person accepting the resignation needed a just and proportionate cause for doing so or was judging the just and proportionate cause alleged by the person resigning. While usually reductively the same, the present wording makes it clear that the latter is the case. Thus, no one can resign an office without stating justifying causes and, when the resignation is not effective without its acceptance by the competent authority, the causes must be such that they persuade the authority to accept it. The one who accepts a resignation cannot do so merely because the resignation was tendered.

The third paragraph addresses the same subject matter as canon 189, §2 of the 1917 Code but significantly modifies it. The former law required that the local ordinary take action within a month on a resignation by accepting it or declining it, but this was not fully compatible with canon 187, §1 therein. The present paragraph provides that if a resignation is not accepted within three months, the law itself refuses the resignation, thus allowing for a pocket veto of the resignation by the higher authority. This also does not allow a resignation submitted without a definite date; this is the case if an officeholder were to submit a written standing resignation that the superior is free to accept at any future date. A resignation that does not require acceptance by anyone is valid when communicated to the proper authority, even though it does not take effect until a future, determined date. In case of ei-

ther kind of resignation, when the one resigning specifies a date for its effect, the authority cannot remove the person from the office prior to that date unless the justifying causes required for removal are certainly already present and the procedure required for removal by universal or particular law is observed.

Paragraph four parallels canon 191, §1 of the previous law but in an important respect contradicts it. The former law stipulated that once a resignation had been submitted it could not be withdrawn. The present paragraph permits withdrawal prior to its taking effect.

ARTICLE 2: TRANSFER
[cc. 190–191]

Canon 190 — §1. **Transfer can be effected only by one who has the right of providing for the office which is being lost as well as for the office which is being conferred.**

§2. If a transfer is to be made when the officeholder is unwilling, a grave cause is required and the procedure prescribed by law is to be observed, with due regard for the right to bring forward arguments against the transfer.

§3. To take effect a transfer must be communicated in writing.

Canon 191 — §1. **In the event of a transfer, the prior office becomes vacant through canonical possession of the other office unless the law provides otherwise or something else has been prescribed by the competent authority.**

§2. The person transferred continues to receive the compensation assigned to the prior office until taking canonical possession of the other office.

The two canons of this article address the subject of canons 193 and 194 of the 1917 Code, but they do so in a different and simplified way. Canon 190, §1 limits transfer in the proper sense to cases in which one and the same higher authority has the competence to provide for both offices. If it is a question of leaving one office and receiving another—which are dependent upon different higher authorities—there is room only for resignation of the former and acceptance of the other.

The second paragraph of canon 190, concerning the transfer of an unwilling incumbent, is substantially the same as canon 192, §2 of the former Code. In transferring an unwilling officeholder from one office to another, the superior must have serious reasons, be certain the incumbent has full opportunity to present reasons against the action, and follow the procedure required by law—whether universal or particular. The transfer of a pastor from one parish to another is governed by canons 1748–1752, while recourse against any other transfer is governed by canons 1732–1739.

The third paragraph of this canon is new and requires that any transfer, whether of a willing or an unwilling incumbent, must be communicated in writing in order to take effect.

Canon 191 substantially repeats canon 194 of the earlier Code and treats both the vacancy of an office as result of a transfer and the financial compensation of the person transferred.

ARTICLE 3: REMOVAL
[cc. 192–195]

Canon 192 — A person is removed from office either by a decree legitimately issued by a competent authority, with due regard for rights which may have been acquired by contract, or by the law itself according to the norm of can. 194.

This canon substantially repeats canon 192, §1 of the previous law. Rights that may have been acquired by a contract of employment may include the rights to health insurance and retirement benefits, housing, and the like. The next canon deals with the right to due process in removal from office.

Canon 193 — §1. A person cannot be removed from an office conferred for an indefinite period of time except for grave reasons and according to the procedure determined by law.
§2. The same holds for the removal of someone from an office conferred for a specified period of time before the term has expired, with due regard for the prescription of can. 624, §3.
§3. When, in accord with the prescriptions of law, an office has been conferred on someone at the prudent discretion of a competent authority, that person can be removed from office for a cause which is, in the judgment of that same authority, considered just.
§4. In order to be effective the decree of removal must be communicated in writing.

This canon addresses the same subject matter as canon 192, §2 of the 1917 Code but it introduces important changes. In the former law the ordinary could remove a cleric from office, bearing in mind that only clerics could hold office, for a just cause and was not required to follow any specified procedure in doing so except in the case of the removal of a pastor. The first and second paragraphs of this canon state that in order to remove a person from an office conferred without a stated term or from an office having a specified term before the expiration of that term, the reasons must be grave and the procedure prescribed by law must be observed. The universal law provides for a procedure that must be followed in the removal both of a pastor who is not a religious or a member of a society of apostolic

life[54] and of the diocesan finance officer before the expiration of his or her term.[55] No procedure is prescribed by the Code for the removal of the following persons: a vicar general,[56] an episcopal vicar who is not an auxiliary bishop before the expiration of his term of office,[57] a parochial vicar,[58] or a religious or a member of a society of apostolic life who holds an ecclesiastical office in a diocese, including that of pastor or parochial vicar, whether with or without a term.[59] Particular law may provide causes and prescribe procedures for the removal of persons from office beyond what is found in the Code.

The reference in the second paragraph to canon 624, §3 concerns religious superiors appointed to their office within the institute for a determined term; this also applies to members of societies of apostolic life.[60]

Canon 194 — §1. One is removed from an ecclesiastical office by the law itself:
1° who has lost the clerical state;
2° who has publicly defected from the Catholic faith or from the communion of the Church;
3° a cleric who has attempted marriage even if only civilly.
§2. The removal from office referred to in nn. 2 and 3 can be enforced only if it is established by the declaration of a competent authority.

This canon corresponds to canon 188 of the earlier Code, which spoke of automatic loss of office in eight instances by reason of tacit resignation. The revised Code more properly identifies this as automatic loss of office by way of removal by the law itself. The three causes listed in paragraph one correspond directly to either one or more canons of the previous law, (i.e., the first to *CIC* 213, §1; the second to *CIC* 188, 4° and 2314, §1, 2°; the third to *CIC* 188, 5°). The other causes of this canon's predecessor (*CIC* 188) are suppressed.

The third cause, a cleric who has attempted marriage even civilly, does not apply to a secular lay person or to a lay religious. Hence, if these persons marry, even invalidly, they do not lose any ecclesiastical office they may hold by reason of the law itself. Particular law, of course, may and should attend to such circumstances.

The second paragraph requires that in the event of public defection from the Catholic faith or from ecclesiastical communion or of attempted marriage on the part of a cleric, the competent authority must establish the fact from certain evidence and declare by decree that the office in question is va-

[54]Cc. 1740–1747.
[55]C. 494, §2.
[56]C. 477, §1.
[57]Ibid.
[58]C. 552.
[59]Cc. 682, §2; 738, §2; 1742, §2; 552.
[60]C. 734.

cant by reason of the law itself. Only then can such authority proceed to provision of the office.[61]

Canon 195 — **If a person is removed from an office which is the source of financial support, not by the law itself, but by a decree of the competent authority, this same authority is to take care such support is seen to for a suitable time, unless it is provided otherwise.**

This canon is new in the Code. This obligation to provide for the financial support of a person removed from an office does not apply in the case of automatic removal by the law itself nor is it applicable to a religious who, by the nature of the religious life, is already otherwise provided for.

ARTICLE 4: PRIVATION
[c. 196]

Canon 196 — **§1. Privation of office, namely removal as a penalty for an offense can be effected only according to the norm of law.**
§2. Privation takes effect in accord with the prescriptions of the canons on penal law.

This canon restricts privation of office to penal removal from office, whereas canon 192 of the 1917 Code applied the expression to removal both as a canonical penalty[62] and for other causes. The present canon can be viewed as redundant with other canons in the Code, but it is appropriately placed here in order to caution ecclesiastical authorities about limitations and procedures found elsewhere in the law. The first paragraph applies the general provision of canon 221, §3 to privation of office as an expiatory penalty for certain crimes.[63] The procedure for inflicting ecclesiastical sanctions is found in canons 1341–1353.

TITLE X
PRESCRIPTION
[cc. 197–199]

Prescription, which can be described as adverse possession by means of which rights can be acquired and obligations can be removed, was treated in the 1917 Code under the rubric of temporal goods of the Church (*CIC* 1508–1512). It more properly belongs among the general norms inasmuch as prescription is not limited to material objects; rather, it is applicable to rights and obligations of the spiritual order. It can be argued, however, that prescription in the latter case is a form of custom (cc. 23–28).

Canon 197 — **The Church accepts prescription as it exists in the civil legislation of the respective nations, as a means of acquiring or losing a subjective right and of freeing oneself from obligations, the exceptions which are determined in the canons of this Code remaining intact.**

This canon, a practically verbatim repetition of canon 1508 of the former Code, canonizes the civil law of the place where it occurs by incorporating through reference the requirements of the secular civil society as normative for the Church.

Canon 198 — **No prescription has any effect which is not grounded in good faith, not only at the beginning but through the entire course of the time required for prescription with due regard for the prescription of can. 1362.**

This repeats canon 1512 of the earlier Code, requiring good faith in order to acquire rights or to be liberated from obligations but adding a reference to canon 1362, considered the canonical statute of limitation for criminal proceedings.

Canon 199 — **Not subject to prescription are:**
1° rights and obligations which are of the divine natural or positive law;
2° rights which can be acquired only from an apostolic privilege;
3° rights and obligations which directly affect the spiritual life of the Christian faithful;
4° the certain and unchallenged boundaries of ecclesiastical territories;
5° Mass stipends and obligations;
6° the provision of an ecclesiastical office which requires the exercise of a sacred order, according to the norm of law;
7° the right of visitation and the obligation of obedience if it should result that the Christian faithful can be visited by no ecclesiastical authority and are no longer subject to any ecclesiastical authority.

This canon substantially repeats canon 1509 of the previous law with clarifications in numbers three and six. The Church considers these matters of such importance or of such a nature that no possession in good faith can acquire or lose a right or free one from an obligation.
Prescription of sacred objects is addressed in canon 1269 and of other material objects or of certain other rights in canon 1270.

TITLE XI
COMPUTATION OF TIME
[cc. 200–203]

Title XI is found in title III of Book I ("General Norms") of the 1917 Code (*CIC* 31–35). Because

---

[61]In the matter of defection from the Catholic faith or from ecclesiastical communion, cf. c. 1364, §1, which does not require that the apostasy, heresy, or schism be public.
[62]Cf. *CIC* 2298, 6°.
[63]C. 1336, §1, 2°.

the law frequently establishes periods of time with respect to rights, obligations, terms of office, age, and the like, the general norms determine how they are to be computed or calculated in order to dispel doubt and to preserve reasonable uniformity. While there is no change in this matter from the former Code, there is remarkable simplification.

Canon 200 — Time is computed according to the norms of the following canons unless otherwise expressly provided by law.

Canon 201 — §1. Continuous time is understood as that which is subject to no interruption.

§2. Available time is understood as that which a person has to exercise or pursue a right but which does not run if the person is unaware or unable to act.

Canon 202 — §1. In the law, a day is understood as a period of time consisting of 24 continuous hours, and it begins at midnight, unless otherwise expressly provided; a week is a period of 7 days; a month is a period of 30 days and a year one of 365 days, unless the month and the year are said to be taken as they appear in the calendar.

§2. If the time is continuous, a month and a year are always to be taken as they appear in the calendar.

Canon 203 — §1. The day from which the computation is to be made is not counted in the total, unless the beginning of the reckoning coincides with the beginning of the day or unless the law expressly provides otherwise.

§2. Unless the contrary is determined the final day is counted in the total, in such a way that, if the total consists of one or more months or years, of one or more weeks, the terminus is reached at the end of the last day of the same number or, if the month lacks a day of the same number, at the end of the last day of the month.

Canon 200, a general canon, repeats canon 31 of the 1917 Code, omitting the latter's reference to liturgical laws. Canon 201, concerning continuous and useful time, repeats canon 35 of the former law in a clearer manner by introducing two paragraphs into the canon. Canons 202 and 203 divide the subject matter of two earlier canons (*CIC* 32 and 34) in a new way, greatly simplifying the complicated latter of the two. Canon 203 completes the simplification of the former canon 34. Canon 33 of the previous law, which permitted some rather complicated, although technically correct, legalistic acrobatics in calculating hours, is fortunately set aside. It is now clear that hours are always computed according to the existing legal time of the place.

Some examples will assist in clarifying what the prose explanation of telling time always seems to obscure. "Continuous time" is the ordinary or usual way of calculating the lapse of time. Terms of office are calculated continuously, as is age; the six-month interval that must be observed between ordination to the diaconate and ordination to the presbyterate is computed continuously, as is the time of temporary religious profession.

"Available time" ("tempus utile"), sometimes referred to as useful time, is a legal fiction devised to safeguard the rights of persons and always refers to a stated period of time within which a person may pursue the acquisition of a full right, e.g., an ecclesiastical office, or defend a right if the person considers himself or herself to have been injured by a judicial sentence or by an administrative decree. If the person in question does not know about a right or is or becomes unable to pursue it, the time within which action on his or her part is required does not run or is interrupted.

Examples of available time are plentiful enough in canon law and a few will be helpful in understanding this concept. If a person has been elected to an office the law provides a period of eight days of available time (*octiduum utile*) from the receipt of notification of election within which to inform the presiding officer whether he or she accepts the election or not. If the person in question does not know about this legal provision or if he or she is or becomes unable to pursue it, the time within which action must be taken does not run or is interrupted.[64] Periods of available time are provided for appeals against judicial sentences and for recourse against administrative decrees.[65]

The provision of canon 203 is alien to modern usage in determining the lapse of time from a specific moment, e.g., from birth or from ordination, and this deserves a few words of explanation. The 1917 Code—when addressing the computation of time—opted for a compromise between the canonical tradition of centuries rooted in the Roman law and the civil practice that prevailed at the time.[66] This canon, like the canon it revises by way of simplification, follows the older canonical usage. A stipulated period of time after a specific event has occurred is not understood to begin until the following midnight. The day from which (*a quo*) is not counted. Thus a person has not completed his or her eighteenth year of age until the actual anniversary of birth has passed, i.e., until midnight when the following day (and year of age) begins. Hence, while in civil law a person is eighteen years of age and thus eligible, for example, to vote on his or her eighteenth birthday, in canon law this same person is said to have achieved his or her majority only on the next day. A man cannot be licitly ordained a

---

[64]Cf. cc. 179, §1; 182, §1; 183, §2.
[65]Cf. 1630, §1; 1734, §2.
[66]F. X. Wernz, *Ius Canonicum*, P. Vidal, ed., 2nd ed. (Rome: Gregorian University, 1952), vol. I, 368–69.

presbyter on his twenty-fifth birthday but only on the next day;[67] a young woman cannot validly marry until the day after her fourteenth birthday;[68] a

[67]C. 1031, §1.
[68]C. 1083, §1.

novice cannot validly make the first profession of vows until at least one full year from the day after he or she was admitted to the novitiate.[69]

[69]Cf. cc. 648, §1; 656, 2°.

BIBLIOGRAPHY

The reader is directed to consult the standard commentaries on the 1917 Code for further examination of the topics covered in titles VII-XI of Book I of the revised Code.

BOOK II
THE PEOPLE OF GOD

[cc. 204–746]

James H. Provost

Book II of the revised Code, as that of the 1917 Code, deals with members in the Church, the structures of ministry and authority, religious life, and the status of Christian lay persons. There is, however, a notable change in perspective evident in the new title and in the new organization of this material.

The previous Code titled the book "On Persons," as if it were dealing with individuals who make up a body politic. The revised Code speaks of the "people of God," focusing on the community of salvation, its members, and its structures. The focus shifts from isolated individuals to persons incorporated within the body of the Church.

The German canonist Klaus Mörsdorf first suggested in 1947 that "people of God" be used in law as one of the two objective descriptions of the Church (the other being "Ecclesia").[1] Vatican II adopted "people of God" as its key description of the mystery of the Church present on earth (*LG,* II). The Council characterized this new people of God as messianic and priestly; it is one and unique; it is gathered together from diverse peoples and is itself the Church and the Body of Christ.[2]

Lumen Gentium 9 identifies four key characteristics of the people of God:

- Christ is its head;
- it is marked by the condition of the freedom of the children of God, in whom the Spirit dwells;
- the law of this new people is to love as Christ loved us;
- its purpose is to promote the Kingdom of God on earth until this is realized fully by Christ's Second Coming at the end of time.

The Council's use of people of God emphasizes the historical character of the Church as the new alliance rooted in the Old Testament Chosen People and on pilgrimage until the full realization of the Kingdom. This people is a communion formed by the action of God, who is a communion in three Persons. The mystery of God revealed in the communion of the human and divine in Christ is continued in this world through the communion of God in the Spirit with the faithful and the communion of the people of God among themselves.[3]

A major tension at Vatican II was the contrast between a "juridical ecclesiology" that understood the Church in terms drawn from civil political theory (a "perfect society," sovereign in the spiritual realm, and structured along the lines of a monarchy based on the primacy of the pope) and this "ecclesiology of communion" that draws on the ancient Christian understanding of the Church as a communion (*koinonia, communio*). Both ecclesiologies can be found in the conciliar documents, but that of *communio* is clearly more influential and provides a more consistent perspective for interpreting the Council's teaching.

The same tension was experienced by the drafters of the revised Code. The juridical ecclesiology was clearly expressed in the 1917 Code, especially in Book II. To revise this Book in terms of an ecclesiology of communion would require a major shift in thinking. Several attempts have been made, but the final product continues to be a compromise—and in that sense faithful to the Council itself. The term "people of God" can be understood with an emphasis on this communion aspect, as above; it can also focus on the organization of this people as a society instituted on this earth by Christ.[4] The two views are complementary rather than exclusive, but the phrase must be read cautiously in a canonical context because here the juridical tradition is so prevalent that an effort is needed at times to appreciate the communion dimension.

For example, "people" is not to be placed in opposition here to hierarchy. It is not the same sense of "people" found, for example, in *Populus* of Senate and People of Rome (SPQR) of Roman law. Rather, it is a theological concept rooted in the teachings of Vatican II, emphasizing the basic unity and social nature of the Church—in which there is an essential equality of all believers within the framework of a hierarchical structure. The "people" are the clergy and lay persons alike.

The title of this Book establishes the conciliar teaching as the controlling context for the canons that it includes. Authority and structures of responsibility within the Church are not independent pow-

[1] K. Mörsdorf in E. Eichmann-K. Morsdorf, *Lehrbuch des Kirchenrechts,* 5th ed. (Paderborn: F. Schöningh, 1947), I, 23.
[2] See A. Grillmeier, "The People of God," in Vorgrimler I, 153–185; J. Komonchak, "A New Law for the People of God: Some Theological Reflections," *CLSAP* (1980), 14–43; O. Semmelroth, "La Chiesa, nuovo populo di Dio," in *La Chiesa del Vaticano II,* G. Barauna, ed. (Florence: Vallecchi, 1965), 439–452.

[3] See J. Hamer, *The Church is a Communion* (London: Geoffrey Chapman, 1964); CLSA Permanent Seminar Studies, "The Church as *Communio*," *J* 36 (1976), 1–245; A. Acerbi, *Due Ecclesiologie: Ecclesiologia giuridica ed ecclesiologia di communione nella Lumen gentium* (Bologna: Dehoniane, 1975).
[4] See, for example, the *Praenotanda* to the 1977 schema, *Comm* 11 (1977), 237, and the discussion by the *coetus* revising this schema in 1979, *Comm* 12 (1980), 50–51.

ers, but they are functions within this organized people, intended to serve the key characteristics identified above. As a mystery or sacrament this people differs from civil social political bodies; it is a unique religious communion, so analogies with democracy, oligarchy, or monarchy are inappropriate. Positions of power are really offices of service within this organized people; those who hold such offices do not possess them as their own but exercise them on behalf of the people and in the name of Christ.[5]

Structure of the Book

Book II is organized into three parts. The first concerns the Christian faithful in general (cc. 204–329), including the basic obligations and rights proper to all Christians (cc. 208–223). The juridic condition of lay persons is detailed (cc. 224–231) as is that of sacred ministers (cc. 232–293). These latter canons (comprising title III) include norms on entrance into sacred ministry, formation for it, and the loss of clerical status. Norms on personal prelatures (cc. 294–297) and associations of the faithful (cc. 298–329) conclude this part.

The second part presents the hierarchical constitution of the Church in two major sections: the supreme authority in the Church (cc. 330–367) and the particular churches and their groupings (cc. 368–572). The third part contains the law on institutes of consecrated life—both religious and secular (cc. 573–730)—and societies of apostolic life (cc. 731–746).

Thus the Book moves from a consideration of the persons who are the people of God, to their constitutional organization, to their special voluntary associations that witness to the holiness to which all in the Church are called and that are engaged in the work of the apostolate.

The present organization is the result of several changes made in the course of drafting the Code, not unlike the movement that took place during the drafting of the *Dogmatic Constitution on the Church* at Vatican II. At the Council, the initial proposal had been to treat of the mystery of the Church, its hierarchical organization, and then of the people of God (understood as laity). A major shift in thinking occurred when the chapter on all the people of God was placed before the chapter on hierarchy, emphasizing that all—hierarchy and lay persons—are equally members of the one people.[6]

Early drafts of the present Code were relatively faithful to the outline of *Lumen Gentium,* treating first the clergy, then lay persons, and finally religious (as *LG* does in chs. III, IV, and VI). This in itself was a major change from the organization of the 1917 Code, which dealt with clergy, then religious, and finally lay persons. The outline, however, still had a problem expressing the common juridic status of all the faithful as called for in the principles for the revision.[7] The organization of the canons failed to give a proper reading of this principle.[8]

By the time the Commission met in 1981, it had been proposed to incorporate the canons of the *Lex Ecclesiae Fundamentalis* concerning membership and rights and duties of Christians into this Book. At the same time, the decision was made to place the treatment on lay persons right after the canons on the common status of all the faithful. The resulting organization emphasizes not only the common juridic status of all the baptized but also the fact that before anything else, every Christian is at least initially a lay person. Sacred ministry is presented, as understood by the structure of the Book, as a further determination for purposes of serving the most common juridic status of Christians—that of being lay persons.

It was proposed initially to treat religious as associations rather than as a distinct status alongside lay persons and clergy. This was the source of some debate by the Commission.[9] The position of Vatican II was influential here. The Council taught (*LG* 43) that religious do not form an intermediary step between lay persons and clergy in the hierarchical constitution of the Church but pertain to the Church's call to holiness. They form a special corporate, voluntary witness to that call. In that sense they are the paradigm of associations within the Church. Yet canonical tradition and practical experience were also considered. The final arrangement is a late compromise, treating associations to which all may belong as part of the law common to all the faithful and separating the special law on institutes of consecrated life and societies of apostolic life into a unique part of the Book.

There is a standard pattern in the documents of Vatican II when addressing church structures. Because of their divine origin, the supreme authority and the local bishop are dealt with prior to considering middle levels of church organization. At the Commission meeting in 1981, it was decided to adopt the same pattern; therefore, canons on the

---

[5]John Paul II highlighted the concepts of people of God, hierarchical authority as service, and the doctrine of the Church as a "communion" as expressing the true and proper image of the Church in the revised Code. See John Paul II, apconst *Sacrae disciplinae leges,* January 25, 1983, 1983 Code, xii.

[6]G. Philips, "History of the Constitution," in Vorgrimler I, 110–120, 127–128.

[7]Principle no. 6 on the protection of the rights of persons, *Comm* 1 (1969), 82–83.

[8]See summary of criticisms in T. Green, "Critical Reflections on the Schema of the People of God," *Stud Can* 14 (1980), 261–262 (cited as Green).

[9]*Rel,* 49.

pope and college of bishops and those who assist in the exercise of supreme power are followed by canons on bishops—only then are the intermediary levels on which bishops act together in conferences and provinces treated. Finally, the internal organization of dioceses and parishes is set forth.

Work of Revision

The canons of this Book are the product of several distinct *coetus* in the revision process. The initial draft published in 1977 contained canons drawn up by five *coetus:* on physical and juridic persons, on the laity and associations of the faithful, on the magisterium, on the sacred hierarchy, and on institutes of perfection.[10] Responding to suggestions from the consultative process, the special *coetus* formed to revise most of the Book moved some of the early canons on physical and juridic persons to Book I as general norms, dropped the canons on rights and duties of all Christians since these would be treated in the *Lex Ecclesiae Fundamentalis,* and made additional changes within the body of the remaining canons.[11] The 1980 version was the product of the special *coetus* that reworked the section on the institutes of consecrated life and the special people of God *coetus.* It was twenty-eight canons shorter than the previous draft.

A later decision not to promulgate the *Lex Ecclesiae Fundamentalis* at this time meant a number of canons had to be added to the Book.[12] The Code Commission debated at its 1981 meeting the organization of the Book and a number of its specific provisions, but it did not debate the *Lex Ecclesiae Fundamentalis* canons that were to be inserted. These were themselves the product of a lengthy process involving two drafts submitted for consultation (1969 and 1971), several other drafts worked on by a reconstituted *coetus* (1972–1976), and a final version put together by a small working group (1977–1979).[13] From this last document, canons on members, rights and duties of all Christians, the supreme authority in the Church, and two *munera* of teaching and sanctifying have been incorporated into the Code. Most of these canons (except those on the two *munera)* are found in Book II.

---

[10]Green, 236, note 4. He does not mention the *coetus* on institutes of perfection because its section had been published separately from the rest of Book II, appearing nearly a year earlier.
[11]*Comm* 12 (1980), 48–129, 236–319; 13 (1981), 111–151, 271–324; 14 (1982), 28–103.
[12]*Rel,* 329–358.
[13]*Comm* 4 (1972), 122–160; 5 (1973), 192–216; 6 (1974), 60–72; 8 (1976), 78–108; 9 (1977), 83–116; 12 (1980), 25–47; 13 (1981), 44–110. See A. Gauthier, "The Progress of the '*Lex Ecclesiae Fundamentalis,*'" *Stud Can* 12 (1978), 377–388.

Part I
THE CHRISTIAN FAITHFUL
[cc. 204–329]

Who is a Christian faithful? Who, in other words, belongs to the people of God, to the Church; who is a "member"? This very basic question has been the subject of considerable study and debate in recent years. Seemingly different answers can be found in the 1917 Code, in Pius XII's encyclical letter *Mystici Corporis* (1943), and in the documents of the Second Vatican Council. The initial canons of Book II provide a nuanced response rooted in the canonical tradition but reflecting the insights and refinements of the Council. Beginning with a statement about all the Christian faithful (c. 204), the Code goes on to provide the criteria for determining full incorporation of a Christian faithful in the Catholic communion (c. 205) and addresses the condition of catechumens who are related to the Church by a specific intention (c. 206). The introductory canons close with a description of the fundamental standings of Christian faithful in the Catholic Church: sacred ministers, lay persons, and religious (c. 207).

Before commenting on the canons themselves, it is necessary to situate them in the context of the discussion on church membership and to explore the various stages through which the canons moved as they were drafted.

a. Membership Concepts

Church law does not use the word "member" in this context. It speaks traditionally of a "person" in the Church, person being a juridic term for the subject of rights and obligations (cf. cc. 96, 113–123). The law also uses the term "Christian faithful" to refer to those who have been established among the people of God (c. 204). This is in keeping with the usage of Vatican II, which preferred this term to Pius XII's encyclical on the Mystical Body which used "membership" in the Church.

Two concepts are at work here. One deals with the human being who is constituted a person, a Christian faithful, or who "belongs." The second concept concerns the Church, that to which the person belongs.

In the 1917 Code it is presumed the Church is the Catholic Church. Baptism constitutes one a person in the Church with all the rights and duties of a Christian. Rights, however, can be restricted if there is an obstacle to ecclesiastical communion or if a penalty (censure) has been imposed (*CIC* c. 87). The baptized who did not belong to the Catholic Church, therefore, were equivalently dealt with as bad Catholics. That Code intended to bind them, except in certain specific cases (*CIC* 12, but see above, c. 11, for the revised Code's provisions).

Pius XII added the profession of true faith to the 1917 Code's requirements of baptism and good standing for one to be truly (*reapse*) a member of the Church. He also made explicit the connection between the Church of Christ and the Catholic Church, declaring one *is* the other. Membership in the salvation community of the Church of Christ is by membership in the Catholic Church.[14] This teaching led to considerable debate over the condition of baptized persons who do not yet profess the true faith (e.g., infants) or who profess the faith but not in its entirety (e.g., other Christians not in communion with the Roman Church); in general, the whole question of membership was debated.[15]

Some canonists distinguished between constitutional membership that comes through baptism and includes all the rights and duties of members, and active membership when one personally assumes the conformity to Christ that was indelibly received in baptism. Some theologians looked to the various levels on which one can belong to the Church, ranging from basic human nature through "anonymous" Christianity, to spiritual and juridical levels of belonging as a baptized person. Others simply took the encyclical as declaring that those who are not Roman Catholics are not in the community of the saved.

Vatican II addressed the questions of the Church and of those who pertain to it. In reference to the Church, it recognized a distinction between the Church of Christ and the Catholic Church, although Christ's Church *subsists in* the Catholic Church (*LG* 8). In deliberately using the phrase "subsists in" rather than "is," the Council nuanced Pius XII's position and opened the possibility for recognizing other Christians and their communities as somehow related to Christ's Church (*UR* 3).

While baptism is the door through which men and women enter the Church of Christ, for full incorporation into the Catholic Church the Council specified something more:

They are fully incorporated into the society of the Church who, possessing the Spirit of Christ, accept her entire system and all the means of salvation given to her, and through union with her visible structure are joined to Christ, who rules her through the Supreme Pontiff and the bishops. This joining is effected by the bonds of professed faith, of the sacraments, of ecclesiastical government, and of communion.[16]

This adds several significant elements to the 1917 Code's view. First, full incorporation is distinguished from the immediate effects of baptism. One can be incorporated into the Church of Christ without thereby being fully incorporated into the visible organization (society) of the Church. It is possible to belong to the Church of Christ and not be a Roman Catholic.

Second, full incorporation requires the presence of the Spirit. The Council deliberately poses this as the first element, focusing on the spiritual and interior dimension of church membership and presenting it as God's continuing action in the Spirit—not just a juridical fact such as citizenship might be considered. This is in keeping with the emphasis on a theological view of the Church as the people of God rather than a solely juridical view of the Church as a perfect society.

Next, personal adhesion is required—not merely the passive reception of baptism. Indeed, the critical element juridically for determining which of the baptized is actually a Roman Catholic comes down to the intention of the individual.[17]

Fourth, that adhesion is to Christ, although mediately it is through the institution of the Catholic Church. The Council again emphasizes the sacramental nature of the Church, i.e., to make Christ present in every age and to all peoples (*LG* 1 and 8). But it is Christ that the Church seeks to make present—not merely itself.

The Council goes on to add three elements drawn from Bellarmine and echoed in Pius XII's *Mystici Corporis*: bonds of professed faith, sacraments, and ecclesiastical government. These are more congenial to a juridical test for membership. The final element, "communion," is drawn from Scripture (Acts 2:42) and relates both to the internal disposition of solidarity among believers and to the external expression of this through the various levels on which the life of the people of God is structured (parish, diocese, and so on).

b. Subsequent Questions

The conciliar teaching cleared the air on some issues, but opened up several others. There is, first of all, the very purpose for talking about membership. Avery Dulles points out that membership connotes different relationships, depending on the context in which it is proposed.[18] From an organic perspective, it means incorporation into the body. Juridically, it implies subjection to the authorities of the organization. In a participatory perspective, membership is voluntary. It may be active or dormant, full or associate, and it can range from nuclear to modal to marginal.[19] Members may be described as active,

---

[14]Pius XII, ency *Mystici Corporis*, June 29, 1943, *AAS* 35 (1943), 201–202.

[15]See Grillmeier, 168–174.

[16]*LG* 14.

[17]See M. Hughes, "The Juridical Nature of the Act of Joining the Catholic Church," *Stud Can* 8 (1974), 45–74, 379–431.

[18]See A. Dulles, "Changing Concepts of Church Membership," *The Resilient Church* (Garden City, N.Y.: Doubleday, 1977), 133–151.

[19]See H. Carrier, *The Sociology of Religious Belonging* (New York: Herder & Herder, 1965), 182–207, who develops these concepts sociologically.

lax, or lapsed. Finally, if one adopts a *communio* point of view, there are various degrees of membership ranging from full to partial, and there can be full or partial communion of communities among themselves as well as of individuals with a specific community.

Traditionally there are various approaches to the basis for religious membership. For some it has been a matter of birth (e.g., born of a Jewish mother). For others, baptism itself is sufficient (e.g., for the Orthodox, Anglicans, and the 1917 Code). In the tradition of the Protestant Reformation one must be inscribed in a local church community to enjoy juridical fellowship, although baptism is considered to give one spiritual fellowship in Christ's Church.

Technically, Roman Catholics are those baptized in the Catholic Church (i.e., with the rites of the Church, or in an emergency when full liturgical rites cannot be used, with the intention that the person be baptized a Catholic) or received into full communion after baptism elsewhere. Membership is always in a Ritual Church (Latin Church or one of the Eastern Catholic Churches—cf. c. 111) and involves membership in a particular church (diocese) and parish (cf. cc. 102–106), although these latter are more easily changed than membership in a Ritual Church (which usually requires a rescript from the Apostolic See—cf. c. 112). To what extent does all this relate to the requirements of professed faith, sacraments, ecclesiastical government, and communion? The practical answer is being developed variously in different pastoral contexts.

Baptism is a sacrament of faith. Yet increasingly the phenomenon of baptized non-believers is encountered pastorally. Are such persons still members of the Church? Here a distinction seems in order. For Roman Catholics, loss of faith does not result in their not being bound by church law (c. 11). This will be discussed more in detail below. If they are in sin, Catholics remain in the Church's body but not in its heart (*LG* 14). It seems possible, therefore, for someone to belong to the structure of the Catholic Church but not to the Church of Christ.

For those who are not Catholics, the fact of their baptism—as for Catholics—has marked them with the character of baptism. This means the sacrament cannot be repeated. If a baptized non-believer later returns to active faith and, perhaps, seeks full communion with the Catholic Church, the person is not to be rebaptized but after suitable preparation is to be received into full communion with a profession of faith (cf. c. 869).

Incorporation into the Church of Christ may be considered from the perspective of communities or from the point of view of individual baptized persons. The Church of Christ is one, although Christians and their communities are currently divided. The Catholic Church professes that the Church of Christ subsists in it. It recognizes closer ties of communion with certain other churches, e.g., the Orthodox. The Anglican communion is considered to have a special place in this relationship (*UR* 13), but this has yet to be more clearly determined and in practice Anglican (Episcopalian) churches are still treated the same as Protestant churches and ecclesial communities.

Some groups have more of the elements necessary to be considered in closer communion with the Church of Christ and are termed "churches" by the Council; others do have some elements, and either by their own desire or by practice of the Council are termed "ecclesial communities." No clarification has been provided as to which groups fit within which categories, however, and the Code sheds no further light on the issue.

The Code considers individuals to be baptized into a community—Roman Catholic or some other. The degree of incorporation into the Church of Christ may vary not only in terms of the degree to which that community is incorporated into Christ's Church but also in virtue of the individual's own spiritual life. Hence, the norms on sacramental hospitality have been revised (cf. c. 844). The Code does not address the rather peculiar situation in some areas where persons are baptized, consider themselves generically Christian, but have never been incorporated into any church or ecclesial communion.

c. Development of Canons

Membership was treated in developing both the *Lex Ecclesiae Fundamentalis* and Book II. The early versions of the *Lex Ecclesiae Fundamentalis* had seven canons that were eventually shortened and reduced to six. The 1977 version of Book II duplicated one of the *Lex Ecclesiae Fundamentalis* canons (on the juridic effects of baptism) and had a descriptive canon concerning who are Christian faithful. The 1980 version dropped the duplication of the *Lex Ecclesiae Fundamentalis* canon and moved the other one to the beginning of the book, where it is now found (c. 204).[20]

The *Lex Ecclesiae Fundamentalis* discussion on membership was in a broader context of various relationships to the Church.[21] The 1980 version began with the relationship of the Church to all people—reaffirming the Church's concern for human rights (*LEF* c. 3). It then addressed the call of all to belong to the Church and their right to do so freely (*LEF* c. 4). Incorporation into the Church of Christ through baptism was stated—together with the attendant provisions on obligations and rights (*LEF* c. 5). This was followed by the requirements for full communion in the Catholic Church (*LEF* c. 6) and

---

[20]See discussion in *Comm* 12 (1980), 55–62.
[21]Ibid., 32–35.

the relationship of other Christians to the Catholic Church (*LEF* c. 7). The section concluded with the situation of non-baptized people and in particular of catechumens *(LEF* c. 8).

When this material was incorporated into Book II to form the present Code, several canons were dropped and only sections of another were taken over.[22] Although it may be regretted that this broader context is no longer expressed in the law, the teaching of the Council must now directly provide the controlling context for understanding the relationship of various persons and communities to the Church of Christ—since the Code is silent on this question.

The Code does raise a different question, however. How is full communion with the Catholic Church lost? Apostasy and schism are clearly attempts to depart from full communion (c. 751). Yet they are punished by a medicinal penalty that applies only to Catholics and is intended to lead the person to both a change of heart and return to the full practice of virtue (cc. 1364, §1; 1331; 1358, §1). Indeed, anyone baptized a Catholic or received into full communion is always bound by church law (c. 11), despite proposals earlier in the revision process to apply the teaching on religious liberty and thereby exempt those who leave by a formal act from merely ecclesiastical laws (see above at c. 11).

Those who do leave the Church by a formal act are, however, no longer bound to the canonical

form of marriage for the validity of their unions (c. 1117) and are not bound by the impediment of disparity of cult (c. 1086, §1). Although they remain bound by other church laws, the exemption places them in a condition not unlike that of non-Catholic Christians under the former Code (cf. *CIC* 1099, §2 and 1070, §1). The question is, what constitutes a formal act of leaving the Church in these restricted cases?

The answer will have to be worked out in practice through the normal channels of jurisprudence. However, two elements do seem required for a person to leave the Catholic Church in even this restricted sense. First, there must be an external, canonically verifiable act. Such an act could be in writing—or at least witnessed by others who can testify to it in the external forum. Second, there must be an intention to leave the Catholic Church. This internal element is required for heresy, apostasy, or schism (c. 1321, §1), and it is parallel to the need for a direct intention to join the Catholic Church of Christ in order for the formal external act of baptism or profession of faith to effect full communion.[23] One should see canon 205 for further discussion on this issue.

---

[22] Dropped were *LEF* cc. 3; 4; 7; and 8, §1.

[23] Thus the question is raised of whether those who declare on a government form that they are leaving the Catholic Church— but do so primarily to avoid paying taxes or being subject to other civil effects—lack the direct intention of leaving full communion itself. See E. Corecco, "Dimettersi della Chiesa per ragioni fiscali," *Apol* 55 (1982), 461–502.

CANONS AND COMMENTARY ————————————

Canon 204 — **§1. The Christian faithful are those who, inasmuch as they have been incorporated in Christ through baptism, have been constituted as the people of God; for this reason, since they have become sharers in Christ's priestly, prophetic and royal office in their own manner, they are called to exercise the mission which God has entrusted to the Church to fulfill in the world, in accord with the condition proper to each one.**

§2. This Church, constituted and organized as a society in this world, subsists in the Catholic Church, governed by the successor of Peter and the bishops in communion with him.

This is a complex, tightly worded canon. Its two paragraphs contain fundamental theological truths expressed in juridical language. As seen earlier, the

question of who is a Christian is intimately linked with the understanding of the nature of the Church. The two paragraphs of this canon address these two issues, making the canon foundational for the rest of the Code. Fittingly, canon 204 introduces Book II and sets the context within which the rest of the canons are to be interpreted. To gain a clearer appreciation of the canon, each paragraph will be analyzed separately, followed by a synthesis of its meaning.

The Christian Faithful

Paragraph one provides a description rather than a definition of who are the Christian faithful. There are several key elements. Baptism is foundational. It produces two effects simultaneously—one personal (incorporation into Christ) and the other social (constitution into the people of God). These two effects have two consequences ("for this reason"). One is that the baptized are made participants in the priestly, prophetic, and kingly functions (*munera*) that Christ continues to exercise in the world. These functions are discussed in greater detail below. The second consequence is to be called to the mission that the people of God carry out as the Church of Christ, a mission God has given the Church to fulfill in this world until the end of time.

The first consequence, participating in Christ's functions, is a personal responsibility and comes unconditionally with baptism. The second, a call to exercise the mission of the Church, is a social responsibility and varies according to one's juridical condition.

For a fuller understanding of this canon, it is necessary to turn to another canon, i.e., canon 96, which also addresses the effects of baptism:

By baptism one is incorporated into the Church of Christ and is constituted a person in it with duties and rights which are proper to Christians, in keeping with their condition, to the extent that they are in ecclesiastical communion and unless a legitimately issued sanction stands in the way.

This canon addresses the juridic consequences of receiving baptism. By baptism a human being receives a new condition in law, that of being a subject of ecclesial duties and rights (a "person," as described above). This condition is proper only to Christians. The non-baptized do not have these ecclesial duties and rights. There is a possible limitation on the duties and rights, depending on the degree of ecclesiastical communion and the good standing of the individual.

Different Sources

These canons were drafted by different *coetus.* Canon 204 was drafted by the *coetus* on the laity and associations of the faithful. The text is drawn primarily from *Lumen Gentium* 31 which dealt with the laity, but here it has been adapted to describe all Christian faithful. Canon 96, which is rooted in canon 87 of the 1917 Code, was proposed in an earlier version by the *coetus* on physical and juridic persons; a similar draft was prepared independently by the *coetus* on the *Lex Ecclesiae Fundamentalis.* The latter version was eventually adopted and reflects the influence of Vatican II (e.g., "incorporated into the Church of Christ") and concerns that surfaced within the *coetus* itself.[24]

The different sources produce some obvious differences between the two canons. Their focus is different: canon 204 looks to the people of God and the social effect of baptism; canon 96 attends to the individual. Their purposes are also different: canon 96 establishes one's juridical status as a person in the Church, while canon 204 describes the Christian faithful in terms of communion (as the people of God) and church mission. These differences are complementary, for they show different effects of the same reality—baptism.

Common Concerns

(1) Baptism is the fundamental juridical event separating Christians from non-Christians. In both canons the law prescinds from the subjective state of soul and attends to the objective facts. This is not to deny the interior dimension—which in the order of salvation is more important. Rather, it is to focus on the external event as the basis for a secure criterion. In keeping with canonical tradition, this criterion is found in the verifiable external event of baptism by water (cf. c. 849). This approach is consistent with the first principle for the revision of the Code, the juridical nature of the law.[25]

(2) A member of the Christian faithful is at the same time incorporated into Christ and into the Church of Christ by baptism. The canons are not contradictory but look at two dimensions of the same event. There is no baptism without the social-juridic effect—at least constitutionally. The actualization of that effect, however, depends on factors beyond the fact of baptism, as both canons imply.

(3) The Christian faithful as persons in the Church have the duties and rights that are proper to Christians in keeping with their "condition." In canon 96 "condition" is that of being baptized, and the distinction is between Christian and non-Christian conditions—not a distinction among Christians themselves. All Christians share the same "freedom of the children of God" that *Lumen Gentium* 9 teaches is their specific condition.

(4) The revised Code provides an important list of duties and rights common to all Christians, proper to their condition as Christians (see below, cc. 208–223). As shall be seen, this listing is not taxative. Another approach is provided by canon 204, which presents the insertion into the

---

[24]The *LEF coetus* concerns are clear from the report in *Comm* 12 (1980), 33. See also the wide-ranging discussion of the people of God *coetus* on the same canon before it was remanded to the *LEF,* ibid., 55–58.

[25]See *Comm* 1 (1969), 78–79. It may be questioned, however, whether the second principle (coordination of internal and external fora, ibid., 79) has been adequately implemented in the decision to prescind from the internal, personal faith disposition of the baptized. As noted earlier, this personal faith act is essential to the juridical act of joining the Church (see note 17 above).

mission of the Church as that which is common to all Christian faithful. The perspectives of duties and rights, and that of insertion into mission, are complementary and will be discussed below in the section on rights in the Church.

(5) Both canon 204 and canon 96 relate to any baptized person. Canon 96 distinguishes incorporation into the Church of Christ and constitution as a person from the duties and rights that may flow from this. These latter are said to be proper to the Christian faithful insofar as they are in ecclesiastical communion and unless there is the obstacle of a sanction. Does this mean that the duties and rights pertain to the baptized in varying degrees within the Church of Christ, such that only those in full communion and without sanctions have these duties and rights fully and simply?[26] Or, does the limitation on duties and rights refer to their exercise, i.e., the extent to which they can be enforced and vindicated in the Catholic Church? These questions arise because a fundamentally theological statement about incorporation into the Church of Christ has been located in a traditionally juridical text concerning the duties and rights of persons in the Catholic Church.

Examining the text of canon 96 itself, several elements argue in favor of the second position. "Ecclesiastical" communion is used rather than the broader "ecclesial" communion. As seen earlier, there can be a distinction between the Church of Christ and the Catholic Church, and a person may belong to the Church of Christ but not be a Catholic. Moreover, the "sanction" mentioned in canon 96 is that of the Catholic Church and in virtue of canons 11 and 18 must be interpreted strictly as applying only to Roman Catholics. On the other hand, it is possible to be in varying degrees of communion with the Church of Christ, and it can be argued that the extent to which one is not in communion with Christ's Church, to that extent a person fails to enjoy the duties and rights of Christians. However, given the fact that canon 96 is within the context of canons on the juridical status of physical persons in the Catholic Church (and indeed, of the Latin Church), it is possible to say at least that the limitations apply to the extent to which duties and rights may be canonically enforced and vindicated in the Catholic Church by those with some degree of communion (full or partial) with it.

Although the original source of canon 204 dealt only with lay persons (*LG* 31) and presumably in that context applied only to Roman Catholics, as it stands this canon also applies to any Christian. It does not distinguish Christian faithful according to the degree of ecclesial communion. Such a distinction appears in the next canon (c. 205), directly with regard to those in full communion and indirectly touching others. In itself canon 204 refers to any baptized person; all, in virtue of baptism, are incorporated into Christ, constituted in some relationship to the people of God (whatever the degree of communion), and on that basis cannot be rebaptized (cc. 845, §1; 864). Indeed, on that basis they also participate in the functions whereby Christ's mission is continued in this world.[27]

The canon does distinguish the degree to which persons are called to participate in the mission of the Church, basing this on their "juridical condition." This is not just the condition of being distinct from the non-baptized: it relates to the degree of communion with the Church of Christ (both personally and ecclesially, as discussed above). It also relates for Catholics to their standing in the Church in terms of good standing (e.g., under sanction or not); basic juridical conditions as determined by age, location, and so forth (cc. 97–112); and the degree of responsibility pertaining to sacred ministers, lay persons, and religious (c. 207).

In effect canon 204 distinguishes the involvement of all Christians in the mission of the Church of Christ according to their degree of communion with the Church and for Roman Catholics also according to their standing in their Church. The earlier impression that only the hierarchy had this mission was corrected at Vatican II (cf. *LG* 10, *AA* 3). The revised Code clearly sets forth the role of all Christians in the Church's mission (cc. 209–211, 216–217) and that of lay persons in particular (c. 225). The notable feature ecumenically is the recognition in law of the legitimate involvement of other Christians in the functions (*munera*) of Christ— carrying out the mission that God gave the Church to be fulfilled in the world. *Unitatis Redintegratio* 3 already laid the foundation for this view. This is not the place to explore the extent to which other churches participate in these *munera* (including that of governance), for the Code addresses directly only the inner operations of the Catholic Church.[28]

---

[26]This would appear to be the opinion of the *LEF* small working group in September 1979, where one consultor (apparently with the agreement of the rest) held that the text is always dealing with "full communion" (*Comm* 12 [1980], 33). Yet the canon itself makes no distinction between baptism into full or partial communion, and to impose such a limitation would go beyond the strict meaning of the law (cf. c. 18).

[27]Some members of the Code Commission objected to the wording of the canon for this very reason. While admitting "Christifideles" applies theologically to all the baptized, the *Relatio* argues that in the context of the Code, especially because of c. 11, "Christian faithful" applies directly only to Catholics (*Rel*, 50). Thus, non-Catholics cannot vindicate their role within the Catholic Church, nor does the Catholic Church claim authority to enforce their participation in the Church's mission.

[28]See P. Krämer, "Die Zugehörigkeit zur Kirche," in *Grundriss des nachkonziliaren Kirchenrechts,* J. Listl et al., eds. (Regensburg: F. Pustet, 1979), 110 and note 43 on the same page.

Munera Christi

The Christian faithful are said to participate in the functions (*munera*) of Christ (c. 204). These functions are an ancient patristic notion that described three dimensions of Christ's mission. He completes the messianic promises (that there would come a great prophet, a new high priest, and a king to rule for all time) through his preaching, sacrifice, and transforming rule over the earth. The threefold description was seldom used in the Middle Ages, but Calvin reintroduced the "prophet-priest-king" trilogy to understand Christ. His usage was picked up later by some German Lutherans, eventually being adopted in the last century by German Catholic authors through whom it entered into current Catholic usage.[29] Vatican II used the threefold division of *munera* as a convenient theological framework to describe not only Christ's mission but also the mission of the Church, using the formula in both a Christological and an ecclesiological sense.[30] The revised Code uses this division in canon 204 through a direct quote from the Council (*LG* 31). It also uses the basic elements of the division in the organization of the Code (Book III on the office or *munus* of teaching, Book IV on the *munus* of sanctifying) but does not make of it the fundamental organizational principle for the entire work (the *munus* of governing, for example, is said to apply to the entire Code).[31]

The application of the *munera* categories has provided a means to evaluate the relationship of the Church and its mission to Christ and his work. It has also been helpful in understanding the active participation by all the faithful in the mission of the Church and in analyzing different aspects of that participation. On the other hand, the limitation of these categories must also be admitted. They are applied unevenly in both the Council and the Code. The most direct usage has been in terms of bishops' powers vis-à-vis orders and jurisdiction (cf. *LG* 21; c. 375, §2). The application has been less clear to the Church at large (*LG*, II) and to lay persons (*LG* 31), for the function of governing relates in different ways to the hierarchy and to others in the Church. The problem has not gone unnoticed, and it was the subject of debate even into the 1981 meeting of the Code Commission. The resolution of the issue is still not entirely satisfactory (see above at c. 129).

Summary

Canon 204, §1 describes who are Christian faithful. Baptism is fundamental to being a Christian

faithful, and by it one is incorporated into Christ and into Christ's Church, with the rights and duties that pertain to those who are in the Church. This description fits any baptized person, but in the context of what is enforceable under the Code it pertains to Catholics in general and to Latin Rite Catholics in particular.

Thus, in law, a member of the Catholic Christian faithful is called to participate in the Church's mission, exercising the threefold functions of teaching, sanctifying, and ruling by which the people of God—the Church—continue Christ's mission. As paragraph two points out, such participation in the Church's mission for a Catholic is within the context of the Catholic Church in which the Church of Christ subsists.

The Church

Paragraph two is a direct quote from *Lumen Gentium* 8. For a fuller understanding of the development of the conciliar text and its implications, one should consult standard commentaries on the Council. As pointed out above there was substantial debate in the Council over this text, especially the statement that the Church of Christ "subsists in" the Catholic Church. The text is nuanced, distinguishing the Church of Christ in this world from the wider communion of saints, which traditionally includes both the saints in heaven and those who have died and await full communion with the Lord.

The text also distinguishes the Catholic Church as the one in which the Church of Christ subsists. It is an observable fact that there are various organized bodies of baptized Christians, and that they are not in full communion with one another. In which, then, does Christ's Church continue, carrying on the mission of Christ as described in paragraph one of this canon? The Council and the Code, by directly incorporating the conciliar text, make a positive claim regarding the Church in which Christ's Church subsists. The text does not make an exclusive or negative judgment on other churches and ecclesial communities. Although the Council did go on to provide an evaluation of these others in terms of the degrees of their communion with the Church of Christ, the Code has a more restricted purpose and focuses on the Catholic Church alone.[32]

Society

The 1917 Code understood the Church as a visible, organized society but based on a civil political

---

[29]See J. Fuchs, *Magisterium, Ministerium, Regimen. Vom Ursprung einer ekklesiologischen Trilogie* (Bonn: Köllen, 1941).

[30]A. Fernandez, *Munera Christi et munera ecclesiae* (Pamplona: EUNSA, 1982) explores the historical development of the formula as well as its use in Vatican II and subsequent writings.

[31]See *Rel*, 47–48.

[32]*LEF* struggled with the formulation of a similar canon and with the relationship of non-Catholics to the Catholic Church. A simpler approach was adopted in the Code, citing *LG* directly without delving into the attached theological issues. See *LEF* c. 1 in its various redactions, and *LEF* c. 7 on those not in full communion.

model of the sovereign state or "perfect society." This latter term means it is a society that contains within itself all the means necessary to achieve its end (hence "perfect"), as contrasted to imperfect societies that are subject to the sovereignty of the State and in some way depend on outside resources (e.g., the State) to achieve their proper end.

The Council did not explicitly reject this position but chose instead to address the Church from a more theological and biblical perspective. The Church is like a sacrament (*LG* 1), and in the intimate connection of the human and divine elements it is compared to the mystery of the incarnate Word (*LG* 8). There is to be no opposition between or separation of the invisible, mystical dimension of the Church from its visible, hierarchically organized dimension. The two form one reality (*LG* 8).

"Society" in this canon, therefore, refers to the visible dimension of the mystery that is the Church—God's people in this world. Just as the Code prescinds from the anomaly of an individual who is baptized but pertains to no ecclesial community, so the Council (and the Code) does not conceive of the Church in this world as anything but visible and in some manner organized, if it is truly Church.

The Code retains the practical conclusions of the previous theory on "perfect society" in that juridic personality is affirmed for the Catholic Church and the Apostolic See by divine institution—and hence as sovereign entities (c. 113, §1). The affirmation that the Church is constituted as an organized society, however, looks more to the sacramental nature of the Church and the necessity for a visible element to be a sacrament in this world.[33]

Catholic Church

This ancient appellation for the true Church comes from the Fathers, beginning with Ignatius of Antioch (early 2nd century). In current usage it refers specifically to those churches in union with the successor of Peter and one another, both Eastern and Western. Because of the significance of union with the bishop of Rome, the Western Church has also been termed the Roman Catholic Church. The Council, however, used the term "Catholic Church" for it refers to the Eastern Catholic Churches as well, particularly in this context.

The Council developed the meaning of catholicity in terms of universality and variety (*LG* 13). The Church is universal both in the sense that it is to spread throughout the world and also because it is for every age, nation, and culture. The Church is

catholic in that it is a communion of various parts of the Church, sharing resources and solicitude for each other and the whole Catholic Church. The Church is also catholic in that it is composed of various ranks, whether of hierarchical service (cf. c. 207 and c. 336 on hierarchical communion) or of spiritual witness (cf. c. 207, §2 on consecrated life).

Synthesis

The two paragraphs of this canon present a highly nuanced position. The Code is not making an exclusive claim that only Catholic Christian faithful share in the functions of Christ and exercise the mission Christ gave the Church; neither is it espousing a vague notion by which all baptized persons would be treated indiscriminately.

Instead, the Code sets two fundamental concepts as foundations for the rest of the law. Christ's Church subsists in the hierarchically organized Catholic Church. The baptized constitute the Church, a people on mission. This does not make of the Church a society founded on the will of the members, for it is based on Christ's action in their baptism. It also, however, does not make of the Church an institution separate from its members, for the people are the Church. The diversity among members does not replace the foundational principle that the members are the Church, but rather it serves to stimulate and call all the Church to be what it truly is—the visible, organized communion of baptized carrying out the mission entrusted to it by Christ. It will be for later canons to specify the requirements for full and partial communion (cf. cc. 205–206), the rights and duties flowing from communion in mission (cf. cc. 208–233), and the diverse ways in which Christian faithful in the Catholic Church carry out the mission of Christ (the concern of much of the rest of the Code).

As Pope John Paul II stressed in promulgating the Code, this vision constitutes part of the newness of the "new" Code and establishes a basic context within which the rest of the canons are to be interpreted. It will take time, however, to appreciate fully the significance of this new way of thinking—and perhaps even longer to put it into practice.

Full Communion

Canon 205 — Those baptized are fully in communion with the Catholic Church on this earth who are joined with Christ in its visible structure by the bonds of profession of faith, of the sacraments and of ecclesiastical governance.

Here the conditions for full communion in the Catholic Church are set forth. The person must be baptized and must be joined to the Church's visible structure by certain visible bonds: profession of faith, the sacraments, and adherence to ecclesiasti-

---

[33]One of the consequences of this shift is that canon law is not to be viewed as parallel to the civil law of a sovereign state but as a legitimate expression of a visible element in the sacramental nature of the Church. In itself, canon law is not sufficient for the Church to be Church, but it serves as a necessary dimension of ecclesial visibility.

cal governance. This full communion with the visible structure of the Church on this earth joins the baptized with Christ. How such joining is effected is not addressed in the canon. Instead, canon 205 restricts itself to the legally verifiable external criteria for determining who is a Roman Catholic.

Sources

The canon is not found in the 1917 Code but is a direct result of the documents of Vatican II: *Unitatis Redintegratio* 3 deals with various elements held in common by some or all Christians; *Lumen Gentium* 14 specifies the elements needed for full communion in the Catholic Church. The text of canon 205 is drawn almost verbatim from *Lumen Gentium* 14 and originally appeared as a canon of the *Lex Ecclesiae Fundamentalis.*[34]

Full Communion

Vatican II developed the expression "full communion" during the debates on *Lumen Gentium.* It has become a technical term and protects the distinction between incorporation into the Church of Christ and degrees of communion with the Catholic Church.[35] Its use here brings this theological precision into the expression of the law.

Full communion is presumed of those who are baptized in the Catholic Church or who are received into such full communion after baptism. For adults, this means a deliberate intention is required to assume such bonds, and even for those who have reached the age of discretion some such intention adapted to their age is necessary (cf. cc. 865, §1; 852, §1). For infant baptism, the situation has not always been clear. Certainly if parents bring their child to the Catholic Church to be baptized as a Catholic, the child becomes a Catholic Christian. The problem arises when under extraordinary circumstances baptism takes place without this ecclesial reference, even if the minister is a priest or deacon. Is the one baptized automatically a Catholic?

The answer is not clear from the Code. According to canon 865, §2, all that canon 205 requires for full communion is not required for an adult to be baptized in an emergency. Canon 861, §2 does not require that the faithful be instructed in the elements of canon 205 but only in the correct manner of baptizing in emergency situations. The bonds of full communion are not necessarily presumed when emergency baptism takes place. Hughes concludes it is the intention of the one responsible for asking for the baptism—the adult personally or parents or others responsible for infants—that determines full communion.[36] Canon 205 specifies what the content of that intention must include.

Full communion signifies that the person enjoys all the duties and rights of a Christian in the Catholic Church (c. 96). In everyday terms such a person is a "member" of the Catholic Church.

Bonds

Three essential bonds are listed in the canon. The first is faith. Those being baptized are to be prepared with regard to the faith (c. 865, §1), normally through the catechumenate (c. 851, 1°). Parents expecting an infant or who have a newborn are to be instructed so they can nurture their children in faith after baptism (cc. 851, 2°; 867). The specific content of what is meant by "faith" here is not spelled out in the Code. Some elements, however, can be gleaned from the canons.

The faith needed for adults to be baptized is referred to in canon 865, §1, which requires that they be sufficiently instructed in the "truths of the faith and in Christian obligations." Canon 212, §1 calls for the Christian faithful to accept what the sacred pastors teach as representatives of Christ, and canon 750 specifies that all that is contained in the deposit of faith and proposed as divinely revealed is to be believed with "divine and catholic faith."

On the negative side, mere doubt in regard to any of these matters is not enough to break the bond required for full communion. This is clear when the limits to the bond of faith are examined. Heresy, the obstinate denial or doubt of a teaching that is to be held with divine and catholic faith, requires pertinacity in addition to denial or doubt (c. 751). Heresy does not apply to doubt or even denial of other types of church teaching, which presumably would not break the bond of full communion. Total denial of faith, i.e., apostasy (c. 751), clearly does break full communion.

Even heretics and apostates remain in some communion with the Catholic Church that is more complete than the partial communion of other Christians with Catholics; even after being excommunicated, they are liable to further sanctions if they do not mend their ways (c. 1364, §2).

The second bond is sacraments. Catholics in full communion are bonded by the same sacraments. There is open communion among Catholics of different particular churches and of the various Ritual Churches in the Catholic communion, expressed in ready access to the Eucharist (c. 923).

Christians in full communion with the Catholic Church have a right to the sacraments there (c. 213), a right that must be respected by sacred ministers when the request is properly made (c. 843, §1). Christians who are not in full communion may be admitted to the sacraments of penance, Eucha-

---

[34]In the 1980 version of the *LEF* it was c. 6; see *Comm* 12 (1980), 33.

[35]See Grillmeier, 173–174, 176–177 for a report on the Council's deliberations.

[36]See Hughes.

rist, and anointing in Catholic churches under certain conditions (c. 844)—thus reflecting the fact that they have some rights to the extent that they are in communion, but these are limited by the degree they lack full communion (cf. discussion under c. 204 above). No matter in what degree of communion Christians may be with regard to the Catholic Church, the marriage of two baptized persons is always a sacrament according to the Code (c. 1055).

The bond of the sacraments is a solidarity with the community that celebrates them (c. 837) and with Christ who acts in them (c. 834). Those who have cut themselves off from Christ by sin remain in the Church but are not to participate in the sacrament of the Eucharist until they have been restored to union with Christ (cc. 915–916). The sacramental bonds are presented by the Council as having a special significance for the reality of the people of God (*LG* 11).

The final bond listed in this canon is ecclesiastical governance. The governance of the Catholic Church is organized hierarchically; it is not just a community church. All the faithful have the duty to maintain the bonds of hierarchical communion. This is usually expressed through a relationship of obedience to the sacred pastors and of communion among the bishops (cf. cc. 212, §1; 333; 336).

Disagreement or even dissent, however, does not in itself break the bond of ecclesiastical government required for full communion (cf. c. 212, §3).[37] The Code does not specify the limits for dissent, whether in matters of doctrine or in questions of church government. Instead, it provides procedures whereby dissent can be addressed and lists guarantees for fair treatment (cf. c. 221 and Book VII on procedures).

The Code does deal with situations in which dissent has gone too far. Schism is withdrawal from subjection to the pope or from communion with members of the Church of Christ subject to the pope (c. 751). Since the dogmatic definitions of Vatican I on papal primacy, it has been difficult to distinguish schism (concerned with church government) from heresy (which deals with matters of the faith). Even those who are subject to sanctions due to schism are still, however, in some manner subject to the Church. The boundaries of full communion, in cases in which they are pushed to the limit, are not as clear cut as would be possible in secular systems of membership.

Spiritual Dimension

This lack of secular-style clarity may be due to factors addressed in the source material (e.g., *LG* 14) but not included in the text of the canon: "possessing the Spirit of Christ" and "bonds of commu-

nion." Both relate to the spiritual nature of full communion, an essential dimension according to the Council document. The Code has tried to include this in the phrase "joined with Christ" (also taken from *LG* 14). A fuller understanding, however, can be developed by considering the conciliar text that controls the interpretation of the canon.

Vatican II emphasized the inner, spiritual reality of communion as well as its external expression. *Lumen Gentium* 14 set as the first criterion for full membership the possession of the Spirit of Christ. Only then did it list the external criteria in bonds such as those found in canon 205. The ultimate reality of full communion transcends legally verifiable bonds. The Church is a mystery, and the fullness of its reality goes beyond what can be expressed in law. Even so, the drafters of the revised Code seem to have had an especially difficult time determining how to include a reference to the essential role of the Spirit in the life of the Church[38] and may have decided to delete the reference to possessing the Spirit because it is too hard to determine externally in law who actually does possess it.

The second phrase dropped from *Lumen Gentium* 14 in drafting canon 205 concerns the bond of communion. The Council added this to the three bonds that have been cited in the canon. In its 1969 and 1971 versions, canon 7, §1 of the *Lex Ecclesiae Fundamentalis* did include all four elements, but subsequent drafts do not mention it. The reason could be this: communion as indicated above is an internal and an external reality, a spirit of solidarity with the other members of the people of God and the living out of that spirit in mutual concern, support, and hierarchical relationships (see c. 209, below). The external, juridically enforceable dimensions of communion may be considered to have been expressed already in the bonds listed in canon 205. The practical, voluntary aspects of communion, however, must not be lost from view; they form the living context in which the other, more juridical bonds are truly effective.

Ultimately, the bond with the Church is rooted in something that can never be lost—baptism. While full communion is expressed in the bonds of profession of faith, sacraments, and ecclesiastical governance, it is fundamentally rooted in the internal commitment of the baptized individual—and in that sense, only the individual can withdraw from full communion. The Church does not expel persons from its midst. Essentially, the heretic, apostate, or schismatic withdraws those bonds by a personal act. The Church recognizes this in declaring the bonds severed, but they are never totally cut. This is why censures such as excommunication are not permanent but must be removed when the

---

[37] See the various studies in *The Right to Dissent,* H. Küng and J. Moltmann, eds., *Con* 158 (New York: Seabury, 1982).

[38] For example, the gifts of the Spirit or charisms were not considered apt matter for juridical formulation; see *Comm* 12 (1980), 43–44.

person has a change of heart and seeks remission of the penalty (cf. c. 1358, §1).

Leaving the Church

Is it then possible for a Catholic to leave the Church? Traditionally, the answer has been no. Baptism irrevocably bonds a person to Christ and the Church, even if that bonding lacks the inner personal commitment of the baptized individual. The radical, constitutional change has been made and is irreversible.

The Council and now the Code have distinguished incorporation into the Church of Christ by baptism and full communion in the Catholic Church by the further bonds listed in canon 205. From this perspective, is it now possible for a Catholic to leave the Church?

The Code does recognize that people do fall away from the Church, not only by slipping from active bonding to the faith, sacraments and ecclesiastical governance (e.g., those who have "notoriously rejected the Catholic faith" in c. 1071, §1, 4°) but also by a formal act declaring they have left the Catholic Church (e.g., cc. 1086, 1117). As discussed earlier, what such a formal act might be is not specified in the law, and in contemporary practice it may be difficult to determine.

However, the Code does not follow its recognition of the factual leaving of the Church to the logical canonical conclusion. Instead, it retains the tradition in law that those who have come into full communion with the Catholic Church are never able to withdraw from the Church's law, even if they do cease to be in full communion (cf. c. 11). They may be exempted from certain regulations (as, for example, the formalities surrounding marriage), but they are considered otherwise bound by Catholic Church law even if the individuals have clearly severed all bonds of full communion.[39]

Purpose of Full Communion

The canon does not indicate the purpose of full communion in the Catholic Church; it is concerned with identifying who are Roman Catholics. However, the purpose of full communion is not an idle question. Why be so concerned about who is a Roman Catholic? The Code's approach to understanding the Church, rooted in the Council's teaching,

goes beyond a view of the Church as a sovereign (or "perfect") society. It addresses the Church as a communion, the people of God, who are engaged in a God-given mission (c. 204). All participate in this mission in their own proper way.

The juridic condition of full communion in the Catholic Church is a specific manner in which Christians participate in the mission God gave the Church. This is the fundamental reason for seeking to identify who are in full communion; thereby, it is possible to specify those who are responsible for carrying out the mission as the Catholic Church, each in keeping with his or her own proper condition in the Church. Full communion also determines the degree to which rights of Christians may be vindicated within the Catholic Church's governmental structure. Finally, full communion is another element in the sacramental nature of the Church, for the Church of Christ can be the light to the nations (i.e., *lumen gentium)* if there are indeed physical persons in full communion who by their lives and their actions carry that light to the people of their day.

Catechumens

Canon 206 — §1. Catechumens are in union with the Church in a special manner, that is, under the influence of the Holy Spirit, they ask to be incorporated into the Church by explicit choice and are therefore united with the Church by that choice just as by a life of faith, hope and charity which they lead; the Church already cherishes them as its own.

§2. The Church has special care for catechumens; the Church invites them to lead the evangelical life and introduces them to the celebration of sacred rites, and grants them various prerogatives which are proper to Christians.

From those in full communion, the Code turns to catechumens—those who have a special relationship with the Catholic Church. Traditionally catechumens are non-baptized persons who seek admission to the Church through baptism. In describing them the Code draws on two conciliar sources (*LG* 14, *AG* 14) that have formed the basis for the renewal of the catechumenate in current liturgical law and practice.[40]

Catechumenate

The Code reflects the structure of the catechumenate as set forth in the *Rite of Christian Initiation of Adults*. It distinguishes pre-catechumenate (c. 787) from the catechumenate properly so called (cc. 788; 851, §1; 865, §1). The latter is a period of time sufficient for three concerns to be addressed:

---

[39]The 1980 schema of the Code was more logical. In its version of c. 11, §3 (now dropped), it exempted from merely ecclesiastical laws those who fell away from the Catholic Church unless the law expressly provided otherwise. The Code has taken the opposite position, binding them unless the law expressly provides otherwise. This raises critical questions beyond the scope of this commentary about the application of the second principle for revision, i.e., the coordination of the internal and external fora. The internal act of intention is essential to the reality of full communion—no less than for the reality of marital consent (see c. 1101, §2).

[40]See *RCIA,* provisional text (Washington: USCC, 1974).

preparation through liturgical rites (c. 788, §1); instruction in the truths of the faith (cc. 851, 1°; 788, §2); and formation in a life lived according to gospel values (cc. 788, §2; 865, §1).

The rite presents two stages in the catechumenate itself: one is a period of general formation; the second is a more intense preparation for baptism as one of the "elect." Finally, after the celebration of the sacraments of initiation (baptism, confirmation, Eucharist—cc. 842, §2; 845, §1; 866) there is a period of "mystagogia" or more complete introduction into the mysteries of faith (c. 789).

Catechumens are distinguished from other non-Catholics by their will to be incorporated into the Church. The Code does not explicitly spell out the relationship of other non-Catholics—not even baptized ones—to the Catholic Church. Technically, baptized non-Catholics who seek full communion with the Catholic Church are not catechumens or "converts," although they are moved by the Spirit and have an explicit will to join the Church. Their baptism is to be recognized (c. 869, §2), and they are eligible for sacramental participation in cases of grave necessity (c. 844)—something to which catechumens are not entitled since they are not yet baptized. In practice, these other Christians who seek full communion with the Church are often treated as catechumens, being provided with the same formation process; they are not, however, to be exorcised or to receive other elements of the liturgical rites involved in baptism, since they are already baptized. No greater burdens are to be imposed on them than are necessary for them to come into full communion.[41]

Catechumens are also distinguished from Catholics and other Christians by the fact that they are not baptized. This poses a special juridical question, for it is only through baptism that one becomes a member of the Christian faithful. How, then, are catechumens to be considered specially related to the Church? The Code adopts the Council's position and looks first to an inner element. Whereas canon 205 dropped a reference to the Spirit of Christ in favor of strictly visible criteria of communion, here the spiritual dimension ("under the influence of the Holy Spirit," "explicit choice") is given prominence along with a visible manner of living in conformity with Christian virtue.

Care of the Church

Cherishing them as already its own even though they are not fully incorporated through baptism, the Church shows a special concern for catechumens. They are invited to lead a life rooted in the gospels, a style of living that is a gift (grace) rather than an imposed discipline. Catechumens—and all Christians—are called fundamentally to discipleship; evangelical discipline is based on Christ's action through faith rather than the strictures of law (cf. Gal 2—5).

Catechumens are also gradually introduced into the liturgical life of the Church. The liturgy is the summit and source of the Church's life (SC 10). Christian initiation is more than an intellectual and behavioral formation; it is initiation into the mystery of the Church itself.

The Council (AG 14) called for the revised Code to spell out the prerogatives proper to Christians that catechumens may enjoy. The task of doing this for a worldwide Church in which even the meaning of "catechumen" may vary depending on culture and religious influences in society left the Code Commission with little choice but to refer further specifics to the various episcopal conferences (c. 788, §3). The revised Code (c. 1183, §1) does repeat its predecessor's permission of Christian burial for catechumens (CIC 1239, §2). It does not repeat the provisions of the Rite of Christian Initiation of Adults that permit catechumens to use the Catholic marriage rites (RCIA 18), but in virtue of canon 2 this prerogative remains in effect.

Pastorally the implementation of the revised Rite of Christian Initiation of Adults can lead to a renewal of parishes as they become welcoming communities for those who seek to join the Church. Frequently the process takes several years and can include all segments of the parish community. The danger of elitism—that tendency to restrict the Church to the select who evidence a greater personal commitment—must also be recognized. Catholic typology has allowed for considerable variety in the intensity of religious commitment among those in full communion, and the Code attempts to balance the concern for internal commitment with visible criteria common to all in terms of what is required for entrance into and for full communion in the Catholic Church.

Clergy, Laity, Religious

Canon 207 — §1. Among the Christian faithful by divine institution there exist in the Church sacred ministers, who are also called clerics in law, and other Christian faithful, who are also called laity.

§2. From both groups there exist Christian faithful who are consecrated to God in their own special manner and serve the salvific mission of the Church through the profession of the evangelical counsels by means of vows or other sacred bonds recognized and sanctioned by the Church. Although their state does not belong to the hierarchical structure of the Church, they nevertheless do belong to its life and holiness.

---

[41]See the principles expressed in the Foreword and Introduction to the Rite of Reception of Baptized Christians into Full Communion with the Catholic Church (Washington: USCC, 1976), 1–7.

The introductory canons on the Christian faithful conclude with the basic groupings of Christians within the Church. These are constituted by the hierarchical constitution of the Church (clergy-laity) and by the distinction of those who by public profession of the evangelical counsels have a distinct role in the life and holiness of the Church. These distinctions are rooted in centuries of tradition, but in recent years they have been the object of questioning in the Church. The revised Code attempts to reflect the nuances introduced by the Second Vatican Council and places in two distinct paragraphs ideas that formed a single sentence in the 1917 Code. The two paragraphs of this canon will be examined in turn.

Sacred Ministers and Laity

Paragraph one makes the following points. Sacred ministers are in the Church by divine institution, that is, it is through the will of Christ that ordained ministers are in the Church, and this distinguishes them from others in the Church. The traditional canonical terms for these two groups are "clergy" and "laity."

The significance of the canon is clearer when contrasted with the corresponding canon of the 1917 Code (*CIC* 107). Nearly all the corresponding words in the earlier canon are found in the revised one: "By divine institution there exist in the Church *clergy* distinct from *laity*" (emphasis in the original). The revised text, however, has some important nuances. Now the distinction is said to be based on sacred ministers—not on the canonically determined status of clergy and laity. Sacred ministers are said to be within ("among") the Christian faithful, i.e., the condition of being a member of the Christian faithful is common to both sacred ministers and the rest of the faithful.

Historical studies[42] have argued that the original distinction in the Church was based on orders—not on class or legal status (clergy-laity). The differentiation of sacred ministers from others does come from Christ, but its legal organization today is more a reflection of the pseudo-Dionysian ideal of *taxis* or perfect order in society, including the society of the Church. Everyone must belong to a certain rank or status, and all must be tightly, hierarchically organized. The attempt to implement this vision has marked medieval and even modern

Catholicism and was clearly expressed in the 1917 Code.

In that Code clergy constituted a special socioeconomic group whose standing was protected by special privileges and whose economic security was assured by canonical title.[43] A man entered this group or class by being tonsured. Tonsure was not an order but a rite by which one was set apart for sacred ministry and became a cleric,[44] just as persons in medieval Europe were designated for certain functions in society by belonging to the various classes or estates (peasantry, nobility, etc.). Only members of the clerical caste could hold office, obtain benefices or pensions in the Church, or exercise the power of ecclesiastical jurisdiction. Only tonsured clerics could be ordained and thus obtain the other power in the Church—that of orders.[45]

Underlying the 1917 Code is an understanding of the Church as composed of two fundamentally distinct and unequal groups—clergy and laity. Lay persons were supposed to support the work of the clergy, receive their ministrations, and obey their orders. In contrast to this passive role, clergy were responsible for church activities ranging from preaching and administering the sacraments, to the apostolate (in which some lay persons could cooperate under certain conditions), to control of church funds and property. The roots of such clerical domination are ancient and varied, ranging from reform efforts and practical necessity to defense of Church interests against the encroachments of lay investiture and state domination. What is significant is that after centuries of attempting to implement such a system, the magisterium at the Second Vatican Council rejected such institutional clericalism and sought to locate sacred ministry within the people of God and the common condition of all the Christian faithful.

The Council affirmed the divinely given nature of sacred ministry. In this sense, the people do not constitute ministers in the Church; Christ does (*LG* 32). The purpose of sacred ministry, however, is service and unity (*LG* 18). Although distinct, ministers and the rest of the Christian faithful are complementary (*LG* 32). The ministers do not take away from the role of the lay persons but are meant to support and promote their role. Other members of the Christian faithful are not to usurp the proper work of sacred ministers, yet they are not by this fact excluded from full participation in the life and work of the Church. The mutual interaction of ministers and people is needed for the Church to accomplish its mission, for all participate in their own way in the saving mission Christ entrusted to the Church. The ministerial and common priesthoods differ in essence and not just degree in their

---

[42]See Y. Congar, *Ministères et communion ecclesiale* (Paris: Cerf, 1971); B. Cooke, *Ministry to Word and Sacraments: History and Theology* (Philadelphia: Fortress Press, 1976); A. Faivre, *Naissance d'une hierarchie. Les premières ètapes du cursus clerical* (Paris: Beauchesne, 1977); J. Fornes, *La nocion de 'status' en derecho canonico* (Pamplona: EUNSA, 1975); B. Marlianges, *Clès pour une théologie du ministère: In persona Christi, In persona Ecclesiae* (Paris: Beauchesne, 1978); E. Nardoni, "Ministries in the New Testament," *Stud Can* 11 (1977), 5–36.

[43]See *CIC* 118–123; 974, §4, 7°; 979–982.
[44]Ibid., 108, §1; 950.
[45]Ibid., 118.

participation in Christ's priesthood, but both are called to mutual effort in the work of the Church (*LG* 10).

Post-conciliar legislation now incorporated in the Code had already implemented key elements of the Council's position. Entrance into the clerical state is by ordination to sacred ministry beginning with the diaconate; it is no longer by tonsure (c. 266, §1). Minor orders have been eliminated, emphasizing in the Latin Church that sacramental ordination as deacon, presbyter, or bishop constitutes one a sacred minister (cc. 1008–1009). Other services may be provided by lay persons—even through permanent installation in those ministries—but this neither makes them sacred ministers nor brings them into a distinct class (c. 230).

It took several efforts for the Code Commission to develop a legal expression of this more balanced position. The 1971 *Lex Ecclesiae Fundamentalis* and 1977 schema *De Populo Dei* based the distinction on the divine institution of the Church. This was later rejected, being replaced in the 1976 *Lex Ecclesiae Fundamentalis* and the 1980 schema by a distinction based on the divine institution of sacred ministers. The 1980 *Lex Ecclesiae Fundamentalis* made it even more explicit that some faithful are ordained and thus constituted sacred ministers distinct from the rest. The final text locates sacred ministers within the people of God as themselves being Christian faithful; therefore, it attempts to express more clearly the Council's view that the distinction is not meant to separate Christians but to lead to closer cooperation and unity within the Church.

It is important to recognize that the 1983 Code affirms that "clergy" is an ecclesiastical law condition for the ordained. It can be lost even though orders are never lost (orders is a "character" sacrament—cf. c. 1008). The purpose of the special legal regulations on the rights, duties, ministerial activities, and private lives of clergy is to promote their ministry of service to all the people of God. The legal status of cleric can be lost (c. 290); yet, the ordained never lose the effects of ordination, and priests who have lost clerical status may still perform certain sacramental functions (e.g., absolution in danger of death—cf. c. 976). Certain legal effects also remain for those who lose their clerical status, even though they are no longer held to clerical obligations (c. 292). For example, a dispensed priest is restricted in activities open to other lay persons; therefore, he has not really regained full lay status in the Church either (see below at c. 229 for an example of these restrictions).

Basis of Difference

In addition to locating sacred ministers within the Christian faithful and emphasizing the divine institution of sacred ministry, the canon makes it clear that "clergy" is a condition based on ecclesiastical law. That is, the *juridical* status of sacred ministers is not necessarily divinely given but is determined in church law and is changeable (as indeed it has been changed in several respects by this Code). On the other hand, the very *existence* of sacred ministers in the Church, whatever their canonical rights and duties, is something divinely given as a permanent element of the Church's constitution.

Beyond this the canon does not go. It attempts neither to define what pertains essentially to clergy or to laity nor to specify further in what they differ. The issue has been the subject of much discussion—even at the Council. Indeed, the Council finally adopted only a typological description of clergy and laity, rather than a strict definition. It described what clergy and laity typically do today. There have been efforts to turn this typological description into an ontological definition, as if this were how clergy and laity ought necessarily to be;[46] however, such efforts break down when faced with overriding pastoral necessities.[47]

The difference, for example, could be placed in the secular character of the lay person ("in the world") and the ecclesial nature of sacred ministers. Yet while sacred ministers are obliged to avoid those activities alien or incompatible with their state (c. 285), the Council admits that they may exercise secular professions and teaches a responsibility of lay persons to act in the Church as well as in the world (*LG* 31).

The difference might also be located in the priesthood, for the priesthood of the ordained differs in essence (or "kind") and not just in degree from that of the common priesthood. Deacons, however, are not ordained unto priesthood but service (*LG* 29) and nevertheless are sacred ministers (c. 1009, §1). Moreover, both the ministerial and the common priesthoods share in the one priesthood of Christ (*LG* 10). It is not priesthood itself that constitutes the difference but something else that differentiates their participation in Christ's priesthood.

The distinction between sacred ministers and lay persons could be sought in their participation in the threefold functions (*munera*) of Christ. The ordained act in the person of Christ as they teach, sanctify, and rule within the people of God (*LG* 32). Such action is not merely an extension of what all are called to do in virtue of baptism—by which each Christian shares in the threefold functions; rather, it is a qualitatively different sharing done on behalf of all in the Church. Yet this distinction could be considered a functional rather than an ontological one, for lay persons can cooperate in this

---

[46]For examples of these positions, see M. Kaiser, "Die Kirchenglieder," *Grundriss*, 120.

[47]See J. Komonchak, "Clergy, Laity, and the Church's Mission in the World," *J* 41 (1981), 422–447. See also discussion below, at c. 228.

service to the rest in the Church and in many instances replace sacred ministers when these are lacking.

This last issue was the object of intense debate in the course of drafting the revised Code, continuing the conciliar debate on the source of power in the Church and whether jurisdiction is a distinct power with a separate source from ordination.[48] The position adopted in the Code (c. 129) does not really solve the theoretical issue, for it is not clear what is meant by lay persons being able to "cooperate" in the power of governance, at least insofar as this affects the specific difference between sacred ministers and the laity.

Perhaps more to the point is the conciliar focus not on the difference but on the interrelationship of sacred ministers and lay persons. The Code has not attempted to go beyond stating the distinction here, and in keeping with the conciliar purpose it proposes elsewhere various ways that the cooperation of all in the Church can promote the accomplishment of Christ's mission.[49]

Consecrated Life

Some sacred ministers and lay persons consecrate themselves in a special way to God and contribute thereby to the saving mission of the Church. They do this by a public profession, recognized and sanctioned by the Church, of the evangelical counsels of chastity, poverty, and obedience. If they are members of religious institutes, this consecration takes the form of public vows (c. 607, §2). Vows or other bonds determined by their statutes are taken by members of secular institutes (c. 712) and some societies of apostolic life (c. 731, §2). Those who make this consecration do acquire a new standing in the Church, but it is one that pertains to the life and holiness of the Church rather than to its hierarchical structure.

Several elements of this second paragraph are noteworthy. First, the terminology has changed from the 1917 Code, which spoke of "religious." No special label is attached to these Christians; rather, there is a description of who they are. Those who make their consecration in recognized institutes form the paradigm for the rest but do not exhaust the possibilities for such consecrated life (cc. 603–605).

Second, the canon adopts the conciliar approach to the question of the place of religious in the structures of the Church. Considered in terms of its hierarchical element, those who make a special consecration of their lives do not form a third state between clergy and laity (LG 43). Viewed from the nature of the Church as a community of holiness and mission, however, they do have a distinct place (LG 44).

What is this status? Common usage refers to clergy, religious, and laity, and the Code Commission stated it did not intend to change this.[50] The 1917 and 1983 Codes are consistent in this treatment: many of the canons on obligations and rights of clergy are extended to lay persons who live a consecrated life in religious institutes, and special obligations and rights are also applied to them (cc. 662–672). In practice they do form a distinct juridical status in the Church.[51]

The basis of this status lies not in the Church's hierarchical structure but in the more complex mystery of the Church itself which combines human and divine elements, hierarchical structure and charisms. Vatican II recaptured the importance of charisms for the mission of the Church (LG 12, AA 3). Institutes of consecrated life are called to respect the spirit of their founders and the graces specific to them (PC 2, c. 577) and have traditionally provided a structure to institutionalize charisms in the Catholic Church. Their corporate and individual witness to evangelical life establishes them in a unique role within the church community. Consecrated life is not an individualistic movement but an intense participation in the spiritual mission of the Church itself; hence, it deserves the special status it enjoys.

Canon 207 concentrates on the verifiable, external elements that constitute consecrated life: profession of the counsels in a form recognized and sanctioned by the Church. These elements, however, must be understood in the context of their conciliar setting—which added the significant interior dimension of a divine call. Greater consideration to the interior element is given when the Code addresses consecrated life in more detail (cc. 573–574). This fact is an important reminder that the canons of this introductory section in Book II provide a valuable synthesis of canonical tradition and conciliar teaching, but it is a synthesis that needs to be placed in broader context to achieve a proper understanding of the law.

Distinctions of clergy, laity, and religious, as well

---

[48] A report on the state of the question together with an extensive bibliography was prepared for the 1981 Code Commission meeting and has been published. See J. Beyer, "De natura potestatis regiminis seu iurisdictionis recte in Codice renovato enuntianda," *P* 71 (1982), 93–145. The Commission adopted the position advocated by Beyer, but the final text evidences some hesitation. For another approach to the issue, see E. Kilmartin, "Lay Participation in the Apostolate of the Hierarchy," *J* 41 (1981), 343–370.

[49] See, for example, cc. 209; 212; 228; 275; 394; 529; 756–759; 835; 843, §2. One conference of bishops did propose to highlight the cooperation of clergy and laity in communion, but after debating the merits of the proposal in a seemingly favorable light, the *coetus* on *De Populo Dei* did not adopt the proposed change. See *Comm* 14 (1982), 29–31.

[50] See *Rel,* 51.

[51] While not bound to all the obligations of members of religious institutes, others who live a consecrated life do receive special attention in terms of obligations and rights; see cc. 718–719 and 723, §4 for secular institutes, c. 737 for members of societies of apostolic life.

as questions of membership and communion are placed in a new setting by this Code. It will take time and patient effort to implement the spirit of these canons and to respect the subtle but substantial changes they imply for Catholic practice. A first and most striking consequence is the increased importance given the fundamental equality of all the Christian faithful and the rights and obligations they share in common. It is to these that the Code and this commentary next turn.

TITLE I
THE OBLIGATIONS AND RIGHTS OF ALL THE CHRISTIAN FAITHFUL
[cc. 208–223]

In promulgating the revised Code, Pope John Paul II identified various reasons for canon law in the Church. Among these he listed safeguarding and defining the rights of each person in the Church.[52] A remarkable feature of papal teaching in the twentieth century has been its concern for the rights of persons,[53] and the application of this concern internal to the Church resonates well with the sensitivities of people today. Such a concern for the rights of all within the Church's legal system has not always been a principal concern of canon law, even though the law has provided for the protection of individual rights in many ways. To appreciate the significance of this new title in the Code, several preliminary comments are in order. They will be arranged in the following manner: (1) the history of the development of the Code's listing of rights for all the Christian faithful; (2) the various statements of obligations and rights in the revised Code; (3) approaches to interpreting rights in the Church; and (4) application of these statements to Catholics and others.

Developing the List

The 1917 Code did indicate that baptism constituted one a person in the Church with all the rights and duties proper to Christians. It did not list what these rights and duties might be, however, except in a passing reference that lay persons were not to be denied the sacraments without cause (*CIC* 682).[54] Rather, that Code concentrated on the rights and duties of certain special groups within the Church, particularly clerics (*CIC* 118–144), religious (*CIC* 592–631), and various officeholders ranging from pastors to cardinals. Intermingled with rights and duties were lists of privileges, a fact that may be a

clue to understanding how the 1917 Code viewed rights as such. Under an absolutist monarchical system of government, rights were considered a concession of the sovereign, and in that sense they were privileges granted to certain persons but not to others. Nineteenth-century political theory recognized other understandings of rights, including rights as based in one's social class rather than in the individual as such. The canonical tradition reflects the experience of the Church in the nineteenth century, warding off the encroachments of liberalism and the *Risorgimento* that deprived the pope of his temporal domain even as it unified the country of Italy. Under such circumstances it would not be unusual to find the law more congenial to theories of rights that resonated with the *ancien régime*.

By the time the Code was promulgated in 1917, the magisterium had already begun to adopt a different view of rights—one based on the dignity of the human person. The dichotomy between church teaching on human rights in society and the provisions of church law did not at first raise serious problems for canonists. The Church is a unique society; thus, it was not at all clear that "subjective rights," as they were termed, pertained to individuals in the Church. The debate even occasioned a major congress on canon law, but the results were inconclusive as far as canonical practice was concerned.[55]

The experience of the Second World War and the subsequent heightened awareness of human rights based on the dignity of persons affected civil society and church leaders alike. The magisterium spoke out forcefully in defense of human rights and in the promotion of human dignity. As Vatican II dawned, voices in the Church were calling for consistency in church teaching and the recognition of rights internal to the Church—based on human dignity and the dignity that comes with regeneration in baptism.

Impact of Vatican II

The Council shifted some basic perspectives that affect the appreciation of rights. The basic paradigm of the Church as a sovereign state, i.e., the paradigm on which the 1917 Code was based, was shifted to a more biblical and theological understanding of the Church as the people of God. All the Christian faithful participate actively in the communion and mission of the Church and based on their baptismal dignity share a common concern for building up the body of Christ (*LG* 32). This equality in dignity and action precedes any differentiation in terms of function and standing in the Church and provides a newly understood basis for addressing fundamental rights in the Church.

---

[52]See John Paul II, *Sacrae disciplinae leges*, xiii.

[53]See D. Hollenbach, *Claims in Conflict. Retrieving and Renewing the Catholic Human Rights Tradition* (New York: Paulist Press, 1979).

[54]Other rights were also guaranteed indirectly. See R. Kennedy, "Canonical Tradition and Christian Rights," in *The Case for Freedom*, J. Coriden, ed. (Washington: Corpus, 1969), 91–106.

[55]See *Acta Congressus Internationalis Iuris Canonici 1950* (Rome: Catholic Book Agency, 1953).

The Council placed the action of Christ as central to the Church. The right and duty of lay persons to the apostolate, for example, are said to arise from their union with Christ (*AA* 3); this is hardly a privilege or concession by ecclesiastical authorities. Christ is also central to the understanding of clergy, who as sacred ministers are transformed by Christ into servants for all in the Church (*LG* 32). While the canonical determination of how duties are to be carried out and what rights are to be enforceable in church law is made by ecclesiastical authority, the foundation for such rights and duties lies deeper than the canonical ordering itself.

Immediately after the Council there were various proposals for a listing of rights in the Church. Some turned to recognized statements of human rights, such as the United Nations' Universal Declaration of Human Rights (1948), and analyzed the Council's documents to see how these rights are found within the Church as well.[56] Others used the conciliar statements directly, developing lists of rights as these were mentioned here and there throughout the various texts.[57] Still others developed their own lists, frequently based on issues of more immediate concern to the authors or to those on behalf of whom they expressed more direct concern.[58]

This latter experience is an important reminder that any listing of rights that has been developed in modern times bears the marks of its historical setting. Those listed in the Declaration of Independence or Bill of Rights of the United States Constitution, or the Rights of Man proclaimed by the French Revolution, very clearly evidence the immediate concerns of those who drew them up. The same is true of the Universal Declaration from the United Nations or, for that matter, of the rights expressed by the Second Vatican Council. None is a comprehensive, exhaustive list of rights; all address real issues of the times but are therefore limited and dated expressions. The same will be true of the listing in the revised Code.

Drafting the List

Protection or respect for rights is listed in four of the ten principles for the revision of the Code.[59] The

first principle, on the juridic nature of the Code, indicates that it should define and protect the rights and obligations of each person toward others and toward society. The next, which looks to fostering pastoral care in the Code, calls for the rights and duties that come within the juridic organization of the Church to be suited to its supernatural end. Canonical norms, therefore, should neither restrict rights nor impose duties unless these are truly necessary for the public good and ecclesiastical discipline. The sixth principle directly addresses the protection of the rights of persons based on the natural law and divine positive law and on what follows in light of the social condition that persons have in the Church. Moreover, this principle calls for the expression of a common juridic status for all in the Church based on their human dignity and the reception of baptism. Finally, the seventh principle looks to procedure for safeguarding and vindicating subjective rights in the Church, eliminating any suspicion of arbitrariness in ecclesiastical administration.

Applying these principles to the practical task of drafting canons proved to be somewhat difficult. Two *coetus* undertook the task independently. Both came up with lists of rights and duties, often mingling rights and duties in the same canon. The *coetus* on the laity and associations of the faithful developed a list of rights and duties common to all the faithful before developing a list applicable specifically to lay persons.[60] This work was taken over into the 1977 schema *De Populo Dei,* canons 16–38.

This *coetus* adopted a sophisticated organization for listing rights and duties in the Church and those the Church proclaims for Christians in the world. Inner church rights and duties were distributed according to a theological system. Rights and duties of communion came first, and those related to the three functions of teaching, sanctifying, and ruling followed. A series of rights relative to one's person was included as was a creative approach to the protection of rights that included redress against administrative excess, a listing of key procedural rights, and provision for legality of penalties. Rights and duties in the world focused on the promotion of human rights and of justice and peace in keeping with the Church's teaching.

The *coetus* on the *Lex Ecclesiae Fundamentalis* also developed a list of obligations and rights. The

---

[56]See J. Beyer, "De iuribus humanis fundamentalibus in statuto iuridico christifidelium assumendis," *P* 58 (1969), 29–58.

[57]The most systematic effort along this line is J. Beyer, "De statuto iuridico christifidelium iuxta vota synodi episcoporum in novo codice iuris canonici condendo," *P* 57 (1968), 550–581. See also P. Viladrich, *Teoria de los derechos fundamentales del fiel. Presupuestos criticos* (Pamplona: EUNSA, 1969); A. del Portillo, *Faithful and Laity in the Church* (Shannon, Ireland: Ecclesia, 1972); J. Kinney, *The Juridic Condition of the People of God* (Rome: Catholic Book Agency, 1972).

[58]See "Toward a Declaration of Christian Rights," in *The Case for Freedom,* 5–14; P. Hinder, *Grundrechte in der Kirche* (Freiburg, Switzerland: Universitätsverlag, 1977); *Le manifeste de la liberté chrètienne,* G. Bessiere, ed. (Paris: Seuil, 1976).

[59]See *Comm* 1 (1969), 79–83.

[60]See report in *Comm* 6 (1974), 50–51. It is significant that this *coetus* undertook such a task, for many of the rights now stated in the Code for all the Christian faithful are found in the documents of Vatican II in specific application to lay persons. Two major breakthroughs have occurred. One is the distinction between *Christifideles* and *laici* (i.e., "faithful" includes more than "lay persons"). The second is a recognition that rights long taken for granted relative to clergy and religious are shared in common with lay persons and can therefore be considered part of the common juridic condition of all the Christian faithful.

organization of the list has undergone various changes as the different drafts were developed.[61] The 1979 meeting of the special *coetus* to revise the schema *De Populo Dei* eventually recommended that the *Lex Ecclesiae Fundamentalis* version be adopted (since it then appeared that the *LEF* would be promulgated separately) and that the listing of rights and duties in Book II be dropped in order to avoid duplication. Suggestions were made for modifying the *Lex Ecclesiae Fundamentalis* version of some canons to benefit from elements only the *De Populo Dei* listing had included, although the promulgated version does not seem to reflect many of these.[62] In 1981, when it was decided not to promulgate the *Lex Ecclesiae Fundamentalis,* the canons on rights and duties were returned to Book II, but this time based on the *Lex Ecclesiae Fundamentalis* listing.

Statements in the Code

The Code contains various lists of rights and duties. The listing of those common to all Christian faithful (cc. 208–223) is basically the organization and content of the 1980 *Lex Ecclesiae Fundamentalis* with some additions based on the *De Populo Dei* list (cc. 209; 220, §2; 222, §2). The list seems to have the following organization. First come four statements relative to the basic equality of Christians—equality, communion, universal call to holiness, and participation in the mission of the Church (cc. 208–211). Next are obligations and rights that arise from the hierarchical differentiation in the Church—obedience, petition, and public opinion (c. 212). The means of sanctification are addressed, including the rights to spiritual goods, to worship according to an approved rite, and to a personal spirituality in keeping with church teaching (cc. 213–214). Four statements relative to the mission of the Church follow—rights to association and assembly, apostolic works, education, and freedom of inquiry and expression in sacred studies (cc. 215–218). Personal rights are listed—freedom from coercion in choosing a state in life, good name, and privacy (cc. 219–220). One canon lists three basic protections of rights—vindication of rights, due process in court, and legality of penalties (c. 221). Finally certain social relationships are specified—support for the Church, promotion of justice, aid to the poor, respect for the common good, and limitations on rights in virtue of the common good (cc. 222–223).

Rights specific to various groups in the Church are also listed. For lay persons, canons 225–231 list seven obligations and rights as well as six capacities recognized in law. The obligations and rights con-

cern participating in the mission of the Church, the vocation of married persons, duties of parents, Christian education, higher theological education, formation for church service, and a just family wage and benefits when employed in church service. Capacities relate to the functions of teaching (a mandate to teach theology), of sanctifying (installed ministries, temporary deputation for liturgical service, and supplying for services of ministers), and of ruling (assignment to church office, service as consultants). Lay persons are explicitly acknowledged to enjoy the obligations and rights of all Christian faithful; this list is considered a further specification in light of their situation in life (c. 224).

These first two lists are new in canon law. They have been developed in light of the teaching of the Council and represent an important new dimension for the canonical tradition. More in line with existing tradition are the next series of lists.

The obligations and rights of clergy are more simplified than in the 1917 Code: the privileges in the former Code have been dropped and several obligations have been revised in light of conciliar teaching or current conditions. Canons 273–289 list five obligations relating to the hierarchical structure of which the cleric is a part, eleven obligations and rights related to his personal development and manner of living, and six obligations and prohibitions affecting his involvement in the world.[63]

The obligations and rights of religious institutes and their members are set forth in canons 662–672. Three statements relate to the pursuit of holiness, six concern the living of religious life, and two address activities that are permissible or prohibited to religious.[64]

The Code contains other lists of rights, including

---

[61]For the final results of the *coetus* work, see *Comm* 12 (1980), 35–44.
[62]See *Comm* 12 (1980), 77–91.

[63]Obligations related to hierarchical structure include reverence and obedience to pope and one's own ordinary; holding of offices requiring power of orders or ecclesiastical governance; accepting and fulfilling an office assigned by an ordinary; a bond of fraternity and cooperation with other clerics; a respect for the role of lay persons. Among the obligations and rights related to personal development and living are the pursuit of holiness; continence and celibacy; association; continuing education; common life; remuneration and benefits; simplicity of life; support for the Church from surplus; residence in diocese; vacation; ecclesiastical garb. Obligations and prohibitions related to involvement in the world encompass prohibited activities; prohibited businesses; promotion of justice and peace; restrictions on political and labor union activities; restriction on volunteering for military service; encouragement to use civil law exemptions.
[64]Among the obligations related to personal holiness are the duties to follow Christ; engage in contemplation; pursue various spiritual and liturgical activities; examine one's conscience and use the sacrament of penance. Obligations and rights related to religious life take in such matters as common life in a religious house; ownership and disposition of personal goods; religious garb; support from the institute. Activities that are permissible or prohibited include the permission to accept a position outside the works of the institute and the prohibitions that apply to clergy in their dealings with the world.

procedural rights (throughout Book VII), rights attached to various offices, and rights inherent in various consultative bodies that must be consulted or even give their consent in accord with provisions in the law (c. 127). A new feature of this Code is a consistent effort to support the obligations and rights of parents. Over twenty canons in various parts of the Code spell out what might be called a bill of parental rights; these will be discussed below at canon 226, §2.

Interpreting Rights

The proper interpretation of these various obligations and rights is not as simple as might first appear. Not unlike the 1917 Code, various terms are used for what might be called "rights," but the nuances in the Latin must be respected for an accurate interpretation. For example, *ius, integrum est, fas est, facultas, potestas,* can each be taken as a right in some sense, as can verbal forms such as *licet* and *possunt.*[65] The proper nuance can only be explored properly in discussing specific canons.

On a broader scale, the basic understanding of rights has become more complicated than the medieval philosophers' approach. For them *ius* could be understood in three dimensions. Objectively it stood for what is just, what must be or can be demanded. The efficient sense referred *ius* to a law or a norm for action. In a subjective meaning, *ius* meant an inviolable moral faculty of doing, omitting, or demanding something.[66]

By the eighteenth century various notions of rights had emerged to explain how the subjective, objective, and efficient meanings of *ius* related to each other. These ranged from natural, to moral, to human rights theories. Fundamental rights were proposed as existing even if the law (the "efficient" *ius*) did not recognize them, and they served as a sort of meta-legal concept that could be used to critique legal systems themselves (as at the Nüremberg trials after World War II).

Subjective rights can be given further classifications based on the distinction between public law and private law. Authors approach the distinction variously, but in general it was held that rights are what a person enjoys in public law where society's interests are at stake. In private law, where individuals' interests are involved, it may be more a question of interests as such rather than rights.[67]

Today three traditions surrounding rights prevail in general usage. These will have a more direct impact on the understanding of the lists of rights in the revised Code. For example, in line with the United States Bill of Rights or the French Declaration of the Rights of Man, rights can be understood as a sphere of free choice in which one is at liberty to act or not. To organize or join an association (c. 215), for instance, is a right that one may choose to exercise or not.

Another approach is to consider rights as entitlements. The individual is not an isolated actor but a member of society; to exercise true liberty may require that society supply for deficiencies in the individual's resources. This approach underlies the United Nations' Universal Declaration of Human Rights and may be found in the canonical right to receive assistance from the sacred pastors out of the spiritual goods of the Church, especially the word and sacraments (c. 213).

A third approach to rights emphasizes the social responsibility that is integral to a right. Rights are not merely claims one can make for isolated freedoms; neither are they only entitlements that one can demand from society. They entail an interaction between individual and society, located in the concept of the common good. The common good is not the sum total of the good of isolated individuals. Rather, the common good is the "sum of those conditions of social life by which individuals, families, and groups can achieve their own fulfillment in a relatively thorough and ready way."[68] This approach is clearly found in the Code (c. 223), although it is applied specifically to the exercise of rights and not to their nature as such.

Obligations and Rights

The headings in the revised Code consistently use the ordering of obligations and rights, whereas the 1917 Code tended to use the reverse—rights and obligations. In some canons that repeat the 1917 Code (e.g., c. 96) the order has clearly been changed—from rights and duties to duties and rights. When queried about the significance of this change, the Code Commission responded that the ordering is not significant, since both rights and obligations come from the sacraments.[69]

This response is significant, for there were some who argued that the theory of rights to be adopted in drafting the Code should be that one's state in life determines the obligations to which one is bound. In order to carry out those obligations, one has corresponding rights. Thus rights will vary depending on one's condition or state in life.[70] While

[65]See P. Ciprotti, "De vocabulorum usu ad ius subiectivum designandum in Codice Iuris Canonici," *Acta Congressus 1950,* 57–61. It will be important to do a similar study on the terms employed in the 1983 Code.

[66]See A. Ottaviani, *Institutiones Iuris Publici Ecclesiastici,* 2 vols., 4th ed. (Vatican City: Typis Polyglottis Vaticanis, 1958), I: 1.

[67]A concise review of these concepts is given by S. Benn, s.v. "Rights," *Encyclopedia of Philosophy* 7, 196–199.

[68]*GS* 74.

[69]See *Rel,* 62.

[70]See, for example, the studies by Hinder and del Portillo cited above, and C. Leitmaier, *Der Katholik und sein Recht in der Kirche. Kritisch-konservative Überlegungen* (Vienna: Herder, 1971).

this approach contains a significant point, for some rights do flow from obligations, it is not accurate when taken as the exclusive understanding of rights. The Church has recognized human nature and the common dignity flowing from it as the bases for fundamental human rights, and within the Church baptism produces other fundamental rights that are prior to any differentiation by states in life.[71]

Rights, on the other hand, give rise to obligations. When the common good calls for one to exercise a right, there is an obligation to do so. Similarly, one person's right produces a corresponding obligation in others to respect that right. Moreover, when one has an obligation to provide something for others, those others have a right to that service. Thus when the Code requires sacred ministers to preach (c. 767) or to provide the sacraments to those who seek them properly (c. 843), it is only expressing the reverse of the right to word and sacrament that is common to all the faithful (c. 213). Or when the Code requires pastors to provide pastoral care (cc. 528–529), bishops to be concerned for the welfare of all the people in their diocese (c. 383), or judges to render judgment (cc. 1453, 1457), it is by that fact assuring a right to those who are entitled to receive that pastoral care, concern, or judgment.

Systems of Interpretation

The common good always regulates the exercise of rights. Rights in this sense are not absolute but relative, for their exercise must respect the rights of others and the conditions needed for all to achieve their fulfillment. This limitation on the exercise of rights is expressed variously in diverse legal systems—systems that are different because of their way of determining how the law is ultimately to be interpreted.

In a system of judicial supremacy, such as exists in the United States, the courts have the final word in determining the meaning of a law or the legitimate exercise of a right. The expression of rights, therefore, can be somewhat brief and to the point. The necessary precautions that regulate their exercise can either be found in other laws or, more likely, in the system of jurisprudence that surrounds the exercise of rights in that society.

In a system of legislative supremacy, on the other hand, such as exists in some other countries and that prevails in the Church, it is the legislator who determines the meaning of the law. The courts are to apply the law in the sense that the legislator determines. In such a system when it is not clear what a law means or how a right may be exercised, recourse is to be taken not to the courts but to the legislator for an interpretation. Others can be designated by the legislator to provide this interpretation. Another possibility is to build into the expression of the law itself the terms of its interpretation.

In an expression of rights, for example, the necessary qualifications to govern this exercise can be found in the system of the courts, or it may be placed in the very wording of the law. Practical examples of such expression of interpretative terms will be found in several canons on the rights common to all the faithful.

One of the most frequently mentioned qualifiers in the Code is "condition." The meaning of this term is not always clear from the context. It could be used to refer to one's state in life in keeping with the theory discussed earlier, by which some proposed to locate the rights of a Christian in his or her state in life rather than in human or baptismal dignity. In such a context, "condition" would be an essential limitation on rights; a person would have the right in question only to the extent that one's condition (the duties of one's state in life) required it.

As indicated, the Code is not to be interpreted in light of such a theory. Instead, it remains within the position taught by Vatican II that rights inhere in the human person (*GS* 29) and, in the Church, also arise from baptism (see discussion on c. 204, above). Determining the meaning of "condition" becomes more complex.

Vatican II used the term at least one hundred ninety-six times. At least sixty percent of the time, it referred to external conditions of time, place, or conditions in the situation. The term was also used with about equal frequency when it related to one's personal abilities or infirmities, a person's social status, the "human condition," the condition of the Church itself, or preconditions for something else to happen. Less frequently it was used to differentiate the condition of Christians from non-Christians, and four times it referred to one's condition or state within the church structure (clergy, religious, laity).

The conciliar usage does not canonize any particular meaning of condition, leaving the possibilities open—depending on the context in which the term is used. Something similar may be said of the Code which is intended to implement the Council.

There is, however, another possible meaning of condition that may be added to the above, that is, the condition of a person who has been graced with a charism. The Council indicated such gifts are the basis for obligations and rights in the Church and in the world (*AA* 3). This is one right within the Church that was considered for inclusion in the

---

[71]Rights that arise from obligations are really "functional" rights—not fundamental or subjective; see H. Coing, "Signification de la notion de droit subjectif," *Archives de philosophie de droit* 9 (1964), 1–15. *DH* 10 and *GS* 26 and 62 present the dignity of the human person as the basis for rights.

Code but is not stated there expressly. Members of *Lex Ecclesiae Fundamentalis coetus* voted to include a statement on the obligations and rights that come from charisms, but they wished to locate it in a theological preamble that was planned for the final document.[72] The *Lex Ecclesiae Fundamentalis* was not promulgated separately, the theological preamble has not appeared; therefore, no expression of this right is found in the revised Code.

However, a charism can be considered to be a condition in which a person is placed by the Holy Spirit. It is a gift given not primarily for the benefit of the individual but for the sake of others. A person in such a condition may have an obligation or be bound to exercise a right more intensely in virtue of the charism received. Final determination of this fact, of course, rests with the pastors of the Church who are to test the true nature of charisms and see to their proper use—not in order to extinguish the Spirit but to test all things and hold to what is good (*AA* 3).

Catholics or All Christians

The fundamental obligations and rights listed in the Code arise variously from human nature, baptism, and positive church law. To what extent are these rights enjoyed in the Church by all the baptized and indeed, insofar as they are human rights, by all humans? An objection to the wording of canon 204 has already been noted, namely, that in itself it includes all the baptized and not just those in full communion with the Catholic Church. In its response, the Code Commission admitted the broad meaning of "Christian faithful" but claimed that in the Code it always means Catholics since this is, after all, the Code for the Catholic Church, and non-Catholics are not bound by merely ecclesiastical laws (c. 11).[73]

The response, however, seems too facile when it comes to such a basic question as rights. Those rights that are expressed in the Code and that arise from human nature—for example, association and assembly (c. 215), freedom of inquiry and expression in the sacred sciences (c. 218), freedom from coercion in choosing a state in life (c. 219), reputation and privacy (c. 220), vindication of rights in the proper forum and due process of law when using the courts (c. 221), and respect for the common good (c. 223, §1)—are not granted by the law. They preexist the law, for they arise from human nature.

Similarly, rights that arise from baptism preexist the law, for they are given not by the legislator but by Christ who acts in the sacrament. The Church can regulate the exercise of those rights, but their existence is given by the Lord. Such, for example,

seem to be the obligations and rights to holiness of life (c. 210), participation in spreading the gospel (c. 211), receiving spiritual help—especially the word and sacraments (c. 213), initiating and promoting apostolic action (c. 216), and Christian education (c. 217).

Certain obligations and rights are clearly rooted in full communion. These pertain to Catholics specifically; for example, the obligations and rights to preserve communion (c. 209), to obey the sacred pastors and participate in the flow of information in the Church (c. 212), to receive the sacraments without restriction when properly disposed (c. 213), to worship God according to an approved rite and pursue a spirituality in keeping with church teaching (c. 214), to engage in the apostolate as a Catholic (c. 216), to legality of church penalties (c. 222, §3), and to be regulated in the exercise of one's rights by church authorities (c. 223, §2).

This is not to claim that non-baptized or even baptized non-Catholics can claim full exercise of rights in the Catholic Church with regard to those matters that arise from human dignity or baptism. The common good of the Church may call for limitations to be imposed. On the other hand, there are times when the Code expressly permits others to exercise certain rights within the Catholic community. For example, anyone—baptized or not—may present a case before a church court (c. 1476), and the object of such a petition may properly be the vindication of rights (c. 1400, §1, 1°). Under certain circumstances, non-Catholic Christians may be admitted to the sacraments of penance, Eucharist, and anointing (c. 844). The preaching of the word is not restricted to Catholic audiences (Book III).

In effect, the Code distinguishes obligations that the Church will enforce only on Catholics (c. 11) and rights that may or may not be able to be exercised in the Church by non-Catholics, depending on the requirements of the common good. In the following discussion on individual obligations and rights common to all the faithful, attention will be focused on Catholics. But this wider application should also be kept in mind where appropriate.

Fundamental Equality

Canon 208 — **In virtue of their rebirth in Christ there exists among all the Christian faithful a true equality with regard to dignity and the activity whereby all cooperate in the building up of the Body of Christ in accord with each one's own condition and function.**

In virtue of baptism there exists a true equality among all Christians. Reborn in Christ, they share a common dignity as children of God. They also have a common responsibility for building up the body of Christ although they carry out that task in

[72]See *Comm* 12 (1980), 43–44.
[73]See *Rel,* 50.

keeping with personal abilities and in light of each one's respective functions.

The canon attempts to reconcile the theological reality of equality in virtue of baptism with the observable fact that people differ in their capacities and involvement in the life of the Church—and indeed in their role in society at large. Children clearly do not carry out the responsibility to build up the body of Christ in the same way that adults do; those who live in areas where the gospel is not known have a different challenge from Christians in already evangelized settings; people who speak publicly for the Church have a different way of carrying out the common task from those not in this limelight. Yet the task is common—to build up the body of Christ; the dignity each shares in virtue of baptism is also common, regardless of other offices and dignities one may have in the Church or civil society.

Vatican II

The source for this canon is *Lumen Gentium* 32. Addressing the relationship of sacred ministers and lay persons, the Council attempted to express both the creative dynamic that exists in their common dignity and responsibility arising from baptism and the differentiation the Lord has placed in the Church by establishing some as sacred ministers. The *coetus* drafting the *Lex Ecclesiae Fundamentalis,* from which this canon is taken, sought to simplify the conciliar language in keeping with the style of a legal Code. This same *coetus* was also concerned to avoid the misunderstanding that claimed there is a democratic-style equality in the Church, as if there were no distinction among the Christian faithful.[74] This was attempted by adding two clauses to the Council's statement and by rearranging the order of the words.

The additions to *Lumen Gentium* 32 are the reference to baptism ("in virtue of their rebirth in Christ") and the qualification "in accord with each one's own condition and function." The first insertion emphasizes the sacramental basis for equality; it does not arise from the people but from Christ. The second is to signal the differences in capacities and ways in which cooperation is carried out in building up Christ's body.

The rearrangement of words has perhaps obscured the Council's points, namely, despite differences between sacred ministers and lay persons all share a common equality, and there is a common activity in building up the body of Christ arising from baptism even before the distinct work of sacred ministers and others in the Church. In the Council's view—which is to control the interpretation of this canon—equality in dignity is not conditioned by a person's condition and function; that

applies only to carrying out responsibilities, which does admit of diversity even though the responsibility itself is common to all the baptized.[75]

The principles for the revision of the Code called for a common juridical state to be expressed in the revised law, based on the radical equality that must exist among all Christians in virtue of both their human dignity and the reception of baptism. This was to precede the delineation of rights and duties proper to diverse ecclesiastical functions.[76] This canon introduces that statement of common juridical state and is to be interpreted as expressing that radical equality. The qualifications relative to condition and function do not detract from this, for they refer to how the common responsibility for action is carried out.

This canon represents a significant change from centuries of canonical tradition. Gratian indicated that there are two types of Christians, clergy and laity.[77] Subsequent authors have constructed a theory of the Church as composed essentially of unequals. This was the standard position of canonists until the Second Vatican Council. It will take time to change such a view, both in canonical expression and in understanding the implications in practice. There is a diversity of functions but a fundamental equality of all in the Church in virtue of baptism. Other dignities, offices, functions, etc., must respect this fundamental equality—something that will take more than one canon in a Code; it calls for a major rethinking of relationships and assumptions in the Church.

Given this fundamental equality, the rights and duties that are based on it are common to all Christians. Accordingly, the section on obligations and rights that begins with this canon on equality, and these rights and duties themselves, are to govern the interpretation of the rest of the law, not vice versa.

Status of Women

A major objection is raised today against the reality of the fundamental equality expressed in this canon, due to discrimination based on sex. The Council quoted Paul's words to the Galatians that in Christ there is no longer Jew or Greek, slave or free, male or female; all are "one" in Christ (*LG* 32). It also proclaimed that "every type of discrimination, whether social or cultural, whether based on sex, race, color, social condition, language, or religion, is to be overcome and eradicated as contrary to God's interest.[78] Admittedly the first cita-

---

[74]See *Comm* 12 (1980), 35–36.

[75]A thorough analysis of the Council's position is provided by F. Retamal, *La igualdad fundamental de los fieles en la Iglesia segun la constitución dogmatica "Lumen gentium"* (Santiago, Chile: Universidad Catholica, 1980).

[76]See *Comm* 1 (1969), 82–83.

[77]C. 7, C.XII, q.1 (Friedberg I: 678).

[78]*GS* 29.

tion refers to inner church life while the second is addressed to the world. But the question can be raised whether discrimination based on sex is justified within the Church both because of the scriptural warrant and because of the need for the Church to be consistent in practicing what it preaches if it is to be credible in its social magisterium.[79]

An earlier version of the listing of rights included a canon based on *Gaudium et Spes* 29, stating that the obligations and rights common to all Christians apply without discrimination on the basis of, among other factors, social condition or sex.[80] This has not been retained in the final listing. There has been, however, a genuine effort in the 1983 Code to eradicate many expressions of sexual discrimination found in the former one. For example, there is no longer discrimination on the basis of sex relative to domicile (c. 104), transfer of rite (c. 112), precautions clerics are to take to protect continence (c. 277, §2), regulations concerning the confessional (c. 964) or the place of marriage (c. 1115) or burial (c. 1177). In cases of converts, polygamists and polyandrists are treated alike (c. 1148, §1). The law concerning religious applies equally to men and women unless the text or nature of the matter evidences otherwise (c. 606). The most notable exception is the regulation on papal cloister, which applies only to monasteries of nuns (c. 677, §3). Women may serve in tribunals even as judges (c. 1421, §2), may be authorized to preach in churches (c. 766), and may be called to exercise pastoral care of local communities (c. 517, §2).

The major discrimination in the Code is between clergy and laity, rather than between men and women. Two exceptions are the restrictions to lay men of formal installation as lectors or acolytes (c. 230, §1), and the impediment of abduction that can be incurred only when a man abducts a woman and not vice versa (c. 1089).

There remains, however, the exclusion of women from ordained ministry (c. 1024), and therefore from the offices, functions, and ministries that are restricted to clerics. Not all of these entail an exercise of the power of orders. For example, only the ordained are capable of exercising the power of governance in the Church (c. 219, §1), and offices that entail the exercise of that power are restricted to clerics (c. 274, §1).

The exclusion of women from orders has been reaffirmed by the Congregation for the Doctrine of the Faith on theological grounds.[81] Canon law is it-self subject to the magisterium and it is not surprising that the revised Code retains the traditional exclusion of women from orders. A legal change could not be anticipated in this regard as long as the magisterial position remains the same.

This does not exclude women from creative, active roles in the Church. To implement the new way of thinking characteristic of the revised Code will take time and effort, providing ample opportunity for all in the Church to explore the full implications of the canons on equality, obligations, and rights. There is need for further theological clarification of the relation between ordained ministry and the power of governance, especially in light of the restriction regarding women being ordained. It must also be admitted, however, that the continued discrimination, even based on theological arguments, may be discouraging to many in the Church.

Obligations of Communion

Canon 209 — §1. The Christian faithful are bound by an obligation, even in their own patterns of activity, always to maintain communion with the Church.

§2. They are to fulfill with great diligence the duties which they owe to the universal Church and to the particular church to which they belong according to the prescriptions of law.

The obligations in canon 209 are based on the bond of communion that incorporates one into the Catholic Church. This bond is an internal reality and has various external expressions. The canon limits itself to obligations relating to the external elements—addressing first the generic expression of communion in whatever a member of the Christian faithful does (§1), then applying this in principle to specific duties within the Church (§2). The actual listing of such duties is not given in this or in any one canon but is contained in various provisions of church law.

The canon is one of the few in this title taken from the 1977 schema *De Populo Dei* rather than from the *Lex Ecclesiae Fundamentalis*.[82] It is based on the general concept of communion which is central to much of the Council's view of the Church and which, in promulgating the Code, John Paul II indicated would be characteristic of the Code as well.[83]

Communion

This is first of all a theological reality. God is a communion of three persons. God's self-revelation is in terms of the communion of the human and divine in Christ. The Spirit is the bond of communion that holds the Church together and bonds each

[79] The 1971 Synod of Bishops recognized in a different context that "anyone who ventures to speak to people about justice must first be just in their eyes" (1971 Synod of Bishops, *Justice in the World* [Washington: NCCB, 1982], 40).

[80] *De Populo Dei*, c. 17, §1; see revised version in *Comm* 12 (1980), 77–78.

[81] See SCDF, *Declaration On the Question of the Admission of Women to the Ministerial Priesthood*, Oct. 15, 1976 (Washington: USCC, 1977).

[82] Schema *De Populo Dei*, c. 19.

[83] John Paul II, *Sacrae disciplinae leges*, xii.

Christian in a divine communion with God and one another. The Church expresses its own structure in the hierarchical communion of the various levels and dimensions of Church, from the most local celebration of the Eucharist to the Church universal.

The sacramental expression of communion is in Holy Communion; therefore, the Eucharist is the source and summit of the Christian life. It expresses the bonds of full communion among those who participate together and provides nourishment to sustain and strengthen their communion locally and universally. Whatever a Christian does is marked by this communion. Religion is not a Sunday-morning-only activity; it touches every aspect of one's life. Whatever a Christian does is done in the power of the Spirit and in solidarity with other Christians (*AA* 18) and therefore always in communion with the Church (c. 209, §1).

Moreover, the Church is a communion of churches. The catholicity of the Church admits a broad spectrum of spiritualities, theological systems, and religious practices. If communion is an obligation, it is also a right to the diversity and breadth of Catholic communion. The law expressly recognizes this in canon 214 in reference to forms of spiritual life and implies it in canon 837 which encourages diversity in liturgical celebrations so that all may participate frequently and actively.

The right to full communion in the Catholic Church based on the obligation to maintain communion must temper the application of decisions by local authorities in particular circumstances. This may pose a problem, for example, either when people hold views that differ from the teaching of their own bishop (c. 753) but are acceptable within the Catholic communion or when parents desire to use catechetical materials acceptable in other particular churches in the Catholic communion but not contained on the list of texts approved by the local bishop (c. 755, §1). The law itself does not resolve these tensions but provides the principle in canon 209 that the application of law in local churches must itself respect the broader communion to which all Catholics are obliged—and to which they have a right.

The Christian faithful cannot be excluded from the communion to which they are obliged unless they themselves break that communion. In other words, the Church cannot break off the communion; only individuals can do so. The procedures surrounding the infliction of censures are one way in which this right and obligation are safeguarded from capricious action while at the same time the Church can legitimately declare the fact of those who do break communion (see cc. 1341–1353).

Duties in Communion

Catholic communion is in a local church (parish or at least diocese: c. 102). Communion with a particular church is the basis for the worldwide Catholic communion that exists in and from the communion of particular churches (*LG* 23; c. 368). The particular church to which one pertains is determined by several canons in the law. It is fundamentally a Ritual Church *sui iuris* (cc. 111–112). For those of the Latin Ritual Church, the Code sets certain other determinants.[84]

Place is used as a basis for determining in law the particular church to which one pertains (c. 102). Those without a domicile or quasi-domicile pertain by law to the place where they are actually present (c. 13, §3). By incardination most clerics are attached in a special way to a diocese (c. 265) even if by domicile they also pertain to some other particular church. Clerics who are members of institutes or societies that have the right to incardinate do not have this special bond to a diocese, but they do pertain by domicile to the diocese where the house to which they belong is located (c. 103). Minors pertain to the particular church of their parents or guardians, but at the same time they can acquire other domiciles or quasi-domiciles (c. 105).

The most fundamental duties toward the Church, universal and particular, are those set down by the Lord: love of God and love of neighbor as Christ has loved us. They arise from God's action in our lives, such as through graces and charisms.[85] Additional duties are frequently specified in general and particular laws or are expressed in customs. It is these duties to which canon 209, §2 binds Christian faithful in a special way.

Some legal duties are common to all Christians, including that of maintaining communion (c. 333, §2 even specifies it for the pope). Other legal duties are singled out in the law in terms of one's standing in the Church (e.g., cc. 273–289 for clergy and cc. 662–672 for religious), position (e.g., c. 145, §2 on duties to be specified for any office), or existential situation (e.g., c. 226, §2 for duties arising from parenthood or c. 225, §1 on evangelization responsibilities in special circumstances). The law also admits that the binding force of some legal duties can be suspended at times depending on a person's actual location (see cc. 12–13) or can vary with the person's age (see c. 97)[86] and mental state (cc. 99; 1323–1324). No one is held to the impossible.

Holiness of Life

Canon 210 — All the Christian faithful must make an effort, in accord with their own condition,

---

[84]In virtue of c. 1, the Code does not set the determinants for other Catholics, only for those in the Latin Church. For others, the law proper to their own Ritual Church is to do this.

[85]See John Paul II, *Sacrae disciplinae leges,* xi.

[86]For obligations determined by age, see cc. 401, 538, 914, 989, 1252, and 1323. For a fuller study, see B. Griffin, "The Ages of Man," *Code, Community, Ministry,* J. Provost, ed. (Washington: CLSA, 1983), 21–23.

to live a holy life and to promote the growth of the Church and its continual sanctification.

All Christians regardless of their state in life are bound by the obligation arising from their union with Christ to live a life worthy of that calling according to their abilities and the circumstances of their lives. They thereby contribute to the growth of the Church in holiness and continue the ongoing work of renewal and conversion of the Church itself.

The canon is drawn from chapter V of *Lumen Gentium* which deals with the call of the whole Church to holiness, a holiness the Council emphasized is common to all. Specifically, sections of *Lumen Gentium* 32, 33, and 40 have been used to compose the wording of the canon. It first appeared as canon 11 in the 1969 *Lex Ecclesiae Fundamentalis* and with only some stylistic modifications now appears as the promulgated text.

Condition

There are not two kinds of holiness in the Church, a higher kind for clergy and a lesser one for laity; there is one common calling to perfection (Mt 5:48 as cited in *LG* 40). This is a reversal of the theory underlying the 1917 Code in which clergy and, by extension, religious were called to live holier lives than lay persons (*CIC* 124 and 592). The revised Code accurately reflects the position of the Council, i.e., whatever one's condition in life, the same holiness is to be pursued in it as in any other situation in life (*LG* 41).

But there can be additional reasons why some Christians are more urgently called to seek holiness. The reception of a charism can impose such a special urgency (*AA* 3). Parents are to work for the sanctification of their children by the witness of their lives (c. 835, §4), and they therefore have a special reason to seek holiness. Those who consecrate their lives through public profession of the evangelical counsels have a special function for the holiness of the Church (c. 574, §1), and clergy are held to seek holiness for the special reason that they are dispensers of divine mysteries to the people of God (c. 276, §1).

Social Dimension

Both the personal and the social dimensions of the pursuit of holiness are stressed in the canon. Holiness, the love of God poured out in our hearts (*LG* 42), has the twofold effect of uniting each person closer with God and bonding all together in that love as God's people. The pursuit of holiness in each person's own life promotes the holiness of all the people of God.

The Church, composed of sinners, "is at the same time holy and always in need of being purified, and incessantly pursues the path of penance

and renewal."[87] The Church itself and hence also its legal structures pertain to the sinful condition of this world under the redemptive cross of Christ. Urging the obligation of Christians to seek holiness is essential for the Church and its law. This is not just a counsel for the personal benefit of individuals, but it is an obligation for the entire body.

Proclaim the Gospel

Canon 211 — All the Christian faithful have the duty and the right to work so that the divine message of salvation may increasingly reach the whole of humankind in every age and in every land.

It is both an obligation and a right for each and every Christian to spread the gospel. This is a universal Christian obligation, binding in all times and places until the final coming. It applies not only to church leaders but to every disciple of the Lord. If the Church is missionary by nature and if all the people of God are the Church, then this obligation and right are but an expression of who we are as Church.

The canon is taken from *Lumen Gentium* 33, a text that originally applied specifically to lay persons. Both *De Populo Dei* (c. 27, §1) and all versions of the *Lex Ecclesiae Fundamentalis* have included it as a fundamental right of all Christians—not only of lay persons. The current text, with some stylistic modifications, is taken from canon 11 of the 1980 *Lex Ecclesiae Fundamentalis.*

Evangelization

This is a foundational canon. It is the basis for a variety of obligations and rights.[88] It locates every Christian in the heart of the mission of the Church—proclaiming the gospel. This work is usually termed evangelization, but that word does not appear in the canon. In church usage it has both broad and narrow senses that may help to clarify the interpretation of this canon.

In the 1917 Code, the work of spreading the gospel was primarily the responsibility of the pope and bishops. Others participated in this work by designation from higher authority, and the presumption was that average Christians had a more passive role of supporting the missionary endeavor and of at least not remaining silent when the faith would be endangered if they did so. Otherwise, the task of

---

[87]*LG* 8. On the sinfulness of the Church, see K. Rahner, "The Pilgrim Church," *Theological Investigations* VI (New York: Seabury, 1974), 253–312.

[88]For example, the rights and obligations related to association and assembly (c. 215); apostolic activity (c. 216); Christian education (c. 217); lay persons' roles in the Church's mission (c. 225); religious education (c. 229); migration of clergy (c. 271); clergy-lay relations (c. 274)—to mention only a few.

spreading the gospel was not specifically theirs.[89] Not only was the responsibility for evangelization understood in a narrow sense, but the work of evangelization was also considered in terms of missionary work to foreign territories whereby a body of truths was to be proclaimed to them, although local ordinaries and pastors were called to show consideration for non-Catholics in their own territories (*CIC* 1350, §1).

At Vatican II there were two senses to "mission" and evangelization. One reflected the traditional meaning of bringing the gospel to areas where it was not yet known and in that sense dealt with missionary lands (see *AG* 6). It broadened the concept of what was involved, however, and included the responsibility of the whole Christian community in those areas—even while recognizing the special role of missionaries (*AG* 19–27).

A second sense of mission, inclusive of the narrower meaning but extended to the entire world, viewed all activity of the Church as in some sense missionary; the Church is missionary by nature (*AG* 2) and even traditionally Christian areas are ever in need of re-evangelization. In this sense "the obligation of spreading the faith is imposed on every disciple of Christ, according to his ability."[90]

Drawing on the deliberations of the 1974 Synod of Bishops as well as on the insights of the Council, Paul VI gave a complex understanding of evangelization in the Church today. It is made up of the renewal of humanity, witness, explicit proclamation, inner adherence to the gospel, entry into the Christian community, acceptance of the signs of salvation, and apostolic activity by those who have been evangelized.[91] All in the Church are called to this work in keeping with the possibilities of their situation; some have special responsibilities because of their role in the Church.[92]

It is this broader understanding of spreading the gospel that applies to canon 211. Drawn from the Council and presented in a Church marked by the teachings of the 1974 Synod of Bishops and papal apostolic exhortation, the canon reinforces the evangelization thrust of the Church as a right and duty of all Christians in every part of the world. It cannot be put off only to those who do expressly missionary work in traditional or new missionary lands.

---

[89]See *CIC* 1327–1328 on the role of the hierarchy in preaching, 1350 on missionary work, and 1325 on bearing witness when the faith was endangered.
[90]*LG* 17.
[91]Paul VI, *EN,* Dec. 8, 1975, nos. 17–24; USCC translation, *On Evangelization in the Modern World* (Washington: USCC, 1976), 15–19.
[92]Paul VI highlighted the roles of the successor of Peter, bishops and priests, religious, lay persons in general, the family in particular, young persons, and those in specialized ministries. See ibid., nos. 67–73, pp. 48–54.

Obligation and Right

Spreading the gospel is not only a duty incumbent upon each of the faithful; it is also a right. As a duty it binds Christians to bear witness to the gospel whenever it is in question or being attacked. It also calls for more active initiative in spreading the good news. The sacrament of confirmation provides the special assistance of the Holy Spirit to enable the confirmed to carry out this duty (c. 879). Parents have the special obligation of proclaiming the gospel to their children (cc. 226, §2; 783), and if they violate this duty they may be subject to sanctions (c. 1366). Similarly, those who actively work against the gospel in a public forum are subject to sanctions (c. 1369).

Yet evangelization is also a right. It extends to all Christians. They need no further authorization or commissioning to exercise this right in the various circumstances of their lives. Unlike many other canons that contain principles of interpretation for moderating the exercise of rights, this canon places no conditions on the right to spread the gospel. This does not mean, of course, that the right can be used contrary to the common good. Its exercise is under the supervision of church authorities (cc. 754, 756), particularly if one were to claim to act in the name of the Church or to carry on evangelization within church property. The revised Code, however, is quite open to competent Christians—whether clergy or lay—doing these very things. It requires for the sake of good order that those who speak in the name of the Church or preach in church buildings obtain the appropriate authorization (see cc. 756–759, 764, 766, 812, 823, 831).

Obedience

Canon 212 — §1. The Christian faithful, conscious of their own responsibility, are bound by Christian obedience to follow what the sacred pastors, as representatives of Christ, declare as teachers of the faith or determine as leaders of the Church.

In imitation of Christ whose obedience unto death opened the way of freedom to the children of God (*LG* 37), the Christian faithful are to obey their bishops when these act specifically in their role as Christ's representatives. The bishops do this when they teach formally, exercising the Church's magisterium, or when they establish binding discipline as pastors of the Church.

The canon in based on *Lumen Gentium* 37 which applied this obligation to lay persons but indicated it was common to all the faithful. Both the *De Populo Dei* schema (c. 23) and the *Lex Ecclesiae Fundamentalis* listed it as a fundamental obligation, although the latter has consistently modified the conciliar source by inserting a qualifier also taken from *Lumen Gentium* 37 ("conscious of their own responsibility") but found in a later context.[93]

Subjective Elements

The canon has subjective and objective elements. Subjectively, it calls for a consciousness of responsibilities and an attitude of Christian obedience.

(1) The phrase on consciousness of responsibilities is used by the Council in the context of emphasizing the familial interaction between lay persons and pastors, part of the give and take of expressing needs and opinions on the one hand and sensitivity to lived experiences on the other. The responsibilities intended in *Lumen Gentium* 37 are those listed in the next paragraphs of canon 212—expressing needs and opinions in the Church.

Consciousness of one's responsibilities, therefore, does not lead to blind obedience but to an obedience in which all Christians have the responsibility to take an active part, expressing their experience of faith and the practical implications of Christian living. Such a responsibility implies a right, as paragraphs two and three indicate; it also implies an obligation on the part of church authorities to consult the faithful before pronouncing on matters of doctrine or establishing church discipline. *Presbyterorum Ordinis* 9, given as a source for the canon in *Lex Ecclesiae Fundamentalis,* calls on priests to listen freely to lay persons, considering their experience and competencies, so that together they may seek to read the signs of the times. It also calls on priests to test, recognize, and encourage the charisms that lay people receive. But this in turn implies mutual cooperation between lay people and priests.

Thus the first subjective element of the canon calls for active participation by all the Church in coming to a determination of what the pastors do teach or establish as discipline. This is further qualified by the attitude of Christian obedience.

(2) *Lumen Gentium* 37 spells out what such an attitude implies. It is based on the obedience of Christ, i.e., an obedience to the will of the Father. This obedience also recognized that the sabbath was made for persons, not the other way around. Christian obedience is rooted in an awareness of God's presence and exercised in the perspective that ours is not a lasting city. It bridges the differences of opinion and outlook not by mindless abdication of personal responsibility but in the freedom of God's children recognizing the situation in this world as transitory and imperfect. It responsibly recognizes the limits in any situation and seeks what is for the common good.

Objective Elements

Canon 212 contains three basic qualifiers as to the object of obedience.

(1) It must be something that comes from the "sacred pastors." This term refers to bishops, including the pope. Obedience is owed to what they intend as specially binding in virtue of their role as representatives of Christ. Not included are personal opinions or matters in which genuine freedom exists within the Catholic communion (see c. 209, §1). To act as Christ's representative is to act with the full responsibility of office (cc. 331, 375) and so too, in keeping with the character of that office, as the source and center of unity in the Church (*LG* 23).

(2) Obedience is owed to what the pastors declare as teachers of the faith. Various degrees of assent are specified in canons 750–754—depending on the qualification of what is taught by the ecclesiastical magisterium. The obedience specified in canon 212, §1 relates to the kind of teaching dealt with in canons 750–754 and not to personal opinions or particular theories that are not included in magisterial teaching.

The purpose of Christian obedience is to imitate Christ in dedication to the truth; hence, the object of that obedience is truth—not the authority of the one teaching it—just as faith primarily relates to the object of what is believed and not merely to its expression.

(3) Obedience is also due to what the pastors determine as leaders of the Church. In one sense this is also an obedience of faith, for the Church is a community of faith. Yet in disciplinary matters the truths of faith are not always directly involved whereas the common good is. Since all are bound to promote the common good (c. 223, §1), it follows that obedience in disciplinary matters is required in the Church. Again, Christian obedience is directed toward what is for the common good and not merely to the authority of the one decreeing something.

Can someone dissent from what the sacred pastors declare or determine? If obedience is in imitation of Christ, then it recognizes that the magisterium is subject to revelation and church governance is meant for the welfare of persons, not vice versa. Dissent on these grounds is possible, but it is to be within the context of one's responsibility to participate in the interaction of pastors and faithful discussed above. On more technical dissent in matters of doctrine, one should see canon 218 below and Book III on the teaching office of the Church.

Petition

§2. The Christian faithful are free to make known their needs, especially spiritual ones, and their desires to the pastors of the Church.

---

[93]See *LEF* c. 12, §1, *Comm* 12 (1980), 37–38.

Christians have the right to petition church authorities, bringing their needs to the attention of those who exercise care for the community. This applies especially but not exclusively to spiritual needs.

The canon is drawn from *Lumen Gentium* 37 in which it applies to lay persons. The canon has extended it to all Christians, clergy as well as laity. Later in the same number of *Lumen Gentium* the pastors are reminded to attend to the experience of lay people in spiritual as well as temporal matters; the canon does not exclude the expression of temporal needs, even though spiritual needs are stressed. Both *De Populo Dei* (c. 28, §1) and the *Lex Ecclesiae Fundamentalis* articulated this petitioning as a fundamental right. The promulgated text is taken from canon 12, §2, of the *Lex Ecclesiae Fundamentalis*.

The conciliar source makes a significant statement about the attitude with which such petitioning is to take place. It is to be done with that freedom and confidence that befit children of God and brothers in Christ (*LG* 37). This implies mutual respect and openness on both parts rather than an adversary situation or one of mutual distrust. Experience indicates that all parties have a responsibility for setting the proper tone in such exchanges.

Public Opinion

§3. In accord with the knowledge, competence and preeminence which they possess, they have the right and even at times a duty to manifest to the sacred pastors their opinion on matters which pertain to the good of the Church, and they have a right to make their opinion known to the other Christian faithful, with due regard for the integrity of faith and morals and reverence toward their pastors, and with consideration for the common good and the dignity of persons.

The right and even at times the duty to express one's opinion about what is for the good of the Church is proclaimed in this canon. Such opinions are especially sought from qualified persons. They are to be expressed to church authorities and, with due regard for public order, may also be made public to other Christians.

The source of this canon is the same paragraph in *Lumen Gentium* 37 as the previous paragraph of canon 212. Some words have been changed and several qualifying phrases added to the conciliar text in keeping with the approach of both the *De Populo Dei* schema (c. 28, §2) and the *Lex Ecclesiae Fundamentalis*. This text is a modification of canon 12, §3 of the *Lex Ecclesiae Fundamentalis*.

This canon is a good example of the influence of a legislative supremacy system of interpretation. The legislator has inserted a number of qualifiers in the conciliar material, considered necessary to provide the basis for a proper legal interpretation when the Council's statement is read as part of canon law. To appreciate the significance of these qualifiers, the substance of the canon must first be understood.

Opinions in the Church

(1) The opinions concern matters that pertain to the good of the Church. These could relate to any of the three functions of teaching, sanctifying, and ruling. They might consider spiritual or temporal matters; they could be favorable or critical.

(2) The right and at times the duty to express an opinion is stated in the conciliar source as pertaining to lay persons and indeed to all the Christian faithful (*LG* 37). Clergy, religious, and lay persons, i.e., persons who have official positions as well as those who do not, are thus included. Clearly an opinion carries greater weight depending both on the competence of the person who expresses it and the soundness of the evidence that supports it. Thus, while all have the right to express an opinion, not all opinions carry the same force.

(3) Opinions may be expressed to those in authority as well as to other Christians. The canon implies a preference that opinions be brought to the attention of church authorities first before they are expressed publicly. This is in keeping with the canonical tradition of approaching the most immediate authority who can do something about a situation before appealing elsewhere—usually to a higher authority, but in this case to the public in the Church. There is much to be said for such a procedure. It brings the issue directly to the attention of someone who can do something about it; this is usually a rather efficient approach. It is conducive to greater communications within the Church. It provides church officials with a better understanding of the attitudes and experiences of all in the Church.

There is another approach to public opinion, one with which people in the United States are quite familiar. This is to test an opinion in public first before authorities take action on it. Sometimes officials themselves, whether in commerce or government, will "float" an idea to see what the public reaction is before acting on it formally. This provides them an opportunity to change an approach in light of the reaction. Similarly, individuals express opinions in many public fora ranging from letters sent to newspapers to conducting meetings and forming organizations. From the interplay of various opinions a consensus may emerge that officials can take into account, or the consensus may challenge the accepted ways of doing things which are no longer in touch with the conditions of the times.

The first procedure tends to control opinion; the second relies on the free exchange of opinion in public to work out its own checks and balances. Problems and successes have been noted with both approaches. What is important is to recognize that people in the Church have different expectations of how public opinion operates, depending on their secular experience in various cultures. This leads to the qualifiers in canon 212, §3.

Qualifiers

(1) The Code distinguishes the expressing of an opinion to pastors and to the rest of the Christian faithful. The Council makes no such distinction, referring instead to "declaring" one's opinion. When the first paragraph mentioned above is taken into account, the canon is indicating how the declaration of opinion is to be done within the framework of canon law.

The Council indicated opinions were to be expressed, if the occasion should arise, through institutions established for such a purpose by the Church. Pastoral councils (*CD* 27) and priests' councils (*CD* 27, *PO* 7) were seen by the Council fathers as examples of such institutions in which opinions on what is for the pastoral good of the Church could be expressed in an orderly fashion. The Code mandates presbyteral councils (c. 495, §1), but it leaves other institutions of this type to local determination (cc. 511, 536). Some might consider that the kind of institution called for by the Council is provided simply by the system of approaching pastors first and then the rest of the faithful; this, however, is to take the term "institution" in a remarkably broad sense. A more traditional reading of "institution" in *Lumen Gentium* 37 would imply that if the councils recommended by Vatican II are not set up, some other institution may have to be established locally if the right to express one's opinion is to be exercised in the Church.

The Council emphasized the personal spirit with which one should express opinions as always "in truth, in courage, and in prudence," whereas the Code focuses on external considerations of "integrity of the faith and morals." Both Code and Council acknowledge the need for reverence toward the pastors when such opinions are expressed.

The Code adds a special qualifier that all this is to be done with due consideration for the common good and the dignity of persons, a reminder that here, too, the provisions of canon 223, §1 apply on concern for the common good.

(2) Both the Code and the Council qualify the right and duty to express an opinion in virtue of the knowledge, competence, and preeminence one enjoys. The degree to which one is informed and expert relates to how well founded an opinion may be. Preeminence (*praestantia*) can refer to "outstanding ability"[94] or an outstanding quality in the individual. All three qualifiers are a question of degree; to the extent that any Christian possesses them, to that extent at least the canon recognizes the right and, at times, the duty to express an opinion.

(3) What is the significance of "at times a duty"? The Council spoke of the faculty (*facultatem*) to express an opinion. This does not require that it be exercised, unless the common good were to require it, and then it would become a duty. The law has replaced faculty with right (*ius*) and retained the rest of the conciliar wording to emphasize that at times the common good does demand that the right be exercised. This would occur especially when failure to speak up would lead to harm to the Church.

(4) The significance of the qualifiers in the canon comes down to this: the right to express opinions in the Church is a fundamental right and, at times, even a duty. But the exercise of this right must be for the common good. It is not to lead to scandal, disrespect for church authorities, libel, or public disturbances. Various qualifiers are used to indicate the interpretation to be given the exercise of the right; of themselves they do not limit its existence—provided a person has some knowledge, competence, and basis for expressing an opinion.

Spiritual Assistance

Canon 213 — The Christian faithful have the right to receive assistance from the sacred pastors out of the spiritual goods of the Church, especially the word of God and the sacraments.

All Christians have a right to receive help from the spiritual goods of the Church. This right is rooted in baptism; it is not a privilege granted by church authorities but a claim rooted in the action of Christ that empowers Christians to seek the services of the sacred pastors. These latter have the obligation to see that this help is made available.

This is the first right mentioned for lay persons and all Christians in *Lumen Gentium* 37, a conciliar statement that is the source for many of the rights in this title. Both *De Populo Dei* (c. 24, §1) and the *Lex Ecclesiae Fundamentalis* considered it a fundamental right for all Christians. The current text is only slightly modified stylistically from canon 13 of the *Lex Ecclesiae Fundamentalis.*

This was the only right (*ius*) directly stated for lay persons in the former Code (*CIC* 682). There it was put in more general terms: lay persons have a right to spiritual goods and to the most powerful helps necessary for salvation. Word and sacrament

---

[94]Abbott, 64 translates it this way, as contrasted to "pre-eminence" in A. Flannery, ed., *Vatican Council II. The Conciliar and Post Conciliar Documents* (Northport, N.Y.: Costello, 1975), 394.

were not specifically mentioned. The Council, building on the concept that word and sacrament are constitutive elements of the Church's mission, listed them as the principal spiritual goods of the Church.

This right of Christians is further supported by the obligation placed on sacred ministers not to deny the sacraments to those who seek them opportunely, are properly disposed, and are not impeded by law (c. 843, §1). Together with the rest of the faithful, clergy are to provide proper preparation for the sacraments (c. 843, §2). Preaching the word of God is a special obligation of clergy (cc. 756–757), and others can be called to help provide this good for the faithful (cc. 758–759).

The Council called for these goods to be made available in abundance (*abundanter*). The Code neither retains this qualification nor specifies the quality of the help received; thus it does not legislate a right to "good" homilies or to the most pastorally satisfying celebration of the sacraments, although these clearly are the ideal. The Code does attempt to make it possible for bishops to provide these helps to Christians more readily despite the growing shortage of clergy relative to the total Catholic population. The potential for non-priests to provide a range of services has been placed in the law, and bishops are empowered to take advantage of these options—especially to provide the necessary help to the faithful entrusted to their care.[95]

While sacred pastors in virtue of their office are responsible to see that these helps are provided (cc. 386–387), they do not have to do it by themselves. The involvement of others is encouraged in order to make word and sacraments more readily available. The bishop can reorganize parishes, structure educational efforts, provide norms for sacramental preparation, and develop whatever else is needed to facilitate the exercise of this right, making it one of the most influential rights in the Church.[96]

Moreover, access to the sacraments cannot be denied someone in full communion without serious cause and due process of law.[97] Even those not in full communion can on occasion seek and receive the sacraments in the Catholic Church; furthermore, Catholics may seek the sacraments wherever they are validly celebrated provided obvious conditions are met (c. 844).

Worship and Spirituality

Canon 214 — The Christian faithful have the right to worship God according to the prescriptions of their own rite approved by the legitimate pastors of the Church, and to follow their own form of spiritual life consonant with the teaching of the Church.

Christians have the right to worship according to the rites approved for their Ritual Church *sui iuris* and to follow a spirituality of their choice provided it is in keeping with the teaching of the Church. The canon refers both to Ritual Churches and to liturgical rites, and it recognizes a variety of spiritualities in the Church.

No one document of Vatican II is the source of this canon. Instead, it is based on a number of conciliar statements. The equality of all Ritual Churches *sui iuris* was declared by Vatican II in *Sacrosanctum Concilium* 4 and *Orientalium Ecclesiarum* 3. The right to a genuine liberty in religious matters was proclaimed in *Dignitatis Humanae* 2 and *Gaudium et Spes* 26. The approval of liturgical rites was restricted to legitimate authorities; individuals are not permitted to tamper with them (*SC* 22). Both *De Populo Dei* (cc. 24, §2; 25; 26) and the *Lex Ecclesiae Fundamentalis* constructed statements of these rights based on the conciliar teaching. The promulgated text is essentially that of canon 14 of the *Lex Ecclesiae Fundamentalis.*

Worship According to Approved Rite

Each person by baptism belongs to a specific Ritual Church *sui iuris* (c. 111). Although any Christian in full communion may worship according to any of the Ritual Churches in communion,[98] the ceremony itself must be in accord with the liturgical law of that particular Ritual Church. For the Latin Church this is emphasized by canon 846.

As indicated in canon 846, the right to worship according to the prescriptions of one's own rite carries with it the obligation on the part of sacred ministers to celebrate that worship in keeping with the appropriate liturgical books. Those who fail to do so may be denying members of the congregation a basic right.

---

[95]For example, non-priests including deacons and lay persons may be authorized to provide pastoral care for communities (c. 517, §2). Lay persons may be authorized to preach in church (c. 766); serve as missionaries (c. 784) and catechists (c. 785); act as extraordinary ministers of baptism (c. 861, §2); be delegated to assist at weddings (c. 1112); and administer some sacramentals (c. 1122).

[96]See c. 381 on the bishop's powers; cc. 515–516 on parish organization; c. 838, §4 on sacramental norms; c. 802 on schools.

[97]See, for example, cc. 912 and 915 on access to the Eucharist; cc. 1341–1363 on the imposition and remission of sanctions.

[98]The obligation of Mass may be fulfilled in any Ritual Church (c. 1248, §1). Certain sacraments may be received in any Ritual Church: baptism (cc. 111; 112, §2), Eucharist (c. 923), and penance (c. 991); some others require the at least presumed permission of the person's own pastor or ordinary: confirmation (c. 886, §1) and anointing (c. 1003). An apostolic indult is needed to confer orders on one of a different rite (cc. 1015, §2; 1021), and at least one of the parties must be of the rite of the assisting minister for a valid celebration of marriage (c. 1110).

Spiritual Life

The Catholic Church has known a great variety of spiritual movements throughout its history. Many of these have traditionally been associated with religious communities and even today constitute a vital dimension of Catholic life. Other forms of spirituality, adapted to varying conditions of time and place, are also evident in the many movements, associations, and personal styles of Catholics. All of these are available for free choice by Catholics; no one spirituality is preferred over the others provided each is in keeping with Catholic teaching.

This can pose a problem at the parochial level. Various types of spirituality seek different forms of public expression. Not all are compatible, at least not at the same time and in the same place. Moreover, various forms of devotion require traditionally that a priest be present either to lead or to supervise the spiritual activity. This is not always possible in the current pastoral situation. Does this in effect mean that parish clergy are denying the right to parishoners to follow their own form of spiritual life in such cases? Hardly, for no one is bound to the impossible, and clergy must observe the priorities for pastoral life as established by the Church. If this means they are not available for certain devotions or spiritual exercises, it may be necessary either for alternative devotional exercises to be developed that do not require clergy or for joint efforts to be developed among various organizations of spiritual life.

On the other hand, provided good order is maintained and nothing is done contrary to church teaching, people are entitled to develop and to participate in spiritual movements of their choice. It is contrary to the right guaranteed in this canon to prohibit a given form of spirituality or to require that only certain ones be observed by people in a given locality. Religious freedom applies within the Church as well as in society, and this is its most visible application.

Association and Assembly

Canon 215 — The Christian faithful are at liberty freely to found and to govern associations for charitable and religious purposes or for the promotion of the Christian vocation in the world; they are free to hold meetings to pursue these purposes in common.

This canon is based on the conciliar recognition of associations organized, joined, and conducted by lay persons (*AA* 19) and by presbyters (*PO* 8). *De Populo Dei* (c. 31) and the *Lex Ecclesiae Fundamentalis* recognized this as a fundamental right of all Christians but had some difficulty in expressing

it satisfactorily. The final text is a modification of canon 15 of the *Lex Ecclesiae Fundamentalis.*

Purpose for Associating

The canon lists three purposes for forming and running associations: charitable purposes, religious purposes, and promoting the vocation of Christians in the world. A different listing of purposes for associations is given in canon 298: perfection of life, public worship, promotion of Christian doctrine, evangelization, works of piety, works of charity, and animation of the temporal order with a Christian spirit. Clearly the listing in canon 215 is not taxative but illustrates some of the purposes for forming associations among Christians.

Vatican II was quite straightforward in asserting the right (*ius*) of lay persons to found, to moderate, and to give their names to associations provided that they maintain the proper relationship with ecclesiastical authorities. Expressing this relationship proved something of a problem in drafting the statement of this right as pertaining to all the faithful. Some early drafts spoke of restricting the organization of some associations to ecclesiastical authorities alone in virtue of their nature. These restrictions have been taken out of the expression of the right and now, in virtue of canon 301, §1, apply only to the exercise of the right for certain types of associations.

The emphasis in the 1917 Code was on the role of ecclesiastical authority in erecting or approving associations (see *CIC* 684, 686). In the 1983 Code the emphasis has shifted to the right of Christians to take the initiative. Although this may result in a multiplicity of associations, it is within the rights of a Christian to organize or join associations as each may desire. It would be a violation of this right to prohibit membership in associations that are established in keeping with the law, even though they are not organized by or under the direction of a pastor or bishop. This is a new way of thinking in some situations, but it reinforces such long-standing organizations as the St. Vincent de Paul Society.

The exercise of this general right to associate is restricted for clergy and religious in certain circumstances. For example, clergy are not permitted to join associations that are not compatible with the obligations of the clerical state or would impede the diligent fulfillment of the duties assigned them by competent ecclesiastical authority (c. 278, §3). Clergy and religious are prohibited from taking an active role in political parties or in governing labor unions unless competent authority judges such is necessary to safeguard the rights of the Church or the common good (c. 287, §2). Permanent deacons are exempted from this latter restriction by canon 288.

While the former excommunication of Catholics

who joined Masonic societies has not been repeated in this Code, a sanction can be imposed on those who join associations that work against the Church, and an interdict can be placed on those who promote or run such groups (c. 1374). Whether Masons fall within these strictures must now be determined by authorities within the particular churches.

Assembly

The right to assemble is a prized value for people in modern times, a right often prohibited by repressive governments. In the Church the affirmation of this right is important not only as a witness to a concern for human rights but also to safeguard the working of the Spirit. Wherever two or three are gathered in Christ's name, Christ is present in their midst.

The law does not specify that church buildings must be made available for those who wish to hold meetings or assemble. It could be argued that if no other location were available, either because of physical restrictions or, for example, because of governmental pressure, the use of church facilities must be permitted if the right to assemble is to be respected. Otherwise, people are free to assemble wherever they wish, provided that good order is maintained; however, they have no specific claim on meeting space within parish or diocesan facilities in virtue of this canon.

The canon does not restrict the right to conduct meetings to a given locality. Hence this fundamental right applies to local, diocesan, national, or international assemblies that Christians are free to conduct on their own initiative in order to pursue those purposes that are appropriate to Christians.

Apostolic Activity

Canon 216 — All the Christian faithful, since they participate in the mission of the Church, have the right to promote or to sustain apostolic action by their own undertakings in accord with each one's state and condition; however, no undertaking shall assume the name Catholic unless the consent of competent ecclesiastical authority is given.

In virtue of baptism every Christian participates in the mission of the Church. This is expressed first and foremost in the apostolic action proper to each person. This activity is rooted in Christ's action in the life of the baptized and so may be initiated by each individual without waiting for further authorization. However, any undertaking that wishes to call itself by the name "Catholic" must receive authorization to use that name from the competent ecclesiastical authority.

The latter provision of the canon is taken directly from *Apostolicam actuositatem* 24. The main part of

the canon, however, is not found verbatim in the conciliar documents but reflects the fundamental teaching of the Council as found in several statements, e.g., *Lumen Gentium* 33; *Apostolicam actuositatem* 3, 15–22, 24; and *Presbyterorum Ordinis* 9. As a fundamental right this has been acknowledged by *De Populo Dei* (c. 27, §2) and the *Lex Ecclesiae Fundamentalis,* the final text being adapted from canon 16 of the latter.

Apostolic activity is discussed in detail in *Apostolicam actuositatem*. Three major forms of the apostolate are indicated therein. The first is that individual apostolic activity is an obligation to which each Christian is called, no matter what condition the person may be in. This is bearing witness to the gospel in each person's situation. *Lumen Gentium* 34 suggests some of the ways in which Christian lay persons carry out this activity. Working together in communities, whether parochial or otherwise, is a second form of apostolic activity. These do not have to be officially organized parochial groups, for parishoners share a common society and hence a common responsibility in witnessing the faith in that society. A third type is an association in which apostolic activity is directly and purposefully carried out. A great variety of apostolic associations exist in the Church. Some have become especially connected with the work of the hierarchy and carry the name "Catholic Action"; however, it must be borne in mind that all associations are worthy means for Catholics to carry out their apostolic responsibilities.

The Code does not go into such detail but presumes the perspective set by the Council. It does indicate that apostolic initiatives are in keeping with each person's condition and status. This is not to limit the right of initiative but rather echoes the Council, which addressed those particular circumstances in which only certain persons can effectively carry on the mission of the Church (*AA* 17–18).

These initiatives are not dependent on the approval or authorization of the hierarchy, whether it be local clergy or the bishops. It is a right that arises from Christ's action in baptism and frequently is reinforced by the reception of charisms which themselves give rise to rights and duties in the Church and in the world (*AA* 3). However, for an initiative to bear the name "Catholic" the Code, repeating the Council, requires the consent of competent ecclesiastical authority.

The authority competent to give such consent is not spelled out in the canon. It may be inferred, however, from parallel places in the Code in keeping with canon 19. When dealing with associations, two specifications are made. Canon 305, §2 entrusts the vigilance of all associations to the Holy See, and to the diocesan bishop for diocesan associations and other associations insofar as they are active in his diocese. As regards the erection of public associations, universal and international ones require action by the Holy See; national associations are erected by conferences of bishops; and diocesan ones are set up by the diocesan bishop (c. 312, §1). While granting the use of the name "Catholic" for apostolic initiatives is not the same as erecting a public association, the apostolic work is often joined to an association or results in one. The authorities specified in canon 312 would at least be competent, although the approval of an individual diocesan bishop may also be sufficient (c. 305, §2).

Christian Education

Canon 217 — **The Christian faithful since they are called by baptism to lead a life in conformity with the teaching of the gospel, have the right to a Christian education by which they will be properly instructed so as to develop the maturity of a human person and at the same time come to know and live the mystery of salvation.**

Christians along with all other people have a right (*ius*) to education. For Christians this includes an education which, as with all education, aims to develop the maturity of human persons; moreover, Christian education also seeks at the same time a knowledge and living of the mystery of salvation. For all persons the right to an education is based on the dignity of the human person. For Christians there is an added basis arising from their baptismal duty to live an evangelical life.

This canon draws on several statements in Vatican II, although most of its actual wording is not traceable to any particular conciliar text. *Gaudium et Spes* 16 and 19 dealt with human rights, including the right to education. *Gravissimum Educationis* 1 and 2 addressed the human right to education and the specific rights of Christians. The understanding of education in the canon is taken from *Gravissimum Educationis* 2 although the conciliar document has been condensed in the interests of a more acceptable juridical statement. This right was listed as a fundamental one belonging to all Christians in *De Populo Dei* (c. 22. §1) and in the *Lex Ecclesiae Fundamentalis*. The present wording is the same as canon 17, §1 of the latter. The second paragraph of canon 17 of the *Lex Ecclesiae Fundamentalis* is now canon 226, §2 discussed below.

The right to education gives rise to various duties in the Church. Parents have the obligation and right to educate their children (cc. 226, §2; 793). The Church claims the right to establish schools, universities, and ecclesiastical faculties to assist the Christian people in exercising their right to a Christian education (cc. 793–821). The understanding of this education in broad terms is repeated in more detail in canon 795.

The right expressed in this canon is to a "Christian" education. The obligations dealt with in Book III relate to "Catholic" education. The difference

seems to be that in dealing with obligations, particularly of parents, the Code is concerned that the education of children include all the elements necessary to embrace full communion in the Church, whereas the overall right applies to deepening any Christian's communion and commitment to Christ. As such it has a broader scope. As based in baptism, it is a right enjoyed by all Christians, although only those in full communion with the Catholic Church can vindicate that right canonically.

The conciliar documents placed greater stress on the religious dimension of Christian education, indicating it has a priority over the development of human maturity. The canon has placed both purposes on a more equal level; this is not to deny the ultimate primacy of the religious but to highlight the fact that both must take place together.

Freedom in Sacred Sciences

Canon 218 — **Those who are engaged in the sacred disciplines enjoy a lawful freedom of inquiry and of prudently expressing their opinions on matters in which they have expertise, while observing a due respect for the magisterium of the Church.**

Those involved in sacred disciplines enjoy the necessary academic freedom for competent research and study as well as the freedom of expression needed to carry on the theological enterprise. Within the context of a believing community, theology maintains due respect for the ecclesiastical magisterium, as that magisterium always retains respect for the revealed truth that it serves.

The canon is drawn from *Gaudium et Spes* 62. Some words of the conciliar text have been simplified (e.g., using prudence for humility and fortitude), and reference to freedom of thought has been dropped, probably as an element that cannot be verified externally the way inquiry and expression of opinion can be. Both *De Populo Dei* (c. 22, §2) and the *Lex Ecclesiae Fundamentalis* included this among the fundamental rights of Christians. The current text with a minor stylistic alteration is the same as canon 18 of the *Lex Ecclesiae Fundamentalis.*

Who are those engaged in sacred disciplines? The canon does not specify, but the conciliar source indicated graduate studies in seminaries and universities. Such persons are presumed to have developed a mature foundation in the faith through catechesis and schooling and are now engaged in theological research and reflection. It is in this activity that the Council recognized a lawful freedom. It did so within the context of ecumenical participation in the theological enterprise—an element not specifically listed in the Code.

The Council further specified that both clergy and laity were included in this freedom, something the Code implies both through canon 229, §2 on lay participation in higher theological studies and through canons 250 and 1032 concerning the theological formation in seminaries of those preparing to become presbyters. In addition to students mentioned in these canons, teachers of theology and its related fields are also included. It would not be possible to posit such liberty for students if their teachers did not also enjoy it.

Neither the Council nor the Code speaks of a right (*ius*) in this context. The Council spoke of recognizing (*agnoscitur*) a lawful freedom; the Code uses the term "enjoy" ("fruuntur"). This is not to say that such freedom is a privilege granted by higher authority that can also be taken away. It is rather an expression of a true right (*ius*) that the Council elsewhere declared to be based not in the subjective disposition of a person but in that person's very nature. Even those who err in their search for truth must be respected because of this; the exercise of their right to religious liberty can be impeded only when the lawful public order is threatened (*DH* 2). Those engaged in sacred disciplines are exercising this right to religious liberty within the context of their faith commitment in the Church.

Earlier drafts proposed to express limitations on the freedom of inquiry, but the promulgated version has dropped these. In seminaries there are certain norms that are to be followed in theological inquiry, rooting the enterprise in Sacred Scripture and requiring dogmatic theology to be rooted in Scripture and tradition. Thomistic theology is given special but not exclusive mention (c. 252, §§2–3), and the implications of canon 218 include the possibility of other theological schools and methods in its place.

The canon provides two touchstones for interpreting the exercise of freedom in the expression of theological opinions. The first is an internal criterion: freedom extends to those matters in which a person enjoys expertise. As noted earlier in commenting on canon 212, §3, this is an appropriate caution that looks to the solidity of the opinion being expressed. The second criterion is rooted in the public order limitation on the exercise of religious liberty. Due respect for the ecclesiastical magisterium is necessary for the public order of the Church.

The canon speaks of "due respect" ("debito . . . obsequio"). Earlier versions would have used "reverence and obedience," but this was dropped in favor of terminology that resonates more accurately with the canons on the magisterium (cc. 750–753). What are the limits to "due respect"? At the very least, the ecclesiastical magisterium must be acknowledged and taken into serious consideration in expressing theological opinions. This does not rule out dissent, however, and several guidelines for theological dissent have included the provision that it must be grounded in a true respect for the magis-

terium even while disagreeing with it on a particular point.[99]

Due respect for the magisterium can also be interpreted in terms of public order in the Church. A theologian should not express opinions that differ from the position of the magisterium in such a way as to lead to disrespect for the magisterium on the part of others. If after observing appropriate procedures, a determination is made that the position of the theologian is not to be taught, due respect for the magisterium includes withholding the expression of the opinion as required.

Yet due respect for the magisterium may at times require a theologian to speak out (see. c. 212. §3). Failure to do so could also be harmful to the Church and a violation of the Christian responsibility theologians have in virtue of their expertise. Freedom is not without responsibility, and this is one of the responsibilities of a person engaged in the sacred discipline.

State in Life

Canon 219 — All the Christian faithful have the right to be free from any kind of coercion in choosing a state in life.

This canon states a basic human right asserted by John XXIII in *Pacem in Terris* and reaffirmed by the Council (*GS* 26, 29, 52). It was phrased in much the same wording as the promulgated version in *De Populo Dei* (c. 30) and the *Lex Ecclesiae Fundamentalis*. Canon 19 of the latter is the precise form adopted in the 1983 Code.

This is not a right to choose whatever state in life one wishes. Rather, it is the right to be free from coercion in selecting a state in life. It is an immunity rather than an entitlement. Its protection is reaffirmed at key places in the Code. No one can be forced to enter marriage, and marriage entered into without free choice is not valid (c. 1103). Orders must be sought freely (c. 1036), and no one is to force another to be ordained or to impede the ordination if the candidate is canonically suited (c. 1026). While a religious community is free to accept or exclude those seeking to enter it (cc. 641, 657), no one can be forced to enter or even be enticed into it (c. 643, §1, 4°).

Reputation and Privacy

Canon 220 — No one is permitted to damage unlawfully the good reputation which another person

---

[99]See International Theological Commission, *Theses on the Relationship Between the Ecclesiastical Magisterium and Theology* (Washington: USCC, 1977); L. O'Donovan, ed., *Cooperation Between Theologians and the Ecclesiastical Magisterium* (Washington: CLSA, 1982).

enjoys nor to violate the right of another person to protect his or her own privacy.

Two rights are expressed in this canon—both in a passive manner. The first is the right to a good reputation, which is not to be damaged unlawfully. The second is the right to privacy, which is not to be violated. Both rights are basic human rights; the first is expressly listed in *Gaudium et Spes* 26. It was listed in *De Populo Dei* (c. 32) and in the *Lex Ecclesiae Fundamentalis,* and the wording of the first part of this canon is taken from canon 20 of the latter. The second, to privacy, is a fundamental right listed in *De Populo Dei* (c. 33) but not found in the *Lex Ecclesiae Fundamentalis.* In its earlier form it referred specifically to privacy in correspondence and other personal matters, but here it is expressed in a more general form.

A good reputation need not be based on fact in order to be enjoyed. The 1917 Code made a distinction between infamy in law—a legal state even though a person's reputation had not suffered in public—and manifest infamy, referring to the loss of reputation for serious reason.[100] The 1983 Code has dropped the sanction of infamy but retains the recognition that some people can lose their reputation with juridic effects.[101]

The canon prohibits unlawfully damaging a good reputation that a person may enjoy. Such a reputation may be lawfully damaged if there is cause, for the reputation may be false. Yet just because a reputation is not warranted is not sufficient reason to damage it; criminal action or other grave sin, admonition by Church authorities, and obstinacy in the wrongful activity would be required for someone to intervene actively with the purpose of damaging another's reputation (cc. 1341; 1717, §2).

The right to privacy is less attended to in the law. Only one other reference is made to it in the Code, at canon 642 on admission to the novitiate, whereby consultation with experts on the suitability of a candidate is subject to the right to privacy. The intimacy of family relations is respected in exempting family members from having to respond as witnesses in a church trial (c. 1548, §2, 2°) and in providing that only spouses can petition a dispensation from non-consummated marriages (c. 1697) or attack the validity of their marriage if the nullity is not already public (c. 1674).

Even in civil law, the right to privacy is a developing area of jurisprudence. Its application in admissions to the seminary, disciplinary action in the

Church, the conduct of ecclesiastical trials, dismissal of teachers, and a host of other concerns will be a source of debate and development over the coming years.

Protection of Rights

Canon 221 — §1. The Christian faithful can legitimately vindicate and defend the rights which they enjoy in the Church before a competent ecclesiastical court in accord with the norm of law.

§2. The Christian faithful also have the right, if they are summoned to judgment by competent authority, that they be judged in accord with the prescriptions of the law to be applied with equity.

§3. The Christian faithful have the right not to be punished with canonical penalties except in accord with the norm of law.

This canon sets down three elements of the protection of rights.

The first provides for Christians to vindicate and defend rights on their own initiative, using the competent forum in the Church to do this. The second is a right of defense, requiring treatment according to due process if one is summoned before church authorities. The third is the legality of penalties so that sanctions are not to be imposed except according to the norms of law.

The Council did not delve into details of the legal protection of rights, but it did declare that effective safeguards for the rights of all citizens and for the peaceful settlement of disputes are part of the fundamental common good in society (*DH* 7). The 1971 Synod of Bishops saw justice in judicial procedure as one of the elements needed for the Church to be credible in its preaching of justice to others.[102]

The *De Populo Dei* schema proposed a statement of the fundamental right of Christians to defend their rights in the judicial and, where permitted, administrative fora of the Church (c. 35). It then listed five procedural rights—including due process of law and the legality of penalties—spelling them out in some detail (c. 36). In revising the draft in 1980, it was decided to situate these rights either in the *Lex Ecclesiae Fundamentalis* or in the appropriate places in procedural law.[103] The *Lex Ecclesiae Fundamentalis* in its various versions has also listed the rights contained in the promulgated version. The final text of canon 221 takes almost verbatim canons 21 and 22 of the *Lex Ecclesiae Fundamentalis,* listing canon 21 of that document as paragraph three.

---

[100]See *CIC* 2293 in which manifest infamy is termed infamy of fact.

[101]See c. 915 in which a person who obstinately perseveres in *manifest* grave sin is to be refused the Eucharist, and c. 1741, 3° in which loss of good reputation is a reason to remove a pastor even without any sin or grave fault.

[102]1971 Synod of Bishops, "The Practice of Justice," in *Justice in the World,* (USCC edition), 41.

[103]See *Comm* 12 (1980), 89–90.

Vindicate and Defend Rights

What forum is competent to hear cases in which Christians prosecute or defend their rights according to the norm of law? The Code urges that people not go to court initially in such circumstances but attempt to resolve their differences equitably. In tribunal cases the judge is first to attempt such an equitable resolution (c. 1446). Administratively the conference of bishops can require each diocese to have a mediation service; if the conference fails to act, the bishop can mandate one for an individual diocese (c. 1733). Such a service may be available through the due process procedures already in place in many American dioceses that provide conciliation and arbitration mechanisms and attend to structuring administrative discretion through various stages of "prior process."[104]

If such mediation does not achieve the desired result, canon 221, §1 clearly provides a right to take recourse in the competent forum. Canonical tradition includes both administrative recourse to superiors and the use of judicial procedures in tribunals as fora for the vindication of rights. At first reading, the Code seems to prefer tribunals. For example, it implies a preference for the judicial forum when penalties are to be inflicted (c. 1342, §1), and penalties are one example of a restriction on rights. It specifies that the first object of a court action is the prosecution or vindication of the rights of physical or juridic persons (c. 1400, §1, 1°). It would seem, therefore, that tribunals of the local diocese or even of the Apostolic See (cc. 1417, 1419) are among the competent fora for vindicating rights—and even to some extent preferred for this.

In practice, however, church courts have been mainly limited to cases involving the right to marry (cc. 1057, §1; 1085, §2). They have not developed the jurisprudence or the expertise to handle more complex cases involving other rights specified in the revised Code—such as reputation, privacy, and education. Church courts do not form an independent judiciary, a fact that further weakens their ability to address issues involving rights—especially when one of the parties is the superior who can remove the judge. The revised Code does attempt to move toward some independence in the system of justice by requiring that judges be appointed for a specified term and by protecting them from removal during their term except for legitimate and grave cause (c. 1422).

Even so, the Church remains within a system of legislative and not judicial supremacy. The courts do not have the role of authentically interpreting the law; this weakens their role in protecting the rights of the Christian faithful. Lower courts cannot judge bishops; such cases must always be heard in Rome. Yet cases involving rights may include bishops as well as the other Christian faithful.

An even more specific limitation on the ability of courts to be an effective forum for the prosecution and vindication of rights is found in canon 1400, §2; this restricts the hearing of controversies arising from acts of administrative power to the administrative forum. They may not be taken to the judicial forum. Since this is a limitation on the right to vindicate one's rights (cf. c. 221, §1) because it restricts the available fora for doing so, it must be interpreted strictly (c. 18). Yet the wording of canon 1400 is not entirely clear—either when dealing with "an act of administrative power" or with "an administrative tribunal."

An initial distinction must be made between administrative acts that are an exercise of executive power of governance (c. 35) and acts of administration that are the work of a good head of the household (c. 1284). Tribunals are competent to decide controversies in regard to acts of administration, as is clear from canon 1413, 1°; it establishes how to determine which tribunal is competent in such cases. Under the revised Code there could be an increase in such cases, for example, dealing with contracts (c. 1290) or labor laws (c. 1286).

Acts of administrative power referred to in canon 1400, §2 are termed "particular administrative acts" in canon 1732 and "decree[s]" in canon 1733. Canon 35 identifies administrative acts as decrees, precepts, and rescripts; canon 59, §2 extends this to permissions and the verbal granting of a favor. One should see above at canons 48–59 for a detailed explanation. It is a reasonable interpretation of canon 1400, §2, therefore, that controversies arising from decrees, precepts, and rescripts and those actions equivalent to them in law are not able to be brought before the judicial forum but must be heard administratively. It is not clear from the Code whether vindicating rights that one considers violated by any other acts is to be considered similarly restricted.

Who might be involved in such a case? The law specifies that an administrative act requires the use of executive power (c. 35), and executive power is a type of power of governance (c. 135) whose exercise is determined by canons 136–144. Clearly ordinaries (c. 134, §1) could be involved in such controversies. Those who are their delegates (cc. 131, 133) may also be involved, although this raises the question of the extent to which the exercise of power of governance can be shared, especially with non-clerics. It could be that controversies with various lay officials in diocesan curias may not involve administrative acts, strictly speaking, and could therefore be taken to the tribunal as well as dealt with through recourse to a superior. Pastors, in those restricted cases in which they can make administrative acts, could also be protected from being taken

[104]See NCCB, *On Due Process* (Washington: USCC, 1971).

to the tribunal in controversies arising from their work. But the instances in which they do exercise executive power appear rather limited, such as granting dispensations (e.g., cc. 1079, §2; 1980, §1; 1245), and hence are not likely to give rise to much controversy over rights.

Could a pastor be taken to court for violation of, for example, the rights protected by canon 213 because of his failure to provide a homily or for denying the sacraments to someone? Theoretically his actions are not an exercise of executive power but of pastoral solicitude and thus amenable to court action under canon 1400. Only the developing jurisprudence of church courts will clarify this.

Nevertheless, a whole class of potential conflicts is clearly removed from the jurisdiction of the courts. While the tribunal is not the competent forum for prosecuting or vindicating rights in these cases, the administrative forum is provided. Traditionally this has meant recourse to the hierarchical superior. Procedures for such recourse are detailed in canons 1732–1739. For those exercising administrative power below the bishop, recourse is to the diocesan bishop; if the bishop himself is involved, recourse is to the Apostolic See (see the commentary on c. 360 below concerning the pertinent office at the Apostolic See).

The canons on administrative recourse were originally found in a more developed part on administrative procedure in the 1980 schema, a procedure that could be carried out either through hierarchical recourse or through administrative tribunals. Administrative courts are still mentioned in the Code but no formal organization for them is found there. The 1980 schema proposed an optional organization of such courts; despite the recommendation of the Commission at its 1981 meeting, these canons were deleted from the promulgated text. Administrative courts are mentioned twice in the 1983 Code: canons 1400, §2 and 149, §2 (where such courts could reverse the appointment to ecclesiastical office of someone lacking the legal qualifications for that office). Currently the only administrative tribunal as such is the Second Section of the Apostolic Signatura, but its competencies are restricted and appeal to the Vatican is cumbersome and expensive. It does not represent a practical alternative as an administrative tribunal.[105]

Experience with due process cases in the United States shows that when a bishop is involved the procedures often do not function effectively, even when there is good will on all sides. Administrative tribunals would provide a more binding resolution to such controversies, yet one in better touch with local conditions and sensitive to the nuances of in-

dividual situations. An episcopal conference could still move to establish such fora either by decree (c. 455) or by legislation at a particular council (c. 445).

Due Process of Law

When one is called to judgment by competent authority, a Christian has the right to be judged according to the prescriptions of law and to have these applied with equity. This applies whether the judgment is in the judicial or administrative forum.

There are various rights guaranteed in the procedures of Book VII, including the rights to notice (c. 1508), to counsel (c. 1481), to see the acts (c. 1598), and so on. Procedures in administrative recourse are simpler and the procedural rights there are less developed, but the revised Code does provide the rights to counsel (c. 1738) and to a speedy hearing of the case (cc. 1734–1735).

Legality of Penalties

In contrast to the broad powers to impose penalties even if they were not previously established in law—something that the former Code permitted (see *CIC* 2222)—sanctions are to be imposed only according to the prescriptions of law. Earlier versions of paragraph three were more specific: no one can be punished except in cases defined in the law itself and in a manner determined by it (1971 *LEF* c. 21), or no one can be afflicted with a sanction unless it is for an offense that at the time it was committed could be punished by that sanction as determined in the law itself with some exceptions (*De Populo Dei* c. 36, §5). While the wording has been simplified in canon 221, §3, the intention remains the same.

Book VI provides a number of norms that must be observed in imposing sanctions in the Church. No sanction can be imposed unless a person has externally violated a law or precept, has done so gravely, and is personally imputable for the act (c. 1321, §1). A sanction can be applied by using either a judicial procedure or an administrative one—only, however, after it is clear that nothing else (e.g., fraternal correction, warning, or pastoral solicitude) will repair scandal, restore justice, or lead to a change in the problematic way of acting (c. 1341).

The protection of rights remains one of the highest ideals in law but also one of the most difficult to implement. The revised Code has expressed the ideal, but the practical mechanisms for implementing it are still in a developmental stage. Without broader experience in procedures other than hierarchical recourse, the law must await the practical evolution of jurisprudence before more refined systems can be adopted for the universal Church. But in a Church that becomes ever more worldwide, reliance on ap-

---

[105]See analysis by T. Molloy, "The Theological Foundation of Ecclesiastical Due Process," *CLSAP* 41 (1979), 63.

peal to Rome as an effective means to prosecute and vindicate rights is increasingly impractical and calls for appropriate alternatives in keeping with the principle of subsidiarity.

Support of the Church

Canon 222 — §1. The Christian faithful are obliged to assist with the needs of the Church so that the Church has what is necessary for divine worship, for apostolic works and works of charity and for the decent sustenance of ministers.

All the Christian faithful are bound to help provide for the needs of the Church in keeping with the basic purposes for which the Church acquires earthly goods. These are to provide what is needed for divine worship, to carry on apostolic and charitable works, and to provide for the honest support of ministers of the Church (c. 1254, §2).

The 1917 Code spoke of the right (*ius*) of the Church to demand from the faithful whatever may be necessary for divine worship, honest support of clergy and other ministers, and for other purposes proper to the Church (*CIC* 1496). Vatican II recalled the obligation that the faithful have to support priests (*PO* 20). Support of the Church was considered a fundamental obligation in keeping with one's possibilities and family condition in the *De Populo Dei* schema (c. 29). The *Lex Ecclesiae Fundamentalis* was less nuanced, and the promulgated text of canon 222, §1, is the same as canon 23 of the 1980 *Lex Ecclesiae Fundamentalis*.

Who Is Bound

The canon speaks directly of the Christian faithful without distinction, in a context of duties and rights common to all the faithful. None are exempted—whatever their position in the hierarchy—whether laity, religious, or clergy. However, elsewhere in the law some qualifications are introduced. Clergy, for example, are encouraged but not obliged to give to the Church or to works of charity what is surplus from their church income (c. 282, §2), although this does not exempt them from supporting the Church from other personal income. Professed members of religious institutes do not have personal administration of their goods. Unless the proper law of their institute determines otherwise, however, they are able to determine what is to be done with income from their goods (c. 668, §1), and the obligation of canon 222, §1 would seem to apply when they make this determination prior to profession.

Although the canon does not include any qualifications to aid in its interpretation, those that were proposed in the *De Populo Dei* version may be understood here, namely, the obligation is according to each person's possibilities since no one is held to the impossible, and family obligations are to be taken into account since the family is the domestic church and as such is the most fundamental unit of ecclesial as well as secular society. Family resources must be safeguarded.

The Obligation

The obligation is to assist with the needs of the Church. Christian stewardship understands this in terms of personal time, talent, and financial support. Even those who lack financial resources are bound by the obligation to provide time and talent to support the purposes of the Church, as is evident from the duties of all the Christian faithful to pursue holiness of life and to participate in the mission of the Church (cc. 210–211).

The Code affirms the right of the Church to demand financial support from the faithful (c. 1260) but prefers that this be in the form of free-will offerings or in response to authorized appeals (cc. 1261–1262, 1265). The diocesan bishop is empowered to tax physical as well as juridic persons, but only an extraordinary and moderate tax can be imposed on physical persons and this only after consultation with the finance and presbyteral councils (c. 1263). It is unlikely that taxation would be effective without some form of civil enforcement such as exists in countries where the tithe or church tax is collected by the government.

The purposes for which the Church acquires temporal goods are spelled out in this canon and again in canon 1254, §2. These purposes limit the extent to which the Church can demand and the Christian faithful are obligated to provide support by canon 222, §1. Traditionally church income was divided three ways (divine worship, support of the clergy, and benefits for the poor) or four ways (an additional part going to the bishop's work of hospitality). Changed social and economic conditions have produced different percentages that are needed for the various categories, but the purposes remain fundamentally the same.

The Church engages not only in divine worship but also in apostolic and charitable works. These vary according to the conditions of time and place but along with word and sacrament are constitutive of the mission of the Church[106] and are to be supported by all. Those who on behalf of the church community and in its name provide ministry in carrying out this mission are also to be supported. It should be noted that "ministers" are specified in canon 222, §1 without further qualification. The 1917 Code was not dissimilar, for it mentioned "other ministers" in addition to clergy (*CIC* 1496). The 1983 Code is more specific, however, for it re-

---

[106]See 1971 Synod of Bishops, "Introduction," *Justice in the World* (USCC edition), 63.

quires adequate support to be provided lay persons who are involved in special service in the Church (c. 231, §2) as well as clergy (c. 281). Both Codes require just wages be paid to employees (*CIC* 1524; c. 1286). However, lay ministers installed on a stable basis as lectors or acolytes do not acquire thereby any claim for such support (c. 230, §1).

Social Justice and Charity

§2. They are also obliged to promote social justice and, mindful of the precept of the Lord, to assist the poor from their own resources.

Christians are bound by a double obligation of promoting social justice by which the systemic injustices in society are addressed and of meeting the practical needs of the poor. The latter obligation is specifically tied in the canon to a precept of the Lord.

This canon is not found in the *Lex Ecclesiae Fundamentalis*. It was added after the 1981 Commission meeting. *De Populo Dei* (c. 38) did cover much of the same concerns, although no mention was made of a dominical precept and the language of the canon was more diffuse. There is no direct source in the texts of Vatican II, although the substance of the canon clearly reflects conciliar doctrine.

Social Justice

Christian social teaching has long presented the dignity of the human person as fundamental to the social order. During the twentieth century various popes emphasized personal dignity over against the pressures in society that would deny or restrict that dignity and the rights that flow from it. In the latter part of the century, Catholic social thought has increasingly pointed to the disorders in the social systems themselves as the object of justice critiques. It is not enough to show charity toward a person who is impoverished; it is necessary to do something about the social system that produces the conditions of poverty. Justice in society extends beyond relations between individuals and includes the whole fabric of societal relationships. Vatican II and recent popes have also stressed the global aspects of social justice, for the interdependence of peoples is an integral element of any social system today.

The canon calls for Christians to "promote" social justice. It does not specify how they are to do this. The possibilities vary depending on the abilities and situation of each person. Some are activists attempting to address social injustice directly. Others participate in organizations and movements that seek to promote social justice through collective efforts (c. 298, §1). For many Christians the obligation of promoting social justice will be fulfilled by responsibly considering the impact on justice in society from their everyday actions.

Charity toward the Poor

Practical concern for less fortunate persons has been a hallmark of Christians from the beginning. Paul took up collections for the Church at Jerusalem in its hour of need. Deacons were instituted specifically to administer care for the poor. Organized distribution of alms has characterized the Church in every age, although it is not intended to relieve individuals of their personal responsibility but rather to provide a channel for this personal concern to be expressed through the Christian community.

By placing together in the same canon the obligations of promoting social justice and meeting the needs of the poor, the Code shows both the intimate connection of justice and charity and the necessity for personal attention to both concerns. Without justice there can be no charity; charity provides the completion and ultimate end of justice. Caring for the needs of the poor from one's own resources provides practical attention to the needs of others and an immediate reminder of one's personal responsibilities but should also enkindle a more positive involvement in works of social justice.

The canon requires the aid to come from one's personal resources. It does not limit this duty to lay persons. Even those with administrative responsibilities in the Church's charitable works are bound to add their own personal contribution as well as their administrative skill. In discussing the criteria for remuneration of clergy, Vatican II included the need for sufficient income so priests can provide personal aid to the poor (*PO* 20).

In doing works of charity, the faithful are directed by the canon to be mindful of the precept of the Lord. No specific precept is cited in the law. The counsel of poverty, one of the evangelical counsels professed by those in consecrated life (c. 600), is to be distinguished from the precept of the Lord to practice charity toward the poor. The Council considered poverty from several angles, including the preaching of the gospel to the poor (*LG* 8), following Christ in poverty of spirit (*AA* 4), and the practical needs of poor people today (*LG* 27) that even call for the transformation of the international social order (*GS* 63, 90). It did not specify a dominical precept as such, but it implied one when addressing the practical consequences of human dignity (*LG* 27).

The precept is not the one given to the rich young man who was told to sell all he had, give the proceeds to the poor, and return to follow Jesus (Mt 19:16–22); that is the evangelical counsel, not a precept for all. For all the Christian faithful the precept is based on the judgment that will be given in accord with Matthew 25:40, where doing to the least of the poor is equivalent to doing to Christ.

Limitations

Canon 223 — §1. In exercising their rights the Christian faithful, both as individuals and when gathered in associations, must take account of the common good of the Church and of the rights of others as well as their own duties toward others.

§2. In the interest of the common good, ecclesiastical authority has competence to regulate the exercise of the rights which belong to the Christian faithful.

Limitations on the exercise of rights by individuals or groups are based on concern for the common good, respect for the rights of others, and one's own duties toward others. These limits should be apparent to the Christian faithful themselves but they can also be spelled out by ecclesiastical authorities.

The canon is drawn from *Dignitatis Humanae* 7 and is a modification of canon 24 of the 1980 *Lex Ecclesiae Fundamentalis.* Whereas the earlier version had specified that authorities could limit by invalidating and incapacitating laws, the promulgated text carries no such mention and clearly applies only to the exercise of rights.

Since the canon does limit the exercise of rights, it is to be interpreted strictly (c. 18). Three types of limitations are given—all apply to the exercise and not to the existence of rights; limits on the existence of certain rights can be set by sanctions (c. 1336, §1).

(1) Common Good

Paragraph one refers to the common good "of the Church" whereas paragraph two relates to the common good without qualifications. Are these the same, or is something special added in paragraph one? Vatican II used the term "common good of the Church" three times; each referred to the common welfare rather than to the technical meaning of "common good" in the Church's social teaching.[107] On the other hand, the Council also distinguished the common good in the temporal order as the concern of civil governments, implying that the common good in the religious order is not subject to civil control but rather is the concern of ecclesiastical authorities.[108]

Dignitatis Humanae 7 is the textual source for the wording in paragraph one. The conciliar text speaks first of the rights of others, then of duties toward others, and finally of the "common good of all." The last item is now placed first in the Code's listing and is changed to the "common good of the Church." Does the phrase now mean the common welfare of the Church (as of an institution), or does it mean the sum of those conditions of life in the church community by which persons can seek their perfection more fully and expeditiously (as *DH* 6 defines "common good")? The difference is that what is necessary for the institution's welfare may not directly affect the conditions in which each of its members seeks perfection. We are faced with the option of adopting an institutional emphasis as the good of the Church or of focusing on the Church as the people of God.

Given the use of common good without qualifiers in paragraph two, the general context of the Book that addresses the Church as the people of God, and the definition of common good in the conciliar document from which the canon is taken, the strict interpretation of the canon requires the technical sense in this use of "common good." That is, it refers to the sum of those conditions within the Church by which persons can seek their perfection. The exercise of rights is to be limited not because of the institution's convenience, but only because such an exercise would harm the conditions within which Christians seek their perfection in the life of the Church.

Christians should be sensitive to these factors themselves. Church authorities can also intervene on this basis to regulate the exercise of rights (§2). That they should do so cautiously while respecting the limits of their authority was spelled out in canon 34 of *De Populo Dei,* which provided for recourse when church authorities went beyond the limits of their competence. This canon was not retained in the promulgated Code, but its substance is covered in the norms on administrative procedure (cc. 1732–1739) and in the sanction for abuse of ecclesiastical power (c. 1389).

(2) Rights of Others

Resolving the conflict of rights is one of the most complex and delicate questions in law. The canon does not propose a norm for handling such conflicts; instead, it proposes an attitude. The exercise of one's rights is limited by the rights that others enjoy. Respect for others should normally lead to restraint in the exercise of one's own rights. Yet conflicts may still arise; the vindication of rights in such situations is covered by canon 221, §2 and the procedures available to implement it. The sensitivity to others enjoined by canon 223, §1, however, remains basic to any resolution of these conflicts. In itself respect for the rights of others is not given as a basis for intervention by ecclesiastical authorities; however, when it reaches the point of affecting the common good, then on that basis the authorities may intervene (§2).

---

[107] *CD* 2 speaks of the pope's role in promoting the good (welfare) common to the Church universal and to each individual church. *AA* 24 indicates some associations are given a special standing in the Church in view of the exigencies of the common good (welfare). *PO* 10 permits priests to belong to personal prelatures or to be trained in special seminaries for the common good (welfare) of the whole Church.

[108] On civil authorities and the common good, see *GE* 3, *DH* 3, and *GS* 78 (in which it is the common good of humankind).

(3) Duties toward Others

Some of the duties listed in this title have been directed toward one's personal life (e.g., duties regarding holiness of life, education); others are duties toward others. A person may also have duties toward others because of a position, office, or function or because of rights that others have. The limitation on the exercise of rights based on this canon is restricted to respecting duties one has toward others, not all duties in general.

Dignitatis Humanae 7 goes on to give the spirit in which limitations on rights are to be considered. While the Code does not incorporate this into the canon, the conciliar text does provide an important source for interpreting the Code. Limitations are not to be imposed arbitrarily or in a manner that favors one person over others. Rather, limitations are to be according to juridic norms in conformity with the objective moral order; they are to be such as are required for effectively protecting the rights of all, promoting an honest public peace, and providing due regard for public morality. Moreover, the Council calls for freedom to be acknowledged as much as possible, with restrictions applied only insofar as necessary.

TITLE II
THE OBLIGATIONS AND RIGHTS OF THE LAY CHRISTIAN FAITHFUL
[cc. 224–231]

The 1917 Code contained two canons directly addressing the rights and obligations of the laity. Canon 682 affirmed the right of the laity (but indeed of all the Christian faithful) to receive the sacraments, and canon 683 prohibited lay persons from wearing ecclesiastical garb. There is a marked change in perspective in the revised Code reflecting the increased awareness of the role of lay persons in the Church and of the equality of all the Christian faithful. Immediately following the canons on the obligations and rights of all the faithful, eight canons delineate in a special way certain major obligations and rights of lay persons and indicate that others are to be found throughout the Code.

To understand this shift in perspective, it will be necessary to explore the meaning of the term "lay person" before examining the development of this title in the Code and the specific canons it contains.

Lay Persons

Who is a lay person? The answer is not easily formulated, as efforts of theologians and the magisterium itself at Vatican II testify.[109] Initially a negative definition is used: a lay person is not a priest or reli-

gious (*AA* 31). Attempts at a more positive understanding have developed three key elements:

- A lay person is a baptized Christian faithful, a member of the people of God. As such, lay persons participate in the mission of the Church in their own proper manner.

- Lay persons' functions in the Church are not as ordained ministers, but they do have legitimate functions within the ecclesial community.

- In contrast with religious, lay persons are in the world and related directly to the secularity of the world.

That is, they are not set apart from the world (as religious are) but are immersed in the secular activities of daily life and precisely there they bear a special Christian role. They are the mustard seed, the leaven, the presence of the Church in the world to transform it into the Kingdom of Christ and of God. This is not something exclusive to lay persons, for all the Church is to carry on this work; however, it is something specific to laity (*AA* 2, 7).

These elements are not to be understood as compartmentalized but as forming one unique reality. Lay persons are Christian faithful; they differ from other Christian faithful in the functions they exercise in the Church and in the world, but all Christian faithful exercise functions in the Church and in the world. There is, as seen above (c. 208), a fundamental equality among all the Christian faithful that is prior to any differentiation in terms of function.

There has been a common practice of using "lay person" and "faithful" interchangeably. The Council attempted to correct this, making the point especially in *Lumen Gentium* by placing the chapter on the people of God ahead of those on the hierarchy, lay persons, and religious life. All are Christian faithful, including hierarchy and religious. The Code attempts to integrate this same point in its organization of canons and by inserting the word "lay" when it means specifically lay Christian faithful. How consistent the effort has been is not clear, and it will still be necessary to evaluate the exact sense of "Christian faithful" in each context. Nevertheless, the position is clear: Christian faithful refers to the common condition of all the baptized whether lay, ordained, or living a consecrated life. So what is specific to lay persons as contrasted with clergy and religious?

Some have attempted to construct a legal understanding of lay persons as a status comparable to clergy and religious. While all are involved in the mission of the Church, each of these three categories is seen as having mutually exclusive, identifiable functions within that mission that give each its proper character. The problem has been to find

---

[109]See survey of literature and analysis of the development in Vatican II by E. Schillebeeckx, *The Mission of the Church* (New York: Seabury, 1973), 90–116.

what is exclusive to lay persons. For example, most of the obligations and rights in the canons that follow are common to all the Christian faithful. Those related to marriage and parenthood, while renounced by clergy and persons who consecrate their lives to evangelical chastity, are common with married ordained deacons; therefore, even these are not exclusively "lay." One should also see the discussion above at canon 207 on efforts to identify the specific difference between clergy and laity.

From a canonical perspective it may be more useful to affirm that lay persons are Christian faithful with all the rights and obligations common to Christian faithful and not to attempt to build a distinct status beyond this. To adopt such a perspective implies a shift in the understanding of the relationship of the Church and the world—even while it continues to recognize the specific place of clergy and religious within the Church.[110] The Code has not adopted this view but reflects an understanding of Church as an entity standing apart from the world. This is perhaps most evident in canons 129–144 on the governance function that is presented in the restricted sense of inner church activities rather than as primarily directed toward establishing the reign of Christ in the world. However, these are theoretical points that must be developed elsewhere and need not impede an understanding of the canons as they stand.

There is, moreover, a point to emphasizing rights and obligations that may be more pressing for the majority of the Christian faithful in the Church today—no matter which theoretical approach is taken to understanding who is a lay person. The various *coetus* that have worked on these canons recognized that many rights of lay persons are scattered throughout the Code. Those that are singled out in this title are not intended to lock lay persons in an enclosed circle, but more simply they are presented in an effort to respond to criticism that the former Code's meagre treatment of lay persons represented a serious deficiency in the Church's law.[111]

Developing the Canons

The *coetus* on the laity and associations of the faithful was among the first to complete its work.[112] The material was later incorporated into the schema for Book II, *De Populo Dei*, at the very end of the book (cc. 523–530). It followed sections on clergy, the hierarchical constitution of the Church, and institutes of consecrated life. This was an organizational scheme similar to that of Book II in the 1917 Code.

An initial canon attempted to specify who are meant by "lay persons": they are all the Christian faithful except those who are ordained ministers or members of an institute of consecrated life. There followed most of the rights and obligations now found in the Code with the exception of the present canon 226. Paragraph one of that canon was added in light of the consultation on *De Populo Dei;* paragraph two was inserted when *Lex Ecclesiae Fundamentalis* was integrated into the Code in the last stages of the revision process.

A special *coetus* reviewed the comments on *De Populo Dei.* The initial canon was replaced by one suggested in the consultation, the forerunner of canon 226 was added, and several other changes were made in individual canons; however, the substance of the earlier draft remained intact.[113] When the various books were combined to form the 1980 schema a new organization was given to Book II as a result of lengthy discussion by this *coetus.*[114] Book II opened with two general canons on the Christian faithful (cc. 204 and 207 in the 1983 Code), a title on sacred ministers (their training, incardination, obligations and rights, and loss of clerical status), and then a second title on the obligations and rights of Christian lay persons. The obligations and rights of all the Christian faithful were to be treated in the *Lex Ecclesiae Fundamentalis.*

Cardinal Willebrands, a member of the Code Commission, proposed the organization of these two titles be reversed, treating the obligations and rights of lay persons immediately after the two general canons. The Commission agreed and added that the obligations and rights of all the Christian faithful would come before those of lay persons when the *Lex Ecclesiae Fundamentalis* was integrated into the Code.[115] This is the organization that now appears in the promulgated text. No significant changes were made in the text of the canons by the *Relatio* or at the 1981 Code Commission meeting. Some stylistic adjustments were made prior to promulgation.

Canon 224 — In addition to those obligations and rights which are common to all the Christian faithful and those which are determined in other canons, the lay Christian faithful are bound by the obligations and possess the rights which are enumerated in the canons of this title.

This introductory canon was added as a result of the consultation on the 1977 *De Populo Dei* schema. It emphasizes that the obligations and rights of lay Christian faithful are actually found in several places in the Code: in this title, in the previous one on the obligations and rights of all Christians, and scattered throughout the Code. The canon does not

---

[110]See ibid.; also Komonchak.
[111]See reports of *coetus* discussions in *Comm* 2 (1970), 95–96, and 13 (1981), 314–315.
[112]*Comm* 2 (1970), 89–98.

[113]*Comm* 13 (1981), 314–322.
[114]*Comm* 12 (1980), 48–54; 13 (1981), 298–302.
[115]*Rel,* 48.

make an exclusive claim that only lay persons enjoy the rights in this title, but clearly they do apply specifically to lay persons. In keeping with the decision to avoid definitions in the Code when possible, no definition or even description of a lay person is given here (although one should see c. 207).

Mission

Canon 225 — §1. Since the laity like all the Christian faithful, are deputed by God to the apostolate through their baptism and confirmation, they are therefore bound by the general obligations and enjoy the general right to work as individuals or in associations so that the divine message of salvation becomes known and accepted by all persons throughout the world; this obligation has a greater impelling force in those circumstances in which people can hear the gospel and know Christ only through lay persons.

§2. Each lay person in accord with his or her condition is bound by a special duty to imbue and perfect the order of temporal affairs with the spirit of the gospel; they thus give witness to Christ in a special way in carrying out those affairs and in exercising secular duties.

The general obligation to carry out the mission of the Church that is common to all the Christian faithful is reaffirmed in a special way for lay persons. The basis for this obligation is sacramental, specifically the sacraments of baptism and confirmation. It may be carried out singly or jointly with others, even in associations. The object of this missionary activity is twofold: to evangelize those who have yet to hear and accept the gospel (§1) and to transform the temporal order with the spirit of the gospel (§2). Lay persons have a special role in this mission at times because it is only through them that the gospel will be heard (§1); at all times, it is through the secular activities typical of lay persons that the temporal order is to be transformed (§2).

The canon is drawn from conciliar sources, particularly *Lumen Gentium* 33 and *Ad Gentes* 21 for paragraph one, and *Apostolicam actuositatem* 7 and *Gaudium et Spes* for paragraph two. Both the *Lex Ecclesiae Fundamentalis* and *De Populo Dei* schema (c. 524) addressed this issue. The promulgated text is adapted from the *De Populo Dei* version that appeared as canon 270 in the 1980 schema.

One should see the commentary above on canons 211 and 216 for the obligations and rights common to all Christians, including lay persons, in their apostolate to implement the Church's mission. Canon 225 reaffirms certain key points as they apply to lay persons.

(1) Source of apostolate. God is the ultimate source for any Christian's involvement in the apostolate. God's action is identified in the canon as coming through baptism and confirmation. *Apostolicam actuositatem* 3 also singled out the Spirit's gifts or charisms as another source of the apostolate, but the canon does not mention this. Participation in the apostolate is not a question of prior deputation by ecclesiastical authorities; it comes from a divine commissioning (sacramental and perhaps also charismatic) that calls for the baptized to act in virtue of their own Christian commitment.

(2) Manner of apostolate. *Apostolicam actuositatem* 15–22 describes the various forms that apostolic effort can take among lay persons. No one is exempt from the individual apostolate. At times this may even be the only way the gospel can be spread (*AA* 17). More effective work is often done either in communities such as a parish, or through organized movements and associations. "Catholic Action" has received special recognition in the Church, but it is not the exclusive way lay persons carry out their apostolate.

(3) Evangelization. As stated earlier (c. 211) this is to be taken in a broad sense. It is not restricted to the ordained, those with a canonical mission or mandate, or professional missionaries (although all these retain a special importance in the work of evangelization—*AG* 23–27). Moreover, this is a "general" obligation. It neither requires nor prohibits lay persons to go to foreign lands or to become full-time evangelists at home. Those who do propose to adopt such a high profile in evangelization are to do so in communion with church authorities and always respecting church teaching (cc. 759, 772, 781–792).

(4) Transform the temporal order. Vatican II repeatedly affirmed the proper autonomy of the temporal order. Christians are to respect its proper laws and competencies. Yet the Church is also called to transform through the spirit of the gospel the sinfulness with which the temporal order is infected (*AA* 7, *GS* 43, etc.). Typically, but not exclusively, this is done through the secular activities of lay persons. Pastors have the responsibility of clearly stating principles concerning the purpose of creation and the proper use of this world's goods, but it pertains to those who are immersed in the secular to develop practical applications (*AA* 7).

Marriage and Family Life

Canon 226 — §1. Lay persons who live in the married state in accord with their own vocation are bound by a special duty to work for the upbuilding of the people of God through their marriage and their family.

§2. Because they have given life to their children, parents have a most serious obligation and enjoy the right to educate them; therefore Christian parents are especially to care for the Christian education of their children according to the teaching handed on by the Church.

Married life constitutes a special vocation. With it comes the special duty of building up the people of God through the witness of married life and the development of a Christian family. Parents in particular have the primary right and duty to educate their children and as Christians to see that their children receive a Christian education.

This canon is drawn from several conciliar sources. *Apostolicam actuositatem* 11 and *Gaudium et Spes* 47–52 deal with marriage and family life; *Lumen Gentium* 11 calls the family the "domestic church"; and marriage is termed a "vocation" by *Lumen Gentium* 35 and *Gaudium et Spes* 48, 49, and 52. Drawing on all these sources but not verbatim, a proposal submitted during the consultation on the 1977 *De Populo Dei* schema was adopted by the *coetus* and became canon 271 in the 1980 schema. It has been adopted in a modified form as paragraph one of this canon, rearranging some of the words in the 1980 schema and dropping a final clause about laws and pastoral action by church pastors in their service to families.

Gravissimum Educationis 3 deals expressly with the rights and obligations of parents for the education of their children; paragraph two is drawn primarily from this source. It was first drafted for the *Lex Ecclesiae Fundamentalis* and appeared as canon 17, §2 in the 1980 version of that document. When the canons of the *Lex Ecclesiae Fundamentalis* were not incorporated into the Code, this section was removed from the general rights and obligations of all Christian faithful and inserted as paragraph two of this canon in the section on lay persons. The phrase qualifying parents as the first and principal educators of their children, taken from *Gravissimum Educationis* 3 in the *Lex Ecclesiae Fundamentalis* text, has been dropped from the final version.

Marriage

Matrimony received special attention at the Council, especially in *Gaudium et Spes* where it was treated as the first of the more urgent concerns of our times. The conciliar teaching has renewed and enriched the Catholic understanding of married life, but there is still need for a fully developed theology on matrimony. This canon does not attempt to make up for the theological work yet to be done, but it does identify certain elements that a theology of matrimony would need to consider.

Marriage is said to be a special calling by God. It is a human reality, but God works within the created order to call couples to a relationship that carries a sacred meaning. Christian marriage establishes the domestic Church, the most fundamental expression of the ecclesial community. It contributes in a special way to building up the people of God, and this is accomplished in a double sense. By their love and fidelity in marriage, cou-

ples make visible in the manner of an ongoing sacramental experience the ever active love and fidelity of Christ for the Church. In addition to this spiritual sense, married couples through their children raise up new members to continue and build up the people of God.

Parents

In its struggle with civil authorities who wish to take over schools and to monopolize the educational enterprise, the Church has insisted that parents are the primary educators of their children and therefore have the primary right and duty to determine how that education will be carried out. The Council applied this position internally in the Church as well as in the Church-State struggle that occasioned it (*GE* passim). Continuing this attention to parents within the Church's own activities, at various stages in the revision process canons have been added until now there is a veritable bill of parental rights and obligations scattered throughout the revised Code.

This canon is the foundation for the rest. Based on *Gravissimum Educationis* 3, it clearly applies within the Church's own legal system the principle that parents have the primary right and duty to see to the education of their own children. While this obligation and right are not absolute but must respect the requirements of the common good (in the temporal order and in the Church), they are so fundamental as to lead to further specifications on behalf of parents.

Parents are to form their children in the faith and in the practice of Christian living (c. 744, §2) and therefore to receive the support of pastors and others involved in religious education (c. 776). The obligation and right to educate their children are repeated in canon 793, §1 with the further specification that Catholic parents have the obligation and right to select the means apt for the Catholic education of their children. Moreover, canon 793, §2 affirms the right that parents have to support from civil authorities in carrying out these obligations. Schools are meant to help parents, and the working together of teachers with parents and parents' associations is called for by canon 796. Parents are free to select the schools where they will send their children (c. 797); in addition, while Catholics are encouraged to send their children to Catholic schools, they are bound to see to the education of their children as Catholics even if they choose other institutions (c. 798).

The role of parents in preparing their children for the sacraments is given repeated emphasis. They have an overall concern (c. 835, §4) as well as specific roles with regard to baptism (cc. 851, 2°; 855; 857; 867–868; 874), confirmation (c, 890), Eucharist (c. 914), and marriage (cc. 1063; 1071, §1, 6°). Christian families are to foster vocations to ordained ministry and religious life (c. 233, §1) and are to receive special attention from parish pastors (c. 529, §1). Couples in ecumenical or religiously mixed marriages are to be given special help (c. 1128).

Parents retain their traditional responsibilities before church courts. In most cases they represent their minor children before an ecclesiastical tribunal (c. 1478). Parents could be exempted from testifying against their children or one another—and vice versa (c. 1548, §2).

The canons already discussed on the right to form associations apply to parents, who are explicitly recognized as able to form associations in dealing with schools and teachers (c. 796, §2). Movements to support marriage and family life such as the Christian Family Movement (CFM), Marriage Encounter, Teams of Our Lady, and others are also given canonical recognition through the canons on associations of the faithful (cc. 298–329).

Whether this increased canonical attention to parents and married couples will make any difference for them in the life of the Church depends both on how seriously these provisions of the revised Code are taken and on what practical efforts are made at the local level to implement them. Parents and married couples themselves have a major responsibility for this in keeping with canons 225 and 228.

Civil Liberties

Canon 227 — Lay Christian faithful have the right to have recognized that freedom in the affairs of the earthly city which belongs to all citizens; when they exercise such freedom, however, they are to take care that their actions are imbued with the spirit of the gospel and take into account the doctrine set forth by the magisterium of the Church; but they are to avoid proposing their own opinion as the teaching of the Church in questions which are open to various opinions.

Christian lay persons are recognized in church law as enjoying the same civil liberties as all citizens enjoy. Their use of this freedom, however, is always as Christians; it is to be imbued with the spirit of the gospel and attentive to the teaching of the Church. In matters in which opinions differ as to how the gospel applies to concrete situations, they are to use their own prudence and faith-filled insight but must not present as official church teaching what is really personal opinion. The canon is drawn from *Lumen Gentium* 37 (on church recognition of the freedom all citizens enjoy) and *Gaudium et Spes* 43 (on applying Christian insight to temporal affairs). *De Populo Dei* (c. 525) contained the first version of this canon. It was modified after the 1977 consultation to insert the term "Christian faithful" since, the *coetus* noted,

the norm applies not only to lay persons but to all Christian faithful.[116] The promulgated version has some stylistic changes from the 1980 schema (c. 272).

The Church has undergone a long and at times painful development to reach the point where this statement can be made in canon law. While the earliest Christians claimed against the Roman Empire the freedom to worship God as they so chose (and not to worship the emperor) and thus made one of the earliest claims for civil liberty in matters of conscience, the Church itself has been slow to recognize modern civil liberties. Even the Magna Carta was rescinded by the pope. Gregory XVI and his successors in the last century condemned many of the civil liberties affirmed by church leaders in this century.[117] More recent popes, however, have proclaimed the fundamental dignity of human persons and supported the basic rights that flow from that dignity. They have called for recognition of fundamental rights in civil legislation and have encouraged Christians to make use of their rights in defense of the Church when necessary. Vatican II confirmed these developments and established them as policy for the Church, not only in the affirmation of *Lumen Gentium* 37 but also in the significant *Declaration on Religious Liberty (DH)*.

The Code's recognition of these liberties for the lay Christian faithful does not imply that clergy and religious are denied these civil rights. The exercise of certain of them is restricted for clergy and religious, but this is in virtue of their special ministry in the Church or, for religious, their living in some way removed from the world.[118] In virtue of canon 18, such restrictions are to be interpreted strictly so that sacred ministers and religious enjoy the same civil liberties recognized for lay persons and all citizens, except in these limited instances.

Gaudium et Spes 43 recognized that there can be various perceptions of how the gospel is to be applied in the temporal order. In addition to the provision not to claim as church teaching what is really one's own opinion, the Council encouraged Christians to engage in sincere dialogue about these matters and to keep in mind mutual charity and concern for the common good.

Official Positions

Canon 228 — §1. Qualified lay persons are capable of assuming from their sacred pastors those ecclesiastical offices and functions which they are able to exercise in accord with the prescriptions of law.

---

[116]*Comm* 13 (1981), 317.

[117]J.C. Murray, "The Problem of Religious Freedom," *TS* 25 (1964), 503–575.

[118]For clergy, see cc. 285, §§3–4; 286; 287, §2. For religious, see cc. 607, §3 (separation from the world) and 672 (certain restrictions on clergy also apply to religious).

§2. Lay persons who excel in the necessary knowledge, prudence, and uprightness are capable of assisting the pastors of the Church as experts or advisors; they can do so even in councils, in accord with the norm of law.

Competent lay persons are capable of being assigned to ecclesiastical offices that the law permits lay persons to exercise. They can also be counselors to the pastors of the Church, even participating in church councils.

The conciliar sources for this canon are found in *Lumen Gentium* 33 and 37. The *De Populo Dei* schema contained two canons, one on lay persons and participation in the hierarchy's apostolate (c. 526) and the other the forerunner of this canon (c. 528). The *coetus* decided that canon 526 duplicated what is in canon 528 and elsewhere in the Code; therefore, the former was deleted. At the same time the *coetus* inverted the original order of the paragraphs in canon 528. The reorganized canon appeared in the 1980 schema as canon 293 and has been promulgated as canon 228 with some stylistic adjustments.

Competence

In both paragraphs of the canon participation by lay persons is said to apply to those who are competent: "qualified" in paragraph one is further specified by "excel in the necessary knowledge, prudence, and uprightness" in paragraph two. Does this exclude the majority of lay persons? It would seem not, for the basis for competence is to be carefully related to the activities to be undertaken. Clearly the person must possess the qualifications required for the office, whatever they are, whether the potential officeholder be cleric or lay (c. 149). These will depend on the nature of the office; for example, more lay persons may be competent for the position of finance officer in virtue of their training and experience than clergy (c. 494, §1).

The knowledge, prudence, and uprightness to serve as counselor depend on the type of counsel sought. Financial counselors, for example, are to be experts in civil law and economic matters (c. 492, §1), whereas advisors on the pastoral situation in the diocese may gain their expertise from the active living of a Catholic life, whatever their educational background. Parents can give counsel about marriage and family life out of their lived experience; so, too, could persons who have received formal training in family studies. The canon does not limit counselors to those who have one or the other background, but it does seek to provide that some criteria be used in selecting counselors.

Ecclesiastical Office

The understanding of ecclesiastical office was modified by Vatican II (*PO* 20) so that the strict sense of the 1917 Code no longer applies (*CIC* 145). For a discussion of the current meaning of office in canon law, one should see above at canon 145. The change has made it possible for lay persons as well as clergy to be considered for some ecclesiastical offices and the Council explicitly sanctioned this (*LG* 37, *AA* 24). The question now is what offices are able to be committed to lay persons, since the Code has specified these as offices that can be committed to their exercise in accord with the law.

The answer is not clear—mainly because there is no consensus yet on the theoretical basis for lay persons to exercise power in the Church. At Vatican II the power of bishops was debated. Its source was located in sacramental ordination to the episcopate rather than in canonical mission from the pope. The conciliar position is that all power in the Church, whether of orders or of governance (jurisdiction), is sacred power that comes from Christ. The understood channel for Christ's action is the sacrament of orders. It would seem that real power must therefore be restricted to the ordained, although lay persons may provide various services in the Church that do not have a binding force or require the power of orders (cc. 129, 273).

In practice, however, lay persons do exercise certain functions in the Church that traditionally have been considered restricted to the power of governance or jurisdiction. The most obvious example is service as a judge in a church court (c. 1421, §2), but there may be other examples as the implications of several provisions in the revised Code are worked out in detail. These could include the power of major superiors in lay religious institutes (c. 620) and the power of vigilance that can be delegated to finance officers (c. 1278).

Earlier versions of canon 129 attempted to provide for this development, but the theoretical debate surrounding the question led to a more hesitant stance in the final text. Lay persons may "cooperate" in the exercise of the power of governance, but only clergy have the capacity for this power. The distinction is not explained further by the Code and will require more discussion before it has the clarity needed to resolve the situation—if that is possible. Some have suggested that the question is poorly posed and needs to be placed in a more satisfactory theoretical framework.[119]

What, then, are the offices that may be entrusted to lay persons? A comprehensive list is not possible at this point since many offices are left to appropriate local authority to develop. Such, for example, are those related to the diocesan curia (c. 469), parish ministry (cc. 516, §2; 517, §2), and various teaching and sanctifying functions. Some offices formerly restricted by law to priests no longer contain such restrictions; therefore, lay persons could conceivably be named diocesan chancellor (c. 483,

---

[119]See Kilmartin.

§2) and to various positions in the diocesan tribunal (cc. 1421, §2; 1428, §2; 1435). Clearly lay persons are not to be named to offices that the law specifies as restricted to priests or clergy.[120] For other offices it will be necessary for the practice of the Church to clarify what are actually not open to lay persons. Recent experience arising from a shortage of clergy and an increased awareness of the responsibilities of the baptized for the mission of the Church have already opened a number of church positions to lay persons. There is nothing to indicate that the Code will reverse this trend, for it arises from pastoral necessity and in the end, no one is held to the impossible (not even bishops when they must fill offices to provide for the pastoral care of God's people).

Counsel

It is an ancient tradition in church law that those exercising executive power seek counsel from others before taking action. The *Regulae Iuris* incorporated this as "what touches all must be approved by all," though not in the sense of democratizing decisions in the Church.[121] Whatever various interpretations might be given this statement, it does reflect concern for drawing on the wisdom that the Spirit has placed within the whole community. The tradition of consulting the faithful in matters of doctrine bears witness to the same concern.[122] Vatican II deliberately set out to restore this ancient practice and repeatedly called for the pastors of the Church to listen and attend to the desires, opinions, and insights of the rest of the Christian faithful. The right and duty of all Christian faithful to participate in this exchange were reviewed above at canon 212, §§2 and 3.

Such counsel may be given in a variety of ways. Personal dialogue and informal contacts are encouraged by the Council (*AA* 10, 25) and can be accomplished during pastoral visitations by bishops and parish pastors (cc. 383, 396–398, 529). The Council recommended certain structures to assure greater consultation of lay persons within the Church, for example, diocesan pastoral councils (*CD* 27, *AG* 30) and apostolic councils at all levels in the Church (*AA* 26). The Code mandates finance councils for dioceses (c. 492), parishes (c. 537), and most juridic persons (c. 1280) on which lay persons

may serve. It may be surmised that lay people will usually serve on such councils given the competence they enjoy in this field. While diocesan and parish pastoral councils are not mandated by the Code, they can be required within individual dioceses (cc. 511, 536); if they exist, they include lay persons.

Perhaps more significant from a theoretical point of view is the opening of traditional councils to lay participation. While only bishops have deliberative vote in such synods, all who are invited participate intimately in the decision-making process and have a right to be heard. Thus lay persons are now authorized to be members of the diocesan synod (cc. 460, 463), provincial and plenary councils (c. 443), and could be invited to ecumenical councils (c. 339, §2). This is certainly in keeping with ancient canonical tradition but is a change from the 1917 Code, which generally restricted participation in such councils to clergy.[123]

These organized opportunities for consultation by lay persons are not mere window dressing. They are to be taken seriously, as canon 127 makes clear. Their effectiveness, however, depends on a number of factors beyond the control of the law.[124]

Theological Formation

Canon 229 — §1. Lay persons are bound by the obligation and possess the right to acquire a knowledge of Christian doctrine adapted to their capacity and condition so that they can live in accord with that doctrine, announce it, defend it when necessary, and be enabled to assume their role in exercising the apostolate.

§2. Lay persons also possess the right to acquire that deeper knowledge of the sacred sciences which are taught in ecclesiastical universities or faculties or in institutes of religious sciences by attending classes and obtaining academic degrees.

§3. Likewise, the prescriptions as to the required suitability having been observed, lay persons are capable of receiving from legitimate ecclesiastical authority a mandate to teach the sacred sciences.

In order to exercise their proper role in the mission of the Church, lay persons have the obligation and right to acquire a formation in Christian doctrine suited to their capacity and condition. This extends to pursuing formal theological studies and degrees in special church institutions. Qualified lay persons may be given the authorization that theologians receive to teach in institutions of higher learning.

The canon is not based on any particular concili-

---

[120]See cc. 150 (office with full care of souls); 378 (office of bishop); 478, §1 (vicar general, episcopal vicar); 517, §1 (several priests *in solidum* in place of pastor); 521, §1 (pastor); 539 (parochial administrator); 546 (parochial vicar); 553, §1 (dean or vicar forane); 556 (rector of a church); 564 (chaplain); 1420, §4 (judicial vicar, adjunct judicial vicar); 1425, §4 (single judge—must be "cleric").

[121]"Quod omnes tangit debet ab omnibus probari," *R.I.* 29 in VI° (from *Reg. Iur. Civ.*, "quod omnes tangit omnibus approbare et tractare debent"). See Y. Congar, "Quod omnes tangit, ab omnibus tractari et approbari debent," *Revue historique de droit français et étranger* 35 (1958), 210–259.

[122]J. Newman, *On Consulting the Faithful in Matters of Doctrine* (1859) (London: Geoffrey Chapman, 1961).

[123]*CIC* 223 (ecumenical councils), 282 (plenary councils), 286 (provincial councils), and 358 (diocesan synods).

[124]See R. Schoenherr and E. Simpson, *The Political Economy of Diocesan Advisory Councils,* CROS Respondents Report 3 (Madison, Wis.: University of Wisconsin, 1978).

ar text, but paragraph one does reflect the concern of both *Christus Dominus* 13 that the faithful be taught to defend and spread the faith and *Apostolicam actuositatem* in general that there be adequate formation for the apostolate. *Gaudium et Spes* 62 and *Gravissimum Educationis* 11 deal with some of the same concerns expressed in paragraphs two and three. For the more proximate source of the wording of this canon, one should see the proposals by A. del Portillo who prepared the background study for the original *coetus* working on the rights of lay persons and who served as *relator* for the group.[125] The canon appeared in *De Populo Dei* (c. 527) and the 1980 schema (c. 274) in much the same wording as it now appears; only minor stylistic adjustments differentiate the various versions.

Formation in Christian Doctrine (§1)

The knowledge to which lay persons are bound, and to which they have a right, is not just a theology abstracted from the rest of human sciences. In dealing with formation for the apostolate, *Apostolicam actuositatem* 29–30 emphasized the need for a well-rounded human formation in the arts and sciences, in theory, and in interpersonal relations in order to place the knowledge of Christian doctrine in its proper setting. Moreover, since this knowledge is required to live and defend the faith as well as to carry out one's apostolate, it is not just a theoretical understanding of church doctrine. As *Apostolicam actuositatem* 29 insists, lay persons are to be gradually led to see all things under the light of faith by practical experiences; they are to be formed to judge and to act on their own and thereby enter into their role in the mission of the Church.

The obligation and right relate to acquiring such knowledge according to the capacity and condition of each person. Natural gifts and talents differ; of those who have received more, more will be expected. Moreover, the Spirit distributes gifts of wisdom, knowledge, understanding, and so on, and the condition of being graced with various charisms will affect this right and duty. Sacramental initiation also marks the condition of Christians; canon 879 indicates that confirmation obliges the confirmed to be witnesses by word and deed to Christ as well as to spread and defend the faith.

Higher Theological Studies (§2)

Until recently, higher theological studies were often considered the domain of the clergy, even though such studies are not necessarily clerical by their nature. However, there has been a steady growth since the Council in the numbers of lay persons engaged in such studies; the canon reaffirms this trend.

One factor in the past that led to the clerical im-

age for such studies was that they were usually part of the preparation for ordination. Seminaries and institutes of higher theological study were treated in the same part IV of Book III in the 1917 Code, and the Council echoed this view of seminaries as related to institutions of higher theological study when it addressed the issue of freedom of inquiry in theology (*GS* 62; see c. 218 above). In the revision of the Code this perspective has changed. Seminaries are no longer treated with educational institutions but as places of formation in preparation for sacred ministry (cc. 232–264). This does not rule out, however, their being places where higher theological studies do take place (c. 252).

Seminaries remain the most widely distributed institutions in which theological formation can be received. The question of admitting students to theological studies in seminaries must be distinguished from admitting persons to formation for sacred ministry—a distinction often expressed in terms of who may live in the seminary (c. 235). Other opportunities for pursuing higher theological studies exist in graduate departments at various universities (c. 811). Canon 229 explicitly opens ecclesiastical universities and faculties erected by the Apostolic See (cc. 815–821) to competent lay students and provides that academic degrees authorized by the Apostolic See may be earned by clergy or lay, male or female candidates.

Teaching Theology (§3)

Lay persons who have the requisite credentials and competence may teach theology in institutes of higher studies. This was long a primarily clerical domain but in recent years has also become more open in practice. The canon reaffirms the correctness of this practice by affirming that lay persons may receive the mandate mentioned in Book III for teachers of theology. One should see below at canon 812 for a fuller explanation of this "mandate." There would also appear to be no obstacle to naming lay men or women with the requisite degrees and competence to teach in seminaries (c. 253).

This more intimate participation by lay persons in the teaching function of the Church does have one exception in current law. Presbyters who are dismissed from clerical status through a rescript of dispensation from celibacy (c. 290, 3°) are once again in the same condition as lay persons canonically (c. 292). Yet the rescript of dispensation requires the bishop to inform the dispensed person that he is restricted from teaching theology in institutes of higher learning. The provision of canon 299, §3 is not, strictly speaking, a right; it is rather a faculty or ability to be authorized. The rescript does not therefore deny a right that might be claimed in virtue of this canon, but it has been argued that the dispensing power of bishops (c. 87,

[125]See del Portillo, 132–137.

§1) could extend to dispensing from this restriction in individual cases provided there is no danger of scandal.[126] This would permit competent theologians in individual cases to continue to provide their services to the Church as lay persons in keeping with canon 229. This opinion, however, is disputed by others in terms of interpreting the extent of the bishop's power to dispense.

Liturgical Functions

Canon 230 — §1. Lay men who possess the age and qualifications determined by decree of the conference of bishops can be installed on a stable basis in the ministries of lector and acolyte in accord with the prescribed liturgical rite; the conferral of these ministries, however, does not confer on these lay men a right to obtain support or remuneration from the Church.

§2. Lay persons can fulfill the function of lector during liturgical actions by temporary deputation; likewise all lay persons can fulfill the functions of commentator or cantor or other functions, in accord with the norm of law.

§3. When the necessity of the Church warrants it and when ministers are lacking, lay persons, even if they are not lectors or acolytes, can also supply for certain of their offices, namely, to exercise the ministry of the word, to preside over liturgical prayers, to confer baptism, and to distribute Holy Communion in accord with the prescriptions of law.

Explicit recognition is given to several ways in which lay persons may exercise prominent roles in liturgical services. Lay men can be installed in a stable manner as lectors and acolytes. Lay persons, whether men or women and of whatever responsible age, may be deputed on a less permanent basis to perform a variety of liturgical functions. In the absence of ministers, lay persons can be authorized to supply for certain of their liturgical services.

Sacrosanctum Concilium, the first constitution issued by Vatican II, called for a broader distribution of roles in liturgical celebrations. While this canon is not taken verbatim from this or any conciliar document, it does reflect the serious efforts that have been made since the Council to implement the conciliar principles. Paul VI provided for lay ministers to be installed on a stable or permanent basis in the *motu proprio Ministeria quaedam* (August 15, 1972);[127] paragraph one is a condensation of the salient provisions of that document. *Sacrosanctum Concilium* 29 first taught the key elements in paragraph two and the canon expresses the liturgical

law found in the *General Instruction to the Roman Missal,* numbers 66–68.[128] *Lumen Gentium* 35 and *Ad Gentes* 16–17 related situations in which lay persons are rightly called on to provide services needed by the community, whether in conditions of persecution or as catechists in missionary lands; paragraph three draws on these sources and subsequent specifications in the revision of the liturgical rites. The canon in its present text is but slightly modified from its two earlier versions, *De Populo Dei* canon 529 and the 1980 schema canon 275.

Installed Ministries (§1)

When Paul VI eliminated tonsure, the minor orders, and subdiaconate from the Latin Church with *Ministeria quaedam,* he likewise provided for a new recognition of lay ministry in the Church. He intentionally took this step to emphasize that ministry is not just ordained or sacred ministry. All participate in the mission of the Church. "Ministry" is one way of carrying out that mission; the Code also speaks elsewhere of the "apostolate" and of "service" by lay persons. Formal recognition of lay ministry was made in terms of the key elements of the Church's mission: word (lector or "reader") and sacrament (acolyte, focusing on the central sacrament—the Eucharist).

The Code continues the canonical provisions from *Ministeria quaedam.* Installation on a permanent or stable basis in these two ministries is limited to men and to those who have reached the age specified by the conference of bishops. In the United States that age is eighteen. A special liturgical rite is to be followed. Installation, however, is not an order. Episcopal orders are not required to install lay men validly in these ministries; this is to be done by the bishop or the major superior of a religious order. By installation a minister does not acquire any claim to financial support in the Church; he does not become a cleric (c. 266, §1).

Lay ministry is not limited to lector and acolyte. *Ministeria quaedam* permitted conferences of bishops to request the installation in other ministries if this was necessary or helpful in their local situation. The revised Code does not abolish this possibility. In principle it would be possible to have a great variety of formally recognized and liturgically instituted ministries within a local church.

Ministry differs from office (c. 145). Installation is to a ministry; a separate determination specifies the community on behalf of whom this service is to be rendered. An installed minister can change offices, as when moving from one parish to another, without the installation in the ministry having to be repeated. It would be necessary, of course, to receive the usual provision of office (c. 146). Yet installation in a lay ministry without reference to a

[126]See J. Provost, K. Lasch, and H. Skillen, "Dispensed Priests in Ecclesial Ministry: A Canonical Reflection," *CS* 14 (1975), 121–133.

[127]*AAS* 64 (1972), 529–534; see Bishops' Committee on the Liturgy, *Ministries in the Church,* Study Text 3 (Washington: USCC, 1974).

[128]See revised text as translated by ICEL, *IGMR,* Liturgy Documentary Series 2 (Washington: USCC, 1982).

specific community on behalf of whom that ministry is to be exercised does seem anomalous and points to one of the limitations in this approach to formalizing lay ministry.

Two problems have surfaced since Paul VI's *motu proprio* in 1972. The first is that the ministries can be exercised by persons who have not been formally installed in them, such as boys under eighteen who normally serve at the altar or men and women who read, distribute the Eucharist, and perform many of the other functions of lectors and acolytes. Moreover, not all lay persons who perform ministry in a stable manner are formally installed liturgically. The Code does not mention liturgical installation for catechists (c. 785)—even though *Ad Gentes* 17 called for them to be given a canonical mission within a local community in a liturgical rite. Why, then, bother with formal installation on a stable basis of men as lectors and acolytes?

Theoretically there could be a significance for such installation if the entire community were conscious of its ministerial role and a variety of persons were providing multiple ministries. Formally installing some who through experience and training evidence an ability to lead and moderate others in these services could strengthen the Church's recognition and awareness of the genuinely ministerial role of all the Christian faithful and the special responsibilities of lay persons.

In practice, however, this vision is rarely encountered. The new ministries were initiated when minor orders and subdiaconate were suppressed, and they combine the functions of these orders in several ways. Although not meant just as steps to sacred orders, candidates for orders are required to be installed and to exercise these ministries before seeking ordination (c. 1035). This could imply that candidates for orders should surface from a broad experience in lay ministry; more frequently it means that the lay ministries are installed as part of the seminary experience and once again take on the flavor that minor orders had before they were suppressed. It is rare to find installed lectors and acolytes as lay men in secular employment, providing volunteer service in the Church—although this is the image in the canon.

The second problem encountered since 1972 is the restriction of installation in these ministries to men. The basis for this restriction has been questioned throughout the process for revising the Code. These are truly lay ministries, are not intended as steps toward sacred orders, and the restriction to males appears an unwarranted discrimination. The limitation, however, has been retained in the canon.

The difficulty in practice is that many of the functions installed lectors and acolytes are to perform have already been entrusted to women as well as men. Women are authorized to proclaim the readings before the gospel, and in some countries such as the United States the conference of bishops has permitted them to read from the same location inside the sanctuary where the gospel will be proclaimed. Women are authorized in many dioceses to distribute the Eucharist as extraordinary ministers. What would be the impact on the community if some who provide these ministries were to be installed but others, equally qualified and experienced, were to be denied installation merely on the basis of sex? It would seem to belie the provisions of canon 208 on the equality of the baptized.

Temporary Deputation (§2)

Recognizing the practical facts and being faithful to the possibilities in *Sacrosanctum Concilium* 29, the *General Instruction on the Roman Missal* (nos. 68–70) has provided for lay persons of either sex and without canonical limitation on age (although clearly they must be old enough to do the service appropriately) to supply some of the same services as installed lectors and acolytes. These additional roles are classified in the pre-Code documents as liturgical ministries; although the canon does not employ the same terminology, these services may still properly be termed "ministries."

The 1917 Code restricted ministry at the altar to males (*CIC* 813). The revised Code does not retain that canon; in virtue of canon 6, §1 it ceases as Code law. However, canon 2 specifies that liturgical law remains in effect. The provisions of the *General Instruction on the Roman Missal* (no. 70) permit women to be appointed to ministries performed outside the sanctuary. They may also be permitted to perform some that are carried on inside the sanctuary; proclaiming the readings before the gospel is explicitly mentioned (no. 70) and distribution of the Eucharist is referred to, implicitly admitting women to the sanctuary (no. 68). Although a subsequent instruction indicated that women are not allowed to serve as altar servers,[129] the Code no longer states this prohibition and the force of this later instruction ceases.[130] The provisions of the *General Instruction on the Roman Missal* need to be interpreted in keeping with conditions of particular churches.[131]

Supplying for Ministers (§3)

The Council (*LG* 35, *AA* 24, *AG* 16–17) had recognized the importance of lay persons' providing certain liturgical services when ministers were unable to do so. This includes both those situations in which clergy are physically absent and those in

---

[129]SCSDW instr On Certain Norms Concerning Worship of the Eucharistic Mystery, *Inaestimabile donum*, April 3, 1980.
[130]See response in *Rel,* 21.
[131]This principle is applied by the *IGMR*, no. 70, to the exercise of these ministries.

which they may be present but their ministerial service is impeded and someone else must supply the basic services permitted to lay persons by law.[132]

The canon permits lay persons to be authorized to exercise the ministry of the word and to preside at liturgical prayer. This could range from Sunday celebrations without a priest to the celebration of the Divine Office or funeral services. The canon also permits the authorization of lay persons to confer baptism and distribute Communion. Through a somewhat complex process, lay persons can also be named to be the official ecclesial witnesses at marriages in fulfillment of the requirements of canonical form (c. 1112).

These authorizations are for cases of necessity. The judgment of what constitutes a case of necessity is left to local authorities. In cases judged to be of necessity, the canon also requires that ministers be "lacking." What kind of ministers are meant here? Clearly sacred ministers would be included, for it was the presupposition of the Council that these were the situations in which lay persons could be so authorized to act. In drafting the Code, however, consideration also had to be given to installed lay ministers who had been introduced since the Council. Initially it was proposed that installed lay ministers as well as sacred or ordained ones be lacking before authorized lay persons could take over. However, this restriction was dropped in the promulgated text. The law now seems to distinguish those who are installed as lectors and acolytes on a stable basis (§1) from lay persons who are authorized to act when sacred ministers are lacking (§3). Of course there is nothing to stop one who is installed as a lector or acolyte from being so authorized; however, one who is not installed could be so authorized and may act even in the presence of a lector or acolyte.

Clearly paragraph three is not a question of someone's acting on his or her own initiative. The regulation of the liturgy and worship life in the diocese is the responsibility of the diocesan bishop (c. 838, §4); normally his authorization is required before a lay person may supply for the minister.[133]

---

[132]This understanding of moral or physical absence is traditionally applied to the conditions needed to use the extraordinary form for marriage (c. 1116, §1). It is reflected elsewhere in the Code; for example, see c. 861, §2 on the minister of baptism.

[133]There is no special authorization needed for a lay person to lead the Divine Office (*General Instruction of the Liturgy of the Hours,* no. 258). In danger of death, any person may baptize (c. 861, §2). The bishop's authorization is needed for lay persons to baptize outside danger of death (c. 861, §2), to assist at marriages (c. 1112), and either directly or through a priest delegated by him for a lay person to be authorized to distribute the Eucharist (*mp Immensae caritatis,* Jan. 29, 1973, no. 1). The bishop sets the general regulations on Sunday celebrations without a priest (c. 1248, §2), but he is not required by general law to specify the lay persons who might be in charge of such celebrations locally.

Employed in Church Service

Canon 231 — §1. Lay persons who devote themselves permanently or temporarily to some special service of the Church are obliged to acquire the appropriate formation which is required to fulfill their function properly and to carry it out conscientiously, zealously, and diligently.

§2. With due regard for can. 230 §1, they have a right to a decent remuneration suited to their condition; by such remuneration they should be able to provide decently for their own needs and for those of their family with due regard for the prescriptions of civil law; they likewise have a right that their pension, social security and health benefits be duly provided.

This canon establishes responsibilities for formation and continued professional competence on the part of lay persons who devote themselves in a special manner to church service, whether permanently or on a temporary basis; it also sets standards for church authorities to meet in terms of providing adequate pay and benefits to such lay persons.

Apostolicam actuositatem 22 set the basic principle, although it applied to church pastors not only the responsibility of providing a just family wage and appropriate benefits but also the duty to aid lay persons in obtaining the necessary instruction, spiritual support, and encouragement. The canon is essentially the same as *De Populo Dei* canon 530 and the 1980 schema canon 276, except that it is now constructed in two paragraphs whereas the earlier versions were only one paragraph; in addition, the promulgated text has added the qualifier "suited to their condition."

Lay persons are here distinguished, according to the special service in the Church that they perform, from the general apostolate and liturgical ministries mentioned earlier (cc. 225, 230). They need not have ecclesiastical offices as such (c. 228, §1), but they may indeed be exercising such an office. Their devotion to such service may be permanent, in the sense of its being without a term, or it may be temporary, i.e., performed only for a time. The canon does not distinguish between full-time and part-time involvement, so both are to be understood as included. The service could be related to the teaching, sanctifying, or governing functions in the Church.

If lay persons are bound to obtain the proper formation to assume a special role in church service, they have a corresponding right to the opportunities in which they can do this. The rights to a Christian education (c. 217) and to theological formation (c. 229) clearly support this. There may also be implications in terms of admission policies to formation programs in seminaries if alternative formation possibilities are not provided in dioceses. The Council source for this canon clearly specified spiritual as well as intellectual formation; admission only to the academic theological programs may not be sufficient to respond to the obligations of the bishops stated by the Council and implied by this canon.

The canon requires that the functions be carried out conscientiously, zealously, and diligently. Given the tendency in other parts of the Code to concentrate on the legally verifiable external elements, these attributes of spirit and attitude are striking. They should be interpreted consistently with other canons relative to the performance of ecclesiastical functions, such as those in which clergy are called to fulfill the functions committed to them "faithfully" (c. 274, §2); bishops are told to remember to set an example of charity, humility, and simplicity of life (c. 387); pastors are said to fulfill their office "in earnest" (c. 529, §1); and administrators of church goods are charged to act with the "diligence of a good householder" (c. 1284, §1).

The provision of a just family wage that respects the standards of civil law and meets the necessities of the person's family applies to both men and women in church service. The canon implements the Church's own social justice teaching internally to church work. It is a further specification of the general principle on employees found in canon 1286, making it clear that these principles apply as well to persons who work without contract and in a more ministerial type of service.

The canon calls not only for a just wage as deter-mined according to Catholic teaching, but it also requires adequate benefits—including health, disability, and retirement insurance. Both the wages and the benefits are characterized as a "right" ("ius"), a claim that can justly be made. In a sense this is stronger than the claim clergy have to honest remuneration (c. 281, §1).

In the consultation prior to the 1981 Commission meeting, an objection was raised that this canon could eliminate a healthy volunteer spirit that has been both characteristic of Catholics and one of the strengths of the Church. The officials of the Commission responded that the right needs to be recognized, although individuals are of course free to renounce the exercise of such a right.[134] Caution must be exercised in taking such an approach lest there be any effort to induce persons to renounce their rights unwittingly. It is one thing to solicit the generous service of volunteers; it is another, and unjust, to impose inadequate wages and benefits just because persons are working for the Church.[135]

---

[134]*Rel,* 74.

[135]The 1971 Synod of Bishops recognized this directly: "Within the Church rights must be preserved. No one should be deprived of his ordinary rights because he is associated with the Church in one way or another. Those who serve the Church by their labors, including priests and religious, should receive a sufficient livelihood and enjoy that social security which is customary in their region. Lay people should be given fair wages and a system of promotion." *Justice in the World* (USCC edition), 40.

BIBLIOGRAPHY

Membership

a. Commentaries on the 1917 Code

Michiels, G. *Principia Generalia de Personis in Ecclesia.* Editio altera. Paris: Desclée, 1955.

Reed, A. *The Juridical Aspect of Incorporation into the Church of Christ—Canon 87.* Cathagena, Ohio: Messenger, 1960.

b. Later Studies

Aymans, W. "Die Kanonistische Lehre von der Kirchengliedschaft im Lichte des II: Vatikanischen Konzils." *AkK* 142 (1973): 387–418.

Carlen, L., ed. *Gliedshaft in der Kirche-Austritt aus der Kirche.* Freiburg, Switzerland: Universitätsverlag, 1982.

Carrier, H. *The Sociology of Religious Belonging.* New York: Herder & Herder, 1965.

Coccopalmiero, F. "Quid significet verba 'Spiritum Christi habentes' Lumen gentium 12:2?" *P* 68 (1979): 253–276.

Congar, Y. "Sur la trilogie: prophète-roi-prêtre." *Revue des sciences philosophiques et théologiques* 67 (1983): 97–115.

Dulles, A. "Changing Concepts of Church Membership." In *The Resilient Church,* 133–151. Garden City, N.Y.: Doubleday, 1977.

Fernandez, A. *Munera Christi et munera ecclesiae. Historia de una theoria.* Pamplona: EUNSA, 1982.

Grillmeier, A. "The People of God." Vorgrimler I: 153–185 (cited as Grillmeier).

Hughes, M. "The Juridical Nature of the Act of Joining the Catholic Church." *Stud Can* 8 (1974): 45–74, 379–431 (cited as Hughes).

Hurley, M. "Baptism in Ecumenical Perspective." *One in Christ* 14 (1978):106–123.

Kaiser, M. "Aussagen des Zweiten Vatikanischen Konzils über die Kirchengliedschaft." In *Ecclesia et Ius,* 121–135. Munich: F. Schöningh, 1968.

Krämer, P. "Die Zugehörigkeit zur Kirche." In *Grundriss des nachkonziliaren Kirchenrechts,* edited by J. Listl et al., 102–110. Regensburg: Pustet, 1980.

Mörsdorf, K. "Persona in Ecclesia Christi." *AkK* 131 (1962): 345–393.

Mosiek, U. *Verfassungsrecht der Lateinischen Kirche.* I: 66–77. Freiburg i. Br.: Rombach, 1975. (*Bibliography*).

Müller, H. "Zugehörigkeit zur Kirche als Problem der Neukodifikation des kanonischen Rechts." *OAKR* 28 (1977): 81–98.

Pototschnig, F. " 'Persona in Ecclesia'—Probleme der rechtlichen Zugehörigkeit zur 'Kirche Christi.' " In *Ex Aequo et Bono,* 277–294. Innsbruck: Universitätsverlag Wagner, 1977.

Rahner, K. "Membership in the Church According to the Teaching of Pius XII's Encyclical 'Mystici Corporis Christi.' " In *Theological Investigations* II: 1–88. Baltimore: Helicon, 1963.

c. Official Code Commission Reports on Membership Canons

Comm 12 (1980): 33–35 (for material now in cc. 205–206); 45–46 (for material now in c. 207); 59–62 (for material now in c. 204).

Comm 14 (1982): 29–31 (for material now in c. 207); 154–158 (for *Rel* on these canons).

d. Commentary on 1983 Code

Bonnet, P., and Ghirlanda, G. *De Christifidelibus. De eorum iuribus, de laicis, de consociationibus.* Rome: Pontificia Universitas Gregoriana, 1983.

Obligations and Rights of Christian Faithful

a. Commentaries on the 1917 Code

Calhoun, J. *The Restraint of the Exercise of One's Rights. Can Law Stud* 462. Washington: Catholic University, 1965.

DeLuca, L. "I diritti fondamentali dell'uomo nell'ordinamento canonico." In *Acta congressus internationalis iuris canonici 1950,* 88–103. Rome: Catholic Book Agency, 1953.

b. Official Code Commission Reports on Rights Canons

Comm 4 (1972): 142–144 (report on bishops' response to 1971 *LEF*).

Comm 5 (1973): 209 (general comments of *LEF coetus*).

Comm 8 (1976): 80–87 (review of some canons on rights in *LEF*).

Comm 12 (1980): 35–44 (*LEF coetus*); 78–91 (*De Populo Dei coetus*).

c. Commentaries on Drafts for the Revised Code

Canon Law Society of America Task Force Committee. "Second Report on the *Schema Canonum Libri II de Populo Dei.*" Washington: CLSA, 1978.

LaDue, W. "A General Analysis of the Proposed Schema On the *Lex Fundamentalis.*" *CLSAP* (1979): 29–46.

————. "A Critique of the Revised Schema of the *Lex Fundamentalis.*" *CLSAP* (1971): 65–77.

Manzanares, J. "De schemate legis Ecclesiae Fundamentalis in Colloquio Hispano-Germanico adnotationes." *P* 61 (1972): 647–662.

Metz, R. "Droits de l'homme ou droits du chrétien dans le projet de la Lex Fundamentalis? Quelques réflexions." In *Ius et Salus Animarum,* 75–91. Freiburg i. Br.: Rombach, 1972.

Vela Sanchez, L. "Christifidelium officia et iura fundamentalia descripta in Legis Fundamentalis schematis textu emendato." *P* 61 (1972): 605–623.

Viladrich, P. "La declaración de derechos y deberes de los fieles." In *El Proyecto de Ley Fundamental de la Iglesia,* 123–159. Pamplona: EUNSA, 1971.

Weber, P. "De Legis Ecclesiae Fundamentalis studio a coetu peritorum Heidelbergensi Iohanne Dombois duce instituto." *P* 62 (1973): 423–466.

d. Other Studies

Benn, S. "Rights." *Encyclopedia of Philosophy* 7: 195–199.

Bertrams, W. "De influxu Ecclesiae in iura baptizatorum" and "Das Wesen des subjektiven Rechtes." In *Quaestiones Fundamentales Iuris Canonici.* Rome: Pontificia Universitas Gregoriana, 1969.

Beyer, J. "De statuto iuridico christifidelium iuxta vota synodi episcoporum in novo codice iuris canonici condendo." *P* 57 (1968): 550–581.

————. "De iuribus humanis fundamentalibus in statu iuridico christifidelium assumendis." *P* 58 (1969): 29–58.

Coing, H. "Signification de la notion de droit subjectif." *Archives de philosophie de droit* 9 (1964): 1–15.

Corecco, E., et al. *Les droits fondamentaux du Chrétien dans l'Eglise et dans la Société.* Fribourg, Switzerland: Ed. Universitaires, 1981.

Coriden, J., ed. *The Case for Freedom: Human Rights in the Church.* Washington: Corpus, 1969.

Gonzalez del Valle, J. *Derechos fundamentales y derechos publicos en la Iglesia.* Pamplona: EUNSA. 1972.

Greinacher, N., and Jens, I., eds. *Freiheitsrechte für Christen? Warum die Kirche ein Grundgesetz braucht.* Munich: Piper, 1980.

Grundhaus, R. "The Individual's Right to Information in the Church: The Development in Papal Thought from Leo XIII to the Present." J.C.L. dissertation, Catholic University of America, 1968.

Hertel, J. "The Legal Implications of the Decree of Vatican II 'Apostolicam actuositatem'; An historical survey of the mission of the people of God." J.C.L. dissertation, Catholic University of America, 1967.

Hinder, P. *Grundrechte in der Kirche. Eine Untersuchung zur Begründung des Grundrechte in der Kirche.* Freiburg/Switzerland: Universitätsverlag, 1977.

Hollenbach, D. *Claims in Conflict. Retrieving and Renewing the Catholic Human Rights Tradition.* New York: Paulist Press, 1979.

Kinney, J. *The Juridic Condition of the People of God. Their Fundamental Rights and Obligations in the Church.* Rome: Catholic Book Agency, 1972.

Leitmaier, C. *Der Katholik und sein Recht in der Kirche. Kritisch-konservative Überlegungen.* Vienna: Herder, 1971.

Lobina, G. *La competenza del supremo tribunale della segnatura apostolica con particolare riferimento alla "Sectio altera" e alla problematica rispettiva.* Rome: Pontificia Universitas Lateranense, 1971.

Neumann, J. *Menschenrechte auch in der Kirche?* Zürich: Benziger, 1976.

Persona e ordinamento nella Chiesa. Atti del II Congresso Internazionale di Diritto Canonico, Milano 10–16 settembre 1973. Milan: Vita e Pensiero, 1975.

Portillo, A. del. *Faithful and Laity in the Church. The Bases of their Legal Status.* Shannon, Ireland: Ecclesia, 1972 (cited as del Portillo).

Prieto, A. "Los derechos subjetivos publicos en la Iglesia." In *Iglesia y Derecho,* 325–361. Salamanca: CSIC, 1965.

Provost, J. "Ecclesial Rights." *CLSAP* (1982): 41–62.

Schwarz, R. "Circa naturam iuris subiectivi." *P* 69 (1980): 191–200.

Viladrich, J. *Teoria de los derechos fundamentales del fiel. Presupuestos criticos.* Pamplona: EUNSA, 1969.

Laity

a. Commentaries on 1917 Code

Champoux, T. *The Juridical Position of the Laity in the Church.* Rome: Pontificia Universitas Gregoriana, 1939.

Sabater March, J. *Derechos y deberes de los seglares en la vida social de la Iglesia.* Barcelona: Herder, 1954.

Schmitz, P. *Das kirchliche Laienrecht nach dem Codex Juris Canonici.* Münster in Westf.: Aschendorff, 1927.

b. Later Studies

Congar, Y. *Lay People in the Church: A Study for a Theology of Laity.* Westminster, Md.: Newman, 1954.

————. "My Path-Findings in the Theology of Laity and Ministries." *J* 32 (1972): 169–188.

Daneels, F. *De subiecto Officii Ecclesiastici attenta doctrina Concilii Vaticani II. Suntne laici officii ecclesiastici capaces?* Rome: Pontificia Universitas Gregoriana, 1973.

Hendren, L. "The Status of Laity in the Church: Their Rights and Duties according to Canon 87 and the Constitution *Lumen Gentium.*" J.C.L. dissertation. Catholic University of America, 1966.

Hervada, J. *Tres estudios sobre el uso del termino laico.* Pamplona: EUNSA, 1973.

Kilmartin, E. "Lay Participation in the Apostolate of the Hierarchy." *J* 41 (1981): 343–370 (cited as Kilmartin). (Also in *Official Ministry in a New Age.* Washington: CLSA, 1982.)

Klostermann, F. "The Laity." In Vorgrimler I: 231–252.

————. "Decree on the Apostolate of the Laity." In Vorgrimler III: 273–404.

Komonchak, J. "Clergy, Laity, and the Church's Mission in the World." *J* 41 (1981): 422–447 (cited as Komonchak). (Also in *Official Ministry in a New Age.* Washington: CLSA, 1982.)

Murray, J. C. "The Problem of Religious Freedom." *TS* 25 (1964): 503–575.

Portillo, A. del. *Faithful and Laity in the Church. The Bases of their Legal Status.* Shannon, Ireland: Ecclesia, 1972.

Power, D. *Gifts That Differ: Lay Ministries Established and Unestablished.* New York: Pueblo, 1980.

Reed, J. "The Laity in Church Law." *TS* 24 (1963): 602–625.

Schillebeeckx, E. *The Mission of the Church.* New York: Seabury, 1973.

c. Official Reports of the Code Commission on Laity Canons

Comm 2 (1970): 89–98 (report of *coetus* on lay persons and associations of the faithful).

Comm 13 (1981): 314–322 (report on discussion by *De Populo Dei coetus* 13 (1981): 314–322 (report on discussion by *De Populo Dei coetus* in 1980).

Comm 14 (1982): 175–179 (1981 *Rel* on these canons).

TITLE III
SACRED MINISTERS OR CLERICS
[cc. 232–293]

CHAPTER I
THE FORMATION OF CLERICS
[cc. 232–264]

The proper training of men for ordained ministry has always been an important experience in the life of the Church. The canons of the revised Code that treat the formation of clerics deserve an appropriate introduction. This introduction will explain how these new canons compare with the corresponding canons of the 1917 Code; the process of revision that they underwent; and the history of training men for ordained ministry.

Comparison with the 1917 Code

There are three significant differences between the revised Code and the 1917 Code in this section. First, the 1917 Code entitled this section "Seminaries" while the 1983 law uses the title "The Formation of Clerics." The revised Code does not want to emphasize the institution of learning but the entire process of preparing a person to be a cleric. The word "formation" (in Latin, *institutio*) is also found in the title of the Vatican II document on the training of priests, *Optatam Totius*. The committee that revised this section of the law based the new canons on this decree.[1]

The second significant change is the location of this section in the Code. The 1983 Code places this legislation in Book II which treats the people of God. It is the first chapter of the third title on sacred ministers or clerics. The 1917 Code located this legislation in Book III, part IV which treated ecclesiastical magisterium. The section on seminaries came between the section on preaching and schools. The revision committee did not judge the section *De magisterio ecclesiastico* appropriate for treating the formation of clerics. It reasoned that there was more to the training of persons for ordained ministry than their doctrinal education.[2] In their critique of the 1977 schema of Book II, the professional canonical societies in Australia, the British Isles, Canada, and the United States were unanimous in their opinion that this material does not belong in Book II but rather in Book III which treats of the Church's teaching office. They rea-

soned that all formation for ministry, including that of clerics, should be viewed in the broader framework of the Church's total educational enterprise.[3]

The third significant difference is the length of the section or the number of canons. The 1917 Code covered this material in twenty canons (*CIC* 1352–1371). The 1983 Code contains thirty-three canons (cc. 232–264).

Principles of Revision

When it began its task, the Pontifical Commission for the Revision of the Code of Canon Law drew up a set of principles to guide it in its work.[4] These criteria were submitted to the First Synod of Bishops for approval. Some of these principles directly guided the revision of the law dealing with the formation of clerics.

The first principle was that the revised Code be a juridical text. The revised Code indeed must have its own spirit, a spirit animated by the gospels, but it is not to be a textbook of theology, exegesis, or spirituality.[5] As a consequence the canons treating the formation of clerics will state clearly the right of the Church to conduct such programs. They will also give clear but general norms on the programs themselves. The revised Code will not be a theological treatise on priesthood nor a treatise on educational theory or methodology.

The third principle addressed the need for the revised canons to foster pastoral care. All laws and precepts, all rights and duties in the Church must be directed to a supernatural end. Consequently the revised Code is to be imbued with a spirit of charity, temperance, humanness, and moderation. The law should not impose obligations when it would be sufficient to give exhortations, instructions, or recommendations.[6] This principle was clearly operative in this section of the revised Code. The whole process of forming a man for the clerical state is a pastoral experience of drawing from him the gifts and talents that the Lord has given for the use of the people of God.

The fifth principle of revision is the last one to be considered in this introduction. It is the principle of subsidiarity. According to this principle, the revised

---

[1]*Comm* 8 (1976), 109.
[2]*Comm* 8 (1976), 108; 13 (1981), 298–302.

[3]T. Green, "Critical Reflections on the Schema of the People of God," *Stud Can* 14 (1980), 236–237, 263.
[4]*Comm* 1 (1969), 77–85. For a fuller explanation of these criteria, see R. Cunningham, "The Principles Guiding The Revision of the Code of Canon Law," *J* 30 (1970), 447–455 and F. Morrisey, "The Revision of the Code of Canon Law," *Stud Can* 12 (1978), 177–198.
[5]*Comm* 1 (1969), 78, 79.
[6]*Comm* 1 (1969), 79.

Code will confine itself to general legislation while entrusting particular laws to national or regional levels of ecclesiastical authority. The Commission judged that the authority to promulgate particular law affords individual institutions a healthy autonomy.[7] These canons therefore make constant reference to conferences of bishops and the local ordinaries. The norms regulating the formation of clerics are general in nature.

The Process of Revision

The initial work on the revised canons on priestly formation was done by the committee charged with the section on the magisterium. The committee met six times between 1968 and 1976. Its discussions and decisions are recorded in the official magazine of the Pontifical Commission of Revision of the Code of Canon Law.[8] The first draft of its work, however, appeared as part of the schema on Book II where it appears today. This draft was sent to all the bishops in 1977. Another draft incorporating the bishops' observations was published in 1980. The 1983 Code is yet another revision based on further comments and recommendations by various people. It was slightly adjusted during the special plenary session of the Code Commission in October 1981.

Historical Background

The Beginning to Trent

Seminaries as we know them today owe their existence to the legislation of the Council of Trent. In fact the word "seminary" was first used in a strictly ecclesiastical document by Reginald Cardinal Pole in a 1556 decree on the reformation of the Church in England.[9] Cardinal Pole played a prominent role in fashioning the decrees of Trent that organized the seminary system. The word comes from the Latin meaning "seed" (*semen*) and indicates primarily a plot of ground where seeds are grown, and from which they are afterward transplanted.[10]

The decrees of the Council of Trent restored to the Church the traditional method of forming men for the priesthood. Basically it presented a return to the concept of the cathedral school. The cathedral school was developed by St. Augustine when he took young men interested in the priesthood into his own episcopal residence. These schools soon spread from Africa through Europe to England and Ireland.[11] Previous to Augustine, the bishops exercised their responsibility to prepare men for sacred

orders. The character or method of this preparation is not known because "no trace can be found of any special institutions for the education of the clergy."[12]

Alongside the episcopal or cathedral schools arose the monastic schools. Primarily intended for boys who would join the monastery, these schools soon became centers for priestly preparation.[13]

The medieval universities always played an important role in the education of the clergy in the Middle Ages. When a university developed a distinct faculty of theology or of canon law, it might attract clerical students from all over the world. The university excelled in offering an academic curriculum that could not be matched by local schools. The training in clerical discipline and religious piety was not the main concern of the university.[14] Clerical hospices and religious houses assisted in these aspects of priestly training. From the number of conciliar decrees addressing the problems of clerical education, one must conclude that the university system was only partially successful in training men for the priesthood.[15]

The laxity of the clergy, both diocesan and religious, was the hallmark of the close of the Middle Ages.[16] Those who were ordained had little or no theological education; did not know how to celebrate the sacraments, including the offering of the Eucharist; and were more interested in their own material well-being than the spiritual well-being of their people. The stage was being prepared for the reforming decrees of the Council of Trent. In terms of clerical education, one of the early significant steps was Paul III's appointment of the commission of reform in July 1536. On March 9, 1537, the commission submitted its report.[17] It recommended that in Rome and in other dioceses three virtuous and learned priests be appointed to supervise ordinations so that no candidate could be ordained except by or with the permission of the diocesan bishop.

Among the many outstanding figures in the formulation of the Tridentine legislation, no one was more significant in drafting the sections on seminaries than Reginald Cardinal Pole. In 1556, having returned to his native England, he issued his famous *Decreta pro Reformatione Angliae*[18] in an effort to reestablish the Catholic Church that had

[7]*Comm* 1 (1969), 81.

[8]*Comm* 8 (1976), 108–166.

[9]Mansi, 23; 1029–1030.

[10]J. Cox, *The Administration of Seminaries* (Washington: Catholic University of America, 1931), 4.

[11]C. Peterson, *Spiritual Care in Diocesan Seminaries* (Washington: Catholic University of America, 1966), 17–27.

[12]*Catholic Encyclopedia,* s.v. "Ecclesiastical Seminary," by A. Vieban.

[13]J. Ellis, "Short History of Seminary Education I and II" in *Seminary Education in a Time of Change,* J. Lee and L. Putz, eds. (Notre Dame, Ind.: Fides, 1965), 5.

[14]Cox, 16.

[15]For example, see The Second Council of the Lateran, c. 9, Mansi, 21, 528; Council of Tours, c. 8, Mansi, 21 1179; Council of Paris, c. 10, Mansi, 22, 831. For further information, see Ellis, 9–12.

[16]Ellis, 12.

[17]"*Consilium detestorium cardionolum et alcorum prelatorum de emendanda ecclesia . . .*" in Mansi, 35, 347–355.

[18]Mansi, 33, 1011–1034.

been so violently shaken by the schism of Henry VIII. The eleventh article of the decree contained norms for the reform of clerical training. When the Council reconvened in Trent for its third and final session in January 1562, the work on the reform of seminaries had hardly begun. In February 1563 a committee of ten bishops was established to address the issue of clerical reform. The first draft was presented to the conciliar fathers in the following May. No historian has ever called the close similarity between this text and the 1556 norms of Cardinal Pole a mere coincidence.[19] In fact the composer of the text did not even adapt the English norms to fit harmoniously with the rest of the draft.

The final draft on the reform of seminaries appeared in the eighteenth chapter of the twenty-third session of the Council. While some alterations were made through the ensuing debates, the approved text remained substantially that of Cardinal Pole. The legislation decreed that every cathedral and metropolitan church should erect a seminary if at all possible. Candidates for the priesthood should be chosen carefully as befits the ministry. These young men were to study—besides grammar, singing, ecclesiastical computation, and other liberal arts—Sacred Scripture, administration of the sacraments, and homilies of the saints. There were detailed canons concerning the use of clerical garb, clerical tonsure, daily Mass, frequent confession, etc. The faculty of a seminary was to be made up of competent persons, i.e., doctors, licentiates, or masters, and they were to be chosen solely by the bishop. The major part of the chapter on seminaries was devoted to administration. It contained detailed directions on how to raise money. The roles of two committees, one for discipline and one for spiritual matters, were clearly delineated.[20]

From Trent to the New World

The decrees of the Council of Trent were implemented immediately in Italy. The first seminary was opened by Cardinal Amulio, the Archbishop of Rieti, in 1564. In the following year Pope Pius IV established the Roman Seminary. In the northern provinces, Charles Borromeo opened several seminaries—the first one in Milan.

The first seminary in Germany was established in Eichstadt in 1564. The decrees of Trent were not immediately accepted in the troubled countries of England, Ireland, and Scotland. Five years after the closing of the Council, however, Douai College was founded. It flourished for centuries as a center of Catholic ecclesiastical and intellectual life.[21]

Although France was slow in officially accepting the decrees of Trent, three Frenchmen distinguished themselves by their work in the formation of the clergy. St. Vincent de Paul began by giving conferences to the priests of Paris, and soon he was instructing those about to be ordained. In 1635 he developed a seminary program in the old College des Bon-Enfants. Before the French Revolution, his congregation (the Vincentians) directed one-third of all French seminaries, i.e., fifty-three major and nine minor seminaries.

St. John Eudes, a member of the Oratory and later the founder of the Society of the Sacred Hearts, erected his first seminary in 1663 at Caen. By the eighteenth century, his priests staffed forty seminaries.

Finally, Jean Jacques Olier, a friend and colleague of both Vincent de Paul and John Eudes, established the famous seminary of St. Sulpice in 1642. The students, soon representing twenty dioceses, attended classes at the Sorbonne. The Sulpicians continued the work of their founder with great success.

The turmoil of the eighteenth century resulted in the closing of many seminaries in Western Europe. The nineteenth century, however, saw the reestablishment of older seminaries and the construction of many new ones. In Ireland, St. Patrick's College at Maynooth was erected in 1795. It became Ireland's national seminary. All Hallows College in Dublin was founded in 1842. It has trained over thirty-five hundred priests, half of whom have served in the United States.[22] Australia's first seminary was opened in 1885 in Sydney by Cardinal Moran. In 1900 Holy Cross College was founded in Dunedin, New Zealand, by Bishop Verdon.

Seminaries in the United States

The first seminary in the New World was established in Baltimore in 1791. At the initiative of Bishop John Carroll, Father Jacques-André Emery, the Superior General of the Sulpicians, commissioned four priests to begin the education of the clergy at St. Mary's Seminary. By 1866, more than twenty-five dioceses had undertaken a seminary foundation with a variety of results. There were also various types of seminaries: the seminary to satisfy the needs of a particular diocese, the seminary conducted by the secular clergy, the house or domestic seminary after the example of St. Augustine, and the national seminary to serve the needs of particular ethnic groups.[23]

---

[19]For a detailed comparison of the two texts, see J. O'Donohoe, *Tridentine Seminary Legislation: Its Sources and Its Formation* (Louvain: Publications Universitaires de Louvain, 1957), 135–139.

[20]For the full text of this chapter, see H. Schroeder, *Canons and Decrees of the Council of Trent* (St. Louis: B. Herder, 1941) 175–179.

[21]Ellis, 30–32.

[22]See *NCE,* s.v. "Seminary," by J. O'Donohoe.

[23]Ellis, 48–52.

The seminary system of the United States was developed through the decrees of the plenary councils of Baltimore. The first council (1852) decreed that there be a major seminary at least in each province. The second council (1866) devoted an entire chapter of its legislative enactment to the organization and administration of seminaries. It stressed the importance of preparatory seminaries as well as major seminaries. It focused on the seminary curriculum by outlining the courses of studies necessary for priestly ministry and prescribing annual examinations, conducted in Latin, in the presence of the bishop or his vicar.[24] The third plenary council (1884) devoted an entire section to seminaries. It promulgated norms in these areas: the establishment of seminaries, the length of the seminary course, the program of studies, admission to the seminary, prayer, vacation times, administration, and a national principal seminary.[25]

The 1917 Code based the section treating seminaries on the decrees of the Council of Trent. A comparison of the 1917 canons and the norms of the councils of Baltimore shows that the American legislation in no place contradicts the universal law of the Church. In only a few instances are the norms of the Baltimore councils more precise and detailed. These would be properly considered *praeter codicem.* Therefore after the 1917 Code, all the norms of the councils of Baltimore were still in effect.[26]

At the time of the promulgation of the 1917 Code, the seminaries in the United States were flourishing. From fifty institutions enrolling nine hundred thirteen students in 1868, the numbers jumped to one hundred nine seminaries enrolling 4,628 students in 1900.[27] In the decade after the Code, there were many important instructions and decrees of the Holy See that addressed the quality of instruction and the accountability of administration.[28] In the main, the Code law remained the guiding norms of seminaries until Vatican II.

In 1960, as the work of the preparatory commission of Vatican II was well under way, the United States counted ninety-six diocesan seminaries and four hundred twenty-nine seminaries for religious. There was a total of 39,896 seminarians.[29] When the Council finished its work, a decline both in seminaries and seminarians had begun. In the last decade the number in all categories has continued to decrease:[30]

	Diocesan Seminaries	Religious Seminaries	Total Seminarians
1972	106	326	22,963
1982	86	217	11,645

---

[24] *Concilii Plenarii Baltimorensis II, Acta et Decreta* (Baltimorae: J. Murphy, 1868), 105–110.

[25] *Concilii Plenarii Baltimorensis III, Acta et Decreta* (Baltimorae: J. Murphy, 1886), 69–94.

[26] J. Barrett, *A Comparative Study of the Councils of Baltimore and The Code of Canon Law* (Washington: Catholic University of America, 1932), 27.

[27] Ellis, 62. For a treatise on the quality of the academic training of priests see, M. Gannon, "Before and After Modernism," in *The Catholic Priest in the United States,* J. Ellis, ed. (Collegeville: St. John's University, 1971), 293–383.

[28] See *CLD* 1, 643–676.

[29] *Official Catholic Directory, Anno Domini 1960* (New York: P.J. Kenedy, 1960), General Summary 1.

[30] *Official Catholic Directory, Anno Domini 1982* (New York: P.J. Kenedy, 1982), General Summary 3. For a more detailed breakdown of these figures by years and by types of seminaries, see *C.A.R.A. Seminary Directory 1979* (Washington: Center for Applied Research in the Apostolate 1979), vii–xxix and *C.A.R.A. Seminary Forum,* A. Fuerst, ed. (Spring, 1981), 9, n. 1.

Right of the Church

Canon 232 — The Church has the duty and the proper and exclusive right to form those who are commissioned for the sacred ministries.

This is substantially the same wording as the initial canon of the 1917 Code (*CIC* 1352). The Church has a mission and both the right and duty to all the means that will assist in fulfilling that mission. Properly trained clerics are essential to the mission. The Church is not dependent on nor can it be regulated by any civil authority in regard to this mission.[31]

The only change from the 1917 Code is the substitution of "those who wish to devote themselves to ecclesiastical ministries" for "those who are commissioned for the sacred ministries." This phrase was changed several times during the Commission's work.[32] The final wording does not seem to carry great significance.

Unlike many other countries, the United States government has never questioned the right of the Church to establish seminaries and to train seminarians. Full freedom of all religious groups to manage their own affairs is guaranteed by the Constitution.

Duty To Foster Vocations

Canon 233 — §1. A duty rests upon the entire Christian community to foster vocations so that sufficient provision is made for the needs of the sacred ministry throughout the entire Church; Christian families, educators and in a special way priests, especially pastors, are particularly bound by this duty. Since it is principally the concern of diocesan bishops to promote vocations, they should instruct the people entrusted to them concerning the importance of the sacred ministry and the necessity of ministers in the Church; therefore they are to encourage and support endeavors to foster vocations by means of projects especially established for that purpose.

§2. Moreover priests, and especially diocesan bishops, are also to be solicitous that men of a more mature age who consider themselves called to the sacred ministries are prudently assisted in word and in deed and duly prepared.

The first paragraph summarizes *Optatam Totius* 2. The 1977 draft had a more extensive canon that explained the activities of the group responsible for fostering vocations.[33] It is significant that the responsibility for priestly vocations clearly belongs to the whole Christian community. There are groups, however, who bear the responsibility in a special way. Bishops have the greatest responsibility by reason of their office. Priests are next, especially pastors. Families and educators are named as people who have great influence in this regard. This is quite in accord with the teachings of Vatican II.[34]

The whole tone of this canon differs radically from its 1917 counterpart. Canon 1353 of the former Code says that priests, especially pastors, must shield boys who show signs of priestly vocation from worldly contagion, train them in piety, educate them, and foster the seed of their vocation. The change from this negative approach to the positive statement of the new canon has also appeared in the many statements of the Holy See concerning vocations.[35]

The second paragraph of the canon reflects the newer and ever-increasing phenomenon of older men who feel called to the priesthood. The published material of the revision committee does not indicate why it decided to include this paragraph nor is its source recorded. The July 14, 1976, private letter of the Sacred Congregation for Catholic Education[36] on delayed vocations was undoubtedly a major source for this norm. The last sentence of *Optatam Totius* 3 as well as number 19 of the *Basic Plan for Priestly Formation* (1970) are also reflected in this canon. The revision committee was careful

[31]In 1864 Pope Pius IX condemned the propositions that the Church did not have exclusive authority over the study of theology (no. 33) and that the Church was subject to civil authority in regard to the seminary curriculum (no. 46). *Ench*, nos. 1733, 1746.

[32]*Comm* 8 (1976), 109, 124, 133.

[33]ComCICRec, *Schema Canonum Libri II de Populo Dei* (Typis Polyglottis Vaticanis, 1977) c. 84, §1 (cited as *Schema de Populo Dei*

[34]*AA*11, *GS*52, *PO*6.

[35]Paul VI, Apostolic Letter *Summi Dei Verbum*, Nov. 4, 1963, *AAS* 55 (1963), 985ff.; *Ratio, AAS* 62 (1970), nos. 5–19; and *Basic Plan*, in *Norms for Priestly Formation: A Compendium of Official Documents on Training Candidates for the Priesthood* (Washington: USCC, 1982), 25–28. See also the many addresses of the Holy Father, particularly the annual statements on the day of prayer for vocations.

[36]*CLD* 8, 946–955.

not to use the term "older" but "more mature age." Some years ago, many bishops would not have allowed someone over thirty-five years old to begin his preparation for the priesthood. This canon is saying that there is no age limit to the possibility of a priestly vocation.

Minor Seminaries

Canon 234 — §1. Wherever minor seminaries or other such institutions exist they are to be maintained and supported; such institutions are those in which, for the sake of fostering vocations, special religious formation along with instruction in the humanities and sciences is provided; whenever the diocesan bishop judges it expedient he should provide for the erection of a minor seminary or a similar institution.

§2. Unless in certain cases circumstances indicate otherwise, young men who intend to be advanced to the priesthood are to be equipped with that training in the humanities and sciences by which young people in their own region are prepared to pursue higher studies.

The documents of the Holy See have historically used the term minor seminary to denote all secondary education previous to the study of philosophy and theology. This corresponded to the European system of education that was also adopted by several English-speaking countries, including the United States. In the early part of this century, the American minor seminary was a six-year program in the understanding of this canon and its counterpart (*CIC* 1354, §2). The major seminary was another six-year program devoted to the study of philosophy and theology. After World War II the American Church aligned itself to the country's educational system. In some places this resulted in calling the high school seminary, "minor," while the four years of college and the four years of theology were both referred to as "major."

The 1917 Code treated the minor seminary in a short paragraph.[37] The law certainly wanted to oblige each diocese to establish a minor seminary if at all possible.[38] The 1983 legislation is careful not to impose such an obligation. Bishops are urged to retain or establish such institutions but are not required to do so.[39]

The purpose of these minor seminaries is clearly

articulated. Following the teaching of Vatican II,[40] these institutions are to assist a young person in initial spiritual formation, while he engages in the same course of studies in humanities and science as other young men in the country. This is strikingly similar to the 1917 Code (*CIC* 1364, 3°).

The 1977 draft of this canon included an additional paragraph on a mixed seminary.[41] The minor seminary could be opened to young men who did not intend to be priests. This paragraph was omitted in the final text because many participants in the final plenary session of the Code Commission were opposed to it.[42] Because this arrangement is not prohibited, a bishop might allow such students to attend the seminary.

Major Seminaries

Canon 235 — §1. Young men who intend to enter the priesthood are to be given a suitable spiritual formation and trained for the duties of the priesthood in a major seminary throughout the entire time of formation, or, if circumstances demand it in the judgment of the diocesan bishop, at least for four years.

§2. Those who legitimately live outside a seminary are to be entrusted by the diocesan bishop to a devout and suitable priest, who is to see to it that they are carefully formed in the spiritual life and in discipline.

Canon 237 — §1. Wherever it is possible and expedient, there is to be a major seminary in every diocese; otherwise the students who are preparing themselves for the sacred ministries are to be entrusted to another seminary, or an interdiocesan seminary is to be erected.

§2. An interdiocesan seminary is not to be erected unless the approval of the Apostolic See has first been obtained for both its erection and its statutes; the approval will be obtained by the conference of bishops if it involves the entire territory, otherwise by the bishops involved.

(Canon 236 treats the preparation of permanent deacons. It will be commented on following the commentary on canon 237.)

The purpose of the major seminary is to form men spiritually, academically, and pastorally for the priesthood.[43] Canon 235, §1 requires at least four years for this instruction while acknowledging

---

[37]*CIC* 1354, §2: "Every effort should be made, especially in larger dioceses to establish two seminaries: a minor seminary where boys may study a literary course, and a major seminary . . ."

[38]G. Cocchi, *Commentarium in Codicem Iuris Canonici ad usum scholarum*, 6 vols., 2nd ed. (Taurinorum Augustae: Officina Libraria Marietti, 1920–1930), 6:86; G. Mahoney, *The Academic Curriculum in Minor Seminaries* (Washington: Catholic University of America, 1965), 46.

[39]*Comm* 8 (1976), 112.

[40]*PO* 3.

[41]"Where minor seminaries or similar institutions exist, if, in the judgment of the Conference of Bishops it is fitting, young men of superior virtue may be admitted to these institutions, even though they do not think they are called to sacred ministry." *Schema de Populo Dei*, c. 85, §2.

[42]*Comm* 14 (1982), 160.

[43]*OT* 4.

that it normally takes longer. Canon 250 indicates how long the academic program should be.

The intent of canon 235 is that priestly training should normally take place in a seminary that provides the entire training program. (This is called a free-standing seminary.) However, exceptions can be made by the local ordinary.[44] This corresponds to its 1917 counterpart (*CIC* 1370) and repeats canon 972 of the former Code in the section on Holy Orders. Today some men are trained for the priesthood by living in a house of formation and attending classes at a university or other theological faculty. (This is called a collaborative seminary.)

Canon 237, §1 repeats the norm of canon 1354, §2 of the 1917 Code: each diocese should have its own major seminary. However, the 1983 law continues to recognize that many dioceses cannot support such an enterprise. Today in the United States there are one hundred seventy-one dioceses, but there are fewer than twenty-five schools of theology owned and supported by dioceses. The other twenty-five free-standing theologates and seventy-five collaborative institutions are, for the most part, owned by religious communities for their own men or for diocesan seminarians of many dioceses. These last are not referred to in these canons. The interdiocesan seminary of canon 237, §2 is the same juridical entity found in canon 1354, §3 of the earlier Code.

Permanent Deacons

Canon 236 — According to the prescriptions of the conference of bishops, aspirants to the permanent diaconate are to be formed to nourish a spiritual life and instructed in the correct fulfillment of the duties proper to this order in the following manner:

1° young men are to live for at least three years in some special house unless the diocesan bishop decides otherwise for serious reasons;

2° men of a more mature age, whether celibate or married, are to spend three years in a program determined by the conference of bishops.

Many canonists were surprised when this single canon on permanent deacons first appeared in the 1980 schema. Logically it belongs here because the section deals with the formation of clerics, and permanent deacons are clerics (c. 266). Because all the remaining canons apply solely to those preparing for the priesthood, it does however seem—practically—to be misplaced.[45]

The 1967 *motu proprio, Sacrum diaconatus ordinem,* of Paul VI is the primary source of legisla-

tion on the restored permanent diaconate.[46] Numbers six and nine of the *motu proprio* are repeated in the first paragraph of this canon. This general legislation of the Church allows a twenty-five-year-old man to be ordained a deacon. However, the bishops of the United States used their option to set a higher age and chose thirty-five years as the minimum.[47] That is the reason there are no "special houses" for the formation of permanent deacons in the United States.

" . . . men of a more mature age" refers to those thirty-five years old.[48] While it has been strongly suggested that these candidates study for three years, this length of time is now required. The American bishops had originally suggested a two-year training program.[49]

Juridic Personality

Canon 238 — §1. By the law itself seminaries legitimately erected possess juridic personality in the Church.

§2. The rector of the seminary represents it in the handling of all matters unless the competent authority has determined otherwise concerning certain matters.

The 1917 Code explicitly stated that seminaries enjoyed juridic or moral personality in the Church (*CIC* 99).

Because a seminary is a non-collegiate juridic person, one physical person must act in its name. The rector is appointed to do so, unless the local ordinary, a regional group of bishops (in the case of an interdiocesan seminary), or the Holy See itself is the duly appointed representative of the seminary in a given juridic act.[50]

Chief Personnel

Canon 239 — §1. Every seminary is to have a rector who presides over it, a vice-rector if necessary, and a finance officer; moreover, if the students pursue their studies within the seminary itself it is also to have teachers who give instruction in the several disciplines in an appropriately coordinated curriculum.

§2. Every seminary is to have at least one spiritual director; the students, however, are free to approach other priests who have been appointed for this function by the bishop.

[46]*AAS* 59 (1967), 697–704; *CLD* 6, 577–584.
[47]"Conditions for Permanent Diaconate in the U.S.," *Catholic Mind* 66 (Nov. 1968), 8. For complete guidelines on the formation of permanent deacons, see *Permanent Deacons in the United States* (Washington: USCC, 1971).
[48]*CLD* 6, 580, n. 12.
[49]*Catholic Mind* 66 (Nov. 1968), 8.
[50]For further information concerning juridic persons, see cc. 113–123.

[44]*OT* 7.
[45]Last-minute attempts to have this canon removed were unsuccessful: *Comm* 14 (1980), 160.

§3. The statutes of the seminary are to provide for ways in which the other moderators, professors, and even the students themselves share in the concerns of the rector especially regarding the observance of discipline.

This canon describes the administrative officers and staff of a seminary. It reflects the content of canons 1357, §3; 1358; and 1359 of the 1917 Code. The *Basic Plan* describes the superiors and professors of the seminary in detail.[51]

The rector is entrusted with the responsibility of administering the seminary as the bishop's representative. It has been traditionally understood that the office of seminary rector is an ecclesiastical office.[52] This canon simply legislates the office. Subsequent canons (cc. 260–261) describe the function of the rector.

A vice-rector would be needed if the seminary were so large that the rector would need such assistance or if he had other responsibilities that took him away from the seminary community for long periods of time (e.g., fund-raising, vocation recruitment, or diocesan administration).

The spiritual director spoken of in paragraph two is the director or administrator of the formation program. In this capacity he would be responsible for the annual retreats; the day of prayer; spiritual conferences; the list of approved spiritual directors; and, in some seminaries, the liturgical celebrations.[53] He may also be chosen by the students as their personal spiritual guide to whom they will manifest their conscience. This spiritual director is also an ordinary confessor. The canon is clear that students are free to choose their personal director from a number of priests appointed by the bishop for this ministry.[54]

Finally this canon calls for statutes that would establish the administrative structure of the seminary under the direction of the rector. In light of canon 243, these statutes should be understood as the basic, constitutional norms and bylaws by which a seminary operates. These would include the charter, the bylaws of the board of directors or trustees, and other fundamental administrative statutes.[55] The 1977 draft retained the two boards of governors found in canon 1359 of the former

Code.[56] The Code Commission decided in its final draft to eliminate these specific boards and simply to require the existence of norms that would cover such administrative functions. It should be noted that, wisely, students are urged to participate in the general administration of the seminary.

Canon 240 — §1. In addition to the ordinary confessors, other confessors are to come regularly to the seminary; moreover, with due regard for the discipline of the seminary, a student is always at liberty to go to any confessor in the seminary or outside of it.
§2. In making decisions concerning the admission of students to orders or their dismissal from the seminary, the opinion of the spiritual director and the confessors can never be sought.

This canon is very similar in scope and content to canon 1361 of the 1917 Code even though the latter had an additional paragraph.

The spiritual director of canon 239 is an ordinary confessor. Canon 240 implies that other priests are also appointed as ordinary confessors. It does not require two or more as did the 1917 Code (*CIC* 1358). The ordinary confessor in a seminary is one who has the primary duty of regularly celebrating the sacrament of reconciliation with the seminarians. The appointment of such confessors does not confer any special jurisdiction because none is needed.[57]

This canon emphasizes the freedom of conscience to which each student has a right. Other priests are to be made available to the seminarians for the purpose of the sacrament whether these confessors reside in the seminary or outside of it. The canon attempts to address possible abuses in the exercise of this freedom by adding "with due regard for the discipline of the seminary." A seminarian, for example, might not invoke this canon as a reason to miss classes, community prayers, or other important exercises of the seminary schedule.

It should be noted that paragraph one does not require these other confessors to be appointed by the bishop. This was explicitly requested during the revision process. The Code Commission responded that it was sufficiently provided for in canon 239, §2.[58]

Paragraph two of this canon protects the forum of conscience. Decisions for advancement or discontinuance of a seminarian are made only with data from the external forum. Not only may internal forum material not be used, but also all suspicion of its use must be assiduously avoided. This new canon includes the spiritual director by name.

[51]*Basic Plan, Norms,* 30–31.
[52]Cox, 82. C. 145 of the 1983 Code continues to support this opinion.
[53]For a detailed canonical description of the spiritual director, see Peterson, 117–155.
[54]This canon limits spiritual directors to priests. The question of deacons and lay people especially women as directors of seminarians is presently being debated in the United States. For the latest official statement see *PPF,* nos. 85–96, 338–348.
[55]While there is no former canon that speaks of this idea, the ap-const, *SapC* of April 15, 1979, uses the word statute in the same sense in nos. 11, 16, 19, 20, *AAS* 71 (1977), 480ff. and *Norms,* 234–235.

He was not named in the 1917 Code (*CIC* 1361, §3) nor was he included in the 1977 draft.[59]

Admission to the Seminary

Canon 241 — §1. The diocesan bishop is to admit to the major seminary only those who are judged capable of dedicating themselves permanently to the sacred ministries in light of their human, moral, spiritual and intellectual characteristics, their physical and psychological health and their proper motivation.

§2. Before they are accepted, they must submit documents certifying that baptism and confirmation have been received and other documents which are required in accord with the prescriptions of the program for priestly formation.

§3. When persons seek admission after they have been dismissed from another seminary or from a religious institute, further testimony is required from their respective superior, especially regarding the cause of their dismissal or their leaving.

This canon deals with the process of admission into the seminary and is a revision of canon 1363 of the 1917 Code. This revised norm applies only to admission into a major seminary, i.e., studies of philosophy and theology, whereas its counterpart applied to both minor and major seminaries.

This canon begins by listing the areas of the candidate's character and life that must be examined before the judgment is made to admit him to the seminary. These areas are found in *Optatam Totius* 6. The revised law no longer requires legitimacy as a condition of admission. This canon, unlike its predecessor, specifies that a person should have proper motivation or the right intention. This had been emphasized by Pope Paul VI in his Apostolic Letter *Summi Dei Verbum,* in which he defined right intention as "a distinct, firm desire to dedicate oneself completely to the service of God."[60] This revised norm reflects the experience and the concerns of modern seminary administrators.

Besides the two certificates of baptism and confirmation, the canon relies on particular law concerning priestly formation to specify other required documents. For the United States, the particular law requires an effective admissions procedure. It indicates that interviews with the candidate and his parents, evaluations from his pastor and teachers, academic records (transcripts) as well as results of standardized tests go together to form an effective procedure.[61] Most seminaries in the English-speak-

ing world require all of the above along with a physical examination and a written report containing the results of psychological testing.[62]

Paragraph three of this canon is substantially the same as its counterpart (*CIC* 1363, §3). The topic is the admission of students who have been dismissed from a seminary or religious institute. The revised canon implies but does not state that the testimony of the former superior contain information on the conduct, character, and temperament of the dismissed person. The revised law also does not prescribe that these superiors are bound to reply truthfully. The Code Commission, in responding to a request to retain these 1917 prescriptions, said that the national programs for priestly formation would address the matter.[63] However, the 1917 law was changed in 1957 by a decree of the Sacred Congregation of Seminaries and Universities.[64] Bishops were discouraged from considering a former seminarian as an applicant to their seminary, whether he was dismissed or departed freely. If they judged such a one to be worthy, they were to apply to the same Sacred Congregation for the authority to admit him.

The revised law does not seem to address the admission of one who previously belonged by any title to a religious family and departed of his own free will. In 1941 a joint decree of the Sacred Congregations of Religious and of Seminaries and Universities prescribed that the bishop must have recourse to the Sacred Congregation of Seminaries and Universities before such an applicant could be admitted.[65] Perhaps this paragraph three intends to cover this situation. While it begins by addressing only those who have been dismissed, it ends by mentioning reasons for dismissal "or leaving." The 1977 draft clearly addressed both dismissal and free departure.[66]

National Program of Priestly Formation

Canon 242 — §1. Each nation should have a program for priestly formation which is to be determined by the conference of bishops in light of

---

[59]*Schema de Populo Dei,* c. 90, §2.

[60]*AAS* 55 (1963), 987; *The Pope Speaks* 9 (1964), 239.

[61]*PPF* 1981, nos. 265–267. For further information on the admission process, see T. Morgen, "Screening Applicants for the Priesthood," *The Priest* 36 (Feb. 1980), 12–15.

[62]While this canon urges the use of testing to determine the fitness of an applicant's mental health, it does not contradict the *Monitum* of the Holy Office prohibiting the use of psychoanalysis as an admission requirement to a seminary; *AAS* 53 (1961), 571 and *CLD* 5, 196. Psychoanalysis is commonly understood as an extended treatment (2 years) for probing the unconscious; it differs from psychological and psychiatric techniques. For an explanation and interpretation of this *Monitum,* see J. Lynch, *TS* 23 (1962), 233–239.

[63]*Rel,* 56.

[64]"*De ratione qua dimissi e Seminariis denuo admitti possint,*" *AAS* 49 (1957), 640 and *CLD* 4, 387.

[65]*AAS* 33 (1941), 371 and *CLD* 2, 426. After the reorganization of the Roman Curia, this Congregation is now called the Sacred Congregation for Catholic Education.

[66]*Schema de Populo Dei,* c. 91, §3.

the norms issued by the supreme authority of the Church and which is also to be approved by the Holy See; when new circumstances require it the program is to be updated with the similar approval of the Holy See; this program is to define the main principles for imparting formation in the seminary as well as general norms which have been adapted to the pastoral needs of each region or province.

§2. The norms of the program mentioned in §1 are to be observed in all seminaries, both diocesan and interdiocesan.

The call for national programs to guide the training of the priests while preserving local needs and customs was voiced first in the conciliar decree on the training of priests.[67] To assist each national conference, the 1967 Synod of Bishops requested the Sacred Congregation for Catholic Education to draw up a basic plan that would serve as a guideline for national programs. This was published in 1970.[68]

Most of the English-speaking national conferences have published at least one edition of a program for implementation in their dioceses.[69] Although the process of composing these documents differed in each country, the seminary community always had considerable input. Each completed national program was submitted to the Sacred Congregation for Catholic Education for approval. This approval has customarily been for five years.[70]

This canon simply prescribes such a national program and determines that it is to be observed by all in the territory. When the suggestion was made to the Code Commission that such a program should not be mandated because of the impossible burden on some conferences of bishops, the Commission replied that if nothing else, a conference could officially adopt the *Basic Plan* with a few adaptations.[71]

[67]*OT* 1.
[68]*Ratio, AAS* 62 (1970), 321–384 and *Basic Plan Norms,* 17–95.
[69]The bishops of the U.S. approved interim guidelines in 1968. The first complete and final *PPF* was approved in 1971. A second edition was published in 1976 and the third edition in 1982. The Australian and New Zealand Conferences published *Preparation for Priesthood* in 1972. It was updated by way of an appendix in 1975. *Norms for Priestly Training in Ireland* was published by the Irish bishops in 1973. A revised document has been prepared but not promulgated. The Canadian Conference published two programs, one for each language community. The English document *Program of Priestly Formation* was approved in 1979. The Conference of the Philippines published its first draft in 1972 for a five-year period.
[70]The American bishops requested that the 1981 program be approved for ten years. The Holy See in its letter of approval did not specify the length of time. In a March 5, 1982, letter to seminary rectors and ordinaries, the chairman of the Committee on Priestly Formation surmised that such a decision would follow the Vatican study of American seminaries.
[71]*Rel,* 56 and *Comm* 14 (1982), 162.

Canon 243 — Furthermore, each seminary is to have its own rule, approved by the diocesan bishop or, in the case of an interdiocesan seminary, by the bishops involved; in the seminary rule the norms of the program for priestly formation should be adapted to particular circumstances, and those areas of discipline which affect the daily life of the students and the order of the entire seminary are to be determined more precisely.

While using entirely different words, this canon repeats the material in canon 1357, §3 of the earlier Code. The seminary rule sets the "order of the day" and other guidelines that explicitate the responsibilities of the students and the expectations of the administration.[72] This rule has again been called for by the *Basic Plan.*[73] In the practical order, the seminary publishes a series of handbooks that are also required by accrediting agencies. These handbooks (student, faculty, administration) contain more than the seminary rule spoken of in this canon.

Integration of Seminary Programs

Canon 244 — The spiritual formation of the students in the seminary and their doctrinal instruction are to be harmonized and arranged so that in accord with the unique character of each student, they acquire the spirit of the gospel and a close relationship with Christ along with appropriate human maturity.

This canon expresses very well the goal of all formation: transformation into Christ as the fullest expression of one's unique self. This canon points out that taking on the spirit of the gospel and forming a close bond with the Lord is accomplished by integrating all academic and spiritual formation components into the student's unique personality which must be brought to the appropriate level of maturity.

There was no canon in the 1917 Code that expressed these ideas. The documents of Vatican II, however, clarify this vision of a well-integrated and fully human minister of the gospel.[74] During the drafting process, it was thought that this canon might be too theological for a juridic document. Finally it was judged appropriate.[75]

Spiritual Formation Program

Canon 245 — §1. Through their spiritual formation the students are to become equipped to exer-

[72]For a brief historical essay on this rule, see *NCE,* s.v. "Rule of Life," by P. Mulhern.
[73]*Basic Plan, Norms,* 30.
[74]*OT* 4, 12; *PO* 8, 12.
[75]*Comm* 8 (1976), 141.

cise fruitfully the pastoral ministry and they are to be formed in a missionary spirit; in the course of their formation they are to learn that a ministry which is always carried out in living faith and in charity fosters their own sanctity; they are to learn to cultivate those virtues which are highly valued in human relations so that they can achieve an appropriate integration of human and supernatural qualities.

§2. The students are to be so formed that, imbued with the love for the Church of Christ, they are devoted with a humble and filial love to the Roman Pontiff, the successor of Peter, are attached to their own bishop as his trustworthy co-workers, and work as companions with their brothers; through the common life in the seminary and through cultivating relationships of friendship and association with others they are to be prepared for fraternal union with the diocesan presbyterate, with whose members they will share in the service of the Church.

This canon, without a counterpart in the 1917 Code, is an excellent summary of the teachings of Vatican II on the spiritual formation of a priest.[76] It emphasizes the pastoral and missionary aspects of spirituality by stating that one's ministry is a means of sanctification.[77] The second paragraph explains the community of brothers that is formed in the priesthood.[78] Both the tone and content of this canon are welcome additions to the juridical norms on seminary formation.

Canon 246 — §1. The celebration of the Most Holy Eucharist is to be the center of the entire life of the seminary, so that daily the students, sharing in the very love of Christ, may draw especially from this richest of all sources the strength of spirit needed for their apostolic work and their spiritual life.

§2. They are to be formed to celebrate the liturgy of the hours by which the ministers of God pray to God in the name of the Church on behalf of all the people committed to them, indeed on behalf of the entire world.

§3. Devotion to the Blessed Virgin Mary, including the rosary, mental prayer and other devotional exercises are to be fostered so that the students acquire a spirit of prayer and gain strength in their vocation.

§4. The students are to become accustomed to

approach the sacrament of penance frequently, and it is also recommended that each one have a director for his spiritual life who has been freely chosen and to whom he can open his conscience with confidence.

§5. Each year the students are to make a retreat.

This is a revision of canon 1367 of the 1917 Code. Both canons treat the spiritual exercises of the seminary, and both have five paragraphs—but the similarities end there. This new canon has totally recast the material.

The 1917 canon began by making the bishop responsible for seeing to it that the seminarians did these experiences of prayer. The new canon properly makes the individual responsible for his own spiritual growth.

The Eucharist should be celebrated daily in the seminary.[79] The Divine Office should be explained and celebrated frequently enough so that, as deacons, they will have accepted it as their form of prayer.[80] The canon does not prescribe how often or when the Office should be prayed in community.

The third paragraph mentions other traditional prayer forms as proven means of strengthening vocations.[81] Devotion to our Blessed Mother has been a tradition among priests. The rosary never appeared in any draft of this canon.

Frequent use of the sacrament of reconciliation replaces the weekly norm of canon 1367, §2, of the former Code. Finally, the length of the annual retreat is not mentioned as it previously had been (*CIC* 1367, §4).

Canon 247 — §1. The students are to be prepared through suitable education to observe the state of celibacy, and they are also to learn to honor it as a special gift of God.

§2. They are to be duly informed of the duties and burdens of sacred ministers of the Church; no difficulty of the priestly life is to be kept back from them.

In the initial drafts of this chapter, this canon was a single paragraph. In 1970 it was divided into two paragraphs in order to emphasize the formation in celibacy.[82] The paragraphs were reversed in 1981. It was noted that it seemed inappropriate to speak of this "special gift of God" after the "duties and burdens" of the ministry.[83]

[76]*OT* 8, 11; *PO* 3, 8, 9.

[77]This theme is fully explained in G. Broccolo, ed., *Spiritual Renewal of The American Priesthood* (Washington: USCC, 1973). For a classical work on the ministry of a priest, see J. Ratzinger, "Priestly Ministry: A Search for Its Meaning," *Emmanuel* 76 (1970), 442–453, 490–505.

[78]This theme is developed in *As One Who Serves* (Washington: USCC, 1977). Also see E. Briere, *Priests Need Priests* (New York: Sentinel Press, 1962).

[79]*Basic Plan, Norms,* 36.

[80]*Basic Plan, Norms,* 36; *SC* 90; *PO* 5. Also see SCSU, *Instruction on the Liturgical Training of Seminarians,* Dec. 25, 1965, *CLD* 6, 766–785; Instruction of SCCE, June 3, 1979, *Norms,* 111–144.

[81]A recent letter of the SCCE expounds on some of these prayer forms and other means of spiritual growth: "Circular letter concerning some of the more urgent aspects of Spiritual Formation in Seminaries," Jan. 6, 1980, *Norms, 209–223.*

[82]*Comm* 8 (1976), 144.

[83]*Rel,* 58 and *Comm* 14 (1982), 164.

In recent years there have been several very fine official documents explaining the nature of priestly celibacy and encouraging a deeper commitment to it as a gift.[84]

Academic Program

Canon 248 — The doctrinal instruction which is to be given has as its goal that the students acquire, along with a general culture which is in accord with the needs of time and place, extensive and solid learning in the sacred disciplines; after they have thereby been grounded and nourished in their own faith, they should be able to announce the teaching of the gospel in a suitable fashion to the people of their times and in a manner which is adapted to their understanding.

The objectives of the academic program of theological education are clearly stated in this canon. Such instruction is to assist the development of the student's faith as well as to equip him for effective preaching and teaching. The canon does not distinguish between different levels of seminary training. It is to be understood, therefore, to apply at all levels. The national programs will specify the objectives for the high school, college, and graduate levels of seminary training.

This canon is a reflection of several documents of Vatican II.[85] It is, however, a repetition of the first paragraph of the *Basic Plan* 59.

Canon 249 — The program for priestly formation is to make provision that the students are not only carefully taught their native language but also that they are well skilled in the Latin language; they are also to have a suitable familiarity with those foreign languages which seem necessary or useful for their own formation or for the exercise of pastoral ministry.

The Holy See has clearly and consistently prescribed the mastery of the Latin language for those studying for the priesthood. Starting with canon 1364, §2 of the 1917 law and ending with the *Basic Plan* 66, numerous documents not only have spoken of the necessity of Latin but have even offered methods of study.[86]

Before the introduction of the vernacular liturgy, all seminaries in English-speaking countries were equally strong in their desire to train seminarians in Latin. Both the discontinuance of Latin in liturgical rites and the increase of older vocations without seminary college experience demanded a change in the tradition. The fact is that the majority of seminarians are not able to understand Latin. Seminary professors have reluctantly tailored their courses and reading lists accordingly. The results have not been disastrous. This new norm, however, demands that the seminary community reexamine its experience. The national program for the United States has the same norm as this canon.[87]

The other languages spoken of in this canon would include Greek and Hebrew for the study of Scripture and a modern language (e.g., Spanish) for the effective exercise of the pastoral ministry.

Canon 250 — Philosophical and theological studies which are conducted in the seminary itself can be pursued successively or conjointly in accord with the program of priestly formation; these studies are to encompass a period of at least six full years in such a way that two full years are devoted to the philosophical disciplines and four full years to theological studies.

The wording of this canon demonstrates clearly the revised law's attempt to be truly a general law. The outside limits of the time to be spent in the study of philosophy and theology are set. The manner of doing this is left up to the national programs with the guideline that philosophical studies should be one-third and theological studies should be two-thirds of the preparation time. There is no change from canon 1365, §1 and §2 of the 1917 Code. The *Basic Plan* 60 offers three models for accomplishing this goal.[88]

The four-year curriculum for the study of theology is very traditional. After the advent of pastoral (field) education, some seminaries have instituted a parish internship before or after diaconate for a period of four to six months; this is to occur during the academic year. Recently seminary administrations have been working toward four full years of academic work (with some field work each week) with the internship as an additional period of time.[89]

---

[84]See Pope Paul VI *On Priestly Celibacy,* June 24, 1967, *AAS* 59 (1967), 657–697 and *The Pope Speaks* 12 (1967), 291–319; SCCE *A Guide to Formation in Priestly Celibacy,* April 11, 1974, *Norms* 155–205; NCCB *Statement on Celibacy,* Nov. 14, 1969 (USCC booklet).

[85]*OT* 13, 14, 17; *GS* 58, 62; *AG* 16.

[86]E.g., the apostolic letter of Pius XI, Aug. 1, 1922, *CLD* 1, 643–647; the letter of the SCSU to the Apostolic Delegate of the U.S., May 26, 1927, and approved by the Holy Father Jan. 25, 1928, *CLD* 1, 647–655; the letter of the SCSU *Latinem excolete,* Oct. 27, 1957, *AAS* 50 (1957), 292–296 and *CLD* 5, 638–642; John XXIII, apconst *Veterum sapientia,* Feb. 22, 1962, *AAS* 54 (1962), 129–135 and *CLD* 5, 642–681; apostolic

letter of Paul VI *Summi Dei Verbum,* Nov. 4, 1963, *AAS* 55 (1963), 993; *OT* 13.

[87]*PPF* no. 411.

[88]Students in seminaries in the U.S.—in accord with its national educational system—study philosophy along with arts and sciences for four years before beginning the study of theology. This arrangement is based on *Basic Plan, Norms,* 42 and SCCE 1972 *Instruction and the Study of Philosophy, Norms,* 95–109.

[89]The national program for the U.S. urges this configuration; see *PPF,* nos. 190, 223.

Canon 251 — Philosophical training ought to be based upon that heritage of philosophy which is perennially valid, and it also is to take into account contemporary philosophical investigation; it is to be so imparted that it perfects the human development of the students, sharpens their minds, and renders them more suitable for pursuing theological studies.

This canon summarizes *Optatam Totius* 15 which treats the study of philosophy. The *Basic Plan* has spelled out more details of the purpose and method of this instruction.[90] When asked in 1965 to explain the meaning of "perennially valid," the Sacred Congregation responded: "the principles of St. Thomas."[91]

The study of the Thomistic synthesis is to be joined to the other valid systems—both historical and contemporary. The purpose is not merely to prepare one for theological studies but to assist students in their personal and human development.

Canon 252 — §1. Theological training is to be so imparted in the light of faith and under the guidance of the magisterium that the students have a thorough understanding of Catholic doctrine in its integrity based on divine revelation, that they gather nourishment from it for their own spiritual lives, and that they can properly announce and safeguard it in the exercise of their ministry.

§2. The students are to be taught Sacred Scripture with special diligence so that they acquire a perception of the whole of Sacred Scripture.

§3. There are to be classes in dogmatic theology which are always to be based upon the written word of God along with sacred tradition, in which the students may learn to penetrate ever more profoundly the mysteries of salvation, with St. Thomas as their teacher in a special way; there are likewise to be classes in moral and pastoral theology, in canon law, liturgy, church history, and other auxiliary and special disciplines; all these classes should be in accord with the prescriptions of the program for priestly formation.

The entire theological curriculum is treated in this canon. Its purpose, the methodology, and the content are summarized. This material was found in canon 1365, §2 of the 1917 Code, which simply listed the topics to be studied.

The first paragraph of this canon almost repeats the first paragraph of *Optatam Totius* 16.

The second paragraph emphasizes the central position of the study of Scripture in the theological curriculum.[92]

The third paragraph lists the classes (or courses) that must be taught in order for students to have a "thorough understanding of Catholic doctrine." There is no attempt to give juridic significance to the ordering of the list.[93] When compared to its 1917 counterpart, this new canon adds pastoral theology and omits sacred eloquence and ecclesiastical music. The former is found in canon 256, §1, but the latter is not mentioned in the 1983 Code. The phrase concerning St. Thomas was included in the last draft.[94] In recent years several documents of the Holy See have described in detail the theological formation of priests.[95]

(The next canons [cc. 253–254] treat the topic of seminary professors. It seems better to continue the theme of seminary programs with the canons on pastoral formation [cc. 255–258] and then return to those on the professors.)

Pastoral Program

Canon 255 — Although the entire formation of the students in the seminary is for a pastoral purpose, strictly pastoral training is also to be arranged by which the students are taught the principles and skills which pertain to the ministry of teaching, sanctifying and ruling the people of God in light of the needs of the place and time.

Canon 256 — §1. The students are to be instructed diligently in those matters which have a special relationship to sacred ministry, especially catechetics and homiletics, the celebration of divine worship, particularly that of the sacraments, the conducting of relationships with people, even non-Catholics or non-believers, the administration of a parish, and the fulfillment of all other duties.

§2. The students are to be instructed in the needs of the universal Church so that they have a concern for the promotion of vocations, for missionary questions, for ecumenical concerns and other more urgent issues including those of a social nature.

These canons on the pastoral formation of seminarians are welcomed. They replace canon 1365, §3 of the 1917 Code, which prescribed "classes in pastoral theology and practical exercises especially on teaching catechism, hearing confessions, visiting the sick and assisting the dying." Encouraged by

---

[90]*Basic Plan, Norms,* 41.

[91]Response of the SCSU, Dec. 20, 1965, *CLD* 6, 252.

[92]*OT* 16 calls Scripture the soul of all theology ("universae theologiae veluti anima"). Also see *Basic Plan, Norms,* 42; *DV* 23.

[93]*Rel,* 60 and *Comm* 14 (1982), 166.

[94]*Comm* 14 (1982), 165.

[95]SCCE, *The Theological Formation of Future Priests,* Feb. 22, 1976, *Norms,* 63–95; *On the Teaching of Canon Law to Those Preparing to be Priests,* April 2, 1975, *Norms,* 147–151; *On Liturgical Formation in Seminaries,* June 3, 1979, *Norms,* 111–144. Also SCSU, *Instruction on Liturgical Training in Seminaries,* Dec. 25, 1965, *CLD* 6, 766–785 and *Basic Plan, Norms,* 42–43.

the teaching of Vatican II, the seminary community has developed programs to assist students in attaining special skills so that the truths of theology can be effectively and adequately communicated to people.[96] These canons describe the general purposes of such training and list the skills that should be developed.[97]

The needs of the Universal Church and the issues of social justice are to be part of the education of a seminarian (c. 256, §2). While not found in the 1917 Code, these same concerns are expressed many times in the teachings of Vatican II and recent writings of the popes.[98]

Canon 257 — §1. The formation of students is to prepare them so that they are concerned not only for the particular church into whose service they are incardinated but also for the universal Church; hence they are to show that they are ready to devote themselves to particular churches which are in serious need.

§2. The diocesan bishop is to take care that the clergy who intend to transfer from their own particular church to a particular church in another region are suitably prepared to exercise the sacred ministry there, namely, that they learn the language of that region and understand the region's institutions, social conditions, usages, and customs.

This canon reflects a strong theme in the teachings of Vatican II. The first paragraph gives a norm for evaluating the readiness of a man for sacred orders. The seminary program should foster this missionary and evangelizing spirit in each candidate. The true minister in the Church will care for the entire Church and will be ready to serve it as needed.[99]

The second paragraph logically follows the first but addresses the question of a cleric transferring to a missionary diocese. This will usually be done following ordination. This canon respects the injunctions found in other documents concerning the necessary training before such a transfer takes place.[100]

Canon 258 — In order that they may also learn through practice the art of exercising the aposto-

late, during the course of their studies and especially during holiday times the students are to be initiated into pastoral practice; this is to be accomplished by means of suitable activities, determined by the judgment of the ordinary and adapted to the age of the students and to local conditions and always under the supervision of a skilled priest.

It has been said that the most significant innovation in seminaries after Vatican II has been the institution of field education programs. This canon lays down the principles that underlie these programs. It is not sufficient for candidates merely to hear about the ministry; they must experience the ministry itself. This must be done under close and proper supervision. These experiences should fit the students' abilities and level of education.[101]

This canon says that the summer months are especially good times for this experiential learning. The *Basic Plan* indicates that the summer months are as good a time as the whole scholastic year.[102] This canon specifies that priests should be the supervisors. The *Basic Plan* leaves room for other supervisors as necessary or appropriate.[103]

Seminary Professors

Canon 253 — §1. Only those persons are to be appointed by the appropriate bishop or bishops to teach the philosophical, theological and juridical disciplines in a seminary who, being outstanding in virtue, have obtained a doctorate or licentiate from a university or faculty recognized by the Holy See.

§2. Care is to be taken that distinct and individual teachers are appointed to teach Sacred Scripture, dogmatic theology, moral theology, liturgy, philosophy, canon law, church history, and other disciplines all of which are to be taught in accord with their own proper methodology.

§3. A teacher who is seriously deficient in his or her duty, is to be removed by the authority mentioned in §1.

Paragraphs one and two of this canon treat the academic qualifications of seminary professors found in canon 1366, §1 and §3 of the 1917 Code. Canon 1360, §1 of the former Code spoke further of the need for professors to be outstanding in virtue and prudence. There are some significant changes, however, in the revised law.

Although the 1917 law preferred professors who had earned their degrees from an institution recog-

[96]*OT* 19; *Basic Plan, Norms,* 48.

[97]For further material on pastoral theology and its relation to academic theology, see SCCE, *The Theological Formation of Future Priests,* Feb. 22, 1976, nos. 102–106, *Norms,* 86.

[98]*OT* 20; *LG* 17, 23; *CD* 6; *AG* 39; and Paul VI, ency *Populorum progressio,* April 2, 1967, nos. 43–55; *Octogesima adveniens,* May 14, 1971, nos. 42–52.

[99]*PO* 10; *OT* 20; *LG* 17, and SCC, *Norms for the Cooperation of the Local Churches Among Themselves and Especially for the Better Distribution of the Clergy in the World,* March 25, 1980 (cited as *Norms for the Cooperation*), *The Pope Speaks* 25 (1980), 234, no. 23.

[100]*AG* 25; *ES* I, 3, nos. 1–4, Aug. 6, 1966, in *AAS* 58 (1966), 759–760 and *CLD* 6, 267; SCC, *Norms for the Cooperation, no. 25.*

[101]*OT* 21; *Basic Plan, Norms,* 48–49; *PPF,* nos. 195–223, 481–492.

[102]*Basic Plan, Norms,* 48.

[103]*Basic Plan, Norms,* 49; *PPF,* no. 217.

nized by the Holy See,[104] it used the phrase "all things being equal" to allow the proper authorities to choose someone without such a degree. This canon does not allow this. The 1977 draft followed the words of the 1917 Code.[105] The *Basic Plan* demands the licentiate or its equivalent, thus leaving more flexibility than this new canon.[106] Seminaries for some years have hired professors, both clerical and lay, who have earned their doctorates and masters in non-pontifical universities. This would be especially true in the areas of philosophy, systematic theology, and Scripture.

This canon extends the academic qualifications to the degree of licentiate, which is not found in the 1917 Code. This canon does not retain the exception for religious nor does it refer to the judgment of the seminary board in appointing professors as is found in the earlier Code (*CIC* 1366, §1).

Paragraph two of this canon addresses the question of the number of professors. Compared to its predecessor (*CIC* 1366, §3), it extends the number of disciplines which should have distinct teachers from four to seven.

Paragraph three is new. It states the right that the appropriate bishop, or bishops, has to remove an incompetent professor. It does not explicitly state the right that a professor has to due process.[107] However, the relevance of canon 221 on the basic procedural rights of Christians should be noted.

Canon 254 — §1. In imparting their disciplines, teachers are to be constantly concerned for the close unity and harmony of the entire doctrine of the faith so that their students experience that they are learning one science; in order for this objective to be more suitably realized, there is to be someone in the seminary who moderates the whole curriculum of studies.

§2. The students are to be instructed so that

they become capable of examining questions in a scientific method through their own qualified research; therefore projects are to be conducted under the supervision of the teachers by which the students learn to pursue certain studies through their own efforts.

This canon is new to canonical literature. It addresses the integration of academic work in the first paragraph and the methods of teaching in the second.[108]

The academic dean fulfills the task set forth in the first paragraph. He is mentioned as an officer in the seminary in the *Basic Plan*.[109] No one would disagree that the goal of equipping students with the skills to do their own research is noteworthy.[110]

Administration of the Seminary

Canon 259 — §1. The diocesan bishop or, if it is a question of an interdiocesan seminary, the bishops involved, are competent to make decisions concerning the above-mentioned governance and administration of the seminary.

§2. The diocesan bishop or if it is a question of an interdiocesan seminary, the bishops involved, are to visit the seminary frequently in person; they are to watch over the formation of the students and the philosophical and theological instruction given them in the seminary; they are also to keep themselves informed concerning their students' vocation, character, piety and progress, especially in view of the conferral of sacred ordination.

The complete jurisdiction of the local ordinary over the administration of the seminary in his diocese was decreed by the Council of Trent, repeated in the 1917 Code (*CIC* 1357, §1), and again prescribed in this canon. This revised canon explicitly mentions the authority of the bishop or group of bishops charged with a regional seminary. It does not refer to the case of a seminary owned and operated by an exempt religious community. The rights of the local ordinary in the governance of such a seminary ought to be specified in a contract following the appropriate norms of the Holy See and the nature of the religious institute that has responsibility for the seminary.[111]

Paragraph two urges the bishop to visit the seminary in order to keep informed of its programs and the progress of his seminarians. This is identical to canon 1357, §2 of the 1917 Code. The bishops usu-

[104]Worldwide there are approximately 200 such faculties in 34 countries. Those in the U.S.: The Catholic University, the departments of theology and canon law of the School of Religious Studies and the School of Philosophy in Washington, D.C.; the theology faculties, St. Mary's Seminary in Baltimore and St. Mary of the Lake in Mundelein, Ill.; the Jesuit Schools of Theology in Berkeley, Calif. and Weston, Mass.; the pontifical faculty of philosophy at Mt. St. Michael's College in Spokane, Wash., and the pontifical faculty of theology at the Dominican House of Studies in Washington, D.C. In Canada, there is the Pontifical Institute for Medieval Studies in Toronto; the faculties of theology at St. Paul's University, the Dominican College, the University of Sherbrooke, and Laval University.

[105]*Schema de Populo Dei*, c. 106, §1. The academic qualifications for a professor of Scripture in a seminary had been further specified by the *mp Bibliorum scientiam* April 27, 1924, *AAS* 16 (1924), 180–182, the Declaration of the Pontifical Biblical Commission, Feb. 26, 1927, *AAS* 19 (1927), 160; and the apconst *Deus scientiarum Dominus*, May 24, 1931, *AAS* 23 (1931), 24lff.

[106]*Basic Plan, Norms*, 31.

[107]The seminary professor is required in c. 833, 6° to make a profession of faith as was required in *CIC* 1406, 7°.

[108]For an extensive description of the role of a seminary professor, see SCCE, "The Theological Formation of Future Priests," nos. 121–127, *Norms*, 89–90 and *OT* 5.

[109]*Basic Plan, Norms*, 30; *PPF*, nos. 258, 454.

[110]*OT* 17 and *Basic Plan, Norms*, 47.

[111]For a clear explanation of this complex relationship, see *Relationship of the Local Ordinary to the Seminary Owned and Operated by Religious, Norms*, 317–326.

ally entrust these tasks to a delegate, for example, the vocation director. Reports on the progress of students are sent annually by the rector. When a seminarian has petitioned for ordination, the report will contain a recommendation of the faculty and rector.

Canon 260 — **In carrying out their duties all are to obey the rector who has the responsibility to see to the daily administration of the seminary in accord with the norms of the program for priestly formation and the rule of the seminary.**

This canon corresponds to canon 1360, §2 of the 1917 Code. A previous canon spoke of the office of the rector.[112] Here the law wishes to indicate that the rector is charged with the daily administration of the seminary under the authority of the bishop. The bishop should appoint someone to this position whom he trusts to make decisions according to the norms of the national program and the guidelines previously approved by him.[113] For the smooth, unified governing of the institution, all professors, staff, and students must obey the rector. This in no way relieves the rector from the responsibility of exercising collegiality and subsidiarity.

Canon 261 — **§1. The rector of the seminary and, under his authority, the moderators and teachers for their part are to see to it that the students exactly observe the norms of the program for priestly formation and the prescriptions of the rule of the seminary.**

§2. The rector of the seminary and the director of studies are carefully to see to it that the teachers duly perform their function in accord with the prescriptions of the program for priestly formation and the rule of the seminary.

These paragraphs repeat the prescriptions of canon 1369, §1 and §3 of the 1917 Code—with the addition of the reference to the program for priestly formation. Canon 1369, §2 of the former law is not retained in the revised law. It prescribed that the rector or his assistants give instructions on urbanity, courtesy, and modesty.

The duties of the rector as prescribed in this canon are clear and fundamental.[114] The faculty handbook should specify the procedures by which professors are evaluated.

Exemption from Parochial Jurisdiction

Canon 262 — **The seminary is to be exempt from parochial governance; the rector of the seminary or**

his delegate is to fulfill the office of pastor for all who are in the seminary, with the exception of matrimonial matters and with due regard for the prescription of can. 985.

This canon is identical to the 1917 Code (*CIC* 1368) with two exceptions: the former law used the word jurisdiction, while this canon uses governance (*regimen*); and the 1917 Code explicitly allowed for another arrangement if so decreed by the Holy See.

Canon 985 mentioned here corresponds to canon 891 of the 1917 Code (mentioned in *CIC* 1368). It forbids the rector from hearing the confessions of students unless a student voluntarily asks him in a particular case.

The scope of the exemption is determined in the same words used in the 1917 Code: "all who are in the seminary." The traditional interpretation continues to be operative. It is a territorial exemption[115] and applies equally to those who remain in the seminary for only a portion of the day, e.g., employees.[116]

The rector, then, has the right and duty to administer the sacrament of the sick and Viaticum, to dispense from the laws of fast and abstinence, and to celebrate funerals. He would also have ordinary power to hear confessions—with the exception mentioned above. The rector would yield to the wishes of parents and relatives to celebrate funerals in their parish churches.[117]

Financial Support and Seminary Tax

Canon 263 — **The diocesan bishop must see to it that provision is made for the establishment and maintenance of the seminary, the support of the students, the remuneration of the teachers, and other needs of the seminary; if the seminary is interdiocesan the bishops involved must make such provisions based upon a mutual agreement worked out by them.**

Canon 264 — **§1. In addition to the collection mentioned in can. 1266 the bishop can impose a tax within the diocese to provide for the needs of the seminary.**

§2. All ecclesiastical juridic persons, even private ones, which have a foundation in the diocese are subject to this tax for the seminary, unless they are maintained through alms alone or they contain a college of students or teachers to promote the common good of the Church; a tax of this type must be general, proportioned to the revenues of those

[112]C. 239, §1.

[113]For a full explanation of the office of rector, see Cox, 81–89 and Peterson, 74–116.

[114]Cox, 83, 85.

[115]W. Onclin, "De Rectoribus Seminariorum" in *IP* 16 (1936), 75.

[116]Cocchi, 108; A. Vermeersch and J. Creusen, *Epitome Iuris Canonici*, 3 vols., 5th ed. (Mechliniae-Romae: H. Dessain, 1934), 2:488.

[117]T.L. Bouscaren, A. Ellis, and F. Korth, *Canon Law*, 4th ed. (Milwaukee: The Bruce Publishing Co., 1963), 762.

who are subject to it, and determined in accord with the needs of the seminary.

These canons replace canons 1355 and 1356 of the 1917 Code.[118] While the general thrust of the revised law in this matter remains the same, the details are significantly simplified. This final text was written subsequent to the 1977 draft.[119]

Canon 263 simply states the obligation to provide financial support for the seminary. While not stated so clearly in the 1917 law, it was certainly implied.

The bishop is empowered by canon 264 to raise money for the seminary by one means: a tax on juridic persons. The 1917 law (*CIC* 1355) gave him three options: collection, tax, and giving the semi-

nary simple benefices. This canon refers to canon 1266 which authorizes the local ordinary to take up a special collection for determined projects. The maintenance of the seminary would be one of these. In many dioceses it is customary to declare one Sunday "Seminary Day" or to give the seminary a share of the annual diocesan campaign.

If the bishop chooses to impose a tax, it will be done differently than allowed by the 1917 Code. The former law allowed benefices to be taxed by a set percent of their income. The revised law states simply that the tax should be proportioned to both the income and the needs of the seminary.

Those subject to such a tax are all juridic persons in the diocese with two exceptions. Those supported solely by alms and those which run a college for the common good are exempted. An example of the former would be nursing homes run by religious women. An example of the latter would be institutions of higher learning owned and operated by a religious community.

[118]*CIC* 1362 authorized the use of funds designed "for the education of clerics" to be used for seminarians who de facto were not yet clerics. This is not retained in the revised law.

[119]*Schema de Populo Dei* cc. 116–119. These draft canons are substantially the same as those of the 1917 Code.

BIBLIOGRAPHY

a. Commentaries on the 1917 Code

Bouscaren, T.L.; Ellis, A.; and Korth, F. *Canon Law.* 4th ed., 756–763. Milwaukee: The Bruce Publishing Co., 1963.

Cocchi, G. *Commentarium in Codicem Iuris Canonici ad usum scholarum.* 6 vols., 2nd ed. Vol. VI, 70–112. Taurinorum Augustae: Officina Libraria Marietti, 1920–1930 (cited as Cocchi).

Vermeersch, A., and Creusen, J. *Epitome Iuris Canonici.* 3 vols., 5th ed. Vol. II, 475–492. Mechliniae-Romae: H. Dessain, 1934.

Woywod, S., and Smith, C. *A Practical Commentary on the Code of Canon Law.* 2 vols., rev. ed. Vol. II, 131–151 (cited as Woywod-Smith).

b. Official Code Commission Reports on the Revision of the Law on the Formation of Clerics

Comm 8 (1976): 108–166 (report on original work of the committee and subsequent meetings spanning 8 years).

Comm 13 (1981): 298–302 (report on decision to restructure Book II).

Comm 14 (1982): 31–71 (reworking of original canons).

Comm 14 (1982): 158–167 (report on observations and recommendations of members of special plenary session, Oct. 1981).

c. Official Documents on the Formation of Clerics

Norms for Priestly Formation: A Compendium of Official Documents on Training Candidates for the Priesthood. Washington: USCC, 1982 (cited as *Norms*).

The Program of Priestly Formation. 3rd ed. Washington: USCC, 1982 (cited as *PPF*).

Enchiridion Clericorum: Documenta Ecclesiae Futuris Sacerdotibus Formandis. Roma: Typis Polyglottis Vaticanis, 1975.

d. Additional Writings on the Formation of Clerics

Cox, J. *The Administration of Seminaries.* Washington: Catholic University of America, 1931 (cited as Cox).

Ellis, J. "Short History of Seminary Education I and II" in *Seminary Education in a Time of Change.* Edited by J. Lee and L. Putz. Notre Dame, Ind.: Fides, 1965 (cited as Ellis).

Peterson, C. *Spiritual Care in Diocesan Seminaries.* Washington: Catholic University of America, 1966 (cited as Peterson).

Chapters II, III, and IV complete the title devoted to sacred ministers or clerics.

The eight canons of chapter II treat the initial affiliation of a cleric with an ecclesiastical structure equivalent to a diocese or a religious community and the conditions under which a temporary or permanent transfer may be effected.[1] In accord with conciliar directives (*PO* 10) the regulations have been revised so that while the ancient principle has been retained, it is adapted to the pastoral needs of the present.[2]

In revising the law dealing with the obligations and rights of clerics (chapter III), most of the pre-

scriptions found in the 1917 Code have been repeated with some notable deletions and additions. The traditional privileges of the clergy are no longer asserted. Clerics are not told that they ought to lead a holier life than the laity and to give a superior example of virtue and right living. All references to tonsure and the wearing of rings have been dropped. On the other hand, a number of conciliar pronouncements on priests have been incorporated. Clerics—in a spirit of fraternity—are to cooperate closely among themselves and to acknowledge and promote the mission of the laity. They are to cultivate a simple life-style and to contribute any surplus income stemming from their ministry to the work of the Church and to charity.

In the final four canons of the title, chapter IV treats the various ways the clerical state may be lost, the effects of the procedure, and the possible readmission to this state.

---

[1]"Opera Consultorum," *Comm* 3 (1971), 189–191; *Comm* 14 (1982), 62–71. In addition to the matters treated in the seven corresponding canons of the 1917 Code (*CIC* 111–117) the 1983 Code provides for a temporary transfer.

[2]J. Hervada, "La Incardinación en la perspective conciliar," *IC* 7 (1967), 479–517.

Canons and Commentary

CHAPTER II
INSCRIPTION OR INCARDINATION OF CLERICS
[cc. 265–272]

Necessity

Canon 265 — Every cleric must be incardinated into some particular church or personal prelature or into an institute of consecrated life or society endowed with this faculty, so that unattached or transient clerics are not allowed at all.

Every cleric without exception must be subject to a definite ecclesiastical superior.[3] The law prohibits a cleric from being unattached or in an itinerant status at any time. The fundamental reason for requiring such a bond is that clerics by definition are public servants; no one should be inducted into the clerical state except for the necessity or utility of

the Church (c. 1025, §2). Private devotion, honor, and convenience are not sufficient justification for ordination as they had been up until the Council of Trent. If, furthermore, clerics were permitted to roam about at will, the spiritual needs of the people could not be provided for properly. As the Church knows well from the experience of the past, ambition and avarice can lure the clergy away from poor areas to more affluent ones.[4] The good order of a diocese or a religious community demands that its ministers not move about capriciously from one apostolic labor to another. In itself the bond is permanent. Clerics may not withdraw from the jurisdiction of their superiors unilaterally or at will but only in accordance with the norms established by the Church. Even when a transfer is legally effected, there is never a moment when the cleric is unattached. The two acts of excardination and incardination coalesce into a single juridical act.

Affiliation also assures the cleric of permanent employment and sustenance in the ministry. Orders are bestowed to be exercised. It would be demoralizing to the individual and scandalous to the laity if

---

[3]The necessity of incardination for all clerics is reaffirmed in almost the terminology of the 1917 Code. For an historical synopsis and commentary on the 1917 Code, see J. McBride, *Incardination and Excardination of Seculars*, CanLawStud 145 (Washington: Catholic University of America, 1941).

[4]Council of Nicaea, c. 15 *(COD,* 12).

a cleric had to wander about seeking an opportunity to carry out his ministry. Through that ministry should come his support—without his being forced to beg or engage in menial tasks. A superior may not arbitrarily cut a cleric loose any more than the cleric may go off on his own. The 1917 Code (*CIC* 979–982), reflecting a centuries-old tradition, required a canonical title as the basis of support for one receiving major orders. In the case of secular clerics, that title was either a benefice, a patrimony (personal property), a subsidy (governmental, ecclesiastical, or private grant), or "the service of the diocese or the missions." For a religious cleric the title was "solemn religious profession," "the common table," or a similar provision. The primary title for ordination under that Code, as it had been in the Tridentine legislation, was the benefice—defined as a sacred office and the right to receive the revenue accruing from the endowment attached to that office (*CIC* 1409). The usual title in the United States, however, was "the service of the diocese." The 1983 Code directs conferences of bishops to supervise the allocation of revenue of benefices (c. 1272). There is now no reference to a title for ordination; all that is required is the judgment of the bishop or major religious superior that the candidate's ministry will be useful to the Church (c. 1025, §2).

With regard to the necessity of clerical attachment there has been no change in the law. A cleric must be incardinated in either a particular church or an ecclesiastical association. Formerly the term "affiliation" (*adscriptio*) was used to apply to all clerics, while "incardination" was reserved for the diocesan clergy. Now both terms are used indiscriminately. Again, whereas the 1917 Code referred simply to a "diocese," the 1983 Code speaks more broadly of a "particular church" (see the commentary on c. 368). Among the associations approved by the Church, some are regarded as clerical and some as lay (c. 588, §§2–3), but the membership need not be composed exclusively of one or the other. As the next canon will specify, there are three types of associations that may have the faculty of incardination: (1) religious institutes whose members live a common life under public vows (c. 607, §2); (2) secular institutes whose members live a consecrated life in the world (c. 710); and (3) societies of apostolic life whose members observe a common life but without religious vows (c. 731). An institute (c. 589) or a society of apostolic life (c. 732) may be either of pontifical law (if established or formally approved by the Holy See) or of diocesan law (if established by a bishop). An institute or society of diocesan law would not as such be able to incardinate (c. 1019, §2).

In addition to particular churches and the associations just described, the Council suggested the establishment of personal prelatures with the right to incardinate (*PO* 10). Pope Paul VI issued experimental norms regarding the personal prelature in which students could be incardinated and promoted to orders under the title of "the service of the prelature" (*mp ES* I, 4). The 1983 Code treats personal prelatures under title IV (cc. 294–297). Their right to incardinate and promote to orders is confirmed. Although the "title" of ordination has elsewhere been suppressed, there is still reference—perhaps by oversight—to the "title of service to the prelature" (c. 295, §1).

Those who seek to be enrolled in the secular or diocesan clergy,[5] according to canon 1016, may apply to the bishop of the diocese in which they have domicile (c. 102) or to the bishop of the diocese to whose service they intend to devote themselves. The provisions of the 1917 Code were considerably more complex (*CIC* 956). If the candidate had a domicile other than that of his birth, he had to take an oath of permanently residing in it. Since, prior to 1972, incardination took place with the reception of first tonsure, there would necessarily be an interval before priestly ordination. It was possible, then, for a bishop to confer tonsure on one of his subjects with the view of later excardination and incardination in an indeterminate diocese, for example, in the foreign missions. The *Schema de Populo Dei* (c. 198) provided that incardination was to take place in the diocese of domicile or the diocese of origin or the diocese to which the candidate wished to devote himself with the consent of the bishop of the diocese of domicile. The 1983 law, however, gives complete freedom for a lay man to affiliate with any diocese whose bishop is agreeable. A previous acquisition of domicile is not required.

Mode

Canon 266 — §1. A person becomes a cleric through the reception of diaconate and is incardinated into the particular church or personal prelature for whose service he has been advanced.

§2. A professed member of a religious institute in perpetual vows or a definitively incorporated member of a clerical society of apostolic life is incardinated as a cleric to the institute or society through the reception of diaconate unless in the case of societies their constitutions establish otherwise.

§3. A member of a secular institute is incardinated into a particular church for whose service he has been advanced through the reception of diaconate unless he is incardinated into the institute itself by virtue of a grant of the Apostolic See.

Certainly from the time of Pope Innocent III (1210) and up to the post-Vatican II era, it was through the reception of first tonsure that an indi-

[5]K. Scanlan, "The Juridical Concept of the Secular Cleric," *J* 19 (1959), 300–308.

vidual became a cleric and was incardinated or affiliated to the diocese for whose service he was promoted. Beginning January 1, 1973, Pope Paul VI by his *motu proprio Ministeria quaedam* suppressed the rite of tonsure and conjoined entrance into the clerical state with the diaconate.[6] At the same time the minor orders of lector and acolyte were transformed into ministries that could be bestowed on lay persons and not reserved to candidates for the sacrament of orders. Under this new arrangement, the pope noted, the distinction between clerics and lay persons would be more readily apparent—as would the distinction between functions proper to the clergy and those that can be entrusted to the laity. Henceforth, no one can be a cleric who has not received diaconal ordination. Since ordination is to be conferred only for service and not for honor or convenience, it is appropriate that incardination occur with the reception of the diaconate that inducts one into the clerical state.

In the case of the secular clergy, then, it is diaconal ordination that incardinates them in the particular church for whose service they are destined. The affiliation is of itself permanent. For the liceity of the diaconal ordination, the individual must previously have been admitted to candidacy through a liturgical rite (c. 1034, §1) and have received the ministries of lector and acolyte (c. 1035, §1). A six-month interval, at least, must elapse between the reception of the acolythate and the diaconate (c. 1035, §2). If the bishop of the diocese is not to perform the ordination, he must authorize by dimissorial letters another bishop to do so (c. 1015, §1). An apostolic administrator and a diocesan administrator with the consent of the board of consultors may also issue such letters of authorization—but not in favor of someone who has been refused by the diocesan bishop (c. 1018). The 1917 Code had restricted the administrator from exercising any faculty regarding ordination, including incardination, during the first year of the vacancy (*CIC* 958, §1, 3°; 113). It is the responsibility of the bishop who is ordaining his own subject for service in another diocese to ascertain that the candidate has been in fact accepted by that diocese.

Through the reception of the diaconate, religious who are already permanently attached to their communities become affiliated with them as clerics. Major superiors of clerical religious institutes or societies of common life of pontifical right may issue dimissorial letters for subjects who are permanently or definitively committed to enable them to receive the diaconate (c. 1019, §1). Major superiors include the moderator of a self-governing house, such as a monastery (c. 613, §2), as well as the supreme moderator of an institute and the moderator of a prov-

ince or its equivalent (c. 620). In clerical societies of apostolic life that have pontifical status, the major superiors may also grant dimissorial letters for subjects who have been definitively incorporated. Under the common law of the 1917 Code, members of societies of the common life without vows had to be incardinated in a diocese; the society itself could not incardinate clerics and its superiors could not issue dimissorial letters. Most societies, however, could do so by privilege in virtue of an exemption or indult.[7] The 1983 Code provides that in clerical societies of apostolic life clerics are incardinated in the society itself unless their constitutions determine otherwise (c. 736, §1).

Those ordained in secular institutes according to canon 266, §3 are incardinated in the particular church that they are going to serve rather than in the institute itself. The diocesan bishop would then have full discretion in approving candidates for orders. By way of apostolic concession, however, these institutes may be given the faculty to incardinate members in the institute (see also c. 715).

Once a cleric is incardinated in a diocese or religious community, the bond of incorporation cannot be broken except as provided by law. A bishop or superior is not permitted to cut him loose without a process of dismissal. The cleric, on the other hand, no matter where he goes or what employment he undertakes remains subject to his proper ecclesiastical superior unless legitimately released. A new affiliation must occur concomitantly with any separation since a cleric may never be unattached or independent of authority.

Permanent Transfer

Canon 267 — §1. In order for a cleric already incardinated to be incardinated validly into another particular church, he must obtain from the diocesan bishop a letter of excardination signed by the bishop; he must likewise obtain from the diocesan bishop of the particular church into which he desires to be incardinated a letter of incardination signed by that bishop.

§2. Excardination thus granted does not take effect unless incardination into another particular church has been obtained.

In order for a cleric incardinated in one particular church to be incardinated in another, he must have written permission from the diocesan bishop of both the place from which he is leaving and the place to which he is going. The prescriptions of the canon are for the validity—not just the liceity—of the process. If one of the requisites is inadvertently

---

[6]*AAS* 64 (1972), 529–534; *CLD* 7, 690–695. The norms for the diaconate were established in *Ad pascendum, AAS* 64 (1972), 534–540; *CLD* 7, 695–698.

[7]J. Nugent, *Ordination in Societies of the Common Life, Can-LawStud* 341 (Washington: Catholic University of America, 1958).

omitted that incardination and any subsequent incardination would be invalid.

A diocesan bishop is understood to be anyone who presides over a particular church (cc. 368; 381, §2). The excardination-incardination of a deacon or priest is of such importance that the decision must rest with the highest authority. The vicar general or the episcopal vicar may not act in this matter without a special mandate.

The 1917 Code (*CIC* 112) stated that the consent given by both bishops had to be permanent (without a time limitation) and absolute (unconditional or irrevocable). Insofar as incardination by its very nature must have these qualities, the revised law does not explicitate them; besides, in a subsequent canon it provides for temporary or limited transfers. Since the destination of the cleric must be indicated in the letter of excardination, the prospective incardinating bishop in a preliminary communication has to inform the excardinating bishop of his readiness to accept the individual. The official letters of excardination and incardination—each of which states the two dioceses involved—are addressed to the cleric concerned. Both letters must be signed personally by the respective bishops. For liceity the incardinating bishop must have certain testimonials described in canon 269, §2 and a written declaration of service from the cleric (c. 269, §3).

The excardination does not take effect until incardination has been effected in the other church. Thus there is no moment when a cleric is without affiliation. Even though the revised law, unlike the former, does not mandate the receiving bishop to notify the dismissing bishop that the incardination has taken place, the good order of the Church seems to call for such notification.

A form of excardination-incardination takes place when a new diocese is established. The decree of erection usually states that the clergy belong to that church in whose territory they are canonically domiciled at the time.[8] The decree may also permit the bishops to arrange the allocation after consulting the clergy concerned.

The *Guidelines* for permanent deacons in the United States recognize a special difficulty. The fact that the majority of these deacons will continue secular work as part of a very mobile secular society qualifies their commitment to the diocese. "With the cooperation and dialogue common among U.S. bishops, a deacon who is transferred into another diocese by his occupation will ordinarily be welcomed into ministry by his new bishop." It may be, however, that that diocese has not exercised its option to implement the permanent di-

aconate. In that case the deacon "will simply not exercise his office."[9]

Ipso Facto Change of Incardination

Canon 268 — §1. A cleric who has legitimately moved from his own particular church into another one is incardinated into this other particular church by the law itself after five years if he made such a desire known in writing both to the diocesan bishop of the host church and to his own diocesan bishop and provided neither of them informed the cleric of his opposition in writing within four months of the reception of his letter.

§2. Through perpetual or definitive admission to an institute of consecrated life or to a society of apostolic life a cleric who is incardinated into that institute or society in accord with the norm of can. 266, §2 is excardinated from his own particular church.

Two further processes of excardination-incardination are provided in the post-conciliar law. The first is known as tacit incardination. After spending five years in another diocese to which he has legitimately transferred, a cleric may seek to be inscribed there. If he expresses his intention in writing to both his own diocesan bishop and the host bishop and neither objects in writing within four months of receiving the notification, then by the law itself the cleric is incardinated in the host diocese. This provision, introduced by the *motu proprio Ecclesiae sanctae* (I, 3, 5), has been taken over unchanged into the 1983 Code. The legislator is concerned lest a protracted indefinite residence in an alien diocese weaken the institute of incardination and lead to uncertainty concerning the cleric's status.

In 1978 the Apostolic Signatura in upholding the appeal of a priest who claimed to be tacitly incardinated presented a detailed jurisprudence. Four conditions are required to effect a change of affiliation in this manner. (1) The cleric must manifest his desire in writing, either during the five-year period or after it has passed. It makes no difference whether or not he does so in formal terminology as long as his meaning is not ambiguous. (2) The written notification must be given both to his own bishop and the host bishop either at the same time or at different times. (3) The cleric must have completed five years of legitimate residence in the host diocese. He need not have discharged any pastoral function in that diocese. The mere fact of residence, however, is not sufficient; it must be formal residence, that is, with the consent of the two bishops. The residence must not have been interrupted by ei-

[8]J. Schmidt, "Status of Incardination at the Establishment of a New Diocese," *J* 21 (1961), 296–310.

[9]U.S. Bishops' Committee on the Permanent Diaconate, *Permanent Deacons in the United States: Guidelines on Their Formation and Ministry* (Washington: USCC, 1971), n. 133.

ther bishop prohibiting it for some reason. (4) Neither bishop has indicated in writing a contrary mind within four months of receiving the petition and the expiration of the five-year period. The manifestation of a contrary mind must be made to the petitioner himself and expressed in clear and certain terms.[10]

The 1917 Code provided for a virtual excardination-incardination through the acquisition of a residential benefice, such as pastorate in another diocese (*CIC* 114). If the priest had the written consent of his ordinary to accept the benefice or to leave the diocese permanently, he would automatically be incardinated in the second diocese. The virtual or implicit incardination has been eliminated insofar as the benefice system has been reformed in the 1983 law (c. 1272).

A third type of excardination-incardination is effected through the perpetual or definitive admission of a cleric to an institute of consecrated life or to a society that enjoys the faculty of affiliation. A cleric incardinated in a particular church who wishes to join a religious community retains his original incardination during the period of the novitiate and temporary profession. The change of affiliation takes place at the moment of final profession.

If, on the other hand, a priest member wishes to leave a religious community, he may not receive an indult to do so until he has found a bishop who will incardinate him or at least receive him on trial. If the bishop does accept him on probation, after five years he is automatically incardinated in the diocese unless the bishop has refused him (cc. 693, 743). A religious who has been legitimately dismissed may not exercise his orders until he finds a bishop willing to receive him by way of experiment or at least permit him to exercise his orders (c. 701).

The 1917 Code provided (*CIC* 641) in the case of a religious in sacred orders who sought an indult of secularization that a benevolent bishop could incardinate him immediately or receive him on probation for three years with the option of extending the period—but not beyond another three years. At the conclusion of the period, the religious, unless dismissed from the diocese, would be ipso facto incardinated in it.[11] Canon 693 of the 1983 Code has instituted a five-year trial period.

Liceity of a New Incardination

Canon 269 — A diocesan bishop is not to allow the incardination of a cleric unless:

1° the necessity or advantage of his own particular church demands it, with due regard for the pre-

[10]*CLD* 9, 52–60; *Comm* 10 (1978), 152–158.
[11]E. Schneider, *The Status of Secularized Ex-Religious Clerics, CanLawStud* 284 (Washington: Catholic University of America, 1948).

scriptions of the law concerning the decent support of clerics;

2° he is certain from a legitimate document that excardination has been granted, and he also has in addition appropriate testimonials from the excardinating diocesan bishop, in secrecy if necessary, concerning the cleric's life, morals, and studies;

3° the cleric has declared in writing to the same diocesan bishop that he wishes to be dedicated to the service of the new particular church in accord with the norm of law.

Certain conditions must be met before a diocesan bishop may proceed to incardinate a cleric. These requisites are for licitness only since the canon does not stipulate any invalidating force. There must be in that particular church some office or position to which the cleric may be assigned so that his time and talents will be spent in the service of religion. Just as orders are not to be conferred on an individual unless in the judgment of the legitimate superior he be considered useful for the ministry of the Church (c. 1025, §2), so, too, a cleric already ordained is not to be added to the diocesan clergy without some ministerial employment being foreseen. Especially since the Council of Trent the Church has sought in its legislation to guard against an idle clergy. Similarly it is important that the clergy have decent sustenance. The bishop, therefore, must be reasonably assured that the new cleric can be adequately supported (c. 281, §1). The 1917 law (*CIC* 117, 1°) referred to supplying a title of ordination since the original one would be lost in the transfer. The 1983 Code has abolished the use of titles as signifying an unfailing source of sustenance.

The receiving bishop needs, furthermore, certain assurances before acting. He must have a legitimately executed document to the effect that the cleric has actually been granted a permanent and unconditional excardination and has not just been promised one. In terms of canon 267 the letter must be signed by the diocesan bishop and in view of canon 270 include the declaration that the excardination is being given for a just cause. (That the incardinating bishop see the document is a matter of liceity; validity depends upon only the issuance of the letter.) Another required document is a testimonial concerning the cleric's life and character as well as a certification of the studies he has completed. If need be, the character reference may be given confidentially (*sub secreto*). It should treat his record of conduct and moral integrity, whether or not he had incurred a canonical irregularity, and the extent to which he spent his time in the diocese. Such traits as zeal, indifference, and selfishness are also to be included. (*CIC* 117, 2° sought, in addition, an appraisal of his parentage, cultural and social background as well as his legitimacy; special care was to be taken in scrutinizing the papers of foreign-born clerics.) The excardinating bishop does not have to draw up the account himself, but he should verify what his staff has prepared. The receiving bishop is to judge the suitability of the cleric petitioning incardination on the same basis as he would a candidate for orders. A mere change of locale does not necessarily lead to moral improvement. Incardination is not to be granted until amendment of life has been established over an appropriate period of time. A pressing need for clergy never justifies the incardination of an unworthy individual.

The final document that the incardinating bishop must have in hand is a written declaration from the cleric that he wishes to dedicate himself to the service of that particular church in accordance with the rule of law. The 1917 law (*CIC* 117, 3°) had prescribed an oath of perpetual service on the occasion of transfer as well as at the time a cleric was ordained to major orders under the title of "service of the diocese." (An oath was also required at tonsure if the candidate had not been born in the diocese [*CIC* 956].) In the spirit of recent legislation a declaration of intention instead of an oath is now sufficient. The declaration concerns present intention; it does not mean that the cleric may not later enter a religious institute or be excardinated again.

Liceity of Excardination

Canon 270 — **Excardination can be granted licitly for just causes only, such as the benefit of the Church or the good of the cleric himself; however, it cannot be denied except for serious reasons; a cleric, however, who thinks that he has been wronged and who has found a bishop to accept him may have recourse against the decision.**

For an excardination to be licit there must be a just cause for it to be granted. The law clearly indicates that the validity of the release is not at stake in this canon;[12] canon 267 has already dealt with the requirements for validity. Such causes may be the good of the Church or the good of the cleric himself. His talents may be better utilized in another diocese because either greater opportunities are offered or because his ministry has become inefficacious through loss of reputation. Health reasons warranting a more favorable climate, for example, would certainly be legitimate. It may even happen that an animosity between the cleric and his bishop suggests a change. Long years of service spent in the host diocese has also been recognized as sufficient. (C. 268, §1 has even established a tacit incardination after five years of service.) Examples of unjust or unworthy reasons would be ambition or avarice. In cases of restlessness or instability, coun-

seling is to be recommended; a transfer will simply postpone facing the problem.

Quite unlike the former law, this canon adds that the bishop cannot deny the request for release except for grave cause. The law thus recognizes a right on the part of a cleric to transfer his affiliation. Neither the Council nor *Ecclesiae sanctae* recognized personal reasons of the cleric as a just cause for excardination.[13] Papal teaching, however, over the past twenty or thirty years has increasingly affirmed as a human right the freedom to develop one's talents and to immigrate to places where a fuller life may be lived.[14] Individuals with their unique endowments cannot be expected to thrive in every physical, social, or cultural environment. By accepting incardination a cleric does not surrender all his human rights. The spiritual good of the faithful is accepted as a canonical reason justifying dispensation from the law (c. 87, §1). The spiritual good of the cleric must also be given due consideration. The welfare of the individual, of course, must be balanced by the community good that is protected through the stability afforded by incardination. The right of the cleric is not automatically to be sacrificed; the law demands that the bishop have grave cause for rejecting a request for transfer.

The universal law must necessarily provide for flexibility. It is left to the bishop to weigh the relative merits of the cleric's petition and the needs of the diocese. Lest discretion become too arbitrary, however, the canon adds that a cleric who considers himself aggrieved and has found a bishop willing to receive him may have recourse against the decision.[15] If a council of arbitration has not been established (c. 1733, §2), then only hierarchical recourse is available; in this case the cleric could communicate with the Sacred Congregation for the Clergy. Should the diocesan bishop not respond at all to a petition for excardination, after three months his response may be presumed negative (c. 57, §2) and recourse may be taken.

Temporary Transfer

Canon 271 — **§1. Outside the case of the true necessity of his own particular church, the diocesan bishop is not to deny clerics permission to move to regions which suffer from a serious dearth of clergy and to exercise the sacred ministry there when he knows that such clerics are prepared and when he judges them fit to do so; he is also to make provision that the rights and duties of these clerics are established through a written agreement with the diocesan bishop of the place where they are going.**

[12]*Comm* 3 (1971), 189-191.

[13]J. Hervada, "La Incardinación," 501.
[14]John XXIII, *Pacem in Terris* 10 (*AAS* 55 [1963], 263); Paul VI, *Octogesima adveniens* n. 17 (*AAS* 63 [1971], 413).
[15]The Secretariat of the Commission noted that the norms for recourse are to be found in Liber VII *De processibus* (*Rel,* 63).

§2. A diocesan bishop can grant his clerics permission to move to another particular church for a predetermined period of time which can be renewed several times; such clerics remain incardinated in their own particular church and, when they return to it, they possess all the rights which they would have had if they had exercised the sacred ministry there.

§3. A cleric who has legitimately moved to another particular church while remaining incardinated in his own church can for a just cause be recalled by his own diocesan bishop provided the agreements made with the other bishop and natural equity are observed; under the same conditions the diocesan bishop of the other particular church can likewise for a just cause deny the same cleric permission for a longer stay in his territory.

The Council was very much concerned about a better distribution of clergy throughout the world. *Christus Dominus* taught that "by divine institution and by virtue of their apostolic office all bishops jointly are responsible for the Church" (*CD* 6). They should arrange as far as possible for some of their priests to minister either permanently or for a fixed perod in regions where the gospel has not yet been proclaimed or where people are in danger of losing the faith—especially on account of the scarcity of priests. *Presbyterorum Ordinis* stressed that the priest, too, has a universal mission insofar as he shares both in the mission entrusted by Christ to the apostles as well as in the priesthood of Christ himself (*PO* 10). Priests are to be solicitous for all the churches. In those areas that are blessed with a greater abundance of vocations they should be prepared to offer themselves gladly for service in countries or missions or tasks that are hampered by a shortage of clergy.

The Council called, therefore, for a revision of rules of incardination and excardination in such a way that, while remaining intact, this ancient institution will better answer the pastoral needs of today. Not only should the better distribution of priests be made easier but also the pursuit of special pastoral projects for different social groups in any region or among any race in any part of the world. The Council suggested that special dioceses, personal prelatures, and other institutions be set up to which priests can be attached or incardinated for the common good of the whole Church (*PO* 10).

In implementation of the conciliar mandate, *Ecclesiae sanctae* directed each episcopal conference to set up a special commission "to study the needs of the various dioceses of the territory and their potential for helping other churches" (*ES* I, 2). While the present laws of incardination and excardination were reaffirmed, the transfer of clerics from one diocese to another was to be facilitated. Except in situations of true need bishops were not to refuse permission to qualified clerics who wished to exer-

cise their ministry in regions suffering from a grave shortage of priests. An ordinary could thus permit a cleric to transfer for a specific period, which could be often extended, while retaining incardination in his own diocese without the loss of any rights whatsoever. After five years the priest could be incardinated in the host diocese if neither his own nor the receiving bishop objected (*ES* I, 3, 5). The Holy See also announced its willingness to establish prelatures "to accomplish special pastoral or missionary tasks for various regions or social groups requiring special assistance." The prelatures would consist of trained secular clergy under their own statutes and prelates (*ES* I, 4).

Pope Paul VI in 1967 set up a commission to "lay down principles to govern a more equitable distribution of the clergy taking into account the needs of the various churches." The Sacred Congregation for the Clergy, which was assigned a coordinating role, consulted with episcopal conferences and arranged an international congress at Malta in 1970.[16] On March 25, 1980 the Sacred Congregation for the Clergy published "Directives for Collaboration among Local Churches and in Particular for a Better Distribution of the Clergy."[17] Ministers need an adequate preparation especially about the culture, language, and customs of the country to which they are going. The rights and duties of priests who volunteer are to be clearly defined in a written agreement between the originating bishop and the host bishop. The priest himself is to assist in drawing up the document and to sign it, if it is to have juridical force. Both curias and the priest are to have copies of the agreement. The following points are to be specified:

(a) the length of time to be spent in the service; (b) the duties of the priest and the location of his residence and ministry, although account must be taken of living conditions in the region to which he is going; (c) the support to be given him, and its source; (d) provisions for care in case of sickness, disability and old age.[18]

It may also be useful to specify the possibility of the priest's visiting his home country after a certain period of time. The agreement cannot be altered without the consent of all concerned, though the host bishop reserves the right to send the priest back if

---

[16]For a report on the Malta conference held from May 24–28, 1970, see F. Romita, "La distribuzione del Clero: "Il mondo e la mia parrochia,' " *ME* 95 (1970), 361–401.

[17]*AAS* 72 (1980), 343–364; *The Pope Speaks* 25 (1980), 219–238. C.A. MacDonald, Executive Director of the Bishops' Committee on Priestly Life and Ministry stated: "The Committee on Priestly Life and Ministry prepared a *Report on the Distribution of Clergy* for the Administrative Committee of the NCCB in 1979, with some revision in 1980. No policy on the question has been developed by the Administrative Committee to this date." (Letter to J.E. Lynch, Sept. 8, 1982.)

[18]No. 27.

his ministry proves harmful, i.e., after advising the original bishop and observing natural and canonical equity.

The present canon thus deals with clerics on loan to another diocese. It incorporates the principal provisions of *Ecclesiae sanctae* and the "Directives" of the Sacred Congregation for the Clergy. The diocesan bishop must allow volunteers from among his clergy, whom he knows to be prepared and fit, to exercise their ministry in areas where there is a serious personnel shortage. Only in a case of real necessity in his own particular church may the bishop deny permission to transfer. The necessity should be weighed with some reference to the needs of the country seeking ministerial assistance. It may happen, however, that the petitioning cleric holds an office requiring talents and professional training not easily replaced. In such instances the bishop would be justified, at least for a time, in refusing to allow a cleric to depart. The burden of proof rests with the bishop; the presumption is in favor of extending aid. If grave reasons are required for a bishop to withhold an excardination that is sought for the good of the Church or of the individual cleric (c. 270), no less can justify opposing a temporary transfer.

The Secretariat of the Code Commission noted that this canon also applies to clerics who are invited to fill a regional or national office or to serve as professors in a Catholic educational institution.[19] Such offices would include regional tribunals, the staff of the episcopal conference, and the military ordinariate among others.

The agreement is to be drawn up in accord with the 1980 "Directives" of the Sacred Congregation for the Clergy; it is important that both bishops and the cleric have a clear understanding of the commitments involved. The proper diocesan bishop may release a cleric for a specified period of time, which can be renewed a number of times, so that he retains his original incardination and upon return enjoys all the benefits he would have had if he had continued to exercise his sacred ministry there. Such rights include seniority and pension benefits. The proper bishop may recall the cleric for just cause provided that written agreement and natural equity are observed. The host bishop may likewise deny for just cause permission for the cleric to dwell any longer in the diocese. Since there has been no change of incardination, the cleric remains legally subject to the original bishop.

Authority Competent To Permit Transfers

Canon 272 — A diocesan administrator cannot grant excardination, incardination or permission to move to another particular church unless the epis-copal see has been vacant for a year and unless he has the consent of the college of consultors.

Excardination, incardination, and permission to transfer to another particular church are the prerogatives of the diocesan bishop. When first drafted the canons of this title referred to the "ordinary" which, according to canon 134, §1, includes vicars general and episcopal vicars. The more restrictive term "diocesan bishop" was substituted because in such important matters it seemed appropriate to reserve the decision to him. This particular canon adds that the diocesan administrator has no authority to act in these matters unless the episcopal see has been vacant for a year—and even then he needs the consent of the board of consultors. By canon 427, §1 the administrator has the power of a diocesan bishop except in those matters that by their nature or by the law are excluded. Here the law does limit his authority to excardinate, incardinate, and permit a transfer. He is not forbidden, as in the 1917 Code (*CIC* 958, §1, 3°) to grant an initial incardination, but he does need the consent of the consultors (c. 1018, §1, 2°). The vacancy of the see is computed from the death of the bishop, not the election of the administrator. If the bishop died on June 15, the authority of the administrator to excardinate would not be effective until June 16 of the following year (c. 203, §1). The consent of the consultors is necessary for the validity of the act (c. 127, §1).

CHAPTER III
THE OBLIGATIONS AND RIGHTS OF CLERICS
[cc. 273–289]

This chapter treats the obligations and rights of clerics in seventeen canons.[20] They are not simple recommendations but binding juridic norms that have validity for the whole Church.[21] The 1917 Code under *De clericis in genere* had two separate titles, one dealing with the rights and privileges, the other with the obligations of the clergy. The revised Code has combined them into one chapter, "The Obligations and Rights of Clerics." The *praeno-*

---

[19] *Rel,* 63. The *Relatio* was subsequently published in *Comm* 14 (1982), 116–230; this citation is on p. 168.

[20] "Opera Consultorum," *Comm* 3 (1971), 192–196; 14 (1982), 71–84. One American archbishop sought to have the title reversed to read *De iuribus et obligationibus,* arguing that this was the traditional way of speaking as evidenced in the corresponding titles of the 1917 Code; furthermore, it is better grounded in the sacramental constitution of the Church itself. The Secretariat of the Commission responded that the proposal could be accepted but did not seem necessary; in fact, both rights and obligations flow from the sacraments. *Rel,* 62.

[21] Cardinal Willebrands thought that counsels and precepts regarding the life of clerics would be better placed outside the Code in special statutes. The Secretariat of the Commission replied that the Code would be very incomplete without such an important chapter and, furthermore, these canons are real juridic norms. *Rel,* 62.

tanda of *Schema de Populo Dei* explained why the titles were combined: in reality the obligations and rights of clerics are very often closely related and therefore more correctly considered within the same title.[22]

Since the four clerical privileges now eliminated had been part of church law for centuries, a brief explanation of their nature is appropriate. The four were known as the *privilegium canonis,* the *privilegium fori,* the *privilegium immunitatis,* and the *privilegium competentis.* Each was discussed in its own canon in the 1917 Code (*CIC* 119–122). The privilege of the canon (*CIC* 119) held that the faithful owe reverence to the clergy according to their various ranks and offices and that one who inflicts a real injury upon a clergyman commits a sacrilege. It is so called because it goes back to canon 15 of the Second Lateran Council (1139) which legislated:

> If anyone prompted by the devil [*si quis suadente diabolo*] shall lay violent hands on a cleric or monk, let him be anathematized so that no bishop may presume to absolve him, except in danger of death, until he be presented to the judgment of the Apostolic See and its mandate received.[23]

(This was the earliest papal reservation of a censure by statute.) While assaults on ecclesiastics had been punished from early times, the council at that moment was attempting a systematic regulation of clerical life. In the anti-clerical disturbances stirred up by Arnold of Brescia, who was condemned by the council, churchmen were particularly vulnerable in that they were forbidden to carry arms and needed protection. Personal violence such as assault or imprisonment was termed a "real" injury as distinct from a verbal attack. The injury of a cleric was considered a "sacrilege," the violation of something sacred. As early as the fourth or fifth century the cultic aspect of ministry predominated.[24] Because the clergy were intimately associated with the Eucharistic sacrifice, a process of sacralization set them apart as guardians of the sacred. Their person was vested with a religious aura so that to harm them was an insult to the divine.

The *coetus* charged with preparing this section of the 1983 Code considered it odious to speak of a right to reverence on the part of the clergy and suggested that if such a norm were retained at all that it be placed under the title defining the obligations of all the faithful.[25] The norm, however, was simply dropped. Although the 1983 Code omits any reference to "sacrilege" and withdraws the automatic excommunication for violence to a priest, deacon, or religious, it does state that anyone who uses physical force against them "out of contempt for the faith, the Church, or ecclesiastical power, or ministry is to be punished with a just penalty" (c. 1370, §3). The same canon imposes automatic penalties, i.e., excommunication for the assault of the Holy Father and interdict for the assault of a bishop (c. 1370, §1–§2).

Another ancient privilege was that of the forum or court. The former Code (*CIC* 120) ruled that in all contentious or criminal cases clerics were to be brought before an ecclesiastical judge unless some other legitimate provision had been made for a particular place. Bishops could not be summoned before a lay judge without permission of the Apostolic See; other clerics were not to be so summoned without the permission of the ordinary of the place where the trial was held. The ordinary was not to refuse permission without a just and grave cause, especially if the plaintiff were a lay man. The canon, it should be noted, forbade the cleric to be summoned as a defendant, not as a witness. The provision that clerics be brought before an ecclesiastical rather than a secular court goes back at least to the fifth century.[26] The dispute between King Henry II of England and Archbishop Thomas Becket in the twelfth century centered largely on this issue.[27] For the most part the special treatment of clerics has had little application in recent times, though some concordats did arrange for the imprisonment of convicted clerics in a monastery.[28] In 1968 the *privilegium fori* was abolished in Spain.[29] The Conference of Spanish Bishops declared in 1973 that, though they were prepared to renounce the privilege, every bishop and priest had the right to preach the full gospel, including social justice issues, without thereby being considered to engage in political matters. It is up to the bishops to decide whether or not a priest is preaching in conformity with the doctrine and mission of the Church; if so, he may not be tried in civil court.[30]

The privilege of immunity in the 1917 Code (*CIC* 121) claimed that clerics were exempt from military service and from those duties and public civil offices alien to the clerical state.[31] While the United

---

[22] *Schema de Populo Dei, Praenotanda,* p. 10.

[23] *COD,* 176.

[24] G. Every, "Sacralization and Secularization in East and West in the First Millennium after Christ," *Sacralization and Secularization,* R. Aubert, ed., *Concilium,* vol. 47 (New York: Paulist Press, 1969), 27–38.

[25] *Comm* 3 (1971), 192.

[26] *Theodosian Code* 16, 2, 41.

[27] C. Duggan, "The Becket Dispute and the Criminous Clerks," *Bulletin of the Institute of Historical Research* 35 (1962), 1–28.

[28] F. Claeys-Bouuaert, "Clerc," *DDC* 3 (1942), 867–868. In 1928 the SCConc declared the *latae sententiae* excommunication of *CIC* 2341 against those who signed the complaint bringing the Bp of Providence, Rhode Island, before the civil court in a school and language dispute (*CLD* 1, 855; *AAS* 29 [1928], 146).

[29] V.M. de Arbeloa, "Los obispos ante le ley de unificación de fueros," *REDC* 29 (1973), 431–455.

[30] J. Eguren, "El fuero eclesiástico, privilegio o derecho del estado clerical?" *REDC* 30 (1974), 131–141.

[31] J. Downs, *The Concept of Clerical Immunity,* CanLawStud 126 (Washington: Catholic University of America, 1941).

States has conferred such exemption, many European countries have not, thus prompting the Holy See to issue regulations for clerics who have been conscripted (*CLD* 1, 98–109). Among alien responsibilities are those connected with a jury member, a magistrate, a police officer, or a notary in a secular court. The incompatibility of the clerical state with certain public duties was recognized as early as 313 A.D. by the Emperor Constantine.[32]

By the privilege of competency, found in the former Code (*CIC* 122), it was maintained that clerics who were forced to satisfy their creditors should be allowed to retain what—in the prudent estimation of an ecclesiastical judge—was necessary for their decent support, with the obligation to repay the debt as soon as possible. This merciful provision goes back to a decretal of Pope Innocent III.[33] The bankruptcy laws afford all citizens similar protection today.

The 1917 Code added (*CIC* 123) that an individual cleric could not renounce these privileges on his own insofar as they belonged to the clergy as a class. The 1983 Code (c. 289) similarly insists that when the civil law provides exemption from military service and certain other civic duties that are incompatible with the clerical state, clerics must take advantage of them.

While the traditional but outmoded privileges no longer find a place in ecclesiastical law, the 1983 Code affirms certain rights belonging to clerics that were unknown in the old Code. These rights were enunciated in the documents of the Second Vatican Council, especially *Presbyterorum Ordinis*. The *coetus* of consultors proposed seven rights:

(1) the right of cooperating with their own bishop in the exercise of the ministry;

(2) the right to obtain some ecclesiastical ministry if they fulfill the conditions required by law;

(3) the right to have sufficient time to use spiritual resources and to perfect their intellectual formation;

(4) the right to form associations with others for promoting the spiritual life or for pursuing ends consonant with the clerical state;

(5) the right to an appropriate vacation as determined by particular law;

(6) the right to receive a fitting and decent remuneration to care for their needs and to make provision for their care in illness, infirmity, or old age;

(7) finally, the right of recourse to competent ecclesiastical authority to vindicate rights proper to the clerical state.

The *coetus* observed that after all the canons of the Code have been revised, it may well be that some rights need not be affirmed under this title as clerical rights, namely, those rights that belong to all the faithful and not to the clergy as such.[34]

The *Schema de Populo Dei* included the first six of these rights under the present title. The *praenotanda* explained that the rights enumerated were "rights which are proper to clerics themselves, especially by reason of the clerical state." They have besides all the rights that are acknowledged to belong to all the Christian faithful.

Certain important and indubitable rights are emphasized as belonging to clerics also; for example, the right of association belongs to clerics as well as to the other Christian faithful, but within certain limits as indicated.[35]

The last of the rights originally proposed, the right of recourse, was not mentioned except in the case of a cleric who was denied permission to transfer to another diocese. Canon 129 of the schema affirmed the right of clerics as co-workers with the bishop to obtain an ecclesiastical office after the conditions required by law were fulfilled. In terms of the previous canon "ecclesiastical office" did not necessarily mean one requiring the power of orders.

The 1983 Code, however, eliminates any reference regarding a right to an office. Nevertheless, every cleric when physically and mentally capable has the right to exercise his orders so long as useful, unless barred by law. Canon 1008 declares that by the sacrament of orders one is deputed to fulfill the *munera* of teaching, sanctifying, and ruling; canon 1025, §2 requires that no one be ordained unless his ministry be considered useful for the Church. Another right omitted from the final text, though in the *Schema de Populo Dei* (c. 138), concerned a right to the time necessary to foster the supernatural life and to carry on the studies necessary for the proper fulfillment of the ministry. In treating the obligation of bishops, on the other hand, the revised Code does direct them to see to it "that means and institutions which they [clerics] need are available to them to foster their spiritual and intellectual life" (c. 384). To the extent, therefore, that the bishop is obliged to provide the means, the priests have the right.

---

[32]*Theodosian Code* 16, 2, 1.
[33]C. 16, X, *De restitutione spoliatorum*, II, 13.

[34]*Comm* 3 (1971), 195–196.
[35]*Praenotanda*, p. 10. *Comm* 9 (1977), 245.

Clerical Reverence and Obedience

Canon 273 — Clerics are bound by a special obligation to show reverence and obedience to the Supreme Pontiff and to their own ordinary.

Unlike in the two previous drafts the 1983 Code gives first place in this chapter to the cleric's obligation of obedience. The canon speaks of a "special" obligation to distinguish the particular duty incumbent upon clerics over and above that of the Christian laity. This theme was emphasized in the Vatican II Decree on "The Ministry and Life of Priests."

Priests for their part should keep in mind the fullness of the sacrament of Order which bishops enjoy and should reverence in their persons the authority of Christ the supreme Pastor. . . . That priestly obedience, inspired through and through by the spirit of cooperation, is based on that sharing of the episcopal ministry which is conferred on priests by the sacrament of Order and the canonical mission (*PO* 7).

This relationship between cleric and bishop arising from the reception of the sacrament of orders requires a spirit of genuine respect and cooperation. Reverence is shown externally through customary signs of respect and deference in recognition of a person's dignity or authority. Such signs would be rising in his presence and according him precedence.[36] The practice of kissing a bishop's ring while dropping to one knee has practically died out, except when meeting the Holy Father. Even in titles of address a simple style has emerged in the United States. The more formal "Your Excellency" or "Your Eminence" is gradually being replaced by "Bishop," "Archbishop," or "Cardinal." Clerics should show singular reverence and obedience to the Holy Father who not only has full and supreme power in the Church but enjoys "the proper, ordinary and immediate power which bishops possess in the particular churches entrusted to their care" (c. 333, §1).

The reverence expected of the clergy hardly differs from that of the well-educated laity. The special character of clerical reverence is to be found rather in the type of obedience rendered. The obedience that a diocesan priest owes his ordinary is called canonical obedience—to distinguish it from the religious obedience owed a religious superior. The obligation of the latter arises from a vow or some other commitment made upon joining a community. Canonical obedience is restricted to those matters that are prescribed by canon law. It is determined by the clerical status and office, on the one hand, and by the extent of episcopal jurisdiction, on the other. The bishop is empowered to enforce the universal law that regulates the clerical state, and the clergy are bound to obey in whatever pertains to their state as such.[37] Religious obedience is more extensive in that it embraces all phases of the subject's life.

The authority of the bishop to enforce the common law regarding clerical discipline (cc. 274–289) includes the right to interpret the law in accordance with local circumstances. His commands must be in conformity with the spirit of the law. He cannot command anything prohibited by it. A deacon, for example, who is unwilling to be promoted to the priesthood cannot be forced to do so, nor, absent grave cause, can he be forbidden to exercise his diaconal orders (c. 1038). Conversely, the bishop cannot prohibit what the Code clearly permits;[38] he cannot, for example, command his priests not to accept Mass offerings (c. 945, §1).

Areas that are not directly connected with the government of the diocese are not inherently within the ambit of episcopal jurisdiction. In civil matters the cleric enjoys all the liberties of every other citizen. (C. 285, §3, however, limits the right to hold public office.) He may join any party, unless it is condemned by the Church; he may vote for any candidate he deems fit. On a debatable issue, such as a specific constitutional amendment, he may sign petitions and take a position that is at variance with that of the bishop.

Private matters, too, are not subject to episcopal direction. Provided that the priest is not incurring debts, the bishop may not interfere in his personal finances or the disposition of his inheritance, let alone dictate his last will and testament. A bishop is exceeding his power when he legislates that assistant pastors are not to own automobiles.[39] Similarly, a bishop has no right to force a cleric before ordination to take a pledge to abstain from alcoholic beverages for a certain period of time, as was commonly done before the Council.

With regard to the personal appearance of clerics, the authority of the bishop is limited to enforcing clerical dress as provided for in canon 284. The 1917 Code required that clerics have a simple hair style (*CIC* 136, §1). The Second Plenary Council of Baltimore in 1886 had legislated in greater detail,

---

[36]For a study on reverence as understood in the 1917 Code see J. Sheehan, *The Obligation of Respect and Obedience of Clerics toward Their Ordinary (Canon 127)*, CanLawStud 344 (Washington: Catholic University of America, 1954).

[37]Even under the 1917 Code the area of canonical obedience was limited. See C. Augustine, *A Commentary on the New Code of Canon Law* (St. Louis: B. Herder, 1919), II, 72.

[38]F. Wernz and P. Vidal, *Ius Canonicum* (Roma: Pontificae Universitatis Gregorianae, 1928) II, no. 599, I. For current thinking, see J. Huels, "Stipends in the New Code of Canon Law," *W* 57 (1983), 215–224.

[39]Sheehan, *The Obligation of Respect*, 113.

forbidding clerics to grow beards.[40] Since this particular legislation was not opposed to the 1917 Code, it remained in effect and could be enforced by the bishop according to a decision of the Sacred Congregation of the Council.[41] The 1983 Code says nothing about hair or beards. In view of widespread acceptance of longer hair and beards, as well as civil court decisions about individual rights in this matter, one may safely say that contemporary custom has prevailed over any restriction. The former prohibition against clerics wearing rings (*CIC* 136, §2) no longer applies. Only in extreme cases in which there is danger of genuine scandal or in which serious consternation can be anticipated may the bishop impose canonical obedience on a cleric to modify his appearance.

Certain Offices Restricted to Clerics/ Duty To Fulfill an Assigned Office

Canon 274 — §1. Only clerics can obtain those offices for whose exercise there is required the power of orders or the power of ecclesiastical governance.

§2. Unless they are excused by a legitimate impediment, clerics are bound to undertake and faithfully fulfill a duty which has been entrusted to them by their ordinary.

The first paragraph, treating the rights of clerics, is a basic statement that offices requiring the exercise of the power of orders or the power of government may be held only by clerics. Canon 129 has already determined that those endowed with sacred orders are capable of the power of governing (jurisdiction); it adds that in the exercise of this power the Christian laity can cooperate "cooperari" according to the norm of law.[42]

The 1983 Code, therefore, goes beyond the 1917 Code in recognizing explicitly that the laity may exercise jurisdiction. The 1917 Code stated that "only clerics can obtain the power either of orders or of ecclesiastical jurisdiction as well as ecclesiastical benefices and pension" (*CIC* 118). The power of or-

ders of its nature directly promotes the sanctification of the faithful through public worship, especially the Mass, and through the administration of the sacraments. Although the 1917 Code did not define "jurisdiction," it equated jurisdiction with the power of ruling: "the power of jurisdiction or of government in the Church, which is of divine institution, extends to both the external forum and the internal forum of conscience" (*CIC* 196). The teaching authority of the Church expressed in official documents was also considered to fall under jurisdiction.[43] As a public power jurisdiction is differentiated from the authority exercised by certain religious superiors or by the father of a family; the latter authority is called dominative. The power of orders according to the 1917 Code comes through the sacrament of ordination, the power of jurisdiction (except for that of the pope) through canonical mission (*CIC* 109). Canonical mission, or the authorization to exercise functions in the name of the Church, is received when an office is conferred to which jurisdiction is annexed (e.g., a bishopric or a pastorate) or when a responsibility is delegated (e.g., to hear confessions).

Commentators, arguing largely on historical precedent, held that the incapacity of the laity to receive jurisdiction was a matter of ecclesiastical law from which the Holy Father could dispense. By way of privilege, then, the pope could permit lay men and even lay women to exercise jurisdiction.[44] The Abbess of the Real Monasterio de las Huelgas near Burgos, Spain, was said to have been given quasi-episcopal jurisdiction so that she could authorize priests to preach and hear confession.[45]

The formulation of canons 129 and 274 of the 1983 Code occasioned considerable debate in the final stages of the revision process.[46] The *Schema de Populo Dei* (c. 128) and the 1980 draft, in seeking to identify governmental power restricted to clerics, referred to the power of ecclesiastical government "founded on sacred ordination" (*ordine sacro innixa*). This phrase was deleted at a plenary congregation of the Commission in October 1981. In preparation for that meeting the Secretariat designated the participation of the laity in the exercise of governmental power as the first special question to be discussed. A dossier sent to all the participants included the following:

(1) observations by several cardinals, most notably Cardinal Ratzinger;

[40]No. 151: "Comam et barbam studiose, aut laicorum more, ne nutriant. Comam alere saepius a Synodis vetitum est. Barbam Clericorum promissam nuper damnavit Pontifex Pius PP. IX. Ecclesiasticis omnibus hac in re morem Romanae Ecclesiae, tanquam normam sequendam, mandamus." *Concilii Plenarii Baltimorensis II . . . Decreta* (Baltimore: John Murphy, 1868), 95.

[41]SCConc, Jan 19, 1920 *(AAS* 12 [1920], 43). J. Barrett, *A Comparative Study of the Councils of Baltimore and the Code of Canon Law,* CanLawStud 83 (Washington: Catholic University of America, 1932), 50–51. By the 1970s, however, the law had fallen into desuetude, *CLSAP* 31 (1969), 132–142.

[42]For recent bibliographies, see: J. Cuneo, "The Power of Jurisdiction: Empowerment for Church Functioning and Mission Distinct from the Power of Orders," *J* 39 (1979), 183–219; J. Huels, "Another Look at Lay Jurisdiction," *J* 41 (1981), 59–80.

[43]F. Claeys-Bouuaert, "Magistère Ecclésiastique," *DDC* 6 (1957), 695–696 presents the arguments for and against considering the teaching power as a power distinct from that of jurisdiction.

[44]M. a Coronata, *Institutiones Iuris Canonici,* 4 ed. (Taurin: Marietti, 1949) I, 181.

[45]*AkK* 88 (1908), 566–567.

[46]*Rel,* 37–41 listed some of the animadversions.

(2) a *votum* of Alfonsus Stickler, Prefect of the Vatican Library; and

(3) a *votum* of Ioannes Beyer, Dean of the Faculty of Canon Law at the Gregorian University.[47]

Cardinal Ratzinger objected: (a) to the distinction in governmental power between that founded on sacred order and that not so founded; (b) to the participation of the laity in the exercise of ruling power not based on order. To say that there was a power not based on sacred order would be inconsistent with *Lumen Gentium* (*LG* 21, 2) which maintained the essential unity of ecclesiastical authority (*sacra potestas*) founded exclusively on the sacrament of order. He thought it a contradiction to hold, furthermore, that an unordained person is incapable of holding a power but that he may participate in the exercise of the power.

The Secretariat and all but two of the consultors on the *coetus* responded that it could safely be affirmed that Vatican II did not abrogate the traditional distinction between the power of order and the power of jurisdiction that was accepted unchallenged for so many centuries; it did not teach, therefore, the origin of all ruling power to be the sacrament of orders. In fact, the Council implied the participation of the laity in such power (*LG* 32, 33, 37; *AA* 24); and the *motu proprio Causas matrimoniales*, furthermore, explicitly gave such power to a lay judge (*CM* V–VII).[48]

According to some theologians the Council was not wholly successful in defining the precise relationship between the powers of order and jurisdiction.[49] In *Lumen Gentium* it taught that through ordination the *munera* of teaching and governing were conferred along with that of sanctifying (*LG* 21, 28). The source of governing authority, then, is ordination and not canonical mission. Canonical mission merely determines the sphere in which jurisdiction may be exercised (*LG* 24). The Council also taught that the ministries of the ordained and of the laity "differ from one another in essence and not only in degree" (*LG* 10); some functions are reserved exclusively to the ordained. The laity through their baptism and confirmation receive "the capacity to assume from the hierarchy certain ecclesiastical *munera* that are to be performed for a spiritual purpose" (*LG* 33).

Since the Council's position is somewhat of a compromise and, therefore, ambiguous, there is no commonly accepted explanation for lay ministry. The Sacred Congregation for the Doctrine of the Faith in its "Declaration on the Question of the Ordination of Women to the Ministerial Priesthood"[50] insisted that "it is the Holy Spirit given in ordination who grants participation in the ruling power of the supreme pastor Christ" (no. 6), but in the same passage acknowledged "the pastoral charge in the Church is normally linked to the sacrament of order." In the official commentary on the document the Congregation noted that the participation of some medieval abbesses in ecclesiastical jurisdiction was an abuse. While canonists in the past had admitted the possibility of separating jurisdiction from order, the Council, the document continued, "has tried to determine better the relationship between the two; the council's doctrinal vision will doubtless have effects on Discipline."[51] One wonders how this position of the Congregation can be reconciled with the fact that the papal *motu proprio Causas matrimoniales* in 1971 permitted a lay man to serve on a panel of three judges in marriage cases. The Pontifical Commission for the Revision of the Code of Canon Law recognized that such lay judges did exercise "jurisdictional power of governing."[52] The Commission argued that classical canonists had held that the pope using his plenary authority could bestow such power and that the lay man's capacity to receive it was affirmed by *Lumen Gentium* 33.

At the final plenary congregation of the Commission the exercise of jurisdiction by lay persons, including a lay associate judge, was recognized in canon 1421, §2 of the 1983 Code; fifty-two out of sixty-three members present voted affirmatively. The definitive formulation of canon 129, however, is deliberately ambiguous, a compromise: "Lay members of the Christian faithful can cooperate in the exercise of this power [of governance] in accord with the norm of law." It may be interpreted either that the laity do not have jurisdiction, that all jurisdiction comes only with the sacrament of orders, or that they can indeed be given jurisdiction by the supreme legislator.

The 1917 Code spoke of the powers of orders and jurisdiction being reserved to clerics (*CIC* 118); canon 274 of the 1983 Code refers to offices that require the exercise of the power of orders or the power of government.[53] An ecclesiastical office is defined in canon 145, §1 as any *munus* stably estab-

---

[47]A. Stickler, "De potestatis sacrae natura et origine," *P* 71 (1982), 65–91; J. Beyer, "De natura potestatis regiminis seu iurisdictionis recte in Codice renovata enuntianda," *P* 71 (1982), 93–145.

[48]March 28, 1971, *AAS* 63 (1971), 441–46; *CLD* 7, 969–974, esp. 971–972.

[49]E. Kilmartin, "Lay Participation in the Apostolate of the Hierarchy," *J* 41 (1981), 343–370.

[50]Oct. 15, 1976, *AAS* 69 (1977), 98–116; *Origins* 6 (1977), 517–524.

[51]*Origins* 6 (1977), 529.

[52]*Comm* 3 (1971), 187.

[53]From a theological perspective the notion of "office" is not a very clear one. David Power has explored "a flexible notion of office which is consonant with tradition and at the same time pertinent to contemporary experience and development," "The Basics for Official Ministry in the Church," *J* 41 (1981), 314–342.

lished by divine or ecclesiastical institution to be exercised for a spiritual purpose (*PO* 20). Among the offices requiring the use of order and governing authority are those of bishop, pastor, and parochial vicar (assistant). The law explicitly demands that the pastor (c. 521, §1) and the parochial vicar (c. 546) must be in presbyteral orders. A deacon, therefore, would not qualify for either appointment. Before the 1917 Code, however, a deacon could be named pastor (*CLD* 1, 246). Presbyteral ordination is also necessary for the office of vicar forane or dean (c. 553, §1) and diocesan administrator (c. 425, §1). To be a member of the presbyteral council (c. 495, §1) or the board of consultors (c. 502, §1) one must also be in priestly orders. Within the diocesan curia the following offices must be filled by priests: moderator of the curia (c. 473, §2), vicar general and episcopal vicar (c. 478, §1), judicial vicar and assistant judicial vicar (c. 1420, §4).

Offices and Functions Open to the Laity

According to the common law diocesan judges are to be clerics (c. 1421, §1); thus deacons are eligible. The episcopal conference, however, is empowered to permit the laity to be named judges (c. 1421, §2). (C. 129 provides that in the exercise of governmental power the laity can cooperate according to the norm of law.) In case of necessity, then, one of these lay judges may be chosen to form a collegiate tribunal. Pope Paul VI in *Causas matrimoniales* first allowed a panel to be composed of two clerics and one lay man (V, I); the Secretariat of the Code Commission affirmed that the lay judge did exercise jurisdiction in his own right. At the final Plenarium Congregation of the Commission an effort was made to eliminate the lay judge on the grounds that he could not in fact exercise jurisdiction. The Plenarium not only retained the lay judge, but by a vote of thirty-six out of forty-eight it deleted the qualification *viri* from *viri laici iudices* of canon 1421, §2, thus enabling women to be associate judges.

The laity are also eligible to be defenders of the bond and promoters of justice (c. 1435), as well as advocates (c. 1483). They may be assessors (c. 1424) and auditors (c. 1428, §2). They may hold the offices of chancellor, vice chancellor, and notary. The chancellor as defined by the law is an archivist. The chancellor in American dioceses has heretofore functioned more as a vicar general and should now be appointed to that office.

In financial matters the expertise of the laity is clearly recognized. They may serve on the finance council that must be established in every diocese (c. 492, §1). A lay person may also be named business manager, a position that every diocesan bishop must fill (c. 494, §1). The laity similarly serve on the financial council required to be set up in every

parish (c. 537). They are to be members of the diocesan pastoral council (c. 512, §1) and the parish council (c. 536, §1) where these groups are established.

In situations in which there is a scarcity of priests, a bishop may entrust a participation in the exercise of pastoral care to a lay person or group of persons (c. 517, §2). The *Annuarium Statisticum Ecclesiae* reported that on December 31, 1980, 80 parishes were entrusted to male religious who were not priests; 552 to sisters (56 in North America); and 472 to lay people. Not counting parishes without permanent priests but served from elsewhere, there were 1,617 parishes—almost all of them in Europe—with no one in charge.[54] The laity are authorized to exercise the ministry of the word, to preside over liturgical prayer, to baptize, and to distribute Holy Communion (c. 230, §3). Lay women are not disadvantaged here as they are in receiving the ministries of lector and acolyte (c. 230, §1). The laity may prepare couples for marriage and formally assist at weddings (c. 1112, §1). They are also allowed to bring Viaticum to the sick and conduct funeral services (*Rite for the Anointing and Care of the Sick*, Praenotanda no. 29 and *Rite for Funerals*, Praenotanda no. 19).

Even in parishes where there is a priest, the laity can be admitted to preach in church if, in certain circumstances, it is necessary or useful (c. 766). In Masses for children, for example, with the consent of the pastor one of the adults may speak after the gospel, especially if the celebrant finds it difficult to adapt to the mentality of children (*Directory for Masses with Children* no. 24). In other liturgies the homily is reserved to the priest and deacon (c. 767, §1).

Clerical Obedience

According to paragraph two of canon 274, clerics must accept and faithfully carry out an assignment given them by their own ordinary. This obligation flows from the fact of incardination and the commitment to serve the diocese;[55] sacred orders are conferred that they may be used. The obligation of canonical obedience may be imposed only by the bishop or the diocesan administrator, since it is the bishop to whom obedience is promised at ordination. The bishop should carefully review decisions of a personnel board. The assignment or office (*munus*) is to be understood broadly, not necessarily limited to the care of souls. It includes such positions as pastor, assistant pastor, chaplain in a hospital, seminary teacher, or director of a religious

[54]*Annuarium Statisticum Ecclesiae* 1980 (Vatican: Libreria Vaticana, 1982), 59, 53.
[55]T. Bouscaren and A. Ellis, *Canon Law: A Text and Commentary* (Milwaukee: Bruce Publishing Co., 1948), 107.

institution. The 1917 law (*CIC* 128) stated that the cleric was bound to accept the assignment as long as the necessity of the Church required it. The Code Commission Secretariat affirmed that the present canon is to be interpreted in terms of the 1917 canon.[56] Utility or the good of the Church is not a sufficient reason to impose the obligation, but there must be a true necessity that cannot be provided for in any other way.[57] The judgment concerning the existence and duration of the necessity belongs to the ordinary. He could, for example, delay for a time the entrance of a cleric into a religious community.[58]

A cleric with a legitimate impediment cannot be forced to accept an assignment. Poor health, whether physical or psychological, as well as a bodily defect or advanced age would be obvious obstacles. The greater the need to be met, the greater should be the excusing cause. Again it is up to the ordinary to judge the validity of the reason. A cleric who thinks that he has been aggrieved may have recourse to the Sacred Congregation for the Clergy,[59] but meanwhile he should accede to the bishop's command. The 1917 law (*CIC* 2399) prescribed that clerics abandoning a charge committed to them by their own ordinary were to be suspended *a divinis*. The 1983 Code (c. 1371, 2°) prescribes that one who does not comply with the legitimate precepts of the ordinary but persists in disobedience after a warning should be punished with a just penalty.

In making assignments, indeed, in exercising authority over his clerics, the bishop is to be guided by the principles of the Second Vatican Council. An intimate relationship is established between them:

> This priestly obedience animated with a spirit of cooperation is based on the very sharing in the episcopal ministry which is conferred on priests

both through the sacrament of orders and the canonical mission (*PO* 7).

The bishop, in turn, is "to regard his priests, who are his co-workers, as sons and friends, just as Christ called his disciples no longer servants but friends" (*LG* 28). Since priests have a joint responsibility to advance the cause of the Church, obedience to Christ demands that they

> confidently propose their plans and urgently expose the needs of the flock committed to them, while remaining ready to submit to the judgment of those who exercise the chief responsibility for governing the Church of God (*PO* 15).

The bishop for his part has a "sacred duty" to know his priests individually and intimately—"their character and talents, their likes and dislikes, their spiritual life, zeal and plans, their health and economic situation, their family and whatever concerns them" (*Directory* III). "In sincere, friendly dialogue, he converses with them about their work, the offices entrusted to them and also about matters pertaining to the life of the whole diocese" (ibid). With a real appreciation of the principles of co-responsibility the bishop must enter into a serious consultation before making an assignment that will have a significant impact on the life of a priest.

Clerical Cooperation

Canon 275 — §1. Since they all work toward one end, the building up of the Body of Christ, clerics are to be united among themselves by the bond of brotherhood and of prayer; they are to strive for cooperation among themselves in accord with the prescriptions of particular law.

§2. Clerics are to acknowledge and promote that mission which lay persons exercise in their own way in the Church and in the world.

This canon, not found in the 1917 Code, urges cooperation among clerics. It is taken from *Presbyterorum Ordinis* which stresses the intimate sacramental bond uniting them; though the conciliar document does not speak of deacons, they, too, share in the same sacrament (*PO* 8). No matter how diverse the apostolates in which they labor, all clerics contribute toward the building up of the Body of Christ. The older should welcome the younger, assisting them to fit into the ministry, and both groups should try to bridge the generation gap through mutual understanding. "They should be particularly concerned about those who are sick, about the afflicted, the overworked, the lonely, in short those experiencing difficulties." The decree notes that it may be necessary to overstep the bounds of a parish or diocese: "no priest is suffi-

---

[56] *Rel*, 63.

[57] F. Cappello, *Summa Iuris Canonici* (Roma: Pontificae Universitatis Gregorianae), I, no. 219. Bouscaren-Ellis, however, distinguished between ordinary and extaordinary employments. The bishop could impose ordinary duties, according to the custom obtaining in the locality, for the good of the Church, even apart from necessity (p. 108).

[58] *CIC* 542, 2° declared unlawful the admission of a cleric in sacred orders to a novitiate against the will of his ordinary if the objection were based on serious harm to souls that would result from his withdrawal that could not be avoided by any other means. The 1983 Code (c. 644) provides only that superiors should not admit secular clerics to the novitiate if the local ordinary has not been consulted.

[59] Since the proposed administrative tribunals were not provided for in the 1983 Code, the only other remedy would be mediation or arbitration (c. 1733). According to the 1917 Code the Sacred Congregation had exclusive right to deal with recourse against the decrees of an ordinary (*CIC* 1601). J. McClunn, *Administrative Recourse: A Commentary with Historical Notes, CanLawStud* 240 (Washington: Catholic University of America, 1946).

ciently equipped to carry out his own mission alone and as it were single-handed" (*PO* 7). Parish priests "should collaborate with other parish priests and with those priests who are exercising a pastoral function in the district such as vicars forane (deans) or who are engaged in works of an extra-parochial nature" (*CD* 30, 1). The precise nature of the cooperation may be worked out in particular law.

Again echoing the Council, the law calls upon the clergy to sincerely appreciate and promote the place of the laity in the mission of the Church (*PO* 9). The *Schema de Populo Dei* in referring to the respect that was to be shown the laity by clerics added "especially priests." This somewhat disparaging emphasis was dropped from the final version. Whereas the earlier schema was satisfied with clerics "recognizing" the role of the laity, the 1983 Code adds the responsibility of positively "promoting" it. The right that the laity have to participate in the Church's mission is paralleled by the obligation of clerics to see that this right is accorded them (c. 225, §1).

In December 1981 the Pontifical Council on the Laity issued a study document explaining the identity and mission of priests within associations of the laity. It sees the priest as the "architect of unity" both within the association and with the Church at large. He is to guarantee that its goals are essentially religious and not political or social or economic.[60]

Holiness of Life

Canon 276 — §1. In leading their lives clerics are especially bound to pursue holiness because they are consecrated to God by a new title in the reception of orders as dispensers of God's mysteries in the service of His people.

§2. In order for them to pursue this perfection:

1° first of all they are faithfully and untiringly to fulfill the duties of pastoral ministry;

2° they are to nourish their spiritual life from the two-fold table of Sacred Scripture and the Eucharist; priests are therefore earnestly invited to offer the sacrifice of the Eucharist daily and deacons are earnestly invited to participate daily in offering it;

3° priests as well as deacons aspiring to the priesthood are obliged to fulfill the liturgy of the hours daily in accordance with the proper and approved liturgical books; permanent deacons, however, are to do the same to the extent it is determined by the conference of bishops;

4° they are also bound to make a retreat according to the prescriptions of particular law;

5° they are to be conscientious in devoting time regularly to mental prayer, in approaching the sacrament of penance frequently, in cultivating special devotion to the Virgin Mother of God, and in using other common and particular means for their sanctification.

The formulation of the basic obligation incumbent upon clerics is taken from the conciliar decree *Presbyterorum Ordinis*. All Christians through their baptismal consecration are "enabled and obliged even in the midst of human weakness to seek perfection." Clerics, consecrated in a new way by the sacrament of orders to be the living instruments of Christ, are bound by a special claim to acquire this perfection (*PO* 12, *LG* 39). The 1917 Code expressed this duty in comparative terms: clerics ought to lead a holier life than the laity, both interiorly and exteriorly, and to excel them by example in virtue and good deeds. The Council, however, insisted that "all Christians in any state or walk of life are called to the fullness of Christian life and to the perfections of love" (*LG* 40). Though the forms and duties of life are many, "holiness is one" (*LG* 41).

Closely following *Presbyterorum Ordinis* 13, the canon indicates the means clerics are to use in striving for perfection.

(1) They do so above all in fulfilling their ministry, the faithful service of the people.

(2) As preachers of the word they must first make it part of their lives by prayerful meditation upon the Scriptures. As dispensers of the mysteries of God it behooves them to seek nourishment at the Eucharistic table.[61] Priests are earnestly recommended to celebrate Mass daily. "Even if the faithful cannot be present, it is the act of Christ and the Church in which priests fulfill their principal function" (c. 904). Deacons are also encouraged to participate in Mass every day.

Sacrosanctum Concilium taught that "communal celebration involving the presence and active participation of the faithful" is to be "preferred," as far as possible, to a celebration that is individual and quasi-private. This rule applies with special force to the celebration of Mass and the administration of the sacraments, even though every Mass has of itself a public and social nature (*SC* 27). Whereas the 1980 draft "commended" concelebration (c. 855), the 1983 Code states merely that priests "may" concelebrate unless the good of the faithful urges otherwise (c. 902).

The Council, too, emphasized that the Mass "is an act of Christ and the Church even if it is impossible for the faithful to be present" (*PO* 13). As Pope Paul VI expressed it, "The Mass, even though

---

60"Identity and Mission of Priests within Associations of the Laity," *Origins* 11 (Feb. 4, 1982), 533–547.

61The expression *ex duplici mensa Sacrae Scripturae et Eucharistiae Verbo Dei nutriuntur* appears several times in Vatican II documents, especially in *PO* 18.

it is celebrated privately, is still not private."[62] He maintained that the communal Mass should not be so emphasized that Mass celebrated privately is thereby discouraged. He said nothing about the preference to be accorded concelebration or whether a priest ought always to celebrate rather than participate in the Eucharist by receiving Communion.

To have said that would have meant a rejection of the ecclesiastical legislation that does not oblige a priest to celebrate Mass daily. What he said was that those who concelebrate or those who participate must not do this from a conviction that Masses celebrated privately are always undesirable.[63]

The *coetus* of the Code Commission noted that this canon juridically or canonically *obligated* priests only to the recitation of the Divine Office and the spiritual retreat.[64] They are *encouraged* to offer Mass daily, even if the faithful are not present. Previously priests had been forbidden to celebrate without a server or without at least someone being present to respond (*CIC* 813). The canonist Coronata noted that the obligation to have a server was a grave one;[65] an instruction of the Sacred Congregation of the Sacraments on October 1, 1949 insisted there were only four exceptional cases that would justify a priest's celebrating Mass without a server. The instruction also called attention to the fact that "all the authors teach unanimously that it is forbidden under pain of mortal sin for women, even nuns, to serve at the altar."[66] The 1983 law, however, requires merely a just and reasonable cause for a priest to celebrate without the participation of at least one member of the faithful (c. 906). A reasonable cause would be the devotion of the priest.

(3) Priests and deacons aspiring to the priesthood are obliged to pray the Divine Office[67] according to proper and approved liturgical books.

By their fulfillment of the Divine Office priests themselves should extend to the different hours of the day the praise and thanksgiving they offer in celebration of the Eucharist. By the Office, they pray to God in the name of the Church for the whole people entrusted to them and in fact for the whole world (*PO* 5).

Sacrosanctum Concilium devoted chapter IV to the Divine Office. One of its main objectives was to restore the traditional sequence of the hours so that the day would be sanctified. "Lauds as morning prayer and Vespers as evening prayer are the two hinges on which the daily office turns. They must be considered as the chief hours and are to be celebrated as such" (*SC* 89). Matins, now called the Office of Readings, is to retain the character of nocturnal prayer when recited in choir but in other circumstances may be carried out at any time. The Middle Hours (Terce, or Midmorning; Sext, or Midday; and None, or Midafternoon) are to be observed in their entirety in choir, but elsewhere one may be chosen suitable to a particular time of day. Compline is to mark the close of day.

The Latin text *Liturgia horarum* was promulgated April 11, 1971;[68] the official English translation was available in 1975. As of November 27, 1977, *The Liturgy of the Hours* became the single official version in English approved by the conference of bishops and confirmed by the Holy See. That translation, as it appears in several authorized editions, or the *Liturgia horarum*, must be used for the liturgical observance whether in common or by individuals.[69] When non-English texts are used in this country for the celebration of the liturgy (the Eucharist, the sacraments, and the Divine Office) they must have the approval of the episcopal conference of the country where published and have been confirmed by the Holy See.[70] One could use, for example, texts in the French, Spanish, Italian, German, or Slovenian languages.

The obligation of clerics to pray the Divine Office daily is canonically or juridically imposed.[71] This duty incumbent upon all clergy in major orders derives from "ancient tradition and immemorial custom"[72] and first became a universal written law with the 1917 Code. The authors interpreted the obligation so strictly that the omission of even one hour was considered a grave sin.[73] A priest would have to be busy with pastoral work practically all day (ten hours) to be excused from the Office.[74] Only the Holy See could dispense from the obligation, but some commentators thought that

---

[62]*Mysterium Fidei, AAS* 67 (1965), 761–762.

[63]K. Seasoltz, *New Liturgy, New Laws* (Collegeville, Minn.: The Liturgical Press, 1980), 102.

[64]*Comm* 3 (1971), 192–193.

[65]Coronata, no. 740.

[66]A priest was permitted to say Mass without a server: (1) for the administration of Holy Viaticum; (2) for the people to hear Mass of obligation; (3) in time of pestilence when the priest would otherwise be obliged to abstain from celebrating for a notable time; (4) if a server who began to serve Mass later departed, *CLD* 3, 335.

[67]"Divine" is used in the sense of "praise of God"; "office" (*officium*) means a "charge, an occupation," a public ritual activity of the community. *Schema de Populo Dei* used the term *horae canonicae* (c. 134, §2, 3°).

[68]*AAS* 63 (1971), 527–535, 712.

[69]*BCLN* 13 (1977), 89.

[70]This is the general principle adopted by the NCCB, *BCLN* 14 (1978), 99.

[71]*Comm* 3 (1971), 193.

[72]Benedict XIV, *Eo quamvis*, May 4, 1745 *CICFontes* I, 900, no. 43. See M. Semple, *The Obligation of the Divine Office in the Latin and Oriental Churches, CanLawStud* 454 (Washington: Catholic University of America, 1967).

[73]Coronata, no. 194, b.

[74]F. Connell, *AER* 148 (1963), 129.

the ordinary could do so for a time in particular cases.[75]

The extravagant claims of the moralists about the gravity of the obligation and the fact that it was said in Latin, little understood by most priests, led to the impression that it was an extrinsic obligation.[76] Since the Council, however, the real meaning of the Office has been found in the category of prayer offered in the name of the Christian community. Far more than a rule of canon law, a specific duty of clerics, it sets up a pattern of prayer in their lives. The fact that a practice has intrinsic meaning and value in itself does not obviate the need for making it a matter of general discipline as well but provides a clear rationale for doing so.

Against this background it is evident that the way in which the scale and relative weighting of the obligation are expressed in the Instruction [on *The Liturgy of the Hours*] ... is far more effective and more reasonable than any effort to assess grave and light matter on a slide rule system.[77]

The Instruction (printed at the beginning of vol. I of *The Liturgy of the Hours*) speaks of the mandate "to recite the whole sequence of Hours each day, preserving as far as possible the genuine relationship of the Hours to the time of day." The "General Instruction" of *The Liturgy of the Hours* introduces distinctions and suggests priorities among the different hours (no. 29). Lauds, or morning prayer, and Vespers, as the two hinges on which this Liturgy turns, are not to be omitted "unless for a serious reason"; certainly their omission is to be exceptional. Clerics are to "carry out faithfully the Office of Readings, which is above all the liturgical celebration of the word of God" in order to become more perfect disciples by welcoming that word into themselves. A lesser reason would justify the omission of this hour. "That the day may be completely sanctified they will desire to recite the middle Hour and Compline, thus commending themselves to God and completing the entire *Opus Dei* before going to bed." The Instruction leaves to the discretion of the ordained minister the judgment of the justifying reasons. "There is of course a danger of self-deception in this kind of decision, but there are certainly reasons or causes which, considered objectively, do excuse from the Office as from other precepts of Church Law."[78]

As for permanent deacons, they are obliged to fulfill the Divine Office as defined by the episcopal conference. The *Guidelines* of the United States Bishops' Committee on the Permanent Diaconate note: "The deacon can very appropriately pray the liturgical hours of Lauds and Vespers as expressing the praise of God from the entire church community."[79] The Bishops' Committee on the Liturgy added: "In view of the particular style of life and circumstances of most permanent deacons, it is appropriate that this be done with their families."[80]

(4) Clerics are obliged to make a retreat in accordance with the prescriptions of particular law.

Like that of the Divine Office the requirement of a retreat is juridically imposed rather than merely commended.[81] The 1917 law (*CIC* 126) stated that secular priests were to make a retreat "at least every three years"[82] at a time and in a pious or religious house designated by their proper ordinary. No one was to be excused except in an individual case and for a just cause by express permission of the ordinary. In the United States, the Third Plenary Council of Baltimore in 1884 decreed that bishops must have retreats for their clergy every year or at least every two years (no. 75). Since the Baltimore legislation was *praeter codicem*, it remained in force after the promulgation of the 1917 Code. It was up to the diocesan bishop, then, to specify the frequency (every year or every two years), the duration, the place, and the method to be followed.[83]

Since the 1983 Code provides that the retreat is to be made in accordance with particular law, the Baltimore norm of a retreat every year or at least every other year would continue in effect. In virtue of his legislative power (c. 391, §2) the diocesan bishop can establish particular law regarding retreats for the clergy. The terminology of the canon, *recessus spirituales,* includes monthly days of recollection as well as formal retreats.[84] In view of the diversity of spiritual needs, it is desirable that some options be made available. Even the former law did not require that the retreat be in common.[85]

(5) Among other individual or common practices of piety, certain ones are recommended to the clergy for attaining holiness of life: mental

[75]Coronata, no. 194, c.

[76]B. Häring, "A Closer Look at the Breviary Obligation," *W* 37 (1962–63), 274–285.

[77]D. O'Callaghan, "The Breviary Obligation," *The Furrow* 29 (1978), 697.

[78]*BCLN* 13 (1977), 88. The law has not been changed regarding the time the hours are to be said. The obligation is from midnight to midnight (E. Regatillo, "Observaciones al estudio sobre el mandato de la Iglesia orante," *Sal Terrae* 60 [1972], 60–62).

[79]*Permanent Deacons in the United States: Guidelines on Their Formation and Ministry,* Bishops' Committee on the Permanent Diaconate (Washington: NCCB Publications Office, 1971), no. 163.

[80]*BCLN* 18 (1977), 88.

[81]*Comm* 3 (1971), 193.

[82]*CIC* 595 obliged religious to make an annual retreat; *CIC* 1367, 4° similarly bound seminarians.

[83]J. Barrett, *A Comparative Study,* 40–41.

[84]*Rel,* 64.

[85]Coronata, no. 188.

prayer, the frequent reception of the sacrament of penance, special devotions to the Virgin Mary.

The 1917 Code placed the responsibility directly on the bishop (*CIC* 125); he was to see that his clergy carried out certain devotional practices. He fulfilled his juridic obligation by exhorting them from time to time at conferences or retreats; he had the authority also to issue a formal precept that would bind in conscience. The eminent canonist Cappello held that he could by strict precept order them to go frequently to confession and to give him proof of having done so but denied that he was able to impose other acts of piety such as daily mental prayer.[86] Some canonists held by analogy with the law referring to religious and seminarians that clerics were to go to confession once a week, others that once a month would be "frequent."[87] The canon in commending devotion to the Blessed Virgin specified the rosary. Other pious practices to be inculcated were visits to the Blessed Sacrament and the examination of conscience.

The 1983 Code properly places the responsibility directly on the clerics. They are to apply themselves regularly to mental prayer. They are to approach the sacrament of penance frequently (*PO* 18). The Code does not offer here or elsewhere any further guideline. The Sacred Congregation for Religious and Secular Institutes in the *Decree on Confession for Religious* on December 8, 1970 did indicate that "frequently" meant "twice a month."[88] In view of the opinion of commentators on the former law, it would seem that once a month could be considered frequent. While special devotion to the Blessed Virgin is recommended, the rosary is not singled out. Other more particular norms may be established by the episcopal conference.[89]

Celibacy

Canon 277 — §1. Clerics are obliged to observe perfect and perpetual continence for the sake of the kingdom of heaven and therefore are obliged to observe celibacy, which is a special gift of God, by which sacred ministers can adhere more easily to Christ with an undivided heart and can more freely dedicate themselves to the service of God and humankind.

§2. Clerics are to conduct themselves with due prudence in associating with persons whose company could endanger their obligation to observe continence or could cause scandal for the faithful.

§3. The diocesan bishop has the competence to issue more specific norms concerning this matter

and to pass judgment in particular cases concerning the observance of this obligation.

This canon represents an important commitment of the Western Church upheld by the Second Vatican Council.[90] The law of celibacy was reaffirmed after considerable discussion in Article 16 of *Presbyterorum Ordinis*. "Perfect and perpetual continence for the sake of the kingdom of heaven was recommended by Christ the Lord" (Mt 19:12). It has "always been highly esteemed by the Church as a feature of priestly life. For it simultaneously signifies and incites pastoral charity as well as being in a special way a source of spiritual fruitfulness in the world." Still, it is not demanded of the priesthood by its nature, as the practice of married clergy in the primitive Church and the tradition of the Eastern Churches bear witness.

The appropriateness of celibacy to the priesthood rests on theological and spiritual grounds. It symbolizes the essence of the ministry in a very effective way. As one entrusted with the ministry of Christ, the more complete is the priest's dedication the more credible is his work. Through celibacy the priest is consecrated in a new and excellent way to Christ, "for his sake and for the sake of the gospel" (Mk 10:29). "It is a special gift of God through which sacred ministers may more readily cling to Christ with undivided heart and dedicate themselves more freely in him and through him to the service of God and of men."[91] The last section of Article 16 attempts to answer the question how the charism of celibacy that God gives to some (Mt 19:11) can be made obligatory for all priests.

This sacred Council approves and confirms this legislation so far as it concerns those destined for the priesthood, and feels confident in the Spirit that the gift of celibacy, so appropriate to the priesthood of the New Testament, is liberally granted by the Father, provided those who share Christ's priesthood through the sacrament of Order, and indeed the whole Church, ask for the gift humbly and earnestly.

In the words of one commentator:[92]

This argumentation makes sense only to the believing Christian; and it becomes all the easier to understand the more one sees the charisma of

---

[86]*Summa Iuris* I, no. 218.
[87]J. Jone, *Commentarium in Codicem Iuris Canonici* (Paderborn: F. Schöningh, 1950), 135.
[88]*AAS* 63 (1971), 318; *CLD* 7, 532.
[89]*Rel*, 64.

[90]J. Lynch, "Marriage and Celibacy of the Clergy, the Discipline of the Western Church: An Historical Synopsis," *J* 32 (1972), 14–38, 189–212; J. Lynch, "Critique of the Law of Celibacy in the Catholic Church from the Period of the Reform Councils," *Celibacy in the Church*, W. Bassett and P. Huizing, eds. 78 (1972), 57–75.
[91]This explanation advanced by the Council did not appear in *Schema de Populo Dei*, c. 135, §1 or in the 1980 text but was added in the promulgated canon.
[92]F. Wulf, Vorgrimler IV, 287.

celibacy as something not extraordinary, but perfectly normal within the framework of God's gracious guidance. Moreover, one may not think of this charisma, that is so deeply embedded in a man's life, as something self-contained, complete, and given all at once, as something a man either has or has not. It should be conceived, rather as something put by God into a man's concrete historical, anthropological and psychological situation, itself possessing a history and being an adventure—the adventure of faith.

The same author observes: "Priestly celibacy cannot be fully explained purely theoretically; in the end it is a matter of faith and spiritual experience, otherwise it cannot be fully lived out."[93]

In this positive presentation, "for the sake of the kingdom of heaven," the conciliar statement as well as the revised law are a great improvement. "All untenable motives for celibacy—arising from notions of cultic purity or from a subliminal depreciation of the body and of sexuality—are avoided, motives still commonly mentioned until quite recently in official documents."[94] The 1917 law (CIC 132) stated that clerics in major orders are barred from marrying and so bound by the obligation of chastity that if they sin against it they are guilty of sacrilege. The Secretariat, while agreeing that the violation of perfect continence is a sacrilege, relegates that issue to moral theology.[95] In view, however, of the abolition of the "privilege of the canon" (CIC 119) which made the physical violation of a cleric or religious a sacrilege (thus with a connotation of cultic purity), it seems more appropriate to refer to the sexual transgressions of celibates not as sacrileges but as violations of a vow. In the past it was controverted whether the obligation of celibacy arose from a vow implicitly taken at the reception of the subdiaconate or from ecclesiastical law.[96] Under the present discipline canon 1037 requires that before the reception of the diaconate a candidate who is not married must, in a prescribed rite, assume publicly before God and the Church the obligation of celibacy—or have made a perpetual vow in a religious institute.

The 1917 Code (CIC 132, §3) ruled that a married man who received major orders without an apostolic dispensation,[97] even in good faith, was prohibited from exercising those orders. The revised new Code does not deal with this situation in the canon on celibacy, but in canon 1042, 1° it declares that a man who has a wife, unless he is legitimately destined for the permanent diaconate, is simply impeded from receiving orders; in canon 1044, §2, 1° it states that a person who illegitimately received orders while bound by an impediment is impeded from exercising those orders. Good faith does not enter into consideration. According to canon 1045 ignorance of the irregularities and of the impediments to ordination does not exempt from them.

Paragraph two of the 1980 draft of canon 250 provided that married men promoted to the permanent diaconate were not bound to the obligation of celibacy. The 1975 Schema de Sacramentis (c. 287, §2), on the other hand, held that deacons who were married were incapable of contracting a new marriage. The 1977 Schema de Populo Dei (c. 135) similarly stated: "Men of more mature age who are living a married life and have been promoted to the permanent diaconate are not obligated to celibacy; but if they lose their wives, they are so bound." The 1980 draft in canon 1040, §1 dealing with the diriment impediment of orders to marriage exempted widowed deacons: "Deacons who were married at the time they received the sacred order are not bound."

Because the arguments for the retention and suppression of the impediment for the widowed deacons were so difficult to evaluate the Secretariat referred the decision to the Plenarium of the Commission in October 1981. The fourth special question posed to the Plenarium concerned permitting widowed deacons who were married at the time they received sacred orders to enter a second marriage. The positive reasons were listed: since these deacons had not chosen celibacy but had manifested a vocation to marriage at the time they were ordained, this burdensome obligation ought not be laid upon them; moreover, since there were often children involved who had to be raised, they could not be taken care of by a hired servant without grave economic difficulty and the danger of incontinence. On the negative side, it was argued that to permit an ordained minister to marry would be going against a millenarian and even an apostolic tradition;[98] it would thus be prejudicial to ecumenism

---

[93]Ibid., 283.
[94]Ibid.
[95]Rel, 64.
[96]Wernz-Vidal, Ius Canonicum II, no. 108.
[97]Pope Pius XII permitted a group of former Lutheran pastors in Germany who were married to be ordained to the priesthood in the 1950s. In December 1967 Pope Paul VI granted a similar dispensation to several married men in Australia who had been Anglican clergymen. In October 1969 Peter Rushton was ordained by Cardinal Gilroy in Sidney (P. Rushton, "A Married Priest in Australia," CR 66 [1981], 383–386). In the U.S. 64 former Episcopal priests by January 1982 had petitioned for ordination in the Roman Catholic Church. (See the

report of Bp Bernard Law, the delegate of the SCDF, on the process in Origins 11 [1982], 517–519.) On June 29, 1982, James Parker was the first former Episcopalian priest to be ordained.
[98]The early councils permitted the ordination of married men but did not allow the ordained to marry. At first there was a temporary concession. The Council of Ancyra (314 A.D.) in c. 10 declared: "If deacons at the time of their ordination declare that they must marry, and that they cannot be continent, and if accordingly they marry, they may continue in their ministry, because the bishop gave them permission to marry; but if at

insofar as it was at odds with the discipline of the Orthodox Churches and at the same time contrary to the practice of the Oriental Catholic Churches. Such an innovation was also seen as gravely injurious to sacerdotal celibacy in that it places in peril that absolute that the sacrament of orders confers as a grace. The Plenarium by a vote of thirty-eight to thirteen affirmed that a widowed deacon could remarry and continue to exercise his order without special permission or dispensation.

The 1983 Code, however, makes no exception for widowed deacons. Canon 1087 states simply: "Persons who are in holy orders invalidly attempt marriage." For a deacon who has lost his wife to marry again a dispensation must be sought from the Sacred Congregation for the Discipline of the Sacraments and Divine Worship. When a bishop presents a petition he may urge personal or pastoral reasons: for example, the need to provide care for the children or the loss to the apostolate if the deacon would seek laicization rather than live celibately.

In paragraph two of canon 277 clerics are warned to be careful about those with whom they associate lest their obligation to continence be endangered and the faithful scandalized. The former law (*CIC* 133) was much more detailed. Clerics were not to live under the same roof with or to frequently visit women so as to give rise to suspicion on the part of others. Clerics were permitted to dwell only with those whose natural kinship (mother, sister, aunt) or whose irreproachable character and maturity obviated any suspicion. Canonists generally understood the advanced age as forty years or older. The revised Code does not single out women as the likely cause of scandal; the association with certain males could be just as harmful.

Paragraph three deals with the authority of the diocesan bishop to safeguard the observance of celibacy. The 1917 law stated that the judgment in an individual case whether there was danger of incontinence or scandal belonged to the bishop who

could forbid such association to his clerics. The 1983 law, while affirming this prerogative of judging particular cases, notes that the bishop has authority to issue specific norms on this matter. The *Schema de Populo Dei* required the bishop before enunciating such rules to first hear the presbyteral council (c. 136, §2). The 1980 draft accorded a greater discretionary power to the bishop; he was to consult the presbyteral council before issuing norms *and* to judge in particular cases. The Secretariat eliminated any reference to the presbyteral council with the following explanation: it is a question of the exercise of the diocesan bishop's legislative power and in a very delicate matter; he may easily have knowledge of circumstances and facts of which the members of the council are ignorant and be unable to communicate them for reasons of justice and prudence.[99] Nothing, furthermore, prevents the bishop, if circumstances warrant, from seeking the opinion of the council in any manner he judges prudent.

Clerical Associations

Canon 278 — §1. Secular clerics have the right to associate with others for the purpose of pursuing ends which befit the clerical state.

§2. Secular clerics are to place great value upon those associations in particular which, having statutes recognized by competent authority, foster holiness in the exercise of the ministry by means of a suitable and properly approved style of life and by means of fraternal assistance, and which promote the unity of the clergy among themselves and with their own bishop.

§3. Clerics are to refrain from establishing or participating in associations whose ends or activity cannot be reconciled with the obligations proper to the clerical state or which could hinder the diligent fulfillment of the duty entrusted to them by competent ecclesiastical authority.

The right of diocesan clerics to form associations is acknowledged for the first time in canon law. Although canon 299, §1 declares that the Christian faithful—which certainly includes clerics—are at liberty to establish organizations, special notice is taken of the clerical right to do so because of the importance of the right and lest there be any doubt about it.[100] Note that the canon includes deacons but pointedly excludes clerics of religious communities.

The right of the faithful to form associations with supernatural objectives was only implicitly recognized in the 1917 Code (*CIC* 684). A decree of the Sacred Congregation of the Council declared that

the time of their ordination they were silent and received the imposition of hands and professed continence, and if later they marry, they ought to cease from their ministry" (*Corpus Iuris Canonici,* c. 8, Dist. 28). Shortly afterwards the Council of Neocaesarea affirmed: "If a presbyter takes a wife, he ought to be deposed from that order" (*Corpus Iuris Canonici,* c. 9, Dist. 28). The Council of Trullo which established the basic law for the Eastern Churches in 692 A.D. legislated: "If any ordained person contracts matrimony, let him be deposed; if he wishes to be married, he should become so before his ordination" (c. 6, *Apostolic Canons* 26).

As of October 31, 1982, the number of permanent deacons in the U.S. was 5,886; there were 2,349 candidates in training. There were no permanent deacons under the age of 32; 4,088 (69%) were between 41 and 60 years of age. As for the marital status, 5,510 (94%) were married; 271 (4%) were celibate; and 105 (2%) were widowers (*Diaconal Quarterly* 9 [1983], 22–23). The U.S. accounted for 62.8% of the world total of permanent deacons, 8,273 (P. Ward, "The Permanent Diaconate after Ten Years," *America* 148 [1983], 475–477).

[99]*Rel,* 65.
[100]*Comm* 9 (1977), 245; *Schema de Populo Dei, Praenotanda,* p. 10.

this was indeed an authentic and natural right.[101] On December 10, 1949, the United Nations in its Universal Declaration of Human Rights asserted: "Every one has the right to freedom of peaceful assembly and association. No one may be compelled to belong to an association" (Art. 21). Pope John XXIII in his 1963 encyclical *Pacem in Terris* offered a fuller explanation.

> From the fact that human beings are by nature social, there arises the right of assembly and association. They have also the right to give the societies of which they are members the form they consider most suitable for the aim they have in view, and to act within such societies on their own initiative and on their own responsibility in order to achieve their desired objectives. . . . It is most necessary that a wide variety of societies or intermediate bodies be established, equal to the task of accomplishing what the individual cannot by himself efficiently achieve. These societies or intermediate bodies are to be regarded as an indispensable means in safeguarding the dignity and liberty of the human person, without harm to his sense of responsibility.[102]

The right of association is a natural right not dependent upon positive law or human concession. The Council, too, insisted that since man is social by nature, there is a fundamental need for Christians to carry out group apostolates (*AA* 18) and that "while preserving intact the necessary link with the ecclesiastical authority, the laity have the right to establish and direct associations, and to join existing ones" (*AA* 19).

During the debate on *Presbyterorum Ordinis*, one of the last council documents to be approved, the competent Commission noted: "Priests cannot be denied what the Council attentive to the dignity of human nature declared as belonging to the laity since it corresponds to natural law."[103] In presenting an intermediate draft of the decree, the conciliar Commission rejected a proposal that associations of priests be placed under the diocesan bishop or the conference of bishops. These associations fall within the area of the personal life of priests and the exercise of their legitimate liberty. From a juridical point of view, furthermore, such exercise of episcopal power would give rise to confusion between the internal and external fora. Practically speaking, also, many priests, out of respect for their ordinary, would be morally forced to join associations directed by him. A polarization would result between diocesan priests who joined associations run by the

bishop and those who did not.[104] In the final draft of the decree, however, associations approved by ecclesiastical authority were especially commended.

Associations of priests are also to be highly esteemed and diligently promoted, when by means of statutes recognized by the competent authority[105] they foster priestly holiness in the exercise of the ministry through a suitable and properly approved rule of life and through brotherly help, and so aim at serving the whole order of priests (*PO* 8).[106]

Paragraph two of the canon, again referring only to diocesan priests, repeats the conciliar text that it is stated in terms of clerics generally and refers to "competent authority" instead of "competent ecclesiastical authority." Clerics are not asked to *promote* approved societies. They are not forbidden to form organizations whose statutes are not submitted to any authority for approval.[107] The unqualified right of clerics to associate for the attainment of goals consonant with their status is recognized in paragraph one. The organizations may be diocesan, national, or international in scope.

The *Schema de Populo Dei* included a rather distrustful paragraph:

> Let secular clergy enroll in only those associations of priests which preserve the proper character of these secular clergy, and whose statutes duly provide that, without respect of persons, harmony among all the members of the presbytery of the particular church is promoted (c. 137, §3).

In eliminating this paragraph the Code assumes the good faith of the clergy and does not suspect them of discrimination or intrigue.

[101]*Corrienten,* Nov. 13, 1920; *AAS* 13 (1921), 139.

[102]Articles 23–24, *AAS* 55 (1963), 262–263. English trans. ed. W. Gibbons, *Pacem in Terris* (Glen Rock, N.J.: Paulist Press, 1963).

[103]*AcSynVat* IV, pars 7, p. 168, *Responsum ad Modum* 129.

[104]*AcSynVat* IV, pars 6, p. 395.

[105]The qualification "statutis ab auctoritate ecclesiastica probatis" was added to distinguish them from so-called "patriotic associations" in socialist states. The Resp. Mod. 30 noted that the associations the decree was referring to had their own juridic journey: they generally began with the approval of the bishop and finally in most instances ended with the sanction of the Apostolic See.

[106]"No reason is given why, when mentioning such associations, the improvement of pastoral opportunities was not more clearly indicated (teamwork, *pastorale d'ensemble*). Suggestions along these lines . . . were reproduced in a very abstract form (*cooperatio*)." Paul-J. Cordes, Vorgrimler, IV, 253.

[107]For the constitution of the Association of Chicago Priests, adopted Oct. 24, 1966, see *Catholic Mind* 65 (Jan. 1967), 55–59. On June 23, 1978, the Association of Chicago Priests wrote to the Sacred Congregation of the Clergy listing grievances and seeking assistance for the solution of problems in the archdiocese. Cardinal Wright, Prefect of the Congregation, responded that the sole "coetus seu senatus sacerdotum, Presbyterium repraesentantium" recognized by the Holy See is precisely the Council or Presbyteral Senate . . . "the Holy See deals directly or through the Ordinary only with the Senate and not with other bodies such as the ACP" (*CLD* 9, 243–244).

Paragraph three of the canon prohibits clerics from establishing or participating in organizations incompatible with the obligations of the ministerial state or the fulfillment of their duties. Certainly groups that advocate or practice violence are antithetical to the clerical commitment. On March 8, 1982, the Sacred Congregation for the Clergy issued a *Declaration on Associations of Priests, Politics and Labor*. It indicates as "irreconcilable with the clerical state, and therefore prohibited to all members of the clergy," those associations of clerics "which directly or indirectly, in a manifest or clandestine manner, pursue aims relating to politics, even if presented under the external aspect of wanting to favor humanitarian ideals, peace and social progress." It saw these groups as sowing division in the Christian community and overshadowing the priestly mission. The declaration also stigmatized as "irreconcilable" those associations

which intend to unite deacons or presbyters in a type of "union," thus reducing their sacred ministry to a profession or career comparable to functions of a profane character. Such associations, in fact, compare the exercise of the functions of the ministerial priesthood to a relationship of work and thus can easily place the clerics in opposition to their holy pastors who become considered only as givers of work.[108]

Certainly today clerics may participate fully in Rotary Clubs, which marks a reversal of policy. In 1929 the Sacred Consistorial Congregation decided that it was "not expedient" for ordinaries to permit clerics to become members or even attend meetings of the Rotary (*CLD* 1, 617); the Holy Office reaffirmed this position in 1951 (*CLD* 3, 284). Paul VI, however, in an allocution to the Rotary Clubs of Italy explained that the "reservations" of the Church were based on a fear that the clubs might be infiltrated by false ideologies or come to conceive themselves as an all-sufficient guide to life, to the exclusion of Christian ideals (*CLD* 6, 511). The Sacred Congregation for the Doctrine of Faith in 1973 indicated that "episcopal conferences have from the Apostolic See the faculty of permitting the inscription of clerics in the Rotary Club" but not in Masonic organizations (*CLD* 8, 456). The same Congregation reaffirmed the next year: "the prohibition remains in every case against clerics and religious as well as members of secular institutes enrolling in any kind of Masonic association" (*CLD* 8, 1211). The 1983 Code in canon 1374 forbids only

in a general way those who plot against the Church and does not single out the Masons. A declaration of the Sacred Congregation for the Doctrine of the Faith, however, reaffirmed the prohibition against joining the Masons (see the commentary on c. 1374).

Continuing Education

Canon 279 — §1. Even after their ordination to the priesthood clerics are to continue to pursue sacred studies; they are to strive after that solid doctrine which is based upon Sacred Scripture, handed down by their predecessors and commonly accepted by the Church and which is contained especially in the documents of the councils and of the Roman Pontiffs; they are to avoid profane novelties and pseudo-science.

§2. In accord with the prescriptions of particular law, priests are to attend pastoral lectures which are to be held after priestly ordination; at times determined by the same particular law they are also to attend lectures and theological meetings or conferences which afford them opportunities to acquire a fuller knowledge of the sacred sciences and of pastoral methods.

§3. They are likewise to pursue a knowledge of the other sciences, especially those which are connected with the sacred sciences, particularly insofar as such knowledge contributes to the exercise of the pastoral ministry.

This canon treats the continuing education of the clergy. The 1917 Code (*CIC* 129) exhorted priests after ordination not to interrupt their studies, especially sacred studies, but to pursue that solid doctrine handed down by the Fathers and received by the Church. They were to avoid profane novelties and pseudo-science known as Modernism.[109] By sacred sciences were meant dogmatic and moral theology, canon law, ecclesiastical history, and Sacred Scripture.[110] Among the other studies the humanities and sciences were considered appropriate and very useful. Special regulations were published for clerics attending a secular university. They had first to be ordained to the priesthood and excel in learning and piety. The necessary approval of the bishop was to be given only for the need and advantage of the diocese, namely, to provide teachers for schools. After finishing their studies the priests remained bound to the service of the diocese and could not accept a professorship or other office against the wishes of their ordinary.[111] Further regulations were made for priests teaching in public schools. In addition to permission from their own ordinary, they

---

[108]*Origins* 11 (1982), 647. "Italian newspapers said the directive was aimed specifically at organizations like Priests for Peace in Hungary, Christian Reality in Yugoslavia, and *Pacem in Terris* in Czechoslovakia. These organizations were said to work in close collaboration with the Communist government and often to be in open conflict with the bishops of the nation" (ibid.).

[109]Cappello, no. 220. The terminology of the canon is taken from *Pascendi* of Pius X, *ASS* 40 (1907), 593.
[110]Cappello, no. 220.
[111]*CLD* 1, 115, Decree of the SCConsist, April 30, 1918.

needed the approval of the ordinary of the place where they were teaching.[112] By the 1970s many of the restrictions regarding the attendance of priests at secular universities were no longer observed.

To ensure that priests would not neglect their intellectual development, the 1917 Code required the junior clergy to take examinations and all priests to attend periodic conferences. For at least the first three years after ordination every priest was to be examined in various sacred disciplines that had been designated in advance. The Third Plenary Council of Baltimore (1884) prescribed that the examinations be extended to five years and include Holy Scripture, dogma, moral theology, canon law, church history, and liturgy (no. 187). If the questions were not answered satisfactorily, the examination could be protracted beyond the five-year period; the grades were to be recorded in the diocesan archives (no. 188). The 1917 Code provided that in the conferring of ecclesiastical offices and benefices, all other things being equal, consideration was to be given to those who scored the highest in these examinations (*CIC* 130, §2). The Sacred Congregation for the Clergy in a circular letter of November 4, 1969 declared that the triennial examinations were still obligatory.[113] With the promulgation of the 1983 Code these examinations are no longer required by the universal law of the Church. The Baltimore legislation has been abrogated either by custom or the reorganization of the matter.

In the 1917 Code, while examinations were required of the junior clergy, all were to attend the clergy conference (*CIC* 131). Several times during the year the ordinary was to convoke meetings in the cathedral city and the rural deaneries for the discussion of moral and liturgical subjects. If it proved difficult to hold such meetings, the solutions of questions were to be submitted in writing according to norms established by the ordinary. Those obliged to attend were: secular priests; religious priests having the care of souls; and other religious with diocesan faculties to hear confessions, if conferences were not held in their own houses. The conferences, very practical in nature, usually included solving problems and cases. The Third Plenary Council of Baltimore (1884) explicitly stated that a case of conscience was to be the obligatory subject matter of the discussion; it also called for papers on Sacred Scripture, dogmatic theology, canon law, and liturgy (nn. 190, 192). The meetings were to be held four times a year in the cities and twice a year in the rural districts (no. 192).[114] Attendance at the conference was juridically prescribed and could be enforced by penalties (*CIC* 2377).

These provisions as such are no longer in effect in that they have been superseded by legislation emanating from Vatican II.

The Second Vatican Council emphasized in several documents the permanent formation of the clergy. *Christus Dominus* urged the bishops

> to encourage institutes and organize special congresses where priests might come from time to time for the purpose of more prolonged retreats ordered to a renewal of life and to acquire a deeper understanding of ecclesiastical studies, especially sacred scripture, theology, the more important social problems and new approaches to pastoral work (no. 16).

Optatam Totius stressed the importance of continuing priestly training after the completion of the seminary course; episcopal conferences have the duty of providing the means.

> Examples of such means are: pastoral institutes cooperating with certain parishes selected for the purpose, the holding of meetings at stated times, and suitable projects by which the junior clergy will be gradually introduced to priestly life and apostolic activity in their spiritual, intellectual and pastoral aspects, with opportunities for constant renewal and progress (no. 22).

The fullest treatment of the subject is given in *Presbyterorum Ordinis* (*PO* 19). Priests are urged to study the Scriptures as the primary source of sacred knowledge. They are to know the tradition of the Church as seen in the teachings of the councils and popes. It is also important for them to keep abreast of developments of secular culture. Various means are suggested to facilitate study: "courses or congresses, the establishment of centers designed for pastoral studies, the founding of libraries and the proper direction of studies by suitable persons" *(PO* 19).

The *motu proprio Ecclesiae sanctae* in August 1966 sought to implement these decrees. Bishops were required to arrange that

> all priests, even if they are actually serving in the ministry, shall follow a course of pastoral lectures for a year after ordination and shall at stated intervals attend other lectures which will provide them the opportunity for acquiring a fuller knowledge of pastoral matters, of the science of theology, of moral theology and of liturgy, of strengthening their spiritual life and communicating their apostolic experience with one another (*ES* I, 7).

This document specifically requires a year of pastoral training for newly ordained priests and a program of lectures on pastoral and theological

---

[112]*CLD* 116–119, Decree of the SCConc, Feb. 22, 1927.

[113]*CLD* 7, 877, no. 18.

[114]L. Hoffman, *Clergy Conferences, CanLawStud* 383 (Washington: Catholic University of America, 1957).

matters for all priests. The Sacred Congregation for the Clergy issued a circular letter on November 4, 1969 treating in more detail the continuing education and formation of clergy, especially junior clergy.[115] The Sacred Congregation for Catholic Education in January 1970 published a *Ratio Fundamentalis Institutionis Sacerdotalis* that included a section on post-seminary training (nn. 100, 101).[116] The Sacred Congregation for Bishops issued a *Directory on the Pastoral Ministry of Bishops* on February 22, 1973 that reminded the bishop of the need for a pastoral year immediately following ordination and periodic renewal courses for all priests (no. 114).

The *Schema de Populo Dei* in canon 138 mandated:

Let diocesan bishops take care that clerics be given necessary time to use means fit for fostering the supernatural life, and that they may be free for study of the sciences, especially the sacred ones, insofar as they are required for due fulfillment of their ministry.

The responsibility of bishops to make it possible for priests to continue their education, as enunciated in *Ecclesiae sanctae*, was thus proposed for the revised Code. This responsibility entailed a corresponding right on the part of the clerics to have sufficient time to make use of the aids to spiritual growth and to develop their intellectual life.[117] This canon was eliminated on the ground that the present canon amply dealt with the matter.[118]

The Program of Continuing Education of Priests, a document published by the United States Catholic Conference in 1972, affirmed:

Every priest has a right and an obligation to continue his spiritual growth and education. He has a right to strong support from his superiors, peers, and the people he serves. He also has an obligation to his superiors and peers, but above all, to his people to continue to grow in grace and knowledge (no. 3).

As One Who Serves: Reflections on the Pastoral Ministry of Priests in the United States, prepared for the Bishops' Committee on Priestly Life and Ministry of the National Conference of Catholic Bishops, 1977 noted:

In practice the strong support mentioned in the document includes not only encouragement but

also financial assistance. Many dioceses have developed continuing education policies which allow for sabbatical periods and include respectable formulas for the financial arrangements (p. 60).

The 1983 Code treats continuing education of the clergy in canon 279. The first paragraph, stating the obligation of clerics to continue sacred studies, is taken almost verbatim from the 1917 Code (*CIC* 129) except for two points emphasized in the Council: that the source of doctrine is Sacred Scripture, and the tradition of the Church is to be found especially in the documents of the councils and of the Roman Pontiffs. The second paragraph requires priests to attend pastoral lectures after their ordination and also to be present at lectures, theological meetings, or conferences that afford the opportunity to develop their knowledge and pastoral techniques. Particular law is to determine the specifics of the program. The last paragraph calls for clerics to cultivate other disciplines especially those that will further their ministerial activity.

The National Conference of Catholic Bishops promulgated in 1971 *The Program of Priestly Formation* for five years *ad experimentum*. After approval by the Sacred Congregation for Catholic Education a second edition was published in 1976 and a third edition in 1982. Every diocese is to have a plan to provide for the continuing education of priests. It may include: clergy conference days, retreat-workshops, pastoral and theological institutes, summer courses, a priests' month after five years of pastoral ministry, and similar opportunities for renewal (nn. 224–225, 3rd ed.).

Common Life

Canon 280 — Some community of life is highly recommended to clerics; wherever such a practice exists, it is to be preserved to the extent possible.

Although common life among diocesan clergy had been encouraged by regional councils and popes from the early Middle Ages,[119] the 1917 Code for the first time recommended it as a universal norm with specific application to the pastor and his assistants. Canon 134 of the former Code stated: "the custom of common life among clerics is laudable and to be encouraged; wherever it exists it is to be maintained as far as possible." In treating the parochial assistant, or curate, the 1917 Code (*CIC* 476, §5) required the bishop "to prudently provide that in accordance with c. 134 he live in the parish rectory." Commentators generally agreed that canon 134 was a counsel rather than a precept, ex-

[115]*CLD* 7, 868–880.
[116]*AAS* 62 (1970), 382–383; *The Pope Speaks* 15 (1970), 313–314. See "Resource Information Booklet on Sabbaticals for the Clergy," National Organization for Continuing Education of Roman Catholic Clergy, 5401 S. Cornell, Chicago, Ill. 60615.
[117]*Comm* 3 (1971), 196.
[118]*Comm* 14 (1982), 79.

[119]See M. Borgman, *The Common Life among Clerics in the Writings of St. Augustine of Hippo and Ecclesiastical Legislation,* CanLawStud 459 (Washington: Catholic University of America, 1968).

cept in cases in which common life had been customary. Some even held that a bishop could not impose it where a contrary custom prevailed.[120]

The common life is generally understood as living under the same roof and sharing the same table. It is not to be confused with the common life of religious that connotes especially a sharing of goods or property. No juridical bond arises as in a society with rules and a superior. The practice of clerics living together is a safeguard of celibacy and a means of fostering other virtues.

The Second Vatican Council, the first ecumenical council to treat the common life of the clergy, took up the subject in *Presbyterorum Ordinis*. The fathers were sharply divided over how strongly to recommend community life. One group pointed out how difficult this type of life would be if love and forbearance were lacking. Thus the proposal that it be observed "to the greatest extent possible" was rejected. Another group sought a more insistent formulation than that in the Code, even if it were not yet possible to prescribe a *vita communis* for all the clergy.[121] The final text read:

> Moreover, in order to enable priests to find mutual help in cultivating the intellectual and spiritual life, to promote better cooperation amongst them in the ministry, to safeguard them from possible dangers arising from loneliness, it is necessary to foster some kind of common life or some other community of life among them (*aliqua vita communis vel aliquod vitae consortium*). This, however, can take different forms according to varying personal and pastoral needs: by priests' living together where this is possible, or by their sharing a common table, or at least by meeting at frequent intervals. (*PO* 8).

The *Schema de Populo Dei* read:

> That clerics may be better able to cooperate in fulfilling the duties of the ministry and that they may have fraternal help in cultivating the spiritual and intellectual life, a certain community life (*quoddam vitae consortium*) is highly recommended to clerics, nay even the practice of life in common (*vitae communis consuetudo*). This practice, where it is in force, is to be preserved as far as possible (c. 140).

The 1980 draft eliminated the rationale and stated simply: "Some community of life (*vitae consortium*), indeed the practice of the common life (*vitae communis consuetudo*) is highly recommended to clerics; wherever such practice exists, it is to be pre-

served as far as it is possible" (c. 254). The Secretariat of the Commission later noted that the words "vitae consortium" were to be suppressed because the expression was used elsewhere in the Code (cc. 1055, §1; 1096, §1) to refer to married life.[122]

Remuneration

Canon 281 — §1. When clerics dedicate themselves to the ecclesiastical ministry they deserve a remuneration which is consistent with their condition in accord with the nature of their responsibilities and with the conditions of time and place; this remuneration should enable them to provide for the needs of their own life and for the equitable payment of those whose services they need.

§2. Provision is likewise to be made so that they possess that social assistance by which their needs are suitably provided for if they suffer from illness, incapacity or old age.

§3. Married deacons who dedicate themselves completely to the ecclesiastical ministry deserve a remuneration by which they can provide for their own support and that of their families; married deacons, however, who receive remuneration by reason of a civil profession which they exercise or have exercised are to take care of their own and their family's needs from the incomes derived from their profession.

The support of the clergy was treated in canons 979 and 981 of the 1917 Code. In order to receive major orders a cleric had to be given a canonical title that signified the source or basis of his livelihood. For a secular cleric the title could be a benefice, personal property, a state subsidy, or the service of the diocese. For religious clerics the title was "solemn religious profession" or the common table. In the United States the usual title by far for secular clerics was the service of the diocese. The 1983 Code makes no reference to a title for ordination; thus the canonical institute is suppressed. The one canon dealing with benefices requires the episcopal conferences, in conformity with the directions

---

[120]Cappello, no. 226; Coronata, no. 193. Voosen, "De residentia parochorum," *IP* 17 (1937), 52–63, esp. 56, held that the bishop needed the permission of the Holy See to impose common life.

[121]Paul-J. Cordes, Vorgrimler IV, 253. *AcSynVat* III, 3, pars 4, 228; IV, 4, pars 4, 350–359.

[122]*Rel*, 67. It is to be noted that the Council spoke of common life assuming different forms: cohabitation, sharing a common table, meeting at frequent intervals. Although the common rectory has been the practice in the United States, according to The Bishops' Committee on Priestly Life and Ministry of the NCCB, "the ability to create a friendly, supportive if not home-like climate has a history of success and failures." The committee noted that some priests were interested in alternatives to the rectory: "Rather steady evidence exists that about one-third of full-time assistants would like separate work and residence areas" (*As One Who Serves* [Washington: NCCB, 1977], 67–68). A later report of the committee recommends: "With regard to a priest's living conditions, a diocese should explore other possibilities in order to eliminate abuses, provide support, and give spiritual witness to the local church" (*The Priest and Stress* [Washington: NCCB, 1982], 21). The National Federation of Priests' Councils lists several dioceses with policies on freedom of residence/alternate residence (*Search and Share* [Chicago: NFPC, 5th ed. 1981], 2).

of the Council (*PO* 20), to consolidate their revenue in a clergy fund (c. 1272).[123]

According to the 1917 Code the title was to be "fully adequate for a fitting livelihood in accordance with norms established by ordinaries based on the varying needs and circumstances of time and place" (*CIC* 979, §2). The ordinary was obligated to see that a cleric promoted for the service of the diocese had adequate support ("sufficiens ad congruam sustentationem," *CIC* 981, §2). Adequate support was understood to include, beyond the necessities of life, "the maintenance of servants according to the status of the beneficiary, decent relaxation, a moderate amount of liberality towards good causes, the demands of sociability, of hospitality that must be shown to friends and to the needy" and provision for the future.[124] There was a dispute about the duty of a cleric to support near-relatives unable to take care of themselves. The amount of income would bear some proportion to the dignity of the individual and his merit or responsibilities. A bishop, for example, should receive more than a pastor; a seminary professor more than an assistant pastor. The standard of living would also vary from place to place depending on economic conditions. What would pass unnoticed in the United States could easily cause scandal in a Third World country. No matter what the wealth of the locality, be it noted, luxurious or extravagant living has always been regarded as abhorrent to the clerical state. "In brief," to cite Archbishop Hannan's doctoral study, "a cleric should receive an income sufficient to enable him to live with fitting dignity in conformity with the general economic conditions of his locality as well as the obligations to which he is subject."[125] If a pastor's salary proved to be more than necessary for his fitting support, he was bound to give the surplus to the poor or to pious causes (*CIC* 1473). It was the prerogative of the ordinary to determine the amount of the income. The Third Plenary Council of Baltimore ordered bishops, with the advice of their consultors, to set the pastor's salary (no. 273).

Although the Church is greatly concerned for the welfare of the clergy, the salvation of souls is its first priority. There may be economic circumstances in which an appropriate income cannot be provided. The 1917 Code (*CIC* 1415, §3) permitted a parish or quasi-parish to be erected even if fitting support of the pastor was unavailable, as long as at least the necessities of life could be met. The Pontifical Commission for the Authentic Interpretation of the Code decided in 1945 that a bishop may not leave a parish unfilled because of the financial diffi-

culties of the diocese.[126] The Third Plenary Council of Baltimore urged priests in charge of missions to be content with their income if it fell below that prescribed by the diocesan statutes. The bishop was not obliged to make up the difference later, if the pastor had received from church income sufficient funds for his shelter and sustenance (no. 273).

Presbyterorum Ordinis affirms that unless otherwise provided "the faithful are bound by a real obligation of seeing to it that the necessary provision for a decent and fitting livelihood for the priests is available." Bishops are to take care that

> rules are drawn up by which due provision is made for the decent support of those who hold or have held any office in the service of God.... Taking into consideration the conditions of different places and times as well as the nature of the office they hold, the remuneration to be received by each of the priests should be fundamentally the same for all living in the same circumstances.

The amount should be in keeping with their status and enough to allow them to provide a proper salary for those who work for them as well as to offer assistance to those in need. The remuneration should be enough to permit a proper vacation each year (no. 20). Diocesan or interdiocesan funds are to be established for health insurance and "for the proper support of priests who suffer from sickness, ill health or old age" (no. 21).

Pope Paul VI in *Ecclesiae sanctae* (1966) sought to implement the conciliar directives. Episcopal conferences were to establish norms "for the provision of a proper living for all clerics."[127] The remu-

---

[123]*Rel*, 283–84.

[124]E. Regatillo, *Institutiones Iuris Canonici*, 2nd ed. (Santander: Sal Terrae, 1946), I, 195.

[125]P. Hannan, *The Canonical Concept of congrua sustentatio for the Secular Clergy, CanLawStud* 302 (Washington: Catholic University of America, 1950), 124.

[126]*AAS* 37 (1945), *CLD* 3, 118.

[127]The NCCB has not published any guidelines on the remuneration of the clergy or on hospitalization and pensions. Practice varies from diocese to diocese. Professional expenses may be included in the salary or may be reimbursed separately. At least one diocese bases salary increases on the Federal Cost of Living Index. Some pensions are funded by the diocese alone; some by priests, parishes and the diocese; still others by the parishes alone. Many pension plans are administered through insurance companies; others are set up locally so that the amounts paid in are used to pay out demands on the system. Almost every diocese in the U.S. has a pension and retirement plan. In 1979 the National Federation of Priests' Councils circulated a survey of clergy remuneration by diocese. In July 1982 one midwest diocese introduced the following salary scale: base pay for parish priests, $4,631 per annum plus $50 increment per year of service through the 25th year; auto allowance of $3,095 per year plus 20 cents per mile in excess of 10,000 *business* miles. Priests in bureaus or institutions receive a base pay of $4,086 plus the yearly increment, no auto allowance unless in excess of 10,000 business miles, but $70 for weekend assignments (Saturday evening and Sunday). Thus the base pay plus allowance or stipends for all priests totals $7,726. Also see J. Kinsella and W. Jenne, *Fullness in Christ: A Report on a Study of Clergy Retirement* (Washington: USCC, 1979).

For civil law issues see K. O'Brien, *The Nature of Support of Diocesan Priests in the United States of America, CanLawStud* 286 (Washington: Catholic University of America, 1949).

neration was to be "on the same scale for all in identical circumstances taking account of the nature of the office and of the conditions of time and place." The income should "be sufficient to permit clerics a decent sustenance and to enable them to assist the poor." Special agencies were to be established to provide for insurance, for health assistance, and for the maintenance of the clergy in sickness and old age" (*ES* I, 8). The 1973 *Directory* also urged bishops to set up mutual benefit societies, "a fund from which priests could borrow at a very low interest," and to establish "some common fund which can take care of the obligations and needs of clergy and people who are serving the Church" (no. 117 c).

The 1983 Code reaffirms the principle of the former Code and of the Second Vatican Council. Since clerics dedicate themselves to the ministry of the Church, they deserve a fitting remuneration that is proportionate to the nature of their office and the conditions of time and place. (Note that the text refers to "ministry of the Church" which is wider than office or *munera*.)[128] Remuneration should be sufficient to provide for their own needs and for the just recompense of those whose services they need. Certainly they must have the means to fulfill their obligations and exercise their rights, such as to take a vacation (c. 283, §2) and to continue their education. They must also have enough to personally assist the poor.

The 1983 Code (c. 281, §2) takes special notice of health and retirement benefits. Clerics are to have enough to take care of their needs during periods of illness, incapacity, and old age. The law is merely applying to the clergy a right which Pope John XXIII said belonged to every human being: "the right to security in case of sickness, inability to work, widowhood, old age, unemployment, or in any other case in which he is deprived of the means of subsistence through no fault of his own" (*Pacem in Terris* 11).

Married deacons are considered in canon 281, §3. Those who work full time in the ministry are to receive compensation sufficient to maintain themselves and their families.[129] The *Guidelines for Permanent Deacons in the United States* provide that in this case they should be "paid an appropriate living wage, with customary fringe benefits and security arrangements" (no. 159). Deacons who continue a secular occupation should take care of their needs and those of their families from the revenue of that work. The *Guidelines* note that part-time deacons should be reimbursed for any expenses incurred in their ministry. If, furthermore, a deacon from a poor community has to forego a necessary second job in order to serve the Church, "some just

compensatory arrangement should be made." Even for deacons in part-time ministry, some dioceses may prefer to articulate financial arrangements in the form of a contract (no. 156). A deacon retired from his secular job may well be able to use a supplement to his pension and social security (no. 158).[130]

Simple Life-Style

Canon 282 — §1. Clerics are to cultivate a simple style of life and are to avoid whatever has a semblance of vanity.

§2. After they have provided for their own decent support and for the fulfillment of all the duties of their state of life from the goods which they receive on the occasion of exercising an ecclesiastical office, clerics should want to use any superfluous goods for the good of the Church and for works of charity.

After affirming their right to a decent livelihood, the law considers how the clergy ought to use temporal goods. This canon is based on Article 17 of *Presbyterorum Ordinis*. Priests are to be thankful "for everything that the heavenly Father has given them towards a proper standard of living." The decree then recommends voluntary poverty that they might

> become more clearly conformed to Christ and more ready to devote themselves to their sacred ministry.... Priests and bishops alike are to avoid everything that might in any way antagonize the poor. More than the rest of Christ's disciples they are to put aside all appearance of vanity in their surroundings. They are to arrange their house in such a way that it never appears unapproachable to anyone and that nobody, even the humblest, is ever afraid to visit it (*PO* 17).

The *Schema de Populo Dei* in canon 142 urged: "Led by the spirit of poverty, let clerics live a simple life and keep themselves from all that smacks of vanity." The 1980 draft, omitting the reference to "the spirit of poverty," stressed a simplicity of life removed from vain luxury. It was thus faithful to the thrust of the conciliar text that viewed poverty as a liberation from all inordinate anxiety and a wholesome detachment from possessions.

[128] *Rel*, 67.
[129] *Sacrum diaconatus ordinem*, nn. 19, 20, 21; *AAS* 59 (1967), 701; *CLD* 6, 581.
[130] In 1979 the Bishops' Committee on the Permanent Diaconate undertook a survey: *A National Study of the Permanent Diaconate in the United States* (Washington: NCCB, 1981). It was determined that deacons spend an average of 14 hours per week in ministry (p. 45). The findings indicated that in some cases the diaconate was placing unfair economic burdens on the deacon or his family. "The economic situation of diaconal candidates must therefore be seriously taken into consideration and the possibility of paid service be further explored" (p. 51).

The second paragraph of the canon echoes the injunction of Vatican II that all monies coming to clerics through the exercise of their office that are over and above what is necessary for their support should be devoted to the work of the Church or for charitable purposes. The *Schema de Populo Dei* included a further admonition from the decree: "Let clerics take care that they never consider an ecclesiastical office as a way of making money nor apply the revenues derived from an ecclesiastical office to the enrichment of their own families" (c. 142, §2). In the interest of brevity, however, the 1983 Code is content to state that surplus income derived from ecclesiastical sources is not to be used for personal enrichment or invested as capital. As has been noted, the former Code (*CIC* 1473) required merely that excess income derived from a benefice was to be distributed to the poor or to pious causes; in the United States only the pastor's salary fell under this category.[131] Under the present law all the emoluments received by every cleric in the performance of his official duties must be dispersed. (For a treatment of "ecclesiastical office" see the commentary on c. 145 [*PO* 20].) The universal law does not speak of the obligation of a cleric to make a will in view of varying circumstances throughout the world;[132] particular law may provide suitable norms. Certainly what a cleric earns by the use of his talents in writing or musical composition may be freely accumulated.

Clerical Absence and Vacation

Canon 283 — §1. Even if they do not have a residential office, clerics nevertheless are not to leave their diocese for a notable period of time, to be determined by particular law, without at least the presumed permission of their proper ordinary.

§2. Clerics are entitled to a due and sufficient period of vacation each year, to be determined by universal or particular law.

Clerics are not to leave the diocese for a notable time without at least the presumed permission of their ordinary. In that the cleric is ordained for the good of the diocese, he is supposed to have some assignment or at least be at the disposition of the bishop should a need for his services arise. It is up to particular law to determine the length of time beyond which permission is necessary. There was a wide discrepancy among commentators on the understanding of "a notable time" in the 1917 law; their views ranged from one month to less than six months, with most opting for three months.[133] Since

the revised law has set the pastor's annual vacation at one month, (c. 533, §2), all clerics may presume permission for an absence of that extent. Clerics who teach in schools without other obligations may presume to travel during vacation periods.[134] The Commission Secretariat noted that this canon also applies to permanent deacons.[135]

The 1917 Code did not recognize a right to a vacation for clerics generally, but it did permit bishops to be absent from their dioceses for three months during the year (*CIC* 338, §2) and pastors for two months (*CIC* 465, §§2–3). Although the universal law made no provision for parish assistants, most diocesan statutes granted them a two- or three-week vacation.[136] The statutes usually allowed substitutes for both pastor and assistants to be compensated from parochial funds.

Presbyterorum Ordinis stated forcefully: "priests' remuneration should be such to allow the priest a proper holiday each year. The bishop should see to it that priests are able to have this holiday" (*PO* 20). The 1983 Code lays down universal laws for those who hold residential offices. It permits a pastor to take a month's vacation every year; the time spent on retreat is not to be counted (c. 533, §2). The same amount of time is granted the parochial assistant (c. 550, §3). The month may be continuous or spread out in several periods over the course of the year. This time is in addition to the one or two days off each week that clerics enjoy by custom, at least in the United States. The diocesan bishop may not be "absent from his diocese beyond a period of one month, whether that period be a continuous one or an interrupted one"; the time spent at bishops' meetings is not counted (c. 395, §2). As for the coadjutor bishop and the auxiliary bishop, "except for the fulfillment of some other office outside the diocese or for the sake of vacation, which should not extend beyond one month, they should not leave the diocese but for a short period of time" (c. 410). Particular law will regulate vacations of those who do not hold residential offices.[137]

Clerical Attire

Canon 284 — Clerics are to wear suitable ecclesiastical garb in accord with the norms issued by the conference of bishops and in accord with legitimate local custom.

Historically, universal legislation on clerical attire has insisted only on its distinctiveness and appropriateness, leaving the specificity to particular custom and statute. The 1917 Code (*CIC* 136) pre-

---

[131]Hannan, *The Canonical Concept of congrua sustentatio*, 133. For some unexplained reason cardinals in the 1917 Code enjoyed the privilege of freely disposing of their income derived from benefices (*CIC* 239, §1, 19°).
[132]*Rel*, 68.
[133]Coronata I, 203.

[134]U. Beste, *Introductio in Codicem* (Neapoli: M. d'Auria, 1961), 204.
[135]*Rel*, 63.
[136]Hannan, *The Canonical Concept of congrua sustentatio*, 115–116.
[137]*Rel*, 68.

scribed generically a "habitus ecclesiasticus decens." By "ecclesiasticus" was meant that the dress had to be distinguished in form or color from secular clothing; "decens" that it was becoming to the clerical state, avoiding elegance as well as sordid negligence. "Habitus" was taken to include both the cassock and street dress. "Legitimate custom and precepts of the local ordinary are to be the guiding norms for this distinctiveness and conformability, and they therefore establish the style of garb to be worn."[138]

The particular law in the United States was established by the plenary councils of Baltimore. The decree of Baltimore II on dress was amplified in Baltimore III (no. 77). The cassock was to be used in church and rectory; outside, a simple black suit was required. With both the cassock and the suit the Roman collar was to be worn.[139] Baltimore II enacted further legislation about the personal appearance of clerics. Elaborate care of the hair and beard in the lay manner was condemned. In fact, clerics were to observe the custom of the Roman Church in being clean shaven (no. 151).[140] These regulations continued after the promulgation of the 1917 Code.

The seriousness of the obligation of wearing clerical garb may be gauged from the penalties that were imposed for its non-observance. The Sacred Congregation of the Council in a decree of July 1931 noted that clerical dress was to be worn "in public always, even during summer vacation."[141] The 1917 Code (CIC 136, §3) decreed an automatic expulsion from the clerical state in the case of someone in minor orders who refused to wear the clerical clothing for one month after a warning by the local ordinary. The former Code (CIC 188, 7°) also provided that all ecclesiastical offices became vacant automatically by tacit resignation when a cleric without justifying cause discards clerical garb on his own authority and does not resume it within a month after being warned by the ordinary. According to the 1917 law (CIC 2379) a cleric in major orders who had thus lost his office should also be suspended from exercising his orders.

With regard to other matters pertaining to personal appearance, by the time of the 1917 Code the practice of the tonsure was far from universally observed; the law (CIC 136) stated that it must be worn except where custom had determined otherwise. Custom was against it in all English and Germanic countries. While there was nothing in the law forbidding the use of a wig or toupee, one could not say Mass with his head covered. The apostolic delegates had the faculty to give permission for the use of a wig during Mass.[142] The 1917 Code neither forbade nor approved the wearing of beards. The particular law of Baltimore II prohibiting beards was still in effect.[143] "Permission is needed regardless of the size or shape of the beard, even for a mustache."[144] The use of rings was specifically forbidden clerics by the 1917 Code (CIC 136, §2) unless the right had been given them by law or apostolic privilege. In addition to bishops, abbots, vicars and prefects apostolic, those who received a doctoral degree from a Catholic or pontifical university were also entitled to wear a ring but not during sacred functions (CIC 1378).

After the Second Vatican Council, significant changes in clerical apparel received ecclesiastical approbation. The Council of the Episcopal Conference of Italy in April 1966 gave its consent for priests when outside of church and ecclesiastical institutions to dress in a black or dark-gray suit with Roman collar.[145] The Council of Spanish Bishops gave similar approval in 1966, thus conforming to the almost universal custom throughout the world.[146] The Prefect of the Sacred Congregation for Bishops in a letter of January 27, 1976 addressed to all papal representatives throughout the world acknowledged: "In order to meet the changed exigencies of attire, the Holy See in her own time has authorized episcopal conferences to introduce in their nations changes, which all are aware of, in the style of ecclesiastical attire."[147] He recognized that it is proper for clergy and religious to wear clothing suitable to the occupation in which they are engaged, for example, recreation.

The 1983 Code repeats verbatim the 1917 law except that, along with local custom, episcopal conferences rather than the local ordinaries are to establish norms for ecclesiastical dress. Quite apart from any initiative or explicit action of episcopal conferences, clerics in many areas of the world have assumed lay attire either completely or under vastly expanded circumstances. Motivated by a genuine desire to enhance communication with the multi-

[138]B. Ganter, *Clerical Attire: A Historical Synopsis and a Commentary,* CanLawStud 361 (Washington: Catholic University of America, 1955). O. Pontal, "Recherches sur le costume des clercs des origines au XIVᵉ siècle d'après les décrets des conciles et des synodes," *AC* 17 (1973), 769–796.

[139]"The painted portraits of the clergy of all denominations in the 19th century up to about 1870 show them wearing a white stock or choker, not the Roman collar. The churches were most thronged during the last quarter of the century, and by then the Roman collar had been widely adopted not only by Catholic priests but by many of the Anglican clergy and even by Nonconformist ministers. Its adoption was largely due to Cardinal Manning from the time that he became the second Archbishop of Westminster in 1865." E.E. Reynolds, "The Roman Collar," *The [London] Tablet* 231 (Sept. 3, 1977), 841.

[140]Barrett, *A Comparative Study,* 50.

[141]*CLD* 1, 124.

[142]*CLD* 182, no. 35.

[143]SCConc, Jan. 11, 1920 in response to an inquiry from Germany regarding the right of the clergy to wear beards. *CLD* 1, 123.

[144]Ganter, *Clerical Attire,* 140.

[145]*CLD* 6, 167–168.

[146]*Sal Terrae* 54 (1966), 608–609.

[147]*CLD* 8, 124–125.

tude, they have sought to eliminate any outward sign of "professionalism"—particularly the Roman collar—that might act as a barrier or appear as a claim to special privilege. It would certainly be within the spirit of the law in the United States today to limit the use of clerical attire to situations in which the cleric is on duty, actually functioning as a cleric, or attending formal gatherings in the diocese. He could, for example, wear sport clothes while traveling or attending class. "Unless in a particular diocese the bishop in accordance with the canon [of the 1917 Code] has regulated clerical dress, it seems that the silence of the Ordinaries is allowing a custom to arise that relaxes the conformity heretofore prevailing."[148]

It does not seem at the present time in the United States that one is justified in giving up clerical garb altogether. Unless specifically approved by the competent legislator, custom contrary to the current canon law does not obtain the force of law until "it has been legitimately observed for a period of thirty continuous and complete years" (c. 26).[149] ("Legitimately" here means that ecclesiastical authority has not protested.) In particular cases the ordinary may dispense from the law. As far as clothing of permanent deacons is concerned, "local custom is to be observed in accordance with the rules laid down by the episcopal conference (*Sacrum diaconatus ordinem* no. 31).[150] The United States *Guidelines* "endorses the hope that deacons will resemble lay people in these matters of lifestyle; however, a fundamental trust on the part of the priests and lay people must rest in the judgment and sensitivity of deacons themselves" (no. 148).[151] The 1917 Code provided as a vindictive penalty applicable to clerics the deprivation of ecclesiastical garb for a time (*CIC* 2298, 9°; 2300) and perpetually (cc. 2298, 11°; 2304). The 1983 Code does not have such a penalty.

On September 8, 1982, Pope John Paul II wrote to the papal vicar of Rome instructing him to promulgate norms regarding the use of clerical and religious garb in the Diocese of Rome. The pope acknowledged that there were "motivations of a historical, environmental, psychological or social order which can be proposed to the contrary" but noted that "motivations of an equal nature exist in its favor." He added that the arguments against clerical garb "appear more of a purely human character than ecclesiological." In the pope's view a distinctive sign is valuable "not only because it contributes to the propriety of the priest in his ex-

ternal behavior or in the exercise of his ministry, but above all because it gives evidence within the ecclesiastical community of the public witness that each priest is held to give of his own identity and special belonging to God." The modern secular city where "the sense of the sacred is so frighteningly weakened" needs the sign value that religious dress constitutes.[152]

On October 1, 1982, the vicar of Rome, Cardinal Poletti, issued a set of norms: "from now on the obligation of clerical or religious garb for both diocesan and religious priests resident in the Diocese of Rome is confirmed in all its force." For secular priests such attire can be the cassock or dark-colored clerical suit with the ecclesiastical Roman collar. Those belonging to religious communities are to wear the habit of their institute or the clerical suit. The law applies to seminarians when they receive the rite of admission of candidates to the priesthood and to religious students from their first religious profession. These norms were approved by the Holy Father on September 27, 1982.[153]

Unbecoming Activity

Canon 285 — §1. In accord with the prescriptions of particular law, clerics are to refrain completely from all those things which are unbecoming to their state.

§2. Clerics are to avoid those things which, although not unbecoming, are nevertheless alien to the clerical state.

§3. Clerics are forbidden to assume public offices which entail a participation in the exercise of civil power.

§4. Without the permission of their ordinary clerics are neither to become agents for goods belonging to lay persons nor assume secular offices which entail an obligation to render accounts; they are forbidden to act as surety, even on behalf of their own goods, without consultation with their proper ordinary; they are likewise to refrain from signing promissory notes whereby they undertake the obligation to pay an amount of money without any determined reason.

The law treats negative clerical obligations. Certain activities are forbidden, not because they are evil in themselves but insofar as they are unbecoming the clerical state. Since the attitude of the people is critical in determining what is unfitting for a cleric, the relativity of time and place must be considered. As "set apart in some way in the midst of the People of God," clerics are "witnesses and dispensers of a life other than that of this earth" (*PO*

[148]N. Halligan, "Clerical Dress," *NCE* Suppl. 17 (1979) 134.
[149]F. Urrutia, "De consuetudine canonica novi canones studio propununtur," *P* 70 (1981), 69–103; *De Normis Generalibus* (Roma: Pontificae Universitatis Gregorianae, 1983), 25–26.
[150]*CLD* 6, 583, no. 31.
[151]A 1979 survey reported that 11.6% of the respondents often wear a Roman collar, 25.3% sometimes do, and 62.5% never do (*A National Study*, p. 15).

[152]*Origins* 12 (Nov. 4, 1982), 344.
[153]Ibid., 343. Religious garb is regulated by c. 669 of the 1983 Code.

3). They must, therefore, maintain a position of dignity in the eyes of the faithful.

The 1917 Code (*CIC* 138), after stating the principle that clerics are to abstain absolutely from all things unbecoming their state, proceeds to list a number of examples.[154] They were not to engage in unfitting trades and professions. (In this country canonists listed such occupations as bartenders, jailers, and taxicab drivers.) They were not to *habitually* gamble or play games with considerable money stakes. (Moderate recreational play was not banned.) They were not to carry arms unless there was just fear for taking such precaution. They were not to indulge in hunting and never participate in "clamorous" hunting, that is, fox hunts or riding to the hounds. Particular law, however, could prohibit priests from hunting at all.[155] They were not to enter taverns or similar places, such as cocktail lounges and hotel bars, without necessity or some just cause approved by the ordinary.

Canon 140 of the 1917 Code forbade the clergy to attend certain entertainments. They were not to be present at spectacles, dances, or festivals—especially in public places—that would be unbecoming the clerical state or give rise to scandal among the people. Among the objectionable spectacles, commentators listed professional prize fights, horse racing, and risqué theatrical productions. Boisterous public celebrations such as New Year's Eve and Mardi Gras parties were likewise considered off limits.

The Third Council of Baltimore (no. 79) prohibited priests from attending all shows in public theaters, spectacles, and horse races. While custom abrogated the complete ban on theatrical performances, horse races remained "absolutely forbidden because of the Holy See's special insistence that this phase of the local law be kept." Two doctoral dissertations reported: "Though there has been no official publication of them, it is a matter of common knowledge that our Bishops have received documents from the Holy See urging the punishment of clerics who attend the races."[156] A number of diocesan synods repeated the injunction against horse racing, even imposing an ipso facto non-re-

served suspension *a divinis*.[157] The Cardinal Vicar of Rome published a sweeping decree approved by the Holy Father on February 1, 1938, which forbade clerics, seminarians, and students in ecclesiastical colleges from attending public theaters, cinemas, or any other public shows such as riding and athletic exhibitions.[158]

The 1983 Code is content with stating the general rule that clerics should wholly avoid all those things that are unbecoming their state according to the prescripts of particular law. Obviously many of the activities once considered inappropriate for clerics ceased to be so—long before the Council. People have grown more tolerant, and clerics are no longer looked upon as semi-cloistered individuals on a pedestal. The Church always expects, however, that they will conduct themselves in such a way as to maintain the respect of the community at large. In their lives they should witness to the higher values and tastes of society. If necessary, particular law can specify what activity in a given locality would threaten clerical esteem.

Worker Priests

An experiment known as the "Worker Priests" and involving about one hundred individuals was carried out in France and Belgium from 1944 to 1959. As a means of evangelizing the lower classes, priests took jobs in factories, at docks, and in the construction industry. They supported themselves by their labor without seeking any privileges. Though such intimate contacts proved beneficial to the cause of religion, they also endangered the spiritual life of the priests. On July 27, 1953 the Sacred Congregation of Seminaries absolutely forbade all seminarians in France as a stage in their training to engage in secular employment. Shortly afterwards the three French cardinals following an interview with the Holy Father declared that the experiment could not be continued in its present form and established several norms. The priests assigned to this apostolate were to be carefully selected and trained. They were to spend only a limited time each day in manual labor "so as to safeguard for them the readiness to meet all the exigencies of their priestly state." They were not to accept any assignments "which might lead to responsibilities in connection with labor unions or other offices which should be left to laymen." Finally, they were not to live by themselves but attached to a parish in which they

---

[154]J. Donovan, *The Clerical Obligation of Canons 138 and 140,* CanLawStud 272 (Washington: Catholic University of America, 1948).

[155]On June 11, 1921, the SCConc responded to an appeal of the priests of Gniezno-Poznan in Poland whose archbishop had forbidden them to hunt. Non-ostentatious hunting is neither absolutely prohibited by *CIC* 138 nor is it declared to be a right of the clergy when done moderately. Strictly speaking, the ordinary has the power to prohibit it entirely. He may impose sanctions according to *CIC* 2221, but they must be proportionate to the offense (*CIC* 2218). Hence he cannot, without grave and special reasons, punish hunting by suspension *latae sententiae* but rather have recourse to *CIC* 2306 and 2313 (*CLD* 1, 125).

[156]Barrett, *A Comparative Study,* 53. This statement was quoted with approval by Donovan, *The Clerical Obligation,* 153.

[157]For example, St. Louis and Cheyenne. In a letter of March 28, 1947, the Archbishop of Baltimore warned that any priest having a domicile or a quasi-domicile in the Archdiocese of Baltimore who attended horse races at a public track incurred ipso facto a non-reserved suspension *a divinis*. The suspension did not apply to horse races at county fairs. These instances are cited by Donovan, *The Clerical Obligation,* 153, no. 47.

[158]*CLD* 3, 67.

were to collaborate. On January 19, 1954, French bishops who had Priest Workers under their jurisdiction further specified these norms "to safeguard that which constitutes the proper mission of the priest. . . . If the Church demands that priests of the Labor Mission work for only a limited time each day, it is to enable them to fulfill all the duties of prayer and the apostolate which they assumed in becoming priests."[159]

On July 3, 1959, in response to Cardinal Feltin's petition that some priests be allowed to work in factories full time, and not as heretofore only three hours a day, the Holy Office decided that the experiment should be ended. Cardinal Pizzardo wrote for the Holy Office that in order to evangelize the workers "it is not absolutely necessary to send priests as workers into the centers of labor, and that it is not possible to sacrifice the traditional concept of the priesthood to this objective, which is nevertheless one to which the Church clings as one of her most cherished missions." Working in factories or yards is "incompatible with the life and duties of a priest." Besides being unable to fulfill all his duties of prayer, "working in factories or even in less important projects exposes the priest little by little to the dangers of being influenced by his surroundings." The Holy See, the letter continued, asks the bishops of France to consider whether the time has not come to supplement various lay apostolates by creating one or more secular institutes composed of both priests and lay members. The latter could work in factories without limitation of time and the priests could provide the necessary spiritual formation. A gradual phasing out was allowed "so as to avoid any hasty and too general change or dangerous disturbance in the workers' apostolate."[160]

The Council, however, contradicted "the alarming arguments which Cardinal Pizzardo had used in his letter."[161] *Presbyterorum Ordinis* observed that although priests are

> assigned different duties, yet they fulfill the one priestly service for people. . . . This is true whether the ministry they exercise be parochial or supra-parochial; whether their task be research or teaching, or even if they engage in manual labor and share the lot of the workers, where that appears to be of advantage and has the approval of the competent authority (*PO* 8).

The reference to worker priests was disputed up to the last draft. Some three hundred sixty-eight fathers wanted the passage deleted; seventy-two asked that the permission for priests to enter this apostolate be given by the local ordinary. The com-

promise formula states that "competent authority has to approve" but does not identify that authority.[162]

On October 23, 1965, two months before the promulgation of the conciliar text, the bishops of France after their plenary assembly in Rome published a communication to the effect that they were proposing to authorize with the consent of the Holy See "a small number of priests to work full time in factories and yards after a suitable period of preparation." The authorization for manual wage-work was called "an essentially priestly mission" and was to be for an initial period of three years. The Holy See laid down three conditions: (1) the priests must not have responsibility for any labor union activity; (2) they are not to live alone but in pairs or groups and together with other priests so as to avoid a contrast between two categories of priests; and (3) there should be in the same place lay members of the Workers' Catholic Action so that the Church may appear to the workers as it really is, "the laity with their temporal engagements and the priests with their spiritual engagement."[163]

The 1971 Synod of Bishops affirmed that as a general rule "the priestly ministry shall be a full-time occupation; sharing in the secular activities of men is by no means to be considered the principal end nor can such participation suffice to give expression to the priests' specific responsibility." In concrete circumstances it is up to the bishop with his presbyterium and, if necessary, in consultation with the episcopal conference to determine whether secular activity is in accord with the priestly ministry.[164]

Alien Activity

In addition to activities that are incompatible with the dignity of the clerical state there are occupations that are foreign to it, but some are not so irreconcilable that they can never be undertaken.

The 1917 Code (*CIC* 139) enumerated some of the professions that, though not considered debasing, were hardly congruous with the spiritual mission of the ministry.[165] Without an apostolic indult clerics were not to practice medicine or surgery, to function in the office of public notary except in ecclesiastical courts, to assume any public office involving the exercise of lay jurisdiction or administration. They were not, therefore, to be magistrates, judges, mayors, governors, or presidents of a country. In certain countries, there was a special prohi-

[159]*CLD* 4, 97–102.
[160]*CLD* 5, 200–205.
[161]P.-J. Cordes, Vorgrimler IV, 251.

[162]Ibid.
[163]*CLD* 6, 168–169.
[164]"The Ministerial Priesthood," Dec. 9, 1971 (*AAS* 63 [1971], 912; *The Catholic Mind* 70 [March 1972], 44–45).
[165]J. Brunini, *The Clerical Obligations of Canons 139 and 142, CanLawStud* 103 (Washington: Catholic University of America, 1937).

bition for clerics to hold legislative offices without permission of the Holy See.[166]

Without the permission of their ordinary, the canon continued, clerics were forbidden: (1) to undertake the administration of property that belongs to lay persons (the executor of a will); (2) to serve in an office that requires the rendering of an account (e.g., the manager of a bank or director of a cooperative union); (3) to act as an attorney in a civil court except in one's own case or in behalf of one's own church; (4) to take any part, even as a witness, without necessity, in a felony criminal trial; and (5) to run as a candidate or to serve in a legislative office. The Code Commission ruled that bishops should be severe in giving permission to priests who seek legislative positions.[167] Note that the 1917 law made a distinction between executive or administrative office and legislative office. Permission of the Holy See was required for a cleric to hold administrative office whereas the ordinary was competent, except where pontifical prohibition intervened, to allow a cleric to be a legislator.

In recent years there have been instances of priests holding public office. The most notable in the United States was Robert F. Drinan, a Jesuit from Massachusetts, who served ten years in the national House of Representatives. In May 1980 he withdrew his candidacy for another term in obedience to an order from the Jesuit superior general, Fr. Pedro Arrupe, which was given "at the express wish of his holiness, Pope John Paul II."[168] A few days later the apostolic delegate to the United States, Archbishop Jean Jadot, "exercising his own authority, barred Norbertine Fr. Robert J. Cornell, a professor at St. Norbert College in De Pere, Wisconsin, from running for Congress. Cornell had served two terms as representative from Wisconsin's Eighth Congressional District, had lost his seat in 1978, and was seeking to regain it."[169] A reporter listed several instances of priests who held political office but were not affected, at least immediately: a member of the Colorado state senate, a member of the county board of representatives in upstate New York, three members of the *Cortes Generales* in Spain, a mayor in a town in the province of Barcelona, and a Maryknoll priest who was foreign minister of Nicaragua.[170]

The question of the secular and political activity of priests was considered at the third general synod of bishops in "The Ministerial Priesthood," which Pope Paul VI made part of the Church's public law in 1971. That document stressed "the priority of the special mission which pervades the total existence of priests" and that "in the ordinary course of events full time should be given to the priestly ministry. . . . By no means is participation in the secular activities which men engage in to be held as the principal objective nor can it suffice to express the particular responsibility of priests." Priests were to be "mindful of the maturity of lay persons" and

highly value it when there is question of a special sphere in which they are versed. . . . Assumption of a role of leadership or a style of active militancy for some political faction must be ruled out by every priest unless in *concrete* extraordinary circumstances this is really demanded for the good of the community and has indeed the consent of the bishop after consultation with the priests' council and, if the case warrants, with the episcopal conference (*CLD* 7, 355–57).

Pope John Paul II indicated his view of such activity in an address to an international gathering of religious-order priests in Mexico City in January 1979: "You are priests and members of religious orders. You are not social directors, political leaders or functionaries of temporal power."[171] He noted that temporal leadership can easily become divisive whereas a priest must be a sign and factor of unity. Just at the time of the Drinan crisis the pope was speaking to the priests of Zaire. He exhorted them:

Leave political responsibilities to those who are charged with them. You have another part, a magnificent part, you are "leaders" by another right and in another manner, participating in the priesthood of Christ, as his ministers. Your sphere of interventions, and it is vast, is that of faith and morals, where it is expected that you

---

[166]The SCConc decreed on July 16, 1957 that priests in Hungary were not "to seek or accept the office of Deputy or any other office whatever." *CLD* 4, 102–103. The SCConc on Feb. 15, 1958 decreed under pain of excommunication ipso facto and specially reserved to the Holy See: "Priests both secular or religious in Hungary are forbidden to seek or accept the office of Deputy or any other office whatever in the Parliament." *CLD* 5, 199.

[167]Apr. 25, 1922, *CLD* 1, 127.

[168]Statement of Fr. Arrupe on May 22, 1980, *Origins* 10 (1980), 16. SCRIS, "Religious and Human Promotion," *CRUX* special edition, Dec. 7, 1981. Msgr. George Higgins has criticized "the precipitous and extremely awkward timing of the directive to Drinan" and "Rome's failure to issue even a brief and perfunctory statement outlining its own theological and pastoral rationale for the Drinan directive." He adds, "Rome also did itself a disservice by failing to explain the Drinan directive in terms that the general public could understand"; "Its failure to make that case pesuasively has also led many Americans . . . to conclude that Rome wants priests to withdraw not only from partisan political activity but from political activity of any kind at all and is opposed to any and all forms of clerical activism, even non-political activism, in support of justice and human rights" (*May Church Ministers Be Politicians? Con* 157, 1982, 82–86).

[169]*The* [*London*] *Tablet* 234 (July 5, 1980), 648.

[170]J. Deedy, "Priests in Politics," *The* [*London*] *Tablet* 234 (July 5, 1980), 648. Three priests in Nicaraguan cabinet posts were ordered to resign, *The Washington Post*, 19 Aug. 1984, p. A 22.

[171]*Origins* 8 (Feb. 15, 1979), 548–549; D. O'Connor, "Religious in Politics," *RfR* 41 (1982), 834–848.

preach at the same time by a courageous word and by the example of your life.[172]

The formulation of the 1983 Code underwent a number of significant changes.[173] The *Schema de Populo Dei* (c. 146, §2) stated: Let not bishops assume public offices, especially those that involve participation in the exercise of lay power without permission of the Holy See; similarly in areas where a pontifical prohibition is in effect other clerics need the license of the Holy See; in other places let clerics obtain the permission of their own ordinary and the ordinary of the place in which they intend to exercise power or administration. The 1980 draft (c. 260, §2) spoke of the "exercise of civil power" rather than "lay power."[174] The 1981 *Relatio* (p. 68) interpreted "civil power" to include legislative, administrative, and judicial authority. The 1983 text, however, rules definitively without qualification: "clerics are forbidden to hold public offices that call for the exercise of civil power." No distinction is made, unlike in the 1917 law, between executive and legislative power, between bishops and other clerics, or between places where a special pontifical prohibition exists and where it does not. The possibility of exceptions is not raised. Members of religious institutes (c. 672) and of societies of apostolic life (c. 739) are also bound by this canon.

In view of the elimination of the provision for an ordinary to grant permission for a cleric to hold public office, does a diocesan bishop have the authority to dispense from the law? According to the principle laid down in canon 87, §1, he may dispense from universal disciplinary laws as often as he judges it is for the spiritual good of the faithful and the matter has not been reserved to the Apostolic See. In the *motu proprio Episcoporum Muneribus,* Pope Paul VI specifically reserved to the Holy See any dispensation from the prohibition upon clerics "to assume public offices which involve the exercise of lay jurisdiction or administration" (IX, 3, b; *CLD* 6, 398). Insofar as the promulgation of the 1983 Code abrogates "other universal disciplinary laws dealing with a matter which is regulated *ex integro* by this Code" (c. 6, §1, 4°), the papal reservation of *Episcoporum Muneribus* ceases. The diocesan bishop is now competent, therefore, to dispense clerics or religious from the law prohibiting them from assuming "public offices which entail a participation in the exercise of civil power." For the present, however, it does seem to be the mind of the Holy See that bishops not exercise this dispensing

power, except perhaps for such local offices as membership on school boards of various comissions.

According to canon 285, §4, without the license of their ordinary, clerics are not to assume financial responsibility for the affairs of others. Since this canon repeats canon 139, §3 of the 1917 Code, it is to be similarly interpreted. The twofold purpose of this regulation, according to the older commentators, is to safeguard clerical decorum and to prevent distractions that would detract from ministerial performance.[175] They are not to manage the money or property of lay men. They need permission, therefore, to be guardians of children, executors of wills, or trustees of funds. They would, of course, be permitted to do so in case of relatives for whom they are responsible.[176] They must also have authorization to hold secular offices for which they are accountable, such as in a savings bank, a cooperative, or a charitable association. "The phrase 'rendering an account' applies not only to a reckoning of the goods or money involved, but may be concerned only with an account of the justice shown by the cleric in exercising such a secular office," as, for example, arbitrator in a labor dispute.[177] The off-cited commentator Cappello understands "secular office" to include in general all municipal duties that do not involve the exercise of lay jurisdiction or administration in the strict sense.[178]

Without consulting the ordinary, clerics are not: (1) to give bail even with their personal property as security and (2) to sign promissory notes obliging themselves to pay money without a determined purpose. The provision is more detailed than the corresponding one in the 1917 Code (*CIC* 137) but is not more extensive. The fact that "consultation" is called for does not mean that the cleric is free to go against the wishes of the ordinary. "It would be wholly novel in canon law for a cleric to be under obligation to seek the opinion of his superior and not to follow it. The authors teach, therefore, that a cleric cannot stand surety against the will of the ordinary."[179]

The *Schema de Populo Dei* included a fourth paragraph[180] inhibiting clerics from hailing anyone before a lay tribunal without the permission of their ordinary. Furthermore, they were to have no part in a lay criminal trial even to the extent of giving testimony without necessity. This prohibition was eliminated from the 1980 draft and the final text. The 1917 Code made no mention of a cleric's taking legal action against a lay man, but Third Baltimore strictly forbade clerics to take a lay man to

[172]*Origins* 19 (May 22, 1980), 11.
[173]The practice of medicine and surgery, proscribed in the corresponding paragraph of the 1917 Code, is not mentioned at all in the 1983 Code.
[174]The *Schema de Populo Dei* spoke of the *exercitio laicalis potestatis* (c. 146, §2). The *Relatio* (68) noted that *potestas civilis* was understood to include legislative, administrative, and judicial power.

[175]Augustine II, 86.
[176]Jone, 147.
[177]Brunini, *The Clerical Obligations of Canon 139*, 30.
[178]Cappello I, no. 233.
[179]Jone, 145.
[180]*Schema de Populo Dei*, c. 146, §4.

civil court for pew rent or any church debt without the written permission of the bishop (no. 84). "This decree seems completely inoperative. When civil action is necessary to insure payment, it is or should be undertaken."[181]

Business or Trade

Canon 286 — **Clerics are forbidden personally or through others to conduct business or trade either for their own benefit or that of others without the permission of legitimate ecclesiastical authority.**

Clerics are barred from engaging in business. An interpretation of this highly technical and complicated canon must begin with the commentators' understanding of the 1917 Code. The 1983 law is the same as the former (*CIC* 142) except for the provision that legitimate ecclesiastical authority may give permission for such activity. Clerics are prohibited from engaging in *negotiatio aut mercatura*.[182] While in practice most canonists treat the terms as synonymous, *negotiatio* refers to all business operations carried on for gain whereas *mercatura* is restricted to trading, i.e., the buying and selling of merchandise. The authors generally list five types of business enterprises.

(1) *Negotiatio lucrativa, mercatura* strictly socalled. Goods are bought with the intention of selling them unchanged for a profit whether or not in smaller quantities or newly packaged. Such activity is not lawful for clerics.

(2) *Negotiatio industrialis* or *artificialis* consists in buying materials with the intention of selling them later at a profit after they have been transformed and improved by one's own labor or by that of one's domestics or hired employees. As distinct from the first type, the intention from the beginning is to effect a change in the item purchased. While clerics are not allowed to profit from the sale of articles produced by paid labor, it is permissible to sell at a profit items made by themselves or by their students at a trade school. It is disputed whether they may own and operate a printing plant employing outside help. One may safely hold that such an enterprise is legitimate if the main objective is not profit but the apostolate of the press. "What is forbidden is not simply buying, nor simply selling, or trading or exchanging, not the making of a profit, but the practice of buying with the intention of selling a thing unchanged or changed by hired labor for profit alone."[183]

(3) *Negotiatio oeconomica* is a permissible activity. It "consists in the profitable manipulation of more or less permanent investments."[184]

Such a prudent management may entail actions which materially do not differ from forbidden acts of business dealing. The actions differ formally in that in illicit commerce there is the intention of profit for profit's sake, while in prudent management there is only the intention of improving or maintaining one's financial position for the sake of proper sustenance or for the support of the works of religion.[185]

It may be helpful to compare "economic" business with the first two categories. In all three there is purchase, sale and profit. In "economic" the article may have been left in its original state or improved before being sold, even with the aid of outside workers. "So the only difference lies in the initial intention when the commodity was bought. Here it is not profit-seeking, whereas that is the case of the other two forms."[186] A religious community, for example, may sell the produce of its land, even if employees do all the work. It may legitimately operate wineries but not if the grapes are purchased elsewhere. Similarly, a cleric is allowed to have his book printed commercially and then market it himself. He may also edit a magazine or newspaper, take charge of its distribution, and enjoy the profit. Land, houses, and farms may be purchased with the intention of renting them out later at a profit.

(4) *Negotiatio politica* or *publica* is

the buying of goods to be sold to a definite community, e.g., a parish, society, or students, not for a profit but for the convenience of the group. Some profit may be made on this material to cover the cost of handling and so on, but if notable profit is made and is not turned back to the benefit of the group, then this would hardly differ from forbidden lucrative business operations.[187]

Bookstores in schools and seminaries, lunchrooms and cafeterias, gift shops in hospitals, religious goods stands in shrines would fall into this category.

(5) *Negotiatio argentaria* includes the buying and selling of currency and of securities. Lucrative "trading in money is forbidden in all its forms: foreign exchange, travellers checks, letters

---

[181]D. Burns, "Committee Report on Legislation of Councils of Baltimore," *CLSAP* 31 (1969), 137.

[182]Members of religious institutes are under the same prohibition (c. 672). They are also bound by the provisions of cc. 285, 287, and 289.

[183]J. Dede, "Business Pursuits of Clerics and Religious: Further Considerations," *J* 23 (1963), 50–60, citation p. 53.

[184]Bouscaren-Ellis, 119.

[185]Dede, "Business Pursuits," 56.

[186]T. Smiddy, "Negotiatio," *J* 11 (1951), 486–519, citation p. 501.

[187]Dede, "Business Pursuits," 56–57.

of credit, etc."[188] With regard to stocks, a distinction must be made between speculation and investment. Investment is the purchase of stocks and bonds with the intention of receiving periodic income. Speculation is done not for the income but with the hope that the item purchased will rather quickly increase in value so that it can be resold for a profit. All speculation is forbidden to clerics, especially such a transaction as short-selling. In certain situations the difference between investment and speculation may not be too evident. "When economic conditions are unsettled one may have to keep a constant eye on the stock market and even be obliged to buy and sell rather frequently in order to protect his original investment. This need not make the operation a case of speculation."[189]

The canon forbids clerics to "conduct" ("exercere") business. According to the commentators the traditional meaning of *exercere* "requires a plurality of acts united morally through the agent's intention or, we might add, through their close proximity to one another. It is on this basis also that they teach that isolated acts do not result in a grave violation of the law."[190] A cleric may not engage in business either personally or through an agent; he is not allowed to commission an agent to carry on the operation in the cleric's name and at his risk. Clerics are forbidden, furthermore, to carry on such activity either for their own benefit or for that of other persons. Pope Clement IX in the seventeenth century inserted this clause in the law when missionaries turned to trading for profit as a means of supporting their work.[191] Even the intention to devote the proceeds to pious or charitable causes does not justify a cleric's engaging in business.

In 1950 the Sacred Congregation of the Council issued a very severe decree dealing with clerics and religious who conduct business or trade.[192] It cited the 1917 Code (*CIC* 2380) which stated: "Clerics or religious who, personally or through others, conduct commerce or trading in violation of the provisions of c. 142 are to be visited with appropriate penalties by the ordinary according to the gravity of the case." Accordingly, in order to establish a firmer and more uniform discipline and to forestall abuses, Pope Pius XII here legislated that all clerics and religious who violate canon 142 of the former law "shall incur, as being guilty of this crime, a *latae sententiae* excommunication specially reserved to the Holy See, and shall in a proper case be further punished by the penalty of degradation." The

promulgation of this automatic excommunication generated an extensive canonical literature.[193]

The 1983 Code dropped the automatic excommunication and has adopted the milder statement of 1917: "Clerics or religious who practice trade or business against the prescriptions of the canons are to be punished in accord with the seriousness of the offense" (c. 1392).

The law now makes explicit reference to the possibility of obtaining permission from "legitimate ecclesiastical authority" to engage in such activity. It was recognized in the past that in cases of necessity, either of the cleric himself or of his family, the ordinary could allow what would otherwise be forbidden.[194] If a cleric inherited or succeeded to a viable business that could not be laid aside without loss, permission of the Holy See should be obtained to continue it.[195] The *motu proprio Episcoporum Muneribus* of Pope Paul VI in 1966 declared reserved to the Holy See any dispensation for a cleric "to practice business or commerce, personally or through others, for their own advantage or that of other persons."[196] Since the restriction is not contained in the 1983 Code, the legitimate authority to grant such permission would be the ordinary.

Signs of Peace

Canon 287 — §1. Most especially, clerics are always to foster that peace and harmony based on justice which is to be observed among all persons.
§2. Clerics are not to have an active role in political parties and in the direction of labor unions unless the need to protect the rights of the Church or to promote the common good requires it in the judgment of the competent ecclesiastical authority.

The clergy are to be especially zealous promoters of peace. This canon is partly based on canon 141 of the 1917 Code, which forbade clerics to participate in any way whatever in civil conflict or public disturbances. The *Schema de Populo Dei* (c. 148) first affirmed the peacemaking obligation of clerics and then repeated the injunction against violence. The 1983 text is content with the positive statement of the clerical role: to foster a peace and concord *based on justice*.

In a new second paragraph, clerics are prohibited from taking part in factional politics and in the direction of labor unions unless necessary to protect church rights or the common good. The competent ecclesiastical authority to judge the necessity is not specified in the 1983 Code. In the *Schema de Populo Dei* (c. 148, §2) and in the 1980 draft (c. 262, §2) permission had to be obtained from the Holy

[188]Smiddy, "Negotiatio," 27.
[189]Ibid., 28.
[190]Ibid., 8.
[191]Clement IX, const. "Solicitudo" June 17, 1669 (*CICFontes* I, 400–401; 465–467).
[192]*CLD* 3, 68–69.

[193]J. Dede, "Business Pursuits," has assembled a bibliography, pp. 61–62.
[194]Bouscaren-Ellis, 119.
[195]Ibid.
[196]IX, 3, d; *CLD* 6, 398.

See in the case of bishops or in places where a pontifical ban is in effect; in other places and in the case of priests and deacons, both their own ordinary and the ordinary of the area where the activity is to occur had to approve. It is reasonable to interpret "competent ecclesiastical authority" in terms of these provisions and the magisterial statements below.

The Third Council of Baltimore legislated that priests were to refrain from discussing publicly, whether from the pulpit or outside, political or merely secular issues. They were not to be silent, however, about the citizen's most grave obligation to labor zealously in public affairs, always and everywhere according to the dictates of conscience, for the greater good of religion and of their country (no. 83). Clerics were recognized, of course, to have the duty of instructing people on religious and moral principles so that they could make informed political decisions.

The 1983 Code restriction on clerical participation in politics must be evaluated in terms of contemporary magisterial pronouncements. As a consequence of its mission to preach the gospel,

the Church has the right, indeed the duty, to proclaim justice on the social, national and international level, and to denounce instances of injustice, when the fundamental rights of man and his very salvation demand it. . . . Of itself it does not belong to the Church, insofar as she is a religious and hierarchical community, to offer concrete solutions in the social, economic and political spheres for justice in the world. Her mission involves defending and promoting the dignity and fundamental rights of the human person.[197]

The 1971 Synod of Bishops affirmed that priests have social and political responsibilities.

Together with the entire Church, priests are obliged, to the utmost of their ability, to select a definite pattern of action, when it is a question of the defense of fundamental human rights, the promotion of the full development of persons and the pursuit of the cause of peace and justice. . . . In circumstances in which there legitimately exist different political, social and economic options, priests like all citizens have a right to select personal options. But since political options are by nature contingent and never in an entirely adequate and perennial way interpret the gospel, the priest, who is the witness of things to come, must keep a certain distance from any political office or involvement. . . . Moreover, care must be taken lest this option appear to Christians to be the only legitimate one or become a cause of division among the faithful. . . . Leadership or active militancy on behalf of any political party is to be excluded by every priest unless, in concrete and exceptional circumstances, this is truly required by the good of the community, and receives the consent of the bishop after consultation with the priests' council and, if circumstances call for it, with the episcopal conference.[198]

Deacon's Obligations

Canon 288 — Permanent deacons are not bound by the prescriptions of cann. 284, 285, §§3 and 4, 286, 287, §2, unless particular law determines otherwise.

Permanent deacons are not bound by the prescriptions of clerical dress (c. 284), occupations foreign to the clerical state such as public office, administration of property belonging to the laity, positions requiring accountability (c. 285, §§3–4), business and trade (c. 286), and participation in partisan politics and acting as officials in labor unions (c. 287, §2). This canon did not appear at all in the *Schema de Populo Dei. Sacrum diaconatus,* the 1967 *motu proprio* restoring the permanent diaconate, provided: "care should be taken that deacons do not carry on a profession or trade which the local ordinary considers unsuitable or which will interfere with the fruitful exercise of their sacred office." The legislation is substantially the same as canon 285, §1 of the 1983 Code dealing with activities unbecoming to the clerical state that does obligate permanent deacons.

A number of objections were raised about including this canon in the Code. It seemed incongruous to some to exempt from clerical obligations those who were clerics. Since permanent deacons are constituted in the hierarchy of the Church, they represent it to the laity. It was proposed to frame the law positively: deacons are bound unless the legitimate authority of the Church in a concrete case should grant an exemption. Another proposal was to say "that they *are not bound* but that the ordinary considering attendant circumstances could prescribe otherwise." A third group thought that the canons dealing with clerical dress and business affairs should not apply but argued that permanent deacons not be involved in partisan politics or in running a union. The Secretariat of the Commission decided to maintain all the exemptions but to add a clause to the effect that these deacons were not bound unless particular law stated otherwise.[199]

[197]The 1971 Synod of Bishops, "Justice in the World," *The Catholic Mind* 70 (March 1972), 58; *AAS* 63 (1971), 932.

[198]"The Ministerial Priesthood," II, 1, 2 b; *AAS* 63 (1971), 912–913; *The Catholic Mind* 70 (March 1972), 44–45.
[199]*Rel*, 69.

Use of Exemptions

Canon 289 — §1. **Since military service is hardly consistent with the clerical state, clerics and candidates for sacred orders are not to volunteer for military service without the permission of their own ordinary.**

§2. Clerics are to make use of those exemptions from exercising duties and public civil offices alien to the clerical state which laws, agreements or customs grant in their favor, unless in particular cases their own proper ordinary has decided otherwise.

Clerics are to take advantage of any exemption granted to the clergy by civil law.

The 1917 Code (*CIC* 121) affirmed as a right or privilege belonging to clerics that they be immune from military service and from public civil offices that are alien to the clerical state. Then a later canon (*CIC* 141) forbade clerics to volunteer for service in the armed forces except in situations in which, with the permission of the ordinary, they could thereby be freed sooner from compulsory service. The *Schema de Populo Dei* (c. 149, §1) repeated the prohibition against clerics' volunteering for such service since it was incongruous with the clerical state. The schema added also that clerics and candidates for ordination must take advantage of any exemption from service that the civil law gives or has recognized in concordats. The 1983 Code states simply, without reference to the civil law, that clerics and candidates for ordination should not volunteer for military service without the permission of the ordinary. This canon applies to deacons as well as priests since no exclusion is made as in the previous canon. Church law in the past and at present does not prevent priests from acting as chaplains in the various branches of the service. Those who volunteer to be chaplains must have the permission of their ordinary or major religious superior.

Clerics are to take advantage also of all other exemptions from civic duties that the secular law, concordats, or custom might grant to the clergy as alien from their state, unless in particular cases their ordinary has judged differently. A cleric, therefore, ought not accept service on a grand or petit jury if federal or state law recognizes the ministry as an excusing cause.[200]

CHAPTER IV
LOSS OF THE CLERICAL STATE
[cc. 290–293]

The corresponding section of the 1917 Code was entitled "The Reduction of Clerics to the Lay State," thus implying the inferiority of the laity.

The insistence of the Second Vatican Council on the fundamental equality of all members of the Church necessitated more appropriate terminology (*LG* 32). The functional diversity among the people of God must be recognized without any trace of disparagement.[201]

In the 1917 Code there were several provisions for reduction to the lay state applicable to clerics in minor orders; however, after the suppression of tonsure and the minor orders by the *motu proprio Ministeria quaedam* in 1972, entrance into the clerical state came only with ordination to the diaconate. Subsequent law, therefore, is concerned only with those diaconal, presbyteral, or episcopal orders.

Under the 1917 Code, furthermore, it was necessary to distinguish three penalties that could be imposed on clerics but only for offenses expressly specified in law: deposition, deprivation of clerical garb, and degradation. Through deposition (*CIC* 2303) one was suspended from office and deprived of all dignities, benefices, and pensions. The penalty of deposition could be inflicted, for example, on a cleric guilty of procuring an abortion (*CIC* 2350, §1). Deprivation of the right to wear ecclesiastical garb, popularly known as defrocking, was either temporary or perpetual (*CIC* 2304); it could be enjoined on a deposed cleric who continued to give scandal and had the effect of revoking all clerical privileges. Degradation, the most serious penalty that could befall a cleric, included, in addition to deposition and deprivation of the right to wear ecclesiastical garb, the reduction to the lay state (*CIC* 2305). Degradation was to be imposed for such crimes as culpable homicide (*CIC* 2354), continuing in a civil marriage after being warned (*CIC* 2388) and publicly joining a non-Catholic sect (*CIC* 2314). The 1983 Code, while it has eliminated the three penalties just described, does provide the penalty of dismissal from the clerical state (c. 290, 2°).

Three Modes

Canon 290 — **After it has been validly received, sacred ordination never becomes invalid. A cleric, however, loses the clerical state:**

1° by a judicial decision or administrative decree which declares the invalidity of sacred ordination;

2° by the legitimate infliction of the penalty of dismissal;

3° by a rescript of the Apostolic See which is granted by the Apostolic See to deacons only for serious reasons and to presbyters only for the most serious reasons.

Canon 291 — **Besides the case mentioned in can. 290, n. 1, loss of the clerical state does not entail a**

---

[200]The scandal arising from the acquiescence of a sister on a jury voting for a death sentence April 6, 1981 is described by J. Betz, "A Sister in the Jury Box," *RfR* 41 (1982), 849–852.

[201]One of the principles guiding the revision of the Code emphasized this fundamental equality (*Comm* 1 [1969], 82–83; *Comm* 9 [1977], 245).

dispensation from the obligation of celibacy, which is granted by the Roman Pontiff alone.

The theological principle is first affirmed that sacred orders once received can never be rendered invalid. The sacrament of orders constitutes a person a sacred minister by conferring an indelible character (c. 1008). The power of orders once bestowed can never be lost or taken away. Though in certain circumstances the exercise of the power may be unlawful, it is never invalid.

One who has been ordained may, however, lose the juridical status of cleric so that he no longer has the right of lawfully exercising the power of orders he possesses. He thus forfeits the privileges of a cleric and reverts to his former condition of lay man. This canon lists three ways in which laicization may take place.

(1) One may lose the clerical state by having his orders declared invalid.

The requisites for valid ordination are specified in theology: the minister must have episcopal orders and the intention to ordain; the candidate must be a baptized male (c. 1024) and, if an adult, have the intention to receive the sacrament; the ordination must consist in an imposition of hands together with the prescribed prayer (c. 1009, §2). For all practical purposes any challenge to the validity of the ordination will focus on the intention of the candidate.[202] The procedure for establishing the nullity of ordination is laid down in canons 1708–1712.

Under the 1917 Code one could impugn not only the validity of the ordination itself but also the obligations that arose from a valid ordination on the ground that the individual had been coerced by grave fear.

In some cases grave fear may be so strong a factor as to preclude the use of reason on the part of the acting subject.[203] In such a case the ordination itself will be invalid, since the man has no free exercise of the will with which he can accept the reception of Orders. Usually, however, grave fear does not take away the use of reason. In consequence of this the will remains fundamentally free in the acceptance of the ordination. Hence the ordination is valid. Still the clear statement of canon 214 indicates that the cleric contracts no obligations from his ordination.[204]

The coercion and lack of subsequent ratification were to be proved in accordance with the 1917 procedure (*CIC* 1993–1998). The Congregation was to decide whether the investigation was to be made in a judicial or administrative form (*CIC* 1993, §1). In 1931 the Sacred Congregation of the Sacraments issued detailed rules to be observed in cases concerning the nullity of ordination or of the obligations inherent in sacred orders (*CLD* 1, 812–833).

To ensure that seminarians were thoroughly prepared for the commitment they were proposing to make, the Sacred Congregation of the Sacraments in 1930 and the Sacred Congregation of Religious in 1931 issued instructions to bishops and religious superiors (*CLD* 1, 463–482). Before presenting himself for each of the orders—subdiaconate, diaconate, and priesthood—the candidate had to make a declaration written in his own hand and confirmed by oath that he was receiving orders altogether freely and that he fully understood all the obligations annexed to the order (p. 469).

Since the instruction was not adequately observed, the Sacred Congregation of the Sacraments in 1955 circulated a letter to all local ordinaries (*CLD* 4, 303–315) in which it listed the principal grounds that were generally alleged when seeking nullity of sacred ordination or of the attached obligations. Some said that they went on to orders "without having duly looked into its prescriptions and without having sufficiently weighed the business of their vocation." Others maintained that coming from a poor family they were sent by their parents or parish priest to the seminary at an early age with the result that they had "a very vague notion of the ecclesiastical vocation" and "accommodated themselves in a bewildered fashion to the state in which they found themselves." Others claimed "undue influence by parents or close relatives: importunate and repeated entreaties, exhortations, and sometimes even serious threats." They were urged to enroll in the ranks of the clergy because of temporal advantages "which would accrue to them and their relatives." "But by far the greater source of complaint is brought out by priests who

---

[202]The Sacred Roman Rota decided in 1928: "For the valid reception of orders a *genuine intention,* at least habitual, is requisite. Hence, if one's intention is simulated, the almost common opinion of theologians holds that the ordination is invalid (contra, Gasparri, *De Ordinatione* I, no. 643). To this common opinion this court adheres" (*CLD* 2, 554).

[203]Again in 1928 the Rota decided: "If one receives sacred orders under grave fear applied by an external agent directly for the purpose of compelling the person to receive orders, the orders are considered valid—since the intention to receive them is not absolutely wanting—but the person will be relieved of the obligations of orders, especially that of chastity.... The canon does not use the term, *ab extrinseco,* but it does say *coactus,* which clearly supposes fear injected from without. It is certain that the fear must be extrinsic" (*CLD* 2, 555–556).

[204]F. Sweeney, *The Reduction of Clerics to the Lay State,* Can-LawStud 223 (Washington: Catholic University of America, 1945), 143. It was the practice of the SCSacr at least since 1960 to consider three questions: (1) whether the *nullity* of sacred orders is established; (2) whether because of *grave fear* the cleric is to be reduced to the lay state without the obligation of celibacy and the Divine Office; (3) whether there is grave *doubt* of the validity of orders or of the grave fear or of other causes so that a recommendation is to be made to the Holy Father for a dispensation from the obligations (*CLD* 5, 211–212).

contend that they have suffered psychic illnesses in the matter of sex. . . . They depict themselves as having an unconquerable and, as it were, a constitutionally bodily proneness toward sensual craving" (p. 308). The document concluded that the earlier instruction was to be read to the seminarians each year, that lectures be given on the instruction, especially by the professors of moral theology when explaining the treatise on orders, and that students be examined on it before receiving the individual orders.

If a priest were later to allege that he took orders under the compulsion of grave fear, he was to be confronted with the sworn declaration in his own hand. Similarly, those who were present at the examination and passed judgment in his favor would have to be questioned (*CLD* 7, 1007–1008).

When after the Second Vatican Council Pope Paul VI reorganized the Roman Curia in the apostolic constitution *Regimini Ecclesiae Universae* (1967), it was provided that the Sacred Congregation for the Discipline of the Sacraments would have competence "to oversee the obligations attached to major orders and to examine questions on the validity of sacred ordination, or to pass such questions on to the competent tribunal, after consulting, if necessary, with the Sacred Congregation for the Doctrine of the Faith."[205] The 1983 Code (c. 360) does not lay down the competency of the various dicasteries of the Curia but leaves the matter to special law. Consequently canon 1709, providing for the resolution of cases regarding the validity of orders, directs simply that the petition be sent to the competent congregation. That congregation will determine whether to handle the case administratively or to designate a tribunal to hear it.

It is to be noted that, unlike in the former Code, this judicial or administrative procedure is limited to cases concerned with the validity of orders, not with the obligations assumed under the pressure of grave fear. The *Schema de Populo Dei* had provided for a dismissal from the clerical state by a judicial sentence or administrative decree in the case of a cleric who because of grave fear or other serious cause did not enjoy due liberty in receiving orders or who is proved to have a serious infirmity that made him incapable of accepting and fulfilling celibacy (c. 151).[206] This canon was eliminated from the 1980 draft. At the final plenarium of the Congregation a proposal was made to reintroduce the provisions of the 1917 Code regarding grave fear upon the reception of orders and the obligations attached. The proposal was overwhelmingly rejected

"since it was considered preferable to leave such a determination to the process of dispensation by the Holy See rather than to a judicial sentence or administrative decree."[207]

(2) A second way the clerical state may be lost is through the penalty of dismissal.

Under the 1917 Code a major cleric could be reduced to the lay state by way of penalty only through degradation; nowhere was reduction to the lay state mentioned as a distinct penalty. (There were instances, however, of the pope's acting over and above the law to do so.)[208] There was no crime in law that automatically effected degradation; the penalty had always to be inflicted.

In the 1983 Code one of the expiatory penalties provided is dismissal from the clerical state (c. 1336, §1, 5°). An expiatory penalty is one that looks not to the correction of the offending party but to the repair or compensation of damage done to the ecclesial order. The penalty of dismissal is never automatic but must always be inflicted (c. 1336, §2). It is limited to those cases explicitly specified in the Code; particular law may not make use of this sanction (c. 1317). Insofar as it is a permanent penalty, it cannot be imposed or declared by a decree (c. 1342, §2). (See the commentary on "Penal Procedure," cc. 1717–1731.) Unlike with other penalties inflicted on a cleric, in situations of penal dismissal the ordinary is not obliged to see that he not lack those things that are necessary for his decent support; but if he is truly in need due to the penalty, the ordinary should see to his care in the best manner possible (c. 1350).

The 1983 Code specifies dismissal from the clerical state for the following crimes: (1) protracted contumacy or grave scandal in connection with apostasy, heresy, or schism (c. 1364, §2); (2) sacrilegious treatment of the consecrated species (c. 1367); (3) the use of physical force against the Roman Pontiff (c. 1370, §1); (4) solicitation in connection with confession (c. 1387); (5) continuance in civil marriage after warnings (c. 1394, §1); (6) concubinage or other state of external sexual sin (c. 1395, §1); (7) sexual sin with force or threats or publicly or with someone under sixteen years of age (c. 1395, §2).

The 1977 *Schema de Populo Dei* provided in addition to an inflicted penal dismissal that the clerical state could be lost "*ipso iure* in cases specified by law" (c. 150, 1°). This clause was suppressed because there are no cases in which one is dismissed from the clerical state *ipso iure* (*Comm* 14 [1982], 86). The 1977 schema also listed "a decree of dismissal from the clerical state *ex officio* issued ac-

[205]*CLD* 6, 336. The practice is for petitions concerning religious clerics to be decided first by the SCSacr. The Congregation reported that in 1981 there was only one petition regarding the nullity of ordination (L'attività della Santa Sede nel 1981, p. 819).

[206]*Comm* 3 (1971), 197.

[207]J. Alesandro, "Summary Report on Plenary Session . . . Oct. 20–29, 1981," p. 5, no. 28.

[208]*AAS* 30 (1938), 274; *CLD* 3, 76–77, 393–394; *CLD* 8, 1199.

cording to the norm of law" (c. 150, 4°). Episcopal conferences were asked to suggest grounds "based on pastoral reasons for concluding that a cleric, even apart from a delict punishable in penal law by dismissal from the clerical state, may be dismissed *ex officio*" (c. 150, 4°, n. 32). It was objected, however, that such a dismissal would be open to abuse; human rights should be safeguarded from administrative discretion; there should be some specificity of cause and procedure (*Comm* 14 [1982], 87). Accordingly, this clause also was eliminated from the 1980 draft and the 1983 Code.

(3) A third way the clerical state may be lost is through a rescript of laicization granted by the Apostolic See.

Although little employed or commented upon, there was provision in the 1917 Code for a reduction to the lay state by means of a rescript from the Holy See (*CIC* 211). This recourse was available, for instance, when it seemed prudent that a subdeacon or deacon should not be advanced to the priesthood (1931 Instr., nn. 14–17; *CLD* 1, 470). The rescript did not necessarily dispense from the obligation of celibacy (*CIC* 213). In fact, the law clearly held that a cleric in major orders who was laicized was still bound by obligations of celibacy (*CIC* 213, §2).

The 1977 schema proposed that upon his request a cleric could lose the clerical state through a rescript of the Apostolic See after consultation with the cleric's proper ordinary; it would be granted in the case of a deacon only for serious reasons and in the case of a priest for the most serious reasons after a suitable time of probation (c. 150, §3). The *Relatio* (p. 70) eliminated the phrase "at the request of the cleric himself" because a rescript can be granted by competent authority no matter who initiates the petition (i.e., the bishop in the case of an unworthy cleric) without the consent of the person involved (c. 61).

The 1983 Code calls for serious reasons in the case of a deacon. Laicizations have been given in situations in which involvement in the ministry threatened to break up a marriage, in cases of sickness and of individuals who were poorly screened, and for widowers who wished to remarry.[209] It should be noted that for permanent deacons celibacy is not usually the issue.

Dispensation from Celibacy

Even though according to canon 291 of the revised Code laicization does not entail a dispensation

from celibacy, a dispensation from celibacy does carry with it a return to the lay state (rescript issued in accordance with the 1980 "Procedural Norms Regarding a Dispensation from Priestly Celibacy" [*CLD* 9, 99]). In the case of priests the two issues can hardly be considered separately. In 1936 a decree of the Sacred Penitentiary stated, "The law of sacred celibacy for the Latin clergy has always been and is now so treasured by the Church that, in the case of priests, dispensation from it was hardly ever granted in times past, and according to present discipline is never given, not even in danger of death" (*CLD* 2, 579–580). Writing in 1963 the American canonist Abbo speculated, "Is there any probability that the Church, in the future, may show greater leniency to lapsed priests, especially those who have attempted marriage and are unwilling to renounce 'conjugal life'?" He concluded that "at present, there is no indication of any substantial change in the praxis followed by the Holy See."[210]

Even as these lines were written, however, the practice of the Holy See had already begun to change. Pope Pius XII after World War II conceded a few dispensations in cases of lapsed priests "who should never have been ordained." Figures later published indicate that dispensations from the obligations of celibacy were being given.[211] From 1939 through 1963 there were 315 instances.[212] In 1962, for example, 31 priests were so released. With the Vatican Council the number exploded, reaching 1,189 in 1965.

The new policy was quietly made known to local ordinaries and superiors general of religious families in a letter of February 2, 1964 (*CLD* 7,1002–1015). A special commission was set up in the Holy Office (later called the Sacred Congregation for the Doctrine of the Faith) with exclusive competence over every case regarding ordination and its obligations. A questionnaire was appended for the type of information to be gathered at the local scene and transmitted to the commission for a solution. The ordinary of the place of habitual residence of the petitioner was to constitute a tribunal composed of a judge, a defender of the bond of sacred ordination, and a recorder to draw up the process in a judicial form. The interrogatory of the petitioner consisted of twenty-seven articles; the "judicial examination" of his parents twenty-two articles and that of the witnesses thirty-two articles.

The commission was also to "consider the cases of those priests who are already involved in concu-

---

[209]In the U.S. as of Oct. 31, 1982 there were 5,886 permanent deacons (*Diaconal Quarterly* 9 [1983], 22). Since the inception of the program in 1971 through July 1983 there have been only 18 laicizations.

[210]J. Abbo, "The Problem of Lapsed Priests," *J* 23 (1963), 153–179, citation at 171.

[211]*AdDocVat* II (*Praeparatoria*), vol. II, pars IV, 409–410. E. Colagiovanni, *Le defezioni da ministerio sacerdotale. Sacra Congregazione per la Dottrina della Fede* (Tipografia Poliglotta Vaticana, 1971), 34, cited in V. Mallon, "Easy Exit for Priests?" *HPR* 78 (May 1978), 14–26.

[212]E. Colagiovanni, "De dispensatione a caelibatu sacerdotali juxta novas normas," *ME* 106 (1981), 227–228.

binage or in attempted civil marriage and whose age is sufficiently advanced and whose true condition is hardly known." Upon favorable recommendation and approval of the Holy Father the commission "will communicate to the said ordinaries the faculty to officiate at a marriage of conscience for such priests." The marriage was to be celebrated "in the presence of the local Ordinary himself without witnesses and notary and its record must be preserved in the secret archives of the curia and notice of it sent to the Holy Office." These provisions were to be "communicated only to the local Ordinaries and the Superiors General of religious families who will use them cautiously and prudently with a serious obligation in conscience to observe secrecy."

The original purpose of the relaxation of discipline seems to have been a pastoral solution for priests who over the years had left without leave, married, and were now anxious to be reconciled. As the number of dispensations increased, it became impossible to keep the new development secret; soon those recently ordained sought to be dispensed. "Whether it had been foreseen that the dispensations offered to forgive mistakes of decades past would be seized upon by priests in active service as a solution of their routine personal problems is a moot question. The fact is they were."[213] Over the next seven years there were roughly thirteen thousand dispensations granted in response to fourteen thousand petitions. Difficulties with celibacy were alleged in eighty-five percent of the cases.[214]

In January 1971 the Sacred Congregation for the Doctrine of the Faith, recognizing that secrecy was impractical, issued "Norms for Preparing in Diocesan and Religious Curias Cases of Reduction to the Lay State Together with a Dispensation from the Obligations Connected with Sacred Ordination" (CLD 7, 110–124). Bishops and superiors were exhorted to try every means to help the petitioner to overcome the difficulties he was experiencing before accepting a petition for laicization. In an accompanying letter the principal differences from the 1964 norms were explained. (1) In place of the "judicial process" a more pastoral and simple investigation is to take place. The purpose is to discover whether the reasons alleged in the petition for a dispensation from celibacy are valid and the assertions based on truth. (2) The ordinary entrusted with the investigation is the proper ordinary of the petitioner, whether diocesan or religious; but if that ordinary is at a distance, he may ask by a formal letter the ordinary of the place where the petitioner resides to carry out the investigation. (3) In the Congregation the documents forwarded will be examined quickly and if ratified a dispensation will be sought at once from the Holy Father. (4) The re-

script will be communicated to the ordinary of incardination or religious profession. (5) The competent ordinary has the faculty to dispense "from the obligation which, to this time, has been exceedingly strict, of maintaining secrecy regarding the dispensation and the canonical celebration of marriage" (p. 120). (6) The conditions to be observed by the dispensed priest were reviewed by several dicasteries and ratified by the Holy Father in a special act. As a general rule, a dispensed priest must stay away from places where his priestly status is known, but the ordinary can dispense if scandal is not feared. In addition to the prohibition to exercise any function of sacred orders, he may not have any liturgical part in celebrations with the people where his condition is known and must never give the homily. He may not function as an administrator or teacher in seminaries, theological faculties, and similar institutions. He may not discharge the functions of director of a Catholic school, or teacher of religion in any kind of school, whether Catholic or not.

On the other hand, the local ordinary, according to his own prudent judgment, can, in particular cases, permit a priest who has been reduced to the lay state and dispensed from the obligations connected with sacred ordination to teach religion in public schools and, by way of exception, also in Catholic schools provided that no scandal or wonderment is to be feared.

Since some questions or difficulties about these norms were raised, the Congregation issued a "declaration" regarding their interpretation on June 26, 1972 (CLD 7, 121–124). The Congregation first expressed concern that petitions were being processed too quickly. There had been instances of the priest's revoking his petition while the case was actually being considered in the Congregation. Other priests did not want to accept the rescript after it had been granted. There were also some who after marriage in the Church had broken their marriage loyalty. "The new norms do not have as their purpose the indiscriminate granting of the favor of dispensation to anyone who requests it but only the reduction to a simpler form of the investigations to be carried out by the Ordinaries" (p. 122).

The Congregation pointed out that the personal interrogation of the petitioner was the main element of the investigation: his difficulties before ordination, mistakes of superiors in judging his vocation; his failure after ordination to adjust to the sacred ministry; crisis in spiritual life, errors regarding celibacy and priesthood.[215] These problems had to be substantiated by other forms of testimony and by the ordinary's own opinion with regard to

---

[213]V. Mallon, "Easy Exit for Priests?" p. 18.
[214]E. Colagiovanni, ME, 227–228.

[215]Approved sample questionnaires for priest-religious may be found in CLD 8, 174–179.

the request itself. The Congregation insofar as it had to consider the good of the Church universal and preserve intact the law of sacred celibacy rejected certain reasons as invalid: (a) the simple wish to marry; (b) contempt for the law of sacred celibacy; (c) attempted civil marriage or a date established for the celebration of marriage with the hope of thus obtaining a dispensation more easily. Ordinaries were told not to submit petitions supported only by these reasons, especially if the priest had received ordination just a few years before.

Ordinaries were told they could not apply canon 81 of the 1917 Code to dispense from celibacy when recourse to the Holy See was difficult and grave harm would result from delay. The dispensation was reserved solely and personally to the Supreme Pontiff (*mp EM*, no. IX, I). Any marriage to a person in Holy Orders, therefore, that was celebrated without a dispensation from the Holy See lacked all validity.

The rescript of reduction and dispensation from clerical obligations took effect from the moment of notification on the part of the ordinary. The Holy See communicated the dispensation to the ordinary, rather than directly to the petitioner, so that the ordinary could take the occasion to encourage the latter to lead a Christian life. If the petitioner expressed a reluctance to accept the rescript, he was still suspended by law and the Congregation had to be consulted for readmission to the clerical state.

The declaration then proceeded to give an interpretation of "similar institutions" in the prohibition of a dispensed priest to function as "rector (or any other administrative officer), spiritual director, or teacher in seminaries, theological faculties, and similar institutions." Included were: faculties, institutes, schools, etc., of ecclesiastical or religious sciences (e.g., faculties of canon law, missiology, church history, philosophy, or pastoral institutes of religious or catechetical education). The dispensation would not be granted until the petitioner retired from any teaching function in such institutions. Also included in the ban were

all other centers of higher studies, even those not strictly dependent upon Church authority, in which theological or religious disciplines are also taught. In these institutes disciplines which are technically theological or closely connected with them (e.g., religious and catechetical education) may not be entrusted to the above-mentioned dispensed priests (pp. 122–123).

The 1971 norms had been in effect for about eight years when John Paul II was elected pope. He was disturbed by the large number of priests requesting dispensation from the obligations that arise from ordination—especially that of celibacy. He, therefore, "from the very beginning of his su-

preme apostolic ministry came to the conclusion that it is necessary to initiate an investigation concerning this situation, its causes, and suitable remedies to be employed for it." As a result of this mature deliberation new norms were promulgated on October 14, 1980. For the first time, in addition to procedural rules, norms are given for the adjudication of this issue. Though more restrictive than the previous practice, there is an element of due process in that criteria are established that had not existed heretofore.

With the exception of cases dealing with priests who have left the priestly life for a long period of time and who hope to remedy a state of affairs which they are not able to quit, the Congregation for the Doctrine of the Faith shall in processing the examination of petitions sent to the Apostolic See accept for consideration the cases of those who should not have received priestly ordination because the necessary aspect of freedom or responsibility was lacking or because the competent superiors were not able within an appropriate time to judge in a prudent and sufficiently fitting way whether the candidate really was suited for continuously leading a life of celibacy dedicated to God.

Care was to be taken that "a dispensation from celibacy not be considered as a right which the Church must recognize indiscriminately as belonging to all its priests. . . . On the other hand, what is to be considered as being a true right is that one which a priest through his oblation has conferred upon Christ and upon all the people of God." Certainly to be avoided is the "notion that a dispensation from celibacy in recent times can be considered to be the result of some quasi-automatic summary administrative process."

As the drafts of the revised law progressed, dispensation from the law of celibacy was tightened. The 1977 *Schema de Populo Dei* stated that a cleric who loses the clerical state according to the norm of law is not bound by any obligations proper to the clerical state (c. 153). The 1980 draft, however, stipulated that loss of the clerical state does not entail dispensation from the obligation of celibacy which only the Roman Pontiff may grant (c. 266).[216] The 1983 Code in canon 291 has definitively determined that one who is laicized is still bound by celibacy unless specifically released by the Holy See.

Even though loss of the clerical state does not in

---

[216]The 1980 draft (cc. 266, 1032) allowed in danger of death for the ordinary or, if he could not be reached, the pastor or other sacred minister to dispense from the impediment of orders to validate a marriage. The 1983 Code (cc. 291, 1079) eliminated any faculty for anyone less than the Holy Father to dispense from the impediment of orders.

itself free one from the obligations of celibacy, the rescript dispensing from celibacy does include laicization. The policy of the Holy See regarding dispensations from celibacy that was announced in October 1980 remains in effect after the promulgation of the 1983 Code (see c. 6). Such dispensations from priestly celibacy are granted in only three situations:

(1) an individual who has been away from the priestly life for a long period and cannot change his condition;

(2) one who should not have been ordained because the necessary freedom or responsibility was lacking;

(3) one whose superior failed to judge that he was unsuited for making a lifelong commitment to celibacy.

The case of one who has been away from the priestly life *for a long time* and who hopes to remedy a state of affairs he cannot quit is precisely the one envisaged by Pius XII and John XXIII in providing a dispensation process. The interpretation of a "long time" (*iamdiu*) is very strict, reportedly twenty years, except in circumstances such as terminal illness. (In danger of death a dispensation has even been granted by telephone.) The refusal to consider a petition unless the priest has been away for a long time is in view of seminary formation. For the good of the program, candidates for the priesthood must be impressed with the firmness of the commitment they are expected to make. Another reason for requiring a lengthy period is that in the past a number of those who sought dispensations later changed their minds.

Procedural norms have been established for petitioning a dispensation from celibacy.[217] The competent authority to initiate the process is the ordinary of the place where the cleric is incardinated or the major superior of the religious institute to which he belongs. If the proper ordinary is unable to handle the case, the ordinary of the place where the petitioner habitually resides can be requested to do so. For a proportionate reason the Sacred Congregation for the Doctrine of the Faith can delegate another ordinary.

The petitioner should first file a signed statement in which he presents general information about himself, indicating the facts and arguments on which he bases his request. The ordinary is then to decide whether to proceed further. If he agrees to do so, he is to prohibit the petitioner from exercising sacred orders unless he judges the reputation of the individual or the good of the community would be harmed. The ordinary is then to carry out an investigation either personally or through a specially designated priest. A notary should be appointed to authenticate the acts of the case.

The bishop or his priest-delegate will interrogate the petitioner under oath according to a questionnaire drawn up for the case at hand. All relevant information with specific dates should be solicited: family background, manner of life, studies, examination before ordination or religious profession, record of priestly ministry, present juridical status (both canonical and civil), the causes and circumstances of leaving the active ministry, and the factors that could have affected the assumption of the clerical obligations. It is significant to note anything in the family background that may suggest instability, such as divorce.

If possible, the superiors of the cleric during his period of formation are to be questioned or required to submit a written deposition. They should be asked whether questions were raised about the candidate's readiness for ordination and what steps were taken to resolve the doubts. In establishing the priest's lack of readiness, a professional psychological evaluation is advisable. Other witnesses suggested by the petitioner or by the one investigating the case are to be heard. Information from seminary professors, priest-peers, and chancery officials may be very useful. Relevant documents relating to the cleric's career are to be assembled.

All the documents are then to be transmitted in triplicate to the Sacred Congregation for the Doctrine of the Faith, along with any notations that might be helpful in assessing the evidence. A statement of the ordinary must be appended in which he states his opinion about the validity of the petition and the likelihood of any scandal.

For those charged with preparing a case of this kind, several practical suggestions may be offered. The petition should be expressed in a suppliant manner, not as if demanding a right. Real proof is needed to substantiate the fact of the unsuitability of the petitioner; the mere endorsement of the bishop is not sufficient. The investigation is to focus on the time frame of the ordination. It must be established that the candidate was not then in a condition to assume the obligations—not that he changed his mind some years later. An analogy may be drawn with the process followed in seeking a dispensation from a non-consummated marriage (cc. 1697–1706). It is recommended to affix a table of contents so that it will be readily apparent that all necessary documentation has been included. The Congregation will then be in a position to respond more expeditiously. In several cases in which the unreadiness for ordination was convincingly presented, the dispensation was granted within two months.

---

[217]*CLD* 9, 96–99. The norms accompanied the announcement of the new policy Oct. 1980.

Effects of Laicization

Canon 292 — **A cleric who loses the clerical state in accord with the norm of law also loses with it the rights which pertain to the clerical state; nor is he bound by any of the obligations of the clerical state, with due regard for the prescription of can. 291; he is prohibited from exercising the power of orders with due regard for the prescription of can. 976; and by the very fact he is deprived of all offices, functions and any delegated power.**

As a result of laicization a cleric loses all rights that pertain to the clerical state; he becomes in the eyes of the Church and for legal effects a lay man. In general he is no longer ranked or recognized as among the sacred ministers of the Church (c. 1008). As the previous chapter indicates, specifically clerical rights are not easily identified. Although no special canon of the 1983 Code forbids the laity to wear clerical garb (unlike *(CIC* 683), for one who has lost the clerical state to dress as a cleric would amount to deception. Similarly, the former cleric must give up use of such titles as "Father" or "Reverend." He can no longer claim financial support from the Church (c. 281); if someone, however, were rendered truly indigent through a penal dismissal, the ordinary should see to it in the best way possible that care is provided (c. 1350, §2). Another right that is lost is that of belonging to clerical associations (c. 278, §1). One who is laicized would also lose any right of suffrage he might have enjoyed as a cleric in a diocese. Obviously any exemptions granted by civil law to clerics, for example, regarding military service, would also cease (c. 289, §§1–2).

The most significant effect of a return to the lay state is the prohibition of exercising the power of orders. As has been noted, the power of orders once received cannot be taken away so as to render the person "unordained." No action can be taken that would make the exercise of orders invalid. In fact, the Church provides in canon 976 that in danger of death anyone who has been ordained a priest may give sacramental absolution of sins and censures even if an approved priest is present. Except in this extreme situation, however, it is unlawful for a laicized cleric to use his orders. He is not, above all, to celebrate the liturgy or confect the sacraments.

While a cleric cannot be deprived of the power of orders but only prohibited from using them (c. 1338, §2), he can be deprived of any offices, functions (*munera*), or delegated power he may possess. Such deprivation occurs automatically with loss of the clerical state. An "office" is a function that is stably or indefinitely constituted for a spiritual purpose (see c. 145). A *munus* is an assignment or task that lacks the permanent quality of an office. In canon 274, §2, for example, it is said that a cleric is bound to undertake any *munus* that the ordinary

commits to him. Delegated power is conveyed apart from orders or office (c. 137, §1). These distinctions are also found in the penalty of clerical suspension that can forbid all or some acts of: (1) the power of orders; (2) the power of governance; (3) the rights or functions (*munera*) inhering in an office (c. 1333, §1). There are also expiatory penalties that can punish a cleric in perpetuity or for a time: deprivation of power, office, function (*munus*), right, privilege, faculty, favor, title, or insignia even honorary (c. 1336, §1, 2°). After the 1980 draft had been critiqued, the Commission Secretariat included the "canonical mission" among those deprivations effected by loss of the clerical state (*Rel,* p. 70). The case in mind was a professor of sacred theology (c. 812). Evidently *munera* in the final text was considered sufficient for the purpose of withdrawing an ecclesiastical mandate to teach.

Another effect of the loss of the clerical state is to free the individual from all clerical obligations except that of celibacy. Canon 291 had already provided that except in a case in which the ordination was declared invalid, the return to the lay state did not include a dispensation from the obligations of celibacy which was reserved to the Roman Pontiff. The previous chapter has treated the special obligations of the clergy (cc. 273–289). A laicized cleric henceforth is bound only by the duties incumbent upon the Christian laity.

Dispensation from Celibacy

When the 1980 norms on the dispensation from celibacy (which entails loss of the clerical state) were circulated to the ordinaries of the world, a sample rescript was attached that listed a number of restrictions on former clerics.[218] Rescripts from the Sacred Congregation for the Doctrine of the Faith continue to use the same formula. Insofar as these prohibitions are not a matter of general law but of administrative decree (c. 59, §1), the diocesan bishop may not dispense from them except where explicitly noted (c. 87, §1).

According to the rescript of dispensation from celibacy currently issued, a dispensed cleric may not give a homily at the liturgy or function as an extraordinary minister of the Eucharist. The 1971 norms[219] forbade him to take *any* liturgical part in celebrations with the people where his condition was known. One of the purposes was to avoid giving rise to confusion among the people as to whether he was functioning as a cleric or as a lay man. Since present policy permits the bishop to dispense from any restrictions on residence in the absence of scandal, the dispensed cleric in that circumstance could fulfill any liturgical function open to a lay

[218]Ibid., 100–101.
[219]*CLD* 7, 116.

man except to distribute Holy Communion; he could now, for example, act as lector.

The rescript also forbids a dispensed cleric to perform any *directive* office in the pastoral field. The previous norms prohibited him from holding *any* pastoral office. Apparently, a dispensed cleric may now be given a pastoral responsibility open to a lay man that does not involve a participation in the power of governance or a leadership position. He could, for instance, teach in the religious education program of a parish but not be the director.

A dispensed cleric may not perform any function whatever in a seminary or equivalent institution, such as a religious house of studies. Here there is no change from the earlier norms. He may not be a rector, spiritual director, professor, or hold any administrative post. Evidently the preparation of candidates to assume the commitment of sacerdotal celibacy would be compromised by having a dispensed priest on the staff.

In other institutions of higher studies[220] under ecclesiastical control, one who is dispensed may not function in a directive office or as a teacher. Here the prohibition is much broader than in the 1971 norms which drew a distinction between faculties, institutes or schools of the ecclesiastical sciences (theology, canon law, missiology, church history, philosophy, religious and catechetical education) and other centers of higher studies.[221] In the former, no teaching function could be entrusted to dispensed priests; in the latter, they could not teach "disciplines which are technically theological or closely connected with them." The current rescript does not make any distinction. In all Church-related institutions of higher learning a dispensed cleric may not perform a directive or teaching function. Unlike in seminaries, however, he may hold a position on the administrative or supportive staff.

The restriction is more limited in institutions of higher learning that are not dependent upon ecclesiastical authority. There the dispensed cleric is excluded only from a discipline that is properly theological or closely connected with the theological disciplines. Nothing prevents him from teaching in the humanities or the social and physical sciences. He may also hold any administrative post.

With regard to elementary or high schools under ecclesiastical control, one who has been dispensed may not exercise a directive or teaching function. The local ordinary may, however, if he judges it will not cause scandal, permit a former cleric to teach but not to be the principal or other administrative official. Here again the present practice is more severe than in 1971 when only the teaching of religion was barred.

In non-Catholic or public schools a dispensed cleric is restricted only in the teaching of religion. Once again the local ordinary in the absence of scandal may allow him to do so.

As previously noted, one dispensed from priestly celibacy, especially a priest who has married, must not live in places where his former status is known. Nevertheless the local ordinary of the place where the petitioner lives, after consulting the ordinary of incardination or the major religious superior, may dispense from this clause of the rescript if no scandal is foreseen.

Return to the Active Ministry

Canon 293 — A cleric who has lost the clerical state cannot become a member of the clergy again without a rescript of the Apostolic See.

The 1917 Code had provision for a cleric in major orders who had been reduced to the lay state to return to the clerical state with the permission of the Holy See (*CIC* 212, §2). Yet it was the practice of the Roman Curia to include in the rescript granting the reduction the phrase "without hope of readmission to the clerical state."[222] The Holy Office did permit a priest who upon an attempted marriage was reduced to the lay status to return to the clerical state after a long period of penance.[223]

With the phenomenal rise in the number of laicizations after Vatican Council II it was inevitable that there would be petitions to reverse the process. The Sacred Congregation for the Doctrine of the Faith in its 1972 declaration warned ordinaries to be very solicitous about priests who were experiencing vocational problems lest they act precipitously and seek a dispensation without objectively serious reasons.

As a matter of fact, especially in the very recent past, some

who had demanded a dispensation because of a sudden crisis, later revoked their own petition when the case was already being considered by this Sacred Department. Yet others, after the rescript of the already granted favor had been communicated to them, moved by divine grace and tortured with pangs of conscience, were unwilling to accept it in order that they might continue to exercise their priesthood. Finally, there are some who after having obtained the dispensation and contracted marriage in the eyes of the

[220]"Institutions of higher studies" are not limited to graduate schools in the American educational system but include colleges that undergraduates attend. See Book III, title III, chapter I "De scholis" and Chapter II "De catholicis universitatibus aliisque studiorum superiorum institutis." This opinion is contrary to that of J. Provost, K. Lasch, H. Skillin, "Dispensed Priests in Ecclesial Ministry: A Canonical Reflection," *CS* 14 (1975), 130.

[221]*CLD* 7, 123; *AAS* 64 (1972), 643.

[222]F. Sweeney, *The Reduction of Clerics to the Lay State*, 171.

[223]U. Lopez, "De reconciliatione sacerdotis qui matrimonium attentare praesumpsit," *P* 26 (1937), 505.

Church, have also broken their marriage loyalty (*CLD* 7, 121–22).

The Congregation announced that if after notification of the rescript the individual changed his mind, a new petition for readmission to the clerical state was to be forwarded to Rome. After the petitioner has spent a "suitable time in probation and after attending to the favorable opinion of the ordinary, the Congregation will decide regarding the opportuneness of suggesting the new favor to the Supreme Pontiff."

The Congregation now processes between twenty to twenty-five cases a year of laicized priests returning to the active ministry. The individual must first find a bishop who is willing to accept him into the diocese. The bishop will then present the case to Rome indicating why the reasons for which the dispensation was granted no longer exist. There is then to be a period of trial lasting from six months to a year during which the petitioner will be assigned to a religious house under the supervision of a prudent priest. The bishop is also to contact the former ordinary to see if he has any objection to the petitioner's resumption of the active ministry. After the Congregation is assured that all these directives have been observed it will issue a *nihil obstat* ("nothing stands in the way") for the petitioner's adoption as a priest of the diocese.[224] Certainly the situation is quite different in the case of a petitioner who has contracted a valid marriage.

A cleric who is dispensed after the 1980 norms have gone into effect is not likely to be eligible for a return to the active ministry. The very terms of the dispensation are that he is unsuitable for the ministry and "should never have been ordained."

[224]CLSA *Roman Replies* 1981, 8.

BIBLIOGRAPHY

Commentaries on the 1917 Code

Dede, J. "Business Pursuits of Clerics and Religious: Further Considerations." *J* 23 (1963), 50–60.

Donovan, J. *The Clerical Obligations of Canons 138 and 140. CanLawStud* 272. Washington: Catholic University of America, 1948.

Hannan, P. *The Canonical Concept of congrua sustentatio for the Secular Clergy. CanLawStud* 302. Washington: Catholic University of America, 1950.

McBride, J. *Incardination and Excardination of Seculars. CanLawStud* 145. Washington: Catholic University of America, 1941.

Smiddy, T. *"Negotiatio." J* 11 (1951): 486–519.

Sweeney, F. *The Reduction of Clerics to the Lay State. CanLawStud* 223. Washington: Catholic University of America, 1945.

Official Code Commission Reports

Comm 3 (1971): 189–197 (Incardination, Obligations and Rights of Clerics, Loss of the Clerical State).

Comm 9 (1977): 243–245 (Incardination, Obligations, etc.).

Comm 14 (1982): 62–88 (Incardination, Obligations, etc.); 167–175 (1981 *Relatio*).

Post-Vatican II Studies

Bassett, W., and Huizing, P., eds. *Celibacy in the Church. Con* 78. New York: Herder and Herder, 1972.

Bassett, W., et al. "Canonical Reflections on Priestly Life and Ministry." *AER* 166 (1972): 363–392.

Colagiovanni, E. *"De dispensatione a caelibatu sacerdotali juxta novas normas." ME* 106 (1981): 209–238.

Ellis, J., ed. *The Catholic Priest in the United States: Historical Investigations.* Collegeville, Minn.: St. John's University Press, 1971.

Hervada, J. "La incardinación en la perspective conciliar." *IC* 7 (1967): 479–517.

Huizing, P., and Walf, K., eds. *May Church Ministers Be Politicians? Con* 157. New York: Seabury Press, 1982.

Kneal, E. "Laicization: CLSA Survey, 1982." *CLSAP* 47 (1982): 247–250.

Larkin, E., and Broccolo, G., eds. *Spiritual Renewal of the American Priesthood*. Washington: USCC Publications, 1973.

Mallon, W. "Easy Exit for Priests?" *HPR* 78 (May 1978): 14–26.

NCCB. *Ad Hoc Committee Report on Priestly Life and Ministry*. Washington USCC, 1974.

––––––. *As One Who Serves: Reflections on the Pastoral Ministry of Priests in the United States*. Washington, USCC, 1977.

––––––. *Studies on Priestly Life and Ministry: Summaries of the Report on the Ad Hoc Bishops' Subcommittees*. Washington: USCC, 1971.

National Federation of Priests' Councils. *Search and Share Directory II*. 1981. "The directory lists categories of programs, policies and plans which have been developed by diocesan councils. ... Many of the programs and plans have been written up so that they can easily be shared with any diocese." 1307 South Wabash Ave., Chicago, Ill. 60605.

O'Reilly, M. "Canonical Procedures for the Laicization of Priests." *CLSAP* 44 (1982): 233–246.

Provost, J. "Toward a Renewed Canonical Understanding of Official Ministry." *J* 41 (1981), 448–479.

Synod of Bishops. *The Ministerial Priesthood*. Washington: USCC, 1972.

Zabla, M. *"De sacerdotalis caelibatus dispensatione normae hodiernae."* P 70 (1981): 237–256.

TITLE IV
PERSONAL PRELATURES
[cc. 294–297]

After three titles treating of the fundamental constitutional elements in the life of the Church (all believers, laity, and clergy), the last two titles of part I consider two forms of the significant (yet not constitutional) phenomenon of ecclesial associations of the faithful (cc. 294–329).

Every believer in full communion with the Church necessarily has his or her place within the Church's constitutional structure. All believers are called to share in the life of communion of the people of God. Within that communion there is a fundamental ministerial differentiation between the laity and the clergy, who participate in the sacrament of order in one grade or another. Although the members of religious communities play a significant role in church life, they are not a middle class between clergy and laity. Rather they follow the way of a special vocation within the framework of the universal vocation to holiness of all believers.

Religious communities are the most noteworthy example of the fundamental will to associate for various ecclesial purposes that has characterized church life since its earliest days. Given the importance of such communities in the mission of the Church and their profound impact on the lives of their members, it is not surprising that they are treated in a separate part III of Book II (cc. 573–746). In a very real sense, however, they are similar to the associations treated in the last two titles of part I. In fact the so-called 1980 schema treated religious together with associations of the faithful in part III of Book II, which was generically entitled "Associations in the Church" (cc. 503–705).[1]

A late addition to the revised Code during the 1982 papal consultation was the present brief title IV on personal prelatures. This is not to say that it was not dealt with in earlier schemata. In fact it prompted a significant amount of discussion in connection with the introductory canons on particular churches (cc. 368–374). That discussion focused on the issue of whether or not such personal prelatures were particular churches.[2] It was ultimately decided that they were not—as is evident from their treatment in this part of the law and not in the section on particular churches. Before commenting on the canons on personal prelatures, some background observations seem appropriate.

The conciliar concern for greater ministerial flexibility in responding to shifting pastoral needs led to a proposal to rethink the institute of incardination and to examine the worldwide distribution of clergy. Vatican II also envisioned the possible establishment of specialized administrative units to incardinate secular priests who would not be linked with any particular church. These personal prelatures would give priests greater flexibility in responding to specialized pastoral needs and exercising the apostolate in various forms (*PO* 10).[3]

This conciliar insight was canonically delineated in *Ecclesiae sanctae* I, 4,[4] which dealt with the following issues affecting the personal prelature: its notion, formation for and incardination in the prelature, the relationship between the prelate heading the prelature and its priests, involvement of the laity, establishment of the prelature and its relationship to local ordinaries and to the conference of bishops. *Ecclesiae sanctae* provided only a skeletal framework for the personal prelature, which would have to be concretized in greater detail in the specific guidelines governing individual institutes.[5] The same is true for the present canons, which largely restate the basic thrust of *Ecclesiae sanctae*.

The original schema on the people of God treated personal prelatures in canon 217, §2 and likened them to particular churches in law unless the contrary was clear from the nature of the matter or the positive prescription of the law. This text was criticized because it tended to treat an association of clerics like a genuine portion of the people of God with its own distinctive hierarchical leader.[6] The so-called 1980 schema reaffirmed the approach of the original schema, for canon 335, §2 stated that personal prelatures were equivalent to particular churches (*aequiparatur*). Canon 337, §2 describing the personal prelature and canon 339, §2 qualifying the basic principle of territoriality reflected the same equation of particular churches and personal

---

[1]For a profitable discussion of constitutional law and the law of association in the revised Code, see Aymans, "Ecclesiological Implications," 51–60.

[2]For a report on the various arguments pro and con in this discussion, see *Comm* 12 (1980), 276–282; *Rel,* 98–101.

[3]For the history of the evolution of the conciliar text, see J. Gutierrez, "De praelatura personali iuxta leges eius constitutivas et Codicis Iuris Canonici normas," *P* 72 (1983), 73–87.

[4]For a discussion of the implications of *ES,* see ibid., 87–97.

[5]For the guidelines governing the publicized personal prelature Opus Dei, see the August 23, 1982 declaration of SCB in *Origins* 12/32 (January 20, 1983), 510–512. See also Gutierrez, 97–104.

[6]See Green, "Critical Reflections," 263–264. This issue is treated in greater detail in Aymans, "Ecclesiological Implications," 58–61.

prelatures in law. This approach was sharply criticized both prior to and at the October 1981 plenary session of the Commission, which voted down the above-mentioned canons. The reworking of the text was left to the Secretariat; however, the Commission clearly intended that such entities not be viewed as similar to particular churches.[7]

Since there has been no published report on the 1982 papal consultation process, it is not entirely clear why the present title and the one following it on associations were separated from the treatment

of institutes of consecrated life and societies of apostolic life contrary to the organization of the 1980 schema. It is neither entirely clear how the present four canons were developed. The following observations, therefore, will be confined to some brief comments on the canons, particularly in terms of their relationship to *Ecclesiae sanctae* I, 4.[8] For the purposes of a concrete illustration of the revised Code, the author will allude to pertinent sections of the August 1982 Sacred Congregation for Bishops' declaration on Opus Dei (cited as Opus Dei).

[7]See Alesandro, 5–6.

[8]See Gutierrez, 104–111.

CANONS AND COMMENTARY

The present title deals with four interrelated issues on personal prelatures:

(a) establishing authority and purposes (c. 294);

(b) government of prelature and relationship of prelate to clerics (c. 295);

(c) lay involvement in prelature (c. 296); and

(d) prelature-local ordinary relationships (c. 297).

Establishing Authority and Purposes

Canon 294 — Personal prelatures which consist of presbyters and deacons of the secular clergy can be erected by the Apostolic See, after consulting the conferences of bishops involved, in order to promote an appropriate distribution of presbyters or to perform particular pastoral or missionary works for various regions or different social groups.

The introductory canon does not describe the prelature but specifies its purpose and highlights the competent authority relative to its establishment. Those purposes are the more equitable distribution of the clergy (not in *ES*) or the pursuit of specialized pastoral goals in various areas or among particular groups of the faithful.[9] While the initial part of the Latin text refers only to priests, toward the end of the text an allusion is made to deacons as well—a change from the first paragraph of *Eccle-*

[9]For the purposes of Opus Dei, see especially IIc.

siae sanctae I, 4. Furthermore, this does not mean that lay persons may not function significantly in such prelatures. The allusion to the Apostolic See should be understood as the Sacred Congregation for Bishops, which is competent in this area in terms of *Regimini Ecclesiae Universae* 49, 1.[10] The prelature is an institutional element pertaining to the Church's hierarchical and pastoral structure—even though it is appropriately distinguished from particular churches. Since the prelature is to serve individual bishops and conferences of bishops, reference is made understandably to consultation with the conferences before the prelature is set up. Especially since the members of the prelatures will frequently function in several particular churches, it is imperative that from the outset there be fostered harmonious relationships between the bishops and the members of the prelatures.[11] This is also true for the necessary interaction between the lay and clerical members of the institute, whose mutual rights and duties need to be clarified in the statutes.

Statutes/Prelate-Cleric Relationships

Canon 295 — §1. A personal prelature is governed by the statutes established by the Apostolic See, and it is presided over by a prelate as its proper ordinary, who has the right to erect a national or international seminary, to incardinate the students,

[10]See ibid., VII–VIII.
[11]See *ES* I, 4e; Opus Dei, V. Although personal prelatures are not particular churches, one sees a comparable concern for consultation between the Holy See and the conferences of bishops in c. 373, §2 on the establishment of personal as distinct from territorial particular churches. Examples of such personal particular churches are ordinariates for the military or for the faithful of a special rite.

and to promote them to orders under the title of service to the prelature.

§2. The prelate must see to the spiritual formation and to the decent support of those whom he will promote by the above-mentioned title.

The prelature is to be governed by statutes drawn up by the Holy See within the framework of the canons of this title (*ES* I, 4a). Hence there is ample room for the development of particular law in this area if various prelatures are formed to meet distinct pastoral needs. The involvement of the Holy See is clear again in this canon since what is envisioned is not an institute tied down to a particular church but rather a pastoral instrument for responding flexibly to the needs of various churches. The whole point of such prelatures is to provide for the undertaking of special missionary or pastoral tasks in areas in need of them.

The key hierarchical figure is the prelate who is the ordinary (c. 134) of the prelature and its primary liaison person with the Holy See and the bishops (*ES* I, 4a). Such an individual is responsible for the formation, incardination, ordination, and ongoing support of the clerics making up the prelature (*ES* I, 4b–c). Although the revised Code does not refer to various titles of ordination in the canons on orders, here one sees a reference to the title of service of the prelature for which the candidates are ordained. The specifics of this ongoing prelate-cleric relationship are to be clarified further in the statutes of the institute.[12]

Lay Involvement in Prelature

Canon 296 — Lay persons can dedicate themselves to the apostolic works of a personal prelature by agreements entered with the prelature; the mode of this organic cooperation and the principal duties and rights connected with it shall be appropriately determined in the statutes.

Though the prelature in law at least is primarily a clerical institute, provision is made for interested lay persons to share in its apostolic work in light of their expertise and experience (*ES* I, 4d). The specifics of such lay involvement are to be articulated in the statutes of the prelature. It is appropriate

[12]See Opus Dei, Ia–b, IIa, and III.

that a contract be drawn up determining the nature of the lay person's commitment to the prelature, which does not change his or her situation theologically or canonically.[13] Even though such laity are committed to the works of the personal prelature, they do not form the "proper people" of the prelature since the prelature is not a portion of the people of God entirely separated from the governmental authority of the local ordinary.

Prelature-Local Ordinary Relationships

Canon 297 — The statutes shall likewise define the relations of the personal prelature with the local ordinaries in whose particular churches the prelature itself exercises or desires to exercise its pastoral or missionary works, with the prior consent of the diocesan bishop.

A major preoccupation of the law here is the organic insertion of prelatures within the pastoral life of the various particular churches, the fostering of legal security, and the minimizing of potential conflicts that would be pastorally counterproductive. The local ordinary and the prelate of such a prelature exercise a cumulative power of government. There is a concern that the legitimate rights of local ordinaries be duly protected in view of their significant leadership role in the particular churches (*ES* I, 4e). This seems particularly true in the areas of worship, education, and general pastoral activity. *Ecclesiae sanctae* I, 22–40 took great pains to deal with various issues of common concern in the relationship between bishops and religious communities. These concerns have also been addressed throughout the revised Code, especially in the law on institutes of consecrated life and societies of apostolic life. An examination of the above-mentioned issues should give one a general idea of the types of concerns to be addressed in the statutes of personal prelatures mutatis mutandis.[14] One notes in conclusion that the consent of the diocesan bishop is required for the missionary or pastoral functioning of a prelature within a given particular church. A local ordinary, such as a vicar general or an episcopal vicar, could not give such authorization without a special episcopal mandate.

[13]See ibid, Ic, II b–d, and IIId. Also cc. 224–231 on the obligations and rights of lay members of the Christian faithful.
[14]See Opus Dei, IV–V.

BIBLIOGRAPHY ─────────────────────────────

The bibliographical material provided at the end of the commentary on "Particular Churches and the Authority Established in Them" (cc. 368–430)

gives a list of significant references regarding this area of canon law.

TITLE V
ASSOCIATIONS OF THE CHRISTIAN FAITHFUL
[cc. 298–329]

The setting of title V, "Associations of the Christian Faithful," and even its introductory language, are interesting and significant. First the setting. Within the very last weeks before promulgation of the 1983 Code, this entire title was transplanted. It had been set up in an entirely different area. It was an adjunct to and a kind of appendix to the canons on religious institutes of consecrated life. In its final form, it stands amidst the area of law dealing explicitly with the rights and duties of the *Christifideles*—whether the Christian faithful be ordained or not.

Second, the language has remained largely unchanged. This history affects the whole interpretation of these canons; it throws considerable light upon the language of the very first canon. It is imperative to recall that these canons describe institutes within the Church that are parallel to, and adjunct to, religious life—despite this new setting. What they describe are groups of non-vowed Christians (usually non-ordained and therefore "lay" —but not necessarily so) who are joined together in associations that have precisely the spiritual aims of varying religious institutes. It is significant to recall that until the last months before the publication of these canons, the title was in fact *"Other* Associations of the Faithful." Those to which they were

contrasted, and to which they were linked both in placement and in spirit, were institutes of consecrated life and societies of apostolic life. This legislation, therefore, has a precise and narrowed intent (that is spelled out in §1).

Therein lies a difficulty. The tendency will be to explore the extent to which certain clearly recognizable and highly visible "associations of the Christian faithful" within the Church can or should be fitted within these canons. Upon that discovery a great deal lies—notably governance and supervision and accountability. To what extent, it may be asked, is a 1980 association, "The Association for the Rights of Catholics in the Church,"[1] to be governed by these norms? The same question may be asked regarding the following: a diocesan hospital; the National Federation of Priests' Councils; contemplative women establishing a new foundation that would be less bound by cloister (and directed by the Holy See to call themselves a "pious union");[2] "Christian life communities," once known as "sodalities"; and the Chicago Association of Priests. The tension between autonomy and governance makes this question critical for such varied associations. Financial assets, appointments of officers, goals, and apostolates themselves will fall under this governance—or will not—according to the norms of title V.

[1] Cf. P.O. Box 3972, Philadelphia, Pa. 19146.
[2] *CLD* 7, 544.

CHAPTER I
COMMON NORMS
[cc. 298–311]

Definition

Canon 298 — §1. In the Church there are associations distinct from institutes of consecrated life and societies of apostolic life, in which the Christian faithful, either clergy or laity, or clergy and laity together, strive by common effort to promote a more perfect life or to foster public worship or Christian doctrine or to exercise other apostolic works, namely to engage in efforts of evangelization, to exercise works of piety or charity and to animate the temporal order with the Christian spirit.

The general characteristic of "associations of the Christian faithful" within the Church is of a group of persons, not under vow—by contrast with the institutes of consecrated life—but nonetheless, they strive to promote "a more perfect life or to foster public worship or Christian doctrine or to exercise other apostolic works" that those other associations also aspire to. The distinction lies primarily in the absence of vows or promises or other "bonds" drawing the members toward the goals of the association. It might be remarked here that the canons of this title suggest a subtle orientation toward the clerical outlook, at least in that only its three final canons are addressed specifically to "Special Norms for Associations of the Laity."[3]

It is interesting also that the three general aims of associations of the faithful described here echo what were indicated in former law as the complete list of *all* associations of the faithful: third orders (toward the perfection of personal life), confraternities (of public worship and Christian doctrine), and pious unions (defined in former law as established for "the exercise of some work of piety or charity,"[4] and broadened in the present law to include works of the apostolate reaching from evangelization to the explicit Christianization of the secular order).[5] The absence in the 1983 law of two of these names —confraternities and pious unions—and the hypothetical list of possible members proposed earlier suggest that the range of potential "associations of the Christian faithful" is enormous. The norms that follow, however, draw limits.

[3]Namely, cc. 327–329. This chapter bears a striking parallel to the same unbalanced proportion found in cc. 224–231, dealing with the *"Christifideles."*
[4]*CIC* 717, §1.
[5]See *CIC* 685.

§2. The Christian faithful should enroll especially in associations which are erected or praised or recommended by competent ecclesiastical authority.

The faithful are exhorted first, as an introduction, to give their allegiance "especially" to those associations that have been either "recommended" by the competent ecclesiastical authority (who will be defined later, in c. 312) or "established" by that authority. That difference is critically important —and will be defined immediately, in the following norms. The unmistakable implication is of a guarded uneasiness regarding membership in any association that has not been granted endorsement or outright establishment by "competent ecclesiastical authority."

Two major classes of associations of the faithful are recognized—based upon either the "establishment" of the association or upon its mere "recommendation" or "commendation" by the authority. The first brings into being a "public" association with certain express rights and limitations of supervision that come with its status as a "juridic person." The second—simple endorsement—brings into being a recognized association of the faithful within the Church; it, however, has only "private" status.

Right To Establish: "Private" Associations

Canon 299 — §1. The Christian faithful are free, by means of a private agreement made among themselves, to establish associations to attain the aims mentioned in can. 298, §1, with due regard for the prescriptions of can. 301, §1.

The right to form a private association is recognized first. Its aims are the three general ones described earlier (perfection of life, public worship, apostolic work). Two qualifications, however, are stated (a third will be added in §3 of this canon). The agreement of the prospective members is *of its nature* "private"—i.e., in the sense of lacking official ecclesiastical establishment. This is not in any sense an indication of its public exposure or secrecy or, above all, of the forbidden "secret societies" of nineteenth-century American church experience. Rather, it is a common covenant agreed upon among members, in a religious matter; it, however, lacks the specific establishment granted by "the authority competent to erect public associations" of canon 312 (the Holy See, national conference, or diocesan bishop). Second, this private agreement may not licitly be one directed toward a specific religious purpose that is of its very nature reserved to the ecclesiastical authority. Canon 301, §1, in turn, will spell this out:

> Competent ecclesiastical authority alone has the right to erect associations of the Christian faithful which set out to teach Christian doctrine in the name of the Church or to promote public worship or which aim at other ends whose pursuit by their nature is reserved to the same ecclesiastical authority.

A private association for the granting of ecclesiastical declarations of nullity would not meet with very high enthusiasm—much less establishment. Less clear would be the legitimacy, as a private association within the Church, of a dissident group establishing within a local church its own school of religion: *is* it proclaiming Christian doctrine "in the name of the Church"?

§2. Such associations are called private associations even though they are praised or recommended by ecclesiastical authority.

The law states that associations remain "private" in nature until they are, technically, "established" by the ecclesiastical authority. Commendation, praise, and even support, do not supply this. The Knights of Columbus, the May Day Rosary Procession, Marriage Encounters national or local, remain essentially private associations within the meaning of church law; they are warmly commended—and indeed recommended—but not established by, the hierarchy. (An earlier view held that the *only* instance of a "public" association—outside the triad of third orders, confraternities, and pious unions—was *Action Catholique* of four decades ago.)[6] The distinction now is critical. With emergence as a *public* association of the Church, in this technical sense, the group becomes a full-fledged ecclesiastical entity, and the civil authority may lack all competence in regard to it—at least in internal matters. Neither can the civil authority interfere in its activity—insofar as the work of the association did not involve some public good. Hospital public health standards, as opposed to, for instance, the designation of a clerical chaplain, may come into play here.

§3. No private association of the Christian faithful in the Church is recognized unless its statutes are reviewed by competent authority.

A minimal level of endorsement from the larger Church is stated here, i.e., a certain level of recognition that is short of full acceptance as a "private"

juridic person but yet beyond mere praise and commendation. It is necessary in every private association, if it is to be "recognized" by the Church, that its statutes be "reviewed by" the competent ecclesiastical authority. Neither of these terms is defined. Generally the first at least implies a somewhat modified acceptance and approval of the condition in which the body presents itself. The second at least implies, and perhaps strongly, careful scrutiny. In any event a direct statement by the authority that the disputed statutes are *not* recognized would effectively deny approval to the petitioning body.

"Catholic" in Title

Canon 300 — **No association shall assume the name "Catholic" without the consent of competent ecclesiastical authority, in accord with the norm of can. 312.**

The name "Catholic" attached to an association, private or public, carries with it an unmistakable connotation of acting in some way for the larger ecclesiastical community. That larger community has a right to demand that those who represent it do so competently, and the name "Catholic" may hence be incorporated into the title of the association *only* with the consent of the competent authorities designated later—Holy See, national conference of bishops, or diocesan bishop. These in turn may legitimately *demand* that the name be removed from the title of an offending association. Judgment in this would seem to rest with the diocesan bishop.

Right To Establish: "Public" Associations

Canon 301 — **§1. Competent ecclesiastical authority alone has the right to erect associations of the Christian faithful which set out to teach Christian doctrine in the name of the Church or to promote public worship or which aim at other ends whose pursuit by their nature is reserved to the same ecclesiastical authority.**

Certain areas of competence in spiritual things are held to be "reserved" to specific ecclesiastical authorities. Where the purpose of a proposed association is of its very nature a function reserved to ecclesiastical authority (and doctrinal teaching and public worship are in this canon specifically instanced as examples of this), the competent authority then "has the right to erect" the proposed association rather than merely *praising* or *recommending* it. The law requires that the authority must thereby bring the association under the multiple requirements for *public* associations, which are the object of this chapter of the law on the People of God. The uneasy conjunction of *magisterium* and academic theological research comes into view here. Must, for example, the Catholic Theological

---

[6]J. Abbo and J. Hannan, *The Sacred Canons*, rev. ed., 2 vols. (St. Louis: B. Herder Book Co., 1957), I:717 (cited as Abbo-Hannan and volume).

Society of America be offered a charter of *establishment* by the National Conference of Catholic Bishops as a "public" association of the faithful and, therefore, a juridic person within the Church? The association certainly acquires juridic, or moral, personality by reason of its civil incorporation. It could correctly claim, however, that it does not "teach Christian doctrine in the name of the Church," and hence would not fall within this framework.[7]

§2. Competent ecclesiastical authority, if it judges it expedient, can also erect associations of the Christian faithful in order to attain directly or indirectly other spiritual ends whose accomplishment has not been sufficiently provided for by the efforts of private persons.

The goals of proclamation of the gospel and of public worship are not the only ones pursued by associations of the Christian faithful that must become "public" juridic persons within the Church. The competent authority reserves the right to establish certain even "indirectly" spiritually oriented public associations in order to attain ends not successfully initiated or accomplished by private enterprises (e.g., the Bishops' Catholic Relief Services).

§3. Associations of the Christian faithful which are erected by competent ecclesiastical authority are called public associations.

The term "public," in short, is attached only to those associations that have been "erected" by competent ecclesiastical authority; this distinguishes them from those "private" associations that are merely "praised or recommended."

Clerical Associations

Canon 302 — Associations of the Christian faithful are called clerical associations when they are under the direction of the clergy, when they presume the exercise of sacred orders, and when they are recognized as such by competent authority.

"Clerical" associations are designated as those governed by clerics (i.e., those of the order of deacon, priest, or bishop), exercising sacred orders, and officially acknowledged as clerical. The intent of this norm is not spelled out—however clear are the terms used to designate the specifically "clerical" association. Since the law recognizes, in canon 298, §1, the possibility of groups of mixed membership as regards clerics or lay persons, it must be assumed that this present norm fixes eligibility for those functions within the Church that are express-

ly to be confined to clerics. In any event, the "exercise of sacred orders" would be confined to the clerical members in a mixed association. The designation of the association as expressly "clerical" would then be dependent upon the function of a cleric as the "moderator"; equally clearly, such a designation would have to be the product of a statutory requirement (e.g., the casual election of a priest to the presidency of the Ushers' Club would not make it thereby an expressly "clerical" association).

Third Orders

Canon 303 — Associations whose members lead an apostolic life and strive for Christian perfection while living in the world and who share the spirit of some religious institute under the higher direction of that same institute are called third orders or some other appropriate name.

It has been noted that earlier legislation recognized only three associations of the faithful—third orders, confraternities, and pious unions.[8] The first alone is now explicitly mentioned in church law. Traditionally, the "first order" was that of men religious—not necessarily ordained—pursuing the evangelical counsels under vow and in common life according to the rule and life-style offered by the founder. The "second order" was of women religious pursuing similar goals, following much the same rule, and normally under the spiritual guidance of a member of the first order. Medieval records show numerous lay persons associating themselves with either institution, sometimes living literally within them or in their shadow, pursuing a life in the spirit of the community but without the bond of vow, and to a greater or a lesser extent still involved in "the world." These "third orders" were initially formalized by Francis of Assisi, although there had been earlier a Benedictine tradition of "oblates." There are now reported to be some nine "third orders" with recognition as juridic persons in the Church—following Benedictine, Franciscan, "Norbertine," Dominican, Carmelite, Augustinian, Francesco de Paolo, Servite, and Trinitarian traditions.[9] (These are third orders *secular*. Third orders *regular* add the formality of vow and common life and become, for all practical purposes, clones of the first order.)

Statutes

Canon 304 — §1. All associations of the Christian faithful, whether public or private, by whatever title or name they are called, are to have their own statutes which define the end of the association or

---

[7] Cf. herein the lengthy detailing of this problem in Book III of the 1983 Code, "The Teaching Office of the Church."

[8] *CIC* 700.
[9] Abbo-Hannan, I, 705.

its social objective, its headquarters, its government, the conditions of membership and by whom
its policies are to be determined, according to the
need or utility of time and place.

Social tranquility demands a measure of guidelines and constitutional limits and privileges. It is
now required that all associations within the
Church, whether public or private, have a clearly
drawn-up constitution by which each may be held
accountable both to the competent superior and to
its own body. Five requisites for this body of statutes are indicated herein: a statement of the association's goals and objectives, the locale of the
association, its rules of governance, the conditions
for membership, and the determiner of its policies.
The final requisite is to be adapted to the culture in
which it is embedded. The competent authority is
quite correct in withholding even an informal endorsement of a group that has not yet clarified its
aims according to these guidelines.

**§2. They are to choose a title or name for them-
selves which is adapted to the usage of their time
and place, selected especially in view of their intended purpose.**

Furthermore, honest representation of the goals
of the association is demanded in the name or title
of the group, as suitable to the culture in which it is
set. The qualification of legitimate use of the term
"Catholic," as stated in canon 300, has already
been seen. It would seem that an ordinary or other
competent superior could require correction of any
false or misleading title—under pain of withdrawal
of approbation.

Vigilance and Accountability

Canon 305 — **§1. All associations of the Christian faithful are subject to the vigilance of competent ecclesiastical authority, whose duty it is to
take care that integrity of faith and morals is preserved in them and to watch lest abuse creep into
ecclesiastical discipline; therefore that authority
has the right and duty to visit them in accord with
the norm of law and the statutes; such associations
are also subject to the governance of the same authority according to the prescriptions of the following canons.**

Central to the concept of associations of the
Christian faithful within the church community is
that there be official recognitioin and endorsement
of the group—whether it has public or private status—by either of the routes already discussed. In
conjunction with becoming either a public or a private juridic entity, however, there comes to either
kind of association a reciprocal relationship of accountability. This is specified here as being directed

to the appropriate ecclesiastical authority that had
either endorsed or established the association. The
thrust of this supervision is clearly twofold: (1)
preservation of the integrity of faith and morals and
(2) verification by the authority that there is no
abuse of ecclesiastical discipline. These guidelines,
from the point of view of the authority, are derived
from those of the general function of the pastor of
the local church (in its broadest sense), i.e., the diocesan bishop. His functions are crystallized in canons 375, 386, 391, and 396, described later in this
volume. There must always be due regard for the
exemption of religious houses—and as is implied in
the above commentary on canon 303, a "third order" might indeed stand at the threshold between
public cult (under a bishop's superintendence) and
internal devotion (under that of the first order).
From the point of view of any association, it is always liable to examination upon the guidelines of
its own internal statutes already described in canon
304, §1, as well as in certain specific areas to be described in the later norms.

**§2. Associations of any kind whatever are sub-
ject to the vigilance of the Holy See; diocesan associations and also other associations to the extent
that they work in the diocese are subject to the vigilance of the local ordinary.**

The range of supervision represents a kind of inverted umbrella: that of the Holy See covers all associations, whether public or private, whether
universal or purely local. Obviously, the latter diocesan associations are under the immediate governance and "vigilance" of the bishop of the
jurisdiction in which they are founded or based.
More importantly, the current guidelines expressly
allow the ordinary of a local church to supervise
those associations whose seat may be elsewhere but
are nonetheless active within the territory of his
own jurisdiction. Again, the norms of public cult
—versus the purely internal devotions of religious
houses—are applicable: that threshold may not be
ignored, and only the public function of the association is liable to supervision and "vigilance."

Benefits

Canon 306 — **In order for a person to enjoy the
rights and privileges, indulgences and other spiritual favors granted to the association, it is necessary
and suffices that the person has been validly received into it and not legitimately dismissed from
it, in accord with the prescriptions of the law and
the proper statutes of the association.**

Only two requirements are stated in the law as
being necessary for participation in the spiritual
benefits of the association: valid reception and continued membership. It is to be noted that these "fa-

vors" granted to the members seem to emphasize the "spiritual" realm exclusively; for example, rights, privileges, indulgences, and other spiritual favors. The canon simply does not address itself to insurance benefits or the right to wear a red cape. These matters are to be settled according to the statutes of the association and adjudicated according to its own internal processes and norms. In addition, the qualifications for "valid" reception are not spelled out—unless that pivotal concept of law is itself addressed within the constitution of the association. In its effect, this means that the "benefits" of the association are not in the least lost either through inactivity within the association or failure to observe other of its statutes. (In addition, obviously, the statutes are not binding in conscience —beyond the demands of the quality of fidelity.) Unless the constitutions and bylaws indicate either expulsion or the penalty of non-participation, the benefits continue to inhere in the members of the association indefinitely.

Membership

Canon 307 — §1. The reception of members is to be done in accord with the norm of law and the statutes of each association.

For membership and its attendant ritual, it has already been noted that the constitution or rule of the association is the determinant. The rule might or might not address itself to the canonical elegances of validating or invalidating circumstances.

§2. The same person can be enrolled in several associations.

Previous concern with multiple and perhaps conflicting association memberships is removed by the present law. Earlier legislation[10] forbade members of one third order to enroll in that of another religious institute. There is no such limitation in the 1983 Code. One person can be ascribed to several associations. There is no contraindication to holding membership in multiple associations within the Church.

§3. Members of religious institutes can enroll in associations in accord with their own law with the consent of their superior.

Members of institutes of consecrated life may also join associations of the faithful. No limitations are stated beyond that of their own statutes. (Theoretically, a devout Jesuit might become, at his own risk and in his own house, a member of the third order of Saint Dominic.) They are referred to their own superior for an appropriate approval and, once

again, to their constitutions, in considering such a group. Former legislation[11] forbade that "which could not be reconciled" with the purposes of the applicant's institute. Contemporary law in effect remands this to the judgment of the superior as he grants or withholds approval.

Dismissal

Canon 308 — No one who has been legitimately enrolled may be dismissed from an association except for a just cause in accord with the norm of law and the statutes.

A proportionate and just cause is required for the dismissal of a duly inscribed member. This may be defined in the statutes of the association; lacking this criterion or in a dispute, recourse might ultimately be made to any of the following: (1) the general standard of "the reasonable judgment of prudent persons"; (2) a process for the settlement of disputes that is expressed in the statutes themselves; or (3) a course of action that is appropriate to the administrative procedures or the Due Process Board.

Rights and Obligations of the Juridic Person

Canon 309 — Legitimately constituted associations have the right, in accord with the law and the statutes, to issue particular norms respecting the association itself, to hold meetings, to designate moderators, officials, other officers and administrators of goods.

Once brought into being by endorsement (private) or establishment (public), an association has a right to the formalities of its own proper norms, to hold assemblies, to designate officers, and so on. The "law and the statutes" that are referred to here are those of the association itself, rather than those of the Code. It is an expression of regard, within the earlier limitations of ecclesiastical "vigilance" (examined in the commentary on c. 305), both for the essential autonomy of the association and for the encouragement of its own spontaneous development and growth within the Church's life. It represents one pole of a tension—of which the other is the primarily spiritual superintendence by the competent ecclesiastical authority. This canon is a bulwark against the intrusion of that authority into the legitimate autonomy of the association.[12] It would seem that only, for instance, where gross fiscal mismanagement by the association or its public utterances are a grave jeopardy to the larger Church might the competent higher authority intervene. This is a difficult minefield lying between the op-

[10]*CIC* 705.

[11]*CIC* 693, §4.
[12]*CIC* 691, §1, 2°.

posing claims of autonomy on the one hand and the common welfare on the other.

Rights and Obligations in Private Associations

Canon 310 — A private association which has not been constituted a juridic person cannot as such be a subject of obligations and rights; however, the Christian faithful associated together in it can jointly contract obligations and acquire rights and possess goods as co-owners and co-possessors; they can exercise their rights and obligations through an agent or proxy.

It has already been indicated that by definition mere praise or recommendation points to a *private* association of the Christian faithful (cf. c. 299). In turn canon 322 will indicate that a private association of the Christian faithful can in no way become an authentic juridic person within the Church until there has been express establishment as such by a decree of the competent authority. Only then will it become capable of rights *as a church body* and a juridic person within it. This canon emphasizes that because it lacks such ecclesial juridic personality, the association cannot as such be a subject of obligations and rights. The canon nonetheless vindicates the capacity of the *members* jointly to contract obligations as co-owners or co-possessors —either upon the part of a group of the members or of all of the members—and even *in solidum.* These modes of possession should be determined in the light of sound moral theological reflections upon justice in cases of both joint ownership and joint possession. In addition, as with former "moral persons," a private association of the Christian faithful may choose a representative or proxy who is empowered to speak and act for the corporate body. There is no specification that he or she must come from within the association itself.

Religious Moderators

Canon 311 — Members of institutes of consecrated life who preside over or assist associations in some way united to their institute are to see to it that these associations give assistance to the works of the apostolate in a diocese, especially cooperating, under the direction of the local ordinary, with associations which are ordered to the exercise of the apostolate in the diocese.

Moderators of third orders or of other associations that are in some way associated with the institute of consecrated life of the moderator must work with the local bishop in guiding their associations toward the general needs of the apostolate of the diocese. Other associations may already be assisting the bishop; the religious moderator may not act independently of them and, in effect, determine his or

her own mission (or that of the association) within the local church. In a positive sense, the moderator is encouraged to stimulate the association to the fulfillment of its own charism by cooperative work in behalf of the apostolic needs of the larger community.

CHAPTER II
PUBLIC ASSOCIATIONS OF THE CHRISTIAN FAITHFUL
[cc. 312–320]

Competent Establishing Authority

Canon 312 — §1. The authority competent to erect public associations is:
1° the Holy See for universal and international associations;
2° the conference of bishops in its own territory for national associations, that is, those which are directed by their founding purpose toward action in the whole nation;
3° the diocesan bishop in his own territory for diocesan associations, but not the diocesan administrator; however, those associations are excepted for whose erection the right has been reserved to others by apostolic privilege.

The appropriate competent ecclesiastical authority for the chartering of public associations of the faithful (and therefore of juridic persons within the Church) is clearly designated. A "universal" or "international" association is established only by the Holy See (1°). The determination of the universal or international character of the proposed association must come from the geographical dispersion of its potential members—not from its aim. The local Rosary Society does not become an international association through its continued support of a distant mission. The membership, further, requires dispersion beyond the national boundary; associations of adjoining *dioceses,* even for an international purpose, come only within the following disposition. National conferences of bishops charter these (2°). The qualification for "national membership" is shifted slightly from the above. "National" associations are defined by the norm as embracing those groups that are destined in their very charter for "action in the whole nation" (to distinguish them from the purely diocesan associations of 3°). What of a national association that intends to have an impact upon the peoples of a distant nation—but *only* through local charitable or even political action? This would still seem to be only a "national" association and, therefore, outside the ambit of the Holy See. If, however, it sends members to work for or, above all, to live in another area, the Holy See, rather than the national conference, then has precedence in chartering the group. Locally, the diocesan bishop—apparently no other ordinary and specifically not the administrator—is empowered to charter local associations. Again the criterion for membership is place of residency as opposed to the reach of the association's goal or mission. The incapacity of the administrator of a diocese, during the vacancy of the episcopal see, is in accord with other restrictions astutely placed upon that incumbent: the concern is that he not burden a future episcopal ordinary with his own caretaker but lasting initiatives (see cc. 428 and 525 for these and other restrictions).

Displacing this right of a local bishop, however, is the right to form public associations of the faithful reserved "by apostolic privilege" to certain "others." It is in virtue precisely of privileges of this kind, i.e., of immemorial duration, that the establishment of sodalities of the Rosary is reserved to the Dominicans, for instance, or of sodalities of the Sorrowful Mother to the Servite Fathers. This right is one only of initiative rather than of charter: the following paragraph places a serious limitation upon it.

§2. The written consent of the diocesan bishop is required for the valid erection of an association or a branch of an association in a diocese, even if this is done in virtue of an apostolic privilege; however, the consent given by a diocesan bishop for the erection of a house of a religious institute also allows for the erection in the same house or church attached to it, of an association proper to the institute.

The allowance of the diocesan bishop to establish public associations of the faithful within his territorial jurisdiction is jealously guarded—and almost absolute: it holds even against those who have the apostolic privilege spoken of above; the written permission of the bishop is necessary for validity even in these cases. The single exception is found in this same §2, in a kind of omnibus law. Permission of a local bishop to an institute of the consecrated life to establish a *house* within the diocese carries with it not only permission to establish a church there (by c. 611, 3°) but also to establish a public association of the faithful. Two requisites must be met: (1) the association must be "in the same house or church attached to it," and (2) it must be "proper to the institute." Forming a chapter of a third order to meet *in various parts of the city or the diocese* therefore requires the explicit permission of the diocesan bishop spoken of in number three of paragraph one. The "proper" connection of the association to the institute is determined either by its being explicitly of the third order of the religious institute (and of the same rule, as adapted) or by its work being, in prudent judgment, "the same" as that of the institute. The association still retains its own autonomy in such matters as observance of its rules or stat-

utes, dispensation within it, admission to membership through a novitiate and profession, if that be required, etc. These are purely "internal" affairs for a third order.

In all of this, the critical point that should be noted in conclusion is that the ultimate criterion of whether an association has been canonically "established" (and is *therefore "public,"* and *therefore* a "juridic person" with rights of ownership and supervision by the competent authority) or has been merely "recommended," must come from the language itself of the document of admission of the association by the competent authority. The line between "recommendation" and "establishment" may be thin; it will reside ultimately in the intent of the authority. This intent in turn should be explicitly stated in the document of foundation spoken of in this canon. In cases in which this has not been done, general principles of law would hold only for "recommendation." None of the burdens or the requirements associated with an officially established public body would be applicable.[13]

Canonical Mission

Canon 313 — A public association as well as a confederation of public associations is constituted a juridic person by the decree by which it is erected by competent ecclesiastical authority in accord with the norm of can. 312; it also thereby receives a mission to pursue the ends which it proposes for itself in the name of the Church, to the extent that such a mission is required.

The equation between a public association and juridic personality is established here: public associations and confederations of them are *ipso iure* constituted as juridic "persons." The implications of this have already been suggested in the opening paragraphs of this commentary regarding associations. To be noted additionally, however, is the interesting fact that there appears here, uniquely, the concept of an association of associations—the National Federation of Priests' Councils has already been instanced as an obvious example. Even apart from civil incorporation (this might appropriately be sought in the U.S.), such confederations also enjoy the juridic rights of voice and ownership within the Church—once they have been granted this truly public personality through "establishment" by the appropriate authority.

The concept of "canonical mission" appears widely, but in indistinct fashion, throughout the structure of the Church. It is associated with the function of governance within the church community; it can be centered around the proclamation of the gospel and teaching; it generally implies a man-

[13]Cf. cc. 10, 14.

date from the competent authority to a Christian to exercise his or her apostolate in some particularized fashion, even beyond that coming from the general call to holiness and mission of all the baptized. Particularly in a catechetical or evangelical context, an express canonical mission confirms the juridic personality of an association. This canon states that the very decree of establishment of a public association carries with it both the canonical mission to its particular charism and to the goals that it proposes for itself in the name of the Church.

Approval of Statutes

Canon 314 — The statutes of any public association as well as their revision or change require the approval of the ecclesiastical authority which is competent to erect the association in accord with the norm of can. 312, §1.

The right to supervise the statutes of an association of the faithful is lodged with that competent authority that established the group officially. More importantly, subsequent modifications to the statutes also require this authoritative approbation. The norm here is clearly concerned with substantive modifications; trivial amendments need not be presented for approval ("the law is not concerned with trifles"). The fashion of such amendments is not indicated. It would seem that a "dialogue committee" should explore the mind of the authority before proposing change within the statutes. The authority in turn should generally cultivate the spirit of individual initiative within the association.

Assigned Tasks

Canon 315 — Public associations on their own initiative can begin undertakings in keeping with their character, and they can direct them in accord with their statutes, but under the further direction of the ecclesiastical authority mentioned in can. 312, §1.

Precisely the initiative just mentioned is here given encouragement with regard to new projects within the ambit of the association; they are to be undertaken spontaneously—yet under the direction of the competent authority. A balance must be struck between merely informing the authority and cooperative, fruitful work with the authority toward the mission of the association.

Ineligibility for Membership

Canon 316 — §1. One who has publicly rejected the Catholic faith or abandoned ecclesiastical communion or been punished with an imposed or declared excommunication cannot be validly received into public associations.

Versions of the Code circulated up to the very time of promulgation contained in canon 307, in what had been paragraph four, a stern rejection of "non-Catholic *Christifideles*" as potential members of public juridic associations. The paragraph was dropped from the Code. There remains ineligibility for membership, however, to Roman Catholics who through one route or another have discontinued their full communion with the Roman Catholic Church. Foremost are those who have "publicly" departed from the Catholic faith. This implies two components: an express disavowal of affiliation with the Catholic faith and the "public" nature of the disavowal.

The criteria of disavowal of "the Catholic faith" might be best found in the criteria for originally becoming a "person" in the Catholic community. The commentary on canons 96, 204, and 205 offer criteria derived from those canons—the touchstones of episcopal hierarchy, the profession of faith, the sacraments, and ecclesiastical governance. What is certain is that the denial of any single component of the complexus of Catholic faith, or of several of them, would not qualify for this exclusion. Holding individual and unacceptable or even unpopular theological stances would not inhibit membership —however strongly some may reject those stances. The "public" departure is more difficult to apply in the concrete. The use of the term is parallel to the popular sense of the word rather than to the technical application of it in penal law, e.g., the popular writer, or the promiscuous public figure. Much more difficult to determine is the nature or gravity of the conduct of the candidate—as to whether it be really contrary to acceptable Catholic teaching (in the first instance) or really the action of a "public sinner" of the former Code of Canon Law (in the second instance).[14] Decision in this requires caution, restraint, and charity; judgment might be deferred, at least in terms of consultation, to the competent authority—who presumably would be endowed with all these felicitous qualities. Public separation from the ecclesiastical community is certainly not present where there has been no external sign of the defection other than mere "non-practice"; even extended attendance at the religious ceremonies of another denomination need not of itself entail positive separation from the Catholic communion. Some objective enrollment, however, would be such an indication. Finally, only the most formal and severe of ecclesiastical penalties (in terms of their manner of imposition) would disqualify a candidate: specifically, (1) only those excommunications that follow upon an explicit public sentence by an ecclesiastical body or ordinary or (2) a similar public, express, declaratory judgment that

[14]Cf., e.g., *CIC* 1240, §1, 6°: the "public and manifest sinners" formerly denied Christian burial, and c. 1184, §1, 3° of the 1983 Code with similar restriction.

such a penalty has been incurred. These are of their nature rare, usually attended by wide media publicity and explicitly condemnatory by name. The most widely known recent American incident was that of the ordinary of New Orleans and the public censure of three persons impeding Catholic school integration, on April 17, 1962.[15]

§2. Those legitimately enrolled who fall into the situations mentioned in §1, are, after a warning, to be dismissed from the association, observing the association's statutes and reserving the right of recourse to the ecclesiastical authority mentioned in can. 312, §1.

The norm suggests an important point. The process of dismissal, in the case in which an accepted member falls within the penalties of paragraph one, may be carried out upon the initiative of the association itself and with due regard for the demands of its own proper statutes; the right of recourse (presumably to both parties, should there be a dispute) is reserved to the competent authority. Two necessary and standard precautions of law are enjoined: as is mandatory in all ecclesiastical penal procedures, there must have been adequate warning and opportunity for repentance; and the requisite formalities of hearing and procedure must have been observed (as far as they are spelled out in the statutes of the association). The first is of even more significance than the second. From analogy to strictly judicial norms for church courts, the failure to observe this deference toward the accused would arguably render the dismissal action of the association itself invalid.

Designation of Supreme Moderator and Chaplain

Canon 317 — §1. Unless otherwise provided in the statutes, the ecclesiastical authority mentioned in can. 312, §1, has the right to confirm as moderator of a public association the person elected by the association or to install the one presented or to name the person by his own right; the same ecclesiastical authority also names the chaplain or ecclesiastical assistant, having heard the major officials of the association where this is expedient.

There are two principal routes by which an incumbent for an office may be designated for a community: by a vote of its own members or by designation by a higher authority. The authority in turn may simply *name* the incumbent, *confirm* (or veto) a candidate elected by the body, or *institute* the incumbent from among a slate of several presented by the body. The statutes of establishment of an association must be very carefully drawn up in

this regard: unless there is *explicit* reservation of the right to elect its own officers, the appointment —based upon one of the three options just enumerated—is to be made by the higher authority. In turn, however, a bishop may never refuse confirmation of a presented candidate, if he or she be "suitable" (c. 179, §2). The judgment of suitability, however, presumably rests with the bishop. Regarding the designation of chaplain, however, the body simply does not have a right to vote upon this officer, although the appointing ecclesiastical authority is to "consult" the officials of the association in making the selection. Good relationships would suggest an informal election by the body, nonetheless, presentation to the authority, and amicable acceptance by the latter.

§2. The norm stated in §1 is also valid for associations erected outside their own churches or houses by members of religious institutes in virtue of apostolic privilege; however, in associations erected by members of religious institutes in their own church or house, the nomination or confirmation of the moderator and chaplain belongs to the superior of the institute, in accord with the statutes.

In cases in which associations have been officially established through apostolic privilege by an institute of consecrated life *outside* their proper churches or houses, principles of law already seen are operative. Even the apostolic privilege does not insulate the selection of the moderator from the hand of the pontifical or national or diocesan authority—nor can the statutes of the associations countermand this. On the other hand, those associations seated *within* the religious house are offered their moderator and their chaplain by the superior of the institute according to its own statutes. The alternative option of election of a candidate by the body and presentation to the superior is preserved, however, by the directives of the canon.

§3. In associations which are not clerical, lay persons can exercise the office of moderator; the chaplain or ecclesiastical assistant shall not assume that role unless the statutes provide otherwise.

This paragraph is the mirror image of canon 302 and directs that lay associations may have lay moderators in their associations, although clerical ones are not excluded. The remainder of the norm is ambiguous: it could imply either that there is not to be a chaplain or that a lay member is not to take the chaplain's position. The implication would seem to indicate that the chaplain should be a cleric, if functions of the sacrament of orders are expected of him. An informal chaplaincy not demanding these functions might still be held as conforming with the norm, however.

[15]Associated Press, in St. Paul (Minn.), *Pioneer-Press,* 4-17-62.

§4. Those who exercise leadership in political parties are not to be moderators in public associations of the Christian faithful which are directly ordered to the exercise of the apostolate.

The uneasy conjunction of "religion and politics" in the United States is directly confronted in the norm of this paragraph. This directs that those in public associations of the Church that are "directly ordered to the exercise of the apostolate" may not present as their moderators those who "exercise leadership in political parties." The earlier qualifications are both careful and exact: *both* public juridic status and direct order "to the exercise of the apostolate" must be present to invoke the injunction. The "directness" of the orientation will be open to the discretionary evaluation of the one appointing the moderator. Open to differing evaluations, however, will be the political connection of the candidate. Two American paradigms come immediately to mind: a priest who was elected a member of the United States House of Representatives and, by contrast, one who is a member of the powerful Rules Committee of the Democratic Party. The concluding qualification of this canon can be read in two ways. It might disallow either (1) the candidate who is a member of a political party and at the same time holds a directing office in government (the U.S. Representative) or (2) the candidate who holds a directing office *in* a political party (the Rules Committee member). By analogy with older law the first would be the intent of the canon. Older law clearly disallowed (without appropriate permission) the first; it never addressed itself to the second. The former has a public character to it. The latter has a certain private dimension. An American political *party* is essentially distinct from the *res publica*.

Special Governance

Canon 318 — §1. In special circumstances where grave reasons require it the ecclesiastical authority mentioned in can. 312, §1, can designate a trustee who is to direct the association temporarily in the name of the authority.

This and the following paragraph deal with urgent and presumably grave situations. The empowering ecclesiastical authority may intrude—in cases in which special and grave circumstances demand it—and appoint a "commissarium" to take over the governance of an association. The appointment is of its nature temporary, and such a provisional or abbreviated term should be designated when the step is taken. A "grave" cause might be serious jeopardy to the public image of the association or to the larger Church, urgent and massive financial crisis, illness or incapacity of the moderator in an association of high importance and visibility, etc. The al-

ternate governor is uncertain in his or her makeup. The term used normally suggests a commission or a committee, although a "trustee" might be argued. The former terms, however, imply a shared and divided responsibility, or widened resources, and may be both the more politic and the more effective in a given emergency. No stipulation is made regarding the displaced moderator; a good document of appointment would make clear, in tactful terms, the temporary status of the "trustee" or committee.

§2. The one who named or confirmed the moderator of a public association can remove the moderator for a just cause, having heard both the moderator and the major officials of the association in accord with the norm of the statutes; however, the one who named the chaplain can remove him in accord with the norm of cann. 192-195.

The summary removal of the moderator of an association for a just cause is remanded to the ecclesiastical authority who (technically) "named" or "confirmed" the moderator. (The authority who "instituted" a candidate from among a presenting slate would certainly also follow this procedure, although he is not expressly named.) This would suggest that there is no place in law for the "de-selection" of an incumbent by a body disgruntled by its former choice of moderator; it also imposes a kind of due process or hearing of both the inadequate incumbent and the major officers of the association. Statutory procedures are to be followed in this matter—if they have been formed. The chaplain may be removed virtually without formality. In both cases, however, the right of recourse remains. The matter is not addressed here, but parallel dispositions of law suggest that the recourse be *in devolutivo tantum*—the incumbent gracefully steps down, until the matter is resolved by the appellate or arbitrating body.

Property of the Juridic Person

Canon 319 — §1. Unless other provision has been made, a legitimately erected public association administers the goods which it possesses in accord with the norm of its statutes under the higher direction of the ecclesiastical authority mentioned in can. 312, §1, to whom the association must render an account of the administration each year.

It has been noted that a "public" association automatically becomes a juridic person (see c. 313). In financial matters, however, unless the statutes of establishment should indicate otherwise, it remains a distinctly minor juridic person, i.e., with administration of its property under the supervision of the enabling competent authority. The intensity or manner of this control is not indicated; the authority is within his rights in demanding complete disclosure and accountability. Good relationships would suggest a workable arrangement that is mutually agreed upon. No form is specified for a required annual report to the appropriate authority: honesty would require that it be complete, if not detailed; and in a major public association, a certified public audit would be in order for the satisfaction of the association, the ecclesiastical authority, and the larger church public.

§2. The association must also render to the same ecclesiastical authority a faithful account of the disposition of offerings and alms which it collects.

Good reporting and good relationships demand also the disclosure of items that are not strictly earned, or income. Foresight suggests spelling out a mutual understanding of what will come within the terms of "offerings" and "alms" and even gifts to the association and are therefore reportable: intangible or at least non-fungible donations may be considerable (the free rent, the amiable discount in a large matter, the "familiarization" trip, etc.).

Suppression

Canon 320 — §1. Associations erected by the Holy See can be suppressed only by the Holy See.
§2. Associations erected by a conference of bishops can be suppressed by the same conference for grave reasons; associations erected by a diocesan bishop can be suppressed by him, and also associations erected through an apostolic indult by members of religious institutes with the consent of the diocesan bishop.

This is subsidiarity in reverse: activity in the opposite direction to the foundational norms of canon 312. The local bishop may not intrude into the national or pontifical association, etc.; the right is affirmed, however, of each seat of empowering authority to recall its own establishment of an association and to suppress it. Grave cause (presumably not required for the Holy See's decision) must underlie such determinations on the part of the national conference or of the diocesan bishop. The latter may even intrude into those associations formed under privilege by institutes of consecrated life, where the same grave cause is present; the right of recourse to the Holy See, i.e., challenging an assertedly unjust or unwarranted suppression, is always open to the aggrieved association.

§3. A public association is not to be suppressed by competent authority without having heard its moderator and other major officials.

The language of this paragraph suggests an invalidating condition: the suppression of an offending public association may not be undertaken *unless*

there has been consultation with the moderator and major officers of the group. This language normally indicates an irreducible condition. Peremptory suppression—without such consultation—would almost certainly be upheld as invalid. Consultation only is demanded; the opinions are consultative and not decisive upon the authority. In addition, there is no demand for a collegiate hearing; a mail census or a series of personal approaches would satisfy the requirement, although a group discussion adds a certain dynamic that the other approaches would not offer.

CHAPTER III
PRIVATE ASSOCIATIONS OF THE CHRISTIAN FAITHFUL
[cc. 321–326]

Self-Direction

Canon 321 — The Christian faithful guide and direct private associations according to the prescripts of their statutes.

The intensity of supervision by the competent ecclesiastical authority of "public" associations is heightened by contrast with the autonomy of those associations that are "private": they may freely direct and guide their own affairs—within the limitations of their founding statutes.

Establishment

Canon 322 — §1. A private association of the Christian faithful can acquire juridic personality by means of a formal decree of the competent ecclesiastical authority mentioned in can. 312.

The way to juridic personality and public establishment is always open to private associations of the Christian faithful by seeking establishment from the appropriate authority. This implies a correlative acceptance of the responsibilities of such a step. The norm requires that establishment be realized through a formal decree; as observed in the commentary on canon 298, §2, that decree should be explicit in stating that the association is being consciously "erected" rather than merely being praised or recommended.

§2. No private association of the Christian faithful can acquire juridic personality unless its statutes have been approved by the ecclesiastical authority mentioned in can. 312, §1; however, the approval of the statutes does not change the private nature of the association.

The review and acceptance of the competent establishing authority must explicitly include an approbation of the statutes of the body, and both should be principally addressed toward them. The language of the norm further safeguards the distinction between public and private bodies: mere approval of statutes alone does not itself constitute public establishment.

Ecclesiastical Supervision

Canon 323 — §1. Although private associations of the Christian faithful enjoy autonomy in accord with the norm of can. 321, they are subject to the vigilance of ecclesiastical authority in accord with the norm of can. 305, and are subject to the governance of the same authority.

Private associations, however autonomous, are still under the concerned pastoral supervision of the competent ecclesiastical authority. The norm both emphasizes the autonomy of the private association within the Church and graciously offers an insight into the intent of canon 305, §1: the supervision or "vigilance" there described is not to be oppressive but identical to the pastoral concern of a bishop for the individuals of his local church, i.e., encouraging, supportive, corrective, stimulative to growth, and demonstrative of leadership.

§2. It is also the responsibility of ecclesiastical authority, while observing the autonomy proper to private associations, to be watchful and take care that their energies are not dissipated and that their exercise of their apostolate is ordered toward the common good.

It is precisely this stimulation toward the work of the apostolate that must be exercised—by focusing the energies of the private association without unduly intruding into its autonomy. The quality of leadership is here challenged in Curia, or national conference, or local bishop, to forestall within the association any aimlessness of its powers, and to guide it toward the larger common good of the people of God.

Selection of Officers

Canon 324 — §1. A private association of the Christian faithful freely selects its own moderator and officials in accord with the norm of its statutes.

Private associations of the Christian faithful may freely designate their own officers within the limitations of their statutes. This function of "private" bodies is in direct contrast to the subjection to the enabling authority in the appointment of officers in "public" associations that is described in canon 317, §1.

§2. A private association of the Christian faithful can freely choose a spiritual advisor, if it desires

one, from among the priests legitimately exercising ministry in the diocese; however, he needs the confirmation of the local ordinary.

The position of "spiritual advisor" in the private association is presumably parallel to that of the "chaplain" described in canon 317, §1, for a public association; the placement is precisely parallel within this area of the Code, and the same norms apply. The requirements are spelled out: the candidate for the office must be a priest (a permanent deacon would not qualify) selected from among those "legitimately exercising ministry in the diocese"; this would be generally verified by his having the faculties of the diocese. An ordinary could, however, in effect extend this legitimate ministry on an ad hoc basis to a priest from another diocese, who has the faculties of that other diocese, for service specifically as the spiritual director or chaplain of the association within his own diocese. "Confirmation" of the candidate must be offered, and it must be expressed; mere failure to reply to a request for confirmation cannot be construed as tacit approval.

Administration of Property

Canon 325 — §1. A private association of the Christian faithful freely administers the goods which it possesses according to the prescriptions of its statutes, with due regard for the right of competent ecclesiastical authority to be watchful that the goods are used for the purposes of the association.

Private associations may freely administer their own property within the requirements of their proper statutes. This norm is a bulwark against intrusion and unsought supervision comparable to canon 309; within the limitations described in the surrounding canons, it can be appealed to as a charter for independence in temporal things. The competent authority may, however, ascertain that the goods of the association are in fact being directed to the goals of the entity.

§2. An association is subject to the authority of the local ordinary in accord with the norm of can. 1301 concerning administration and disposition of funds which have been donated to it or left to it for pious causes.

An important exception to the foregoing relative fiscal autonomy of a private society is the right of the ordinary to supervise the execution of bequests in behalf of pious causes. Canon 1301 jealously protects the intent of the testator and states there the requirement that the local ordinary (who is automatically the executor of such last wills and testaments in this regard, at least within the boundaries of the worshiping community itself) verify the carrying out of the bequest. He may therefore legitimately inquire whether the private association has carried out the intent of bequests made to it, and the association has a corresponding obligation to yield to and to cooperate with such requests.

Dissolution

Canon 326 — §1. A private association of the Christian faithful ceases to exist in accord with the norm of its statutes; it can also be suppressed by competent authority if its activity causes serious harm to ecclesiastical doctrine or discipline or is a scandal to the faithful.

The extinction of a private association should be foreseen in its own constitution and statutes and comes about through their prescriptions. Its suppression, however, comes from external initiative and agencies that are beyond the control of the statutes and lies with the establishing authority. The grave causes necessary for suppression to occur are parallel to those discussed in the commentary on canon 320. Three are named: serious jeopardy to doctrine or to ecclesiastical discipline or scandal to the faithful.

§2. The allocation of the goods of an extinct association is to be determined in accord with the norm of its statutes, with due regard for acquired rights and the will of the donors.

It is hoped that the constitution, in its foreseeing a possible future dissolution of the association, as suggested in paragraph one, will also have indicated a prior disposition of the assets of the entity. They are to be so disbursed according to those statutes. If it has not been determined—always within pertinent requirements of civil law—the enabling competent ecclesiastical authority should equitably determine the disposition of the assets. Two qualifications upon this are stated in the canon. Already-existing contractual obligations and other "acquired rights" (e.g., in an insurance program) must be honored; as with reference to canon 325, §2, assets acquired through a last will and testament must be disposed of according to the intentions of the testator. The supervising authority has no option in this—other than to carry out the already-stated intent in the contract or the will.

CHAPTER IV
SPECIAL NORMS FOR
ASSOCIATIONS OF THE LAITY
[cc. 327–329]

Foundation

Canon 327 — Lay members of the Christian faithful are to esteem greatly associations estab- lished for the spiritual purposes mentioned in can. 298, and especially those which propose to animate the temporal order with the Christian spirit and in this way greatly foster an intimate union between faith and life.

This and the following two canons offer a curious, truncated parallel to all that has gone before. It has already been noted (cf. the commentary on c. 298, §1) that the cast of all the intricate legislation on associations of the Christian faithful that precedes this point is clerical. These three canons intensify that impression. This first canon indicates that even lay Christians may form associations with the same ends as those of canon 298 (even though *that* had suggested that associations of the faithful may be clerical or lay or mixed in their memberships). The implications here are of a stratified ecclesiology and a seemingly pejorative stance. A proper understanding of the role of the laity makes it difficult to see the intent of this conscious subdivision within this entire set of norms; it seems to contradict the whole thrust of *Lumen Gentium,* especially chapter V, on the call to holiness and to the apostolate of all baptized believers. It is not clear in the present formulation of law whether *"Christifideles"* means all believers or refers to the laity alone or even to clerics alone. Some norms (as this one) seem to differentiate laity from hierarchy; others suggest in appropriate places equality through baptism with differing ministries. The commentary on canons 204 to 207 addresses itself to some of the most profound underlying questions of the 1983 Code that are implied in the very existence of this brief chapter.

Cooperation with Other Associations

Canon 328 — Those who preside over associations of the laity, even those associations erected in virtue of an apostolic privilege, are to see to it that they cooperate with other associations of the Christian faithful, where it is expedient, and willingly assist the various Christian works especially those in the same territory.

This norm is precisely parallel—for lay associations of the faithful—to what was expressly said for *public* (but not specifically lay) associations in canon 311; it repeats almost verbatim the injunction that associations of members of institutes of consecrated life should cooperate with and pursue the apostolic ends of already-existing associations within a diocese. The implication is that the earlier canon excluded lay persons from consideration (although it did not say that) and that this supplies for that exclusion and formalizes it.

Aims

Canon 329 — Moderators of associations of the laity are to see to it that the members of the association are duly formed for the exercise of the apostolate which is proper to the laity.

The moderator of lay associations should see to it that the members are encouraged and "formed" to apostolates appropriate to the laity. The entire question of diverse ministries within the contemporary Church underlies this directive. Determination of this "apostolate which is proper to the laity" must await further clarification in the reflections of theologians and the guidance of the magisterium.

BIBLIOGRAPHY

The bibliographical material provided at the end of the commentary on canons 96–123 of Book I gives a thorough list of significant references regarding this area of canon law.

Part II
THE HIERARCHICAL CONSTITUTION OF THE CHURCH
[cc. 330–572]

Book II is divided into three parts; this is the second. The Book began with who are the people of God, those who are in communion and live the life of the Church as Christian faithful, whether lay or clerical. It also explored their free association within the Church. Now the Code turns to the institutional structures that support and serve those people, whether at the most local level of parish and diocese or at the more general level of province, nation, and international communion.

The Church is organized universally as a communion of particular churches. There are various bonds that form this communion, among which are the visible, juridical ties of hierarchical communion by which bishops are joined with one another and with the head of the college of bishops, the pope (*LG* 23). This second part of Book II on the people of God addresses the Church's hierarchical constitution principally in terms of those whose ministry it is to assure the continuance of unity in communion.

There are two sections to this part. The first deals with supreme authority in the Church (cc. 330–367). The second addresses particular churches and their groupings and the authority established in them (cc. 368–572). Supreme authority rests with the pope and the college of bishops (cc. 330–341); it is exercised by them in various ways and with the help of various institutions pertaining to the Church universal (cc. 342–367). Particular churches, primarily dioceses, are the key elements in the communion of churches. The law views them first in themselves and in terms of the ministry of bishops within them (cc. 368–430). It then takes up the interrelationship of various churches in provinces, conferences of bishops, and the juridic institutions pertaining to them (cc. 431–459). Finally, the canons address the inner structuring of the particular church at the diocesan level, in parishes, and as individual churches (cc. 460–572).

Comparison with the 1917 Code

The material in these canons reflects one of the major shifts in thinking that according to Paul VI should characterize the revised Code in light of the Second Vatican Council. Vatican I had begun a doctrinal treatment of the Church but was cut short, issuing only a document on the pope and not able to complete its teaching with a consideration of the bishops and of the ecclesial setting in which the Petrine ministry and the episcopal ministry are exercised.[1] Vatican II deliberately set out to complete the work of Vatican I, seeking to provide the broader ecclesial context for understanding supreme authority in the Church (*LG* 18).

The 1917 Code was a faithful reflection of Vatican I's teaching and of the consensus among theologians and canonists about the hierarchical structure of the Church.[2] It organized its treatment in terms of power: supreme power and those who by ecclesiastical law participate in it, and episcopal power and those who participate in that power.[3] These were not equal powers. Canon 108, §3 of the former law indicated that the hierarchy of jurisdiction consisted of the "supreme pontificate and subordinate episcopate."

The 1983 Code adopts a moderated approach. It focuses on authority rather than power: supreme church authority, and authority in relationship to particular churches.[4] Authority is the legitimate exercise of power, and law is concerned with addressing how such an exercise is legitimate. Moreover, the Vatican II teaching on the college of bishops places the episcopate in a different light vis-à-vis the pope, the head of that college, than was apparent in the organization of the 1917 Code.

This new way of thinking has also affected the revised Code's organization of various canonical institutes. The 1917 Code presented metropolitans, plenary and provincial councils, and other authorities above the level of the diocese as participating in supreme power. Now they are presented as elements of the relationships between particular churches, i.e., part of their mutual cooperation and functioning. This does not detract from the authority of metropolitans or particular councils, but it places a different light on the source of that authority: it is rooted in the communion of churches and collegial interaction of bishops and does not strictly devolve directly from the pope.

[1] Vatican I, First Dogmatic Constitution on the Church of Christ *Pastor aeternus*, July 18, 1970, *COD*, 788–792. For details on this council, see C. Butler, *The Vatican Council 1869–1870* (Westminster, Md.: Newman, 1962).
[2] V. Walsh, "The Theological and Juridical Role of the Bishop: Early Twentieth Century and Contemporary Views," *Apol* 44 (1971), 39–92.
[3] See the rubrics in *CIC* for Book II, part I, section II, titles VII and VIII.
[4] See the rubrics of the 1983 Code for Book II, part II, section I, and section II, title I.

Finally, given the peculiar nature of certain institutes and the fact that the Code is directed toward the Church universal and not just its central administration, a number of institutes that received lengthy treatment in the 1917 Code are now referred to particular legislation appropriate to them. Thus, for example, there are few canons on the Roman Curia, and the treatment of cardinals has been shortened. Other institutes express the collegiality of bishops and greater involvement of particular churches in the universal communion, with canons added on the synod of bishops and on conferences of bishops—both new institutes since the 1917 Code.

Sources

The key sources for these canons are found in the conciliar documents *Lumen Gentium* and *Christus Dominus,* especially chapter III of *Lumen Gentium* and its accompanying "Explanatory Note," and chapters I and III of *Christus Dominus.* In addition, a number of canons from the 1917 Code have been retained or at least appear in a form modified on the basis of post-conciliar legislation. Key documents since the Council for this part of the law include the *motu proprio Apostolica sollicitudo* of September 15, 1965 on the synod of bishops,[5] a series of practical directives by Paul VI on matters affecting cardinals, the apostolic constitution *Regimini Ecclesiae Universae* of August 15, 1967 governing the reorganized Roman Curia,[6] the *motu proprio Sollicitudo omnium ecclesiarum* of June 24, 1969 regulating papal legates,[7] and the provisions of the *motu proprio Ecclesiae sanctae* of August 6, 1966 on conferences of bishops, metropolitans, and related matters.[8]

Significant Changes

At least five significant changes deserve mention in setting the context for these canons.

First, the organization of the material was the subject of considerable debate even through the 1981 meeting of the Code Commission. The approach proposed earlier would have begun with the Church universal, then dealt with regional structures, and finally addressed the particular church or diocese. This was eventually replaced with a style more in tune with the pattern followed at Vatican II. This begins with the Church universal, then deals with the particular church, and finally addresses particular churches in relationship to one another and in their own inner structures. As noted

above, this is an important expression of the "new way of thinking" that characterizes the Code. It also constitutes the context within which the canons are to be interpreted (c. 17).

Second, in keeping with the Second Vatican Council's effort to complete the work of the First Vatican Council, the pope and the college of bishops are said to exercise supreme authority in the Church—not the pope alone. In presenting this material, the Code remains faithful to Vatican II as it stands, without attempting to resolve points the Council did not resolve and without entering the subsequent discussions on theories that would explain the relationship of pope and college. The Code, therefore, should not be used as a pretext to foreclose the various legitimate theological positions that have emerged during and since the Council.

Third, the presentation on supreme authority also limits its consideration to the universal Church level in law. This is in contrast to the 1917 Code which extended participation in universal power even to metropolitans. In the 1983 Code the structures above the level of a diocese but below that of the Church universal are considered groupings of particular churches, i.e., expressions of ecclesial communion rather than exercises of primatial power. The precise nature of this authority and the theoretical explanation for its place in the Church are open to further discussion and refinement. Again, the Code is not intended to foreclose such theoretical development.

Fourth, the synod of bishops, a new institute established during Vatican II, is given detailed treatment. While the Code does not present any significant development in this structure beyond existing norms, it does highlight the place of the synod by treating it before the canons on the cardinals or Roman Curia. In law, the context is a significant consideration for interpreting the meaning and relative importance of an institute.[9]

Finally, conferences of bishops, whose juridic status was given a new focus and force during Vatican II, receive renewed treatment in the Code. As with the synod of bishops, the Code does not break new ground in this area, but it does systematize what has been existing law and evidences the importance conferences have achieved in the pattern of Catholic life since the Council.

Also to be noted is the continuation of some traditional canonical institutes that may seem to have fallen into desuetude in recent times. Consistories of cardinals are provided with a new look even though they have become quite formalized in prac-

---

[5]*CLD* 6, 388–393.
[6]Ibid., 324–357.
[7]*CLD* 7, 277–284.
[8]*CLD* 6, 264–298.

[9]This point was raised in objection to the present ordering but the Code Commission reported that the pope himself had asked for the present arrangement; see *Rel. Comm* 14 (1982), 180.

tice. Provincial and even plenary councils are continued as major structures of church life, and indeed they are updated to provide for participation by a cross-section of the people of God.

Drafting the Canons

These canons are the product of two distinct lines of development in the Code revision process. The canons dealing with the pope and the college of bishops, including the norms on ecumenical councils, were developed by the *Lex Ecclesiae Fundamentalis coetus.* There was some refinement between the 1969 to 1971 versions of the *Lex Ecclesiae Fundamentalis* (cc. 30–45) and the 1980 *Lex Ecclesiae Fundamentalis* text (cc. 29–42) submitted to the pope but not promulgated. The development involved giving greater emphasis to the conciliar teaching on the role of the college of bishops and the pope's relationship to it, and an attempt was made to state the doctrinal basis for the apostolic succession of pope and bishops in line with the teaching of Vatican I and Vatican II. After the 1981 meeting of the Code Commission, much of this material was inserted in the Code. Dropped in the transition were an introductory section (1980 *LEF* c. 19, §1)—replaced by canon 330 in the promulgated text—and a section on the solicitude of bishops for the welfare of the Church at large (1980 *LEF* c. 34, §2). With some modifications, the rest of the 1980 *Lex Ecclesiae Fundamentalis* text on these issues is now law.

The remainder of the canons under consideration here are drawn from the work of the *coetus De clericis,* whose name was later changed to *De sacra hierarchia.* Its work was first published in the 1977 schema *De Populo Dei* (cc. 155–216), later revised and somewhat reorganized in the 1980 schema (cc. 277–334). As a result of discussion at the Code Commission meeting in 1981, the organization of the material was further revised to reflect the Vatican II approach, as explained above. In the promulgated text a canon that referred to the *Lex Ecclesiae Fundamentalis* for the law on the supreme authority in the Church (1980 schema c. 277) was replaced by the insertion of the *Lex Ecclesiae Fundamentalis* canons described above (cc. 330–341).

Section I: SUPREME CHURCH AUTHORITY
[cc. 330–367]

This section is organized into five chapters preceded by an introductory canon. It addresses supreme authority in the Latin Church, for that is the subject matter of this Code (c. 1); as such, however, supreme authority is often considered supra-ritual. Certainly the treatment of the pope and the college of bishops is not limited to the Latin Church. To the extent that the other institutes covered in this section apply to the communion of Ritual Churches *sui iuris* that forms the general Catholic Church, they also pertain to more than the Latin Church. For purposes of this commentary, however, their significance in the Latin Church will be the prime consideration.

Supreme Authority

As noted above, this Code deals with supreme "authority" rather than supreme "power" as the 1917 Code termed it. The difference is more than semantics, for it reflects a renewed approach to the role of power and authority in the Church. This was highlighted by Pope John Paul II in promulgating the Code when he stressed that hierarchical authority is to be considered as service. To appreciate the newness involved here, it will be important to consider briefly the historical development of "power" in the Church.[10]

1. Early Christendom

In the primitive Church, power and function were one. As a result of disputes over the value of functions performed by unworthy ministers, the concept of power in the Church began to emerge as something beyond the work of individual persons and was seen as Christ's power continuing to work among His people.

With the development after Constantine of Christendom as a single society formed by Church and State, the theory of two powers took shape. The Church exercised a spiritual power (*potestas spiritualis*) while civil authorities exercised a secular power (*potestas laicalis*). Spiritual power had Christ for its source, contained all that was needed for the Church to do its mission, and was exercised by various vicars: bishops as vicars of Christ, the pope as vicar or successor of Peter.

2. Middle Ages

Distinctions became more common from the ninth century. As a result of the lay investiture controversy and the rise of missionary priests who were not limited to a fixed place for ministry, the exercise of power was gradually distinguished from the power itself. Early reform movements frequently sought to enforce church renewal by appealing to central authorities and thereby developed increased

[10]See U. Navarette, "Potestas Vicaria Ecclesiae. Evolutio historica conceptus atque observationes attenta doctrina concilii Vaticani II," *P* 60 (1971), 414–486; R. Schwarz, "De potestate propria Ecclesiae," *P* 63 (1974), 429–455; P. Krämer, *Dienst und Vollmacht in der Kirche. Eine rechtstheologische Untersuchung zur Sacra Potestas-Lehre des II Vatikanischen Konzils* (Trier: Paulinus, 1973).

centralization around the Roman See. Innocent III crowned all this by two major developments. He authorized absolute ordinations, which meant the reception of power in the Church without any necessary connection to its exercise in a particular place. He also transformed the general title of "Vicar of Christ" from one formerly applied to all bishops, to a special expression for the fullness of power enjoyed by the pope.[11]

Medieval theories of power moved from the unitary spiritual power concept of the early Church to a concept of two powers within the Church. One power is that of orders that comes from ordination; the other is the power of jurisdiction that comes from the pope through the granting of a canonical mission. As Vicar of Christ the pope held the fullness of jurisdiction; other jurisdictional power was derived from him. According to some, even the jurisdiction of civil authorities was derived from the pope. Among the complex issues of conciliarism in the late medieval period was the debate over supreme power in the Church in the form of "supremacy"—supremacy of the pope over council, or of the council over pope.

3. Reformation

With the late medieval breakup of Christendom and the rise of nation-states, the power of the Church remained as a "proper jurisdiction" exempt from the new civil authorities. One of the Reformers' claims was for a truly spiritual Church devoid of the earthly trappings of power accumulated in the Church. They called for civil authorities to resolve questions of church order as part of national sovereignty.

The Catholic response was to emphasize the visible dimension of the Church, a society as visible as any nation, and to assert the "proper power" of the Church. Against the claims of secular authorities and the Reformers, this was a power as proper to the Church in the spiritual realm as the power natural to civil governments in the secular realm.

The exercise of this power was located ultimately in the pope, sovereign in the Church. Reform efforts and the reorganized Roman Curia heightened the practical effects of this centralization despite efforts by Gallicans, Josephinists, and others to highlight the role of the local churches.

Perfect Society

This polemical emphasis on the Church's own power in the Church-State issue produced a shift in how that power was described within the Church

itself. The two hierarchies of orders and jurisdiction, formerly distinguished according to their source (ordination or canonical mission), were now distinguished according to their object. Orders, a sacramental power, was directed toward the true Body of Christ, the Eucharist, and other sacraments; jurisdiction, on the other hand, was concerned with the mystical Body of Christ, or church life and order. Its source was seen to be native to the Church, as with any sovereign society that has all the powers needed to achieve its mission (i.e., a "perfect society," as contrasted to dependent or imperfect societies like the family). A perfect society has the "proper power" Catholics claimed in their debates with the Reformers. In addition to this proper power of jurisdiction that was natural to the Church as a perfect society, it also possessed the sacramental power of orders as a special power from Christ.

The earlier concept that those who exercised power in the Church did so as Christ's vicars gave way to a new notion—that they exercised the proper power of the Church in their own name when using jurisdiction but by special commission from Christ when using power over sacramental matters. Ultimately, of course, even jurisdiction was derived from Christ for it came through His vicar, the pope, but the nature of the power was viewed in frankly secular terms.

The debates between ultramontanes and those who sought a more collegial approach to church government were framed in these terms, both sides operating within the same basic categories. Thus the teaching of Vatican I must be placed within this context of "perfect society" theory or an understanding of church power in terms taken from civil governmental theory.

Sacred Power

The debates at Vatican II touched on several key elements of this history of power in the Church. To begin with, the Council appreciated the Church as an ecclesial reality—more dissimilar from a civil society than it is like one. Power in the Church is that of Christ, which means *all* power in the Church is truly vicarious, even that which the pope and bishops exercise properly as ordinaries (i.e., in virtue of their offices). The question is now about authority—the legitimate exercise of Christ's power—rather than about power native to church government.

The source of this power is Christ. For the pope this has been clear, since even his primacy of jurisdiction is given by the Lord upon his acceptance of legitimate election. The Council wrestled with how to explain the power exercised by bishops as coming from Christ while still maintaining good order and structure in the Church. The solution of *Lu-*

---

[11]M. Maccarrone, *Vicarius Christi: Storia del titolo papale* (Rome: Pontificia Universitas Lateranense, 1953).

men Gentium and its "Explanatory Note" is this.[12] Bishops receive the functions (*munera*) by which they participate in Christ's mission as teachers, sanctifiers, and pastoral rulers with episcopal consecration, which the Council taught is a sacramental act and hence one in which Christ acts directly (*LG* 21). By their very nature, however, these *munera* are to be exercised only in hierarchical communion with the other members of the college of bishops, including its head (*LG* 21). This is because these *munera* are those of Christ, not personal possessions of the pope or bishops; they are by nature to be exercised only in an ecclesial context, the context of communion.

This conciliar teaching reverses the 1917 Code provision whereby episcopal consecration conferred the power of orders (the *munus* of sanctifying), but canonical mission conferred the ruling function of which teaching was a part. Thus before the Council, a priest named to be bishop could take possession of his see and exercise jurisdiction and magisterium there even before he was consecrated a bishop (*CIC* 332, 334). Since the Council and explicitly in the revised Code (c. 379), it is required that he receive episcopal consecration before taking possession of a diocese.

The ultimate purpose of church law, and therefore of power and authority within that law, is the salvation of souls (*salus animarum;* cf. *LG* 18). This applies to all authority in the Church. The specific purpose of supreme authority as expressed in both Vatican I and Vatican II is the unity of the Church (*Pastor aeternus*) in faith and fellowship (*LG* 18). Since the agents of supreme power, according to *Lumen Gentium,* are multiple (i.e., the pope and the rest of the bishops as a college in communion with him), the issue of their relationship in the exercise of supreme authority is crucial. Otherwise, what is intended for the unity of the Church could seem to lead to disunity.

Church Teaching

In line with a long historical development having special affinity to medieval controversies and to reform movements spearheaded by popes (e.g., Gregory VII [pope: 1073–1085], Innocent III [pope: 1198–1216], and Boniface VIII [pope: 1294–1303]), Vatican I addressed the supreme power of the pope. In the dogmatic constitution *Pastor aeternus,* his

primatial role was set forth in three stages. Chapter I focused on Peter as the prince of the apostles and head of the Church who received directly from Christ a primacy not only of honor but of jurisdiction. Chapter II argued that what Christ established in Peter is to remain in the Church; that it remains in Peter's successor; and that his successor is the "Roman See" which, by that fact, has the more powerful principality in the Church and from it the rights of communion flow to all.

The third chapter discussed the content of the primacy, which embraces a superiority of ordinary power by the Roman See over all other churches. The jurisdiction of the Roman Pontiff is characterized as truly episcopal (i.e., it comes with his being bishop of Rome) and immediate (not subject to any intermediaries, whether civil or ecclesiastical). In virtue of hierarchical subordination and true obedience, all are bound to submit to his jurisdiction in matters of faith and morals as well as in issues of discipline and church government. The purpose of this primacy of jurisdiction is that the Church may be one.

The fourth chapter of the conciliar document addressed the teaching authority of the pope. This is treated in the present commentary in the discussion of Book III and will not be developed further here.

Although *Pastor aeternus* appears sweeping in its claims, it was a carefully nuanced document resulting from debates in the First Vatican Council. Its drafters were conscious of the major objections of those not sharing ultramontanist sentiments and made an effort to meet them. That it was not intended to have the pope replace the legitimate role of bishops in the Church is expressly stated in the document. Vatican I was unable to finish its projected fuller treatment of the Church due, in part, to external historical circumstances, so this statement is not developed further. However, the German bishops in 1875 issued a clarification that does give some insight into the meaning of pope-bishop relationships as understood at the time.[13] Since their statement received explicit approbation by Pius IX, it is worth considering.

In response to Bismarck's claims that in virtue of the conciliar definitions the bishops in Germany were now agents of a foreign power, the bishops reaffirmed that the First Vatican Council had changed nothing in terms of the traditional role of bishops as constitutional in the Church. Vatican I, they pointed out, was an ecclesial, not a civil law, event; the episcopate is of divine right in the Church; and the pope's powers, while truly primatial within the Church, are nevertheless limited by what Christ set for the Church. Bishops, therefore,

---

[12]The "Explanatory Note" originally prefaced the report of the doctrinal commission about its handling of the recommendations (*modi*) from the Council members for changing the draft text of *LG.* It was announced to the Council that this explanatory note provided the proper understanding of the conciliar text and was to be published whenever the text of *LG* itself was published. See detailed commentary by J. Ratzinger, "Announcements and Prefatory Note of Explanation," Vorgrimler I, 297–305.

[13]F. Logan, "The 1875 Statement of the German Bishops on Episcopal Power," *J* 21 (1961), 285–295.

are not his agents but truly pastors in their own right within their own dioceses.

Vatican II attempted to complete the treatment begun by Vatican I by turning to the other dimension of agents of supreme authority in the Church, the episcopate. Explicitly reaffirming the teaching of Vatican I on papal primacy, Vatican II developed a parallel argument to explain the role of bishops (*LG* 18–24).

Where Vatican I began with the special role of Peter, Vatican II commenced with the apostles. Christ, the Council taught, called the apostles and formed them in the manner of a college or stable group. From among their midst He selected Peter, setting him over them. All the apostles, however, were sent by Christ on mission. Next Vatican II turned, as did Vatican I, to the question of their successors. Dealing with the apostles' successors, the Council focused on their mission. The two concepts are integrally connected: it is to continue their mission that the apostles needed successors. There are two senses in which the Council proposed that bishops succeed the apostles: in function, and as a college. First, just as the successor of Peter continues Peter's function, so the successors of the apostles continue the apostles' pastoral function; second, as Peter and the rest of the apostles formed one college, so the successor of Peter and the apostles' successors form one college.

The content of supreme authority is discussed in terms drawn from Vatican I but without mentioning the word "jurisdiction." The focus in Vatican II is more on pastoral authority, but this is truly a binding authority—as realistically binding as that expressed in more juridic terms under "jurisdiction." So the Roman Pontiff is acknowledged as exercising full, supreme, and universal power over the whole Church—which he can always use freely. The college of bishops is likewise the subject of supreme, full power over the whole Church; however, it must always act in communion with its head, the pope. This power is sacramental, for its source is Christ acting through sacramental ordination to the episcopate. It is episcopal, pertaining to the order of bishops for both the pope's power and that of the rest of the members of the college. It is an authority always exercised in hierarchical communion of head and members within the college. Religious assent of soul (rather than the "hierarchical subordination and true obedience" of Vatican I) is said to characterize how all in the Church are bound to this supreme authority.

Theoretical Questions

While *Lumen Gentium* makes major strides in placing the role and exercise of supreme power in a larger perspective, it left some critical issues unresolved. At the time of the Council and continuing since then, there are at least three major schools of thought on how the pope and bishops relate to each other in terms of supreme authority.[14]

The first focuses solely on the pope.[15] No act of supreme authority can take place without his involvement. If the bishops were to attempt to act without him, their action would count for nothing—even if it were to take place in the most solemn setting of an ecumenical council. Hence, according to this view, the true subject of supreme authority is the pope alone. On occasion, he joins to himself the other bishops, but this is more for the solemnity of the act than adding another subject of supreme power.

The second view, reflected quite explicitly in the "Explanatory Note" published with *Lumen Gentium,* holds that there are two subjects of supreme authority, although these are inadequately distinct.[16] That is, the pope can act alone as Vicar of Christ, exercising the fullness of supreme power in the Church in his own right and not involving the college of bishops; he can also act together with the other bishops in a collegial act, and in this case there is a second subject of supreme power—the college of bishops acting with its head. This view sees papal and collegial exercises of supreme power as distinct, but inadequately so, because in either case it is the one power of Christ that is being exercised, and in both cases the pope is personally involved. It is not a question of two subjects who might be opposed, and hence lead to disunity; rather, it is a matter of two different modalities in which the unifying power of Christ can be legitimately exercised as the supreme authority in the Church.

A third view also seeks to protect the unity of the Church but takes the role of the college of bishops (and of the apostolic college before it) as more central in the plan of salvation.[17] It locates the subject of supreme power in the college of bishops alone. The pope functions authentically not as an independent agent but as successor of Peter, i.e., head of the college. It is in virtue of this role that he is able to act sometimes without the rest of the college (but never independent, as it were, of communion in the college of bishops) and at other times with the rest of the members of the college. This view holds that

---

[14]Y. Congar, "Le problème ecclésiologique de la papauté après Vatican II," in *Ministères et communion ecclésiale* (Paris: Cerf, 1971), 167–186.

[15]This was the position defended by the minority at Vatican II. See A. Acerbi, *Due Ecclesiologie: Ecclesiologia giuridica ed ecclesiologia di communione nella "Lumen Gentium"* (Bologna: Dehoniane, 1975), 243–245, 444–447.

[16]K. Mörsdorf, "Bishop: Canon Law," *SacM* I, 231–232; W. Bertrams, *Quaestiones fundamentales iuris canonici* (Rome: Pontificia Universitas Gregoriana, 1969), 325–527.

[17]K. Rahner, "On the Relationship Between the Pope and the College of Bishops," *Theological Investigations* 10 (New York: Herder & Herder, 1973), 50–70.

even when the pope freely determines to act without involving other members of the college, he is still exercising the supreme power that Christ gave the college, a college that Peter was designated to head but not to replace or duplicate.

Two comments may be made about this theoretical debate. The first is that it continues to focus on individuals (pope and bishops) rather than on ecclesial realities (particular churches). There is as yet an unresolved tension between perceiving the Church in terms of the hierarchy and grasping the Church as the people of God, a worldwide communion of persons. Are the pope and the bishops to be understood first as existing in some way abstracted from diocesan churches or the church communities in which they serve, and only secondarily as ministering within God's people; or, is their function so intimately tied to the service of the people of God that they make sense only in the context of that ministry? In the first view, the subjects of supreme authority begin to distance themselves from the churches in which they serve and are seen in relationship to the abstraction of "universal Church." In the second view, they are rooted in the particular churches where they minister, and as Vatican I was careful to point out, it is the relationship of those churches to one another that is the foundation of the *munus* that one bishop has in regard to others (whether as pope, or as patriarch, metropolitan, etc.).[18]

The second remark that can be made about the theoretical debate is that it does have certain practical consequences. For example, to what extent are certain institutes in the Church expressions of papal or of collegial authority? To the extent that they are viewed as exclusively papal (in the sense of the pope acting independently of the college of bishops), they remain exempt from considerations of sensitivity to all the bishops that would have to be made were they to be considered expressions of the episcopal college. Two examples may help to clarify this point: the college of cardinals, and a new canonical institute—the synod of bishops.

The college of cardinals was considered by some in medieval times to succeed the apostles in the dimension of college even as bishops were successors of the apostles in terms of pastoral rule.[19] While this view is clearly superceded by the magisterium's teaching about the college of bishops, the college of cardinals can still be viewed either as a creation of

the papacy or as an expression of the collegial nature of church government (cf. c. 351, in which cardinals are appointed freely by the pope yet are to be members of the college of bishops). To what extent are the actions of the college of cardinals expressive in the collegiality of all bishops in the exercise of supreme authority in the Church?

The synod of bishops is perhaps an even clearer example of the issue. As will be seen below, when it was originally created, the synod was said to act on behalf of the world's bishops—a statement many took as alluding to the synod as a form of representative action by the college of bishops. In the Code, however, the synod is not so characterized and can be viewed more as an agent of papal power (c. 334), even though it may still be given the authority to take decisive action (c. 343).

Some institutes such as particular councils and the functions of metropolitans, which were presented in the 1917 Code as participating in papal power, are seen in the 1983 Code as expressions of the collegial relationships among bishops (or more accurately, as arising from the collaboration of various particular churches among themselves: cc. 431–459).

Although Vatican II called for the reform of the Roman Curia and of the legates of the Apostolic See in order to reflect more clearly their role of services to all the bishops, subsequent norms and those contained in the 1983 Code present these institutes as strictly papal institutes, directly subject to the pope and with little if any reference to the college of bishops.

Although the cardinals, the synod of bishops, the Roman Curia, and legates of the Roman Pontiff are commonly understood as assisting the Roman Pontiff specifically, and canon 334 presents them in the context of a papal rather than a collegial exercise of supreme power, nevertheless only legates are necessarily papal by definition. Even though current practice seems not to recognize the synod, the cardinals, and the Curia as exercises of collegial solicitude and responsibility in the universal Church, this does not rule out the theoretical possibility that such is indeed their nature, particularly if the theory about the college of bishops being the ultimate agency of supreme authority were adopted. Bishops are involved in each of these institutes (except legates), participating in the concern for the unity and life of the Church universal. Their involvement in virtue of the functions of Christ, in which they share by episcopal consecration, is more than as mere delegates of the pope—however undefined that something "more" may be.

Organization of the Canons

After an introductory summary on the successors of Peter and of the apostles (c. 330), the canons on supreme authority are divided into five chapters.

[18]Y. Congar, "La consécration épiscopale et la succession apostolique constituent-elles chef d'une Eglise locale ou membre du collège?" in *Ministères et communion ecclésiale,* 123–140; K. Rahner and J. Ratzinger, *The Episcopate and the Primacy* (New York: Herder & Herder, 1962); J.M.R. Tillard, *The Bishop of Rome* (Wilmington, Del.: Michael Glazier, 1983).

[19]Y. Congar, "Notes sur le destin de l'idée de collégialité épiscopale en Occident au Moyen Age (VIIe–XVIe siècles)," in *La collégialité épiscopale: Histoire et théologie* (Paris: Cerf, 1965), 118–128.

The first deals with the subjects of supreme authority, i.e., the Roman Pontiff (cc. 331–335) and the college of bishops (cc. 336–341). Ecumenical councils are dealt with as an expression of episcopal collegiality in keeping with *Lumen Gentium* 22. The remaining four chapters address specific agencies through which the exercise of supreme authority is carried out on a more frequent or regular basis in the Church universal: the synod of bishops (cc. 342–348), cardinals of the Holy Roman Church (cc. 349–359), the Roman Curia (cc. 360–361), and legates of the Roman Pontiff (cc. 362–367).

In general the canons cover the same material as the corresponding sections in the 1917 Code, frequently drawing on conciliar decrees or more recent particular legislation. The synod of bishops is new to this Code, not having existed at the time of the 1917 Code; the canons on the cardinals have been reduced, those on the Roman Curia even more dramatically—leaving much of the detail found in the former Code to particular law.

CANONS AND COMMENTARY _____

CHAPTER I
THE ROMAN PONTIFF AND THE
COLLEGE OF BISHOPS
[cc. 330–341]

Introductory Canon

Canon 330 — Just as, by the Lord's decision, Saint Peter and the other Apostles constitute one college, so in a similar way the Roman Pontiff, successor of Peter, and the bishops, successors of the Apostles, are joined together.

The relationship of pope and college of bishops is based on the relationship the Lord established between Peter and the other apostles. As explained above, Vatican II taught that the Lord constituted the apostles as a stable body or college and selected Peter from among their number as head of the group. This canon is a statement about both the college of bishops and the primacy of the pope, basing the foundation for their roles in the Church on the extent to which bishops are successors of the apostles and the pope is the successor of Peter.

The source for this canon is *Lumen Gentium* 22. It is repeated here verbatim, except for one omission. The Council presented Peter and the other apostles as constituting one *apostolic* college, but the canon has dropped the qualifier "apostolic." The conciliar text did appear fully in early versions of the *Lex Ecclesiae Fundamentalis* (1969: c. 31, §3; 1971: c. 32, §3) but was dropped from later versions of the *Lex Ecclesiae Fundamentalis* in favor of a longer and more theological statement about the same matters. The current text reappeared in this form only with the promulgation of the Code in 1983.

The canon makes several significant affirmations.

1. *College.* Peter and the other apostles were constituted as one college. This contains two major points. The first is that Peter is not separate from the rest of the apostles, as if they formed a college and Peter was not part of it. The apostolic college consisted of all the apostles, Peter included.

The second point is one expressed by the "Explanatory Note" published with *Lumen Gentium.* The term "college" is not to be understood in a strictly juridical sense, but analogically. Words such as "order" and "body" are also used to refer to the same reality as "college" in this context. Hence the "college" is not a "group of equals who entrust their power to their president" but "a stable group whose structure and authority are to be deduced from revelation."[20] Standard norms for collegial action, such as canon 119, do not apply strictly when examining how the apostolic college acted or how the college of bishops is to act today.

2. *Constitutional.* The formation of the apostolic college was by the Lord's design. It was not mere chance, nor a purely practical arrangement in imitation of some secular prototype, even if such prototypes existed. Rather, it is by Christ's design that the college came to be.

As established by the Lord, both the college and Peter's role in it are divine law (*iure divino*); hence, they are constitutional for the Church. They cannot be changed. Moreover, for the Church to be true to its own nature, they must be operable. One cannot extinguish the other, in theory or in practice.

3. *Proportionality.* The similarity of the relationship between Peter and the apostles and the relationship of the successor of Peter and the bishops is

_____
[20]"Explanatory Note," 1; Abbott, 98–99.

one of proportionality. That is, as the "Explanatory Note" published with *Lumen Gentium* states, to be successors does not "imply any transmission of the extraordinary power of the apostles to their successors" but rather that the "proportionality between the first relationship (Peter/apostles) and the second (pope/bishops)" is affirmed.[21]

The apostles are commonly considered to have enjoyed certain extraordinary powers in addition to those they received for pastoring the Church. These were in virtue of their roles as founders of the Church; these extraordinary powers are not considered to have survived them. Thus, for example, public revelation closed with the death of the last apostle. However, other functions necessary for the ongoing mission of the Church were designed to remain, and these are held to include the pastoring functions of teaching, sanctifying, and governing within the Church.

Vatican II taught that these pastoring functions continue in the body of bishops. The emphasis is on the succession by the entire body. Bishops as a body are successors to the pastoring function of the apostles; in the college of bishops the apostolic college continues.

Similarly, those extraordinary powers that the apostle Peter enjoyed along with the other apostles were not transmitted to his successors. But the special role committed to Peter within the apostolic college has continued in the Church through Peter's successors; for it is a continuing function within the college, designed for the pastoring of the Church and hence to last beyond the founding period of church history.

The canon therefore proposes that the relationship of the Roman Pontiff to the rest of the bishops is similar to that which existed between Peter and the rest of the apostles: they constitute, by the Lord's will, one single college that continues the mission given to the apostolic college. Within the college of bishops the pope continues the functions that Peter exercised within the apostolic college. The proportionality implies not only the significant role of the pope—in line with that entrusted to Peter—but it also limits the pope's role to that which Peter had among the apostles. The pope does not succeed to the role Christ had vis-à-vis the apostles but to that which Peter was given within the group.

Vatican I presented the See of Peter as the successor of Peter.[22] Vatican II has modified this by specifying the successor as the bishop of the See of Rome. *Lumen Gentium* uses in this connection the appellation taken from ancient Rome, *pontifex,* to designate the bishop of Rome. This title does not convey something new to Peter's successor, but it is an ancient custom of Christianizing titles and practices that were prevalent in pre-Christian times when these proved to be apt expressions for Christian realities. The word itself means one who builds bridges. It resonates well with the role of the bishop of Rome in maintaining the unity of the college of bishops and through that role the unity of the Church by bridging the differences that exist inevitably within a worldwide communion. For more discussion on this title, see below at canon 331.

This canon introduces the entire section on supreme authority in the Church, one of the fundamental elements in the hierarchical constitution of the Church but not its only element. Indeed, one of the purposes of the college of bishops is to express the diverse particular churches that are not dealt with under the section on supreme authority, but that are themselves constitutional elements of the Church.[23] Supreme authority, on the other hand, is not presented here as a secular power organized along some political model, whether that be the model of a confederation, an empire, or some other civil law scheme. Rather, it is a unique ecclesial reality established by the Lord, based on the apostles, and organized along the manner of a college in a special sort of way. The next two articles detail the specifics of this organization.

ARTICLE 1: THE ROMAN PONTIFF
[cc. 331–335]

Bishop of the Church of Rome

Canon 331 — The bishop of the Church of Rome, in whom resides the office given in a special way by the Lord to Peter, first of the Apostles and to be transmitted to his successors, is head of the college of bishops, the Vicar of Christ and Pastor of the universal Church on earth; therefore, in virtue of his office he enjoys supreme, full, immediate and universal ordinary power in the Church, which he can always freely exercise.

This canon is an effort to synopsize the carefully worded descriptions of the pope found in the documents of Vatican I and Vatican II without taking sides in current debates over the source of the pope's role or how to explain his relationship with the college of bishops in the supreme power of the Church. It deals with the pope as successor of Peter (in the first clause up to the semicolon) and characterizes the power of his office (in the remainder of the canon).

The text is drawn verbatim from the 1980 version of the *Lex Ecclesiae Fundamentalis* (c. 29, §2). The

---

[21]Ibid.; Abbott, 99.

[22]*Pastor aeternus* 2 refers both to the bishop of the See of Rome and to the Roman Church itself. Whoever succeeds in this chair of Peter obtains the primacy over the universal Church. The emphasis is on the relationship of primacy to the church of Peter's successor, Rome, which has thereby the "greater principality over all the churches." Cf. *COD,* 789.

[23]See *LG* 23; cc. 368–369.

reference to succeeding Peter is taken from *Lumen Gentium* 20 and the terms that characterize the nature of the power of his office and his freedom to exercise it are drawn from texts in *Lumen Gentium* 22 and 27, and *Christus Dominus* 2. These in turn are based on chapter three of *Pastor aeternus* of Vatican I. Canon 218 of the 1917 Code is comparable, although obviously it does not reflect the Vatican II phrases.

Bishop of the Church of Rome

The terms used to name the pope vary. This is the one place in the Code where he is named in reference to his diocese, Rome. Elsewhere in the Code the title drawn from pre-Christian Rome of "Roman Pontiff" (*Romanus Pontifex*) is preferred. At times he is termed the Supreme Pontiff (*Summus Pontifex*), a term that Vatican II applied primarily to Christ, the supreme High Priest (*LG* 21) and by analogy to the pope who is supreme among the pontiffs or bishops of local churches (*LG* 21). All represent Christ in their own churches; as head of the college of bishops, the Roman Pontiff is supreme among the pontiffs.

The analogy by which this last title is applied to the pope must be properly understood. In any analogy there is something similar that is used to compare two elements that are not similar. If Christ is the supreme High Priest (*Summus Pontifex* par excellence), then the application of this title to the pope must respect what the "Explanatory Note" published with *Lumen Gentium* presents as the proportionality to be observed. It is not the relation of Christ to the apostles but of Peter among the apostles that explains the relationship between pope and bishops.[24]

At Vatican I it was clearly in virtue of being bishop of Rome that the pope was presented as exercising a special role within the communion of churches, for it was stated that the See of Rome holds the principality over all other churches.[25] This reflected the ancient Christian emphasis on the Church and on the officeholder as intimately tied to his church. Vatican II shifted the emphasis to the apostles as a body and to those who succeed in their place for continuing the mission given them by Christ. This, in one sense, abstracts from the local church or ecclesial focus and concentrates more on the person.[26] The canon attempts to bridge these two approaches by beginning with the traditional formula "bishop of the Church of Rome," and then

relating this immediately to the successor of Peter and head of the college of bishops.[27]

Office of Peter

The office (*munus*) that the Lord gave in a singular way to Peter is said to continue in the bishop of Rome as the successor to whom this office was intended to be transmitted. As noted earlier, this office was within the college of the apostles; that of the pope is always within the communion of the college of bishops (c. 333, §2). This college, however, has a mission that goes beyond itself and beyond the inner concerns of the Church: to proclaim the gospel everywhere and at all times (a mission that all Christians share: cc. 756, 211). The function of unifying the college of bishops extends to providing for unified effort in its mission. Hence the role of the pope extends beyond the immediate confines of intra-ecclesial concerns, and as the head responsible for unity, it extends to the entire mission that the college was commissioned to carry out.

It is not as if the bishop of Rome were also the local bishop of every other local church. Rather, in virtue of the role of the Church of Rome, where the apostles Peter and Paul gave the ultimate witness of their lives, the bishop of that See has a special role within the communion of all the churches that form the Catholic communion (c. 368). This is further spelled out in the other titles in canon 331.

Papal Titles

The titles applied to the pope in one sense express his various functions. In another way they represent the differing views of the relative position of the pope and the college of bishops as the subject of supreme power. Each has its own history; only when taken as a whole do they present a comprehensive view of the role of the pope.

1. Head of the college of bishops (*caput collegii*) is clearly a Vatican II appellation, although it comes to the Council with a long history already and can hardly be considered an innovation.[28] It states directly what *Lumen Gentium* 22 and canon

---

[24]Congar, "Le problème ecclésiologique," 181.

[25]*Pastor aeternus* 2.

[26]In another sense Vatican II reflected a renewed ecclesiology. The Church appears in *LG* as a communion of churches (dioceses) rather than as a universal entity with dioceses as administrative subdivisions. See Tillard, 36–41, 68–69.

[27]Scholars argue that it is not necessarily a question of linear descent from Peter to one individual after another serving as bishop of Rome. It is possible that for some time the Church of Rome was governed not by a single individual bishop but by a college of church elders. The second-century letters of Clement, for example, are viewed by many scholars today, Catholic as well as Protestant, as bearing witness to more of a collective than an individual leadership in the Roman See at that time. The function (*munus*) of Peter, however, continued in the Roman See even under this arrangement, as those same letters attest. See J. Fuellenbach, *Ecclesiastical Office and the Primacy of Rome* (Washington: Catholic University, 1980).

[28]See historical studies in Congar et al., *La collégialité épiscopale*.

330 express concerning the pope succeeding to the place of Peter as head of the college of bishops.

2. Vicar of Christ (*Vicarius Christi*) has a rather complex history.[29] For the first millennium of Christian history the term regularly applied to bishops in their dioceses. Vatican II again employs the term for bishops in their own dioceses, where they are truly vicars of Christ in governing the flock committed to their care (*LG* 27). All power in the Church is truly that of Christ. Church authorities, whether as diocesan bishops or head of the college of bishops, exercise Christ's power as vicars and legates of the Lord, not as earthly rulers wielding a type of secular power.

Innocent III (pope: 1198–1216) is said to have been the first to restrict the use of "Vicar of Christ" to the pope as an expression of the fullness of power that the pope, as Peter's successor, had received from Christ. From the thirteenth century the term has been amplified, even inflated, to indicate the pope's absolute jurisdiction over civil rulers as well as within the Church. In more recent times its genuinely spiritual meaning is being recovered. It is difficult to demonstrate how this title in itself establishes any greater authority for the pope in the Church than is already his as bishop of Rome and, therefore, head of the college over which he presides as Peter's successor.

3. Pastor of the universal Church on earth (*universae Ecclesiae his in terris Pastor*) represents a modification of earlier formulae.[30] The Council of Florence and, citing it, Vatican I had referred to the pope as the head of the whole Church (*totiusque ecclesiae caput*).[31] The formula in canon 331 is taken from *Lumen Gentium* 22 where "head" (*caput*) was changed to "pastor." This shift is significant. It indicates the pastoral nature of the pope's authority: it is not a civil jurisdiction but an authority directed toward the salvation of souls.

The pope's power is that of a bishop or chief pastor. Vatican I painstakingly characterized papal power as "episcopal."[32] What a bishop is responsible to do for the salvation of souls in his own diocese, the pope is responsible to assure as to all the Church. As canon 333, §1 emphasizes, this does not in any way detract from the authority of bishops in their own dioceses but is intended to support and strengthen them. As head of the college, the pope has the office of being pastor to the pastors,

hence also of all the flock. The exercise of this office is further specified below (c. 333).

It should be noted the canon does not relate other titles appropriate to the bishop of Rome within the communion of Ritual Churches *sui iuris* and within the Latin Church. For example, the bishop of Rome is metropolitan of the province of Rome, primate of the country of Italy, and patriarch of the Western or Latin Church. The Code does not attempt to distinguish between his functions internal to the Latin Church (to which the Code applies directly—c. 1) and his functions within the communion of Ritual Churches *sui iuris*. This assumption of all his responsibilities into the highest ones can at times leave some confusion as to the exact basis on which the pope or those acting in his name become involved in a particular case, resulting in some tension particularly in dealing with Eastern Catholic Churches.

Papal Power

Drawing on the statements of Vatican I and *Lumen Gentium* 22 and *Christus Dominus* 2 of Vatican II, the canon goes on to detail the power that comes in virtue of the pope's office (*vi muneris sui*).

1. Power, in this context, always exists. The relationship to others that is constituted in virtue of the pope's office is a stable element in the Church's constitutional structure, even though that power may not be put into action at every moment (*in actu*). This power becomes supreme authority when it is used legitimately, for as noted above authority is the legitimate use of power.

2. Supreme power (*suprema*) means there is no power in the Church above this power. It is not subject to any other power on this earth, although it is always subject to Christ. Vatican I applied this directly to the relationship between the Church and civil governments, some of which at that time claimed their approval was needed before papal decrees could affect citizens subject to them. In *Pastor aeternus* III, the First Vatican Council denied these civil leaders' claims to an authority over the pope's, affirming papal power to be supreme in the Church. Similarly, Vatican I emphasized that the pope constitutes the court of ultimate appeal in the Church, to which any Christian may have recourse at any time, and from whose judgment there is no further appeal (see c. 333, §3 below).

The college of bishops is also said to be the subject of supreme power (c. 336). See the discussion above for the various theories that attempt to explain the relationship between pope and college in the exercise of supreme power.

3. Full (*plena*) indicates supreme power is not parceled out, as if the pope had only a piece of supreme power. Supreme power is indivisible, for it is the power of Christ in and over the Church that is

[29]M. Maccarrone, *Vicarius Christi: Storia del titolo papale.*

[30]On the historical development of this title, see H. Marot, "Note sur l'expression 'Episcopus Ecclesiae Catholicae,' " in *La collégialité épiscopale,* 94–98; R. Minnerath, *Le pape: Evêque universel ou premier des évêques?* (Paris: Beauchesne, 1978).

[31]Council of Florence, Session 6, *COD* 504; Vatican I, *Pastor aeternus* 3, *COD,* 789.

[32]Tillard, 142–150.

exercised by those who act in the person of Christ, vicariously exercising Christ's pastoral care for God's people. Whether the pope alone, or the college in a collegial act of head and members, exercises supreme power, it is always complete, lacking in nothing that pertains to it, and hence full.

4. Immediate (*immediata*) power is one that is not subject to any intermediaries or mediation. There is no middle party in the exercise of this power, and the pope can relate directly to any member of the Church—whether bishop or religious, cleric or lay—without being constrained to specific channels of civil authorities or ecclesiastical structures. As with the affirmation of supreme power, so the "immediate" character of papal power denies claims of civil powers to stand between the pope and some of the Christian faithful. Ecclesial power is a spiritual reality unlimited by national boundaries or civil jurisdictions.

While it is also true that papal power is immediate in the ecclesiastical sense so that the pope is not bound a priori by specific structures of ecclesiastical law, this does not mean that the pope should not or does not follow proper procedure. His very function of promoting the unity and good order of the Church binds him morally to observe procedures established by custom and by the Church's own law. His power to intervene directly in a local ecclesial situation is always to be used as a support to the proper and immediate authority that the local bishop exercises in virtue of his office, and not as a replacement or diminution of the local bishop's role (c. 333, §1).

5. Universal (*universali*) power is unlimited by the confines of the diocese of Rome, its province, or even the Latin Church. It extends to the full communion of the Catholic Church in all its Ritual Churches *sui iuris*, for the pope is head of the college and the See of Rome is to provide the service of unity to all the churches.

6. Ordinary power (*ordinaria potestate*) comes with the office. It is not something delegated personally to the pope as an individual, but it pertains to the office of the See of Peter as such. It is important to respect this traditional canonical meaning of "ordinary" as found in canon 131, §1 of the revised Code, for the term can be confused at times with an everyday use of the term that contrasts "ordinary" with "extraordinary." The canon does not claim, as Vatican I and Vatican II did not claim, that the pope exercises the daily care in all the churches. It does assert that his role comes with the office and is not a delegated power to a particular individual.[33] As ordinary power, it is limited to the purposes and nature of the office; but the presumption behind ordinary power is that the one who exercises it does

so properly when acting in virtue of his office, and need not adduce further proof of his authority to act (as contrasted to delegated power; cf. c. 131, §3).

7. Church (*in Ecclesia*) power is distinct from civil jurisdiction. The pope's power is truly "in the Church" for it binds only those who are subject to Peter and the apostolic college he headed. Christ's kingdom is not of this world, he informed Pilate, and the authority of his followers is in view of the kingdom of heaven—not in view of an earthly kingdom. The power of the pope is in keeping with the nature of the Church, limited therefore by the constitution of the Church itself, revelation and dogma, and the salvation of souls for which the Church exists. It is a power that is in this world but not of it. It does not claim, as once was attempted in medieval times, to be a superior jurisdiction to civil authorities in the secular sphere, for it is of an entirely different nature, truly ecclesial.

8. Free exercise (*quam semper libere exercere valet*) can be another way of expressing what is meant by "immediate" in this context. *Lumen Gentium* 22, for example, uses the same phrase about "which he can always freely exercise" as the canon, but it does not use the word "immediate" to characterize papal power. *Christus Dominus* 2, on the other hand, does the reverse. However, the term does mean more than just "immediate," for the pope is the one who determines how supreme power is to be exercised—whether collegially or by the head of the college alone (c. 333, §2).

The phrase has at least the following meanings. First, the pope cannot be forced to act, and when he does act it is always done freely. The use of ecclesiastical power which results from force or fear is null (c. 125, §1), and this applies as much to forcing the pope to act as it does to any minister of the Church. Second, the pope's actions cannot be legitimately stopped when he does act in virtue of his office. There is no authority that can impede his action, and an attempt to do so would be a crime—as is any illegitimate attempt to hinder the exercise of ecclesiastical power (c. 1375).

The phrase, however, does not mean the pope can act capriciously or without regard for the Scriptures, doctrine, the constitution of the Church, the sacraments, or a multitude of other limitations too numerous for even the doctrinal commission of Vatican II to attempt to mention.[34]

The Code spells out in several places the practical implications of this papal power. Some of these involve the pope's office as final arbiter in maintaining the unity of the Church's communion. So, no appeal is possible from a decision or decree of the pope (c. 333, §3), and the procedures for recourse

---

[33]G. Thils, *Primauté pontificale et prérogatives épiscopales: "Potestas Ordinaria" au Concile du Vatican* (Louvain: E. Warny, 1961).

[34]*AcSynVat*, vol. III, pars I, 247; see also K. Rahner, "The Hierarchical Structure of the Church, with Special Reference to the Episcopate," in Vorgrimler I, 202.

against an administrative decree do not apply to his actions (c. 1732). Other canons focus on his exercise of supreme power for the mission of the Church in spreading the gospel. He can exercise the infallibility of the Church in teaching doctrine (c. 749) and express the ordinary magisterium of the Church (cc. 752, 754). Together with the college of bishops he is responsible for the supreme direction and coordination of missionary work (c. 782). See below (c. 333) for a more detailed examination of the exercise of the primacy.

Papal Election and Resignation

Canon 332 — §1. The Roman Pontiff obtains full and supreme power in the Church by means of legitimate election accepted by him together with episcopal consecration; therefore, one who is already a bishop obtains this same power from the moment he accepts his election to the pontificate, but if the one elected lacks the episcopal character, he is to be ordained a bishop immediately.

§2. If it should happen that the Roman Pontiff resigns his office, it is required for validity that he makes the resignation freely and that it be duly manifested, but not that it be accepted by anyone.

The papal office is so significant within the Church that it is of critical importance to know when it is filled and by whom. Because there is no one superior to the pope who could confer the office or confirm his election to it, the pope takes office canonically by accepting legitimate election. If he is not already a bishop, he must receive episcopal consecration before his acceptance of the election has full effect. If he should decide to resign the papal office, a pope need only act freely and properly manifest his decision; the effectiveness of his resignation does not depend on its acceptance by any other authority.

This canon repeats provisions of the 1917 Code with some modifications. Canon 219 of the former Code is the basis for paragraph one, with the addition from Paul VI's apostolic constitution *Romano Pontifici eligendo* (n. 88) of the requirement for consecration if the one elected is not already a bishop;[35] paragraph two is modified from canon 221 of the earlier law.

There are detailed norms for the election of a pope. Originally the bishop of Rome was selected according to the common practice of the early Church, with election by the clergy of the diocese assisted by neighboring bishops and affirmed by the people. By the eleventh century secular political interests and divisions within the Roman Church itself led to a needed reform of the selection process.

Nicholas II in 1059 defined the role of the cardinals in this electoral process, and during the Third Lateran Council in 1179 Alexander III restricted papal elections solely to the cardinals.[36] The norms for the election of a pope have been modernized by Pius XII, John XXIII, and Paul VI.[37]

After the death or resignation of a pope, the cardinals must wait fifteen days, and may wait as long as twenty, before beginning the conclave, or secret retreat, during which the election takes place. This is usually held in the Vatican palace in Rome. Only cardinals and certain aides can attend. Election can be by one of three methods: acclamation (unanimous consensus or "inspiration"); "compromise" worked out by a group delegated to come to a decision on behalf of the rest; or balloting. If the latter form is used, ballots are cast and counted according to a detailed, formal procedure with a two-thirds vote required for election. No more than four ballots are taken daily. After each session the ballots are burned, giving rise to the watch for the color of the smoke (white for an election, black if the ballot was without result)—the most characteristic feature of conclaves in the popular mind.

The candidate who receives the necessary two-thirds vote is asked if he will accept the position. If he does, he indicates what name he will use as pope, and the cardinals individually promise him obedience. If he is not already a bishop, his episcopal consecration takes place right away. Then the result of the election is announced to the world.

The new pope acquires full, supreme, and immediate power upon acceptance of the election, or if not yet a bishop, upon episcopal consecration following the acceptance of the election. The ceremonial announcement of the election results or the liturgical celebration whereby he takes possession of the papal office (formerly called a coronation) is not essential, for upon acceptance of the election the bishop has become "the bishop of the Church of Rome and, at that same instant, the true pope and the head of the episcopal college."[38]

Resignation by a pope is rare, but it is not unknown. Celestine V in 1294 resigned after five months as bishop of Rome. Other precedents are debated by scholars because of questions about the facts in each case.[39] The law continues to provide for the possibility of papal resignation.

There is no authority who confirms a papal election; similarly, there is no authority needed to accept a papal resignation. The revised Code does clarify the evident requirement that resignation

[35]Paul VI, apconst *Romano Pontifici eligendo,* Oct. 1, 1975, *CLD* 8, 167.

[36]Ibid., *CLD* 8, 134.

[37]Pius XII, apconst *Vacantis Apostolicae Sedis,* Dec. 8, 1945; John XXIII, *mp Summi Pontificis electio,* Sept. 5, 1962; Paul VI, apconst *Romano Pontifici eligendo,* Oct. 1, 1975. This last is the law in force at the time the 1983 Code was promulgated: *CLD* 8, 133–169.

[38]Paul VI, *Romano Pontifici eligendo,* 88; *CLD* 8, 167.

[39]P. Granfield, "Papal Resignation," *J* 38 (1978), 118–131.

must be free, as with any resignation (c. 188). It must also be properly manifested (c. 332, §2). The canon makes no further specification as to what "proper" manifestation of the resignation would require, but general law states it is to be communicated to those responsible for filling the resulting vacancy, and it must be done either in writing or orally in the presence of two witnesses (c. 189, §2). In the case of a pope this means it must be communicated to the cardinals. The resignation takes effect from the moment it is communicated to them (c. 189, §3), but a pope who resigns could be eligible for reelection (c. 189, §4).

Exercise of Primacy

Canon 333 — §1. The Roman Pontiff, by virtue of his office, not only has power in the universal Church but also possesses a primacy of ordinary power over all particular churches and groupings of churches by which the proper, ordinary and immediate power which bishops possess in the particular churches entrusted to their care is both strengthened and safeguarded.

§2. The Roman Pontiff, in fulfilling the office of the supreme pastor of the Church is always united in communion with the other bishops and with the universal Church; however, he has the right, according to the needs of the Church, to determine the manner, either personal or collegial, of exercising this function.

§3. There is neither appeal nor recourse against a decision or decree of the Roman Pontiff.

This canon deals with the complex relationship known as the primacy. Three key concepts are addressed in separate sections: the primacy itself (§1); the communion that must always exist between the pope and the rest of the bishops in the college of bishops (§2); and the obverse of primacy, namely, that the pope is the court of last appeal and from his decisions or decrees there is no further appeal or recourse (§3).

The canon is taken primarily from canon 31 of the 1980 *Lex Ecclesiae Fundamentalis,* with some slight modification. Paragraph one is rooted in Vatican I, i.e., in *Pastor aeternus* III, and in *Lumen Gentium* 22, 25, and 27, with special emphasis on *Lumen Gentium* 27 (which repeats many of the same terms used in *Pastor aeternus* in this context). *Lumen Gentium* 22 and the "Explanatory Note" published with that document provide the sources for paragraph two; paragraph three is taken from canon 227, §2 of the 1917 Code, where appeal to an ecumenical council was explicitly mentioned.

The canon attempts to follow a careful course through the complex issues involved. Some initial comments on individual elements are needed before an overall appreciation of the text can be attempted.

The Primacy

In his role in the universal Church the pope enjoys a juridic independence and a special power over all others in the Church. He is not subject by right to any other ecclesial authority. He would be considered subject to another if his office were only on a par with others (e.g., the first among equals or *primus inter pares*), for then peer pressure would have legal significance. Similarly he would be considered subject or in some way lacking supreme authority if by law some aspect of episcopal jurisdiction were to escape his jurisdiction.

The canon expresses the basis for the primacy, its extent, and its relationship to the role of diocesan bishops in their own particular churches.

1. Basis. It is "by virtue of his office" that the pope has this primacy. The canon does not specify further what is meant by "his office." The *Lex Ecclesiae Fundamentalis* had proposed to indicate that it is in virtue of his role as pastor of all the faithful. *Lumen Gentium* 18 refers to the office of Peter and his successors as the perpetual and visible principle and foundation for the unity of faith and communion. *Lumen Gentium* 18 also refers to his office as Vicar of Christ and pastor of the whole Church (as does *LG* 22; see above on the titles of the pope).

In light of this it can be asserted that by the office of the pope the canon includes at least his function of providing for the unity of the Church, his service as head of the college of bishops, and his episcopal role within the Church universal. As a bishop he is vicar of Christ; as head of the episcopal college he is pastor of the bishops who form the college. The college of bishops is the principal expression and instrument of the communion of churches that form the Church universal (*LG* 23); as pastor of the bishops, therefore, the pope has a special episcopal role within the communion of churches.

2. Extent. In virtue of his office the pope holds primacy not only over the universal Church but also as pastor of the pastors over them and over the particular churches committed to their care. These are dioceses or equivalent portions of God's people (c. 368). Since groupings of particular churches are either elements of the Church universal or groupings of particular churches themselves (cc. 431, 447), the pope's authority extends to them as well.

These are not merely administrative structures; they are portions of God's people. Hence the primacy extends to individual Catholics, members of the hierarchy as well as all other faithful.

3. Relationship to diocesan bishops. In the particular churches committed to their care the diocesan bishops have power (c. 381) that is proper (i.e., in their own name—c. 131, §2), ordinary (i.e., in virtue of their office—c. 131, §1), and immediate (i.e., direct, not legally bound to any intermediaries). In virtue of his office the pope also has proper, ordinary, and immediate power over each particu-

lar church. As indicated above, Vatican I went to great pains to indicate that these are not conflicting authorities but mutually supportive.

Pastor aeternus III, and *Lumen Gentium* 27 which explicitly reaffirms it, present the primacy as asserting, strengthening, and safeguarding the power that bishops have in their particular churches. The canon repeats this affirmation, though without the reference to asserting the bishop's power since this is already provided for elsewhere in the Code (c. 381, §1). Papal primacy does not deny, weaken, or replace the role of diocesan bishops. In making this affirmation the canon does not provide legal norms to implement it. Instead it relies on the Vatican II notion of communion within the college of bishops to set the context and to provide the basic structure whereby papal primacy and the role of diocesan bishops are harmonized.

Communion

This is an ancient concept for expressing relations among particular churches and within the hierarchy.[40] Turning from a way of thinking more characteristic of civil politics, Vatican II adopted this early church concept to express the bonding together of Christians in various ways to form the Church of Christ. See the discussion above on ecclesial and full communion at canons 204 and 205.

1. Hierarchical communion. Full communion in the Catholic Church is achieved by bonds of faith, sacraments, and governance (c. 205). This is an organic reality expressed in many different ways.[41] Among bishops it is by their common solicitude for the welfare of all God's people and the mission of the Church, and by their pastoral care for the particular churches committed to them *(LG* 23).

The concept of communion is central to the college of bishops. One becomes a member through episcopal consecration together with communion with the head and other members of the college (c. 336). This is a "hierarchical communion" for it is a communion of the hierarchy and is itself lived in a hierarchical relationship of head and members in the college.[42]

2. Relationship of communion. Whether we advert to it or not, the bond of communion is always

in existence and provides the basic substratum of Catholic life. This is true of the general communion of the faithful in the Church; it is also true of the hierarchical communion within the college of bishops. Thus the canon points out (§2) that the pope is always in communion with the other bishops and with all the faithful (the universal Church) when he exercises his office as supreme pastor.

Communion becomes a crucial issue when it is threatened or even lost. This occurs especially through heresy, apostasy, and schism. Classical canonists discussed the question of whether a pope, in his private or personal opinions, could go into heresy, apostasy, or schism.[43] If he were to do so in a notoriously and widely publicized manner, he would break communion and, according to an accepted opinion, lose his office ipso facto (c. 194, §1, 2°). Since no one can judge the pope (c. 1404) no one could depose a pope for such crimes, and the authors are divided as to how his loss of office would be declared in such a way that a vacancy could then be filled by a new election.

The canon (§2) does not state an inevitable fact but a basic presumption when it says that the pope always acts in communion. Indeed, if a pope were not in communion, he would not be fulfilling his office as supreme pastor.

3. Papal role in communion. The manner in which the pope exercises his function as supreme pastor within hierarchical communion is something he himself determines. He has several options. As supreme pastor he may act personally, such as when he travels to various countries, gives personal witness to the faith in speeches or writings, or otherwise involves himself in the pastoral activity of the Church. He may act through others, particularly through the offices of the Roman Curia or other institutions that have developed to assist him in his pastoral role (c. 334). He may act collegially, calling on other members of the college of bishops to participate with him in his role of supreme pastor. This, of course, is different from his determination of how the college as such will act (c. 337, §3): here it is a question of how the primatial power will be exercised; there it is one of how collegial actions are organized.

Highest Appeal

A final dimension of primacy is expressed in paragraph three. There is no appeal from a decision of the pope in a particular matter, nor is there recourse against a decree he may issue. This does not mean, of course, that the pope is above judgment.

---

[40]J. Hamer, *The Church is a Communion* (London: Geoffrey Chapman, 1964); CLSA Permanent Seminar, "The Church as a Communion," *J* 36 (1976), 1–245.

[41]"Explanatory Note," 2.

[42]G. Ghirlanda, *"Hierarchica Communio": Significato della formula nella "Lumen Gentium"* (Rome: Pontificia Universitas Gregoriana, 1980) holds hierarchical communion is the juridic missioning of a bishop and constitutes the key element of membership in the college of bishops. Others correctly observe that the Council specifically made sacramental consecration the foundation for membership in the college and understood hierarchical communion in broader than strictly juridic terms; cf. G. Thils, *La Primauté pontificale* (Gembloux: Duculot, 1972), 202; Tillard, 47–48.

[43]S. Sipos, *Enchiridion Iuris Canonici,* 7th ed. (Rome: Herder, 1960) cites Bellarmine and Wernz in support of his position; this view, however, is termed "antiquated" by F. Cappello, *Summa Iuris Canonici* (Rome: Pontificia Universitas Gregoriana, 1961), 297.

He is always subject to the judgment of God; he cannot go beyond the limits of his office, and he may not betray the constitution of the Church.[44] But if one is not satisfied with a decision or decree of the pope, there is no higher authority that can reverse his decision or rescind his decree.

Primacy has traditionally meant that the pope serves as a court of last appeal. It is not possible to be a court of last appeal if there can be a further appeal or recourse. The canon, therefore, states not only a tradition of long standing in the Church but also a truism—given the function of the pope within hierarchical communion.

Meaning of Primacy

Having considered the several issues involved in papal primacy it may now be possible to attempt a synthesis of the meaning of primacy in canon law.

Papal primacy is a function entrusted to the office of Peter and his successors for building up the Church: it is pastoral in nature. It is exercised in an ecclesial context; hence, it is essentially a relationship in communion for safeguarding the unity of the Church and providing for the effective exercise of the Church's mission.

While it means that the pope can intervene in any case, at any time, or in any place in the Church for the purpose of the pastoral life and welfare of the people of God, it does not make the pope a "super bishop" or replace the role of bishops and others in the Church. Instead, it is meant to affirm, strengthen, and safeguard their offices.

The primacy is expressed in various ways in the canons. At times matters are referred directly to the pope under one of his titles, usually as Roman Pontiff. In these instances he must intervene personally in the exercise of the office of primacy. At other times the canons state the need for action by the Apostolic See. "Apostolic See" and "Holy See" include the pope himself and those offices of the Roman Curia that assist him in his primatial ministry (c. 361).

The pope is mentioned specifically in reference to a number of issues. For example, clergy are bound to special obedience toward him (c. 273), and religious are held to obey him in virtue of the vow of obedience (c. 590, §2). The pope may celebrate the sacraments, including penance (c. 967, §1) anywhere; he may dispense private vows of anyone, anywhere (c. 1196); appeal to him at any stage of a process is always permitted in virtue of his primacy (c. 1417, §1). Indeed, he is the supreme judge for the whole Catholic world (c. 1442).

The pope has a special role in the acts of the college of bishops (cc. 337–338, 341) and in admitting new members to the college through the nomination of bishops or the confirmation of their election (c. 377). Bishops are to report to him every five years on their ministry in pastoring a diocese (c. 399, §1), and he can send legates of his own to any place or person. Through his primatial power the pope can limit the competence of diocesan bishops, reserving certain matters to himself or other authorities (c. 381, §1) or exempting religious from the bishops' authority (c. 591).

In virtue of the primacy, the pope is the supreme administrator and dispenser of ecclesiastical goods (c. 1273), and those who exercise the right of ownership over church goods always do so under his authority (c. 1256).

Dispensing clergy from celibacy is restricted to the pope (c. 291), as is dispensation from a ratified but not consummated marriage (cc. 1142; 1698, §2). The judgment of certain cases is reserved to him (c. 1405, §1). His acts or specially approved documents are not subject to review by a judge (c. 1405, §2), and his decrees are not subject to administrative recourse (c. 1732; cf. c. 333, §3). No one can judge the First See (c. 1404).

Even more extensive are the references to the Apostolic See, requiring its involvement in a great variety of ecclesiastical activities—ranging from reviewing the acts of a particular council or episcopal conference (cc. 446, 455), to dispensing from various irregularities and impediments for orders and marriage (cc. 1047, 1078), to a number of elements in religious life. In the exercise of the pope's primatial office, the Apostolic See is involved in setting general norms for the teaching, sanctifying, and ruling functions in the Church. Examples are too numerous to list here.

Central to these canonical provisions, however, is the purpose for the primacy. It is not meant to complicate or restrict Christian life but to assert, strengthen, and safeguard that life as it is lived in particular churches throughout the world. The primacy is directed toward stimulating an active life by Catholics, the evangelization of the world, and the Church's action on behalf of the kingdom of justice and peace whose coming Christ came to announce. It is limited, as noted earlier, by those divinely given elements that limit supreme power. It is eminently pastoral in its nature, and the many provisions for its exercise contained in the Code are reminders of its use in specific pastoral situations in the past that continue to exemplify the purpose for this power today.

Assistance in Exercising Primacy

Canon 334 — In exercising his office the Roman Pontiff is assisted by the bishops who aid him in various ways and among these is the synod of bishops; moreover the cardinals assist him as do other

---

[44] The doctrinal commission of Vatican II expressly affirmed this when Paul VI proposed *LG* should state that the pope is "answerable to the Lord alone." See discussion in Rahner, "The Hierarchical Structure," 202; Tillard, 41–42.

persons and other institutes according to the needs of the times; all these persons and institutes, in his name and by his authority, carry out the task committed to them for the good of all the churches, according to the norms defined by law.

The Roman Pontiff is aided in the exercise of his office by other members of the college of bishops, particularly through certain institutions and groups. Preeminent among these is the synod of bishops (see fuller discussion below at cc. 342–348). Ongoing assistance is provided by the cardinals (cc. 349–359) and by various offices and services, including the Roman Curia (cc. 360–361) and papal legates (cc. 362–367). These persons and institutions are to work with a service orientation for the good of all the churches in keeping with the role of the pope in whose name and authority they carry out the functions committed to them.

In the 1980 *Lex Ecclesiae Fundamentalis* this canon appeared as canon 32; it had two paragraphs: the first dealing with the service of bishops and especially the synod of bishops; the second concentrated on the cardinals and the Roman Curia. The first portion of the present canon is drawn from *Christus Dominus* 9 and Paul VI's *motu proprio Apostolica sollicitudo* setting up the synod of bishops.[45] The latter portion expresses traditional teaching and practice.

Inclusion of the synod of bishops in this listing of agencies that operate on the basis of papal authority has been debated; see below for a discussion on the nature of the synod. Whatever the result of that debate, in practice the synod does include within its competence the task of assisting the Roman Pontiff in his office, and the Roman Pontiff can determine whether to exercise his office collegially (c. 333, §2).

At the time of Vatican II there were various proposals to replace the college of cardinals with a more representative group—either the synod of bishops or a regular meeting of the heads of episcopal conferences. Paul VI himself admitted to considering the inclusion of others besides the cardinals even in the process of electing a pope.[46] However, the decision has been made to retain the college of cardinals, and efforts to internationalize the body have in some measure attempted to respond to earlier criticisms that it had too narrow a base for what has become a worldwide Church.

Vatican II expressly called for the reform of the Roman Curia (*CD* 9) that it might provide suitable aid to the Roman Pontiff and the pastors of the Church (i.e., the bishops as a body). Considerable tension has existed for centuries between those who assist the pope in the various Roman offices and the bishops who pastor particular churches. The reform of the Curia under Paul VI was designed to respond to this desire of the Council, but the tension remains and perhaps is not resolvable because of differences in perspective between central administrators and local pastors.

The canon, in any event, based on the text of *Christus Dominus* 9, attempts to stress four elements in this regard. First, the agencies that assist the pope do so in his name and with his authority. A practical result of this is the broad understanding of the Apostolic or Holy See (c. 361). Second, these agencies operate with a specific task that has been committed to them; their competence is supposed to be limited and defined, and their authority is to be circumscribed thereby. Third, they act according to norms established in law, providing a stability and continuity in the service they render. Finally, their purpose is to work for the good of all the particular and Ritual Churches that compose the Catholic communion and not specifically for their own power or influence. The *Christus Dominus* text added "and in the service of the sacred pastors," a phrase that must be understood in interpreting canon 334 since the pastors represent the particular churches that they pastor (*LG* 23; c. 393).

The practical applications of this canon are spelled out in greater detail in the remaining chapters of this section.

Interim Governance of Apostolic See

Canon 335 — When the Roman See is vacant or entirely impeded nothing is to be innovated in the governance of the universal Church; however, special laws enacted for these circumstances are to be observed.

The general principle that there is to be no change in the condition of a diocese while the see is vacant (c. 428, §1) is applied to the governance of the universal Church when the Roman See is vacant or even impeded. The See is vacant when there is no pope; it is impeded when the pope is hindered from exercising his office (in parallel with impeded diocesan sees—c. 412). Special laws governing this situation are contained in the norms on the election of a pope; at the time this Code was promulgated these laws were found in Paul VI's apostolic constitution *Romano Pontifici eligendo,* part I.[47]

A similar provision appeared in canon 241 of the 1917 Code, but it made specific mention of Pius X's apostolic constitution *Vacante Sede Apostolica* of

---

[45]Paul VI, *mp Apostolica sollicitudo,* Sept. 15, 1965, *CLD* 6, 388–393.

[46]See report on two March 1973 allocutions by Paul VI, *CLD* 8, 130–133.

[47]*CLD* 8, 136–146. *Romano Pontifici eligendo,* however, does not address the complex issue of the impeded see, for example, when a pope might suffer a coma or other total disability, become insane, or be otherwise truly incapacitated from either exercising his office or resigning.

December 25, 1904. The revised Code adopts a more general manner of citing the particular law in question, given the experience of recent modifications in the laws on papal elections. The revised Code adds mention of the impeded see, a condition that is not expressly addressed even in Paul VI's apostolic constitution.

Romano Pontifici eligendo specifies that the government of the universal Church is in the hands of the college of cardinals during a vacancy of the Apostolic See. Key administrator is the Camerlengo or Chamberlain, assisted by three other cardinals (initially, those who are senior in each of the three ranks of cardinal bishops, presbyters, and deacons; later, however, three are elected by the general sessions of cardinals on a rotating three-day basis). He handles the practical affairs for the governance of the universal Church, while the Vicar for the Diocese of Rome automatically serves as administrator of the diocese during the vacancy.

Cardinals who head the various departments of the Roman Curia cease from their offices, as does the Cardinal Secretary of State. The services of the Roman Curia, including the Secretariat of State, are continued by their respective staffs but only for routine matters. Any issues requiring specific approval of the pope must be put off until a new pope is elected.

The cardinals in Rome meet daily before the conclave begins. These are called general sessions and handle the more important ordinary business or matters that cannot wait until a new pope is elected; they also advise the Camerlengo on various issues. The cardinals as a body are responsible for preparing what is needed to elect a new pope, though they use committees of their members for this; they also interpret the law concerning papal elections if any doubts arise. They cannot, however, change, dispense from, or in any way alter laws passed by a Roman Pontiff and have no power over matters that belong to the Roman Pontiff personally while he is alive. They cannot dispose of or detract from the rights that belong to the Apostolic See.

Once a new pope is elected and accepts the election, he immediately assumes governance of the universal Church, and the rights cardinals have during the vacancy cease.

ARTICLE 2: THE COLLEGE OF BISHOPS
[cc. 336–341]

Description

Canon 336 — The college of bishops, whose head is the Supreme Pontiff and whose members are the bishops by virtue of sacramental consecration and hierarchical communion with the head and members of the college, and in which the apostolic body endures, together with its head, and never without **its head, is also the subject of supreme and full power over the universal Church.**

The canon affirms that the college of bishops is also the subject of supreme and full power in the universal Church. It further clarifies that members of this college are those who have been consecrated sacramentally as bishops and who are in hierarchical communion with the head of the college and other members. Repeating what was stated earlier (c. 331), the Supreme Pontiff is head of the college and his involvement is required for any action of the college as such. In the college of bishops the apostolic body continues to be present and effective in the world.

The canon is a simplified version of canon 29, §3 of the 1980 *Lex Ecclesiae Fundamentalis.* Drawing on terminology from *Lumen Gentium* 20 and 22, from its "Explanatory Note" 3 and 4, and from *Christus Dominus* 4, the canon is nevertheless a new creation rather than a verbatim quote of conciliar material.

Four topics are covered here: the conditions for membership in the college; the relationship of the college to its historical roots; the special role of the head of the college; and finally, the authority of the body.

Membership in the College

One of the major developments at Vatican II was the affirmation that episcopal consecration is a sacrament—the fullness of the sacrament of orders—and that in this sacramental consecration the new bishop receives the three *munera* of Christ: to teach, to sanctify, and to govern (*LG* 21). As noted earlier, this represents a new way of considering the source for a bishop's authority. There was considerable controversy over this point during the Council, a controversy that the "Explanatory Note" published with *Lumen Gentium* attempts to resolve or at least to assuage. It does this by explaining that hierarchical communion is essential for a sacramentally consecrated bishop to be a member of the college of bishops. A definition of "hierarchical communion," however, is not given in either the "Explanatory Note" or the text of *Lumen Gentium* itself.

Hierarchical communion has a practical significance when it comes to the question of who has a right to be involved in the exercise of the teaching, sanctifying, and ruling offices of the Church. As far as exercising these with authority on behalf of a portion of the people of God, a canonical determination is needed since there are many bishops; without some delimitation of which bishop is accountable for what portion of God's people, chaos could result. *Lumen Gentium* 24 and the "Explanatory Note" explain that the canonical determination (or "canonical mission") by which a bishop is named pastor of a particular diocese is to be understood in this light. Such a canonical mission always includes communion with the Apostolic See (*LG* 24).

With regard to the universal Church, however, it is not a question of canonical mission or juridical delimitation. Any bishop in communion—whether he governs a diocese, has a special office, or is retired—has a right to participate in strictly collegial actions of the college of bishops. Hierarchical communion, therefore, has a broader meaning than the canonical mission or juridical determination of a portion of God's people for whom one is responsible; more fundamentally, it looks at the bonds of communion that exist among the bishops and, in particular, with the head of the college. The source of hierarchical communion is the internal bond within each member of the college, i.e., head and members. It is not a question of a juridical relationship only—one, for example, that could be granted by an individual within the college (such as the pope as head). Rather, it is an "organic reality which demands a juridical form, and is simultaneously animated by charity."[48] To be an organic reality it must be the work of all the members, one with another, the pope's role being central but not exclusive.

The practical implication is, for example, that for a bishop to be called to an ecumenical council does not depend on whether he has a canonical mission—this was something that was debated prior to Vatican I and Vatican II and certainly was not clear in the 1917 Code (*CIC* 223, §3). It does depend on valid sacramental consecration as a bishop and perseverance in hierarchical communion with the other members of the college—including but not limited to the head of the college (see below, c. 339, §1).

This leaves open the question of the relationship of bishops who are validly consecrated but not in hierarchical communion, such as the Orthodox. The Catholic position recognizes that they do exercise true governance over their own subjects;[49] it also holds that some communion with the Apostolic See is necessary to exercise governance in a local church (*LG* 24). Are Orthodox, for example, to be considered in some degree of hierarchical communion with the college of bishops—even though not full communion—analogous to the fact that Christians can be in some but not full communion with the Church of Christ? This is a complex question that goes beyond the scope of this commentary.[50]

Apostolic College

The apostolic college endures in the college of bishops. Three observations may be made here. First, the college continues the mission that Christ committed to the body of the apostles. The orientation is toward the work to be done, preserving the apostolic faith, and continuing the work of evangelization down through the centuries. Second, apostolic succession is presented as the continuation of the apostolic body in the college of bishops. It is not phrased so much in terms of individuals passing on to other individuals what they have received from a specific apostle, although consecration by a validly consecrated bishop is essential (c. 1012); rather, the focus is on the mission to be done and on the continuation of the bishops' collegial responsibility for that mission. Third, the college of bishops cannot be more than the body of the apostles. Its role and authority are determined by the role and authority of the apostles. Thus it is essentially religious and ecclesial, not a secular or civil power.

Head of the College

The canon repeats several cautionary phrases found in the conciliar documents. The pope is the head of the college; the college cannot act without its head but only together with him. How this is supposed to work in practice is explained later (cc. 337, 338, 341). As indicated earlier it is not a question of the pope over against the college but of the pope's role within and in reference to the college. As a sacramentally consecrated bishop in hierarchical communion, the pope is a member of the college; as bishop of Rome he is its head. See above for various theories about the relationship of pope and college in the exercise of supreme power. What should be noted here is the sui generis nature of this college and the inadequacy of any secular parallels to explain how this relationship is supposed to work.

The 1980 *Lex Ecclesiae Fundamentalis* addressed the relationship of pope and college in one canon (c. 29), but out of the same material the Code has made two canons in separate articles of this chapter. This could seem to separate the pope from the college, something that the *Lex Ecclesiae Fundamentalis* attempted to avoid through the organization of the material. The close interrelatedness of pope and college was a recurring concern of the Council, even by means of the cautionary phrases repeatedly stressing the headship of the pope. This conciliar teaching on their interrelatedness must govern the interpretation of this canon.

Authority of the College

The college of bishops has both a moral authority and a juridical one. The Vatican II documents term the moral authority "solicitude" and refer to the at-

[48]"Explanatory Note," n. 2; Abbott, 99.

[49]*UR* 16. This has been applied on a juridic level by the Roman Rota in determining the validity of marriages; see *coram* Abbo, Feb. 5, 1970; *J* 31 (1971), 392–402; *coram* Canals, Oct. 21, 1970, *CLD* 7, 10–14.

[50]Vatican II purposely left this question open; see the "N.B." at the conclusion of the "Explanatory Note" published with *LG*.

titude of concern and mutual support that bishops are to show for one another and for the work of the Church throughout the world. This is not a binding juridical authority, but nevertheless it results in real action on the part of individual bishops that affects various parts of the world. The popes and the Council have encouraged this, particularly in terms of sharing personnel and material resources, but also in terms of the solidarity bishops ought to express for particular churches in need.[51]

In addition to the worldwide concern expressed in solicitude, the college of bishops also is the subject of supreme and full power in the universal Church. The Code deals only with this type of authority although the *Lex Ecclesiae Fundamentalis* had spoken of both types (1980 *LEF* c. 34, §2).

As with the pope, the power addressed here is for the pastoral welfare of God's people. It is supreme; there is no appeal from a decree of the college of bishops passed in ecumenical council (c. 1732). It is likewise full; therefore, it is not a question of the college having only a part of supreme power. It is not characterized as immediate, however, perhaps because it does require the mediating intervention of the head of the college to take full effect (c. 341). The remaining canons in this article specify how the college exercises its power.

Exercise of Power

Canon 337 — §1. The college of bishops exercises power over the universal Church in a solemn manner in an ecumenical council.

§2. The college exercises the same power through the united action of the bishops dispersed in the world, which action as such has been inaugurated or has been freely accepted by the Roman Pontiff so that a truly collegial act results.

§3. It is for the Roman Pontiff, in keeping with the needs of the Church, to select and promote the ways by which the college of bishops is to exercise collegially its function regarding the universal Church.

The college of bishops exercises the supreme power of the Church in several ways. In a strictly collegial act it does so solemnly when gathered in an ecumenical council and in a less solemn manner when dispersed throughout the need. As its head the pope has the responsibility to determine in which manner the college will act, and both types of action require the involvement not only of the members themselves of the college but also of the head of the college who either initiates the action or freely accepts it.

The first two paragraphs of this canon are taken from *Lumen Gentium* 22, which is also quoted by

Christus Dominus 4. The third paragraph is drawn from the third part of the "Explanatory Note" published with *Lumen Gentium*.

The canon does not address another type of collegial action alluded to in the Code. In addition to strictly collegial action, which is covered in this article and in which the entire college itself is engaged, there is a broad sense of action by the college of bishops in which members act in virtue of their membership in the college but do not engage the authority of the entire college as such. Examples of such action include collegial participation in the exercise of primatial power (c. 333, §2) and individually assisting the Roman Pontiff in his service on behalf of the college and all the Church (c. 334). The office of metropolitans, the work of particular councils, and that of conferences of bishops can be understood as actions in virtue of being members of the college although the authority of the college itself is not engaged. Vatican II declared that governing their own dioceses well is an act reflective of bishops' membership in the college *(LG* 23).

The canon does address strictly collegial actions. There are three topics to be discussed: ecumenical councils; dispersed action by the college; and the role of the pope.

Ecumenical Councils (§1)

These are the most solemn assemblies in the Christian world. Vatican II is considered by the Catholic reckoning to be the twenty-first ecumenical council. The first four (Nicaea, Constantinople I, Ephesus, and Chalcedon) are generally recognized as normative by all orthodox Christians of East and West, and indeed in many ways constitute the touchstone of orthodoxy in ecumenical relations.[52] See the accompanying table (after the commentary on c. 367) for a list of the twenty-one councils.

Some councils were called by persons other than the pope; most commonly it was done by the emperor. Beginning with the Lateran Councils in the twelfth century, ecumenical councils were increasingly under papal control—an issue of special importance in the long-running and frequently transferred gathering known as the Council of Florence (1431–1445). Some were attended only sparsely by bishops from distant parts of the world. For example, early councils had practically no European bishops present except legates from the pope, and it was only with Vatican II that there were bishops from every corner of the world.

Councils, even a pastorally oriented one such as Vatican II, generally have addressed major doctrin-

---

[51]Pius XII, ency *Fidei donum*, Apr. 21, 1957; *LG* 23, *CD* 6.

[52]A brief description introducing each council is provided in *COD*. See also B. Botte, et al., *Le concile et les conciles* (Paris: Cerf, 1960); P. Huizing and K. Walf, eds., *The Ecumenical Council*, Con 167 (New York: Seabury, 1983).

al questions. Frequently before Vatican II they condemned those who denied the doctrinal positions adopted by the council, and at times were called specifically to issue such condemnations. Ecumenical councils have also been concerned with matters of church discipline. Much of practical Catholic life has been influenced by decisions concerning the sacraments, organization of pastoral care, life-style of the clergy, etc., from councils down through the ages. A major interest beginning with the first council (Nicaea) has been to restore the unity of the Church. Lyons II, Florence, even Trent, and especially Vatican II have had this as a major concern.

In a council the college of bishops exercises the supreme power of the Church both in teaching and for pastoral governance. However, this does not mean that the head and members have always been involved personally and concomitantly. For example, many early councils were not attended by popes but by their legates; the Roman Pontiff later received the decrees of the council. The Council of Vienne (1311–1312) was attended by only a few of the world's bishops, and these appear to have been selected according to a system as if they were representatives of groups of bishops. After Vatican I it was even questioned if a future council would ever be needed—given the clarification on the pope's primacy at that council; after Vatican II, some have wondered if another such gathering would ever be possible—given the expense!

Vatican II was the first council to be attended by bishops from virtually every area of the world, many of them native to their culture.[53] Only in the twentieth century has the Catholic Church become a truly worldwide Church. Even at Vatican I most of the bishops were Europeans. The indigenization of the Church and of its hierarchy on a truly universal geographic basis presents church authorities with a new, cross-cultural phenomenon that cannot be addressed successfully by merely repeating structures and procedures developed when the Catholic Church, indeed the Latin Church, was a more homogeneous cultural unit.

Some have proposed to understand the basic structure of the Church as an ongoing ecumenical council.[54] This perhaps stretches the point; it could seem to identify the Church itself too closely with the hierarchy who serve the Church. The point, however, is that councils cannot be ruled out for the future. Similarly, not every council could be rated a "success," and even those that have had significant effects in church life are limited by the time and circumstances in which they were held and because they needed later updating.

The basic norms affecting the convening, conduct, and results of ecumenical councils are discussed below (cc. 338–341).

Dispersed Action (§2)

This is a less evident exercise of supreme power by the college of bishops. When votes are taken at an ecumenical council, it is clear enough what action the bishops are taking. Dispersed around the world, there is no usual way in which their common decision is evident. The canon specifies that the initiation or at least reception of the bishops' dispersed common action by the pope is the key to determining whether the college as such has actually acted.

The point is not only a practical one for determining that this particular action is an exercise of supreme authority by the college; it is also a juridical one. The law distinguishes identifying an action of the bishops dispersed around the world as truly collegial (c. 333, §2) from the binding force that that action may eventually have in the Church (c. 341, §2). Even if all the bishops of the world were to take a particular stand, it would not necessarily entail the exercise of full and supreme power in the Church; it could be a common opinion that they all hold but does not thereby become a position of the college itself, binding on the Church universal. The intervention of the head of the college provides a juridically verifiable element for the action to be clearly collegial and determines when that action binds the Church universal.

In explaining this point the Council approached the issue with considerable nuance. It declared that the college exercises its power dispersed around the world together with the pope either because he initiates the action, or because he approves it, or because he freely receives it even though he may not issue a formal approbation (*LG* 22). It is not always possible, for example, to find a formal papal approbation even for decrees of some early ecumenical councils. The favorable use by later popes of those decrees has been taken to indicate papal reception. A similar set of options is provided for collegial action outside an ecumenical council.

The Code presents two approaches to this issue. In this canon it refers to the inauguration of collegial action by the pope or at least to his free acceptance of it (presumably, if the action were initiated by someone else). Later, in dealing with the effect of collegial action, the Code drops any reference to free acceptance and requires papal approval (c. 341). The point was debated by the *coetus* in drafting these canons. It decided intentionally to leave "free acceptance" out of the later canon.[55] When

---

[53]Rahner remarks that this has brought the Catholic Church to a new stage of its catholicity, something not experienced in this way in the previous nineteen centuries of Christianity. See K. Rahner, "Towards a Fundamental Theological Interpretation of Vatican II," *TS* 40 (1979), 716–727.

[54]H. Küng, *Structures of the Church* (New York: Thomas Nelson & Sons, 1964).

[55]*Comm* 8 (1970), 102–104.

two canons differ on such a significant point, however, the issue must be resolved by returning to the
conciliar source that provides for all three eventualities.

Role of the Pope (§3)

The pope determines the way in which the college will act collegially. That is, when strict collegial action such as this canon describes is
considered, the pope determines which manner is to
be followed.

The text of paragraph three is drawn from the
"Explanatory Note" (n. 3) published with *Lumen
Gentium*. In that document two qualifications are
added that help to interpret the meaning of the
canon. When he determines the way the college will
act, the pope does not act arbitrarily but within
definite parameters. The "Explanatory Note"
indicates that he does this in virtue of his responsibility for the whole flock of Christ; hence, it is within an eminently pastoral context rather than in a
power struggle or political setting. Second, the
"Note" explains that the determination is done in
light of the good of the Church. It is not a question
of convenience or personal desire, but it is a decision based on the overriding good of the Church
for which the college—both head and members—
exists.

Papal determination does not have to be in advance of the action. It could come later, so that an
action at first not clearly understood to be strictly
collegial could later be clarified as such by subsequent approval or free acceptance by the pope.

Ecumenical Council

The Code provides a basic framework to clarify
key roles relative to an ecumenical council. Rules of
order themselves are set at each ecumenical council. Key roles dealt with in the Code are those of the
pope as head of the college of bishops, participation
by bishops and others at a council, what happens if
during a council the Roman See becomes vacant,
and how binding force is given to whatever the
council decides.

Role of the Pope

**Canon 338 — §1. It is for the Roman Pontiff
alone to convoke an ecumenical council, to preside over it personally or through others, to
transfer, suspend or dissolve it, and to approve its
decrees.**

**§2. It is for the same Roman Pontiff to deter-
mine matters to be treated in a council and to establish the order to be followed in a council; to the
questions proposed by the Roman Pontiff the fathers of a council can add other questions, to be approved by the same Roman Pontiff.**

The pope's role in an ecumenical council results
from being the head of the college of bishops. His is
the right and responsibility to convoke a council; to
preside over (personally or through others) and
otherwise govern the location, continuation, and
conclusion of a council; and to approve its decrees.
He is responsible for the rules of order that will be
used in the council and for the agenda followed.
Items for the agenda are determined by the pope or
added by him at the suggestion of the council's
members.

This canon is a revised version of canon 222 of
the 1917 Code. It reflects the position of *Lumen
Gentium* 22. The canonical position it states, however, is relatively recent in light of the history of
councils in the Church.

Convoking an ecumenical council was originally
the work of Roman emperors, although usually
with the advice or encouragement of bishops. At
times it was done despite the misgivings of the
Roman Pontiff (e.g., Pope Leo I with regard to
Chalcedon). Even some medieval councils such as
Constance and Basle/Florence were not truly papal initiatives. The 1917 Code decreed that there
could not be an ecumenical council unless the
pope convoked it, but the revision of that canon in
this Code adopts a less absolute position. In practice, recent councils have been the work of popes;
Vatican II was a surprising and strictly papal
initiative.

Presiding over a council does not necessarily
mean chairing the sessions. At Vatican II, for example, various arrangements were adopted for
chairing the sessions, although whoever chaired always did so under the authority ("presidency") of
the pope. The canon indicates this explicitly by
adding that the pope presides either personally or
through others.

To transfer a council means to move the location
where it is being held. This happened a number of
times in the past; the Council of Trent, for example,
was moved for a time to Bologna. Suspending a
council, on the other hand, refers to a temporary
cessation of the work. The council continues to exist legally and at the current location, but it is not
at work and no decrees can be issued until it is reconvened. This is also different from interrupting a
council, which occurs automatically if the Apostolic See becomes vacant during the course of a council (c. 340). Dissolution of a council means
termination of it. This can happen when the agenda
has been completed, or even before then. Once a
council is declared dissolved, it cannot perform any
further actions or issue any decrees with supreme
authority; however, if a large portion of the episcopal college desired to continue to act and later their
action was received by a pope (the pope at the time
or a subsequent pope), it would be truly a collegial
act of supreme power (c. 337, §2).

While under current law the pope determines the

agenda and rules of order for a council, in practice he does not do this alone. Preparatory commissions were established for both Vatican Councils; they drew up numerous draft documents (schema, or in the plural, schemata) on the basis of suggestions from bishops around the world, the Roman Curia, Catholic universities, religious superiors, etc.[56] The rules of order were worked out in the preparatory process as well and then promulgated by the pope.[57] When Vatican II convened, the members of the Council asked for time to consider some of their options under the rules and during the course of the Council the rules were changed—in part because of requests by the Council fathers.

The usual problem at a council is the volume of material to be considered. It just is not possible to take up every suggestion that the members would like to cover. As head of the college, the law gives the pope the final decision on what will be included in the agenda. He can also keep certain issues off the agenda. At Vatican II, Paul VI reserved to himself the volatile issues of birth control and clerical celibacy, precluding their discussion by the Council itself.

Participants at a Council

Canon 339 — §1. It is the right and duty of all and only the bishops who are members of the college of bishops to take part in an ecumenical council with a deliberative vote.

§2. The supreme authority of the Church can call others who are not bishops to an ecumenical council and determine the degree of their participation in it.

Those with a right to be members of an ecumenical council are bishops—and only bishops. They must be invited when a council is convened, whether they are diocesan bishops, auxiliaries, performing some special office, or retired. Other persons can be invited by the supreme authority of the Church, but otherwise they have no legal right to participate.

This canon is a revised version of canon 223 of the 1917 Code. It expressly includes the provision of *Christus Dominus* that all bishops have a right to participate in an ecumenical council.

When the canon mentions "deliberative vote" it means those votes that determine the position of the council as such. To have a consultative vote means one has a right to be heard in the debate, but only those with a deliberative vote cast a ballot to determine the final outcome of the debate. All bishops are recognized as having a deliberative vote to determine the positions adopted by a council; this is

something not guaranteed titular bishops in the 1917 Code (*CIC* 223, §2).

Others who are invited may be granted a deliberative or a consultative vote. The invitation is by the "supreme authority of the Church," without further qualification. This supreme authority is the pope, but it is also certainly the council (bishops and pope acting together) once the council convenes (c. 337, §1). There is no limitation on who may be invited. In the past, emperors, princes, and other lay persons have not only been invited but even presided. The Empress Irene convoked and with her son presided at Nicaea II. At Vatican II superiors general of clerical religious institutes were invited with a deliberative vote. A large number of experts (*periti*) were invited as consultors but did most of their work in committee or subcommittee sessions. Non-Catholic observers were invited; while they did not have a vote of any kind, they frequently participated as observers in study sessions and were a notable influence on the thinking of many Council members. The Council was addressed by non-members, including some of the lay Catholic and non-Catholic observers.

In the future it would be possible to have an ecumenical council composed of lay persons as well as clerics who are not bishops. A council is not only where the college of bishops exercises supreme power in the Church; it is an event of the whole Church.

Automatic Interruption

Canon 340 — If the Apostolic See becomes vacant during the celebration of a council, it is interrupted by the law itself until a new Supreme Pontiff orders it to be continued or dissolves it.

Upon the death of the pope or his resignation, the Apostolic See becomes vacant and no innovations are to be made in the governance of the universal Church until a new pope is elected (c. 335). Therefore an ecumenical council, which exercises governance in the Church universal, is interrupted until a new head of the college of bishops is selected.

This canon is a revised version of canon 229 of the 1917 Code.

It is a practical norm. The canon does raise some questions, precisely the kinds of cases for which some advance provisions would be advisable. For example, should an ecumenical council be interrupted if the Apostolic See becomes vacant because of the total mental disability of the pope, even though he is still physically alive (e.g., in a permanent coma, or goes insane)? What of a situation in which the Apostolic See is vacant because of loss of communion through heresy or similar crime (c. 194, §2, 2°; c. 333, §2)? These may be precisely the

[56]*AcDocVat, Antepreparatoria.*
[57]See initial rules in *CLD* 5, 246–267.

moments when a council is needed. The Council of Constance, for example, was the instrument for resolving a long and dangerous schism within the Western Church and saw the replacement of three contenders for the chair of Peter and the election of a commonly accepted successor. The law, however, says nothing about these matters and there are no extant special norms to cover such eventualities.

Binding Force of Decrees

Canon 341 — §1. Decrees of an ecumenical council do not have obligatory force unless they are approved by the Roman Pontiff together with the fathers of the council and are confirmed by the Roman Pontiff and promulgated at his order.

§2. For decrees which the college of bishops issues to have obligatory force this same confirmation and promulgation is needed, when the college takes collegial action in another manner, initiated or freely accepted by the Roman Pontiff.

For decrees of the episcopal college to have obligatory force, whether they are issued in an ecumenical council or through a less solemn manner, they must be approved and promulgated by the Roman Pontiff.

The canon restates canon 227 of the 1917 Code and applies its provisions not only to an ecumenical council but also to other forms of collegial action by the college of bishops. As explained above (c. 33), *Lumen Gentium* 22 deals with some of the same issues.

There were three steps followed in the formula concluding the decrees adopted at Vatican II. The first was the result of the voting in public session at which the Council members gave their formal approval to the text. This was followed by the approbation of the document by the pope. Finally, there was a phrase by which the pope ordered the promulgation of the text.[58] All three juridical acts were needed for the conciliar document to have full binding force in the Church.

Drawing on this experience the canon applies the same requirements to any other collegial acts before they can have binding force in the Church. This provision goes beyond the conditions stated in *Lumen Gentium* 22 (or even c. 337, §2) by adding the requirement of promulgation. It is also more restrictive than *Lumen Gentium* 22 or canon 337, §2; approbation is mentioned without adding the additional possibility of free reception. As discussed

above, the canon must be interpreted in light of the conciliar constitution; it is clearly not a constitutive law but a disciplinary one.

CHAPTER II
THE SYNOD OF BISHOPS
[cc. 342–348]

The "synodal principle" is an ancient one in the Church. It means that people come together to discuss major issues in the Church and at times make practical determinations about those issues. The principle is applied analogously in different settings. An ecumenical council is a "synod." So, too, are a particular council, a diocesan synod, and today, a special body of bishops who meet with the pope to review issues of major significance to the Church universal.

The present "synod of bishops" is an innovation from the Second Vatican Council.[59] Some have seen its roots in the "permanent synods" held in former times by some of the Oriental Patriarchates, especially Constantinople, but its more immediate cause was the experience of free and open discussion on issues of considerable importance in the presence of the pope. This began with the meetings of the preparatory commissions for Vatican II when a new spirit began to be felt even among the bishops in the Church, a spirit of dialogue and honest searching for pastorally effective approaches to the issues of the times.

When he became pope, Paul VI called on the bishops to aid him in his office. He made a special appeal to this effect at the opening of the second session of the Council in 1963.[60] At the conclusion of that session, with its heated debates over the relationship of pope and bishops and the role of members of the college of bishops in the central administration of the Church, there was a move among the bishops to see if something could be set up that would continue the beneficial impact of the Council even after Vatican II would close. Others, particularly officials in the Roman Curia but not exclusively they, questioned the possibility of the college of bishops—even in an ecumenical council—placing some sort of limit on the pope's freedom to act, extending also to anything that might limit the freedom of those who acted in his name.

A proposal was moving through the conciliar drafting process to include in the document on the bishops' pastoral office in the Church a provision for an ongoing gathering of bishops to represent the world's hierarchy. Before this could be acted on by the Council, Paul VI issued the *motu proprio Apos-*

---

[58]Abbott translates: "Each and every one of the things set forth in this [document] has won the consent of the Fathers of this most sacred Council. We, too, by the apostolic authority conferred on us by Christ, join with the Venerable Fathers in approving, decreeing and establishing these things in the Holy Spirit, and we direct that what has thus been enacted in synod be published to God's glory."

[59]D. Foley, *The Synod of Bishops: Its Canonical Structure and Procedures* (Washington: Catholic University, 1973).
[60]Paul VI, allocution opening second session of Vatican II, Sept. 24, 1963, *AAS* 55 (1963), 849–850.

tolica sollicitudo.[61] In this document he established the "synod of bishops," defined its nature and authority, and provided for its basic structure. Some interpreted this as an effort to preempt the Council; others pointed to it as a move to ease the concern of the minority while at the same time providing for the kind of agency desired by the majority. In any event, the Council seconded Paul VI's action when it adopted *Christus Dominus* by making explicit reference to it and drawing on the wording of *Apostolica sollicitudo* to describe the synod (*CD* 5).

The first meeting of the synod of bishops took place in 1967. The next, an extraordinary one, was held in 1969. Since that time ordinary meetings have been held regularly: 1971, 1974, 1977, 1980, and 1983. Two special sessions have also been held: one for the church in The Netherlands and the other for the Ukrainian Church.

Apostolica sollicitudo defines the synod of bishops as a central ecclesiastical institute that acts on behalf of the whole Catholic episcopate; by nature it is permanent ("perpetual"), but it meets only occasionally (is not in continuous session). As a central ecclesiastical institute it pertains to the governance of the Church universal rather than to a local area, even though it can be utilized to express the solicitude of the Church universal for a limited area or group of people.

Its members act on behalf of the whole Catholic episcopate.[62] This is a very significant statement, for the debate at the time of the synod's creation centered around whether it would be an extension of the papal office or an exercise of the collegiality of bishops. Those who hold it is essentially a papal institution (similar to other papal structures such as legates, the Roman Curia, etc.) point out that it was created by the pope and must be convened and address the agenda proposed by the pope; in addition, its members must be confirmed by the pope, and the pope is to decide what will be made public of the results of the synod. They see it as fundamentally an advisory group which collegially assists the pope (which is how *CD* 5 describes it) but not a collegial act of the college of bishops.[63]

Others point to the characteristic that the members of the synod are selected as representatives of all the bishops of the Catholic Church, or in other words as representatives of the college of bishops. Even the rules on selecting members indicate that they should be chosen in light of their ability to reflect the thinking of the bishops whom they represent on the topic to be discussed at the synod. At the synod they are supposed to be concerned for the whole Church in terms that are equivalent to the pastoral office in which the college of bishops succeeds the apostolic body. This implies that the synod is a true exercise of the college of bishops, either in a wide sense (those participating do so in virtue of their membership in the episcopal college and not as delegates of the pope) or even in the strict sense of genuinely collegial action, since there is nothing to preclude a strictly collegial act from being conducted in a representative manner. *Christus Dominus* is taken as reinforcing this view for it says that the synod signifies that all the bishops in hierarchical communion participate in solicitude for the universal Church (*CD* 5).[64]

The Code does not enter into these debates. Likewise, it does not provide a legal definition of the synod of bishops that might resolve the question. Instead, in keeping with the revised Code's general practice of giving descriptions rather than definitions, it describes the synod in terms drawn from *Apostolica sollicitudo* but reflects the experience of the various synodal sessions held in the meantime. In addition to this description, the canons of this chapter deal with the authority of the synod, the role of the pope in it, the types of sessions and the membership proper to each, concluding a synod, and the effect of the vacancy of the Roman See during a synod session. They close with norms on the administrative structure or secretariat that serves the synod.

Description

Canon 342 — The synod of bishops is that group of bishops who have been chosen from different regions of the world and who meet at stated times to foster a closer unity between the Roman Pontiff and the bishops, to assist the Roman Pontiff with their counsel in safeguarding and increasing faith and morals and in preserving and strengthening ecclesiastical discipline, and to consider questions concerning the Church's activity in the world.

This description focuses on the purposes for the synod. There are three given in this canon: to foster a closer unity within the college of bishops between

[61] Paul VI, *mp Apostolica sollicitudo*, Sept. 15, 1965, *CLD* 6, 388–393. See R. Trisco, "The Synod of Bishops and the Second Vatican Council," *AER* 161 (1967), 145–160.

[62] *Apostolica sollicitudo* I; *CLD* 6, 389. See A. Anton, "Episcoporum Synodus: partes agens totius catholici episcopatus," *P* 57 (1968), 495–527.

[63] V. Ferrara, "Il Sinodo dei Vescovi tra ipotesi e realtà. Natura teologico-giuridica del Sinodo," *Apol* 42 (1969), 491–556. Although he recognizes the role of the college at the synod, Bertrams places it as a participation in the primacy (or role of the head of the college) rather than in the college itself: W. Bertrams, "De Synodi Episcoporum potestate cooperandi in exercitio potestatis primatialis," *P* 57 (1968), 528–549. Foley, observing the early experiences of the synod, sees it as de facto a participation in primatial power even though it has the potential to become strictly collegial (217–234).

[64] Anton, "Episcoporum Synodus"; E. Schillebeeckx, "The Synod of Bishops—One Form of Strict but Non-Conciliar Collegiality," *IDO-C Dossier* 67–9 (Mar. 12, 1967).

head and members; to advise the pope regarding pastoral governance in the Church; and to address the role of the Church in the contemporary world.

The canon is drawn from *Apostolica sollicitudo* II. However, the organization of the purposes as expressed in the *motu proprio* has been changed, and some of the practical provisions (which in fact do take place at synods) have not been included in the canon.

The first purpose given in the canon is to foster a closer unity or joining together between the pope and the bishops. The *motu proprio* added that this should provide for greater mutual aid between the parties. The Catholic Church has become a truly worldwide Church only in this century, and the problems of maintaining close ties of communion and solicitude on such a scale are indeed enormous. The regular exchange of views and personal contacts between bishops that was found to be so important at Vatican II is continued in the synod so as to benefit both the pope in his office and, through their representatives, the bishops dispersed throughout the world.

The second purpose looks toward the pastoral welfare of the Church. Particular emphasis is placed on safeguarding and increasing faith and morals, and on maintaining and strengthening church discipline. It is interesting to note that the canon looks only toward presenting advice to the pope in these matters; the *motu proprio* focused on developing consensus on the part of all.

The third purpose addressed the role of the Church in the modern world. As a worldwide Church it is not always easy to have a thorough and accurate grasp of what is happening. In addition to the traditional sources of information developed by the Vatican, the synod provides a truly unique opportunity for bishops from every part of the globe to report on significant developments in their areas and to explore together how the mission of the Church can be carried out effectively under such circumstances.

The *motu proprio* looked not only to addressing the Church's role in the world but also to developing more accurate information and a sense of direction on issues relating to the inner life of the Church. This in fact is how the synods have developed, and it is regrettable that the canon falls short of the vision described in the *motu proprio*. The Code does not abrogate the *motu proprio*, however, for it explicitly refers to the special law by which synods are governed, a law contained in the *motu proprio* and in the special *Ordo* for the conduct of a synod.[65] In virtue of canon 21 (and indeed, in light

of the facts of experience) the broader sense of the synod's role remains in effect.

Authority of the Synod

Canon 343 — It is the role of the synod of bishops to discuss the questions on their agenda and to express their desires about them but not to resolve them or to issue decrees about them, unless the Roman Pontiff in certain cases has endowed the synod with deliberative power, and, in this event, it is his role to ratify its decisions.

Expressive of the solicitude that forms the foundational role of the college of bishops, the synod does not meet as a legislative body but within the rich Catholic tradition of consultative organs. Its meetings can be given deliberate weight; this means that its decrees would become binding upon confirmation and promulgation by the pope (c. 341, §2).

The canon rephrases the provisions already contained in *Apostolica sollicitudo* II.

In addition to the distinction of consultative and deliberative vote discussed earlier (c. 339), the law also distinguishes consultation as a process to be used by executives in the Church (c. 127). The distinction between these two senses of "consultation" can at times become blurred. This seems to be the case in the debate over the nature of the synod as an exercise of collegial or primatial power.

If, as some claim, the synod is really an agency of the papacy, it is in effect a delegated group to provide advice. It would have no special claim relative, for example, to the offices of the Roman Curia and no particular claim to have its advice be considered any differently from that of those who act in virtue of delegation from the Supreme Pontiff. The synod's consultative role would be in line with the consultation an executive undertakes, non-binding but at times useful.

On the other hand, if as others claim the synod is truly a collegial action by the college of bishops, even if only in the broad sense, then it participates in supreme power not by delegation but in virtue of office. It would have a basis in law for asserting its advice to be based on a different kind of warrant, that of the college of bishops itself, than that which supports departments whose purpose is to serve the pastors of the Church. Its consultative role would count for something even though it did not, with supreme power, make the final decision in the issue.

Canon 334 can be taken to imply the first view, for it lists the synod among those advisors whose counsel the pope, as the executive authority in question, can find useful but is not bound to follow. Indeed, the law does not even require him to consult the synod. Canon 343, however, clearly places the synod in a different context, that of consultative or deliberative vote in the exercise of supreme pow-

---

[65]Council for the Public Affairs of the Church, *Ordinem Synodi Episcoporum celebrandum recognitum et auctum,* June 24, 1969, *CLD* 7, 323–327; further revised Aug. 20, 1971, *CLD* 7, 338–341.

er—an exercise that is proper to the college of bishops (c. 336).

It seems in practice that the theoretical debate becomes more heated when it touches on the very real issue of whose views will prevail on what is to be done in a practical matter. It may be an oversimplification, but the impression is sometimes given that it comes down to whether the bishops of the world or the officials of the Curia are to have more impact on the direction the Church is to take in a given issue.

Role of the Pope

Canon 344 — A synod of bishops is directly under the authority of the Roman Pontiff whose role it is to:

1° convoke a synod as often as he deems it opportune and to designate the place where its sessions are to be held;

2° ratify the election of those members who are to be elected in accord with the norm of special law and to designate and name its other members;

3° determine topics for discussion at a suitable time before the celebration of the synod in accord with the norm of special law;

4° determine the agenda;

5° preside over the synod in person or through others;

6° conclude, transfer, suspend and dissolve the synod.

The role of the pope in the synod of bishops is quite parallel to his role in an ecumenical council. That is, it is up to him to determine when to convoke a synod; to set the agenda; to preside in person or through others; and to conclude, transfer, suspend or dissolve the synod. For parallels with the ecumenical council, one should see canon 338. In addition, the pope ratifies the synodal members selected by bishops around the world and may add a certain number (up to 15% of the total, according to *Apostolica sollicitudo* X). He also sets the topic or topics for discussion at the synod well in advance so that the conferences of bishops around the world will have an opportunity to engage in preliminary discussions to prepare the synodal members for the meeting.

The provisions of the canon are essentially those in *Apostolica sollicitudo*. The provision of number six is an addition.

As with an ecumenical council, the pope does not carry out these various responsibilities in isolation but is aided by others; in this case, it is the general secretariat with its council (c. 348). The advice of conferences of bishops is regularly sought to determine what topics seem most timely for a future synod.

The provision to ratify the members selected seems somewhat incongruous in light of the fact that only bishops in communion with the Apostolic See and other members of the college of bishops can be elected by the conferences of bishops to attend the synod. This provision may betray an attitude on the part of the drafters of both *Apostolica sollicitudo* (where it appears as III, 2) and the Code to see the synod as ultimately an agency of the primacy rather than of the college as a whole. On the other hand, it may be a credentialling provision not commonly understood outside this context.

Membership and Sessions

Canon 345 — A synod of bishops can meet in a general session, which deals with matters which directly concern the good of the entire Church; such a session is either ordinary or extraordinary; a synod of bishops can also meet in a special session, which deals with matters which directly concern a definite region or regions.

Canon 346 — §1. The membership of a synod of bishops gathered in ordinary general session consists of the following: for the most part, bishops elected to represent their individual groups by the conferences of bishops in accord with the special law of the synod; other bishops designated in virtue of this law itself; other bishops directly named by the Roman Pontiff. To this membership are added some members of clerical religious institutes elected in accord with the norm of the same special law.

§2. A synod of bishops is gathered in extraordinary general session to deal with matters which require a speedy solution; its membership consists of the following: most of them are bishops designated by the special law of the synod in virtue of the office which they hold; others are bishops directly named by the Roman Pontiff. To this membership are added some members of clerical religious institutes elected in accord with the same law.

§3. The membership of a synod of bishops gathered in special session consists of those who have been especially selected from the regions for which the synod has been convoked, in accord with the norm of the special law which governs such a synod.

Three types of synods are possible (c. 345); the purpose and membership for each are specified in canon 346. The provisions of the canons are basically those of *Apostolica sollicitudo* IV–VIII. Ordinary and extraordinary sessions are also called "general sessions," distinct from "special sessions" which are more restricted in purpose and membership.

Ordinary sessions meet now every three years. They address one or more special topics whose subject matter makes it advisable to consult the doctrine, prudence, and wishes of the bishops of the whole Catholic world. The topics are selected in advance by the pope and discussed by the conferences of bishops prior to the meeting of the synod. Topics covered in the ordinary sessions through 1983 have included:

- 1967 – five questions arising from the conditions of the times: dangers to the faith, revision of the Code of Canon Law, seminaries, mixed marriages, and the liturgy;

- 1971 – ministerial priesthood, justice in the world;

- 1974 – evangelization;

- 1977 – catechetics;

- 1980 – the role of the family;

- 1983 – reconciliation.

Some participants at ordinary and extraordinary synods are the same: patriarchs, major archbishops, and metropolitans of the Eastern Catholic Churches; and cardinals who head departments of the Roman Curia. In ordinary sessions, bishops are elected by their respective conferences according to a graduated scale: one bishop from conferences with up to twenty-five members; two from conferences with between twenty-six and fifty members; three from conferences with between fifty-one and one hundred members; and four from conferences with over one hundred members. In addition, ten religious men elected by the Union of Superiors General are members of the synod, and the pope can add up to fifteen percent more.

Extraordinary sessions are designed to give special attention to a subject of high importance to the universal Church that calls for a speedy solution. In addition to the officials of Eastern Catholic Churches and cardinals who head departments in the Curia, extraordinary synods are attended by the presidents of the various conferences of bishops and by three religious superiors of men.

The only extraordinary synod held up to 1984 took place in 1969 to explore the relationship between the episcopacy and the primacy. This issue was one of the major ones dealt with at Vatican II, but by 1969 there were still a number of significant issues unresolved on the practice of collegiality. The synod came to a number of decisions to improve communications between the Vatican and bishops in various parts of the world, especially in terms of major policy statements (such as the ency *Humanae Vitae*) which had at times come without advance warning to the bishops, and yet which they were supposed to be able to interpret to the people of their local areas.

Special sessions are designed for issues affecting one or more particular regions. The first two such

sessions were convoked by John Paul II in 1980: the first to treat of issues affecting the church in The Netherlands; the second to address issues of concern to Ukrainian Catholics.

Members of a special synod are bishops of the region—whether all of them or (at least theoretically) those elected to represent the region. The two special sessions held in 1980 involved all the bishops of the two areas concerned. In addition, religious can be named, and heads of curial departments attend for discussion of issues that relate to their competence.

Conclusion or Suspension

Canon 347 — §1. When a session of a synod of bishops is concluded by the Roman Pontiff, the responsibility entrusted to the bishops and other members in the synod ceases.

§2. If the Apostolic See becomes vacant after a synod has been called or during its celebration the meeting of the synod is suspended by the law itself as is the responsibility which had been entrusted to its members in connection with it; such a suspension continues until a new Pontiff decrees either that the session be dissolved or continued.

Members are elected for a particular synod only; once that synod has concluded, its members have finished their office and have no further responsibility as synod members. If, however, the Roman See becomes vacant after a synod has been convoked or during its meeting, the synod and the responsibility of its members are automatically suspended until the new pope determines whether to continue or to end the synod.

These provisions are based on *Apostolica sollicitudo* XI and on the general provision that no innovations are to be made in the governance of the universal Church when the Roman See is vacant (c. 335).

It is interesting to note that the canon makes a specific point about the pope concluding a synod, whereas the *motu proprio* merely says that when the work is done, the members have concluded their responsibilities.

The suspension of a synod during the vacancy of the Apostolic See is meant to leave the new pope a free hand in determining whether to continue or to call off the synod at this time. Similar provisions are made for other assemblies in the Church, ranging from ecumenical councils when the Roman See becomes vacant (c. 340) to diocesan synods if the diocesan see should fall vacant while a synod is in session (c. 468, §2).

Synod Secretariat

Canon 348 — §1. The synod of bishops has a permanent general secretariat presided over by a gen-

eral secretary who is appointed by the Roman Pontiff; he is assisted by the council of the secretariat; this council consists of bishops, some of whom are elected in accord with the norm of its special law by the synod of bishops itself while others are appointed by the Roman Pontiff; the responsibility of all these members ceases when a new general session begins.

§2. Furthermore one or several special secretaries are established who are named by the Roman Pontiff for each session of a synod of bishops, but they remain in the role entrusted to them only until the session of the synod has been completed.

Staff services to the synod as an institution are provided by a permanent secretariat headed by a general secretary appointed by the pope. In addition, special secretaries are named by the pope for each session of the synod of bishops, but they function only during that synod session itself. There is also a council that advises the secretariat between synod sessions. Its members, who serve only between one general assembly and the next, are bishops elected at the just concluded synod and others added by the pope.

The canon reflects changes made in the *Ordo* for the celebration of synods after the 1969 extraordinary session.[66] The addition of the council to advise the secretariat was considered an important step in assuring better communications with the bishops of the world concerning synodal matters.

The general secretariat, working with its council, canvasses the conferences of bishops for potential topics for the next synod. They present a report to the pope, who selects the actual topic to be discussed. The secretariat is then charged with drafting a discussion document (*instrumentum laboris*) to aid the conferences of bishops in their discussion of the topic. The results of discussions are collected and given to bishops who will be synod members; they are asked to summarize the reports and provide an overview for the opening portion of the synod meeting. Practical details for the preparation of the synod session are also handled by the secretariat.

CHAPTER III
THE CARDINALS OF
THE HOLY ROMAN CHURCH
[cc. 349–359]

The cardinals are a unique feature of Roman Catholicism. They exercise major influence in the Church, not only because they form the college that elects the bishop of Rome, but also because they occupy major positions in the central administration of the Church and, increasingly, are the diocesan bishops of major sees around the world. To under-

stand this unique institution it will be helpful to know something of its history before exploring the provisions of the Code.[67]

Name

"Cardinal" comes from the Latin word for hinge (*cardo*). A hinge has a double function. It serves as a pivot on which, for example, a door swings in a doorjamb; it also attaches the door (something from outside the doorjamb itself) to the wall.

In the early Church a cleric was ordained to a particular post, and this was for life. This position was termed the cleric's "title" and he was called a "titular" there. When a cleric changed his attachment from the title to which he was ordained to some other position, he was said to have been inserted or "incardinated" in the new post, drawing on the sense of "cardo," or hinge, that attaches a door to the wall. Clergy in this situation were not said to be "titulars" but "cardinals." This term was used in many dioceses in the Western Church and was accepted as a technical canonical term by the time of Gregory the Great (pope: 590–604).

One reason some clerics were transferred (becoming "cardinals" instead of "titulars") was their outstanding ability. Bishops wanted to take advantage of what these clergy had to offer, and gradually they became the most significant advisors or aides to the bishop. In this sense "cardinal" gradually took on the other meaning of hinge, namely, the pivot or key element on which the outcome of an issue might swing.

In Rome a rather unique use of "cardinal" developed on the basis of liturgical practice. Priests assigned to the various house churches ("titles") that had come down from the very earliest years of the Church in Rome were asked to provide liturgical services at the shrines built over the tombs of the martyrs. Most significant among these shrines were the basilicas at the tombs of Peter, Paul, and Lawrence, and the basilicas of St. Mary Major and the Lateran. When they were providing liturgical services at these basilicas, the priests were known as "cardinals" for they were inserted there temporarily, acting outside their proper church or "title." This is the origin of the "cardinal presbyters" of today.

The bishops of the neighboring towns or suburbs of Rome helped out with episcopal services at the Lateran, the cathedral church of Rome. In their own dioceses they were "titulars," but when providing episcopal functions at the Lateran they were "cardinals." This is the origin of today's "cardinal

---

[66]*CLD* 7, 338–341.

[67]See C.G. Fürst, *Cardinalis: Prolegomena zu einer Rechtsgeschichte des römischen Kardinalskollegiums* (Munich: W. Fink, 1967); S. Kuttner, "*Cardinalis*: The History of a Canonical Concept," *Traditio* 3 (1945), 129–214; P. van Lierde and A. Giraud, *What is a Cardinal?* (New York: Hawthorn, 1964).

bishops," who are attached to the seven suburbicarian sees around Rome.

Gradually the popes began to rely on the pastors or priests of the titles and on the neighboring bishops as their chief advisors among the clergy of the area. The meaning of "cardinal" in Rome, as elsewhere, gradually took on the sense of being among the pivotal aides to the bishop—in this case to the pope not only in his local responsibilities but also in his role as head of the college of bishops. They served as envoys and legates to carry out special papal commissions, including that of representing the pope at an ecumenical council.

Rise of the Cardinalate

Reform popes beginning with Leo IX (pope: 1048–1054) wanted to eliminate simoniacal clergy from Rome. Since cardinals were the key pastors and neighboring bishops as well as the chief advisors and assistants to the popes, they became the cornerstone of the reform. Naming reform-minded clerics as cardinal priests and bishops, the popes began to transform "cardinals" in Rome into a cadre of clergy to improve the pastoral life of the city and to carry the renewal of Christian life to other places in the Church. The restriction of the election of the bishop of Rome to the cardinals of the Holy Roman Church further enhanced their role.

At the same time, a new rank was added to the cardinals, i.e., the "cardinal deacons." Social services in Rome, especially after the papacy took over governance of the city from the Empire, had been provided by deacons. Initially organized as direct aides to the popes and attached to the papal palace at the Lateran, deacons were later sent also to "diaconia" or social service centers in various districts of the city, each with a chapel attached. Since deacons had also been key advisors to the popes in virtue of their involvement in the administration of church goods for the care of the poor, the reforming popes used the "diaconia" as places to locate additional reforming clergy, naming them "cardinal deacons" and including them within the college of cardinals.

In the Middle Ages cardinals were the key advisors to the pope. They were organized into a canonical college, similar to the chapter of canons at a cathedral or collegiate church. Theories developed as to the divine right of the cardinalate, some even holding that the cardinals succeed to the collegiate aspect of the apostles just as bishops who head dioceses succeed to the apostles' pastoral role.[68] The cardinals also formed the papal court, similar to the courts that secular rulers held with the princes of their kingdoms (hence the title "prince of the Church" which is still used for cardinals).

Reforms of the College of Cardinals

Sixtus V in 1586 and Innocent XII in 1692 attempted to reform the college of cardinals. Sixtus fixed the number of cardinals at seventy, a figure that remained in effect until John XXIII changed it by naming more. Sixtus also set various qualifications to improve the quality of members of the college and opened selection to every Christian nation, marking a significant effort to internationalize the college. Innocent restricted the pastoral role of cardinals in their titles in order to open the way for local clergy to provide more effective pastoral care of the people.

John XXIII and Paul VI in more recent years have made several reforms affecting the cardinals. In addition to increasing the number of cardinals, John decreed that all of them should be ordained bishops.[69] Paul VI reorganized the internal governance of the college of cardinals and imposed age restrictions, the most significant of which was to limit the right to enter the conclave to elect a pope to those who were not yet eighty years old.[70]

The revised Code reflects many of these reforms, although not the eighty-year-old limit on papal electors. It gives the basic structures for the college of cardinals but leaves the details of the inner operations of the college generally to the college's statutes or particular law. The canons provide a description of what is the college of cardinals, their ranks and how to move from one rank to another, the creation of cardinals, the organization of their college, resignation from curial offices, and the relationship of cardinals with the pope.

College of Cardinals

Canon 349 — The cardinals of the Holy Roman Church constitute a special college whose responsibility is to provide for the election of the Roman Pontiff in accord with the norm of special law; the cardinals assist the Roman Pontiff collegially when they are called together to deal with questions of major importance; they do so individually when they assist the Roman Pontiff especially in the daily care of the universal Church by means of the different offices which they perform.

Three major functions of cardinals are described. First and specific to them is the duty of electing the

[68]G. Alberigo, *Cardinalato e collegialità: Studi sull'ecclesiologia tra l'XI e il XIV secolo* (Florence: Vallecchi, 1969); Y. Congar, "Notes sur le destin de l'idée de collégialité épiscopale en occident au moyen age (VIIe–XVIe siècles)," in *La collégialité épiscopale: Histoire et théologie*, 99–129 (Paris: Cerf, 1965).

[69]John XXIII, *mp Cum gravissima*, Apr. 15, 1962, *CLD* 5, 273–274.
[70]Paul VI, *mp Sacro Cardinalis consilio*, Feb. 26, 1965, *CLD* 6, 312–313; idem, *mp Ingravescentem aetatem*, Nov. 21, 1970; *CLD* 7, 143–145.

bishop of Rome. They also provide a special advisory body that the pope can call on to deal with questions of major importance. Finally, they individually assist the pope in various ways—but particularly in performing special offices (such as in the Roman Curia) for the daily care of the universal Church.

This canon replaces canon 230 of the 1917 Code with a more precise description of the functions of the cardinals. It refers to them as a "special college" rather than the "senate of the Roman Pontiff," and includes the mention of their responsibility to elect the pope.

The use of "college" rather than "senate" deserves a comment. In the Middle Ages the college of cardinals was considered to succeed not only to the apostolic college insofar as it was a college but also to the Senate of ancient Rome for the governance of Rome and the Papal States as well as the universal Church.[71] From this comes the use of the color purple, also characteristic of the Roman Senate, and the patrician rank of cardinals (equal to kings, above secular princes). These secular analogues are replaced in the revised Code with language drawn more from an ecclesial setting. Although "college of cardinals" means a specific juridic collegial body in keeping with the law on collegiate juridic persons (c. 115, §2), the wording of the canon appears more influenced by the norms on the college of bishops than it is by the norms on juridic persons. Members of this college, as with the college of bishops, assist the Roman Pontiff collegially in advising on matters of major importance and individually in regard to the daily care of the universal Church—but as members of the college of cardinals.

Cardinals provide their advice to the pope collegially in consistories (c. 353) and collectively in general meetings of the cardinals; they also head various offices of the Roman Curia or serve on the various congregations of the Curia even if their full-time responsibility is to pastor a particular church elsewhere in the world.

Ranks

Canon 350 — §1. The college of cardinals is divided into three ranks: the episcopal rank which consists of both the cardinals to whom the Roman Pontiff assigns the title of a suburbicarian church and the oriental patriarchs who have become members of the college of cardinals; the presbyteral rank; and the diaconal rank.

§2. The Roman Pontiff assigns to each of the cardinals of presbyteral or diaconal rank his own title or *diaconia* in the city of Rome.

§3. The oriental patriarchs who have become members of the college of cardinals have as their title their own patriarchal see.

§4. The cardinal dean holds as his title the diocese of Ostia along with the other titular church which he already holds.

§5. With due regard for priority in rank and in promotion, through an option made during a consistory and approved by the Roman Pontiff, cardinals from the presbyteral rank can transfer to another title, and cardinals from the diaconal rank can transfer to another *diaconia*, and if they have remained in the diaconal rank for a period of ten full years they can transfer also to the presbyteral rank.

§6. A cardinal from the diaconal rank who transfers through option to the presbyteral rank precedes all those cardinal presbyters who became cardinals after him.

There are three ranks in the college of cardinals, corresponding to the historical roots for the cardinals of the Holy Roman Church (see introductory material at the beginning of this chapter). All cardinals are bishops (c. 351, §1), but their rank within the college of cardinals is characterized in terms of one of the clerical ranks of bishop, presbyter, or deacon. Cardinals have the choice of opting to change the church to which they are assigned or of moving from the rank of deacons to that of presbyters; they are to do so in consistory and require the approval of the pope for the change to take effect.

The canon combines provisions contained in canons 231 and 236 of the 1918 Code, as well as changes made by John XXIII[72] and Paul VI.[73]

There are two types of cardinal bishops: those who are appointed by the pope to one of the six suburbicarian dioceses and oriental patriarchs who have been named to the college of cardinals. There are actually seven suburbicarian sees: Albano, Ostia, Porto and Santa Rufina, Palestrina, Sabina and Mentana, Frascati, and Velletri. However, the cardinal elected as dean (c. 352, §2) also holds the title of Ostia. Title to a suburbicarian diocese gives no pastoral authority over that diocese (c. 357, §1), and there are bishops named to those sees to provide for the pastoral care of the people there.[74]

Cardinals of presbyteral rank, or cardinal priests, are assigned one of the *tituli* in Rome when they are created cardinals. In consistory they can later opt to change to a vacant title; this requires the approval of the pope. As with cardinal bishops, cardinals

[71]C. Lefebvre, "Les origines et la role du cardinalat au moyen age," *Apol* 41 (1968), 59–70.

[72]John XXIII, *mp Ad suburbicarias Dioeceses,* Mar. 10, 1961, *CLD* 5, 275–276.
[73]Paul VI, *mp Ad purpuratorum patrum,* Feb. 11, 1965, *CLD* 6, 310–311.
[74]John XXIII, *mp Suburbicariis Sedibus,* Apr. 11, 1962, *CLD* 5, 270–272.

of presbyteral rank have no pastoral authority in the church of their title (c. 357, §1), but they are expected to aid the church of their title and have often provided it with major financial support.[75]

Cardinals of diaconal rank are assigned one of the *diaconia* or aid stations that used to be staffed by deacons in early medieval Rome. Their relationship to the church is the same as for cardinals of the other ranks (c. 357, §1). Cardinal deacons are officials of the Roman Curia, and prior to 1965 they were often not bishops. In consistory and with the pope's approval they can change the *diaconia* to which they were assigned and, after ten years as a cardinal deacon, they can opt to transfer to the presbyteral rank. If they do so, they are listed in rank of precedence before cardinal presbyters who were created after they were named cardinal deacons.

Since the reform of John XXIII in 1961, the right of option of cardinal presbyters to the rank of cardinal bishops has been dropped. The pope alone determines who will be cardinal bishops.

Creation of Cardinals

Canon 351 — §1. Those promoted as cardinals are men freely selected by the Roman Pontiff, who are at least in the order of the presbyterate and are especially outstanding for their doctrine, morals, piety and prudence in action; those, however, who are not yet bishops must receive episcopal consecration.

§2. Cardinals are created by a decree of the Roman Pontiff, which is published in the presence of the college of cardinals; from the time of this publication they are bound by the duties and possess the rights defined in law.

§3. When a person has been promoted to the dignity of cardinal and his creation has been announced by the Roman Pontiff who, however, reserves the person's name *in pectore*, he is not bound by any of the duties of cardinals nor does he possess any of their rights in the meantime; however, after his name has been made public by the Roman Pontiff he is bound by those duties and possesses those rights; but he enjoys his right of precedence from the day on which his name was reserved *in pectore*.

The pope freely selects who will be cardinals and announces this formally in a consistory with the existing members of the college of cardinals. Usually the pope announces the names of those he is naming to the college, but on occasion he may decide to withhold the name, holding it to his heart (*in pectore*). The canon specifies that to be named a cardi-

nal one must be a priest or bishop and be outstanding in various qualities.

The canon simplifies the provisions of canons 232 and 233 of the 1917 Code and incorporates the reforms of John XXIII's *motu proprio Cum gravissima.*[76]

The qualifications to be selected are stated broadly. The 1917 Code had more detailed requirements, excluding those who were not of legitimate birth and who had incurred various irregularities (*CIC* 232, §2). These are vestiges of reform efforts that were needed to avoid some of the difficulties encountered when the selection of cardinals could be influenced by existing members of the college or other sources. With the reservation to the pope of free selection, even the qualifications listed in the canon can be dispensed and provide more of a guideline than a constitutive law.

The announcement of new cardinals is done in a consistory held in secret. It is a vestige of the time when the college served as the papal court, and appointments to cardinalatial dignity were subject to debate and required the consent of the college. Today this is more of a formality.

From the moment of the announcement the new cardinals enjoy the full rights of cardinals, including that of electing a pope. They are also bound by various obligations as specified in the special law for the college of cardinals. Those whose names are not published, however, gain no rights and are not bound by the duties of cardinals. If the pope dies without revealing the name, the appointment ceases. If, however, the pope later reveals the name, the cardinal enjoys the rights of precedence as if his name had been published on the date the appointment *in pectore* was announced.

The Code has dropped a listing of several obligations and privileges of cardinals (*CIC* 234, 235, 239),[77] and only the faculty to hear confessions everywhere in the world with no restrictions (c. 967, §1) and the personal exemption of cardinals from the jurisdiction of local bishops (c. 357, §2) are expressly retained in the Code.

Dean of the College

Canon 352 — §1. The dean presides over the college of cardinals; if he is impeded from doing so, the assistant dean takes his place; the dean or assistant dean does not possess any power of governance over the other cardinals but is considered to be first among equals.

§2. When the office of dean becomes vacant, the cardinals who possess a title to a suburbicarian

[75]Paul VI, *mp Ad hoc usque tempus,* Apr. 15, 1969, *CLD* 7, 146–147.

[76]John XXIII, *mp Cum gravissima,* Apr. 15, 1962, *CLD* 5, 273–274.

[77]H. Hynes, *The Privileges of Cardinals: Commentary with Historical Notes* (Washington: Catholic University, 1945).

church and they alone elect someone from their own number to act as dean of the college; this election is to be presided over by the assistant dean if he is available or by the oldest elector; they are to take the name of the person elected to the Roman Pontiff who is competent to approve the one elected.

§3. The assistant dean is elected in the same manner described in §2, with the dean himself presiding over the election; the Roman Pontiff is also competent to approve the election of the assistant dean.

§4. The dean and the assistant dean are to acquire a domicile in the city of Rome if they do not already have it there.

As a collegiate juridic person the college of cardinals has its own officials. Chief among these are the dean and assistant dean. They are elected by and from among the cardinal bishops who possess a title to a suburbicarian diocese, and the pope must confirm the election. Thereafter they are to reside in Rome and carry out various functions in the college of cardinals—with the dean serving as first among equals.

The canon revises canon 237 of the 1917 Code in light of Paul VI's reform, *motu proprio Sacro Cardinalium consilio.*[78]

In addition to the various internal functions within the college that are governed by its own norms, the dean has several key functions when the Apostolic See is vacant.[79] He convenes the regular meetings of cardinals prior to the conclave, sends the notice to all the cardinals to come to the conclave, and, if he is not over eighty years old himself, he also chairs the conclave. If he is over eighty, the assistant dean takes his place in the conclave. If he, too, is over eighty, then the cardinal elector who is first in rank and age takes their place. If the dean is in the conclave, he has the right to consecrate the newly elected pope if the electee is not already a bishop.

Paul VI changed the former provision by which the dean was automatically whoever had been cardinal bishop the longest. Now the selection is by vote, but the vote and the candidates are restricted to the cardinals who have a title to a suburbicarian diocese. This excludes the oriental patriarchs who are cardinals, even though they are cardinal bishops.

Consistories

Canon 353 — §1. The cardinals are of special assistance to the Supreme Pastor of the Church

through their collegial activity in consistories to which they are called by order of the Roman Pontiff who also presides over them; consistories are ordinary or extraordinary.

§2. All the cardinals, at least all those present in the city of Rome, are called together for an ordinary consistory to be consulted on certain serious matters which nevertheless occur rather frequently, or to carry out certain very solemn acts.

§3. All the cardinals are called together for an extraordinary consistory which is celebrated when the special needs of the Church or the conducting of more serious affairs suggests that it should be held.

§4. Only the ordinary consistory in which some solemnities are celebrated can be public, that is, a consistory to which, in addition to the cardinals, there are admitted prelates, legates of civil societies, or others who are invited to it.

A consistory is a formal gathering of the college of cardinals, chaired by the pope, and originally a meeting in which open debate and discussion took place. Over the centuries it became highly formalized in the manner of a European royal court, and today it serves more of a ceremonial purpose.

This is a new canon. The 1917 Code did not describe consistories. This canon may be an effort to revitalize an institution that has become so formalized that John Paul II avoided it when he wished to obtain the serious advice of the cardinals on issues of finance and restructuring the Roman Curia. In November 1979 he held a general assembly of the cardinals—instead of a consistory—and he did the same in December 1982.[80]

The new organization of consistories provides both for ordinary sessions that deal with serious matters or carry out certain more solemn acts, and extraordinary ones that are held when the special needs of the Church suggest it or to conduct more serious affairs. All the cardinals are to be called to an extraordinary consistory; only those present in Rome at the time of an ordinary one need be called to it. Normally a consistory is held in secret, although the press and various dignitaries can be invited to certain ordinary ones, such as those involved with canonizations, the conferral of the pallium, or the public celebrations when new cardinals have been created.

Resignation

Canon 354 — Cardinals who preside over the dicasteries and other permanent institutions of the Roman Curia and Vatican City and who have completed their seventy-fifth year of age are requested to tender their resignation from office to the Ro-

---

[78]Paul VI, *mp Sacro Cardinalium consilio,* Feb. 26, 1965, *CLD* 6, 312–313.
[79]Paul VI, apconst *Romano Pontifici eligendo,* Oct. 1, 1975, *CLD* 8, 133–169.

[80]See reports in *Origins* 9 (1979), 356–359, 371–374; 12 (1982), 411–418.

man Pontiff, who will decide on the matter after he has weighed all the circumstances.

This canon does not concern resignation from the college of cardinals but applies to cardinals the regulations that apply to other officers of the Roman Curia concerning resignation at age seventy-five. The Code deals with this matter in the same manner as the resignation of bishops (c. 401) and pastors (c. 538, §3) at age seventy-five. They are requested to submit their resignation; it is not a question of automatically losing the office because an age limit has been reached (c. 184, §1).

This is an innovation introduced by Paul VI in the *motu proprio Ingravescentem aetatem*.[81] That document also prescribed that when cardinals reach the age of eighty they automatically cease being members of curial congregations and can no longer be electors for a new pope. The Code Commission debated this at some length in its 1981 plenary session and finally agreed not to include this latter provision in the Code itself but to leave it to the particular law for the college of cardinals.

Relationship with the Pope

Canon 355 — §1. The cardinal dean is competent to ordain to the episcopate the person elected to be Roman Pontiff if that person requires ordination; if the dean is hindered from doing so the assistant dean has the same right; if the assistant dean is likewise hindered from doing so then the oldest cardinal from the episcopal rank has this right.

§2. The first cardinal deacon announces to the people the name of the newly elected Supreme Pontiff; he likewise invests metropolitans with the pallium or hands it over to their proxies in place of the Roman Pontiff.

Canon 356 — Cardinals are obliged to cooperate assiduously with the Roman Pontiff; therefore cardinals who exercise any office in the Curia and who are not diocesan bishops are obliged to reside in Rome; the cardinals who care for a diocese as diocesan bishops are to come to Rome whenever they are called there by the Roman Pontiff.

Canon 357 — §1. The cardinals who have been assigned title to a suburbicarian church or to a church in Rome are to promote the good of these dioceses and churches by their counsel and patronage after they have taken possession of them; they do not, however, possess any power of governance over them; nor are they to intervene in any way in matters which concern the administration of their goods, their discipline or the service of the churches.

§2. The cardinals who are staying outside Rome and outside their own diocese are exempt from the power of governance of the bishop of the diocese in which they are staying in those matters which concern their own person.

Canon 358 — At times the Roman Pontiff commissions a cardinal to represent him in some solemn celebration or in some group of persons as his *legatus a latere*, that is, as his alter ego; likewise at times the Roman Pontiff commissions a cardinal to fulfill a certain pastoral duty as his special envoy (*missus specialis*); such cardinals possess competence only over those matters entrusted to them by the Roman Pontiff.

Canon 359 — When the Apostolic See becomes vacant the college of cardinals possesses only that power in the Church which is given to it in special law.

The college of cardinals has a special relationship with the Roman Pontiff. These canons spell out certain aspects of this relationship as they affect the vacancy of the Apostolic See, the election of the pope, personal contact with the Roman Pontiff, and special missions they perform on his behalf. In light of this relationship cardinals also enjoy a special personal exemption from local bishops.

These canons cover the issues dealt with in the 1917 Code in canons 239, §§2 and 3; 240; and 241—as modified by John XXIII[82] and Paul VI.[83]

1. Election

When the Apostolic See is vacant, the college of cardinals has a special role (see above at cc. 332, 335). This is a limited role, however, and cannot go beyond what is contained in the special law governing that situation (c. 359).

In addition to the privilege mentioned above that the dean of the college may have to consecrate the electee if he is not already a bishop, the senior cardinal deacon has the privilege of announcing the good news of the election of a pope. This is traditionally done from the balcony above the main entrance to Saint Peter's Basilica with the formula: "I announce to you a great joy, we have a pope," followed by the name taken by the new pontiff.

2. Personal Contact

Cardinals are to provide advice and assistance to the pope in his service to the universal Church. To assure that they are able to do this, the traditional norm has required them to reside in Rome, excep-

---

[81] Paul VI, *mp Ingravescentem aetatem*, Nov. 21, 1970, *CLD* 7, 143–145.

[82] John XXIII, *mp Suburbicariis Sedibus*, Apr. 11, 1962, *CLD* 5, 270–272.

[83] Paul VI, *mp Ad hoc usque tempus*, Apr. 15, 1969, *CLD* 7, 146–147.

tions being made for cardinals who are diocesan bishops elsewhere; even they, however, were obliged to obtain the pope's permission to leave Rome when they came to the city (*CIC* 238). This is now revised, but some of the same concern continues to be expressed in canon 356. The special tie of cardinals to the Holy Roman Church requires them to come to Rome whenever the pope calls them.

3. Special Missions

In addition to the regular service of legates (cc. 362–367), special missions are often entrusted by the pope to members of the college of cardinals. Canon 358 spells out two types of missions: one is of a more ceremonial nature (*"legatus a latere"*), literally, legate from the side [of the pope], or as his alter ego; the other is more pastoral in nature (*"missus specialis,"* or specially sent). An example of the former is the cardinal who represents the pope at a major celebration such as a Eucharistic Congress.

4. Personal Exemption

Although cardinals have no pastoral jurisdiction in the churches that are their title in Rome or the suburbicarian dioceses, when they are outside Rome and outside their own dioceses if they are diocesan bishops, they enjoy a personal exemption from the local authorities. This is not so broad as the privileges in liturgical matters that cardinals enjoyed under the 1917 Code (*CIC* 239, §1), and it is more in keeping with the general norm that pastoral activities are always subject to the diocesan bishop even though some persons may be exempt in their personal lives (e.g., religious institutes also enjoy an autonomy of life, c. 586, §1).

CHAPTER IV
THE ROMAN CURIA
[cc. 360–361]

The Roman Curia is composed of the various offices and related services that assist the supreme authority of the Church in its ministry of service and governance in the Church. The Curia has a rich and varied history, has been cast as both hero and villain at various stages in the history of the Church itself, and today continues to be a major factor in pope-bishop relationships. While the Code leaves most details concerning the Curia to particular law, it is important to have some understanding of its history and operations. This introductory material will discuss both the history of the Curia and the reforms of Paul VI. The commentary on the canons proper will give a brief description of the various offices in the Curia at the time the 1983 Code was promulgated.

History

The use of the term "Roman Curia" seems to have come into vogue in the twelfth century. Prior to that time the offices assisting the bishop of Rome were all grouped under the title "Roman Church" (*Ecclesia Romana*). "Curia" itself has unclear roots, perhaps beginning as a term for the "assembly" in early Rome, later being applied to the hall in which an assembly met, and in particular to the building where the Roman Senate met. During the Empire it referred to both the Senate and the Imperial Court.

In church usage "curia" can mean a judgment, a major gathering, or the hall used by church leaders (bishop, eparch, patriarch, etc.). In this latter sense it has referred to both the building itself and the people who work there.

By whatever title, the offices that assist the pope in his functions beyond the diocese of Rome have undergone development. These can be divided into three stages, corresponding to the specific characteristic of each period.[84]

1. Ecclesial Organization of a Patriarchate (1–11 centuries)

Three elements characterized the organization of the Roman Church at this time: the presbyterium, synods or councils, and the offices staffed by the palace clergy.

The presbyterium consisted of all the presbyters and deacons during the first five centuries; later it was restricted to the presbyters of the *tituli* (cardinal presbyters) and the seven regional deacons. Visiting bishops were also welcome to attend the meetings of the presbyterium, where ordinary matters were reviewed and decided.

More serious business was conducted in a synod or council attended by the bishops of neighboring cities, other bishops who may have been called to the meeting, and any bishops who happened to be in the city when the meeting took place. Presbyters and deacons also participated. These more solemn gatherings met annually from the fourth century.

The clergy attached to the papal palace at the Lateran developed specialties. In addition to the archpriest and archdeacon (heads respectively of the presbyters and deacons in the diocese), there were notaries whose job eventually evolved into the Apostolic Chancery and various officials in charge of running the household, the treasury, and vest-

---

[84]N. del Re organizes this history into five periods, considering the reforms of Pius X and Paul VI as distinct stages. But these were reforms in the bureaucracy and retained the basic approach systematized by Sixtus V. N. del Re, *La Curia Romana: Lineamenti storico-giuridici,* 3rd rev. ed. (Rome: Ed. di Storia e Letteratura, 1970). See also J. Sanchez y Sanchez, "La Curia Romana hasta Pablo VI," *REDC* 32 (1976), 439–458.

ments; all were under the archdeacon. These latter eventually became the Apostolic Camera ("camera" being the word for "rooms").

Such an organization was not unique to Rome, and seems to have been fairly typical of how the various patriarchates functioned at the time. When East and West became separated in the eleventh century, Rome was already beginning to develop a new style of organization.

2. Medieval Court (11–16 centuries)

The practices of royal courts in the Middle Ages provide a pattern for understanding the structures in effect for the medieval papacy. Three major elements can be identified: the cardinals, consistories, and the development of various offices and tribunals.

As noted earlier, rather than drawing on clergy with local pastoral interests, medieval popes developed a professional executive group for purposes of fostering church reform and renewal. These became the key figures in Roman Church government especially after Nicholas II and Alexander III increased their role in papal elections.

Consistories were meetings of cardinals to discuss faith, morals, and church discipline; they also provided the advice to the pope that a secular prince would seek "at court." Consistories gradually replaced meetings of the presbyterium and synods or councils—at first on a monthly basis and then by the time of Innocent III (died 1216) on the average of three times per week.

Major decisions were made in consistories that were initially an opportunity for serious debate as well as a setting of greater formality for acts of some special significance. As with secular courts, judicial as well as administrative decisions could be reached in consistory.

The Middle Ages saw the development of various stable offices in the Roman See. In addition to the chancery and apostolic camera, tribunals developed. Papal chaplains developed reports for consistories when cases were appealed there; later, these chaplains were called "auditors" for they were to listen to the case and report. Innocent III authorized them to make decisions subject to his confirmation. This became the special judicial organ of the Sacred Roman Rota.

From the seventh century there had been a "cardinal penitentiary" to whom matters of conscience could be brought; this had become an important function by the thirteenth century. Services for expediting the increasing correspondence of the popes were developed: the apostolic datary, the apostolic signatura (to handle requests for favors or justice), and the "secret camera" to handle diplomatic correspondence (eventually, the secretariat of state).

By the late Middle Ages the increasing complexity and volume of issues were taxing this system to the limit. There were civil issues for the Papal States, ecclesiastical ones for the Western and universal Church, and concerns related to international diplomacy. Consistories were too unwieldy for this situation. They had developed highly complex procedures that delayed their taking action. Advance study groups of cardinals (called "congregations") were formed to review various issues and to brief them in consistory as one means to speed up the work. Eventually, however, a new system of bureaucracy was installed as a more efficient and effective way to operate.

3. Bureaucracy (16–20 centuries)

In response to the growing threat of heresy in the sixteenth century, Paul III drew on the traditional idea of working groups of cardinals that had prepared cases for discussion in consistory. He named a special congregation and gave it an independent authority to act in his own name without going through the complexities of the consistory. It was known as the "Congregation of the Universal Inquisition or Holy Office." Pius IV drew on this pattern to set up an instrument to oversee the implementation of the Council of Trent when he established the Sacred Congregation of the Council in 1564. Three additional congregations were set up between 1571 and 1582 by Pius V and Gregory XIII.[85]

However, it was Sixtus V (pope 1585–1590) who gave the bureaucracy a systematic organization and established it firmly as the pattern of operations in Rome. In 1588 he suppressed the general consultation of cardinals in consistory and established instead nine congregations to deal with the government of the universal Church and six to handle the government of the Papal States.[86] Each congregation was composed of cardinals who were to address the issues of their competency at regular meetings, a sort of government by committee. He defined the competencies of each congregation in order to avoid, if possible, interference betweeen them.

Subsequently the various congregations developed professional staffs who themselves prepared issues for discussion by the committee of cardinals who formed the congregation. The word for a law court in Athens, "dicastery," was applied to these agencies of church government.

By the end of the nineteenth century the system suffered from several problems. The number of dicasteries had been multiplied—often by popes seeking to circumvent inaction by an entrenched body

---

[85]Congregation of the Index (1571) by Pius V; Congregations on consultation of bishops (1571) and of regulars (1582) by Gregory XIII.

[86]Sixtus V, apconst *Immensa aeterni Dei,* Jan. 22, 1588.

that refused to address issues or failed to act. As a result, several dicasteries could be competent in the same matter, making it a question of politics rather than justice to get a favorable hearing in Rome. The loss of the Papal States in 1870 meant several dicasteries were no longer needed and resulted in a corps of unemployed prelates who formerly had served in civil capacities for the government of the Papal States. Leo XIII put the prelates to work as a sort of middle management in the other dicasteries. Financial problems were increased, however, by the large number of dicasteries and the loss of income from the Papal States.

Pius X reorganized the Roman Curia in 1908 into eleven congregations, three tribunals, and five offices.[87] He standardized procedures and attempted to abolish cumulative competencies. He separated the internal and external fora and distinguished contentious cases (which were referred to tribunals) from voluntary or administrative ones. With some slight revisions, Benedict XV adopted this reform into the 1917 Code (*CIC* 242–264).

Reform of Paul VI

Although both Pius XI and Pius XII are reported to have considered further reforms in the Roman Curia, it was John XXIII who took action for reform, but this was on a broader scale with Vatican II. Bishops before and during the Council called for a reform of the Curia. They complained about the way the Curia dealt with bishops, about the need for frequent recourse to Rome for those things needed to run a diocese, about the fact that the Curia was a "closed" shop, and about the number of titular bishops in the Curia.[88]

Some specific reform proposals were made at the time. These included the idea of adding residential bishops to the direction of congregations, a greater internationalization of the staff, new organization to the dicasteries, reducing the number of titular bishops, and clarifying the relationship of papal legates with bishops. Clarification was asked of both the functions proper to the Curia and the nature of the power of the dicasteries.

Paul VI was able to draw on recommendations contained in conciliar documents (especially *CD* 9, 10) and unpublished ones collected during the Council, especially in appendices to some of the drafts discussed at the Council.[89] He was also faced with certain internal management difficulties. Ple-

nary meetings of cardinals (the "congregation" strictly speaking) were not being held; cardinal prefects, who held office for life, dominated their dicasteries; and the regular meetings of major officials were more of a rubber stamp affair than the effective consultation they were supposed to be. Staff were promoted as part of the "carriere" or careerism within the Curia rather than by examinations as required by law. Although curial officials took oaths not to accept gifts, the practice of accepting gifts was widespread. Many also served as "agents" for interested dioceses, compromising the impartiality of the system, and the system of taxes for curial services varied considerably.[90]

Through a series of documents, Paul VI renamed the Holy Office and revised its functions,[91] added diocesan bishops as members of the congregations,[92] gave a general reorganization to the Curia and its inner operations,[93] reformed the norms governing legates,[94] and set age limits on the membership of cardinals in congregations.[95] Most of these reforms had been promulgated by the time the synod of bishops met in 1969. This synod called for greater contacts between the Curia and the conferences of bishops;[96] it reflected a concern more with the style of operation of the curial offices than with the inner reform of the Curia itself.

Additional reforms have been considered by John Paul II and the question of such reform was on the agenda for the 1982 meeting of cardinals. However, it is the reform of Paul VI that characterizes the Roman Curia at the time of the promulgation of the 1983 Code.[97] Although the Code leaves details of the operations of the Curia to particular law, it sets the basis for that law and the key to its interpretation in two significant canons.

The Roman Curia

Canon 360 — **The Supreme Pontiff usually conducts the business of the universal Church by means of the Roman Curia, which fulfills its duty in his name and by his authority for the good and the service of the churches; it consists of the Secretariat of State or the Papal Secretariat, the Council for**

---

[87]Pius X, apconst *Sapienti Consilio*, June 29, 1908, *AAS* 1 (1909), 7–19.

[88]I. Gordon, "De Curia Romana renovata: renovatio 'desiderata' et renovatio 'facta' conferuntur," *P* 58 (1969), 60–70; K. Mörsdorf, "Decree on the Bishops' Pastoral Office in the Church," in Vorgrimler II, 171–175.

[89]Appendices to schema *De Cura Animarum, AcSyn Vat*, vol. II, pars IV, 771–826, and to schema *De Pastorali Munere Episcoporum in Ecclesia*, ibid., 382–392.

[90]J. Sanchez y Sanchez, "Pablo VI y la reforma de la Curia Romana," *REDC* 21 (1966), 461–478.

[91]Paul VI, *mp Integrae servandae*, Dec. 7, 1965, *CLD* 6, 353–359.

[92]Paul VI, *mp Pro comperto sane*, Aug. 6, 1967, *CLD* 6, 322–324.

[93]Paul VI, apconst *RE*, Aug. 15, 1967, *CLD* 6, 324–357.

[94]Paul VI, *mp Sollicitudo omnium Ecclesiarum*, June 24, 1969, *CLD* 7, 277–284.

[95]Paul VI, *mp Ingravescentem aetatem*, Nov. 21, 1970, *CLD* 7, 143–145.

[96]E. Farhat, "De Primo Extraordinario Synodi Coetu (1969)," *ME* 97 (1972), 3–23.

[97]For descriptions of the major elements of this reform, see "Curia, Reform and Present Structure," in *SacM* 2, 52–55; historical notes in *Annuario Pontificio*; and *Regimini Ecclesiae Universae*.

the Public Affairs of the Church, congregations, tribunals and other institutions, whose structure and competency are defined in special law.

The canon describes the Curia as the instrument through which the pope usually conducts the business of the universal Church. Drawing on the words of *Christus Dominus* 9, it indicates that the Curia exists for the good and the service of the particular churches that form the communion of the universal Church. The chief categories of dicasteries are named, and reference is made to particular law for the structure and competence of these offices.

Canon 242 of the 1917 Code gave a much briefer description with no reference to the purpose for the Curia, merely stating that it consists in congregations, tribunals, and offices. The revised Code draws on the discussions at Vatican II and the wording of *Christus Dominus* 9, although it modifies this wording in a notable manner. The Council taught that the Curia fulfills its duty for the good of the churches and in service to the sacred pastors. The canon has dropped any reference to the Curia providing ministry to the bishops and retains reference only to the churches. Since bishops head and represent the particular churches, the conciliar teaching remains the proper interpretation for this canon. Even though the Curia is presented as a participation in primatial service (in both *CD* and the canon), this is always in communion with the rest of the bishops (c. 333, §2) and for the good of the college that the pope heads.

The classification of dicasteries is taken from Paul VI's reorganization of the Curia. A supervising and coordinating function is carried out by the Secretariat of State or Papal Secretariat for inner church concerns, and by the Council for the Public Affairs of the Church for concerns external to the Church. All the various congregations are considered to be on an equal footing, each with its own competence. Three types of tribunals exist, and a large number of offices have been established as well as councils, commissions, etc., to address various needs. The major organizations are described below.

Secretariat of State or Papal Secretariat

If an organizational chart were to be drawn of the Roman Curia, the Secretariat of State would appear as the chief middle manager in the Curia. As reorganized under Paul VI, the Secretariat of State is responsible for aiding the pope in his relationships with the universal Church and in dealing with the other departments of the Roman Curia. It is responsible for coordinating the work of the various curial offices, and regular meetings of the heads of the dicasteries are presided over by the Secretary of State. Matters not clearly within the competence

of one or another dicastery are handled by the Secretariat. In principle, direct access to the pope himself is through the Secretariat.

Together with the Council for the Public Affairs of the Church, the Secretariat supervises the work of papal legates around the world, and the two offices are responsible for the Pontifical Commission for Social Communications. The Secretariat is also responsible for editing the official gazette or register of the Holy See, *Acta Apostolicae Sedis* (cf. c. 8, §1).

The Secretary of State, a cardinal, is in charge of the Secretariat. He is assisted by a *sostituto,* or deputy, and by staff drawn from the papal diplomatic corps as well as the civil service of the Roman Curia itself. Its offices are located in the Vatican Palace near those of the pope.

Council for the Public Affairs of the Church

Formerly a section of the Secretariat of State, Paul VI reorganized this agency responsible for diplomatic relations with civil governments. It is still headed by the Secretary of State; but, unlike the Secretariat that is run directly by him, there is a council of cardinals that shares the responsibility for overseeing the work of this office.

While in theory the council deals with Church-State relations and matters touching on civil governments, in practice the distinction has not always been that clear; for example, the *American Procedural Norms* were approved by the council rather than by the Secretariat of State.[98]

The council examines questions submitted to it by the pope, has responsibility for the diplomatic relations of the Holy See with various nations, and together with the Secretariat of State oversees the operations of the papal diplomatic corps.

Congregations

The congregations have a distinctive organization. Technically the "congregation" consists in the committee of cardinals and bishops who are charged with the responsibility of caring for a particular concern on behalf of the supreme authority of the Church and in service to the churches. Each congregation is chaired by a "prefect," called a "pro-prefect" if he is not a cardinal, who is assisted by a secretary (usually a titular archbishop) and a staff of varying proportions.

The full membership of the congregation includes cardinals resident in Rome and cardinals from dioceses around the world. Paul VI, in response to requests from Vatican II, enlarged the congregations by the addition of up to seven diocesan bishops.[99] This full membership gathers annual-

---

[98]Council for the Public Affairs of the Church, rescript, Apr. 28, 1970, *CLD* 7, 950–966.

[99]Paul VI, *mp Pro comperto sane,* Aug. 6, 1967, *CLD* 6, 322–324.

ly for a plenarium, or plenary meeting, to discuss matters of major importance and either approve or make policy decisions on matters within the congregation's competence.

"Ordinary" meetings of all the members who are in Rome at the time are held regularly throughout the year. Theoretically all major decisions implementing policy are made or affirmed at these sessions. Agenda for the meetings is developed with accompanying documentation by the congregation's staff.

The cardinal prefect, secretary, and major staff personnel meet frequently (how frequently depends on the congregation) to carry on the ordinary business of the dicastery within the policy set by the plenary session and in keeping with decisions reached in the ordinary meetings. This group, known as the *congressus,* also decides what to do with issues that are brought to the congregation's attention: whether to submit them to the pope directly, to place them on the agenda for a plenary session, or to handle them in an ordinary session.

The congregations draw on experts in their respective fields, usually from among those living in Rome but also calling on the help of others around the world. Consultors can be asked their advice by mail. They can also be called to meetings of the "council" of consultors where their advice is sought as a body.

At the time the 1983 Code took effect there were nine congregations. Their responsibilities are not always clearly in line with the title of the congregation; catechetics, for example, is under the Sacred Congregation for the Clergy rather than the Sacred Congregation for Catholic Education. These differences are often based on historical circumstances as will be evident in reviewing each congregation.

Finally, a word needs to be said about the practice of referring to the congregations as "sacred." When the reform of the Curia was first announced, the term "sacred" was not in the title of the various congregations. But years of customary use in calling them by this name are not overcome by a stroke of the pen, and by the time the document was officially published each congregation was once again "sacred." The practice can be understood in light of the fact that these congregations deal with sacred matters, i.e., religious ones. They are not involved in civil governance issues, nor are they responsible for Church-State relations (which pertain to the Council for the Public Affairs of the Church, a dicastery which is not termed "sacred").

1. Sacred Congregation for Bishops. This dicastery is responsible for the erection, division, suppression or other changes in dioceses, ecclesiastical provinces, regions, military vicariates, and personal prelatures. Likewise, it cares for the process of selecting bishops, apostolic administrators, military vicars, and other vicars or prelates with personal jurisdiction. It receives the five-year report (c. 399)

submitted by diocesan bishops, orders apostolic visitations of dioceses, and deals with whatever else touches bishops personally, in their ministry, or retirement. It may issue directories on the pastoral ministry of bishops.[100]

The congregation used to be called the Consistorial Congregation and still retains competence for whatever touches consistories, ranging from setting the agenda for them to various matters normally dealt with in consistory, including conferral of the pallium on metropolitans (c. 437). It also deals with the work of metropolitans, and in places not subject to the congregations for oriental churches or evangelization of nations, it is competent to handle matters concerning particular councils and conferences of bishops.

Within the Roman Curia the prefect of the Sacred Congregation for Bishops is charged with convening periodic meetings of the prefects of other congregations responsible for questions concerning the clergy: congregations for clergy, religious and secular institutes, and Catholic education. The Sacred Congregation for Bishops also works with various commissions and secretariats dealing with specialized ministries: emigration, apostolate of the sea and of the air, migrants, the Commission for Latin America, and the General Council for Latin America which is made up of representatives of various groups working in or for Latin America.

2. Sacred Congregation for Catholic Education. This congregation was formerly called the Sacred Congregation for Seminaries and Universities and retains some of that former identity in two of its three offices.

The first office is competent for matters dealing with seminaries, except for those seminaries under the Sacred Congregation for the Oriental Churches and the Sacred Congregation for the Evangelization of Peoples. Its responsibility includes vigilance over the direction, discipline, and temporal administration of seminaries; the education of diocesan clergy; and the systematic education of religious clergy. The congregation also relates to the Pontifical Works for Priestly Vocations.

The second office has competency over universities and other institutes of higher education. These include ecclesiastical institutions established by the authority of the Holy See (cc. 815–821), Catholic colleges and universities (cc. 807–814), and similar institutions. It is concerned as well with Catholic presence at institutions not directly related to the Church. This office also has competence concerning scholarly institutes and associations.

The third office looks after matters affecting Catholic schools, both parochial and diocesan, except those subject to the Sacred Congregations for

---

[100]A major directory on pastoral ministry by bishops was published in 1973; see *Directory.*

the Oriental Churches and for the Evangelization of Peoples.

3. Sacred Congregation for the Clergy. This was formerly the Sacred Congregation of the Council, established to implement and interpret the decrees of the Council of Trent. This explains why the congregation has extensive responsibilities beyond the concerns that would usually seem to pertain to the clergy as such.

Three offices exist within this congregation. The first deals with the life and ministry of the clergy, ranging from their holiness of life to their continuing education and pastoral ministry. It exercises vigilance over pastors and other priests in pastoral ministry, and over presbyteral councils.[101] Although they involve more than the clergy, this congregation also is competent to oversee pastoral councils (diocesan and parish).[102]

The second office addresses questions of preaching and catechetics. It is to promote and approve pastoral and catechetical directories that may be prepared by the various conferences of bishops and may itself indicate opportune norms for the religious instruction of children, youth, and adults.[103] An international council for catechetics is annexed to this office.

The third office is competent for matters of temporal administration. When permission of the Holy See is needed to alienate ecclesiastical goods (c. 1292, §2), the matter is handled through this office. Similarly it oversees matters relating to pious foundations, wills and legacies, the condition of church buildings, sanctuaries and artistic patrimony, taxes, pensions, and the proper support for the clergy.

4. Sacred Congregation for the Doctrine of the Faith. This was the original congregation in the present-day sense of the word, formed as the Inquisition in response to the threats of heresy in the sixteenth century. Known also as the Holy Office, its name was changed by Paul VI prior to the full reorganization of the Curia.[104] Prior to this reform it was termed the "supreme" congregation and technically was headed by the pope himself although a cardinal served as secretary.[105] Since the general reform of the Roman Curia it has been headed by its own cardinal prefect and is juridically equal to all the other congregations.[106]

This dicastery is to examine new teachings and opinions, promote their study and, if necessary, condemn those opposed to the principles of the faith after hearing the bishops of the region affected. It examines books and other writings and may condemn those opposed to the faith after following a process made public for the first time in 1971.[107] Privilege of the faith marriage cases and petitions for dispensations from celibacy and loss of clerical state are handled by this congregation. It also is responsible for defending the sacrament of penance, including judgment in cases in which the seal of the confessional has been violated or in which solicitation in the confessional has been alleged.

The congregation is responsible for the Pontifical Biblical Commission and the International Theological Commission.

5. Sacred Congregation for the Oriental Churches. The name of this dicastery was changed from "Oriental Church" to "Oriental Churches" (in the plural) to reflect the teaching of Vatican II on the equality of the various Ritual Churches *sui iuris* that form the worldwide communion of the Catholic Church. In addition to the assigned cardinals, the various patriarchs and major metropolitans of the Eastern Catholic Churches are automatically members of the congregation as is the president of the Secretariat for Promoting Christian Unity. There is a distinct office within the congregation for each of the Eastern Catholic Churches.[108]

For members of the Eastern Catholic Churches (bishops, clergy, religious, and lay persons) this congregation has all the faculties that are exercised for the Latin Church by the congregations for bishops, clergy, religious and secular institutes, and Catholic education—even in mixed matters where Catholics of the Latin as well as Eastern Catholic Churches are involved. In addition, it has exclusive responsibility for activities of the Church in specific geographic areas traditionally ministered to by Eastern Catholic Churches.

6. Sacred Congregation for the Evangelization of Peoples or for the Propagation of the Faith. The earlier title was simpler: Sacred Congregation for the Propagation of the Faith. However, given the pejorative meaning "propaganda" has in the modern world, a more descriptive name has been given to this dicastery. Its organization and functions were given more specific attention at Vatican II than any other agency of the Roman Curia (*AG* 29).

In addition to the cardinal members of the congregation, bishops from around the world and in particular from missionary territories have been included together with some directors of national missionary societies and superiors general of religious institutes engaged in missionary work.

The congregation traditionally had full jurisdiction over territories considered still to be "missionary" (originally much of Protestant Europe as well

---

[101]SCC, circular letter, Apr. 11, 1970, *CLD* 7, 383–390.

[102]SCC, circular letter, Jan. 25, 1973, *CLD* 8, 280–288.

[103]SCC, *GCD,* Mar. 18, 1971 (Washington: USCC, 1971).

[104]Paul VI, *mp Integrae servandae,* Dec. 7, 1965, *CLD* 6, 358–359.

[105]Ibid.; cf. *CIC* c. 247.

[106]Paul VI, apconst *RE* I, 1, §2, *CLD* 6, 324.

[107]SCDF, *Nova agendi ratio in doctrinarum examine,* Jan. 15, 1971, *CLD* 7, 181–184.

[108]The *Annuario Pontificio* lists twenty Eastern Catholic Churches according to five Oriental ritual families: Alexandrian, Antiochene, Byzantine, Chaldean, and Armenian.

as the "foreign missions" outside of Europe). When the revised Code took effect, the congregation was responsible for certain regions of southeast Europe, parts of the Americas, almost all of Africa, the Far East, New Zealand and Oceania (with the exception of Australia and most of the Philippine Islands). The congregation has traditionally granted special faculties and norms that simplify the provisions of the general law of the Church for the area subject to it. It would appear that in virtue of canon 6 these special laws, if they are contrary to the provisions of the revised Code, are no longer in effect unless specifically renewed by the congregation.

Its competence is quite broad, extending not only to the direction of specifically missionary activities but also to the development and governance of pastoral life in dioceses located in the territories subject to it. There are, however, some exceptions to this competence. It does not replace the competence of the Sacred Congregations for the Doctrine of the Faith, for the Causes of Saints, or for Oriental Churches. Similarly, competence is retained for these areas by the Sacred Congregation for Catholic Education insofar as universities are concerned, and by the Sacred Congregation for Sacraments and Divine Worship in regard to questions of rites and liturgical texts, and for cases of non-consummated marriages. Otherwise, from issues involving religious congregations founded and working primarily in the missions to the erection of dioceses and the naming of bishops, this congregation is competent for the territories under its charge.

7. Sacred Congregation for Religious and Secular Institutes. This congregation is often referred to by its Latin abbreviation "SCRIS" (Sacred Congregation . . .). In addition to the cardinals and diocesan bishops assigned to the congregation, three superiors general of clerical religious institutes participate at the plenary sessions. The congregation has two sections: the first deals with religious institutes (cc. 607–709) and the second has competence for secular institutes (cc. 710–730).

The first section is competent for all religious of the Latin Church (the Sacred Congregation for Oriental Churches carries that competency for religious of those churches). Included with religious are societies of apostolic life (cc. 731–746) and third orders (cc. 311, 312, 317). Not included, however, are religious institutes founded in mission areas and working principally there (these are under the Sacred Congregation for the Evangelization of Peoples).

This section of the congregation is responsible for permission to establish, suppress, or change an institute. It supervises questions of government, looks toward safeguarding the specific purpose of each institute, approves the constitutions and discipline for individual institutes, and is to encourage the adaptation and renewal of religious life. This section also is concerned with the property and privileges of re-

ligious. When permission of the Holy See is required for a business transaction or to alienate ecclesiastical goods held by religious, the permission comes through this section of the congregation (c. 638, §3). Finally, this section establishes or approves councils of major superiors.

The second section performs similar functions for secular institutes, adapted to their specific nature.

8. Sacred Congregation for Sacraments and Divine Worship. This congregation has undergone some additional changes since the general reform of the Roman Curia. In addition to the existing Sacred Congregation for the Discipline of the Sacraments (*CIC* 249) and the Sacred Congregation of Rites (*CIC* 253), a special commission (*consilium*) was set up during Vatican II to oversee the implementation of the reforms mandated by the Council.[109] It worked in conjunction with the existing congregations but brought to the task a staff who shared the renewed vision of liturgy taught by the Council. The three bodies were retained in the 1967 general reform. In 1969 the Sacred Congregation of Rites was reorganized into two congregations, the Sacred Congregation for Causes of Saints, and the Sacred Congregation for Divine Worship.[110] This latter subsumed into it the commission for implementing the reforms of Vatican II. Later, in 1975, the current Sacred Congregation for Sacraments and Divine Worship was formed by amalgamating the existing Sacred Congregations for Sacraments and for Divine Worship.[111] The new dicastery has two sections, one each for the former separate congregations.

The section on sacraments looks after the discipline of the seven sacraments with the exception of privilege of the faith cases, dispensations from celibacy for priests, and the validity of marriage (which is the responsibility of courts such as the Roman Rota: cc. 1443–1444). Dispensations from celibacy for deacons, cases of non-consummation of marriage (cc. 1697–1706), and cases of nullity of sacred ordination (cc. 1708–1712) are sent to the Sacred Congregation for Sacraments and Divine Worship and are processed by this section. It also has a special role in matters pertaining to the Eucharistic fast and the celebration of Mass.

Pastoral and liturgical concerns relative to divine worship are the competence of the other section. It prepares liturgical texts and calendars for the universal Latin Church as well as those proper for specific dioceses and religious institutes. It approves, dispenses and interprets texts and translations, governs the veneration of relics, confirms patrons (of dioceses, etc.), and confers the title of "minor basili-

---

[109]Paul VI, *mp Sacram Liturgiam*, Jan. 25, 1964, *CLD* 6, 69.
[110]Paul VI, apconst *Sacra Rituum Congregatio*, May 8, 1969, *CLD* 7, 238–245.
[111]Paul VI, apconst *Constans Nobis*, July 11, 1975, *CLD* 8, 224–227.

ca" on noteworthy churches. This section also confirms the acts of conferences of bishops relative to liturgical matters and is supposed to maintain contact with national liturgical commissions and liturgical institutes.

This congregation is competent for all the Latin Church, including areas under the Sacred Congregation for the Evangelization of Peoples.

9. Sacred Congregation for Causes of Saints. This congregation was formed when the Sacred Congregation of Rites was reorganized in 1969.[112] It carries the responsibility for beatification and canonization of saints in the Latin and Eastern Catholic Churches and is competent in matters concerning the authentication of relics.

The congregation works through three offices. The first one (called the "judicial office") establishes the procedures for beatification and canonization and carries them out. The second office is that of the promoter general of the faith who acts as the so-called "devil's advocate," investigating any objections and assuring the integrity of the procedure. A third office, the historico-hagiographical office, investigates cases for which there are no living witnesses and is to use careful historical research to determine the heroic virtue of persons whose causes have been presented long after their death.

Secretariats

Three permanent secretariats were established in the 1960s. The Secretariat for Promoting Christian Unity was originally organized by John XXIII to facilitate the relationships of non-Catholics with the Second Vatican Council. The other two secretariats—the Secretariat for Non-Christians, and the Secretariat for Non-Believers—were established by Paul VI in light of discussions at the Council. All three were incorporated into the Roman Curia by Paul VI as part of his general reform of the Curia.

Secretariats have an organizational pattern similar to congregations. That is, cardinals and bishops from around the world are named to the secretariat; a cardinal serves as president ("pro-president" if he is not a cardinal), chairing the commission and heading the staff. He is assisted by a secretary, undersecretary, and appropriate staff.

1. Secretariat for Promoting Christian Unity. The secretariat has the competence specified by its title and carries this out in two offices; one deals with relations with Eastern Christians (e.g., Orthodox) and the other deals with Western Christians (e.g., Anglicans, Protestants, etc.). In addition, this secretariat was given the responsibility of relations on a religious level with the Jews, something it carries out through a special commission.

2. Secretariat for Non-Christians. This secretariat is charged with developing relations with non-Christian believers and with promoting a greater esteem among Christians for believing non-Christians. The secretariat has a special office for religious relations with the Moslems.

3. Secretariat for Non-Believers. The study and development of relations with atheists is the charge given this secretariat. It has carried on dialogues with Marxists and studies on the meaning of atheism and religious indifference in the world today.

Tribunals

There are three tribunals as part of the dicasteries of the Roman Curia. Each has a unique organization and specialized competence.

1. Apostolic Penitentiary. From the early Middle Ages there has been a practice of naming a cardinal to provide absolution of censures reserved to the pope. Over the centuries his competence has been gradually restricted to the internal forum, and today he functions at the level of the universal Church in many ways similar to the canon penitentiary at the diocesan level (c. 508). The cardinal penitentiary is assisted by a regent and other prelates who make up the "major penitentiary" and decide issues submitted in the internal forum.

The Penitentiary grants favors, absolutions, dispensations, commutations, sanations, and condonations for the internal forum. For example, if a confessor remits a censure reserved to the Apostolic See for a person in danger of death (c. 976) who later recovers, or for a person in grave spiritual need (c. 1357, §1), recourse is to be taken to the Apostolic Penitentiary without revealing the name of the person involved. Similar recourse to the Penitentiary is to be made in occult cases involving certain irregularities for the exercise of orders (c. 1048). The Penitentiary has also granted radical sanation for second marriage in cases in which the invalidity of the first marriage cannot be proven in a church court.[113]

2. Supreme Tribunal of the Apostolic Signatura. This is the supreme court of the external forum in the Church. It is composed of a panel of cardinals who are judges, presided over by one of their number as prefect. These are assisted by a secretary and subsecretary, promoter of justice and defender of the bond, chancellor, and staff. Two types of consultors are also used by the Signatura: voters (*votantes*) and referees (*referendarii*) who provide their expert opinions to assist in clarifying the law or evaluating a particular case.

The Signatura has its own special rules of procedure[114] and for judicial actions works through two sections. The first section carries out the competen-

---

[112]Paul VI, apconst *Sacra Rituum Congregatio,* May 8, 1969, *CLD* 7, 238–245.

[113]*CLD* 5, 712–713.

[114]Apostolic Signatura, *Normae Speciales in Supremo Tribunali Signaturae Apostolicae ad experimentum servandae,* Mar. 25, 1968, *CLD* 7, 246–272.

cies listed in canon 1445, §1, and the second section is responsible for those listed in canon 1445, §2.

3. The Roman Rota. The word "rota" is the Latin word for wheel and is applied to this court, the main appellate court of the Roman Curia, because of the system for determining the composition of various panels of judges (or *ternus*). Rotal judges are called auditors and serve in panels of three, five, seven, or as a panel of the whole body (*videntibus omnibus*).

The Rota also has its own special rules of procedure[115] and is competent for the cases listed in canons 1443–1444.

Councils and Commissions

Several councils and commissions carry on important work in the Roman Curia. Some are temporary, carrying out the revision of the Church's law for the Latin Church or the Eastern Catholic Churches, or the revision of the Vulgate. Others are scholarly, dealing with biblical studies, sacred archeology, history, and sacred art in Italy. Others have more pastoral ends, such as the pontifical commissions for justice and peace, the laity, the family, and social communications media. There are also commissions for the ecclesiastical archives in Italy and for certain Italian shrines.

Offices

Operations of the Roman Curia and services directly connected with the pope's household are carried on by several offices. Some have important historical roots, such as the Apostolic Camera in charge of the temporal goods of the Holy See. Others are of more recent origin. The Apostolic Chancery was replaced by several of these offices as well as services provided through the Secretariat of State and was suppressed in 1973.[116]

Apostolic See

Canon 361 — In this Code the term "Apostolic See" or "Holy See" applies not only to the Roman Pontiff but also to the Secretariat of State, the Council for the Public Affairs of the Church and other institutions of the Roman Curia, unless the nature of the matter or the context of the words makes the contrary evident.

This canon provides a clarification for the various times "Apostolic See" or "Holy See" appears elsewhere in the Code or in other church documents. Unless the words clearly restrict the case to the Roman Pontiff, Supreme Pontiff, etc., then the

various dicasteries and services of the Roman Curia are included.

This is a slightly revised version of canon 7 of the 1917 Code, reflecting the reorganized structure of the Roman Curia but retaining the same basic identification of the offices of the Curia with the Apostolic See.

A major question has been the authority with which the Roman Curia carries on its tasks. Benedict XIV clearly restricted the Curia to administrative actions, excluding legislative power from their competence.[117] Yet the instructions and regulations issued by curial offices form the bulk of legislation since the 1917 Code. The apostolic constitution *Regimini Ecclesiae Universae* repeats the traditional norm that "nothing important and out of the ordinary is to be done unless it has first been made known to the Supreme Pontiff" and "all decisions require pontifical approval" with the exception of those for which special faculties have already been given by the pope, or tribunal decisions.[118] The observance of this norm places decisions by curial dicasteries within the provisions of canon 30, so that in each particular case they can become legislative.

The long-term effect of this practice has been to produce administrative law rather than legislation as the consistent source for canonical development. This is not unlike developments under various civil governments, but it carries with it the danger of replacing the theologically sound foundation of church law, based on bishops as legislators and synods or councils as the principal forum for legislating, with administrators acting as delegates.[119]

On the other hand, the identification of the Curia with "Apostolic See" provides a simplified way of identifying the agencies to which recourse must be made when a matter is reserved to the Apostolic See. From a canonical rather than theological perspective, the canon is quite adequate.

CHAPTER V
THE LEGATES OF THE ROMAN PONTIFF
[cc. 362–367]

The practice of churches sending representatives to other communities or even to civil authorities has its roots in the earliest traditions of the Church. Barnabas was sent to represent the Jerusalem church to Christians in Antioch (Acts 11), for example. The practice was adopted early by the Ro-

---

[115]*Normae S. R. Rotae tribunalis,* Sept. 1, 1934, *AAS* 26 (1934), 449–491. The first two titles have been replaced by experimental norms approved by Paul VI, *Nuove norme del tribunale della Sacra Romana Rota,* May 27, 1969; *CLD* 8, 1055–1078.

[116]Paul VI, *mp Quo aptius,* Feb. 27, 1973; *CLD* 8; 229–233.

[117]J. Schmidt, "The Juridic Value of the *Instructio* Provided by the Motu Proprio *'Cum Iuris Canonici'* September 15, 1917," *J* 1 (1941), 289–316.

[118]Paul VI, apconst *RE* 136, *CLD* 6, 356.

[119]See discussion of the issues in del Re, 47–50; J. Sanchez y Sanchez, "La constitution apostolique 'Regimini ecclesiae universae' six ans après," *AC* 20 (1976), 39–41; J. Lecuyer, "The Place of the Roman Curia in Theology," in *The Roman Curia and the Communion of Churches,* ed. by P. Huizing and K. Walf, *Con* 8–9 (New York: Seabury, 1979); J. Souto, "La Reforma de la Curia Romana," *IC* 8 (1968), 547–568.

man church, which not only sent letters (e.g., those attributed to Clement) but also individuals, particularly priests and deacons. At the Council of Arles in 312 there were two priests and deacons "sent from the City of Rome by Sylvester, Bishop." The right of the Roman church to send legates to any church was affirmed in 343 by the Council of Sardica, although it must be admitted that only the Western bishops remained when this decree was adopted.

Individual representatives are an outgrowth of the concept of communion that bonded together the early churches. Letters of communion were, of course, more practical and frequent than individual envoys. Such letters normally are concerned with doctrine, discipline, and mutual exhortation in the faith. Examples in recent practice are not only the letters from the Apostolic See (encyclicals, apostolic letters, apostolic exhortations), but also the statements by various conferences of bishops about issues that are of concern to more than just their individual dioceses.

In addition to this literary exchange, patriarchal churches developed the practice of sending representatives to each other. These ecclesiastical ambassadors were important channels of information and communication within the Catholic communion. By the fifth century, when the bishop of Rome had taken on responsibility for the civil as well as the religious life of the city, the Roman church began to send permanent representatives or "apocrisiaries" to the Imperial Court at Constantinople. This was the beginning of the current practice of nuncios who represent the Holy See not only to local churches but also to civil governments.

In the Middle Ages the popes granted to certain residential bishops special powers over neighboring bishops that went beyond the prerogatives of metropolitans: Thessalonika in Illyricum, Arles in Gaul, Tarragona and Seville in Spain. They were "Apostolic Vicars," a title that gradually changed in the ninth century to *legatus natus,* or legates born with the naming to that particular see. Eventually persons occupying such positions become known as primates.

A person sent on a more transitory mission was known as a *legatus missus* or legate sent for a specific purpose. When such an envoy was a cardinal, he was known as a *legatus a latere,* sent from beside the pope.[120] Selected for the specific task and more closely allied to the pope, legates of this type gradually took on a more stable function in the places to which they were sent. There was a corresponding diminishing of the significance of the *legatus natus* bishops, so that by the 1917 Code they are said to

have no special right because of such a title attached to their see (*CIC* 270).

In the sixteenth century Gregory XIII reorganized the system of legates and established permanent nunciatures with the principal task of implementing the Council of Trent. This system was given further recognition at the Congress of Vienna in 1815, where special prerogatives were accorded papal nuncios in virtue of the spiritual mission of the Holy See. The Vienna Convention in 1961 modified this special status but retained recognition of the right of the Holy See to send representatives under international law.

The system of legates was criticized during the Second Vatican Council—mainly from the viewpoint of pastoral concerns. Bishops complained that legates were acting as "superbishops" over the local ordinaries, lacked pastoral formation, and lived a life-style out of keeping with the conditions in the local churches. Concern was also expressed about their political activities. Some even questioned the idea of legates today, pointing instead to the role of conferences of bishops as the appropriate agents of the Church in dealing with local governments.

Responding to these criticisms, and in light of the directives of the Council that the office of legates be more precisely defined (*CD* 9), Paul VI issued a new particular law for papal representatives in 1969.[121] Arguing that the function of these representatives is to bring the pope closer to the local churches and the various nations closer to the pope, Paul VI affirmed the importance of legates but also more clearly spelled out their role. This *motu proprio* forms the major source for the canons in this section, although they evidence some further development as will be pointed out below.

Right to Legates

Canon 362 — The Roman Pontiff possesses the innate and independent right to nominate, send, transfer and recall his own legates to particular churches in various nations or regions, to states and to public authorities; the norms of international law are to be observed concerning the sending and the recalling of legates appointed to states.

The Roman Pontiff as a spiritual leader has the right to use legates in his relationships with local churches and with civil governments, without any other power having the right to interfere with this activity. The only limitations recognized by the canon are the norms of international law.

The canon is based on *Sollicitudo omnium Ecclesiarum* III, 1 and replaces the less detailed provisions of canon 265 of the 1917 Code.

---

[120]Even today cardinals are sent as special envoys, either to some solemn celebration (in which case they are titled *legatus a latere*) or on a special pastoral duty (as a *missus specialis*); see c. 358.

[121]Paul VI, *mp Sollicitudo omnium Ecclesiarum,* June 24, 1969, *CLD* 7, 277–284.

The right of the Roman Pontiff to send legates is said to be innate, that is, it comes with the office rather than as something conceded by other (e.g., civil) authorities to the pope. The basis for this international role of the Holy See is its worldwide spiritual mission—making it an international entity with a different nature than that of a civil government but giving the Holy See a genuine standing in international law. The diplomatic relations of the pope are always carried on in light of this spiritual mission, hence legates represent the Holy See—not the State of Vatican City; civil governments enter into relations not with the State of Vatican City but with the Holy See itself. Even the title given representatives of the Holy See ("nuncios" rather than "ambassadors") is intended to underscore the particular nature of their mission.

The right is also an independent right, so that its exercise is not limited or in any other way circumscribed by other authorities when legates to local churches are concerned—and only by the norms of international law when representatives to civil governments are considered. The canon is a clear affirmation of the Church's independence from civil authorities insofar as its inner life and structures are concerned, an affirmation that reflects years of struggle to keep civil authorities from attempting to control the naming of legates to the church in their countries.

The sending and recalling of legates appointed to civil governments are governed by diplomatic norms, treaties, and conventions, most particularly the Vienna Convention of 1961. Earlier diplomatic norms (e.g., the Congress of Vienna in 1815) had granted the special privilege to papal legates to serve automatically as dean of the diplomatic corps in the capital to which they were posted, rather than the dean's post being filled by the diplomat longest in service in that capital. The 1961 norms do not require this privilege, and the Holy See has accommodated to this reality so that a legate who is not automatically dean of the diplomatic corps where he is assigned is now called a "pro-nuncio" instead of the traditional "nuncio."

Types of Legates

Canon 363 — §1. To legates of the Roman Pontiff is entrusted the responsibility of representing him in a stable manner to particular churches and also to states and public authorities to which they are sent.

§2. They also represent the Apostolic See who are appointed to a pontifical mission as delegates or observers at International Councils or at conferences and meetings.

There are three basic types of legates: those who represent the pope to particular churches; those

who represent him to particular churches and to civil governments; and those who represent the Apostolic See in international organizations or at various conferences and meetings.

The canon is a simplification of *Sollicitudo omnium Ecclesiarum* I and II. Canon 267 of the 1917 Code presented the basic distinction between representatives to civil governments and those who were sent only to churches in an area.

The canon does not give detailed descriptions of the various types of legates but leaves this to the particular law contained in *Sollicitudo omnium Ecclesiarum*. This *motu proprio* remains in effect, since the Code has not reordered the material *ex integro* (c. 6) and the details in the *motu proprio* are particular law for this specific legal institute (c. 20).

As noted above, legates who represent the pope to the local churches in an area, but not to the civil government, are known as "apostolic delegates." Representatives to the civil government have various titles. A "nuncio" holds the rank of ambassador and enjoys the privilege of being automatically the dean of the diplomatic corps in the capital where he serves. A "pro-nuncio" is also an ambassador but without the special privilege. An "internuncio" is an extraordinary envoy and minister plenipotentiary, a rank used in diplomatic norms when relations have not yet been raised to the ambassadorial level. In addition, "regents" and "chargés d'affaires with special instructions" can serve as permanent legates below the ambassadorial level under certain circumstances.

Sollicitudo omnium Ecclesiarum I limits these positions to "ecclesiastical men," or clerics, many of whom are bishops. This norm remains in effect as particular law for legates. The *motu proprio* II permits lay men as well as clerics to serve as representatives of the Apostolic See to various international organizations or at conferences and meetings.

If the Apostolic See has voting status, this kind of legate is termed a "delegate"; if the status does not include the right to vote, the legate is an "observer." The Apostolic See maintains such legations at the United Nations, in various United Nations-related international organizations, at the Organization of American States, etc. It has also participated in various international meetings, such as the Helsinki meeting on European security that produced the so-called Helsinki Accords.

Ecclesial Responsibilities

Canon 364 — The principal duty of a pontifical legate is to work so that day by day the bonds of unity which exist between the Apostolic See and the particular churches become stronger and more efficacious. Therefore, it belongs to the pontifical legate for his area:

1° to send information to the Apostolic See on the conditions of the particular churches and all

that touches the life of the Church and the good of souls;

2° to assist the bishops by action and counsel, while leaving intact the exercise of the bishops' legitimate power;

3° to foster close relations with the conference of bishops by offering it assistance in every way;

4° to transmit or propose the names of candidates to the Apostolic See in reference to the naming of bishops and to instruct the informative process concerning those to be promoted in accord with the norms given by the Apostolic See;

5° to strive for the promotion of matters which concern peace, progress and the cooperative efforts of peoples;

6° to cooperate with the bishops in fostering suitable relationships between the Catholic Church and other churches or ecclesial communities and non-Christian religions also;

7° in concerted action with the bishops to protect what pertains to the mission of the Church and the Apostolic See in relations with the leaders of the state;

8° to exercise the faculties and fulfill the other mandates committed to him by the Apostolic See.

All legates are bound to these responsibilities; particularly bound, however, are those who represent the pope to local churches and those who also are accredited to local governments, for whom these are common tasks.

The canon is based on *Sollicitudo omnium Ecclesiarum* IV–VIII. It is a less detailed listing than in the *motu proprio*, but it is a more specific and Church-centered one than that found in canon 267 of the 1917 Code.

The listing of responsibilities has been altered from the 1980 schema by the insertion of number one concerning sending information to the Apostolic See, a new item overall even in comparison with the *motu proprio*—although in fact it has always been a significant function of legates.

Their principal duty is to promote the unity of the Church, in keeping with the key role of the Petrine ministry in the Church as a service of unity. The eight specific functions are all to be interpreted and carried out with the promotion of that unity in mind. They do not represent, therefore, an effort to replace the rightful role of diocesan bishops (which is clearly affirmed in 2°) or the competence of the conference of bishops (3°). The *motu proprio* (VIII, 2) calls for the legate to attend the opening session of the annual meeting of a conference of bishops even though he is not a member of the conference by law (c. 450, §2).

In practice, one of the most significant aspects of a legate's work is the selection of bishops (4°). The procedures for this are spelled out below at canon 377. The key link in the process is the legate, who submits not only the list of names or *ternus* of those proposed for the office but also his own evaluation of the situation. As number one indicates, his first job is to inform the Apostolic See on local conditions, and it is in reference to selecting bishops that this can become especially sensitive and influential in the life of the local churches to which he is the papal representative.

The promotion of peace and the development of peoples (5°) is in keeping with the active role taken by recent popes in this regard. It is also a significant function of the papal representatives in more troubled parts of the world, and it is one of the reasons why various nations have sought to maintain diplomatic relations with the Holy See.

The task of fostering ecumenism and interreligious relations (6°) also reflects an important aspect of the work of recent popes. This is to be done in cooperation with the local bishops, for they are the ones who must deal with the situation practically and are also supposed to be well informed about local conditions.

Even if a legate is not posted to a country as representative to the government, he is to work with the bishops of the area to protect the Church's mission as well as the interests of the Apostolic See in dealing with local civil leaders (7°). This effort, even for a legate who has such a civil diplomatic role, is to be carried out in concerted action with the bishops—not as a separate political power.

Finally, legates can be given special faculties for matters that would otherwise have to be sent to Rome (8°).[122] They can also be charged to carry out investigations of local questions that are brought to the attention of the Apostolic See, whether of a doctrinal or disciplinary nature.

The canons do not mention the special relationship that should exist between legates and religious in the country. *Sollicitudo omnium Ecclesiarum* IX calls on legates to foster the development of conferences of major superiors (cc. 708–709) and to be present for at least the first session of their annual meetings. The legate together with the diocesan bishop of the principal house of an institute are to give their advice whenever a diocesan institute seeks to become pontifical (IX, 3; cf. c. 589).

Diplomatic Responsibilities

Canon 365 — §1. It is the special responsibility of a pontifical legate who also exercises a legation to states in accord with the norms of international law:

1° to promote and foster relations between the Apostolic See and the authorities of the state;

2° to deal with questions concerning the relations between the Church and the state; and in a special manner to deal with the drafting and imple-

[122]See the report of faculties granted to legates in *CLD* 9, 172–192.

mentation of concordats and other agreements of this type.

§2. **In conducting the negotiations mentioned in §1, as circumstances suggest, the pontifical legate is to seek out the opinion and counsel of the bishops of the ecclesiastical jurisdiction and also inform them on the progress of these negotiations.**

As representatives of the Apostolic See, legates deal directly with civil governments concerning interests of the Holy See itself and in regard to Church-State relations within the country. Often these latter are worked out in treaties or concordats between the civil government and the Apostolic See. The bishops of the local country are not directly involved in this, although the legate is instructed to draw on their advice and to keep them informed as the circumstances may suggest.

This canon is taken, with a few stylistic changes, from *Sollicitudo omnium Ecclesiarum* X. It is more explicit than the corresponding provisions of canon 267, §1, 1° of the 1917 Code.

The interests of the Holy See can be of a purely religious or moral nature, such as questions of justice, development of peoples, world peace, etc. They can also be of a material nature, ranging from seeking aid for needy areas and relief for disaster victims to special support for the Church in its ministry and various apostolates. These interests also relate to the good of the local churches in the area.[123]

Concordats or international pacts existing before the Code took effect remain intact, even if they contain provisions contrary to the Code (c. 3). These are bilateral pacts entered into on behalf of the Church by the Apostolic See—not as a civil power but in virtue of its character as a spiritual entity in international law. The civil government that enters the concordat can be a national government (e.g., Italy, Spain, Colombia) or a subdivision of a country, such as the concordats that exist with certain states within the Federal Republic of Germany.[124]

One of the more significant concordats in history was the Concordat of Worms to settle the lay investiture controversy in 1122. This was a simultaneous pair of actions in which Callistus II issued an eccle-

siastical decree and Henry V issued an imperial edict.[125] More recent concordats take the form of bilateral treaties or contracts between the two parties.

In addition to the mutual recognition that such concordats contain, they often make provision for state support for Catholic schools, the teaching of Catholic religion courses within state-supported schools, theological faculties in state-supported universities, the support of the clergy, maintenance of church buildings (especially in countries where church real estate has been nationalized), various aspects of the apostolate, etc. In past concordats the State has been given certain rights in the naming of bishops for the area, but since Vatican II (*CD* 20) the Church has been attempting to rescind such privileges so that the selection of bishops is entirely in the hands of the Church. This position is reaffirmed in the present Code (c. 377, §5).

There could be an inconvenience in the Code's provision that relations between Church and State can be worked out from the Catholic Church's point of view without the direct involvement of the bishops in the country. This approach made especially good sense in situations in which religious liberty was not the position of the State nor in fact the actual practice there. However, where a sound tradition of religious liberty exists and may be reinforced by a civil doctrine on the separation of Church and State that is not inimical to the Church, local bishops who are also local citizens may be the most effective persons for dealing with Church-State relations. The canon does not rule out consulting local bishops and indeed calls for it when the circumstances warrant, but the Code is especially mindful of those situations in which religious liberty is denied in practice and in which an international presence is needed to protect the interests of the local churches as well as the concerns of the Holy See.

Privileges

Canon 366 — In view of the special character of a legate's role:

1° the headquarters of a pontifical legation is exempt from the power of governance of the local ordinary unless it is a question of celebrating marriages;

2° after he has previously advised the local ordinaries insofar as this is possible, a pontifical legate is allowed to perform liturgical celebrations, even in pontificals, in all the churches within his legation.

The ecclesiastical privileges of a legate apply both to the seat of the legation and to the liturgical functions that a legate may carry out, even in ponti-

---

[123]In the U.S., the apostolic delegate became a pro-nuncio in 1984. This changed the nature of the apostolic delegation from a strictly ecclesiastical presence for the Church in the U.S. to the status of an embassy accredited to the U.S. government. It also changed the norms concerning Church-State relations that must be observed by the pro-nuncio from those of delegates, who work always "in concerted action with the bishops" (c. 364, 7°) to those of diplomats who have in addition an independent base for dealing with the civil government.

[124]Texts of concordats are published in the appropriate issues of the *AAS*. Modern concordats have been collected by A. Mercati, *Raccolta di Concordati su materie ecclesiastiche tra la Santa Sede e le Autorità Civili* (Rome: Tipografia Polyglotta Vaticana), and L. Schoppe, *Konkordate seit 1800* and *Neue Kondordate und konkordatare Vereinbarungen*.

[125]See B. Tierney, *The Crisis of Church & State 1050–1300* (Englewood Cliffs: Prentice-Hall, 1964), 89–91.

ficals according to the liturgical books if he is a bishop.

The canon is a simplified statement of the provisions of *Sollicitudo omnium Ecclesiarum* XII and represents a revised approach to the matter dealt with in canon 269, §§2 and 3 of the 1917 Code.

The exemption of the legation from the power of governance of the local ordinary does not exempt it from liturgical norms that are in force in the country. The *motu proprio* XII, 2 provides that the legate can give faculties to priests to hear confessions in the chapel of the legation, can exercise his own faculties there, and can carry on sacred functions there; this, however, must be in keeping with the norms in force for that territory. Other disciplinary norms of the local ordinary that go beyond the general law of the Church, however, do not have to be followed in the legation.

The legate does not enjoy the right in law to assist at marriages, so for weddings in the legation or for the legate himself to assist at marriages elsewhere, delegation from an appropriate authority is needed (c. 1108, §1). For other liturgical functions he does not need delegation, but if possible he is to notify the local ordinaries before conducting services in a church outside the seat of the legation.[126]

Duration in Office

Canon 367 — The function of pontifical legate does not cease when the Apostolic See becomes vacant unless the contrary is determined in the pontifical letters; it does cease, however, when his mandate has been fulfilled, when he has been informed of his recall, or when his resignation has been accepted by the Roman Pontiff.

Although a legate of the Roman Pontiff, a pontifical representative does not cease from office when the Apostolic See falls vacant, unless specific provisions have been made in the letter of appointment. The office of legate is lost, however, according to procedures in keeping with the nature of his office as a delegate.

The canon is based on *Sollicitudo omnium Ecclesiarum* III, 2, although it has added the exceptive clause concerning restrictions imposed by the pontifical letters. This clause did appear in canon 268, §1 of the 1917 Code, which was also more explicit than the present canon in reference to the faculties of a legate (which do not cease when the Apostolic See is vacant).

During the vacancy of the Apostolic See, nothing is to be innovated in the governance of the universal Church (c. 335). However, legates carry out ordinary business and, similar to the offices of the Roman Curia below the rank of prefect, retain their responsibilities during the vacancy.[127] Any matters for which they need special approval from the pope, or which must be referred to him personally, must wait until a new pope is elected.

A legate ceases from office in the same manner as anyone with delegated authority (c. 142). If the legation was for a specific purpose, once that purpose has been achieved the function of legate ceases. Legates can also be recalled, and their functions cease upon receipt of notification of such recall. If a legate desires to resign, the resignation takes effect upon receipt of notification of its acceptance.

The *motu proprio* also applies to legates the norms for officials of the Roman Curia, so that when they reach seventy-five they cease from office (III, 3).

---

[126]This is similar to the right of a metropolitan within the province, except that the metropolitan does not need to notify the local bishop of his liturgical activities in that bishop's diocese unless he is going to use the cathedral church, in which case he must notify him (c. 436, §3). The legate does not have to notify the bishop even if he is using the cathedral church, although if possible he should do so when using any church in a diocese.

[127]The apconst *Romano Pontifici eligendo* specifies that curial officers below the prefects remain in service and carry out routine functions of their dicasteries (25), and that the functions and powers of papal legates do not cease during the vacancy (21).

Council	Dates
1. Nicaea	325
2. Constantinople I	381
3. Ephesus	431
4. Chalcedon	451
5. Constantinople II	553
6. Constantinople III	680–681
7. Nicaea II	787
8. Constantinople IV	869–870
9. Lateran I	1123
10. Lateran II	1139
11. Lateran III	1179
12. Lateran IV	1215
13. Lyons I	1245
14. Lyons II	1274
15. Vienne	1311–1312
16. Constance	1414–1418
17. [Basle/Ferrara] Florence [Rome]	1431–1445
18. Lateran V	1512–1517
19. Trent	1545–1563
20. Vatican I	1869–1870
21. Vatican II	1962–1965

BIBLIOGRAPHY

Chapter I:
The Roman Pontiff and the College of Bishops

a. Historical Studies

Alberigo, G. *Lo Sviluppo della dottrina sui poteri nella Chiesa universale: Momenti essenziali tra il XVI e il XIX secolo.* Rome: Herder, 1964.

Botte, B., et al. *Le concile et les conciles: Contribution à l'histoire de la vie conciliaire de l'église.* Chevetogne and Paris: Cerf, 1960.

Butler, C. *The Vatican Council 1869–1870.* Westminster, Md.: Newman, 1962.

Fuellenbach, J. *Ecclesiastical Office and the Primacy of Rome.* Washington: Catholic University, 1980.

Maccarrone, M. *Vicarius Christi: Storia del titolo papale.* Rome: Pontificia Universitas Lateranense, 1953.

Marthaler, B. "The Councils in History: A Survey of Selected Literature." *TS* 26 (1965): 393–406.

Navarette, U. "Potestas Vicaria Ecclesiae. Evolutio historica conceptus atque observationes attenta doctrina concilii Vaticani II." *P* 60 (1971): 414–486.

Schwarz, R. "De potestate propria Ecclesiae." *P* 63 (1974): 429–455.

————. *Die eigenberechtige Gewalt der Kirche.* Rome: Pontificia Universitas Gregoriana, 1974.

Thils, G. *Primauté pontificale et prérogatives épiscopales: "Potestas Ordinaria" au Concile du Vatican.* Louvain: E. Warny, 1961.

Tierney, B. *Foundations of the Conciliar Theory.* Cambridge, England: University Press, 1955.

Tierney, B., and Linehan, P., eds. *Authority and Power: Studies in Medieval Law and Government.* Cambridge, England: University Press, 1980.

Walsh, V. "The Theological and Juridical Role of the Bishop: Early Twentieth Century and Contemporary Views." *Apol* 44 (1971): 39–92.

b. Official Code Commission Reports on Supreme Authority Canons

Comm 4 (1972): 144–145 (report on bishops' response to 1971 *LEF*).

Comm 8 (1976): 87–98, 102–108 (general comments of *LEF coetus*).

Comm 9 (1977): 83–91, 114–116 (review of some canons in *LEF*).

Comm 13 (1981): 45–53 (1979 *LEF*).

Comm 14 (1982): 89–90 (*LEF coetus*), 179–180 (1981 *Rel*).

c. Other Studies

Acerbi, A. *Due Ecclesiologie: Ecclesiologia giuridica ed ecclesiologia di communione nella "Lumen Gentium."* Bologna: Dehoniane, 1975.

Anton, A. *Primado y colegialidad: Sus relaciones a la luz del primer Sinodo extraordinario.* Madrid: B.A.C., 1970.

Bertrams, W. *The Papacy, the Episcopacy, and Collegiality.* Westminster, Md.: Newman, 1964.

————. *Quaestiones fundamentales iuris canonici.* Rome: Pontificia Universitas Gregoriana, 1969.

Congar, Y. *Ministères et communion ecclésiale.* Paris: Cerf, 1971.

Congar, Y., and Dupuy, B.-D., eds. *L'episcopat et l'Église universelle.* Paris: Cerf, 1962.

Congar, Y., et al. *La collégialité épiscopale: histoire et théologie.* Paris: Cerf, 1966.

Coriden, J., ed. *The Once and Future Church: A Communion of Freedom.* New York: Alba, 1971.

Empie, P., and Murphy, T.A., eds. *Papal Primacy and the Universal Church.* Minneapolis: Augsburg, 1974.

Fagiolo, V., and Concetti, G., eds. *La collegialità episcopale per il futuro della Chiesa.* Florence: Vallecchi, 1969.

George, J. *The Principle of Subsidiarity—With Special Reference to Its Role in Papal and Episcopal Relations in the Light of "Lumen Gentium."* Washington: Catholic University, 1968.

Ghirlanda, G. *"Hierarchica Communio": Significato della formula nella "Lumen Gentium."* Rome: Pontificia Universitas Gregoriana, 1980.

Granfield, P. "Papal Resignation." *J* 38 (1978): 118–131.

Kramer, P. *Dienst und Vollmacht in der Kirche. Eine rechtstheologische Untersuchung zur Sacra Potestas-Lehre des II Vatikanischen Konzils.* Trier: Paulinus, 1973.

Küng, H., ed. *The Petrine Ministry in the Church. Con* 64 (New York: Herder & Herder, 1971).

Minnerath, R. *Le Pape: Evêque universel ou premier des évêques?* Paris: Beauchesne, 1978.

Chapter II: The Synod of Bishops

a. Official Documents

Paul VI. *Mp Apostolica sollicitudo.* Sept. 15, 1965. *AAS* 57 (1965): 775–780; *CLD* 6: 388–393.

Council for the Public Affairs of the Church. *Ordinem Synodi Episcoporum celebrandum recognitum et auctum.* June 24, 1969. *AAS* 61 (1969): 525–539; *CLD* 7:323–337.

———. *Ordo Synodi Episcoporum celebrandae recognitus et auctus nonnullis additamentis perficitur.* Aug. 20, 1971. *AAS* 63 (1971): 702–704; *CLD* 7:338–341.

b. Studies

Anton, A. "Episcoporum Synodus: partes agens totius catholici episcopatus." *P* 57 (1968): 495–527.

Bertrams, W. "Motu proprio 'Apostolica Sollicitudo' (15/9/65): Synodus Episcoporum pro universa Ecclesia constitutur." *P* 55 (1966): 108–132.

———. "De Synodi Episcoporum potestate cooperandi in exercitio potestatis primatialis." *P* 57 (1968): 528–549.

Ferrara, V. "Il Sinodo dei Vescovi tra ipotesi e realtà. Natura teologico-giuridica del Sinodo." *Apol* 42 (1969): 491–556.

Foley, D. *The Synod of Bishops: Its Canonical Structure and Procedures.* Washington: Catholic University, 1973.

Laurentin, R. *Le Synode permanent: naissance et avenir.* Paris: Seuil, 1970.

Schillebeeckx, E., "The Synod of Bishops—One Form of Strict but Non-Conciliar Collegiality." *IDO-C Dossier* 67–9 (March 12, 1967).

Trisco, R. "The Synod of Bishops and the Second Vatican Council." *AER* 161 (1967): 145–160.

Zurowski, M. "Synodus Episcoporum in quantum 'partes agens totius catholici episcopatus.'" *P* 62 (1973): 375–391.

Chapter III: The Cardinals of the Holy Roman Church

a. Commentaries on the 1917 Code

Belardo, M. *De Iuribus S.R.E. Cardinalium in Titulis.* Rome: Pontificium Institutum Utriusque Iuris, 1938.

Hynes, H. *The Privileges of Cardinals: Commentary with Historical Notes.* Washington: Catholic University, 1945.

Saco, C. "Regimen juridico vigente del colegio cardenalicio." *IC* 8 (1968): 223–266.

van Lierde, P., and Giraud, A. *What is a Cardinal?* New York: Hawthorn, 1964.

b. Official Documents

John XXIII. *Mp Ad suburbicarias Dioeceses.* Mar. 10, 1961. *AAS* 53 (1961): 198; *CLD* 5: 275–276.

John XXIII. *Mp Suburbicariis Sedibus.* Apr. 11, 1962. *AAS* 54 (1962): 253–256; *CLD* 5: 270–272.

John XXIII. *Mp Cum gravissima.* Apr. 15, 1962. *AAS* 54 (1962): 256–258; *CLD* 5: 273–274.

Paul VI. *Mp Ad purpuratorum patrum.* Feb. 11, 1965. *AAS* 57 (1965): 295–296; *CLD* 6: 310–311.

Paul VI. *Mp Sacro Cardinalium consilio.* Feb. 26, 1965. *AAS* 57 (1965): 296–297; *CLD* 6: 312–313.

Paul VI. *Mp Ad hoc usque tempus.* Apr. 15, 1969. *AAS* 61 (1969): 226–227; *CLD* 7: 146–147.

Paul VI. *Mp Ingravescentem aetatem,* Nov. 21, 1970. *AAS* 62 (1970): 810–813; *CLD* 7: 143–145.

c. Studies

Alberigo, G. *Cardinalato e collegialità: Studi sull' ecclesiologia tra l'XI e il XIV secolo.* Florence: Vallecchi, 1969.

Congar, Y. "Notes sur le destin de l'idée de collégialité épiscopale en occident au moyen age (VIIe–XVIe siècles)," in *La collégialité épiscopale: Histoire et théologie.* (Paris: Cerf, 1965): 99–129.

Fürst, C. *Cardinalis: Prolegomena zu einer Rechtsgeschichte des römischen Kardinalskollegiums.* Munich: W. Fink, 1967.

Kuttner, S. "*Cardinalis:* The History of a Canonical Concept." *Traditio* 3 (1945): 129–214.

Lefebvre, C. "Les origines et la role du cardinalat au moyen age." *Apol* 41 (1968): 59–70.

Snodgrass, T. "Cardinals: A Textual Analysis of Changes in Legislation," J.C.L. dissertation, Catholic University of America, 1983.

Chapter IV: The Roman Curia

a. Commentaries on the Curia prior to Vatican II

Berutti, C. *De Curia Romana notulae historico-exegetico-practicae.* Rome: Officium Libri Catholici, 1952.

Bouix, D. *Tractatus de Curia Romana.* Rev. ed. Paris: Perisse Frères, 1880.

Cappello, F. *De Curia Romana iuxta reformationem a Pio X sapientissime inductam.* 2 vols. Rome: F. Pustet, 1911–1912.

Martin, M. *The Roman Curia As It Now Exists.* New York: Benziger Bros., 1913.

Sanchez y Sanchez, J. "Pablo VI y la reforma de la Curia Romana." *REDC* 21 (1966): 461–479.

———. "La Curia Romana hasta Pablo VI," *REDC* 32 (1976): 439–458.

Schmidt, J. "The Juridic Value of the *Instructio* Provided by the Motu Proprio '*Cum Iuris Canonici*' September 15, 1917." *J* 1 (1941): 289–316.

b. Official Documents

Paul VI. *Mp Sacram Liturgiam.* Jan. 25, 1964. *AAS* 56 (1964): 139–144.

Paul VI. *Mp Integrae servandae.* Dec. 7, 1965. *AAS* 57 (1965): 952–955; *CLD* 6: 353–359.

Paul VI. *Mp Pro comperto sane.* Aug. 6, 1967. *AAS* 59 (1967): 881–884; *CLD* 6: 322–324.

Paul VI. Apconst *Regimini Ecclesiae Universae.* Aug. 15, 1967. *AAS* 59 (1967): 885–928; *CLD* 6: 324–357.

Paul VI. *Mp Sacra Rituum Congregatio.* May 8, 1969. *AAS* 61 (1969): 297–305; *CLD* 7: 238–245.

Paul VI. *Mp Sollicitudo omnium Ecclesiarum.* June 24, 1969. *AAS* 61 (1969): 473–484; *CLD* 7: 277–284.

Paul VI. *Mp Ingravescentem aetatem.* Nov. 21, 1970. *AAS* 62 (1970): 810–813; *CLD* 7: 143–145.

Paul VI. *Mp Quo aptius.* Feb. 27, 1973. *AAS* 65 (1973): 113–116; *CLD* 8: 229–233.

Paul VI. Apconst *Constans Nobis.* July 11, 1975. *AAS* 67 (1975): 417–420; *CLD* 8: 224–227.

Secretary of State. *Regolamento Generale della Curia Romana.* Feb. 22, 1968. *AAS* 60 (1968): 130–176; *CLD* 7: 147–176.

c. Studies

Bassett, W., and Huizing, P., eds. *The Finances of the Church. Con* 117. New York: Seabury, 1979.

Delgado, G. *La Curia Romana: El gobierno central de la Iglesia.* Pamplona: EUNSA, 1973.

del Re, N. *La Curia Romana: Lineamenti storico-giuridici.* 3rd rev. ed. Rome: Ed. di Storia e Letteratura, 1970.

Gordon, I. "De Curia Romana renovata: renovatio 'desiderata' et renovatio 'facta' conferuntur." *P* 58 (1969): 59–116.

Hamer, J. "In the Service of the Magisterium: Evolution of a Congregation." *J* 37 (1977): 340–357.

Huizing, P., and Walf, K., eds. *The Roman Curia and the Communion of Churches. Con* 127. New York: Seabury, 1979.

Jimenez Urresti, T., ed. *Structures of the Church. Con* 58. New York: Herder & Herder, 1970.

McReavy, L. "Reorganization of the Roman Curia." *CR* 53 (1968): 306–313.

Miller, R. *The Congregation for the Doctrine of the Faith: Its Origin, Concept, and the Development of Its Competency.* Washington: Catholic University, 1975.

Sanchez y Sanchez, J. "La constitution apostolique 'Regimini ecclesiae universae' six ans après." *AC* 20 (1976): 33–66.

Zizola, G. "The Reformed Roman Curia." In *We, the People of God.* Ed. by J. Coriden, 49–77. Huntington, Ind.: Our Sunday Visitor, 1968.

Chapter V: The Legates

a. Commentaries prior to Vatican II

Paro, G. *The Right of Papal Legation.* Washington: Catholic University, 1947.

Staffa, D. *Le Delegazioni Apostoliche.* Rome/New York: Desclée, 1959.

Walf, K. "Der Apostolische Pronuntius: Neue Sinngebung für einen alten Terminus technicus." *AkK* 134 (1965): 376–381.

b. Official Documents

Mercati, A. *Raccolta di Concordati su materia ecclesiastiche tra la Santa Sede e le Autorità Civili.* Vol. 1 (1908–1914); vol. 2 (1915–1954). Rome: Tipografia Polyglotta Vaticana, 1919 and 1954.

Paul VI. *Mp Sollicitudo omnium Ecclesiarum.* June 24, 1969. *AAS* 61 (1969): 473–484; *CLD* 7: 277–284.

Schoppe, L. *Konkordate seit 1800. Originaltext und deutsche Übersetzung der geltenden Konkordate.* Frankfurt: A. Metzner, 1964.

———. *Neue Konkordate und konkordatare Verinbarungen. Abschlüsse in den Jahren 1964 bis 1969.* Hamburg, 1970.

c. Studies

Cardinale, H. *The Holy See and the International Order.* Gerrards Cross, England: Van Duren, 1976.

deEcheverria, L. "Funciones de los Legados del Romano Pontifice." *REDC* 25 (1969): 581–636.

———. "The Pope's Representatives." In *The Roman Curia and the Communion of Churches.* Ed. by P. Huizing and K. Walf, 56–63. *Con* 127. New York: Seabury, 1979.

Hennesey, J. "Papal Diplomacy and the Contemporary Church." In *The Once and Future Church.* Ed. by J. Coriden, 179–204. New York: Alba House, 1971.

Jimenez-Urresti, T., ed. *Structures of the Church.* *Con.* 58. New York: Herder & Herder, 1970.

Lallou, W. *The Fifty Years of the Apostolic Delegation Washington, D.C. 1893–1943.* New Jersey: St. Anthony Guild, 1943.

Marini, L. "The Apostolic Delegate: His Role in Ecclesiastical Law." J.C.L. dissertation, Catholic University of America, 1983.

Minnerath, R. *L'Eglise et les Etats concordataires (1846–1981): La souveraineté spirituelle.* Paris: Cerf, 1983.

Oliveri, M. *The Representatives: The Real Nature and Function of Papal Legates.* Gerrards Cross, England: Van Duren, 1981.

Wister, R. *The Establishment of the Apostolic Delegation in the United States of America: The Satolli Mission, 1892–1896.* Rome: Pontificia Universitas Gregoriana, 1981.

Section II: PARTICULAR CHURCHES AND THEIR GROUPINGS
[cc. 368–572]

TITLE I
PARTICULAR CHURCHES AND THE AUTHORITY ESTABLISHED IN THEM
[cc. 368–430]

One of the areas of the revised Code reflecting the most significant change from its 1917 predecessor is the structuring of the life and ministry of the particular church. This in turn manifests the shift in focus throughout Book II from an overly institutional ecclesiology characterizing the 1917 Code to a more communitarian emphasis in the present law. Instead of concentrating on isolated individuals like the 1917 Code ("De personis"—"Persons") did, the present law stresses the sacramentally grounded community of believers ("De Populo Dei"—"People of God"). Instead of focusing primarily on certain individuals exercising power over other individuals, it stresses the common mission of all believers and the special roles of service which some fulfill for others. Only within this broader frame of reference can one properly appreciate the specific canons on the particular church, the bishop, and other significant leadership figures at the diocesan, parish, and deanery level.

Before discussing those canons it seems advisable to comment briefly on some noteworthy themes underlying legal reform in this area. Then some brief observations will be made on the work of the Code Commission and on some noteworthy changes from the 1917 Code. Subsequently, the individual canons of this title will be examined; particular attention will be devoted to those canons especially reflecting the orientations of Vatican II.

Key Theological—Canonical Themes

Identifying the values underlying a given legal institute or cluster of institutes is not always easy, but it can help to understand individual canons. Accordingly one may note that the revised law on the particular church reflects among other things the influence of three theological-canonical values: the principle of communion, the principle of subsidiarity, and the principle of qualified territoriality.[1] Some observations about each are in order.

One may use various models in attempting to conceptualize the Church, none of which is entirely satisfactory. However, the *communio* model seems particularly relevant in clarifying recent developments in ecclesiastical organization.[2] The Church is a sign and instrument of the intimate union of God and human persons and of human persons among themselves. It is a communion of life, love, and truth originating in God's redemptive love, established by the ministry of Christ, and enlivened by his Spirit. The notion of communion expresses the union of the members of the people of God among themselves and with Christ their head. It also clarifies the union of the particular churches among themselves and with the Church of Rome.

A significant dimension of the revised law is its recognition of the importance of the particular churches, in which and out of which the universal Church of Christ exists. The highly centralized preconciliar ecclesiology and legal system highlighted the universal Church and tended to view the particular churches merely as useful administrative subdivisions of that universal Church. On the contrary the revised law reflects a central feature of conciliar ecclesiology, namely, that the particular churches are not field offices of a giant multi-national corporation, but local realizations of the one Church of Christ (*LG* 23; *CD* 11; *UR* 15; *AG* 19). Hence there is a movement back toward a view of the universal Church as a communion of communions, each of which is Christ's Church. In light of the diversity of the people of God, there are diverse forms of particular churches, among which the diocese is the most noteworthy and on which this commentary concentrates nearly exclusively (c. 368). However, in all of these churches the one, holy, catholic, and apostolic Church is present, active, and growing.

Not surprisingly this shift in emphasis affects the structuring of the revised law. A separate chapter is devoted to the various particular churches and their corresponding subdivisions (cc. 368–374). The 1917 Code had no corresponding section even though it contained several canons on various administrative subdivisions such as dioceses, parishes, and deaneries (*CIC* 215–217). Interestingly enough this material was situated not in the canons on diocesan and parish organization (*CIC* 329–486) but rather immediately following the treatment of clerics in general and just preceding the canons on the Roman Pontiff.

---

[1]See J. Komonchak, "A New Law for the People of God: A Theological Evaluation," *CLSAP* (1980), 14–43.

[2]For an exploration of various theological-canonical implications of the notion of the Church as a communion, see *J* 36 (1976), 1–245.

Another principle whose implications in the revised Code are undeniable is that of *subsidiarity*. It can mean various things, however; here it refers to the post-conciliar movement toward decentralized decisional processes in the Church. The basic orientations of Church discipline need to be adapted to the diversity of peoples and cultures making up the Catholic community. There are to be more options for decisional initiatives to be taken by the individual particular churches; in other words, canonical pluralism is to be admitted along with theological, liturgical, and ascetical pluralism. Principle five for the revision of the Code was the first official recognition of the applicability of subsidiarity in canon law;[3] this subsidiarity is meant to strengthen and confirm legislative unity while at the same time doing justice to the reasonableness and need of individual institutions to provide for themselves by particular law.[4]

The principle of subsidiarity is reflected in part in the increased decisional freedom of conferences of bishops and diocesan bishops. A noteworthy point of tension throughout the revision process was the difficulty of structuring the law so as to do justice to the values of coordinating pastoral activities in a given region and enhancing the legitimate integrity of the episcopal office. Whenever conflicts arose in this connection, the Code Commission generally tended to protect the autonomy of the diocesan bishop in the exercise of his office. Accordingly the decisional competence of the conference of bishops was gradually reduced during the revision process.

The 1917 Code tended to view the bishop as empowered for his leadership role by delegation of supreme church authority. On the contrary both Vatican II and the revised law see him as sacramentally empowered by episcopal consecration to carry out the threefold *munus,* or function of Christ (ruling, teaching, and sanctifying) (*LG* 21; c. 375). In the particular church entrusted to him the bishop possesses all the ordinary and immediate power he needs to represent Christ; and he is said to be a vicar, not of the Roman Pontiff, but of Christ himself (*LG* 27). The authority of the bishop is said to be "proper," i.e., it is presumed to exist whenever he must fulfill his pastoral responsibilities; it is restricted only when limitations are explicitly stated (c. 381, §1). Granted, no individual particular church is an island unto itself. However, such limitations on the pastoral autonomy of the diocesan bishop should seemingly be restricted to those matters on which a common approach is necessary for the unity or advantage of the universal Church or the churches in a given area (*CD* 8a).

Besides the pope, the bishop is the most significant leadership figure in the revised Code. To a certain extent the revised Code is an episcopal Code inasmuch as it contains over four hundred fifty references to the bishop in one form or another. And yet the conciliar enhancing of the status of the bishop must not lead to his becoming an isolated monarch out of touch with the dynamics of the particular church entrusted to him. In light of the above-mentioned principle of communion, he is viewed as the leader of a sacramental community in mission (*kerygma, diakonia, koinonia*). He is considered a principle of unity in catalyzing the ministerial resources of the particular church in service to the world. While the 1917 Code tended to view the bishop as pursuing the mission of the Church on his own with some trusted advisors, the revised law sees him as fostering various corporate processes whereby different members of the people of God can share actively in the realization of that mission. Finally, one can properly appreciate the varied dimensions of the episcopal office only by examining the whole Code and not simply the canons in Book II to be treated in this part of the commentary.[5]

The final noteworthy point is the principle of *qualified territoriality*. Principle eight for the revision of the Code stated that the pastoral purpose of the diocese and the good of the entire Church required clear and definite territorial divisions. Nevertheless, weighty reasons at times may justify other forms of jurisdictional units for specific pastoral ministries. The revised Code does not include territory as an essential or constitutive element in describing the particular church (c. 369). However, it is viewed as the ordinary means of identifying that portion of the people of God which will be recognized as a particular church (c. 372, §1). The relative permanency of geographical bonds suggests that territory be the ordinary criterion of determining ecclesiastical pastoral units. However, the importance of adapting to shifting pastoral needs in a changing, pluralistic world makes advisable the utilization of other organizational criteria, e.g., rite, nationality, language, occupation, etc. (c. 372, §2).

After the consideration of some key themes that underlie the revised law, some brief observations are in order on the activity of the Code Commission in formulating this section of the law. Lest the following comments be unduly repetitious of comparable introductory remarks in other areas of Book II, the author limits his focus to the formulation of the canons on bishops and on the impeded and vacant see.

---

[3]See *Comm* 1 (1969), 80–82. English translation is in J. Hite, G. Sesto and D. Ward (eds.), *Readings Cases Materials in Canon Law* (Collegeville, Minn.: The Liturgical Press, 1980), 73–75 (cited as Hite, *Readings*).

[4]See F. Morrisey, "The Importance of Particular Law in the New Code," *CLSAP* (1981), 1–17 *passim*.

[5]For a brief overview of various aspects of the episcopal office in the revised Code, see T. Green, "The Diocesan Bishop in the Revised Code: Some Introductory Reflections," *J* 42 (1982), 320–349 *passim*. For a more detailed discussion of various aspects of the episcopal office in the particular church, see SCB, *Directory on the Pastoral Ministry of Bishops* (Ottawa: Canadian Catholic Conference 1974) (cited as *Directory*).

Revision of 1917 Code

The original schema on the people of God,[6] forwarded to the bishops and others for evaluation in January 1978, was the work of various Code Commission committees. However, the canons on bishops were formulated by the committee on the sacred hierarchy.[7] The introductory norms (cc. 217–224) clarified the basic elements of diocesan organization, describing the diocese, parish, and deanery in light of *Christus Dominus* 11 and 30 and *Ecclesiae sanctae* I, 21. The norms on bishops were arranged somewhat differently from the bipartite structure of the 1917 Code, which treated of bishops in one unit (*CIC* 329–349) and of coadjutor and auxiliary bishops in another (*CIC* 350–355). The original schema was organized in a tripartite fashion, encompassing norms on all bishops (cc. 225–232), norms on residential bishops (cc. 233–260), and norms on coadjutors and auxiliaries (cc. 261–269).

The original schema largely systematized the sacramental, magisterial, and pastoral governance aspects of the episcopal office in light of *Christus Dominus* 11–21 and the 1917 Code. The norms on coadjutor and auxiliary bishops attempted to implement *Christus Dominus* 25–26 and *Ecclesiae sanctae* I, 13. Finally the norms on the impeded and vacant see (cc. 330–348) basically restated the 1917 Code (*CIC* 429–444). Like the 1917 Code they were separated from the canons on bishops, yet they immediately preceded the canons on the parish and not those on the deanery as in the 1917 Code. The basic structure of the original schema has been largely maintained in the present law, which will be discussed shortly.

A special committee was established to review the evaluations of the original people of God schema. The canons on bishops and on the impeded or vacant see were discussed at two sessions in March and April 1980.[8] After all of the original schemata were revised, the Commission issued the so-called 1980 schema,[9] which was discussed by the members of the Code Commission during 1980 and 1981. Canons 335–341 of this schema dealt with the particular churches; canons 342–347 with all bishops;

canons 348–369 with residential bishops; canons 370–378 with coadjutor and auxiliary bishops; and canons 435–453 with the impeded or vacant see. Certain changes were introduced into this schema either prior to or during an October 1981 plenary session of the Commission. Then it was forwarded to Pope John Paul II for promulgation.[10] His own personal consultation during 1982 led to several changes being incorporated in the schema prior to the promulgation of the present law in January 1983.

Noteworthy Changes in Revised Code

While noting certain similarities to the 1917 Code, the following reflections will generally highlight some principle differences between the revised Code and the former law. First a basic organizational difference will be noted. Then some noteworthy changes from the 1917 Code will be briefly indicated. This will help to put in perspective subsequent comments on individual canons.

In the 1917 Code certain legal institutes at the intermediate level of Church government such as metropolitans and plenary and provincial councils (*CIC* 271–292) were placed before the institutes of diocesan and parish law (*CIC* 329–486). The former were viewed as sharing in the exercise of supreme church authority, whereas the latter were viewed as different ways of sharing in the exercise of subordinate episcopal authority. The revised law reflects the conciliar teaching on the basic unity of episcopal authority that transcends the somewhat dualistic 1917 Code distinction between supreme papal authority and subordinate episcopal authority (*CIC* 108, §3). The present law also correctly understands intermediate level institutes such as metropolitans and plenary and provincial councils as sharing in the exercise of genuinely episcopal authority. A question still remains, however, about the precise relationship between the canons on the particular churches (bishops and various diocesan and parish institutes) and the canons on the intermediate level of church government involving groupings of the particular churches (metropolitans, particular councils, and conferences of bishops).

The original schema treated the intermediate level of church government (cc. 185–216) prior to the particular church (cc. 217–397). This arrangement was questioned by some critics because the particular church and the diocesan bishop are divine law realities and thereby enjoy a certain preeminence over ecclesiastical law realities such as the metro-

[6]ComCICRec, *Schema Canonum Libri II de Populo Dei* (Rome: Typis Polyglottis Vaticanis, 1977).

[7]For pertinent reports of the committee on its work leading up to the original schema, see *Comm* 4 (1972), 40–50; 5 (1973), 216–235 (clerics in particular); and 7 (1975), 161–172 (coadjutor and auxiliary bishops). For an overview of criticisms of the original schema by canon law societies largely in the English-speaking world, see T. Green, "Critical Reflections on the Schema on the People of God," *Stud Can* 14 (1980), 235–322 *passim.*

[8]For pertinent reports on the revisions of the original schema by this special committee, see *Comm* 12 (1980), 275–314; 13 (1981), 140–146.

[9]ComCICRec, *Schema Codicis Iuris Canonici* (Rome: Libreria Editrice Vaticana, 1980).

[10]For a helpful overview of the 1980 schema, which takes cognizance of official changes in the text up to and including the October 1981 plenary session of the Commission, see J. Alesandro, "Law and Renewal: A Canon Lawyer's Analysis," *CLSAP* (1982), 1–40 *passim.*

politan and the conference of bishops. Furthermore, placing the canons on the particular church before those on the intermediate level of church government would correspond to the structuring of conciliar documents such as *Christus Dominus* and post-conciliar documents such as the *Directory on the Pastoral Ministry of Bishops*. Such a change was initially rejected by the Commission. Hence the 1980 schema was organized like the original schema with the canons on the intermediate level of government (cc. 306–334) preceding those on the particular church (cc. 335–502). Nevertheless, the October 1981 plenary session of the Commission voted overwhelmingly to place the canons on the particular church before those on the intermediate level of church government. Somewhat surprisingly, however, the revised law inserts the material on the intermediate level of church government (cc. 431–459) between the initial treatment of the bishop and the impeded or vacant see (cc. 368–430) and the other institutes of the particular church (cc. 460–572).

In comparing the revised Code and the 1917 Code, one finds points of continuity but especially points of discontinuity largely reflecting the impact of Vatican II on the revised Code.

By way of continuity the general issues treated in both the revised Code and the 1917 Code are fundamentally the same despite significant differences in approach in the former document. The basic structures at the diocesan, deanery, and parish levels are fundamentally the same in both Codes. The basic rules on the qualifications for bishops, on their designation, and on their taking possession of the diocese are fundamentally the same. However, the process for surfacing names of episcopal candidates is developed more extensively in canon 377 than in the 1917 Code. The various aspects of episcopal governmental authority articulated in the 1917 Code are largely reaffirmed in the revised Code although the latter more clearly differentiates the various forms of the exercise of that authority (legislative, executive, and judicial). Certain episcopal obligations in the 1917 Code are simply reaffirmed in the revised Code (cc. 388; 395–400). Finally the canons on the impeded or vacant see (cc. 412–430) largely restate the 1917 Code. This trend is more noticeable here than in any other part of title I.

By way of discontinuity, the following changes in the revised Code are noteworthy. Various canons describe the notion of the diocese (c. 369) and other particular churches such as territorial abbeys or prelatures (c. 370), apostolic vicariates or prefectures (c. 371), and an apostolic administration (c. 372). In the 1917 Code various elements of such particular churches could be discerned from an examination of various canons; however, no one canon succinctly clarified their nature. Likewise

two new canons list various types of particular churches (c. 368) and bishops (c. 376).

Certain other points give the revised Code a greater legal clarity than its 1917 predecessor. The territoriality of particular churches is affirmed as a matter of principle although there may be exceptions (c. 372, §1). The juridic personality of such entities is explicitly affirmed (c. 373) as is the status of the diocesan bishop as the legal representative of the diocese (c. 393).

As noted earlier, unlike the 1917 Code, the revised law incorporates a new section on the law applicable to all bishops (cc. 375–380) before it deals with diocesan or residential bishops (cc. 381–402) and coadjutor and auxiliary bishops (cc. 403–411). Furthermore, unlike the 1917 Code it also treats of the impeded or vacant see in this initial title I (cc. 412–430) rather than immediately prior to the deanery as in the former law or the parish as in earlier schemata. This makes good sense systematically since the ordinary and extraordinary forms of diocesan government at the highest level are dealt with in the same general context.[11]

Several canons reflect the richness of the conciliar teaching on the episcopal office. The introductory canon 375 speaks of bishops as successors of the apostles and clarifies the magisterial, cultic, and governance dimensions of the pastoral office. It also highlights the significance of episcopal consecration in empowering bishops to exercise their office while drawing attention to the hierarchical communion into which they are incorporated. Canon 379 requires them to be consecrated before they officially take possession of the diocese while canon 381, §1 clarifies their possession of ordinary, proper, and immediate power to govern their dioceses except in those areas reserved to supreme church authority or another higher level of church government. The conciliar efforts to upgrade the status of coadjutor and auxiliary bishops are evident especially in canon 406 on their being named either vicar general or episcopal vicar and canon 409 on the auxiliary's continuance in office even during the vacancy of the see.

There are certain new developments regarding appointment to office. Canon 377 treats in more detail than the 1917 Code the role of the papal legate, the provincial bishops, and the diocesan bishop in the designation of episcopal candidates. Following the orientation of *Christus Dominus* 20, the new canon prohibits granting civil authorities any rights or privileges of designating bishops in the future. A new canon 413 requires the bishop shortly after taking possession of the diocese to draw up a list of

[11]See alternative organizations of the original schema proposed by the aforementioned canon law societies in Green, "Critical Reflections," 315–322. All of them suggested an organization of the law in this area comparable to the definitive text.

persons to succeed him in the government of the diocese if the see is impeded.

Finally *Christus Dominus* 12–18 significantly influence the specification of various dimensions of the episcopal office. First of all, as regards the strictly pastoral governance aspects of episcopal ministry, one might observe various exhortations regarding the bishop's solicitude for various groups in the diocese including those not fully members of the Roman communion (c. 383), his responsibility to foster close relationships with his priests (c. 384), his obligation to be the primary diocesan figure in fostering vocations (c. 385), and his responsibility to coordinate the exercise of the apostolate and encourage all the faithful to be involved in the fulfillment of the Church's mission (c. 394).

Canon 386 highlights different aspects of the bishop's magisterial office, both his own personal preaching and teaching and his supervision of the exercise of the Church's teaching ministry. He is called to foster doctrinal integrity while allowing appropriate freedom in clarifying the mysteries of faith. Finally canon 387 clarifies various aspects of the bishop's sanctifying office. First of all he is to set an example of Christian holiness. Furthermore, he is to ensure that the celebration of the sacraments is conducive to an ever deeper insight into and living of the paschal mystery by those entrusted to his pastoral care. Canon 389 stresses the importance of his personally presiding at the celebration of the Eucharist especially on holy days and other solemnities.

CANONS AND COMMENTARY

CHAPTER I
PARTICULAR CHURCHES
[cc. 368–374][12]

These introductory canons clarify the basic elements of the organization of the particular churches somewhat comparably to canons 215–217 of the 1917 Code. However, for a complete discussion of these issues, one must also consult canons 515–518 on the parish. After listing the diocese and other particular churches (c. 368), the law describes the diocese, the preeminent form of the particular church (c. 369). Then follow brief descriptions of territorial prelatures and abbacies (c. 370), apostolic vicariates and prefectures (c. 371, §1), and an apostolic administration (c. 371, §2). A subsequent canon affirms the basic principle of the territoriality of the particular church while admitting exceptions for reasons of more effective pastoral care of the faithful of a different rite or other comparable factors (c. 372). Only the supreme church authority may establish particular churches, which enjoy juridic personality (c. 373). Finally the particular churches in turn are to be subdivided into parishes; these units may be joined in vicariates forane (deaneries) if it is pastorally advisable (c. 374). Generally

speaking, this part of the revised law is notably streamlined in contrast to earlier schemata.

Types of Particular Churches

Canon 368 — Particular churches in which and from which exists the one and unique Catholic Church are first of all dioceses; to which unless otherwise evident are likened a territorial prelature, a territorial abbacy, an apostolic vicariate, an apostolic prefecture, and an apostolic administration which has been erected on a stable basis.

This partly theological canon reflects the shift in conciliar ecclesiology from a Church understood in almost exclusively universalist terms (1917 Code) to the vision of a variety of communities in vital relationship with one another. The canon reflects the teaching of *Lumen Gentium* 23 that the Church is truly universal only insofar as it is particularized in the different cultures of the world.[13] The self-realization of the Church requires an exchange between the gospel and the life, traditions, and customs of the people to whom it is preached. The particular churches are not merely administrative regions of the "perfect society" of the Church. Rather they are formed in the image of the universal Church; and it is precisely in them and from them that the

[12]For official Code Commission reports on the formulation of these canons, see *Comm* 4 (1972), 39–43; 12 (1980), 275–285. For some useful reflections on the issues treated in these canons, see Abbo-Hannan I, 272–279, 333–348; *Directory,* pars. 171–189.

[13]For some theological reflections on these issues, see J. Komonchak, "Ministry and the Local Church," *CTSAP* 36 (1981), 56–82; K. Rahner in Vorgrimler I, 205–207. See also 1980 *CTSAP* for various articles on the local church.

one and unique Catholic Church exists. The canon does not explicitly restate the conciliar teaching that the pope and the bishop are the visible source and foundation of church unity in their respective spheres of influence. The Spirit is obviously the invisible and most significant principle of unity in the multiplicity of the churches.

The term "particular church," which is so fundamental to the revised Code, is actually used in various senses in Vatican II. In *Christus Dominus,* the conciliar document with the most direct legal implications for diocesan and parish law, it means the diocese; and that is how it will be interpreted in this part of the commentary. However, in *Orientalium Ecclesiarum* it means the individual autonomous Ritual Churches of the East. In *Ad Gentes* it means all the churches in a given socio-cultural context. In *Lumen Gentium* it means the diocese in some instances and a grouping of dioceses in other instances.

In the fullest and proper canonical sense the term "particular church" means the diocese, that portion of the people of God entrusted to the bishop to be nurtured in faith along with the presbyterate (c. 369). However, other configurations of the "particular church" are mentioned in this canon and will be briefly described in subsequent canons. Whatever theological-canonical points are made subsequently relative to the bishop and the diocese can be applied mutatis mutandis to these other configurations.[14]

Notion of Diocese

Canon 369 — A diocese is a portion of the people of God which is entrusted for pastoral care to a bishop with the cooperation of the presbyterate so that, adhering to its pastor and gathered by him in the Holy Spirit through the gospel and the Eucharist, it constitutes a particular church in which the one, holy, catholic and apostolic Church of Christ is truly present and operative.

The canon simply restates *Christus Dominus* 11 in describing the diocese—another theological canon with no parallel in the 1917 Code. A word or two about the constitutive elements of the diocese are in order since this basic notion of a "portion of the people of God" is the dominant theological-canonical construct, in light of which the various provisions for intra-ecclesial relationships are formulated.[15]

---

[14]In this connection it might be noted that one of the most strongly debated issues during the revision process was whether so-called "personal prelatures" were to be considered particular churches. It was finally decided that they are not particular churches. Hence they are dealt with elsewhere in the revised law. See the commentary on cc. 294–297.

[15]Canon 515, §1 describes the parish in comparable terms.

First of all, the diocese is not primarily a subdivision of the universal Church but rather a community of the baptized confessing the Catholic faith, sharing in sacramental life, and entrusted to the ministry of the bishop. The territorial factor to be mentioned later is not constitutive of the people of God but merely determinative, however convenient an organizing principle it may be.

Secondly, the portion of the people of God is entrusted to the bishop as the visible principle and foundation of its unity. In this connection one needs to see canon 381, §1 as intimately related to this canon. The former canon states that the bishop is the ordinary, proper, and immediate pastor of the church entrusted to him. The bishop governs and represents the particular church and acts in its name in the communion of churches. He also represents the universal Church among his fellow believers; the universal Church is present through the preaching of the gospel and the celebration of the sacraments mediated by the bishop.

Thirdly, despite his preeminent status, the bishop does not function as an isolated figure in the pastoral ministry. Somewhat comparable to his relationship to his brother bishops in the college of bishops, he functions with his fellow presbyters in a hierarchically structured exercise of the priestly, teaching, and pastoral ministries of the Lord. His relationship with the presbyters will vary, depending on whether they are formally incardinated in the diocese or whether they belong to a religious community or a personal prelature. In any event the collaborative efforts of bishop and presbyters are geared to fostering the union of the faithful with the Lord in such a way that the one, holy, catholic, and apostolic Church is truly active and present in the particular church. The modalities of the bishop's relationships with his presbyters, either individually or corporately, will be clarified in subsequent canons.

Finally the canon and the conciliar text allude to a significant patristic theme in highlighting the gospel, the Eucharist, and the Spirit as the fundamental constitutive principles of the Church's life and ministry.

The next two canons briefly describe five ecclesiastical structures comparable to a diocese, most of which have parallels in the 1917 Code. They reflect a certain organizational flexibility and a concern to provide for certain ecclesiastical situations in which the ordinary ecclesiastical organization cannot be established for one reason or another.

Notion of Territorial Prelature/Abbacy

Canon 370 — A territorial prelature or territorial abbacy is a certain portion of the people of God which is established within certain territorial boundaries and whose care, due to special circum-

stances, is entrusted to some prelate or abbot who governs it as its proper pastor, like a diocesan bishop.

The 1917 Code (*CIC* 319–327) referred to certain jurisdictional figures called abbots or prelates *nullius,* who in the name of the pope governed certain territories set apart from dioceses with quasi-episcopal jurisdiction. The Latin term *nullius* meant that the territory belonged to no diocese and that its clergy and people were subject to the abbot or prelate in question. Such authority figures were called abbots or prelates depending on whether their church was abbatial or prelatial.

Unlike the 1917 Code, the present law does not discuss the legal status of such prelates in detail, but it simply describes the prelature or abbacy as a variant form of a particular church entrusted to an abbot[16] or prelate for special reasons. For example, the committee clearly had in mind special pastoral provisions for military forces such as the Military Ordinariate in referring to prelatures here.[17] The hierarchical figure in question functions like a bishop, hence such an ecclesiastical structure is logically dealt with in the present section of Book II. This represents a change from the 1917 Code, which treated such prelates under the general rubric of supreme (papal) church authority.

Apostolic Vicariate/Prefecture Administration

Canon 371 — §1. An apostolic vicariate or an apostolic prefecture is a certain portion of the people of God which is not yet erected into a diocese, due to particular circumstances, and whose pastoral care is entrusted to an apostolic vicar or to an apostolic prefect who governs it in the name of the Supreme Pontiff.

§2. An apostolic administration is a certain portion of the people of God which is not erected into a diocese by the Supreme Pontiff due to particular and very serious reasons and whose pastoral care is entrusted to an apostolic administrator who governs it in the name of the Supreme Pontiff.

Traditionally there has been a legal distinction between regions affected by the general law of the Church and those subject to missionary law. The former refers to places in which the church hierarchy has been perfectly established; the latter to places in which the church hierarchy has been only

imperfectly or inchoatively established. The first paragraph of this canon reflects that traditional distinction in dealing with two organizational configurations proper to the missions. Generally speaking before a missionary territory becomes a diocese, the following process normally occurs: first a mission is set up; subsequently the mission is changed to an apostolic prefecture; and then finally the latter becomes an apostolic vicariate usually governed by a titular bishop.

Like the preceding canon, the present law does not specify in detail the legal status of the apostolic vicar or prefect as was done in the 1917 Code (*CIC* 293–311). Rather the present law simply describes the ecclesiastical structures in question as variant forms of particular churches and highlights the pastoral role of the vicar or prefect. Explicit reference is made to their functioning in the name of the pope, who normally acts through the Sacred Congregation for the Evangelization of Peoples.

Paragraph two of the canon refers to an ecclesiastical structure for which there seems to be no direct 1917 Code parallel.[18] For particularly serious reasons it may be impossible to set up a diocese in a given area. For example, Church-State conflicts may preclude normal organizational developments. In such instances the pope may establish an apostolic administration to provide for appropriate pastoral care on an interim basis. The apostolic administrator functions in a way comparable to the apostolic vicar or prefect mentioned above.

Territoriality of Particular Church

Canon 372 — §1. As a rule that portion of the people of God which constitutes a diocese or some other particular church is limited to a definite territory so that it comprises all the faithful who inhabit that territory.

§2. Nevertheless, there can be erected within the same territory particular churches which are distinct by reason of the rite of the faithful or some similar reason when such is deemed advantageous in the judgment of the supreme authority of the Church after it has listened to the conferences of bishops concerned.

Reference was made earlier to the principle of qualified territoriality as a basic theme underlying the renewed diocesan and parish law. That principle with its qualification is affirmed here for the particular churches as such, and it is also operative in the structuring of parishes (c. 518).

[16]One might note the October 23, 1976 *mp* of Paul VI *Catholica Ecclesia* which barred the future establishment of abbacies *nullius* except in extraordinary circumstances. It also stated that the rules of *CD* 23 relative to diocesan boundaries were to be implemented in the case of those abbacies continuing to exist. See *AAS* 68 (1976), 694ff. English translation is found in *CLD* 8, 236–238.

[17]See *Comm* 4 (1972), 41.

[18]The 1917 Code contained several canons on apostolic administrators (*CIC* 312–318). However, such persons governed an *already existing diocese* either during its vacancy or if the bishop were unable to fulfill his office. This provision was viewed as a somewhat extraordinary measure to be taken only for rather serious reasons.

Paragraph one states that normally a particular church is territorially established, i.e., those Christians living in a precisely defined area are formed into a community whose spiritual head is the bishop or other church authority assigned to it. Thus the individual Christian is given his or her pastor,[19] and such territorial limits foster the orderly exercise of episcopal authority. While this was an operative principle in the 1917 Code, no canon succinctly stated the point comparably to the present text.

Paragraph two reflects the insight that exceptionally weighty pastoral factors such as sensitivity to the spiritual needs of faithful of different rites may suggest establishing a particular church based principally though not exclusively on non-territorial considerations. This provision in part is an effort to implement some of the concerns expressed in *Christus Dominus* 22–24, which dealt with the revision of diocesan boundaries. That such a non-territorial particular church is seen as an exception to the rule seems evident from the reference to the intervention of supreme church authority after consultation with the interested conferences of bishops. The "supreme authority of the Church" referred to here would normally be the Sacred Congregation for Bishops unless it is a question of a missionary particular church, in which case the Sacred Congregation for the Evangelization of Peoples would be competent. If negotiations with civil governments are called for, the Council for the Public Affairs of the Church also plays a significant role in handling the matter.[20]

Unlike the somewhat lengthy conciliar treatment of diocesan boundaries, the revised law does not go into detail on the various criteria for structuring the particular churches. The Council was especially concerned that particular church boundaries be such that the nature and mission of the Church could be realized fully and that the bishop or other church authority presiding over it could be able to carry out his pastoral duties effectively. Particularly important in this connection are adequate institutional and personnel resources to facilitate the pursuit of ecclesial goals in light of the diversity of the people of God in a given setting.[21]

Competent Authority/Juridic Personality

Canon 373 — It is within the sole competence of the supreme authority of the Church to erect particular churches; once they have been legitimately erected these churches enjoy juridic personality by reason of the law itself.

The establishment of particular churches is one of the most significant administrative issues addressed in the Code. Hence not surprisingly, competence in this area rests with the supreme church authority functioning through the above-mentioned congregations. Though the history of this development is not entirely clear, the popes have apparently vindicated exclusive competence in this area since the beginning of the eleventh century. The revised law largely restates canon 215, §1 of the 1917 Code although in somewhat simpler form. No explicit reference is made to the dividing, uniting, or suppressing of particular churches as was true in the earlier Code; yet, such administrative options are clearly within the competence of church authority.[22]

The revised Code explicitates the juridic personality of legitimately erected particular churches. A juridic person is a legal entity distinct from physical persons which enjoys an independent existence and is endowed with the capacity of acquiring and exercising rights as well as contracting obligations according to the norms of law.[23] In this connection one might note that the bishop is technically the legal representative of the diocese in its various juridic affairs (c. 393); the same would be true mutatis mutandis for authority figures presiding over other particular churches.

Parishes and Vicariates

Canon 374 — §1. Each and every diocese or other particular church is to be divided into distinct parts or parishes.

§2. In order to foster pastoral care through common action several neighboring parishes can be joined together into special groups such as vicariates forane.

The revised law mandates the subdivision of particular churches into parishes (§1) and indicates as an option the possible joining of several parishes into groupings such as vicariates forane (deaneries) for more effective pastoral action (§2). Unlike the 1917 Code which dealt with parishes in some detail (*CIC* 216) in this section, the revised law considers parish structures in some detail more logically in the section on parishes (cc. 515–518). Unlike the 1917 Code which required either the establishment of such vicariates (*CIC* 217, §1) or consultation with the Holy See if this were impossible (*CIC* 217,

---

[19]In this connection, see cc. 102–107 on the influence of such territorial factors as domicile and quasi-domicile on the legal status of believers.

[20]See *RE* 49, 1–3; 28.

[21]For some reflections on the conciliar discussion of diocesan boundaries, see Moersdorf in Vorgrimler II, 238–242. On the responsibility of conferences of bishops to examine existing territorial boundaries, see *ES* I, 12. One might note that there is a standing NCCB Boundaries of Dioceses and Provinces Committee.

[22]Canon 515, §2 on episcopal authority vis-à-vis parishes refers to a bishop's establishing, modifying, or suppressing them.

[23]For the general norms on juridic persons, see cc. 113–123.

§2), the revised law reflects a greater flexibility[24] and a sensitivity to the extraordinary diversity of pastoral situations throughout the Church. It further bespeaks enhanced episcopal discretion in structuring the particular church since no reference is made to consultation with the Holy See in this connection (c. 515, §2).[25]

CHAPTER II
BISHOPS
[cc. 375–411]

ARTICLE 1: BISHOPS IN GENERAL
[cc. 375–380][26]

This article, like the following one, integrates distinctly conciliar insights on the episcopal office and elements found in the 1917 Code. The article itself is new since the 1917 Code did not differentiate organizationally between those issues pertinent to all bishops and those relevant specifically to diocesan bishops and coadjutor/auxiliary bishops.

The initial canon deals with the divine institution of the episcopate, the sacramental basis of episcopal ministry, and the reality of hierarchical communion (c. 375). After the types of bishops are briefly described (c. 376), the law clarifies certain aspects of the process whereby bishops are designated (c. 377) as well as the qualifications for the episcopal office (c. 378). Finally two obligations of the bishop-designate are specified: the reception of episcopal consecration before taking possession of a diocese (c. 379) and the making of a profession of faith and the taking of an oath of loyalty to the Holy See (c. 380).

Bishops exercise their episcopal ministry on two related levels: *individually* as the heads of particular churches and *collegially,* i.e., primarily with their brother bishops in serving the universal Church but also secondarily with certain of their brother bishops in serving a group of particular churches. The canons in this part of the Code deal almost exclusively with bishops as individual leaders of particular churches. For the bishops in their collegial functioning, one should consult the prior section on supreme church authority (cc. 330–367) or the fol-lowing title on groupings of the particular churches (cc. 431–459).

Institution and Functions of Episcopate

Canon 375 — §1. Through the Holy Spirit who has been given to them, bishops are the successors of the apostles by divine institution; they are constituted pastors within the Church so that they are teachers of doctrine, priests of sacred worship and ministers of governance.

§2. By the fact of their episcopal consecration bishops receive along with the function of sanctifying also the functions of teaching and of ruling, which by their very nature, however, can be exercised only when they are in hierarchical communion with the head of the college and its members.

This theological canon is a particularly clear example of the need constantly to interpret the revised law in light of Vatican II, the historical and doctrinal event which still provides the norm by which even the revised law must be understood and reformed where necessary.[27] The canon reworks canon 329, §1 of the 1917 Code in light especially of *Lumen Gentium* 20–21.

Paragraph one clarifies the divine institution of the episcopate and the triple aspect of the bishop's pastoral role as teacher of doctrine, priest of sacred worship, and minister of church government. In referring to the bishops as successors of the apostles by divine institution, the canon implies that the episcopate is not an element of purely human and variable church law in the sense that the post-apostolic Church might have also given itself a non-episcopal constitution. The text also implies some sort of apostolic succession of a sacramental and juridic nature in virtue of divine institution. However, neither *Lumen Gentium* 20 nor the present canon indicates how this divine institution came about.

This paragraph speaks rather cryptically of the Spirit's empowering the bishops to fulfill the varied dimensions of their pastoral office. Understandably it does not specify those dimensions in any detail. Accordingly one must examine other parts of the revised Code. For the bishop's role as a teacher of doctrine, one should consult especially Book III on the Church's teaching function and especially canon 756, §2 on the bishop as moderator of the Church's ministry of the word. For the bishop's role as a priest of sacred worship, one should consult especially Book IV on the Church's sanctifying function and especially canon 835, §1 on the bishop's personal priestly role and his responsibility of supervising the liturgical life of his diocese. The bishop's role as a minister of church government is treated extensively throughout the revised Code.

---

[24] For various examples of the pastoral flexibility of the revised law, see Alesandro, 12–13.

[25] For prior provisions for such episcopal discretion, see *CD* 32 and *ES* I, 21.

[26] For official Code Commission reports on the formulation of these canons, see *Comm* 5 (1973), 217–219; 12 (1980), 285–293. For some useful reflections on the legal status of bishops see K. Moersdorf, "Bishop," in K. Rahner (ed.), *Encyclopedia of Theology* (New York: Seabury, 1975), 151–157. For an overview of the rights and responsibilities of bishops in the revised Code, see T. Green, *A Manual for Bishops: Rights and Responsibilities of Diocesan Bishops in the Revised Code of Canon Law* (Washington: USCC: 1983). For some helpful reflections on historical changes in the episcopal office, see J. Lynch, "The Changing Role of the Bishop: An Historical Survey," *J* 39 (1979), 289–312.

[27] The literature on the teaching of *LG* on the episcopate is extensive. For example, see Rahner in Vorgrimler I, 186–217.

However, one might note that the subsequent article 2 on diocesan bishops deals largely with this dimension of the episcopal office.

Paragraph two articulates one of the most significant conciliar developments in affirming the foundation of the various functions of the bishop in his sacramental consecration. The issue of the relationship between orders and jurisdiction is an extremely complex one which cannot be addressed here.[28] Suffice it to note that in the 1917 Code the justifiable distinction between the power of orders and the power of jurisdiction was interpreted as meaning that the power of orders came from sacramental ordination whereas the power of jurisdiction came exclusively and ultimately from a canonical mission from the pope or some other supra-episcopal authority (*CIC* 108, §3). This somewhat dualistic viewpoint did not do justice to the intrinsic unity of the two powers and the oneness of their nature. However, *Lumen Gentium* 21 and the present text affirm that all three functions (the power to sanctify, teach, and govern) are conferred by episcopal consecration itself. This is true for all bishops and not simply for diocesan bishops. Hence, at least in terms of consecration and membership in the college of bishops, prescinding from further determinations, there is a basic equality among all bishops. This accounts for all bishops having a right to take part in an ecumenical council (c. 339, §1). It probably accounts for the insertion of the present article in the revised Code.

A respect for the integrity of the communion of churches seemingly underlies the clause stating that the functions of teaching and governing can be exercised only in hierarchical communion with the head and members of the college. This condition for the valid exercise of the episcopal office reflects its twofold character; it is both personal and collegial. The bishops have a twofold representative function. They represent the universal Church, a communion of many particular churches, and they also represent the individual particular churches in which the universal Church is actualized. There is a reciprocal connection between the personal and collegial elements, each becoming operative in the other; to play one off against the other would violate the unity of Christ's Church.

Types of Bishops

Canon 376 — Bishops are called *diocesan* when the care of a diocese has been entrusted to them; all others are called *titular.*

Although all bishops have the same sacramental power in virtue of episcopal consecration, there are nevertheless various gradations within episcopal ministry which cannot be accounted for in terms of orders but only in terms of the Church's power to organize itself in various offices. This canon reflects the fact that the primary analogate as regards the episcopal office is the *diocesan* or residential bishop to whom a particular church is entrusted. Article 2 of this section of the Code is devoted entirely to such a bishop as are most of the canons of the Code dealing with bishops. All other bishops receive *titular* sees in view of the necessary connection between the bishop and a distinct portion of the people of God; however, they do not exercise the power of government in such situations.

Earlier drafts of the law had specified certain titular bishops, e.g., coadjutor or auxiliary bishops, bishops exercising some other function for the good of a particular church or a group of particular churches. However, it was finally decided to simplify the canon by dropping all such references.

Designation of Bishops

Canon 377 — §1. The Supreme Pontiff freely appoints bishops or confirms those who have been legitimately elected.

§2. At least every three years the bishops of an ecclesiastical province or, if circumstances suggest this, the bishops of a conference of bishops are to compose in common counsel and in secret a list of presbyters, including members of institutes of consecrated life, who are suitable for the episcopacy and send it to the Apostolic See; each bishop retains the right to make known to the Apostolic See on his own the names of presbyters whom he thinks worthy and suitable for the episcopal office.

§3. Unless other provisions have legitimately been made, whenever a diocesan bishop or a coadjutor bishop is to be named, in regard to the *ternus,* as it is called, to be proposed to the Apostolic See it is the responsibility of the pontifical legate to seek out individually the suggestions of the metropolitan and the suffragans of the province to which the diocese to be provided for belongs or with which it is joined and of the president of the conference of bishops and to communicate them to the Apostolic See together his own preference; moreover, the pontifical legate is to hear some members of the college of consultors and of the cathedral chapter, and if he judges it expedient, he shall also obtain, individually and in secret, the opinion of other members of the secular and religious clergy as well as of the laity who are outstanding for their wisdom.

§4. Unless other provisions have been legitimately made, a diocesan bishop who judges that an auxiliary bishop ought to be given to his diocese is

[28]For a comparison of Vatican II and the 1917 Code on certain key aspects of papal-episcopal relationships, see V. Walsh, "The Theological and Juridical Role of the Bishop: Early 20th Century and Contemporary Views," *Apol* (1971), 39–92.

to propose to the Apostolic See a list of at least three priests who are quite suitable for this office.

§5. No rights and privileges of election, nomination, presentation, or designation of bishops are hereafter granted to civil authorities.

One of the most significant administrative acts in the life of the Church is the designation of a bishop.[29] This noteworthy canon deals with various aspects of the designation process. Paragraph one reaffirms the preeminent role of the Roman Pontiff in the process. Paragraph two treats of the periodic preparation of lists of acceptable episcopal candidates. Paragraphs three and four deal with the designation of diocesan/coadjutor bishops on the one hand and auxiliary bishops on the other hand. Finally paragraph five treats of the future involvement of civil authorities in the designation process.

By way of introduction it should be noted that the process of becoming a bishop involves several distinct but interrelated steps. First there is the designation of a particular person for the episcopal office, which can take place in various ways; the present canon deals almost exclusively with this initial stage of the process. Then there is the actual conferral of the office, which is presently reserved to the pope although there is no explicit statement of this as was true in canon 332, §1 of the 1917 Code. Then there is the consecration of the bishop-designate and finally his taking possession of office, both of which are mentioned in canon 379.[30]

The first paragraph reaffirms the 1917 Code's emphasis on the preeminent role of the pope in the designation of bishops process. Canon 329, §2 of the former Code is somewhat modified in that the present law refers not simply to the free conferral of office by the pope but also to his confirming candidates who have been legitimately elected in virtue of particular law. By "free conferral" is meant that the pope chooses episcopal candidates without the necessary involvement of others in the process even though he will conduct an information-gathering effort through his advisors. One form of necessary involvement of others in the candidate-designation process is the election of episcopal candidates, to which the 1917 Code alluded (*CIC* 329, §3). Although it is not common in the United States, in various places throughout the Church, such as Germany and Switzerland, certain groups such as chapters of canons (c. 503–510) have long enjoyed such electoral rights.[31]

The canons on the designation of bishops reflect an effort to integrate various values; the success of this integration effort varies from period to period in the life of the Church. The preeminent role of the pope reflects a gradual centralization of the process historically, at least in part to cope with certain abuses. It also reflects his mission to promote the common good of the universal Church and the particular good of all the churches (*CD* 2). The qualification of papal candidate-designation prerogatives by certain electoral rights is a vestige of an earlier church practice when the presbyterate especially played a much larger part in the selection process.[32]

Paragraph two focuses on the regular updating of lists of potential episcopal candidates. This paragraph and the two following ones deal exclusively with the prior consultation process whereby the Holy See examines the merits of such candidates in light of the general qualifications for office specified in canon 378 and other specific requirements related to the office in question.

The provincial bishops are seen as the key figures in the preparation of such lists; this reflects the March 1972 norms on the selection of bishops issued by the Council for the Public Affairs of the Church.[33] It also reflects a tendency during the revision process to restrict the role of conferences of bishops, which is said to be dependent on particular circumstances. This probably reflects a realistic assessment of the differences among episcopal conferences not only in terms of the number of their members but also in terms of the resources available to them to deal with this and other responsibilities.[34]

Paragraph two also restates the continuing con-

---

[29]The significance of this issue accounts for the noteworthy efforts of the CLSA during the 70's to develop appropriate procedures for the selection of bishops in light of the orientations of Vatican II. Some works published in this connection may prove helpful in understanding the broad theological-canonical-historical dimensions of this question, which can hardly be explored in this commentary. See W. Bassett (ed.), *The Choosing of Bishops* (Hartford: CLSA, 1971); CLSA, *Procedure for the Selection of Bishops in the United States* (Hartford: CLSA, 1973).

[30]For various aspects of the legal process of acquiring an ecclesiastical office, see the commentary on cc. 146–183.

[31]For some information on particular law provisions in recent times, see R. Trisco, "The Variety of Procedures in Modern History," in Bassett, *Choosing of Bishops,* 33–60.

[32]See J. Lynch, "Co-responsibility in the First Five Centuries: Presbyteral Colleges and the Election of Bishops," *J* 31 (1971), 14–53.

[33]See Council for the Public Affairs of the Church, *Episcoporum delectum,* March 25, 1972, *AAS* 64 (1972), 386–391. English translation is found in *CLD* 7, 366–373. Article II, 2 is especially significant in this connection. These norms will probably continue to be operative except where they are specifically modified by the present law. This does not seem to be one of those areas in which the revised Code *ex integro* or completely reworks prior universal norms (c. 6, §1, 4°). The revised law simply specifies an obligation of the provincial bishops; however, it goes into no detail on the formalities of their fulfilling such an obligation as is true in articles III–IX of said norms.

[34]One might note that *ES* I, 10 called for conferences of bishops to propose episcopal candidates to the Holy See on a yearly basis. One might also note that the NCCB maintains a standing committee on the nomination of bishops (see article X, 2 of the March 1972 norms).

cern for the secrecy to be observed in connection with such provincial meetings, which are to take place every three years and not annually as proposed in earlier schemata. It also explicitly refers to religious priests as eligible for the episcopate (cc. 705–707) to respond to concerns that such eligibility was not highlighted strongly enough in earlier schemata. Another late insertion in the text restates the right of individual bishops to forward names of suitable episcopal candidates to the Holy See even apart from the above-mentioned provincial meetings.[35] This is another instance of the committee's efforts to highlight the important role of individual bishops even apart from their collegial undertakings.

Paragraph three treats of the naming of a diocesan bishop or a coadjutor bishop in a particular diocese.[36] Contrary to the general character of the information-gathering effort mentioned in paragraph two, this paragraph focuses on the specific concerns of a particular diocese. The special importance of the office of diocesan bishop or coadjutor, which automatically implies the right of succession when the see is vacant (c. 403, §3), accounts for the differentiation between this paragraph and the following one on auxiliary bishops. Another key difference is the source of initiative in proposing a candidate. In the case of the auxiliary, it is usually but not always the diocesan bishop (c. 403, §§1–2); in the case of the coadjutor it is the Holy See (c. 403, §3).

The present text significantly modifies earlier schemata by highlighting the role of the papal legate (apostolic delegate) in the information-gathering process. Those schemata had emphasized the role of the provincial bishops, comparable to the preceding paragraph on the updating of lists of candidates. This is not to say that the papal legate was not envisioned as being part of the consultative process; however, his role was not explicitly alluded to in those schemata, which, like the present law, did not deal with all the ramifications of the selection process in any event. The present text should also be viewed in relationship to canon 364, 4°, which succinctly treats of the role of the legate in this process.

The legate is expected to consult individually with various persons before formulating a list (ternus) of candidates for the Holy See. Presumably such persons reflect certain insights and experience that need to influence the process. The legate is expected to consult the metropolitan and the suffragan bishops who head the other dioceses in the province in question; this reflects the traditionally significant involvement of the provincial bishops in the selection process. He is also expected to consult

the president of the conference of bishops, presumably to profit from the latter's insights on the significance of the episcopal choice in light of the concerns of the whole Church in a given country.[37] A concern to incorporate the wisdom of the local presbyterate in the process seems to underlie the requirement that certain members of the college of consultors (c. 502) and the chapter of canons (cc. 503–510) be consulted. One might have thought that an explicit reference to the whole presbyteral council (cc. 495–501) might have been pertinent in this connection although technically it ceases functioning during the vacancy of the see (c. 501, §2).

Besides the above-mentioned individuals, the legate may consult other clerics or knowledgeable lay persons; this seems necessary if he is to benefit from the diversified insights of a reasonably broad cross-section of the people of God of a particular church. In a matter of such noteworthy importance for the life and mission of that church the informed involvement of at least select clergy, religious, and laity seems indispensable. This seems to be a concrete implication of the basic Christian right to be involved in the Church's mission (c. 211) and to express one's opinion on issues affecting its life (c. 212, §3).[38]

Despite criticism expressed during the revision process, consultation regarding episcopal candidates is to be carried out on an individual basis and not corporately even for collegial bodies such as the college of consultors. This provision and the requirement of secrecy presumably are to preclude any semblance of political campaigning that might violate the proper integrity of the process. They also are to protect the value of confidentiality and respect for persons in such a delicate area. Despite such legitimate concerns one may wonder whether the benefits frequently flowing from corporate deliberations are unfortunately lost due to the present norms.

Finally, the initial clause of the paragraph refers to the possibility that other provisions may be made in particular law for the filling of a particular see. This reflects the de facto diversity characterizing the designation process at present. There is no reason to believe that such diversity will be curtailed in the future or that there might not be special provi-

---

[35]See article II, 1 of the March 1972 norms.

[36]This paragraph seems to be a somewhat modified version of article XIII, 2 of the March 1972 norms.

[37]See articles X and XIII, 2 of the March 1972 norms. This reference to the president of the conference of bishops was also a relatively late addition to the final text.

[38]Probably the main purpose of the proposed CLSA procedures for the selection of bishops was to structure a systematic way of providing for informed and genuinely representative ecclesial involvement in the selection process. See note 29. One of the major criticisms of the prior law and the present Code has been their failure to do justice to the value of such broad-based ecclesial involvement despite the practical problems it would pose. See Green, "Critical Reflections," 269–271. Also P. Huizing and K. Walf, (eds.), *Electing our Bishops*, vol. 137, *Con* (New York: Seabury, 1980); J. Provost, "Selection of Bishops—Does Anybody Care?" *CS* 18 (1979), 211–222.

sions for the United States reflecting its distinctive legal-pastoral experience somewhat comparable to the special procedural norms in effect from 1970 to 1983.

Paragraph four on the designation of an auxiliary bishop is much less complex than the preceding paragraph though some of the concerns raised in that connection are relevant here as well. Like paragraph three, the law refers to the possibility of special particular law provisions in this area as well. The focus here is entirely on the diocesan bishop and on his perception of the need for an auxiliary in light of the pastoral needs of the diocese and his own ability to meet them (c. 403, §1). Unlike the requirement of paragraph two that the provincial bishops update the general list of candidates every three years, this paragraph leaves the matter of proposing candidates to the Holy See entirely up to the discretion of the diocesan bishop. Interestingly enough, a proposal to refer explicitly to input from the provincial bishops in this matter was rejected by the Code Commission although it had been provided for in some circumstances in the original schema.

The final paragraph of the canon deals with the involvement of civil authorities in the designation process. It responds to the conciliar desire that in the future no rights or privileges be granted to civil authorities regarding the election, nomination, or presentation of episcopal candidates (*CD* 20). The Council Fathers judged that the freedom of the Church and the spiritual good of the faithful could best be served by reaffirming the proper and exclusive right of ecclesiastical authority to appoint and install bishops and by curtailing the formal involvement of civil authorities. Such involvement was normally sanctioned by concordats or bilateral Church-State agreements on various issues of common concern. The history of Church-State relations in this area is a complex one, but it is clear that there have been notable abuses by civil authorities that have impaired the integrity of the designation process. This accounts for the continuing Holy See effort to persuade civil authorities to waive their rights in this matter and thereby enable this crucial legal-pastoral matter to be completely under church control. This effort has not been entirely successful, and there are areas of continuing Church-State conflict still to be resolved.[39]

Qualifications for Episcopate

Canon 378 — §1. In order for a person to be a suitable candidate for the episcopacy it is required that he be:

1° outstanding for his solid faith, good morals, piety, zeal for souls, wisdom, prudence and human virtues and endowed with the other talents which make him fit to fulfill the office in question;

2° in possession of a good reputation;

3° at least thirty-five years of age;

4° ordained a priest for at least five years;

5° in possession of a doctorate or at least a licentiate in sacred scripture, theology, or canon law from an institute of higher studies approved by the Apostolic See or at least truly expert in these same disciplines.

§2. The definitive judgment concerning the suitability of the person to be promoted belongs to the Apostolic See.

Paragraph one of this canon largely restates the qualifications for the episcopate specified in canon 331, §1 of the 1917 Code.[40] Two notable differences are the following: there is no special reference to the legitimacy of the candidate but rather simply to his good reputation; furthermore, the minimum age for promotion to the episcopate is thirty-five rather than thirty. A proposal to raise the age to forty was rejected by the committee.

Canon 378, §1, 1° speaks in part of the talents that make a candidate suitable for a given episcopal office. This presupposes a knowledge not simply of the particular qualifications of a candidate but also of the distinct needs of a given diocese in light of the diverse conditions of various dioceses even in the same country. The original schema, in paragraph three of the preceding canon, referred explicitly to the needs of the diocese as an integral part of the consultative process. Even if the present law does not explicitly call for such an examination of diocesan needs, it is still an extremely important concern, which can be met only through a serious effort to involve a fairly broad cross section of the people of God in a particular church. This might be expedited in connection with the quinquennial report which the bishop must make to the Holy See according to canon 399, §1.

Paragraph two is another example of the preeminent role of the Holy See in the designation process. It largely restates canon 331, §3 of the 1917 Code regarding the judgment whether a particular candidate meets the legal requirements for the episcopal office. However, it modifies the 1917 Code in two respects. It indicates that the Holy See expresses the "definitive" judgment, which implies that other judgments are also relevant during the process. Furthermore and more significantly, it drops the adverb *unice,* which seems to imply that the Holy See might not always make the definitive judgment on suitability for the episcopal office. Such judgments might possibly be made at the level of the conference of bishops or perhaps at the level of the province with a Holy See ratification finalizing the decisional process.

---

[39]See Moersdorf, in Vorgrimler II, 236–237.

[40]For another formulation of the qualifications for the episcopate, see article VI, 2 of the March 1972 norms.

When reference is made to the Holy See in the canons on the designation of bishops, it usually means the Sacred Congregation for Bishops unless one is dealing with the missionary churches when the competent congregation is the Sacred Congregation for the Evangelization of Peoples.[41] However, if the selection of bishops involves negotiations with civil governments, the Council for the Public Affairs of the Church is competent.[42]

Finally one might note that two canons of the 1917 Code are dropped: canon 330 of the 1917 Code on Holy See determination of the suitability of a candidate, which is duly dealt with in the present norms and canon 331, §2 of the 1917 Code requiring that candidates not subject to free conferral by the pope fulfill the same requirements as candidates chosen by the pope. The general rule stated at the beginning of the present canon makes that latter canon superfluous.

Requirement of Consecration

Canon 379 — Unless he is held back by a legitimate impediment, whoever is promoted to the episcopacy must receive episcopal consecration within three months from the reception of the apostolic letter and before he takes possession of his office.

The present canon attempts to expedite the bishop-designate's assumption of episcopal responsibilities by requiring his consecration normally within three months of his nomination and prior to his taking possession of office. This somewhat modifies canon 333 of the 1917 Code that required the bishop-designate to be consecrated within three months of his nomination and to go to the diocese for which he was appointed within four months. In requiring consecration prior to the taking possession of office (*LG* 21), the present canon reflects the conciliar emphasis on the significance of episcopal consecration for the conferral of the power of government.

One might also note canon 1013 on the necessity of a papal mandate for an episcopal consecration and canon 1014 on the consecrating bishops. Also relevant is canon 1382 excommunicating a bishop consecrating another bishop without a papal mandate; this is one of the few excommunications whose remission is reserved to the Holy See—an indication of the seriousness with which the legislator takes this legal violation.

Profession of Faith/Loyalty Oath

Canon 380 — Before he takes canonical possession of his office, the person promoted is to make a profession of faith and take an oath of fidelity to

the Apostolic See in accord with a formula approved by the same Apostolic See.

The exigencies of ecclesial communion as understood by the legislator seem to underlie this twofold obligation of a profession of faith (c. 833, 3°) and an expression of loyalty to the Holy See on the part of the bishop-designate.

ARTICLE 2: DIOCESAN BISHOPS
[cc. 381–402][43]

This article of the revised Code attempts to integrate various provisions on episcopal rights and obligations from the 1917 Code (*CIC* 334–349) and from Vatican II especially *Christus Dominus* 11–21. Accordingly one must have recourse to standard commentaries on the 1917 Code and on *Christus Dominus*[44] for a proper understanding of the pertinent canons on the diocesan bishop as distinct from the coadjutor or auxiliary bishop.

The initial canons in this section deal with the scope of episcopal authority (c. 381) and the way the bishop takes possession of the diocese (c. 382). A general canon on the bishop's pastoral role toward various groups of people (c. 383) is followed by provisions on the bishop's relationship to his priests (c. 384) and his responsibility to foster various types of vocations (c. 385). After a brief statement of the bishop's teaching office (c. 386), several canons treat of various aspects of his sanctifying ministry (c. 387): the obligation of Mass for the people (c. 388), the bishop's Eucharistic presidency role (c. 389), and his exercise of pontificals (c. 390).

Subsequently a general canon clarifies his threefold legislative, administrative, and judicial role and the way he exercises it (c. 391). The bishop is called upon to foster common discipline and curb various abuses (c. 392), and he is also said to be the official legal representative of the diocese (c. 393). His responsibility to supervise the apostolate and to encourage the faithful to participate in it (c. 394) is followed by a series of obligations specified in the 1917 Code: residence (c. 395), visitation of the diocese (cc. 396–398), quinquennial report (c. 399), and *ad limina* visit (c. 400). Finally in light of Vatican II, the final two canons articulate a commendation of retirement (c. 401) and specify provisions for the retired bishop (c. 402).

Scope of Episcopal Power

Canon 381 — §1. A diocesan bishop in the diocese committed to him possesses all the ordinary,

---

[41]See *RE* 49, 1.
[42]See *RE* 28.

[43]For official Code Commission reports on the formulation of these canons, see *Comm* 5 (1973), 219–224; 12 (1980), 293–308. For some reflections on the 1917 Code, See Abbo-Hannan II, 358–374.
[44]For a commentary on these paragraphs, see Moersdorf, in Vorgrimler II, 232–235.

proper and immediate power which is required for the exercise of his pastoral office except for those cases which the law or a decree of the Supreme Pontiff reserves to the supreme authority of the Church or to some other ecclesiastical authority.

§2. Unless it appears otherwise from the nature of the matter or from a prescription of the law, persons who head the other communities of the faithful mentioned in can. 368 are equivalent in law to a diocesan bishop.

The first paragraph of this canon reaffirms a noteworthy point of conciliar teaching on the episcopal office: the bishops govern their churches as vicars and ambassadors of Christ, not as vicars of the Roman Pontiff (LG 27). Accordingly, they have all the power necessary for the exercise of their pastoral office by divine right; such a power has an existence of its own apart from the papacy (CD 8a). This power is ordinary, i.e., related to his office; immediate, i.e., directly exercised over those entrusted to his care without an intermediary; and proper, i.e., exercised in his own name. This power of the bishop, which is operative in legislative, judicial, and administrative matters (c. 391, §1) is not confined to the sphere of government; it is operative throughout the whole range of the Church's work, which includes the threefold office of teaching, sanctifying, and governing.

The above-mentioned conciliar development underlying the revised law means that the former system of granting faculties to bishops has been replaced by a system of papal reservations, which is alluded to in the last part of the paragraph with its indication of certain matters which may be reserved by law or by decree of the Roman Pontiff to the supreme church authority or to some other supra-episcopal authority.[45] The relationship between the pope and the bishop has been significantly altered: the latter is now presumed to have all the power necessary for his ministry. The implications of this shift in legal relationships can be clarified only by a thorough examination of the revised Code regarding the episcopal office.

The present canon reflects an ongoing tension in the constitutional life of the Church: the bishop is to enjoy increased decisional discretion in the daily exercise of his office; yet, he is still situated within a hierarchical structure, which stretches both above and below him. The pope's prerogatives must be

safeguarded if he is to exercise properly his role of fostering the unity of all the churches. Furthermore, the bishop's rule must not degenerate into arbitrary government, for he is at the center of a ministry of service within the particular church. Hence he is called to foster the conditions necessary for all believers to exercise their sacramentally grounded mission in the Church and in the world. Accordingly he is to fulfill the various dimensions of his office constantly according to the norm of law.

The second paragraph of the canon applies the principle of enhanced episcopal discretion to comparable authority figures presiding over particular churches other than dioceses. Occasionally, however, the nature of the matter or a specific legal prescription might preclude such persons' enjoying equivalent canonical status. For example, such an authority figure who was not a bishop would not be empowered to ordain.

Taking Possession of Diocese

Canon 382 — §1. A bishop promoted to a diocese cannot exercise the office entrusted to him unless he has first taken canonical possession of the diocese, but he can exercise the offices which he already had in the same diocese at the time of promotion, with due regard for the prescription of can. 409, §2.

§2. Unless he is held back by a legitimate impediment, a person promoted to the office of diocesan bishop must take canonical possession of his diocese within four months from the reception of the apostolic letter if he has not yet been consecrated a bishop or within two months if he has already been consecrated.

§3. A bishop takes canonical possession of a diocese as soon as he personally or through a proxy has presented within the diocese the apostolic letter to the college of consultors, in the presence of the chancellor of the curia who officially records the event; in newly erected dioceses, however, he takes canonical possession as soon as he has seen to the communication of the apostolic letter to the clergy and the people present in the cathedral church, with the senior presbyter among those present officially recording the event.

§4. It is strongly recommended that the act of taking canonical possession occur within a liturgical act in the cathedral church with the clergy and people assisting.

The present canon largely reflects the 1917 Code relative to the significant step of the bishop's officially taking possession of the diocese (CIC 334, §§2–3); however, there are some noteworthy changes. The canon deals with the obligation of taking possession of the diocese prior to the bishop's exercising his office (§1), the time within

---

[45]As examples of areas withdrawn from the competency of the bishop, one might note certain irregularities for orders (c. 1047) or marriage impediments whose dispensation is reserved to the Holy See (c. 1078, §2). Furthermore, in the structuring of pastoral ministry, the bishop may introduce a system of limited tenure for pastors only after authorization by the conference of bishops (c. 522). Finally, in the tribunal arena, the bishop may authorize tribunals with one clerical judge in first instance (c. 1425, §4) or lay judges (1421, §2) only with the permission of the conference of bishops.

which he is to fulfill this obligation (§2), the way in which he is to fulfill this obligation (§3), and the importance of a properly liturgical act of taking possession of the diocese (§4).

The canon primarily clarifies the fact that the valid exercise of the episcopal office presupposes the formal taking possession of the diocese through the presentation of the papal letter of appointment to the appropriate persons. Such a measure is required in the interests of juridical clarity lest there be any doubt about the validity of episcopal acts. However, paragraph one notes that if the bishop-designate exercises another office during the vacancy of the diocese, he may continue to function validly in that capacity prior to his taking possession of the see.

The revised Code differs from the 1917 Code in several respects. First of all it differentiates between the bishop-designate who is already a bishop (two months) and the one who is not yet a bishop (four months) regarding the time for fulfilling the obligation of taking possession (§2). Secondly, the corporate body to whom the letter of appointment is to be presented either personally or by proxy is the college of consultors (cc. 502; 501, §2) instead of the cathedral chapter as in the 1917 Code (§3). The college represents the presbyterate of the diocese and replaces the presbyteral council during the vacancy of the see; it also replaces the cathedral chapter unless in a given area the chapter becomes the college of consultors (c. 502, §3). Thirdly, the revised Code differentiates between an established diocese and a newly created one regarding the mode of taking possession. In the latter instance the letter of appointment is to be presented to the clergy and people of the diocese at the cathedral—an interesting way of symbolizing the unity in diversity of the people of God in a particular church. Finally the revised Code reflects a more refined liturgical sensitivity by strongly encouraging that the taking possession of the diocese occur during a liturgical celebration at the cathedral so that this significant act may not be seen purely as a bureaucratic formality but rather as a duly ecclesial reality.

The Bishop as Pastor

Canon 383 — §1. In the exercise of his pastoral office a diocesan bishop is to show that he is concerned with all the Christian faithful who are committed to his care regardless of age, condition or nationality, both those who live within his territory and those who are staying in it temporarily; he is to extend his apostolic spirit to those who cannot sufficiently make use of ordinary pastoral care due to their condition in life and to those who no longer practice their religion.

§2. If he has faithful of a different rite within his diocese, he is to provide for their spiritual needs ei-

ther by means of priests or parishes of that rite or by means of an episcopal vicar.

§3. He is to act with kindness and charity toward those who are not in full communion with the Catholic Church, fostering ecumenism as it is understood by the Church.

§4. He is to consider non-baptized as being committed to him in the Lord so that there may shine upon them the charity of Christ for whom the bishop must be a witness before all.

This conciliar-inspired canon on various aspects of the bishop's pastoral office is one of a number of new texts in this section of the revised Code. Although some committee members were hesitant about including such exhortatory canons in the revised Code, the majority judged that selected conciliar texts were quite appropriate in clarifying various dimensions of the episcopal office. This is especially true for those dimensions not explicitly mentioned in the 1917 Code.

The present canon integrates various parts of *Christus Dominus* 16, 18, and 23. It stresses the comprehensive scope of the bishop's pastoral solicitude and highlights certain groups of people who might not ordinarily be thought of as being within the scope of his pastoral care:[46] those deprived of ordinary pastoral care because of their way of life such as migrants, refugees, tourists, etc., the faithful of a different rite, members of other Christian communions,[47] and those who are not baptized.

Bishop's Relationship to Priests[48]

Canon 384 — The diocesan bishop is to attend to presbyters with special concern and listen to them as his assistants and advisers; he is to protect their rights and see to it that they correctly fulfill the obligations proper to their state and that means and institutions which they need are available to them to foster their spiritual and intellectual life; he is also to make provision for their decent support and social assistance, in accord with the norm of law.

---

[46]See *Directory,* pars. 153–161.

[47]See also c. 755 on the bishop's responsibility to foster the ecumenical movement and to formulate appropriate norms. Among other canons pertinent to the bishop's ecumenical responsibilities are the following: 844 (sacramental sharing), 933 (celebration of the Eucharist in a non-Catholic church), 1124–1129 (ecumenical marriages), and 1183 (burial of a member of another Christian church). See also Alesandro, 6–8. One should especially note the responsibility of bishops individually and the conference of bishops to consult with hierarchs of other churches before policies on sacramental sharing are finalized (c. 844, §5). This principle should be operative in other areas as well, e.g., norms on ecumenical or mixed marriages.

[48]See *Directory,* pars. 107–117.

The indispensable role that the presbyters of a diocese play in assisting the bishop to fulfill the varied aspects of his pastoral office underlies this strong exhortation. The bishop is to be attentive to his priests, to take seriously their contributions to the pastoral life of the diocese, to protect the exercise of their rights, and to ensure that they are able to fulfill the obligations proper to their distinctive place in the Christian community (cc. 273–289). This canon, taken from *Christus Dominus* 16, makes special reference to the bishop's responsibility to support the ongoing spiritual and intellectual development of priests (c. 279) and to ensure their decent support including appropriate pension and health insurance provisions (c. 281). In this connection one might stress the importance of an enlightened personnel policy respecting individual talents and professional goals and fostering appropriate pastoral adaptation and personal satisfaction.

Explicit reference is not made to presbyteral councils and to the college of consultors (cc. 495–502); but, when the canon refers to the bishop's listening to priests as his assistants and advisors, this certainly is not limited to priests as individuals. Rather the legislator clearly envisions corporate groups such as the presbyteral council, which is one noteworthy form of institutionalizing that dialogue between bishop and presbyters that is at the heart of the Church's public life (*PO* 7, *CD* 11). In this connection it should be emphasized that the bishop is to hear his presbyteral council not simply in the particular issues specified in law but in general in all matters of significant pastoral importance (c. 500, §2).

Fostering of Vocations

Canon 385 — As much as is possible the diocesan bishop is to foster vocations to the different ministries and to the consecrated life, with special care shown for priestly and missionary vocations.

In light of the bishop's responsibility to foster a climate in which the diverse gifts of the Spirit can be exercised, this new canon forcefully emphasizes his responsibility to foster various types of vocations within the people of God.[49] While the original text based on *Christus Dominus* 15 had spoken of religious, priestly, and missionary vocations, the present law also speaks more comprehensively of vocations to all ministries. Furthermore, reference should also be made to canon 233, which speaks of the special episcopal responsibility to foster priestly vocations, especially so-called late vocations. The bishop's missionary responsibility is also highlighted in canon 782, §1 on his solicitude for the work of

the missions and canon 791, 1° on his task of fostering missionary vocations.

Finally, it is important to note the episcopal responsibility to see to it that all ecclesial gifts are duly recognized and utilized for the service of the particular church. In view of the present pressures experienced by numerous dioceses regarding priestly personnel, every effort should be made to see to it that no genuine ministerial gift is not employed for church service.

The Bishop as Teacher

Canon 386 — §1. The diocesan bishop is bound to present and explain to the faithful the truths of the faith which are to be believed and applied to moral issues, frequently preaching in person; he is also to see to the careful observance of the prescriptions of the canons concerning the ministry of the word, especially those concerning the homily and catechetical formation, so that the whole of Christian doctrine is imparted to all.

§2. Through suitable means he is strongly to safeguard the integrity and unity of the faith to be believed while nevertheless acknowledging a rightful freedom in the further investigation of its truths.

This canon is a perfect example of the need constantly to situate the canons on bishops in this title within the broader context of the whole Code. It summarizes certain aspects of *Christus Dominus* 12–14 on the bishop's teaching office, highlighting the importance of communicating Christian doctrine and fostering the integrity of the faith. Its reference to recognizing rightful freedom in the investigation of revealed truths is the other side of the coin of the basic right of the Christian scholar to freedom of inquiry in the sacred disciplines. Such scholars also enjoy a basic right to express their opinions in areas of their competency with due regard for the Church's hierarchical magisterium (c. 218).[50]

To evaluate properly the teaching office of the bishop[51] in the Code, one must take due cognizance of Book III on the Church's teaching office in its

---

[49]See ibid., pars. 196–197.

[50]For some insightful reflections on the relationship between bishops and Catholic theologians and other scholars, see L. O'Donovan (ed.), *Cooperation between Theologians and the Ecclesiastical Magisterium* (Washington: CLSA, 1982). Two articles of particular interest are J. Boyle, "The Rights and Responsibilities of Bishops: A Theological Perspective" (1–30) and R. Carlson, "The Rights and Responsibilities of Bishops: A Canonical Perspective" (31–52).

[51]For some useful reflections on the bishop's teaching office, see J. Hickey, "The Bishop as Teacher," in *The Ministry of Bishops: Papers from the Collegeville Assembly* (Washington: USCC, 1982), 15–20; R. Sanchez, "The Bishop as Evangelizer," ibid., 21–26. Also *Directory,* pars. 55–74.

entirety and not simply the specific references to preaching (cc. 762–772) and catechetics (773–780) made in the present canon.

The Bishop as Sanctifier

Canon 387 — Since the diocesan bishop is mindful that he is obliged to set a personal example of holiness, in charity, humility and simplicity of life, he is to make every effort to promote the holiness of the Christian faithful according to each one's own vocation; since he is the foremost dispenser of the mysteries of God, he is constantly to endeavor to have the Christian faithful entrusted to his care grow in grace through the celebration of the sacraments and both understand and live the paschal mystery.

Once again one sees the influence of conciliar texts on this new canon on the bishop's sanctifying office. It directly reflects *Christus Dominus* 15 in stressing that the bishop is first and foremost bound to set an example of personal sanctity and then to foster the sanctity of his fellow believers in accord with his role as principal dispenser of the mysteries of God. The primary goal of his liturgical efforts is to facilitate the process whereby the members of the people of God deepen their life of faith and come to an ever richer understanding of the paschal mystery, which they are to live in their daily lives.

Like the preceding canon on the bishop's teaching office, this text can be properly appreciated only by seeing it in relationship to the rest of the Code, especially Book IV on the Church's sanctifying office. Particularly significant canons in that Book are canon 835, §1 on the bishop's sanctifying function and his role as moderator, promoter, and protector of the Church's liturgical life and canon 838, §1 on the bishop's responsibility of issuing liturgical norms within the limits of his competency. Those canons constitute the broad frame of reference within which the specific provisions on the bishop's liturgical supervisory role can be adequately assessed. This represents a noteworthy change from the 1917 Code that viewed the bishop's liturgical responsibility in terms of his implementing universal norms in his diocese while according him no real discretionary authority in shaping liturgical discipline in light of the needs of his own particular church.

Mass for the People

Canon 388 — §1. After he has taken possession of his diocese the diocesan bishop must apply a Mass for the people committed to him on Sundays and the other holy days of obligation within his region.

§2. The bishop himself must personally celebrate and apply Mass for the people on the days men-tioned in §1; but if he is legitimately hindered from such celebration, he is to apply Mass on these days through another priest or personally do so on other days.

§3. A bishop satisfies this obligation by applying one Mass for all the people entrusted to him if, besides his own diocese, other dioceses are entrusted to him, even under the title of administration.

§4. A bishop who has not satisfied the obligation mentioned in §§1-3 is to apply as many Masses for the people as he has missed as soon as possible.

Here the revised Code restates somewhat more simply a fundamental episcopal obligation articulated in the 1917 Code (*CIC* 339). The bishop's role as high priest of the diocese presumably implies this special obligation to celebrate the Eucharist for the people of the diocese on Sundays and holy days of obligation (c. 1246).[52] A comparable obligation binds pastors in light of their liturgical presidency role within their parishes (c. 534).

The canon clarifies the scope of the obligation (§1) while dropping a somewhat detailed 1917 Code discussion of its implications if a holy day occurs on Sunday or is transferred (*CIC* 339, §§2–3). It specifies the personal nature of the obligation, which means that it must be fulfilled by the bishop himself or another priest on the day it occurs or by the bishop on another day if he is legitimately prevented from celebrating such a Mass (§2). Should the bishop be administering a diocese other than his own, he need offer only one Mass to observe the law (§3). Finally, the gravity of the obligation is clear from the fact that the bishop is required as soon as possible to apply any Masses that he may have omitted in dereliction of his responsibilities (§4). The seriousness with which the law takes this obligation is comparable to the strictness of the law on Mass offerings (cc. 945–958).

Bishop's Eucharistic Presidency Role

Canon 389 — He is to preside frequently over the celebration of the Eucharist in the cathedral church or in another church of his diocese, especially on holy days of obligation and other solemnities.

This new canon highlights the bishop's personal Eucharistic presidency role in virtue of his status as the first liturgist of the particular church specified in *Sacrosanctum Concilium* 41. The central role of the bishop in Eucharistic celebrations is forcefully highlighted as well in canon 899, §2 on the diversity of roles within the Eucharistic celebration and in

---

[52]Another significant conciliar text regarding the bishop's sanctifying office is *LG* 26. For some helpful reflections on this issue, see R. Weakland, "The Bishop as Sanctifier," in *The Ministry of Bishops*, 43–48. Also *Directory*, pars. 75–91.

canon 837, §1 on the Church itself as a sacrament of unity, a holy people gathered around and guided by the bishop. The liturgical centrality of the cathedral church is reaffirmed as well in the present canon, which suggests that every effort be made to see to it that the celebrations there reflect the very best of the Church's liturgical tradition.[53]

Exercise of Pontificals

Canon 390 — A diocesan bishop can conduct pontifical functions throughout his entire diocese; he cannot do so, however, outside his own diocese without the express or at least reasonably presumed consent of the local ordinary.

Certain sacred functions proper to a bishop require the use of pontifical insignia, i.e., mitre and crozier; this is what is technically meant by conducting pontifical functions.[54] The present canon simplifies canon 337, §§1–3 of the 1917 Code by indicating simply that the bishop can conduct pontifical functions in his own diocese without any restrictions. This provision seems to be another concrete implication of his liturgical presidency role in his diocese. However, the law's respect for the comparable role of other diocesan bishops accounts for the second part of the canon requiring at least the presumed consent of the competent local ordinary if the bishop is to conduct pontifical functions outside his diocese.

The present canon drops the 1917 Code's description of the meaning of conducting pontifical functions (*CIC* 337, §2) and its reference to the possible use of a throne and baldachino in such functions (*CIC* 337, §3).

Aspects of Bishop's Governmental Role

Canon 391 — §1. The diocesan bishop is to rule the particular church committed to him with legislative, executive and judicial power in accord with the norm of law.
§2. The bishop personally exercises legislative power; he exercises executive power either personally or through vicars general or episcopal vicars in accord with the norm of law; he exercises judicial power either personally or through a judicial vicar and judges in accord with the norm of law.

This canon succinctly expresses the legislative, executive, and judicial aspects of the bishop's pastoral governmental role and those institutes and persons through which he normally exercises governmental power. The present law updates

canon 335, §1, of the 1917 Code, particularly through a clearer statement of the respective competencies of the bishop and those assisting him in diocesan government. This newer conceptual clarity reflects the committee's effort to respond to a concern of the 1967 Synod for a more precise differentiation of those exercising legislative, executive, and judicial functions in the Church.[55] The reference in paragraph one to the "norm of law" indicates that what is envisioned here is the bishop's ordinary pastoral care. His power is neither unlimited nor arbitrary but is to be exercised with a sensitivity to the competency of higher authority and the legitimate role in the mission of the particular church to be played by other individuals and groups.

Like numerous other canons in this part of the Code, the present canon can be correctly understood only in relationship to other parts of the revised Code. The legislator here affirms certain basic legal principles whose implications are concretized throughout the whole Code. The following brief observations attempt to highlight certain key aspects of the bishop's pastoral governmental office with particular emphasis on his legislative function.

First of all, paragraph two of the canon deals with the bishop's legislative function. An earlier version of the canon stated that the bishop alone exercised legislative power in the diocese either personally or through the diocesan synod. However, the present law states simply that the bishop himself exercises legislative power. This seems to reflect a fear on the part of the Commission that the bishop's pastoral discretion would be unduly curtailed if explicit reference were made to other individuals or institutes being involved in the exercise of legislative authority. The Commission apparently feared that undue pressure might be brought to bear upon the bishop in formulating diocesan policies in various areas. However, it never really clarified the basis for such fears. Nor did it really attempt to explain the law's restrictiveness on delegating legislative authority on the one hand and its openness to the bishop's delegating executive and judicial authority on the other. One might also note the relevance of the general principle on legislative authority expressed in canon 135, §2. Legislative power is to be exercised in accord with the prescription of the law, and a legislator below the level of the supreme legislator may not validly delegate it unless the law explicitly provides for this. There seems to be no place in the revised Code where such an explicit provision is made in the case of bishops.

Despite the somewhat questionable restraints on episcopal discretion in this area, the issue may not be such a major concern in pastoral practice. The revised Code does provide for a diocesan synod to assist the bishop in his legislative responsibilities

[53]See *The Cathedral: A Reader* (Washington: USCC, 1979).
[54]For some reflections on the contemporary revision of the Roman Pontifical, see K. Seasoltz, *New Liturgy New Laws* (Collegeville, Minn.: Liturgical Press, 1980), 125–131.

[55]See Hite, *Readings,* 76.

should he choose to utilize it (cc. 460–468). Furthermore, much will depend in the future on the evolution of mature relationships between the bishop and various consultative bodies such as presbyteral councils which are mandatory (cc. 495–501) and diocesan pastoral councils which are optional (cc. 511–514). Practically speaking, the bishop might simply ratify the decisions of such groups and the policy determinations of a diocesan synod. Frankly it would have been more satisfactory if the law had been more open to broader deliberative options for such bodies. However, the law can still be creatively and responsibly interpreted, especially by placing the legal texts within the broader theological-pastoral context, in which alone they can be knowledgeably interpreted.[56]

One might also note that canon 135, §2 states that a lower-level legislator can never validly pass a law contrary to the law of a higher authority. This higher authority usually refers to the revised Code itself; however, it might conceivably refer to policies determined by the conference of bishops in an area of its competence. For example the National Conference of Catholic Bishops might determine certain norms on the qualifications for lay judges in tribunals or on the exercise of judicial authority by one judge in first instance. The diocesan bishop could not make any laws contrary to such conference norms any more than he could issue legislation contrary to the revised Code. The diocesan bishop may not permit something prohibited by a higher legislative authority. For example, he may not issue diocesan personnel guidelines permitting deacons to be appointed pastors in the technical sense of the term since this would contradict canon 521, §1 prohibiting such an option. Nor may a bishop prohibit what is permitted by a higher legislative authority. For example, he may not issue diocesan guidelines on the sacramental preparation of children prohibiting parents from having an integral role in that enterprise even though he may specify the concrete implications of their role in practice. Such a prohibition would be contrary to various provisions of the revised Code such as canon 226, §1 on the basic educational right of parents vis-à-vis their children, canon 774, §2 further reaffirming parental educational obligations, canon 776 on the responsibility of pastors to promote and foster parental catechetical involvement, and canon 913 on the preparation of children for first Communion.

The bishop's laws may be in accord with the universal law or they may concretize it, particularly in those areas where the revised Code offers latitude for particular legislation. The bishop may also at-

tach penalties to the existing law, be it to universal law where perhaps no penalty is specified or to diocesan law. While Book VI on penal law has significantly reduced the number of penalties in universal law, it has enhanced the options for establishing particular law penalties.

As the author of his own diocesan legislation, the bishop is competent to interpret, apply, abrogate, or dispense from it (c. 88). Where there is no Holy See reservation, he may legislate without papal approval. Furthermore, he may determine the mode of promulgating such norms, e.g., synodal statute book, diocesan newspaper, etc.; such laws one month after promulgation bind those affected by them unless the bishop determines otherwise (c. 8, §2).

The revised Code is quite open to the bishop's exercising his broad executive authority either personally or through vicars, be they vicars general or episcopal vicars (cc. 475–481), despite certain limitations on their authority and certain areas where they require a special episcopal mandate to act.[57] The bishop might well take advantage of the legal options afforded him by vicars in different areas of diocesan life, e.g., administration of property, education, liturgy, ecumenism, and personnel policy. The breadth of episcopal responsibilities in those areas is awesome; they can probably be responsibly fulfilled in most dioceses only through the judicious use of vicars with appropriate accountability controls. It is impossible to specify all the various aspects of the bishop's executive authority. Suffice it to note that, except for Book VII on the exercise of judicial authority, most of the revised Code deals with the administrative arena, be it in terms of personnel policy, educational policy, sacramental discipline, or the administration of church property to name only a few. When all is said and done, the church administrator is to humanize and accommodate the principles laid down by the legislator, set them in their proper context, apply them equitably, and dispense from them wherever necessary (cc. 85–93). Generally speaking, there are relatively few legal restrictions on the bishop's functioning in this area, contrary to the situation in the judicial arena.

Before concluding these reflections, it should be noted that the area of church life occasioning the most conflicts is the broad area of administrative discretion. Reference is made at the end of Book VII to a process of administrative recourse if one feels aggrieved by administrative discretion of one

[56]See Green, "Diocesan Bishop," 333–339. On the increasing importance of particular law such as various types of diocesan statutes, guidelines, etc., see Morrisey, *passim*. See also E. Correcco, "The Bishop, Head of the Local Church and its Discipline," *Con* 38 (1968), 88–104.

[57]Technically speaking, whenever the law refers explicitly to "diocesan bishop" and not to "local ordinary" or "ordinary" simply, the vicar general or episcopal vicar needs a special mandate or authorization from the bishop to act (c. 134, §3). This usually refers to especially significant administrative acts such as incardinating or excardinating a cleric (cc. 265–272), establishing a parish (c. 515, §2), permitting the alienation of church property (c. 1292, §1).

type or another, e.g., the removal of a pastor, the dismissal of a teacher, the imposition of a diocesan tax on a parish (cc. 1732–1739). However, perhaps still more significant than such *post-factum* recourse procedures is a systematic effort to eliminate unnecessary discretionary power and to control necessary discretionary power in the life of the Church. If it is a special responsibility of bishops to preclude conflicts within the Church and to help resolve them justly (c. 1446, §1), then it seems pertinent to stress certain tasks of bishops in monitoring administrative discretion in their dioceses.

Three points that seem especially relevant in this connection are: (1) ensuring that the competencies of administrative organs and individual administrators are reasonably and precisely delineated; (2) seeing to it that the criteria of administrative decision-making in various areas are clarified, e.g., personnel policy; and (3) insisting on the issuing of written opinions supporting administrative decisions, especially when the rights of individuals are adversely affected.[58]

Finally, the bishop is said to exercise judicial authority either personally (c. 1419) or through the vicar judicial (officialis) (c. 1420) and the judges (c. 1421) in accord with the norm of law. Practically speaking, if the bishop is the sole legislator and if he functions fairly frequently in the executive arena even while utilizing vicars, he hardly ever functions directly in the judicial arena. The elaborate set of rules for judicial activity in Book VII reflects a lengthy process of refining the procedures for judicial decision-making, which is largely geared to the resolution of conflicts of rights at least theoretically.[59] While the bishop may theoretically judge any cases not reserved to higher authority (cc. 1419, 1405), his role in practice usually is confined to supporting and ensuring a certain accountability from those officials he has appointed to the tribunal staff.

Fostering of Common Discipline

Canon 392 — §1. Since he must protect the unity of the universal Church, the bishop is bound to promote the common discipline of the whole Church and therefore to urge the observance of all ecclesiastical laws.

§2. He is to be watchful lest abuses creep into ecclesiastical discipline, especially concerning the ministry of the word, the celebration of the sacra- ments and sacramentals, the worship of God and devotion to the saints, and also the administration of property.

The bishop's responsibility to foster the good of the whole Church along with his brother bishops in the college of bishops underlies this traditional expectation that he promote the common discipline of the Church in his diocese (*CIC* 336). He is thereby to foster the observance of all ecclesiastical laws, universal and particular (§1). Likewise he is to see to it that abuses are precluded in certain particularly important areas such as the ministry of the word (cc. 756–780), the celebration of the sacraments and sacramentals (cc. 840–1172), the worship of God and the veneration of the saints (cc. 1186–1190), and the administration of church property (cc. 1254–1310) (§2).[60]

Representation of Diocese

Canon 393 — The diocesan bishop represents his diocese in all its juridic affairs.

In accord with the concern of the revised Code to specify legal representatives of juridic persons, the bishop is understandably said to be the official representative of the diocese. This is a new canon even though it was implicitly understood in the 1917 Code.[61]

Fostering of Apostolate

Canon 394 — §1. The bishop is to foster the various aspects of the apostolate within his diocese and see to it that within the entire diocese or within its individual districts all the works of the apostolate are coordinated under his direction, with due regard for their distinctive character.

§2. He is to urge the faithful to exercise the apostolate in proportion to each one's condition and ability, since it is a duty to which they are bound; he is also to recommend to them that they participate and assist in the various works of the apostolate in accord with the needs of place and time.

Most of the obligations of bishops articulated in the remaining canons of this article reflect traditional legal expectations stated in the 1917 Code. However, there are a couple of exceptions to that

---

[58]See NCCB, *On Due Process,* rev. ed. (Washington: NCCB, 1972), 31–34. For some general principles on pastoral government, see *Directory,* pars. 93–98.

[59]Judicial processes are structured theoretically according to a contentious or conflict of rights model whereas practically speaking most cases in church courts are marriage cases, which do not really involve such conflicts of rights for the most part. See the observations of Wrenn at the beginning of the commentary on Book VII.

[60]At times it may be pastorally advisable to dispense from church law in a given instance. See c. 87 on dispensations from universal laws and c. 88 on dispensations from diocesan laws, laws of provincial or plenary councils, or laws of the conference of bishops. For the most significant post-conciliar document in this area, see Paul VI *mp De episcoporum muneribus,* June 15, 1966, in *AAS* 58 (1966), 467–472. English translation is in *CLD* 6, 394–400.

[61]There are comparable provisions in the revised Code for seminary rectors (c. 238, §1) and pastors of parishes (c. 532).

rule: this canon on the exercise of the apostolate and canon 401 on resignation of office.

The present canon reflects the conciliar teaching that the bishop and other clerics are not the only ones responsible for carrying out the Church's mission. Rather all believers are called upon to share in the realization of that mission in one form or another. This is rooted ultimately in the fact that as regards certain basic ecclesial realities there is a fundamental equality of all believers preceding all types of structural differentiations within the community. We all share the same baptism, destiny, Lord, and mission (*LG* 9, 32). Consequently the revised law should reflect the values of both fundamental equality and functional diversity within the Church. The present canon embodies that concern and calls upon the bishop to foster the involvement of a broad cross section of the people of God in fulfilling its mission.

The immediate conciliar source of this canon seems to be *Christus Dominus* 17, which can be properly appreciated only by being situated within the broad context of the ecclesiological developments embodied in other conciliar documents such as *Lumen Gentium* and *Apostolicam actuositatem*.

The first concern of the canon is that the bishop actively encourage the various aspects of the apostolate throughout the diocese. The canon itself does not specify this further; but, the conciliar text and the original schema had spoken of catechetical, missionary, charitable, social, family, educational, and other pastoral undertakings. Secondly, the legislator is understandably concerned about the coordination of these apostolic activities, which becomes more pressing an issue as more apostolic initiatives are undertaken. There is a legitimate fear of a duplication of efforts and a dissipation of resources without some kind of coordination of pastoral enterprises. As the key figure in realizing the mission of the particular church, the bishop has the principal responsibility in this area.[62] However, this does not mean that he himself must personally undertake this coordinating function. He might well make use of his vicar general or an episcopal vicar in this connection. Canon 493 on the diocesan curia addresses various dimensions of the broad issue of coordinating different diocesan activities, be they pastoral or administrative. That canon among other things refers to the possible appointment of a so-called moderator of the curia and the possible establishment of an episcopal council of vicars to realize such coordination objectives.

Paragraph two of the canon calls for the bishop to remind the faithful of their apostolic responsibilities and to encourage them to share in the Church's apostolate according to their personal status, talents, and the distinctive circumstances of place and time. This is a concrete implication of the basic Christian duty to foster the growth of the Church (c. 210) and the basic right and duty to participate in the task of communicating the divine message of salvation to all persons (c. 211). The present canon does not explicitly allude to the establishment of associations for pastoral purposes as did *Christus Dominus* 17 and the original schema in a separate canon. However, in this connection one should take cognizance of canons 215–216 on the basic Christian right to form associations for various spiritual purposes with due regard for the requirement of the approval of church authority if a given association is to call itself a Catholic association.[63] In closing, one might note the important responsibility of the bishop and other church leaders to foster a climate conducive to the development of various pastoral enterprises lest the invitation to participate in the apostolate in the Church and in the world be perceived merely as a pro forma reality whose implications are not taken seriously.

Obligation of Residence

Canon 395 — §1. Even if he has a coadjutor or an auxiliary bishop, a diocesan bishop is bound by the law of personal residence within his diocese.

§2. Provided provision is made that the diocese not suffer any disadvantage through his absence from it, he can be absent from his diocese for a just cause but not for more than one month, whether continuous or interrupted; this period does not include the time spent on his *ad limina* visit, or at councils, at a synod of bishops or at a conference of bishops, whenever he must be present, or the time spent on another office which has been legitimately entrusted to him.

§3. Except for a serious and urgent reason he is not to be absent from his diocese on Christmas, during Holy Week, on Easter, Pentecost, or Corpus Christi.

§4. If the bishop has been absent illegally from his diocese beyond six months, the metropolitan is to inform the Apostolic See; the senior suffragan is to do so if the metropolitan is illegally absent.

The first of a series of canons reaffirming traditional episcopal obligations somewhat modifies canon 338 of the 1917 Code regarding residence in the diocese. Paragraph one reaffirms the personal obligation of residence even if the bishop has a coadjutor or auxiliary. This obligation, rooted in Tridentine legislation,[64] is related to the necessity of the bishop's being available to his people in the exercise of his teaching, sanctifying, and governing role. The obligation of residence means not simply physical presence in the diocese but also fulfilling

---

[62]See *Directory*, pars. 103–105.

[63]See cc. 298–329 on associations of the faithful.
[64]See Conc. Trident., sess. XXIII *de ref.*, c. 1.

the various episcopal responsibilities clarified in the canons and elsewhere. Furthermore, this pastoral concern is also clear from the fact that he is to ensure that the pastoral good of the diocese is not jeopardized even by his legitimate absence. It is not specified in law how he is to fulfill this expectation; however, one might assume that he can achieve this goal in part through the appropriate use of vicars.

Paragraph two somewhat simplifies canon 338, §2 of the 1917 Code on various excusing causes warranting the bishop's absence from the diocese. It also significantly reduces the amount of time of such absence from two to three months to a month, be it continuous or interrupted. Though there is no official explanation for this change, one may assume that it reflects the increased conciliar and post-conciliar emphasis on the status of the diocesan bishop and the multiplication of episcopal responsibilities. The reasons permitting the bishop's absence are partially those specified in the 1917 Code (*ad limina* visit[65] and attendance at councils[66]) and partially new considerations (attendance at synod of bishops[67] or conference of bishops[68] or exercise of an extra-diocesan office[69]).

Paragraph three offers the bishop more options for the time of such legitimate absence than the 1917 Code since the former prohibits his absence only on certain significant holy days and not during the whole period of Advent and Lent as did the latter.

Paragraph four reflects the legislator's concern for accountability in the fulfillment of this obligation. Should the bishop violate the law and be absent for more than six months, the metropolitan is to refer the matter to the Holy See in virtue of his somewhat circumscribed pastoral oversight role in the province (c. 436). If the metropolitan himself violates the residence obligation, the senior suffragan bishop in terms of appointment is to refer the matter to the Holy See. This senior suffragan functions in a comparable fashion if the metropolitan wishes to dissolve the presbyteral council in his archdiocese since normally a bishop must consult the metropolitan before he dissolves the presbyteral council (c. 501, §3).

It is somewhat surprising that the law here takes effect only after six months' absence comparable to the 1917 Code even though the present law notably abbreviates the permissible time of episcopal absence. One might also note in this connection the possibility of a just penalty including privation of

office for grave violations of this and other residence obligations (c. 1396).[70]

The next three canons deal with various aspects of the bishop's responsibility to visit the diocese at least every five years in view of ensuring a certain accountability in meeting various diocesan goals and objectives and fulfilling the varied dimensions of the Church's mission.

Obligation of Visitation

Canon 396 — §1. The bishop is obliged to visit his diocese annually, either in its entirety or in part, in such a way that the entire diocese is visited at least every five years; he may make this visitation personally or if he is legitimately hindered from doing so personally, he may do so through the coadjutor or auxiliary bishop, through a vicar general or episcopal vicar, or through another presbyter.

§2. The bishop has the right to choose for himself those clerics he prefers to be his companions and assistants on the visitation; any other contrary privilege or custom whatsoever is reprobated.

The present canon simplifies canon 343 of the 1917 Code on the obligation of making the visitation. It drops the latter's specification of certain reasons for the visitation[71] in line with the general tendency of not explicitating the reason(s) for a law within the canon. Although the obligation is a personal one like the others specified here, the canon permits other clerics to fulfill it. Unlike the 1917 Code the present canon mentions the coadjutor or auxiliary bishop first in this connection—another example of the effort to enhance the status of such hierarchs in the revised Code. One would think that this is a responsibility that should be carried out by the bishop personally if possible so that he might gain a first-hand insight into the pastoral state of the diocese and thereby be better able to see to the preparation of a truly accurate quinquennial report (c. 399). The personal carrying out of the visitation might be a significant problem in large dioceses; however, elsewhere it would seem to be a fine opportunity for the bishop to support and challenge those engaged in various pastoral ministries throughout the diocese. Vicars might profitably be employed not so much to carry out the visitation proper but rather to free the bishop from various

---

[65]See c. 400.

[66]This presumably refers to ecumenical councils (cc. 337–341) and particular councils, i.e., plenary and provincial councils (cc. 439–446).

[67]See cc. 342–348.

[68]See cc. 447–459.

[69]This might refer to service in one of the dicasteries of the Roman Curia, See Paul VI, *mp Pro comperto sane,* Aug. 6, 1967, *AAS* 59 (1967), 883, n. III. English translation is in *CLD* 6, 322–324 (esp. 322).

[70]One might also note the residence obligations of coadjutor and auxiliary bishops (c. 410), pastors (c. 533), and parochial vicars (c. 550).

[71]Among the reasons for the visitation in *CIC* 343, §1 were the following: "the preservation of sound and orthodox doctrine, the defense of morality, the correction of abuses, the promotion of peacefulness, simplicity, piety, and docility among the clergy and laity, and the inauguration of any and all measures that seem, from the circumstances, profitable for religion." (Abbo-Hannan I, 369) See also *Directory,* pars. 166–170.

administrative commitments that might otherwise prevent him from making the visitation or would lead to its being a largely pro forma experience on the occasion of confirmation or some other ceremony.

The present canon simplifies canon 343, §2 of the 1917 Code on those accompanying the bishop during the visitation and omits canon 343, §3 of the former law on provisions in case of the bishop's dereliction of his duty. For that, one must turn to canon 436, §1, 2° indicating that with Holy See approval the metropolitan is to carry out the visitation in case of episcopal neglect.

Scope of Visitation

Canon 397 — §1. Persons, Catholic institutions, and sacred things and places are subject to the ordinary episcopal visitation if they are located within the area of the diocese.

§2. The bishop can visit members of religious institutes of pontifical right and their houses only in those cases expressly mentioned in law.

In two paragraphs this canon briefly indicates the subjects of the ordinary episcopal visitation (§1) and the limitations of episcopal visitation prerogatives in the case of religious of pontifical right (§2). A few words on the general scope of the visitation and on its implications for religious seem sufficient especially since the latter issue is treated in more detail in the commentary on religious law.

The bishop has the right and duty to visit various persons, institutions, and sacred things and places in the diocese as a matter of principle. Without going into exhaustive detail on the point, one might note that the following *persons* are subject to the visitation: secular clergy, religious fulfilling pastoral offices in the diocese in matters pertinent to those offices, members of associations of the faithful (c. 305), etc. The *institutions* subject to the visitation would be schools and other educational institutions, hospitals, nursing homes, etc. The sacred *things* subject to visitation would be sacred vessels and vestments, altars, relics, etc.; the sacred *places* subject to visitation would be churches, oratories, cemeteries, etc.

The second paragraph of the canon needs to be read in connection with canons 628, §2 and 683 of the section on institutes of consecrated life. The present law seems to reflect especially *Christus Dominus* 35 and *Ecclesiae sanctae* I, 38 and 39, 2 with their enlarging of the right of episcopal visitation regarding various institutions of religious. This development envisions the fostering of the good of the particular church and the harmonious collaboration of religious and other pastoral ministers in various areas of the apostolate, especially education, worship, and pastoral care. The right of visitation largely concerns the observance of general laws and

the bishop's directives in the above-mentioned areas of the apostolate.

The law distinguishes between religious institutes[72] of pontifical right and other institutes of consecrated life (c. 589). This implies in practice that institutes established by the Holy See or approved by it with a formal decree are less subject to episcopal supervision than other religious, especially regarding the internal life of the community. Accordingly, canon 683, §1 states that the general right of episcopal visitation embraces churches and oratories which the faithful regularly frequent, schools, and other works of religion or spiritual or temporal charity entrusted to religious. It explicitly excludes his visiting schools attended only by members of the religious community. If certain abuses are pointed out and the religious superior does not take appropriate action, the bishop himself may deal with the issue (c. 683, §2). Besides this visitation right, canon 628, §2 states that the bishop may visit autonomous monasteries (c. 615) and religious institutes of diocesan right in his own diocese even in matters of internal religious discipline. However, this is not permitted in religious institutes of pontifical right.

Style of Visitation

Canon 398 — The bishop is to strive to complete his pastoral visitation with due diligence, and he is to take care lest anyone be imposed upon or burdened by unnecessary expenses.

This canon notably simplifies canons 345–346 of the 1917 Code on the paternal approach and simplicity that should characterize the visitation as well as on recourse taken against administrative decrees issued on the occasion of the visitation. Interestingly enough, the original schema had basically restated the 1917 Code with its prohibition against the visitors taking any special gifts on the occasion of the visitation. However, the committee felt that the text should be simplified. Hence the present canon basically restates the initial part of canon 346 of the former law with slight modifications.

Quinquennial Report

Canon 399 — §1. The diocesan bishop is bound to present a report to the Supreme Pontiff every five years concerning the state of the diocese committed to him, according to a form and at a time determined by the Apostolic See.

§2. If the year set for the presentation of this report falls entirely or in part within the first two-

---

[72]The committee explicitly changed the original formulation of this canon which spoke more generically of "institutes of consecrated life" (cc. 573–730) thereby including secular institutes (cc. 710–730). The present text referring to "religious institutes" (cc. 607–709) is meant to exclude secular institutes.

year period of his governance of the diocese, the bishop can omit the composition and presentation of the report on this one occasion.

A concern for ecclesial accountability and the papal responsibility to promote the good of all the churches seem to underlie this episcopal responsibility to forward to the Holy See every five years a detailed report on the state of the diocese. The report of most particular churches is forwarded to the Sacred Congregation for Bishops, which has drawn up a detailed form according to which it is to be prepared.[73] In missionary territories the competent dicastery is the Sacred Congregation for the Evangelization of Peoples. Pertinent information is shared with other Roman dicasteries and with the Vatican Statistics Office. The present canon largely restates canon 340, §1 and §3 of the 1917 Code while dropping canon 340, §2 of the former law which listed in detail the various quinquennia when bishops and other hierarchs in different parts of the world were to forward their reports. The present law continues the rather benign approach of the 1917 Code toward new bishops by exempting them from preparing a report if it is due during the first biennium after their taking possession of the diocese.

While the quinquennial report could be prepared in a somewhat pro forma fashion, it might occasion a truly serious effort to clarify the state of the diocese in various pastoral areas. It might be an appropriate opportunity to call a diocesan synod (cc. 460–468) or to make a creative use of the diocesan pastoral council (cc. 511–514). In any event it seems indispensable that there be a serious effort to elicit insights from a broad cross section of the people of God in a diocese—whatever the institutional vehicle chosen to achieve this purpose.[74]

Ad Limina *Visit*

Canon 400 — **§1. During the year in which he is bound to present his report to the Supreme Pontiff and unless other provisions have been made by the Apostolic See, the diocesan bishop is to come to Rome to venerate the tombs of the blessed apostles Peter and Paul and is to appear before the Roman Pontiff.**

§2. Unless he is legitimately hindered from doing so, the bishop is to satisfy this aforementioned obligation personally; if he is so hindered, he is to satisfy this obligation through his coadjutor, if he has one, through an auxiliary bishop, or through a suitable priest of his presbyterate who resides in his diocese.

§3. An apostolic vicar can satisfy this obligation through an agent, even through one living in Rome; an apostolic prefect is not bound by this obligation.

This institute, which originally involved only the bishops of the province of Rome, was gradually extended to all bishops throughout the world by the thirteenth century. Its main purpose today is to foster close contact between the pope and the bishops, to enable them to present their quinquennial reports to the appropriate authorities, and to facilitate contacts between the bishops and various officials of the Roman Curia. Generally speaking, the papal legate in consultation with the president of the conference of bishops coordinates the details of such visits, be it by individual bishops or by groups of bishops. The present law largely restates canons 341–342 and 299 of the 1917 Code.

The obligation of making the *ad limina* visit is a personal one in light of the importance of fostering direct pope-bishop relationships. However, paragraph two of the canon indicates that the coadjutor or an auxiliary bishop or another suitable priest may be delegated to fulfill this obligation.

An awareness of the difficulties that may impede the fulfillment of such an obligation by missionary hierarchs accounts for the flexibility of paragraph three permitting apostolic vicars to meet their responsibilities through a proxy, even one residing in Rome. The fact that apostolic prefects are not bound to make such a visit is an example of the provision of canon 381, §2 that hierarchs presiding over particular churches comparable to dioceses are equivalent to bishops unless the law specifically provides otherwise.

Retirement from Office

Canon 401 — **§1. A diocesan bishop who has completed his seventy-fifth year of age is requested to present his resignation from office to the Supreme Pontiff who will make provisions after he has examined all the circumstances.**

§2. A diocesan bishop is earnestly requested to present his resignation from office when he has become less able to fulfill his office due to ill health or another serious reason.

A concern to foster ministerial accountability and protect the best interests of the particular church seems to underlie this canon on episcopal

---

[73]See SCB, decr *Ad Romanam Ecclesiam,* June 6, 1975, in *AAS* 67 (1975), 674–676. English translation is in *CLD* Supplement through 1980 at *CIC* 340, §§1–13. Among the areas of inquiry in the SCB form are the following: pastoral and administrative organization of the diocese; general religious situation; economic situation of the diocese; liturgy; clergy; religious and secular institutes; cooperation with the missions, seminaries, and universities; Catholic education; the laity; ecumenism, social assistance, and various other pastoral questions. There is also a section of the form that seeks statistical information about some of the above areas of inquiry.

[74]A possible model for such a data-gathering and evaluating enterprise is the special diocesan committee for the selection of bishops referred to in the CLSA procedure indicated in note 29.

retirement—the first time in church history that one finds a comparable universal norm. The issue of episcopal retirement was discussed at some length at Vatican II, and *Christus Dominus* 21 earnestly requested the bishop to resign his office if old age or another serious reason made it advisable. Undoubtedly the conciliar emphasis on the episcopal office and an awareness of the pressing demands of ministerial leadership in a changing world focused attention on the possible problems of fulfilling the responsibilities of such an office for various reasons. The post conciliar *motu proprio Ecclesiae sanctae* I, 11 further concretized this conciliar concern by asking all diocesan bishops voluntarily to retire at seventy-five years of age. However, it made no reference to other reasons perhaps because it was judged difficult or possibly unnecessary to specify a detailed list of reasons.

There was somewhat of a tempering of the force of the legislator's intent regarding retirement during the revision process. Canon 259, §1 of the original schema stated forcefully that at seventy-five years of age all diocesan bishops and those equivalent to them in law must submit their resignation to the competent authority. Canon 259, §2 of the original schema strongly encouraged bishops to retire if they were unable to fulfill their responsibilities due to ill health or some other reason, prescinding from any consideration of age. It is not clear what reasons prompted a change in this text at the end of the revision process. However, the present canon recommends but does not strictly require a bishop to retire. The second paragraph dealing with ill health or a comparable serious reason expresses the commendation a bit more strongly ("enixe") than the first paragraph treating of the age factor alone. Since the pope appointed the bishop, the resignation is understandably presented to the former functioning through the congregations mentioned earlier in the discussion of the designation of bishops (c. 377). The pope is to decide whether or not to accept the resignation and if so how best to provide for the retired bishop in light of the next canon. This is a specific example of the applicability of canon 189 on the competent authority regarding resignation from office.[75]

Status of Retired Bishop

Canon 402 — §1. A bishop whose resignation from office has been accepted retains the title of bishop emeritus of his diocese and can retain a place of residence in his diocese if he so desires, unless other provisions have been made by the

Apostolic See in certain cases due to special circumstances.

§2. The conference of bishops must see to it that suitable and decent support is provided for a resigned bishop, with due regard for the primary obligation which rests upon the diocese which he has served.

The first paragraph, dealing with the title and residence of the retired bishop, envisions his continuing relationship with the diocese. He retains the title of bishop emeritus of the retired see, and he may continue to live in the diocese if he chooses unless the Holy See makes other provisions. The retired bishop is technically a titular bishop in the sense of canon 376. This first paragraph seems to reflect a sensitivity to the patristic emphasis on the bishop as permanently spiritually wedded to his diocese.

As regards the support of the retired bishop, the second paragraph understandably highlights the primary responsibility of the diocese from which he has retired. However, one practical implication of episcopal collegiality is a concern for the situation of retired bishops. Hence, not surprisingly, the law obliges the conference of bishops to see to it that its retired members are duly provided for. The conference itself is not precisely obliged to provide such support, but, rather, to see to its availability in one form or another. Individual dioceses, especially in the missions, might conceivably find it difficult to meet this responsibility; perhaps the conference could provide alternative avenues of such support.

Before closing this section it might be noted that three canons of the 1917 Code have been dropped from the revised law. These canons discussed the precedence of bishops (*CIC* 347), the status of titular bishops in their titular dioceses (*CIC* 348), and the privileges of bishops (*CIC* 349). In this last connection it might be noted that changes in the law itself have made somewhat unnecessary specific provisions for episcopal faculties and privileges such as were contained in the November 1963 *motu proprio Pastorale Munus*.[76]

ARTICLE 3: COADJUTOR AND AUXILIARY BISHOPS
[cc. 403–411][77]

The following article reworks canons 350–355 of the 1917 Code in light of *Christus Dominus* 25–26

---

[75]For examples of other canons on the retirement of various church leaders, see c. 332, §2 (pope); c. 354 (cardinals); c. 411 (coadjutor and auxiliary bishops); and c. 538, §3 (pastors). For the general rules on retirement, see cc. 187–189.

[76]See *AAS* 56 (1964), 5–12. English translation is in *CLD* 6, 370–378.

[77]For official Code Commission reports on the formulation of these canons, see *Comm* 5 (1973), 223–224; 7 (1975), 161–172; 12 (1980), 309–314. For a helpful discussion of *CD* 25–26, see Moersdorf in Vorgrimler II, 242–249. For a useful discussion of the similarities and differences between the 1917 Code and

and *Ecclesiae sanctae* I, 13. It strives to enhance the status of both coadjutor and auxiliary bishops in diocesan life. The initial canon discusses the ways in which such bishops are appointed (c. 403). After considering the formalities for taking possession of office (c. 404), the law clarifies their rights and obligations and their replacing the diocesan bishop who is absent from the diocese or impeded from functioning within it (c. 405). Canon 406 specifies that coadjutor or auxiliary bishops are to be appointed vicars general or at least episcopal vicars; furthermore, the diocesan bishop is to consult them in various undertakings and they are to function in union with him (c. 407). After clarifying how they can help the diocesan bishop (c. 408), the law articulates their status when the see is vacant (c. 409). Finally, two canons deal with their obligation of residence (c. 410) and their retirement (c. 411).

Among the general principles underlying the reformulation of the canons on coadjutor and auxiliary bishops are the following: the need to provide for the pastoral needs of the diocese; the importance of respecting the integrity of the episcopal status of the coadjutor or auxiliary; and the necessity of fostering unified diocesan government and a close working relationship between the diocesan bishop, the key authority figure, and his coadjutor and/or auxiliaries.

Appointment of Coadjutor/Auxiliary

Canon 403 — §1. When the pastoral needs of the diocese warrant it one or several auxiliary bishops are to be appointed at the request of the diocesan bishop; an auxiliary bishop does not possess the right of succession.

§2. An auxiliary bishop equipped with special faculties can be given to a diocesan bishop in more serious circumstances even of a personal character.

§3. If it appears more opportune to the Holy See, it can ex officio appoint a coadjutor bishop who is also equipped with special faculties; a coadjutor bishop does possess the right of succession.

The initial canon clarifies a certain "hierarchy of auxiliaries" in ascending order as it deals successively with the simple auxiliary bishop (§1), the auxiliary endowed with special faculties (§2), and the coadjutor with special faculties who enjoys the right of succession (§3).[78] While the initiative regarding the appointment of the simple auxiliary rests with the diocesan bishop, the initiative in ap-

pointing an auxiliary with special faculties probably rests with the Holy See; and it certainly does in the appointment of a coadjutor with the right of succession. This modifies the 1917 Code, which did not speak explicitly of the initiative of the diocesan bishop in any event and distinguished among coadjutors given to the person of the bishop enjoying the right of succession, coadjutors given to the person of the bishop without the right of succession (auxiliaries), and coadjutors given to the see itself (*CIC* 350).

It seems that the auxiliary is normally appointed in view of distinctly diocesan considerations, somewhat prescinding from the personal situation of the diocesan bishop. From the conciliar discussion, it seems that such considerations might be the size of the diocese, the large number of its inhabitants, the presence of a significant number of the faithful of a different rite or language than the majority, or the presence of a significant pastoral concern, e.g., specialized needs of urban ministry or a ministry to migrants. It might be noted that the appointment of an auxiliary was discussed in *Christus Dominus* 25 immediately following the consideration of the revision of diocesan boundaries for various reasons (*CD* 22–24).

On the contrary, the coadjutor and probably the auxiliary with special faculties are appointed normally because of certain personal problems experienced by the diocesan bishop in adequately meeting the varied responsibilities of his office. Among other things this may be due to age, ill health, or time-consuming extra-diocesan responsibilities such as holding an office in the conference of bishops or being a member of a dicastery of the Holy See.

An extensively discussed issue during the revision process was whether the coadjutor should automatically enjoy the right of succession or whether this was unduly circumscribing the administrative freedom of the Holy See.[79] Ultimately the committee decided that it was inappropriate for the coadjutor not to enjoy the right of succession as envisioned by *Christus Dominus* 26, contrary to the original schema which had made the right of succession optional. The various options afforded by the canon were judged sufficient to preserve the proper freedom of the Holy See. If a diocesan situation were viewed as particularly serious yet the Holy See did not wish to appoint a coadjutor, it could always name an auxiliary with special faculties.

Taking Possession of Office

Canon 404 — §1. A coadjutor bishop takes possession of his office when he personally or through

---

Vatican II on coadjutor and auxiliary bishops, see A. Vallini, "De figura episcopi coadjutoris et auxiliaris secundum doctrinam Concilii Oecumenici Vaticani II recognoscenda," *Apol* 40 (1967), 177–214. See also *Directory*, par. 199.

[78]At times in referring generically to coadjutor bishops, auxiliaries with special faculties, and simple auxiliaries, the author uses the term "auxiliaries."

[79]For a detailed discussion of this issue, see *Comm* 7 (1975), 161–172.

his proxy has presented the apostolic letter of appointment to the diocesan bishop and the college of consultors in the presence of the chancellor of the curia who officially records the event.

§2. An auxiliary bishop takes possession of his office when he has presented the apostolic letter of appointment to the diocesan bishop in the presence of the chancellor of the curia who officially records the event.

§3. If, however, the diocesan bishop is completely hindered, it is sufficient for both a coadjutor bishop and an auxiliary bishop to present the apostolic letter of appointment to the college of consultors in the presence of the chancellor of the curia.

The provisions for taking possession of office are comparable to those for the diocesan bishop (c. 382). They also reflect the preeminent status of the coadjutor in comparison with the auxiliaries. While the auxiliaries normally present their letters of appointment to the diocesan bishop along with the chancellor, the coadjutor presents his letter of appointment to the diocesan bishop and the college of consultors in a manner comparable to that of the diocesan bishop himself. By way of exception, if the diocesan bishop is prevented from accepting the credentials of his brother bishops, all three types of auxiliaries may present them to the college of consultors representing the presbyterate. This canon is somewhat comparable to canon 353 of the 1917 Code.

Rights and Obligations in General

Canon 405 — §1. A coadjutor bishop and an auxiliary bishop have the obligations and rights which are determined in the prescriptions of the following canons as well as those which are defined in the letter of their appointment.

§2. A coadjutor bishop and the auxiliary bishop mentioned in can. 403, §2, aid the diocesan bishop in the entire governance of the diocese and take his place if he is absent or impeded.

This canon reflects a committee decision to differentiate between the generic rights and duties of coadjutor and auxiliary bishops (§1) and the specific duties of the coadjutor and the auxiliary with special faculties, who enjoy a somewhat more significant status than the simple auxiliary (§2). If one is to understand the legal status of coadjutors and auxiliaries correctly, the present canon needs to be seen in relationship to the three following ones.

The Council Fathers wished to enhance the status of coadjutor and auxiliary bishops so that they would be viewed not simply as confirmation helpers but rather as vital sharers in the threefold function of teaching, sanctifying, and governing. However, there was also a preoccupation that the unity of di-

ocesan government not be jeopardized by possible conflicts between the diocesan bishop and his auxiliary bishops. The harmonizing of these values was a major objective of the committee in formulating these canons.

First of all, it should be noted that membership in the college of bishops into which the coadjutor or auxiliary is incorporated through consecration does not of itself grant any specific rights or powers in the diocese. Hence the particular "job description" of the coadjutor or auxiliary must be determined from his letter of appointment and from the concrete implications of the office of vicar general or episcopal vicar to which he is appointed (cc. 475–481). The law clearly intends that coadjutor and auxiliary bishops function as significant administrative leaders in the diocese, that the diocesan bishop consult them frequently and assign significant responsibilities to them in preference to other priests, that coadjutors and auxiliaries work willingly with the diocesan bishop in various ways, and that there be an ongoing effort to foster a meeting of minds and genuine collaboration on all pastoral concerns. However, when all is said and done, the actual status of the coadjutor and auxiliary will probably depend greatly on the nature of their personal working relationship with the diocesan bishop.

Paragraph two of the canon as well as canons 406 and 407, §1 differentiate between the coadjutor and the auxiliary with special faculties on the one hand and the simple auxiliary on the other. However, besides the fact that the former bishops must be appointed vicars general and should be entrusted with tasks requiring a special episcopal mandate (c. 406, §1), it is not entirely clear how their preeminent status will be evident in the practical daily functioning of a diocese. This is true whether the diocesan bishop is actually present in the diocese or is absent for some reason (e.g., fulfilling some extra-diocesan commitment) or is impeded from fulfilling his office (c. 412). In fact there may be relatively few situations in which there is such a varied configuration of auxiliary bishops in one diocese.

Appointment as Vicar General/Episcopal Vicar

Canon 406 — §1. A coadjutor bishop as well as the auxiliary bishop mentioned in can. 403, §2, is to be appointed a vicar general by the diocesan bishop; moreover the diocesan bishop is to commit to such a bishop rather than to others those matters which by law require a special mandate.

§2. Unless another provision has been made in the apostolic letter and with due regard for the prescription of §1, the diocesan bishop should appoint his auxiliary or auxiliaries as vicars general or at least episcopal vicars, dependent upon his authority alone, or that of a coadjutor bishop or the auxiliary bishop mentioned in can. 403, §2.

Given the conciliar emphasis on the preeminence of the vicar general in the diocesan curia (*CD* 27) and the stress on episcopal vicars' fulfilling different noteworthy episcopal responsibilities, it is not surprising that *Christus Dominus* 26 and *Ecclesiae sanctae* I, 13 required the coadjutor to be named vicar general and the auxiliaries to be named vicars general or at least episcopal vicars. This would institutionalize the concern for enhancing the status of such bishops expressed in various conciliar interventions. At least they would enjoy a minimum of faculties in the diocese.

The present canon reflects the same preoccupations, differentiating between coadjutors and auxiliaries with special faculties (§1) and simple auxiliaries and once again reaffirming the dependence of the latter on the former (§2). As noted earlier, the practical situation in individual dioceses may vary somewhat from the general thrust of these canons. Furthermore, whatever may be the technical legal situation, the preeminent position of the vicar general may be a distinctly European phenomenon not always corresponding to the de facto experience of churches in the United States and elsewhere where the chancellor or a comparable officeholder may be the most significant figure in the diocesan curia.[80]

Episcopal Consultation and Collaboration

Canon 407 — §1. In order to foster the present and future good of the diocese as much as possible, the diocesan bishop, the coadjutor and the auxiliary bishop mentioned in can. 403, §2, are to consult with one another on matters of major importance.

§2. In considering matters of major importance, especially of a pastoral character, the diocesan bishop is to consult his auxiliary bishops before others.

§3. Because they have been called upon to share part of the concerns of the diocesan bishop, a coadjutor bishop and an auxiliary bishop are so to fulfill their duties that they proceed in harmony with him in their efforts and intentions.

Among the concerns explicitated by *Ecclesiae sanctae* I, 13 regarding the appointment of auxiliaries were the unity of diocesan government and effective collaboration between the diocesan bishop and the auxiliaries. This canon expresses a similar preoccupation although it stresses somewhat more forcefully consultation with the coadjutor and the auxiliary with special faculties ("consulant") than with simple auxiliaries ("consulere velit"). The canon envisions both consultation before policies are articulated and collaboration in the exercise of

the episcopal office. The underlying rationale for the canon is the present and future good of the diocese specified in the first part of paragraph one. Once again the specifics of this consultation and collaboration will have to be worked out in practice since the law itself does not indicate specific pastoral issues in which such consultation and collaboration are called for. Furthermore, despite the welcome stress on such consultation, this provision does not alter the legal position of the diocesan bishop or his auxiliaries. The former is still the key decisional figure in the diocese unless the coadjutor or the auxiliary with special faculties has been granted faculties by higher authority to act independently of the diocesan bishop, e.g., in the administration of church property.

Assistance Rendered Diocesan Bishop

Canon 408 — §1. Unless they are prevented from doing so by reason of a just impediment, a coadjutor bishop and an auxiliary bishop are obliged to perform the pontifical and other functions to which the diocesan bishop is bound whenever he requests them to.

§2. The diocesan bishop is not to entrust habitually to another those episcopal rights and functions which the coadjutor or auxiliary bishop can exercise.

While the two preceding canons have no precedents in the 1917 Code, the present text synthesizes two complementary provisions of that earlier source while modifying them somewhat. The auxiliaries are normally obliged to perform pontifical and other episcopal functions when asked to do so by the diocesan bishop (*CIC* 351, §4). Likewise the diocesan bishop is strongly encouraged not to delegate habitually to other clergy distinctly episcopal rights and functions (*CIC* 351, §3). This understandable provision takes on even greater force in light of the conciliar emphasis on episcopal collegiality and its fostering a special respect for coadjutor and auxiliary bishops.

Vacancy of See

Canon 409 — §1. Upon the vacancy of the episcopal see the coadjutor bishop immediately becomes the bishop of the diocese for which he had been appointed provided he has legitimately taken possession of it.

§2. Unless other provisions have been made by the competent authority, upon the vacancy of the episcopal see an auxiliary bishop retains all and only those powers and faculties which he possessed as vicar general or as episcopal vicar while the see was filled until a new bishop takes possession of the see; if, however, he has not been designated diocesan administrator, he may exercise this same pow-

---

[80]For an overview of some different approaches to diocesan organization, see J. Provost, "Diocesan Administration: Reflections on Recent Developments," *J* 41 (1981), 81–104.

er, conferred by law, under the authority of the diocesan administrator who presides over the governance of the diocese.

This canon deals with the status of the coadjutor bishop (§1) and that of the auxiliary with special faculties or the simple auxiliary (§2) when the diocese is vacant[81] (c. 416). The difference in status between these auxiliaries is eminently clear here for the coadjutor immediately assumes the government of the diocese if he has legitimately taken possession of office (c. 404, §1). This assures a desirable continuity in government for the good of the diocese comparable to that expressed in the 1917 Code (*CIC* 355, §1). On the contrary, the situation is more complex for the auxiliary with or without special faculties; yet, the 1917 Code is somewhat modified (*CIC* 355, §2).

In upgrading the status of auxiliaries, Vatican II and the committee faced the problem that when the see was vacant the office of auxiliary ceased (*CIC* 355, §2). At times a priest would be chosen diocesan administrator[82] and would thereby exercise authority over the auxiliary bishop until the see was filled; to some Council Fathers and committee members this seemed inappropriate. However, on the other hand, a long-standing unrestricted right of electing the administrator was enjoyed by the diocesan consultors (chapter of canons). Two values seemed in conflict: a respect for the dignity of the auxiliary and an acknowledgment of the electoral right of the consultors (chapter)—one of the few vestiges in the Code of such corporate presbyteral decision-making.

Ecclesiae sanctae I, 13 dealt with the issue by expressing a desire that the auxiliary (one of the auxiliaries) be elected diocesan administrator during the vacancy of the see. However, this was not required, and hence the freedom of the appropriate electoral body was maintained. Nevertheless, even if he were not elected administrator, the auxiliary maintained all the powers he formerly enjoyed as vicar general or episcopal vicar, and he was to exercise them in accord with the administrator.[83]

Paragraph two largely reaffirms *Ecclesiae sanctae* I, 13. Although the revised Code indicates that the auxiliary is to assume the leadership of the diocese prior to the election of the administrator (c. 419), the committee rejected a proposal to express a preference that the auxiliary (one of the auxiliaries) be elected administrator. Furthermore, the auxiliary

not elected administrator enjoys only and all those powers he possessed when the see was filled. Hence the status quo is reaffirmed; the non-episcopal diocesan administrator may not curtail the auxiliary's powers even though the latter functions under the authority of the former until the see is filled. Surely the non-episcopal administrator may confer additional authority upon the auxiliary to facilitate their working together.

Accordingly, contrary to the usual rule that the power of vicars general or episcopal ceases during the vacancy of the see (c. 481, §1), the legislator's respect for the dignity of the auxiliaries accounts for this exception here. This situation continues only until the diocese is filled; then, technically the powers of the auxiliary cease, and new provisions must be made by the new bishop according to law, especially canon 406. Finally, one might note that the initial phrase of the canon provides for possible Holy See initiatives that might affect the status of the auxiliary differently.

Obligation of Residence

Canon 410 — A coadjutor bishop and an auxiliary bishop are obliged to reside within the diocese like the diocesan bishop and they are not to leave the diocese except for a short time, unless they are fulfilling some other office outside the diocese or they are on vacation, which is not to exceed one month.

The good of the diocese and the demands of the episcopal office underlie this provision obliging coadjutor and auxiliary bishops to reside in the diocese, comparable to the residence obligation of the diocesan bishop. Unlike the provision for diocesan bishops (c. 395), the present canon refers explicitly only to vacation time and the fulfillment of a given office as reasons for legitimate absence for no more than a month each year. However, one should take cognizance also of the required presence of coadjutors and auxiliaries at various supra-diocesan councils, at meetings of the conference of bishops, and perhaps at the synod of bishops.[84] Furthermore, the fact that no explicit reference is made to vacation time for diocesan bishops hardly means that they do not enjoy that basic clerical right, the exercise of which should enhance the fulfillment of their minis-

---

[81]No reference is made here to the impeded as distinct from the vacant see. For this issue, see commentary on cc. 412–415.

[82]The term used in the 1917 Code was the "vicar capitular" since this interim diocesan leader was chosen by the chapter of canons (*CIC* 432, §2).

[83]An April 25, 1975 response of the Pontifical Commission for the Interpreting of the Decrees of Vatican II confirmed the derogation from *CIC* 355, §2. See *AAS* 67 (1975), 348. English translation is in *CLD* 8, 253–254.

[84]As regards the role of coadjutor and auxiliary bishops outside the diocese, one might note their right and duty to be present at an ecumenical council with a deliberative vote (c. 339, §1), their participation in particular (plenary or provincial) councils with a deliberative vote (c. 443, §1, 2°), and their membership in the conference of bishops, the coadjutors with a deliberative vote (c. 454, §1) and the auxiliaries with a deliberative or consultative vote depending on the statutes (c. 454, §2). However, only the diocesan and coadjutor bishops and not the auxiliary bishops enjoy a deliberative vote in the drawing up of or modifying of the conference statutes (c. 454, §2).

try (c. 283, §2). Unlike the law on diocesan bishops (c. 395, §4), no explicit provision is made for the violation of the law on residence by auxiliaries. However, the appropriate penal canon (c. 1396) would still be operative.

Resignation from Office

Canon 411 — The prescriptions of cann. 401 and 402, §2 on resignation from office are applicable to a coadjutor and an auxiliary bishop.

The law on retirement for coadjutors or auxiliaries is basically the same as that for diocesan bishops mutatis mutandis. Yet, the provisions for the diocesan bishop's title of bishop emeritus and his maintaining diocesan residence (c. 402, §1) are not explicitly restated here. However, as regards the latter issue, the option of continued residence in the diocese by the coadjutor or auxiliary would probably be part of the conference of bishops' guidelines mentioned in canon 402, §2. Or it would probably be provided for in diocesan personnel policy.

CHAPTER III
THE IMPEDED SEE AND THE VACANT SEE
[cc. 412–430][85]

ARTICLE 1: THE IMPEDED SEE
[cc. 412–415]

This article like the following one deals with various contingencies that prompt special legal provisions for the extraordinary exercise of diocesan government. First of all, the law articulates the notion of the impeded see (c. 412); subsequently, it specifies the procedure to be followed when the bishop is prevented from exercising his normal diocesan leadership role (c. 413). The status of the one exercising diocesan leadership in such a contingency is then clarified (c. 414). Finally the legislator considers the special situation in which the bishop is impeded in his leadership role because he has incurred an ecclesiastical penalty (c. 415). These canons are generally comparable to the 1917 Code, which treated this issue in only one canon (CIC 429).

Notion of Impeded See

Canon 412 — An episcopal see is understood to be impeded if by reason of captivity, banishment, exile or incapacity, the diocesan bishop is wholly prevented from fulfilling his pastoral function in the diocese, and cannot communicate with the people of his diocese even by letter.

[85]For official Code Commission reports on the formulation of these canons, see *Comm* 5 (1973), 233–235; 13 (1981), 140–146. For some helpful reflections on the 1917 Code, see Abbo-Hannan I, 427–439.

Contrary to the 1917 Code, the present law devotes a separate canon to the notion of the impeded see; however, the basic concept is the same in both Codes. This bishop cannot carry out the basic functions of his office for reasons of personal health or more likely because of socio-political factors resulting in the bishop's captivity, imprisonment, or exile. Interestingly enough, the present law seems to have its remote origins during the troubled times of the fourth and following centuries when various invasions disrupted both the civil and ecclesiastical orders. At one time one might have thought such a canon somewhat of an outdated relic of the past; however, contemporary Church-State conflicts may make this and subsequent canons seem rather useful in assuring some measure of stability in church government. While this canon refers to a physical impediment preventing the bishop's exercise of his office, canon 415 refers to a canonical impediment barring the bishop's ordinary functioning in the diocese.

Determination of Interim Diocesan Leadership

Canon 413 — §1. When the see is impeded the governance of the diocese, unless the Holy See provides otherwise, belongs to the coadjutor bishop if there is one; if there is none or if he is impeded, it belongs to an auxiliary bishop or the vicar general or the episcopal vicar or to another priest, following the order of persons determined in a list to be composed by the diocesan bishop immediately upon taking possession of the diocese, which list is to be communicated to the metropolitan and renewed at least every three years; it is to be preserved in secret by the chancellor.

§2. If there is no coadjutor bishop or he is impeded, and the list mentioned in §1 is also lacking, the college of consultors is to select a priest who is to govern the diocese.

§3. Whoever assumes the governance of the diocese according to the norms of §1 or §2 shall immediately advise the Holy See of the see's being impeded and of his assuming the function.

The law provides in various ways for the exercise of interim diocesan leadership when the see is impeded. First of all, paragraph one indicates that such leadership should normally be exercised by the coadjutor bishop as the most significant official other than the diocesan bishop. If there is no such bishop or if he also is impeded from functioning, diocesan leadership passes to some other significant diocesan official according to the order determined in a list to be prepared by the bishop soon after taking possession of the diocese (c. 382). This other diocesan official could be the auxiliary bishop, the vicar general, an episcopal vicar, or another priest. While the requirement of such a list is new in the revised Code, the bishop was to delegate the vicar general, another cleric, or even several clerics in succession even in the 1917 Code (*CIC* 419, §§1–2). This list is to be kept secret by the chancellor of the diocese; however, it is to be communicated to the metropolitan[86] presumably in the interests of provincial accountability and in light of his supervisory function. Finally, it is to be reviewed and either confirmed or modified every three years, somewhat comparable to canon 377, §2 regarding potential episcopal candidates.

Paragraph two deals with the exceptional situation in which there is neither a coadjutor nor the list referred to in paragraph one. Like the provisions on the vacant see, it calls for the election of a diocesan administrator by the college of consultors (c. 502); this is also comparable to the 1917 Code (*CIC* 429, §3).

Paragraph three reflects a concern that the Holy See be informed of the impeded see and the provisions taken for interim diocesan leadership. Presumably this is related to the pope's responsibility to care for all the churches; it also embodies a concern for the impact of significant developments in one particular church on other churches in the communion.

Finally, the Holy See might make certain provisions for the impeded see in light of the exceptive clause specified at the beginning of paragraph one ("Nisi . . . providerit"). This would be comparable to canon 419 on the vacant see.

Status of Interim Diocesan Leader

Canon 414 — Whoever is called to exercise temporarily the pastoral care of a diocese according to the norm of can. 413 is bound by the obligations and enjoys the power which belong by law to a diocesan administrator only for the time during which the see is impeded.

The bishop or priest governing the impeded see enjoys the same rights and is bound by the same obligations as the diocesan administrator mentioned in the following canons on the vacant see. This is presumably because of the parity of legal situations. These rights and obligations will be clarified in greater detail in the commentary on the vacant see.

Penalizing of Bishop

Canon 415 — If the diocesan bishop is prohibited from exercising his function by an ecclesiastical penalty, the metropolitan is to make recourse immediately to the Holy See in order that it may provide; if there is no metropolitan or if he himself is

the penalized bishop, the senior suffragan in terms of promotion is to make such recourse.

At times the normal functioning of diocesan government is impaired not because of some physical factor precluding the bishop's communication with the people of the diocese but because of his incurring a canonical penalty for some serious canonical violation. The fact that this situation is viewed differently from other examples of the impeded see is clear from the fact that reference is made to a report by the metropolitan to the Holy See, which is to make appropriate provisions for interim diocesan government. If there is no metropolitan or if he himself is penalized, the senior suffragan in terms of appointment reports to the Holy See. This provision is comparable to the 1917 Code, which, however, explicitly referred to the censures of excommunication, suspension, or interdict unlike the present law which speaks generically of a penalty (*CIC* 429, §5). While one should refer to the pertinent commentary on penal law to clarify the issues raised here, one possible example of the applicability of this canon is the situation of the bishop who would consecrate another bishop without a pontifical mandate and thereby incur excommunication reserved to the Holy See—one of the few excommunications reserved to the Holy See (c. 1382).

ARTICLE 2: THE VACANT SEE
[cc. 416–430]

The initial canon briefly indicates the notion of the vacant see (c. 416). Subsequent canons regulate the validity of the acts of the vicars until they are aware of the vacancy of the see (c. 417) and the situation of the diocesan bishop transferred from one see to another (c. 418). After indicating who governs the diocese prior to the election of the administrator (c. 419), the law specifies those governing the particular church in an apostolic vicariate or prefecture during a vacancy (c. 420). Canon 421 regulates the election of an administrator while canon 422 specifies the obligation of notifying the Holy See about pertinent developments. Canon 423, §1 prohibits the election of more than one administrator while canons 423, §2 and 425 indicate certain qualifications for office; the rules for the election are stated in canon 424. While canon 426 clarifies the legal status of the person governing the vacant see before the choice of the administrator, canon 427 does the same for the latter. Canon 428 reaffirms the traditional prohibition of diocesan innovations during the vacancy and prohibits the administrator's prejudicing episcopal or diocesan rights or tampering with official diocesan documents. The administrator is bound by the ordinary episcopal obligations of residence and Mass for the people (c. 429). Finally, the law describes the cessation of office by the administrator (c. 430). Most of

---

[86]Explicit provision is not made here for the person to whom the metropolitan communicates such a list. However, in light of parallel canons, it would seem to be the senior suffragan in terms of appointment to office. See c. 415.

the canons in this article like the preceding one are comparable to the 1917 Code; significant changes will be noted during the commentary.

Notion of Vacant See

Canon 416 — An episcopal see is vacant upon the death of the diocesan bishop, upon his resignation accepted by the Roman Pontiff, and upon transferral or deprivation of office made known to the bishop.

The present Code restates the reasons for the vacancy of the see specified in the 1917 Code (*CIC* 430, §1): death, retirement, transferral, or deprivation of the episcopal office.[87] The first factor (death) is self-evident. The second (retirement) is somewhat more relevant than in the 1917 Code, given the current provisions for episcopal retirement (c. 401); it should be noted, however, that the see is vacant only when the pope has accepted the bishop's resignation. The third factor (transferral) is also reasonably self-evident; however, one might note that the following canon treats of the status of the transferred bishop in the diocese from which he is being transferred. The final point (privation) presupposes the commission of an ecclesiastical offense for which deprivation of office is the appropriate penalty. This largely refers to situations of persistent resistance to higher authority in a serious matter. In this instance the "higher authority" would be the Holy See, which alone is competent to issue a decree of privation of the episcopal office.

Validity of Vicars' Acts

Canon 417 — All those things done by the vicar general or episcopal vicar have full force until they have received certain notice of the death of the diocesan bishop; likewise, those things done by the diocesan bishop or the vicar general or episcopal vicar have full force until they have received certain notice of the above-mentioned pontifical actions.

A concern to ensure the continuity of diocesan administration and provide for legal security accounts for this provision affirming the validity of the acts of vicars until they are certain of the bishop's death. At this point they lose their authority, which is normally linked to the authority of the bishop whose vicars they are. By way of exception, the auxiliary bishop retains his authority as vicar general or episcopal vicar during the vacancy (c. 409, §2). The canon is also relevant to the acts of the diocesan bishop himself until he has been duly informed of the Holy See's acceptance of his resig-

nation, of his transferral, or of his privation of office. Unlike the 1917 Code (*CIC* 430, §2), this canon deals with all episcopal acts or acts of vicars and does not exempt such provisions as the conferral of ecclesiastical offices from its rather comprehensive scope. Realistically, this would be pertinent only to bishops unless certain episcopal vicars for personnel were empowered to confer ecclesiastical offices in virtue of a special mandate.

Status of Transferred Bishop

Canon 418 — §1. Upon certain notice of transferral the bishop must go to the new diocese within two months and take canonical possession of it; and from the day he takes possession of the new diocese his former diocese is vacant.

§2. From the reception of certain notice of transferral until taking canonical possession of the new diocese, the transferred bishop in his former diocese:

1° obtains the power of a diocesan administrator and is bound by those obligations; all authority of the vicar general and episcopal vicars ceases, with due regard for can. 409, §2;

2° continues to receive the entire salary proper to this office.

The law makes special provisions for the vacant diocese when the bishop is transferred rather than having died, resigned, or been deprived of office.

Until he formally takes possession of the new diocese (*CIC* 430, §3), the bishop functions as diocesan administrator in the diocese from which he is being transferred and enjoys his regular income in that connection. In such a situation his former vicar general and/or episcopal vicars lose any power they might have exercised unless they are auxiliary bishops (c. 402, §2). The revised law is somewhat more stringent than the 1917 Code in requiring the transferred bishop to take possession of his new diocese within two months of his appointment rather than four months as was formerly true.

Interim Government before Administrator

Canon 419 — When the see is vacant, until the establishment of a diocesan administrator, the governance of the diocese devolves upon the auxiliary bishop or if there are several, upon the senior auxiliary bishop in terms of promotion, or if there is no auxiliary bishop upon the college of consultors, unless the Holy See has provided otherwise; whoever assumes the governance of the diocese in this fashion is to convoke without delay the college which is competent to designate the diocesan administrator.

If the diocese is not vacant due to the transfer of the bishop, ordinary episcopal authority passes immediately to the auxiliary bishop (or to the senior

---

[87]In this general connection it would be good to consult the general canons on loss of ecclesiastical office (cc. 184–196).

auxiliary in terms of appointment if there are several) until the election of the administrator.[88] This also presupposes that no coadjutor bishop assumes the leadership of the diocese. The present law somewhat modifies the former Code, which provided that such authority passed immediately to the chapter/diocesan consultors unless special provisions had been made by the Holy See or an apostolic administrator (*CIC* 312–318) had been appointed (*CIC* 431, §1). If there is no auxiliary, however, the above-mentioned authority passes to the college of consultors as had been the case in the former Code. This new provision may be another effort to enhance the status of the auxiliary and perhaps ensure that he is chosen administrator by the college of consultors. In any event the key function of diocesan leadership at this point is expediting the arrangements for the election of the diocesan administrator by the competent group. This is usually the college of consultors, but it may be another corporate body if special provisions are made in particular law.[89] The reference to convoking the competent college "without delay" is further specified by canon 421, §1, which requires the election of the administrator within eight days of the vacancy of the see.

Interim Government in Missions

Canon 420 — Unless the Holy See has determined otherwise, when the see is vacant in an apostolic vicariate or prefecture, its governance is assumed by a pro-vicar or pro-prefect named for this purpose by the vicar or prefect immediately after taking possession.

The needs of missionary churches are addressed by this canon, which requires the apostolic vicar or prefect to name a pro-vicar or pro-prefect to succeed the former when the see is vacant in order to provide for continuity in government. A comparable provision of the 1917 Code (*CIC* 309) treated this issue more extensively. Such a canon may be used as a point of reference in dealing with certain issues not explicitly addressed in the present law, e.g., the procedure to be followed if no pro-vicar or pro-prefect is named. As is true for all of the above-mentioned situations, the Holy See may always intervene and make special provisions.

Election of Administrator

Canon 421 — §1. Within eight days of receiving the notice of the vacancy of the episcopal see, the diocesan administrator, that is, he who governs the diocese in the interim, must be elected by the college of consultors, with due regard for the prescription of can. 502, §3.

§2. If within the prescribed time the diocesan administrator for any reason at all has not been legitimately elected, the choosing of the same devolves upon the metropolitan, and if the vacant see is itself the metropolitan church or the metropolitan church is vacant as well as the suffragan, it devolves upon the senior suffragan bishop in terms of promotion.

The present law reaffirms the traditional approach to interim diocesan government dating back especially to the Council of Trent. Prior to Trent the chapter of canons was generally free to determine how the diocese was to be governed during the vacancy: corporately by the chapter or through its members succeeding one another in turn or through a representative completely dependent on its will. Trent curtailed the chapter's freedom in this regard and required its choosing a vicar capitular who would govern the diocese until the see was filled. Although he was chosen by the chapter, the vicar was independent of it and could not be removed by it. This approach reflects the preference for monarchical as distinct from collegial government patterns that has characterized much of the Church's legal history.

The 1917 Code embodied that Tridentine requirement of a vicar capitular normally chosen by the chapter in its treatment of the vacant see (*CIC* 430–444). The present Code somewhat simplifies the prior law but maintains its fundamental thrust. Paragraph one states that within eight days of notification of the vacancy of the see, the college of consultors is to elect the diocesan administrator for the duration of the vacancy (*CIC* 432, §1). The preeminent role of the college is highlighted; however, its authority during the vacancy is restricted, particularly regarding its relationship to the administrator, who generally functions independently of it. Canon 502, §3 alludes to the possibility that a conference of bishops may determine that the cathedral chapter is to function as the college of consultors. If an auxiliary bishop has assumed the leadership of the diocese according to canon 419, he presides at the meeting of the college to elect the administrator; otherwise, it is the senior member of the college of consultors in terms of ordination.

The supervisory role of the metropolitan in the province (c. 436, §1, 3°) is exemplified again in paragraph two, providing for his choosing the administrator if the college fails to do so within the re-

---

[88]For the legal status of this interim leadership figure, see c. 426. This is also true if the college of consultors functions in this role.

[89]One might note that *CIC* 431, §2 mentioned the possibility of a special Holy See provision for the archbishop or another bishop to choose the diocesan administrator. However, this canon was dropped in the revised Code. See Abbo-Hannan II, 432.

quired eight-day period.[90] The metropolitan remedies the deficiencies of the suffragan diocese in fulfilling the requirements of law. If the metropolitan see itself is vacant, the senior suffragan of the province chooses the administrator of the archdiocese if its college of consultors is derelict in its electoral duty for whatever reason.

Notification of Holy See

Canon 422 — The auxiliary bishop, or if there is none, the college of consultors, is to inform the Holy See immediately of the death of the bishop; the one elected diocesan administrator is to do the same concerning his own election.

As was true for the impeded see (c. 413, §3), there is a concern that the Holy See be notified of the vacancy if its action has not occasioned the vacancy in the first place. Practically speaking, the only situation in which the present canon is operative is the case of the death of the bishop when the auxiliary bishop mentioned in canon 419 or the college of consultors is to notify the Holy See of such a development. Likewise the importance of ongoing communications between the Holy See and the particular church underlies the requirement that the administrator-elect notify the Holy See of his election (*CIC* 432, §4).

Only One Administrator/ Distinction from Finance Officer

Canon 423 — §1. One person is to be chosen diocesan administrator, and all contrary customs are revoked; otherwise the election is invalid.

§2. The diocesan administrator is not to be the finance officer at the same time; accordingly if the finance officer of the diocese has been elected administrator another temporary finance officer is to be chosen by the finance council.

This and the following two canons deal with the election of the administrator and certain qualifications for office, some for validity and some for liceity.

Like the 1917 Code (*CIC* 433, §1) the present law prohibits electing more than one administrator, presumably in the interests of unified diocesan government. Apparently this had been a disputed issue before the 1917 Code, and there were contrary customs involving the election of more than one administrator. The law does not simply prohibit the election of more than one administrator; it also invalidates any such election (§1).

A concern for fiscal accountability seems to underlie the prohibition of the administrator's simultaneously functioning as diocesan finance officer.[91] Hence, if the diocesan finance officer (c. 494) is chosen diocesan administrator, the diocesan finance council (cc. 492–493) is to choose another finance officer pro tempore until a new bishop is appointed. The importance of the council's role here is clear from the fact that normally the bishop alone appoints all significant diocesan officers (§2).

Election of Administrator

Canon 424 — The diocesan administrator is to be elected according to the norms of cann. 165-178.

The election of the diocesan administrator is a true canonical election and is therefore governed by canons 165–178. Whatever the law requires for a valid and licit election is required for the valid and licit election of the administrator. Of course if the requirements for liceity alone are violated, the administrator-elect may still assume the office and function in accord with the subsequent canons.

The 1917 Code required an absolute majority of the electors for one to be chosen diocesan administrator (vicar capitular) (*CIC* 433, §2). This requirement was somewhat stricter than the ordinary rules on elections in canons 174 and 101, §1, 1° of the 1917 Code which permitted certain elections without such an absolute majority after several ballots. That 1917 Code requirement of an absolute majority is dropped in the present law; hence, canons 178 and 119, §1, 1° providng for other options as well are the operative laws in this respect.[92]

Qualifications of Administrator

Canon 425 — §1. To be validly chosen diocesan administrator one must be a priest of at least thirty-five years of age who has not been elected, nominated or presented for the same vacant see.

§2. A priest who is outstanding in doctrine and prudence is to be elected diocesan administrator.

§3. If the conditions previously mentioned in §1 have been neglected, the metropolitan, or if the metropolitan church itself is vacant, the senior suffragan bishop in terms of promotion, having ascertained the truth of the matter, is to appoint an administrator in his stead; the acts of the one who

---

[90]This should be understood as "useful time" in accordance with c. 201, §2.

[91]This incompatibility of offices differs from the 1917 Code which did not view the roles of administrator and finance officer as incompatible (*CIC* 433, §3). However, the notion of "finance officer" meant something different in the 1917 Code than it does in c. 494 and elsewhere. In the former law it referred to a situation in which the chapter was in some way responsible for the collection of revenue. However, this was not true for the diocesan consultors in the U.S.; hence, those provisions of law on the finance officer (econome) were not really relevant in the American context.

[92]See the commentary on cc. 119; 165–178.

was elected contrary to the prescriptions of §1 are invalid by law.

Paragraph one requires that the validly elected administrator be a priest who is at least thirty-five years of age and has not been elected, nominated, or presented for the see in question, all preliminary steps requiring the subsequent intervention by higher authority. The revised Code thereby raises the minimum age from thirty years of age (*CIC* 434, §1). This corresponds to the raising of the minimum age for the episcopate from thirty (*CIC* 331, §1, 2°) to thirty-five (c. 378, 3°). Paragraph two indicates that for the liceity of the election the priest elected should be outstanding in learning and prudence. No other requirements are specified in universal law for the eligibility of candidates for administrator. Particular law may add its own specifications provided they do not contradict the Code.

The surrogate role of the metropolitan in certain instances of legal violations in the suffragan churches (c. 436, §1, 3°) is exemplified once again in paragraph three, treating of the college's election of a candidate not meeting the requirements for validity specified in paragraph one. The metropolitan may choose the administrator in such an instance once he is aware of the situation. If the metropolitan see is affected, the senior suffragan fulfills the surrogate electoral role. Such a surrogate function is exercised only in this instance; no ordinary right of electing an administrator is acquired either by the metropolitan or the senior suffragan. If for some reason neither the metropolitan nor the senior suffragan is aware of the invalid election, this does not change the legal situation; any acts of the invalidly elected administrator would be null. Interestingly enough, the revised Code does not explicitly require the metropolitan or the senior suffragan to be informed of the election of the administrator although the Holy See is to be notified (c. 422). On the contrary, canon 467 requires the declarations and decrees of a diocesan synod to be forwarded to the metropolitan.

Status of One Governing Diocese before Administrator

Canon 426 — **Whoever governs the diocese while the see is vacant and before an administrator is designated enjoys the power which the law grants to the vicar general.**

This provision on the status of the one governing the diocese immediately upon its being vacant should seemingly have been situated along with canon 419 on interim diocesan government prior to the election of an administrator. However, comparable to the 1917 Code (*CIC* 435, §1), it is treated in the immediate context of the next canon on the

legal status of the administrator (c. 427). Whoever governs the vacant diocese before the administrator is chosen is comparable to a vicar general when the see is filled; hence, one should consult the commentary on canons 475–481 to clarify the full implications of this canon. Certain canons of the 1917 Code are dropped in light of this general provision, e.g., canon 435, §2 of the former law on the execution of pontifical rescripts sent to the bishop and the possession of habitual faculties.[93]

Status of Administrator

Canon 427 — **§1. The diocesan administrator is bound by the obligations and enjoys the power of the diocesan bishop, excluding those things which are excepted by their very nature or by the law itself.**
§2. Once the diocesan administrator has accepted the election he obtains power; no further confirmation is required, but the obligation of can. 833, §4, remains.

This noteworthy canon treats of the obligations and power of the diocesan administrator (§1) and the point at which he technically obtains such authority (§2). Like canons 381, §1 and 391, §1 on the diocesan bishop, this text cryptically affirms the administrator's rights and obligations, the scope of which can be appreciated properly only through a detailed examination of the revised Code.

In general, the fact that the administrator fulfills the most significant leadership position in the particular church means that he normally enjoys a legal status comparable to the diocesan bishop himself (§1). Hence where the law reads "diocesan bishop," one can usually substitute the term "diocesan administrator." However, since the administrator functions only on an interim basis until the see is filled, the law at times explicitly prohibits his functioning like the diocesan bishop; this normally happens in fairly significant issues of diocesan government.[94] Furthermore, if the administrator is not a bishop, certain distinctly episcopal prerogatives especially in the sacramental arena are outside his sphere of competence. These limitations on the office of the administrator need to be seen in connection with the following canon prohibiting

---

[93]Furthermore, a reference to permitting another bishop to exercise pontifical functions in the diocese is also dropped (*CIC* 435, §2).

[94]At times the administrator is barred from acting at all. For example, he may not establish public associations of the faithful (c. 312, §1, 3°). He may not convoke a diocesan synod (c. 462, §1). He may not entrust a parish to a religious community (c. 520, §1). He may not grant dimissorials to a candidate who has been denied them by the bishop (c. 1018, §2). At times he may function but subject to restrictions not normally binding the bishop. He may remove the chancellor or the notaries only with the consent of the college of consultors (c. 485). He may permit the secret diocesan archives to be opened but only in

significant innovations in the diocese during the vacancy.

The legislator's intention to stress the independence of the administrator is clear from the fact that he obtains his office simply by the acceptance of his election without there being a need for anyone to confirm that election (*CIC* 438).[95] The administrator is obliged to make a profession of faith in the presence of the college of consultors (c. 833, 4°). This is comparable to the bishop's obligation to make a similar profession of faith though there is no reference to an oath of loyalty to the Holy See in this context (c. 380).

One might note the dropping of an explicit 1917 Code prohibition of the chapter's retaining any jurisdiction for itself, limiting the term of the diocesan administrator (vicar capitular), or placing any other restrictions on the exercise of his office. Apparently it is judged that the legal situation has sufficiently changed so that there is no longer any need for such a canon, which referred to certain pre-1917 Code problems in chapter-vicar capitular relationships (*CIC* 437).

No Innovations during Vacancy

Canon 428 — **§1. When the see is vacant there are to be no innovations.**

§2. Those who temporarily govern the diocese are prohibited from doing anything which could in any way be prejudicial to the diocese or episcopal rights; they themselves and any other persons are specifically prohibited from removing, destroying or altering any documents of the diocesan curia, whether personally or through another.

Two canons of the 1917 Code are reaffirmed here in an apparent effort by the legislator to preclude noteworthy problems for the future bishop and to protect the diocese against the administrator's making unwise decisions with possibly adverse long-term implications. The two paragraphs of the canon are interrelated since the second helps to clarify the meaning of the first.

The first paragraph restates the general principle of canon 436 of the 1917 Code; there are to be no innovations in the diocese during the vacancy of the see. This does not mean that the administrator may

not make decisions that would redound to the benefit of the diocese or the future bishop. Rather, in light of paragraph two, what is envisioned is the administrator's doing something that could be detrimental to the diocese or the future bishop. What is prohibited is the administrator's prejudicing the diocese or episcopal rights by his actions (*CIC* 435, §3). More specifically, the law prohibits the administrator or anyone else from tampering with official diocesan documents in view of their relevance in clarifying diocesan and episcopal rights especially. Such tampering may involve removing such documents from the archives, destroying them, or in any way altering them. Such violations can make the administrator or another individual liable to a just penalty (c. 1391, especially 1°).

Residence/Mass for People

Canon 429 — **The diocesan administrator is obliged to reside in the diocese and to apply Mass for the people according to the norm of can. 388.**

Like the diocesan bishop, the administrator is bound by the obligations of residence (c. 395) and Mass for the people of the diocese (c. 388). The explicit affirmation of such obligations here indicates the seriousness with which the legislator takes their observance (*CIC* 440).[96]

Cessation of Administrator's Office

Canon 430 — **§1. The responsibilities of the diocesan administrator cease with the taking possession of the diocese by the new bishop.**

§2. The removal of the diocesan administrator is reserved to the Holy See; any resignation must be presented in authentic form to the college which is competent to elect but it does not have to be accepted by this body; if the diocesan administrator has been removed or resigned or dies another administrator is to be elected according to the norm of can. 421.

Somewhat comparable to the canons on the impeded (c. 412) and vacant (c. 416) see, this canon summarizes in two paragraphs the various ways in which the administrator ceases functioning in the diocese. The first paragraph might be said to be the ordinary way that the office ceases while the second indicates somewhat extraordinary ways of its cessation.

The normal way that the administrator ceases functioning is when the vacant see is filled and the new bishop takes possession of the diocese (*CIC* 443, §2) (§1). Even if the administrator himself is the new bishop, he can function only as the admin-

---

case of necessity (c. 490, §1). He may issue dimissorials but only with the consent of the college of consultors (c. 1018, §1, 2°).

  At times he may act only after the see has been vacant for a year. With the consent of the college of consultors, he may grant letters of excardination or incardination or permit a cleric to migrate to another particular church (c. 272). He may name pastors on his own whereas during the first year of the vacancy he can only install or confirm pastors who are presented (e.g., religious pastors) or elected in virtue of special legal provisions (c. 525, 1°–2°).

[95] A comparable legal situation is the election of the pope, which is not confirmed by anyone (c. 332, §1).

[96] For further explanations of the two obligations, the commentary on the relevant canons should be consulted.

istrator until he formally takes possession of the diocese (c. 382).

The independence of the administrator is clear from the second paragraph on various ways that he may cease functioning prior to the filling of the vacant see. His removal from office is reserved to the Holy See; the college of consultors which elected him has no power in this respect. However, no criteria warranting his removal are specified in law unlike the provisions for due cause in the removal of pastors (c. 1741). Furthermore, the administrator may resign his office. Although his resignation is to be submitted to the college which elected him, it is not necessary that this college formally accept it.[97] It is sufficient that it be done in writing or orally before two witnesses (c. 189, §1).

Finally, the interests of continuity in diocesan government underlie the provision that the competent college elect another administrator in place of the removed, retired, or deceased administrator. Canon 421 and the other relevant norms on the election of the administrator are operative in this connection.

Before finishing this part of the commentary, it would be appropriate to note that certain canons of the 1917 Code have been omitted in the present law. In light of the separate provisions for the diocesan finance officer (c. 494), certain canons on the activities of the finance officer (econome)[98] and his relationship to the vicar capitular are presumably unnecessary (*CIC* 441–442). Somewhat surprisingly the revised law drops canon 444 of the former law requiring the new bishop to request a report on the activities of the administrator, the finance officer (econome), the chapter, and other officials appointed to act during the vacancy. The 1973 report of the committee indicated that a reworked version of canon 444 of the 1917 Code would be part of the revised law.[99] However, this decision was apparently changed during the revision process. The norm might not be relevant if the administrator becomes the new bishop; however, it seems to serve the best interests of ecclesial accountability if the new bishop is from outside the diocese or perhaps is from within the diocese but has not been significantly involved in its functioning during the vacancy.[100]

---

[97]This provision is also comparable to c. 332, §2 on the papal resignation which need not be accepted by anyone. See also c. 189, §1.

[98]See note 91.

[99]See *Comm* 5 (1973), 235.

[100]Interestingly enough, c. 540, §3 provides for the parish administrator's presenting such a report to the new pastor.

BIBLIOGRAPHY

Commentaries on the 1917 Code

Abbo, J., and Hannan, J. *The Sacred Canons.* 2 vols. Vol. I, 353–377, 427–439. St. Louis: B. Herder Book Co., 1952 (cited as Abbo-Hannan and volume).

Bouscaren, T., and Ellis, A. *Canon Law.* 150–153, 173–178, 184–187. Milwaukee: The Bruce Publishing Co., 1946.

Vermeersch, A., and Creusen, I. *Epitome Iuris Canonici.* 3 vols., editio septima. Vol. I, 284–287, 347–360, 393–397. Mechliniae-Romae: H. Dessain, 1956.

Commentaries on Pertinent Conciliar Documents

Moersdorf, K. "Decree on the Bishops' Pastoral Office in the Church," in Vorgrimler II, 165–301.

Rahner, K. "Dogmatic Constitution on the Church: Chapter III, articles 18–27," in Vorgrimler I, 186–217.

Official Code Commission Reports on the Formulation of This Part of the Revised Code

Onclin, W. "De clericis—de sacra hierarchia." *Comm* 5 (1973): 216–224, 233–235.

Pavoni, N. "Coetus studiorum 'De Populo Dei'." *Comm* 12 (1980): 275–314 (cc. 368–411).

———. "Coetus 'De Populo Dei'." *Comm* 13 (1981): 140–146 (cc. 412–430).

Pontificia Commissio Codici Iuris Canonici Recognoscendo. *Relatio complectens synthesim animadversionum ab em.mis atque exc.mis patribus Commissionis ad novissimum schema Codicis iuris Canonici exhibitarum, cum responsionibus a Secretaria et consultoribus datis.* Rome: Typis Polyglottis Vaticanis, 1981, 47–49, 98–109.

Insights on the Revised Code

Alesandro, J. "Law and Renewal: A Canon Lawyer's Analysis." *CLSAP* (1982): 1–40.

Aymans, W. "Ecclesiological Implications of the New Legislation." *CLS-GBIN* (June–September, 1982): 38–73.

Green, T. "Critical Reflections on the Schema on the People of God." *Stud Can* 14 (1980): 235–322 (cited as Green, "Critical Reflections").

———. "The Diocesan Bishop in the Revised Code: Some Introductory Reflections." *J* 42 (1982): 320–349 (cited as Green, "Diocesan Bishop").

Komonchak, J. "A New Law for the People of God: A Theological Evaluation." *CLSAP* (1980): 14–43.

Legrand, H. "The Revaluation of Local Churches: Some Theological Implications." *Con* 71 (1972): 53–64 (American ed.).

Mallet, J. "Diocesan Structure and Governance." *CLSAP* (1980): 151–160.

Morrisey, F. "The Importance of Particular Law in the New Code." *CLSAP* (1981): 1–17.

Provost, J. "The Impact of the Proposed Book II 'De Populo Dei' on the Local Church." *Stud Can* 15 (1981): 371–398.

TITLE II
GROUPINGS OF PARTICULAR CHURCHES
[cc. 431–459]

The Catholic Church is a communion of churches. Vatican II notes that one of the earliest expressions of this was found in the groupings of particular churches within a territory, and eventually within a larger cultural unit (*LG* 23). This development was given formal recognition and legal support by the early ecumenical councils. Today the structural organization of the Catholic Church still retains the basic structures developed under the Roman Empire of dioceses and provinces, and the special role of the bishop of the principal city or "metropolis" as metropolitan.

Vatican II called for a revitalization of these supradiocesan structures that involve the active and regular participation by the bishops of the area (*CD* 36, 40). It also introduced into formal church structures a practice that had been developing especially in recent decades, i.e., bishops in a nation or similar territory coming together in conferences for purposes of mutual support and to address certain common concerns (*CD* 37–38). Conferences of bishops were a major factor in implementing the reforms of Vatican II and constitute one of the new structures of the Church designed to express the spirit of the Council.

Following after the canons about particular churches themselves, this title addresses the structuring of such particular churches below the level of the universal Latin Church. The title itself is organized into four chapters. The first deals with territorial groupings of particular churches. The next three address bishops as metropolitans, as gathered in particular councils, and as working together in conferences of bishops.

The treatment here has some important differences from the 1917 Code (*CIC* 271–292). In the previous Code metropolitans and particular councils were viewed as participating in the supreme power of the Church, and conferences of bishops were periodic gatherings within provinces for inner-church business. In the revised Code these various structures are seen as groupings of particular churches, expressive of the solicitude of the bishops who pastor them. Conferences of bishops have a new and significant role within these structures, following on the determinations made in Vatican II and subsequent developments.

Major sources for these canons continue to be the 1917 Code's provisions on provinces, metropoli-

tans, and particular councils. *Christus Dominus* 36–41 dealt with these intermediary supradiocesan structures, and in particular established the basis for norms concerning conferences of bishops in *Christus Dominus* 37–38. Paul VI in *Ecclesiae sanctae* I, 41 provided some further refinements.

The canons themselves were drafted initially by the *coetus De clericis,* later named the *coetus De sacra hierarchia.* They were first published as canons 185–216 of the schema *De Populo Dei* in 1977. Revised in February 1980 in light of comments received on that draft, they were presented in revised form and in a slightly different organization as canons 306–334 of the 1980 schema. Further comments on both their content and their place in relationship to the canons on dioceses were made in the *Relatio* prepared for the 1981 meeting of the Code Commission, and at the meeting itself even further determinations were made as to their location in Book II.

It had been proposed earlier to organize this part of the Code by beginning with canons on structures of the universal Church, then canons on groupings of particular churches, and finally canons on particular churches themselves and their own internal organization. This was questioned, particularly at the 1981 meeting of the Code Commission, as not being faithful to Vatican II. The Council consistently dealt with the Church at the universal and particular levels and then with groupings of particular churches. This is the order adopted in the promulgated Code.

Within the canons on groupings of particular churches, it had first been proposed to deal with particular councils and conferences of bishops, then with metropolitans and primates. The role of conferences of bishops had been somewhat prominent in the 1977 draft *De Populo Dei,* a fact objected to by some bishops.[1] The revision of the canons which resulted in the 1980 schema produced the internal organization found in the final text: a description of the groupings of churches themselves, then a discussion of the episcopal leadership within these. That leadership is presented primarily in traditional terms of individuals (metropolitans), then collective leadership in particular councils and finally in conferences of bishops. The organization appears to reflect the criticism of the role assigned to conferences of bishops in the first (1977) draft.

---

[1]The criticism continued despite a more restricted approach adopted in the 1980 schema. See 1981 *Rel, Comm* 14 (1982), 124.

As to the content, there have been two major shifts. The first concerns the basic concept of how particular churches are grouped. The 1977 and 1980 drafts had both spoken of "ecclesiastical regions" as well as provinces. This was in keeping with *Christus Dominus* 40, 3°, which called for ecclesiastical provinces to be grouped into regions if this seemed useful. In an effort to avoid reliance on civil political divisions, which can themselves be in dispute, and to stress the ecclesial nature of the divisions being proposed in canon law, "ecclesiastical regions" were considered to be the grouping of ecclesiastical provinces either within a larger territory or coterminous with the ecclesiastical province. This was a roundabout way of describing a national conference of bishops, for example, without using the term "national." From a practical point of view this would respect the fact that in some nations there can be more than one conference of bishops; e.g., in the United States there are the National Conference of Catholic Bishops and the Conferencia Episcopal Puertorriquena, given that Puerto Rico is part of the United States.

The concept proved to be too unwieldy and the final text has dropped any reference to ecclesiastical regions in this sense.[2] Instead it retains ecclesiastical provinces as the primary grouping of dioceses and uses "nation or certain territory" to refer to the grouping of dioceses whose bishops form a conference. Ecclesiastical regions are now groupings of provinces within a nation, the understanding being that they are an intermediate level between the national and the provincial.

The second substantive shift that has taken place during the drafting process was mentioned earlier, namely, the respective importance of conferences of bishops. Not only has their placement been changed to come after the more traditional structures of metropolitans and particular councils, but also their competence has been diminished, at least insofar as items mentioned in the law itself are concerned.

---

[2]See discussion which led to the change, *Comm* 12 (1980), 244–251.

CANONS AND COMMENTARY ————————————

CHAPTER I
ECCLESIASTICAL PROVINCES AND ECCLESIASTICAL REGIONS
[cc. 431–434]

The Code retains the general principles of a territorial rather than a personal organization of the Church. For the first thousand years this applied to the organization of Ritual Churches as well as to the territorial divisions (provinces, dioceses, etc.) within them. While today rite is a personal division acquired through baptism (c. 111), Ritual Churches *sui iuris* are themselves organized primarily along territorial lines. This was a principle discussed and adopted anew at the beginning of the period of revision, and while it does admit of some exceptions within a diocese (e.g., personal parishes, c. 518), the basic organization of the Church above the level of diocese is still territorial.[3]

The basic territorial grouping of particular churches is the ecclesiastical province. It is com-

posed of neighboring dioceses—one of which is designated as the archdiocese whose bishop, the metropolitan, has a special role within the province. In about half the nations of the world there is only one province, coterminous with the national boundaries. In some parts of the world, the province includes several countries (e.g., Suva in the South Pacific). There are also other, larger and more populous areas where several provinces are found within a nation. If there are a number of provinces within the country, these can be organized into regions, so that there would be several regions within the one country. An example of this is the United States where the conference of bishops has, on an administrative basis, organized itself into thirteen regions, most of which include several provinces.

The law provides for various activities to be conducted on a provincial level. Provincial councils are the legislative body for an entire province. The bishops of the province meet even outside a provincial council to carry out various responsibilities, from proposing names of candidates for episcopal office (c. 377, §2) to setting certain fees and offerings (c. 1264) and determining Mass stipends (c. 952, §1). In some areas the churches of the prov-

---

[3]Principles for the Revision of the Code, 8: *Comm* 2 (1969), 84; English translation is in J. Hite et al., eds., *Readings, Cases, Materials in Canon Law* (Collegeville, Minn.: The Liturgical Press, 1980), 77.

ince coordinate various pastoral and evangelization activities on a provincial level.

Ecclesiastical Provinces

Canon 431 — **§1. Neighboring particular churches are to be brought together into ecclesiastical provinces limited to a certain territory in order that the common pastoral activity of the various neighboring dioceses may be promoted in accord with the circumstances of persons and places and in order that the relationships of the diocesan bishops among themselves may be more suitably fostered.**

§2. As a rule exempt dioceses are no longer to exist; individual dioceses, therefore, and the other particular churches which exist within the territory of an ecclesiastical province must belong to this ecclesiastical province.

§3. The supreme authority of the Church alone is competent to establish, suppress or change ecclesiastical provinces, after hearing the bishops involved.

The organization of neighboring particular churches into provinces has eminently pastoral purposes: to promote their common pastoral activity in a way suited to the particular circumstances of the area, and to develop the spirit of collegiality among the bishops involved. Because of these pastoral purposes, every diocese is to belong to an ecclesiastical province. However, since the determination of provinces goes beyond the authority of any individual bishop, the bishops involved are asked their advice, but the final decision to establish, suppress, or change an ecclesiastical province pertains to the supreme authority of the Church.

The canon is drawn from *Christus Dominus* 39 and 40; 39 is the source for much of paragraph one and 40, 2° provides the rule contained in paragraph two. Paragraph three finds its source in the 1917 Code (*CIC* 215, §1).

The Church is more than small groupings or even dioceses; it is God's people as they live in the specific circumstances of time and place, and these often cross the boundaries of dioceses as such. The larger pastoral zone of a province provides the possibility for coordinated pastoral planning and action while retaining the more local identity of diocese and parishes. Similarly the bishops of an area know by experience the conditions of the Church in that area and the persons who make up the Church there. For the various matters on which provinces must act or when their advice is sought, this more immediate knowledge is important for the welfare of the Church universal.

Provinces, therefore, are not to be merely formal entities, i.e., paper organizations without an effect on the life of the people of God. They are groupings of churches, not just bishops; the people of the various particular churches have a right to provincial

and not just diocesan involvement. This is formalized in a special manner in the regulations on particular councils (cc. 443–445), but the informal and ongoing relationships within the province are presumed not only for the effective functioning of a council but by the very spirit and description of a province found in this canon.

Exempt dioceses are those that are exempt from any province and the supervision of a metropolitan (archbishop) and are directly subject to the Holy See. For example, the dioceses of Switzerland are each subject directly to the Holy See; there is no ecclesiastical province there. The same is true of the dioceses of the Scandinavian countries and of certain other individual dioceses for various historical circumstances. The Council called for an end to this practice (*CD* 40, 2°), unless unusual factors argued otherwise.

Both the Council (*CD* 41) and *Ecclesiae sanctae* (I, 42) called for a revitalization of provinces and asked that the conferences of bishops examine whether more suitable boundaries should be set for provinces in their area. The results of such study were to be forwarded to the Holy See which would make the final determination.

Authority in Province

Canon 432 — **§1. In accord with the norm of law the provincial council and the metropolitan possess authority within the ecclesiastical province.**

§2. An ecclesiastical province enjoys juridic personality by the law itself.

There are two agents of authority in the province: the metropolitan and the provincial council. Their authority is in reference to the province as such, which by law is a juridic person (hence, a public juridic person: c. 116, §2).

The authority which a metropolitan and a provincial council have within the province is that which is specified in law. The law is quite specific about the limits to this authority, that is, on the limits to the ability to bind others by their decisions. One should see discussion below on each for further details.

Ecclesiastical Regions

Canon 433 — **§1. If it appears useful, especially in nations where particular churches are more numerous, neighboring ecclesiastical provinces can be united into ecclesiastical regions by the Holy See at the proposal of the conference of bishops.**

§2. An ecclesiastical region can be erected into a juridic person.

Canon 434 — **The gathering of the bishops of an ecclesiastical region is to foster cooperation and common pastoral action in the region; however, the** powers which are given in the canons of this code to the conference of bishops do not belong to such a gathering, unless some of them shall have been specially granted to it by the Holy See.

Vatican II called for provinces to be joined together into ecclesiastical regions, where this seemed useful (*CD* 40, 3°). It did not give any further specification of what such regions might be. The Code now identifies them as groupings of provinces within nations where there are a number of particular churches. Such regions may be erected as juridic persons, but they need not be. The authority of the bishops within them is not the same as that belonging to the conference of bishops, which includes the bishops of all the ecclesiastical regions within the nation or similar territory (c. 447).

As discussed earlier, the concept of ecclesiastical region has gone through several stages in the process of drafting the Code. At first it appeared as the territory which served as the basis for determining the conference of bishops, and special rules were made in cases in which provinces and regions were coterminous with each other, i.e., where the province included the entire nation. The more simplified notion in the final text is closer to the administrative divisions developed by the National Conference of Catholic Bishops in the United States, for example, which groups bishops according to various geographical regions of the country.

However, the canonical concept of "region" is still different from the administrative practice in the United States. Ecclesiastical regions include several provinces, whereas some of the National Conference of Catholic Bishops regions are coterminous with a particular province. Ecclesiastical regions can be erected only by the Holy See, at the suggestion of the conference of bishops, whereas the administrative regions of the National Conference of Catholic Bishops are a practical arrangement determined by the bishops themselves.

CHAPTER II
METROPOLITANS
[cc. 435–438]

From the earliest days of the Church a special relationship existed between "mother" and "daughter" churches, that is, between churches which had evangelized other communites which hence were considered to be their "daughters." This relationship existed between larger towns in an area, where the faith first took hold, and the smaller towns in that region. In the Eastern Empire, which was divided into provinces, this led by the fourth century to the name "metropolitan" being applied to the mother church (the "metropolis" of the area) and its bishop. Early councils confirmed the authority of metropolitans in the surrounding churches.

The West did not have the same organization into provinces as in the Eastern Roman Empire, but the older and more active churches in evangelization were recognized as "metropolitan." By the sixth century the bishops there were called archbishops, and by the eighth century the bishops subject to them became known as "suffragans" because they could vote (*suffragio*) in a provincial council. The metropolitans exercised important authority in their area: they confirmed the election of suffragan bishops and consecrated them, convened and presided over provincial councils, maintained discipline over their suffragans and supplied for their ministry in cases of negligence, and served as a court of appeal from decisions in the diocesan courts of their suffragans.

Abuses occurred over the course of centuries and gradually the rights of metropolitans were restricted, primarily by the Roman Pontiff who reserved many of these functions to himself. The Council of Trent reorganized the role of metropolitans (sess. XXIV, cc. 2 and 3 *de ref.*), further restricting their functions but calling on renewed coordination within the province through regular provincial councils.

The 1917 Code further restricted the rights of metropolitans and clarified their prerogatives (*CIC* 272–280). The revised Code further simplifies the norms concerning metropolitans (cc. 435–438).

Determination

Canon 435 — **The metropolitan, who is the archbishop of the diocese which he heads, presides over an ecclesiastical province; this office is connected with an episcopal see which has been determined or approved by the Roman Pontiff.**

The office of metropolitan is tied to a particular see. The bishop of that see is called an archbishop, but within his own diocese he has only the usual powers of a diocesan bishop; in addition, he exercises certain other powers over the neighboring dioceses which with his own form an ecclesiastical province.

The canon is based on canon 272 of the 1917 Code. There are two notable changes. The first distinguishes between the titles "metropolitan" and "archbishop," which the 1917 Code had made synonymous. There are some archbishops who are not metropolitans, so there is indeed a distinction between the two titles.

The second change makes reference to the metropolitan as having an "office," whereas the 1917 Code termed it a "dignity." The emphasis, in keeping with the spirit of the revised Code, is on the service which a metropolitan is to provide rather than on his privileges (which are dealt with in a very cursory fashion in the revised Code).

The office of metropolitan is fixed to a particular diocese rather than depending on the qualities of the individual who exercises the office. He is not elected as a chairman of the province by the bishops of the area, but in virtue of the pope's designation or approbation his diocese always serves as the metropolitan see for the province.

Presiding over an ecclesiastical province may mean quite a bit in some parts of the world, i.e., where the province is coterminous with the national boundaries. In other areas, where several provinces exist within a single nation, the conference of bishops tends to be more significant and to have a more organized staff than the individual provinces.

Authority over Suffragans

Canon 436 — §1. Within the suffragan dioceses the metropolitan is competent:

1° to be vigilant that the faith and ecclesiastical discipline are carefully preserved and to inform the Roman Pontiff of abuses if there are any;

2° to perform the canonical visitation if the suffragan bishop has neglected it, after the reason for doing so has first been approved by the Apostolic See;

3° to appoint a diocesan administrator in accord with the norm of cann. 421, §2 and 425, §3.

§2. Where circumstances demand it a metropolitan can be invested by the Apostolic See with special duties and power to be determined in particular law.

§3. The metropolitan possesses no other power of governance within the suffragan dioceses; he can, however, perform sacred functions in all the churches as if he were a bishop in his own diocese, but he is to inform the diocesan bishop if it is the cathedral church.

The power of metropolitans is strictly limited to those items specified in the canon (§3), although special powers can be delegated to a metropolitan by the pope under certain circumstances (§2). This limitation is in keeping with the tradition of putting a check on the authority of metropolitans—a development begun in the Middle Ages.

The canon is drawn from canon 274 of the 1917 Code, but with several changes. The previous Code dealt with supplying for installation of those presented by patrons for a benefice if the suffragan omitted doing so without cause, granting indulgences, serving as a court of second instance and even as a court of first instance for certain types of contentious cases involving suffragan bishops. It also provided considerable detail about what the metropolitan could do when authorized to conduct a visitation of a suffragan's diocese. Many of these have been dropped or significantly changed in the revised Code.

Vigilance over faith and morals has traditionally been a responsibility of metropolitans. In the early Church this was accomplished at the regular meetings of provincial councils during which the bish-

ops of the area worked together to see to proper faith and morals in their churches. Such councils were enjoined by the Council of Trent for the same purpose (sess. XXIV, c. 2 *de. ref.*). They are given renewed form in the revised Code (cc. 439–446) with a more pastoral emphasis on safeguarding faith and morals (c. 445).

The metropolitan's vigilance, however, does not give him any governing power over the suffragan dioceses. He is rather to report any difficulties to the Apostolic See, so that his role is more an information gathering one than one of active intervention.

Continuing an ancient tradition, the metropolitan may supply for the visitation of a suffragan's diocese if that bishop fails to accomplish this responsibility (see cc. 396–398 on the bishop's visitation). However, the metropolitan needs the prior approval of the Apostolic See before he undertakes such a task, emphasizing again that his own office is more a coordination and communications function than one of governance within the dioceses of suffragans.

The metropolitan may appoint the diocesan administrator in a suffragan diocese if the consultors (or where they have this right, the chapter of canons) have failed to elect the administrator within the prescribed time (c. 421, §2) or have elected someone who lacks the necessary qualifications for the position (c. 425, §3).

Other duties and powers can be granted by the Apostolic See under circumstances which demand it and which would give the metropolitan extraordinary authority within the province. This is not further specified in the Code but is left to particular law.

The canon does not mention other governmental functions that the metropolitan exercises within the province, although not directly within the dioceses of suffragans. With the consent of a majority of the suffragan bishops he has a special role in regard to provincial councils (c. 442), and he convenes meetings of the bishops of the province to determine various financial matters such as Mass stipends (c. 952, §1), stole fees and the tax for acts of discretionary executive power, etc. (c. 1264).

The metropolitan's tribunal is the usual court of second instance for the tribunals of the suffragan dioceses (c. 1438, 1°) and serves as the court of first instance in actions concerning the rights or temporal goods of a juridic person represented by a suffragan bishop (c. 1419, §2, an exception to the usual norm that bishops are judged in contentious cases by the Roman Rota: c. 1405, §3, 1°).

In addition to the governmental powers listed above, the metropolitan has liturgical prerogatives within the suffragan dioceses, performing sacred functions (pontificals) in those dioceses as if he were the local bishop. The only restriction is that to do so within the cathedral church of a suffragan's diocese, he must first notify the local diocesan bishop. Usual courtesy among bishops provides for such advance communication in all other cases of an archbishop's exercising pontifical functions in a suffragan's diocese, although this is not required by law.

Pallium

Canon 437 — §1. Within three months from the reception of episcopal consecration or from the time of canonical provision if he has already been consecrated a bishop, a metropolitan is obliged personally or through his proxy to request the pallium of the Roman Pontiff; the pallium signifies the power with which the metropolitan is invested by law within his own province in communion with the Roman Church.

§2. In accord with the norm of liturgical laws a metropolitan can use the pallium in any church whatsoever within the ecclesiastical province over which he presides, but not outside it, even if the diocesan bishop gives his assent.

§3. A metropolitan requires a new pallium if he is transferred to another metropolitan see.

The pallium is a circular band of white woolen cloth with two hanging strips, worn by an archbishop over his shoulders on top of the vestments at Mass and in other solemn liturgical celebrations. It is marked by six dark purple crosses. The pallium is a symbol of the metropolitan's authority in communion with the Church of Rome; it pertains to the metropolitan see he occupies, so that if he is transferred to a new metropolitan see he must obtain a new one.

The canon is a much simplified set of provisions drawn on canons 275–279 of the 1917 Code, and it reflects the reforms made by Paul VI in the *motu proprio Inter eximia episcopalis.*[4] The former norm restricting the exercise of certain archiepiscopal functions until after the pallium had been obtained in Rome (*CIC* 276) has been dropped, as have certain other details found in the former Code.

The origins of the pallium are obscure.[5] It may be derived from festive garb worn by nobles in the Roman Empire at various feasts. It was first adopted by bishops in the East and is retained in the "omophorion" worn by them at the Eucharist. Patriarchs conferred it on their metropolitans, and these latter did likewise on their suffragans. In the West it was first adopted by the popes, who later began sending it to certain bishops as a sign of esteem. In the ninth century it became mandatory for metropolitans to

petition the pallium from the pope to confirm the authority they held within their provinces. In the Middle Ages it was seen as a sign of the "plenitude of pontifical power" and considered a delegation of authority from the pope. The 1917 Code continued to view the role of metropolitans as a participation in papal power; hence, there developed the restriction on carrying out certain archiepiscopal functions until the pallium had been obtained, unless a special indult permitted otherwise (*CIC* 276).

The role of the metropolitan in the revised Code is not seen as a direct participation in papal authority. Restrictions based on obtaining the pallium have been dropped, but the pallium remains a symbol of authority and the requirement to petition it is retained. This must be done either personally or through a proxy within three months of taking possession of the metropolitan see (or being consecrated).

The pallium is made from wool shorn from sheep presented to the pope each year on the Feast of St. Agnes. It is to be petitioned formally at a consistory, but the actual conferring of it has become a privilege of the senior cardinal deacon.

Liturgical law governs the use of the pallium. It may be used only within the ecclesiastical province over which the metropolitan presides. It is particular to that province; therefore, a new one would have to be petitioned if the metropolitan is transferred to a new metropolitan see.

Patriarchs and Primates

Canon 438 — The title of patriarch or primate besides being a prerogative of honor, carries with it no power of governance in the Latin Church unless the contrary is clear in some instances in virtue of apostolic privilege or approved custom.

The pope is the traditional "Patriarch of the West." All other bishops within the Western Church are subject to him, so even those with the honorary title of "patriarch" have it in a somewhat analogous sense, not in the same sense as the traditional patriarchs of the early Church. Similarly, primates within nations have only an honorary title unless special provisions are made otherwise.

This canon is similar to canon 271 of the 1917 Code, which additionally made mention of the rights of precedence. All questions of precedence have been removed from the revised Code and pertain to liturgical law.

The title "patriarch," which was one common term for a bishop in some areas of the early Church, was gradually reserved to the three major sees recognized in canon 6 of the Council of Nicaea: Rome, Alexandria, and Antioch. The title was also applied to the bishop of Jerusalem because of the special honor in which that see was held (c. 7 of the

[4] Paul VI, *mp Inter eximia episcopalis,* May 11, 1978, *CLD* 9, 192–194.

[5] See H. Orioli, "La collazione del pallio," *Nu* 4 (1976), 88–96; S. Sipos, *Enchiridion Iuris Canonici,* 7th ed. (Rome: Herder, 1960), 184–186.

Council of Nicaea), and later the bishop of Constantinople acquired its use.

After the schism between East and West and following the Crusades, Latin patriarchs were established in traditional Eastern patriarchal sees, particularly Jerusalem. The Latin Patriarch of Jerusalem is a title still in use. Venice, because of its contacts with the East, was later granted the title of Patriarch which is also still in use. During the voyages of exploration certain new patriarchates were established, at first with considerable authority over the new lands: Lisbon in Portugal, and patriarchs for the East and West Indies. These titles also remain, but none of them carries a special jurisdiction any longer.

Primatial sees are those with a special historical and, at times, jurisdictional importance within a nation. Carthage was a primatial see in North Africa in the early Church. During the Middle Ages a number of primatial sees were established in Europe—several of which survive to this day—ranging from Armagh in Ireland to Warsaw in Poland.

A primatial see has no particular jurisdiction attached to it; it is a designation of honor. However, particular law or custom has given to some primatial sees a special responsibility for the Church within that country. For example, the Primate of Poland exercises special faculties in marriage cases and for other internal affairs of the Church in that country.

CHAPTER III
PARTICULAR COUNCILS
[cc. 439–446]

Particular councils have been an important feature of Catholic life from the earliest centuries. Bishops of an area gathered to discuss common concerns in regard to faith and discipline. Such councils assumed a special importance as the Church expanded to new areas and proved so useful that Constantine drew on their example in convening the first ecumenical council.

Councils in the early Church were legislative and judicial bodies as well as occasions when the bishops exercised their teaching office. At times the gathering included bishops of a restricted area, such as a province; at other times a larger territory was included, involving several provinces (as in the councils in North Africa by the time of Augustine). These latter became known as plenary councils; the former are provincial councils.

Legislation governing the holding of councils dates from some of the earliest ecumenical councils. This was especially true of provincial councils. The first ecumenical council (Nicaea, 325 A.D.) mandated that provincial councils be held twice a year (c. 5). This rule was reaffirmed in 451 by the Council of Chalcedon (c. 19) but reduced to once a year by Nicaea II in 787 (c. 6), and then determined at once

every three years in 1515 by Lateran V.[6] The practice of regular provincial councils fell into disuse despite the detailed prescriptions of the Council of Trent in 1563,[7] and the 1917 Code required them only once every twenty years (CIC 283).

There is no similar legislation governing the larger or "plenary" councils, which in more recent centuries have sometimes been called "national" councils. The practice, however, is evident from the early centuries of the Church. They were important to the life, doctrine, and discipline of the Church in North Africa, Spain, and later in Charlemagne's empire. England and various areas of Europe held these sessions well into the Middle Ages. Efforts by Gallicans and Febronians to use such national councils to deny the primacy of the Holy See led to the prohibition of national gatherings in later centuries.[8] In the nineteenth century plenary councils were once again employed to enact laws for establishing the Church in new areas (e.g., the Plenary Councils of Baltimore) or for restoring Catholic life in areas disrupted by the Reformation or the French Revolution. Even after the 1917 Code there have been plenary councils in Ireland (1927), China (1929), Poland (1936), the Philippines (1953), and in several South American countries.

Councils represent not only the ancient and ongoing tradition of the Church; they are an important expression of the collegial relationships among bishops and the Church's very nature as a communion. Dioceses are not isolated units operating on their own but exist in close interdependence with neighboring dioceses and other particular churches in the same ethnic, cultural, or political setting. Councils provide an orderly and visible expression of this interdependence of particular churches in the same ethnic, cultural, or political setting. They have also provided an opportunity for others in the Church to express both their experience and concern for the matters under discussion, as well as a public forum where issues can be debated and resolved for the welfare of all the churches involved.

The practice of recent years, particularly since the 1917 Code, has been to rely more on the administrative decisions of bishops than on the deliberations of particular councils. The growth of conferences of bishops bears witness to this restriction to an administrative approach and even to the exclusion from the decision-making process of others who by law would have been entitled to address the issues at a particular council. This trend can also be traced to the requirement, in force since the decree of Sixtus V in 1589,[9] that the decrees of a

---

[6]Session 10, "Bulla contra exemptos," COD 607.

[7]Session 24, de ref., c. 2, COD 737.

[8]Sipos, 186.

[9]Sixtus V, Immensa Aeterni, Jan. 22, 1589, Magnum Bullarium Romanum II, 670. The decrees of provincial and plenary councils were to be reviewed by the Congregation of the Council be-

particular council be "reviewed" by the Holy See before they can take effect. In practice this "review" has resulted in decrees being changed contrary to the decisions of the bishops, raising the question of whether there was much point to the conciliar process itself.[10]

While retaining the requirement that decrees be reviewed by the Holy See, the revised Code does attempt to provide both for a revitalization of particular councils through broader participation of a cross section of the local churches and for greater initiative by the bishops involved. Given the traditional canonical adage that what touches all should be treated by all,[11] this revised law on particular councils presents the churches with a unique opportunity to carry out the adaptation of general law to local circumstances to address those concerns that affect the mission of the Church across diocesan boundaries.

The canons are an effort to implement the desire of Vatican II that councils flourish with new life in the Church. "Thus, faith will be spread and discipline preserved more fittingly and effectively in the various churches, as the circumstances of the times require."[12] The actual text of the revised Code is a modification of canons 218–292 of the 1917 Code.

Plenary Councils

Canon 439 — §1. A plenary council, that is, one which is held for all the particular churches belonging to the same conference of bishops, is to be celebrated as often as it seems necessary or advantageous to the conference of bishops, with the approval of the Apostolic See.

§2. The norm established in §1 is also valid for the celebration of a provincial council in an ecclesiastical province whose boundaries coincide with the territory of a nation.

Plenary councils involve all the bishops belonging to the same conference of bishops. If there are several provinces in the area, a plenary council is clearly distinct from the provincial councils each of those provinces might hold; if the area covered by an ecclesiastical province coincides with the territory of a nation, a provincial council for that area has the same significance as a plenary council since it covers a geopolitical unit similar to what a plenary council would involve. The two, therefore, are

treated the same, such that councils under these circumstances may be held if these three criteria are met: (1) the council would be necessary or advantageous for the welfare of the churches involved; (2) the conference of bishops of the area decides this to be the case; (3) the Apostolic See approves the decision to convene such a council.

The canon is based upon, but amounts to a major modification of, canon 281 of the 1917 Code. The former Code's understanding of a plenary council did not deal with situations in which there is only one province for a nation or similar geopolitical unit; it required that the bishops petition for permission from the Roman Pontiff (rather than receive approval for their own decision from the Apostolic See), and the Roman Pontiff designated a legate to convene and preside at a plenary council (whereas in the revised Code the conference of bishops has these responsibilities: c. 441).

In the preliminary drafts of this canon an ecclesiastical region was used to determine the territory involved in either a plenary council or a provincial council that is equivalent to a plenary one. As discussed above, the concept of ecclesiastical region has been changed from the equivalent of a geopolitical unit, such as a nation, to an ecclesiastical subdivision within a conference of bishops. The determination of the area included in a plenary council is now based on membership in a conference of bishops, although consideration of national boundaries has been retained for those provinces which cover an entire nation. This amounts to nearly half the conferences of bishops in the world, including such obvious examples as Belgium and The Netherlands.

Plenary councils can be convened by conferences of bishops which do not include the whole national territory; for example, Puerto Rico is not an independent nation but has its own conference of bishops and could hold its own plenary council.[13] Some conferences of bishops do not include a province (e.g., Switzerland, Bulgaria) so that any council they might convene would automatically be plenary rather than provincial.

The initiative for convening a plenary council is left to the conference of bishops. There is no requirement for periodic convening of such councils, only "as often as it seems necessary or advantageous." In the past, plenary councils have been held in the United States, for example, to assess the new condition of the Church after the erection of several provinces, or in light of changed civil circumstances (such as the American Civil War). Similarly, plenary councils could be held because of the significance of civil or ecclesiastical developments for the life of

---

fore they could be promulgated. The review was done by the Congregation "Fide" Propaganda for areas subject to it.

[10]See J. Provost, "Preparing for Particular Legislation to Implement the Revised Code," *J* 42 (1982), 358–359.

[11]While the phrase is applied most properly to collegial bodies (c. 119, 3°), historically it has a much richer application within the life of the Church. See Y. Congar, "Quod omnes tangit, ab omnibus tractari et approbari debet," *Revue historique de droit français et étranger* 35 (1958), 210–259.

[12]CD 36.

[13]Although part of the U.S., Puerto Rico is treated in the diplomatic structure of the Church as a Central American country, the Apostolic Nuncio to the Dominican Republic serving as Apostolic Delegate to Puerto Rico.

the Church in the area. The decision to convene one is not necessarily predicated on crises in the Church, nor does it have to wait for calamities. It could also seem advantageous to convene plenary councils to develop long-range planning on a coordinated national basis or to provide a meaningful forum for the involvement of clergy, religious, and lay persons in developing continued efforts at mission by the Church in the area.

Provincial Councils

Canon 440 — §1. With due regard for can. 439, §2, a provincial council for the various particular churches of the same ecclesiastical province is to be celebrated as often as it seems opportune in the judgment of the majority of the diocesan bishops of the province.

§2. When the metropolitan see is vacant a provincial council is not to be convoked.

Provinces not coterminous with national boundaries are free to conduct provincial councils whenever it seems opportune to the bishops of the province, although not when the metropolitan see is vacant. There is no requirement for prior approval of the Apostolic See to act on the decision to convene such a council.

This is a modification of canons 283–284 of the 1917 Code, which mandated provincial councils every twenty years and provided for circumstances when the metropolitan see happened to be vacant at the time that the provincial council was to be celebrated.

How frequently provincial councils are to be held has changed from twice a year (Councils of Nicaea and Chalcedon), to once a year (Nicaea II), to once every three years (Lateran V), to once every twenty years (*CIC* 283). The revised Code adopts a new approach to determining how frequently such councils should be held: a pastoral determination rather than a calendar one. This is partially due to the fact that the old system was not followed in practice anyway and partially to the increased emphasis in the revised Code on the responsibility of local bishops for the adaptation of Catholic life to the conditions of their areas. They are the ones who should be most concerned and best qualified to determine that a particular council—provincial or plenary—is needed to meet the needs of their churches.

The danger in this approach is that provincial councils will not be held at all. However, the previous norms requiring their celebration at stated intervals were ineffective and the new, more pastoral norm may offer a more realistic approach to such councils. Perhaps as all the Christian faithful assume more actively their responsibilities and rights in regard to the mission of the Church (cc. 211–225) and seek more effective means to exercise their rights to petition and expression of opinion (c. 212, §§2–3), the ancient tradition of councils may find renewed usefulness for the life of the Church.

Authority over Particular Councils

Canon 441 — It is the role of the conference of bishops:

1° to convoke a plenary council;

2° to select the place in which to celebrate a council within the territory of the conference of bishops;

3° to select the president of the plenary council from among the diocesan bishops, but he is to be approved by the Apostolic See;

4° to determine its agenda and the questions to be treated; to establish the date for the opening and closing of the plenary council; to transfer, prolong and dissolve it.

Canon 442 — §1. With the consent of the majority of the suffragan bishops, it is the role of the metropolitan to:

1° convoke a provincial council;

2° to select the place in which to celebrate a provincial council within the territory of the province;

3° to determine its agenda and the questions to be treated; to establish the date for the opening and closing of the provincial council; to transfer, prolong and dissolve it.

§2. It is the role of the metropolitan to preside over a provincial council; if he is legitimately hindered from doing so this role devolves upon the suffragan bishop elected by the other suffragans.

The conference of bishops exercises direct authority over plenary councils—determining whether to convoke one, where and when it will meet, who will preside, and what matters will be treated in it. The approval of the Apostolic See is needed for only two of these decisions: the determination to hold a plenary council and the election of the president. For provincial councils, this collegial approach is replaced by the role of the metropolitan, but the consent of a majority of the suffragan bishops in the province is needed. Moreover, the presidency of provincial councils is not determined by the bishops of the province unless the metropolitan is hindered from assuming the presidency himself.

Canon 441 represents a major shift from canons 281 and 288 of the 1917 Code by giving the conference of bishops the authority that formerly was reserved to the legate of the Apostolic See who convened, presided over, determined the agenda and various matters concerning time, place, duration, suspension, transfer and closing of a plenary council. In canon 442 greater voice is given to the suffragan bishops than that provided by canon 284 of the former Code relative to convening a provincial council and determining its location (before they had only to be consulted, now a majority must consent). Likewise the determination of who will preside at a provincial council if the metropolitan is hindered from doing so is changed; the earlier norm (*CIC* 284) required the replacement be the senior suffragan bishop in order of promotion, whereas the revised Code provides for the suffragans to elect the replacement from among their number.

There are some limitations on the respective authorities in terms of the decisions they can make: a plenary council must be held within the territory of the conference of bishops, a provincial council must take place within the territory of the province. Only a diocesan bishop can preside at either a plenary or provincial council. In the case of a plenary council, the election must also be approved by the Apostolic See, although now the choice of the president is left to the free determination of the bishops in the conference.

In reference to provincial councils, canon 442, §2 does not indicate what the legitimate hindrances might be which would keep a metropolitan from presiding at a provincial council. Although such a council cannot be convoked when the metropolitan see is vacant (c. 440, §2), the metropolitan might have died after the council was convoked and therefore a replacement would be necessary. The metropolitan might also be ill, incapacitated, or hindered by some other physical reason. Could a moral reason also be invoked? That is, under certain circumstances the metropolitan might judge that he ought not to preside, but that the bishops of the province would be able to determine someone more suited for the rigors of presidency or more skilled at presiding at such a meeting. "Legitimate" reasons are not necessarily physical;[14] given the pastoral emphasis in the Code, pastoral reasons may be sufficient for a metropolitan to consider himself legitimately impeded. Short of his physical incapacitation or death, however, it would seem the suffragans would not be authorized to elect a president for a provincial council to replace the metropolitan if the latter were opposed to their action, even if he were morally impeded from presiding.

Participants at Particular Councils

Canon 443 — §1. The following are to be called to particular councils and have the right of a deliberative vote in them:

1° diocesan bishops;

2° coadjutor and auxiliary bishops;

[14]For example, a priest may be physically present but legitimately impeded from witnessing a marriage, and the extraordinary form may then be used. (c. 1116, §2); moral as well as physical factors can justify a Catholic's receiving sacraments from a non-Catholic minister in whose church that sacrament is valid (c. 844, §2).

3° other titular bishops who fulfill within the territory a special function committed to them by the Apostolic See or by the conference of bishops.

§2. Other titular bishops who are living in the territory, even if they be emeriti, can be called to particular councils and they have the right of a deliberative vote.

§3. The following are to be called to particular councils but they have only a consultative vote:

1° the vicars general and the episcopal vicars of all the particular churches in the territory;

2° the major superiors of religious institutes and societies of apostolic life; the number of men and women, however, is to be determined by the conference of bishops or by the bishops of the province; and the superiors are in turn to be elected by all the major superiors of the institutes and societies which have their headquarters within the territory;

3° rectors of ecclesiastical and Catholic universities and the deans of faculties of theology and of canon law which are located within the territory;

4° some rectors of major seminaries; their number is to be determined in accord with n. 2 above; and they are elected by the rectors of the seminaries which are located within the territory.

§4. Presbyters and other members of the Christian faithful can also be called to particular councils with only a consultative vote; their number is not to exceed half of the number of those mentioned in §§1-3.

§5. The cathedral chapters, the presbyteral council and the pastoral council of each of the particular churches are likewise to be invited to provincial councils in such a way that each sends two of its members as representatives; these should be selected in a collegial manner by each of these bodies; they possess only a consultative vote.

§6. Others also can be invited to particular councils as guests if it seems advantageous in the judgment of the conference of bishops in regard to a plenary council or in the judgment of the metropolitan along with his suffragan bishops in regard to a provincial council.

There are two types of categories for participants. The first type relates to who must be and who may be invited to attend. The second type of category relates to whether they have a deliberative vote (may participate in the discussion and are counted among those determining the final outcome of the council), a consultative vote (may participate in the discussion but do not determine the final outcome), or are guests (observers). In addition to bishops, the canon provides for participation by a cross section of the Church: lay persons and religious as well as clergy. Even non-Catholics may be invited, although they would be among the guests.

Three distinct canons regulated participation at particular councils in the former Code: one on plenary councils (*CIC* 282) and two on provincial councils (*CIC* 285–286). In addition to bishops, clergy or religious men were the only others mentioned in law who could participate at particular councils under the former Code. The revised Code broadens participation considerably, dropping the restriction to males and including lay persons as well as religious and clergy.

Deliberative Vote

These participants not only participate by right in the discussions that take place during a council; they also are the ones who determine the final outcome of the discussion. Their votes (or "voices") are not the only ones heard at a particular council, but theirs are the only ones counted when the council finally determines the position it will adopt on a given issue.

Those with a deliberative vote who must be called to particular councils are diocesan bishops, auxiliary and coadjutor bishops, and titular bishops who exercise a special function at the request of the Apostolic See or the conference of bishops. These latter would include bishops attached to the military vicariate, for example. Titular bishops who serve as territorial prelates, apostolic vicars, apostolic prefects, or apostolic administrators in the sense of canon 368 would also be included here.

Whether titular bishops who perform the function of legate within the territory have a right to be called to a particular council is not clear from the canon. By particular law an apostolic delegate, or nuncio, is not a member of the local episcopal conference; by analogy, it would seem he is also not a participant by right at a particular council in the territory where he serves.

Those who are not bishops but who head particular churches equivalent to dioceses (territorial prelatures or abbacies, apostolic vicariates, prefectures, or administrations established on a stable basis: cc. 368; 381, §2) are by law members of the conference of bishops (c. 454, §1). However, these are not mentioned in terms of participants at particular councils, even though for plenary councils they are included in the conference that has authority over the plenary council (c. 441). This would appear to be a lacuna in the law, and they should be called and participate with a deliberative vote at a plenary council, since they are included among those with authority over the council. Since the purpose for provincial councils is the same as that for plenary councils (c. 445), it would appear that these persons who are considered equivalent to diocesan bishops should also be called and exercise a deliberative vote there as well.

Although they do not have to be called to a particular council, other titular bishops living in the territory may be called to it. If they are, the law gives them a deliberative vote. The revised Code

does not have the option given in the former Code (*CIC* 282, §2; 286, §2) of deciding whether these bishops would have a deliberative or consultative vote at a particular council; if called, they enjoy a deliberative vote.[15] Retired (emeritus) bishops are specifically included in this category (§2).

Consultative Vote

These participants have the right to participate in the discussion, but they do not share in making the final determination of the council's position. Sometimes this is called having voice but no vote (whereby "vote" is meant what the canons refer to as a deliberative vote). The presence of participants with a consultative vote is one of the features that distinguishes a particular council from a meeting of the conference of bishops (c. 454). Such participants are to express the wisdom which resides within the people of God, voicing the experience of Catholic life and the needs and desires of the faithful. They may also bring specific expertise in terms of pastoral work, theology, canon law, and the other sciences needed to make provision for the needs of the people of God in that area (c. 445).

The canon distinguishes between those having a consultative vote who must be called and others who may be called to the council. By law, some individuals are specifically to be called: all the vicars general (c. 475) and vicars episcopal (c. 476) within the territory, rectors of ecclesiastical universities and faculties (cc. 815–821) and of Catholic universities (cc. 807–814) as well as the deans of theology and canon law in the territory. The law determines that two representatives are to be selected collegially by each of the presbyteral councils and diocesan pastoral councils in the territory. The bishops (conference of bishops for plenary council, bishops of the province for provincial council) specify the number of certain other persons to be selected by designated groups: major superiors of religious institutes and societies with headquarters in the territory elect the number of major superiors of men and women set by the bishops; rectors of major seminaries elect the rectors to fill the number set by the bishops.

In addition to these various categories of persons who must be invited, the law allows for additional clergy and lay persons to be invited. It sets a proportion which must be observed for the overall membership: these additional invitees cannot exceed one-half the number of bishops, vicars general, episcopal vicars, religious superiors, rectors, and deans. No other norms are given for determining how these additional participants with a consultative vote are to be selected.

[15] This differs from the norm concerning their participation in meetings of the conference of bishops, where the option of determining whether theirs is to be a consultative or deliberative vote is retained: c. 454, §2.

Guests

A final category of "guests" is given in the canon (§6), with no specification that they have or are denied a consultative vote. The intention of the canon, however, is that they be observers and not enter into the discussion. This is clear from the percentage limitation placed on additional invitees in paragraph four. If in addition to this limited number of invitees with a consultative vote the bishops desire to admit other Catholics or even non-Catholics, they are free to do so, but these additional persons are not entitled to participate in the discussions. The limitation is designed to assure good order, and also to keep certain pressure groups from packing the house and pressuring the free exchange of views in the discussion itself.

The distinction into consultative and deliberative vote reflects the hierarchical nature of the Church. But the addition of a cross section of the people of God is an effort to reflect in councils themselves the communal nature of the Church which John Paul II has highlighted as characteristic of the revised Code.[16]

Attendance

Canon 444 — §1. All who are invited to attend particular councils must attend them unless they are detained by a just impediment about which they are bound to inform the president of the council.

§2. Those who are invited to attend particular councils and who have a deliberative vote in them can send a proxy if they are detained by a just impediment; however, the proxy has only a consultative vote.

Attendance at a particular council is an important responsibility (c. 209, §2) and not just a privilege. It concerns the welfare of the people of God within the council's territory. Its participants are held accountable for this responsibility by the council itself, so they must inform the president of a just impediment which may detain them. Participation in such a council is a personal responsibility: those with a consultative vote are either to attend or their place is vacant; those with a deliberative vote, if impeded, can send a proxy but the proxy has only a consultative vote.

The requirement to notify the council president of the reason for one's absence is made general in the revised Code. In the former Code it applied specifically only to religious who could not attend a provincial council (*CIC* 286, §4). Those who were impeded from coming but would have a deliberative vote if they could come were to send a proxy and prove the cause which impeded them from attending, but the proxy did not exercise the missing

16John Paul II, *Sacrae disciplinae leges.*

person's deliberative vote (*CIC* 287). Under the former Code specific mention was made of using another council member as proxy, but this has not been retained in the revised Code. Its absence from the canon, however, would not rule out the possibility unless the statutes drawn up for the specific council were to determine otherwise.

The former Code also had restrictions on leaving a council and required permission to absent oneself once the council had begun. This permission was granted by the president after the reason for leaving had been demonstrated (*CIC* 289). This provision is not continued in the revised Code; unless statutes for a specific council were to repeat it, participants would not be so bound by law, although the commitment to their responsibilities in the council must be carried out.

Purpose and Authority

Canon 445 — A particular council sees to it that provision is made for the pastoral needs of the people of God in its own territory, and it possesses the power of governance, especially legislative power, so that with due regard always for the universal law of the Church it can decree what seems appropriate for increasing faith, organizing common pastoral activity, directing morals and preserving, promoting or protecting common ecclesiastical discipline.

In keeping with ancient tradition, a council is called to make provision for the pastoral needs of the people of God. It is an authoritative gathering, such that it possesses governance authority particularly in the area of legislation. A council looks to promoting faith and morals, organizing common pastoral work, and providing for ecclesiastical discipline in the territory.

The purposes listed in the former Code tended to look more toward problem-solving than toward promoting pastoral life and development. Those former purposes included looking into what would lead to increasing the faith, moderating mores, correcting abuses, resolving controversies, and fostering the observance of a common ecclesiastical discipline (*CIC* 290).

A council exercises the power of governance not as a cumulation of the governance power of its individual members but as an entity in its own right. Thus auxiliary bishops and others without the power of governing a diocesan church participate in a council in the exercise of a power of governance over the particular churches involved in the council. The decision-making process in a council permits lay persons to cooperate in the power of governance by law (c. 129, §2).

Councils characteristically, but not exclusively, are legislative bodies. They issue decrees which have the force of law (c. 29). In keeping with the principle of subsidiarity which is to guide not only the drafting of the Code but also its interpretation and implementation,[17] conciliar decrees should not become mired in details best left to local dioceses or even parishes. But conciliar legislation can establish the broad framework within which pastoral work will be carried out and can supply the vision and thrust which will stimulate further initiatives at the local level.

Legislation from a particular council is always subject to the general law of the Church; therefore, a particular council cannot enact legislation contrary to the laws issued by higher authorities (c. 135, §2). Its legislation is particular law; unless otherwise specified, it is binding only in that territory (c. 13, §1) and only on those actually in the territory with a domicile or quasi-domicile there (c. 12, §3). It can be dispensed in individual cases by a local ordinary (diocesan bishop, vicar general, episcopal vicar within his area of competence: c. 134, §1) whenever he judges such a dispensation will contribute to the good of the faithful (c. 88).

Even with all these cautions, however, the actions of a particular council are very significant for the life of the churches participating in it. This is evident from past experience (e.g., the remarkable significance of the Councils of Baltimore for the Church in the United States and of other plenary councils in various parts of the world for ecclesial practices there). It is also evident from the broad pastoral concerns expressed in this canon. These councils are to look toward promoting the faith, the first and most fundamental task of the Church. They work to provide common approaches to the mores of Christians (the moral life but also the manner of behavior), pastoral action in the Church, and the observance of ecclesiastical discipline. They constitute a significant opportunity to read the signs of the times, respect the conditions of local culture, and present the Church in that part of the world as a true light to all peoples there. Considering the publicity possible from such councils, they have an important role in making the Church more visible in local society.

Promulgation

Canon 446 — At the conclusion of a particular council the president is to see to it that all the acts of the council are sent to the Apostolic See; decrees issued by the council are not to be promulgated until after they have been reviewed by the Apostolic See; it is the role of the council itself to define the manner of the promulgation of its decrees and the time at which the promulgated decrees begin to oblige.

Laws come into existence when they are promulgated (c. 7); the promulgation of the laws of particular councils is governed by several conditions. The council itself must decide on what decrees it intends to issue; it must also specify the manner of promulgation (c. 8, §2). However, before the promulgation can take place, the decrees must be reviewed by the Apostolic See which will consider them in light of the acts of the council, which its president is to forward.

This canon repeats the basic provisions of canon 291, §1 of the 1917 Code. It does not specify, as the former law did, which dicastery of the Apostolic See is to receive the documents and review the decrees. The special norms for the Roman Curia in force at the time the Code was promulgated indicate this is the competence of the Sacred Congregation for Bishops except for areas under the authority of the Sacred Congregation for the Evangelization of Peoples (Propagation of the Faith).

Sixtus V (pope: 1585–1590) first instituted the requirement that all decrees be reviewed in Rome prior to promulgation, even though they are promulgated not by authority of the Apostolic See but rather by authority of the council which drew them up. In the past this provision has caused delay and tension between the bishops of various parts of the world and the Apostolic See. It is designed as a safeguard to assure that decisions of particular councils are not contrary to general church law. It has also been used, however, for other purposes, including that of imposing on local churches a discipline which they themselves had not voted to assume, for in the "review" of the decrees changes have been made which were not the work of the council in question but which must be promulgated with the authority of that council since they appear in the final version of the decrees.[18]

When a council determines the manner and time for promulgation, it may use any method it deems appropriate, provided it respects the time needed to obtain a review of the decrees by the Apostolic See. If the council has not specified otherwise in its decrees, they begin to bind one month from the date of promulgation (c. 8, §2).

---

[17]Principles for the Revision of the Code, 5: *Comm* 2 (1969), 80–82; Hite, 73–75. See also the Preface to the Latin edition of the Code.

[18]Benedict XIV explicitly stated that review (*recognitio*) was to include corrections to the text adopted by the bishops; see his *De Synodo Dioecesana*, Liber III, Capitulum III. Detailed instructions for correcting the Third Plenary Council of Baltimore were issued by the Congregation "Propaganda Fide" and are published in J. Mansi, ed., *Sacrorum Conciliorum Nova et Amplissima Collectio* (Paris: Welter, 1901–1927), tome 48, columns 880–884. There is at least one case in which decrees of a council which had received a favorable *recognitio* were later rescinded by the Apostolic See; see report in F. Murphy, *Legislative Powers of the Provincial Council: A Historical Synopsis and a Commentary* (Washington: Catholic University, 1947), 50, note 95.

CHAPTER IV
CONFERENCES OF BISHOPS
[cc. 447–459]

Conferences of bishops, as contrasted to particular councils of bishops, are a relatively recent development in church structures.[19] Their early growth seems to have been occasioned partly by the restrictions placed on particular councils, both by local civil governments and by the requirement that conciliar decrees be reviewed in Rome. One way to circumvent these restrictions was to hold a conference rather than a council. At a conference no decisions could be made which would be binding on bishops who did not agree, but at the same time if the bishops could agree on something together they would not need to obtain "recognition" of their decision by the Apostolic See but could act on their own. Councils, on the other hand, required strict canonical procedures and their decisions had to be reviewed in Rome before they could take effect.

Between 1561 and 1788 the archbishops of France held regular conferences. These addressed issues of Church-State relations, common issues of church discipline, and the relations between the bishops and the Apostolic See. The meetings were colored by Gallican influences as were similar meetings held less regularly in Germany and Northern Italy (where the influence was through Febronianism).

Less polemic settings marked more recent developments.[20] The bishops of Belgium began meeting regularly from the time of the country's independence in 1830, with specific rules of order being drawn up in 1842. German bishops held a very significant conference in 1848 in Würzburg and from 1867 started holding regular sessions at Fulda. At the invitation of the government, the bishops of Austria met regularly from 1849 to 1856. Rome objected to the government's role, but under Leo XIII the Holy See later tried to encourage the Austrian bishops to begin meeting again. In the United States, regular meetings of the archbishops were held after the Third Plenary Council of Baltimore in 1884.

The 1917 Code addressed conferences of bishops only in light of meetings within a province (*CIC* 292). While for about half the nations of the world in which there is one province for the whole country this would be equivalent to a national conference of the bishops, in other areas there was no provision in the Code for regular gatherings of bishops apart from the provincial level. The Code viewed these conferences as primarily consultative, i.e., to discuss issues related to the good of religion in the dioceses of the province and to prepare matters for treatment in future provincial councils. There were two areas in which the provincial council took binding action: setting the fees for acts of voluntary jurisdiction and related matters (*CIC* 1507) and fixing judicial fees for tribunals in the province (*CIC* 1909).

The development of national conferences of bishops took on a new form after the First World War and promulgation of the Code. In the United States a "National Catholic War Council" had been organized during the First World War by the archbishops and four bishops selected by them. The four bishops were deputed to care for United States Catholics involved in the war effort. After the war, all the bishops met in 1919 and decided to continue the organization as part of the post-war effort. At their meeting the following October (1920) the bishops changed the name to the "National Catholic Welfare Council."[21]

The Consistorial Congregation intervened and two years later (1922) decreed the dissolution of the National Catholic Welfare Council. The Curia was opposed because of what some perceived as a threat to central ecclesiastical authority, and it was encouraged in its opposition by some individual bishops who saw the group as a threat to their local autonomy. After intense negotiations the organization was reestablished under the name of "National Catholic Welfare Conference" in May of 1923. The term "council" was dropped to make it clear that the agency was not a canonical body and had no authority over local dioceses. It provided services primarily for refugees, concern in social justice questions, news (National Catholic News Service), and education.

In 1919 the cardinals and archbishops of France began regular assemblies again. The regular sessions of bishops in Belgium and Germany continued after the war. Following the Second World War a new impetus was felt for building interdiocesan collaboration. In 1947 the metropolitans began meeting regularly in Spain; in 1955 C.E.L.A.M. was founded.[22]

At Vatican II the bishops of the various countries formed caucuses within the first week of the opening session, and throughout the Council they built on the pre-conciliar experiences of so many nations. The bishops saw this type of cooperation as

---

[19]F. Carroll discusses the forerunners of conferences: *The Development of Episcopal Conferences* (Sydney: Catholic Press Newspaper, 1965), 4–6.

[20]P. Huizing, "The Structure of Episcopal Conferences," *J* 28 (1968), 164–165; see history of early conferences in Carroll, 6–64, and R. Kutner, *The Development, Structure and Competence of the Episcopal Conference* (Washington: Catholic University, 1972), 3–37.

[21]E. McKeown, "The National Bishops' Conference: An Analysis of Its Origins," *The Catholic Historical Review* 66 (1980), 565–583.

[22]Consejo Episcopal Latino-Americano. See J. Soria-Vasco, "Le C.E.L.A.M. ou Conseil Episcopal Latino-Americain," *AC* 18 (1974), 179–220.

a practical structure for continuing the work they were beginning at the Council. The first decree of the Council, *The Constitution on the Sacred Liturgy,* provided for "various kinds of competent territorial bodies of bishops [to be] legitimately established" (*SC* 22). Later documents on liturgical reform and the *Decree on Ecumenism* (*UR* 8) developed the concept further. It received direct attention in *Christus Dominus* 37–38, and further legal specifics were added by Paul VI in the *motu proprio Ecclesiae sanctae* I, 41. The revised Code consolidates much of this development in canons 447–459.

The relations between conferences of bishops and the Vatican have not always been as harmonious as all would desire. The issue came to a head over the reaction of the conferences to the encyclical *Humanae Vitae.* An extraordinary synod was convened (see cc. 345; 346, §2) in 1969 and determined the need to clarify the application of the principle of subsidiarity to the relations between conferences of bishops and the Holy See. Agreement was reached on better communications, especially concerning major statements the Holy See planned to issue, and the synod of bishops itself was recognized as an important vehicle for strengthening the ties between conferences of bishops and the Apostolic See. The synod also proposed steps for closer cooperation of the conferences among themselves.[23]

The norms for the reorganization of the Curia called on dicasteries to foster good relations with conferences of bishops.[24] While this has generally been attempted, tension continues to exist between curial officials and the conferences of bishops. Bishops themselves are divided on how much importance should be given to conferences, continuing the suspicions voiced in the early 1920s toward the National Catholic Welfare Council. In response to comments from bishops in various countries,[25] the number of items to be committed to conferences of bishops by law was reduced in the drafting of the revised Code from around one hundred twenty-eight in the pre-1980 schemata to around seventy-six in the 1980 schema. There are approximately eighty-two instances in the final text where the competence of conferences of bishops is mentioned.

The deletions included some items agreed upon at the 1969 extraordinary synod (e.g., pre-promulgation communication to conferences of laws about to be issued by the Apostolic See) as well as areas in which conferences would have provided some limitation on the autonomy of individual bishops (e.g., vigilance over finances). Reflecting an opinion that conferences of bishops do not participate in the teaching function of the Church, a number of items

relating to that function were dropped, although the final text retains reference to bishops gathered in conferences as exercising the ordinary teaching function of the Church (c. 753). The canons on conferences were also relocated from their placement in earlier drafts. They had preceded the traditional structures of metropolitans and particular councils; they are now placed after these, even though in contemporary practice conferences represent the more common way in which bishops work together for the welfare of the churches.

The canons are organized as follows. Conferences are described, and the manner in which they are established is given. Canons follow on membership in conferences, their statutes, internal organization and meetings, and the conditions under which conferences may exercise binding authority. The roles of the permanent council and general secretary are described, and the canons conclude by dealing with the question of relations among conferences.

Description

Canon 447 — The conference of bishops, a permanent institution, is a grouping of bishops of a given nation or territory whereby, according to the norm of law, they jointly exercise certain pastoral functions on behalf of the Christian faithful of their territory in view of promoting that greater good which the Church offers humankind, especially through forms and programs of the apostolate which are fittingly adapted to the circumstances of the time and place.

The conference is described in terms of what and who it is as well as the purpose for its existence. It is a permanent institution of ecclesiastical law which does not go out of existence when its membership changes, but it is an institution which remains even as members are replaced. Its members are bishops determined according to territory, usually the territory of a nation but not necessarily so (c. 448, §2). Its purpose is to provide a means whereby the bishops can exercise certain pastoral functions both internal to the life of the Church ("on behalf of the Christian faithful") and external in terms of the Church's service to humankind. The conference is presented as especially a practical institution, conducting apostolic programs and providing structures useful to the existing conditions in which the Church is called to minister.

There is no comparable canon in the 1917 Code. This canon was added during the consultation process and first appeared in the 1980 schema. Much of the text of the canon is taken verbatim from *Christus Dominus* 38. There are some stylistic changes, but there have been some substantive

[23]E. Farhat, "De primo extraordinario synodi coetu (1969)," *ME* 97 (1972), 3–13.
[24]Paul VI, *RE* 8; see above under Roman Curia at c. 360.
[25]*Rel, Comm* 14 (1982), 199.

changes as well. Characterizing the conference as a "permanent institution" was added by the *coetus*[26] to provide juridical clarity; "exercise certain pastoral functions" changes the conciliar text's "exercise their pastoral functions"; "on behalf of the Christian faithful of their territory" is an addition of the *coetus*.

There are two visions of the role of the conference of bishops. One sees it as an intermediary structure between the Holy See and diocesan bishops, a kind of "intermediate curia" between the Roman Curia and diocesan curias.[27] From this perspective the conference is either feared or touted, but its role is placed in the context of tensions between the universal and particular church. The other perspective is to see it as a pastoral endeavor arising from the common concerns of bishops as members of the college of bishops, expressing their solicitude and indeed providing occasionally for strict collegial action as a portion of the college of bishops. In this sense it is not an intermediate structure but part of the concentric circles of the ecclesiology of communion presented by the pope as characteristic of the revised Code.

There also seem to be two perspectives on what is the major focus of the work of the conference. The text of *Christus Dominus* sees the conference as part of the apostolic, missionary thrust of the Church, bringing to humankind the greater good which the Church has to offer. The canon concentrates instead on the exercise of pastoral functions on behalf of the Christian faithful and sees this as how the bishops work to provide the greater good which the Church has to offer. The difference in these perspectives may lie in differing understandings of the relationship of the Church with the world.[28] The conciliar text appears to present the Church as present in the world, whereas the canon distinguishes the pastoring role as internal to the Church and only indirectly (i.e., through the ministry to Christians) acting in the world.

In both the conciliar text and the canon, the major concern is to see the conference as apostolic and pastoral in nature. In keeping with its origin, it is primarily concerned with applying the life of the gospel to local conditions. This is done, however, through the full pastoral function in which the bishops succeed to the apostolic body, although primarily under the form of solicitude and only rarely as an exercise of the power of governance.

[26]See report in *Comm* 12 (1980), 263.
[27]See report on discussion by *coetus, Comm* 12 (1980), 263; also, J. Listl, "Plenarkonzil und Bischofskonferenz," *Handbuch des katholischen Kirchenrechts* (Regensburg: Pustet, 1983), 309.
[28]See discussion on the differing understandings in J. Komonchak, "Clergy, Laity, and the Church's Mission in the World," *J* 41 (1981), 431–444.

Establishment of Conferences

Canon 448 — §1. Generally the conference of bishops encompasses all who preside over particular churches of the same nation according to can. 450.

§2. If, however, in the judgment of the Apostolic See, having consulted the diocesan bishops who are involved, circumstances of persons or things suggest it, a conference of bishops may be erected for a smaller or larger territory so that it takes in either the bishops of some particular churches constituted in a given territory or those presiding over particular churches in different nations; it is for the same Apostolic See to determine special norms for individual conferences.

Canon 449 — §1. After hearing the bishops involved, it pertains to the supreme church authority alone to erect, suppress or change the conferences of bishops.

§2. The conference of bishops once legitimately erected enjoys a juridic personality by the law itself.

Canon 449 restricts to the Apostolic See the authority to erect, suppress, or change conferences of bishops. In taking these actions the Apostolic See is bound by the law to consult the bishops involved. The basis on which conferences are determined is territorial. Normally the territory which is used is that of a nation, but at times other territorial bases may be used. For these kinds of arrangements the Apostolic See will issue special norms in addition to the general norms governing conferences contained in the Code. No matter what territorial basis is used, once a conference of bishops is established, it has public juridic personality (c. 116) in virtue of the law itself.

Canon 448, §2 is based on *Christus Dominus* 38, 5° and Paul VI's *motu proprio Ecclesiae sanctae* I, 41, §4. An earlier draft of the canons presented conferences as established by the law itself, the Apostolic See becoming involved only when a proposed conference included bishops of several nations (*Schema De Populo Dei* 199, §2). That draft even proposed that conferences exist at the regional level (national or its equivalent), district level (a division of a region), and for provinces that were not part of a larger region (c. 199, §1). The concept of region has been changed, as noted above—so, too, has the concept of the juridic origin of conferences of bishops.

The *coetus* argued that since the Apostolic See must be involved in establishing conferences that include several nations (as *CD* 38, 5° and *ES* I, 41, §4 state), it must be involved in establishing any conference. This hardly matches the history of conferences and represents a significant shift from the conciliar perspective. The Council (*CD* 38, 3°) and post-conciliar legislation (*mp ES* I, 41, §§1–2) had required the approval of statutes by the Apostolic See but had left the authority to establish a conference in the hands of the participating bishops. The provision for the involvement of the Apostolic See can be justified from the perspective of providing for unity within the Church, but this is only one of several possible ways in which such a service can be provided; the law as it now stands is not a dogmatic statement but a practical norm which admits of further development.[29]

A conference of bishops is a juridic person. Established by law and competent to act in the name of the Church, it is a public juridic person (c. 116, §1). By nature collegial (c. 115, §2), it is governed by the norms for collegial acts (c. 119). A conference may hold property and own temporal goods, and these are ecclesiastical goods subject to the norms of Book V (c. 1258). Suit against a conference of bishops can be brought only before the Roman Rota (c. 1405, §3, 3°), but administrative recourse can be taken against its decrees and administrative acts (c. 1732).

Membership

Canon 450 — §1. The members of the episcopal conference are, by law, all diocesan bishops and those equivalent to them in law, also coadjutor bishops, auxiliary bishops and other titular bishops who fulfill within the same territory a particular function for which they are mandated by the Apostolic See or by the conference of bishops; ordinaries of another rite may also be invited, however in such manner that they enjoy only consultative vote, unless the statutes of the conference of bishops determine otherwise.

§2. The other titular bishops and the legates of the Roman Pontiff are not by law members of the conference of bishops.

Membership is determined by two major criteria: membership in the college of bishops and pastoral responsibility. The two are not coterminous, but generally they are closely interrelated. Thus members of the college of bishops who exercise a pastoral responsibility as diocesan bishops, coadjutor

[29]Although most conferences are national, there are a number of exceptions. At the time the Code was promulgated, there were 84 conferences of bishops which were coterminous with the commonly accepted civil boundaries of nations. Four were for portions of nations (separate conferences for Puerto Rico and the rest of the U.S.; distinct conferences for Scotland and for England and Wales in Great Britain). Twelve included more than one national unit (including the Irish Bishops' Meetings for Northern Ireland and the Republic of Ireland). There were also 10 organizations of conferences of bishops within larger areas, 6 in Africa and 1 each for Asia, Europe, Central America, and Latin America.

and auxiliary bishops, or a particular function within the territory are by law members of the conference. Others who are not bishops but who are equivalent to them in law in virtue of their pastoral responsibilities (cc. 368; 381, §2) are also made members by the law itself. Bishops whose pastoral ministry is in a different Ritual Church *sui iuris* (or rite) are not subject to this Code, but the statutes of individual conferences of bishops can provide for them to be invited as members and even to have a deliberative vote. Finally, bishops who do not have a pastoral function in the territory as well as legates of the Roman Pontiff are not members by law, although the statutes may provide for their participation in individual conferences.

The canon is drawn from *Christus Dominus* 38, 2° but with a notable change. The conciliar decree provided for membership in a conference by all the diocesan bishops in the territory, no matter what their rite. In drafting the canon this was reversed, but after objections from several sources this compromise was included in the law; therefore, a conference may choose to remain faithful to the letter of the conciliar document, although for various reasons it may also choose to make exception to it.

The canon, in keeping with the Council, mentions only "ordinaries," i.e., diocesan bishops, of other rites; both documents are silent concerning coadjutors and auxiliaries. It would be within the spirit of the documents, however, for the statutes of an individual conference to allow for the participation by diocesan bishops, coadjutors, and auxiliaries from other rites on the same basis as for Latin Rite bishops. The Apostolic See's approval of statutes including these bishops might be considered to supply for any absence of mention of them in the Code itself.

The role of titular bishops mentioned in paragraph two has been a source of some concern given the increased numbers of retired bishops. The Apostolic See has encouraged conferences of bishops to restrict deliberative votes to those exercising a pastoral function and to provide only a consultative vote to these other titular bishops.

Statutes

Canon 451 — Each conference of bishops is to prepare its own statutes, which must be reviewed by the Holy See, and which among other things are to provide for the holding of plenary meetings of the conference as well as a permanent council of bishops, a general secretary of the conference, and other offices and commissions, which in the judgment of the conference will help it fulfill its purpose more effectively.

Every juridic person must have its own statutes (c. 117), which define its purpose, constitution, government, and operation (c. 94, §1). The canon specifies certain elements which are to be covered in the statutes (plenary meetings, a permanent council, general secretary, other offices and commissions) but leaves it to the individual conferences to make specific determinations in these matters. The statutes must be reviewed by the Apostolic See, but they bind on the authority of the conference which adopts them, not on the authority of the Apostolic See.

This canon repeats the provisions of *Christus Dominus* 38, 3°, with the addition of requiring mention of plenary meetings in the statutes.

In addition to the items listed in this canon, the statutes are also to determine whether to invite ordinaries of other rites and with what type of vote (c. 450, §1); the type of vote to be extended to auxiliary bishops (c. 454, §2); the status of those other titular bishops mentioned in canon 450, §2 and their vote if they are members (c. 454, §2); the relationship of the conference and the legate of the Roman Pontiff (c. 450, §2); and the administration of goods belonging to the conference (cc. 1279, 1281).

A conference is free to determine in its statutes what type of vote (majority, two-thirds) is to be required on the various matters which come before it, except in those matters in which it proposes to issue a general decree which has the force of law (in which a two-thirds vote is required: c. 455, §2) or in voting to adopt or amend the statutes (in which case voting is limited to those with a deliberative vote by law, but no restriction is given on the size of the majority to be required: c. 454, §2). If the statutes do not specify otherwise, the provisions of canon 119 on collegial acts would apply in all other votes.

Statutes drawn up by conferences after Vatican II were reviewed and "approved" experimentally for a limited period of time; subsequent revisions have also been "approved" although technically "review" is all the conciliar text and canon require. The Sacred Congregation for Bishops is the competent dicastery for this, except for those conferences in territories subject to the Sacred Congregation for the Evangelization of Peoples (Propagation of the Faith).

Internal Organization and Meetings

Canon 452 — §1. Each conference of bishops is to elect a president for itself; it is also to determine who is to serve in the role of pro-president when the president is legitimately impeded; and it is also to appoint a general secretary of the conference, according to the norm of the statutes.

§2. The president of the conference, and the pro-president when the former is legitimately impeded, preside not only at the general meetings of the conference of bishops but also over its permanent council.

Canon 453 — The plenary sessions of the conference of bishops are to be held at least annually, and additionally as often as special circumstances require, according to the prescriptions of the statutes.

Canon 454 — §1. Diocesan bishops, those equivalent to them in law and also coadjutor bishops have a deliberative vote in plenary sessions of the conference of bishops by the law itself.

§2. Auxiliary bishops and other titular bishops who are members of the episcopal conference enjoy either a deliberative or consultative vote according to the prescriptions of the statutes of the conference; however, only those mentioned in §1 enjoy a deliberative vote when it is a question of drawing up or modifying the statutes.

Three major organizational elements are required by the Code: officers (president, vice-president, or "pro-president," and general secretary); permanent council (board, administrative committee, executive: see c. 457 below); and meetings of the full conference (plenary meetings). While further details are to be worked out by each conference in its statutes, the canons do require certain key elements to be included.

The Council left such details up to conferences to work out in drafting their respective statutes (*CD* 38, 3°), as did the *motu proprio Ecclesiae sanctae* (I, 41, §§1–2). There was some discussion in drafting the canons about how detailed they ought to be, but even the requirement of an annual meeting was retained lest the canons have no practical effect.[30]

The legal minimum for the role of the president is to preside over the plenary meetings of the conference and over its permanent council or executive board and to forward to the Apostolic See a report of the acts and a copy of any decrees from each plenary meeting (c. 456). He may have other responsibilities in keeping with the statutes, but he cannot act in the name of all the bishops unless it is a matter for which special competence has been given, or each and every bishop consents (c. 455, §4). The pro-president, or vice-president, as he is more commonly termed in English, fills in for the president when the latter is impeded. The general secretary's responsibilities are detailed below at canon 458.

As is implied by their very name, conferences are intended to be meetings of bishops, opportunities for personal interchange and discussion so that the personal insights and experiences of the bishops can be shared and brought to bear on the pastoral conditions in which they minister. Hence there is a requirement that they gather as a body at least once a year; plenary sessions can be held more often, as determined in the statutes of the respective conferences. The canons do not mandate particular

---

[30]*Rel, Comm* 14 (1982), 198.

agenda for such meetings but leave this up to the permanent council (c. 456).

Voting membership is spelled out as discussed above, so that a deliberative vote by law belongs to diocesan bishops, those equivalent to them, and co-adjutor bishops.[31] The statutes are to determine the voting status of other bishops who are members of the conference, but they are not authorized to vote on the statutes themselves, whether the statutes are being drawn up or amended. Only those who have a deliberative vote in virtue of the law can adopt or modify the statutes.

Although this seems to establish a two-tiered system within a conference, it does provide assurance that those with primary pastoral responsibilities among the bishops will have the more serious voice insofar as the structure and operations of the conference are concerned. This has already been in practice for other matters in some countries, such as the United States, where only diocesan bishops vote on matters of budget since they will have to provide the financial support for that budget.

Binding Authority

Canon 455 — §1. The conference of bishops can issue general decrees only in those cases in which the common law prescribes it, or a special mandate of the Apostolic See, given either *motu proprio* or at the request of the conference, determines it.

§2. The general decrees mentioned in §1 can be validly passed in a plenary session only if two-thirds of the members of the conference having a deliberative vote approve them; such decrees do not have binding force, unless they have been legitimately promulgated, after having been reviewed by the Apostolic See.

§3. The manner of promulgation and the time from which the decrees take effect are to be determined by the conference of bishops itself.

§4. In the cases where neither the universal law nor a special mandate of the Apostolic See has granted the conference of bishops the power mentioned above in §1, the competence of individual diocesan bishops remains intact; and neither the conference nor its president may act in the name of all the bishops unless each and every bishop has given his consent.

Canon 456 — When the plenary session of the conference of bishops has been completed, a report

of the acts of the conference and its decrees are to be sent to the Apostolic See by the president, so that these acts may be brought to its attention and it may review the decrees, if there be any.

General decrees issued by a conference of bishops in accord with canon 455 have the force of particular law for the territory represented in the conference (c. 29). The authority of the conference to issue general decrees extends to those matters specified in general law or for which special authorization has been given by the Apostolic See. Two-thirds of the voting members, whether present for the vote or not, must adopt such a general decree, and their action must be reviewed by the Apostolic See before it can be promulgated and have binding effect for the area. In all other matters, a conference can act in the name of all the bishops only if all the members agree unanimously.

Canon 455 is based on the provisions of *Christus Dominus* 38, 4° and the general provisions for promulgation of a law (c. 8, §2). Both the final paragraph of this canon and canon 456 are new with the Code.

Canon 455 gives rise to six topics of study: decrees which the conferences can issue; cases in which such decrees can be issued; voting on the decrees; review of conference action by the Apostolic See; promulgation of the decrees; and other conference actions.

Decrees

Two types of general decrees are described in Book I of the Code: "general decrees" (c. 29) and "general executory decrees" (c. 31). General decrees are laws properly speaking, while general executory decrees are more precise determinations of how to observe laws. Conferences are competent to issue both types of decrees.

a. General decrees can be issued by a competent legislator (c. 29) and by those who have executive but not legislative authority if they have special authorization for this (c. 30). There is a theoretical question as to whether episcopal conferences issue general decrees as legislative or executive bodies. The canons do not specify the conference as either but as a body exercising "certain pastoral functions" for the faithful of their territory. The pastoral function *(munus pastorale)* is understood generally to include all three functions of teaching, sanctifying, and governing. It, therefore, could be argued that as part of its pastoral function the conference of bishops is properly a legislative body; however, the Code places certain restrictions on its exercise of the legislative aspect of that pastoral function. On the other hand, it could be argued that since paragraph one of this canon grants to conferences of bishops the right to issue general decrees

---

[31]Coadjutors in the revised Code have the right of succession and will automatically become diocesan bishops when the see becomes vacant (cc. 403, §3; 409, §1). They are instructed with special faculties and are already involved in the governance of the diocese as vicars general (cc. 403, §3; 406, §1). This pastoral responsibility may explain why the canon places them automatically in the category of members with a deliberative vote by law.

and that otherwise they do not have that right (§4), conferences have only executive authority. From this perspective paragraph one represents an application of canon 30 rather than a limitation applied to actions carried out in accord with canon 29.

b. General executory decrees can be issued to determine more precisely how a law is to be observed. Such decrees are not laws but have to be promulgated in the manner of laws since they bind not only those who are charged with seeing that laws are observed (which would be an instruction: c. 34, §1) but also the entire community (c. 31). Legislative power is not required to issue this type of decree; executive authority is sufficient.

c. Which decrees of a conference of bishops require the full procedure specified by this canon? Clearly the first do, for they are mentioned by name ("general decrees"); they establish particular law, and the procedures are similar to those which apply to legislative bodies such as particular councils (cf. cc. 445–446).

It can be questioned whether the Code requires the formalities of this canon to be observed in issuing the second type of decree. A general executory decree does not add a new source of binding authority to what has already been legislated; it is limited to executing or urging the observance of the law, not making a law. If a general executory decree is contrary to the law, or if the law is later changed, the decree stands or falls depending on the law and not on the decree or the authority of the one who issued it.

An example of such decrees in the Code may be those instances in which a decree of the conference of bishops may *permit* something, for this establishes how something already contained in the law is to be put into action. An example is canon 522 (concerning term appointments for pastors) in which the law authorized the diocesan bishop to name a pastor for a limited term if the conference of bishops has issued a decree (i.e., a general executory decree) permitting this provision of the law to be put into practice.

The restriction of canon 455 is clearly that—a restriction on the exercise of the "pastoral function" which is the proper obligation and right of a conference of bishops (c. 447). As a law which restricts the free exercise of rights, it must be interpreted strictly (c. 18); therefore, when canon 455 uses the technical term "general decrees" and not the technical term "general executory decrees," the precision of the Code in canons 29 and 31 is to be respected and the restrictions in canon 455 are to be considered as applying only to "general decrees." A conference of bishops may issue general executory decrees following the voting procedures established in its own statutes and without such decrees having to be reviewed by the Apostolic See prior to their taking effect. As with all actions of a conference of bishops, the Apostolic See is to be notified of such general executory decrees (c. 456).[32]

Cases in which Decrees Are Authorized

The Code indicates a number of situations in which conferences of bishops are authorized to issue general decrees, general executory decrees, or individual decrees (administrative acts: c. 35). In a letter issued shortly before the Code went into effect, the Secretary of State identified twenty-one cases in which conferences were required to act either if they had not already done so or if their earlier actions were contrary to the provisions of the Code and twenty-two cases in which conferences had the option to act.[33] The concern of the Secretariat was to avoid any legislative vacuum which could result when the Code took effect. While the letter failed to differentiate between general decrees and general executory decrees, it did give an informative listing of issues on which conferences are authorized to act by law. Other listings have been developed from other analyses of the Code.[34]

It is important to apply carefully the criteria established in Book I for differentiating general decrees (c. 29), general executory decrees (c. 31), individual decrees (including those which request a rescript from the Apostolic See: c. 48), individual precepts (c. 49), rescripts (c. 59), and various collegial actions such as elections (cc. 164–179). Only general decrees require the limited process spelled out in this canon; the others are regulated by the general norms in Book I and the statutes of the individual conferences.

The Code has not used a standard vocabulary to identify technically the type of decree which is intended in the various canons each time a conference is authorized to act. In order to determine if the conference issues a general decree (which is subject to all the limitations of c. 455) or a different type of decree, it is necessary to evaluate each case in light of the descriptions of the various decrees given in Book I. Even then, however, it is not always clear from the texts of the various canons if the conference is being authorized to determine a more pre-

---

[32]This opinion seems to be confirmed by a response from the SCB (Prot. 388/83) to an inquiry from the NCCB in 1983. The congregation distinguished between "the choice of possibilities already indicated in the law (e.g., c. 522)" and instances in which "the Conference is asked to establish norms (e.g., c. 1126)."

[33]Secretariat of State, letter to Presidents of Episcopal Conferences (no Prot. given), Nov. 8, 1983. The letter is so concerned about a "legislative vacuum" at the time the revised Code took effect that it authorized conferences to adopt interim provisions even without review by the Apostolic See, but these would be in effect only until January 1, 1985.

[34]For example, J. Listl, 314–320; G. Melguizo Y., "Las conferencias episcopales en el nuevo Codigo de Derecho Canonico," *Universitas Canonica* 3 (1983), 41–61; unpublished listing developed by NCCB Canonical Affairs Committee.

cise way of observing the law or setting a new law in itself. For example, does canon 1126 authorize the conference to determine how the general law for the declaration and promises in a mixed marriage is to be applied in its territory, or, does it make a new particular law for this subject matter? If it is the former (a general executory decree), the conference need not follow all the restrictions in canon 455 but can adopt the "norms" according to the procedures it has determined for itself in drafting its statutes. If it is the latter (a general decree or particular law), then the special provisions of canon 455 apply.[35]

Some of these distinctions are newly organized in this Code; applying them to determine which cases are within the restrictions of canon 455 will be the source of some debate and research for the foreseeable future. For the purposes of this study, those canons which obviously call for the conference to establish particular law or prescriptions or those which seem to go beyond determining more precisely the methods to be observed in applying the law already given in the Code are considered as calling for general decrees in the sense of canon 455. From this initial analysis, there seem to be at least twenty-nine cases in which the Code authorizes (and at times requires) conferences to adopt this kind of general decree:

1. qualifications for installation as a lector or acolyte (c. 230, §1);

2. norms for the formation of candidates for the permanent diaconate (c. 236);

3. norms on presbyteral councils (c. 496);

4. authorization for cathedral chapters to take the place of the college of consultors (c. 502, §3);

5. sacramental books to be maintained by parishes (c. 535, §1);

6. determination of standards for the care of retired pastors (c. 538, §3);

7. norms for preaching by lay persons in churches (c. 766);

8. norms for preaching on radio and television (c. 772, §2);

9. regulations on the catechumenate (c. 788, §3);

10. norms on religious education in schools and on the media (c. 804, §1);

11. norms for clergy and religious appearing on radio and television (c. 831, §2);

12. adaptation of the adult catechumenate and norms for conducting it (c. 851, 1°);

13. norms on the administration of baptism (c. 854);

14. norms on recording the baptism of adopted children (c. 877, §3);

15. decision to require parishes to keep a record of confirmations in addition to the diocesan record (c. 895);

16. norms concerning the arrangement of confessionals (c. 964, §2);

17. setting an older age for ordination to the diaconate or presbyterate (c. 1031, §3);

18. particular law governing the promise to marry or engagements (c. 1062, §1);

19. norms on pre-nuptial investigation and banns (c. 1067);

20. setting an older age to enter marriage licitly (c. 1083, §2);

21. determination of how marriages are to be noted in parish registers (c. 1121, §1);

22. decision to abolish or transfer the observance of holy days (c. 1246, §2);

23. determination of a different food besides meat from which faithful are to abstain on days of penance (c. 1251);

24. norms on contributions given to the Church (c. 1262);

25. norms on fund-raising (c. 1265, §2);

26. regulations on benefices where benefices are still in effect (c. 1272);

27. norms on leasing church property (c. 1297);

28. norms for conciliation and arbitration of disputes (c. 1714);

29. decision to require each diocese to have an office of mediation (c. 1733, §2).

Other situations, aside from canons 447–459 on conferences as such, in which conferences of bishops are mentioned in the Code are these:

1. establishing interdiocesan seminaries, with the approval of the Apostolic See (c. 237, §2);[36]

---

[35] This latter is the opinion offered by the SCB cited above. However, this interpretation could be based primarily on the use of the term "norms" in the canon and not on a careful analysis of whether the canon calls for new law or directions on how to apply existing law in local circumstances.

[36] C. 455 requires review ("recognitio") of a conference's general decrees, not formal "approval" of them. Canons which call for the approval of the Apostolic See can be dealing with individual decrees rather than general ones. Such decrees would be

2. setting a program of priestly formation, with the approval of the Apostolic See (c. 242, §1);

3. determining the participation expected of permanent deacons in the liturgy of the hours (c. 276, §2, 3°);

4. specifying clerical garb for the area (c. 284);

5. being consulted before the Apostolic See erects a personal prelature in the area (c. 294);

6. erecting public associations for the area (c. 312, §1, 2°; cc. 313, 314, 316, 318, and 319 are included in this authority);

7. suppressing public associations erected by the conference (c. 320, §2);

8. granting juridic personality to private associations (c. 322);

9. suppressing private associations (c. 326, §1);

10. electing representatives to the synod of bishops (c. 346, §1);

11. being consulted by and receiving cooperation from the papal legate (c. 364, 3°);

12. being consulted before the Apostolic See erects a particular church for a special rite or group of persons in the territory (c. 372, §2);

13. cooperating in drafting lists of potential candidates for the episcopacy (c. 377, §2);

14. seeing to support of retired bishops (c. 402, §2);

15. proposing erection by the Apostolic See of regions within the conference (c. 433, §1) which have canonical status even though not the same power as a conference of bishops (c. 434);

16. calling a plenary council, with the approval of the Apostolic See (c. 439);

17. determining the place for a plenary council; setting the rules of order, agenda, and meetings; and with the approval of the Apostolic See, selecting the council's president (c. 441);

18. determining certain numbers of participants at a plenary council (c. 443);

19. receiving copies of decrees from diocesan synods (c. 467);

20. authorizing bishops to set a limited term in the appointment of pastors (c. 522);

21. cooperating with conferences of major religious superiors (c. 708);

22. exercising authentic magisterium (c. 753);

23. promoting Christian unity (c. 755, §2);

24. issuing catechisms for their territory, with the prior approval of the Apostolic See (c. 755, §2);

25. establishing a catechetical office for the conference (c. 755, §3);

26. providing for the care of visitors from missionary areas (c. 792);

27. providing for Catholic universities and faculties (c. 809);

28. exercising vigilance over doctrine in the territory (c. 810, §2);

29. establishing higher institutes for religious studies (c. 821);

30. exercising vigilance, passing judgment, and even taking corrective action concerning publications and media (c. 823, §2);

31. approving editions and translations of the Sacred Scriptures (c. 825, §1);

32. permitting ecumenical translations of the Sacred Scriptures with notes (c. 825, §2);

33. developing a list of censors for books or even establishing a commission of censors (c. 830, §1);

34. preparing adaptations and translations of liturgical books and, with prior approval from the Apostolic See, publishing them (c. 838, §3);

35. determining cases of "other grave necessity" when baptized non-Catholics may receive Catholic sacraments of Eucharist, penance, and anointing (c. 844, §4);

36. developing norms on such sacramental sharing after consulting the appropriate authorities of other churches (c. 844, §5);

37. determining another age for confirmation than the age of discretion (c. 891);

38. determining whether it is acceptable for lay persons to assist at marriages (for which individual bishops must seek permission from the Apostolic See) (c. 1112, §2);

39. drawing up a marriage ritual for the area, to be approved by the Apostolic See (c. 1120);

40. determining how the declarations and promises for a mixed marriage are to be made (c. 1126);

adopted according to the statutes of the conference, not necessarily with the full formalities called for in c. 455 (two-thirds vote, etc.).

41. establishing common norms for dispensation from canonical form (c. 1127, §2);

42. approval for a shrine to be called "national" (c. 1231);

43. approving statutes of a national shrine (c. 1232, §1);

44. permitting use of materials other than stone for altars (c. 1236, §1);

45. determining the laws of fast and abstinence more precisely or substituting other penitential practices (c. 1253);

46. where social security does not care for the clergy, seeing that some institute does provide for this (c. 1274, §2);

47. defining acts of extraordinary administration for dioceses (c. 1277);

48. defining minimums and maximums on values for alienation of church goods (c. 1292, §1);

49. permitting lay persons to serve as judges (c. 1421, §2);

50. permitting bishops to use single-judge courts if collegiate tribunals cannot be formed (c. 1425, §4);

51. forming a tribunal of second instance with the approval of the Apostolic See, if the Apostolic See has allowed an interdiocesan tribunal of first instance (c. 1439, §1);

52. establishing tribunals of second instance in other situations, with the approval of the Apostolic See (c. 1439, §2);

53. exercising certain powers relative to interdiocesan tribunals of second instance (c. 1439, §3);

In addition, several canons refer to actions being taken with reference to the conference of bishops as determining the extent of action (e.g., federation of diocesan institutes for social security and other financial matters: c. 1274, §4; competence in certain marriage cases provided both parties live within the territory of the same conference: c. 1673, 3°) or specifying actions of individual bishops (who may be absent from their diocese for meetings of the conference: c. 395, §2; and who are to consult other members of the conference before setting norms for general absolution: c. 961, §2).

Voting

Two-thirds of those with a deliberative vote in the conference must approve a general decree for it to be adopted. Since general decrees are particular laws which bind throughout the territory of the

conference, this provision is intended to protect against a small majority imposing its will on a large minority. At the same time, it seems to represent a serious reserve about the decisions reached in the conference in which only bishops participate as compared with the particular council in which a larger cross section of the Church has engaged in the discussions and preparations for the decree.

Canon 119, 2° indicates that—as a general norm for collegial acts—if there is a quorum of a majority of those who must be convoked, then an absolute majority of those present (i.e., over half) can adopt a decree. Both conferences of bishops and particular councils are collegial bodies and are governed by this norm "unless provision is made otherwise by law or statutes" (c. 119). The bishops of a conference who are convened as a plenary council, therefore, could adopt by majority vote of those present a decree which, if considered instead in the setting of a plenary meeting of the conference, would require a two-thirds vote of those entitled to vote even if not all were present. The differences are obvious: at a council, a quorum is required, but once that is present only an absolute majority of those present is needed (hence a bit over 25% of the bishops). For a conference of bishops, two-thirds of those entitled to a deliberative vote must approve, whether they are present or not.

The result has been that for conferences in which a vote is taken and the two-thirds majority is not reached with the votes of those present, a ballot must be taken of the absent members to determine if a two-thirds majority appproves, even though the absent members missed the discussion which preceded the vote and therefore have not been part of the full decision-making process. At a council, such is not the case, and the vote of those who participated in the full decision-making process is all that is considered.

As to the question of what bishops are considered to have a deliberative vote, one should see above at canon 454.

Review by Apostolic See

A general decree adopted by the necessary two-thirds majority of bishops with a deliberative vote must next be sent to the Apostolic See for review. The president is responsible to see that a report of the acts is sent to the Apostolic See to enable such a review to take place. This is a provision similar to that stated for the acts and decrees adopted by particular councils (c. 446). The same concern over the meaning of "reviewed" ("recognita") for decrees of particular councils discussed above applies to decrees adopted by conferences of bishops.

Promulgation

General decrees are laws. They must be promulgated to take effect (cc. 455, §2; 7). The conference itself determines the manner by which such general decrees are to be promulgated, and unless the conference specifies otherwise these decrees take effect one month after promulgation (cc. 455, §3; 8, §2).

Universal laws are normally promulgated in the *Acta Apostolicae Sedis* which provides an official source for the text of the law. It is up to particular legislators to determine whether to adopt a similar procedure so the law can be readily known. To date this has not been done, for example, in the United States where decisions of the conference of bishops are not published in any official organ, nor are they collected in any official collection so they can be readily consulted. If particular laws, especially decrees adopted at periodic meetings by conferences of bishops, are to have any lasting force, it is imperative that some form of regular reporting be established by the respective conferences.

It should also be noted here that general executory decrees, even though they do not require review by the Apostolic See, must be promulgated to take effect (c. 31, §2). Thus, decisions by conferences which implement or further specify how the general law is to be observed must be promulgated, and it is important that they also be included in any official publication or collection of conference decisions.

Other Conference Actions

A conference of bishops is not able to require a particular course of action or mandate that a particular position be followed by individual bishops except in the cases specified in accord with paragraph one. The liberty of individual bishops is upheld by the Code in keeping with the ecclesiological reality that the Church exists in and from the particular churches or dioceses; they are not administrative subdivisions of a larger organization, even of conferences of bishops.

There are some limits to this provision, however. First, in those cases in which the conference is to adopt general executory decrees, these are binding as specifications of how the law is to be observed and bishops are bound by the general law to obey such decrees. As indicated above, these are different from general decrees which are actually new laws.

Moreover, if all the bishops unanimously agree to a particular course of action or position, it is in effect a position of the conference for it is the position of all its members. It has binding force not as an imposition or restriction on the individual members but as an agreed-upon decision which in virtue of that agreement has binding effect. This applies to actions taken by the president of the conference on behalf of the members as well as to actions of all the members.

Permanent Council and General Secretary

Canon 457 — The permanent council of bishops is to prepare the agenda for the plenary meeting of the conference and see to it that the decisions made during the plenary sessions are properly implemented; it is also to care for other matters which are entrusted to it according to the norm of the statutes.

Canon 458 — It is the responsibility of the general secretary:
1° to prepare a report of the acts and decrees of the plenary meeting of the conference, and also the acts of the permanent council of bishops and to communicate the same to all the members of the conference; he is also to draw up the other acts which are entrusted to him by the president of the conference or by the permanent council;
2° to communicate to neighboring conferences of bishops those acts and documents which the conference in plenary session or the permanent council of bishops decided to send to them.

The ongoing operations of a conference between sessions are assured by a permanent council and the services of a general secretary and appropriate staff. The law specifies what their responsibilities are in general but leaves further details up to the statutes and to practical decisions in keeping with local situations.

The canons are based on the provisions of *Christus Dominus* 38, 3° and add practical descriptions of the functioning of these agencies in line with experience since the Council.

The permanent council is composed of bishops. It serves as a board on which normally the officers of the conference serve together with other members, whether ex officio or elected to it. The president of the conference also chairs the permanent council (c. 452, §2). It pertains to this council, rather than to the president personally, to prepare the agenda and to see that the decisions made during plenary conference sessions are properly implemented. The statutes are to clarify other responsibilities for the council, including its relationship to the officers and to the general secretary.

The permanent council is presented in the law as a service of conference members to the conference itself. It is not a sort of "super conference," and accountability for its work is to the full conference. Its minutes are shared with all members of the conference, not only with the members of the permanent council (c. 458, 1°). The decision-making authority of the conference does not belong to the permanent council but to the conference as a whole.[37]

---

[37]The Central Commission for the Coordination of Postconciliar Work and for the Interpretation of Conciliar Decrees respond-

The general secretary provides essential staff services to the conference. The law does not specify qualifications for this position, but obviously the person must be competent to carry out the duties listed in canon 458 as well as any others which may be attached to the office by the conference or its permanent council. The law does not require that this office be conferred upon a cleric, and since the position does not in itself entail the exercise of the power of governance it would appear to be open to lay persons—men and women—as well as clergy, unless the statutes provide otherwise.

The responsibilities of the general secretary fall into three categories. The first relates to meetings of the conference in plenary session or of the permanent council. The general secretary draws up reports ("minutes") of such meetings and distributes these to all the members.

The second category of responsibilities is broader; other acts entrusted by the president of the conference or by the permanent council can include the drafting of reports and study projects or the implementation of various programs being conducted by the conference. In the United States, for example, the general secretary is responsible for a large staff that is charged with implementing conference activities in a wide range of concerns, including both civil and ecclesiastical matters.

A third category addresses the practicalities of relating conferences with one another. The general secretaries are the main channel of communications between conferences. The canon does not require that all documents, minutes, etc., of a conference be shared with neighboring ones, but neither does it prohibit this. Rather, it leaves the determination of what information is to be shared either to the conference itself or to its permanent council.

Relations among Conferences

Canon 459 — §1. Mutual relationships are to be fostered between the conferences of bishops of different regions, especially those who are neighbors, for the promotion and protection of the greater good.

§2. Whenever the actions or programs entered into by the conferences take on an international aspect it is necessary to consult the Apostolic See.

Conferences of bishops are encouraged to develop good relations among themselves. This obviously applies to those conferences which are neighbors, but it is not limited to them. However, if actions and programs which the conferences propose to undertake go beyond the borders of the individual conferences and become interna-

tional, the Apostolic See is to be consulted.

The canon is based on *Christus Dominus* 38, 5° and the *motu proprio Ecclesiae sanctae* I, 41, §5. The statement in the latter source is much more detailed than the canon itself concerning areas of cooperation and the means to achieve it.

Cooperation among conferences has taken various forms. It has been institutionalized, with the approval of the Apostolic See, in various conferences of conferences. In Africa, in addition to S.E.C.A.M. (Symposium of Episcopal Conferences of Africa and Madagascar) there are regional groupings such as I.M.B.I.S.A. (Inter-Regional Meeting of Bishops of Southern Africa), A.E.C.A.W.A. (Association of the Episcopal Conferences of Anglophone West Africa) and A.M.E.C.E.A. (Association of Member Episcopal Conferences in Eastern Africa). Two other associations bring together conferences from various French-speaking areas in Africa. In Asia, there is the Federation of Asian Bishops' Conferences (F.A.B.C.); in Europe, there is the Consilium Conferentiarum Episcopalium Europae (C.C.E.E.); and in Latin America, there are the Consejo Episcopal Latinoamericano (C.E.L.A.M.) and Secretariado Episcopal de America Central y Panama (S.E.D.A.C.).

Regular meetings are held between the officers of the conferences of bishops in North America as well as between those in North and South America. Ad hoc gatherings have been held to discuss various issues, either by officers of the conferences involved (e.g., to discuss the "peace pastoral" developed by the bishops in the U.S., a meeting that involved bishops from various parts of Europe and the U.S.) or by representatives of conferences (several sessions of representatives were held in the process of preparing responses to drafts for the revised Code).

The purposes of such contacts are to promote and to protect the greater good. The canon does not limit this to the greater good of the individual conferences, and it may be understood as applying to the greater good of the Church universal as well as the greater good of humankind.

The Apostolic See requires that it be consulted before conferences move from exchanging information about their respective activities and concerns to engaging in actions or programs which would take on an international character. This is in keeping with a general position adopted in practice and expressed elsewhere in the Code (e.g., c. 312, §1, 1° on universal or international public associations) that anything which goes beyond the territory of a particular conference of bishops requires the approval of the Apostolic See. It is not always clear in practice, however, when an action or program no longer is the coordinated effort of individual conferences within their respective territories and becomes international in itself.

ed in the negative to an inquiry as to whether the legislative power of conferences could be delegated to conference commissions. See response of June 10, 1966, *CLD* 7, 131.

Special Church Structures

1. National Conference of Catholic Bishops (NCCB)/ United States Catholic Conference (USCC)

In the United States there are two organizations for the bishops: one is an ecclesiastical juridic person (National Conference of Catholic Bishops, the conference of bishops in a canonical sense); the other is a civil corporation (United States Catholic Conference). The two bodies are composed of the same members and share the same authorities: officers, general secretary and associate general secretaries, and basic staff offices. They differ in operations and in spheres of interest.

The NCCB is principally a bishops' organization. Its committees are composed of bishops aided by a small staff; however, the principal work is done by bishops themselves. Its concerns are usually intraecclesial, although they may extend to the Church beyond the boundaries of the conference's own territory as an expression of solidarity and solicitude.

The USCC maintains many of the services originally developed under the National Catholic Welfare Conference, ranging from the National Catholic News Service and important work among refugees and immigrants to major divisions dealing with education and social concerns. The USCC committees are made up of bishops and other faithful, and they serve as policy supervisory bodies. Basic policies are set by the full conference, but supervising their implementation is left to the committees. The work, however, is carried out by a technical staff headed by executives who are expert in their respective fields.

USCC concerns are more program-oriented: some are in service within the Church (e.g., education); others deal with Church-State relations (especially legislation and administrative policies); and still others address Church-world issues (social justice).

Both conferences meet in annual meetings in November; usually one day of the bishops' meeting is devoted to USCC activities and the other days deal with NCCB affairs. There is an Administrative Committee which serves for the NCCB as the permanent council mentioned in canon 457. The same members serve as the Administrative Board and Board of Trustees of the USCC. A National Advisory Council has been formed to advise the Administrative Committee/Board and to propose items for their consideration. It is composed of bishops, clergy, members of institutes of consecrated life, and lay persons selected within the various administrative regions of the NCCB.

2. Other Supra-Diocesan Structures

In addition to the structures listed in the Code (provinces, metropolitans, particular councils, and conferences of bishops), various other structures have developed particularly since the Second Vatican Council.

In Europe there have been various approaches to interdiocesan meetings in the process of implementing the decisions of Vatican II.[38] The first such effort was held in The Netherlands and took the form of a National Pastoral Council. This was originally an effort to consult on a broad basis, both with full publicity and possibility for suggestions and comments by an interested faithful as well as with a view to working out the proper implementation of the conciliar documents in the quite unique situation of the Church in Holland. Later developments led to controversy concerning topics being discussed and the way the role of the bishops at the Pastoral Council was understood, particularly by observers outside the process itself. It was eventually suspended by order from the Apostolic See, and a circular letter from the Sacred Congregation for the Clergy advised other national hierarchies against instituting national pastoral councils.[39]

Especially in the German-speaking countries various synods were held to implement the Council, retaining the nature of diocesan synods while being conducted on a national basis. For example, in Germany the dioceses in both East and West Germany held "common synods" for their respective territories. A "common synod" is one at which the diocesan synods were held as a synod of all the dioceses meeting in common at one location, the business being carried on according to special norms approved by the Apostolic See. The dioceses in Switzerland coordinated the agenda and procedures of their respective diocesan synods, meeting first in each diocese (all on the same dates), and then for a "second reading" of the synodal documents at a common session of all the synodal members. This provided for coordinated implementation of conciliar decrees while retaining the distinct characteristics of the various language and cultural groupings in the country. Although these were not designed as events to be repeated on a regular basis, they do provide alternatives to provincial or plenary councils and illustrate creative approaches to expressing the communion of churches in specific territories.

Other supra-diocesan structures have not been directed toward making binding decisions but have explored significant alternatives to the traditional canonical structures. In England and Wales a Convention of the Catholic Church was held in Liverpool in 1980 which provided an important pastoral

[38]See J. Provost, "Preparing for Particular Legislation," 370–379.

[39]SCC, circular letter, Jan. 25, 1973; *CLD* 8, 288. On the Dutch experience, see J. Coleman, *The Evolution of Dutch Catholicism 1958–1974* (Berkeley: University of California, 1978).

emphasis to the development of the Church there.[40] In Latin America various national sessions have been held in preparation for the general conferences of Latin American bishops at Medellin (1968) and Puebla (1979).[41] The "Call to Action" process and conference (1976) in the United States is still another example of an interdiocesan structure not specifically covered in the Code.[42]

In the United States, a number of dioceses within the same state have formed organizations known as State Catholic Conferences.[43] For the most part, these have addressed Church-State issues ranging from abortion and education questions to taxes and legislation at the state level. Some have formed departments which coordinate the efforts of the various dioceses regarding inner-church activities, and a few provide some direct services in the area of benefits for church employees. There has been no effort to form these into canonical bodies; instead, they are civil corporations carrying on the work of the Church within the context of the various states in the United States.

[40]See P. Jennings. "A Signpost for the Pilgrim Church? An Assessment of the National Pastoral Congress," *CR* 65 (1980), 233–239.

[41]Final documents of both meetings have been published in English: Second General Conference of Latin American Bishops, *The Church in the Present-Day Transformation of Latin America in the Light of the Council, II: Conclusions,* 2nd ed. (Washington: USCC, 1973); Third General Conference of Latin American Bishops, *Evangelization at Present and in the Future of Latin America: Conclusions* (Washington: NCCB, 1979).

[42]J. Finnegan, "The Detroit Conference—'A Call to Action'—as a Model of Church Governance," *CLSAP* 39 (1977), 10–18.

[43]M. Sheehan, "State Catholic Conferences," *J* 35 (1975), 431–454.

BIBLIOGRAPHY

Groupings of Particular Churches

a. Studies on Pre-Vatican II Law

Barrett, J. *A Comparative Study of the Councils of Baltimore and the Code of Canon Law.* Washington: Catholic University, 1932.

Bouix, M.D. *De Concilio Provinciali.* 2nd ed. Paris: Ruffet, 1862.

Corecco, E. *La Formazione della Chiesa Cattolica negli Stati Uniti d'America attraverso l'Attività Sinodale.* Brescia: Morcelliana, 1970.

Griffin, B. *The Provincial Councils of Portland in Oregon.* Rome: Pontificia Universita Lateranense, 1964.

Guilday, P. *A History of the Councils of Baltimore (1791–1884).* New York: Macmillan, 1932.

Hennesey, J. "The Baltimore Conciliar Tradition." *Annuarium Historiae Conciliorum* 3 (1971): 71–88.

Morrisey, F. "The Development of Particular Canonical Legislation in Canada." *Église et Théologie* 11 (1980): 223–245.

Murphy, F.J. *Legislative Powers of the Provincial Council.* Washington: Catholic University, 1947.

Orioli, H. "La collazione del pallio." *Nu* 4 (1976): 88–96.

Poblete, E. *The Plenary Council: A Historical Synopsis and a Commentary.* Washington: Catholic University, 1958.

Popek, A. *The Rights and Obligations of Metropolitans: A Historical Synopsis and Commentary.* Washington: Catholic University, 1947.

Schiefen, R.J. "The First Provincial Synod of Westminster (1852)." *Annuarium Historiae Conciliorum* 4 (1972): 188–213.

b. Official Code Commission Reports

Comm 4 (1972): 39–50 (report on *coetus De sacra hierarchia*)

Comm 12 (1980): 244–275 (revision of 1977 *De Populo Dei* schema)

Comm 14 (1982): 187–200 (1981 *Rel*)

c. Other Studies

Aymans, W. *Das Synodale Element in der Kirchenverfassung.* Munich: Max Hueber, 1970.

———. "Wesenverständnis und Zustandigkeiten der Bischofskonferenz im Codex Iuris Canonici von 1983." *AkK* 152 (1983): 54–61.

Carroll, F. *The Development of Episcopal Conferences.* Sydney: Catholic Press Newspaper, 1965.

Congar, Y. "Quod Omnes Tangit, Ab Omnibus Tractari et Approbari Debet." *Revue historique de droit français et étranger* 35 (1958): 210–259.

Farhat, E. "De Primo Extraordinario Synodi Coetu (1969)." *ME* 97 (1972): 3–23.

Feliciani, G. *Le Conferenze Episcopali.* Bologna: Il Mulino, 1974.

Finnegan, J. "The Detroit Conference—'A Call to Action'—as a Model of Church Governance." *CLSAP* 39 (1977): 10–18.

George, J. *The Principle of Subsidiarity—With Special Reference to its Role in Papal and Episcopal Relations in the Light of "Lumen Gentium."* Washington: Catholic University, 1968.

Huizing, P. "The Structure of Episcopal Conferences." *J* 28 (1968): 163–176.

Jennings, P. "A Signpost for the Pilgrim Church? An Assessment of the National Pastoral Congress." *CR* 65 (1980): 233–239.

Klostermann, F. "Supra-National Episcopal Conferences." *Con* 38 (October, 1968).

Kutner, R. *The Development, Structure, and Competence of the Episcopal Conference.* Washington: Catholic University, 1972.

Legrand, H.M. "Synodes et conseils de l'après-concile." *Nouvelle revue théologique* 98 (1976): 193–216.

Lettmann, R. "Episcopal Conferences in the New Canon Law." *Stud Can* 14 (1980): 347–367.

Listl, J. "Plenarkonzil und Bischofskonferenz." In *Handbuch des katholischen Kirchenrechts,* 304–324. Ed. J. Listl, et al. Regensburg: Pustet, 1983.

Maritz, H. "Die Kirchenprovinz. Provinzialkonzil und Metropolit." In *Handbuch des katholischen Kirchenrechts,* 325–329. Ed. J. Listl, et al. Regensburg: Pustet, 1983.

McKeown, E. "The National Bishops' Conference: An Analysis of Its Origins." *The Catholic Historical Review* 66 (1980): 565–583.

McManus, F. "The Scope of Authority of Episcopal Conferences." In *The Once & Future Church: A Communion of Freedom,* 129–178. Ed. J. Coriden. New York: Alba House, 1971.

Melguizo Y., G., et al. "Las conferencias episcopales en el nuevo Codigo de Derecho Canonico." *Universitas Canonica* 3/7 (1983): 41–61.

Morrisey, F. "The Significance of Particular Law in the Proposed New Code of Canon Law." *CLSAP* 43 (1981): 1–17.

Onclin, W. "The Power of Decision in the Church at the Supra-Diocesan Level." *Stud Can* 4 (1970): 279–296.

Pesendorfer, M. *Partikulares Gesetz und partikularer Gesetzgeber im System des geltenden lateinischen Kirchenrechts.* Vienna: Herder, 1975.

Provost, J. "Preparing for Particular Legislation to Implement the Revised Code." *J* 42 (1982): 348–382.

Sheehan, M. "State Catholic Conferences." *J* 35 (1975): 431–454.

Soria-Vasco, J. "Le C.E.L.A.M. ou Conseil Episcopal Latino-Americain." *AC* 18 (1974): 179–220.

TITLE III
THE INTERNAL ORDERING OF
PARTICULAR CHURCHES
[cc. 460–572]

Diocesan Organization

This contribution addresses the various organizational structures found at the diocesan level (cc. 460–514). These canons are contained in title III of section II of the part of Book II that describes the Church's hierarchical structure. In this part on hierarchical structure, the treatment of particular churches (section II) is divided into three titles. The canons of title III considered here are closely related to the canons of title I ("Particular Churches and the Authority Established in Them"), especially the latter's treatment of the diocesan bishop and his auxiliaries (cc. 381–411).

This contribution does not comment on all of the canons of title III. Its last three chapters (cc. 515–572) contain norms about structures that are below the diocesan level such as parishes and deaneries; these are treated elsewhere. This contribution limits intself to the first five chapters, those that deal with structures situated at the diocesan level itself. Chapter I on the diocesan synod immediately sets forth the norms for a special *legislative* activity (cc. 460–468). Chapter II describes the basic *administrative* structure of the diocese (cc. 469–494); it contains three separate articles on vicars general and episcopal vicars, on notarization and archives, and on the finance council and finance officer. Chapter III introduces into the Code norms on the presbyteral council and the college of consultors (cc. 495–502); chapter V does the same for the diocesan pastoral council (cc. 511–514). These two chapters thereby establish firmly in law the structures of consultation at the diocesan level called for by Vatican II. Chapter IV treats chapters of canons (cc. 503–510); its norms (except perhaps for c. 508, §2) do not apply to dioceses in some parts of the world.

CANONS AND COMMENTARY

CHAPTER I
THE DIOCESAN SYNOD
[cc. 460–468]

The diocesan synod as a canonical institute dates from the fourth century although its composition and purpose have evolved considerably since then. The first gathering of clergy similar to a synod seems to be that convoked by Pope Siricius in Rome (387).[1] As early as the sixth century, synods of priests and/or abbots were quite frequent in the Frankish kingdom. It was not long before a notion of "Christendom" developed in which the affairs of Church and State were often intermingled. During this period many synods addressed both ecclesiastical and secular matters. Local synods truly flourished during the Middle Ages. Innocent III is known to have convoked them quite frequently.

Lateran Council IV (1215) decreed that synods should be held annually to promulgate to the clergy the decrees of provincial councils. A similar disciplinary norm was issued by the Council of Trent.[2]

The 1917 Code (*CIC* 356–362) retained the notion of the diocesan synod as a convocation by the bishop of certain of his priests to address the needs of the diocese. Although the Code mandated its observance in each diocese at least every ten years, the synod fell into desuetude in many areas of the world. The revised Code, recognizing this historical development, has broadened the consultation process of the diocesan synod and at the same time left many specific determinations to the local level. The chapter's nine canons treat the following aspects of the diocesan synod: notion; convocation; participation; legislation; and cessation.

[1] Benedict XIV, *De Synodo Dioecesana*, I, 1, 6.

[2] Sess. XXIV, *de ref.*, c. 2.

The Notion of the Diocesan Synod

Canon 460 — A diocesan synod is a group of selected priests and other Christian faithful of a particular church which offers assistance to the diocesan bishop for the good of the entire diocesan community according to the norm of the following canons.

One of the aims of the Code's revision was to clarify the exercise of the power of governance according to its three functions: legislative, executive, and judicial (c. 135). On the diocesan level, legislative power is exercised solely by the diocesan bishop—either within or outside of a synod.[3] Canon 460 is a new text; it has no counterpart in the former Code. It describes the diocesan synod without even mentioning the bishop's legislative activity as its primary purpose. Legislation is presumed to be the principal aim of the synod, given the references at the end of the chapter (cc. 466–467), but such a conclusion relies more on the synod's recent history as a legislative forum than on anything explicitly contained in the text. Canon 460 simply identifies the synod as a "group . . . which offers assistance to the diocesan bishop for the good of the entire diocesan community."

The synod has been, historically, an exclusively clerical institute. This restricted concept of membership has been altered in the revised Code in which the synod is identified as a group of "selected priests and other Christian faithful of a particular church." The Commission rejected the use of the term "meeting" (*conventus*) and chose instead the word "group" ("*coetus*"). The synod is not simply an ad hoc convocation but an identifiable entity with particular members selected to assist the bishop in exercising his legislative office. In this sense, although they are not juridically deputized "representatives of the whole people of God," the members of the synod participate in an exercise of community reflection and discussion about matters of ecclesial concern.[4] This revision represents the law's commitment to utilize the gifts of the entire Christian community. While the bishop is the legislator, other members of his particular church perform the critical tasks of guiding and facilitating his legislative action (*adiutricem operam*).

The Convocation of a Synod

Canon 461 — §1. A diocesan synod is to be celebrated in each of the particular churches when cir- cumstances warrant it in the judgment of the diocesan bishop, after he has consulted the presbyteral council.

§2. If a bishop has the care of several dioceses or if he has the care of one as its proper bishop and of another as its administrator, he can convoke one diocesan synod for all the dioceses entrusted to him.

In the past millennium, diocesan synods were celebrated frequently. They came under suspicion, however, as a possible form of "conciliarism." The "Council of Pistoia" (1786), for instance, issued certain decrees, claiming independent authority for synods, which were found unacceptable and subsequently condemned by Pius VI.[5] The 1917 Code urged the convocation of synods by setting ten years as the maximum interval between synods (*CIC* 356). This norm, however, had little success in promoting synods; in many countries they were hardly, if ever, held. The Code Commission had an opportunity to revive and modernize this canonical institute. In the original draft (1977 schema) the ten-year interval was retained, but a second clause stated the bishop's right to defer its celebration for an additional ten years, a recognition of the practical state of affairs in many dioceses. During the consultation on this text, several groups urged a more frequent celebration of the synod as a desirable form of legislative activity in the Church, but the Commission refused to change the text in the 1980 schema. It reasoned that the synod is "the normal institute for the updating of the diocese's particular legislation" and should therefore have sufficient flexibility to fulfill its function without the need for constant and frequent revisions.[6] Moreover, canon 380 of the 1980 schema was even more drastically altered by the Commission to leave matters totally in the hands of the diocesan bishop.[7] The final text retains the obligation to convoke a synod ("*celebretur*") but leaves its timing completely to the discretion of the diocesan bishop in consultation with his presbyteral council.

The promulgation of the revised Code creates circumstances in which many dioceses might find a synod useful after a suitable period of reflection and implementation. The many changes in universal law and the Code's stress on particular legislation have created a need for more finely adapted diocesan norms. While frequent synods did not materialize after the 1917 Code, the 1983 Code may very well revive this institute as a responsible form of episcopal legislative leadership.

The second paragraph of the canon repeats substantially the stipulation of the 1917 Code (*CIC* 356, §2) permitting one synod to be held for two or

---

[3]*Comm* 5 (1973), 221. C. 391, §2 concerning the diocesan bishop's exercise of legislative power makes no reference to the synod. There was a reference in c. 244, §3 of the original 1977 schema, but it was deleted by the consultors without any explanation. *Comm* 12 (1980), 301.

[4]*Comm* 12 (1980), 314–315.

[5]*Auctorem fidei*, Aug. 28, 1794, nos. 9–11.

[6]*Comm* 12 (1980), 315.

[7]Cf. *Rel*, 109.

more dioceses which have been committed to the same bishop, even if he acts only as diocesan administrator. This is simply an option and is not urged by the canon. In practice, an interdiocesan synod might be counterproductive since the resulting legislation might not be "particular" enough, that is, accommodated to the concrete circumstances in the individual dioceses. Before holding such a unified synod, the diocesan bishop should consult with the presbyteral council in each of the affected dioceses. The "administrator" referred to in this canon is not the administrator *sede vacante* (c. 421) but a bishop of one diocese assigned to administer another diocese indefinitely.[8]

Canon 462 — §1. Only the diocesan bishop convokes the diocesan synod, not however one who presides over a diocese *ad interim*.

§2. The diocesan bishop presides over the diocesan synod; he can, however, delegate the vicar general or an episcopal vicar to fulfill this office for individual sessions of the synod.

A vicar general or episcopal vicar cannot *convoke* a synod even if he has received a special mandate for all acts reserved by universal law to the diocesan bishop. The word "only" prohibits the conferral of such a mandate even ad hoc.[9] Convocation in this sense, however, is effected simply by a decree. The preliminary work (e.g., the selection of participants, their deputation, the procedures to be followed) can be entirely delegated to a vicar general or episcopal vicar (c. 463). The diocesan administrator *sede vacante* is explicitly prohibited from convoking a synod; the same restriction applies a fortiori to an auxiliary bishop who, while retaining his powers and faculties of governance, must exercise them under the authority of the administrator (c. 409, §2).

The 1917 Code distinguished the sessions of the synod itself (sometimes called *solemn sessions*) from preparatory sessions. A delegate of the bishop could preside over preparatory sessions (*CIC* 361). The revised Code avoids this distinction, stating simply that a vicar may be delegated to preside at individual sessions (§2). No one other than a vicar may be delegated to fulfill this office; nor may the vicar be delegated at the start of the synod to preside at *all* the sessions. This would frustrate the intent of the institute, which is designed to bring the diocesan bishop as legislator together with many responsible clerics, religious, and lay persons in order to hear

open discussion and ponder the acts of governance which will prove most beneficial to the diocese.

Participation in the Synod

Canon 463 — §1. The following persons are to be called to the diocesan synod as its members and are obliged to participate in it:

1° the coadjutor bishop and the auxiliary bishops;

2° the vicars general, the episcopal vicars and the judicial vicar;

3° the canons of the cathedral church;

4° the members of the presbyteral council;

5° lay members of the Christian faithful and members of institutes of consecrated life, to be selected by the pastoral council in a manner and number to be determined by the diocesan bishop or, where such a council does not exist, in a manner determined by the diocesan bishop;

6° the rector of the diocesan major seminary;

7° the vicars forane;

8° at least one presbyter to be selected from each vicariate forane by all who have the care of souls there; also to be selected is another presbyter who would take the place of the first one selected if he were impeded;

9° some superiors of the religious institutes and societies of apostolic life which have a house in the diocese, to be selected in a manner and number determined by the diocesan bishop.

§2. Others can be called as members to the diocean synod by the diocesan bishop; these can be clerics, members of institutes of consecrated life, or lay members of the Christian faithful.

§3. If he should judge it opportune, the diocesan bishop can invite as observers to the diocesan synod some ministers or members of churches or ecclesial communities which are not in full communion with the Catholic Church.

A diocesan synod is not simply a group of persons freely selected by the bishop. While there is flexibility in composing the synod, certain obligations are clearly specified. The first two paragraphs of the canon indicate respectively those who *must* be called and those who *can* be called to serve as synodal members. Paragraph three provides the option of inviting ecumenical guests to attend the sessions as observers, a role distinct from that of synodal members.

The first paragraph lists nine categories of persons whom the diocesan bishop must call to participate in the synod. This episcopal obligation to call such persons is complemented by a similar obligation on their part to participate. Both the convocation and the acceptance should be in writing in order to verify precisely those who are officially "members of the synod" ("sodales") with the right of free discussion and consultative vote. This list of

---

[8]Cf. c. 428. This interpretation is consistent with *CIC* 356, which uses the phrase "in perpetuam administrationem," and with the prohibition against the convocation of a synod by one who has *interim* charge of a diocese (c. 462, §1).
[9]*CIC* 357, §1 mentioned both "convoking" and "presiding," thus implying that both acts could be performed by a vicar general with a special mandate. The revised Code treats them separately: "convoking" in c. 462, §1 and "presiding" in c. 462, §2.

priests, religious, and laity revises canon 358, §1 of the 1917 Code, which was exclusively clerical. It adds the following to the 1917 list: the auxiliary bishops; the vicars episcopal; the judicial vicar; the members of the presbyteral council; lay persons and members of lay institutes of consecrated life selected by the pastoral council or, in its absence, by a special process established by the bishop; one priest and a substitute from each deanery; some superiors of religious institutes and societies of apostolic life selected in accord with a process determined by the bishop. The list retains the following from the former Code: the rector of the major seminary (both college seminary and theologate, c. 250); the deans; the canons of the cathedral chapter.

The first paragraph fails to mention lay representatives of societies of apostolic life, deacons, or the moderators of secular institutes. Such persons can be included, however, on the basis of the second paragraph which permits the bishop to convoke others to serve as synodal members. Although societies of apostolic life are overlooked in this second paragraph, their members can be called since they would qualify as either clerics or lay persons. These persons do not have the same obligation to participate as those listed in paragraph one, but they have some responsibility to accept the bishop's designation since they are not simply *invited* but *convoked.*

Paragraph three states the option of *inviting* leaders and other representatives of the Orthodox and Protestant Churches to participate in the synod as ecumenical observers. This list is not taxative but simply exemplificative of those who might be interested in the synodal proceedings. Unbaptized persons, though not mentioned in paragraph three, could also be invited as observers.

Canon 464 — A member of the synod who is hindered by a legitimate impediment cannot send a proxy to attend in his or her name; such a member is to inform the diocesan bishop of this impediment.

Those called to synod on the basis of canon 463, §§1 and 2 are members with the right to speak and vote. Even if legitimately unable to attend, they cannot send representatives to take their place. The only exception in universal law is that of the priest representing a deanery. If he is canonically impeded, his alternate can substitute for him. The diocesan bishop himself, however, may include in his determination of the process for selecting representative laity and religious superiors (c. 463, §1, 5° and 9°) a provision for substitution modeled after the arrangement for deanery representation. Since synodal observers are not officially members of the synod, they too can send substitutes unless the diocesan bishop decrees otherwise.[10]

Canon 465 — All the proposed questions are to be subject to the free discussion of the members during the sessions of the synod.

The method of celebrating the synod is left completely in the hands of the diocesan bishop and the synodal members. The revised Code has deleted all references to preparatory commissions and schemata[11] and retained solely the general principle that the sessions must be marked by "free discussion." This phrase, preserved from the 1917 Code, is given added significance by many of the rights articulated at the beginning of Book II: for example, the right to make one's opinion known (c. 212), the right to be educated in the faith (c. 217), the right to freedom of inquiry (c. 218), and the right to one's good reputation (c. 220). The process for a successful synod must seek to promote the exercise of these and other human and ecclesial rights by careful planning, the collection of accurate data and its communication to all members, procedures to facilitate collegial discussion and the drafting of background papers and proposed decrees, and a process of interaction with the diocesan bishop to assist him in making the final legislative decisions.

Synodal Legislation

Canon 466 — The diocesan bishop is the sole legislator at a diocesan synod while the remaining members of the synod possess only a consultative vote; he alone signs the synodal declarations and decrees which can be published only through his authority.

The diocesan bishop is identified as a member of the synod and its sole legislator.[12] The "consultative vote" of the other members, however, should not be demeaned. The intent of the synodal process is not merely the articulation of advice. It is a collaborative effort to arrive at acceptable statements and decrees which will be truly beneficial for the diocese. In this sense *consultation* means more than simply *advice;* it implies mutual responsibilities on the part of all the people of God gathered together in synod. The diocesan bishop cannot at the outset delegate the synodal members to legislate on his behalf (c. 135, §2). Nevertheless, he can indicate that he will rarely reject recommendations overwhelmingly approved by the synod unless he has compelling reasons to do so, an attitude encouraged by the Code

---

[10]Cf. *Comm* 12 (1980), 317.

[11]*CIC* 360–361. The deletions were approved by the Commission regarding c. 384 of the 1980 schema which had retained the details of CIC 360 *(Rel,* 111).

[12]The "free discussion" urged in the canon refers solely to the official members of the synod, not to the ecumenical or other observers who may be present. Nevertheless, nothing prevents the presiding officer from recognizing observers and permitting them to voice their reactions or even to submit written comments for the benefit of the members, (Cf. *Rel,* 111 *ad c. 385.*)

(c. 127, §2). While only the bishop promulgates the synodal documents, they are truly the product of all the representatives of the community.[13]

When the bishop signs the synodal documents, he should explicitly state the laws he is promulgating as well as the date on which they begin to bind; otherwise, diocesan laws will automatically begin to be in effect one month after promulgation (c. 8, §2).

Canon 467 — The diocesan bishop is to communicate the texts of the synodal declarations and decrees to the metropolitan and to the conference of bishops.

This new canon recognizes the need for the sharing of information at the level of the province and the conference of bishops. Copies of the synodal issuances should be sent to the metropolitan and to the general secretary of the conference. If not otherwise disseminated, the documents should at least be kept on file so that other bishops will be able to benefit from valuable developments in individual dioceses. Earlier versions of this canon required the communication of the synodal declarations and decrees to the Apostolic See.[14] In the final stages of the revision process, however, it was decided that the collection of such diocesan legislation at the universal level reflected an overly centralized approach.[15] The final text, therefore, limits the sharing of information to the national and provincial levels. It should be noted that the *communication* of texts in no way implies the need for acceptance or approval by the recipients.

Cessation of a Synod

Canon 468 — §1. It is within the competence of the diocesan bishop to suspend or dissolve a diocesan synod in accord with his own prudent judgment.

§2. If the episcopal see should become vacant or impeded, a diocesan synod is interrupted by the law itself until the succeeding diocesan bishop has decreed that it is to continue or that it is terminated.

This canon, which has no counterpart in the 1917 Code, states that a bishop may suspend or dissolve the synod. A decree of suspension, sent to all the synodal members, should indicate whether the synod's activity is halted indefinitely or only for a specific period of time. The reference to "prudent judgment" implies that the bishop must have a just cause to suspend or dissolve the synod.

The episcopal see becomes vacant by the death, resignation, transfer, or removal of the bishop (c. 416). It is impeded if all communication between

him and the diocese is disrupted because of physical separation or physical or mental incapacity (c. 412). In such cases the law itself *interrupts* the synod, i.e., suspends its activity until the see is unimpeded or a successor takes office. Physical or mental incapacity in this case is any condition which prevents the diocesan bishop from exercising his legislative authority, thereby nullifying the very purpose of the synod.

When a synod is suspended, either by decree or by law, the members of the synod may not meet formally even if, prior to the suspension, a vicar was given a special mandate to preside at individual synodal sessions. When the new bishop takes possession of his office, he may simply reconvene the synod as it is, dissolve it outright, dissolve it and call another, or alter the existing synod in his decree of continuation in regard to such points as membership, matters under discussion, or the procedures being followed.

CHAPTER II
THE DIOCESAN CURIA
[cc. 469–494]

The initial six canons of this chapter define the diocesan curia, the method of appointment, the coordination of diocesan administration, and the formalities for juridic documents. The chapter then treats, in separate articles, three institutes of administration: vicars general and episcopal vicars, notarization and archives, the finance council and finance officer.

Definition of the Diocesan Curia

Canon 469 — The diocesan curia consists of those institutions and persons which furnish assistance to the bishop in the governance of the entire diocese, especially in directing pastoral activity, in providing for the administration of the diocese and in exercising judicial power.

The canon expands the definition of the diocesan curia of canon 363 of the 1917 Code, which left the phrase "the governance of the whole diocese" unexplained. The revised version specifies that such governance includes especially the direction of pastoral activity, the administration of the diocese as a juridic person, and the exercise of judicial power. In doing so, it recognizes that the curia consists not only of persons but of institutes or structures[16] and includes among its officers lay persons and religious as well as clerics. The canon refrains from identifying the elements of the curia by name as did the 1917 Code (*CIC* 363, §2) (vicar general, chancellor, tribunal officials, examiners, and parish priest consultors). Instead, it leaves their identification to the

---

[13]The phrase "remaining members" was inserted deliberately to distinguish the diocesan bishop from the other members of the synod. *Comm* 12 (1980), 318.

[14]Cf. c. 279 of the 1977 schema and c. 387 of the 1980 schema.

[15]Cf. *Rel,* 111 *ad c. 387.*

[16]The word "institutis" was inserted in the revision of *CIC* 363.

diocesan bishop.[17] The curia certainly includes the vicars general and episcopal vicars, the chancellor and other notaries, the tribunal personnel, and the finance officer. It would also seem to include the finance council, specifically treated in article 3. The three articles of this chapter, however, do not offer a taxative list. Given the Code's concept of ecclesiastical office (c. 145), all those who participate in the overall administration of the diocese should be considered members of the diocesan curia, especially those who direct diocesan departments such as education, religious education, liturgy, charity, social concerns, temporalities, and the other facets of ecclesial life organized and promoted at the diocesan level.[18] The presbyteral council and the college of consultors, which are treated in a separate chapter, are not, strictly speaking, institutes of the curia although they are closely associated with it insofar as their counsel assists the bishop in the governance of the diocese (c. 495).[19] Synodal examiners and parish priest consultors (*CIC* 385–390) are deleted from the Code. Those appointed to such offices prior to the promulgation lost all rights and were no longer bound by their obligations when the revised Code became effective (11/27/83) since the offices themselves were suppressed. Pastors constituted by the presbyteral council to advise the bishop regarding the administrative removal or transfer of a pastor (cc. 1740–1752), are similar to the examiners and parish priest consultors of the former Code. They too are considered members of the diocesan curia even though their involvement in diocesan administration will be rather infrequent.

Appointment to Curial Offices

The next two norms reinforce the expanded notion of the curia found in canon 469. While canon

[17]The canon uses the phrase "the bishop" instead of "the diocesan bishop" which is the more precise term according to cc. 134 and 381. The word *Episcopus* was repeated from *CIC* 363 which also had a reference to those who govern the diocese *loco Episcopi,* a phrase deleted by the revised canon as superfluous. In several canons in this section and, in fact, throughout the Code, the single word *episcopus* is used when the norm should more precisely state *episcopus dioecesanus.* Sometimes, the canon has already referred to the diocese and therefore avoids repeating the word in adjectival form (e.g., c. 369). In other places, however, there seems to be no justification for the imprecision other than an oversight caused by reproducing too literally the text of the 1917 Code (e.g., c. 487 which relies on *CIC* 377.

[18]Cf. *Directory:* "To the extent that he is able, the bishop establishes in the curia pastoral, social-charitable, and liturgical departments with the responsibility of directing the many services of the apostolate, as well as the councils, offices, standing and temporary committees for transacting particular and current business, secretaries, and such like" (no. 200).

[19]The distinction between curia and councils is concisely described in the *Directory:* "The curia, therefore, ought to be the means for studying, planning and carrying through the pastoral program which the bishop weighs and ponders together with his councils" (no. 200).

364 of the 1917 Code dealt with the appointment of persons to those offices specifically mentioned in the canon (*praedicta*), canons 470 and 471 apply to all those who exercise offices within the curia.

Canon 470 — **The diocesan bishop appoints those who exercise offices within the diocesan curia.**

Since curial offices are not limited to those treated in this chapter, the canon states a general principle that all officeholders are appointed by the diocesan bishop.[20] The vicar general or episcopal vicar, even with ordinary executive power, may not appoint members of the curia to their offices unless the former has received a special mandate to this effect (c. 134).

Some curial offices are fully described in universal law; others are not. In appointing persons to the latter offices, it is important to refer to the canons on ecclesiastical offices for guidance (cc. 145–196). Some of these norms deserve special mention. The obligations and rights of an office should be defined by the authority who constitutes the office (c. 145, §2). A candidate for appointment must be in communion with the Church and qualified for the office according to law (c. 149, §1). Any office which requires the exercise of priestly orders cannot be validly conferred on anyone other than a bishop or a priest (c. 150). No one can be appointed to two or more offices which are incompatible, that is, which cannot be fulfilled properly by one person (c. 152). Every appointment to an office should be in writing (c. 156). This last provision, explicitly contained in canon 364 of the 1917 Code, was deleted from canon 470 only because it was repetitious. Since such appointments are meant to have juridic effect, the norm of canon 156 should be scrupulously followed; in addition, the letter of appointment should be notarized in accord with canon 474.

Canon 471 — **All persons who are admitted to offices within the curia must:**
1° promise to fulfill their function faithfully according to the manner determined by law or by the bishop;
2° observe secrecy within the limits and according to the manner determined by law or by the bishop.

The canon creates a twofold canonical obligation for those appointed to a curial office: (a) to carry out their duties faithfully, a legal duty to be reinforced by a personal promise; and (b) to respect confidentiality required by law or by the bishop. The canon has simplified canon 364, §2 of the 1917

[20]Cf. c. 157. This specification was missing in *CIC* 364 since it was addressed in the separate canons describing the appointment of the various officeholders listed in *CIC* 363, §2.

Code and changed its emphasis. It no longer speaks of taking an oath in the hands of the bishop. Instead, the obligations of service and secrecy, attached to the acceptance of the office, are reinforced by the ecclesiastical law itself.

By omitting a reference to the bishop, however, the canon leaves a lacuna regarding the promise of faithful service. Since it is not an oath, it is not made directly to God. The final phrase of the first paragraph ("or [determined] by the bishop") does not refer to the method of making such a promise but to the determination of one's duties.[21] It is not clear, therefore, whether the promise is made to the diocesan bishop or simply to the Church in general. The most reasonable interpretation seems to be that the promise can be made to the diocesan bishop in person, before his delegate, or simply in writing. A written record of the promise should be retained since it provides proof of the intimation of the appointment to the officeholder and his or her personal acceptance of the rights and duties attached to the office.

Tribunal Personnel

Canon 472 — The prescriptions of Book VII: *Processes* are to be observed concerning cases and persons which refer to the exercise of judicial power in the curia; the prescriptions of the following canons are to be observed concerning those matters which involve the administration of the diocese.

Since Book VII describes the rights and responsibilities of those who exercise judicial authority, the remainder of the canons in this chapter do not apply to tribunal personnel as such. The first three canons do apply to them, however, including the need to be appointed by the diocesan bishop, the promise of service, and the obligation of secrecy—matters also treated in canons 1454–1455. If some elements of tribunal activity apply to the general administration of the diocese, these would be regulated by the canons in Book II unless they touch on the internal workings of the tribunal. For example, the salaries of all tribunal personnel are not regulated by canon 1649 on tribunal fees and would normally be governed by the administrative norms common to the entire diocesan curia.

Coordination of the Curia

Canon 473 — §1. The diocesan bishop must see to it that all matters which concern the administra-

tion of the entire diocese are duly coordinated and arranged in such a manner that the good of the portion of God's people entrusted to him is more suitably attained.

§2. It is the responsibility of the diocesan bishop himself to coordinate the pastoral activity of the vicars general or episcopal vicars; whenever it is expedient he can appoint a moderator of the curia, who ought to be a priest, and whose task it is, under the authority of the bishop, to coordinate the exercise of administrative responsibilities and to see to it that the other members of the curia duly fulfill the office entrusted to them.

§3. Unless in the judgment of the bishop local circumstances warrant otherwise, the vicar general or, if there are several, one of the vicars general is to be appointed moderator of the curia.

§4. If he judges it expedient in fostering more suitable pastoral activity, the bishop can establish an episcopal council consisting of the vicars general and the episcopal vicars.

The need to coordinate diocesan administration exists in every diocese, but it is especially critical in larger dioceses where many vicars and other personnel may be appointed to direct and promote pastoral activity. This new canon addresses such a need, at least in principle. It refers to four distinct offices and institutes: the diocesan bishop, the vicars general and episcopal vicars, the moderator of the curia, and the episcopal council.

The *diocesan bishop* has the ultimate responsibility for coordinating and regulating diocesan activities. This responsibility will be exercised solely in regard to offices explicitly contained in the Code if no other offices are established on the diocesan level. In other cases, however, the curia is far more complex and includes many additional offices and departments which assist him in fulfilling his duties as head of the portion of the people of God entrusted to his pastoral care. The diocesan bishop can cede neither his duty nor his authority over all diocesan agencies and personnel, a factor which can be significant when someone's rights have allegedly been violated by an agent of the diocese.[22]

Vicars general and episcopal vicars are a form of shared responsibility in the Church. They participate in executive (administrative) governance with ordinary power and are regulated not only by the will of the diocesan bishop but by the universal law as well. If there is more than one vicar general or if several episcopal vicars are named to meet the needs of the diocese, their own activity must be coordinated; otherwise, there would be no hope of unified pastoral action among those subject to the individual vicars. Paragraph two of the canon states that the coordination of vicars is the diocesan bishop's task. The paragraph then addresses the possi-

---

[21]The comma between "adimplendo" and "secundum" in the first paragraph might raise doubts about this interpretation, especially since no such comma is found in the second paragraph. The record of the Commission's discussion of this canon, however, suggests that the comma was retained as a typographical error caused by the deletion of an intervening phrase "addito etiam iuramento." Cf. *Comm* 13 (1981), 114.

[22]Cf. c. 1734, §3.

ble need for a moderator of the curia. It should be noted that the canon does not state that a vicar general, as vicar general, is responsible for such coordination. The Code generally presumes that the vicar general is concerned with *centralized administration* of a bureaucratic nature while the episcopal vicars specialize in *pastoral work*. Because of this distinction, the vicar general is not granted by the universal law itself the vicarious charge to coordinate the work of colleagues, the episcopal vicars. This remains the personal responsibility of the diocesan bishop unless he specifically determines otherwise.[23]

The *moderator of the curia* is an optional office ("he *can* appoint"). An earlier draft mandated the office for all dioceses, but the Commission subsequently decided that it would be of only limited value in a smaller diocese in which coordination is more easily and effectively achieved by the diocesan bishop himself.[24] The moderator must be a priest or bishop and should be a vicar general unless the diocesan bishop makes an exception because of local circumstances. The Code's notion of a moderator of the curia may not be entirely compatible with existing attempts at coordination in individual dioceses. On the one hand, in some dioceses coordination is a separate and integral function, for example, in the form of a lay administrative director without the general responsibility or administrative authority of a vicar general or of a priest as an episcopal vicar for solely canonical or administrative affairs. On the other hand, the moderator of the curia is not supposed to be a "super vicar general," somehow "more" an alter ego of the bishop than the other vicars. Neither approach is consistent with the notion of moderator found in the Code. The canon restricts the office to a priest or bishop since the moderator is expected to possess and exercise ordinary executive power and be able to make pastoral decisions affecting the entire diocese. Nevertheless, if there are other vicars general or episcopal vicars, his duties as moderator do not extend to them as such. He is concerned primarily with administrative matters and with the supervision of those working in the curia (§2). Of course, an individual episcopal vicar may be directly accountable to the moderator if the former happens to head an agency or office in the curia (e.g., vicar for religious or for priest personnel). Because of the comprehensive nature of his responsibilities, it is appropriate for the moderator of the curia to be a vicar general rather than an episcopal vicar (§3), for his duties refer to the centralized administrative offices rather than to pastoral activity in a particular region or apostolate. The norm in paragraph three underscores the above-mentioned distinction of the Commission between the activity of vicars general and episcopal vicars.

The coordination of the activity of the *vicars* is the responsibility of the diocesan bishop himself, not specifically of the vicar general or the moderator of the curia (at least by universal law).[25] To assist him in this task, however, he may constitute an *episcopal council* to foster pastoral activity more suitably (§4). The final version of paragraph four restricts quite considerably the scope of this council. The text excludes not only lay persons but also any cleric who is not a vicar. The purpose of this council is not the *collegial governance* of the diocese (a concern voiced by some drafters of the law) but the furtherance of pastoral activity by *coordinating the work of the vicars* among themselves under the direction of the diocesan bishop. The constitution of such a council is optional.[26]

While the underlying theory of canon 473 is fairly plain, the canon itself is rather open-ended. It is an important addition to the Code since it recognizes the critical need for coordination at the diocesan level, a need which the diocesan bishop may not be able to meet without special help. It fosters the exercise of ordinary power by those in charge of such coordination and yet it does not impose structures unnecessarily.

The Acts of the Curia

Canon 474 — Those curial acts which are to have a juridic effect must, for their validity, be signed by the ordinary from whom they emanate; likewise they are to be signed by the chancellor or the notary of the curia; the chancellor is bound to inform the moderator of the curia concerning such acts.

This new norm reflects a prevalent concern of the Code that acts of ecclesiastical authorities be put in writing. The following are some examples: appointment to any ecclesiastical office (c. 156); incardination/excardination (c. 267, §1); consent of the diocesan bishop for the establishment of a religious house in his diocese (c. 609); and general delegation to assist at marriages (c. 1111). These are just a few instances of the requirement of documentation in matters which have longstanding juridic effects. This canon seeks to guarantee the authen-

---

[23]Cf. *Comm* 13 (1981), 116. The task is that of the diocesan bishop; if he needs help, he may appoint a moderator of the curia.
[24]*Comm* 13 (1981), 115–116.

[25]This is even clearer when one notices the *deletion* of c. 293, §2 of the 1977 schema: "In order to foster harmonious pastoral activity and unity of discipline throughout the diocese, vicars general and episcopal should frequently confer with the vicar general who is the moderator of the curia in accord with the determinations of the diocesan bishop." Cf. also *Comm* 13 (1981), 120.
[26]Cf. the deletion of the phrases "and certain other clerics chosen by him" and "the orderly governance of the diocese" from canon 285, §3 of the 1977 schema, the discussion in *Comm* 13 (1981), 116–117 and in *Comm* 5 (1973), 225, and the response concerning c. 393 in the *Rel*, 112.

ticity of such documentation by certain official signatures. The intent is straightforward and simple enough, but questions are raised by the wording of the canon.

a. An extremely important distinction must be noted at the outset between *curial acts* which are meant to have a juridic effect and *juridic acts* (cc. 124–128). A curial act (*actum curiae*) is a *document.* It may be a rescript, a decree, a letter, or some other form of writing. When the document has juridic consequences, it must be signed by the ordinary who issues it in order to be a valid *document.* A juridic act (*actus iuridicus*) is the *action of a person.* If the person has proper authority, posits what the act essentially requires, and observes the formalities and conditions required by law for validity, the juridic act is valid (c. 124). The validity of an *actum curiae* (the document itself) can affect the validity of an *actus iuridicus* (the authority's action) if, as canon 124, §1 prescribes, the *written form* is a formality required by law for the *juridic act's* validity. If, on the other hand, a juridic act need not be in writing in order to be valid, the invalidity of the written document would not invalidate the juridic act itself. Two examples may help to clarify this distinction. A matrimonial dispensation is a juridic act which can be posited by the vicar general (c. 1078, §1). Although dispensations should normally be communicated through a written rescript, this is not a requirement for the validity of the dispensation itself. If a vicar general grants such a dispensation, instructs his secretary to prepare the rescript, and then fails to sign it, the rescript is invalid but the dispensation is valid. In order to prove the validly posited juridic act in the external forum, however, it will be necessary to obtain the vicar's signature or verification by a notary that the juridic act was in fact posited. Incardination/excardination, however, is a juridic act in which the written form is required for validity (c. 267, §1). If the bishop indicates to his chancellor that he has decided to incardinate a particular priest, orders a decree of incardination to be drawn up, but neglects to sign it, the document itself is invalid (*actum curiae*) and, since no written form of incardination validly exists, the juridic act of incardination (*actus iuridicus*) is also invalid. The chancellor's verification of the bishop's decision does not suffice. There is no juridic act until a valid written instrument exists. Canon 474 refers *directly* to a *document* (*actum*) and only *indirectly* affects the exercise of governance in a *juridic act* (*actus*).

b. Does the phrase "curial acts" include the written acts of the diocesan bishop himself? The diocesan bishop is distinct from the curia and yet, if the documents of those who assist him must be signed and countersigned, it seems logical that the one with ultimate responsibility for diocesan administration should be no less obliged to certain formalities than are his collaborators. Furthermore, to

hold the more restrictive interpretation of "curial acts" would mean that documents signed by the diocesan bishop are not the concern of the chancellor's archival duties since the same phrase is used in this context in canon 482. Although conditions for validity require a strict interpretation, to exempt the acts of the diocesan bishop from the phrase "curial acts" would be not only strict but also unreasonable and contrary to the intent of the law.[27]

c. Another question is raised by the use of the word "ordinary." According to canon 134, an "ordinary" refers to the diocesan bishop and his vicars general and episcopal vicars. A definite distinction is made between "ordinaries" and those who act by generally delegated executive power (*ad universitatem casuum*).[28] In many dioceses several types of juridic acts are posited by those enjoying only delegated authority (e.g., chancellors). Certainly, the intent of the canon is to require on every curial act the signature of the person issuing it. Nevertheless, the technical wording of canon 134 justifies the strict interpretation that the requirement of the signature *for validity* applies only to acts placed by the diocesan bishop or one of his vicars. Those acting by delegated authority are obliged to put juridic acts in writing and sign them; their failure to sign, however, would not invalidate the document.

d. The countersignature by the chancellor or notary obliges all those issuing curial acts, but it is not a condition of validity.[29] If the chancellor issues a curial act on the basis of delegated authority (e.g., a dispensation rescript), he should sign it personally and arrange for it to be countersigned by the vice-chancellor or another notary.

Two of the values promoted by the maintenance of a written record are consistency and accountability. Without written policies and procedures, unity and coordination in today's complex world are not likely to be achieved. Writings represent decisions and commitments and offer the administrator a secure data base for consistent action and pastoral planning. The verification of data and information-sharing are functions quite distinct from decision-making. The chancellor's notarization and data storage responsibilities are meant to stabilize such functions in a diocese. Decision-makers will turn to archives to refresh their memories and provide a history upon which to base present action. The written records found in archives are especially important for those concerned primarily with coordination, such as the moderator of the curia. The canon notes, therefore, that a close collaboration must exist between chancellor and moderator so that all curial acts having a juridic effect will immediately be made known to the moderator who can

[27] Cf. J.E. Prince, *The Diocesan Chancellor. An Historical Synopsis and Commentary, CanLawStud* 167 (Washington, D.C.: Catholic University, 1942), 66–68.
[28] Cf. cc. 137–138.
[29] *Comm* 5 (1973), 226 and *Rel,* 113 *ad c. 394.*

then integrate such information into the overall plan of organization at the diocesan level. If the diocese has no moderator of the curia, the chancellor should create a similar relationship with the vicar general overseeing diocesan administration.

ARTICLE 1: VICARS GENERAL AND EPISCOPAL VICARS
[cc. 475–481]

This article retains the traditional notion of the vicar general as the most important office of the diocesan curia and adds to it the concept of the episcopal vicar established by the Second Vatican Council (*CD* 23, 26, 27).

The vicar general is a diocesan figure which evolved during the last millennium. Some have suggested that the office was developed to replace that of the archdeacon since the latter began to cause considerable dissension, particularly in the twelfth and thirteenth centuries. Others conclude that the vicar was used solely to supplement the work of archdeacons, many of whom were unable or neglected to fulfill all their responsibilities. During the Middle Ages various titles identified a figure similar to today's vicar general: *procurator, provisor, adiutor,* and *episcopalis officii vices.* For example, a text in the *Decretals* of Gregory IX refers to *vicarii et procuratores generales.* At the start, such authorities governed the diocese only when the bishop was absent from his see or when the see was vacant. By the fourteenth century, however, the vicar was recognized as possessing comprehensive jurisdiction within the diocese even when the bishop was present. His jurisdiction extended *tam in spiritualibus quam in temporalibus,* to all aspects of life in the diocese, including at times authority over the officialis. In certain cases, the same cleric served as both vicar and officialis. The 1917 Code implemented the directives of Vatican I by stabilizing the office of vicar general as the alter ego of the diocesan bishop, prohibiting the use of the title for honorary purposes, limiting the number of vicars general, and defining their jurisdiction.[30] The 1983 Code retains substantially the same description and strengthens it by explicitating the vicar's governance as executive in nature and requiring that every diocese have at least one vicar general.

The same article introduces into the Code the figure of the episcopal vicar who is likened in all things to the vicar general but who functions only in regard to "a certain part of the diocese, or for a determined type of activity, or for the faithful of a determined rite" (*CD* 27). The conciliar imperative to establish this office was implemented in *Ecclesiae*

sanctae I,14, whose norms are here incorporated into the Code.

The Definition of Vicars General and Episcopal Vicars

Canon 475 — §1. A vicar general is to be appointed in each diocese by the diocesan bishop; he is to assist the diocesan bishop in the governance of the entire diocese and is endowed with ordinary power according to the following canons.

§2. As a general rule only one vicar general is to be appointed unless the size of the diocese, the number of its inhabitants or other pastoral reasons warrant otherwise.

The revision makes the office of vicar general *mandatory* for every diocese (§1). The 1917 Code (*CIC* 366, §1) had *urged* the appointment of a vicar general "whenever the proper governance of the diocese" required it. This qualifying phrase (now used in c. 476 regarding episcopal vicars) left the decision to establish the office of vicar general in a particular diocese to the bishop. The deletion of the phrase makes the office an unqualified requirement. This was the explicit intention of the Code Commission based on its reading of Vatican II.[31]

The use of the phrase "as a general rule" in the second paragraph permits the diocesan bishop to appoint more than one vicar general. The 1917 Code mentioned only two reasons to justify more than one vicar general: diversity of rites and the size of the diocese (*CIC* 366, §2). The revised Code adds the notion of a large number of inhabitants and "other pastoral reasons." In dioceses with an extensive Catholic population, it may be pastorally helpful to the diocesan bishop to appoint more than one vicar general, particularly if the former has been assigned auxiliary bishops to assist in the overall office of pastoral care (cf. c. 406). In many cases, however, the possibility of appointing episcopal vicars and the very concept of the vicar general as a director of central administration should dissuade the diocesan bishop from multiplying many vicars general. Pastoral effectiveness may very well suffer and ecclesial unity be impaired if too many persons exercise executive governance over the entire diocese. In such cases, the office designed to facilitate and unify diocesan administration would have the very opposite effect. The practice of naming honorary vicars general is also alien to the Code. It diminishes the important role of the vicar general as one with ordinary universal executive power since those with the title never in fact exercise such authority.

Canon 476 — As often as the correct goverance of the diocese requires it the diocesan bishop can

---

[30]Cf. T.D. Dougherty, *The Vicar General of the Episcopal Ordinary, CanLawStud* 447 (Washington, D.C.: Catholic University, 1966).

[31]*Comm* 5 (1973), 226 and 13 (1981), 118.

also appoint one or several episcopal vicars, who possess the same ordinary power which the universal law gives to the vicar general according to the following canons either in a determined section of the diocese or in a certain type of business or over the faithful of a determined rite or over certain groups of persons.

Episcopal vicars are *optional.* The qualifying phrase from canon 366 of the 1917 Code, which had applied to the vicar general, is now used as a rationale for episcopal vicars: "as often as the correct governance of the diocese requires it." Even then, the revised Code states not that a bishop *must* appoint an episcopal vicar when the need is present but that he *can* do so.

The episcopal vicar is equated to the vicar general in all ways except the extent of his responsibilities and authority. While the vicar general possesses executive authority in all aspects of diocesan administration not reserved to the bishop himself, the episcopal vicar enjoys ordinary executive authority solely in regard to a specific type of activity or a particular group of persons identified by some objective criterion such as territory, rite, or ethnic background. It is important to clarify the special field of endeavor proper to the episcopal vicar since there should be no doubt about the area in which he exercises ordinary power of executive governance.[32] This determination should be included in the document constituting the office of the episcopal vicar or in the letter of appointment itself. The same document should also indicate explicitly any matters reserved to the diocesan bishop or the vicar general and any additional mandates to act which would not normally be considered part of the episcopal vicar's ordinary power of governance.

The Appointment of a Vicar

Canon 477 — **§1. With due regard for the prescription of can. 406, the diocesan bishop freely appoints and freely removes a vicar general and an episcopal vicar; an episcopal vicar who is not an auxiliary bishop is to be appointed only for a time to be determined in the act of appointment.**

§2. When a vicar general is absent or legitimately impeded the diocesan bishop can appoint another to take his place; the same norm applies to an episcopal vicar.

Vicars general and episcopal vicars are appointed at the discretion of the diocesan bishop. They do not have even the qualified independence of the officialis who may be removed only for a "legitimate

[32]"In appointing an episcopal vicar, the bishop will be concerned to define accurately the area of his authority lest the jurisdiction of several persons should overlap or become doubtful." *Directory,* no. 202.

and serious cause" (c. 1422). One who serves as the alter ego of the bishop must have his complete and continued confidence. Total dependence on the diocesan bishop, while making the office somewhat precarious in nature, also reinforces its authority. When one can so easily be removed, one's continued presence and action are all the more authoritative. (The same rule can sometimes be seen in the business world where the authority and power of executives are often matched by lack of job security.) While the diocesan bishop has complete discretion in the appointing and removing of priests as vicars, the same does not hold true in regard to auxiliary bishops. By law coadjutors and auxiliaries with special papal faculties must be appointed as vicars general and all other auxiliaries must be appointed as episcopal vicars if not vicars general (c. 406).

A priest who is appointed an episcopal vicar may not be given a permanent or indefinite appointment. He must receive a term of office although there is no prohibition against repeatedly renewing such a term. A priest can be appointed as vicar general indefinitely or for a limited term. Because of canon 406 (mentioned above), an auxiliary bishop is appointed as vicar general or episcopal vicar indefinitely. In all cases the juridic act constituting the office in the diocese and/or the letter of appointment should state whether the office is assigned indefinitely or for a specific period of time and whether the stated term is renewable. The appointment must be in writing, signed by the diocesan bishop, and notarized (cc. 156, 474).

The second paragraph of this canon, which restates substantially canon 366, §3 of the 1917 Code, provides for the occasion when the vicar general is away from the diocese. It is usually most helpful in situations in which both the diocesan bishop and the vicar general are absent at the same time, leaving no one in the diocese with ordinary universal power of executive governance. In a sense, the norm is superfluous, considering the complete discretion given to the diocesan bishop about both vicars general and episcopal vicars in canons 475–477. It is important to note that, although such an appointment may be for only a short time—even a few days—the conditions and formalities of the universal law for these offices must be observed (e.g., minimum age, pastoral qualifications, appointment in writing).

The Qualifications of a Vicar

Canon 478 — **§1. A vicar general and an episcopal vicar are to be priests, not less than thirty years of age, holding a doctorate or licentiate in canon law or in theology or at least being truly expert in these disciplines, as well as being recommended by reason of their sound doctrine, integrity, prudence, and experience in handling matters.**

§2. The role of vicar general and episcopal vicar cannot be assumed by the same person who functions as canon penitentiary; nor is this office to be entrusted to persons who are related by blood to the bishop up to the fourth degree.

The qualifications for both vicars general and episcopal vicars are identical; they repeat almost *verbatim* those found in the 1917 Code (*CIC* 367). The most fundamental requirement is that of priesthood. For the validity of the appointment the candidate must be a validly ordained priest or bishop. This condition is necessary because of the vicar's responsibility to exercise complete power of executive governance, including those acts for which the priestly character is required (cc. 129, §1; 150). The canon, however, does not limit candidates to *diocesan* priests. The 1917 Code required that the vicar general be a priest from the diocesan clergy even though incardinated in another diocese. A religious priest could be assigned as vicar only if the diocese itself had been committed to a particular religious community (*CIC* 367). The revised Code permits the diocesan bishop to appoint any priest or bishop to the post although the heightened emphasis given to the bishop's own presbyterate would suggest that the candidate should normally be selected from the clergy already serving the diocese, whether diocesan or religious.

Vicars must be thirty years old, an age requirement raised by the 1917 Code from that of twenty-five established by the Council of Trent. They must also be learned in the ecclesiastical sciences and possess those personal qualities which such a position of authority demands. In regard to academic qualifications, the canon retains the "equivalency clause" of canon 367, §1 of the 1917 Code ("or at least being truly expert"), similar to the norm on the bishop (c. 378, §1, 5°) and unlike the stricter qualifications for the officialis (c. 1420, §4) and the seminary professor (c. 253, §1).

The second paragraph of the canon retains two traditional disqualifications: the mixture of the fora and consanguinity. The exclusion of the canon penitentiary arises from the incompatibility of the two offices, a prohibition based on the general principle of canon 152. Since one office deals totally with the internal forum and the other with the external forum, insoluble conflicts would inevitably occur.

Close relatives of the diocesan bishop are excluded from the office to avoid any appearance of nepotism. Actually, the revised Code expands and strengthens the disqualification. The 1917 Code restricted the prohibition to those related to the bishop in the second grade mixed with the first (uncle-nephew) (*CIC* 367, §3). Using the Roman method of computation (c. 108), the revised Code prohibits relatives of the fourth grade, which would include first cousins or granduncle-grandnephew. On the other hand, the revised text omits the word

"especially" found in its predecessor (*CIC* 367, §3) which had implied that no blood relatives should be appointed as vicars without a special reason even if they were not within the grades specified by law. The present norm makes no such statement or implication of disqualification for anyone related more distantly than the fourth grade.

Finally, the revised Code omits the former prohibition (*CIC* 367, §3) against a pastor or anyone else exercising an office of pastoral care. The office of pastor and vicar are therefore recognized as essentially compatible although in practice the diocesan bishop must decide whether the responsibilities of the one office may seriously hamper the fulfillment of the responsibilities of the other. While a pastor might be able to serve effectively as the episcopal vicar of a local region without neglecting his parish duties, it seems unlikely—except in smaller dioceses—that he could function well as both a full-time pastor and a vicar general.[33]

The Vicar's Authority

Canon 479 — §1. In virtue of his office the vicar general possesses that executive power in the entire diocese which belongs to the diocesan bishop in law, that is, he possesses the power to place all administrative acts with the exception of those which the bishop has reserved to himself or which in law require the special mandate of the bishop.

§2. The episcopal vicar possesses by the law itself the same power mentioned in §1 but only over that determined section of territory, that type of business, or those faithful of a determined rite or group for which he was appointed, with the exception of those cases which the bishop has reserved to himself or to the vicar general or which in law require the special mandate of the bishop.

§3. Within the limits of their competency the vicar general and episcopal vicar also possess the habitual faculties granted to the bishop by the Apostolic See as well as the power to execute rescripts, unless other provisions have been expressly made or unless the diocesan bishop has been chosen to act because of some personal qualification.

The power of the vicar general is ordinary since it is by universal law attached to his office; it is vicarious since he exercises it on behalf of the diocesan bishop (who possesses ordinary and *proper* power of governance) (c. 131). While the vicar general is empowered to govern throughout the entire

---

[33]Cf. *Comm* 13 (1981), 119. While two *full-time* offices may not be compatible, all priests in the curia are not only permitted but encouraged by the *Directory* "to exercise some ministry for the care of souls, lest the curia become a merely administrative and juridical staff—which certainly will happen if the officials have almost no experience or understanding of pastoral work or of the needs of the faithful and of their spiritual life" (no. 200).

diocese, he does not have complete power of governance since he is limited to the executive area. He is not a legislator nor can legislative power be delegated to him by the diocesan bishop. Thus, he has no authority to pass laws or even general decrees, which are similar to laws (c. 30). He may, however, issue general executory decrees which determine ways in which laws are to be applied and their observance promoted (c. 31). The vicar general is not authorized to exercise judicial power; such power is reserved to the diocesan bishop and his officialis (judicial vicar). The officialis constitutes one tribunal with the diocesan bishop and he must be completely distinct from the vicar general (c. 1420, §1). In exercising ordinary executive power of governance the vicar general is bound by the general norms found in canons 136–144, which should be carefully studied by him upon acceptance of his office. He should note in particular the rules concerning those subject to him (c. 136), his right to delegate even "ad universitatem casuum" (c. 137), and his right to interpret his executive power broadly (c. 138).[34]

While the vicar general's executive power is considerable, it is not as extensive as that of the diocesan bishop since the latter may reserve certain administrative acts to himself or the law itself may prohibit the vicar general from acting in a particular matter without a special episcopal mandate. In the 1917 Code the requirement of a special mandate by universal law caused some confusion. Twenty-three canons explicitly called for a special mandate to enable the vicar general to act. Other canons, however, though not explicitly requiring a special mandate, dealt with serious matters more appropriately reserved to the bishop of the diocese.[35] This led commentators to conclude that the explicit references to a special mandate in the 1917 Code were not all-inclusive and represented only a demonstrative list. Debate ensued on what the vicar general could or could not do on the basis of ordinary power. The revised Code seeks to dispel this confusion by a stricter use of vocabulary. Although the diocesan bishop and the vicar general are both "ordinaries of the place," any canon which uses the words "diocesan bishop" applies *only* (*dumtaxat*) to the diocesan bishop and not to the vicar general or episcopal vicar unless the vicar has received a special mandate to act (c. 134, §3). If a canon uses the phrase "ordinary of the place," the vicar general is authorized to act even without a special mandate.

An example of this distinction can be seen in canon 87: the *diocesan bishop* can dispense from all universal disciplinary laws which are not reserved to the Apostolic See (§1); *every ordinary* (both the diocesan bishop and the vicar general) can dispense from the same laws as well as those reserved to the Apostolic See (except celibacy) when recourse to Rome is difficult and grave harm would result from the delay (§2). In normal circumstances (no difficulty of recourse or grave harm), the vicar general can dispense only from diocesan laws and those passed by a provincial or regional council or by the conference of bishops (c. 88), not from universal disciplinary laws. If the diocesan bishop wants the vicar general to be able to dispense from universal disciplinary laws under normal circumstances, he must grant him a special mandate to do so.[36]

The episcopal vicar has the same authority as the vicar general except for the more restrictively determined scope of his jurisdiction (by territory, activity, or group of persons). He is an ordinary of the place (c. 134, §1) and needs a special mandate if the universal law uses the term "diocesan bishop." One other difference between the vicar general and the episcopal vicar is the fact that the diocesan bishop can limit the episcopal vicar's power of governance by reserving some acts not only to himself but to the vicar general while the latter's power can be limited by the diocesan bishop's reservation of such acts to himself alone, not to someone else.

Similar to canons 66 and 368 of the 1917 Code, the third paragraph of this canon states that, in general, vicars receive all faculties habitually conceded to the diocesan bishop and may execute all apostolic rescripts unless a particular rescript was expressly assigned to the diocesan bishop because of his personal qualifications ("industria personae"). It should be noted that canon 134 applies only to the Code of Canon Law and does not affect subsequent documents granting such habitual faculties. If habitual faculties are conceded to the "diocesan bishop," they are nonetheless received by the vicars as well. If a Roman document wishes to restrict a particular faculty to diocesan bishops alone, it must explicitly state this fact (e.g., by a phrase such as

---

[34] The use of the term "executive" clarifies *CIC* 368, §1 which simply stated the vicar general's universal jurisdiction "in spiritualibus ac temporalibus, quae ad Episcopum iure ordinario pertinet."

[35] One example is the readmission to the clerical state of one who had returned to the lay state after receiving minor orders (*CIC* 212) (Dougherty, 63).

[36] The change in vocabulary will dispel some confusion although cases of doubt will remain. Some canons use different phrases such as *Episcopus* (c. 479, §§2–3), *auctoritas competens ecclesiastica* (c. 812), *Episcopus loci* (c. 763). In fact, the change in vocabulary did not provide the vicar general with many more faculties. Of the twenty-three norms explicitly calling for a special mandate for the vicar general in the 1917 Code, eleven use the phrase "diocesan bishop" in the 1983 Code (thus still requiring a special mandate for the vicar general), nine were completely abrogated or the institute gradually suppressed (e.g., benefices), and only three retained the term "ordinary of the place" (permission for a secret marriage in c. 1130 [*CIC* 1104]; permission to establish a public oratory in c. 1223 [*CIC* 1191]; the remission of penalties in the external forum in c. 1355 [*CIC* 2314, §2]).

exclusis vicariis generalibus et episcopalibus); otherwise, the norm found in this third paragraph will be operative and no special mandate will be needed for the vicars to exercise the faculty.

Finally, it should be noted that, although the canons, by using the phrase "diocesan bishop," require a special mandate for the vicars to act, the diocesan bishop can grant such a mandate in his letter of appointment without specifying every canon to which it applies. He can grant the mandate "for all matters in which it is required by universal law" and then reserve any particular matter to himself if he so wishes.

Canon 480 — **The vicar general and the episcopal vicar must report to the diocesan bishop on the principal matters which are to be treated and which have been treated, and they are never to act contrary to his will and mind.**

Vicars have considerable authority, but it must be understood in light of their relationship to the diocesan bishop. This norm is quite similar to canon 369 of the 1917 Code and is based on the need for close coordination between the diocesan bishop and his vicars. Vicars share in the bishop's responsibility (*sollicitudo*), but they neither "multiply" the diocesan bishop nor participate with him in some sort of collegial diocesan governance. They are directly responsible to him and must keep him completely informed about their actions on serious matters. If the diocesan bishop has already denied a favor, no vicar—whether informed of the denial or not—can grant the favor validly (c. 65, §3).

The Cessation of the Vicar's Office

Canon 481 — **§1. The power of a vicar general or of an episcopal vicar ceases when the time of their mandate has expired, when they resign and with due regard for cann. 406 and 409, when they are informed of their removal by the diocesan bishop and when the episcopal see is vacant.**

§2. Unless they possess the episcopal dignity the power of the vicar general and of the episcopal vicar is suspended with the suspension from office of the diocesan bishop.

The canon repeats substantially canon 371 of the former Code, listing several ways in which the vicars may lose the power of governance attached to their office. The 1917 Code did not conceive of appointment to the office of vicar for a limited term. The revised Code, therefore, adds to the former text another occasion on which a vicar's power ceases: when his term of office expires (§1). The word "mandate" may apply to his appointment to the office itself or to any special faculties attached tempo-rarily to his office. In the former case, the expiration of the term causes the vicar to lose the office itself; in the latter case, only the special faculties cease. Even though the vicar's term lapses on a certain date, the loss of the office does not take effect juridically until this fact is stated to him in writing by the diocesan bishop (c. 186).

Vicars may resign from office voluntarily. The vicar should have a just reason for resigning and, for validity, must inform the diocesan bishop about the resignation in writing or before two witnesses. The resignation does not take effect until the diocesan bishop is duly informed (cc. 187, 189). The resignation does not require acceptance by the diocesan bishop in order to take effect.

A priest can be freely removed from the office of vicar by the diocesan bishop provided that natural and canonical equity is observed.[37] The removal requires only a just reason (c. 193, §3). No particular procedure is required other than informing the vicar in writing. The priest does not lose the office until he receives the written decree of removal, signed by the diocesan bishop and properly notarized (cc. 193, §4; 474). If the episcopal see becomes vacant, the priest serving as a vicar automatically loses his office. Without a diocesan bishop there can be no alter ego. His powers do not cease, however, until he is morally certain (not necessarily through a written instrument) that the diocesan bishop has died or that the pope has accepted the bishop's resignation, transferred him to another office, or removed him from the office of diocesan bishop (cc. 416–417).

An auxiliary bishop can be removed from the office of vicar general, but the explicit reference to canon 406, §1 suggests that he must at least be appointed as an episcopal vicar. A coadjutor bishop or auxiliary with special papal faculties can be removed from the office of vicar general only for grave reasons (c. 193, §1). The same holds for the removal of any auxiliary bishop from the office of episcopal vicar. When the episcopal see becomes vacant for any reason, auxiliary bishops lose the office of vicar general or episcopal vicar but retain all their powers of governance attached to the office, including any special mandates granted by the diocesan bishop; they exercise these powers and faculties under the authority of the diocesan administrator until the succeeding bishop takes possession of the episcopal see (c. 409). As soon as the auxiliary bishop is certain that this has occurred, he loses the powers and faculties which he originally received as vicar general or episcopal vicar; he must be reinstated to his office by the new diocesan bishop if he is to continue to exercise such responsibilities (cf. cc. 406, 409).

[37]Cf. the response to Cardinal König on this point concerning c. 189 of the 1980 schema in *Rel,* 45.

ARTICLE 2: THE CHANCELLOR,
OTHER NOTARIES
AND THE ARCHIVES
[cc. 482–491]

This article simplifies the norms found in the corresponding canons of the 1917 Code (*CIC* 372–384) yet maintains the Church's traditional care for the major documents of ecclesiastical governance. *Archives* began at an early stage of the Church's history. Even during the first three centuries, bishops preserved in their residences baptismal records called *diptychs,* and by the fourth century more developed forms of archives appeared. These were invaluable before the invention of mechanical printing since they safeguarded a record of not only the Church but the secular society within which it existed. As the diocesan curial system evolved, archives became indispensable tools of ecclesiastical governance, concerned with maintaining and indexing documents for future reference.

Notaries existed in the earliest days of the Church. The first notaries wrote the acts of the martyrs. Later, they were charged with transcribing and preserving documents for papal and diocesan archives. They were called by various names (*notarii, scrinarii, chartularii*) and were accorded high dignity in the papal household. In subsequent centuries, notaries were used not only to transcribe writings but to sign certain documents, thereby certifying them as authentic.

The office of *chancellor* developed from a secular model, combining archival preservation and notarization. The *cancellarius* was the doorkeeper at the grille of the Roman law court who eventually assumed the duties of secretary to the magistrate. After the decline of the Roman Empire, a similar office of great dignity was held by the royal chancellor, the keeper of the king's seal. In the twelfth century the bishop's chancellery was developed particularly through the activity of the cathedral chapter. The office of chancellor (similar to that in the royal court) was assigned to a member of the chapter. He was responsible for signing and preserving the letters of the bishop. The title was soon applied in ecclesiastical circles to the figure who was in charge of the entire documentary system of the diocese as distinct from ordinary notaries or transcribers. During the thirteenth century, the chancellor assumed the regulation of teaching and lecturing in the newly founded universities. This academic function eventually evolved into a separate office of considerable importance and the title is used to the present day in both Catholic and secular universities. The Council of Trent made no mention of the office of chancellor, but it did confirm the right of the bishop to establish a notary in his curia.[38] After Trent, the diocesan chancellor was rec-

ognized as the bishop's principal notary and, as such, the authenticator of legitimate documents. To this responsibility was soon joined that of custodian of the diocesan archives. This twofold office developed in particular legislation and diocesan practice, which "gradually attributed the name of *chancellor* to the one who was the notary of the episcopal curia, and specifically to that notary who had care of the safe-keeping of the documents drawn up by all the notaries of the diocese."[39] It was incorporated into universal legislation for the first time in 1917 (*CIC* 372). The 1983 Code has retained this notion in the second article on the diocesan curia.

The Chancellor

Canon 482 — §1. In every curia, a chancellor is to be appointed whose principal task is, unless particular law determines otherwise, to see to it that the acts of the curia are gathered, arranged and safeguarded in the archive of the curia.

§2. If it seems necessary the chancellor can be given an assistant, whose title is vice-chancellor.

§3. The chancellor and vice-chancellor are automatically notaries and secretaries of the curia.

Every diocesan curia must have a chancellor whose principal function is that of custodian and organizer of the official archives (§1). The archives are to maintain in systematic fashion the "acts of the curia." The canon omits the former Code's instruction to order such acts chronologically. In many cases, such a systematic arrangement would be imprudent. To determine which acts of the curia should be preserved in this manner is no easy task, especially when one considers the expanded notion of the curia found in canon 469. Certainly, curial acts which have a juridic effect should be deposited in the archives (c. 474) and retained at least as long as proof of the juridic effect is needed. Many curial acts, however, have no strictly juridic effect. For example, every diocesan bishop and his vicars send and receive numerous letters which, though not simply personal, deal solely with advice or encouragement rather than an official decision. Nevertheless, they should be preserved, at least for a reasonable period of time. Memoranda internal to the curia may have no juridic effect and are rarely notarized, but they may represent extremely important sources of verbal exchange and administrative policy.

The canon wisely allows for local adaptation in fulfilling this responsibility ("unless particular law determines otherwise"; also cf. c. 491, §3). In larger dioceses it may be impossible for the chancellor to retain and order all the acts of the curia as it is now defined—for example, the material generated by offices dealing with catechesis, Catholic education,

[38]Sess. XXII, *de ref.,* c. 10.

[39]Prince, 35.

construction, central purchasing, and other administrative areas. While such departments will individually maintain extensive active and research files, they should also send to the chancellor their more important documentation for storage in a central place for long-term preservation or the coordination of policy with other pastoral agencies. Since so many determinations about archives are left to diocesan policy, it is important for the diocesan bishop and the chancellor to study the situation carefully and to set down in writing the process which the latter will follow to fulfill the task of the acts of the curia being "gathered, arranged and safeguarded."

The second paragraph of the canon retains the option of appointing a vice-chancellor to assist the chancellor (the alternate title, *vice-tabularius,* is dropped). Although nothing is said about the office, certain conclusions can be drawn. The close connection between chancellor and vice-chancellor implies that the qualifications for both are the same. They are both appointed by the diocesan bishop[40] and can be freely removed by him (c. 485). Their rights and duties are parallel except that the vice-chancellor, as an assistant, acts at the direction of the chancellor. These are separate offices rather than two persons appointed to the same office *in solidum.* Although the canon uses the singular, there is no prohibition against the appointment of two or more vice-chancellors to assist the chancellor.

The quasi-equality of the two offices is supported by the third paragraph of the canon which speaks of both officeholders as notaries and secretaries of the curia by reason of the law itself.[41] The word *secretaries* (which was added to the text of the 1917 Code) is meant simply to clarify their work as notaries, not to imply an additional function.[42]

One of the most important changes in canon 482 is the abrogation of the requirement that the chancellor be a priest (*CIC* 372, §1). The revised Code permits the diocesan bishop to appoint any person—lay, religious, or cleric—to the office. While

this canon does not specify that the candidate must be a Catholic, full communion with the Church is required in accord with canon 149. A lay or religious chancellor, however, cannot exercise the office of notary in cases involving the reputation of a priest; such cases are reserved to a priest-notary (c. 483, §2). While the broadened eligibility for the office of chancellor may seem striking to some, one must bear in mind that, in universal legislation, the office involves little, if any, exercise of ordinary governmental power. In some dioceses, particularly in the United States, the chancellor exercises considerable authority but only in virtue of delegated power; the faculties are not intrinsically attached to the office itself.[43]

The delegation of broad powers of governance to the diocesan chancellor is alien to the concept of the office found in the Code. It is contrary to the emphasis on the ordinary power of governance and harmful to the system of vicars which the Code promotes and, in fact, requires. The possibility of appointing deacons, religious, and lay persons as "simply" chancellors (archivists-notaries) may have the beneficial side-effect of separating in practice the exercise of overall governance from the office and returning it to the vicar general or episcopal vicar. In cases, however, where the title is retained for a position of governance, it must be admitted that the offices of vicar general and chancellor are not incompatible and a priest or bishop could be appointed to both, thus permitting the "chancellor" to exercise ordinary power of executive governance (i.e., as "vicar general"). This solution, however, may, in retaining a title, have the undesirable effect of obscuring the office of chancellor as official notary and archivist.

Notaries

Canon 483 — §1. Besides the chancellor other notaries can be appointed, whose writing or signature establishes the authenticity of any acts whatsoever, of judicial acts only or of the acts of a certain case or transaction only.

§2. The chancellor and the notaries must be of good character and above reproach; a priest must be the notary in cases in which the reputation of a priest can be called into question.

This canon reproduces substantially the prescriptions found in canon 373, §§1–4 of the 1917 Code. Notaries differ from the chancellor and vice-chancellor in two points: (a) they receive the office of notary by episcopal appointment while the chancellor and vice-chancellor receive it from the law itself; and (b) the chancellor and vice-chancellor are au-

---

[40]C. 482 neglects to identify the authority who appoints the chancellor. From the parallel with the appointment of the vicar general (c. 475, §1) and the finance officer (c. 494, §1), the omission is most likely an unintentional oversight in simplifying *CIC* 372. The diocesan bishop is the proper authority to appoint the chancellor and vice-chancellor and to remove them from office (cc. 157, 470, 485).

[41]The revised text remedies a lacuna in *CIC* 372, §3, which failed to name the vice-chancellor as a notary by law. This led to a discussion about whether the vice-chancellor was to assist the chancellor in only his archival responsibilities unless he was explicitly appointed a notary by the bishop.

[42]This interpretation is supported by the consistent and unopposed use of the phrase "notarii seu secretarii Curiae" in all the schemata. The word "seu" was changed to "et" after the final plenary session of the Commission, presumably for the sake of Latin style. The word "secretary" does not *completely* describe the function of the "notary" (which "seu" would suggest). It clarifies *part* of the chancellor's task as a notary, a part for which not every notary is responsible.

[43]The phrase requiring the moderator of the curia to be a priest was added to c. 473, §2 specifically to address the situation in the U.S. (*Comm* 13 [1981], 122. Cf. also cc. 129 and 228.)

thorized by law to notarize all curial acts while notaries may be restricted to judicial acts, or a specific type of case or transaction, or even a single case or document. The notary's letter of appointment should state his or her competence and should be signed by the bishop and notarized (cc. 156, 474).

Notaries need not be clerics; they must, however, be Catholic (c. 149). Since their primary function is to certify the authenticity of curial acts, they should be chosen for their honesty, integrity, and exemplary reputation in the community, qualities which should exceed even the requisites for ecclesiastical offices of other types (§2).[44] It is often helpful for an ecclesiastical notary to become a notary public so that certain church documents may be easily certified in a manner acceptable in civil law.

Cases involving the reputation of a priest (§2) would include matters such as the imposition or declaration of an ecclesiastical penalty, the instruction of a petition for laicization, or the administrative removal or transfer of a pastor. If no priest holds the office of notary, one can be appointed to function in this capacity even for an individual case. Since the use of a priest as notary is not a requisite for validity and is intended principally to protect the reputation of the priest in question, he would be permitted to waive the privilege, especially considering the obligation of secrecy assumed by anyone accepting the office of notary (c. 471, 2°).

Canon 484 — The duties of notaries are:

1° to write the acts and instruments relating to decrees, dispositions, obligations and other tasks required of them;

2° to record faithfully in writing what has taken place and sign the record with a notation of the place, day, month and year;

3° with due consideration of all requirements, to furnish acts or instruments to one legitimately requesting them from the files and to declare copies of them to be in conformity with the original.

This canon repeats canon 374 of the 1917 Code almost verbatim and is self-explanatory.

The Removal of Chancellors and Notaries

Canon 485 — Chancellors and notaries can be freely removed from office by the diocesan bishop, but not by the diocesan administrator except with the consent of the college of consultors.

The diocesan bishop needs a just reason to remove the chancellor, vice-chancellor, or notary; the decree of removal should be in writing and notarized (cc. 193, §§3–4; 474). When the episcopal see is vacant, the diocesan administrator cannot validly

remove chancellors and notaries from office without the consent of the college of consultors. If a chancellor is exercising the power of governance by delegated authority, his powers remain in effect *sede vacante* (c. 142, §1). If a priest received such delegated powers because he was chancellor, his valid removal from office by the diocesan administrator would also cause his delegated powers to cease. Such removals must be in writing, signed by the diocesan administrator, notarized, and based on a just reason (cc. 193, §§3–4; 474). When the offices of chancellor, vice-chancellor, and notary are occupied by lay persons, civil contracts of employment should be worded in accord with the canonical right of removal expressed in this canon.[45]

Archives

The last six canons of the article treat three types of diocesan archives: the general archives, the secret archives, and the historical archives. Diocesan archives seem to have been formally instituted by Charles Borromeo in the first provincial Council of Milan (1565). Legislation for Italy was promulgated by Benedict XIII (1727)[46] and for the vicariate of Rome by Pius X (1912).[47] The 1917 Code incorporated the fundamental obligation to maintain diocesan archives (*CIC* 375) and specified several details about archival content, use, and methods of preservation (*CIC* 376–384). The revised Code, while retaining some specific norms, simplifies the canons by expressing general principles and leaving specification to individual diocesan policy.

In this area, the spare canonical obligations must be understood in the light of practical norms developed by modern archival science. The task of *gathering* requires the development of an effective records management program that provides reasonable schedules of retention and disposal of current records at the level of the individual diocesan agencies. Before records can be *arranged,* an organizational chart of the diocese and its various departments and agencies must be created. Records should be arranged according to groups that reflect the functions of these departments or agencies so that, by observing the archival arrangement, one can easily see a fairly accurate reflection of the diocesan organizational chart. Records are not *safeguarded* simply by being stored. They should be kept in acid-free folders, in acid-free boxes, on steel shelving, with proper environmental controls of temperature (approximately 68° F.) and relative humidity (about 45%), and in a secure location equipped with adequate smoke detection devices. These, and many other norms developed by archi-

---

44Cf. *Comm* 13 (1981), 112–113 on the suppression of c. 282, §1 of the 1977 schema.

45*Rel,* 114.
46*Maxima vigilantia,* June 14, 1727, *Bullarium Romanum XXII,* 560–567.
47*Etsi nos, AAS* 4 (1912), 5.

vists, will be important aids in drawing up the diocesan policy needed to concretize the principles of the Code.

Canon 486 — **§1. All diocesan and parochial documents must be protected with the greatest care.**

§2. In every curia, there is to be established in a safe place a diocesan archive or storeroom in which the instruments and writings which refer to both the spiritual and temporal affairs of the diocese, properly arranged and diligently secured, are to be safeguarded.

§3. There is to be an inventory or catalog of the documents contained in the archive, with a brief synopsis of the contents of each one.

The first paragraph expresses the general principle that all documents dealing with the diocese and its parishes must be safeguarded. This is a serious obligation ("custodiri debent") which binds not only the diocesan bishop but the pastor as well (cf. cc. 491, §1; 535, §4). At times, it may be prudent to copy and retain on the diocesan level certain documents deposited in parish archives in order to provide a duplicate system of preservation.[48] For example, some dioceses may wish to make microforms of parochial sacramental records in order to facilitate the issuance of documents and at the same time minimize the physical handling of aging registers.

The second paragraph specifies that a diocesan archives should be located in each curia, a phrase not found in canon 375, §1 of the 1917 Code upon which the canon is based. It also states that the archives should be situated in a safe place, a slight change from the former Code's "safe and convenient place." No rationale is given for these changes by the Code Commission. They may have been made in order to explicitate the importance of physically locating the archives in the building which houses the diocesan curia. This interpretation was given to the 1917 Code.[49] The revised Code supports it by replacing "convenient" ("commodo") with "in every curia" ("in unaquaque curia"). Nevertheless, the principal obligation affirmed by the canon is the constitution of a diocesan archives, not the choice of place, which should admit of accommodation to local circumstances.

The third paragraph repeats substantially canon 375, §2 of the 1917 Code, calling for a cataloging system to permit information-retrieval and accountability for deposited documents. The technological breakthroughs of microprocessing facilitate the fulfillment of this obligation considerably. Rather elaborate indexing systems, which would have been impossible by hand only a short time ago, are now quite simple. In recognition of advances in this field, canon 376 of the 1917 Code concerning yearly inventories, transfer of files, and the technical care of paper documents has been deleted.

Canon 487 — **§1. It is necessary that the archive be locked and that only the bishop and the chancellor have a key to it; no one may licitly enter it without the permission either of the bishop or of both the moderator of the curia and the chancellor.**

§2. It is a right of interested parties to obtain personally or through their proxy an authentic written copy or a photocopy of documents which are public by their nature and which pertain to the status of such persons.

This canon revises canon 377 of the 1917 Code. The latter stated that only the chancellor should possess the key to the archives and that permission to enter must be granted by the bishop or the vicar general *and* the chancellor. The meaning of this phrase was debated, with some authors concluding that the permission of the chancellor was always needed even if the bishop himself had given permission.

It may happen that the bishop or vicar-general has given permission unaware of certain circumstances connected with the party to whom it was conceded, which circumstances, being known to the chancellor, strongly prompt him to refuse. In such an event the chancellor would have to be guided by the grave obligation of guarding the archives which is placed upon him directly by the Code and which he must regard as one of the principal duties of his office.[50]

While the revised wording does not settle the question definitively, it seems to support the notion that the permission of the chancellor is needed only when the moderator of the curia grants permission. If the diocesan bishop grants permission, the chancellor's additional permission is not required. This interpretation is supported by the insertion of the word "simul," the parallelism with the more clearly worded canon 488, and the decision to place the key to the archives in the custody of both the diocesan bishop and the chancellor. If the chancellor objects to the entrance into the archives of a particular person who has episcopal permission, he can, before complying with the request, consult the diocesan bishop to make certain that all pertinent information about the person has been shared with the bishop. The vicar general or episcopal vicar is not authorized to grant permission, nor can the

[48]*Comm* 13 (1981), 123.

[49]Wernz-Vidal, *Ius Canonicum,* vol. 2 (1923), no. 647.

[50]W.F. Louis, *Diocesan Archives. A Historical Synopsis and Commentary, CanLawStud* 137 (Washington, D.C.: Catholic University, 1941), 62.

chancellor alone grant permission unless delegated to do so by the diocesan bishop. If there is no moderator of the curia in a particular diocese and the vicar general fulfills a similar role without use of the title, it seems reasonable that he should be able to grant permission together with the chancellor. The diocesan bishop can grant general permission to those working in his curia to have access to the archives; he may also attach specific conditions to such access. One approach would be to grant to all department heads who have a need to know the permission to consult the diocesan archives, provided that both the chancellor approves and the consultation is in accord with the chancellor's directions. The permission of the bishop or the moderator of the curia can be reasonably presumed in ordinary circumstances. The diocesan bishop could also delegate the chancellor outright to grant permission without the corresponding permission of the moderator of the curia.

Although the paragraph uses the word "key," any modern method of security may be employed. If index information is stored in a computer, the "key" may be the entrance code. A safe may be used in which the combination is known only to the diocesan bishop and the chancellor. Prudence should be exercised in this matter since at times neither the bishop nor the chancellor may be available. Certainly, the moderator of the curia, the vicars general and episcopal vicars, and the vice-chancellors should have access to the "key" even if they do not possess it normally. The intent of the canon is to promote security, not to frustrate use of the archives.

This goal is exemplified in the second paragraph which recognizes the documentary service archives should perform. This represents a different attitude from the 1917 Code in which the archives were seen foremost as depositories and quite secondarily as active instruments of information-retrieval. It should be noted that the paragraph refers solely to public documents concerning a person's ecclesiastical state. This would include, for example, letters of appointment or sacramental information such as a certificate of ordination or a laicization decree. Whether a party can be considered to have an interest in the document in a technical sense must be determined by the chancellor before responding to a request. This question sometimes arises in regard to genealogical searches of baptismal and marriage records. The use of the word "authentic" implies that the copy, whether written or photocopied, should be certified by a notary before release.

Canon 488 — **It is not permitted to remove documents from the archives, except for a brief time only and with the consent either of the bishop or of both the moderator of the curia and the chancellor.**

The canon reproduces canon 378 of the 1917 Code in more general form. Instead of specifying three days for the use of a document and stating the ordinary's right to extend the time period, it prescribes that a document may be absent from the archives for "a brief time only." The detail about requiring a receipt is omitted. The word "writing" ("scripturas") is changed to "documents" ("documenta") as a more all-inclusive term. As in the previous canon, if no moderator of the curia has been appointed in a particular diocese, the vicar general who fulfills such a coordinating function could grant permission together with the chancellor for the temporary removal of archival documents. The diocesan bishop can grant such permission on his own. The permission of the bishop or the moderator of the curia can be reasonably presumed in ordinary circumstances, and the bishop can also delegate the chancellor to grant permission without his consent or that of the moderator of the curia. General permission to use documents can be given to curial officers such as, e.g., the director of priest personnel and his secretary regarding the files of individual priests. With the ease of photocopying today, there is little call for the removal of documents except perhaps to consult a file during working hours. For longer use, the originals should be retained in the archives and copies sent to the interested party (notarized if necessary).

Canon 489 — **§1. There is also to be a secret archive in the diocesan curia or at least a safe or file in the ordinary archive, completely closed and locked which cannot be removed from the place, and in which documents to be kept secret are to be protected most securely.**

§2. Every year documents of criminal cases are to be destroyed in matters of morals in which the criminal has died or in which ten years have passed since the condemnatory sentence; but a brief summary of the case with the text of the definitive sentence is to be retained.

The detailed legislation of the 1917 Code concerning the secret archives (*CIC* 379–382) has been reduced to two canons (cc. 489–490). Every diocesan curia must have a secret archives, at least in the form of an especially secure safe or file cabinet. The canon does not specify all of the documents which should be stored in this archives although the second paragraph mentions one category, i.e., criminal cases involving questions of morals.[51] The acts of such "penal procedures"[52] should be destroyed when the guilty person has died or the case has

---

[51]"Penal procedures" is a more accurate term than "criminal cases." (Cf. cc. 1387, 1390, 1394, 1395, 1398.)
[52]Cf. cc. 1717–1731.

been completed for ten years.[53] Until they are destroyed, the acts are retained in the secret archives; after they have been destroyed, a summary of the case with the definitive sentence should be kept in the secret archives. Other confidential documents are also normally stored in the secret archives: matrimonial dispensations in the non-sacramental internal forum (c. 1082); the register for secret marriages (c. 1133); dispensations from impediments and irregularities to orders (cc. 1047, 1048); decree of dismissal from a religious institute (c. 700); and documents relating to the loss of the clerical state by invalidity, penalty, or dispensation (cc. 290–293). Very few canons explicitly require storage in the secret archives. It is left to the discretion of the diocesan bishop to determine which matters should be placed in the general archives and which relegated to the secret archives. This task will normally be delegated to the chancellor. In this area, it is important for dioceses to investigate the civil laws of their particular region in order to protect all their archives, especially this secret archives, from subpoena and other legal invasive strategies.

Canon 490 — §1. Only the bishop may have the key to the secret archive.

§2. When the see is vacant the secret archive or safe is not to be opened, except in a case of true necessity by the diocesan administrator himself.

§3. Documents are not to be removed from the secret archive or safe.

The detailed norms concerning two separate keys for the secret archives are omitted (*CIC* 379–381); they are replaced by the simple statement that the diocesan bishop alone should have the key to the secret archives (§1). The implication of the second paragraph is that the key would normally be given to the diocesan administrator *sede vacante.* The third paragraph explicitates the inference of canon 379, §4 of the former Code that no document should be removed from the secret archives even for a brief period of time. The diocesan bishop can dispense from these universal disciplinary norms (c. 87). Thus, he might wish to consign a duplicate key to the vicar general or the chancellor with authority to permit access to the secret archives for legitimate reasons. A distinction should be drawn between documents deposited in the secret archives because of the requirement of law (e.g., matrimonial dispensations in the internal forum) and those placed there at the discretion of the bishop or chancellor. The prohibition against removal of the latter from the archives should not be interpreted as strictly as the removal of the former. Photocopying is equivalent to removal since the intent of the norm is not simply to preserve the original (as in c. 488) but to avoid dissemination of the information contained in the document. Nonetheless, if necessity warrants it, the diocesan bishop may permit certified copies to be made for legitimate confidential use. In such cases, however, the copies should be returned to the chancellor for filing or destruction.

The principles of the Code concerning general and secret archives need accommodation and concretization. The canons address only two levels of confidentiality (normal records and secret records). In fact, however, there are many grades of confidentiality attached to the various documents preserved in curial archives. While the canons provide flexibility through the use of authoritative permissions, a curia with an organized system will need to draft written policy and procedures for the many levels of access and information-sharing which administration requires, possibly adopting in some cases even the governmental model of variously "classified" documents.

Canon 491 — §1. The diocesan bishop is to see to it that the acts and documents of the archives of cathedral, collegiate, parochial and other churches in his territory also are diligently preserved; also, inventories or catalogs are to be made in duplicate, one of which is to be kept in the church's own archive and the other in the diocesan archive.

§2. The diocesan bishop is also to see to it that there is an historical archive in the diocese in which documents having an historical value are diligently preserved and systematically arranged.

§3. In order to inspect or remove the acts and documents spoken of in §§1 and 2 above, the norms established by the diocesan bishop are to be observed.

The first paragraph states more clearly than did canon 383, §1 of the 1917 Code that the diocesan bishop is responsible for the establishment and upkeep of archives in those juridic persons which are subject to him, particularly parishes. The canon does not require that copies of the documents in such archives be sent to the curial archives, but it does demand that an inventory of these documents in the form of a catalog or index be kept on file at the diocesan level. This is an area of parochial responsibility which can be of great importance for a parish and yet one which may often be sadly neglected or poorly implemented. The universal law does not constitute a separate archival officer at the parish level, and there are frequent changes of administration in parishes. There is more likelihood, therefore, that parish records will be treated haphazardly. The canon provides for norms to be issued by the diocesan bishop concerning the inspection and removal of documents (§3). Such norms would do well to include guidelines for par-

[53]The 1917 Code had specified destruction by burning (*CIC* 379, §1).

ish archives in order to provide a common system of preserving documents throughout the diocese.

While all archives contain some historically significant material, the second paragraph of this canon specifies the responsibility of the diocesan bishop to establish an historical archives in the diocese in order to preserve documents valuable to posterity. Such an endeavor is a specialized field in itself and requires the assistance of experts. This historical archives differs from the general archives since it will rarely be consulted for anything other than research while the general archives is meant to facilitate administration through information-retrieval. Some important documents are hardly ever consulted, e.g., the papal decree establishing the diocese or appointing the diocesan bishop; these should immediately be stored in the historical archives. Other documents are important but must be available for consultation, e.g., synodal legislation or the constitution of the presbyteral council; the originals of these documents should be deposited in the historical archives and a master copy kept in the general diocesan archives for ready reference.

ARTICLE 3: THE FINANCE COUNCIL AND THE FINANCE OFFICER
[cc. 492–494]

The final three canons of chapter II treat the curial *structure* of financial administration and accountability at the diocesan level although the overall norms on finance are found in Book V (cc. 1254–1310).

The Finance Council

Canon 492 — **§1. In each diocese a finance council is to be established by the bishop, over which he himself or his delegate presides, and which is to be composed of at least three members of the Christian faithful truly skilled in financial affairs as well as in civil law, of outstanding integrity and appointed by the bishop.**

§2. Members of the finance council are to be named for a five year term; but having completed this term they may be named to other five year terms.

§3. Those persons are excluded from the finance council who are related to the bishop up to the fourth degree of consanguinity or affinity.

The finance council is similar to the administration council (*Consilium administrationis*) in canon 1520 of the 1917 Code although certain differences should be immediately noted. The diocesan bishop is obliged to establish the finance council and may freely select its members (§1) while the 1917 Code required the ordinary to consult the cathedral chapter or the diocesan consultors before appointing members to the administration council. After the

1917 Code was promulgated, the diocesan consultors themselves were appointed as the council of administration in many dioceses to facilitate consultation on temporal matters.

At least three persons must be appointed to the finance council (the former Code required a minimum of two); no maximum number of members is expressed. The diocesan bishop may preside over the council directly or through a delegate. The members of the council must be Catholic and may be lay persons, religious, or clerics. Since the role of presider involves no pastoral care requiring the sacrament of orders (c. 150), the diocesan bishop can name a lay person to serve as his presiding delegate. The members of the council should be learned in both civil law and finances (§1).

The original drafts of this canon called for a close connection with the presbyteral council and affirmed the right of the conference of bishops to issue norms. Both clauses were deleted after the consultation process,[54] leaving greater discretion to the diocesan bishop. Since the consent and/or advice of both the finance council and the presbyteral council or college of consultors are sometimes required together, it would not be proper to identify the finance council completely with either of the other two consultative bodies.[55] Nevertheless, it would be prudent to have representatives from the presbyteral council and college of consultors on the finance council to foster coordination and information-sharing. This is critical in regard to temporal matters such as real estate transactions and construction projects which often have significant pastoral implications. The advice of qualified accountants and attorneys may be insufficient or even inadequate to address such situations properly. The topic often requires an "interdisciplinary" approach best effected by a mixture of "technical" and "pastoral" advisors.

The members of the council, like the consultors (c. 502), have a five-year term which is renewable indefinitely (§2). Besides expertise, they must possess outstanding integrity, since financial administration must be marked by scrupulous honesty (§1); no member may be related to the diocesan bishop within the fourth grade of consanguinity or affinity (i.e., the bishop's first cousin, grandniece, grandnephew, granduncle, grandaunt, or their spouses) (§3). The council members hold an ecclesiastical office in the curia and should therefore receive a signed and notarized letter of appointment (cc. 156, 474) and make the usual promise of service and confidentiality (c. 471).

Canon 493 — **In addition to the duties committed to it in Book V: *The Temporal Goods of the Church*, the finance council is to prepare each year**

---

[54]*Comm* 13 (1981), 127.
[55]Cf. cc. 1263 and 1277.

according to the directions of the diocesan bishop a budget of the income and expenditures foreseen for the governance of the entire diocese in the coming year; moreover at the close of the year it is to examine a report of receipts and expenditures.

The position of the finance council in the diocesan structure is more significant than that of the council of administration in the former Code. The finance council is not solely an advisory group to be consulted at the discretion of the bishop but a council with specific rights and duties, most of which are found in Book V. The finance council (unlike the presbyteral council) does not cease *sede vacante* (cc. 423, 501).

Two of the council's important responsibilities are contained in canon 493, which has no counterpart in the 1917 Code. The council is charged with preparing the annual diocesan budget and approving the annual finance report. This twofold task is under the direction of the diocesan bishop; the council does not act independently of him. It is an important project, integral to sound management. In practice, the finance officer or even a team of curial officers may actually prepare the budget, but such work should be pursued in accord with instructions approved by the finance council; in addition, the finished product should be presented to the diocesan bishop for final authorization through the finance council and with its endorsement. Similarly, the diocesan financial report for the previous year will most likely be prepared by the finance officer and staff together with professional auditors, but it should be submitted to the finance council for approval before being sent to the diocesan bishop for his consideration.

Although parish finance councils are mandated in canon 537, the determination of their activity is left to the pastor and to diocesan norms. Canon 493 and the other norms concerning the diocesan finance council offer a model for parallel activity on the parish level, and it would be prudent to consult the diocesan finance council as well as the presbyteral council before issuing such norms for parishes.[56]

The Finance Officer

Canon 494 — §1. In each diocese, after listening to the college of consultors and also the finance council, the bishop is to name a finance officer who is to be truly skilled in financial affairs and absolutely distinguished for honesty.

§2. The finance officer is to be appointed for a five year term but, having completed this term, may be reappointed for other five year terms; during the term of office the finance officer may not be removed except for a grave cause, to be assessed by

the bishop after listening to the college of consultors and the finance council.

§3. It is the role of the finance officer to administer the goods of the diocese under the authority of the bishop in accordance with the budget determined by the finance council; from the income of the diocese the finance officer is to meet the expenditures which the bishop or others deputized by him have legitimately authorized.

§4. At the end of the year the finance officer must give to the finance council a report of receipts and expenditures.

The finance officer is a new figure of the diocesan curia. Some precedent is found in the 1917 Code in the work of the cathedral chapter or the diocesan consultors in the administration of temporalities. When the see became vacant, such collegial groups were required to elect a procurator or *oeconomus* to administer the temporalities of the diocese along with the vicar capitular (*CIC* 432). In many dioceses, however, temporalities were not administered by the chapter or consultors but by the bishop himself. In such cases, the *oeconomus* was not elected *sede vacante;* instead, the vicar capitular assumed all responsibilities, spiritual and temporal. The concept now found in canon 494, therefore, is almost completely new and without counterpart in the former Code since it involves a stable office within every curia *sede plena* or *sede vacante*.

The finance officer may be a lay person, religious, or cleric. The diocesan bishop has the duty to appoint someone to the post after consulting both the college of consultors and the finance council. This consultation should deal with the job description and the candidates for the position. The office is mandatory, not optional (*nominetur*) (§1).

The candidate for the office must be a Catholic (cc. 129, 149) and respected for financial expertise, uprightness, and honesty. The precise duties of the office will vary among dioceses; in many cases, however, the officeholder should be a certified public accountant and capable of working well with the many different people affected by diocesan payrolls and program budgets. There is no explicit prohibition against close relatives of the diocesan bishop (as is the case with the vicars and the members of the financial council [cc. 478, 492]); it would be imprudent, however, to appoint a close relative since the general intent of the Code is to avoid any appearance of nepotism in diocesan governance.

Since this position is an office of the diocesan curia, the appointment should be in the form of a signed and notarized letter and the officeholder is required to make the customary promise of service and confidentiality (cc. 156, 471, 474). The appointment is for a five-year term which can be renewed indefinitely (§2).[57] Six months prior to the expira-

---

[56]For the activity of the finance council, consult the following: cc. 423, 494, 1263, 1277, 1281, 1287, 1292, 1305, 1310.

[57]Cf. *Rel,* 114 *ad c. 414.*

tion of the term, the same finance officer or a new one may be appointed by the diocesan bishop, the new appointment taking effect on the day that the original term lapses (c. 153, §2). Although the canon is explicit about the quinquennial term, this does not mean that the diocese must enter a five-year civil contract with the finance officer.

Civil contracts must take into account the canonical right of removal. While a fairly stable figure in the Code, the finance officer is removable. The canon prescribes a "grave cause" and prior consultation (not consent) with the college of consultors and finance council (§2). The finance officer is actually a more stable position than the vicars or chancellor who can be "freely" removed for only a "just reason." The diocesan bishop judges whether the reason for removal is sufficiently serious. The finance officer's stability in office is similar in many ways to that of the judicial vicar and the other tribunal judges. They also can be removed by the bishop only for a "legitimate and serious cause" (c. 1422). Another sign of similar stability is the retention of office *sede vacante*. In fact, if the finance officer should be elected diocesan administrator when the see is vacant, the finance council must appoint another finance officer to serve temporarily (c. 423). Unlike the judicial vicar, however, the finance officer can be removed for a grave cause by the diocesan administrator *sede vacante* after consulting the college of consultors and the finance council (cc. 1420, §5; 427, §1).

The consultation with the finance council required for appointment and removal points to the accountability of the finance officer not only to the diocesan bishop but to the council as well. This relationship is exemplified by the finance officer's duty to administer diocesan monies in accord with the annual budget prepared by the finance council (§3) and the obligation to report to the council each year about diocesan receipts and expenditures (§4). The finance officer's principal accountability, of course, is directly to the diocesan bishop (§2), but the special relationship with the finance council should not be overlooked.

While the concrete rights and duties of the finance officer will be specified at the diocesan level, the juridic figure described in the canon seems to be primarily a comptroller, exercising discretionary authority within certain clear limits. These limits are determined not by the finance officer but by the bishop in consultation with his finance council, his curial officials, and other consultative groups such as the presbyteral council and college of consultors. Thus, the finance officer defrays diocesan expenses not by personal authority but on the basis of authorization. Such authorization occurs in three different ways: (a) the budget, developed by the finance council and approved by the bishop, sets parameters within which the finance officer is authorized

to act; (b) curial officials authorize the finance officer to defray expenses for their administrative activity in accord with budgetary constraints; and (c) the bishop himself or his delegate may authorize expenditures which exceed the budget (§3). The finance officer, as described in the canon, neither makes policy nor authorizes expenditures but applies stated policy and controls receipts and expenditures in accord with proper authorization. This, however, is only a general principle; it must be carefully tailored to local circumstances. In every case, the finance officer's rights and duties should be precisely determined, preferably in writing. Appropriate civil instruments should also be drawn up to provide legal recognition of these powers and the ability to exercise these canonical responsibilities in the marketplace. This last task, like most temporal matters, requires careful study and collaboration by canon and civil lawyers.[58]

CHAPTER III
THE PRESBYTERAL COUNCIL AND THE COLLEGE OF CONSULTORS
[cc. 495–502]

The presbyteral council is rooted in the desire of Vatican Council II to reform the already-existing presbyteral consultative bodies, namely, the cathedral chapter and the diocesan consultors. The theological basis for such reform is the conciliar notion of the presbyterium:

Priests, prudent cooperators with the episcopal order as well as its aids and instruments, are called to serve the People of God. They constitute one priesthood (*unum presbyterium*) with their bishop, although that priesthood is comprised of different functions.... Intent always upon the welfare of God's children, they must strive to lend their effort to the pastoral work of the whole diocese and even of the entire Church (*LG* 28).

Collaboration with the bishop in one presbyterium requires a regular exchange of ideas, consultation and advice.

Included among the collaborators of the bishop in the government of the diocese are those priests who constitute his senate or council, such as the cathedral chapter, the board of consultors, or other committees established according to the circumstances or nature of various localities. To the extent necessary, these institutions, especially the cathedral chapters, should be reorganized in keeping with present-day needs (*CD* 27).

[58]For example, cf. cc. 22; 1284, §2, 2°; 1290.

The implications of these insights were then articulated in terms of a senate of priests:

> Therefore, on account of this communion in the same priesthood and ministry, the bishop should regard priests as his brothers and friends. . . . He should gladly listen to them, indeed, consult them, and have discussions with them about those matters which concern the necessities of pastoral work and the welfare of the diocese. In order to put these ideals into effect, a group or senate of priests representing the presbytery (*presbyterium*) should be established. It is to operate in a manner adapted to modern circumstances and needs and have a form and norms to be determined by law. By its counsel, this body will be able to give effective assistance to the bishop in his government of the diocese (*PO* 7).

The conciliar mandate was implemented juridically through *Ecclesiae sanctae* (August 6, 1966), which required the establishment in every diocese of a presbyteral council, i.e., "an assembly or senate of priests who represent the body of priests (*presbyterium*) and who by their counsel can effectively assist the Bishop in the government of the diocese" (*ES* I, 15, 1). The *motu proprio* set down norms on membership, authority, and cessation of the council (*ES* I, 15, 2–4), noting that chapters and consultors, until canonically reformed, would remain in existence together with the new presbyteral councils (*ES* I, 17, 2). This document thereby raised a question about the interrelationship of these various groups, a question which the revised canons have sought to answer, though not always with complete success.

The circular letter of the Sacred Congregation for the Clergy (April 11, 1970) is not a separate legislative text but an authentic interpretation of *Ecclesiae sanctae,* clarifying the meaning of the institute and fostering its establishment in every diocese. The letter traces the history of the formation of presbyteral councils in the Council and *Ecclesiae sanctae.* The obligation to constitute such a council arises from the hierarchical communion between bishops and priests. Its composition should be such as to represent the whole presbyterium. The council, "preeminent among other organs of the same kind," assists the bishop in the government of the diocese through consultation and advice (no. 9). In individual cases the bishop may voluntarily grant his council a deliberative vote. In conclusion, the letter urges the establishment of presbyteral councils in all dioceses, their development of written statutes for approval by the bishop, action by the conferences of bishops to develop operating norms for councils, and a decision by each episcopal conference about the revision of cathedral chapters and boards of consultors.

The canons of this chapter firmly establish the presbyteral council as the principal consultative group concerned with pastoral governance and explicitate in universal norms some of the matters addressed only in general terms in prior legislation. The first seven canons treat the establishment of the council, its statutes, membership, authority, and cessation; the final canon describes the college of consultors and its relationship to the presbyteral council.

The Establishment of the Presbyteral Council

Canon 495 — §1. A presbyteral council is to be established in each diocese, that is, a body of priests who are to be like a senate of the bishop, representing the presbyterate; this council is to aid the bishop in the governance of the diocese according to the norm of law, in order that the pastoral welfare of the portion of the people of God entrusted to him may be promoted as effectively as possible.

§2. In apostolic vicariates and prefectures the vicar or the prefect is to establish a council of at least three missionary presbyters whose opinion is to be heard in more serious matters, even by letter.

Every diocese must have a presbyteral council; its establishment is mandatory, not optional ("constituatur"). The council is composed of bishops and priests ("sacerdotum"); deacons, religious and lay persons may not be members. This group of priests has a twofold relationship—to the bishop for whom it serves as a type of senate, and to the presbyterium of the diocese who are represented by it. There was much debate during the revision process about the use of the terms "senate" and "representing." Some were concerned about the "democratization" of diocesan governance;[59] others felt that any notion of "representation" would lead to a division between the bishop and his presbyterium.[60] In fact, at the April 1980 meeting of the committee reworking this canon, the consultors agreed to suppress the phrase "qui tamquam senatus Episcopi."[61] Despite the staff's vote however, the 1980 draft (c. 415) and the promulgated text (c. 495, §1) retained the description of the presbyteral council as similar to a senate and deliberately avoided using the same term

[59] *Comm* 13 (1981), 128.
[60] *Rel,* 115 (comments of Cardinal Wyszynski).
[61] The secretary made the surprising statement that the phrase could be deleted since the college of consultors would be fulfilling this function and such an amendment would be in accord with those organs of consultation which expressed the desire that the competence of the presbyteral council not be broadened. *Comm* 13 (1981), 129. In the 1917 Code the phrase "tanquam senatus" was applied to the chapter of canons (*CIC* 391, §1) and in a transferred sense to the diocesan consultors (*CIC* 423).

regarding the college of consultors (c. 502) or the chapter of canons (c. 503).

Another indication of the concern of some about this new canonical institute is the insertion of the phrase "ad normam iuris" into the canon, emphasizing the council's competence to address questions of governance only in cases permitted by universal or particular law.[62] The universal law itself, however, urges the diocesan bishop to seek the advice of the council in any significant matter (c. 500, §2). Despite the reservations of some of the consultors of the Commission and the concerns of some conferences of bishops, the promulgated text clearly supports the role of the presbyteral council as the primary consultative group regarding matters of diocesan governance (§1).

The second paragraph of the canon makes provision for apostolic vicariates and prefectures which are similar to dioceses and are treated as particular churches (c. 368). Since it would be difficult to set up a presbyteral council in such missionary lands, the vicar or prefect is obliged instead to appoint at least three priests to advise him in more serious matters. Since the Latin term "presbyteris" is used, the appointees must be priests—not bishops, deacons, or lay persons.[63] Unlike the presbyteral council, which must be called together to offer advice collegially (c. 127), these appointed missionary advisors can be consulted by letter (§2).

The Statutes of a Council

Canon 496 — **The presbyteral council is to have its own statutes approved by the diocesan bishop, in light of the norms issued by the conference of bishops.**

The statutes (c. 94) should be drafted and approved by the presbyteral council itself or at least by an initial steering group.[64] The conference of bishops can issue norms to guide the drafting of statutes. The council's statutes (or *constitution* as it is sometimes called) are not in effect until they are explicitly approved by the diocesan bishop. The written form of the statutes should contain the bishop's approval in writing, his signature, and that of the chancellor or notary since the document has the juridic effect of governing the activity of the council (c. 474). To establish a presbyteral council

prior to any statutes, the diocesan bishop must issue a decree of constitution, also signed and notarized. If the initial steering committee develops the statutes, the presbyteral council can be constituted and the statutes approved in the same decree. Bylaws to guide the internal workings of the council in accord with its approved constitution do not require episcopal approval. Changes in the constitution (official statutes) must be approved by the diocesan bishop to become effective.

The Membership of the Presbyteral Council

The next three canons of this chapter offer general principles about the composition of the council, the right to elect and to be elected, and the method of election. These principles admit of many different models of membership and must therefore be concretized in the individual council's own statutes.

Canon 497 — **With regard to the designation of the members of the presbyteral council:**
1° about half the members are to be freely elected by the priests themselves according to the norm of the following canons as well as the council's statutes;
2° some priests, according to the council's statutes, ought to be ex officio members, that is, members of the council in virtue of their office;
3° the diocesan bishop is free to name some others.

After much debate and the consideration of several options, the Code Commission finally settled on the phrase "about half the members" ("dimidia circiter pars") to describe the portion of the council which should be freely elected by the presbyterium (§1).[65] Not every member of a presbyteral council can be elected; such a statute would be contrary to the universal law which calls for some ex officio members. The use of the word "circiter," however, would permit the vast majority of members to be elected. The statutes must designate which priests (or bishops) are members ex officio. It would seem appropriate to include all vicars general and perhaps all episcopal vicars in this category unless there are too many in a particular diocese. In making this determination, the statutes should take into consideration the purpose of the council (diocesan governance, the pastoral good of the people), its position as the bishop's senate, and the importance of

---

[62]This point is even clearer when one reads the account of the committee debating the concept of a deliberative vote at the session of April 17, 1980 concerning c. 314, §2 of the 1977 schema. The result of the discussion was a revised paragraph which indicated that the diocesan bishop should hear the presbyteral council or obtain its consent "only in cases expressly defined by law." *Comm* 13 (1981), 133.

[63]Cf. *Rel, 115 ad c. 415.*

[64]Cf. conclusion 1(b) of the circular letter of the SCC (4/11/70), which urged each presbyteral council to "prepare its own statutes which must be approved by the bishop."

[65]The SCC had specified that the majority of the members of the council should be elected by the priests (circular letter, no. 7; cf. also *Directory*, no. 203d). The drafts of the Code used the phrase "appropriate part" of the membership ("congrua pars" in *Comm* 13 [1981], 130 and the 1980 schema, c. 417), leaving it to the diocesan bishop to approve statutes which would determine the phrase more precisely. The Code Commission rejected this approach and settled on the phrase found in the promulgated text (*Rel*, 115–116).

structuring the membership in such a way as to represent the presbyterium (c. 499).

The diocesan bishop has the right to appoint members to the council. While he is not required to exercise this right, the council's statutes cannot deny the right. It is appropriate for the statutes to indicate how many members may be appointed by the bishop and even under what conditions, provided that such determinations are simply norms for the exercise of his right (which he accepts by approving the statutes) and not a denial of the right itself. In no case, however, may the statutes provide for episcopal appointment of so many members that half of the total membership ceases to be freely elected by the priests.

Finally, it should be noted that the canons do not determine any minimum or maximum number of members. This is left entirely to the statutes which should take into consideration the purpose of the council and the rules for its composition (cc. 495, 497, 500). The fact that the members of the college of consultors must be appointed from the membership of the presbyteral council implies that six is the minimum for both groups (c. 502).

Canon 498 — **§1. The following have the right to both active and passive vote in constituting the presbyteral council:**

1° all secular priests incardinated in the diocese;

2° secular priests not incardinated in the diocese, and priests who are members of an institute of consecrated life or a society of apostolic life, who live in the diocese and exercise some office for the good of the diocese.

§2. To the extent the statutes provide for it, the same right of election can be extended to other priests who have a domicile or quasi-domicile in the diocese.

This canon establishes certain rights regarding the election of the priests described in canon 497, 1°. All priests incardinated in the diocese have a right to vote and to be elected. Priests incardinated in another diocese or belonging to a religious institute or apostolic society have the same rights if they dwell within the confines of the diocese and at the same time exercise some ecclesiastical office on behalf of the diocese.

The universal law makes no exceptions in regard to incardinated priests. Even those exercising their ministry outside the diocese retain their rights.[66] This active and passive right, however, is not absolute; it can be restricted for a proportionately grave reason. For example, a priest who is away from the diocese illegitimately or one who is no longer exercising his priestly ministry may have this right inhibited by the

diocesan bishop.[67] Such norms can be incorporated into the statutes of the council (c. 497, 1°).

Religious priests (in vows), priests of societies of apostolic life (e.g., Maryknoll Fathers, Sulpicians), and visiting diocesan priests are not technically required to have even a quasi-domicile but simply to be "dwelling" within the diocese.[68] For them, the more important criterion is the requirement that they "exercise some office for the good of the diocese," a phrase which should be carefully determined in the council's statutes.

The priests named in the first paragraph have the right by the universal law itself to vote and be elected. The second paragraph permits the approved statutes to extend this right to other priests who possess at least a quasi-domicile in the diocese, e.g., a retired priest living in a diocese other than that of his incardination. The right may not be extended to those who exercise some ministry in the diocese without residing there, e.g., priests from a nearby diocese who assist regularly at a parish on weekends.[69]

Canon 499 — **The manner of electing members of the presbyteral council is to be determined in the statutes in such a way that, insofar as it is possible, the priests of the presbyterate are represented, taking into account especially the diversity of ministries and various regions of the diocese.**

The precise method of election is left to the council's statutes. The canon states only the general criterion, a council which is representative, especially in the light of the various ministries and regions of the diocese. In some dioceses with small land areas and homogeneous populations, the diversity of regions will be miniscule and require little, if any, representation in comparison to the various ministries present in the area. Furthermore, the representative character of the council will be achieved in part by the naming of ex officio members (c. 497, 2°). The canon should certainly not be interpreted as requiring election by regional groupings and/or by categories of ministry.

While using the governmental model of election districts is one way of ensuring representation, it is not the only way; perhaps it is not even the best way. Those who are elected by a small constituency

---

[66] The committee rejected the additional requirement of domicile or quasi-domicile for incardinated priests. *Comm* 13 (1981), 130.

[67] Cf. *Rel*, 117 *ad c. 418.*

[68] Cf. the deletion of this requirement from c. 312 of the 1977 schema (*Comm* 13 [1981], 130). Since a quasi-domicile is acquired simply by living in a place with the intention of remaining there three months or by de facto residing there for three months (c. 102, §2), it is not likely that such a priest will qualify for the right to vote and be elected without at least a quasi-domicile.

[69] The committee deleted the phrase of c. 312, §2 of the 1977 schema permitting the right to be extended to priests who exercise some office for the good of the diocese without actually residing in the diocese. *Comm* 13 (1981), 130.

consider themselves "representatives" of that constituency. The notion of representation in canon 499 implies a mix of priests who are "representative" of the entire presbyterium rather than delegates of one part. A way of ensuring such overall unity is to provide for all priests to vote for all elected council members while nominating candidates through some objective criterion, e.g., region of residence, ministry, age. In this way, the "representative" character of the council (the mix) is achieved, but the elected members consider themselves "representatives" (i.e., electees) of the entire presbyterium rather than of simply one segment.

The Authority of the Presbyteral Council

Canon 500 — §1. It pertains to the diocesan bishop to convoke the presbyteral council, to preside over it, and to determine the questions to be treated by it or to receive proposals from its members.

§2. The presbyteral council enjoys only a consultative vote; the bishop is to listen to it in matters of greater moment, but he needs its consent only in cases expressly defined by law.

§3. The presbyteral council is never able to act without the diocesan bishop who alone can divulge what was determined in keeping with §2.

The role of the presbyteral council was discussed at great length, particularly the possibility of granting it a deliberative vote. The final version of the Code views the council as completely consultative in nature and without authority to act on its own. Its function is not to exercise governance directly but to assist the bishop in his exercise of governmental authority.

The early drafts of the revised Code represented a more nuanced position: the council would enjoy purely consultative vote, but exceptions could be made by the universal law or by the diocesan bishop himself in accord with determinations of the conference of bishops.[70] At the committee meeting of April 17–18, 1980, this approach met with great resistance. It was not supported by either the conciliar documents or *Ecclesiae sanctae* I, 15. Its only textual justification was the circular letter of the Sacred Congregation for the Clergy, which was not legislation but a document of interpretation. The consultors rejected the notion that a deliberative vote could be authorized by the conference of bishops or by the diocesan bishop himself. The presbyteral council could enjoy a deliberative vote only on the basis of universal law (§2).[71]

These deliberations led to a very restrictive wording in the 1980 schema stating that the diocesan bishop is obliged to consult the council or to obtain its consent "solely in cases expressly defined by the law."[72] The effect of this revision was to limit radically the competence of the presbyteral council. Not only would it rarely be granted a deliberative vote, but the bishop had no obligation even to consult it except in specific cases. Although the Code Commission itself did not change this text,[73] it was amended prior to promulgation to the wording found in the second paragraph. The diocesan bishop has a general obligation to consult the presbyteral council in more important matters ("negotiis maioris momenti"); his obligation is not limited merely to those cases explicitated in the law. Thus, the preeminent place of the presbyteral council as the chief consultative body for matters of governance was restored by the pope's final revision.

"Matters of greater moment" is a general phrase which must be interpreted according to local circumstances. The *Directory on the Pastoral Ministry of Bishops* offers the following examples:

> . . . the holiness of life, sacred science, and other needs of the priests, or the sanctification and religious instruction of the faithful, or the government of the diocese in general. . . . It is the task of this council, among other things, to seek out clear and distinctly defined aims of the manifold ministries in the diocese, to propose matters that are more urgent, to indicate methods of acting, to assist whatever the Spirit frequently stirs up through individuals or groups, to foster the spiritual life, in order to attain the necessary unity more easily. They ought, finally, to deal with equal distribution of funds for the support of clerics, and also with the erection, suppression and restoration of parishes (no. 203b).[74]

If the presbyteral council is truly consulted on "matters of greater moment," it will certainly earn its title as the primary consultative body concerning diocesan governance.[75] Although its agenda will vary with changing circumstances, the council's re-

---

[70]Cf. *Comm* 5 (1973), 230, c. 314 of the 1977 schema, and the circular letter of the SCC, no. 9, which recognized the bishop's right to grant a deliberative vote to the council in specific cases.

[71]*Comm* 13 (1981), 133. It is interesting to read the rationale of one consultor who felt that the Congregation's circular letter was issued at a time of "crisis when there was pressure in various parts of the world from 'senates' or presbyteral councils, both national and provincial, to possess many of the faculties of the bishop." *Ibid.*

[72]"Episcopus dioecesanus illud audire debet vel etiam eius consensu eget solummodo in casibus iure expresse definitis." C. 420, §2 of the 1980 schema.

[73]Cf. *Rel,* 117 *ad c. 420,* in which a deliberative vote is equated with a bishop's "renouncing his power." The possibility of the bishop's permitting a deliberative vote was suppressed because of the "overwhelming" advice received in the consultation.

[74]In this description, which is not taxative, the *Directory* relies on the 1970 circular letter and on the 1971 Synod of Bishops (*De sacerdotio ministeriali,* Part 2, II), both of which should be consulted in determining the competence of the presbyteral council in the diocese.

[75]Cf. *Directory,* no. 203c.

sponsibilities are not left totally to the bishop's discretion. The canons explicitly require episcopal consultation of the presbyteral council in regard to several issues: the advisability of a diocesan synod (c. 461, §1); the modification of parishes (cc. 515, §2; 813); offerings of the faithful on the occasion of parish services (c. 531); norms for parish councils (c. 536); the construction of a church or the conversion of a church to secular use (cc. 1215, §2; 1222, §2); and the imposition of a diocesan tax (c. 1263). In all of these instances, the advice, not the consent, of the presbyteral council is needed. Only one canon seems to call for its consent. Canon 1742, §1 instructs the diocesan bishop to submit a list of pastors from which the presbyteral council selects the membership of a standing committee to serve as advisors to the bishop whenever a pastor is administratively removed from office or transferred against his will.

Canon 500 might seem overly restrictive if one thinks of the presbyteral council as separate from the diocesan bishop. Such an image may arise from the civil model of government in which a "balance of powers" is struck to protect and promote the common good. The canon, in fact, is not based on such a secular model but on the uniqueness of the Church as a hierarchical communion.[76] The unity of priests and bishop should make the debate over consultative and deliberative vote an academic issue, at least in the best of circumstances.[77] The norms are meant to stabilize the relationship of the council and the bishop and foster their harmonious collaboration for the overall pastoral good of the diocese.

The bishop convokes the presbyteral council, presides over it, and determines its agenda (§1). Such duties need not be carried out personally. The diocesan bishop can approve regularly scheduled meetings stated in the council's statutes. He may also delegate someone to call individual meetings on an ad hoc basis. To "preside" over the council does not mean that the bishop must chair the individual sessions, although he may wish to do so at times. There is no prohibition against creating an office of chairman in the statutes, which can also formalize the council's agenda-setting procedure. The council is to be both the "senate" of the bishop and "representative" of the presbyterium. As such, therefore, it is desirable for items to be initiated by the bishop as well as by council members. The tasks mentioned in paragraph one are not only the bishop's right but also his obligation ("Episcopi dioecesani est"). The intent of the canon is not to burden the bishop unduly but to ensure that he realizes

that the proper functioning of the council is ultimately his responsibility.

It is in this sense that the council cannot act apart from the diocesan bishop. Its advisory function is directly related to him and only indirectly to the pastoral benefit of the diocese. It is therefore the bishop's right and responsibility ("cura spectat") to publicize the activity of the council (§3). Once again, this obligation need not be exercised personally by the bishop in every instance. He will normally arrange for a regular method of publication to be written into the statutes. If the bishop is to be more closely united with the presbyterium, he should inform the priests of his diocese on a regular basis about the discussions and resolutions of the council and his own reaction to them. Such sharing should be the general rule although certain matters will on occasion be kept in executive session either temporarily or indefinitely. In such cases all the members of the council are bound to secrecy (c. 127, §3).[78]

The Cessation of the Presbyteral Council

Canon 501 — §1. Members of the presbyteral council are to be designated for a term determined in the statutes in such a way that the full council or some part of it is renewed within a five year period.

§2. When the see is vacant the presbyteral council ceases and its functions are fulfilled by the college of consultors; within a year of taking possession of the diocese the bishop must establish the presbyteral council anew.

§3. If the presbyteral council is no longer fulfilling the function committed to it for the good of the diocese or is gravely abusing it, the diocesan bishop can dissolve it after consulting with the metropolitan or, if it is a question of the metropolitan see itself, with the suffragan senior by promotion, but the bishop must establish it anew within a year.

All priests who are not members ex officio should be elected or appointed to the presbyteral council for a term (§1). The term is not specified in the universal law. The statutes of the council may, therefore, establish any term of office or even several types of terms. The only obligation is that the whole council or at least part of it be "renewed" every five years. "Some part" does not necessarily

---

[76]Cf. comments on the differences between canon and common law in the General Introduction to this commentary, 10–14.

[77]Cf. R. Kennedy, "Shared Responsibility in Ecclesial Decision-Making," *Stud Can* 14 (1980), 5–24; and F. McManus, "Canonical Consultation," *AER* 166 (1972), 368–370.

[78]Although one might argue that the presbyteral council eminently meets the criteria for institutes which are to be considered part of the diocesan curia (c. 469), there has been a traditional distinction between the bishop's councils and his curia. Thus, strictly speaking, the members of the council are not required to make the twofold promise of c. 471. Nevertheless, it would be appropriate for the statutes to incorporate such a requirement insofar as the members of the council are accepting an office to assist the bishop in the governance of the diocese, even though it is on the level of policy and consists in dialogue and advice rather than in some form of administration.

mean a majority. The renewal of a third of the membership would certainly fulfill the intent of the canon. The renewal is a juridic, not a factual, reality and it need not result in different members. There is no prohibition against indefinitely successive terms. Thus, although the entire council or a large part of it was reelected or reappointed (juridically renewed), the actual membership might be practically the same.

Ex officio members lose their membership on the presbyteral council when they lose the office which was the basis of their membership. Other members cease when their terms, as defined by the statutes, expire. In the latter case, the diocesan bishop should inform them in writing of the loss of membership (c. 186).

Since the presbyteral council cannot act without the bishop, the vacancy of the episcopal see (c. 416) causes the group to cease as a juridic institute (§2). The succeeding bishop must establish a new council within one year by issuing an appropriate decree and approving the statutes. These acts should be in writing, signed by him, and notarized (c. 474). Since the council is not simply suspended *sede vacante* but ceases, the members lose their office and are not automatically reinstated by the new bishop's appointment. Thus, if he wishes to continue the prior council, he must indicate this in his decree of establishment.

The members of the presbyteral council appointed to the college of consultors retain the office of consultor *sede vacante*. If one's term of office as consultor expires during the vacancy of the see, the law provides for its automatic extension until the new bishop reappoints or replaces the consultor in question (c. 502, §1).

The diocesan bishop must consult with the metropolitan (or the metropolitan with his senior suffragan) before dissolving the presbyteral council for dereliction of duty or grave abuse. The council may not be dissolved for any other reason. Similar to its establishment, the dissolution must be in the form of a signed and notarized decree (c. 474). This condition affects the validity of the dissolution since the act is equivalent to the removal of all members from their offices (c. 193, §4). Within a year, the bishop must establish a new presbyteral council. Its reconstitution should follow the same formalities described above regarding its reconstitution when a new bishop takes possession of the see. When the see is vacant, the council ceases by law; in the case of a dissolution, the council ceases by authoritative decree. In both cases, however, the constitution of a new council requires an authoritative decree; it is never reconstituted by law.

The College of Consultors

Canon 502 — §1. Some priests are to be freely selected by the diocesan bishop from among the members of the presbyteral council to constitute a college of consultors; their number is to be not less than six nor more than twelve; the college is established for a five year term, and is responsible for the functions determined in the law; when the five year term is over, the college continues to exercise its proper functions until a new college is established.

§2. The diocesan bishop presides over the college of consultors; if the see is impeded or vacant, the one who takes the place of the bishop in the interim presides, or, if such a person has not yet been established, the priest who is oldest in ordination in the college of consultors.

§3. The conference of bishops can determine that the functions of the college of consultors be committed to the cathedral chapter.

§4. In apostolic vicariates and prefectures the functions of the college of consultors belong to the mission council mentioned in can. 495, §2, unless the law determines otherwise.

The Vatican Council spoke of the "reorganization" of cathedral chapters (*CD* 27) and *Ecclesiae sanctae* of the "revision" of both chapters and consultors (I, 17, 2). These documents did not clarify whether the groups would continue to exist alongside the newly established presbyteral council. The 1970 circular letter of the Sacred Congregation for the Clergy, therefore, called upon conferences of bishops to submit their "motions relative to the revision of the cathedral chapter and the reformation or confirmation of the board of consultors" (no. 10). The present law seeks to determine the proper status of each of these consultative bodies.

The cathedral chapter is reduced primarily to a liturgical function with some flexibility to introduce other duties. The consultors are closely attached to the presbyteral council and given certain duties by universal law. The relationship between the chapter and the consultors reverses that of the former Code. The 1917 Code provided for consultors in the event that a diocese did not have a cathedral chapter (*CIC* 423) and authorized the consultors to act in place of the chapter (*CIC* 427). In the revised Code, however, the consultors are a stable college involved in governance. Its duties can be assumed by the cathedral chapter only if so stated by the conference of bishops (§3).[79] While the 1917 Code decreed that every diocese must have either a chapter of canons or a board of consultors, the 1983 Code determines that every diocese must have a college of consultors unless its duties have been transferred to the cathedral chapter by particular law. In some

---

[79]In fact, this option was inserted into the text between the 1977 and 1980 schemata because of the importance which cathedral chapters still have in Germany and Austria. *Comm* 13 (1981), 135.

countries, therefore, dioceses may have both a college of consultors and a cathedral chapter in addition to the presbyteral council.[80]

The first paragraph of this canon describes the establishment of the college of consultors. Its members must be priests or bishops ("sacerdotes") who are, at the time of their appointment as consultors, already members of the presbyteral council. They are appointed for a five-year term. If, during that period, they cease to be members of the presbyteral council, they do not thereby cease to be members of the college of consultors. The two groups, though closely linked, are canonically independent entities.[81]

In order to keep the college from competing with the presbyteral council, the law not only requires membership on the presbyteral council as a qualification for appointment to the college but adds to the minimum number of six (found previously in *CIC* 425, §1) a maximum number of twelve. Although the five-year term is applied to the college as a unit, nothing prevents the diocesan bishop from appointing the individual members to the college for a five-year term commencing on different dates. If he neglects to reappoint consultors after their terms have expired, they retain the right to exercise their office until officially replaced. The bishop must appoint consultors by a signed and notarized letter (cc. 156, 474). Although, strictly speaking, they are not part of the curia, it would be appropriate, in the light of their important responsibilities, to ask duly-appointed consultors to make the twofold promise of canon 471 (cf. c. 127, §3). When a consultor's term of office expires, he must be so informed by the diocesan bishop in writing (c. 186).

One of the most important phrases of paragraph one is that which limits the competence of the college of consultors to those "functions determined in the law." The college does not have any general functions as does the presbyteral council (c. 500, §2); its functions are solely those explicitly stated in the law.[82] These functions include the following: the election of the diocesan administrator when the see becomes vacant (c. 421, §1); other duties when the see is impeded or vacant (cc. 272, 413, §2, 419, 422, 485, 501, §2); and certain financial duties such as advice regarding the hiring and firing of the finance officer (c. 494), consent for acts of extraordinary administration (c. 1277), and consent for the alienation of certain ecclesiastical property (c. 1292, §1).

The college of consultors is presided over by the diocesan bishop or, when the see becomes vacant, by the diocesan administrator unless the latter has not yet been chosen by the consultors (§2). When the see becomes vacant, the senior auxiliary bishop presides over the consultors until they elect the administrator, who then begins to preside (c. 419). If the diocese has no auxiliary bishop, the senior consultor presides until the administrator is elected.

In apostolic vicariates and prefectures (c. 368) the three or more priests appointed to serve as a missionary council in accord with canon 495, §2 also fulfill all the duties assigned to the college of consultors unless some other provision is made in a particular case (§4).

CHAPTER IV
CHAPTERS OF CANONS
[cc. 503–510]

The chapter of canons has evolved over the centuries. It seems to have arisen from the practice of priests living according to the "canonical rule," the norms found in various canons of church councils. During the Merovingian period there were many attempts to promote this type of discipline, encouraging priests to live the "canonical life" within the cloister of the bishop's residence. Eventually, however, priests whose benefices required them to live elsewhere remained outside the bishop's residence. The aspect of common life receded, but priests still sought to live the "canonical life." They continued therefore to meet regularly in the chapter (*capitulum*).

The origin of the title "chapter" is not clear. It may have arisen from a reference to the group as a *caput parvum* in comparison to the bishop as the *caput maius,* from the practice of deciding matters by individual vote (*capitatim*), or from the tradition of reading a chapter of the rule (*capitulum regulae*) at meetings. During the Middle Ages the chapter became a very significant group in the diocese, controlling episcopal elections and governing the diocese when the see was vacant. Certain canons became important officials, e.g., the canon theologian (*canonicus theologus*) and the canon penitentiary (*canonicus poenitentiarius*), both of whom were given canonical status by the Council of Trent and singled out more recently in canons 398–401 of the 1917 Code.

The revised Code, while retaining this ancient canonical institute, revises it considerably. Chapter IV contains only eight canons in contrast to the thirty-two canons of the 1917 Code (*CIC* 391–422), since the norms have only limited applicability throughout the world. Many countries have never established chapters and in other areas they have diminished in importance. Dioceses which have no chapter of canons are affected only by canon 508, §2 which requires a substitute for the canon penitentiary.

---

[80]The U.S. was one of the first regions to introduce consultors, an advisory group without benefices, as a substitute for chapters. This practice was later recognized in the 1917 Code as an option and given a fixed status for all dioceses in the 1983 Code. Cf. *Concilii Plenarii Baltimorensis II. Acta et Decreta* (1868), 53ff.

[81]*Rel,* 118 *ad c. 422* and *AAS* 76 (1984), 747.

[82]*Rel,* 119 *ad c. 422.*

Canon 503 — The chapter of canons, whether cathedral or collegial, is a college of priests whose responsibility it is to perform the more solemn liturgical functions in the cathedral or collegial church; moreover, the cathedral chapter is to fulfill the duties which have been committed to it by the law itself or by the diocesan bishop.

The canon limits the role of the chapter to solemn liturgical functions, omitting the former Code's description of the chapter as the bishop's "senate and counsel" (*CIC* 391, §1). The bishop is permitted to commit other duties to the cathedral chapter, but these must be in accord with its liturgical character. The duties of the diocesan consultors cannot be committed to the chapter unless the bishops of a particular region are authorized to do so by a legislative decree of the conference of bishops (cc. 502, §3; 455).

Canon 504 — The erection, change or suppression of a cathedral chapter is reserved to the Apostolic See.

Cathedral chapters are not promoted by the canon. The Code Commission purposely deleted a paragraph which would have required that existing chapters be retained and new chapters founded where possible.[83] This deletion was based on the close connection between chapters and benefices, which themselves are discouraged and require careful supervision (c. 1272). Canon 504 reserves the erection, change, or suppression of cathedral chapters (not collegial chapters) to the Apostolic See. The 1917 Code (*CIC* 392) and earlier drafts of this had applied this reservation to all chapters, even collegial.[84]

Canon 505 — Each and every chapter, whether cathedral or collegial, is to have its own statutes, drawn up by a legitimate capitular act and approved by the diocesan bishop; these statutes are not to be changed or abrogated without the approval of the same diocesan bishop.

The canon repeats substantially canon 410, §2 of the 1917 Code. Since the diocesan bishop's approval has a juridic effect (i.e., constituting, amending, or abrogating statutes), it must be in written form, signed, and notarized (c. 474). The legitimate capitular act of approving statutes must be posited by a majority vote of the canons assembled in chapter and in accord with universal law and existing statutes of the chapter.

Canon 506 — §1. With due regard always for the laws of its foundation, the statutes of the chapter

are to determine the constitution of the chapter and the number of canons, define which things must be done by the chapter and which by the individual canons in the performance of divine worship and the ministry, schedule the meetings in which the business of the chapter is taken care of, and, with due regard for the prescriptions of universal law, determine the conditions required for valid and legitimate transactions.

§2. The statutes are also to define, having observed the norms laid down by the Holy See, the proper insignia of the canons and their financial compensation, whether stable or to be given on the occasion of the performance of duty.

The first paragraph identifies the matters to be determined by the statutes: constitution, membership, meetings and formalities and, most important, the acts of divine worship and ministry to be carried out by the chapter as a whole and by individual canons. The second paragraph notes that the statutes must determine the canons' insignia, in accord with pontifical norms, and their financial remuneration. This canon radically simplifies the complicated rules found in the former Code, which particularly addressed the financial rights and duties of the chapter (e.g., *CIC* 393, 394, 395, 397).

Canon 507 — §1. One of the canons is to preside over the chapter, and other offices are also to be established according to the norm of the statutes, taking cognizance as well of the usages prevailing in the region.

§2. Other offices which may aid the canons can be entrusted to clerics who do not belong to the chapter, according to the norms of the statutes.

The revised Code simplifies considerably the norms concerning the various offices fulfilled by canons. The chapter is free to determine who will preside over it (§1), a change in emphasis from canon 397 of the 1917 Code which prescribed a certain order of precedence unless the statutes decreed otherwise. The chapter's statutes may establish other offices for canons (§1). The text omits all mention of the canon theologian (*CIC* 398–400).

The second paragraph states that clerics (a term which includes deacons) may be appointed to fulfill certain chapter offices even though they themselves are only auxiliary to, not members of, the chapter. The concept of honorary canons which was specified in canons 406–407 of the 1917 Code has been deleted from the universal law and left to particular law.[85]

[83]C. 318, §1 of the 1977 schema; cf. *Comm* 13 (1981), 135.
[84]Cf. *Comm* 13 (1981), 135.

[85]Cf. the suppression of c. 325 of the 1977 schema, which had permitted conferences of bishops to decide whether their regions should have honorary canons. *Comm* 13 (1981), 137–138.

Canon 508 — §1. The canon penitentiary, both of a cathedral church and of a collegial church, in virtue of his office has the ordinary faculty, which nevertheless he cannot delegate to another, of absolving in the sacramental forum from undeclared *latae sententiae* censures not reserved to the Apostolic See, even outsiders within the diocese and members of the diocese outside it.

§2. Where there is no chapter the diocesan bishop is to appoint a diocesan priest to fulfill this same function.

Although the office of canon theologian has been omitted from the Code, that of canon penitentiary is retained and some of his duties are to be discharged even in dioceses without chapters. The first paragraph of the canon attaches to the office of the canon penitentiary the ordinary power to absolve in the sacramental forum from all undeclared automatic censures not reserved to the Apostolic See. Even though it is ordinary in nature, this power cannot be delegated to others. Bishops have the same faculty and can delegate it (c. 1355, §2). The canon penitentiary may exercise this faculty on behalf of all penitents subject to him, even those who are not experiencing special hardship by remaining in the state of grave sin until competent authority can absolve from the censure in the external forum; nor is it necessary for the penitent to have recourse to the competent superior in the external forum within one month (c. 1357, §2). These conditions must be met when a similar faculty is used by a confessor who is not a canon penitentiary (c. 1357).

When there is no chapter in a diocese, the bishop has the obligation of designating a priest to fulfill this office (§2). The designated priest ("sacerdotem") should not be an auxiliary bishop since he would already have the faculty for the sacramental forum, nor any of the vicars general or episcopal vicars since they have the faculty for the external or internal, non-sacramental forum (c. 1355, §2). While the diocesan bishop is instructed to designate a single priest as a substitute for the canon penitentiary, he could also approach this pastoral need in a different manner. Instead of solving it on the basis of canon 508, §2, he could grant to all his priests the faculty to absolve by delegated power from all unreserved and undeclared automatic penalties in the external forum on the basis of canon 1355, §2.

Canon 509 — §1. It is for the diocesan bishop, having listened to the chapter, but not for the diocesan administrator, to confer each and every individual canonry whether in the cathedral church or in the collegial church, every contrary privilege being revoked; it is for the same bishop to confirm the election by the chapter of the one who shall preside over it.

§2. The diocesan bishop is to confer the canonry only upon priests outstanding in doctrine and integrity of life who have exercised the ministry in a praiseworthy manner.

The first paragraph substantially repeats canon 403 of the 1917 Code, omitting any reference to the conferral of benefices, adding the right of the diocesan bishop to confirm the election of the president of the chapter, and specifying that the diocesan administrator *sede vacante* does not receive the right to confer canonries.

The second paragraph repeats canon 404, §1 of the 1917 Code, adding the stipulation that those to be appointed canons should be priests "who have exercised the ministry in a praiseworthy manner," another example of the Code's stress on the chapter of canons as a liturgical and ministerial group, rather than an institute of diocesan governance.

Canon 510 — §1. Parishes are no longer to be joined to a chapter of canons; those which are united to some chapter are to be separated from the chapter by the diocesan bishop.

§2. In a church which is at the same time parochial and capitular, a pastor is to be designated, whether chosen from among the members of the chapter or not; this pastor is bound by all the duties and enjoys all the rights and faculties which are proper to a pastor according to the norm of law.

§3. It is for the diocesan bishop to establish definite norms by which the pastoral duties of the pastor and the responsibilities proper to the chapter are to be fittingly integrated; these norms are to preclude the pastor's impeding capitular functions or the chapter's impeding parochial functions; the diocesan bishop is to resolve conflicts, should any arise; his first concern will be seeing to it that the pastoral necessities of the faithful are fittingly provided for.

§4. Any alms which are given to a church which is at the same time parochial and capitular are presumed to be given to the parish unless otherwise evident.

The final canon treats the situation in which the chapter is connected with a parish church. In the 1917 Code the chapter itself could be the pastor of a parish (*CIC* 471, §1). In this case, the parish was fully united to the chapter, and one of the canons was appointed as a parochial vicar to carry out the pastor's duties and exercise rights on behalf of the chapter (*CIC* 402). The revised Code prohibits this arrangement in canon 520, §1, requiring even a parish committed to a religious institute to have a personal pastor, rather than a vicar. The same canon omits all reference to the chapter of canons, indicating that no parish may be committed to a chapter for pastoral care (even apart from *pleno iure* union).

This approach is confirmed by canon 510 which instructs the diocesan bishop to separate parishes formerly united to chapters (§1). If the chapter's church (the cathedral for the cathedral chapter or another notable church for a collegial chapter) is also a parish church, a pastor is assigned to it independently of the chapter. He may or may not be one of the canons since there is no formal connection between the parish and the chapter (§2). In any conflict or question, the presumption is always in favor of the pastoral needs of the faithful (§3) and the rights of the parish (§4). In other words, the chapter is located in the church of a particular parish, not vice versa.

CHAPTER V
THE PASTORAL COUNCIL
[cc. 511–514]

The Second Vatican Council strongly recommended the establishment of councils in each diocese to study and deliberate on pastoral matters and make practical suggestions for the benefit of the particular church.

It is highly desirable that in each diocese a pastoral council be established over which the diocesan bishop himself will preside and in which specially chosen clergy, religious, and lay people will participate. The function of this council will be to investigate and to weigh matters which bear on pastoral activity, and to formulate practical conclusions regarding them (*CD* 27).

As spare as this reference may seem, it initiated an important canonical institute based on the *communio* model of the Church expressed by the phrase "people of God." By baptism and confirmation *all* are called to share in the threefold office of Christ as priest, prophet, and king, in accord with their respective roles in the Church. It is fitting therefore that a diocesan structure represent the organic reality of the particular church.

The conciliar text contained certain key principles: (a) the pastoral council is established to serve the needs of the entire particular church; (b) it is not a group apart from the bishop but one closely joined with him, over which he himself presides; (c) it is not a lay association but a group which represents a cross section of the diocese; and (d) it is neither a decision-making body nor a study club but a set of advisors who will investigate the diocese's pastoral life and recommend concrete steps to promote and improve it.

Ecclesiae sanctae I, 16–17 took these principles and implemented them canonically: (a) *purpose*—promote conformity to the gospel in the life and actions of the people of God; (b) *method*—examine all matters relative to pastoral activity, weigh them carefully, and propose practical steps to be taken; do detailed research before discussing an issue, especially by consulting offices which specialize in the area under consideration; (c) *authority*—consulta-

tive; (d) *stability*—a permanent institution but with terms for its members; (e) *meetings*—at the discretion of the bishop; (f) *membership*—clergy, religious, and lay persons; (g) *coordination*—with presbyteral council and other episcopal councils by carefully defining respective competencies, sharing members, setting up joint sessions, and other forms of collaboration.

The pastoral council, while not involved in the governance of the diocese, should address any pastoral matters which call for study and practical recommendations. It is totally under the authority of the bishop and does not act apart from him. He should therefore look upon it as one of his closest collaborators in the development of pastoral policy and planning. It is highly recommended for every diocese.[86]

These principles are preserved only in general form in the four canons of chapter V. In practice, the existence and operation of a pastoral council will depend chiefly on its statutes as approved by the diocesan bishop.

The Establishment of a Pastoral Council

Canon 511 — **In each diocese, to the extent that pastoral circumstances recommend it, a pastoral council is to be established whose responsibility it is to investigate under the authority of the bishop all those things which pertain to pastoral works, to ponder them and to propose practical conclusions about them.**

The establishment of a pastoral council is not entirely optional; it might be called a qualified obligation. It *should* be established *if* pastoral circumstances call for it. This canon should be read in the light of the conciliar directive that a pastoral council in each diocese is "highly desirable."[87]

The council is under the authority of the diocesan bishop and may be constituted by no one else. Its area of competence is broadly described as anything which can be termed "pastoral." Its method, specified in *Christus Dominus* 27 and *Ecclesiae sanctae* I, 16, is threefold: to gather data, strive to understand it, and make conclusions and proposals.

The pastoral council is constituted for the individual diocese. Since members of the Code Com-

---

86Although not legislative in character, two other important documents which treat the pastoral council are the report of the 1971 Synod of Bishops (*De Sacerdotio ministeriali*, Part 2, II, 3) and the *Directory*. The latter document, which draws from *CD* 27, *ES* I, 16 and the 1971 Synod of Bishops, presents the principles in a narrative and interpretative format, explicitly pointing up the planning function: "By its study and reflection, the council furnishes the judgments necessary to enable the diocesan community to plan its pastoral program systematically and to fulfill it effectively" (no. 204).

87*Optatur ut constituatur Consilium pastorale* (*Comm* 5 [1973], 231). Cf. *Rel*, 120 *ad c. 431*, responding to Cardinal König on this point, and the *Directory*, no. 204.

mission were concerned about *supra-diocesan* pastoral councils, certain words were carefully chosen in order to avoid any interpretation that the pastoral council could be anything other than a form of *diocesan* consultation.[88]

The Membership of a Pastoral Council

Canon 512 — §1. The pastoral council consists of Christian faithful who are in full communion with the Catholic Church, clerics, members of institutes of consecrated life and especially lay persons, who are designated in a manner determined by the diocesan bishop.

§2. The Christian faithful who are appointed to the pastoral council are to be so selected that the entire portion of the people of God which constitutes the diocese is truly reflected, with due regard for the diverse regions, social conditions and professions of the diocese as well as the role which they have in the apostolate, either as individuals or in conjunction with others.

§3. No one except Christians of proven faith, good morals and outstanding prudence are to be appointed to the pastoral council.

The council membership should be representative of all the people of God and should therefore include priests, deacons, men and women religious, and especially lay persons,[89] all of whom must be Catholic (§1). The manner in which they are designated to serve on the council is left completely to the discretion of the diocesan bishop. This does not mean that all must be personally appointed by him. In fact, he might arrange for none to be appointed by him. It is the *manner* of designation which he must determine. He may decide that the members should be elected, or appointed, or ex officio, or any mixture of the three. In short, as the first paragraph indicates, the universal law sets down no norms about the method of designation; it is concerned solely with the results of the method, the representative quality of the council described in the second paragraph.

The pastoral council is meant to be *representative* of the whole people of God without the members being considered necessarily as *representatives* (deputees) of a specific constituency. There is no prohibition against the election of members—even of all the members—provided that the result of the election is a council which reflects as much as possible the entire people of God of the particular church. With this goal in mind, the varied methods of designation prescribed for the presbyteral council (c. 497) may serve as a model for the pastoral council. Any method chosen must seek to form a cohesive group, and each member in the group should have the sense of being a servant of the entire diocese rather than simply a representative of any particular sector.[90]

Given the important role of the pastoral council, the qualifications mentioned in the third paragraph (faith, moral integrity, and prudence) can hardly be questioned. They should, however, be concretized more precisely in the council's statutes, which may also add other qualifications to those of universal law.[91]

The canons do not indicate how many persons should serve on a pastoral council. There is no minimum or maximum number; the matter is therefore left entirely to the diocesan bishop (§1). It would be impossible to have fewer than three since the membership should include at least a priest, a religious, and a lay person. Even three could hardly fulfill the council's objectives, except in the most extreme circumstances. On the other hand, the council cannot be so large as to frustrate the exchange of ideas among the members. The determination of the number should be based on the need to fulfill the council's work of studying pastoral questions, effectively deliberating on them in a collegial manner, and forming practicable recommendations.

Canon 513 — §1. The pastoral council is to be established for a period of time according to the prescriptions of the statutes which are issued by the bishop.

§2. When the see is vacant the pastoral council ceases to exist.

The pastoral council as a juridic institute is in itself permanent. The canon does not suggest that the council is a temporary or passing reality. It is not a task force which receives its commission, completes its charge, and dissolves. The phrase "ad tempus"

---

[88]Cf. the use of the phrase "in singulis dioecesibus" in *Comm* 5 (1973), 231 and the insertion of the phrase "in dioecesi" after "opera pastoralia" in *Comm* 13 (1981), 138 and *Rel,* 120 *ad cc. 431–434.*

[89]The text stresses the involvement of lay persons by the use of the word "especially," which replaced earlier suggestions that the *majority* of the members should be lay persons. Cf. the deletion of c. 327, §2 of the 1977 schema and the insertion of "praesertim" in §1 in *Comm* 13 (1981), 139.

[90]Cf. *Comm* 13 (1981), 139; "From a juridical point of view, the members of such a council are not deputized or elected by the other faithful of the diocese." The Code Commission's approach varies somewhat from that found in the *Directory* which speaks of constituencies as well as the entire diocese. It raises the notion of parish pastoral councils and suggests the following model for the designation of the members of the diocesan pastoral council: "These [parish] councils, grouped together according to areas, could choose their representatives to serve on the diocesan council, so that the whole diocesan community may feel that it is offering its cooperation to its bishop through the diocesan council" (no. 204). Even so, the concept should not be equated with the governmental model of legislative deputees. The *method* of election provides broader participation and ownership but, once elected, the members must be concerned with the particular church as one people of God.

[91]Cf. *Comm* 13 (1981), 139 in which the paragraph was criticized by some of the consultors as not properly juridic.

refers not to the juridic institute as such but to the term of the members to be fixed by the statutes (§1). The entire membership need not end their terms at the same time, nor is it necessary for all members to have equal terms.

The establishment of the council as a juridic entity and the approval of its statutes should be in writing, signed by the diocesan bishop, and notarized (c. 474). Members of a pastoral council assume an ecclesiastical office (c. 145). They should therefore receive a written recognition of this fact, whether they are designated ex officio, by appointment or by election (c. 156). The expiration of a member's term should also be intimated in writing (c. 186). The office held by the members is a consultative pastoral office, which is not part of the diocesan curia.

Since the pastoral council is totally dependent on the diocesan bishop, it ceases to exist when the episcopal see becomes vacant (§2). All members, with or without terms, lose their office and all rights and duties articulated in the statutes. The decree of establishment and the approved statutes cease to have any juridic effect. the council does not revive automatically when the succeeding bishop takes possession of the diocese. To do so would infringe on his administrative discretion as expressed in canon 511. He must therefore issue a new decree of establishment and approval of statutes and confirm the former members in their positions, if he wishes to carry on the pastoral council in the form in which it existed before the see became vacant.

The Authority of a Pastoral Council

Canon 514 — §1. It pertains exclusively to the diocesan bishop to convoke the pastoral council according to the necessities of the apostolate and to preside over it; the pastoral council enjoys only a consultative vote; it is for the bishop alone to make public what has been done in the council.

§2. The pastoral council is to be convoked at least once a year.

Consistent with *Ecclesiae sanctae* I, 16, 2, the first paragraph of this canon identifies the council's authority as solely consultative. Because of the nature and purpose of the council as a study and planning group, this point was not extensively debated as it was in regard to the presbyteral council.[92]

[92]Cf. commentary on c. 500 above.

The diocesan bishop has the right and responsibility to convoke the council (§1). He is obliged to arrange at least one meeting each year (§2), although the canon urges meetings whenever pastoral needs warrant them. The bishop can exercise his responsibility in this regard by approving in the council's statutes a regular schedule of meetings or some other method of calling meetings.

Although the bishop presides over the council (§1), this does not require him to chair the meetings. The statutes can constitute a chairperson and other officers to facilitate the work of the council prior to and during the meetings. The council may even meet without the bishop, provided that it has been properly convoked in accord with its statutes. If the statutes do not provide a method of calling meetings, the council may not meet without the bishop's at least implicit approval.

The statutes should also determine the method of publicizing the activity of the council. This determination is the right and responsibility of the diocesan bishop (§1). He may require that specific matters be kept confidential or perhaps released to only certain persons.[93] Given, however, the pastoral purpose of the council and its specialty of planning, publicity will normally be widespread in order to obtain as much feedback as possible regarding major projects and policies.

Although the Code offers little guidance regarding the coordination of councils, it remains an important need in any diocese.[94] It is especially critical to foster information-sharing and collaboration between the pastoral council, the presbyteral council, other *praeter legem* consultative bodies, and the central administrative offices. In universal law, the diocesan bishop himself is the point of reference and the presumed coordinator. In practice, however, he cannot accomplish this on his own. Systems of coordination should be built into the statutes and working policies of all these councils and offices.

[93]Since neither the consent nor the counsel of the pastoral council is required by law and the council is not part of the curia, the members are not directly bound by the secrecy of cc. 127, §3 and 471. Nevertheless, the bishop's right to moderate publicity creates a corresponding obligation on their part to maintain confidentiality. It would seem appropriate to articulate in the statutes the members' obligation to fulfill their office and maintain confidentiality when needed. The statutes could require a promise of service and secrecy modeled on c. 471.
[94]Cf. *ES* I, 17, §1.

Collins, P. "The Diocesan Synod—An Assembly of the People of God." *J* 33 (1973): 399–411.

Comm 5 (1973): 314–319.

Comm 12 (1980): 219–235.

Comm 13 (1981): 111–146.

Coriden, J.A. "The Diocesan Synod: An Instrument of Renewal for the Local Church." *J* 34 (1974): 68–93.

Donnelly, F.B. *The Diocesan Synod. An Historical Conspectus and Commentary. CanLawStud* 74. Washington D.C.: Catholic University, 1932.

———. "The New Diocesan Synod." *J* 34 (1974): 396–402.

Dougherty, T.D. *The Vicar General of the Episcopal Ordinary. CanLawStud* 447. Washington, D.C.: Catholic University, 1966 (cited as Dougherty).

Hamel, J.R. "Une chancellerie après Vatican II." *Stud Can* 12 (1978): 81–91.

Kennedy R. "Shared Responsibility in Ecclesial Decision-Making." *Stud Can* 14 (1980): 5–24.

Louis, W.F. *Diocesan Archives. An Historical Synopsis and Commentary. CanLawStud* 137. Washington, D.C.: Catholic University, 1941.

McManus, F. "Canonical Consultation." *AER* 166 (June 1972): 368–370.

Prince, J.E. *The Diocesan Chancellor. An Historical Synopsis and Commentary. CanLawStud,* 167. Washington, D.C.: Catholic University, 1942 (cited as Prince).

Provost, J. "The Working Together of Consultative Bodies—Great Expectations." *J* 40 (1980): 257–281.

Purcell, J.W. "The Institute of the Senate of Priests." *J* 38 (1978): 132–152.

Rossi, B.A. *Priests' Senates. Canadian Experiences.* Roma: Edizione dell 'Urbe, 1979.

SCC. Circular letter on priests' councils. April 11, 1970. *CLD* 7: 383–390.

Swift, T.P. "The Pastoral Office of Episcopal Vicar—Changing Role and Powers." *J* 40 (1980): 225–256.

The following is a commentary on canons 515–572. These canons comprise chapters VI, VII, and VIII of Book II ("De Populo Dei"), part II, section II, title III.

History

The schema on the people of God represents the work of several *coetus,* or committees, of the Pontifical Commission for the Revision of the Code of Canon Law.[1] The sections on parishes, pastors, and parochial vicars; vicars forane; and rectors of churches and chaplains (chaps. VI–VIII) are the work of the *coetus* on the Sacred Hierarchy.[2] The initial draft of the schema was sent for study to all the bishops, the Roman Curia, pontifical faculties, and the Union of Superiors General in January 1978. Their resulting evaluation and comments were due in Rome by the end of that same year. Because of the shortness of time, a number of the episcopal conferences relied in part on critiques prepared by professional canonical societies. For example, in the United States the Canon Law Society of America assisted the National Conference of Catholic Bishops in preparing its comments. Many of the individuals and groups involved in this year-long evaluation expressed the hope that a second consultation would take place. However, this never happened, and the revisions based on the evaluation were compiled into what became the 1980 schema.[3]

The final study and revision of this schema were undertaken by the Pontifical Commission for the Revision of the Code of Canon Law, enlarged by fifteen members, at their plenary session, October 20–28, 1981 at Rome.[4] In the section of the law which this commentary treats, twenty-six canons were discussed and although there was some re-wording, the only major alterations that occurred were the addition of a new section on chaplains which then followed the one on rectors of churches. After the plenary session, the various sections of the proposed law were synthesized by the Pontifical Commission for the Revision of the Code of Canon Law and the definitive schema was entrusted to the Holy Father with the request that it be promulgated as soon as possible. The Holy Father decided to study the text personally before promulgating it. The episcopal conferences were informed that the Holy Father was prepared to accept any suggestions or proposals which the bishops thought should still be presented. When the revised Code was promulgated on January 25, 1983 (to be effective the first Sunday of Advent, November 27, 1983), there were no substantive changes in this section of the law (cc. 515–572) except for the new section on chaplains (cc. 564–572).

Relation to 1917 Code

In general it can be said that this section of the new law corresponds to the basic structure of the 1917 Code, namely, Book II, part I, section II, title VIII, chapter VIII: vicars forane (*CIC* 445–450); chapter IX: pastors (*CIC* 451–470); chapter X: parochial vicars (*CIC* 471–478); and chapter XI: rectors of churches (*CIC* 479–486).[5]

Noticeable changes in this area from that of the 1917 Code involve a redefinition of parish (c. 515) and pastor (c. 519) according to *Christus Dominus* 30–31.[6] Team ministry for parishes (c. 517) is now permitted as are terms of office for pastors with the approval of the conference of bishops (c. 522). Parish finance councils are mandatory (c. 537), and pastoral councils are permitted at the discretion of the local bishop after consulting the presbyteral council (c. 536). Non-priests and even non-clerics may function (with a priest's supervision) in significant pastoral offices in case of a shortage of priests (c. 517, §2). The former distinction between removable and irremovable pastors has been eliminated from the law, and all pastors are asked to submit their resignations at age seventy-five (c. 538).

The section on parochial vicars simplifies the 1917 Code. The various types of parochial vicars are reduced and more is said regarding their office, rights, and obligations. Furthermore, the parochial

---

[1] On January 25, 1959, Pope John XXIII called for the *aggiornamento* of canon law; at the same time he announced he would convoke an ecumenical council. The Pontifical Commission for the Revision of the Code of Canon Law was instituted by the same pope on March 23, 1963 with Cardinal Pietro Ciriaci named as its president. Succeeding popes have continued the work begun by John XXIII and gradually expanded the Commission.

[2] See *Comm* 8 (1976), 23–31.

[3] This revision was drafted at Rome by the Code Commission during its eighth session, May 8–16, 1980. See *Comm* 13 (1981), 146–151; 271–314.

[4] See *Comm* 13 (1981), 256–270.

[5] Because of the similarity to the 1917 Code it is helpful to consult such commentaries as Abbo-Hannan, Ayrinhac, Bouscaren-Ellis, and Woywod-Smith. These English commentaries are based on and refer in many instances to such classical commentaries as Wernz-Vidal, Cappello, etc.

[6] See T. Green, "Critical Reflections," 246–247; J. Provost, "Revising Canon Law," 277–278; Initial CLSA Report (1978).

vicar cannot be removed except for a just cause (c. 552).

The vicar forane (dean) is now treated in the canons following parishes and parish personnel (c. 553–555) rather than in the canons preceding them as in the 1917 Code. Now the vicar forane is considered a coordinator and facilitator of pastoral activity rather than a supervisor for the bishop. An extensive job description for the office is included in these canons.

CANONS AND COMMENTARY

CHAPTER VI
PARISHES, PASTORS, AND PAROCHIAL VICARS
[cc. 515–552]

Parishes

Canon 515 — §1. A parish is a definite community of the Christian faithful established on a stable basis within a particular church; the pastoral care of the parish is entrusted to a pastor as its own shepherd under the authority of the diocesan bishop.

§2. The diocesan bishop alone is competent to erect, suppress or alter parishes; he is not to erect, suppress or notably alter them without hearing the presbyteral council.

§3. A legitimately erected parish has juridic personality by the law itself.

Etymologically "parish" is derived from the Greek *paroikia,* which in the early Church meant a pilgrim people, whose real country and citizenry is in heaven.[7] For approximately the first four centuries parish and diocese were coextensive. With the end of the persecutions and the increasing spread of the faith, it became necessary to establish permanent outposts in the country to which bishops at first deployed some of the cathedral clergy. Up to the eleventh century the medieval feudal system heavily influenced the structure of the parish (it was the goal of the Emperor Charlemagne to have a church with its own parish priest in every village and town). Because of the feudal system the clergy became dependent on the support of the landowner, and the bishop's authority began to be diminished. This, however, was corrected during the Gregorian reform when Gregory VII reconstituted the parish into a structure which has remained substantially unchanged to the present.

Marcuzzi contends that rather than defining "parish," the 1917 Code (*CIC* 216) contained a number of juridic terms which together described the then contemporary notion of parish. Thus, a parish was understood to be a (1) *territorial section of the diocese,* with a (2) *proper church edifice* to which a (3) *Catholic population was assigned* under the leadership of a (4) *proper pastor* who was removable or irremovable and who was responsible for the (5) *care of souls.*[8] A parish was also considered to be a parochial benefice primarily for the determination and assignment of revenue to the pastor.[9] From the standpoint of the 1917 Code the parish was understood to be an organization or institution to serve the spiritual needs of the faithful.

Vatican II (*SC* 42, *AA* 20) shifted the concept of parish from that of an organization or institution to one of community.[10] Underpinning this notion of parish as a community of the Christian faithful[11] is the theological principle of *communio* (Greek *koinonia*), a scripturally oriented concept which can be applied analogously to various facets of the Church including the parish.[12] This idea is a key to understanding the intent and thrust of Vatican II. The need for parish structures, however, should not be minimized. Pope Paul VI pointed out that "communion in Christ" could not effectively operate were it not for ecclesial structures.[13] Therefore, in the conciliar documents the traditional descriptions of territoriality, pastoral office, stability, and care of souls are applied to parish; however, now there is a distinct stress on the personalistic rather than the institutional aspect. Vatican II also emphasized the purpose for which a parish exists: to provide pastoral care for the Christian faithful. "Pastoral care" is broadly described as teaching, sanctifying, and gov-

---

[7]See C. Riege, "Parish," 1017–1019.

[8]See P. Marcuzzi, "Verso una nuova definizione," 833.
[9]*CIC* 1409–1488 contained the provisions for benefices in general, some of which are applicable to parishes. Vatican II (*PO* 20) called for a reform of the benefice system so that the emphasis would be placed on the ecclesiastical office rather than on revenues.
[10]See A. Dulles, *Models of the Church,* 43–57.
[11]C. 204 describes the "Christian faithful."
[12]See L. Hertling, *Communio: Church and Papacy in Early Christianity,* 102; see also *J* 36 (1976), 1–245.
[13]See *The Pope Speaks* 18 (1973), 282.

erning in such a manner that parishioners and parish communities will really see that they are members of both the diocese and the universal Church. Therefore, they should work together with other parishes, vicars forane, and those engaged in supra-parochial ministry so that all pastoral work will be unified and more effective.[14]

Post-conciliar legislation flowing from Vatican II contained no significant variations regarding the juridic description of the parish.[15] However, this interim legislation prepared the way for some modifications of terms relating to the parish which now appear in the revised law. *Ecclesiae sanctae* treated of the establishment, change, and suppression of parishes (*ES* I, 21); parishes entrusted to religious (*ES* I, 33); and the modification of the benefice system (*ES* 18). The *Directory* synthesized conciliar and post-conciliar concepts pertaining to parishes.[16]

The present law incorporates in this canon the concepts and emphasis of Vatican II and post-conciliar legislation. The major change in the juridic notion of parish is its description as a community of the Christian faithful ("communitas christifidelium"). By treating the territoriality of parishes in canon 518 and not in this initial canon, the law clarifies the fact that, however important territorial factors are in parish organization, what really is constitutive of the parish is its being a community of persons. Likewise a diocese is primarily described as a "portion of the people of God" (c. 369).[17]

Another change from the 1917 Code can be seen in the second paragraph of this canon. Now the competency of the diocesan bishop to establish, suppress, or notably alter parishes is completely recognized even in the case of non-territorial parishes, a right formerly reserved to the Holy See (*CIC* 216, §4). In establishing a new parish some of the principles suggested for establishing a diocese can be applied by analogy, i.e., territorial continuity, an adequate number of inhabitants, and sufficient human and temporal resources.[18] A diocesan commission on parish modifications comprised of resource persons with expertise in the art, architecture and construction of churches is important in

this regard.[19] When the diocesan bishop permanently closes a parish, adequate provision must be made for the continuity of spiritual service to the remaining parishioners. This is usually taken care of by surrounding parishes. Also, care must be taken for the proper disposition of parish registers and other historical records. Sometimes a parish can be transferred effectively to another part of the diocese. A variety of possibilities exist with regard to the notable alteration of parishes.

> At times, for the good of the souls, it will be necessary to change the boundaries of parishes either by uniting several into one, or by dividing larger parishes, or to establish new parishes or centers for non-territorial communities and also to give a new internal organization to parishes of a single city, or by adapting the buildings to suit the needs of the congregation, allowing everyone a view, keeping organic unity, and permitting easy access for everyone (*CD* 32; *ES* I, 21).[20]

Such alterations would include changes regarding the external structure of the parish but not internal changes such as building a new church or rectory.[21] Before the local bishop can validly establish, suppress, or change a parish, he has to consult his presbyteral council.[22] While he is not legally obliged to follow that advice he should take such counsel seriously. In countries where agreements exist between the Apostolic See and the civil government or if there is a question of rights acquired in this manner by physical or juridic persons, the matter is to be settled with those parties by competent authority.[23]

Finally, in the third paragraph of this canon a legitimately established parish is classified as a juridic (formerly "moral" "non-collegiate") person. It is, therefore, the subject of rights and obligations and can be established, suppressed, or otherwise changed only by competent ecclesiastical authority. It must be supervised by a physical person (proper pastor) who represents the parish in all juridic affairs (c. 532).

Quasi-Parishes/Other Communities

Canon 516 — §1. **Unless the law provides otherwise, a quasi-parish is equivalent to a parish; a quasi-parish is a definite community of the Christian faithful within a particular church which has been entrusted to a priest as its proper pastor but due to**

[14]*CD* 30, 1: The commentary on cc. 529–537 further specifies the parameters of pastoral care.

[15]See Marcuzzi, "Verso una nuova definizione," 837.

[16]See *Directory*, 174–183. The *Directory* envisioned a further directory to be drawn up for the use of pastors; however, such a directory has not yet been published.

[17]See Marcuzzi, "Verso una nuova definizione," 838–839. The change in terminology from the 1977 schema of the IV *coetus De Sacra Hierarchia* is reflected in the term "portio populi Dei" which was discarded in favor of "communitas" to show more accurately that persons rather than territory constitute the parish.

[18]See *CD* 22–24; the *Directory* contains a number of practical suggestions regarding the establishment of new parishes (174–183); see also K. Mörsdorf, in Vorgrimler II, 241.

[19]See *Directory*, 178, 181.

[20]*Directory*, 177.

[21]See Mörsdorf, 274; see also A. Bevilacqua, "Selected Questions in Chancery Practice," 103–106. Bevilacqua presents an extensive and eminently practical approach to parish mergers including what specific items ought to be included in the bishop's decree.

[22]See *ES* I, 15, 3.

[23]See *ES* I, 21, 3.

particular circumstances has not yet been erected as a parish.

§2. When certain communities cannot be erected as a parish or quasi-parish, the diocesan bishop is to provide for their pastoral care in another manner.

The 1917 Code considered quasi-parishes to be divisions of apostolic vicariates and prefectures in mission territories which had not yet been established as dioceses (*CIC* 216, §2). Their parish priest was called a quasi-pastor (*CIC* 451, §2) and possessed full pastoral faculties and powers as well as legal obligations described by law.[24] No mention of quasi-parishes was made in the 1977 schema on the people of God. In the 1980 schema, however, the concept was reinstated but with a juridic content altogether different from the preceding one.[25]

The present law no longer identifies a quasi-parish specifically with the mission territory. Now in a broader sense it is connected with a "particular church"[26] and its priest is called a proper pastor. In certain dioceses, especially in the United States, "missions" are attached to some parishes under the care of their pastors. As such, these fit the new description of quasi-parishes. Ordinarily, a quasi-parish is equivalent in law to a parish unless the law provides otherwise. A quasi-parish is one which has not been established as a parish because it lacks one or more qualifications, e.g., resident pastor; necessary financial resources; territorial boundaries or a natural grouping by way of rite, nationality, or language. Presumably, quasi-parishes could eventually become parishes in their own right.

The diocesan bishop is expected to provide for the pastoral needs of those communities which cannot become parishes or quasi-parishes, e.g., hospitals, prisons, migrant camps, homes for the elderly, airport oratories, and similar institutions.[27] These are distinct from quasi-parishes which are always capable of reaching the full status of parish. Ordinarily, pastoral care for these unique communities will be rendered by the territorial parish within whose boundaries the institution is located. However, if this is not feasible, a chaplain (cc. 564–572) or rector (cc. 556–563) can be appointed by the diocesan bishop. Also, in accord with canon 517, §2 the community could be entrusted to a person or community of persons who are not priests when there is a shortage of priests. In such an instance a priest is designated to supervise the parish's pastoral care. It is important that the Christian faithful who belong to these kinds of communities be made increasingly aware of the fact that they are members of the diocese and, in turn, of the universal Church.[28]

Team Ministry

Canon 517 — §1. When circumstances require it, the pastoral care of a parish or of several parishes together can be entrusted to a team of several priests in solidum *with the requirement, however, that one of them should be the moderator in exercising pastoral care, that is, he should direct their combined activity and answer for it to the bishop.*

§2. If the diocesan bishop should decide that due to a dearth of priests a participation in the exercise of the pastoral care of a parish is to be entrusted to a deacon or to some other person who is not a priest or to a community of persons, he is to appoint some priest endowed with the powers and faculties of a pastor to supervise the pastoral care.

This canon has no precedent in the 1917 Code. "Team ministry" is a concept that is new to the church law since Vatican II.

Team ministry is an emerging form of parish service and administration. . . . It represents a marked change from the traditional form of pastoral ministry and is designed to provide for the voluntary sharing of authority and responsibility by the priests assigned to a parish. The priest members of a pastoral team jointly plan the ministry they are to undertake, and by mutual consent they establish their individual areas of responsibility within that ministry. It is primarily through the equal distribution of authority that this team ministry is distinguished from the traditional pastorate.[29]

According to Cora, team ministry is rooted historically in the ancient presbyterium gathered around the bishop. Vestiges of such collegiality are evident today institutionally in cathedral chapters and the college of cardinals and liturgically in the imposition of hands at ordination and concelebration.[30] R. Duffy holds that theologically the thrust of team ministry is ecclesial and eschatological.

The ecclesial concern of ministry is to build a credible church community that constantly renews itself by the way it evokes the charism of all its members. This involves a growing eschatological responsibility for building the Kingdom. Such complementary concerns restore a scriptural sense of salvation, rooted in the shared redemptive needs of the world as well as those of

---

[24]For historical data on the development of parishes and quasi-parishes, see H. Ayrinhac II, 17–26.
[25]See Marcuzzi, "Verso una nuova definizione," 846–847.
[26]A "particular church" could be either a diocese, abbey, apostolic vicariate, or a prefecture (c. 368).
[27]See *Directory*, 180, 183.

[28]Ibid., 174.
[29]Archdiocese of Hartford, "Team Ministry: The Hartford Model," 194–195.
[30]See G. Cora, "Team Ministry: Theological Aspects," 685–687.

the individual. Given such a two-fold task, team ministry must, first of all, be a model of what it proclaims; a core community shaped by Gospel values and concern. Such a disciple community provides the necessary and challenging symbol of Gospel commitment constantly renewed. For this is not only sociologically but theologically true that the characteristic of a healthy community is renewed commitment. Team ministry must be tested by its ability to evoke such commitment from its own members and thus be a credible symbol to the larger Christian community.[31]

In the United States following Vatican II several dioceses allowed experimentation in team ministry to take place.[32]

The diocesan bishop is to determine the feasibility of team ministry. He might be motivated by a concern for the individual needs of the priests who comprise the team as well as the exigencies of pastoral ministry to a specific parish or group of parishes served by one team. Although members of the team are to act as one ("*in solidum*"), one priest has to be named the "moderator." Canonically speaking, he represents the parish(es) in all juridic affairs according to law (c. 532). Ideally, the moderator will truly represent the pastoral team and will never act in any formal matter until the team has reached a consensus. The team is accountable directly to the bishop through the moderator. Subsequent canons describe the qualifications (c. 542), functions, and duties (c. 543) of team members. Because all team members are equivalently pastors, by law they must be priests.

The second paragraph of the canon contains provisions for administering a parish when there is a shortage of priests. In such a case the diocesan bishop may place a parish in the care of one who is not a priest—at least to a certain extent. Such a person could be preferably a deacon,[33] a religious sister, brother, lay person, or a community of such individuals. Pastoral leadership would mean providing at least minimal pastoral care so that the parish would not have to be closed. Canonically, this includes all areas except the specific duties of an or-

dained priest. One who is not ordained could be deputed to proclaim the gospel and preach the word (cc. 758–759, 765–766), to baptize (c. 861, §2) and to assist at marriages (c. 1112).[34]

> [The diocesan bishop] requires and willingly employs suitable, chosen collaborators—clerics, religious, or lay people—whom he makes his associates in some areas of his charge, but by various titles and in different degrees; with them he shares the apostolic mission and to them he entrusts responsibilities, according to the norms of prudent pastoral cooperation.[35]

Strangely, for such a significant pastoral leadership position the law does not assign a title.[36] When one who is not a priest administers a parish, the diocesan bishop must appoint a priest to supervise the parish's pastoral care. This priest would have full pastoral powers and faculties to conduct the juridic affairs of the parish as prescribed by law (cc. 530, 532). Presumably, he would not reside at the parish but would be available periodically to celebrate the Eucharist and administer other sacraments. He and the deacon or non-ordained person mentioned above presumably are jointly accountable to the diocesan bishop for the welfare of the parish. The fact that one who is not ordained can function in such a significant parish leadership role departs from the legal tradition of the recent past and is a significant step in the direction of providing continued pastoral service for the people of God as well as recognizing the role of religious and lay people in pastoral ministry.

Types of Parishes

Canon 518 — As a general rule a parish is to be territorial, that is it embraces all the Christian faithful within a certain territory; whenever it is judged useful, however, personal parishes are to be established based upon rite, language, the nationality of the Christian faithful within some territory or even upon some other determining factor.

As in the former law (*CIC* 216, §1), normally a parish is territorial, and its geographic boundaries are determined by the diocesan bishop. Whenever a parish is significantly altered as by establishment or changing of boundaries, the bishop must consult the presbyteral council (c. 515, §2). Some hold that strictly territorial groupings of the faithful are fre-

---

[31]R. A. Duffy, "Team Ministry," 640–641.

[32]See R. Kennedy, "Experimental Parishes and the Law of the Church," 314–327. In each instance it would have been necessary for the diocesan bishop employing the faculties of *EM* to dispense from certain legal requirements, e.g., *CIC* 460, §2 which prohibited a parish from having more than one pastor. In 1974 CARA evaluated the team ministry experiment of the Hartford Archdiocese to test whether the team ministry goals were being reached and whether the experiment was a success. The study proved that these goals were indeed being met and that the plan was achieving a balance between a concern for the faithful and the psychological needs of priests. See Archdiocese of Hartford, "Team Ministry: The Hartford Model," 193–202.

[33]See J. Lynch, "Parochial Ministry," 391.

[34]The conference of bishops regulates the norms for preaching by lay persons. In order to delegate a religious sister, brother, or a lay person to assist at marriages, the diocesan bishop needs a special faculty from the Holy See along with the approval of the conference of bishops.

[35]*Directory*, 198.

[36]The title "administrator" in canonical terminology refers specifically to the juridic figure mentioned in c. 540.

quently artificial and deadening as the territorial principle as a norm for a parish affiliation becomes increasingly obsolescent.[37] The advantages of territorial boundaries are that they define pastoral jurisdiction, e.g., assistance at marriages, and can unify the community. Vatican II (*CD* 30), however, recognized the limitation of territorial boundaries and exhorted parish priests to cooperate with others beyond the limits of their territories. One of the duties of the vicar forane is to coordinate such supra-parochial cooperation.[38]

The *Directory* offers the following general norm for establishing territorial limits in a given situation:

> . . . that the area and number of people belonging to a parish be such that there can be sufficient pastoral assistance, mutual knowledge and cooperation between the pastor and his other helpers in the ministry and the people, and also the immediate and continuing care of souls.[39]

Conciliar and post-conciliar norms (*CD* 32; *ES* I, 21) called for reconsidering parish boundaries so that in cases where too great a population or too large a territory rendered the exercise of pastoral activity difficult and less effective a parish might be suitably divided or united to another parish. A diocesan commission on the establishment of new parishes and the construction of churches might be helpful to the diocesan community.[40]

Following Vatican II, the First Synod of Bishops (1967) recognized the need to constitute personal jurisdictions although it confirmed the principle of territoriality in church organization. This meant that territory no longer is considered a constitutive element but only a determining element of the community of the faithful although the traditional territorial arrangement remains normative for parishes.[41] Personal parishes are determined by the diocesan bishop on the basis of pastoral criteria other than strictly territorial ones; e.g., specialized groupings of persons with particular pastoral needs. Four such groups are specifically mentioned in the law:

1. Personal parishes for persons of existing rites,[42] particularly for Catholics of the Eastern Rites (*OE* 4), can be established when the spiritual good of the faithful requires this. Normally, Eastern Rite Catholics do not fall within the jurisdiction of a Latin Rite diocesan bishop. However, when this is the case, the diocesan bishop is charged with their spiritual care.

2. Parishes for persons of a common language need to be established when their spiritual needs cannot be met adequately otherwise. The particular church needs to show special concern for persons in a foreign country who wish to preserve their language and customs.

3. Persons who speak a language common to several countries may still need a personal parish based on their national origins. In such instances the present law empowers the diocesan bishop to establish such parishes.[43] The 1917 Code (*CIC* 216, §4) forbade the establishment of parishes based on language or nationality without special permission from the Holy See.

4. Various other groups could include college and university personnel,[44] military forces, charismatic groups, etc. Following Vatican II a number of bishops dispensed from the provisions of canon 216, §4 of the 1917 Code in light of *De Episcoporum Muneribus* and thereby allowed certain experimental parishes to develop under their supervision. They did this to meet the spiritual needs of various groups which did not fit the categories mentioned above.[45]

Pastor

Canon 519 — The pastor is the proper shepherd of the parish entrusted to him, exercising pastoral care in the community entrusted to him under the authority of the diocesan bishop in whose ministry of Christ he has been called to share; in accord with the norm of law he carries out for his community the duties of teaching, sanctifying and governing, with the cooperation of other presbyters or deacons and the assistance of lay members of the Christian faithful.

This canon, which modifies the 1917 Code, defines the meaning of a pastor of a parish. Historically, the concepts "pastor" and "parish" have been intertwined ever since the fifth century when pastors began to reside at parishes in outlying areas, al-

---

[37]Although the territorial principle makes for good order, the needs of modern Christians have become so varied and their styles of commitment have expanded so much that a new approach today is important. See W. LaDue, "Structural Arrangements of the Parish," 325.

[38]See cc. 553–555.

[39]*Directory*, 176.

[40]See *Directory*, 178.

[41]See J. Lynch, "Canon Law," 47.

[42]For the possibility of more rites developing in the future see J. Jungmann, "Constitution on the Sacred Liturgy," 105.

[43]See W. Nessel, "The National Parish Revisited," 89–92. Nessel holds that in those cases in which an existing national parish no longer serves its intended purpose, the diocesan bishop ought to consider seriously either moving it to another location or closing the parish.

[44]C. 813 emphasizes the need for the pastoral care of students even through the establishment of specific (personal) parishes for them.

[45]See R. Kennedy, "Experimental Parishes," 323–324.

though city parishes began to develop only in the tenth century. The law on pastors and parishes in the 1917 Code dates from the Council of Trent.[46]

Three theological-canonical themes seem to underlie the revised law:

1. The focal point of this chapter is the parish as a community of persons. The pastor exists for the parish community which gives meaning to his office.[47]

2. Vatican II (*CD* 30–31) has clearly outlined the theological dimensions of the pastorate, comparing it to the biblical shepherding office which the priest shares with his bishop in the name of Christ.[48]

3. The pastoral service aspect of the office of pastor has replaced the prior overemphasis on the temporal benefice dimension of the office.

The term "parish priest" (*parochus*) distinguishes this concept from the diocesan bishop as pastor although there is a parallel between their respective offices. What is essential here is that the parish priest is a shepherd in his own right. It also means that he is the *ordinary* and *immediate* pastor who feeds his sheep in the name of the Lord.[49] The diocesan bishop has received his mission directly from the Lord through the fullness of orders and thereby becomes the vicar of Christ in the particular church assigned to him (*LG* 37). Although the parish priest is sent by the bishop and depends on him in the exercise of his office, he is not merely a kind of extension of the bishop. On the contrary, the parish priest is the spiritual head of the parish and truly represents the invisible Lord, and it is his duty to unite the individual faithful in a community founded in and for Christ. He is prepared sacramentally for this ministry by ordination and is authorized to exercise it for a given community through the appointment of the bishop.

The parallel between the office of bishop and that of the pastor of a parish can be seen particularly in their ministerial duties. Because he participates in the ministry of the bishop, the pastor's primary role is to teach, sanctify, and govern, a threefold function (*munus*) rooted basically in holy orders and determined by his canonical mission. According to Ratzinger the pastoral office is the all-embracing and fundamental office from which the other two (the ministry of the word and the priestly ministry) emerge as two modes of articulating its implications.[50] The meaning of "pastoral care" referred to in this canon has been clarified in the preceding commentary on canon 515, §1, and a specific list of

pastoral duties is found in canons 528–530. Another similarity between the bishop and parish priest is their sacramentally grounded responsibility to be concerned about the people of God beyond the limits of their diocese or parish. Hence, Vatican II (*CD* 30, 1) emphasized the importance of pastors of parishes being sensitive to the supra-parochial implications of their ministry.[51] Finally, both bishop and parish priest are not the only ones who are responsible for the missionary duties of their respective communities. Other ordained ministers, religious and laity, who form the individual community also have a right and duty to assist in promoting pastoral action. Priests and deacons who are assigned to the parish (not to the pastor) are to be regarded as the pastor's co-workers. The use of this term in the present law is praiseworthy because it reflects the ideas of collegiality and co-responsibility. Vatican II (*AA* 10, *SC* 42) insisted that the action of the laity is so necessary that without it the apostolate of pastors will frequently be unable to obtain its full effect. Therefore, the diocesan bishop is expected to collaborate closely with others through such consultative bodies as the presbyteral council, the diocesan finance council, etc. Even more explicit now is the obligation of the parish priest to collaborate with similar structures on the parish and diocesan levels, i.e., parish council, diocesan pastoral council, deanery council, presbyteral council, parish finance council. Such collaboration envisions the welfare of the Christian faithful of the parish and diocese.

Subsequent canons in this section of the law further specify the implications of the office of pastor. However, from a critical standpoint there appears to be an overly hierarchial stress in some of these canons. For example, the law dealing with the participation of non-clerics in pastoral activity (c. 517, §2) seems to be an appendage not well integrated into the mainstream of this section. Such an approach is unfaithful to the intent and thrust of *Apostolicam actuositatem* regarding the duties and charisms of the laity. Moreover, while the law emphasizes the liturgical and magisterial role of the pastor, it is less than satisfactory in regard to his pastoral leadership role. By contrast, little attention is given to other members of the parish in the law. The role of the deacon in parish life is hardly mentioned. The theological principle of the Church as a real communion of Christians (*communio*) central to the ecclesiology of *Lumen Gentium* has not been applied adequately in these canons.

Parishes Entrusted to Religious

Canon 520 — §1. A juridic person is not to be a pastor; however, the diocesan bishop, but not the

[46]See Bouscaren-Ellis, 186–187.

[47]See article by Lynch in note 33.

[48]See F. Wulf, in Vorgrimler IV, 233–236.

[49]See Mörsdorf, in Vorgrimler II, 105.

[50]Ibid., 231.

[51]Church law, however, specifies certain areas of jurisdiction that a pastor can exercise only within his parish, e.g., delegation for marriages (c. 1111).

diocesan administrator, with the consent of the competent superior, can entrust a parish to a clerical religious institute or to a clerical society of apostolic life, even erecting the parish in a church of the institute or society, with the requirement, however, that one presbyter should be the pastor of the parish or one presbyter should act as the moderator mentioned in can. 517, §1, if its pastoral care is entrusted to a team.

§2. The assignment of the parish mentioned in §1 can be permanent or for a definite predetermined period of time; in either case the assignment should be made by means of a written agreement between the diocesan bishop and the competent superior of the institute or society; among other matters this agreement is expressly and carefully to determine the work to be done, the persons to be attached to the parish and the financial arrangements.

A change from the 1917 Code allows the diocesan bishop but not the diocesan administrator[52] to entrust a parish to a religious community with the consent of the respective superior but without an apostolic indult, which was required according to canon 452 of the 1917 Code. The law now gives the diocesan bishop broad authority to change parishes after consulting with the presbyteral council (c. 515. §2). In light of increasing pastoral demands due to the lack of diocesan clergy, Vatican II (CD 33–35) urged religious priests to give more help to diocesan bishops in pastoral ministry with due consideration for the special character of their religious institute. Post-conciliar legislation (ES I, 33) enabled the diocesan bishop to expedite such arrangements.

The revised law prohibits the uniting of parishes with juridic persons pleno jure as had been permitted by the 1917 Code.[53] Formerly, when a parish was joined pleno jure to a religious institute, that institute which was a juridic person became the pastor of the parish. Now only physical persons can technically be pastors of parishes. The reason for this is the right of the Christian faithful to have a proper pastor, immediately available to them who, like the diocesan bishop, represents the invisible Lord.[54] Prior to the 1917 Code, religious were not supposed to assume the pastoral care of persons. Where a parish had been united with a religious house, a diocesan priest was retained to exercise the

care of souls.[55] The present law is even more explicit than the 1917 Code (CIC 452, §2) in providing for one of the priests to be the pastor or the moderator among a team of priests (c. 517). In this way pastoral activity is best coordinated and accountability achieved.

The assignment of a parish to a religious community can be permanent (in perpetuum)[56] or for a predetermined period of time. A written agreement should be made between the diocesan bishop and the religious community so that the provisions are clearly stated and misunderstandings are prevented. The following should be clarified:

1. The work to be fulfilled, i.e., any special mission in addition to the normal pastoral duties prescribed by law.

2. Persons to be attached to the parish. This pertains especially to the pastor and parochial vicar(s), who need the faculties of the diocese. In addition, the pastor needs formal confirmation by the diocesan bishop (c. 682).

3. Finances. In the 1917 Code such a union entitled the religious community to receive the major portion of parish revenue (CIC 1423). The present law does not explicitate this matter. Hence, there is a need to clarify the assignment of revenues in the agreement.

4. Time framework if the parish is assigned for a predetermined length of time.

In all other matters universal law does not exempt parishes entrusted to religious from particular diocesan law, e.g., norms for parish councils, finance councils, etc.

Qualifications for Pastors

Canon 521 — §1. To assume the office of pastor validly one must be in the sacred order of the presbyterate.
§2. He should also be distinguished for his sound doctrine and integrity of morals and endowed with a zeal for souls and other virtues; he should also possess those qualities which are required by universal and particular law to care for the parish in question.
§3. For the office of pastor to be conferred on someone, it is necessary that his suitability be clearly evident by means of some method deter-

[52]Like CIC 432, c. 428, §1 reaffirms the rule that when the office of bishop is vacant, no innovations are to be made. Temporary provisions need to be made for the spiritual care of persons until the appointment of the new bishop, who then will make the major decisions. The diocesan administrator is accordingly limited in his decision-making ability.
[53]See Woywod-Smith II, 176.
[54]See CD 11; see also Mörsdorf, "Decree on the Bishop's Pastoral Office in the Church," 230.

[55]See Woywod-Smith II, 165.
[56]The term "permanent" (in perpetuum) in church law means that the assignment is irrevocable until such time as the competent authority or one's successor(s) determines otherwise. Hence, perpetuity is determined by the will of the competent superior.

mined by the diocesan bishop, even by means of an examination.

By requiring that a pastor be a priest,[57] the law reflects a theological value proposed in Vatican II (*PO* 6) in the sense that the sacrament of orders especially empowers the priest to reflect the image of the Good Shepherd to the people he serves. Universal law expects a pastor among other things to be able to administer the sacraments (cc. 835, §2; 843; 530), to preach the gospel (cc. 757, 762), and to undertake general parish administration (c. 532). Particular law (diocesan regulations and lawful customs) might also impose special continuing education requirements, language requirements, or special skills in founding a parish or in ministering to parishes with special problems.[58]

In certain regions to ensure suitability for office the former law (*CIC* 459, §4) required either a competitive or non-competitive examination (*concursus*) to determine fitness for the pastorate. However, in some countries, e.g., the United States, this had fallen into desuetude.[59] Vatican II (*CD* 31) called for the elimination of this competitive exam. The law retains the idea of an examination as a tool the diocesan bishop may want to employ to determine pastoral fitness, yet he is free to employ some other method. The post-conciliar era has witnessed some experiments in developing clergy evaluation/accountability instruments not only for pastors but for associate pastors and priests in other forms of ministry.[60]

Term of Office for Pastors

Canon 522 — **The pastor ought to possess stability in office and therefore he is to be named for an indefinite period of time; the diocesan bishop can name him for a certain period of time only if a decree of the conference of bishops has permitted this.**

Limitations on the term of an ecclesiastical office are not entirely new to church law. Certain offices, e.g., diocesan consultors, have always had a limited term. However, the term of office for pastors has never been limited before by the general law of the Church. Stability in the pastoral office has always been the norm so that the pastor could exercise the

parochial office, get to know his people well, and receive adequate sustenance. The former provision for removable and irremovable pastors was linked to the benefice system, which envisioned in part the support of priests. Vatican II (*PO* 20, *CD* 31) called for a complete revision of the benefice system and eliminated the distinction between removable and irremovable pastors. In the former law the processes for removing and transferring pastors (*CIC* 2147–2167) safeguarded the value of pastoral stability against arbitrary episcopal discretion. While the revised law retains the idea of pastoral stability from canon 454 of the 1917 Code, it also permits the bishop's limiting the term of office of the pastor under some circumstances.

The approval of the conference of bishops is a prerequisite for the implementation of a term of office for pastors. Canon 455, §2 further specifies the competence of conferences of bishops and requires that certain actions on the part of a conference be ratified by the Holy See for their validity. Although nothing is explicitly stated in law, a healthy uniformity of practice seems to require that the conference of bishops determine such matters as the number of years for a term of office, the number of times a term is renewable, how the presbyteral council is to be consulted, and norms for exceptions to the rule. Once the conference of bishops sanctions a term of office for pastors, a diocesan bishop can undertake the practice if he deems it necessary and valuable. In November 1983, the National Conference of Catholic Bishops voted to allow diocesan bishops the option of adopting term of office policies for the assignment of pastors; they also voted to leave it up to the diocesan bishop to determine the length and renewability of such terms. The Holy See approved of this action but stipulated that the term must be six years; such a term may be renewed. This policy became effective on September 24, 1984.

"Term of office," "tenure," and "limited tenure"[61] are common terms for a practice begun in several parts of the world immediately following Vatican II. Ordinarily, the procedure had been implemented by an indult from the Holy See which generally contained four conditions:

1. The term for a pastor was to be six years, renewable once.

2. The process was to be experimental until the 1917 Code was revised.[62]

---

[57]By way of exception c. 517, §2 allows non-ordained personnel to exercise the pastoral office to a limited degree when a shortage of priests exists.

[58]Various American dioceses have expanded the list of expected qualifications for the pastorate above and beyond those mentioned in the Code. See J. Teixeira, *Personnel Policies,* 32–34.

[59]See *CLD* 1, 249.

[60]Consult the National Association for Church Personnel Administrators, 100 East Eighth Street, Cincinnati, Ohio 45202 for an up-to-date list of these experiments, e.g., Periodic Review Program of the Milwaukee Archdiocese.

[61]The term "tenure" is a misnomer because it refers primarily to the academic world, namely, for a professor tenure means an unlimited term of office, barring certain factors that may be due cause for removal.

[62]Terms of office according to indults granted before the revised law became operative remain in effect until those terms expire, and it will be up to the conference of bishops in each region to determine whether terms of office for pastors will continue to be legitimate.

3. Permission was contingent upon the diocesan bishop consulting with his council of priests.

4. Terms of office were not to be retroactive for those already assigned to pastorates.

Vatican II did not specify a term of office for pastors. Rather this concept was derived from a series of sound legislative changes which can be summed up in two basic principles:[63]

1. According to *Christus Dominus* 30 the bishop must be free to make good assignments. This allows him to anticipate and plan for future assignments, and it facilitates difficult transfers and assignments.

2. According to the *Directory* (98), a key principle of personnel policy is placing the right person in the right place.

Limited terms of office for pastors make sense for various reasons. From the standpoint of the parish, it prevents the deleterious effects of long-term appointments, gives relative stability to parishes, and provides new leadership. For the priest a limited term of office can lessen the burdens of the pastorate, permit a graceful exit at times from a difficult situation, prevent personal stagnation, and provide stimulation and job satisfaction. However, there are definite risks to a limited term of office. Moving is always difficult and can lead to an emotional crisis in a priest's life and an unwillingness to undertake needed programs and decisions; furthermore, it may prevent the pastor from knowing his people well. The present law retains the transfer and removal process (cc. 1740–1752) so that the general norm of pastoral stability does not admit of irremediable abuses.

Assignment of Pastor

Canon 523 — With due regard for the prescription of can. 682, §1, the diocesan bishop is the person competent to provide for the office of pastor by means of free conferral unless someone possesses the right of presentation or of election.

As was the case in canon 455 of the 1917 Code, assignment to the pastoral office[64] is made by the diocesan bishop. Appointment to such an office is a significant administrative act[65] and, as in the past,

requires a special episcopal mandate for a vicar general or an episcopal vicar to expedite this, e.g., a vicar for personnel.[66] An exception to episcopal freedom in the assignment process occurs in the case of religious. The diocesan bishop assigns the office of pastor to a member of an institute of consecrated life or a clerical society of apostolic life only after this priest has been named, presented, or approved by his proper superior (c. 682).

In general, the law affords the diocesan bishop maximum freedom in conferring the office of pastor (c. 157). Following the statement of this principle of requisite liberty by Vatican II (*CD* 28) and subsequent legislation (*ES* I, 18), the Apostolic See began to relinquish various rights and privileges pertaining to the reservation of benefices so that former restrictions on the diocesan bishop are no longer present in the revised Code. In the past, certain privileges and customs sometimes gave to certain physical or juridic persons the right to elect, nominate, or present candidates for the office of pastor. Ordinarily, this happened in countries where, by custom, this right fell to the ruler or governor of the nation. When such an election, nomination, or presentation was carried out according to law, the diocesan bishop had to confer the appointment. Post-conciliar legislation (*ES* I, 18, 1), however, abrogated those privileges wherever possible. In the few remaining places where popular elections still exist[67] the respective episcopal conferences are to propose to the Apostolic See the approach that seems best to them in view of abolishing such practices if possible. If the rights and privileges in this same area have been established by agreement (concordat) between the Apostolic See and the State or by agreement with either physical or juridic persons, their termination should be discussed with the interested parties. Hence, in some instances these rights and privileges still exist, and in such cases the diocesan bishop must acknowledge them until they are rescinded.

In recent years, particularly in the United States, personnel boards consisting of elected, representative clergy have assisted the diocesan bishop in selecting candidates for the pastorate and other offices. Although these boards are not mentioned in the revised law, there is no reason why they cannot continue in the future. Existing boards function ac-

---

[63]See J. Janicki, "Limited Term of Office and Retirement," 39–59; see also J. Janicki, "Limited Term of Office for Pastors," 42–51.

[64]Appointment to the pastorate is subject to the general provisions for acquiring and losing such an office as specified in cc. 146–196.

[65]See cc. 35–47 for the general norms on administrative acts, cc. 48–58 on individual decrees and precepts, and cc. 59–75 on rescripts.

[66]See c. 479 on the status of the vicar general and/or episcopal vicars.

[67]*CIC* 160–178 regulated canonical elections. The 1917 Code did not abrogate the custom of popular elections, e.g., for the pastorate, but restricted the practice to a choice of three candidates proposed by the diocesan bishop (*CIC* 1452). In this century popular elections existed by custom in certain European and Middle East countries. See Wernz-Vidal II, 185; Woywod-Smith II, 1458; and J. Neumann, "Election and Limitation of Term of Office in Canon Law," 58–59. The custom of canonical elections never developed significantly in the United States because of trusteeism; see J. Lynch, "Parochial Ministry," 392–397.

cording to policies which indicate that they are consultative bodies whose advice ultimately does not bind the bishop although he should take it seriously. Moreover, priests can appeal to the diocesan bishop directly.

Suitability of Pastor

Canon 524 — After he has weighed all the circumstances, the diocesan bishop is to confer a vacant parish on the person whom he judges suited to fulfill its parochial care without any partiality; in order to make a judgment concerning a person's suitability he is to listen to the vicar forane, conduct appropriate investigations and, if it is warranted, listen to certain presbyters and lay members of the Christian faithful.

The diocesan bishop is conscientiously obliged to follow the principle of placing the right person in the right place (*Directory* 98). In the post-conciliar period some bishops have announced parochial vacancies in such a way that priests who deem themselves qualified can apply for the position. This is done by means of an "open listing" or advertising in the diocesan newspaper or through a circular letter. This method helps bishops select the right person and also enhances the morale of the clergy. The diocesan bishop, however, cannot be constrained to choose only those priests who apply for a given position. Ayrinhac holds that the diocesan bishop must take means to find out the moral worth, executive ability, and intellectual aptitude of the intended pastor.[68] Vatican II (*CD* 31) expects the bishop to take into consideration the priest's learning, piety, zeal for the apostolate, and other gifts and qualities which are necessary for the proper spiritual care of persons.

In formulating a judgment of suitability, the bishop is to consult the vicar forane (dean), who presumably knows well the parish needs and the character/suitability of individual priests—especially those of his deanery. Besides the vicar forane many dioceses have priest personnel boards, whose elected members gather data to help the bishop determine pastoral fitness. Also, the advice of other priests or groups such as the presbyteral council or the college of consultors could be sought. Lay persons should be prudently consulted individually about their knowledge of a particular candidate for the pastoral office; however, they may be consulted collectively, e.g., through a representative body such as a parish council. Such lay persons may also be profitably consulted about the overall needs of the parish. In certain cases the bishop may have to consult persons outside the diocese.

Pastoral Appointments During Impeded/Vacant Diocese

Canon 525 — When a see is vacant or impeded the diocesan administrator or another person who is ruling the diocese in the meantime is competent:
1° to install or confirm presbyters who have been legitimately presented or elected for a parish;
2° to appoint pastors if the see has been vacant or impeded for a year.

According to canon 412, the see (office of the diocesan bishop) is impeded when the bishop is in captivity, banished, exiled, incapacitated, or otherwise cannot communicate with his people. It becomes vacant on the death of the diocesan bishop or when his resignation from office is accepted by the Roman Pontiff or when he is transferred or deprived of office (c. 416). The law provides for the continuity of diocesan governance in both instances by empowering the diocesan administrator or another person ruling the diocese in the meantime to act in personnel matters.[69] It should be noted that if the diocese is vacant, the office of vicar general or episcopal vicar ceases (c. 481, §1); this is important in cases where the vicar general or episcopal vicar had been assigning pastors.[70]

The diocesan administrator or other person in charge can appoint or confirm as pastors those members of a religious community who have been presented by their respective superiors in accord with canon 682. He can also appoint others to the pastoral office who have been legitimately elected.[71] However, he can appoint other pastors only if the see has been vacant or impeded for one year.[72] During the first year of a parish vacancy, the law adequately provides for its temporary administration (c. 539).

The former law (*CIC* 455, §2) explicitly stated that the diocesan administrator or other person in charge of a vacant diocese could appoint pastors in the same manner as mentioned above and also parochial vicars. The present law does not explicitly authorize the administrator to appoint parochial vicars. However, he is clearly able to do so because he enjoys legal authority equivalent to that of the diocesan bishop unless the law explicitly forbids a certain legal act; in this instance, it does not do so.[73]

[68]See Ayrinhac II, 322.

[69]See cc. 412–430 for procedures to follow when the diocese is impeded or vacant.
[70]See previous commentary on c. 523.
[71]Ibid.
[72]Innovations are prohibited at the time of a vacant or impeded see (c. 428).
[73]See cc. 427, §1; 547.

One Pastor Only

Canon 526 — §1. A pastor is to have the parochial care of only one parish; however the care of several neighboring parishes can be entrusted to the same pastor due to a dearth of priests or in other circumstances.

§2. In the same parish there is to be only one pastor or one moderator in accord with can. 517, §1; any custom contrary to this is reprobated and any privilege contrary to this is revoked.

The ideal of a pastor's being assigned to only one parish is carried over from the 1917 Code (*CIC* 460, §1). This was based on the prohibition against holding two incompatible offices (*CIC* 156). The law allowed only one exception in the case of two parishes which had been united but whose individual identities had been preserved completely ("aeque principaliter unitis"). On the other hand, the former law forbade more than one pastor for each parish (*CIC* 460, §2). In this way the law sought to correct the abuse in some places of appointing to one parish several pastors who would exercise authority alternately or divide it among themselves.[74] In these cases, some of which antedated the Council of Trent, pastoral responsibilities were not clearly defined, and this led to jurisdictional confusion and the neglect of souls.[75]

The present canon envisions that a pastor normally will be assigned to only one parish. An exception to this can be made when there is an insufficient number of priests or other circumstances warrant it. Rather than close a parish and suspend pastoral services, the law now permits the diocesan bishop to entrust its care to a priest who is already the pastor or moderator of another parish(es). Canon 517, §2 provides for the administration of parishes by those who are not priests; however, in each case the diocesan bishop must appoint some priest to supervise the pastoral care. The present canon allows a priest to care for or supervise multiple parishes. He would have all the rights and duties of a pastor in each parish he serves. Since the financial arrangements of benefices do not apply any longer, the diocesan bishop is to determine how the priest is to be reimbursed. The present canon further parallels the former law by mentioning that there should be no more than one pastor in each parish nor more than one moderator in every parish that is staffed by a team of priests (c. 517, §1).

The canon reprobates (abolishes) any contrary custom and revokes any contrary privilege. Such an explicit statement of a reprobation or revocation is

necessary to achieve the effects of law according to custom (c. 28) and privilege (c. 79). A similar reprobation and revocation was made in the former law (*CIC* 460, §2).

Installation of Pastor

Canon 527 — §1. The person who has been promoted to carry out the pastoral care of a parish acquires that care and is bound to exercise it from the moment he takes possession of the parish.

§2. While observing the method accepted by particular law or legitimate custom, the local ordinary or a priest delegated by him places the pastor in possession of the parish; for a just cause, however, the same ordinary can dispense from such a method of installation; in such a situation the notification of the dispensation communicated to the parish replaces the formal taking of possession.

§3. The local ordinary is to define a period of time within which the parish is to be taken possession of; if the time lapses needlessly and there be no legitimate impediment, he can declare the parish vacant.

The wording of this canon reflects the 1917 Code regarding taking possession of a benefice conferred on a person (*CIC* 1443–1445). Ordinarily, the effective date of the appointment is specified in the letter of appointment by the diocesan bishop. Pastoral rights, obligations, and authority are operative on that date. Woywod notes that in the United States the Plenary Councils of Baltimore had not prescribed a special form of taking possession of the parish. Therefore, diocesan statutes or customs determined the manner of taking possession.[76] The provisions of the Council of Trent[77] and canon 461 of the 1917 Code whereby the pastor made the profession of faith before the diocesan bishop or his delegate are retained in the present law and could form an integral part of the installation (c. 833). However, should the pastor fail to make this profession for whatever reason, he would not be deprived of the office as was formerly specified in the 1917 Code (*CIC* 2403).

The diocesan bishop could delegate the vicar forane or another representative to install a pastor in a paraliturgical or liturgical ceremony, which would include among other things the reading of the letter of appointment and the profession of faith. The former law allowed the pastor to be installed by proxy although he could not make the profession of faith in this manner (*CIC* 1443–1445; 1407). Today it seems fitting for the diocesan liturgical commission or others to devise a suitable ceremony of installa-

74See Lynch, "Parochial Ministry," 395.
75Similarly Abbo-Hannan notes that the practice of the plurality of diocesan bishops in a single diocese was condemned as early as the Council of Trent (I, 455).

76See Woywod-Smith I, 190.
77Session XXIV, c. 12; see H. Schroeder, *Canons and Decrees of the Council of Trent,* 206–207.

tion for pastors to be celebrated at a principal Sunday liturgy. For a just cause the diocesan bishop can dispense a pastor from an installation ceremony; such a dispensation suffices for the pastor to assume his office.

The Pastor as Teacher and Sanctifier

Canon 528 — §1. The pastor is obliged to see to it that the word of God in its entirety is announced to those living in the parish; for this reason he is to see to it that the lay Christian faithful are instructed in the truths of the faith, especially through the homily which is to be given on Sundays and holy days of obligation and through the catechetical formation which he is to give; he is to foster works by which the spirit of the gospel, including issues involving social justice, is promoted; he is to take special care for the Catholic education of children and of young adults; he is to make every effort with the aid of the Christian faithful, to bring the gospel message also to those who have ceased practicing their religion or who do not profess the true faith.

§2. The pastor is to see to it that the Most Holy Eucharist is the center of the parish assembly of the faithful; he is to work to see to it that the Christian faithful are nourished through a devout celebration of the sacraments and especially that they frequently approach the sacrament of the Most Holy Eucharist and the sacrament of penance; he is likewise to endeavor that they are brought to the practice of family prayer as well as to a knowing and active participation in the sacred liturgy, which the pastor must supervise in his parish under the authority of the diocesan bishop, being vigilant lest any abuses creep in.

This and the following two canons deal with the obligations and functions of pastors. Although they are not exhaustive, the lists contained in the law provide a rather comprehensive job description, which is also used for team ministers (c. 543), temporary administrators of parishes (c. 540), and parochial vicars (c. 549).[78]

The conciliar teaching on pastors (*CD* 30, *LG* 28) emphasizes that their ministry is intrinsically bound up with that of their bishop and that they cooperate with him in a special way and make him present in a certain sense to the individual local congregations as far as possible. Hence, priests in parochial ministry assume practically the same duties and functions as their bishop in their part of his larger mission. The threefold teaching, sanctifying, and governing functions (*munera*) of the bishop are applicable to the pastor mutatis mutandis.

The present canon highlights the teaching and sanctifying roles of the pastor. Both roles were

treated in the 1917 Code (*CIC* 467–469), but now they are nuanced by conciliar ideas and expressions (*CD* 30, *LG* 28). The pastor's role as teacher begins with announcing the word of God, which, in turn, is to penetrate his homilies, his efforts at catechetical formation, and other magisterial projects. The pastor is to be especially attentive to the education of children and young adults as well as lapsed Catholics and non-Catholics. In the spirit of Vatican II (*AA* 6), it is recommended that he employ the Christian faithful in his ministry.

The second paragraph of the canon highlights the pastor's sanctifying role. Here the emphasis is on the Eucharist as central to parish life. Besides celebrating the sacraments for his people, he should encourage participation in the liturgy and family prayer. He is obliged to supervise the liturgy in his parish so that it is authentically celebrated (*SC* 19).

The pastor's magisterial and cultic roles are further explicitated in Books III and IV of the 1983 Code.

Pastoral Obligations: Governance

Canon 529 — §1. In order to fulfill his office in earnest the pastor should strive to come to know the faithful who have been entrusted to his care; therefore he is to visit families, sharing the cares, worries, and especially the griefs of the faithful, strengthening them in the Lord, and correcting them prudently if they are wanting in certain areas; with a generous love he is to help the sick, particularly those close to death, refreshing them solicitously with the sacraments and commending their souls to God; he is to make a special effort to seek out the poor, the afflicted, the lonely, those exiled from their own land, and similarly those weighed down with special difficulties; he is also to labor diligently so that spouses and parents are supported in fulfilling their proper duties, and he is to foster growth in the Christian life within the family.

§2. The pastor is to acknowledge and promote the proper role which the lay members of the Christian faithful have in the Church's mission by fostering their associations for religious purposes; he is to cooperate with his own bishop and with the presbyterate of the diocese in working hard so that the faithful be concerned for parochial communion and that they realize that they are members both of the diocese and of the universal Church and participate in and support efforts to promote such communion.

This new canon clarifies the pastor's role of governance, again borrowing conciliar ideas and expressions (*CD* 30, *PO* 28). The first paragraph of the canon stipulates that the pastor must get to know his people. This includes visiting their homes; seeking out the poor, sick and disturbed; counseling married people; and promoting family life in general.

---

[78]It should be noted that when a parish is vacant a parochial vicar is not obliged to offer the "Mass for the people" (c. 549).

The second paragraph of the canon refers to the pastor's duty to consider the needs of the broader Church beyond the parameters of his parish and to help his people do the same. This section is firmly grounded on the principle of *communio*.[79] The pastor is supposed to cooperate with his bishop and his fellow priests through such structures as the presbyteral council. He is also to promote lay involvement in the Church's mission by fostering their religious associations[80] and encouraging their participation in the life of the parish and of the diocese as individuals and as members of consultative bodies such as the parish council, the parish finance council, and the diocesan pastoral council. The pastor is supposed to enable the people to see themselves as concerned members both of a parochial community and also of larger communions at the diocesan and universal levels.[81]

Functions of the Parish Priest

Canon 530 — The following functions are especially entrusted to the pastor:
1° the administration of baptism;
2° the administration of the sacrament of confirmation to those who are in danger of death, according to the norm of can. 883, 3°;
3° the administration of Viaticum and the anointing of the sick with due regard for the prescription of can. 1003, §§2 and 3, as well as the imparting of the apostolic blessing;
4° the assistance at marriages and the imparting of the nuptial blessing;
5° the performing of funerals;
6° the blessing of the baptismal font during the Easter season, the leading of processions outside the church and the imparting of solemn blessings outside the church;
7° the more solemn celebration of the Eucharist on Sundays and holy days of obligation.

The functions of the pastor listed in the present canon are essentially the same as those listed in the former Code (*CIC* 462). They center primarily on administering the sacraments, officiating at funerals, blessing the baptismal font at Easter, conducting processions, and imparting solemn blessings. Formerly, these functions were reserved ("reservatae") to the pastor in an exclusive sense so that no one else was able to perform them without his permission.[82] Now the word entrusted ("commissae")

is used, which mitigates the above-mentioned reservation. With the exception of assisting at marriages, other priests do not need special faculties to administer the sacraments validly, especially in time of significant pastoral need, e.g., confirmation in danger of death (c. 883, 3°), anointing of the sick (c. 1003, §2). Also, since Vatican II, some lay ministers share in functions once reserved to the parish priest, e.g., ministers of the Eucharist, lectors, officiants at baptism and marriage.

Stole Fees

Canon 531 — **Although another person may have performed some parochial function, that person is to put the offerings received from the Christian faithful on that occasion into the parish account, unless it is obvious that such would be contrary to the will of the donor in the case of voluntary offerings; after he has listened to the presbyteral council, the diocesan bishop is competent to issue regulations which provide for the allocation of these offerings and the remuneration of clerics who fulfill the same function.**

In order to understand this canon, which significantly modifies the former law, it is essential to distinguish between stipends for the celebration of the Eucharist and voluntary offerings, or stole fees, as they are popularly called. According to canon 945, §1 the priest who celebrates or concelebrates the Eucharist has the right to receive a stipend for that celebration, whose amount is set either by a provincial council, a meeting of the bishops of the province, or local custom (c. 952).[83] The present canon refers only to voluntary offerings, or stole fees.

According to canon 1264, 2° the amount of the offerings to be given on the occasion of the administration of certain sacraments and sacramentals is to be set by the bishops for a province. Current custom would prevail where this has not been done. Formerly, canon 463 of the 1917 Code held that a pastor had a right to receive all the legitimate offerings (stole fees) for services performed by him or by another. Vatican II (*PO* 20–21) accentuated the idea that the Church is to remunerate the clergy adequately for ministerial work so that they will be less dependent on voluntary offerings.[84] However,

---

[79]See Hertling, *Communio*. This work discusses the history of *communio (koinonia)* in the Church and shows its many implications and applications at the local and universal level. *Communio* was one of the basic principles underlying the major documents of Vatican II; see also *J* 36 (1976), for a series of articles on *communio*.

[80]These associations, private and public, universal and local, are now delineated in a new section of the Code (cc. 298–329).

[81]This part of the canon is taken almost verbatim from *CD* 30, 1.

[82]See Bouscaren-Ellis, 200.

[83]See J. Challencin, "Mass Stipends—Embarrassing?," 415–422. This article highlights the theology and history of Mass stipends.

[84]See Bouscaren-Ellis, 207. Historically, in the U.S. the Second and Third Councils of Baltimore recommended that diocesan regulations should be enacted which would provide for the distribution of stole fees among all the priests who reside in the same house. C. 281, §1 guarantees a cleric's right to remuneration in return for the ecclesiastical ministry he renders. C. 1274 specifies the obligations of the diocese and the conference of bishops to provide the financial structures that will help meet the temporal needs of the clergy, particularly since the benefice system has been suppressed in most instances.

in those places where clergy support depends completely or to a great extent on such offerings, e.g., mission territories, the Council called for a more equitable sharing of voluntary offerings from the faithful. The present canon, reflecting the spirit of Vatican II, states that all such offerings received by another cleric (priest or deacon) who may have performed some parochial ministry are to be deposited in the parish fund unless it is clear that the donor wanted the offering to be a personal gift. It is up to the diocesan bishop in consultation with his presbyteral council to decide how these offerings are to be used and how the priests and deacons who engage in parochial ministry are to be remunerated.[85] Besides priests and deacons who are assigned to parishes, these regulations will have to apply to priests who supply part-time services to the parishes as well as to permanent deacons, religious, and lay persons who may be authorized to baptize (c. 861, §2) and/or delegated to witness marriages (c. 1112, §1). The diocesan regulations will also have to address situations in which the sacraments are celebrated outside of the parish church.

The spirit of the present law as well as time-honored principles of moral theology dictate that spiritual ministry is never contingent upon such remuneration.[86]

Juridic Representation of the Parish

Canon 532 — **The pastor represents the parish in all juridic affairs in accord with the norm of law; he is to see to it that the goods of the parish are administered in accord with the norms of cann. 1281-1288.**

Each parish has a juridic personality of its own according to canon 515, §3. This means that each parish is the subject of rights and obligations. The pastor represents the parish in all legal matters, according to law. The change in law that this canon reflects is due to the revision of the benefice system. Formerly, because the pastor held "title" to the parish (a benefice), he automatically became its juridic representative (*CIC* 451).

In most dioceses particular law would stipulate some of the duties of pastors in regard to legal matters pertaining to the parish. The pertinent civil law would differ from place to place. In some places civil law allows a parish to be incorporated as a corporation sole. In such a case the pastor in effect becomes a juridic person from the standpoint of civil law. In other places the custom is to incorporate the parish as a corporation aggregate in which elected members of the parish join with the pastor

as a juridic person to conduct civil law matters for the parish.[87] The ecclesiastical laws on custom would apparently allow this to continue according to the present canon.

The pastor is bound by church laws regarding the administration of parish property as found in canons 1281–1288. Canon 532 is an example of the general principle specified in canon 1279, §1 to the effect that the (physical) person (pastor) who immediately governs the (juridic) person (parish) to whom ecclesiastical goods belong is responsible for their administration.

Residency, Vacation, and Absence of Pastors

Canon 533 — **§1. The pastor is obliged to reside in a parish house close to the church; in particular cases, however, the local ordinary can permit him to live elsewhere, especially in a house shared by several presbyters, provided there is a just cause and suitable and due provision is made for the performance of parochial functions.**

§2. Unless there is a serious reason to the contrary, the pastor may be absent each year from the parish on vacation for at most one continuous or interrupted month; the days which the pastor spends once a year in spiritual retreat are not counted in his vacation days; if the pastor is to be absent from the parish beyond a week he is bound to inform the local ordinary of this.

§3. The diocesan bishop is to issue norms which provide for the care of a parish by a priest possessing the needed faculties during the absence of the pastor.

The first paragraph of this canon basically restates the 1917 Code (*CIC* 465). The obligation of pastoral residency dates from the Council of Trent.[88] It has been customary in the United States to build the rectory close to the church if not on the same property. However, this is not always the case in other countries, and priests often live in houses, apartments, or condominiums rented by the parish.

Exceptions to this rule are to be determined by the diocesan bishop. A diocesan policy on alternate living should indicate the causes which justify such residences as determined by the local bishop. In providing for such exceptions, the law shows a concern for both priests and parishioners. From the standpoint of the parishioners, access to their pastor is a basic value; hence, his having to travel excessive distances could lessen his pastoral effectiveness. From the standpoint of the parish priest, there is a need for adequate room and board, secretarial service, transportation, etc. One positive reason for an exception to the law on residency is to

---

[85]C. 281 specifies the general principle regarding the remuneration of priests and deacons (permanent and transitional).

[86]See c. 848; c. 1181 specifically applies this principle to funeral rites; see also Bouscaren-Ellis, 207.

[87]See Woywod-Smith II, 204.

[88]Session XXIII, c. 1; see H. Schroeder, *Canons and Decrees of the Council of Trent*, 206–207.

facilitate a priest's living with other priests. This may aid the priest's apostolic work and serve as an example of fraternal charity and unity to the faithful.[89]

The second paragraph of this canon further specifies the general norm (c. 283, §2) that clerics are to have an adequate vacation.[90] It modifies the 1917 Code which permitted a pastor to have a two-month vacation, unless this were restricted by the local bishop (*CIC* 465, §2). One reason for this was to compensate for inordinately long travel time years ago. Nowadays, it is the custom in many dioceses that priests have a day off each week, in which case the aggregate period for vacation would amount to approximately two and one-half months per year. According to the present law the pastor may choose to plan his vacation for his entire month or for several periods throughout the year which together add up to one month. The one-month period could be extended or restricted for a grave reason. The priest's annual retreat is not to be counted in this time. In the past the pastor needed written permission if he were to be absent beyond a week. Nowadays, it is customary for the pastor to notify the chancery office about his absence. Presumably, no objections will be forthcoming if the needs of the parish are provided for. The prime reason for a vacation is to maintain one's proper health, physically and psychically, especially in light of contemporary pastoral pressures in many parishes. The pastor is to be adequately compensated so that he has enough money for an annual vacation.[91]

The third paragraph of this canon calls for diocesan norms to provide for those instances in which a pastor is absent from the parish, e.g., vacations, retreats, illnesses, and emergencies. Canon 539 covers some of these contingencies of a longer duration or a more permanent nature. Canon 541, §1 provides for the absence of the pastor in parishes where there is one or more parochial vicars. Practically speaking, diocesan norms should indicate who is to provide the substitute and that person's faculties during the absence. According to canon 1111, §1, the substitute could be delegated the faculty for witnessing specific marriages or even given a general delegation for all marriages in the parish by the diocesan bishop or the pastor. Diocesan norms could also provide for instances when the pastor must leave suddenly and unannounced.

By way of analogy of law (c. 19), this canon can help one clarify the rules on vacations of team members who are equivalent to pastors. Although it does not specifically refer to provisions for the absence of the moderator of a parochial team, this author judges that since a parish team acts *"in solidum,"* the senior priest on the team in terms of assignment could fulfill the office of moderator until the latter returns.[92]

Mass for the People

Canon 534 — §1. After he has taken possession of his parish the pastor is obliged to apply Mass for the people entrusted to him each Sunday and holy day of obligation within the diocese; if he is legitimately prevented from this celebration, he is to apply Mass on these same days through another priest or he himself is to apply it on other days.

§2. A pastor who has the care of several parishes is obliged to apply only one Mass for all the people entrusted to him on those days mentioned in §1.

§3. A pastor who has not satisfied the obligation mentioned in §§1 and 2 is to apply as many Masses for his people as he has missed as soon as possible.

The former law on the pastor's obligation to celebrate the Mass for the people (*CIC* 466) is substantially unchanged although it is limited to Sundays and holy days in a particular diocese.[93] This law applies only to pastors of parishes and quasi-parishes, not to rectors, chaplains, parochial vicars, or moderators of religious communities.[94] Canon 388 imposes a similar obligation on the diocesan bishop. A pastor is legitimately excused from this obligation in cases of captivity, exile, banishment, incapacity, ill health, or for some other reason (c. 539). In such cases it should be fulfilled through another priest, e.g., a parish administrator (c. 540, §1). The obligation also applies to team ministry parishes (c. 543, §2, 2°). However, the obligation does not apply in the case of a parochial vicar who acts as a substitute for the pastor in accord with canon 549. For a legitimate reason, e.g., illness or unavailability of another priest, the obligation can be transferred to another day if necessary. When a priest is in charge of several parishes, he is bound to apply only one Mass on the assigned days for all the people entrusted to his care.

---

[92]There is a legal analogy to this in c. 549.

[93]*CIC* 339 obliged pastors to offer the "Mass for the people" on approximately eighty-eight days of the year (see Bouscaren-Ellis, 210). On July 25, 1970 this was reduced by the SCC to Sundays and holy days of obligation, effective Jan. 1, 1971 (*CLD* 7, 393).

[94]See Ayrinhac II, 341. Abbo-Hannan notes that the Mass for the people is a grave obligation that binds in justice (I, 464)/ Bouscaren-Ellis holds that the obligation is attached to the pastoral office and is not excused by the scarcity of revenue (210). An authentic interpretation of the Code Commission declared that this obligation is seriously binding on bishops by reason of divine law. Although pastors are hypothetically bound by divine law, they can be dispensed from the obligation depending on certain conditions which are under the control of the Church (*CLD* 1, 254).

---

[89]See *CD* 28; NCCB, *As One Who Serves,* 67–68.

[90]C. 281, §1 requires a priest to be adequately remunerated for the necessities of life; nowadays, a vacation is such a necessity.

[91]Ibid.; see also *PO* 20.

Parish Registers

Canon 535 — §1. **Each parish is to possess a set of parish books including baptismal, marriage and death registers as well as other registers prescribed by the conference of bishops or the diocesan bishop; the pastor is to see to it that these registers are accurately inscribed and carefully preserved.**

§2. In the baptismal register are also to be noted the person's confirmation and whatever affects the canonical status of the Christian faithful by reason of marriage, with due regard for the prescription of can. 1133, adoption, reception of sacred orders, perpetual profession in a religious institute, and change of rite; these notations are always to be noted on a document which certifies the reception of baptism.

§3. Each parish is to possess its own seal; documents which are issued to certify the canonical status of the Christian faithful as well as all acts which can have juridic importance are to be signed by the pastor or his delegate and sealed with the parish seal.

§4. Each parish is to have a registry or archive in which the parish books are kept along with episcopal letters and other documents which ought to be preserved due to necessity or usefulness; all these are to be inspected by the diocesan bishop or his delegate during his visitation or at another suitable time; the pastor is to take care that they do not come into the hands of outsiders.

§5. The older parish books are also to be carefully preserved in accord with the prescriptions of particular law.

The former law (*CIC* 470) is hardly changed here. The present canon adds a number of details which were found in various places in the 1917 Code. In the past, details to be included in the parish registers could be found in the *Roman Ritual.*[95] Nowadays, for practical purposes, religious goods stores carry blank registers which are set up in the required manner. Besides baptism, marriage, and death registers, the parish may be required to have others if prescribed by the conference of bishops or the diocesan bishop, e.g., a census book. The pastor is accountable for the care and accuracy of these records. In parishes entrusted to one who is not a priest in virtue of canon 517, §2, that person presumably bears the responsibility.

This canon gives special attention to the baptismal register since it is the chief locus for requisite information on every Catholic. To be noted in each case is a record of confirmation, marital status (except for marriages celebrated secretly [c. 1133]),

adoption, reception of holy orders, religious profession, and change of rite. When a baptismal certificate is required, the above information should always be written on the document. It would follow from natural equity that if this appended information were of a delicate nature, e.g., adoption, and the person reading the document could be injured, it would be sufficient to issue the certificate with the following or similar words, preferably in Latin: "If marriage is to be contracted, consult the place of baptism."[96] If the record is needed for marriage, it will alert the priest arranging the marriage that he needs to obtain further information privately.

The parish seal, usually the embossing type rather than a rubber stamp, is to be used on all documents, especially ones that have legal importance. Ordinarily the seal is placed over the signature of the parish priest or his delegate. The canonical status of the Christian faithful is signified through testimonial letters of freedom issued on the occasion of a pending marriage, ordination, etc. These should bear the signature of the parish priest and the seal.

Each parish should have a safe place to keep the parish registers along with all other important documents, historical records, and other valuable items. Again, the parish priest is responsible for the safekeeping of these items. Most of the records are confidential and access to them should be granted only with due care. The diocesan bishop should inspect the records during his visitation or at another suitable time. He can delegate this task to another, e.g., vicar forane (c. 555, §1, 3°).

Older parish books including historical records and old parish registers, particularly those that cannot be duplicated, should be preserved with special care. There should be diocesan guidelines in regard to this. Many dioceses require that in addition to a fireproof vault or safe a microfilmed copy of all parish books be kept on file at the chancery office. As more parishes turn to computer systems for storing and processing sacramental data, suitable backup methods will be needed to insure the safekeeping of such records.

Parish Councils

Canon 536 — §1. **After the diocesan bishop has listened to the presbyteral council and if he judges it opportune, a pastoral council is to be established in each parish; the pastor presides over it, and through it the Christian faithful along with those who share in the pastoral care of the parish in virtue of their office give their help in fostering pastoral activity.**

§2. This pastoral council possesses a consultative vote only and is governed by norms determined by the diocesan bishop.

---

[95]The *Roman Ritual* referred only in general terms to the recording of sacramental records. The 1917 Code specified in greater detail the manner of recording the reception of the various sacraments.

[96]"In casu de matrimonio consulenda est ecclesia baptismi."

A parish council is a parochial structure consisting of representative members of the parish who form one body with the pastor in fulfilling the Church's ministry.[97] This new and evolving concept in church law results from the conciliar emphasis on the expanding role of the laity. Conciliar texts stressing the collaboration of clergy and faithful in the evangelization and sanctification tasks of the Church provide the broad context within which the concept of parish councils can best be understood.[98] Although parish councils are not specified in detail in the conciliar documents, *Apostolicam actuositatem* 26 promotes the idea of councils at the parochial level.

Theologically, the right and duty of the laity to participate in parish councils are founded in the grace of baptism and confirmation.[99]

Prior to the Council, the Church perceived God's guidance and direction as flowing almost entirely through the leaders—the hierarchy: pope, bishop, pastor—finally to be activated in parishes through programs and other projects. The concept of shared responsibility changed that thinking. The theological meaning of shared responsibility is that God's truth, which provides the guidance for the Church, comes not only through the leaders but also through the people. In order for the Church to have the fullness of God's light and guidance, the people must be consulted. Thus, a totally new ministry of the People of God was born—a special ministry of people and pastor together reflecting on the parish's ministerial activity and on the basis of that reflection, discerning what needs to be changed or developed in the parish to make it more faithful to what God is calling it to be. It is this ministry that is specifically and particularly the ministry of the parish council.[100]

Born out of the need for co-responsible leadership, the parish council is the locus for the effective participation of clergy and laity in the total mission of the parish as called for in Vatican II.

It would be hard to express with greater frankness, clarity and precision the rights and duties of the laity within the Church's mission. If one may so put it, the Council here [*GS* 43, ed.] utters a warning against 'clericalism,' which may consist not only of the clergy encroaching on aspects of the Church's activity that are beyond their competence, but also in the laity shirking their responsibilities and throwing them onto the clergy.

According to Vatican II, one of the chief principles of the apostolate of the Church is that the laity should shoulder all the tasks that belong to their vocation in the Church and in the world. This does not by any means imply disrupting the community, but rather strengthening it. The Council mentions this in several places.[101]

Representative spiritual leadership, efficiency in accomplishing pastoral goals, spiritual growth and renewal, as well as the utilization of sound administrative procedures are some values that indicate a need for parish councils today. The parish council is considered to be a vital component of each parish.[102]

... A parish needs a council in order to insure that it is truly faithful to God's call. Catholics have always cherished the idea of obedience and fidelity to God's word spoken in and through the Church. It is that same Church that is calling its people now to listen for God's words spoken not only through the leadership, but through fellow Christians as well. But to hear that word spoken through the people requires a new structure, a new way. A council united with the pastor provides by design that way, because its representative nature insures that every voice is heard, not just those that are the loudest, or the most powerful or the most traditional.[103]

Vatican II has affirmed that the diocesan bishop has ample freedom to structure parishes so as to provide the best possible service to the people in his care. Hence, after consulting his presbyteral council, he may require parish councils to be established in all parishes, and he may indicate the parameters of authority of such bodies.

The presence of both pastor and council members is necessary for the council to be effective. Because he is ultimately responsible for the care of the parish, the pastor presides at the parish council in a way strikingly similar to his presidency at the Eucharist.

In the past the priest was the only person who ministered in the celebration of the Eucharist. Since Vatican II, the celebration of the liturgy recognizes many other ministries: the ministry of reading, singing, of planning the liturgy, of serving, of distributing the Eucharist, the liturgical ministry of the diaconate. The priest presides over the liturgy of the word and does not begin his special ministry until the Eucharistic prayer. So the shift in the priest's liturgical role is from being the only minister to being the presider over

[97]See T. Early, "Parish Councils," 330–332.

[98]See *LG*, chapter IV; see also W. Rademacher, *The Practical Guide for Parish Councils,* 14–25.

[99]See *AA* 3.

[100]Diocese of Columbus, "Parish Council Rationale," 244.

[101]K. Wojtyla, *Sources of Renewal,* 386–387.

[102]See *Directory,* 179.

[103]Diocese of Columbus, "Parish Council Rationale," 243–244.

the people's ministry and the celebrant of the Eucharistic faith.

So, too, with respect to the rest of the parish's ministry, the pastor's role is changing. While he continues to bear the final responsibility for the total parish ministry, he carries out that responsibility less and less as the one and only minister and increasingly as the presider over the ministry of the people and the sharer with the people in that ministry.[104]

The pastor's ex officio role would not preclude an elected member's conducting regular meetings of the council; in fact, such an approach may be preferred. The presiding role of the pastor has to be seen within the context of the process of decision-making which involves many stages. Kennedy distinguishes between decision-making (a process) and choice-making (a part of the process). He traces several stages of this process which include producing creative ideas, gathering factual data, making a choice among alternative options, implementing and evaluating the choice.[105] Integral to each stage of parish decision-making is the collaboration of the pastor and the parish council. In virtue of his office the pastor presides over and ratifies those stages of the process leading up to and including the final choice and its implementation. This role cannot be surrendered or diminished[106] nor should authority be viewed as personal power, but rather as genuine service to the Christian faithful exercised in a collegial way.

The fundamental role of the leader is to make collegiality possible. He is its guarantee. He is there primarily so that each member may be a part of a whole, and thus assume full responsibility within and toward a common effort. The role of the one in charge is not that of making a "personal" decision after having taken the advice of others into account. For in that case it would still be "his" decision. His role is rather to make it possible, in so far as this depends upon him, for there is to be a common decision which commits each member to the decision, in such a way that they are solidly behind it and willing to accept all the consequences of what has been decided together.[107]

For the sake of accountability to the diocesan bishop whom he represents and the people of God whom he serves, the pastor must ratify the recommendations of the parish council before they can be implemented. Likewise, the pastor must prevent the parish council from endorsing proposals which would be contrary to universal church law, diocesan statutes, or civil law.[108]

Besides the pastor, others who share in the pastoral care of the parish in virtue of their office would include: the associate pastor(s), the moderator and members of a team ministry, deacons, lay ministers, directors of religious education, teachers, and other hired personnel—some of whom may not actually be members of the parish. Not all of these would necessarily be ex officio members of the parish council. The forum provided by the council enables all to collaborate in fostering pastoral activity, i.e., an organized, unified endeavor, which broadly includes liturgy, education, social service, evangelization, mission activity, family life, communications, ecumenism, and administration. Parish council committees frequently correspond to these areas of concern. According to Rodimer, the ministry of the parish council is coextensive with the total mission of the parish.

1. The first thing a council must do is pray that with the grace of God they may discern the voice of the Holy Spirit and try to be one with Christ to acknowledge his presence in their midst.

2. The second need of a parish is conversion to a sense of community.

3. The third need of a parish is for growth, maturity, the need to change, to accept the importance of change.

4. The fourth need is for planning, i.e., statements of its mission, vision, goal setting, objectives.[109]

The second paragraph of this canon states that the parish council is a consultative body.

Categories such as "deliberative" or "consultative" have often been used to identify what stage in the process is filled by various agencies, organizations or individuals. When taken in isolation, however, these terms may not be adequate to the reality of church life as projected by the Second Vatican Council. Shared responsibility within the respective competency of the structured commu-

[104]Ibid.

[105]See R. Kennedy, "Shared Responsibility in Ecclesial Decision-Making," 5–23.

[106]For example, c. 1289 emphasizes that the pastor may not relinquish his administrative duties arbitrarily.

[107]See L. Suenens, *Co-Responsibility in the Church,* 132.

[108]Sometimes this is referred to as the pastor's duty to veto a proposal. Arbitrary use of such authority should be able to be appealed to the diocesan bishop. See c. 1737 which deals with recourse against administrative decisions of those in authority subject to the bishop.

[109]F. Rodimer, "Are Parish Councils on the Right Track?," 728–729.

nity is a more complex and less easily categorized experience. Assuring the accountability of those who have the responsibility to serve the community is more difficult than determining who has the final say, but in the last analysis it will provide more effective structuring of the exercise of power in the Church.[110]

In this regard the parish council is analogous to structures such as the diocesan or deanery council, the presbyteral council, and the college of consultors, which must be consulted in certain instances specified by law for an action to be valid. Similarly, the bishop could determine that in certain instances the parish council would have to be consulted.[111]

The diocesan norms which regulate parish councils have to be ratified and promulgated by the diocesan bishop. If individual parish councils are to have constitutions tailored to their unique makeup and needs, diocesan norms could indicate the necessary components of each constitution. These norms could regulate such considerations as the age of elected membership, membership selection, terms of office, the scope of the parish council, its basic structure, manner of voting, etc. Diocesan norms could also indicate those instances in which the pastor must consult the council for the validity of an action.

Parish Finance Council

Canon 537 — **Each parish is to have a finance council which is regulated by universal law as well as by norms issued by the diocesan bishop; in this council the Christian faithful, selected according to the same norms, aid the pastor in the administration of parish goods with due regard for the prescription of can. 532.**

It is a new concept in the law that every parish must have a finance council.[112] Its counterpart on the diocesan level is seen in canons 492–493 among others. The parish finance council is a specific example of the general principle in canon 1280 that every juridic person must have a council or at least two consultors who will assist the administrator in fulfilling his or her responsibilities.

Unlike the law regulating the diocesan finance council, this canon does not specify the constitutive

elements of the parish finance council other than by referring generically to universal law and episcopal norms. Therefore, since every legitimately established parish bears a juridic personality (c. 515, §3), the provisions of Book V, title II ("The Administration of Goods") apply. Other norms are relegated to particular law and need to be issued by the diocesan bishop to regulate uniformly the composition of the finance council and its duties. The diocesan bishop, for example, could determine the instances in which the administrator of a parish needs to consult the parish finance council for the validity of a financial action. The bishop also could set limits for financial actions which could not be exceeded on the parish level without his written permission. In some instances there could be some overlapping with the parish council and/or civil corporation structures of the parish, and it would seem advantageous for the diocesan norms to specify these relationships.

Cessation from the Pastoral Office and Retirement

Canon 538 — **§1. A pastor ceases from office by means of removal or transfer by the diocesan bishop which has been done in accord with the norm of law, by resignation of the pastor submitted for a just cause and accepted by the same diocesan bishop for validity and by lapse of time if the pastor has been appointed for a definite period of time in accord with the prescriptions of particular law mentioned in can. 522.**

§2. A pastor who is a member of a religious institute or a society of apostolic life is removed in accord with the norm of can. 682, §2.

§3. When a pastor has completed his seventy-fifth year of age he is asked to submit his resignation from office to the diocesan bishop, who, after considering all the circumstances of person and place, is to decide whether to accept or defer the resignation; the diocesan bishop, taking into account the norms determined by the conference of bishops, is to provide for the suitable support and housing of the resigned pastor.

One ceases to exercise the pastoral office in various ways, three of which are carried over from the 1917 Code to the present law: removal, transfer, and resignation. The present law adds a new one: expiration of term (c. 184).

After Vatican II both the administrative removal and transfer processes have been simplified for the good of the parish. Canons 1740–1747 should be consulted about the removal procedure.[113] Basically, it is the same as the 1917 Code process for the removal of *removable* pastors *(CIC 2157–2161),*

---

[110]J. Provost, "Structuring the Community," 276; see also J. Provost, "Consultative Bodies," 261.

[111]This means that in those instances which are specified by the bishop, a pastor could not make a decision alone. C. 127 addresses in general the issue of actions which are dependent for their validity on a superior's obtaining the consent or counsel of certain persons before acting.

[112]See Lynch, "Parochial Ministry," 402. Lynch sees this new law as applying in a very noteworthy way the principles of co-responsibility and accountability so highly esteemed in the post-conciliar Church.

[113]See commentary on Book VII, part V, section II, regarding the removal and transfer of pastors.

which was substantially shorter than the process for irremovable pastors. It is essential that a genuine cause exist for removal and that the process be followed exactly. Recourse against administrative removal is to the Sacred Congregation for the Clergy. When recourse has been taken, the pastor is obliged to leave the parish, but the bishop may not appoint a successor although an administrator may be appointed pending the outcome of the appeal. The administrative transfer process for pastors is supplied in canons 1748–1752. Again due cause must be present and the process followed. If a pastor will not accept a transfer, the diocesan bishop can declare the parish presently occupied by the pastor vacant at a certain point (c. 1751, 2°).

Resignation from office might occur for a number of reasons, e.g., retirement, poor health, scandal, incompetency, etc. It is up to the diocesan bishop to accept the resignation if he deems the reason to be valid.

The expiration of term provision follows from the new rule on a possible term of office (c. 522). If a pastor were appointed for a predetermined time, the office ceases immediately upon completion of said term. According to canon 522 the conference of bishops will determine the norms for a term of office policy, which will thereby permit the local bishop to implement such an approach in his diocese.

The second paragraph of the canon refers to the removal of religious pastors according to canon 682, §2. In such a case either the diocesan bishop or the superior of the clerical institute or apostolic society can initiate the process for removal. The diocesan bishop can remove such a pastor after notifying his superior, and the diocesan bishop must remove the pastor when asked to do so by his superior. Neither the bishop nor the superior is obliged to disclose to the other the reason for his decision. In the former law (*CIC* 454, §5) a religious pastor removed in this way had the right of recourse to the Holy See without a suspensive effect, which meant that the parish could be assigned to a new pastor even though the recourse had been made.

The third paragraph of the canon contains another change in law reflecting Vatican II (*CD* 30) and post-conciliar legislation (*ES* I, 20). Because of advanced years or other grave reasons, some pastors may be unable to perform their duties adequately. Accordingly, pastors at the age of seventy-five are requested to resign from pastoral office only, but not from priestly ministry. Yet, retirement at the age of seventy-five is not automatic and must be examined in each case by the diocesan bishop especially since some priests are able to function administratively well beyond the age of seventy-five while others are impaired for reasons of health or other serious causes. Individual differ-

ences must be taken into consideration.[114] Another consideration for the diocesan bishop is the availability of clergy. Depending on the shortage of priests in certain areas, the diocesan bishop might not be able to afford to allow some priests to retire at the age of seventy-five.

When retirement occurs, the diocesan bishop must provide suitable room and board for the priest. Vatican Council II prescribed that adequate support be given those who retire from office after a long life of priestly ministry (*PO* 21). Wholistic needs of retired priests should be taken into consideration.[115] In countries where social security may be lacking, programs of adequate remuneration and health assistance may need to be drawn up by the conferences of bishops either on a national scale or for groups of dioceses (c. 1274, §2). A comprehensive study of retirement has already been begun in the United States by the National Conference of Catholic Bishops.[116]

Impeded or Vacant Parish

Canon 539 — **When a parish becomes vacant or when the pastor is prevented from exercising his pastoral office in the parish due to captivity, exile, banishment, incapacity, ill health or some other cause, the diocesan bishop is to appoint as soon as possible a parochial administrator, that is, a priest who substitutes for the pastor in accord with the norm of can. 540.**

A parish becomes vacant if the pastor dies or if his office ceases according to canon 538 with his removal, transfer, resignation, or expiration of term. A pastor is hindered in the exercise of his ministry when he is captive, exiled, banished, incapacitated, or ill.[117] Whether the parish is impeded or vacant, the bishop is to appoint a parochial administrator as soon as possible. The need to continue spiritual service to the people is even more urgent if the parish is not served by a parochial vicar(s) or team member(s) who can substitute in the interim according to canon 541. Should no priest be available, the bishop could assign a person who is not a priest to function in a leadership role with a neighboring pastor supervising pastoral care (c. 517, §2) so that the responsibility for pastoral administration is shared.

This canon is not substantially different from canon 472 of the 1917 Code although that canon dealt only with vacant parishes.

[114]See G. Bootz, P. Murphy, and J. Zeurcher, "Pre-Retirement and Retirement for Religious," 98.
[115]See Janicki, "Limited Term of Office and Retirement," 48–50.
[116]See NCCB, *Fullness in Christ.*
[117]See cc. 412–430. There are certain similarities between the vacant/impeded diocese and parish.

Parochial Administrator

Canon 540 — §1. A parochial administrator is bound by the same duties and enjoys the same rights as a pastor unless the diocesan bishop determines otherwise.

§2. A parochial administrator is not permitted to do anything which can prejudice the rights of the pastor or harm parish goods.

§3. After he has fulfilled his function the parochial administrator is to render an account to the pastor.

The duties and rights in law of a parochial administrator are generally the same as those of a pastor, particularly as delineated in canons 528–530. Also, he validly assists at the celebration of marriages. For good reason, however, the bishop could restrict some of the administrator's powers. Ayrinhac observes that the actual pastor could choose to discharge personally some pastoral duties even during his absence, e.g., Mass for the people.[118] One might wonder what is to be done in the case of a pastor who is incapacitated by reason of age or mental illness. Can he be prevented by the ordinary from exercising his ministry when an administrator has already been appointed to substitute for him? The bishop could certainly prevent him from exercising his office, at least in part. However, if the pastor is intransigent, the ultimate step might have to be removal from office.

While in office a parochial administrator should not make major changes or innovations without consulting the bishop.[119] The parochial administrator should render an account either to the pastor who is resuming parish leadership or to a newly appointed pastor. This reflects a concern for pastoral accountability and is basically the same provision as in the prior law *(CIC 473)*.

Parish Vacancy/Pastor Impeded: Interim Governance

Canon 541 — §1. When a parish becomes vacant or when the pastor is hindered from exercising his pastoral duty the parochial vicar is to assume the governance of the parish in the meantime until a parochial administrator is appointed; if there are several parochial vicars, the senior vicar in terms of appointment assumes the governance; if there are no parochial vicars, then a pastor specified by particular law assumes the governance.

§2. The person who has assumed the governance of a parish in accord with the norm of §1 is to in- form the local ordinary immediately that the parish is vacant.

Canon 539 specifies that when a parish is vacant or a pastor is hindered in exercising his pastoral duties, a parochial administrator is to be appointed. The present canon specifies further that until such a parochial administrator is appointed the parochial vicar automatically assumes the governance of the parish. If there is more than one vicar, the senior vicar in terms of appointment assumes such a role. The 1917 Code made this same provision (*CIC* 472). Logically, it is assumed that the parochial vicar is most knowledgeable about parish needs. Accordingly, uninterrupted service to the people is maintained. The former law further provided that where there was no parochial vicar the nearest pastor should take charge.[120] The nearest pastor was to have been determined in advance by the diocesan bishop to obviate doubts in an emergency (*CIC* 472). Since the present law does not provide for this contingency, one might apply the comparable law in the 1917 Code in light of the general principles of law (c.19) governing such a situation unless they are superseded by the particular law of the diocese. The interim administrator should notify the bishop at once that he is assuming the governance of the parish.

Qualifications of Team Members

Canon 542 — The priests who as a team have been entrusted with the pastoral care of some parish or group of different parishes in accord with the norm of can. 517, §1:

1° are to be endowed with the qualities mentioned in can. 521;

2° are to be appointed or installed in accord with the prescriptions of cann. 522 and 524;

3° are responsible for pastoral care only from the moment of taking possession; their moderator is to be placed in possession of the parish in accord with the prescriptions of can. 527, §2; for the other priests a legitimately made profession of faith substitutes for taking possession.

This and the following canon refer to priests who comprise a parish team (c. 517, §1). Because team members are equivalent in law to pastors, their qualifications, powers, obligations, etc., are the same as those specified for pastors. The present canon directs attention to the corresponding requirements for pastors. For example, team members are affected by the same laws as pastors regarding qualifications (c. 521), possible term of

---

[118]See Ayrinhac II, 358.
[119]This follows from the axiom "sede vacante, nihil innovetur." See c. 428 regarding vacant dioceses.

[120]See Abbo-Hannan I, 470. The nearest pastor is determined by a moral, not a mathematical computation.

office (c. 522), appointment (c. 524), taking possession of the parish (c. 542, 3°), profession of faith (c. 833, 6°), and inception of duties (c. 527, §1). The entire team is required to make the profession of faith, but the moderator is singled out in the investiture ceremony (c. 542, 3°), presumably to indicate that he represents the rest of the team.

Functions and Duties of Team Members

Canon 543 — **§1. Each of the priests who as a team have been entrusted with the pastoral care of some parish or group of different parishes is obliged to perform the duties and functions of the pastor which are mentioned in cann. 528, 529 and 530 in accord with an arrangement determined by themselves; all these priests possess the faculty to assist at marriages as well as all the faculties to dispense which are granted to the pastor by the law itself, to be exercised, however, under the direction of the moderator.**

§2. All the priests of the team:

1° are bound by the obligation of residence;

2° through common counsel are to establish an arrangement by which one of them celebrates Mass for the people in accord with the norm of can. 534;

3° in juridic affairs only the moderator represents the parish or parishes entrusted to the team. [Apparently 3° should read §3.]

The functions and duties of priests who comprise a parish team (c. 517, §1) are equivalent to those which pertain to pastors. These would include preaching, instructing, and celebrating the sacraments (c. 529); meeting human concerns and collaborating with the bishop as well as with their parishioners (c. 530); offering the assigned Mass for the people (c. 534); and representing the parish in juridic affairs (c. 532) if one is the moderator and residing within the parish (c. 533). To enable team members to fulfill some of the above obligations, they would have, by law, the general delegation needed to assist at marriages within the parish (c. 1111) as well as certain dispensing faculties, e.g., regarding holy days (c. 1245), fast and abstinence (c. 1245), certain marital impediments in danger of death (c. 1079, §2), and private vows (c. 1196, 1°).

This canon stresses the role of the moderator as the one who coordinates, organizes, and unifies the pastoral action of the team. Because they act as one (*"in solidum"*), there should be a consensus among all the team members regarding their respective duties and functions so that these are exercised in harmony. Team members do this by sharing information equally and by fostering unified action. Theologically speaking, this becomes in the broad sense a sacramental sign of unity and service for the community they serve.

Team Ministry Vacancy

Canon 544 — **When one of the priests in the team mentioned in can. 517, §1 or its moderator ceases from office or when one of them becomes incapable of exercising pastoral duties the parish or parishes entrusted to the care of the team do not become vacant; however, the diocesan bishop is to name another moderator; the senior priest on the team in terms of assignment is to fulfill the office of moderator until another is appointed by the diocesan bishop.**

Since every team member is equivalent to a pastor, the provisions of canon 538 apply regarding removal, transfer, resignation, retirement, and expiration of term.

However, the provisions of canon 544 differ significantly from those concerning the vacant parish or impeded pastor in canon 539. The law does not envision the case of all members of the team ceasing from office at the same time, which could happen if all are appointed at the same time and for a specified term of office. Nor does it provide for an instance in which all team members would at the same time become incapable of exercising pastoral duties. By analogy of law, in this case the parish(es) indeed would be vacant and the governance would have to be provided for by the diocesan bishop or according to the provisions of particular law (c. 541). Normally, however, the parish(es) does not become vacant because the moderator's office is automatically assumed by the other team member or the older by reason of assignment if there are two. In the absence of more precise specifications, the provisions of law in the parallel situation of parochial vicars would apply. Hence, if the remaining team members were all equal in terms of the length of their assignment, the oldest of the group in age would be in charge until another moderator is appointed (c. 541, §1).

Parochial Vicars

Canon 545 — **§1. A parochial vicar or several of them can be associated with the pastor whenever it is necessary or suitable for duly implementing the pastoral care of the parish; parochial vicars are priests who render their services in pastoral ministry as co-workers with the pastor in common counsel and endeavor with him and also under his authority.**

§2. A parochial vicar can be assigned to assist in fulfilling the entire pastoral ministry on behalf of an entire parish, a definite part of the parish, or a certain group of the Christian faithful of the parish; he can also be assigned to assist in fulfilling a certain type of ministry in different parishes concurrently.

The ecclesiastical office of parochial vicar is treated extensively in this and the succeeding seven canons. The former law has been changed considerably but not substantively. The complicated provisions of the 1917 Code for different types of vicars assisting the pastor, i.e., vicar *oeconomus* (*CIC* 473), vicar *substitutus* (*CIC* 474), vicar *adjutor* (*CIC* 475), and vicar *cooperator* (*CIC* 476–477) are simplified in this reworked section of the law.[121] The title "parochial vicar" is now used exclusively for vicar *cooperator*. "Associate pastor," "assistant pastor," and "curate" are the equivalent terms used in English-speaking countries.

The preeminent value of the spiritual care of persons is the norm governing the need for parochial vicars. Depending on the size of the parish and other needs including that of the parish priest (pastor), one or more parochial vicars may be necessary. In the spirit of Vatican II (*CD* 30), the present law has designated the parochial vicar and pastor as fraternal co-workers. Both possess the same "shepherding authority," i.e., the spiritual functions (*munera*) to teach, to sanctify, and to direct the people entrusted to their care in their individual and communal exercises of the corporal and spiritual works of mercy. The difference between the pastor and the parochial vicar lies only in the administrative powers of the pastor. The parochial vicar is subject to this administrative authority and in this way differs from members of a team who share that authority "*in solidum.*"[122] The spirit of the law suggests that they work together in an atmosphere of mutual trust, acceptance, understanding, and fraternity.[123]

A parochial vicar can be appointed for full or specialized services to the parish. If his letter of appointment states that he is to help carry out the total pastoral ministry for the entire parish, he shares completely in the ministry of the pastor except for the administrative responsibilities. He may also be assigned to a determined section of the parish. This might refer to a specific geographical area and could include a mission or outlying sector of he parish. He might also be assigned for a specific ministry, e.g., religious education, youth ministry, etc. A new feature of the law states that he may be assigned to fulfill a certain type of ministry in several determined parishes concurrently. There is a great amount of flexibility here. In an age of specialization and in an area where there is a dearth of priests, one associate pastor might move from parish to parish to conduct youth ministry or ministry to the sick or a religious education ministry. In

such a case his scope of accountability, remuneration, and similar matters would have to be specified further.

Ordination Required for Parochial Vicar

Canon 546 — To be validly named parochial vicar one must be constituted in the sacred order of the presbyterate.

Although this canon is new in formulation, it conveys an idea that was contained at least implicitly in the former law.[124] In recent years there has been a growing movement in some areas of the Church to suggest broadening the ministerial roles of women including their admission into all forms of ministry in the Church, including the diaconate and ordained priesthood.[125] At the same time the Holy See has resisted this movement on theological grounds.[126] While the present canon clearly precludes women from being parochial vicars, a number of parishes today have non-ordained "pastoral associates" fulfilling many of the parochial vicar's functions.[127] Canon 517, §2 provides that when there is a dearth of priests in a given diocese, the pastoral care of a parish may be exercised by a man or woman who is not a priest under the direction of a priest-supervisor.

Appointment of Parochial Vicar

Canon 547 — The diocesan bishop freely names a parochial vicar, having heard, if he judges it opportune, the pastor or pastors of the parishes for which he is appointed and the vicar forane, with due regard for the prescription of can. 682, §1.

Its emphasis on the importance of the episcopal office prompted Vatican II (*CD* 31) to stress the need for the local bishop to be as free as possible in assigning priests so that he could place the most qualified person in a given assignment.[128] This canon reinforces the bishop's right regarding the appointment of parochial vicars. At the same time it changes the previous law (*CIC* 476, §3), which required the bishop always to consult with the pastor before assigning a parochial vicar. This seems a bit regressive, however, in contrast to the 1917

---

[121]See Initial CLSA Report (1978); see also Green, "Critical Reflections," 246–247.

[122]See previous commentary on c. 542.

[123]C. 548, §3 specifies that the pastor and parochial vicars are co-responsible for the pastoral care of the parish. Brotherly understanding and not subservience should be the basic guide for authority.

[124]*CIC* 476, §§3–4 referred to parochial vicars as members of the diocesan or religious clergy, and *CIC* 478, §2 referred to them as priests. The former law explicitly stated that pastors had to be ordained priests (*CIC* 453, §1).

[125]See USCC Task Force, "Identifying Women's Concerns," 69–73.

[126]See *Origins* 6 (1977), 517–524 for an English translation of the "Declaration on the Question of the Admission of Women to the Ministerial Priesthood" of the SCDF.

[127]See R. Weakland, "The Bishop and the Sacraments," 125.

[128]See *Directory*, 98.

Code. To understand this abrupt shift, one must realize that the former law had attempted to correct certain abuses involving the benefice system, some of which antedate the Council of Trent.[129] However, the present law does not discourage the bishop from consulting the pastor(s) of the parish(es) to which the parochial vicar is to be appointed as well as the vicar forane or dean. Nor does this canon prevent the bishop from conferring with a personnel board. The point here is that in the final analysis the bishop is responsible for whoever is appointed.

An exception to the general rule occurs in the case of the appointment of a parochial vicar who is a member of an institute of consecrated life or a clerical society of apostolic life. In this case, canon 682, §1 states that the appointment is made by the bishop following the presentation of the candidate by the superior of the respective institute or society similar to the provision for the appointment of a pastor (c. 523).

The diocesan bishop could delegate a vicar general or episcopal vicar to assign parochial vicars. In such a case the bishop should issue a mandate as described by canon 479, §§1–2.[130]

Rights and Obligations of the Parochial Vicar

Canon 548 — §1. The obligations and rights of the parochial vicar are defined in the canons of this chapter, in the diocesan statutes, in the letter of the diocesan bishop and more specifically in the mandate given him by the pastor.

§2. Unless the letter of the diocesan bishop expressly states otherwise the parochial vicar is obliged by reason of his office to assist the pastor in fulfilling the total parochial ministry, except for the obligation to apply Mass for the people, and if circumstances warrant it, to substitute for the pastor in accord with the norm of law.

§3. The parochial vicar is regularly to consult with the pastor on planned or existing programs so that the pastor and the parochial vicar or vicars can provide through their combined efforts for the pastoral care of the parish for which they are responsible together.

This canon and those that follow (cc. 549–551) articulate various obligations, rights, and a job description of the parochial vicar. Some of the ideas are innovative, but no substantive changes have taken place since the 1917 Code.

The obligations of the parochial vicar in this chapter are as follows: (1) supply general pastoral care (c. 545, §1); (2) cooperate with the pastor of

the parish (cc. 545, §1; 548, §3); (3) substitute the same services as the pastor must provide (cc. 549; 528–530); and (4) reside within the parish (c. 550, §1). The same chapter delineates the right of the parochial vicar to a vacation (c. 550, §3) and to a retreat.[131]

Other rights and obligations may be prescribed in the diocesan statutes and/or in the letter of appointment from the diocesan bishop.[132] The job description of the parochial vicar for a specific parish can be further specified by the pastor depending on such conditions as the needs of the parish, the availability of the pastor, etc.

Presumably, a parochial vicar will exercise his office in fulfilling the total parochial ministry stated in canon 545, §2 except for the obligation to apply Mass for the people (c. 534). However, the bishop could alter this in the letter of appointment and assign the parochial vicar to a specific portion of the parish or for a specific work within the parish in accord with canon 545, §2. The parochial vicar might be assigned the same type of ministry in a number of parishes. In such an instance, the local pastors could not require the parochial vicar to undertake more tasks than are specified in his appointment by the bishop.

If the parish becomes vacant or if the pastor is hindered in exercising his duty, the parochial vicar should assume the general governance of the parish until an administrator is appointed. Canon 541 deals with the latter contingency and provides that the senior parochial vicar in terms of appointment could assume parish governance if there are several vicars. In this way uninterrupted spiritual service can be given to the people. The law stresses the relationship between the parochial vicar and the pastor as one of fraternal collaboration. This reflects the principles of collegiality and co-responsibility which have somewhat shaped the revised law.[133] There is a vast difference between the spirit of the present law and that of the 1917 Code, which spoke of the docile subjection of the parochial vicar to the pastor and of the pastor's duty of paternal vigilance and direction vis-à-vis the parochial vicar (*CIC* 476, §7). Therefore, the law clearly indicates that pastors, parochial vicars and team members alike are co-responsible for the service they render to the people of God.

Parochial Vicar as Substitute

Canon 549 — Unless the diocesan bishop has provided otherwise in accord with the norm of can. 533, §3, and unless a parochial administrator has

---

[129]See Ayrinhac II, 359–369; see also Woywod-Smith I, 199.

[130]See the previous commentary on c. 523. The delegation to appoint parochial vicars is comparable to the delegation to appoint pastors.

[131]Although the present law does not explicitly grant to the parochial vicar the right to a retreat, there is an analogy of law (c. 17) with specific reference to c. 533, §2.

[132]E.g., delegation for marriage (c. 1111, §1); the faculty of subdelegating with the power to subdelegate again (c. 137, §3).

[133]See Green, "The Revision of Canon Law," 645.

been appointed, the prescriptions of can. 541, §1, should be observed during the absence of the pastor; in this case the parochial vicar is bound by all the obligations of the pastor with the exception of the obligation to apply Mass for the people.

This canon provides for the operation of a parish when the pastor is absent for whatever reason. The 1917 Code provided for a vicar *substitutus* when a pastor was absent from a parish due to some foreseen or unforeseen event; if the substitute were appointed by the pastor, he had to be approved by the bishop and then he had all the powers of the pastor (*CIC* 474).

The law now empowers the parochial vicar to be the substitute in cases of the foreseen and unforeseen absence of the pastor unless the local bishop makes other provisions. Such provisions might be necessary in individual cases if the parochial vicar is advanced in age, incapable, or unwilling to assume the pastoral obligations. In cases of such pastoral absence, canon 541, §1 places the responsibility of substituting for the pastor on the parochial vicar who is senior in terms of his appointment.

Canon 533, §2 states that a pastor may be absent from the parish for one month each year not including his spiritual retreat. However, if the absence is more than one week, the bishop is to be informed. This canon would transfer the needed faculties of the pastor to the parochial vicar during such an absence. At this time the parochial vicar is bound by all the obligations of the pastor except for that of applying Mass for the people.[134]

Residency of Parochial Vicar

Canon 550 — §1. The parochial vicar is obliged to reside within the parish, or, if he has been appointed to different parishes concurrently, he is obliged to live in one of them; however, the local ordinary can permit him to reside elsewhere, especially in a house shared by several priests provided there is a just cause and such an arrangement does not hinder the discharge of his pastoral duties.

§2. The local ordinary is to see to it that some community of life is fostered between the pastor and the parochial vicars within the rectory whenever this can be done.

§3. The parochial vicar possesses the same rights as the pastor in the matter of vacation time.

There is a striking parallel between this canon and the one on the residency of pastors (c. 533). Both canons reflect the spirit of the 1917 Code, i.e., reasonable service to the people presupposes that the parochial vicar live in the parish or at least in

one of them if he serves more than one parish (*CIC* 476, §5).

In the United States and some other countries, it has been customary to construct a rectory near the church. However, this is not the case in many parts of the world where the priest does not necessarily live where he works. Both systems have advantages and disadvantages to the priest personally and ministerially. In certain United States dioceses there is a growing concern to provide for alternatives to the church rectory arrangement. The present canon leaves the determination of this up to the bishop but encourages the idea of living in a residence shared by other priests. Such an arrangement could help to promote the welfare of the priest as a celibate individual in need of fraternal support within an environment conducive to spiritual growth.

Nowadays, the quality of priestly relationships, especially at the parish level, is pastorally significant. The second paragraph of this canon charges the bishop to promote some type of community life between the pastor and parochial vicars, presumably where they do not live together. In places where the priests live in a rectory, the bishop is to promote common life. While this could include shared meals, community prayers, recreation, etc., due consideration must be given to the different life-styles of diocesan and religious clergy.[135]

The final paragraph of this canon reflects the parity between the pastor and parochial vicar in regard to vacation time. Vatican II (*PO* 20) indicated that bishops are to see to it that their priests are to have a proper vacation each year. Given contemporary stress and strain, a regular vacation as well as days off are necessary for the physical, emotional, and spiritual health of the priests in view of an effective ministry. The equation of vacation time for pastor and parochial vicar implicitly reflects the co-responsible nature of both offices. By contrast the 1917 Code did not provide for the parochial vicar's vacation.

Voluntary Offering/Stole Fees

Canon 551 — The prescriptions of can. 531 are to be observed concerning the offerings which the Christian faithful give to the parochial vicar on the occasion of his performing his pastoral ministry.

The reader should see the commentary on canon 531 since the provisions of the present canon are the same.

Removal of Parochial Vicar

Canon 552 — With due regard for the prescription of can. 682, §2, the parochial vicar can be re-

---

[134]See Bouscaren-Ellis, 219. This clarifies what had been a doubt of law in the 1917 Code.

[135]See *PO* 8; see also NCCB, *As One Who Serves*, 67–68.

moved by the diocesan bishop or by the diocesan administrator for a just cause.

This canon somewhat improves the 1917 Code regarding the protection of human rights. In the former law two categories of parochial vicars could be removed from office. The first was the "perpetual vicar," who was very much like a pastor with regard to removal from office (*CIC* 471). Usually, the perpetual vicar held a benefice and, therefore, was subject to the same process of removal as a pastor (*CIC* 471, §3). The second category, which included all other types of parochial vicars, e.g., *oeconomus, substitutus, adjutor,* and *cooperator,* could be removed at the will of the bishop (*CIC* 472–476). Commentators like Wernz-Vidal and Ayrinhac held that although a canonical cause was not necessary in such cases of removal, there had to be some real existential cause in keeping with canonical equity.[136] In addition, a recourse to a higher authority was always allowed but only after the priest was removed from office (*in devolutivo*).[137]

The present canon requires that there be a "just cause" objectively before the parochial vicar can be removed. This improves the 1977 schema which viewed the "just cause" in terms of the prudent judgment of the diocesan bishop or diocesan administrator with due regard for natural equity.[138] Canon 1741 lists five causes for which a pastor can be removed from his office. They include bringing grave harm to the ecclesial community, permanent illness of mind or body rendering his ministry ineffective, hatred of the people, grave neglect of office, and poor administration. This list is not taxative, but it illustrates some of the objectively just causes that are proportionate to the removal of a priest from office. The bishop should probably consider these and similar causes before removing a parochial vicar from office although he is not strictly obliged to act only in light of the causes for removal of pastors. Unlike the case of a pastor, there is no legal process for the removal of a parochial vicar. However, a truly equitable procedure would minimize the suspicion of arbitrariness or supposed injustice. If the parochial vicar felt that he had been dealt with unjustly, that his good name had been impaired, or that he had suffered some other damage in being removed from office, he could take re-

course (*in devolutivo*) to the Sacred Congregation for the Clergy.

A parochial vicar who is a member of an institute of consecrated life or a society of apostolic life can be removed in accord with canon 682, §2 either by the local bishop or the religious superior. This provision, which restates canon 454, §5 of the 1917 Code, offers less protection of rights for members of an institute of consecrated life or a society of apostolic life than for diocesan priests. This is related to the nature of the ties binding religious to their community as distinct from those binding diocesan clergy to the diocese.

This section of canons explicitly refers to the removal of pastors and parochial vicars; however, there is no explicit mention of the removal of team members. Nevertheless, because team members are equivalent to pastors, the law on the removal of pastors would be applicable to them.[139]

CHAPTER VII
VICARS FORANE
[cc. 553–555]

Vicars Forane

Canon 553 — §1. A vicar forane, who is also called a dean or an archpriest or some other name, is a priest who is placed over a vicariate forane.

§2. Unless particular law determines otherwise the vicar forane is named by the diocesan bishop after, in accord with his own prudent judgment, he has consulted the priests who exercise ministry within the vicariate in question.

In this and the following canons, the institute of vicar forane is basically unchanged from the 1917 Code (*CIC* 445–450). However, the revised law explicitly links the title of "dean" with that of the fourth-century "archpriest."[140] The modern idea of vicar forane dates back to the First Provincial Council of Milan in 1565 under the direction of St. Charles Borromeo. At that time the office was introduced, and it subsequently spread to other parts of Italy and the rest of the world.[141] The title reflects the older idea of those rural or outlying (forane) parts of the diocese where the bishop's presence and concern can be made visible by a dean. More recently, certain dioceses have appointed deans to urban and metropolitan districts with the title of "urban vicar."[142] Deacons, non-ordained

---

[136]Technically, curates did not exercise an office according to the former law. Ayrinhac, however, held that a curate could appeal to higher authority if, for instance, his reputation was damaged in being removed from his assignment; see Ayrinhac II, 365–366; see also, Wernz-Vidal II, 805.

[137]Recourse *in devolutivo* means that the parochial vicar must vacate his office pending the results of the recourse. Should the ordinary's decision be reversed, the parochial vicar's office can be restored to him.

[138]See c. 384 of 1978 schema.

[139]See previous commentary on c. 538, §1; see also commentary on Book VII (removal and transfer of pastors) (cc. 1740–1752).

[140]See B. Forshaw, "Archpriest," 772–773.

[141]See P.W. Rice, "Rural Dean (Vicar Forane)," 682.

[142]See R. Howes, "Regional Pastor: Regional People," 19–24. Howes describes how this office may be effectively adapted to present-day needs.

members of an institute of consecrated life or a clerical society of apostolic life, and lay persons are excluded from the office of vicar forane.

Canon 374 requires that a diocese be divided into parishes, and it permits parishes in a certain vicinity to be grouped together in a vicariate forane or deanery to promote better pastoral care. However, this is not necessarily the same as an episcopal vicariate since recently a number of dioceses have appointed episcopal vicars in addition to or in place of the traditional vicars forane.[143] The *Directory* (184) suggested that, in addition to territorially defined deaneries, there can be personal, ritual, or functional deaneries not restricted to territorial groupings, e.g., a deanery consisting of hospital chaplains in one region or city.

A counterpart to vicars forane in the Eastern Church are the protopresbyters. These offices in both the Eastern and Western rites were recognized by Vatican II (*CD* 30) and subsequent legislation (*ES* I, 19), which saw a value in promoting pastoral action through such supra-parochial structures.

A vicar forane is appointed by the diocesan bishop. Since the term "diocesan bishop" rather than "ordinary" is used here, a vicar general, or episcopal vicar could not appoint a vicar forane without a special mandate. A new feature in the law is its recommendation that before appointing vicars forane bishops consult with the priests who exercise their ministry within the respective vicariates. This reflects a sensitivity to the wisdom of such presbyteral input in such a significant decision.

This canon permits particular law to determine another way of naming the vicar forane. The vicar forane might be elected by his fellow priests or even by all the Christian faithful in a specific vicariate. Following such an election the bishop would finalize the appointment. A broader selection process might foster better relationships and more fruitful collaboration between the vicar forane and the other members of the people of God he is to serve.

The general law does not define the manner in which vicars forane are accountable to the bishop whereas the *Directory* (188) states that at fixed times the bishop is to convoke meetings of the vicars forane to discuss particular diocesan affairs with them and receive information on the condition of the diocese. Accountability to others, e.g., fellow priests or people of the vicariates, could also be fostered through regular meetings of the presbyteral council, the diocesan pastoral council, or the deanery pastoral council, especially if all or some of the vicars forane were ex-officio members of such bodies.

*Qualifications/Term of Office/
Removal of Vicar Forane*

Canon 554 — §1. For the office of vicar forane, which is not linked to the office of pastor of a certain parish, the bishop is to select a priest whom he has judged suitable after he has considered the circumstances of place and time.

§2. A vicar forane is to be appointed for a certain period of time determined in particular law.

§3. The diocesan bishop can freely remove a vicar forane from office for a just cause in accord with his own prudent judgment.

This canon slightly modifies the 1917 Code which encouraged the appointment of pastors to the office of vicar forane. Here it is explicitly stated that a vicar forane does not have to be a pastor. This seems to be more realistic than the former law since, if the job description of vicar forane is fairly extensive, one who is not a pastor may have the best chance of fulfilling such responsibilities easily. Suitability for this office ought to be judged in terms of a candidate's fulfilling the job description indicated in the following canon.

The *Directory* (187) suggests general criteria for the candidates for this office. Each one is to: (1) exercise personally the spiritual care of persons; (2) reside in the deanery and command the highest respect of the clergy and people by his learning, prudence, piety, and apostolic work; (3) be a person to whom the bishop may suitably grant faculties for the entire deanery, unless he prefers to appoint him an episcopal vicar with certain specified duties; and (4) be able to foster and supervise the joint pastoral program in his territory.

Like certain other ecclesiastical offices, a vicar forane is to be appointed for a specified term of office.[144] Such a term is to be determined by particular law, e.g., episcopal decree, diocesan synod, or even the conference of bishops.[145]

To afford the bishop the requisite liberty he deserves in making appointments, the vicar forane can be removed from office by the bishop according to his prudent judgment. The law itself requires that there be a just cause. One might envision those grave causes which warrant the removal or transfer of a pastor as indicated in canon 1741 mutatis mutandis; but the bishop is not limited to those reasons. The fact that the vicar forane is not fulfilling his job description or that he may be urgently needed to fill another office would be examples of other

---

[143]See W. Bassett, "The Office of Episcopal Vicar," 285–313.

[144]The same is true for episcopal vicars who are not bishops and members of the college of consultors (c. 502, §1); pastors can be but are not required to be appointed for a term of office (c. 522).

[145]See *Directory*, 187.

reasons which might impel the bishop to remove a vicar forane.[146]

Powers, Duties, Rights of Vicar Forane

Canon 555 — §1. In addition to the faculties legitimately granted him in particular law, a vicar forane has the duty and right:

1° to promote and coordinate the common pastoral activity within the vicariate;

2° to see to it that the clerics of his district lead a life which is in harmony with their state of life and diligently perform their duties;

3° to see to it that religious functions are celebrated in accord with the prescriptions of the sacred liturgy, that the good appearance and condition of the churches and of sacred furnishings are carefully maintained especially in the celebration of the Eucharist and the custody of the Blessed Sacrament, that the parish books are correctly inscribed and duly cared for, that ecclesiastical goods are carefully administered, and finally that the rectory is maintained with proper care.

§2. Within the vicariate entrusted to him the vicar forane:

1° is to see to it that clerics, in accord with the prescriptions of particular law and at the times stated in such law, attend theological lectures, meetings or conferences in accord with the norm of can. 279, §2;

2° is to take care that the presbyters of his district have ready access to spiritual helps and is to be particularly concerned about those priests who find themselves in rather difficult circumstances or who are beset with problems.

§3. The vicar forane is to take care that the pastors of his district whom he knows to be seriously ill do not lack spiritual and material aids, while seeing to it that the funerals of those who die are celebrated with dignity; he is likewise to make provision that when they are sick or dying, the books, documents, sacred furnishings or other things which belong to the Church are not lost or transported elsewhere.

§4. The vicar forane is obliged to visit the parishes of his district in accord with the regulations made by the diocesan bishop.

This canon contains an extensive job description of the vicar forane, clarifying his powers, duties, and rights. It is much broader than the 1917 Code, which largely classified his duties in terms of the supervision of priests, the custody of the Blessed Sacrament, and the care of church appurtenances and records (*CIC* 447). Many of the powers/faculties of the vicar forane come from particular law.

This is understandable in light of variations from place to place. Among the faculties of vicars forane might be the granting of faculties for confessions to visiting priests and the dispensing of certain matrimonial impediments. The vicar forane might also be given the faculty to administer confirmation as an extraordinary minister (c. 884, §1).

Three preeminent rights and duties of the vicar forane are stated in the law: (1) He is to promote and coordinate the general pastoral activity[147] in his vicariate. This is not restricted to the activity of the clergy, but it extends to the active involvement of all the people of God in the mission of the Church. Its scope needs to be clarified and described in more detail by particular law. (2) He is to supervise the life-style and ministry of the clergy. While the implications of this duty are multifaceted, the thrust of the revised Code is more toward positive leadership of the clergy in a given area rather than pastoral surveillance as emphasized in the 1917 Code. (3) He is to supervise liturgical functions, the care of churches, sacramentals, custody of the Blessed Sacrament, ecclesiastical records, and church administration in general. There is a definite value in having someone perform these important duties for the diocesan bishop at the regional level.

The second paragraph of the canon mentions more duties related to the supervision of the clergy. The first of these duties involves promoting the continuing education of the clergy. The reference to canon 279, §2, 1° implies that the vicar forane is to remind priests of their continuing education obligations; but, at the same time it might mean that he should arrange for conferences or study days within his vicariate or elsewhere so that the above-mentioned obligations could be met. Secondly, he is expected to be concerned about the spiritual needs of the clergy of his vicariate and help priests experiencing problems. By reason of his proximity to the priests of the vicariate, the vicar forane can anticipate problematic situations as well as provide crisis intervention.

In its solicitude for priests who are ill, elderly, or dying the Church assigns to the vicar forane the obligation of looking after their spiritual and material welfare. He is also charged with seeing to the details of their funerals. He is to make sure that when priests are sick or dying, articles belonging to the church are not lost or transported elsewhere either through accident or the foibles of human nature.

Finally, the law states that the diocesan bishop is to prescribe the number of times per year as well as the manner in which the vicar forane is to visit the parishes in his district. Obviously, this would be to foster parish accountability in relationship to diocesan goals and objectives. Interestingly enough,

---

[146]C. 194 indicates the instances in which an ecclesiastical office is lost *ipso iure.*

[147]The term "pastoral activity" is described at greater length in *Directory*, 103–105.

there is no reference to the dean's reporting to the bishop each year as was previously the case (*CIC* 449).

CHAPTER VIII
RECTORS OF CHURCHES AND CHAPLAINS
[cc. 556–572]

ARTICLE 1: RECTORS OF CHURCHES
[cc. 556–563]

Rectors of Churches

Canon 556 — Rectors of churches are understood to be priests to whom is given the care of some church which is neither parochial nor capitular nor connected with a house of a religious community or of a society of apostolic life which celebrates services in such a church.

The former law on rectors (*CIC* 479–486) is basically unchanged in the following canons. Wernz notes that in every diocese certain churches exist for the convenience of all or for a certain class of Christian faithful. These are entrusted to the care of "rectors" who have a certain affinity to chaplains of institutes of consecrated life, pious associations, hospitals, prisons, shrines, etc.[148]

Although both rectors and pastors exercise the spiritual care of persons, these canons generally subordinate the ministry of the rector to that of the local pastor so as not to detract from the preeminent role of the parish. Hence, this canon explicitly excludes from the governance of rectors all parochial and capitular churches or those connected with a house of a religious community or a clerical society of apostolic life in which the community celebrates services. In the United States priests have been and continue to be named rectors of cathedrals; however, they are not included in this canon since their ministry is clearly parochial. It should be noted that the rector of a church must be a priest.

Appointment of Rectors

Canon 557 — §1. The diocesan bishop freely names the rector of a church, with due regard for the right of election or of presentation if someone legitimately possesses it; in this case the diocesan bishop is competent to confirm or to install the rector.
§2. Even if the church belongs to some clerical religious institute of pontifical right the diocesan bishop is competent to install the rector presented by the superior.
§3. Unless the diocesan bishop has determined otherwise, the rector of a church which is connect- ed with a seminary or other college which is governed by clerics is the rector of that seminary or college.

This canon stipulates that the diocesan bishop is competent to appoint the rector. On the other hand, there are three possibilities regarding the naming, electing, or presenting of a rector.

1. The bishop himself could name and appoint the rector. This is the normal situation and reflects the Vatican II emphasis on episcopal discretion in various appointments within the diocese.[149]

2. In other instances someone other than the bishop might possess by custom the right of election or of presentation, e.g., a juridic person such as a university. In these cases the bishop confirms the election or installs the candidate who is presented.

3. In the case of rectors of churches belonging to clerical institutes of consecrated life, the bishop installs the candidate who is presented. This is parallel to the presentation of a pastor by the superior of such an institute (c. 682, §1).

This canon further states that ordinarily when a church is connected with a seminary or college run by clerics, the rector is the same for both. However, the law leaves it up to the bishop to make an exception to this rule if it is expedient, thereby preserving his requisite liberty.

Rights of Rectors

Canon 558 — With due regard for the prescription of can. 262, a rector is not allowed to perform the parochial functions mentioned in can. 530, nn. 1-6, in the church committed to him unless the pastor consents or delegates the rector if the matter warrants it.

As was the case in the former law (*CIC* 481), the thrust of this canon is to prevent any encroachment on the local parish, e.g., loss of lay participants, revenues, etc., by a church or chapel of lesser rank. Therefore, the rector is not allowed to perform the pastoral functions mentioned in canon 530, 1°–6° without the permission of the local pastor. In addition, proper delegation is required for the celebration of marriage by the rector (c. 1111).

The one exception to this general norm is the rector of the seminary because a seminary is exempt from parochial jurisdiction (c. 262) except in two instances: (1) in the case of marriage which always

---

[148]See Wernz-Vidal II, 806–807. The norms on chaplains are specified in cc. 564–572.

[149]See c. 157; *CD* 28; *ES* I, 18; a vicar general or episcopal vicar could be given a mandate to appoint rectors (c. 479, §§1–2).

requires proper delegation (c. 1111); and (2) in regard to the prohibition of the rector's hearing the confessions of seminarians (c. 985). Otherwise, the rector or his delegate has complete pastoral authority in the seminary committed to him.

Liturgical Celebrations by Rector

Canon 559 — A rector can perform liturgical celebrations, even solemn ones, in the church committed to him with due regard for the legitimate laws of the foundation and as long as they do not harm the parochial ministry in the judgment of the local ordinary.

The celebrations mentioned in this canon refer primarily to the Eucharist since other liturgical functions mentioned in canon 530, 1°–6° require the local pastor's permission. The only limitations on these celebrations occur when the legitimate laws of foundations[150] could be broken or when the local parish might be harmed, e.g., loss of lay participants, revenue, etc.[151]

Extended Services of the Rector

Canon 560 — Where he thinks it advisable, the local ordinary can order the rector to celebrate within the church particular functions, even parochial ones, for the people and to make the church available to certain groups of the Christian faithful for the conducting of liturgical celebrations.

This canon seems to be motivated by a concern for the common good when the local ordinary judges that the rector of a certain church should provide specific services including parochial functions for the people of the surrounding environment or even for certain groups of the faithful, e.g., ethnic groups lacking a national parish in the diocese.

Formerly, the law in this regard (*CIC* 483) specified that a rector was to provide liturgical and catechetical service for persons who lived so far from their parish church that it was more convenient for them to utilize the nearer, though non-parochial, church to which the rector was assigned.

Permission of Rector

Canon 561 — Without the permission of the rector or of another legitimate superior no one is al-

lowed to celebrate the Eucharist, administer the sacraments or perform other sacred functions in the church; this permission is to be granted or denied in accord with the norm of law.

This canon restricts the use of a non-parochial church to those who have obtained the permission of the rector or other legitimate superior, e.g., the rector's delegate, local pastor, or diocesan bishop.[152] The reason for this could stem from the fact that the rector himself must obtain the permission of the local pastor for most sacred functions particularly in the case of the celebration of marriage (c. 558).

Duties of Rectors

Canon 562 — Under the authority of the local ordinary with due regard for legitimate statutes and vested rights, the rector of a church is obliged to see to it that the sacred functions are celebrated with dignity in the church in accord with the liturgical norms and the prescriptions of the canons, that obligations are faithfully fulfilled, that its goods are carefully administered, that the maintenance and the good appearance of sacred furnishings and buildings are provided for and that nothing whatever is done which is in any way out of harmony with the sanctity of the place and the reverence due to a house of God.

This canon clarifies the different aspects of the rector's accountability to the local ordinary. It is interesting to note that the rector is directly accountable to the local ordinary rather than to the pastor of the parish. The rector is to take into consideration legitimate diocesan statutes which affect non-parochial churches as well as vested rights acquired by means of apostolic indults or legitimate customs regarding a specific non-parochial church.

The rector's first obligation is to see to it that sacred functions are celebrated with the dignity they deserve according to the liturgical norms and the prescriptions of the canons. He is also required to see to the fulfillment of Mass obligations (cc. 956–958), e.g., foundation Masses (c. 1303, §1, 2°). He is responsible further for the administration of the church's goods as well as the maintenance of the furnishings and buildings. These responsibilities parallel the obligations of pastors of parishes (c. 532) and are founded upon the general canonical obligations of administrators (cc. 1281–1289). Finally, he is to see to the adequate supervision of the church particularly if he does not live there.

---

[150]Foundation laws are regulations drawn up and approved by the bishop and the patron who built or endowed the church. Where these foundation laws still exist, they must be observed even if they preclude the celebration of certain liturgical functions. See Woywod-Smith I, 202.

[151]The former law (*CIC* 482) stipulated that in case of doubts on this point the local ordinary should settle controversies between rector and pastor and make proper provisions to avoid such difficulties in the future.

[152]Certain commentators on the 1917 Code like Ayrinhac (II, 368) and Abbo-Hannan (I, 477) held that reasonably presumed permission sufficed.

Removal of Rector

Canon 563 — For a just cause and in accord with his own judgment the local ordinary can remove from office a rector of a church, even if he had been elected or presented by others, with due regard for the prescription of can. 682, §2.

This canon clearly indicates that although the rector of a non-parochial church holds a canonical office in the strict sense, he enjoys no right of permanence in that office. Therefore, he can be removed at any time by the local ordinary[153] for a just cause even if the latter had appointed the rector for a specified term. Abbo-Hannan holds that the removal is valid even without the justifying cause.[154] The just cause is specified to respect the value of canonical equity and to protect rights.

The local ordinary can remove the rector of a non-parochial church even if he has been elected or presented by others, e.g., physical or juridic persons who have that acquired right (c. 557, §1). However, the removal of a rector who is a member of a religious institute or society of apostolic life is analogous to one who is pastor of a parish.[155]

ARTICLE 2: CHAPLAINS
[cc. 564–572]

Description of Chaplains

Canon 564 — A chaplain is a priest to whom is entrusted in a stable manner the pastoral care, at least in part, of some community or particular group of the Christian faithful, to be exercised in accord with universal and particular law.

This new canon clearly indicates that a chaplain serves "some community" or "particular group" of the faithful rather than a parish or quasi-parish. Therefore, although the office is pastoral by nature, a chaplain is not a pastor. Nor is he a rector of a church except when a non-parochial church is attached to the house of a community or group.[156] This law specifies that there should be some degree of stability which would attach to the office more so than to the community or group the chaplain serves, which is often of an itinerant nature. Hence, he could be given a term of office to insure stability.[157]

Universal and particular law are to regulate the exercise of this office. Universal law provides a basic framework within which more specific provisions are to be formulated.

Appointment of Chaplain

Canon 565 — Unless the law provides otherwise or special rights belong legitimately to someone, a chaplain is appointed by the local ordinary, who is also competent to install one who is presented or to confirm one who is elected.

Normally, a chaplain is appointed by a local ordinary, which includes the diocesan bishop or a vicar general or episcopal vicar. However, there are other provisions in the law for this type of appointment, e.g., military chaplains are governed by special laws (c. 569). It could also be that by custom, vested rights, or special agreements with the Holy See (concordats) persons other than the local ordinary could elect or present chaplains for special communities or groups. However, the local ordinary is to confirm those elected and install those presented.

The chaplain could be installed in office in a manner similar to the provisions for pastors (c. 527).

Faculties of Chaplains

Canon 566 — §1. A chaplain ought to be given all the faculties which proper pastoral care requires. Besides those which are granted by particular law or special delegation, a chaplain in virtue of his office enjoys the faculty to hear the confessions of the faithful entrusted to his care, to preach the word of God to them, to administer Viaticum and the anointing of the sick, and to confer the sacrament of confirmation on those who are in danger of death.

§2. In hospitals, prisons and on sea journeys a chaplain, moreover, has the faculty, to be exercised only in those places, to absolve from censures latae sententiae which are not reserved nor declared, with due regard for the prescription of can. 976.

The emphasis in this canon is on pastoral care. While the faculties given to chaplains by general law are very similar to the faculties of pastors (c. 530), solemn baptism, the witnessing of marriages, and the conducting of funerals seem to be excepted. Where the need exists, particular law could provide for these cases.

The second paragraph of the canon grants the faculty to absolve from certain *latae sententiae* censures (cc. 1331–1335) in hospitals, prisons, and on ocean voyages under ordinary circumstances above and beyond danger-of-death situations in which cases every priest can absolve from all censures and

---

[153]The use of the broader term "local ordinary" here is inconsistent since c. 557 specifically mentions the diocesan bishop as the one who is competent to appoint a rector. It is understood, however, that the diocesan bishop could extend his authority for assigning and removing a rector to a vicar general or episcopal vicar in accord with c. 479, §§1–2.

[154]See Abbo-Hannan I, 478.

[155]see commentaries on c. 538, §2 and c. 682, §2.

[156]See commentary on c. 572.

[157]The term of office would not prevent the diocesan bishop from transferring or removing a chaplain as long as it is done for a just cause and prudently (c. 572).

sins (c. 976). The faculty granted by this canon refers specifically to non-declared and non-reserved censures, and it is limited to the above-mentioned situations.

Chaplain of Lay Religious

Canon 567 — §1. The local ordinary is not to proceed to the appointment of a chaplain for the house of a lay religious institute without consulting the superior who has the right to propose a priest after hearing the community.

§2. It is the chaplain who celebrates or moderates liturgical functions; but he is not allowed to involve himself in the internal governance of the institute.

Although the former law considered lay religious to be in the care of the local pastor, canon 464, §2 of the 1917 Code allowed the diocesan bishop to withdraw such non-exempt religious from the pastor's jurisdiction and commit them to the care of a chaplain. Such a chaplain was much like a rector of a non-parochial church.[158] Also, the former law distinguished between a chaplain and a confessor to lay religious even though a priest could have been named the group's confessor as well as its chaplain. Finally, the former law forbade the confessor to meddle in the internal affairs of the religious community so as to preserve a clear delineation between the internal and external fora.[159]

The present law does not distinguish between the chaplain and the confessor.[160] The local ordinary must consult with the superior of the lay religious institute before appointing its chaplain. The superior, in turn, must consult with the religious community, and the law implies that the superior could refuse a chaplain who is being presented for consideration. The revised law retains the rule prohibiting the chaplain from interfering in the internal government of the institute.

Chaplains to Migrants

Canon 568 — To the extent it is possible, chaplains are to be appointed for those who cannot avail themselves of the ordinary care of a pastor because of the condition of their life, such as migrants, exiles, refugees, nomads, sailors.

This canon exhibits a concern for meeting the pastoral needs of persons outside the mainstream of parish life through chaplains. There is a real parallel between a chaplain in this sense and a pastor of a personal parish (c. 518). The canon mentions sail-

ors, but these may be covered by the special laws that govern military chaplains and personnel (c. 569). Migrants,[161] exiles, refugees, and nomads represent a truly mobile population. Although it is not specifically mentioned, campus ministry is a type of pastoral area that could warrant a chaplain where such ministry has not become parish based (c. 813).

Military Chaplains

Canon 569 — Military chaplains are governed by special laws.

In some, if not most, parts of the world, e.g., the United States[162] and Canada, apostolic vicariates (c. 372, §2) have been established by the Holy See to provide for the pastoral needs of military personnel. Military chaplains, like pastors, have ordinary jurisdiction although it is personal rather than territorial.[163] Military chaplains ordinarily do not serve for a lifetime but rather retain their affiliation with their diocese or religious institute.

Special legislation regulates military chaplaincies. Usually the Holy See (SCB) would help develop such legislation together with the proper military ordinary in a given country.

Besides the faculties mentioned in canon 566, military chaplains could be given those special faculties which their ministry demands, especially for solemn baptism, assisting at marriage, and conducting funerals. In the United States the Military Vicariate has its own chancery and tribunal. Its sacramental records are kept in central archives.

Chaplain of a Non-Parochial Church

Canon 570 — If the headquarters of a community or group is attached to a non-parochial church the chaplain is to be the rector of that church, unless the care of the community or church requires otherwise.

In this canon the "headquarters of a community or group" refers to a religious community, secular institute, society of apostolic life, or other association of the Christian faithful. Where a non-parochial church is attached to such a group, its chaplain becomes the rector of that church. Some of the preceding norms for rectors could be applicable here.

Basically, this canon imposes the responsibility for the church building and its use in addition to the chaplain's ministry to a specific community or group of persons. However, the last part of the canon allows another to function as rector if neces-

---

[158]See Woywod-Smith I, 231; Wernz-Vidal III, 165.
[159]Wernz-Vidal III, 155.
[160]C. 630, §3 requires that sufficient and suitable confessors be provided for religious by their superiors.

[161]See *CLD* 7, 209–215 for an English translation of the "Instruction on the Pastoral Care of Emigrants" of the SCB (Aug. 22, 1969).
[162]See J. Marbach, "Military Ordinariate," 847–849.
[163]See *CLD* 7, 391–392.

sary. This author judges that where there is a dearth of priests, a deacon, religious sister or brother, or a lay person could be assigned the duties of the rector under the supervision of a priest similar to the provisions of canon 517, §2.

Chaplain's Relation to Local Pastor

Canon 571 — In exercising his pastoral office a chaplain is to maintain an appropriately close relationship with the pastor.

This canon seeks to promote an amicable relationship between a chaplain and the local pastor(s) especially when their ministries might overlap at times. This means the chaplain should clarify his assignments, duties, faculties, and the people who comprise the community or group he is to serve so that possible misunderstandings about these matters might be avoided. Also, the chaplain and pastor need to work out an agreement on such matters as weddings, funerals, baptisms, sacramental records, and the public celebration of Mass. Should a conflict arise between the chaplain and local pastor(s), it should be referred to the local ordinary for resolution if necessary.

Removal of Chaplains

Canon 572 — In regard to the removal of a chaplain the prescription of can. 563 shall be observed.

At this point the law indicates that the norm for the removal of a rector (c. 563) is pertinent to the removal of a chaplain. Even if a chaplain has been assigned for a specified term of office, he does not have a vested right to the office; he could be transferred or removed as long as there is a just cause prudently determined by the local ordinary or the chaplain's superior. In such a case the law seeks to protect the chaplain's reputation as far as is possible. Religious chaplains can be removed from office by the local ordinary or superior by notifying the other but without necessarily receiving the other's consent (c. 682, §2).

BIBLIOGRAPHY

Articles

Archdiocese of Hartford. "Team Ministry: The Hartford Model." *Origins* 5 (1975), 194–195.

Bassett, W. "The Office of Episcopal Vicar." *J* 30 (1970), 285–313.

Bevilacqua, A. "Selected Questions in Chancery Practice." *CLSAP* (1981), 103–106.

Bootz, G.; Murphy, P.; and Zeurcher, J. "Pre-retirement and Retirement for Religious." *RfR* 29 (1970), 94–103.

Challencin, J. "Mass Stipends—Embarrassing?" *Emmanuel* (1979), 415–422.

Cora, G. "Team Ministry: Theological Aspects." *AER* 167 (1973), 684–690.

Diocese of Columbus. "Parish Council Rationale: New Level of Ministry." *Origins* 7 (1977), 244 (cited as "Parish Council Rationale").

Green, T. "Critical Reflections on the Schema on the People of God." *Stud Can* 14 (1980), 235–322 (cited as "Critical Reflections").

———. "The Revision of Canon Law: Theological Implications." *TS* 40 (1979), 593–679 (cited as "Revision of Canon Law").

———. "The Use of Vatican II Texts in the Draft *De Populo Dei.*" Huizing, P., and Walf, K. *The Revised Code of Canon Law: A Missed Opportunity? Con* 147 (1981), 45–53.

Howes, R. "Regional Pastor: Regional People." *The Priest* 36 (1980), 19–24.

Janicki, J. "Limited Term of Office and Retirement." *CLSAP* (1979), 39–59.

Jungmann, J. "Constitution on the Sacred Liturgy." *Commentary on the Documents of Vatican II.* H. Vorgrimler, ed. 5 vols. Freiburg: Herder, 1968. (Vol. I, 1–87.)

J 36 (1976), 1–245 (series of articles on the ecclesial understanding of *communio-koinonia*).

Kennedy, R. Commentary in *On Due Process.* (Washington: USCC, 1979).

———. "Experimental Parishes and the Law of the Church." *Dunwoodie Review* 12 (1972), 123–134.

———. "Shared Responsibility in Ecclesial Decision-Making." *Stud Can* 15 (1980), 5–23.

LaDue, W. "Structural Arrangements of the Parish." *J* 30 (1970), 314–327.

Lynch, J. "The Parochial Ministry in the New Code of Canon Law." *J* 42 (1982), 383–421 (cited as "Parochial Minstry").

McBrien, R. "A Theologian's View of the New Code." *Origins* 11 (1918), 431–456.

Marcuzzi, P.G. "Verso una nuova definizione giuridica di parrocchia." *Salesianum* 43 (1981), 831–844 (cited as "Verso una nuova definizione").

Morrisey, F. "The Importance of Particular Law." *Origins* 11 (1981), 421–430.

Mörsdorf, K. "Decree on the Bishop's Pastoral Office in the Church." *Commentary on the Documents of Vatican II*. H. Vorgrimler, ed. 5 vols. Freiburg: Herder, 1968. (Vol. II, 165–300.)

Nessel, W. "The National Parish Revisited." *J* 28 (1968), 82–92.

Neumann, J. "Election and Limitation of Term of Office in Canon Law." *Bishops and People*. A. Swidler and L. Swidler, eds. and trans. Philadelphia: The Westminster Press, 1970, 54–70.

NCE, 1st. ed., s.v. "Team Ministry," by R.A. Duffy; "Parish Councils," by T. Early; "Archpriest," by B. Forshaw; "Canon Law," by J. Lynch; "Rural Dean (Vicar Forane)," by P.W. Rice; "Parish," by C. Riege.

Pope Paul VI "Address to the Second International Congress of Canonists." *The Pope Speaks* 18 (1973), 275–283.

Potz, R. "Is the Language of the Draft Codex Intelligible and Contemporary?" *The Revised Code of Canon Law: A Missed Opportunity?* P. Huizing and K. Wolf, eds. *Con* 147. Edinburgh: T. and T. Clark, 1981, 82–87.

Provost, J. "Revising Canon Law: Where Do We Stand?" *America* 145 (1981), 277–278 (cited as "Revising Canon Law").

———. "Structuring the Community." *CS* 15 (1976), 269–280.

———. "The Working Together of Consultative Bodies—Great Expectations." *J* 40 (1980), 257–281 (cited as "Consultative Bodies").

Rodimer F. "Are Parish Councils on the Right Track?" *Origins* 6 (1977), 728–729.

USCC Task Force. "Identifying Women's Concerns." *Origins* (1976), 69–73.

Weakland, Rembert. "The Bishop and the Sacraments." *Origins* 12 (1982), 121–126.

Wulf, F. "Commentary on the Decree on the Ministry and Life of Priests." *Commentary on the Documents of Vatican II*. H. Vorgrimler, ed. 5 vols. Freiburg: Herder, 1968. (Vol. IV, 210–236; 267–287.)

Reference Works

Abbo, J., and Hannan, J. *The Sacred Canons*. 2 vols. St. Louis: Herder, 1962 (cited as Abbo-Hannan and volume).

Ayrinhac, H.A. *Constitution of the Church in the New Code of Canon Law*. 5 vols. New York: Longmans, Green and Company, 1930 (cited as Ayrinhac and volume).

Bouscaren, T.L., and Ellis, A. *Canon Law*. Milwaukee: The Bruce Publishing Co., 1960 (cited as Bouscaren-Ellis).

Bouscaren, T.L., and O'Connor, J.I. *Canon Law Digest*. 7 vols. Milwaukee and New York: Bruce, 1934–1969; Chicago: Province of Society of Jesus, 1975.

Dulles, A. *Models of the Church*. Garden City, New York: Doubleday, 1974.

Hertling, L. *Communio: Church and Papacy in Early Christianity*. Chicago: Loyola University, 1972 (cited as *Communio*).

Janicki, J. "Limited Term of Office for Pastors." J.C.L. dissertation, Catholic University of America, 1977.

NCCB. *As One Who Serves*. Washington: USCC, 1977.

———. *Fullness in Christ: A Report on the Study of Clergy Retirement*. Washington: USCC, 1979 (cited as *Fullness in Christ*).

Rademacher, W. *The Practical Guide for Parish Councils*. St. Meinrad, Ind.: Abbey Press, 1979.

Suenens, L. *Co-responsibility in the Church*. New York: Herder and Herder, 1968.

Teixeira, J. *Personnel Policies: A Canonical Commentary on Selected Current Clergy Personnel Policy in the United States of America*. CanLawStud 503. Washington: The Catholic University of America, 1981 (cited as *Personnel Policies*).

Wernz, F., and Vidal, P. *Ius Canonicum*. 7 vols. Rome: Apud Aedes Universitatis Gregorianae, 1928 (cited as Wernz-Vidal and volume).

Wojtyla, K. *Sources of Renewal—The Implementation of Vatican II*. New York: Harper & Row, 1980 (cited as *Sources of Renewal*).

Woywod, S., and Smith, C. *A Practical Commentary on the Code of Canon Law.* 2 vols. New York: Joseph F. Wagner, 1952 (cited as Woywod-Smith and volume).

Sources

CLSA. "Initial Report of Task Force Committee on the Draft of the Canons of Book Two: The People of God." Washington, June 13, 1978 (cited as Initial CLSA Report).

Comm 8 (1976), 23–31.

Comm 13 (1) (1982), 146–151.

Comm 13 (2) (1982), 271–314.

Pontificia Commissio Codici Iuris Canonici Recognoscendo. *Relatio.* Typis Polyglottis Vaticanis, 1981.

SCB. *Directory of the Pastoral Ministry of Bishops.* (English translation of May 31, 1973 official Latin text.) Ottawa: Canadian Catholic Conference, 1974 (cited as *Directory*).

SCDF. "Declaration on the Question of the Admission of Women to the Ministerial Priesthood." *Origins* 6 (1977), 517–524.

Schroeder, H.J. *Canons and Decrees of the Council of Trent.* (Original text with English translation.) St. Louis: Herder, 1950.

Part III
INSTITUTES OF CONSECRATED LIFE AND SOCIETIES OF APOSTOLIC LIFE
[cc. 573–746]

History

Within the history of the renewal of the Church called for by Vatican II and the renewal of church law begun by Pope John XXIII in 1959 is contained the renewal of the law for institutes of consecrated life and societies of apostolic life.

The promulgation of *Perfectae Caritatis* in 1965 initiated the process. The decree was implemented by the norms set forth in *Ecclesiae sanctae* in 1966 which called upon institutes to renew their life including their legislation. Thus updating constitutions and proper law was only one aspect of the larger goal of a renewal of life. Particular efforts were directed at renewing both formation in *Renovationis Causam* and institutes of cloistered nuns in *Venite Seorsum,* both in 1969, and then finally the evangelical witness of institutes in *Evangelica Testificatio* in 1971.

During the same period the Pontifical Commission for the Revision of the Code of Canon Law established principles to direct the revision of the Code, which needed to be made more precise to better fit the formulation of law for institutes and societies. Thus, the subcommission for institutes and societies developed four subprinciples to direct its work.[1]

The first was that the law should have both a spiritual and juridical foundation. The law should have a balance that recognizes that the spirit gives life to the law while at the same time clearly and precisely states rights and obligations.

Second, the law should foster the spirit of the founder or foundress and the specific character of each institute and society. Thus, the universal law should contain only general principles leaving the specifics to the law of the institute or society. The canons should avoid a "leveling off" while promoting the uniqueness of each institute or society.

Third, the canons should be flexible so that institutes and societies may easily adapt the general norms to the diverse situations and needs of the institute or society and the areas where they serve. Further, the law of the institute or society is to reflect this subsidiarity. Each is to establish constitutions which contain the fundamental norms of the institute or society along with lesser norms that can be easily changed and adapted to time, culture, apostolate, and locale.

Fourth, the canons regulating government should provide for the cooperation and representation of members in the governing process. The provision to establish chapters so that the entire institute or society is represented and allowing for a variety of organs of consultation are ways in which the canons fulfill this principle.

In addition, inequality of treatment between institutes or societies of men and women is to be avoided, except where necessary because of the nature of the matter or due to some particular situation.

The first draft of the law appeared in 1977[2] with its helpful introduction and was received as one of the sections of the law that was more than just a modification or adaptation of the 1917 Code.

The 1977 schema began with six preliminary canons which specified the essential elements of consecrated life both theologically and juridically. These fundamental norms were drawn primarily from *Lumen Gentium.* The greater part of the schema was composed of eighty-two canons which were common to all institutes. The schema concluded with a section on matters proper to individual institutes which was intended to explain and distinguish the various forms of consecration by means of public profession, which are recognized by the Church. It was divided into three sections: the first entitled religious institutes which was subdivided into monastic institutes (monks and nuns) and institutes dedicated to the works of the apostolate (canonical, conventual and apostolic); the second, institutes of associated apostolic life; and the third, secular institutes.

However, the organization of the draft and the lack of sufficient particulars stimulated objections which led to modifications in the 1980 draft. Specifically the section on matters proper to individual institutes was eliminated. New canons on general chapters and the apostolate of religious were added while other canons were made more specific. The 1983 Code, for the most part, follows the 1980 draft.

---

[1]ComCICRec, "Schema of Canons on Institutes of Life Consecrated by Profession of the Evangelical Counsels," USCC, 1977, 13–15.

[2]Id. for the full text of the 1977 schema in English.

Theology

The theology of the revised law is drawn from the gospel and Vatican II, often using conciliar wording in the text of canons. The foundation of the law is a call to follow Christ led by the Holy Spirit according to the gospel. The law recognizes that institutes and societies originate as a response to the Holy Spirit. Those who respond to the prompting of the Holy Spirit go to the Church which confirms the response. One aspect of this confirmation is to present to the institute or society a certain ordering of the gifts in the form of law which is based on the experience of the Church. This ordering in law is intended to enhance rather than restrict the gift. Over the years the law changes to better take account of the work of the Spirit.

The canons are permeated by evangelical terminology with over forty references to Christ, the Lord, God, the Holy Spirit, the gospel and the Kingdom of God which reflects the gospel theology and spirituality of the law.[3] In addition, spread throughout the canons are spiritual exhortations that provide a gospel atmosphere and spirit to the law.

Structure

Part III of Book II on the people of God is entitled "Institutes of Consecrated Life and Societies of Apostolic Life." These terms describe all those who commit themselves to live the evangelical counsels in an institute or society approved by the Church. This structure reflects the inclusion of institutes and societies first as members of the people of God with a special calling within their vocation as Christians.

Part III is divided into two sections. Section I is entitled "Institutes of Consecrated Life" and section II "Societies of Apostolic Life." Section I is divided into three titles: title I contains the common norms for all institutes of consecrated life; title II, those for religious institutes; and title III, those for secular institutes. In addition, the canons on secular institutes apply fourteen of the canons on religious institutes to secular institutes and the canons on societies of apostolic life apply twenty-one of the common norms and forty-six of the canons on religious institutes to societies of apostolic life.

There are fewer total canons in the revised law. Some matters such as dowry and studies in clerical institutes are omitted. Other canons are less detailed than in the 1917 Code since they simply call for the institute or society to legislate in a particular area while additional canons are an invitation to develop proper law although they do so without spe-

cifically stating it. There are about one hundred matters that are specifically left to the constitutions or proper law of institutes and societies. This reflects the intent of the law to transfer the primary focus for legislation from the universal law to institutes and societies.

Characteristics

The revised law acknowledges that consecrated life is a gift of the Holy Spirit to the Church and in leaving the preponderance of legislative work to institutes and societies, it recognizes that the Vatican II directive to return to the spirit of the founder or foundress and to renew and adapt in accord with that spirit will be accomplished most appropriately within the institute or society.

The revised law also transfers to the institute or society authority that was previously reserved to the Apostolic See such as granting exclaustration[4] or dividing an institute or society into parts.[5]

The law recognizes that the institutes and societies have a proper autonomy of life especially regarding the internal life of the institute or society while at the same time understands that institutes and societies are part of the Church and subject to church authority. The canons foster dialogue between bishops and institutes and societies to aid them to better serve the people of God.

Members of religious institutes are to profess their commitment by means of vows while secular institutes may use other sacred bonds. In addition, the 1983 Code omits the distinction between solemn vows and simple perpetual vows since the law uses only the term perpetual vows.

Consecrated life now includes hermits who profess the evangelical counsels by vow or other sacred bond and virgins who are consecrated to God. In addition, bishops are to strive to discern new gifts of consecrated life that may not fall into the categories although approval of new forms of consecrated life is reserved to the Apostolic See.

Conclusion

A revised church law and new constitutions and proper law are not guarantees of renewal. As the Fathers of Vatican II noted, institutes and societies must honestly face the fact that the most desirable changes, including church law and proper law, will fail to achieve their purposes unless a renewal of spirit gives life to the changes. In fact, interior renewal must always be accorded a leading role in order to bear fruit in the visible life of institutes and societies.

[3]The 1917 Code had only a few similar references.

[4]C. 686.
[5]C. 581.

It should be recognized that no law is perfect. Some of the important questions are not answered by the revised law, if indeed those questions are capable of legal resolution. The law is always open ended in the sense that experience will show what lies ahead for its proper understanding and development. With this in mind the imperfections that remain form the agenda for the coming years in the ongoing response of institutes and societies to the Spirit of God.

Section I: INSTITUTES OF CONSECRATED LIFE
[cc. 573–730]

TITLE I
NORMS COMMON TO ALL INSTITUTES OF CONSECRATED LIFE
[cc. 573–606]

These initial canons regulating institutes of consecrated life are unique since they apply equally to religious and to secular institutes. Their terminology is general, avoiding expressions historically associated with religious life as such. The body of norms in title I must be supplemented by the particular canons of titles II or III for religious or secular institutes respectively. Further, these common norms will be considered basic for newly emerging forms of consecrated life (cf. c. 605).

The section as a whole is of critical theological importance, resting heavily on texts from the Second Vatican Council.[1] The concrete use of certain theological or pastoral texts should be understood as pointing to the fuller theology provided by these documents as a background for the law, rather than as a selection of specific texts to be used juridically.

Besides the key theological canons (cc. 573–578), this introductory section presents the general juridical principles governing the erection, division,

union, and suppression of institutes (cc. 579–585), their governmental autonomy and proper law (cc. 586–587), various types of institutes and their relationship to ecclesial authority (cc. 588–595), the authority of superiors and chapters (c. 596), general requirements for admission (c. 597), and essential norms for the observance of the evangelical counsels and the life of the institute (cc. 598–602). Entirely new to the law are the canons recognizing the eremetical life (c. 603), the order of virgins (c. 604), and provision for the emergence of new forms of consecrated life (c. 605). The final canon of title I repeats the 1917 Code's provision for the greatest possible equality of treatment between institutes of men and women (c. 606).

The draft of the revised law circulated in 1977 contained a much larger section of common norms. There were, at that time, seven titles which included eighty-eight canons. This was an attempt to emphasize in the structure of the law the essential unity of the consecrated life that lies beneath the diversity of the religious and secular charisms. It proved difficult, however, to speak of such topics as temporal goods, incorporation, and separation in ways which fully preserved the integrity of both religious and secular institutes. Furthermore, those critiquing the draft were not satisfied.

The subsequent draft preserved the principle of norms common to all institutes of consecrated life but in a much abbreviated form. This dimension of the law's structure is a significant change from the 1917 Code which was structured to reflect religious life only.

---

[1]In particular, *PC* and *LG* VI.

Canon 573 — §1. **Life consecrated by the profession of the evangelical counsels is a stable form of living by which faithful, following Christ more closely under the action of the Holy Spirit, are totally dedicated to God who is loved most of all, so that, having dedicated themselves to His honor, the upbuilding of the Church and the salvation of the world by a new and special title, they strive for the perfection of charity in service to the Kingdom of God and, having become an outstanding sign in the Church, they may foretell the heavenly glory.**

§2. Christian faithful who profess the evangelical counsels of chastity, poverty and obedience by vows or other sacred bonds according to the proper laws of institutes freely assume this form of living in institutes of consecrated life canonically erected by competent church authority and through the charity to which these counsels lead they are joined to the Church and its mystery in a special way.

Canon 573 stands as a capstone upon which this section of the law is built. Above all it seeks to give a comprehensive description of the consecrated life which will be regulated by the subsequent canons. It is, fundamentally, a life consecrated through profession of the evangelical counsels. In harmony with the Council's emphasis on the radical consecration of every Christian in baptism,[2] the canon notes that this is a dedication by a new and special title. This new and special consecration is rooted in, and more fully expresses, that of baptism.[3] It may be seen as a further specification of the Christian vocation.

The canon also notes that this new step in the Christian life is a vocation—a life entered under the influence of the Holy Spirit. This concept of divine calling has long been taught by the Church, but it did not appear in the 1917 Code's treatment of religious life.[4] This was largely due to the fact that vocation was considered to be a theological or spiritual concept, not a juridical one. The commission rewriting this section of the law, however, committed itself to the principle of writing juridic norms which would "promote God's gift of a divine calling, assist the work of grace in souls dedicated to God so that they may attain the perfection of charity . . . ."[5] In a word, the commission would attempt an intermingling of the spiritual and the juridical.[6]

It is clear from this initial canon that the law is concerned with a permanent way of life. In an era of instability and transitoriness, the new canons speak of what has traditionally been called a "state of life" (*CIC* 487). There are, of course, a wide variety of kinds of associations in which the faithful may seek their own spiritual advancement and work for the accomplishment of diverse works of charity and piety.[7] These, however, require no permanent commitment of one's total life and being. Life consecrated through profession of the evangelical counsels demands precisely that.

When the canon speaks of this life as a closer following of Christ, it echoes the Council's sentiment when it spoke of following with greater liberty and imitating Christ more closely.[8] Further, the concept speaks of a new and deeper insertion into the paschal mystery of Christ—an insertion begun radically at baptism. By sacrament, the Christian is baptized into Christ, entering His redemptive dying and rising. Religious profession has long been viewed in the Church as a sort of second baptism, an entering more profoundly into Christ's dying and rising, and so an entering into a more radical identification with Him. In professing a life of evangelical poverty, chastity, and obedience, the consecrated Christian—either religious or secular—takes up this closer following.

All of this, the canon recognizes, is motivated by charity. Love of God is supreme and total, yet simultaneously linked with the love which is expressed in prayer for and service of others. The life of consecration is seen as honoring God and furthering the mission of the Church. The terminology of perfection of charity is frequently avoided today. There is a concern that it could suggest a pride quite unsuitable to Christians. At root, however, the canon deals with the fundamental law of the gospel which requires of every Christian a constant growth in the twofold love of God and others. As they pursue this in their lives of poverty, chastity, and obedience, the members of institutes of consecrated life become signs of the life to come. The de-

---

[2]*LG* 10, *AA* 3.
[3]*LG* 44, *PC* 5.
[4]*CIC* 538 speaks of admitting persons of right intention.
[5]*Comm* 2 (1970), 170.

[6]This approach was criticized by those convinced that the law's expression should be more exclusively juridical, e.g., J.F. Gallen, "The Proposed Spiritual Canons," *RfR* 37 (1978), 294–302.
[7]Book II, part I, title V, "Associations of the Christian Faithful."
[8]*PC* 1.

gree of this eschatological witness will vary according to the nature of the institute.

The second paragraph of the canon specifies the context in which this life is lived. With the exception of canons 603 and 604 on hermits and the order of virgins, respectively, the law is concerned with institutes erected by the competent ecclesial authority. This initial canon emphasizes the historical fact that consecrated life is born of the Spirit and has been approved by church leadership throughout the centuries, under the inspiration of the same Spirit. The dynamic of consecrated life is seen as an integral part of church life. Within the experience of each foundation, the fundamental charism has been received and has evolved; constitutions and statutes based upon that lived charism have been presented to the Church for approval, rather than the Church's first having developed norms by which the institutes must organize. This principle is important to understanding the revised laws great emphasis on the proper law of the institute.

Since the Council, that proper law has been under revision and is the instrument through which each institute receives its initial or continued approbation from the Church. The canon also stresses another link between members of institutes and the Church. The charity which is fostered by a life of the counsels links them to the mystery of the Church.

Because the canon applies to all institutes of consecrated life, it speaks of both vows and other sacred bonds. The evangelical counsels are the same: poverty, chastity, and obedience; the bonds by which they are undertaken vary according to the kind of institute and its proper law.

The enumeration of the three traditional counsels recognizes these as essential aspects of Christ's own total self-oblation. Since this offering is one and integral in consecration, it remains true that some institutes may actually pronounce fewer or more vows or other bonds. Nevertheless, the totality of their gift, given according to the approved proper law, includes the same three dimensions. Additional specific vows, in accordance with an institute's charism and legitimate heritage, may be defined in proper law.

Canon 574 — §1. The state of those who profess the evangelical counsels in institutes of this kind pertains to the life and sanctity of the Church and for this reason is to be fostered and promoted by all in the Church.

§2. Certain Christian faithful are specially called to this state by God so that they may enjoy a special gift in the life of the Church and contribute to its salvific mission according to the purpose and spirit of the institute.

The place within the Church of those who live this consecrated life is expressed in the terminology of the Council. They are not living some state between clergy and laity within the hierarchical structure of the Church. Rather, both clergy and laity may be given this gift of grace in the Church's life and contribute in their own way to the Church's mission.[9] This is consistent with the principle that consecrated life grew up within the Church, not as a part of the structure but as a gift of the Spirit within that structure. This gives institutes a certain freedom and autonomy within the Church similar to that of an individual family.

In the second paragraph of the canon the doctrine of charism is linked with the gift of vocation to a particular institute. According to its founding spirit, each institute serves the mission of the Church in a particular way. Throughout the centuries, diverse kinds of institutes have been raised up by the Spirit: the monastic, the mendicants, institutes of simple vows dedicated to a wide variety of works, missionary societies, and secular institutes.

Canon 575 — The evangelical counsels, based on the teaching and examples of Christ the Teacher, are a divine gift which the Church has received from the Lord and always preserves through His grace.

The counsels themselves are viewed as gifts of Christ to the Church—based as they are on His own life and teaching.[10] While a reading of the gospel can yield many other counsels given by Jesus to His followers, a deeper reflection on the attitude of His own consecration in the paschal mystery[11] and on the long evolution of consecrated life under the guidance of the Spirit in the Church gives deeper insight into the particular relevance of these three counsels in expressing the total consecration of life. A life of radical following of Christ is intimately caught up in His own total love of the Father and total dependence and trust which ultimately led to an obedience even unto death.[12] Total commitment to the way of Christ in the paschal mystery involves all gospel values and all counsels of the Lord.[13]

Canon 576 — It belongs to the competent authority of the Church to interpret the evangelical counsels, to regulate their practice by laws, to constitute therefrom stable forms of living by canoni-

[9]*LG* 43.
[10]*LG* 43, *PC* 1.
[11]Jn 17, 18–19.
[12]Phil 2, 8.
[13]The 1917 Code singled out these traditional counsels (*CIC* 487) without commenting on their source; without explicit statement, it assumed the Church's right and responsibility to legislate.

cal approbation, and, for its part, to take care that the institutes grow and flourish according to the spirit of the founders and wholesome traditions.

The Church's responsibility with regard to the evangelical counsels exists precisely because the life of the counsels is a charism, a gift of the Spirit to and for the Church. The modality in which the counsels are lived varies according to the nature of diverse institutes. These ways are examined and approved by the Church, thereby designating institutes in which the faithful, so drawn by the grace of vocation, can enter securely on a path of following Christ more closely. The specific areas of church authority are outlined: (1) to interpret the evangelical counsels; (2) to regulate the practice of the counsels by legislation; (3) to establish stable forms of life by canonical approval; and (4) to see that these institutes develop and flourish according to the spirit of their founder or foundress, and their sound traditions.

The Church's role in establishing institutes of consecrated life is normally by way of approval of a founding charism, although certain institutes have grown out of needs perceived by church authority. The responsibility to maintain this form of life means that the Church has the duty to point out to an institute when its way of life seems to have drifted outside the gospel or its own particular charism. This is to be accomplished by church authority without blocking the growth and development of the charism of the institute from within.[14] This in no way diminishes the primary responsibility of the members of an institute for their own fidelity. Rather it focuses the universal nature of the Spirit's gifts to the Church.

Canon 577 — **In the Church there are very many institutes of consecrated life which have different gifts according to the grace which has been given them: they follow Christ more closely as He prays, announces the Kingdom of God, performs good works for people, shares His life with them in the world, and yet always does the will of the Father.**

The notion of the diverse charisms of institutes, given in broad strokes, is based essentially on the Council.[15] However, the notion of Christ remaining with people in the world was added to the conciliar text to give clearer reference to the nature of the secular institutes. Each charism expresses a particularly nuanced way of following Christ in fulfillment of the Father's will, whether by lives wholly dedicated to contemplation (c. 674), to diverse apostolic ministries and charitable works (c. 675), or to the less visible apostolate of consecrated secularity lived in the midst of others (c. 710).

Canon 578 — **The intention of the founders and their determination concerning the nature, purpose, spirit and character of the institute which have been ratified by competent ecclesiastical authority as well as its wholesome traditions, all of which constitute the patrimony of the institute itself, are to be observed faithfully by all.**

The Council's call for religious renewal stressed a return by each institute to its spiritual patrimony.[16] For many, this has meant a profound new study of the life and writings of a founder or foundress, within his or her own historical context. The heritage which unfolds from this kind of research usually reveals the general nature of the institute (i.e., religious or secular), an emphasis in apostolate (e.g., contemplation, education, health care, service to the poor), an orientation of spirituality (e.g., Franciscan, Teresian, Ignatian, Alphonsian), and an organizational principle (e.g., centralization, autonomy of houses). Experience has shown that this is both difficult and rewarding; it is a labor which does not yield clear-cut answers, once and for all.

In the course of history, it is possible that an original founding intention was not faithfully reflected in the type of approbation granted at a given time.[17] It is also possible that in the course of time, changes occurred which called for reexamination in the light of the founding charism and the general nature of the institute. Nevertheless, legitimate evolution in fidelity to an institute's heritage would rarely call for a radical change of identification within the general types of institutes (e.g., a change from religious to secular institute).

An important part of the process of studying an institute's heritage and making contemporary adaptations is the writing of constitutions and the related documents of proper law (c. 587). These, in all aspects, must be informed by the institute's spiritual heritage; according to these constitutions, members make their profession of the evangelical counsels.

Erection and Suppression

The group of canons which follows (cc. 579–585) provides for the erection, structural organization, and suppression of institutes. The principle of subsidiarity has clearly been applied in granting greater autonomy to the internal authority of institutes. Nevertheless, the broad responsibility of the Church ,with regard to consecrated life is exercised at critical moments such as initial erection or final suppression of an institute. Further, in decisions which affect the very identity and autonomy of an institute such as certain kinds of mergers or unions,

---

[14]*LG* 43, 45.
[15]*LG* 46.

[16]*PC* 2.
[17]Secular institutes were not formally recognized as a distinct form of consecrated life in the Church until 1947.

reservation to the Holy See better guarantees the rights of individual members as well as justice and equity in the disposition of temporal goods.

Canon 579 — Diocesan bishops each in his own territory can erect institutes of consecrated life by a formal decree, provided that the Apostolic See has been consulted.

Ordinary procedure over the years has been that a new institute begins its life in a diocese quite informally. In time, it is erected as a pious union or association (cc. 298–329), until such time as its numbers and situation suggest sufficient stability for further approbation. The approval of a pious union and its statutes is within the authority of the diocesan bishop for a group within his territory, without previous permission from the Holy See. It is then his responsibility to continue to follow the life and work of such an association and to provide it assistance in the development of statutes. The local vicar for religious often provides this ongoing assistance. Such groups are technically subject to the canons for associations of the faithful, but they may develop and seek approval of statutes which closely resemble the constitutions of a religious or secular institute in preparation for the desired future status.

It is the erection as a diocesan institute which requires previous consultation with the Holy See. When the *nihil obstat* has been received from the Sacred Congregation for Religious and Secular Institutes, the diocesan bishop issues a Decree of Erection. The Church's regard for the life of the counsels encourages bishops to be alert to, and supportive of, new gifts of the Spirit, even in terms of new forms of consecrated life (c. 605), but it is also wary of a proliferation of institutes which might have the same purpose or end.[18] From time to time, the Sacred Congregation for Religious and Secular Institutes publishes guidelines for those seeking erection as institutes of consecrated life, indicating those documents which must be submitted with the bishop's request for the *nihil obstat* to proceed.[19]

Canon 580 — The aggregation of one institute of consecrated life to another is reserved to the competent authority of the aggregating institute, always safeguarding the canonical autonomy of the aggregated institute.

This canon on aggregation deals specifically with an affiliation between two institutes of consecrated

life, both of which remain distinct and autonomous.[20] The competent authority here is that of the aggregating institute, respecting the canonical autonomy of the institute aggregated. This does not mean, however, that the aggregating institute has jurisdiction over the aggregated institute.

Aggregation is a way in which institutes of common spirit may be more closely bonded; for example, related religious institutes of men and of women have often been referred to as first, second, and third orders. Similarly, there could be the aggregation of a religious institute and a secular institute of the same spirituality, even though they remain autonomous and distinct in the nature of their particular vocation.

Canon 581 — Dividing an institute into parts, whatever the parts are called, erecting new ones, joining previously erected parts or defining them in another way pertains to the competent authority of the institute, in accord with the norm of the constitutions.

The law of the Church now gives full authority to each institute for deciding internal, structural changes: division into parts (e.g., provinces,[21] regions), erection of new parts, fusion of existing parts, or the realignment of boundaries. Suppression of parts is governed according to canon 585. The principle of subsidiarity is evident from the fact that all of these determinations in pontifical institutes were reserved previously to the Holy See (*CIC* 494, §1).[22] It is significant, however, that the designation of the competent authority of the institute is to be placed in the constitutions, rather than any other part of proper law.

Some religious institutes have reserved this authority to the general chapter. However, others have found it more effective to assign this to the general council which meets more frequently and may be expected to be better informed on the affairs and well-being of the institute as a whole.

Canon 582 — Mergers and unions of institutes of consecrated life are reserved to the Apostolic See alone; confederations and federations are also reserved to it.

Mergers and unions, federations and confederations are all reserved to the Apostolic See. This res-

---

[18]The 1917 Code's prohibition against a new institute assuming the name or habit of an institute already established *(CIC 492, §3)* is not repeated in the revised law, although its principle remains sound. In actual practice many institutes are distinguished from one another by the use of a place name in their official title.

[19]*ComRelMiss* 52 (1971), 191; *CLD* 7, 458.

[20]The special relationship between some institutes of consecrated life and certain other types of association is referred to in cc. 677 and 725. This kind of aggregation was also the focus of *CIC* 492, §1.

[21]Provinces in religious institutes are defined in c. 621.

[22]The SCRIS decree *Ad instituenda experimenta* gave the general chapter of pontifical religious institutes, within their own law, the authority to reunite existing provinces or otherwise change their boundaries, to erect new provinces, or to suppress others. *AAS* 62 (1970), 549–550.

ervation avoids the complications which can arise in cases in which several bishops and institutes are involved. The practice of the Sacred Congregation for Religious and Secular Institutes illustrates at least two types of merger—the term "union" sometimes being used interchangeably: (a) a smaller institute merges with a larger, the former becoming extinct; and (b) two or more institutes merge, forming an entirely new institute.[23] This latter form calls for new constitutions and new elections. In each case of a merger or union between institutes, the details must be spelled out clearly and there must be careful spiritual, psychological, and juridical preparation. Individual members of institutes entering a merger must be allowed to freely choose to belong to the new entity, to seek transfer to another institute, or to request dispensation from their sacred bonds. Part of each merger agreement must also provide for the disposition of temporalities within the norms of universal and proper law. The Council suggested that such mergers might take place when there seems to be no reasonable hope for growth and development of an institute.[24]

Federations and confederations are moral unions in which each institute keeps its identity and juridical autonomy. In such a coming together, institutes which share a common heritage may join in common research and study of their charism and spirituality. The statutes of such affiliations do not touch upon the internal governance of any member institute.

With regard to federations of monasteries of nuns of the same order, the 1950 constitution *Sponsa Christi* stated: "the principal end is fraternal help, not only in fostering the religious spirit and regular monastic discipline, but also advancing economic matters."[25] Contemporary federations such as the Federation of the Sisters of St. Joseph have made great contributions toward a study of their common heritage and to a sense of unity among the members of many autonomous congregations of St. Joseph Sisters.

Canon 583 — Changes in institutes of consecrated life which affect matters which have been approved by the Apostolic See cannot be made without its permission.

Once erected and approved by the competent church authority, an institute of consecrated life is an ecclesial entity, with particular accountability to the erecting authority. The canon enunciates the basic principle of competency: the authority approving an action or making a law has the competency for changing or dispensing from the same.

This principle is clearly applied with regard to the authority competent to approve constitutions and to authorize change in them (c. 587, §2). Canons 593 and 594 further develop the relationship between ecclesiastical authority and pontifical and diocesan institutes respectively.

Canon 584 — Suppressing an institute pertains to the Apostolic See alone, to whom also it is reserved to determine what is to be done with the temporal goods of the institute.

As is the case of mergers and unions (c. 582), the complete suppression of any institute and the disposition of its temporal goods are reserved to the Holy See. Similarly there must be great care for the individuals involved.

Canon 585 — Suppressing parts of an institute pertains to the competent authority of the institute itself.

The suppression of parts of an institute is within the competency of its internal authority and must be provided for in proper law. In view of the provisions of canon 581, it would seem wise to provide for the suppression of parts such as provinces or regions in the same section of the proper law which provides for their erection and realignment. Canon 616 gives further directives for the suppression of religious houses.

Canon 586 — §1. For individual institutes there is acknowledged a rightful autonomy of life, especially of governance, by which they enjoy their own discipline in the Church and have the power to preserve their own patrimony intact as mentioned in can. 578.

§2. It belongs to local ordinaries to safeguard and protect this autonomy.

In harmony with the Council's expressed respect for diverse charisms, the revised law affirms the right of each institute to its own autonomy—especially with regard to governance. This internal autonomy was first officially recognized for religious congregations of simple vows by Pope Leo XIII in *Conditae a Christo* (1900)[26] and for secular institutes by Pope Pius XII with *Provida Mater Ecclesia* (1947).[27] This autonomy assures, for example, that the competent authority of the institute receives new members, admits to profession or incorporation, receives sacred bonds, gives apostolic assignments, and supervises the administration of goods.[28]

---

[23] *CLD* 8, 324; *ComRelMiss* 55 (1974), 87*fn*3.
[24] *PC* 21; *ES* II, 39–40. The parallel canon in the 1917 Code (*CIC* 494, §1) envisioned unions of monasteries as monastic congregations.
[25] *AAS* 43 (1951), 19–20.

[26] *CICFontes* III, 562.
[27] *AAS* 39 (1947), 14–24.
[28] Although the 1917 Code warned against the interference of the local ordinary in the internal affairs of a pontifical institute, it singled out numerous areas for his vigilance over lay institutes (*CIC* 618, §2, 2°).

The appropriate balance between the spheres of authority of diocesan bishops and major moderators of institutes of consecrated life was called for in both earlier documents and occurs frequently throughout the revised law. Canons 593 and 594 refer back to the principle of autonomy when speaking of the Apostolic See and the diocesan bishop in relationship to pontifical and diocesan institutes respectively.

Besides governance, the particular discipline and heritage of each institute, referred to in canon 578, are to be respected, protected, and fostered by the bishops. A particularly significant sphere in which the respective authority of bishops and of religious superiors intersect is that of apostolate within the local church. Canons 678–683 give guidelines for collaboration in these matters. Both collaboration and the rightful autonomy of each institute were given emphasis in the 1978 document "Directives for the Mutual Relations between Bishops and Religious in the Church."[29] The role of the bishop, expressed in the canon's second paragraph, is further developed in the document:

> Bishops, along with their clergy, should be convinced advocates of the consecrated life, defenders of religious communities, promoters of vocations, firm guardians of the specific character of each religious family both in the spiritual and in the apostolic field (no. 28).

Canon 587 — **§1. In order to protect more faithfully the particular vocation and identity of each institute, its fundamental code or constitutions must contain, besides what must be observed according to can. 578, fundamental norms about the governance of the institute and the discipline of members, the incorporation and formation of members, and the proper object of sacred bonds.**

§2. A code of this kind is approved by the competent authority of the Church and can be changed only with its consent.

§3. In this code spiritual and juridical elements are to be suitably joined together; however norms are not to be multiplied unless it is necessary.

§4. Other norms established by the competent authority of the institute are to be suitably collected in other codes, which can moreover be fittingly reviewed and adapted according to the needs of places and times.

In speaking of institutes of consecrated life, the canons consistently employ two terms in reference to the law which is specific to each institute. The more general term, proper law (*ius proprium*), includes the institute's fundamental code or constitutions and any other supplementary collections of norms or statutes by which a given institute is governed or ordered. The names of these books vary from institute to institute; that book which corresponds to the matter described in canon 587, §1 is intended whenever the universal law uses the term constitutions.[30]

The first paragraph of the canon gives a broad outline of the contents of each institute's fundamental code, or constitutions.[31] Of prime importance are the expression and preservation of that unique patrimony which characterizes each institute (cf. c. 578). In the other expressions of fundamental norms, those which are essential to the institute as religious or secular in general as well as those which characterize its particular spirit, nature and end must be included.

With regard to governance, an institute's basic structures must be outlined: general chapter or its equivalent; major moderators, their authority, and terms; councils and their key roles in decision-making; intermediate structures if they exist; and essential provisions for local governance in the case of religious institutes. Optional structures of participation in governance such as advisory bodies may well be left to supplementary documents which are more readily changed. In general, structures and areas of competency which are called for in universal law should be provided for and protected by inclusion in the fundamental code of the institute. Sometimes this is handled by reference to the observance of canonical norms, without a repetition of the canons in the text. An appendix of pertinent canons may be attached to the constitutions for convenience and clarity.

In matters of formation, each stage should be mentioned, with its purpose, minimum and maximum lengths, and a statement of who has the authority to admit or dismiss from each stage. Greater detail must be present regarding the religious novitiate and the equivalent time of probation in secular institutes. This is because of their key importance and the canonical requirements for validity. Less detail need be included of pre-novitiate programs since canon law requires only that there be suitable preparation before admission (c. 597, §2). The rights and obligations which accompany each stage of formation should be made clear.

The way in which incorporation takes place in

---

[29]*AAS* 70 (1978), 473–506.

[30]Although the term particular law technically is used, in contrast to universal law, to designate the law governing a particular local church, the term sometimes appears in translations and commentaries in place of *ius proprium*.

[31]Following the recognition of institutes of simple religious vows, a set of norms was published which included a specific outline to be followed in preparing constitutions: "Normae 28 iunii 1901," in P.T. Schaefer, *De Religiosis*, Rome, 1947, 1102–1135. Following the 1917 Code, another set of norms, without detailed outline, was published to assist new institutes in preparing constitutions adapted to the Code. *AAS* 13 (1921), 312–319. Following the Council, the Church deliberately urged religious to proceed with their revision, without awaiting the publication of the revised universal law.

the institutes must be specified: who admits, the kind of bonds used, the minimum and maximum lengths of temporary incorporation, the rights and obligations attached. The inclusion of these matters is important, not only because of canonical requirements but in justice to prospective members.

Similarly the constitutions must contain the essential elements of the religious or secular life-style of the institute, the particular way of observing the counsels (cf. c. 598, §1), and key elements of the spiritual life. Constitutions must also contain provision for the handling of temporalities and of separation from the institute.

This principal code, as paragraph two of the canon notes, is the instrument through which an institute's existence and role in the Church are given formal approbation. This approbation says to members and prospective members that the spirituality described in the constitutions is according to church teaching, that the authority contained in them is recognized by the Church, and that the apostolic works outlined in them are mandated by the Church. The authority which grants this formal approbation is the Apostolic See in the case of pontifical institutes and the diocesan bishop in the case of diocesan institutes (c. 589).

Since Vatican II, virtually all approved religious institutes have been engaged in the revision of constitutions called for by *Perfectae Caritatis* (no. 3) and *Ecclesiae sanctae* (II, 6). The general principle was that this work would be completed by the second regular chapter following the special renewal chapter. In many cases this work took longer than was originally intended and extensions of time were granted. When submitting documents for this renewed approbation, both the fundamental code and supplementary documents—following the general chapter's approval of texts—had to be submitted so that an overview of the institute and its law could be seen. In the future, only changes in the fundamental code will require approval from the competent ecclesial authority, following a request from the general chapter, usually with a two-thirds vote.

The third paragraph of the canon calls for the difficult blending of spiritual and juridical norms within the constitutions. Thus, for example, the same document will contain the spiritual principle of servant leadership and the juridical requirements for valid elections of the superior. In dealing with the counsels there will be expressions of the gospel inspiration for following Jesus Who was poor, chaste, and obedient as well as the juridical requirements which flow from permanently undertaking the life of these counsels by sacred bonds. Stylistically this is difficult, but a purely spiritual document would not adequately constitute proper law, and a purely juridical expression would not be faithful to the spiritual renewal initiated by the Council.

The supplementary collections of norms and pol-

icies referred to in the canon's fourth paragraph are subject to the competent bodies or persons within the institute. This does not imply, however, that these codes—dealing, for example, with particulars of entrance, formation, finances, and elections—are less a part of the institute's proper law, or that they are not similarly binding as long as they are in effect. According to their nature, these codes may be changed by the general chapter, provincial chapter, or the bodies or persons responsible for making such statutes, policies, or procedures. The competent authority and the required vote for making changes should be stated in their text.

Within the 1917 Code, there was explicit reference to the effect the revised universal law would have on existing rules and constitutions. Contrary matter was abrogated (*CIC* 489). There is no such special canon in the 1983 law, although essentially the same provision regarding contrary matter is in canon 6. Since constitutions of many congregations, at the time of promulgation, did not have definitive approbation, there was time to adjust to the revised norms. In cases in which definitive approbation was already granted, a subsequent chapter would have to deal with any discrepancies. (Note: Provision for interim solutions was provided in a decree from the Sacred Congregation for Religious and Secular Institutes [Feb. 2, 1984]. This allowed supreme moderators, acting collegially with their councils, to define matters of great importance if the constitutions had lacunae due to the revised Code. *Informationes,* [Dec., 1983], 115–116; also in *Origins* 13 [1984], 602).

Canon 588 — §1. The state of consecrated life by its very nature is neither clerical nor lay.

§2. An institute is said to be clerical if, by reason of the purpose or design intended by its founder or in virtue of legitimate tradition, it is under the supervision of clerics, it assumes the exercise of sacred orders, and it is recognized as such by church authority.

§3. An institute is called lay if recognized as such by church authority, by virtue of its nature, character and purpose it has a proper function defined by the founder or by legitimate tradition which does not include the exercise of sacred orders.

That institutes, by nature, are neither clerical nor lay is a new principle in the law, and the definitions of those two types of institutes are new. In the 1917 Code, a numerical dominance of priest members was the criterion given to determine that an institute was clerical (*CIC* 488, 4°). In the present canon, an institute is clerical when, by reason of the purpose or aim intended by the founder, or in virtue of legitimate tradition, three characteristics are simultaneously present: it is under the direction of clerics, takes up the exercise of sacred orders, and is recognized as clerical by the authority of the Church. Again, reverence for the intention of the founder and the legitimate traditions of institutes are evidenced, combined with the recognition of the Church.

There is an effort in the third paragraph of the canon to give a positive definition to the lay institutes, rather than the customary formula "otherwise, it is lay." Again, the intent of the founder or foundress is mentioned as is that portion of the Church's mission which is the institute's rightful function according to approbation by the Church. This function, however, characteristically does not include the exercise of sacred orders.

These provisions do not negate the permission which has been given to institutes with both clerical and lay members, to grant lay members certain administrative roles. However, it seems to leave in place the prohibition against lay members of clerical institutes holding moderators' offices without special permission.[32] Similarly, it does not alter the provision which has been made for congregations of brothers to put forth certain of their members for the reception of orders, particularly in service of their own institute's need of ministerial priesthood.[33]

The significance of distinguishing clerical and lay institutes arises in other parts of the law, particularly with reference to participation in ecclesial governance (c. 596, §2). The canon's reference to the intent of the founder could urge some institutes to examine under which title they have sought approbation from the Church.

Relationship to Ecclesiastical Authority

Canons 589–595 further explore the relationship between institutes of consecrated life and ecclesiastical authority. The special position of these institutes in the Church has already been noted in earlier theological canons: by means of a new and special title, members are given over to the building up of the Church (c. 573, §1); they are associated with the Church and its mystery in a special way through charity (c. 573, §2); by their state, they pertain to the life and holiness of the Church (c. 574, §1); and they possess a special gift in and for the Church (c. 574, §2).

In more juridic terminology, the subsequent canons indicate the following: the authority having competency (c. 589), the special obedience due the Sovereign Pontiff (c. 590), the institute of exemption (c. 591), the necessity of periodic reports (c. 592), and the parameters of ecclesial authority (cc. 593–594) with respect to the autonomy of institutes (c. 586).

Canon 589 — **An institute of consecrated life is said to be of pontifical right if it has been erected by the Apostolic See or approved by a formal decree of the Apostolic See; on the other hand an institute is said to be of diocesan right if, after having been erected by a diocesan bishop, it has not obtained a decree of approval from the Apostolic See.**

Essentially it is the erection or formal approbation of an institute which establishes it as pontifical or diocesan. An institute may, after establishment as a diocesan institute (c. 579), later seek recognition as a pontifical institute. Normally this takes place after considerable growth and the spread of the institute into various dioceses. Some institutes, however, choose to remain diocesan.[34]

Canon 590 — **§1. Institutes of consecrated life, inasmuch as they are dedicated in a special way to the service of God and of the entire Church, are subject to the supreme authority of this same Church in a special manner.**
§2. Individual members are also bound to obey the Supreme Pontiff as their highest superior by reason of the sacred bond of obedience.

In expressing institutes' special relationship to the Holy Father, the present canon expands the comparable canon from the 1917 Code (*CIC* 499, §1). Not only do members, by virtue of their vow, owe obedience to the Sovereign Pontiff, but institutes as well, being juridic persons in the Church, are uniquely subject to his authority. The expression of rationale provided in paragraph one of the canon is also new in the law[35] and recalls the ecclesial dimensions of this life so frequently mentioned in the canons.

It may be noted that the matter of this canon is quite different from the preceding and later canons which parallel the authority of the Apostolic See and the diocesan bishop for respective types of institutes. There is no parallel statement here regarding bishops. The authority dealt with in the canon is the unique role of the papacy, which indeed extends in a particular way to all the faithful.[36]

---

[34]SCRIS reported the approbation, as pontifical, of 30 institutes (28 religious, 2 secular) which were formerly diocesan, between the years 1979–1982. *Informationes* 5, 6, 7, 8 (1979, 1980, 1981, 1982). While in some cases less than twenty years had elapsed, it was not uncommon that forty or fifty years passed before the change to pontifical status. A 1981 study published by SCRIS encouraged all religious institutes to eventually seek pontifical status, in order to better emphasize the universal nature of their vocation within the Church. "Dimensione Teologico-Giuridica dell'Approvazione Pontificia," *Informationes* 7 (1981), 57–71.
[35]*Comm* 11 (1979), 63.
[36]It is for this reason that some would have preferred omitting the phrase "tamquam supremo eorum Superiori." However, this part of the *CIC* expression was retained. *Comm* 15 (1983).

[32]"Clericalia instituta," *AAS* 61 (1969), 739–740.
[33]*PC* 10.

461

Canon 591 — **In order to provide better for the good of institutes and the needs of the apostolate, the Supreme Pontiff, by reason of his primacy over the universal Church and considering the common good, can exempt institutes of consecrated life from the governance of local ordinaries and subject them either to himself alone or to another ecclesiastical authority.**

The law continues to allow for the historic institution of exemption, but now it is understood in the light of the Council. While the 1917 Code merely defined exempt institutes as those removed from the jurisdiction of the local ordinary (*CIC* 488, 2°),[37] the present canon gives rationale. The pope, in view of his primacy in the universal Church, may exempt an institute in order to better provide for the good of the institute and the needs of the apostolate. The general good spoken of in the canon is taken from *Lumen Gentium* 45, which does not mention the good of the institute. By placing an institute specifically under his own jurisdiction or that of another ecclesiastical authority such as a patriarch,[38] the Sovereign Pontiff removes it from the jurisdiction of the local ordinary. Nevertheless, the Council clearly called upon members of exempt institutes to show "respect and obedience towards bishops in accordance with canon law."[39] This kind of cooperation is required for the good of the local church.

The institution of exemption has had a long and varied existence in the Church. The first statement of exemption seems to have been granted to the Monastery of Bobbio in 628. At times, this status served to protect and insure the possibility of a peaceful religious life; in another era it became essential to the centralized apostolate of the Mendicants. History has shown that exemption can be of service to the public good as a protection against illegitimate interference with institutes and as promotion of universal Church reform. When, however, it becomes an instrument of power and competition, it is abusive.

The fact that the law recognizes the possibility of exemption for institutes of consecrated life does not mean that in the present era it will be broadly invoked. The Council's strong emphasis on the role of bishops in the Church includes the provision in *Christus Dominus* that religious, exempt or not, are subject to the diocesan bishop in public worship, the care of souls, preaching to people, religious and moral education, catechetical instruction, liturgical formation, diocesan rules regarding behavior proper to the clerical state and various activities related to the exercise of the sacred apostolate, Catholic schools' policy and supervision, and legitimate decrees of episcopal councils and conferences which bind all.[40]

In the past, commentators spoke of a strict or broad sense of exemption, including status as a pontifical institute in the broad interpretation. The current restrictions of exempt privilege in the law would suggest that there is no longer a great distinction. Those who now possess exempt status—religious of solemn vows or those of simple vows by special privilege—know from their own statutes and practice the meaning of this in their particular case. An application of exemption today would most probably be in very particular circumstances that are to be made clear in the decree granting the exempt status.

Canon 592 — **§1. In order that the communion of institutes with the Apostolic See be better fostered each supreme moderator is to send a brief report on the status and life of the institute to the Apostolic See in a manner and at a time determined by the latter.**
§2. The moderators of every institute are to promote knowledge of the documents of the Holy See which affect members entrusted to them and be concerned about their observance of them.

The rapport between institutes and the hierarchy involves a two-directional flow of information and interest. Moderators will be asked periodically to report on the state of their institute. Explicit reference is made to this in canon 704 which requires that the report include an account of those who in any way have left the institute. The 1917 Code (*CIC* 510) called for a written report every five years from monastic congregations and all religious of pontifical right. This requirement was suppressed in 1967, but the obligation to send the acts of general chapters to the Sacred Congregation for Religious and Secular Institutes remained in effect.[41]

Regarding communication from the sacred congregation to institutes, today's religious are much more apt to have personal access to ecclesial documentation affecting their lives. Nevertheless, since moderators of institutes have a particular responsibility for the common good, paragraph two of the canon charges them with keeping their members informed. Examples of this kind of publication are found in the documents from the Sacred Congregation for Religious and Secular Institutes on Religious and Human Promotion and the Contemplative Dimension of Religious Life.[42] The efforts of institutes to provide for the education of their mem-

---

[37]*CIC* 615 further defined those who were exempt: regulars (i.e., religious of solemn vows) including their novices, except nuns not subject to regular superiors. See also Vermeersch-Creusen, *Epitome,* 1963, 625–630.
[38]*LG* 45.
[39]Ibid.

[40]*CD* 45.
[41]*ComRelMiss* 46 (1967), 406–407.
[42]*Origins* 10 (1981), 529–541; 550–555.

bers in the revised law shows the exercise of this responsibility as well.

Canon 593 — **With due regard for the prescription of can. 586, institutes of pontifical right are immediately and exclusively subject to the power of the Apostolic See in internal governance and discipline.**

Canons 593 and 594 clearly must be read in conjunction with canon 586 which preserves the just autonomy of every institute. What is described here is distinct from exemption; it is in matters of internal governance and discipline that pontifical institutes come directly under the Apostolic See. The point of the norm is that the diocesan bishop does not relate to the affairs of these institutes as he does to those of diocesan institutes (c. 595). The canon is more a protection of the institute's internal autonomy than a declaration of external authority.

Canon 594 — **With due regard for can. 586, an institute of diocesan right remains under the special care of the diocesan bishop.**

As noted above, canon 594 explicitly includes reference to a diocesan institute's autonomy while establishing that it remains under the particular care of the diocesan bishop. The implications of this are developed in the following canon.

Canon 595 — **§1. It belongs to the bishop of the principal seat of the institute to approve the constitutions and confirm any changes legitimately introduced into them, except in those matters in which the Apostolic See has intervened; it also belongs to him to deal with business of greater importance which affects the whole institute and which are beyond the power of its internal authority; he does so after consulting other diocesan bishops if the institute has spread to several dioceses.**

§2. The diocesan bishop can grant dispensations from the constitutions in particular cases.

Institutes of diocesan right have a rapport with the bishop of the diocese in which their principal center is located, comparable to the relationship of pontifical institutes with the Apostolic See.

It is from the diocesan bishop that these institutes seek the initial approbation of their constitutions once the *nihil obstat* has been received for their erection. Subsequent changes in those constitutions also are approved by the bishop. When exercising authority in this and in other matters beyond the competency of the internal authority of the institute, this bishop must be in consultation with the bishops of other dioceses into which the institute has spread.

The dispensations which the local bishop may give are limited: they are from provisions of constitutions, not universal law, and they are granted in particular cases, not general dispensations.

Canon 596 — **§1. Superiors and chapters of institutes enjoy that power over members which is defined in universal law and the constitutions.**

§2. Moreover, in clerical religious institutes of pontifical right they also possess ecclesiastical power of governance for both the external and the internal forum.

§3. The prescriptions of cann. 131, 133 and 137-144 are applicable to the power referred to in §1.

The canon's general statement regarding superiors and chapters[43] again recognizes the autonomy of internal governance enjoyed by institutes of consecrated life. Sections of the universal law referred to would, in particular, include canons 617–640 for religious and canon 717 for secular institutes. The canons no longer use the 1917 Code's term, dominative power (*CIC* 501). The constitutions of each type of institute should carefully define the authority of moderators and chapters or the comparable structures.

The second paragraph of the canon repeats the former Code's recognition of an additional power held by members of clerical institutes of religious. The work commission engaged in considerable discussion over limiting this statement to religious institutes. It was finally decided that the statement was sufficient for the common norms, since only the moderators of clerical secular institutes with the faculty of incardination have this same share in the ecclesiastical power of governing, and such institutes are few in number.[44] The same matter is further specified by canon 266, §3 on incardination and canon 715 on secular institutes.

When the commission was reworking this section of the law in April of 1979, the first two paragraphs of canon 596 were joined and composed the entire canon. The opinion was expressed by one consultor that all institutes share in the same authority:

> . . . The power of all institutes, including lay, is in some way ecclesiastical, derived, that is, from ecclesiastical power; it is not that of friendship, private, nor dominative (a term already superceded). Even in the case of laity, there can be a certain participation in the power of governing.[45]

Although the group did not feel it could adequately deal with that issue at the time, there were later developments in the canon following the 1980

[43]These terms are usually reserved to religious, but the intent of the canon includes the comparable persons and bodies in secular institutes. The presence of these terms is perhaps explained by the fact that the first two paragraphs were originally combined.

[44]*Comm* 11 (1979), 307.

[45]Ibid., 306.

schema. The original text was divided so that paragraph two recognized the unique governing power of clerical religious institutes. Paragraph three was added, referring to certain canons from the law's section on the ecclesiastical power of governing and applying these to the power mentioned in paragraph one.

In brief, the canons referred to deal with ordinary and delegated power for governing (c. 131); the meaning of the term ordinary (c. 134); the delegation of ordinary executive power and its exercise (cc. 136–141); and the cessation of delegated and ordinary power (cc. 142–143). Canon 144 extends the principle of "supplet Ecclesia" to executive acts of governing.

Some of these canons, of their nature, apply only to clerical institutes, but others are not so limited as is evidenced by the new location of this whole body of canons in Book I, "General Norms," rather than in the section on the clergy as was the case in the 1917 Code. The issue raised by the consultor will continue to be studied and discussed until greater clarity is achieved.

Canon 597 — §1. Any Catholic, endowed with a right intention, who has the qualities required by universal and proper law and who is not prevented by any impediment can be admitted to an institute of consecrated life.

§2. No one can be admitted without suitable preparation.

The law here states only the generic qualifications for admission. These are supplemented in each particular section of the law: for religious in canons 641–645 and for secular institutes in canons 720–721.

The term "right intention," familiar from the 1917 Code, now cannot be read apart from other clear references in the law to divine vocation. It is the role of the various institutes' probationary periods to facilitate mutual discernment of the presence of vocation in those who have been admitted. Particular impediments—simplified in the revised law—appear in the sections pertaining to each type of institute.

The second paragraph contains a significant change introduced since the Council. The universal law now specifies nothing of the preparation to be given candidates prior to the canonical period of formation. It states simply that no one is to be admitted without fitting preparation. The duration and circumstances of this could be quite diverse depending upon the type of institute, its particular circumstances, and the candidate seeking admission. All of this should be clearly expressed in the institute's proper law.

Canon 598 — §1. Each institute, keeping in mind its own character and purposes is to define in its constitutions the manner in which the evangelical counsels of chastity, poverty and obedience are to be observed for its way of living.

§2. All members must not only observe the evangelical counsels faithfully and fully, but also organize their life according to the proper law of the institute and thereby strive for the perfection of their state.

In calling upon every institute to specify the way in which its members observe the evangelical counsels, the law fulfills its own guiding principles and recalls ancient practice in the Church. In establishing guidelines for itself, the work commission had determined to make the universal law the guardian of essential principles of consecrated life, leaving to proper law the specifications required by the diverse charism, nature, spirit, and end of each institute.[46]

While these counsels are considered of the very essence of consecrated life (c. 573), there can be considerable diversity in the emphasis placed on one or another of them by particular institutes. The manner of living obedience and poverty will be quite diverse for secular and for religious institutes. In all cases, the way of living the counsels is to be developed in the constitutions.

The importance of the proper law in this matter is as ancient as monasticism. Whether the formula of profession included one vow or four was of minimal importance because everything essential was included in the rule. The second paragraph of the canon further develops this notion indicating the role of proper law in the fulfillment of one's vocation. Not only will these documents go beyond the letter of the law regarding the counsels, they will describe the other essential elements of life in the institute. This highlights the significance of making professions "according to the constitutions" of the particular institute.

The Evangelical Counsels

The three counsels which are the subject matter of the three subsequent canons form the familiar threefold expression of consecration. Actually the present terminology goes back only as far as the thirteenth century, when the Franciscan formulary became more or less an exemplar for later foundations.[47] Even in that tradition, however, the term poverty was not used at first. There was rather an expression of living without possessing anything of one's own. Other formularies frequently expressed stability, obedience, life in common, conversion of life, and having nothing of one's own. Except for the earliest centuries during which occurred the

46*Comm* 2 (1970), 170–176.
47Monastic orders, canons regular and Dominicans continued to follow their own formularies.

consecration of virgins and ascetics, explicit reference to a vow of chastity also appeared later.

A strong influence on the threefold expression of poverty, chastity, and obedience becoming normative was the doctrine developed by St. Thomas Aquinas. Aquinas's theories of ridding oneself of the threefold impediments to perfection and of giving over one's threefold goods as a means to perfection in charity have, until recent times, been the customary way of explaining the three counsels.[48] From his conclusions[49] came the general practice of expressing these three counsels where, in the past, it had seemed unnecessary to include all three in the formulary since their content was preserved in the rule.

The teaching of the Council has shifted the contemporary approach to the counsels; the focus is now, as it was in the very first century, on the following of Jesus (c. 573, §1). The canons recognize the counsels as a divine gift based in the very life, as well as in the teachings, of Jesus (c. 575). The texts treating each of the three counsels rely heavily on *Perfectae Caritatis* 12, 13, and 14.

There was difference of opinion within the commission over how juridical these canons should be. The more strictly juridical 1917 Code had no canon on chastity. Some who studied the 1977 draft for the revised law proposed a fuller expression of the motivation and spiritual meaning of each of the counsels. In the end, however, the canons remained quite brief,[50] and there was a change in their location. The three canons, situated in the section on religious in the 1977 draft, were moved into the common norms of the 1980 schema.

Each of the three counsels is given a brief gospel context as the foundation for its fundamental juridical obligation. When developing the expression of the counsels in constitutions, as called for in canon 598, it is helpful to return to the complete conciliar texts and the proven traditions of the institute as well as sound contemporary literature on the counsels.

Canon 599 — **The evangelical counsel of chastity assumed for the sake of the kingdom of heaven, as a sign of the future world and a source of more abundant fruitfulness in an undivided heart, entails the obligation of perfect continence in celibacy.**

This brief canon states both the motivation and the effect of observing this counsel's juridical obligation—perfect continence in celibacy. Distinct from the chastity required of all Christians, this is lived out in celibacy. Distinct from other motivations and life-styles of remaining unmarried, this state is chosen for the kingdom and is lived out in perfect continence. These three terms—chastity, perfect continence, and celibacy—are deliberately employed in the canon to identify more clearly the object of a sacred bond to live the evangelical counsel which has traditionally been called chastity. The members of the commission chose to avoid phrases more proper to moral theology than to canon law.[51]

The interrelatedness of the concepts of chastity, its sign value, and its fruitfulness are found more clearly in the conciliar text than in the synthetic form of the canon:

> Chastity "for the sake of the kingdom of heaven" (Mt. 14:22) . . . uniquely frees the heart of man (cf. 1 Cor. 7:32–35), so that he becomes more fervent in love for God and all men. For this reason it is a special symbol of heavenly benefits, and . . . a most effective means of dedicating themselves wholeheartedly to the divine service and the works of the apostolate.[52]

The proper law of institutes further develops the way of living and preserving the counsel of chastity. There is direction given in the conciliar text when it refers to the value of prayer, mortification, health care, and sincere love between the members. Recognizing the challenges to fidelity, the Council also speaks of the careful selection and preparation of candidates.

Canon 600 — **The evangelical counsel of poverty in imitation of Christ who, although He was rich became poor for us, entails, besides a life which is poor in fact and in spirit, a life of labor lived in moderation and foreign to earthly riches, a dependence and a limitation in the use and disposition of goods according to the norm of the proper law of each institute.**

As in the case of chastity, the canon on the counsel of poverty gives a gospel motivation; this is followed by a sort of description of what is involved and the juridical obligation. The counsel is taken up in imitation of Christ with the example from His life being the supreme act of divestiture: the Incarnation. The canon alludes to a part of the scripture text which the Council cited more fully: "Remember how generous the Lord Jesus was: he was rich, but he became poor for your sake, to make you rich out of his poverty."[53]

The conciliar text also gives fuller explanation to the canon's statement that the counsel is not merely "poverty of spirit." It is not enough to be dependent on superiors in the use of things; there must be a poverty in fact as well as the essential spirit of detachment.

[48]*Summa* I[a]II[ae] q. 108, art. 4.
[49]*Summa* II[a] II[ae] q. 186 art 7.
[50]*Comm* 11 (1979), 311.
[51]Ibid.
[52]*PC* 12. A further part of this text, more proper to religious life, is picked up in c. 607.
[53]2 Cor 8, 9. *PC* 13.

On the other hand, while the term simplicity of life—which has come into popular use—expresses much of the same ideal in the following of Christ, it does not coincide perfectly with the concept of the counsel. The key differentiating factor in institutes of consecrated life lies in the principle of dependency or limitation. This, it must be noted, varies significantly from the common life of religious to the more individualized life-style but often demanding accountability of secular institutes.

Further specifications of the meaning of poverty and the meaning of limitation in use for secular institutes are left to their constitutions. The universal law for religious gives further detail. Canon 668 deals with the specifics of religious dependence: cession papers, wills, earnings, acts of renunciation, and changes in legal documents. Canon 635, §2 calls upon religious institutes to use or administer communal goods in a way consonant with, and expressive of, their poverty. A part of this expression is to be through contribution to the needs of the Church and care for the poor (c. 640).

During the consideration of the canon there was much discussion over this matter of giving to the poor. In the end this was seen to be an institutional obligation—at least among religious—rather than one of the individual's vow of poverty.[54]

Another point of discussion was over reference to work. The Council had spoken of religious as being bound by the common law of labor.[55] Some consultors saw this more as a result of poverty than an essential element of the counsel. Others feared an interpretation which would stress remunerative labor too much. There was an effort at clarification in changing the Latin text from "vitam in labore et omnimodo sobrietate ducendam" to "vitam . . . operose in sobrietate ducendam . . . ."[56] A statement of Pope Paul VI, referred to during the commission discussions, was used to put the matter in perspective:

It will therefore be an essential aspect of your poverty to bear witness to the human meaning of work which is carried out in liberty of spirit and restored to its true nature as the source of sustenance and of service.[57]

A difficulty in writing the canon, as one applicable to both religious and secular institutes, was the real difference between them. The historical antecedent of the religious vow of poverty was the vow to share all in common, i.e., to have nothing of one's own. This latter concept does not apply at all to secular institutes, yet it is perhaps closer to the essence of religious poverty than the word "poverty" itself.

Canon 601 — **The evangelical counsel of obedience, undertaken in a spirit of faith and love in the following of Christ who was obedient even unto death requires a submission of the will to legitimate superiors, who stand in the place of God when they command according to the proper constitutions.**

The canon's brief expression must again be read in the context of *Perfectae Caritatis* where it is more explicit that the fundamental motivation for the sacred bond of obedience is the love of the will of God.[58] It is to this end that members follow the obedient Christ. The thing which is characteristic of the obedience in institutes of consecrated life is the way in which the will of God is mediated. The canon, expressing a juridical principle, speaks of the submission of one's will toward legitimate superiors—acting in the place of God—according to constitutions.

The role of religious superiors is further outlined in canons 618 and 619 where the spirit of service and a pastoral kind of concern are included. It is critical for both religious and secular institutes to give clear expression to the role of moderators and the way of observing obedience in their proper law. The canon surely does not preclude dialogue and mutual discernment, but it does recognize real authority which comes with office.

The concept of the superior acting in the place of God is very old in religious tradition. The Rule of St. Benedict clearly saw the abbot as taking the place of Christ in the monastery. However, the same rule made clear that he was no arbitrary tyrant because he too was subject to the same rule. In the course of commission discussion, the wisdom of including the phrase "vices Dei gerentes" was questioned. It was observed that this was in the conciliar document but had not been repeated in *Evangelica Testificatio*. There was awareness of the concept being both traditional and much under discussion. The question was raised, too, as to its appropriateness for secular institutes.[59] In the final decision on a text from among many offered, the matter was not raised again for specific vote.

In the apostolic exhortation of Pope Paul VI, the relationship between authority and obedience is expressed in these terms:

Consequently, authority and obedience are exercised in the service of the common good as two complementary aspects of the same participation in Christ's offering. For those in authority, it is a matter of serving in their brothers the design of the Father's love; while, in accepting their directives, the religious follow our Master's example and cooperate in the work of salvation. Thus, far from being in opposition to one another, author-

[54]*Comm* 11 (1979), 312.
[55]*PC* 13.
[56]*Comm* 11 (1979), 312.
[57]*ET* 20.

[58]*PC* 14.
[59]*Comm* 11 (1979), 314.

ity and individual liberty go together in the fulfillment of God's will, which is sought fraternally through a trustful dialogue between the superior and his brother, in the case of a personal situation or through a general agreement regarding what concerns the whole community.[60]

In each of the three preceding canons on the evangelical counsels, there were two very significant tensions in play. First, it was difficult to find the proper balance of theological and juridical content. Some of the consultors favored a more juridical text while others wished to include more of the Council's motivational rationale for each counsel. In the end, the theological was reduced to what seemed most essential, but in the course of rewording various drafts, the full impact of the conciliar teaching was inevitably lessened.

Second, there was the tension of seeking a wording suitable to both religious and secular institutes. Although *Perfectae Caritatis* includes reference to all consecrated life, it was written with much greater consciousness of religious life. As a result its texts, as incorporated into the law, sometimes need even further interpretation for secular institutes.

The basic juridical content is presented: perfect continence in celibacy, dependent and limited use of temporalities, and a certain form of mediation of the will of God. The deeper motivations and the more concrete implications of these must be found in the conciliar documents, other parts of the law, and in the constitutions according to which members make their commitment in an institute of consecrated life.

Canon 602 — The life of brothers or sisters proper to each institute, by which all members are united together like a special family in Christ, is to be determined in such a way that it becomes a mutual support for all in fulfilling the vocation of each member. Moreover by their communion as brothers or sisters, rooted in and built on love, the members are to be an example of universal reconciliation in Christ.

The canon's Latin expression "vita fraterna" presents difficulties in translation. This is not the common life or even life in community: it is rather the spirit of oneness, rooted in baptism, binding together even more closely in Christ those who have been called in a common vocation of charism, life, and mission. In this case the conciliar expression has been changed in order to speak of the bonding spirit of both kinds of institutes.[61]

The common heritage and spirituality of each institute is shared as is a genuine care of the members for one another. For religious this takes place with-

in the context of the common life (cf. cc. 607, §2; 665, §1). In secular institutes, the genuine communion of spirit is an obligation incumbent upon all (c. 716) but not through common life as lived by religious (c. 714).

Other Forms of Consecrated Life

The law next speaks formally of two of the most ancient forms of consecrated life and expresses openness to the development, under the Spirit, of new forms. The uniqueness of the inclusion of hermits and virgins here is that these persons are not members of institutes and thus are not bound by the subsequent laws for religious or secular institutes.

Canon 603 — §1. Besides institutes of consecrated life, the Church recognizes the eremitic or anchoritic life by which the Christian faithful devote their life to the praise of God and salvation of the world through a stricter separation from the world, the silence of solitude and assiduous prayer and penance.
§2. A hermit is recognized in the law as one dedicated to God in a consecrated life if he or she publicly professes the three evangelical counsels, confirmed by a vow or other sacred bond, in the hands of the diocesan bishop and observes his or her own plan of life under his direction.

The eremetical life, also called anchoritism, has its roots in the third century with such desert fathers as St. Paul (c. 234–342) and St. Anthony (251–356). The solitude, prayer and penance of the hermits are recognized as the beginning of the monastic life of both men and women in the Church. Their search for solitude distinguished them from the cenobitic form of life which gathered around St. Pachomius in the same era.

In the 1977 schema of the revised law, the eremetical life was mentioned along with the cenobitic life as a form of monasticism. This seemed to envision a monk or nun, receiving permission to live apart from the community in greater solitude. Benedict had foreseen the possibility of this in his rule but permitted it only after the religious was well formed in the spiritual life.

In the same schema, the canon explicitly dealing with hermits was in a set of preliminary canons, just before the section dealing with religious, societies, and secular institutes explicitly. The relocation of the canon further clarifies that these persons are not members of institutes. The rules of institutes provide adequately for members who seek greater solitude; reference to this has been removed from the universal law. The hermits spoken of in the canon relate directly to the diocesan bishop, making their public profession of the counsels in his

---

[60]*ET* 25.
[61]*PC* 15. This text uses the expression "vita in communi agenda."

hands. Such persons are recognized in law as living a consecrated life.

For centuries the eremetical life was less known and practiced than cenobitic monasticism. Today increased interest is evident. Beyer speaks of the diverse possibilities of this life, within the essential elements listed in the canon:

> The description of the eremetical life can be the norm in light of which all hermits discern and carry out their vocation wherever they live it: in the desert, the forests, the mountains or in the solitude of the modern city. Today, besides the public witness of the hermits through their abandonment of the world, austerity of life, and external solitude, there are also hermits who remain in the world, live in reserve, supporting themselves by common manual labor. They are almost unknown, and in their cities they pray and work to the praise of God and for the salvation of the world . . . some, even, live in a *laura* (or colony of hermits) under the direction of a spiritual director without being bound to the same rule or institute and without constituting a community.[62]

Canon 604 — §1. Similar to these forms of consecrated life is the order of virgins, who, committed to the holy plan of following Christ more closely, are consecrated to God by the diocesan bishop according to the approved liturgical rite, are betrothed mystically to Christ, the Son of God, and are dedicated to the service of the Church.

§2. In order to observe their commitment more faithfully and to perform by mutual support service to the Church which is in harmony with their state these virgins can form themselves into associations.

Also of ancient origin in the Church is the order of virgins. In the earliest centuries of Christianity, both men (ascetics) and women (virgins) dedicated themselves permanently in a life of virginity in the following of Christ and the service of others. Accounts of the early virgins are most familiar; they came to be an order of persons in the Church, preceding the concept of institutes of consecrated life.

The Council's first promulgated document, *The Constitution on the Sacred Liturgy* stated simply that the rite of the consecration of virgins contained in the *Roman Pontifical* should be revised.[63] In 1970, a revised rite was published under the authority of Pope Paul VI.[64]

The canon itself notes the two elements of consecration and service. The introduction to the rite

states: "Those who consecrate their chastity under the inspiration of the Holy Spirit do so for the sake of more fervent love of Christ and of greater freedom in the service of their brothers and sisters" (no. 2). In this form of consecrated life there is not necessarily any profession of vows. Consecration is received through the ministry of the diocesan bishop, who with extended hands, pronounces the prayer of consecration over the candidate. In cases of nuns receiving this consecration, it is an act distinct from their profession although it may take place within the same ceremony. The requirements are listed in the ritual.

The consecration, however, is once again a reality available to women living "in the world." Again, the ritual states the requirements:

> (a) that they should always have been unmarried, and never lived in public or open violation of chastity;

> (b) that by their age, prudence, and universally approved character they should give assurance of perseverance in a life of chastity dedicated to the service of the Church and of their neighbor;

> (c) that they should be admitted to the consecration by the bishop who is ordinary of the place (no. 5).

The imagery of the ritual, as the canon suggests, is strongly nuptial and there is provision for the giving of the veil and ring if this is according to local custom.

Unlike the canon on hermits, this canon did not appear in the 1977 schema but was added later. A great deal of discussion took place over the second paragraph on association of consecrated virgins. There was concern that this might appear to be legislation for a new form of institute. While the matter could have been omitted since all in the Church have the natural right of association, it was decided to make just the brief statement of their freedom to come together, leaving the rest to future developments.[65]

Canon 605 — Approving new forms of consecrated life is reserved to the Apostolic See alone. Diocesan bishops, however, should strive to discern new gifts of consecrated life granted to the Church by the Holy Spirit and they should aid their promoters so that they can express their proposals as well as possible and protect them with suitable statutes, utilizing especially the general norms contained in this section.

The present canon is unprecedented in the Code but reflects what has taken place in the Church,

[62]J. Beyer, *Verso un Nuovo Diritto degli Istituti di Vita Consacrata* (Milan: Àncora, 1976), 124–125.

[63]*SC* 80.

[64]*AAS* 62 (1970), 650; *ComRelMiss* 51 (1970), 373–375. Quotes are taken from the authorized translation published in 1975 by ICEL.

[65]*Comm* 11 (1979), 331–334.

most recently in the case of the secular institutes. It is now clear that a life of total consecration according to the evangelical counsels can be fulfilled in concretely diverse ways. The present law recognizes two types of institutes of consecrated life: (a) diverse forms of religious institutes, and (b) consecrated secularity in secular institutes. Aware that the Spirit breathes continually, bishops are charged with both openness and care in helping promote potential new gifts to the Church. This canon does not refer to the approval of new institutes which are religious or secular (cc. 579, 589) but to possible distinct new forms. The present structures of the law provide the basic guidelines for any such new forms in this first title on general norms (cc. 573–606).

Canon 606 — **Whatever is determined about institutes of consecrated life and their members applies equally to either sex, unless the contrary is apparent from the context of the wording or nature of the matter.**

Although the text of the canon is substantially the same as its parallel in the 1917 Code *(CIC* 490), there is a greater equality achieved between men and women in the revised law. A notable exception in the law for religious is the regulation of cloister for nuns (c. 667, §§3–4). In general, however, distinction arises from the clerical or lay states of the members or institutes.

BIBLIOGRAPHY

Bibliographical material for part III of Book II can be found after the commentary on canon 746.

TITLE II
RELIGIOUS INSTITUTES
[cc. 607–709]

Title II consists of the canons that govern religious institutes. It specifies the principles and directions of the common norms while at the same time offers specific legislation for religious institutes.

Title II begins with an introductory canon which describes religious life followed by eight chapters, six of which apply directly to institutes while two refer to related areas. The six which apply to institutes directly cover the erection and suppression of houses, the governance of institutes, the admission and formation of members, the rights and obligations of members, the apostolate of institutes, and separation from the institute. The two short chapters which apply to related areas cover the raising of a religious to the episcopate and conferences of major superiors.

CANONS AND COMMENTARY

Canon 607 — **§1. Religious life, as a consecration of the whole person, manifests in the Church a wonderful marriage brought about by God, a sign of the future age. Thus religious bring to perfection their full gift as a sacrifice offered to God by which their whole existence becomes a continuous worship of God in love.**

§2. A religious institute is a society in which members, according to proper law, pronounce public vows either perpetual or temporary, which are to be renewed when they have lapsed, and live a life in common as brothers or sisters.

§3. The public witness to be rendered by religious to Christ and to the Church entails a separation from the world proper to the character and purpose of each institute.

The title on religious is introduced by this short theological description of religious life. The canon focuses on some of the important characteristics of religious life, namely, consecration, public vows, life in common, and bearing witness to Christ.

Paragraph one which is based on *Lumen Gentium* 44 understands consecration in terms of living the fullness of the gospel life by means of the evangelical counsels. There is a greater accent on the worship element of the consecration so that religious life has a value in itself aside from the various means of apostolic service. The thrust of this paragraph can have importance when religious institutes develop a ritual of consecration. Thus, each institute may express in its own way its particular concept of consecration, its view of the intimate union between God and the consecrated person, and the manner in which the institute manifests that it is a sign of the risen life.

Paragraph two defines two characteristics of religious life:

1. It is a society in which members profess public vows which are perpetual.

2. The members live a common life.

The form of consecration is that of public vow which according to canon 1192, §1 is a vow accepted in the name of the Church by a legitimate ecclesiastical superior. The legitimate superior would be the person designated in the constitutions to accept the vows or the delegate of that person in accord with canon 656, 5° which requires profession to be received by the lawful superior, personally or through another.

This paragraph has a juridical aspect since it allows the final form of profession to be perpetual vows or perpetually renewed temporary vows. In either case, profession is for life regardless of the form.

The use of vows rather than other sacred bonds as a means of consecration is a change from the practice introduced by many religious institutes after the Council of using promises or other forms of commitment. It should be noted that in the common norms total consecration of life according to the evangelical counsels can be accomplished by means other than vows. However, for religious, public vows are the norm for the profession of both temporary and perpetual vows.

The law does not change the content of the vows since the life of the evangelical counsels is to be delineated in the proper law of the institute. Canon 1191, §1 defines a vow as a deliberate and free promise made to God concerning a better and possible good which must be fulfilled by reason of the virtue of religion. For religious, it is the consecration of life as a total self-gift to God in response to the divine call which expresses the "virtue of religion."

The prescription of the common life incorporates the norm of canon 602 which recognizes some form of common life as necessary to all institutes of consecrated life. The meaning of common life is reflected more fully in canons 608 and 665. An institute's expression of its concept of the common life is left to the proper law of the institute.[1]

Paragraph three has its roots in *Lumen Gentium* 46 which would balance "separation from the world" with the note that religious are not to be strangers to their brothers and sisters while pursuing separation from the world.[2] The "separation" called for in this paragraph as a part of the public witness of religious is to be lived according to the nature and end of the institute. The concept is a flexible one providing for wide parameters that are applicable to the lives of those totally given over to the contemplative life and those involved in widely diverse apostolic and missionary activities. It especially means separation from the life of the sinful world while at the same time ministering in and to the same sinful world. The very fact of living the common life constitutes a form of separation which should not be viewed negatively as separation from others but positively as a form of witness not only of total dedication to God but also to the unity in Christ that is at the heart of all Christian community.

The common life and communal efforts at evangelical simplicity, consecrated celibacy, and religious obedience result in social patterns, economic interests, and professional attitudes which tend to "separate" the religious from much in the world without separating them from the persons with whom and for whom they minister. It is the communal dimension of their lives which makes their witness more public.

---

[1]See the SCRIS discussion of small communities in *Con Life*, vol. I, no. 2 (1975), 141–145, and religious who live alone in apartments, *Con Life*, vol. III, no. 2 (1979), 164–168. Religious living apart from their community, except for the serious reasons provided for by law, are considered as not corresponding to the idea of common life.
[2]See c. 667 for a description of physical separation from the world by means of canonical cloister.

CHAPTER I
RELIGIOUS HOUSES AND THEIR ERECTION AND SUPPRESSION
[cc. 608–616]

This chapter expresses the norm that religious are to live in a legitimately constituted house under the authority of a superior. It provides for the erection and suppression of the houses of religious, giving general criteria for the erection of a house, the procedure for its erection, and the rights of religious after a house is established. The houses of canons regular, monks, and nuns are described in separate canons.

Canon 608 — A religious community must live in a house legitimately constituted under the authority of the superior designated according to the norm of law; each house is to have at least an oratory in which the Eucharist is celebrated and reserved so that it truly is the center of the community.

A religious community is to live in a legitimately established house. The law does not define the term "house" nor does it make distinctions in types of houses as did the previous law.[3] A house can be a juridic person if it meets the requirements of canon 115, with all the rights and responsibilities of a juridic person including the right to acquire, possess, administer, and alienate temporal goods (c. 634, §1). The house is to be legitimately established under the authority of a superior designated according to the norm of the law (see cc. 625, §3; 629).

Since the law contains no definition of the canonical term "house," an institute may define the term or describe what it means by a house in its proper law. Concepts that developed under the previous Code such as principal house (a house that had another house or houses subject to it) and filial house (a house which is subject to another house and therefore not established as a separate juridic person) may provide helpful parallels in organizing a religious institute, or present needs may call for the development of a new method of organization. The law in omitting definitions of types of houses allows each institute the necessary flexibility to develop its own structure.

The provision for at least an oratory in every house focuses on the centrality of Christ for the life of the community and its worship. Eucharistic presence is the norm. At the same time, it is realized that certain living situations may make the reservation of the Sacrament imprudent or impractical because of considerations of safety and reverence. It may be most prudent to rely on reservation of the Sacrament at the local church.[4] Because of the tra-

---

[3]*CIC* 488, 5°.
[4]*CLD* 8 (1978), 327–328.

dition of Eucharistic worship in some institutes, the reservation of the Sacrament should not be denied them without grave reason. In most cases the law regulating the reservation of the Eucharist should not present difficulties (cc. 934–944). The preference for the celebration of the Eucharist at least twice a month (c. 934, §2) should not be strictly called for, especially in the case of lay religious in areas where there are few clergy or where this would impose an undue burden. The law's provision for a lay minister of the Eucharist to provide exposition (c. 943) should facilitate this devotion among religious.

Canon 609 — **§1. Houses of a religious institute are erected by the competent authority according to the constitutions with the previous written consent of the diocesan bishop.**

This paragraph sets out the two requirements for the erection of a house:

    1. the previous written consent of the diocesan bishop;

    2. the action of the competent authority of the institute in accord with its constitutions.

Practically, this paragraph means that an institute has considered or been invited by the bishop to consider establishing a house in a diocese. If the institute desires to establish a house, it should then petition the bishop for his written consent. Upon receiving the written consent, the institute should follow the norms in its constitutions for erecting a house. Canon 610 sets out the basic matters to be considered before an institute erects a house.

The process of erecting a house would not seem to be required when religious are serving in a diocese where the institute is already established and the religious are merely changing residence. Change of residence would require only the authorization of the institute's competent authority.

This paragraph does not mention the role of the pastor in establishing a house within parish boundaries. However, it would be prudent to inform the pastor in order to promote a harmonious relationship between the pastor and the religious institute.

§2. In order to erect a monastery of nuns the permission of the Apostolic See is also required.

Paragraph two repeats the norm of canon 497, §1 of the 1917 Code requiring the permission of the Apostolic See and the consent of the diocesan bishop in order to erect a monastery of nuns. Canon 488, 7° of the former law defined nuns as religious women who professed solemn vows or those whose vows would normally be solemn but who by disposition of the Holy See were permitted

to profess simple vows because of their situation. The present law omits both these definitions and eliminates the distinction between solemn and simple vows. Thus, it seems that those who have been previously designated as nuns will continue to be covered by those portions of the law referring to nuns since the law does not provide any definition of the term.

Canon 610 — **§1. The erection of houses takes place with due regard for their usefulness for the Church and the institute and safeguarding those things which are required for the correct living out of the religious life of the members according to the specific purposes and spirit of the institute.**

This paragraph requires the institute and the bishop to keep two matters in mind when considering the erection of a house:

    1. The house should be useful for the Church and the institute.

    2. The members of the house should be able to live the religious life according to the spirit of the institute.

The first requirement touches on the authority of the bishop over the works of the apostolate in the diocese and his decision on whether there is a need for the members of a particular institute in the diocese. The second requirement is more the responsibility of the institute. It must decide if its particular life can be properly lived within the diocese.

This paragraph calls for the attention of both the bishop and the institute to ensure that the needs of the members assigned to the house can be met. In addition, the bishop should ascertain that the erection of another house will not infringe on the availability of support for religious already living in the area. This would be especially true of an institute that does not engage in an apostolate that provides sufficient income for support.

Many institutes have internal criteria for accepting a mission which takes into account the needs of the local church, particular apostolates, and the living situation and thereby determine if they will establish new houses. These norms are better placed in their proper law rather than the constitutions.

§2. No house is to be erected unless it can be prudently judged that the needs of the members will be suitably provided for.

Very early in church law it was established that religious should be able to support themselves. This canon extends that concept to the present law by requiring that a house should not be erected unless it can suitably provide for the members. The language is broad and covers not only the temporal needs of religious (income for food, lodging, medical care, etc.) but also the spiritual needs of the members (see cc. 630, 663).

Canon 611 — The consent of the diocesan bishop to erect a religious house of any institute brings with it the right:

1° to lead a life according to its own character and the purposes of the institute;

2° to exercise the works proper to the institute according to the norm of law, with due regard for any conditions attached to the consent;

3° for clerical institutes to have a church, with due regard for the prescription of can. 1215, §3, and to perform sacred ministries, observing what is by law to be observed.

Canons 609 and 610 state the requirements for the erection of a house while canon 611 deals with some of the same matters in terms of the rights of the institute when a bishop consents to the erection of a house.

Number one is similar to the final clause of canon 609, §2. Once a house has been erected, religious have the right to lead a life according to the particular nature and purpose of the institute. For example, if a contemplative institute established a house in a diocese it would not be proper for the bishop to pressure the institute to change its lifestyle to that of an apostolic institute because of the ministerial needs of the diocese.

Since each institute has its own charism and sometimes its own particular apostolates (especially apostolic institutes) the consent given by the bishop to establish a house would apply to all the works usually engaged in by the institute, unless some of these were excluded by the consent of the bishop. The bishop and the institute should engage in dialogue leading to the bishop's written consent (c. 609, §1) so that the bishop understands the nature and purposes of the institute and that the institute understands any specific conditions the bishop wishes to place on the institute in his diocese. The specific conditions should be clearly expressed in the written consent of the bishop. A bishop needs to know the plans of an institute in his diocese so there is not a duplication of services between religious institutes or between religious and the diocese (see commentary on c. 612).

When the bishop consents to the erection of a house by a clerical institute, the consent includes the right to have a church and to perform the sacred ministries. Canon 1215, §1 requires the written consent of the bishop to establish a church. Canon 1215, §3 further requires an institute to obtain the consent of the bishop to build a church in a particular place even though the institute has already received consent to establish a new house in the diocese.

Canon 612 — **In order that a religious house be converted to apostolic works different from those for which it was established the consent of the diocesan bishop is required; but this is not so if it is a matter of a change which refers only to internal government and discipline, with due regard for the laws of the foundation.**

This canon illustrates the balance between the authority of bishops over apostolic works in the diocese and the autonomy of institutes over their own internal government and discipline. It applies to a situation in which the consent of the bishop did not cover the new work the house wishes to undertake. However, even if a bishop has consented generally to the works of the institute as described in the constitutions, if the new work is a major undertaking it would be prudent to consult the bishop.

If, for example, the institute wanted to convert the novitiate into a place of retreat for its own members or a provincial house, this would be a matter of internal governance or discipline and would not need the consent of the bishop although the intention to do so should be made known to him. If, however, the institute had a novitiate in the diocese and because of a lack of novices wanted to open a retreat center and this was not included in the original consent, the consent of the bishop should be obtained.

Canon 613 — **§1. A religious house of canons regular and monks under the governance and care of its own moderator is autonomous unless the constitutions state otherwise.**

Historically monks and canons regular have lived in autonomous houses. This meant especially that there was no higher authority than the abbot or superior of that autonomous house. There can be lesser houses associated with an autonomous monastery under the jurisdiction of a local moderator, but they are subject to the moderator of the autonomous house. Such autonomous houses may form confederations of monasteries (c. 582), but the governance and care of each house is autonomous unless its constitution provide otherwise.

This paragraph refers only to male religious (monks and canons regular), however, canon 616, §4 on the suppression of houses refers to an autonomous monastery of nuns. Thus, although this paragraph explicitly mentions only male religious as being autonomous, canon 616, §4 envisages autonomous female religious.[5]

§2. A moderator of an autonomous house is by law a major superior.

---

[5]The 1977 schema, c. 105, §2 was more clear in providing that whatever applied to monks also applied to nuns.

This paragraph makes the moderator of an autonomous house a major superior with all the prerogatives of a major superior (see c. 620 describing the office of major superior).

Canon 614 — Monasteries of nuns which are associated with an institute of men maintain their own order of life and governance according to the constitutions. Mutual rights and obligations are to be so defined that the association is spiritually enriching.

This canon protects the independence of monasteries of nuns attached to an institute of men in regard to their own order of life and governance.[6] The particulars of the mode of attachment are to be outlined in the constitutions of both institutes (see c. 580 on aggregation). This canon specifies that the areas of attachment are intended to advance the spiritual good, thereby eliminating areas of governance (see c. 586). Areas of association could include mutual sharing of spiritual documents, appropriate rituals, confessors, and spiritual direction. Except for confessors, these can be areas of mutual exchange.

Canon 615 — An autonomous monastery which has no other major superior beyond its own moderator and is not associated with any other institute of religious in such a way that the superior of the latter enjoys true power over such a monastery determined by the constitutions is committed to the special vigilance of the diocesan bishop according to the norm of law.

When an autonomous monastery has no major superior except its own moderator nor is joined to another institute that exercises jurisdiction (governing power) over it, its superior enjoys true power as determined by the constitutions. Although "true power" is not clarified in this canon or elsewhere, it apparently refers to the power given in law to a superior. This canon applies to monasteries of pontifical right, since if the monastery were of diocesan right it would already be under the jurisdiction of the bishop. This canon is consistent with the principles of canon 589 which gives the Supreme Pontiff the right to subject institutes to himself or another ecclesiastical authority. In this case the universal law commits these monasteries to the special vigilance of the diocesan bishop. This is a non-jurisdictional phrase which preserves the autonomy of the monastery. Canons 678, 681, and 683 already give the bishop specific responsibilities toward all religious in the diocese. Special vigilance in the context of this canon appears to refer to pastoral concern by the bishop for autonomous monasteries since his rights and responsibilities toward religious are de-

fined elsewhere in the law. This would fulfill the idea of the last clause of the canon which speaks of special vigilance according to the norm of law.

Canon 616 — §1. A legitimately erected religious house can be suppressed by the supreme moderator according to the norm of the constitutions after having consulted the diocesan bishop. The proper law of the institute is to provide for the goods of the suppressed house, with due regard for the wills of the founders and donors or for legitimately acquired rights.

In general, the provisions of canon 616 follow the principle that the authority to suppress a house belongs to the authority competent to erect a house. Canon 616 further specifies the prescriptions of canons 584 and 585 which give the general norms for the suppression of institutes or their parts.

The power to suppress a house belongs to the supreme moderator in accord with the constitutions of the institute. The process implied in paragraph one is that the supreme moderator consider the question of the suppression of a house. If the decision is in favor of suppression, the diocesan bishop should be consulted. The diocesan bishop should then express his opinion to the supreme moderator after which the supreme moderator can make a decision whether or not to suppress the house. Suppression requires consultation with the bishop while erection of a house requires the consent of the bishop.

In institutes composed of provinces, the constitutions or proper law may provide that the initiative to close a house come from the province government since they have more direct authority over and better knowledge of their houses. Constitutions may also provide for the consent or the consultative vote of the council of the supreme moderator in order to suppress a house; however, the act of suppression belongs to the supreme moderator.

Again, suppression of a house, being analogous to erection of a house does not refer to every residence of a religious. The move of religious from one dwelling to another or their departure from a dwelling owned and furnished by a parish does not constitute the "suppression" of a house, just as their movement there, in and of itself, did not constitute the erection of a house.

The proper law of the institute is to provide for the disposition of the goods of the suppressed house. In institutes with houses in different countries, it may be better to provide for the disposition of goods according to the law of the nation in which the house is located so it can be accomplished in accord with the civil law of that country. This would be true in the United States where most religious institutes, some local houses, and/or the apostolates sponsored by the institute are tax exempt and may only distribute their goods upon le-

[6]*CLD* 8 (1978), 328–329.

gal dissolution in accord with certain tax-exempt purposes. Many religious institutes and religious institutions substantially restate the federal tax regulation on the disposition of goods upon dissolution in their articles of incorporation or bylaws. The federal tax law requires the goods be dedicated to another tax-exempt (religious or charitable) purpose which is the usual disposition of goods by a house of a religious institute. In doing so, the institute or another house or work of the institute may be named the beneficiary upon dissolution.

Canon 123 provides that upon the extinction of a public juridic person the allocation of its goods, rights, and obligations is governed by its statutes; however, if there are no statutes governing their distribution, they go to the immediately superior juridic person. As a practical matter, religious houses and residences should keep an up-to-date inventory of goods belonging to the religious house, diocese, or parish so that when a change of residence or suppression of a house occurs, the ownership of goods may be easily determined.

Goods that come to a house through a will or gift are to be disposed of in accord with the intent of the testator or donor. Usually, this will occur when the testator or donor makes the legacy or gift with attached conditions, such as limiting the use of the legacy or gift to certain purposes. For example, a house may be the beneficiary of the income of stocks and bonds placed in trust as long as the religious house uses the income to feed or clothe the poor of a particular city. If the house in that city is suppressed and there is no other house to do the work, the income may be lost. However, if the trust income may be used for the care of the poor in any area, the house may be suppressed and the income transferred to a similar work. If the institute is to give up the care of the poor entirely, then none of its houses would meet the conditions of the gift. Institutes should consult an attorney when receiving legacies and gifts so any conditions for use are understood; thus, if a house is suppressed and the house is the beneficiary of conditional gifts, the proper disposition of the goods may be made.

§2. The suppression of the only house of an institute pertains to the Holy See, to which is also reserved the right to determine what is to be done in that case with its goods.

The suppression of the only house of an institute is equivalent to suppression of the institute, thus this paragraph repeats the provision of canon 584, making the Holy See the competent authority to suppress. The Holy See also reserves the right to dispose of the goods of the institute in such a case. In these cases, property of members such as dowries should be restored to them. The status of former members of a suppressed institute would pertain to the Holy See. In most cases transfer to another institute or dispensation from vows would be granted to former members.

§3. The suppression of an autonomous house, such as that described in can. 613, belongs to the general chapter, unless the constitutions state otherwise.

This paragraph is part of the special legislation that appears throughout the law applying to autonomous houses. In this case, unless the constitutions state otherwise, the right to suppress an autonomous house belongs to the general chapter. Since this paragraph does not mention the disposition of goods upon suppression, this matter should be provided for in the constitutions.

§4. The suppression of an autonomous monastery of nuns pertains to the Apostolic See, with due regard for the prescriptions of the constitutions with regard to its goods.

This paragraph reflects the special relationship the Apostolic See has reserved to itself for autonomous monasteries of nuns (see c. 609, §2); therefore, the suppression of such a monastery belongs to the Apostolic See. The disposition of goods is to be in accord with the constitutions.

CHAPTER II
THE GOVERNANCE OF INSTITUTES
[cc. 617–640]

Chapter II on the governance of institutes is divided into three articles. The first two concern governance, namely article 1 on superiors and councils and article 2 on chapters. The third article on temporal goods and their administration is a specific application of the power of governance.

Article 1 on superiors and councils is composed of fourteen canons with the majority being devoted to the ministry, authority, selection, and removal of superiors at all levels from the supreme moderator to the local superior. Although the role of the superior is given more specific attention, the important and complementary role of both councils and members of institutes balances the section.

Article 2 contains the norms for general chapters and chapters of limited jurisdiction such as a province chapter. It also provides for other organs of participation and consultation. The fundamental responsibilities of a general chapter are outlined as well as norms for its composition. Because of the unique nature of each institute, the details for chapters and other organs of participation and consultation are left to the constitution and proper law.

Article 3 on temporal goods and their administration describes what parts of a religious institute are capable of exercising power over temporal goods; defines the goods of the institute as ecclesiastical goods; provides for the acquisition, use, and disposition of goods, the making of contracts, and the contracting of debt. It concludes with an exhortation regarding the use of temporal goods.

ARTICLE 1: SUPERIORS AND COUNCILS
[cc. 617–630]

Canon 617 — **Superiors are to fulfill their duty and exercise their power according to the norm of universal and proper law.**

This is an introductory canon which directs all superiors to the legal sources of the power of their office which is the universal law of the Church and all the levels of law regulating the life of an institute. The scope and limits of the power of a superior are contained in the universal and proper law. This would also imply the power to interpret the law subject to appeal to higher authority if an interpretation were disputed. There is no terminology in this Code parallel to that of "dominative power" used in canon 501, §1 of the 1917 Code.[7]

Canon 618 — **Superiors are to exercise their power, received from God through the ministry of the Church, in a spirit of service. Therefore, docile to the will of God in carrying out their duty, they are to govern their subjects as children of God and, promoting their voluntary obedience with reverence for the human person, they are to listen to them willingly and foster their working together for the good of the institute and of the Church, but with the superiors' authority to decide and prescribe what must be done remaining intact.**

This canon recognizes the principle that there is one authority in the Church. It is the power of Christ poured forth on the Church by the gift of the Holy Spirit at Pentecost. Thus, ecclesial authority is all spoken of as received from God. Since it is one, it is transmitted through the Church and, in imitation of Christ the Head, is exercised in a spirit of service. Those who exercise this authority in religious institutes do so according to the universal law and the proper law of the institute approved by the Church. Having been legitimately designated for a role of authority, they have that "personal" authority necessary for the exercise of their office.[8] The member's vow of obedience corresponds to and complements the authority of the superior in a mutual cooperation with the will of God.

While maintaining the principle of authority vested in persons, the Church in the spirit of the Council (*PC* 14) calls for the active participation on the part of all members of an institute toward a relationship of collaboration, cooperation, and mutual concern. Respect by members for those holding positions of authority is not meant to limit or excuse them from the requirement of personal responsibility for the life of the institute.

Superiors are called on to listen to the will of God both personally and with the members of the institute so that their actions will always flow from God's plan. Thus, authority and individual liberty go together in seeking and fulfilling God's will.[9] There may be particular structures established at all levels of the life of the institute to aid the superiors in listening to their members in order to better serve God, the people of God, and the institute.

Canon 619 — **Superiors are to devote themselves to their office assiduously and, together with the members entrusted to them, they should be eager to build a community of brothers or sisters in Christ in which God is sought after and loved before all else. Therefore, they are to nourish the members frequently with the food of the word of God and lead them to the celebration of the sacred liturgy. They are to be an example to the members in cultivating virtues and in the observance of the laws and traditions of the particular institute; they are to meet the personal needs of the members in an appropriate fashion, look after solicitously and visit the sick, admonish the restless, console the faint of heart, and be patient toward all.**

This canon emphasizes the pastoral role of superiors toward the members of the institute. It is based on *Perfectae Caritatis* 6 which applies to all members but which is here used as a guide for the superior in fulfilling the pastoral role of the office. Since it is basically a pastoral canon, it can be understood both as a balance to the specific juridical obligations of a superior and also as a guide to the way in which the superior exercises juridical responsibilities.

In selecting language from *Perfectae Caritatis* 6 that applies to each member of an institute, the canon emphasizes that the superior is not solely responsible for building a communion in Christ. Rather the superior does this with all the members of the institute. The emphasis is now on fraternal or sisterly caring rather than on a paternal or maternal superior role.[10] Nevertheless, while all share in this responsibility, the superior is designated as

[7]See c. 596 and cc. 617–619 on the authority of superiors.

[8]SCRIS has addressed the issue of the "personal" authority of a superior in *ET* 25, and *Experimenta Circa, AAS* 64 (1972), 393 and *CLD* 7 (1975), 484–485. See also *CLD* 8 (1978), 329–330.

[9]*ET* 25. This same section further states that "this labor of seeking together must end, when it is the moment, with the decision of the superiors whose presence and acceptance are indispensable in every community."

[10]C. 618 refers to members as "children of God" not as children of the superior. See also *ET* 25 which describes superiors as those who exercise responsibility among their brothers and sisters.

having a specific role of leadership in building up the community.

Although this summary of important responsibilities plus those enumerated in proper law might seem to place an impossible burden on superiors, it must be kept in mind that the same responsibilities also belong to the members to be exercised along with and in accord with superiors as members designated for leadership.

Canon 620 — Major superiors are those who govern a whole institute, a province of an institute, some part equivalent to a province, or an autonomous house, as well as their vicars. Comparable to these are the abbot primate and superior of a monastic congregation, who nonetheless do not have all the power which universal law grants major superiors.

The superiors in law who have the office of major superior are listed in this canon.[11] This canon identifies all those who exercise the responsibilities referred to in the canons that specifically mention the major superior.[12] It includes both the superior and vicar who govern:

1. a whole institute;

2. a province of an institute;

3. a part of an institute equivalent to a province;

4. an autonomous house.

The vicar is included as a major superior because the vicar has the power of the major superior when the major superior cannot exercise the responsibilities of office. It may be helpful to state the occasions when a vicar exercises the office of major superior in the proper law.

An abbot primate and the superior of a monastic congregation are included with certain limitations. To ascertain the responsibilities of a specific office, both universal law and the laws of the monastic institute must be consulted.

Canon 621 — The grouping of several houses under the same superior which constitutes an immediate part of the institute and which has been canonically erected by the legitimate authority is called a province.

A province is defined by this canon as a:

1. union of several houses;

2. under the same superior;

3. constituting an immediate part of the institute;

4. erected by the legitimate canonical authority of the institute.

This definition is related to canon 620 which defines one who governs a province or its equivalent as a major superior. The erection of a province belongs to the competent authority of the institute (c. 581), which is a change from the 1917 Code (*CIC* 494) which reserved the right to erect a province to the Holy See. The proper law of the institute should set forth the criteria to be used in erecting a province which may include a minimum number of members, a specific geographical locale, or a similar culture or language.

The term "immediate" appears to mean the first or primary organizational unit of an institute that exists without some intervening unit of organization between it and the highest authority of an institute. This should be interpreted flexibly so as not to interfere with commissions, special groups, etc., that are formed to serve an institute at the highest level.

Canon 622 — The supreme moderator holds power over all provinces, houses and members of the institute, which is to be exercised according to proper law; other superiors enjoy power within the limits of their office.

The supreme moderator of an institute has authority which extends to a variety of circumstances defined by the common law and power which extends to all provinces, houses, and members and is exercised according to the law of the institute. This canon pertains to the power which the supreme moderator has by virtue of proper law. Within the general principles of church law, each institute—consistent with its own charism, tradition, and ongoing renewal—is to establish the power a supreme moderator has in regard to provinces, houses, and members. The powers given to a supreme moderator in proper law can cover a wide range since some institutes prefer a highly centralized form of government which gives the supreme moderator extensive power even in a province or over houses and members, while other institutes are very decentralized, with the supreme moderator providing a base of unity for the entire institute, exercising power periodically in a province—usually centering on the time of visitation, election, and chapter—and very little power over individual houses or members.

---

[11] The superiors listed in c. 620 are comparable to those listed in *CIC* 488, 8°.
[12] In certain cases such as that of an institute which has no provinces or equivalent structure, the same person may be both a supreme moderator and a major superior according to canon law.

Canon 623 — **In order that members be validly appointed or elected to the office of superior, a suitable time is required after perpetual or definitive profession, to be determined by proper law, or if it is a question of major superiors, by the constitutions.**

The 1917 Code (*CIC* 504) required a particular age and time in vows for a member to be designated a superior general or major superior. This canon which applies to all levels of superiors requires only a suitable time after perpetual profession to be a superior although institutes are free to have an age requirement. Because of the later age of entrance into religious life in some institutes, age may not be a relevant concern, while in other institutes, where age of entrance is early, age may be a consideration and an appropriate matter for proper law.

Both later age of entrance and transfers of religious between institutes make the focus of this canon on time in perpetual commitment a prudent provision for insuring sufficient experience in the life of the institute and commitment to it, a requirement before assuming a role of leadership and responsibility. The requirement of a suitable period of time after perpetual commitment to be appointed or selected as superior is necessary for validity, thus it may not be omitted in the constitutions for major superiors or proper law for other superiors. For local superiors, time after perpetual commitment or the retention of an age requirement may be more suitably regulated by the proper law of provinces or other divisions that can take into account national and cultural situations of experience in religious life and age.

In addition, since exceptional people may not be eligible for the office of superior because they do not meet the requirement for a suitable time after perpetual commitment, an institute may wish to provide for a waiver of its requirements. A regulation on waiver should be suitably phrased to designate who has the right to waive and the procedure for waiver. Waiver should not be used as a method of bypassing important requirements for office or appointing personal choices to the office of superior.

Canon 624 — **§1. Superiors are to be constituted for a certain and appropriate amount of time according to the nature and needs of the institute, unless the constitutions state otherwise for the supreme moderator and for superiors of autonomous houses.**

This paragraph states the principle that superiors at all levels should hold office for a specified period of time. Two exceptions are allowed which show deference to approved traditions of religious institutes. These are the supreme moderator and the superiors of autonomous houses. Traditionally, these institutes have provided that such offices be for life, although some have now changed this practice. Institutes which prefer to retain superiors in office for life must provide for it in their constitutions.

§2. Proper law is to provide in suitable norms that superiors constituted for a definite time do not remain too long in offices of governance without an interruption.

This paragraph is related to canon 624, §1. Even though there is to be a certain term of office for superiors, there is also to be a limit on the amount of time, or consecutive terms, a superior holds office. The provision seems intended to provide a healthy turnover of superiors so that one person does not continue too long in office with the potential negative effects to the person and the institute. One who has served a defined amount of time in office as superior may be reelected or reappointed after an intermission in office according to the proper law of the institute.

Institutes may make these provisions to cover time in a particular office or to cover time in all like offices of governance. For example, there may be a limit of two consecutive terms as superior of a particular local community and no more than three consecutive terms as superior of all local communities.

§3. Nevertheless they can be removed from office during their term or transferred to another office for reasons determined in proper law.

Two separate situations are covered by this paragraph. First, removal of a superior from office must be for cause stated in proper law. Appropriate reasons would be bad health, malfeasance, serious incompetence, repeated serious violations of the constitutions, or other serious causes. Institutes should also develop a procedure for removal which would protect both the institute and the superior whose removal is proposed.[13] As a matter of practice, voluntary resignation—especially in cases of bad health—is usually the preferred process.[14]

Transfer usually occurs when a person is more needed in another office of the institute. The reasons for transfer might be to start a new province or work of an institute or to engage in some service to the whole institute. Again, the causes and process should be stated in proper law.[15]

Canon 625 — **§1. The supreme moderator of an institute is to be designated by canonical election according to the norm of the constitutions.**

---

[13]See cc. 192–195.
[14]See cc. 187–189.
[15]See cc. 190–191.

The supreme moderator must be chosen through canonical election, i.e., according to canons 164–179 which contain the general norms for election to an ecclesiastical office, and in accord with the norm of the constitutions of the institute. Except for the general norms on canonical elections, the method of election is determined by the institute as stated in the constitutions. For the majority of institutes, the election is accomplished by the general chapter; however, certain institutes have received approval for the direct election of the supreme moderator.[16]

§2. The bishop of the principal seat presides at elections of the superior of an autonomous monastery, mentioned in can. 615, and of the supreme moderator of an institute of diocesan right.

This paragraph is a change from canon 506 of the 1917 Code since the bishop of the principal seat of the institute presides at the election of the supreme moderator only for diocesan institutes and autonomous monasteries. The bishop may appoint a delegate to preside at such elections.

This paragraph is in accord with canon 586 regarding the internal life of institutes since it omits the discretionary power of a bishop to nullify or ratify elections for diocesan institutes and to preside at the elections of pontifical institutes of women.

§3. Other superiors are to be constituted according to the norm of the constitutions, but in such a way that if they are elected they need the confirmation of the competent major superior; if they are appointed by the superior, a suitable consultation is to precede.

All other superiors are constituted according to the constitutions of the institute. Thus, each level (province, region, local) may elect a superior provided that election is confirmed by the competent major superior. Conversely, if a superior is to be appointed by a higher superior, the appointment is to be preceded by sufficient consultation with the members, i.e., to let the superior know the thoughts of the members. The principle is established in this paragraph of communicating the selection of superiors to both higher authority and to members to ensure that all who are affected by the designation of superior may be heard.

Both the method of consultation by the competent major superior and the method of confirmation should be outlined in the proper law of the institute. For example, confirmation could be by a competent major superior alone, with the consent of the council, or with a consultative vote. Suitable consultation could be by discussion with chapter members, members of a local community, or even by a consulting vote.

Canon 626 — **Superiors in the conferral of offices and members in elections are to observe the norms of universal and proper law, abstain from any abuse or partiality and name or elect those whom they know in the Lord to be truly worthy and suitable having nothing in mind but God and the good of the institute. Moreover, in elections they are to avoid any procurement of votes either directly or indirectly for themselves or for others.**

Elections and appointments to offices in religious institutes[17] are to be characterized by members seeking the will of God and the good of the institute. This should be understood from the perspective of the teaching of the Church that authority in the Church is a share in the authority of Christ participated in through the various structures and institutions in the Church with an emphasis on service rather than power.

Superiors in conferring offices, and members in elections are to nominate or elect those whom they believe in the Lord to be worthy and suitable. Thus, dialogue, prayer, and reflection all form part of the process of discernment which should characterize the selection or election of leaders in religious institutes.

Nominating and electing worthy and suitable people require knowledge of the persons being considered and the kind of discussion that promotes adequate knowledge. This is especially true in large and/or international institutes in which qualifications for office may not be well known. Discussion and consultation among members and chapter delegates of the qualifications of members for office are not prohibited by the canon and is a method of gaining the necessary knowledge to cast a vote. Some institutes in their proper law provide appropriate forms of discussion and consultation on the qualifications of members for office. A community may have a nominating or preference ballot to guide chapter members in casting their vote.

The means of obtaining helpful information and electing worthy and suitable people is limited by the prohibition not to procure votes. This limitation excludes asking for votes or making promises to receive a vote. It would not exclude asking people who are nominated or being considered for office to present their views on a particular matter or arranging a forum or means for the presentation of such views; however, there would be no obligation on the part of a religious being considered for office to present his or her views or opinions. In addition, it would not exclude the necessary consultation re-

---

[16]*CLD* 8 (1978), 354–357, *CLD* Supp. through 1980, c. 506 (1981), 1; *RR* (1982), 35–36.

[17]Cc. 164–179.

ferred to above to gain the requisite knowledge to cast a vote.

The canon does not state the effect of the determination that procurement occurred during an election. An institute may wish to invalidate an election in the case of procurement or provide for a commission to investigate whether procurement affected the results of an election before declaring it invalid since holding a new election or reconvening a chapter may be a difficult and expensive undertaking.

Canon 627 — §1. According to the norm of the constitutions, superiors are to have their own council, whose assistance they are to use in carrying out their office.

This paragraph of the law providing that superiors at all levels have a council establishes both a form of participation in government by the members of the institute and a way of guarding against any overly autonomous exercise of authority. The emphasis is on the help a council can provide superiors in fulfilling their role.

The composition of the council at each level in the institute is a matter to be provided for in the constitutions. It would also be proper for each institute to describe the role of the council and the election or selection process in the proper law. In addition, it would be appropriate to note the instances in which the local community could be constituted as a house council or the prerogative of the appropriate authority to do so because of the small number of members assigned to a house[18] or when it may not be practical to have a house council.

The law does not determine the number of councillors nor the requirements to be a councillor. These are both matters for proper law. However, if a general council is not composed of four members in addition to the superior, there should be a provision in proper law for gathering such a body in the event of a dismissal of a member.[19]

The responsibilities of councillor are a matter for both universal and proper law. Canon 627, §2 refers to the cases in which the universal law requires the consent or consultation of the council, and proper law can do the same. The primary role of the councillor is to offer honest and sincere advice as well as to raise important issues before the superior and council. In the organization of many institutes, councillors also have administrative roles in the governance or service of the institute that need to be clearly stated in proper law. Job descriptions together with an organizational chart and lines of communication and accountability will help to ensure the proper functioning of the unit.

§2. Besides the cases prescribed in universal law, proper law is to determine cases in which consent or counsel is required in order to act validly, which must be obtained in accord with the norm of can. 127.

This paragraph enumerates the two cases in which a superior needs to seek the consent of the council for the validity of an act. The first is the matter prescribed in the universal law, and the second is the matter prescribed in the proper law of the institute.

The universal law requires the superior to seek the consent of the council or vote collegially in certain instances[20] and to seek consultation, hear the opinion, or act with the council in other instances.[21] In some matters the decision is left to the competent authority which gives institutes the right to decide the method by which a decision is to be made.[22] The methods chosen should be stated in proper law. There is no legal limitation on the matters for which proper law might require consent or consultation for validity, except those matters that are reserved to a particular superior. There are, however, the traditions of the institute and the practicality of apportioning decisions requiring the consent of the council, the consultative vote of the council, or the decision of the superior so that the proper balance of deliberation, votation, flexibility, and speed of response occurs in a given situation.

The reference to canon 127 on juridic acts is a significant one involving the validity of actions which are to be taken with the advice or consent of a "collegial body." Canon 127, §2, 1° invalidates actions of a superior requiring consent if the superior did not seek consent or acted against the vote of the body required to give consent. Canon 127, §2, 2° invalidates actions of a superior that require counsel if the superior has not sought counsel or listened. Although the superior is not required to follow the result of a consultative vote, the superior should not depart from the vote without some persuasive reason. In accord with canon 127, §1 the council must be called together when consent or consultation is required, and if no opportunity is given council members to manifest consent or opinion the action of the superior is invalid. In addition, when consent or counsel is required, the council is obliged to secrecy by canon 127, §3 if in the judgment of the superior the matter requires it.

This paragraph also allows for further determinations regarding consent that may be added to proper law. Such a matter might include a requirement for a unanimous vote or a certain number or

---

[18]*CLD* 7 (1975), 480; *CLD* 8 (1978), 333.
[19]See c. 699, §1.

[20]See cc. 638, §3; 647, §1; 647, §2; 665, §1; 684, §1; 684, §3; 686, §1; 686, §3; 688, §2; 690, §1; 690, §2; 699, §1; and 703.
[21]See cc. 656, 3°; 689, §1; 691, §1; 694, §2; and 697.
[22]See cc. 580; 581; 585; 587, §4; 609, §1; 616, §1; and 641.

percent of the council in matters considered to be of great importance.

Deliberative vote means a superior may not place a certain act without the consent of the council. There is no obligation on the part of a superior to act after having obtained the consent of the council. For instance, if a superior has the consent of the council to sell a property that requires the consent of the council, the superior is not obligated to sell the property after obtaining the consent of the council. If, however, the council has advised the sale of the property, the superior should not, without good cause, act contrary to the advice.

Consulting a council may take the form of a consultative vote which as stated above does not oblige the superior but which the superior should not act contrary to unless there is very serious reason to do so, especially when the vote is unanimous. Consulting the council members can also mean listening to them and then acting after hearing their advice. This mode is often expressed in the terms "with the advice of council," "having consulted wih the council," or "having heard the council." It is important that the nature of the vote or consultation be clearly stated in the constitutions or proper law and that the vote or consultation be recorded accurately in the minutes.

Canon 628 — **§1. Superiors who are designated for this function by the proper law of the institute are to visit the houses and members entrusted to them at the times designated by the norms of this same proper law.**

The institution of visitation is ancient in religious life. It dates from the earliest days when institutes established more than one house subject to the same higher superior. Without doubt, one of the purposes of this practice was to promote fidelity and to guard against abuses whether on the part of members or on the part of superiors. More positively, however, particularly with regard to large, widely spread institutes engaged in works of the apostolate, the visitation can serve as a source of unity, inspiration, and a mutual exchange of ideas and experiences. Further, it can be an invaluable source of information and understanding for those who carry particular responsibility for the mission of the institute. It is intended to provide a forum in which each member of an institute may offer observations on the state of life in the institute and the local community. Visitation is a privileged moment in which a superior may come to know the members of the institute. As large institutes, particularly those which are international, seek to practice more effectively the principle of subsidiarity, they will find the experience of visitation in diverse cultures and circumstances essential for knowing how to apply this principle.

The person given the charge to make the visitation and the frequency of visitations are left to proper law. The scope and number of visitations should be arranged so as not to burden an institute with too many visitations nor to make them so infrequent that important matters are not easily addressed. The coordination of visitations in multilevel institutes is necessary to promote order in governance and management of institute affairs.

§2. It is the right and the duty of the diocesan bishop to visit even with respect to religious discipline:

1° autonomous monasteries mentioned in can. 615;

2° individual houses of an institute of diocesan right situated in his territory.

The bishop has the right and duty to visit autonomous monasteries and houses of institutes of diocesan right in his territory even regarding matters of religious discipline. Since such institutes have their own visitation which covers matters of religious discipline, the superior of the institute and the bishop should coordinate the scope and timing of their visitations so as not to duplicate work or overburden the members of the institute.[23]

§3. Members are to deal in a trusting manner with a visitator, whose legitimate questions they are obliged to answer according to truth in love; moreover no one is permitted in any way to divert members from this obligation or otherwise to impede the scope of the visitation.

Trust is a necessary characteristic if the purpose of a visitation is to be accomplished. The demeanor of the visitator should promote trust and a member should come to the visitator in a trusting manner. A visitation can be an effective instrument of promoting fidelity and unity and of correcting abuses only if members are trustful. This trustfulness should find its source in the obligation of each member to promote the growth of the institute.

Since members are normally obliged to answer legitimate questions, the visitator should phrase questions in a sensitive manner, so as not to accuse anyone or to betray a source of information. In addition, members are protected from being induced to make a manifestation of conscience to superiors and by analogy this would also apply to visitators.

Canon 629 — **All superiors are to reside in their respective houses and not absent themselves from it, unless according to the norm of proper law.**

---

[23]See c. 396 and c. 683 regarding visitation by the diocesan bishop; also *Venite Seorsum,* nos. 8, 9, and 14 regarding cloistered nuns and visitation.

Each religious house is to have a superior (c. 608). Superiors are to reside in their own house and are not to be absent from the house except as proper law allows. The requirement of residency for superiors is meant to promote availability and accessibility since being present to the community is certainly an effective means of discharging the pastoral responsibility of a superior. Superiors are absent for a variety of valid reasons including apostolate, recreation, retreat, vacation, etc. This canon puts superiors on notice that constant absence limits their availability to truly serve the members of the community.

Institutes may find it impractical to have a superior at every residence, especially in the case of small communities; thus, designating a regional superior may be more practical. This canon does not restrict such flexibility in accord with the proper law of the institute.[24]

Canon 630 — §1. Superiors are to recognize the due freedom of their members concerning the sacrament of penance and the direction of conscience, with due regard however for the discipline of the institute.

Canon 630 on the sacrament of penance combines the principles of freedom of conscience and the value of the sacrament. It is drawn from *Perfectae Caritatis* 14 obliging the superior to make a special point of allowing members to have freedom with regard to the sacrament of penance and the direction of conscience. This is important since rapport between the confessor or spiritual director and the individual is such an important element in an ongoing relationship with a confessor or spiritual director. The language "with due regard however for the discipline of the institute" allows institutes to adopt their own norms regarding the sacrament of penance and spiritual direction. These regulations should likewise not infringe on the freedom of members in regard to the sacrament of penance or spiritual direction.

§2. According to the norm of proper law superiors are to be solicitous that suitable confessors to whom they can confess frequently be available to members.

This paragraph which describes the obligations of superiors to see that confessors are available should be read with canon 664 regarding the responsibility of members to receive the sacrament of penance. Although the paragraph applies to all superiors, it has a special application to superiors of

houses where it may be more difficult for members to receive the sacrament of penance such as houses of retirement or infirmaries.

§3. In monasteries of nuns, in houses of formation and in more numerous lay communities there are to be ordinary confessors approved by the local ordinary after consultation with the community; members nevertheless have no obligation to approach them.

The law specifies certain houses, which because of their nature, are to have ordinary confessors approved by the local ordinary after having consulted with the community. These are the following:

1. monasteries of nuns;

2. formation houses;

3. larger communities of lay religious.

In the case of monasteries of nuns, the reason clearly is regard for cloister. With regard to formation houses, the reason for an ordinary confessor would flow from the special nature of this period of religious life. The provision for an ordinary confessor for larger houses of lay religious would seem to be one of consideration for the needs of these religious, especially if it would be difficult for them to travel to see a confessor or if their number would work a hardship in the local situation. No one is obliged to approach such confessors.

The key principle remains, in all cases, the availability of the sacrament through confessors suited to the needs of the religious. There is no longer a provision in the law requiring that priests have special faculties in order to hear the confessions of religious.

§4. Superiors are not to hear the confessions of their subjects unless the latter request it of their own initiative.

The norm that superiors should not hear the confessions of subjects unless they request it of their own free will is intended to protect superiors from any implication that they might have consciously or inadvertently used internal forum knowledge in their role as superior. The exception is made so that subjects cannot be denied the sacrament of penance at a time when only the superior is available or when the superior is the one the subject feels is to be most trusted.

§5. Members are to approach superiors with trust, to whom they can express their minds freely and willingly. However, superiors are forbidden to induce their subjects in any way whatever to make a manifestation of conscience to them.

---

[24]See the SCRIS reply in *CLD* 7 (1975); 467, stating "the office of superior cannot be dispensed with in local houses" and *CLD* 8 (1978); 347 allowing for a non-resident superior in small communities.

Paragraph five is meant to balance the pastoral role of the superior as one who can be trusted and freely approached with the superior's role of governing in which the member is to be protected from the coercion that may issue from a person in authority and used to gain knowledge of matters of conscience.

Manifestation of conscience includes all matter of the interior life from the highest grace to sinful matters. It does not include the external conduct of the member, most especially that required for fidelity to the life of the community contained in the proper law of the institute. At the same time, a member may voluntarily make a manifestation of conscience to a superior, but a superior may not reveal this matter in the external forum without the consent of the subject.[25]

ARTICLE 2: CHAPTERS
[cc. 631–633]

The general chapter is the highest authority in an institute whose supreme authority should be described in the constitutions. In order that the actions of the institute be truly representative of the entire institute, the chapter is to be formed so that this representation is ensured.

Canon 631 — §1. The general chapter, which holds supreme authority in the institute according to the norm of the constitutions, is to be so formed that, representing the entire institute, it should be a true sign of its unity in love. Its foremost duty is this: to protect the patrimony of the institute mentioned in can. 578, and promote suitable renewal in accord with this patrimony, to elect the supreme moderator, to treat major business matters and to publish norms which all are bound to obey.

The general chapter, recognized as having supreme authority according to the constitutions, is to be representative of the total institute and a sign of its unity in charity. This quality of being representative suggests broad membership from throughout the institute, as opposed to the chapter appearing as the privileged domain of any particular group. The chapter should not have an excessively large number of ex officio members so that broad representation is diluted. The notion of representation, however, does not mean that delegates are elected to "represent" certain ideas, works, or theologies. As a delegate, the religious is of and for the whole institute and is not to be thought of as bound in any way by the thinking of a "constituency" by whom the delegate was elected, even if delegates are nominated or elected from a particular

group within the community such as age groups, apostolates, or geographical areas.[26]

The canon sets forth some of the principal responsibilities of the general chapter: to preserve the institute's particular patrimony and promote appropriate renewal according to that patrimony; to elect the supreme moderator; to deal with major affairs; and to publish norms binding on all. This is the one governmental body in religious life which truly operates on a collegial model in the sense that all persons participating have equal voice. Those who are in positions of authority in the institute have no higher authority in or over the chapter and should not try to exercise special influence by virtue of their elected or appointed position. Superiors as well as all other members of the institute are bound by the acts of a chapter that is legitimately held and concluded. Proper law, however, should make some provision for the interpretation of doubtful matters which might arise in chapter acts.

It will be noted that the law continues to maintain that the highest superior of the institute is elected within the general chapter. There have been instances of exceptions allowing for direct election in small institutes.[27]

§2. The composition and the extent of the power of the chapter is to be defined in the constitutions; proper law is to determine further the order to be observed in the celebration of the chapter, especially regarding elections and procedures for handling various matters.

In the light of some years of experimentation under the guidance of *Ecclesiae sanctae*'s[28] directives of more participative chapter preparation, the law calls for proper law to define and develop its own norms regarding the general chapter. It will be noted that a distinction is made here: the composition of the chapter and the scope of its power are to be in the constitutions; other matter may be in the institute's proper law.

There are different methods of ordering a chapter, especially in regard to timing the elections and adopting resolutions or statutes for the institute. In some institutes the election precedes consideration of substantive matters, while others consider the substantive matters first in order to commit the newly elected superior and council to the directives of the chapter.

It is of particular importance in nations where religious are accustomed to the ways of participative democracy that proper law express clearly both the spiritual ideals of such a collegial body and the broad responsibilities and obligations for active participation in the overall work of the chapter. Many

[25]See *PC* 14 fostering respect for direction of conscience.

[26]*CLD* 8 (1978); 332.
[27]See commentary on c. 625, §1 and footnote 16.
[28]*ES* 11, 1–4 and 6.

decisions must be made according to the nature of the institute and serious effort made, especially in international institutes, to provide for adequate representation of diverse cultures and for appropriate degrees of subsidiarity in the implementation of chapter decisions.

§3. According to norms determined in proper law, not only provinces and local communities but also any member at all can freely send his or her wishes and suggestions to the general chapter.

This paragraph is intended to protect the access of not only provinces and local communities to a chapter but also individual members. This is important since the collating and consolidating of pre-chapter suggestions may lose the import and direction of particular suggestions which can be presented in their particularity by any member of an institute.

Canon 631 does not touch on the subject of active and passive voice in the election of chapter delegates. The 1917 Code left the matter to proper law except for excluding those in temporary vows from active or passive voice unless the constitutions determined otherwise.[29] For the most part, institutes restricted active and passive voice to perpetually professed members. However, the guidelines of the Sacred Congregation for Religious and Secular Institutes have approved granting active voice to members in temporary vows and passive voice to those professed for more than three years.[30]

Canon 632 — Proper law is to determine clearly what pertains to other chapters of the institute and other similar gatherings, namely, regarding their nature, authority, composition, mode of procedure and time of celebration.

The canons do not regulate similar bodies at a lower level of government within the institute. The regulation of chapters or similar gatherings at the provincial or other levels is left to proper law. Where chapters at diverse levels are traditionally built into proper law, these should be examined in the light of the principles of participation, representation, and subsidiarity. Proper law should determine the nature, authority, composition, manner of proceeding, and time for such other gatherings. The responsibilities of chapters at each level need to be clearly stated in order to avoid confusion.

The decisions regarding the diverse types of gatherings (e.g., chapters, assemblies of the whole, etc.) should be made so that members understand the role of the body, what sort of decisions are to be made (if any), and how this body is related to other levels of government. Proper law should be sufficiently concrete as to what will take place, what authority, if any, the body has, and whether the outcome will be decisions, recommendations, or reports so that excessive amounts of energy do not have to go into such decisions every time there is occasion for such a gathering. Members must be able to become familiar with the processes so that they can participate more actively.

Canon 633 — §1. Organs of participation or consultation are to carry out faithfully the duty entrusted to them according to the norm of universal and proper law and to express in their own way the concern and participation of all members for the good of the entire institute or community.

All organs of participation, chapters at all levels, councils, assemblies, senates, commissions, etc., should carry out the duties entrusted to them in the law. Since only the general chapter and general council are governed specifically but not totally by universal law, the completion of regulations for these bodies and regulations for all other organs of participation and consultation are to be determined by proper law.

Ecclesiae sanctae[31] provided that each institute was to ensure the participation of all the members for the good of the entire community. It further noted that this will be the case if members have a real and effective part in the choice of chapter and council officials. The same principle applies by analogy to all the institute's organs of participation and consultation.

§2. Wise discretion is to be used in establishing and using these means of participation and consultation, and their procedures are to conform to the character and purpose of the institute.

In order to provide appropriate means of participation and consultation, religious institutes have used a wide variety of methods such as pre-chapter surveys, local community meetings, and open forum meetings for whole institutes or parts of an institute. These methods have been used for various purposes including formulating a chapter agenda, discussing important matters on a chapter agenda, or broader purposes such as discussing the charism of the institute or redefining the mission of the institute. Discretion is urged because institutes have had varying degrees of success in employing different means of participation and consultation.

---

[29]*CIC* 578, §3.
[30]*Con Life*, vol. II, no. 1 (1977); 59–62. See also *CLD* 8 (1978); 368–369.

[31]*ES* 11, 18.

ARTICLE 3: TEMPORAL GOODS AND
THEIR ADMINISTRATION
[cc. 634–640]

The canons of article 3 further specify the Church's general law on temporal goods as it applies to religious institutes and their parts insofar as they are juridic persons. Thus, in order to understand the law, reference must be made to canons 1254–1310 on temporal goods and canons 113–123 on juridic persons.

Canon 634 — **§1. Institutes, provinces and houses, insofar as they are juridic persons by the law itself, are capable of acquiring, possessing, administering and alienating temporal goods, unless this capacity has been excluded or restricted in the constitutions.**

This paragraph enumerates the parts of a religious institute that are capable of acquiring, possessing, administering, and alienating temporal goods. This capability belongs to institutes, provinces, and houses insofar as they are juridic persons. It would likewise apply to institutions separate in civil law such as schools and hospitals that are part of a juridic person. The capacity can be limited or excluded in the constitutions for the whole institute (some mendicant institutes) or for a part of the institute (a province or a house). With regard to houses, recognition by law as a juridic person would seem to apply only to those erected in accord with canon 609.

Religious institutes and their parts also need to select an appropriate form of civil legal existence in order to effectively perform their mission. In addition, administrators are required by canon 1284, §2, 2° to see that ownership of ecclesiastical goods is safeguarded in civilly valid ways. In the United States this frequently means incorporation as a nonprofit corporation. Incorporation does not add to or diminish the powers of a juridic person, although corporate documents that do not clearly address canonical responsibilities can sometimes negate or cause difficulty in the exercise of canonical powers. Canonical responsibility for the alienation and administration of goods always belongs to the appropriate juridic person. Usually, this is the supreme moderator and council or the major superior and council whether it be for the institute itself or one of several apostolic works of the institute such as schools or hospitals. In a non-profit corporation this can be accomplished by reserving the civil powers that parallel canonical responsibility to the superior and council. Thus, it is appropriate for the institute to devise the civil law organization in such a way that its canonical responsibilities can be easily exercised.

It should also be recognized that when religious undertake an apostolate, there is no canonical obligation to own or completely control the organization or institution through which the apostolate is accomplished, which means there may be no goods to administer; thus, the canons on temporal goods would not apply. At the same time, a religious institute may decide that ownership or complete control is the best method of accomplishing their particular apostolate or mission. Decisions regarding the structure used to engage in a specific apostolate should be made with due consideration for the consequences of the use of that structure for a particular mission.[32]

§2. Nevertheless, they are to avoid all appearance of luxury, immoderate wealth and amassing of goods.

This paragraph is based on *Perfectae Caritatis* 13 exhorting institutes to avoid all semblance of luxury, excessive wealth, and accumulation of property because of the scandal to others when institutes live in a manner inconsistent with their way of life. This paragraph should be read with canon 635, §2 which encourages institutes to use and administer goods so that their corporate poverty is fostered and canon 640 which expresses the positive responsibility to contribute goods to care for the needs of the Church and the poor.

Canon 635 — **§1. The temporal goods of religious institutes, since they are ecclesiastical goods, are regulated by the prescriptions of Book V,** *The Temporal Goods of the Church,* **unless it is expressly stated otherwise.**

The general norms on the temporal goods of the Church regulate ecclesiasical goods; therefore, insofar as the temporal goods of a religious institute are ecclesiastical goods, they are regulated by that law. This paragraph provides for exceptions that would either appear in the common law or in particular regulations approved for an institute by the Apostolic See. For example, the law on temporal goods states the right of juridic persons to own and administer property. In areas where this is prohibited by civil law or practice, the Apostolic See can make appropriate exceptions for the institute. Canon 1280 provides that each juridic person should have

---

[32]For example, religious institutes can insure and protect the mission of an institution by several means such as clearly stating the purpose of an institution in the articles of organization, by making the council corporate members, by reserving a certain number of places on the board of trustees, by ongoing financial contributions that continue only so long as the mission of the organization is being fulfilled, by exercising a priority option to fill designated positions in the organization, or by contracting to fill certain positions in the organization.

its own finance council or at least two advisors that assist the administrator in meeting the important responsibilities of stewardship which will apply to each institute and its parts that are juridic persons.

§2. Nevertheless, each institute is to determine appropriate norms for the use and administration of goods so that the poverty appropriate to the institute is fostered, protected and expressed.

This paragraph is based generally on *Ecclesiae sanctae* 11, 23. Each institute is to develop norms so that the institute can nourish, protect, and express its way of living poverty. This is an all-encompassing and important regulation. It may be comparatively easy to make norms that apply to property or money. It is more difficult to provide norms that dovetail the use and administration of goods with the religious heritage of poverty. Yet, that is the meaning of this paragraph.

Canon 636 — **§1. In each institute and likewise in each province which is governed by a major superior there is to be a finance officer, distinct from the major superior and constituted according to the norm of proper law, who carries out the administration of goods under the direction of the respective superior. Even in local communities there is to be a finance officer distinct from the local superior to the extent that it is possible.**

Treasurers are provided for from the highest level of an institute to the local community level. The superior and the treasurer should be different persons at the higher levels of government, but in the local community it is only required that the treasurer should be distinct from the local superior where possible. In situations in which a superior has a full schedule of pastoral and administrative duties, it is doubtful if such a superior should be treasurer as well.

The treasurer is to be constituted according to proper law wherein the requirements and general duties of the office should be stated. A more particular job description should also be developed for each level of treasurer. The treasurer is an administrative officer under the direction of the moderator or superior. Proper law or a job description should outline the actions a treasurer may perform without seeking the permission of the superior.

§2. At the time and in the manner determined by proper law finance officers and other administrators are to render an account of their administrative actions to the competent authority.

Treasurers and other administrators are to render an account to the competent superior at the time and in the manner stated in proper law. These reports may be weekly, monthly, annually (or all three) depending on the frequency of transactions and the necessity of up-to-date reports. Other administrators might include someone in charge of property, pensions, trust funds, or investments.

Canon 637 — **Autonomous monasteries mentioned in can. 615 must render an account of their administration once a year to the local ordinary; moreover, the local ordinary has the right to know about the financial reports of religious houses of diocesan right.**

An autonomous monastery is to render an annual account to the local ordinary. The monastery and the bishop should develop norms for the report. It would normally include a statement of income and expenses for the year, a balance sheet, and a narrative report on important transactions and the financial condition of the monastery. The local ordinary also has the right to know about the economic affairs of religious houses of diocesan right. This would include statements similar to those mentioned above.

Canon 638 — **§1. It is for proper law, within the scope of universal law, to determine acts which exceed the limit and manner of ordinary administration and to determine those things which are necessary to place an act of extraordinary administration validly.**

This paragraph governing the administration of goods in religious institutes is similar to canon 1281 on the administration of goods in the Church.[33] First, an institute is to determine which acts exceed the limit and manner of extraordinary administration. The limit refers to the dollar amount and the type of transaction.

The judgment as to what is ordinary or extraordinary in regard to the limit and manner must take into account the nature of the institute and its apostolates which are covered by this paragraph. Religious institutes and their works range from the simple to the very complex. Proper law will need to account not only for the transactions of the institute and its houses but also institutions which daily deal in a variety of transactions that involve large amounts of money and may in certain instances require a speedy decision. Thus, that which is extraordinary for the institute may be ordinary for its educational institutions or hospitals.

The majority of institutional apostolic works in the United States are non-profit corporations. Whether the work is a separate corporation or part

---

[33]See the commentary on c. 1281 describing ordinary and extraordinary administration.

of a multilayered corporate system, the corporate charter, bylaws, or other legal documents should take account of the canonical requirements.[34]

This paragraph also looks to proper law to describe the process for validly placing an act of extraordinary administration. Such processes may include the consent of the council; a report or recommendation from the local house, the trustees, advisors, or governing board of an apostolic work, pension committee, or investment committee.

The investment of money should also be subject to internal policy. What is needed is a practical, prudent approach to investments such as a finance or investment committee that is empowered to make purchases and sales up to a certain amount and beyond that to seek the permission of the superior and the council. It is also wise to have the advice of experts who are knowledgeable about investments. An annual accounting that lists all investments (real estate, stocks, bonds, etc.) with their purchase price, current market value, and annual income or yield made to the superior and distributed to the members would be appropriate so that members know the current financial status of the institute and can make recommendations regarding the use of the resources of the institute.

§2. Besides superiors, officials who are designated for this purpose in the proper law can validly incur expenses and perform juridic acts of ordinary administration within the limits of their office.

Those other than superiors who may perform acts of ordinary administration would be treasurers; investment officers or committees; fund-raisers; a president, chief executive officer, or director of a school, hospital, or retreat center. The officers should be named and the acts they can perform should be defined in the appropriate proper law or civil documents if applicable.

Since soliciting resources is an important work of most institutes in order to further their particular missions, it is important that this work reflect the principle of Christian stewardship. Thus, the principles and guidelines for fund-raising in the United States should be followed and supplemented by internal guidelines where necessary to meet the responsibilities the institute has to its donors and the public at large.[35]

§3. For the validity of alienation and any other business transaction in which the patrimonial condition of a juridic person can be affected adversely, there is required the written permission of the competent superior with the consent of the council. If, moreover, it concerns a business transaction which exceeds the highest amount defined for a given region by the Holy See, or items given to the Church in virtue of a vow, or items of precious art or of historical value, the permission of the Holy See is also required.

The written permission of the competent superior and the consent of the council according to the norm of law (both universal and proper) are required for a valid alienation or any other transaction which may adversely affect the patrimony of a juridic person. The Holy See establishes the amount for each region of institutes, thus institutes are an exception to canon 1292, §1, which gives the conference of bishops the right to establish the maximum amount for alienation.[36]

Institutes should refer to canons 1290–1298 for a complete description of the law regarding such transactions.

§4. For the autonomous monasteries mentioned in can. 615 and for institutes of diocesan right it is additionally necessary to have the written consent of the local ordinary.

This paragraph applies canon 638, §§1–3 to autonomous monasteries and institutes of diocesan right and adds the requirement of the written consent of the responsible local ordinary. It is complementary to canon 1276, §1 which requires the ordinary to watch over the administration of goods which belong to public juridic persons subject to him.

Canon 639 — §1. A juridic person which has contracted debts and obligations even with the permission of the superior is bound to answer for them.

Normally a juridic person (institute, province, local house) contracts a debt with the permission (express or implicit) of the superior or the authorized agent (delegate of the superior, treasurer, etc.). When such permission is secured, the juridic person must answer for the debt. The intent of this paragraph is that only authorized persons make contracts.

§2. If a member with permission of the superior has made a contract concerning personal goods, the

---

[34]This is often done by reserving certain corporate powers to the council of the institute which parallel the council's canonical responsibilities such as the power to sell, lease or encumber property and to merge or dissolve the corporation. Other powers not directly related to property such as establishing the philosophy or mission, amending the corporate charter or bylaws, and confirming the selection of trustees and certain officers are often used to support the mission of canonical stewardship.
[35]See *CLD* 8 (1975), 415–421 or *Origins* 7 (1977–1978), 378–380.

[36]The present ceiling on alienation is $1,000,000.00 for the U.S. *RR* 1982, 34.

member must answer for it, but if the business of the institute was conducted by order of the superior, the institute must answer.

Members who are capable of acquiring and owning property, even with the permission of the superior, are personally responsible for the contract, but if the member is conducting the business of the institute, the institute is responsible. However, it is probably difficult for a third party to know when a member is acting on his or her own behalf or in behalf of the institute. Thus, in some cases, it may be helpful to designate the authorized personnel to banks, stores, wholesalers, etc.

§3. A religious who has made a contract without any permission of superiors must answer for it, but not the juridic person.

A member is personally responsible for a contract made without the permission of the superior. Institutes should be made aware that in cases in which a religious has a history of making certain contracts on behalf of the institute, it may be held civilly liable even if a particular contract was made without the permission of the superior, unless the other party to the contract was given notice that the member was making a contract for which the member was taking personal responsibility.

§4. It shall be a fixed rule, nevertheless, that an action can always be brought against one who has profited from the contract entered into.

This paragraph would apply to parties who accept church court jurisdiction. The appropriate civil law would apply in the several United States jurisdictions to recover contested money or goods arising out of a contract.

§5. Religious superiors are to be careful that they do not permit debts to be contracted unless it is certain that the interest on the debt can be paid from ordinary income and that the capital sum can be paid off through legitimate amortization within a time that is not excessively long.

It is a practical rule of finance to require that interest on a debt be able to be repaid from ordinary income and that the capital be repaid from income within not too long a time. This is a flexible norm which obligates superiors to engage in planning in regard to debts in order to allocate the financial resources of the institute so that it is not overextended and unable to meet debt repayment.

Canon 640 — Taking into account local conditions institutes are to strive to give, as it were, collective witness of charity and poverty and are to contribute what they can of their own goods for the needs of the Church and the sustenance of the poor.

The issue of a collective witness to charity and poverty has been the subject of intense discussion by institutes. This canon reminds institutes of their responsibility to see to it that the life of the institute bears witness to charity and poverty, since the failure to do so renders a corporate negative witness to values that institutes publicly profess.

The question of the contribution by religious is a practical one. Some institutes are poor and their contribution is their labor. Others are able to make donations of money, property, or services (without pay or less than normal compensation). This canon should be read in conjunction with canon 634, §2 prohibiting the appearance of luxury, immoderate wealth, and amassing of goods. In a sense, it is a concrete suggestion regarding the disposition of surplus goods.

BIBLIOGRAPHY

Bibliographical material for part III of Book II can be found after the commentary on canon 746.

CHAPTER III
ADMISSION OF CANDIDATES AND
FORMATION OF MEMBERS
[cc. 641–661]

Chapter III begins with the admission to the novitiate, leaving the suitable preparation required in canon 597, §2 to the proper law of the institute. This is a departure from the 1917 Code which required a six-month postulancy for all women religious of institutes with perpetual vows and for lay brothers.[1] In some instances, the postulancy, which could not be prolonged beyond a year, began to be identified too closely with the novitiate experience and afforded neither the opportunity for a gradual transition from secular to religious life nor an ob-

jective experience of the life and apostolate of the religious institute.[2]

The proper law of the institute should determine the length of time, the place, and the content of the preliminary preparation period.[3] The purposes of this period are the following: (a) to judge the disposition and vocation of the candidate, (b) to determine if the candidate possesses the qualities requisite for the life and obligations of the particular institute, (c) to assess the religious formation of the candidate, and (d) to provide for a gradual transition from secular to religious life.[4] During this time, the candidates should be under an experienced religious of the institute who works closely with the director of novices to insure continuity in the formation program.

---

[1]*CIC* 539, *RC* 4, 10 (2), 11–12, 14. The discussion of the special *coetus* on admission to the novitiate can be found in *Comm* 12 (1980), 185–187, and 13 (1981), 151–156.

[2]*CLD* 6, 481–488.
[3]*RC* 12, 1–3.
[4]Ibid., 4, 11.

CANONS AND COMMENTARY

ARTICLE 1: ADMISSION TO THE NOVITIATE
[cc. 641–645]

Canon 641 — **The right of admitting candidates to the novitiate pertains to major superiors according to the norm of proper law.**

The right or the juridic act of admitting to the novitiate or beginning of religious life belongs to major superiors (c. 620) according to the proper law of the institute. The proper law can require the advice or consent of the council.[5] The major superior who decides and the members of the council who share in the decision-making process should consult with the religious charged with the candidates and study pertinent records to apprise themselves of the potential and qualifications of the candidates. The nature, spirit, and end of the particular institute should be the objective criteria in admitting candi-

dates. Irreparable harm can be done to a candidate, the novitiate community, and/or the religious institute by receiving unsuitable candidates.[6]

Canon 642 — **Superiors are to be vigilant about admitting only those who, besides the required age, have health, suitable character and sufficient qualities of maturity to embrace the particular life of the institute; this health, character, and maturity are to be attested to, if necessary by using experts, with due regard for the prescription of can. 220.**

A Catholic with the right intention, having the qualities required by the universal and proper law and not held back by an impediment, can be admitted to an institute of consecrated life (c. 597, §1). Besides the completion of seventeen years of age, the law prescribes the health, character, and maturity necessary to enter a particular institute. To de-

---

[5]Gallen, *RfR* (1976/5), 782. Gallen recommends a consultative vote for admission to the novitiate and the renewal of temporary profession.

[6]*RC* 4, 14.

termine the sufficient health of a candidate, it would be wise to require candidates to undergo a physical examination by a doctor recommended by the institute and familiar with its life and apostolate. Interviews with the candidate, a visit to the home, and testimonials from former employers and teachers can help to determine the character of the person for religious life. The academic record of the candidate will determine the aptitude for the formation program and the works of the institute.[7] Those involved in the decision process should be privy to these records and know the recommendations of the religious responsible for the candidate during the probationary period.

Difficult cases may require the services of an approved specialist in the behavioral sciences of high moral standards and familiar with the demands and responsibilities of religious life. This help can only be employed with the knowledge and consent of the candidate in keeping with the provisions of canon 220. The vigilant care required of superiors in their efforts to determine suitable health, character, and maturity for admission will preclude future unhappiness and difficulties for the individual and other members of the institute.

Canon 643 — §1. One is invalidly admitted to the novitiate:

1° who has not yet completed the seventeenth year of age;

2° who is a spouse, during a marriage;

3° who is presently held by a sacred bond with any institute of consecrated life or who is incorporated in any society of apostolic life, with due regard for the prescription of can. 684;

4° who enters the institute as a result of force, grave fear or fraud, or whom the superior receives induced in the same way;

5° who has concealed his or her incorporation in any institute of consecrated life or society of apostolic life.

A person bound by one of the five impediments would invalidly enter a novitiate of a religious institute. Such an invalid act would render subsequent acts invalid, e.g., profession in the institute. It is wise to include the invalidating impediments within the constitutions of the proper law or at least in the appendix.[8] Major superiors, formation personnel, and secretaries involved in collating the required records for admission to the institute should be knowledgeable and alert to invalidating conditions.

A person cannot be admitted to a religious institute unless he or she has observed the seventeenth birthday. This requirement differs from the former law which required the completion of fifteen years of age.[9] Prolonged schooling with the subsequent

delay in assuming vocational and professional obligations would seem to be a consideration in this revision. As in the former Code, no age limit is set beyond which a person cannot enter a religious institute.

Marriage, presumed to be valid until declared invalid by the Church, exists until the death of either spouse or dissolution by the Church. Separation from a partner or a civil divorce would not remove this impediment. A petition for dispensation of this nature should include an account of the marriage, the provisions for the children involved, and the reasons for the marital breakdown. A civil divorce would be necessary to settle financial issues and prevent the partner from forcing a return.[10]

A person incorporated into a society of apostolic life or bound by sacred bonds, temporary or perpetual, in an institute of consecrated life is invalidly admitted to the novitiate of a religious institute. The only exception is the person seeking a transfer according to the provisions of canon 684. The former Code included those who had been in temporary or perpetual profession in a religious institute even though they had been legitimately separated from the institute.[11] The requirement of testimonials from major superiors in such cases is required in canon 645, §2.

A person coerced through force or grave fear enters a novitiate invalidly. Examples of fraudulent entrance would be the concealing of physical disability or psychiatric disorders, the hiding of a police record, or a dishonorable discharge from military service. The withholding of such pertinent information and its nature would place the integrity and suitability of the candidate in serious doubt. The candidate is admitted invalidly to the novitiate if the competent major superior in one of these same dispositions receives him or her.[12]

Note that it is the hiding or concealing of the incorporation in an institute of consecrated life or a society of apostolic life which effects the invalid admission to the novitiate, and not the previous incorporation. If a person inadvertently failed to mention such a previous incorporation, he or she would not be invalidly admitted to the novitiate. Canon 690 provides for one being readmitted to the same religious institute after having legitimately departed after the novitiate or profession.

§2. Proper law can establish other impediments to admission, even for validity, or can add other conditions.

The universal law requires seventeen years of age, freedom from sacred bonds, free will, and probity of life. The proper law of the institute can add other invalidating impediments to admission to the

[7]SCRIS, June 4, 1970, *CLD* 7, 81, c. 66.
[8]SCRIS, May 8, 1970, *CLD* 8, 374, c. 593.
[9]*CIC* 542, §1, 2°.

[10]*CLD* (1979 Supp.), 1, c. 542; *RR* (1982), 28–29.
[11]*CIC* 542, §1, 5°.
[12]*CIC* 542, §1, 3°.

novitiate.[13] It seems unwise both for the good of the institute and the rights of the candidate to multiply invalidating impediments needlessly.

Canon 644 — Superiors are not to admit to the novitiate secular clerics if their local ordinary has not been consulted or those who, burdened by debts, cannot repay them.

A secular cleric is incardinated into a diocese and assumes certain ministerial obligations to the people of God in the particular church. A failure to consult the proper ordinary of the candidate would not invalidate the admission of the secular cleric; however, the testimony of the local ordinary could prove helpful in determining the candidate's stability and suitability for the life and apostolate of the institute.

A person burdened by considerable debt may be liable to judicial action. Those obliged to render an account, e.g., administrators of property, treasurers, or guardians should settle such affairs prior to entering a novitiate. Such serious obligations would certainly distract from if not conflict with the formation of the person in religious life. Superiors should be careful to avoid placing the institute in a position of accountability for such financial burdens.

Canon 645 — §1. Before they are admitted to the novitiate, candidates must show proof of baptism, confirmation and free status.

Before admission, the candidate is required to submit certificates of baptism and confirmation. Ordinarily, the fact of marriage or religious profession is noted on the baptismal record. Great distance from the place of baptism, improper recording, or loss of records through damage may preclude the availability of the certificates. In such instances, the testimony of a trustworthy witness or the word of the candidate, if baptized and confirmed after reaching the age of reason, would suffice. Other testimonials and the home visit would further attest to the free state of the candidate.

§2. If it is a question of admitting clerics or those who have been admitted to another institute of consecrated life, a society of apostolic life or a seminary, there is further required the testimony of the local ordinary or major superior of the institute or society or of the rector of the seminary respectively.

This provision repeats the former law.[14] Testimony from such persons is significant in determining the candidate's character, stability, and suitability for the religious institute.

§3. Proper law can demand other testimonies about the requisite suitability of candidates and their freedom from impediments.

The proper law of the institute can require more testimony of the candidate's character and free state than that required in the universal law for religious. Employers and teachers have experience of the character, capabilities, adaptability, and perseverance of the candidate in demanding circumstances.

§4. If it appears necessary superiors can ask for other information, even with the obligation of secrecy.

Superiors have serious obligations both to their religious institutes and to the candidates seeking admission. They should be reasonably certain of the candidate's health, character, and maturity. To this end, they may obtain pertinent information even secretly to remove doubts as to the person's suitability. The confidential nature of such information demands discretion and sensitivity.

ARTICLE 2: THE NOVITIATE AND
FORMATION OF NOVICES
[cc. 646–653]

The novitiate or formation in a specific religious life-style was initiated by St. Benedict and adapted by the Church for all religious institutes during the Council of Trent.[15] This principal period of formation for religious enables the novice to do the following: (a) grow in love of God and neighbor, (b) study and live the special charism approved by the Church, and (c) experience life in community and the practice of the evangelical counsels.[16] This initial formation should be planned in keeping with the nature, spirit and end of the religious institute.[17] Under an experienced director, the novice begins a study of the history and spirit of the institute, the practice of daily personal and communal prayer, and an education in Sacred Scripture and theology, particularly the theology of religious life.

Canon 646 — The novitiate, by which life in the institute begins, is ordered to this, that the novices better recognize their divine vocation and one which is, moreover, proper to the institute, that they experience the institute's manner of living, that they be formed in mind and heart by its spirit, and that their intention and suitability be tested.

---

[13]The former law provided that the constitutions of religious institutes could have impediments in addition to those indicated in the universal law. See *CIC* 542, §1.
[14]*CIC* 544, §§3–7.

[15]SCR, March 7, 1967; *CLD* 6, 483–486. The discussions of the special *coetus* can be found in *Comm* 13 (1981), 156–168.
[16]*RC* 13.
[17]*PC* 2; *ES* II, 16; *RC* 5, 10 (1), 13, 15–33.

Pius XI stated that to make a novitiate poorly was to build on sand.[18] The former law required a retreat of at least eight full days before beginning the novitiate.[19] Post-conciliar legislation left to the proper law of the religious institute the amount of time for retreat before candidates begin their novitiate, provided that the retreat be a minimum of five full days and that it be made in an appropriate manner.[20] The novitiate environment should be conducive to the recollection and leisure necessary to respond to a divine vocation to the particular institute. Novices should come to know and appreciate the special charism which they are called to live. They should recognize its articulation in the history, tradition, law, customs, and above all in the members of the institute. Both the novices and their director must test their call and evaluate their capability to live the particular charism with enthusiasm and fidelity.

Canon 647 — §1. The erection, transfer and suppression of a novitiate house are to take place through a written decree of the supreme moderator of the institute with the consent of his or her council.

The former Code required the permission of the Apostolic See for the erection of a novitiate of an institute of pontifical right.[21] In the revised law, the supreme moderator, after procuring the consent of the council, through a written decree can erect, transfer, and/or suppress a novitiate house. Novitiate houses should not be uselessly multiplied, inasmuch as there is great advantage to the novices living community life under an experienced director who instructs and forms them in the nature, spirit, and end of the institute.

§2. In order to be valid a novitiate must be made in a house properly designated for this purpose. In particular cases and as an exception, by concession of the supreme moderator with the consent of the council, a candidate can make the novitiate in another house of the institute under the guidance of an approved religious who assumes the role of director of novices.

For validity, a novitiate must be made in the house designated for this purpose. The transition from secular to religious life and the formation in the charism of the institute require a special environment free from the tension and distraction of the apostolic commitment of religious.[22] Only in a particular case and by way of exception, e.g., one novice entering the religious institute or a novice requiring special consideration because of cultural background, can the supreme moderator with the consent of the council permit the novice to make the novitiate in another house of the institute. In such a case, an exemplary and experienced religious should be assigned to direct the novice in the place of the director of novices. This person should have the time and leisure necessary to devote to this responsible task. The house designated for the novice should be chosen wisely and noted for religious discipline and an atmosphere conducive to nurturing the charism in the novice.

§3. A major superior can permit a group of novices to live for a stated period of time in another house of the institute, designated by the same superior.

The decision is made by the competent major superior, and the proper law of the institute can require the advice or consent of the council. The provision is qualified: (a) a group of novices, (b) a house of the institute, and (c) a prescribed period of time. Such a decision could be made to provide community life for a small number of novices or time for vacation or recreation for the novices.

Canon 648 — §1. In order that the novitiate be valid it must include twelve months spent in the community of the novitiate itself, with due regard for the prescription of can. 647, §3.

In addition to a novitiate house, twelve months in the novitiate community are prescribed for the validity of the novitiate. Besides a designated place for the purpose of forming the novices, a period of time is established in order that the novices can integrate the instruction they receive, learn the nature and spirit of the institute, and acclimate to the responsibilities of community life.[23]

§2. To complete the formation of the novices, in addition to the time mentioned in §1, the constitutions can determine one or several periods of apostolic exercises to be spent outside the novitiate community.

Over and above the twelve months in the novitiate community required for validity, the constitutions of the religious institute can provide one or more times of apostolic activity carried on outside the novitiate community for perfecting the formation of the novices. Such a provision may afford the novices the opportunity to further integrate the spirit and values of the institute in the midst of apostolic activity. The term "constitutions" is used in

[18]SCR, March 7, 1967; *CLD* 6, 483–486.
[19]*CIC* 541.
[20]SCRIS, June 4, 1970; *CLD* 7, 81.
[21]*CIC* 554, §1. At first supreme moderators of religious institutes received faculties to transfer the novitiate. Sec. State, Nov. 6, 1964, *CLD* 6, 155; SCR, May 31, 1966; *CLD* 8, 359.
[22]This section repeats *CIC* 555, §1, 3°. See also *RC* 5, 15–19.
[23]*RC* 12.

the canon rather than proper law which includes both the constitutions and the directory. This time outside the novitiate house and the novitiate community is not required for a valid novitiate unless stated in the proper law of the institute.

§3. The novitiate is not to extend beyond two years.

The religious formation of the novices needs to be integrated with apostolic experience and professional training. It is unjust to both the individual and to the institute to extend any probationary period indefinitely. The time spent in the novitiate should not exceed two years, but this provision would not prejudice the six-month extension permitted in canon 653, §2 in an individual case.

Canon 649 — **§1. With due regard for the prescriptions of cann. 647, §3, and 648, §2, absence from the novitiate house which lasts more than three months, either continuous or interrupted, renders the novitiate invalid. An absence of more than fifteen days must be made up.**

In the former law, an absence of more than thirty days, consecutive or otherwise, invalidated the novitiate.[24] In the revised law, absences of more than three months, continuous or intermittent, invalidate the novitiate. This prescription does not prejudice the provisions of canons 647, §3 and 648, §2. Absences exceeding fifteen days must be made up.[25] If a novice was absent for seventeen days during the period of novitiate, he or she would have to make up two days of the novitiate. Absences because of dismissal from the institute or legitimate departure according to the free will of the novice would seem, as in the former law, to invalidate the novitiate.

§2. With the permission of the competent major superior first profession can be anticipated, but not by more than fifteen days.

In the former law, only the renewal of temporary profession could be anticipated but not beyond one month.[26] The former Code required a full and uninterrupted year of novitiate before first profession.[27] The provision for the competent major superior to permit first profession to be anticipated by not more than fifteen days allows some flexibility regarding a significant liturgical feast, a common day of profession for novices beginning the novitiate

within a few days of each other, and/or travel times for guests.[28]

Canon 650 — **§1. The scope of the novitiate demands that the novices be formed under the guidance of a director according to the program of training to be defined by the proper law.**

The purpose of the novitiate is to form the novices according to the nature and end of the institute as defined in the proper law. The director of novices and the assistants should possess wisdom, charity, prudence, and piety. They should have a great knowledge and love of the institute, be familiar with the formation program, and form the novices through personal witness and instruction.

§2. The governance of novices is reserved to one director under the authority of the major superiors.

This provision safeguards the unity and harmony so necessary for good formation, while avoiding the ambiguity and dissension following from multiplicity of directors. The director has the responsibility for governing the novitiate and is accountable to the major superior as indicated in the proper law of the institute.

Canon 651 — **§1. The director of novices is to be a member of the institute who has professed perpetual vows and is legitimately designated.**

Perpetual or definitive profession in the institute and proper designation indicate that the person appointed director of novices has the knowledge and experience necessary to form others in the life of the institute. The proper law of the institute should state the process for the designation of the director. Adequate consultation should take place before the appointment or confirmation of the director of novices, and the proper law of the institute can require the advice or consent of the council. Requirements of age, years of perpetual profession, and specialized training can be required by the proper law of the institute.[29] It would be wise not to require too specialized skills for such a position in the proper law. Teachers or specialists can be brought into the novitiate. The director possesses a personal witness of the charism and a love and knowledge of the institute.

§2. If there is a need, assistants can be given to the director to whom they are subject regarding the

---

[24]*CIC* 556, §1.
[25]This is a change from *RC* 22 (2), which provided that the major superior after consultation with the novice director decided in an individual case for absences lasting less than three months.
[26]*CIC* 577, §2.
[27]*CIC* 555, §1, 2°; 572, §1, 3°.

[28]*RC* 26.
[29]The former law required 35 years of age and 10 years professed from first profession for the master of novices (*CIC* 559, §1) and 30 years of age and 5 years professed from first profession for the assistants (*CIC* 559, §2). Age requirements were left to particular law for these offices in post-conciliar legislation. See SCRIS, June 4, 1970; *CLD* 7, 81, c. 66.

governance of the novitiate and the program of training.

In case of necessity, assistants can be given to the director of novices. They are subject to the director in all that pertains to the novices and the formation program. These assistants should be exemplary religious of the institute who recognize the importance of formation and their cooperation with the director.[30]

§3. Members who have been carefully prepared and who, not impeded by other duties, can carry out this duty fruitfully and in a stable manner are to be in charge of the training of novices.

The provision shows the priority given to formation in the universal law. The members designated for this important task should be carefully prepared and unimpeded by other duties in order that they carry out their office fruitfully and in a stable manner.[31]

Canon 652 — §1. It is for the director and assistants to discern and test the vocation of the novices and to form them gradually to lead correctly the life of perfection proper to the institute.

The director of novices and the assistants gradually form the novices in a life of perfection suitable to the nature and spirit of the institute. While engaged in this task, formation personnel are obliged to study and to test the vocation of the novices. These responsibilities are important, as recommendations based on objective criteria should be made to the major superior who admits to first profession according to the proper law.[32]

§2. The novices are to be led to cultivate human and Christian virtues; they are to be introduced to a fuller way of perfection by prayer and self-denial; they are to be instructed to contemplate the mystery of salvation and to read and meditate on the Sacred Scriptures; they are to be prepared to cultivate the worship of God in the sacred liturgy; they are to be trained in a way of life consecrated by the evangelical counsels to God and humankind in Christ; they are to be educated about the character and spirit, purpose and discipline, history and life of their institute; and they are to be imbued with a love for the Church and its sacred pastors.

The formation program attempts to integrate the spiritual, intellectual, and affective qualities of the novices. The novitiate program should include

the areas of study prescribed in this paragraph of the canon and could be outlined in the directory of the proper law of the institute. The studies in the novitiate contribute to the foundation for religious life. While the novices can earn credits for such studies, the primary purpose is not the attainment of a degree.

§3. Conscious of their own responsibility, the novices are to collaborate actively with their director so that they may faithfully respond to the grace of a divine vocation.

The novices should be conscious of their obligations and respond to their divine vocation through an active cooperation with the director. They should determine their own willingness and suitability to persevere in the life of the particular religious institute, since they will eventually ask to be admitted to first profession. Cooperation with experienced directors, an honest self-evaluation in light of objective criteria, and the virtues of humility, perseverance, and prudence will assist the novices in their deliberations.

§4. Members of the institute are to take care that on their part they cooperate in the work of training novices by the example of their life and by prayer.

Only a few members of a religious institute are designated to form the novices through their witness and instruction in the novitiate house. However, all members have the obligation to promote the spirit and end of the institute. All members can cooperate in the apostolate of formation through prayer and example.

§5. The time of novitiate mentioned in can. 648, §1, is to be employed properly in the work of formation and therefore the novices are not to be occupied with studies and duties which do not directly serve this formation.

This paragraph emphasizes the purpose of the novitiate and repeats the former law.[33] The twelve months required for the validity of the novitiate are reserved for the formation of the novices in the life and spirit of the institute. Studies geared toward attaining professional degrees or training in one of the institute's apostolates should not be undertaken by the novices at this time. If initial formation is poor or there is a lack of concentration on the purpose of the novitiate program, the novice will be unable to assume the greater responsibility of integrating formation in religious life with apostolic responsibility.

[30]RC 30; SCRIS, May 8, 1974; CLD 8, 374–375.
[31]CIC 559, §3; RC 30–32; SCRIS, June 9, 1976, CLD 8, 374–375.
[32]CIC 563; RC 30, 32.
[33]CIC 565, §3; RC 5, 15, 18, 25, 28, 29, 31.

Canon 653 — **§1. A novice can freely leave an institute; moreover the competent authority of the institute can dismiss a novice.**

The canon shows the freedom of a novice to leave the institute and the authority of the competent superior according to the proper law to dismiss a novice. A novice should make the decision to leave only after serious consideration and the counsel of a confessor, spiritual director, or one of the formation personnel. The competent authority would seem to be the same major superior who admits to the novitiate, prolongs the novitiate, admits to or excludes from profession. Before dismissing a novice, the same competent authority should consult qualified persons, e.g., the formation personnel. The proper law of the institute may require the advice or consent of the council. Encouraging the novice to leave or excluding him or her from first profession would be more sensitive and appropriate than dismissal in some cases. Such difficult situations can be avoided through a careful scrutiny of candidates at the time of application and during the preliminary probation period before entrance to the novitiate. While the former Code indicated that the competent authority was not obliged to give reasons for the dismissal,[34] the revised law is silent in this matter. It would seem just to present the novice with the objective criteria on which the decision was based. The fact of departure and the reasons should be recorded in the file of the novice in the event that he or she decides to seek readmission or admission to another institute of consecrated life, a society of apostolic life, or a seminary.

§2. When the novitiate is completed, a novice, if judged suitable, is to be admitted to temporary profession; otherwise the novice is to be dismissed. If there is a doubt about the novice's suitability, the time of probation can be extended by the major superior according to the norm of proper law, but not more than six months.

The proper law of the institute should indicate the competent major superior who prolongs the novitiate in an individual case, admits to or excludes a novice from profession, or dismisses a novice from the institute. The advice or consent of the council can be required in such cases. The major superior and council should study the recommendations of the formation personnel before making the decision. Sickness during the time of the novitiate may prompt the competent authority to extend the novitiate in a particular case. A novice may request an extension of the novitiate, or a prolongation may be recommended by the formation personnel, if the novice has not met their expectations. It may be unrealistic to expect substantial improvement within

six months. It may be wiser to counsel the novice to leave religious life in order to gain the objectivity necessary to evaluate a religious vocation. The revised law does not mention the privilege of a novice in danger of death to make profession granted by Pius X, September 10, 1912.[35]

ARTICLE 3: RELIGIOUS PROFESSION
[cc. 654–658]

The rite for religious profession approved by Pope Paul VI and entered into the *Roman Ritual* reflects the esteem the Church has for the faithful, both cleric and lay, called by God to consecrate themselves in a special way to the glory of God and the service of His people.[36] Religious profess to live out their baptismal promises more intensely by following Christ more closely through the profession of the evangelical counsels according to the proper law of a particular religious institute. The Church intercedes for religious in its public prayer, blesses them, and associates their self-offering with the sacrifice of Christ in the Eucharist.[37]

Canon 654 — **By religious profession members assume by public vow the observance of the three evangelical counsels, are consecrated to God through the ministry of the Church, and are incorporated into the institute with rights and duties defined by law.**

It is important to note the words profession, consecration, and incorporation. While all Christians through their baptism are called to practice the evangelical counsels, religious profess by public vow to observe the three counsels according to the law of a religious institute. Promises or sacred bonds other than public vows as set down in *Lumen Gentium* 44, *Renovationem Causam* 2, 7, 34–37 and canon 573, §2 are no longer permitted for temporary or perpetual profession in religious institutes.[38] The universal law no longer uses the terminology of "solemn" and "simple" profession of vows in religious institutes. Religious institutes which had solemn profession prior to the revision of the universal law of the Church can continue to

---

[34]*CIC* 571, §1.

[35]Gallen, *RfR* (1979/5), 711–712.
[36]*SC* 80; SCDW, Feb. 2, 1970; *AAS* 62, 553. The rite with accompanying norms can be found in *ComRelMiss* 51 (1970), 186–189. *CIC* 571, §3 required eight full days of retreat before temporary profession. Post-conciliar legislation leaves the determination of the amount of time of retreat to the proper law, on the conditions that a minimum of five full days be stipulated and the retreat be made in a suitable manner. SCRIS, June 4, 1970; *CLD* 7, 81, 5.
[37]*LG* 44–45. The discussion of the special *coetus* on the revision of the law on religious profession can be found in *Comm* 13 (1981), 169–175.
[38]The promises or other sacred bonds were permitted to apostolic religious institutes but not to contemplative religious institutes. SCRIS, July 24, 1976; *CLD* 8, 364–365.

use the term in their proper law, and the effects of solemn vows can be attributed to the profession by the proper law of the institute.[39]

Through their profession, religious strive to live a life of great charity, and the Church consecrates them as witnesses of the love of Christ for His people in contemplating the Father, proclaiming the Kingdom, healing the sick, converting sinners, and doing good to all. The religious exemplifies Christ and continues His work on earth. A religious is incorporated into a particular institute which has been given legal sanction and canonical status in the Church. With incorporation, the religious assumes certain rights and obligations according to the universal law of the Church and the proper law of the institute.[40]

Canon 655 — **Temporary profession is made for the time defined in proper law, which may not be less than three years and no longer than six.**

This canon follows the general principle of setting a prescribed period of time for a probationary period. The time given to temporary profession continues the formation begun in the novitiate and provides the religious with the lived experience of the evangelical counsels according to the law of the institute prior to perpetual or definitive profession. For the validity of perpetual profession, temporary profession must last for at least three years. Temporary profession may be made up to six years but no longer unless permitted in an individual case by the competent superior (c. 657, §2). This provision of minimum and maximum time for temporary profession insures a lived experience of the vowed life with its obligations, protects the rights of the religious who anticipates perpetual profession, and provides adequate time for evaluation of those in the formation process by the competent formation personnel prior to admission to perpetual profession. Temporary profession is made according to the proper law of the institute, and the religious should express in the formula of profession the time for which the obligation binds. The first profession need not be made for the entire length of time required in the institute. For example, if temporary profession is required for a period of three years in a religious institute, the proper law can provide that the profession be made for one year and repeated for three; for two years and then for one, vice versa; or for the three years. This provision permits those who have made temporary vows in a religious institute the freedom to leave, if they wish, when the time of profession expires. The proper law of a religious institute could permit the flexibility allowed in the universal law, i.e., temporary profession could extend from three to six years, depending on

the readiness of the religious and the formation program.

Canon 656 — **For the validity of temporary profession, it is required that:**
1° the person who is about to make the profession shall have completed at least the eighteenth year of age;
2° the novitiate has been validly completed;
3° admission has been freely given by the competent superior with the vote of the council in accord with the norm of law;
4° the profession be expressed and made without force, grave fear or fraud;
5° the profession be received by the legitimate superior personally or through another.

The conditions required for the validity of temporary profession are similar to those in the former Code.[41] The two differences are that the present law requires the completion of eighteen years rather than sixteen years, and the vote of the council, according to the proper law rather than the decisive vote of the council for first profession required in the 1917 Code.[42]

The novice must have completed eighteen years of age, i.e., observed the eighteenth birthday. This requirement for the validity of first profession would not seem to pose a problem today, inasmuch as the candidates for religious life seem to be older in years than previously.

The novice must have completed a valid novitiate (cc. 643; 647: §2, 648, §1; 649, §1). One invalid act renders all subsequent acts invalid. It is important that those interviewing candidates, collating records, recommending or admitting to the novitiate or profession take care that the person meets the conditions of the universal law of the Church and the proper law of the institute for a valid admission, novitiate, or profession.

The proper law of the religious institute should indicate the competent superior who admits to temporary profession and whether the vote of the council is deliberative or consultative.[43]

The profession must be expressed, i.e., the public declaration or statement of intention is required for validity. No action is free if it is impeded by force or grave fear. The act of profession must contain the essential elements (name of the person, the religious institute, the profession of the vows of consecrated chastity, poverty and obedience, the time for which this profession is made, and the name of the superior of the institute who represents the Church and the institute in receiving the profession). The formulation of the act of profession should be in-

---

[39]*PC* 13; *ES* II, 24.
[40]*PC* 4; *ET* II, 13–29; cc. 662–672.

[41]*CIC* 572.
[42]*CIC* 572, §1, 1°; 575, §2.
[43]Gallen recommends a deliberative vote of the council for admission to first profession as required in *CIC* 575, §2.

cluded in the proper law and not be left to the free initiative of the candidates.[44] The permission for additions of personal piety to the profession formula is left to the competent authority in the religious institute.

The proper law of the institute should indicate the superior competent to receive the profession. This superior acts in the name of the Church and the institute and may not be the same superior who admits the novice to temporary profession.[45] This superior can delegate another member to receive the profession, and this provision would cover exceptional circumstances which prevent the superior from being present to receive the profession. The relationship formed by the act of profession between the newly professed and the religious institute is reflected in the receiving of the profession by the competent authority. This reception is reserved to the proper internal superiors of the religious institute, and the name of the superior should be included in the record of profession. The minister of the Eucharist brings to completion the sacrifice which the novice makes in the hands of the designated superior of the institute by uniting it to the sacrifice of Christ.[46]

Canon 657 — §1. When the time for which the profession has been made has elapsed the religious who freely requests it and is judged suitable is to be admitted to a renewal of profession or to perpetual profession; otherwise the religious is to leave.

This provision reflects the contractual nature of the profession and the testing of the vocation which continues during the entire probationary period. The directory section of the law of the religious institute should contain a carefully delineated program for the period of temporary profession. The religious is free to leave the institute with the expiration of temporary profession. Likewise, the legitimate superior (c. 656, 3°) can admit the religious, who freely requests and is judged suitable, to the renewal of temporary profession or to perpetual profession. The decision to permit or to refuse subsequent profession should be based on objective criteria derived from the formation program, and justice would warrant that reasons based on the criteria be given to the member judged unsuitable. In cases in which temporary profession is not renewed annually, it would seem wise to review periodically the progress of the member in temporary profession.

§2. If it seems opportune the period of temporary profession can be extended by the competent superior, according to proper law, but in such a way that the entire time in which the member is bound by temporary vows does not exceed nine years.

This paragraph of the norm reflects the general principle of law that a period of time should be set for any probationary period, while allowing some flexibility for difficult cases in which an extension of time would prove beneficial. This may happen in the case of illness or when a temporary professed member is receiving counsel or assistance in remedying a behavioral problem that places admission to subsequent profession in doubt. Too prolonged a period of temporary profession can stifle enthusiasm and encourage a lack of decisiveness for permanent commitment. Permitting a person to remain in religious life for considerable time on probation without evaluation and then refusing perpetual profession are unjust actions and can promote bitterness in the person as well as a difficult return to secular life.

§3. Perpetual profession can be anticipated for a just cause, but not by more than three months.

This provision of three months allows for some flexibility as does the provision for first profession (c. 649, §2). Examples of a just cause for anticipating perpetual profession are the following: (a) a feast day of the religious institute, (b) the missioning of religious to a particular apostolate or program, and (c) danger of death. There is no mention of anticipating the renewal of temporary profession, but this would seem permissible. It is to be noted, however, that the anticipated renewal does not begin until the time for which the former profession was made has expired.

Canon 658 — Besides the conditions mentioned in can. 656, 3°, 4° and 5° and others attached by proper law, for the validity of perpetual profession the following are required:
1° the completion of at least the twenty-first year of age;
2° previous temporary profession for at least three years, with due regard for the prescription of can. 657, §3.

Some religious institutes have temporary profession only, and the proper law of such institutes should establish the time at which the bond between the member and the institute becomes definitive or the person is fully incorporated into the institute. This is important with regard to juridical effects and the assuming of rights and responsibilities. Examples would be the requirement of a will before definitive profession and the right of passive

---

[44]See SCRIS, Feb. 14, 1973; *CLD* (1973 Supp.), c. 576.
[45]For example, the superior general could be the competent authority in the proper law who, with the advice or consent of the council, admits a novice to temporary profession, while the provincial superior could be the competent authority in the proper law who receives the profession.
[46]SCRIS, Oct. 14, 1974; *CLD* 8, 361–364.

voice or eligibility for a position of authority in the institute.

For the validity of perpetual profession, in addition to the prescriptions of canon 656, 3°–5° and the norms in the proper law of the institute, the universal law for religious includes two requirements.

The first is that one has attained the twenty-first birthday. This would not seem problematic, inasmuch as canon 656, 1° requires the completion of the eighteenth year for the validity of temporary profession and a minimum of three years in temporary vows before being validly admitted to perpetual or definitive profession.

The second requirement is that one has spent at least three years in temporary profession with allowance made for the anticipation of perpetual profession as provided in canon 657, §3. The minimal requirement of temporary profession in canon 655 is for the validity of perpetual profession. This requirement is the same as that of the former Code.[47]

ARTICLE 4: THE FORMATION OF RELIGIOUS
[cc. 659–661]

Religious profession obliges a person to a lifelong process of conversion to Christ according to the nature and spirit of a particular institute. This responsibility of continuous renewal and adaptation rests with both the individual religious and the competent superiors of the institute.

Canon 659 — §1. In individual institutes after first profession the formation of all members is to be continued so that they may lead more fully the proper life of the institute and carry out its mission more suitably.

From incorporation or first profession, the formation program should be geared to integrating the professional and experiential training of the member with the religious and spiritual training of the novitiate.[48]

§2. Therefore, proper law must define the program of this formation and its duration, keeping in mind the needs of the Church and the circumstances of human persons and times to the extent this is required by the purpose and character of the institute.

An outline of the content and time of the formation program should be included in the directory of the proper law of an institute. The outline can be revised and updated periodically in keeping with the needs of the Church, the nature and end of the institute, and the signs of the times.

§3. The formation of members who are preparing to receive holy orders is regulated by universal law and by the program of studies proper to the institute.

Members of religious institutes preparing for sacred orders are instructed according to the prescriptions for the formation of priests in the universal law and the proper law of the institute.[49]

Canon 660 — §1. The formation is to be systematic, adapted to the capacity of the members, spiritual and apostolic, doctrinal and at the same time practical, and when it seems opportune, leading to appropriate degrees both ecclesiastical and civil.

The formation program should be gradual, adapted to the aptitude of the religious, and directed toward an integration of the doctrinal, spiritual, and apostolic training. Religious should acquire appropriate degrees indicating competence in respective fields of service, since religious formation is no substitute for professional competence. Teachers and resources for such technical training could be shared or pooled by religious institutes in certain areas.[50] Here it may be noted that the local ordinary exercises authority with regard to the admission of men and women religious to state and non-confessional universities.[51]

§2. During the time of this formation duties and jobs which would impede the formation are not to be assigned to members.

Such integration takes time, leisure, and reflection. A full apostolic schedule with the accompanying serious responsibility given to a member still in a formation program would drain the energies needed to integrate the spiritual and professional aspects of religious life.

Canon 661 — Throughout their entire life religious are to continue carefully their own spiritual, doctrinal, and practical formation, and superiors are to provide them with the resources and time to do this.

---

[47]*CIC* 574. *RC* left to the general chapter of the religious institute to decide the time of temporary profession within the framework of from 3 to 9 years continuously.
[48]*ES* II, 35–36; *RC* 7–9.

[49]*OT; ES* II, 34; *Ratio,* Jan. 6, 1970, *AAS* 62, 321. See *CLD* 7, 883–884. See also cc. 232–264.
[50]*PC* 18; *ES* II, 37.
[51]SCR, Jan. 10, 1967; *CLD* 6, 448. SCRIS, July 2, 1971; CLD 7, 527, *VR* 31 (1971), 370.

In addition to the formation program, planning should take place for the renewal and adaptation of the members at critical stages in human development. The time, finances, and other resources should be provided by those in authority for renewal and updating in accord with church teaching, the nature of the institute, and the particular aposto-lates of the religious.[52] The norm emphasizes the personal responsibility for continual formation in Christ according to the nature and end of the institute.

[52]*LG* 47; *PC* 4; *ET* IV, 42–50.

BIBLIOGRAPHY

Bibliographical material for part III of Book II can be found after the commentary on canon 746.

The next two chapters of this title discuss the obligations and rights of institutes and their members and the apostolate of institutes, respectively.

Chapter IV covers a variety of obligations and rights including the following: the spiritual life; the sacrament of penance; presence and absence in community; cloister; use, administration, and renunciation of personal goods; the religious habit; and providing for the spiritual and material necessities of life for members. For the most part the norms are more general and flexible than the previous law, leaving the application of the norms to the individual institute.

Chapter V, after stating that the primary apostolate of all religious is the witness to a consecrated life and noting the special apostolate of contemplative religious, devotes itself primarily to apostolic institutes. The canons root apostolic endeavors in a relationship with God and communion with the Church at large. Both bishops and superiors have particular and mutual obligations that require cooperation in order to best serve the people of God.

CANONS AND COMMENTARY

CHAPTER IV
THE OBLIGATIONS AND RIGHTS OF INSTITUTES AND THEIR MEMBERS
[cc. 662–672]

Canon 662 — **Religious are to have as their highest rule of life the following of Christ as proposed in the gospel and expressed in the constitutions of their institute.**

This canon recognizes that the fundamental norm of the religious life is the following of Christ as proposed by the gospel and that the Holy Spirit has inspired a variety of ways of following the gospel which has resulted in the special charism of the many religious institutes in the Church.[1] The special charism of the institute is to be expressed in its constitutions.

Basing the canon on *Perfectae Caritatis* 2 was meant to open up the vision of the theological foundation of religious life. The origin and the center of religious life is Christ and the way of life presented in the gospel. In some ways, this canon is meant to guard against the conditions of legalism and narrowed vision that precipitated the call for renewal initiated by the Church in Vatican Council II. Thus, this canon is a theological and legal principle that is offered to help focus the attention of religious institutes on Christ, the fundamental norm of religious life, and to guide institutes in expressing the thrust of their gospel commitment and charism in a way that centers on Christ.[2]

Canon 663 — **§1. Contemplation of divine things and assiduous union with God in prayer is to be the first and foremost duty of all religious.**

§2. Members are to participate in the Eucharistic Sacrifice daily if possible, receive the Most Sacred Body of Christ and adore this same Lord present in the Sacrament.

§3. They should apply themselves to the reading of Sacred Scripture and to mental prayer; they are to celebrate the liturgy of the hours worthily according to the prescriptions of proper law, with due regard for the obligation of clerics in can. 276, §2, 3°, and they are to perform other exercises of piety.

§4. They are to cultivate a special devotion to the Virgin Mother of God, model and protector of all consecrated life, including the Marian rosary.

§5. They are faithfully to observe an annual period of spiritual retreat.

Canon 663 is a series of exhortations which are intended to direct religious—both individual members and communities—to the sources of the spiritual life.[3] Since each paragraph recommends rather than commands a particular practice, it will be left up to individual institutes to specify the manner of practicing these exhortations. In the previous Code a series of similar practices were made the responsibility of the superior with regard to the religious in

---

[1] *PC* 2 (a) and (b).

[2] See also cc. 575–577 and 598.

[3] The exhortations are based on *PC* 5, 6, 15, and 25.

their care while this canon places primary responsibility on the individual religious.[4] The focus on union with God in prayer is consistent with the emphasis in the canons that religious life is a consecration of the whole person to God whose life is to be a continuous adoration in love of God (c. 607) and that the apostolate of religious is in their witness to the consecrated life (c. 673).

The second paragraph which covers participation in the Eucharist is worded so that the expectation is daily participation while understanding that religious may be in circumstances in which the expectation need not be met. This would include assignments in which the daily celebration of Eucharist is such a distance that it would take too much time to travel back and forth or where the only celebration of Eucharist is at a time when ministry does not permit attendance.

The decision regarding the ability to attend the Eucharist should be grounded in an appreciation of the Eucharist as the center of the life of a community and the nourishment offered to individual religious by receiving the Body and Blood of the Lord.

The final three paragraphs focus on spiritual exercises that have always held an important place in the lives of religious, namely, the Sacred Scriptures, mental prayer, the liturgy of the hours, devotion to Mary, and the annual retreat. All of these are appropriate matter for the proper law of the institute to apply the recommendations according to its own spiritual tradition, while in canon 663, §3 the celebration of the liturgy of the hours is specifically left to the proper law of the institute.

Canon 664 — Religious are to apply themselves to conversion of heart to God, examine their conscience even daily, and frequently approach the sacrament of penance.

This is another theological, spiritual exhortation which focuses on the initial call of the gospel, namely, to reform, change, or convert one's life. It then names two specific means of conversion, a daily examination of conscience and the sacrament of penance.

This canon changes both the previous law and the 1970 decree issued by the Sacred Congregation for Religious and Secular Institutes providing for the sacrament of penance at specific intervals of one or two weeks.[5] Thus, the law now promotes the sacrament while leaving it to the individual religious to decide when the sacrament is to be received.

Each institute has its own spiritual heritage as to the practices or attitudes which aid personal conversion. This canon fosters that heritage without limiting its application.

Canon 665 — §1. Observing a common life, religious are to live in their own religious house and not be absent from it without the permission of their superior. However, if it is a question of a lengthy absence from the house the major superior for a just cause and with the consent of the council can permit the member to live outside a house of the institute, but not for more than a year, except for the purpose of caring for poor health, for the purpose of studies or of undertaking an apostolate in the name of the institute.

This paragraph addresses the subject of common life as a norm of religious life and the exceptions to the norm. The norm is that religious should live in their own houses and not be absent from them without the permission of the superior. Common life is part of the Church's understanding of religious life. Unity in Christ and mutual support are the primary reasons for the common life.[6]

To have permission of the superior for absence from the house is practical and courteous from the standpoint of the religious, the superior, and the people served by the individual and community. It does not refer to ordinary absence but only those which because of their nature or length should be brought to the superior. Proper law may identify some of the situations in which permission is needed; however, institutes should be careful not to overregulate a subject which requires practical solutions and adjustments.

This canon recognizes two situations of extended absence. Both require the permission of the major superior and the consent of the council.

The first is absence for just cause. Examples of just cause would be caring for a close family member[7] who is ill or vocation difficulty. In cases of just cause, the absence can be permitted for up to a year. In such cases this canon should be read along with canon 686 as providing a series of steps available to religious institutes in aiding their members to resolve whether or not they have a vocation or attending to the reasons that meet the concept of just cause.

The meaning of extended absence is not defined. Therefore, an institute may decide for itself the minimum length of extended absence which would require the permission of the superior and the consent of the council. Although a shorter period may be appropriate, a contemplated absence beyond three months would seem lengthy enough for a superior to bring the matter to the council.

The second is absence for the causes permitted in

---

[4]*CIC* 595.
[5]See *CIC* 595, §1, 3° and *Dum Canonicorum, AAS* 63 (1971), 318–319 and *CLD* 7 (1975), 531–533.

[6]C. 602. The common life has been a consistent theme in documents directed to religious. *PC* 15; *ES* 11, 25; *ET* 39, *Con Life*, vol. 1, no. 2 (1975), 141–145 and *Con Life*, vol. III, no. 2 (1977), 164–168.
[7]In appropriate cases caring for a family member who is sick can be accomplished by an assignment that offers opportunity to care for the relative.

the law, namely, the illness of a member, pursuing a course of studies, or exercising an apostolate in the name of the institute. In such cases the absence may be in excess of one year. Since many institutes serve in ministries where it is their custom to assign only one person or where it is practical to assign only one person, an exception is made to the norm of living in a house of the institute to fulfill the mission of the Church and the institute. Examples of such assignments are pastorates, parish administrators, home and foreign missions, and intercommunity houses.

The Sacred Congregation for Religious and Secular Institutes described the status of religious living outside their house in explaining the meaning of the former legislation and since the language of the present law is similar, the guidelines of the sacred congregation remain appropriate.

These religious remain members of their community; they are bound to observe their vows: consecrated chastity, obedience to their superior, and according to circumstances, the vow of poverty. If they require financial assistance, the community should provide what they require. Such religious retain active and passive voice. They continue to wear their religious habit, that external sign by which they bear witness to their status as persons consecrated to God by religious profession.

When permission is granted religious to live outside a house of their institute, it is advisable that an agreement be made regarding contracts to be maintained with their congregation, the exercise of their religious rights and duties and the financial assistance they may require. They should give their superior an account of monies received and spent. Serious failure to comply with their religious duties as far as possible under the circumstances and according to the terms of the agreement would justify the superior to take corrective measures regarding these religious.[8]

§2. Members unlawfully absent from the religious house with the intention of withdrawing from the power of their superiors are to be solicitously sought after by them and aided to return and persevere in their vocation.

This paragraph seems to be based on the biblical injunction to seek out those who are "lost" and emphasizes the pastoral role of superiors toward those who have withdrawn unlawfully from the religious house. The tone is solicitous and caring toward the departed member and no penalties are attached to

the unlawful absence. Emphasis is on the value that the Church and the institute place on the vocation of the member in aiding the member to return and persevere in his or her calling.

Canon 666 — **Necessary discretion is to be observed in the use of media of social communication, and whatever is harmful to one's vocation and dangerous to the chastity of a consecrated person is to be avoided.**

The Vatican decree on social communication and the instruction of the Pontifical Council for the Instruments of Social Communication, *Communio et Progressio,* form the underlying basis of this canon and it should be read in that perspective.[9]

Since religious institutes often use the media to advertise for vocations, fund-raising, and other activities, they should be careful to promote a proper image and not demean themselves in the media.

In addition, there is a warning concerning materials that are harmful to the religious vocation, especially chastity. The impact and influence of media deserve serious consideration regarding their effects on the personal and communal life of religious. Discretion, prudence, and wisdom are needed in order to develop guidelines in this area.

Canon 667 — **§1. In all houses cloister adapted to the character and mission of the institute is to be observed according to the determinations of proper law, with some part of the religious house always being reserved to the members alone.**

Each institute is to develop proper law concerning the cloister in accord with its own character and mission. Part of each house is always to be reserved to members alone to ensure them personal privacy and privacy for their life of prayer, study, and leisure.

§2. A stricter discipline of cloister is to be observed in monasteries ordered to the contemplative life.

A stricter cloister which should be described in proper law is to be observed in contemplative monasteries in order to safeguard their life of prayer and separation from the world. This paragraph along with canon 667, §1 applies to all contemplative institutes while the following two paragraphs apply only to nuns.

§3. Monasteries of nuns which are totally ordered to the contemplative life must observe *papal* cloister, namely according to norms given by the Apostolic See. Other monasteries of nuns are to observe cloister adapted to their own character and defined in the constitutions.

---

[8]*Con Life,* vol. II, no. 2 (1977), 167–168. The guidelines treat further of requests for extension of time beyond that granted by the superior and the council.

[9]*IM* 9 and *Communio et Progressio* 21–22.

This paragraph covers two different monasteries of nuns. First, it discusses monasteries of nuns completely ordered to the contemplative life. Such monasteries are to observe the cloister according to the norms of the Apostolic See.[10] Second, other monasteries, presumably those not completely ordered to the contemplative life, should accommodate their cloister to their own character and define it in the constitutions. This seems to refer to the former minor enclosure of nuns suppressed by *Ecclesiae sanctae* 11, 32 which stipulated as this paragraph does that nuns, who though contemplative have adopted some external works, must define the nature of their enclosure in the constitutions.[11]

§4. For a just cause the diocesan bishop has the faculty of entering the cloister of monasteries of nuns which are in his diocese, and, for a grave cause and with the consent of the superior, of permitting others to enter the cloister and nuns to leave the cloister for a truly necessary period of time.

The diocesan bishop has the right to enter a cloister of nuns located in his diocese and to allow others to enter for just cause. Such cause may be a dispute which the bishop or his delegate is trying to help resolve. The permission of the bishop (at least habitual) is necessary for others to enter the cloister and for nuns to leave the cloister. *Venite Seorsum* 7 and 8[12] lists many of the causes for which entrance to the cloister has been allowed and for which leaving the cloister has been permitted. These will serve as appropriate guidelines until new norms are issued or existing ones affirmed. Monasteries of nuns may present to the local bishop causes based on their experience that call for entrance of others into or egress of members from the cloister so that such matters may be facilitated.

Canon 668 — **§1. Members are to cede the administration of their goods to whomever they prefer before first profession, and unless the constitutions state otherwise, they are freely to make disposition for their use and their revenues. Moreover, they are to draw up a will, which is also valid in civil law, at least before perpetual profession.**

The five lengthy paragraphs of canon 668 give the norms regarding the relationship of the individual religious to property. Led by the gospel spirit of poverty and detachment, all religious are to reduce their involvement concerning the goods they own while some may even renounce ownership completely. The purpose of the detachment and renunciation is to become dependent on God and the community while becoming free from the false security possessions have to offer. This canon is related to canon 670 which requires the institute to furnish all things necessary for the life of its members.

The first paragraph requires that members cede administration of their goods prior to first profession and freely dispose of use and usufruct unless the constitutions state otherwise.[13] An example will help to understand the meaning of the term. If a member owns an apartment house, to cede administration means to appoint someone to care for it, its physical upkeep, and the payment of expenses; to dispose of use means to decide who shall use or live in the building; and usufruct means to dispose of the rent or income, for example, donate it to a charity or keep it in an account in the member's name. Normally, one person would be empowered to perform all three tasks.

The cession may be made to the institute if the institute is willing to receive it.

During this period legal title is retained by the member. Thus, the person designated in the cession need not add his or her name to any title, deed, bank or securities account. If during temporary profession, members have the option to transfer their goods to a community account, appropriate records should be kept to ensure the member's property is protected and able to be identified.

Although the form of cession used by many communities is or could be construed as civilly valid, the document is intended to have significance only within the life of the institute. The paragraph does not require a cession be civilly valid as it does a will; however, in appropriate cases it may be helpful to execute a power of attorney or some other similar document to make the cessation effective civilly.

The final requirement is to make a will, valid in civil law, at least before final profession. The time at which the will is to be made is left to proper law, however, it would be more prudent to do so prior to temporary profession providing a member is civilly of age.[14] Since the civil requirements for a valid will differ from state to state (and country to country), an attorney should be consulted to aid members in drawing up a will or at least in providing models of wills for their use, provided the wording of the

---

[10] *Venite Seorsum* 7.

[11] See the comment of Dammertz, V, "The Juridical Structure of Contemplative Life," *Con Life*, vol. VI, no. 1 (1982), 33–39 on "papal enclosure and constitutional enclosure," 37–38.

[12] Id. at p. 37 questioning the norms of *Venite Seorsum* 7b.

[13] Unlike the previous law (*CIC* 568) a novice is not prevented from renouncing goods or assuming obligations affecting them. The rationale for the previous law was to protect the novice from imprudently disposing of property so that a decision to remain or depart would not be dependent on the disposing of goods. Such a rationale may be cause to regulate the matter in proper law.

[14] In the previous law (*CIC* 569, §3) a will was to be made prior to the profession of temporary vows. The present law changes the time to at least before final profession for which a person must be at least 21 years old (c. 658) which would meet the highest age requirements in the U.S.

models does not subtly influence the disposition of property. For instance, a model paragraph could indicate how to make a bequest to parents, relatives, or charities.

In case a member has no property, a valid will can still be made which would provide for the disposition of any property that may come into the possession of the member.

§2. In order to change these dispositions for a just cause and to place any act whatsoever in matters of temporal goods they need the permission of the superior who is competent according to the norm of proper law.

This paragraph covers two situations. The first is that of changing a cession or altering or making a new will. These actions require a just cause such as aiding a family member, supporting charitable work, providing for newly acquired goods, or protecting goods from dissipation.

The second is placing any act in regard to a member's temporal goods. These would be actions that do not involve the cession or will but may be necessary or helpful to protect property or provide for its better use or investment such as a sale or exchange of property, transfer of title, or establishment of a trust. Normally a member should have freedom in choosing whether to perform such actions. The law is intended only to act as a check so that the contemplated action is consistent with canon law, proper law, the witness value of religious life, and the providing of protection for the member so that the full implications of the proposed action are understood. This may involve referring a member to an attorney or business counsellor to receive appropriate advice.

Proper law is to determine the appropriate superior to approve all the above-mentioned actions. Normally this would be a major superior, however, in certain cases a regional or local superior may be appropriate.

§3. Whatever a religious acquires through personal work or by reason of the institute is acquired for the institute. Unless it is otherwise stated in proper law those things which accrue to a religious by way of pension, subsidy or insurance in any way whatever are acquired for the institute.

After profession, whatever a member acquires through his or her own work is acquired for the institute. Institutes may require a member to sign an agreement or understanding to this effect to preclude later disagreement or misunderstanding about the meaning of the law. This paragraph would not include an inheritance or gifts to the member personally as opposed to a gift to the person as a member of the institute. Unless it is otherwise stated in proper law, pensions, subsidies, and insurance are acquired for the institute. Since in civil law many of these benefits are in the name of the individual such as social security and retirement benefits the disposition of them should be a matter of agreement between the member and the institute.

§4. Those who must renounce their goods completely because of the nature of the institute are to make a renunciation before perpetual profession in a form which, if possible, is also valid in civil law and takes effect from the day of profession. Religious in perpetual vows who wish to renounce their goods either in part or totally according to the norm of proper law and with permission of the supreme moderator are to do the same thing.

This paragraph gives each institute the right to provide in proper law for the renunciation of the right to own property. If because of the nature of the institute it should take place prior to perpetual profession, it would be valid from the day of profession. This paragraph also states if possible the renunciation should be valid in civil law. It is an open question whether such a renunciation would be valid in United States' jurisdictions.[15] In general it can be said that courts are reluctant to enforce such an agreement.

§5. Professed religious who have fully renounced all their goods because of the nature of the institute lose the capacity of acquiring and possessing, and therefore invalidly place acts contrary to the vow of poverty. Moreover, those things which accrue to them after the act of renunciation belong to the institute, according to the norm of proper law.

This paragraph defines the meaning of renunciation and applies it to members who renounce their goods because of the nature of the institute.[16] Renunciation means that a member cannot acquire or possess property and to do so is an act contrary to the vow. In addition, those things which accrue to the member after the renunciation belong to the institute in accord with the proper law of the institute. There is, however, no obligation to accept a

---

[15]There has been little litigation on the subject concerning religious; however, courts are reluctant to enforce an agreement in which someone gives up a basic civil right such as the right to own property. See, *Order of St. Benedict of New Jersey* v. *Steinhauser* 179 F. 137 (D. Minn. 1910), 194 F. 289 (8th Cir. 1912), 234 U.S. 640 (1914) in which the federal appeals court held the vows of a monk to be an unenforceable agreement to forfeit the right to own property which was reversed by the U.S. Supreme Court based on the language of the civil corporate documents. See also the discussion in J. Hite, "The Status of the Vows of Poverty and Obedience in the Civil Law," *Stud Can* 10 (1976), 131–193.

[16]The 1980 schema did not restrict the application of the canon to religious who made a renunciation because of the nature of the institute.

gift or an inheritance.[17] This puts the institute at no advantage in regard to gifts since a donor can always make the institute the donee. It is a different matter with an inheritance and a member should carefully discern if refusal of an inheritance is wise. If, for instance, there is a needy member of a family, a member could always obtain permission for his or her share to go to that member of the family. The member should realize that refusing an inheritance will result in that inheritance being disposed of according to other provisions of the will of the testator or according to the laws of intestacy in the state. It would be wise to know the result of refusing before making the refusal.

Another question that has arisen concerns relatives or friends of religious who wish to provide for them even if that religious has renounced the capacity to own property. The member should realize that a relative or friend can do this regardless of the wishes of the member. It can be done, for example, by setting up a trust that may be in effect until a religious dies or until a certain age or time. Since a member can do nothing about this, except persuade the person otherwise, such an arrangement by a relative or friend does not violate church law.

Canon 669 — §1. Religious are to wear the habit of the institute made according to the norm of proper law as a sign of their consecration and as a testimony of poverty.

This paragraph summarizes the basic elements regarding the habit for religious institutes. First, the purpose of a habit is twofold: it is a sign of the religious life and a testimony of poverty. Second, norms regarding the habit are left to proper law. The paragraph is worded similarly to the 1917 Code in that there is no requirement that an institute have a habit since a few institutes have never had a habit.[18]

According to *Perfectae Caritatis* 17 since a habit is a sign of consecrated life it should be simple, modest, and at the same time both poor and becoming. In addition, a habit should meet the requirements of health and be suited to the time, place, and needs of the apostolate.

In 1972 a letter of the Sacred Congregation for Religious and Secular Institutes addressed inquiries being made regarding the habit.[19] In its reply it offered the principle that a habit should be such that it distinguishes the religious person who wears it, but it did not present any specific description of a habit. The letter further stated that secular clothes are permitted when wearing a habit would impede the normal activities of the religious. In such a case, the clothing should in some way be different from forms of dress that are clearly secular.[20]

The question has been raised as to what constitutes a religious habit.[21] Since the law itself makes no specific requirement but is worded so as to leave the particulars concerning a habit to the institute, it seems in accord with the spirit of the revised law for an institute to examine its own charism, tradition, present requirements, and apostolates and develop norms which best suit the institute.[22]

§2. Clerical religious of an institute which does not have its own habit are to wear clerical dress according to the norm of can. 284.

Clerical religious who are members of an institute which does not have a habit are to follow the norms for clerical dress in canon 284 which provide that religious wear suitable ecclesiastical garb in accord with the norms issued by the conference of bishops and legitimate local custom.

Canon 670 — An institute must furnish for its members all those things which are necessary according to the norm of the constitutions for achieving the purpose of their vocation.

Each institute in accepting members has the responsibility of furnishing all the spiritual and material resources necessary for fulfilling their vocation. This canon offers an important balance to all the canons that enumerate the specific obligations of members. In this canon, superiors and councils are given notice they must provide that which is necessary to the vocation of their members. This requires planning and budgeting of time and finances to see that each member has access to adequate spiritual and material resources. This canon is complementary to canon 661 concerning the ongoing formation of religious. This may include retreats, days of recollection, conferences, adequate housing, cloth-

---

[17]The right of a testamentary beneficiary to renounce or decline a devise or bequest is generally recognized. *Am Jur* 2nd, Wills, 80 (1975), §1597. See §§1601 and 1606 on exercising the right to renounce within a reasonable time and the time in which title passes.

[18]This has been attributed to the fact that the habit was so common that there was no need to make a law requiring a habit. E. Gambari, "Unfolding the Mystery of Religious Life," (Boston: St. Paul Editions, 1970; 148–151).

[19]*CLD* 7 (1975), 534–535.

[20]*ET* 22.

[21]For an example of one opinion see J. Gallen, "Questions and Answers," *RfR* 32 (1973), 174–176, who states SCRIS "evidently does not hold that a religious habit is retained when one uses a pin, a cross, or a religious symbol," and for another opinion see, P. Boyle, "Understanding Legislation for Religious," *Sisters Today* 44 (1972), 70–83 at p. 77, "Since purely secular clothes, without any apparent sign of commitment, are permitted for particular reasons, it is clear that no particular reason is required to justify purely secular clothes worn with some readily exterior sign. This combination constitutes a religious habit."

[22]The language of the canon was intentionally modeled on *PC* 17 since there were amendments offered to make the canon more restrictive and more flexible and both were rejected. *Rel,* 151.

ing, education, professional updating, counseling, etc.

Canon 671 — A religious is not to accept duties and offices outside the institute without the permission of the legitimate superior.

The purpose of this canon is to safeguard the primary commitment of a member to the life and works of the institute. There are many offices and duties for which religious may be well suited because of training and experience. In requiring the permission of the superior prior to such an undertaking, the opportunity is provided for the member and superior to discuss the responsibilities of such offices and duties to determine if they are consistent with the religious commitment of the member. Important areas of discussion would include the nature of the office or duty and the time commitment. For example, membership in professional societies and associations that would not substantially take up the time of the religious would not be covered by this canon. Offices and duties which a religious could prudently bring to the superior would include both religious or secular offices such as an appointment to a diocesan or supra-diocesan office or the acceptance of a position with an organization that advocates special causes or has the purpose of influencing legislation. This should not be understood to deter religious from appropriate expression of religious, social, and political beliefs or limit their ability to join groups that take a religious, social or political stance. This canon applies only when an office or duty is being offered.

Canon 672 — Religious are bound by the prescriptions of cann. 277, 285, 286, 287, and 289, and, moreover, religious clerics are bound by the prescriptions of can. 279, §2; in lay institutes of pontifical right, the permission mentioned in can. 285, §4 can be granted by the proper major superior.

This canon applies certain rules of conduct or prohibitions regarding clerics to religious. In summary, canon 277 requires prudence when associating with people who are dangerous to celibacy or cause scandal to the faithful; canon 285 prohibits conduct unbecoming to the clerical (religious) state; canon 286 enumerates certain occupations, offices, and financial arrangements that may not be entered into without permission;[23] canon 287 prohibits an active role in political parties and labor unions unless certain conditions are present; canon 289 forbids volunteering for military service and certain civil duties and offices without permission; and canon 279, §2 obligates religious clerics to pursue

studies after ordination to acquire a better knowledge of the sacred sciences and pastoral methods.

In order for a religious to accept a public office, it will be necessary to obtain a dispensation. Canon 285, §3 does not indicate the appropriate authority to grant dispensations. This needs to be clarified so that requests for dispensation may be made to the appropriate authority, whether it be the diocesan bishop, religious superior, the Holy See, or some combination thereof.[24]

The question of whether a religious can be an executor of a will, guardian, trustee, or have a power of attorney is raised by canon 285, §4, which requires permission before a religious may accept an office which includes the obligation to render an account. In lay pontifical institutes the permission needed to exercise such powers is to be granted by the major superior. The same would be true for pontifical clerical institutes since canon 285, §4 requires the permission of the ordinary of the cleric who would be the religious cleric's major superior. In addition, the obligations of the vow of poverty are important since one of the reasons a religious cedes the power of administration over property is to be free from such responsibilities in order to be more fully committed to his or her calling. There are situations in which a religious may be asked to undertake such responsibilities. For example, a religious may be the only one left in a family or the one best suited to exercise such responsibilities toward a sick or aging parent or relative. Canon 285, §4 would require permission to do so. In arriving at a decision a member and superior should review the expected responsibilities. If the office will require a substantial commitment of time and energy, it would be appropriate to look for another solution. If it can be easily accomplished or most of the work delegated to others (accountants, lawyers), these responsibilities should not interfere with a member's religious commitment.

CHAPTER V
THE APOSTOLATE OF INSTITUTES
[cc. 673–683]

Although some of the material of this chapter was addressed in the 1917 Code, it now appears as a separate and distinct chapter. The chapter relies substantially on *Perfectae Caritatis, Christus Dominus, Ecclesiae sanctae,* and *Mutuae Relationes.* Thus, these canons will be more completely understood when read against the background of the above documents.

Canon 673 — The apostolate of all religious consists first in their witness of a consecrated life

---

[23]SCRIS, "Religious and Human Promotion," 11–12, *CLD* 9 (1983), 379–410, and SCC, "Declaration on Associations of Priests, Politics and Labor," *Origins* 11 (1982), 645–647.

[24]See S. Holland, *National Catholic Reporter,* vol. 19, no. 31, May 27, 1983, p. 19, stating that it is likely members of pontifical institutes would petition the Holy See for the dispensation.

which they are bound to foster by prayer and penance.

By making the witness of living the consecrated life the primary apostolate of religious, this canon focuses on the consecration of a religious to God rather than on the service element so often connected with the idea of apostolate. The canon is broadly worded to include institutes primarily dedicated to the active life or the contemplative life. The very fact that a religious is consecrated is an act that has value in itself and gives witness to God's presence. The service aspect of the apostolate is emphasized in canon 675, but it is based on the witness of the religious being consecrated to God. The commitment made by a religious is fostered by prayer and penance (conversion) which are the foundation of the consecrated life of every institute without regard to whether it is dedicated primarily to prayer, service, or a particular combination of those two elements.

Canon 674 — Institutes which are wholly ordered to contemplation always retain a distinguished position in the mystical Body of Christ: for they offer an extraordinary sacrifice of praise to God, they illuminate the people of God with the richest fruits of their sanctity, they move it by their example, and extend it through their hidden apostolic fruitfulness. For this reason, however much the needs of the active apostolate demand it, members of these institutes cannot be summoned to aid in various pastoral ministries.

This canon which is directed to contemplative institutes is based on *Perfectae Caritatis* 7 and 9 and explains the role of contemplative institutes in the Church. The theological/juridical principle of the canon is that because of the nature of the contemplative vocation, members of these institutes are not to be summoned to pastoral ministries. This principle is to be adhered to even though there is great need for ministry in the active apostolate. Within prudent bounds, so as to keep the nature of the contemplative life intact, members of contemplative institutes have always carried out a pastoral ministry such as offering hospitality or of being spiritual guides, counsellors, and confessors. These ministries would not be prohibited by this canon insofar as they do not interfere with the basic calling of the members of the institute. The ministries that are envisioned as consistent with the life of the institute can be outlined in the proper law.

Canon 675 — §1. In institutes dedicated to works of the apostolate, apostolic action pertains to their very nature. Hence, the whole life of members is to be imbued with an apostolic spirit, indeed the whole apostolic action is to be informed by a religious spirit.

This paragraph adopts the words of *Perfectae Caritatis* 8 in describing institutes dedicated to the works of the apostolate. The description is based on the idea that "apostolic action" pertains to the very nature of such an institute. This has its roots in the charism of the institute and the fact that an institute's ministry is entrusted to it by the Church.[25] Mentioning that the entire religious life of members is to be imbued with an apostolic spirit is to recognize that the spirituality of such institutes will have its foundation in its apostolic nature. In a complementary sense, the apostolic activity of its members is to be informed by a religious spirit which is a reference to the primary witness of the apostolate of all religious, namely, the witness of their consecrated life (c. 673). Thus, there is to be no division or dualistic approach to life in institutes dedicated to the works of the apostolate. It is one life with two dimensions that complement each other rather than causing division.

§2. Apostolic action is always to proceed from an intimate union with God, and it is to confirm and foster that union.

This paragraph is adapted from a further statement of *Perfectae Caritatis* 8. In that document a member is seen as being able to answer the call to follow and serve Christ only if his or her apostolic activity finds its source in intimate union with Him. As one commentator puts it:

There can be no doubt that the survival of the active communities in the future depends upon their foundation upon a deep spiritual life, and upon the guarantee of prayer and meditation; for the enormous demands by the present-day apostolate, in whatever form, upon the whole man and his time, and the circumstances of modern life, are far from conducive to corporate life and prayers.[26]

§3. Apostolic action, to be exercised in the name and by the mandate of the Church, is to be carried out in its communion.

The apostolic action has three related characteristics. First, it is exercised in the name of the Church and is not an independent exercise of ministry by religious institutes or one of its members. Second, it is exercised by the mandate of the Church. This may occur because a bishop has granted permission to an institute to erect a house and perform the works of the institute; because the bishop has entrusted a particular work to an institute; or because religious recognized a need and re-

[25]*PC* 8.
[26]F. Wulf, "Commentary on the Appropriate Renewal of the Religious Life," in Vorgrimler, 353.

ceived approbation to engage in a certain work. Third, the principle of ecclesial communion reflects the spirit of obedience, interdependence and co-responsibility a religious institute has for apostolic works in regard to authority, co-workers, and those served. The Church, which encompasses religious institutes, is to give witness to the living body of Christ, and through all its parts work toward a pastoral action that reflects its ecclesial communion.[27]

Canon 676 — Lay institutes, whether of men or women, share in the pastoral office of the Church through spiritual and corporal works of mercy and offer the most diverse services to men and women; therefore they are to persevere faithfully in the grace of their vocation.

The majority of religious in the Church are members of lay institutes, most of whom are engaged in apostolic action. The Code follows the format of *Perfectae Caritatis* in devoting special attention to lay institutes. The scope and depth of the apostolic action of lay institutes are recognized; however, the canon is not juridical since it places no special legal responsibilities on such institutes. It is more of a word of encouragement with a vote of gratitude for the blessing that these institutes have been for the Church.

This canon does not legislate regarding the matter of the ordination of some members of lay institutes of men. *Perfectae Caritatis* 10 states that lay institutes of brothers may admit some members to holy orders to meet the need for priestly ministry in their houses. Such a provision requires the approval of the general chapter. The lay character of the institute is not affected by the provision.

Canon 677 — §1. Superiors and members are faithfully to retain the mission and works proper to the institute; nevertheless they are to accommodate these prudently to the needs of times and places, including the use of new and appropriate means.

This paragraph is a two-pronged exhortation asking institutes to continue to serve in the valuable manner in which they have served in the past but to be prepared to change and serve in new ways according to the needs that are brought to their attention. These two important interests may be difficult for an institute to balance. The decreasing number of religious has led many institutes to establish their priorities by reviewing their present apostolates; listening closely to the call of the pope, the bishop, and the people; and making the very difficult decision to retain some apostolates, abandon some, and open new ones. It is rare that everyone will be satisfied with such decisions. The issues should be well studied and everyone affected should be communi-

cated with so that decisions will be as well received as possible.[28]

§2. Moreover, if they have associations of the Christian faithful related to them, institutes are to assist them with special care so that they are imbued with a genuine spirit of their family.

There has been a long and rich tradition of religious institutes and associations of the faithful sharing the heritage of a founder or foundress or a common spiritual tradition. This paragraph, without offering any particular norms, exhorts institutes to recognize their special obligation to care for the associations of the faithful attached to them. The proper law of institutes and associations may set out in further detail the mutual responsibilities and privileges of the institute and the association.

Two canons in the section on associations mention the relationship between institute and associations. Canon 311 provides that members of institutes which preside over or assist associations should see to it that the associations furnish assistance to the apostolic works of the diocese. For public non-clerical associations, canon 317, §3 provides that lay persons can exercise the office of moderator, and the chaplain or ecclesiastical assistant should not fill that office unless the statutes provide otherwise.

Canon 678 — §1. Religious are subject to the authority of bishops, whom they are obliged to follow with devoted humility and respect, in those matters which involve the care of souls, the public exercise of divine worship and other works of the apostolate.

This paragraph describes the authority of the bishop over the works of the apostolate.[29] It specifies that religious are under the authority of the bishop in those matters which involve the care of souls, public worship,[30] and the exercise of the apostolate. This is a broad area which is best served by ongoing communication between bishop and religious so that there is true balance between the legally recognized role of the bishop as pastor of the diocese and the autonomy granted by law to a religious institute.

§2. In exercising an external apostolate, religious are also subject to their own superiors and

[27]*PC* 8, *MR* 20.

[28]*MR* 40–42 focuses on the need for constant dialogue between bishops and religious superiors to provide new models of apostolic presence while retaining and updating traditional apostolates. These sections emphasize the need for study beforehand followed by review of the results.
[29]*CD* 35 (4); *ES* 1, 25–26; and *MR* 53. See also cc. 375 and 392.
[30]The question of liturgical abuse was given consideration in *MR* 43 wherein religious superiors and members were reminded to be faithful to the laws and directives of the Holy See and the decrees of the bishops in regard to the exercise of public worship.

must remain faithful to the discipline of the institute, which obligation bishops themselves should not fail to insist upon in cases which warrant it.

This paragraph describes the balance of authority exercised in regard to religious who engage in the external apostolate. It focuses on the obligation of religious to their institutes both in regard to fidelity to the discipline of their institute and obedience to superiors. Institutes in their proper law often have guidelines concerning both spirit and practice in regard to apostolic work.

Primary responsibility for religious discipline belongs to the superiors of the institute.[31] Bishops are also asked to understand the responsibility of a member to the institute and if a case arises, a bishop is to urge the members to be faithful to the discipline of the institute. This is most appropriately done by the bishop's first contacting the superior since for the most part even major superiors are mobile enough to visit and care for the fidelity of their members.

§3. In organizing the works of the apostolate of religious, it is necessary that diocesan bishops and religious superiors proceed after consultation with each other.

This paragraph recognizes the need for cooperation and discussion between the bishop and religious superiors regarding the works of the apostolate. The clarification of expectations and responsibilities and the cooperative planning that take place during such discussion should be most helpful in ordering the relationship between the bishop and the institute regarding the apostolate of the religious in the diocese.

This paragraph is related to canon 677, §1 which covers the responsibility of religious relating to works proper to the institute and the call to undertake works that meet the needs of the Church. Bishop and superiors should try to ascertain together the apostolic needs in their area to study means to provide new ways of meeting needs.[32]

Canon 679 — **When a most serious reason demands it a diocesan bishop can prohibit a member of a religious institute from living in his diocese; if the major superior of that religious has been advised and neglects to act, the matter is to be referred to the Holy See immediately.**

The bishop has the authority to prohibit a religious who has an assignment in his diocese from remaining there. This is a power complementary to but broader than that of canon 678, §2 which al-

lows bishops to urge fidelity to the discipline of the institute. This canon does not specify the nature of the cause but only that its seriousness must be grave. In accord with the subject of this chapter of the law, it will at least apply to all matters under the care of the bishop, especially delicts or transgressions involving the care of souls, public worship, and the works of the apostolate. It might also be applied to matters such as publicly contradicting church teaching, publicly violating church laws for which a penalty is incurred, or engaging in civilly criminal conduct.

The canon contains three steps. First, the bishop must notify the major superior of the conduct of the religious. Second, the major superior must fail to act. Third, the bishop is to refer the matter to the Holy See.[33]

The language of the canon presents some questions. First, when the bishop referrs the matter to the Holy See is it merely a report of the events or does the Holy See respond by confirming or reversing the actions of the bishop? Second, must the religious move immediately upon receiving the prohibition from the bishop? Third, is there a specific avenue of appeal for the religious? It would seem helpful in such cases for the bishop to notify the major superior of his referral of the matter to the Holy See so that the major superior could provide the Holy See with his or her opinion regarding the prohibition.

Canon 680 — **Among the various institutes and also between them and the secular clergy, orderly cooperation as well as a coordination of all apostolic works and activities, under the direction of the diocesan bishop, with due regard for the character and purpose of individual institutes and the laws of the foundation, is to be promoted.**

Two areas of cooperation that are to be encouraged under the moderation of the bishop are described in this canon.[34] The first is cooperation among the various institutes of the diocese. Although it may be appropriate to continue some of the separate diocesan organizations of men and women religious because of their particular interests, this canon looks to a way of encouraging cooperation among all religious. *Mutuae Relationes* 59 encourages the formation of associations of religious at the diocesan level because they have been useful as organisms of mutual liaison promoting the renewal of religious life, discussing the mutual concerns of bishop and religious, and coordinating the

---

[31] C. 586.
[32] *MR* 41 envisions apostolic innovations and launching experiments to care for important apostolic needs.

[33] *CIC* 617, §1 had a similar procedure except that it provided for notification of the superior instead of specifying the major superior. However, *CIC* 617, §1 applied to exempt religious.
[34] *CD* 35 (5).

activities of the various institutes serving in the diocese.[35]

The second is cooperation between religious and secular clergy since each has a special mission of service in the diocese. For the most part, secular clergy and religious have had separate diocesan organizations with representatives on pastoral councils where they exist. This area of cooperation could be fulfilled by a separate organization of clergy and religious or by a committee of the diocesan pastoral council.[36]

Finally, the canon provides for the coordination of the apostolates of all the religious in a diocese by the bishop. In doing so the bishop is to respect the nature of each institute so that the needs of the diocese do not result in a religious institute being asked to violate its essential character.

Canon 681 — **§1. Works which are entrusted to religious by the diocesan bishop are subject to the authority and direction of this same bishop, with due regard for the right of religious superiors according to the norm of can. 678, §§2 and 3.**

Certain works are entrusted to religious such as a parish, school, retirement home, etc., in which the bishop employs the religious for a certain work, as compared with erecting a house to which an apostolate of the institute is attached.[37] When such an arrangement is made, religious are engaged to perform a particular work and do not have the permission to engage in all the works proper to the institute as allowed in canon 611. These works are properly under the direct care and supervision of the bishop reserving the right of religious superiors regarding their own discipline (c. 678, §§2–3).

§2. In these cases a written agreement is to be drawn up between the diocesan bishop and the competent superior of the institute, which, among other things, expressly and accurately defines what pertains to the work to be carried out, the members to be devoted to this, and economic matters.

This paragraph specifies that there should be a written agreement drawn up between a bishop and the competent superior which is to define accurately the work(s) to be carried out, the members designated to carry it (them) out, and financial matters.[38] Such an agreement is an advantage to both the bishop and the institute in clarifying the duties and responsibilities of each.

Some agreements are for a particular work, a parish, a school, a spiritual center, etc., and these agreements may be for a specific length of time. This necessarily involves assignment of personnel such as nominating a pastor or associate, a principal of a school, or a director of a spiritual center for approval by the bishop or one of his delegates. Most dioceses have a specific salary scale for such appointments, but some dioceses also provide living accommodations, car or travel allowances, etc. All this needs to be expressed in an agreement and signed by the competent authorities.[39]

Individual religious may be hired for a particular diocesan ministry which would include agreement on the same matters between both the member and the competent authority of the institute. An agreement is helpful in preventing misunderstanding regarding important areas in which a ministry is entrusted to a religious, even though individual contracts are not covered by canon 681.[40]

Canon 682 — **§1. If there is a question of conferring an ecclesiastical office in the diocese upon a certain religious, the religious is appointed by the diocesan bishop, following presentation by or at least assent of the competent superior.**

If a religious is appointed to an ecclesiastical office[41] in a diocese, the religious is to be presented by or have the assent of the competent superior and then be named by the bishop. Such offices may include that of pastor, episcopal vicar, or vicar for religious. *Mutuae Relationes* 58 in discussing offices that may be entrusted to religious notes that a written agreement may be necessary for certain offices to protect the stability of the office and the devolution of goods in case the office or undertaking should be suppressed or discontinued.

§2. A religious can be removed from the office entrusted to him or her either at the discretion of the authority who entrusted it, after having notified

---

[35]See J. Vilnet, "Common Responsibilities of Bishops and Major Superiors," *Con Life,* vol. IV, no. 1 (1979), 271–287 at p. 279 wherein he envisages three types of associations: (1) an office of religious which may be formed by religious to coordinate their activity in the diocese; (2) an association of major superiors who with the bishop and his council treat legal questions which concern the institutes and the diocese; and (3) a diocesan pastoral council of men and women religious to examine and orient the participation of religious in the diocese.

[36]MR 55–56. See also c. 512 which provides for religious to be represented on the diocesan pastoral council; c. 463 which provides for the representation of religious on the diocesan synod; and c. 498 providing for religious priests to be represented on the priests' council or senate of priests.

[37]MR 57 (a) "the difference existing between the *distinctive works* of an institute and *works entrusted* to an institute should be kept in mind by the local ordinary. In fact, the former depend on the religious superiors according to their constitutions, even though in pastoral practice they are subject to the jurisdiction of the local ordinary according to law (cf. *ES* 1, 29)."

[38]*ES* 1, 30 (2); *MR* 57 (b).

[39]Such agreements may also provide for the resolution of disputes under the contract within the church by use of existing means or special processes described in the agreement such as mediation or binding arbitration. This can be helpful in avoiding civil suits in such matters.

[40]MR 58. See *Reardon* v. *Lemoyne* 452 A 2d 428 (N.H., 1982), for a dispute involving religious, the bishop, the diocesan superintendent of schools, the diocesan school board and members of a parish school board.

[41]See cc. 145–196 on ecclesiastical office.

the religious superior, or at the discretion of the superior, having notified the authority; and neither requires the consent of the other.

Either the authority who committed the office to the religious or the competent superior can remove a religious from office without the consent of the other party, after having notified the other party. The dual authority to remove represents the competency of the diocese over the job and the superior over the member.

This paragraph is silent on the matters of cause for removal and notification of the cause to the religious being removed. *Ecclesiae sanctae* 1, 32 cited by *Mutuae Relationes* 58, which is the source of this paragraph, was also silent on the questions of cause and notification although it did contain a right to appeal to the Apostolic See.

Possible causes for removal might be misconduct, incompetency, or even the need for a religious to accept an important assignment in the institute. In this sense it would be comparable to canon 624, §3.

Canon 683 — **§1. At the time of the pastoral visitation and also in case of necessity the diocesan bishop, either in person or through someone else, can make a visitation of the churches of religious or of their oratories, which the Christian faithful habitually attend, schools and other works of religion or charity, whether temporal or spiritual, entrusted to religious; however he may not visit schools which are open only to students belonging to the institute.**

There are two instances when a bishop may visit the churches, oratories, schools, and works of religious institutes.[42] The first is the time of the pastoral visitation of the bishop which is to occur so that the bishop visits all the places in his diocese every five years. The second covers cases of necessity which may be initiated because a matter has come to the attention of the bishop or the institute has brought the matter to the attention of the bishop. There is an express exemption for schools which are open to students of a particular institute. This canon does not enumerate any of the instances referred to in canon 397, §2 which allows the bishop to visit members of houses of pontifical religious institutes only in the cases expressly provided for by law.

§2. But if by chance he discovers abuses and has advised the religious superior in vain, he himself can provide for it on his own authority.

When the bishop discovers an abuse by virtue of visiting the places mentioned in canon 683, §1, he is to notify the superior. He may advise the local superior, but the notification required by this paragraph would most suitably be the major superior who has the primary responsibility within the institute to correct the abuses of members. If the notification of the religious superior has no effect, the bishop may correct the abuse on his own authority.

---

[42]The specific places of visitation, churches, and oratories which the faithful habitually attend, and schools and works, all flow from the areas of the bishop's authority stated in c. 678, §2, namely, the care of souls, public worship and other apostolic works.

BIBLIOGRAPHY

Bibliographical material for part III of Book II can be found after the commentary on canon 746.

This portion of commentary covers the last three chapters of title II. While chapter VI applies directly to institutes in its provisions for separation therefrom, chapters VII and VIII apply to areas related to institutes in their provisions for the elevation of a religious to the episcopate and for the conferences of major superiors, respectively.

CANONS AND COMMENTARY

CHAPTER VI
SEPARATION OF MEMBERS FROM THE INSTITUTE
[cc. 684–704]

Canons 684–704 apply to members of religious institutes—both clerics and lay—and to members of secular institutes and societies of apostolic life according to the norm of canon law (cc. 726–730; 742–746) and the proper law of the institute. The processes for separation should be followed meticulously so as to protect both the rights of the individual member and those of the institute, and to avoid an invalid separation. For example, if the consent of the council is required, the councillors should be assembled by the appropriate major superior, and the same superior cannot act without an absolute majority vote of those present (c. 127).

Religious who are clerics (c. 266, §1) must be accepted probationally or unconditionally by a diocesan bishop before receiving an indult of exclaustration or departure from a religious institute. Canons 290–293 of the Code apply to religious who are clerics and request or are forced to return to the lay state in addition to separation from a religious institute.

ARTICLE 1: TRANSFER TO ANOTHER INSTITUTE
[cc. 684–685]

The first article of chapter VI deals with the transfer of a member from one institute of consecrated life or society of apostolic life and the immediate entrance to another institute. A transfer occurs when a member of an institute of consecrated life or a society of apostolic life becomes so attracted to the nature, spirit, and end of another institute that he or she initiates the process to move to the new institute. A transfer should not be con-fused with the seeking of admission to an institute of consecrated life or a society of apostolic life after one legitimately leaves an institute during or at the termination of noviceship or temporary profession, after perpetual profession through an indult of departure, or by a decree of dismissal.[1]

Canon 684 — **§1. A member in perpetual vows cannot transfer from one religious institute to another without the permission of the supreme moderator of each institute given with the consent of their respective councils.**

Canon 684 specifies members in perpetual profession, but this would not seem to preclude one in temporary profession. The revised law employs the principle of subsidiarity in the process for transfer, inasmuch as the former law required the permission of the Holy See for a transfer, even in cases in which the transfer was from one autonomous monastery to another in the same institute.[2] *Pastorale Munus* 38 granted the faculty to the local ordinary to permit a religious to transfer from one religious institute of diocesan right to another institute of diocesan right. The revised law permits the supreme moderators of the religious institutes with the consent of their respective councils to effect the transfer of a member from one institute of religious life to another. The superior interviewing the member petitioning a transfer should be careful to ascertain the reasons prompting the request, and those coun-

---

[1]For a study of transfer from one religious institute to another, see J. G. Konrod, J.C.L., diss., *The Transfer of Religious to Another Community. CanLawStud* 278 (Washington, D.C.: The Catholic University of America, 1979). See also Gallen, *RfR* 38 (1979/6), 882–885.
[2]*CIC* 632.

seling such a religious should determine if the person is knowledgeable and attracted to the nature, spirit, and end of the new institute.

The supreme moderator of the institute to which the religious wishes to transfer has the right and duty to request testimony and the necessary information regarding the member before putting the issue before the council. The supreme moderator of the institute from which the person wishes to transfer should testify as to the suitability of the transferring religious and be most sincere in appraising the reasons for the request for the supreme moderator of the new institute. Sometimes, a member wishing to transfer is granted a leave of absence (c. 665, §1) for a time of pre-probation, e.g., a religious in an apostolic institute transferring to an institute of contemplative life. This time affords the member an experience of the life and provides the competent authority of the new institute the opportunity to form a better judgment on the suitability of the candidate for admission to the probation program. The transfer should be issued before the beginning of the formal probation, and a copy of the documents should be kept in the personnel file of each institute.

§2. After completing a probationary period which is to last at least three years, the member can be admitted to perpetual profession in the new institute. However, if the member refuses to make this profession or is not admitted to making it by competent superiors, the member is to return to the former institute, unless an indult of secularization has been obtained.

A new novitiate was required in the former law, unless the transfer was from one monastery to another of the same institute.[3] The formal probationary period provides the instruction and experience which introduces the transferring religious into the history, nature, tradition, and law of the new institute. The transferring religious has probably had courses in the theology of religious life and the vows. An outline of the objectives and goals of this probationary period could be placed in the directory of the institute. The period must extend for at least three years, and the proper law of the institute can require more time than this minimal requirement in the universal law. During this probationary period, the member can decide against profession, or the competent authority can refuse the candidate admission to profession. In either case, the person is obliged to return to the former institute unless an indult of departure has been petitioned, or in the case of one in temporary vows, the time for which the profession was made has expired.

Admission to perpetual profession after the three-year probationary period refers to a member transferring after perpetual profession, and repeats the former law in not requiring temporary profession in the new institute.[4] The proper law of the institute could require the consent of the council before admitting a transferring religious to perpetual profession. A religious transferring while in temporary profession is obliged to fulfill the requirement of at least three years of temporary profession before being validly admitted to perpetual profession (c. 658, 2°). It is left to the proper law or the competent authority of the institute to determine the amount of time the religious transferring in temporary vows remains in temporary profession. Some consideration should be given to the time spent in temporary profession in the former institute. Prolonged periods of probation and/or temporary profession can violate justice, stifle enthusiasm, and encourage indecisiveness regarding permanent commitment.

§3. For a religious to transfer from an autonomous monastery to another of the same institute or federation or confederation, it is required and is sufficient to have the consent of the major superior of both monasteries and the chapter of the receiving monastery, with due regard for other requirements determined in proper law; a new profession is not required.

The former law required the permission of the Holy See for this transfer, but neither a new novitiate nor a new profession was required.[5] The superior of the monastery from which the member is transferring should be most sincere with the superior of the monastery to which the member is transferring regarding the member's potential to live monastic life and the reasons for the transfer. The proper law of monastic institutes can require a period of probation in the new monastery before a definitive decision is made regarding the transfer.

The consent of both or either of the councils can be required in the proper law in addition to the consent of both major superiors and the consent of the chapter of the receiving monastery. A new profession is not required, since the member has already made profession according to the proper law of the institute.

§4. Proper law is to determine the time and mode of probation which is to precede the profession of a member in the new institute.

It is left to the proper law of the institute to provide for the manner and time of this probationary period. While this period can extend beyond the three-year minimum in the universal law, justice

[3] *CIC* 633, §1–§3.

[4] *CIC* 634; see discussion of special *coetus Comm* 13 (1981), 325–329.
[5] *CIC* 632; 633, §3.

warrants that it should not be unduly prolonged. Some consideration should be given to the formation in the theology of religious life and the vows already given in the former institute.

§5. For one to transfer to a secular institute or a society of apostolic life or from them to a religious institute permission of the Holy See is required, and its mandates are to be observed.

Permission for such transfers is reserved to the Holy See, and this provision reflects the essential differences in these canonical institutes and the more fundamental reorientation of a person's divine vocation.

Canon 685 — §1. Until the religious makes profession in the new institute, while the vows remain, the rights and obligations which the member had in the former institute are suspended; however, the religious is obligated to observe the proper law of the new institute from the beginning of the probationary period.

The effects of the transfer are similar to those in the former law.[6] The member remains obligated by the vows; the rights and obligations in the former institute are suspended during the probationary period and cease with profession in the new institute. From the time of admission, the transferred member is obliged to observe the proper law of the new institute and to obey the competent superiors and formation personnel.

§2. By profession in the new institute the member is incorporated into it, while the preceding vows, rights and obligations cease.

The effects of the new profession are similar to those in the former law.[7] The religious professes to live the evangelical counsels according to the proper law, is incorporated into the new institute, and assumes the rights and obligations accorded at membership. The former vows, rights, and obligations cease with the new profession. The religious who transfers from one monastery to another of the same federation or confederation loses the rights and obligations peculiar to the former monastery and assumes the rights and obligations of the new monastery at the time of transfer.

There is nothing stated regarding temporalities in the case of a transfer. The former institute has the right to whatever it acquired by reason of the member's work or whatever was given to the member during incorporation in the institute according to the universal law and the proper law of the institute. The new institute would seem to have a right

to some remuneration from the former institute for the room and board during the probationary period. In the case of a religious with a dowry, the same should be given to the new institute at the time of the profession without the accrued interest.

ARTICLE 2: DEPARTURE FROM THE INSTITUTE
[cc. 686–693]

For a grave cause, usually a crisis or questions concerning vocation, an indult of exclaustration is petitioned by a member and given by the competent authority. Exclaustration provides time and distance to the religious in order to evaluate the gift of a divine vocation. The competent authority, the time, the effects, and the accountability during the process and duration of exclaustration differ from leave of absence given for a just cause by a major superior with the consent of the council according to canon 665, §1.[8]

Canon 686 — §1. With the consent of the council the supreme moderator for a grave reason can grant an indult of exclaustration to a member professed of perpetual vows, but not for more than three years, and with the prior consent of the local ordinary where he must remain if this concerns a cleric. Extending the indult or granting it for more than three years is reserved to the Holy See or, if there is question of institutes of diocesan right, to the diocesan bishop.

The revised law reflects the conciliar principle of subsidiarity; in the former law, an indult of exclaustration was granted to a member of a religious institute of pontifical right by the Apostolic See and to a member of an institute of diocesan right by the local ordinary.[9] For a grave cause, e.g., a vocational crisis, the supreme moderator with the consent of the council can grant an indult of exclaustration to a perpetually professed member which must not exceed three years. A religious who is a cleric must first procure the consent of the ordinary of the place wherein he will reside.

The former law did not qualify the member as perpetually professed.[10] While the present law does not seem to exclude a member in temporary profession from petitioning for an indult of exclaustration, serious problems with a vocation during the formative and probationary time of religious life

---

[6]*CIC* 633, §1.
[7]*CIC* 635, §1.

[8]SCRIS *Con Life* 2 (1977–1978), 164–169. See also *Comm* 13 (1981), 329–330. The difference between simple exclaustration and qualified exclaustration was raised by a consultor in the discussion but does not appear in the revised law. An explanation of *exclaustratio qualificata* can be found in *ComRelMiss* 34 (1955), 374–377. *CLD* 4, c. 638, 240–244.
[9]*CIC* 638.
[10]Ibid.

might be better resolved through the process in canon 688.

An indult of exclaustration can be granted for three years, two years and one year, vice versa, or for one year and renewed annually. It is well to set up periodic meetings with the exclaustrated member in order to evaluate the resolution of the grave cause which prompted the request. For a prolongation beyond three years or for a petition for an indult of more than three years, the permission of the Apostolic See for institutes of pontifical right or of the diocesan bishop for institutes of diocesan right is required. Neither the interests of the member nor those of the institute are served in unduly prolonging the period of exclaustration. In cases which exceed the three-year period, the Apostolic See usually indicates a date of termination at which time the petitioner would have to come to a decision.[11] It must be noted that a religious in voluntary exclaustration is free to return at any time to the institute. In such a case, the superior general should require the religious to cancel the indult so as to preclude instability. When the reasons for the indult cease or the time expires, the member is obliged to return to the institute or petition for an indult of departure.

§2. It belongs to the Apostolic See alone to grant an indult of exclaustration for nuns.

This norm provides greater objectivity in the decision to grant an indult of exclaustration to a religious whose major superior is at once the local superior. The petition of the member and the supporting statement of the superior are sent to the Apostolic See.

§3. If a supreme moderator with the consent of the council petitions, exclaustration can be imposed by the Holy See on a member of an institute of pontifical right or by a diocesan bishop on a member of an institute of diocesan right for grave reasons, with equity and charity being observed.

Imposed or enforced exclaustration (*Exclaustratio Ad Nutum Sancte Sedis*) was introduced by the Apostolic See prior to the revised law.[12] For a grave cause, the enforced exclaustration is imposed by the Apostolic See at the request of the supreme moderator with the consent of the council, whether the member consents, is opposed, or is indifferent to the decree. This action is taken both for the good of the member and of the institute. Grave causes prompting such serious action would be the following: (a) continual refusal to obey legitimate requests of superiors in serious matters, (b) disruptive behavior promoting disharmony in community life, or (c) a derogatory witness to religious life causing scandal. The supreme moderator should follow most exactly the process for the dismissal of a member in canon 697, apprising the member of the reasons for the action, allowing time for the modification of behavior, and informing the member of the right to defense. Failure to follow one or more steps in the process would jeopardize the rights of the member and could result in the denial of the petition by the Apostolic See.

The provisions of the rescript must be fulfilled, and the religious institute is obliged to support the member on enforced exclaustration if circumstances so warrant. A cleric on imposed exclaustration must find a bishop who will accept him into the diocese.

The member on enforced exclaustration cannot return to the religious institute without a decree of revocation from the authority that issued the decree. This process is a more charitable way of dealing with a member whose offenses are not so grave as to prompt dismissal yet are so serious as to provoke disharmony in community life and to jeopardize the peace of other members of the institute.

Canon 687 — Exclaustrated members are free from obligations which are incompatible with their new condition of life and at the same time remain dependent on and subject to the care of their superiors and also the local ordinary, especially if the member is a cleric. The members may wear the habit of the institute unless it is determined otherwise in the indult. However, they lack active and passive voice.

This canon greatly simplifies the former law.[13] While the member on exclaustration is obliged to live the vows, he or she is free from obligations of religious life (communal prayer, common life) incongruent with the present living conditions. The member is obliged to self-support, and the vow of poverty requires a simple life-style. Whatever the member earns belongs to the institute, but the person on exclaustration must provide for himself or herself. If the member cannot provide a decent living, the institute should assist. The vow of chastity does not preclude social contacts and healthy interpersonal relationships. If the member on exclaustration begins to move from the evaluation of religious vocation to the possibility of intimacy with another in marriage, he or she should petition for an indult of departure from the institute.

The religious is subject to the competent superior according to the law of the institute or to the local ordinary of the place of residence, particularly if the religious is a cleric. Since the religious seeks time and distancing to make a decision regarding

[11]Schumacher, ed. *RR* (1981), 38–39.

[12]Gutierrez, *ComRelMiss* 32 (1953), 336–339; Schumacher, ed. *RR* (1982), 38–40.

[13]*CIC* 639.

vocation or is forced to leave the community life of the institute, he or she is not obliged to represent the institute as a public person in wearing the habit of the institute, unless the rescript so states. The right to active and passive voice, which gives the member responsibility for the internal government of the institute, is suspended. The member is free to concentrate on the grave cause which prompted the petition for exclaustration.

Canon 688 — §1. Whoever wishes to leave an institute when the time of profession has expired can depart from it.

This provision repeats the former law and reflects the probationary nature of temporary profession.[14] The time for which the profession is made affords the member the experience of living the evangelical counsels according to the proper law of the institute. With the termination of this time and the fulfillment of temporary commitment, the religious is free to leave the institute, and all rights and obligations assumed at temporary profession cease. One contemplating so decisive a step should seek the advice of religious superiors, the formation personnel, and other competent persons.

§2. During the time of temporary profession whoever asks to leave the institute for a grave reason can be granted an indult to leave by the supreme moderator in an institute of pontifical right with the consent of the council; in institutes of diocesan right and in monasteries mentioned in can. 615, the indult, in order to be valid, must be confirmed by the bishop of the house of assignment.

The obligation to live the vows according to the law of the institute for a prescribed period of time is a serious responsibility, and a religious should not request to leave the institute before the temporary profession has expired without a grave cause. Serious familial problems or obligations, extreme difficulty in living the vowed life, unsuitability, and failure to adapt to the works of the institute are sufficiently grave causes which may prompt this request. With the consent of the council, the supreme moderator of an institute of pontifical right can grant the indult.[15] The indult would not be valid in institutes of diocesan right or in the *sui iuris* monasteries of canon 615, unless confirmed by the bishop of the place where the religious is assigned. A valid indult to depart frees the person from the obligation of the vows and the rights and duties assumed at profession.

Canon 689 — §1. If just causes are present, when temporary profession has expired a member can be excluded from making a subsequent profession by the competent major superior after listening to the council.

This paragraph of the canon is similar to the former law and reflects the contractual nature of a religious vocation.[16] As the member is free to leave with the expiration of temporary profession (c. 688, §1), so the competent major superior, for a just cause and after hearing the council, can exclude a member in temporary profession from making subsequent profession, temporary or perpetual. The proper law should specify the competent major superior who admits to profession and whether the advice or the consent of the council is required. Such action should be undertaken with equity and charity, and the member should be apprised of the reasons for exclusion from subsequent profession.

Periodic evaluations by the formation personnel shared with the temporary professed member should prevent shock or surprise at the decision of the superior. Apparent lack of vocation, unsuitability for the life and/or works of the particular institute, laziness or failure to apply oneself, and responsibility for serious disharmony in community living are sufficiently just causes warranting such action. A record of the reasons for exclusion from subsequent profession should be kept in the personnel file for reference in the event that the member seeks to return to the institute or applies to another institute of consecrated life or society of apostolic life. Such a record would assist those who admit in determining growth and maturity.

§2. Even if it is contracted after profession, physical or psychic illness which in the judgment of experts renders the member mentioned in §1 unsuited to lead the life of the institute, constitutes a reason for not admitting such a person to a renewal of profession or to making perpetual profession, unless the infirmity had been incurred through the institute's negligence or through work performed in the institute.

This paragraph differs from the former law which prohibited a religious institute from excluding a temporary professed member from subsequent profession because of ill health, unless it was proved that the member had fraudulently concealed or hidden the illness before profession.[17] In the present law, a temporary professed member can be excluded from subsequent profession by the competent major superior with the advice or consent of the council according to the proper law, if in the judg-

[14]*CIC* 637; *Comm* 13 (1981), 331–333.
[15]Provision was made for the granting of this indult by the supreme internal authority of religious institutes with the consent of the council prior to the revision of canon law. See Sec. of State, *Cum Admotae* I, 14, Nov. 6, 1964, *AAS* 59–374. SCRIS, *Cum Superiores,* Nov. 27, 1969, *AAS* 61–738.

[16]*CIC* 637.
[17]Ibid.

ment of experts, i.e., a doctor, psychiarist, psychologist, the physical or psychic disorder prevents the person from living the life of the institute. Justice and charity should be observed in such a case. Counseling during the time of temporary profession would help prevent shock at exclusion from subsequent profession. Note that the illness could have been contracted before as well as after the profession. The exception would be if the infirmity resulted from negligence on the part of the institute or from labor performed in the institute.[18]

§3. A religious, however, who becomes insane during temporary vows, even though unable to make a new profession, cannot be dismissed from the institute.

This paragraph did not appear in the 1980 draft.[19] The religious in temporary profession who becomes insane is not responsible for his or her actions, and there can be no valid subsequent profession. It is the degree of psychic disorder which makes this case different from cases covered by paragraph two of this canon.[20] A disturbed person can be capable of living apart from the demands of community life in a religious institute, while a psychotic person could not.

Canon 690 — **§1. A religious who after completing the novitiate or after profession has left the institute legitimately, can be readmitted by the supreme moderator with the consent of the council without the burden of repeating the novitiate; it is up to the same moderator to determine a suitable probationary period before temporary profession and a time in such vows prior to perpetual profession according to the norm of cann. 655 and 657.**

Canon 690 differs from the former law which required a dispensation from the impediment of previous profession from the Apostolic See before a former member legitimately separated from a religious institute could be readmitted or admitted to another institute. Such a person was required to make a new novitiate and profession and his or her place was determined by the new profession.[21] The canon reflects *Renovationes Causam* 38 and includes all legitimate departures from a religious institute upon completion of the novitiate or after

profession.[22] The supreme moderator with the consent of the council can readmit such a person, and the novitiate need not be repeated. The law leaves to the same moderator to decide an appropriate period of probation for the person returning to the institute. The time spent in religious life before the legitimate departure, the time away, the maturity, experience, and background of the candidate should all be factors in determining the probationary period. Canons 655 and 657, i.e., the time in temporary profession before a valid perpetual or definitive profession must be observed.

§2. With the consent of the council, the superior of an autonomous monastery enjoys this same faculty.

The superior of a *sui iuris* monastery defined in canon 615 enjoys this same faculty. The consent of the council is required, and the proper law may require the advice or consent of the chapter in order to avoid readmitting one who provokes or experiences serious difficulties in the necessarily confined life of the monastery.

Canon 691 — **§1. One who is professed in perpetual vows is not to seek an indult to leave the institute without very grave reasons weighed before the Lord; such a petition is to be presented to the supreme moderator of the institute, who is to transmit it to the competent authority with a personal opinion and that of the council.**

The indult of departure from a religious institute after perpetual profession was formerly called an indult of secularization.[23] It should be petitioned only for a grave reason, such as the following: (a) conviction that one has lost the vocation and can no longer live the life with integrity; (b) grave familial obligations resulting from sickness or death which cannot be adequately responded to within the institute; or (c) the life-style of the member is no longer congruent with the nature and end of the institute. The member should weigh the decision in prayer and seek the advice and direction of experienced persons. It is wise to petition a year of exclaustration (c. 686, §§1–2) before coming to a final decision. With the opinion of the council, the supreme moderator sends the petition of the member with a supporting statement to the competent external authority for a decision. The petition should contain such pertinent data as the name of the person and years professed, the name of the diocese,

---

[18]Post-conciliar legislation derrogated from c. 637. See SCRIS, *Dum Canonicarum,* Dec. 8, 1970, *AAS* 63–318. This decree did not contain the exceptions in the case of infirmity resulting from negligence on the part of the institute or from work performed for the institute. See also Gutierrez, *ComRelMiss* 52 (1971), 350–360.

[19]The legislation repeats a ruling of SCRIS on c. 647, §2, 2° of the 1917 Code. See SCRIS, Feb. 5, 1925. *AAS* XVII, 107.

[20]Insanity is a legal term. Psychologists and psychiatrists refer to the person as psychotic.

[21]*CIC* 542, §1, 5°; 640.

[22]SCRIS has applied *RC* 38 only to those who legitimately departed from a religious institute after completion of the novitiate while in temporary vows. See *RR* (1981), 36–37. According to the discussion of the consultors in the special *coetus,* the canon could be applied to those in both temporary and perpetual profession. See *Comm* 13 (1981), 336.

[23]*CIC* 640, §1, 1°–2°. See *Comm* 13 (1981), 333–335; 337–339.

and the reasons prompting the request. If professional opinion(s) has been sought in the process, e.g., the advice of a psychologist or psychiatrist, it is well to include the same.

§2. An indult of this kind in institutes of pontifical right is reserved to the Apostolic See; but in institutes of diocesan right the diocesan bishop of the house of assignment can also grant it.

The gravity of such a reorientation of one's calling is reflected in the reservation of the power to grant an indult of departure to the Apostolic See for a religious in an institute of pontifical right and to the bishop of the diocese in which the house where the religious resides is located for a religious in an institute of diocesan right.[24]

Canon 692 — **Unless it has been rejected by the member in the act of notification, an indult legitimately granted and made known to the member brings with it, by the law itself, a dispensation from vows and from all obligations arising from profession.**

Once the indult is granted and the petitioner is notified, dispensation from the vows and from all other obligations of religious life is effected. In such a delicate and important matter, every effort should be made to communicate the contents of the rescript within the context of a personal interview to the petitioner. If the religious refuses the indult at the time of notification, the effects do not take place, and the rescript should be returned to the Apostolic See or the diocesan bishop with a notation of the petitioner's refusal. The indult is void, and a new one must be petitioned if the member decides later to depart. Whether the indult is accepted or refused, a copy of the rescript with the signature of the petitioner or a note of the refusal should be kept in the personnel file of the institute.

Canon 693 — **If the member is a cleric, the indult is not granted before he finds a bishop who will incardinate him into a diocese or at least receive him experimentally. If he is received experimentally, he is incardinated into the diocese by the law itself after five years have passed, unless the bishop has refused him.**

The indult to depart religious life does not free a religious who is a cleric from the obligation he assumed at ordination. Such a cleric must find a diocesan bishop who will incardinate him or at least

receive him on probation.[25] If the cleric is received on probation and five years elapse, he is incardinated into the same diocese by law, unless the bishop refuses him.

ARTICLE 3: DISMISSAL OF MEMBERS
[cc. 694–704]

The dismissal process for delicts indicated in the law and for other grave, external, imputable, and juridically proved reasons has been greatly simplified in the revised law.[26]

Canon 694 — **§1. A member is to be held to be ipso facto dismissed from the institute who:
1° has notoriously abandoned the Catholic faith;
2° has contracted marriage or has attempted it, even only civilly.**

Canon 694 repeats the former Code and applies to a member in temporary or perpetual profession.[27] Public defection from the Catholic faith or an attempted or contracted marriage effects immediate dismissal from a religious institute, inasmuch as these actions are totally incompatible with consecrated life.

Public desertion of the Catholic faith through apostasy, heresy, or schism incurs dismissal.[28] It is not necessary that the member have joined a non-Catholic or non-Christian sect to prove desertion.

An attempted or contracted marriage, even a civil marriage, by a member of a religious institute effects dismissal. The dismissal is effective even if the marriage is invalid. A religious who is a cleric incurs suspension, and could be dismissed from the clerical state. A perpetually professed lay religious incurs an interdict.[29]

§2. In these instances the major superior with the council without any delay and after having col-

---

[24]The local ordinary of the place where the religious lives rather than the ordinary of the place of the principal house of the religious institute continues the decision of the Committee for the Authentic Interpretation of the 1917 Code. See *AAS* XXI, 321.

[25]*ES* I, 3 (5). See SCRIS, May 28, 1974. *CLD* 8, 423–424, 456 for the case of a priest who received an indult of departure from his institute and was permitted to exercise sacred orders without being incardinated or accepted by a diocesan bishop into his diocese. He could not, however, exercise sacred orders outside his religious institute without the express permission of the diocesan bishop of the place he was residing. See *RR* (1982), 37–38.

[26]The 1917 Code contained norms for the dismissal of a religious in temporary profession (*CIC* 647–648), for those in perpetual profession in non-exempt clerical and lay institutes of men religious (*CIC* 649–650), for those in institutes of women religious (*CIC* 651–652), and for religious in clerical exempt religious institutes (*CIC* 654–658). Gradually, the dismissal process was made simpler. See SCRIS, Nov. 25, 1969. *CLD* 7, 563–569; SCRIS, Mar. 2, 1974. *CLD* 8, 430, 453–455. For the discussion of the *coetus* on the revised law for dismissal, see *Comm* 12 (1980), 341–362.

[27]*CIC* 646.

[28]C. 751.

[29]C. 1394.

lected proofs should issue a declaration of the fact so that the dismissal is established juridically.

Aware of such action on the part of a member, the major superior with the council immediately collects the proofs and declares the fact that juridically constitutes dismissal. Note that it is the action of the member and not that of the major superior and council which effects the dismissal. The urgency required in the canon would help to avoid the scandal arising from the person's affiliation with the religious institute.

Canon 695 — §1. A member must be dismissed for the offenses in cann. 1397, 1398 and 1395, unless in the delicts mentioned in can. 1395, §2, the superior judges that dismissal is not entirely necessary and that the correction of the member and restitution of justice and reparation of scandal can be sufficiently assured in some other way.

A member must be dismissed for the delicts stated in these canons, since they are crimes against human life and liberty and bring infamy on the religious institute. In the case of a sexual offense committed by a religious (c. 1395, §2) the competent superior may decide against dismissal and deal with the issue in a more effective way. It is important that reparation for scandal be made and that there be restitution for any injustice.

§2. In these cases the major superior, having collected proofs about the facts and imputability, is to make known the accusation and the proofs to the member who is about to be dismissed, giving the member the opportunity of self-defense. All the acts, signed by the major superior and a notary, along with the written and signed responses of the member, are to be transmitted to the supreme moderator.

The major superior collects proof of both the fact of the delict and the imputability of the member. The member about to be dismissed is informed of the accusation and proofs and advised of the right of defense. Legal counsel should be offered to assist in this defense. All of these acts signed by the major superior and a notary are sent to the supreme moderator. The defense of the member should be written and signed by him or her. The religious has the right to send the defense directly to the supreme moderator (c. 698).

*Canon 696 — §1. A member can also be dismissed for other causes, provided that they are grave, external, imputable and juridically proven, such as: habitual neglect of the obligations of consecrated life; repeated violations of the sacred bonds; pertinacious disobedience to lawful prescrip-*tions of superiors in a serious matter; grave scandal arising from the culpable behavior of the member; pertinacious upholding or spreading of doctrines condemned by the magisterium of the Church; public adherence to ideologies infected by materialism or atheism; unlawful absence mentioned in can. 665, §2 lasting six months; other causes of similar seriousness which may be determined by the proper law of the institute.

Note that the member can be dismissed and that the cause prompting the dismissal process must be grave, external, imputable, and juridically verifiable. These are the same qualities for a delict, and there could be mitigating circumstances with regard to imputability which should be considered.[30] The first four reasons indicate a neglect of the more serious obligations of consecrated life and a lack of the spirit of religious vocation. The next two show a disdain for the Church and its teachings and a contempt for Christian values. One illegitimately absent for six months lacks a sense of responsibility and accountability for the duties assumed at incorporation into the particular institute. The proper law can include other grave causes prompting the dismissal process, but it seems wise in this area as in penal law to adhere strictly to the universal law in order to avoid violating the rights of the member.

§2. Even causes of lesser seriousness determined in proper law suffice for the dismissal of a member in temporary vows.

The probationary period in a religious institute extends from candidacy to perpetual or definitive profession. The member in temporary vows continues to be formed in the spirit of the institute and is obliged to cooperate with superiors and formation personnel. The proper law of an institute can state less grave reasons for dismissing a member in temporary profession. In such cases, the cause should be external, imputable, and juridically proved. These offenses, while less grave, raise serious doubts as to the singleness of purpose of the member and the wisdom of the legitimate superiors in admitting such a person to subsequent temporary or perpetual profession. In such cases, the competent major superior can refuse subsequent profession according to the norms of canon 689, §1.

Canon 697 — In the cases mentioned in can. 696, if the major superior, after having heard the council, believes the process of dismissal is to be begun:
1° the major superior is to collect or complete proofs;

_____

[30]See commentary on c. 1321, §1.

2° the major superior is to warn the member in writing or before two witnesses with an explicit threat of subsequent dismissal unless the member reforms, the cause of the dismissal is to be clearly indicated and the member is to be given the full opportunity of self-defense; but if the warning is in vain the superior is to proceed to a second warning, after an intervening time of at least fifteen days;

3° if this warning also has been in vain and the major superior with the council believes that there is sufficient proof of incorrigibility and that the defenses of the member are insufficient, and fifteen days have elapsed since the last warning without any effect, the major superior is to transmit to the supreme moderator all acts, signed by the major superior and a notary, along with the signed response of the member.

It would be well to advise the member of the option of petitioning for an indult of departure from the institute. If the member refuses to take this action, the process for dismissal must be followed exactly in order to avoid jeopardizing the rights of the religious and to prevent the refusal of confirmation by the proper external authority due to faulty process.

The major superior apprises the council of the reason and the proofs and seeks its advice before deciding to initiate the process.

In the presence of two witnesses or in writing, the major superior: (a) admonishes the member for the grave violation, (b) warns the religious to remedy his or her behavior, (c) threatens the religious with dismissal if there is no improvement, and (d) advises the member of the right to defense. If the warning is given verbally, a written account should be drawn up and signed by the major superior and two witnesses. The major superior can take appropriate measures to assist the religious in remedying behavior, e.g., a change of residence or apostolate. If there is no evidence of improvement at the termination of fifteen days, a second warning is issued by the major superior.

If the second warning goes unheeded, the major superior with the council decides the incorrigibility and insufficient defense on the part of the member. It is important that at least fifteen days have elapsed since the second warning before the major superior sends the acts of the case signed by himself or herself and a notary with the defense signed by the member to the supreme moderator of the institute. In some institutes, the superior issuing the canonical warnings is the supreme moderator.

Canon 698 — **In all cases mentioned in cann. 695 and 696, the right of a member to communicate with and offer a defense directly to the supreme moderator always remains intact.**

The member should be made aware of this right to communicate with and to send the defense directly to the supreme moderator of the institute.

Canon 699 — **§1. With the council, which must have at least four members for validity, the supreme moderator is to proceed collegially to the careful weighing of the proofs, arguments and defenses; if it has been so decided by a secret ballot, the supreme moderator is to issue the decree of dismissal, with the motives in law and in fact expressed at least in summary fashion for validity.**

Note that there are two requirements for the validity of the dismissal: (a) that the council of the supreme moderator be composed of at least four members, and (b) that the decree of dismissal contain at least in summary the reasons for dismissal in law and in fact. If there are not four members on the council, the supreme moderator with the consent of the council should appoint a member(s) of the institute to meet the requirement of law. The superior general and the council act collegially studying the acts of the case and deciding by secret vote on the dismissal.

§2. In autonomous monasteries mentioned in can. 615 the decision on dismissal pertains to the diocesan bishop, to whom the superior is to submit the acts examined by the council.

This provision for the monasteries of canon 615 allows greater objectivity in the decision and protection to a member when the local superior of the monastery is at once the major superior. When the council studies and approves the acts of the case, the superior sends them to the diocesan bishop.

Canon 700 — **A decree of dismissal does not take effect unless it has been confirmed by the Holy See to whom the decree and all the acts are to be transmitted; if it is a question of an institute of diocesan right, the confirmation belongs to the bishop of the diocese where the house to which the religious is assigned is situated. The decree, for validity, must indicate the right which the dismissed religious enjoys to have recourse to competent authority within ten days from receiving the notification. The recourse has a suspensive effect.**

A decree of dismissal for a member in an institute of pontifical right has no force unless it is confirmed by the Apostolic See. Therefore, once the decision to dismiss is reached by the supreme moderator and council, the acts of the case should be sent to the Apostolic See. In the case of a member of a diocesan institute, the decree of dismissal is confirmed by the bishop of the diocese in which the house where the member resides is located.[31] For validity, the decree must contain the information that the member has the right to appeal the decision to the competent authority within ten days from receiving notification. An appeal suspends the effects of the dismissal indicated in canon 701, until a reply is received from the Apostolic See. The member retains all the rights and responsibilities assumed at incorporation into the institute.[32]

Canon 701 — Vows, rights and obligations derived from profession cease ipso facto by legitimate dismissal. However, if the member is a cleric, he cannot exercise sacred orders until he finds a bishop who receives him after a suitable probationary period in the diocese according to can. 693 or at least allows him to exercise sacred orders.

The vows, rights, and obligations assumed at profession cease with the legitimate dismissal from an institute. A cleric, however, is not free from the obligations assumed at sacred orders. He cannot exercise the same until he finds a bishop who receives him into the diocese on probation or at least permits him to exercise the duties of sacred orders.

Canon 702 — §1. Those who have legitimately left a religious institute or have been legitimately dismissed from one can request nothing from it for any work done in it.

Canon 702 repeats the former law.[33] A person becomes a member of a religious institute to dedicate himself or herself freely and completely to God and to the service of His people. Such a person, having legitimately departed or been dismissed from the institute does not have a claim to compensation for services rendered while in the institute.

§2. The institute however is to observe equity and evangelical charity toward the member who is separated from it.

While there is no obligation in justice to provide for those legitimately separated from a religious in-

stitute, the law directs the competent authority to observe evangelical charity and equity toward these former members.[34] The assistance should embrace not only economic or material needs but also the spiritual, moral, and social dimensions of the person's life.[35] The competent authority of the institute can benefit both members and former members by enrolling in social security and utilizing programs offering counsel and economic assistance to those separated from the institute. With the dispensation from vows, the former member regains the right of ownership and/or administration of temporalities. The institute is not obliged to return what was given to it while the person was a member, but charity would prompt a return of at least some portion of the gift.

Canon 703 — In the case of serious exterior scandal or very grave imminent harm to the institute a member can be immediately expelled from the religious house by the major superior, or, if there is a danger in delay, by the local superior with the consent of the council. If it is necessary the major superior should see that the process of dismissal is begun according to the norm of law or refer the matter to the Apostolic See.

This canon repeats the former law[36] and provides protection for members of a religious institute in drastic situations requiring immediate decision because the action(s) of a member incurs grave external scandal or very grave and imminent harm to the institute. The major superior—and even a local superior if there is danger in delay—with the consent of council can expel the member from the house. An expulsion does not have the effects of an ipso facto dismissal, and the major superior should initiate the dismissal process according to the law or refer the matter to the Apostolic See.

Canon 704 — The report to be sent to the Apostolic See referred to in can. 592, §1 is to mention members separated from the institute in any way whatsoever.

The supreme moderator is obliged to send to the Apostolic See a report of the state of the religious institute in a specified manner and time. An account of those members separated from the institute should be given in the report. The information

---

[31]The confirmation of a dismissal from a religious institute was discussed by the *coetus*, but at the plenary session of the ComCICRec in Rome, Oct. 20–29, 1981, the Commission decided by a vote of 36 to 19 on the requirement of confirmation from the competent external authority in order to protect religious particularly in Third World countries. This requirement prevents arbitrary dismissal by a superior of a religious who may be unaware of the right of recourse against such an administrative decision.

[32]Violations of personal rights, including right of recourse, in the dismissal process can result in the lack of confirmation by the competent external authority. See Sig. Apost., June 1, 1974; Nov. 8, 1975. *CLD* 8, 430–488; *ComRelMiss* 57 (1976), 373–381 and 60 (1979), 275–278; *RR* (1981), 43–46.

[33]*CIC* 643, §1.

[34]While the former law (*CIC* 643, §2) dealt with the woman religious leaving the institute without financial means, commentators applied the principles of charity and equity to both men and women religious in a similar situation. See Woywod, I, 323.

[35]SCRIS, Jan. 25, 30, 1974 *CLD* 8, 424–427. See also Gutierrez, *ComRelMiss* 53 (1972), 289–301; Ricceri, CL1 (1977), 161–170; *RR* (1981): 39–42.

[36]*CIC* 653. See *Comm* 13 (1981), 361.

is helpful in determining the quality of life and governance in the institute as well as the regard for the rights of the members. The data should not be reported generally but should indicate illegitimate as well as legitimate departures, the time at which separation occurred (temporary or perpetual profession), and the type of separation (transfer, voluntary or enforced exclaustration, departure, or dismissal).

CHAPTER VII
RELIGIOUS RAISED TO THE EPISCOPATE
[cc. 705–707]

At times a religious is named a bishop by the Holy Father. In such cases, adjustments are made because of the obligations of the religious to the traditions of a particular institute, to community and common life, and to the practice of the evangelical counsels according to the proper law of a religious institute. The universal law of the Church makes provisions in order that these obligations do not impede the greater responsibilities of the religious ordained a bishop for service to the people of God in a particular church.[37]

Canon 705 — **A religious raised to the episcopate remains a member of his own institute but is subject to the Roman Pontiff alone in virtue of his vow of obedience and is not bound by obligations which he himself prudently judges cannot be reconciled with his position.**

This canon is similar to the former law.[38] A religious elevated to the episcopate remains a member of the religious institute with modified rights and obligations. While the religious remains subject to the pope by the vow of obedience, he is exempt from the legitimate authority of the religious institute. The religious ordained a bishop can dispense himself from any obligation of the proper law or custom of the institute which would impede the fulfilling of the obligations of the episcopate. It would seem that any position of authority such a religious would have in the religious institute would cease with his ordination.

Canon 706 — **As regards the above-mentioned religious:**
1° if through profession he has lost the ownership of goods, he has the use of goods which come to him as well as their revenues and administration; however the diocesan bishop and those mentioned

in can. 381, §2 acquire the ownership for the particular church; all others, for the institute or the Holy See depending on whether the institute is capable of ownership or not;
2° if through profession he has not lost the ownership of goods, he regains the use, revenues and administration of the goods which he had; he fully acquires for himself those which come to him afterwards;
3° in either case, however, he must distribute goods coming to him according to the will of the donors when they do not come to him for personal reasons.

This canon is similar to the former law and modifies the obligations of the vow of poverty for a religious ordained a bishop.[39] If the religious has renounced the capacity for ownership through religious profession, he does not regain this capacity, and any acts contrary to the vow would be invalid. However, the same religious has the right of administration, use, and usufruct of the temporal goods which now accrue to him. In such a case, the ownership is acquired by the particular church of which the religious is the diocesan bishop or equivalent in law to the diocesan bishop (cc. 368; 381, §2). If the religious is not a diocesan bishop, his proper religious institute would acquire ownership. If the religious institute is incapable of ownership, it is acquired by the Apostolic See.

A religious appointed to the episcopacy, who has not lost ownership through religious profession, regains the use, usufruct, and administration of the temporal goods already owned. Likewise, anything gained personally or as remuneration for labor belongs to this religious in episcopal office. He has full title and control of temporalities acquired after being raised to the episcopate. He can sell, donate, alienate, or enter contractual agreements in any licit way and dispose of personal property by means of a will.

The juridical effects of the vow of poverty cease for a religious who has not renounced ownership and is ordained a bishop. The same person is free from seeking the permission of superiors and other obligations regarding the vow of poverty according to the proper law of the institute. However, such a religious is bound by the spirit of the vow of poverty in the use of temporal goods and should avoid luxuries and superfluous expenditures.

All bishops are obliged to use donations and dispose of goods according to the intentions of the donors, when the goods are not intended for them personally or as a recompense for their labors. In such cases, the bishop acts as the administrator of church property and is bound to fulfill the will and intention of the donors.

[37]The discussion of the special *coetus* on this chapter can be found in *Comm* 13 (1981), 363–364. The historical background for this topic can be found in J. J. Marositz, *Obligations and Privileges of Religious Promoted to the Episcopal or Cardinalitial Dignities, CanLawStud,* 256 (Washington, D.C.: The Catholic University of America, 1948).
[38]*CIC* 627.

[39]*CIC* 628.

Canon 707 — §1. A retired religious bishop may choose a place to live for himself even outside the houses of his institute unless something else has been provided by the Apostolic See.

Canon 707 differs from the former law. Canon 629 of the 1917 Code required the retired religious bishop to return to his religious institute. He could choose any house of the institute in which to live but lost active and passive voice. The revised law permits the retired religious bishop to choose a residence either within or beyond the religious institute, unless the residence is provided by the Holy See. The same religious does not lose active and passive voice in the proper institute as formerly. With the right to active and passive voice, there is a corresponding obligation to be thoroughly informed regarding the persons and issues in the religious institute. This may be problematic if the retired bishop decides to live outside the religious institute.

§2. If he has served a certain diocese, suitable and worthy sustenance is to be his according to can. 402, §2 unless his own institute wishes to provide that sustenance; otherwise the Apostolic See is to provide.

The primary obligation of providing appropriate sustenance for the retired bishop rests with the diocese he served (c. 402, §2). In some cases, the religious institute of the retired bishop provides the support. If no provision is made by either the particular church or the religious institute, the Apostolic See provides.

CHAPTER VIII
CONFERENCES OF MAJOR SUPERIORS
[cc. 708–709]

Conciliar and post-conciliar teachings emphasize the Church as *communio,* the people of God baptized into Christ, inspired by His Spirit, and sharing in Christ's mission. This understanding of the Church has great implications for the unity, collaboration, and cooperation of the people of God in building up the Body of Christ. The conferences of major superiors encouraged in the universal law foster mutual relations among religious and between them and ecclesiastical authorities at universal and national levels.[40]

Canon 708 — Major superiors can usefully associate in conferences or councils so that joining forces they can work toward the achievement of the purpose of their individual institutes more fully, always with due regard for their autonomy, character and particular spirit, transact common business and foster suitable coordination and cooperation with conferences of bishops and also with individual bishops.

The conferences and councils are encouraged; they are not obligatory. A religious institute is free to join or not in such associations, and the religious composing the conferences or councils are major superiors (c. 620). The canon emphasizes the importance of safeguarding the particular character and spirit of a religious institute which has been approved and canonically erected by competent ecclesiastical authority. Participation in such conferences or councils should help to strengthen the identity, autonomy, and goals of each institute, while enabling it to relate with other religious institutes, the conference of bishops, and individual bishops for the good of the Church.

Canon 709 — Conferences of major superiors are to have their own statutes approved by the Holy See, by which alone they can be erected, even as a juridic person, and under whose supreme governance they remain.

The conferences of major superiors are subject to the Holy See, and they are governed by the universal law for juridic persons (cc. 113–123) and their own statutes approved by the Holy See. Two international unions, the Union of Superiors General canonically erected May 29, 1967,[41] and the International Union of Superioresses General canonically erected December 8, 1965,[42] were established to promote the life of religious institutes for the service of the Church through greater collaboration among the institutes themselves and more direct contact with the Holy See. A council of major superiors of men and women from these two unions acts as a consultative body to the Sacred Congregation for Religious and Secular Institutes.[43]

In the United States, the Conference of Major Superiors of Men and the Conference of Major Superiors of Institutes of Women Religious were organized in 1956. Both conferences were canonically erected by the Sacred Congregation for Religious and Secular Institutes in 1959. The Conference of Major Superiors of Men was incorporated as a non-profit corporation in the District of Columbia in 1963. The Conference of Major Superiors of Institutes of Women Religious was incorporated as a civil body in the State of Missouri, April 24, 1962, and in the District of Columbia in December 1971, under the title of Leadership Confer-

---

[40]CD 35, 50; AG 33; PC 23; ES II, 42–43; MR 41–45; Comm 13 (1981), 365.

[41]CLD 7, 462–467; VR 25 (1968), 179.
[42]CLD 6, 448–455; 472–476; Apol 49 (1976), 133–162.
[43]ES II, 42; CLD 8, 348–351, c. 501; TPS 18 (1973), 314–316.

ence of Women Religious of the United States of America.[44]

The Canadian Religious Conference, an associa-

tion of major superiors of men and women religious was established in Canada in 1954. It is to be noted that the men and women religious in Canada associate together, rather than in separate conferences.[45]

[44]Information regarding the two conferences can be procured from the Secretariats at 8808 Cameron Street, Silver Spring, Maryland 20910.

[45]The address of the Canadian Religious Conference is 324 Laurier E., Ottawa, Ontario KIN 6P6.

BIBLIOGRAPHY

Bibliographical material for part III of Book II can be found after the commentary on canon 746.

TITLE III
SECULAR INSTITUTES
[cc. 710–730]

In 1947, secular institutes were formally recognized by Pope Pius XII, as a state of perfection—a true form of consecrated life in the Church. The Apostolic Constitution *Provida Mater Ecclesia*[1] expressed this recognition and gave the institutes their proper name and their own particular law. One year later, the *motu proprio Primo feliciter*[2] more clearly stressed the uniqueness of the institutes' character—a secular character—and their role as Christian leaven in the world. Immediately following *Primo feliciter,* was the Instruction *Cum Sanctissimus*[3] which further developed and clarified points, particularly from *Provida Mater.*[4]

Historically, the institutes date back to at least the sixteenth century. In Italy, St. Angela Merici envisioned a group of women who were consecrated to God in a life of the counsels but who lived and exercised their apostolate in the world without habit or life in common. Later, during the troubled times of the Revolution and the suppression of the Society of Jesus in France, French Jesuit Père Pierre-Joseph Picot de Clorivière (1735–1820) was inspired to found societies which, at first, he envisioned as a new type of religious. He believed that religious life consisted essentially in the profession of the three evangelical counsels. Observances, cloister, habit, and common life were seen as secondary. Consequently, members of his societies could fully live in the world and exercise civil professions. Later however, Père de Clorivière reflected that these were not, in fact, religious societies.

His members were religious before God but not before men.[5]

In still another century and nation, the Polish Capuchin priest Onorato Kozminski (1829–1916) is credited with the foundation of twenty-six institutes following the ideal of the hidden life of the Holy Family of Nazareth.[6] Conceived in a time of religious persecution, the institutes of Kozminski were designed in part to keep persons desiring a consecrated life from leaving Poland. It was the founder's conviction that the practice of the counsels and the work of the apostolate could be carried on in every sector and that this was the future way and the only way of Christian renewal after the collapse of the faith.[7]

Examples of pioneering foundations can be multiplied, especially in nineteenth century Italy and France. Outstanding among these is the Italian Franciscan Agostino Gemelli (1875–1959), founder of the Missionaries of the Kingship of Christ. Gemelli envisioned associations of laity, consecrated to God in the world.[8] His classic *Pro Memoria* (1939), an apologia for this new form of consecrated life in the Church, expressed its uniqueness in a phrase later to be echoed in papal and conciliar documents. Members of institutes, stated Gemelli, did not work from "outside the world"; they rather worked on the world from, "as it were, within the world."[9]

This phrase appeared later in *Primo feliciter,* which spoke of the apostolate of members being exercised "not only *in the world,* but as it were, as *originating in the world.*"[10] Therefore it must correspond to their secular condition. At the time of the Second Vatican Council, this phrase again appeared in *Perfectae Caritatis,*[11] and now appears essentially intact, in the canons.[12]

[1]*AAS* 39 (1947), 114–124.
[2]*AAS* 40 (1948) 283–286.
[3]Ibid., 293–297.
[4]Statistics published in 1978 showed the existence of 125 institutes approved by the Church: 37 pontifical and 88 diocesan. M. Albertini, "A trent'anni dal Motu proprio *Primo feliciter,*" *Dialogo* 6 (1978), 33. An estimate of membership made at the time of the 1970 International Congress of Secular Institutes reported approximately 30,000 women members, 3000 priests, and 400 lay men. A. Oberti, "Preparazione significato e prospettive del Convegno Internazionale degli Istituti Seculari," *VC* 7 (1971), 151, fn. 1.

The 1984 *Annuario Pontificio* listed 8 pontifical secular institutes of men and 39 of women. The *Official Catholic Directory* for 1983 lists 17 institutes of pontifical or diocesan right which have members in the U.S.

[5]F. Morlot, "Consacrazione sacerdotale e consacrazione nei consigli evangelici," *VC* 7 (1971), 639, fn. 5.
[6]F. DaRiese, "Onorato Kozminski animatore di vita consacrata precursore degli Istituti secolari," *VC* 12 (1976), 610–611, fn. 9.
[7]Ibid. 613–615.
[8]Gemelli later accepted the notion of institutes of secular priests and became the founder of one.
[9]"Operando, per così dire, sul mondo *dal di dentro del mondo.*" "Le associazioni di laici consacrati a Dio nel mondo," in *Secolarità e Vita Consacrata* (Milan: Àncora, 1966), 424.
[10]"Non tantum *in saeculo,* sed veluti *ex saeculo . . . ,*" *PF* II.
[11]"Apostolatum in saeculo ac veluti ex saeculo," *PC* 11.
[12]"Sodales laici, munus Ecclesiae evangelizandi, in saeculo et ex saeculo, participant . . . ," c. 713, §2.

Canon 710 — **A secular institute is an institute of consecrated life in which the Christian faithful living in the world strive for the perfection of charity and work for the sanctification of the world especially from within.**

Secular institutes share with religious that total consecration of life recognized by the Church. Their distinguishing characteristic, consecrated secularity, is reflected by speaking of members living in the world, and seeking its sanctification from within. The latter phrase suggests the image of leaven which appears explicitly in canon 713, §1. The notion of consecrated secularity was highlighted by Pope Paul VI in addressing the institutes on the twenty-fifth anniversary of *Provida Mater.* He wished them to be an example and model of the spirit the Council wished to infuse in the Church— overcoming secularism and rendering the Church leaven and soul in the world:

> The Church has need of your witness! Humanity is waiting for the Church to increasingly incarnate this new attitude before the world, which in you, in virtue of your consecrated secularity must shine forth in a most special way.[13]

The same theme was picked up by Pope John Paul II, addressing institute members in 1980. He spoke of their "hallmark . . . to change the world from the inside."

> You are in the world, but not just in the social sense, classified as secular, but put there, personally, every bit of you. Being there must be a thing of the heart, what you really mean and want. So you must consider yourselves part of the world, committed to the sanctification of the world, with full acceptance of its rights, its claims upon you, claims inseparable from the autonomy of the world, of its values, of its laws.[14]

Canon 711 — **The consecration of a member of a secular institute does not alter the member's proper canonical condition among the people of God, whether lay or clerical, with due regard for the prescriptions of law affecting institutes of consecrated life.**

In the limited canonical sense in which the terms "religious" and "secular" are mutually exclusive, the terms secular institute and secular consecration are given legal clarity by the canon. A member's canonical condition within the people of God is not changed. Members of institutes remain lay persons or secular clerics, sharing in the mission of the Church, proper to their respective conditions. By assumption of the evangelical counsels in a manner approved by the Church, they are totally consecrated but they do not become religious nor are their institutes religious.[15] Consequently, the canons common to all institutes of consecrated life (cc. 573–606) apply equally to secular institutes. However, the canons for religious (cc. 607–709) are not to be applied to them except in the case of explicit references. Examples of this kind of reference are found in canon 727, §2 on clerics incardinated in the institute, canon 729 on dismissal, and canon 730 regarding transfers.

Canon 712 — **With due regard for the prescriptions of cann. 598-601, the constitutions are to determine the sacred bonds by which the evangelical counsels are taken in the institute and are to define the obligations flowing from these same bonds, while always preserving, however, in its way of life the distinctive secularity of the institute.**

The canons referred to are those which speak of each of the evangelical counsels and the necessity of constitutions more fully expressing the mode of observing them in each institute. *Provida Mater,* in providing the institutes' *Lex Fundamentalis,* clarified that they might employ diverse forms of bonds: for chastity, a vow, oath, or consecration binding in conscience; for poverty and obedience, vows or promises.[16]

It was carefully stated in the papal document that the vows taken by these members were not the "public vows of religion."[17] Ensuing discussion and interpretations, however, demonstrated the inadequacy of speaking of purely private vows in any institute of consecrated life formally recognized and approved by the Church.

In 1949, Canals commented on vows taken in secular institutes:

> These vows, even if they are not public in the specific sense of public vows . . . nevertheless are not strictly private vows which pertain to the in-

[13]"In questo giorno," *AAS* 64 (1972), 212.

[14]"To Change the World from Inside," *Secular Institutes,* (Rome: Conference Mondiale Des Instituts Seculiers–CMIS–, 1981), 109–110. Addressing the 1983 SCRIS Plenaria on Secular Institutes, John Paul II spoke of the institutes as "eruptions of grace" for which God is to be praised. *Informationes* 9 (1983), 122.

[15]A phrase clearly stating this was inserted in *PC* 11 just prior to the final vote on the document.

[16]*PM* III, 2.

[17]*PM* II, 1.

ternal forum—ignored by the Church in the external forum. . . . They can, with merit, be called
semipublic vows, *recognized private* vows, or *social* vows.[18]

Although the law's definition of a public vow has
not changed (c. 1192, §1), it is clearer today than in
the past that there can be more than one form of
public vow according to diverse types of institutes.
The law now regulating dispensations from sacred
bonds made in secular institutes points to the public
nature of these bonds in the technical sense of their
being verifiable, without compromising the discretion and confidentiality frequently practiced by institute members.

In view of the life-style of the institutes, their
mode of living the counsels, particularly poverty
and obedience, must be given clear expression in
their proper law. Since common life is not characteristic of the institutes[19] those portions of universal
law designed to foster, protect, or ensure that dimension of religious life may not be imposed on
members of secular institutes.

*Canon 713 — §1. The members of these insti-
tutes express and exercise their own consecration
in their apostolic activity and like a leaven they
strive to imbue all things with the spirit of the gospel for the strengthening and growth of the Body of
Christ.
§2. Lay members share in the Church's evangelizing task in the world and of the world through
their witness of a Christian life and fidelity toward
their consecration, and through their efforts to order temporal things according to God and inform
the world by the power of the gospel. Also, they cooperate in serving the ecclesial community, according to their particular secular way of life.
§3. Clerical members through the witness of
their consecrated life, especially in the presbyterate, help their brothers by their special apostolic
charity and in their sacred ministry among the people of God they bring about the sanctification of
the world.*

This canon provides for the existential reality of
a wide diversity among secular institutes, some being engaged in works explicitly related to the apostolic activity of the Church, and others acting
silently and invisibly as leaven by the fact of their
presence as consecrated persons in the midst of
their daily professional, social, and political milieu.
Provida Mater described the apostolate of the institutes, in these words:

. . . They can act as the leaven of rechristianiza-
tion for families, professions and civil society by

reason of their close and daily contact with a life
of complete and perfect dedication to holiness;
they can exercise the apostolate in many ways
and carry out manifold ministerial tasks that
place, time or circumstances forbid or render
very difficult for priests and religious.[20]

Some were disappointed in the latter part of this explanation, seeing in it a supplementary, rather than
a proper role.

Pope Pius XII was more explicit about the institutes' uniqueness the following year. After referring
to the members as light and salt in a dark and sa-
vorless world, he spoke of them again as leaven:

. . . small in quantity yet ever active, which always and everywhere at work, mingled with all
grades of society, from the highest to the lowest,
strives by work, example and in every way to
reach and permeate them each and all until the
whole mass is transformed and wholly leavened
in Christ.[21]

Further, the entire life of the members of secular institutes must become apostolate.

This apostolate of the secular institutes is to be
faithfully exercised not only *in the world,* but as it
were, as *originating in the world* and consequently in its profession, activities, forms, places and
circumstances it must correspond to the secular
condition.[22]

The canon's second paragraph, in focusing the
role of lay institutes, uses terminology familiar from
Lumen Gentium's chapter on the laity. It is theirs
in a particular way to order the temporal in the way
of Christ (*LG* 31); they make the Church present in
places and circumstances where they alone allow it
to be salt of the earth (*LG* 32); all that they do—
work, prayer, family life, recreation—done in the
Spirit, becomes spiritual sacrifice (*LG* 34).

While some institutes have a specific work (e.g.,
catechetics, the medical profession) most frequently
the lay institute members are immersed in the midst
of others as farmers, lawyers, teachers, nurses, fac-
tory workers, civil servants. The quality of their
consecrated life is brought to bear on their everyday
situation. What pertains to the role of the laity in
the Church is theirs. This became increasingly clear
in the years following approbation. Addressing directors of institutes in 1976, Pope Paul VI invited
them to hear the words of *Evangelii Nuntiandi* 70
as theirs.[23]

[18]S. Canals, "De Institutis Saecularibus: Doctrine et Praxis," *ME*
74 (1949), 156.
[19]*PM* III, 4.

[20]*PM* Intro.
[21]*PF* Intro.
[22]*PF* II.
[23]"C'est bien volontiers," *ComRelMiss* 57 (1976), 368–370.

That article, addressed to the laity, notes that their condition demands a particular form of evangelization. Theirs is a wide field embracing the realms of politics, society, and economics; culture, the sciences, and arts; international relations and the mass media. It is through working in the midst of these things, stated the Holy Father, that the laity contribute to building the Kingdom and bringing others to salvation in Christ.

At the same time, he noted that this was not the work of the institutes as institutes; theirs was to form their members' consciousness to maturity and openness. In this way, members would prepare themselves in their professions with great zeal and so be enabled to approach in a spirit of evangelical detachment the burdens and joys of the social responsibility toward which Providence has directed them.[24] While the gospel values which inform their lives are apt to involve them, as Christians, more totally in spheres of labor, society, and politics which are not visibly related to works of the Church as such, all roles which are possible for lay involvement in the Church's mission and worship are also theirs.

Just as lay institute members take up the role of the laity in the Church, so members of clerical institutes share the role of the secular clergy. As the third paragraph of the canon suggests, they are leaven within the diocesan presbyterate. The secularity of priest members must be understood differently than that of lay members in reference to a relationship with the "world."

In the technical sense of their not being religious, these priests are secular. Their role in the sanctification of the world is through the sacred ministry. Although in a less direct way, these institute members contribute to the building of the earthly city through their roles as teachers of faith and offerers of the spiritual gifts of the faithful. The Council provided for those in holy orders to engage in secular activities and professions only as an exception.[25]

At the 1970 International Congress of Secular Institutes, a French-speaking group of priest members reflected on their secularity in these words:

> To build the world is, therefore, to make a more fraternal, free, and joyous humanity. The priest participates in this construction and he is thus secular—in the sense that we have said of proximity to the world—in the measure in which he works in close communion with the laity.[26]

In a 1972 address to secular institutes, Pope Paul VI stated:

> In himself, the priest as such has also, like the Christian layman, an essential relationship with the world, which he must realize in an exemplary way in his own life, in order to carry out his own vocation for which he was sent into the world as Christ was sent by the Father (cfr. Jn. 20, 23). But as priest he assumes a specifically priestly responsibility for the proper formation of the temporal order. Unlike the layman—apart from exceptional cases, as expressed in a vote of the recent Episcopal Synod—he does not exercise this responsibility with direct and immediate action in the temporal order, but through his ministerial action and through his role as educator in the faith (cfr. *Presbyterorum Ordinis,* 6). This is the highest means to ensure that the world should constantly be perfected, according to the order and the significance of creation.[27]

Canon 714 — Members are to lead their life according to the norm of the constitutions, in the ordinary conditions of the world, either alone or each in their respective families, or in a group of brothers or sisters.

The canon's positive expression of diversity for members' living situations has its roots in the original document of approbation. *Provida Mater* described the institutes in negative terms, as those who neither take the public vows of religion "nor impose community life or domicile in common on all their members. ... "[28] Similarly, the 1948 instruction from the Sacred Congregation for Religious listed the exclusion of "a common life that is externally organized" as part of a checklist for examining the true nature of secular institutes.[29]

Although *Provida Mater* had called for institutes to have some common house, these were clearly for the purpose of providing housing for leaders, for those ill or unable to provide for themselves otherwise, or for purposes of formation and spiritual exercises.[30] The options of living alone, with family, or with others provide for diverse personal, cultural, and societal factors.

Canon 715 — §1. Clerical members incardinated in a diocese depend on the diocesan bishop, with due regard for those things which pertain to consecrated life in their particular institute.

§2. If those who are incardinated in an institute according to the norm of can. 266, §3, are appointed to particular works of the institute or to the gov-

---

[24]Ibid., 369.
[25]*LG* 31.
[26]*Acta Congressus Internationalis Institutorum Saecularium.* Milan, 1971, 204.

[27]*Secular Institutes in the Magisterium of the Church.* (Rome: CMIS, 1974), 71–72. In the preliminary report of a research committee on clerical secular institutes, the following observation is made. "Their consecrated secularity makes them understand that they are neither laymen nor monks, but missionaries *of* the people of God and *in* the people of God. . . ." "The Secular Character of Priests: Why and How" (CMIS, August, 1984).
[28]*PM* II, 1.
[29]*CS* 7d *(Cum Sanctissimus).*
[30]*PM* III, 4.

ernance of the institute, they depend on the bishop in a way comparable to religious.

In his address on the twenty-fifth anniversary of *Provida Mater,* Pope Paul VI spoke of a threefold requirement in considering difficulties of priest members of institutes: (a) the secularity of the priest, (b) the necessity of maintaining close contact with the institute for spiritual sustenance, and (c) the requirement of remaining in close dependence on the diocesan bishop.[31] Such considerations have a bearing on incardination.

The first paragraph of the canon calls for the balance between the priest's dependence on the diocesan bishop, as are other clerics incardinated in the diocese, and dependence on his institute in those spheres of personal life and spirituality which fall within the realm of the counsels and the institute's proper law. Such matters as the observance of poverty, an orientation in spirituality, and times of retreat will be governed by the life of the institute. The diocesan bishop knows of the priest's membership in the institute, even though others may not.

The reference in paragraph two, to canon 266, §3 clarifies that the norm for clerical institutes is diocesan incardination; incardination in the institute is by concession of the Apostolic See. In those cases in which members are designated for roles of governing the institute or for works particular to the institute and thus are not equally available for works in the diocese, their dependence on the bishop is like that of religious priests. For example, canon 678 speaks of the two interrelated spheres of authority with regard to ministry.

Canon 716 — §1. All members are to share actively in the life of the institute according to proper law.

§2. Members of the same institute are to maintain communion among themselves, carefully fostering unity of spirit and genuine relationship as brothers or sisters.

The notion of "vita fraterna" spoken of in canon 602 recurs here for the secular institutes. Proper law must delineate how members participate in governance and what is expected with regard to gatherings, retreats, and accountability. Through the means proper to the institute, a spirit of care and unity focused by a shared charism is fostered. As seen in canon 714, this does not imply cohabitation or the holding of goods in common.

Canon 717 — §1. The constitutions are to prescribe a particular manner of governance and define the time during which moderators hold their office and the way in which they are chosen.

§2. No one is to be chosen supreme moderator who is not definitively incorporated.

§3. Those who are put in charge of the governance of the institute are to take care that the unity of its spirit is kept and that active participation of the members is encouraged.

The universal law stipulates very little regarding the governance of secular institutes. The canon explicitly states that the constitutions—not proper law in general—must provide the following: the mode of governance, the term of directors, and the way of designating these. The one detail specified by the canon's second paragraph is the definitive incorporation of the highest moderator. Legislation from religious law is not to be transferred to secular institutes; as has been noted, the common norms (cc. 573–606) do apply.

The responsibilities assigned to those in roles of governance correspond with the responsibilities listed for members in the previous canon: the promotion of a spirit of unity and active participation in the life of the institute.

Canon 718 — The administration of the goods of the institute, which should express and foster evangelical poverty, is ruled by the norms of Book V, *The Temporal Goods of the Church,* and by the proper law of the institute. Likewise the proper law is to define especially the financial obligations of the institute toward members who carry on work for it.

The administration of temporal goods in secular institutes—as for any public juridic person in the Church—is regulated by Book V of the Code[32] and by proper law. Institutional ownership however, generally is minimal and the form of evangelical poverty fostered and expressed is usually individual.

A working paper by a special Pontifical Commission for Secular Institutes reads:

> The consecrated lay person who, because of his social condition usually renounces neither the possession nor the free use of his goods, achieves poverty above all by an inner detachment and by a limited and conditioned use of them, according to the rules of his Institute.

> Although retaining as a rule his rights of possession and of gain the consecrated lay person endeavors in every situation to consider himself a "steward" of the goods he owns and acquires; he feels there is nothing that really belongs to him, but everything must serve him as a "sign" of charity and justice among his brothers.[33]

---

[31]*SI in Magisterium,* 72–73.

[32]Cc. 1254–1310.
[33]"Riflessioni sugli istituti secolari desunte dall'esperienza di vita," *Informationes* 3 (1977), 45.

The proper law is to define the obligations of the institute—especially economic obligations—toward members who work for it. Since members are usually self-supporting, provision must be made for the living expenses including such things as insurance, social security, and retirement benefits for those who work on behalf of the institute itself.

Canon 719 — **§1. In order that members may respond faithfully to their vocation and that their apostolic action may proceed from their union with Christ they are to be diligent in prayer, concentrate in a fitting manner on the reading of Sacred Scripture, make an annual retreat and carry out other spiritual exercises according to proper law.**

§2. The celebration of the Eucharist, daily if possible, is to be the source and strength of the whole of their consecrated life.

§3. They are freely to approach the sacrament of penance, which they should receive frequently.

§4. They are freely to obtain necessary guidance of conscience and should seek counsel of this kind even from their moderators, if they wish.

The spiritual life proposed for the institutes has the twofold purpose of aiding the members' faithful response to vocation and of insuring that their apostolic actions flow from their union with Christ. The key fonts of all spiritual life in the Church are listed: prayer, scripture, retreat, spiritual exercises, Eucharist, the sacrament of penance, and spiritual direction. It is the role of proper law to give more specific orientation to this dimension of the members' lives, always preserving the freedom of conscience referred to in paragraphs three and four.

Canon 720 — **The right of admission into the institute, whether for probation or for the assumption of sacred bonds, whether temporary or perpetual or definitive, pertains to the major moderators with their council according to the norm of the constitutions.**

The right of admitting members to probation in the institute and to the assumption of any sacred bonds, belongs to major moderators with their councils, according to the institute's constitutions. As noted in canon 712, the kind of bonds used is also in the constitutions. Following the period of temporary commitment, the lifelong assumption of sacred bonds in secular institutes may be "perpetual" or "definitive," as explained in canon 723, §3–4.

Canon 721 — **§1. One is invalidly admitted to the initial probation:**

1° who has not yet reached the age of majority;

2° who is still bound by a sacred bond in some institute of consecrated life or who is incorporated in a society of apostolic life;

3° who is married while the marriage lasts.

§2. The constitutions can establish other impediments, even for the validity of admission, or place certain conditions.

§3. Moreover, for one to be received it is necessary to have the maturity to lead the life proper to the institute.

The universal law lists only three invalidating impediments to admission to initial probation in secular institutes: (a) not having reached the age of majority, (b) being bound by sacred bonds in an institute of consecrated life or by incorporation in a society of apostolic life, and (c) being bound by the bonds of marriage. Canon 97, §1 states that majority in the Church is reached with the completion of one's eighteenth year.

Persons legitimately dispensed from the bonds of incorporation in another institute or society or whose temporary bonds of incorporation have expired are free of impediment. Admission to a novitiate or other form of initial probation does not constitute an impediment.

With regard to marriage bonds, the death of the spouse or the issuance of a decree of nullity ends the impediment. Cases of divorced persons seeking entrance must be considered individually. Dispensation from the impediment of marriage bonds is possible but granted cautiously. Matters which must be taken into consideration, in addition to the usual requisites for membership, include the following: any hope of marital reconciliation, the status and attitude of the former spouse, and provision for children.

The second paragraph of the canon notes that constitutions may state other impediments to valid admission to initial probation. This should not be done without very serious consideration of the requirements for membership and the possibility of objectively evaluating the matter in question. Other conditions for admission may be added without reference to validity.

While the canon's third paragraph does not attempt to make the level of maturity a measurable juridical element for validity, its extreme importance for the life of the institutes is stressed by its inclusion here. The life of consecration, lived individually and often observing discretion, makes unique demands on personal maturity.

Canon 722 — **§1. The initial probation is to be so arranged that the candidates may understand more fittingly their divine vocation and indeed the vocation proper to the institute and may be trained in the spirit and way of life of the institute.**

§2. The candidates are to be properly formed in living according to the evangelical counsels and taught to translate this life completely into the apostolate, using those forms of spreading the gospel which better respond to the purpose, spirit and character of the institute.

§3. The manner and time of this probation before first undertaking sacred bonds in the institute are to be defined in the constitutions; yet it is to be no less than two years.

The canon's first two paragraphs focus on the importance of initial formation and its various components. This stress also appeared in *Perfectae Caritatis,* following its description of the institutes' special secular character and apostolate in, and from, the world.

> Let them know quite clearly, at the same time, that they will be unable to accomplish so great a task unless the members have so thorough a grounding in matters divine and human that they will be truly leaven in the world, for the strengthening and increase of the Body of Christ. Superiors therefore should devote great care to the formation, especially the spiritual formation, of their subjects, and also to the promotion of their higher studies.[34]

Initial formation is to be ordered toward helping the candidate achieve fuller knowledge of his or her particular vocation and toward giving an experience of living according to the spirit and way of life of the institute.

The reference in paragraph two to the whole life of members being converted into apostolate is directly taken from Pope Pius XII's expression in *Primo feliciter.*[35] The forms of evangelization proper to secular institutes are given generically in canon 713 for lay and clerical institutes respectively.

The formation of members will be more specifically focused by proper law. The canon's third paragraph specifies that it is the constitutions which must indicate the length and manner of fulfilling the initial probation. In keeping with the institute's secular nature there is no required house or community for formation. The minimum time of two years is stated, but no maximum is expressed.

Canon 723 — §1. After the time of the initial probation has passed, the candidate who is judged worthy is either to take on the three evangelical counsels strengthened by a sacred bond or to depart from the institute.

§2. This first incorporation, no shorter than five years, is to be temporary according to the norm of the constitutions.

§3. When the time of this incorporation has passed, the member who is judged worthy is to be admitted to perpetual or definitive incorporation, that is, with temporary bonds always to be renewed.

§4. Definitive incorporation is equivalent to perpetual incorporation as far as certain juridic effects are concerned, to be determined in the constitutions.

At the end of the period of initial formation, candidates are admitted to sacred bonds (cf. c. 720) or they leave the institute. The first act of incorporation must be temporary, i.e., for a specified amount of time. The specifics of this incorporation are regulated by the constitutions of each institute, but a minimum of five years must be spent in temporary incorporation. As in the case of initial formation, the required length of time exceeds that required of religious.

Following temporary incorporation, members may be admitted to an incorporation called either perpetual or definitive. The latter term may be traced to *Provida Mater's* treatment of bonds in secular institutes:

> As regards the incorporation of members in their Institute and the bond resulting therefrom: the bond joining the Secular Institute and its members properly so called must be: 1° Lasting (*stabile*) according to the Constitutions, either for life or for a determined period, and in the latter case it must be renewed on expiry.[36]

In definitive incorporation, temporary clearly does not mean provisional or probationary but merely that the bonds are made continually for specified periods of time.

The fourth paragraph on the juridical effects of definitive incorporation then follows logically. The universal law makes a similar application in requiring definitive incorporation for supreme moderators (cf. c. 717, §2).

Canon 724 — §1. After the sacred bonds are first taken formation is to be continued according to the constitutions.

§2. Members are to be formed in divine and human matters equally; the moderators of the institute are to take seriously the continuing spiritual formation of members.

Constitutions must make provision for the ongoing formation of members. The second paragraph of the canon takes its terminology from *Perfectae Caritatis* 11 cited above.

Canon 725 — The institute can associate to itself, by some bond determined in the constitutions, other members of the Christian faithful who strive

---

[34] *PC* 11.
[35] " ... integra vita sodalium Institutorum Saecularium, professione perfectionis, Deo sacra, in apostolatum converti debet ... ," *PF* II.

[36] *PM* III, 3.

toward evangelical perfection according to the spirit of the institute and share its mission.

The existence of various forms of association with the institutes preceded their formal recognition by the Church. *Provida Mater,* in approving secular institutes as a true and complete form of consecrated life, refers to members in the strict sense:

> Associates who desire to belong to the Institute as members in the strict sense, in addition to the exercises of piety and mortification undertaken by all those who aspire to perfection of Christian life, must effectively tend to the same perfection by the special means here enumerated. . . . [37]

There follows the provision for undertaking each of the counsels—chasity, obedience, and poverty.

Persons not permanently bound to the evangelical counsels may be linked to an institute, sharing its spirit and mission in a way defined in constitutions. Such persons, however, are not bound by canons of universal law for consecrated life and cannot be considered members in the strict sense.[38]

Canon 726 — §1. **When the time of temporary incorporation has elapsed, the member can leave the institute freely or be excluded from renewal of the sacred bonds for a just cause by the major moderator after hearing the council.**

§2. For a serious reason the temporarily incorporated member can freely petition and obtain from the supreme moderator with the consent of the council an indult to leave.

Members in temporary incorporation may leave when their bonds expire, or they may be excluded from the renewal of those bonds for a just cause. The latter is within the competency of a major moderator, hearing his or her council. A real inability or unwillingness to observe any of the counsels or to live the life of the institute according to its constitutions would constitute such a cause.

Permission to leave the institute during temporary incorporation is reserved to the highest moderator with his or her council's consent. The request must be freely made by the member for reasons which are deemed grave or serious. All of these factors signal the greater seriousness of leaving while bonds are still in effect. As is clear from canon 728, the moderator does not dispense from sacred bonds, but by the legitimate granting of an indult to leave, bonds and rights and obligations are said to cease.

---

[37] *PM* III, 2.

[38] A study conducted by SCRIS and published in 1976 reiterated these conclusions. "Married People and Secular Institutes," *SI,* 281–302.

Canon 727 — §1. **The perpetually incorporated member who wishes to leave the institute, having thought seriously about this before God, may seek an indult to leave from the Apostolic See through the supreme moderator if it is an institute of pontifical right; otherwise from the diocesan bishop as it is defined in the constitutions.**

§2. If it is a question of a cleric incardinated in the institute, the prescription of can. 693 is to be observed.

In the case of perpetually incorporated members, the request for separation is made through the highest moderator who forwards the request to the Apostolic See or the diocesan bishop, according to whether the institute is pontifical or diocesan. The seriousness with which the Church views consecrated life and the existence and stability of sacred bonds is reflected in the gravity of causes required and the sphere of authority with competency in each case.

The usual procedure is that the member's request, addressed to the proper ecclesial authority, is sent to the head of the institute, who is to forward it with his or her own letter. While the moderator may express support of the member's request or objection to it, the necessary letters should be sent on without undue delay. The role of the highest moderator's council is not expressed in the canon and should be clarified in proper law.

In the canon's second paragraph, special provision is made for perpetually incorporated clerics incardinated in the institute (cf. c. 715, §2). In a rare reference to religious law, the canon states that these cases are treated as are those of religious priests leaving their institute without leaving the ministerial priesthood (c. 693). The similarity is due to incardination in the institute and calls for incardination, or at least experimental reception, into the diocese before the indult is granted. In turn this fulfills the requirements of canon 265 which legislates some form of incardination against the existence of *clerici vagi.*

Canons 726 and 727 provide for separation of temporarily and perpetually incorporated members. Presumably in the latter case the sense of canon 723 would be invoked, equating the juridical effects of perpetual and definitive incorporation.

Canon 728 — **When the indult to leave has been legitimately granted, all bonds, rights and obligations emanating from incorporation cease.**

The juridical effect of legitimately granted separation from an institute is the dissolution of bonds and the cessation of all rights and obligations flowing from incorporation. The canon is not explicit, but presumably the official indult is effective upon notification of the requesting member, unless he or she explicitly rejects it when notified (cf. c. 692).

Canon 729 — **A member is dismissed from the institute according to the norm established in cann. 694 and 695; furthermore, the constitutions may determine other causes of dismissal, provided they are proportionately serious, external, imputable, and juridically proven and the procedure determined in cann. 697-700 shall be observed. The prescription of can. 701 applies to the dismissed member.**

The dismissal of a secular institute member is covered in this one canon, by referring to other sections of the law. Cases of ipso facto dismissal (c. 694) and dismissal due to specific offenses (c. 695) are borrowed from religious law and involve very particular causes. The canon listing general causes for dismissal from religious institutes is not repeated here. Further determination is left to constitutions, with the usual requirements, i.e., that such causes be proportionately grave, external, imputable, and juridically proven. Proportionate gravity, in this context, would seem to refer to the matter in preceding canons; it could also be read in reference to the seriousness of the action under consideration.

The procedure to be followed in cases other than those provided for in canons 694–695 is that explained in the law for religious (cc. 697–700). The reference to canon 701 indicates the juridical effects of dismissal and provides for the particular circumstances of priests.

Canon 730 — **In order that a member of a secular institute may transfer to another secular institute, the prescriptions of cann. 684, §§1, 2, and 4 and 685 are to be observed. In order that a transfer be made to a religious institute or to a society of apostolic life or from these to a secular institute, the permission of the Apostolic See is required and its mandates are to be obeyed.**

The final canon in this title specifies the transfer process, once again borrowing from religious law. In principle, the greater the similarity between institutes, the simpler the process. Here, transfers between two secular institutes are arranged between the institutes (cf. c. 684, §1). Paragraphs two and four of canon 684 and canon 685 are invoked to provide for the time of probation in the new institute, the juridic condition of the member, and the effect of profession in the new institute. The omission of canon 684, §3 is logical since it speaks of monastic transfer. The canon's parallel (c. 684, §5) requires permission of the Apostolic See for transfers to or from religious institutes and societies of apostolic life.

BIBLIOGRAPHY

Bibliographical material for part III of Book II can be found after the commentary on canon 746.

Section II: SOCIETIES OF
APOSTOLIC LIFE
[cc. 731–746]

Immediately following the Code's treatment of institutes of consecrated life, section II continues with the societies of apostolic life. In the past, these have been known variously as Societies of Men or Women Living in Community without Vows (title XVII, *CIC*), as Institutes of Associated Apostolic Life (title II, 1977 schema), or simply as missionary societies.

Although the history of such societies is sometimes traced back to such groups as the Beguines of the twelfth century, more familiar society names appeared in the sixteenth and seventeenth centuries: e.g., St. Philip Neri's Institute of the Oratory (1575); St. Charles Borromeo's Oblates of St. Ambrose (1578); the Congregation of the Mission (1625) and the Daughters of Charity (1933) of St. Vincent de Paul and St. Louise de Marillac; and the Priests of St. Sulpice (1642) founded by Jean-Jacques Olier.

Prior to the 1917 Code, societies of this type were sometimes called "secular congregations." While their members lived in community the absence of a religious vow of poverty avoided legal problems of land ownership in nineteenth-century Europe. Societies continued to come into existence, sometimes more closely resembling religious congregations in situations in which legal problems could be averted.

In 1868, the White Fathers were founded in Algeria, and in 1892, Cardinal James Gibbons founded the Society of St. Joseph of the Sacred Heart. Twentieth-century foundations included the Maryknoll Foreign Mission Society (1911), the Society of St. Columban for the Chinese Missions (1917), and the Foreign Mission Society of Scarboro (1918).

At the time of the 1917 Code, many so-called secular congregations opted for recognition as societies under that Code's title XVII. They were described there as "imitating" the way of life of religious, and the law for societies drew heavily on religious law. The accent placed by the Code on the absence of vows in the societies tended at times to obscure the fact that many constitutions required a life of the evangelical counsels. They used different forms of bonds, however, for making that commitment. The placement of societies with religious in the law and in church directories and the strong similarities which do exist in many cases have made it all the more difficult to express their unique identity. The relocation of the societies in the present law was the result of lengthy Commission discussion.

In the 1977 schema for the revision of the law, societies were included among institutes of consecrated life. In part I of that schema, the canons common to all institutes including societies, were eighty-eight in number. Besides the four general canons introducing part II of the schema, there were four canons which were particular to the societies. These dealt with their nature as apostolic, but not religious, and their obervance of the counsels; the apostolic ordering of their fraternal life; their use of temporalities; and their relationship to the local ordinary and practice of incardination.

During Commission meetings in 1980, some consultors felt strongly that the societies should remain under "Institutes of Consecrated Life." The opinion was expressed that most founders of societies intended consecration.[1] Many societies however, particularly missionary societies of priests, did not wish to be situated in that portion of the law. Although all societies are ordered toward the apostolate and have community life, a key difficulty remained in the diversity of meaning given to consecration and the means of undertaking it.[2] It was noted that the six pontifical societies of women have consecration through vows clearly spelled out in their constitutions.[3]

A proposal to juridically recognize two types of societies was not accepted.[4] In the final Commission decision on whether to place the societies with institutes of consecrated life, there were no positive votes.[5]

[1] *Comm* 13 (1981), 377.
[2] Ibid., 381–382.
[3] In 1980 these were said to number about 40,000. Ibid., 383.
[4] Ibid., 386.
[5] Seven consultors voted against the proposal and four abstained. Ibid., 387.

Canon 731 — **§1. Comparable to institutes of consecrated life are societies of apostolic life whose members without religious vows pursue the particular apostolic purpose of the society, and leading a life as brothers or sisters in common according to a particular manner of life, strive for the perfection of charity through the observance of the constitutions.**

§2. Among these there are societies in which the members embrace the evangelical counsels by some bond defined in the constitutions.

The opening canon on societies continues the practice of recognizing their similarity to institutes of consecrated life. The present law, however, avoids earlier problems by stating precisely that members do not take religious vows, i.e., vows which incorporate them into a religious institute, with the juridical content and effects described in religious law. There may, in fact, be vows, depending on the society's constitutions, but these do not make the members religious, even if they are not viewed as purely private vows.[6]

The aspect of the societies now stressed in their title and their end is their apostolic nature. Also characteristic of the societies are their striving for the perfection of charity and the fraternal or community spirit led in common according to their own way of life and constitutions. While the phrase used repeats wording used in religious law,[7] the societies' style of community life will be characteristic of them and should be expressed in each society's proper law.

The second paragraph of the canon reflects the rationale for not having included societies among institutes of consecrated life. The recognition that members of some societies assume the evangelical counsels by a bond defined in their constitutions clarifies that this is not a general obligation for all societies. The canon speaks simply of bonds and makes no reference here to permanence.

A wide diversity in types of bonds used by societies (vow, oath, promise), the number and content of these bonds, and their temporal character are longstanding historically. As bonds taken in a society publicly recognized by the Church, these are usually not regarded as purely "private" bonds, binding only in the internal forum—even if, according to constitutions, they are not formally received by a superior in the name of the Church. The circumstances surrounding a society's foundation may well have shaped the form used for incorporation or for the undertaking of the evangelical counsels. The

classic example of this is the Daughters of Charity of St. Vincent de Paul, whose apostolic labors dictated using forms carefully distinct from those of religious life in an era when all women religious professed solemn vows and were strictly cloistered.

Canon 732 — **Whatever is determined in cann. 578-597 and 606 is applicable to societies of apostolic life, with due regard for the nature of each society; in addition, cann. 598-602 are applicable to the societies mentioned in can. 731, §2.**

Despite the new organization of the law, the section on societies continues to draw heavily on canons regulating consecrated life in general, or religious life, in particular. Rather than repeat principles already enunciated in the law, the second canon of this section refers back to several canons from the title which introduces institutes of consecrated life.[8]

The first reference, canon 578, speaks of fidelity to the intent of the founder or foundress. This is followed by the norms regulating the following: erection, aggregation, divisions, mergers, changes subject to the Holy See, suppression, autonomy, proper law, types of institutes, exemption, communication with the Holy See, relationship to ecclesiastical authority, the authority of superiors and chapters, and general norms for admission.[9] The inclusion of canon 606 invokes the principle of equal application of the law to societies of men and of women.

In this way, many juridical areas are covered without repetition but with the added caution that the particular character of each society is to be respected. Further, it is significant that those canons which define consecrated life, as such, are not invoked.[10]

The societies of canon 731, §2 however, are bound also by the canons on the counsels and on communitarian life.[11] Since all Christians are obliged in some way by the evangelical counsels and all society members are called to strive for the perfection of charity (cf. c. 731, §1), it is characteristic of the societies spoken of in this second paragraph that these undertake the counsels by a bond which is to be defined in their constitutions. The great diversity between societies highlights the critical importance of their proper law.

[6] Ibid., 383, 385.
[7] "Vitam fraternam in communi," canon 607, §2.

[8] Cc. 573–606.
[9] Cc. 579–597.
[10] Cc. 573–577.
[11] Cc. 598–602.

Canon 733 — **§1. A house is erected and a local community is established by the competent authority of the society with the prior written consent of the diocesan bishop, who must also be consulted for its suppression.**

§2. Consent to erect a house entails the right of having at least an oratory in which the Most Holy Eucharist is celebrated and reserved.

The erection of houses, the establishment of local communities, and the suppression of either of these are within the competency of the society's authority, acting in conjunction with the diocesan bishop. For the erection of houses and constituting of local communities, his previous consent in writing is required; in cases of their suppression, the bishop is consulted. The distinction between houses and communities is not delineated. Canon 740, however, states the obligation of members to live in such houses or communities.

With the bishop's consent to erect a house comes the right to have at least an oratory in which the Blessed Sacrament can be celebrated and reserved. According to canon 741, §1, houses may also have the status of juridic persons. It was with particular consciousness of women's societies that the second paragraph was added, assuring the right to at least an oratory.[12]

Canon 734 — **The governance of a society is determined by the constitutions, with due regard for cann. 617-633, according to the nature of each society.**

The constitutions of each society must clearly determine its governance. As a guideline to be used according to each society's nature, they are given the entire first two sections from the religious law's chapter on governance, namely, superiors and councils (cc. 617–630) and chapters (cc. 631–633). Since all societies do not formally assume the evangelical counsels, their proper law must adequately express the implications of obedience such as is referred to in canon 618. Canon 738, §1 also deals with the relationship of society members to their own moderators. Significantly, the other article on religious governance, that on temporal goods, is not cited here for the societies.

Canon 735 — **§1. The admission, probation, incorporation and training of members are determined by the proper law of each society.**

§2. In respect to admission into the society, the conditions established in cann. 642-645 are to be observed.

§3. Proper law must determine especially the doctrinal, spiritual and apostolic method of probation and training suited to the purpose and charac-

ter of the society, in such a way that the members, recognizing their divine vocation, may be fittingly prepared for the mission and life of the society.

Each society's proper law must determine its own norms for the admission, probation, incorporation, and formation of members. The earlier reference to canon 597 states the general requirements for admission. Again in the second paragraph of the canon, the societies are given religious law as a guideline in developing their proper law. The canons cited comprise the entire section on admission to the novitiate, with the exception of canon 641 which states the right of major superiors to admit candidates according to the institutes' proper law. The societies' own law must provide for who admits candidates.

A great flexibility is left to the society's proper law with regard to probation and formation. The end and nature of the society shape these, especially the doctrinal, spiritual, and apostolic formation of members. The goal is to help candidates recognize their divine vocation and to offer suitable preparation for the life and mission of the society. The diversity of societies leaves room for significant diversity in programs of formation. This third paragraph of the canon goes significantly beyond the 1917 Code's treatment of formation for society members.

Canon 736 — **§1. In clerical societies the clerics are incardinated in the society itself, unless the constitutions provide otherwise.**

§2. In those matters which pertain to the course of studies and the reception of orders the norms for secular clerics are to be observed with due regard however for §1.

The norm stated for clerical societies is incardination in the society. Constitutions can provide the exception to this—i.e., diocesan incardination. Besides the intent of the founder and legitimate tradition, the norm flows from the fact that societies have particular missions or apostolic works. When these are proper to the society rather than to the diocese, incardination in the society follows logically. There may, however, be clerical societies whose members are in service of a diocese, receive their sustenance through the diocese, and so logically follow the practice of diocesan incardination.

Aside from this practice of incardination in certain societies, clerical members follow the norms for secular clergy regarding programs of studies and the reception of orders. Proper law must harmonize this specifically clerical training with canon 735, §3's provision for particular programs of formation.

Canon 737 — **Incorporation entails obligations and rights for the members defined in the constitu-**

12*Comm* 13 (1981), 391.

tions as well as a concern on the part of the society to lead the members to the end of their particular vocation, according to the constitutions.

The particular constitutions of each society govern the mutual rights and obligations of members and society after incorporation. The diversity of societies, particularly with regard to the evangelical counsels, leaves the universal law vague here and emphasizes the importance of clarity in proper law. It is noted explicitly, however, that the society is responsible for leading members toward the fulfillment of their particular vocation. By canon 732's inclusion of canon 587, it is clear that society constitutions must contain certain matters and are subject to approval by the competent ecclesiastical authority.

Canon 738 — §1. **All the members are subject to their particular moderators according to the norm of the constitutions in those matters which affect the internal life and discipline of the society.**
§2. They are subject also to the diocesan bishop in those matters which affect public worship, the care of souls and other works of the apostolate, with due regard for cann. 679-683.
§3. The relations of a member incardinated in a diocese with his proper bishop are defined by the constitutions or particular agreements.

Society members must relate to various spheres of authority. The autonomy of moderators is preserved in matters relating to the internal life and governance of the society. The earlier inclusion of canon 586 also assures this.

Members are also subject to the authority of the diocesan bishop in the usual spheres of public worship, the care of souls, and other apostolic works. Once again, canons from the law for religious are given as an additional guide. These canons deal further with competent spheres of authority, cooperative efforts within the diocese, works committed to a society by the bishop, the conferral of ecclesiastical office, and episcopal visitation.

In the case of clerics incardinated in the diocese, the relationship with the bishop must be defined in the constitutions or in particular agreements. This necessity always arises in cases in which clerics have two sets of obligations and rights due to membership in a society and incardination in a diocese. A further complication can arise in the case of societies if a member is incardinated in one diocese and works in another. For this reason it seemed in the best interest of all that there be clarity of mutual responsibilities and lines of accountability expressed in constitutions and particular agreements.

Canon 739 — **Besides the obligations which they have as members according to the constitutions the members are bound by the common obligations of**

clerics, unless something else is evident from the nature of the matter or from the context.

The canon clearly is addressed only to clerical societies. Although it does not expressly say so, this is in fact evident from the nature of the matter. The content of the canon supplements the provisions of canon 738, making explicit that clerics who are society members are also under the obligations common to all clerics in the Church except when they clearly do not apply. Such obligations must be considered when writing and approving constitutions of societies. Significant areas of difference from other clerics can come in cases of incardination in the society and in cases in which a society has its own proper apostolic works. The obligation to the same course of studies was already expressed in canon 736, §2.

Canon 740 — **Members must live in a house or community legitimately established and observe common life according to the norm of proper law, by which absences from a house or community are also governed.**

The canon focuses on that communal aspect of the societies which has traditionally been characteristic of them, and it supplements the earlier reference to canon 602. Members must live in legitimately constituted houses or communities and their observation of a common life is according to proper law. Once again, diversity with regard to the assumption of the evangelical counsels and the fact that these societies are not canonically religious warn against reading this canon as requiring the common life of religious where all is held in common. Proper law must provide for absences from these houses and communities. It is perhaps significant that this is an area in which the law for religious life is not cited as a further guideline.

Canon 741 — §1. **Societies and, unless the constitutions state otherwise, their parts and houses are juridic persons, and, as such, capable of acquiring, possessing, administering and alienating temporal goods according to the norm of the prescriptions of Book V, *The Temporal Goods of the Church,* cann. 636, 638 and 639 and the norm of proper law.**
§2. According to the norm of proper law the members are also capable of acquiring, possessing, administering and disposing of temporal goods, but whatever comes to them in consideration of the society belongs to the society.

Although their constitutions may state otherwise, the norm for societies is to enjoy the status of juridic persons in the Church. This is noted for the society as a whole and for its parts and houses. From this follows the usual capacities with regard to temporal goods and the consequent application of the norms of Book V of the universal law.[13] Societies are also subject to their own proper law in such matters and to canons 636, 638, and 639, again canons borrowed from religious law. The first of these provides for finance officers and reports; the second deals with ordinary administration and valid alienation; and the last explains spheres of responsibility for debts contracted.

The second paragraph of the canon deals with individual members and temporal goods. It is a distinctive mark of societies that members may administer and dispose of goods as well as acquire and own them. These matters are further regulated by proper law, the one general limitation being that whatever comes to a member for the society is acquired by the society and does not become the property of the individual member. Proper law does well to clarify which things accrue to the members and which to the society (e.g., pensions, insurance) and to state the society's requirements, if any, regarding wills. Any such wills must be valid according to civil law as well.

Canon 742 — The departure and dismissal of a member not yet definitively incorporated is governed by the constitutions of each society.

The constitutions of each society must provide norms for the voluntary departure and the dismissal of members not yet definitely incorporated. The universal law gives no norms in this instance, however, both justice and the overall tenor of similar laws require that constitutions be very clear so that the rights and well-being of both members and society are safeguarded. Particularly in cases of dismissal, it should be stated who is the competent authority and what causes are sufficient for dismissal.

The 1917 Code did not have a canon such as this regarding the departure of those not definitively incorporated. Canon 681 of the 1917 Code covered all separation including the matter treated in the next four canons.

Canon 743 — A member definitively incorporated can obtain an indult of departure from the society from the supreme moderator with the consent of the council, unless it is reserved to the Holy See by the constitutions; the rights and obligations flowing from incorporation cease, with due regard for the prescription of can. 693.

Those definitely incorporated require an indult to leave the society. This can be granted by the supreme moderator with consent of the council, unless this is reserved by the constitutions to the Holy See. This latter is more apt to be the case in societ-

ies of women with vows.[14] Although at the time of their foundation such vows may have been thought of as private, in recent decades there has been increased acceptance of the theory that bonds cannot be strictly private in institutes and societies publicly erected and approved by ecclesiastical authority. If a society does not have bonds which effect definitive incorporation, the canon would not apply.

Proper law should clarify when the indult takes effect. Through it, all rights and obligations flowing from incorporation cease. The reference to canon 693 applies in cases in which members are not already incardinated in a diocese.

Canon 744 — §1. It is reserved to the supreme moderator also with the consent of the council to grant permission to a member definitively incorporated to transfer to another society of apostolic life; in the meantime the rights and obligations associated with the prior society are suspended, and the member has the right to return before definitive incorporation into the new society.

§2. In order to transfer to an institute of consecrated life or from that to a society of apostolic life, the permission of the Holy See is required and its mandates must be observed.

It is also within the competency of the highest moderator with consent of the council to grant the indult of transfer to another society, in the case of definitively incorporated members. With such an indult the rights and obligations of the first society are suspended, but the right to return remains throughout the time prior to definitive incorporation in the new society. This law, while similar to that provided for institutes of consecrated life, omits details which surely must be provided for in proper law: e.g., the length and nature of probation for those transferring and the assumption of rights and obligations in the new society. It is understood that the receiving society must also consent to the transfer.[15]

Transfers involving a society and an institute of consecrated life, i.e., a religious or secular institute, require recourse to the Apostolic See. Essentially the same statement is made in canon 684, §5 of religious law and canon 730 of the law for secular institutes. The difference in procedure is due to the diversity of types of institutes. It is simpler to transfer between societies than to move between societies and institutes of consecrated life because of the greater similarity.

Canon 745 — The supreme moderator with the consent of the council can grant to a definitively incorporated member an indult of living outside the society, not however beyond three years, with

[13]"Temporal Goods of the Church," cc. 1254–1310.

[14]*Comm* 13 (1981), 397.
[15]Ibid., 399.

the rights and obligations which are not suitable for the new condition being suspended; the member remains however under the care of the moderators. If it is a question of a cleric there is required in addition the permission of the ordinary of the place in which he must dwell, under whose care and dependency he also remains.

Permission to live outside the society can be granted by the highest moderator with consent of the council. The maximum length of this permission is three years, during which the rights and obligations not consonant with the member's new condition are suspended. Such persons remain under the responsibility of society moderators. Although the canon is less explicit, its reference to living "extra societatem" is comparable to canon 686, §1 on exclaustration and not to canon 665, §1 on living outside a house of the institute. The status comparable to the latter is treated in canon 740.

In the case of a cleric, there is the added requirement of the consent of the bishop where the cleric will reside and to whom he will be accountable. In cases in which society members are incardinated in a diocese and this permission to live outside of the society involves a change of diocese, consultation with the first bishop would also be required.

Canon 746 — **For the dismissal of a member definitively incorporated, cann. 694-704 are to be observed with due adaptations being made.**

The entire matter of the dismissal of members is to be handled by societies according to the law for religious, "congrua congruis referendo." This qualifying phrase would seem to call for minor adjustments such as understanding bonds of incorporation, where the law speaks of vows, or society, where it speaks of religious institute. Further, canon 696, §1's reference to habitual neglect of the obligations of consecrated life, must be understood as the obligations of universal law for societies, and the proper law of the particular society. Canon 696, §2 regarding those in temporary commitment does not apply since this matter is left to each society's constitutions by canon 742.

BIBLIOGRAPHY

(The material listed below serves as a comprehensive bibliography for part III of Book II.)

Sources

Acta Congressus Internationalis Institutorum Saecularium. Milan, 1971.

Acta Synodalia Sacrosancti Concilii Oecumenici Vaticani II. Romae: Typis Polyglottis Vaticanis, 1970–1978.

Codex Iuris Canonici Pii X Pontificis Maximi Iussu digestus Benedicti Papae XV auctoritate promulgatus. Romae: Typis Polyglottis, Vaticanis, 1917.

Communicationes, Commentarium Pontificiae Commissionis Codici Iuris Canonici Recognoscendo. Rome, 1969–.

Pontificia Commissio Codici Iuris Canonici Recognoscendo. *Schema Canonum de Institutis Vitae Consecratae per Professionem Consiliorum Evangelicorum.* (Reservatum). Romae: Typis Polyglottis Vaticanis, 1977.

Secular Institutes in the Magisterium of the Church. Rome: CMIS, 1974.

Secular Institutes: The Official Documents. Rome: CMIS, 1981.

Reference Works

Beyer, J. *Verso un Nuovo Diritto degli Istituti di Vita Consacrata,* Milan: Àncora, 1976.

Dinn, M.J., ed.; Tessier, Louise, P.M.; Courneene, E. *Canonical Documentation on Consecrated Life (1963–1976).* Ottawa: Faculty of Canon Law, Saint Paul University, 1977.

Holland, S. *The Concept of Consecration in Secular Institutes.* Rome, 1981.

Morlot, F. *Bibliographie sur Instituts Séculiers (années 1891–1972).* Rome, 1973.

Oberti, A., ed. *Nel Mondo per il Mondo. Gli Istituti Secolari Oggi.* Rome, 1972.

Olmsted, T.J. *The Secularity of Secular Institutes.* Rome, 1981.

Secolarità e Vita Consacrata. Milan: Àncora, 1966.

Vorgrimler, H., ed. *Commentary on the Documents of Vatican II.* 5. vols. New York: Herder and Herder, 1967–1969.

Articles

Albertini, M. "A trent'anni dal Motu proprio *Primo feliciter.*" *Dialogo* 6 (1978): 30–35.

Beyer, J. "Ad documentum 'Notae Directivae' pro mutuis relationibus inter Episcopos et Religiosos, annotationes." *P* 68 (1979): 564–611.

———. "De Institutorum vitae consecratae novo jure." *P* 63 (1974): 145–168; 178–222. 64 (1975): 363–392; 533–588.

———. "De Instructione 'Renovationis Causam' Commentarium." *P* 59 (1970): 21–75.

———. "Gli Istituti Secolari, oggi." *VC* 11 (1975): 386–394; *VC* 12 (1976): 96–103; 175–182.

———. "Institutes of Perfection in the New Law of the Church." *Way* 13 (1971): 87–115.

———. "L'Avenir des Instituts Séculiers." *Gregorianum* 46 (1965): 545–594.

———. "Le deuxieme project de droit pour la vie consacree." *Stud Can* 15/1 (1981): 87–134.

———. "Religious Life or Secular Institute." *Way* 7 (June 1969): 112–132.

———. "Review of Work, De Vita per Consilia Evangelica Consecratae." *J* 30 (19—): 511–512.

———. "The new law of the Church for Institutes of Consecrated Life." *Way* 23 (Autumn, 1974): 75–96.

Boucher, Marie-Alice. "Un nouveau droit propose aux Institutes religioux." *Stud Can* 11/2 (1977): 351–388.

Boyle, P.M. "Understanding legislation for Religious." *Sisters Today* (1972–1973): 70–83.

Canals, S. "De Institutis Saecularibus: Doctrina et Praxis." *ME* 74 (1949): 151–163.

Conference of Major Superiors of Men. "Survey Results on Schema of Canon Law." Washington, D.C., December 15, 1977.

Conference Mondiale des Instituts Seculiers. "The Secular Character of Priests: Why and How." Research Committee Report. Rome, August, 1984.

Courel, F. "Apostolic Religious: One End." *Way* 15 (Autumn, 1971): 46ff.

Cunningham, R. "The Principles Guiding the Revision of the Codes." *J* 30 (1970): 447–455.

Da Riese, F. "Onorato Kozminski animatore di vita consacrata precusore degli Istituti secolari." *VC* 12 (1976): 608–621.

de la Croix Bonadio, J. "Notes towards a definition of the Secular Institutes." *Way* 12 (Spring, 1971): 16ff.

Dufault, W.J. "The Superiors General and 'Renovationes Causam.'" *Stud Can* 3/2 (1969): 269–275.

Fuertes, J.B. "De valore et significatione Constitutionis Apostolicae 'Provida Mater Ecclesia.'" *ComRelMiss* (1972): 52–72.

———. "Instituta Saecularia et consecratio." *ComRelMiss* (1975): 3–36; 97–122; 197–224; 289–314.

———. "Los Institutos Seculares. El fenómeno y su norma." *ComRelMiss* (1972): 162–176.

———. "Motu Proprio 'Primo Feliciter.'" *ComRelMiss* (1973): 12–39.

———. "Motu Proprio 'Primo Feliciter' contrarium Constitutioni 'Provida Mater?'" *ComRelMiss* (1971): 60–67.

———. "'Professio' et 'Cooptatio.' De usu et significatione verborum in schemate De Religiosis novi CIC." *ComRelMiss* (1977): 356–362.

———. "Vocatio religiosa." *ComRelMiss* (1971): 147–166.

Gallen, J.F. "Budget, Principles with regard to (C)." *RfR* (1974): 966–969.

———. "Canon Law for Religious after Vatican II." *RfR* (1972): 949–966. (1973): 1273–1287. (1975): 50–70. (1976): 75–101. (1978): 294–302. (1979): 48–77.

———. "Comments on the Instruction on Formation." *RfR* 28 (1969): 886–906.

———. "Decree on Confessions of Religious." *RfR* 30 (1975): 420–464.

———. "Formation Principles in 'Renovationis Causam.'" *RfR* (1970): 298–304.

———. "Impediments to the Noviceship in the New Canon Law." *J* 37 (1977): 160–167.

———. "Religious Poverty Re-Examined." *RfR* (1978): 736–747.

———. "The General Chapter of Affairs." *RfR* (1974): 294–307.

———. "The Proposed Spiritual Canons." *RfR* 37 (1978): 294–302.

———. "Typical Constitutions." *RfR* (1975): 191–223.

Gambari, A.E. "Elementi costitutivi e caratteristici della vita religiosa." *VC* (1969): 581–589. (1970): 98–106; 157–165.

———. "I fratelli negli Istituti clericali oggi." *VC* (1970): 229–233.

———. "La Sacra Congregazione per i Religiosi e gli Istituti Secolari." *VC* (1973): 823–845.

Garvey, T.J. "The Religious Brother in the Clerical Community." *RfR* (1972): 206–209.

Gorricho, C. "La renovacion de la vida contemplativa." *VR* 28 (1970): 30–41.

———. "Pequena historia de la 'Evangelica Testificatio.'" *VR* 28 (1970): 180–182.

———. "Potestad de la Superiora general durante el Capitulo (C)." *VR* 28 (1970): 261–262.

Green, T.J. "The Revision of the Code: The First Decade." *J* (1976): 353–451.

Gutierrez, A. "Apostolatus Institutorum Saecularium." *ComRelMiss* (1970): 208–222.

———. "Consecratio et saecularitas in Institutis Saecularibus." *ComRelMiss* (1970): 193–207.

———. "Decretum circa usum et administrationem sacramenti paenitentiae diei 8/12/70." *ComRelMiss* (1971): 350–360.

———. "De demissione Religiosorum iurisprudentia recens, 'Processus iudicialis' ... " *ComRelMiss* (1974): 222–243; 313–322.

———. "Facultas Superiorum laicalium dispensandi vota subditorum." *ComRelMiss* (1970): 6–19.

———. "Laicitas et pluralismus Institutorum Saecularium." *ComRelMiss* (1971): 3–24.

———. Ob XXV anniversarium a promulgatione Constitutionis Apostolicae 'Provida Mater Ecclesial.'" *ComRelMiss* (1972): 97–123.

———. "Participatio Laicorum in regimine religionis clericalis." *ComRelMiss* (1970): 97–114.

———. "Profession temporal sin intencion de perseverar?" *Sacra Congregatio pro Religiosis et Inst. Saecul. Informationes* (1977): 73–79.

———. "Vicarius episcopalis pro Religiosis." *ComRelMiss* (1979): 105–117.

Guy, J-C. "Religious Costume Yesterday and Today." *Way* 4 (Nov. 1964): 66ff.

Hayes, J.M. "Religious and the Diocese Administration." *Stud Can* 3/2 (1969): 251–258.

Hill, R.A. "Religious." *CS* 15 (Fall, 1976): 319–322.

Hite, J. "The Status of the Vows of Poverty and Obedience in the Civil Law." *Stud Can* 10/1 (1976): 131ff.

Hostie, R. "Vie et mort des Ordres religieux." *Con* (1974): 21–30.

Huizing, P. "A Methodological Reflection on the Section 'Institutes of Consecrated Life' in the *Schema Codicis Iuris Canonici.*" *J* 42 (1982): 80–191.

Leadership Conference of Women Religious. "Recommendations: Schema of Canons on Religious Life." Washington, D.C. 1977.

Leo XIII. "Conditae a Christo." *CICFontes* III, 562–566.

Lesage, G. "Evolutio et momentum vinculi sacri in professione vitae consecratae." *Periodica de re morali, canonica et liturgica* (1978): 413–445. *VC* (1979): 74–95.

———. "Le principe de susidiarite et l'etat religieux." *Stud Can* 2 (1968): 99–123.

Midali, M. "Secolarità, laicità, consacrazione e apostolato." *Salesianum* 36 (1974): 261–311.

Moncion, R.P. Jean, O.M.I. "Budget, personnel et etat religieux." *Stud Can* 4/1 (1970): 147–153.

———. "Should a Religious Congregation Provide a Reserve Fund or a Pension Plan for its Members?" *Stud Can* 3/1 (1974): 183–190.

Morlot, F. "Consacrazione sacerdotale e consacrazione nei consigli evangelici." *VC* 7 (1971): 638–657.

Morrissey, F. "The Spirit of the Proposed New Law for Institutes of Consecrated Life." *Stud Can* 9 (1975): 77–94.

Muller, H. "Secular Institutes for Priests." *Way* 12 (Spring, 1971): 81–89.

Nardin, G. "Le Conferenze dei Religiosi e la Chiesa locale." *Sacra Congregatio pro Religiosis et Inst. Saecul. Informationes* (1978): 167–207.

Oberti, A. "Preparazione significato e prospettive del Convegno Internazionale degli Istituti Secolari." *VC* 7 (1971): 151–154.

Ochoa, X. "De Ratione Generali Accomadatae Renovationis Statum Perfectionis." *ComRelMiss* 37 (1958): 323–332. 38 (1959): 79–93; 191–204.

O'Connor, D.F. "Guidelines and Practical Issues in the Drafting of New Constitutions." *RfR* (1978): 753–776.

———. "Some Observations on Revised Constitutions." *RfR* (1979): 771–779.

O'Reilly, M. "Faculties in Form of Religious." *Stud Can* 7/1 (1973): 93–111.

O'Rourke, K.D. "The New Law for Religious: Principles, Content, Evaluation." *RfR* 34 (1975): 23–49.

Orsy, Ladislas, S.J. "Government in Religious Life." *Way* 2 (May, 1966): 105–106.

Paul VI. "C'est bien volontiers." *ComRelMiss* 57 (1976): 368–370.

———. "In questo giorno." *AAS* 64 (1972): 206–212.

Pennington, M.B. "Renovationis Causam: Instruction on the Renewal of Religious Formation—A Practical Commentary." *Stud Can* 3/1 (1969): 107–124.

———. "The Evolution of Monastic Law." *Stud Can* 8/2 (1974): 349–362.

———. " 'Venite Seorsum'—An Evaluation." *Stud Can* 5/2 (1971): 245–257.

———. "The New Code of Canon Law and the New Legislation of the Religious Institute." *J* 42 (1982): 192–196.

Pichard, D. "Renouveau de la consécration des Vierges." *Vie Spirituelle* 205 (1974): 576–587.

Pinto, Pio Vito. "Exclaustratio et Absentia a domo des religieuses." *Stud Can* 11/2 (1977): 389–402.

Pius XII. "Primo feliciter." *AAS* 40 (1948): 283–286.

———. "Provida Mater Ecclesia." *AAS* 39 (1947): 114–124.

———. "Sponsa Christi." *AAS* 43 (1951): 5–24.

Regan, C. "The schema of Canons on Institutes of Life Consecrated by Profession of the Evangelical Counsels." *Proceedings of the Thirty-ninth Annual Convention.* CLSA (1977): 98–111.

Rothluebber, S.F.B. "The Power of Decision in Religious Communities." *Stud Can* 4/2 (1970): 297–307.

Sacra Congregatio pro Religiosis et Inst. Saecul. "Ad instituenda experimenta." *AAS* 62 (1970): 549–550.

———. "Clericalia instituta." *AAS* 61 (1969): 739–740.

———. "Contemplative Dimension of Religious Life." *Origins* 10 (1981): 550–555.

———. "Dimensione Teologico-Giuridica dell'Approvazione Pontificia." *Informationes* 7 (1981): 57–71.

———. "Directives for the Mutual Relations between Bishops and Religious in the Church." *AAS* 70 (1978): 473–506.

———. "Identità e Missione degli Istituti Secolari, Oggi." *Informationes* (1983): 121–142.

———. "Il Vicario episcopale per i Religiosi e le Religiose." *Informationes* (1979): 35–68.

———. "La formazione negli Instituti Secolari." *Informationes* (1979): 285–290.

———. "Leave of Absence or Exclaustration?" *Informationes* (1976): 204–210.

———. "May the Temporarily Professed Be Granted Active and Passive Voice in the Election of Delegates to the General Chapter and May They Be Appointed Local Superiors?" *Informationes* (1976): 69–73.

———. "Religious and Human Promotion." *Origins* 10 (1981): 529–541.

———. "Secular Institutes." Jan. 6, 1984. Informative Document Sent to Bishops of the World.

———. "The Rite of Consecration to a Life of Virginity." ICEL, 1975.

———. "Voting Rights of Those Who Are Living Outside the Community." *Informationes* (1975): 157–161.

Said, M. "De vita consecrata per consiliorum evangelicorum: Eius relatio ad baptisma, ad charisma, ad missionem Institutorum." *Periodica de re morali, canonica et liturgica* (1978): 361–371. *VC* (1979): 27–34.

———. "Particular Law of Institutes in the Renewal of Consecrated Life." *RfR* (1977): 924–947.

———. "The New Law versus the Gospel." *RfR* (1975): 888–896.

———. "The Present State of the Reform of the Code Concerning the Section 'De Institutis Perfectionis.' " *Stud Can* 8 (1974): 213–235.

Tresalti, Emilio. "The Identity of the Secular Institute." *Way* 33 (Spring, 1978): 133–140.

BOOK III

THE TEACHING OFFICE OF THE CHURCH

[cc. 747–833]

INTRODUCTION

James A. Coriden

The holy People of God shares in Christ's prophetic office. It spreads abroad a living witness to Him. . . . By the sense of faith which is aroused and sustained by the Spirit of truth, God's People accepts . . . the very Word of God, clings without fail to the "faith once delivered to the saints" (Jude 3), penetrates it more deeply by means of accurate insights, and applies it more thoroughly to life. (*LG* 12; cf. also 35).

The People of God believes that it is led by the Spirit of the Lord, who fills the earth. Motivated by this faith it strives to discern the authentic signs of God's presence and purpose among the events, needs and desires which this People shares with the others of our time. For faith casts a new light on everything, reveals God's plan for the integral human calling, and directs the mind toward solutions which are fully human (*GS* 11).

The office of educating belongs to the Church by a unique title . . . most of all because it has the duty of announcing the way of salvation to all people, of communicating the life of Christ to those who believe, and of assisting them with continual concern so that they may grow into the fullness of that life (*GE* 3).

Among the principal duties of bishops, the preaching of the gospel holds the preeminent place. For bishops are the heralds of the faith who lead new disciples to Christ, and authentic teachers who, with the authority of Christ, preach to the people entrusted to them the faith they are to believe and put into practice. By the light of the Holy Spirit they make that faith clear . . . and cause it to bear fruit . . . (*LG* 25).

These four quotations from the Second Vatican Council illustrate why the teaching office of the Church has been given a place of increased importance in the revised Code of Canon Law. The matters pertaining to the teaching office have been gathered into one distinct Book of the Code, and that Book has been placed immediately after the Book on "The People of God" and ahead of the Book on "The Office of Sanctifying in the Church." In comparison with the 1917 Code, in which the materials on teaching were buried in titles XX, XXII, XXIII, and XXIV of the Book on "Things," their treatment has been enhanced and placed in a new balance with the other traditional *munera* of the Church, namely, sanctifying and ruling. This elevation of the teaching office reflects a new con-

sciousness of the primacy of proclamation of the word among all of the Church's missions and ministries. It corrects a distortion or devaluing of this role which was rooted in the Catholic reaction to the Protestant Reformation.

Within this Book on "The Teaching Office of the Church" the ordering of the five titles also signals ministerial priorities. The ministries of the word, namely, preaching and catechetics, are first and foremost (cf. c. 761, *CD* 13). The second title is on the missionary activity of the Church, a treatment much heightened and expanded from that in the 1917 Code. This reflects a new awareness of the fact that the Church is missionary in its very essence, and that this task belongs to every one of its members (c. 781, *LG* 17, *AG* 2). These two areas are integral to the very nature and mission of the Church, and hence of much greater import than the three other titles: "Catholic Education," "Instruments of Social Communication and Specifically Books," and "The Profession of Faith."

Much of the material in this Book on the teaching office is new, that is, without counterpart in the 1917 Code. And most of the new legislation is derived directly from the documents of the Second Vatican Council, especially *Ad Gentes, Christus Dominus, Dei Verbum, Gravissimum Educationis, Inter Mirifica,* and *Lumen Gentium.* A large number of these canons are exhortatory or declaratory rather than directly regulatory or prohibitory.

A few of the significant changes which this Book of the revised Code introduces in comparison with the 1917 Code of Canon Law are the following:

- the regulation of seminaries has been shifted from the section on the teaching authority to the chapter on "The Formation of Clerics" in the title on "Sacred Ministers or Clerics" in the Book on "The People of God";

- the whole institute of the prohibition of books has been eliminated;

- the title on missionary activity has been enlarged and its importance emphasized;

- the role of lay persons in preaching, catechesis, missionary work, education, and the communications media is more explicitly acknowledged and encouraged;

- parental rights and responsibilities for the education of their children are strongly emphasized;

- Catholic schools in general and colleges and universities in particular receive much more attention, and some of the innovations are restrictive;

- the importance of the modern media of communications to the mission of the Church is acknowledged;

- the range of religious writings which are to be submitted for approval before publication is greatly reduced.

CANONS AND COMMENTARY

Introductory Canons

These nine general canons, which serve as a preface to this Book of the Code, make doctrinal assertions, assign certain responsibilities, claim some basic rights, and define a few terms related to the Church's teaching authority.

Canon 747 — §1. The Church, to whom Christ the Lord entrusted the deposit of faith so that, assisted by the Holy Spirit, it might reverently safeguard revealed truth, more closely examine it and faithfully proclaim and expound it, has the innate duty and right to preach the gospel to all nations, independent of any human power whatever, using the means of social communication proper to it.

§2. To the Church belongs the right always and everywhere to announce moral principles, including those pertaining to the social order, and to make judgments on any human affairs to the extent that they are required by the fundamental rights of the human person or the salvation of souls.

This is a statement of the Church's conviction about its own relationship to revealed truth and the responsibilities which flow from that relationship. The source and language of the first paragraph are from the First Vatican Council (a. 1870, Dogmatic Constitution *Dei Filius*, ch. 4); perhaps it is unfortunate that the outdated expression "deposit of faith" was retained because of the closed, static impression it conveys. (However, *LG* 25 quotes the same language from Vatican I.) This paragraph closely parallels canon 1322 which opened the section on the Ecclesiastical Magisterium in the 1917 Code (cf. *LG* 24; *DV* 7, 8 on this theme).

The second part of this paragraph simply states the responsibility and right, which pertain to the whole Church, to proclaim the gospel to all people. This follows from the first part of the paragraph which states that the Church is to expound faithful-

ly revealed truth. The affirmation that the right and duty are independent of any human power means that they are native and proper to the Church; the Church requires no empowerment, warrant, or commission from any human source in order to carry out this solemn charge. The mandate is from Christ Himself (Mt 28: 19–20).

Four changes distinguish this part of the paragraph from its predecessor, canon 1322, §2 of the 1917 Code: the Church is to "announce the gospel" rather than "teach gospel doctrine"; it is independent of "any human power" rather than just "any civil power" in so doing; the Church is to make use of all appropriate media in carrying out its proclamatory task; and the final section, which stated the obligation of everyone to learn the gospel doctrine and embrace the true Church, has been omitted. It is treated in the following canon.

It must be borne in mind that when the canon states that the "Church" is to safeguard and expound revealed truth and to announce the gospel to all people, it means the entire church membership, not only the hierarchy or clergy. It is the people of God who share in the prophetic office of Christ, as the Second Vatican Council repeatedly taught (*LG* 12, 31, 35; *AA* 2, 6, 10 *et passim*).

The second paragraph, like the latter part of the first, was transferred into the final version of the Code from the 1980 schema of the *Lex Ecclesiae Fundamentalis* (c. 57). It is part of a larger vision of the relationship between the Church and the political order which is described in *Gaudium et Spes* 76 (the source for the paragraph). It asserts the Church's basic right to teach about the moral order, especially in its social dimensions. Note that the canon speaks in terms of announcing "moral principles" rather than discerning particular moral situations. The second part of the paragraph defends the right of the Church to pass judgment on any human concerns when such assessment is demanded by the "fundamental rights of the human person or the salvation of souls." This should neither be read as an arrogant claim of omniscience nor a license to meddle in anyone's affairs; it is an assertion of the Church's legitimate concern about the human condition, especially in matters bearing on salvation, and of its freedom to express itself on such issues.

Canon 748 — §1. All persons are bound to seek the truth in matters concerning God and God's Church; by divine law they also are obliged and have the right to embrace and to observe that truth which they have recognized.

§2. Persons cannot ever be forced by anyone to embrace the Catholic faith against their conscience.

This new canon reinterprets the obligation to seek and embrace religious truth in the light of the Second Vatican Council's teachings on religious freedom; the language is that of the *Declaration on Religious Liberty* (*DH* 1). The dignity of the human person is placed in balance with the duty to search for the truth about God.

In paragraph two the principle of religious freedom and immunity from coercion are applied to the Catholic faith. In words taken from *Dignitatis Humanae* 2 and 4, the canon affirms the primacy of conscience. The act of faith must be free to be salvific.

Canon 749 — §1. The Supreme Pontiff, in virtue of his office, possesses infallible teaching authority when, as supreme pastor and teacher of all the faithful, whose task is to confirm his fellow believers in the faith, he proclaims with a definitive act that a doctrine of faith or morals is to be held as such.

§2. The college of bishops also possesses infallible teaching authority when the bishops exercise their teaching office gathered together in an ecumenical council when, as teachers and judges of faith and morals, they declare that for the universal Church a doctrine of faith or morals must be definitively held; they also exercise it scattered throughout the world but united in a bond of communion among themselves and with the successor of Peter when together with that same Roman Pontiff in their capacity as authentic teachers of faith and morals they agree on an opinion to be held as definitive.

§3. No doctrine is understood to be infallibly defined unless it is clearly established as such.

This canon is a brief statement of the Church's doctrinal position regarding the inerrancy of two of its own organs of teaching authority. The special prerogative of teaching infallibly which is here ascribed, under certain very specific conditions, to the papal office and to the college of bishops, must be seen within the context of the entire Church, that is, within "the infallibility promised to the Church" (*LG* 25). "The holy people of God shares in Christ's prophetic office . . . the body of the faithful, anointed as they are by the Holy One (1 Jn 2:20, 27) cannot err in matters of belief" (*LG* 12).

The first paragraph of the canon is derived from the Dogmatic Constitution *Pastor aeternus* (ch. 4) of the First Vatican Council and from *Lumen Gentium* 25; the second is based on *Lumen Gentium* 25 and Vatican I's other Dogmatic Constitution, *Dei Filius* (ch. 3). They should be interpreted in the theological context of those sources.

The third paragraph, which closely parallels canon 1323, §3 of the 1917 Code, sounds the important cautionary note that no teaching is ever to be viewed as infallibly defined unless it is clearly and firmly shown to have been authentically proposed in that manner. In fact the exercise of the infallible teaching authority is extremely rare.

Canon 750 — All that is contained in the written word of God or in tradition, that is, in the one deposit of faith entrusted to the Church and also proposed as divinely revealed either by the solemn magisterium of the Church or by its ordinary and universal magisterium, must be believed with divine and catholic faith; it is manifested by the common adherence of the Christian faithful under the leadership of the sacred magisterium; therefore, all are bound to avoid any doctrines whatever which are contrary to these truths.

Here is described the appropriate response of the Christian faithful to God's holy word. Those things which God has revealed about Himself are to be believed with "divine and catholic faith." The canon is similar to canon 1323, §1 of the 1917 Code, and it is taken from the Dogmatic Constitution *Dei Filius* (ch. 3) of the First Vatican Council; it is also related to the teachings of *Lumen Gentium* 25 and *Dei Verbum* 10.

Those matters to be believed with "divine and catholic faith" are (1) contained in the word of God, written or handed down, and (2) proposed as divinely revealed by the teaching authority of the Church, either by solemn judgment or by the ordinary and universal magisterium. The final part of the canon warns that believers are to shun teachings which are opposed to those which are divinely revealed.

Canon 751 — Heresy is the obstinate post-baptismal denial of some truth which must be believed with divine and catholic faith, or it is likewise an obstinate doubt concerning the same; apostasy is the total repudiation of the Christian faith; schism is the refusal of submission to the Roman Pontiff or of communion with the members of the Church subject to him.

The canonical definitions of heresy, apostasy, and schism given here closely resemble the definitions of the 1917 Code (except that *CIC* 1325, §2 defined *persons* rather than *acts*, i.e., heretics, apostates, and schismatics). Since these are the most serious offenses against a community of faith, these concepts must be understood exactly and construed strictly. When public, manifest, and formal, these actions can involve grave consequences, including loss of office and possible excommunication (cf. cc. 194, §1, 2° on removal from office; 1336 on punishments for clerics; 1364 on excommunication).

All of these actions, if they are to fulfill these canonical definitions, must be born of "bad faith." (Those speaking for the Commission for Revision were insistent on this point; cf. *Comm* 7:2 [1975], 150 and the *praenotanda* to the 1977 *schema*, p. 3.) Whatever else "mala fide" means, it is clearly the opposite of "good faith." It implies not only knowledge—that the positions taken are knowingly, consciously, and intentionally espoused, with full cognizance that they are in opposition to what is to be held "fide divina et catholica"—but also defiance—that the beliefs are denied or repudiated in rejection of the authority of God revealing or the church teaching.

The canon refers to "post-baptismal" events, and presumably this means after Catholic baptism or after reception into the Catholic Church. Catechumens or baptized members of other churches or ecclesial communities are excluded. The text omits the qualifying phrase "while still calling themselves Christians" which was in the corresponding 1917 canon. The obstinate ("pertinax") denial or doubt which defines heresy implies both the passage of time and a process of challenge or dialogue. It means that the denial or doubt is persistent and tenacious, i.e., held after long consideration and serious attempts to wrestle with the truth. Heresy refers only to doubt or denial of these things which "must be believed with divine and Catholic faith," that is, contained in divine revelation and proposed as such by the Church's teaching authority (cf. c. 750). It does not apply to a rejection or denial of lesser doctrines, much less theological interpretations or disciplinary legislation.

Apostasy is described in even stronger terms than in the 1917 Code. It implies more than simply withdrawing from the Christian faith, i.e., more than a distancing, separation, or abandonment. Similarly, the definition of schism is slightly sharpened; instead of a simple *refusal* of subjection to the papal authority or of communion with the members of the Church, the revised canon speaks of a rejection ("detrectatio"), an adamant refusal to submit to the pope or to remain in communion, comparable to a refusal to serve in the military (cf. c. 209, §1 on the basic Christian obligation to remain in commmunion).

Heresy, apostasy, and schism are harsh words to the ear of a believer; the canonical realities are harsher still, and must be judged with the utmost care and reserve.

Canon 752 — **A religious respect of intellect and will, even if not the assent of faith, is to be paid to the teaching which the Supreme Pontiff or the college of bishops enunciate on faith or morals when they exercise the authentic magisterium even if they do not intend to proclaim it with a definitive act; therefore the Christian faithful are to take care to avoid whatever is not in harmony with that teaching.**

This canon describes the appropriate response of the Christian faithful to the teachings of the Church. In doing so, it carefully distinguishes this level of response from that described in canon 750, namely a respect rather than the assent of faith ("religiosum obsequium," as over against "assensus fidei"). In the language of *Lumen Gentium* 25, the canon speaks of "religious respect" as the proper response to what legitimate church authority teaches in matters of faith and morals. This is a general guideline which incorporates a healthy respect for and acceptance of sound teaching in the Church. It calls for a basic attitude of religious assent based on a presumption of truth and good judgment on the part of the teaching authority. However, since teachings are included which are not infallible and can be erroneous, the principles of the pursuit of truth and the primacy of conscience still come into play. In other words, dissent is possible because the teachers mentioned in the canon can be and de facto have been mistaken. To search for the truth is everyone's duty and right (c. 748).

Canon 753 — **Although they do not enjoy infallible teaching authority, the bishops in communion with the head and members of the college, whether as individuals or gathered in conferences of bishops or in particular councils, are authentic teachers and instructors of the faith for the faithful entrusted to their care; the faithful must adhere to the authentic teaching of their own bishops with a religious assent of soul.**

The ordinary teaching authority of bishops and the appropriate attitude of the faithful toward it are outlined in this canon. It is derived from *Lumen Gentium* 25, and should be read in that context. When teaching the faithful entrusted to their care, individually or in groupings (episcopal conferences and particular councils are mentioned explicitly), bishops are not infallible, but they do act as authentic teachers. For that reason, Christian believers are to give "religious respect" to their teachings. What was said in the commentary on the preceding canon about dissent and the necessary quest for truth also applies here. However, because of their special share in Christ's prophetic office and their duty to witness to His truth, bishops deserve the respect due to witnesses of the faith. The explicit inclusion in the canon of the authentic teaching role of bishops gathered in conferences is a very significant addition; the earlier draft of the canon (c. 61 of the 1980 schema *LEF*) mentioned synods and particular councils, but not conferences.

Canon 754 — All the Christian faithful are obliged to observe the constitutions and decrees which the legitimate authority of the Church issues in order to propose doctrine and proscribe erroneous opinions; this is especially true of the constitutions and decrees issued by the Roman Pontiff or the college of bishops.

This canon speaks of the appropriate response of the faithful to "constitutions and decrees" (e.g., such as those issued by the Second Vatican Council) which propose teachings or proscribe errors. They do not necessarily call for the assent of faith or "religious respect," but they are to be observed. They are pastoral documents by which legitimate teaching authorities reassert accepted doctrines or warn of dangerous errors, and, as such, they deserve a respectful reception. The canon is based on canon 1324 of the 1917 Code, but it is cast much more positively. It draws attention to the special level of respect due to the decrees of the highest authority: the pope or the college of bishops. It is also broader in scope; it includes the doctrinal documents of individual bishops, whereas *CIC* 1324 was limited to those of the Holy See.

Canon 755 — §1. It is within the special competence of the entire college of bishops and of the Apostolic See to promote and direct the participation of Catholics in the ecumenical movement, whose purpose is the restoration of unity among all Christians, which the Church is bound by the will of Christ to promote.

§2. It is likewise within the competence of bishops and, in accord with the norm of law, of conferences of bishops to promote the same unity and to issue practical norms for the needs and opportunities presented by diverse circumstances in light of the prescriptions of the supreme church authority.

This new canon assigns responsibility for Catholic participation in the ecumenical movement to the highest authorities in the Church. It is cast in very positive terms, e.g., "to promote . . . the ecumenical movement, whose purpose is the restoration of unity among all Christians," and the mandate is the strongest known to us: we are bound by the will of Christ to promote it. The broader context and richer meaning for this terse canon are found in the *Decree on Ecumenism* (*UR* 4) from the Second Vatican Council.

The second paragraph assigns a similar responsibility for promoting Christian unity to the bishop for his diocese and to the episcopal conference for its region. It urges them to promote Christian unity and to establish guidelines for action toward that end, depending on local needs and opportunities. This mandate seems to coincide well with the provisions for diocesan and territorial ecumenical commissions contained in the May 14, 1967 *Ecumenical Directory* from the Secretariat for Promoting Christian Unity (nos. 3–8). (The anti-ecumenical provisions of *CIC* 1325, §3, which prohibited discussions with non-Catholics about matters of faith, has been suppressed.)

TITLE I
THE MINISTRY OF THE DIVINE WORD
[cc. 756–780]

Canon 756 — §1. As regards the universal Church the duty of proclaiming the gospel has been especially entrusted to the Roman Pontiff and to the college of bishops.

§2. As regards the particular church entrusted to them the individual bishops exercise this responsibility since within it they are the moderators of the entire ministry of the word; sometimes, several bishops simultaneously fulfill this office jointly for various churches at once in accord with the norm of law.

This canon assigns responsibilities to certain officeholders for seeing that the first duty of the whole Church, namely, proclaiming the gospel, is carried out. In a special way the pope and the college of bishops have that responsibility jointly for the universal Church. This first paragraph is based on canon 1327, §1 of the 1917 Code, *Lumen Gentium* 25, and *Christus Dominus* 3 and 4. The significant change from the previous law is the explicit inclusion of the college of bishops as the subject of this solemn responsibility; the earlier canon spoke only of the papal "munus" for the Church universal.

The second paragraph assigns the parallel responsibility for announcing the gospel to the individual bishops in the particular churches (i.e., dioceses) which are under their care (c. 386 further specifies the bishop's duties); it further describes their duty as "moderators" of the entire ministry of the word. This seems to imply a general oversight and a singular responsibility, but certainly neither a monopoly nor a rigid control. As the following canons point out, all members of the Church share this blessed burden of proclaiming the good news of Christ. This paragraph is drawn from canon 1327, §1 of the 1917 Code, with regard to the individual bishops (based on the reform decrees of the Council of Trent, especially c. 4 of the *decretum de reformatione* of Sess. 24) and on *Christus Dominus* 3. It is from this Second Vatican Council decree that the most important innovation is derived: the warrant for several bishops to fulfill their responsibility for preaching the gospel *together*, for example, the bishops of a state or province or region or country. There have been many recent, powerful examples of this collegial or joint proclamatory effort.

Canon 757 — It is proper for presbyters who are co-workers with the bishops to proclaim the gospel of God; pastors and others entrusted with the care of souls are especially bound to this office as regards the people entrusted to them; deacons also are to serve the people of God in the ministry of the word in communion with the bishop and his presbyterate.

This new canon sets forth the special responsibilities of presbyters and deacons in announcing the gospel of God, and it does so with carefully nuanced clarity. The sources, besides canon 1327, §2 of the 1917 Code, are *Presbyterorum Ordinis* 4, *Lumen Gentium* 28 and 29, and *Christus Dominus* 30, and the canon accurately reflects the rich theology of those documents. The canon indicates that presbyters, who are "cooperatores" of the bishop and share the same priesthood with him, have as their own proper role ("proprium") or peculiar prerogative to preach the gospel. And all presbyters, especially those to whom the care of souls has been assigned (e.g., pastors, vicars, chaplains, etc.; see c. 528, §1) are bound to this grave responsibility and joyful duty on behalf of their people. Deacons are treated differently in the canon: they too are to serve the people of God in the ministry of the word, and they are to do so in communion with the bishops and the *presbyterium*. The mode of this service is left undetermined in the canon; it invites specification and designation based on talent and training.

Canon 758 — In virtue of their consecration to God, members of institutes of consecrated life give testimony to the gospel in a special manner, and they are appropriately enlisted by the bishop to assist in proclaiming the gospel.

Religious have a special role in the spread of the gospel by the very fact that they have consecrated their lives to God. This new canon grounds the evangelizing mandate of religious on the very fact of their consecration; they have a special role in the living witness to the gospel because of the nature of the lives they have chosen. For this reason the bishop is instructed to enroll members of religious in the great work of proclaiming the gospel. A corollary would be the willingness of the religious, depending on their abilities and availability, to collaborate with the bishop in this task. The canon appears to be based on the teachings of *Christus Dominus* 33–35; *Lumen Gentium* 44–46; *Perfectae*

Caritatis 1 and 5; *Mutuae Relationes* 10 and 14; and *Evangelii Nuntiandi* 69.

Canon 759 — In virtue of their baptism and confirmation lay members of the Christian faithful are witnesses to the gospel message by word and by example of a Christian life; they can also be called upon to cooperate with the bishop and presbyters in the exercise of the ministry of the word.

The proper and inalienable role of lay persons as witnesses to the gospel message is asserted clearly in this new canon. The right and responsibility of the laity to give testimony to the gospel—by their words and by their lives—is squarely based on their reception of the sacraments of initiation and commitment. This role cannot be denied them, but it also makes it most appropriate that they be called upon to share in the ministry of the word along with the bishop and presbyters. The canon thus distinguishes the obligation and privilege of witnessing to the gospel, incumbent on every baptized Christian (cf cc. 211, 225) from the more public and official "ministry of the word." (This revised law makes no distinction between men and women; *CIC* 1327 stated that "worthy men" could be asked to aid in preaching the gospel.) The canon is drawn from *Evangelii Nuntiandi* 70; *Lumen Gentium* 33 and 35; *Apostolicam actuositatem* 3, 6, 10, and 25; *Ad Gentes* 41; and *Gravissimum Educationis* 7.

Canon 760 — The mystery of Christ is to be expounded completely and faithfully in the ministry of the word, which ought to be based upon sacred scripture, tradition, liturgy, the magisterium and the life of the Church.

The canon gives the object, or goal, of the ministry of the word, namely, a full and faithful exposition of the mystery of Christ, and the sources from which it is to be drawn. The list of five sources, or bases, on which the ministry of the word is to rest includes the obvious and traditional ones. They are not sharply or narrowly conceived, nor are they mutually exclusive. And the list is neither exhaustive nor taxative. The final category, "the life of the Church," would encompass, for example, the history of God's people, its order and discipline, its individual and corporate witness, and its present activities. The canon itself is new; it had no parallel in the 1917 Code, and it was not contained in the earlier drafts of this revision. It seems to be based on the rich teaching of the Second Vatican Council on the ministry of the word (*DV* 10; *SC* 7, 10, 35; *PO* 4; *CD* 12; *OT* 16).

Canon 761 — The various means which are available are to be employed to proclaim Christian teaching, especially preaching and catechetical formation, which always hold the primary place; other

means to be employed, however, are the exposition of doctrine in schools, academies, conferences and meetings of every type, and its spreading by means of public declarations by legitimate authority made on the occasion of certain events, by the press, and by the other instruments of social communication.

This canon is a nearly verbatim quotation from *Christus Dominus* 13, with further roots in *Inter Mirifica* 13 and 14. In essence, the canon simply urges that any and every means available be used to transmit the message of Christ. No one office or person is given this charge; it is the responsibility of all members of the Church. The fact that "Christian teaching" is used here instead of the "gospel," or "gospel message," or "word," which the foregoing canons used, is not significant; it simply reflects the language of *Christus Dominus.* Preaching and catechetical instruction are given pride of place among all the various media for disseminating the word. Their primary importance dictates the structure of the remainder of title I, namely the two following chapters: "The Preaching of the Word of God" and "Catechetical Instruction."

CHAPTER I
THE PREACHING OF THE WORD OF GOD
[cc. 762–772]

Canon 762 — Since the people of God are first brought together by the word of the living God, which it is altogether proper to require from the mouth of priests, sacred ministers are to value greatly the task of preaching since among their principal duties is the proclaiming of the gospel of God to all.

This canonical clarion, partly quoted from *Presbyterorum Ordinis* 4, and directly rooted in the scriptures, places the duty of preaching the gospel as the first responsibility of the Church's ministry. Following the Vulgate translation of the prophet Malachi (2:7) the canon uses the word "sacerdotum," the generic term for priest which includes both bishops and presbyters. "Sacred ministers," however, covers all those who have received ordination, that is, it includes deacons. All these ministers are not only to value and highly esteem the duty of preaching, but they also are to consider it their primary responsibility. It is both the direct mandate of the Lord (Mk 16:15), and the generative and unifying force which builds up the people of God. The proclamation of the gospel is what *makes* the Church; nothing can be placed ahead of it among the priorities of its ministers.

Canon 763 — It is the right of bishops to preach the word of God everywhere, including the churches and oratories of religious institutes of

pontifical right, unless the local bishop has expressly refused this in particular cases.

This new canon states the right of all bishops to preach anywhere in the world. It is a specification and application of the principle stated in canon 756, §1, namely that the college of bishops is responsible for the proclamation of the gospel in the universal Church. Canon 349, §1, 1° of the 1917 Code granted to bishops the *privilege* of preaching anywhere with the presumed consent of the local ordinary. The Apostolic Letter *Pastorale Munus* of Pope Paul VI (Nov. 30, 1963; II, 1; *AAS* 56 [1964] 5; *CLD* 6, 376) broadened the privilege to do so "unless a local ordinary expressly disapproves." This canon states it as a "right" which is proper to every bishop, residential or titular, presumably stemming from his sacramental ordination by which he becomes a member of the episcopal college (*LG* 21; *CD* 3, 4; see also c. 375, §2). The right may be exercised in the churches and oratories of religious, but its exercise can be limited in particular instances by the express refusal of the local diocesan bishop.

Canon 764 — With due regard for the prescription of can. 765, presbyters and deacons possess the faculty to preach everywhere, to be exercised with at least the presumed consent of the rector of the church, unless that faculty has been restricted or taken away by the competent ordinary or unless express permission is required by particular law.

Those who share the sacrament of orders with bishops, namely presbyters and deacons, are here granted by the law itself the "faculty" of preaching anywhere in the world. The faculty is given them by the general law of the Church in virtue of their sacramental ordination, and not because of an appointment to an office. The canon provides for four possible *limitations* on the preaching faculty or its exercise:

(1) the competent ordinary can restrict or remove the faculty; the "competent ordinary" could include the ordinary of the place wherein the priest or deacon is incardinated, the major superior of the religious institute to which the priest or deacon belongs, or the ordinary of the place in whose territory the priest or deacon proposes to preach. The restriction or withdrawal of the faculty to preach can be temporary or permanent, partial or total. Obviously the length of time or conditions of the limitation should be made clear in the letter of decree or precept. Since it involves a matter that is both at the very heart of ministry and vital to the life of the Church, the reasons for limiting or withdrawing a person's faculty to preach must be very serious and carefully weighed; normally they should be expressed in writing;

(2) particular legislation, e.g., at the national or diocesan or religious institute levels, may require a permission ("licentia") to preach in addition to the general faculty. Such particular laws (or general decrees) could establish conditions, qualifications, and processes for receiving permission to preach. See canon 772, §1 on the bishop's authority to issue such norms. Some regulations enacted by the conference of bishops may be advisable in order to insure that the people are well served by good preaching. (Since such laws would be restrictions on the minister's free exercise of rights, they are to be interpreted strictly; c. 18.);

(3) the refusal of the rector of the church whose presumed consent is necessary to preach. Those charged with pastoral care, e.g., a pastor, the moderator of a team of ministers, a parish administrator, or the rector of a church, have the responsibility to see that the word of God is preached to their people with integrity (c. 528, §1), and thus they have a right of vigilance over the preaching that takes place in their churches. They may refuse their consent for a priest or a deacon to preach therein. Clearly, this must be done only for a serious reason, based on a sure knowledge, and after careful deliberation. All caprice, whimsy, or arbitrariness must be absent from such a grave decision;

(4) the necessary permission of the religious superior, mentioned in the following canon, when it is a question of preaching to religious in their own churches or oratories.

This canon represents a radical restructuring and simplifying of the whole institute of preaching faculties (cf. *CIC* 1337–1342).

Canon 765 — **Preaching to religious in their churches or oratories requires the permission of the superior who is competent in accord with the norm of the constitutions.**

It is for the constitutions of the individual religious institutes to designate the competent superior whose permission must be obtained before a priest or deacon may preach to the members of that institute in one of their own churches or oratories. This is a simplification of the provisions of canon 1338 of the 1917 Code. No distinction is made between clerical and lay religious, nor between institutes of diocesan or pontifical right.

Canon 766 — **Lay persons can be admitted to preach in a church or oratory if it is necessary in certain circumstances or if it is useful in particular cases according to the prescriptions of the confer-ence of bishops and with due regard for can. 767, §1.**

This canon provides a broad warrant for lay preaching. It is a complete about-face from the stern prohibition of canon 1342, §2 of the 1917 Code. And that prohibition of lay preaching had a long history: it originated in a letter of Pope Leo the Great in the year 453, and was reiterated in various forms by popes of the thirteenth and fifteenth centuries. It was aimed at those who usurped the role of preacher, those self-appointed evangelists who were often in rebellion against the communion of faith or its teachings.

Today's situation and needs are quite different, and that is why the prohibition has been dropped and a positive, permissive posture has replaced it. The Second Vatican Council reminded us that all of the baptized must concern themselves with the proclamation of the gospel (e.g., *LG* 12, 31, 33, 35; *AA* 3, 6, 10, 25), and that there is a widespread need for more persons to do the preaching—persons who are committed to the ministry of the word, trained in the scriptures and theology, and skilled in communication; these are the reasons for the dramatic change in the Church's discipline. (Also cf. cc. 211, 225, 229.)

The canon permits the admission of lay persons to preach in churches or oratories (and, a fortiori, in other places where preaching takes place) in either of two circumstances: (1) when in certain circumstances necessity requires it, e.g., when a parish or mission is entrusted to a lay catechist or pastoral associate, or (2) in particular cases when utility urges it, i.e., when it appears pastorally useful in this instance. The first circumstance seems to envision a permanent or habitual state of need; the latter may apply to ad hoc or unusual situations or ordinary convenience or suitability, e.g., a special appeal.

There is no hint of any distinction between lay women and lay men in the canon.

No faculties are required. But the expression "can be admitted" ("admitti possunt") does imply that someone does the admitting or gives permission. The permission or consent could be presumed or implicit in an appointment to a pastoral office, or it could be explicit and given for one specific event. Who can give permission or admit the lay person to preach? Obviously the bishop can do so; he is the moderator of the entire ministry of the word in the diocese (c. 756, §2). But also the pastors or rectors who are in charge of the churches and oratories (whose consent is presumed by priests and deacons [c. 764] and whose obligation it is to see that homilies are delivered [c. 767, §4]) could grant approval for lay persons to preach. They have the responsibility of providing for the proclamation of the word of God to the people (c. 528, §1).

The canon presumes that the episcopal conference will issue norms for the admission of lay persons to preach, and it orders those regulations to be followed.

Finally, the canon refers to canon 767, §1, which states that the "homily" is reserved to a priest or deacon, thereby implying that lay persons are not ordinarily to preach in that particular form.

Canon 767 — §1. Among the forms of preaching the homily is preeminent; it is a part of the liturgy itself and is reserved to a priest or to a deacon; in the homily the mysteries of faith and the norms of Christian living are to be expounded from the sacred text throughout the course of the liturgical year.

§2. Whenever a congregation is present a homily is to be given at all Sunday Masses and at Masses celebrated on holy days of obligation; it cannot be omitted without a serious reason.

§3. If a sufficient number of people are present it is strongly recommended that a homily also be given at Masses celebrated during the week, especially during Advent or Lent or on the occasion of some feast day or time of mourning.

§4. It is the duty of the pastor or the rector of a church to see to it that these prescriptions are conscientiously observed.

This entire canon on the homily is new; it results from the *rediscovery* of the scriptures and the liturgical renewal. It is the enactment of *Sacrosanctum Concilium* 52, *Dei Verbum* 24, and *Inter Oecumenici* 53–55.

The first paragraph states that the homily, in which "the mysteries of faith and the norms of Christian living are to be expounded from the sacred text [of scripture] throughout the course of the liturgical year," is "preeminent" among all forms of preaching, is an integral part of the liturgy, and is reserved to the priest or deacon.

The 1964 Instruction provides a fuller description: "By a homily derived from the sacred text is understood an explanation either of some aspect of the readings from holy scripture or of another text from the Ordinary or Proper of the Mass of the day, taking into account the mystery which is being celebrated and the particular needs of the hearers" (SCRit, *IO*, 26 Sept. 1964, no. 54).

The homily referred to in this canon is that preached within the Eucharistic celebration. This is clear from the context (i.e., §§2–3 refer explicitly to the Mass), from the sources (both the *SC* 52 and pars. 53–55 of the 1964 Instruction are in the chapters on the Eucharistic mystery), and from the explanation given by the Code Revision Commission (*Comm* 7:2 [1975], 152 and the *praenotanda* of the 1977 schema, p. 4). This is worth noting because lay persons are permitted to read a homily at sacred celebrations of the word of God when there is no priest or deacon available (*IO* 37).

The General Instruction of the *Roman Missal* (SCRit, 3 April 1969, no. 42) states that "the homily should ordinarily be given by the celebrant himself." The Commission for Interpretation of the Decrees of the Second Vatican Council (11 Jan. 1971; *AAS* 63 [1971], 329; *CLD* 7, 633) decided that these words must not be interpreted to mean "that those who are neither priests or deacons but are men and women who participate in the liturgy" can give the homily. Apparently the commission intended to show disapproval of dialogue homilies. Similarly, the Third Instruction on Implementation (SCDW, 5 Sept. 1970; *AAS* 62 [1970], 692; *CLD* 7, 43) stated: "The purpose of the homily is to explain to the faithful the proclaimed word of God and to adopt it to the thinking of this age. This, therefore, is the responsibility of the priest. The faithful, however, are to refrain from comments, dialogue, and similar activities."

Normally, then, the homily at Mass is the obligation and prerogative of the celebrant. When the celebrant does not preach the homily, it is reserved to another priest or to a deacon. This does not militate against various other forms of preaching by lay persons, when necessity requires it or usefulness urges it, even in the context of the eucharistic celebration. (See J.T. Henderson, "The Minister of Liturgical Preaching," *W* 56:3 [1982], 214–230.)

The second paragraph of this canon is a direct quote (nearly verbatim) from *Sacrosanctum Concilium* 52. It is a serious mandate to have a homily at all Sunday Masses (including the Saturday evening celebration) and Holy Day Masses. It is to be omitted only for a very serious reason. For example, if the celebrant is morally or physically unable to preach a homily, it would be preferable to have someone else preach it than to omit it.

Paragraph three, based on *Sacrosanctum Concilium* 49, and the 1964 Instruction 53, is an extremely strong recommendation ("valde commendatur") that homilies be preached whenever Mass is celebrated with people present. Weekday Masses in Advent and Lent as well as festive celebrations or times of mourning are singled out as especially appropriate occasions for homilies.

The final paragraph assigns responsibility. It is the pastor or rector of the church (or the one who has these duties, e.g., parochial administrator or moderator of a team ministry) who is to take care that the aforementioned directives regarding the homily are carefully observed. Canon 528, §1 places this responsibility at the very top of the list of pastoral teaching tasks.

Canon 768 — §1. It is necessary that those who proclaim the word of God to the Christian faithful are first of all to propose those things which one ought to believe and do for the glory of God and for the salvation of humankind.

§2. They are also to impart to the faithful the

teaching which the magisterium of the Church proposes concerning the dignity and freedom of the human person, the unity and stability of the family and its duties, the obligations which men and women have from being joined together in society, and the ordering of temporal affairs according to God's plan.

This canon speaks of the content of preaching. Although it contains an echo of canon 1347, §1 of the 1917 Code, it is drawn directly from *Christus Dominus* 12. The first paragraph is a very general statement of basic priorities: before all else, those things which we are to believe and do for God's glory and our salvation. *Christus Dominus* further describes this primal goal of preaching as "the integral mystery of Christ," those truths without which one cannot know Christ.

The second paragraph is more specific and entirely new. It highlights the importance of preaching on human dignity, social responsibility, and the right ordering of temporal goods. The terms are drawn from the fuller expression in *Christus Dominus* 12; that full paragraph is a very valuable source. Some of the changes made in the canon's shorter version are worth noting: in *Christus Dominus* the "teachings of the Church are to be taught" was changed to "teaching which the magisterium of the Church proposes" is to be imparted; in the canon many of the specifics of Vatican II's decree, e.g., bodily life, labor and leisure, poverty and affluence, just distribution of material goods, peace and war, have been reduced and condensed into such general expressions as "the obligations which men and women have from being joined together in society." The terseness of the canon may be admirable, but the original text is a much more direct and helpful guide.

Canon 769 — Christian doctrine is to be proposed in a manner accommodated to the condition of its listeners and adapted to the needs of the times.

This canon replaces canon 1347, §2 of the 1917 Code, and it is drawn from *Christus Dominus* 13 and *Gaudium et Spes* 4. Though it is much more positive than the canon it replaces, it is much more bland than its sensitive and eloquent sources. It is little more than a common truism about any preaching or teaching. *Christus Dominus* 13 speaks of the need of Christian teaching to "respond to the difficulties and problems by which people are most burdened and anguished," and of the special concern which teachers must have for the poor and weak to whom the Lord has sent them to preach the gospel. The passage goes on to speak of the need for seeking and fostering dialogue with the people among whom we live. Only in this way can preach-

ing be accommodated to their situations and adapted to their needs.

Canon 770 — At certain times according to the prescriptions of the diocesan bishop, pastors are to arrange for those types of preaching which are called spiritual exercises or sacred missions or for other types of preaching adapted to their needs.

The mandate for parish missions or spiritual exercises originated in two encyclical letters of Pope Pius IX in the middle of the nineteenth century (to the bishops of Italy in 1849 and to the bishops of the Austrian Empire in 1856). Such missions or exercises were among the means of reinvigorating the Church, which he strongly recommended. The 1917 Code (*CIC* 1349) required bishops to see that such missions were held for their people at least every ten years and ordered pastors to cooperate in this.

The present canon puts the responsibility on pastors to arrange for these extraordinary preaching and teaching events. No time frame or schedule is suggested, but the canon infers that diocesan norms should be issued to regulate or guide the practice. The canon is a broad, open mandate for whatever forms of parish renewal are judged to be opportune and effective. It provides an invitation for diocesan encouragement and support for such programs at the parish level (e.g., cf. *Parish Development: Programs and Organizations. A Directory*. Washington: The Parish Project, NCCB, 1980).

Canon 771 — §1. Pastors of souls, especially bishops and pastors, are to take care that the word of God is proclaimed also to those members of the faithful who do not enjoy sufficiently or who lack completely common and ordinary pastoral care due to their condition of life.

§2. They are also to make provision for the message of the gospel to come to non-believers who live in their territory, since the care of souls must embrace them as well as the faithful.

Those who are not reached by ordinary pastoral care are to be the object of special solicitude. This new paragraph draws the attention of bishops (see c. 383, §1) and pastors (see c. 529, §1) to those among the faithful who are not touched by the usual structures of the preaching ministry; special provision must be made for them to hear the word of God. The exhortation is taken directly from *Christus Dominus* 18 (which, in turn, is based on Pius XII, Apostolic Constitution *Exsul Familia*, 1 Aug. 1952; *AAS* 44 [1952], 649; *CLD* 3, 84–98), which provides these examples of those whose "condition of life" makes them hard to care for pastorally: migrants, exiles, refugees, voyagers by sea and air, nomads, nursing home patients, prisoners, the retarded, military personnel, immigrants, and others.

According to paragraph two, non-believers also command pastoral attention; the message of the gospel must be made known to them as well. The pastoral "care of souls" includes them just as it does the faithful. The paragraph is a restatement of canon 1350, §1 of the 1917 Code, which used the term "non-Catholics" rather than "non credentes." Thus the canon reflects an ecumenical awareness; it does not presume to equate non-Catholics with non-believers. It resonates with the exhortation of *Christus Dominus* 13, which speaks of the Church's maternal solicitude for all persons, believers and non-believers, and with the rich mission theology of *Ad Gentes* 2–8. Current efforts to reach out to the unchurched, inspired by Paul VI, Apostolic Exhortation *Evangelii Nuntiandi* (8 Dec. 1975; *AAS* 68 [1975], 5) are clearly in the spirit of this provision.

Canon 772 — §1. The norms issued by the diocesan bishop concerning the exercise of preaching are to be observed by all.

§2. The prescriptions of the conference of bishops are to be observed in giving radio or television talks on Christian doctrine.

The first paragraph simply calls for the observance of whatever rules the diocesan bishop issues on the exercise of the preaching ministry in addition to the foregoing canons. Now that he no longer grants preaching faculties to priests and deacons (because they have them by law [c. 764], in virtue of their ordination), the diocesan bishop may still regulate and direct the preaching in his territory by issuing suitable norms. This paragraph serves also as a reminder that the diocesan bishops (not the other ordinaries) are the "moderators of the entire ministry of the word" in the particular church (c. 756, §2).

Paragraph two calls for the observance of whatever norms the episcopal conference might issue regarding preaching on radio or television. It recognizes both the tremendous influence of these modern media and the fact that they often carry a message well beyond the territorial boundaries of one diocese or even of a large region. This provision, new in this revision of the Code, does not demand national legislation, but it suggests that the episcopal conference may issue guidelines on radio and television discourses on Christian doctrine if it sees the need. It is the kind of authorization to issue general decrees that the conference requires according to canon 455, §1 and §2. Compare this with canon 831, §2. The conciliar background on the Church's use of the media can be found in *Inter Mirifica* 13–22.

CHAPTER II
CATECHETICAL INSTRUCTION
[cc. 773–780]

Canon 773 — There is a proper and serious duty, especially on the part of pastors of souls, to provide for the catechesis of the Christian people so that the faith of the faithful becomes living, explicit and productive through formation in doctrine and the experience of Christian living.

One function of church law is to assign responsibilities and describe relationships among various members of the Church so that it might be built up and effectively pursue its mission. Here the grave responsibility for catechetical instruction is assigned in an ultimate way to the "pastors of souls," i.e., bishops, pastors of parishes, vicars, chaplains, etc. It is "proper" to them, that is, the catechetical task is part and parcel of their pastoral charge. The first part of the canon, the basic assignment of responsibility, is virtually the same as canon 1329 of the 1917 Code. The second part of the canon, taken from *Christus Dominus* 14, helps us understand what catechesis means and how it is accomplished. Catechesis is that form of the ministry of the word directed toward those who have been evangelized, who have heard the gospel, and who have responded in faith. The aim of catechetical instruction is to render that faith lively, conscious, and effective ("viva . . . explicita atque operosa"); in other words, to help faith develop and grow so that it can be a real guiding force in the believer's life. Pope John Paul II stated that "the name catechesis was given to the whole of the efforts within the Church to make disciples, to help people to believe that Jesus is the Son of God, so that believing they might have life in his name (Jn 20:31), and to educate and instruct them in this life and thus build up the Body of Christ" (*CT*, p. 1).

The canon calls for this to be accomplished by means of doctrinal instruction and (here the canon goes beyond *CD* 14 in a significant way) the experience of Christian living. Faith is nurtured, in other words, by observing the actions of other Christians and interacting with them—in families, neighborhoods, parishes, schools, clubs, etc.—as well as by more formal education in the teachings of the gospel.

The following canons make explicit what is implicit in this one, namely, that the responsibility for catechetical formation of adults and children is shared by many others in addition to "pastors of souls" and that these others are to collaborate with them in carrying out this central task of ministry.

Canon 774 — §1. Under the supervision of legitimate ecclesiastical authority this concern for catechesis pertains to all the members of the Church in proportion to each one's role.

§2. Parents above others are obliged to form their children in the faith and practice of the Christian life by word and example; godparents and those who take the place of parents are bound by an equivalent obligation.

Every member of the Christian community shares in the responsibility for the catechetical effort; so vital is this activity to the health and vigor of the Church that it must be the concern of every believer. This new canon, which is based on the participation of all believers in the prophetic office of Christ (*LG* 12, 35; *CT* 16; cc. 211, 225, §1) also points out that this catechetical solicitude is to be exercised under the guidance of church authority and shouldered to the extent and in the manner that each person is able.

Parents have a primary responsibility for the growth in faith and Christian living of those to whom they have given the gift of life. The substance of paragraph two was contained in canon 1335 of the 1917 Code, but the *primacy* of the parental role has now been made explicit. It is further emphasized by the canon's location ahead of those which specify the responsibilities of the bishop, pastor, religious, etc. The revised canon finds its roots in conciliar and post-conciliar teaching: *Lumen Gentium* 11 and 35; *Gravissimum Educationis* 3; *Catechesi Tradendae* 16 and 68; and *Familiaris Consortio* 36–39. Paragraphs 68 of *Catechesi Tradendae* and 39 of *Familiaris Consortio* provide expanded descriptions of this familial catechesis. See also canons 226, §2; 776; 851, §2; 890; 914; and 1136.

Those who function "in loco parentis," either temporarily or permanently, share the same responsibility. This might include adoptive parents, foster parents, custodians, directors of boarding schools, and others entrusted with the care of children. It also applies to those who volunteered at the children's baptisms to serve as their sponsors (cf. c. 872).

Canon 775 — **§1. While observing the prescriptions of the Apostolic See it is the responsibility of the diocesan bishop to issue norms concerning catechetics and to make provision that suitable instruments for catechesis are available, even by preparing a catechism, if such seems appropriate, and by fostering and coordinating catechetical endeavors.**

§2. It is within the competence of the conference of bishops, with the prior approval of the Apostolic See, to see to it that catechisms are issued for its territory if such seems useful.

§3. There can be established within the conference of bishops a catechetical office whose princi-

pal task would be to furnish assistance to the individual dioceses in catechetical matters.

This canon spells out the responsibilities of the diocesan bishop and of the bishops' conference in reference to the catechetical task. It has no parallel in the 1917 Code; it is based on conciliar and post-conciliar instructions: *Christus Dominus*; the Encyclical *Catechesi Tradendae* of 1979; and the *General Catechetical Directory* of 1971.

The first paragraph itemizes three responsibilities of the individual diocesan bishop: (1) to issue norms for the catechetical effort within the diocese—this looks to the organization and guidance of the catechetical apostolate, so that it might be an effective ministry of the word; (2) to see to it that appropriate catechetical materials are made available for the task—this has general reference to all sorts of physical equipment and aids, and extends even to the preparation of catechisms, if that seems to be advantageous; and (3) to promote and coordinate the various catechetical undertakings in the diocese—teacher training, religious instruction, schools, catechumenate, etc.—all need continual encouragement and careful integration.

Usually the bishop will carry out these responsibilities through an office of religious education or the diocesan catechetical office, which was called for by the decree of the Sacred Congregation of the Council's *Provido Sane* (12 Jan. 1935; *AAS* 27 [1935], 151) and by the *General Catechetical Directory* 126. The office itself is not mentioned in the revised Code (although it was in c. 27, §2 of the 1977 schema), but its functions are warmly encouraged.

The first paragraph is based on *Christus Dominus* 14, on *General Catechetical Directory* 125–126, and on *Catechesi Tradendae* 63. In the latter document Pope John Paul II wrote:

I know that your ministry as Bishops is growing daily more complex and overwhelming. A thousand duties call you: from the training of new priests to being actively present within the lay communities, from the living, worthy celebration of the sacraments and acts of worship to concern for human advancement and the defense of human rights. But let the concern to foster active and effective catechesis yield to no other care whatever in any way. This concern will lead you to transmit personally to your faithful the doctrine of life. But it should also lead you to take on in your diocese, in accordance with the plans of the Episcopal Conference to which you belong, the chief management of catechesis, while at the same time surrounding yourselves with competent and trustworthy assistants. Your principal role will be to bring about and maintain in your Churches a real passion for catechesis, a passion embodied in a pertinent and effective organization, putting into operation the necessary personnel, means and equipment, and also financial resources.

The new second paragraph of this canon assigns the responsibility to the national conference of bishops of seeing that catechisms are published for use in its territory. It is clearly facultative, not mandatory ("if such seems useful"), and implies that the conference could publish catechisms itself or would encourage others to do so, e.g., individual authors, associations, agencies, religious communities, or private publishers. Anomalously the canon calls for the conference to obtain the prior approval of the Apostolic See if it does publish a catechism or cause one to be published; whereas if others publish them, only the approval of the local ordinary is required (c. 827, §1). Apparently the reason for this greater caution and higher review is the official or semi-official status that might be attached to a publication which emanates from an episcopal conference.

Paragraph two seems to be based on the Encyclical *Catechesi Tradendae* 50, which also reminds us that the *General Catechetical Directory* is the standard of reference for catechisms. It does not mention the publication of catechetical *directories* by episcopal conferences (although c. 26, §1 of the 1977 schema did); these were called for by the *General Catechetical Directory* foreword and 117.

The final paragraph simply suggests that the episcopal conference may set up a catechetical office to be of aid to the catechetical ministry of the individual dioceses. This was recommended in the *General Catechetical Directory* 128 which describes possible functions of such an office in greater detail.

Canon 776 — **In virtue of his office the pastor is bound to provide for the catechetical formation of adults, young people and children, to which end he is to employ the services of the clerics attached to the parish, members of institutes of consecrated life and of societies of apostolic life, with due regard for the character of each institute, and lay members of the Christian faithful, above all catechists; all of these are not to refuse to furnish their services willingly unless they are legitimately impeded. The pastor is to promote and foster the role of parents in the family catechesis mentioned in can. 774, §2.**

This canon specifies the responsibilities of the pastor in reference to the religious education of his people. It is an explication of the general mandate contained in canon 773. This canon replaces and improves upon canons 1333 and 1334 of the 1917 Code. It is based on *Lumen Gentium* 28–29, *Christus Dominus* 30 and 35, *Gravissimum Educationis* 3, and *Catechesi Tradendae* 67–68.

The canon begins by establishing the pastor's obligation which stems from the office he holds (cf. c. 528, §1). Many others share this responsibility for the religious formation of the people—in fact, every baptized person does (see c. 774, §1)—but the law fixes the central and coordinating responsibility at the parish level on the pastor. The accountability is clear beyond question.

Three groups of people are mentioned as the objects of the pastor's catechetical concern, namely, adults, young people, and children. *(CIC* 1333 spoke of children.) This itemization clearly implies the need for different kinds of instructional programs for each of the age groups, appropriately adapted to their needs and abilities. Adults are put in first place probably because of the more recent recognition of their central role. Pope John Paul II wrote of adult catechesis in 1979: "This is the principal form of catechesis, because it is addressed to persons who have the greatest responsibilities and the capacity to live the Christian message in its fully developed form" *(CT* 43). (Cf. also *CD* 14, *AG* 14, *GCD* 20, *RCIA* 37–40.)

The canon enumerates three groups whose aid the pastor is to enlist in accomplishing the ongoing catechetical task:

(1) clerics attached to the parish, that is, priests and deacons who have been assigned or have assumed pastoral activity in the parish—the suitability of their involvement is mentioned in canon 757 above;

(2) religious, that is, male or female members of institutes of consecrated life (c. 573) or of societies of apostolic life (c. 731), when the nature of their religious community, its life, and apostolates, do not militate against such catechetical involvement. The dedication of religious men and women to the task of religious instruction is appropriate because of their consecration to God (c. 758) and their life of witnessing to Christ *(LG* 44, 46; *CD* 33, 35; *PC* 1);

(3) lay persons, all of whom in virtue of their baptism and confirmation (c. 759) share in the concern for deepening and developing the faith of the believing community (c. 774). Among the laity, the canon singles out two groups for special mention:

(a) catechists, i.e., those trained for and dedicated to the task of explaining and expounding the word of God (cf. c. 785, §1);

(b) parents, whom the pastor is to encourage and support in their singularly vital and effective "family catechesis" (cf. c. 774, §2 above).

Finally, the canon urges all of the above persons to be generously cooperative when called upon to collaborate with the parish pastor in catechetical endeavors. All have an obligation—at least of support and concern—and, unless there are good reasons why they are not able to help, they should willingly assist. Naturally, in all of the above categories of potential helpers, consideration must be given to natural talent, aptitude, strength of faith, knowledge, training, and ability in addition to willingness.

Canon 777 — **In accord with the norms established by the diocesan bishop, the pastor is to make particular provision:**

1° that suitable catechesis is given for the celebration of the sacraments;

2° that children are properly prepared for the first reception of the sacraments of penance and Most Holy Eucharist and the sacrament of confirmation by means of a catechetical formation given over an appropriate period of time;

3° that children are more fruitfully and deeply instructed through catechetical formation after the reception of First Communion;

4° that catechetical formation also be given to those handicapped in body or mind insofar as their condition permits;

5° that the faith of young people and adults be fortified, enlightened and developed through various means and endeavors.

This canon gathers together for special attention several pastoral situations which have peculiar catechetical requirements. It serves as a reminder or checklist for pastors of some teachable moments or special groups which call for suitable religious instruction. The canon does not imply that the pastor must give these instructions personally; it is his duty to see that they are provided. It is a new canon, but numbers two and three are taken from canons 1330 and 1331 of the 1917 Code.

1°–appropriate instruction for the celebration of the sacraments

This refers to the general and continuous catechesis which must go on in support of the sacramental life of the parish. These are the instructions and explanations given in preparation for or on the occasion of sacramental celebrations. They may be long or short, e.g., a six-week series in preparation for confirmation or a few words before Mass or the anointing of the sick. It is an ongoing and challenging form of pastoral catechesis, and one of the most important. The faithful must understand what they celebrate in the sacraments so that they may participate actively and intelligently. This point appears to be based on *Sacrosanctum Concilium* 19 and 35; *Inter Oecumenici* 19; *General Catechetical Directory* 25; and *Catechesi Tradendae* 67. (Cf. also c. 851 on baptism and c. 1063 on marriage.)

2°–preparation of children for the first reception of penance and Eucharist

Number two reaffirms the substance of canon 1330 of the 1917 Code. It envisions a catechetical instruction in preparation for these two sacraments which extends over some considerable but unspecified period of time and which is appropriately adapted to the age, development, and culture of the children. It omits any reference to the preparation for the sacrament of confirmation (which *CIC* 1330, §1 included), but certainly does not thereby imply that a careful and thorough catechesis should not precede the reception of that sacrament as well (see c. 890). The law mentions the sacrament of penance before the Eucharist, but this does not seem to be significant. That is, it does not address the controversy over the children's reception of first penance before First Communion. (Cf. c. 914 and its explanation.) The Holy See, conference of bishops, individual bishops, catechetical and liturgical journals have generated statements in quantity on the issue, e.g., see *Canon Law Digest* 7, 834–839; 8, 563–608; *Sharing the Light of Faith: An Official Commentary* (Washington: USCC, 1981), 56–68; K. Seasoltz, *New Liturgy, New Laws* (Collegeville: Liturgical Press, 1980), 63–67.

3°–further religious instruction of children after their First Communion

This point restates canon 1331 of the 1917 Code, but its emphasis falls on the continuing and deepening formation of children in faith rather than on the more immediate completion of the catechism by those who recently received their First Holy Communion. The canon provides legal incentive for the ongoing programs of religious instruction for children and young people, which are such a vital factor in our Christian communities. It speaks in terms of a lengthier, richer, and more profound cultivation or refinement of the child's catechetical formation as the child continues to develop after becoming a communicant.

4°–catechetical instruction for the retarded and handicapped

This difficult and important pastoral responsibility is an entirely new provision of the law; it was not even included in the earlier drafts of this revised Code. It springs from a heightened awareness of the special needs of those who suffer from various mental or physical handicaps; they can no longer be neglected in society or in the Church. This conviction found expression in the 1977 synod of bishops and was restated in the subsequent Apostolic Exhortation of John Paul II, *Catechesi Tradendae* (1979), 41. The canon calls for instruction to be imparted to the extent that the condition of the handicapped persons permits.

5°–growth in faith of the adult members of the community

The sources for this new point are the same as those mentioned in the commentary on canon 776 above. It reflects the recently rediscovered awareness of the adult members of our faith communities, the centrality of their role, and, consequently the primacy of their growth in faith. Catechesis for adults, said the *General Catechetical Directory,* must be considered the chief form of catechesis. All other forms are in some way oriented to it (*GCD* 20). The canon hints at the variety of the forms and methods, the continual efforts and undertakings, which are required to reach adult believers. Its aim is that their faith be strengthened, illumined, and developed, so that their adherence to it may be fully responsible.

Canon 778 — Superiors of religious institutes and of societies of apostolic life are to see to it that catechetical formation is diligently imparted in their churches, schools and in other works entrusted to them in any manner.

Religious superiors of men and of women are here assigned a direct responsibility for the catechetical instruction of the people. This is in addition to the cooperation which religious are expected to offer to pastors in fulfilling the catechetical task in local parishes (c. 776). The sense of the canon is to make religious superiors directly responsible for the religious formation of those faithful whom they serve in their own churches, chapels, schools, colleges, missions, hospitals, and various other apostolic enterprises, no matter how the apostolate was assigned to them (e.g., by their own initiative, by request of the local bishop, by directive of the Holy See, for a long time or only temporarily, etc.). Since the canon does not distinguish, the "superiors" referred to include both local and major superiors. It is a grave and sweeping charge, a further indication of the seriousness with which both the Second Vatican Council and the revised Code view the catechetical function. The canon is based on *Christus Dominus* 35, 1 and on *Catechesi Tradendae* 65.

Canon 779 — Catechetical formation is to be given by employing all those helps, teaching aids and instruments of social communication which appear to be more effective in enabling the faithful in light of their characteristics, talents, age and conditions of life, to learn the Catholic teaching more fully and practice it more suitably.

This canon is a wise pastoral exhortation about the means to be used in the catechetical ministry, the necessary adaptation of the methods to the au-

dience, and a reminder of the goals which the ministry strives to achieve. It had no counterpart in the 1917 Code; it is derived from *Christus Dominus* 14, *Inter Mirifica* 16, and *Catechesi Tradendae* 45–50.

The canon urges the use of the full panoply of the means of communication which the modern world has made available, e.g., television, radio, the press, records, tape recordings, as well as the various forms of catechetical literature. We must search unceasingly for the most suitable and effective methods to accomplish this vital task. Their suitability implies their adaptation to those being reached. The canon lists four measures of the human situation of the faithful to be considered: natural disposition, abilities, age, and circumstances of life. Finally, the canon states the aim of the catechetical enterprise: believers are to learn the teaching of their religion more fully and reduce that teaching to practice more aptly.

Canon 780 — Local ordinaries are to see to it that catechists are duly prepared to fulfill their task correctly, namely, that continuing formation is made available to them, that they acquire a proper knowledge of the Church's teaching, and that they learn in theory and in practice the norms proper to the pedagogical disciplines.

The final canon in the section on catechetical instruction stresses the need for the suitable preparation and continuing education of catechists. It is without parallel in the 1917 Code, is drawn from *Christus Dominus* 14, and mirrors the concern of *Catechesi Tradendae* 71 (cf. cc. 219; 229, §1; 785, §2).

Local ordinaries (cf. c. 134) bear the responsibility for making available both the initial preparation and ongoing formation which catechists need for their task. But *Catechesi Tradendae* 71 stresses the importance of interdiocesan cooperation in sponsoring training institutes and catechetical centers. "What better assistance can one church give to another than to help it grow as a church with its own strength?" The canon, echoing *Christus Dominus* 14, calls for the formation of catechists in both the doctrine of the Church and in the theory and practice of teaching. (*CD* added the "laws of psychology.") It is clear that for the work of the religious educator to be successful, he or she must be genuinely knowledgeable in the faith and possess authentic pedagogical skill. Surely a firm faith and the example of a Christian life are also essential for success.

TITLE II
MISSIONARY ACTION OF THE CHURCH
[cc. 781–792]

The second major section of this Book on the Church's teaching office is concerned with the

Church's missionary activity. The material is almost entirely new, that is, the 1917 Code contained no section on missionary activity (only the tersest of references were found in *CIC* 1350–1351 in addition to the provisions for apostolic vicars and prefects, *CIC* 293–311, *CIC* 252 on the SCProp). For the most part missionary law was considered particular legislation, i.e., for some designated areas of the Church, not for the Church universal. The insertion of these twelve canons in the revised Code is a recognition of the missionary *nature* of the Church; missionary action is incumbent upon every member of the Church in every land.

The main sources for these new laws are the conciliar documents *Lumen Gentium, Ad Gentes,* and *Christus Dominus.* These documents and *Ecclesiae sanctae* III contain more detailed and explicit discipline on missionary matters than does this section of the Code. Also confer the Instruction of the Sacred Congregation for the Evangelization of Peoples, *Quo Aptius,* on cooperation between bishops and Pontifical Missionary Works (24 Feb. 1969; *AAS* 61 [1969] 276; *CLD* 7, 839–845), the Sacred Congregation for Bishops' *Directory on the Pastoral Ministry of Bishops* (22 Feb. 1973; *AAS* 65 [1973], 46), and the Apostolic Exhortation of Paul VI *Evangelii Nuntiandi* (8 Dec. 1975; *AAS* 68 [1976], 5).

Since missionary activity comprises far more than teaching, it might be asked why this section is inserted in the Code's Book on the Church's teaching office. The answer is that the principal missionary activity is seen to be the preaching of the gospel by the testimony of life and word, and for that reason its disciplinary rules follow after those on the ministry of the divine word.

Canon 781 — Since the entire Church is missionary by its nature and since the work of evangelization is to be viewed as a fundamental duty of the people of God, all the Christian faithful, conscious of their own responsibility in this area, are to assume their own role in missionary work.

The canon is a clear proclamation of the fundamental missionary nature of the Church, and a strong assertion of the consequent missionary responsibility which falls upon each and every member of the Church. Christ's mandate to "proclaim the good news to all creation" (Mk 16:15) was intended for all of His followers. This canon reminds the entire Church that the task of evangelization does not belong only to the hierarchy or to foreign missionaries but to all of God's people. This basic assertion at the outset of the section on missionary activity helps to put in context the assignment of the more specific responsibilities in the canons which follow. The canon is drawn from *Lumen Gentium* 17, *Ad Gentes* 2 and 35, and *Dignitatis Humanae* 13—it finds fuller expression in *Evangelii*

Nuntiandi 13–16 and 59–66. It states the theological reason for all forms of participation in the great work of evangelization, from personal conversion and public witness to financial support for and exchange with missionaries.

Canon 782 — §1. The supreme direction and co-ordination of endeavors and activities which deal with missionary work and missionary cooperation belong to the Roman Pontiff and the college of bishops.
§2. Since they are the sponsors for the universal Church and for all the churches, individual bishops are to have a special concern for missionary work especially by initiating, fostering and sustaining missionary endeavors in their own particular church.

The two paragraphs of this canon make explicit the hierarchical responsibility for stimulating and supervising the official missionary efforts of the Church; the college of bishops with the pope are to direct and coordinate the missionary task, and the individual bishops are to arouse, foster, and sustain missionary projects in their own dioceses. The canon is drawn from the rich teaching of the Second Vatican Council, especially *Lumen Gentium* 23; *Christus Dominus* 6; and *Ad Gentes* 6, 29, 31, and 38. It is a vast improvement over the terse canon 1350 of the 1917 Code. *Ad Gentes* 29 speaks of the roles of the Sacred Congregation for the Evangelization of Peoples and the Secretariat for Promoting Christian Unity in directing and coordinating the Church's missionary activity worldwide (cf. *RE* 83–95 and compare *CIC* 252). A peculiar omission from this canon is any mention of the role of the episcopal conferences. *Lumen Gentium* 23, *Ad Gentes* 31 and 38, and *Ecclesiae sanctae* III, 3–11 assign serious roles to the conferences, and, of course, these responsibilities remain even though not contained in the Code. (An admonition to extend hospitality to those from mission lands is contained in c. 792.) The conscious omission of the general competence of the episcopal conferences in missionary matters was made because of the "often repeated concerns that the excessive power of episcopal conferences would redound to the detriment of the proper authority of diocesan bishops" (*Rel* 177). Just as the vigorous involvements of episcopal conferences are not foreclosed by the absence of any explicit authorization in the Code, so too individual and private group initiatives and ventures of a missionary or evangelizing nature are certainly not prohibited or discouraged. The doctrinal assertion of canon 781 provides adequate theological warrant for such activities (cf. also cc. 211, 215, 216).

The stated foundation for the special solicitude which individual bishops are to show for missionary activity is the fact that "they are the sponsors for the universal Church and for all the churches." The expression "sponsores" implies a serious commitment, like that of marriage partners or of guarantors (*CD* 6). Some of the ways in which the solicitude is to be exercised are contained in canon 791.

Canon 783 — **Since members of institutes of consecrated life dedicate themselves through their consecration to the service of the Church they are obliged in a special manner to engage in missionary work in accord with the character of the institute.**

This canon speaks of the serious obligation which rests upon individual religious men and women to share in the missionary activity of the Church. The rationale given is that by reason of their religious consecration of life they are to dedicate themselves to the service of the Church. For this reason, in ways which are in keeping with their own religious community's character and charism, they are to devote themselves to that work which is both central and vital to the Church: its great task of evangelization. This missionary effort may find expression in myriad forms, but the canon poses a challenge to each religious which is not to be ignored. The canon is based on *Lumen Gentium* 44, *Ad Gentes* 40, and *Perfectae Caritatis* 20.

Canon 784 — **Missionaries are those persons who are sent to engage in missionary work by competent ecclesiastical authority; they can be chosen from among those who are native or non-native to the country; they may be secular clerics, members of institutes of consecrated life or of societies of apostolic life, or other lay members of the Christian faithful.**

This canon gives the Code's new definition of those who are "missionaries" in a strict or legal sense. They are simply believers in Christ who are sent for missionary work by competent ecclesiastical authority. They may be lay men or women, members of religious communities, or members of the secular clergy (deacons, priests, or bishops), and they may be indigenous to the missionary area or from elsewhere. By focusing almost exclusively on the etymological and extrinsic sense of "those persons who are sent," the Code's definition is simple but relatively impoverished when compared to the richly nuanced description of *Ad Gentes* 23, from which it is drawn. The latter includes the additional elements of a calling by Christ; and gifting by the Spirit; natural dispositions, character, and talents; preparation for mission work; being sent to those who are far from Christ; and serving in faith and obedience. Missionaries are all called ministers of the gospel.

Who is the "competent ecclesiastical authority" empowered to send missionaries? The Code does not say, but in addition to the Apostolic See and diocesan bishops (and those who are their equivalents, such as apostolic administrators, prefects, or vicars; see c. 381 §2), those who are ordinaries and possess executive authority (c. 134), those delegated by them, major superiors of men's and women's religious institutes (for their own subjects), and probably vicars general and episcopal vicars would be included. The ordinary of the place to which the missionary is being sent should obviously be consulted well in advance.

Canon 785 — **§1. Catechists are to be employed in carrying out missionary work; catechists are those lay members of the Christian faithful who have been duly instructed, who stand out by reason of their Christian manner of life, and who devote themselves to expounding the gospel teaching and organizing liturgical functions and works of charity under the supervision of a missionary.**

§2. Catechists are to be educated in schools destined for this purpose or, where such schools are lacking, under the supervision of missionaries.

This canon describes lay catechists and strongly encourages their employment in missionary work. Three elements are included in the description of lay catechists: (1) their formation—they are to be suitably instructed; (2) the quality of their lives—they are to be outstanding in their Christian lifestyle; and (3) their works—they are to help spread the gospel and organize liturgical celebrations and works of charity. These activities are to be carried out under the direction of a missionary, so the lay catechists are to be the assistants or associates of missionaries; no other limit, however, is put on the autonomy or range of their work. *Ad Gentes* 17, which is the principal source for this canon, recognizes the maximum importance of the catechists' role and recommends that they should receive a canonical mission in a public liturgical celebration so that their service among the people might be enhanced by a greater authority.

The second paragraph of the canon details the above mentioned need for catechists to be suitably prepared for their work; their formation is to take place in special schools or under the guidance of individual missionaries in cases where such schools are lacking. *Ad Gentes* 17 states that the training of catechists is to be thorough and adapted to cultural advances, that more schools should be established for this purpose, and that spiritual sustenance and continuing education for the catechists must also be provided (cf. also *EN* 73). It also insists that full-time catechists be paid a just wage, so that they may have a decent standard of living and social security.

Canon 786 — **Missionary activity, properly so-called, by which the Church is implanted among** peoples and groups in which it has not yet taken root, is accomplished by the Church especially by sending heralds of the gospel until the young churches are fully established to the point that they are able to perform the work of evangelization on their own with their own resources and sufficient means.

This canon attempts to define missionary activity and to describe the principal way in which it is carried out. It also provides a criterion by which a church is judged to be no longer a "mission." "Missionary activity," properly speaking, is defined in terms of the spread of the Church, i.e., planting it where it has not yet been rooted. (The term is used here in a much narrower and stricter sense than that stated in the heading for the title or in c. 781. See *Rel* 177.) This is accomplished chiefly by the Church sending heralds to the peoples or groups until a new church is fully established among them. And this "fully established" status is measured by the new church's possession of its own means and resources which enable it to carry on the work of evangelization by itself.

These descriptive terms are borrowed directly from *Lumen Gentium* 17 and *Ad Gentes* 6 which are strong, carefully nuanced, theological explanations of the Church's missionary task. In the conciliar statements the aim of missionary action is more evenly balanced between the proclamation of the good news of Christ and the establishment of new churches. In this canon the emphasis is almost exclusively on the implantation and growth of new churches. This shift may not be without ecumenical ramifications. (Cf. *EN* 17–24 for a much broader vision.)

Canon 787 — §1. By the witness of their life and words missionaries are to establish a sincere dialogue with those who do not believe in Christ in order that through methods suited to their characteristics and culture avenues may be open to them by which they can be led to an understanding of the gospel message.
§2. Missionaries are to see to it that they teach the truths of faith to those whom they judge to be ready to accept the gospel message so that these persons can be admitted to the reception of baptism when they freely request it.

A further delineation of the activity and striving of missionaries is stated in this canon. The two paragraphs suggest two stages in this effort: (1) sincere dialogue with non-believers so that they might be led to an understanding of the Christian gospel message—missionaries are to open this dialogue by the testimony of their lives and by their words; they are to set forth the gospel in ways suited to the abilities and background of their partners in dialogue; and (2) instruction in the faith for those judged

ready to accept the gospel message, so that they might be admitted to baptism if they so desire—their request for membership in the Church through baptism must be entirely free. This final assertion about the freedom of those accepting the faith and deciding to join the Church is a restatement of canon 1351 of the 1917 Code and is also firmly rooted in the theological teaching of *Dignitatis Humanae* 2 and 3 and *Ad Gentes* 13. The main part of the canon, on mission work, is derived from *Ad Gentes* 11 and 12. However, the conciliar document contains a far richer and more nuanced analysis than that represented in this attenuated statement. The same themes are also given broader treatment in *Evangelii Nuntiandi* 17–24.

Canon 788 — §1. After a period of pre-catechumenate has elapsed, persons who have manifested a willingness to embrace faith in Christ are to be admitted to the catechumenate in liturgical ceremonies and their names are to be registered in a book destined for this purpose.
§2. Through instruction and an apprenticeship in the Christian life catechumens are suitably to be initiated into the mystery of salvation and introduced to the life of faith, liturgy, charity of the people of God and the apostolate.
§3. It is the responsibility of the conference of bishops to issue statutes by which the catechumenate is regulated; these statutes are to determine what things are to be expected of catechumens and define what prerogatives are recognized as theirs.

This canon is basically an admonition to follow the process of the catechumenate when persons have manifested their desire to enter the Church; it also empowers the conference of bishops to issue regulations on the rights and duties of catechumens. The restoration of the catechumenate is one of the positive liturgical reforms stemming from the Second Vatican Council (see *SC* 64–65). The support and example offered to new Christians by the entire community of faith is proving to be a powerful source of deepening and renewal for local congregations as well as for the individuals directly involved. The entire process is thoroughly explained in the landmark document, *Rite of Christian Initiation of Adults* (cf. the Introduction especially). This canon is based directly on *Ad Gentes* 13–14, which sets forth the steps on the path from conversion to full initiation. *Ad Gentes* 14 concludes by directing that "the juridical status of catechumens should be clearly defined in the new Code of Canon Law." That difficult directive has not been followed; instead it has now been passed on to the episcopal conferences. It is a serious and delicate task since catechumens are joined to the Church, are of the household of Christ, and "with love and solicitude Mother Church already embraces them as her own" (*LG* 14; cf. cc. 206; 851, §1; 1183).

Canon 789 — Through a suitable instruction neophytes are to be formed to a more thorough understanding of the gospel truth and the baptismal duties to be fulfilled; they are to be imbued with a love of Christ and of His Church.

Those newly incorporated into the Church are not to be viewed as finished or perfect; rather their formation and deepening are to continue. The canon calls for more than further instruction; it asks for a Christian formation which engenders love for Christ and His Church. This canon is a pale shadow of *Ad Gentes* 15 from which it is drawn. The conciliar text, headed "Forming the Christian Community," is a rich and beautiful instruction to missionaries on "raising up congregations of the faithful who will walk in a manner worthy of the vocation to which they have been called" (Eph 4:1). Among other valuable elements it urges the encouragement of an ecumenical spirit; this ecumenical note was also contained in an earlier draft of this canon but unfortunately omitted from the final version.

Canon 790 — §1. It is the responsibility of the diocesan bishop in missionary territories:
1° to promote, supervise and coordinate endeavors and works which concern missionary activity;
2° to provide that the necessary contracts are entered into with the moderators of institutes which dedicate themselves to missionary work and that relations with them redound to the good of the mission.
§2. All missionaries living in his jurisdiction, including religious and their assistants, are subject to the prescriptions issued by the diocesan bishop mentioned in §1, n. 1.

Because the diocesan bishop is the guide and center of unity of the diocesan apostolate, he is to coordinate the missionary effort in the whole diocese (c. 394). This canon makes that responsibility explicit for diocesan bishops (not for all local ordinaries) in those regions designated by the Apostolic See as missionary territories. The canon is derived directly from *Ad Gentes* 30 and 32, and contains three prescriptions: (1) it delineates the supervisory role of the diocesan bishop in all missionary matters (but it omits the admonition of *AG* 30 that he is to do so "in such a way that the spontaneous zeal of those who share in the work will be preserved and fostered"); (2) it admonishes *all* missionaries, even religious and those working under their authority, to heed the regulations on mission matters issued by the diocesan bishop—*Ad Gentes* 30 calls for the establishment of a pastoral council on which clergy, religious, and laity are to be represented for the bet-

ter coordination of the missionary apostolate of the diocese; and (3) it instructs the bishop to see to it that formal agreements are made with the superiors of religious missionary communities so that relations with such religious groups are such as to advance the welfare of the mission. Presumably this call for specific, written agreements is in the interests of clear and lasting understandings. Verbal arrangements or vague promises have often led to conflicts, misunderstandings, and disruption of the apostolate. Items such as how many persons, with what kind of preparation, for how long a time, in what kind of apostolate, and other conditions of ministry should be made explicit from the outset in these agreements with religious communities. Confer the Instruction, *Relationes in territoriis*, of the Sacred Congregation for the Evangelization of Peoples (24 Feb. 1969; *AAS* 61 [1969], 281; *CLD* 7, 845–861), with suggested forms of contracts appended.

Canon 791 — To foster missionary cooperation in the individual dioceses:
1° missionary vocations are to be promoted;
2° a priest is to be appointed to promote effectively endeavors on behalf of the missions, especially the *Pontifical Missionary Works*;
3° an annual missions' day is to be observed;
4° every year a suitable monetary contribution for the missions is to be forwarded to the Holy See.

In contrast with the foregoing canon, this one refers to all of the dioceses of the world, not only those in mission territories. It specifies some of the ways in which the local churches are to foster missionary cooperation. This responsibility stems from the fact that bishops are consecrated not just for one diocese, "but for the salvation of the entire world," and that communion and cooperation between churches are necessary for carrying on the work of evangelization. "In virtue of this communion, individual churches carry a responsibility for all others" (*AG* 38). The canon is based on *Christus Dominus* 6, *Ad Gentes* 38, and *Ecclesiae sanctae* III. It calls for four different actions on behalf of the missions in every diocese:

> 1°–encouraging missionary vocations among both clerics (deacons, presbyters, and bishops) and laity

This includes the Second Vatican Council's entreaty that bishops send some of the better priests who offer themselves for missionary work to those dioceses in need at least for a time (*AG* 38); it also means that lay missionaries are to be found and fostered.

> 2°–a priest is to be appointed to promote activities for the benefit of the missions, especially the diocesan collection for the official papal program (*AG* 29; *RE* 85)

Why the missionary director needs to be a priest (*sacerdos*) is not at all clear (although priests' [*presbyteri*] responsibilities in support of missionary activity are spelled out in *AG* 39), and it seems that a non-priest could fill the position; the key requisite is for someone who can do it *effectively*; the person should be a member of the diocesan pastoral council (*ES* III, 4).

3°–an annual mission day is to be celebrated

Its purposes are prayer, a heightened mission awareness, and the solicitation of funds.

4°–a suitable sum of money is to be sent to the Holy See each year to help support the missions

This envisions both the direct voluntary offerings of the faithful and contributions from parishes and other institutions (*ES* III, 7–8); confer the Instruction, *Quo Aptius*, from the Sacred Congregation for the Evangelization of Peoples (24 Feb. 1969; *AAS* 61 [1969], 276; *CLD* 7, 839–845).

Canon 792 — **The conferences of bishops are to establish and promote works through which persons who come to their territory from missionary lands for the sake of work or study may be received like family and assisted with adequate pastoral care.**

This unusual canon is another manifestation of the communion of the churches. It envisions a warm and supportive reception of those from the young churches when they come for work or study to the established churches. But it also infers that great benefits will accrue to *both* partners in this missionary dialogue. The older churches are often rejuvenated and invigorated as well as challenged by close personal contacts with those from mission lands. The canon is taken directly from *Ad Gentes* 38 which also admonishes the episcopal conferences to initiate and foster the ways and means for the welcome and assistance of these temporary immigrants or reverse missionaries.

It is somewhat strange that only this responsibility (and that of regulating the catechumenate, c. 788, §3) of the episcopal conferences in regard to the missions found its way into the revised Code. The other important functions of the conferences mentioned in *Ad Gentes* 38 and *Ecclesiae sanctae* III, especially the role of the "episcopal commissions for the missions," have been omitted from the Code. Needless to say, these grave missionary responsibilities remain.

TITLE III
CATHOLIC EDUCATION
[cc. 793–821]

Catholic education receives an expanded (29 canons as compared with 12 in the 1917 Code) and up-

dated (it strongly reflects the teachings of Vatican II's *Declaration on Christian Education*) treatment in the revised Code. Symbolic of its new direction is the fact that the very first word of the first canon is "parents." It clearly asserts the rights of parents in the educational process. The entire comparable section in the 1917 Code was entitled "Schools" (*CIC* Book III, title XXII, 1372–1383). Here the entire section is given the title of "Catholic Education": its three subdivisions (chapters) are "Schools," which refers to elementary and secondary schools (cc. 796–806); "Catholic Universities and Other Institutes of Higher Studies," covering post-secondary education, i.e., Catholic colleges and universities (cc. 807–814); and "Ecclesiastical Universities and Faculties," which are those erected or approved by the Holy See for the "sacred disciplines" (cc. 815–821). The section begins with three introductory canons which state some basic principles.

Canon 793 — **§1. Parents as well as those who take their place are obliged and enjoy the right to educate their offspring; Catholic parents also have the duty and the right to select those means and institutions through which they can provide more suitably for the Catholic education of the children according to local circumstances.**

§2. Parents also have the right to make use of those aids to be furnished by civil society which they need in order to obtain Catholic education for their children.

The first paragraph contains two fundamental assertions of parental rights and responsibilities (for parallels see cc. 226, §2; 774; 776; 851, §2; 890; 914; 1136) regarding their children:

(1) parents have both the obligation and the right to educate their offspring; this is a simple statement of the natural law, and it is derived from the fact that the parents conferred life on their children; the right and obligation also devolve upon those who legitimately take the place of the parents, e.g., adoptive parents, foster parents, guardians, etc.;

(2) Catholic parents have the duty and the right to select the most appropriate means and schools for the Catholic education of their children; the duty ("officium") implies both the grave obligation to see to the formation of their children in the Catholic faith in the best way open to them, and the right to make the determination, among the means or schools available, of those which are most suitable for their children. For this duty and right of selection to be meaningful, there must exist some options from which to make choices. Does this imply that the local Catholic community is responsible for providing

not only schools or other instructional facilities but also some *alternative* means of Catholic education, so that the parents can make real choices? It is an interesting question, but the more basic responsibility of the local church is to see that effective Catholic education is made genuinely available to the parents in their midst, taking into consideration their economic and social conditions.

Paragraph one, with its central focus on the parental role in children's education, is drawn from *Gravissimum Educationis* 3, 6, and 7 and from canon 1372 of the 1917 Code (cf. also *LG* 11, *GS* 48, *AA* 11).

In paragraph two the parental claim on the help they need to educate their children properly falls on the State, even when it is a question of religious education. The language is quite general: "aids to be furnished by civil society which they [parents] need in order to obtain Catholic education for their children." There is no attempt to specify exactly what the responsibilities of civil governments are in this regard, but it is an assertion that the civil society *has* responsibilities even in the matter of religiously oriented education. "Parents have the right to determine, in accordance with their own religious beliefs, the kind of religious education that their children are to receive. Government, in consequence, must acknowledge the rights of parents to make a genuinely free choice of schools and of other means of education. The use of this freedom of choice is not to be made a reason for imposing unjust burdens on parents, whether directly or indirectly" *(DH* 5). The nature and extent of the assistance which civil society should make available to parents for the religious education of their children is a matter of lively debate in modern pluralistic societies.

The second paragraph is based on *Gravissimum Educationis* 3, 6, and 7 as well as on *Dignitatis Humanae* 5.

Canon 794 — §1. The duty and right of educating belongs in a unique way to the Church which has been divinely entrusted with the mission to assist men and women so that they can arrive at the fullness of the Christian life.

§2. Pastors of souls have the duty to arrange all things so that all the faithful may enjoy a Catholic education.

The appropriateness of the Church's role in education is stated in paragraph one, and it is based on the God-given mission to aid everyone in finding their way to Christ. The canon thus grounds the Church's duty and right to educate on a supernatural warrant alone, namely, its divine mission to evangelize. But *Gravissimum Educationis* 3, which is the source for this canon, bases it on a purely nat-

ural claim as well: the Church is a human society capable of educating. The latter argument should not be lost sight of; it could have value in a secular context. In the 1917 Code the Church simply claimed the right to establish any kind of school at any level (*CIC* 1375); no basis for the claim was presented.

Paragraph two states that the responsibility for trying to arrange things so that all the Catholic faithful might have the benefit of a Catholic education is laid upon the "pastors of souls, " i.e., bishops and parish priests. It is a heavy burden indeed, and it is reminiscent of the similar charge given at the Third Plenary Council of Baltimore (a. 1884, no. 199) to establish a school in every parish within two years. The real responsibility for making Catholic education available clearly rests on everyone in the community of faith; the pastors are to be the stimulators and coordinators of the effort. Some of the means by which Catholic education is provided to the members of the Church are enumerated in *Gravissimum Educationis* 4, namely, catechetical formation, media of communication, groups, associations, and schools.

Canon 795 — Since a true education must strive for the integral formation of the human person, a formation which looks toward the person's final end, and at the same time toward the common good of societies, children and young people are to be so reared that they can develop harmoniously their physical, moral and intellectual talents, that they acquire a more perfect sense of responsibility and a correct use of freedom, and that they be educated for active participation in social life.

This splendid statement of educational goals is distilled from the rich first paragraph of *Gravissimum Educationis*. That paragraph opens with a ringing declaration of the inalienable right to an education and then goes on to elaborate some of the key characteristics of education in today's world. The summary given in this canon stresses four elements of education:

(1) holistic—it seeks the integral formation of the whole person and concerns itself with the development of physical, moral, and intellectual endowments;

(2) developmental—conscious of the changes and growth which children and young people are experiencing, it fosters a sense of gradual formation, an evolution of talents, and a heightened sense of responsibility and use of freedom;

(3) social—far from an individualistic or privatistic orientation, it aims at the common good of society, and it insists on a refined sense of responsibility and right use of freedom for active

participation in the life of the human community;

(4) personal—it strives for the formation of the human person, fully endowed with responsibility and freedom, and directed toward that person's final destiny—life with God.

The canon and its source document both merit the educator's frequent reflection.

CHAPTER I
SCHOOLS
[cc. 796–806]

Canon 796 — **§1. Among educational means the Christian faithful should greatly value schools, which are of principal assistance to parents in fulfilling their educational task.**
§2. It is incumbent upon parents to cooperate closely with the school teachers to whom they entrust their children to be educated; in fulfilling their duty teachers are to collaborate closely with parents who are to be willingly heard and for whom associations or meetings are to be inaugurated and held in great esteem.

Paragraph one simply points out the primacy of schools among all the various means of education, and it urges the faithful to esteem them highly. It is careful to describe them as auxiliary to the children's parents, because the primary duty to educate remains theirs (cf. c. 793, *GE* 3). The first paragraph is drawn from *Gravissimum Educationis* 5, which more fully describes the advantages of the schoolplace.

Both parents and teachers are admonished in the second paragraph to work as partners in the educational process; parents are urged to cooperate with the schoolteachers, and the teachers to collaborate with the parents, listening to them and starting associations for them. This mutual collaboration is often difficult, but it can bring rich rewards for the students. *Gravissimum Educationis* 8 is the source of this exhortation.

Canon 797 — **It is necessary that parents enjoy true freedom in selecting schools; the Christian faithful must therefore be concerned that civil society acknowledge this freedom for parents and also safeguard it with its resources in accord with distributive justice.**

The canon is a strong and clear assertion of the parental prerogative of choosing their children's schools, and it admonishes all the faithful to insist that their civil governments recognize and protect this important freedom in practice. The resources of the State in support of education are not to be distributed in such a way as to penalize those parents who exercise their right to choose suitable schools for their children. Distributive justice demands that parents not suffer economic detriment for their decision to send their children to schools which reflect their religious convictions. In a complex, pluralistic society this governmental duty is both hotly disputed and difficult to fulfill, but believers are here urged to press their case for a just distribution of educational subsidies.

The canon is taken directly from *Gravissimum Educationis* 6 and reflects the teaching of *Dignitatis Humanae* 5; the Second Vatican Council's instruction is derived in part from the Third Provincial Council of Cincinnati (a. 1861).

Canon 798 — **Parents are to entrust their children to those schools in which Catholic education is provided; but if they are unable to do this, they are bound to provide for their suitable Catholic education outside the schools.**

This canon enunciates the basic obligation of parents to see to the Catholic education of their children. They are to send the children to schools wherein Catholic education is provided, when such schools are available to them. Obviously the law envisions either Catholic schools (cf. c. 803) or other public or private schools in which Catholicism is lived and taught. This should not be narrowly construed; many acceptable arrangements exist for genuine Catholic education.

The second part of the canon states the parents' obligation to provide for the Catholic education of their children when they are not able to send them to the schools described above. The inability to enroll the children in such schools is not specified, that is, it might arise from any one of several sources, e.g., the schools do not exist, they are too distant or too costly, language or ethnic or political barriers exist, etc. No matter what prevents the parents from sending their children to schools which provide Catholic education, the parents are still obliged to see that the children actually do receive an appropriate Catholic education outside of school. This process may take many forms, from the atmosphere and interaction within the family itself (*GE* 3) to highly developed and effective liturgical and catechetical programs within the community of the Church (*GE* 4, 7). The parental responsibility is a serious one, and the entire community of faith should reach out generously to assist parents in fulfilling it.

The canon is derived from the teachings of *Gravissimum Educationis* 3 and 8, and canon 1372, §2 of the 1917 Code; it modifies in a positive way the prohibitions of canon 1374 of the 1917 Code.

Canon 799 — **The Christian faithful are to strive so that in civil society the laws which regulate the formation of youth provide also for their religious**

and moral education in the schools themselves in accord with the conscience of the parents.

This canon is another exhortation for action in the civil sphere which would provide for positive public policies in education. The faithful are urged to strive for educational laws which provide for religious and moral formation, along with the other facets of education, in the schools which are regulated by the State. However, such moral and religious instruction is to be given in accord with the conscience of the parents. This is obviously a very difficult task in a modern, religiously pluralistic society. The canon is drawn from *Gravissimum Educationis* 7 and is concerned with public school education. It favors retaining the moral and religious aspects of education within such schools, even in pluralistic societies, rather than to abandon the attempt at moral and religious formation in the schools and thereby assume a completely neutral or secular stance. The Second Vatican Council text expresses the intent of the canon: "The Church gives high praise to those civil authorities and civil societies that show regard for the pluralistic character of modern society, and take into account the right of religious liberty, by helping families in such a way that in all schools the education of their children can be carried out according to the moral and religious convictions of each family" (*GE* 7). The canon does not imply that Catholics should try to make public schools into Catholic schools; rather it advocates the retention of some moral and religious training in public schools so that, with further and fuller formation in "the teachings of salvation," children might advance their "development as Christians along with their growth as citizens of the world" (*GE* 7).

Canon 800 — §1. The Church has the right to establish and supervise schools of any discipline, type and grade whatsoever.

§2. The Christian faithful are to foster Catholic schools by supporting their establishment and their maintenance in proportion to their resources.

In paragraph one the Church asserts its right to establish and run schools of all kinds. The claim is more sweeping and inclusive than those expressed in canon 1375 of the 1917 Code and in *Gravissimum Educationis* 8, from which the canon is drawn. It extends to schools of all levels (e.g., elementary, secondary, college, postgraduate, etc.), of any kind (e.g., general, professional, technical, etc.), and of any discipline (e.g., religion, theology, humanities, science, agriculture, etc.), and it mentions both the founding and control of such schools. Clearly the Church is convinced that, in pursuit of its teaching, missionary, and salvific goals, it must be free to launch educational efforts across a very broad spectrum, depending on the needs of the

apostolate. Vatican II drew attention to assessing contemporary needs when the establishment of Catholic schools is being considered, for example, the need for professional and technical schools, for adult education, for social service education, for schools for the handicapped, and for preparing religious educators (*GE* 9).

The second paragraph of this canon urges the members of the Church to encourage Catholic schools and to support them to the extent of their abilities. This familiar but necessary exhortation is drawn from *Gravissimum Educationis* 8 and 9, and canon 1379, §3 of the 1917 Code. The appeal is made not only to the parents whose children attend Catholic schools, but to all of Christ's faithful; it also implies support and assistance of all kinds, not only financial aid and moral support. The language of the Second Vatican Council is extremely earnest: "This sacred synod strongly exhorts . . . to spare no sacrifice. . . ." In this context the Council also entreats Catholics to show special concern for the poor, for those deprived of family assistance and affection, and for those without the gift of faith (*GE* 9).

Canon 801 — Religious institutes whose proper mission is that of education, while faithfully retaining this mission of theirs, are also to devote themselves to Catholic education through their schools established with the consent of the diocesan bishop.

This new canon warmly encourages those religious communities whose apostolates include Catholic education, and, at the same time, it reminds them that their schools are to be established with the permission of the local diocesan bishop. The longtime commitment and effective service of men and women religious in the various levels and kinds of Catholic education are here recognized and encouraged. Far from abandoning this difficult but eminently valuable form of apostolate, religious communities are urged to devote themselves to it. Special mention is made of their labors within their own schools. The final admonition of *Gravissimum Educationis* 9, mentioned above, applies also to those religious engaged in education. The canon depends in part on *Christus Dominus* 35, and *Ecclesiae sanctae* I, 29, 30, and 39.

Canon 802 — §1. If schools imparting an education imbued with the Christian spirit are not available the diocesan bishop is to see to it that they are established.

§2. The diocesan bishop is to provide for the establishment of professional schools, technical schools and other schools required by special needs whenever such would be advantageous.

This statement of the diocesan bishop's responsibility to see to the establishment of schools is a close parallel to canon 1379, §1 of the 1917 Code. However, there are two significant changes from the former law: (1) canon 1379 spoke only of the absence of "Catholic elementary and secondary schools" whereas this canon states that the bishop has the obligation when "schools imparting an education imbued with the Christian spirit" are lacking. Consequently, the bishop might satisfy himself that a genuinely Christian education may be available in other schools besides those which are solely under Catholic auspices, e.g., ecumenical schools, released time arrangements, or various other forms of cooperation; (2) it is the "diocesan bishop" alone who bears the responsibility rather than the more inclusive "ordinary of the place." Both the first and second paragraphs of canon 802 are derived from *Gravissimum Educationis* 9.

In paragraph two the canon speaks of the various kinds of special schools which might be responsive to local, contemporary needs. Two examples are offered, namely, professional and technical schools, but many others may be imagined, e.g., the others mentioned in *Gravissimum Educationis* 9. In this case it is not simply the absence of such schools which should trigger the bishop's action, but also when they are truly needed and the bishop has some way of providing for their establishment, in other words "whenever such would be advantageous."

Canon 803 — §1. That school is considered to be Catholic which ecclesiastical authority or a public ecclesiastical juridic person supervises or which ecclesiastical authority recognizes as such by means of a written document.

§2. It is necessary that the formation and education given in a Catholic school be based upon the principles of Catholic doctrine; teachers are to be outstanding for their correct doctrine and integrity of life.

§3. Even if it really be Catholic, no school may bear the title *Catholic school* without the consent of the competent ecclesiastical authority.

This canon attempts to answer this question: What makes a school Catholic? The legal response to the question is in terms of the intervention, either direct or indirect, of church authority. To be considered Catholic a school must be under the direction of church authority or a public juridic person (cf. cc. 113–123), or it must be recognized in writing as Catholic by a church authority. Furthermore, the third paragraph of the canon provides that no school, even though it really *is* Catholic may *call* itself Catholic without the consent of competent church authority. Among the many possible criteria of a school's Catholicity, e.g., name, recognition, origin, stated purpose, ownership, operating authority, faith commitment of teachers or students, spirit and atmosphere, orthodox teaching, or

actual inculcation of gospel values, the Code has chosen what is perhaps the simplest and most verifiable criterion: operation or recognition by church authority (either directly, or indirectly exercised in the establishment of a public juridic person). The canon rescues itself from pure extrinsicism by the addition of paragraph two, which declares that both the formation (of character) and education in a Catholic school is to be grounded upon the basics of Catholic teaching, and that the teachers are to be outstanding for their correct teaching and moral probity. However, this is clearly neither a part of the legal criterion of Catholicity nor a requisite for the use of the name "*Catholic school*"; it is an expectation, a characteristic which should not be absent. Those within the school itself, the community of administrators and teachers, should be the monitors of quality Catholic teaching and of the example of Christian living.

Religious communities which have been approved by the Holy See or by a diocesan bishop are public juridic persons, hence schools operated by them can be considered Catholic schools in the sense of paragraph one of the canon.

Who is the competent ecclesiastical authority whose permission is required for a school to call itself Catholic? Certainly the Holy See, diocesan bishops, and other local ordinaries (cf. c. 134); nothing prevents the authority from being delegated, e.g., to a superintendent of schools (cf. c. 137). It can be argued that in the case of schools owned and operated by clerical religious communities, the major religious superiors of those groups as possessors of ordinary power are also competent authorities for their own schools (cf. c. 801). However, the bishop, as coordinator of apostolic works within each diocese, is the higher authority (*CD* 17, 35; *ES* I, 39).

Canon 804 — §1. Catholic religious formation and education which are imparted in any schools whatsoever as well as that acquired through the various media of social communications are subject to the authority of the Church; it is the responsibility of the conference of bishops to issue general norms in this area, and it is the responsibility of the diocesan bishop to regulate such education and be vigilant over it.

§2. The local ordinary is to be concerned that those who are assigned as religion teachers in schools, even in non-Catholic ones, be outstanding for their correct doctrine, their witness of Christian living and their pedagogical skill.

Paragraph one states that even when they are carried on in schools which are not Catholic or by means of radio, television, and the print media, Catholic formation and education remain subject to ecclesiastical authority. The episcopal conference is to issue general regulations for such educational efforts, and the diocesan bishop is to watch over and supervise them in the local church. The canon applies to those situations in which Catholic religious education is made available in private schools, those sponsored by public authority, or those conducted through the various communications media; such education is still subject to the Church, in virtue of its sacred teaching mission, and therefore subject in some measure to those entrusted with authority in the Church. The delicate issue of exactly how that control or surveillance is to be exercised in each civil jurisdiction and cultural setting is to be determined by the bishops' conferences. The canon is an updated and expanded statement of canon 1381, §1 of the 1917 Code.

The second paragraph narrows and specifies the general concerns stated in the first, and at the same time it spreads the responsibility from the diocesan bishop to the ordinary of the place (i.e., more encompassing; cf. c. 134; would include, e.g., an episcopal vicar for education). The concern is for the quality of the teachers of religion, even in schools which are not Catholic; the ordinaries are to be solicitous that the teachers be distinguished in three areas: a proper grasp of church doctrine, the witness of a Christian life, and the art of teaching. The canon does not say how the local ordinaries are to give expression to this pastoral concern; that must vary according to the situation, and will likely be addressed by the norms issued by each bishops' conference. It seems obvious that both fundamental fairness in employment practices and the autonomy of the school's internal regimen should be respected.

This canon is apparently based on canon 1381, §2 of the 1917 Code and on *Gravissimum Educationis* 7, which suggests a positive attitude of affection and assistance for those many Catholic children in non-Catholic schools; it infers that the most effective means of helping them may be through the living witness of their teachers, the zeal and example of their schoolmates, and the efforts of the priests and lay persons who offer them spiritual aid.

Canon 805 — **For his own diocese the local ordinary has the right to name or approve teachers of religion and likewise to remove or to demand that they be removed if it is required for reasons of religion or morals.**

The pastoral solicitude for the quality of teachers of religion mentioned in the previous canon (§2) is here sharpened to a right of the ordinary of the place to appoint and remove teachers of religion. Since this canon replaces canon 1381, §3 of the 1917 Code, which referred to "schools of whatever kind," presumably it applies to teachers in all schools in the ordinary's territory, both Catholic (cf. c. 803) and those not operated or authorized by

the Church. It would extend to schools operated privately or by public authority so long as the Catholic faith is taught in them. (Obviously the ordinary has no rights over the teachers of other faiths or of comparative religions.) It is difficult to imagine how the ordinary will exercise or vindicate this right in schools which are not directly under ecclesiastical control. The authority can be delegated, and it may be both fairer and wiser to continue to allow the school administrators to exercise the function in accordance with the normal procedures for appointment and removal of teachers. The canon itself opens the way to the use of an intermediary or delegate when it uses the language "name or approve," and "remove or to demand that they be removed." The 1981 *Relatio* of the Code Commission confirms this and states that local practice is to be respected: "It is to be noted that the canon looks to either nomination *or approval* as an appropriate equivalent where it is not the custom to nominate" (p. 180).

The basis for removing teachers of religion from their positions is stated most generally: "for reasons of religion or morals" ("religionis morumve ratio"), but it must be related to the function of teaching the Catholic religion. The offenses or deficiencies would have to be very serious to justify such drastic action, and all procedures of civil law, fundamental fairness, and natural equity should be observed.

Canon 806 — **§1. The diocesan bishop has the right of vigilance over and visitation of the Catholic schools located in his territory, even those schools which have been established or are being directed by members of religious institutes; he is likewise competent to issue prescriptions dealing with the general regulation of Catholic schools; such prescriptions are also operative for those schools which are directed by religious, with due regard for their autonomy regarding the internal management of their schools.**

§2. The directors of Catholic schools, under the vigilance of the local ordinary, are to see to it that the instruction given in them is at least as academically distinguished as that given in the other schools of the region.

Part one of the first paragraph states the diocesan bishop's right of vigilance over and visitation of the Catholic schools (cf. c. 803) in his territory. (Cf. also cc. 396–398.) Note that the right belongs to the diocesan bishop alone—not to other local ordinaries—but the right can be exercised through delegates of the bishop. Those schools founded or operated by religious communities are not exempt from this right of oversight and visitation. The privilege granted before the 1917 Code and in effect after its promulgation, which exempted the schools of some religious (regulars) from this right of visitation has been revoked. (Cf. Bouscaren, *Canon Law*, pp. 766–767 and *CD* 35, 4.)

Both sections of paragraph one are derived from *Christus Dominus* 35, 4 and *Ecclesiae sanctae* I, 39, and they replace canons 1381 and 1382 of the 1917 Code. These sources are helpful for interpretation.

What kinds of Catholic schools are subject to the bishop's right of vigilance and visitation? Only primary and secondary schools, or are colleges, seminaries, and other types also included? Since the text of the canon says simply "Catholic schools," the context gives the answer to the question, namely, that this chapter of the Code is focused on elementary and secondary Catholic education; colleges, universities, and seminaries are regulated elsewhere in the Code (i.e., in the following chapter). It is true that some canons of this chapter, e.g., canons 800 and 804, use language that is quite sweeping, but the revised Code, unlike the 1917 Code, distinguishes clearly between its chapters on schools and those on other levels of educational institutions. This line of reasoning is confirmed by the Code Commission in its 1981 *Relatio*, "Universities and Institutes of higher studies do not come under the chapter on schools." ("Sub capite 'De scholis' non veniunt Universitates neque Instituta Studiorum Superiorum," p. 179.) An argument might be made from the sources that the purpose of the law is more broad, e.g., extending to the oversight of all Catholic education in the diocese, but the rules of interpretation (namely, c. 17—laws are to be understood in accord with proper meaning of the words taken from text and context, and c. 18—laws which restrict the free exercise of rights are to be interpreted strictly) seem to compel a limited understanding of the word "schools" here and hence a limitation of the bishop's right of vigilance and visitation to primary and secondary schools.

Are the other institutions mentioned in *Ecclesiae sanctae* I, 39 or in canon 1382 of the 1917 Code, e.g., oratories, recreation centers, hospitals, orphanages, etc., also subject to the bishop's right of vigilance and visitation? Here the language of the canon itself seems to answer the question. It states simply "schools," and those other institutions are clearly not schools in the way that term is used in this chapter. The bishop may well have both legitimate interest in and authority over those other institutions, e.g., in virtue of his duty to coordinate the pastoral activity of the diocese, or the right of visitation contained in canon 397, but they are not subject to the vigilance and visitation set forth in this canon.

Are the "internal schools" of religious communities which are open only to the community's own students exempt from the bishop's right of vigilance and visitation? They were exempted in canon 1382 of the 1917 Code and in *Ecclesiae sanctae* I, 39, and they are explicitly excluded by canon 683, §1.

What is the scope of the bishop's right of vigi-

lance and visitation? Again the canon sets no parameters or guidelines in its wording, but such oversight has always been limited (e.g., *CIC* 1381, §2 spoke of "anything taught or done against faith or good morals"), and a canonical visitation is not a fishing expedition. The context here is the bishop's responsibility for the quality of Christian education in his diocese, i.e., how effectively the children and young people are being formed in the faith and helped to a healthy Christian maturity. Many factors impinge upon that central project in a school, e.g., finances, buildings, administration, spirit, etc., but the bishop's vigilance and visitation should be focused on those which affect it most directly. The scope of the visitation authorized by this canon, for example, should not extend to all of the matters mentioned in *Christus Dominus* 35, 4, because some of them are unrelated to the educational task, even though they are matters in which religious are accountable to the bishop.

The second part of paragraph one authorizes the diocesan bishop to regulate the educational policies of Catholic schools (those described in c. 803, §1), and those schools operated by religious are declared to be subject to those policies. The language used, "general regulation" ("generalem ordinationem," taken from *CD* 35, 4), seems to imply policies or general guidelines rather than detailed regulations. The canon adds that in those schools run by religious, their legitimate autonomy in regard to the internal management of the schools must be respected; this would certainly extend, for example, to the employment of instructors.

If the issuance of these Catholic school policies is considered to be lawmaking in a strict sense, they must be given by the bishop himself because his legislative authority cannot be delegated (c. 135, §2). However, there is no reason why such policy statements cannot be considered a less formal kind of rule making—e.g., general executory decrees (c. 31) or instructions (c. 34) or guidelines—for which executive authority, which can be delegated (c. 137), suffices.

Perhaps more important than the exact legal nature of these educational policies is the process which leads up to their promulgation. It is an area of the Church's life which is well suited to collegial decision making. Catholic school boards have functioned very effectively; they embody the principle of shared responsibility for the Church's teaching office. The process of consultation and discussion before school policies are issued should be thorough and open.

The second paragraph of canon 806 is a mandate for quality in Catholic education; those responsible are to see that the instruction imparted in Catholic schools is at least as scientific and excellent as in the other schools in the same area. The canon reflects the high ideals for Catholic schools so eloquently stated in *Gravissimum Educationis* 8 and 9.

CHAPTER II
CATHOLIC UNIVERSITIES AND
OTHER INSTITUTES OF HIGHER STUDIES
[cc. 807–814]

A preliminary question of a very serious nature must be raised about this set of canons on higher education, namely, whether or not they are applicable to most of the Catholic colleges and universities in the United States. Our Catholic institutions of higher learning are both distinctive and diverse in character, and they are the most numerous—with the largest number of students—in the world.

Both historically and in contemporary practice, the Catholic colleges and universities of the United States are considered as related to or affiliated with the Church rather than as "canonically Catholic." Except in the case of the very few diocesan colleges and The Catholic University of America, ties with the institutional Church have generally been informal and implicit at most; even diocesan colleges have been incorporated civilly, and the sponsorship and church responsibility, although of the greatest moral weight and significance, have not ordinarily been made a matter of canonical formality or determination. The vast majority of the colleges and universities in the United States have been sponsored by religious institutes of women or of men; these have been characterized by the proportion of religious, very great in the past, who serve as members of the governing boards, faculty, and administration. Generally these institutions have been without canonical ties to the local church or diocese, although again the moral weight and significance of their relationship to the church community cannot be overestimated.

The diversity among the Catholic colleges and universities in the United States further underlines a basic difference from the patterns in European countries and in countries whose educational systems are under European influence. This diversity ranges from small four-year liberal arts colleges to major universities with a comprehensive offering of graduate, professional, and undergraduate programs. There are many variations and combinations, for example, colleges with baccalaureate programs and one or more graduate programs added at the master's degree level.

In the United States there are some institutions that are considered *non-sectarian* at civil law, despite their original and continuing Catholic sponsorship and their present and continuing maintenance of the Catholic educational tradition, the presence of strong departments of religious studies, including Roman Catholic theology, close collaboration with the diocesan bishop, etc. Other institutions lack a formal policy affirming their Christian and Catholic nature, but de facto perpetuate, as a result of their foundation and sponsorship, a strong Christian and Catholic presence. Still others, and perhaps the considerable majority, express official policies—differing greatly in language and style—that assert their Catholic mission. It is difficult if not impossible to apply the canons as such to such divergent situations of the Catholic colleges and universities in the Fifty States of the United States.

The Catholic character and mission of all these American institutions are not at question. The character and mission have been maintained in different ways, but any kind of formalization of canonical status has been generally avoided, the recognition of the Catholic character and mission by church authorities has been implicit, and the relationships of the institutions to the total church community and to church authorities have instead been cooperative and collaborative. (Unlike the institutions sponsored by some other religious bodies in the U.S., the Catholic colleges and universities do not enter into formal covenants or the like with ecclesiastical authorities nor do they, with certain exceptions, receive any direct church support.)

The question of the applicability of the canons to Catholic colleges and universities in the United States has other important facets:

First, it is evident that the canons are designed for systems of higher education in situations considerably different from those in North America. The pattern of post-secondary institutions which are publicly chartered but still retain their private and independent character is not known in most countries. Similarly, academic acceptance by private accrediting associations and other professional agencies and by voluntary educational associations is not significant elsewhere; in the United States it is of primary significance for the evaluation of institutions of higher learning and indeed for their impact upon human society, that is, for that very "public, persistent, and universal presence [of the Christian mind] in the whole enterprise of advancing human culture" of which Vatican II spoke (*GE* 10). Again, the location of the ultimate institutional authority in a governing board or board of trustees, which holds a public trust under the charter of incorporation, is a distinctive feature of institutions that is not contemplated in the canons.

The Catholic institutions in the United States, in order to satisfy the nature and purpose of higher education, follow the distinctive American pattern. At the same time they remain completely free to conduct instructional and research programs in the light of Catholic faith and with the interaction of all academic disciplines. This pattern differs so greatly in style of academic governance and in cultural and social dimensions from the European system of higher education that it is seriously questionable whether the canons are indeed applicable in the United States.

A second and related element is the purpose of canons 810, §2 and 812, which seek to assure the integrity of Catholic teaching. The historical background of such legislation, and specifically the background of the "canonical mission," which in turn is related to the mandate required of teachers of theological disciplines (c. 812), is found in nineteenth-century efforts to protect the Church's teaching office and the freedom of teachers of theology from the hostile interference of civil states and secular political control. To the extent that this is the purpose of the law, it has no application at all in the United States. In this country both ecclesiastical authorities and teachers of theological disciplines are protected by the provisions of the First Amendment, prohibiting a governmental establishment of religion and protecting the free exercise of religion, and by similar provisions in the constitutions of the Fifty States. In other words, the absence of this rationale for the law, a rationale which may remain a genuine concern in some countries today, makes the law inapplicable in the United States. The other evident purpose of the law, namely, the safeguarding of doctrine within the church community, appears to be adequately assured by the exercise of moral rather than canonical authority.

Still another, and third, consideration has already been suggested by the absence of formal juridical or canonical ties—in most instances—between the American Catholic post-secondary institutions and church authorities. The revised Code of Canon Law has refined the definitions of institutions which are considered as having juridical personality at canon law, namely, as subjects of canonical rights and obligations (see c. 113, §2). The determination whether an individual institution is a juridical person would have to be made. None of the Catholic colleges and universities would be considered a public juridical person, that is, with the capacity of acting "in the name of the Church" (c. 116, §1). In other matters also, even apart from the canons on Catholic higher education, the institutions are not touched directly by the canon law. For example, see canon 1257, §2 concerning property: this is not governed by the canon law even in the case of those institutions which might have been constituted as private juridical persons. These principles hold despite the fact that the canon law is understood as applicable to Catholic members of the college or university community, whether faculty members or administrators or students.

This point is made because in fact the canons concerning Catholic colleges, universities, and other institutions of higher studies—when read carefully—appear to avoid imposing norms or obligations upon the institutions as such, beyond stating what would be otherwise evident from the nature of their identity, precisely because without juridical personality the institutions do not have any standing in the canon law. This becomes especially important in the case of canon 812, which is later commented upon at some length.

The aforementioned considerations about applicability are sound and have led some to the conclusion that the canons are inapplicable to most American institutions of higher education. They do not, however, diminish either the need to examine the canons carefully or the significance of the ministry of higher education within the Church. Such a ministry demands that, in accord with the fundamental purpose of the canons, those Catholics who teach or who exercise other positions of responsibility in Catholic colleges and universities act in full communion with the Church. This does not contravene in any way the right to academic freedom, which the canons expressly uphold in accord with the explicit teaching of Vatican II (see cc. 809 and 218). (These observations on the applicability of the canons are derived from a memorandum drawn up by Frederick R. McManus with the assistance of other canonists and circulated to Catholic college presidents on 3 Aug. 1983 by the Association of Catholic Colleges and Universities.)

Canon 807 — The Church has the right to erect and to supervise universities which contribute to a higher level of human culture, to a fuller advancement of the human person and also to the fulfillment of the Church's teaching office.

The opening canon both reasserts the Church's right to be involved in higher education and offers a brief rationale for that involvement. The Church may establish and run colleges and universities; in so doing, they contribute to: (1) the advancement of culture; (2) the development of the human person; and (3) the fulfillment of the Church's teaching office. *Gravissimum Educationis* 10, from which this canon is drawn, speaks eloquently of the Church's intention to have the individual disciplines studied according to their own principles and methods and with proper freedom of scientific investigation (cf. c. 218) so that a deeper understanding may result, and so that faith and reason will be seen to be at one in the harmony of truth.

Pope John Paul II said to the presidents of Catholic colleges and universities in the United States:

As one who for long years has been a university professor, I will never tire of insisting on the eminent role of the university, which is to instruct but also to be a place of scientific research. In both these fields, its activity is closely related to the deepest and noblest aspiration of the human person: the desire to come to the knowledge of truth. No university can deserve the rightful esteem of the world of learning unless it applies the highest standards of scientific research, constantly updating its methods and working instruments, and unless it excels in seriousness, and therefore, in freedom of investigation (Oct. 7, 1979; *Pilgrim of Peace*, USCC, p. 165).

No authority is designated for the establishment or governance of these institutions; per se they do not require the intervention of any ecclesiastical authority. *Gravissimum Educationis* 8 and canon 1375 of the 1917 Code are also among the sources for this canon; canon 800 of the revised Code is its parallel.

Canon 808 — **Even if it really be Catholic, no university may bear the title or name *Catholic university* without the consent of the competent ecclesiastical authority.**

Anyone in the Catholic Church can establish a Catholic college or university. The action of a church authority is required if it is canonically erected as a public juridic person (c. 116; cf. 1981 *Rel* 181). But for the college or university to bear the *title* or *name* "*Catholic*" the permission of a competent ecclesiastical authority must be received, even though the institution is already really Catholic. (Cf. the remarks at the beginning of this chapter of the Code about the applicability of these canons to U.S. institutions.)

This preoccupation with the use of the name "*Catholic*," both here and in reference to elementary and secondary schools in canon 803, §3, is difficult to understand. It goes beyond the restrictions on the canonical establishment of Catholic universities and faculties and the approval of statutes by the Holy See called for in canon 1376 of the 1917 Code. It is echoed in canon 300 on associations of the faithful and canon 216 on apostolic enterprises. Its root is in *Apostolicam actuositatem* 24, which is far removed from higher education. It may reflect a desire to prevent the use of the title "*Catholic*" by institutions which are perceived not to be authentically Catholic. But the words of Pope John Paul II to the presidents of Catholic colleges and universities place the concern in a more positive light:

A Catholic university or college must make a specific contribution to the Church and to society through high quality scientific research, in-depth study of problems, and a just sense of history, together with the concern to show the full meaning of the human person regenerated in Christ, thus favoring the complete development of the person. Furthermore, the Catholic university or college must train young men and women of outstanding knowledge who, having made a personal synthesis between faith and culture, will be both capable and willing to assume tasks in the service of the community and of society in general, and to bear witness to their faith before the world. And finally, to be what it ought to be,

a Catholic college or university must set up, among its faculty and students, a real community which bears witness to a living and operative Christianity, a community where sincere commitment to scientific research and study goes together with a deep commitment to authentic Christian living.

This is your identity. This is your vocation. Every university or college is qualified by a specific mode of being. Yours is the qualification of being Catholic, of affirming God, his revelation and the Catholic Church as the guardian and interpreter of that revelation. The term "Catholic" will never be a mere label, either added or dropped according to the pressures of varying factors (Oct. 7, 1979; *Pilgrim of Peace*, USCC, pp. 164–165).

No definition of a Catholic college or university is given in the Code; the following canon (c. 809) and the place in *Gravissimum Educationis* 10 from which it is drawn, and the foregoing words of Pope John Paul II help us to understand what the Church considers them to be.

Who are the ecclesiastical authorities competent to give permission for a college or university to call itself "*Catholic*"? Earlier drafts of this same canon mentioned the Apostolic See and the episcopal conference, and surely both of them are included here; diocesan bishops who are given the right and duty of vigilance in canon 810, could also grant permission, personally or through a delegate, for institutions within the diocesan territory. It might be argued that major superiors of clerical religious communities devoted to the educational apostolate might also grant such permission for an institution founded and operated by their community, based on their status as ordinaries (c. 134) and their communities' special participation in the teaching office of the Church (cc. 758, 801). Normally the executive authority of such ordinaries is limited to the members of their communities.

It is difficult to imagine very many Catholic colleges or universities in the United States actually requesting the permission suggested in this canon. Most such institutions are already confident in their Catholic identity. And the canons do not have retroactive effect (c. 9); an institution which used "*Catholic*" in its title or description before November 27, 1983, is not subject to the new provision of this canon.

Canon 809 — **If it is possible and advantageous the conferences of bishops are to see to it that universities or at least faculties are established, suitably distributed throughout their territory, in which the various disciplines are to be investigated and taught with due regard for their academic autonomy, and with due consideration for Catholic doctrine.**

This canon, echoing the teaching of *Gravissimum Educationis* 10 and canon 1379, §2 of the 1917 Code, obliges the bishops' conference to be concerned about the establishment of Catholic colleges and universities and their appropriate distribution throughout the territory of the conference. The conference is to see to their establishment if it is judged possible and expedient. The brief statement of the purpose of these institutions of higher learning also reflects *Gravissimum Educationis* 10: the various disciplines may be investigated and taught, observing the scientific autonomy of each, and with due regard for Catholic teaching. Their proper educational function is given clear priority.

As Pope John Paul II said,

The relationship to truth explains therefore the historical bond between the university and the Church. Because she herself finds her origin and her growth in the words of Christ, which are the liberating truth (cf. Jn 8:32), the Church has always tried to stand by the institutions that serve, and cannot but serve the knowledge of truth (Oct. 7, 1979; *Pilgrim of Peace*, USCC, p. 165).

Canon 810 — §1. It is the responsibility of the authority who is competent in accord with the statutes to provide for the appointment of teachers to Catholic universities who besides their scientific and pedagogical suitability are also outstanding in their integrity of doctrine and probity of life; when those requisite qualities are lacking they are to be removed from their positions in accord with the procedure set forth in the statutes.

§2. The conference of bishops and the diocesan bishops concerned have the duty and right of being vigilant that in these universities the principles of Catholic doctrine are faithfully observed.

In treating of the appointment and removal of teachers in Catholic colleges and universities in paragraph one, the revised Code *canonizes* the statutes of the institution. It respects the legitimate autonomy of each academic setting. These critical and sensitive processes are to be governed by the internal regulations of each school. The authorities responsible and the procedures to be followed are those which the institution has established for itself; this paragraph simply recognizes those statutes as the law to be applied. The statutes should embody the standards of fairness and good practice which are accepted in the academic community of the country or culture. The institutional authority is addressed in the first paragraph; the second paragraph speaks to episcopal responsibilities.

In addition, paragraph one gives an indication of the qualities to be sought in those who are candidates for teaching positions in Catholic colleges or universities: (1) capability in knowledge and in teaching; and (2) integrity of doctrine and upright-

ness of life. These are very general guidelines; they simply point in the direction of the kind of scholarly excellence and personal example which should characterize Catholic college faculty members. They cannot be applied to teachers employed because of their doctrinal divergence (e.g., for ecumenical reasons) or where the discipline is devoid of doctrinal implications.

In its 1981 *Relatio* (pp. 182–183) it is clear that the Code Commission feels that this paragraph applies to administrators as well as to the teaching faculty.

The duty and right of vigilance over Catholic colleges and universities stated in the second paragraph is concurrent, that is, it belongs both to the episcopal conference and to the diocesan bishop. The interested diocesan bishop (presumably the one in whose territory the college or university is located) acts by his own authority and not as the agent for the conference, but his action does not prevent the conference from also exercising vigilance, that is, from also overseeing the same institution. The canon does not provide for the resolution of the possible conflicts which could arise out of this double concession of authority (but cf. cc. 1732–1739 on administrative recourse).

What is the duty and right of vigilance? It does *not* imply ownership, governance, jurisdiction, control, intervention, or even visitation—all of those levels of authority and responsibility are distinct from the "ius invigilandi." It does mean a pastoral watchfulness, a benign surveillance, a solicitous oversight. It implies information and communication, inquiry, advice, sharing of concerns, even perhaps friendly persuasion. But it is not an adversarial relationship; it is neither inquisitorial nor authoritarian.

What is the *scope* of this duty and right of vigilance over Catholic colleges and universities? "That . . . the principles of Catholic doctrine are faithfully observed," says the canon. It is an interest which stems from the bishop's teaching office, a concern which is related to the ministry of the word in his diocese (cf. c. 386). The scope of vigilance is limited then to the basics of Catholic teaching and the way they are communicated and witnessed in the context of and in accord with the methods of an institution of higher education.

The bishop or the conference may exercise this duty of vigilance by delegation.

Earlier drafts of the second paragraph provided that bishops could remove teachers for reasons of faith or morals. The deletion of that provision is most worthy of note. It was removed as both unnecessary and inappropriate, an improper external intervention in the internal affairs of an institution of higher education.

Canon 811 — §1. The competent ecclesiastical authority is to provide that at Catholic universities there be erected a faculty of theology, an institute of theology, or at least a chair of theology so that classes may be given for lay students.

§2. In the individual Catholic universities classes should be given which treat in a special way those theological questions which are connected with the disciplines of their faculties.

The first paragraph of this canon makes it incumbent upon ecclesiastical authorities to promote the teaching of theology in Catholic colleges and universities, especially so that lay students will benefit from it. It is taken directly from *Gravissimum Educationis* 10, and it is also related to *Gaudium et Spes* 57, which is concerned with the necessary dialogue between faith and culture. The bishops of the United States spoke to the value of theological studies in this context in 1980:

> It is advisable, however, that students be encouraged to cope with their personal problems of faith and to consider the religious dimensions of the major issues in our contemporary culture and society. Theology should enable students to think and to act within a vision of life that includes religious values. A truly liberating and elevating education is incomplete without the study of theology or religion ("Catholic Higher Education and the Pastoral Mission of the Church," USCC, 1981, p. 5).

The competent ecclesiastical authority is not specified, but it would include the Holy See, episcopal conferences, diocesan bishops, and might possibly extend to major religious superiors of clerical congregations which are devoted to Catholic higher education. Three forms of theological presence are suggested in the canon: a faculty (i.e., a school or department), an institute, or at least a chair; the choice depends on the situation within the college or university and the funds which can be raised to support the theological enterprise.

Paragraph two is an attempt to promote the dialogue between theology and the other disciplines on campus, and to promote theological reflection on the issues raised by those disciplines. The canon is drawn from *Gravissimum Educationis* 10, and *Gaudium et Spes* 36; both insist on the value of genuine scientific investigation in all branches of learning. Catholic colleges and universities are to stimulate the exchange between theology and the other disciplines by seeing that the theological questions related to those other disciplines are publicly discussed.

Canon 812 — **It is necessary that those who teach theological disciplines in any institute of higher studies have a mandate from the competent ecclesiastical authority.**

This terse, new canon caused more apprehension and provoked more opposition during the drafting stages of the revised Code than probably any other provision of the law. The requirement of an ecclesiastical mandate to teach theology is found nowhere in the 1917 Code nor in the teachings of the Second Vatican Council. It originated in Germany in 1848 when the hierarchy was struggling to retain some control over the teaching of religion in the newly secularized schools. The German bishops ruled that no one could teach the Catholic religion at any level of the educational system unless he or she had a "canonical mission" from the local bishop. This provision was later included in the various concordats between the Vatican and the German State. It was taken over into the regulations for "pontifical faculties" (i.e., those erected or approved by the Holy See) in the Apostolic Constitution *Deus Scientiarum Dominus* (24 May 1931; *AAS* 23 [1931], 241). This authorization ("missio canonica") to teach was to be given and could be withdrawn by the chancellor of the pontifical university (arts. 21, 22). When these norms for pontifical schools were reissued in 1979 (Apostolic Constitution *Sapientia Christiana*, 15 Apr. 1979; *AAS* 71 [1979], 469) this provision was retained (art. 17). Now, with this present canon, the ecclesiastical authorization process is extended to all teachers of theology in all Catholic colleges and universities. (Cf. what was said at the outset of this chapter of the Code on the applicability of these canons to the North American context.)

When the canon was proposed in the 1977 draft of the revised Code, it raised a storm of opposition in North America. The Association of Catholic Colleges and Universities, the Catholic Theological Society of America, and the "Bishops and Presidents Committee" all made strong representations for its deletion. The grounds for their opposition, briefly, were these: (1) this mode of ecclesiastical control would have a chilling and stifling effect on theological investigation; (2) it represents an unwelcome intrusion into the normal academic procedures by an outside authority, i.e., a violation of the legitimate autonomy of educational institutions; (3) this sort of control may well cause conflicts with teachers' unions or government regulations; (4) this new form of church involvement might jeopardize financial assistance from the government; (5) the canon contains no provision for the customary procedures in cases of removal of professors; (6) it may cause a major administrative burden on some bishops; (7) the purpose which the law seeks is presently being accomplished within the academic institutions by the judgment of peers and by conscientious administrators; and (8) the canon is superfluous, because adequate provision is already made in canon 810. This concern was carried by prelates from Canada and the United States to the Code

Commission (cf. 1981 *Rel*, p. 183), and in person to Pope John Paul II by delegates of the Association of Catholic Colleges and Universities (audience of March 18, 1982). Concern remains at such a level in North America that the United States and Canadian bishops are being urged to request an indult dispensing these territories from the obligation of canon 812.

The canon proposed by the Code Commission in 1977 and again in 1980 was changed significantly but not essentially when it was presented to the plenary meeting of October 1981. The earlier version read: "Those who teach courses in theology or courses related to theology in any kind of institute of higher studies require ("egent") a canonical mission." Four significant changes appear in the present canon 812: (1) the level of exigency was moderated from "require" ("egent") to "should have" ("habeant oportet"); (2) the authorization was changed from a "canonical mission" ("missio canonica") to a "mandate" ("mandatum")—the Code Commission said that it was not the same as a real canonical mission (*Rel*, p. 184); (3) the granting authority is named, at least generically, the "competent ecclesiastical authority"; and (4) it is limited to "theological disciplines"—the "courses related to theology" are omitted.

As it now stands, what institutions are referred to by the canon? All and only Catholic colleges and universities are included, that is, all Catholic institutions of post-secondary education, including academies, institutes, etc., but excluding seminaries because they are specifically regulated by another section of the Code, namely, canons 232–264. Institutions erected or approved by the Holy See, "ecclesiastical universities and faculties," are included by canon 818. But the canon is not directed to the institutions; its obligation falls upon the individual teacher to have a mandate.

Which instructors in those institutions are covered by this regulation? Those who will be added to faculties to teach theology on a full-time basis as their chief faculty responsibility. One-time, part-time, or occasional theology teachers are probably not included because the canon is concerned with ongoing, long-term instruction. Since the Code is not retroactive (cf. c. 9), those who held academic appointments at the time it became effective are not affected. Similarly not affected are those who are teaching or will teach theology who are not Catholics or not in the Latin Church; they are not bound by the Code (cf. cc. 1, 11). Finally, what is meant by "theological disciplines"? Since the law is clearly restrictive of "the free exercise of rights" it is subject to strict interpretation (c. 18). The "theological disciplines" certainly refer to dogmatics or systematics as well as historical, moral, and sacramental theology. Church history, liturgical studies, canon law, and sacred scripture, while not—strictly

speaking—"theology," are probably included in the meaning of "theological disciplines" (cf. c. 252). However, catechetics, many areas of pastoral studies, comparative religions, history or sociology of religion are not considered "theological disciplines."

Who is the "competent ecclesiastical authority"? The Apostolic See and the local diocesan bishop are surely capable of granting the mandate to teach theology. Probably the other ordinaries listed in canon 134 could also do so, and it might be argued that the major religious superiors of clerical communities which own and operate Catholic colleges could give mandates for their own members teaching in their own institutions. The episcopal conference is probably not included.

The "mandate" is simply a recognition that the person is properly engaged in teaching the theological discipline. It is not an empowerment, an appointment, or a formal commission. It is disciplinary, not doctrinal. It does not grant approval of what is taught nor is it a formal association with the Church's mission or ministry of teaching. There is no requirement that the mandate be in writing or even explicit, nor that it be received more than once.

Those ordinaries who are competent to grant the mandate may delegate that authority to others (e.g., an administrative officer of the college, the faculty of a department, etc.). Before issuing any such mandates for teaching theology (if a dispensation from the law is not obtained), it might be well to consider the following: (1) delegating an academic administrator within each institution to grant such mandates, following the school's usual procedures for appointments of and, when necessary, removal of instructors; and (2) establishing procedural safeguards so that the customary peer review and due process protection are afforded and all appearances of arbitrary action avoided.

Canon 813 — **The diocesan bishop is to have serious pastoral concern for students by erecting a parish for them or by assigning priests for this purpose on a stable basis; he is also to provide for Catholic university centers at universities, even non-Catholic ones, to give assistance, especially spiritual to young people.**

This canon fixes on the diocesan bishop the pastoral responsibility for providing campus ministry. It is taken directly from *Gravissimum Educationis* 10 where the motivation is stated: "the lot of society and of the Church itself is intimately connected with the development of those young people who are engaged in higher studies." The pastoral concern is for students at both Catholic and non-Catholic colleges and universities, and the bishop is instructed to set up a parish for their benefit or at least permanently assign priests for their ministry. Colleges and universities, both Catholic and non-Catholic, are to have "Catholic university centers," like the Newman Foundations, for the aid, especially spiritual help, of the young people studying there. The Second Vatican Council spoke of the "carefully selected and prepared priests, religious and lay persons providing both intellectual and spiritual assistance" to the students. It is indeed a critical apostolate.

Canon 814 — The prescriptions established for universities are equally applicable to other institutes of higher studies.

This canon simply clarifies terminology. In the foregoing canons the term "universities" was used to stand for all sorts of post-secondary educational institutions: colleges, universities, academies, institutes, etc. (but not seminaries; they are separately regulated by cc. 232–264). The canon states that what was prescribed for universities applies to the other institutions as well.

CHAPTER III
ECCLESIASTICAL UNIVERSITIES AND FACULTIES
[cc. 815–821]

Canon 815 — Ecclesiastical universities or faculties are proper to the Church in virtue of its duty to announce revealed truth; they serve to investigate the sacred disciplines or those disciplines related to the sacred, and to instruct students scientifically in those same disciplines.

The Church has its own schools for the advanced study of the sacred sciences for the twin purposes of exploring them more profoundly and instructing students in them. The canon simply states the appropriateness of the Church's sponsoring such universities and faculties and relates them to its basic mission of proclaiming what has been revealed. The canon is derived directly from *Gravissimum Educationis* 11.

Canon 816 — §1. Ecclesiastical universities and faculties can be established only through erection by the Holy See or through its approval; the Holy See also has a supervisory role with respect to them.
§2. Individual ecclesiastical universities and faculties must have their statutes and plan of studies approved by the Apostolic See.

The establishment and regulation of these ecclesiastical schools is closely controlled by the highest authority in the Church; they must be founded or approved by the Holy See alone (even though it would be necessary to consult the local conference

of bishops before doing so, as the Code Commission agreed in the 1981 *Rel*, p. 185). In addition, detailed norms for their operation are issued by the Holy See. The Apostolic Constitution *Deus Scientiarum Dominus* was issued for this purpose in 1931 (24 May; *AAS* 23 [1931], 241); it was replaced in 1979 by another Apostolic Constitution, *Sapientia Christiana* (15 Apr.; *AAS* 71 [1979], 469).

The second paragraph of the canon describes a further means of close supervision of these schools by the Holy See: their statutes, educational philosophy, and programs of study are subject to the approval of the Sacred Congregation for Catholic Education.

This canon replaces canon 1376 of the 1917 Code.

Canon 817 — No university or faculty which has not been erected or approved by the Apostolic See can grant academic degrees which have canonical effects in the Church.

Academic degrees which have canonical effects in the Church may be granted only by these official ecclesiastical faculties. The degrees in question are the licentiate (*licentia*) and doctorate (*laurea*) in the sacred disciplines, i.e., in theology, sacred scripture, canon law, etc. These credentials are mentioned in the Code and elsewhere as either required or recommended qualifications for certain positions or offices in the Church; for example, canon 253, §1, for teachers in seminaries; canon 378, §1, 5°, for bishops (either the academic degrees or expertise in one of the disciplines); canon 478, §1, for vicars general and episcopal vicars; canon 1420, §4, for vicar judicial (*officialis*); and canon 1421, §3, for other judges in church courts. Canon 817 is substantially the same as canon 1377 of the 1917 Code. It has been a frequent practice to accept equivalent degrees in teaching positions and equivalent expertise in other church offices for these ecclesiastical degree requirements. (Cf. the *Ordinationes* [*AAS* 71 (1979) 500, n. 17], which implements the apconst *SapC* [1979] in regard to teachers on ecclesiastical faculties.)

Canon 818 — The prescriptions for Catholic universities specified in cann. 810, 812 and 813 are also applicable to ecclesiastical universities and faculties.

The canon simply provides that what was prescribed for Catholic colleges and universities in canons 810 (internal procedures for faculty appointments and the concurrent vigilance by episcopal conference and diocesan bishop), 812 (mandate for teachers of theology), and 813 (pastoral care of students) applies to ecclesiastical universities and faculties as well.

Canon 819 — **Insofar as the good of a diocese, a religious institute or indeed the universal Church itself requires it, diocesan bishops or the competent superiors of institutes must send to ecclesiastical universities or faculties young people, clerics and members who are outstanding for their character, virtue and talent.**

This canon warmly encourages church leaders, both local ordinaries and religious superiors, to sponsor promising people for studies at ecclesiastical universities and faculties. The measure of need is broadly stated: "Insofar as the good of a diocese, a religious institute [including its apostolates] or indeed the universal Church itself requires it." Persons of outstanding natural talent, personal goodness, and mental ability are to be chosen to pursue further studies; they may be young men and women, priests, and members of the religious communities. The canon is derived from *Optatam Totius* 18 and *Gravissimum Educationis* 10, but these conciliar documents simply encourage higher studies in the sacred sciences and other areas; the canon directs attention to the ecclesiastical universities or faculties as places to pursue them.

Canon 820 — **The directors and professors of ecclesiastical universities and faculties are to see to it that the various faculties of such universities mutually assist one another insofar as their objectives permit this; they are also to see to it that mutual cooperation exists between their own university or faculty and other universities and faculties, even non-ecclesiastical ones; through their combined efforts, meetings, coordinated scientific research and other means, they are to work together for the greater advance of the sciences.**

This is a plea for collaboration among the various departments of ecclesiastical universities and faculties and for cooperation between these institutions and others, so that from these common efforts human knowledge might be advanced. The canon attempts to overcome academic isolation by urging administrators and faculty members to promote various kinds of mutual assistance, projects, meetings, and coordinated research. It is taken directly from *Gravissimum Educationis* 12 and has further background in *Gaudium et Spes* 62; both provide a persuasive rationale for this interaction.

Canon 821 — **The conference of bishops and the diocesan bishop are to provide, wherever possible, for the establishment of higher institutes for the religious sciences, namely institutes in which the theological disciplines and other disciplines pertaining to Christian culture are taught.**

This is an encouragement for the establishment of institutes for advanced religious studies. It is aimed at enabling adults to achieve more profound formation in their Christian faith. The responsibility is jointly shared: the episcopal conference and the diocesan bishop are both to provide such schools or opportunities. Their scope is described in terms of the "theological disciplines and other disciplines pertaining to Christian culture."

In two earlier drafts of the revised Code this canon was placed in the previous section, with Catholic colleges and universities, but the Code Commission moved it to this chapter on ecclesiastical institutions because such institutes "ought to depend entirely on ecclesiastical authority, otherwise they inevitably produce serious disagreements" (*Rel*, 184).

TITLE IV
INSTRUMENTS OF
SOCIAL COMMUNICATION
AND SPECIFICALLY BOOKS
[cc. 822–832]

This material on the use of the media in the service of the Church's teaching office and on the prior censorship of books represents a major change from the corresponding title of the 1917 Code (*CIC* Book III, title XXIII, 1384–1405). That title contained two sections: one on the censorship of books by ecclesiastical authority prior to their publication—this has been retained in the revised Code, but in a modified and attenuated form; and the other on the prohibition against publishing, reading, keeping, or selling certain large categories of religion-related writings—this latter section has been entirely eliminated in the revised Code.

The prohibition of books, along with the *Index of Prohibited Books*, was effectively repealed by two decrees of the Sacred Congregation for the Doctrine of the Faith in 1966 (14 June; *AAS* 58 [1966], 1186; *CLD* 6, 817–818).

The prior censorship of books was reordered by another decree of the Sacred Congregation for the Teaching of the Faith, "On the Vigilance of the Church's Pastors Regarding Books" (*De ecclesiae pastorum vigilantia circa libros*, 19 Mar. 1975; *AAS* 67 [1975], 281; *CLD* 8, 991–996), and this section of the revised Code, except for the first canon, is derived almost verbatim and in sequence from that document. The range of publications required to have ecclesiastical approval by this revised legislation has been drastically reduced: from the whole gamut of writings on religious or moral topics to those publications most closely related to the Church's teaching and worship, namely, the scriptures, liturgical and devotional books, catechisms, and theological textbooks. Thus the purpose of this legislation has partially changed, from a rather paternalistic attempt to protect the faith and morals of the people by safeguarding them from harmful religious publications, to a more restrained and positive effort to assure that those writings which express the Church's prayers and beliefs do so accurately.

Canon 822 — §1. **The pastors of the Church, employing a right which belongs to the Church in fulfilling its responsibility, are to endeavor to make use of the instruments of social communication.**

§2. These same pastors are to see to it that the faithful are taught that they are bound in duty to cooperate so that the use of the instruments of social communication is animated with a human and Christian spirit.

§3. All the Christian faithful are to be concerned about furnishing assistance in this pastoral activity in such a way that the Church effectively fulfills its responsibility through such instruments; this is especially true for those who in any way have a role in the regulation or use of these instruments.

The opening canon of this title is positive in tone; it encourages the use of the media for the good purposes of the Church and of humankind. Most of the subsequent canons are negative, pertaining to various kinds of restrictions on the use of the media. The first paragraph admonishes the pastoral leaders of the Church (here meaning the bishops) to do their best to use the instruments of social communications (the press, cinema, radio, television, and similar mass media) as aids in carrying out the Church's mission of teaching. At the same time, the paragraph claims that the Church has every right to use such media in fulfillment of its mission (just as it has the right to use schools, for example).

This entire canon is directly derived from *Inter Mirifica* 3. The attention given to these modern means of social communication, both by the Second Vatican Council and now here in the Code, is a recognition by the Church of their vital importance and powerful influence (cf. *IM* 1, 2).

The bishops are urged in paragraph two to enlist the aid of the faithful in making communications media true instruments of human development and Christian salvation. Clearly the members of the Church have more influence over the media, and are probably more affected by them, than are the Church's pastoral leaders. Hence, echoing the Second Vatican Council (*IM* 3) this paragraph recalls this particular obligation of lay persons.

In the final paragraph of the canon Christ's faithful are exhorted to lend a hand with the whole Church's pastoral activity in and through the media, so that the Church might employ these modern means in carrying out its mission. The focus of this paragraph, reflecting *Inter Mirifica* 13, is on the media in support of the Church's pastoral action rather than the more general benefits to humankind targeted in paragraph two. But the task here is not described as narrowly catechetical nor simply evangelistic; it is broadly pastoral, looking to the health of the media and their positive cultural impact as well as to the ways that they might serve the Church's teaching office. Those involved in the arrangement and use of the media are especially singled out and called to lend their expertise to the Church's efforts, which are truly their own.

Canon 823 — §1. **In order for the integrity of the truths of the faith and morals to be preserved, the pastors of the Church have the duty and the right to be vigilant lest harm be done to the faith or morals of the Christian faithful through writings or the use of the instruments of social communication; they likewise have the duty and the right to demand that writings to be published by the Christian faithful which touch upon faith or morals be submitted to their judgment; they also have the duty and right to denounce writings which harm correct faith or good morals.**

§2. The bishops as individuals or gathered in particular councils or conferences of bishops have the duty and the right mentioned in §1 with regard to the Christian faithful committed to their care; the supreme authority of the Church has this duty and right in regard to the whole people of God.

Three distinct and separable sets of duties and rights are claimed for the pastors of the Church in the first paragraph. They share a unity of purpose: the preservation of "the integrity of the truths of the faith and morals." Beyond that they are quite different:

(1) the duty and right of vigilance lest harm come to the faith or morals of Christ's faithful by means of books or other media. It is a general charge to pastoral watchfulness in order to prevent the believing people from being misled in a world of easy, open, and free communications. The positive support and encouragement of good books, periodicals, and programs is one important way of exercising the responsibility while another is the attempt to point out, criticize, and even discourage publication and media presentations which are perceived to be detrimental;

(2) the duty and right to require that the writings of the faithful which treat of faith or morals be submitted for their evaluation. This is a general claim to the right of prior censorship—it is focused and applied to some specific kinds of publications in the canons which follow. The same claim was made in canon 1384, §1 of the 1917 Code. Note that it applies only to *writings* (not oral or electronic communications) for *publication* (not for private use or circularization) by *Catholics* (not by persons who are not members of the Church) which touch on *faith* or *morals* (not on secular or even broadly religious topics). The claim for any kind of prior censorship must

be seen in the context of and limited by the fundamental freedom of inquiry and expression (c. 218);

(3) the duty and right to reprove writings which are harmful to the true faith or good morals. This speaks of expressing disapproval of someone's written work, offering a critique, and pointing out errors or inadequacies; it does not imply the authority to prevent publication or prohibit use. It would apply to books or articles written by anyone, Catholic or non-Catholic, which are seen to be actually hurtful to faith or morals.

The second paragraph makes clear who the "pastors of the Church" are who possess these duties and rights, and on whose behalf they are to exercise them. They are episcopal prerogatives which can be exercised either individually or collegially when the bishops are gathered in council or in conference. The canon implies that it is the diocesan bishop alone (not retired or titular bishops) who possess this authority, because of the expression "with regard to the Christian faithful committed to their care." But there is nothing to prevent it from being exercised by delegation to others. The highest authority (i.e., that of the pope and college of bishops) in this matter is asserted for the benefit of all the people of God.

Canon 824 — §1. Unless otherwise established, the local ordinary whose permission or approval to publish books is to be sought according to the canons of this title is the proper local ordinary of the author or the ordinary of the place in which the books are published.

§2. Unless otherwise evident, the prescriptions of the canons of this title concerning books are to be applied to any writings whatsoever which are destined for public distribution.

When approval is needed to publish a book, according to the canons which follow, it may be sought from the ordinary of the place where the author resides (cf. cc. 102–106 on domicile and quasi-domicile) or where the publisher's place of business is located. Since the canon uses "local ordinary" rather than "diocesan bishop," the permission could be asked of the vicar general or episcopal vicar as well. The third option given in the 1917 Code, namely, the ordinary of the place of *printing* (*CIC* 1385, §2) has been eliminated. The other requirement stated in the 1917 law and in *Ecclesiae Pastorum* 1, namely, that if the permission is denied by one competent ordinary, a person must not seek it from another without letting him know of the denial, is not restated here. While courtesy or complete candor might counsel that the earlier denial of approval should be brought to the attention of the

second ordinary, canon 65 would not require it because it is not a favor ("gratia") which is being requested but simply a condition for the exercise of a right.

These canons use two words to describe what is asked of the ordinary: "permission" ("licentia") to publish and "approval" ("approbatio") of a publication. *Permission* is required by certain persons (e.g., clerics or religious, cc. 831 and 832) to publish some kinds of writings or to publish in certain periodicals (c. 831) or for books and pamphlets to be displayed or sold in churches (c. 827, §4). *Approval* is required for some specific categories of writings (e.g., editions of the scriptures, c. 825; liturgical books and prayer books, c. 826; catechisms, and some kinds of textbooks). This "approbatio" does not really mean "approval" of the book by the ordinary who grants it, rather it simply signifies that he has found nothing in it which he perceives to be harmful to faith or morals. It is an essentially negative judgment of non-offensiveness, and not an endorsement or recommendation of the book. This "approval," therefore, does not enhance the book or authenticate its contents; it only permits the author to publish the book and, if it is inserted in the book, informs the prospective reader that a pastor of the church deemed the book not to be a danger to faith or morals. It also permits the book to be used as a textbook in a Catholic school or displayed and sold in churches (c. 827).

The mere absence of an "approbatio" from a book which is required to have it does not make that work suspect, much less harmful or erroneous. The author may have neglected to seek the approval; it may have been long delayed or wrongly denied; or it may have been granted but not printed in the book.

Paragraph two states that for the purposes of this title of the Code, unless otherwise evident, the term "books" is understood to include all manner of writings which are to be publicly distributed. It would *not* include materials for private use or for limited circulation, for example, the notes an instructor gives to a class of students, committee reports sent to members of professional societies, study texts, or draft documents of limited circulation, etc. So it is not the size or form of the publication (e.g., book, pamphlet, newspaper, etc.) nor the mode of production (i.e., printed, multilithed, mimeographed, etc.) which matters; the quality which brings the writing within the scope of these canons is its availability to the general public. The source for this paragraph is article 1 of *Ecclesiae Pastorum*; it modified canon 1384, §2 of the 1917 Code.

Canon 825 — §1. Books of the Sacred Scriptures cannot be published unless they have been approved either by the Apostolic See or by the conference of bishops; for their vernacular translations to be pub-

lished it is required that they likewise be approved by the same authority and also annotated with necessary and sufficient explanations.

§2. With the permission of the conference of bishops Catholic members of the Christian faithful can collaborate with separated brothers and sisters in preparing and publishing translations of the Sacred Scriptures annotated with appropriate explanations.

These restrictions are not intended to discourage or impede the publication and distribution of the sacred scriptures; the Second Vatican Council fathers spoke to the contrary: "Easy access to sacred scripture should be provided for all the Christian faithful . . . since the word of God should be available at all times, the Church with maternal concern sees to it that suitable and correct translations are made into different languages, especially from the original texts of the sacred books" (*DV* 22). The concern is for the accuracy of the translations and the adequacy of the accompanying explanations. The first part of paragraph one is concerned with editions of the scriptures in their original languages. The latter part covers translations into modern languages: they are to be approved by the Holy See or an episcopal conference, and they are to be furnished with "necessary and sufficient" explanations.

The first paragraph closely resembles canons 1385, §1 and 1391 of the 1917 Code; it is also based on *Dei Verbum* 22 and 25, and on *Ecclesiae Pastorum* 2.

According to paragraph two of this canon, the ecumenical enterprises, encouraged by *Dei Verbum* 22, are required to receive the permission ("licentia") of the episcopal conference, but no approval of the completed work is necessary.

Canon 826 — §1. The prescriptions of can. 838 are to be observed concerning liturgical books.

§2. For the reprinting in whole or in part of liturgical books as well as their vernacular translation, the ordinary of the place in which they are published must attest that they correspond with the approved edition.

§3. Prayer books for the public or private use of the faithful may not be published without the permission of the local ordinary.

The first paragraph refers to canon 838, §2 which reserves to the Apostolic See the right to publish official liturgical books (in Latin) and to approve their translation into vernacular languages. Episcopal conferences have the authority to prepare translations of liturgical books in their proper languages and to publish them after their approval by the Holy See (c. 838, §3; cf. *SC* 39; Decree of the SCRit on the publication of liturgical books, 27 Jan. 1966; *AAS* 58 [1966], 169–171; *CLD* 6, 811–814; and a

circular letter from the SCDW on translations of sacramental formulas, 25 Oct. 1973; *AAS* 66 [1974], 98–99; *CLD* 8, 67–69). The liturgical books enumerated in the 1966 decree follow: *Roman Breviary, Roman Missal, Roman Ritual, Roman Pontifical, Roman Martyrology,* the *Ceremonial* of Bishops, and books of Gregorian chant.

The second paragraph explains that when liturgical books, or any part of them, are republished or issued in new editions, the ordinary of the place of publication must attest to their fidelity to the original text and/or to the approved edition of the translation. This verification of the accuracy of the liturgical texts is not the same as a permission to publish; there are also the proprietary concerns of copyrights. Paragraph two replaces canon 1390 of the 1917 Code and *Ecclesiae Pastorum* 3.

"Prayer books," as discussed in paragraph three, are non-liturgical devotional books and pamphlets but probably do not include meditation books or reflections written to assist mental prayer or growth in the spiritual life. This paragraph, which requires the ordinary's permission to publish such prayer books, is drawn from canon 1385, §1, 2° of the 1917 Code and from *Ecclesiae Pastorum* 3.

Canon 827 — §1. With due regard for the prescription of can. 775, §2, catechisms and other writings dealing with catechetical formation or their translations need the approval of the local ordinary for their publication.

§2. Books which treat questions of sacred scripture, theology, canon law, church history or which deal with religious or moral disciplines cannot be employed as the textbooks on which instruction is based in elementary, middle or higher schools unless they were published with the approval of the competent ecclesiastical authority or subsequently approved by it.

§3. It is recommended that books which deal with the matters mentioned in §2 be submitted to the judgment of the local ordinary even if they are not employed as textbooks for teaching; the same is true for writings in which something is found to be of special concern to religion or to good moral behavior.

§4. Books and other writings which treat of questions of religion or morals cannot be exhibited, sold, or distributed in churches or oratories unless they were published with the permission of the competent ecclesiastical authority or they were subsequently approved by it.

Canon 775, §2 authorizes episcopal conferences to publish catechisms for their territory, if that seems useful, after the Holy See has given approval to the catechisms. Respecting that prerogative of the conferences, the first paragraph of the canon calls for other catechisms and catechetical writings for instructional use to be approved by the local ordinary before they are published. The "writings dealing with catechetical formation" include workbooks, pamphlets, teachers' manuals, etc., but not writings *about* catechetics or the teaching of religion such as those found in professional journals or periodicals. The canon requires that translations of catechisms from other languages be approved even though the original has already received approval. The apparent reason for this is that the cross-cultural transfer and use of teaching materials may present problems of adaptation and these prospective problems deserve pastoral attention. Paragraph one is based on canon 1385, §1, 2° of the 1917 Code and on *Ecclesiae Pastorum* 4.

Paragraph two says that certain textbooks are required to have the approval of an ordinary in order to be used in Catholic schools. The approval may be given prior to their publication or afterward. Books on sacred scripture, theology, canon law, church history, and those dealing with "religious or moral disciplines" on which classroom instruction is based in elementary and secondary schools and even in colleges are included. The canon envisions manuals or texts which are written and structured so that they serve as the framework and basic reference for courses in these subjects. It does not include other books written on these same topics, even if they are occasionally referred to or assigned as required readings in school courses. The operative category is "textbooks." The vast majority of theology-related writings are neither published as nor actually used for textbooks.

The disciplines enumerated in the canon are to be strictly, not broadly, interpreted because the law itself is clearly one which restricts the free exercise of rights (c. 18). And the textbooks in those disciplines must treat of them entirely or principally, not merely tangentially, in order to fall under the law's requirement.

It can be argued that this requirement (only textbooks in these theology-related areas which are published with ecclesiastical approval can be used in Catholic schools) does not apply to seminaries. Seminaries are not mentioned in the canon, and they are regulated by entirely distinct legislation, both in the 1917 Code (*CIC* Book III, titles XXI, XXII) and in the revised Code (Book II, part I, title III, chapter I). However, the contrary is also arguable (see Urrutia, *P* 65:2–3 [1976], 567–569).

The second paragraph is a modification of canon 1385, §1, 2° (which extended to a far wider range of works) of the 1917 Code, and is taken from *Ecclesiae Pastorum* 4.

Paragraph three encourages those who are publishing in the far wider field of religiously related writings also to seek an ordinary's approval of their works. It imposes no obligation to do so; it is purely a recommendation. And it extends to a wide range of writings: works of sacred scripture, theology, canon law, church history, "religious or moral dis-

ciplines," even when they are not used as instructional textbooks in schools, as well as those "writings in which something is found to be of special concern to religion or to good moral behavior."

This too repeats *Ecclesiae Pastorum* 4, and represents a mitigation of canon 1385, §1, 2°, of the 1917 Code (which *required* previous censorship for all such writings). Since the submission of these writings for ecclesiastical approval is now purely voluntary, the approval itself has little juridic effect (cf. §4). However, it is here encouraged in order to assist the local ordinary in his duty of safeguarding the truths of faith and integrity of morals, in order to assist authors who might profit from such a review of their writings, and in order to give some assurance to prospective readers that nothing doctrinally or morally harmful is contained in those books which have received approval.

Paragraph four states that for books and pamphlets which treat religious or moral issues to be displayed, offered for sale, or given away in churches they must be published with ecclesiastical permission (see c. 824, §1) or approved by such authority subsequent to their publication. Here it is apparently the casual assumption that whatever is displayed or distributed at the church door must be in some sense *official* or *approved* which has led to this requirement for ecclesiastical permission or approval. The permission ("licentia") to publish or the subsequent approval ("approbatio") means no more in these instances than elsewhere; that is, they are essentially negative judgments that the works are not harmful to faith or morals, rather than positive endorsements or recommendations (cf. commentary on c. 824, §1). This final paragraph of canon 827 had no parallel in the 1917 Code; it is taken directly from *Ecclesiae Pastorum* 4.

Canon 828 — It is unlawful to reprint collections of decrees or acts issued by some ecclesiastical authority unless prior permission of this same authority has been obtained and its conditions observed.

The prohibition concerns only the republication of collections of decrees or official acts which have already been published by some church authority. It refers only to collections as such, i.e., a systematically ordered series of documents, and not to individual decrees or instructions. The corresponding canon in the 1917 Code, canon 1389, applied only to collections of the decrees of the Roman Congregations. Here the scope has been expanded to include not only the Roman Congregations, but also particular councils, episcopal conferences, diocesan synods, bishops, general and provincial chapters of religious communities, etc. The purpose of the law apparently is to give the responsible authorities the opportunity to review the republished collection for completeness and accuracy.

Canon 829 — **The approval or permission to publish some work applies to its original text, but not to new editions or translations of it.**

When, in accord with the foregoing canons, a written work is accorded either approval ("approbatio") or permission ("licentia") to be published, these authorizations pertain only to the original text; if the work is translated into another language or reissued in a new edition, these must receive separate authorization. This requirement of a new approval or permission does not apply to reprints of a work which contain no consequential changes from the original. This canon reinstates the law of the 1917 Code, canon 1392, §1, which had been relaxed by *Ecclesiae Pastorum.*

Canon 830 — **§1. The conference of bishops can compile a list of censors known for their knowledge, correct doctrine and prudence who could aid diocesan curias, or it can establish a commission of censors which local ordinaries can consult; however, the right of each local ordinary to entrust the judging of books to persons approved by him still remains intact.**

§2. In undertaking the office, the censor, laying aside any respect for persons, is to consider only the teaching of the Church concerning faith and morals as it is proposed by the ecclesiastical magisterium.

§3. The censor's opinion must be given in writing; if it is favorable, the ordinary, in his own prudent judgment, is to grant the permission to publish, giving his own name and the time and place of the granting of the permission; if, however, he does not grant the permission, the ordinary is to communicate the reasons for his refusal to the author of the work.

This canon regulates the operation of the censorship process for granting ecclesiastical approval or permission to publish written works, when it is required or requested. It does not preclude the ordinary himself from reviewing the materials submitted; he has that authority. But it sets forth the norms for the following: (1) who are to function as censors, (2) the criteria by which they are to make judgments, (3) the communication of that judgment, and (4) the ordinary's consequent concession or denial of the approval. This canon modifies canons 1393 and 1394 of the 1917 Code in several significant ways, and it is taken from *Ecclesiae Pastorum* 6.

According to paragraph one, censors, who can be lay persons, religious, or clerics, may be designated in three different ways:

(1) the conference of bishops may compile a list of persons, outstanding for their knowledge, correct doctrine, and prudence, and make it available to the dioceses in their territory so that those individuals might be employed individually as censors when needed. Such a list should contain persons of diverse expertise (e.g., scripture, theology, canon law, catechetics, etc.) and considerable diversity of background and viewpoint within each discipline, lest a harmful bias or narrowness be imposed on the process because of the limited choice of censors;

(2) the conference of bishops may establish a commission of censors, presumably of persons with the same qualities as aforementioned, which the ordinaries might then consult. This envisions some form of collegiate action and corporate responsibility on the part of the commission; that is the way canonical commissions function (cf. c. 127, §1), otherwise it would not differ from the list of individual censors. Again, the diversity of expertise and background of the persons on such a commission would be vital to its fair and equitable performance;

(3) each local ordinary may commit the judgment about books to persons who are simply approved by him—great freedom is given to the ordinary to choose someone in whom he has confidence to make the necessary evaluation.

These three ways of designating censors are not necessarily disjunctive alternatives; they could and perhaps should function simultaneously and concurrently. Those dioceses which experience a large demand for book approvals and have adequate personnel resources could well rely on the ordinary's own appointed censors. The list provided by the episcopal conference might be of help to those whose resources are more limited, and who receive requests less frequently. A national commission might well be entrusted to review major publications of national significance, e.g., a new biblical translation, a series of catechisms, or religious textbooks, etc. (See Urrutia, *P* 65 [1976:2-3], 544-555.)

Paragraph two presents two criteria for the censor to follow when evaluating a written work, one negative and one positive:

(1) all personal considerations are to be excluded—that is, the censor's favorable or unfavorable disposition toward the author, his or her reputation, school of thought, or previous writings are not to be permitted to enter into the judgment of the book;

(2) the censor is to be mindful only of the Church's teaching on faith and morals as proposed by its teaching authorities—that is, the censor is to judge the book in relationship to the teaching of the Church. Do its contents conform to that teaching, go beyond it, contradict it, ques-

tion it, or are they in areas in which authors are free to disagree, i.e., matters not finally settled or beyond dispute? (See c. 386, §2.) The criterion is more succinctly stated than in the 1917 Code (cf. *CIC* 1393, §2, which comes from Pope Benedict XIV's Apostolic Constitution *Sollicita ac provida*, 9 July 1753, #17, *CICFontes* II, 411, a passage on the distinction between firm teachings and variable opinions that is well worth reading), but the aim is the same; it comes directly from *Ecclesiae Pastorum* 6. Lest this simple criterion lead censors to harsh and narrow judgments, it is important to recall the Second Vatican Council's teachings on the critical need for dialogue with various cultures and with "the many voices of our age," for new theological investigations (*AG* 22; *GS* 44, 54, 62), and on the hierarchy of truths (*UR* 11).

The censor's role is limited to this doctrinal evaluation; normally he or she is not called upon to express opinions on the opportuneness or propriety of permitting the work to be published. A somewhat wider range for discretionary judgment might be permitted to the ordinary.

Paragraph three states that the censor is to give his or her judgment about the book to the ordinary in writing. The importance of this written record is obvious, especially in the event that approval is not given, because then the reasons for the denial must be given to the author.

If the censor's opinion is favorable, the ordinary then makes his own prudent judgment about permitting the publication of the work. This, too, is to be given in writing, with the name of the ordinary and the time and place of the concession mentioned, so that it may be printed in the book, if that is the author's wish. The name of the censor need not appear either in the grant of permission or in the book.

Is the ordinary bound by the judgment of the censor? No, his is an independent, prudential judgment and it may override the view of his appointed censor (or even of the national commission of censors, if he consulted it, in accord with §1). Indeed, he may act as his own censor.

May the ordinary deny the permission to publish for reasons other than the doctrinal content of the work? Commentators on the 1917 Code thought so, and this revised law speaks of "his own prudent judgment," but it is hard to imagine a concern that would justify such an action. Publishing one's written works is closely allied to a very basic freedom of investigation (cf. c. 218) and discussion (*GS* 62), and any restriction or inhibition of the free exercise of rights must be strictly interpreted (c. 18). Similarly, when there is a matter of delay on the part of the censor or the ordinary in rendering their decisions or a question of a fee for the process or a burden of proof when the decision is a difficult or doubtful one, every consideration must be given to the author; the fundamental freedom of expression must be honored in practice.

Canon 831 — §1. Without a just and reasonable cause the Christian faithful are not to write anything for newspapers, magazines or periodicals which are accustomed to attack openly the Catholic religion or good morals; clerics and members of religious institutes are to do so only with the permission of the local ordinary.

§2. It is the responsibility of the conference of bishops to establish norms concerning the requirements for clerics and members of religious institutes to take part in radio or television programs which deal with questions concerning Catholic teaching or morals.

Catholics should not write in papers, magazines, or periodicals which openly attack the Church or good moral life, unless there is some just and reasonable cause for doing so. The canon makes explicit what is only common sense—one ought not cooperate with or lend one's name to those who are actively opposed to our faith community or the good of society, unless there is some good reason for doing so, e.g., refuting errors or arguing for the truth. Lay persons may make their own responsible judgment about the justifying reasons; clerics and religious are to ask permission of the ordinary of the place. This does not refer to the approval ("approbatio") of what the cleric or religious is going to write; it is simply a permission to write (cf. c. 824, §1). The first paragraph of the canon is a modification of canon 1386 of the 1917 Code, and is taken directly from *Ecclesiae Pastorum* 5. This revised law adds the word "openly" ("manifesto") to the descriptive phrase "accustomed to attack" when describing the publications. This limits it somewhat; it applies to only those publications which are well known for their stance, about whose character there can be no doubt.

Paragraph two recognizes the importance of the electronic media as well as the fact that they transcend diocesan boundaries. It asks the bishops' conferences to issue norms on the requirements for clerics and religious to take part in radio and television programs about Catholic teaching or morals. The norms are not to be for lay persons even though engaged in the same enterprises. The canon refers to those who conduct or appear on such programs regularly; it does not seem to include interviews or occasional appearances. (Compare with c. 772, §2.)

Canon 832 — In order for members of religious institutes to publish writings dealing with questions of religion or morals they also need the permission of their major superior in accord with the norm of their constitutions.

This canon requires religious to obtain permission of their superiors (whoever is designated in the constitution of the community) when they wish to publish something on religion or morality. It does not imply prior censorship and approval of the writings; it is simply permission ("licentia") to write. The canon parallels the even more restrictive canon 1385, §3 of the 1917 Code, and comes from *Ecclesiae Pastorum* 5. The purpose of the law seems to be more the good order of religious life than the safeguarding of the faithful in matters of doctrine; it serves to undergird the requirements of community constitutions rather than to impose new obligations. *Ecclesiae Pastorum* 5 contained a prior section pertaining to clerics, who, "because of their office and special responsibility" were earnestly requested to obtain permission from the ordinary for such writings, but that section was eliminated and this rule for religious retained.

TITLE V
THE PROFESSION OF FAITH*
[c. 833]

Canon 833 — The following persons are obliged to make a profession of faith personally in accord with a formula approved by the Apostolic See:

1° in the presence of its president or his delegate, all persons who take part with either a deliberative or consultative vote in an ecumenical or particular council, in a synod of bishops, or in a diocesan synod; the president takes it in the presence of the council or synod;

2° those promoted to the cardinalatial dignity, in accord with the statutes of the sacred college;

3° in the presence of one delegated by the Apostolic See, all persons promoted to the episcopacy and those who are equivalent to a diocesan bishop;

4° in the presence of the college of consultors, a diocesan administrator;

5° in the presence of the diocesan bishop or his delegate, vicars general, episcopal vicars and vicars judicial;

6° in the presence of the local ordinary or his delegate and at the beginning of their term of office, pastors, the rector of a seminary, and the professors of theology and philosophy in seminaries; those to be promoted to the order of diaconate;

7° in the presence of the grand chancellor or, in his absence, in the presence of the local ordinary, or in the presence of their delegates, the rector of an ecclesiastical or Catholic university at the beginning of the rector's term of office; in the presence of the rector, if the rector is a priest, or the local ordinary, or their delegates and at the beginning of their term of office, teachers in any universities whatsoever who teach disciplines which deal with faith or morals;

8° the superiors in clerical religious institutes and societies of apostolic life in accord with the norm of the constitutions.

The public manifestations of personal belief, of which this canon speaks, are acts of prayerful worship arising from the gift and virtue of faith, but they are here made juridical requirements on the occasion of the assumption of certain offices or functions related to the Church's teaching mission. The outward expression of faith in the form of a recital of a creed gives witness to the community of the authentic belief of the person who is to perform the teaching role. The practice is rooted in the ancient custom of requiring a profession of faith before ordination; it was greatly expanded by the Council of Trent (a. 1563; cc. 1, 12 of the *decretum de reformatione* of Sess. 24; c. 2 of the *decretum de reformatione* of Sess. 25) as an instrument of the counter-Reformation in an effort to safeguard and build up the Catholic faith. This single canon replaces and modifies canons 1406–1408 of the 1917 Code.

The obligation to make the required profession of faith falls directly on those persons listed in the canon; however, commentators on the 1917 Code thought that those who are to witness or receive the professions were also obliged by the law to do so. The list of those obliged to make the profession is obviously taxative, and should not be expanded or extended to others by analogy; it is also to be strictly interpreted (c. 18).

The formula for the profession of faith was printed in the front of the 1917 Code. An abbreviated formula for the profession of faith was issued by the Sacred Congregation for the Doctrine of the Faith in 1967 (*AAS* 59 [1967], 1058). It eliminates the elements of an oath or promise and returns the profession to an affirmation of belief based on the Nicene-Constantinopolitan Creed. (See profession at end of this volume.)

The profession is made orally in the presence of the one designated to witness it, or a delegate of that person when the canon permits. It may be made individually or in a group, and when several are making the profession at the same time, either they may all read through it together or one may read it aloud and all affirm it at the end.

---

*A note on the "Oath Against Modernism": Pope Pius X in 1910 ordered that an oath against modernism and a profession of faith be made by many of the same persons mentioned in c. 833 and others (*Motu proprio Sacrorum Antistitum*, 1 Sept. 1910, *AAS* 2 [1910], 655). It was not contained in the 1917 Code, but a decree of the Sacred Congregation of the Holy Office in 1918 declared that the prescriptions "are not mentioned in the Code because they are of their nature temporary and transitory; but that, since the virus of Modernism has not ceased to spread, these prescriptions must remain in full force until the Holy See decrees otherwise" (*AAS* 10 [22 March 1918], 136; *CLD* 1, 50). Some seventy-five years later the "virus" seems to have run its course, and the observance of the prescriptions seems to have fallen into desuetude.

Perhaps the most significant change in this revised canon is its extension, in number seven, to the presidents and teachers in Catholic colleges and universities; canon 1406, §1, 8° of the 1917 Code pertained only to "pontifical," i.e., canonically established, universities and faculties. The instructors covered are only those teaching disciplines related to faith or morals. (Cf. the comments on the applicability of cc. 807–814 to North American institutions of higher education.)

The seminary personnel subject to this law in number six are the rector and professors of theology and philosophy. This may be interpreted strictly so as to exclude these in the auxiliary disciplines, e.g., scripture, canon law, church history, liturgy, pastoral studies, etc., but the Code Commission intended for the term "theology" to include areas related to theology; for that reason they eliminated the explicit mention of canon law (cf. 1981 *Rel*, p. 188).

The law obliges neither non-Catholics (c. 11) nor those already holding offices or appointments at the time the revised Code went into effect (c. 9).

Lay persons and women and men religious can be delegated to witness the professions of faith by the ordinary of the place or the chancellor of the university in numbers six and seven, because the canon does not limit the delegation; canon 1407 of the 1917 Code which excluded lay witnesses, has been dropped; and the act of witnessing a profession of faith is not an exercise of jurisdiction. (Some authors thought it was a juridical act. Cf. Canavan, *Profession of Faith*, p. 56.) Rectors, provosts, deans, and department chairpersons would appear to be the most appropriate delegates for this purpose.

There is no penalty attached to the omission of this profession of faith. Canon 2403 of the 1917 Code, which threatened loss of income and of office for neglecting the profession of faith, is not part of the revised Code, and no other penalty is even suggested.

Finally, the obstacle to contrary custom in this matter has been removed. Canon 1408 of the 1917 Code reproved any contrary customs, thus preventing the emergence of a legitimate practice of noncompliance with this law. The omission of this provision from the revised law leaves open the possibility of particular (local) customs presently in existence (cc. 5, 28) or to arise in the future (cc. 24–25), contrary to these requirements for professions of faith.

BIBLIOGRAPHY

(In addition to the sources cited in the commentary, the following works might prove helpful.)

On Vatican II Council Documents

Vorgrimler, H. *Commentary on the Documents of Vatican II.* 5 vols. New York: Herder & Herder, 1967–1969.

On the Canons

Connolly, M. "Some Orientations on De Munere Docendi." *CLSAP* (1982): 219–232.

Nedungatt, G. "The Schema De Magisterio Ecclesiastico." *Nu* (1980): 55–75.

Schmitz, H. "Die Beauftragung zum Predigtdienst." *AkK* (1980): 45–63.

Urrutia, F.J. *De Ecclesiae Munere Docendi.* Rome: Gregorian University, 1983.

———. "De magisterio ecclesiastico." *P* 68 (1979): 2, 327–367.

On the Teaching Authority

Alberigo, G. "Dal bastone alla misericordia: Il magistero nel cattolicesimo contemporaneo, 1830–1980." *Cristianesimo nella Storia* (1981): 487–521.

Crowley, L.J. "The Teaching Power and Mission of the Church." *Stud Can* (1975): 215–234.

Directory on the Pastoral Ministry of Bishops. SCB, 31 May 1973. Ottawa: Canadian Catholic Conference, 1974.

Dulles, A. "The Magisterium in History: A Theological Reflection." *CS* 17 (1978): 2, 264–281.

——— "The Teaching Authority of Bishops' Conferences." *America* 148 (1983): 453–455.

Horvath, T. "A Structural Understanding of the Magisterium of the Church." *Science et Esprit* (1977): 283–311.

Huizing, P. "Magistère: Pouvoir ou Témoignage?" *RDC* (1975): 199–206.

Peters, E. *Heresy and Authority in Medieval Europe.* Philadelphia: University of Pennsylvania Press, 1980.

Vela Sanchez, L. "De Magisterio Ecclesiastico en Derecho Canonico." *Con* 117 (1976): 117–127.

Weis, N. "Quaedam de laicorum prophetico munere in Ecclesia iuxta Concilium Vaticanum II." *P* 70 (1981): 429–448.

On Infallibility

Chirico, P. *Infallibility: Crossroads of Doctrine.* Kansas City: Sheed, Andrews & McMeel, 1977.

Empie; Murphy; and Burgess, eds. *Teaching Authority and Infallibility in the Church.* Minneapolis: Augsburg, 1978.

Kirvan, J., ed. *The Infallibility Debate.* New York: Paulist Press, 1971.

Tierney, B. *Origins of Papal Infallibility, 1150–1350.* Leiden: Brill, 1972.

Title I: The Ministry of the Divine Word

Preaching

Foley, N., ed. *Preaching and the Non-Ordained.* Collegeville, Minn.: Liturgical Press, 1983.

Fulfilled in Your Hearing: The Homily in the Sunday Assembly. Washington: USCC, 1982.

Catechetics

Dalglish, W. *Models for Catechetical Ministry in the Rural Parish.* Washington: NCDD, 1981.

General Catechetical Directory. SCC, 17 June 1971. Washington: USCC, 1971.

Hater, R. *The Role of a Diocesan Religious Education/Catechetical Office.* Washington: NCDD, 1981.

Marthaler, B. *Catechetics in Context: Notes and Commentary on the General Catechetical Directory.* Huntington, Ind.: Our Sunday Visitor, 1973.

———. *Sharing the Light of Faith: An Official Commentary.* Washington: USCC, 1981.

Mayr, M., ed. *Modern Masters of Religious Education.* Birmingham, Ala.: Religious Education Press, 1983.

Parent, N., ed. *Christian Adulthood: A Catechetical Resource.* Washington: USCC, 1982.

Sharing the Light of Faith: National Catechetical Directory for the Catholics of the United States. Washington: USCC, 1979.

Sharing the Light of Faith: Norms and Guidelines for Catechetical Planners. Washington: USCC, 1980.

Title II: Missionary Action of the Church

Dammertz, V. "Die Ausführungsbestimmungen zum Konzilsdekrete über die Missionstätigkeit der Kirche." *AkK* (1967): 45–67.

Greco, J. "De ordinatione activitatis missionalis." *P* 55 (1966): 289–314.

Jacqueline, B. "L'Organisation de la coopération missionaire après le Concile Oecuménique Vatican II." *AC* (1974): 125–142.

Lombardia, P. "El estatuto jurídico del catecumeno segun los textos del Vaticano II." *IC* (1966): 529–562.

Nebreda, A. "The Mission of the Church and Missionary Activity." *Teaching All Nations* (1972): 163–177.

Reuter, A. "De novis rationibus iuris missionalis a Concilio Vaticano II inductis vel indictis." *Euntes Docete* (1975): 293–315.

Rossignol, R. "Vatican II and the Missionary Responsibility of the Particular Church." *Indian Theological Studies* (1980): 34–46.

Urrutia, F.J. "Catechumenatus iuxta Concilium Oecumenicum Vaticanum secundum." *P* (1974): 121–144.

Title III: Catholic Education

Carrier, H. "Scholarum libertas in societate hodierna." *P* (1973): 467–484.

Catholic Higher Education and the Pastoral Mission of the Church. Washington: USCC, 1981.

The Catholic School. SCCE, 19 March 1977. Washington: USCC, 1977.

"Déclaration, L'Université Catholique dans le monde moderne." Congres des Univ. Cath. *P* (1973): 625–657.

McGrath, J. *Catholic Institutions in the United States: Canonical and Civil Law Status.* Washington: Catholic University Press, 1968.

Maida, A. *Ownership, Control and Sponsorship of Catholic Institutions: A Practical Guide.* Harrisburg, Pa.: Pennsylvania Catholic Conference, 1975.

Moots, P., and Gaffney, E.M. *Church and Campus: Legal Issues in Religiously Affiliated Higher Education.* Notre Dame: University of Notre Dame Press, 1979.

Schmitz, H. "Revision des Kirlichen Hochschulrechts." *AkK* (1974): 69–100.

Sullivan, F. "Universitas Catholica in mundo hodierno." *P* (1973): 609–623.

To Teach as Jesus Did: A Pastoral Message on Catholic Education. Washington: NCCB, 1972.

Wade, F. *The Catholic University and the Faith.* Milwaukee: Marquette University Press, 1978.

On the Magisterium and Theologians

Alfaro, J. "Problema theologicum de munere Theologiae respectu Magisterii." *Gregorianum* 57 (1976): 39–79.

Congar, Y. "Bref historique des formes du 'magistère' et des ses relations avec les docteurs." *Revue des sciences philosophiques et théologiques* 60 (1976): 99–112.

Curran, C. "Academic Freedom: The Catholic University and Catholic Theology." *The Furrow* (1979): 739–745.

Curran, C., and Hunt, R. *Dissent In and For the Church: Theologians and Humanae Vitae.* New York: Sheed & Ward, 1969.

Hamer, J. "In the Service of the Magisterium: The Evolution of a Congregation." *J* (1977): 340–357.

Hunt, J., and Connolly, T. *The Responsibility of Dissent: The Church and Academic Freedom.* New York: Sheed & Ward, 1969.

The Magisterium, The Theologian and The Educator. CS 17 (1978): 2, 147–309.

O'Donovan, L., ed. *Cooperation Between Theologians and the Ecclesiastical Magisterium.* Washington: CLSA, 1982.

Potvin, T. "Guidelines for a Working Relationship between the Pastoral Magisterium and the Theologians in the Church." *Stud Can* 15 (1981): 13–43.

Provost, J. "Canonical Mission and Catholic Universities." *America* 142 (1980): 22, 475–477.

Rahner, K. "The Teaching Office of the Church in the Present-Day Crisis of Authority." *Theological Investigations,* vol. 12, 3–30. New York: Seabury, 1974.

———. "Theology and Teaching Office." *Doctrine and Life* (1981): 622–634.

Sulumeti, P. "The Juridical System of 'Mandatum.'" *African Ecclesiastical Review* (1973): 316–328.

"Theses de Magisterii Ecclesiastici et Theologiae ad invicem relatione." Commissio Internationalis Theologiae, 6 June 1976. *Gregorianum* 57 (1976): 549–563.

Thompson, W. "Authority and Magisterium in Recent Catholic Thought." *CS* (1977): 278–298.

Title IV: Instruments of Social Communication and Specifically Books

Baragli, E. "Una constante preoccupazione pastorale della Chiesa." *La Civiltá Cattolica* 126 (1975): 2, 436–449.

Bortolotti, R. "Librorum prohibitio iuxta notificationem S.C. Pro D.F., die 14 iunii 1966." *P* (1967): 116–138.

Echeverría, L. "La vigilancia episcopal sobre la publicación de libros." *Revista española de Derecho canónico* (1975): 341–372.

Nessels, W. "Prior Censorship and Human Rights." *J* (1967): 58–67.

Toconel, P. "S.D. pro D.F. decretum de Ecclesiae Pastorum vigilantia supra libros." *Apol* (1975): 5–11.

Urrutia, F.J. "De limitibus libertatis scribendi fidelium iuxta legem canonicam." *P* 65 (1976): 529–583.

Title V: The Profession of Faith

Canavan, W.J. *Profession of Faith.* Catholic University Canon Law Dissertation No. 151. Washington: Catholic University, 1942.

Lahache, J. "Profession de Foi." *DDC* 7:342–345.

Madden, J. "The Profession of Faith." *Australasian Catholic Record* (1968): 137–146.

BOOK IV

THE OFFICE OF SANCTIFYING IN THE CHURCH

[cc. 834–1253]

Frederick R. McManus

The canons of this Fourth Book of the Code govern the liturgical life and celebrations of the Latin Church. A small number of canons refer to other devotional practices of the Christian community; these practices are understood to be closely related to the liturgy, but they are not a formal part of the Church's public and official corporate worship.

Although Book IV may be seen as a very selective collection of liturgical laws, that term is generally reserved, somewhat more narrowly, for the juridic norms that govern the actual celebration of the sacraments and other services. This is the sense of canon 2 (of both the 1917 Code and the 1983 Code): for the most part the Code does not define or determine the rites themselves, and all the liturgical laws falling outside the Code retain their full canonical force—unless they are contradicted, and so abrogated, by the Code.

The liturgical laws common to the universal Latin Church are to be found chiefly in the official Roman liturgical books, both in their introductions, or *praenotanda,* and in the rubrical directives which describe the rites and accompany the appointed texts. They are also in related juridic documents, e.g., apostolic constitutions and letters.[1] Particular liturgical laws are found in the corresponding liturgical books of various nations and regions, as well as in decrees and statutes of dioceses and bodies or groups of particular churches which follow the Roman rite. In addition, although the Code does not regularly advert to this, there are non-Roman rites of the Latin Church, the most notable now being the Ambrosian rite of Milan.[2] Such non-Roman Western rites, whether of particular churches or of religious orders,[3] were preserved in the post-Tridentine reform of the Roman liturgical books, provided they had at least two hundred years' standing. Today, although diminished in number and in influence, these rites too may have their own liturgical books and laws. Together the Roman rite and the non-Roman rites of the Latin Church are called the Latin rites.

The norms of Book IV, unlike the larger body of uncodified liturgical legislation, are more often concerned with the liturgy from the viewpoint of its extrinsic discipline, e.g., canonical requirements for ministers or recipients of sacraments or for proper times or places of celebration. In other words, the canons are generally not ritual regulations and are distinct from them. As is evident, however, such a distinction can be made only imperfectly, and many canons of Book IV (as in the corresponding parts of *CIC*)[4] do affect liturgical celebrations directly. Such canons are somewhat basic norms rather than rubrical directions.

The distinction explains why Book IV does not deal with all parts of the liturgy. Such significant elements as the church year, music, and art are not directly touched, nor is there any effort to give a balanced or proportionate treatment of each sacrament or other rite. Because the canons do not include the body of liturgical laws, the commentary that follows offers some guidance to such norms, so that the canons themselves may be understood in their broader context.

Comparison with the 1917 Code

Book IV is a radical departure from the corresponding Book III of the 1917 Code, not so much in the content of the canons themselves as in their selection and arrangement.

Following the medieval categories of the canon law, which treated persons and things separately, Book III of the 1917 Code (*CIC* 726–1551) dealt with such diverse "things" as simony, sacraments, sacred places (including funeral rites) and sacred times, divine worship, the Church's teaching office, benefices, and church property. The revised codification follows instead the categories accepted by Vatican II, namely, the *munera,* or offices, of (1) teaching (now Book III), (2) sanctifying (Book IV), and (3) ruling (Book II, principally in part II); the canons on church property now constitute Book V.

This pattern of the revised Code confines Book IV, selectively, to the church order affecting the total liturgical and sacramental life of the Christian people, with the important exception already mentioned: the largest number of liturgical laws lies entirely outside the Code.

Second, Book IV reflects a major simplification in the quantity as well as in the substance of the canons; it reduces about six hundred canons of the 1917 Code to little more than four hundred, and this despite the fact that the number of canons on marriage is only slightly smaller than before.

---

[1] The source material for existing, postconciliar liturgical legislation of the universal Latin Church is collected and translated into English in: International Commission on English in the Liturgy, *Documents on the Liturgy, 1963–1979: Conciliar, Papal, and Curial Texts* (Collegeville: Liturgical Press, 1982), from which translations below are taken.

[2] See A.A. King, *Liturgies of the Primatial Sees* (Milwaukee: The Bruce Publishing Co., 1957).

[3] See A.A. King, *Liturgies of the Religious Orders* (Milwaukee: The Bruce Publishing Co., 1955).

[4] *CIC* is used in this commentary to refer to the 1917 *Codex Iuris Canonici.* Canons which are referred to *without CIC* are those of the present, revised Code of 1983.

Much of this simplification has been achieved by the elimination of minute prescriptions and by leaving to the liturgical laws outside the Code (and/or to particular law) matters not necessary in the codification. Sometimes the reduction in the number of canons suggests the lesser significance of the matter treated or the changed circumstances of Christian life. For example, canons on indulgences have been reduced from twenty-six (*CIC* 911–936) to six (cc. 992–997); the eight canons on the reservation of sins or cases in the sacrament of penance (*CIC* 893–900) have been suppressed.

In general, the revision of the canons has been influenced by the decrees of Vatican II, by the reformed liturgical books, or *Ordines,* of the 1960s and 1970s and other implementing documents of the postconciliar period, and by the pastoral and other principles which governed the whole revision.[5] The most significant departure from the 1917 Code, however, is the rearrangement, or reordering, of canons.

Order of the Canons

The sequence of canons in the 1917 Code treated the seven sacraments of the Church, not as the liturgical mysteries celebrated by the Christian community but almost exclusively as the means of sanctification provided by God through the ministry of the ordained. Thus it was only after the canons on the sacraments (and sacred places and times) that divine worship itself was taken up (beginning with *CIC* 1255).

A similar sequence was originally planned for the revised Code. In the first schema circulated for comment by the episcopate, the seven sacraments were again treated as in the 1917 Code.[6] An initial canon identified them as "the principal means of sanctification and salvation" but made no reference to their being liturgical acts of worship. Another schema, for sacred places, sacred times, and divine cult, again retained the sequence (and orientation) of the former Code.[7]

In the light of comments regarding the schemata and, even more significant, the explicit teaching of Vatican II, the sequence was reversed. The liturgy is first treated as a whole, then (1) "The Sacraments" (cc. 840–1165), (2) "Other Acts of Divine Worship" (cc. 1166–1204), and (3) "Sacred Places and Times" (cc. 1205–1253). These three headings constitute the three parts of Book IV.

This order flows from a critical correction and amplification of the earlier teaching of Pius XII on the liturgy that occurred during Vatican II. In the 1947 encyclical *Mediator Dei,* the liturgy was defined principally in terms of the public worship offered to the Father by the Church, that is, by Christ and his members.[8] The 1963 conciliar constitution on the liturgy, *Sacrosanctum Concilium*—which along with the 1965 pastoral constitution *Gaudium et Spes* (for the canons on marriage) mainly influenced Book IV—enlarged this definition to embrace both the sanctification of humankind and the ecclesial acts of cult offered by Christ the Head and his members.[9] Moreover, it formally redefined the seven sacraments not only as signifying the divine grace which they impart by the action of Christ (*ex opere Christi*) but as sacraments of faith, which "make people holy, build up the Body of Christ, and give worship to God." They were described as celebrations (as well as ministrations) which "most effectively dispose the faithful to receive this [divine] grace in a fruitful manner, to worship God rightly, and to practice charity."[10]

This development is reflected in the fundamental doctrinal canons of Book IV, 834, §1 and 840, which are derived from *Sacrosanctum Concilium* 7 and 59 respectively. It is reflected to a lesser degree in the title of Book IV, "The Office of Sanctifying in the Church." While this phrasing may at first glance appear to restrict the canons to the action of God through the Church upon the faithful, the canons themselves embrace both sanctification and worship, or cult—that is, the totality of public liturgy. The Latin expression in the title (*munus sanctificandi*) is intended to include the entirety of the Church's "exercise of the priestly office of Jesus Christ." This office of sanctifying, which is regularly mentioned in conciliar documents along with the office of teaching and the office of ruling, has itself a twofold meaning: *sanctificare* means both "to make holy" and "to glorify the Holy [God]" and was thus considered a suitable term for the divine liturgy as defined by Vatican II. In the title of Book IV, as well as in the arrangement and content of the canons, sanctification is understood to include worship, or cult.

Nature of Liturgical Law

In recent years there has been considerable discussion, especially among English-speaking commentators, about the nature (or style) and weight of the liturgical law. In part this is a response to the greater flexibility and openness to adaptation that have been written into the liturgical norms themselves; in part it reflects the pastoral situation can-

[5] "Principia Quae Codicem Iuris Canonici Recognitionem Dirigant," *Comm* 1 (1969), 77–85.

[6] ComCICRec, *Schema documenti pontificii quo disciplina canonica de sacramentis recognoscitur* (Typis Polyglottis Vaticanis, 1975).

[7] ComCICRec, *Schema canonum libri IV de Ecclesiae munere sanctificandi* (Typis Polyglottis Vaticanis, 1977).

[8] Nov. 30, 1947: *AAS* 39 (1947), 528–529.

[9] *SC,* Dec. 4, 1963, n. 7: *DOL* 7. (Since *SC* is the first document in *DOL*, numbers 1–131 of *DOL* correspond to numbers of articles of *SC.*)

[10] *SC* 59.

onized in the conciliar texts and especially the style of the constitution on the liturgy.

First of all, it is clear and certain that the canons (including the seminal c. 2, which indicates that liturgical laws, though outside the codification, continue in full canonical force) and the liturgical books themselves consider such norms as an integral and preceptive part of the ecclesiastical or canon law. The ordinary canonical principles of promulgation and interpretation and the canonical institutes such as custom and dispensation are equally applicable to the liturgical laws. At the same time many of the liturgical laws may be categorized in traditional terms as non-preceptive or directive only (or even as simply descriptive of rites) or as facultative, that is, as offering choices and options. Their great number and diversity—one reason why they are not easily subject to codification or inclusion in the Code of the Latin Church—require, even more than other parts of the canon law, an appreciation of the comparative weight of the form they take: all the way from a conciliar constitution to minor instructions and even simple declarations of an authoritative kind.[11] These forms seem to go far beyond the relatively simple forms determined in the general norms in the titles of the Code on laws (cc. 7–22), custom (cc. 23–28), and general decrees and instructions (cc. 29–34). This is especially true because of the characteristic form of the liturgical books, their introductions (praenotanda), and rubrics which are considered below.

Nevertheless the liturgical law is considered to be almost radically different from other parts of the canon law, both in the matters affected and in its style. This is suggested even by the titles of recent studies: New Liturgy, New Laws[12] by R.K. Seasoltz and Liturgical Law: New Style, New Spirit by T. Richstatter.[13]

The liturgical celebrations of sacraments and other services are actions implicating the whole person of each member of the Christian assembly; they are matters of the most intimate faith and piety, which are articulated communally. The norms that govern them are more aesthetic and artistic than juridic or canonical. Since the celebrations are to be the authentic worship of the Church as it is gathered in a particular place at a particular time, accomplished in forms and words that are both personal and impersonal, individual and common, the liturgical norms easily come into conflict with actual situations. The constitution on the liturgy followed the traditional pattern of expository and doctrinal introduction followed by dispositive

norms, and the norms themselves were frequently hortatory and broadly stated. This pattern has been followed in the revised liturgical books and norms which the constitution mandated. Thus, along with the historical, ecclesiological, and theological reappraisal of the Church's liturgy, it was inevitable that a different spirit would inform the liturgical laws themselves.

Whether the axiom "lex orandi, lex credendi" is taken to mean that the liturgy is a norm of faith—as it is surely a principal theological source—or is taken to mean, according to Pius XII, that the law of belief should determine the liturgical text and rite,[14] it is evident that the liturgy is a fit subject for authoritative legislation: at every point it involves the Christian faith which it proclaims; it is a touchstone of the communion of churches and of the congregations of the particular or local church; it is the preeminent social and public action of the Christian community; it is of the nature of rite or ritual, with recurring forms and patterns that are evidently subject to canonical discipline and normative custom.

In summary, while the liturgical celebration is not easily governed or moderated because it is ultimately the celebration of the mysteries in the Spirit, the laws affecting this celebration are urged with all the force of the rest of the canon law. The renewed tone and spirit that infuse them, however, and the relative weight of their demands in the face of conflicting pastoral expectations have led to a legitimate openness, a recognition of the religious value of diversity, and an invitation to cultural and other adaptation. All this must be kept in mind in the interpretation of the canons themselves and all other kinds of liturgical law, with a special concern not only for the immediate text and context but also for the larger context of celebration.

Liturgical Books

The recurrent sources listed for the canons on divine worship and sacraments in the 1917 Code are the Roman liturgical books "restored by decree of the holy council of Trent and issued by command of" several popes after that council. The norms of those modern liturgical books became in some instances the canons of the 1917 Code. After its promulgation, it became necessary to revise the introductory notes, or praenotanda, of the Roman Ritual, in instances where the canon law had been changed; this was done in an edition of 1925. Once again in the present codification, the Roman liturgical books, this time as "restored by decree of the holy ecumenical council of Vatican II and promulgated by authority of Pope Paul VI," are a major source for the canons of Book IV, along with papal

[11]F.R. McManus, "Liturgical Law and Difficult Cases," W 48 (1974), 347–366.

[12]Collegeville: Liturgical Press, 1980.

[13]Chicago: Franciscan Herald Press, 1977. See also W. Kelley, "The Authority of Liturgical Laws," J 28 (1968), 397–424; J.M. Huels, "The Interpretation of Liturgical Law," W 55 (1981), 218–237.

[14]Mediator Dei: AAS 39 (1947), 540–541.

and curial documents issued during the period beginning in 1964.

The post-Tridentine liturgical books, exclusive of the books of chant such as the *Roman Gradual* and the *Roman Antiphonal,* were formally enumerated in 1946 as the *Roman Breviary, Roman Missal, Roman Ritual, Roman Pontifical, Roman Martyrology, Ceremonial of Bishops, Memoriale Rituum* (for smaller churches), *Octavarium* (for the offices of local octaves), and the collection of *Decreta Authentica* of the Congregation of Sacred Rites.[15] Of these the *Roman Missal* for the Eucharist (1570), the *Roman Pontifical* (1596) and *Roman Ritual* (1614) for the other sacraments and rites, and the *Roman Breviary* for the daily prayer of the Church (1568) were the most important and basic.

These four Roman liturgical books, with the exception of the ritual, had been imposed as binding upon the whole Latin Church. An exception, to preserve the other major rites of the West such as Ambrosian, Mozarabic, and Gallican, as well as the uses of many particular churches and religious orders, was made in cases in which a different rite had been in use for at least two hundred years.

Aside from the considerable increase in the number of saints' feasts, the four principal liturgical books of the post-Tridentine period were not greatly altered until the beginning of the twentieth century. Even then, in the reform initiated by Pope Pius X, the revisions were principally by way of the simplification of regulations, and no significant ritual changes were made in the celebrations which the liturgical books govern by their texts and rubrics. The reform was taken up again by authority of Pius XII with the establishment of a commission for this purpose in 1948, and a series of revisions resulted in the publication of several sections of liturgical books. When John XXIII undertook the convening of Vatican II, he placed the unfinished work of the reform commission on the conciliar agenda. Finally, in the conciliar constitution on the liturgy a reform of all the Roman liturgical books was formally decreed, along with specific norms and directives for that reform and laws governing the further adaptation of the liturgical books, once the revision could be completed.[16]

The several parts of the Roman liturgical books were prepared by the Consilium for the Implementation of the Constitution on the Liturgy (1964) and promulgated by authority of Paul VI, in decrees of the Congregation of Sacred Rites (until 1969), later by the Sacred Congregation for Divine Worship (1969–1975), and still later by the Sacred Congregation for Sacraments and Divine Worship.

The revised *Roman Missal* appeared in three parts: the *Order of Mass* (promulgated April 6, 1969), the *Lectionary for Mass* (order of readings,

May 25, 1969), and *Missal* (presidential prayers or sacramentary, April 3, 1969). The Roman Calendar, for both the Eucharist and the Liturgy of the Hours, was promulgated March 21, 1969.

The *Roman Ritual* includes several parts (formerly called titles in the one-volume ritual of 1614): *Rite of Marriage* (March 19, 1969), *Rite of Baptism for Children* (May 15, 1969), *Rite of Funerals* (August 15, 1969), *Rite of Religious Profession* (February 2, 1970), *Rite of Christian Initiation of Adults* (January 6, 1972), *Rite of Anointing and Pastoral Care of the Sick* (December 7, 1972), *Holy Communion and Worship of the Eucharist outside Mass* (June 21, 1973), and *Rite of Penance* (December 2, 1973). The section on blessings has not yet appeared.

The *Roman Pontifical* includes the *Ordination of Deacons, Priests, and Bishops* (August 15, 1968), *Rite of Consecration to a Life of Virginity* (May 31, 1970), *Rite of Blessing an Abbot or Abbess* (November 9, 1970), *Rite of the Blessing of Oils, Rite of Consecrating the Chrism* (December 3, 1970), *Rite of Confirmation* (August 22, 1971), *Rite of Institution of Readers and Acolytes, etc.* (December 3, 1972), and *Dedication of a Church and an Altar* (May 29, 1977). The related volume, the *Ceremonial of Bishops,* has not yet appeared.

The Liturgy of the Hours was promulgated April 11, 1971. It replaces the *Roman Breviary* and gives the Divine Office according to the Roman rite.

Corresponding liturgical books in English and in the other languages have been published, those in English ordinarily prepared by the International Commission on English in the Liturgy, a joint commission of Catholic bishops' conferences.[17] Each vernacular liturgical book has the approbation of the conference of bishops for its territory and the confirmation of the Apostolic See.

Liturgical Laws and the Code

The contents of the liturgical books have their own canonical significance because of their inclusion of liturgical laws. They provide, moreover, interpretative background for the pertinent canons of the Code which have been revised in the light of the liturgical books or which are derived from them. Since their contents do not ordinarily follow the style of canons, they are able to provide, sometimes at length, the *ratio,* or rationale, for the laws. This includes doctrinal, catechetical, pastoral, historical, and other information and, according to circumstances, may be important in understanding the canons of Book IV.

There is a theoretical question about the possible conflict between the liturgical laws outside the Code, particularly those in the liturgical books re-

[15]SCRit, decr, Aug. 10, 1946: *AAS* 38 (1946), 371–372.
[16]*SC* 21–40.

[17]Established 1963; see F.R. McManus, *ICEL: The First Years* (Washington, 1981).

cently revised by decree of Vatican II, and the canons of Book IV. Such a question of conflict must be resolved in the individual case, but the principles are relatively simple.

First, the liturgical laws (in the liturgical books and other sources, including the documents of Vatican II and postconciliar legislation) retain their force, in accord with canon 2, unless abrogated by a contrary prescription of the Code.

Second, a later law (in this hypothetical instance, a prescription of a canon) abrogates or derogates from an earlier law, in accord with canon 20, in three instances: if it expressly so states (which does not occur in the canons of Book IV), if it is directly contrary to the earlier law (which must be established in the individual case), or if it entirely rearranges the subject matter of the earlier law (which

does not occur in Book IV in relation to uncodified liturgical laws).

Third, in the examination of an instance of apparent conflict or contradiction, the presumption is in favor of the continuance of the existing liturgical law. In accord with canon 21, in a case of doubt the revocation of an existing (liturgical or other) law by a subsequent canon or other law is not presumed: the later law is to be related to the former and, to the extent possible, harmonized with it. Thus the resolution of conflicts between the norms of the liturgical books will be made, in case of doubt, in favor of the liturgical law. (The very few instances in which the revised canons have caused a change in the liturgical law are mentioned in the commentary below.)

CANONS AND COMMENTARY

Introductory Canons

Six introductory canons (cc. 834–839) govern Book IV as a whole, which includes sacraments, other acts of divine worship, and sacred places and times. The six canons are both explanatory or doctrinal and normative: they include (1) a definition of the liturgy; (2) liturgical offices and ministries; (3) the responsibility of the ordained to arouse the faith that is necessary for the exercise of the common priesthood; (4) a norm of preference for communal celebration of the liturgy; (5) a determination of the ecclesiastical authorities who have power to moderate or regulate the liturgy; and (6) the responsibility for non-liturgical practices.

These canons replace the basic norms of 1255–1264 of the 1917 Code, which were the introductory canons of the title on divine worship. Certain of those canons, those which do not appear here or elsewhere in the codification, are simply abrogated. In particular this is true of the old canons on the desirability of the separation of women and men in church or at sacred rites[18] (women with heads covered, men bareheaded),[19] and the norm that women religious permitted to sing in church not be visible to the congregation.[20] On the other hand, canons 1261, §1 (concerning abuses in divine worship) and 1264, §1 (concerning improper music in church) of the 1917 Code, while formally and canonically abrogated, continue to oblige morally, quite apart from positive ecclesiastical law.

Definition of the Liturgy

Canon 834 — §1. The Church fulfills its office of sanctifying in a special way in the sacred liturgy, which is indeed the exercise of the priestly office of Jesus Christ; in it through sensible signs the sanctification of humankind is signified and effected in a manner proper to each of the signs and the whole of the public worship of God is carried on by the mystical Body of Jesus Christ, that is, by the Head and the members.

§2. This worship takes place when it is carried out in the name of the Church by persons lawfully deputed and through acts approved by the authority of the Church.

The text of paragraph one, which has no precedent in the 1917 Code, is derived from *Sacrosanctum Concilium* 7. It is slightly rephrased from the constitution to make it serve as an explanation of the way in which the ecclesial office of sanctifying is accomplished, namely, in the liturgy. Since the latter does not exhaust the entire life of the Church[21] nor is it the entirety of ecclesial sanctification (which includes other prayers and devotional exercises not strictly assimilated to the official liturgy),[22] the liturgy is said to fulfill this office of the

---

[18]*CIC* 1262, §1.
[19]*CIC* 1262, §2.
[20]*CIC* 1264, §2.

[21]*SC* 9.
[22]See c. 839.

Church in a special way, indeed in an entirely special way that "far surpasses any others."[23] This concept is explained by Vatican II as "the summit toward which the activity of the Church is directed; at the same time it is the fount from which all the Church's power flows."[24]

The definition of the liturgy from *Sacrosanctum Concilium* 7 is partially derived from Pius XII (*Mediator Dei*), as already noted, but it has been considerably modified and amplified, especially to include the sacramental concept of signs and the action of divine sanctification as well as worship offered to God by and in Christ. Although the explanation of signs perceptible to the senses, as signifying and bringing about sanctification, is directly and primarily applicable to the seven sacraments, the statement is made of the liturgy as a whole, which has innumerable signs over and above those central to the seven sacraments.

The language of paragraph two occurs in canon 1256 of the 1917 Code but in a somewhat different context. There it was a definition of public cult (other than sacraments) offered to God and the saints, as opposed to private cult. Here, however, paragraph two provides instead a canonical distinction between liturgical services and other cultic activity of the church community or of individual Christians. There are two elements to the distinction.

First and of less practical significance, in order to be considered liturgy the activity must be "carried out in the name of the Church by persons lawfully deputed." This deputation comes primarily from baptism and is enjoyed by all the faithful; it is the sharing in the common priesthood mentioned in canon 836 and described by Vatican II: "The faithful are deputed by the baptismal character to the worship of the Christian religion."[25] In this primary sense, the canon means that the liturgy is carried out by the baptized members of the Christian community.

At times this element has been understood as referring to the presidency of the ordained that is requisite for certain but not all liturgical celebrations. In other instances, it has been understood as referring to the liturgical presidency of the non-ordained, who may be deputed, in a manner not determined by the canon, for this purpose.[26] Examples of the latter include the non-ordained who lead services of the word of God, preside at funeral services, etc.

A particular question has arisen in the past about the liturgical nature of the individual praying of the Liturgy of the Hours by a person who does not possess the explicit deputation or mandate given to the

ordained, to religious, etc. This question has been effectively resolved by the conciliar decision that all lay persons should be encouraged to celebrate the liturgical office of prayer, preferably "with the priests, or among themselves, or even individually."[27] This decision has been formally incorporated in the revised Liturgy of the Hours[28] and is a specific application of the deputation to (public) cult of all the baptized (above).

The second element of the distinction in paragraph two is more useful as a canonical means to determine liturgical actions, namely, that these be "approved by the authority of the Church" (replacing the stricter formulation of *CIC* 1256: "by institution of the Church"). The usual but not exclusive means of approbation is by way of inclusion of rites in official liturgical books, as determined in canon 838, §§2 and 3. Thus it is possible to define as liturgical, in the sense of this canon, any rite which appears in an approved liturgical book and to define as non-liturgical or extra-liturgical all other prayers and devotional practices. Nonetheless, since such other practices may themselves have various degrees of ecclesiastical approbation, it may be expected that the competent authority will indicate whether a rite, approved but not included in an official book, is formally recognized as part of the liturgy of the Church.

It is important to add that the revised liturgical books of the Roman rite themselves include by reference many services, the specific elements of which (texts, order of parts) may not be formally prescribed or described. This inclusion, as a means of approbation, makes such services properly liturgical. Examples are the penitential services for which the *Rite of Penance* gives examples and the services of the word of God on the occasion of the visitation of the sick or exposition of the Blessed Sacrament. Another instance of inclusion in the liturgy by reference is found in *Sacrosanctum Concilium* 98: the approved short offices of religious and other institutes, which are obligatory for the members, satisfy the requirements of being "the public prayer of the Church."[29]

Liturgical Offices and Ministries

Canon 835 — **§1. First and foremost, the bishops exercise the office of sanctifying; they are high priests, principal dispensers of the mysteries of God and moderators, promoters and custodians of the whole liturgical life of the church committed to them.**

§2. The presbyters also exercise this office; they are in fact sharers of the priesthood of Christ Him-

---

[23]*SC* 13.
[24]*SC* 10.
[25]*LG* 11: *DOL* 141; *SC* 14.
[26]*SC* 35, 4.

[27]*SC* 100.
[28]General Instruction of the Liturgy of the Hours, Feb. 2, 1971, nos. 20–32: *DOL* 3450–3462.
[29]*DOL* 98.

self so that they are consecrated as his ministers under the authority of the bishop to celebrate divine worship and sanctify the people.

§3. Deacons have a part in celebration of the divine worship in accord with the prescriptions of the law.

§4. The rest of the Christian faithful by active participation in celebrations of liturgy especially in the Eucharist in their own way also have their own part in the office of sanctification; parents share in the office of sanctification in a particular way by leading a conjugal life in the Christian spirit and by seeing to Christian education of their children.

This canon, with the exception of the final clause of paragraph four, was inserted from the proposed *Fundamental Law of the Church*.[30] It is doctrinal rather than preceptive. The definition of the role of the ordained ministers in paragraphs one through three reflects a more tentative statement in the conciliar constitution on the Church: "The divinely instituted ecclesiastical ministry is exercised in different orders by those who, already in antiquity, are called bishops, presbyters, and deacons."[31] Although the canon might have been logically added after canons 836–837, in which the total Church is understood as celebrating the liturgy, the norm affecting sacred (ordained) ministers in canon 837 is preceded by an explanation of their liturgical function. Nonetheless it should be clear that, in accord with canon 834's definition, radically and fundamentally it is the whole community of the faithful, the Church itself, which celebrates the liturgy in union with its Head, the Lord Jesus, and that the common priesthood of all the baptized, mentioned in canon 836, is logically prior to the ordained priesthood.

In paragraph one the sanctifying role of the bishop, most evident when he presides at the liturgy and especially at the Eucharistic liturgy, is seen to extend to his authoritative governance of the liturgy as moderator, promoter, and guardian. This responsibility is rooted in his sacramental ordination. On the one hand, Vatican II formally taught that "episcopal consecration bestows the fullness of the sacrament of orders . . . the high priesthood, the summit of the sacred ministry."[32] Thus it put an end to theories which challenged the sacramentality of episcopal ordination and saw the episcopate only as the highest degree of the ordinary or simple priesthood of presbyters.[33] On the other hand, the conciliar fathers saw the sacramental ordination, or consecration (the terms are interchangeable), of a bishop as the source, or root, of the "offices of teaching and governing" as well as of sanctifying,

while insisting that these other offices "of their very nature, can be exercised only in hierarchic communion with the head of the college and its members."[34] In direct relation to the liturgical presidency of the bishop, the constitution on the liturgy gives the central definition:

The bishop is to be looked on as the high priest of his flock, the faithful's life in Christ in some way deriving from and depending on him. Therefore all should hold in great esteem the liturgical life of the diocese centered around the bishop, especially in his cathedral church; they must be convinced that the preeminent manifestation of the Church is present in the full, active participation of all God's holy people in these liturgical celebrations, especially in the same eucharist, in a single prayer, at one altar at which the bishop presides, surrounded by his college of priests and by his ministers.[35]

The (diocesan) bishop is described as the moderator of the entire liturgical life of the particular church, an expression used in the liturgical books as well,[36] because the moderation or regulation of the liturgy pertains to him. He is described as the promoter of the liturgy,[37] whether directly or through commissions and other means. He is described as guardian, or custodian, of the liturgy in that he safeguards its integrity and authenticity within the particular church. This canonical responsibility in turn is founded in the liturgical presidency of the diocesan bishop.

Again following the *Dogmatic Constitution on the Church*, paragraph two sees the members of the presbyterate as participants in the (special or ordained) priesthood but dependent upon the bishop: the members of the order of presbyters are seen as having "a limited share of the full priesthood [of the bishops]: episcopal consecration is the primary and comprehensive instance of sacramental ordination to office."[38] (The Latin texts are generally careful to use *presbyter* for presbyters or priests of the second order, *sacerdos* in reference to both bishops and presbyters; in English the context usually permits the word "priests" to be used and understood as referring either to members of both orders or to presbyters alone.)

The bishops, as "sharers in [Christ's] consecration and mission . . . in turn have lawfully handed on to different individuals in the Church [namely, presbyters and deacons] in varying degrees a participation in this ministry."[39] In direct reference to the

---

[34]*LG* 21: *DOL* 145.
[35]*SC* 41. The language is derived from Saint Ignatius of Antioch.
[36]E.g., *RPenance*, n. 9: *DOL* 3074.
[37]In the sense of *SC* 14–19, 41–46.
[38]Vorgrimler 1:193.
[39]*LG* 28: *DOL* 148.

[30]*LEF* n. 67.
[31]*LG* 28: *DOL* 148.
[32]*LG* 21: *DOL* 145.
[33]Vorgrimler 1:193.

principal liturgical role of presiding at the Eucharist, the *Roman Missal* explains: "Every authentic celebration of the eucharist is directed by the bishop, either in person or through the presbyters, who are his helpers."[40]

With regard to the order of deacons, paragraph three uses only general language, leaving to the liturgical books the determination of specific parts to be taken by the deacons. These functions had been defined (and enlarged) by Vatican II, not only in connection with the restoration of the permanent diaconate but also in reference to all deacons,[41] who share in

the *diaconia* of liturgy, word, and charity. Insofar as competent authority assigns them [i.e., either in the law generally or in the case of the individual deacon], the [liturgical] duties of the deacon are to: administer baptism solemnly; care for the eucharist and give holy communion; assist at and bless marriages in the name of the Church; carry viaticum to the dying; read the Scriptures to the people and exhort and instruct them; preside over worship and prayer; administer sacramentals; officiate at funeral and burial rites.[42]

One should see canon 1169, §3 for a limitation upon the liturgical office of deacons that was introduced after Vatican II.[43] It is understood, moreover, that deacons preside at the liturgy only in the absence of the bishop and presbyter.

The rest of the Christian faithful by active participation in celebrations of liturgy . . . have their own part in the office of sanctification. The concept *participatio actuosa* is ultimately derived from a statement of Pius X in 1903 about the primary and indispensable source of the Christian spirit, namely, "active participation [*la partecipazione attiva* in the original and authentic text] in the sacred mysteries and in the public and solemn prayer of the Church."[44] The concept is the recurring theme of the constitution on the liturgy and all the liturgical books. In the context of paragraph four, the other members of the Church are contrasted with the ordained ministers in the preceding paragraphs and their role is said to be carried out in their own manner, or mode ("suo modo").

In the first place, the role of the faithful is that of the members of the praying people assembled in a congregation; their common or congregational parts are defined in the liturgical books, both in

principle and in particular instances. Canon 836 gives the fundamental principle in virtue of which all the faithful (including the ordained) share, namely, the common priesthood; canon 837 enlarges somewhat upon communal participation. "Suo modo" in canon 835, §4 thus refers to the hierarchic and communal nature of the liturgy in the full assembly of the Church.

In addition, there is indirect reference (as there is direct reference in c. 837, §1) to special liturgical roles, or ministries, which some of the faithful, other than the ordained, may and should perform. These include those for which liturgical institution is required (at present only the lay ministries of reader and acolyte in the Latin Church, mentioned in c. 230, §1; other lay ministries with liturgical institution were originally contemplated); those for which some deputation or commission is expected (such as the ministry of reader on a less stable basis, as in c. 230, §2); and the very many specific ministries referred to in the introductions to the liturgical books, both during the liturgical rites themselves and in preparation for them.[45]

The final clause of paragraph four, which did not appear in the drafts of the *Fundamental Law of the Church* from which the canon is derived, deals with a very different if related matter: the sanctifying office of parents in relation to their children, both through the Christian style of their married life and through the Christian upbringing of the children that they undertake. (See also c. 774, §2.) In this context the clause can best be understood as a single and significant illustration of the breadth of the sanctifying office which every Christian believer enjoys in relation to others (children to parents, spouse to spouse and to other members of families, neighbor to neighbor, worker to worker, etc.) not only in the liturgical and other celebrations of the Church but in every dimension of Christian living.

Responsibility of Ordained Ministers

Canon 836 — Since Christian worship, in which the common priesthood of the Christian faithful is exercised, is a work which proceeds from faith and is based on it, sacred ministers are to strive diligently to arouse and enlighten that faith, especially through the ministry of the word by which faith is born and nourished.

The canon, without direct precedent in the 1917 Code, first expounds the need for faith for the exercise of the common (general, universal, primary) priesthood of the Christian faithful, then enjoins the ordained to support the faith of others, especially through the ministry of the word.

The expository part of the canon flows from the

[40]*IGMR* 59: *DOL* 1449.

[41]Commission for Interpretation of Decrees of Vatican II, March 26, 1968: *AAS* 60 (1968), 363; *DOL* 2547.

[42]*LG* 29: *DOL* 149.

[43]Commission for Interpretation of Decrees of Vatican II, Nov. 13, 1974: *AAS* 66 (1974), 667; *DOL* 2592.

[44]*Mp Tra le sollecitudini*, Nov. 22, 1903: *ASS* 36 (1903–1904), 329–339.

[45]E.g., for the Eucharist, *IGMR*, nos. 67–70: *DOL* 1457–1460; for initiation, *RCIA*, nos. 41–48: *DOL* 2368–2375.

definition in canon 834 ("the exercise of the priestly office of Jesus Christ") and is an assertion of the relation of faith to liturgical celebration. "Before people can come to the liturgy they must be called to faith and to conversion."[46] Not only must the church community proclaim the gospel to non-believers, it must "ever preach faith and penance to believers, prepare them for the sacraments, teach them to observe all that Christ has commanded, and invite them to all the works of charity, worship, and the apostolate."[47] In particular, the chief liturgical celebrations are called "sacraments of faith" because they "not only presuppose faith, but by words and objects they also nourish, strengthen, and express it.[48] In turn, the common priesthood is defined:

> By rebirth and the anointing of the Holy Spirit the baptized are consecrated as a spiritual house and a holy priesthood. . . . Though they differ from one another in essence and not only in degree, the universal priesthood of believers and the ministerial or hierarchic priesthood are nonetheless interrelated: each of them in its own special way is a sharing in the one priesthood of Christ.[49]

The second element of the canon, and the first explicit norm for conduct in Book IV, is directed to the members of the hierarchic priesthood, the ordained ministers. They are bound to arouse and illumine the faith of the other sharers in the common priesthood, specifically in relation to the liturgical celebrations. A similar conciliar injunction is:

> Pastors must therefore realize that when the liturgy is celebrated something more is required than the mere observance of the laws governing valid and lawful celebration; it is also their duty to ensure that the faithful take part fully aware of what they are doing, actively engaged in the rite, and enriched by its effects.[50]

The reference to the ministry of the word as the special means to stimulate and nourish faith is a specific application, here in the context of the faith needed to exercise the common priesthood, of the many canons of Book III, title I, which speak of the responsibility of the ordained in relation to the word of God.[51] It has particular significance for the liturgy, in which the celebration of the word is intimately and inextricably related to the celebration of the Eucharist and the other sacraments. The liturgical reform itself is based in part on norms derived from the formative (or didactic) nature of the liturgy, in which the ministry of the word of God is to be better integrated, enlarged, and enriched. While the ministry of the word is very evident in the homily, it is exercised in other ways liturgically, both in preparation for the celebration (liturgical catechesis) and in the rites themselves, all in support of the faith that is celebrated.

Common Celebration and Participation

Canon 837 — §1. Liturgical actions are not private actions but celebrations of the Church itself, which is "the sacrament of unity," namely, a holy people assembled and ordered under the bishops; therefore liturgical actions pertain to the whole body of the Church and manifest and affect it, but they affect the individual members of the Church in different ways according to the diversity of orders, functions and actual participation.

§2. Liturgical actions, to the extent that by their proper nature they involve a common celebration, are to be celebrated where possible with the presence and active participation of the Christian faithful.

The first paragraph is, like canon 834, a description or definition of liturgical celebrations; it is directly quoted from *Sacrosanctum Concilium* 26, where it introduces the norms for liturgical change which are drawn from the hierarchic and communal nature of the liturgy. In the present context it is the reason for the norm given in paragraph two; in *Sacrosanctum Concilium* it precedes a series of liturgical principles and/or laws which it was not necessary to include in the canons, although they remain in force: each person should perform his or her own role in the liturgy; those with special liturgical ministries (servers, readers, commentators, choir members, etc.) should perform their offices with piety and decorum, be imbued with the spirit of the liturgy, and be properly prepared; the people should take part by acclamations, responses, psalmody, antiphons, and songs, as well as by actions, gestures, postures, and, at proper times, reverent silence, the roles of the people being specified in the liturgical books; only distinctions based upon liturgical function, holy orders, and honor to civil authorities may be attended to in the liturgy.[52]

Unlike paragraph one, which is descriptive and defining, paragraph two is an explicit norm for conduct; it is derived from the conciliar decree:

> . . . whenever rites, according to their specific nature, make provision for communal celebration involving the presence and active participation of the faithful, it is to be stressed that this way of celebrating them is to be preferred, as far as possible, to a celebration that is individual and, so to

---

[46]*SC* 9.
[47]Ibid.
[48]*SC* 59; see c. 840.
[49]*LG* 10: *DOL* 140.
[50]*SC* 11.
[51]See cc. 756–757, 762–764, 767–773, 776–777.

[52]*SC* 26–32.

speak, private. This applies with especial force to the celebration of Mass and the administration of the sacraments, even though every Mass has of itself a public and social character.[53]

The canon expresses the conciliar injunction even more forcefully, but without altering it; the present canonical context does not demand that the public and social character of the so-called *Missa privata,* auricular confession, or individual praying of the Liturgy of the Hours be formally vindicated. The circumstances, whether of sacramental penance or the celebration of a minor sacramental blessing, which may give a quasi-private appearance to an ecclesial rite are acknowledged, but the preference in all cases possible is for communal celebration, with the presence and active participation of the faithful.

Regulation of the Liturgy

Canon 838 — §1. The supervision of the sacred liturgy depends solely on the authority of the Church which resides in the Apostolic See and, in accord with the law, the diocesan bishop.

As a whole, this fundamental canon is intended to determine the place within the church community where the power to govern, regulate, or moderate the liturgy resides.

With the clarifying addition of the word "diocesan," paragraph one is taken verbatim from *Sacrosanctum Concilium* 22, §1. The first clause, vindicating the right of the Church to regulate the liturgy, is a matter of public ecclesiastical law and appeared in canon 1260 of the 1917 Code in a different form but with a similar purpose: "In the exercise of worship the ministers of the Church must depend exclusively on ecclesiastical superiors." This language opposed attempts at civil intervention in the governance of the liturgy, especially during the nineteenth century. In paragraph one of the present canon, the first clause serves to introduce the specific places within the Church where canonical power over the liturgy is found, namely, in the Bishop of Rome and the diocesan bishop (as well as in the respective conferences of bishops); it denies any competence in matters of liturgy to those outside the church community.

The second and more significant clause of paragraph one is based upon, but radically derogates from, canon 1257 of the 1917 Code, which attributed the regulation or ordering of the liturgy exclusively to the Apostolic See. Although the parallel might have been more precise had Roman Pontiff and diocesan bishop (or even Apostolic See and episcopal see) been used, the conciliar intent is clear: to remove the reservation of the regulation of

the liturgy to the Apostolic See as a "major cause" and to acknowledge that the regulation of the liturgy pertains also to the diocesan bishop.

That some elements in the governance of the liturgy are nonetheless removed from the authority of the diocesan church is indicated by the expression, in relation to the individual bishop, "ad normam iuris." The liturgical law will therefore determine whether the bishop may act or is limited, for example, by the common liturgical law of the Latin Church or the particular law of the conference of bishops.

The principle of *Christus Dominus* 8, a (and of c. 381, §1) is applicable: there is a presumption that the bishop has all the power over the governance of the liturgy that is required for the exercise of his pastoral office, always excepting cases reserved to the supreme authority or other ecclesiastical authority. (The responsibility of the diocesan bishop is further described in §4 of the canon.)

Apostolic See

§2. It is for the Apostolic See to order the sacred liturgy of the universal Church, to publish the liturgical books, to review their translations into the vernacular languages and to see that liturgical ordinances are faithfully observed everywhere.

While recognizing the modification required by *Sacrosanctum Concilium* 22, §1 (chiefly the omission of the adverb "exclusively"), paragraph two of the canon retains the intent of canon 1257 of the 1917 Code: to reserve to the Apostolic See the right to publish the liturgical books of the universal (Latin) Church. These are the liturgical books in Latin, now revised by decree of Vatican II and promulgated by papal authority. It is in harmony with these that the particular liturgical books, generally in the vernacular languages, are prepared and issued by the respective territorial authority.[54]

As explained at the beginning of this commentary, the principal liturgical books of the Roman rite were issued in official form during the decades following the Council of Trent, which in 1563 had entrusted their revision to the Roman See. The *Roman Breviary, Roman Missal, Roman Pontifical,* and *Roman Ritual,* along with ancillary volumes such as the *Roman Martyrology* and *Ceremonial of Bishops,* remained substantially unchanged until the present century. Increasingly they displaced the liturgical usages of particular churches within the Latin Church. The canon now refers directly to the new Roman liturgical books issued in sections beginning in 1968 with the *Ordination of Deacons, Priests, and Bishops* (a part of the *Roman Pontifical*) and completed for the most part in the 1970s. These official books, issued in Latin, are published

---

[53]*SC* 27.

[54]*SC* 63, b.

in a basic and exemplary edition, called the *editio typica*, by the Apostolic See itself (that is, by decree of the appropriate dicastry, now the SCSDW); the republication of such Latin editions in whole or part requires an attestation of the ordinary of the place of publication, in accord with canon 826, §2.

The canon next speaks of the power of the Apostolic See with respect to the vernacular versions of official liturgical books, which are primarily the responsibility of the conferences of bishops. This is explained below under paragraph three of the canon. The Apostolic See reviews such editions and accords them confirmation, or *recognitio*.[55] Finally, paragraph two speaks of the broad power and responsibility of the Roman See to see to the observance of the liturgical law throughout the Church.

Conferences of Bishops

§3. It pertains to the conferences of bishops to prepare translations of the liturgical books into the vernacular languages, with the appropriate adaptations within the limits defined in the liturgical books themselves, and to publish them with the prior review by the Holy See.

The third paragraph of the canon represents a succinct conflation of several norms of *Sacrosanctum Concilium* and retains their force: it is the responsibility of the conferences of bishops (or other territorial bodies such as councils) to determine the use and extent of the introduction of the vernacular into liturgical celebrations, the decisions being subject to approval, that is, confirmation, by the Apostolic See;[56] it is the responsibility of the conferences to approve the translations (nothing being said in *SC* about confirmation by the Apostolic See);[57] adaptations of the revised Roman liturgy are to be indicated in the rubrics of the (Latin) liturgical books themselves;[58] it is the responsibility of the conferences to specify such potential or anticipated adaptations (again, nothing being said in *SC* about confirmation by the Apostolic See);[59] and, finally, the conferences are to prepare particular rituals adapted to the needs of their territories and to introduce them after prior review (*recognitio*) by the Apostolic See.[60]

The summary of these norms in paragraph three leaves intact the several elements of the conciliar constitution. In any event, these retain their force as part of the liturgical law and are to be understood in the same sense as before.[61] In particular,

paragraph three preserves the relationship of the canonical action of the conferences of bishops in the publication of vernacular liturgical books to the canonical action of the Apostolic See. The former is described as the preparation and publication of the books; *Sacrosanctum Concilium* speaks to the same effect but, in clearer harmony with *Christus Dominus* 37, 4, the constitution refers to the conferences of bishops the approbation of texts and the preparation and introduction of the ritual books themselves. The canonical action of the Apostolic See, on the other hand, is described alternatively as approving (in the sense of confirming)[62] and as reviewing (*recognitio*) prior to promulgation.[63] The language of the canon is an application of what is stated in canon 455, §2, itself based upon *Christus Dominus* 38, 4: the approval of particular liturgical books is an instance of the cases, referred to in canon 455, §1, where the conference of bishops has primary competence.

In explaining this relationship more precisely, the conciliar commission on the liturgy stated that a law enacted by the conference of bishops is subsequently acknowledged and completed by the Apostolic See; while this subsequent action, called *recognitio* in the canon, adds juridic and moral weight, it does not change the nature of the law.[64] The latter proceeds from the legislative power of the conference rather than from that of the Apostolic See.

This third paragraph of canon 838 appears to limit, but does not limit, the power of the conferences of bishops to the approval of vernacular liturgical books and to adaptations foreseen in the Latin books. Despite its omission at this point, *Sacrosanctum Concilium* 22, §2 remains in effect: "In virtue of power conceded by the law, the regulation of the liturgy within certain defined limits belongs also to various kinds of competent territorial bodies of bishops lawfully established." Primarily this regulation pertains to the conferences, in accord with canons 447–459; a fortiori it is applicable to other bodies of particular churches such as councils, in accord with canons 439–446. The conciliar constitution deliberately avoided deciding whether this right belongs to the conferences of bishops by divine or human law,[65] but it is an expression of the collegiality (*affectus collegialis*) of the bishops of a given territory or region.[66]

The revised liturgical books list in their introductions (*praenotanda*) the liturgical adaptations that are foreseen as falling within the competence of the respective conferences of bishops, depending upon the culture and traditions of various peoples (as well as adaptations or accommodations which lie

---

[55]*SC* 36, §3 speaks only of the confirmation of the *acta* of the episcopal conferences concerning the vernacular; *SC* 63, b speaks of confirmation of the rituals.
[56]Ibid.
[57]*SC* 36, §4.
[58]*SC* 38.
[59]*SC* 39.
[60]*SC* 63, b.
[61]C. 6, §2.

[62]*SC* 36, §3.
[63]*SC* 63, b.
[64]*AcSynVat* 1, 4:288.
[65]Ibid.
[66]*LG* 23.

within the competence of the diocesan bishop or even the presiding minister); both *Sacrosanctum Concilium* and postconciliar liturgical legislation not found in the liturgical books indicate further areas of competence of the conferences. It is to adaptations of this sort or at this level that paragraph three refers.

Over and above such matters, the possibility of the conferences initiating "more profound liturgical adaptations" (i.e., those not anticipated in the Latin liturgical books) is also within their competence, in accord with the conciliar constitution:

1. The competent, territorial ecclesiastical authority mentioned in art. 22 §2 [of *SC*] must, in this matter, carefully and prudently weigh what elements from the traditions and culture of individual peoples may be appropriately admitted into divine worship. They are to propose to the Apostolic See adaptations which are considered useful or necessary that will be introduced with its consent.

2. To ensure that adaptations are made with all the circumspection they demand, the Apostolic See will grant power to this same territorial ecclesiastical authority to permit and to direct, as the case requires, the necessary preliminary experiments within certain groups suited for the purpose and for a fixed time.

3. Because liturgical laws often involve special difficulties with respect to adaptation, particularly in mission lands, experts in these matters must be employed to formulate them.[67]

The canon does not refer to a final possibility, namely, the role of the conferences of bishops or other bodies in the development of a new rite, i.e., a new non-Roman rite of the Latin Church, which may be acknowledged in the future as being of equal right and dignity with the Roman liturgy.[68]

Diocesan Bishop

§4. It pertains to the diocesan bishop in the church entrusted to him, within the limits of his competence, to issue liturgical norms by which all are bound.

This final paragraph enlarges the simple reference to the diocesan bishop in paragraph one of canon 838.

It belongs to the bishop to enact liturgical norms within the limits of his competence, that is, unless circumscribed or restricted in some way.[69] A similar

[67]*SC* 40.
[68]*SC* 4; see *AcSynVat* 1, 3:121.
[69]See "ad normam iuris" of §1 of this canon; also *CD* 8, a and c. 381, §1.

norm is found in canon 1261, §2, of the 1917 Code; there, however, the enactment of laws was in terms of the observance of the existing (and common) prescriptions of the canons on worship, the avoidance of superstitious practice in the daily life of the faithful, and the exclusion of anything alien to the faith, out of harmony with ecclesiastical tradition, or commercialization.[70] The acknowledgment in *Sacrosanctum Concilium* 22, §1 and also in paragraph one of this canon that the regulation of the liturgy pertains to the bishop radically changes the sense of canon 1261, §2 of the 1917 Code: the regulation of the liturgy is no longer exclusively or uniquely the responsibility of the Apostolic See, as was the case in canon 1257 of the former Code.

The final clause of paragraph four, stating that all are bound by diocesan liturgical law, is an inclusive statement; unlike canon 1261, §2 of the 1917 Code, it avoids the possibility of exceptions to or exemptions from the binding force of such laws. This is in harmony with the conciliar decree that religious exemption from diocesan authority is not applicable to "the public exercise of divine worship," unless the religious are of a different canonical or liturgical rite.[71]

Prayers and Devotions

Canon 839 — §1. The Church carries out the office of sanctification in other ways also, whether by prayers by which God is asked that the Christian faithful be sanctified in truth, or by works of penance and charity which greatly help to root and strengthen the kingdom of Christ in souls and contribute to the salvation of the world.

§2. Local ordinaries are to see to it that the prayers and other pious and sacred exercises of the Christian people are fully in harmony with the norms of the Church.

The first paragraph of this canon, which is doctrinal rather than normative, was added in the final stages of the revision process. Like the concluding clause of canon 835, §4, it serves to broaden the concept of the sanctifying office, in accord with the conciliar constitution on the liturgy. It also introduces paragraph two, directly derived from the constitution, which governs the Church's diverse acts and services of prayer and piety that are not considered liturgical in the strict sense.

The second paragraph replaces canons 1259 (prohibiting prayers and exercises of piety in churches or oratories without the express permission of the local ordinary) and 1261 of the 1917 Code (requiring local ordinaries to exclude abuses from public and private divine cult and from the daily life of the faithful) but does so with more posi-

[70]*CIC* 1261, §1.
[71]*CD* 35: *DOL* 197.

tive language. It is concerned with prayers and devotional exercises which are not strictly liturgical in the sense of canon 834.

Pious exercises are communal celebrations (or even individual practices) which lack authoritative recognition as liturgical; sacred exercises are such observances which have "special dignity if they are undertaken by mandate of the bishops according to customs or books lawfully approved."[72] These latter, while not formally admitted into the liturgy of the Roman or non-Roman rites of the Latin Church, are formally recognized by particular churches; thus they are closely analogous to the liturgy as it is understood in the strict and usual sense but differ from pious devotions in general, which receive only a more general approval or encouragement. The theoretical question whether such sacred services at some point become a kind of diocesan liturgy is not resolved either by *Sacrosanctum Concilium* 13 or the canon.[73] For the publication of prayer books that contain pious and sacred exercises, one should see canon 826, §3.

The norms of the Church, with which the prayers and practices in question must be in harmony, are basically the following: "These devotions should be so fashioned that they harmonize with the liturgical seasons, accord with the sacred liturgy, are in some way derived from it, and lead the people to it, since, in fact, the liturgy by its very nature far surpasses any of them."[74] The conformity of contemporary services of the word of God commanded by these norms is evident;[75] it is the responsibility of local ordinaries to see that all other services be reappraised in the light of the conciliar norm.

It is no longer necessary that prayers and exercises of piety be reviewed and expressly approved by the local ordinary for use in churches or oratories,[76] nor are local ordinaries prohibited from approving new litanies for public recitation.[77]

Part I
THE SACRAMENTS
[cc. 840–1165]

The canons on the seven sacraments of the Church constitute well over three-quarters of Book IV. The number of canons is large, partly because the sacraments are the principal elements of the liturgy, partly because the discipline of the sacraments, in varying degree, has given rise to special needs for order and regulation in the Church. After nine preliminary canons of an introductory or general character, this first part of Book IV is divided straightforwardly into seven titles corresponding to the seven sacraments. In this it differs from the arrangement of the constitution on the liturgy, which has one chapter devoted to the Eucharist alone, another chapter on the other sacraments and the sacramentals. (The latter are treated in *SC* as lesser signs or sacraments; in the canons they are treated among other actions of divine worship, in part II of Book IV.) The arrangement of the titles in the codification gives emphasis to the sequence of the initiatory sacraments: baptism, confirmation, and Eucharist, in accord with the basic statement in canon 842, §2.

Aside from the very first canon of part I and single introductory canons for each title, no formal theological statements about the sacraments are given. There is no need from a disciplinary viewpoint to enter into theological questions about the greater or lesser significance of individual sacraments, e.g., the complementary and subordinate nature of confirmation in relation to baptism.

Matter and Form

The canons of Book IV assume the scholastic doctrine of matter and form, especially in relation to the seven sacraments, even though these distinctions are not readily accommodated to penance and matrimony. They are concerned, at least for canonical purposes, with what is minimally necessary for validity in the Latin Church, without touching such questions directly for the other Churches. This minimal demand, however, is never to be taken to be what is usual or desirable, and such an understanding of the canons (and of the liturgical books in cases like celebrations in circumstances of emergency) must be avoided. On the contrary, the liturgical books go to great pains to express the fullness of celebration, insisting upon the offices and ministries of the entire community and seeking always the fullness of signs, not only the signs that are central and considered operative and essential but also all signs and elements.

The canons do not enter into theological discussions of divine determination or institution of those elements without which these would not be Christian sacraments in the understanding and acceptance of the Church. They take for granted that the central form of words must indeed be those prescribed in the liturgical books of the Latin Church but that these are not only different in other Churches, including those in full communion with the Catholic Church, but are subject to change and determination by ecclesiastical authority. This has been amply demonstrated by the reform of Paul VI, who formally introduced new consecratory prayers for holy orders, new forms for confirmation and anointing of the sick, etc. Moreover, he introduced authorized new Eucharistic prayers with a variety

72*SC* 13.
73Vorgrimler 1:16–17.
74*SC* 13.
75*SC* 35, 4.
76*CIC* 1259, §1.
77*CIC* 1259, §2.

605

of epicleses, albeit a single (but revised) form of institutional narrative or consecration.

In connection with this, the teaching of Pius XII in 1947 has been followed,[78] namely, that the (verbal) *form* of a sacrament is not the minimal formula that is essential; as reiterated by Paul VI in the revision of the rites of ordination: "the form consists in the words of the consecratory prayer, of which the following belong to the essence and are consequently required for validity:"[79] (there follow the short formulas for the respective orders of deacons, presbyters, and bishops). The same principle is observed in the rite of penance, when again a distinction is made between the integral form of sacramental absolution ("God the Father of mercies . . .") and the essential words, traditional in the Latin Church since the sixteenth century ("I absolve you . . .").[80] This question is not unrelated to ecumenical considerations, because of long-standing disputes between East and West about the central and minimal form required in the anaphora or Eucharistic prayer. A recent initial attempt to speak of this in a joint statement of delegates of the Roman and Orthodox Churches reads:

> . . . The eucharistic mystery is accomplished in the prayer which joins together the words by which the Word made flesh instituted the sacrament and the epiclesis in which the Church, moved by faith, entreats the Father, through the Son, to send the Spirit so that in the unique offering of the incarnate Son, everything may be consummated in unity.[81]

A similar recognition of a changed ecclesiastical discipline underlies the canons in respect to the central and essential *matter* or action of the sacraments. The minimal requirement for validity is specified by the canons, but without entering into past disputes. This position too derives from Pius XII who, in relation to the matter of the sacrament of orders, declared that, whatever had been required or had been taught to be required in the past (at least within the Latin Church) as essential for validity, henceforward the ritual laying on of hands would suffice.[82] The possibility of change is likewise illustrated in the ritual of Paul VI, for example, in the case of confirmation, where the essential matter is described, for the Latin Church, as "anointing

with chrism on the forehead, which is done by the laying on of the hand"—but not to the denigration of the full laying on of hands which takes place before the anointing, "even if it is not of the essence of the sacramental rite."[83]

In summary, the canons are careful to determine, generally in the language already used in papal documents or the liturgical books, the matter and form minimally essential but do not (1) enter into theological or other questions more deeply, (2) overstate the laws, which may affect the Latin Church only, or (3) propose that the celebration is in any way integral or complete merely by the satisfaction of the minimal requirement.

For the responsible authority in the determination of what is necessary for valid sacraments, one should see canon 841.

Introductory Canons

The preliminary canons on the sacraments (cc. 840–848) correspond to canons 731–736 of the 1917 Code and are general in character, affecting all the titles and canons of part I. The more notable changes introduced in the revision of the preliminary canons are the following: (1) the definition of sacraments in general; (2) an explicit norm on the initiatory sacraments of baptism, confirmation, and Eucharist; and (3) the new discipline on sharing in worship (*communicatio in sacris*) with other Christians.

Definition of Sacraments

Canon 840 — **The sacraments of the New Testament, instituted by Christ the Lord and entrusted to the Church, as they are the actions of Christ and the Church, stand out as the signs and means by which the faith is expressed and strengthened, worship is rendered to God and the sanctification of humankind is effected, and they thus contribute in the highest degree to the establishment, strengthening and manifestation of ecclesial communion; therefore both the sacred ministers and the rest of the Christian faithful must employ the greatest reverence and the necessary diligence in their celebration.**

The norm contained at the end of this canon, about reverent and careful celebration, is derived from canon 731, §1 of the 1917 Code. The former Code's reference to "administering and receiving" sacraments, however, has been changed to "celebrating." Although the giving of a sacrament by a Christian minister and the receiving of a sacrament by another Christian remain correct expressions, preference is given here and elsewhere in the canons (as in the revised liturgical books) to "celebration"

[78] Apconst *Sacramentum Ordinis,* Nov. 30, 1947: *AAS* 40 (1948), 6; see *DOL* 2608.

[79] Apconst *Pontificalis Romani,* July 18, 1968: *AAS* 60 (1968), 372–373; *DOL* 2609–2611.

[80] *RPenance* 19: *DOL* 3084; n. 40: *DOL* 3105. Declarative or indicative formulas of absolution were gradually introduced in the Middle Ages under the influence of the Scholastics.

[81] Joint Roman Catholic-Orthodox Commission for Theological Dialogue, "The Mystery of the Church and of the Eucharist in the Light of the Mystery of the Holy Trinity," July 6, 1982, *Origins* 12 (1982), 157–160.

[82] See above, notes 78 and 79.

[83] Apconst *Divinae consortium naturae,* Aug. 15, 1971: *AAS* 63 (1971), 663–664; *DOL* 2507.

of sacraments by the whole Christian community. For the same reason the formulation of the canon is explicit in speaking of both the ordained ministers and the rest of the faithful as engaged in common celebration.

The more significant part of the canon is its explanation of the nature of sacraments (which were described merely as "the principal means of sanctification and salvation" in *CIC* 731, §1). This is in accord with *Sacrosanctum Concilium* 59:

> The purpose of the sacraments is to make people holy, to build up the Body of Christ, and, finally, to give worship to God; but being signs they also have a teaching function. They not only presuppose faith, but by words and objects they also nourish, strengthen, and express it; that is why they are called "sacraments of faith." They do indeed impart grace, but, in addition, the very act of celebrating them disposes the faithful most effectively to receive this grace in a fruitful manner, to worship God rightly, and to practice charity.[84]

The influence of the conciliar statement on the canon is seen in the understanding of sacraments (1) as signs and means of expressing and strengthening faith, (2) as actions (of Christ and the Church) of worship as well as of sanctification,[85] and (3) as constitutive of the Church. The first two of these elements were entirely missing from earlier drafts of the new canon. As explained at the beginning of the commentary on Book IV, the inclusion of references to faith and to worship reflects a major development in the canonical (and doctrinal) understanding of the sacramental signs of faith, which are both ecclesial celebrations of worship and means of grace.

Requisites for Validity

Canon 841 — Since the sacraments are the same for the universal Church and pertain to the divine deposit, it is for the supreme authority of the Church alone to approve or define those things which are required for their validity; it is for the same supreme authority of the Church or other competent authority in accord with the norm of can. 838, §§3 and 4 to determine what pertains to their lawful celebration, administration and reception and also the order to be observed in their celebration.

This canon was derived from the draft of the proposed *Fundamental Law of the Church*[86] and was added in the final stages of the revised codification.

It locates the ecclesial authority responsible for (1) the determination of matters requisite for the validity of sacraments and (2) the determination of all other matters of celebration of sacraments.

With regard to the first element, one should see the commentary above on matter and form as determined by the Church and also the concern lest, because the minimal requisites need to be determined, these should be thought to suffice doctrinally, liturgically, or pastorally. The present canon is concerned to reserve the approval or definition of what is necessary for validity, genuineness, or reality of sacraments to "the supreme authority of the Church." This terminology is used to refer to the body or order of bishops as "the subject of supreme and full power over the universal Church, together with the Roman Pontiff and never without this head, a power which it cannot exercise without the consent of the Roman Pontiff."[87] The expression is likewise used of the Bishop of Rome himself acting as head of the order of bishops; he is said to have "a full, supreme, and universal power, which he is always able to exercise freely."[88] This supreme authority of the college of bishops, of the Roman Pontiff, and of the other bishops in hierarchic communion is stated canonically in canons 330, 331, and 336.

The second part of the canon treats all else which may be decreed for the lawful celebration, ministration, and reception of sacraments as well as the order of their celebration. This may be decreed by either the supreme authority already mentioned or the other authorities named in canon 838, §§3 and 4, namely, the conferences of bishops and the diocesan bishops, as the canon law of the liturgy may determine. The canon thus has the effect, with regard to the seven sacraments, of clarifying and reinforcing canon 838.

Sacraments of Initiation

Canon 842 — §1. One who has not received baptism cannot be validly admitted to the other sacraments.

§2. The sacraments of baptism, confirmation, and the Most Holy Eucharist are so interrelated that they are required for full Christian initiation.

No exception is made to the norm of paragraph one. The sacraments may be received only by Christian believers, those who have and profess the Christian faith. But the believer, before he or she may be admitted to any other sacrament, must first be baptized. As canon 1170 indicates, this norm does not hold true of other rites of the Church, such as sacramentals, which may be given to catechumens and also to non-Catholics.

---

[84]*DOL* 59.
[85]*SC* 7: *DOL* 7.
[86]*LEF* 68, §2.

[87]*LG* 22.
[88]Ibid.

Although it was understood in canon 737, §1 of the 1917 Code, the explicit statement of paragraph one is new. In earlier drafts of the canons, paragraph one was related to the prescriptions on sacraments to be received by Christians who are not Catholics (now c. 844); here it stands as a basic norm. On the question of valid baptism, one should see canon 849.

Without any direct precedent in the 1917 Code, paragraph two summarizes the doctrine that the three sacraments of baptism, confirmation, and Eucharist are so closely related as to be necessary for full Christian initiation. As is evident, the completion of initiation through full participation in the Eucharistic celebration continues through the Christian life, unlike baptism and confirmation which may be celebrated by and for an individual only once.[89]

The sequence of the initiatory sacraments had to be stated at this point, in accord with tradition and the conciliar efforts at restoration of that tradition, because pastoral circumstances and other causes generally disrupt the order in which the sacraments are celebrated for most Catholics of the Latin Church. In the Latin Church the interrelation of the initiatory sacraments is most clearly seen only when the sacraments are celebrated, as the climax of the catechumenal formation of new believers, i.e., persons who become Christians after reaching the age of reason, in accord with canon 852, §1.

The widespread practice of postponing the sacrament of confirmation beyond the age of reason, despite canon 788 of the 1917 Code (and now c. 891), coupled with the practice (since the beginning of the 20th century) of receiving the Eucharist at about the age of reason, has given rise to an entirely different sequence in the case of those baptized in infancy: baptism, Eucharist, confirmation. If, in addition, the baptized child receives the sacrament of penance before the Eucharist, a still further alteration in the sequence occurs: baptism, penance, Eucharist, confirmation.

In those parts of the Latin Church where baptized children are confirmed either as infants or at least before their first admission to Eucharistic Communion, the question does not arise in the same way, although the relation of the three sacraments to which the canon refers may be less evident because of the considerable interval between baptism and confirmation. Nor does the question arise at all in the practice of the Eastern Churches where, according to a still more venerable tradition, the children of Christian families are fully initiated in infancy, receiving the sacraments in a single rite as does an adult neophyte (c. 866).

Both the 1917 Code and the present codification respect the traditional sequence of the initiatory sacraments by the order of the titles on these sacraments. The same is true of the conciliar documents and the revised liturgical books, in which the following explanation is given:

> Through baptism men and women are incorporated into Christ. They are formed into God's people and they obtain forgiveness of all their sins. They are rescued from the power of darkness and brought to the dignity of adopted children.... Signed with the gift of the Spirit in confirmation, Christians more perfectly become the image of their Lord and are filled with the Holy Spirit.... Finally, they come to the table of the eucharist to eat the flesh and drink the blood of the Son of Man so that they may have eternal life and show forth the unity of God's people.... Thus the three sacraments of initiation closely combine to bring the faithful to the full stature of Christ and to enable them to carry out the mission of the entire people of God in the Church and in the world.[90]

Vatican II and the revised liturgical books are realistic about restoring the complete tradition of the initiatory sacraments, celebrated together or at least in sequence. Even if the sequence is upset in practice, *Sacrosanctum Concilium* 71 provided that the relationship and sequence of the sacraments should be clearly manifested at least at the celebration of confirmation:

> The rite of confirmation is also to be revised so that the intimate connection of this sacrament with the whole of Christian initiation may stand out more clearly; for this reason it is fitting for candidates to renew their baptismal promises just before they are confirmed.

> Confirmation may be conferred within Mass when convenient ...

The revised rites make the point even more effectively and paragraph two of the canon states the norm which has application to the first three titles of part I. Nevertheless the norm may appear to be only an ideal in places where the sequence of sacraments indicated by the canons is not observed, as is permitted by canon 891.

Duties of Ministers and Others

Canon 843 — §1. The sacred ministers cannot refuse the sacraments to those who ask for them at appropriate times, are properly disposed and are not prohibited by law from receiving them.

§2. Pastors of souls and the rest of the Christian faithful, according to their ecclesial function, have the duty to see that those who seek the sacraments

[89]See c. 845, §1.

[90]*IGIC*, n. 2: *DOL* 2251.

are prepared to receive them by the necessary evangelization and catechetical formation, taking into account the norms published by the competent authority.

Canon 213 asserts the right of the faithful to receive spiritual goods, especially the word of God and the sacraments. These are elements of the full liturgical participation by the Christian people that is "their right and duty by reason of their baptism."[91] From this right flows the norm of paragraph one, prohibiting any denial of the sacraments by the ordained ministers of the Church without cause.

The disqualifications for which people may be denied the sacraments are clear enough when specified in the law, e.g., irregularities for orders in canon 1041, or denial of the Eucharist in canon 915. It is less clear when a request for sacramental ministrations is to be judged opportune or inopportune, reasonable or unreasonable; the latter question arises, e.g., in connection with auricular confession in canon 986, §1. Similarly, the proper disposition of faith and devotion can be judged adequately only by the person who seeks the sacrament. Although a judgment can and sometimes must be made by the minister, the canon establishes a presumption in favor of the Christian person.

There is a parallel to paragraph two of this canon in canon 836, which speaks of the obligation of ordained ministers to arouse and strengthen the faith of others for the exercise of the common priesthood in the liturgy. Here the responsibility is, first, that of those who exercise a pastoral office and, second, that of all members of the Church, lay and ordained, depending upon their ecclesial office or function of whatever kind. The duty, moreover, is specifically in relation to preparation for the sacraments.

The intent of paragraph two is best illustrated in the repeated admonitions of the liturgical books, which describe the appropriate preparation for those who are to receive sacraments and the means to provide it. Such explanations are generally contained in sections of the *praenotanda* of the respective books entitled "Offices and Ministries." These speak in detail of pastors, other ordained ministers, catechists, parents, and families, indeed the Christian community at large, as having a role in the preparation of others for the sacraments. Such *praenotanda* are examples of norms issued by competent authority; others include diocesan norms and guidelines, pastoral directories, and the like.

Sharing in Sacraments

The next canon treats sacramental or liturgical sharing (*communicatio*) in the reception of sacra-

[91]*SC* 14.

ments (1) in the case of Catholics who may receive the sacraments from ministers not in full communion with the Catholic Church and (2) in the case of Christians who are not themselves in full communion with the Catholic Church but who may seek the sacraments from its ministers. It does not treat other kinds of sharing in worship or spiritual things, i.e., those not involving the reception of sacraments. Canon 1258 of the 1917 Code is abrogated by omission: it prohibited all active participation by Catholics in non-Catholic sacred rites; it tolerated passive or merely material presence under specified conditions.

Canon 844 — **§1. Catholic ministers may licitly administer the sacraments to Catholic members of the Christian faithful only and, likewise, the latter may licitly receive the sacraments only from Catholic ministers with due regard for §§2, 3, and 4 of this canon, and can. 861, §2.**

§2. Whenever necessity requires or genuine spiritual advantage suggests, and provided that the danger of error or indifferentism is avoided, it is lawful for the faithful for whom it is physically or morally impossible to approach a Catholic minister, to receive the sacraments of penance, Eucharist, and anointing of the sick from non-Catholic ministers in whose churches these sacraments are valid.

§3. Catholic ministers may licitly administer the sacraments of penance, Eucharist and anointing of the sick to members of the oriental churches which do not have full communion with the Catholic Church, if they ask on their own for the sacraments and are properly disposed. This holds also for members of other churches, which in the judgment of the Apostolic See are in the same condition as the oriental churches as far as these sacraments are concerned.

§4. If the danger of death is present or other grave necessity, in the judgment of the diocesan bishop or the conference of bishops, Catholic ministers may licitly administer these sacraments to other Christians who do not have full communion with the Catholic Church, who cannot approach a minister of their own community and on their own ask for it, provided they manifest Catholic faith in these sacraments and are properly disposed.

§5. For the cases in §§2, 3, and 4, neither the diocesan bishop nor the conference of bishops is to enact general norms except after consultation with at least the local competent authority of the interested non-Catholic church or community.

This canon, which is the result of Vatican II's deliberations on ecumenism, replaces canon 731, §2 of the former Code. The latter contained an absolute prohibition of sacramental ministrations to "heretics or schismatics, even those erring in good faith and asking for the sacraments," without prior reconciliation. (Even under that canon, which admitted no exceptions in the text, it was understood that in danger of death, penance and anointing might be given conditionally under certain circumstances.)

With paragraph one of the new canon the intent is clear, namely, to define the outer limits of permissible sharing in sacraments. (C. 861, §2 is treated as an exception because it contemplates the giving of baptism by "any person with the right intention in case of necessity.") It is concerned only with licit giving and receiving of sacraments, the question of validity having been determined in principle by canon 842, §1. It is concerned, moreover, with exceptions in the cases of penance, Eucharist, and anointing of the sick only. The sacraments received but once, as determined in canon 845, §1, are not at issue since these may be received only within one's own communion, although in an earlier and more severe redaction of the canon it was proposed to introduce an explicit prohibition. The sacrament of marriage is treated elsewhere and specially in the canons, in part because of the common teaching of the Latin Church that the spouses are the ministers of this sacrament; thus there are distinct considerations of giving and receiving the sacrament when one of the persons is a baptized non-Catholic.

Although the canon provides specific norms, the underlying principles remain those of Vatican II's *Decree on Ecumenism:* Sharing in sacred things (*communicatio in sacris*)

> may not be regarded as a means to be used indiscriminately toward restoring Christian unity. Such sharing is dependent mainly on two principles: the unity of the Church, of which it is a sign, and the sharing in the means of grace. Its function as a sign often rules out *communicatio in sacris.* Its being a source of grace sometimes favors it. Unless the conference of bishops, following the norm of its own statutes, or the Holy See has ruled otherwise, the local bishop is the authority competent to decide with prudence what the right course of action should be in view of all the circumstances of time, place, and people.[92]

In effect the present canon provides a ruling on behalf of the Apostolic See, but this determination too is derived from Vatican II, specifically from its norms affecting the Catholic Eastern Churches:

> . . . when Eastern Christians separated in good faith from the Catholic Church request it of their own accord and are rightly disposed, they may be admitted to the sacraments of penance, eucha-

rist, and anointing. Moreover, Catholics may request these same sacraments of ministers of other Eastern Churches having valid sacraments on any occasion of need or genuine spiritual benefit when access to a Catholic priest is physically or morally impossible.[93]

As is clear from its text, paragraph two of the canon follows the conciliar norm just quoted for Catholics, adding only the caution "provided that the danger of error or indifferentism is avoided." It extends the possibility, however, of Catholics receiving the sacraments beyond the Eastern Churches to any other churches in which "these [three] sacraments are valid." No determination is made concerning what churches are meant, although postconciliar directives from the Secretariat for Promoting Christian Unity explain that the problem or hesitation arises because of the failure of some Western churches and ecclesial communities to share "the same ecclesiological and sacramental bases that particularly unite us to the Churches of the East."[94] More specifically, the expectation, spelled out in greater detail in the ecumenical dialogue, is that a church is to "have kept the substance of eucharistic teaching, the sacrament of orders, and apostolic succession,"[95] i.e., in order to be judged as having valid sacraments of penance, Eucharist, and anointing of the sick.

In paragraphs three and four, the conciliar norm quoted above is applied to other Christians who may seek the sacraments of penance, Eucharist, and anointing from a Catholic minister. Again the conciliar decree is followed, but the more irenic and precise language, "members of the Eastern Churches who do not have full communion with the Catholic Church," replaces "Eastern Christians separated in good faith." And again an extension is made, beyond Eastern Christians, to members of other churches which in the judgment of the Apostolic See are in the same situation as regards the (validity of the) three sacraments. Some guidance in this matter is provided by Vatican II's *Decree on Ecumenism,* which singles out the Anglican communion among Western churches and ecclesial communities as one occupying "a special place among those communions in which Catholic traditions and institutions in part continue to exist."[96] There has been, however, no formal judgment published by the Apostolic See concerning the Anglican or other communions as a church or churches "in the same situation as the Eastern Churches."

The canon makes a clear distinction between those covered by paragraph three, who have only to

[92]*UR* 8: *DOL* 186. For complete documentation (1964–1980) of ecumenical documents of the Apostolic See, in English translation, see T.F. Stransky and J.B. Sheerin, eds., *Doing the Truth in Charity* (New York: Paulist Press, 1980).

[93]*OE* 27: *DOL* 179; *ED* I, 55: *DOL* 1009.
[94]SPCU, decl, Jan. 7, 1970, n. 6: *AAS* 62 (1970), 184–188; *DOL* 1029.
[95]SPCU, communication, Oct. 17, 1973, n. 9: *AAS* 65 (1973), 616–619; *DOL* 1061.
[96]*UR* 13.

ask for one of these sacraments of their own accord and be properly disposed, and those named in paragraph four. With regard to the latter, who are neither Eastern Christians nor in the same situation, it is first required that there be a serious need (whether danger of death or other need) in the judgment of the diocesan bishop or the conference of bishops, next that they be unable to approach their own minister, and, finally, that they manifest the Catholic faith concerning the sacraments in question.[97] With regard to the serious need, the Secretariat for Promoting Christian Unity has given as examples the situation of persons in prison or under persecution or, aside from such cases of suffering and danger, the situation of persons who live at some distance from their own communion; this is not an exhaustive indication of such cases.[98]

All this is of course in addition to the usual requirement, repeated from paragraph two, that the individual seek the sacrament of his or her own accord and be properly disposed.

Since, if possible, the principle of reciprocity should be respected in ecumenical relationships,[99] paragraph five has been added so that no general norms will be issued on the matters in the three preceding paragraphs without consultation with at least a local authority of the respective church or community and preferably with some superior authority. The language of paragraph five is carefully constructed to leave the diocesan bishop (and the conference of bishops, which has preemptive power in accord with Vatican II's *Decree on Ecumenism*)[100] free to act in individual cases or in issuing general norms even if the consultation with the competent authority of the other communion is not favorable.

Neither the canon nor the extensive elaborations of the problem address such particular questions as the seriousness of the need, all other conditions being verified, in cases of proposed sacramental sharing on occasions of legitimate and desirable presence and other participation in the Eucharistic celebration of other communions, e.g., in connection with a marriage or ecumenical dialogue. The language of the conciliar decree itself remains somewhat negative: such sharing "may not be regarded as a means to be used indiscriminately toward restoring Christian unity."[101] In resolving individual cases and in the issuance of norms of a more general nature, both diocesan bishops and conferences should take into account the successive statements of the Secretariat for Promoting Christian Unity. The ecumenical directory of 1967 in particular, upon which later statements comment,

is to be considered "not as a collection of advisory principles which one can freely accept or ignore but as an authentic instruction, an exposition of the discipline to which all who wish to serve ecumenism truly should submit themselves."[102]

For the special question of concelebration of priests under the presidency of a bishop or priest of another church, one should see canon 908.

Repetition of Sacraments

Canon 845 — §1. The sacraments of baptism, confirmation and orders cannot be repeated since they imprint a character.

§2. If, after diligent investigation, there is still a prudent doubt whether these sacraments mentioned in §1 have been truly or validly conferred, they are to be conferred conditionally.

The canon does not enter into a doctrinal or theological exposition of the "character" of the three sacraments,[103] which explains their permanent effect (membership in the Church in the case of baptism and confirmation, the pastoral office in the case of orders), but paragraph one states both the tradition and the discipline that they cannot be repeated. It follows canon 732, §1 of the 1917 Code almost verbatim.

The language of canon 732, §2 of the former Code, however, has been carefully rephrased to avoid even suggesting a "repetition" of these sacraments, which would be null and sacrilegious. In the 1917 Code the text read: "But if a prudent doubt should exist whether they were in fact or validly conferred, they should be conferred again conditionally."

The revised paragraph two omits "again" for the sake of precision, since a conditional celebration or ministration of one of these sacraments ("if you were not baptized . . . " etc.) is not by definition a second conferral of the sacrament. More important, the introduction of a requirement of a diligent investigation stresses that these sacraments may not be given indiscriminately under condition.

The principal instance of this possibility is in the reception of Christians into full communion with the Catholic Church. In reference to this, the *Roman Ritual* is explicit:

The sacrament of baptism may not be repeated and conditional baptism is not permitted unless there is a prudent doubt about the fact or validity of the baptism already received. If after serious investigation it seems necessary—because of such prudent doubt—to confer baptism again conditionally, the minister should explain beforehand

[97]*ED* I, 55: *DOL* 1009.
[98]Ibid.; SPCU, instr, June 1, 1972, n. 6: *AAS* 64 (1972), 518–525; *DOL* 1050.
[99]*ED* I, 43: *DOL* 997.
[100]*UR* 8: *DOL* 186.
[101]*ED* I, 42: *DOL* 996.

[102]SPCU, decl, Jan. 7, 1970, n. 8: *DOL* 1031.
[103]Trent, sess. VII, *de sac. in genere,* can. 9: *COD* 685; sess. XXIII, *de ordine,* c. 4, can. 4: *COD* 742–744.

the reasons why baptism is conferred conditionally in this instance and he should administer it in the private form.[104]

This norm is itself dependent upon the careful exposition in the 1967 ecumenical directory on the subject, which again is most explicit: "The practice of the conditional baptism of all without distinction who desire to enter full communion with the Catholic Church cannot be approved";[105] the directory discusses in detail the matters to be inquired into.[106] The matter is taken up again in canon 869.

Observance of the Liturgical Laws

Canon 846 — §1. The liturgical books approved by the competent authority are to be faithfully observed in the celebration of the sacraments; therefore no one on personal authority may add, remove or change anything in them.

§2. The ministers are to celebrate the sacraments according to their own rite.

This canon has a complex history. On the one hand, paragraph one is unequivocal in requiring that the approved liturgical books be followed in the celebration of the seven sacraments; on the other hand, the reprobation of contrary customs in the 1917 Code[107] has been suppressed. The text of the first clause of paragraph one is a simplified redaction, reflecting a new style of liturgical law, of canon 733, §1 of the 1917 Code: "in making (*conficiendis*), administering, and receiving the sacraments the rites and ceremonies which are prescribed in the ritual books approved by the Church should be carefully observed." The substance of this norm remains unchanged, and it thus leaves open the traditional possibility of distinguishing the binding (preceptive) norms of the liturgical books affecting sacraments from those which are merely directive or even descriptive.

The second clause of paragraph one is derived literally from the conciliar constitution on the liturgy and, remotely, from the teaching of Pius XII, who denied the right to moderate the liturgy to anyone other than the Roman Pontiff or to introduce change "at the decision of private persons, even if they belong to the orders of the clergy."[108] Having recognized that the regulation of the liturgy pertains to the Apostolic See *and* the diocesan bishop, and indeed also to bodies of bishops of particular churches, summed up now in canon 838, *Sacrosanctum Concilium* 22, §3 reads: "no other person,

not even if he is a priest, may on his own add, remove, change anything in the liturgy." The text is here applied to the seven sacraments only.

The prohibition of additions, omissions, and changes in the celebrations of the sacraments is made without qualification, but it must be qualified by the fact that the revised liturgical books themselves incorporate very numerous instances of accommodation (often at the discretion of the minister), i.e., permitted substitutions and choices, alternative texts, etc. The norm, moreover, does not speak to the possibility of contrary liturgical customs or pastoral situations in which the liturgical laws may not bind.[109]

In paragraph two of the canon, which is partially derived from canon 733, §2 of the 1917 Code, the practical determination of the rite to be followed (Roman, Ambrosian, Byzantine, etc.) is made in accord with the proper rite of the (presiding) minister. In this case the text speaks of sacraments only, not of other liturgical services. The authentic ritual traditions of the different churches are to be respected;[110] if a minister has or may have the care of a community which is of a rite different from his own, he may be permitted by indult to preside according to that rite. In concelebration, the rite to be followed is that of the presiding celebrant.

One important difference from canon 733, §2 of the 1917 Code is that the former law applied the norm to everyone (*unusquisque*), not merely to the minister. This is now an unrestricted matter for persons other than the minister of a sacrament, although conciliar injunctions about the preservation of the several rites, especially those of the Eastern Churches, which are in every way equal to the Roman and other Latin rites, remain in full force.[111]

Holy Oils

Canon 847 — §1. In the administration of sacraments in which the sacred oils are to be used, the minister must use oils pressed from olives or from other plants that have been recently consecrated or blessed by the bishop, with due regard for the prescription of can. 999, n. 2; he is not to use old oils unless there is some necessity.

§2. The pastor is to obtain the sacred oils from his own bishop and keep them carefully in a fitting manner.

This canon replaces canons 734–735 of the 1917 Code, permitting part of their prescriptions to fall into disuse and introducing into the Code the possibility of using plant oils other than olive oil in the celebration of the sacraments. The required use of olive oil or, in the case of chrism, of olive oil and

[104]*RCIA*, appendix, "Rite of Receiving Baptized Christians into the Full Communion of the Catholic Church," n. 7: *DOL* 2482.

[105]*ED* I, 14: *DOL* 968.

[106]*ED* I, 9–20: *DOL* 963–974.

[107]*CIC* 818, with reference to the Eucharistic celebration.

[108]*Mediator Dei: AAS* 39 (1947), 544.

[109]See the treatment of the nature of liturgical law at the beginning of the commentary on Book IV.

[110]*SC* 4; *OE* 6: *DOL* 165.

[111]Ibid.; also *OE* 3: *DOL* 163.

balsam, was altered in the revision of the pertinent part of the *Roman Pontifical:*

> The matter suitable for a sacrament is olive oil or, according to local conditions, another oil extracted from plants.

> Chrism is made of [olive or other plant] oil and some aromatic substance,[112]

that is, perfume or other sweet-smelling matter.

The same change was affirmed formally by Paul VI, in reference to the sacrament of anointing of the sick:

> Since olive oil, which has been prescribed until now for the valid celebration of the sacrament, is unobtainable or difficult to obtain in some parts of the world, we have decreed, at the request of a number of bishops, that from now on, according to circumstances, another kind of oil can also be used, provided it is derived from plants and is thus similar to olive oil.[113]

Although the actual use of the oil of catechumens is much diminished in the revised Roman rite, its significance is described traditionally along with the more important chrism and oil of the sick:

> The Christian liturgy has adopted the Old Testament usage of anointing kings, priests, and prophets with consecratory oil because they prefigured Christ, whose name means "the anointed of the Lord."

> Similarly, chrism is a sign that Christians, incorporated by baptism into the paschal mystery of Christ, dying, buried, and rising with him [see *SC* 6], are sharers in his kingly and prophetic priesthood and that by confirmation they receive the spiritual anointing of the Spirit who is given to them.

> The oil of catechumens extends the effect of the baptismal exorcisms: it strengthens the candidates with the power to renounce the devil and sin before they go to the font of life for rebirth.

> The oil of the sick, for the use of which James [see 5:14] is the witness, provides the sick with a remedy for both spiritual and bodily illness, so that they may have strength to bear up under evil and obtain pardon for their sins.[114]

The requirement that the oil of the sick be blessed by the bishop is mitigated by canon 999.

According to that canon those who in law are equivalent to a diocesan bishop and, in case of necessity, any priest may bless this oil; the latter may do so only in the actual celebration of the sacrament (that is, not as a part of the Holy Thursday ritual or on other occasions). A further exception, not mentioned in the canon, is that "in the case of the baptism of adults, priests have the faculty to bless [the oil of catechumens] before the anointing at the designated stage of the catechumenate."[115] Moreover, the very use of the oil of catechumens in the baptism of children and in the Christian initiation of adults is dependent upon its continuance by decision of the conference of bishops;[116] it is no longer used in the ordination of priests, whose hands are now ritually anointed with chrism instead.

Canon 734, §1 of the 1917 Code was somewhat more specific about the use of oils recently blessed, speaking of those blessed by the bishop on the preceding Holy Thursday, but the substance of this prescription remains unchanged: for the worthy signification of the oils, they should be fresh and free flowing. The codification suppresses the practice of adding unblessed oil to the blessed oils when the supply ran low.[117]

Canon 735 of the former law may be quoted to indicate how the worthy custody of the blessed oils has now been expressed only in general terms:

> The parish priest must seek the holy oils from his Ordinary and keep them carefully in the church in a safe and becoming place under lock; nor should he keep them at home, unless with the Ordinary's permission, because of necessity or other reasonable cause.

The requirement of obtaining the oils from one's own bishop is retained: it is a sign of communion of the local parishes and congregations with the bishop and with one another. The keeping of the oils in church in the traditional ambry remains appropriate but is no longer specified, the canon asking only for a diligent and becoming custody. For the carrying of the oil of the sick on one's person and the like, one should see canon 1003, §3.

In this connection the *Roman Pontifical,* after giving the rite for the blessing and consecration of the oils in the chrism Mass, concludes: "In the sacristy the bishop may instruct the priests about the reverent use and safe custody of the holy oils."[118]

Offerings for Sacraments

Canon 848 — The minister should ask nothing for the administration of the sacraments beyond the

---

[112]*ROils* 3–4: *DOL* 3863–3864.
[113]Apconst *Sacram Unctionem infirmorum,* Nov. 30, 1972: *AAS* 65 (1973), 5–9; *DOL* 3317.
[114]*ROils* 2: *DOL* 3862.

[115]Ibid., n. 7: *DOL* 3867.
[116]Ibid.; also *RBaptC* 24, 2: *DOL* 2308; *RCIA* 65, 7: *DOL* 2392.
[117]*CIC* 734, §2.
[118]*ROils* 28.

offerings defined by the competent authority, always being careful that the needy are not deprived of the help of the sacraments because of their poverty.

Although the canons on simony in the 1917 Code[119] no longer precede the canons on the sacraments, the present canon (corresponding to *CIC* 736) indicates a concern for the reverence due to sacred things, and especially the reverence due to sacraments, and the need to avoid even the appearance of profit-seeking from sacramental ministrations. Any request (or, a fortiori, exaction) of payment for the giving of a sacrament over and above the established offerings is prohibited. According to canon 1264, 2°, the offering should be determined by the meeting of bishops of each ecclesiastical province; this is understood to be a limit imposed by decision of the provincial meeting, not a tax which must be exacted on the occasion of the celebration of sacraments (and sacramentals). Canon 952, §§1 and 2, makes a similar rule for the determination of the offering for Mass, which is the responsibility of the provincial council or the meeting of bishops of the province; in the absence of such a decree, the offering is left to diocesan custom. The canon does not prohibit offerings or gifts that are entirely voluntary, but there may be particular law on this matter.

The clause proscribing abuses by which the poor may be deprived of the sacraments because of their lack of offerings is new. Although the canon does not apply the principle to sacramentals and other acts of worship, the obligation exists apart from positive ecclesiastical law.

For the application of this norm to funeral rites one should see canon 1181.

TITLE I
BAPTISM
[cc. 849–878]

The thirty canons devoted to baptism are introduced by a single canon of definition. They are then divided, according to a pattern followed in several other titles on the sacraments, into chapters on (1) the celebration of the sacrament (cc. 850–860, some basic and general norms), (2) the minister (cc. 861–863), (3) those to be baptized (cc. 864–871), (4) sponsors (872–874), and (5) proof and recording of the sacrament (cc. 875–878).

It is important to refer again to canon 842, §2 on the interrelatedness of baptism, confirmation, and (first) Eucharist as initiatory sacraments. Although the disciplinary norms on baptism, which is generally celebrated separately in the case of infants in the Latin Church, are given by themselves, their relationship to title II on confirmation and title III on

the Eucharist is always to be kept in mind, since these sacraments are necessary for complete Christian initiation.

Nature of Baptism

Canon 849 — **Baptism, the gate to the sacraments, necessary for salvation in fact or at least in intention, by which men and women are freed from their sins, are reborn as children of God and, configured to Christ by an indelible character, are incorporated in the Church, is validly conferred only by washing with true water together with the required form of words.**

This doctrinal canon has been rephrased from the text in canon 737, §1 of the 1917 Code, and a summary of the effects of the sacrament has been added to the original. The liturgical books, quoted above in the commentary on canon 842, §2, use somewhat different language to the same purpose, i.e., laying stress on incorporation in Christ and the formation of God's people, the element with direct social and thus canonical significance. Similarly, the conciliar constitution on the Church explains the sacrament:

> Incorporated into the Church through baptism, the faithful are deputed by the baptismal character for the worship of the Christian religion. Reborn as children of God, they must confess before men the faith they have received from God through the Church.[120]

This is fully elaborated in the general introduction (*praenotanda*) to Christian initiation in the *Roman Ritual* under the heading "Dignity of Baptism."[121]

The canon speaks of the forgiveness of sins first, relying upon the expression in the creed, "one baptism for the forgiveness of sins," and the exposition of newness of life as freedom from sin in Romans 8. The mention of baptism of desire ("in voto"), namely, when the sacrament itself is not received, is included for doctrinal completeness rather than canonical significance.[122] The doctrine of baptism by desire has had a recent exposition by Vatican II:

> Those who without fault of their own do not know the gospel of Christ and his Church, yet seek God sincerely and try, moved by grace, to do his will as it is known to them through the dictates of conscience, may attain eternal salvation. Divine Providence does not deny the help necessary for salvation to those who without blame have not yet come to the express knowl-

[119]*CIC* 727–730.

[120]*LG* 11: *DOL* 141; see *AG* 14: *DOL* 246.
[121]*IGIC* 3–6: *DOL* 2252–2255.
[122]Trent, sess. VI, *de iustificatione*, c. 4: *COD* 672.

edge of God and strive to live a good life with the help of his grace.[123]

The language of the canon referring to what is necessary for the valid reception of the sacrament may be compared with canon 737, §1 of the former Code: "washing ["ablutio"] with true and natural water with the prescribed form of words." "Ablutio" has been replaced by "lavacrum" ("the bath of water by the power of the word" of Eph 5:26), and "natural" has been omitted as possibly unclear or redundant: the water must be true water as commonly or ordinarily understood. The use of distilled water or even a mixture in which water predominates, and which would still be considered true water, is lawful depending on circumstances and does not affect the validity of the sacrament. It is not necessary in this canon to be more specific, e.g., to indicate the importance of using clean water or blessed water; the mention of blessed water in canon 853 rather than in this canon removes the element of blessing from the present context of requirements for validity.

The form or formula needed for the valid celebration of baptism is described as the necessary, required, or requisite form rather than as the "prescribed" form (CIC 737, §1). This change mitigates slightly the earlier text and in some degree recognizes that, important as are the precise prescriptions of words, the form necessary for a real or valid celebration is not so exacting as to make a slight alteration a cause of invalidity. In the Latin Church the central, operative, and essential words are "I baptize you in the name of the Father, and of the Son, and of the Holy Spirit."[124] This form, in use since the Middle Ages, replaced the threefold profession of faith by way of questions and responses as an accompaniment to the washing with water; this threefold profession of faith now precedes the washing in the rite and is somewhat distinct from it. In the Eastern rites, the corresponding form is different, e.g., "The servant of God N. is baptized in the name of the Father, and of the Son, and of the Holy Spirit."

At this point a distinction found in canon 737, §2 of the 1917 Code between solemn baptism (with all prescribed rites and ceremonies) and non-solemn or private baptism (without all such rites and ceremonies) is suppressed. Instead, it is left to the liturgical books to describe the rites of baptism according to circumstances; it is left to canon 850 to indicate the minimal rite in case of urgent necessity. The term "private baptism" continues to be used, differently from canon 737, §2 of the former law, in reference to the conditional baptism of persons to be received into full communion whose baptism is found upon investigation to be doubtful. In individual cases of

this kind, it is for the local ordinary to determine "what rites are to be included or excluded in conditional baptism,"[125] since "private" is then understood in its usual sense: removed from or out of public view.

Finally it should be added that the canon, in speaking of what is necessary for valid or real baptism, takes for granted the intention of the one to be baptized (if an adult, in accord with c. 852) and the baptizing minister. This is adverted to in canon 869, §2.

CHAPTER I
THE CELEBRATION OF BAPTISM
[cc. 850–860]

This chapter, which includes eleven canons, more than one-third of the canons on baptism, deals with diverse aspects of the discipline of this sacrament: (1) the rite to be followed in the celebration (c. 850); (2) those to be baptized (cc.851–852); (3) the water of baptism and the manner of baptizing (cc. 853–854); (4) the baptismal name (c. 855); (5) the time for baptismal celebration (c. 856); and (6) the place for baptism (cc. 857–860).

The canons in this first chapter about the persons to be baptized have to be understood in relation to Chapter III (cc. 864–871), which elaborates further on the same matter.

Rite of Baptism

Canon 850 — Baptism should be administered in accord with the order prescribed in the approved liturgical books, except for the case of urgent necessity when only what is required for the validity of the sacrament must be observed.

The rite, or order (Ordo), to be followed for the celebration of baptism is given in the revised Roman Ritual and in particular rituals drawn up in harmony with it.[126] All the rites except that for the baptism of infants (i.e., in accord with c. 852, those who have not attained the use of reason) include confirmation and Eucharist as integral parts of the order.

The principal and basic rite, on which the other rites depend, is entitled the "Rite of the Catechumenate Arranged in Stages," in which the celebration of the three sacraments is the third stage. Variants of this are the "Simple Rite for the Initiation of an Adult," "Short Rite for the Initiation of an Adult in Danger of Death or at the Point of Death," and "Rite of Initiation for Children of Catechetical Age." (The ritual also includes a chapter on "Preparing Uncatechized Adults for Confirmation and the Eucharist" and an appendix, "Rite of

[123]LG 16.
[124]IGIC 23: DOL 2272.
[125]RCIA, appendix, n. 7: DOL 2482.
[126]See SC 63, b.

Receiving Baptized Christians into the Full Communion of the Catholic Church." Both of these rites, or orders, are distinct from baptism and are for those who have not been fully initiated or for those whose Christian initiation has taken place out of full communion with the Catholic Church.)[127]

Next, for infants, there is the "Rite of Baptism for Several Children," the basic rite for communal celebration in accord with canon 837, §2. The variants include the "Rite of Baptism for One Child," "Rite of Baptism for a Large Number of Children," "Rite of Baptism for Children Administered by a Catechist when No Priest or Deacon Is Available," and "Rite of Baptism for Children in Danger of Death when No Priest or Deacon Is Available." (Also included is the related "Rite of Bringing a Baptized Child to the Church," when the baptism itself has already been celebrated in circumstances of urgency. It takes the place of the order of "supplying ceremonies" in such cases. The latter was revised to "manifest more clearly and fittingly that an infant who was baptized by the short rite has already been received into the Church"[128] and is now welcomed into the local parish community.)[129]

The approved liturgical books give these rites in full detail, with extensive directions about accommodations to pastoral and other circumstances. The canon, however, goes on to mention only the exception of urgent necessity, e.g., danger of death, a period of religious persecution, serious family disagreement about the baptism, and other circumstances which may make it impossible to celebrate the appropriate and prescribed rite in its fullness. Even in such circumstances it may be possible and is surely desirable to celebrate several other parts of the rite, since baptism is more than the essential washing with water; the canon states what *must* be observed as a minimum in cases of urgent necessity, namely, only what is required for the validity of the sacrament of baptism; for this, one should see canon 849. The matter is explained more fully in the ritual, which gives emergency rites that include the general intercessions, profession of faith, baptismal washing, and the Lord's Prayer but adds that "when a person is at the point of death or when time is pressing because death is imminent" the minister omits all but the pouring of the water and the customary sacramental form. Even in urgent necessity priests and deacons may be able to use the simple rite with adaptations, and a priest should also confer the sacrament of confirmation (in this

case omitting the postbaptismal anointing with chrism).[130]

For another instance in which the full rite is not followed, namely, conditional baptism, one should see the commentary on canons 849 and 869.

Preparation for Baptism

Canon 851 — It is necessary that the celebration of baptism be properly prepared. Thus:

1° an adult who intends to receive baptism is to be admitted to the catechumenate and, to the extent possible, be led through the several stages to sacramental initiation, in accord with the order of initiation adapted by the conference of bishops and the special norms published by it;

2° the parents of an infant who is to be baptized and likewise those who are to undertake the office of sponsor are to be properly instructed in the meaning of this sacrament and the obligations which are attached to it; personally or through others the pastor is to see to it that the parents are properly formed by pastoral directions and by common prayer, gathering several families together and where possible visiting them.

This canon has no direct precedent in the 1917 Code and was introduced only after the consultation of the episcopate and others, in which the absence of all reference to the catechumenate and the preparation for the baptism of infants was pointed out. A slightly expanded exposition of the catechumenate is given in canon 788.

The first part of this canon is concerned with the preparation and formation of adults for baptism and indeed for complete Christian initiation. It is applicable, in accord with canon 852, to all who have reached the age of reason, although the rites may be considerably adapted for children "unbaptized as infants, who have reached the age of reason and are of catechetical age and who have been brought by their parents or guardians for Christian initiation or have come of their own accord with parental permission."[131] The canon reflects the restoration of the catechumenate, officially acknowledged and introduced in 1962 with the revised rite for the baptism of adults "arranged according to the stages of the catechumenate"[132] and formally mandated by Vatican II as part of the liturgical reform:

The catechumenate for adults, divided into several stages, is to be restored and put into use at the discretion of the local Ordinary. By this means

---

[127]These rites were published by decree of SCDW *Ordinis Baptismi adultorum,* Jan. 6, 1972 (*AAS* 64 [1972], 252: *DOL* 2327). The section of the *Roman Ritual* is entitled *Ordo Initiationis Christianis Adultorum.*

[128]*SC* 69.

[129]Although logically and in other ways dependent upon the rite of adult initiation (note 127), these rites for children appeared earlier, by decree of SCDW *Ordinem Baptismi parvulorum,* May 15, 1969 (*AAS* 61 [1969], 548: *DOL* 2248) in *Ordo Baptismi Parvulorum.*

[130]*RBaptC 21–22: DOL* 2305–2306; *RCIA* 280–281: *DOL* 2444–2445.

[131]*RCIA* 306: *DOL* 2458.

[132]SCRit, decr, Apr. 16, 1962: *AAS* 54 (1962), 310. The *Ordo Baptismi Adultorum per Gradus Catechumenatus Dispositus* of 1962 divided the rite of the 1614 ritual into 7 stages.

the time of the catechumenate, which is intended to be a period of well-suited instruction, may be sanctified by sacred rites to be celebrated at successive intervals of time.[133]

As is clear, the period of the catechumenate is not merely a time of pedagogical instruction or successive liturgical celebrations:

those who through the Church have accepted from the Father faith in Christ[134] should be admitted to the catechumenate by means of liturgical ceremonies. The catechumenate means not simply a presentation of teachings and precepts, but a formation in the whole of Christian life and a sufficiently prolonged period of training; by these means the disciples will be become bound to Christ as their master. Catechumens should therefore be properly initiated into the mystery of salvation and the practice of gospel living; by means of sacred rites celebrated at successive times,[135] they should be led gradually into the life of faith, liturgy, and charity belonging to the people of God.[136]

Although the series of rites is not itself the catechumenate of Christian formation, the rites do define the successive periods of the catechumenate:

The first period consists of inquiry on the part of the candidates and of evangelization and the pre-catechumenate on the part of the Church. It ends with the [rite of] entrance into the order of catechumens.

The second period, . . . which may last for several years includes catechesis and the rites connected with catechesis. It comes to an end on the day of the [rite of] election.

The third period, shorter in length, ordinarily co-incides with the Lenten preparation for the Easter celebration and the sacraments. It is a time of purification and enlightenment.

The final period [after the sacraments of initiation are celebrated] goes through the whole Easter season and is devoted to the postbaptismal catechesis or mystagogy.[137]

The length of the catechumenate is not determined by the common law, but may be a matter of particular law. It is anticipated, however, that, after initial conversion and acceptance as catechumens, the period of catechesis will be extensive ("which

may last for several years"; the initiation of children of catechetical age "is to be extended over several years, if need be, before they receive the sacraments")[138] prior to the final preparation during the Lenten season. Unlike canon 788, this canon does no more than mention the institute of the catechumenate, although attention is given elsewhere to the status of the catechumens, e.g., in canons 206 and 1170, in accord with the conciliar teaching:

Catechumens who, moved by the Holy Spirit, seek with explicit intention to be incorporated into the Church are by that very intention joined to it. With love and solicitude Mother Church already embraces them as her own.[139]

The new code of canon law should set out clearly the juridic status of catechumens; they are already joined to the Church, already part of Christ's household, and are in many cases already living a life of faith, hope, and charity.[140]

For the full implications of the catechumenate, the *Rite of Christian Initiation of Adults* must be studied in detail, in particular, the ministries and offices of the whole people of God, "represented by the local Church," which is to "understand and show that the initiation of adults is its concern and the business of all the baptized."[141] The circumstances which may make the complete catechumenate impossible, referred to in the canon, are recognized by the inclusion of a "Simple Rite for the Initiation of an Adult" which may be permitted by the local ordinary "in extraordinary circumstances when a candidate has been unable to go through all the stages of the catechumenate or when the local Ordinary, convinced that the candidate's Christian conversion is sincere and that he or she is religiously mature, decides that the candidate may receive baptism without delay."[142] This rite, the use of which is reserved to exceptional cases permitted by the local ordinary, allows for the celebration of the entire rite at once or for one or more of the rites of initiation prior to the celebration of the sacraments.

In the initial conciliar decision to restore the catechumenate the actual practice was left to the discretion of the local ordinary in *Sacrosanctum Concilium* 64, and he may indeed "set up the formation program of the catechumenate and lay down norms according to local needs."[143] Elsewhere this is explained: "The bishop, in person or through his delegate, sets up, regulates, and promotes the pastoral formation of the catechumens and admits

---

[133]*SC* 64; see also *CD* 14: *DOL* 193; *AG* 14: *DOL* 246.
[134]See *LG* 17: *DOL* 144.
[135]See *SC* 64–65.
[136]*AG* 14: *DOL* 246.
[137]*RCIA* 7: *DOL* 2334.

[138]Ibid., 307: *DOL* 2459.
[139]*LG* 14.
[140]*AG* 14: *DOL* 246.
[141]N. 41: *DOL* 2368.
[142]N. 240: *DOL* 2433.
[143]N. 66: *DOL* 2393.

the candidates to their election and to the sacrament."[144] Nevertheless the conference of bishops has preemptive power, not only in the liturgical adaptations foreseen in the ritual,[145] but also in the general discipline of the catechumenate (the "special norms" mentioned in this canon).

In number two of canon 851, a summary statement is given of the pastoral responsibility for the preparation of parents and also sponsors in the case of the baptism of infants. This is explained at slightly greater length in the ritual, in accord with the conciliar decision[146] to clarify the roles of parents and sponsors:

> Before the celebration of the sacrament, it is of great importance that parents, moved by their own faith or with the help of friends or other members of the community, should prepare to take part in the rite with understanding. They should be provided with suitable means such as books, letters addressed to them, and catechisms designed for families. The parish priest (pastor) should make it his duty to visit them or see that they are visited; he should try to gather a group of families together and prepare them for the coming celebration by pastoral counsel and common prayer.[147]

This norm is satisfied by parochial and other programs of preparation and formation, both before and after the baptism of the child; this is a duty of priests, deacons, and lay people and "it is the duty of the bishop to coordinate such pastoral efforts in the diocese."[148] It is related to the involvement of the community:

> The people of God, that is, the Church, made present by the local community, has an important part to play in the baptism of both children and adults.

> Before and after the celebration of the sacrament, the child has a right to the love and help of the community. During the rite . . . the community exercises its duty when it expresses its assent together with the celebrant after the profession of faith by the parents and godparents. In this way it is clear that the faith in which the children are baptized is not the private possession of the individual family, but the common treasure of the whole Church of Christ.[149]

An earlier version of number two of the canon spoke directly to the nature of the obligations of parents (and sponsors) in the Christian upbringing of the baptized child; on this point one should see canons 774, §2 and 835, §4. Although the baptism of infants has been a matter of controversy at various periods, the ritual is clear that, while the full rite of Christian initiation (of adults) is basic, the tradition is to be maintained: the children of a Christian family that is properly prepared "are baptized in the faith of the Church."[150] Although they are incapable of undergoing a catechumenal preparation, its place is taken by subsequent Christian upbringing that is in some sense analogous to the postbaptismal catechesis or mystagogy of the adult neophyte.

Definition of Adults and Infants

Canon 852 — §1. What is prescribed in the canons on the baptism of an adult is applicable to all who are no longer infants but have attained the use of reason.

§2. One who is not of sound mind (*non sui compos*) is equated with an infant so far as baptism is concerned.

The canon is based on the principle that the rite of baptizing infants is for "those who have not yet reached the age of discernment and therefore cannot profess personal faith."[151] Any who have left infancy are considered to be adults for the purposes of the canons on baptism. For the age at which the baptism of adult candidates should be deferred to the bishop, one should see canon 863.

So far as the rite for the celebration is concerned, the modern *Roman Ritual* of 1614 distinguished (1) an order for the baptism of children, which was in effect an abbreviated version of the rite for the baptism of adults and which therefore had to be revised so as to be "suited to the fact that those to be baptized are infants"; (2) an order for the baptism of adults, which until the partial revision of 1962[152] combined on a single occasion the several rites from the distinct stages of the catechumenate. (It was on this account that local ordinaries formerly employed the power of *CIC* 755, §2 and permitted "for grave and reasonable cause" the use of the rite for children in the baptism of adults. In the U.S. this was the general practice, arising from indults granted on several occasions at the request of national councils.)[153]

The revision of the entirety of the liturgical celebration and the corresponding restoration of the catechumenate, first, make the adult rite basic and

[144]N. 44: *DOL* 2371.
[145]N. 65: *DOL* 2392.
[146]*SC* 67.
[147]*RBaptC* 5, 1: *DOL* 2289.
[148]N. 7, 1: *DOL* 2291.
[149]N. 4: *DOL* 2288.

[150]N. 2: *DOL* 2286.
[151]N. 1: *DOL* 2285.
[152]See above, note 132.
[153]The American bilingual ritual (*Collectio Rituum ad Instar Appendicis Ritualis Romani,* Washington: National Catholic Welfare Conference, 1961) did provide the rite for adult baptism (pp. 59–181).

primary and, second, reserve the rite for children to those who have not reached the age of reason (or are "*non sui compos*") and are thus unable to profess faith and undergo the catechumenal formation.

Baptismal Water

Canon 853 — Outside a case of necessity the water to be used in the conferral of baptism should be blessed in accord with the prescriptions of the liturgical books.

The baptismal water is ordinarily blessed in the course of the rite of baptism except during the Easter season, when the water blessed at the Easter Vigil is used.[154] In the Latin Church the water is no longer blessed at the vigil of Pentecost. During the Easter season, the relationship between baptism and the paschal mystery is signified more clearly by the practice of keeping the baptismal water from the Vigil; at other times the blessing "expresses the mystery of salvation that the Church recalls and programs. If the baptistery is supplied with running water, the blessing is given to the water as it flows."[155]

A minister of the sacrament who may not himself or herself bless the water should, apart from necessity, use water already blessed. A priest or deacon who ministers the sacrament should bless the water except in cases of necessity when there is not sufficient time.

The ritual adds that the water should be "clean, both for the sake of the authentic sacramental symbolism and for hygienic reasons." Depending on the climate, moreover, the water should be heated beforehand.[156]

Immersion and Infusion

Canon 854 — Baptism is to be conferred either by immersion or by pouring, the prescriptions of the conference of bishops being observed.

The canon differs from its predecessor, canon 758 of the 1917 Code, in two ways: (1) Sprinkling as a mode of baptism has been omitted lest it appear to be as appropriate and fitting as immersion or pouring. (2) The preference is given to immersion, in accord with the ritual: it is "more suitable as a symbol of participation in the death and resurrection of Christ."[157]

With regard to the choice of immersion or pouring, which the ritual indicates is a matter of local custom,[158] the individual case may be determinative

but always "so that in different traditions and circumstances there will be a clear understanding that this washing is not just a purification rite but the sacrament of being joined to Christ."[159]

The canon does not speak explicitly, as did its predecessor, of a combination of immersion and pouring, in which the candidate stands in a pool of water and, thus partially immersed, has water poured on his or her head. The ritual, however, does allow either total or partial immersion, namely, the immersion of the whole body or, especially in the case of adults, the immersion of the head only.[160]

The modes of baptizing may be further determined and refined by the prescriptions of the conference of bishops, which will take into account the cultural and other circumstances and the significance, whatever mode is chosen, of the sign of a cleansing bath which expresses entrance into the paschal mystery of the death and resurrection of Jesus.

Baptismal Name

Canon 855 — Parents, sponsors and the pastor are to see that a name foreign to a Christian mentality is not given.

The prior norm of canon 761 of the 1917 Code obliged the pastor to require that a Christian name (i.e., ordinarily the name of a saint or sometimes the name of a virtue or the like) be given or at least added to the name chosen by the parents. In the revision the responsibility in this matter belongs to the parents (of an infant) and the sponsors as well as the pastor, and the substance of the norm is different: a Christian name in the sense of a saint's name is not required but only one that is not alien or offensive to Christian sensibilities. This amelioration of the law may permit many names that are neutral in character or have been considered as pagan or non-Christian; it excludes names chosen deliberately by parents (or even by an adult candidate) that are offensive to Christian belief or practice.

This relaxation of the law should not be understood as a denigration of Christian names or the religious and cultural significance attached to a ritual designation of names. The *Roman Ritual* had already derogated from canon 761 of the former Code, at least for non-Christian regions, describing the name which might be chosen by a catechumen as "a Christian name or one in use in that part of the world, so long as it has a Christian meaning."[161] Canon 855 enlarges upon this freedom and puts the matter negatively.

---

[154]*SC* 70.
[155]*IGIC* 21: *DOL* 2270.
[156]Ibid., 18: *DOL* 2267; 20: *DOL* 2269.
[157]Ibid., 22: *DOL* 2271.
[158]*RBaptC* 18, 2: *DOL* 2302.

[159]*RCIA* 32: *DOL* 2359.
[160]Ibid., 220.
[161]*RCIA* 203, 205; 26, 2: *DOL* 2353.

Day of Baptismal Celebration

Canon 856 — Although baptism may be celebrated on any day, it is recommended that ordinarily it be celebrated on a Sunday or if possible at the Easter Vigil.

This canon is concerned with the time or day appropriate for the liturgical celebration of baptism, not directly with the period of time which may elapse between birth and infant baptism.

In the liturgical books the Easter Vigil is considered as the ordinary time for the baptism of both adults and infants, Sunday as the ordinary time for the baptism of infants. A stronger preference for the Easter Vigil had been proposed for this canon, but it was not accepted because of the actual practice in the case of infant baptism and the possibility of some conflict with canon 867. In effect, canon 867 requires that the baptism of infants not be postponed for a full year or for many months until the next Easter Vigil. The choice of Sunday as a preferred baptismal day is intended to give greater prominence to the paschal nature of the sacrament.[162] (*CIC* 772, in accord with the very ancient usage of the Church, prior to the development of the norm of c. 867, considered it fitting that adults be baptized on the vigils of Easter and Pentecost, especially in cathedral and metropolitan churches, if this could be conveniently done.)

With regard to the choice of the day of baptism for infants, the ritual provides greater detail: "To bring out the paschal character of baptism, it is recommended that the sacrament be celebrated during the Easter Vigil or on Sunday, when the Church commemorates the Lord's resurrection."[163] This may appropriately take place at the Sunday Eucharist so the entire community may be present, but it is not desirable as a weekly practice.[164] With regard to the Christian initiation of adults, "as a general rule, pastors should make use of the rite of initiation in such a way that the sacraments themselves are celebrated at the Easter Vigil ...," but other possibilities are considered: if the number of candidates is very large, the majority should be initiated at the Easter Vigil, others during the Easter octave, e.g., at a mission station if not at the principal church; for "unusual circumstances and pastoral needs," the sacraments of initiation may be celebrated outside the Easter Vigil or Easter Sunday, but as far as possible on Sunday. The ritual also goes into detail about the time for the celebration of the other rites of initiation, particularly their scheduling during the period of the catechumenate and final preparation (i.e., during Lent, after the rite of election).[165] Canon 856 is in harmony with these norms, which have to be taken into account in understanding it.

As already mentioned, the distinct question of the early baptism of infants, in canon 867, has also to be considered. It is no longer tenable, however, that adults (those who have reached the use of reason) should, aside from necessity, be baptized "as soon as is possible worthily and conveniently, since baptism is the gate to the Church and the latter is the necessary society."[166]

Place of Baptism

Canon 857 — §1. Outside a case of necessity, the proper place for baptism is a church or oratory.

§2. As a rule adults are to be baptized in their own parish church and infants in the parish church proper to their parents, unless a just cause suggests otherwise.

This and the following three canons deal with the place of baptism. Canon 858 considers the baptismal font, which should be located in a place proper for baptism; canons 859–860 consider exceptions to the basic norm of canon 857. In general, the former law was principally influenced by the desire to protect parochial rights; the revised law is largely concerned with the more important consideration of baptism as entrance into the parish community.

Canon 857, §1 repeats the norm of canon 773 of the 1917 Code, but adds the possibility of exceptions in case of necessity. Although historically baptism has been frequently celebrated outside churches, e.g., in rivers and open pools,[167] it is a very strong tradition that the sacrament, as a sign of entrance into the Christian community, should be celebrated in the place where that community assembles for worship. Only in the place of assembly can the sign of incorporation into the ecclesial body be fully manifested. That this should be the local ecclesial body is the intent of paragraph two. A distinction is made: only in case of necessity should baptism take place outside a church or oratory; the baptism should be celebrated in the candidate's parish church, but an exception can be made for a lesser or just cause. (For the proper pastor—or, this instance, parish—by reason of domicile or quasi-domicile, one should see c. 107; here the rule is to be applied analogously to the candidate for baptism.)

In paragraph one the principle is that the sacraments are ordinarily to be celebrated in sacred places, as described in canon 1205; in paragraph two the principle is that, since incorporation into the Church is by means of incorporation into the

[162]*IGIC* 28: *DOL* 2277.
[163]*RBaptC* 9: *DOL* 2293.
[164]Ibid.
[165]*RCIA* 49–62: *DOL* 2376–2389.

[166]A. Vermeersch-I. Creusen, *Epitome Iuris Canonici,* vol. I, editio septima (Mechliniae-Romae: H. Dessain, 1974, n. 52).
[167]J.G. Davies, *The Architectural Setting of Baptism* (London: Barrie and Rockliff, 1962).

local community, the parish church is the place of baptism. Among the "lesser groupings of the faithful [i.e., lesser than the particular or diocesan church] . . . parishes, set up locally under a pastor, taking the place of the bishop, are the most important: in some manner they represent the visible Church established throughout the world."[168]

An apparent exception to paragraph two, for which no cause is needed, is the celebration of the initiatory sacraments under the presidency of the bishop in the cathedral church. This holds true in the case mentioned in canon 863 and indeed in any case since "the liturgical life of the diocese is centered around the bishop, especially in his cathedral church," and it is "because it is impossible for the bishop always and everywhere to preside over the whole flock of his Church" that lesser groupings, and principally parishes, exist."[169]

The liturgical books parallel these norms: "So that baptism may clearly appear as the sacrament of the Church's faith and of incorporation into the people of God, it should normally be celebrated in the parish church. . . ."[170] This should, moreover, be at a communal celebration, as asserted in canon 837, §2 and repeatedly in the ritual, where it is made specific for the baptism of infants: "As far as possible, all recently born babies should be baptized at a common celebration on the same day. Except for a good reason, baptism should not be celebrated more than once on the same day in the same church."[171]

Baptismal Font

Canon 858 — §1. Every parish church is to have a baptismal font, with due regard for the cumulative right already acquired by other churches.

§2. The local ordinary, after hearing the pastor of the place, may permit or order for the convenience of the faithful that there be a baptismal font in another church or oratory within the boundaries of the parish.

The *Roman Ritual* gives a definition of the place where a font is located:

The baptistery is the area where the baptismal font flows or has been placed. It should be reserved for the sacrament of baptism and should be a place worthy of Christians to be reborn in water and the Holy Spirit. It may be situated either inside or outside the church or in some other part of the church easily seen by the faithful; it

should be large enough to accommodate a good number of people.[172]

(For the baptismal liturgy of the word "a suitable place should be provided in the baptistery or in the church.")[173]

The font itself, as a physical structure, may take any appropriate form with either flowing water or some part of the structure, pool or basin in form, that will hold the baptismal water; it "should be spotlessly clean and of pleasing design."[174]

The direct concern of the canon, however, is with the font not as a physical structure but as the regular place for baptism, although on occasion some smaller and movable vessel may be used for the sacrament, e.g., in the sanctuary of the church. It is considered, moreover, to be the principal indication of the right of a church or oratory to celebrate the sacrament, in accord with canon 857, §1. Therefore paragraph one requires a font in every parish church even if there may be some existing and vested right in another church or churches to be the alternative place for baptisms in the area; this is what is meant by a cumulative right of such a church, a right which never excludes that of the parish church. This alternative is retained from canon 774, §1 of the 1917 Code, where it was understood as respecting such rights, perhaps of very lengthy usage, but also as inhibiting them for the future as abuses (i.e., as weakening the parish as liturgical community); that canon of the former Code had revoked and reprobated all statutes, privileges, and customs contrary to the possession of a font by a parish church.

A further exception is made in paragraph two, following canon 774, §2 of the 1917 Code. This permits baptisms to be celebrated outside the principal parish church by way of a permission from the local ordinary for cause (namely, the convenience of the people) to erect a font in a (secondary) church or oratory within the territorial confines of the parish. He is first bound to consult the pastor, according to a new provision of the law, already mentioned in the *Roman Ritual,* which adds: "In these places too, the right to celebrate baptism belongs ordinarily to the pastor."[175]

This exception may be a common occurrence in parishes with very large territory, where there are natural subcommunities in particular areas or neighborhoods or even along other lines. On the one hand, the concession of one or more additional places for baptism should not work against the development and maintenance of a lively sense of

[168]SC 42.
[169]SC 41–42.
[170]RBaptC 10: DOL 2294.
[171]IGIC 27: DOL 2276.

[172]Ibid., 25: *DOL* 2274. On these and similar questions, see (U.S.) Bishops' Committee on the Liturgy, *Environment and Art in Catholic Worship* (Washington: USCC, 1978), nos. 76–77.
[173]*IGIC* 24: *DOL* 2273.
[174]Ibid., 19: *DOL* 2268.
[175]*RBaptC* 11: *DOL* 2295.

community within the one parish; on the other hand, there may be divisions within the larger parochial community which constitute true local congregations, although not recognized canonically as parishes. For the meaning of oratories, one should see canon 1223; the distinction between public and semi-public oratories, which was employed in canon 774, §2 of the 1917 Code, is no longer made.

Baptism in Other Churches

Canon 859 — If due to grave inconvenience because of distance or other circumstances a person to be baptized cannot go or be taken to the parish church or to the other church or oratory mentioned in can. 858, §2, baptism may and must be conferred in some nearer church or oratory, or even in some other fitting place.

Although this canon corresponds to canon 775 of the former Code and has the same purpose, some of the earlier restrictions are removed: there is no mention of the pastor as minister of baptism in these circumstances; the "serious inconvenience or danger" (understood as danger to an infant) is reduced to "grave inconvenience"; and the possible use of a fitting place (i.e., not a church or oratory) is included. The last provision was introduced to allow for needs in mission territory. More precise determinations may be made in particular law or decree, protecting both the ecclesial nature of baptism celebrated within the parish community and the special circumstances of individual parishes or localities.

Baptism outside Churches

Canon 860 — §1. Outside the case of necessity, baptism is not to be conferred in private homes, unless the local ordinary has permitted this for a grave cause.
§2. Baptism is not to be celebrated in hospitals unless the diocesan bishop has decreed otherwise, except in case of necessity or some other compelling pastoral reason.

Although a reference to some place of baptism other than a church or oratory has been introduced into the preceding canon, both paragraphs of canon 860 are directed toward avoiding abuses and safeguarding signs of the (parochial) community's role in the celebrating of baptism. In summary, baptism should take place in a church or oratory except in case of necessity (c. 857, §1), in the parish church except for just cause (c. 857, §2) or alternatively in a church or oratory lawfully possessing a baptismal font (c. 858, §2) or in a church with a vested and cumulative right to celebrate baptisms (c. 858, §1), or finally because of "distance or other circumstances" and to avoid serious inconvenience, in the

church, oratory, or other fitting place mentioned in canon 859.

Canon 860 refines this last matter further, dealing in paragraph one with baptism in private homes. Canon 776 of the 1917 Code had described different circumstances which would permit baptism at home: the first involved a concession in favor of the families of rulers, a concession that is abrogated in the revision; the second allowed the local ordinary to grant permission "in accord with his prudent judgment and conscience, for a just and reasonable cause, in some extraordinary case." This has now been reframed so that the local ordinary may grant the permission, which is not needed in case of necessity, for a grave cause. The case of necessity is strictly explained in the ritual as danger of death; the ritual also omits the possibility of permission by the local ordinary, preferring to insist upon community and parochial celebration of the sacrament.[176]

The case mentioned in paragraph two has arisen in urban situations in which births regularly take place in hospitals and in which the celebration of baptism, although it may be a sign of pastoral solicitude on the part of the hospital chaplain, runs counter to the development of strong ecclesial communities. A new norm has therefore been introduced in paragraph two, derived from an early draft of the conciliar constitution on the liturgy and more immediately from the ritual:

Unless the bishop decides otherwise, baptism should not be celebrated in hospitals, except in cases of emergency or for some other compelling pastoral reason. But care should always be taken that the parish priest is notified and that the parents are suitably prepared beforehand.[177]

CHAPTER II
THE MINISTER OF BAPTISM
[cc. 861–863]

The three canons of this chapter deal with (1) the minister in both usual and exceptional circumstances, (2) the right to baptize in a given territory, and (3) the (diocesan) bishop as minister of the sacrament.

Minister of Baptism

Canon 861 — §1. The ordinary minister of baptism is a bishop, presbyter or deacon, with due regard for the prescription of can. 530, n. 1.
§2. If the ordinary minister is absent or impeded, a catechist or other person deputed for this function by the local ordinary confers baptism licitly as does any person with the right intention in

---

[176]Ibid., 12: *DOL* 2296.
[177]Ibid., 13: *DOL* 2297.

case of necessity; shepherds of souls, especially the pastor, are to be concerned that the faithful be instructed in the correct manner of baptizing.

The 1917 Code had mentioned only the priest as ordinary minister of the sacrament. With the restoration of the diaconate, the fundamental determination in paragraph one has been fully spelled out, and canon 741 of the 1917 Code (which considered the deacon as extraordinary minister, acting only with permission) has been abrogated.[178] All the non-ordained would be considered as extraordinary ministers, that is, outside the regular and customary order, should such terminology be employed. The cross-reference to canon 530, 1°, indicates that the ministry of baptism is entrusted or committed especially to the pastor (and a fortiori, but in a different way, to the bishop, as in c. 863). This replaces the stricter formulation of canon 738 of the former Code, which reserved baptism to the pastor or a priest with the pastor's permission or the permission of the local ordinary. Despite this relaxation, the next canon of this chapter insists upon the right and responsibility to baptize in a given territory.

The minister is here understood as the presiding minister or celebrant. The offices and ministries of others in the celebration, including the parents and sponsors, are elaborated upon in the introduction to the ritual.[179] When the baptism is celebrated during the Eucharist, the presiding priest administers the sacrament itself, but he may be assisted by other priests or by deacons, e.g., if the number of infants is very large.[180]

In paragraph two rather distinct cases are treated. First, it is understood that in many situations catechists or others who are not ordained may be regularly and commonly deputed by the local ordinary as ministers of baptism, and a somewhat simpler rite is provided for such circumstances when a priest or deacon is not available.[181] (It was intended in an earlier draft of the canon to specify instituted acolytes and readers ahead of catechists, but they are now included among any others who may be deputed.) The second case is that of necessity when any person who has the right intention may baptize; again a rite is provided, with the understanding that in extreme emergency, i.e., at the moment when death is imminent, the simple washing with water while saying the baptismal formula suffices.[182]

On this point, the *Roman Ritual* has this explanation:

In imminent danger of death and especially at the moment of death, when no priest or deacon is available, any member of the faithful, indeed anyone with the right intention, may and sometimes must administer baptism. If it is a question only of danger of death [i.e., if death is not imminent], then the sacrament should be administered by a member of the faithful if possible, according to the shorter rite. Even in this case a small community should be formed or at least one or two witnesses should be present if possible.[183]

This last provision is, first, to make the celebration genuinely ecclesial even in the most difficult circumstances and, second, to strengthen the proof of baptism, as in canons 875–876.

Although it is anomalous that the minister of baptism in extreme circumstances should be a non-believer, paragraph two expresses both the importance of the sacrament and the concern that no person, otherwise ready to be baptized, should be deprived of the sign and sacrament of cleansing and incorporation in the Church. The norm is applicable equally to the baptism of adults, although the occasion of principal concern (see c. 867, §1) is the baptism of infants. Again the ritual elaborates on the preparation of persons who must be ministers of baptism in danger of death:

All laypersons, since they belong to the priestly people, and especially parents and, by reason of their work, catechists, midwives, family or social workers, or nurses of the sick, as well as physicians or surgeons, should be thoroughly aware, according to their capacities, of the proper method of baptizing in case of emergency. They should be taught by parish priests, deacons, and catechists. . . .[184]

Among the related canons of the 1917 Code (*CIC* 738, §1; 741–743), the preferences among those who should baptize in danger of death (cleric preferred to a lay person, man preferred to a woman, etc.)[185] have been suppressed along with the prohibition of parents baptizing their children except in danger of death when no one else is present to baptize the child.[186]

Right To Baptize

Canon 862 — Outside the case of necessity, it is not lawful for anyone, without the required permis-

---

[178]*LG* 29: *DOL* 149; *IGIC* 11: *DOL* 2260.
[179]*IGIC* 7–17: *DOL* 2256–2266; *RCIA* 41–48: *DOL* 2368–2375; *RBaptC* 4–7: *DOL* 2288–2291.
[180]See *RBaptC*, "Rite of Baptism for a Large Number of Children," n. 124.
[181]*RBaptC*, "Rite of Baptism for Children Administered by a Catechist when No Priest or Deacon Is Available."
[182]*RCIA*, "Short Rite of Adult Initiation in Proximate Danger of Death or at the Point of Death"; *RBaptC*, "Rite of Baptism for Children in Danger of Death when No Priest or Deacon Is Available."

[183]*IGIC* 16: *DOL* 2265.
[184]Ibid., 17: *DOL* 2266.
[185]*CIC* 742, §2
[186]*CIC* 742, §3.

sion, to confer baptism in the territory of another, not even upon his own subjects.

The previous canons on the right of the pastor to baptize the infants and adults of his parish (*CIC* 738, §§1–2; 739; 740) have been reduced to the present formulation. The canon is derived from canon 739 of the 1917 Code, with the addition of the phrase "outside the case of necessity." It is parallel to canon 530 in which the special role of the pastor in relation to the faithful of the parish is mentioned. Although the permission, even aside from necessity, may be given readily, the underlying principle is the significance of baptism as entrance into the local community or congregation, which will be one's own or, in the case of infants, is already the Christian community of one's parents. Another purpose is to assure the proper recording of baptism, as in canons 877–878.

The canon requires that permission be obtained in all instances except necessity, even when the minister might feel justified in baptizing persons of his own parish or territory ("subjects") in another territory.

Bishop as Minister

Canon 863 — **The baptism of adults, at least those who have completed fourteen years of age is to be referred to the bishop so that it may be conferred by him, if he judges it expedient.**

The reference here is to the diocesan bishop, and the canon is a minimal norm to strengthen what is determined more broadly in the *Roman Ritual*. In itself the Christian initiation of all adults, and not merely or at least those who are more than fourteen years of age, is reserved to the bishop, as was stated in similar language in canon 744 of the 1917 Code.

The canon was prepared to be in harmony with the existing liturgical law, despite the addition of the reference to those over fourteen years. The bishop's responsibility for all baptisms[187] is the greater in the case of adults:

> The bishop, in person or through his delegate, sets up, regulates, and promotes the pastoral formation of catechumens and admits the candidates to their election [ordinarily at the beginning of Lent] and to the sacraments. It is to be hoped that, presiding if possible at the Lenten liturgy, he will himself celebrate the rite of election and, at the Easter vigil, the sacraments of initiation. Finally, as part of his pastoral care, the bishop should depute catechists, truly worthy and properly prepared, to celebrate the minor exorcisms.[188]

(The adaptations in the rites of Christian initiation, beyond those decreed by the conference of bishops, which pertain to the diocesan bishop are enumerated in the *Roman Ritual*.)[189] The positions of authors who attempted to minimize the sense of canon 744 of the 1917 Code, which had the same effect as the revised canon, seem to be inadequate.[190]

Although the bishop is not bound by the canon to celebrate the baptism, others are bound to refer the baptism of adults to him so that, if possible and expedient in his judgment, he may be the presiding minister of baptism (and also confirmation, in accord with cc. 842, §2; 884, §1).

CHAPTER III
THOSE TO BE BAPTIZED
[cc. 864–871]

The eight canons of this chapter deal with (1) the fundamental capacity for baptism (c. 864), (2) the particular requirements for adults who are to be baptized (cc. 865–866), (3) the parallel requirements for infants (cc. 867–868), and (4) special situations in the case of conditional baptism, the baptism of foundlings, and the baptism of aborted fetuses (cc. 869–871). The language of the earlier law, "the subject of baptism" or even "recipient" of baptism was considered to be an inadequate expression of the action of the (adult) candidate who seeks the sacrament and has been avoided in favor of the neutral *baptizandi*, those to be baptized.

The sequence of the canons was changed from the earlier draft in which the special cases of an aborted fetus and a foundling were considered first, then the baptism of infants, and finally the baptism of adults. The altered sequence stresses the exemplary nature of adult initiation as fundamental to the meaning and discipline of the sacrament of baptism.

Capacity for Baptism

Canon 864 — **Every person not yet baptized and only such a person is able to be baptized.**

Although the canon may appear to be stating the obvious, it is a fundamental affirmation that all human beings, including infants (and indeed, as theologians and canonists have discussed at length, the unborn), are capable of being baptized, but that those who have died are incapable. Although slightly rephrased, the revision does not alter canon 745 of the former Code. The reference to "not yet baptized" is another assertion of what is said in canon 845, §1. In the 1917 Code, the basic norm of this

---

[187]*IGIC* 12: *DOL* 2261.
[188]*RCIA* 44: *DOL* 2371.

[189]Ibid., 66: *DOL* 2393; *RBaptC* 26: *DOL* 2310.
[190]Vermeersch-Creusen, *Epitome,* n. 28; J. Abbo-J. Hannan, *The Sacred Canons,* 2nd ed., (St. Louis: B. Herder Book Co., 1960), 1:750.

canon was followed directly by three canons (*CIC* 746–748) about several circumstances in which it might be possible to baptize a fetus within the womb or during delivery or to baptize an aborted or abnormal fetus; these norms were largely derived from the *Roman Ritual* of 1614.[191] In the revision, this question has been stated simply and in principle only in canon 871 at the end of the chapter; the revised ritual does not touch the question.

Qualifications for Adult Baptism

Canon 865 — §1. To be baptized, it is required that an adult have manifested the will to receive baptism, be sufficiently instructed in the truths of faith and in Christian obligations and be tested in the Christian life by means of the catechumenate; the adult is also to be exhorted to have sorrow for personal sins.

§2. An adult in danger of death may be baptized if, having some knowledge of the principal truths of faith, the person has in any way manifested an intention of receiving baptism and promises to observe the commandments of the Christian religion.

Assuming the canonical definition of an adult in canon 852, §1 ("[one who has] attained the use of reason"), this canon enlarges upon canon 752, §1 of the 1917 Code ("An adult may not be baptized unless knowingly, willingly, and properly instructed") in conformity with the requirement of catechumenal formation (c. 851, 1°) and the treatment of the catechumenate given in canon 788. The mention of knowledge and intention requisite in the candidate for baptism is now supplemented by direct reference to the formative and probationary character of the period of preparation for Christian initiation. The concluding clause of paragraph one is repeated from canon 752, §1 of the former Code; it explicitly adds the notion of repentance and conversion to the paschal and initiatory dimensions of the sacrament.

With regard to paragraph two, the use of "aliquam . . . cognitionem" and "quovis modo" describes, for the circumstances of danger of death, the minimal knowledge and intention sufficient on the part of the adult who may then be baptized. (The question of the unconscious adult who might earlier have given "some probable indication" of an intention to be baptized, which was the subject of *CIC* 752, §3, is suppressed in the revision of the Code.)

The canon does not offer further detail about the "principal" truths of faith; in decrees of the Apostolic See addressed to missionary circumstances the reference is to "the mysteries of faith the knowledge of which is necessary for salvation."[192] The person

who is not a catechumen should be able to make some rudimentary profession of baptismal faith, namely, a "serious indication of being converted to Christ and having given up attachment to pagan worship or immoral conduct; such a person should be willing to go through the cycle of initiation if he or she recovers"; similarly, a catechumen should make "a promise to complete the usual catechesis upon recovering."[193] In these circumstances, the person in danger of death or at the point of death should also receive the sacraments of confirmation and Eucharist in accord with canon 866.[194] For the case of an infant who has not reached the age of reason, one should see canons 889, §2 (confirmation) and 913, §2 (Eucharist).

Completion of Sacramental Initiation

Canon 866 — Unless a grave reason prevents it, an adult who is baptized is to be confirmed immediately after baptism and participate in the celebration of the Eucharist, also receiving Communion.

The canon repeats the norm of canon 753, §1 of the 1917 Code (which speaks of "grave and urgent reasons" which might excuse a person from completing sacramental initiation at once), but adds that confirmation as well as Communion are to be received immediately by the neophyte, that is, ordinarily as part of the single liturgical celebration. This addition is possible because the priest who baptizes an adult is now likewise empowered to celebrate the sacrament of confirmation, in accord with canon 883, 2°.

An attempt to minimize the significance of the completion of initiation by substituting simple "just reason" as sufficient to delay confirmation and Eucharist was rejected by the plenary commission during the process of revising the canon. This is not to deny the possibility of separating the sacraments for serious reason, when the confirmation and Eucharistic Communion have to be delayed,[195] but rather to enforce the doctrine of canon 842, §2. The position of canonists that the norm of this canon is not a significant precept is no longer tenable.[196]

The former exhortation in canon 753, §1 of the 1917 Code that the priest minister and those to be baptized should be fasting, although comformable to ancient tradition, has been suppressed. In relation to initiation at the Easter Vigil, however, the conciliar constitution urges that the paschal fast of Good Friday be prolonged throughout Holy Saturday.[197]

191Title II, c.1.
192SCOf, decr, Jan. 25, 1703: *CICFontes* 764.

193*RCIA* 279: *DOL* 2443.
194Ibid., 280: *DOL* 2444.
195Ibid., 56: *DOL* 2383.
196Abbo-Hannan, *Sacred Canons* 1:755.
197*SC* 110.

Time of Infant Baptism

Canon 867 — §1. Parents are obliged to see to it that infants are baptized within the first weeks after birth; as soon as possible after the birth or even before it parents are to go to the pastor to request the sacrament for their child and to be prepared for it properly.

§2. An infant in danger of death is to be baptized without any delay.

The canon represents, in paragraph one, a substantial departure from canon 770 of the former Code ("Infants should be baptized as soon as possible"), which itself reflected a norm introduced in the Middle Ages. Prior to that period there was greater concern, even in the case of infants, that baptism should be celebrated at the appropriate times, principally Easter and Pentecost; the "quam primum" of the Council of Florence[198] was itself understood in different ways, requiring infant baptism to be celebrated soon after birth but allowing this to be within a few days or even a month. This requirement, moreover, was more specifically determined by particular law, for example, the Second Plenary Council of Baltimore (1866), which required baptism of infants "at once."[199]

Distinguishing carefully the case of the infant in danger of death (§2), the canon recognizes several developments, chiefly that the baptism of infants should not be celebrated indiscriminately but rather with the necessary preparation of the parents, even when these are Christian and Catholic. It summarizes what is expressed more diffusely in the postconciliar legislation but removes the term "quam primum" from its reference to the time of baptism and employs it instead with reference to the requisite preparation for baptism. Such preparation should begin promptly after the birth and preferably in the period before the birth.

According to the ritual,

the first consideration is the welfare of the child, that it may not be deprived of the benefit of the sacrament; then the health of the mother must be considered so that, if at all possible, she too may be present. Then, as long as they do not interfere with the greater good of the child, there are pastoral considerations, such as allowing sufficient time to prepare the parents. . . .[200]

The chief addition made in the ritual to the norm in paragraph one is found in the statement:

An infant should be baptized within the first weeks after birth. The conference of bishops may,

for sufficiently serious pastoral reasons, determine a longer interval of time between birth and baptism. When the parents are not yet prepared to profess the faith or to undertake the duty of bringing up the children as Christians, it is for the pastor, keeping in mind whatever regulations may have been laid down by the conference of bishops, to determine the time for the baptism of infants.[201]

Again, the point is repeated with reference to the adaptation of the sacramental discipline:

In many countries parents are sometimes not ready for the celebration of baptism or they ask for their children to be baptized even though the latter will not afterward receive a Christian education or will even lose the faith . . . the conference of bishops may issue pastoral directives, for the guidance of pastors, to determine a longer interval between birth and baptism.[202]

A tension is thus evident between the medieval and modern usage of prompt baptism of infants and the importance that the infant be from a truly Christian family or at least be assured of Christian upbringing, in accord with canon 868, 2°. The second consideration is also supported by the older tradition of baptizing infants only at the appointed liturgical times; the canon, however, would not permit the postponement of baptism beyond a few weeks for the sole reason of permitting the celebration, otherwise appropriate, at the Easter Vigil, unless the conference of bishops determines an interval longer than the canon contemplates.

All this, however, is carefully distinct from paragraph two, with its provision that an infant in danger of death should be baptized without delay. This norm, moreover, is not affected by the contemporary development of a funeral rite for the infant who dies before he or she can be baptized.[203]

Requirements for Infant Baptism

Canon 868 — §1. For the licit baptism of an infant it is necessary that:

1° the parents or at least one of them or the person who lawfully takes their place gives consent;

2° there be a founded hope that the infant will be brought up in the Catholic religion; if such a hope is altogether lacking, the baptism is to be put off according to the prescriptions of particular law and the parents are to be informed of the reason.

§2. The infant of Catholic parents, in fact of non-Catholic parents also, who is in danger of death is licitly baptized even against the will of the parents.

[198]Eugene IV, bull *Cantate Domino* (sess. XI): *COD* 576.
[199]*Acta*, n. 225.
[200]*RBaptC* 8: *DOL* 2292, n. 5: *DOL* 2289. See also c. 851, 2°.

[201]*RBaptC* 8, 3–4: *DOL* 2292.
[202]Ibid., 25: *DOL* 2309.
[203]*Rite of Funerals*, n. 82, 231–237.

This canon is a new redaction of norms found in the 1917 Code (*CIC* 750–751). It states in stricter terms the requirement that an infant be baptized only with (1) the consent of the parent(s) or responsible guardian and (2) the assurance of Catholic upbringing. The child who is baptized before he or she can profess Christian faith is baptized in the faith of the Church as this is expressed by parents or others within the Catholic community who take their place, such as guardians of orphaned children or sponsors who are in a position to be responsible for Catholic upbringing.

The possibility of deferring baptism, as mentioned in the ritual and described in the commentary on canon 867, §1, is based upon the fear that the child will not be supported in the Christian faith subsequently. The norms of postponing baptism in such circumstances, ordinarily until the parent(s) can be adequately moved or instructed so that they can give an assurance or hope of Catholic upbringing, may be specified in particular law. The additional note that the reasons should be explained to the parents is intended to avoid the risk of further alienating parents who are themselves deficient in the practice of the Catholic religion.

In 1980 the Sacred Congregation for the Doctrine of the Faith issued an instruction on the baptism of infants which (1) vindicated the Christian tradition of infant baptism and (2) summarized contemporary difficulties, including those arising in pluralistic societies.[204] The instruction is completed with pastoral-directive norms; these had already been anticipated in a private response of 1970, in which "non-practicing" Christian parents were defined as those "who are polygamous, unmarried, married lawfully but lapsed altogether from the regular practice of the faith, or those who request their child's baptism as a purely social convention." With regard to these, the response offered the following summary:

a. It is essential to bring the parents to a recognition of their responsibilities.

b. It is also essential to evaluate the sufficiency of the guarantees concerning the Catholic upbringing of the children. These guarantees are given by some member of the family or by the godfather or godmother or by the support of the Christian community. (By guarantees we mean that there is a well-founded hope of a Catholic upbringing.)

c. If the conditions are sufficient in the judgment of the pastor, the Church can go ahead with the baptism, because the children are baptized in the faith of the Church.

d. If the conditions are insufficient, there is the possibility of proposing to the parents: the enrollment of the child with a view to its being baptized later; further pastoral meetings as a way of preparing them for the rite of reception of their child for baptism.[205]

Although in this 1970 response the Congregation contemplated an enrollment of the child with the possibility of a rite of reception of the child who would later be baptized (which would offer some analogy to a period of "catechumenate" during which the parents would receive Christian formation), in the instruction of 1980 the Congregation affirmed the need for dialogue with the parents and their adequate preparation before the baptism, but rejected the proposal of a rite of enrollment which might easily be confused with the sacrament of baptism. It proposed two pastoral principles, first, that the divine gift of baptism for the child should not *ex sese* be deferred, but, second, that:

Guarantees are to be made that this gift can so grow through genuine upbringing in the faith and Christian life that the sacrament may attain its total "truth." These guarantees are regularly to be offered by the parents or relatives, even if they can be supplied in various ways in the Christian community. If, however, these guarantees are not truly serious, this can be reason to defer the sacrament; if, finally, they are certainly null, the sacrament is to be denied.[206]

As already noted, it is for particular law to determine further the norm of paragraph one, number two, but paragraph two is a summary rule for the special circumstance of any child in danger of death. It had originally been intended to limit the norm of paragraph two, dealing with the sensitive matter of baptizing a child against the will of its parents, by the clause "unless from this [the baptism] the danger of hatred of religion may arise."

Conditional Baptism

Canon 869 — §1. If there is a doubt whether one has been baptized or whether baptism was validly conferred and the doubt remains after serious investigation, baptism is to be conferred conditionally.

§2. Those baptized in a non-Catholic ecclesial community are not to be baptized conditionally unless, after an examination of the matter and the form of words used in the conferral of baptism and after a consideration of the intention of an adult

---

[204]Oct. 20, 1980: *AAS* 72 (1980), 1137–1156.

[205]July 13, 1970: *N* 7 (1971), 69–70; *DOL* 2317–2318.
[206]*AAS* 72 (1980), 1151.

baptized person and of the minister of the baptism, a serious reason for doubting the validity of the baptism is present.

§3. If the conferral or the validity of the baptism in the cases mentioned §§1 and 2 remains doubtful, baptism is not to be conferred until the doctrine of the sacrament of baptism is explained to the person, if an adult, and the reasons for the doubtful validity of the baptism have been explained to the adult recipient or, in the case of an infant, to the parents.

This canon enlarges upon canon 845, §2, which treats the possibility of celebrating conditionally, in case of doubt, the three sacraments which may not be validly received a second time. For the postconciliar development in relation to the reception of Christians concerning whose baptism there is doubt, one should see the commentary on that canon.

With direct reference to baptism, paragraph one indicates two instances in which baptism may be celebrated with the condition, "If you are not [already] baptized, . . . " These are (1) a doubt of the fact of baptism, which cannot be resolved after serious investigation, e.g., no record or witnesses can be found; and (2) a doubt whether the baptism, which can be established to have occurred, was valid in view of a defect of the elements mentioned in canon 849—again if the doubt cannot be resolved after serious investigation. Ordinarily an inquiry into the records and ritual of a Christian church or ecclesial community should make it possible to avoid conditional baptism.

In paragraph two, the implications of the presumption set up in the "Rite of Receiving Baptized Christians into the Full Communion of the Catholic Church" are drawn out to indicate the nature of the inquiry that is to be made:

The sacrament of baptism may not be repeated and conditional baptism is not permitted unless there is prudent doubt of the fact or the validity of the baptism already received. If after serious investigation it seems necessary—because of such prudent doubt—to confer baptism again conditionally, the minister should explain beforehand the reasons why baptism is conferred conditionally in this instance and he should administer it in the private form.[207]

The pastoral norm in paragraph three, derived from the text of the ritual just quoted, will avoid needlessly calling into question the practices of other churches and ecclesial communities, for which

there should be "just esteem."[208] In the case of children, the correct instruction of the parents or others will avoid giving the false impression that a repetition of the sacrament is involved. As the reference in paragraph three to both of the preceding paragraphs of the canon indicates, this reasoning is equally applicable in all cases of conditional baptism.

It is for the local ordinary to determine, in individual cases, what rites are to be included or excluded in conditional baptism.[209]

Special Cases of Baptism

Canon 870 — A foundling or abandoned child is to be baptized unless upon diligent investigation proof of baptism is established.

This canon has to be understood in conjunction with canon 868, §1, 2°, that is, the infant may be baptized only when there is the assurance of Catholic upbringing, in this instance an assurance from those who will have the care of the abandoned infant or foundling.

The canon differs from canon 749 of the 1917 Code, from which it is derived, only by suppressing the former reference to conditional baptism. It sets up a presumption, unless upon careful investigation there is proof of baptism, that the infant is unbaptized and therefore should be baptized unconditionally.

Canon 871 — If aborted fetuses are alive, they are to be baptized if this is possible.

The revised text differs from canon 747 of the former Code, which required that "all aborted fetuses, at whatever stage of gestation, should be baptized absolutely, if certainly alive, and conditionally if there is doubt." The norm is now stated simply: whatever the reason for the abortion, if possible a living fetus should be baptized unconditionally. For this reason the liturgical law, in accord with canon 861, §2, mentions specifically those who should be instructed in the manner of baptizing in such circumstances: parents, catechists, midwives, family or social workers, nurses of the sick, physicians, and surgeons.[210]

Other special cases, such as baptism in the womb or in the course of delivery or the baptism of abnormal fetuses, are no longer mentioned, canons 746 and 748 of the 1917 Code being suppressed and such questions left to pastoral theory and practice.

---

[207]*RCIA*, appendix, n. 7: *DOL* 2482.

[208]*ED* I, 18: *AAS* 59 (1967), 574–592; *DOL* 972. The *Directory* is the source for the norm of the ritual, the ritual is the source for the canon (see nos. 12–19: *DOL* 966–973).

[209]*RCIA*, appendix, n. 7: *DOL* 2482.

[210]*IGIC* 17: *DOL* 2266.

**CHAPTER IV
SPONSORS
[cc. 872–874]**

The three canons of this chapter replace eight canons of the 1917 Code (*CIC* 762–769), suppressing the distinction between valid and lawful sponsorship along with the canonical institute of spiritual relationship, which gave rise to a matrimonial impediment (*CIC* 1079). This does not diminish either the significance or the responsibility of sponsors within the community of faith, but it does away with the previous canonical effects of spiritual relationship.

Responsibiity of Sponsors

Canon 872 — **Insofar as possible one to be baptized is to be given a sponsor who is to assist an adult in Christian initiation, or, together with the parents, to present an infant at the baptism, and who will help the baptized to lead a Christian life in harmony with baptism, and to fulfill faithfully the obligations connected with it.**

The liturgical books define in fuller terms the function of godparents (i.e., "sponsors," as used here in canon 872 and subsequently), within the offices and ministries of the Church:

It is a very ancient custom of the Church that adults are not admitted to baptism without a godparent, a member of the Christian community who will assist them at least in the final preparation for baptism [i.e., from their election, ordinarily at the beginning of Lent] and after baptism will help them to persevere in the faith and in their lives as Christians.

In the baptism of children, as well, a godparent is to be present in order to represent the expansion of the spiritual family of the one to be baptized and the role of the Church as a mother. As occasion offers, the godparent helps the parents to lead the child to profess the faith and to show this by living it.

At least in the final rites of the catechumenate and in the actual celebration of baptism the godparent's part is to testify to the faith of the adult candidate or, together with the parents, to profess the Church's faith, in which the child is being baptized.[211]

The term "sponsor" is used for godparent ("patrinus") in translating the revised Code. It serves to indicate the dimension of the godparent's role by which he or she testifies before the Christian community to the adult candidate's faith and probity of life. In the liturgical books, however, "sponsor" is the term used for the person who accompanies the candidate seeking admission to the catechumenate. Such a sponsor "stands as a witness to the candidate's moral character, faith, and intention";[212] he or she may or may not also serve as godparent ("patrinus") during the subsequent periods leading up to sacramental initiation and during the post-baptismal period. The godparent of an adult is thus understood as the one who is chosen by the candidate, delegated by the local Christian community, and approved by the priest to testify, from the time of election, to the community about the candidate. He or she is "to show the candidate how to practice the Gospel in personal and social life and to be for the candidate a bearer of Christian witness and a guardian over growth in the baptismal life."[213]

Number of Sponsors

Canon 873 — **Only one male or one female sponsor or one of each sex is to be employed.**

Although the language of the canon differs somewhat from canon 764 of the 1917 Code, the substance remains unchanged, with the purpose of excluding multiplication of sponsors. The norm of the ritual is similar: "Each child may have a godfather and a godmother."[214] It is assumed that an adult will have only one sponsor, as explained in the commentary on canon 872, but a second sponsor is not excluded.

Qualifications of Sponsors

Canon 874 — **§1. To be admitted to the role of sponsor, a person must:
1° be designated by the one to be baptized, by the parents or the one who takes their place or, in their absence, by the pastor or minister and is to have the qualifications and intention of performing this role;
2° have completed the sixteenth year, unless a different age has been established by the diocesan bishop or it seems to the pastor or minister that an exception is to be made for a just cause;
3° be a Catholic who has been confirmed and has already received the sacrament of the Most Holy Eucharist and leads a life in harmony with the faith and the role to be undertaken;
4° not be bound by any canonical penalty legitimately imposed or declared;**

---

[211]Ibid., 8–9: *DOL* 2257–2258.

[212]*RCIA* 42: *DOL* 2369.
[213]Ibid., 43: *DOL* 2370.
[214]*RBaptC* 6: *DOL* 2290.

5° not be the father or the mother of the one to be baptized.

§2. A baptized person who belongs to a non-Catholic ecclesial community may not be admitted except as a witness to baptism and together with a Catholic sponsor.

The suppression of the canonical effects of serving as sponsor, specifically the spiritual relationship that was an impediment to marriage, made unnecessary the distinct series of requirements for validity and licitness for sponsors (*CIC* 765–767). Instead the simple listing in paragraph one of this canon replaces the old canons and supplements the more general statement of the ritual, which speaks of godparents as having sufficient maturity for the responsibility, being themselves fully initiated, and being Catholics who are canonically free to serve.[215]

In addition to what is said in number one of paragraph one, the sponsors of adults are understood to be delegated by the Christian community and approved by the priest (pastor), who is the one competent to judge the qualifications which are required.[216]

Number three requires that the sponsor be himself or herself a fully initiated Catholic Christian, having received the three sacraments of initiation; paragraph two deals with the possible role of a Christian who is not in full communion with the Catholic Church. It is clear that a person who has not been initiated as a Christian cannot appropriately fulfill such responsibilities as testifying to the community about a catechumen's faith and goodness of life or of undertaking, in the case of a child, the role of assisting in Catholic upbringing. Particular law may be more specific about the moral or other qualifications of sponsors.

Number five is a traditional norm, indicative of the distinction between natural parenthood and spiritual parenthood. It takes on greater significance because of the greater insistence upon the primary role of natural parents in the revised ritual.[217]

Other disqualifications from service as sponsor (affecting religious, those in sacred orders, spouses of the candidates, etc.) have been suppressed.

With regard to paragraph two, the rationale is explained in the 1967 *Directory on Ecumenism*:

For it is not simply as a relative or friend of the one to be baptized or confirmed that the godparent has responsibility for the Christian upbringing of the recipient; in acting as the guarantor of the faith of the candidate, the godparent is also the representative of the community of faith,[218]

and in particular the Catholic community. The admission of the baptized person belonging to a non-Catholic ecclesial community to serve as a Christian witness to a baptism is on account of that person's "having a convinced faith in Christ."[219] The canon does not suppress, but does not advert to, the special case of a Christian of a separated Eastern Church (not directly referred to in the expression "ecclesial community"). Such a person may be admitted not only as a Christian witness but also as a sponsor in the proper sense, along with the Catholic sponsor, who has "the duty of looking out for the Christian upbringing of the baptized."[220]

CHAPTER V
THE PROOF AND RECORD OF CONFERRED BAPTISM
[cc. 875–878]

The four canons of this chapter treat, as the heading indicates, (1) the means of establishing the fact of baptism (cc. 875–876) and (2) the recording, or registration, of baptisms (cc. 877–878).

Proof of Baptism

Canon 875 — One who administers baptism is to see to it that, unless a sponsor is present, there be at least a witness by whom the conferral of baptism can be proved.

Canon 876 — If it is not prejudicial to anyone, to prove the conferral of baptism, the declaration of a single witness who is above suspicion suffices or the oath of the baptized person, if the baptism was received at an adult age.

The two canons expand what is found in canon 779 of the 1917 Code, without altering the substance of that canon. The only addition is the obligation placed upon the minister to see that there be a witness in addition to himself or herself; ordinarily the principal witness is the sponsor, but canon 875 is concerned with the special circumstances when baptism is celebrated without any assembly of the Christian community.

Ordinarily the record of baptism (cc. 877–878) should be available as proof that the baptism has taken place. In the absence of such a public document, the testimony of a single witness or of the person baptized will suffice, e.g., to establish baptism so that one may be admitted to other sacraments. Greater proof may be needed when the rights of another person may be adversely affected, e.g., if the fact of baptism must be established or disproved in a cause for the declaration of nullity of marriage.

---

[215]*IGIC* 10: *DOL* 2269.
[216]See above, note 213.
[217]*SC* 67; see *RBaptC* 5: *DOL* 2289.
[218]*RBaptC* 57: *DOL* 1011.

[219]Ibid.
[220]Ibid., n. 48: *DOL* 1002; see *RBaptC* 10, 3: *DOL* 2259.

Registration of Baptism

Canon 877 — §1. **The pastor of the place where the baptism is celebrated must carefully and without delay record in the baptismal book the names of those baptized making mention of the minister, parents, sponsors, witnesses if any and the place and date of the conferred baptism, together with an indication of the date and place of birth.**

§2. If it is a question of a child born of an unmarried mother, the name of the mother is to be inserted if there is public proof of her maternity or if she asks this willingly, either in writing or before two witnesses; likewise the name of the father is to be inserted if his paternity has been proved either by some public document or by his own declaration before the pastor and two witnesses; in other cases, the name of the one baptized is recorded without any indication of the name of the father or the parents.

§3. If it is a question of an adopted child, the names of the adopting parents are to be recorded, and also, at least if this is to be done in the civil records of the region, the names of the natural parents, in accord with §§1 and 2, with due regard for the prescriptions of the conference of bishops.

Canon 878 — **If baptism was administered neither by the pastor nor in his presence, the minister of baptism, whoever it is, must inform the pastor of the parish in which the baptism was administered, so that he may record it in accord with can. 877, §1.**

The text of the two canons, derived in substance from canons 777–778 of the former Code, is clear. Canon 877, §1 adds to the earlier norm the inclusion of the date and place of birth of the neophyte and the reference to witnesses, in accord with canons 875–876. The requirement of registration of baptisms is parallel to the norms for certain other sacraments, but the baptismal record is primary both in itself and as the place for additional annotation of confirmation (c. 895), orders (c. 1054), and marriage (c. 1122), as well as of validations, declaration of nullity, and dissolution of marriage (c. 1123). This requirement of additional annotations is summed up in canon 535, §2.

As is evident, the purpose of canon 877, §2 is to protect the reputation of the parents of an illegitimate child. The norm of paragraph three, which is new, recognizes both the desirability of a complete record in the case of an adopted child and also the legitimacy of concealing the names of the natural parents in such a case, in accord with the civil practice in the region and any more precise determinations of the conference of bishops.

With regard to canon 878, a second paragraph had originally been proposed, which would have required that the proper pastor of a neophyte be in-

formed of a baptism celebrated elsewhere, but this was suppressed as too great a burden on priests.

TITLE II
THE SACRAMENT OF CONFIRMATION
[cc. 879–896]

This second title of part II, on the sacrament of confirmation, follows a pattern similar to that of the title on baptism. Thus it has successive chapters on (1) celebration (cc. 880–881), (2) minister (cc. 882–888), (3) those to be confirmed (cc. 889–891), (4) sponsors (cc. 892–893), and (5) proof and record (cc. 894–896).

The canons are considerably fewer in number than those on baptism, partly because it was possible to incorporate some parallel norms on baptism by reference, partly because confirmation is secondary and complementary to baptism in Christian initiation. Traditionally, confirmation looks to the completion of initiation in the Christian's (first) sharing in the Eucharist. Recognizing but prescinding from the complexities and pastoral exceptions, the constitution on the liturgy decreed a ritual reform of the sacrament of confirmation so that its full celebration—even when not part of the single rite of initiation—would still be closely related to baptism and Eucharist:

> The rite of confirmation is also to be revised in order that the intimate connection of this sacrament with the whole of Christian initiation may stand out more clearly; for this reason it is fitting for candidates to renew their baptismal promises just before they are confirmed.

> Confirmation may be conferred within Mass when convenient; as for the rite outside Mass, a formulary is to be composed for use as an introduction.[221]

This conciliar decree has been carried out fully in the reform of the Roman liturgy, not only in the distinct rite for the celebration of confirmation in the *Roman Pontifical*[222] but also in the more fundamental and integral rite of full Christian initiation. The complete and basic rite explains the rationale of confirmation within sacramental initiation in this way:

> According to the ancient practice preserved in the Roman liturgy, adults [i.e., all who are no longer infants but have attained the use of reason][223] are not to be baptized without receiving

---

[221]*SC* 71.
[222]The *RConf* as a distinct liturgical service forms part of the *Roman Pontifical*, but it appears also, and indeed more basically, as a part of the *Roman Ritual*, in *RCIA*.
[223]C. 852, §1.

the sacrament of confirmation immediately afterward . . . , unless serious reasons prevent this. This combination signifies the unity of the paschal mystery, the link between the two sacraments through which the Son and the Spirit come with the Father to those baptized.[224]

Neither the canonical definition of the sacrament (c. 879, which introduces this title of 18 canons) nor the norms themselves, however, can be understood except as principally concerned with the more common situation of the separate confirmation of those who had been baptized as infants some years earlier. While the canons are ordinarily applicable also to the case of neophytes who are initiated after reaching the age of reason (and who are then confirmed in the same rite),[225] they are chiefly directed to the celebration of confirmation on a separate occasion from—and regularly several years later than—baptism.

In addition, the canons of this title take for granted that confirmation, even in the case of those baptized as infants, will be received before participation in the Eucharist, in accord with the tradition of both sacraments. Where it is determined that confirmation should be postponed further for cause, as canon 891 allows under certain circumstances, this practice is treated in the canons as exceptional. Common as this practice is in many regions, it does invert the sequence of confirmation and Eucharist that is clearly indicated in the canons and in the liturgical books.

Nature of Confirmation

Canon 879 — The sacrament of confirmation impresses a character and by it the baptized, continuing on the path of Christian initiation, are enriched by the gift of the Holy Spirit and bound more perfectly to the Church; it strengthens them and obliges them more firmly to be witnesses to Christ by word and deed and to spread and defend the faith.

The progressive sequence of the three sacraments of Christian initiation, even though they are celebrated together when an adult is initiated, is explained by this doctrinal or expository canon, which contains no norm. As the language of the (revised) rite of confirmation makes explicit, the gift received is the Holy Spirit of God, with an increment of enrichment, incorporation in the Church, the gifts of the Spirit, and greater conformity to Christ in witness to the faith.

Because the canon does not enter into theological speculation, it simply repeats from canon 845, §1 the reference to the character impressed by the sac-

rament, because of which it is not repeatable. It does not deny or minimize the coming of the Spirit upon those who are only baptized or the force of one's baptismal commitment to the gospel, which is renewed and deepened in the celebration of the sacrament of confirmation. Again, the canon is not concerned with the historical development of this sacrament from baptism and its relation to the "explanatory" postbaptismal anointing in the baptism of children.[226] (The ritual, however, is careful to suppress the postbaptismal anointing if indeed the newly baptized persons are to be confirmed, lest there be any confusion.)[227]

A similar exposition of the special nature of confirmation is contained in the introduction to the rite itself:

Those who have been baptized continue on the path of Christian initiation through the sacrament of confirmation. In this sacrament they receive the Holy Spirit whom the Lord sent upon the apostles on Pentecost.

This giving of the Holy Spirit conforms believers more fully to Christ and strengthens them so that they may be witnesses to Christ for the building up of his body in faith and love. They are so marked with the character or seal of the Lord that the sacrament of confirmation cannot be repeated.[228]

CHAPTER I
THE CELEBRATION OF CONFIRMATION
[cc. 880–881]

Rite of Confirmation

Canon 880 — §1. The sacrament of confirmation is conferred through anointing with chrism on the forehead, which is done by the imposition of the hand, and through the words prescribed in the approved liturgical books.

§2. The chrism to be used in the sacrament of confirmation must be consecrated by a bishop, even if the sacrament is administered by a presbyter.

As already noted, the ritual for confirmation appears, in the reformed Roman liturgy, as a distinct part of the *Roman Pontifical,* as well as in the *Rite of* [complete] *Christian Initiation of Adults.* The present canon in paragraph one follows canon 780[229] of the 1917 Code, but rephrases it to conform with an apostolic constitution of Paul VI. This document summarized the historical evolution of the sacrament and then made a formal determination:

---

[224]*RCIA* 34: *DOL* 2361.
[225]Ibid.; *RCIA* 35: *DOL* 2362; c. 866.

[226]*RBaptC* 18, 3: *DOL* 2302.
[227]*RCIA* 263.
[228]*RConf* 1–2: *DOL* 2510–2511.
[229]". . . by the laying on of the hand with the anointing with chrism. . ."

From what we have recalled, it is clear that in the administration of confirmation in the East and West, though in different ways, the most important place was occupied by the anointing, which in a certain way represents the apostolic laying on of hands. . . .

As regards the words pronounced in confirmation, we have examined with the consideration it deserves the dignity of the respected formulary used in the Latin Church, but we judge preferable the formulary belonging to the Byzantine Rite. This expresses the Gift of the Holy Spirit himself and calls to mind the outpouring of the Spirit on the day of Pentecost (see Acts 2:1–4, 38). . . .

The sacrament of confirmation is conferred through the anointing with chrism on the forehead, which is done by the laying on of the hand, and through the words: Be sealed with the Gift of the Holy Spirit.[230]

Thus paragraph one of the canon refers, without elaboration, to the reform by which (1) the very act of anointing was described and defined as a laying on of the hand of the minister and (2) the traditional Roman formulary for the anointing, dating from about the twelfth century, was replaced by an adaptation of the Byzantine "The seal of the Gift of [i.e., which is] the Holy Spirit."

With regard to the central and essential action of the rite, when it was felt in the eighteenth century that the simple anointing with the minister's thumb did not adequately express the apostolic laying on of hands, a slight addition was made in the appendix of the *Roman Pontifical*. This directed the minister of the sacrament to lay his [open or outstretched] right hand on the candidate's head during the act of anointing the forehead.[231] The revised rite has suppressed this rubric, following the exposition of Paul VI, which in effect again equated the anointing itself with a laying on of the hand.[232] The text of the apostolic constitution, however, went on immediately to speak of the significance of the additional (and more evident) laying on or extension of hands which precedes the actual anointing:

But the laying of hands on the elect [i.e., with both hands of the minister extended over the person or persons to be confirmed], carried out with the prescribed prayer before the anointing, is still

to be regarded as very important, even if it is not of the essence of the sacramental rite: it contributes to the complete perfection of the rite and to a more thorough understanding of the sacrament. It is evident that this prior laying on of hands differs from the laying on of the hand in the anointing of the forehead.[233]

The revised rite of the sacrament retains the traditional consignation or signing of the forehead with chrism in the form of the cross, although the essential formulary now used in the Latin Church no longer refers to the sign of the cross.

The consecration or blessing of chrism, the principal holy oil used in the celebration of sacraments, is reserved in paragraph two to a bishop, ordinarily the diocesan bishop, who consecrates the chrism at the annual Mass of the Chrism. No exceptions are made in the common law to allow the consecration of chrism by a priest, as is the case with the oil of catechumens (if its liturgical use is retained) and the oil of the sick: "Consecration of the chrism belongs exclusively to the bishop."[234] Nonetheless indults are granted to permit the consecration of chrism by presbyters.[235]

The validity of the sacrament of confirmation conferred by a presbyter in danger of death, in accord with canon 833, 3°, with oil not consecrated by a bishop is not called directly into question by this canon, although in the past the use of consecrated chrism has been commonly understood as essential.[236] In the consecration of chrism by the diocesan bishop, moreover, there is sign of communion within the particular church. For this reason, even in the Eastern Churches where chrismation or confirmation is normally conferred by presbyters, the consecration of chrism is reserved to the bishop.

The required composition of the chrism was formerly described strictly as consisting of olive oil with the addition of a quantity of balsam. It is now described simply as "made of oil and some aromatic substance." The oil itself may be either "olive oil or, according to local conditions, another oil extracted from plants."[237]

Canon 881 — It is desirable that the sacrament of confirmation be celebrated in a church and during Mass, but for a just and reasonable cause it may be celebrated outside Mass and in any worthy place.

This canon contains no strict or formal injunction, but its appropriateness is self-evident. With regard to place, it substantially repeats canon 791 of

---

[230]Apconst *Divinum consortium naturae*, Aug. 15, 1971: *AAS* 63 (1971), 657–664; *DOL* 2506–2507.
[231]Part III, *Additamenta, Pontificalis Ritus pro Confirmationis Sacramento;* see I. Nabuco, *Pontificalis Romani Expositio Iuridico-practica*, 2nd ed. (Paris: Desclée, 1962), 46.
[232]Commission for Interpretation of Decrees of Vatican II, June 9, 1972: *AAS* 64 (1972), 526: *DOL* 2529.

[233]Apconst *Divinum consortium naturae*, loc. cit.
[234]*ROils* 6: *DOL* 3866.
[235]SCProp, Feb. 17, 1973: *CLD* 8:472.
[236]I.A. de Aldama *et al., Sacrae Theologiae Summa IV* (Madrid: B.A.C., 1953), 204.
[237]*ROils* 3–4: *DOL* 3683–3684.

the 1917 Code; the norm of that canon about confirmation celebrated in exempt places is now covered by canon 888, in the next chapter of this title.

When celebrated together with baptism, confirmation falls under the same norms for the place of celebration as baptism; one should see canons 857–860. That confirmation be celebrated in a church, even if apart from baptism, expresses the public and communal nature of this and all sacraments. That it be celebrated during Mass can be, according to circumstances, a sign that it properly leads to the (first) participation in the Eucharist by the Christian believer.

As to time of celebration, that is, the appropriate day or season, the recommendation of Pentecost week in canon 790 of the 1917 Code has been suppressed. It is left to the liturgical books to indicate the appropriateness of confirmation (if it cannot be celebrated at the Easter Vigil) during or toward the end of the Easter season, e.g., Pentecost Sunday itself.[238]

In its positive recommendation of the celebration of confirmation during the Eucharistic celebration, which is now given as the primary rite for confirmation in the *Roman Pontifical,* the canon reflects some development since *Sacrosanctum Concilium* 71. The conciliar decree had encouraged confirmation within Mass, but spoke only in cautious terms ("permitted when convenient") because of the difficulties that were anticipated when very large numbers of persons are to be confirmed.[239] In such circumstances it was reasonably felt that the rite of confirmation might be out of proportion to the Eucharistic liturgy itself, besides being greatly burdensome because of its own length.

The subsequent change is stated in the introduction to the revised rite:

Confirmation takes place as a rule within Mass in order that the fundamental connection of this sacrament with all of Christian initiation may stand out in clearer light [see *SC* 71]. Christian initiation reaches its culmination in the communion of the body and blood of Christ. The newly confirmed therefore participate in the eucharist, which completes their Christian initiation.[240]

This development was made possible in part by a concession, first made on the occasion of the publication of the rite and repeated in canon 884: any minister of confirmation may associate presbyters with him as concelebrants in the rite of anointing, thus allowing the confirmation of even large numbers within Mass.

The *Roman Pontifical* now provides a rite of confirmation outside Mass as well (chapter II), with not only the introductory formulary decreed by *Sacrosanctum Concilium* 71 but also a full liturgy of the word, which is to be given great emphasis even when the sacrament must be celebrated outside Mass.[241]

CHAPTER II
THE MINISTER OF CONFIRMATION
[cc. 882–888]

The substantial disciplinary change in this chapter from the corresponding norms of the 1917 Code is a major extension to presbyters of the faculty to confirm in many circumstances. Although the bishop is still considered to be the ordinary minister of the sacrament in the Latin Church, the canons sum up a radical change in this pastoral office in recent decades.

The seven canons of the chapter deal in succession with (1) the ordinary and special minister (cc. 882–884), (2) the responsibility to minister the sacrament (c. 885), and (3) the licitness and validity of ministering the sacrament in particular circumstances (cc. 886–888).

Ordinary and Special Ministers

Canon 882 — The ordinary minister of confirmation is the bishop; a presbyter who has this faculty by virtue of either the universal law or a special concession of competent authority also confers this sacrament validly.

It had been anticipated at certain stages of the revision of canon 792 of the 1917 Code that the bishop would be called the "original" minister of confirmation, since this terminology had been deliberately chosen by Vatican II.[242] That terminology signifies that the bishop is the primary minister of confirmation as indeed he is of all the sacraments of Christian initiation; at the same time it acknowledges that in most rites of the Church the presbyter rather than the bishop is the regular and usual minister of confirmation. Since, however, the present Code affects only the Latin Church, the expression "ordinary minister" was retained for the bishop, while the usage *minister extraordinarius* in reference to presbyters (*CIC* 792, §2) was suppressed.

In this connection, Vatican II strongly reaffirmed the usage of presbyteral confirmation in the Eastern Churches and added interritual norms pertinent also to the Latin Church:

Regarding the minister of confirmation the practice existing in the Eastern Churches from the most ancient times is to be fully restored. Priests, therefore, using chrism blessed by a patriarch or

---

238*RCIA* 56: *DOL* 2683.
239*AcSynVat* 2, 2:567.
240*RConf* 13: *DOL* 2522.
241Ibid.
242*LG* 26: *ministri originarii;* Vorgrimler 1:217.

a bishop, are empowered to confer this sacrament.

All Eastern rite priests, either in conjunction with baptism or separately from it, can confer this sacrament validly on the faithful of any rite, including the Latin; however, for lawfulness they are to follow the regulations of both the general and particular law. Latin rite priests, in accordance with the faculties they have for the administration of this sacrament, may also administer it to the faithful of the Eastern Churches, without prejudice to the rite and, in what concerns lawfulness, observing the regulations of both the general and particular law.[243]

These interritual norms, which remain in effect, are not adverted to in this chapter of the Code, but the divergent prescriptions of canons 782, §4 (on Latin presbyters confirming non-Latins) and 782, §5 (on Eastern presbyters confirming Latins) of the 1917 Code were suppressed in favor of the conciliar decree.

The second clause of the canon distinguishes between presbyters who confirm validly by virtue of a faculty conceded by the law (in effect, by the law of the liturgical books or by the Code, specifically cc. 883–884) and presbyters who confirm validly by virtue of a faculty specially conceded to them. The same distinction was made in canon 792, §2 of the former Code. The revised text differs, however, in speaking of the latter faculty as coming from competent authority, thus including not only the Apostolic See but also the diocesan bishop[244] or indeed any minister of the sacrament who, for cause, associates presbyters with him in the celebration of the sacrament.[245]

Neither this canon nor a later canon[246] referring to the valid ministration of confirmation by presbyters enters into the theological question, much discussed in the past, regarding how the presbyter may confirm validly only if he has a faculty or some other concession. The attempted solutions to this question vary, e.g., that every presbyter has a remote but not proximate power to confirm or that the ordained presbyter has the power to confirm but its valid exercise has been withdrawn or limited, etc.[247] These considerations do not affect the clarity of the canons which follow.

Presbyteral Ministers by Law

Canon 883 — The following have the faculty of administering confirmation by the law itself:

1° within the limits of their territory, those who are equivalent in law to the diocesan bishop;

2° with regard to the person in question, the presbyter who by reason of office or mandate of the diocesan bishop baptizes one who is no longer an infant or one already baptized whom he admits into the full communion of the Catholic Church;

3° with regard to those in danger of death, the pastor or indeed any presbyter.

This canon picks up the reference in canon 880 and enumerates those, other than bishops, who have the faculty to confirm in virtue of the common law.

First are included those presbyters who govern a particular church, not a diocese, which is assimilated to or equated with a diocese: territorial prelatures, territorial abbacies, vicariates and prefectures apostolic, and apostolic administrations erected in stable fashion, as listed in canon 368.[248] In this connection the liturgical law explicitly lists diocesan administrators (formerly called vicars capitular).[249] The phrase "within the limits of their territory" has to be specially noted, first, because unlike bishops the faculty of such presbyters to confirm is restricted territorially and, second, because canon 887 makes this territorial restriction a condition for the validity of the sacrament.

The second of the three categories of presbyters is that most recently added in the revised liturgical books and flows from the principle of reform: it clarifies and strengthens the relationship of the sacraments of initiation.[250] The office of the presbyter who baptizes or admits into full communion is not specified: it is generally that of pastor, parochial vicar, rector of a church, chaplain, indeed any priest with some pastoral office who may baptize adults or receive baptized adults into full communion; those without any such office require a mandate from the bishop, namely, a mandate either to baptize or to receive into full communion. In neither case is any office or distinct mandate to *confirm* needed: this is a faculty conceded by the law itself, and the presbyter is bound by canon 885, §2 to use the faculty.

As is evident from the liturgical books, the canon does not permit the priest to confirm on an occasion other than the rite of baptism or reception into full communion.[251] Unlike the case mentioned in number one of this canon, it is not a matter of celebrating confirmation by itself, nor is the concession lawfully applicable, in the Latin Church, to the case of infants (except in danger of death).

---

[243]*OE* 13–14: *DOL* 167–168.
[244]C. 884, §1.
[245]C. 884, §2.
[246]C. 887.
[247]De Aldama, *Sacrae Theologiae Summa IV* 216–218.

[248]See c. 381, §2.
[249]*RConf* 7a: *DOL* 2516; see c. 427, §1.
[250]*RCIA* 46: *DOL* 2373; *RCIA*, appendix, n. 8: *DOL* 2483; *RConf* 8: *DOL* 2483.
[251]See Commission for Interpretation, Apr. 25, 1975: *AAS* 67 (1975), 348; *DOL* 2532.

The question arises whether the bishop may, in apparent contravention of the common law, prohibit a presbyter from exercising the faculty of number two. The resolution of the question seems to be that, while the bishop may not so act, he may very properly reserve the baptism of adults, including all who are no longer infants, to himself and thus in effect reserve their confirmation to himself.[252] The same would hold for the rite of reception into full communion, of which confirmation is an integral part unless the person has already been validly confirmed.[253]

The faculty to confirm, under the same heading, belongs also to the presbyter in "the case of readmission of an apostate from the faith who has not been confirmed."[254] This authentic interpretation of the faculty, made in 1975, was later elaborated in a second interpretation, to the effect that the presbyter may confirm, in the rite of readmission to full communion, the baptized Catholic adult who after baptism "has without fault been instructed in a non-Catholic religion or adhered to a non-Catholic religion.[255] This further interpretation appears to exclude only the case of confirmation of the baptized Catholic who through his or her own fault has been instructed in or adhered to a non-Catholic religion; in such cases any doubt of culpability should be resolved in favor of the person.

In the case of adults, however, "who were baptized as infants but did not receive further catechetical formation and did not receive confirmation and the eucharist,"[256] the ritual has a different disposition:

> The climax of their entire formation will normally be the Easter Vigil. At that time the adults will make profession of their baptismal faith, receive the sacrament of confirmation, and take part in the eucharist. If, because the bishop or special minister of that sacrament is not present, confirmation cannot be given at the Easter Vigil, it is to be celebrated as soon as possible and, if this can be arranged, during the Easter season.[257]

The language of the ritual thus excludes the case in question, namely, the baptized Catholic who has simply never been catechized or admitted to the other sacraments. The ritual was thus interpreted, in 1980, to deny the presbyteral faculty to confirm "an adult who, having received baptism in the Catholic Church, afterwards without his or her fault never put the faith into practice, namely, on the occasion when he or she is admitted to full practice."[258] This limitation, unaffected by the canon, creates an anomalous situation at the Easter Vigil, if such persons are then admitted to full practice. Bishops have therefore sought indults from the Apostolic See to permit presbyteral confirmation for this occasion or have invoked other principles of the canon law.[259] The norm, however, is as stated above.

In summation of number two, by law presbyters have the faculty to confirm (1) adults, including all who are no longer infants and have attained the use of reason, on the occasion and in the rite of their baptism; (2) baptized adults who are admitted into full communion, in the rite of admission; (3) baptized Catholics who have apostasized from the faith, upon their readmission to full communion; and (4) baptized Catholics who have been instructed in or adhered to a non-Catholic religion, without fault of their own, upon their readmission to full communion. They do not, however, have the faculty to confirm baptized Catholics who have not been catechized or previously admitted to confirmation and the Eucharist, upon their admission to full practice of the faith.

The third and final category of presbyters with the faculty by law to confirm is more easily explained. It has its origin in a limited concession, beginning with a curial decree of 1946, in which the faculty to confirm persons in danger of death was given to pastors and to some, but not all, parochial vicars.[260] Successive extensions of the faculty were reflected in the revised *Roman Pontifical:*

> in danger of death, provided a bishop is not easily available or is lawfully impeded: pastors and parochial vicars; in their absence, their associate pastors; priests who are in charge of special parishes lawfully established; administrators; substitute and assistant priests (coadjutors); in the absence of all of the preceding, any priest who is not disqualified by censure or canonical penalty.[261]

Even this slight limitation has now been removed by the present canon, and the pastor or indeed any presbyter has the faculty to confirm a person in danger of death. The danger of death is not to be understood as the moment when death is imminent, but simply when the danger of death is present. In such circumstances, infants also should be confirmed in accord with canon 889, §2. The integrated rites for the several sacraments in all such cases

---

[252]C. 863 speaks of "at least" those who are 14 years old.

[253]*RCIA,* appendix, n. 8: *DOL* 2483.

[254]"Commission for Interpretation of Decrees of Vatican II, loc. cit.

[255]Commission for Interpretation of Decrees of Vatican II, Dec. 21, 1979, I, 2: *AAS* 72 (1980), 105.

[256]*RCIA* 295: *DOL* 2447.

[257]*RCIA* 304: *DOL* 2456.

[258]Commission for Interpretation of Decrees of Vatican II, loc. cit., I, 1.

[259]See c. 884, §1 ("if necessity requires") or even c. 144, §1 ("in factual or legal common error, and also in positive and probable doubt . . .").

[260]SCSacr, Sept. 14, 1946: *AAS* 38 (1946), 349.

[261]*RConf* 7: *DOL* 2516.

of danger of death are found in *Pastoral Care of the Sick: Rites of Anointing and Viaticum,* approved for use by the conferences of bishops in countries where English is spoken.[262]

In cases of error or doubt about the possession of the faculty to confirm that is mentioned in canons 882 and 883, canon 144, §2 applies the norm of paragraph one of canon 144: the faculty to confirm (although not an executive power of governance) is supplied by the Church "in common error about fact or about law, and also in positive and probable doubt about law or about fact." One should see the commentary on canon 144.

Presbyteral Ministers by Concession

Canon 884 — §1. The diocesan bishop is to administer confirmation personally or see that it is administered by another bishop, but if necessity requires he may give the faculty to administer this sacrament to one or more specified presbyters.

§2. For a grave cause, a bishop and likewise a presbyter who has the faculty to confirm by virtue of law or special concession of competent authority may in individual cases associate presbyters with themselves so that they may administer the sacrament.

A further extension of the presbyteral faculty to confirm is made in paragraph one, a matter formerly reserved in the Latin Church to the Apostolic See. There is no determination of the nature or degree of the necessity required for the diocesan bishop to concede the faculty to one or more presbyters, but it is present at least in such circumstances as the illness of the bishop, his necessary absence from the diocese for an extended period, a large number of parishes where confirmation is to be celebrated, etc. No restriction is placed upon the bishop in his selection of presbyters to be ministers of confirmation, but it may be appropriate to choose a vicar general, episcopal vicar, pastor, etc.[263]

The case mentioned in paragraph two is quite distinct and is derived from the introduction, in the revised *Roman Pontifical,* of a kind of concelebration of the sacrament of confirmation.[264] In this the principal and presiding minister of the sacrament is joined by one or several presbyters; they lay hands upon all the candidates (by extending their hands over them) in silence during the prayer which is said before the anointing by the principal minister alone. The latter then hands the vessels of chrism to the associate or concelebrating presbyters, who,

along with him, perform the anointing of the individual candidates in the usual way.[265]

Any minister of the sacrament of confirmation, bishop or presbyter, may concede the faculty mentioned in paragraph two. The "grave cause" required for this concession is described in somewhat more cautious language in the *Roman Pontifical:* "On the basis of true need and a special reason, as sometimes is present because of the large number of those to be confirmed."[266] The previous requirement that the concelebrating presbyters be chosen on the basis of diocesan, parochial, or other office or consideration, while appropriate, no longer binds in view of the simpler statement of the canon. Ordinarily the presence of a large number of persons to be confirmed, which both lengthens the rite itself unduly and also makes it disproportionate to the Eucharistic rite within which confirmation is celebrated, is the sufficient grave cause of paragraph two but other grave causes are not excluded.

Obligation To Confirm

Canon 885 — §1. The diocesan bishop is obliged to see that the sacrament of confirmation is conferred on his subjects who properly and reasonably request it.

§2. A presbyter who has this faculty must use it for those in whose favor the faculty was granted.

This canon follows canon 785 of the 1917 Code but omits, as no longer needed in the law, such prescriptions as these: (1) the ordinary if lawfully impeded should see that confirmation is conferred if possible at least within each five-year period and (2) the metropolitan should report any negligence in this matter to the Roman Pontiff. The simplification of the canon, which is possible because such abuses in the episcopal ministry are now rare, does not lessen the weight of the obligation of paragraph one.

In paragraph two the corresponding norm of the former Code (*CIC* 782, §2) is rephrased to oblige all presbyters who have the faculty to confirm by law (c. 883) or special concession (c. 884) to exercise the faculty. Thus the presbyter who baptizes a person who is no longer an infant or receives a baptized person of such an age into full communion should not fail to confirm him or her on that occasion.

Right To Confirm

Canon 886 — §1. In his own diocese the bishop legitimately administers the sacrament of confirmation even to the faithful who are not his subjects,

[262]This edition, incorporating liturgical rites and texts from several parts of the *Roman Ritual,* was prepared by ICEL and issued by publishers in Canada, England, Australia, United States, etc., in 1983.
[263]See *RConf* 8: *DOL* 2517.
[264]Ibid.

[265]*RConf* 25–28.
[266]*RConf* 8: *DOL* 2517.

unless there is an express prohibition by their own proper ordinary.

§2. To administer confirmation licitly in another diocese, the bishop needs at least the reasonably presumed permission of the diocesan bishop, unless it is a question of his own subjects.

Canon 887 — A presbyter who has the faculty to administer confirmation licitly confers this sacrament even on externs in the territory designated for him, unless there is a prohibition of their own proper ordinary; but such a presbyter may not validly confer the sacrament on anyone in another territory with due regard for the prescription of can. 883, n. 3.

Canon 888 — The ministers may administer confirmation even in exempt places within the territory where they are able to confer the sacrament.

These three canons are clearly stated and deal with the place of confirmation in a sense different from canon 881, which is concerned with the significance of its celebration taking place in a church.

Canon 886 is concerned entirely with the lawfulness of celebration of the sacrament. It is first presumed that the bishop legitimately confirms all persons who are within his own diocese, although it will be unlawful for him to confirm a person from another diocese contrary to an express prohibition by that person's own bishop. In paragraph two it is presumed that a bishop may lawfully confirm outside his own diocese: always in the case of persons from his own diocese and regularly in other cases unless the local bishop prohibits him from celebrating the sacrament. This canon is little changed from canon 783 of the 1917 Code, except that paragraph two of that canon required the bishop who confirmed his own subjects in another diocese against the diocesan bishop's will to do so privately.

Canon 887 has a special importance because it determines not only the licitness but also the validity of confirmation by presbyters. Whether he has the faculty to confirm by law or by special concession, a presbyter always confirms validly within his own territory, although it is unlawful for him to confirm an extern contrary to a prescription of that person's ordinary. On the other hand, the text is explicit that in the Latin Church those who are not in episcopal orders may not validly confirm outside their own territory. This applies equally to presbyters who head particular churches equated to dioceses and others mentioned in canon 883. On the other hand, a presbyter outside his own territory has the faculty to confirm if he baptizes an adult or receives a baptized adult into full communion by mandate of the diocesan bishop (c. 883, 2°) or if he receives the faculty from the diocesan bishop in virtue of canon 884, §1 or from the principal minister

of the sacrament in virtue of canon 884, §2. Likewise, as the concluding phrase of canon 887 notes, any presbyter validly confirms a person in danger of death anywhere.

The final canon of this chapter, canon 888, is derived from canon 792 of the 1917 Code, which stated that the diocesan bishop had the right to administer confirmation in places of his diocese otherwise exempt from his jurisdiction. Canon 888 applies this norm to all ministers of the sacrament.

CHAPTER III
THOSE TO BE CONFIRMED
[cc. 889–891]

This brief chapter, which corresponds to canons 786–789 of the 1917 Code, deals in succession with (1) the capacity to be confirmed (c. 889), (2) the obligation of the sacrament and preparation for it (c. 890), and (3) the age of those to be confirmed (c. 891).

Capacity for Confirmation

Canon 889 — §1. All baptized persons who have not been confirmed and only they are capable of receiving confirmation.

§2. Outside the danger of death, to be licitly confirmed it is required, if the person has the use of reason, that one be suitably instructed, properly disposed and able to renew one's baptismal promises.

Canon 842, §1, on baptism as a prerequisite for the valid admission to the other sacraments, and canon 845, §1, which includes confirmation among the sacraments that cannot be repeated, are the basis for paragraph one of this canon.

In paragraph two, the common discipline of the Latin Church, which is to postpone the sacrament of confirmation until about the age of discretion, is explained in terms of the required preparation, disposition, and personal renewal of baptismal commitment. For the norm concerning the age of those to be confirmed, one should see canon 891.

The first exception is in favor of those in danger of death, where the possibility of preparation may be extremely limited or, in the case of infants, may not be present at all. In addition, the clause "if the person has the use of reason" may be understood to permit the confirmation of those who, although not in danger of death, lack the capacity to be adequately instructed or are not in possession of their faculties.[267]

The *Roman Pontifical* elaborates on the appropriate preparation and disposition for the sacrament:

---

[267]See c. 852, §2.

Persons who are to receive confirmation must already have received baptism. Moreover, those possessing the use of reason must be in the state of grace, properly instructed, and capable of renewing the baptismal promises.

In the case of adults [i.e., those who are no longer infants but have attained the use of reason], those principles are to be followed, with the required adaptations, that apply in the individual dioceses to admitting catechumens to baptism and eucharist. Measures are to be taken especially for catechesis preceding confirmation and for the association of the candidates with the Christian community and with individual Christians. Such association is to be of a kind that is effective and sufficient for the candidates to achieve formation toward both bearing witness by Christian living and carrying on the apostolate. It should also assist the candidates to have a genuine desire to share in the eucharist. . . .

If one who has the use of reason is confirmed in danger of death, there should, as far as possible, be some spiritual preparation beforehand, suited to the individual situation.[268]

In this connection, the rite of the Christian initiation of children of catechetical age should be consulted, especially the introductory paragraphs concerning the kind of formation necessary for initiation and applicable, with the necessary adaptations and depending on the age of the candidate, to preparation for confirmation.[269]

Obligation of the Sacrament

Canon 890 — The faithful are obliged to receive this sacrament at the appropriate time; their parents and shepherds of souls, especially pastors, are to see to it that the faithful are properly instructed to receive it and approach the sacrament at the appropriate time.

This canon constitutes a radical revision of canon 787 of the 1917 Code: "Although this sacrament is not necessary for salvation with the necessity of means, nevertheless it is not lawful for anyone, who has the opportunity to receive it, to neglect it; indeed, pastors should see that the faithful approach this sacrament at the opportune time." The revised canon retains the concept of the appropriate time, taken up directly in the next canon, but states the obligation more firmly and explicitly. The responsibility of pastors is enlarged but made secondary to

that of parents, who are the guardians of children (and of young people, when the sacrament is postponed beyond the age of discretion).

As in other instances, the treatment of "offices and ministries" in the introduction to the *Rite of Confirmation* offers both the background and the explicitation of responsibility, beginning with that of the whole Christian community:

One of the highest responsibilities of the people of God is to prepare the baptized for confirmation. Pastors have a special responsibility to see that all the baptized reach the completion of Christian initiation and therefore that they are carefully prepared for confirmation. . . .

The initiation of children into the sacramental life is ordinarily the responsibility and concern of Christian parents. They are to form and gradually increase a spirit of faith in the children and, at times with the help of catechism classes, prepare them for the fruitful reception of the sacraments of confirmation and the eucharist. The role of the parents is also expressed by their active participation in the celebration of the sacraments.[270]

Age for Confirmation

Canon 891 — The sacrament of confirmation is to be conferred on the faithful at about the age of discretion unless the conference of bishops determines another age or there is danger of death or in the judgment of the minister a grave cause urges otherwise.

The 1917 Code preferred that confirmation in the Latin Church be postponed until about the seventh year of age, but it permitted earlier confirmation in two cases: if an infant were in danger of death or if the minister judged an earlier age to be expedient for just and grave causes. Canon 788 of the former Code, however, did not contemplate in any way the deferral of the sacrament, common in many regions, beyond the seventh year. In accord with canon 5 of the 1917 Code, a centennial or immemorial custom of an early age for confirmation (or, for that matter, a later age) could be tolerated by ordinaries, despite the Code's preference; a similar toleration is allowed in canon 5, §1 of the revised Code.[271]

Prior to Vatican II, there had been limited Roman recognition of the actual pastoral situation in many places, e.g., that one admitted to the Eucharist before confirmation, because of the lack of an

[268]*RConf* 12: *DOL* 2521.
[269]*RCIA* 306–369, esp. 306–308: *DOL* 2458–2460.

[270]*RConf* 3: *DOL* 2512.
[271]See SCSacr, June 30, 1932: *AAS* 24 (1932), 271; *CLD* 1:348–349.

639

opportunity to be confirmed beforehand, should not on that account be kept from frequenting the Eucharist.[272] Nevertheless an authentic interpretation of canon 788 of the former Code had stated that an episcopal law postponing the age of confirmation to the tenth year could not be sustained.[273]

In the revision of the rite of confirmation, a broad concession was made to diverse pastoral practice in these terms:

With regard to children, in the Latin Church the administration of confirmation is generally delayed until about the seventh year. For pastoral reasons, however, especially to implant deeply in the lives of the faithful complete obedience to Christ the Lord and a firm witnessing to him, the conferences of bishops may set an age that seems more suitable. This means that the sacrament is given after the formation proper to it, when the recipients are more mature.

In this case every precaution is to be taken to ensure that in the event of danger of death or serious problems of another kind children receive confirmation in good time, so that they are not left without the benefit of this sacrament.[274]

(In the light of this norm of the *Roman Pontifical*, the NCCB decreed that the norm be adopted as stated, but that a bishop of an individual diocese of the U.S. might "set a later age [for confirmation] as normative in his jurisdiction.")[275]

In the redaction of canon 891, it was proposed that the reference to the seventh year (*CIC* 788) be suppressed and the question of age be left to local custom or the decree of the conference of bishops.[276] The promulgated text, however, rejected this position and retained the earlier norm, now rephrased as "about the age of discretion," stating it as not only preferable but normative for the Latin Church. At the same time it allows for the several exceptions that permit confirmation at a still earlier age, as did its predecessor. The canon recognizes, moreover, as had the revised *Roman Pontifical*, the right of the conferences of bishops to determine a different age. While it is to be expected that this determination, if made, will be of a later age, in accord with the practice in many places, there is nothing in the canon to prevent a conference of bishops from establishing an age earlier than the one normative in the Latin Church.

In summary, this canon leaves open to further development in the particular churches a contro-

verted and uncertain question. In every case the norm of the interrelatedness (and indeed sequence) of the three sacraments of Christian initiation has to be taken into account, as this is stated in canon 842, §2. The juridical development in the twentieth century has had three principal stages: (1) the 1917 Code, in which the seventh year is preferred for confirmation as appropriate or suitable; (2) the revised *Roman Pontifical*, in which the same age is merely described as the general practice in the Latin Church, but for pastoral reasons the juridical determination is left to the conferences of bishops —and this despite the doctrinal position of the liturgical books on the interrelatedness and sequence of the sacraments of initiation; and (3) canon 891, in which the norm, and not merely the preference, is decreed: the age for confirmation is "about the age of discretion," but again with exceptions, and primarily with the recognition of the right of the conferences of bishops to make a further and different decision.

Although the future development may make difficult the liturgical catechesis on the nature of confirmation, it is clear in the canons that, even if delayed, this sacrament is to be understood as embracing a renewal and deepening of baptismal commitment. This should be inculcated in any event, at least from the age of discretion, and is regularly renewed and deepened at each Sunday Eucharistic celebration—as well as annually at the Easter Vigil (and, in the dioceses of the U.S., at all the Eucharistic celebrations of Easter Sunday).[277] Thus, even if the pastoral reason for delaying the sacrament of confirmation is to provide an occasion for a more mature acceptance and manifestation of Christian faith and witness, this aspect of confirmation is in continuity with the same baptismal commitment which all the baptized, including unconfirmed children past the age of discretion and unconfirmed young people, are expected to renew regularly within the Christian community during the Eucharist, which is both the completion and the continuing renewal of initiation.

CHAPTER IV
SPONSORS
[cc. 892–893]

This brief chapter of two canons corresponds to, and is dependent upon, the chapter on the sponsors for baptism (cc. 872–874). It is concerned only with the sacrament of confirmation when it is celebrated separately from baptism; when the sacraments of Christian initiation are celebrated together, the same persons serve throughout the rite as sponsors. (The Latin term is *patrinus* or *patrina* in the case of both sacraments; the Latin *sponsor* is usually re-

[272]Ibid.
[273]CodCom, Mar. 26, 1952: *AAS* 44 (1952), 496: *CLD* 3:314.
[274]*RConf* 11: *DOL* 2520.
[275]NCCB, April 1972: *BCLN: 1965–1975* (May–June 1972), 327–328.
[276]Schema (1980), c. 845.

[277]NCCB, November 1970: *BCLN, 1965–1975* (Nov. 1970), 252.

served for the member of the community who presents an adult candidate for admission to the catechumenate but may not always serve as sponsor during the final Lenten preparation for sacramental initiation.)

The codification does not take up, as did canon 795, 5° of the 1917 Code, the possibility of sponsorship by proxy, nor does it formally limit the number of sponsors, as did canon 794 of the former Code, although clearly it contemplates a single sponsor for each candidate. In the past it was not uncommon, in the case of a large number of persons to be confirmed, for one to four persons —either as proxies for others or on their own behalf—to serve as sponsors for all the candidates. This, however, was regarded as an evasion of the norm of canon 794 of the 1917 Code.[278]

Responsibility of Sponsors

Canon 892 — As far as possible a sponsor for the one to be confirmed should be present; it is for the sponsor to see that the confirmed person acts as a true witness to Christ and faithfully fulfills the obligations connected with this sacrament.

The qualifying clause, "as far as possible," derived from canon 793 of the former Code (which referred to "a very ancient custom of the Church"), suggests that a sponsor is not strictly required for confirmation. In almost all circumstances, however, the participation of a sponsor for each one to be confirmed is possible and customary.

The general statement of responsibility of sponsors in this canon is parallel to what is said in canon 872, in the case of baptism. It is elaborated upon in the *Roman Pontifical:*

> As a rule there should be a sponsor for each of those to be confirmed. These sponsors bring the candidates to receive the sacrament, present them to the minister for the anointing, and will later help them to fulfill their baptismal promises faithfully under the influence of the Holy Spirit whom they have received.[279]

Qualifications of Sponsors

Canon 893 — §1. To perform the role of sponsor, it is necessary that a person fulfill the conditions mentioned in can. 874.
§2. It is desirable that the one who undertook the role of sponsor at baptism be sponsor for confirmation.

By cross-reference, paragraph one of this canon incorporates all the conditions for sponsorship mentioned in canon 874 in the case of baptism. The present canon is perhaps better understood by speaking first of the norm of paragraph two, as does the *Rite of Confirmation:*

> In view of contemporary pastoral circumstances, it is desirable that the godparent at baptism, if available, also be the sponsor at confirmation; *CIC* can. 796, no. 1 is therefore amended. This change expresses more clearly the link between baptism and confirmation and also makes the function and responsibility of the sponsor more effective.[280]

Thus, in view of the problem of relating confirmation to baptism adequately in the usual pastoral situation, this particular link is proposed.

Nevertheless the usages and sensibilities of persons and families are respected as the text quoted continues:

> Nonetheless the option of choosing a special sponsor for confirmation is not excluded. Even the parents themselves may present their children for confirmation. It is for the local Ordinary to determine practice in the light of local conditions and circumstances.

It is thus in accord with such a determination within the local church—or, of course, if the sponsor at baptism is simply not available at the time of confirmation—that the norm of paragraph one of this canon comes into play. The liturgically and theologically desirable practice is the one recommended in paragraph two.

One should see canon 874 for a commentary on the conditions requisite in a sponsor at confirmation who has not served as a sponsor at baptism. Since the cross-reference is to the entirety of canon 874, the special case of paragraph two of that canon (the service as witness by a baptized person who belongs to a non-Catholic ecclesial community) is also applicable to sponsorship at confirmation.

There is only one apparent conflict to be mentioned, namely, the norm excluding the father or mother of the candidate from sponsorship, which is explicitly allowed by the *Roman Pontifical* (above). The question will not arise if canon 893, §2 is observed, but wherever the practice of parents presenting their children for confirmation is followed, the difference between canon 874, 5° and the existing liturgical norm must be resolved.

The discrepancy was adverted to in a report to the Code Commission. The report held that the exclusion of parents from sponsorship was appropriate "since the function [of sponsorship] is adjunctive and quasi-suppletory, namely, to assist the parents in the Christian upbringing of their

[278] Abbo-Hannan, *Sacred Canons,* 1:788–799.
[279] *RConf* 5: *DOL* 2514.
[280] Ibid.

children." The report immediately added, however, that (in accord with the *Roman Pontifical*) "the parents may certainly present their children [for confirmation], but then it must be said that sponsors are lacking, for it is proper that the parents name the sponsors."[281] The Commission accepted this explanation and did not feel it necessary to alter the canon to include explicitly this possibility of parents presenting their children. From this it is evident that the norm in the *Roman Pontifical* may continue to be followed, despite the judgment submitted to the Commission that the parents in such instances would not be sponsors in the strictest sense.

CHAPTER V
THE PROOF AND RECORD OF CONFERRED CONFIRMATION
[cc. 894–896]

Proof of Confirmation

Canon 894 — The prescriptions of can. 876 are to be observed for the proof of the conferral of confirmation.

This was formally spelled out separately for confirmation in canon 800 of the 1917 Code.

Although the occasion for establishing juridical proof of the conferral of confirmation may be rare, the terms of the corresponding canon on baptism are incorporated here by reference. Canon 875, which requires at least a witness to baptism, is not explicitly mentioned in the case of confirmation, but is taken for granted and is implicit in canon 894.

Record of Confirmation

Canon 895 — The names of the confirmed with mention of the minister, the parents and the sponsors, the place and the date of the conferral of confirmation are to be noted in the confirmation register in the diocesan curia, or, where the conference of bishops or the diocesan bishop has prescribed it, in a book kept in the parish archive; the

[281]*Rel,* 209.

pastor must advise the pastor of the place of baptism about the conferral of confirmation so that notation be made in the baptismal register, in accord with the norm of can. 535, §2.

Canon 896 — If the pastor of the place were not present, the minister either personally or through another is to inform him of the confirmation as soon as possible.

The meaning of these two canons is self-evident, and the first of them, which parallels canon 877, §1 on baptism, formally prescribes what is anticipated in canon 535, §2, namely, that the sacramental and other elements of the status of a person should be maintained in the records of the place of one's baptism.

The norm of canon 895, however, differs from the prescription of the 1917 Code, which required simply a parochial confirmation register (*CIC* 798) and did not mention a diocesan or curial register of confirmation. The present law offers an alternative: either a register of confirmation maintained in the diocesan curia or, depending on the prescription of the conference of bishops or of the diocesan bishop himself, in accord with canon 535, §1, a register maintained in the parish archives.

Although the introduction of a diocesan register of confirmation may appear superficially to add a complex element of diocesan centralization (and even to create a certain disjunction of confirmation from the sacrament of baptism, which it should complement), contemporary technological developments in record keeping facilitate such central recording and the like. As the canon reads, such a register should be established unless either the conferences of bishops or the diocesan bishop determines otherwise.

Canon 896 repeats the norm of canon 799 of the 1917 Code with a slight modification. If he is absent from the confirmation, the pastor of the place (of confirmation) is to be notified of the fact of confirmation rather than the proper pastor of the one confirmed (as *CIC* 799 had required). This is in harmony with the reasoning which prompted the omission from canon 878 of any requirement to send notification of baptism to the proper pastor of a neophyte.

BIBLIOGRAPHY

Bibliographical material on baptism and confirmation is incorporated in the bibliography that can be found after the commentary on canon 1007.

John M. Huels, O.S.M.

TITLE III
THE MOST HOLY EUCHARIST
[cc. 897–958]

The third and final sacrament of full Christian initiation is the Eucharist, the subject of the sixty-two canons of this title. The canons are arranged in three chapters: "The Eucharistic Celebration," "The Reservation and Veneration of the Most Holy Eucharist," and "Offerings Given at the Celebration of Mass." This division better integrates the various aspects of Eucharistic discipline than did the former Code which dealt with reservation and worship of the Eucharist not in the section on the sacraments but in that on divine worship which in-cluded such topics as sacred furnishings and vows and oaths. The new arrangement bespeaks the essential unity of the Eucharist celebrated, received, and reserved. Some members of the *coetus* (committee) of the Pontifical Commission for the Revision of the Code of Canon Law which prepared this title of the Code believed that the section on Mass offerings should be treated in Book V on church property, but it was decided to leave it in this title given its special relation to the celebration of the Eucharist.[1]

---

[1]ComCICRec, *Schema Documenti Pontificii quo Disciplina Canonica de Sacramentis Recognoscitur* (Romae: Typis Polyglottis Vaticanis, 1975), 8.

CANONS AND COMMENTARY

CHAPTER I
THE EUCHARISTIC CELEBRATION
[cc. 899–933]

This chapter of thirty-five canons—more than half of all the canons on the Eucharist—is divided into four articles: "The Minister of the Most Holy Eucharist," "Participation in the Most Holy Eucharist," "Rites and Ceremonies of Eucharistic Celebration," and "The Time and Place of Eucharistic Celebration." The former Code treated the Eucharist in two chapters, one on the Eucharistic sacrifice and one on the sacrament. The more integral approach of the revised Code better manifests the continuity and unity of the sacrificial and sacramental dimensions of the Eucharistic action. The doctrinal canon (c. 899) which introduces the chapter on the Eucharistic celebration is preceded by two other foundational canons (cc. 897–898) governing the title on the Eucharist as a whole.

Foundational Canons

Canon 897 — The Most Holy Eucharist is the most august sacrament, in which Christ the Lord himself is contained, offered and received, and by which the Church constantly lives and grows. The Eucharistic Sacrifice, the memorial of the death and resurrection of the Lord, in which the sacrifice of the cross is perpetuated over the centuries, is the summit and the source of all Christian worship and life; it signifies and effects the unity of the people of God and achieves the building up of the Body of Christ. The other sacraments and all the ecclesiastical works of the apostolate are closely related to the Holy Eucharist and are directed to it.

Canon 898 — The faithful are to hold the Eucharist in highest honor, taking part in the celebration of the Most August Sacrifice, receiving the sacrament devoutly and frequently, and worshiping it with supreme adoration; pastors, clarifying the doctrine on this sacrament, are to instruct the faithful thoroughly about this obligation.

Canon 899 — §1. The celebration of the Eucharist is the action of Christ Himself and the Church; in it Christ the Lord, by the ministry of a priest, offers Himself, substantially present under the forms of bread and wine, to God the Father and gives Himself as spiritual food to the faithful who are associated with His offering.

§2. In the Eucharistic banquet the people of God are called together, with the bishop or, under his authority, a presbyter presiding and acting in the person of Christ; and all the faithful present,

whether clergy or laity, participate together in their own way, according to the diversity of orders and liturgical roles.

§3. The celebration of the Eucharist is to be so arranged that all who take part receive from it the many fruits for which Christ the Lord instituted the Eucharistic Sacrifice.

Canons 897 and 898 introduce the entire title on the Eucharist, including the chapters on reservation and worship and on Mass offerings. Canon 899 is an additional introductory canon for the first chapter on the Eucharistic celebration. Canons 897 and 899 establish the doctrinal foundations for the disciplinary canons which follow, i.e., they are doctrinal in the broad sense, including statements of dogma as well as authoritative teachings which lack a strictly dogmatic character. The canons manifest an effort to harmonize past doctrine, such as the real presence and the sacrificial nature of the Mass, with Vatican II emphases such as the Eucharist as meal as well as its celebrational and memorial character. The ecclesial dimensions of the Eucharist which were highlighted at the Council are also evident: the Eucharist as source and sign of the unity of the Body of Christ; as source and summit of the Church's life and worship, its nourishment and growth; and as action of the whole people of God participating in the sanctifying function of the Church and reflecting its hierarchical structure through diverse and distinct liturgical roles and ministries.

Canon 898 is an exhortation on the general obligations of the faithful regarding the Eucharist and on the duty of pastors ("animarum pastores") to elucidate Eucharistic doctrine. This duty, which binds all ecclesiastical officeholders who exercise pastoral care, is also stated in canon 843, §2 for the sacraments in general. More specific directives on the obligation of pastors per se ("parochi") to provide catechetical and experiential formation in the Eucharist are found in canons 528, §2; 777, 2°; and 914. Canon 898 also introduces three principal aspects of the Eucharist which are treated in the Code: the Eucharistic action or celebration, Holy Communion, and the veneration of the Eucharist.

The history of these three canons is rather complex. A major part of canon 897 was derived from canon 66, §1 of the proposed *Lex Ecclesiae Fundamentalis;* the original version of canon 898 was canon 72 of the 1975 schema introducing the proposed section on the "subject of the holy Eucharist"; the core of canon 899, §§1–2 was canon 61 of the schema. Major revisions in the formulation and positioning of the canons were made by the *coetus* on the sacraments in response to critiques received during the consultation process, and final changes were made before the 1981 plenary session of the Pontifical Commission for the Revision of the Code

of Canon Law.[2] The immediate and proximate sources of the canons are chiefly certain texts of Vatican II, but the canons also draw on pre-conciliar sources such as the Council of Trent and the 1917 Code, as well as post-conciliar sources such as the *General Instruction of the Roman Missal.*[3]

ARTICLE 1: THE MINISTER OF THE MOST HOLY EUCHARIST
[cc. 900–911]

The twelve canons of this article deal with a wide variety of issues relative to the minister of the Eucharist, who includes the celebrant and concelebrants at Mass, and the ordinary and special ministers of Communion and Viaticum. The canons establish the discipline for the following matters: (1) valid and licit celebration (c. 900); (2) Mass intentions (c. 901); (3) concelebration (c. 902); (4) the celebret (c. 903); (5) the frequency of celebration (cc. 904–905); (6) the necessity of the presence of some faithful (c. 906); (7) functions restricted to the priest (c. 907); (8) the prohibition of interdenominational concelebration (c. 908); (9) the personal prayer of the priest (c. 909); (10) Eucharistic ministers (c. 910); and (11) ministers of Viaticum (c. 911).

Valid and Licit Celebration

Canon 900 — §1. The minister, who in the person of Christ can confect the sacrament of the Eucharist, is solely a validly ordained priest.

§2. A priest who is not canonically impeded celebrates the Eucharist licitly observing the prescriptions of the following canons.

The 1917 Code (*CIC* 802) spoke of the priest's having the "power to offer the sacrifice of the Mass," whereas this canon speaks of validly confecting ("conficere") the sacrament of the Eucharist. Despite the change in terminology, the meaning remains the same: only a validly ordained priest may preside at the Eucharist and validly consecrate the bread and wine. Lay persons who attempt the liturgical action of the Eucharist automatically incur the penalty of interdict and deacons the penalty of suspension (c. 1378, §2, 1°).

The second paragraph of the canon, which is new in the revised Code, deals with the licit celebration of the Eucharist. While any priest may validly consecrate the sacrament, some priests may not do so licitly, such as those who have been deprived of the

---

[2] *Comm* 13 (1981), 233–238, 408–410; *Rel,* 209–210.
[3] See, e.g., *SC* 14, 26, 28, 41, 47, 48; *LG* 11; *PO* 2, 5, 6; Trent, sess. XIII, cap. 1, c. 1, *Ench* 1636, 1651; sess. XXII, cap. 1, cc. 1–2, *Ench* 1739–1742, 1751–1752; *CIC* 801; Intro. to *IGMR* 1–15; *IGMR* 1–5, 7, 48, 58–62, 74, 326.

exercise of their order by a penalty (cc. 1331, §1, 2°; 1332; 1333, §1, 1°; 1338, §2) or who have lost the clerical state (cc. 290; 292; 1336, §1, 5°). Other requirements for the licit celebration of the Eucharist are specified in the canons which follow.

Mass Intentions

Canon 901 — A priest may apply the Mass for anyone, living or dead.

A Mass may be applied for anyone, [4] living or deceased, baptized or non-baptized, sinner or saint. The canon is totally open-ended and unequivocal in marked contrast to the 1917 Code (*CIC* 809), which said that Mass may be applied for the dead in purgatory or for the living with the exception of public Masses for the excommunicated. Private Masses could be applied for tolerated excommunicates ("excommunicati tolerati"), which included baptized non-Catholics, but for the excommunicates who must be avoided ("excommunicati vitandi"), a private Mass could be applied only for their conversion (*CIC* 2262, §2, 2°). A "private Mass" excluded any publicizing of the name of the person for whom the Mass was being applied. A 1976 decree of the Sacred Congregation for the Doctrine of the Faith derogated from the 1917 Code to permit public Masses to be applied for deceased non-Catholic Christians when their families, friends, or subjects expressly request it and the ordinary judges that scandal is absent. [5] These conditions no longer bind since the revised Code does not mention them.

This canon was dropped from the second draft of the schema on the sacraments in 1978 because it was considered more theological than juridical, but it was reinstated in 1981. [6]

Concelebration

Canon 902 — Priests may concelebrate the Eucharist unless the welfare of the Christian faithful requires or urges otherwise but with due regard for the freedom of each priest to celebrate the Eucharist individually, though not during the time when there is a concelebration in the same church or oratory.

Various forms of concelebration have existed in the Western and Eastern Churches since at least the third century. Even before the liturgical reforms decreed by Vatican II, the *Roman Pontifical* had prescribed concelebration at Masses for the ordination of priests and the consecration of bishops. *The Constitution on the Sacred Liturgy* derogated from canon 803 of the 1917 Code to permit much wider opportunity for concelebration. [7] It also directed that a new rite for concelebration be prepared, and this was accomplished already by 1965. [8] The liturgical laws governing concelebration are found principally in the *General Instruction of the Roman Missal* 153–208. Number 153 of this instruction states that concelebration is required at the ordinations of bishops or priests and at the Chrism Mass. It recommends concelebration, unless the needs of the faithful require otherwise, at: (a) the evening Mass of Holy Thursday; (b) the Mass for councils, meetings of bishops, or synods; (c) the Mass for the blessing of an abbot; (d) the conventual Mass and the principal Mass in churches and oratories; (e) the Mass for any kind of gathering of priests, either secular or religious. Number 155 states further that the bishop, in accord with the law, has the right to regulate concelebration in his diocese, even in the churches and oratories of the exempt.

The first part of the canon is based substantially on a statement of the 1967 Instruction on the Worship of the Eucharistic Mystery. [9] Concelebration is preferred over multiple private Masses because it manifests the Church gathered "in the unity of the sacrifice and the priesthood, in one act of thanks, around one altar with ministers and holy people." [10] However, priests should not insist on concelebration at the expense of the welfare of the faithful, such as when more than one Mass is required to meet pastoral needs. [11]

The second part of the canon is based on a statement from *The Constitution on the Sacred Liturgy* which may have been necessary to promote consensus among the Fathers at Vatican II in favor of concelebration and, therefore, to contribute ultimately to the movement away from private Masses. The document said that each priest should have the "opportunity" ("facultas") to celebrate an individual Mass, [12] and the canon reaffirms this by saying that priests are at complete liberty to celebrate the Eucharist individually. This does not apply to Holy

---

[7] *SC* 57.

[8] Ibid., 58; *Ritus servandus in concelebratione Missae et Ritus Communionis sub utraque specie* (Romae: Typis Polyglottis Vaticanis, 1965); P. Jounel, *The Rite of Concelebration of Mass and of Communion under Both Species* (New York: Desclée, 1967). (Cited as either *Rite of Concelebration* or *Rite of Communion under Both Kinds*.)

[9] SCRit, instr *Eucharisticum mysterium*, May 25, 1967, *AAS* 59 (1967), 539–573, n. 47.

[10] SCRit, decr *Ecclesiae semper*, Mar. 7, 1965, *AAS* 57 (1965), 410. See also *IGMR* 59.

[11] See the critiques of concelebration by R.K. Seasoltz, *New Liturgy, New Laws* (Collegeville, Minn.: The Liturgical Press, 1980), 87–90, and R. Taft, "Ex Oriente Lux? Some Reflections on Eucharistic Concelebration," *W* 54 (1980), 308–324.

[12] *SC* 57, 2, n.2.

---

[4] See the commentary on c. 945 for an explanation of what it means to apply a Mass.

[5] SCDF, decr, June 11, 1976, *AAS* 68 (1976), 621; *CLD* 8, 864.

[6] *Comm* 13 (1981), 244; *Rel*, 209.

Thursday, however, when liturgical law prohibits all Masses without a congregation. Furthermore, priests are forbidden from celebrating an individual Mass at the time when there is a concelebration occurring in the same place, and they are also subject to the prohibition of canon 906 against celebrating without at least some of the faithful present. The canon must not be understood as encouraging priests to celebrate private Masses whenever they wish, because the intent of the liturgical reform is that the whole local community, including priests, should participate "in the same Eucharist, in one prayer, at one altar."[13]

The Celebret

Canon 903 — **A priest is to be permitted to celebrate even if he is unknown to the rector of the church provided he presents a letter of recommendation issued by his ordinary or superior within the year or provided it can be prudently judged that the priest is not prevented from celebrating.**

The law on the celebret from the 1917 Code (*CIC* 804) is retained here but is greatly simplified. A celebret is a letter of recommendation from a priest's ordinary or superior which attests to the priest's ordination and good standing. Its chief purpose is to protect the faithful from impostors. Secular priests obtain the celebret from their local ordinary, and priests who are religious or members of clerical societies of apostolic life may obtain it from their local ordinary or major superior or even from their local superior. To be valid it must be dated within a year of its presentation to the rector of the church where the priest wishes to celebrate. In this canon the term "rector" includes anyone who has the care of a church or oratory, such as a pastor or religious superior, and not only the rector mentioned in canon 556. In many places the celebret is not requested of visiting priests, and the canon states that it is not necessary when the rector prudently judges that a priest should not be prevented from celebrating.

Frequency of Celebration

Canon 904 — **Remembering that the work of redemption is continually accomplished in the mystery of the Eucharistic Sacrifice, priests are to celebrate frequently; indeed daily celebration is strongly recommended, since even if the faithful cannot be present, it is the act of Christ and the Church in which priests fulfill their principal function.**

Canon 905 — **§1. It is not licit for a priest to celebrate the Eucharist more than once a day except**

for certain instances when the law permits such celebration or concelebration more than once.
§2. If priests are lacking, the local ordinary may permit priests, for a just cause, to celebrate twice a day and even, if pastoral need requires it, three times on Sundays and holy days of obligation.

The daily celebration of the Eucharist by each priest was not an ancient practice in the Church, nor was it required by universal law even when it became common. The 1917 Code obliged priests to celebrate several times a year, which the commentators interpreted as only three or four times a year. The former law also directed bishops and religious superiors to see that their priests celebrated Mass at least on Sundays and holy days of obligation (*CIC* 805).

Canon 904, in effect, mitigates the 1917 Code because it no longer speaks of a binding obligation to celebrate but instead uses exhortatory language: "priests are to celebrate frequently," not *must* celebrate. Priests are also encouraged to celebrate Mass even daily or, as canon 276, §2, 2° puts it, they are earnestly invited to offer the Eucharist daily. Clearly there is no legal obligation for priests to celebrate daily Mass, but it is highly commended for the reasons adduced in the canon.

The wording of canon 904 is very similar to that of a norm of the 1967 Instruction on the Worship of the Eucharistic Mystery which in turn draws on the conciliar *Decree on the Ministry and Life of Priests* and Paul VI's encyclical "On the Doctrine and Worship of the Holy Eucharist."[14] The statement that "priests fulfill their principal function" by celebrating the Eucharist originates in *Presbyterorum Ordinis* 13 and must be interpreted in that context where the Council was speaking expressly of the priests' *sanctifying* function only. The same article also develops the priests' functions of ruling (in the broad sense of pastoral care) and teaching.

Bination and Trination

While priests may celebrate daily, they are forbidden from celebrating or concelebrating more than once each day except when the law permits it. The purpose of canon 905, §1 is to prevent the abuse of priests' celebrating multiple Masses for inadequate reasons or from improper motives, such as the desire for Mass offerings or superstition. Similar prohibitions have been a part of church law since the eleventh century.[15]

The principal occasions when the law permits a priest to celebrate or concelebrate more than once a

---

[13]Ibid., 41.

[14]*PO* 13; *Eucharisticum mysterium* 44; ency *Mysterium fidei,* Sept. 3, 1965, *AAS* 57 (1965), 762, *Documents on the Liturgy 1963–1979* (Collegeville, Minn.: The Liturgical Press 1982), 176; see also *PO* 2, 5; *LG* 28; *AG* 39.

[15]C. 53, D. I, *de cons.;* c. 3, 12, X, *de celebratione missarum,* III, 41; *CIC* 806.

day are: (1) on Holy Thursday at the Chrism Mass and at the evening Mass of the Lord's supper; (2) at the Easter Vigil and the second Mass of Easter; (3) at the three Masses of Christmas, provided that the Masses are at their proper times according to the liturgical books; and (4) at concelebrations with the bishop or his delegate at a synod or pastoral visitation, or on the occasion of a meeting of priests, or gatherings of religious—and another Mass celebrated for the benefit of the people.[16]

The 1917 Code (*CIC* 806, §1) permitted trination on All Souls' Day, a practice that has existed in the universal Church only since 1915.[17] The revised Code has abolished this practice since the former Code is explicitly abrogated (c. 6, §1, 1°). However, the *Roman Missal* provides three separate Mass texts for November 2, which may hinder complete discontinuation of the All Souls' trination.

In 1963 Paul VI granted to residential bishops the faculty to permit priests to celebrate twice on weekdays for a just cause and when there is a shortage of priests, and even three times on Sundays and holy days of obligation when there is true pastoral need.[18] Canon 905, §2 extends this faculty as a general law to all local ordinaries, not only residential bishops. The law permits bination and trination only for priests who preside at the Eucharist but not for concelebration except in the cases mentioned above. Local ordinaries may permit a priest to binate when there is a just cause, such as to provide for the needs of the faithful, and only when there is an insufficient number of priests available. For permission to trinate on Sundays and holy days, there must be a case of genuine pastoral need as, for example, when a priest has the care of more than one church or when the church is unable to accommodate all the faithful who wish to attend. The mere convenience of the faithful would not be an adequate reason to trinate unless a sufficient number of them could not otherwise attend Mass. The Apostolic See discourages the multiplication of Masses when a church is large enough to accommodate the faithful at a smaller number of Masses. According to the Instruction on the Worship of the Eucharistic Mystery, the pastoral effort is weakened by multiple Masses because the participation of the people in a scattered congregation is diminished and the effectiveness of overworked priests is reduced.[19] The same document adds that small religious communities and other groups should take part in the parish Mass on Sundays and feast days rather than at separate celebrations. Multiple

Masses attended by a few and small group Masses on the Lord's Day tend to detract from the value of the Eucharist as a sign and source of ecclesial unity. Local ordinaries should observe strictly the requirements of a just cause and pastoral need in allowing bination and trination so that the quality of participation and the unity of the community do not suffer.

Those who have permission to trinate on Sundays and holy days need not observe the norm that specifies that the three Christmas Masses be celebrated only at the proper times. A priest who celebrates more than once a day may not retain more than one Mass offering except on Christmas in accord with the norm of canon 951. If pastoral need requires that a priest regularly celebrate more than three Masses on Sundays and holy days, an application for an indult should be made to the Sacred Congregation for the Discipline of the Sacraments. This congregation has been accustomed to granting indults for a period of three years to ordinaries to allow their priests to celebrate three Masses on Saturdays and the day before a holy day of obligation provided one of the Masses is the anticipated evening Mass of the day of precept.[20]

Presence of Faithful Necessary

Canon 906 — A priest may not celebrate without the participation of at least some member of the faithful, except for a just and reasonable cause.

The prohibition against celebrating the Eucharist without the presence of some member of the faithful has been a part of church law at least since the pontificate of Alexander III in the twelfth century, and it was reaffirmed in the 1917 Code in terms of the requirement of a server for every Mass.[21] Vatican II insisted that

rites which by their proper nature are to be celebrated in common with the presence and active participation of the faithful should be celebrated that way insofar as possible rather than individually or quasi-privately. This applies especially to the celebration of Mass. . . . [22]

Despite the preference for communal celebration, the Council admitted the possibility of individual celebration, and Paul VI taught that such celebrations are permissible "for a just cause . . . even if only a server assists and makes the responses."[23]

The Sacred Congregation for the Discipline of the Sacraments in 1949 stated that according to the

---

[16]*IGMR* 158. See also SCSacr, rescript, Mar. 10, 1970, *CLD* 7, 38–39, which permits priests who celebrate a Mass for the faithful on Holy Thursday to concelebrate at the evening Mass.

[17]Benedict XV, apconst *Incruentum,* Aug. 10, 1915, *AAS* 7 (1915), 401.

[18]*PM* I, 2.

[19]*Eucharisticum mysterium* 26.

[20]A similar indult granted to the NCCB for all U.S. ordinaries expired in 1979 and was not renewed, so each ordinary must apply individually for this faculty.

[21]C. 6, X, *de filiis presbyt. ord. vel non,* I, 17; *CIC* 813, §1.

[22]*SC* 27.

[23]*Mysterium fidei, AAS* 57 (1965), 761–762.

approved authors there are only four cases in which Mass may be celebrated without a server: when it is necessary to give Viaticum to a sick person; to enable the people to satisfy the precept of hearing Mass; in time of pestilence, when a priest would otherwise be obliged to abstain from celebrating for a notable time; and when the server leaves during the course of the Mass.[24] Pius XII would not even grant an indult for Mass to be said without a server unless some member of the faithful were present to assist.[25] The server in the former law was required not primarily for the material assistance of the priest but because the Eucharist is essentially an action of the whole Church, priest and people. In the words of Thomas Aquinas, the server "represents the whole Catholic people, and in that capacity answers the priest in the plural."[26]

Canon 906 alters the previous discipline in two ways. First, the server is no longer necessary, but there must be the *participation* of at least some member of the faithful, i.e., of at least one other Christian who can make the responses in place of the congregation. For individual celebration the *Roman Missal* provides a "Rite of Mass Without a Congregation," and the server's responses in it can now be made by any member of the faithful. Second, the requirement that there be serious necessity for a priest to celebrate alone is changed to a just and reasonable cause. Such a cause would be demonstrated whenever a member of the faithful is unavailable and when the priest is unable to participate in a communal celebration, e.g., as result of illness, infirmity, or travel. A just and reasonable cause would not be the mere convenience of the priest or his preference for celebrating alone. Canon 902, while granting priests the freedom of celebrating individually instead of concelebrating, does not excuse the priest from the law requiring the presence of at least some member of the faithful.

Female Altar Servers

The revised Code, unlike the 1917 Code (c. 813, §2), does not prohibit females from serving Mass. Nevertheless, the *General Instruction of the Roman Missal* 70 states: "At the discretion of the rector of the church, women may be appointed to ministries outside the sanctuary." Despite the seeming finality of this norm, it has been abrogated implicitly by subsequent law and practice. Although women are excluded from being instituted into the ministry of permanent acolyte, canon 230, §2, 3° permits them to be deputed for a time as readers, commentators, cantors, leaders of liturgical prayers, ministers of baptism and Communion, all of which almost necessarily require their presence at some point within the sanctuary. Furthermore, canon 930, §2 expressly allows a lay man or woman to assist at the celebration of the Mass of a blind or infirm priest. The 1975 revised edition of the *General Instruction of the Roman Missal* 70 allows episcopal conferences to designate "a suitable place for a woman to proclaim the word of God in the liturgical assembly," and the exercise of liturgical ministries by women within the sanctuary is explicitly permitted by many local churches, including the dioceses of the United States.[27] Therefore, the prohibition of that norm has been abrogated by subsequent law and practice which, while not literally contrary to it, render its observance morally or physically impossible.[28] Hence, there is no solid legal basis for excluding female altar servers. The 1970 instruction, *Liturgicae instaurationes,* and the 1980 instruction, *Inaestimabile donum,* had each reaffirmed the prohibition against female altar servers, but neither document has any force beyond that of the former law.[29]

Functions Restricted to the Priest

Canon 907 — In the celebration of the Eucharist it is not licit for deacons and lay persons to say prayers, in particular the Eucharistic prayer, or to perform actions which are proper to the celebrating priest.

In the tradition of Jewish ritual meals and of the Last Supper, certain functions in the Eucharist have always been reserved to a presider, who as leader of the community prays and acts in its name. The Second Vatican Council established the general principle that those who have a liturgical ministry should perform only and all those functions which pertain to them according to the nature of the rite and the liturgical norms.[30] The hierarchical structure of the liturgy flows from the hierarchical ordering of the people of God who, "in their own way, have their own part to play in the liturgical action."[31] The more the faithful clearly understand their proper role in the liturgical community and in the Eucharistic action, "the more conscious and fruitful will be that active and proper participation of the community."[32]

---

[24]Instr *Quam plurimum,* Oct. 1, 1949, *AAS* 41 (1949), 507; *CLD* 3, 318.
[25]Ibid., 508.
[26]*Summa Theologiae,* III, q. 83, art. 5, ad 12.
[27]Appendix to the *IGMR* for the Dioceses of the U.S.A., Appendix 1, 66d.
[28]*Comm* 13 (1981), 242.
[29]SCDW, instr *Liturgicae instaurationes,* Sept. 5, 1970, *AAS* 62 (1970), 692–704, n. 7; SCSDW, instr *Inaestimabile donum,* Apr. 3, 1980, *AAS* 72 (1980), 331–343, n. 18; *Origins* 10 (1980), 41–44. Cf. c. 34, §3.
[30]*SC* 28.
[31]*LG* 11.
[32]*Eucharisticum mysterium* 11; see also n. 12.

The Eucharistic prayer is the preeminent prayer of the priest.[33] In this central prayer of praise and thanksgiving the priest unites the community with himself as he addresses the Father through the Son in the name of all, and "the entire congregation joins itself to Christ in acknowledging the great things he has done and in offering the sacrifice."[34] The priest's voice alone must be heard "while the community gathered for the celebration of the sacred liturgy religiously observes silence."[35] When non-priests join in the Eucharistic prayer or when concelebrants are more than barely audible, the sign of the celebrant as leader of worship and president of the community is diminished and the role of silence, fostered by *The Constitution on the Sacred Liturgy,* is neglected.[36] Moreover, the common recitation of the Eucharistic prayer destroys its dialogical character whereby the priest proclaims and the people listen attentively and respond. Among the most important responses of the people is the "Amen" when they affirm the whole prayer at its end. To accentuate its importance, the "Amen" should be embellished with song and never overwhelmed by reciting the doxology in common.[37]

Besides the Eucharistic prayer, the other prayers and actions in the Eucharist proper to the celebrating priest are specified in the *Roman Missal.* Although canon 970 is new, it is related to canon 818 of the 1917 Code which stated that the priest celebrant must observe accurately and devoutly the rubrics of the liturgical books and beware of adding other ceremonies or prayers on his own. The canon is closely related to the basic principle expressed in canons 835, §4 and 899, §2 that the faithful have their proper part to play in the sanctifying office and actively participate in liturgical celebrations, especially the Eucharist, in their own way.

Interdenominational Concelebration Prohibited

Canon 908 — It is forbidden for Catholic priests to concelebrate the Eucharist with priests or ministers of churches or ecclesial communities which are not in full communion with the Catholic Church.

Two decrees of Vatican II and several post-conciliar documents issued by the Secretariat for Promoting Christian Unity considered the question of sacramental sharing in general and of common participation in the Eucharist in particular.[38] A 1970 declaration of the secretariat specifically mentions the issue of "common Eucharistic celebration jointly celebrated by ministers belonging to separated churches and ecclesial communities."[39] A 1972 instruction of this same secretariat affirmed the basic principle that "of its very nature, the celebration of the Eucharist signifies the fullness of the profession of faith and ecclesial communion."[40] This canon does not change this discipline. Unlike canon 844 on interdenominational sacramental sharing, however, there are no special provisions for concelebration between those churches—such as the separated Eastern Churches—which have preserved the substance of the Eucharist, the sacrament of orders, and the apostolic succession.

Inter-Ritual Concelebration

Concelebration among Catholics of diverse rites is not excluded by this canon, and permission for it can be obtained from the apostolic pro-nuncio or other papal legate. Only the rite of the host church may be used, but concelebrants may wear the vestments of their own rite.[41]

Personal Prayer of Priest

Canon 909 — The priest is not to fail to make the required prayerful preparation for the celebration of the Eucharistic Sacrifice or the thanksgiving to God upon its completion.

The appendix to the *Roman Missal* provides several optional prayers of preparation for and thanksgiving after Mass. The priest may use these prayers or choose other ways to observe this canon. Canon 909 is substantially the same as canon 810 of the 1917 Code.

Eucharistic Ministers

Canon 910 — §1. The ordinary minister of Holy Communion is a bishop, a presbyter or a deacon.
§2. The extraordinary minister of Holy Communion is an acolyte or other member of the Christian faithful deputed in accord with can. 230, §3.

Ordinary Ministers

Canon 845 of the 1917 Code stated that the priest alone is the ordinary minister of Commu-

---

[33]*IGMR* 10.
[34]*IGMR* 54.
[35]SCDW, littcirc, *Eucharisticae participationem* 8, Apr. 27, 1973, *AAS* 65 (1973), 343.
[36]*IGMR* 170; BCL, *Study Text 5: Eucharistic Concelebration* (Washington, D.C.: USCC, 1978), 25, n. 6; *SC* 30.
[37]*IGMR* 191, *Inaestimabile donum* 4; BCL, *Music in Catholic Worship* (Washington, D.C.: USCC, 1972), 53, 54; *BCLN* 16 (1980), 230.

[38]*OE* 27–29; *UR* 8, 14, 22; *ED* 42–44, 55, 59; SPCU, decl *Dans ces derniers temps,* Jan. 7, 1970, *AAS* 62 (1970), 184–188; SPCU, instr *In quibus rerum circumstantiis,* June 1, 1972, *AAS* 64 (1972), 518–525; SPCU, interpretation *Dopo la pubblicazione,* Oct. 17, 1973, *AAS* 65 (1973), 616–619; SPCU, *Ecumenical Collaboration at the Regional, National and Local Levels,* IIIa; *CLD* 8, 879–880.
[39]*Dan ces derniers temps* 1.
[40]*In quibus rerum circumstantiis* 4a.
[41]*J* 42 (1982), 168.

nion, and the deacon is the special minister ("minister extraordinarius") who could exercise this ministry only with permission of the local ordinary or the pastor, and for a grave reason. This canon states the discipline of the Church that has been in effect since 1967 when the permanent diaconate was restored and deacons were made ordinary ministers of the Eucharist.[42]

Special Ministers

Minister extraordinarius was at first generally translated as "extraordinary minister," but since the publication by the International Commission on English in the Liturgy of the *Rite of Commissioning Special Ministers of the Eucharist* in 1978,[43] the term "special minister" has become the more acceptable. This change not only represents a more nuanced rendering of the Latin word, but it also recognizes the fact that these ministers typically function today on a regular, and, therefore, non-extraordinary, basis.

In 1966 special Eucharistic ministers were first provided for when Paul VI derogated from canon 845 of the 1917 Code by enabling heads of local churches to petition the Apostolic See for a three-year faculty which would permit them to mandate qualified religious men and women and qualified lay men to distribute the Eucharist.[44] The principal condition for granting the faculty was that there be just cause, such as the scarcity of priests in mission lands. During the next few years numerous indults were granted to individual bishops and to entire bishops' conferences, including the National Conference of Catholic Bishops.[45] When the minor orders were abolished by Paul VI in 1972, the new lay ministry of acolyte was created, among whose duties is that of distributing the Eucharist whenever ordinary ministers are not available or the number of communicants is great.[46]

The January 29, 1973 instruction of the Sacred Congregation for the Discipline of the Sacraments, *Immensae caritatis,* provided for the creation of special ministers without the necessity of the competent authorities' applying for particular indults.[47] With the appearance of the instruction, all local ordinaries have the faculty to appoint qualified persons of either sex to serve as special ministers for a given occasion, for a stated period of time, or even permanently, if needed. *Immensae caritatis* noted three circumstances, each of which would warrant the exercise of this ministry: (1) the absence of a

priest, deacon, or acolyte; (2) the inconvenience or inability of these same persons in distributing Communion due to some other pastoral ministry or due to ill health or advanced age; and (3) the presence of so many people who wish to receive Communion that the celebration of Mass or the distribution of Communion outside Mass would be protracted too long. Although it is not stated in the instruction, another appropriate reason for the use of special ministers is to promote a more active role by the laity in the liturgy as desired by Vatican II.

Local ordinaries also have the faculty to permit individual priests to appoint a qualified person to distribute Communion for a specific occasion when there is a genuine need. This faculty provides for the exceptional case when the number of available ordinary ministers and regularly deputed special ministers is insufficient to meet pastoral needs. Those who would make use of the provision are required to obtain advance permission from their local ordinary, who may also give general permission. In cases of great need, tacit permission for such ad hoc delegation should often be presumed.

Paragraph two of the canon requires that the special minister be deputed in accord with canon 230, §3. While not required by the common law, it is pastorally desirable to provide a suitable period of formation or instruction for the candidates who are to be commissioned as special ministers.[48] Local ordinaries are free to mandate special ministers as they see fit provided that the individual candidates' names are approved by the local ordinary himself. *Immensae caritatis* recommends that the mandate be given by the local ordinary (or by the priest deputing the minister on an ad hoc basis) according to the *Rite of Commissioning Special Ministers of Holy Communion.*

According to canon 230, §2 acolytes and other special ministers of the Eucharist may distribute Communion when the needs of the Church require it and when (ordinary) ministers are lacking. This may be either during the celebration of Mass or outside Mass, and they may administer either the bread or the cup. The requirements of need and a lack of ordinary ministers should be interpreted broadly. It sometimes happens, especially at large celebrations when sufficient concelebrants and deacons are present, that the service of the assigned special ministers may not be needed. Pastors prudently should preclude the problems that arise in such situations by ensuring that their special ministers are aware of the auxiliary nature of this ministry and the preference that the law gives to the service of the ordinary ministers. However, if such an understanding is lacking in a particular case, it

---

[42]Paul VI, *mp Sacrum diaconatus ordinem,* V, 3, June 18, 1967, *AAS* 59 (1967), 702; *CLD* 6, 577.

[43]This is the provisional translation of the *editio typica* which appeared in 1973.

[44]SCSacr, letter *Fidei custos,* Mar. 10, 1966, *CLD* 7, 645–648.

[45]*CLD* 7, 648–652.

[46]Paul VI, *mp Ministeria quaedam,* Aug. 15, 1972, *AAS* 64 (1972), 532–533; *CLD* 7, 690.

[47]*AAS* 65 (1973), 265–266.

[48]Some worthwhile instructional aids are W.J. Belford, *Special Ministers of the Eucharist* (New York: Pueblo, 1979) and BCL, *Study Text I: Holy Communion, Commentary on the Instruction Immensae Caritatis* (Washington, D.C.: USCC, 1973).

may be preferable to allow the special ministers to fulfill their duties rather than abruptly dismiss them just before or during the liturgy. In such a case a genuine need of the Church—that of harmony and charity—is served better when the special ministers are permitted to assist.

Ministers of Viaticum

Canon 911 — §1. The pastor and parochial vicars, chaplains and, for all who live in the house, the superior of the community in clerical religious institutes or societies of apostolic life have the right and the duty to bring the Most Holy Eucharist to the sick in the form of Viaticum.

§2. In case of necessity or with at least the presumed permission of the pastor, chaplain, or superior, who should later be notified, any priest or other minister of Holy Communion must do this.

The minister of Viaticum in the 1917 Code was principally the pastor; other priests could administer it only in necessity or with at least the presumed permission of the pastor or ordinary.[49] The chief change in the law governing the minister of Viaticum occurred in the 1972 revision of the rites of anointing and Viaticum, which added as ordinary ministers both assistant pastors—now called parochial vicars—and priests who care for the sick in hospitals.[50] This canon includes all chaplains as ordinary ministers of Viaticum and not only those who care for the sick in hospitals. General norms governing chaplains are found in canons 564–572, and canon 566, §1 specifically mentions the administration of Viaticum as one of the chaplain's duties. The right of the pastor to administer Viaticum is also enunciated in canon 530, 3°, where it is listed as one of the functions specially committed to the pastor.

The ordinary ministers of Viaticum for religious remain nearly the same as in the 1917 Code (*CIC* 514). For clerical religious institutes and clerical societies of apostolic life, the ordinary minister of Viaticum is the superior of the house. He has the right and duty to administer the sacrament to all who live in the house, including boarders who are not members of the institute. The ordinary minister for houses of lay religious is the pastor, parochial vicar, or chaplain of the house. The ordinary minister of Viaticum for a diocesan seminary is the seminary rector or his delegate in accord with canon 262.

The administration of Viaticum by the ordinary minister is both a right and a duty. By making it a duty incumbent on priests who have positions of pastoral care, the legislator assures that the faithful have access to the full benefits of spiritual comfort provided by the Church, including penance and anointing. The administration of Viaticum is also a right. For the pastoral good of the dying person, however, priests who enjoy this right should not insist on its exercise if another minister is requested.

The 1972 *Rite of Anointing,* number 29 permitted deacons and special ministers to give Viaticum if no priest is available. One reason for this restriction is to encourage the distribution of Viaticum during the Eucharistic celebration.[51] Ministers of Viaticum other than the ordinary ministers may be used either in case of need or if the minister has at least the presumed permission of the ordinary minister. A case of need is demonstrated when someone is in danger of death and the ordinary minister is unavailable. One can always presume the permission of the ordinary minister in cases of danger of imminent death because the right of the faithful to receive the last sacrament supercedes the right of the ordinary minister to give it. Since the administration of Viaticum is a canonical duty of the ordinary minister, he should be notified when this duty is fulfilled by another. A deacon follows the rite of Viaticum outside Mass prescribed for priests in the *Rite of Anointing,* numbers 101–114.[52] Lay ministers follow numbers 68–78 of the *Rite of Holy Communion and Worship of the Eucharistic Mystery Outside Mass.*[53]

ARTICLE 2: PARTICIPATION IN THE MOST HOLY EUCHARIST
[cc. 912–923]

The twelve canons of this article treat various aspects of participation in the Eucharist, all of which are related to the reception of Holy Communion. The norms regulate the following: (1) the recipient of Communion (c. 912); (2) reception of Communion by children (cc. 913–914); (3) the prohibition of the Eucharist to grave sinners (cc. 915–916); (4) Communion twice a day (c. 917); (5) Communion outside Mass (c. 918); (6) the Eucharistic fast (c. 919); (7) the Eucharistic precept (c. 920); (8) the recipient of Viaticum (cc. 921–922); and (9) the reception of the Eucharist in other rites (c. 923).

Recipient of Communion

Canon 912 — Any baptized person who is not prohibited by law can and must be admitted to Holy Communion.

Eligible baptized persons may and *must* be admitted to the Eucharist because they have a right to the sacrament in accord with canon 213. According

---

[49]*CIC* 850; see also *CIC* 397, 3°; 464, §2; 1368.
[50]*Rite of Anointing* 29.
[51]Ibid., 26.
[52]*Pastoral Care of the Sick; Rites of Anointing and Viaticum,* nn. 197–211.
[53]*Rite of Anointing* 29; 112. See also commentary on cc. 910 and 921–922.

to canon 842, §1, which is considered divine law, the recipient of Communion must be baptized. For good reason, however, the Church can prohibit persons from receiving the sacrament or limit their reception of it. The law greatly restricts access to the Eucharist by baptized non-Catholics (c. 844, §§3–4). Further restrictions are specified in the canons which follow.

Reception of Communion by Children

Canon 913 — §1. For the administration of the Most Holy Eucharist to children, it is required that they have sufficient knowledge and careful preparation so as to understand the mystery of Christ according to their capacity, and can receive the Body of the Lord with faith and devotion.

§2. The Most Holy Eucharist may be given to children who are in danger of death, however, if they are able to distinguish the Body of Christ from ordinary food and to receive Communion reverently.

Canon 914 — It is the responsibility, in the first place, of parents and those who take the place of parents as well as of the pastor to see that children who have reached the use of reason are correctly prepared and are nourished by the divine food as early as possible, preceded by sacramental confession; it is also for the pastor to be vigilant lest any children come to the Holy Banquet who have not reached the use of reason or whom he judges are not sufficiently disposed.

Since 1910 it has been the practice of the Latin Church to give Communion to children from the age of seven.[54] The ancient custom of giving Communion to infants had largely ceased in the West by the twelfth century, but it is still maintained in Eastern Churches. The Council of Trent decreed that it is not necessary to give the Eucharist to children before they have reached the age of discretion, but it did not condemn the practice.[55]

The intent of canon 913 is to ensure that children who receive the Eucharist have adequate catechetical and spiritual preparation. Paragraph one states in broad terms the minimal requirements for admitting children to the Eucharist in ordinary circumstances. It does not specify what constitutes sufficient knowledge or how much faith and devotion is expected of the child but rather allows the persons mentioned in canon 914 to make such decisions while advising that the preparation be according to the child's capacity. The careful preparation required is something more than the intellectual preparation indicated by the words

"sufficient knowledge." It includes formative experiences in faith such as are promoted by active participation in the Eucharist even before the children receive their first Holy Communion. The liturgy itself has formative value,[56] especially when it is adapted to the children's level as suggested by the principles contained in the *Directory on Children's Masses.*[57] The use of the approved Eucharistic prayers for children can also encourage greater participation in and a fuller understanding of the "mystery of Christ" referred to in the canon.

Children who are in danger of death may receive Communion even if they do not have the sufficient knowledge and careful preparation specified in paragraph one. However, paragraph two requires that they be able to distinguish the Body of Christ from ordinary food and to receive it reverently. The latter requirement is a change from the 1917 Code (*CIC* 854, §2), which stated that the child must be able to "reverently adore" the Host. The change reflects an emphasis of the liturgical reform that the primary purpose in reserving the Eucharist is for Viaticum, not for adoration.[58]

Canon 914, a corollary of canons 528; 777, 2°; 843, §2; and 898, gives greater responsibility to parents and guardians in the preparation of children for the Eucharist than did the 1917 Code (*CIC* 854, §5) which saw this principally as the pastor's duty.[59] Once the children have attained the use of reason and are judged sufficiently prepared and disposed, parents (or guardians) and pastors are responsible for seeing that children receive Communion as early as possible so that they not be deprived of a sacrament to which they have a right in law. The pastor has an additional obligation to see that children who do not have the use of reason or who are not sufficiently disposed do not receive the Eucharist. The canon gives broad discretionary latitude to the pastor for determining whether the child meets these requirements. However, in view of the right of the baptized to receive the sacraments, a doubt about the use of reason or sufficient disposition should be resolved in favor of the child's receiving Communion.

The Mentally Handicapped

The issue of the use of reason is especially problematic in the case of the mentally handicapped. Other than the presumption that it is attained at the age of seven (c. 97, §2), the Code does not define the "use of reason" or limit the understanding of it to any one epistemology, such as that of Aristotle

---

[54]SCSacr, decr *Quam singulari,* Aug. 8, 1910, *AAS* 2 (1910), 577–583.

[55]Sess. XXI, *Decr. de comm.,* c. 4, *Ench* 1734.

[56]*SC* 33.

[57]SCDW, *Directory on Children's Masses,* Nov. 1, 1973, *AAS* 66 (1974), 30–46.

[58]*Eucharisticum mysterium* 49; *Rite of Holy Communion and Worship of the Eucharistic Mystery Outside Mass* 5. (Cited as *Rite of Holy Com. and Worship.*)

[59]See *Directory on Children's Masses* 10.

and the Scholastics. Traditionally the use of reason has been viewed in terms of the acquisition of abstract, cognitive skills, but the law does not exclude a broader definition which places primacy on symbolic and intuitive ways of knowing. For example, mentally handicapped persons may not be able to conceptualize and articulate the difference between the Body of Christ and ordinary food, but they can sometimes appreciate the sacredness of the Eucharistic food in the context of the reverence shown the sacrament by their families and the Christian community. Some dioceses and conferences of bishops have policies which permit the distribution of Communion to such persons.[60] In the absence of a local policy, pastors should not arbitrarily deny the sacraments to the mentally handicapped who are suitably prepared and disposed "according to their capacity" (c. 913, §1) and who are supported by the faith of family or community.[61]

Penance before First Communion

In the years following Vatican II there was rather widespread experimentation with the practice of delaying first penance until after first Communion, but the Apostolic See repeatedly ordered that these experiments be halted.[62] Nevertheless, canons 988 and 989, based on the discipline of the Council of Trent,[63] require only those conscious of serious sin to confess before receiving Communion, and this also applies to children receiving first Communion. It does not seem that the intention of this canon is to subrogate this long-standing discipline but rather to suggest that the right of children to the sacrament of penance can be served best when pastors and catechists offer formation for penance appropriate to the level of the child making first Communion and provide the opportunity for penance before first Communion for those children who need or desire the sacrament. Hence, children who do not approach the sacrament of penance should not be deprived of their right to make first Holy Communion.

Prohibition of Eucharist to Grave Sinners

Canon 915 — Those who are excommunicated or interdicted after the imposition or declaration of the penalty and others who obstinately persist in manifest grave sin are not to be admitted to Holy Communion.

Canon 916 — A person who is conscious of grave sin is not to celebrate Mass or to receive the Body of the Lord without prior sacramental confession unless a grave reason is present and there is no opportunity of confessing; in this case the person is to be mindful of the obligation to make an act of perfect contrition, including the intention of confessing as soon as possible.

Canon 915, based on canon 855 of the 1917 Code, prohibits giving the Eucharist to anyone who obstinately perseveres in manifest, serious sin. A manifest sin is one which is publicly known, even if only by a few; obstinate perseverance is indicated when a person persists in the sin or sinful situation and does not heed the warnings of church authorities or adhere to church teachings. Clearly, those who are excommunicated or interdicted by an inflicted or declared sentence are regarded by the Church as grave and manifest sinners, and they are excluded from the sacraments by penal law as well (cc. 1331, §1, 2°; 1332). Other categories of manifest and grave sins are not so neatly discernible. The minister cannot assume, for example, that the sin of public concubinage arising from divorce and remarriage is always grave in the internal forum. Any prudent doubt about either the gravity or the public nature of the sin should be resolved by the minister in favor of the person who approaches the sacrament.

Canon 916, a composite of canons 807 and 856 of the 1917 Code, is based on Tridentine doctrine. Citing the Scriptures (1 Cor 11:28–29), Trent confirmed the Church's teaching that one who is conscious of grave sins may not receive the Eucharist.[64] The 1967 Instruction on the Worship of the Eucharistic Mystery affirmed this discipline, adding that confessions should not be heard during the celebration of Mass.[65] Canon 916 adds nothing new to past discipline in requiring those who are conscious, i.e., *certain* of having committed a grave sin, to return to the state of grace by sacramental confession or a perfect act of contrition when sacramental confession is not possible. However, unlike canon 856 of the 1917 Code, this canon makes it explicit that a perfect act of contrition includes the intention to confess as soon as possible.

Communion Twice a Day

Canon 917 — A person who has received the Most Holy Eucharist may receive it again on the same day only during the celebration of the Eucha-

[60] See, e.g., the pastoral statement of the Roman Catholic Bishops of England and Wales, *All People Together* (London: CSP Studios, 1981), nn. 15–19.

[61] On the right of the mentally handicapped to the Eucharist, see D. Wilson, "The Church, the Eucharist, and the Mentally Handicapped," *CR* 60 (1975), 69–84; J. Huels, "'Use of Reason' and Reception of the Sacraments by the Mentally Handicapped," *J* 44 (1984), 209–219.

[62] SCSacr and SCC, decl *Sanctus Pontifex*, May 24, 1973, *AAS* 65 (1973), 410; *CLD* 8, 563; SCSDW, letter, Mar. 31, 1977, *CLD* 8, 603; SCSDW and SCC, reply, May 20, 1977, *AAS* 69 (1977), 427; *CLD* 8, 607.

[63] Sess. XIII, *De euch.*, cap. 7, c. 11, *Ench* 1646–1647, 1661.

[64] Ibid.

[65] *Eucharisticum mysterium* 35.

rist in which the person participates, with due regard for the prescription of can. 921, §2.

The purpose of this canon is twofold: on the one hand, to promote active participation in the Eucharist including the full sacramental sharing in the Lord's Body and Blood; on the other hand, to prevent the abuse of receiving multiple Communions out of superstition, ignorance, or misguided devotion.

The 1917 Code (*CIC* 857) forbade the reception of Communion more than once a day except in danger of death or in need of impeding irreverence. The law was mitigated repeatedly after Vatican II to allow more frequent opportunities to receive twice on the same day.[66] This canon greatly simplifies the post-conciliar legislation by permitting the reception of Communion twice in a day for any reason, provided the second reception occurs in the context of the Eucharist at which one is actually participating. Such participation implies minimally one's physical presence at the Eucharist. It excludes a second Communion outside of Mass except as Viaticum, and it also excludes a second Communion during a Mass at which one is not participating, such as when one enters in the course of the Mass only to receive Communion.

Communion Outside Mass

Canon 918 — **It is highly recommended that the faithful receive Holy Communion during the celebration of the Eucharist itself, but it should be administered outside Mass to those who request it for a just cause, the liturgical rites being observed.**

The 1917 Code was rather liberal in its provision for Communion outside Mass. In addition to Communion for the sick and dying, any priest could give Communion outside Mass in a church at the hours during which Mass could be celebrated and even at other times for a reasonable cause; it could also be given immediately before or after a private (low) Mass.[67] Beginning with Vatican II the Church's attitude toward Communion outside Mass became more restrictive. The Council decreed that Communion received during the Eucharistic celebration is "the more perfect form of participation in the Mass."[68] The 1967 Instruction on the Worship of the Eucharistic Mystery said that it is greatly recommended ("valde commendatur") that the faithful receive Communion during Mass. It also stated that it is

necessary to accustom the faithful to receive Communion during the Eucharist, and that there must be a just cause for distributing Communion outside Mass.[69] The canon reflects this change in attitude, and it even more strongly ("maxime commendatur") recommends that the faithful receive Communion during the Eucharistic celebration. Because the mind of the Church is that Communion be given primarily during Mass, the requirement of a just cause for Communion outside Mass should be strictly observed. Some examples of a just cause include the inability to participate in the Eucharistic celebration due to illness or old age or the absence of a priest who can preside at Eucharist. Liturgical law requires pastors to see to it that the sick and aged be given every opportunity to receive the Eucharist frequently, especially during the Easter season.[70]

The liturgical rites to be observed in distributing Communion outside Mass are contained in the *Roman Ritual* under the title, "Holy Communion and Worship of the Eucharist Outside Mass." The ritual prescribes an introductory rite and a celebration of the word preceding the distribution of Communion. Options are provided for a shorter reading of the word when the entire service of the word is pastorally unsuitable, such as when there are only one or two communicants. The Eucharistic prayer may never be said in Communion services outside Mass, although a reading of the Last Supper narrative is permissible.[71]

Communion may be given outside Mass on any day and at any hour, with several exceptions. On Holy Thursday and Good Friday the sacrament may be administered only during the Eucharist or the celebration of the Lord's passion, respectively; Communion may be given to the sick at any time on these days. On Holy Saturday only Viaticum may be administered. In this way the ancient tradition of the single Eucharist of a community is maintained at least on the principal days of the church year.

Eucharistic Fast

Canon 919 — **§1. One who is to receive the Most Holy Eucharist is to abstain from any food or drink, with the exception only of water and medicine, for at least the period of one hour before Holy Communion.**

§2. A priest who celebrates the Most Holy Eucharist two or three times on the same day may take something before the second or third celebra-

---

[66]SCRit, instr *IO*, Sept. 26, 1964, *AAS* 56 (1964), 877–900, n. 60; *Rite of Concelebration* 15; SCRit, instr *Tres abhinc annos,* May 4, 1967, *AAS* 59 (1967), 442–448, n. 14; *Eucharisticum mysterium* 28; SCDW, instr *Immensae caritatis,* Jan. 29, 1973, *AAS* 65 (1973), 264–271, pt. 2.

[67]*CIC* 846; 867, §4.

[68]*SC* 55.

[69]*Eucharisticum mysterium* 31; 33a.

[70]*Rite of Anointing* 46. *Pastoral Care of the Sick: Rites of Anointing and Viaticum,* provides rites of Communion outside Mass for the sick in ordinary circumstances. See also commentary on cc. 921–922.

[71]*Liturgicae instaurationes* 6e.

tion even if the period of one hour does not intervene.

§3. Those who are advanced in age or who suffer from any infirmity, as well as those who take care of them, can receive the Most Holy Eucharist even if they have taken something during the previous hour.

The ancient custom of fasting before the Eucharist arose in the Church after the third century and was mandated by early councils. The Church considers fasting a means of spiritual preparation for the Eucharist and a way of showing reverence for the sacrament.

Paragraph one of the canon reflects the discipline of the Church that has been in force since 1964. The traditional total fast from midnight, prescribed in the 1917 Code (*CIC* 808, 858), was reduced to a three-hour fast in 1957[72] and to a one-hour fast in 1964.[73] In 1953 permission was granted to take water and medicine anytime before reception of Communion.[74] The medicine may be in solid or liquid form, and it need not be prescribed by a physician.

Paul VI allowed residential bishops to permit priests who binate or trinate to take nourishment in liquid form before the celebration of the next Mass.[75] Paragraph two of this canon extends this to all priests even without the bishop's permission, and it also allows the taking of solid foods. Priests therefore need observe the Eucharistic fast only for their first Mass of the day. Even if the subsequent Mass is much later in the day, such as an evening Mass after dinner, the fast of paragraph one does not oblige the priest. The word "celebrates" in paragraph two should be understood also as including priests who concelebrate.

Paragraph three represents a change from the previous law which required a fast of about a quarter of an hour for the sick in hospitals or at home, for those who are confined to their homes because of old age, or for those who live in a nursing home. Those who care for the sick and aged and their families were bound to a fast of about fifteen minutes if they could not observe the one hour fast without inconvenience.[76] The sick were able to take non-alcoholic drink anytime before Communion.[77] According to paragraph three of the canon, those who are advanced in age or who suffer from any infirmity and those who care for the sick and aged are not bound by any fast. The terms "advanced age" and "infirmity" are subject to broad interpretation. Certainly anyone too old or too infirm to go to

church need not fast. Those who care for the sick or aged are exempted from the fast only when they are actually caring for the sick or aged at the time they receive Communion, such as when Communion is given in a home or an institution. This category of persons may also be broadly interpreted to include those who contribute in non-material ways to the care of the sick, such as visitors and family members who provide moral and emotional support.

By specifying that the fast is to be *at least* one hour, the legislator appears to be encouraging the faithful to fast for a longer period, if they desire. The one-hour fast is computed from the time of the completion of the consumption of food or drink until the reception of Communion, not the onset of Mass. Prior to the 1983 Code dispensations from the Eucharistic fast were reserved to the Apostolic See;[78] now the diocesan bishop may dispense.

Eucharistic Precept

Canon 920 — §1. All the faithful, after they have been initiated into the Most Holy Eucharist, are bound by the obligation of receiving Communion at least once a year.

§2. This precept must be fulfilled during the Easter season unless it is fulfilled for a just cause at some other time during the year.

As a result of widespread neglect of the sacrament in the Middle Ages, various church councils from the sixth century onward enacted disciplinary laws obligating the faithful to receive the Eucharist, especially on the principal feasts. Lateran IV in 1215 established a general law for the Latin Church requiring the reception of Communion at least once a year at Easter by those who had attained the age of discretion, unless for some reasonable cause one's priest has advised against it for a time.[79] This law, confirmed by Trent,[80] is basically the same as that incorporated into the 1917 Code (*CIC* 859, §1). The 1983 Code retains the annual precept but with some changes.

One change is greater latitude for the fulfillment of the Eucharistic precept besides Easter time. The *coetus* which prepared the original draft of this canon understood Easter time as the period from Palm (Passion) Sunday to Pentecost Sunday.[81] The dioceses of the United States have an indult which allows the Easter duty to be satisfied from the First Sunday of Lent to Trinity Sunday.[82] The satisfaction of the Eucharistic precept outside this period requires a just cause, such as illness, but it must be satisfied within the space of one year. The year in

---

[72]Pius XII, *mp Sacram Communionem,* Mar. 19, 1957, *AAS* 49 (1957) 177; *CLD* 4, 286.

[73]Paul VI, decr, Nov. 21, 1964, *AAS* 57 (1964) 186; *CLD* 6, 566.

[74]Pius XII, apconst *Christus Dominus,* Jan. 6, 1953, *AAS* 45 (1953) 15; *CLD* 4, 269.

[75]*PM* I, 3.

[76]*Immensae caritatis* pt. 3.

[77]*Sacram Communionem* 4.

[78]*EM* IX, 20.

[79]Cap. 21, *Ench* 812.

[80]Sess. XIII, *De euch.,* c. 9, *Ench* 1659.

[81]*Comm* 13 (1981), 417–418.

[82]Second Plenary Council of Baltimore, n. 257.

question is a period of three hundred sixty-five days continuous time which is reckoned from the previous Communion in accord with canon 203.

Another change from the former law is the elimination of the exception which allowed the *sacerdos proprius,* understood as one's pastor or confessor, to permit an individual to postpone satisfaction of the Eucharistic precept for a reasonable cause. The annual precept is now absolute, barring excusing causes such as physical or moral impossibility.

Under the former law all who had attained the use of reason were bound by the Eucharistic precept. The revised law specifies that all the faithful who have been initiated into the Eucharist are bound, i.e., those who have made their first Communion. Unlike the 1917 Code (*CIC* 859, §3), the pastor of one's parish need not be notified when the Eucharistic precept is fulfilled outside one's own parish.

Also dropped in the present law are canons 860 and 861 of the earlier Code. The former canon specified the duty of those who have the care of children to see that they fulfill the paschal precept, while the latter stated that a sacrilegious Communion did not satisfy the precept. Such concerns need not be expressed in a book of law, but they still bind morally.

Recipient of Viaticum

Canon 921 — §1. The Christian faithful who are in danger of death, arising from any cause, are to be nourished by Holy Communion in the form of Viaticum.

§2. Even if they have received Communion in the same day, those who are in danger of death are strongly urged to receive again.

§3. While the danger of death lasts, it is recommended that Holy Communion be given repeatedly but on separate days.

Canon 922 — Holy Viaticum for the sick is not to be delayed too long; those who have the care of souls are to be zealous and vigilant that they are nourished by Viaticum while they are fully conscious.

Viaticum is the last sacrament of Christian life, the Eucharist meant for those at or near the time of death. Vatican II called for the revision of the rite of Viaticum and for a new continuous rite of penance, anointing, and Viaticum, and this was implemented in 1972.[83] The revised rite recommends that Viaticum be given during Mass when possible and that it be given under both kinds.[84] It is advisable to reserve in the tabernacle a properly sealed vessel of the Precious Blood for Viaticum in emergencies

outside Mass.[85] The dying who are unable to receive under the form of bread may receive under the form of wine alone (c. 925).

The 1917 Code (*CIC* 864) considered the reception of Viaticum by the faithful in danger of death as a "precept" to which they were bound by law. By contrast, the 1983 Code uses exhortatory language which better suggests the voluntary faith response that should characterize the reception of any sacrament, but this should not be understood as a change in law. The obligation still exists in liturgical law as found in the *Rite of Anointing,* which states that "all baptized Christians who can receive communion are bound to receive viaticum" in danger of death.[86] Children in danger of death who are able to distinguish the Body of Christ from ordinary food and receive it reverently may, but are not obliged to, receive Viaticum (c. 913, §2).

The Code does not define "danger of death" but, given the Church's desire that Viaticum be the final sacrament of passage from death to eternal life, a strict interpretation is in order. Viaticum should be received only by those who are in some real danger of dying, whether from intrinsic causes such as a grave illness or extrinsic sources such as a criminal execution. In doubt about the degree of danger, Viaticum may be given.

Viaticum should be received as soon as possible after the faithful fall into the danger of death, even if they have already received Communion that day. Terminally or seriously ill persons, although not in immediate danger of death, should not postpone its reception too long lest they lose consciousness or die. Canon 921, §3 recommends that "Holy Communion" be given each day while the danger lasts, whereas canon 864, §3 of the 1917 Code said it was fitting to give "Holy Viaticum" in these same circumstances. The change indicates that those who have the duty of administering Viaticum according to canon 911, §1 fulfill this duty if they administer it but once to a person in mortal danger, even if this danger persists for many days. Deacons, special ministers, and other priests who are not obliged to administer Viaticum may bring daily Communion to those in danger of death.[87]

Eucharist in Other Rites

Canon 923 — The Christian faithful may take part in the Eucharistic Sacrifice and receive Communion in any Catholic rite, with due regard for the prescription of can. 844.

This canon is substantially the same as canon 866 of the 1917 Code, but there are some differences. The former law did not mention explicitly the par-

---

[83]*SC* 74.
[84]*Rite of Anointing* 26.

[85]*Pastoral Care of the Sick* 181.
[86]N. 27; *Pastoral Care of the Sick* 237.
[87]See commentary on cc. 910, 911, and 918.

ticipation in the Eucharist but only the reception of Communion. Communion could be received "for reasons of piety" in another rite, but the law urged that the paschal precept be satisfied and Viaticum received in one's own rite. Now there are no qualifications concerning the participation in and reception of the Eucharist in other Catholic rites. However, the faithful may not receive the Eucharist of a church or ecclesial community which is not in full communion with the Catholic Church except for the case mentioned in canon 844, §2.

ARTICLE 3: RITES AND CEREMONIES OF EUCHARISTIC CELEBRATION
[cc. 924–930]

The seven canons of this article treat the following matters: (1) the matter of the Eucharist (c. 924); (2) Communion under one or both kinds (c. 925); (3) the requirement of unleavened bread (c. 926); (4) serious abuses (c. 927); (5) the language of the Eucharist (c. 928); (6) vestments (c. 929); and (7) aged and infirm celebrants (c. 930).

Matter of the Eucharist

Canon 924 — §1. The Most Sacred Eucharistic Sacrifice must be offered with bread and wine, with which a small quantity of water is to be mixed.

§2. The bread must be made of wheat alone and recently made so that there is no danger of corruption.

§3. The wine must be natural wine of the grape and not corrupt.

In keeping with the Last Supper narratives, the Church has always regarded bread and wine as the only matter essential for the Eucharistic meal and sacrifice. A small quantity of water ("modica aqua") is to be added to the wine by the deacon or priest at the preparation of the gifts. Cyprian of Carthage saw in this ritual mixing of water and wine a sign of the unity between Christ and his people, a tradition also reflected at the Council of Trent.[88] The *General Instruction of the Roman Missal* 133 and the *Order of Mass* 20 speak of a "little water" ("parum aquae"), while the 1917 Code (*CIC* 814) required a "very small quantity" ("modicissima aqua"). This change should discourage the scrupulous measuring of drops of water as sometimes occurred in the past. Omission of the water in the cup is considered illicit. When more than one vessel of wine is to be consecrated, liturgists recommend that the water be poured into the central cup and not into any additional cups or flagons.

In a 1929 instruction, the Sacred Congregation for the Discipline of the Sacraments taught that bread made of any substance other than wheat is invalid matter, as is bread to which has been added such a great quantity of another substance that it can no longer be considered wheat bread in the common estimation. The requirements that the bread be recently made and not corrupt are for liceity; however, if the bread is so corrupt that it is no longer considered as bread in the common estimation, it is invalid matter.[89] The *General Instruction of the Roman Missal* 283 stipulates that the bread for the Eucharist should have the appearance of real food and be made in such a way that the priest is able to break it into parts and distribute them to at least some of the faithful. Subsequent instructions from the Apostolic See have attempted to clarify the meaning of this law by indicating that the "appearance" of bread applies to its color, taste, and thickness rather than to its shape.[90]

Wine not made from grapes is considered invalid matter for the Eucharist, as is wine to which water has been added in greater or equal quantity.[91] The *General Instruction of the Roman Missal* 284 says the wine should be natural and pure, i.e., not mixed with any foreign substance. Wine may be corrupt in several ways: that which has totally turned to vinegar is invalid matter; that which has partially become vinegar, or contains unapproved additives or foreign matter, or which loses most of its alcohol, is used illicitly. Over the course of time, the Apostolic See has established specific regulations governing the wine-making process, alcoholic content, and use of additives.[92]

Alcoholic Priests

Canonists and theologians have commonly held that must, or the unfermented juice of ripe grapes, is valid matter for the Eucharist but is gravely illicit except in necessity.[93] In 1974 the Sacred Congregation for the Doctrine of the Faith authorized ordinaries in the United States to grant to priests who request it permission to concelebrate without receiving from the cup or, when concelebration is not possible, to preside at the Eucharist using unfermented grape juice instead of wine.[94] The permission was granted only to those priests who were being treated or who had been treated for alcoholism and only to those who requested such permission.[95] In 1983 the Sacred Congregation for the

---

[88]*Epistula 63 ad Caecilianum,* 13, *PL* 4:395–396; Trent, sess. XXII, *Decr. de Missa, Ench* 1748.

[89]*Dominus Salvator Noster* I, Mar. 26, 1929, *AAS* 21 (1929) 632; *CLD* 1, 353; Roman Missal of Pius V, De defectibus, III.

[90]*Liturgicae instaurationes* 5; *Inaestimabile donum* 8.

[91]*Dominus Salvator Noster* I.

[92]E. Regatillo, *Ius sacramentarium,* 3rd ed. (Santander: Sal Terrae, 1960), 110–112.

[93]The chief authorities for this view are Pope Julius I, C. 7, D. II, *de cons.,* and Thomas Aquinas, *Summa Theologiae* 3, q. lxxiv, art. V ad 3.

[94]Letter of Cardinal Seper, May 2, 1974, *CLD* 8, 517.

[95]Clarification of Bishop J. Rausch, NCCB General Secretary, May 23, 1974, *CLD* 8, 519.

Doctrine of the Faith revoked all general faculties relative to the use of grape juice at Mass which had been given to episcopal conferences or individual ordinaries by that congregation or by the Sacred Congregation for the Sacraments and Divine Worship. Permissions previously granted to priests to use grape juice at Mass were not affected by this decision. The congregation further decided that a solution for alcoholic priests who concelebrate is to receive Communion by intinction; individual celebrants may receive by intinction and let another participant at Mass consume the remainder of the consecrated wine.[96]

Communion under One or Both Kinds

Canon 925 — Holy Communion is to be given under the form of bread alone or under both kinds in accord with the norm of the liturgical laws or even under the form of wine alone in case of necessity.

In contrast to the 1917 Code (*CIC* 852) which prescribed that Communion be given only in the form of bread, this canon reflects the restored practice of Communion under both kinds and the revised liturgical law permitting Communion under the form of wine alone in cases of need.

Communion under Both Kinds

Throughout the history of the Church, Communion under both kinds was always the ideal in keeping with the Lord's Supper, but the Church also permitted Communion under one kind for "just causes and reasons."[97] For the first twelve centuries, Communion under both kinds was the general practice of the Church. Communion under one kind was given in special cases, such as to the sick, and it could even be given under the form of wine alone when the communicant was unable to consume bread. By at least the thirteenth century, the custom of administering only the Eucharistic bread had become dominant in the West, and the Council of Constance in 1415 decreed that this custom should be considered as law.[98] With few exceptions, the distribution of Communion under the form of bread alone remained the practice of the Latin Rite until the liturgical renewal following Vatican II. In *Sacrosanctum Concilium* 55b, the Council took the first step toward a return to the Church's earlier practice of giving both kinds to all communicants. The 1965 *Rite of Communion under Both Kinds*

permitted the practice in specified cases with the consent of the bishop, and this and later developments were included in the 1970 *Roman Missal.*

Communion under both kinds is permitted in accord with the liturgical laws which chiefly appear in the *General Instruction of the Roman Missal* 240–252. Communion under both kinds is said more fully to express the sign of the Eucharistic meal; of the new and eternal covenant ratified by the Blood of the Lord; and of the relationship between the Eucharistic Banquet and the eschatological banquet (*IGMR* 240). The clear implication is that Communion under both kinds is the ideal, i.e., normative, practice.

The *General Instruction of the Roman Missal* 242 enumerates the cases for which ordinaries may permit Communion under both kinds, adding that episcopal conferences may establish guidelines for the ordinaries to concede the faculty on other occasions as well. In the United States the National Conference of Catholic Bishops has extended the list of cases to all Masses, including Sundays and holy days. The ordinaries are to determine the extent of the practice within their respective jurisdictions, namely, local ordinaries for their territories and pontifical right major superiors of clerical religious institutes and societies of apostolic life for their subjects.

The final paragraph of the *General Instruction of the Roman Missal* 242 places certain limits on the kinds of occasions and the nature of the groups for which ordinaries may permit the distribution of Communion under both kinds. It says the faculty should not be conceded indiscriminately but for celebrations which are well defined, with proper precautions indicated, and not on occasions when there are a great number of communicants. It further states that the groups who receive under both kinds should be well determined, orderly, and homogeneous. In enforcing these norms, ordinaries should understand that the underlying motivation is not to restrict the practice unnecessarily, but rather to ensure proper catechetical preparation and good order, and to preclude abuses. The restrictive norms first appeared in *Sacramentali communione,* the June 29, 1970 instruction of the Sacred Congregation for Divine Worship.[99] The only problem addressed in this instruction that was considered an abuse by the congregation is that of the communicants' passing the cup from hand to hand or taking it without the assistance of a minister. The minister is part of the sign of Communion, signifying Christ's giving Himself through the ministry of the Church; it is important, therefore, to have a sufficient number of ministers of the cup.

In interpreting the restrictions mentioned above, it should be noted that their origin in *Sacramentali*

---

[96]Letter of Cardinal J. Ratzinger to pontifical representatives, private, Sept. 12, 1983, Prot. n. 89/78. See also SCDF, *Responsa ad proposita dubia,* Oct. 29, 1982, *AAS* 74 (1982), 1298.

[97]Trent, sess. XXI, *Ench* 1732. See J. Huels, "Trent and the Chalice: Forerunner of Vatican II?" *W* 56 (1982), 386–400.

[98]Sess. XIII, *Ench* 1198–1200.

[99]*AAS* 62 (1970), 664–666.

communione antedated the 1973 provision for lay ministers of the Eucharist.[100] Since there were generally not enough *ordained* ministers available for efficient administration of the cup to large congregations before 1973, the Sacred Congregation for Divine Worship in 1970 understandably would see this fact as a just reason to restrict the types of groups and the occasions for which the faculty could be conceded. However, with the potential for an adequate number of ministers of the cup in every congregation and community, the problems addressed in the 1970 instruction are considerably diminished if not eliminated.[101]

Although the *General Instruction of the Roman Missal* recognizes four different ways of administering Communion under both kinds (*IGMR* 244–252), *Sacramentali communione* teaches that the mode of direct reception from the chalice is optimal. The reason is undoubtedly that this mode best witnesses to the dominical command to "take and drink." Practical problems in administering the cup to large congregations can be overcome with proper preparation and catechesis, a sufficient number of Eucharistic ministers, and the knowledge that comes with experience.

A chief problem that has arisen in some places with general use of the practice for large congregations is the cluttering of the altar with multiple chalices that detract from the sign of the one bread and the one cup. On this point Pope Gregory II taught that it is "not fitting to place two or three chalices on the altar when one celebrates Mass."[102] A recommended solution is to use a flagon, keeping the chalices of administration at a separate place.[103]

Hygienic factors are the principal reason for the reluctance of many to receive from the chalice. In their catechesis, pastors and religious educators need not emphasize this issue. The most convincing demonstration of the safety of the practice is the witness of others in the assembly who suffer no ill effects from it.

Wine Alone

In the late 1950's and early 1960's, the Holy Office granted indults for the reception of Communion under the form of wine alone on behalf of persons who were medically unable to consume the bread; permission was even granted to take the Precious Blood through a stomach tube.[104] The 1967 Instruction on the Worship of the Eucharistic Mystery (n. 41) derogated from canon 852 of the 1917 Code by allowing Communion to be given under the form of wine alone to those who are unable to receive it under the form of bread in case of need and in the judgment of the bishop. The instruction directed the priest to celebrate the Eucharist in the house of the sick person or to bring the Blood of the Lord to the sick person in a sealed vessel. Since the appearance of the 1972 *Rite of Anointing* (n. 95), the judgment of the bishop is not required.

The canon requires that there be a case of need for administering Communion under the form of wine alone. This is demonstrated whenever a person is physically or psychologically unable—whether permanently or temporarily—to consume the Eucharistic bread.

Unleavened Bread

Canon 926 — In accord with the ancient tradition of the Latin Church, the priest is to use unleavened bread in the celebration of the Eucharist whenever he offers it.

The requirement of unleavened bread is for liceity.[105] In the early centuries, both Eastern and Western Churches used leavened bread for the Eucharist, but in the eighth and ninth centuries the use of unleavened bread became the general custom in the West. In keeping with the limited scope of the Code, the canon properly addresses only the practice of the Latin Rites, unlike the 1917 Code (*CIC* 816) which alluded to the Eastern usage.

Serious Abuses

Canon 927 — It is sinful, even in extreme necessity, to consecrate one matter without the other or even both outside the celebration of the Eucharist.

Theological opinion has not been in agreement on whether the consecration of only one of the elements[106] suffices for the validity of the Mass. Neither the 1917 Code (*CIC* 817) nor the revised Code resolves the issue of validity, but instead both use the moral authority of the Church to forbid under penalty of sin the consecration of only one element in or outside of Mass, or the consecration of even both elements apart from the Eucharistic celebration. While the use of moralistic language ("nefas est") is rare in the 1983 Code and in contemporary liturgical law, it conveys how strongly the Church desires to maintain the integrity of the Eucharistic

---

[100]*Immensae caritatis* pt. 1.

[101]For a detailed treatment of these issues, see J. Huels, *The Interpretation of the Law on Communion under Both Kinds,* CanLawStud 505 (Washington, D.C.: Catholic University of America, 1982); see also *idem,* "Communion under Both Kinds on Sundays—Is it Legal?" *J* 42 (1982), 70–106.

[102]*Epistula 14 ad Bonifacium, PL* 89: 524.

[103]BCL, *Environment and Art in Catholic Worship* (Washington, D.C.: USCC, 1978), 47.

[104]*CLD* 5, 434; *CLD* 6, 562–65.

[105]Council of Florence, Decree for the Greeks, *Ench* 1303; Pius X, apconst *Tradita ab antiquis,* II, Sept. 14, 1912, *AAS* 4 (1912), 614–616.

[106]Regatillo, *Ius sacramentarium,* 178–179.

celebration and the two signs of bread and wine. Excluded are even cases of extreme necessity, such as lack of time to celebrate an entire Eucharist in the case of a person in danger of death, or lack of bread or wine due to war or persecution. The Church prefers that there be no Mass or Communion at all rather than allow the sacramental action to be distorted by minimalistic practices.

Language of Eucharist

Canon 928 — The Eucharist is to be celebrated in the Latin language or in another language provided the liturgical texts have been legitimately approved.

Latin is the "typical" language of the Latin Rites, but experience has shown that the use of the vernacular allows for greater participation in the Eucharist and a fuller appreciation of it. Although the vernacular is generally pastorally preferable, the Eucharist may be celebrated in Latin provided the revised texts are employed, and in special cases it may even be genuinely advantageous to do so.[107] Local ordinaries are encouraged by the Apostolic See to provide Masses in Latin in at least some churches, especially in areas where groups of people speak different languages.[108] The use of music with Latin texts, particularly Gregorian chant, is often suitable even in Masses in the vernacular.[109] Sign language may be used in Masses at which deaf persons are present.[110] Translations of liturgical texts are prepared and approved according to the norm of canon 838, §§2–3.

Vestments

Canon 929 — In celebrating and administering the Eucharist, priests and deacons are to wear the liturgical vestments prescribed by the rubrics.

The rubrics governing Mass vestments are chiefly found in the *General Instruction of the Roman Missal* 297–310. The principal changes from past liturgical law are the elimination of the maniple and the optional use of amice and cincture when the design of the alb does not functionally require them. A cassock or habit need not be worn under the alb. Unlike the 1917 Code (*CIC* 136, §2; 811, §2), the revised Code does not exclude priests from wearing

rings, even when they preside at the Eucharist, although liturgists point out that celebrants' rings can be a source of distraction.

Conferences of bishops may determine adaptations regarding the material and form of vestments.[111] The National Conference of Catholic Bishops allows both natural and artificial fabrics for sacred vesture provided that they are suitable for liturgical use, subject to the further judgment of the local ordinary in doubtful cases.[112] In many regions, including the United States and Canada, the Apostolic See has approved the use of the chasuble-alb at concelebrations, Masses for special groups, celebrations outside a sacred place, and similar occasions. The stole is worn over the chasuble-alb and should be the color appropriate to the Mass being celebrated.[113] The vestment color for funerals is violet or black, but conferences of bishops may determine their own color in accord with popular sentiment, human sorrow, and Christian hope. The liturgical color for funerals of children should be festive with a paschal significance. The approved colors for funeral vesture in the United States are white, violet, or black.[114]

When Communion is given in a church or oratory, the appropriate vesture for the ordinary ministers of Communion is alb and stole, or a surplice and stole over a cassock or habit. Special ministers should wear whatever is customary in the region or whatever has been approved by the ordinary. For Communion outside a church, the vesture of the ministers should be appropriate and in accord with local circumstances.[115]

Aged and Infirm Celebrants

Canon 930 — §1. If a sick or aged priest is unable to stand, he may celebrate the Eucharistic Sacrifice while seated, observing the liturgical laws, but not with the people present unless by permission of the local ordinary.

§2. A blind priest or one with some other infirmity celebrates the Eucharistic Sacrifice licitly by using the text of any approved Mass, with another priest, deacon or even properly instructed lay person present to help him, if needed.

Paragraph one provides for priests who by reason of age or illness are unable to stand while presiding at Eucharist. The incapacitating illness may be of any nature or origin, either temporary or permanent. The favor may be interpreted broadly as, for example, on behalf of a priest who suffers discomfort while standing, even though he is capable of it.

[107]SCRit, instr *Musicam sacram* 48, Mar. 5, 1967, *AAS* 59 (1967), 314; John Paul II, letter *Dominicae cenae* 10, Feb. 24, 1980, *N* 16 (1980), 143; *Origins* 9 (1980), 661.

[108]SCDW, notification, June 14, 1971, *AAS* 63 (1971), 714; *CLD* 7, 54. For the text of the Oct. 3, 1984 circular letter of the SCDW on the restricted use of the "Tridentine Mass," see *BCLN* 20 (1984), 37–38.

[109]*Musicam sacram* 51.

[110]Consilium for the Implementation of the Constitution on the Sacred Liturgy, letter, Dec. 10, 1965, *CLD* 6, 552–553.

[111]*SC* 128; *IGMR* 304, 308.

[112]Appendix to the *IGMR* for the Dioceses of the U.S.A. 305.

[113]*CLD* 8, 528.

[114]*Tres abhinc annos* 23; *Rite of Funerals* 22, 6; 81. *IGMR* 308 d, e; *IGMR* U.S. Appendix, 308.

[115]*Rite of Holy Com. and Worship* 20.

The intent of paragraph two is to provide for celebrants who are blind or who have disorders which would make it difficult to follow diverse Mass texts, such as a priest who is disoriented as a result of illness or old age. The prior law required the permission of the priest's bishop or general superior before making use of provisions similar to those which this canon grants outright to the priests in question.[116]

ARTICLE 4: THE TIME AND PLACE OF
EUCHARISTIC CELEBRATION
[cc. 931–933]

The three canons of this article treat the proper times for the Eucharist (c. 931) and the place of celebration (cc. 932–933).

Proper Times for the Eucharist

Canon 931 — **The celebration and distribution of the Eucharist may take place on any day and at any hour, except for those times excluded by the liturgical norms.**

The discipline on the proper time for the celebration of the Eucharist and the distribution of Communion is much simpler in canon 931 than it was in the former Code (*CIC* 820, 821, 867). The Eucharist may be celebrated and Communion may be distributed at any hour with several exceptions. The anticipated Mass of Sunday and holy days of obligation may be celebrated only in the evening (c. 1248, §1). In many places "evening" is understood in a broad sense as including late afternoon from about 4:00. When anticipated Masses are held before this time, it is doubtful whether the precept to attend Mass on the day of obligation has been satisfied. Moreover, anticipated Sunday Masses held too soon lessen the value of the Lord's day as "the original feast day" and the "foundation and kernel of the whole liturgical year."[117]

The other exceptions for the time of celebration and the distribution of the Eucharist are for the days of the Easter triduum. On Holy Thursday the Mass of the Lord's Supper is celebrated in the evening at a convenient hour. In cases of true necessity the local ordinary may permit an earlier Mass but only for those who find it impossible to participate in the evening Mass. Where pastoral reasons require it, the local ordinary may also permit a second evening Mass. Holy Communion may be given to the faithful only during Mass, but it may be taken to the sick at any time of the day. According to the Church's ancient tradition, the sacraments are not celebrated on Good Friday or Holy Saturday. Holy Communion may be given to the faithful only

at the celebration of the Lord's passion on Good Friday, but it can be brought to the sick who cannot participate in this service at any time that day. On Holy Saturday Communion may be given only as Viaticum. The liturgy of the Easter Vigil takes place at night and should not begin before dark on Saturday nor go beyond sunrise on Sunday.[118]

Canon 931 represents little change from the previous discipline since canons 821 and 867 of the 1917 Code already had been derogated from or mitigated by Pius XII in 1953 and 1957 and later by Paul VI.[119]

Place of Celebration

Canon 932 — **§1. The celebration of the Eucharist is to be performed in a sacred place, unless in a particular case necessity demands otherwise; in such a case the celebration must be done in a respectable place.**

§2. The Eucharistic Sacrifice is to be performed upon a dedicated or blessed altar; a suitable table can be used outside a sacred place, always retaining the use of a cloth and corporal.

Canon 933 — **For a just cause and with the express permission of the local ordinary it is licit for a priest to celebrate the Eucharist in a sacred edifice of another church or ecclesial community that does not have full communion with the Catholic Church, scandal being avoided.**

The Eucharistic celebration should take place in a church, oratory, or other sacred place that has been appointed for divine cult by dedication or blessing in accord with canons 1205–1209. The altar may be fixed or movable and should be dedicated or blessed in accord with canon 1237. In particular cases of need the Eucharist may be celebrated in some other becoming place, especially one that does not unduly hinder the participation or attentiveness of the people as a result of undesirable distractions.[120] A particular case includes not only a single occasion but also the case of an individual priest who must regularly celebrate outside a sacred place by reason of necessity. Cases of need include sickness, old age, distance from a church, and in general whenever there is some pastoral advantage to celebrating outside a sacred place, such as at occasional Masses for children and for other particular groups.[121] At Masses outside a sacred place any

---

[116]*PM* I, 5, 6, 10; Secretary of State, rescript *Cum admotae* I, 2, 3, 5, Nov. 6, 1964, *AAS* 59 (1967), 374–375; *CLD* 6, 147.

[117]*SC* 106; c. 1246, §1.

[118]These norms are found in the *Roman Missal* in the rubrics for the triduum.

[119]Pius XII, *Christus Dominus* VI; *Sacram Communionem* 1; *PM* I, 4; *Cum admotae* I, 1.

[120]*IGMR* 253.

[121]*Directory on Children's Masses* 25; SCDW, instr *Actio pastoralis*, May 15, 1969, *AAS* 61 (1969), 806. A. Kavanaugh emphasizes that Masses for special groups outside a sacred place are "abnormal" and should be done rarely, and that even children should regularly attend Mass with the entire local community. See *Elements of Rite* (New York: Pueblo, 1982), 13–14, 67–68.

suitable table may be used instead of an altar.[122] By analogy with the *General Instruction of the Roman Missal* 268, the shape, size, and decoration of the cloth to cover the table should be in keeping with the table's design.

For a just cause the Eucharist may also be celebrated in a church of a non-Catholic Christian denomination with the express permission of the local ordinary, provided there is no scandal. The local ordinary is the final judge of whether there may be scandal, but in many areas, especially where non-Catholic Christians are numerous, the possibility of scandal is remote. Also required for this permission is a just cause, such as pastoral advantage or ecumenical good will. Since the phrase, "another church or ecclesial community that does not have full communion with the Catholic Church," refers only to separated Christian churches, canon 933 makes no provision for the celebration of the Eucharist in non-Christian churches. Hence, there is no strict obligation to obtain the local ordinary's permission to celebrate in such places, especially in interdenominational chapels at hospitals, universities, military bases, and at other places of worship where the possibility of scandal is slight.

Canons 932 and 933 principally alter the previous discipline in the following ways: (1) permission of the ordinary is no longer required to celebrate the Eucharist outside a sacred place with the exception of canon 933;[123] (2) permission of the diocesan bishop is no longer required to celebrate Mass at sea and on rivers;[124] (3) the specific prohibition against celebrating Masses in bedrooms has been removed;[125] and (4) the prohibition against celebrating Mass in the churches of heretics or schismatics is abrogated.[126]

CHAPTER II
THE RESERVATION AND VENERATION OF
THE MOST HOLY EUCHARIST
[cc. 934–944]

The custom of reserving the Eucharist originated in the ancient Church primarily to provide for the administration of Viaticum. Other purposes for reservation included providing Communion to those absent from the assembly, particularly the sick, and for the liturgy of the presanctified during Lent. Frequently the Eucharistic wine was reserved as well as the bread so that Communion could be given under both kinds. The place of reservation varied according to period, locale, and circumstances; and it included private houses, the dwellings of eremitical religious, and the sacristy or similar place in a church. It was also the custom of many centuries for priests and monks to carry the Eucharist with them on journeys. By the end of the ninth century, regulations in some areas directed that the Eucharist be reserved within the church itself in close proximity to the altar; this had become the rule in many places by the twelfth century. The practice of burning a continuous light, or sanctuary lamp, near the reserved Eucharist began toward the end of the twelfth century and became widespread by the sixteenth. The use of a tabernacle on the altar did not become a general practice in the Western Church until the post-Tridentine period.[127]

The Council of Trent upheld the legitimacy of reserving the Eucharist for administration to the sick, and it also defended the adoration of the Eucharistic species in general and Eucharistic processions in particular.[128] The veneration of the Eucharist outside Mass was actually a rather late development in the life of the Church. Eucharistic processions, particularly on the feast of Corpus Christi, and visits to the Blessed Sacrament were derived from practices originating in the eleventh century, and the first reliable evidence for exposition and benediction comes from the fourteenth century. It was only in the seventeenth and subsequent centuries that benediction became prevalent.[129]

Vatican II decreed that popular devotions

> should be so drawn up that they harmonize with the liturgical seasons, accord with the sacred liturgy, are in some way derived from it, and lead the people to it, since in fact the liturgy by its very nature is far superior to any of them.[130]

In accordance with this conciliar principle and the norms of the 1967 Instruction on the Worship of the Eucharistic Mystery,[131] the revised *Roman Ritual* provides several forms of worship of the Eucharist outside Mass: (1) exposition of the Blessed Sacrament for a lengthy period or a brief period and adoration by religious communities; (2) a rite of Eucharistic exposition and benediction; (3) Eucharistic processions; and (4) Eucharistic congresses. The canons of this chapter are based chiefly on the norms of this and of other parts of the section of the *Roman Ritual* entitled, "Holy Communion and Worship of the Eucharist Outside Mass"; the *General Instruction of the Roman Missal* is also a key source.

In addition to the conciliar principle of the primacy of the liturgy over popular devotions, several principles specifically on Eucharistic devotions

---

[122]*IGMR* 260.
[123]*Cum admotae* I, 4; *Actio pastoralis* 4; *Liturgicae instaurationes* 9.
[124]*PM* I, 8.
[125]*CIC* 822, §4; *PM* I, 7; *Cum admotae* I, 4; *Actio pastoralis* 4.
[126]*CIC* 823, §1.

[127]See A. King, *Eucharistic Reservation in the Western Church* (New York: Sheed and Ward, 1965).
[128]Sess. XIII, cap. 6, c. 7, *Ench* 1645, 1657; cap. 5, c. 6, *Ench* 1643–1644, 1656.
[129]See N. Mitchell, *Cult and Controversy: The Worship of the Eucharist Outside Mass* (New York: Pueblo, 1982).
[130]*SC* 13.
[131]*Eucharisticum mysterium* 49–67.

from the 1967 instruction, *Eucharisticum mysterium,* provide the doctrinal foundation for the liturgical law and the canons of this chapter. The chief principles are these:

(1) The celebration of the Eucharistic sacrifice is the origin and consummation of Eucharistic worship outside it.

(2) The Eucharist is no less an object of adoration because it was instituted by Christ to be eaten.

(3) The primary and original purpose for reserving the Eucharist is the administration of Viaticum; the secondary reasons are the giving of Communion and the adoration of the sacrament.

(4) The Eucharistic presence of Christ is the real presence par excellence, but Christ is also present in the assembly of the faithful, in the word, and in the person of the minister.

(5) Prayer before Christ the Lord sacramentally present, no less than the reception of the sacrament, should move the faithful to lead lives of witness and service in human society.[132]

Canons 934–940 treat the reservation of the Eucharist, including: (1) obligatory and facultative reservation (c. 934); (2) personal retention of the Eucharist (c. 935); (3) religious and pious houses (c. 936); (4) accessibility to churches (c. 937); (5) the tabernacle (c. 938); (6) the quantity and renewal of Hosts and vessels for reservation (c. 939); and (7) the sanctuary lamp (c. 940). Canons 941–944 treat the worship of the Eucharist. Canons 941–943 regulate Eucharistic exposition and benediction and canon 944 is concerned with Eucharistic processions.

Obligatory and Facultative Reservation

Canon 934 — §1. The Most Holy Eucharist:
1° must be reserved in the cathedral church or its equivalent, in every parish church and in the church or oratory attached to the house of a religious institute or society of apostolic life;
2° it can be reserved in the chapel of a bishop and, with the permission of the local ordinary, in other churches, oratories or chapels.
§2. In sacred places where the Most Holy Eucharist is reserved there must always be someone who has the care of it, and, insofar as possible, a priest is to celebrate Mass there at least twice a month.

This canon specifies those sacred places in which the Eucharist must be reserved and those in which it may be reserved, and it establishes the conditions for Eucharistic reservation. The first condition is that there be someone who has charge of the place where the Eucharist is reserved. This person need not have any ecclesiastical office or be a cleric since the chief purpose of this law is to prevent the desecration of the Blessed Sacrament. The second condition is that a priest celebrate Mass in that place at least twice a month, as far as this is possible. This ensures the frequent renewal of the consecrated Hosts in accord with canon 939 and, even more importantly, it reinforces the primacy of the Eucharistic action and its intimate connection to the sacrament reserved. The phrase, "insofar as possible," permits a broad interpretation of the norm; however, there still should be some provision for the regular celebration of Mass even if it always cannot be done at least twice a month. Canon 1265, §1 of the former Code required that Mass be celebrated at least once a week as a condition for reservation.

When the two conditions of paragraph two are met, the law mandates Eucharistic reservation in specified sacred places where pastoral care is usually exercised and where there would be need for Communion for the sick and dying. The Eucharist must be reserved in: (1) the cathedral church; (2) a church equated with a cathedral, including the principal church of a territorial abbey or prelature, or an apostolic vicariate or prefecture, or an apostolic administration; (3) every parish church; and (4) the church or oratory attached to the house of a religious institute or society of apostolic life. This latter requirement is also found in canon 608. A church is a sacred place which the faithful have a right to attend and in which they have a right to participate in divine worship (c. 1214). An oratory is a sacred place to which they may go with the consent of the competent superior (c. 1223). However, the Eucharist must be reserved in an oratory of a house of a religious institute or a society of apostolic life even if it is not open to members of the faithful.

The Eucharist may be reserved in the private chapel of a bishop and in any other churches, oratories, and chapels with the permission of the local ordinary provided the conditions of paragraph two are satisfied. This is a change from canon 1265, §2 of the 1917 Code which specified that an apostolic indult was necessary for Eucharistic reservation in any sacred place other than those mentioned in that canon.

It is desirable when possible to reserve the Eucharistic wine as well as bread so that Communion can be given under the two kinds outside Mass, especially as Viaticum.[133]

---

[132]Ibid., 3e; 3f; 49; 55; 13; *Rite of Holy Com. and Worship* 2; 3; 5; 6; 81.

[133]*Comm* 13 (1981), 425.

Personal Retention of the Eucharist

Canon 935 — It is not licit to keep the Most Holy Eucharist on one's person or to carry it on a journey unless there is an urgent pastoral need and the precepts of the diocesan bishop are observed.

The retention of the Eucharist by private persons was common in the ancient Church, especially in times of persecution, but by the fifth or sixth centuries the practice had died out and was forbidden in places. In contrast to canon 1265, §3 of the 1917 Code, which absolutely prohibited the personal retention of the Eucharist and the carrying of it on a trip, this canon allows some flexibility. Normally the Blessed Sacrament may not be kept in one's private possession, either on one's person or in a fixed place. However, there may be times when this is necessary, such as in remote areas where no sacred place is available for reservation. In such cases of urgent pastoral need, the permission of the diocesan bishop must be obtained to reserve the Eucharist in one's home or other place. The bishop may also establish regulations regarding the renewal of Hosts, the tabernacle, and similar matters. The canon refers only to the habitual retention of the Eucharist but not to its legitimate possession such as when Communion is brought to the sick or dying.

As noted above, it was the practice for many centuries for priests, monks, and others to carry the Eucharist with them on long journeys so that they could be refreshed by the sacrament and receive Viaticum if needed. Today such a practice is both unnecessary and undesirable due to modern means of transportation, the accessibility of churches, and the primacy of receiving Communion during the Eucharistic celebration, even as Viaticum.

Religious and Pious Houses

Canon 936 — In the house of a religious institute or in any other pious house the Most Holy Eucharist is to be reserved only in the church or principal oratory attached to the house, but, for a just cause the ordinary can permit that it be reserved in another oratory of the same house.

The purpose of this canon is to prevent the duplication of places for Eucharistic reservation in the same house. The Eucharistic action is the preeminent source and sign of ecclesial unity as well as the origin of the sacrament reserved. Therefore, the reservation of the "one bread and the one cup" in a single place better preserves this sign of unity and better recognizes the close association between Eucharistic celebration and reservation. The Eucharist should be reserved only in the principal church or oratory attached to the house of a religious institute or other house of piety, namely, the church or oratory frequented by the faithful and the members of

the house. If the members of the house worship in an oratory separate from the church or oratory attended by the faithful, the Eucharist may be reserved in each. If there is more than one distinct community under the same roof, there may be reservation in the oratory of each community.[134] In all other cases permission of the ordinary and a just cause are required for reserving the Eucharist in a second oratory of the same house. Permission is not needed to reserve the Eucharist in a Blessed Sacrament chapel connected to the principal church or oratory provided that it is the exclusive place of reservation.

The specific prohibition of canon 1267 of the 1917 Code against reserving the Eucharist inside the choir or enclosure in convents of nuns is abrogated, and this matter is governed by canons 934 and 936 as well as by the relevant proper law of the religious institute.

Accessibility to Churches

Canon 937 — Unless a grave reason prevents it, the church in which the Most Holy Eucharist is reserved should be open to the faithful for at least some hours each day so that they are able to spend time in prayer before the Most Blessed Sacrament.

This canon refers only to churches in the strict sense of canon 1214 but not to oratories and other sacred places. In contrast to canon 1266 of the 1917 Code, the canon, for a grave reason, allows exceptions to the rule that churches which reserve the Eucharist should be open to the faithful for at least some hours each day.[135] In some areas it is necessary to lock the church in order to prevent vandalism and burglary. This alone constitutes a sufficiently grave reason, especially if no one is available to guard the church for at least some hours each day, i.e., for more than one hour. In any case, the canon appears to be more a pastoral recommendation than a true legal obligation. It is desirable that churches *should* be open for some hours each day, but the canon does not say that they *must* be open.

The Tabernacle

Canon 938 — §1. The Most Holy Eucharist is to be reserved regularly in only one tabernacle of a church or oratory.
§2. The tabernacle in which the Most Holy Eucharist is reserved should be placed in a part of the church that is prominent, conspicuous, beautifully decorated, and suitable for prayer.

---

[134]Pontifical Commission for the Authentic Interpretation of the Canons of the CIC, interpretation, June 3, 1918, *AAS* 10 (1918), 346; *CLD* 1, 53.
[135]See also *Eucharisticum mysterium* 51.

§3. The tabernacle in which the Eucharist is regularly reserved is to be immovable, made of solid and opaque material, and locked so that the danger of profanation may be entirely avoided.

§4. For a grave cause, it is licit to reserve the Most Holy Eucharist in another safer and becoming place especially during the night.

§5. The person who has charge of the church or oratory is to see to it that the key of the tabernacle in which the Most Holy Eucharist is reserved is safeguarded most diligently.

This canon regulates the place, construction, and custody of the tabernacle, somewhat simplifying canons 1268–1269 of the 1917 Code. The norms largely repeat some of the liturgical laws on this matter found in the *General Instruction of the Roman Missal* 276–277 and the *Roman Ritual* under the title, "Holy Communion and Worship of the Eucharist Outside Mass," numbers 6, 9, and 10.

With its insistence on a single focus for the reserved Eucharist, paragraph one is a corollary of canon 936. The Eucharist must be reserved regularly, i.e., habitually, in a single tabernacle of a church or oratory. Liturgical law provides an exception for the Easter triduum when the Blessed Sacrament is transferred ritually to another chapel or side altar after the celebration of the Lord's Supper on Holy Thursday. However, no duplicate reservation in the same church or oratory is permissible as a rule.

Paragraph two suggests broad guidelines for the place of reservation, but liturgical law is more specific. The *General Instruction of the Roman Missal* states: "It is strongly recommended that the blessed sacrament be reserved in a special chapel. . . ." The *Roman Ritual* adds that the chapel should be "separate from the body of the church, especially in churches where marriages and funerals are celebrated frequently and churches which are much visited by pilgrims or because of their artistic and historical treasures."[136] The Bishops' Committee on the Liturgy offers a rationale for these exhortations:

A room or chapel specifically designed and separate from the major space is important so that no confusion can take place between the celebration of the Eucharist and reservation. Active and static aspects of the same reality cannot claim the same human attention at the same time.[137]

If it is not possible to have a separate place for reservation, the Eucharist may be reserved in the sacred place where Mass is celebrated. The Bishops' Committee on the Liturgy directs that the tabernacle be positioned in a wall niche, on a pillar, or in a Eucharistic tower, but it discourages placing it on the altar because "the altar is a place for action and

not for reservation."[138] In 1983 the Sacred Congregation for Sacraments and Divine Worship dropped from the *Roman Ritual* the express mention of an altar as a possible place for the tabernacle, but this provision remains in the *General Instruction of the Roman Missal* 276.[139]

Paragraph three treats the design of the tabernacle. Wood, marble, and metal are traditionally acceptable materials for the construction of tabernacles, but the canon says that any solid and opaque material can be used. Like this canon, liturgical law leaves much leeway for determining the shape, size, and ornamentation of the tabernacle according to pastoral need and artistic tastefulness. Paragraphs four and five treat the custody of the tabernacle. For a grave cause, such as danger of profanation, the Eucharist may be reserved in some place other than the tabernacle especially at night.

Liturgical law states that the presence of the Eucharist in the tabernacle is to be shown by a veil or in another suitable way determined by the competent authority.[140] The use of the tabernacle veil is no longer universal or insisted upon by the competent authority in the dioceses of the United States.[141]

Quantity and Renewal of Hosts

Canon 939 — Consecrated hosts are to be reserved in a ciborium or vessel in sufficient quantity for the needs of the faithful; they are to be frequently renewed and the old hosts properly consumed.

This canon, a simplification of canons 1270 and 1272 of the 1917 Code, treats the quantity and renewal of the reserved Eucharist and the vessels for it. The number of consecrated Hosts which are to be reserved is dependent on the needs of the faithful. Liturgical law is more specific in saying that there should be sufficient Hosts for the Communion of the sick and others outside Mass.[142] The same principle holds true for the quantity of consecrated wine for reservation. In order for the sign of Communion to be expressed more clearly as a sharing in the sacrifice actually being celebrated, Communion should not be given during Mass from the reserved elements but from the bread and wine consecrated at the Mass.[143] The quantity of the reserved elements always should be kept to the minimum needed for Communion outside Mass, and this will facilitate the requirement of frequent renewal.

The renewal of the reserved Eucharistic bread is accomplished by consuming it and replacing it with

[136]*IGMR* 276; *Rite of Holy Com. and Worship* 9.
[137]*Environment and Art in Catholic Worship* 78.

[138]Ibid., 80.
[139]Decr, *Promulgato Codice,* Sept. 12, 1983, *N* 20 (1983), 543.
[140]*Rite of Holy Com. and Worship* 11.
[141]J. Champlin, *The Proper Balance* (Notre Dame, Ind.: Ave Maria, 1981), 131.
[142]*Rite of Holy Com. and Worship* 7.
[143]*SC* 55; *IGMR* 56h.

newly consecrated breads. The canon does not indicate how often this should occur, and variations in climatic and other conditions preclude any specific rule on frequency of renewal. However, the *General Instruction of the Roman Missal* states that the bread should not spoil or become too hard and easily broken.[144]

The breads should be reserved in a ciborium or other suitable vessel such as a pyx. The vessel may be made from any materials that are prized in a region, including ebony or other hard woods, as long as they are suited to sacred use.[145] The consecrated wine should not be reserved except for Communion of the sick. It should be kept in a properly covered chalice and placed in the tabernacle after Mass until it is needed. When Communion or Viaticum is brought to the sick under both kinds or under the form of wine alone, the wine must be carried in a vessel so secured as to eliminate all danger of spilling.[146]

The Sanctuary Lamp

Canon 940 — A special lamp to indicate and honor the presence of Christ is to burn at all times before the tabernacle in which the Most Holy Eucharist is reserved.

The canon speaks only of a "special lamp" without specifying a wax candle or a lamp fueled by olive oil as did canon 1271 of the 1917 Code. Nevertheless, liturgical law prefers an oil lamp or a lamp with a wax candle.[147] The oil may be of any kind, although the law traditionally favored vegetable oil, especially olive oil. Under the former law the candle was to be made at least in part from beeswax, olive oil, or another kind of vegetable oil.[148] Ordinaries were able to permit substitutions for oil lamps and wax candles when these were unavailable or could not be obtained without grave inconvenience or expense. In such a case any oil, especially vegetable oil, could be substituted, or even an electric light as a last resort.[149] Such substitutions may now freely be made by the persons in charge of sacred places. In choosing any kind of sanctuary lamp they should be guided by the principles of "quality" and "appropriateness" which are conditions that must be met in the selection of all church furnishings.[150]

Exposition and Benediction

Canon 941 — §1. In churches or oratories where it is permitted to reserve the Most Holy Eucharist, there can be expositions either with the ciborium or with a monstrance, observing the norms prescribed in the liturgical books.

§2. Exposition of the Most Holy Sacrament is not to be held in the same part of the church or oratory during the celebration of Mass.

Canon 942 — It is recommended that in these same churches and oratories an annual solemn exposition of the Most Holy Sacrament be held during a suitable period of time, even if not continuous, so that the local community may meditate and may adore the Eucharistic Mystery more profoundly; but this kind of exposition is to be held only if a suitable gathering of the faithful is foreseen and the established norms are observed.

Canon 943 — The minister of exposition of the Most Holy Sacrament and the Eucharistic benediction is a priest or deacon; in particular circumstances the minister of exposition and reposition only, without benediction, is an acolyte, an extraordinary minister of Holy Communion or another person deputed by the local ordinary observing the prescriptions of the diocesan bishop.

The liturgical law on exposition of the Eucharist is found in the *Roman Ritual* under the title, "Holy Communion and Worship of the Eucharist Outside Mass," numbers 82–100. The *Roman Ritual* provides a rite of simple exposition and a rite of exposition and benediction. Several introductory principles from the *Roman Ritual* governing the relationship between exposition and the Mass are noteworthy:

(1) Exposition stimulates the faithful to spiritual union with Christ which culminates in sacramental Communion.

(2) The arrangements for exposition must carefully avoid anything which might obscure the principal desire of Christ in instituting the Eucharist, namely, to be received as food, healing, and consolation.

(3) The celebration of the Eucharistic Mystery includes in a more perfect manner the spiritual communion to which exposition is intended to stimulate the faithful.[151]

The *Roman Ritual* distinguishes three kinds of exposition: that for a lengthy period, that for a brief

---

[144]*IGMR* 285.
[145]*IGMR* 292.
[146]*Rite of Holy Com. and Worship* 55; *Rite of Anointing* 95; *Inaestimabile donum* 14.
[147]*Rite of Holy Com. and Worship* 11.
[148]SCRit, decr, Dec. 13, 1957, *AAS* 50 (1960), 50; *CLD* 5, 613.
[149]SCRit, decr *Urbis et orbis*, Aug. 18, 1949, *AAS* 41 (1949), 476; *CLD* 3, 518.
[150]*Environment and Art in Catholic Worship* 18–23.
[151]*Rite of Holy Com. and Worship* 82–83.

period, and that for adoration by religious communities. Brief periods of exposition must always include time for readings of the word of God, hymns, prayers, and a period of silent prayer. Exposition merely for the purpose of giving the benediction is forbidden. There may never be exposition, whether lengthy or brief, in the same part of the church or oratory where Mass is being celebrated. Exposition should be interrupted during Mass unless the Mass is celebrated in a chapel apart from the exposition and at least some of the faithful remain in adoration.[152]

Canon 942 deals with the lengthy period of exposition and recommends that it take place solemnly once a year in churches and oratories where the sacrament is reserved. There is no mention of the Forty Hours' Devotion required by canon 1275 of the former law. Hence, the recommendation of this canon could be fulfilled by any annual period of exposition held for a protracted time, i.e., longer than the brief period mentioned in the *Roman Ritual*. However, the annual lengthy exposition should not be held unless it is foreseen that there will be a suitable number of people who will be present for it.[153] Exposition is an optional devotion which may not be suitable when it is not a true expression of popular piety. Exposition need not be continuous during this extended period, especially when it goes beyond one day, and the Eucharist may be replaced in the tabernacle at times which have been prearranged and duly announced. This may not be done more than twice in the day, e.g., at midday and at night.[154]

Canon 943 basically restates the liturgical law on the ministers of exposition and of benediction.[155] The ordinary minister of exposition is a priest or deacon who may also bless the people with the sacrament at the end of the period of adoration. In the absence of a priest or deacon, an acolyte, special minister of Communion, or another person deputed by the local ordinary may publicly expose for adoration and later repose the Eucharist. These ministers may open the tabernacle and place the vessel containing the Eucharist on the altar or place of exposition or put the Host in the monstrance. At the end of the adoration they replace the Eucharist in the tabernacle, but they may not give the blessing. The canon broadens the former liturgical law which restricted the special minister of exposition and reposition to an acolyte, a special minister of Communion, or a member of a religious community or of a lay association of men or women which is devoted to Eucharistic adoration. Now any member of the faithful may be deputed for this ministry

by the local ordinary who may also establish further prescriptions regarding specific matters.

Canon 1274, §2 of the former Code limited the minister of exposition and reposition to the priest or deacon, and only the priest could give the benediction. This law was derogated from in 1967 to permit deacons to give the blessing and in 1972 to allow acolytes to expose and repose the Eucharist.[156]

Eucharistic Processions

Canon 944 — §1. When it can be done in the judgment of the diocesan bishop, as a public witness of the veneration toward the Most Holy Eucharist, a procession is to be conducted through the public streets, especially on the solemnity of the Body and the Blood of Christ.

§2. It is for the diocesan bishop to enact regulations which concern the participation in and the dignity of the processions.

There is little evidence for Eucharistic processions before Pope Urban IV established the feast of Corpus Christi in 1264, but in the fourteenth century such processions became widespread. As noted above, the Council of Trent approved this custom in response to Protestants who denied the legitimacy of various forms of Eucharistic cult outside Mass.

The revised Code significantly deemphasizes sacred processions in comparison with the 1917 Code where the subject occupied an independent title consisting of six canons (*CIC* 1290–1295). However, a deemphasis was seen already in the 1967 Instruction on the Worship of the Eucharistic Mystery which stated that "it is for the local ordinary to decide whether such processions are opportune in present-day circumstances."[157] The canon strengthens this restriction by relegating this judgment to the diocesan bishop who may enact his own regulations which, according to the *Roman Ritual*, "determine the time, place, and order of such processions."[158] The liturgical laws governing Eucharistic processions are quite broad and allow great latitude for local customs provided that they are in accord with the directives of the competent authority.[159] In many parts of the world, including the United States, it is not customary to hold public Eucharistic processions. The intent of church law is to encourage such processions in those areas where it is customary and "when today's circumstances permit it and when it can be a true sign of common faith and adoration."[160]

---

[152]Ibid., 83.
[153]Ibid., 86.
[154]Ibid., 88.
[155]Ibid., 91.

[156]*Sacrum diaconatus ordinem* V, 3; *Ministeria quaedam* VI.
[157]*Eucharisticum mysterium* 59.
[158]*Rite of Holy Com. and Worship* 101.
[159]Ibid., 101–108.
[160]Ibid., 102.

CHAPTER III
OFFERINGS GIVEN AT THE
CELEBRATION OF THE MASS
[cc. 945–958]

The custom of accepting Mass offerings arose in the Western Church as a result of several key developments. In the ancient Church the faithful brought gifts to the Sunday assembly, especially the bread and wine for the Eucharist, and the excess was distributed to the Church's ministers and to the poor. By the seventh or eighth century, gifts of money were frequently substituted and their purpose became chiefly the support of the clergy. Other contributing factors included the spread of votive Masses, which were offered for the intentions and desires (*vota*) of a group or an individual, and of private Masses, which were celebrated without a congregation out of a priest's personal devotion. By the Carolingian period all three of these developments had taken hold and contributed to the custom of the priest's accepting a single stipend for each Mass in return for remembering a special intention. This practice became widespread in the eleventh and twelfth centuries. Scholastic theologians attempted to provide a rationale for Mass offerings by devising a theory of the threefold fruits of the Mass, of which the celebrant applies the "special fruit" for the intention of the stipend donor. The Council of Constance in 1415 and Pope Pius VI in 1794 upheld the practice against adversaries who opposed it on theological grounds and who charged that it was simoniacal.[161] Canons 945–958 principally reflect the discipline enacted by various popes over three centuries, including the 1974 apostolic letter of Paul VI, *Firma in traditione.*[162]

Perhaps the most important change in the revised Code's treatment of Mass offerings occurs in the title of this section which in the 1917 Code was "Mass Alms or Stipends." No longer does the law refer to the donation for the application of Mass as a "stipend" (*stipendium*), but rather as an "offering" (*stips*) given by one of the faithful. The word "stipend" suggests a mercantile exchange of goods for services or the remuneration of a *do ut facias* contract. By contrast, the word "offering" clearly signifies that it is given freely by the faithful primarily out of their concern for the Church and their desire to support its material needs. Mass offerings properly can be understood as gifts to the Church or its ministers on behalf of some intention, much as a donation or bequest is made to any charitable institution *in the name of* some person, living or deceased. A Mass offering is totally gratu-

itous. The only obligation a priest assumes in accepting an offering is to apply a Mass according to a definite intention. Indeed, the present Code eliminates canons 833–834 of the 1917 Code, which spoke of the donor's being able to place conditions on the celebration of the Mass and of the obligation of the priest to satisfy any such mutually acceptable conditions, such as the time for the celebration of the Mass. Obviously, even under the revised law, a priest who agrees to celebrate a Mass at a certain time is bound in justice to do so, but the fact that the Code deemphasizes such conditions by not mentioning them indicates the legislator's desire to remove contractual and mercantile associations from the treatment of Mass offerings and to consider them the wholly gratuitous gift of the donor for the welfare of the Church.

Another significant change is the elimination of the three kinds of stipends distinguished in canon 826 of the former Code, namely, *stipendia manualia, ad instar manualium,* and *fundata,* or *Missae fundatae.* Canon 825 of the 1917 Code, which forbade certain abuses, is also dropped, apparently because it is superfluous to condemn specific infractions when the law is clearly stated and its implications evident. With the exception of the four canons already mentioned that have been suppressed, all other canons of the former Code, or at least parts of them, are retained and usually reworded in the revised Code.

The fourteen canons of this chapter treat the following matters: (1) Mass offerings and intentions (cc. 945–946); (2) basic regulations governing Mass offerings (cc. 947–951); (3) the amount of the Mass offerings (c. 952); (4) the satisfaction and transference of Mass obligations (cc. 953–956); and (5) the duties of ecclesiastical officials regarding the satisfaction of Mass obligations (cc. 957–958).

Mass Offerings and Intentions

Canon 945 — §1. In accord with the approved usage of the Church, it is lawful for any priest who celebrates or concelebrates Mass to receive an offering to apply the Mass according to a definite intention.

§2. It is strongly recommended that priests celebrate Mass for the intention of the Christian faithful, especially of the needy, even if no offering has been received.

Canon 946 — The Christian faithful who make an offering so that the Mass may be applied for their intention contribute to the good of the Church and by their offering take part in the concern of the Church for the support of its ministers and works.

Canon 945, §1 like canon 824, §1 of the 1917 Code, does not explain what it means "to apply the Mass according to a definite intention." The tradi-

---

[161]Constance, sess. VIII, errors of J. Wycliff, nn. 19 and 25, *Ench* 1169, 1175; Pius VI, const. *Auctorem fidei,* Aug. 28, 1794, nn. 30 and 54, *Ench* 2630, 2654.

[162]Innocent XII, const. *Nuper,* Dec. 2, 1697; Pius X, decr *Ut debita,* May 11, 1904; *CIC* 824–844; Paul VI, *mp Firma in traditione,* June 13, 1974, *AAS* 66 (1974), 308–311; *CLD* 8, 530.

tional theory of the special fruit of the Mass which the priest applies for the benefit of the donor's intention is widely discredited by contemporary theologians and, moreover, is not fostered in recent ecclesiastical documents on the subject.[163] No reference was made to any special fruit of the Mass accruing to the donor's intention either in the report of the Code Commission *coetus* which prepared the draft of canons on sacraments or in the 1974 *motu proprio Firma in traditione*.[164] Nevertheless, the canons of this chapter set forth disciplinary norms whose observance does not depend on any particular theological theory but which are simply regulations intended to avoid abuses. From a canonical viewpoint, "to apply the Mass according to a definite intention" means only that the celebrant or concelebrant cannot accept more than one offering for one Mass, and consequently no other than the donor's intention or intentions can be conjoined with that offering. This neither precludes other intentions being prayed for which are not conjoined with an offering, nor does it even imply that the priest must know what the specific offering-intention is. However, justice would seem to require that priests who celebrate Masses which are applied for intentions should resolve to include these intentions habitually in their prayers at Mass at least in a general fashion, even when they do not know the specific intention.

Canon 945, §1 states that *it is lawful* for a priest who celebrates or concelebrates Mass to receive an offering. This means that the priest *may,* but does not have to, receive an offering. In some parts of the world the custom of accepting Mass offerings has never thrived, and in other areas it has died out or is dying out. The laws of this chapter do not impose the practice but only seek to regulate it in those areas where it legitimately exists. Individual priests, or even whole groups of priests, such as the members of an ecclesiastical province or a religious institute, are not prevented from voluntarily refusing to accept Mass offerings or from giving them to the parish or other apostolate if they are accepted.

The norm of canon 945, §2, which was not found in the prior law, recommends that priests pray at Mass for the intentions of the faithful, especially of the needy, even without accepting an offering. The meaning of the phrase, "celebrate Mass for the intention of the Christian faithful," can be determined from similar phrases contained in the Eucharistic prayers which speak of offering the Eucharistic Sacrifice for the Church, the pope, bishops, clergy, the faithful, and other intentions. The liturgy itself demonstrates that the Eucharist is celebrated for many intentions and is never limited to

any one intention of the priest. The "intention" spoken of in this norm refers therefore to a special intention for which the priest may pray in addition to the intentions of the entire assembly, but one need not infer that the priest's prayer has any special efficacy different from the prayers of the community. In many places the priest's intention is included in the prayers of the faithful. While this can be a worthy practice, it is inadvisable for the leader of prayer to conclude the intention with the phrase, "for whom this Mass is offered," since the Mass is offered for many intentions as the Eucharistic prayers explicitly state. It is inadvisable, moreover, to mention the intention in the memento of the dead in the Eucharistic prayer because the inclusion of the special intention disproportionately stresses its role and, in the case of intentions conjoined with offerings, suggests that special consideration in the Mass can be obtained by the payment of money.

Canon 946, which appears for the first time in the revised Code, provides a practical rationale for the custom of accepting Mass offerings. Such offerings contribute to the good of the Church and enable the donors to participate in some small way in the Church's concern for its ministers and ministries. Like the change in title from "stipends" to "offerings," this canon evidences a new understanding of the system of Mass offerings, namely, that it is primarily a means of church support which does not need to be justified by any particular theological rationale such as the medieval theory of the threefold fruits of the Mass.

Basic Regulations

Canon 947 — **Any appearance of trafficking or commerce is to be entirely excluded from Mass offerings.**

Canon 948 — **Separate Masses are to be applied for the intentions for which an individual offering, even if small, has been made and accepted.**

Canon 949 — **One who has the obligation of celebrating Mass and applying it for the intention of those who made the offering is bound by the same obligation even if the offerings received have been lost, through no fault of his own.**

Canon 950 — **If the sum of money is offered for the application of Masses without an indication of the number of Masses to be celebrated, the number is to be computed in view of the offering established in the place where the donor resides unless the donor's intention must be lawfully presumed to have been different.**

Canon 951 — **§1. A priest who celebrates Mass more than once on the same day may apply the in-**

---

[163]See M.F. Mannion, "Stipends and Eucharistic Praxis," *W* 57 (1983), 194–214; J. Huels, "Stipends in the New Code of Canon law," ibid., 215–224.
[164]*Comm* 4 (1972), 58.

dividual Mass for the intention for which the offering is made, but with the law that, except on Christmas, he may retain the offering for only one Mass, giving the other offerings to purposes prescribed by the ordinary, except for some recompense by reason of an extrinsic title.

§2. A priest who concelebrates a second Mass on the same day may not take an offering for it under any title.

Canons 948–951 are basic regulations which follow from the guiding rule of canon 947 forbidding any trafficking in Mass offerings. This canon, identical to canon 827 of the 1917 Code, sums up numerous disciplinary measures enacted over the centuries, including a reform decree of the Council of Trent.[165] Since the acceptance of Mass offerings has frequently led to accusations of simony, the Church understandably wishes to regulate the practice strictly to avoid all appearances of commercialism. According to canon 1385, those who illegitimately profit from Mass offerings is to be punished with a censure or another just penalty. These and the following canons of this chapter are intended to preclude profiteering and other abuses connected with Mass offerings.

Canon 948 is worded somewhat differently than canon 828 of the 1917 Code, but the meaning is the same: the celebrant and concelebrants each may accept only one offering for one Mass, even if a smaller amount than customary is accepted. Although the donor's intention can include more than one person, only one offering can be taken. The obligation to apply the Mass according to the intention requested by the donor does not cease even though the offering may have been lost. This rule of canon 949 was also found in canon 829 of the former Code. Likewise, canon 950 is very similar to canon 830 of the previous law: if the number of Masses to be applied is not specified, the number is computed on the basis of the amount which is customary in the territory of the donor. For example, if a donor makes an offering of $100 for Masses to be celebrated, and the customary Mass offering of that place is $10, then ten Masses are to be applied for the requested intention.

The norm of canon 951 forbidding priests from retaining more than one Mass offering each day is a long-standing disciplinary measure intended to prevent any appearance of clerical avarice.[166] On Christmas priests may trinate and keep the three Mass offerings. Unlike canon 824, §2 of the former Code, the present law permits the acceptance of offerings for any number of Masses celebrated by a priest in one day, provided that the priest personally retains no more than one offering. The offerings

from subsequent Masses must be given to the cause prescribed by the priest's ordinary. This change in discipline was made originally by Paul VI in 1974, but it was only for binations and trinations.[167] While the priest may not retain more than one offering each day, he may be compensated for celebrating additional Masses by virtue of some extrinsic title. For example, the priest can be paid for his services in celebrating the Mass even though he may not keep personally the offerings from any extra Masses celebrated in one day. However, pastors who must celebrate Mass more than once a day to provide for the needs of the faithful in their care may not receive additional remuneration because this is a service which they are obliged to offer in virtue of their office.[168] Unlike canon 824, §2 of the 1917 Code, the present law permits pastors and others who are obliged to celebrate the *Missa pro populo* on Sundays and holy days to take an offering for a second Mass which they celebrate that day.

The norm of canon 951, §2 was first established by the Sacred Congregation for Divine Worship in 1972 and was affirmed by Paul VI in 1974.[169] A priest may not take another offering, even one on behalf of his ordinary, when he concelebrates on the same day that he celebrates or concelebrates another Mass. For example, if a priest concelebrates a funeral in the morning and celebrates a Mass later in the day for the faithful, he may accept an offering for only one of those Masses. However, if the priest *presides* at a concelebrated Mass and must also preside at one or more additional Masses that day, he may receive offerings for each Mass, though retaining only one for himself and giving the others to the cause prescribed by his ordinary.

Amount of Offering

Canon 952 — §1. It is for the provincial council or a meeting of the bishops of the province to determine by decree for the whole province what offering is to be made for the celebration and application of a Mass and it is not licit for a priest to ask for a larger sum; nevertheless it is lawful for a priest to accept for the application of a Mass a voluntary offering that is larger or even smaller than the one determined.

§2. Where there is no such decree the custom in effect in the diocese is to be observed.

§3. Members of any religious institutes of any kind must also observe the decree or custom of the place mentioned in §§1 and 2.

This canon makes two significant changes in canons 831–832 of the former law. The competent au-

---

[165]Sess. XXII, *de observandis et evitandis in celebratione missae.*
[166]D. I, c. 53, *de cons.;* Benedict XIV, const. *Quod expensis,* Aug. 26, 1738.

[167]*Firma in traditione* IIIa.
[168]SCConc, resolution, Nov. 13 and 18, 1937, *AAS* 30 (1938), 101–103; *CLD* 2, 204.
[169]*In celebratione Missae* 3b; *Firma in traditione* IIIa.

thority for determining the amount of Mass offerings is no longer the local ordinary but the provincial council or the meeting of bishops of a province, a change which promotes uniformity of practice between neighboring dioceses. A second change from the former law is the absence of any provision allowing the local ordinary to prevent priests from accepting an offering that is lower than the defined or customary amount. While a priest may not demand a larger amount than that defined or customary in the province, he may accept an offering in any amount that is freely given.

Satisfaction and Transferal of Mass Obligations

Canon 953 — It is not lawful for anyone to accept more stipends for Masses to be applied by himself than he can satisfy within a year.

Canon 954 — If in certain churches or oratories Masses are requested for celebration in larger numbers than can be celebrated there, they may be celebrated elsewhere unless the donors have expressly indicated a contrary intention.

Canon 955 — §1. One who intends to entrust to others Masses to be applied, is to entrust their celebration as soon as possible to priests acceptable to him, provided it is clear to him that they are entirely above suspicion; he must transmit the entire stipend he received unless it is established with certainty that the excess over the appropriate amount in the diocese was given for personal reasons; he is also obliged to see to the celebration of the Masses until he has received notification that the obligation has been accepted and the stipend received.
§2. The time within which the Masses are to be celebrated begins on the day on which the priest who is to celebrate them receives them unless otherwise indicated.
§3. Those who entrusted to others Masses to be celebrated are to note in a book without delay both the Masses received and those sent to others, as well as their stipends.
§4. Every priest must accurately note Masses which he has accepted to celebrate and which have been satisfied.

Canon 956 — Each and every administrator of pious causes or those obliged in any way to see to the celebration of Masses, whether clergy or laity, are to give to their ordinaries, in a manner to be determined by the latter, Mass obligations which have not been satisfied within a year.

Canons 953–956 consolidate and reformulate canons 835–841 and 844 of the 1917 Code but without significant alteration. Since, according to canon 953, a priest may not retain any Mass obligations

beyond those which he is able to satisfy personally within the course of a year, the following canons provide norms for the transferal of Mass offerings to other places and priests. Canon 954 allows Mass offerings to be transferred from one place to another unless the donor expressly indicates the contrary. In other words, when the one who accepts the offering agrees to have the Mass celebrated in a specific place, the Mass obligation cannot be satisfied elsewhere without the donor's permission or without the permission of the competent authority according to canon 1309.

Canon 955, compiled from five different canons of the 1917 Code (*CIC* 837–840, §1; 844), provides straightforward rules for the transferal and recording of Mass offerings. When a priest has more Mass obligations than he can satisfy personally in the course of one year, he should give them to other priests of his choice who are above suspicion, i.e., who are priests in good standing whose reliability is not in doubt. The entire offering must be given unless it is clear that the excess over the customary amount of a Mass offering was given for personal reasons. Frequently one can presume that any excess is indeed meant as a personal gift to the priest or the institution accepting the offering.

The time referred to in canon 955, §2 is the period of one year that each priest has to satisfy all Mass obligations. Likewise, the year referred to in canon 956 is not the calendar year but one year from the acceptance of the offering. Any Mass obligations which have not been satisfied within a year after they have been accepted must be transmitted to the ordinary.

Duties of Ecclesiastical Officials

Canon 957 — The duty and right of seeing to it that Mass obligations are fulfilled belong to the local ordinary in the churches of secular clergy and to the superiors in the churches of religious institutes and societies of apostolic life.

Canon 958 — §1. The pastor and rector of a church or other pious place where Mass offerings are usually received are to have a special book in which they list accurately the number of Masses to be celebrated, the intention, the stipend given and their celebration.
§2. The ordinary is obliged to examine these books each year either personally or through others.

While canon 842 of the 1917 Code spoke of the "right and duty" of seeing that Mass obligations are fulfilled, the inverted word order of canon 957 of the present Code better reflects the reality of this task as more an obligation than a privilege. For the secular clergy, this role of vigilance belongs to local ordinaries, including vicars general and episcopal vicars, and for the clergy of religious institutes or societies of apostolic life, it belongs to superiors, including local superiors.

Canon 958 obliges pastors and rectors of churches and other places where Mass offerings are usually received to keep an accurate record of the number of Masses, the intentions, the amount of the offerings, and the satisfaction of the obligation to celebrate the Masses. Every year this Mass record must be checked by the ordinary or his delegate, whether cleric or lay person. This is a slight change from canon 843 of the former law, which stated that the Mass book should be reviewed *at least* once a year. Ordinaries may also reduce and transfer Mass obligations in accordance with canons 1308–1309.

BIBLIOGRAPHY

Bibliographical material on the Most Holy Eucharist is incorporated in the bibliography that can be found after the commentary on canon 1007.

TITLE IV
THE SACRAMENT OF PENANCE
[cc. 959–997]

The thirty-nine canons of this title are distributed in four chapters, the first three of which deal with the sacrament of penance or reconciliation, the fourth with indulgences. After a single introductory canon, the title treats the following: (1) the celebration of the sacrament (cc. 960–964); (2) the minister (cc. 965–986); and (3) the penitent (cc. 987–991), along with (4) indulgences (cc. 992–997). A quantitatively disproportionate number of canons treats the priest who acts as a minister of the Church in the sacrament, partly because of the detailed norms that govern the faculty or capacity to minister. The addition of six basic norms on indulgences, related to but carefully distinct from sacramental reconciliation, will be considered below.

Vatican II mandated, as in the case of all liturgical services, a reform of the rite for celebrating the sacrament of penance: "The rites and formularies for the sacrament of penance are to be revised so that they more clearly express both the nature and effect of the sacrament."[1] In this text of *The Constitution on the Sacred Liturgy* the reference is to the social and ecclesial nature of sacramental reconciliation,[2] an aspect which is less apparent in the ordinary circumstances of individual or auricular confession than in the other sacraments.[3]

The constitution, treating penance also as a dimension of the church year, introduces and stresses the same neglected ecclesial aspect: "The baptismal and penitential aspects of Lent are to be given greater prominence in both the liturgy and liturgical catechesis." Hence:

a. More use is to be made of the baptismal features proper to the Lenten liturgy; some of those from an earlier era are to be restored as may seem advisable.

b. The same is to apply to the penitential elements. As regards catechesis, it is important to impress on the minds of the faithful not only the social consequences of sin but also the essence of the virtue of penance, namely, detestation of sin as an offense against God; the role of the Church is not to be neglected and the people are to be exhorted to pray for sinners.

During Lent penance should be not only inward and individual, but also outward and social. . . .[4]

The liturgical reform carried out this mandate, specifically in the 1973 *Rite of Penance* of the *Roman Ritual*. This includes not only the three rites and texts for the sacrament itself, mentioned below, but also an appendix of exemplars for communal penitential celebrations, including those that are seasonal in orientation.[5] These services are also the occasion of conversion and reconciliation but in themselves are distinct from the sacrament itself. The possible combination of such freely developed services with celebration of the sacrament is also contemplated:

Sometimes these services will include the sacrament of penance. In such cases after the readings and homily the rite for reconciling several penitents with individual confession and absolution is to be used (*Rite of Penance* nos. 54–59) or, in those special cases for which the law provides, the rite for general confession and absolution (*Rite of Penance* nos. 60–63).[6]

The canons of this title of the Code on penance do not address directly the enhanced ecclesial dimension of the liturgical reform except in passing. Nor is the nature of the sacrament of penance as public cult offered to God formally treated; this is left to canon 840.[7] The discipline of the 1917 Code is generally retained, especially the traditional norms of conduct affecting the ministers of the sacrament, bishops and presbyters, and the avoidance of misconduct and abuse. The major developments may be summarized as follows:

(1) The few norms for celebration include new canons on general sacramental absolution when individual, auricular confession of sins has not preceded the absolution or reconciliation. Under this heading, too, the norms on the lawful place of celebration have been included and certain re-

---

[1] *SC* 72.
[2] *SC* 27.
[3] *AcSynVat* 1, 2:567. See pp. 558–559 on the restoration of the laying on of hands, "even if without physical contact," as "a sign of reconciliation and of restored communion with the Church" (Cyprian).

[4] *SC* 109–110; see cc. 1249–1253 on days of penance, although neither the social and ecclesial nor the liturgical elements of penance are stressed in those canons.
[5] *RPenance*, Appendix II: "Samples of Penitential Services," n. 1–73. Another appendix gives a "Form of Examination of Conscience."
[6] Ibid., 4: *DOL* 3109.
[7] *Rel*, 224–225.

strictions lifted. Most of the liturgical law on the sacrament remains outside the Code, in accord with canon 2.

(2) Proposals that those ordained to the presbyterate should by the very fact of ordination be empowered to minister the sacrament were rejected.[8] Instead the requisite faculty over and above holy orders was retained, but a radical extension or enlargement of this faculty was introduced in canon 967, §§2–3. This was done in accord with the basic pastoral purposes of the recodification. Thus, although the norms on faculties remain substantially intact, most priests with a regular or habitual faculty to minister may exercise it everywhere unless canonically prohibited.

(3) The chapter of the 1917 Code on the reservation of sins (*CIC* 893–900) has been abrogated, at the recommendation of the Apostolic Penitentiary,[9] and along with it the canonical institute whereby the minister of the sacrament could be limited or restricted in his canonical and sacramental power with regard to reserved cases of sins. The institute of reservation of sins, which had been rigorously limited by the 1917 Code to "very grave and atrocious" cases and hemmed in by restraints against excessive or abusive reservations,[10] was pastorally obsolescent or obsolete.

Liturgical Reform

Because the canons are almost entirely concerned, in accord with canon 2, with the extrinsic discipline affecting the celebration, minister, and penitent, it is necessary to refer to the *Rite of Penance* for a broader treatment of the canonical discipline of celebration. The 1973 revision of the ritual provides three distinct rites for the celebration of sacramental reconciliation, all of them enhanced with prayers, biblical readings, and other elements as part of the general reform of the liturgical books of the Roman liturgy, in accord with *Sacrosanctum Concilium* 25:[11]

(1) Rite for Reconciliation of Individual Penitents

The first rite, although historically and traditionally derivative, is treated as primary and basic because it has been the common usage of the Church in medieval and modern times. As the rite for individual or auricular confessions of sins followed by individual absolution, it is the celebration with which the canons are almost exclusively concerned.

It was the only rite treated, in its unrevised form, in the 1917 Code.

(2) Rite for Reconciliation of Several Penitents with Individual Confession and [Individual] Absolution

In its present form—as a communal celebration which constitutes a framework for individual confession and individual absolution—the "second" rite is an innovation. Aside from the individual absolution of sins, however, it follows in the more venerable tradition of the general or communal reconciliation of penitents by the bishop on Holy Thursday—any individual confession of sins to presbyters having taken place earlier and traditionally prior to the Lenten observance. This older rite of reconciliation was retained in the 1596 *Roman Pontifical* but had become obsolete; the liturgical revision follows this tradition except that it requires individual absolution.[12]

The canons do not refer to this new second rite of the *Roman Ritual*, although it was this rite which Paul VI anticipated might become common:

> It [the second rite] combines the two values of being a community act and a personal act. It is a preferable form of reconciliation for our people when it is possible but it usually presupposes the presence of many ministers of the sacrament and this is not always easy. Still, we hope that especially for homogeneous groups—children, youth, workers, the sick, pilgrims, etc.—it may become the normal way of celebration, since it involves a more complete preparation and a more structured service.[13]

(3) Rite for Reconciliation of Several Penitents with General Confession and Absolution

This rite is new. Prior to the publication of the *Rite of Penance,* general or communal absolution without previous individual confession of sins had to be celebrated according to the ritual for individual penance, with the liturgical texts changed to the plural, as explained below. Canons 961–963 determine the limited conditions under which the new rite may be used.

As a whole, the *Rite of Penance* is characterized by greater openness to adaptation than other sections of the *Roman Ritual*. This results from a recognition that (1) the public and ecclesial nature of penance is fundamentally the same as that of the other sacraments, but (2) the sacrament has been

---

[8]*Comm* 10 (1978), 56.

[9]*Rel,* 230–231.

[10]*CIC* 897; see also *CIC* 895, 898, 900.

[11]For the complex history of the reform, see A. Bugnini, *La Riforma Liturgica (1948–1975)* (Rome: CLV-Edizioni Liturgiche, 1983), 646–664.

[12]In the Roman Pontifical, part three: "De expulsione publice poenitentium ab ecclesia, in feria quarta cinerum"; "De reconciliatione poenitentium, quae fit in feria quinta Coenae Domini." An early redaction of the second rite in the liturgical reform of the *RPenance* followed the tradition of communal absolution.

[13]Address, April 3, 1974: *N* 10 (1974), 225–227; *DOL* 3112. The text did not appear in *AAS*.

celebrated ordinarily in quasi-private circumstances in which only two members of the Christian community are present, namely, the penitent and the minister.

With regard to ritual adaptation to circumstances, no matter which of the three rites is followed, it is for priests and especially pastors

> in celebrating reconciliation with individuals or with a community to adapt the rite to the concrete circumstances of the penitents. They must preserve the essential structure and the entire form of absolution, but if necessary they may omit some parts of the rite for pastoral reasons or enlarge upon them, may select texts of readings or prayers, and may choose a place more suitable for the celebration according to the regulations of the conference of bishops, so that the entire celebration may be enriching and effective.[14]

Unlike the law on several other sacraments, there is no canon on the required form of words for the sacrament of penance, as approved in the liturgical books. With certain variants for communal absolution, this formulary is, for the Latin Church:

> God the Father of mercies, / through the death and resurrection of his Son / has reconciled the world to himself / and sent the Holy Spirit among us / for the forgiveness of sins; / through the ministry of the Church / may God give you pardon and peace, / and I absolve you from your sins / in the name of the Father, and of the Son, / and of the Holy Spirit. / R. Amen.[15]

This is the integral text which may not be altered and is referred to as the "entire form of absolution" in the text quoted above; the essential words begin "I absolve you . . . " and suffice in emergency circumstances.

Although a restoration of the more traditional and venerable deprecative form of reconciliation was not included in the *Rite of Penance,*[16] the above formulary was newly introduced for the following reasons:

> The form of absolution indicates that the reconciliation of the penitent comes from the mercy of the Father; it shows the connection between the reconciliation of the sinner and the paschal mystery of Christ; it stresses the role of the Holy Spirit in the forgiveness of sins; finally, it underlines the ecclesial aspect of the sacrament, because reconciliation with God is asked for and given through the ministry of the Church.[17]

One should see the introduction to the *Rite of Penance* for a summary but important treatment of the mystery of reconciliation in the history of salvation, the reconciliation of penitents in the Church's life, and the several offices and ministries of reconciliation, including the role of the community:

> The whole Church, as a priestly people, acts in different ways in the work of reconciliation that has been entrusted to it by the Lord. Not only does the Church call sinners to repentance by preaching the word of God, but it also intercedes for them and helps penitents with a maternal care and solicitude to acknowledge and confess their sins and to obtain the mercy of God, who alone can forgive sins. Further, the Church becomes the instrument of the conversion and absolution of the penitent through the ministry entrusted by Christ to the apostles and their successors.[18]

Remission of Canonical Censures

The canons of this title are of course concerned with the sacramental remission of sins. This is kept distinct from the remission of canonical sanctions—both the medicinal penalties or censures enumerated in canons 1331-1333 and the expiatory penalties of canon 1336—with which Book VI is concerned. The remission or cessation of censures (excommunication, interdict, and the suspension of ordained ministers) may, however, take place in connection with and on the occasion of sacramental reconciliation. The minister of the sacrament, if he is empowered by the law to remit censures (in particular by c. 1357), must observe the norms of Book IV, title VI.

While the act of remitting canonical censures is distinct from the sacramental absolution of sins and is defined rather as the remission of an ecclesiastical penal sanction, the *Roman Ritual* makes special provision for the case:

> The form of [sacramental] absolution is not to be changed when a priest, in keeping with the provision of law, absolves a properly disposed penitent from a censure *latae sententiae.* It is enough that he intend also to absolve from censures. Before absolving from sins, however, the confessor may [separately and distinctly] absolve from the censure, using the formula which is given below for absolution from censure outside the sacrament of penance.
>
> When a priest, in accordance with the law, absolves a penitent from a censure outside the sacrament of penance, he uses the following formula: By the power granted to me, / I absolve

[14]*RPenance* 40: *DOL* 3105.
[15]*RPenance* 46; ibid., 19, 21: *DOL* 3084, 3086.
[16]See Bugnini, 648–650.
[17]*RPenance* 19: *DOL* 3084.

[18]*RPenance* 8: *DOL* 3073. See Mt 18:18, Jn 20:23.

you / from the bond of excommunication (*or* suspension *or* interdict). / In the name of the Father, and of the Son, + / and of the Holy Spirit. The penitent answers: Amen.[19]

[19]*RPenance,* Appendix I, 1–2. The text of the first paragraph, as it appeared in the *RPenance,* has been altered slightly (omitting "Until other provision is made and as may be necessary, the present regulations which make recourse to the competent authority obligatory are to be observed") in the light of the recodification. See SCSDW decr *Promulgato Codice Iuris Canonici,* Sept. 12, 1983: *N* 20 (1983), 540–555 [cited as *Variationes*]; translation, *Emendations in the Liturgical Books Following upon the New Code of Canon Law* (Washington: ICEL, 1984), 20.

Thus, with reference to the celebration of the sacrament of penance for one who is also under canonical censure, two possibilities are envisioned. (1) The minister of the sacrament, if the law permits him to do so, remits the censure in the very act of absolving from sin. (2) Alternatively, the minister, again if permitted by the law, first remits the canonical censure in a distinct act—using the extra-sacramental formula given above—before the absolution from sin.

CANONS AND COMMENTARY ────────────────────

Nature of the Sacrament

Canon 959 — In the sacrament of penance the faithful, confessing their sins to a legitimate minister, being sorry for them, and at the same time proposing to reform, obtain from God forgiveness of sins committed after baptism through the absolution imparted by the same minister; and they likewise are reconciled with the Church which they have wounded by sinning.

The text considerably enlarges canon 870 of the 1917 Code, which it replaces, deliberately removing the description of absolution as "judicial" but adding a specific mention of the several acts of the penitent: confession of sins, sorrow for the sins confessed, proposal or resolution to reform—the latter corresponding to the nature of penance as conversion or change. Moreover, the text mentions, as its counterpart did not, that the forgiveness is from God (alone) and adds the concept of reconciliation with the church community, as intended by the conciliar Fathers of Vatican II.[20]

This succinct doctrinal canon may be supplemented by the introduction to the *Rite of Penance* already mentioned in this commentary.

CHAPTER I
THE CELEBRATION OF THE SACRAMENT
[cc. 960–964]

This brief chapter of five canons treats in succession the following: (1) individual and integral confession of sins and absolution (c. 960); (2) general absolution without previous individual confession (cc. 961–963); and (3) the place for the celebration of the sacrament with individual confession (c. 964). Nothing is said directly about the liturgical celebration itself, aside from the penitent's confession of sins and the discipline affecting absolution or reconciliation; the norms for celebration are left to the *Rite of Penance* in the *Roman Ritual.* Nor is there reference to the second rite of reconciliation, namely, communal celebration of the sacrament with individual confession and individual absolution, or to communal penitential celebrations without sacramental reconciliation—both of which are significant elements in the revised Roman liturgy of penance.

Canons 961–963 have no counterparts in the 1917 Code; they have been introduced in the light of the greater possibility of general sacramental absolution, to which the *Roman Ritual* devotes a full rite of song and opening prayer, celebration of the word of God with homily, general confession and absolution, and concluding thanksgiving, song or hymn, and blessing—but only "for cases foreseen in the law."[21]

Individual Reconciliation

Canon 960 — Individual and integral confession and absolution constitute the only ordinary way by which the faithful person who is aware of serious sin is reconciled with God and with the Church; only physical or moral impossibility excuses the person from confession of this type, in which case reconciliation can take place in other ways.

[20]*SC* 72; see the beginning of the commentary on this sacrament.

[21]*RPenance* 60–63.

The first clause of the canon, in dealing with individual reconciliation of penitents, does so in contrast to the following three canons. The mention of integral confession of sins to the minister of the sacrament is based upon the teaching of the Council of Trent. Reflecting the developed Scholastic doctrine of the sacrament, the Council anathematized those who held

> that in the sacrament of penance for the remission of sins it is not necessary by divine law to confess each and every mortal sin, which one recalls upon due and diligent prior reflection, even occult sins and those which are against the two final precepts of the decalogue, and the circumstances which change the species of the sin. . . . [22]

Although there has been some dispute concerning the expression "iure divino" in this text, since the traditions of penitential discipline were so diverse in earlier centuries, the present canon does not depart from the expectation of the integrity and specificity of the confession of sins.

The statement of the canon has been rephrased somewhat from canon 901 of the 1917 Code, which explained the meaning of integral confession as requiring mention of all sins of which the penitent is conscious and of the circumstances which make a specific change in the sin. This has been understood, again in accord with Tridentine teaching, not in reference to aggravating circumstances but only to circumstances which make the sin a violation of a specifically different precept or virtue.[23]

These elements of the canon anticipate what is determined in greater detail in chapter III on the penitent, especially canons 987–989. What is different in the present canon is the limited acknowledgment that this primary manner of celebration of the sacrament, with full and individual confession of sins prior to absolution or reconciliation, is only the ordinary means or mode by which a believer conscious of a grave sin committed after baptism is reconciled to God and the Christian community. This provides an opening to canons 961–963 on the exceptional, or out-of-the-ordinary, mode of reconciliation.

In addition, the language of the first part of the canon reflects contemporary theology and the teaching of Vatican II, which have recovered the tradition that sacramental penance involves ecclesial reconciliation. This was of course more evident in antiquity and the early medieval period, for example, when one acknowledged his or her grave (and public) sins at the beginning of Lent and was reconciled publicly on Holy Thursday in the common assembly.

The second part of canon 960 introduces the common teaching of moral theology which recognizes excuses from individual and integral confession because of physical or moral impossibility, a matter not mentioned in this context by the 1917 Code. These kinds of impossibility may embrace a variety of physical and moral (even psychological) incapacities on the part of the penitent, the latter's relationship to the only available minister, circumstances of time or place, etc. The alternative means of sacramental reconciliation which are referred to include a less than complete individual confession of sins followed by individual absolution and, most obviously, the exceptional mode regulated by the three canons which follow. Reconciliation with God and the Church may of course also be accomplished by means of sacraments other than penance, above all through the Eucharistic celebration, as well as by non-sacramental penance and contrition.

The succinct statement of this canon is enlarged upon in the introduction to the *Rite of Penance* where, after a doctrinal exposition of the mystery of reconciliation, there is a section on "Reconciliation of Penitents in the Church's Life."[24] This section of the *Roman Ritual* deals successively with the Church itself as both holy and always in need of purification; penance in the Church's life and liturgy; reconciliation with God and with the Church; the traditional "parts" of the sacrament: contrition, confession, the act of penance or expiation, and the actual absolution or reconciliation; and the need and benefit of sacramental penance as the celebration of the Church's faith, thanksgiving, and sacrifice.

General Reconciliation

Canon 961 — §1. Absolution cannot be imparted in a general manner to a number of penitents at once without previous individual confession unless:

1° the danger of death is imminent and there is not time for the priest or priests to hear the confessions of the individual penitents;

2° a serious necessity exists, that is, when in light of the number of penitents a supply of confessors is not readily available rightly to hear the confessions of individuals within a suitable time so that the penitents are forced to be deprived of sacramental grace or holy communion for a long time through no fault of their own; it is not considered a sufficient necessity if confessors cannot be readily available only because of the great number of penitents as can occur on the occasion of some great feast or pilgrimage.

§2. It is for the diocesan bishop to judge whether the conditions required in §1, n. 2, are present; he can determine general cases of such necessity in the

---

[22]Sess. XIV, *de poenitentia,* c. 7: *COD* 712.
[23]Abbo-Hannan, *Sacred Canons* II, 28–29 (cited as Abbo-Hannan).

[24]*RPenance* 3–7: *DOL* 3068–3072.

light of criteria agreed upon with other members of the conference of bishops.

The immediate antecedent of the three new canons on general sacramental absolution without previous individual confession of sins is the *Rite of Penance* of 1973. The third rite, as given in the *Roman Ritual,* appears to be an ordinary mode of communal reconciliation, but the introduction, based on *Normae pastorales* issued in the preceding year,[25] severely restricts its "ordinary" celebration. As published, the norm immediately prior to the promulgation of the Code was as follows.

Special, occasional circumstances may render it lawful and even necessary to give general absolution to a number of penitents without their previous individual confession.

In addition to the danger of death, general absolution for many of the faithful who have confessed generically, but have been rightly disposed for penance, is lawful if there is a serious need. This means a case in which, given the number of penitents, not enough confessors are available to hear the individual confessions properly within a reasonable time, with the result that, through no fault of their own, the faithful would be forced to be for a long time without the grace of the sacrament [of penance] or without communion. Such a situation may occur in mission lands particularly, but in other places as well and in groups of people to whom the serious need mentioned clearly applies.

When confessors can be made available, however, the procedure is not lawful solely on the basis of a large number of penitents, for example, at some great festival or pilgrimage.

It belongs exclusively to the local Ordinary, after consultation with other members of the conference of bishops, to make the judgment on whether the conditions stated already are verified and therefore to decide when it is lawful to give general absolution.

If, apart from the instances established by the local Ordinary, any other serious need arises for general absolution, a priest is bound first, whenever possible, to have recourse to the local Ordinary in order to give the general absolution. If this is not possible, he is to inform the same Ordinary as soon as possible of the need in question and of the fact of the absolution.[26]

The terms of this pre-codal law reflect in part the existing discipline before 1973, i.e., even before the issuance of the *Rite of Penance.* During World War II, the Apostolic Penitentiary issued an instruction on the subject, indicating that (1) general sacramental absolution is permissible for serious and urgent cause even in circumstances other than the danger of death; (2) local ordinaries are competent to permit this absolution; and (3) the rite for the sacrament of penance in the 1614 *Roman Ritual* should be followed but with the liturgical texts in the plural—since the existing ritual did not contain a special rite for these circumstances.[27]

As already mentioned, the revised *Rite of Penance* does provide such a rite, relying upon the canonical discipline in force but prefixing the new pastoral norms of 1972. It also includes a very brief rite for general absolution in emergency circumstances, such as the danger of death.[28]

When the norms of the *Roman Ritual* quoted above are compared with canon 961, several changes are evident: (1) greater specificity concerning the danger of death as one of the reasons permitting the use of the rite; (2) suppression (but not denial) of the ritual's positive observation concerning instances in mission lands and elsewhere where the serious need "clearly applies"; (3) restriction of the permission to diocesan bishops rather than local ordinaries; (4) requirement that the bishop's decision be made in the light of criteria agreed upon with the other members of the conference of bishops (and not merely after consultation with them); and (5) omission of a possible judgment by a priest minister of the sacrament that general absolution may be given when recourse to the diocesan bishop is impossible.[29]

With regard to this last matter, the possible decision of the minister himself, the ordinary principles of moral theology about impossibility of recourse in situations of necessity may be applied.[30] The other changes listed above, especially (3) and (4), are further restrictions placed by the canon upon the celebration of general reconciliation. This has been recognized in variants to be introduced into the *Rite of Penance,* so that its norms will conform literally with the present canon.[31] The Apostolic See

[25]SCDF, June 16, 1972: *AAS* 64 (1972), 510–514: *DOL* 3038–3051.

[26]*RPenance* 31–32: *DOL* 3096–3097.

[27]Apostolic Penitentiary, instr Mar. 25, 1944: *AAS* 36 (1944), 155–156. The development of the third rite of penance, although introduced in the light of recommendations by the conciliar Fathers of Vatican II, was closely tied to the discipline of this document. See Bugnini, 651–655.

[28]*RPenance* 64–65.

[29]The dispositions of cc. 961–963 will replace, to the extent necessary, the corresponding norms of the introduction to the *RPenance* 31–34 (and also the *Normae pastorales* of 1972, from which cc. 961–963 likewise differ, as noted in the text). See *Variationes,* as cited above; *Emendations,* 17–20, as cited above, note 19.

[30]*Rel,* 228.

[31]See note 29, above.

has repeatedly expressed concern lest the restricting norms for general sacramental absolution be exceeded to the (further) diminution of auricular confession.[32]

The language of the canon, even with these further inhibitions, continues to permit the celebration of the third rite if the conditions are fulfilled. As Paul VI explicitly asserted, the enlarged discipline was introduced "with our special approval and by our mandate."[33] With particular reference to the language of canon 961, the availability of confessors is a relative matter: it depends on the size of the congregation of penitents, the period of time needed for the proper celebration of the sacrament of penance (i.e., in accord with the revised ritual), the remoteness of the community and its size, which might deny freedom of choice of confessors or desired anonymity to penitents, etc. The extended deprivation of sacramental grace mentioned in the canon as justifying general absolution refers to the grace of the sacrament of penance;[34] this deprivation may create a spiritual hardship to those not conscious of grave sin as well as to those who are conscious of grave sin and who would therefore be deprived not only of sacramental penance but also of sacramental Communion. Finally, the lengthy period of time has to be understood relatively, as in other instances, in terms of a rather limited time, even a day's deprivation of the sacrament.[35]

The canon thus balances carefully the rather exceptional character of the rite of general absolution with the pastoral criteria, to be judged by the diocesan bishop in harmony with the criteria that may have been approved by the conference of bishops. The judgment of the bishop or the criteria of the conference may justify or require the celebration even though the serious need cannot be characterized as creating an emergency situation.

It is of course true that, even in the circumstances in which the law permits the celebration of general reconciliation without prior individual confession of sins, those conscious of grave sin may indeed receive divine pardon in view of the degree and kind of their contrition ("perfect contrition") without the sacrament.[36] Such persons are nonetheless deprived of the grace of the sacrament of pen-

ance[37] and share less perfectly in the dimension of ecclesial reconciliation. The same is true of those who are conscious only of lesser or venial sins, which may indeed be remitted in ways other than the sacrament, but who in the circumstances are likewise deprived of sacramental reconciliation.

Canon 962 — §1. **For a member of the Christian faithful validly to enjoy sacramental absolution given to many at one time, it is required that this person not only be suitably disposed but also at the same time intend to confess individually the serious sins which at present cannot be so confessed.**

§2. As much as can be done, the Christian faithful are to be instructed concerning the requirements specified in §1, also on the occasion of receiving general absolution; an exhortation that each person take care to make an act of contrition is to precede general absolution, even in danger of death if time is available.

The disposition to which paragraph one of this canon refers includes the inner conversion which "embraces sorrow for sin and the intent to lead a new life ... expressed through confession made to the Church, due expiation, and amendment of life. God grants pardon through the Church, which works by the ministry of priests."[38] The *Rite of Penance,* prior to the revised codification, had specified these dispositions in relation to general sacramental absolution: that those present "repent individually of their sins, have the intention of refraining from them, are resolved to rectify scandal or injuries they may have caused. ... "[39] The purpose of paragraph one is to repeat, under pain of invalidity of the absolution (which the *Roman Ritual* had not mentioned), a disposition special to the exceptional circumstances of general sacramental reconciliation. This disposition is the intent to confess individually in due time the grave sins which could not be confessed individually on the occasion of general absolution.

The due time to which paragraph one refers for individual confession is further specified in the next canon ("as soon as there is an opportunity") and, more generally, by the traditional precept of at least annual confession of grave sins in canon 989.

The norm of paragraph two may be seen as a

[32]SCDF letter Jan. 14, 1977: *BCLN,* Nov. 13, 1977, 57–58; *DOL* 3127–3132. Paul VI, address April 3, 1974: *N* 10 (1974), 225–227: *DOL* 3110–3113.

[33]Paul VI, address April 20, 1978: *AAS* 70 (1978), 328–332; *DOL* 3138–3139.

[34]" ... gratia sacramentali aut sacra communione diu carere cogantur; ... "

[35]See E.F. Regatillo-M. Zalba, *Theologiae Moralis Summa,* III (Madrid: BAC, 1954), n. 1052, p. 917 (cited as Regatillo-Zalba).

[36]International Theological Commission, report "Penance and Reconciliation," 1983, C, II, 4: *Origins* 13 (1984), 513–524.

[37]The various redactions of this text (*Normae pastorales, RPenance,* and the several schemata of the Code) differ but always refer to *gratia sacramentalis* and place it in some distinction from (the deprivation of) Holy Communion, a deprivation which affects only those conscious of the continuing guilt of grave sin. See also the commentary on c. 988, §2, below.

[38]*RPenance* 6: *DOL* 3071; on the Church's ministry, see the revised formula of the sacrament, at the beginning of the commentary on this title.

[39]*RPenance* 33: *DOL* 3098.

specification of canon 988, §1, which speaks of the fundamental obligation to confess grave sins committed after baptism that have not yet been confessed in individual or auricular confession. In this way the usual canonical discipline is maintained. The mention of "danger of death if time is available" is applicable to the short rite of general absolution[40] rather than the complete and lengthy "third rite" of reconciliation of several penitents with general confession and absolution.

This paragraph is derived immediately from a similar injunction in the *Rite of Penance* and the specific norm that, after the homily of the third rite, there be a brief instruction or *monitio* concerning the requisite and special dispositions of penitents. The act of contrition, which is called simply a "general confession," follows this pattern in the full rite of general absolution:

> The deacon, another minister, or the priest then [after the homily and instruction] calls upon the penitents to show their intention by some sign (for example, by bowing their heads, kneeling, or giving some other sign determined by the conference of bishops). They should also say together a form of general confession (for example, the prayer *I confess to almighty God*), which may be followed by a litany or a penitential song. Then the Lord's Prayer is sung or said by all. . . .
>
> Then the priest pronounces the invocation that expresses prayer for the grace of the Holy Spirit to pardon sin, the proclamation of victory over sin through Christ's death and resurrection, and the sacramental absolution given to the penitents.[41]

For the United States, the National Conference of Catholic Bishops decreed in 1974 that the sign of penance before general sacramental absolution should be determined and announced by the minister, namely, an "appropriate external sign of penance to be shown, e.g., kneeling, bowing of the head, bowing deeply, standing (if the penitents have been kneeling), a gesture such as the sign of the cross, etc."[42]

Canon 963 — With due regard for the obligation mentioned in can. 989, a person who has had serious sins remitted by a general absolution is to approach individual confession as soon as there is an opportunity to do so before receiving another general absolution unless a just cause intervenes.

The canon contains a precept distinct from that of canon 989, in which the annual confession of grave sins is prescribed as a minimum. In other words, the present norm may oblige even before the lapse of a year's time, i.e., as soon as possible after the celebration of general sacramental reconciliation. Since the divine and ecclesial sacramental reconciliation has already taken place, the norm must be considered an ecclesiastical law specifying when the intention to confess individually (c. 962) should be fulfilled.

Nonetheless the language of the canon recognizes, as did the *Rite of Penance* and the *Normae pastorales* which preceded it, that there may be a just cause which may excuse from individual confession "as soon as there is an opportunity." This cause may be the same as that justifying the general sacramental absolution in the first place, such as the remoteness of the area and the lack of ministers of the sacrament, so long as that condition or cause continues. There is of course no obligation to confess sins which are not grave, as canon 989 indicates.

Canon 964 — §1. The proper place to hear sacramental confessions is a church or an oratory.

§2. The conference of bishops is to issue norms concerning the confessional, seeing to it that confessionals with a fixed grille between penitent and confessor are always located in an open area so that the faithful who wish to make use of them may do so freely.

§3. Confessions are not to be heard outside the confessional without a just cause.

The final form of this canon, which replaces canons 908–910 of the 1917 Code, is the result of several variant redactions. In particular, canons 909–910 of the former Code had singled out women for special restrictions, indicating that the confessional for their celebration of the sacrament should be in an open and conspicuous place, while permitting the sacrament to be celebrated for male penitents even in private homes. In some places, moreover, it was customary and acceptable for the confessions of men to take place regularly in rooms, sacristies, and other areas without the use of a special confessional. It was (and is) always understood, finally, that in many circumstances such as sickness the sacrament is properly celebrated in any opportune or available place.

In the revised *Roman Ritual* the prescriptions of the 1917 Code were referred to as continuing in force,[43] but it was left to the conferences of bishops to make further (and different) determinations "about the place proper for the ordinary celebration of the sacrament of penance" and to priests

---

[40]*R Penance* 64–65.
[41]*R Penance* 35: *DOL* 3100
[42]*BCLN 1965–1975* (Dec. 1974), 450; see R. Keifer-F.R. McManus, *The Rite of Penance: Commentaries,* I, *Understanding the Document* (Washington: The Liturgical Conference, 1975), 128–129.

[43]*R Penance* 12: *DOL* 3077.

and especially pastors to "choose a place more suitable for the celebration according to the regulations of the conference of bishops, so that the entire celebration may be enriching and effective."[44] In the light of this, with the development of chapels or rooms of reconciliation as alternatives to the modern style of confessional (or in combination with such a confessional), the conference of bishops in 1974 decreed for the United States that it is

> considered desirable that small chapels or rooms of reconciliation be provided in which penitents might choose to confess their sins through an informal face-to-face exchange with the priest, with the opportunity for appropriate spiritual counsel. It would also be regarded as desirable that such chapels or rooms be designed to afford the option of the penitent's kneeling at the fixed confessional grill in the usual way, but in every case the freedom of the penitent is to be respected.[45]

A further elaboration was later given by the United States Bishops' Committee on the Liturgy:

> A room or rooms for the reconciliation of individual penitents may be located near the baptismal area (when it is at the entrance) or in another convenient place. Furnishings and decoration should be simple and austere, offering the penitent a choice between face-to-face encounter or the anonymity provided by a screen, with nothing superfluous in evidence beyond a simple cross, table and bible. The purpose of this room is primarily for the celebration of the reconciliation liturgy; it is not a lounge, counseling room, etc. The word "chapel" more appropriately describes this space.[46]

Early drafts of the recodification left the matter generally to the conference of bishops, with the provision that there be available a confessional with a fixed screen or grille. Subsequently a norm was introduced or reintroduced to require that the confessions of women take place in a confessional with a fixed screen "except by reason of infirmity or other necessity."[47] In the final text, the present form of paragraph three appears without reference to or restriction upon the confessions of women.

Thus paragraph one of the present canon follows canon 908 of the 1917 Code, except for the distinction, now suppressed, between public and semipublic oratories.[48] The reason for paragraph one is that the sacrament, even though celebrated regular-

ly in a rather individualized and private rite, is an ecclesial celebration for which the place of the communal liturgical assembly is appropriate.

The provision of the confessional or confessional seat is retained in paragraphs two and three. The common form of booth, with a place for the penitent (either open to public view or enclosed but) separate from the seat of the minister, is not prescribed, unless by particular law. Confessionals in one or other of these styles, e.g., with or without a door or doors, were introduced after the Council of Trent and spread widely in the Latin Church.[49] The canon, however, prescribes only that the seat of the confessor be in an open place and that there be a screen or grille between the penitent and the confessor; no norm is given concerning the style or form of the fixed dividing barrier.

The purpose of the norm is to afford the penitent anonymity if he or she desires and to make certain that there is no suspicion of confessor or penitent because of a privacy which might otherwise be desired. The room or chapel of reconciliation in which a "confessional" area with a fixed screen is incorporated fully satisfies the norm. If the room or chapel does not itself incorporate an area with a fixed screen, the latter must be available elsewhere.

In accord with paragraph three, the use of the usual confessional remains prescribed, but for a lesser reason than "necessity" (as earlier intended by the codifiers) the confession may take place elsewhere. The reasons given, for example, by the National Conference of Catholic Bishops (above) are a just cause for that body's encouragement and preference for the rooms or chapels in which the penitent remains free to choose face-to-face confession or the anonymity provided by the confessional screen.

CHAPTER II
THE MINISTER OF THE SACRAMENT OF PENANCE
[cc. 965–986]

The first half of this chapter deals directly with the priest as minister of this sacrament and with his faculty to minister. After an introductory canon (c. 965), the acquisition of the faculty (cc. 966–969) is treated, along with special qualifications in those who may have the faculty and the terms of the faculty itself (cc. 970–973), and finally the cessation of the faculty (cc. 974–975).

The other eleven canons of the chapter deal with several matters closely related to the exercise of this sacramental ministry by priests: (1) special cases of

---

[44]*RPenance* 38b: *DOL* 3103; 40: *DOL* 3105.

[45]*BCLN 1965–1975* (Dec. 1974), 450.

[46]*Environment and Art in Catholic Worship* (Washington, 1978), n. 81.

[47]*Comm* 10 (1978), 68–69.

[48]C. 1223.

[49]On the introduction of such confessionals, and the several styles, see J.B. O'Connell, *Church Building and Furnishing: The Church's Way* (Notre Dame, Ind.: University of Notre Dame Press, 1955), 72–73.

absolution (cc. 976–977); (2) the manner of receiving the confession of sins, the absolution, and the imposition of an act of penance (c. 978–981); (3) the false denunciation of confessors (c. 982); (4) confidentiality (cc. 983–985); and (5) the responsibility to exercise the ministry of reconciliation (c. 986).

There is relatively little on the faculty to minister in the revised *Roman Ritual,* except for a brief pastoral exhortation to priests[50] and a basic statement in which the priest's ministry is placed in an ecclesial context:

> The whole Church, as a priestly people, acts in different ways in the work of reconciliation that has been entrusted to it by the Lord. . . .
>
> The Church exercises the ministry of the sacrament of penance through bishops and priests. By preaching God's word [newly introduced as a formal element of the actual rite of sacramental reconciliation] they call the faithful to conversion; in the name of Christ and by the power of the Holy Spirit they declare and grant the forgiveness of sins.
>
> In the exercise of this ministry priests act in communion with the bishop and share in his power and office as the one who regulates the penitential discipline.
>
> The competent minister of the sacrament of penance is a priest who has the faculty to absolve in accordance with canon law. . . .[51]

Thus the role of the priest as minister is asserted to include both declaring and granting the forgiveness of sins. This is in accord with the teaching of Trent which repudiated any assertion that ecclesial reconciliation was merely one of declaring God's forgiveness or was void of judgmental (as well as other) dimensions.[52] The relationship of the presbyter to the bishop, who is the moderator of the liturgy and of the penitential discipline in the local church, is expressed in two ways: fundamentally as communion within the presbyterate and canonically as possession of the faculty to reconcile or absolve sinners.

The faculty to minister this sacrament to penitents is generally referred to in the canons as the faculty to "hear" confessions, although such terminology refers to only part of the rite. The terminology has to be understood always as referring to the authorization to minister the sacrament, to absolve as well as to receive ("hear") the confession of sins. A similar usage is found in the canonical reference to the minister as "confessor," which is regularly retained in the canons. It corresponds also to the popular and even traditional practice of referring to the sacrament as "confession" rather than penance or reconciliation, although the revised ritual is careful to retain "penance" and to introduce "reconciliation."[53] The popular and canonical emphasis upon the confessional dimension of the sacrament has been explained as reflecting a modern concentration upon this aspect, which was less prominent in ancient and medieval times:

> The form of the acts of the penitent was also subject [in the historical development of the sacrament] to a noteworthy change. It often happened that one of these was emphasized so much that the others were relegated to the background. Public penance in the primitive Church stood under the sign of public satisfaction which lasted for a set period of time; private penance in the Middle Ages and in the modern period, on the other hand, underlined the importance of contrition; in our own time, the accent is more on confession. . . .[54]

The accent on confession is indeed greater in the canons of this chapter and the next, in which the terminology is largely unchanged from the 1917 Code, than it is in the ritual. The latter's emphasis is on divine and ecclesial reconciliation as well as on contrition and confession.

This chapter corresponds closely to canons 871–892 of the 1917 Code. It introduces, however, a more generous recognition of confessional faculties, already mentioned at the beginning of the commentary on the sacrament of penance. More important, it suppresses all jurisdictional language in relation to confessional faculties.

A certain analogy with the sacrament of confirmation is possible: over and above sacramental ordination or participation in the ordained presbyterate, some faculty or capacity or concession to absolve is needed. The analogy with confirmation is supported by canon 144, §2, which applies the institute of supplied executive power of governance or jurisdiction equally to both sacraments (as well as to the faculty to assist at marriage). In the case of confirmation, the addition to the power of holy orders has been variously explained; in the case of penance the addition to the power of holy orders

---

[50]*RPenance* 10: *DOL* 3075.

[51]*RPenance* 8–9: *DOL* 3073–3074. On the bishop of the particular church as *moderator* of penitential discipline, see *LG* 26: *DOL* 146.

[52]Sess. XIV, *de poenitentia,* c. 9: *COD* 712.

[53]The preference of the revisers of the ritual of Paul VI is evident in the use of "reconciling" in the name of each of the three rites of the sacrament.

[54]International Theological Commission, report, 1983, B, IV, 6, 5: *Origins* 13 (1984), 520.

has been explicitly described in the past as an augmentation of jurisdiction or the power of governance.[55] The recodification, however, carefully avoids jurisdictional language in this connection. At the same time it is clear that the church authority which is the ultimate source of the faculty to absolve or reconcile is a person, ordinarily the bishop, who exercises a power of governance or jurisdiction.

The minister of reconciliation in these canons is the priest (bishop or presbyter) who may absolve from sins in the celebration of the sacrament of penance. Insofar as the remission of canonical sanctions is concerned, one should see canons 1354–1363 and, with specific reference to confessors and the remission of censures, canon 1357. Distinct in itself from the remission of sins, this discipline has been explained briefly at the beginning of the commentary on the present title on the sacrament of penance.

Sacerdotal Ministry of Reconciliation

Canon 965 — Only a priest is the minister of the sacrament of penance.

Canon 966 — §1. For the valid absolution of sins it is required that, besides the power received through sacred ordination, the minister possess the faculty to exercise that power over the faithful to whom he imparts absolution.

§2. A priest can be given this faculty either by the law itself or by a concession granted by competent authority in accord with the norm of can. 969.

In the first of the canons of this chapter, the Latin "sacerdos" is used to refer to both bishops and presbyters. Like canon 871 of the 1917 Code, the text follows the Council of Trent, which condemned the doctrine of those who held that

> priests are not the only ministers of absolution but it was said to each and every Christian: "Whatever you declare bound on earth shall be held bound in heaven, and whatever you declare loosed on earth shall be held loosed in heaven" and "For those whose sins you forgive, they are forgiven; for those whose sins you retain, they are retained."[56]

As already suggested, the faculty or capacity to absolve or remit sins through the celebration of sacramental reconciliation is understood as rooted in holy orders—and thus is a power for which presby-

teral ordination is necessary—but it is also understood as requiring a distinct, additional concession which permits the valid exercise of the ministry on behalf of God and the Church. This is the sense of canon 966.

Vatican II refrained from using the medieval distinction between the power of orders and the power of jurisdiction (now alternatively and preferably called the power of governance or governing).[57] Nonetheless the distinction between the power of orders and the capacity to exercise that power is retained in relation to sacramental absolution. With significant rephrasing to avoid the reference to jurisdiction, the text of canon 966 follows canon 872 of the former Code, which spoke of (confessional) jurisdiction as ordinary or delegated.

In principle, the determination of the faculty to absolve is based on the relationship of the minister to the penitents, namely, the particular members of the faithful who seek reconciliation. Thus in succeeding canons the faculty is related either to the office of ministry which the priest has in respect to the penitents or to the jurisdictional power which the grantor of the faculty has in respect to the penitents.

In paragraph two of canon 966 the distinction between ordinary and delegated jurisdiction, the categories employed by canon 872 of the 1917 Code, has been replaced by a distinction between a faculty from the law and a faculty from a concession or grant.

In cases of error or doubt concerning the possession of the faculty of canon 966, the Church supplies the faculty, in accord with canon 144, §2. One should see the commentary on instances of "common error about fact or about law, and also in positive and probable doubt about law or about fact," according to the doctrine of paragraph one of that canon. In effect, canon 144, §2 employs the institute of supplied jurisdiction (now called and limited to supplied executive power of governance) to the faculty of the minister of the sacrament of penance, although it is no longer called or considered a jurisdictional faculty.

Faculty from the Law

Canon 967 — §1. Besides the Roman Pontiff, cardinals by the law itself possess the faculty to hear the confessions of the Christian faithful anywhere in the world; likewise, bishops possess this faculty and licitly use it anywhere unless the diocesan bishop denies it in a particular case.

§2. Those who enjoy the faculty of hearing confessions habitually whether in virtue of office or by

[55]E.g., Regatillo-Zalba, 280; see *CIC* 872–881, all speaking of jurisdiction.

[56]Sess. XIV, *de poenitentia*, c. 10: *COD* 713. The biblical texts are Mt 18:18 and Jn 20:23.

[57]See *LG* 18–29 (ch. III); the jurisdictional terminology is used only once (*LG* 23) in treating the hierarchical constitution of the Church.

grant from the ordinary of the place of incardination or the place in which they have a domicile can exercise the same faculty everywhere unless the local ordinary denies it in a particular case, with due regard for the prescriptions of can. 974, §§2 and 3.

§3. Those who have been granted the faculty to hear confessions in virtue of an office or by a grant from the competent superior in accord with the norms of cann. 968, §2 and 969, §2 can by the law itself use the faculty anywhere in respect to members and others who stay day and night in a house of the institute or society; such persons also exercise this faculty licitly unless some major superior has denied it concerning his own subjects in a particular case.

As in most instances in the canons and in the 1917 Code, the faculty to "hear" confessions is understood as the faculty to exercise the power of orders to "absolve" penitents from their sins, as already noted. This usage is without prejudice to the natural meaning of hearing a confession of sinful actions, which may be done by anyone. Here and in succeeding canons it is simply a canonical usage referring to the sacerdotal ministry of presiding over all the elements of the sacrament of penance. The present canon replaces canon 873 of the 1917 Code, clarifying and expanding the terms of the earlier text.

A distinction is made in paragraph one. The bishop of Rome himself, as head of the college of bishops, and the cardinals, as the principal ministers of the Roman diocese, absolve both validly and licitly everywhere and without restriction. Bishops, whether diocesan bishops or not, absolve validly everywhere, but it is illicit for them to absolve if the diocesan bishop refuses to permit this in a particular case. This acknowledgment of the faculty from the law for all members of the order of bishops is new in the revision of the Code.

A more substantial reform of the discipline of confessional faculties is found in paragraph two. The text anticipates what is determined in detail in succeeding canons and makes a broad, general determination in favor of those presbyters whose faculty is derived from their office or granted by the local ordinary—of the place of their incardination or, if they are incardinated elsewhere or are religious or others who lack diocesan incardination, from the ordinary of their place of domicile—provided always that the faculty is habitual or regular, that is, not conceded for a particular occasion or for particular circumstances. Once they possess the faculty under these conditions, such presbyters may validly and licitly absolve everywhere unless in a particular case the local ordinary refuses to permit this; they have this faculty from the law, i.e., from canon 967, §2.

A local ordinary may not, in contravention of the common law, refuse to permit all priests from other dioceses or priests in general to exercise the faculty, as granted here, but for cause (not specified in the canon) he may deny it to an individual priest or on an individual occasion. Thus the presbyters enumerated in paragraph two have a status parallel to that of bishops mentioned in paragraph one: the presumption always favors the right of the minister, who possesses the faculty according to the terms described here, to exercise it everywhere.

The pastoral and practical advantages of this broadening of the discipline are evident, and the concession is related to recent, limited developments: for the convenience of penitents and ministers alike, some bishops had agreed to concede confessional faculties to all the priests of the same province or region who had the faculty within their own particular church. An underlying reason for such concessions, including the one made in the canon, is a more authentic recognition of the communion of local or particular churches.

Nothing is said expressly in paragraph two concerning the validity of sacramental absolution by a priest who has been denied the right to exercise his faculty by a local ordinary. According to the principle set down in canon 10, an express determination of the law is needed to render an act invalid, and thus the priest in these circumstances would appear to act validly but illicitly. Nevertheless canon 974, §2–3, to which reference is made, equates this denial or refusal by the local ordinary with the revocation of the faculty. It is stated in canon 974, §2 that the priest whose faculty is revoked by a local ordinary (other than the ordinary of his place of incardination or domicile) loses the faculty but only in the territory of the revoking ordinary. As paragraph two of canon 967 indicates, its terms must be understood in conjunction with the later canon, both as to loss of the faculty (c. 974, §2) and the notification of the priest's own ordinary or superior (c. 974, §3). Moreover, a comparison with paragraph three of the present canon, to be discussed next, supports the position that the priest who is denied the faculty by a particular local ordinary absolves invalidly in the latter's territory.

The final paragraph of canon 967 extends a similar concession, by operation of the law, to confessors who are superiors or who have received the faculty from a competent superior of a religious institute or society of apostolic life, if it is a clerical institute of pontifical right or status. In this case, however, the faculty is limited to the absolution of penitents who are members of the institute or society or who live regularly ("day and night") in a house of the institute or society. As in paragraph two, the faculty may be exercised everywhere in respect to the penitents who are mentioned; it is exercised illicitly but validly if in a particular case the competent major superior denies the right to absolve.

A comparison of paragraphs two and three reveals that the cases are indeed analogous, but, according to the fundamental principle affecting confessional faculties, the concession within institutes and societies is restricted to the benefit of those penitents who are subject in some way—as members or as those living in religious or similar communities—to the authorities of the individual institute or society. More notably, in paragraph three it is clear that the absolution given in contravention to the will of a major superior is valid if illicit, whereas in paragraph two this more generous expression is not present.

Faculty from Office

Canon 968 — §1. In virtue of their office any local ordinary, canon penitentiary, as well as the pastor of a parish and those who take the place of the pastor of a parish possess the faculty to hear confessions within their jurisdiction.

§2. In virtue of their office superiors of a clerical religious institute or society of apostolic life of pontifical right who in accord with the norms of their constitutions possess executive power of governance enjoy the faculty to hear the confessions of their subjects and others staying in the religious house day and night, with due regard for the prescription of can. 630, §4.

As the preceding canon indicates in general those who have the faculty to absolve from the law, this canon determines those who have the faculty, again from the law, in virtue of an office which they hold.

The enumeration in paragraph one includes the local ordinaries named in canon 134, §1-2 (over and above bishops, already covered by c. 967, §1) for the particular church as defined in canon 368; the canon penitentiary of canon 508, again for the particular church; and the pastor and those who take the place of a pastor, as determined in the canons of Book II, title III, chapter VI (cc. 515-552), for the parish or quasi-parish. Since the officeholders so indicated have the faculty to absolve from the law on a habitual basis, they possess it elsewhere and indeed everywhere in accord with canon 967, §2.

In paragraph two a similar determination is made in favor of superiors of clerical religious institutes and societies of apostolic life of pontifical right, but it is limited to the celebration of the sacrament for the members and those who live regularly in their religious houses. Again, canon 967, §3 provides that the superiors in question have the same faculty throughout the institute or society. (Superiors are reminded, however, that canon 630, §4 prohibits them from hearing confessions of the members subject to their authority "unless the latter request it of their own initiative.")

Faculty from Concession

Canon 969 — §1. The local ordinary alone is competent to confer upon any presbyters whatsoever the faculty to hear the confessions of any of the faithful; however, presbyters who are members of religious institutes should not use such a faculty without at least the presumed permission of their superior.

§2. The superior of a religious institute or of a society of apostolic life of pontifical right mentioned in can. 968, §2, is competent to confer on any presbyter whatsoever the faculty to hear the confessions of his subjects and others staying day and night in the house.

The two paragraphs of the present canon rest on the principle or rule already stated: the concession of the faculty (to those who do not have it in virtue of their office or by the operation of the law itself) depends upon a power residing in the grantor over those to whom or for whom the priest ministers the sacrament. Thus, although the faculty itself is no longer considered a governing or jurisdictional power, its concession to another demands (executive) power of governance[58]—ordinary or delegated—in the grantor, and this power in respect to the penitents rather than the minister.

In paragraph one the usual situation in the particular church is envisioned in which the diocesan bishop (or one equated in law to a diocesan bishop)[59] or other local ordinary grants the faculty. The terms or conditions under which this is to be done are determined in subsequent canons (especially cc. 970-973), and paragraph one requires only that, while they may possess the faculty by concession of the respective local ordinary, priests who are members of religious institutes should not use it without the permission of their own superior. This permission they may presume unless the contrary is established.

Although the language of canon 874, §1 of the 1917 Code, to which this canon corresponds, has been simplified, there is no restriction placed on the extent of the faculty; it is applicable for the benefit of all members of the faithful who fall within the authority of the grantor of the faculty. The required "special jurisdiction to hear, validly and licitly, the confessions of any women religious and novices whatsoever" of canon 876 of the former Code has simply been suppressed. Moreover, as already noted, once a priest receives the faculty from the local ordinary of his place of incardination or domicile on a habitual or regular basis, he possesses the faculty everywhere, in accord with canon 967, §2 and with the restriction mentioned there.

In paragraph two the same principle is applied to

[58] See cc. 135-144.
[59] C. 381, §2 collated with c. 368.

determine who, in addition to the local ordinary, may grant the faculty in the case of penitents who are (1) members of a religious institute or of a society of apostolic life of pontifical right or (2) persons, not members of the particular institute or society, who live in the house of the institute or society. The norm follows canon 875 of the 1917 Code, which spoke only of exempt clerical institutes but which also embraced, for obvious reasons of convenience, the case of persons who live "day and night" in a house of an institute or society. Canon 514, §1 of the former Code had explained this concept of dwelling in such a house as "by reason of service, education, hospitality, or illness," but this further explanation is not necessary. The period of one's stay in the house of an institute or society need not be protracted—a single day suffices—in order to render operative the terms of the canon by which the superior may grant the faculty or, in the usual situation, by which the priest who has received such a faculty from his superior may exercise it to minister to an individual.[60]

The common law does not limit the concession of this faculty to major superiors, as defined in canon 620, but the constitutions may do so, since by cross reference paragraph two incorporates the full terms of canon 968, §2: "superiors of a clerical religious institute or society of apostolic life of pontifical right who in accord with the norms of their constitutions possess executive power of governance." As in the parallel case of paragraph two of the present canon, once a priest—whether a member of the institute or society or not—receives the faculty, he possesses it throughout the institute or society, in accord with canon 967, §3 and with the restriction mentioned there.

Qualifications of Ministers

Canon 970 — The faculty to hear confessions is not to be granted to presbyters unless they are found to be qualified by means of an examination or their qualifications are evident from another source.

The 1917 Code required, as does the present canon, an examination of the applicant prior to the concession of the faculty. Canon 877, §1 of the former Code also added the possibility of omitting the examination in the case of a priest "whose theological doctrine they [the grantors of the faculty] consider established from other sources." In paragraph two (of *CIC* 877), the possibility of a later, new examination was raised if there were prudent doubt about the continuing qualifications of a confessor—even of a pastor or a canon penitentiary; this norm has been suppressed but might have some applicability in principle in cases of revocation or other

[60]Abbo-Hannan, I, 524.

cessation of the faculty, as treated in canons 974–975.

The form of examination, written or oral, is not prescribed, nor is its precise content (moral and sacramental theology, with some attention to the priest's pastoral capabilities). In addition to the requisite knowledge, the minister must of course satisfy the other expectations of the law, such as the discretion and prudence mentioned in canon 979, the integrity of character which confidentiality (cc. 983–984) demands, etc., along with a willingness to observe the canons and the liturgical law on the sacrament. On the other hand, in countries like the United States where it is usual that all priests be conceded the faculty upon ordination or upon undertaking any pastoral responsibility, without restriction as to the persons to be absolved or as to the occasions for the celebration of the sacrament, the evidence of qualification for presbyteral ordination may serve the same purpose as the examination referred to here. One should see canons 1050–1052, especially canon 1051 concerning the testimonial to and inquiry into an ordinand's doctrine, piety, morals, suitability, and state of physical and psychological health. In other circumstances it is for the local ordinary to determine the form of examination, if necessary, and the persons to conduct the examination (the office of synodal examiners of *CIC* 385–390, especially 389, §2, having been suppressed in the recodification); in the case of externs or religious he may be satisfied with the evidence of qualifications submitted by the respective ecclesiastical superiors.

Concession to Externs

Canon 971 — The local ordinary is not to grant the faculty to hear confessions habitually to a presbyter, even one who has a domicile or quasi-domicile in his jurisdiction, without first consulting with his ordinary, if possible.

The canon envisions the common situation in which the local ordinary confers the faculty upon priests incardinated elsewhere or upon priests who are members of religious institutes and societies of apostolic life. It does not demand that the priest have a domicile or quasi-domicile within the territory of the local ordinary—although it is only in the case of the concession to priests who do have a domicile in the grantor's territory that the terms of canon 967, §2 become operative. In the present canon consultation with the priest's own ordinary is required, if possible, before the concession of the faculty. Even if the priest's own ordinary advises against the grant, the local ordinary may concede the faculty, provided the other canons, and especially canon 970, are observed; in the case of a religious, however, although the local ordinary may grant the faculty, the priest should not use it "without at least the presumed permission" of his superior, in accord with canon 969, §1.

The norm of canon 874, §2 of the 1917 Code has been suppressed: on the one hand, it obliged local ordinaries not to give the faculty to religious who had not been formally presented by their own superior; on the other hand, it required local ordinaries not to deny the faculty, without grave cause, to religious thus presented.

Period of Concession

Canon 972 — The faculty to hear confessions can be granted by the competent authority mentioned in can. 969 for an indefinite or for a definite period of time.

The distinction between an indefinite and a definite period of time is different from the concept of a habitual or regular concession of the faculty in the following canon and in canon 967, §2. The grant of the faculty for an extended period of time, but still limited ("definite"), may be considered a habitual faculty, as of course is any concession for an indefinite period.

A limitation of time may be in relation to a specified period, for example, for a year or for a specified number of months; such a limitation may be more likely in the case of priests who are not incardinated in the diocese of the grantor or in the case of religious who serve during a protracted but not indefinite period in the diocese. Or the limitation of time may be in such terms as "for as long as you remain in the diocese." If no such limitation is expressed, the concession is presumed to be for an indefinite period, as is usual in the case of members of the diocesan presbyterate, whose incardination is permanent or indefinite.

In the 1917 Code a similar norm was included, but it spoke rather of a possible concession of the faculty "circumscribed by some definite limits," whether of time or penitents (*CIC* 878, §1). The exhortation of canon 878, §2 of the 1917 Code, that grantors of the faculty not impose excessive restrictions without reasonable cause, has been omitted as no longer necessary.

Concession in Writing

Canon 973 — The faculty to hear confessions habitually is to be granted in writing.

This canon represents a somewhat stricter norm than the corresponding canon 879, §1 of the former Code, which demanded only an express concession of the faculty whether in writing or orally ("for the valid hearing of confessions"). The revision makes a written grant obligatory if the faculty is to be habitual in character, but the requirement of a written concession is not for the validity of the faculty. The

canon is of course not retroactive in the case of those who have received the faculty by oral concession.

Canon 879, §2 of the 1917 Code, which prohibited any charging of a fee for the faculty, has been suppressed, but such a charge would be simoniacal.

Revocation and Cessation

Canon 974 — §1. The local ordinary as well as the competent superior is not to revoke the faculty to hear confessions habitually except for a serious cause.

§2. When the faculty to hear confessions is revoked by the local ordinary who granted it as mentioned in can. 967, §2, the presbyter loses that faculty everywhere; when this faculty is revoked by another local ordinary, the presbyter loses it only in the territory of the revoking ordinary.

§3. Any local ordinary who has revoked a presbyter's faculty to hear confessions is to inform the latter's own ordinary by reason of incardination or his competent superior in the case of a member of a religious institute.

§4. When the faculty to hear confessions is revoked by his own major superior, the presbyter loses the faculty to hear the confessions of the members of the institute everywhere; when the faculty is revoked by another competent superior, the presbyter loses it only as regards the subjects of the superior's jurisdiction.

Canon 975 — Besides by revocation, the faculty referred to in can. 967, §2 ceases by loss of office, excardination or loss of domicile.

The principal concern of these two canons is the possible revocation of the faculty for cause. Although not mentioned here, the faculty also ceases, as is evident, either upon loss of office, if in accord with canon 968 the minister possesses the faculty by reason of his office, or upon completion of the period, if in accord with canons 969–973 he possesses it by concession and the concession has been made for a definite period of time.

With regard to revocation for cause, canon 974, §1 is substantially the same as canon 880, §1 of the 1917 Code, although the former norm mentioned also the possibility of suspension of the faculty (i.e., suspension for a definite or indefinite period). The omission of language referring to suspension of the faculty removes any possible dispute about validity or invalidity of the exercise of a suspended faculty. In effect, "suspension" may now be equated with revocation; a subsequent concession of the faculty, after the reasons for revocation have ceased, may be treated as a new grant.

The grave cause for revocation includes such matters as the transgression of the norms of the subsequent canons on the proper conduct of the minister, if the transgression is serious, and the loss of the qualifications mentioned in canon 970.

Both paragraphs two and four of canon 974, the meaning of which is evident, are new norms made necessary by the introduction of the concession of the faculty by law in canon 967, §2 and §3 respectively. On the other hand, paragraph three of the canon simply imposes upon local ordinaries an obligation of notification should they, for grave cause, revoke the faculty of an extern or of a member of a religious institute. The prescriptions of canon 880, §§2–3 of the 1917 Code, concerning revocation or similar action in the case of a pastor, of the canon penitentiary, or of all the confessors of a religious house have been omitted as unnecessssary or otherwise covered; a proposed paragraph five of canon 974, on loss of the faculty because of deprivation of office and the like, was not introduced.[61]

Finally, canon 975 treats the specific case of canon 967, §2, in which ministers "can exercise the same faculty everywhere unless the local ordinary denies it in a particular case." If the ministers who enjoy this faculty habitually in virtue of office or by grant of the ordinary of the place of incardination or the place where they have a domicile lose that office, incardination, or domicile respectively, they also lose the faculty in other places. (The analogous case of canon 967, §3 is not mentioned in canon 975 because, in the situation in question, the loss of the faculty comes about by revocation, a matter specifically covered in canon 974, §4.)

Absolution in Danger of Death

Canon 976 — Even though he lacks the faculty to hear confessions, any priest validly and licitly absolves from any kind of censures and sins any penitent who is in danger of death, even if an approved priest is present.

As noted at the beginning of the commentary on this chapter, the second half of the norms, beginning with canon 976, deal with the exercise of the ministry by the priest who has the requisite faculty and with certain special cases and abuses.

Canon 976 is derived from canon 882 of the 1917 Code, from which it does not differ substantially. The absolution from the ecclesiastical sanction of censure in the internal forum of the sacrament of penance has been mentioned at the beginning of the commentary on this title; although it is distinct from the absolution of sins and in ordinary situations requires that the minister have a special faculty to remit a censure or censures, the present canon is all embracing: it attributes to every ordained priest the capacity to remit censures as well as to absolve from sins if a penitent is in danger of death.

As understood in other contexts,[62] the danger of death does not mean that the person is at the point of death or *in extremis*. As is evident, the final clause of canon 976 assures to the penitent in danger of death complete freedom in the choice of the available ministers of the sacrament. Finally, the revised canon has suppressed the norm that the absolution of an accomplice in these circumstances would be valid but illicit (*CIC* 884)[63] or that the penitent upon recovery would in certain circumstances be obliged to have further recourse (*CIC* 2252).

For the case of the penitent in danger of death seeking reconciliation from a minister who is not a Catholic, one should see canon 844, §2.

Absolution of an Accomplice

Canon 977 — The absolution of an accomplice in a sin against the sixth commandment of the Decalogue is invalid, except in danger of death.

As noted under the preceding canon, the norm of canon 977, while derived from canon 884 of the 1917 Code, no longer declares illicit the absolution of an accomplice who is in danger of death.[64] In all other cases it is both illicit and invalid for a priest to absolve an accomplice, female or male, from a sin against the sixth commandment in which he and the penitent have been accomplices. There is no further restriction under pain of invalidity of absolution, whatever may be the impropriety of the confessor's absolving an accomplice from other sins. The matter is treated in detail by moral and pastoral theologians.

Ministry of the Confessor

Canon 978 — §1. In hearing confessions the priest is to remember that he acts as a judge as well as a healer and is placed by God as the minister of divine justice as well as of mercy, concerned with the divine honor and the salvation of souls.

§2. In the administration of the sacrament, the confessor, as a minister of the Church, is to adhere faithfully to the doctrine of the magisterium and the norms enacted by competent authority.

Canon 979 — The priest in posing questions is to proceed with prudence and discretion, with attention to the condition and age of the penitent, and he is to refrain from asking the name of an accomplice.

---

[61]*Comm* 10 (1978), 63.

[62]See c. 1004, §1.
[63]Benedict XIV, apconst *Sacramentum Poenitentiae,* June 1, 1741: Document III among the documents appended to the 1917 Code.
[64]Ibid.

Canon 980 — **If the confessor has no doubt about the disposition of a penitent who asks for absolution, absolution is not to be refused or delayed.**

The three canons quoted above form a unit to describe and direct the exercise of the ministry of reconciliation by priests.

Canon 978 corresponds verbatim to canon 888, §1 of the former Code, giving equal weight to the minister's role as judge and as healer. The *Roman Ritual* enlarges upon the conduct of the minister, placing the judgmental role in a somewhat secondary position:

In order that he may fulfill his ministry properly and faithfully, understand the disorders of souls and apply the appropriate remedies to them, and act as a wise judge, the confessor must acquire the needed knowledge and prudence by constant study under the guidance of the Church's magisterium and especially by praying fervently to God. For the discernment of spirits is indeed a deep knowledge of God's working in the human heart, a gift of the Spirit, and an effect of charity. . . .

By receiving repentant sinners and leading them to the light of the truth, the confessor fulfills a paternal function: he reveals the heart of the Father and reflects the image of Christ the Good Shepherd. He should keep in mind that he has been entrusted with the ministry of Christ, who accomplished the saving work of human redemption by mercy and by his power is present in the sacraments.[65]

An earlier version of a revised canon 888, §1 of the former law was replaced during the process of codification by a return to the 1917 Code, as noted above. At the same time paragraph two was added; it is without direct precedent in the 1917 Code but reflects the text of the ritual.[66]

In paragraph two of canon 978, the magisterium referred to is presumed to be the official or episcopal magisterium, as exercised by the pope and the other bishops, singly or together, in ordinary or more solemn mode. In some sense the concern for orthodox doctrine, especially as regards moral teaching, in the context of sacramental confession and ministerial counsel differs from the concern for orthodoxy in preaching, catechesis, or other teaching. On the occasion of the sacrament of penance, and specifically on the occasion of auricular confession, there is a special importance to avoiding any disturbance of the penitent's conscience by the aberrant opinions of the minister, whether these are rigid or lax. The mention of the norms issued by authority refers to the juridical norms emanating, for example, from the diocesan bishop or the conference of bishops or found in the common law.

The second of the three canons is derived from, and is a simpler version of, canon 888, §2 of the 1917 Code: The priest "is to avoid entirely any inquiry concerning the name of the [penitent's] accomplice, pressing anyone with prying or useless questions, above all those concerned with the sixth commandment, and especially imprudent questions addressed to young persons about matters of which they are ignorant." Though stated more briefly, the intent of the norm and exhortation in canon 979 remains the same as before.

Although inquiry in the course of sacramental confession about the identity of an accomplice was not uncommon in some places during the eighteenth century, it could easily lead to violation of confidentiality, as demanded in canons 983–984, and was therefore condemned as a serious abuse on the part of confessors.[67]

Finally, canon 980 repeats, with only formal changes of language, the injunction of canon 886 of the former Code. The presumption is that the penitent has confessed his or her sins in good faith and has the requisite disposition. This does not restrict the judgmental authority of the minister in the case of the penitent who refuses to expresss sorrow or resolution of amendment of life. Even in these circumstances, however, the minister should exert every effort to move and assist the penitent to the proper dispositions, namely, a true conversion of life.

Penances or Acts of Satisfaction

Canon 981 — **The confessor is to enjoin salutary and suitable penances in keeping with the quality and number of the sins but with attention to the condition of the penitent; the penitent is obliged to perform the penances personally.**

The act of the penitent called satisfaction or, commonly, the "penance" was required to take place, in the older tradition and in the case of grave and public offenses, during the period between the act of confession and the later reconciliation and absolution. In the development of the sacrament the act came to be postponed until after the sacra-

---

[65]*RPenance* 10, a and c: *DOL* 3075; on the presence of Christ, see *SC* 7.
[66]*Comm* 10 (1978), 65–66.
[67]Among the sources of *CIC* 888, §2: Benedict XIV, ency *Suprema*, July 7, 1745; apconst *Ubi primum*, June 2, 1746; *Ad eradicandum*, Sept. 28, 1746; *Apostolici ministerii*, Dec. 9, 1749: *CIC Fontes* 360, 370, 373, 405, respectively. These documents and *Sacramentum Poenitentiae* (above, note 63) indicate the extreme seriousness of violations or potential violations of the discipline of this sacrament, and specifically of the sacramental seal.

mental absolution; instead the imposition of the act of satisfaction and its acceptance (i.e., the stated or implied will to fulfill the penance) suffices before sacramental reconciliation. The doctrine is expressed in the *Rite of Penance* of the *Roman Ritual:*

> True conversion is completed by expiation for the sins committed, by amendment of life, and also by rectifying injuries done. The kind and extent of the expiation must be suited to the personal condition of penitents so that they may restore the order they have upset and through the corresponding remedy be cured of the sickness from which they have suffered. Therefore, it is necessary that the act of penance really be a remedy for sin and a help to renewal of life. Thus penitents, "forgetting the things that are behind" (Phil 3:13), again become part of the mystery of salvation and press on to the things that are to come.[68]

Aside from the kind of restitution or reparation for the evil that has been directly done by the sinful act of the penitent, the choice of the act or satisfaction is left to the discretion of the minister (who may, according to circumstances, leave the further choice of a specific and appropriate act to the penitent). It may be a charitable or other virtuous action, prayer, or fasting, but its correspondence to the extent and character of the sins confessed and the particular capacity of the individual penitent must be judged by the confessor.

The present canon follows canon 887 of the former law with slight changes of language. In the 1917 Code there was explicit mention of the penitent's "willing acceptance" of the penance or act of satisfaction directed by the confessor. Although this has been suppressed, the refusal of the penitent to perform the proposed penance would, in the case of the confession of grave sins, be reason for the minister not to absolve. In both former and revised law the mention of "suitable penances" and the "condition of the penitent" suggests that the confessor not excessively burden the penitent whose resolution seems weak or who is otherwise limited and, of course, the penitent who is sick or dying.

This whole matter is summed up and explained in the *Rite of Penance:*

> A penitent who has been the cause of harm or scandal to others is to be led by the priest to resolve to make due restitution.

Next, the priest imposes an act of penance or expiation on the penitent; this should serve not only as atonement for past sins but also as an aid to new life and an antidote for weakness. As far as possible, therefore, the penance should correspond to the seriousness and nature of the sins. This act of penance may suitably take the form of prayer, self-denial, and especially service to neighbor and works of mercy. These will underline the fact that sin and its forgiveness have a social aspect.[69]

False Denunciation of Confessors

Canon 982 — One who confesses the false denunciation of an innocent confessor to ecclesiastical authority concerning the crime of solicitation to sin against the sixth commandment of the Decalogue is not to be absolved unless that person has first formally retracted the false denunciation and is prepared to repair damages, if they have occurred.

Both the crime of solicitation, as here defined, and the false denunciation with which the canon is concerned are also the subject of canonical sanctions. The priest who is guilty of the crime of solicitation "in the act or on the occasion or under the pretext of confession" is to be punished in accord with canon 1387 (suspension, prohibitions, and deprivations in accord with the seriousness of the offense and, in more serious cases, dismissal from the clerical state). The penitent, female or male, who falsely accuses a confessor of this crime before ecclesiastical authority is punished, in accord with canon 1390, §1, with an interdict *latae sententiae* and, if a cleric, by suspension as well.

Canon 982, however, deals only with the absolution from sin of a penitent who has confessed having committed false denunciation. It is an instance in which the law requires that the act of satisfaction—here formal retraction of the denunciation before an ecclesiastical authority—must have taken place before the confessor may absolve; it is not necessary that other elements of damage to the falsely denounced confessor be repaired before absolution, but the penitent must declare himself or herself prepared to make such reparation.

Formerly the absolution from false denunciation was the only instance of an absolution from sin reserved by the common law to the Apostolic See, and canon 894 of the 1917 Code on this matter appeared in the now suppressed chapter on the reservation of sins. The reservation has ceased in virtue of the present canon and has been replaced by the stated condition for absolution.

A related canon of the 1917 Code, on the obligation of reporting an actual case of solicitation to the local ordinary or to the Apostolic See, has also been suppressed, and the relevant constitution of Bene-

---

[68] *RPenance* 8c: *DOL* 3071; see Trent, sess. XIV, *de poenitentia,* cap. 8: *COD* 708–709; Paul VI, apconst *Indulgentiarum doctrina,* Jan. 1, 1967, nn. 2–3: *AAS* 59 (1967), 5–24; *DOL* 3156–3157.

[69] *RPenance* 18: *DOL* 3083.

dict XIV, *Sacramentum Poenitentiae*,[70] which was incorporated in the canons as an appendix by reference in canon 904 of the former law, is no longer a part of the common law. These changes, however, do not alter the gravity or nature of the sin of solicitation or of false denunciation, as treated by moral theologians in the light of the teaching of Benedict XIV.

Confidentiality of Confession

Canon 983 — §1. The sacramental seal is inviolable; therefore, it is a crime for a confessor in any way to betray a penitent by word or in any other manner or for any reason.

§2. An interpreter, if there is one present, is also obliged to preserve the secret, and also all others to whom knowledge of sins from confession shall come in any way.

Canon 984 — §1. Even if every danger of revelation is excluded, a confessor is absolutely forbidden to use knowledge acquired from confession when it might harm the penitent.

§2. One who is placed in authority can in no way use for external governance knowledge about sins which he has received in confession at any time.

The two canons deal with distinct aspects of the confidentiality which the minister—and others who may obtain similar knowledge from the celebration of this sacrament—must maintain with regard to matters learned from the individual confession of sins by penitents. Canon 983 is concerned with any kind of betrayal of a penitent, whose confession of sins is said to be under or protected by an inviolable sacramental seal. Canon 984 is concerned with other use of knowledge obtained in the course of the individual celebration of the sacrament, even when there is no disclosure of a person's sins. The canons do not touch extra-sacramental confidentiality, to which the ordained minister is bound as is any recipient of confidences, but bound even more so when the relationship of the minister to the individual is analogous to that of a professional counselor.

Canon 983, §1, which gives a definition of the seal of the sacrament, is derived from canon 889, §1 of the former Code. There the identical obligation was expressed positively ("the confessor is to take care diligently lest he betray . . ."). In order to stress the gravity of the violation of the norm, without entering into the question of the gravity of the moral guilt which is left to moral theologians, the revised canon uses the strong word "nefas." Neither the canon nor earlier interpretations admit exceptions to the norm: this is the meaning of the expression "in any way . . . by word or in any other manner or for any reason." No distinction is made

among the matters confessed, whether the sinful action itself or attendant circumstances, or the acts of satisfaction or penances imposed, etc. The secrecy concerning the penitent and his or her confession of sins that is to be maintained is properly described as total.

In another context, that of ecclesiastical sanctions, without lessening the obligatory force of canon 983, §1, a distinction is made between direct and indirect violation of sacramental confidentiality. A direct violation, namely, one in which the penitent's identity is known or may readily become known (e.g., from the circumstances described or by implication) is punished by the *latae sententiae* excommunication of the minister, with remission of the penalty reserved to the Apostolic See, in accord with canon 1388, §1. The same canon states that an indirect violation of the seal, namely, when there is only some slighter possibility or danger that the penitent may be betrayed, "is to be punished in accord with the seriousness of the offense." Canon 983, §1 proscribes both direct and indirect violations of sacramental confidentiality.

The sacramental seal is referred to briefly but forcefully in the ritual: "Conscious that he has come to know the secret of another's conscience only because he is God's minister, the confessor is bound by the obligation of preserving the seal of confession absolutely unbroken."[71]

The obligation of the canon is not affected by a contrary disposition of civil law in jurisdictions where communications to an ordained minister, whether sacramental or extra-sacramental, are not considered privileged at law.

Since canon 990 permits penitents to confess their sins through interpreters, the latter are mentioned explicitly in paragraph two of canon 983, although the inviolability of the sacramental secrecy extends equally to all who, deliberately or indeliberately, accidentally or in any other way, come to a knowledge of sins from confession. Canon 889, §2 of the 1917 Code has been somewhat rephrased so that the obligation of confidentiality which persons other than the minister have is no longer called the sacramental seal.

In this case the canonical sanction differs from that incurred by the minister himself, as mentioned above. Other persons who betray a penitent "are to be punished with a just penalty, not excluding excommunication," in accord with canon 1388, §2.

In canon 984, the second of the two related canons, other use of knowledge gained from a penitent's confession of sins may be permitted—or, according to a more prudent judgment, tolerated—only if there is no danger of revelation (i.e., of the matters disclosed in the confession and the identity of the penitent) and if no harm will come to the penitent from the confessor's use of information.

[70]June 1, 1741; Doc. III of *CIC.*

[71]*RPenance* 10d: *DOL* 3075.

Any other use of such knowledge, even if it does not constitute a direct or indirect violation of the sacramental seal of canon 983, §1, is entirely prohibited by canon 984, §1.

The sense of paragraph one of canon 984 is that the confessor may come to the knowledge of various incidental information in the course of confessions. It may not be disclosed or even used in any way that may be detrimental to the penitent; an instance might be the use of such information in a way advantageous to the confessor, always excluding any hurt or disadvantage to the penitent. An older instruction of the Holy Office counseled against even references in preaching to matters learned in confession: although all danger of disclosure or injury might be absent, the broad confidence of penitents in the inviolability of the sacramental secrecy might be lessened.[72]

In paragraph two the prohibition against the use of knowledge about sins, as distinct from any other knowledge, is directed toward ecclesiastical authorities, lest they employ such knowledge, apart from any disclosure of sins, in external governance. As is evident from a reading of the text, the norm is applicable whether the action of the superior is to the advantage or disadvantage of the penitent.

In substance canon 984 follows canon 890 of the 1917 Code.

Restriction of Confessors

Canon 985 — A director of novices and his associate, the rector of a seminary or other institution of education are not to hear the sacramental confessions of their students living in the same house unless the students in particular cases spontaneously request it.

The purpose of the prohibition contained in the present canon is evident: to assure the freedom of penitents, in accord with canon 991, in the case of special relationships which might be intimidating to a penitent or create a needless burden for a penitent. Canon 985 does relax somewhat the norm of canon 891 of the former law, which it otherwise follows: the 1917 Code permitted the persons named in the canon to hear confessions only if requested "spontaneously, in particular cases, and for a grave and urgent cause." The third of these conditions has been suppressed. Canon 240, §2 deals with a related matter in the formation of ordained ministers.

Responsibility for Ministry

Canon 986 — §1. All to whom the care of souls is committted by reason of an office are obliged to provide that the confessions of the faithful entrusted to their care be heard when they reasonably ask

to be heard and that the opportunity be given to them to come to individual confession on days and hours set for their convenience.

§2. In urgent necessity any confessor is obliged to hear the confessions of the Christian faithful, and in danger of death any priest is so obliged.

The canon corresponds to canon 892 of the 1917 Code, except that a moral distinction of obligations, out of justice (*CIC* 892, §1) or out of charity (*CIC* 892, §2), has been omitted; the distinction is not a matter for canonical determination. In addition, paragraph one reflects a recent pastoral concern that generous opportunities for auricular confession be available. Thus there is new language in the text: "and that the opportunity be given to them [the faithful] to come to individual confession on days and hours set for their convenience."

A similar but briefer statement appears in the *Rite of Penance:* "The confessor should always show himself to be ready and willing to hear the confessions of the faithful whenever they reasonably request this."[73] More directly, the pastoral norms on general absolution of 1972 state: "To enable the faithful to fulfill without difficulty the obligation of individual confession, steps are to be taken to ensure that there are confessors available in places of worship on days and at times assigned for the convenience of the faithful."[74]

Although the practice of establishing fixed times for the celebration of individual reconciliation is required by paragraph one of the canon, this does not satisfy the obligation of those mentioned in paragraph one and, in urgent necessity, those mentioned in paragraph two, to hear the confessions of any of the faithful who reasonably seek this at times other than those established. On the other hand, the otherwise appropriate practice of scheduling appointments for individual confessions does not excuse from the requirement of the designated "days and hours set for their [the faithful's] convenience," for example, before Sundays and feasts and on penitential occasions. The scheduled times should not be during the Eucharistic celebration, and the following norms of the liturgical law are pertinent:

The reconciliation of penitents may be celebrated in all liturgical seasons and on any day. But it is right that the faithful be informed of the day and hours at which the priest is available for this ministry. They should be encouraged to approach the sacrament of penance at times when Mass is not being celebrated ["so that the administration of the sacrament may be unhurried and that people will not be impeded from active par-

---

[72]June 9, 1915: *ME* 29 (1917), 199–201.

[73]*RPenance* 10b: *DOL* 3075.
[74]N.IX: *DOL* 3047. See also n. XII: Priests "are to extol its ['devotional' confession's] great benefits for the Christian life and to make it clear that they are always ready to hear such confessions whenever the faithful request": *DOL* 3050.

ticipation in the Mass"] and preferably at the scheduled times.

Lent is the season most appropriate for celebrating the sacrament of penance. Already on Ash Wednesday the people of God hear the solemn invitation, "Turn away from sin and be faithful to the Gospel." It is therefore fitting to have several penitential services during Lent, so that all the faithful may have an opportunity to be reconciled with God and their neighbor and so be able to celebrate the paschal mystery in the Easter triduum with renewed hearts.[75]

CHAPTER III
THE PENITENT
[cc. 987–991]

Only five canons treat the member of the faithful who confesses his or her sins and seeks absolution: a single canon on the penitent's disposition (c. 987) is followed by two canons on the obligation to confess (cc. 988–989), a canon on the possibility of confessing with the intervention of an interpreter (c. 990), and a final canon on the penitent's freedom of choice in the selection of a minister (c. 991).

The canons correspond rather closely to the chapter of the 1917 Code (*CIC* 901–907) entitled, "The Subject of the Sacrament of Penance," with some omissions: (1) canon 902, which defined "sufficient but not necessary matter" for the sacrament, namely, mortal sins already confessed and venial sins—the definition remains accurate but is not needed canonically; (2) canon 904, as already noted in the commentary on canon 982, so that the canonical obligation to denounce a confessor guilty of the crime of solicitation in confession is now suppressed; and (3) canon 907, which stated that one could not satisfy the precept of confessing sins by a sacrilegious or voluntarily null confession.

As in the 1917 Code, these norms—aside from oblique references to general confession and absolution—are for the case of individual confession of sins. For norms affecting the penitent in the case of general absolution without prior specific confession of sins, one should see canons 961–963. The exposition of the *Roman Ritual,* over and above what is said about the penitential ministry of the whole Church (quoted at the beginning of the commentary on this title of the Code), may serve as introduction to the canons:

The parts that penitents themselves have in the celebration of the sacrament are of the greatest importance.

When with the proper dispositions they approach this saving remedy instituted by Christ and confess their sins, their own acts become part of the sacrament itself, which is completed when the words of absolution are spoken by the minister in the name of Christ.

In this way the faithful, even as they experience and proclaim the mercy of God in their own life, are with the priest celebrating the liturgy of the Church's self-renewal.[76]

In this connection, the revision of the rite of individual confession, as decreed by Vatican II in *Sacrosanctum Concilium* 72, embraces liturgical elements not found in the 1614 *Roman Ritual.* These directly affect the penitent and make the celebration a prayerful act of public worship as well as a healing source of grace for the penitent:

(1) A less formal welcome to the penitent has been introduced so that the priest may greet penitent Christians "with fraternal charity and, if need be, address them with friendly words." The sign of the cross is followed by some form of exhortation by the priest to the penitent to have confidence in God. Then "penitents who are unknown to the priest are advised to inform him of their state of life [for example, if they are ordained ministers, married persons, or religious], the time of their last confession, their difficulties in leading the Christian life, and anything that may help the confessor in the exercise of his ministry."[77]

(2) A brief reading of the word of God by the priest or the penitent is an optional part of the rite at this point: "For through the word of God Christians receive light to recognize their sins and are called to conversion and to confidence in God's mercy."[78]

(3) After the confession of sins and acceptance of penance, a distinct prayer for forgiveness, in the penitent's own words or in some set form of prayer, is singled out in the revised rite as a distinct ritual element: "Next, through a prayer for God's pardon the penitent expresses contrition and the resolution to begin a new life. It is advantageous for this prayer to be based on the words of Scripture."[79] For this reason examples or models of such a prayer are given in the *Rite of Penance.*[80]

---

[75]*RPenance* 13: *DOL* 3078; the words quoted in brackets are the explanation given in SCRit, instr *Eucharisticum Mysterium,* May 25, 1967: *AAS* 59 (1967), 539–573; n. 35: *DOL* 1264.

[76]*RPenance* 11: *DOL* 3076.
[77]*RPenance* 16: *DOL* 3081.
[78]*RPenance* 17: *DOL* 3082.
[79]*RPenance* 19: *DOL* 3084.
[80]*RPenance* 45, 85–92.

(4) After the form of absolution (explained above at the beginning of this commentary on the sacrament), accompanied by the ritual laying on of hands, the celebration concludes with a proclamation of praise by the minister and the penitent ("Give thanks to the Lord, for he is good." R. "His mercy endures for ever.") and a liturgical dismissal. Finally, "the penitent continues the conversion thus begun and expresses it by a life renewed according to the Gospel and more and more steeped in the love of God, for 'love covers a multitude of sins' (1 Pt 4:8)."[81]

Because the sacrament of penance, as a liturgical celebration, involves priest and penitent in a dialogue, the canons on the penitent have to be understood in the context of the preceding chapter on the minister. In that chapter, for example, the minister's imposition of an act of penance or satisfaction, in accord with canon 981, must be understood as coupled with the penitent's acceptance of this act and resolution to carry it out.

Disposition of the Penitent

Canon 987 — In order to receive the salvific remedy of the sacrament of penance, the Christian faithful ought to be so disposed that, having repudiated the sins committed and having a purpose of amendment, they are converted to God.

As is evident, the canon, which was newly redacted for the codification, can only sum up the requisite conditions of disposition that the penitent must have. Under the consideration of the parts of the sacrament prior to the ecclesial act of absolution and reconciliation, the ritual enlarges upon the requisite elements—both of spiritual disposition and of submission to the Church's ministry:

The most important act of the penitent is contrition, which is "heartfelt sorrow and aversion for the sin committed along with the intention of sinning no more."[82] "We can only approach the Kingdom of Christ by *metanoia*. This is a profound change of the whole person by which we begin to consider, judge, and arrange our life according to the holiness and love of God, made manifest in his Son in the last days and given to us in abundance" (see Heb 1:2; Col 1:19 and passim; Eph 1:23 and passim).[83] The genuineness of penance depends on this heartfelt contrition. For conversion should affect a person from within toward a progressively deeper enlightenment and an ever-closer likeness to Christ.

The sacrament of penance includes the confession of sins, which comes from true knowledge of self before God and from contrition for those sins. However, the inner examination of heart and the outward accusation must be made in the light of God's mercy. Confession requires on the penitent's part the will to open the heart to the minister of God and on the minister's part a spiritual judgment by which, acting in the person of Christ, he pronounces his decision of forgiveness or retention of sins in accord with the power of the keys.

True conversion is completed by expiation for the sins committed, by amendment of life, and also by rectifying injuries done. The kind and extent of this expiation must be suited to the personal condition of the penitents so that they may restore the order that they have upset and through the corresponding remedy be cured of the sickness from which they suffered [see c. 981]. Therefore, it is necessary that the act of penance really be a remedy for sin and a help to renewal of life. Thus penitents, "forgetting the things that are behind" (Phil 3:13), again become part of the mystery of salvation and press on to the things that are to come.[84]

Finally the ritual attempts to balance the more evident effects of the sacrament upon the penitent as an individual and the ecclesial significance referred to in canons 959–960:

Just as the wounds of sin are varied and multiple in the life of individuals and the community, so too the healing that penance provides is varied. Those who by grave sin have withdrawn from communion with God in love are called back in the sacrament of penance to the life they have lost. And those who, experiencing their weakness daily, fall into venial sins draw strength from a repeated celebration of penance to reach the full freedom of the children of God. . . .

In order that this sacrament of healing may truly achieve its purpose among the faithful, it must take root in their entire life and move them to more fervent service of God and neighbor.

The celebration of this sacrament is thus always an act in which the Church proclaims its faith, give thanks to God for the freedom with which Christ has made us free (see Gal 4:31), and offers its life as a spiritual sacrifice in praise of God's glory, as it hastens to meet the Lord Jesus.[85]

---

[81] *R Penance* 20 (*DOL* 3085), 47, 93.
[82] See Trent, sess. XIV, *de poenitentia*, cap. 4: *COD* 705.
[83] Paul VI, apconst *Paenitemini*, Feb. 17, 1966: *AAS* 58 (1966), 179; *DOL* 3017–3030.

[84] *R Penance* 6: *DOL* 3071.
[85] *R Penance* 7: *DOL* 3072.

Obligation of Penitent To Confess

Canon 988 — §1. A member of the Christian faithful is obliged to confess in kind and in number all serious sins committed after baptism and not yet directly remitted through the keys of the Church nor acknowledged in individual confession, of which one is conscious after diligent examination of conscience.

§2. It is to be recommended to the Christian faithful that venial sins also be confessed.

Canon 989 — After having attained the age of discretion, each of the faithful is bound by an obligation faithfully to confess serious sins at least once a year.

The first of these canons is derived from canons 901–902 of the 1917 Code, but with considerable reworking of the texts and, as already noted, without an explicit definition of "sufficient but not necessary matter" for the sacrament.[86]

In paragraph one of canon 988 the phrase "in kind and in number" has been added to the earlier text, in order to make explicit the obligation of the penitent to inform the minister of the nature and number of grave sins being confessed so that the minister may make his judgment with sufficient knowledge. The phrase in question replaces the norm of canon 901 of the 1917 Code, which required the penitent to "explain in confession the circumstances which may change the species of sin." Thus the penitent is not directly obliged to indicate in themselves the circumstances of the sins, provided that he or she expresses clearly the nature and kind of sin that is confessed.

The reference, unchanged from canon 902 of the former law, to sins "not yet directly remitted through the keys of the Church," i.e., through the power and ministry of the Church, indicates the precise nature of the confessional obligation. The divine forgiveness may indeed have taken place, and the contrition of the penitent may have been such that he or she has indeed been pardoned by God. Nevertheless the obligation remains to submit oneself to the power and ministry of the Church in the sacrament of reconciliation. Moreover, although grave sins forgotten in confession are indirectly remitted, the canon indicates that these must be confessed when remembered and thus be submitted for "direct remission." No judgment is made in the canon (or elsewhere in the law) whether such grave sins may be few or many; the distinction is at another level, namely, that grave sins committed after baptism must at some point be confessed. One should see the commentary on canon 960 for the recognition in the law that there may be a physical or moral impossibility which excuses from the obligation expressed in canon 988, §1.

Finally, the phrase "nor acknowledged in individual confession" has been added to the original language of canon 901 of the former Code to emphasize, in accord with canons 962, §1 and 963, that, despite the generic confession of sins before general sacramental absolution, the obligation of individually confessing grave sins remains—although they have been already remitted in the sacrament in the manner of general absolution.[87]

The norm of canon 988, §1 is expressed in the ritual in less juridic terms but to the same effect: "To obtain the saving remedy of the sacrament of penance, according to the plan of our merciful God, the faithful must confess to a priest each and every grave sin that they remember after a diligent examination of conscience."[88]

In accord with canon 916, those conscious of grave sin not yet confessed are not to celebrate Mass or receive Holy Communion "without prior sacramental confession unless a grave reason is present and there is no opportunity of confessing; in this case the person is to be mindful of the obligation to make an act of perfect contrition, including the intention of confessing as soon as possible."

It is not for the canon law to determine what sins, including transgressions of the ecclesiastical law itself, are grave, what sins are non-grave or venial.[89] A recent statement of the International Theological Commission is to the point:

Already in the parenesis and the practice of the early Christian communities distinctions were made:

a. sins which exclude from the Kingdom of God, such as leading an immoral life, idolatry, adultery, pederasty, avarice, and so on (cf. 1 Cor 6:9f.), and which also lead to exclusion from the community (cf. 1 Cor 5:1–13);

b. the so-called daily sins (*peccata quotidiana*).

The fundamental difference between grave and non-grave sins is taught by the entire tradition of the Church, even if important differences in terminology [e.g., grave, mortal, lethal, etc.] and in the appraisal of individual sins occur.[90]

A careful distinction is drawn between the two paragraphs of canon 988. Any obligation to confess

---

[86]See *Comm* 10 (1978), 70–71.

[87]Ibid.

[88]*RPenance* 7a: *DOL* 3072; see Trent, sess. XIV, *de poenitentia*, cc. 7–8: *COD* 712.

[89]See *Rel,* 234.

[90]Report, 1983, C, III, 2: *Origins* 13 (1984), 523; see also, on the canonical avoidance of distinctions between "grave" and "mortal" sins, *Comm* 10 (1978), 70.

is limited to grave sins, in accord with paragraph one. In paragraph two there is a recommendation that venial sins (and, as is understood, grave sins that have already been directly remitted) be confessed, either in so-called confessions of devotion or in connection with the confession of a grave sin.

The *Rite of Penance* enlarges upon this recommendation:

> ... The frequent and careful celebration of this sacrament is also very useful as a remedy for venial sins. This is not a mere ritual repetition or psychological exercise, but a serious striving to perfect the grace of baptism so that, as we bear in our body the death of Jesus Christ, his life may be seen in us ever more clearly [see 2 Cor 4:10]. In confession of this kind, penitents who accuse themselves of venial faults should try to be more closely conformed to Christ and to follow the voice of the Spirit more attentively. ... [91]

It is in accord with this understanding of the sacrament, as remedy for sins both grave and lesser, that penitents are encouraged to repeat at least generically the confession of past venial (or even grave) sins and to follow on occasion the practice of a general confession, in the sense of the confession of the sins of one's life or of an extended period of one's life.

The forgiveness of venial sins may of course be sought and obtained in many non-sacramental ways, aside from the Eucharist or penance, through both individual and communal acts, none of which is excluded by the exhortation of the canon. The recommendation of paragraph two of canon 988, however, is based upon an understanding of the altogether distinct (and superior) nature of sacramental reconciliation with God and the Church, a special appreciation of the doctrine of sacramental grace, and the teaching of Vatican II. In another context, while praising extra-liturgical communal and individual acts of devotions, the Council asserted that the liturgy (above all, the Eucharist and the other sacraments) "by its very nature far surpasses any of them."[92] Similarly, without denigrating any of the means or occasions of divine forgiveness, the canon urges the celebration of the sacrament of penance even in the case of the confession of venial sins only.

For related norms concerning ordained ministers, one should see canon 276, §2, 5°; concerning students for the ordained ministry, one should see canon 246, §4; concerning religious, one should see canon 664; concerning members of secular institutes, one should see canon 719, §3. Also related to canon 988 is the reference in canon 915 to sacramental confession preceding the first Communion

of children who have reached the use of reason. If the child is conscious of grave sin, he or she is bound by canon 988, §1 (and c. 916); otherwise the reference in canon 915 may be understood in the light of canon 988, §2.

Canon 989 specifies the time when the obligation of canon 988, §1 is to be fulfilled, without suggesting that it is desirable to postpone the confession of a grave sin for a period of an entire year. The canon is rephrased from canon 906 of the 1917 Code, itself based upon the norm introduced by the Fourth Lateran Council in 1215.[93] The former norm was somewhat more specific, defining the age of discretion in terms of attaining the use of reason; in effect, the obligation begins when one becomes capable of committing grave sin. Should one then commit a grave sin, the canon requires that he or she confess at least within a year. The failure of canon 906 of the former Code (and the earlier law) to make clear that the obligation of annual confession is applicable only in the case of grave sins has now been remedied.[94]

Confession through an Interpreter

Canon 990 — No one is prohibited from confessing through an interpreter, avoiding abuses and scandals; the prescription of can. 983, §2 is to be observed.

The canon, which is in substance the same as canon 903 of the 1917 Code, permits, but does not require, that a penitent make use of the service of an interpreter if the minister, for example, does not know the penitent's language. The former norm had made this point explicitly: "if penitents wish, they are not prohibited ... ," but the choice still remains that of the penitent. The cross reference to canon 983, §2 is concerned with the obligation of secrecy incurred by an interpreter.

Freedom To Choose a Confessor

Canon 991 — The Christian faithful are free to confess to a legitimately approved confessor of their choice, even one of another rite.

The final canon of the chapter, which follows canon 905 of the 1917 Code, articulates and assures a right of the Christian believer to a free choice of a confessor or, put negatively, not to be obliged to confess to a confessor designated by an ecclesiastical superior and not to be coerced in any way in the

---

[91] *RPenance* 7b: *DOL* 3072.
[92] *SC* 13.

[93] Const. 21: *COD* 245: "Each member of the faithful, of both sexes, after he or she has reached the years of discretion, is to confess individually [*solus*] all his or her sins at least once a year. ..."
[94] See *RPenance* 34: *DOL* 3099, where the mention of annual confession is also referred explicitly to "all those grave sins not hitherto confessed one by one."

choice of a minister of individual confession. One should see canon 240, §1 for an application of this norm to seminaries.

Since in this matter there is no distinction of rites, one bound by the Code of Canon Law for the Latin Church may celebrate the sacrament with a minister of any of the Eastern Churches. It was proposed that the canon should speak only of a legitimately approved confessor of another Catholic rite.[95] Such a qualification of the text was unnecessary since the question is adequately covered by canon 844, §2.

CHAPTER IV
INDULGENCES
[cc. 992–997]

The six canons of this chapter remain from a major simplification of the former discipline on indulgences, which was found in canons 911–936 of the 1917 Code. This simplification was mostly achieved, however, by the exclusion of other norms, which are still in force, from the codification. The revised canonical discipline of the institute of indulgences—found principally in the apostolic constitution *Indulgentiarum doctrina* of 1967[96] and the norms of the *Enchiridion indulgentiarum* of 1968[97]—is still in effect for the Latin Church. (The Eastern Churches do not have a corresponding institute in their tradition, but those churches in full communion with the Roman See may have adopted, under Latin influence, a parallel devotional discipline.) Thus the few canons on the subject remaining in the revised Code are simply the basic norms on this subject: (1) definitions of indulgences (cc. 992–993); (2) applicability of indulgences (c. 994); (3) right to grant indulgences (c. 995); (4) capacity to gain indulgences (c. 996); and (5) canonical prescriptions outside the Code (c. 997).

The chapter on indulgences appears within the title on the sacrament of penance because of their historical development in the medieval period as a parallel to the remission of canonical penances and with some relationship to sacramental reconciliation. Because of both controversy and abuse, however, indulgences are now carefully and absolutely distinguished from sacramental reconciliation itself and from the forgiveness of sins: while the act of piety or prayer to which an indulgence is attached may indeed be an act of reconciliation with God and the Church, an indulgence, in the refined doctrine elaborated in late medieval and modern times, is understood as a remission of temporal or purgatorial punishment still due *after* the forgiveness of sins. For this reason the definitions of indulgences

speak of remission of punishment for sins already forgiven insofar as culpability or guilt is concerned; the indulgence itself is not a remission or absolution of sin.

A month before the conclusion of Vatican II in 1965, at two meetings the conciliar Fathers heard reports from the conferences of bishops on a document about indulgences that had been drawn up by the Apostolic Penitentiary.[98] This draft was not intended for conciliar debate or action but only as a means of general consultation in preparation for a papal document on the subject. The reactions of the bishops to the proposed simplification of the canonical discipline were mixed, and the apostolic constitution of Paul VI which appeared at the beginning of 1967 included a doctrinal and historical exposition preceding its twenty norms in order to introduce changes "that are suited to the times and take into account the wishes of the conferences of bishops."[99] The norms, which otherwise left intact canons 911–936 of the 1917 Code, were summarized as

> concerned mainly with three points: to fix a new measure for partial indulgences [in place of the ancient measure in days and years]; to lessen the number of plenary indulgences; to reduce and organize into a simpler and worthier form the matters related to indulgences attached to objects and places ("real and local" indulgences).[100]

A rationale for limiting the number of plenary indulgences was given by the pope: " . . . the usual receives scant attention; the plentiful is not highly valued. Also many of the faithful need time sufficient for a right preparation to gain a plenary indulgence." Similarly, the suppression of the very terms, "real" and "local" indulgences, was explained as making it clear "that the Christian's acts are the subject of indulgences, not things and places; these are merely the occasions for gaining indulgences."[101] "An [indulgenced] act sometimes has a connection with a particular object or place."[102]

These steps to elevate the doctrine and practice of gaining indulgences to a spiritual and religiously virtuous plane, while eliminating the apparently mechanistic or quantitative elements, were carried forward in the 1968 publication of a radically reduced collection or enchiridion of indulgences (once called a *raccolta*) by the Apostolic Penitentiary.[103] This collection of indulgenced acts and prayers was prefaced by thirty-six norms, embracing both the papal norms of the preceding year and a revision of the remainder of canons 911–936 of

[95]*Rel,* 234.

[96]Paul VI, apconst, Jan. 1, 1969: *AAS* 59 (1967), 5–24; *DOL* 3155–3187.

[97]Apostolic Penitentiary, June 29, 1968 (Vatican Polyglot Press, 1968): *DOL* 3193–3228.

[98]*AcSynVat* 4, 6: 131–197, 292–307, 315–335.

[99]*ID* 12: *DOL* 3166.

[100]Ibid.

[101]Ibid.

[102]*ID,* norm 12: *DOL* 3178; *EI* 7: *DOL* 3199.

[103]See note 97, above.

the 1917 Code. The norms of the 1968 enchiridion remain in force, as will be mentioned again in the commentary on canon 997.

Of specific historical interest are the suppression of the so-called *toties quoties* plenary indulgences,[104] understood as available with unlimited frequency, and the suppression of the so-called privileged altar, to which plenary indulgences for the dead were attached on the occasion of Eucharistic celebrations. The privileged altar had been defined in canons 916–918 of the former Code. Instead, "Like a devoted mother, the Church in its special concern for the faithful departed establishes that in every sacrifice of the Mass suffrages are most lavishly offered on behalf of the dead; any privilege in this matter is suppressed."[105]

Definitions of Indulgences

Canon 992 — An indulgence is a remission before God of the temporal punishment for sin the guilt of which is already forgiven, which a properly disposed member of the Christian faithful obtains under certain and definite conditions with the help of the Church which, as the minister of redemption, dispenses and applies authoritatively the treasury of the satisfactions of Christ and the saints.

Canon 993 — An indulgence is partial or plenary in as far as it frees from the temporal punishment due to sin either partly or totally.

The first of these canons gives a definition from Paul VI's constitution on indulgences. It follows canon 911 of the 1917 Code: "All shall hold in high esteem indulgences or remission before God of the temporal punishment due to sins, whose guilt has already been removed. This remission is granted by the ecclesiastical authority from the treasury of the Church, for the living by way of absolution [of penalty or punishment], for the dead by way of suffrage." The text is now more carefully nuanced to summarize the doctrinal exposition in the 1967 apostolic constitution, which offers the following statement of the Church's purpose in this institute:

An indulgence has certain features in common with other methods and means of taking away the remnants of sin, but at the same time is clearly distinct from the others.

This means that in the case of an indulgence the Church, using its power as minister of Christ the Lord's redemption, not only offers prayers, but authoritatively dispenses to the faithful rightly disposed the treasury of expiatory works of

Christ and the saints for the remission of temporal punishment.

The purpose intended by ecclesiastical authority in granting indulgences is not only to help the faithful to pay the penalties due to sin, but also to cause them to perform works of devotion, repentance, and charity—especially works that contribute to the growth of faith and the good of the community.[106]

Although not expressed in the canon, the underlying doctrine on indulgences, so often articulated almost exclusively in terms of the authoritative intervention of church authority, is equally or more significantly one of the communion of saints:

The life of each of God's children is in Christ and through Christ conjoined with the life of all other Christians. . . .

This is the basis of the "treasury of the Church." The treasury of the Church is not to be likened to a centuries-old accumulation of wealth. It means rather the limitless and inexhaustible value that the expiation and merits offered by Christ have in the eyes of God for the liberation of all humanity from sin and for the creation of communion with the Father. . . . Added to this treasure is also the vast, incalculable, ever increasing value in God's eyes of the prayers and good works of the Blessed Virgin Mary and the saints. . . .

The union between those who are still pilgrims and their brothers and sisters who have died in the peace of Christ is therefore not broken, but rather strengthened by a communion in spiritual blessings. . . . [107]

Canon 993, also derived directly from the papal document,[108] radically changes the measure of indulgences, formerly related to the period of days or years (or, until recent times, the "quarantines" or Lenten periods) of canonical penances or indeed a specified period of punishment in purgatory. On the contrary, the partial character of most indulgences is now defined indefinitely, i.e., simply as less than full or plenary indulgence or remission of temporal punishment. A further authoritative elaboration of this concept is as follows: "Any of the faithful who, being at least inwardly contrite, perform a work carrying with it a partial indulgence, receive through the Church the remission of temporal punishment equivalent to what their own act already receives."[109] In this language there is an effort to

---

[104]*ID*, norm 19: *DOL* 3185; *EI* 30: *DOL* 3222.
[105]*ID*, norm 20: *DOL* 3186; *EI* 21: *DOL* 3213.

[106]*ID* 8: *DOL* 3162.
[107]*ID* 5: *DOL* 3159.
[108]*ID*, norm 2: *DOL* 3168; *EI* 2: *DOL* 3194.
[109]*ID*, norm 5: *DOL* 3171; *EI* 6: *DOL* 3198.

maintain fully the medieval and traditional doctrine of remission of punishment but to relate it directly to the goodness of the act or work for which the indulgence is conceded.

The requisite conditions are stated more forcefully in the current law with regard to the plenary indulgence, which except in the case of persons on the verge of death may be gained only once on any single day. These conditions attempt to avoid any mere multiplication of acts or, as it were, frequent and repeated "total remissions of temporal punishment":

The requirements for gaining a plenary indulgence are the performance of the indulgenced work and the fulfillment of three conditions: sacramental confession; eucharistic communion; prayer for the pope's intentions. A further requirement is the exclusion of all attachment to sin, even venial sin.

Unless this unqualified disposition and the three conditions are present, the indulgence will be only partial. . . .

Several plenary indulgences [on different days] may be gained on the basis of a single sacramental confession; only one may be gained, however, on the basis of a single communion and prayer for the pope's intention.

The condition requiring prayer for the pope's intentions is completely satisfied by reciting once the Our Father and Hail Mary for his intentions; nevertheless all of the faithful have the option of reciting any other prayer suited to their own devotion and their reverence for the pope.[110]

Applicability of Indulgences

Canon 994 — The faithful can gain partial or plenary indulgences for themselves or apply them for the dead by way of suffrage.

The text of the canon needs no interpretation; it follows the norm of canon 930 of the 1917 Code. The concept of applying indulgences for the dead was explained by Paul VI: "The faithful who apply indulgences as suffrages for the dead are practicing charity in a superior way and with their thoughts on the things of heaven are dealing more virtuously with the things of earth."[111]

The traditional reference to indulgences for the dead as granted only by way of suffrage, prayer, or petition indicates that the Church asserts no power of authoritative declaration concerning the extent of purgatorial punishment of those who have already died.

A corollary of this canon is that "no one gaining an indulgence may apply it to other living people."[112]

Right To Grant Indulgences

Canon 995 — §1. Besides the supreme authority of the Church, only those can grant indulgences to whom this power has been given by the law or granted by the Roman Pontiff.

§2. No authority beneath the Roman Pontiff can commit to others the power to grant indulgences unless it was expressly given to him by the Apostolic See.

Since the 1967 norms of Paul VI on indulgences did not suppress all the canons of the 1917 Code on the subject, it was only in the following year that canons 911–924 of the former Code (which treated the concession of indulgences and constituted article I of the chapter on indulgences in the 1917 Code) were revised.

The general reference in paragraph one of the present canon has to be enlarged by listing those now permitted by the law to grant indulgences:

Diocesan bishops and their equivalents in law possess from the outset of their pastoral office the right to:

§1. grant partial indulgences to persons or in the places subject to their jurisdiction;

§2. bestow the papal blessing with a plenary indulgence, using the prescribed formulary, three times a year on solemn feasts that they will designate, even if they only assist at the solemn Mass.

Metropolitans may grant partial indulgences in their suffragan dioceses just as in their own.

Patriarchs may grant partial indulgences in every place, even those exempt, of their patriarchate, in churches of their own rite outside the boundaries of their patriarchate, and everywhere in the world in favor of their own people. Archbishops major [of the Eastern Churches] have the same power.

Cardinals possess the power to grant partial indulgences in every place or institution and in favor of those persons subject to their jurisdiction or protection. They may do so elsewhere, but only regarding indulgences to be gained by the people present on each occasion.[113]

---

[110]*ID*, norms 7, 9, 10: *DOL* 3173, 3175, 3176; *EI* 26, 28, 29: *DOL* 3218, 3220, 3221.
[111]*ID* 8: *DOL* 3162.

[112]*EI* 3: *DOL* 3195.
[113]*EI* 11–14: *DOL* 3203–3206.

Capacity To Gain Indulgences

Canon 996 — §1. In order that one be capable of gaining indulgences one must be baptized and not excommunicated and in the state of grace at least at the completion of the prescribed works.

§2. In order that one be a capable subject for gaining indulgences one must have at least the intention of receiving them and fulfill the enjoined works at the stated time in due fashion, according to the tenor of the grant.

This canon states the fundamental requisites in the person who is desirous of gaining a plenary or partial indulgence; it replaces canons 925–936 of the 1917 Code, with the understanding that the 1968 norms on the subject also remain in effect. According to paragraph one, catechumens may not gain indulgences.[114] It has been usual to commend to the faithful that they have a general intention of gaining indulgences in order to satisfy paragraph two of this canon.

These qualifications are in addition to those dispositions mentioned above in the commentary on canon 993.

Special Laws on Indulgences

Canon 997 — In regard to the granting and use of indulgences other prescriptions contained in the particular laws of the Church must be also observed.

Earlier redactions of this canon referred to the 1968 *Enchiridion indulgentiarum* by name, but this reference was too particularized.[115] There is a certain parallel between this canon and canon 2, since it incorporates by reference extra-codal norms on indulgences as canon 2 affirms the canonical force of extra-codal laws on liturgical celebration.

As already noted, the principal current, universal law on indulgences was established by Paul VI's 1967 constitution. With the exception of some interim provisions, however, the twenty norms of Paul VI were included among the thirty-six norms of the enchiridion. With regard to the latter, it should be pointed out that, aside from the reform of the canonical discipline of indulgences, the collection itself was radically changed. This was done principally by a major reduction in the number of indulgenced works and prayers. There are now some seventy such indulgences, a few of which are attached to good works in broad terms, for example, to acts of charity for those in need; the majority of the listed indulgences are attached to traditional and devotional prayers.

The following are the principal norms of the enchiridion, not mentioned already and not touched directly by the canons, which remain in effect in virtue of canon 997:

15. §1. No book, booklet, or pamphlet listing indulgences granted is to be published without the permission of the local Ordinary or local [Eastern] Hierarch.

§2. The publication, in no matter what language, of an authentic collection of prayers and devotional works to which the Apostolic See has attached indulgences requires the express permission of the same Apostolic See. . . . [116]

32. An indulgence annexed to any prayer may be gained no matter what the language of recitation, provided the accuracy of the translation is supported by a declaration either of the Apostolic Penitentiary or of one of the Ordinaries or Hierarchs in the region where the language of the translation is in general use.[117]

From norm 32 it is clear that devotional prayers, even if they carry indulgences, are carefully distinguished from liturgical prayers and other liturgical texts in the vernacular, for which the approbation is conceded solely by the respective conference of bishops for the churches of its territory, in accord with canon 838, §§2–3; such decrees of the conferences must be confirmed by the Apostolic See. On the contrary, any diocesan bishop or other (local) ordinary of a region where the language is one of those in general use may declare that a vernacular translation of an indulgenced prayer, originally in Latin or some other language, is accurate.

As far as English versions of indulgenced prayers are concerned, there are often several texts in legitimate use, texts which have been approved at different periods. Some are variants of traditional or archaic forms; others are in modernized form or in new and contemporary translation. No uniformity of such devotional prayers is required, although on occasion liturgical texts will have indulgences attached for devotional use; in such cases the texts will already have a single official version for a given territory, with the canonical approbation and confirmation referred to above.

A new translation of the devotional prayers to which indulgences are attached has been provided for members of the conferences of bishops in countries where English is spoken. Prepared by the International Commission on English in the Liturgy, these alternatives to the (various) translations already in use are available for inclusion in devotional books, along with other contemporary trans-

---

[114]See c. 1170 on blessings for catechumens (and persons who are not Catholics).

[115]For a contrary opinion, see *Rel,* 235.

[116]*DOL* 3207.

[117]*DOL* 3224.

lations.[118] The publication of all such texts for the use of the church community is governed by canon 826, §3, which requires the permission of a local ordinary for the publication of "prayer books for the public or private use of the faithful." Such books (or booklets, pamphlets, leaflets, etc.; see c. 824, §2) ordinarily contain both indulgenced texts and other devotional material.

The other, related norm of the enchiridion quoted above (n. 15) is distinct from but in harmony with what has been said. In paragraph one of norm 15, books (or other publications) listing indulgences are required to have the permission of the local ordinary, just as is expected by canon 826,

§3 for books of prayers in general. In paragraph two of norm 15, however, any authentic collection of (all the) prayers and devotions to which the Apostolic See has attached indulgences requires express permission of that See, namely, a permission given by the Apostolic Penitentiary.[119] In effect, this refers to any integral and official version, in any language, of the *Enchiridion indulgentiarum* itself; it does not refer to the publication of the indulgenced prayers in other kinds of collections, listing of the indulgences or indulgenced prayers, publication of prayers or indulgences from sources other than the Apostolic See, etc., for all of which local ordinaries remain competent.

---

[118]*A Book of Prayers* (Washington: ICEL, 1982).

[119]*EI* 9: *DOL* 3201.

BIBLIOGRAPHY

Bibliographical material on the sacrament of penance is incorporated in the bibliography that can be found after the commentary on canon 1007.

TITLE V
THE SACRAMENT OF
THE ANOINTING OF THE SICK
[cc. 998–1007]

After an introductory canon, the remaining nine canons of this title treat in separate chapters the celebration of the sacrament of the anointing of the sick (cc. 999–1002), the minister of anointing (c. 1003), and those to be anointed (cc. 1004–1007).

Without entering into complex historical, liturgical, and theological questions concerning this sacrament, the conciliar Fathers of Vatican II in 1963 proposed to reform and strengthen its discipline as well as its ritual celebration:

"Extreme unction," which may also and more properly be called "anointing of the sick," is not a sacrament for those only who are at the point of death. Hence, as soon as any one of the faithful begins to be in danger of death from sickness or old age, the fitting time for that person to receive this sacrament has certainly already arrived.

In addition to the separate rites of the sick and for viaticum, a continuous rite shall be drawn up, structured so that the sick person is anointed after confessing and before receiving viaticum.

The number of anointings is to be adapted to the circumstances; the prayers that belong to the rite of anointing are to be so revised that they correspond to the varying conditions of the sick who receive the sacrament.[1]

Several distinct pastoral and doctrinal questions were addressed in this decree.

(1) The nature of the sacrament—a healing anointing of those seriously ill—had been compromised by the almost universal pastoral practice which treated it principally as the sacrament for the dying, principally or even exclusively for those whose death was imminent or almost certain. This in turn had diluted the significance of Eucharistic Viaticum as the sacrament of the dying; the name of extreme, final, or last anointing, and the inclusion of anointing among "last rites" had contribut-

ed to this confusion. On the Eucharist as Viaticum, one should see canons 921–922.

(2) The medieval practice and doctrine of anointing clearly distinguished sacramental from other anointings of the sick and also distinguished anointings of the sick by ordained ministers from anointings by lay persons, common in the earlier period. The close association of anointing with (final) penance helped in turn to create a requirement that the gravity or perilous situation of the sick person had to be certain or proved. Modern ecclesiastical documents which spoke to the contrary and permitted or encouraged a broader use of the sacrament, while recognizing the more common usage, were not widely accepted in church practice.[2] Prior to Vatican II, a certain recovery of much older traditions had been initiated, especially when particular rituals returned to the sequence of anointing before Viaticum.[3] (This is the "continuous rite" mentioned in *Sacrosanctum Concilium* 74, quoted above.) Such rituals accepted the fact that in very many circumstances the person to be anointed might be close to death or even at the point of death, but they moved in the direction of celebrating anointing as soon as the seriousness of the illness became evident.

(3) Although not directly touched in the conciliar constitution or in the canons, an underlying question is the relation of the sacrament, as understood in medieval and modern times, to the anointing described in the Letter to James: "Is there anyone sick among you? Let him send for the presbyters of the Church and let them pray over him, anointing him with oil in the name of the Lord. The prayer of faith will save the sick man and the Lord will raise him up. If he has committed any sins, they will be forgiven him."[4] Before the medieval period this text was very broadly understood in reference to various anointings, e.g., by Pope Innocent I (401–417): "There is no doubt that these words [of the Letter of James] are to be understood of the faithful who are sick, and who can be anointed with the holy oil of chrism, which has been prepared by

---

[1]*SC* 73–75. For a commentary on these articles, see F.R. McManus, "The Sacrament of Anointing: Some Ecumenical Considerations," in *Miscellanea Liturgica in onore di S. E. il Cardinale Giacomo Lercaro* II (Rome: Desclée, 1967), 809–840.

[2]This was true of papal letters which sought to encourage the celebration of the sacrament without any scruple over the perilous state of the sick person: Benedict XV, *Sodalitatem,* May 31, 1921: *AAS* 13 (1921), 345; Pius XI, *Explorata res,* Feb. 2, 1923: *AAS* 15 (1923), 105.

[3]E.g., *Collectio Rituum ad Instar Appendicis Ritualis Romani pro Omnibus Germaniae Dioecesibus* (Ratisbon: Pustet, 1950), 50–64; *Collectio Rituum ad Instar Appendicis Ritualis Romani pro Dioecesibus Statuum Foederatorum Americae Septentrionalis* (Milwaukee: The Bruce Publishing Co., 1954), 64–82.

[4]5:14–15.

the bishop, and which not only priests but all Christians may use for anointing, when their own needs or those of their family demand."[5]

The healing effect of this anointing is mentioned first in the biblical text, without primary reference to the conditional effect of the forgiveness of sins. Nevertheless the integral healing (physical and spiritual) and raising up by the Lord and indeed the relationship to sickness (physical healing) were relegated both in pastoral practice and in theory to a secondary place: emphasis was placed almost entirely upon spiritual healing of sin and final anointing for glory. This was in direct contradiction to the (ancient) prayers for anointing retained in the modern *Roman Ritual;* their lack of suitability, on the occasion when the person is not anointed until all human hope of survival is gone, is one of the reasons for the reform decreed in *Sacrosanctum Concilium* 73, quoted above.

(4) *The Constitution on the Sacred Liturgy* does no more than recover a simpler and older tradition. It deliberately leaves open, by its declaration that it is "certainly" and "already" time for the sacrament when the person "begins" to be in danger, the question whether a wider opening can legitimately develop. In this, the language of *Sacrosanctum Concilium* 71 does not propose or insinuate any trivialization of the sacrament or its indiscriminate celebration in cases of lesser or slight illness. In the period after Vatican II, however, papal and curial documents, to be mentioned under canon 1004, §1, entertained and supported a further development in full harmony with the conciliar decision.

The Roman rite for the sacrament of the anointing of the sick (simply called "the oil of the sick" in some Eastern rites) is given, in revised form, in the *Rite of Anointing and Pastoral Care of the Sick.* This section of the *Roman Ritual* not only deals with anointing and other elements of sacramental and pastoral ministry to the members of the Christian community who are sick but also includes rites for the sacrament for the dying, the Eucharist as Viaticum. The introduction (*praenotanda*) has an important treatment of sickness in relation to the paschal mystery of the death and resurrection of the Lord Jesus.[6]

For countries where English is spoken, the several conferences of bishops have approved, and the Apostolic See has confirmed, the liturgical book, *Pastoral Care of the Sick: Rites of Anointing and Viaticum.*[7] The title reflects both the breadth of the Latin edition, affecting the total ministry of the Church to its sick members, and the distinct significance of the two sacraments: (1) anointing for the sick who are not "dying" (but also for the sick who are close to death and could not be anointed earlier, at a more fitting time) and (2) Viaticum for the dying. A rearranged format, along with additional pastoral notes, supports more clearly the necessary distinctions made in the conciliar reform of the sacramental celebration of anointing of the sick.

[6]*RAnointing* (1972), nos. 1–7: *DOL* 3321–3327.
[7]This ritual is arranged, as mentioned earlier in this commentary, to include not only the section of the *Roman Ritual* cited in the preceding note but also excerpts from other rites, as appropriate. The Roman introduction (*praenotanda*) is included in its entirety, in accord with *SC* 63b, and is cited by the same numbers as the Latin text; since all editions but one published in several English-speaking countries follow both the text and the design (including pagination) prepared by ICEL, references to it can be made by page number.

[5]Ep. 25, 8: *PL* 20:559; trans. P. Palmer, *Sacraments and Forgiveness,* Sources of Christian Theology, vol. II (Westminster, Md.: Newman Press, 1959), 283.

Nature of Anointing

Canon 998 — The anointing of the sick by which the Church commends to the suffering and glorified Lord the faithful who are dangerously sick so that He relieve and save them, is conferred by anointing them with oil and using the words prescribed in the liturgical books.

Compared with the introductory canon on this sacrament in the 1917 Code (*CIC* 937), this text replaces the former name of the sacrament (final or extreme anointing or unction), adds a brief doctrinal exposition of the nature of the sacrament, and excises the specific mention of olive oil. The development is based upon the conciliar decree, *Sacrosanctum Concilium* 73, already quoted; the doctrinal language of the canon was used in the *Dogmatic Constitution on the Church* (1964):

> By the sacred anointing of the sick and the prayer of priests the entire Church commends the sick to the suffering and glorified Lord, asks that he lighten their suffering and save them (see Jas 5:14–15); the Church exhorts them, moreover, to contribute to the welfare of the whole people of God by associating themselves freely with Christ's passion and death (see Rom 8:17; Col 1:24; 2 Tm 2:11–12; 1 Pt 4:13).[8]

This conciliar text was quoted by Paul VI in the apostolic constitution on the revised rite of the sacrament of anointing, in which the required use of blessed olive oil was modified:

> Since olive oil, which has been prescribed until now for the valid celebration of the sacrament, is unobtainable or difficult to obtain in some parts of the world, we have decreed, at the request of a number of bishops, that from now on, according to circumstances, another kind of oil can also be used, provided it is derived from plants and is thus similar to olive oil.[9]

Parallel to the norm given in reference to the essential formula for other sacraments, canon 998 speaks of the words prescribed in the liturgical books. In this case the same apostolic constitution altered, for the Latin Church, the medieval form found in the *Roman Ritual* ("May the Lord forgive you by this holy anointing and his most loving mercy whatever sins you have committed by the use of your sight. . . . "): "We have thought fit to modify the sacramental form in such a way that, by reflecting the words of James, it may better express the effects of the sacrament."[10]

The revised form—the first clause of which is said by the minister while anointing the forehead of the sick person, the second while anointing the hands—is: "Through this holy anointing / may the Lord in his love and mercy help you / with the grace of the Holy Spirit. / R. Amen. May the Lord who frees you from sin / save you and raise you up. / R. Amen."[11] This is the integral formula referred to in canon 1000, §1 and replaces the formulas for the anointing of each of the senses.

CHAPTER I
THE CELEBRATION OF THE SACRAMENT
[cc. 999–1002]

This first chapter includes the determination of the minister of the blessing of oil for the sick (c. 999), a general canon on the rite of anointing (c. 1000), and norms affecting both the responsibility to see to the celebration of the sacrament (c. 1001) and the special case in which several or many sick persons are to be anointed together (c. 1002).

Blessing of Oil

Canon 999 — Besides a bishop those can bless the oil to be used in the anointing of the sick:
1° who are equivalent in law to a diocesan bishop;
2° in case of necessity, any priest but only in the celebration of the sacrament.

The canon speaks in terms of what is considered the usual situation: the use of oil blessed by the diocesan bishop at the annual Mass of the Chrism, celebrated ordinarily on Holy Thursday, in accord with the rite of the *Roman Pontifical.*[12]

Although there is a special significance to the use of oils blessed by the bishop who presides over the local church and is its principal moderator of liturgical celebration and discipline,[13] this canon does not exclude the possibility that another bishop may be deputed to bless the oils. The *Roman Ritual* adds that the minister of anointing "should make

---

[8]*LG* 11: *DOL* 141.
[9]*Sacram Unctionem infirmorum,* Nov. 30, 1972: *AAS* 65 (1973), 5–9; *DOL* 3317; see *ROils* 3: *DOL* 3863.
[10]Ibid.; *DOL* 3318; also *RAnointing* 25: *DOL* 3345.
[11]Ibid.; also *Pastoral Care,* 94 (n. 124).
[12]*ROils* 9–10: *DOL* 3869–3870.
[13]C. 835, §1.

sure that the oil remains fit for use and should replenish it from time to time, either yearly when the bishop blesses the oil on Holy Thursday or more frequently if necessary."[14]

As indicated in canon 368 together with canon 381, §2, the law equates with the diocesan bishop those persons who preside over portions of the flock (particular churches) that are not formally constituted as dioceses: territorial prelatures and abbacies, vicariates and prefectures apostolic, and apostolic administrations established in a stable manner. Like diocesan bishops, they bless the oil for the sick in the Mass of the Chrism and require no additional faculty to do this.

The second category of ministers of the blessing of oil, however, is treated as an exception, i.e., when oil blessed by the bishop is not available.[15] Blessing of the oil by the minister of the sacrament during the actual celebration is considered not uncommon by the ritual, which provides alternatives: either the blessing by the minister of anointing or a prayer of thanksgiving over the oil (in effect, another style of blessing) if it has already been blessed by the bishop.[16] This practice of blessing by the minister himself is followed in some other, non-Roman rites; it has a certain parallel in the blessing of the baptismal water in the course of the celebration of that sacrament and as in that case permits a fuller liturgical catechesis about the oil.[17]

Canon 999 permits the minister to bless the oil for the sick "in case of necessity" but does not determine the nature or degree of this necessity, given the fact that the minister may judge the practice to be liturgically and spiritually suitable. The ritual explains that, in this case, the minister "may bring the unblessed oil with him, or the family of the sick person may prepare the oil in a suitable vessel. If any of the oil is left after the celebration of the sacrament, it should be absorbed in cotton or cotton wool and burned."[18] The canon does lessen the degree of necessity stressed in the ritual, which speaks of "true necessity,"[19] but still looks upon the blessing of the oil by the minister as exceptional.

The reference, in this connection, to the actual celebration of the sacrament has been added to the canon for clarity. It is only a bishop or one equated with a diocesan bishop who blesses the oil during the Mass of the Chrism, i.e., apart from the celebration of the sacrament of anointing.

One should see canon 847 for norms concerning the holy oils in general, norms which are not repeated here. Older authors discussed related questions: the possibility of using other blessed oils for anointing the sick and the validity or invalidity of

the sacrament if unblessed oil were used, as well as the addition of unblessed oil in smaller quantities (as a kind of blessing by contact). These questions no longer arise.

Manner of Anointing

Canon 1000 — §1. The anointings are to be carefully performed while observing the words, the order and the manner prescribed in the liturgical books; but in case of necessity it is sufficient that one anointing be made on the forehead, or even on another part of the body, while saying the entire formula.

§2. The minister is to perform the anointing with his own hand unless a serious reason persuades him to use an instrument.

Although the entire rite for the anointing of the sick—including introductory rites and brief liturgy of the word, laying on of hands, and concluding prayers—is of significance, the canon (like *CIC* 947, which it revises) concentrates on the anointing with oil and the required sacramental form. On the latter, one should see the commentary on canon 998.

The modern *Roman Ritual* (1614) had prescribed the anointing of eyes, ears, nose, hands, feet, and (until prohibited by *CIC* 947, §2) loins. The 1925 edition permitted the anointing of the feet to be omitted for a reasonable cause (in accord with *CIC* 947, §3)[20] and also added or restored a ritual laying on of hands because of the repeated examples of this healing gesture in the New Testament.[21] Vatican II decreed that, in the course of the revision of all Roman liturgical rites, "the number of the anointings is to be adapted to the circumstances."[22] Thus, in the revised ritual of Paul VI the anointings were simplified, as described in the canon, and the accompanying formula altered for the Latin Church, as noted in the commentary on canon 998. The conferences of bishops remain free, in the preparation of particular rituals for their territories, to make further adaptations of the anointings: "Depending on the culture and traditions of different peoples, the number of anointings may be increased and the places to be anointed may be changed."[23]

Although paragraph one of this canon follows the language and intent of canon 947, §1 of the 1917 Code and a reference to the order or sequence of anointings is retained, it is now ordinarily a matter of anointing forehead and hands only. In effect the present canon allows the anointing of the hands to be omitted in case of necessity, e.g., if the person

[14] *RAnointing* 22: *DOL* 3342.
[15] *RAnointing* 21: *DOL* 3341.
[16] *RAnointing* 75–75bis; *Pastoral Care,* 92–93 (n. 123).
[17] *RCIA* 215; *RBaptC* 54–55.
[18] *RAnointing* 22: *DOL* 3342.
[19] *RAnointing* 21: *DOL* 3341; *ROils* 8: *DOL* 3868.

[20] Title VI, c. 2, n. 11.
[21] See Mk 6:5; 16:18; Lk 13:11–13; Acts 9:12, 17; 28:8; *Roman Ritual,* title VI, c. 2, n. 7.
[22] *SC* 75.
[23] *RAnointing* 24: *DOL* 3344.

is in imminent danger of death (when Viaticum should be given immediately after the single anointing), if there is some physical obstacle to the anointing of the hands, if there is a large number of persons to be anointed and time in short, etc. Similarly, paragraph one recognizes the situation in which even the single anointing of the forehead is not possible, e.g., if in case of accident the head is not accessible, and indicates that another part of the body be anointed "because of the particular condition of the sick person."[24] It says nothing, however, about the style of anointing, e.g., the use of sufficient oil, so that the sacramental sign may be perceived as an authentic gesture of healing, as contemporary authors urge.[25]

The serious reason which, according to paragraph two, may permit the minister to use an instrument to avoid direct physical contact with the body of the sick person may be danger of infection or even extreme repugnance. Ordinarily, however, whatever the sick person's condition, the minister will be able to take the same safeguards against infection as do nurses and doctors in their ministry to the sick.[26]

Responsibility to the Sick

Canon 1001 — Pastors of souls and persons who are close to the sick are to see to it that they are supported by this sacrament at an appropriate time.

The thrust of this canon, which does not have a direct counterpart in the 1917 Code, is to establish the responsibility for celebrating the sacrament of the anointing of the sick at an opportune time. This time is related to the question, treated in canons 1004–1006, of those who may and should be anointed. Vatican II explicitly defined the appropriate, proper, and ideal time: "*As soon as* any one of the faithful *begins* to be in danger of death from sickness or old age, the fitting time for that person to receive this sacrament has *certainly already* arrived" (emphasis added).[27] Thus, in its desire to broaden the interpretation of the sacramental discipline of anointing,[28] the conciliar Fathers determined that—leaving open the possibility of an even earlier time—it is certainly opportune at the very beginning of serious illness.

The responsibility at this point in the Christian's illness rests with those who have the pastoral office and those who are close to the sick person by family relationship, friendship, or the ministry of healing (such as nurses and doctors). The canon does not mention, since it is sufficiently obvious, that the sick person should ask for the sacrament if those who have the responsibility are negligent.[29]

Anointing of Several Persons

Canon 1002 — The communal celebration of the anointing of the sick for many of the sick at the same time who are duly prepared and rightly disposed can be performed according to the prescriptions of the diocesan bishop.

This canon, which did not appear in most drafts of the recodification, does not have reference to the communal celebration of the sacrament for a single person (or of a very few persons), for which it is always desirable that at least some small community of the Christian people assemble and participate;[30] this dimension of communal celebration is always stressed in the revised ritual.[31] The canon is instead concerned with cases in which there are several or many persons to be anointed together in a single rite, and it is based on the *Roman Ritual:* "The local Ordinary has the responsibility of supervising celebrations at which sick persons from various parishes or hospitals may come together to receive the sacrament."[32] (The text of the canon employs "diocesan bishop" rather than "local Ordinary" to indicate the role of the bishop as president and moderator of the liturgy in the particular church.)[33]

Directions are therefore provided in the ritual for the "Celebration of Anointing in a Large Congregation," for occasions such as pilgrimages or other large gatherings of a diocese, city, parish, or society for the sick.[34] The contemporary exemplar of such celebrations of the sacrament was a gathering at Lourdes in 1969, at which a trial use of the rite was allowed.[35] A pastoral note is added in English-language editions of the ritual: "In particular, the practice of indiscriminately anointing large numbers of persons on these occasions simply because they are ill or have reached an advanced age is to be avoided. Only those whose health is seriously impaired by sickness or old age are proper subjects for the sacrament."[36] For this question, one should see the commentary on canon 1004, below.

CHAPTER II
THE MINISTER OF
THE ANOINTING OF THE SICK
[c. 1003]

Canon 1003 — §1. Every priest, and only a priest, validly administers the anointing of the sick.

---

[24]*RAnointing* 23: *DOL* 3343.
[25]See L. Bouyer, *Rite and Man* (Notre Dame, Ind.: University of Notre Dame Press, 1963), 212.
[26]Abbo-Hannan, II, 69.
[27]*SC* 73.
[28]*AcSynVat* II, 2:568–569; 5:653–654.

[29]*RAnointing* 13: *DOL* 3333.
[30]In accord with *SC* 26–27 and c. 837.
[31]*RAnointing* 35–36: *DOL* 3355–3356.
[32]*RAnointing* 17: *DOL* 3337.
[33]C. 835, §1.
[34]*RAnointing* 83–85.
[35]*N* 6 (1970), 13–33; *CLD* 7, 687.
[36]*Pastoral Care*, 78.

§2. All priests to whom the care of souls has been committed have the duty and the right to administer the anointing of the sick to all the faithful committed to their pastoral office; for a reasonable cause any other priest can administer this sacrament with at least the presumed consent of the aforementioned priest.

§3. Every priest is allowed to carry blessed oil with him so that he can administer the sacrament of the anointing of the sick in case of necessity.

The first two paragraphs of this canon distinguish between validity and licitness: the ministration of the anointing of the sick may be done validly by any priest; out of respect for those exercising the pastoral office in a particular place or community, not every priest acts lawfully in the celebration of the sacrament.

In the last stages of the revision an unsuccessful effort was made to remove the words "valide" (much debated in the process of revision) and "omnis et solus" from the text of paragraph one, which follows canon 938, §1 of the 1917 Code closely. The omission was proposed on the grounds that the statement cannot be supported historically, at least for the first eight centuries; the *Roman Ritual* does not refer to validity in this connection; and the Council of Trent used the expression "proper minister" in regard to the priest.[37] The Code Commission preferred to retain the 1917 text. The Latin canon has "sacerdos," which includes both bishops and presbyters.

This action appears to preclude, at least for the present time and discipline, the celebration of the sacrament by deacons, although this concession is widely desired in the United States, Germany, and other countries. This restriction is partly because of a desire to retain the relationship of the sacrament to the anointing mentioned in the Letter of James, which speaks of presbyters or elders, understood as those in positions of authority in the local Christian community.[38] The anathema of Trent, concerned with those who held that lay persons could administer anointing, did not speak directly to the question of validity nor did it have any direct bearing upon the possibility of anointing by deacons.[39] The extent to which the question may remain open to future development depends upon the complex relation of sacramental anointing to other kinds of anointing, whether by lay persons or by the ordained, referred to in the commentary at the beginning of this title of canons.

In paragraph two, the obligation of those who

have the pastoral office (pastors, parochial vicars, chaplains, etc.) to administer the sacrament is coupled with a right. This right excludes other priests, who do not have a reasonable cause, from intervening in this sacramental ministry to the sick of a given parish or community. It is generally not difficult to presume the permission of those who have the pastoral responsibility, but this presumption should not result in a needless repetition of the sacrament, in accord with the limitation prescribed in canon 1004, §2. Canon 939 of the 1917 Code was suppressed in the revision; it dealt with the moral question of the obligation, in justice, of the local pastor and the obligation, in charity, of any other priest.

The ritual, which is not affected by the canon, enlarges upon the ministry of the priest in relation to anointing of the sick. The ministers

have the pastoral responsibility both of preparing and helping the sick and others who are present, with the assistance of religious and laity, and of celebrating the sacrament.

The local Ordinary [more precisely, the diocesan bishop] has the responsibility of supervising celebrations at which sick persons from various parishes or hospitals may come together to receive the sacrament.

Other priests also confer the sacrament of anointing with the consent of the minister mentioned [bishops, pastors, vicars, priests responsible for the sick or aged in hospitals, and superiors of clerical religious institutes]. Presuming such consent in a case of necessity, a priest need only inform the parish priest (pastor) or hospital chaplain later.

When two or more priests are present for the anointing, one of them may say the prayers and carry out the anointings, saying the sacramental form. The others may take the remaining parts, such as the introductory rites, readings, invocations, etc. Each priest may lay hands on the sick person.[40]

Given the reduction in the number of anointings, it is not feasible to follow the Eastern usage, in which several priests participate in the several anointings of a single person; as noted above and in the commentary on canon 1002, if there are several or many sick persons, a number of priests may perform the anointing of individual persons. The ritual, moreover, treats at length the offices and ministries of Christians other than the ordained to the sick.[41]

Canon 947 of the 1917 Code, on the custody of

---

[37] *Rel.* 237; Trent, sess. XIV, de extr. unctione, c. 3: *COD* 710–711.

[38] *Jerome Biblical Commentary* (Englewood Cliffs, N.J.: Prentice-Hall, 1968), 2:377, K. Condon, "The Sacrament of Healing," in T. Worden (ed.), *Sacraments in Scripture* (Springfield, Ill.: Templegate, 1966), 176–179.

[39] Loc. cit., can. 4: *COD* 713.

[40] *RAnointing* 17–19: *DOL* 3337–3339.

[41] *RAnointing* 32–37: *DOL* 3352–3357.

the oils, is omitted from the revised canons, although the keeping of the oils in a suitable and worthy manner is required by canon 847, §1. In particular, the prohibition of keeping of the oils in the parochial residence, mentioned in canons 735 and 946 of the former law, is replaced by the concession of paragraph three of the present canon. This change had been anticipated along the same lines in a decree of 1965, which gave local ordinaries power to allow priests "the permission to carry the oil of the sick with them, especially when using the various means of transportation to travel."[42] As is evident from canon 999, this 1965 concession and that of paragraph three are now less significant since any priest may bless any (plant) oil in case of necessity when he is to minister the sacrament of anointing of the sick.

CHAPTER III
THOSE ON WHOM THE ANOINTING OF THE SICK IS TO BE CONFERRED
[cc. 1004–1007]

The four canons give, first, the basic norm for the celebration and even repetition of the sacrament (c. 1004), then special cases of somewhat doubtful capacity to receive the sacrament (cc. 1005–1006) and of persons who persist in public circumstances of sinful life (c. 1007).

In particular, the chapter, while providing adequate clarity for canonical purposes, represents a development and broadening with regard to those who may and should be strengthened spiritually, physically, and psychologically by anointing, both the changes directly sought by Vatican II and the further changes found in post-conciliar papal and curial documents. As commented upon at the beginning of the title on anointing of the sick, this reflects the contemporary sense of the Church to enlarge the occasions when the sacrament may and should be celebrated.

Those To Be Anointed

Canon 1004 — §1. The anointing of the sick can be administered to a member of the faithful who, after having reached the use of reason, begins to be in danger due to sickness or old age.

§2. This sacrament can be repeated whenever the sick person again falls into a serious sickness after convalescence or whenever a more serious crisis develops during the same sickness.

From one viewpoint, paragraph one determines what Christian believers are eligible to receive, or

are capable of receiving, the anointing of the sick; in this, paragraph one follows canon 940, §1 of the former law, although the 1917 text was phrased negatively, stating that the sacrament might not be given to those incapable of receiving it. From another viewpoint, by the phrase, "begins to be in danger," paragraph one specifies what is called in canon 1001 the appropriate time to celebrate this sacrament, namely, at the beginning of serious illness. The reference to the Christian's having reached the use of reason is a concern because of the aspect of anointing as consummating or completing Christian penance,[43] namely, in the divine forgiveness of (personal) sin; on this question, however, one should see the commentary on canon 1005.

The nature of the illness is not addressed in the canon, only its seriousness. This leaves open to further development the question of serious psychological illness. Although the sacrament has ordinarily been associated with physical impairment, the gravity and even peril or danger of some psychological disorders are undeniable, and thus English-language rituals, without attempting to give a final resolution to this issue, have the following pastoral note: "Some types of mental illness are now classified as serious. Those who are judged to have a serious mental illness and who would be strengthened by the sacrament may be anointed."[44]

During the process of drafting paragraph one of this canon, it was planned to add, in slightly adapted form, but explicitly, the following norms from the revised ritual:

"A sick person may be anointed before surgery whenever a serious illness is the reason for the surgery."

"Elderly people may be anointed if they have become notably weakened even though no serious illness is present."

"Sick children may be anointed if they have sufficient use of reason to be strengthened ["confortari"] by this sacrament."[45]

It was determined, however, that these paragraphs should be deleted from the draft on the grounds that the matter was already regulated adequately by the (revised) liturgical books. In the final stages of consideration by the Code Commission, attempts to add these references and to add the mention of danger "of death" to paragraph one of this canon were not successful.

Thus it becomes important to refer to the introduction to the section of the *Roman Ritual* on the sacrament. This took as its starting point the con-

---

[42]SCRit, decr *Pientissima Mater Ecclesia,* Mar. 4, 1965: *AAS* 57 (1965), 409; *DOL* 3314; see also SCC, general directory *Peregrinans in terra,* Apr. 30, 1969: *AAS* 61 (1969), 3605; *DOL* 2616.

[43]*RAnointing* 6: *DOL* 3327 (following the Tridentine teaching on anointing, in the places cited above in notes 37 and 39).
[44]*Pastoral Care,* 27 (n. 53).
[45]*RAnointing* 10–12: *DOL* 3330–3332.

ciliar intent to improve pastoral practice and, without transgressing the traditions of anointing that were judged sound, to expand the potential occasions for its celebration in the Christian community.[46]

Both in the ritual and in the apostolic constitution introducing it, the degree of gravity or seriousness of the illness is left somewhat open, without explicit mention of the relationship of this seriousness to death, which may be a rather remote danger. This was done not to minimize the seriousness of the condition which calls for the celebration of the sacrament but to remove all hesitation about anointing when it will be proper and fruitful. It also serves to correct what are now considered abuses[47] or aberrations in the tradition: to reserve the sacrament for cases of persons *in extremis,* to postpone the celebration until there is a high likelihood or near certainty of death, or to consider the anointing in itself or primarily the sacrament of the dying.

The Council of Trent, reflecting the problematical traditions and the pastoral practice of the period, recognized in effect two possibilities, giving primacy to anointing as the sacrament of the sick but attributing to it a secondary "name" of sacrament of the departing[48] because of the frequent (and, in later centuries, usual and almost exclusive) occasions when the sacrament was given to the dying. The recovery of an older and sounder tradition, and indeed an enlargement of that tradition, is demanded by the other post-conciliar expositions of the matter, in particular that of the *Roman Ritual:*

The Letter of James states that the sick are to be anointed in order to raise them up and save them. Great care should be taken to see that those of the faithful whose health is seriously impaired by sickness or old age receive this sacrament.

A prudent or reasonably sure judgment, without scruple, is sufficient for deciding on the seriousness of the illness; if necessary a doctor may be consulted.[49]

Commenting upon this development on the occasion of a communal anointing of a large number of sick persons, Paul VI explained:

Here as in the other sacraments the Church's main concern is, of course, the soul, pardon for sin, and the increase of God's grace. But also, to the extent that it is up to the Church, its desire

and intent is to obtain relief and, if possible, even healing for the sick. . . . The revision's intent was to make the overall purpose of the rite clearer and to lead to a wider availability of the sacrament and to extend it—within reasonable limits—*even beyond cases of mortal illness* (emphasis added).[50]

The careful balance between the wrongful restriction of the sacrament and its celebration for those not seriously ill is reflected also in an explanatory note attached, in English-language rituals, to the text of the *praenotanda* which refers to health as "seriously impaired by sickness or old age":

The word *periculose* has been carefully studied and rendered as "seriously," rather than as "gravely," "dangerously," or "perilously." Such a rendering will serve to avoid restrictions upon the celebration of the sacrament. On the one hand, the sacrament may and should be given to anyone whose health is seriously impaired; on the other hand, it may not be given indiscriminately or to any person whose health is not seriously impaired.[51]

The same introduction of the *Roman Ritual* enlarges pastorally upon what is in paragraph one (and also in c. 1001):

In public and private catechesis, the faithful should be educated to ask for the sacrament of anointing and, as soon as the right time comes, to receive it with full faith and devotion. They should not follow the wrongful practice of delaying the reception of the sacrament. All who care for the sick should be taught the meaning and purpose of the sacrament.[52]

Less commentary is required by paragraph two of the present canon; it is derived from canon 940, §2 of the 1917 Code, which in turn was based upon the teaching on the repetition of the sacrament (in the same illness) by the Council of Trent.[53] In the preparation of *The Constitution on the Sacred Liturgy,* it was intended to remove this restriction; after the conciliar debate, any mention of repetition of anointing was omitted from the constitution because of uncertain historical and theological precedents.[54]

The text of paragraph two also represents developments since Vatican II in its reworking of its counterpart (*CIC* 940, §2: "In the same illness this sacrament may not be repeated unless the sick per-

---

[46]*AcSynVat* II, 5:654, which seeks an *interpretatio latior.*

[47]The conciliar commission on the liturgy was explicit: "We intend to suppress the abuse of administering this sacrament only to those *in articulo mortis* or extreme danger to life" (*AcSynVat* II, 2:568).

[48]Sess. XIV, de extr. unctione, c. 3: *COD* 711.

[49]*RAnointing* 8: *DOL* 3328.

[50]Homily, Oct. 5, 1975: *N* 11 (1975), 257–258; *DOL* 3365.

[51]*Pastoral Care,* 13 (n. 8).

[52]*RAnointing* 13: *DOL* 3333.

[53]Sess. XIV, de extr. unctione, c. 3: *COD* 711.

[54]*AcSynVat* II, 2:569 ("lest the Council enter into disputed questions").

son has recovered after being anointed and has again fallen into another danger of death"). This language had been altered by Paul VI to read: "The sacrament may be repeated if the sick person recovers after being anointed and then again falls ill or if during the same illness the person's condition becomes more serious."[55]

Even before the broadening statement quoted, the text of canon 940, §1 of the 1917 Code had been understood to permit the repetition of the sacrament "through the mere lapse of a long time without recovery,"[56] thus creating the presumption that a newly critical or more seriously impaired condition is present. This presumption in favor of celebrating the sacrament is analogous to those situations mentioned in canon 1005, that is, the sacrament may be administered in case of doubt of a new seriousness of condition. It does not mean, however, that the sacrament should be administered on some regular basis, such as weekly or monthly, to the ill person, without any reference to the progress of the illness.

Special Cases

Canon 1005 — This sacrament is to be administered when there is a doubt whether the sick person has attained the use of reason, whether the person is dangerously ill, or whether the person is dead.

The canon differs from canon 941 of the former law principally by the omission of a reference to *conditional* ministration in these instances of doubt. To avoid scruple on the part of the minister—and thus to correct pastoral abuses which had denied the sacrament to some of the faithful who were seriously ill—the condition attached to the formula of anointing ("If you have attained the use of reason . . . ," "If you are living . . . ") is simply suppressed. In addition, the second of the three doubtful situations has been rephrased from the somewhat narrower text of the earlier Code (doubt "whether he or she is truly in danger of death"). The canon, it should be noted, goes beyond the ritual and retains the language of obligation ("ministretur") in all the cases of doubt which are mentioned.

With regard to the first case of doubt, the canon enlarges upon canon 940, §1 of the 1917 Code and its reference to the use of reason in the sick person, whether a small child or one who is mentally retarded. The norm of the ritual, left intact by the canon, may be somewhat clearer: "Sick children may be anointed [in accord with the canon: are to be anointed] if they have sufficient use of reason to

be strengthened ["confortari"] by this sacrament."[57] Canon 1005 in effect adds that the sacrament is to be administered even if it remains doubtful whether the child (or the retarded person) has sufficient reasoning power to be (spiritually, physically, and/or psychologically) strengthened by anointing. Although the limited requirement of the use of reason is related to the forgiving nature and effect of the sacrament, there is no demand that the child should have committed any sin or be repentant for any sin. Finally, there is no application of this canon (or of c. 1004, §1) to those who have had the use of reason and then become mentally incompetent; no doubt whatever exists in such cases, and such persons are to be anointed, much the same as those persons referred to in canon 1006.

With regard to the second case of doubt, canon 1005 simply extends the norm of canon 1004, §1 to all cases in which the seriousness of impaired health is doubtful. With regard to the third case, a doubt whether the person is dead, some additional explanation is needed.

It is certain that the sacrament of the anointing of the sick—which is also the sacrament of the dying who were unable to be anointed or in fact were not anointed at an earlier and proper time in the illness—may not be given to a dead person. This would be improper; none of the seven sacraments may be given to a person who is dead. The norm of the *Roman Ritual* is explicit on this point: "When a priest has been called to attend those who are already dead, he should not administer the sacrament of anointing. Instead he should pray for them, asking that God forgive their sins and graciously receive them into the kingdom."[58] For this reason, English-language rituals add a number of appropriate prayers, psalms, and biblical readings so that the minister may follow the direction just quoted.[59] Some of these texts are taken from the *Rite of Funerals,* as is suggested by the *Roman Ritual* itself.[60]

The canon, however, rephrases the liturgical law ("But if the priest is doubtful whether the sick person is dead, he may give the sacrament conditionally") to reinstate the language of obligation. If there is doubt whether death has occurred, the person should be anointed. The judgment is one that it should be possible for the minister himself to make; by analogy with the norm for judging the seriousness of illness, he should be able ordinarily to rely upon medical judgment.[61]

Canon 1006 — This sacrament is to be conferred upon sick persons who requested it at least implicitly when they were in control of their faculties.

[55]*Sacram Unctionem infirmorum: DOL* 3318; *RAnointing* 9: *DOL* 3329.
[56]Abbo-Hannan II, 63.

[57]*RAnointing* 12: *DOL* 3332.
[58]*RAnointing* 15: *DOL* 3335.
[59]*Pastoral Care,* 189–198 (nos. 223–231).
[60]*RAnointing* 151.
[61]*RAnointing* 8: *DOL* 3328.

Since sometimes the nature of a serious illness is such that the person is unable consciously to ask for the sacrament, the canon repeats, in simpler form, the norm of canon 943 of the 1917 Code. (*CIC* 944, which had among other things strongly urged that the sick be anointed while still fully conscious, was not included in the revision; its concern is adequately covered by the reformed discipline of the sacrament, which restores the tradition of anointing the sick at the very onset of illness.)

This canon is substantially the same as the current liturgical and pastoral norm: "The sacrament of anointing may be conferred [in accord with the canon: is to be conferred] upon sick people who, although they have lost consciousness or the use of reason would, as Christian believers, probably have asked for it were they in control of their faculties."[62] In effect, a presumption is established that the Christian believer is desirous of receiving the sacrament of anointing of the sick—unless there is contrary evidence such as that described in canon 1007. In the past the desire of the believer to receive the sacrament has been called an implicit habitual intention, sufficient if it is internal.

[62]*RAnointing* 14: *DOL* 3334.

Canon 1007 — The anointing of the sick is not to be conferred upon those who obstinately persist in manifest serious sin.

The canon is derived from canon 942 of the 1917 Code: "The sacrament is not to be conferred upon those who, impenitent, contumaciously persist in manifest serious sin; if this is doubtful, it should be conferred conditionally." A comparison of the language of the former and revised canons indicates substantial agreement. As in other cases in which doubt exists, the presumption favors the celebration of the sacrament but—again, as in other doubtful cases such as those mentioned in canon 1005—the revised law suppresses the reference to conditional anointing. This change may be attributed to a development that sees no need for the minister of the sacrament to advert to a potential invalidity of the sacrament because of lack of intention on the part of the one to be anointed. In any event, the prohibited case is that of a public sinner whose obstinate perseverance in a sinful life is known;[63] the contemporary judgment of the Christian community will almost always appreciate and accept the likelihood of repentance.

[63]For similar cases, see cc. 915; 1184, §1, 3°.

BIBLIOGRAPHY

(The following bibliographical material provides further information regarding the sacraments discussed in the first five titles of Book IV: baptism, confirmation, the Eucharist, penance, and the anointing of the sick.)

Abbo, J., and Hannan, J. *The Sacred Canons.* 2 vols., 2nd ed. St. Louis: B. Herder Book Co., 1960.

BCL. *Environment and Art in Catholic Worship.* Washington: NCCB, 1978.

————. *Ritual Revision: A Status Report.* Washington: NCCB, 1981.

Bugnini, A., ed. *Documenta Pontificia ad Instaurationem Liturgicam Spectantia (1903–1953).* Rome: Edizioni Liturgiche, 1953. II (1953–1959), Rome, 1959.

————. *La Riforma Liturgica* (1948–1975). Rome: CLV-Edizioni Liturgiche, 1983.

Callevaert, C. *Liturgicae Institutiones.* 2 vols. Bruges, 1925–1929.

Chupungco, A. *Cultural Adaptation of the Liturgy.* New York: Paulist Press, 1982.

Crichton, J. *The Ministry of Reconciliation.* London: Geoffrey Chapman, 1974.

Gordon, I. "Constitutio de S. Liturgia et canones 1256–1257," *P* 54 (1964): 89–140.

Green, T. "The Revision of Sacramental Law: Perspectives on the Sacraments Other than Marriage," *Stud Can* 11 (1977): 261–327.

Gusmer, C. *And You Visited Me: Sacramental Ministry to the Sick and the Dying.* New York: Pueblo, 1984.

Hovda, R., ed. *Made Not Born: New Perspectives on Christian Initiation and the Catechumenate.* Notre Dame, Ind.: University of Notre Dame Press, 1976.

Huels, J. "The Interpretation of Liturgical Law," *W* 55 (1981): 218–327.

———. *The Interpretation of the Law on Communion under Both Kinds. CanLawStud* 505. Washington, D.C.: Catholic University of America, 1982.

ICEL. *Documents on the Liturgy, 1963–1979: Conciliar, Papal, and Curial Texts.* Collegeville, Minn.: The Liturgical Press, 1982.

———. *Pastoral Care of the Sick: Rites of Anointing and Viaticum.* Collegeville, Minn.: The Liturgical Press, 1983.

———. *The Rites of the Catholic Church.* 2 vols. New York: Pueblo, 1976–1980.

Jones, C.; Wainwright, E.; and Yarnold, E., eds. *The Study of Liturgy.* New York: Oxford University Press, 1978.

Kaczynski, R., ed. *Enchiridion Documentorum Instaurationis Liturgicae, I (1963–1973).* Turin: Marietti, 1975.

Kavanagh, A. *The Shape of Baptism: The Rite of Christian Initiation.* New York: Pueblo, 1978.

Keifer, R., and McManus, F. *The Rite of Penance: Commentaries; I, Understanding the Document.* Washington: The Liturgical Conference, 1975.

Kelley, W. "The Authority of Liturgical Laws," *J* 28 (1968): 397–424.

King, A. *Eucharistic Reservation in the Western Church.* New York: Sheed and Ward, 1965.

McManus, F. "Liturgical Law and Difficult Cases," *W* 48 (1974): 347–366.

Manzanares Marijuan, J. *Liturgia y Decentralizacion en Concilio Vaticano II.* Rome, 1970.

Martimort, A. *The Church at Prayer,* Part I. New York: Desclée, 1968. Part II, New York: Herder and Herder, 1973.

———. *The Signs of the New Covenant.* 2nd ed. Collegeville, Minn.: The Liturgical Press, 1963.

Martos, J. *Doors to the Sacred: A Historical Introduction to Sacraments in the Catholic Church.* Garden City, N.Y.: Doubleday, 1981.

Mitchell, N. *Cult and Controversy: The Worship of the Eucharist Outside Mass.* New York: Pueblo, 1982.

Oppenheim, P. *Institutiones Systematico-historicae in Sacram Liturgiam;* Tom. II–IV, *Tractatus de Iure Liturgico.* Turin: Marietti, 1939–1940.

Orsy, L. *The Evolving Church and the Sacrament of Penance.* Denville, N.J.: Dimension Books, 1978.

Palmer, P., ed. *Sources of Christian Theology;* I, *Sacraments and Worship* [baptism, confirmation, and Eucharist]; II, *Sacraments and Forgiveness* [penance, anointing of the sick, indulgences]. Westminster, Md.: Newman Press, 1955.

Regatillo, E. *Ius Sacramentarium.* 3rd ed. Santander: Sal Terrae, 1960.

Richstatter, T. *Liturgical Law: New Style, New Spirit.* Chicago: Franciscan Herald Press, 1977.

Schillebeeckx, E., ed. *Sacramental Reconciliation* (*Con* 61). New York: Herder and Herder, 1971.

Searle, M. *Christening: The Making of Christians.* Collegeville, Minn.: The Liturgical Press, 1980.

Seasoltz, R.K. *The New Liturgy: A Documentation, 1903–1965.* New York: Herder and Herder, 1966.

———. *New Liturgy, New Laws.* Collegeville, Minn.: The Liturgical Press, 1980.

Wagner, J., ed. *Adult Baptism and the Catechumenate* (*Con* 22). Glen Rock, N.J.: Paulist Press, 1967.

TITLE VI
ORDERS
[cc. 1008–1054]

In the development of any legal system the principle of continuity is much more evident than the principle of change. The law on orders in the revised Code of Canon Law follows this general rule of continuity. To understand effectively the revised law on orders, the reader must be in control of some introductory material which summarizes the continuity and indicates the reasons for change. A context for this introductory ecclesiological material is provided by an address of Pope Paul VI to the 1973 Canon Law Congress in Rome. In his address, Pope Paul made it very clear that canon law reflects theology. It is conditioned by institutional necessity and pastoral circumstance. He taught that the canonist must seek the reasons for his or her own doctrine more deeply in the Scriptures and theology. He stressed that with the Second Vatican Council there has ended once and for all the time when certain canonists refused to consider the theological aspects of the disciplines studied or the laws they applied.[1] The methodology of the commentary on orders will flow from this context. It will be not only canonical but also theological and pastoral. The introductory material logically divides itself into the following categories:

(1) the theological foundation and pastoral context of the law on orders in the 1917 Code of Canon Law;

(2) the theological foundation and pastoral context of the changes in the law on orders from the Second Vatican Council to the 1983 Code of Canon Law;

(3) the theological foundation and pastoral context of the deliberations by the *coetus* (committee) on the sacrament of orders and the Code Commission itself which resulted in the text of the revised law on orders.

The 1917 Code

The major source of understanding the theological foundation and pastoral context of the 1917 Code is of course the text itself, in particular the in-troductory canons on clerics and orders. As the footnotes of these canons indicate, the law on orders comes from the *Corpus Iuris Canonici* and the Council of Trent.[2] The 1917 legislation was not very new; it simply organized an enormous amount of material on clerics and orders into a code format. There are two major premises in these two sections of the Code which flow from its theological base and perception of ministry:

(1) The Church is hierarchical in nature and only clerics can obtain jurisdiction.

(2) Ministry is viewed as fundamentally sacramental and clerical. The role of non-clerics including religious is to assist the cleric in fulfilling the responsibilities of ministry.

Accepting these premises in the much broader context that everything must be understood in its proper history, it must be concluded that the 1917 Code was a remarkable document which simply communicated the unchallenged ecclesiology of the time. The vertical lines of jurisdiction, whether ordinary or delegated, became the means of perceiving and implementing ministry "in the name of the church."

The Law on Clerics

The introductory canon on clerics defined a cleric as one who had been bound to divine ministry by at least the reception of first tonsure. The hierarchical principle contained in this canon was applied to the varied grades of orders which are conferred by ordination and to jurisdiction which is obtained ordinarily by canonical mission. The law distinguished the hierarchy of orders and jurisdiction from the viewpoint of divine and ecclesiastical institution. By divine institution the hierarchy of jurisdiction consisted in the supreme pontificate and a subordinate episcopacy. All other levels of orders and jurisdiction were of ecclesiastical institution and by implication could be changed by the Church. Using this hierarchical model of the Church as a base, the law logically considered the essential question of how a person would enter this hierarchy of orders and jurisdiction. The response was twofold: (1) a person entered into orders through sacred ordination and (2) with the exception of the pope who obtained jurisdiction when he

---

[1]Paul VI, "The Juridical Structure of the Church as Protection of Spiritual Order," *OssRomEng* (Oct. 4, 1973), 2.

[2]*CIC* 108–109, 948–950.

accepted a legitimate election, all other clerics obtained jurisdiction through canonical mission.[3] While the statement was very traditional, the counter-reformational context of the canon was recognized from what it excluded as legitimate means for entering the hierarchy of orders and jurisdiction, namely, the will of the people or secular authority. This conclusion was confirmed by the footnote of the canon, which quoted in part the Council of Trent reacting to the claims of the reformers.[4]

If the reader is to understand the practical consequences of the law on orders and jurisdiction, the concept of canonical mission must be understood. The Code itself defined canonical mission as the conferral of an ecclesiastical office by competent ecclesiastical authority according to the norms of the sacred canons. Canon 109 together with canon 118 which limited ecclesiastical jurisdiction to clerics effectively controlled both admission to the hierarchy of orders and jurisdiction and the exercise of orders and jurisdiction.[5]

The Law on Orders

The introduction to the law on orders reflected even more intensely the theological foundation and perception of ministry of the 1917 Code. It stated that the sacrament of orders distinguishes clerics from the laity for the purposes of governing the faithful and for the ministry of divine cult.[6] The sixty-four canons which dealt with the sacrament (CIC 948–1011) were organized under six different chapters.

The chapter on the minister of the sacrament (CIC 951–967) followed the traditional distinction between major and minor orders and presented the law on the ordination of bishops and on dimissorial letters for diocesan candidates and candidates from religious institutes. The chapter concluded by specifying when dimissorial letters may be sent to a bishop other than the diocesan bishop for ordination.

The chapter on the subject of ordination (CIC 968–991) had two articles. It contained the norms for the valid and lawful celebration of the sacrament. It considered the norms for the education/formation of the candidate, the conferral of minor orders, the age of the candidates for major orders, the canonical title of ordination for diocesan candidates and candidates from religious institutes with either solemn or simple vows. The chapter concluded with a lengthy consideration of impediments and irregularities along with the norms for dispensation.

The chapter on the prerequisites for orders (CIC 992–1001) dealt with the intention of the candidates, testimonial letters, dimissorial letters, competency exams, and consultation about the worthiness of the candidate through a public announcement.

The law on orders concluded with three brief chapters: chapter IV on the rites and ceremonies for ordination (CIC 1002–1005); chapter V on the time and place for ordination (CIC 1006–1009); and finally chapter VI on the records for all ordinations (CIC 1010–1011).[7]

The Second Vatican Council to the 1983 Code of Canon Law

During this period a number of legislative developments have had a significant effect on the law on orders. Before considering the content of the material, this commentator would like to use the method of the first section of this introduction and begin with the reason for legislative changes in the law on orders. The reason is found in the development of the theological base and pastoral context of the former law which in fact necessitated change. The heavy stress in the former law on the hierarchical nature of the Church and the law's perception of ministry as fundamentally clerical and sacramental have been modified by the ecclesiology of the Council. The Council contextualized the teaching on the hierarchy by understanding the Church as a community of God's people.[8] The Council saw ministry as rooted in baptism, making it a vocational responsibility of all God's people and not just the ordained.[9]

It would be helpful to consider the legislative changes in the chronological order of their appearance.

The Restoration of the Permanent Diaconate

The first of these changes originated at the Council itself with the call for the restoration of the permanent diaconate.[10] This was followed by an apostolic letter of Pope Paul VI in 1967, in which he issued general norms for restoring the permanent diaconate.[11] The restoration was rooted in the ministerial structures of the early Church, and it restored to the Church its fullness as the sign of salvation. The exclusively functional interpretation of the restoration of the permanent diaconate was rejected by Pope Paul when he noted that some of the diaconal functions have already been given to lay persons especially in missionary countries. The theological reason for the restoration of the perma-

---

[3]CIC 108, 147.
[4]CIC 109.
[5]CIC 109, 147, 196, 219, 332.
[6]CIC 948.

[7]For the complete text of the law on orders, confer CIC 948–1011.
[8]LG, II.
[9]SC 6, 14; LG 10–14; AA 3.
[10]LG 29.
[11]Paul VI, mp, General Norms for Restoring The Permanent Diaconate in the Latin Church, June 18, 1967 (Washington, D.C.: USCC, 1967)

nent diaconate according to the pope was "that the special nature of this order will be shown more clearly."

Reformation of First Tonsure, Minor Orders, Subdiaconate

This reformation came through a 1972 apostolic letter of Pope Paul VI[12] responding to two separate but interrelated issues. The first was a pre-conciliar concern of the bishops for a renewal of the subdiaconate and minor orders. The second was a conciliar concern that the liturgical rites be restructured so that the Christian people could understand them with ease and take part in them fully as befits a community.

In presenting reasons for the reformation, Pope Paul VI noted that many of the ministerial functions attached to minor orders are already being exercised by the laity and that baptism gives the Christian people the right and obligation to participate in liturgical celebration. Concentrating on offices related to the ministry of the word and altar, the pope retained two: the office of lector and the office of acolyte. The term minor orders was replaced by ministries and the conferral of ministries was called installation not ordination. The aim of this change was to allow the distinction between clergy and laity to emerge with greater clarity. Ministries are reserved to men. Prior to being admitted to ministries, the candidates are obliged to complete certain steps to insure they have the qualities and intention to fulfill the responsibilities of these offices. When both ministries are to be conferred on the same candidate, an interval of time is required between the conferral of lector and acolyte to allow for the exercise of the ministry. Finally, unless a dispensation is given, candidates for orders must receive both ministries.

In retrospect the following observations can be made on this apostolic letter:

(1) Its structural goal has been achieved through the reformation and the liturgical rites around the reform have been completed.

(2) The pastoral goal of having the laity exercise the rights flowing from their baptism has been achieved in a very limited manner because the ministries have been limited to men. As a result most local churches have avoided ministries in the sense of this document and have substituted analogous rites for "installing" men and women to fulfill the functions of the offices of lector and acolyte. The result is that ministries in the canonical sense are received by one class of people in the Church—those entering the clerical

state. This situation is practically the same as the former law when the only persons who received minor orders were those proceeding toward major orders. In the opinion of this commentator, the basic reason why conferences of bishops have not requested other ministries as allowed in the apostolic letter is simply because the same difficulty would result—these ministries would also be limited to men.

Norms for the Order of Deacon

Pope Paul VI issued a second letter on August 15, 1972 on the diaconate.[13] After a brief review of the historical developments regarding that office, Pope Paul promulgated three significant changes:

(1) Admission to Candidacy. Since the rite of first tonsure was abrogated, a new rite was introduced whereby the candidate manifests his will to offer himself to God and the Church so that he may exercise a sacred order. Religious are exempt from this rite.

(2) Ministries. The ministries of lector and acolyte should be given to those who are candidates for the diaconate and priesthood so that through the gradual exercise of the ministry of the word and altar they may reflect and understand the double aspect of the priestly office.

(3) Celibacy. A rite of consecration to celibacy has been added to the ordination ceremony. The rite binds candidates for the priesthood and unmarried candidates for the diaconate. It also binds religious. Married deacons who have lost their wives cannot marry.

Theological-Pastoral Foundation of Revised Law

Two issues are to be addressed under this heading. The first is that the theological foundation of the Code Commission's deliberations was necessarily the theology of the Council and of post-conciliar legislation. Admittedly it is another question whether or not the Commission was faithful to the principles of conciliar and post-conciliar renewal. The second issue is the pastoral context of the Commission's deliberations. The pastoral perception of the commission on clerics, ministry, and orders can be deduced from the international consultation process on the revised Code. A brief word on the history of that process may help the reader understand more effectively the canonical commentary on the text.[14]

In 1963 Pope John XXIII established the Pontifi-

---

[12]Paul VI, *mp, First Tonsure, Minor Orders and the Subdiaconate,* August 15, 1972.

[13]Paul VI, *mp, Norms for the Order of Diaconate,* August 15, 1972.

[14]J. Alesandro, "Background on the Canon Law Code's Revision," *Origins* 12 (Feb. 3, 1983), 541–544.

cal Commission for the Revision of the Code of Canon Law. Pope Paul VI enlarged its membership in 1964 and it began its formal work in 1965. The consultors were initially divided into ten study groups; however, the number was increased to sixteen in 1966. The work of the Commission was presented to the 1967 Synod of Bishops. The latter approved ten guiding principles for the revision and restructuring of the 1917 Code in the light of the Second Vatican Council.

The process of revision can be summarized as follows: the Commission would examine the draft texts of the study groups and if it approved the text as a definitive draft, the text should be submitted to the pope. After the pope approved the text, it was sent to the conferences of bishops, the Curia, the Union of Superiors General and the faculties of Catholic universities around the world. After these groups submitted their observations, each study group would consider the observations and make further revisions in the text. The final draft would be submitted to the Commission of Cardinals for approval prior to submitting it to the pope for his study, approval, and promulgation.

One study group was given the responsibility to revise the law on all the sacraments with the exception of marriage. It is possible to follow the progress of each group through the journal of the Pontifical Commission, appropriately called *Communicationes*. The material on orders, the subject of this commentary, appeared in the 1978 edition of *Communicationes*.[15] The material, which was considered in two different *coetus* meetings—February and March—became the substance of the 1980 draft of the revised Code of Canon Law. The final source of documentary information on the development of the revised law on orders was the report of the Commission's reaction to the 1980 schema of the revised Code. This material was considered at the 1981 plenary session of the Commission.[16]

The content of the Commission's work will be included in the commentary on each canon. However, a final introductory note may be helpful to the reader. The law on orders—probably more than any other sacrament—had already been significantly changed due to legislation promulgated by Pope Paul VI. In part, the work of the Commission was to incorporate this material into the revised law in the form of canons.

---

[15]M. de Nicolò, "Coetus studiorum de Sacramentis: 'de ordine,' " *Comm* 10 (1978), 179–208. All subsequent Code Commission references will be to this volume.
[16]ComCICRec, *Relatio* (Typis Polyglottis Vaticanis, 1981).

CANONS AND COMMENTARY

There are two prenotes to this section.[17] The first is on the title of the section. Some consultors preferred the title *De Ordinatione* since that is the term consistently used in the canons. However, that opinion was not sustained because it was thought that the reason for the suggested change was not sufficient in view of the long tradition of using *De Ordine* as a title for this sacrament. The second prenote deals with the seven general observations made on the entire draft text of the law on orders. These observations expressed concern over the ecclesiological, collegial, and liturgical aspects of the draft. There was a concern for a clearer distinction between bishops and priests on one hand and deacons on the other since deacons do not participate in the power of governing. Some consultors wanted more emphasis on the fact that bishops and priests not only celebrate the liturgy and govern but are also a part of God's people and form God's people.

There were suggestions that the text define the essential elements of the conferral of the episcopacy. There was a request that attention be given to episcopal ordination since practically all the canons consider ordination to the diaconate and priesthood. Some consultors felt that the law should refer to the fact that a vocation is from God. Furthermore, the law should deal with fitness for the apostolate and not limit itself to discussing the human qualities of those to be ordained. Finally it was suggested that only the dispensations for major issues should be reserved to the Holy See.

The decision of the sacramental law *coetus* was that these concerns should be considered on a canon by canon basis and not taken as a unit. Two observations, however, have a special value regarding the mentality of the consultors. They did not respond to the ecclesiological objections to the draft because they thought too much stress on the power of the people could blur the distinction between the ministerial priesthood and the priesthood of the

---

[17]*Comm*, 179–180.

faithful. The same basic mentality was present in not accepting the objection concerning a lack of collegiality. It was thought that stressing collegiality could challenge the authority of the hierarchy.

Nature of Sacrament of Orders

Canon 1008 — By divine institution some among the Christian faithful are constituted sacred ministers through the sacrament of orders by means of the indelible character with which they are marked; accordingly they are consecrated and deputed to shepherd the people of God, each in accord with his own grade of orders, by fulfilling in the person of Christ the Head the functions of teaching, sanctifying and governing.

The revised Code follows the methodology of the 1917 Code and introduces each sacrament with canons summarizing the theology of the Church on the sacrament along with a statement on the matter and form of the sacrament. Canons 1008–1009 fulfill this function in the revised law. Canon 1008 articulates the theology of the sacrament of orders. It has three important elements.

(1) "By divine institution." There is no need to repeat the content of the theological commentaries on the question of institution.[18] However it is important to note that the original draft of this canon had the words "by the institution of Christ." The consultors decided that the traditional terminology was more precise theologically since Christ did not directly institute priesthood and diaconate as such.[19] From a canonical viewpoint the divine institution terminology is used in contradistinction to ecclesiastical institution. This distinction was the basis of the action of Pope Paul VI in 1972 when he abrogated the minor orders and established ministries.[20] Logically and theologically there is no reason why a new structure could not be established in the future if the legislator's perception of the Church's needs changes. However, due to divine institution, the episcopacy, priesthood, and diaconate will always be the permanent realities in the life of the Church.

(2) "The indelible character with which they are marked." Again it is not necessary to repeat here the content of the theological commentaries on the question of sacramental character.[21] From a canonical viewpoint the indelible sacramental character has the following effects: (a) the ordained person is so configured to Christ that he acts in the person of Christ; (b) the ordained person is distinguished from other non-ordained persons among the people of God; and (c) once validly conferred the sacrament cannot be repeated.

(3) "In accord with his own grade of orders." There is one sacrament of order. However, there are three grades of order, the fullness of the priesthood being obtained in episcopal ordination.[22] The original draft of this canon did not include the words "in accord with his own grade of order." The words were added by the consultors to make more clear the basic distinction of the episcopacy, priesthood, and diaconate.[23] Each level of order has its own responsibilities for the mission of the Church. These responsibilities have been discussed by the Council and have been structured into the canons of this Code. The episcopacy and priesthood participate in the threefold office of Christ: to sanctify, to teach, to shepherd.[24] Priests are united to their bishop in priestly dignity and together with him form a sacerdotal college.[25] Deacons "on whom hands are laid not for priesthood but for ministry"[26] are joined to the bishop and priests and to a degree they are authorized to exercise ministry in the service of the liturgy, of the gospel, and of works of charity.[27]

Grades of Order/Matter and Form

Canon 1009 — §1. The orders are the episcopacy, the presbyterate, and the diaconate.
§2. They are conferred by an imposition of hands and by the consecratory prayer which the liturgical books prescribe for the individual grades.

This canon simply lists the grades of order. Some consultors thought that the canon should be expanded to include a separate section on each grade of order. The opinion was not accepted because this suggestion is already contained in other parts of the Church's legal system. However, a second paragraph was added to the canon to describe how the

---

[18]For a summary of some material on "institution" in English from a variety of theological viewpoints, confer *NCE*, s.v. "Sacraments, Theology of," by J. Quinn; *SacM*, s.v. "Orders and Ordination," by P. Fransen; L. Ott, *Fundamentals of Catholic Dogma*, trans. by P. Lynch (Rockford, Ill.: Tan, 1954), 336; R. McBrien, *Catholicism* (Minneapolis, Minn.: Winston, 1981), 743–744; A. Dulles, *A Church To Believe In* (New York: Crossroad Press, 1982), 80–102.

[19]*Comm*, 181.

[20]Paul VI, *First Tonsure, Minor Orders and the Subdiaconate*, passim, but especially nos. 1–4.

[21]For a summary of some material on sacramental character in English, confer Ott, 457; *NCE*, "Sacramental Character," by P. Hanley; P. Fransen, passim; McBrien, 739–740; Synod of Bishops, *The Ministerial Priesthood* (Washington, D.C.: USCC, 1971), 14; SCDF, *Declaration in Defense of Catholic Doctrine on the Church against Certain Errors of the Present Day*, June 24, 1973 (Washington, D.C.: USCC, 1973), 11.

[22]Paul VI, apconst, *Approval of New Rites of the Ordination of Deacons, Presbyters and Bishops*, June 18, 1968, in *The Rites*, 2 vols. (New York: Pueblo, 1976–1981) 2:44.

[23]*Comm*, 181.

[24]*LG* 20.

[25]*PO* 28.

[26]*The Rites*, 2:46.

[27]*LG* 29.

sacrament is conferred.[28] The theological commentaries contain material on the matter and form of the sacrament,[29] and the apostolic constitution of Pope Paul VI which promulgated the approved revised rites for ordination is a valuable commentary on the liturgical changes.[30]

CHAPTER I
THE CELEBRATION AND MINISTER OF ORDINATION
[cc. 1010–1023]

This chapter is a combination of two separate chapters of the 1917 Code. At the suggestion of the *coetus* responsible for this section, what had been chapter IV of the original schema on the time and place of ordination was combined with chapter I on the minister of ordination.[31]

Time of Ordination

Canon 1010 — Ordination is to be celebrated within the solemnities of Mass on a Sunday or on a holy day of obligation; for pastoral reasons, however, it can take place on other days, even on ordinary weekdays.

This canon was transferred from the former division of this material in chapter IV and made the first canon in chapter I. Originally the canon contained two paragraphs (c. 237 of original schema). The first paragraph considered episcopal ordination while the second paragraph was concerned with "other ordinations." The *coetus* recommended that the two paragraphs be combined into one. The recommendation was followed, and the canon is one paragraph which considers all ordinations.[32]

The canon continues the tradition of the Church that ordinations be celebrated within Mass. However, it simplifies the former law on the time for ordination by listing in a context of pastoral realism the preferences for the time of ordination: Sundays, holy days, and, for pastoral reasons, weekdays. As a matter of fact, the practice of using weekdays for ordinations was authorized by the Holy See for the United States in 1940.[33]

Setting for Ordination

Canon 1011 — §1. As a rule ordination is to be celebrated in the cathedral church; for pastoral reasons, however, it can be celebrated in another church or oratory.

§2. The clergy and other members of the Christian faithful are to be invited to the ordination so that a large congregation may be present for the celebration.

Originally this canon contained one paragraph (c. 239 of original schema). However, the *coetus* recommended that the canon be divided into two paragraphs to allow for the separate consideration of the place for ordination and those to be invited to the ordination.[34] The first paragraph of the canon deals with the place for ordination. It simplifies the former law (*CIC* 1009). The canon gives a juridic basis for alternatives to the cathedral church as the traditional place for ordination, thereby reflecting a developing practice in many local churches. Not only are ordinations celebrated in oratories or seminaries and religious communities as allowed in the former law, but this canon allows for ordinations in other churches of the diocese. In the United States there is a growing practice to have ordinations in the parish church of the candidate or in the parish where the candidate as a transitional deacon exercised his ministry in either a deacon internship program or in an extended diaconate program.

The second paragraph of the canon is a recognition of the teaching of the Church that an ordination is not only a celebration for an individual or group of individuals, it is a celebration of the Church. The presence of the clergy and other members of the Christian faithful make visible this theology. The importance of the believing community worshiping and celebrating together as a community is one of the reasons why canon 1010 of this revised Code specifies times when the believing community would be free from their ordinary responsibilities to celebrate the ordination ceremony. The pastoral situation in the United States is such that most ordinations are celebrated on weekdays. This is actually the third preference of canon 1010. However, it is a day when both clergy and other members of the Christian faithful are more free to participate than they would be on a Sunday or holy day.

Minister of Ordination

Canon 1012 — The minister of sacred ordination is a consecrated bishop.

---

[28]*Comm,* 181.

[29]For a summary of some material on the matter and form of orders, confer Ott, 454–455; Quinn, 807–808; *The Rites,* 2:46–48.

[30]*The Rites,* 2:44–48.

[31]*Comm,* 206. The original sacramental law schema dealt with the sacrament of orders in cc. 190–241. See ComCICRec, *Schema Documenti Pontificii quo Disciplina Canonica de Sacramentis Recognoscitur* (Typis Polyglottis Vaticanis, 1975).

[32]*Comm,* 206.

[33]SCSacr, *Indult to the Bishops of the United States,* May 18, 1940, *CLD* 2, 249.

[34]*Comm,* 206.

The apostolic letters of Pope Paul VI *First Tonsure, Minor Orders, and the Subdiaconate* and *Norms for the Order of Diaconate* have contributed to a rather simple interpretation of this canon. Since 1972, minor orders and the subdiaconate no longer exist in the Latin Church, and the clerical state begins with the diaconate. In the former law there was never any doubt about the necessity of having a bishop or bishops ordain to the episcopacy, priesthood, or diaconate (*CIC* 951). The tradition is clear on this point.[35] The only point of discussion in the former law concerned the extraordinary minister of ordination as applied to minor orders and the subdiaconate. Since these no longer exist in the Latin Church, there is absolute clarity that the bishop is the minister of ordination.

In the development of the final text of this canon there were two suggestions for change:

(1) The adverb "only" should be added to the text. The suggestion was not accepted because the consultors thought that the present text clearly reflected the tradition.

(2) It was suggested that the text of the canon be changed to be more in accord with the liturgical terminology, i.e., "consecrated bishop" should read "ordained bishop." The suggestion was not accepted by the consultors.[36]

Pontifical Mandate for Episcopal Ordination

Canon 1013 — No bishop is permitted to consecrate anyone a bishop unless it is first evident that there is a pontifical mandate.

The original form of this canon contained introductory theological material which was intended to provide a context for the norm of law (c. 193 of original schema). However, in the discussions among the consultors there was no agreement on the practical effects of the first part of the canon. The *Praeses* recalled the Prefatory Note of Explanation to *Lumen Gentium* 22, in which the questions of validity and lawfulness were left to the debate of theologians. The intervention implied that the consultors were trying to settle these questions. As a result, the first part of the canon was suppressed.[37]

The present text of the canon essentially repeats canon 953 of the 1917 Code. In accord with the norm of interpretation which states that material which is the same as the former law is interpreted within the canonical tradition, it can be stated that this canon concerns lawfulness and prohibits the consecration of a bishop without a mandate from the Holy Father.[38] If a bishop were consecrated without the required mandate, the ordination would be valid but unlawful. The consecrating bishops and the newly consecrated bishop would be automatically excommunicated according to the present law.[39]

Co-Consecration of Bishop-Elect

Canon 1014 — Unless a dispensation has been granted by the Apostolic See, the principal consecrating bishop in an episcopal consecration is to associate to himself at least two other consecrating bishops; but it is especially appropriate that all the bishops who are present should consecrate the bishop-elect along with the bishops mentioned.

The draft text of this canon was substantially sustained by the *coetus* (c. 194 of original schema). However two small changes were incorporated into the text:

(1) The appropriateness of having all the bishops present consecrate the bishop-elect was emphasized by the adding of the word "valde" to the text.

(2) The word "ordain" was replaced by "consecrate" to make this canon consistent with the decision of the consultors on terminology, which had been mentioned in this commentary under canon 1012.

This canon basically repeats canon 954 of the 1917 Code. The custom of co-consecrators, which originated prior to the Council of Nicaea and which symbolizes the unity of the episcopacy, is extended and thereby strengthened by this canon. This is not surprising since the Second Vatican Council stressed collegiality and taught that a bishop becomes a member of the episcopal college by his ordination and through hierarchical communion.[40] In terms of validity, it is clear that the consecration of a bishop by one bishop is valid.[41] In terms of lawfulness, co-consecrators are required. If there are insurmountable difficulties in observing this requirement, a dispensation must be obtained.

The canons now move from the consideration of ordinations to the episcopacy to ordinations to the priesthood and diaconate.

[35]*Ench*, nos. 1326, 1768, 1777.
[36]*Comm*, 182.
[37]Ibid.

[38]"Ordination of a Bishop," *The Rites*, 2:87.
[39]C. 1382.
[40]Prefatory Note of Explanation to *LG* 22.
[41]M. Conte A. Coronata, *Institutiones Iuris Canonici, De Sacramentis*, 3 vols. (Torino: Marietti, 1943–1946), 2:24; S. Woywod, A *Practical Commentary on the Code of Canon Law*, 2 vols. (New York: Wagner, 1929), 1:495.

Dimissorial Letters

Canon 1015 — §1. Each candidate is to be ordained to the presbyterate or the diaconate by his own bishop or with legitimate dimissorial letters from him.

§2. The candidates' own bishop is to ordain his own subjects personally unless he is impeded from doing so by a just cause; he cannot, however, licitly ordain a subject of an oriental rite without an apostolic indult.

§3. The person who can grant dimissorial letters to receive orders can also confer these same orders personally provided he possesses the episcopal character.

The first paragraph of this canon contains the two traditional norms for lawful ordination: each candidate should be ordained by his own bishop; if for some reason this is not possible, the candidate should be ordained with legitimate dimissorial letters. The first of these norms does not present any difficulty for interpretation. However, the second norm requires some explanation because it presupposes the reader understands the meaning of dimissorial letters. By definition dimissorial letters are letters by which a proper ordinary permits another bishop to ordain one of his subjects and presents a recommendation of the candidate's worthiness to the ordaining bishop.[42] All major superiors of clerical religious institutes of pontifical right and clerical institutes of apostolic life are considered ordinaries and therefore have the right to issue dimissorial letters for their subjects.[43]

The second paragraph of this canon simply affirms one of the many responsibilities of the residential bishop. If the office is accepted, the bishop should do his best to fulfill the responsibilities of the office. The traditional reasons which would justify a bishop from personally ordaining his subjects are poor health, distance, and the expenses involved in traveling long distances if the diocese is large. Unacceptable reasons would be laziness or mere inconvenience.[44]

The second part of this paragraph concerns candidates of the Oriental Rite. It is not lawful for a bishop of the Latin Rite to ordain them without an apostolic indult. There was a discussion among the consultors whether this question should be included in the revised Code since it states explicitly that it is concerned exclusively with the Latin Church.[45] However, the text was sustained. The prohibition is consistent with the prior law and the theology of the Second Vatican Council that the Oriental Rite should be respected by the Latin Rite and retain its own traditions as an equal.[46] A pastoral problem regarding the implementation of this canon is rooted in the individual candidate's lack of awareness that he is a member of the Oriental Rite. This lack of awareness is frequently traceable to an error at the time of his baptism. Consequently there are no records available which indicate the candidate is not a member of the Latin Rite.

Paragraph three of this canon was a separate canon in the 1917 Code (*CIC* 959). The consultors retained the text but transferred it to this canon as a third paragraph. The canon brings together two separate issues:

(1) Since the granting of dimissorial letters is an act of jurisdiction, it is necessary that the grantor have jurisdiction. For example, a titular bishop without subjects (an auxiliary bishop) could not grant dimissorial letters. On the other hand, a titular bishop with jurisdiction (one elected as a vicar capitular) could issue dimissorial letters.

(2) To ordain validly the person must be a bishop. This point has already been discussed under canon 1012. The conclusion is clear: when an individual is a bishop and possesses jurisdiction, he can not only issue dimissorial letters for his subjects who are candidates for orders, but he may ordain them himself. As the authors say, nothing further is required.[47]

Proper Bishop for Ordination

Canon 1016 — As regards the diaconal ordination of those who intend to become members of the secular clergy, the proper bishop is the bishop of the diocese in which the candidate has a domicile or the diocese to which he intends to devote himself; as regards the presbyteral ordination of secular clerics, the proper bishop is the bishop of the diocese into which the candidate has been incardinated through the diaconate.

The draft text of this canon followed the text of canon 956 of the 1917 Code (c. 198 of the original schema). However, in the discussions of the *coetus* textual changes were made. The first change entirely eliminated the place of origin as one of the criteria for determining the proper bishop for

---

[42]J. Quinn. *Documents Required for the Reception of Orders,* CanLawStud 266 (Washington, D.C.: Catholic University of America, 1948), 130.

[43]C. 134.

[44]Coronata, *De Sacramentis,* 26; J. Abbo and J. Hannan, *The Sacred Canons,* 2 vols. (St. Louis: Herder 1960), II: 29.

[45]*Comm,* 183; c. 1.

[46]*OE* 1–5.

[47]Coronata, *De Sacramentis,* 44, U. Beste, *Introductio in Codicem* (Naples: D'Auria, 1956), 553; E. Regatillo, *Ius Sacramentarium* (Santander: Sal Terrae, 1949), 483.

ordination. Second, in a concern for clarity, it was decided to consider ordination to the order of deacon first and then ordination to the order of priest. Finally, for reasons of logical development within the law on orders, the placement of this canon was also changed.[48] This canon exclusively considers the ordination of diocesan candidates for orders. It begins with a consideration of the proper bishop for the order of deacon. The two criteria for judging who is the proper bishop are: (1) the bishop of the diocese in which the candidate has a domicile; and (2) the bishop of the diocese to which the candidate intends to devote himself. The case covered by the first criterion is clear. However, as regards the second criterion, the candidate must manifest his intention in writing. The written statement is very important now since entrance into the clerical state and incardination into a diocese come through ordination to the order of deacon.[49] The proper bishop for ordination to the priesthood flows from the norm contained in the first part of the canon: the proper bishop for ordination to the priesthood is the bishop of the diocese into which the candidate was incardinated through diaconate. If there are changes of intent for whatever reason by either the bishop or the deacon, the deacon would have to remain as deacon until the bishop approves his priestly ordination, institutes excardination-incardination procedures, or requests an indult of laicization.

Territoriality of Ordination Prerogatives

Canon 1017 — A bishop can confer orders outside his own jurisdiction only with the permission of the diocesan bishop.

This canon is a simple conclusion from the traditional principle of law that the residential bishop is the head of the local church and ministry in the local church is exercised in union with him.[50] Since the authority of a residential bishop is limited to his territory, when he leaves his diocese he must have the permission of the bishop of the diocese into which he enters to ordain lawfully.[51] When a visiting bishop has received the required permission, he may ordain his own subjects and the subjects of others if he has legitimate dimissorial letters. This norm of law is quite practical due to the growing custom in many regional seminaries of inviting one of its sponsoring bishops to ordain at the seminary. Since the ordaining bishop is not in his jurisdiction, he would need the permission of the bishop in

whose diocese the seminary is situated. Undoubtedly, however, the bishop would ordain validly if for any reason he did not have permission.

Dimissorial Letters for Seculars

**Canon 1018 — §1. The following can grant dimissorial letters for the secular clergy:
1° the proper bishop mentioned in can. 1016;
2° an apostolic administrator and, with the consent of the college of consultors, the diocesan administrator; and with the consent of the council mentioned in can. 495, §2, an apostolic pro-vicar and pro-prefect.
§2. A diocesan administrator, a pro-vicar apostolic, and a pro-prefect apostolic are not to grant dimissorial letters to those who have been denied access to orders by their diocesan bishop, vicar apostolic, or prefect apostolic.**

This canon lists those who can issue dimissorial letters for the diocesan clergy. The final draft text has been simplified, and this paragraph has been reduced from four parts to two (c. 198 of original schema). Those listed in the canon possess jurisdiction. Those who possess jurisdiction permanently, e.g., a diocesan bishop, and those appointed by the Holy See, e.g., an apostolic administrator, can issue dimissorial letters without conferring with the college of consultors. Those who administer a diocese, a vicariate, or a prefecture during a vacancy must consult the appropriate council before issuing dimissorial letters.

This commentator judges that the draft text of this canon was more complete and precise than the present text. It seems that not mentioning vicars and prefects apostolic in the text and then explicitly referring to pro-vicars and pro-prefects apostolic creates an unnecessary need for interpretation. The canonical tradition is clear that apostolic vicars and prefects can issue dimissorial letters without consulting their councils. They have the same rights for their territories as residential bishops. The former law and the draft of this canon presented to the *coetus* on the sacraments stated this point very clearly in the text.[52] In this canon it is not clearly stated. Further, neither the animadversions of the *coetus* nor the final report of the Code Commission explains the reasons for the change of text.

The second paragraph of the canon repeats a traditional principle of law that what has been denied by a higher authority cannot be granted by a lower authority. This point is important in practice since the diocesan bishop, vicar apostolic, or prefect apostolic presumably had good reasons for denying access to orders. For the good of the particular church, the final judgment on access to orders in

---

[48]*Comm,* 198.
[49]Paul VI, *Norms for the Order of the Diaconate,* 9; N. Halligan, *Sacraments of Community Renewal,* 3 vols. (Staten Island, New York: Alba House, 1974), 3:7 (cited as Halligan).
[50]*CD* 11–15; c. 381.
[51]*CIC* 1008; Woywod, 1:556.

[52]*CIC* 958; *Comm,* 185.

these cases should be left to the judgment of the new bishop, vicar apostolic, or prefect apostolic.

Dimissorial Letters for Religious

Canon 1019 — §1 The major superior of a clerical religious institute of pontifical right or the major superior of a clerical society of apostolic life of pontifical right is competent to grant dimissorial letters for the diaconate and for the presbyterate on behalf of the subjects who have become perpetually or definitively members of the institute or society in accord with their constitutions.

§2. The ordination of all other members of any institute or society is governed by the law for seculars; any other indult whatsoever which has been granted to superiors is revoked.

This canon specifies who may issue dimissorial letters for religious and members of clerical societies of apostolic life. There was little discussion in the *coetus* on the canon. The suggestion of not using the word "subjects" in the text was not accepted. However, the word "clerical" was added before "society" for reasons of precision.[53]

The first paragraph clarifies who has the right to issue dimissorial letters for candidates who are members of pontifical right clerical institutes of consecrated life or societies of apostolic life. The right to issue dimissorial letters belongs to the major superiors of religious institutes or societies of apostolic life. However, they cannot issue them unless the candidates have become members of the institute or society perpetually and definitively according to the constitutions. This restates the former law.[54] The practice of the Holy See is to allow a candidate to anticipate perpetual profession rather than dispense him so he could be ordained in temporary vows. This policy is consistent with the canonical tradition that there be no unattached clerics in the Church.[55]

The second paragraph covers the ordinations of all other members of religious institutes and societies of apostolic life. Candidates for orders from these institutes or societies are governed by the law for diocesan candidates. This question has already been considered in the commentary on canon 1018. Any indult which has been granted to major superiors of non-pontifical right religious clerical institutes or non-pontifical right societies of apostolic life is revoked by this canon. The reference to indults in this canon is the same as in the former law, which concerned the right to issue dimissorial letters for members of these institutes or societies who had not been definitively incorporated.[56]

Necessary Testimonials and Documents

Canon 1020 — Dimissorial letters are not to be granted unless all the testimonials and documents which are demanded by law in accord with cann. 1050 and 1051 have been obtained beforehand.

This canon was transferred almost verbatim from the 1917 Code of Canon Law (*CIC* 960). Therefore, it is to be interpreted in the same manner as the former law. Dimissorial letters are based on testimonial letters and should not be issued by the proper authority unless all the testimonial letters and other required documents are completely in order. This commentary will consider these documents under the proper heading; however, it should be mentioned here that the obligation of the competent authority to verify the truthfulness and accuracy of the testimonial letters and other documents is a grave one.

Eligibility To Receive Dimissorials

Canon 1021 — Dimissorial letters can be sent to any bishop who is in communion with the Apostolic See with the exception of a bishop who is of a rite different from the rite of the candidate, which requires an apostolic indult.

This canon also repeats the 1917 Code (*CIC* 961). It contains two basic norms. First, to be eligible to receive legitimate dimissorial letters, the bishop must be in union with the Holy See. This norm is consistent with the theology of *Lumen Gentium* 22 and its authentic interpretation contained in the Prefatory Note of Explanation published as an appendix to the *Dogmatic Constitution on the Church.*[57] The second norm of the canon contains an exception. Even though the bishop is in union with the Holy See, an apostolic indult is necessary if he is of a different rite than the candidate for orders. This norm is consistent with both the theology of the Second Vatican Council and the first canon of the revised Code of Canon Law.[58]

Authenticity of Dimissorials

Canon 1022 — After he has received legitimate dimissorial letters, the ordaining bishop is not to proceed to the ordination unless there is clear proof that they are genuine.

There was some discussion of the *coetus* about the draft text of this canon. The discussion centered on whether the ordaining bishop in addition to verifying the authenticity of the dimissorial letters had

[53]*Comm,* 185.
[54]*CIC* 964, §3; SCRIS, *Instruction on the Renewal of the Religious Life,* Jan. 6, 1969, n. 37, 2.
[55]*CIC* 111; c. 265.
[56]*CIC* 964, §4; Coronata, *De Sacramentis,* 56; Beste, 556.

[57]Prefatory Note of Explanation to *LG* 22.
[58]*OE* 1–5.

a further obligation to inquire about the qualities of the candidate and discover whether the dimissorial letters were granted according to the norms of law. As a result of the discussion, a decision was made to return to the text of the 1917 Code.[59]

This canon is simply a prudential norm to protect the bishop and, by implication, the Church from forgeries. As is true for academic transcripts, the proper procedure is to have the letters delivered directly from the competent authority to the ordaining bishop. If the letters are delivered by the candidates themselves, the ordaining bishop must examine them carefully and, if necessary, verify them by contacting the authority who issued them. Once the dimissorial letters are verified as authentic, the bishop can presume the testimonial letters are truthful and accurate, and he may ordain the candidate without further investigation.[60]

Conditions Regarding Validity of Dimissorials

Canon 1023 — Dimissorial letters can be circumscribed with restrictions or revoked by the one who granted them or his successor; but once they have been granted, they do not cease to be operative when the authority of the one granting them ceases.

There are two parts to this canon. The first part concerns the right of the one who issued the dimissorial letters or his successor to restrict the dimissorial letters in some way. For example, the candidate must be ordained within a certain period of time or by a particular bishop or after an examination of his worthiness and fitness. By implication, if the dimissorial letters are issued without any limitations, they are valid indefinitely.[61]

The second part of the canon concerns continuity of government. It considers the status of the dimissorial letters when the grantor loses his authority. This could happen in a number of ways, e.g., death, transfer, or retirement. The canon applies the general norms of law on a vacant office to this question and concludes that the dimissorial letters continue to be valid as written.[62]

CHAPTER II
CANDIDATES FOR ORDINATION
[cc. 1024–1052]

The title of this chapter was changed from "The Subject of Ordination" to the present title "Candidates for Ordination." The suggestion of one consultor that the chapter should be divided into the headings of diaconal ordination, priestly ordination, and episcopal ordination was not sustained. The traditional order of considering the sacrament, although modified, was basically retained.[63]

Requisites for Valid Ordination

Canon 1024 — Only a baptized male validly receives sacred ordination.

This canon originally had two paragraphs (c. 206 of original schema). However, the second paragraph was transferred to the following canon and became the first paragraph of that canon. The present text of this canon was sustained without discussion. The reason for the change was to separate the requirements for the validity and those for the lawfulness of orders.

This canon concerns the validity of the sacrament. It restates verbatim the first section of canon 968 of the 1917 Code. The criteria listed in the canon are clear and the interpretation is the same as that in the former law: only a validly baptized male can be ordained.[64] Although the interpretation of this canon is traditional and clear, the literature on this canon during the revision process exceeds the total amount of literature on all the other canons on orders. This commentator judges that the question of the formulation of this canon was settled when Pope Paul VI promulgated *First Tonsure, Minor Orders and the Subdiaconate* in 1972 and limited the installation of persons in the ministries to men.[65] While there is no intrinsic connection between ministries and orders, the document made the mind-set of the legislator very clear. An a fortiori dynamic was established, and its effect on the revision process was so efficacious that there is no recorded discussion of this canon in either the *coetus* or the *Relatio* of the commission. It was simply accepted as presented. Since this commentary is on the law as written, it is not the place to discuss the allegations of sexism in the Church. However, to provide the reader with a context for further study, references to the discussion are included in the footnotes and bibliography.[66] A final note is in order. The present text of the canon certainly settles the question for the government of the Church. However, it should neither discourage those who are working for equal rights for women in the Church

[59]*Comm*, 186.
[60]*CIC* 962; Coronata, *De Sacramentis*, 47; Regatillo, 484.
[61]Coronata, *De Sacramentis*, 45–46.
[62]*CIC* 61, 207; cc. 46; 132, §2.

[63]*Comm*, 187.
[64]Coronata, *De Sacramentis*, 69; Beste, 558.
[65]Paul VI, *First Tonsure, Minor Orders and Subdiaconate*, n.7.
[66]NCCB, Committee on Pastoral Research and Practice, "Theological Reflections on the Ordination of Women," *RfR* 33 (March 1973), 218–222. For an excellent survey of the literature on the question along with documents from the Pontifical Biblical Commission and the SCDF, confer J. Coriden, ed., *Sexism and Church Law* (Ramsey, New Jersey: Paulist Press, 1977).

nor limit in any way their efforts to raise the consciousness of people on this fundamental and sensitive issue within the believing community.

Requirements for Licit Ordination

Canon 1025 — **§1. In order for one to be ordained licitly to the presbyterate or to the diaconate, it is required: that the candidate having completed a period of probation according to the norm of law is endowed with the required qualities in the judgment of the proper bishop or competent major superior; that he is not restrained by any irregularity or by any impediment; that he has fulfilled the prerequisites according to the norms of cann. 1033-1039; in addition the documents mentioned in can. 1050 have been obtained, and the investigation mentioned in can. 1051 has been conducted.**

§2. Furthermore, it is required that in the judgment of the same legitimate superior he is considered to be useful for the ministry of the Church.

§3. The bishop who ordains his own subject who is destined for the service of another diocese must be sure that the person to be ordained is going to be assigned to the other diocese.

The first paragraph of this canon provides the agenda for the four articles which form the content of the chapter. In essence, these articles represent the concern of the Church that only fit candidates will be approved for orders. Each area contained in the first paragraph of the canon will receive individual attention under the appropriate article.

The second paragraph contains a traditional teaching of the Church regarding orders: "No person becomes a priest for himself" or "Candidates are ordained for God's people."[67] There is an interesting change in this text when compared to the 1917 Code (*CIC* 969). Formerly, the prohibition applied to diocesan candidates for orders. In the revised Code the prohibition has been extended to candidates from religious institutes or societies of apostolic life. The wording of the canon has been broadened to include bishops and major superiors. In an age in which vocation shortages are extensive, the implementation of this canon will present little difficulty. However, the principle still stands that fit candidates should be ordained only when they are considered useful for the ministry of the Church.

The final paragraph of this canon considers a bishop's ordaining his own subject who is committed to the service of another diocese. As in the former law, it is required that the candidate through a prior written agreement be incardinated into the diocese he has agreed to serve.[68]

[67]Coronata, *De Sacramentis,* 73; Beste, 561.
[68]C. 266.

ARTICLE 1: REQUIREMENTS IN THE CANDIDATES
[cc. 1026–1032]

Freedom of Candidates for Orders

Canon 1026 — **In order for one to be ordained he ought to possess the required freedom; it is unlawful to force someone to receive orders or to deter one who is canonically suitable from receiving them by whatever means and for whatever reason.**

This canon repeats canon 971 of the 1917 Code and is concerned with the liberty of the candidate for orders. It considers such liberty from the viewpoints of his being forced to receive orders or of his being prevented from receiving orders. The canon applies to anyone who could influence a candidate, e.g., parents, relatives, teachers, and superiors.[69] If the candidate is forced to receive orders, the question of the invalidity of orders arises and would have to be examined according to ecclesiastical procedures.[70]

Formation of Candidates for Orders

Canon 1027 — **Those who aspire to the diaconate or the presbyterate are to receive an accurate formation in accord with the norm of law.**

This canon reflects the concern of the Church that candidates for orders be properly formed for the exercise of ministry. While the formulation of the canon is new, the concern of the Church is traditional. The wording of the canon "in accord with the norm of law" includes both universal and particular law. Since the Second Vatican Council, decentralization and subsidiarity have played significant roles in the governmental system of the Church. Therefore, it is to be expected that particular law will be more prominent for the formation of the clergy.[71]

Instruction on Obligations of Orders

Canon 1028 — **The diocesan bishop or the competent superior is to see to it that candidates are**

[69]Beste, 561.
[70]Coronata, *De Sacramentis,* 76–77; cc. 290, 1°; 1708–1712.
[71]The conciliar and post-conciliar directives on theological education/formation are good examples of the contemporary importance of particular law in the Church. While the Council and the Holy See made certain determinations, each national conference of bishops was mandated to develop a program of priestly formation for its territory. Confer *OT* 1. The following documents are pertinent and are available from the USCC Publications Office: SCCE, *The Basic Program of Priestly Formation,* March 30, 1970; idem, *The Theological Formation of Future Priests,* February 2, 1976; NCCB, *The Program of Priestly Formation,* June 18, 1971; 2nd ed., March 3, 1976; 3rd ed., November 30, 1981.

duly instructed concerning those matters which pertain to the order to be received and its obligations before they are promoted to that order.

This canon contains an admonition to the diocesan bishop or competent major superior which particularizes the general nature of the prior canon. The bishop or major superior is required to certify that the candidate is correctly instructed on the nature and obligations of the order he is to receive. In practice this responsibility is fulfilled through the programs of theological education/formation used by the competent authority to prepare candidates for ministry.

Requisites for Orders

Canon 1029 — After all circumstances have been taken into account in the prudent judgment of the proper bishop or the competent major superior, only those should be promoted to orders who have an integral faith, are motivated by a right intention, possess the required knowledge, and enjoy a good reputation, good morals, and proven virtues, and other physical and psychological qualities which are appropriate to the order to be received.

The draft of this canon was not accepted by the *coetus* (c. 213 of original schema). It was thought to be incomplete. As a result of the discussion within the *coetus,* the following points were added to the text: (1) specific references to the supernatural dimensions of qualifications for orders—correct faith and approved virtues; and (2) a reference to required knowledge. Two additional suggestions were not included in the text of the canon, namely, a reference to theological and pastoral training and consultation on the candidate with the presbyteral and parochial councils. Presumably it was thought that theological and pastoral training was already included under required knowledge and since consultation in any form was the right of the competent authority, it was already implicitly contained in the canon.[72]

In a very real sense this canon is the heart of the law on candidates for orders. Even with a shortage of vocations, the Church insists on a thorough testing of its future ministers.[73] A brief word on each criterion in the canon will be helpful.

(1) "The prudent judgment of the proper bishop or the competent major superior." In all cases those who are responsible for the immediate training of the candidates for orders are required to make recommendations to the proper bishop or competent major superior. This recommendation is consultative in character, for the competent authority must carefully consider the reports on all the points men-

tioned in this canon and then make a judgment on the promotion of a candidate to orders.

(2) "An integral faith." This means that the candidate has not only accepted the faith as taught by the Church[74] but is a believer who lives the faith and, obedient to the Spirit, commits himself to an unending process of conversion.[75]

(3) "A right intention." This is a key area both for the candidate and for those judging his fitness for orders. An individual must choose to live his life imitating the example of the Lord as teacher, priest, and shepherd. The candidate must choose to be a co-worker with the bishop in fulfilling the mission the Lord has entrusted to His Church. Experience has shown that an error in this area can lead to unfortunate results for the life of the individual and not infrequently for the ministry of the Church.[76]

(4) "Possess the required knowledge." A presumption is established that when the individual has completed the courses required by universal and particular law, this requirement has been fulfilled.

(5) "Good reputation." This is a very important factor in approving a candidate for orders. Ordination makes a person a public figure in the Church. The ordained person must be a credible figure to the people of God.

(6) "Good morals, and proven virtues." Since the ordained are called by a special title to holiness, their lives should reflect their vocational decision.[77]

(7) "Physical and psychological qualities." Due to the unfortunate number of priests who have been laicized, the Church has learned to give serious attention to the health of the candidates, especially emotional health. The Church has initiated psychological testing as part of the admissions procedures to seminaries. This practice is the result of laicization indults granted for psychological reasons which antedated ordination but of which the candidate was unaware when he petitioned for orders. This commentator judges that with the consent of the candidate, the results of the admissions testing and interview should be used in the seminary program of human growth and development, which is so important for spiritual growth and so necessary to make a free and informed decision for orders. This is a serious responsibility of the seminary's formation program.[78]

Denial of Presbyterate

Canon 1030 — Only for a canonical reason, even if it be occult, can the proper bishop or the compe-

---

[72]*Comm,* 190–191.
[73]*OT* 4.

[74]*LG* 25; *Program of Priestly Formation,* 1981, nos. 115–118.
[75]*SC* 9; *OT* 8; *PO* 12.
[76]*OT* 4; *PO* 2.
[77]*LG* 41; *OT* 8–12; *PO* 15–19.
[78]*Program of Priestly Formation,* 1981, nos. 94, 272; SCCE, "A Guide to Formation in Priestly Celibacy," *Norms for Priestly Formation* (Washington, D.C.: USCC, 1982), 165–173.

tent major superior forbid access to the presbyterate to deacons destined for the presbyterate subject to them and with due regard for recourse in accord with the norm of law.

This canon is a logical consequence of the prior canon. It affirms the right of the proper bishop or competent major superior to prohibit a transitional deacon from being promoted to the priesthood for a canonical reason. The canonical reason would be the non-fulfillment of one of the criteria of the prior canon even if such a factor is occult. It is very important to understand that the serious responsibility of the competent authority to approve fit candidates for orders never ceases. If new evidence becomes available, the competent authority must fulfill its responsibility to the Church. The deacon has the right to have recourse according to the norms of law. This point was stressed by the members of the *coetus*. They thought that the competent authority was obliged to inform the deacon of the reasons for the prohibition and that he be given the opportunity to respond.[79]

Age for Orders

Canon 1031 — §1. The presbyterate is not to be conferred upon those who have not yet completed the age of twenty-five and who do not possess sufficient maturity; an interval of at least six months is to be observed between the diaconate and the presbyterate; men destined for the presbyterate are to be admitted to the order of diaconate only after they have completed the age of twenty-three.

§2. A candidate for the permanent diaconate who is not married is not to be admitted to the diaconate unless he has completed at least twenty-five years of age; if the candidate is married, he is not to be admitted to the permanent diaconate unless he has completed at least thirty-five years of age and has the consent of his wife.

§3. The conference of bishops may determine a norm by which an older age is required for the presbyterate and the permanent diaconate.

§4. The Apostolic See reserves to itself the dispensation from the age required in §§1 and 2 when it is a question of more than one year.

The canon establishes the age for orders and mentions some points of pastoral prudence for those candidates for the permanent diaconate who are married.

According to paragraph one, the required age for priesthood is the completion of the twenty-fifth year. The candidate must also possess sufficient maturity. This simply intensifies the importance that the revised Code gives to psychological maturity already mentioned in canon 1029. The required age for the transitional diaconate is the completion of the twenty-third year. The reader should be aware that church law contains special norms for the computation of time. Technically, the phrase "the completion of" means that the civil birthday of a person is not counted in the computation, and a person has not completed his twenty-fifth year or twenty-third year until the day after his civil birthday. Practically speaking, a candidate is eligible for the priesthood at the beginning of his twenty-sixth year and for the transitional diaconate at the beginning of his twenty-fourth year.[80]

There is also a required period of time between the reception of the diaconate and the priesthood. The period stated in the law is six months. This stipulation is totally consistent with the mind-set of the Church that formation not be rushed and that candidates be given the opportunity to exercise the order they have received before advancement to higher orders. This also applies to ministries.[81]

The second paragraph considers the permanent diaconate and distinguishes between permanent deacons who are married and those who are not married. Those who are not married are not to be ordained until they have completed their twenty-fifth year. On the other hand, those who are married shall not be ordained until they have completed their thirty-fifth year. In both cases these norms are minimum norms. One might ask why a difference exists. Apparently there is a concern that the marriage of the candidate is stable. The consent of the wife is important because the diaconal ministry of the husband can put pressures on the marriage. The experience of permanent deacon programs has been that when the married couple feels called to ministry they exercise team ministry quite successfully with minimal pressure on the marriage.

According to the norm of paragraph three, the law respects local conditions and gives the right to conferences of bishops to require an older age for orders.

The last paragraph of canon 1031 is simply a norm of control by the Holy See. If a dispensation from the age requirements of paragraphs one and two of this canon involves more than one year, the dispensation is reserved to the Holy See.

Academic-Pastoral Prerequisites for Ordination

Canon 1032 — §1. Candidates for the presbyterate can be promoted to the diaconate only after they have completed a five-year curriculum of philosophical and theological studies.

§2. After he has completed the curriculum of studies and before he is promoted to the presbyterate, a deacon is to participate in pastoral care, ex-

---

[79]*Comm*, 188.

[80]C. 202.
[81]Paul VI, *Norms for the Order of the Diaconate*, n. 2.

ercising his diaconal order for a suitable period of time, to be determined by the bishop or by the competent major superior.

§3. An aspirant to the permanent diaconate is not to be promoted to that order unless he has completed the time of formation.

This canon specifies the general requirement of canon 1029 on studies. A candidate for the priesthood must complete a five-year course of philosophical/theological studies prior to ordination to the diaconate. The conference of bishops has the responsibility of planning a program for priestly formation based on the universal law. The program must be approved by the Holy See.[82]

Paragraph two combines universal law with the principle of subsidiarity. It requires a deacon to exercise his diaconal ministry after the completion of his studies and before his ordination to the priesthood. The competent authority must determine the length of time during which the diaconal ministry is to be exercised.

The formation programs for the permanent diaconate vary from diocese to diocese. This canon seems to indicate the question is not sufficiently mature to allow for universal legislation.[83]

ARTICLE 2: PREREQUISITES FOR ORDINATION
[cc. 1033–1039]

Canon 1033 — One is licitly promoted to orders only if he has received the sacrament of confirmation.

The requirement that the candidates for orders be confirmed is a traditional one. It is based on a motivation of theological fitness, namely, it is not proper for a person to be ordained for ministerial service if he has not completed his Christian initiation.[84]

Admission to Candidacy

Canon 1034 — §1. An aspirant to the diaconate or to the presbyterate is not to be ordained unless he has first been inscribed as a candidate by the authority mentioned in cann. 1016 and 1019 in a liturgical rite of admission; this is done after he has submitted a signed petition written in his own hand and accepted in writing by the aforementioned authority.

§2. A man who has been admitted through vows to a clerical institute is not bound to obtain this type of admission.

This canon is the result of the legislation promulgated by Pope Paul VI in 1972. Since first tonsure was abrogated, a new rite was introduced called admission to candidacy, in which the candidate publically manifests his intention to offer himself to God and the Church in orders.[85] The Church in the person of the proper bishop or competent major superior must accept in writing the written petition of the candidate. This provision facilitates the process whereby the candidate consciously prepares himself for ordination. He is also reminded that he must care for his vocation in a special way.[86]

According to paragraph two, those who have been admitted through vows to a clerical religious institute are exempt from this requirement. However, members of clerical institutes of apostolic life must follow the canon. This is the reason for the reference in the first paragraph to canon 1019, which deals in part with major superiors in clerical institutes of apostolic life.

Exercise of Ministries

Canon 1035 — §1. Before anyone is promoted to either the permanent or the transitional diaconate he is required to have received the ministries of lector and acolyte and to have exercised them for a suitable period of time.

§2. Between the conferral of acolyte and diaconate, there is to be an interval of at least six months.

This canon incorporates a provision of the apostolic letter of Pope Paul VI on ministries as it applies to orders. The pope said that candidates for diaconate, whether transitional or permanent, must receive both ministries and exercise them for a fitting period of time. The purpose of the latter requirement is to give the candidates the opportunity of becoming more comfortable with the service of the word and altar. It also provides the Church with the opportunity of judging the performance of the candidates as they exercise the ministries.[87]

The second paragraph specifies the time period between the conferral of the ministry of acolyte and the reception of the diaconate. A period of six months is required.

Declaration of Candidate's Freedom

Canon 1036 — In order to be promoted to the order of diaconate or of presbyterate the candidate is to give to his own bishop or to the competent major superior a signed declaration written in his own hand, testifying that he is about to receive sacred

[82]*Program of Priestly Formation,* 1981, 36–53, 147–150.
[83]Confer Bishops' Committee on the Permanent Diaconate, *Permanent Deacons in the United States* (Washington, D.C.: USCC, 1971).
[84]Beste, 570.

[85]"Admission to Candidacy for Ordination of Deacons and Priests," *The Rites,* 2:39–43.
[86]Paul VI, *General Norms for the Order of Diaconate,* n. 1, c.
[87]Paul VI, *Norms for the Order of Diaconate,* n. 2.

orders of his own accord and freely and that he will devote himself perpetually to the ecclesiastical ministry; this declaration is also to contain his petition for admission to the reception of orders.

This canon is another example of legislation promulgated by Pope Paul VI being incorporated into the revised Code. The canon considers the intention of the candidate for orders and requires that he state in writing that he is freely and of his own accord about to take orders and that he will devote himself perpetually to ecclesiastical ministry. In addition he must petition to be admitted to the reception of orders. As mentioned in canon 1029, advancing to orders with the right intention is absolutely essential. One purpose of the admission to candidacy ceremony required by canon 1034 and the signed declaration of this canon is to help the candidate carefully discern his intention. The repetition of this type of requirement in the revised law is at least partially due to the data compiled in the laicization processes in which the candidates alleged a lack of understanding and insufficient freedom at the time of their ordination. From that viewpoint these requirements are helpful. However, they are also external to the individual as legal requirements must be. If the difficulties blocking an appreciation of and/or a free commitment to ordination and its obligations are not conscious to the individual, these requirements will not be efficacious. This very important factor must be dealt with in the formation programs of the seminary through psychological testing, quality programs of self-understanding and development, and trusting and honest dialogue between the candidates and their advisors.[88] Laicization procedures are not unlike annulment procedures in the sense that the reasons for failure are not malicious intentions but a personal incapacity to perceive and fulfill obligations of a particular state of life. Consequently the remedy is to improve as far as possible the preparation process.

Consecration to Celibacy

Canon 1037 — An unmarried candidate for the permanent diaconate and a candidate for the presbyterate is not to be admitted to the order of diaconate unless in a prescribed rite he has assumed publicly before God and the Church the obligation of celibacy or professed perpetual vows in a religious institute.

This canon concerns the special consecration to celibacy required of unmarried candidates for the permanent diaconate and candidates for the priesthood (c. 277). The canon is the result of the legislation of Pope Paul VI in 1972. The obligation to

make this special consecration to celibacy also binds religious unless they have made perpetual profession in a religious institute. It must take place prior to the ordination to the diaconate.[89] It is another example of the Church's efforts to raise the consciousness of the candidate regarding the obligations contained in his decision for orders. This ceremony, which is contained in the rite of ordination for the diaconate,[90] reflects the concern of the Church over the unfortunately high departure rate among priests. When this canon is joined to the present policy of the Holy See on laicization, a strong message is sent to potential unmarried permanent deacons and priests. Consequently the commitment to celibacy should be made with careful discernment and be responded to with sustained generosity.

Denial of Exercise of Diaconate

Canon 1038 — A deacon who refuses to be promoted to the presbyterate cannot be forbidden the exercise of the order he has received unless he is prevented from exercising it by a canonical impediment or some other serious cause to be evaluated in the judgment of the diocesan bishop or competent major superior.

This canon considers two issues. The first issue is the case of a deacon who refuses to be promoted to the priesthood yet wishes to continue functioning in ministry as a deacon. The law protects his right to continue in ministry. The second issue is the case of a deacon candidate who has been prohibited access to the priesthood by the competent authority because it has become clear that an impediment or some other grave canonical reason prohibiting priesthood is present. In this case the deacon candidate can be prohibited from the exercise of his diaconal ministry. The due process observations in the commentary on canon 1030 would also apply here.

Pre-Ordination Retreats

Canon 1039 — All those who are to be promoted to some order are to make a retreat for at least five days in a place and in a manner determined by the ordinary; before he proceeds to the ordination, the bishop must be certain that the candidates have duly made this retreat.

The final canon in this article concerns obligatory retreats prior to ordination. The law requires all candidates for orders to make a retreat of at least five days prior to the reception of orders. The ordinary[91] has the right to determine the time and

---

[88]*Program of Priestly Formation,* 1981, 90–93.

[89]Paul VI, *Norms for the Order of Diaconate,* n. 6.
[90]"Ordination of Deacons and Priests," *The Rites,* 2:73–74.
[91]C. 134.

the place. The ordaining bishop must be certain that this requirement has been fulfilled.

ARTICLE 3: IRREGULARITIES AND OTHER IMPEDIMENTS
[cc. 1040–1049]

Three significant decisions were made regarding this article by the *coetus.* The first decision was to leave the authority to dispense from major impediments with the Holy See. Second, it was decided to suppress the traditional distinction between irregularities from crime and from defect. Finally, it was decided to retain the term "irregularity" for perpetual impediments since this is the technical term in the canonical tradition.[92]

Prohibitions on Reception of Orders

Canon 1040 — **Persons who are affected by a perpetual impediment, which is called an irregularity, or a simple impediment are prevented from receiving orders; the only impediments which can be contracted are contained in the following canons.**

This canon is quite traditional. It contains two norms and two simple definitions. The two norms are:

(1) Impediments prevent candidates from receiving orders. A later canon will discuss how impediments will prevent the exercise of orders already received.

(2) The candidate for orders contracts no impediment or irregularity unless it is listed in the subsequent canons. This second norm is important because the revised law has simplified the former law on irregularities and impediments.

The definitions are traditional. An irregularity is a perpetual impediment. An impediment is a temporary disqualification.

Irregularities for Reception of Orders

Canon 1041 — **The following are irregular as regards the reception of orders:**
1° a person who labors under some form of insanity or other psychic defect due to which, after consultation with experts, he is judged incapable of rightly carrying out the ministry;
2° a person who has committed the delict of apostasy, heresy or schism;
3° a person who has attempted marriage, even a civil one only, either while he was impeded from entering marriage due to an existing matrimonial bond, sacred orders or a public perpetual vow of chastity, or with a woman bound by a valid marriage or by the same type of vow;
4° a person who has committed voluntary homicide or who has procured an effective abortion and all persons who positively cooperated in either;
5° a person who has seriously and maliciously mutilated himself or another person or a person who has attempted suicide;
6° a person who has performed an act of orders which has been reserved to those who are in the order of episcopacy or presbyterate while the person either lacked that order or had been forbidden its exercise by some declared or inflicted canonical penalty.

This canon lists six irregularities which affect the reception of orders. A brief word on each irregularity will be helpful.

(1) Insanity or some other psychic defect. This irregularity contains two parts: (a) Insanity. Insanity was a heading in the 1917 Code under irregularity from defect (*CIC* 984, 3°). It is to be understood in the same way as in the former law, i.e., a disorder which habitually impairs the use of reason. Commentators on the irregularity were consistent in stating that each case must be judged individually by experts.[93] (b) Psychic defect. This is a new heading which for this commentator refers to the category of personality disorders.[94] The addition of this category to the canon probably reflects not only the Church's acceptance of progress in the psychological sciences but also its experience in caring for priests who have resigned or who are so troubled that they have been advised by experts to petition for laicization. Since the canon deals with the reception of orders, it will be used by the National Conference of Catholic Bishops to reinforce its policy of requiring psychological testing as part of the admissions process for candidates for orders. Further, it is consistent with its requirement that a psychological staff be available for faculty/staff referrals and for the continued evaluation of students whenever necessary.[95] It is important to note that the experts do not make decisions on vocations but are part of the discernment process used by the Church.[96]

(2) The crime of apostasy, heresy, or schism. The second category of irregularity restates the 1917

---

[92]*Comm,* 195–196.

[93]Coronata, *De Sacramentis,* 143; Beste, 576; Regatillo, *Ius Sacramentarium,* 518.

[94]While it is beyond the scope of this commentary to discuss in detail the questions of insanity and psychic defect, it is important for the reader to understand the question. The canonical literature on insanity-psychic defect is usually listed in connection with marriage nullity processes. For an explanation of the terms and a general bibliography, confer L. Wrenn, *Annulments,* 4th ed. (Washington: CLSA, 1983); G. Graham, "Personality Disorders and their Effect on the Validity of Marriage," *CLSAP* (1976), 138–149.

[95]*Program of Priestly Formation,* 1981, nos. 94, 272, 347.

[96]*Comm,* 197.

Code verbatim (*CIC* 985, 1°). The terms are defined in the 1983 Code in the same way as they were in the 1917 Code.[97] The traditional interpretation of this canon applies this irregularity to those who have committed the crime of apostasy, heresy, or schism after the reception of baptism and in particular to those who were converted to the Catholic faith then left the Church and now have returned to the Church. The traditional opinion also taught that in practice a dispensation should even be obtained for precautionary reasons for those who were born in apostasy, heresy, or schism or whose baptism was doubtful.[98] The reason given was that it is very difficult to prove in the external forum the good faith which would exempt from the notion of crime. A decision of the Code Commission stated that this irregularity also extends to those who have belonged to an atheistic sect.[99] It is important not to get lost in legalism on this question and lose sight of the real issue. The law exists because of the importance of a stable faith in candidates for orders.

(3) Attempted marriage. This third cause of irregularity concerns an attempted marriage even if it is only a civil ceremony. The canon covers five possible situations, three involving the man and two involving the woman with whom he has attempted marriage. The bases of the law are an abuse of the sacrament of marriage and the incongruity that a person in this situation would be an apt candidate for orders.

This irregularity provides an opportunity to consider an increasingly common situation, which is not itself an irregularity. Many seminaries are beginning to receive applications of those who have been married and divorced but whose marriages were declared null by an ecclesiastical tribunal. This commentator judges that the admissions board has a serious responsibility to contact the tribunal and not only verify the authenticity of the annulment but also request information on the reasons for it. In some cases the reasons for the annulment are rooted in insanity or a psychic defect which, as noted, could disqualify the applicant from being a candidate for orders.

(4) Homicide and abortion. The fourth cause of irregularity is voluntary homicide and effective abortion. It extends not only to the principals but to all those who cooperate in the commission of the crime. Death resulting from an accident or legitimate self-defense is not a cause of the irregularity.[100] There was a discussion among the consultors concerning the question of abortion. Some wanted a stricter norm applied to candidates for orders so

that even an attempt at abortion would result in the irregularity. However, the suggestion was not accepted, and the traditional text was retained. The effect must follow if the irregularity is to be incurred.[101]

(5) Mutilation and attempted suicide. This commentator judges that the problems with reality perception and depression which affect persons who mutilate themselves or others or who have attempted suicide suggest that this issue be addressed in connection with the first category in this canon—insanity or psychic defect. The problems are psychological and should be considered in a psychological context. It is somewhat surprising that the revised law considers mutilation and attempted suicide under a separate heading and uses the phrase "seriously and maliciously." As suicide is no longer a reason for denying a person Christian burial[102] because of presumed inculpability rooted in personal incapacity, temporary or permanent, it is difficult to understand why the same norm of psychological incapacity should not be applied to mutilation or attempted suicide. This is not an argument for accepting such persons as fit candidates for orders but for considering them under the first category of this canon.

(6) Abuse of sacred order. The final category of irregularity for the reception of orders is the abuse of sacred order. It covers two cases: (a) placing an act of orders when the person lacks that order; and (b) placing an act of orders when the person has been prohibited its exercise.[103] The cases are different. To incur the irregularity in the first case, the action must be performed in a solemn manner, i.e., with vestments and in a function reserved to those in orders. If the person is not responsible, the irregularity is not incurred.[104] The second case requires some distinctions. If the penalty which prohibits the exercise of orders is non-declared, the cleric may exercise the order to protect his reputation; the irregularity would not be incurred. If the penalty is a censure, the penalized cleric may exercise orders for those in danger of death. If it is not a declared censure, the cleric may also respond to requests from the faithful for the sacraments.[105]

Impediments to Reception of Orders

Canon 1042 — The following are simply impeded from receiving orders:

1° a man who has a wife, unless he is legitimately destined for the permanent diaconate;

2° a person who holds an office or position of administration which is forbidden to clerics by cann.

[97]Cc. 751, 1364; *CIC* 1325, §2; 2314.
[98]Coronata, *De Sacramentis,* 156; Beste, 577; Regatillo, *Ius Sacramentarium,* 524–525.
[99]Pontifical Code Commission, "Atheistic Sect: Effect of Membership as Regards Ordination and Marriage," July 30, 1934, *CLD* 2, 286.
[100]Coronata, *De Sacramentis,* 162; Beste, 577.

[101]*Comm,* 199.
[102]C. 1184. See *CIC* 2350, §2.
[103]Coronata, *De Sacramentis,* 180–182; Regatillo, *Ius Sacramentarium,* 529.
[104]Beste, 575; Halligan, 3:38.
[105]Cc. 1335; 1352, §2.

285 and 286 and for which he must render an account until he becomes free by relinquishing the office and position of administration and has rendered an account of it;

3° a neophyte, unless he has been sufficiently proven in the judgment of the ordinary.

This canon lists three impediments.

(1) Marriage. Normally marriage is an impediment to orders in light of canon 277. However, in light of the legislation of Pope Paul VI on the permanent diaconate which has been included in the revised Code, permanent deacons who are married are not bound by the impediment. The impediment binds as long as the marriage bond exists. Therefore, it does not bind widowers or those who have obtained an annulment. In some cases the Holy See will dispense from this impediment if the wife consents, seeks admission to a religious institute, or at least gives assurance she will not interfere with her husband's priestly vocation.[106]

(2) Offices and duties forbidden to clerics. Those who exercise offices or have duties listed in canons 285–286 are impeded from receiving orders unless they are destined to be permanent deacons, who are normally not bound by such prohibitions (c. 288). From the viewpoint of the law on orders, these impediments do not present an overwhelming problem. As soon as the candidate gives up the forbidden office or duties, he is free from the impediment and from that viewpoint is eligible for the reception of orders.

(3) Neophytes. A neophyte traditionally has been understood as one who has been baptized absolutely in the Catholic Church as an adult. In this context it would refer to converts and also to those who have recently been received into full communion. The law prohibits their ordination until in the judgment of the ordinary they have proven themselves to be firm in the faith. A rule of thumb being used by many seminaries in the United States is that a candidate must live the faith for three years prior to his admission to the seminary.

Notification of Impediments

Canon 1043 — The Christian faithful are obliged to reveal impediments to sacred orders, if they know of any, to the ordinary or to the pastor before ordination.

This canon reminds the Christian faithful of their obligation to inform church authority of any impediments regarding the candidates for ordination. It is another example of the Church's concern that only apt candidates be ordained. In an age in which mobility is a way of life, the cooperation of the

Christian faithful in this matter has taken on a significant degree of importance.

Irregularities/Impediments to Exercise of Orders

Canon 1044 — §1. The following are irregular as regards the exercise of orders already received:

1° a person who has illegitimately received orders while he had an irregularity precluding his receiving orders;

2° a person who has committed a delict mentioned in can. 1041, n. 2 , if the delict is public;

3° a person who has committed a delict mentioned in can. 1041, nn. 3, 4, 5, 6.

§2. The following are impeded from exercising orders:

1° a person who has illegitimately received orders while he was bound by an impediment precluding his receiving orders;

2° a person who is afflicted with insanity or some other psychic defect mentioned in can. 1041, n. 1, until the time when the ordinary, after consultation with an expert, permits him the exercise of that order.

This canon lists those who are declared irregular or impeded from the exercise of orders already received. The first paragraph of the canon concerns irregularities; the second paragraph considers impediments. The revised Code is more explicit than the 1917 Code in the sense that it lists in separate canons what affects the lawful reception of orders and what affects their lawful exercise. The canon simply applies the categories of canons 1041–1042 to the question of the exercise of orders. In summary, whatever prohibits the reception of orders also prohibits their exercise. The reader is referred to the commentary on those canons for pertinent explanations. The only change in this canon is that the category of insanity-psychic defect which was listed as an irregularity for the reception of orders is now categorized as an impediment in the second paragraph. The impeding effect ceases when the ordinary, after consulting experts, judges that the candidate is fit to exercise orders.

Ignorance of Irregularity/Impediment

Canon 1045 — Ignorance of the irregularities and impediments does not exempt from them.

Ignorance of irregularities and impediments does not exempt from them. This canon is consistent with the law of the Church on ignorance contained in canon 15 of the revised Code. Even though the law no longer explicitly distinguishes irregularities from crime and from defect, the text and context of the canons seem to allow the traditional interpretation of the canon to stand. That interpretation stated that irregularities from crime would not take

---

[106]Coronata, *De Sacramentis,* 191; Beste, 580; Regatillo, *Ius Sacramentarium,* 532.

effect unless there was grave culpability. Irregularities from defect would bind because they are primarily for the protection of the Church and are intended to exclude from ministry those who through no fault of their own would hinder that ministry.[107]

Multiplication of Irregularities/Impediments

Canon 1046 — Irregularities and impediments are multiplied when they arise from different causes. They are not multiplied by the repetition of the same cause except in the case of the irregularity arising from voluntary homicide or the effective procuring of an abortion.

This canon considers the multiplication of irregularities and impediments. It basically restates the 1917 Code (*CIC* 989). Irregularities and impediments are multiplied only for different causes, not for a repetition of the same cause. The two exceptions to this norm are voluntary homicide and effective abortion. The only change in the text from the 1917 Code is the addition of the second exception, namely, effective abortion. Although no explanation of the addition was given by the *coetus,* the reason is undoubtedly the Church's reaction to the increasingly common acceptance of abortion in civil legislation and secular value systems.

The practical implications of this canon will be evident in subsequent canons on dispensations from irregularities and impediments. On the basis of this canon, the only time a number must be included in the petition for a dispensation is when the two exceptions stated here constitute the substance of the petition for the dispensation.

Dispensation from Irregularities/Impediments

Canon 1047 — §1. A dispensation from all irregularities is reserved to the Apostolic See if the fact upon which they are based has been brought to the judicial forum.
§2. A dispensation from the following irregularities and impediments to receiving orders is also reserved to the Holy See:
1° from the irregularity arising from the public delict mentioned in can. 1041, nn. 2 and 3;
2° from the irregularity arising from the public or occult delict mentioned in can. 1041, n. 4;
3° from the impediment mentioned in can. 1042, n. 1.
§3. Also reserved to the Apostolic See is a dispensation from the irregularities precluding the exercise of an order already received which are mentioned in can. 1041, n. 3, but only in public cases, and in can. 1041, n. 4, even in occult cases.
§4. The ordinary can dispense from irregularities and impediments not reserved to the Holy See.

This canon states precisely who can dispense from irregularities and impediments.

The first paragraph repeats the traditional norm of the 1917 Code that whenever the fact on which an irregularity rests is brought to the judicial forum, the dispensation is reserved to the Holy See (*CIC* 990, §1). The judicial forum can be either ecclesiastical or secular.[108]

The second paragraph of the canon lists irregularities for and an impediment to the reception of orders which are also reserved to the Holy See. The canon does not explicitly state the causes of the irregularities/impediments. It simply refers back to canons 1041–1042. The reservations are the following:

(1) Irregularities arising from *public* crimes of apostasy, heresy, schism, and attempted marriage. The word "public" is important for the interpretation of this canon. In the canonical tradition, the word public means that the criminal action has already been divulged or happened in such circumstances that it can be prudently judged that it can and will become known; otherwise, it is occult. If the crime itself is hidden, it is considered materially occult. It is formally occult if the imputability is hidden.[109] Unless the crime is public, the reservation does not take effect.

(2) Irregularities arising from public or occult crimes of voluntary homicide and effective abortion. There are no exceptions to the binding force of this reservation.

(3) The final reservation concerns a man having a wife. As mentioned under canon 1042, in very rare cases and under very limited circumstances the Holy See will dispense in this case.

The third paragraph of the canon considers reservations of irregularities which prohibit the exercise of orders already received. The canon specifies two cases: public cases of attempted marriage and public or occult cases of voluntary homicide or effective abortion.

The final paragraph of the canon specifies that the ordinary may dispense from all irregularities and impediments not reserved to the Holy See. It is important to note that the term "ordinary" includes major superiors of pontifical right clerical religious institutes of consecrated life and major superiors of pontifical right clerical societies of apostolic life.[110]

Exercise of Prohibited Order

Canon 1048 — If, in more urgent occult cases access to the ordinary cannot be had or when it is a question of the irregularities mentioned in can. 1041, nn. 3 and 4, access to the Sacred Penitentiary

[107]Beste, 581; Regatillo, *Ius Sacramentarium,* 535.

[108]Coronata, *De Sacramentis,* 210.
[109]*CIC* 2197; Regatillo, *Ius Sacramentarium,* 536.
[110]Cc. 134, 368.

cannot be had and if there is a danger of serious harm or infamy, the person who is impeded by an irregularity from exercising an order can exercise it, with due regard, however, for the responsibility of making recourse as soon as possible to the ordinary or Sacred Pentitentiary through a confessor and without mentioning the name of the person who has the irregularity.

This canon deals with the very important question of the exercise of a prohibited order in certain urgent occult cases. When the ordinary cannot be reached *or* when the irregularities of attempted marriage, voluntary homicide, or effective abortion are involved *and* the Sacred Penitentiary cannot be approached *and* there is imminent danger of grave harm or infamy, *then* the person impeded from exercising an order can exercise it. However, he still has the responsibility to have recourse as soon as possible to the ordinary or the Sacred Penitentiary through a confessor who shall not mention the name of the former. In the revised law the confessor does not have the right to dispense (*CIC* 990, §2). The confessor is merely the instrument of recourse for the cleric who is prohibited from the exercise of the order.

One consultor on the *coetus* requested that a distinction be made between the faculties to dispense which belong to bishops and other ordinaries and the faculties which belong to confessors. He judged that the confessor was in a preferential position. The response to this request was that the canon does not consider faculties for confessors at all. It simply gives the person subject to the irregularity the right to exercise the order with the obligation to have recourse.[111] In essence this canon places a double responsibility on the person who has incurred the irregularity. He must make the decision to exercise orders, and he must take the necessary steps to have recourse.

Dispensation Procedure

Canon 1049 — §1. In the petition to obtain a dispensation from irregularities and impediments, all the irregularities and impediments are to be indicated; nevertheless, general dispensation is valid even for those which have been omitted in good faith with the exception of the irregularities mentioned in can. 1041, n. 4, or others which have been brought to the judicial forum; however, a general dispensation is not valid for those which have been omitted in bad faith.

§2. If it is a question of the irregularity arising from voluntary homicide or from procuring an abortion the number of the delicts is also to be mentioned for the dispensation to be valid.

§3. A general dispensation from the irregular-

ities and impediments to receive orders is valid for all the orders.

The final canon in this article deals with the procedure for obtaining a dispensation. It formulates the procedural implications of the prior material on irregularities and impediments.

The first paragraph begins by stating that petitions for a dispensation must indicate all irregularities and impediments involved in a particular case. Consistent with the law on *subreptio* and *obreptio,* the canon stipulates that a general dispensation is valid for omissions made in good faith except for irregularities based on voluntary homicide, effective abortion, and other factors brought to the judicial forum. A general dispensation is not valid for omissions made in bad faith.[112]

Paragraph two reinforces that part of the commentary on canon 1046 that stated when the petition for a dispensation concerns voluntary homicide or effective abortion, the number of delicts must be mentioned for the validity of the dispensation.

The final paragraph states that a general dispensation from irregularities and impediments which prohibit the reception of orders is valid for all orders. In other words once the dispensation has been obtained, the effect is final. There is no need to request another dispensation for subsequent orders.

ARTICLE 4: REQUIRED DOCUMENTS AND EXAMINATION
[cc. 1050–1052]

This article considers a very important responsibility for the administration of any seminary or school of theology. The required documents and the inquiry constitute proof that the requirements of the law have been fulfilled and the suitability of the candidate for orders has been established. The canons are not difficult to interpret. In fact they are a simple and practical checklist for the administrators of seminaries and schools of theology.

Documents for Ordination

Canon 1050 — For one to be promoted to sacred orders the following documents are required:
1° certification that the studies prescribed by can. 1032, have been duly completed;
2° certification that the diaconate has been received if it is a question of those to be ordained to the presbyterate;
3° certification that baptism and confirmation have been received and that the ministries mentioned in can. 1035 have been received if it is a question of those to be promoted to the diaconate; also, certification that the declaration mentioned in can. 1036 has been made; and, if the ordinand who

---

[111]*Comm,* 202.

[112]C. 63.

is to be promoted to the permanent diaconate is married, certification of the marriage that was celebrated and of the wife's consent.

This canon exclusively considers required documents. It demands that documentary proof be available for all the requirements of the law. There must be documentary proof of the completion of studies, prior orders, reception of baptism and confirmation, reception of ministries, the signed declarations of freedom and if the candidate is a permanent deacon, a certificate that the marriage was celebrated and that his wife consents to the ordination.

Pre-Ordination Inquiries

Canon 1051 — As regards the inquiry concerning the qualities required of an ordinand the following prescriptions are to be observed:

1° a testimonial is to be furnished by the rector of the seminary or the house of formation concerning the qualities required for the reception of orders; that is, the candidate's correct doctrine, genuine piety, good morals and his suitability for exercising the ministry; and, after a duly executed inquiry, the state of his physical and psychological health;

2° in order that the inquiry may be properly conducted, the diocesan bishop or the major superior can employ other means which seem useful in accord with the circumstances of time and place, for example testimonial letters, public announcements or other means for gaining information.

In the former law and in the final draft of this canon for the revised Code, this canon was a part of the prior canon. However, it was judged that the question of the inquiries should be considered as a separate issue. In addition, two paragraphs were eliminated from this canon.[113]

The canon requires the rector of the seminary or house of formation to issue testimonial letters regarding the qualities required for the reception of orders. The required areas are listed in the canon. Furthermore, the proper bishop or major superior has the right to use other means to gather information on the suitability of the candidates.

Responsibilities of Ordaining Bishop

Canon 1052 — §1. In order for a bishop conferring an ordination in virtue of his own proper right to proceed to the ordination, he must be certain that the documents mentioned in can. 1050 have been furnished and that the suitability of the candidate has been proved through positive arguments

after the inquiry has been conducted in accord with the norm of law.

§2. In order for a bishop to proceed to the ordination of one who is not his own subject, it is sufficient that the dimissorial letters refer to the fact that such documents have been furnished, that the inquiry has been conducted in accord with the norm of law and that the suitability of the candidate has been proved; but if the candidate is a member of a religious institute or a society of apostolic life, the dimissorial letters must also certify that he has definitively become a member and that he is a subject of the superior who grants the letters.

§3. If despite all the above considerations the bishop has certain reasons for doubting the suitability of the candidate for ordination, he is not to ordain him.

If the bishop is ordaining one of his own subjects, he must be certain that the required documents are available and that the suitability of the candidate has been established by positive arguments.

If the bishop is ordaining a subject of another ordinary, then the dimissorial letters must indicate that the documents are available, the inquiry has been completed, and the candidate is suitable. If the candidate is a member of a religious institute or a clerical society of apostolic life, the dimissorial letters must also certify that he is definitively incorporated and a subject of the superior who issued the letters.

Finally if, after all of the above information, the bishop still has a doubt about the fitness of the candidate, he is not to ordain him.

CHAPTER III
REGISTRATION AND CERTIFICATION
OF ORDINATION CONFERRED
[cc. 1053–1054]

Canon 1053 — §1. After the ordination has been conferred, the names of those ordained and the ordaining minister, along with the place and date of the ordination, are to be noted in a special register which is to be carefully kept in the curia of the place of ordination; all the documents for each ordination are also to be carefully preserved.

§2. The ordaining bishop is to give each of the ordained an authentic certificate of the ordination which was received; those who have been promoted through dimissorial letters by a bishop other than their own are to show this certificate to their own ordinary so that the registration of the ordination is recorded in the special register to be kept in the archives.

This canon requires that the data of the ordination should be entered into a special register which is to be kept in the *curia* of the place of ordination.

---

[113]*CIC* 993; see c. 233 of the original schema; *Comm,* 203–204.

Each candidate should receive a certificate of the ordination. Those promoted through dimissorial letters should show the certificate to their own ordinaries for registration in the archives.

Canon 1054 — **In the case of seculars the local ordinary and in the case of those who are subject to him the competent major superior, are to send notification of every ordination celebrated to the pastor of the place where the ordained person has been baptized so that a notation may be made in the baptismal register according to the norm of can. 535, §2.**

The final canon in the law on orders concerns the church of baptism of those who have received orders. The local ordinary for diocesan clergy and the major superior for his subjects should notify the church of baptism of the ordained of every order he receives. This canon is more strict than the 1917 Code, which explicitly required notification only of the subdiaconate.[114] The revised law is still concerned with diriment impediments to marriage and also seems to be insisting on complete records in the church of baptism.

[114]*CIC* 1011.

BIBLIOGRAPHY

Sources

Bouscaren, T., and O'Connor, J. (eds.). *The Canon Law Digest.* 8 vols., nos. 1–6, Milwaukee: The Bruce Publishing Co., 1934–1969; nos. 7–8, Mundelein: St. Mary of the Lake Seminary, 1975–1978.

Codex Iuris Canonici. Pii X Pontificis Maximi iussu digestus Benedicti XV auctoritate Promulgatus. Romae: Typis Polyglottis Vaticanis, 1917.

Codex Iuris Canonici. Ioannis Pauli II auctoritate promulgatus. Vatican City: Libreria Editrice Vaticana, 1983.

ComCICRec. *Relatio.* Romae: Typis Polyglottis Vaticanis, 1981.

de Nicolò, M. "Coetus studiorum de Sacramentis: 'de ordine.' " *Comm* 10 (1978), 179–208.

Denzinger, H., and Schönmetzer, A. *Enchiridion symbolorum definitorum de rebus fidei et morum.* 35th ed., June 15, 1973.

NCCB. *The Program of Priestly Formation,* June 18, 1971; 2nd ed., March 3, 1976; 3rd ed., November 30, 1981 (cited as *Program of Priestly Formation* and year).

Paul VI. *Mp, General Norms for Restoring the Permanent Diaconate in the Latin Church.* June 18, 1967 (cited as *General Norms for Restoring the Permanent Diaconate*).

————. Apconst, *Approval of New Rites for the Ordination of Deacons, Presbyters and Bishops.* June 18, 1968 (cited as *The Rites*).

————. *Mp, First Tonsure, Minor Orders and the Subdiaconate.* August 15, 1972 (cited as *First Tonsure, Minor Orders and the Subdiaconate*).

————. *Mp, Norms for the Order of the Diaconate.* August 15, 1972 (cited as *Norms for the Order of the Diaconate*).

Pontifical Code Commission. *Atheistic Sect: Effect of Membership as Regards Ordination and Marriage.* July 30, 1934.

Rites of the Catholic Church as Revised by the Second Vatican Ecumenical Council. 2 vols. New York: Pueblo, vol. I, 1976; vol. II, 1980.

SCCE. *The Basic Program of Priestly Formation.* March 30, 1970.

————. *A Guide to Formation in Priestly Celibacy.* April 11, 1974.

————. *The Theological Formation of Future Priests.* February 2, 1976.

SCDF. *Declaration in Defense of Catholic Doctrine on the Church Against Certain Errors of the Present Day.* June 24, 1973.

SCSacr. *Indult to the Bishops of the United States.* May 18, 1940.

Synod of Bishops. *The Ministerial Priesthood.* 1971.

Reference Works

Abbo, J., and Hannan, J. *The Sacred Canons.* 2 vols. St. Louis: Herder, 1960.

Beste, U. *Introductio in Codicem.* Naples: D'Auria, 1956 (cited as Beste).

Coriden, J., ed. *Sexism and Church Law.* Ramsey, N.J.: Paulist Press, 1977.

Coronata, M. *Institutiones Iuris Canonici, De Sacramentis.* 3 vols. Torino: Marietti, 1943–1946 (cited as *De Sacramentis*).

Dulles, A. *A Church To Believe In.* New York: Crossroad Press, 1982.

McBrien, R. *Catholicism.* Minneapolis, Minn.: Winston Press, 1981 (cited as McBrien).

Ott, L. *Fundamentals of Catholic Dogma.* Trans. by P. Lynch. Rockford, Ill.: Tan, 1954 (cited as Ott).

Quinn, J. *Documents Required for the Reception of Orders. CanLawStud* 266. Washington, D.C.: Catholic University of America, 1948.

Regatillo, E. *Ius Sacramentarium.* Santander: Sal Terrae, 1949 (cited as Regatillo).

Woywod, S. *A Practical Commentary on the Code of Canon Law.* New York: Wagner, 1929 (cited as Woywod).

Wrenn, L. *Annulments.* 4th ed. Washington: CLSA, 1983.

Articles

Alesandro, J. "Background on the Canon Law Code's Revision." *Origins* 12 (Feb. 3, 1983), 541–544.

Fransen, P. "Orders and Ordination." *SacM* 4, 305–308, 324–325 (cited as Fransen).

Graham, G. "Personality Disorders and their Effect on the Validity of Marriage." *CLSAP* (1976), 138–149.

Hanley, P. "Sacramental Character," *NCE* 12, 786–789.

NCCB, Committee on Pastoral Research and Practice. "Theological Reflections on the Ordination of Women." *RfR* 33 (1973), 218–222.

Paul VI. "The Juridical Structure of the Church as Protection of Spiritual Orders," *OssRomEng* (Oct. 4, 1973), 2.

Quinn, J. "Sacraments, Theology of," *NCE* 12, 810–811 (cited as Quinn).

Thomas P. Doyle, O.P.

TITLE VII
MARRIAGE
[cc. 1055–1165]

Early Development of Marriage

More canons are devoted to marriage in the Code of Canon Law than to any other single subject. This extensive concern for marriage reflects the importance of this sacrament in the life of the Church. The formulation of the canonical dimensions of marriage is the result of centuries of study and experience. Nevertheless, the canonical is but one dimension of this complex human, social, and ecclesial reality.

The Church's concern for marriage has spanned its history. The earliest Christians lived in the Roman world. Although these early Christians followed civil customs and legal requirements for entrance into marriage, the inner morality was at odds with that of the pagan Roman society. Christians were asked to commit themselves to an indissoluble union and to mutual fidelity. The marital relationship was based upon the belief that it reflected the union of Christ and His Church. For the Romans, marriage was important because of its relationship to the welfare of society and the patriarchal family. For the Christians, its value was intrinsic. Another important difference between the two concepts of marriage was the fact that Christians believed that the spouses were spiritually equal.

The earliest evidence of a normative regulation for marriage is found in the Pauline epistles, especially 1 Corinthians 7 and Ephesians 5:21–33. Paul refers to various aspects of the husband-wife relationship such as mutual respect and fidelity, the relationship of celibacy to marriage, and marital permanence. The passage from Corinthians also contains the reference to the Pauline privilege.

The synoptic gospels also contain references to marriage in terms of its permanence (Lk 16:18; Mk 10:1–12; Mt 5:31–32 and 19:3–12). All of the synoptic citations deal with the Lord's response to the question of whether or not a man may divorce his wife and remarry if she commits adultery. The treatment of marriage by the early Christian writers was, for the most part, apologetic. It was not an indepth theological or legal treatment. Rather, these early authors simply defended the Christian approach to marriage against the slanderous attacks of non-believers.

Serious consideration of the theological dimensions of Christian marriage began with the Fathers of the Church. Origen, Tertullian, Jerome, Cyprian, and Ambrose, among others, studied marriage as a theological reality. In certain cases, the treatises written were replies to the teachings of the Gnostics and in others to the teachings of heretical Christian sects. Augustine made the greatest and most far-reaching contribution with his many treatises and sermons on the nature of Christian marriage.

Contemporary with Augustine, the bishops of the various churches began to enact legislation concerning marriage. Gathered in local councils and synods throughout the Christian world, church leaders considered disciplinary problems relative to marriage and enacted legislation in the form of canons aimed at counteracting behavior and beliefs which were believed to be contrary to the Christian concept of marriage.

The legislative activity of the first millennium of Christian history was almost totally devoted to the inner morality or living out of marriage. It was not until the eleventh and twelfth centuries that a shift to the canonical dimension took place. By this time, the Church had "acquired competence" over marriage. Many of the bishops found themselves in positions of authority, not only over the spiritual lives of the faithful, but their civic lives as well. Church authorities were faced with determining when marriage began and what acts constituted a true marriage. The *consensus-copula* debate of the twelfth century was precisely over what made a *marriage*, the consent of the parties or sexual consummation. The debate was settled by Pope Alexander III early in the thirteenth century by means of a series of tribunal, or church court, decisions.[1] Once consent had been freely exchanged by the parties who were baptized, a true sacramental marriage existed. The attribute of absolute indissolubility was added when the marriage was consummated by sexual intercourse. This understanding of when marriage came into being has remained the teaching of the Church to the present day.

Many aspects of the canonical framework of marriage were substantially formulated during this late medieval period. Further development took place at the Council of Trent. Marriage was officially listed as one of the seven sacraments. The obligation of canonical form was introduced as well in the wake of the problem of clandestine marriages.

---

[1] T. Mackin, *What Is Marriage?* (New York: Paulist Press, 1982), 158–172.

Marriage in the 1917 Code

In the 1917 Code, the canons on marriage were contained in title VII of Book III ("Things") (*CIC* 1012–1143). The one hundred thirty-two canons began with a canon that stated that every marriage between the baptized is ipso facto a sacrament. Subsequent canons in the introductory section listed procreation and education of children as the primary ends of marriage with mutual assistance and the remedying of concupiscence as the secondary ends (*CIC* 1013, §1). The essential properties of marriage were listed as unity and indissolubility (*CIC* 1013, §2). Nevertheless, no attempt was made to offer a definition of marriage. Subsequent attempts at definitions were made by canonical commentators and moral theologians, yet no consensus was ever reached.

The 1917 Code did not present a theological treatise on the nature of marriage. The section on preparatory steps leading to marriage stressed the investigation into the freedom to marry and the publication of the banns of marriage. The following section dealing with impediments distinguished between impedient impediments which made a marriage valid but illicit and diriment impediments which made a marriage invalid.

The canons on matrimonial consent made no mention of the effect of mental or emotional disturbance on marital validity. Invalidating factors included in this section all were grounded in the intellect and the will, e.g., error of person, simulation of consent, force, and fear. The remaining sections on marriage dealing with canonical form, marriages of conscience, the effects of marriage, marital separation, convalidation, and second marriages were all based on the formulations of the twelfth and thirteenth centuries and the Council of Trent; yet, at the same time they reflected the sociocultural context of the late nineteenth and early twentieth centuries.

The Contemporary Revision of Marriage Law

The Work of the Code Commission

Although marriage was included with the other sacraments in Book IV of the proposed Code, a special committee was named to revise the marriage canons of the 1917 Code. This committee met seventeen times between October 1966 and January 1973. A draft of canons reflecting its work and that of a committee on the other sacraments was circulated to the episcopal conferences and other interested bodies and persons in March 1975. The purpose of this process was to allow for study, critique, and suggestions on the proposed revision.

A special commission met twenty-four times between February 1977 and February 1978 to revise the draft canons in the light of the observations and suggestions submitted. The revised canons for the entire Code were circulated again in 1980.[2]

Pope John Paul II appointed an expanded commission of cardinals, archbishops and bishops to study the 1980 schema in 1981. The commission met from October 20 to 28, 1981. Numerous changes in the marriage canons were proposed and discussed. Finally, the commission's report with the final text of the suggested canons was sent to the Holy Father on April 22, 1982. When the definitive version of the Code was promulgated on January 25, 1983, it was evident that several canons were altered in some form or another from the 1980 schema.

Basic Structure of the 1983 Canons on Marriage

There are one hundred eleven canons on marriage in the revised Code (cc. 1055–1165). The basic structure follows that of the 1917 Code with the material divided into ten chapters. Two entire chapters have been dropped, namely, those dealing with impedient impediments and second marriages. The chapter on the time and place of marriage has been dropped and pertinent canons included in the chapter on the form of marriage.

Although the impediment of mixed marriage (marriage between a Catholic and baptized non-Catholic) has been dropped, such marriages are considered as a special pastoral problem warranting special treatment. Mixed marriages are now treated in a separate chapter.

Noteworthy Changes from the 1917 Code

Before mentioning the more important changes in the 1983 Code, it is important to indicate certain of the sources for the revised legislation.

While much of the 1917 Code has been retained, if in modified form in many instances, the influence of the conciliar constitution *Gaudium et Spes* is obvious. Among other principal sources for the revised legislation are the encyclical *Humanae Vitae* and decisions of the Roman Rota which interpreted the conciliar doctrine in the judicial sphere.

Although a comprehensive definition of marriage is avoided, canon 1055 reflects *Gaudium et Spes* 48 in that it states that the agreement by which spouses marry is a covenant. Marriage itself, the *consortium* or community of the whole of life, comes into being through this convenant.

This canon reflects a personalist approach by stating further that the marital consortium is ordered by its very nature to the good of the spouses and the procreation and education of children. A restating of the hierarchy of ends as in the 1917

Code is avoided. Rather, the canons speak first of the *essence* of marriage and then of its *purpose*.

The object of marital consent was the *ius in corpus,* or right to the body for sexual acts apt for procreation, according to the 1917 Code. The revised Code expands on this and sees the object of consent as the giving and receiving of the whole person for the purpose of establishing marriage.

The introductory canons (cc. 1055–1062), which give some general definitions about the canonical understanding of marriage, reflect a juridical concern for the canonical elements and for the substance or inner value of marriage as well. This is reflected in the very first canon on marriage but also in later canons on consent. The Code canonizes Rotal jurisprudence developed since the Council, which stated that consent could be nullified if persons suffered from a serious psychological disorder which rendered them incapable of assuming the obligations of marriage. A subsequent canon on simulation (c. 1101) indicates that the spouses must not exclude marriage itself or the marital community in their consent as well as the essential elements and properties of marriage.

More attention is given to pre-marital preparation than in the 1917 Code. The thrust of the canons differs as well. The episcopal conference is to determine norms for establishing freedom to marry which could include some form of marriage banns. The extensive treatment of the banns found in the 1917 Code has been dropped. The first chapter of the marriage canons is concerned with the pastoral care of those entering marriage. Pastors have the obligation of involving the Christian community in seeing to it that both the community as a whole and individual couples receive adequate preparation and assistance for marriage. The canons acknowledge the fact that the marital relationship can have an effect on the wider Christian community. This is especially true in the enumeration of certain cases which must be referred to the bishop (mixed marriages or marriages with Catholics who have notoriously left the faith or are under ecclesiastical censure) (cc. 1124, 1071).

The impedient impediments have been dropped as has been the former distinction of minor and major grade impediments. Although the impedient impediments have been dropped as such, the circumstances which gave rise to the impediments are still considered in the Code. Simple vows, if temporary, have no effect on marriage, but if they are perpetual the marriage is invalid. Mixed marriage, although not an impediment, requires the permission of the bishop. The requirements for re-

ceiving this permission are outlined in the chapter entitled "mixed" marriages rather than "interfaith" or "ecumenical" marriages.

The only marriage impediments are diriment or invalidating impediments. Some changes were made in the canons on the impediments of public vows, crime, consanguinity, affinity, and legal adoption. The impediment of spiritual relationship arising from baptism has been entirely dropped. The dispensation from impediments of ecclesiastical law may be given by the local ordinary with certain cases reserved to the Holy See. In the 1917 Code dispensations were given by the Holy See, although the power to grant certain dispensations was regularly delegated to local bishops.

There are significant changes in the legislation on the form of marriage. Although the official witness for the Church is ordinarily to be a bishop, priest, or deacon, with proper delegation when needed, provision is made for a lay person to act as the official witness. When there is need, such as scarcity of sacred ministers, the local bishop may petition the Holy See for permission to delegate lay persons in countries where the episcopal conference has authorized such procedures. A Catholic entering a mixed marriage or one involving the impediment of disparity of cult may receive a dispensation from the obligation of canonical form from his or her bishop if necessary.

The canons on the Pauline privilege have remained substantially unchanged. A proposed canon on the dissolution of marriages in favor of the faith, known as privilege of the faith cases, was dropped in the promulgated version.

Reference to three papal constitutions in canon 1125 of the 1917 Code has been dropped. These dealt with the application of canonical norms to situations of polygamy in mission lands. Yet the provisions made in these constitutions have been partially included in canons 1148 and 1149 of the 1983 Code.

In five instances the episcopal conference may enact particular legislation. These include norms for the premarital examination and the publication of the banns (c. 1064); raising the required age for licit entrance into marriage (c. 1083, §2); deciding whether or not individual bishops will be permitted to petition to allow lay persons to witness marriage (c. 1112); drawing up proper rituals for the celebration of marriage subject to the approval of the Holy See (c. 1120); and finally, determining the means by which the declaration and promise required for mixed marriages will be fulfilled (c. 1126).

The Fundamental Nature of Marriage

Canon 1055 — §1. The matrimonial covenant, by which a man and a woman establish between themselves a partnership of the whole of life, is by its nature ordered toward the good of the spouses and the procreation and education of offspring; this covenant between baptized persons has been raised by Christ the Lord to the dignity of a sacrament.

§2. For this reason a matrimonial contract cannot validly exist between baptized persons unless it is also a sacrament by that fact.

The first paragraph of the canon which sets forth the fundamental nature of Christian marriage is grounded in *Gaudium et Spes* 47–52, with particular emphasis on paragraph 48. The conciliar description of marriage in turn draws on the rich biblical and theological traditions on the meaning of Christian marriage, beginning with the creation account of Genesis 2:24.

The spouses commit themselves to each other by means of a *covenant.* A covenant, or *b'rith,* was, in Jewish tradition, an agreement which formed a relationship which was equal in binding force to a blood relationship. Consequently, the relationship does not cease even if the consent to the covenant is withdrawn by one or both of the parties. The most profound type of covenant, aside from that which exists between God and His people, is the covenant between spouses.

The notion of covenant best describes the theological dimension of marriage. Its use reflects the personalist approach of conciliar theology and most post-conciliar jurisprudence.[3] It is a relationship which recognizes the spiritual equality of the spouses and their capacity to enter into an agreement which demands the gift of the whole person, one to another.

The covenant, based on the free election of the spouses, involves an interpersonal relationship which is total, that is, involving their spiritual, emotional, and physical joining. Aided by grace, the two are able to give themselves to one another on a day-to-day basis, thus bringing the object of the covenant, the community of the whole of life, into reality.

The term *covenant* replaces the term *contract,* generally used in the 1917 Code and related literature, to describe the nature of marital consent. Since the sacramental dimension of marriage is grounded in the belief that the marital relationship reflects the totally faithful and unending relationship of Christ to His Church, *covenant* is a more accurate theological description of marriage consent.

On a juridical level, covenant more clearly describes what results from the exchange of consent. The spouses enter the covenant with a specific purpose: the creation of the "most intimate communion of the whole of life." The use of the term "communion of life" is not new. It formed the basis for the classical Roman law definition of marriage[4] and is consistently used in canonical and theological treatises on marriage from the Middle Ages to the present.[5] Although most of the nineteenth- and twentieth-century commentators understood the term to mean sexual union or mere cohabitation, the legislator clearly means much more in this canon. The marital community is unique in that it involves a union of the spouses on all levels of human activity. It is based on their equality and gives rise to and depends on a lasting pledge of complete fidelity to one another.

The establishment of this community is prompted by a special kind of love, conjugal love. Though this love may be experienced and expressed in a variety of ways, it is essentially rooted in the will. It prompts the spouses to give themselves to one another. As a will act it is aimed not at self-fulfillment but the good of the other.[6] This community of the whole of life is not simply an attribute of marriage; it is marriage.

Unlike canon 1013 of the 1917 Code, *Gaudium et Spes* avoided setting forth a hierarchy of ends of marriage. This omission does not mean that the purposes of marriage are arbitrarily determined by the spouses. By natural and divine determination marriage is ordered to the good of the spouses (*bonum coniugum*) and the procreation and education of children. The two ends are intimately related. They are what marriage is about. The unselfish giving in the context of the marital community promotes the natural and spiritual good of the spouses. Naturally, one may ask what acts or attitudes are

---

[3]See *GS* 12, 14; John Paul II to the Secretariate of the Synod, 2–23–80 in *La documentation catholique* 77 (1980), 225; Mackin, 248–282.

[4]Modestinus D 23 2 1. "Nuptiae sunt coniunctio maris et feminae et consortium omnis vitae, divina et humana iuris communicatio."

[5]See Z. Grocholewski, "De communione vitae in novo schemate *de matrimonio* et de momento iuridico amoris coniugalis," *P* 68 (1979), 438–480.

[6]Pius XI, *Casti Connubii* 12–31–30, translation in Mackin, 217. Official Latin text in *AAS* 22 (1930), 549. "This mutual interior molding of husband and wife, this determined effort to protect one another, can, in a real sense, as the Roman Catechism teaches, be said to be the chief reason and purpose of matrimony, provided matrimony not be looked at in the restricted sense as instituted for the proper conception and education of children, but more widely as a blending of life as a whole and the mutual interchange of sharing thereof."

necessary for the community of life. An exhaustive list is not possible since much depends on society, culture, and personality. Yet certain basic attributes are to be expected: heterosexual companionship, interpersonal friendship, spiritual and material support. Here we find that mutual assistance, formerly considered a secondary end, is now rightly included in the very essence of marriage.

The *good of the spouses,* grounded in conjugal love, is, according to *Gaudium et Spes* " . . . rooted in the will and embraces the good of the whole person."[7] By natural inclination the marital community is ordered to cooperation in God's work of creation not only by means of physical procreation but the human and Christian formation of the children as well. While the existence of a true marriage does not depend on procreation (marriages of the aged and sterile), there must nevertheless be an openness to procreation by all who choose this sacrament.

The fulfillment of this purpose of marriage is not exhausted with physical procreation. The spouses are obligated to see that the children procreated receive a Christian education. This formation takes place primarily in the context of the marital community wherein the children learn the meaning of love of God and neighbor through the loving example and instruction of their parents. Such an understanding of the comprehensive nature of the purpose of marriage is rooted in Augustinian and Thomistic theology.[8]

The sacramental character of marriage was fully recognized only after a long period of time, and the understanding of this character is still evolving. Christians have always seen a sacred dimension to marriage. Early Christian writers referred to marriage as *sacramentum* or *mysterion.* Yet only in the thirteenth century was marriage defined by the Church as one of the seven sacraments of the new law.[9] Although there is no scriptural evidence of direct institution by Christ, the sacramentality of marriage is grounded in His saving work. It images His union with the Church and is a means for bringing about Christian peace through the growth of unselfish love, which in turn transcends the couple and reaches out to the community. Christ enhanced the goodness of marriage as a natural institution with sacramental dignity because of the potential for growth in true charity for the spouses.

The second paragraph of the canon sets forth a fundamental juridical truth about marriage. Every valid marriage entered into between two certainly baptized persons, be they Catholic or not, is of its nature a sacrament. The term "contract" is used in

connection with marriage only in this canon. This reflects the fact that a natural marriage contract becomes, by reason of the baptism of the spouses, a sacramental covenant.

The law presumes that valid baptism means a living faith and a commitment to the Christian (usually Catholic) community. Because this is not always the case, the canon refers only to the validity of marriages of the baptized and not to their fruitfulness. Validity refers to the juridically verifiable existence of a marriage. The fruitfulness of a marriage is a category which extends beyond the legal and social fact of its existence. It depends on the actual degree of faith, the quantity and quality of which cannot be definitively measured by the law. This dimension involves the unselfish growth of the parties in the marital community and the positive influence their relationship has on one another and on the community.

The identification of contract with sacrament was prompted in part by the attempts of certain European civil governments to gain absolute authority over marriage. The Church wished to avoid any semblance of a belief that the sacrament was added to the marriage contract as a kind of pious superstructure with marriage remaining essentially a secular affair. The canonical development of this question culminated in canon 1012, §2 of the 1917 Code. Since the spouses themselves are both the ministers and the recipients of the sacrament insofar as they give and accept one another's consent, the agreement or covenant is itself sacramental if both are baptized. Marriage as a sacrament is thus seen as an action of the Church by which the spouses, in view of their baptismal commitment, express their willingness to enter into a new dimension of their relationship with the Church.

By baptism the Church means *valid* baptism, that is, the pouring, sprinkling, or immersion with water accompanied by the Trinitarian formula. All persons, Catholic or not, who are baptized in this manner are capable of a sacramental marriage. If consent is exchanged prior to baptism and one or both of the spouses are baptized subsequent to the wedding, the marriage becomes sacramental at that time.[10]

---

[7] *GS* 49.

[8] Augustine, *De civitate Dei* 15 16; Thomas Aquinas, *Summa Theologiae* 111 29 2; Raymond of Penafort, *Summa de matrimonio* 11 12.

[9] Decree for the Armenians, *Ench* 695; Trent, session VII, c. 1.

[10] Raymond C. Finn, *Towards a Reinterpretation of Canon 1012: A Study of its Theological and Canonical Foundations* (Rome: University of St. Thomas, 1977). For a further discussion of the relationship between faith and the sacrament of marriage, one of the most controverted issues during the Code revision process, see W. Cuenin, "The Marriage of Baptized Non-Believers: Questions of Faith, Sacrament and Law," *CLSAP* (1978), 38–48; R. Cunningham, "Marriage and the Nescient Catholic: Questions of Faith and Sacrament," *Stud Can* 15 (1981), 263–284; W. LaDue, "The Sacramentality of Marriage," *CLSAP* (1974), 25–35; L. Orsy, "Christian Marriage: Doctrine and Law: Glossae on Canons 1012–1015," *J* 40 (1980), 282–348 especially 284–299; idem, "Faith, Sacrament, Contract and Christian Marriage: Disputed Questions," *TS* 43 (1982), 379–398.

The Essential Properties of Marriage

Canon 1056 — The essential properties of marriage are unity and indissolubility, which in Christian marriage obtain a special firmness in virtue of the sacrament.

The essential properties of marriage, unity and indissolubility, must be understood in the context of sacramental marriage defined as the intimate community of the whole of life.

Natural marriage has always tended toward unity, that is, toward marriage involving two spouses and not one spouse with a plurality of partners as in polygamy. This is true in spite of instances of polygyny and polyandry in various societies, both past and present. In certain primitive societies marriage as a partnership did not have an intrinsic value. Its importance was relative to the needs of the wider social group such as the tribe or clan. In Christian marriage the conjugal relationship has an intrinsic importance. The total self-giving which is essential to marriage is impossible with a plurality of husbands or wives. Likewise, the complete nurture of children is impossible except in the context of the community of life since this nurture transcends the material welfare of the children. It includes their spiritual and emotional welfare as well.

The community of life is based on and needs total human fidelity for its existence and growth. This is not simply the absence of extramarital sexual involvement but fidelity to the interpersonal relationship. The total gift of self cannot be divided. It must be given and continuously expressed to one person. Fidelity is not possible without unity, that is, one partner with whom to share one's life.

Indissolubility is not only an essential property but a necessity for a covenant marriage. Christians believed in marital indissolubility from the beginning of the Church. This was in opposition to Roman marriage which was intrinsically dissoluble simply by the withdrawal of consent by a spouse. In this context the radical nature of indissolubility is obvious. It is based on gospel teaching and is not merely an ideal but a norm of life.[11] Nevertheless the meaning of the gospel statement and the nature of indissolubility have been subject to debate and study from the earliest years of the Church. In the pre-medieval Church the so-called Matthean exceptive clause (Mt 19:9) of no divorce except for *porneia* gave rise to the conviction in a few isolated instances that divorce with remarriage was permitted in cases of adultery. Yet contemporary biblical scholarship seems to hold that *porneia* referred to marriages within forbidden degrees of blood relationship and not to adultery.[12]

Prior to the twelfth century the Church viewed indissolubility as a moral demand and surrounded it with disciplinary legislation. From this period on, canonists and theologians began to refer to indissolubility not as a matter of "should not" but "cannot" be dissolved. The bond of marriage which came into existence with a valid, sacramental marriage was seen not simply as a moral obligation but as an ontological reality. From the thirteenth century on, the Church taught that a valid marriage covenant, consummated by sexual intercourse, was absolutely indissoluble by any earthly power. Even if the existential relationship ends, the spouses are called to ongoing fidelity to the indissoluble covenant. A subsequent marriage is not only forbidden, but it would be invalid.

Marital Consent—the Beginning of the Covenant

Canon 1057 — §1. Marriage is brought about through the consent of the parties, legitimately manifested between persons who are capable according to law of giving consent; no human power can replace this consent.

§2. Matrimonial consent is an act of the will by which a man and a woman, through an irrevocable covenant, mutually give and accept each other in order to establish marriage.

The marital covenant begins with the exchange of consent between the spouses. Since marriage is a specific way of life which demands a total gift of self, the mutual exchange of consent must be a free act of the will on the part of each party. Consent may be given only by the spouses. It may not be given on their behalf by any outside source such as parents, guardians, etc.[13]

The Roman law tradition held that consent alone made marriage, while the Germanic tradition held that sexual consummation was necessary for a true marriage. Hincmar of Rheims and, later, Gratian held to this latter view. In opposition to this, Peter Lombard of the School of Paris held to the "consent alone" theory. The lengthy debate was settled in 1181 by Alexander III, who stated that while consent alone made marriage, subsequent consummation added the element of absolute indissolubility to the covenant.

It is clear that consent must be for marriage, that is, consent to the covenant between the spouses for

---

[11]Lk 16:18; Mk 10:9–12; Mt 5:32, 19:9.
[12]J. Fitzmyer, "The Matthean Divorce Texts and Some New Palestinian Evidence," *TS* 37 (1976), 197–226.

[13]While this has been the constant teaching of the Church, it was emphasized in law by a series of decretals issued by Alexander III in the 12th century. Prior to this period there was growing tension between the secular model of marriage, by which consent was supplied by parents or secular authorities for purposes of securing economic, familial, or political gain, and the ecclesiastical model, which stressed the sacred dimension of marriage. See G. Duby, *Medieval Marriage* (Baltimore: Johns Hopkins, 1978).

the specific purpose of creating and sustaining the marital community.

The canon further states that consent must be legitimately manifest. The internal act of the will must not only be expressed by external signs such as words or gestures, but it must take place within the context of certain prescribed formalities. These formalities are set forth in canon law and, for most secular societies, in civil law as well. Civil and canon law manifest the community interest in the marital relationship. Marriage is not a purely private affair but a relationship which affects both ecclesial and civil society. Nearly every society has surrounded marriage with norms or regulations. Both custom and law have decreed that there be some formality involved in the entrance into marriage.

As early as the first century St. Ignatius of Antioch required that Christians submit themselves to the authority of the bishop to receive his blessing prior to entering marriage.[14] Although this action was not required for validity at the time, it was an external sign of the spouses' acceptance of the Christian morality of marriage.

Legitimate manifestation of consent for Catholics involves the prescribed canonical form. This is treated in chapter V, canons 1108–1123.

The Right to Marriage

Although the right to marriage is one of the most fundamental human rights, it is not absolute. Potential spouses are subject to civil and canonical requirements which have been justly enacted for their good, the good of possible children, and the good of the community. In short, the basic requirements of law envision spouses capable not only of a wedding ceremony but also of a marital relationship.[15]

To be capable according to canon law means freedom from the impediments. In addition to the impediments set forth in the canons, ecclesiastical jurisprudence has developed an understanding of sacramental marriage which gives rise to certain volitional, intellectual, and psychological requirements commensurate with the nature of the intimate communion of the whole of life.

The spouses must have a fundamental understanding of the obligations of marriage and freely choose to assume them. They must possess the emotional stability and spiritual and psychological capacity to establish and nourish a true marital community.

The formal object of consent is referred to in the second paragraph of the canon. Consent is exchanged between a man and a woman, clearly meaning that no other human combination is possi-

ble. It is a free act of the will by which the spouses commit themselves to each other by means of a covenant, that is, a total and undying agreement or pact. Once consent is expressed, it cannot be withdrawn.

The covenant involves a gift of persons and not merely the exchange of rights for one or the other aspect of marriage. Restating *Gaudium et Spes,* the canon states that by this agreement the spouses give and accept one another. This involves a twofold action: first, each of the spouses make an unqualified gift of himself or herself to the other. This in turn calls for an unqualified acceptance of the other by each spouse.

The purpose of this mutual gift of self is specified in the law: the establishment of matrimony, understood in terms of the communion of life of canon 1055. Matrimony thus understood implies an acceptance of a relationship ordered to the procreation and education of children and marked by total fidelity and permanence.

The Right To Marry

Canon 1058 — All persons who are not prohibited by law can contract marriage.

The right to marriage is fundamental, grounded in human nature itself. This right is protected by both civil and canon law. For Christians, marriage exists for the good of the individuals and for the good of the community as well. Accordingly, prospective spouses are subject to certain regulations.

In both civil and canon law certain prohibitions or impediments have been enacted in view of the effect a prohibited marriage would have on the spouses, the children, and the community. These are not an unjust denial of individual freedom but a limitation placed on the right to marry for the good of all concerned.

Throughout history both secular society and the Church have recognized not only a right but an obligation to provide either customary or legal structures which in certain instances restrict the exercise of the right to marry. These restrictions respond in the first place to the natural law requirements for a true marital community. In addition, certain restrictions have been enacted in response to particularly critical problems experienced by the Church with respect to marriage (clandestine marriages, arranged marriages, incestuous marriages).

The canon states a broad principle of freedom. All persons not prohibited by divine or ecclesiastical law are free to enter a marriage covenant.

The Church's Authority over Marriage

Canon 1059 — Even if only one party is Catholic, the marriage of Catholics is regulated not only by divine law but also by canon law, with due re-

[14]Ignatius of Antioch, *Epistula ad Polycarpum PG* 5 723.
[15]T. Doyle, "The Individual's Right to Marry in the Light of the Common Good," *Stud Can* 13 (1979), 245–301.

gard for the competence of civil authority concerning the merely civil effects of such a marriage.

As a natural yet God-given institution marriage is obviously regulated by divine law. The Church, as the visible structure of Christ's Body on earth, claims authority over marriage. This authority is manifested in canonical legislation which embraces sacramental marriages of the baptized and extends to non-sacramental marriages in which only one party is baptized. This includes sacramental marriages in which both parties are baptized non-Catholics and non-sacramental marriages in which only one party is a baptized Catholic or non-Catholic.

While this authority (also known as competence) is comprehensive regarding Catholics, it also extends to baptized non-Catholics as well. While non-Catholics are not bound by merely ecclesiastical laws (c. 11) in general, the Church makes an exception to this rule in regard to marriage at least in situations in which non-Catholics marry Catholics.

From the primitive Church to the twelfth century, Catholics followed secular legislation for entrance into marriage. Ecclesiastical authorities sought to make genuinely Christian perspectives prevail over the contrary views of the Romans and others. This was achieved through teaching and preaching, yet there was a great deal of legislative activity (e.g., dealing with adultery, divorce), all of which was disciplinary in nature.

The role of the Church in Western society changed dramatically during the eleventh and twelfth centuries. It acquired competence or control over the legal complexities of entrance into marriage. It was also faced with making decisions on the invalidity of marriage. The matrimonial legislation enacted in this period pertained to the substance and structure of marriage as the Church began to refine the idea of what marital consent actually was and who was capable of exchanging this consent.

The importance of marriage in the life of the Church justifies its exercising authority over the sacrament. Hence, one can see the rationale for the establishment of impediments, requirements for entrance into marriage, and canonical form. Furthermore, the Church alone is competent to legislate about or interpret the meaning of marriage itself and its essential properties.

While secular society specifies certain requirements for civil marriage (blood tests, residence, license), these laws cannot conflict with either divine or ecclesiastical law concerning marriage or its essential properties. For example, some countries require a civil marriage ceremony. Yet this does not suffice for Catholics who must also exchange consent according to canonical form in order to be validly married. Similarly, while a civil divorce may decree that the civilly recognized dimension of the marriage no longer exists, the parties are still con-

sidered bound by the marriage unless the Church either dissolves the bond (in cases of non-sacramental marriages or non-consummated sacramental unions) or declares it null and void.

This canon states that civil authority maintains its competency only over those effects which do not touch the substance, essential properties, or canonical form of marriage. What the canon refers to as "merely civil effects" would include such matters as change of name for the wife, succession, inheritance, and tax regulations, to name a few.

The Favor of the Law

Canon 1060 — Marriage enjoys the favor of the law; consequently, when a doubt exists the validity of a marriage is to be upheld until the contrary is proven.

To state that marriage enjoys the favor of the law means simply that a legally recognized marriage is presumed to be a valid union. When validity is doubtful, invalidity must be proven according to the norms of law for the marriage to be declared invalid.

This canon reflects the legal axiom "in case of doubt the validity of the action stands." It is more than a procedural canon in that it is based on the concept of indissolubility as well as the fact that a marriage once validly entered does not depend on the will of the parties for its ongoing existence. This canon seeks to balance the good of the parties with the good of the community as well as to affirm the sanctity and stability of the institution of marriage.

This presumption of law presupposed an "appearance of marriage," that is, a wedding ceremony according to canonical form for Catholics and some indication of publicly recognized exchange of consent for non-Catholics. In other words, there must be an objective reason to presume that an exchange of consent took place.

This presumption is known in canon law as a simple presumption. This means that it can be overturned by canonically acceptable proof of the contrary being true. The method and nature of contrary proof is determined by procedural law.

Most commentators hold that this canon is valid for both the external forum and the forum of conscience, or internal forum. In the public, or external, forum this presumption is necessary, for without it one could reach the conclusion that marriages are dissoluble by the parties themselves. To say that the presumption holds for the internal forum means that spouses, even though they may be subjectively convinced of invalidity, must respect the law which presumes the contrary.

This canon is related to canon 1085, §2, which deals with the celebration of second marriages. A second marriage may not be celebrated even though the first is null or dissoluble until nullity or dissolution is declared by a competent church authority. Marriages celebrated without a proper church decree may be valid but would not be licit.

Definitions of Matrimony

Canon 1061 — §1. A valid marriage between baptized persons is called ratified only if it has not been consummated; it is called ratified and consummated if the parties have performed between themselves in a human manner the conjugal act which is per se suitable for the generation of children, to which marriage is ordered by its very nature and by which the spouses become one flesh.

§2. After marriage has been celebrated, if the spouses have cohabited consummation is presumed until the contrary is proven.

§3. An invalid marriage is called putative if it has been celebrated in good faith by at least one of the parties, until both parties become certain of its nullity.

When two baptized persons exchange consent in a valid marriage ceremony, the union is called *matrimonium ratum*, or ratified marriage, if it has not been consummated by sexual intercourse after consent. The term *ratum* means that the union is approved by the Church as a valid sacramental covenant.[16] It makes no judgment on the internal quality of the interpersonal relationship.

A ratified marriage is called *consummatum*, or consummated, if sexual intercourse takes place *after* the exchange of consent. The act of intercourse is more than sexual contact. It is the most intimate expression of human love. *Gaudium et Spes* 49 states that "married love is uniquely expressed and perfected by the exercise of acts proper to marriage." Thus there is a direct relationship between consummation and the conjugal society. This canon states that marriage is ordered to the act of consummation. Yet the preceding canons, especially canon 1055, indicate that the marital covenant consists in a total joining of persons and not merely a physical joining. By their initial act of intercourse, the spouses express their covenantal joining in the most profound manner and become one flesh in the physical sense. This is the most expressive sign of the fact that they have committed themselves to one another for the creation of the community of the whole of life. In this community they will grow to become "one flesh" in all dimensions of their humanity.

Although the canonical notion of consummation has been criticized as being overly biological and inadequately personalistic in light of the fact that marriage involves the whole person, it is also true that the law must have some standard by which to make a juridical determination. Yet the fact that sexual consummation must be accompanied by a spiritual joining was recognized as early as Gratian who stated in his *Decretum* that those who become one in body must also become one in mind.[17] The concern for the human quality of sexual consummation is long-standing in the Church's canonical tradition. Gratian devotes an entire section (*causa*) to the inadmissibility of violent consummation.[18]

The *quality* of sexual consummation is important insofar as this act reflects the nature of the marital covenant. Consummation must take place in a human fashion (*humano modo*), that is, willingly and lovingly on the part of each party.[19] If consummation takes place in an atmosphere or as a result of physical or moral violence or coercion, it cannot be said to have occurred in a human fashion.

The consultors who discussed the canons favored the notion that natural sexual intercourse constituted consummation and that use of contraceptives did not prevent true completion of the act as long as the device used did not interfere with the physical act of intercourse.[20] The question thus posed is practical and the response framed in terms of the biological dimension of consummation. Whether or not any type of artificial contraception impedes the sexual act as an effective sign of the complete gift of one spouse to the other is primarily a theological issue.

The second paragraph states simply that if the spouses have lived together, intercourse or consummation is presumed to have occurred. This canon has a practical importance in cases of alleged non-consummation. The presumption must then be overturned by contrary evidence to show that although there had been cohabitation, consummation did not in fact take place.

A *putative* marriage is a marriage that is presumed valid but in fact is invalid. Although there is an appearance of marriage since a wedding ceremony took place, the presence of a nullifying factor results in actual invalidity. The nullity may be due to an undispensed impediment, a defect in consent, or a condition which causes an incapacity to fulfill marital obligations. In such cases, at least one of the parties is presumed to have exchanged consent in good faith, that is, with no idea of the invalidating factor.

The theory of the putative marriage has its ori-

---

[16]Gratian c. 34, c. 27, q. 2 *CorpusIC* 1, 1073; Gasparri, *De Matrimonio* (Vatican: Typis Polyglottis Vaticanis, 1932), 1, n. 41, 38.

[17]Gratian c. 3, c. 31, q. 2, *CorpusIC* 1, 1113. "Quorum unum futurum est corpus unus debet esse et animus: atque ideo nulla invita est copulanda alicui."

[18]Gratian c. 36, q. 1, *CorpusIC* 1, 1288–1289.

[19]*GS* 49. "Hence the acts in marriage by which the intimate and chaste union of the spouses takes place are noble and honorable; the truly human performance of these acts fosters the self-giving they signify and enriches the spouses in joy and gratitude."

[20]Ibid; *Comm* 6 (1976), 180.

gins in the Middle Ages when the extension of the impediments of consanguinity and affinity caused some marriages to be invalid without the spouses' knowledge. Such cases were not uncommon due to the complex nature of the above-mentioned impediments. Numerous people were invalidly married because of varying degrees of blood or legal relationship. This gave rise to problems of legitimacy of children, succession, inheritance, and support. Alexander III gave the putative marriage theory the force of law in a series of decretals.[21] Gradually the notion was extended to include impediments other than consanguinity and affinity.

The concept of the putative marriage is significant in that it provides certain juridical effects in favor of one or both of the spouses and the children. In the present Code the primary effect is the provision for legitimacy of children born of or conceived during a putative marriage (see c. 1137).

For a marriage to be considered putative there must have been an appearance of marriage. This implies a ceremony according to canonical form for marriages involving at least one Catholic and some sort of legally accepted ceremony for non-Catholics. Marriages which are invalid due to a lack of canonical form are not considered putative.

The Betrothal or Engagement

Canon 1062 — §1. **A promise of marriage, be it unilateral or bilateral, called an engagement, is regulated by particular law which has been established by the conference of bishops after it has taken into consideration any existing customs and civil laws.**

§2. A promise to marry does not give rise to an action to seek the celebration of marriage; an action for reparation of damages, however, does arise if it is warranted.

Although the betrothal or engagement is primarily a social affair in most contemporary societies, there are still instances wherein it has social and even legal importance. In most ancient societies, marriage was concluded by means of a process as opposed to a single, legally recognized act. In the Mosaic law the rite of betrothal carried all of the juridic force of marriage. The same was true for the Germanic law of the Early Middle Ages. Infidelity by the woman was considered to be adultery if committed during the engagement period. The early Church accepted the more lenient Roman law concept of the engagement as a promise to marry in the future as opposed to the traditional notion which saw engagement as a form of wife purchase. In spite of the gradual emancipation of the Roman woman, the engagement still involved monetary transactions between the groom and the father of the bride. The custom of payment of a dowry prior to marriage still exists in certain countries.

By the Late Middle Ages child betrothal was customary in order to secure marriages for economic gain. This led to the actual supplying of consent by the families, a practice contrary to the developing theology of marriage. Alexander III challenged this system by declaring that child betrothals were invalid unless followed by the consent of the betrothed after they came of age.[22]

The present legislation uses the term "promise" rather than contract or covenant when referring to the engagement. It is a promise that a marriage will take place in the future and has moral force but does not legally bind one to marry against his or her will.

The regulation of betrothals is left to the particular legislation of episcopal conferences. This legislation could conceivably include such matters as a liturgical rite, the form by which the promises are made, witnesses, and even dowry.

If the engagement is broken for either just or unjust reasons, neither party may institute an action or suit to compel the other to marry. If there was an exchange of monetary or other gifts in view of the wedding, suits for reparation of damages may be lodged before ecclesiastical courts. Several civil jurisdictions regulate betrothals and permit actions for fraud, breach of promise of marriage, and compensation for material loss.

CHAPTER I
PASTORAL CARE AND WHAT MUST PRECEDE CELEBRATION OF MARRIAGE
[cc. 1063–1072]

Catechesis and Preparation for Marriage

Canon 1063 — **Pastors of souls are obliged to see to it that their own ecclesial community furnishes the Christian faithful assistance so that the matrimonial state is maintained in a Christian spirit and makes progress toward perfection. This assistance is especially to be furnished through:**

1° preaching, catechesis adapted to minors, youths and adults, and even the use of the media of social communications so that through these means the Christian faithful may be instructed concerning the meaning of Christian marriage and the duty of Christian spouses and parents;

2° personal preparation for entering marriage so that through such preparation the parties may be predisposed toward the holiness and duties of their new state;

3° a fruitful liturgical celebration of marriage clarifying that the spouses signify and share in that mystery of unity and of fruitful love that exists between Christ and the Church;

---

[21]See X 4 17 *Qui filii sint legitimi, CorpusIC* 2, 709–717.

[22]X 4 2 6, *CorpusIC* 2, 674–675.

4° assistance furnished to those already married so that, while faithfully maintaining and protecting the conjugal covenant, they may day by day come to lead holier and fuller lives in their families.

Pastors have a most serious obligation to insure that various forms of assistance are provided for those preparing to marry and for those already married. By "pastors of souls" the Code refers to bishops and priests upon whom rests the primary obligation of the spiritual care of persons. The Code further states that pastors should draw on the resources of the entire Catholic community. This could involve marriage preparation programs utilizing the assistance of married couples and other experts (physicians, psychologists, lawyers), post-marital support and study groups, as well as groups or individuals trained to assist married couples who are experiencing problems.

The most important point to be made about this canon is the gravity of the obligation, especially in light of serious contemporary problems facing Christian marriage. Some of the threats posed to Christian marriage are mentioned in *Gaudium et Spes* 47.[23] The Papal Commission on Marriage and the Family states:

> The crisis which gravely affects the family in those countries [European and North American] arises directly from the development of a mentality which stresses material success, individualism, efficiency, technology that is becoming more and more refined, and the development of a lifestyle that stresses money, action and power.[24]

Since marriage and family life are necessary for the well-being of the Christian community and the evangelization of society,[25] the importance of this obligation cannot be overstressed. A variety of means of assistance are possible in responding to the spiritual needs of those preparing for marriage as well as those already married.

The community has a right to expect maturity and true Christian commitment from those who marry. The gravity of the obligation to provide assistance should be understood in light of this right of the community.

After the general introduction the canon gives four examples of how this assistance may be furnished. The three major areas of concern are stated,

namely, *general catechesis of all the faithful on marriage, proximate preparation and catechesis of individual couples preparing to marry, and post-marital help and support.*

General Catechesis

The detailed approach of this canon responds to the urgent need for comprehensive marriage and family life preparation. The Papal Commission on Marriage and the Family stated that there are widespread deficiencies in such preparation. John Paul II's allocution on the family further stressed this point:

> More than ever necessary in our times is preparation of young people for marriage and family life. . . . But the changes that have taken place within almost all modern societies demand that not only the family but also society and the Church should be involved in the effort of properly preparing young people for their future responsibilities. Many negative phenomena which are today noted with regret in family life derive from the fact that, in the new situations, young people not only lose sight of the correct hierarchy of values but, since they no longer have certain criteria of behavior, they do not know how to face and deal with the new difficulties. But experience teaches that young people who have been well prepared for family life generally succeed better than others.[26]

Marriage preparation begins with the general education of the faithful on the meaning of marriage, its importance in the life of the Christian community, and the nature of its obligations and responsibilities. It is especially important that the sacramental or faith dimension of marriage be stressed in such a way that it be understandable and attractive to people. The conditions of the society and even the particular community must be taken into consideration, particularly the effect of secular value systems on the formation of marital and family values.

Church leadership has recognized the intense need for effective means of promoting education and support for marriage and the family. Numerous resources are available on a diocesan and national level to assist in the formulation and execution of programs especially on a parish level.[27] General preparation must not be limited to an isolated sermon but should be an integral part of catechetical and adult education programs, Catholic school curricula, and other forms of parish and diocesan programs.

The 1917 Code spoke of general education but

---

[23]*GS* 47. " . . . This happy picture is not reflected everywhere but is overshadowed by polygamy, the plague of divorce, so-called free love, and similar blemishes; furthermore, married love is too often dishonored by selfishness, hedonism and unlawful contraceptive practices. Besides, the economic, social, psychological and civil climate of today has a severely disturbing effect on family life."

[24]Papal Committee on the Family, "The Family in the Pastoral Activity of the Church" (Washington, D.C.: USCC, 1978), 5.

[25]John Paul I, "On The Family," 9–21–1975 (Washington, D.C.: USCC, 1975).

[26]*FC* 120–121.

[27]*Families in the Eighties* (Washington, D.C.: USCC, 1981).

stressed the issue of freedom from impediments. The present Code emphasizes a broader approach. The nature and demands of the interpersonal relationship, nurture of children, and the responsibilities of marriage as a Christian vocation in the community are vital elements to be seriously considered.

Proximate Preparation for Marriage

The preparation of individual couples planning marriage is far more important today than in the past. This preparation involves several elements. The first is the determination that both parties are ready for marriage. This must be considered from the point of view of the resources of the parties in light of the demands placed on married persons in contemporary society. Some form of pre-marital inventory or psychological assessment tool can be helpful as a starting point in determining fitness for marriage. Since more maturity is required for a successful marriage today than in the past, it follows that the psychological and emotional requirements are raised as well. On the other hand, it is to be remembered that marriage involves growth. What should be sought is some evidence of a basic degree of maturity and the potential for continued growth as well as the ability to cope with the expected stresses and strains of a developing marital relationship.

The parties' understanding of the commitment to sacramental marriage must be assessed as well as their willingness to live out the implications of this commitment. Marriage is referred to as a "vocation" in canon 226, §1 and not simply a state of life.

Once basic readiness is determined, the next step in the process should be a consideration of the interpersonal dimension of marriage. Certain questions are fundamental: personal goals in marriage; expectations of one another; real awareness of the other person, including strengths and weaknesses; acceptance of faults and foibles; ability to enunciate and evaluate reasons for marriage; etc. On this level the concern is for the ability not only to make the required gift of self but to accept the same from the other.

Since Christian marriage is a sacrament and a vocation, the parties should then be led to a deeper understanding and appreciation of their role in fostering the well-being and growth of the Christian community. This will include the procreation and education of children as an especially important element. It should also include worship, service to the community and, most important, the example of a well-ordered Christian life.[28]

Proximate preparation involves diocesan-wide programs utilizing the talents of priests, deacons (especially married deacons), lay married couples, religious, and professionally trained counselors. It involves the necessary dynamic of guided interpersonal communication with the parties as well as group presentations and discussions. The number and variety of programs which have been initated in North America and Europe in the recent past reflect a recognition of the serious need in this regard. The demand for adequate education and preparation for marriage cannot be met by a few sessions with the parish priest; thus there is the necessity of community involvement.[29]

Preparation programs for prospective spouses which are mandatory and not optional neither infringe upon nor violate the right to marriage. Although they are mandatory in some cases, such programs cannot be made a condition for the validity of the marriage. Nevertheless, participation in them may be a necessary requirement for permission to marry. The mandatory nature of such programs reflects the Church's awareness of the serious problems facing marriage in contemporary society. They are also a response to the right of the spouses to receive adequate direction and preparation relative to their decision to marry. The exercise of the right to marry is relative to the capacity and willingness to live out the obligations of the sacrament.

Since proximate preparation is not limited to completion of the required forms, but rather is a much more complex reality, it must begin some time before the planned wedding date. This will ensure that the engagement period is truly a preparation period for marriage and not simply for a wedding.[30]

The Liturgical Celebration

The fact that this canon mentions the liturgical celebration indicates that it is not only a means of sanctification of the spouses and the celebration of their consent but a source of instruction for all present in the theological significance of the marriage covenant.

Since the wedding liturgy is an act of the Church's public worship, it must conform to the general norms for liturgical celebration. Particular norms are found in the *Introduction* of the revised rite of marriage.

The liturgical celebration should manifest the fact that the spouses are undertaking a special vocation in the Christian community. It is not a personal or private affair in which the bride and groom express their love by means of gestures or words which have a special significance only to them or to a select few. The entire liturgy must reflect the fact that they consider their love to be sacred and there-

---

[28]*FC* 81–116.

[29]See M. Thomas, "An Analysis and Critique of Marriage Preparation Programs," *Marriage Studies* 1:1–64.

[30]See T. Doyle, "The Individual's Right to Marry in the Context of the Common Good," *Stud Can* 13 (1979), 246–301.

fore make their commitment to each other in light of the Church's understanding of marriage.

Marriage is a universal human institution to which Christ gave a profound sacramental dignity. Throughout the centuries the liturgical rites connected with marriage gradually evolved in their expression of the notion of marriage unique to Christians. Prior to the liturgical reforms of Vatican II the exchange of vows took place before the beginning of the Eucharist. While retaining a separate liturgical ritual for the exchange of consent outside of Mass (as in the case of mixed marriages), the celebration of the sacrament between two Catholics is now placed within the Mass just after the homily. This change no doubt reflects the sacred character of marriage and its ecclesial significance.

The *Introduction* of the revised rite states that local customs may be introduced into the ritual provided these continue to express the meaning of the sacrament. The composition of particular marriage rituals is left to the conference of bishops and subject to the approval of the Holy See. The use of particular gestures, words, readings, or music should not obscure the religious nature of the celebration.

The spouses are both the ministers and recipients of the sacrament. Their exchange of consent should express their commitment not only to each other but to their ecclesial faith. Any request by the bride and groom to compose their own vows should be carefully scrutinized. Whatever form the vows take, they must explicitly state the full commitment until death. The traditional English expression of the vows, which originated in the ancient Sarum rite, remains one of the clearest renditions of the nature of the marriage covenant.

Post-Marital Assistance

The absence of societal supports for marital and family stability is also recognized by the Church. The ecclesial community is to compensate for this by providing sources of support and renewal for married couples. The many challenges facing married persons and their families demand not only encouragement by the Church but resources upon which they may draw in times of need.

This is especially true for couples and families in crisis. Many troubled marriages can be saved with competent intervention before the relationship has totally disintegrated. This intervention can be offered in the form of counseling agencies, support groups, and referral services.

Post-marital support should also be directed to those not in a state of crisis. Numerous groups and movements have been founded to provide positive support for spouses and families. The Christian Family Movement, Teams of Our Lady, and Marriage Encounter are but three examples of movements which have been especially influential in promoting growth in the sacramental and ecclesial dimensions of marriage.

The Obligation of the Local Ordinary

Canon 1064 — It is up to the local ordinary to make provisions that such assistance is duly organized, even after consulting men and women of proven experience and skill, if it seems appropriate.

The local ordinary has the primary obligation of providing for the various forms of pre-marital and post-marital assistance. This obligation binds the diocesan bishop and all those equivalent to him in law.

Local ordinaries must make provisions for various ethnic and social groups of the diocese. They should also take into consideration the state of family life as it actually exists in the diocese as well as the customs of the various economic and social strata of the diocese.

The local ordinary is advised to formulate diocesan programs in light of advice offered by qualified lay persons who possess particular expertise in those areas noted in the preceding canon. This should pertain especially to those programs which require the skills of professionally trained persons such as psychiatrists, psychologists, and other counselors. This is in keeping with canon 212, §3 which states that properly qualified believers have a right and duty to offer advice to their pastors as well as canon 228, §2 which similarly states that qualified lay persons may be called upon as experts in various areas of assistance to the community.

In conclusion, it should be mentioned that the bishop has always been called upon to exercise special leadership in regard to marriage in virtue of his responsibility for the sacraments and for the spiritual life of the faithful.

The Reception of Confirmation, Penance, and the Eucharist

Canon 1065 — §1. If they can do so without serious inconvenience, Catholics who have not yet received the sacrament of confirmation are to receive it before being admitted to marriage.
§2. It is strongly recommended that those to be married approach the sacraments of penance and the Most Holy Eucharist so that they may fruitfully receive the sacrament of marriage.

The reception of baptism is necessary for the valid reception of the sacrament of matrimony. The reception of the sacraments of confirmation, penance, and Eucharist is strongly recommended for Catholics who enter a sacramental marriage (including a mixed marriage) as well as those who enter a disparity of cult marriage. Although following this recommendation is not necessary for the validity of the marriage, it is urged in virtue of the faith dimension of marriage as well as the ecclesial obligations.

Confirmation

The present Code repeats the legislation of the 1917 Code (*CIC* 1021, §2) which urged the reception of confirmation before marriage. Commentaries on the 1917 Code and the marriage law committee which helped to formulate the present Code say little about canon 1065. Mention is limited to concern for the nature of the obligation and reasons for allowing non-confirmed persons to marry. In any event a willingness to be confirmed is presumed.

Some commentators hold that receiving confirmation is a grave obligation and others state that it is light. Those who hold to the gravity of the obligation relate confirmation to the strengthening of faith needed to respond to the graces of the sacrament of marriage. Cappello relates the obligation to the fulfilling of the purpose of marriage. Since this includes the acceptance of children and their education in the worship of God, parents must be confirmed in the same faith in which they will raise their children.[31]

The confirmed Catholic is charged with communicating the faith by word and example. In marriage this is primarily realized through the community of the whole of life wherein the spouses assist each other by mutual sanctification and growth in faith. It is also accomplished by the nurture of the life of faith of their children.

Penance

Prior legislation treated the question of confession before marriage from a juridical and theological viewpoint. Prior to the 1917 Code, particular legislation in certain dioceses made confession before marriage an absolute requirement.[32]

The 1917 Code (*CIC* 1033) used the words "strongly exhort" since confession (and communion) are not strictly a matter of precept in the context. It is "strongly recommended" (*enixe commendatur*) in the present canon that penance be received prior to marriage; however, it is not an absolute requirement for the sacrament of marriage.

Theologically, penance is recommended in view of the traditional teaching that marriage is a sacrament of the living. In this context the law is concerned with the proper dispositions of those about to marry. Since the marital covenant requires a selfless commitment of the parties one to another in view of their special role in the life of the community, those who make this commitment should be in the state of grace, having been reconciled to God and His Church.

Eucharist

Prior to the revised rite of marriage, the Eucharist was celebrated after the wedding itself had taken place. The exchange of consent within the Mass in marriages of two Catholics and a Catholic and a baptized non-Catholic emphasizes the intimate relationship of the Eucharist to the sacrament of marriage.

Marriage is a human reality founded on reciprocal love. As a sacrament, marriage reflects the covenant between Christ and His Church and is the efficacious sign of this New Covenant. It is symbolized in marriage by the reciprocal and indissoluble commitment of the spouses. Since the Eucharist is the nuptial banquet of those sharing in the covenant between Christ and His Church, it is fitting that Catholic spouses partake in it at their wedding since they are committing themselves to a life which should reflect the reality of the union of Christ and His Church.

Sacramental marriage is more than an example of the New Covenant. It is also a means of accomplishing it. Like the Eucharist, marriage is ordered to the building up of the Body of Christ. The place of the Eucharist in a marriage relationship is made clear when marriage and the family are considered as the basic Christian community or a "little Church." Conciliar and post-conciliar documents refer to the role of the spouses in building up the Church.[33] The Eucharist, the center of the Church, should also be the center of the marital community.[34]

The exhortation to receive the Eucharist is more a pastoral than legal concern. It is included under proximate preparation for marriage because of the importance of spiritual preparation for marriage.

Although marriage cannot be prohibited or delayed solely because one or both spouses refuse to receive the Eucharist, the reasons for such a refusal should be carefully examined by the pastoral minister as he assesses the overall readiness for marriage. It is somewhat incongruous for certain Catholics habitually to reject the Eucharist from their lives and at the same time request sacramental marriage, which is so intimately related to the Eucharist.

Certitude of Valid and Licit Celebration

Canon 1066 — Before marriage is celebrated, it must be evident that nothing stands in the way of its valid and licit celebration.

---

[31]F. Cappello, *Tractatus Canonico-Moralis de Sacramentis,* V, *De Matrimonio,* (Romae: Marietti, 1947), n. 150, 152. See also *The Rites* (New York: Pueblo, 1976), 298.

[32]P. Gasparri, *Tractatus Canonicus de Matrimonio,* ed. 1932 (Romae: Typis Polyglottis Vaticanis, 1932), 1, n. 198, 118.

[33]*LG* 41. " . . . Because in this way they present to all an example of unfailing and generous love, they build up the brotherhood of charity, and they stand as witnesses and cooperators of the fruitfulness of Mother Church, as a sign of, and a share in that love with which Christ loved His bride and gave Himself for her." See also *FC* 81–119.

[34]See A. Ambrosiano, "Mariage et Eucharistie," in *Nouvelle revue théologique* 98 (1976), 289–305.

This canon is situated between those which deal with a basic readiness for marriage and those directly concerned with freedom to marry. Directly related to canon 1066 are canons 1058 (the right to marry) and 1077 (temporary prohibition of marriage). This canon is a reminder that the right to marry is contingent on fulfilling certain legal prerequisites.

This canon enunciates a basic fact about marriage. It states that a wedding cannot take place unless the pastoral minister is morally certain that it will be valid and licit. Practically speaking, this type of certitude means that there is no reason to believe that the marriage would be invalid or at least illicit. Knowingly to permit or witness a wedding if one is aware of the presence of a diriment impediment or other invalidating factor is to permit an invalid marriage. This same obligation was contained in the 1917 Code (*CIC* 1019, §1). Nevertheless, it appears to have been rarely invoked due to the difficulties involved in determining when a proposed marriage would certainly be invalid.[35]

The pastoral minister must arrive at this certainty by means of positive and morally certain arguments and not mere conjecture, hypothesis, or negative arguments. In short, all prudent doubt that the union would be invalid must be removed.[36]

This canon is concerned not only with impediments which may be present but with any factor which would render the marriage invalid or illicit. With reference to invalidity, of particular importance are the many invalidating factors arrived at by developing matrimonial jurisprudence. One might note the various kinds of emotional and psychological disorders, rejection of the Catholic concept of marriage, and seriously inadequate consent which reflects a desire for a wedding but does not include true marriage.

When the pastor applies this canon, he must objectively study the facts of the case. The parties have a right to a thorough, unbiased investigation of their readiness for marriage grounded in their fundamental right to marriage as well as their right to adequate pastoral care (c. 213). If the pastoral minister is certain of invalidating factors such as the outright rejection of children, fidelity, or perpetuity or the presence of an impediment or serious psychological disorder, he may not witness the union. If he has serious doubts about the union, the prudent approach would be to consult the local ordinary out of respect for the parties' rights. The local ordinary could in turn invoke canon 1077 and study the matter and perhaps prohibit the marriage temporarily.

The Investigation of Freedom To Marry

Canon 1067 — The conference of bishops is to issue norms concerning the examination of the parties, and the marriage banns or other appropriate means for carrying out the necessary inquiries which are to precede marriage. The pastor can proceed to assist at a marriage after such norms have been diligently observed.

Since marriage is not a private possession of the two parties but a matter of public interest, both ecclesial and secular societies have traditionally enacted legislation concerning basic requirements for marriage. Such legislation is aimed at assuring that the parties will not enter a relationship that would be detrimental to themselves, possible children, or the community. Church legislation in this regard has always involved some form of pre-nuptial investigation. Thus church authorities would be satisfied that both positive and natural law demands would be met.

Prior to the fifth century this inquiry was conducted by the bishop and was originally prompted by a concern about incestuous marriages or marriages with infidels. From that time on, the obligation was incumbent upon the parish priest. General legislation enacted at ecumenical councils (especially Lateran IV and Trent) referred to pre-nuptial investigations, public solemnization of marriages and the banns. These provisions reflected a concern for marriage in relation to the welfare of the parties, family life, and the community.[37]

Two matters are dealt with: the examination of the parties by the pastoral minister in order to determine freedom to marry and the traditional publication of the proposed marriage by means of the banns. The latter amounted to an inquiry within the community to discern possible impediments.

The Examination of the Parties

The preparatory steps alluded to in canon 1063 should have indicated a general readiness for marriage. Next there follows the examination of the parties aimed primarily at:

(a) determining that the parties are free of impediments;

(b) ascertaining that they have sufficient knowledge of Christian doctrine;

(c) determining that their consent is free.[38]

The episcopal conference is charged with issuing norms on how the investigation is to be carried out

---

[35]T. Doyle, 298–300.
[36]F. Wernz and P. Vidal, *Ius Canonicum*, V, *De Matrimonio* (Romae: Apud Aedes Universitatis Gregorianae, 1925), n. 112, 130.

[37]T. Fulton, *The Pre-nuptial Investigation* (Washington, D.C.: Catholic University of America, 1948), 1–50.
[38]Wernz-Vidal, 143.

while the obligation itself rests with the local ordinary. Given the diversity of the population in many countries, especially the United States, it seems that broad norms on a national level would enable the local ordinary to make appropriate adaptations for his own situation.

In the past the examination often consisted simply in filling out certain forms. More recently dioceses have expanded the approach to include various tools such as the pre-marriage inventory. Conceivably some form of examination concerned with the spiritual or faith capacity of the parties could be included as well. The examination is concerned with the couple's awareness of the ecclesial dimension of marriage as well as their willingness to follow the Church's teaching.

The Obligation for the Examination

The obligation to see that the examination is carried out is incumbent upon the local ordinary. The ultimate responsibility for conducting it belongs to the pastor who has the canonical right to assist at marriages in his parish (c. 530, 4°). In other words, a pastoral assistant or other minister or lay person may in fact conduct the preparatory steps and the examination, yet it is the pastor's responsibility to see to it that this is done correctly.

The gravity of the obligation is obvious both from the nature of sacramental marriage and its relation to the life of the community. Past legislation seriously admonished priests and bishops to examine carefully those planning marriage. Penalties were attached to the neglect of this obligation, including suspension from the benefice and even suspension from office. The obligation then is not simply to conduct the investigation but to conduct it well.

The Inquiry

The Church has conducted an inquiry among the members of the community by means of the banns since Lateran Council IV. The 1917 Code contained detailed legislation on the banns (*CIC* 1023–1028). Its purpose was to uncover impediments or other circumstances which would impede a valid and licit marriage. Although it was effective in the past, the institute of banns has presently become something similar to an ecclesiastical social register in many places. Consequently, the conference of bishops is charged with enacting legislation on banns which will respond to distinct pastoral needs.

The inquiry must be structured to protect the rights of the parties and preserve confidentiality. On the other hand, it must provide a realistic avenue for people to present to the proper authorities serious objections to the marriage or important knowledge about the parties.

Procedure in Danger of Death

Canon 1068 — Unless contrary indications are present, in danger of death, if other means of proof cannot be obtained, it is sufficient that the parties affirm—even under oath, if the case warrants it— that they have been baptized and that they are not held back by any impediment.

The Code makes one exception to the obligation of conducting a full examination and that is when there is danger of death. Such situations would normally involve persons who are in irregular marriages or living together. Danger of death here means probable danger arising from intrinsic (illness) or extrinsic (war, natural disaster) causes. If it is a question of intrinsic causes, this can be on the part of either or both parties.

The canon presumes that there is no other means of ascertaining freedom to marry except for the statement of the parties themselves. They *both* must affirm that at least one was baptized and both are free of impediments and other possible invalidating factors. Although the 1917 Code stated that the affirmation was to be given under oath, the present law indicates that this is considered an exceptional way of affirming freedom to marry. Thus the word of the parties would suffice if there were no legitimate reason to doubt their veracity.

This canon may not be used if there is certain knowledge of an impediment or other invalidating factor. This is especially true in cases of people living in unions which are irregular due to a prior marriage on the part of at least one party.

The Obligation of the Faithful To Reveal Impediments

Canon 1069 — All the faithful are obliged to reveal any impediments they are aware of to the pastor or to the local ordinary before the celebration of marriage.

The obligation to reveal impediments binds all the faithful and is related to a concern for the common good. It concerns certain or highly probable knowledge of an impediment and not mere suspicion. Family members and other close acquaintances are generally those most significantly affected by this obligation. This obligation includes impediments as well as other invalidating factors such as serious mental illness or invalidating intentions hidden from the examining priest.

Knowledge obtained in sacramental confession can never be used and in certain cases knowledge revealed under the auspices of professional confidence or secrecy, such as medical or counseling information, cannot be revealed. According to certain civil laws such information can be revealed with the written release of the person involved.

If an impediment is revealed to the pastoral minister, his or her first obligation is to verify it. If indeed a diriment impediment is present, either it must be dispensed by the competent authority or the wedding must be canceled. The course of action taken depends on the nature of the impediment (see c. 1080).

Notification of the Parties' Completed Examination

Canon 1070 — If someone other than the pastor who is to assist at the marriage has conducted the investigations, that person is to notify the pastor of the results as soon as possible through an authentic document.

The pre-marriage preparation and examination may take place under the direction of someone other than the pastor of the parish where the wedding will take place. This would happen if the spouses live in one parish or town and will be married in another. The results of the preparatory process, that is, the assurance that both parties are free to marry, must be communicated by the person who conducted the process to the pastoral minister responsible for witnessing the wedding by means of an authentic document, i.e., one that is signed and sealed. This information is then included in the marriage file.

Situations Requiring the Local Ordinary's Permission

Canon 1071 — §1. Except in case of necessity, no one is to assist at the following marriages without the permission of the local ordinary:

1° the marriage of transients;

2° a marriage which cannot be recognized or celebrated in accord with the norm of civil law;

3° a marriage of a person who is bound by natural obligations toward another party or toward children, arising from a prior union;

4° a marriage of a person who has notoriously rejected the Catholic faith;

5° a marriage of a person who is bound by a censure;

6° a marriage of a minor child when the parents are unaware of it or are reasonably opposed to it;

7° a marriage to be entered by means of a proxy, mentioned in can. 1105.

§2. The local ordinary is not to grant permission for assisting at the marriage of a person who has notoriously rejected the Catholic faith unless the norms of can. 1125 have been observed, making any necessary adaptations.

This canon is a taxative list of marriages which cannot be witnessed without the permission of the local ordinary. These situations do not constitute impediments since objectively they do not alter the basic right to marry. Yet they involve situations which may possibly endanger the spouses, potential children, or the community. The law gives special consideration to these cases because experience has shown that they present particular problems.

Transients

A transient (*vagus*) is one who has no fixed abode (c. 100), that is, no domicile, quasi-domicile, or fixed residence. This situation may be temporary or the person may be a habitual transient. Such persons may well be unstable, suffering from some form of mental or character disorder. They require an especially thorough preparation and examination, particularly regarding their stability and freedom to marry.

Many kinds of persons could fit into this category: perpetual wanderers, those temporarily homeless, migrant workers, immigrants.[39] Some of these may be homeless through no fault of their own, yet they are capable of marriage. Others may be quite unstable and consequently not capable of the stability required for marriage.

Marriages Prohibited by Civil Law

In the United States civil authority over marriage is left to the individual states, hence the requirements may vary from state to state. In other countries the legislation may be more uniform.

Civil law impediments have two possible effects: the marriage is either absolutely void, or it is voidable. To be voidable means that it is considered valid until attacked in civil court and declared void. A civil annulment does not mean that the Church considers the marriage null as well, since civil authorities have no jurisdiction over the sacrament of marriage.

Among the civil law impediments are the following: prior marriage; lack of minimum age by at least one party; blood relationship within specified degrees; adoptive relationship; severe mental disorder; and venereal disease. In most jurisdictions one (or more) of the above factors results in absolute invalidity. Civil annulments may also be granted in marriages entered through fraud or duress.

If a civil impediment corresponds to a canonical impediment, the matter is subject to the appropriate canons and requires a dispensation if possible. Other civil impediments may have no bearing on canonical validity, e.g., residency requirements or interracial marriage.[40]

Except in rare circumstances the pastor is bound in conscience and by civil law to respect the civil

---

[39]"Instruction," SCSacr, in *CLD* 1, 498. Marriages of emigrant workers were to be considered marriages of transients (*vagi*).

[40]H.D. Krase, *Family Law Cases and Materials.* American Casebook Series (St. Paul: West, 1976).

legislation. Ordinarily marriage so impeded should be postponed until the impediment ceases or the marriage is allowed by court order.

Natural Obligations Arising from a Previous Union

Even though a prior union is declared invalid (including invalidity due to defect of form) or dissolved by the Church, there may still be natural obligations to a former spouse or children born of the union. A subsequent union, though ecclesiastically valid, may pose serious difficulties to the fulfillment of these obligations. They may also place serious strains on such a second marriage.

A divorced spouse continues to bear certain responsibilities to children, including financial obligations. It is more difficult to determine natural obligations to an ex-spouse although serious illness or financial destitution may create such obligations.

Theoretically, this canon would require the local ordinary's intervention in every case of remarriage of a divorced person. Practically speaking, it applies only to cases wherein natural obligations had been neglected or would be seriously endangered by a second marriage.

Marriages with Those Who Have Notoriously Rejected the Faith

One who *notoriously* rejects the faith does not merely neglect its practice, but professes openly that he or she is no longer a Catholic and refuses obedience to the Church and its laws. This differs in law from those who have simply abandoned the faith without positively rejecting it or those who are temporarily non-practicing. They may be unsuitable for marriage for other reasons.

The law presumes that those who have notoriously rejected the faith are hostile to it, pose a danger to the believing party and/or to the Catholic nurture of children, and may be a scandal to the community. It is also difficult to envision a faith sharing in the marital community with one hostile to Catholicism.

The Church's long history of legislative concern for such marriages is grounded in its experience of their negative effect on the Catholic spouse and children and the belief that strong Catholic family life is necessary for the well-being of the Church.

The law includes a rejection of Christianity as well as rejection of Catholicism. It is not necessary to embrace another religion. The primary danger is to the believing party and possible children. Consequently, there must be grave reasons to permit the marriage and certain assurance that the believing party will be allowed to practice the faith and that any children born will be baptized and raised as Catholics.

The 1917 Code defined notoriety of fact in terms of ecclesiastical offenses. It is an act publicly known and committed under such circumstances that it

can neither be concealed nor legally excused.[41] Although notorious abandonment of the faith is not in itself an offense in the present Code, this definition assists in understanding its meaning. The person in question may well admit to having rejected the faith or may have done so by one or a series of public acts which lead to presumption of rejection of the faith. It is important that the matter be clarified at the outset of the pre-marital preparation process.

Marriages of Those Bound by Censure

Persons who are excommunicated or under interdict are forbidden to receive any of the sacraments.[42]

The solution to the problem depends on the nature of the censure and the offense upon which it is based (cc. 1331–1335). Reconciliation to the Church and remission of the censure prior to the marriage suffice to rectify the situation. The law is concerned, however, with those who are not reconciled.

The problem is twofold: it is presumed that the person will receive the sacrament of marriage while in a state of serious sin. Second, the offense itself may well pose a serious threat to a successful marriage covenant. Since this covenant implies a sharing of faith and some degree of participation in the life of the Church, the couple is placed in an incongruous situation: the person under censure is at the same time requesting marriage which presumes a special relationship to the Church and refusing to rectify a serious situation which makes the aforementioned relationship impossible.

Marriage of Minors

A person who has not completed his or her eighteenth year is considered a minor (c. 97, §1). If one or both parties are under this age, the case must be referred to the local ordinary.

Marriages of the young have always posed special problems for ecclesiastical and civil legislators. Prior to the 1917 Code the ages for validity were fourteen and twelve for males and females respectively. The ages were raised to sixteen and fourteen in the 1917 Code. In his commentary on this, Gasparri states that a certain maturity of judgment (*mentis discretio*) is needed which is lacking in those of a young age.[43] While marriages above the minimum age were considered valid, the 1917 Code (*CIC* 1067, §2) strongly discouraged the marriages of minors.

Such marriages are discouraged because of the presumption that minors lack the emotional stability and maturity to handle the difficulties of married life. In contemporary society many of the

---

[41] *CIC* 2197, §3.
[42] Cc. 1331, §1, 2°; 1332.
[43] Gasparri 2, n. 783, 12.

traditional familial and societal supports for marriage have disappeared. While minors are socially emancipated at an earlier age, experience shows that many lack the inner strengths which enable married persons to make the needed sacrifices and adjustments.

The law subjects minors to the judgment of parents or guardians in the exercise of their rights. Parents can neither force their children to marry nor absolutely forbid them to marry. The law presumes that parents will have sufficient knowledge of their children as well as concern for their welfare. Therefore, they should be in a position to estimate their readiness for marriage.

The pastor may not proceed with the marriage if the parents of the minor party are unaware of the intended marriage. In such cases he should see that they are informed and then ask their opinion of the situation. If the minor has a serious reason for not consulting his or her parents, the pastor must carefully weigh all the circumstances before deciding not to consult them.

If the parents oppose the union, the pastor should thoroughly examine their reasons. If their opposition appears to be reasonable, the canon is clear. If the pastor questions the validity of parental opposition, the prudent approach would be to submit the matter to the local ordinary, since this would amount to a doubt of fact.

If resources are available, the parties to the marriage should be referred for pre-marital counseling. A competent counselor will be able to help them to clarify their motivation to marry and discover their strengths and weaknesses. If the couple is truly immature and unprepared, expert counseling should help them to discover this themselves.

Marriage by Proxy

A proxy marriage is one which takes place without the parties being physically present to each other. One or both are represented by persons who must be duly mandated to exchange consent on behalf of the parties themselves. The procedural implications of proxy marriages are treated in canon 1105. In all cases of proxy marriage the local ordinary's permission is required.

Only under the most extreme circumstances should a proxy marriage be considered. When it is next to impossible for the parties to be together and a delay would cause grave harm, there might be sufficient reason for such a marriage. When a marriage is to take place by proxy, the parties must, nevertheless, be properly prepared and the inquiry into freedom to marry carried out. For this, the physical presence of the parties is required since the very nature of marital preparation demands interpersonal dialogue. Permission for a proxy marriage does not constitute an exemption from any of the requirements for a valid and licit union.

Although proxy marriages are rare, they may occasionally be justified. Military service may prevent the physical presence of both parties at the marriage. In cases involving immigrants a proxy marriage might be necessary for one party to obtain a visa. In such cases it must be certain that the primary intent is to marry and not simply to enter the country.[44]

Marriages with Former Catholics

If the local ordinary allows a marriage with one who has notoriously abandoned the faith, the norms for mixed marriages must be applied.

Although the 1917 Code did not specifically state that marriages with such persons were to be treated as mixed marriages, it did state that there was to be an assurance that the children would be educated and dangers to the other party be removed (CIC 1065, §2). Also, some commentators felt that such marriages should be treated as mixed marriages if the lapsed Catholic had embraced another sect.[45] If he or she had not, the case was not treated as a mixed marriage, yet the pastor was to do all in his power to prevent the union. It was common practice under the 1917 Code to treat marriages involving Catholics who had embraced other sects as mixed marriages requiring dispensation from the ordinary.

The present law states that all marriages with Catholics who have notoriously left the Church are to be treated as mixed marriages. It is especially important that the baptism and education of children be discussed and reasonably guaranteed. Furthermore, the lapsed Catholic may have rejected the Church's teaching on the ends and essential properties of marriage. The pastor should carefully consider these matters with the parties in order to determine that they are entering the union with proper intentions.

If the local ordinary is not satisfied that the legal requirements will be fulfilled, he may refuse the requested permission. In dealing with such cases the local ordinary may adapt the norms for mixed marriages. He might require an oral or written assurance by the lapsed Catholic concerning any of the above-mentioned significant legal-pastoral concerns.

The Meaning of Necessity

One is not to assist at any of the above-mentioned marriages without permission of the local ordinary except in case of necessity. All of these situations presumably pose a threat to the establishment of a true conjugal community. The gravity of the necessity required to justify assisting at the mar-

---

[44]Cappello, n. 330, 338.
[45]Gasparri 1, nn. 492–494, 291–293.

riage without the ordinary's permission will vary depending on the particular circumstances.

This canon is a clear example of the Church's awareness of the effect of a marriage not only on the parties themselves but on the community. The necessity for proceeding without permission must clearly outweigh the possible dangers which may arise in each case.

Extra-marital pregnancy should not be considered a sufficient reason to proceed without permission. On the contrary, it demands even greater caution since there is a tendency to focus on the pregnancy alone, without a proper consideration of the other factors needed to establish a stable marriage.

Marriages of the Young

Canon 1072 — **Pastors of souls are to take care to prevent youths from celebrating marriage before the age at which marriage is usually contracted in accord with the accepted practice of the region.**

By "marriages of the young" the law means marriages of minors and marriages entered before the customary age of the region. However, local custom or opinion may hold that marriages of those who are a few years older than eighteen are still "marriages of the young."

The mention of such marriages in two canons reflects the Church's grave concern for the problems they pose. This concern is not new since there was an unsuccessful move at the Council of Trent to raise the ages for validity. Some Fathers suggested that no one below the ages of eighteen and sixteen for males and females respectively be allowed to marry validly without parental consent, and others suggested the age of twenty-five for both.

In his commentary on the similar canon in the 1917 Code, Gasparri argued that maturity of judgment does not necessarily come with the minimum age for validity.[46] Attainment of the minimal age at which one can exercise the right to marry does not automatically mean that a person is capable of exercising the right.

The customary practice of the region is not always reflected in the civil law requirements for minimum age. In some cases civil law requirements are lower and in others higher than canonical requirements.

Much more is required for a successful marriage than the ability to procreate. The consenting parties must give and receive each other for the purpose of constituting the community of life. Since the present Code presents marriage in terms of a comprehensive, interpersonal relationship, the capacities of the young must be measured in light of these criteria.

Cultural and social mores which supported marital stability for so long a time cannot be generally presumed in contemporary Western society. There is a widespread social and legal philosophy which no longer supports the concept of a committed, life-long marriage. Often the reasons for marital breakdown can ultimately be traced to ideological factors such as social and economic forces which undermine the values of Christian marriage. This causes undue pressure on those entering marriage, especially if they are young.

The assessment of a person's readiness for marriage and ability to fulfill the demands of the covenant relationship must take cognizance of the social milieu. For various reasons there has been a kind of isolation of the individual and a breakdown of the true sense of community. The resulting cult of the individual makes it all the more difficult for persons to grasp the meaning of the unqualified gift of self needed for marriage. Materialism and excessive economic demands have caused many to define themselves and their personal success in terms of possessions or economic power.

Societal mobility and occupational pressures promoting frequent moves make it difficult for many young married couples to establish roots in a community. They may be removed from their families as well. Consequently, they do not benefit from the support which can come from close relationships with friends and families. Spouses must now meet a wider and more complex variety of emotional and psychological needs in each other. At one time many of these needs were met to a degree by the extended family and the community. While the ability to meet the emotional needs of the marriage partner is required for marriage, many young people lack the capacity for the kind of emotional intimacy required. As a result, marital unions which are fragile from the beginning often break down rapidly and end in divorce.

Adolescent Marriage Today

The presumption that adolescents lack the maturity for marriage today is reinforced by current divorce statistics as well as the findings of social scientists and psychologists. Approximately 48% of divorces occur between couples who married before the age of twenty. Likewise, only 18.7% of those marrying between the ages of sixteen and eighteen and 42% of those marrying between the ages of nineteen and twenty-one did *not* experience marital breakdown.[47]

The high rate of breakdown of adolescent marriages is more clearly understood if the reasons which often motivate such marriages are studied. Tribunal experience has pointed to the following

---

[46]Ibid., 1, 291–292.

[47]See T. Doyle, "Why Some Catholics Get Divorced," *U.S. Catholic* 45 (1980), 32–27.

reasons among others: pre-marital pregnancy; rebellion against parents or authority in general; false expectations of marital happiness and success; reaction to an unhappy home life; lack of awareness of personal strengths and weaknesses; peer pressure and general encouragement of early marriage. Often marriage is looked upon as an answer to problems rather than a commitment to a new way of life.[48]

Although adolescent marriage may be customary in some regions and acceptable in some families, this in itself does not justify such marriages. The social and legal emancipation of adolescents has weakened parental control. Consequently, many important life decisions are made in spite of and often contrary to prudent and objective guidance.

The quality of marriage must also be considered. The high divorce rate, the phenomena of abortion and birth control and relaxed standards of sexual morality have contributed to a redefinition of the meaning of marriage for many, especially the young.[49]

In an effort to provide a support system, numerous dioceses have drawn up pre-marriage guidelines. These are generally geared to two things: to discern readiness for marriage and to prepare for a marriage. The pastor is no longer isolated in his dealings with adolescent marriages since he can often invoke the support of a diocesan-wide policy. Ideally, the decision to cancel or postpone a wedding should be made by the parties themselves as an important step in their maturation process.[50]

CHAPTER II
DIRIMENT IMPEDIMENTS IN GENERAL
[cc. 1073–1082]

The Definition of an Impediment

Canon 1073 — A diriment impediment renders a person incapable of contracting marriage validly.

An impediment to marriage is a circumstance or condition which directly affects a marriage in such a way that the law forbids such a marriage. It is a circumstance which is directly related to a person. It may arise from the person's relationship to another or it may rest in his or her very nature.

The 1917 Code contained two kinds of marriage impediments: impedient, which rendered a marriage illicit but not invalid; and diriment, which rendered a marriage invalid. The present Code contains only diriment impediments. The impedient

impediments have been dropped as such, and the circumstances upon which these impediments were based (simple vows, mixed religion, legal adoptive relationship) are treated differently.[51]

Historical Synopsis

Since marriage has always been geared in part to the propagation of the race and the well-being of the community, it has been the subject of legal regulation. Marriage legislation has included impediments based on moral or physical circumstances which the community considered to be detrimental to the parties, possible children, or the community.

There is evidence of prohibited marriages in the Pauline epistles. Such prohibitions included incestuous marriages, marriages with non-believers, and second marriages after divorce. The various post-apostolic synods and councils regularly passed legislation concerning marriage impediments. Much of this legislation was in response to community needs or abuses.

There has never been a systematic organization of impediments based on a fundamental set of principles. The number, nature, effects, and cessation of impediments have changed in the course of history in order to respond to the Church's needs. This evolution has also reflected a developing understanding of the nature of marriage as a social and ecclesial reality.[52]

Origin of Impediments

Canonical literature has consistently distinguished between impediments which are based on divine law and those grounded in ecclesiastical law. Divine law impediments are based on marriage as a natural institution and affect all persons, baptized or not. Ecclesiastical law impediments are based on the sacramental nature of marriage and its relation to the believing community. As such, these impediments affect only baptized Catholics (c. 11) although in the 1917 Code they also bound non-Catholics except for disparity of worship (*CIC* 1070). Canonical commentators generally agree that the divine law impediments include prior bond, impotence, and consanguinity in the direct line and in the second degree of the collateral line. However, certain commentators view disparity of cult, sacred orders, and perpetual vow of chastity as divine law impediments.

The Holy See alone is competent to interpret

---

[48]"The western family and the future of the Church," *Pro Mundi Vita* 41 (1974), 13.

[49]See J. McAreavy, *North American Diocesan Pastoral Directives for Marriages of the Young and Immature* (Rome: Gregorian University, 1976).

[50]See M. Thomas, "An analysis and critique of marriage preparation programs," *Marriage Studies* 1, 1980, 1–22.

[51]Simple vows in a religious institute, if perpetual and public, are considered a diriment impediment (c. 1088). Mixed religion is considered in a special chapter (cc. 1124–1129). If the relationship is in the direct line or second degree of the collateral line, legal adoption is always a diriment impediment (c. 1094).

[52]See J. O'Rourke, "The Scriptural Background of the Marriage Impediments," *J* 20 (1960), 29–41, and A. Bride, "Empêchements de mariage," *DDC* 5, col. 266.

which impediments are of divine origin. It alone can also enact new ecclesiastical law impediments and authentically interpret impediments of either kind.

Some Distinctions

Certain distinctions based on the different kinds of impediments assist in understanding them. *Absolute* impediments affect a marriage with all persons, baptized or not. A *relative* impediment affects marriages only with certain persons. Some impediments are *perpetual* since the circumstances which cause them always remain while others are *temporary* since their causes may disappear in time.

Cessation of Impediments

An impediment itself is a law which is based on certain existing circumstances. The binding force of the law may be *dispensed* by the competent ecclesiastical authority even though the circumstances do not change. Thus a person may be allowed to marry in certain cases in spite of the existence of an impediment.

An impediment can also cease by the passage of time or by some act or event which changes the circumstances upon which the impediment is based. It may cease by a voluntary act on the part of one of the parties or by a change in the law itself. For example: lack of age ceases with time; prior bond can cease with the death of a former spouse; and disparity of cult ceases with the baptism of the non-baptized party.

Public and Occult Impediments

Canon 1074 — An impediment which can be proven in the external forum is considered to be a public impediment; otherwise, it is an occult impediment.

An impediment is considered *public* if its existence can be proved in the external forum. An *occult* impediment is one which cannot be proven in the external forum. This distinction is important in discussing dispensation from impediments.

Public Impediments

The circumstances which cause certain of the impediments may be a matter of public record such as prior bond of marriage, sacred orders, perpetual vows, and legal adoption. Consequently, these are always considered public impediments since they can be proven by ecclesiastical or civil documents which are open to the public. Other impediments may be based on circumstances that are commonly known but not verifiable by a civil or canon law document.

Some impediments may be either public or occult

depending on whether or not the circumstances are known. Crime and abduction may exist in fact, yet they may not be publicly known and therefore be considered occult.

If an impediment cannot be proven in the external forum, it is considered occult. This is important in those cases in which the circumstances are not a matter of public record and are not well known or known at all. For instance, a person may be unaware of the fact of a blood relationship with a spouse; yet the impediment exists and the marriage is invalid.

Authority To Establish Impediments

Canon 1075 — §1. The supreme authority of the Church alone has the competency to declare authentically when divine law prohibits or voids a marriage.

§2. Only the supreme authority has the right to establish other impediments for the baptized.

The question of who could establish impediments was settled with the 1917 Code which stated that the Holy See alone is capable of declaring when the divine law prohibited marriage or when certain circumstances would be considered an ecclesiastical law impediment (*CIC* 1038). In short, the Holy See alone can establish diriment impediments. Prior to the 1917 Code the matter was unclear and canonists debated whether bishops or other ecclesiastical authorities could establish at least impedient impediments.

Also, the Holy See alone is competent to define the meaning of an impediment, e.g., determining which degrees of consanguinity invalidate or what exactly constitutes impotence.

Although the Church holds that certain impediments are of divine law origin, the precise nature and effects of these impediments have not been clear throughout history. There has also been a debate over the dispensing power of the bishops and even the Holy Father in certain cases. For instance, although the Holy Father can dissolve non-sacramental marriages and non-consummated but sacramental unions, it is commonly taught that he cannot dispense from the impediment of a valid prior sacramental bond in cases of consummated marriages.

When the Holy See interprets a divine law impediment, it does so for all persons, baptized or not. However, ecclesiastical law impediments bind only baptized Catholics unless the contrary is stated in law.

The Holy Father alone has the authority to establish or authentically interpret an impediment. Interpretations issued by dicasteries of the Roman Curia are made on delegated authority from the Holy Father.

Custom and Impediments

Canon 1076 — A custom which introduces a new impediment or which is contrary to existing impediments is reprobated.

A custom is a practice or way of acting common to a community. The earliest laws grew out of customs which in time became officially recognized by a legislator. According to canon law a custom never attains the force of law except through an act of the legislator. Theoretically, a custom may attain the force of law provided it corresponds to the principles in canons 23–28. This is not so with marriage impediments.

No community may introduce or maintain a custom which introduces a new ecclesiastical law impediment. The commentators point out that the impediment of disparity of cult grew out of custom. While this may have been true in the past, custom may no longer introduce any such impediment. Also, it is not permissible to interpret an ecclesiastical law impediment according to local custom nor are customary practices with regard to dispensation allowed.

This canon prohibits the creation of impediments based on local customs which could possibly be detrimental or contrary to the fundamental nature of marriage, e.g., customs which introduce sterility as an impediment. Such impediments could also unjustly circumscribe the right of the Church to regulate marriage or the rights of the parties to marriage itself.

The Ordinary's Right To Prohibit Marriage

Canon 1077 — §1. In a particular case the local ordinary can prohibit the marriage of his own subjects wherever they are staying and of all persons actually present in his own territory, but only for a time, for a serious cause and as long as that cause exists.

§2. Only the supreme authority of the Church can add an invalidating clause to a prohibition.

The power to prohibit a particular marriage temporarily flows from the Church's right to enact impediments and determine other conditions necessary for a valid marriage. The Church can dispense from the law in view of the individual or common good and for the same reasons it can strictly enforce the law. Consequently, the local ordinary is empowered to prohibit a union which could probably cause harm to the parties themselves or to the community.

Since this canon limits the individual's right to marry, the use of a prohibition must be based on the positive probability that the union would cause serious problems. The power to prohibit a marriage differs from the obligation of not witnessing a marriage, mentioned in canon 1066, since this latter obligation is grounded in the moral certitude that a marriage would be invalid.

Historical Synopsis

The power to prohibit a marriage is well founded in the Church's legislative history. In the earliest centuries certain marriages were forbidden under pain of penance and excommunication. The prohibition of marriage emerged as a canonical institute in the twelfth century and was not limited to the pope but was extended to bishops and, in certain cases, to priests.[53]

The marriage prohibition has always been disciplinary in nature and never was considered an impediment in itself. Also, a marriage celebrated in spite of a prohibition was never considered invalid for that reason alone. Although prohibitions were generally placed when there was a strong suspicion of an impediment, they were also placed for reasons other than possible invalidity. The most significant reason was the belief that the proposed marriage would be a source of scandal.

In addition to possible scandal or the probability of an impediment, prohibitions were urged whenever there was a doubt that one or both of the parties were freely entering the marriage.

Present Legislation

History indicates that the power to prohibit a marriage was related to the welfare of the marrying individuals, the good of the community, and the dignity of the sacrament. The present legislation is similar to that of the 1917 Code in that the local ordinary must have a serious cause to prohibit a marriage. This is not limited to a suspicion of an impediment or to the seven cases mentioned in canon 1071, §1 but may be any circumstance that the local ordinary deems serious. If there is a doubt about a party's capacity to fulfill the obligations of marriage, the strength of his or her commitment, or the motivating factors for the marriage, a prohibition may be imposed.

Marriage prohibitions may be imposed only in particular cases and not as a general rule, e.g., for all marriages of a certain type. A prohibition may be imposed for as long as the serious cause for deferring the marriage exists, and it may not be imposed for punitive reasons.

The decision to prohibit a marriage should be made only after a thorough examination of the case involving a weighing of the possible harm that the parties might experience if the union is postponed against the probable future harm if it is permitted. It is always advisable to take counsel with qualified

---

[53]See J. Waterhouse, *The Power of the Local Ordinary to Impose a Matrimonial Ban* (Washington, D.C.: Catholic University of America, 1952).

experts such as psychiatrists or psychologists if the case involves a question of emotional stability. The advice of the pastoral minister involved should also be given due consideration.

The local ordinary's power to prohibit a marriage extends to his own subjects anywhere, even if the proposed marriage will take place in another diocese. He may prohibit the marriage of persons actually in his diocese even though they are subjects of another bishop.

Present law restricts this power to the local ordinary although in the past it was often delegated to pastors. Consequently, while the pastor may refuse to witness a marriage he is certain will be invalid or even illicit, he may not prohibit a marriage according to this canon. The power to prohibit is shared by all local ordinaries, e.g., the bishop, vicars general and others equivalent to the bishop in law (c. 134). Ecclesiastical judges may also be given delegated power to issue prohibitions at the conclusion of marriage annulment processes. If a judge prohibits a marriage, the power to lift this prohibition is usually restricted to the local ordinary or his delegate.

A prohibition issued by the local ordinary or his delegate is never binding under possible invalidity. Only the Holy See can add an invalidating clause to a prohibition.

Dispensation from Impediments

Canon 1078 — §1. The local ordinary can dispense his own subjects wherever thay are staying as well as all persons actually present in his own territory from all the impediments of ecclesiastical law with the exception of those impediments whose dispensation is reserved to the Apostolic See.

§2. A dispensation from the following impediments is reserved to the Apostolic See:

1° the impediment arising from sacred orders or from a public perpetual vow of chastity in a religious institute of pontifical right;

2° the impediment of crime mentioned in can. 1090.

§3. A dispensation is never given from the impediment of consanguinity in the direct line or in the second degree of the collateral line.

A dispensation is a relaxation of the obligation of the law when there is a just and reasonable cause. The special legislation concerning dispensation from matrimonial impediments is understood in the context of the general norms for dispensation (cc. 85–93).

It has been stated that the purpose of the legislation on the impediments is to protect the parties, the community, and the dignity of the sacrament. Yet cases may arise when a relaxation of the law would be more beneficial to the parties while at the same time not harmful to the community or the sacrament.

In the 1917 Code the power to dispense from impediments was reserved to the Holy See, yet for certain impediments this power was regularly delegated to the bishops. Prior to the promulgation of the present Code, the Holy See extended the power to dispense from the general laws of the Church to the bishops except in specifically reserved cases.[54]

In the present law (c. 87) the diocesan bishop has the ordinary power to dispense from all non-reserved disciplinary laws of the Church. This canon applies the general principle to marriage impediments: the diocesan bishop can dispense all those staying in his territory and his own subjects anywhere from all non-reserved impediments of ecclesiastical law. Since this canon uses the term "local ordinary" and not "diocesan bishop" it includes the bishop and all those who are equivalent to him in law (c. 134, §§1–2). In practice, such dispensations are usually granted by vicars general or others with delegated power to do so.

Impediments of divine law origin can be dispensed neither by the local ordinary nor by the Supreme Pontiff because of their origin. Certain ecclesiastical law impediments are reserved to the Supreme Authority of the Church and cannot be dispensed by a lower authority. Those so reserved are the impediments arising from sacred orders or a public perpetual vow of chastity in institutes of pontifical right and the impediment of crime. This reservation also applies to permanent deacons who are unmarried at the time of ordination or to married permanent deacons who for some reason seek to marry a second time. The local ordinary may dispense from a vow of chastity if it was taken in an institute of diocesan right.

The canon specifically mentions that the impediment of consanguinity in the direct line and in the second degree collateral line is never dispensed.

Local ordinaries cannot dispense from reserved impediments except in urgent cases mentioned in the following canons. If there is grave harm in delay, the local ordinary may proceed according to canon 87, §2, that is, in cases in which the Holy See usually grants the dispensation. It is specifically stated, however, that this provision does not apply to dispensations from the obligation of clerical celibacy.

It appears clear that dispensations would be invalid and not merely illicit, when one is not legally authorized to grant them.

If there is a doubt about whether or not the circumstances of the case constitute the matter for an impediment (e.g., a doubt about whether a person is

[54]*Pastorale Munus,* November 30, 1963 in *CLD* 6, 370–378 and *De Episcoporum Muneribus,* June 15, 1966 in *CLD* 6, 394–400.

perpetually impotent), it may be dispensed in vir-
ture of canon 14, provided that it is not reserved.
The only exception to this rule involves the reserved degrees of consanguinity (c. 1091, §4). If
there is a doubt, the impediment is not dispensed.
This is known as a "doubt of fact," and it is verified
if it is unclear that the circumstances which give
rise to the impediment actually exist in a particular
case. Such a doubt could exist in cases of impotence, abduction, lack of age, public propriety, and
disparity of cult. It is less probable but still possible
that such a doubt could exist in cases of impediments which involve publicly recognized acts. This
would be very rare in cases of sacred orders, vows,
or prior bond, yet it is conceivable in cases of legal
adoption.

While the local ordinary can dispense from non-
reserved public and occult impediments, recourse
may also be had to the Sacred Penitentiary[55] for a
dispensation from occult impediments. In a given
case there may be both public and occult impediments. Dispensations must be granted for each impediment. This may be done by the local ordinary if
it is within his competence; otherwise recourse
must be had to the Sacred Penitentiary for any reserved occult impediments.

Under ordinary circumstances a dispensation
from reserved impediments is sought from the competent congregation of the Holy See, e.g., for the
priesthood, the Sacred Congregation for the Doctrine of the Faith; for diaconate, the Sacred Congregation for the Sacraments; and for public vows, the
Sacred Congregation for Religious and Secular Institutes.

A Just and Reasonable Cause

A just and reasonable cause is required for the
validity of any dispensation given by an ecclesiastical authority other than the legislator (c. 90, §1). If
there is doubt about the sufficiency of the cause, a
valid dispensation may be granted (c. 90, §2). Some
commentaries on the 1917 Code contained lists of
canonical reasons sufficient for granting dispensations from the impediments.[56] These lists were issued by the Holy See in the last century but may
not be considered taxative since the notion of sufficient cause may be more broadly interpreted under
the present law.

The nature of the just and reasonable cause
should be considered in the context of the impediment to be dispensed. Due consideration should be
given to the possible effect of the circumstances in
question on the proposed marriage.

Reserved Cases

Further clarification is needed concerning reserved impediments. First, a distinction must be
made between the impediments arising from sacred
orders and perpetual vows of chastity and the obligations attached to them. Once validly received, sacred orders never become invalid even though the
ordained person loses the clerical state and becomes
a lay man. Loss of the clerical state does not in itself constitute a dispensation from the obligations
of celibacy. This dispensation is separate and is reserved to the pope (cc. 290–292). The ordinary
practice of the Holy See is not to grant a dispensation from the impediment itelf but to consider a dispensation from the obligation of celibacy as part of
the process of laicization.[57]

If the vow of perpetual chastity is dispensed by
the Holy See, the impediment ceases to exist and
the person is free to marry.

The reservation of the impediment of crime includes both aspects, that is, murder of a spouse and
conspiracy to murder. Under the 1917 Code the
third degree of the impediment, murder, was reserved to the Holy See. There is no record of a dispensation ever having been granted if the
impediment were public.

Dispensation in Danger of Death

**Canon 1079 — §1. In danger of death, the local
ordinary can dispense his own subjects wherever
they are staying as well as all persons who are actually present in his territory both from the form prescribed for the celebration of matrimony and from
each and every impediment of ecclesiastical law,
whether it be public or occult, except the impediment arising from sacred order of the presbyterate.**

**§2. In the same situation mentioned in §1 and
only for cases in which the local ordinary cannot be
reached, the pastor, the properly delegated sacred
minister and the priest or deacon who assists at
matrimony in accord with the norm of can. 1116,
§2, also possess the faculty to dispense from the
same impediments.**

**§3. In danger of death a confessor enjoys the
faculty to dispense from occult impediments for the
internal forum, whether within or outside the act of
sacramental confession.**

**§4. In the case mentioned in §2, the local ordi-
nary is not considered to be accessible if he can be
contacted only by means of telegraph or telephone.**

The local ordinary can dispense his own subjects
anywhere or anyone in his territory if there is a
probability of death for either party in the relation-

---

[55]Bouscaren-Ellis, 168–169: "The Sacred Penitentiary . . . has
jurisdiction for the internal forum only. It grants dispensations, absolutions, faculties and decides questions of conscience."

[56]Cappello 5, n. 231, p. 227.

[57]Bouscaren-Ellis, 545–546.

ship or if one is actually dying. This power may also be used for the revalidation of a marriage.

According to Cappello, the probability of death in this context means a situation in which a person is in circumstances wherein he or she may probably die.[58] The probable cause of death can be intrinsic (illness) or extrinsic (outside cause). Hence the commentators refer to such examples as an imposed death sentence, impending surgery, and wartime military service. The most common application is in cases of serious illness or impending surgery.

In danger of death there must be a concomitant cause for seeking the dispensation. The 1917 Code mentioned the two most common causes as peace of conscience of the parties or legitimation of children (c. 1043). Although they are not mentioned in the present law, these causes are certainly sufficient. If it is a matter of peace of conscience, it does not matter whether it is the party facing probable death or the other party.

Author of the Dispensation

The power to dispense in danger of death is given by law to local ordinaries. Since it is ordinary power, it may be delegated to others.

If the local ordinary cannot be reached, a pastor or another priest or deacon delegated to perform the marriage may also dispense. If none of the above is available, a non-delegated priest or deacon may dispense (as in c. 1116, §2 on extraordinary form cases).

The last paragraph of the canon states that the local ordinary is considered unavailable if he can be reached only by telegraph or telephone. This means that he is considered available if he can be reached by mail or in person within a reasonable amount of time.

A confessor may dispense from occult impediments in the internal forum. A confessor is considered to be any priest with the faculty to hear confessions or the priest actually hearing the confession of the person in question. This provision is included for cases wherein one of the parties is conscious of an occult impediment but wishes it to remain confidential.

The confessor may use this power even outside of sacramental confession. Prior recourse to the local ordinary is not needed for occult impediments nor is there an obligation to inform him of a dispensation.

If there is a question of both public and occult impediments, the attending priest may act as confessor and dispense from the occult impediment, and he may also dispense from the public impediment if recourse to the local ordinary is impossible.

Scope of the Dispensing Power

In danger of death the law allows for dispensation from each impediment of ecclesiastical law with the exception of the impediment arising from the priesthood, which is reserved to the Holy See. The divine law impediments cannot be dispensed under this canon.

The obligation of canonical form may also be dispensed from. This includes not only the requirement of a duly authorized priest or deacon but that of witnesses as well. Although it is difficult to conceive of a situation in which no possible witnesses would be available, commentators have studied the question and concluded that if such were the case and a grave need existed, consent could be validly exchanged without witnesses.[59]

Since it is clear that divine law impediments may not be dispensed, it follows that a prior bond of marriage can neither be dispensed nor a kind of emergency annulment be given without due regard for the requirements of procedural law.

Dispensation When All Is Prepared for the Wedding

Canon 1080 — §1. Whenever an impediment is discovered after all the wedding preparations are made and the marriage cannot be deferred without probable danger of serious harm until a dispensation can be obtained from competent authority, the following persons enjoy the faculty to dispense from all the impediments with the exception of the ones mentioned in can. 1078, §2, n. 1: the local ordinary and, as long as the case is an occult one, all persons mentioned in can. 1079, §§2 and 3, observing the conditions prescribed in that canon.

§2. This power is also operative for the convalidation of a marriage if the same danger exists in delay and there is insufficient time to have recourse to the Apostolic See, or to the local ordinary concerning impediments from which he is able to dispense.

A situation of true urgency could arise other than in danger of death. A dispensation from certain ecclesiastical law impediments is possible if the impediment is discovered after all wedding preparations have been made and delaying the wedding would cause serious harm. Commentators on canon 1044 of the 1917 Code state that a dispensation can be granted even if the impediment is known to the parties and revealed to the priest only shortly before the wedding. This is true even if the impediment was concealed in bad faith.[60] Thus the

[58]See Cappello, n. 232–234, p. 229–234.

[59]J. Carberry, *The Juridical Form of Marriage* (Washington, D.C.: Catholic University of America, 1934), 155.
[60]Cappello, n. 234bis, 235.

dispensation is not to be denied as a punishment for such bad faith, but it should be granted if it will be to the spiritual benefit of the parties and the other conditions are met.

The law is clear that the impediment must be discovered by the priest or deacon after all is prepared for the wedding. When does the law consider that all is prepared? The commentators do not agree on the exact meaning, some holding to a strict interpretation meaning *all* preparations. Others hold that it is not required that all of the preparations be made, yet some should have been made at least by the parties themselves.[61] Practically speaking, several factors enter into the discussion: the nature of the preparations made, the time left before the wedding, and the kind of impediment. A reading of several canons from Book I assists in interpreting this canon. A strict interpretation is to be given to a dispensation and to the faculty to dispense in particular cases (cc. 36, §1; 92). Also, laws which contain an exception to the law are to be strictly interpreted (c. 18), and dispensations are exceptions to the law. In short, the faculty to dispense should be strictly interpreted, the good of the parties and the requisite cause for the dispensation being carefully considered.

What Can Be Dispensed

Ecclesiastical law impediments may be dispensed with the clear exception of those mentioned in canon 1078, §2, 1°. Consequently, the impediments arising from any sacred order or from perpetual vows in a pontifical institute may not be dispensed. The remaining ecclesiastical law impediments, including consanguinity in the fourth degree collateral line and crime may be dispensed under the proper conditions.

Who May Dispense

Urgent cases when "all the wedding preparations are made" differ from danger-of-death situations in that only the local ordinary may dispense from public impediments.

The pastor or duly delegated priest or deacon may not dispense if the impediment is publicly known. Their power is restricted to *occult cases* when recourse to the local ordinary is impossible. An occult case differs from an occult impediment. It refers to situations which involve circumstances which are perhaps public by nature (capable of external forum proof) yet are in fact secret, i.e., known only to the parties or to a very few people. For example, the non-baptism or blood relationship (first cousins) may be unknown to all and discovered only at the last moment. These may be considered public impediments, but they are occult cases.

[61]Bouscaren-Ellis, 506–509.

If the circumstances of the impediment are generally known or will shortly become such, then it is not considered an occult case and it cannot be validly dispensed except by the competent authority, i.e., the local ordinary.

The use of this canon by an undelegated priest or deacon has practical application only when the extraordinary form of marriage is used (c. 1116) since this canon does *not* give the power to dispense from canonical form. Thus the undelegated priest or deacon may validly dispense in occult cases if the extraordinary form is legitimately used. If, however, the marriage is to take place before witnesses only, there is no possibility of a dispensation.

The confessor can dispense from occult impediments and in occult cases. His power to dispense is limited to the internal forum as in the foregoing canon. One or both of the parties may be conscious of an occult impediment which cannot be disclosed without grave harm. Thus the confessor may dispense and retain the needed secrecy.

Cause for the Dispensation

The law states that a dispensation may be granted if there is danger of grave harm in delaying the wedding until a dispensation from the proper authority is received. For reserved cases publicly known and included in the canon, the proper authority is the Holy See. For other public impediments, it is the local ordinary and for occult impediment, the local ordinary or the Sacred Penitentiary.

When recourse to the proper authority is impossible, a dispensation is justified largely in terms of the harm which could result from a delay. Commentators on canon 1045 of the 1917 Code do not give a taxative list of such instances of harm given the variety of possible cases. However, one must note such matters as loss of reputation of the parties, serious family rifts, financial loss, possible loss of employment, or even deportation.

Needless to say, this canon is open to a variety of abuses if it is not interpreted prudently and with a view to the overall good of the parties and the welfare of the community. The grave pastoral obligation to see that the requirements for a valid marriage are met remains. Consequently, the pastoral minister must see to it that all of the requirements for pre-marriage preparation and examination are fulfilled. If these were properly carried out, there would normally be no need to invoke this canon.

If an impediment has been concealed, it is most important that the pastoral minister determine the reason. The law emphasizes readiness for marriage; therefore, the primary issue is not the celebration of the wedding as a social reality but the probability that it will be the beginning of a stable and fruitful marital relationship. The possible loss of money invested in the wedding celebration or the fear of temporary embarrassment is not sufficient reason to dispense from an impediment *if* it appears that the relationship will be seriously imperiled.

The dispensing powers of this canon apply also to revalidation of marriages. If an impediment is discovered shortly before the revalidation and the obtaining of a dispensation would result in a delay and consequent grave harm to the parties themselves or to the children, then the canon may be used. In any case, the normal procedures required for entrance into marriage are applicable for revalidations.

Some concluding qualifications are necessary relative to the dispensing power of this canon. It cannot be broadly interpreted so as to allow for the dissolution of a non-sacramental marriage in favor of the faith[62] or of a sacramental but non-consummated union.

Under special conditions a lay person may be delegated to act as the official witness at marriages (c. 1112). Nevertheless, he or she has no power to grant dispensations from impediments or form. The power of government required to grant a dispensation is enjoyed by those in sacred orders and may be exercised by lay persons when the law provides (c. 129). No such provision is included in canon 1112 nor is any mention made of lay witnesses in canons 1079 and 1080.[63]

Recording Dispensations for the External Forum

Canon 1081 — The pastor or the priest or deacon mentioned in can. 1079, §2, is immediately to inform the local ordinary of a dispensation granted for the external forum; it is also to be recorded in the marriage register.

The pastor or other sacred minister who grants a dispensation in virtue of canon 1079, §2 must see that it is recorded in the marriage register of the parish in which the marriage took place. This is a disciplinary law and the validity of the dispensation is not affected if this obligation is neglected.

This obligation applies *only* to dispensations granted in the external forum. Those granted in the internal forum are neither to be communicated to the local ordinary nor recorded in the marriage register.

Recording Internal Forum Dispensations

Canon 1082 — Unless a rescript from the Penitentiary states otherwise, a dispensation from an occult impediment granted in the internal non-sacramental forum is to be recorded in a book which is to be kept in the secret archive of the curia; if the occult impediment becomes public later on, no other dispensation is necessary for the external forum.

If an occult impediment is dispensed in the non-sacramental internal forum, it is to be recorded in a special book kept in the diocesan secret archives.

If the circumstances giving rise to the impediment become public after a dispensation has been granted in the non-sacramental forum, no further dispensation for the external forum is necessary. If, however, a dispensation has been granted in the sacramental forum there will be no record nor will the priest who granted it be able to discuss it since it will be covered by the seal of the confessional. Consequently, if such an occult impediment becomes public, there may be a need to grant a dispensation from it in the external forum.

CHAPTER III
DIRIMENT IMPEDIMENTS SPECIFICALLY
[cc. 1083–1094]

Lack of Age

Canon 1083 — §1. A man before he has completed his sixteenth year of age, and likewise a woman before she has completed her fourteenth year of age, cannot enter a valid marriage.

§2. It is within the power of the conference of bishops to establish an older age for the licit celebration of marriage.

This canon affects all Catholics. A male cannot enter a valid marriage before he has completed his sixteenth year nor can a female before she has completed her fourteenth year. Although there was a proposal to raise the minimum ages for validity, the committee decided against it, given the difficulty of deciding upon an advanced age which would be acceptable for the universal Church.[64] The law balances the basic right to marry, however, with the realization that more maturity is required than that which is presumed at puberty. In two earlier canons the marriages of the young are discouraged (cc. 1071, §1, 6°; 1072).

The non-baptized are not bound by this impediment since it is of ecclesiastical law origin. They are, however, bound by civil laws which include minimum age requirements. A marriage between a baptized person and a non-baptized person who is under the legal age for validity would probably be considered valid in canon law in virtue of past debate on the question.[65] A marriage between two

---

[62]SCDF, Dec. 18, 1968, private, in *CLD* 7, 765.

[63]SCSacr, instr *Sacramentalem indolem,* May 15, 1974, in *CLD* 8, 817–818.

[64]*Comm* 9 (1977), 360.

[65]Holy Office, March 1, 1961, *CLD* 5, 502–503.

non-baptized persons which is considered civilly invalid due to lack of age of at least one of them would also be considered invalid in canon law.

The conferences of bishops are permitted to enact legislation requiring an age higher than that mentioned in the canon, but this can be done only for liceity.[66] If such legislation is enacted, permission from the local ordinary would be required to marry below the age for liceity. Presently, certain dioceses have established guidelines which set a minimum age below which the parties must obtain the local ordinary's permission.

Dispensation from the Impediment

The local ordinary may dispense from the impediment of age. To do so, however, would certainly require a most serious reason given the high rate of divorce for marriages entered into by teenagers.

Most states in the United States have minimum age requirements for marriage. In some instances these are below the canonical ages for validity, yet in most the minimum legal age is the same or above the canonical age.[67]

Historical Background

Canonical legislation on minimum age for a valid marriage has been influenced to an extent by Roman law which determined that puberty was necessary for such a union and presumed that puberty had been reached at the ages of fourteen and twelve for males and females respectively.

The medieval canonists referred to a minimum age but did not specify a particular age and emphasized the fact of puberty instead. While church legislation referred to the presumed ages of puberty as fourteen and twelve, this presumption yielded to contrary proof. If the parties were capable of physical consummation before these ages, the marriage was considered valid. This remained the basis of the law on the minimum age until the 1917 Code.[68]

The 1917 Code raised the minimum age to sixteen for males and fourteen for females (CIC 1067). A dispensation was granted only by the Holy See. Furthermore, the ability to consummate the marriage prior to the minimum age was no longer sufficient to enable parties to contract marriage validly. Consequently, any marriage attempted by parties below the specified age was invalid.

---

[66]For information on the discussion concerning the role of the conferences of bishops in establishing impediments, see T. Green, "The Revised Schema de matrimonio," J 40 (1980), 62.

[67]CBS News Almanac (Maplewood, N.J.: Hammond Almanac, 1978), 230. The minimum age is below that of canon law in Kansas, Louisiana, Maine, Massachusetts, Mississippi, Missouri (males only), New Hampshire, Rhode Island, and Washington.

[68]See J. O'Dea, The Matrimonial Impediment of Non-Age (Washington, D.C.: Catholic University of America, 1944).

Physical Impotence

Canon 1084 — §1. Antecedent and perpetual impotence to have intercourse, whether on the part of the man or of the woman, which is either absolute or relative, of its very nature invalidates marriage.

§2. If the impediment of impotence is doubtful, either by reason of a doubt of law or a doubt of fact, a marriage is neither to be impeded nor is it to be declared null as long as the doubt exists.

§3. Sterility neither prohibits nor invalidates marriage, with due regard for the prescription of can. 1098.

The impediment of impotence arises from the inability of a man or a woman to have sexual intercourse. Although the impediment itself is of divine law origin, the question of what precisely constitutes impotence has been a matter of dispute. The pertinent questions raised in this dispute include the following: Is procreative sexual intercourse necessary or only the ability to complete the sexual act? What are the elements that constitute complete sexual intercourse? What are the elements of functional and organic impotence? The committee spent a good deal of time discussing these and other relevant questions before formulating the canons.[69]

Impotence means the incapacity for normal sexual intercourse. This involves the ability on the part of the man to sustain an erection, penetrate the woman's vagina, and ejaculate. It is not necessary that the ejaculation consist of semen elaborated in the testicles.[70]

On the part of the woman it is necessary that she have a vagina capable of receiving the male organ. It is not necessary that she have a uterus, ovaries, and fallopian tubes. In fact, a woman fitted with an artificial vagina prior to marriage is not considered impotent, provided it is constructed of natural, human material.[71]

The inability to complete the act of intercourse may be due to organic problems, such as the lack of or an injury to a genital organ considered indispensable for normal intercourse. It may also be the result of serious malformation of either the male or female organs, making the completion of intercourse impossible.

Impotence may be due to a functional disorder, that is, an incapacity to complete the physical act caused by a psychological or nervous condition even though the genital organs are intact. This is sometimes known as psychic impotence. There is a conflict between the sexual instinct and its expression because of fear, anxiety, or anger which usually manifests itself by an inability to have an erection

---

[69]Comm 6 (1974) 177–198, and, CLA 34 (1975), 3–8.
[70]SCDF, May 13, 1977, in CLD 8, 676–677.
[71]Comm 6 (1974), 196–197.

or an ejaculation on the part of the man, and frigidity or vaginismus on the part of the woman.[72]

The Impediment

The inability to complete the act of intercourse must be *antecedent* and *perpetual,* that is, it must have existed prior to the marriage and it must be incurable by natural human means. If a person becomes impotent after a marriage has been contracted, this is known as subsequent impotence and has no effect on marital validity.

The condition may be *relative,* making the person incapable of intercourse with some but not all persons or *absolute,* rendering the person incapable of intercourse with all persons.

Doubt of Fact or Law

If a doubt exists about the existence of impotence or its perpetual and irremediable nature, the parties are not to be prevented from marrying. If there is a possibility of creating a community of life and completing sexual intercourse, the marriage is to be permitted even though it is unlikely that its procreative dimension will be fulfilled. If afterward the marriage breaks down, it may not be declared null on the grounds of doubtful impotence at the time of the wedding. In cases of such a doubt, the parties' basic right to marry prevails.

Sterility

Sterility is the inability to beget children even though one is capable of complete sexual intercourse. At the time of the wedding the parties exchange the right to the community of life which includes the right to natural heterosexual intercourse. The parties do not exchange the right to have children since the exchange of consent includes the right to *acts* per se apt for generation of children and not to children themselves. The parties must be capable of sexual intercourse since this is fundamental to the unitive and generative dimensions of marriage. Procreation is an action of nature and an effect of sexual intercourse, yet it does not result from every act of intercourse. Since marriage is "by nature ordered to the good of children" (*GS* 49), the spouses must be open to procreation and capable of sexual acts which are needed for procreation. Yet they do not have complete control of fecundation.

Sterility is not an impediment to marriage: hence the sterile may marry both validly and licitly. It is not an impediment because fecundity is not absolutely necessary for the community of the whole of life. Sterility does not deprive marital consent of its proper object (the community of life) nor does it impede sexual intercourse.

On the other hand, sterility is a quality that could have a seriously detrimental effect on the marriage if fraudulently concealed. The ability to procreate is a quality justifiably expected in spouses. Its absence could radically change the expectations and nature of the marital commitment. Consequently, although sterility itself does not impede one from marrying, fraudulently to conceal it under certain circumstances would be grounds for challenging the validity of the marriage.[73]

Prior Marriage Bond

Canon 1085 — §1. A person who is held to the bond of a prior marriage, even if it has not been consummated, invalidly attempts marriage.

§2. Even if the prior marriage is invalid or dissolved for any reason whatsoever, it is not on that account permitted to contract another before the nullity or the dissolution of the prior marriage has been legitimately and certainly established.

The *marriage bond* is the ontological reality which exists between two persons who have exchanged marital consent. It begets a juridical obligation of mutual fidelity for as long as the bond exists. The bond is not simply an attribute of the relationship which gives rise to a moral obligation of fidelity as long as the spouses are together as husband and wife. It is a reality that comes into existence with consent and no longer depends for its continued existence on the will of the spouses alone (*GS* 49). Between two non-baptized persons or a baptized and non-baptized person there exists a *natural bond.* If both parties are baptized (Catholic or not) it is a *sacramental bond.* In either case the bond is by nature exclusive, thus ruling out more than one spouse at a time.

The marriage bond is also perpetual by nature. It continues to exist until it is legitimately terminated. Since it does not depend on the will of the spouses, it continues to exist even if one or both withdraw consent, thus ending the existential marital relationship.

A natural or sacramental bond gives rise to an impediment of divine law which renders persons already married incapable of entering a subsequent marriage while the prior bond is still intact. Insofar as it is of divine law origin, the impediment cannot be dispensed by any earthly power.

Marriage and especially sacramental marriage is monogamous by nature. The community of the whole of life is intimately related to the essential properties of unity and indissolubility. The spouses make their complete and unqualified gift of self to

---

[72]A. Freedman, *Modern Synopsis of Psychiatry* (Baltimore: Williams and Wilkins, 1976), 765; E. Hudson, ed., *Handbook II for Marriage Nullity Cases,* (Ottawa: St. Paul's University, 1980), 245; and L. Wrenn, *Annulments,* 3rd ed., (Toledo: CLSA, 1978), 7–21.

[73]See commentary on c. 1098.

one another for a relationship that will last until death. It is because of this complete fidelity to one another in an indissoluble union that the marriage reflects the Christ-Church relationship. The impediment serves as a sanction for monogamy and the fulfillment of the purposes of marriage as well. The proper education of children depends on the loving community of life which exists between the parents. The total gift of self required of the spouses and the sharing of their complete love with their children are not possible if monogamy is not preserved.

The early Church spoke of the bond of marriage in terms of a moral imperative or solemn commitment. From the twelfth century on, the prohibition against second marriages was known as the impediment of *ligamen*. By this time the concepts of validity and invalidity had become juridical categories. Persons already married were not only prohibited from attempting a second marriage while both spouses were still alive, they were incapable of a second marriage in virtue of the impediment.[74]

Cessation of the Impediment

The impediment ceases only when the bond itself ceases to exist. A valid sacramental bond which is consummated ceases only with the death of one of the parties. A sacramental yet non-consummated bond may be dissolved by the Supreme Pontiff (c. 1142). A natural but non-sacramental bond ceases with the death of one of the parties. It also ceases through dissolution by means of the Pauline privilege (c. 1143).

By death, canon law refers to natural death and not legal death as described in some civil law codes.[75] In the absence of direct proof of death, canon law provides procedures for arriving at a morally certain presumption that natural death has occurred (c. 1707). If a spouse presumed dead according to canon law is actually alive and reappears, the second marriage is in fact invalid.

Marriages Declared Null

If a marriage is declared invalid for any reason, a subsequent valid marriage is possible since the invalidity of the prior union means that no marriage bond ever existed and hence there is no diriment impediment. The invalidity of a marriage is always established by means of canonical procedures since

marital validity is presumed unless the contrary is proven according to law. The invalidity of a marriage may not be arbitrarily declared by the parties themselves.

The second paragraph of the canon states that a second marriage may not be licitly entered into until the prior union has been declared invalid by a competent tribunal or dissolved by the proper authority.

The dissolution of a valid but non-sacramental bond depends on an act of the Holy See in the case of sacramental but non-consummated marriages. The dissolution of a marriage in favor of the faith (the privilege of the faith dissolution) also requires an act of the Holy See. In the case of a Pauline privilege, a marriage between two non-baptized persons is dissolved by a subsequent marriage but normally only after the baptism of one party and the conducting of interpellations to verify the departure of the other party.[76] In these three instances a valid bond is dissolved by means of a power which the parties themselves lack.

A case involving invalidity presents another set of circumstances. The marriage may be invalid, a fact of which one or both of the parties may be convinced, yet the canonical presumption of validity has not been objectively overturned and the declaration of nullity issued. The intervention of the competent authority is necessary for the good order of the community and, above all, for the stability of marriage. There always remains a chance that the prior marriage is valid in spite of the opinions of the parties about it.

Disparity of Cult

Canon 1086 — §1. Marriage between two persons, one of whom is baptized in the Catholic Church or has been received into it and has not left it by means of a formal act, and the other of whom is non-baptized, is invalid.

§2. This impediment is not to be dispensed unless the conditions mentioned in cann. 1125 and 1126 are fulfilled.

§3. If at the time the marriage was contracted one party was commonly considered to be baptized or the person's baptism was doubted, the validity of the marriage is to be presumed in accord with the norm of can. 1060 until it is proven with certainty that one party was baptized and the other was not.

A sacramental marriage means that both parties are baptized. Consequently, a marriage between a Catholic and a non-baptized person is not a sacrament. Such a relationship is classified as an impediment because of the difficulties the Catholic spouse may encounter both in practicing the faith and in baptizing and raising as Catholics children who

---

[74]G. Joyce, *Christian Marriage* (London: Sheed and Ward, 1933), 377–426.

[75]H. Black, *Black's Law Dictionary,* revised 4th ed. (St. Paul: West, 1968), 488: "*Civil death.* The state of a person who, though possessing natural life has lost all his civil rights, and as to them, is considered as dead. . . . *Presumptive death.* That which is presumed from proof of a long, continued absence unheard from and unexplained. The general rule as now understood, is that the presumption . . . ceases at the expiration of seven years from the time the person was last known as living; and after the lapse of that period there is a presumption of death."

[76]See commentary on c. 1144.

may be born of the union. In this regard, the Council says:

> The Christian family springs from marriage, which is an image and a sharing in the partnership of love between Christ and the Church; it will show forth to all men Christ's living presence in the world and the authentic nature of the Church by the love and generous fruitfulness of the spouses, by their unity and fidelity and by the loving way in which all members of the family cooperate with each other (GS 48).

Those Bound by the Impediment

Those baptized in the Catholic Church or received into it are bound by this impediment. Baptized non-Catholics, however, are not bound by the impediment, therefore, their marriages with the non-baptized are not presumed invalid.

Children born of Catholic parents and baptized Catholics in infancy as well as those born of mixed marriages and baptized in infancy are bound by the impediment. If a child of a mixed or disparate marriage is baptized but not raised Catholic in violation of the promise made by the Catholic party, he or she is still bound by the impediment.

Although the canon states clearly that those baptized in the Catholic Church are bound by the impediment, what of children of non-Catholic parents baptized by Catholic ministers contrary to the provisions of canon 868, §1, 2°? There is neither an intention on the part of the parents to raise the children Catholics nor a founded hope that this will in fact happen. Are such children bound by the impediment? Commentators who studied the question under the 1917 Code held that they were not bound.[77]

If, on the other hand, a child of non-Catholic parents who is in danger of death is baptized by a Catholic minister or one who intends to confer Catholic baptism, he or she is considered bound by the impediment.[78]

Those who have left the Church by a formal act are not bound by the impediment. Although the Code does not define a formal act of defection, it can be presumed that some act of embracing a non-Catholic religion is sufficient. Participation in a reception ceremony, re-baptism, confirmation, or a similar form of adherence to the non-Catholic religion would constitute a formal act. Regular attendance and participation in liturgical services as well as involvement in other church activities could also be considered presumptive of a formal act of defection. Signing an abjuration of the faith, however, is

certainly such a formal act even without transfer to another sect.

Definitive departure from the Church need not include embracing another religious sect. An avowed Communist or member of another explicitly anti-Catholic organization is presumed to have left the Church by a formal act.

Departure from the faith by a formal act is not the same as not practicing the faith. Those who rarely or never receive the sacraments, yet still consider themselves at least nominally Catholic, would be bound by the impediment.

The impediment arises when a Catholic marries a person who is certainly not baptized. Included among the non-baptized are members of certain Christian denominations who do not practice baptism or whose form of baptism is considered invalid by the Church.[79]

Valid baptism consists in the pouring of natural water over the subject while pronouncing the Trinitarian formula. In emergency situations it is necessary that water be poured and that the person administering the sacrament intend to do what the Church intends.

Doubt about Baptism

If a marriage between a Catholic and a doubtfully baptized person has taken place, the marriage is presumed to be valid. The doubt about baptismal validity is resolved in favor of the validity of the marriage. The same is true for marriages of two Catholics, one or both of whom are doubtfully baptized. If a person is commonly believed to be baptized but no documentary proof can be found, the presumption is in favor of baptism and, therefore, the validity of the marriage. This presumption yields to contrary proof; therefore, definite evidence of the non-baptism of at least one party would overturn the presumption in favor of the validity of the marriage.

If the doubt about the baptism arises before marriage, the usual practice is to resolve it or seek a dispensation from the impediment.

Dispensation from the Impediment

Dispensation from the impediment of disparity of cult is subject to the same canonical conditions as permission for a mixed marriage (cc. 1125–1126). The canon states that the dispensation is not to be granted unless these conditions are fulfilled. This

---

[77] F. Schenk, *The Matrimonial Impediments of Mixed Religion and Disparity of Cult* (Washington, D.C.: Catholic University of America, 1929), 106–107.

[78] Ibid., 112.

[79] Private and unpublished research by J. Dolciamore and J. Rolek of the Chicago Metropolitan Tribunal indicate that baptism in the following denominations is not considered valid Catholic baptism: Apostolic Church, Bohemian Free Thinkers, Christian Science, Church of Divine Science, People's Church of Chicago, Quakers, Universalists, Salvation Army, Pentecostal Church, Christadelphians, Jehovah's Witnesses.

phrasing differs from that of the 1980 schema which put the obligation in a positive light, stating that the prescriptions of the canons on mixed marriages are to be applied here.[80] In light of this change it appears obvious that a dispensation granted without the fulfillment of the conditions would be invalid (c. 39).[81] If the dispensation from a diriment impediment is invalid, a subsequent marriage would likewise be invalid.

Sacred Orders

Canon 1087 — Persons who are in holy orders invalidly attempt marriage.

The impediment arising from sacred orders is of ecclesiastical law origin insofar as clerical celibacy is an essential requirement for the liceity of orders according to Latin disciplinary law. In the 1917 Code the impediment arose with the subdiaconate, at which time clerics in the Latin Church implicitly assumed the obligation of celibacy. Although the order of subdeacon has been abolished in the Latin Church,[82] those who have received it remain bound by the obligation unless they are dispensed even though they have received no other orders. Under the present law bishops, priests, and deacons incur the impediment (cf. c. 1394, §1 for the penal implications of a violation of the law).

The impediment to marriage and the obligation of celibacy (c. 277) do not exist unless three conditions are fulfilled: (a) the order must be validly received; (b) it must be received with full knowledge of the obligations attached; and (c) the order must be freely received without grave force or fear being inflicted on the candidate.[83] Since the obligation of celibacy is attached to sacred orders, if the orders are invalid there is no impediment.

The process of declaring the invalidity of sacred orders differs from the process of laicization with a dispensation from the obligation of celibacy (cc. 290–292). If this obligation is dispensed, the basis for the impediment disappears, rendering it inoperative. The process whereby a deacon is laicized and dispensed is conducted by the Sacred Congregation for the Sacraments, while the same process for priests is conducted by the Sacred Congregation for the Doctrine of the Faith. The rescript of laicization and the dispensation are distinct and need not be granted together. Both are granted by the Supreme Pontiff alone. Dispensations from celibacy for deacons and priests were granted more readily during the pontificate of Paul VI than at present.

There is no record of the Holy See ever dispensing a bishop.[84]

Dispensation from the Impediment

Although a dispensation from the obligation of celibacy occurs from time to time, dispensation from the *impediment* itself is rare. Ordinarily such dispensations are reserved to the Holy See (c. 1078, §2, 1°). In danger of death, the local ordinary may dispense only deacons from the impediment (c. 1079, §1).

Permanent Deacons

Men ordained to the permanent diaconate incur the impediment arising from orders as do transitional deacons. Married men who are ordained permanent deacons may not validly marry if they are widowed or receive an ecclesiastical annulment. Single men who aspire to the permanent diaconate are obliged to perpetual celibacy (c. 1037).

Public Perpetual Vow of Chastity

Canon 1088 — Persons who are bound by a public perpetual vow of chastity in a religious institute invalidly attempt marriage.

Men and women who take a public vow of perpetual chastity in a religious institute are bound by the impediment which arises from the vow and thus may not validly marry (cf. c. 1394, §2 for the penal implications of a violation of the law). A *public* vow is one taken in a religious institute which is recognized and approved as such by the Holy See (pontifical right) or by a diocesan bishop (diocesan right) (cf. c. 1192, §1). The impediment is attached to a public vow of perpetual chastity and to no other form of commitment to the evangelical counsel, although other forms of commitment are allowed for other types of institutes of consecrated life (c. 573, §2). On the contrary, simple vows, whether temporary or perpetual, and private vows of chastity or virginity, not to marry, to receive sacred orders, and to embrace the religious life gave rise to an impedient impediment under the 1917 Code (*CIC* 1058). Solemn vows of chastity gave rise to a diriment impediment in the 1917 Code (*CIC* 1073). The simple, perpetual vow of chastity gave rise to a diriment impediment only in those institutes to which this effect has been attached by the Holy See.

Under the present Code it is still possible to take private vows, yet these have no canonical effects (cf. c. 1192, §1). Those who take public temporary

---

[80]1980 schema, c. 1083.
[81]Bouscaren-Ellis, 525–543.
[82]Paul VI, *MP Ad pascendum,* August 5, 1972, *CLD* 8, 695–698.
[83]Cappello, n. 437, 420.

[84]J. Lynch, "Critique of the Law of Celibacy in the Catholic Church from the Period of the Reform Councils," in F. Böckle and P. Huizing, *Celibacy in the Church, Con* 78 (New York: Herder and Herder, 1972), 66.

vows of chastity will not be bound by an impediment. However, those who take a public perpetual vow of chastity, whether it is a simple vow or a solemn vow (cf. c. 1192, §2), will be bound by the diriment impediment.

A perpetual vow is distinguished from a temporary vow in that the former is taken until death while the latter is taken for a determined period of time, defined in law as no less than three and no more than six years (c. 655). The 1917 Code distinguished between simple perpetual and solemn vows. This distinction no longer exists as to legal effects of the vow of chastity.

Dispensation from the Impediment

As in the case of the impediment arising from sacred orders, a dispensation from the vow itself differs from dispensation from the impediment. If the vow itself is dispensed, the impediment ceases. If the vow is taken in an institute of pontifical right, a dispensation from the impediment is reserved to the Holy See (c. 1078, §1, 2°) except in cases of danger of death. If the vow is taken in an institute of diocesan right, the local ordinary may dispense under ordinary circumstances and in cases of danger of death.

Under the provisions of canon 1080 (when all is prepared for the wedding) the pastor, delegated sacred minister, or non-delegated sacred minister may dispense if it is an occult case.

Abduction

Canon 1089 — No marriage can exist between a man and a woman abducted or at least detained for the purpose of contracting marriage with her, unless the woman of her own accord chooses marriage after she has been separated from her abductor and established in a place where she is safe and free.

A man who has abducted, kidnapped, or even detained a woman for the purpose of marrying her may not do so validly since a diriment impediment arises from the very fact of the abduction. The basis of the impediment is the presumption that, although the woman may agree to marriage, she is not doing so freely.

The essential elements of the impediment are the abduction or retention of a *woman* for the purpose of contracting marriage with her. Abduction differs from elopement since it involves actions perpetrated against the will of the woman. The fact of her free choice to marry is negated precisely because she was abducted for this very purpose.

The impediment arising from abduction applies only to a woman since this is most often the case. If, on the contrary, a man were abducted, the valid-

ity of the marriage might be challenged on the canonical grounds of force and fear (c. 1103).

Abduction or retention may result from physical or moral violence such as actual physical harm or force, threats, intimidation, blackmail, or some other form of force which the woman cannot reasonably resist. The abduction may be conducted by a man through others whom he employs to abduct physically or otherwise unduly influence the woman. The result is the same for he is holding her against her will in order to force her into marriage.

A woman might willingly go with a man but then be held against her will after learning of his intentions. This amounts to forceful detention and is equivalent to abduction. Even if the woman is the man's fiancée, the impediment exists as long as she is held against her will.

Although the abduction or retention must be for the purpose of marriage, it is not necessary to prove that this was the man's intention from the outset. A woman might go freely with a man, have sexual intercourse, and then be held with a view to marriage under threat of disclosure.

Cessation of the Impediment

The impediment ceases only when the woman is separated from the man and is situated in a place or situation wherein she can make a decision free from all hint of coercion. The impediment remains even if the woman declares that she is making a free decision to marry while still with the man. The difference between force and fear, properly speaking, and the impediment of abduction lies in the fact that with the former, consent to marry is a direct result of the force and/or fear. With abduction, the force compelling the woman to remain with the man may have been removed, yet the fact that she is still with him causes the strong presumption that her consent would not be free. The impediment based on this presumption safeguards the institution of marriage and protects the personal freedom of the woman.

Since this impediment is of ecclesiastical law origin and is not reserved, it may be dispensed by the local ordinary. Nevertheless, it would be unrealistic to expect such a dispensation even in cases of danger of death. A dispensation could only be given while the woman is still with the man, otherwise the impediment ceases. Even if granted, there would be a strong presumption of consent under duress.

Crime

Canon 1090 — §1. A person who for the purpose of entering marriage with a certain person has brought about the death of that person's spouse or one's own spouse, invalidly attempts such a marriage.

§2. They also invalidly attempt marriage between themselves who have brought about the death of the spouse of one of them through mutual physical or moral cooperation.

The impediment of crime arises between a man and a woman if either one murders his or her own or the other's spouse for the purpose of marriage to one another. It also arises if they cooperate with one another in bringing about a spouse's murder even prescinding from an actual marriage. In either case there is an obvious incompatibility between the taking of a life and entrance into marriage as a result of that prior crime.

In the 1917 Code the impediment included adultery as a degree of crime. Hence, a marriage was invalid if it took place between two persons who had committed adultery with one another with a promise or hope of marriage to each other (*CIC* 1075, 1°). This degree of the impediment has been dropped in the present Code.

Coniugicide

The first degree of this impediment involves the actual murder of one's own spouse or the spouse of another. A mutual promise of marriage is not required and the intent to marry may be on one side only. Thus, if a man murders his wife and intends to marry another woman, the impediment is present even though the other woman is ignorant both of his intention to marry and of the murder. A valid marriage is required, however; otherwise, the murder would be homicide and not coniugicide.

If the murder is not carried out directly by one of the involved parties but by another (a hired killer) acting on behalf of the party, the impediment exists.

The second degree involves conspiracy on the part of both of the parties. If the man and woman cooperate in bringing about the death of one of their spouses, they are impeded from marriage. As in the first degree, they may cooperate either physically or morally in the murder.

Proof

Proof of the impediment requires two things: the direct or indirect murder of a spouse and an intention to marry on the part of at least one party. The key factor is the murder since any subsequent marriage, whether intended at the time of the murder or not, fulfills the requirements of the canon.

Since the impediment depends on coniugicide for its existence, an actual murder must have taken place. This is to be distinguished from a civil conviction for murder although such a conviction would cause a presumption of a public impediment. If in fact the parties directly murdered or conspired to murder a spouse, the impediment exists even though it is occult.

Cessation and Dispensation

The impediment of crime never ceases of itself. Under ordinary circumstances its dispensation is reserved to the Holy See (c. 1078, §2, 2°). Under the 1917 Code the first degree of crime (adultery with a promise of marriage) was regularly dispensed by the Holy See when it dissolved a non-consummated marriage. A dispensation was easier to obtain for the first degree of the impediment than for the second and third degrees (murder either direct or by conspiracy). However, even here dispensations were sometimes granted if the murder was not publicly known, but there is no record of a dispensation having been granted if the murder was publicly known.[85]

In danger of death the impediment may be dispensed by the local ordinary or those mentioned in canon 1079, §§2–3. It may also be dispensed in cases in which all is prepared for the wedding (c. 1080). If it is publicly known, only the local ordinary may dispense. If it is an occult case, it may be dispensed by the other sacred ministers mentioned in canon 1079.

In light of the crime upon which the impediment is based and the possible scandal, it would be incongruous to dispense a publicly known impediment in any circumstances save danger of death. Although a dispensation is possible in occult cases outside of danger of death, it would be imprudent for one to be granted.

Consanguinity

Canon 1091 — **§1. In the direct line of consanguinity, marriage is invalid between all ancestors and descendants, whether they be related legitimately or naturally.**

§2. In the collateral line of consanguinity, marriage is invalid up to and including the fourth degree.

§3. The impediment of consanguinity is not multiplied.

§4. If there exists any doubt whether the parties are related through consanguinity in any degree of the direct line or in the second degree of the collateral line, marriage is never permitted.

Consanguinity means the blood relationship between two persons. This relationship is based on the descent from one person to another (direct line) or on the descent of various persons related to a common ancestor (collateral line). This relationship is based on a true blood relationship and, therefore, does not depend on the marital status of the com-

---

[85]Bouscaren-Ellis, 551.

mon ancestor. Consequently, it exists between a person and all of his or her direct descendants even though he or she may not have been married to the natural parent.

Prohibitions against marriages between blood relatives have existed since primitive times although the extent of the prohibition has varied. Legal and cultural prohibitions are essentially based on the incest taboo. Societies have generally condemned sexual relations between blood relatives as a kind of perversion. Marital relationships between related persons become socially more acceptable as they become more distant.

Sexual and marital relationships between close relatives have generally been thought to have negative genetic consequences. In addition, they are highly disruptive of the family unit.

Extent of the Impediment

Marriage is prohibited by divine law to all persons related in the direct line (parent-child, grandparent-grandchild, etc.) and to persons related in the second degree of the collateral line (brother-sister). The impediment also prohibits marriages between persons related in the third and fourth degrees of the collateral line (uncle-niece, first cousins). In this regard it is of ecclesiastical law origin and therefore not binding on non-Catholics.

The degrees of consanguinity are computed according to the Roman system which has been used in most civil law systems. In the direct line each person or generation is a degree, not counting the ancestor (cf. c. 108). Thus children would be first degree, grandchildren, second. In the collateral (also called indirect) line there are as many degrees as there are persons on each side of the line, omitting the common ancestor. Brother and sister are related in the second degree, aunt and nephew in the third, first cousins in the fourth, and second cousins in the sixth degree. The 1917 Code extended the impediment to second cousins (sixth degree), but the present Code extends it only to first cousins.

Consanguinity depends on descent from a common ancestor. Although the common ancestor is usually two people (a mother and father), it may be one if a parent has children by different spouses. Nevertheless, a half-blood relationship alters neither the computation of degrees nor the existence of the impediment. Thus a man could not marry his half-sister.

Under the 1917 Code the impediment of consanguinity was multiplied when the relationship was multiplied. This happened in three ways: (a) if two persons who were related married, (b) if two brothers married two sisters, and (c) if a man married two sisters or woman married two brothers successively and had children with each. Under the present law, the impediment is *not* multiplied. Consequently the complicated task of determining

degrees of consanguinity with multiple relationships is no longer a problem.

It is also important to note that the method of computation of degrees of the collateral line was different in the 1917 Code. Each branch counted for a degree. Thus brother and sister were first degree, first cousins were second degree, second cousins were third degree. An uncle-niece relationship was referred to as second degree touching on the first. As noted earlier this is changed in the present Code.

Doubt of Fact

The ordinary rule of seeking a dispensation if there is a doubt about the facts of the case does not hold in the case of the impediment of consanguinity if the doubt concerns the possibility of a relationship in the direct line to any degree and in the collateral line to the second degree. Because of the potential negative consequences of such unions, the Church does not dispense even in case of doubt.

Dispensation

Since a blood relationship is permanent, the impediment does not cease but may be dispensed in certain degrees of the collateral line. It is dispensed neither in any degree of the direct line nor in the second degree of the collateral line. Since these degrees are of divine law origin they bind the nonbaptized as well as baptized non-Catholics.

The local ordinary may dispense from the third degree of the collateral line (uncle-niece, aunt-nephew). Under the 1917 Code the practice of the Holy See was to grant such dispensations very rarely and then for extraordinarily grave reasons.[86] The impediment in the fourth degree of the collateral line should be dispensed rarely and only for grave reasons. In degrees other than those of divine origin, the impediment may also be dispensed from in those urgent cases mentioned in canons 1079–1080.

Although the ecclesiastical impediment of consanguinity may be dispensed, civil law may prohibit such unions. Certain states in the United States prohibit marriages within specified degrees of consanguinity. All states prohibit marriages of persons related in the direct line and in the second and third degrees of the collateral line. A number permit marriages between first cousins and numerous states permit marriages between second cousins.[87] Accordingly it is important to check pertinent civil law statutes if questions arise in this connection.

---

[86] SCSacr, instr, August 1, 1931, in *CLD* 1, 514.
[87] The various state law digests indicate that marriages of first cousins are permitted in the following states: Alabama, California, Connecticut, District of Columbia, Florida, Georgia, Kentucky, Maine, Maryland, Massachusetts, New Jersey, New York, Rhode Island, South Carolina, Texas, Vermont, Virginia.

Affinity

Canon 1092 — Affinity in the direct line in any degree whatsoever invalidates matrimony.

The relationship which exists between one spouse and the blood relatives of the other spouse (in-laws) is known as affinity. Just as with consanguinity, marriage is prohibited within certain degrees in both civil and canon law.

In the 1917 Code the impediment included the second (fourth) degree of the collateral line and it was multiplied. In the present law it includes all degrees in the direct line, but it omits degrees in the collateral line and it is not multiplied.

The impediment prohibits marriages between one spouse and all of the other spouse's relatives in the direct line. This includes the descendants of a spouse by another marriage such as stepchildren, stepgrandchildren, etc.

Affinity is defined in canon 109 as the relationship arising from a valid marriage even if it is non-consummated. Since the impediment is of ecclesiastical law origin, it does not affect marriages of the non-baptized or of baptized non-Catholics. If one or both of the parties are baptized Catholics after the marriage, a relationship of affinity becomes an impediment.

Affinity arises only between the spouse and the blood relatives of the marriage partner and not between the blood relatives of one spouse and those of the other, e.g., a man's brothers and sisters are not related by affinity to his wife's brothers and sisters. Also, the relationship affects blood relatives and not relatives by adoption. Since the relationship does not cease, one is still bound by affinity to the relatives of one's spouse even after he or she dies.

The impediment of affinity has had a long and complex history in canon law. In the medieval Church the impediment was based on licit or illicit intercourse and not marital consent. Hence it arose from intercourse and not marriage. Prior to Lateran Council II the invalidating degrees were similar to those of consanguinity and went as high as the fourteenth degree collateral line. In the eleventh century the scope of the impediment became even more complicated with the introduction of the second and third classes of affinity. Second class involved the relationship of a spouse with the relatives of a person who married a blood relative of his or her marriage partner. The third class involved the relationship between a person who married a widow or widower and the relatives of the deceased spouse. The computations of prohibited relationships became quite complex for the married and nearly impossible if affinity arose from illicit intercourse.

Certain ecumenical councils (Lateran II, Trent) attempted to simplify the basis for the impediment. Finally the 1917 Code changed the basis to a valid, ratified marriage and stated that the prohibited degrees were all those in the direct line and second degree (or fourth in the revised Code) of the collateral line (*CIC* 1077).[88]

Dispensation

A dispensation is needed to marry anyone related in the direct line of affinity but not in the collateral line. Under the 1917 Code dispensations from the first degree of the direct line (stepchild with mother- or father-in-law) were reserved to the Holy See and granted only very rarely. Under the present law a dispensation from the impediment may normally be granted by the local ordinary or by others in urgent situations specified in canons 1079–1080.

Public Propriety

Canon 1093 — The impediment of public propriety arises from an invalid marriage after common life has been established or from notorious and public concubinage; it invalidates marriage in the first degree of the direct line between the man and the blood relatives of the woman, and vice-versa.

The impediment of public propriety (sometimes known as public honesty or public decency) is based on a more or less stable but non-marital relationship between a man and a woman. The impediment makes it impossible for the man or the woman to marry validly the blood relatives of the other in the first degree of the direct line. Thus a man could not validly marry the daughter of his mistress nor could the woman validly marry the son or father of her lover.

The impediment is based either on an invalid marriage or on public or notorious concubinage. By an invalid marriage the law includes those marriages which are in fact invalid, yet have the appearance of marriage, i.e., marriages declared invalid for one reason or another. The impediment does not arise from non-sacramental or non-consummated marriages which are dissolved since these are considered valid. Marriages invalid due to a defect of form are not considered putative marriages and, therefore, do not in themselves give rise to the impediment. Nevertheless, if cohabitation occurs, this could be considered a basis for the impediment.[89]

Concubinage is the cohabitation of a man and a woman on a more or less stable basis, perhaps a not uncommon phenomenon in contemporary society. It is considered to be public or notorious if it is well known to the community and cannot be hidden.

---

[88]For historical background, see G. Joyce, 538 and F. Wahl, *The Matrimonial Impediments of Consanguinity and Affinity* (Washington, D.C.: Catholic University of America, 1934), 77–79.

[89]Code Commission, March 12, 1929, in *CLD* 1, 516–517.

The impediment does not arise from illicit intercourse without concubinage.

Cessation and Dispensation

The commentators debate whether the impediment ceases if the parties to the relationship marry validly. Some hold that it gives rise to the impediment of affinity since this is considered a more firm impediment, while others hold that it does not cease since a person may incur more than one impediment. The more probable opinion is that which holds the impediment to be permanent, continuing even with the impediment of affinity.[90]

As with the other impediments of ecclesiastical law origin, it may be dispensed by the local ordinary and others in urgent situations (cc. 1079–1080).

Legal Relationship

Canon 1094 — They cannot validly contract marriage between themselves who are related in the direct line or in the second degree of the collateral line through a legal relationship arising from adoption.

A legal relationship between persons arises from the act of legal adoption by which a person receives as his or her child one who is not so by nature. In most civil jurisdictions a legally adopted child acquires the status of a legitimate child. Some civil codes provide for restricted adoption by which only certain rights and duties are established between adopter and adoptee.

The 1917 Code contained two canons on legal adoption. It was an impedient impediment in those places where the civil law impediment was prohibitive (*CIC* 1059) and a diriment impediment in those places where the civil law impediment was invalidating (*CIC* 1080).

Certain countries have no civil legislation prohibiting marriages between persons who are legally related. In others the impediment either invalidates the marriages or simply prohibits but does not invalidate them. It may extend to any or all of the following persons: adopted person and (a) adopter, (b) adopter's spouse, (c) natural children of adopter, (d) other adopted children of adopter, (e) descendants and ascendants of adopter.[91]

France, England, and West Germany are among the countries where the impediment is invalidating. In Canada, each province has revised statutes according to which adoption does not constitute an impediment to marriage. The United States has no uniform legislation and only two states have some form of prohibition: Massachusetts prohibits marriages between adoptive parents and children; Mississippi prohibits marriages between a father and his adoptive daughter.[92]

Present Canon Law

Ecclesiastical legislation depends on the civil law to decide what determines an adoptive relationship. It does not depend on civil legislation concerning the canonical impact on marriage as in the 1917 Code. Marriage is invalid between an adoptive person and his or her adoptive parent, as well as between adoptive siblings.

The impediment depends on a true legal relationship, therefore it does not arise if a person lives with a family but is never legally adopted. The relationship between a parent and his or her non-adopted stepchildren (the children of his or her spouse by another marriage) gives rise to the impediment of affinity.

If the legal adoptive relationship ceases by action of a civil court, the basis for the impediment is removed and it ceases.[93]

The impediment may be dispensed by the local ordinary and others in urgent situations (cc. 1079–1080). It should be noted that the ecclesiastical impediment invalidates a marriage whether or not the comparable civil impediment prohibits or invalidates. The impediment does not bind non-Catholics.

CHAPTER IV
MATRIMONIAL CONSENT
[cc. 1095–1107]

Although canon 1057, §2 positively defines matrimonial consent, its meaning is further clarified by the canons which deal with factors which render consent invalid. In scholastic categories, consent results from the combined actions of the cognitive, deliberative or critical, and volitional faculties. Yet these faculties cannot act in isolation of one another for the act of matrimonial consent is not simply an act of the will but an act of the person. The essential concept of marriage proposed by Vatican II is personalist in nature:

> ... It is rooted in the contract (*foedus*) of the partners, that is, in their irrevocable personal consent. It is an institution confirmed by divine law and receiving its stability, even in the eyes of society, from the human act by which the partners surrender themselves to each other.[94]

---

[90]J. Gallagher, *The Matrimonial Impediment of Public Propriety* (Washington, D.C.: Catholic University of America, 1952), 140–141.

[91]M. Wojnar, "Legal relationship and guardianship as matrimonial impediments," *J* 30 (1970), 343–355, 465–497.

[92]M. Ploscowe and H. Foster, *Family Law: Cases and Materials,* 2nd ed., (Boston: Little Brown, 1977), 1084.

[93]Wernz-Vidal, n. 196, p. 235.

[94]*GS* 48.

It is not simply a juridic act whereby spouses exchange rights for specific things. It is their freely chosen entrance into a covenant of the whole of life.[95]

In the past the law tended to isolate the intellectual and volitional elements of the consenting process, while the behavioral sciences, especially contemporary psychiatry and psychology, stressed the action of the total personality. Just as the formation of the personality is influenced by extrinsic factors such as society, culture, and family, so also the consenting process is influenced by factors and forces which exist outside the person.

The person who chooses marriage does not do so isolated from the influences of his or her socio-cultural environment and familial development. One's concept of marriage and personal commitment will have been influenced by what has been experienced and learned from family and society. The motivation to marry will be influenced by the personal relationship that exists between the persons themselves. It will also be influenced by what each one perceives marriage to be as well as by their personal expectations of each other and marriage in general.

The validity of marital consent depends on a minimal degree of knowledge of what marriage is and the free acceptance of its responsibilities. Marital validity also depends on the psychological capacity to evaluate the personal choice, elicit the human act of consent and, finally, fulfill the obligations involved.

Consensual Capacity

Canon 1095 — **They are incapable of contracting marriage:**

1° who lack the sufficient use of reason;

2° who suffer from grave lack of discretion of judgment concerning essential matrimonial rights and duties which are to be mutually given and accepted;

3° who are not capable of assuming the essential obligations of matrimony due to causes of a psychic nature.

Consensual capacity touches on three capacities: (a) to make a responsible human act; (b) to evaluate sufficiently the nature of marriage and, consequently, choose it freely; and, finally, (c) to assume its essential obligations.

Number one of this canon is based on the fact that the marriage covenant comes into existence by means of the valid exchange of consent (c. 1057). If a person lacks sufficient use of reason so as not to know what he or she is doing at the time consent is exchanged, then there is no true consent.

Until the mid-twentieth century, ecclesiastical jurisprudence recognized the invalidating effect of mental illness only when it precluded the possibility of a responsible human act at the time of consent. Traditionally, the ground of nullity was known as *amentia* or insanity. This is a legal rather than medical term having no precise diagnostic meaning in either discipline. Civil courts usually use it to convey either a type of mental affliction or the degree of mental affliction required for certain legal consequences. Canonical jurisprudence has been more consistent in its use of the term, usually understanding it to mean a permanent or temporary state of mind attributed to a variety of causes. If the cause of *amentia* were a psychotic disorder, it was necessary to prove that the person was afflicted prior to the wedding. Canonists also debated whether a person could validly contract marriage during a so-called lucid interval. Although early writers (18th century) argued affirmatively, Gasparri held that it was theoretically possible, yet practically improbable; in case of doubt, it was presumed that the marriage was contracted in insanity.[96] Contemporary advances in medical science have reduced the debate to near irrelevance.

One may be incapable of a human act at the time of consent for various reasons. The first broad category is mental illness which the Rota usually understands as a psychotic disorder.[97] Consensual incapacity may also be due to what the European psychologists and psychiatrists refer to as "psychopathies" commonly known by their North American colleagues as personality or character trait disorders.[98] Consensual incapacity may also be caused by certain psychoneuroses.

Whatever the disturbance, it must be so severe as to impede the use of reason. The person suffering from a permanent disorder is presumed to be habitually incapable of an internal will act. Conceivably, a temporary disorder could impede the use of reason for a time but not permanently. Not only must the person be capable of an internal will act but also there must be an awareness of what is being done at the time of the wedding.[99] A series of Rotal decisions in the twenties and thirties held that the parties must be capable of *manifesting* their consent. Those who, at the time of the wedding, lacked consciousness due to alcoholic intoxication, drug-induced state, sleep, or epilepsy, marry invalidly

[95]Mackin, 293–294, and P. Palmer, "Christian Marriage: Contract or Covenant," *TS* 33 (1972), 617–665.

[96]Gasparri 2, n. 785, pp 14–15.
[97]L. Hinslie and R. Campbell, *Psychiatric Dictionary* (New York: Oxford University, 1970), 619; and E. Hudson, 187–189.
[98]E. Egan, "Psychopathy and the Positing of an Act of Matrimonial Consent," *Stud Can* 10 (1976), 308.
[99]W. Doheny, *Canonical Procedure in Matrimonial Cases* (Milwaukee: The Bruce Publishing Co., 1938), 507. "Canonists uniformly teach that persons who are asleep, intoxicated or unconscious are not capable of contracting marriage validly, as they do not enjoy the use of reason at the time. . . . "

although they had the intention of marrying (habitual intention) prior to the ceremony.[100]

The important question is whether or not the disorder or state is so severe that the person did not know right from wrong, not the determination of the correct clinical classification. If a person does not know right from wrong, valid consent is impossible. The jurisprudence is usually concerned with cases of consent supposedly exchanged during a lucid interval or alcoholic or drug-induced blackout. The person may appear somewhat alert but actually is not aware of his or her surroundings or actions.

Lack of Due Discretion

The ability to form an adequate will act at the time of marriage is not sufficient in itself for a valid marriage. It must be preceded by sufficient deliberation or critical judgment about the implications of the act of consent for the person at that particular time. The person does not only consent to a wedding but makes a decision about his or her life and the life of the marriage partner. If there is a serious inability to evaluate critically the decision to marry in light of the consequent obligations and responsibilities, then consent may well be invalid. A person must be able to evaluate his or her motivation for the wedding, personal strengths and weaknesses, as well as those of the other party, and his or her ability to live up to the demands of the marriage.[101]

This evaluation is governed by the person's *critical faculty,* an ability that differs from mere intellectual apprehension of the situation. For the psychiatrist and the jurist this means " . . . the ability to form judgments, that is, the capacity to draw correct conclusions from the material acquired by experience."[102]

The critical faculty depends first on the mature ability to grasp what the marital relationship entails. The person must then be able to relate marriage as an abstract reality, i.e., what it theoretically involves, to his or her concrete situation. This requires insight and the application of one's actual situation and abilities to the theoretical demands of marriage.

The critical faculty involves existential judgments. It depends on a person's emotional and psychological state and an appreciation of the lessons learned from life experiences. It also presupposes freedom from mental confusion, undue pressure, or fear in contemplating marriage.

Jurisprudence refers to *due* discretion which is discretion proportionate to the consequences of the decision to be made. In the case of marriage, it must be proportionate to the requirements of the interpersonal relationship needed to create and sustain the community of the whole of life. The responsibilities of being a marriage partner and a parent must be evaluated in the context of one's emotional and psychological state as well as that of the other party. A person may be capable of right judgment in areas of life such as business, personal health, etc., but generally incapable of good judgment in regard to interpersonal relationships and specifically in regard to the special relationship demanded for Christian marriage.[103]

Poor judgment at the time of consent often results from an impairment or lack of internal freedom. This may be rooted in psychological or emotional problems which do not impede the intellect but have a significant influence on the will, or it may result from existential factors such as grave fear prompted by external pressure which a person cannot withstand. Thus marriage is chosen in a true state of mental confusion.[104] It is one thing to understand sufficiently what marital consent means in the practical order and quite another to make this consent with sufficient freedom.

The test of sufficient or due discretion is necessarily vague since the areas of understanding, evaluation, and decision are somewhat intangible, as are many of the responsibilities of marriage. Marital consent is an act of the person, and the success of the marriage depends on the resources of the person. Since persons differ, these intangible factors cannot be objectively measured for all persons of all backgrounds and cultures.

Usually the serious lack of discretionary ability is due to some form of psychopathy or personality disorder which has a grave affect on the intellect. Similarly, the exercise of judgment, while not totally impaired, may be significantly diminished due to a nervous disorder.[105] This disorder may be permanent or transitory. In either case, it must be so serious that at the time of consent the person affected is incapable of *marital* consent. The mere fact of a personality or nervous disorder in itself does not necessarily lead to the conclusion of a lack of due discretion; rather, what must be determined is the gravity of the condition and its actual effect on the intellectual capacity to evaluate the decision or the ability of the will to choose freely.

The development of the notion of the formal ob-

[100]This is confirmed by decisions c. Heard, December 4, 1943, *SRRDec* 35 (1943), 885–903; Grazioli, July 1, 1933, *SRRDec* 25 (1933), 403–419; and Jullien, July 30, 1932, *SRRDec* 24 (1932), 364–382.

[101]C. Pinto, Feb. 4, 1974, *CLD* 8, 727: "A person is also incapable of giving matrimonial consent if he, although actually possessing the use of reason, nevertheless, is lacking the discretion of judgment proportionate to the marriage contracted."

[102]Hinslie and Campbell, 419.

[103]C. Anné, Oct. 26, 1972, *EIC* 29 (1973), 109–117, and Hudson, 203–207.

[104]M. Ahern, "Psychological Incapacity for Marriage," *Stud Can* 7 (1973), 230–231.

[105]C. Fagiolo, Jan. 23, 1970, *EIC* 27 (1971), 147–151; c. Pompedda, Apr. 28, 1971, *ME* 97 (1972), 787–796. Also, Wrenn, 92–93.

ject of marital consent as the community of the whole of life has affected the development of the jurisprudence on lack of due discretion. Deliberation must be proportionate to the demands of the interpersonal relationship. Since this relationship is not lived in the abstract, the various socio-cultural factors which either weaken or support the Christian concept of marriage must also be considered.

Incapacity To Assume Obligations

In addition to the capacity for a deliberate act of the will, spouses must be psychologically capable of assuming and carrying out the essential obligations of marriage. One cannot validly exchange consent to marriage if it is beyond one's capacity. A person may be capable of understanding the nature of marriage and of making a deliberate act of the will while at the same time being radically incapable of assuming its obligations.[106]

Traditionally, psychological incapacity was tied directly to the ability to give consent. Cases submitted to the Rota alleging incapacity to fulfill the obligations assumed were routinely given negative decisions. An advance was made in 1957 with a decision which held that although a nymphomaniac was capable of eliciting a will act, she was nevertheless incapable of fulfilling the essential obligations of fidelity and, therefore, her consent was invalid.[107] Decisions based on similar jurisprudence were rendered in 1961 and 1967, the latter of which declared null a marriage in which the husband was incapable of fulfilling the marital obligations due to homosexuality.[108]

The development of the jurisprudence in this area expanded with scientific advances in understanding the nature and effects of the personality disorders. The classification and nomenclature used for the different disorders vary; yet the essential conclusions remain the same: a person gravely afflicted has a severely weakened or non-existent freedom of choice and of control over his or her affective-impulsive life. Since the sixties, an abundant jurisprudence has developed concerning the effect of the personality disorders on the ability to assume and fulfill marital obligations.

Early jurisprudence related incapacity either to the ability to exchange the right to the body for heterosexual acts or to the essential obligations arising from the three goods of marriage: children, fidelity, and permanence. As the object of marital consent was expanded to include the right to the communi-

ty of the whole of life, so the understanding of marital incapacity has expanded to include other essential obligations of marriage.[109]

The Essential Obligations of Marriage

Marriage consent involves the exchange of certain rights between the parties, rights which are related to the essential obligations of marriage. In his famous 1969 Rotal decision, Anné held that the formal object of marital consent to which the parties commit themselves was more than the right to the body for heterosexual acts (*ius in corpus*). It was, in its totality, the right to the community of the whole of life. This is more than cohabitation but, rather, is a developing, lifelong relationship.[110] This decision was followed by others which further developed this concept. In none of the above-mentioned decisions, however, does one find an exhaustive and detailed list of the elements essential to the community of life. To compile such a list is virtually impossible since every marital relationship is unique given the differences of couples in terms of backgrounds, personalities, and culture. Nevertheless, there are certain basic aspects of a covenant marriage which one is expected to be capable of fulfilling. The most obvious one is the heterosexual dimension of the marriage, to which the spouses have a right. Yet the joining together in the marital community is more than just a physical reality; it involves a true intertwining of the personalities. The capacity for marriage involves the capacity for an interpersonal relationship. This concept has been refined by various Rotal decisions since 1973.[111] The spouses must be capable of giving themselves and accepting the other as a distinct person. They must be capable of relating to each other in a manner that is unique to marriage. The parties must be "other oriented" since the obligations of marriage are rooted in a self-giving love. According to Serrano, the capacity for a marital relationship presupposes the development of an adult personality.[112]

Serrano and other Rotal judges who have been instrumental in developing the notion of marital capacity all point out that the interpersonal relationship can reach a greater or lesser degree of

---

[106]Hudson, 200–203.

[107]C. Sabattani, June 21, 1957, *SRRDec* 49 (1957), 500–513.

[108]C. Lefebvre, Dec. 2, 1967, *SRRDec* 59 (1967), 803. See also J. Schmidt, "Homosexuality and the Validity of Matrimony—A Study in Homo-psychosexual Inversion," *J* 32 (1972), 381–399, 494–530, and Hudson, 224–225.

[109]See D. Fellhauer, "*The Consortium omnis vitae* as a Juridical Element of Marriage," *Stud Can* 13 (1979), 7–171. See also W. Schumacher, "The Importance of Interpersonal Relations in Marriage," *Stud Can* 9 (1975), 5–21.

[110]C. Anné, Feb. 25, 1969, *ME* 96 (1971), 21–39. Also, W. LaDue, "Conjugal Love and the Juridical Structure of Christian Marriage," *J* 34 (1974), 36–67.

[111]See Decisions c. Serrano, Apr. 3, 1973, *CLD* 8, 692–724; Apr. 30, 1974, *EIC* 31 (1975), 191–202; July 9, 1976, *ME* 102 (1977), 363–381. C. Anné, Mar. 11, 1975, *CLD* 8, 739–754; Raad, Apr. 15, 1975 unpublished; Staffa, Nov. 29, 1975, *CLD* 8, 768–790; Lefebvre, Jan. 31, 1976, *ME* 102 (1977), 363–381; and Ewers, Jan. 15, 1977, *EIC* 33 (1977), 354–356.

[112]C. Serrano, July 9, 1976, *ME* 102 (1977), 369–371.

perfection in different spouses. The external manifestations of the developing community of life will necessarily differ from couple to couple. According to Anné:

> At the core . . . is the state of mind of husband and wife, by which the spouses, despite human frailty and the grave, even very grave fault of one or the other, constantly strive in their concrete circumstances to bring into effect that indefinable sum of attitudes, of behavior and of actions, varying in its concrete expressions in different cultures, without which it would be impossible to bring into being and keep in being that communion of life, which is necessary for the achievement in a truly human way, of the ends which marriage is destined to achieve.[113]

Perhaps one of the most succinct expressions of the meaning of this capacity is found in Panormitanus' comment on the medieval concept of *affectio maritalis:* "It is the will to treat one's spouse as a spouse should be treated."

The fulfillment of the obligations flowing from the three goods of marriage (children, fidelity, permanence) depends on the strength of the interpersonal relationship. A serious incapacity for interpersonal sharing and support will impair the relationship and consequently the ability to fulfill these obligations. Marital capacity cannot be considered in isolation but in reference to the fundamental relationship to the other party.

Serious Psychic Causes

The incapacity to assume the essential obligations of marriage differs from an unwillingness to do so in that one or both of the parties suffers from a debilitating psychological condition to such an extent that it is impossible to begin and sustain a marital relationship. The psychic factor itself is not the cause of invalidity, rather the gravity of the affliction is the root of the incapacity.

The law does not specify which types of psychic causes can incapacitate one for marriage nor does it give a partial listing of disorders which have a detrimental effect on the marital community. However, the marriage committee clearly intended to include not simply sexual anomalies but also other psychological disorders which affect the personality.[114]

The diagnosis of a disorder, even a tentative one, is a clinical and not a juridical issue. The classification of and terminology related to the various disorders change, and court experts themselves often differ about the precise classification of an obvious disorder.[115]

The phrase "of a psychic nature" includes a wide range of possibilities. Marital incapacity can result from a psychotic disorder or a personality disorder, provided the disorder is a true constitutional impairment which prevents the person from improving his or her situation. A personality disorder is a very complex and elusive phenomenon which resists easy analysis.[116] Although the Rota has generally demanded a clearly diagnosed disorder in incapacity cases, continuing research developments, changing terminology, and the elusive nature of the disorders themselves make exact diagnoses difficult. One important Rotal decision states that marital incapacity can result from an abnormality which is not really an illness but which is caused by various factors which preclude one's entering into an interpersonal relationship. The abnormality is referred to as "emotional immaturity."[117]

When canonists use the term "immaturity" they use it in a specific sense and not in reference to ordinary chronological immaturity which affects everyone at one time in his or her development. Rather, immaturity is a psychological condition which affects the ability to make judgments, to control one's actions, and to relate to another. As such, it is not a temporary condition but a permanent one.

Some canonists refer to absolute and relative incapacity, indicating that a person may be incapable of marriage to anyone or only to certain persons. In cases involving a psychotic disorder, a person may be incapable of marriage to anyone at any time, yet a similar incapacity is not as easily demonstrated with a personality disorder. According to Serrano, it is not necessary to prove that a person is incapable of any marriage but, rather, that he or she is incapable of the marriage being adjudicated by the court.[118] Psychiatrists and psychologists are frequently reluctant to pronounce on a person's abso-

[113]C. Anné, Dec. 4, 1975, *EIC* 33 (1977), 176–177, trans. from Fellhauer, 139–140.
[114]*Comm* 7 (1975), 50.

[115]M. Pompedda, "Neuroses and psychopathic personalities in relation to consent." Lecture notes from the *Cursus Renovationis,* given in Rome at the Gregorian University, 1973, in H. McMahon, "The Role of Psychiatric and Psychological Experts in Nullity Cases," *Stud Can* 9 (1975), 66.
[116]Egan, 313.
[117]C. Lefebvre, January 31, 1976 *ME* 102 (1977), 285. See *DSM III,* 90–92 on "Childhood Onset Pervasive Developmental Disorder." This is a clinical description of the disorder referred to by Lefebvre. On p. 91 the diagnostic criteria include: "Gross and sustained impairment in social relationships, e.g., lack of appropriate affective responsivity, inappropriate clinging, asociality, lack of empathy."
[118]C. Serrano, Apr. 5, 1973 in *CLD* 8, 718: "It is not necessary to maintain that this man is incapable of any possible marriage. Whatever may be the case for other interpersonal relationships which he could have or would have formed . . . it is sufficiently clear that we must judge that this concrete marriage was null from the beginning."

lute incapacity for marriage but prefer to limit their opinions to the case before them.[119]

For the canonist, the object of primary concern is not the psychic disorder but, rather, its effects upon the interpersonal relationship. What is sought is a clear-cut pattern of behavior which leads to a judgment that a psychic disorder has prevented the community of life from coming into being. Occasional acts of irresponsibility, be they grave or light, do not in themselves constitute proof either of incapacity or of the existence of a psychic disorder. Yet a pattern of such behavior can and usually does provide evidence of such a disorder.

Ignorance

Canon 1096 — §1. For matrimonial consent to be valid it is necessary that the contracting parties at least not be ignorant that marriage is a permanent consortium between a man and a woman which is ordered toward the procreation of offspring by means of some sexual cooperation.

§2. Such ignorance is not presumed after puberty.

Ignorance about the essential nature of marriage is best understood in the Thomistic sense. It is the privation or lack of knowledge in a person who is naturally capable of such knowledge. It is, therefore, distinguished from ignorance about the nature of marriage due to psychic causes or a total lack of the use of reason.

A minimal knowledge of the nature of marriage is required by the natural law itself, since one cannot intend or will to enter the marriage covenant without knowing what it is. A detailed and sophisticated knowledge of the essence of marriage is not required. Yet a person should have more than an abstract notion of marital consent: there should be a realization of the personal implications of that to which he or she is consenting.

The law specifies a minimal awareness required for valid consent. The spouses must know that marriage is a permanent relationship of a special nature between a man and a woman. They must also know that this relationship is ordered to the procreation of children through sexual cooperation.

The *consortium* referred to in the canon is understood not simply as the context within which procreative sexual acts take place. It is the partnership of the spouses. This requires the knowledge that some mutual cooperation, support, and companionship is required. They must also know that the relationship is of its nature permanent and cannot be terminated by the parties themselves.[120]

The spouses should also know that the sexual dimension of marriage is ordered to procreation and not solely to sensual pleasure. Although commentators on the 1917 Code disputed whether knowledge of sexual intercourse was required, recent jurisprudence holds that it is, and this opinion is embodied in the present canon.[121]

The Cause of Ignorance

Ignorance of the nature and purpose of marriage may result from the human inability to learn, such as retardation or severe learning disability. A person may be so impaired that he or she fails to grasp the meaning of interpersonal relationships, the permanence of marriage, or the connection between procreation and sexual activity. This type of ignorance of marriage, if caused by psychological or emotional deficiencies, would also be related to incapacity.

Ignorance is more properly ascribed to those who have the basic capacity for knowledge but lacked the opportunity rather than the capacity to learn. Knowledge is obtained through formal instruction, observation of others, and experience. People learn about marriage to a great extent from the society and immediate environment in which they live. Contemporary Western society no longer provides a consistent example of stable marriage. Numerous people are raised in single-parent homes, never living in the context of a community of life. Confusing and conflicting social customs and value systems can prevent a person from learning that the notions of permanent commitment and self-sacrifice are acceptable facets of life. Because of these social realities, canonical jurisprudence no longer presumes that all persons marry in the manner intended by God.[122] Consequently, a person could go through a wedding ceremony yet be ignorant of the fact that the subsequent marriage involves a self-sacrificing community of life ordered to the good of the spouses and the procreation and education of children.

The law presumes that all persons have the requisite knowledge of the nature and purpose of marriage after they attain puberty. This presumption is formulated negatively, that is, ignorance is presumed prior to but not after puberty.

[119]J. Higgins, "Psychological Influences on the Matrimonial Bond," in *The Bond of Marriage*, W. Bassett, ed. (Notre Dame, Ind.: University of Notre Dame, 1968), 208: "It is strongly questioned whether a finding of total incapacity is either necessary or real. Except in very extreme cases, can a psychiatrist so clearly define and so absolutely diagnose general mental or emotional inability to marry? Would it not be preferable to limit the decision only to the relationship of the individual in question?"

[120]C. Serrano, Apr. 25, 1975, *EIC* 31 (1975), 173–176.
[121]C. Mattioli, Nov. 25, 1965, *CLD* 6, 623–625.
[122]C. Ewers, May 16, 1968, *SRRDec* 60 (1968), 346–347.

Error about the Person

Canon 1097 —§1. Error concerning the person renders marriage invalid.

§2. Error concerning a quality of a person, even if such error is the cause of the contract, does not invalidate matrimony unless this quality was directly and principally intended.

The law holds that acts placed in ignorance or error about that which constitutes their substance are invalid, otherwise, the act is valid unless the law specifies that this is not the case (c. 126). Error may influence marital consent either regarding the person whom one is marrying or regarding the nature of marriage itself.

Error is a false judgment about something or someone and as such it is a defect of the intellect. The person in error is not devoid of knowledge but possesses erroneous knowledge about a person or a thing. The person then makes a judgment or forms an opinion based on what is erroneously perceived.

Error of Person

The reality of marital consent as a gift of one's self to another requires a knowledge of the person with whom consent is exchanged. Consent is exchanged with a specific man or a woman. If an error is made about the identity of the marital partner, consent is invalid. This kind of error is also known as substantial error, since the substance of the matrimonial covenant is invalidated. No one can give true marital consent unless the other party is the person he or she intends to marry (§1).

Error of Quality of the Person

A quality is some aspect of the person that contributes to the shaping of the overall personality. Such qualities may be moral, physical, social, religious, or legal. Some examples are honesty, freedom from disease, social status, appearance, marital status, education, religious convictions, etc. An error about a quality of a person, even if marital consent is exchanged precisely because of this quality, does not invalidate marriage unless that quality is directly and principally intended (§2). A woman may marry a man because of some quality she finds particularly attractive or even necessary such as wealth, social rank, occupation, or even religion. If she is actually in error and the quality does not exist, the marriage is still valid.

Since matrimonial consent is exchanged with a person and not with a quality of the person, it is presumed that the essence of consent remains despite the error about the quality.

The canon makes a distinction, however. If a person makes an error about a quality that he or she directly and principally intends, the consent could be invalid. In the above-mentioned examples, it is presumed that the person can distinguish between the person to whom consent is made and the desired quality. Here the person gives consent precisely and only because of a perceived quality.

If the quality is such that it is equivalent to the person, then the error would be substantial and not merely accidental. This notion was introduced by St. Thomas Aquinas and was interpreted strictly by Sanchez and broadly by St. Alphonsus of Liguori.[123]

Sanchez held that the quality about which the error is made must be unique and proper only to the individual believed to possess it. As such it determines this person and no other, and marital consent is directed primarily to the quality and secondarily to the person. St. Thomas gives the example of one's being the only son of the king.

St. Alphonsus, however, taught that the quality need not be unique to one person only; it might be common to many, yet it is the primary interest of the person exchanging consent. Although canonists have traditionally accepted Sanchez's view, a recent trend in jurisprudence has applied St. Alphonsus' interpretation.[124] This trend was based on an approach to defining a person which is not restricted to the "substance and accidents" model. The person is also a composite of social, physical, cultural, and civil qualities. In recent jurisprudence, nullity was based on the fact that the quality, even though common to many, was truly grave, discovered after the marriage, and when discovered resulted in a serious disruption of marital life.

The two interpretations of error of quality have been debated by jurists and members of the marriage committee.[125] The broad interpretation of error of quality amounting to an error of the person proposed by the Rotal judges Canals and DeFelice has been criticized as going beyond the traditional meaning of the law. At the conclusion of his articles on the subject, Dalton states:

> At this point it should be clear that the interpretation of "error redundans" being proposed by Canals-DeFelice is in open conflict with existing law. It flies in the face of the general principle that error concerning accidental qualities does not affect the validity of juridical acts or contracts.[126]

The wording of the present canon resolves the difficulty. The wording of the 1917 Code stated

[123]*Suppl.* Q. 51, art. 2; T. Sanchez, *De Matrimonio* Lib. 7, 18, 38; and Liguori, *Theologia Moralis* 5, 6, 31.

[124]C. Canals, Apr. 21, 1970, *CLD* 8, 796–801; c. Ferraro, July 18, 1972, *EIC* 30 (1974), 278–292; c. DeFelice, Mar. 26, 1977, *CLS-GBIN* 40 (1979), 38–39; c. DeFelice, Jan. 14, 1978, ibid., 50–59; cf. M. Reinhardt, "Error qualitatis in errorem personae redundans," *CLSAP* (1973), 55–69.

[125]*Comm* 9 (1977), 371–372.

[126]W. Dalton, "Error redundans: a look at some recent jurisprudence," *CLS-GBIN* 50 (1981), 32.

that error of quality invalidated "if the error of quality amounts to (*redundet*) an error of the person" (*CIC* 1083, §2, 1°). The present wording avoids equating an error of quality with an error of person. It refers directly to a quality "directly and principally intended." This is not an antecedent error about an accidental quality of the person or an error about the cause of the marriage, e.g., the man who marries a woman because she is pregnant and later finds out she is not. The quality must be directly intended and the primary concern of the person to the extent that the principal reason for the marriage is the quality and not the other person. This quality need not be unique to the person but, even if common to many, must be of such subjective magnitude in the mind of the person marrying that it almost completely overshadows the person of the other party.

When a person directly and principally intends a quality which is the reason for the marriage, he or she implicitly conditions the marriage upon the existence of that quality. When the error is discovered and the person finds that the quality does not exist, the marital relationship is destroyed. Actually, there is no conjugal community (*consortium vitae*) in the true sense because this community depends on the gift of the persons. This gift is presumably not made if a quality of the partner is the overriding concern of one of them as noted above.

Fraud

Canon 1098 — A person contracts invalidly who enters marriage deceived by fraud, perpetrated to obtain consent, concerning some quality of the other party which of its very nature can seriously disturb the partnership of conjugal life.

Fraud or deceit is a deliberate act of deception by which one person hides a significant fact from another to achieve a given end. In this case, one party to the marriage deliberately deceives the other about the presence or absence of a certain quality about himself or herself. The presence or absence of the quality is of such significance that the discovery of the truth of the situation could destroy the marital relationship.

Juridic acts placed as a result of fraud are generally valid unless the contrary is specifically stated in the law (c. 125, §2). This canon is such an exception. Although the 1917 Code did not contain a similar canon, the developing jurisprudence concerning error of quality gradually led to the clarification of the effect on marital validity of fraud about an important quality.

The marital community depends on the honesty of the spouses for its successful development. Marital consent is not simply an exchange of abstract rights but an exchange of the persons themselves. Honesty about one's identity and total personality

is essential because marriage involves the emotional and psychological union of the parties. The process whereby the two become one may be impeded or made impossible by the presence or absence of a significant quality of one of the parties. Deceit about such a quality negates the gift of self since the person presented is not the true and complete self; and, therefore, the very essence of consent is radically altered. If there is deceit about an essential or significant quality, then there is no true joining of wills; rather one party manipulates the will of the other.

There are certain essential elements to be proved if fraud is to invalidate a marriage:

(a) *It is deliberately perpetrated in order to obtain consent.* The deceiver believes that if the other party knew the truth regarding the object of the deceit, he or she would not give consent. The truth about the quality need not be hidden through malice since the canon does not qualify the motivation for the fraud in the sense that it is good or bad (*dolus malus* or *dolus bonus*). This could be the case with a person who is ambivalent about his or her sexual orientation. He or she may truly love the deceived party and feel that the marriage will solve the problem of his or her sexual identity. The deceiver may in fact not realize the seriousness of the deception.

(b) *The quality is real, grave, and present at the time of consent.* The quality must be an actual feature of the individual and not an isolated action from the past which is no longer relevant to the person. It must be *grave,* either objectively or subjectively. This means that it is so serious that its concealment would be commonly accepted as an injustice to the other party (objective) or so serious in the estimation of the other party that, although it might not adversely affect others, it causes profound reaction on the part of the person deceived (subjective). Finally, the quality must actually be present or absent at the time of the marriage and neither an isolated past incident that has no bearing on the person in the present nor a future quality, detached from who the person is now. The deceived must obviously make an error about the present and not the future if it is to affect marital consent.

(c) *The quality must be unknown to the other party.* The deceit must cause an error on the part of the deceived. If the latter knows about the presence or absence of the quality from one or another source, then error cannot be alleged. The deceit or fraud *must* precipitate an *error* about an important *quality.*

(d) *The discovery of the absence or presence of the quality must precipitate the end of the marriage.* When the deceived person discovers the error, it significantly alters the relationship to the extent that he or she realizes that there actually is no community of life. The breakdown of the marriage must be directly related to the discovery of the absence or presence of the quality. The person of the deceiver is radically altered because of the deception *and* the quality to the extent that the deceived would not have given consent had he or she known of the truth of the situation.

Reference has been made to the *presence* or *absence* of certain qualities. A prospective spouse may implicitly expect certain qualities such as heterosexuality, fertility, acceptance of one's religious beliefs, etc. If a quality expected in a spouse does not exist and its non-existence is fraudulently concealed, then one has been deceived about the absence of an expected quality. If, on the other hand, a person conceals the presence of a quality that is not commonly expected, or at least not subjectively (on the part of the deceived) expected, then it is a case of deceit about a quality that is present. Some examples of such qualities are: homosexuality; alcoholism; drug addiction; sexual dysfunction; previous marriage, even though invalid due to lack of canonical form; prior criminal record; mental illness; or sterility.

The introduction of fraud into the marriage canons is an example of the personalist approach of the law. It recognizes the fact that the creation of the marital community depends on a person's spiritual, psychological, intellectual, and physical maturity. The law presumes that the parties to a marriage are willing and capable of accepting certain defects in each other as well as unpleasing factors in each other's personalities. Altogether different, however, are those qualities which so change the identity of the person that consent itself would not have taken place had they been known.[127]

Simple Error

Canon 1099 — Error concerning the unity, indissolubility or sacramental dignity of matrimony does not vitiate matrimonial consent so long as it does not determine the will.

The process whereby spouses exchange Christian marital consent involves the intellectual apprehension of the nature and essential elements of Christian marriage. A person's concept of marriage may be marred by error, i.e., a false judgment about factors essential to the marriage covenant.

The 1917 Code stated that simple error about the properties of unity and indissolubility did not invalidate consent (*CIC* 1084). Simple error is that which remains in the intellect but does not influence the will. Thus simple error and valid consent coexist.

This coexistence is based on the presumption that all Christians have a general intention to marry according to the mind of Christ. This presumption is grounded in the fact that in Christian society

there is a kind of reinforcement of basic Christian values.

Simple error is, therefore, understood to mean false notions about marriage which are superceded by the acceptance of true Christian marriage. If, however, the error about one of the essential properties of marriage is such that it causes the person to reject this property by a positive act of the will, then it is no longer simple error but simulation.

The law now refers to error in a general way, no longer qualifying it as "simple." It admits that it may well influence the will, since it implicitly distinguishes between error which remains in the intellect and that which influences the will. Error about unity or indissolubility does not invalidate if it is such that the prevailing intention is to enter marriage as it is understood by the Church. If the error is such that it precludes not only an awareness but also an acceptance of the true nature of marriage, then it could well influence the person to choose a model of marriage contrary to Christian marriage. Thus consent would be invalid.

The Process of Consent

Marital consent is a unique act or peak moment in a process whereby two persons decide to commit themselves to each other for marriage. The process itself begins with speculative or abstract knowledge of marriage as a desirable institution. The next step is critically evaluating the decision to marry a specific person. Marriage now becomes more than an abstract reality. It is a real possibility in one's life and will involve potential change and adjustment.

As the parties reflect on marriage, they will no doubt think about the ramifications of such a decision in their own personal lives. To reflect on the effects of marriage there must be a frame of reference. A person's awareness of marriage and its effects on people are influenced by how one sees marriage in a particular society or culture. Other influential factors are the predominant or popular attitudes toward sexual morality and personal commitment. At one time, Western societies had great respect for Christian marriage. People learned from life itself that marriage was for life and involved total fidelity. A variety of social and economic factors have caused a change in attitudes toward Christian marriage and family life.

The crisis which gravely affects the family in these countries [Europe and North America] arises directly from the development of a mentality which stresses material success, individualism, efficiency, technology that is becoming more and more refined, and the development of a lifestyle that stresses money, action and power. More and more, the authentic values of family life: love as a gift of self, the generous acceptance of life, the spirit of sacrifice, are being regarded

[127]See P. Sumner, *"Dolus as a Ground for Nullity of Marriage," Stud Can* 14 (1980), 171–194, and Wrenn, 82–84.

as less important and are being relegated to a secondary level. The stress placed on individual fulfillment, the strong pressures placed by the mass media on public opinion have weakened the impact of the teaching of the Church.[128]

The sexual revolution and the rapid rise of divorce have resulted in widespread attitudes toward marriage that are contrary to those held by the Church. Some persons believe that marriage is not indissoluble. For still others, sexual activity is not restricted to marriage either in theory or in practice. A contraceptive mentality has caused the planned childless marriage to be a real option. Although these factors have always existed, they have become socially acceptable and have affected the formation of attitudes toward the obligations and essential properties of marriage.[129]

A person may well approach marriage with seriously erroneous ideas about the fundamental nature of sacramental marriage and the marital properties of unity and indissolubility. These erroneous notions enter the process of consent, since they become determining factors in what the intellect presents to the will. The choice of marriage with a specific person is then based on what is erroneously understood to be marriage and not the true concept espoused by the Church.

An error about the nature or obligations of marriage does not affect validity unless it determines the will. Otherwise it remains a disposition and does not result in a new model of marriage.

The probability that erroneous notions will determine the will is recognized by the Church to be much higher today than ever before. The Rota has studied changing social conditions and attitudes toward marriage and rendered a series of recent decisions which indicate that the presumption that all marry as Christ intends is increasingly questionable. One decision stated that it is impossible to distinguish between erroneous notions of marriage and a positive rejection of an essential property by the will.[130]

The Object of Error

Three aspects of marriage are mentioned as the possible objects of erroneous opinions: unity, indissolubility, and the sacramental dignity of marriage.

Error concerning unity could include the opinion that polygamy is possible, yet this is not a common option in Western society. Error about unity would more likely affect one's notion of the obligation of marital fidelity.

Error about indissolubility includes the belief that once the existential relationship itself is dead, the marriage is completely ended and the parties are free to marry again. Such an error includes the belief that there is no such thing as an indissoluble bond to which the parties are obliged to remain faithful, even after civil divorce. Another aspect of this type of error would be the belief that the State has the power to dissolve the marriage bond.

Error about the sacramental dignity of marriage concerns the fact that a marriage between two baptized persons is a sacramental marriage. In order to invalidate, an error about the sacramental dignity of marriage would have to consist in a belief that marriage, even though performed in a Catholic church, is merely a civil affair. Closely related to an error about the sacramental dignity is an erroneous notion of absolute indissolubility. St. Augustine referred to absolute indissolubility as the "good of the sacrament" because of its relationship to the sacred dimension of marriage. Marital indissolubility becomes absolute precisely because of the sacramental dimension. If a person is in error about the sacramental dignity of marriage, he or she will probably not hold for absolute indissolubility.

The relationship between error about the sacramentality of marriage and the determination of the will must be properly understood. Here the distinction between simple error and an error which does influence the will is most important. If any error about the sacramental dignity of marriage were considered invalidating, the majority of marriages would be null since most people do not consider marriage to be a sacrament. An error about the sacramental dignity of marriage is more than a confused or imprecise idea of why it is a sacrament or why it has a religious dimension. Rather, such an error must be about the fundamental sacramentality of marriage and must be so deeply rooted that the person conceives of it exclusively as a human enterprise governed solely by civil law or local custom.

If the person's erroneous opinion about any of these three aspects of marriage is such that he or she can conceive of and give consent to marriage in no other way, then the will is compelled to choose a model of marriage which is inimical to that of the sacramental covenant.

Knowledge or Opinion of Nullity

Canon 1100 — The knowledge or opinion of the nullity of a marriage does not necessarily exclude matrimonial consent.

This canon covers situations in which one or both of the parties know that the marriage is null or have an opinion that it is null even though such an opinion is erroneous. In spite of this knowledge or opinion, consent is exchanged. The marriage is not

---

[128]Papal Committee for the Family, *The Family in the Pastoral Activity of the Church* (Washington, D.C.: USCC, 1978), 6. See also A. Cherlin, *Marriage, Divorce and Remarriage* (Cambridge: Harvard University, 1981), 33–68.

[129]*FC* 12–14.

[130]C. Ewers, May 16, 1968 (see note 123).

invalid by this very fact, although it may well be invalid for some other reason. In other words, consent exchanged in spite of knowledge or opinion of nullity does not render the consent defective.

If one or both parties believe that an impediment exists yet want to enter a valid marriage, the consent itself is not defective. If there really is no impediment, the marriage is valid. On the other hand, if an impediment does exist and it can be dispensed, the renewal of consent is not obligatory. Rather, a sanation can be granted to resolve the situation (cf. c. 1163). One party may believe seriously that the other party's intentions are lacking in some way and, therefore, the union will be invalid. If this person desires a valid union, the consent would be valid and proof of nullity would depend on a sentence of a competent tribunal. The same would hold true in those cases wherein the belief or opinion of nullity is based on the presence of a psychic cause that could possibly be a cause of invalidity.

If the knowledge or opinion of nullity causes the person to go through an ecclesiastical ceremony with the belief that consent is merely a civil formality lacking all sacramental value, then the situation is different. Here the party is actually feigning or simulating consent, since there is no will to enter a true marriage. Rather, there is the belief that the consent itself has no religious or sacramental value.

Simulation of Matrimonial Consent

Canon 1101 — §1. The internal consent of the mind is presumed to be in agreement with the words or signs employed in celebrating matrimony.

§2. But if either or both parties through a positive act of the will should exclude marriage itself, some essential element or an essential property of marriage, it is invalidly contracted.

The concept of simulation is important because it touches on the very act of the will by which marriage comes into being. A historical synopsis will elucidate some of the complexities of the subject. Simulation must be about something, consequently an understanding of the object of simulation is as vital as an understanding of the process itself. The object of simulation is multifaceted and has a definite meaning in canon law.

The marriage covenant begins with the exchange of consent by the spouses. Consent is an act of the will and as such it is internal. The spouses must express their commitment to each other by means of words or signs which are perceivable to the senses, usually by pronouncing the marriage vows. Presumably the external expression is sincere and the spouses fully intend to give and accept each other as they begin their marriage. They are also presumed to understand and accept the obligations of marriage even though the marriage ritual does not mention them in detail.

This presumption of the validity of an act is a commonsense part of human experience, operative in civil law as well as in canon law (e.g., contracts). With marriage there must be a presumption of conformity between the internal intention and the outward expression because no one but the spouses can give consent to marriage, i.e., consent cannot be supplied by a parent or anyone else.

The Simulation of Consent

Up to the thirteenth century it was always presumed that the intention of the will was in conformity with the outward expression of consent. However, a papal decree in 1212 declared invalid a marriage in which the man exchanged consent, not for the purpose of marriage, but for reasons which the pope deemed contrary to marriage.[131] This was what later jurisprudence referred to as simulation.

Marital consent is simulated when there is a contradiction between the external manifestation of consent and the internal intention of the will. Traditional Rotal jurisprudence explains simulation as the coexistence of two acts of the will: the external act which says "I will" and the internal act which says "I won't" to marriage. To simulate, one must be aware of the nature and obligations of marriage and knowingly reject or exclude either marriage itself or one of its essential elements or properties. The canon refers to exclusion by a positive act of the will, since the simulator internally rejects marriage outright while participating in the marriage ceremony for ulterior motives contrary to marriage. A person may also express consent yet intend his or her own idea of marriage which excludes the true nature of Christian marriage.

Since simulation involves an internal act, its external proof is difficult. Basically, simulation involves a person's taking a definite stand contrary to the Church's view of marriage. The intention presumed by the Church is replaced by a contrary intention.

The development of the notion of simulation has involved the refinement of the juridic proofs of simulated consent. Prior to the 1917 Code a contrary intention had to be formulated as an expressed condition which thus became part of consent. Mentally retained conditions or contrary intentions were not presumed to be invalidating because of the difficulty in proving them. Following the 1917 Code the Rota began to accept Gasparri's theory that a mentally retained intention against an essential element of marriage invalidated consent, even though it was not an expressed part of the manifestation of consent.[132]

There have been several interesting developments

[131]*Tua nos* X 4 1 26, *CorpusIC* 2, 670–671.

[132]C. Lefebvre, "De bonorum matrimonii exclusione secundum Card. Gasparri opera," *Apol* 33 (1960), 143.

regarding simulation in recent years. A person who exchanges consent yet substitutes his or her concept of marriage is considered to have simulated as is a person who simply refuses to bind himself or herself to the Church's concept of marriage. This is more than a simple non-inclusion of the Church's concept of marriage since there is a degree of rejection of marriage or one of its essential elements or properties.[133]

Another recent development in jurisprudence has been called either "inadequate consent" or "lack of commitment amounting to simulation." Here, the issue is not precisely the rejection of marriage by a positive act of the will but the failure to include a true understanding of marriage in one's consent. This evolving jurisprudence is based on several factors:

(a) the weakness of the presumption that all marry according to the mind of Christ or the Church;

(b) the expanded notion of the formal object of marital consent from the right to potentially procreative acts to the right to a procreative community of the whole of life;

(c) the realization that consent may be weak or non-existent yet not the result of lack of a due discretion or various psychic causes.

The point of departure is the person giving consent and the motivation for this consent. A person may not specifically reject marriage yet at the same time not intend a true lifelong union. Such a person may want a wedding ceremony for a number of reasons, yet none of these includes the creation of the conjugal community.

Conceivably, a person could use the wedding celebration and exchange of consent to achieve other ends, as in a wedding of convenience.[134]

The notion of simulation admits of various distinctions. The Rota has consistently distinguished between *total simulation* and *partial simulation*. The former is best described as the complete rejection of marriage, while one participates in the wedding ceremony to achieve an end other than true marriage. An example would be a person who goes through a marriage ceremony to obtain a civil law benefit such as citizenship or extended residency in a country.

Partial simulation is the acceptance of marriage in general but with a rejection of one or more of the

essential obligations or properties. It has traditionally been formulated in terms of the rejection of one of the three goods of marriage: children, fidelity, or permanence.

The Object of Simulation

Consent is invalid if one or both of the parties exclude *marriage itself,* be it marriage in general or the Church's concept of marriage.

To reject the Church's concept of marriage is to reject marriage as a community of the whole of life. This is a unique kind of marital relationship which presumably includes certain elements such as cohabitation, mutual support, respect, and stability of conduct. Yet it is difficult to enumerate those things necessary for a true community of life since one can confuse essential elements with culturally and socially acceptable ways of expressing the gift of self which constitutes marriage.

Since a fundamental aspect of marriage is the interpersonal relationship between the spouses, the rejection of such a relationship would obviously constitute a rejection of marriage itself.[135]

Essential Elements of Marriage

There is a close relationship between the rejection of marriage itself and the rejection of an essential element of marriage. The essential elements are distinguished from the essential properties, which will be considered below.

Foremost among the essential elements of marriage is its ordination to the good of children. This includes the right to the conjugal act. The denial of this right has been understood under a double aspect in traditional jurisprudence: the exclusion of the right to sexual intercourse and the exclusion of children. Although traditional Rotal jurisprudence held that an intention contrary to the good of children was limited to the denial of the perpetual and exclusive right to sexual acts, contemporary jurisprudence has added another dimension. If one or both parties frustrate the purpose of marriage itself, this amounts to simulation.

The sexual act and procreation are intimately related to conjugal love and the marital community. The sexual act is the most intimate expression of conjugal love, which, according to *Humanae Vitae,* is a fruitful love which does not exhaust itself in the communion of the spouses but is destined to perpetuate itself by cooperating in the work of creation.[136] The right to the conjugal act is denied if one party intends to restrict it in such a way that intercourse itself or non-contraceptive intercourse is refused ei-

[133]C. Anné, Nov. 8, 1963, *SRRDec* 55 (1963), 764; C. Lefebvre, Feb. 19, 1965, *SRRDec* 57 (1965), 176.

[134]See R. Brown, "Inadequate Consent or Lack of Commitment: Authentic Grounds for Nullity," *Stud Can* 9 (1975), 249–265; idem, "Total Simulation: a Second Look," *Stud Can* 10 (1976), 235–250; and J. Humphreys, "Lack of Commitment in Consent," ibid., 345–362; "Activity in the Roman Rota," *CLS-GBIN* 47 (1980), 26–29.

[135]C. Serrano, Apr. 5, 1973, *CLD* 8, 693–694; *Comm* 9 (1977), 375, and Serrano, "Le droit à la communauté de vie et d'amour conjugal comme l'objet du consentement matrimonial: aspects juridiques et l'evolution de la jurisprudence de la Sacrée Rote romain," *Stud Can* 10 (1976), 276–277.

[136]*GS* 49–50; *HV,* n. 9.

ther completely or systematically to avoid conception. The right to the conjugal act cannot be restricted to certain times under certain circumstances nor can persons validly marry on the condition that intercourse never take place. The right to the conjugal act must be acceded to whenever it is reasonably requested.[137]

More important for contemporary society is the question of the direct exclusion of children from marriage. Advances in contraceptive methods make the total exclusion of children possible with no interruption in regular sexual intercourse. Socio-economic conditions and a widespread secularist-materialist philosophy have resulted in the childless union as a preferable model of marriage for many.[138]

The relationship between the conjugal community and the openness to procreation is fundamental. The obligation to accept children is essential to the marriage covenant. Those who consent to marriage with a firm purpose of avoiding all children or restricting their number consent invalidly.[139]

A careful distinction must be made between a temporary exclusion of children which invalidates and such an exclusion which does not. Numerous couples marry with a plan to avoid children for a time. The morality of artificial contraception notwithstanding, such exclusions become invalidating factors only when they are so firmly held that they take precedence over the marriage covenant.

Essential Properties

The essential properties of marriage are unity and indissolubility. An "essential property" is an aspect of marriage which is grounded in the covenantal relationship itself. It is essential because it is grounded in the essence of marriage itself. This is true of both natural and sacramental marriage, although the property of indissolubility is absolute in sacramental marriages (c. 1056).

Simulation regarding the property of unity has traditionally been understood within the context of marital fidelity. Strictly speaking, unity means having only one spouse. One who enters marriage with an intention of taking more than one spouse at the same time denies the right to unity. Such a formulation of an intention against unity is rare.

Simulation of marital unity can also take the form of an intention against marital fidelity. To exclude fidelity in this way means that a person enters marriage with a firm belief that he or she has a right to sexual relations with someone other than one's spouse.

Yet marital fidelity involves more than refraining from extra-marital sexual intercourse. It is an obligation which involves the whole person since the "one flesh" relationship which results from consent is neither limited to nor dependent on sexual intercourse alone. A division of this union can result from a deep interpersonal relationship with someone other than one's spouse if it amounts to emotional, psychological, spiritual, and sexual alienation from the spouse.

Although the exclusion of the obligation of fidelity has traditionally been understood in terms of a rejection of the right to sexual fidelity, the conciliar definition of the fundamental nature of marriage indicates that the exclusivity of the commitment needs to be viewed in broader terms. In short, fidelity involves not simply an exclusive right to intercourse but also a total commitment to the person of the spouse.[140]

The denial or exclusion of marital fidelity must be framed in terms of an absolute rejection of its obligations at the time of consent. The exclusion of the right and obligation of fidelity is distinct from acts which violate these rights and obligations. A person may violate fidelity, especially through adultery, yet the violation itself does not constitute proof of simulation. Being unfaithful may result from weakness, sin, or the psychological incapacity to be true to one person (e.g., hyperaesthesia). It may also result from the fact that the person was convinced from the beginning of the marriage that he or she had a right to adulterous relations.

Traditionally, jurisprudence has held to the distinction between the will to assume the obligations of fidelity and the will to assume but not to fulfill them. Persons who assumed these obligations, yet at the same time decided that they would not fulfill them, were not considered to have excluded fidelity. In light of the present understanding of marriage, the object of fidelity is not simply the right to intercourse but the right to the community of life. Consequently, this distinction is questionable. A person who assumes the obligation of fidelity but decides at the same time that he or she will not always fulfill it brings a destructive element to the community of life. The fidelity required must be total and directed to the person.

The property of indissolubility refers to the perpetual bond by which a man and woman are united in marriage for life. It is intrinsic to the marriage covenant and cannot be qualified in any way. A person cannot marry (validly) with the condition that he or she is obliged to remain married only as long as love lasts or there is human satisfaction. Indissolubility is excluded if a person firmly believes that he or she has a right to a subsequent marriage if the first union ends or that there is no obligation

[137]See M. Ahern, "The Marital Right to Children: a Tentative Re-examination," *Stud Can* 8 (1974), 91–108.

[138]For an attempt to justify childless marriages, see D. Doherty, "Childfree Marriage—a Theological View," *CS* 18 (1979), 137–145.

[139]Hudson, 134–137.

[140]See T. Doyle, "A New Look at the 'Bonum Fidei,'" *Stud Can* 12 (1978), 5–40.

of fidelity to the first bond. Unlike the values of fidelity and openness to children, there is no distinction between indissolubility itself and acts which might violate it. The very intent to enter a dissoluble union constitutes an exclusion of this property.

A person can exclude indissolubility in more than one way. He or she can explicitly reject it as an essential property of marriage. There can also be an implicit rejection based on an erroneous understanding of the nature of marriage. A deep-seated error which influences the will can be the basis for a denial not only of the right to indissolubility but also of the rights to marital fidelity and potentially procreative intercourse.[141]

Conditional Marriage

Canon 1102 — §1. Marriage based on a condition concerning the future cannot be contracted validly.

§2. Marriage based on a condition concerning the past or the present is valid or invalid, insofar as the subject matter of the condition exists or not.

§3. The condition mentioned in §2 cannot be placed licitly without the written permission of the local ordinary.

Since marriage begins by means of a contract or agreement between the parties, it is possible to place conditions on this agreement. A historical overview of the Church's canonical treatment of condition assists in understanding the present legislation. The 1917 Code and the present Code speak of three kinds of condition: past, present, and future. Each has a different effect on the validity of consent.

A condition in a legal agreement is a circumstance attached to it in such a way that the validity of the agreement depends on the fulfillment of the condition. The contract may be dissolved upon non-fulfillment of the condition or suspended until the condition is fulfilled. Since the marriage covenant begins with a bilateral agreement, it too has been subjected to conditions, at least in the Latin Church.

A true condition is a circumstance that directly influences marital consent and the conjugal community. A conditional consent is verified when a spouse places more importance on the fulfillment of the condition than on marriage itself. Thus the commitment to the marital community depends on the verification of the condition rather than on the free gift of self and the complete acceptance of the other.

For a circumstance to be a true condition, it must ordinarily have real and objective importance and touch upon the marital relationship. Yet a cir-

cumstance can be so subjectively important to a person that the validity of consent is affected if it is not verified.

A true condition is traditionally distinguished from:

> (a) a *mode* which is an accessory clause attached to consent which has already been given, e.g., "I now marry you, but afterward you must start going to church";

> (b) a *cause* which is a reason for the marriage but upon which free consent does not depend, e.g., "I am marrying you because you will become wealthy";

> (c) a *demonstration* which highlights some quality that is presumed in a future spouse, e.g., "I marry you who are Caucasian."[142]

In all of the above examples, the circumstance accompanies consent in some way; yet, the consent does not depend upon it.

Canon law refers to conditions based on circumstances in the *past, present,* and *future*. A future condition is related to a circumstance that must happen after consent is exchanged. Present and past conditions are based on circumstances which already exist at the time of the marriage.

Historical Synthesis

An overview of the historical development of the law on conditioned marriage is helpful in understanding the contemporary legislation. It is also closely related to the evolution of the law on simulation.

The controversy on conditioned marriage began with Gratian's mention of it in the *Decretum*. He stated that the validity of marriage should not be contingent on some future event. Therefore, it was to be contracted absolutely or not at all.[143]

Later, Raymond of Penafort inserted into the Gregorian collection a general decretal which was intended to clarify all legal doubts and summarize the Church's law on the matter.[144] This decretal distinguished between honest conditions, shameful or impossible conditions, and conditions contrary to the substance of marriage. The canonists immediately began to study the decretal and agreed that

---

[142]Wrenn, *Annulments,* 220–221.

[143]c 8 C 27 q 2, *CorpusIC* 1, 1064.

[144]x 4 5 7, *CorpusIC* 2, 684: "Inasmuch as the marriage contract is favored, if conditions are inserted which are contrary to the substance of marriage, for example, if one says to the other: 'I contract with you if you avoid children,' or 'until I find another more suitable in honor or wealth,' or 'if you sell yourself for adultery,' it lacks no effect. Should other conditions be placed in marriage, if they are shameful or impossible, it is as if they were not added because of the favor of marriage" (author's translation).

---

[141]See D. Fellhauer, "The Exclusion of Indissolubility: Old Principles and New Jurisprudence," *Stud Can* 9 (1975), 135–152.

honest conditions concerning the future suspended the validity of marriage until they were fulfilled. Impossible, immoral, or sinful conditions which were contrary to the substance of marriage were considered as not having been made and, therefore, had no effect on validity. Future conditions contrary to the substance of marriage made consent invalid. The decretal lists three examples of conditions contrary to the substance of marriage, each being an example of violation of one of the goods of marriage.

What exactly constituted the substance of marriage? This question was not answered in the decretals, therefore, the commentators took it up. Although there was no agreement on a definition, many writers equated the substance of marriage with the three goods of marriage.

The 1917 Code retained the prior legislation on conditioned marriage and added a paragraph concerning past and present conditions (*CIC* 1092). The canon may be summed up as follows:

(a) Conditions based on future circumstances or events which are necessary, impossible, or immoral but not contrary to the substance of marriage have no effect on validity since they are considered not to have been made.

(b) A future condition which is contrary to the substance of marriage makes the marriage invalid while future conditions which are considered licit and not contrary to the substance of marriage suspend its validity until the condition is fulfilled.

(c) If conditions are made based on past or present circumstances, the validity of the marriage depends on whether or not they actually exist. If they do not, the marriage is invalid.

The present legislation is simpler than that of the 1917 Code. Future conditions of any kind may not be attached to marital consent. If such a condition is attached, even though it not be contrary to the substance of marriage, consent is invalid. Past and present conditions affect validity, depending on whether or not they actually are or were fulfilled. If a person wishes to attach a present or past condition to consent licitly, the local ordinary must grant permission to do so in *writing*.

Future Conditions

Conditioning a marriage on a future circumstance is a subtle matter insofar as the condition will sometimes be implicit. In spite of the invalidating prohibition against such marriages, people will probably continue to insert future conditions into marital consent.

Why would a person marry conditionally? One

of the parties might have doubts about the strength of the relationship and condition the marriage on future happiness. A prospective spouse might be in serious error about the nature or obligations of marriage, attaching a condition against future children, for example. Conceivably, an individual's personal value system is such that he or she implicitly conditions the marriage on the fulfillment of certain values. Here the value system of the society is highly significant in forming the individual's values.[145]

Wrenn's study of the effect of societal and personal value systems on conditioned marriages suggests that there may be a sizable number of invalid marriages as a result:

When all of these observations are taken together and when one realizes that a person may make a condition implicitly, that he can be motivated to do so not by any specific doubt but simply by objective circumstances, that he need not realize that by doing so he is vitiating or suspending the marriage, that his own value system and that of his peers is extremely important in precipitating the placing of the condition, and that the condition itself need only be something moderately specific to occur within a few years' time, when all of this is realized, it cannot but occur to us that there must be a fair number of conditioned marriages in our time that are going undetected.[146]

What is the circumstance underlying such a condition? Basically, it may be summed up as self-fulfillment.

In light of past jurisprudence, only true conditions contrary to the substance of marriage invalidate. Invalidity depends on proof that such a condition actually existed at the time of consent. Illicit future conditions may also be considered in terms of the exclusion of an element essential to marital consent. A future condition seriously modifies the free gift of self which is needed for consent. The existence and growth of the interpersonal conjugal community depend on the generosity of the spouses and not on the previous fulfillment of a condition.

It is significant that the present canon does not permit licit future conditions even though this had been possible in the Latin Church for centuries. The reasons for this change are not officially recorded, so one can only hypothesize what might have been the rationale of the marriage law committee. It is reasonable to believe that the canons on the nature of marriage (c. 1055) and consent (c. 1057) present an understanding of the marriage covenant that precludes even licit future conditions.

---

[145]Wrenn, "A New Condition Limiting Marriage," *J* 34 (1974), 292–315.

[146]Ibid., 307.

Past and Present Conditions

Past and present conditions do not have the same effect on consent as future conditions since they neither rule out the complete gift of self nor make the marital commitment contingent on some future event. A *past* condition is a circumstance that occurred prior to the time of consent which influences the perception, estimation, or identity of one spouse in the eyes of the other, e.g., "I marry you provided you have never been married before." A past condition refers to the existence or non-existence of a historical fact which has at least grave subjective importance for one of the spouses.

A *present* condition is based not on something that happened in the past or will happen in the future but on a circumstance directly related to a person at the time of consent. Such conditions are usually made in the form of implicit expectations, e.g., "I marry you if you are not an alcoholic, or terminally ill, or immoral." Such expectations could also be related to such factors as physical virginity, good family, legitimacy, practice of religion, particular occupation, etc.[147]

A person could be so influenced by life experiences that what would normally be an expected quality in a spouse becomes a condition sine qua non. A child of alcoholic parents could conceivably condition marriage on the fact that a spouse not drink. While legitimacy, family background, or virginity, for example, are not factors that are objectively necessary for a successful marriage, these or similar circumstances may be very important subjectively for a particular spouse.

The validity of a marriage which is based on a past or present condition depends on whether or not the reason for the condition exists. If it is an implicit condition and the discovery of its non-fulfillment alters a person's commitment to the extent that it is withdrawn, then the marriage was probably directly connected to the condition. If the discovery does not have a significant effect on one person's commitment to the other, then it cannot be said that the marriage was truly conditioned.

Although the canon does not distinguish between implicit and explicit conditions, past jurisprudence allows for both.[148] If one party insists on a past or present condition, then it is expressed explicitly after the written permission of the local ordinary is obtained. It should be noted that this requirement affects the liceity of the marriage only. The obvious reason for this regulation is to discourage conditioned marriages. Nevertheless, most such conditions will be placed implicitly, often without the realization that they may well have an effect on the validity of the union.[149]

[147]Doheny, 640–644.
[148]Wrenn, "A New Condition," 299–300.
[149]Wrenn, *Annulments,* 76–78.

Force and Fear

Canon 1103 — **A marriage is invalid if it is entered into due to force or grave fear inflicted from outside the person, even when inflicted unintentionally, which is of such a type that the person is compelled to choose matrimony in order to be freed from it.**

The marriage covenant can come into existence only through the free consent of the parties. Marital consent is not merely a contract like other contracts, but it is an act whereby the spouses freely commit themselves to each other totally. Therefore, it is improbable that true consent be the result of force and fear. In the first place, the consent is not free and in the second place, the marital community is based on a loving mutual commitment and not on aversion.

Legal acts which result from external force which cannot be resisted are invalid (c. 125, §1). *Force* is generally understood to be a physical or moral coercion from without which the person cannot resist. In this context the person chooses marriage in order to avoid the greater evil. If there were no outside force, the person would not choose marriage.

The threat may include bodily harm, or it may be moral pressure such as the threat of lawsuits, imprisonment, loss of reputation, employment, etc. Because of the presence of this force and the subsequent fear it induces in the person, freedom is so diminished that consent to the marriage appears to be the only possible way to escape the pressure.

Persons subject to grave force may consent by means of some external sign; but, if they otherwise would not have chosen marriage, it is highly doubtful that they are interiorly consenting to it.

Fear, on the other hand, comes from within. It is the intimidation of the mind which comes about precisely because of the external force. While fear can be so overpowering as to render a person temporarily irrational, it ordinarily diminishes but does not totally suppress the freedom to act. The law presumes a minimal degree of freedom in marriages entered because of force and fear, yet because of the nature of the marriage covenant, the consent is considered invalid.

In order to be invalidating, fear must be grave, extrinsic, and inescapable except through the marriage. The 1917 Code also demanded that it be *unjust* (*CIC* 1087); however, this requirement has been dropped in the present law. Whether fear is justly or unjustly inspired is of secondary importance if it is so strong that the person sees marriage as the sole and undesirable way of escaping the pressure.

Grave fear is that which compels a person to give consent which he or she would ordinarily not give. It may be objectively grave in that it arises from a source which would intimidate any reasonable person, e.g., loss of life or grave bodily harm. Such fear can also be subjectively grave, arising from a source which might sufficiently intimidate some but not others.

Extrinsic fear is that which is caused from a source outside of the person. It is not conjured up in the mind or imagined as a result of scrupulosity, autosuggestion, or even real circumstances. An unmarried pregnant teenager usually experiences fear simply because of the pregnancy. This fear is intrinsic; yet, if her parents threaten her with some form of force unless she marries, then her fear becomes extrinsic.

The person who exerts pressure, resulting in grave fear in another, need not intend to compel the person to marry. The fear then need not be inspired with a particular marriage in view but any marriage.

A related issue is the requirement that the fear be inescapable except through marriage. In the mind of the person experiencing the fear, the only possible relief is through marriage.

One of the indicators of fear is aversion for the marriage. There need not be an aversion to the spouse as such, but there must be an aversion to the marriage. Aversion is a strong dislike or repugnance for marriage since it is not freely entered.

There are numerous situations wherein some type of pressure inspires a grave fear compelling a person to marry. The usual example is the pressure experienced when a woman finds herself pregnant out of wedlock. Aside from this, persons have been forced to marry irrational suitors out of fear inspired by the threat of violence, blackmail, loss of reputation, etc.

Reverential Fear

Common fear is that which is inspired by a force or agent hostile to the person. It is distinguished in canon law from reverential fear, which is that by which a person is afraid to resist someone to whom he or she is subject. While there may well be a certain amount of hostility on the part of the person inducing the fear, this is not the overwhelming motivation.

In any relationship between parent and child, subject and superior, there is always the potential for fear on the part of the child or subject that he or she will incur the anger, disappointment, or rejection of the parent or superior as a result of certain kinds of behavior. If this is qualified by the threat of long-standing rejection or estrangement, this may prompt a fear which will induce the child or subject to act against his or her will to avoid what appears to be a greater evil.

The key factors in determining whether reverential fear seriously diminishes the freedom of the will are: (a) the nature of the relationship between the inferior and the superior, (b) the manner in which the fear is induced, and (c) the gravity of the resulting evil.

The freedom of the will is more easily diminished in a person having an unusually docile personality with a strong emotional or psychological dependence on a parent or superior than in a person exhibiting a marked degree of independence. The fear must not be imagined or anticipated, but must result from some form of pressure from the superior. It is not enough that the parent or superior simply ask the person to marry. This should be accompanied by such tactics as excessive cajoling, threats of disinheritance, expulsion from the home, loss of support and the like, or even threats of physical restraint or violence. The person need not be terrified but fearful to the extent that marital consent is seen as the only way to avoid the greater evil. Whatever the nature of the force which induces the fear, even if it amounts to a threat of permanent estrangement or indignation, if it weakens personal resolve against the marriage it can amount to invalidating fear.

Again, the most common example of invalidating reverential fear is that induced by parents over pregnancy out of wedlock. It can also be caused by anyone in authority for whom a person has respect. This respect need not be for the person precisely but for the office the person holds.

Cultural factors also affect the issue, particularly in societies or communities that still have arranged marriages. If the parent-child relationship is marked by a degree of subservience and unquestioning obedience, there is a high possibility of marriages entered into because of reverential fear.[150]

In all cases of invalidating reverential fear, the ordinary jurisprudential principles are operative: the fear must be grave and extrinsic. Furthermore, it must be at least subjectively escapable only by giving consent to marriage.

Presence of Spouses Required at Exchange of Consent

Canon 1104 — §1. In order for marriage to be contracted validly, it is necessary that the contracting parties be present together, either in person or by proxy.

§2. Those to be married are to express their matrimonial consent in words; however, if they cannot speak, they are to express it by equivalent signs.

Since the ministers of the sacrament of marriage are the spouses themselves, it follows that they must be present to one another when consent is ex-

[150]See R. Knopke, *Reverential Fear in Matrimonial Cases in Asiatic Countries: Rota Cases* (Washington, D.C.: Catholic University of America, 1949). Reverential fear is examined in pre-Communist China in the context of the still-existing patriarchal family.

changed. This mutual presence is required in non-sacramental marriages as well.

Prior to the 1917 Code marriage could be validly contracted by letter, usually for a grave reason.[151] The 1917 Code required the presence of the parties themselves, or their proxies, for validity. A survey of canonical literature does not reveal evidence of a dispensation having been granted from this law since the promulgation of the 1917 Code. The present canon repeats the prior law.

The spouses or their proxies must be present to each other at one and the same time so that consent may be given and received mutually in one ceremony. Consent may not be given by one party on one day in one place and received and then offered by the other party at another time in another place.

The spouses must manifest their consent by words if they can speak. If one or both are deaf and/or dumb, consent may be expressed by signs or written notes which express the intention of the will. In any case, there must be some visible sign of assent by both spouses.

Marriage rituals contain the formula ordinarily used in the exchange of consent.[152] The use of this formula is not binding for validity or liceity, thus allowing for formulas which may be more fitting or expressive in various cultural settings. The spouses may also ask to compose their own vow formula. This is permissible as long as the personalized vows express the basic essentials required for the exchange of consent, namely, the nature of the marriage covenant and the properties of unity and indissolubility without condition.

Marriages by Proxy

Canon 1105 — §1. In order for marriage to be entered validly by proxy, it is required that:

1° there be a special mandate to contract marriage with a certain person;

2° the proxy be appointed by the person who gave the mandate and that the proxy fulfill this function in person.

§2. To be valid a mandate must be signed by the person who gave it as well as by the pastor or the local ordinary where the mandate was issued, or by a priest delegated by either of these, or at least by two witnesses, or it must be arranged by means of a document which is authentic according to civil law.

§3. If the person giving the mandate cannot write, this is to be noted in the mandate itself and another witness is to be added who also must sign the document; otherwise, the mandate is invalid.

§4. If the person who gave the mandate revokes it or becomes insane before the proxy has contract- **ed the marriage in that person's name, the marriage is invalid even though either the proxy or the other contracting party was unaware of these developments.**

A proxy is an agent who expresses the will of a person or otherwise acts on a person's behalf after being duly appointed. Marriage by proxy is permitted when one or both of the spouses cannot be present to one another.

When marriage takes place by proxy, all other canonical and civil requirements for valid and licit marriage must be met. If consent is in any way withdrawn by either party prior to the proxy marriage, even though the proxy is not aware of it, the union is invalid since the validity depends on the actual consent of the parties themselves and not that of the proxies. The parties must meet all canonical requirements regarding an awareness of the nature of marriage and a willingness and capacity to accept its obligations. The intentions of the proxies have no bearing on marital validity.

The permission of the local ordinary is necessary for a licit proxy marriage (c. 1071, §1, 7°). Marriage by proxy usually takes place when it is impossible for the parties to be present to each other and there is an urgent need for the exchange of consent without delay. This could be the case in marriages involving soldiers during wartime or immigrants.

Although canon law permits proxy marriages, few states in the United States allow them.[153] Since the permission of the local ordinary is required for marriages not in conformity with civil law (c. 1071, §1, 2°), the civil status of proxy marriages must be investigated before one proceeds further.

Canon law requires no special ceremony for a proxy marriage, although the manifestation of consent is to take place before a duly authorized priest, deacon, or delegated lay person and two witnesses.[154] It is sufficient that the Church's official witness ask for and receive the consent which the proxies express in the name of the parties. It is not necessary that the parties be actually aware that consent is being exchanged by proxy at the time it is happening, provided they have not withdrawn consent. The proxies may be of either sex. They do not contract a legal relationship with the spouses or with each other by acting as agents nor does the validity of the marriage depend in any way on their personal intentions. The nuptial Mass and blessing are not explicitly forbidden in the *Rite of Marriage* or the *Sacramentary* as they were in the Tridentine Missal.[155] Nevertheless, the very nature of a proxy

[151]Ayrinhac-Lydon, 214.

[152]*The Rite of Marriage* (New York: Catholic Book, 1970), 24–25.

[153]Ploscowe and Foster: proxy marriages are allowed in Florida, Kansas, Oklahoma, Idaho, Iowa, Montana, Nebraska, Nevada and New Mexico. They are permitted in Texas only if the couple is separated because of military service. They are not authorized in the remaining states.

[154]DeSmet, 1, 79.

[155]*Missale Romanum*, xxvi, nn. 379–381.

marriage makes the full liturgical celebration out of place. It would be more fitting that the spouses participate in a special ceremony and receive the nuptial blessing when it is convenient for them to do so.

The Mandate

The canonical regulations concerning the mandate by which the proxy is appointed are binding for validity. Therefore, if the mandate is invalid, so is the marriage.

The mandate must be given in writing and must clearly state that the prospective spouse appoints a specific person to exchange consent with the other party to the marriage who is also specifically named. The proxy must express consent in person and cannot delegate this duty to someone else even though the party has agreed to this. In such cases another mandate is needed.

The mandate must be signed by the prospective spouse and the witness or witnesses specified in the canon. The prescribed witnesses are either the prospective spouse's parish priest or the local ordinary of the place where the mandate is issued. It may also be signed by another priest who has been delegated by either one of the above. In the absence of the pastor, local ordinary, or delegated priest, the mandate may be signed by two lay witnesses. The mandate can also take the form of a commission following a recognized civil law formula.[156] If the prospective spouse cannot write, this fact is to be noted in the mandate. Another witness must then sign the document, attesting to the fact that the person cannot write.

Consent Expressed through an Interpreter

Canon 1106 — Marriage can be contracted through an interpreter; however, the pastor is not to assist at such a marriage unless he is convinced of the interpreter's trustworthiness.

If the official minister and/or the witnesses cannot understand the language of the parties, an interpreter may be used. The minister is to be sure of the interpreter's trustworthiness so that what the parties are expressing is accurately conveyed to him.

The parties might not be able to communicate with each other in the same language and, therefore, need an interpreter to make themselves understood to each other. While this is theoretically possible, it poses certain pastoral problems. If they cannot speak the same language, then the ability to communicate is either impaired or practically nonexistent. In such cases the wisdom of the marriage itself should be seriously questioned.

Consent in Certain Invalid Marriages

Canon 1107 — Even if a marriage was entered invalidly by reason of an impediment or defect of form, the consent which was furnished is presumed to continue until its revocation has been proved.

If true consent is given in a marriage that is later declared null because of the presence of an impediment or a lack of canonical form, the consent itself is presumed to endure. The withdrawal of consent must be proved for it is not presumed. This canon is relevant to the institute of the *sanatio in radice* (cc. 1161–1165). If a marriage invalid due to an undispensed impediment or a lack of form is validated by a *sanatio,* the renewal of consent is not required (c. 1163).

CHAPTER V
THE FORM OF THE CELEBRATION OF MARRIAGE
[cc. 1108–1123]

The form for the celebration of marriage means the external formalities which accompany the exchange of consent. In the Latin Rite the spouses themselves are the ministers of the sacrament. In marriages of those not bound by the form, the consent of the spouses alone makes the marriage. By the requirement of form, the Church holds that certain formalities must be present when the exchange of consent takes place.

Since the Council of Trent canonical form has normally been required for the validity of marriages involving at least one Catholic. There is ample historical evidence to show that Christian marriages were often celebrated with religious ceremonies from the first century on. Prior to Trent the civil form of marriage sufficed for validity. Yet to ensure that the spouses accepted the Church's teaching on marriage, they were asked to go to the church for a blessing, and in time to exchange their consent before a church official.[157]

With the Middle Ages came the problem of clandestine, or secret, marriages. Since consent alone sufficed in the absence of rules for witnesses or the recording of the marriage, numerous marriages took place that could not be proven. This led to the problem of multiple marriages with no recorded proof of the true union. The solemnization of marriage was urged and even mandated during this time, but it was never necessary for validity. Consequently, the problems posed by clandestine marriages remained unresolved.

The Tridentine legislation (*Tametsi*) required that marriages be celebrated before the proper pastor of at least one of the parties or another priest

---

[156]Vicariate of Rome, private, 1953, *CLD* 4, 338–339. A proxy marriage was declared invalid due to the lack of the signatures of the witnesses.

[157]See J. Carberry, *The Juridical Form of Marriage* (Washington, D.C.: Catholic University of America, 1934), 7–20.

delegated by him. The presence of at least two witnesses was also necessary. Although this legislation was intended for the entire Church, it had binding force only in those countries where it was promulgated. Consequently, canonical form was initially required for validity only in certain dioceses.

After the decree *Tametsi* was issued, certain problems arose that necessitated a further clarification. The requirement of marriage before a proper pastor was one problem since it severely restricted where people could marry. The method of promulgation was another since entire countries were unaffected by the decree. The marriages of non-Catholics among themselves and mixed marriages posed certain other problems.

Heeding the requests of many bishops, the Holy See modified the Tridentine decree with the decree *Ne temere* of August 7, 1909. This decree extended the requirement of canonical form to the entire Latin Rite Church. The rule for valid assistance was modified by making territory its basis. Consequently, a bishop in his diocese or a pastor in his parish could witness the marriages of anyone actually in the territory. Also, the law of form bound all who were baptized in the Catholic Church or later converted to it, irrespective of whether or not they had been raised in the faith.

The 1917 Code retained the requirement of canonical form for validity but modified the rule on those who were bound (*CIC* 1099). Those who were baptized but never raised in the faith were not bound. This in turn caused problems in determining what was meant by Catholic upbringing. Pius XII settled the issue on August 1, 1948 by abrogating the last portion of the canon ("item . . . contraxerint"), thus restoring Catholic baptism alone as the basis for one's being bound by canonical form.

The obligation to observe canonical form serves a purpose beyond providing a means of proof that consent has been exchanged. The ancient tradition of urging Catholics to have their marriages solemnized as a sign of their willingness to live by the Church's teaching on marriage is also important. Furthermore, the fulfillment of this obligation puts the couple in contact with the Church prior to the wedding. Consequently, the canonical requirements regarding pre-marital investigations and preparation can be more effectively fulfilled.

The Meaning of Canonical Form

Canon 1108 — §1. Only those marriages are valid which are contracted in the presence of the local ordinary or the pastor or a priest or deacon delegated by either of them, who assist, and in the presence of two witnesses, according to the rules expressed in the following canons, with due regard for the exceptions mentioned in cann. 144, 1112, §1, 1116 and 1127, §§2 and 3.

§2. The one assisting at a marriage is understood to be only that person who, present at the ceremony, asks for the contractants' manifestation of consent and receives it in the name of the Church.

This canon explains the meaning of canonical form and the role of the Church's official witness. Canonical form is distinguished from liturgical form, the latter being the rites and ceremonies which accompany the exchange of consent. As will be seen, it is possible to observe the liturgical form without observing canonical form.

Marriages involving at least one Catholic must normally take place in the presence of three persons: the Church's official witness and two other witnesses.

The official witness is usually the local ordinary, the pastor, or a priest or deacon delegated by either one. He is to observe the subsequent canons on canonical form. This canon also mentions those instances in which the absence of the Church's official witness does not result in marital invalidity.

In addition to the official witness, two other witnesses are required. They must have the use of reason and be capable of comprehending what is happening in the exchange of consent. Although a minimum age is not mentioned, witnesses cannot be below the presumed age of reason. There appear to be few other restrictions on the witnesses. They may be of the same or of different sexes. While the witnesses are usually lay persons, clergy and religious may act in this capacity. They need not be Catholic or even baptized, since their sole function is to attest to the fact that the marriage took place. The witnesses are not required by canon law to sign any documents, although their names must be inscribed in the marriage register. In some civil jurisdictions they may be required to sign a civil register or a marriage certificate.

Since the witnesses must be capable of comprehending what is happening, those who are incapable, even if temporarily, may not be witnesses. This would include the intoxicated, the insane, infants, or the deaf and dumb.[158]

The Church's official witness has an active role to play in the ceremony. He *must* ask for and receive the consent of the parties in the name of the Church. This is provided for in the revised ritual wherein the celebrant asks the parties three questions and then asks them to express their consent.

The official witness must always ask for and receive the consent of *both* parties and not merely one of them.[159] One may envision situations in which other priests or deacons are present or mixed marriages with a non-Catholic minister present. In such cases those other than the official witness merely observe the exchange of consent, although they may fulfill other liturgical roles.

[158]Wernz-Vidal 5, 685–686.
[159]SCDF, private reply, Nov. 28, 1975, *CLD* 8, 820–822.

The Official Witness

Canon 1109 — **Unless through a sentence or decree they have been excommunicated, interdicted or suspended from office or declared such, in virtue of their office the local ordinary and the pastor validly assist within the confines of their territory at the marriages of their subjects as well as of non-subjects provided one of the contractants is of the Latin rite.**

Functioning as an official witness at marriages is a quasi-jurisdictional act. Ordinarily it is based on the concept of territory. The local ordinary and the pastor of a parish have the ordinary power to witness marriages of their own subjects and anyone else actually in their territory. Non-subjects need not even have a quasi-domicile or temporary residence. They must merely be physically present for the wedding. The notion of territory is not restricted to the parish church but includes the extent of the area within the defined boundaries of the diocese or parish.

Included under the category of local ordinary are all the authority figures equivalent to them in law. Therefore, vicars general, apostolic administrators, diocesan administrators, vicars apostolic, and prefects apostolic have this power. The same is true of those equivalent to pastors, namely, administrators, quasi-pastors, and all priest members of parochial teams (c. 543).

Those who have the power to witness marriages by reason of the office they hold (local ordinary, pastor, etc.) do so validly only after they have assumed it and for as long as they hold it. Those who leave their office through retirement or expiration of the office obviously lose the power to witness marriages. If the officeholder is under sentence or decree of excommunication, interdict, or suspension, he loses the power to assist validly at marriages. However, automatic penalties which are not declared do not suspend the power to witness marriages. A cleric who attempts marriage incurs an automatic suspension (c. 1394, §1) and loses any ecclesiastical office he holds as well (c. 194, §1, 3°). Consequently, priests or bishops who attempt marriage lose the power to assist validly at marriage.

At least one party to the marriage must be a member of the Latin Rite. A Latin pastor cannot validly witness a marriage between two Oriental Rite Catholics or a mixed marriage if the Catholic party is a member of an Oriental Rite. For the validity of such marriages, the ordinary of at least one of the parties must delegate the faculty to assist to the Latin Rite minister. Furthermore a Latin or Oriental priest must seek the permission of the Apostolic Pro-Nuncio, besides the appropriate faculty from the proper ordinary, if the former wishes to assist at the marriage of two people, neither of whom is a member of his rite. This requirement does not affect the validity of the union, provided the priest is properly delegated.

If, however, both parties to the marriage belong to an Oriental Rite that has no organized hierarchy in the country, they are subject to the jurisdiction of the local Latin ordinary. In such cases the Latin ordinary or pastor may validly assist at marriage.

Presently the faithful of the following Oriental Rites have ordinaries (Eparchs or Exarchs) in the United States: Byzantine-Ruthenian, Byzantine-Ukrainian, Byzantine-Rumanian, Melkite, Maronite, Chaldean, and Armenian. Members of the other Oriental Rites are under the jurisdiction of the Latin ordinaries.

It is important to understand the principles of acquisition of membership in Ritual Churches. In the 1917 Code a person automatically became a member of the rite of his or her parents. If the parents were of two different rites, the child took the rite of the father (*CIC* 98, 756). Although children were to be baptized in their proper rite, baptism by a sacred minister of another rite did not affect membership in the child's proper rite, e.g., a child of Byzantine parents baptized by a Latin priest is still a member of the Byzantine Rite.

In the present Code one's rite is determined by parentage. If the parents are of different rites, they may mutually decide upon the rite of baptism. If they cannot agree, the child is to be baptized in the father's rite and hence acquires membership in that rite (c. 111, §1). A person may also transfer from one rite to another by apostolic indult (c. 112, §1). A convert may choose the rite to which he or she wishes to belong.

This point is important since members of Oriental Rites often do not know that they are such if they have been raised in a Latin Rite setting.

Personal Ordinaries and Pastors

Canon 1110 — **In virtue of their office and within the limits of their jurisdiction an ordinary and a personal pastor validly assist only at marriages involving at least one of their subjects.**

A personal ordinary or pastor is one whose jurisdiction is not based on territory but is related to a specifically determined class of people. Such jurisdiction could include people of a specific rite, language, or nationality, or it could be based on some other criterion (c. 518). Consequently, military ordinaries and chaplains can be included in this category since their jurisdiction and pastoral care are limited to specific classifications of persons.

Those ordinaries and pastors with personal jurisdiction may validly assist at the marriages of their subjects only within the limits of their jurisdiction. These limits can be geographical if a personal parish is so established that it includes all the persons of a given language or nationality within specified boundaries. This would be the case if more than one personal parish exists in a given territory. The pastor or ordinary may assist at marriages if at least one party is his subject.

A personal pastor apparently cannot delegate another priest or deacon to witness a marriage in his church if neither of the parties is subject to him. This is because his jurisdiction is limited to his subjects only.

Delegation

Canon 1111 — §1. As long as they validly hold office, the local ordinary and the pastor can delegate to priests and deacons the faculty, even a general one, to assist at marriages within the limits of their territory.

§2. To be valid the delegation of the faculty to assist at marriages must be given expressly to specified persons; if it is a question of a special delegation, it is to be granted for a specific marriage; however, if it is a question of a general delegation, it is to be granted in writing.

Those who have the power to assist at marriage because of the office they hold may delegate this power as long as they hold the office. This delegation may be general, for all marriages in the territory, or for a specific marriage only.

General delegation is the grant of delegation to a specific priest or deacon to assist at all marriages within the territory. It may be given by the local ordinary or by the pastor and must be in writing. If general delegation is not given in writing, it is presumed not to have been granted.

Specific delegation is that granted to a specific priest or deacon for a specific marriage. Such delegation need not be given in writing, yet the fact must be noted in the marriage register.

Those with delegated faculties may also subdelegate, that is, empower still another priest or deacon to witness the marriage for which they had been given delegated authority. There are limits, however, on the power to subdelegate validly. Those with general delegation may subdelegate but only to a specific priest or deacon for a specific marriage. One who has subdelegated power may not again subdelegate another priest or deacon. If, however, the person who delegates by reason of office or general delegation specifically states that subdelegated power may be again subdelegated, then this may be done validly (c. 137, §4).

Lay Persons as Official Witnesses

Canon 1112 — §1. With the prior favorable opinion of the conference of bishops and after the permission of the Holy See has been obtained, the diocesan bishop can delegate lay persons to assist at marriages where priests or deacons are lacking.

§2. A suitable lay person is to be chosen who is capable of giving instructions to those to be wed and qualified to perform the marriage liturgy correctly.

The power to act as an official witness at a marriage is a commission to witness the exchange of consent in the name of the Church. It is not an act that requires sacred orders nor is it an act of jurisdiction in the strict sense. In cases of true pastoral need the law provides for the delegation of lay persons to act as official witnesses to marriage. Lay men and women and non-clerical religious may be delegated to act as official witnesses.

There are certain restrictions on delegating lay persons. First, the conference of bishops must vote to allow individual bishops to request the power to delegate. If the conference of bishops votes favorably, the bishop must then request the permission of the Holy See to delegate a person specifically chosen by him to assist at marriages within his territory. The lay person is delegated by the bishop and not by the Holy See, however, without permission of the Holy See, a bishop cannot do so validly.

This permission is to be requested only when a priest or deacon cannot be present to witness the ceremony. This includes those who would officiate by reason of office as well as delegated priests or deacons. While this usually applies to situations in which the scarcity of sacred ministers renders their presence physically impossible, such as in mission territories, there are other possibilities. There might be no priests or deacons capable of communicating with immigrant groups. In such cases pastoral needs might well be met by the delegation of lay persons from within the group. The delegation of lay persons to officiate at marriages is an exceptional option and is not intended as an alternative to priests and deacons as ordinary official witnesses for marriage.

Lay persons may be given delegation for a specific marriage or they may be given general delegation. The individual to be delegated must be personally selected by the ordinary who may not delegate the power of selection.[160] The lay person must first of all be suitable, that is, a respected member of the Catholic community. He or she must be capable of fulfilling the requirements for pre-marital investigation and preparation and of conducting the special wedding liturgy.

Lay persons acting as official witnesses may preside at a liturgy of the word and give an exhortation on Christian marriage. They also ask for and receive the consent of the parties. However, because they lack sacred orders, they can neither give the nuptial blessing nor bless wedding rings. Since this concession is solely to act as an official witness, the

---

[160]SCSacr, *Sacramentalem indolem*, May 15, 1974, *CLD* 8, 817.

lay person cannot dispense from any of the matrimonial impediments.[161]

Obligations of the Delegated Witness

Canon 1113 — **Before special delegation is granted, all the legal requirements for establishing freedom to marry are to have been fulfilled.**

Whenever special delegation is granted, the usual requirements for freedom to marry must be met. Since the delegated witness acts in the name of the Church, those whose consent they witness must be free to marry and willing and capable of fulfilling the marital obligations.

Responsibilities of the Official Witness

Canon 1114 — **The person who assists at the celebration of a marriage acts illicitly unless the freedom of the contracting parties has been established in accord with the norm of law and the permission of the pastor has been obtained, if possible, when one is functioning in virtue of general delegation.**

This canon reinforces the obligation to determine that the prospective spouses are free to marry. The priest or deacon delegated to witness the marriage must first be certain that the parties are free to marry. Even though the pre-marital investigation might be conducted by someone else, the priest or deacon who will witness the marriage is responsible.

Before the wedding, those who assist by reason of general delegation should also obtain the permission of the pastor of the parish where the wedding will take place. This permission is not delegation, for it is presumed that the assisting priest is already delegated. This permission reflects a deference to the pastor, whose right it is to witness marriages in his parish (c. 530, 4°). Failure to obtain permission does not affect the validity and probably not even liceity of the marriage, since the canon includes the qualifying words "if possible."

The Place of Marriage

Canon 1115 — **Marriages are to be celebrated in the parish where either of the contractants has a domicile, quasi-domicile or month-long residence; the marriages of transients are to be celebrated in the parish where they actually reside; marriages can be celebrated elsewhere with the permission of the proper ordinary or pastor.**

If both parties to the marriage are Catholic, the celebration may take place in the parish church where either party has a domicile, quasi-domicile, or a month's residence. Mixed marriages are ordi-

narily celebrated in the parish church of the Catholic party unless the local ordinary or the pastor has granted permission for the marriage to take place elsewhere (c. 1118, §1) or a dispensation from canonical form has been obtained (cf. c. 1127, §2).

While the marriages of transients are to be celebrated in the parish where they are actually staying, such marriages are subject to the approval of the local ordinary (c. 1071, §1, 1°).

In mixed rite marriages, Oriental law stipulates that the celebration is to take place in the church of the groom (*Crebrae allatae*, c. 88, 3). Marriages celebrated in the church of the bride are both valid and licit but ordinarily require the permission of the groom's pastor.

Extraordinary Form of Marriage

Canon 1116 — **§1. If the presence of or access to a person who is competent to assist at marriage in accord with the norm of law is impossible without serious inconvenience, persons intending to enter a true marriage can validly and licitly contract it before witnesses alone:**
1° in danger of death;
2° outside the danger of death, as long as it is prudently foreseen that such circumstances will continue for a month.
§2. In either case and with due regard for the validity of a marriage celebrated before witnesses alone, if another priest or deacon who can be present is readily available, he must be called upon and must be present at the celebration of the marriage, along with the witnesses.

The Church recognizes that there may be circumstances when it would be difficult, if not impossible, to have a sacred minister or delegated lay person present to witness a marriage officially. Since the spouses themselves are the ministers, the law provides for the extraordinary form of marriage. Under certain circumstances, only if an official witness cannot be present, the spouses may validly exchange consent in the presence of two witnesses.

The use of the extraordinary form presupposes that the parties are free to marry, capable of sustaining a marital covenant, and not otherwise bound by a diriment impediment. Use of the extraordinary form does not include an implicit dispensation from impediments. The parties must intend to enter a valid marriage even though they may not be fully aware of the meaning of the extraordinary form.

Grave Inconvenience

If either party is in danger of death, a valid marriage may be contracted before witnesses alone. This does not mean imminent death but danger of death; a situation wherein there is a reasonable chance that death may occur due to illness, im-

[161]Ibid., 818.

pending surgery, war, or even execution. The key point is that an official witness cannot be contacted or approached without grave inconvenience. It must be difficult *both* for the parties to approach a sacred minister and for the minister to go to the parties.

The grave inconvenience may be due to distance, lack of means of communication, or lack of transportation. In this case it amounts to physical impossibility. The inconvenience may also be caused by the moral impossibility of the official witness being present. This could be true during wartime or in areas where Catholics are persecuted. Civil laws may forbid any religious marriages or a given marriage itself. If such a sanction were unjust, e.g., legislation forbidding interracial marriages, it could be construed that the official witness cannot be present due to grave inconvenience. There is no taxative list of circumstances which constitute grave inconvenience and justify use of the extraordinary form. However, grave inconvenience does not include those situations in which an official witness is prevented from being present due to an ecclesiastical prohibition of the marriage in question, i.e., prior bond or undispensed impediment.

The extraordinary form may be used outside of danger of death if it is foreseen that an official witness cannot be contacted or approached without grave inconvenience for a period of one month. If the parties are morally certain that the situation which prevents the official witness from being present will not change, they may exchange consent before the other witnesses alone. Even if the parties err in the assumption and an official witness may be conveniently had within a month, the marriage is still valid. It is also valid if through their own fault, the parties find themselves in a situation requiring the extraordinary form.

Two Witnesses

The canon states that marriage may be contracted before witnesses alone. Accordingly, it envisions two witnesses of either the same or of different sexes. They must have the use of reason and be capable of attesting to the fact that consent was exchanged.

In spite of the clarity of the canon, some commentators on the 1917 Code believed that in extreme circumstances a marriage would be valid before one witness or even no witnesses.[162]

[162]Carberry, 142; 155. The author cites three canonists who hold the probable opinion that in extreme circumstances marriages contracted with no witnesses would be valid: Gasparri, Vromant, and Wouters. In his concluding comments on the section, the author states on p. 155: "In extraordinary circumstances if no witnesses are available marriage would be validly celebrated without them. In such cases a marriage is valid because the natural right to marry will prevail over the ecclesiastical law which prescribes the canonical form; in such circumstances its validity does not arise from the use of the canon 1098."

The second paragraph refers to the availability of an undelegated, and therefore unauthorized, priest or deacon. If such a minister is available, he is to be summoned even though he is not delegated to witness the marriage. His presence is not required for the validity of the exchange of consent. He may, but is not bound to, interrogate the parties and ask for and receive their consent. Such a priest or deacon does, however, enjoy the faculty to dispense from certain ecclesiastical law impediments according to canons 1079–1080.

Those Bound by the Form

Canon 1117 — With due regard for the prescriptions of can. 1127, §2, the form stated above is to be observed whenever at least one of the contractants was baptized in the Catholic Church or was received into it and has not left it by a formal act.

Latin Rite Catholics are normally bound to observe the canonical form of marriage as outlined in the above-mentioned canons. This includes those who are baptized in the Catholic Church and those baptized in another Christian denomination but later received into the Catholic Church as converts. Catholics who were baptized but not raised in the Church and those who later ceased practicing the faith are also bound by this obligation.

Baptized Catholics who have left the Church by a formal act are not bound to observe the form of marriage. Consequently their marriages are considered valid and cannot be declared null due to defect of canonical form if they do not observe it.

Since the canon does not define precisely the meaning of departure by a formal act, there are various possibilities. Those who become members of another Christian or non-Christian denomination or make a formal profession of atheism are considered to have left by a formal act. To prove such adherence it is not necessary to produce a written document but merely evidence by which they may be considered to have definitely left the Catholic Church.

The Place of Celebration

Canon 1118 — §1. Marriage between Catholics or between a Catholic and a baptized non-Catholic party is to be celebrated in a parish church; with the permission of the local ordinary or the pastor, it can be celebrated in another church or oratory.

§2. The local ordinary can permit marriage to be celebrated in some other suitable place.

§3. Marriage between a Catholic party and a non-baptized party can be celebrated in a church or in some other suitable place.

The canons have already referred to marriage within a parish (c. 1115) but not to the place of the celebration itself. The proper and ordinary place for the celebration of marriage is the parish church.

The celebration of marriage between Catholics or between a Catholic and a baptized non-Catholic is a sacramental celebration and not merely a public witnessing of a private commitment between two persons. It is also a special commitment to a new dimension of life within the Christian community. This is especially true if both parties are Catholics, yet two baptized Christians who may not share the same religious tradition presumably also make such a commitment. Because of the relationship of the marriage covenant to the local Christian community or parish, it is most fitting that the ceremony take place in the parish church.

Marriages between two Catholics may take place in the parish church of the groom or the bride. A marriage between a Catholic and baptized non-Catholic should take place in the parish church of the Catholic party unless a dispensation from canonical form has been granted (cf. c. 1127, §2). Until the *motu proprio Matrimonia mixta* (March 31, 1970), marriages between Catholics and non-Catholics were to take place outside of the parish church, usually in the rectory.

Marriages may also be celebrated in churches or oratories other than the parish church, including private oratories. This refers to Catholic churches or oratories and includes shrines, non-parochial churches, and chapels of religious houses, colleges, seminaries, and hospitals. The permission of the local ordinary or pastor is required: the permission of the pastor of one of the parties to celebrate a marriage in another parish church (and presumably that of the pastor of the other church) and the local ordinary's permission to celebrate in a non-parochial church or oratory. In all such cases the officiating minister must obtain the required delegation to assist either from the pastor of the territorial parish within which the marriage will be celebrated or from the local ordinary.

The local ordinary may also permit a marriage to be celebrated in another suitable place other than a Catholic church or chapel. The determination of what is suitable is left to the local ordinary. One might envision here churches of other denominations, halls, or even private homes. The choice of place must always take into consideration the fact that the celebration of marriage is a sacred event which should not be secularized by the surroundings of the ceremony. Again, the proper delegation from the territorial pastor or local ordinary is always required.

Although marriages between Catholics and non-baptized persons are not sacramental, they are nevertheless religious events in which Christ the Lord is called upon to witness the exchange of consent. Such marriages should ordinarily be celebrated in the parish church of the Catholic party or in another suitable place. In the latter case, the local ordinary's permission is not required, yet the officiating minister should act prudently in light of the sacred character of the ceremony and any diocesan guidelines on this subject.

The Liturgical Form of Marriage

Canon 1119 — Outside of a case of necessity, the rites prescribed in the liturgical books approved by the Church or received through legitimate customs are to be observed in the celebration of marriage.

The liturgical form of marriage is the ceremonial context in which the canonical form is expressed. The rite of marriage as contained in the liturgical books of the Latin Church is to be followed.[163] The revised rite contains certain options which afford greater latitude in the choice of prayers, blessings, and readings than in the past.

The essential element of the ritual is the exchange of consent. Except in those cases in which canonical form has been dispensed from or the parties marry according to extraordinary form, the official witness must ask for and receive the exchange of consent. In addition to the exchange of consent, the ritual stresses the liturgy of the word which should usually be celebrated even if the ceremony takes place without a Mass.

If the ceremony takes place within the Mass, the nuptial Mass with its particular readings is to be used. If, however, the wedding takes place on a Sunday or solemnity, the Mass of the day is celebrated. On Sundays during the Christmas season, as well as ordinary Sundays throughout the year, the readings from the nuptial Mass may be used.

The norms for the nuptial blessing are contained in the rite of marriage. These no longer restrict the giving of the nuptial blessing as in the past. Hence it may be given to the same person more than once, at marriages celebrated outside of Mass, and during any liturgical season.

Local liturgical customs may be followed, provided these are approved by the competent authority. A legitimate custom must be distinguished from either an ad hoc adaptation of the ritual in whole or in part or the substitution of purely secular practices for elements of the liturgy.

In case of necessity, all elements of the ritual may be eliminated with the exception of the exchange of consent. There must always be some expression of consent since this is the essential means whereby the marriage covenant comes into existence. Among the cases of necessity one might note marriage in danger of death, the use of the extraordi-

---

[163] *The Rite of Marriage*, Mar. 19, 1969 (New York: Catholic Book, 1970).

nary form, or situations in which there has been a dispensation from canonical form.

Particular Rituals

Canon 1120 — **The conference of bishops can draw up its own marriage ritual, to be reviewed by the Holy See; such a ritual, in harmony with the usages of the area and its people adapted to the Christian spirit, must provide that the person assisting at the marriage be present, ask for the manifestation of the contractants' consent and receive it.**

Both the present Code and the liturgical books mention the competence of the conference of bishops to compose and approve of a particular ritual for the celebration of marriage. Such local or particular rituals must embody the Christian spirit and provide for the role of the Church's official witness in the exchange of consent. The *Rite for the Celebration of Marriage* (introduction, nn. 12–18) contains guidelines for composing such rituals. Particular care must be taken when non-Christian symbolism is considered, lest it detract from the overall Christian significance of the ceremony.

If more than one particular ritual is composed for a given region, it is within the competence of the conference of bishops and not the local ordinary to grant the appropriate approval.

Registration of Marriages

Canon 1121 — **§1. After a marriage has been celebrated, the pastor of the place of celebration or the person who takes his place, even if neither has assisted at the marriage, should as soon as possible note the following in the marriage register: the names of the spouses, the person who assisted and the witnesses, the place and date of the marriage celebration; these notations are to be made in accord with the method prescribed by the conference of bishops or the diocesan bishop.**

§2. Whenever a marriage is contracted in accord with can. 1116, if a priest or deacon was present at the celebration he is bound to inform the pastor or the local ordinary concerning the marriage entered as soon as possible; otherwise, the witnesses jointly with the contractants are bound to do so.

§3. If the marriage has been contracted with a dispensation from canonical form, the local ordinary who granted the dispensation is to see that the dispensation and the celebration are inscribed in the marriage register at the curia and at the parish of the Catholic party whose pastor made the investigation concerning their free state; the Catholic spouse is bound to inform the same ordinary and pastor as soon as possible of the celebration of the marriage, the place of celebration and the public form that was observed.

The pastor of the parish in which the marriage takes place is responsible for seeing that the required information is inscribed in the parish marriage register. If there is no pastor, it is the responsibility of the one who takes his place.

The official witness at the marriage is not responsible for its registration if he is one other than the pastor. If the marriage is performed in a parish church or within a parish other than the proper parish of the bride or groom, the pastor who registers the marriage need not notify the proper parish of either the bride or groom.

The conference of bishops or the diocesan bishop can decide on the manner of registering marriages, that is, on the proper formularies or registry books to be used.

When marriage is celebrated according to the extraordinary form, the non-delegated priest or deacon who may be present (c. 1116) is to inform the pastor of the place where the marriage took place or the local ordinary, who in turn is to see to it that the marriage is properly registered in that parish.

If no priest or deacon were present at the celebration, the witnesses (or at least one of them) are to inform the pastor of the place or the local ordinary, attesting to the fact that the marriage took place.

If a dispensation from canonical form has been granted, the local ordinary who granted the dispensation is to see to it that the marriage is registered in the diocesan archives and in the parish of the Catholic party. The local ordinary is understood to be the ordinary of the Catholic party since he alone may grant such a dispensation (c. 1127, §2).

The local ordinary must also inform the pastor of the parish where the pre-marriage investigation took place. Even if this investigation is carried out by a priest or deacon not assigned to parish ministry or by a visitor, the marriage must be registered in the parish.

The local ordinary of the Catholic party is the ordinary of the diocese in which the person has either domicile or quasi-domicile (c. 107). The local ordinary of the place where the Catholic party is staying temporarily is not considered his or her own ordinary, unless he or she has only a diocesan domicile or quasi-domicile or has no domicile or quasi-domicile at all.

After a marriage has been celebrated with a dispensation from canonical form, the Catholic party is obliged to inform his or her local ordinary and the above-mentioned pastor of the fact and place of the marriage, and the public form observed in the ceremony.

Usually this information is required in the petition for the dispensation, yet it is to be verified afterward by the Catholic party. It is the responsibility of the priest or deacon who conducts the pre-marital investigation to advise the Catholic of this obligation.

Notification of Church of Baptism

Canon 1122 — §1. The contracted marriage is also to be noted in the baptismal register in which the baptism of the spouses has been inscribed.

§2. If the marriage was contracted in a parish where a spouse was not baptized, the pastor of the place where it was celebrated is to send a notice of the contracted marriage as soon as possible to the pastor where the baptism was conferred.

The pastor of the place where the marriage took place is also responsible for notifying the pastor of the church of baptism of the Catholic parties of the fact of the marriage. This is to be done when marriage is celebrated according to form and with a dispensation from form. It is not necessary to notify the church of baptism of baptized non-Catholics, although this may be done as a courtesy.

The baptismal register should indicate not only the fact of baptism but also the reception of confirmation, profession of perpetual religious vows, and the reception of sacred orders. One step in the investigation of freedom to marry is the obtaining of a recently issued certificate of baptism. This certificate should mention the specifics of baptism as well as other pertinent notations such as marriage.

Other Information for the Baptismal Register

Canon 1123 — Whenever a marriage is convalidated in the external forum, is declared null or is legitimately dissolved other than by death, the pastor of the place where it was celebrated must be informed so that a notation may be duly made in the marriage and baptismal registers.

The baptismal register is to contain other notations pertinent to the person's marital status. If a marriage is dissolved by the Pauline privilege or the privilege of the faith, this fact is to be noted along with the date of the dissolution and the protocol number of the official document. So too the dissolution of ratified but non-consummated marriages is to be noted.

If a putative marriage is declared null by an ecclesiastical tribunal, this too is to be noted in the baptismal register with the date, protocol number of the document, and name of the tribunal which declared the nullity. Marriages convalidated in the internal forum are registered only in the diocesan secret archives, noting the fact of convalidation and whether it was by simple convalidation or radical sanation (cf. cc. 1156–1165). It is not necessary to make a notation of marriages terminated by death.

Usually the diocesan curia handling either a dissolution or a nullity case sends these notices directly to the churches of baptism. A similar notification is sent to the parish where the marriage took place to be entered in the marriage register.

This information is required only when it refers to marriages which were attempted or celebrated in the Catholic Church or with a dispensation from form. Marriages which are null by reason of simple defect of form are not considered putative. There is no obligation to inform the churches of baptism when such marriages are declared null.

CHAPTER VI
MIXED MARRIAGES
[cc. 1124–1129]

The term "mixed marriages" refers in the broad sense to marriages between Catholics and non-baptized persons (disparity of cult marriages) and those between Catholics and baptized non-Catholics. In the strict sense the term refers to a sacramental union between a Catholic and baptized non-Catholic. The 1917 Code referred to these marriages as those involving the impediment of "mixed religion" (*CIC* 1061).

The Church has always shown concern for marriages between Catholics and members of other Christian denominations. The question first arose with the problem of marriages between Catholics and members of heretical or schismatic sects. Certain early church councils legislated against marriages with Jews or heretics.[164]

During the twelfth and thirteenth centuries marriages of Catholics with heretics were clearly forbidden, yet they were considered to be valid unions, based on the baptism of each party.[165] During this period there is no evidence either of papal or episcopal dispensation for mixed marriages. This question apparently did not arise until after the Council of Trent.

Trent did not address mixed marriages directly, yet they were indirectly prohibited by the decree *Tametsi*. Pastors were forbidden to witness the marriages of Catholics and heretics unless the heretic had formally abjured his or her errors.

In the eighteenth century the Church began to grant dispensations to allow Catholics to enter mixed marriages. At first these were reserved to the pope and were contingent on the renunciation of the heresy. The elements of grave cause and required promises of the parties regarding the practice of the faith and the raising of the children were prerequisites for the dispensation. By the end of the eighteenth century, bishops, especially those in mission territories, were receiving the faculties to dispense.

The fundamental reason for prohibiting marriages with non-Catholics, whether baptized or not,

---

[164]Elvira, c. 16, Mansi 2, 8; Laodicaea, c. 10, Mansi 2, 585; Chalcedon, c. 14, Mansi 7, 388.

[165]See X.4.19.7, *CorpusIC* 2, 722 and Thomas Aquinas, *Supl.* Q. 59, art. 1.

has been the belief that such unions posed a serious threat to the continued practice of the faith by the Catholic party and to the baptism and Catholic upbringing of any children born of the union.[166]

In recent decades, particularly the period following Vatican II, there have been extensive changes in the canonical and theological attitudes toward mixed marriages. This change is partly rooted in the sociological reality of large numbers of non-Catholic Christians living in many areas of the world, thus making mixed marriages more commonplace and socially acceptable. With the Second Vatican Council there also came an acceptance of the ecumenical movement as well as advances in the Church's teaching on religious freedom. The change in ecclesiological emphasis from the Church as a perfect society to the Church as the people of God embodying various levels of communion has also affected the official attitude toward members of other Christian denominations in many areas including marriage.

The changes regarding mixed marriages are most evident in three major areas: (a) the nature of the prohibition against them; (b) the formulation of the required promises; and (c) the liturgical form.

Although mixed religion is no longer an impedient impediment as in the 1917 Code (*CIC* 1060), mixed marriages are still considered special types of marriages. The 1917 Code stated that such marriages were "severely prohibited" and required a dispensation. The present Code simply states that they are prohibited without the permission of the local ordinary.

The two post-conciliar decrees on mixed marriages[167] engendered much research, writing, and dialogue among Catholics and non-Catholics alike. For non-Catholic scholars, the problems with the Catholic position centered on two areas: the requirement of canonical form (or a dispensation) for validity and the requirement of the declaration and promise by the Catholic party (cf. c. 1125, 1°).[168]

A more lenient attitude toward mixed marriages posed theoretical and practical problems for Catholic scholars. The first and most obvious one is a difficulty in reconciling the "community of the whole of life" and its corresponding shared practice of the faith with a marriage in which the partners belong to different denominations. Other questions concern differences in the theology of marriage, particularly in respect to indissolubility. A third area of concern is the reconciliation of the doctrine on religious freedom with the obligation of sharing one's faith with one's children.

Mixed Marriage: Notion and Permission

Canon 1124 — Without the express permission of the competent authority, marriage is forbidden between two baptized persons, one of whom was baptized in the Catholic Church or received into it after baptism and has not left it by a formal act, and the other of whom is a member of a church or ecclesial community which is not in full communion with the Catholic Church.

A mixed marriage is one in which one party has been either baptized in the Catholic faith or converted to it after baptism and the other party has been baptized into another Christian denomination. For the Catholic, baptism alone is required, not the fact of having been raised in the practice of the faith. The non-Catholic is one who has been validly baptized in another Christian denomination according to Catholic standard. This includes both Protestants and Eastern Orthodox.

Those who were members of the Catholic Church, yet have departed by a formal act, are not bound by this legislation just as they are not bound by the requirement of canonical form. Consequently they need not obtain permission to marry non-Catholics. On the other hand, Catholics who marry former Catholics who have departed by a formal act must obtain permission since these marriages are considered to be mixed marriages (cf. c. 1071, §2).

While the present legislation certainly mitigates prior discipline, mixed marriages still require special pastoral concern and are not to be equated with the marriages of two Catholics.

Unlike *Matrimonia mixta* which stated that a mixed marriage "may not be contracted,"[169] the present legislation uses the stronger phrase "is forbidden." This prohibition is based on the presumption that a marital relationship between persons of different denominations will impede their spiritual communion. Although the prospective spouses may profess a common belief in Jesus Christ, the expression of this belief can vary greatly.

The Catholic party must obtain the permission ("licentia") of the local ordinary. This may be his or her own local ordinary, the local ordinary of the place where the Catholic party is staying temporarily, or the local ordinary of the place where the marriage is to take place. The power to grant this permission may be delegated even to pastors. There

166See F. Schenk, *The Matrimonial Impediments of Mixed Religion and Disparity of Cult* (Washington, D.C.: Catholic University of America, 1929) xiii–xvi.

167SCDF, instr *Matrimonii sacramentum,* Mar. 18, 1966, *AAS* 58 (1966), 235, *CLD* 6, 592–596, and Paul VI, *mp, Matrimonia mixta,* Mar. 31, 1970, *AAS* 62 (1970), 257; *CLD* 7, 711–718.

168See E. Sunderland, "The Pastoral Care of Ecumenical Marriages—The Episcopal Perspective," and T. Lull, "Ecumenical Marriages: Pastoral Problem or Opportunity," *Journal of Ecumenical Studies* 16 (1979), 619–628, 643–650; M. Hurley, ed. *Beyond Tolerance* (London: Geoffrey Chapman, 1975), 79–121; and J. Lynch, "Ecumenical Marriages," *CLSAP* 5 (1973), 33–54.

169*Matrimonia mixta, CLD* 7, 712, 715.

are no restrictions on the local ordinary's competence to permit mixed marriages.[170]

Mixed marriages celebrated without the local ordinary's permission or in contravention of his refusal to grant permission are valid as long as both parties are baptized. Under the 1917 Code mixed marriages involving the impediment of mixed religion which were celebrated without a dispensation from the impediment were illicit but not invalid. Such marriages that take place now without the required permission are also illicit since they are celebrated without the proper observance of the law; however, no canonical penalties are incurred. The question is more pastoral than canonical since the prohibition is intended to insure proper pastoral preparation of a couple in light of problems facing them in a mixed marriage. Two important questions which must be faced are: (a) ensuring a respect for the rights of each party to practice his or her faith, and (b) recognizing the Catholic party's grave obligation to see that any children are baptized and educated in the faith.

Conditions for Granting Permission

Canon 1125 — The local ordinary can grant this permission if there is a just and reasonable cause; he is not to grant it unless the following conditions have been fulfilled:

1° the Catholic party declares that he or she is prepared to remove dangers of falling away from the faith and makes a sincere promise to do all in his or her power to have all the children baptized and brought up in the Catholic Church;

2° the other party is to be informed at an appropriate time of these promises which the Catholic party has to make, so that it is clear that the other party is truly aware of the promise and obligation of the Catholic party;

3° both parties are to be instructed on the essential ends and properties of marriage, which are not to be excluded by either party.

Before permission is given for a mixed marriage there must first be a "just and reasonable cause" for permitting the union. Certain conditions must also be fulfilled.

Matrimonia mixta introduced a new and different attitude toward mixed marriages by stating that the Church " . . . does not refuse a dispensation . . . provided that a just reason is had."[171] This reflected the practice of readily dispensing from the impediments of disparity of cult and mixed religion. The present legislation reflects a more cautious attitude.

The permission is not to be automatically presumed even if the conditions are fulfilled. The competent authority may exercise some discretion in determining whether such a permission will better serve the parties or be a detriment to the faith of the Catholic. The canon states that the competent authority "can" grant permission ("concedere potest") yet he "is not to grant it" ("eam ne concedat") unless the conditions are fulfilled.

The pastor of the parish where the marriage preparation takes place is responsible for determining the authenticity of the reason for the mixed marriage as well as the fulfillment of the other conditions.

A just and reasonable cause is more than the parties' desire to marry. It need not be a negative reason such as danger of civil marriage or defection from the faith. If the parties' maturity, awareness of the responsibilities of a sacramental marriage, and commitment to their respective churches indicate that the presumed dangers of a mixed marriage are offset by the strengths of the parties, then a sufficient cause for the permission is had.

The assessment of the sufficiency of the cause should be done in conjunction with a consideration of the conditions required for granting permission. The entire matter must be taken seriously by the parties and the pastoral minister in view of the successful establishment and nurture of the sacramental union.

The first condition involves the declaration and promise given by the Catholic party. This is a modified version of the *cautiones* required under the 1917 Code. The non-Catholic party is no longer required to make any promises. Rather, the Catholic party is to declare that he or she is prepared to remove all danger of departing from the faith and promise to do all in his or her power to see that any children are baptized and raised as Catholics. The responsibility for fidelity to the Church rests with the Catholic party and not the non-Catholic spouse, although the non-Catholic is obliged to respect the Catholic's situation. The Church's caution in this area is not without foundation since recent studies indicate that a high percentage of Catholics who enter mixed marriages eventually stop practicing their faith.[172]

The Catholic party should first acknowledge any potential dangers of defection from the faith. A strong anti-Catholic sentiment or aversion to regular worship on the part of the non-Catholic should be recognized as a potential danger. There is also a possible danger when two committed people arrive at the point when they feel that they can no longer worship apart. These and any other potential dangers to the Catholic party should be openly dis-

[170]Under the 1917 Code the Holy See reserved to itself such dispensations when the petitioner had received a papal dissolution and wished to enter a subsequent marriage.
[171]*Matrimonia mixta*, n. 3, *CLD* 7, 715.

[172]S. Butler, "Interchurch Marriage: Problems and Prospects," *CS* 19 (1980), 209.

cussed between the parties. They should do all that is possible to arrive at a point of understanding lest the source of the contention pose a danger of defection from the faith or jeopardize the growth of the marital relationship itself.

The Catholic party must also make a promise concerning the Catholic baptism and nurture of children. Since this is a stated purpose of marriage itself (*GS* 48), it follows that a Catholic intends to fulfill it in requesting a marriage sanctioned by the Church. This promise applies to all children yet to be born of a proposed union. It does not technically extend to children born to the couple out of wedlock nor to children born in an invalid union.[173]

Not allowed are prearrangements between parties whereby some of the children will be baptized and raised in one denomination and others in the Catholic faith. Likewise, it is not permissible to baptize the children in one denomination and either raise them in the other or in none at all. There is a continuity between baptism, education, and participation in the life of the Catholic Church. This is grounded in the ecclesial dimension of baptism and the presumption that parents who present their children for Catholic baptism understand and accept the responsibility of providing for their Catholic nurture.

Baptizing the children in different denominations may appear to be an equitable solution, yet it does violence to the notion of the family as a united community. Although superficially ecumenical, such a solution not only perpetuates but deepens the already existing divisions.[174]

Clearly the most difficult problem is the understanding and practical application of the Catholic party's obligation to "do all in his or her power" to see to the Catholic baptism and nurture of the children. The canon's phrasing reflects an evolution in the Church's approach to the question. Past legislation on this point reflects a preoccupation with the faith of the Catholic party and that of the children. This is in part based on what Orsy calls a "war psychology" between Catholics and Protestants as well as a strict interpretation of the doctrine of "no salvation outside the Church."[175]

Present legislation acknowledges the right and duty of the Catholic party to fulfill the obligation, yet at the same time it takes into account the principles of religious liberty and the corresponding rights of the non-Catholic party to practice his or her faith and transmit this faith to the children. It also considers the right to a stable and happy marriage and recognizes the tensions that denominational divisions bring to the marital community.

After the promulgation of *Matrimonia mixta,* the various conferences of bishops issued guidelines adapting the general legislation to their particular circumstances. None of these guidelines offered a precise interpretation of the phrase "to do all in one's power" since the very wording eludes such a definition. Many highlighted the concrete circumstances of the situation, i.e., good will of the parties, absence of an unwilling spirit on the part of the non-Catholic. Several also stated that the promise does not involve an absolute obligation to baptize and educate the children in the Catholic faith.[176]

A series of Roman decisions based on the instruction *Matrimonii sacramentum* of 1966 gives some insight into the mind of the Holy See at the time and aids in clarifying the force of the promise required in the present law.

In assessing the cases, the Sacred Congregation for the Doctrine of the Faith emphasized the strength of the marriage itself and the grave risk posed to it by a conflict between the spouses. The sincerity and faith of the Catholic party were also important factors in granting requested dispensations. Thus even when the Catholic party could not in conscience promise to raise the children as Catholics because of the opposition of the non-Catholic party, the dispensation was granted, based on the sincerity and active faith of the Catholic and the presumption that he or she would do all possible to see that the children were raised in the Catholic faith.[177]

"To do all in one's power" does not mean an absolute promise at the risk of jeopardizing the marriage itself. While the rights of the non-Catholic party are considered, preference is apparently given to the Catholic party's right and obligation to provide for the Catholic nurture of any children born of the union.

The pastoral minister should guide the couple in a thorough discussion of the question prior to the marriage. This should include a discussion of each party's denomination's commitment and his or her attitude and understanding of the faith of the other. The nature of possible objections to the Catholic nurture of the children should be explored along with possible ways to avoid undue tension in this regard.

If there is no resolution to the problem but the beginnings of a rift that may well grow and imperil the marriage itself, the couple should be directed to consider the wisdom of questioning the decision to marry. At times, the Catholic either will not or cannot make either the declaration or the promise. In

[173]Holy Office, Jan. 16, 1942, *AAS* 34 (1942), 22.

[174]L. Orsy, "Religious Education of Children in Mixed Marriages," *Gregorianum* 45 (1964), 739–760.

[175]Ibid., 743.

[176]J. Lynch, "Mixed Marriages in the Aftermath of '*Matrimonia Mixta,*'" *Journal of Ecumenical Studies* 11 (1974), 643–646.

[177]See decisions SCDF, May 17, 1966, June 18, 1966, July 9, 1966, Dec. 10, 1966, Dec. 12, 1966, Feb. 27, 1967, *CLD* 6, 597–604.

this case the wisdom of a Catholic marriage should be discussed.

The Non-Catholic Party's Obligation

The non-Catholic party is not obliged to make any promises or guarantees concerning the faith of the Catholic party or the raising of children. However, he or she is to be informed of the declaration and promise required of the Catholic party. This should be done early in the preparation period to allow time to explain and discuss their meaning and the reasons for the requirement.

Education in the Nature of Marriage

The third condition to be fulfilled is the instruction of the parties in the essential ends and properties of marriage. This should be done in the context of the introductory canons on marriage (cc. 1055–1061) with a full explanation of the theological nature of the community of the whole of life, the purpose of marriage, and the properties of fidelity and indissolubility. While this instruction should be conducted in a positive manner, differences in the understanding of these points should be examined especially if they could pose a threat to the marriage. This last point is important since neither party may exclude any of the essential ends or properties of marriage if they are to be admitted to marriage in the Church.

The Competence of the Conference of Bishops

Canon 1126 — The conference of bishops is to establish the way in which these declarations and promises, which are always required, are to be made, what proof of them there should be in the external forum and how they are to be brought to the attention of the non-Catholic party.

The conference of bishops is to determine by statute the specific manner in which the declaration and promise are to be made. It is clear that they are always required and may not be excluded nor left optional at the discretion of the pastoral minister or local ordinary.

The declaration and promise may be made in writing by the Catholic party in the presence of the pastoral minister. They may also be made orally and attested to by the pastoral minister's signature or the signatures of witnesses. A prepared formulary could be used to which necessary signatures are affixed. In any case, there must certainly be some indication that the declaration and promise were sincerely made. Although the canon does not refer to an oath, this could be required of the Catholic party should the conference of bishops so decide.

The conference is also to decide how and when the declaration and promise is to be brought to the attention of the non-Catholic party.

Canonical and Liturgical Form

Canon 1127 — §1. The prescriptions of can. 1108 are to be observed concerning the form to be employed in a mixed marriage; if a Catholic party contracts marriage with a non-Catholic of an oriental rite, the canonical form of celebration is to be observed only for liceity; for validity, however, the presence of a sacred minister is required along with the observance of the other requirements of law.

§2. If serious difficulties pose an obstacle to the observance of the canonical form, the local ordinary of the Catholic party has the right to dispense from the form in individual cases, but after consulting the ordinary of the place where the marriage is to be celebrated and with due regard, for validity, for some public form of celebration; the conference of bishops is to issue norms by which such a dispensation may be granted in an orderly manner.

§3. Before or after the canonical celebration held in accord with the norm of §1, it is forbidden to have another religious celebration of the same marriage to express or renew matrimonial consent; it is likewise forbidden to have a religious celebration in which a Catholic and a non-Catholic minister, assisting together but following their respective rituals, ask for the consent of the parties.

Those entering a mixed marriage are bound by the norms of canon 1108 regarding canonical form. The liturgical form is found in the *Rite of Marriage.*

The exchange of consent is to take place during a liturgical ceremony in the church or other suitable place (cf. c. 1118). Although the rite of marriage is generally to be performed outside of Mass, the local ordinary may permit its celebration within the Mass.[178] Permission to celebrate mixed marriages in church with sacred rites was first given in a general manner in the instruction *Matrimonii sacramentum* (1966) and stated again in *Matrimonia mixta* (1970). The latter decree included the possibility of marriage within the Mass. As in the past, the local ordinary may require that permission be granted for each case or he may grant a general permission, leaving the final decision to the discretion of the pastor or pastoral minister.

Canonical form (or an appropriate dispensation) is required for the validity of marriages between Catholics and Protestants. It is required for liceity only in marriages between Latin or Oriental Rite Catholics and non-Catholic Orientals (Orthodox) provided the marriage takes place before a sacred minister.[179]

---

[178] *The Rite of Marriage,* n. 8.

[179] The conciliar decree *Orientalium Ecclesiarum,* Nov. 21, 1964, n. 18 legislated that Oriental Catholics marrying Oriental Orthodox before an Orthodox sacred minister were bound to canonical form for liceity only. This was extended to Latin Rite Catholics marrying Oriental Orthodox on Feb. 22, 1967, SCOC, decr *Crescens matrimoniorum, CLD* 6, 605–606.

A Catholic who marries an Orthodox Christian before an Orthodox priest is bound to all of the canonical requirements concerning freedom and capacity to marry. He or she should also petition for a dispensation from canonical form even though this is not required for validity.

Dispensation from Canonical Form

The Catholic party in a mixed marriage or disparity of cult marriage has a right to petition his or her local ordinary for a dispensation from canonical form. If granted, the marriage may take place validly before a non-Catholic minister or civil official.

When canonical form is dispensed, the non-Catholic officiant acts as the official witness and receives the exchange of consent according to the particular religious or civil form. If a Catholic priest or deacon is present, he may assist to some degree, but he may not ask for and receive the consent.

A dispensation from canonical form should not be confused with permission to celebrate a marriage in a non-Catholic church or other suitable place (cf. cc. 1118, 933). In such cases, the requirements of canonical form are to be followed with the duly delegated priest or deacon acting as official witness.

The competent authority to grant a dispensation from form is the local ordinary of the Catholic party, that is, the ordinary of the place where he or she has domicile or quasi-domicile. He may grant such dispensations in individual cases but not in a general way. If the marriage is to take place in another diocese, the local ordinary of that diocese does not grant the dispensation but is to be consulted by the local ordinary of the Catholic party. However, the former does not have to approve the granting of the dispensation.

Requirements for the Dispensation

First, there must be serious difficulties blocking the observance of the canonical form. Some possible examples are:

(a) when the non-Catholic party has a conscientious objection to a Catholic celebration;

(b) when there is a possibility of the non-Catholic party's estrangement from family or religious denomination;

(c) when the non-Catholic party requests that a parent or other close relative officiate at the ceremony;

(d) when a Catholic officiant cannot conveniently be present;

(e) when the only church in the vicinity is a non-Catholic church;

(f) when a nominal Catholic marries a devout non-Catholic.[180]

The second requirement is that some form of public celebration take place. A public celebration is one which conforms to some type of religious or civil regulation with subsequent public recognition provided for. Most civil jurisdictions require some form of public recognition of a marriage including the presence of a duly authorized official witness. Although common law marriages are recognized as valid in some places, these do not satisfy the requirement precisely because they do not involve any kind of public celebration.

The public form of celebration is required for the validity of the marriage. Consequently, marriages celebrated in such a way that the form is not considered public or civilly valid would be considered invalid in canon law as well. Care must be taken that the requirements of both canon law and civil law be fulfilled.

The conferences of bishops are empowered to establish norms concerning the granting of dispensations from the form. Such norms may be enacted for validity as well as liceity. They could include requirements regarding a specific date, place, and official witness with a new dispensation needed for any change.

Dispensations from canonical form may normally be granted *only* for mixed or disparity of cult marriages and not for marriages in which both parties are Catholic. The only exception is a dispensation from form in danger of death (c. 1079). A dispensation from canonical form may be granted to a Catholic who is marrying a former Catholic who has left the Church by a formal act. Dispensation from form for marriages of two Catholics is granted only by the Holy See.[181]

Double Ceremonies

After a mixed marriage is celebrated according to canonical form, it is forbidden to have another religious celebration according to a non-Catholic rite at which consent is exchanged or renewed. To permit such a duplication of the exchange of consent would indicate a non-acceptance of its validity by at least one of the parties.

This prohibition does not include civil ceremonies prior to religious ceremonies in countries where this is required by civil law. In such cases the couple is not considered to be truly married according to canon law until after the religious ceremonies. Also, a dispensation from form is not required when civil law requires this procedure.

---

[180]See *Mixed Marriages: Particular Norms for South Africa,* South African Bishops' Conference, Jan. 9, 1970, *CLD* 7, 729.
[181]SCSacr, reply, June 6, 1973, *CLD* 8, 818–820. Dispensation from form was granted to two Catholics. The bride was a recent convert from Lutheranism. Her family refused to attend the marriage unless it was held in a Lutheran church.

The canon does not specifically forbid another religious ceremony during which a blessing is imparted but without an exchange or renewal of consent. This problem may arise in marriages with the Orthodox. In such cases a Catholic ceremony may not be considered valid for the Orthodox party, who may then be deprived of the sacraments of his or her church. Since the blessing by a sacred minister is essential for Orthodox Christians, the Holy See has permitted a second religious ceremony at which the Orthodox priest imparted the sacred blessing.[182]

The Catholic minister is also forbidden to ask for and receive the consent of the Catholic party while the non-Catholic minister asks for and receives the consent of the non-Catholic. When ministers of both denominations assist at a mixed marriage ceremony, only one is to ask for and receive the consent of both parties.

Marriages celebrated with a dispensation from canonical form are to be recorded according to the prescriptions of canon 1121, §3.

Pastoral Care for Mixed Marriages

Canon 1128 — Local ordinaries and other pastors of souls are to see to it that the Catholic spouse and the children born of a mixed marriage do not lack spiritual assistance in fulfilling their obligations and are to aid the spouses in fostering the unity of conjugal and family life.

The Church acknowledges the special problems which may result from mixed marriages. In addition to special pastoral care in preparation for such marriages, local ordinaries and other pastors are to provide some form of post-marital pastoral care for the Catholic spouse and the children. They should be given help in fulfilling their obligations as Catholics. The law also urges assistance for both spouses in strengthening their marital covenant and their family life.

In order to provide this care, special preparation is needed for priests and others involved. Ecumenical programs conducted by pastoral ministers of Catholic and other faiths have been developed to provide realistic assistance to those in mixed marriages. In this regard, it is important to provide for the continuing education of both spouses in each other's faith and to see that the children are given the opportunity to develop an understanding and respect for the faith of the non-Catholic spouse.[183]

Application of the Canon to Disparity of Cult Marriages

Canon 1129 — The prescriptions of cann. 1127 and 1128 are also to be applied to marriages involving the impediment of disparity of cult mentioned in can. 1086, §1.

The prescriptions of canons 1127 and 1128 concerning the canonical and liturgical forms of marriage apply also to disparity of cult marriages.

If canonical form is observed, it is to follow the *Rite of Marriage* which states that the ceremony is to take place outside of Mass.[184] If a dispensation from canonical form is sought, the provisions of canon 1127 apply equally to marriages with the non-baptized.

CHAPTER VII
MARRIAGES SECRETLY CELEBRATED
[cc. 1130–1133]

The celebration of marriage is always a matter of the external forum. Furthermore it is a public event at which the parties begin a state of life recognized as such by both civil and religious societies. Marriage in the Christian tradition implies a relationship between two people to be lived out in a special way in the Christian community.

Nevertheless the Church permits the secret celebration of marriages when the greater spiritual good of the parties demands it. A marriage celebrated in secret is one which is celebrated according to all the norms of law but without any of the usual publicity so that it remains unknown to the public.

The somewhat ambiguous terminology for such marriages in the 1917 Code, "marriages of conscience," has been replaced by the more accurate phrasing of the present Code. Consequently it cannot be construed that such marriages are allowed simply because the consciences of the parties compel them to marry.

The first legislation concerning secret marriages was enacted by Benedict XIV. The 1917 Code included canons on secret marriages based on Benedict XIV's legislation with some minor changes (*CIC* 1104–1107).[185]

Secret Marriages

Canon 1130 — For a serious and urgent reason the local ordinary can permit a marriage to be celebrated secretly.

A marriage celebrated in secret must be celebrated according to canonical form, that is, before a

---

[182]SCDF, replies, June 16, 1966, Oct. 26, 1964, *CLD* 6, 22–23. A double ceremony was permitted provided the vows were exchanged before the Catholic priest and the sacred blessing only given by the Orthodox priest in the second ceremony.

[183]See B. Schiappa, *Mixing: Catholic-Protestant Marriages in the 1980's,* (New York: Paulist Press, 1982), and S. Sandmel, *When a Jew and a Christian Marry,* (Philadelphia: Fortress Press, 1977).

[184]*Rite of Marriage,* intro., n. 8.

[185]For a complete historical and canonical treatment of secret marriages, see V. Coburn, *Marriages of Conscience* (Washington, D.C.: Catholic University of America, 1944).

duly authorized sacred minister or lay officiant and two witnesses. The parties must be free to marry according to the law.

The major differences between secret marriages and other marriages are simply that the banns, if they are in force in the area, are not announced, the ceremony takes place in secret, and all involved must keep the fact of the marriage a secret.

The permission of the local ordinary is necessary to celebrate a marriage in secret. Since no restriction is made on which local ordinary may grant permission, the local ordinaries of the domicile, the quasi-domicile or temporary residence of either party, or the local ordinary of the place of marriage are competent.

There must be a serious and urgent reason for permitting such marriages. The seriousness of the situation should be such that the good achieved by a public celebration is sufficiently offset by the good to be achieved by a secret celebration. In addition, there must be an element of urgency, i.e., there will be possible harm to the parties if there is a delay.

Some examples of serious reasons which have appeared in commentaries on the 1917 Code are marriages of those living in concubinage, marriages contrary to civil law if the prohibition is contrary to natural or ecclesiastical law such as interracial marriages, and marriages in countries where the Church is persecuted and religious marriages are forbidden.

Requirements for Secret Marriages

Canon 1131 — The permission to celebrate a marriage secretly also includes:
1° permission that the pre-matrimonial investigation be made secretly;
2° the obligation that secrecy concerning the marriage be observed by the local ordinary, the assisting minister, the witnesses and the spouses.

Permission to celebrate a secret marriage does not exempt one from the obligation of the pre-marital investigation and instruction. All canonical norms must be followed with the exception of the banns, if they are in force in the area. If one or both of the parties is a minor, the parents should be consulted unless there is a most serious reason for not doing so. If the parental objections to the marriage are clearly unjust and serious harm would come to the minor if the parents discovered the proposed marriage, then consultation with them could be omitted but only after discussing the matter with the local ordinary (cf. c. 1071, §1, 6°).

Those who know about the secret celebration of a marriage, including, of course, all who participate in the ceremony, are bound to observe secrecy about the matter. Although the canon mentions the local ordinary, officiant, witnesses, and spouses, anyone else who is aware of the marriage is also bound to secrecy.

The local ordinary has the right to exercise discretion in the choice of the witnesses. He should take care that those chosen are persons who will understand the nature of the secret celebration and will observe secrecy.

Naturally, the spouses themselves are obliged to secrecy. In fact, the obligation which binds the others involved is inserted in the law to protect the parties. If *both* parties agree to make the fact of their marriage known at some time after its celebration, the obligation of secrecy ceases for all the others.

Cessation of the Obligation of Secrecy

Canon 1132 — The obligation to observe secrecy mentioned in can. 1131, n. 2, ceases on the part of the local ordinary if serious scandal or serious harm to the sanctity of marriage is threatened by observing the secret and this is to be made known to the parties before the celebration of the marriage.

The local ordinary alone may cease to observe the secrecy without the consent of the parties. He may do so if he judges that continued secrecy will cause serious scandal which could be averted by publicizing the marriage, e.g., when the parties are known to be living together and at the same time actively participating in the life of the Church. He may also publicize the marriage if he judges that serious harm will be done to the sanctity of marriage by continued secrecy about a marriage.

Recording Secret Marriages

Canon 1133 — A marriage celebrated secretly is to be noted only in the special register which is to be kept in the secret archive of the curia.

Secret marriages are to be recorded *only* in the special register kept for this purpose. This register is retained in the secret archives of the diocesan curia. The marriage is not to be recorded in the local parish register where it is performed nor are the customary notifications sent to the places of baptism.

It is left to the discretion of the local ordinary to decide if and when copies of the marriage record may be issued. The spouses may need a record of their marriage for various legal purposes or to assure the legitimacy of their children.

CHAPTER VIII
THE EFFECTS OF MARRIAGE
[cc. 1134–1140]

The exchange of marital consent and the creation of the marriage covenant bring about certain effects derived from the nature of marriage both as a natural institution and as a sacramental reality. As a natural institution marriage introduces an added element of stability into the relationship and provides the foundation for the family.

Some of the effects of natural marriage are determined by socio-cultural factors in different societies and in different periods of history. For example, the degree of stability has varied. In Roman law, marriage was intrinsically dissoluble, i.e., it could be terminated by the spouses at will without the intervention of civil authorities. For most contemporary civil societies, marriage is intrinsically indissoluble yet extrinsically dissoluble: the spouses may not declare themselves to be no longer married, but a civil official may do so by means of a decree of divorce.[186]

The canonical and theological tradition of the Catholic Church ascribes varied effects to valid but non-sacramental unions, non-consummated sacramental unions, and consummated sacramental unions. This is especially true regarding the stability of the relationship and its degree of indissolubility.

The canons in this chapter treat the major canonical effects of marriage: the bond, the rights and duties of spouses toward each other and to their children, and the legitimacy of children. The indissoluble nature of the bond and the above-mentioned rights and duties are rooted in divine law as interpreted by the Church's magisterium. Legitimacy of children is an effect rooted in positive ecclesiastical law.

The Marriage Bond

Canon 1134 — **From a valid marriage arises a bond between the spouses which by its very nature is perpetual and exclusive; furthermore, in a Christian marriage the spouses are strengthened and, as it were, consecrated for the duties and the dignity of their state by a special sacrament.**

The primary effect of the valid exchange of marital consent is the constitution of the marriage bond. The bond is the unique relationship between a man and a woman by which they are constituted husband and wife.[187] According to Vatican II, the bond is rooted in the consent of the partners:

The intimate relationship of life and love which constitutes the married state . . . is rooted in the contract of the partners, that is, in their irrevocable personal consent. It is an institution con-

firmed by the divine law, and receiving its stability, even in the eyes of society, from the human act by which the partners mutually surrender themselves to each other; for the good of the partners, the children, and of society this sacred bond no longer depends on human decision alone.[188]

The Church has always taught that the bond comes into existence at the time valid consent is exchanged. At that moment the bond is an integral and not a partial reality. The bond cannot be equated with the existential quality of the human relationship. It does not depend on the strength of this relationship for its existence or its perpetuity, since it receives these from the essence of marriage itself.

By their mutual consent the spouses enter into a covenant. Once entered into it no longer depends on the will of the spouses for its existence nor is it simply the sum total of the marital obligations. With the covenant the spouses become "two in one flesh" in the biblical sense: a total enmeshing of persons.

From the age of the Fathers to the twelfth and thirteenth centuries, the bond meant a strong obligation to lasting fidelity, based on the New Testament sayings about marital indissolubility. In spite of the long-standing Roman tradition of marital dissolubility by the spouses themselves, the Church consistently taught that Christians were forbidden to remarry after divorce.[189]

When the Church acquired competence over marriage in the Middle Ages (the authority to declare when marriage began or ended), the understanding of the bond shifted from that of its being purely a moral obligation to that of its being a separate reality. It was something that *could* not be terminated or dissolved rather than a relationship that *should* not be terminated. Schillebeeckx holds that both understandings of the bond are mutually inclusive and rooted in Sacred Scripture.[190]

A marriage bond comes into being with the *valid* exchange of consent. Once the marital relationship begins, the bond is perpetual and not merely long lasting. It is also exclusive in that it exists between the two spouses and not three or more. If marital consent is presumed valid but in fact is not, for some reason, the bond does not come into existence.

A bond arises with every valid marriage. It is referred to as a *natural* bond if consent takes place between two unbaptized persons or a baptized and non-baptized person.

If both parties are baptized, the marriage is a sacrament by the very fact that consent was ex-

[186]See the following historical studies: P. Corbett, *The Roman Law of Marriage* (Oxford: Clarendon, 1930); M. Forbes, ed., *Marriage in Tribal Societies* (Cambridge: Oxford University, 1962); and E. Westermarck, *The History of Human Marriage,* 3 vols., 5th ed. (New York, 1922).

[187]U. Navarette, "De vinculo matrimonii in theologia et iure canonico," in *Vinculum Matrimonii,* 100.

[188]*GS* 48.

[189]See A. Bevilacqua, "The History of the Indissolubility of Marriage," *CTSAP* 22 (1972), 253–308, and H. Crouzel, *L'Eglise primitive face au divorce* (Paris: Beauchesne, 1971).

[190]E. Schillebeeckx, 203; 388–391.

changed. This includes Catholics who are married according to canonical form as well as baptized non-Catholics who marry among themselves.

The baptismal status of the parties determines the degree of indissolubility of the bond. If the marriage is non-sacramental (involving at least one non-baptized person), the natural bond may be dissolved by the power of the Church through the Pauline privilege or the privilege of the faith. The bond arising from a sacramental marriage may likewise be dissolved by the Supreme Pontiff if it has not been consummated. Once a sacramental union has been consummated by sexual intercourse, the bond takes on the character of absolute indissolubility beyond the power of any earthly authority.

The concept of a marriage bond is related to the need for stability in the marriage relationship. Civil societies have always demanded some degree of stability and termination of marriage. At times these have been purely customary in nature and at other times they have taken the form of civil legislation. The difference between cohabitation and marriage is the public commitment made by the spouses to remain true to one another. The stability of Christian marriage is grounded only secondarily in its usefulness to society. Rather it is rooted in the nature of the relationship itself. Since the sacrament of marriage reflects the Christ-Church union, it follows that it must have a high degree of stability. The marriage covenant then imposes total and lasting fidelity, the primary obligation and sustaining element of the existential dimension of the marriage bond.

The Mutual Obligations of the Spouses

Canon 1135 — Each of the spouses has equal obligations and rights to those things which pertain to the partnership of conjugal life.

Marital consent is a mutual gift of persons which imposes certain fundamental obligations on each party and accords each fundamental rights. These rights and duties are grounded in the marriage covenant as a unique way of life.

Christianity introduced the element of equality between the spouses into marriage, an element which distinguished it from other cultural approaches to marriage. When Christianity came into existence the position of the wife was culturally inferior to that of her husband. This cultural and societal inequality had a legal corollary with unequal duties and especially rights between the spouses. This was especially true regarding marital fidelity in that absolute fidelity was usually only demanded of the wife.

In spite of social and cultural inequalities which may be imposed from without, Christian marriage imposes equal obligations of the spouses toward one another.

One must distinguish between the conjugal rights and duties and the many ways of expressing them. Expressions of love, partnership, sharing, etc., can vary from culture to culture and from personality to personality. Nevertheless there are certain basic elements which the spouses have a right to expect from one another. First there is the right to heterosexual acts. The sexual act is the most intimate and complete expression of conjugal love, yet it is not the only aspect of the conjugal community.

Obviously it is not possible to compile an inclusive list of the essential rights and duties of marriage. Their implications have been partially clarified through the jurisprudence of the Church's courts. Various court decisions have concluded that, among other things, the spouses are entitled to mutual respect and support, cohabitation, and an interpersonal relationship.[191]

Duties of Parents toward Children

Canon 1136 — Parents have the most serious duty and the primary right to do all in their power to see to the physical, social, cultural, moral and religious upbringing of their children.

By its very nature the institution of marriage and married love is ordered to the procreation and education of children and it is in them that it finds its crowning glory.[192]

The procreative dimension of marriage has a twofold dimension which includes openness to procreation and is fulfilled by the education of children. This educative dimension cannot be radically separated from procreation itself.[193]

When two people marry they assume the obligation of properly raising any children that may be born of the union. They cannot absolve themselves of this responsibility. It extends to all essential aspects of human and Christian nurture. Fundamental to this obligation is the conduct of the spouses toward one another. Their example of unselfish love in itself teaches the children the meaning of charity. The religious formation of the children is particularly important. It begins with the baptism of children born of the union and extends to sharing the practice of the faith with them and providing for their Christian instruction. While other persons or agencies may assist the parents in providing this instruction, the basic obligation rests with the parents and may not be transferred to others.

Along with the duty of providing for their children's education, the law also states that parents have a *right* to do so. This right is grounded in the

---

[191]See Hudson, 141–147.
[192]*GS* 48.
[193]See Aquinas, *Summa Theologiae*, III, Q. 29.

essence of marriage itself and may not be usurped or curtailed by others, including the State. Only in extreme cases, when parents are incapable of fulfilling their duties to the extent that the good of the children is seriously threatened, is this right forfeited. It must always be remembered that the child, too, has a right to nurture, support, and formation (c. 217).

The rights and obligations of parents to their children are specifically mentioned in other canons of the Code. These canons relate primarily to the religious education of the children.[194]

Parents must also provide for their physical, social, and cultural nurture as well as their moral and religious formation. Physical nurture is not satisfied simply by allowing the child to be born but entails providing that which is needed for healthy growth. The social and cultural nurture of children implies that they not be isolated from society but guided in such a way that they will learn their roles and responsibilities as citizens.

Legitimacy of Children

Canon 1137 — Children conceived or born of a valid or putative marriage are legitimate.

A legitimate child is defined in both civil and canon law as one born of lawful wedlock. The term describes the child's legal standing but it has no moral or spiritual implication. In the 1917 Code legitimacy was required for nomination to the cardinalate (*CIC* 232, §2, 1°) and the episcopate (*CIC* 331, §1, 1°), for appointment as a prelate or abbot nullius (*CIC* 320, §2), and for the reception of sacred orders (*CIC* 984, 1°). Since all of these restrictions have been dropped in the present Code, there are no canonical effects of illegitimacy.

Children conceived or born of a valid or putative marriage are considered legitimate. A putative marriage is one that is presumed valid by at least one party but which is in fact invalid (c. 1061, §3). If a putative marriage is subsequently declared null by an ecclesiastical court, children conceived or born of it are legitimate.

If both parties are aware of the fact that their marriage is certainly invalid, due for instance to the presence of a diriment impediment or lack of canonical form, children born of it are considered illegitimate.

[194]C. 793: obligation to form children in the faith and in the practice of the Christian life; c. 797: right and obligation to educate children and to choose appropriate means for Catholic education; c. 798: parents should choose Catholic schools or if not possible they are bound to provide Catholic education; c. 867: parents' obligation to provide for baptism for children; c. 890: obligation to provide preparation for confirmation; c. 914: obligation to provide preparation for Holy Communion.

Presumptions concerning Legitimacy

Canon 1138 — §1. The father is he whom a lawful marriage indicates unless evident arguments prove otherwise.

§2. Children are presumed to be legitimate if they are born at least 180 days after the celebration of the marriage or within 300 days from the date when conjugal life was terminated.

This canon contains two basic presumptions of law concerning legitimacy. They are interrelated in that they seek to establish legitimacy in situations of doubt of fact.

The father of children born of a valid or putative union is the man indicated as the husband of the mother. This presumption, derived from Roman law, subsequently passed into the legal systems of most countries as well as canon law. However this presumption can be overturned by contrary proof.

It must be demonstrated that during the period of time when conception was possible, intercourse between the husband and wife was impossible due to physical separation, male impotence, or some other legally sufficient reasons. The admission of adultery on the part of the mother with the consequent suspicion that another man is the father is not sufficient to prove illegitimacy.

The second paragraph is self-evident. Although its scientific basis may be disputed in individual cases, it is a presumption of law whose effects are purely legal.

Legitimation of Children

Canon 1139 — Illegitimate children are rendered legitimate through the subsequent valid or putative marriage of their parents, or through a rescript of the Holy See.

Children born of an invalid (and not merely putative) marriage become legitimate upon the validation or radical sanation of the marriage. This of course presumes that any existing invalidating impediments to the marriage are either removed or dispensed. Similarly, children born out of wedlock become legitimate upon the marriage of their parents. In either case, even if the validation or subsequent marriage is putative and therefore in fact invalid, the children are legitimate.

Legitimacy may also be attained by a rescript of the Holy See. Such a rescript legitimizing children has no effect on the marriage of their parents, that is, it does not validate an invalid marriage.

Foundlings and adopted children are presumed to be legitimate until the contrary is proved.

Effects of Legitimation

Canon 1140 — Insofar as canonical effects are concerned, legitimized children are equivalent in

everything to legitimate children unless the law expressly states otherwise.

Children who are born illegitimate and are later legitimized are equal in law to those born or conceived of a valid or putative marriage, unless the contrary is expressed in law. While there were exceptions to this rule in the 1917 Code (nomination to the episcopate and cardinalate), none are expressed in the present Code.

CHAPTER IX
THE SEPARATION OF THE SPOUSES
[cc. 1141–1155]

ARTICLE 1: DISSOLUTION OF THE BOND
[cc. 1141–1150]

When marital consent is exchanged, the already existing human relationship takes on a new dimension with the creation of the marriage bond. If the spouses separate and the existential relationship ends, the marriage still exists as a civil and canonical reality. If the union is terminated by a civil divorce, the canonically recognized bond continues to exist.

Nevertheless, the Church acknowledges the fact that in some instances the separation of the spouses may be justified. However, because of the principle of indissolubility and the relationship of marital stability to the Church's life, the instances of separation are regulated.

The Church also acknowledges the fact that the degree of indissolubility differs because of the relationship of baptism to marital consent. Since the marital relationship is not an exclusively private matter, the spouses may never declare themselves divorced and the marriage bond dissolved (intrinsic indissolubility). In some cases, however, the bond can be dissolved by the Church and the parties declared free to marry. A dissolution is distinguished from a declaration of nullity. In the former case, an existing bond is dissolved. In the latter, a judicial or administrative declaration of a competent ecclesiastical authority states that a valid bond never existed, even though there may have been an appearance of marriage. By an appearance of marriage is meant a wedding ceremony that the Church would consider presumably valid. In marriages invalid due to simple lack of canonical form, there is no appearance of marriage.

Absolute Indissolubility

Canon 1141 — A ratified and consummated marriage cannot be dissolved by any human power or for any reason other than death.

A ratified or sacramental marriage is one between two baptized persons. The law includes other Christians who are validly baptized such as most Protestants and all Orthodox whose marriages, when contracted among themselves, are ratified unions.

When a ratified marriage is subsequently consummated by sexual intercourse, performed in a human manner, the union becomes absolutely indissoluble. No human power, civil or ecclesiastical, is capable of dissolving a ratified, consummated marriage. Death alone can dissolve such a bond. While all marriages are indissoluble to a certain degree, only the ratified, consummated marriage is absolutely so.

The theological argument for indissolubility is based on the sayings of Jesus in the synoptic gospels,[195] yet these sayings do not mention the degrees of indissolubility, the nature of sacramentality, or the effect of consummation. It was left to the Church to determine the limits of indissolubility. Although some studies have argued that even a ratified, consummated marriage could theoretically be dissolved by the Supreme Pontiff, the present Code restates the position which the Church has consistently held throughout its history.

The concept of marital indissolubility has had a complex history. Numerous pre-medieval councils and synods enacted legislation forbidding Christians from remarrying after divorce. In order to uphold the teaching on indissolubility, severe penances were imposed on those who remarried contrary to church law.[196] These councils did not deal with the issue of the validity of second marriages, which leads to the presumption that indissolubility was viewed largely in terms of a moral obligation attached to the marriage bond. Although the Church proclaimed indissolubility from the earliest times, it remains unclear whether or not marriages concluded contrary to ecclesiastical prohibitions were considered null.[197]

In spite of the consistency of church teaching in this early period, certain questionable texts have formed the basis for an argument that the Church has, in fact, allowed remarriage after divorce.[198] Al-

---

[195] Mk 10:9, 11–12; Mt 5:32, 19:9; Lk 16:18. See T. Doyle, "Select Bibliography on the Sacrament of Marriage," *Marriage Studies* 1, 83–85.

[196] For example: the Synod of Elvira (306), cc. 8, 9, 47, 64, 70; Carthage XI, c. 8; Angers (453), c. 6; Vannes (465), c. 2; Fruili (796), c. 10. For more information on this period, see Joyce, 301–376.

[197] C. Lefebvre, "L'evolution de l'action de nullité," *RDC* 26 (1976), 25, and J. Gaudemet, "Le lien matrimoniale," *RDC* 21 (1971), 81–105.

[198] Ambrosiaster, *Commentaria in XIII Epistolas Beati Pauli, PL* 17, 218; Origen, *In Matthaeum Commentaria,* 14, 23, *PG* 13, 1246; *Penitential of Theodore,* I, 14; II, 12 in MacNeill and Gamer, *Medieval Handbooks of Penance* (New York: Octagon, 1965), 184–186, 195–197, 208–211; Council of Verberies, c. 9, *MGH Leges* sect. 2, 40 and Council of Compiegne, c. 11, 19, *MGH Leges,* sect 2, 37. See also N. Jung, *Evolution de l'indissolubilité: remariage religieux des divorcés* (Paris: P. Lethielleux, 1974), 65–92.

though some argue that these texts indicate that the Church does have the power to dissolve ratified, consummated marriages, most scholars hold the opposite opinion. While some of the texts certainly indicate that remarriage was allowed, it did not necessarily mean that the Church was dissolving a ratified, consummated bond and amounted to a rare exception which does not lead to a solid basis for such a practice.[199]

Further development of the meaning of absolute indissolubility took place in the eleventh to thirteenth centuries. By this time, church authorities had full jurisdiction over marriage and family life. The Church was now faced with deciding divorce questions. Its teaching on indissolubility had to be upheld; yet, it also had to respond to those who approached the church courts, asking if they were married or not. Imposing penances on the remarried was not sufficient. The question was precisely what made a marriage and when did it become indissoluble. Ethnic diversity in the European world made the question more difficult to answer:

> The conflict between Christian peoples whose resolution produced the medieval refinement of the inherited definition of marriage arose from a conflict between the Roman law on marriage and the laws and customs of the major ethnic groups of the West. . . . This conflict was inevitable . . . for each of the major ethnic groups entering the inclusive Christian community had its own traditional understanding of the nature of marriage.[200]

Although the debate among the scholars as to what actually made a marriage had its remote beginnings in the ninth century, it reached its major proportions in the eleventh and twelfth centuries and was finally settled in the thirteenth century. It is known as the *consensus-copula* debate and was dominated by the theologians of the University of Paris, led by Peter Lombard, and the canonists of the University of Bologna, led by Gratian.

The debate is so-called because the Paris school taught that consent alone was necessary for a true marriage, while the Bologna school held that consent was the beginning of marriage, but only with sexual consummation did a true marriage come into existence.[201]

The question was never definitively answered by the theologians and canonists. Instead the dispute was resolved by three popes, Alexander III

(1159–1181), Urban II (1185–1187), and Innocent III (1189–1216) whose decretal letters on marriage cases presented to them answered the question but did not explain it. Alexander III first decreed that spouses could remarry after consent if the marriage had not been consummated. In his *Compilatio Prima* he stated: "God's command that a man and a woman not dismiss the spouse refers only to a consummated marriage."[202] The opinions of Alexander III and his two successors dominated the section on marriage in the Church's first officially approved book of laws, the *Decretals of Gregory IX*.[203]

The resolution of the dispute can be summarized in this way: true marriage exists from the moment of consent; when this consent is completed with sexual intercourse, the property of absolute indissolubility is added. Consummation symbolizes the two becoming one flesh and is the sign that the union has become absolutely unbreakable.[204] Thus the juridical reality of the absolutely indissoluble bond is fixed with consummation even though the spouses' consciousness of being truly one in mind and spirit as well as in body depends on a variety of human factors. Even when this consciousness ceases to exist and the spouses no longer feel that they are one, the indissoluble bond perdures.

The Meaning of Consummation

In spite of the succinct wording of the canon, the exact nature of consummation has also been subject to development.[205] Essentially consummation has always been defined as the complete act of sexual intercourse taking place after the exchange of consent. Intercourse prior to consent is not considered to be consummation and therefore has no effect on subsequent consent.

The questions which have arisen about the more precise meaning of consummation have concerned two things: the biological components of the act of intercourse and the manner in which intercourse is completed.

The essential biological components are discussed in the commentary on impotence (c. 1084). One additional issue is worth mentioning in this regard: Was a marriage truly consummated if the male ejaculation was not of testicular origin? The Holy See resolved this long-standing question by affirming that semen of testicular origin is not required for complete consummation.[206]

The present Code further defines the quality of sexual intercourse required for consummation by stating that it must take place in a human fashion

---

[199]For two excellent studies of this question, see H. Crouzel, and A. Bevilacqua, 253–308.

[200]Mackin, 147.

[201]For studies of the debate, see Mackin, 145–171; W. O'Connor, "The Indissolubility of a Ratified, Consummated Marriage," *Ephemerides Theologiae Lovaniensis* 13 (1936), 692–722; W. Bassett, "The Marriage of Christians: Valid Contract, Valid Sacrament?" in *The Bond of Marriage* (Notre Dame, Ind.: University of Notre Dame, 1968), 117–180.

[202]Cited in Mackin, 169.

[203]Ibid., 170.

[204]J. Alesandro, *Gratian's Notion of Marital Consummation* (Rome: Catholic Book Agency, 1971), 213.

[205]See E. Hudson, "Marital Consummation according to Ecclesiastical Legislation," *Stud Can* 12 (1978), 93–123.

[206]SCDF, decr, May 13, 1977, *CLD* 8, 676.

(*humano modo*). This is a most important qualification in that it clearly reflects the conciliar teaching about sexual intercourse in marriage.

Married love is uniquely expressed and perfected by the exercise of the acts proper to marriage. Hence the acts in marriage by which the intimate and chaste union of the spouses takes place are noble and honorable; the truly human performance of these acts fosters the self-giving they signify and enriches the spouses by joy and gratitude (*GS* 49).

Negatively speaking this means that sexual consummation does not result from either physical or moral violence which is of such a degree as to remove the freedom of one of the parties.[207] The use of aphrodisiacs, drugs, or intoxicants does not necessarily destroy the true nature of consummation even though their use may diminish the freedom of the will and its assent to the sexual act.[208] If the freedom of the will is not merely diminished but removed to the point that one of the parties either does not know what he or she is doing or submits to intercourse almost totally out of fear, then the sexual intercourse which may take place does not amount to true consummation. In short, a marriage is not consummated through rape.

Consummation in a human fashion implies more than the absence of force, coercion, or violence. Interpreted within the broad context of marriage as a gift of persons, it implies that the act by which the marriage is consummated and subsequent sexual acts are true acts of love by which the spouses express this gift. Clarifying the precise juridical meaning of true human consummation is difficult since the concept eludes such juridical categories. It is easier to determine when consummation has *not* taken place in a human manner than positively to evaluate the positive degrees of consummation as an act of love.

Dissolution of a Ratified but Non-Consummated Marriage

Canon 1142 — A non-consummated marriage between baptized persons or between a baptized party and non-baptized party can be dissolved by the Roman Pontiff for a just cause, at the request of both parties or of one of the parties, even if the other party is unwilling.

The bond of a non-consummated sacramental marriage is not absolutely indissoluble. If the consent has not been consummated by sexual intercourse in a human fashion, the Supreme Pontiff can dissolve the bond, permitting the parties to marry

again. In doing so, the Pope uses his vicarious power which cannot be delegated.[209]

The dissolution of the bond of marriage first took place in the twelfth century when Pope Alexander III first granted a series of dissolutions precisely because the marriages had not been consummated. Since the exact basis for doing this was not clarified to the satisfaction of successive popes, the practice of dissolving non-consummated marriages declined during the pontificates of several of Alexander's successors. Finally Pope Benedict XIV declared in 1767 that the pope undoubtedly possessed the power to dissolve non-consummated marriages.[210]

The 1917 Code described the papal action as dissolution by dispensation (*CIC* 1119, "dissolvitur per dispensationem"). Some members of the marriage committee suggested that this phrase be retained. They argued that the marriage was not actually dissolved but rather that the obligations flowing from it were dispensed or suspended. However the committee as a whole rejected this opinion, stating that it lacks foundation.[211] The wording of the canon appears to indicate that the intent of the legislator is to show that the Supreme Pontiff actually dissolves the bond.

The petition for dissolution may be submitted by either spouse even though one spouse may be unwilling. The power to dissolve extends both to sacramental marriages of Catholics and non-Catholics and to non-sacramental marriages in which one spouse is baptized. Canon 1142 does not extend it to marriages in which neither spouse is baptized.

The dissolution depends on two things: the non-consummation of the marriage and the presence of a just cause for the dissolution.

It must be demonstrated that complete sexual intercourse did not take place at any time after consent. The petitioner may also allege that although physical intercourse did take place, it was not completed in a human fashion but by force or otherwise against the will of the spouse. Whether or not intercourse had taken place prior to the marriage does not affect the indissolubility of the bond.

Since the marriage bond, whether ratified or natural, actually exists, there must be a proportionately just cause for its dissolution. A greater pastoral good should result from the dissolution than from the marriage's continued existence. Commentators list several examples of acceptable causes such as the irreconcilable breakdown of the marriage, the possibility of scandal, or the danger of moral or religious perversion.[212]

---

[207]*Comm* 6 (1974), 187.
[208]Ibid., 191–192.

[209]*EM,* V, *CLD* 6, 397: " . . . but not the divine laws, natural or positive from which the Supreme Pontiff alone, using his vicarious power, can dispense . . . " *Comm* 10 (1978), 108.
[210]See Joyce, 430–437.
[211]*Comm* 10 (1978), 108.
[212]W. Doheny, *Canonical Procedure in Matrimonial Cases: Informal Procedure* (Milwaukee: The Bruce Publishing Co., 1944), 197.

The process for obtaining a dissolution is found in Book VII, canons 1697–1706. The competent local ordinary accepts the petition and initiates the gathering of proofs. After the case has been prepared, the acts are submitted to the Sacred Congregation for the Sacraments for further study. The final decision is made by the Supreme Pontiff himself. Several noteworthy changes in the process are explained in the commentary on the procedural canons.

The 1917 Code also stated that a ratified, nonconsummated marriage could be dissolved by the profession of solemn religious vows by one of the spouses. This has been dropped in the present Code.

The Pauline Privilege

Canon 1143 — §1. A marriage entered by two non-baptized persons is dissolved by means of the pauline privilege in favor of the faith of a party who has received baptism by the very fact that a new marriage is contracted by the party who has been baptized, provided the non-baptized party departs.

§2. The non-baptized party is considered to have departed if he or she does not wish to cohabit with the baptized party or does not wish to cohabit in peace without insult to the Creator unless, after receiving baptism, the baptized party gave the other party a just cause for departure.

The Pauline privilege is the dissolution of a natural bond marriage between non-baptized parties. It takes place when one of the parties to the marriage is baptized and then enters a subsequent marriage. The first marriage is dissolved by the second marriage. It is not brought about by direct action on the part of the Church as in the dissolution of a nonconsummated marriage since the Church has no jurisdiction over the marriages of two non-baptized persons.

The dissolution by means of the Pauline privilege is based on an interpretation of the passage of St. Paul (1 Cor 7:12–15) in which the Apostle advises converts to depart if their unbelieving spouses refuse to continue married life in peace. The canonical understanding of the privilege is based on the particular interpretation of the phrase "the brother or sister is not bound." This is understood to mean that the convert is not obliged to remain living with the non-believer but is free to marry another.

There are occasional references to the Pauline saying in the patristic writings in conjunction with the dissolution of marriage, yet there is no conclusive evidence that the Pauline privilege was understood then as it is now. By the high Middle Ages, Gratian and Peter Lombard both spoke of the right of remarriage of the convert if the non-baptized party remarried after separation. The Pauline privilege became part of the Church's canonical legisla-

tion in 1199, [213] yet the way in which and the time when the first marriage was dissolved were only clarified in the 1917 Code (*CIC* 1126).

The marriage to be dissolved must be one in which both of the parties were certainly non-baptized. The dissolution depends on two conditions: that one of the parties is baptized before the second marriage and that the non-baptized party departs. The separation of the spouses in itself does not dissolve the natural bond; rather, the entrance into a new marriage accomplishes the dissolution. Conversion to Catholicism is not required; rather, conversion to Christianity suffices for the use of the privilege. Consequently the privilege can be applied in the following cases:

(a) A Catholic seeks to marry a convert to Catholicism, who was formerly non-baptized and married to a non-baptized person.

(b) A Catholic seeks to marry a convert to another Christian Church who was formerly non-baptized and married to a non-baptized person.

(c) A convert to Catholicism who was formerly non-baptized and married to a non-baptized person seeks to marry a baptized or non-baptized person. In this case the dissolution is granted in virtue of canon 1147.

The Departure of the Non-Baptized Party

The departure is required in order to preclude the convert's using baptism as an excuse for separation. The dissolution is based on the fact that the non-baptized party will not remain with the baptized spouse or will not do so peacefully, allowing the other spouse to fulfill his or her Christian responsibilities. While in the Pauline community the baptism of the convert caused the separation or the hostility of the non-baptized party made conjugal peace nearly impossible, the contemporary situation is somewhat different. In most cases separation and divorce have already occurred prior to a consideration of conversion and the application of the privilege.

The second paragraph of the canon further explains the meaning of departure. It applies to situations in which a married couple are still together and one of the parties is baptized. If the non-baptized spouse leaves, this may result from the baptism of the other spouse, who may not, however, be the culpable cause of the separation. The canonical requirement is not fulfilled if the baptized party is the culpable cause of the separation. If, for instance, the baptized party commits adultery or has an affair and is baptized with the intention of dissolving the marriage, the privilege cannot be applied.

---

[213]X. 4.19.7, *CorpusIC* 2, 722; see also Joyce, 467–475.

The requirement of a departure is fulfilled if the non-baptized party leaves with no intention of returning. The termination of conjugal life may be a direct result of the other spouse's baptism or some other cause, provided it is not the fault of the baptized spouse.

If the non-baptized party refuses to depart yet refuses to live with the baptized spouse peacefully "without insult to the Creator," the departure of the baptized spouse is justified and the privilege may be applied. The phrase "insult to the Creator" refers to conditions which make fulfillment of the obligations of the Christian life difficult or impossible for the baptized party.

The Interpellations

Canon 1144 — §1. In order for the baptized party to contract a new marriage validly, the non-baptized party must always be interrogated on the following points:

1° whether he or she also wishes to receive baptism;

2° whether he or she at least wishes to cohabit in peace with the baptized party without insult to the Creator.

§2. This interrogation must take place after baptism; for a serious reason, however, the local ordinary can permit this interrogation to take place before the baptism, or even dispense from this interrogation either before or after the baptism, provided it is evident in light of at least a summary and extra-judicial process that it cannot take place or that it would be useless.

Proof of departure is canonically demonstrated if the non-baptized spouse manifests an intention: (a) not to be baptized, or (b) not to live peacefully with the baptized party. Ordinarily these intentions are made known in response to the interpellations.

The interpellations are questions posed to the non-baptized party concerning his or her intentions. They are ordinarily made after the baptism of the other spouse; however, the local ordinary clearly has rather extensive discretionary power in this regard. If it is certain that the conversion will take place, the ordinary may permit the interpellations to take place before the baptism. A serious reason is required for this departure from the ordinary procedure.

Formerly the Holy See reserved to itself the right to dispense from the interpellations altogether. This power was extended to diocesan bishops in *De Episcoporum Muneribus* and is theirs by general law in the present Code. Before granting such a dispensation, the local ordinary must objectively determine that the interpellations would either be useless or cannot be made. The summary, non-judicial process mentioned in the canon implies some form of investigation by the ordinary or his delegate to as-

certain if the reasons given for a dispensation are true.

The interpellations are required for the validity of the second marriage since the use of the privilege depends on the verification of the above-mentioned conditions. Yet the interpellations are a means to an end and not an end in themselves. If the whereabouts of the non-baptized spouse are unknown and some form of search turns up no information, the interpellations obviously cannot be made. If, however, it is certain from sources other than the word of the baptized spouse that the other spouse will not convert or live peacefully with the baptized spouse, then a dispensation can be granted. The object of the interpellations and the other processes is to determine the non-baptized spouse's intentions concerning baptism and conjugal life with the baptized spouse. If a civil divorce has already been granted to the spouses, it may be presumed that there is no reasonable hope for reconciliation. In spite of the civil divorce, the common practice in the past was at least to attempt the interpellations.

There are several possible responses to the interpellations:

(a) If the non-baptized party indicates a willingness to be baptized but is unwilling to live in peace with the baptized party, the former's sincerity is doubtful given the ambiguity of the answers. The baptized party is to be allowed to enter a second marriage.[214]

(b) If the non-baptized party does not want to be baptized but indicates a willingness to live in peace with the baptized party, several possibilities arise. Their marital life may be continued with no possibility of a second marriage; or, depending on the circumstances, the baptized party may be allowed to separate with no possibility of a second marriage using the privilege. In this case, if the local ordinary is informed that the non-baptized party may well indicate a willingness to live in peace but is not sincere, he may dispense with the second question regarding peaceful cohabitation and ask only the first concerning baptism.

(c) The non-baptized party may acknowledge the interpellations but at the same time refuse to answer the questions. Such a refusal can be interpreted as a negative response to both questions.

If the spouses have been separated, especially for a long time and the non-baptized party responds affirmatively to one or both of the questions, the response should be carefully evaluated in the light of all of the relevant circumstances and the possible

---

[214]A. Abate, *The Dissolution of the Matrimonial Bond* (Rome: Desclée, 1962), 75.

motivation for such responses. The facts of the case may point to an entirely different conclusion about the departure than the non-baptized party's answers.

Making the Interpellations

Canon 1145 — §1. As a rule, the interrogation is to take place on the authority of the local ordinary of the converted party; if the other spouse asks for a period of time during which to answer, the same ordinary is to grant it while warning the party that after this period has elapsed without any answer, the person's silence will be considered to be a negative answer.

§2. An interrogation carried out privately by the converted party is also valid and is indeed licit if the form prescribed above cannot be observed.

§3. In either case the fact that the interrogation took place and its outcome must legitimately be evident in the external forum.

The interpellations are made by the local ordinary of the baptized party after he first ascertains that the marriage took place while both parties were unbaptized. The usual method is by letter sent by the ordinary or his delegate. A less common method is the actual interrogation of the non-baptized party.

Although the interpellations are regularly to be made by the ordinary, the baptized party may validly do so privately. The fact that the interpellations have been made must be established as well as the authenticity of the responses. The simplest way of proving a private interpellation is for the baptized party to forward a registered or certified letter to the other party with a return receipt requested.

When the questions are posed, the non-baptized party is also to be informed that a reasonable period of time will be allowed for the responses. A set time limit should be stated with a reminder that a failure to respond will be interpreted as a negative answer. Even if the interpellations are privately made, they are a matter of the external forum. There must always be proof that they have been made or attempted as well as proof of the other party's responses.

The law does not state how many times the interpellations are to be made; therefore, it is presumed that they are to be made at least once. Repeated attempts should be made if there is some reason to believe that the other party will respond.

The Second Marriage

Canon 1146 — The baptized party has the right to contract a new marriage with a Catholic party:

1° if the other party answered negatively to the interrogation or if the interrogation has been legitimately omitted;

2° if the non-baptized party, interrogated or not,

at first peacefully cohabited without insult to the Creator but afterwards departed without a just cause, with due regard for the prescriptions of cann. 1144 and 1145.

The baptized party has a right to enter a second marriage once the departure of the non-baptized party has been proven through negative responses to the interpellations or by other means which satisfy the requirements for a dispensation from interpellations.

Rather than enter a second marriage, the baptized party may reconcile with the non-baptized party and reestablish common life. If this reconciliation is unsuccessful and the parties subsequently separate, the baptized party may still use the privilege and enter a second marriage even if sexual relations have occurred between them. Even though one party has been baptized, the union does not become sacramental.

If the baptized party wishes to enter a second marriage after a reconciliation and second separation from the non-baptized party, the interpellations need not be repeated. Nevertheless the usual conditions for the use of the privilege remain and the baptized party is not to have been the cause of the separation. Although the interpellations need not be repeated, there must be some proof of departure.

Entering a Mixed Marriage

Canon 1147 — For a serious cause the local ordinary can permit the baptized party who employs the pauline privilege to contract marriage with a non-Catholic party, whether baptized or not, while observing the prescriptions of the canons on mixed marriages.

If the party using the privilege is a baptized Catholic, he or she may enter a second marriage with a baptized person of another Christian denomination and even with a non-baptized person. The Catholic party must obtain the local ordinary's permission if it is a mixed marriage and a dispensation from the impediment if it is a disparity of cult marriage. In either case the canons on mixed marriages are to be fulfilled (cc. 1124–1129).

The local ordinary may permit such marriages for a grave cause. In both cases the privilege is applied as a favoring of the faith of the newly baptized Catholic. An assurance that the permission or dispensation will not endanger this faith but will in fact serve to strengthen it combined with the Catholic's basic right to marriage provide a basis for the requisite cause.

Special Provisions for Polygamous Marriages

Canon 1148 — §1. After he has received baptism in the Catholic Church, a previously non-

baptized man who simultaneously has several non-baptized wives can keep one of them as his wife while dismissing the others if it is difficult for him to remain with the first. The same is true for a non-baptized woman who simultaneously has several non-baptized husbands.

§2. In the situations mentioned in §1, marriage is to be contracted according to the the legitimate form after the reception of baptism, while observing the prescriptions on mixed marriages if necessary, as well as the other requirements of law.

§3. After considering the moral, social and economic situation of the area and of the persons, the local ordinary is to take care that sufficient provision is made in accord with the norms of justice, Christian charity and natural equity for the needs of the first wife and of the other wives who are dismissed.

During the period of missionary expansion, particularly in the sixteenth century, missionaries frequently encountered prospective converts who were in complicated marital situations which were incompatible with the Church's teaching on marriage. Consequently three papal constitutions issued in 1537, 1571, and 1585 dealt with the procedures to be followed particularly in cases of polygamy.[215] These provisions were issued specifically for certain mission territories in which these circumstances were encountered. The 1917 Code extended the provisions so that they could be applied to similar circumstances encountered anywhere (*CIC* 1125).

The present canon is a practical refinement of the provisions of these constitutions. It incorporates some of their principles as well as the principles of the Pauline privilege.

If a convert has several wives or husbands, he or she may not remain in a polygamous marriage. If it can be done without difficulty, the convert should remain with the first person he or she married. If not, one of the spouses is to be chosen by the convert and the others dismissed. The spouse chosen by the convert is not required to accept baptism.

The subsequent marriage is to be contracted according to canonical form. Permission for a mixed marriage or a dispensation from the impediment of disparity of cult is to be obtained from the local ordinary if either is needed. The permission for the convert to choose a spouse and enter a Catholic marriage does not implicitly contain any needed dispensations.

The usual provisions of law concerning the premarital examination and instruction are to be followed as well as the other provisions of law concerning marriage. If some of the children already born to the union remain with the convert

and his or her spouse, they are not required to convert. However the spouses are required to have baptized and raised in the Catholic Church any children born of the second union.

Finally, the local ordinary of the converting party is to make sure that provision is made for the dismissed wives. No such provision is required for the dismissed husbands. The ordinary himself does not have to provide for the dismissed wives, but he is to do what he can to see that this obligation is fulfilled, presumably by the husband who converted.

Although no mention is made of any children who may be involved, the convert, especially if he is the father of the children is bound in justice to see that they are provided for. Although canon 1071, §1, 3° is not mentioned, the obligations to which it refers apply here as in any other marriage.

Separation Due to Captivity or Persecution

Canon 1149 — A non-baptized person who, once having received baptism in the Catholic Church, cannot restore cohabitation with a non-baptized spouse due to captivity or persecution can contract another marriage even if the other party received baptism in the meantime, with due regard for the prescription of can. 1141.

This canon is based on the papal constitution *Populis* (January 25, 1585). It applies to situations in which two non-baptized parties to a marriage are separated from each other due to captivity or persecution. A party baptized during the separation may enter a subsequent marriage even with a non-baptized person. The law presumes that a reconciliation between the original spouses is either impossible or not desired by them.

If only one spouse converts, the case resembles a Pauline privilege although the canon does not specifically state that the second marriage dissolves the first. Nevertheless this can be presumed since the circumstances are the same. Yet this canon makes an interesting exception to the requirements of the Pauline privilege. If the other spouse also is baptized during the separation, the first spouse may still enter a second marriage. If both parties are baptized during the separation and before a subsequent marriage by either one, their union becomes sacramental though non-consummated. In this case the canon contains an implicit dissolution of the ratified but non-consummated bond. Why is the normal process for such dissolutions not required in such cases? The discussions of the marriage committee reveal little more than the fact that this question came up.[216] Nevertheless the circumstances in which the canon may be applied are such that it is presumed that contact or communication between the separated spouses is difficult if not impossible.

[215]*Altitudo* of Paul III, June 1, 1537; *Romani pontificis* of Pius V, Aug. 2, 1571 and *Populis* of Gregory XIII, Jan. 25, 1585. See F. Woods, *The Constitutions of Canon 1125* (Milwaukee: The Bruce Publishing Co., 1935).

[216]*Comm* 10 (1978), 116.

The canon implies that even if the other spouse is baptized there is no way of knowing this for certain. This is a case of doubt in which the faith of the convert as well as his or her right to marry are favored (cf. c. 1150).

The canon does admit of the possibility of reconciliation of the separated spouses. If both have been baptized and sexual intercourse occurs, the marriage becomes consummated as well as ratified and an absolutely indissoluble bond exists. Consequently no second marriage is possible for either party.

The application of this canon presupposes that the convert entering a second marriage fulfills the usual canonical requirements for entrance into marriage.

The Favor of the Law

Canon 1150 — In a doubtful matter the privilege of the faith enjoys the favor of the law.

This canon is an exception to the presumption in favor of marital validity contained in canon 1060. If a positive and insoluble doubt exists about certain facts in a privilege case, the law favors the dissolution and privilege of the faith rather than the validity of the prior marriage.

This presumption is applied only to non-sacramental marriages which may be dissolved by the Pauline privilege or in virtue of canons 1148 and 1149.[217] In these cases a presumably valid but non-sacramental marriage is dissolved in favor of a sacramental marriage or to preserve the faith of a Catholic party even in a non-sacramental marriage. Even if the second marriage is non-sacramental, the Catholic party's faith is favored precisely because his or her new marital status is recognized by the Church.

The canon is best understood in terms of the kinds of doubts which may arise. These concern most of the conditions under which the non-sacramental marriage may be dissolved. Nevertheless certain of these conditions must be verified and are not open to doubt, namely, the non-baptism of at least one of the parties and the nature of the marriage to be dissolved. Other conditions related to the dissolution concern the departure of the non-baptized party, the interpellations, the sincerity of the replies, the baptismal status of the other party, etc.

Baptism

If a doubt arises about the baptismal status of one or both of the parties, special circumstances are present. If an insoluble doubt about the non-baptism of each of the parties arises, the Pauline privilege may not be applied. If there is an insoluble doubt about one of the parties, the case is to be referred to the Holy See.[218] The exception to this situation is the possible baptism of the other party mentioned in canon 1149. Here, even if it is certain that the other is baptized, the second marriage is permitted.

Validity of the Non-Sacramental Marriage

If there is a question about the validity of the marriage, such as the presence of an impediment, lack of sufficient consent, etc., the privilege may be applied even though the doubt cannot be resolved.

The Interpellations

Several doubts could arise about the interpellations such as the sufficiency of the reason for dispensing from them, the sincerity of the replies of the departed party, or the length of time allowed for the replies. If such a doubt cannot be objectively resolved, the second marriage may be permitted.

The Cause of Departure

If there is a doubt about who was the cause of the departure with the possibility that the baptized party was the cause, the matter should be looked into. If the question cannot be resolved or if the other party is unconcerned that the convert may have been at least partially responsible for the separation, then the privilege may be applied.[219]

The dissolution of the first marriage depends on its non-sacramental nature (with the exception mentioned in c. 1149). Consequently this point is not open to doubt.

If a positive but insoluble doubt arises about one or more of the above-mentioned factors and remains even after serious attempts have been made to resolve it, the presumption of the canon may be applied in favor of the dissolution of the marriage. Except for a doubt about the baptismal status of the parties, the local ordinary is competent to decide when a doubt is insoluble and hence when the privilege may be applied.

The Privilege of the Faith

While the 1917 Code was in force, marriages between a baptized and non-baptized party were regularly dissolved in virtue of what was commonly known as the privilege of the faith. This type of dis-

---

[217]Certain canonists have recently debated whether or not the presumption of *CIC* 1127 (c. 1150) is applicable to all marriages (including sacramental) and not merely Pauline privilege cases. For the broad approach, see R. Carney, "New Applications of Canon 1127," *CLSAP* (1977), 49–52; J. Provost, "Some Approaches to the Applications of Canon 1127," *J* 40 (1980), 426–434. For the traditional interpretation, see L. Orsy, "An Evaluation of 'New Applications of Canon 1127,'" *J* 38 (1978), 163–170; L. Orsy, "More about Canon 1127: The Power of the Diocesan Tribunal," *J* 39 (1979), 447–455.

[218]Holy Office, June 10, 1937, *CLD* 2, 343.
[219]Bouscaren-Ellis, 630.

solution differed from the Pauline privilege in that it involved direct action by the Supreme Pontiff, who dissolved such marriages in virtue of his vicarious ministerial power. Although there was no provision for such dissolutions in the 1917 Code, the pope first dissolved such a marriage in 1924.[220]

At first, dissolutions were granted only to baptized non-Catholics who had been married to non-baptized persons and later converted to Catholicism and sought to marry a Catholic. In time, the privilege of the faith was extended to non-baptized persons who wished to marry Catholics and finally to either party of a non-sacramental marriage entered into with a dispensation from the impediment of disparity of cult.

Although the 1917 Code contained no canons pertaining to privilege of the faith dissolutions, they regularly took place. The Holy See issued two sets of instructions concerning privilege of the faith dissolutions, one in 1934 and the other in 1973. The 1980 schema contained one proposed canon dealing with them (c. 1104), which was dropped in the final version of the Code. Nevertheless the institution of the privilege of the faith will continue, administered according to the 1973 norms.[221]

ARTICLE 2: SEPARATION WHILE THE BOND ENDURES
[cc. 1151-1155]

The Obligation of Living the Common Life

Canon 1151 — Spouses have the duty and the right to preserve conjugal living unless a legitimate cause excuses them.

The common life or actual living together of the spouses is essential if the purposes of marriage are to be attained. The community of the whole of life depends on living arrangements facilitating the spouses actually being together since this community involves the joining of the persons in the total union which is the essence of marriage (c. 1055). The common life (*convictus coniugalis*) is a fundamental obligation of marriage; the spouses must be present to each other in order to bring about each other's good and to nurture any children born of the union. The gravity of the obligation is related to the nature of marriage itself.

Nevertheless marital discord is a reality. Situations may arise which make the harmonious living of married life impossible. While the spouses have the obligation to do all in their power to foster the

common life, a separation may be the more prudent way of dealing with a relationship that has deteriorated to the point where it actually is the opposite of what true marriage is supposed to be.

The canon states that a legitimate cause excuses the spouses from maintaining the marital community. The procedural norms on marital separation (cc. 1692–1696) provide the means of determining if there is such a cause. Most civil jurisdictions also have processes whereby spouses are legally separated but not divorced. In any case of separation the indissoluble bond remains intact. Although the spouses do not share a life together, they are still married to one another and are bound to the obligation of fidelity.

The Role of Church Authority

While the initial marriage canons present a decidedly personalist view of the sacrament, it is also true that the public commitment, once made, is subject to the laws of a higher authority than the spouses themselves. Because of the indissoluble nature of marriage and its ecclesial role, ecclesiastical authority gives practical witness to the seriousness of the marital covenant by requiring couples to submit their case to the Church when separation is contemplated.

Although the Code presents separation primarily as a judicial and administrative matter, it also incorporates two other vital elements: charitable forgiveness of a spouse which is rooted in the very nature of the conjugal covenant, and the value of involving a third party in the process of discerning whether or not counseling or some other form of intervention will assist in restoring marital life.

These two elements are essential to understanding the Church's role when a spouse presses his or her right to terminate common life. Church authorities must balance the welfare of the spouses, the practical obligation of cohabitation, and the good of any children involved. The right to separate is not to be taken lightly. Whether or not a permanent separation is allowed or whether the parties are encouraged to work at a reconciliation depends greatly on the cause of the discord and the quality of their relationship.

The Complexity of Marital Separation

Marital separation is far from a simple matter. It produces various effects on the spouses and the children since it is usually a peak moment in a process of gradual disintegration of the marital relationship. It is not an end or solution to the problems of a troubled marriage but the beginning of a new stage in the relationship.

A separation can have a positive outcome if the spouses have a basic commitment to one another and use the occasion to examine their relationship. Since serious marital problems can rarely if ever be

---

[220]Holy Office, Nov. 5, 1924, *CLD* 1, 553. This is the famous Helena case.

[221]Holy Office, May 1, 1934, unpublished in English; SCDF, *Norms,* Dec. 6, 1973, *CLD* 8, 1177–1185. The fact that the 1973 norms continue to be operative was communicated to the Apostolic Delegate in the U.S. by the SCDF in a private but unrestricted response dated Sept. 8, 1983.

solved by the spouses themselves, the help of a counselor is essential. Depending on the circumstances of the separation and the effectiveness of the counseling, the separation can bring about a stronger marital relationship.

The initial separation may be a prelude to divorce if the relationship has deteriorated to such an extent that there is no commitment of the spouses to each other or to their marriage. In this case they must realize that the separation will have a variety of psychological effects on them[222] as well as social, familial, and economic effects.[223] The separation itself and the entire process of marital disintegration have a profound effect on the children of a marriage.[224]

Separation because of Adultery

Canon 1152 — **§1. Although it is earnestly recommended that a spouse, moved by Christian charity and a concern for the good of the family, not refuse pardon to an adulterous partner and not break up conjugal life, nevertheless, if the spouse has not expressly or tacitly condoned the misdeed of the other spouse, the former does have the right to sever conjugal living, unless he or she consented to the adultery, gave cause for it, or likewise committed adultery.**

§2. Tacit condonation exists if the innocent spouse, after having become aware of the adultery, continued voluntarily to live with the other spouse in marital affection. Tacit condonation is presumed if the innocent spouse continued conjugal living for a period of six months and has not had recourse to ecclesiastical or civil authority.

§3. If the innocent spouse spontaneously severed conjugal living, that spouse within six months is to bring a suit for separation before the competent ecclesiastical authority; this authority, after having investigated all the circumstances, is to decide whether the innocent spouse can be induced to forgive the misdeed and not to prolong the separation permanently.

Historically in Christian and non-Christian tradition adultery has been considered the ultimate offense against a marriage relationship. In Roman law and in earlier legal systems, adultery was generally treated as a grave offense against the proprietary rights of the husband. It was also surrounded by various religious and cultural taboos.

In the Christian tradition with its radically different understanding of marital fidelity, sexual intercourse outside of marriage by either partner is an offense against the right to fidelity which is enjoyed by both husband and wife. It is also a grave offense against the covenant relationship itself. Just as the union of the two in one flesh is effected and symbolized by sexual consummation, so too the rupture of this union is symbolized by intercourse with a third party.

In spite of the gravity of adultery, the law appeals to the essential covenant element of forgiveness. The marital union is not grounded in sexual union but on a more comprehensive joining of the spouses grounded in charity. The law also appeals to the good of the family as a motivation for forgiving an adulterous spouse. One of the challenging aspects of marital fidelity is a love for the other which enables a spouse to overcome unfaithfulness. Because of this appeal to forgiveness, the right to separation as a result of adultery is not absolute.

The first paragraph of the canon qualifies the exercise of the right to separate. The innocent spouse loses this right, barring forgiveness, if he or she condoned the adultery, gave cause for it, consented to it, or committed adultery himself or herself. The canon refers to the right to separate and not to the solution of the problems in the relationship since the spouses still have an obligation to try to heal the marriage.

Although the innocent spouse loses the right to separate if he or she condoned the adultery or was adulterous, this does not mean that they are to remain together, continuing this kind of married life. Cooperation in adultery or condoning extra-marital relationships is a serious perversion of the covenant. It is an offense against the Christian dignity of the spouses and the sacrament as well. It may also be construed to be an offense against any children of the marriage since they too have a right to expect stability and honesty in their parents' relationship.

"Tacit condonation" is defined as knowing of a spouse's adultery yet remaining with him or her and continuing to engage in sexual relations. This condonation is presumed if the innocent spouse remains with the adulterous spouse for six months or more without recourse to ecclesiastical or civil authority. The innocent party must remain of his or her own accord in order to forfeit the right of separation. If it is not morally or physically possible to leave or if the innocent spouse unwillingly assents to sexual intercourse, then condonation is not presumed.

Within six months after a separation due to adultery, the innocent spouse should approach the ecclesiastical authority for a consideration of the case. The separation is already a fact. The authority's role is to decide whether permission should be given for an indefinite separation or whether reconciliation should be urged.

A truly innocent spouse is gravely offended by adultery and hence should not be made to bear the

[222]R. Weiss, *Marital Separation* (New York: Basic, 1975), 36–68.

[223]A. Cherlin, *Marriage, Divorce and Remarriage* (Cambridge: Harvard University, 1981), 69–92.

[224]T. Doyle, "The Effects of Marital Disintegration on Children," *Priest* 37 (1981), 10–17. See also Weiss, 167–204, and J. Desperts, *Children of Divorce* (New York: Doubleday, 1962).

entire burden of trying to repair the rupture of the marital community. The ecclesiastical authority, after carefully considering all of the circumstances of the case, may see possibilities for a reconciliation. He should then try to convince the innocent party to forgive the other spouse and work toward a reconciliation, usually through some form of counseling. Nevertheless the ecclesiastical authority may not force this point if it appears to be a moral impossibility.

Although the canon does not mention it, the errant spouse should be approached by the ecclesiastical authority either by mail or through some other form of contact. The former should be encouraged to participate in the process since this will enable the authority to assess the possibilities of reconciliation more realistically.

Separation for Other Causes

Canon 1153 — §1. If either of the spouses causes serious danger of spirit or body to the other spouse or to the children, or otherwise renders common life too hard, that spouse gives the other a legitimate cause for separating in virtue of a decree of the local ordinary, or even on his or her own authority if there is danger in delay.

§2. In all cases, when the reason for the separation ceases to exist, conjugal living is to be restored unless ecclesiastical authority decides otherwise.

The 1917 Code listed adultery as the only cause for permanent separation; it also gave other causes for temporary separation (*CIC* 1131). The present Code does not give examples of other causes. Rather, it states that situations which result in serious danger "of spirit or body" to the innocent spouse or children can justify a separation. In such cases it is urged that recourse to the ecclesiastical authority be made prior to the actual separation. Nevertheless, if there is danger in delay, the innocent spouse may act on his or her own authority.

It is impossible to provide a taxative list of situations or actions which could cause serious danger to "spirit or body" or otherwise make the common life too difficult to sustain. The law refers here to serious problems which are not easily resolved and not to situations which cause surmountable tensions in a marriage. Part of the process of growing together in the marital community is learning to confront and overcome misunderstandings and tensions.

Although the canons use language which implies guilt and innocence, marital discord may not always result from morally culpable acts. One or the other party may be afflicted with a serious mental disorder or character disturbance which results in bizarre behavior endangering the other party and common life. In such cases the right of separation is also applicable.

If the cause for the separation ceases, the parties must restore the common life. This statement appears simple enough, yet in reality marital rifts are rarely so uncomplicated. If the cause of the discord is truly serious, the spouses will probably be incapable of working out a true reconciliation on their own. The ecclesiastical authority should allow protracted separation only after attempts at counseling have been made. If the parties agree to resume common life, they should be strongly encouraged to enter into a counseling program in order to examine the cause of the problem and strengthen the relationship.

The ecclesiastical authority mentioned in the canons is either the diocesan bishop, who may authorize a separation by decree, or a competent judge, who issues a sentence of separation at the conclusion of a judicial process (c. 1692). A spouse may initiate a temporary separation on his or her own authority (cc. 1152–1153), but a permanent separation may be authorized only by a competent ecclesiastical authority.

Provision for the Children

Canon 1154 — After the separation of the spouses, suitable provision is to be made for the adequate support and education of the children.

This canon dealing with the provision for the care and education of the children in cases of separation is considerably simpler than prior legislation (*CIC* 1132). The appropriate decisions in this regard are to be made by the spouses themselves.

When a separation occurs the spouses usually resort to civil action leading to a legal separation. A key part of this process is working out legally enforced details about the support of the children, terms of custody, visitation rights, etc. In addition to those more practical matters it is essential that the spouses be guided in relating to each other and to their children. All too often the children can become pawns in the continued struggle between the parents thus causing them additional emotional and psychological trauma and perhaps even permanent damage. Some civil and ecclesiastical jurisdictions provide counseling services aimed specifically at helping separated parents to deal positively with their children.

Resumption of the Common Life

Canon 1155 — The innocent spouse can laudably readmit the other spouse to conjugal life, in which case the former renounces the right to separate.

A spouse given permission for a permanent separation is not obliged to reestablish common life. If, however, the spouse who exercised the right to separate admits the other spouse to common life again, the right is renounced. Any subsequent separation must take place according to the norms of law.

Ecclesiastical Penalties and Separation

There are no ecclesiastical penalties for failure to observe the canons on separation. Spouses who separate without ecclesiastical permission may not be deprived of the sacraments unless one or the other enters a subsequent marriage without ecclesiastical approval.

Also, the canons on separation apply to marriages in which only one party is Catholic or baptized as well as to marriages between two Catholics.

Civil Divorce Action

Although Catholics should obtain ecclesiastical permission to initiate civil divorce action, in fact a good number do not seek such a permission. If a divorce is obtained, the spouses are prohibited from a subsequent marriage since the marriage bond is presumed to perdure even though common life has been definitively terminated. On the other hand, they are neither excommunicated nor prohibited from receiving the sacraments or fully participating in the Church's life.

The proliferation of divorce in contemporary society is an unfortunate reality which the Church has dealt with in a positive and pastoral manner. Many dioceses have offices or programs for the pastoral care of the separated and divorced including those who have remarried without ecclesiastical approbation. The existence of these programs does not indicate a change in the Church's teaching on the indissolubility of marriage or its stress on the obligations of spouses to maintain common life. They do, however, acknowledge the complex reality of marital breakdown and the need for comprehensive pastoral action for those who have experienced it.[225]

The high incidence of divorce among Catholics in recent years has also prompted a good deal of research in the causes of marital breakdown.[226] As the ecclesiastical tribunals and other Church authorities have studied this phenomenon on a case by case basis, they have been able to arrive at a deeper and more comprehensive understanding of the nature of the marital relationship. This in turn has prompted a heightened appreciation for the value of more thorough preparation for marriage.

---

[225]See M. Durkin and J. Hitchcock, *Catholic Perspectives: Divorce* (Chicago: Thomas More, 1979); J. Rue and L. Shanahan, *The Divorced Catholic* (New York: Paulist Press, 1972); J. Young, ed., *Ministering to the Divorced Catholic* (New York: Paulist Press, 1979).

[226]T. Doyle, "Marital Breakdown: the Experience of the Tribunal," *Priest* 37 (1981), 16–20, and Cherlin, 33–68.

CHAPTER X
CONVALIDATION OF MARRIAGE
[cc. 1156–1165]

ARTICLE 1: SIMPLE CONVALIDATION
[cc. 1156–1160]

A valid marriage comes into existence with the exchange of consent by the spouses. If at least one of the spouses is Catholic, consent must be exchanged according to canonical form. If an undispensed impediment is present, if the consent of at least one of the parties is deficient for a canonically recognized reason, or if canonical form is not observed, the consent is invalid. Consequently no marriage covenant comes into existence.

If the consent is invalid and the spouses continue to share a common life, the law provides a remedy for making the consent valid. This is called convalidation, and it may be applied when the marital relationship exists despite the lack of a juridically recognized marital covenant. Convalidation is a legal remedy by which the original consent, invalid in itself, is subsequently made valid. Convalidation always presupposes that the consent of the parties, though canonically invalid, continues to exist.

The convalidation of a marriage may take place in a number of ways. The two major categories are:

(a) simple convalidation which may take place by a private renewal of consent or public renewal according to canonical form, and

(b) *sanatio in radice,* or radical sanation, which literally means a "healing in the root."

The most common manner of convalidation is the renewal of consent according to canonical form. Although this is commonly known as the "blessing" of a marriage, this term is inaccurate and misleading because it implies that the renewed consent was actually valid from the beginning but given the added religious or sacramental dimension through the convalidation. Another term often used is "validation" which while technically correct is less accurate than "convalidation." This latter term is preferred because it connotes the making valid of an act which had some appearance of validity the first time it was performed. Convalidation always presupposes that marital consent has been expressed in a recognized ecclesiastical or civil forum. It is never applied if the parties have been simply living together or living in a common law marriage.

Simple Convalidation and Sanation

There is a basic difference between the two forms of convalidation. In either case the initial exchange of consent was evidently invalid for one reason or another. In spite of this a human commitment of the spouses to one another still exists whereby they do not consider themselves to be simply living together. Although their union is canonically invalid, it is usually if not always recognized in civil law. This degree of civil formality indicates a marital state of mind which in turn adds an aura of marriage to the relationship. In short, there is a marital commitment of the spouses to one another despite the lack of ecclesiastical recognition.

If the marriage is convalidated by a renewal of consent, the spouses, or at least one of them, is required to make a new marital consent. When this is done, the covenant comes into existence, and the effects of marriage begin with this exchange of consent. In effect the convalidation is brought about by the parties themselves if there is a mutual exchange of consent, or by at least one of them if it is a unilateral expression of consent, presuming always that the consent of the other party continues.

The other manner of convalidation is by radical sanation. This does not involve an exchange of consent or any other action by the parties themselves. It is an action taken by the Holy See, the local ordinary, or others delegated by either of the above. The act of sanation makes the original consent valid. Thus the marriage itself is considered valid from the moment of the initial consent. When a radical sanation is granted, the marriage covenant is considered in law to have existed from the very beginning, and the effects of marriage are retroactive to the moment of the initial consent.

Historical Development

There is some controverted evidence that the Church issued a kind of convalidation for invalid marriages as early as the sixth century. Certain early councils attempted to provide a remedy for converts who entered marriage in good faith prior to conversion yet whom the Church considered invalidly married due to the existence of an impediment. The Council of Orleans III (538) stated that such marriages were to be regarded as valid marriages since they were entered into in good faith.[227]

From the tenth to the thirteenth centuries the popes occasionally dispensed from impediments that had existed at the time consent was exchanged. These dispensations did not include the requirement that consent be renewed.[228] Although there was some insistence upon the renewal of consent

early in the fifteenth century, there was no uniform practice until after the Council of Trent.[229]

The first grant of a radical sanation appears to have been issued by Pope Boniface VIII (1294–1303).[230] In addition to individual sanations, there were also general grants of sanation to remedy large numbers of marriages which were invalid for one or another reason. The first of these took place upon the reception of English Catholics back into union with Rome early in the reign of Mary Tudor (1553–1558).[231]

Simple Convalidation

An invalid union may be convalidated by the renewal of consent either privately or according to canonical form. Simple convalidation takes place when consent is invalid for the following reasons: (a) the presence of an undispensed impediment, (b) defective consent, or (c) lack of canonical form.

Marriages Invalid Due to an Impediment

Canon 1156 — §1. To convalidate a marriage which is invalid due to a diriment impediment, it is required that the impediment cease or that it be dispensed and that at least the party who is aware of the impediment renew consent.

§2. This renewal of consent is required by ecclesiastical law for the validity of the convalidation even if both parties furnished consent at the beginning and have not revoked it later.

If a diriment impediment were present and not dispensed at the time of the original consent, it must either have ceased or been dispensed before the marriage can be convalidated by a renewal of consent.

Certain impediments cease with time or the change of circumstances: lack of age ceases with time, and prior bond (*ligamen*) ceases with the death of a former spouse or the dissolution of the bond. The impediments of sacred orders and public vows themselves are not dispensed. Rather the obligation of celibacy is dispensed.

Any other impediment must be dispensed at the time of convalidation. If it cannot be dispensed, consent cannot be renewed since it would be invalid as was the original consent.

The essential element for a simple convalidation, presuming that the impediment ceases or is dispensed, is the *renewal of consent*. This is an act of the will whereby the party or parties conscious of the impediment consent to marriage with the other.

227Bruns, *Canones Apostolorum et Conciliorum Saeculorum IV-VII*, 2 vols. (Berolini, 1839), 2, 194.

228J. Brennan, *The Simple Convalidation of Marriage* (Washington, D.C.: Catholic University of America, 1937), 18: "It was late in the thirteenth century when the renewal of consent was demanded for the first time in the simple convalidation of marriage.... The early councils merely issued permission to those living in invalid marriages to continue in them."

229Ibid., 19.

230T. Ryan, *The Juridical Effects of the 'Sanatio in Radice'* (Washington, D.C.: Catholic University of America, 1955), 13.

231Ibid., 14–16.

The parties may well recognize that their marriage is invalid according to ecclesiastical law but valid under civil law. Their original consent may not have changed because of the knowledge of the impediment, but in fact it may have become stronger by the passage of time. In spite of this, a new act of consent and not simply a reaffirmation of the original consent is required at least by the party who is aware of the impediment.

Although the original consent is juridically invalid, it must still exist if the union is to be convalidated. This means that the original marital intention, based on the spouses' commitment to each other, still exists. It would be absurd to expect two persons to elicit a new act of consent if their commitment to each other had died.

Application to Non-Catholics

The obligation to renew consent is of ecclesiastical law, therefore non-Catholics are not bound by it. If a marriage is to be validated after the cessation or dispensation of an impediment and both parties are Catholic, then both must renew consent. If, however, one party is not a Catholic then that party *may* renew consent but is not bound to do so. He or she must affirm that the original consent still exists.

Before a marriage is convalidated, the pastoral minister must be certain that the party or parties who will renew consent understand what is happening. There must be an intention to create a sacramental or natural bond covenant based on the spouses' enduring commitment to each other. It is certainly unwise to encourage or even allow a convalidation if the sole motivation is to please parents or family members, salvage a troubled relationship, or attain some other end which is quite distinct from entrance into a true marriage.

Even though the non-Catholic is not bound to renew consent, if he or she is aware of the presence of an impediment, its nature should be explained. Also the concept of validity and invalidity as it applies to marriage should be clarified. If the question of the legitimacy of children arises, the pastoral minister should refer to canon 1137 which explains that children born of a putative marriage are legitimate.

A New Act of the Will

Canon 1157 — The renewal of consent must be a new act of the will concerning a marriage which the person who is renewing consent knows or thinks was null from the beginning.

If one or both of the parties are not aware that their first exchange of consent is invalid, they can hardly be expected to give new consent. It is not necessary that they have certain knowledge of nullity, yet upon explanation of the situation by the pastoral minister, they must at least accept the possibility that the first consent is juridically invalid. Knowledge of nullity may not have been present from the beginning of the union but is somehow verified at the time of the validation. The pastoral minister should distinguish between the spouses' sense of commitment and love for each other, present at the time of the original consent, and the canonical requirements for a valid consent leading to a valid marriage.

The term "renewal" of consent may appear misleading. The original consent may be naturally sufficient, resulting in the spouses' enduring commitment to each other. Yet it is juridically ineffective. The new consent must be a new act of the will, distinct from the first consent. Furthermore, it must relate to marriage here and now with the acknowledgment of the fact that it will result in a new sacramental or natural bond.

Non-Catholics may well consider the first exchange of consent to have been sufficient and still effective. Under the 1917 Code they were required to elicit a new act of consent and not merely reaffirm perduring consent. Consequently the acceptance of the true nature of convalidation posed a serious problem. Recent studies have indicated that most of the simple convalidations later declared to have been invalid were so because of the failure of at least one party to elicit a true act of consent. This failure was based on the often-held conviction that the convalidation was actually a blessing and not really a marriage.[232]

If the non-Catholic party truly accepts the force of canon law and believes that the original consent is invalid, then he or she would be required to renew consent.

Public and Occult Impediments and Renewal of Consent

Canon 1158 — §1. If the impediment is a public one, the consent is to be renewed by both parties according to the canonical form, with due regard for the prescription of can. 1127, §2.

§2. If the impediment cannot be proven to exist, it is sufficient that the consent be renewed privately and in secret by the party who is aware of the impediment, provided the other party perseveres in the consent already given, or by both parties when each of them knows about the impediment.

---

[232]See L. Bogdan, *Renewal of Consent in the Simple Validation of Marriage* (Rome: Lateran University, 1979), especially chap. V, "Summary report of the survey of American Viewpoints regarding the simple validation of marriage," 89–103, and J. Johnson, "The 'Simple' Convalidation as a Pastoral Problem," *Stud Can* 15 (1981), 462–479.

The Code distinguishes between public and occult impediments. If the impediment can be proved in the external forum, it is public. If it cannot be so proved, it is considered occult (c. 1074).

It is important to understand that a *public impediment* may not be publicly known. Nevertheless it is still treated as a public impediment despite the lack of publicity. If it is unknown to one of the parties, he or she is to be made aware of it prior to the exchange of consent.[233]

Renewal by canonical form involves all the requirements mentioned by the law with due regard for canon 1127, §3 with its prohibition of two distinct religious ceremonies or the observance of both a Catholic and non-Catholic expression of consent. The pre-nuptial investigation and instruction are to be conducted and the convalidation duly registered.

Occult Impediments

An impediment may be known to one party only and not provable in the external forum. Some examples of occult impediments best illustrate the meaning of the law:

(a) lack of age; if no records or witnesses are available, the party may be aware of the lack of age at the time of the marriage, but there is no way to prove it.

(b) crime in the first degree (*CIC* 1075, 1°), i.e., adultery with a promise to marry. It is possible but highly improbable that the other two degrees (murder, murder by conspiracy) could be unprovable as well.

(c) abduction, provided the force used to retain the woman has ceased and she remains with the abductor of her own free will.

Although the legislation on certain impediments has been changed from the 1917 Code, this does not alter the invalidity of a marriage entered into before the present Code with an undispensed diriment impediment which is not found in the present Code. The diriment impediments or degrees of impediments invalidating marriage in the 1917 Code but which are not included in the present one are as follows:

(a) crime in the first degree (*CIC* 1075, 1°);

(b) sacred order of subdeacon (*CIC* 1072);

(c) consanguinity, third degree of the collateral line (second cousins) (*CIC* 1076, §2);

(d) affinity, first and second degrees of the collateral line (*CIC* 1077, §1);

(e) spiritual relationship (*CIC* 1079).

Private Renewal of Consent

If the marriage is invalid due to an occult impediment, it may be convalidated by the private renewal of consent. This means that the spouses exchange marital consent privately, by some sign, verbal or otherwise. It is also to be done secretly, that is, without making the fact known to anyone else. Consent which is renewed privately does not involve canonical form. There is no need for the presence of a priest and witnesses are *not* to be present nor is the private renewal recorded in the marriage register. The pastoral minister the couple consults should explain the meaning of private and secret renewal to them.

If only one party is conscious of the presence of an undispensed occult impediment, he or she is bound neither to inform the other party nor to tell the other that the marriage is invalid. The party conscious of the impediment is bound to renew consent even though the other party does not know why. This can be done by some manifestation to the other of the person's commitment to marriage. It may be verbal but it also may be in the form of sexual intercourse performed as an expression of love and commitment.[234] The party may, however, choose to inform the other spouse of the impediment but should do so in a way that will not disrupt marital life. In any case, the convalidation requires that the occult impediment must have ceased or been dispensed and the original commitment and consent still be in existence.

Invalidity Due to Defect of Consent

Canon 1159 — §1. A marriage which is invalid due to a defect of consent is convalidated when the party who had not consented now gives consent, provided the consent given by the other party still exists.

§2. If the defect of consent cannot be proven it is sufficient that the party who did not consent gives consent privately and in secret.

§3. If the defect of consent can be proven it is necessary that the consent be given according to the canonical form.

Marital consent may also be invalid due to a substantial defect of consent. This would be true of marriages entered into because of force and fear, marriages entered into with an attached invalidating condition, or marriages in which one or both

---

[233]J. Chelodi, *Ius Matrimoniale iuxta Codicem Iuris Canonici*, 3rd ed. (Trent: 1921), n. 164.

[234]Bouscaren-Ellis, 641.

parties simulated consent. One or both parties may be conscious of having entered the union with a definite intention against children, fidelity, or permanence and later, having matured, renounced the formerly held attitude. Even if this contrary intention or condition is withdrawn, the consent which it affected remains invalid and must be renewed. The same is true of forced or conditioned marriages. The original circumstances may have changed and the parties' commitment to each other become truly marital, yet the original consent remains invalid.

First, it is necessary that there be knowledge of nullity by at least one of the parties. Furthermore a valid renewal presupposes an intention to marry according to the mind of the Church and perduring consent on the part of both parties.

If the defect of consent cannot be proved in the external forum as with simulation, the party or parties may renew consent privately and secretly. This may be accomplished by a direct, verbal expression of renewal or by an act or acts which manifest a conscious intention to enter a true marriage. If both parties are aware of the defect of consent and consequent nullity, then both must exchange consent. If the situation is known only to one and he or she does not want to disclose it to the other, then consent is renewed by this party only (c. 1158).

If the defect of consent can be proved in the external forum or if it has been proved in the external forum, the renewal must take place according to canonical form. This would be true in cases of marriages entered into by force and fear which are known to others or marriages already declared null by a tribunal.

Private renewal of consent is urged by the law in order to avoid scandal or embarrassment to the parties. Nevertheless they are free to request that renewal take place according to canonical form.

Invalidity Due to Defect of Form

Canon 1160 — **With due regard for the prescription of can. 1127, §2, marriage which is invalid due to a defect of form must be contracted anew according to canonical form in order to become valid.**

A marriage may be invalid due to defect of form in two ways: total lack of form and lack of substantial form. There is a total lack of form if the marriage involves at least one Catholic and takes place before a non-Catholic minister or civil official without a dispensation from form. This does not apply to Latin or Oriental Catholics who marry before an Oriental Orthodox bishop or priest without a dispensation from form. Such marriages are illicit but valid (c. 1127, §1).

A lack of substantial form means that the parties exchanged consent according to what appeared to be canonical form but which is actually invalid due to the absence of an essential element. This would

be the case if the priest or deacon lacked the faculties to witness the union, if there were no witnesses or only one witness, if the officiant did not ask for and receive the vows, or if the exchange of vows was omitted altogether.

For the validation of marriages invalid due to defect of canonical form for any reason, it is necessary that the former ceremony be recognized as invalid (at least by the Catholic party in mixed marriages) and that new consent be exchanged. Furthermore, this new consent must be expressed according to canonical form.

Since this is a matter of ecclesiastical law, non-Catholics are not obliged to recognize the invalidity of the former consent nor are they bound to give new consent. They must however, express to the sacred minister the fact that their original consent perdures.

ARTICLE 2: RADICAL SANATION
[cc. 1161–1165]

The Nature of Radical Sanation

Canon 1161 — **§1. The radical sanation of an invalid marriage is its convalidation without the renewal of consent, granted by competent authority and including a dispensation from an impediment, if there was one, and from the canonical form, if it was not observed, and the retroactivity into the past of canonical effects.**

§2. The convalidation occurs at the moment the favor is granted; it is understood to be retroactive, however, to the moment the marriage was celebrated unless something else is expressly stated.

§3. A radical sanation is not to be granted unless it is probable that the parties intend to persevere in conjugal life.

Radical sanation, or the healing of a marriage, is the act of a competent ecclesiastical authority which renders valid the consent which was invalid from the beginning. No renewal of consent is required although the original consent, though juridically invalid, must still exist on the part of each spouse.

Radical sanation has three effects:

(a) The invalid consent is made valid from the very moment it was exchanged.

(b) The impediment which made the consent invalid is automatically dispensed (see c. 1163).

(c) The canonical effects of a valid union are applied retroactively to the beginning of the union.

The principal canonical effects mentioned above are the sacramentality of the union (provided both parties were baptized at the time of consent) and the legitimation of any children born of the union. The children are considered legitimate from the time of their birth and not from the time of the act of sanation.

Ordinarily a marriage convalidated by sanation becomes valid from the very beginning once the sanation is granted by the legitimate authority. The spouses need not be present and often are not present when it is granted. In extraordinary situations the sanation may be *imperfect,* that is, not retroactive to the time of the original consent. This is the case if naturally sufficient consent did not exist at the time of entrance into the marriage but was expressed only later on in the relationship. In such cases the competent authority granting the imperfect sanation is clearly to indicate the time from which the consent is to be considered valid.

Theoretically a sanation may also be granted if one of the parties is dead. Although the marriage bond is not brought into existence, the other effects of validity, principally the legitimation of children, can be effected.

The last paragraph of this canon mentions an absolute requirement for a radical sanation: the perduring marital consent of the spouses. If one of the spouses refuses to renew consent either privately or according to canonical form but certainly intends to stay married, the sanation can be granted.

Sanation of Defective Consent

Canon 1162 — §1. A marriage cannot be radically sanated if consent is lacking in either or both of the parties, whether the consent was lacking from the beginning or was given in the beginning but afterwards revoked.

§2. If, however, consent was indeed lacking in the beginning but afterwards was given, a sanation can be granted from the moment the consent was given.

If the original consent was invalid due to a defect such as simulation, force and fear, or an invalidating condition, it cannot be sanated unless the defect has been removed. The consent must have been naturally sufficient at the time it was exchanged in order to be sanated. A consent which is defective due to one of the above-mentioned reasons cannot be made valid since the sanation neither supplies for the defect nor removes it. This can be done only by the party or parties responsible for it. Consequently the defect must be removed if the consent is to be sanated.

Defective consent is convalidated by sanation from the moment the defect is removed or the true consent is furnished. Thus it is not "radical" in that it is not retroactive to the time of the first invalid consent but only to the moment when true consent was furnished.

The canon also states that a sanation cannot be granted if the consent was naturally sufficient in the beginning but afterward removed. Thus if the original consent was free of defect but later on one or both of the parties introduced an intention against children, fidelity, or permanence, a sanation would not be possible since there would not be naturally sufficient consent upon which to base it.

Sanation and Diriment Impediments and Lack of Form

Canon 1163 — §1. A marriage which is invalid due to an impediment or due to defect of legitimate form can be sanated provided the consent of each party continues to exist.

§2. A marriage which is invalid due to an impediment of the natural law or of divine positive law can be sanated only after the impediment has ceased to exist.

A principal effect of radical sanation is the dispensation from impediments which rendered the consent invalid from the beginning.

If the impediment ceased to exist in time, the original consent remains invalid. For retroactive validity it is necessary that the impediment be dispensed from the time of the original consent. The sanation carries an implicit dispensation only from impediments of ecclesiastical law: lack of age, disparity of cult, sacred orders, public vows, abduction, crime, consanguinity in the collateral line after the second degree, affinity, public propriety, legal adoption, and the former impediment of spiritual relationship. The dispensation of certain of these impediments is reserved to the Holy See. This question will be considered under canon 1165.

If the consent is invalid due to an impediment of natural law or divine positive law, the sanation does not grant an automatic dispensation. The impediment must first have ceased in order for the marriage to be sanated. These impediments are prior bond, absolute and perpetual impotence, consanguinity in the direct line and in the second degree of the collateral line. Of these three, only the impediment of prior bond can actually cease either by death or dissolution. Absolute and perpetual impotence and consanguinity do not cease by their very nature.

Defect of Canonical Form

If a marriage is invalid due to a total lack of form or lack of substantial form, it may be sanated. The sanation also carries with it an implicit dispensation from observing the canonical form.

In all cases of sanation the consent of the parties must still exist at the time the sanation is granted.

Awareness of the Parties of the Sanation

Canon 1164 — A sanation can be granted validly even when one or both of the parties are unaware of it, but it is not to be granted except for serious reason.

Since a radical sanation depends primarily on the perduring consent of the parties and the other requirements mentioned above, it is not necessary that both parties know that it has been granted. One party may want a sanation for reasons of conscience while the other party, though committed to the marriage, is unwilling to renew consent. The spouse conscious of the nullity may seek and receive a sanation without the other spouse's ever knowing about it. This is done only for a grave reason and with the assurance that the other party's consent still exists and is free of defects.

A sanation may also be granted if *neither* party is aware of it. Since a sanation is actually a favor, it is not necessary that the spouses request it or even consent to it. The validity of the sanation depends on the perduring consent and the will of the competent authority who grants it. Generally a sanation is not granted if both parties are unwilling to receive it.[235] Nevertheless it could happen in order to legitimate children born of the union. It could also happen that one or more marriages are invalid because of a defect of canonical form. These could be sanated without the spouses ever knowing about it.[236]

The Authority Competent To Grant a Sanation

Canon 1165 — §1. Radical sanation can be granted by the Apostolic See.

§2. In individual cases radical sanation can be granted by the diocesan bishop, even if several reasons for nullity exist in the same marriage, provided the conditions mentioned in can. 1125 concerning the sanation of a mixed marriage are fulfilled. The diocesan bishop cannot grant radical sanation, however, if there is present an impediment whose dispensation is reserved to the Apostolic See in accord with can. 1078, §2, or if it is a question of an impediment of the natural law or of the divine positive law which has ceased to exist.

In the 1917 Code only the Holy See was competent to grant sanations (*CIC* 1141). Nevertheless papal nuncios and apostolic delegates as well as local ordinaries were commonly delegated this faculty.

The Holy See is competent to grant radical sanations either in singular cases or in general, that is,

to whole groups of people. However, there are few examples of general sanations.[237]

The Holy See alone is competent to grant radical sanations in cases involving reserved impediments and in cases of mixed marriages when the requirements of canon 1125 have not been met. Also, the Holy See alone grants sanations in cases involving natural or divine positive law impediments when the impediment has ceased to exist. Consequently marriages invalid due to the following impediments are sanated only by the Holy See "even if the basis for the impediment has ceased to exist": sacred orders, public vow of perpetual chastity in a pontifical institute, crime (c. 1078, §2), and prior bond.

It is clear that the Holy See does not grant sanations for marriages invalid because of consanguinity in the direct line or second degree of the collateral line nor in cases of perpetual impotence.

The Diocesan Bishop

The diocesan bishop is competent to grant sanations in individual cases if the cause of nullity was due to a defect of form, a defect of consent, or an undispensed impediment.

The diocesan bishop may grant sanations in cases involving impediments which are not reserved to the Holy See. He may not grant sanations in cases involving impediments of natural or divine positive law when the impediment has ceased to exist. This limitation of the diocesan bishop's power affects the validity of the sanation.

Mixed Marriages

If the diocesan bishop sanates a mixed marriage, he must be certain that the conditions required for mixed marriages are met (c. 1125). If these conditions are not fulfilled, the sanation may be granted only by the Holy See.

While this canon mentions mixed marriages, it includes disparity of cult unions as well as those of the baptized.[238]

Procedural Notes

A petition for a sanation should be directed to the competent authority, i.e., the diocesan bishop of the place where the parties live or the Holy See. Although the diocesan bishop alone is competent (and not other local ordinaries), he can delegate this power to others.

The petition should contain the pertinent facts of the case as well as the reasons why the original consent was invalid. It should also contain the reasons why a sanation is being requested as opposed to an ordinary convalidation involving a renewal of con-

---

[235]Cappello 5, n. 852, 855.
[236]The diocesan bishop can grant sanations in individual cases only. Group sanations must be referred to the Holy See.

[237]Cappello 5, n. 858, 865–866.
[238]*Comm* 10 (1978), 124.

sent. Finally, there must be assurance that marital consent still exists on the part of both parties and that this consent is free of defects.

If the cause of invalidity is an impediment of natural or divine positive law, proof of its cessation must be provided either by an authentic document

or by the testimony of witnesses. If it is a case of prior bond and proof of death such as a death certificate or its equivalent is not available, the parties should have recourse to the presumed death process in canon 1707.

BIBLIOGRAPHY

Preliminary Norms

Books

Bassett, W. *The Bond of Marriage.* Notre Dame, Ind.: The University of Notre Dame, 1968.

Bassett, W., and Huizing, P. *The Future of Christian Marriage.* Con. 87. New York: Herder and Herder, 1973.

Bouscaren, T., and Ellis, A. *Canon Law: A Text and Commentary.* Milwaukee: The Bruce Publishing Co., 1963.

Cappello, F. *Tractatus Canonico-Moralis De Sacramentis.* 5th ed. Vol. 5. *De Matrimonio.* Rome: Marietti, 1945.

Doms, H. *The Meaning of Marriage.* New York: Sheed and Ward, 1939.

Duby, G. *Medieval Marriage.* Baltimore: Johns Hopkins University, 1978.

Esmein, A. *Le Mariage en droit canonique.* 2 vols. Paris, 1891. Reprinted, New York: Burt Franklin, 1968.

Gasparri, P. *Tractatus Canonicus de Matrimonio.* 2 vols. Rome: Typis Polyglottis Vaticanis, 1932.

Heaney, S. *The Development of the Sacramentality of Marriage from Anselm of Laon to St. Thomas Aquinas.* Washington, D.C.: Catholic University of America, 1963.

Joyce, G. *Christian Marriage.* London: Sheed and Ward, 1933.

Kasper, W. *Theology of Marriage.* New York: Abingdon, 1980.

LeClercq, J. *Monks on Marriage: A Twelfth Century View.* New York: Seabury, 1982.

Mackin, T. *What is Marriage?* New York: Paulist Press, 1982.

———. *Divorce and Remarriage.* New York: Paulist Press, 1984.

Ôueré-Jaulnes, F. *Mariage dans l'Eglise Ancienne.* Paris: Centurion, 1972.

Sampley, J. *And the Two Shall Become One Flesh: A Study of Traditions in Eph. 5:21–33.* Cambridge: University, 1971.

Schillebeeckx, E. *Marriage: Human Reality and Saving Mystery.* New York: Sheed and Ward, 1965.

Articles

Ambrozic, A. "Indissolubility of Marriage in the New Testament: Law or Ideal." *Stud Can* 6 (1972): 269–288.

Ashdowne, M. "The Sacramentality of Marriage: When is it Really Present? Future Dimensions." *Stud Can* 9 (1975): 287–304.

Benoit, P. "Christian Marriage According to St. Paul." *CR* 65 (1980): 309–321.

Bevilacqua, A. "The History of the Indissolubility of Marriage." *CTSAP* 22 (1972): 253–308.

Brueggemann, W. "Of the Same Flesh and Bone." *Catholic Biblical Quarterly* 32 (1970): 532–542.

Doyle, T. "The Relationship of Canon Law to the Catholic Family." *Priest,* 39, no. 2 (Feb. 1983): 37–42.

Gallagher, C. "Marriage and Family in the Revised Code." *CLS:GBIN* (Sept. 1982): 96–118.

Green, T. "The Revision of Marriage Law: An Exposition and Critique." *Stud Can* 10 (1976): 363–410.

Häring, B. "Fostering the Nobility of Marriage and the Family." *Commentary on the Documents of Vatican II.* H. Vorgrimler, ed. Vol. 5. New York: Herder and Herder, 1969, 225–245.

Jossua, J. "The Fidelity of Love and the Indissolubility of Christian Marriage." *CR* 56 (1971): 172–181.

Kordorf, W. "Marriage in the New Testament and the Early Church." *Journal of Ecclesiastical History* 20 (1969): 193–210.

LaDue, W. "Conjugal Love and the Juridical Structure of Christian Marriage." *J* 34 (1974): 36–67.

O'Connor, W. "The Indissolubility of a Ratified, Consummated Marriage." *Ephemerides Theologiae Lovaniensis* 13 (1936): 692–722.

Orsy, L. "Christian Marriage: Doctrine and Law. Glossae on Canons 1012–1015." *J* 40 (1980): 282–348.

Palmer, P. "Christian Marriage: Contract or Covenant." *TS* 33 (1972): 617–665.

Chapter I

Books

Cherlin, A. *Marriage, Divorce, Remarriage: Social Trends in the United States.* Cambridge, Mass.: Harvard University, 1982.

Donovan, J. *The Pastor's Obligation in Pre-Nuptial Investigations.* Washington, D.C.: Catholic University of America, 1938.

Heneghan, J. *The Marriages of Unworthy Catholics.* Washington, D.C.: Catholic University of America, 1949.

Marriage Preparation Resource Book. Washington, D.C.: USCC, 1976.

O'Donnell, C. *The Marriage of Minors.* Washington, D.C.: Catholic University of America, 1945.

Waterhouse, J. *The Power of the Local Ordinary to Impose a Matrimonial Ban.* Washington, D.C.: Catholic University of America, 1952.

Articles

Ambrosiano, A. "Mariage et Eucharistie." *Nouvelle revue théologique* 98 (1976): 289–305.

Carter, M. "Teen-age Marriage: A Diocesan Policy." *J* 35 (1975): 276–295.

Cunningham, R. "Marriage and the Nescient Catholic." *Marriage Studies* 2 (1982): 20–37.

DeNaurois, L. "Marriages of Catholics Who Have Lost the Faith." *Marriage Studies* 2 (1982): 38–59.

Doyle, T. "The Individual's Right to Marry in the Context of the Common Good." *Stud Can* 13 (1979): 245–301.

Hunt, R., and King, M. "Religiosity and Marriage." *Journal For the Scientific Study of Religion* 17 (1978): 379–405.

Jermann, T. "Can the Young Make Good Marriages?" *America* (April 15, 1973): 329–330.

Lynch, T. "Policy on Teen-age Marriages," *CLSAP* (1973): 62–69.

McAreavy, J. "Emotional Immaturity and Diocesan Pre-Marriage Policies," *Stud Can* 16 (1982): 283–330.

Martimort, A. "Contribution de l'histoire liturgique à lá théologie du mariage." *N* 14 (1978): 516–533.

"Parish Weddings." *Pastoral Music* (entire issue) 3 (1978).

Schmeiser, J. "Welcomed Civil Marriage: Canonical Statements." *Stud Can* 14 (1980): 49–88.

Serrano-Ruiz, J. "Values in the Formation of Christian Marriage." *Vidyajoti* (1978): 150–161.

Thomas, M. "An Analysis and Critique of Marriage Preparation Programs." *Marriage Studies* 1 (1981): 1–64.

Villain, A. "Matrimony" Chapter VII in *The History and Liturgy of the Sacraments.* New York: Benziger, 1932, 276–334.

Vogel, C. "The Role of the Liturgical Celebrant in the Formation of the Marriage Bond." *Marriage Studies* 2 (1982): 67–87.

Wrenn, L. "A New Condition Limiting Marriage." *J* 34 (1974): 292–315 (cited as "A New Condition").

Chapter III

Books

Cloran, O. *Previews and Practical Cases on Marriage: Preliminaries and Impediments.* Milwaukee: The Bruce Publishing Co., 1963.

Donohue, J. *The Impediment of Crime.* Washington, D.C.: Catholic University of America, 1944.

Fair, B. *The Impediment of Abduction.* Washington, D.C.: Catholic University of America, 1944.

Gallagher, J. *The Matrimonial Impediment of Public Propriety.* Washington, D.C.: Catholic University of America, 1952.

O'Dea, J. *The Matrimonial Impediment of Non-Age.* Washington, D.C.: Catholic University of America, 1944.

Schenk, F. *The Matrimonial Impediments of Mixed Religion and Disparity of Cult.* Washington, D.C.: Catholic University of America, 1929.

Articles

Bride, A. "Empêchements de mariage." *DDC.* Paris: Letouzey et Ané, 1949, vol. 5, col. 266.

O'Rourke, J. "The Scriptural Background of the Marriage Impediments," *J* 20 (1960): 29–41.

Chapter IV

Books

Burns, D. *Matrimonial Indissolubility: Contrary Conditions.* Washington, D.C.: Catholic University of America, 1963.

Chatham, J. *Force and Fear as Invalidating Marriage: The Element of Injustice.* Washington, D.C.: Catholic University of America, 1950.

Courtemanche, B. *The Total Simulation of Matrimonial Consent.* Washington, D.C.: Catholic University of America, 1948.

Freedman, A.; Kaplan, H.; and Sadock, B. *Modern Synopsis of Psychiatry: A Comprehensive Textbook.* 2nd ed. Baltimore: Williams and Wilkins, 1976.

Hudson, J. *Handbook II for Marriage Nullity Cases.* Ottawa: St. Paul University, 1980.

Keating, J. *The Bearing of Mental Impairment on the Validity of Marriage.* Rome: Gregorian University, 1973.

Rimlinger, H. *Error Invalidating Marital Consent.* Washington, D.C.: Catholic University of America, 1932.

Sangmeister, J. *Force and Fear as Precluding Matrimonial Consent.* Washington, D.C.: Catholic University of America, 1932.

Timlin, B. *Conditional Matrimonial Consent.* Washington, D.C.: Catholic University of America, 1934.

Wrenn, L. *Annulments.* 3rd ed. Toledo, Ohio: CLSA, 1978 (cited as *Annulments*).

Articles

Ahern, M. "Error and Deception as Grounds for Nullity," *Stud Can* 11 (1977): 225–260.

———. "Psychological Incapacity for Marriage." *Stud Can* 7 (1973): 227–251.

———. "The Marital Right to Children: A Tentative Re-examination." *Stud Can* 8 (1974): 91–107.

Arena, A. "The Jurisprudence of the Sacred Roman Rota: Its Development and Direction after the Second Vatican Council." *Stud Can* 12 (1978): 265–293.

Brown, R. "Inadequate Consent or Lack of Commitment: Authentic Grounds for Nullity." *Stud Can* 9 (1975): 249–265.

———. "Total Simulation: A Second Look." *Stud Can* 10 (1976): 235–249.

Corcoran, P. "Marriage Theology Today: Breakthrough or Breakdown." *Stud Can* 7 (1973): 39–48.

Daley, R. "The Distinction between Lack of Due Discretion and the Inability to Fulfill Obligations of Marriage." *Stud Can* 9 (1975): 153–166.

Doyle, T. "A New Look at the 'Bonum Fidei' " *Stud Can* 12 (1978): 5–40.

Egan, E. "Psychopathy and the Positing of an Act of Matrimonial Consent." *Stud Can* 10 (1976): 303–313.

Fellhauer, D. "The 'Consortium Omnis Vitae' as a Juridical Element of Marriage." *Stud Can* 13 (1979): no. 1.

———. "The Exclusion of Indissolubility: Old Principles and New Jurisprudence." *Stud Can* 9 (1975): 105–133.

Lesage, G. "The 'Consortium Vitae Coniugalis': Nature and Applications." *Stud Can* 6 (1972): 99–113.

Mendonça, A. "Antisocial Personality and the Nullity of Marriage." *Stud Can* 16 (1982): no. 1.

Murtagh, C. "The Jurisprudential Approach to the *Consortium Vitae.*" *Stud Can* 9 (1975): 309–323.

Reinhardt, M. "Error qualitatis in errorem personae redundans." *CLSAP* (1973): 55–69.

Sumner, P. " 'Dolus' as a Ground for Nullity of Marriage." *Stud Can* 14 (1980): 171–194.

Wegan, M. "La distinction entre ius et usus iuris dans la jurisprudence recente de la Rote." *RDC* 29 (1979): 92–113.

Chapter V

Books

Carberry, J. *The Juridical Form of Marriage.* Washington, D.C.: Catholic University of America, 1934.

Articles

Bernhardt, J. "Evolution du sens de la forme de célébration du mariage dans l'église d'occident." *RDC* 30 (1980): 187–205.

Dunderdale, E. "The Canonical Form of Marriage: Anachronism or Pastoral Necessity." *Stud Can* 12 (1978): 41–55.

Chapter VI

Books

Hurley, M., ed. *Beyond Tolerance. The Challenge of Mixed Marriage: A Record of the International Consultation Held in Dublin.* London: Geoffrey Chapman, 1975.

Schiappa, B. *Mixing: Catholic-Protestant Marriages in the 1980's.* New York: Paulist Press, 1982.

Articles

Bhaldraithe, K. "Joint Pastoral Care of Mixed Marriages." *Furrow* 22 (1971): 124–133.

Duffy, P. "The Sociology of Mixed Marriages." *Australasian Catholic Record* 49 (1972): 40–54.

Fagan, S. "Inter-Church Marriage: Gift or Threat." *Doctrine and Life* (1974): 608–615.

Hardon, J. "Mixed Marriages: A Theological Analysis." *Église et Théologie* 1 (1979): 229–260.

Knox, L. "Marriage and Ministry: Some Ecumenical Considerations." *J* 32 (1972): 463–478.

Lynch, J. "Ecumenical Marriages." *CLSAP* (1973): 33–54.

Mahfoud, P. "Les mariages mixtes: Etude historico-canonique." *Apol* 38 (1976): 84–95.

Orsy, L. "The Religious Education of Children Born of Mixed Marriages." *Gregorianum* 45 (1964): 739–760.

Chapter VIII

Books

Crouzel, H. *L'Eglise primitive face au divorce.* Paris: Editions Beauchesne, 1971.

Jung, N. *Evolution de l'indissolubilité: remariage réligieux des divorcés.* Paris: P. Lethielleux, 1975.

McDevitt, G. *Legitimacy and Legitimation.* Washington, D.C.: Catholic University of America, 1941.

Robleda, O. *Vinculum Matrimoniale.* Rome: Universitá Gregoriana Editrice, 1973.

Chapter IX

Books

Abate, A. *The Dissolution of the Matrimonial Bond in Canonical Jurisprudence.* New York: Desclée, 1962.

Casoria, J. *De Matrimonio Rato et Non-consummato.* Rome: Catholic Book Office, 1959.

Cherlin, A. *Marriage, Divorce, Remarriage.* Cambridge: Harvard University, 1981.

Doheny, W. *Canonical Procedure in Matrimonial Cases—Informal.* Vol. 2. Milwaukee: The Bruce Publishing Co., 1944.

Forbes, E. *The Canonical Separation of Consorts.* Ottawa: University of Ottawa, 1948.

Gregory, D. *The Pauline Privilege.* Washington, D.C.: Catholic University of America, 1931.

Kearney, F. *The Principles of Canon 1127.* Washington, D.C.: Catholic University of America, 1942.

King, J. *The Canonical Procedure in Separation Cases.* Washington, D.C.: Catholic University of America, 1952.

Weiss, R. *Marital Separation.* New York: Basic Books, 1975.

Woods, F. *The Constitutions of Canon 1125.* Milwaukee: The Bruce Publishing Co., 1935.

Articles

Bouscaren, T. "An Inquiry into the Practical Application of Canon 1125 Outside Mission Countries." *Analecta Gregoriana* IX: 279.

Declau, P. "The Pauline Privilege: Is it Promulgated in the First Epistle to the Corinthians?" *Catholic Biblical Quarterly* 13 (1951): 146–152.

Demuth, P. "The Nature and Origin of the Privilege of the Faith." *Resonance* 4 (1967): 60–73.

Denis, J. "La portée du canon 1127." *RDC* 10/11 (1960–1961): 126–135.

Donnelly, F. "The Helena Decision of 1924." *J* 36 (1976): 442–449.

Genuario, W. "Rotal Criteria for Granting Separations." *J* 22 (1962): 333–345.

Greco, J. "Le pouvoir du Souverain pontife à l'égard des infidèles." Rome, 1967.

Grenier, H. "Can We Still Speak of the Pauline Privilege?" *J* 38 (1978): 158–162.

Kelly, J. "Separation and Civil Divorce." *J* 6 (1946): 187–238.

Kuntz, J. "The Petrine Privilege: A Study of Some Recent Cases." *J* 28 (1968): 486–496.

Navarette, U. "Indissolubilitas matrimonii rati et non-consummati: Opiniones recentiores et observationes." *P* 58 (1966): 415–489.

O'Rourke, J. "The Faith Required for the Privilege of the Faith Dispensation." *J* 36 (1976): 450–455.

Orsy, L. "An Evaluation of 'New Applications of Canon 1127.' " *J* 38 (1978): 163–170.

——. "More About Canon 1127: The Power of the Diocesan Tribunal." *J* 39 (1979): 447–455.

Provost, J. "Some Approaches to the Application of Canon 1127." *J* 40 (1980): 426–434.

Chapter X

Books

Bogdan, L. *Renewal of Consent in the Simple Validation of Marriage.* Rome: Pontificia Universita Lateranense, 1979.

Brennan, J. *The Simple Convalidation of Marriage.* Washington, D.C.: Catholic University of America, 1937.

Harrigan, R. *The Radical Sanation of Invalid Marriages.* Washington, D.C.: Catholic University of America, 1938.

Ryan, T. *The Juridical Effects of the "Sanatio in Radice."* Washington, D.C.: Catholic University of America, 1955.

Articles

Bastnagel, C. "Sanatio in Radice." *J* 5 (1945): 265–268.

Bernhardt, J. "Propos sur la nature juridique de la 'Sanatio in Radice' dans le droit canonique actuel." *EIC* 4 (1948): 389–406.

Ganter, B. "Problems of Simple Convalidation and Sanatio in Radice." *J* 21 (1961): 57–74.

Walker, E. "The Invalid Convalidation: A Neglected 'Caput Nullitatis.' " *Stud Can* 9 (1975): 325–336.

Wrenn, L. "Invalid Convalidations." *J* 32 (1972): 253–265.

Part II
OTHER ACTS OF DIVINE WORSHIP
[cc. 1166–1204]

Part II of Book IV is divided into five titles, dealing with certain acts of divine worship other than sacraments. This part consists of thirty-nine canons which are gathered from various parts of Book III of the prior Code. The title dealing with sacramentals now contains seven canons. In the prior Code there were ten (*CIC* 1144–1153). This topic is the first one dealt with in this part; formerly it was title VIII of part I of Book III, coming immediately after the seven titles on the individual sacraments. The title on the liturgy of the hours contains three canons which are new to this Code. The treatment of ecclesiastical burial is reduced from forty canons to ten. Formerly this material was treated in part II of Book III under sacred places (*CIC* 1203–1242). The present Code contains five canons dealing with the cult of the saints, sacred images, and relics. The prior Code treated these issues in fourteen canons in part III of Book III on divine cult (*CIC* 1276–1289). The title on vows and oaths now contains fourteen canons, which is one less than the 1917 Code (*CIC* 1307–1321).

This portion of the law reflects a codification of present practice in light of the relevant conciliar and post-conciliar documents.[1]

[1]For a discussion of the work of the original Code Commission subcommittee revising this section of the law, see *Comm* 4 (1972), 160–165; 5 (1973), 44–46. For the revision of the original schema, see *Comm* 12 (1980), 319–324; 345–347; 350–357; 372–387. Among the various significant changes in this section of the law, one may note the reduction in the number of reserved blessings, a new title on the liturgy of the hours, and increased options for cremation.

CANONS AND COMMENTARY

TITLE I
THE SACRAMENTALS
[cc. 1166–1172]

Definition of Sacramentals

Canon 1166 — Somewhat in imitation of the sacraments, sacramentals are sacred signs by which spiritual effects especially are signified and are obtained by the intercession of the Church.

Sacramentals are no longer defined as things or actions (*CIC* 1144) but rather as sacred signs (*SC* 60). They are differentiated from the sacraments in that the grace is obtained through the intercession of the Church and not through the action itself.[2] By expanding the definition from things or actions to the all-inclusive "signs," the Council indicated that every event in life can be sanctified. There is scarcely any proper use of a material thing which cannot be directed toward the sanctification of people and the glory of God (*SC* 61).

Establishment, Interpretation, Administration of Sacramentals

Canon 1167 — §1. The Apostolic See alone can establish new sacramentals, authentically interpret those already accepted, abolish or change any of them.

§2. The rites and formulae approved by church authority are to be carefully observed in confecting or administering the sacramentals.

This canon combines canons 1145 and 1148 of the 1917 Code. In the earlier ages of the Church this authority was not necessarily reserved to the Holy See. However, the Council of Trent anathematized anyone who would ignore the rites approved by the Church or substitute others for them.[3] Since Trent the Holy See has retained this authority.[4] The secretariat of the Commission rejected the objection that such a law does not take into account the diverse socio-cultural situations in

[2]Woywod 1, 734.

[3]Sess. VII, *De sacramentis in genere,* c. 13.
[4]Abbo-Hannan 2, 415.

the world and that it excludes local adaptations.[5] This is true even though the Council had empowered local authorities to adapt sacramentals to local situations (*SC* 39, 62). Rome will honor requests made by individual bishops and conferences of bishops, but it is concerned about practices which may give the appearance of magic or superstition.[6]

Formerly a distinction was made between invocative blessings (the blessing of a house, a car, etc.) and constitutive blessings (those which made an object or a place sacred) (*CIC* 1148, §2). This distinction is no longer found in the Code since everything which is blessed should be treated with respect.

Minister of Sacramentals

Canon 1168 — **The minister of the sacramentals is a cleric who has been given the necessary power; in accord with the norm of the liturgical books and according to the judgment of the local ordinary, some sacramentals can also be administered by lay persons who are endowed with the appropriate qualities.**

This canon is less restrictive than the former law (*CIC* 1146). Formerly only clerics could be legitimate ministers. Now lay persons can administer sacramentals in accord with the judgment of the local ordinary and the norms of the liturgical books (*SC* 79). Some examples would be the distribution of ashes on Ash Wednesday, parents blessing their children, a special minister of the Eucharist blessing a communicant.[7]

Minister of Consecration, Dedication, and Blessings

Canon 1169 — **§1. Persons who possess the episcopal character as well as presbyters to whom it is permitted by law or by legitimate concession can validly perform consecrations and dedications.**

§2. Any presbyter can impart blessings, except those which are reserved to the Roman Pontiff or to bishops.

§3. A deacon can impart only those blessings which are expressly permitted to him by law.

Like other canons in this Code this particular canon is not as restrictive as the former law (*CIC* 1147). The Council wished that reserved blessings be relatively few in number and in favor of bishops or ordinaries (*SC* 79). According to the *Roman Ritual* the reserved blessings are: the blessing of bells for use in a church or an oratory, the foundation stone of a church, a new church or public oratory, an antimension, a new cemetery, blessing and erection of stations of the cross, and papal blessings (*IO* 77). The enhanced power of local ordinaries is clear from the fact that the power to consecrate or dedicate does not presuppose an apostolic indult (*CIC* 1147, §1) but simply a legitimate concession.

Paragraph three does not mention lectors among those persons who may give blessings; this is a change from the former law, which permitted lectors to bless bread and new fruits.[8] Since they are not clerics, lectors are governed by canon 1168 on lay persons as ministers of sacramentals.[9] Deacons, on the contrary, may perform only those blessings which are in the rituals (*LG* 29) such as the blessing of rings at a wedding, exorcism at baptism, blessing at benediction.[10]

Recipients of Blessings

Canon 1170 — **Blessings, to be imparted especially to Catholics, can also be given to catechumens and even to non-Catholics unless a church prohibition precludes this.**

Formerly (*CIC* 1149) sacramentals could be given to non-Catholics only to strengthen their faith or improve their physical health when no law prohibited it. The present Code does not retain these causes for administering a sacramental to non-Catholics. The Code Commission judged that if a blessing can be given to animals and to inanimate objects, such as cars, it could also be given to persons.[11]

Since those who are not in full communion with the Church might confuse sacraments and sacramentals, the Church has retained the qualification that non-Catholic reception of a sacramental not be contrary to an ecclesiastical prohibition. This fear of *communicatio in sacris* has been the primary reason for prohibitions in this area.[12]

Although the faithful have the right to spiritual assistance from their pastors from the spiritual goods of the Church (c. 213), the diocesan bishop can issue norms on their reception (c. 838, §4). Traditionally, it has been recommended that people be in the state of grace when receiving a sacramental.[13]

Reverence for Sacred Things

Canon 1171 — **Sacred things which are destined for divine worship through dedication or a blessing**

---

[5]*Rel*, 268.

[6]Ibid.

[7]*Holy Communion Outside Mass* 2, 16.

[8]"The Ordination of Lectors," in *The Rite of Ordination and Episcopal Consecration* (Washington: USCC, 1967), 11.

[9]*Holy Communion Outside Mass* 3, 10.

[10]Ibid.

[11]*Rel*, 269.

[12]Abbo-Hannan 2, 421.

[13]Ibid.

are to be treated with reverence and not be employed for improper or profane use even if they are under the control of private individuals.

Sacred things are defined as those which have been blessed, consecrated, or dedicated for divine worship. The object or place should not be so dedicated if it appears that profane use cannot be avoided.[14] Those who have in their possession sacramentals or other sacred objects are obliged to treat them with care (*CIC* 1150). When sacramentals can no longer be used, they are usually destroyed, e.g., pouring of holy water into a sacrarium, the burning of holy oils. The law provides that anyone who profanes a sacred object is to receive a just penalty (c. 1376).

Performance of Exorcisms

Canon 1172 — §1. No one can legitimately perform exorcisms over the possessed unless he has obtained special and express permission from the local ordinary.

§2. Such permission from the local ordinary is to be granted only to a presbyter endowed with piety, knowledge, prudence and integrity of life.

This canon replaces canons 1151–1153 of the 1917 Code. It empowers the local ordinary to decide when an exorcism may be given to someone who is demoniacally possessed. The Church wishes to guard against two extremes: those who would see demonic possession in every bizarre behavior pattern and those who would say a priori that demonic possession never takes place.[15]

Some members of the Commission felt it unnecessary to include the required qualities for an exorcist; however, the secretariat decided that from past experience the expression of the qualities of piety, integrity of life, prudence, and knowledge is necessary.[16]

The law makes no mention of any restrictions regarding the faith or religious conviction of the one to be exorcised.[17] Nor does the canon refer to the exorcism within the rite of baptism as did canon 1153 of the former Code.

TITLE II
THE LITURGY OF THE HOURS
[cc. 1173–1175]

This short title of three canons is an innovation of this Code. Like the preceding treatment of the sacraments and sacramentals, the opening canon is theological in tone, describing the nature and purpose of the prayer; the second canon indicates who

is to pray the liturgy of the hours; and the third indicates when it is to be prayed. This title was a late addition to the Code. It was not found in the approved text of the so-called 1980 schema which was submitted to the Holy Father for his approval. However, the canons are basically those proposed at the 1980 *Plenarium* session.[18] They represent the restoration of this form of prayer called for by the Council (*SC* 86–87).

Purpose of the Liturgy of the Hours

Canon 1173 — The Church, fulfilling the priestly function of Christ, celebrates the liturgy of the hours, whereby hearing God speaking to His people and memorializing the mystery of salvation, the Church praises Him in song and prayer without interruption and intercedes for the salvation of the whole world.

The liturgy of the hours prayed throughout the day throughout the world is a sign of the Church continually praying and praising God. It is the commingling of songs, psalms, and prayers which petition and praise the Lord. The canons speak of the liturgy of the hours although popularly the prayer is known as the Divine Office (*Officium* in Latin means service among other things)[19] or breviary.[20]

Clerical Obligation and Lay Participation

Canon 1174 — §1. Clerics are obliged to perform the liturgy of the hours according to the norm of can. 276, §2, n. 3; members of institutes of consecrated life and societies of apostolic life are bound according to the norm of their constitutions.

§2. Other members of the Christian faithful according to circumstances are also earnestly invited to participate in the liturgy of the hours inasmuch as it is the action of the Church.

Priests and transitional deacons are to pray the liturgy of the hours daily. The corresponding obligation for permanent deacons is to be determined by the conference of bishops (c. 276, §2, 3°). Religious are bound according to their constitutions. However, clerics and religious should pray the liturgy of the hours not merely from obedience to the law but because of its pastoral value for their lives (*LC* 8). Since the liturgy of the hours is the prayer of the Church, the whole Church is encouraged to participate (*LC* 1, *SC* 100).

---

14 Ibid., 423.
15 Woywod 1, 736.
16 *Rel*, 269.
17 Abbo-Hannan 2, 425.

18 *Rel*, 269. In this connection, see "The Liturgy of the Hours and Other Liturgical Books" in R.K. Seasoltz, *New Liturgy, New Laws* (Collegeville, Minn.: Liturgical Press, 1980), 112–141, 221–222, 241.
19 *LOTH*, 53.
20 Ibid., 46.

Observance of True Time

Canon 1175 — In performing the liturgy of the hours the true time of each hour is to be observed as much as possible.

The liturgy of the hours is to be prayed at the appropriate times (*SC* 88, 94). In the past it was not uncommon for people to pray the breviary all at once. Sometimes it would be said at 11:45 p.m.; and then immediately upon being completed it would be prayed for the following day. Since the liturgy of the hours is to be prayed continually throughout the day (c. 1173), it is to sanctify the whole day. Just as there is no material thing which cannot be used for the sanctification of persons,[21] there also is no time of day which is not made holy by this prayer.[22]

TITLE III
ECCLESIASTICAL FUNERAL RITES
[cc. 1176–1185]

This title is considerably shortened and re-organized in comparison to the 1917 Code. Instead of being entitled "ecclesiastical burial" (*CIC* 1203–1242), its new title emphasizes the rites surrounding burial. The consultors chose the term "exequiae" over "sepultura" because of its more comprehensive meaning. Were this material treated in the part on sacred places and times rather than in the part on other acts of divine worship, the term *sepultura* would have been more appropriate.[23] The forty canons of the 1917 Code (*CIC* 1203–1242) have been reduced to ten. The former section on cemeteries (*CIC* 1205–1214) has been shortened and placed in the section on sacred places (cc. 1240–1243). There is greater latitude for particular law and the judgment of the local ordinary. Most dioceses have policies concerning burials already, and the National Catholic Cemetery Conference has also published recommended policies which are compatible with these canons.[24]

Definition and Purpose of Funeral Rites

Canon 1176 — §1. The Christian faithful departed are to be given ecclesiastical funeral rites according to the norm of law.

§2. Through ecclesiastical funeral rites the Church asks spiritual assistance for the departed, honors their bodies, and at the same time brings the solace of hope to the living; such rites are to be celebrated according to the norm of liturgical laws.

§3. The Church earnestly recommends that the pious custom of burying the bodies of the dead be observed; it does not, however, forbid cremation unless it has been chosen for reasons which are contrary to Christian teaching.

This canon states the right which the Christian faithful have to Christian burial. The second paragraph of the canon explicitly mentions the various purposes of the ecclesiastical funeral rites. An earlier version of the canon had made explicit reference to the competence of the conference of bishops in making certain determinations regarding funeral rites. However, the committee judged that such a reference was unnecessary since it is implicitly contained in the allusion to the appropriate liturgical laws.[25]

The third paragraph of the canon restates the Church's preference that bodies be buried; however, cremation is no longer forbidden unless it is chosen for reasons contrary to Christian teaching. The former law was quite forceful and restrictive in its opposition to cremation (*CIC* 1203). Actually, the Church has never been against cremation as such but discouraged it because of the reasons people used to justify it. The Holy See has said that permission for cremation is to be denied only when it is based on a sectarian spirit, hatred of the Catholic religion or the Church, or a denial of Christian doctrine. Funeral rites are not to be performed at the place of cremation.[26]

CHAPTER I
THE CELEBRATION OF FUNERAL RITES
[cc. 1177–1182]

Place of Funeral Rites

Canon 1177 — §1. As a rule the funeral rites for any of the faithful departed must be celebrated in his or her own parish church.

§2. However, any member of the Christian faithful or those commissioned to arrange for his or her funeral may choose another church for the funeral rites with the consent of its rector and after informing the departed person's pastor.

§3. If death has occurred outside the person's own parish, and the corpse has not been transferred

---

[21]See c. 1166 above.
[22]*LOTH,* 20.
[23]*Comm* 12 (1980), 346. For some pertinent references on funeral rites, see Seasoltz, 225–226, 242.
[24]National Catholic Cemetery Conference, *Christian Burial Guidelines,* Jan. 28, 1975. Reported in *CLD* Supp. through 1979 at *CIC* 1203.

[25]*Comm* 12 (1980), 346. See also SCDW, *Ordo Exsequiarum* (Rome: Typis Polyglottis Vaticanis, 1969). English trans.: *Rite of Funerals* (Washington: USCC/ICEL, 1971). For some perceptive reflections on this whole issue, see R. Rutherford, *The Death of a Christian: The Rite of Funerals* (New York: Pueblo, 1980).
[26]Holy Office, instr. on cremation of corpses, May 8, 1963, in *AAS* 56 (1964), 822–823. English trans. in *CLD* 6, 666–668. On the issue of funeral rites at the place of cremation, see SCDF on funeral services at a crematory chapel, July 9, 1966 in *CLD* 8, 851.

to that parish and another church has not been legitimately chosen for the funeral, the funeral rites are to be celebrated in the church of the parish where the death occurred unless another church has been designated by particular law.

The parish church is normally the center of the person's life of faith. It is there that both the sacraments are celebrated and the person grows in closeness with the Lord through the reception of the Holy Eucharist. It is only fitting that at the time of passage from this world to the next the appropriate rites should be celebrated in the parish church. The expression "parish church" indicates any church serving a geographical territory; that is, a mission or a station is included in this term.[27] "Parish church" would also include non-territorial parishes. The word "propriae" is understood to mean the place of domicile or quasi-domicile.[28] However, everyone enjoys the right to choose another church. The notifications of the rector of the chosen church as well as the proper pastor are matters of practicality and courtesy, but no one is to be denied Christian burial unless prohibited by law.

Rites for the Diocesan Bishop

Canon 1178 — The funeral rites of a diocesan bishop are to be celebrated in his own cathedral church unless he has chosen another church.

This canon is basically the same as in the prior law (*CIC* 1219, §2); however, it is much more simplified. Since the law states that the principle of selecting one's place of burial applies also to bishops, it would also apply to cardinals and the other ecclesiastical authorities mentioned in the prior law.[29]

Rites for Religious

Canon 1179 — As a rule the funeral rites of religious or members of societies of apostolic life are to be celebrated in their own church or oratory by their superior if it is a clerical institute or society, otherwise by the chaplain.

In the prior Code the corresponding canon (*CIC* 1221) referred only to male religious since canon 1230, §5 of the 1917 Code referred to women. However, the differences have been suppressed in this Code. The word "generatim" indicates that religious too can choose the place of their funeral. If they die outside their house, they would probably follow the rule of canon 1177, §3. Members of secular institutes are ruled by the common law.[30]

Place of Burial

Canon 1180 — §1. If a parish has its own cemetery, the faithful departed are to be interred in it unless another cemetery has been legitimately chosen either by the departed person or by those who are responsible to arrange for his or her interment.
§2. However, everyone, unless prohibited by law, is permitted to choose a cemetery for burial.

Generally "ubi funus ibi tumulus." If the funeral takes place in the parish church, the burial would normally take place in the parish cemetery, but this need not be the case. This canon lists a basic right which is not found in those listed in canons 208–231. The law here restates canon 1223, §1 of the 1917 Code, which gave everyone the right to choose his or her place of funeral and burial unless prohibitied by law. The term "cemetery" is understood in the broadest sense to include mausolea, places where ashes are kept, etc.[31]

Offerings for Funerals

Canon 1181 — The prescriptions of can. 1264 are to be observed in regard to the offerings given on the occasion of funerals; precautions are nevertheless to be taken in funeral rites against any favoritism toward persons and against depriving the poor of the funeral rites which are their due.

Canon 1264 states that the bishops of the province should fix the amount or set a limit on the amount to be given on these occasions. Scandal is always to be avoided, and no one is to be denied Christian burial because of a lack of money. In light of the spirit of the Council and the canon, there should be no distinctions or exceptions for private persons or classes of persons (*SC* 32). Likewise canon 848 forbids the denial of the sacraments to persons who lack money.

Death Register

Canon 1182 — After the interment an entry is to be made in the death register in accord with the norm of particular law.

The death register is one of the books which every parish should have (c. 535, §1). Such a book is to be kept in every church from which people are buried. The appropriate entry is to be made in the register of the church from which the person is buried, not necessarily in the register of his own parish church. However, the pastor of the deceased should be notified of the death and burial.[32]

---

[27] Abbo-Hannan 2, 478.
[28] *Rel,* 269–270. See also c. 102.
[29] Abbo-Hannan 2, 481.
[30] *Rel,* 270.

[31] Ibid.
[32] Woywod 2, 46.

CHAPTER II
THOSE TO WHOM ECCLESIASTICAL
FUNERAL RITES
ARE TO BE GRANTED OR TO BE DENIED
[cc. 1183–1185]

*Rites for Catechumens, Non-Baptized Children,
Non-Catholics*

Canon 1183 — §1. **As regards funeral rites catechumens are to be considered members of the
Christian faithful.**

**§2. The local ordinary can permit children to be
given ecclesiastical funeral rites if their parents intended to baptize them but they died before their
baptism.**

**§3. In the prudent judgment of the local ordi-
nary, ecclesiastical funeral rites can be granted to
baptized members of some non-Catholic church or
ecclesial community unless it is evidently contrary
to their will and provided their own minister is unavailable.**

The catechumenate is more notably emphasized
in the present Code than in its 1917 predecessor.
The catechumenate, described in canon 788, is the
normal way of admitting non-baptized adults into
the Church (cc. 851, §1; 865). This is one of the few
instances in the revised Code in which the legal status of the catechumen has been changed. The
Council called for a clarification of that status (*AG*
14), and canon 206, §2 states that certain prerogatives proper to the Christian faithful are also to be
granted to catechumens. The present canon attempts to specify one such prerogative. Once inscribed into the book of catechumens, a person has
a special relationship to the Church; according such
an individual Christian burial is a way of highlighting that relationship.

The *Sacramentary* contains a Mass for a child
who dies before baptism.[33] The rubrics state that
the doctrine of the necessity of baptism should not
be weakened in the catechesis of the faithful. The
requirement of the local ordinary's permission reflects the concern that someone might doubt the
Church's constant teaching on infant baptism. The
unbaptized child may receive these rites if the parents intended to have the child baptized. In no way
does the Church want to encourage procrastination
about such an important action as baptism.[34]

There are three conditions for a non-Catholic to
be given an ecclesiastical burial: (1) the prudent
judgment of the local ordinary, (2) the absence of a
contrary intent on the part of the deceased, and (3)
the unavailability of the proper minister of the deceased. If a person is unchurched or has dropped

out of a particular ecclesial community, and at the
same time attends Catholic services on a regular basis, the minister would be unavailable. The Church
respects the wishes of the deceased and wants to
avoid any appearance of proselytizing.

*Those to Whom Ecclesiastical Funeral Rites Are
Denied*

Canon 1184 — §1. **Unless they have given some
signs of repentance before their death, the following are to be deprived of ecclesiastical funeral rites:
1° notorious apostates, heretics and schismatics;
2° persons who had chosen the cremation of their
own bodies for reasons opposed to the Christian
faith;
3° other manifest sinners for whom ecclesiastical
funeral rites cannot be granted without public scandal to the faithful.**

**§2. If some doubt should arise, the local ordi-
nary is to be consulted; and his judgment is to be
followed.**

The preceding canon listed those to whom ecclesiastical funeral rites could be conceded, while this
canon speaks of those to whom they are to be denied. The penalty of denial of Christian burial has
largely been dropped from this Code. However, this
canon indicates the few times when burial is to be
denied. It reflects the committee's effort to respond
to requests that the law offer a listing of sins warranting denial of burial even if such a listing were
not a taxative one.[35] In applying this canon, one
should follow canon 18 which states that laws
which restrict rights should always be interpreted
strictly.

The first number of paragraph one mentions
apostates, heretics, and schismatics. Canon 751 defines apostasy as the total post-baptismal repudiation of the Christian faith. Heresy is the obstinate
post-baptismal denial of or doubt about some truth
which is to be believed as part of divine and Catholic faith. Schism is the post-baptismal refusal of
submission to the Holy Father or of communion
with the members of the church subject to him. Notoriety is not discussed in the revised Code; however, in light of the prior Code, it may be understood
in two different ways. Notoriety in law follows the
sentence of a competent judge or a judicial confession. Notoriety in fact means that an action is publicly known or has been committed in such
circumstances that it is entirely impossible to conceal it or offer any legal justification for it (*CIC*
2197). A properly strict interpretation of the canon
seems to require that notoriety in law be verified before ecclesiastical burial is denied. Furthermore, it
should be noted that those who are baptized into

---

[33]"Funeral Mass of a Child Who Died Before Baptism," in the
Sacramentary (New York: Catholic Book, 1974), 986–987.
[34]*Comm* 12 (1980), 354.

[35]Ibid., 355–356.

non-Catholic churches are not technically considered heretics or schismatics (*UR* 3).

While the former law (*CIC* 1240, §1, 5°) forbade ecclesiastical funeral rites for all persons who were cremated, the present law limits the prohibition to those who choose cremation for reasons opposed to the Christian faith (§1, 2°).

The final category of those to be deprived of Christian burial is a somewhat generic one, i.e., other manifest sinners who may not be given ecclesiastical burial without public scandal to the faithful (§1, 3°). A manifest sin is one for which there are eyewitnesses who can give testimony about it. If there is no public scandal, the right of burial is not to be denied even to manifest sinners. The local ordinary should always be consulted if there is any doubt about the appropriateness of denying Christian burial. This is to protect persons against possibly arbitrary pastoral discretion at the local level.

The consultors on the committee judged that those who were notoriously excommunicated would not be explicitly mentioned in the canon as in the former law (*CIC* 1240, §1, 2°); however, they are understood as being included under the general rubric of "public sinner." Those subject to an interdict are not technically included here.

Certain categories of persons mentioned in the former law are not explicitly included in the prohibition of this canon, e.g., members of forbidden societies (*CIC* 1240, §1, 1°), those who deliberately commit suicide (*CIC* 1240, §1, 3°), those who are killed in a duel or die from a duel-related wound (*CIC* 1240, §1, 4°). The only situation about which there was any discussion was the case of a member of a forbidden society. In view of the difficulty of determining the degree of adherence of an individual to the doctrine of such a society, the committee judged it best not to make an explicit mention of such individuals in the canon. Only if they are manifest sinners does the issue of a possible denial of Christian burial arise.[36]

In conclusion it might be noted that the present mitigated discipline was anticipated by a private 1973 letter of the Sacred Congregation for the Doctrine of the Faith on the burial of Catholics in irregular marriages:

... The celebration of religious obsequies will not be prohibited for the faithful who, although finding themselves before death in a situation of manifest sin, have preserved their attachment to the Church and have given some sign of penitence and on condition that public scandal on the part of other members of the faithful has been removed.

In the meantime, scandal on the part of the faithful or of the ecclesiastical community will be able

to be lessened or avoided to the extent that pastors will explain the viewpoint which befits the meaning of Christian obsequies and in which many see an appeal to the mercy of God. ...[37]

Denial of Funeral Mass

Canon 1185 — Any funeral Mass whatsoever is also to be denied a person excluded from ecclesiastical funeral rites.

Canon 18 on the strict interpretation of laws which deny or restrict a right should also be followed in this case. Although the previous law (*CIC* 1241) prohibited anniversary Masses and any type of public ceremony for those to whom ecclesiastical burial rites were denied, the present Code does not restate that prohibition.

Oftentimes Masses are requested for non-Catholics who would not be allowed a Catholic funeral in accord with canon 1183, §3. The Sacred Congregation for the Doctrine of the Faith has ruled there is no problem with private Masses. As regards the public celebration of Mass it stated:

The current discipline ... must be retained as a general norm. ... The reason for this is consideration due to the conscience of such deceased persons who have not made full profession of the Catholic faith. ... This norm can be derogated from whenever the following conditions are simultaneously verified:

(1) A public celebration of masses is expressly requested by members of the family, by friends or by subjects of the deceased out of a genuinely religious motive.

(2) In the judgment of the ordinary, scandal on the part of the faithful is absent.

... In those cases public mass may be celebrated on condition, however, that the name of the deceased not be mentioned in the eucharistic prayer since such commemoration presupposes full communion with the Catholic Church.[38]

TITLE IV
THE VENERATION OF THE SAINTS, SACRED IMAGES AND RELICS
[cc. 1186–1190]

This title, which corresponds to part III of Book III of the prior Code which dealt with divine cult, contains two canons dealing with devotion to the

---

[36]Ibid., 356.

[37]SCDF, private letter, May 29, 1973. Reported in *CLD* 8, 862–863. See also idem, decr of Sept. 20, 1973. Reported in *CLD* 8, 864.

[38]SCDF, "Decree on the Public Celebration of Mass in a Catholic Church for Deceased Non-Catholic Christians," June 11, 1976, in *AAS* 68 (1976), 621. Reported in *CLD* 8, 864–866.

saints [cc. 1186–1187], two canons regulating images in churches and precious images (cc. 1188–1189), and one canon dealing with relics (c. 1190).

Objects and Purpose of Veneration

Canon 1186 — **To foster the sanctification of the people of God the Church recommends to the particular and filial veneration of the Christian faithful the Blessed Mary ever Virgin, the Mother of God, whom Christ established as the Mother of the human race; it also promotes true and authentic devotion to the other saints by whose example the Christian faithful are edified and through whose intercession they are sustained.**

This canon is lengthier and more comprehensive in its reasons for veneration of the Blessed Mother and the saints than its 1917 Code counterpart (*CIC* 1276). Its emphasis on devotion to the Blessed Virgin Mary echoes *Lumen Gentium* 66 and *Sacrosanctum Concilium* 103, and its stress on the honor due the saints, which must always be kept in its proper perspective, reflects *Sacrosanctum Concilium* 111.

Public Cult of Saints/Blessed

Canon 1187 — **Veneration through public cult is permitted only to those servants of God who are listed in the catalog of the saints or of the blessed by the authority of the Church.**

This canon eliminates the distinction between the veneration which is permissible to the saints and to the blessed. Formerly, the blessed could normally not be patrons (*CIC* 1278), nor could their statues normally be carried in procession (*CIC* 1287, §3). These distinctions are now left to other legislation. The Sacred Congregation for Divine Worship stated that only images of the Blessed Virgin Mary may be crowned, while excluding images of a given saint or blessed.[39]

Displaying of Images

Canon 1188 — **The practice of displaying sacred images in the churches for the veneration of the faithful is to remain in force; nevertheless they are to be exhibited in moderate number and in suitable order lest they bewilder the Christian people and give opportunity for questionable devotion.**

The canon restates *Sacrosanctum Concilium* 125 almost verbatim. Also relevant are *Sacrosanctum Concilium* 123 and 124, which declare that the Church has not adopted any one type of art form but has admitted styles from every period. The art should be beautiful and appropriate, not repugnant to faith, morals, or piety.

An original paragraph two of this canon had explicitly indicated the right and duty of the local ordinary to ensure the authenticity of images presented for public veneration. However, it was dropped in view of the reference to the liturgical oversight role of the diocesan bishop in the initial canons of Book IV (c. 838, §4).[40]

Restoration of Valuable Images

Canon 1189 — **Whenever valuable images, that is, those which are outstanding due to age, art or cult, which are exhibited in churches or oratories for the veneration of the faithful need repair, they are never to be restored without the written permission of the ordinary who is to consult experts before he grants permission.**

This canon is practically the same as canon 1280 of the 1917 Code. It recognizes the Church's artistic heritage and the fact that certain objects have been used by God in his providence to grant special favors and blessings. It is natural and normal that these objects should be protected.

The Council envisioned the experts to be consulted according to this canon to be a commission or standing committee (*SC* 126), but the Code Commission did not want to list this council on the arts and not name others; however, the law does intend such a group.[41] The Sacred Congregation for the Clergy has issued a statement concerning the historico-artistic heritage of the Church which any commission would do well to consult.[42]

Alienation of Relics and Images

Canon 1190 — **§1. It is absolutely forbidden to sell sacred relics.**

§2. Significant relics or other ones which are honored with great veneration by the people cannot in any manner be validly alienated or perpetually transferred without the permission of the Apostolic See.

§3. The prescription of §2 is also applicable to images in any church which are honored with great veneration by the people.

[39]SCDW, "Norms Regarding Crowning Images of the Blessed Virgin," Mar. 25, 1973, in *AAS* 65 (1973), 280. Reported in *CLD* 8, 908–909.

[40]*Comm* 12 (1980), 373.
[41]*Rel*, 272–273. One might note that the reference to "men" experts in *CIC* 1200 ("peritos viros") is dropped in the present law.
[42]SCC, "Address to the Presidents of the Episcopal Conferences," Apr. 11, 1971 in *AAS* 63 (1971), 215. Reported in *CLD* 7, 821–824.

It is strictly forbidden to sell relics. Any transfer of relics from one place to another without the permission of the Holy See is only temporary regardless of how long the second party possesses the relics.

Ecclesiastical authorities must exercise great care lest relics or other sacred images fall into the wrong hands. This vigilance also involves ensuring that the people who have relics in their possession take proper care of them. An especially sensitive time would be when estates are being settled. Authorities should be watchful lest relics or sacred images fall into the hands of those who do not appreciate them or who might even ridicule them. Although the Code forbids the selling of sacred relics, it does not forbid buying them. This might be necessary in order to redeem a relic or a sacred image from a pawnshop or from someone who is not showing proper respect for it. Just penalties are to be inflicted on those who profane a sacred thing or illegally alienate an ecclesiastical good (cc. 1376–1377).

TITLE V
A VOW AND AN OATH
[cc. 1191–1204]

CHAPTER I
A VOW
[cc. 1191–1198]

Some consultors wanted these canons situated in Book I on general norms,[43] but the Code accepts the common doctrine that vows and oaths constitute acts of worship,[44] and thus they are included in this part. These canons on vows generally considered private vows only. Public vows are treated in other places such as religious law, e.g., canons 654–658.

Definition and Conditions of Vows

Canon 1191 — §1. A vow is a deliberate and free promise made to God concerning a possible and better good which must be fulfilled by reason of the virtue of religion.

§2. Unless they are forbidden by law, all who have the suitable use of reason are capable of making a vow.

§3. A vow made through grave and unjust fear or fraud is null by the law itself.

This initial canon is almost the same as canon 1307 of the 1917 Code except for the addition of the invalidating element of fraud in paragraph three. This is an exception to the general law on the validity of such acts (c. 125, §2). Fraud and fear are not to be interpreted in exactly the same way as in the

marriage canons (cc. 1098, 1103). For as regards a vow, the fear must still be unjustly induced; whereas for marriage, fear must merely be grave and come from outside the person. The fear must also be the cause of the vow and not merely the occasion of it.[45]

Distinction of Vows

Canon 1192 — §1. A vow is *public* if it is accepted in the name of the Church by a legitimate superior; otherwise, it is *private*.

§2. A vow is *solemn* if it is acknowledged as such by the Church; otherwise, it is *simple*.

§3. A vow is *personal* if an act of the vowing person is promised; it is *real* if something is promised; it is *mixed* if it shares the nature of a personal and real vow.

The reserved vows of canon 1308, §3 of the 1917 Code have been omitted from the 1983 law. In religious law a simple vow formerly made acts contrary to the vows illicit but not invalid unless the constitution stated otherwise; solemn vows made such acts invalid (*CIC* 579). This distinction has been dropped in the revised Code. There was some discussion about whether another classification was necessary, since some consultors felt that the distinction between public and private vows was too restrictive. For example, secular institutes and societies of common life did not technically profess public vows. Yet what they did profess seemed in the opinion of the consultors to be more than merely private vows. The consultors felt the question concerning the vows of secular institutes is still being discussed, and rather than prejudice the outcome of the discussion, they let the distinction stand.[46]

Obligation of a Vow

Canon 1193 — By its nature a vow obligates only the person who makes it.

This canon simply restates canon 1310, §1 of the 1917 Code. The second paragraph of this prior canon has been dropped.

Cessation of a Vow

Canon 1194 — A vow ceases when the time appointed for the fulfillment of its obligation has passed, when there is a substantial change in the matter promised or when the condition on which the vow depends or the purpose for which it was made no longer exists; it also ceases through dispensation or commutation.

---

[43]*Comm* 12 (1980), 374–375.
[44]St. Thomas II–II[ae], q. 88, a. 5 et q. 89, a. 4.

[45]Bouscaren-Ellis, 671.
[46]*Comm* 12 (1980), 375–376.

The notion of a direct annulment of a vow mentioned in canon 1311 of the former Code is omitted here. The first part of the canon deals with matters which are intrinsic to the vow, such as its conditions, the matter which is promised, or the time for its fulfillment; the last two ways of cessation, namely, dispensation and commutation, are extrinsic causes of its cessation.[47]

Suppression of a Vow

Canon 1195 — **A person who has power over the matter of the vow can suspend its obligation for as long as its fulfillment would prejudice such a person.**

In the former law (*CIC* 1312), someone who had dominative power over another could annul a vow. However, such an annulment is no longer mentioned regarding the cessation of a vow. A person who has power over the matter which has been vowed can suspend the obligation. An example would be a religious superior suspending the vows of a novice if they interfered with the good order of the religious house.[48]

Dispensation of a Vow

Canon 1196 — **Besides the Roman Pontiff, the following persons can dispense from private vows for a just reason provided a dispensation does not injure a right acquired by others:**
1° the local ordinary and the pastor as regards all their own subjects as well as travelers;
2° the superior of a religious institute or society of apostolic life if they are clerical of pontifical right as regards members, novices, and persons who stay day and night in a house of the institute or society;
3° persons to whom the power of dispensation has been delegated by the Apostolic See or by the local ordinary.

The canon speaks only of private vows, i.e., not accepted in the name of the Church (c. 1192, §1). Number one adds the pastor to the list of those who may dispense according to canon 1313 of the 1917 Code. However, this does not include the confessor unless the power is delegated to him by one who has it.[49]
The dispensing power here presupposes the possession of executive power which can be delegated according to the norms of law (c. 137). The only limitation on dispensing from private vows is the right of a third party, who is not allowed to be injured by the dispensation.

Commutation of the Works Promised

Canon 1197 — **The work promised in a private vow can be commuted to a greater or an equal good by the person who makes the vow; however, a person who has the power of dispensation according to the norm of can. 1196 can commute it to a lesser good.**

Canon 1314 of the former Code is changed here to refer to a private vow instead of a non-reserved vow. The individual himself or herself may commute the vow in favor of a greater or equal good. Those who have the power to dispense in accordance with canon 1196 may commute the vow in favor of a lesser good.

Effects of Religious Profession

Canon 1198 — **Vows made before religious profession are suspended as long as the person who makes the vow remains in a religious institute.**

Religious profession does not annul or eradicate the vows made prior to profession; rather the effects of the vow are suspended. Thus if a person left religious life, such vows would be binding. Upon making religious profession, however, a person could commute all his or her private vows in favor of the vows of the religious institute (c. 1197).[50]

CHAPTER II
AN OATH
[cc. 1199–1204]

Definition of an Oath

Canon 1199 — **§1. An oath, that is the invocation of the divine name as a witness to truth, cannot be taken unless in truth, in judgment and in justice.**
§2. An oath which the canons demand or admit cannot be taken validly through a proxy.

Commentators describe oaths as "assertory" if they affirm a truth or "promissory" if they affirm the sincerity of a promise. These latter can be absolute or conditional.[51] Nothing prevents an oath from being taken validly by proxy, unless the law requires its being taken personally,[52] e.g., the oath of office for tribunal officials in canon 1454, the oath for witnesses in canon 1562, and the oath by parties in a trial in canon 1532. The norm is basically the same as that of canon 1316 of the 1917 Code.

[47]Abbo-Hannan 2, 552.
[48]Bouscaren-Ellis, 675.
[49]*Comm* 12 (1980), 377.

[50]Woywod 2, 92.
[51]Abbo-Hannan 2, 555.
[52]Ibid.

Obligation of an Oath

Canon 1200 — §1. A person who freely swears to do something in the future is bound by a special obligation of religion to fulfill what has been affirmed by oath.

§2. An oath extorted through fraud, force, or grave fear is null by the law itself.

The first paragraph of the canon deals only with promissory oaths, whereas the second paragraph deals with all oaths.[53] The canon does not explicitly demand that the force or fear which nullifies an oath be unjust, which would technically be an exception to canon 125. However, the use of the word "extortum" seems to indicate that unjust force or fear is envisioned.[54] An oath binds only the person who swears and is not passed on to his or her descendants.

Promissory Oaths and Harmful Effects

Canon 1201 — §1. A promissory oath follows the nature and the condition of the act to which it is attached.

§2. If an oath is attached to an act which directly tends towards the injury of others or towards the prejudice of the public good or of eternal salvation, the act is not reinforced by the oath.

Basically the norm is the same as that of canon 1318 of the former Code. The law refers to an oath which is accessory to other actions. It follows the nature of a promise. It can be retracted before it is accepted by the other party.[55] Obviously, one would not call on the Divine Name to aid one in doing something which would prejudice the common good, eternal salvation, or the welfare of others.

Cessation of Obligation of Oaths

Canon 1202 — The obligation arising from a promissory oath ceases:

1° if it is remitted by the person for whose advantage the oath has been taken;

2° if the thing sworn to is substantially changed or if, due to changed circumstances, it becomes either evil or entirely indifferent or, finally, if it would impede a greater good;

3° if the final purpose for or condition under which the oath may have been taken no longer exists;

4° through its dispensation or commutation in accord with the norm of can. 1203.

This canon is very much like canon 1194 which treats of the cessation of a vow. Except for the elimination of the word "irritatio," it basically restates canon 1319 of the 1917 Code.

Suspension, Dispensation, and Commutation of Oaths

Canon 1203 — The persons who can suspend, dispense or commute a vow have the same power over a promissory oath for the same reasons; but if the dispensation from the oath tends to prejudice others who refuse to remit its obligation, only the Apostolic See can dispense the oath.

As in the case of vows (c. 1196), the only limitation on the dispensation of an oath is the right of a third party (parties), who might be jeopardized by the dispensation. If such a party is unwilling to remit the obligation because of its prejudicial effects, only the Holy See may grant the dispensation. The canon drops the term "irritare" and the phrase "propter necessitatem aut utilitatem Ecclesiae" which were part of canon 1320 of the former Code.

Interpretation of Oaths

Canon 1204 — An oath is to be strictly interpreted according to the law and the intention of the person taking the oath, or if that person acts out of fraud, according to the intention of the person to whom the oath is made.

The canon restates canon 1321 of the prior law and affirms three principles. An oath is to be interpreted strictly. The intention of the person taking the oath is to be understood in terms of the way it was expressed. If an intention contrary to what was sworn can be proved, it must prevail. If a person acted fraudulently in the external forum, the oath is to be interpreted according to the mind of the person who received it.[56]

53Bouscaren-Ellis, 677.
54*Comm* 12 (1980), 378.
55Bouscaren-Ellis, 678.

56Ibid., 679.

BIBLIOGRAPHY

Commentaries on the 1917 Code

Abbo, J., and Hannan, J. *The Sacred Canons*. 2 vols. St. Louis: Herder, 1952 (cited as Abbo-Hannan and volume).

Bouscaren, L., and Ellis, A. *Canon Law*. Milwaukee: The Bruce Publishing Co., 1948 (cited as Bouscaren-Ellis).

Woywod, S. *A Practical Commentary on the Code of Canon Law*. 2 vols. New York: J. Wagner, 1926 (cited as Woywod and volume).

Post-Conciliar Documents

Paul VI. Apconst *Laudis Canticum*. Nov. 1, 1970. *AAS* 63 (1971): 527–535. English trans. in *The Pope Speaks* 16 (1971): 129–131.

————. *Mp Ministeria Quaedam*. Aug. 15, 1972. *AAS* 64 (1972):529–534. SCDW. *Ordo Exsequiarum*. Aug. 15, 1969. Rome: Typis Polyglottis Vaticanis, 1969. English trans. as *Rite of Funerals*. BCL-USCC. ICEL. Washington: USCC, 1971.

SCRit. Instr *Inter Oecumenici*. Sept. 26, 1964. *AAS* 56 (1964): 712–718.

On the Proposed Texts of the Revised Code

Comm 12 (1980): 319–387.

Comm 13 (1981): 441–443.

Books and Periodicals

BCL. *Liturgy of the Hours Text VII*. Washington: USCC, 1976 (cited as *LOTH*).

"Funeral Mass of a Child Who Died Before Baptism," in the *Sacramentary*. New York: Catholic Book, 1974.

Manzanares, J. "In schema de locis et temporibus sacris deque cultu divino animadversiones et vota." *P* 68 (1979): 139–158.

"The Ordination of Lectors," in *The Rite of Ordination and Episcopal Consecration*. Washington: USCC, 1967.

Rutherford, R. *The Death of a Christian: The Rite of Funerals*. New York: Pueblo, 1980.

SCDW. *Holy Communion Outside of Mass*. June 21, 1973. Trans. and pub. by ICEL. 3 vols. Washington: USCC, 1974 (cited as *Holy Communion Outside Mass* and volume).

Seasoltz, R. K. *New Liturgy, New Laws*. Collegeville, Minn.: Liturgical Press, 1980.

Part III
SACRED PLACES AND TIMES
[cc. 1205–1253]

The part of the Code on sacred places and times has been reduced from one hundred one canons in the 1917 Code (*CIC* 1154–1254) to forty-nine canons here. The material is simplified. The liturgical ceremonies are left to the liturgical books and not put into the Code; the terminology of the Code is brought into harmony with the reformed liturgical books. Some items of the former Code, such as asylum in churches, the ringing of church bells, and details of church construction, are omitted from the revised Code. Other items are taken from this section and placed where they more logically belong, e.g., the legislation concerning funerals is not placed here but in part II of Book IV, "Other Acts of Divine Worship"; only the legislation concerning the place itself, the cemetery, is found in these canons on sacred places and times.[1]

[1]For an official Code Commission report on the formulation of the original draft of this part of the law see *Comm* 4 (1972), 160–168; for a report on the revision of the original draft see *Comm* 12 (1980), 319–367.

CANONS AND COMMENTARY

TITLE I
SACRED PLACES
[cc. 1205–1243]

Notion of Sacred Places

Canon 1205 — Sacred places are those which have been designated for divine worship or for the burial of the faithful through a dedication or blessing which the liturgical books prescribe for this purpose.

Places become sacred places by their dedication or blessing. The terminology (the word "consecration" is no longer used) is brought into harmony with that of the liturgical books to which this canon refers: *Dedication of a Church and an Altar* (see the bibliography following c. 1253) and *Rite of Blessing a Cemetery* (see the commentary on c. 1240). The introductions to these two rites give the theological context for the legislation in this portion of the Code and are the source for understanding these canons.

Minister of Dedication/Blessing

Canon 1206 — The dedication of any place is within the competency of the diocesan bishop and those who are equivalent to him in law; they can commission any bishop or, in exceptional cases, a presbyter to perform a dedication within their own territory.

Canon 1207 — Sacred places are blessed by an ordinary; the blessing of churches, however, is reserved to the diocesan bishop; but either one of these can delegate another priest for this purpose.

Canons 1206 and 1207 speak of the minister of the dedication (c. 1206) or blessing (c. 1207). The rite of dedication is to be used when the place is destined for sacred purposes *permanently;* if because of special circumstances the designation is *only for a time,* the rite of blessing is to be used. The rite of dedication is distinguished by the wealth of its rites and symbols.[2]

Since the bishop has been entrusted with the care of the particular church, it is his responsibility to dedicate to God new churches built in his diocese. If he cannot himself preside at the rite, he shall entrust this function to another bishop, especially to one who is his associate and assistant in the pastoral care of the community for which the church has been built; or, in altogether special circumstances, to a priest to whom he shall give a special mandate.[3]

[2]*Dedication of a Church and an Altar,* 83.
[3]Ibid., 12.

Certification of Dedication/Blessing

Canon 1208 — A document is to be drawn up attesting that the dedication or blessing of a church or the blessing of a cemetery has been performed; one copy is to be kept in the diocesan curia and another copy in the church's archive.

Proof of Dedication/Blessing

Canon 1209 — Provided no one suffers damage from it, the dedication or blessing of any place is sufficiently proven even through one witness who is above all suspicion.

Secular Use of Sacred Place

Canon 1210 — Only those things which serve the exercise or promotion of worship, piety and religion are to be admitted into a sacred place; anything which is not in accord with the holiness of the place is forbidden. The ordinary, however, can permit other uses which are not contrary to the holiness of the place, in individual instances.

Canon 1210 is new to the Code. The local ordinary has the power, for example, to permit a musical presentation or secular drama to be presented in a sacred place or allow the place to be used as a shelter or hospital in time of emergency, etc.

Violation of Sacred Places/Reparation

Canon 1211 — Sacred places are violated through seriously harmful actions posited in them which scandalize the faithful and are so serious and contrary to the holiness of the place, in the judgment of the local ordinary, that it is not licit to perform acts of worship in them until the harm is repaired through a penitential rite in accord with the norm of the liturgical books.

In the 1917 Code the focus of this canon was on the *act* which violated the holiness of the sacred place (*CIC* 1165); here, the emphasis is on the scandal for the faithful. It is not a question of the sacred place losing its dedication or blessing as in canon 1212; this canon concerns actions which are so contrary to the nature of the sacred place that the faithful who worship there would see the need for public penance before the place is again used for their acts of cult.

The Sacred Congregation of Rites in an instruction of September 26, 1964 revoked canon 1176 of the 1917 Code and stated that any priest can reconcile a church that has been violated, whether the church had been consecrated or only blessed. The March 1983 draft edition of the *Rituale Romanum: De benedictionibus* contained an appendix, *Publica supplicatio peragenda cum gravis iniuria domui ec-*

clesiae est illata ("The Public Period of Prayer in the Case of Grave Injury to a Church Building"). The final text of the *De benedictionibus,* promulgated by the Sacred Congregation for Divine Worship in May 1984, does not contain this rite, and (insofar as this commentator is able to determine) no revision of title IX, chapter 9, number 18 of the former *Roman Ritual* currently (1984) exists.

It is to be noted that the terms "desecration," "reconciliation," and "pollution" are no longer used in this context. The public nature of the penitential rite follows upon the public nature of the crime and the scandal.

Loss of Sacred Character

Canon 1212 — Sacred places lose their dedication or blessing if they suffer major destruction or if they have been permanently given over to profane uses, de facto or through a decree of the competent ordinary.

Canon 1205 states how a place *becomes* sacred; canon 1212 states how a place *loses* this quality. The words "desecration" or "secularization" are no longer used by the Code.

"Major destruction" means that the place cannot function according to the definition of "sacred place," namely, a place for divine cult or for the burial of the faithful. If after the destruction the place is to be restored and again used for cult, it would be dedicated or blessed anew.

If a sacred place is to undergo extensive restoration, the question to be asked is whether the restored place is a *new* place and therefore to be dedicated or blessed anew, or whether it is the former place restored. If the latter is true, it would not be dedicated or blessed anew (for it never ceased to be sacred), and the completion of the work would be marked by some other celebration of gratitude and praise. Important in this decision would be whether or not the exercise of cult continued in the place during the renovation.

The mobility of population centers, the changing financial situation of neighborhoods, the growth of parishes, and the decrease in membership of others: these and many other factors may determine that a place once used exclusively for cult be given another use. This canon allows the competent ordinary to do this. For example, the diocesan bishop could issue a decree allowing a parish to build a new church and to use the former church for a parish hall. The decree is sufficient to cause the place to lose its dedication or blessing; no further "ceremony" is needed.

The Sacred Congregation for the Council decreed on July 31, 1961 that a sacred place could be sold and used as a "sacred place" by non-Catholics provided there is no danger of scandal.

Canon 1213 — **Ecclesiastical authority freely execises its powers and functions in sacred places.**

While the content of this canon is the same as canon 1160 of the 1917 Code, the tone of the canon reflects a different and more harmonious relationship between the power of the Church and that of the State than expressed in the former Code.

CHAPTER I
CHURCHES
[cc. 1214–1222]

Notion of Church

Canon 1214 — **The term church signifies a sacred building destined for divine worship to which the faithful have a right of access for divine worship, especially its public exercise.**

This canon defines the use of the word "church"; the fact that a church is intended for *all the faithful* distinguishes it from an oratory or private chapel. The Code no longer speaks of "public oratories." The most common examples of churches in this canon will be the cathedral of a diocese and the parish church.

Building of Church

Canon 1215 — **§1. No church is to be built without the expressed written consent of the diocesan bishop.**
§2. The diocesan bishop is not to furnish this consent unless he judges that a new church could serve the good of souls and that the means necessary for building the church and for divine worship would not be lacking in the future; he is to make this judgment after listening to the presbyteral council and the rectors of neighboring churches.
§3. Even religious institutes must obtain the permission of the diocesan bishop before they build a church in a certain and determined place even if they have received the consent of the diocesan bishop to establish a new house in the diocese or city.

The diocesan bishop is concerned with the building of a new church because this would ordinarily also involve the establishment of a new parish.

Building and Repair of Church

Canon 1216 — **The principles and norms of the liturgy and of sacred art are to be observed in the building and repair of churches; the advice of experts is also to be employed.**

The norms referred to can be found in the introduction to *Dedication of a Church and an Altar,*

General Instruction of the Roman Missal 253–280, and in the United States Bishops' Committee on the Liturgy's 1978 statement *Environment and Art in Catholic Worship.* The detailed legislation of the 1917 Code is now left to the liturgical books.

Dedication/Blessing of Church

Canon 1217 — **§1. As soon as its construction is properly completed, a new church is to be dedicated or at least blessed as soon as possible, observing the laws of the sacred liturgy.**
§2. Churches, especially cathedral and parochial churches, are to be dedicated with a solemn rite.

In order that the faithful may benefit from the full effect of the symbolism and the significance of the rite of dedication, the opening of a new church and its dedication should take place at one and the same time. "For this reason care should be taken that, as far as possible, Mass is not celebrated in a new church before it is dedicated."[4] When the church to be dedicated has already been in use, a different rite is used, namely, that given in chapter three of the rite of *Dedication of a Church and an Altar,* "Dedication of a Church Already in General Use for Sacred Celebrations."

The "solemn rite" referred to in paragraph two is that found in chapters one through four of the 1978 text. A blessing is given in chapter one for the "Laying of a Foundation Stone or Commencement of Work on the Building of a Church" which is an important part of the Church's liturgy, even though not mentioned in the Code.

The phrase "or at least blessed . . . observing the laws of the sacred liturgy" found in paragraph one refers to the rites found in chapter five of the *Dedication:*

> It is desirable that sacred buildings of churches which are destined for the celebration of divine mysteries in a stable manner should be dedicated to God. Such a dedication takes place according to the rite of dedication described in Chapters Two and Three, which is distinguished by the wealth of its rites and symbols. It is fitting that private chapels or sacred buildings which, because of special circumstances, are destined for divine worship only for a time, should be blessed according to the rite which is described below.[5]

Title of Church

Canon 1218 — **Each church is to have its title which cannot be changed after its dedication.**

[4]Ibid., 41.
[5]Ibid., 83.

Although this canon speaks only of "dedication," churches which are merely blessed are also to have a title.[6]

The detailed prescriptions of the 1917 Code are not repeated here; one is to follow the directives of the current liturgical books. Concerning titles, the rite states:

When a church is to be dedicated it must have a titular. Churches may have for their titular: the Blessed Trinity, our Lord Jesus Christ invoked according to a mystery of his life or a title already accepted in the sacred liturgy, the Holy Spirit, the Blessed Virgin Mary, likewise invoked according to some appellation already accepted in the sacred liturgy, one of the angels, or, finally, a saint inscribed in the Roman Martyrology or in an Appendix duly approved; but not a blessed, without an indult of the Apostolic See. A church should have one titular only, unless it is a question of saints who are inscribed together in the Calendar.[7]

The titular feast of the church is celebrated annually with the rank of solemnity.[8] Churches named after the Blessed Virgin Mary without the addition of a particular mystery or title or under a title which does not have its own liturgical day celebrate their titular feast on August 15, the Assumption.[9]

Performance of Acts of Worship

Canon 1219 — All acts of divine worship can be performed in a church legitimately dedicated or blessed, with due regard for parochial rights.

Care for Churches

Canon 1220 — §1. All whose concern it is are to take care that such cleanliness and propriety is preserved in churches as befits the house of God and that anything which is out of keeping with the sanctity of the place is precluded.

§2. Ordinary concern for preservation and appropriate security measures are to be used to protect sacred and precious goods.

Free Access to Church

Canon 1221 — Entrance to a church during the time of sacred celebrations is to be free and gratuitous.

[6]Ibid.

[7]Ibid., 12.

[8]*Roman Calendar,* Table of Liturgical Days, I 4 c.

[9]SCSDW, *Decreta Authentica,* 2529.

Church's Loss of Sacred Character

Canon 1222 — §1. If a church can in no way be employed for divine worship and it is impossible to repair it, it can be relegated to profane but not sordid use by the diocesan bishop.

§2. Where other serious reasons suggest that a church no longer be used for divine worship the diocesan bishop, after hearing the presbyteral council, can relegate it to profane but not sordid use with the consent of those who legitimately claim rights regarding the church and as long as the good of souls is not thereby impaired.

Canon 1222 takes the general norms given in canon 1212 and applies them to churches.

CHAPTER II
ORATORIES AND PRIVATE CHAPELS
[cc. 1223–1229]

Notion of Oratory

Canon 1223 — The term oratory signifies a place designated by permission of the ordinary for divine worship for the benefit of some community or assembly of the faithful who gather there; other members of the faithful may also have access to it with the consent of the competent superior.

The 1917 Code defined three kinds of oratories: public, semi-public, and private (or domestic) (*CIC* 1188). In the present Code, the former "public oratory" is absorbed into the notion of a "church"; the former "semi-public oratory" is now simply "an oratory"; the former "private (or domestic) oratory" is now called a "private chapel" (see c. 1226 below).

The principal difference in the definitions of church and oratory in the present Code is the fact that the church is for the use of *all the faithful* whereas an oratory is "for the benefit of some community or assembly of the faithful."

Permission for Oratory

Canon 1224 — §1. The ordinary is not to grant the permission required to establish an oratory unless he first visits the place destined for the oratory himself or through another and finds it suitably constructed.

§2. Once this permission is granted, however, the oratory cannot be converted to profane uses without the authority of the same ordinary.

Performance of Sacred Celebrations

Canon 1225 — All sacred celebrations can be carried out in oratories legitimately established unless liturgical norms prevent this or the law or a prescription of the local ordinary has made certain exceptions.

Notion of Private Chapel

Canon 1226 — The term private chapel signifies a place designated for divine worship for the advantage of one or several physical persons with the permission of the local ordinary.

The 1917 Code (*CIC* 1188) used the term private (or domestic) oratory for what the present Code in canon 1226 calls a private chapel.

Establishment of Private Chapel

Canon 1227 — Bishops can establish for themselves a private chapel which enjoys the same rights as an oratory.

"Cardinals" are omitted from the canon for the law presumes that each individual is a bishop (*CIC* 1189).

Sacred Celebrations in Private Chapel

Canon 1228 — With due regard for the prescription of can. 1227, the permission of the local ordinary is required for Mass and other sacred celebrations to take place in a private chapel.

Blessing of Oratories/Private Chapels

Canon 1229 — It is fitting that oratories and private chapels be blessed according to the rite prescribed in the liturgical books; they must, however, be reserved only for divine worship and be free from all domestic uses.

The solemn rite in chapters one through four of the *Dedication of a Church and an Altar* is intended for churches; the rite referred to in canon 1229 is that found in chapter five: "Blessing of a Church." The introduction to this rite states that it is for "private oratories, chapels. . . ." The words "private" and "oratories" should be transposed to bring the phrase into harmony with the present Code and should read "oratories, private chapels."

CHAPTER III
SHRINES
[cc. 1230–1234]

Notion of Shrine

Canon 1230 — The term shrine signifies a church or other sacred place to which the faithful make pilgrimages for a particular pious reason with the approval of the local ordinary.

This chapter on shrines is new and was not found in the 1917 Code. The distinguishing mark of a shrine is that it is a place to which the faithful "make pilgrimages."

Authorization of Shrine

Canon 1231 — For a shrine to be called a national one, the conference of bishops must approve; for it to be called an international one, the Holy See must approve.

This new canon will in the future prevent several shrines in honor of the same mystery or saint from claiming for themselves the name "the National Shrine of . . . " as is currently the case. Canon 9 states that "laws deal with the future and not the past, unless specific provision be made in the laws concerning the past" which this canon does not.

Statutes of Shrines

Canon 1232 — §1. The local ordinary is competent to approve the statutes of a diocesan shrine; the conference of bishops for a national shrine; the Holy See alone for an international shrine.
§2. These statutes are to determine especially the purpose of the shrine, the authority of its rector and the ownership and administration of goods.

Privileges of Shrines

Canon 1233 — Certain privileges can be granted to shrines as often as local circumstances, the large number of pilgrims and especially the good of the faithful seem to suggest it.

Pastoral Service of Shrines

Canon 1234 — §1. At shrines more abundant means of salvation are to be provided the faithful; the word of God is to be carefully proclaimed; liturgical life is to be appropriately fostered especially through the celebration of the Eucharist and penance; and approved forms of popular piety are to be cultivated.
§2. Votive gifts of popular art and piety are to be displayed in shrines or adjacent places and kept secure.

CHAPTER IV
ALTARS
[cc. 1235–1239]

Notion of Altar

Canon 1235 — §1. An altar or a table on which the Eucharistic Sacrifice is celebrated is said to be *fixed* if it is so constructed that it is joined to the

floor and therefore cannot be moved; it is *movable* if it can be transferred.

§2. It is fitting that there be a fixed altar in every church; in other places designated for sacred celebration, a fixed altar or a movable altar.

The complex and technical definitions of the 1917 Code (*CIC* 1197) are replaced with terminology which is immediately understandable. There is no longer any mention of an "altar stone"; the term "movable altar" refers to the altar itself and not to an altar stone as in the previous legislation.

This legislation speaks of *one* altar; the former legislation presumed there would be several altars in a church. The rite of *Dedication* states that "in new churches it is better to erect one altar only, so that in the one assembly of the people of God the one altar may signify our one Savior Jesus Christ and the one eucharist of the Church."[10]

Construction of Altar

Canon 1236 — **§1. According to church custom the table of a fixed altar is to be of stone, in fact of a single natural stone; nevertheless, even another material, worthy and solid, in the judgment of the conference of bishops also can be used. The supports or the foundation can be made of any material.**

§2. A movable altar can be constructed from any solid material appropriate for liturgical use.

The symbolic meaning of an altar and the liturgical legislation regarding its construction and use are given in the *General Instruction of the Roman Missal* (nn. 259–267) and in the *Dedication of a Church and an Altar* (pp. 59–81).

The appendix to the *General Instruction* for the dioceses of the United States indicates that "materials other than natural stone may be used for fixed altars provided these are worthy, solid and properly constructed, subject to the further judgment of the local ordinary in doubtful cases" (n. 263).

Dedication/Blessing of Altar

Canon 1237 — **§1. Fixed altars are to be dedicated; movable altars, however, are to be dedicated or blessed according to the rites prescribed in the liturgical books.**

The rites mentioned in this paragraph are to be found in the *Dedication of a Church and an Altar* in chapter four, "Dedication of an Altar" and chapter six, "Blessing of an Altar."

The fact that the altar is used for the Eucharistic banquet is its principal dignity and the most ancient

part of the whole rite of its dedication or blessing; therefore, an altar should not be used for Mass until it is dedicated or blessed.

A portable altar may be *dedicated* even if it is not made of natural stone.

Relics

§2. The ancient tradition of keeping the relics of martyrs and other saints under a fixed altar is to be preserved according to the norms given in the liturgical books.

This paragraph is notably different from its corresponding paragraph in the 1917 Code. The former legislation spoke of a small space (sepulchre) cut into the altar or altar stone which contained the (usually very small) relics of saints (*CIC* 1198, §4). The *General Instruction* of 1970 speaks of maintaining the practice of *enclosing in* the altar or of placing *under* the altar the relics of saints."[11] In the rite of *Dedication* there is no longer any mention of enclosing the relics in the altar. The present Code repeats the legislation found in the rite of *Dedication* and states that the relics are to be placed *under* the fixed altar. Furthermore, the rite states that "the relics intended for deposition should be of such a size that they can be recognized as parts of human bodies. Hence excessively small relics of one or more saints must not be deposited."[12]

The entire dignity of an altar consists in this: the altar is the table of the Lord. It is not, then, the bodies of the martyrs that render the altar glorious; it is the altar that renders the burial place of the martyrs glorious. However, as a mark of respect for the bodies of the martyrs and other saints, and as a sign that the sacrifice of the members has its source in the sacrifice of the Head, it is fitting that altars should be constructed over their tombs, or their relics placed beneath altars, so that "the triumphant victims may occupy the place where Christ is victim: he, however, who suffered for all, upon the altar; they, who have been redeemed by his sufferings, beneath the altar." This arrangement would seem to recall in a certain manner the spiritual vision of the apostle John in the Book of Revelation: "I saw underneath the altar the souls of all the people who had been killed on account of the word of God, for witnessing to it." Although all the saints are rightly called Christ's witnesses, the witness of blood has a special significance, which is given complete and perfect expression by depositing only martyrs' relics beneath the altar.[13]

---

[10]*Dedication*, 12.

[11]*IGMR* 266.
[12]*Dedication*, 61.
[13]Ibid., 60–61.

Loss of Sacred Characters

Canon 1238 — §1. An altar loses its dedication or blessing according to the norm of can. 1212.

§2. Altars, be they fixed or movable, do not lose their dedication or blessing through the reduction of a church or other sacred place to profane uses.

In the 1917 Code an immovable altar lost its consecration in many ways, for example, if the top was separated from the support even for a moment's interval (*CIC* 1200). In the current legislation the altar must suffer "major destruction," that is, no longer be usable as an altar, or be *permanently* given to profane uses. The terms "execration" and "desecration" are not used in the present Code.

Exclusively Cultic Use of Altar

Canon 1239 — §1. Both a fixed and a movable altar are to be reserved exclusively for divine worship and entirely exempt from profane use.

§2. No corpse may be buried beneath the altar; otherwise Mass may not be celebrated on it.

Only the relics of saints may be placed beneath an altar. The bodies of the Roman Pontiff, cardinals, and diocesan bishops (c. 1242) may be buried in their proper churches but not beneath an altar.

CHAPTER V
CEMETERIES
[cc. 1240–1243]

Establishment of Cemeteries

Canon 1240 — §1. The Church is to have its own cemeteries wherever this can be done, or at least spaces in civil cemeteries destined for the faithful departed and properly blessed.

§2. If however, this cannot be achieved, individual graves are to be properly blessed as often as needed.

The canons on cemeteries in the 1917 Code (*CIC* 1205–1214) formed the first chapter on ecclesiastical burial (*CIC* 1203–1242), and the entire body of canons was placed within the treatment on sacred places. In the present Code these two topics are separated: cemeteries (cc. 1240–1243) are treated here with sacred places; the legislation regarding ecclesiastical burial (cc. 1176–1185) is contained earlier in Book IV on the Church's office to sanctify, part II: "Other [than the Sacraments] Acts of Divine Worship." In both cases the legislation has been considerably reduced and simplified.

The revised rite for blessing a cemetery is contained in the *Ordo ad coemeterium benedicendum* which is found in part III, chapter 34 of the *Rituale*

Romanum: De benedictionibus promulgated by the Sacred Congregation for Divine Worship in May 1984. The English translation of this rite is being prepared by the International Commission on English in the Liturgy and will be issued in 1986.

The blessing mentioned in paragraph two of this canon is found in the *Rite of Funerals* 53 and 71.[14]

Authorization of Cemeteries

Canon 1241 — §1. Parishes and religious institutes can have their own cemetery.

§2. Other juridic persons or families can also have their own particular cemetery or burial place to be blessed according to the judgment of the local ordinary.

Burial in Churches

Canon 1242 — Corpses are not to be buried in churches unless it is a question of interring in their proper church the Roman Pontiff, cardinals or diocesan bishops, even those who are retired.

Canon 1242 repeats the 1917 Code (*CIC* 1205) with the omission of "abbots, prelates nullius, and royal personages." The prohibition extends to the interment of bodies in a vault built under the floor of the church if this space is an oratory or a chapel which is blessed and devoted to divine worship and not merely a burial vault.[15] It is not permitted to place memorial tablets with the names of the departed in churches.[16]

Particular Law on Cemeteries

Canon 1243 — Particular law is to determine appropriate norms on the discipline to be observed in cemeteries, especially regarding the protecting and fostering of their sacred character.

This canon is another example of the Code's emphasis on subsidiarity, leaving details of the legislation to local churches.

Examples of this legislation for the United States can be found in the National Catholic Cemetery Conference's "Christian Burial Guidelines."[17] A good model for local legislation is found in *Funeral Guidelines: Diocese of La Crosse.*[18]

---

[14]ICEL, *Rite of Funerals* (Washington: USCC Publications, 1971), 53 and 71. See also 193 and 230.

[15]Oct. 16, 1919. *AAS* 11 (1919), 478.

[16]SCRit. *AAS* 14 (1922), 556.

[17]National Catholic Cemetery Conference, "Christian Burial Guidelines, Jan. 28, 1975. See: *CLD* Supp. through 1979, c. 1203.

[18]Office of Sacred Worship, *Funeral Guidelines,* Diocese of La Crosse, 1982.

TITLE II
SACRED TIMES
[cc. 1244–1253]

Determination of Feast Days/Penitential Days

Canon 1244 — §1. It is within the competence of the supreme ecclesiastical authority alone to establish, transfer or abolish feast days or days of penance which are common to the universal Church, with due regard for the prescription of can. 1246, §2.

§2. Diocesan bishops can determine special feast days or days of penance for their dioceses or places but only *per modum actus*.

Dispensation from Observance of Sacred Times

Canon 1245 — With due regard for the right of diocesan bishops which is mentioned in can. 87, for a just reason and in accord with the prescriptions of the diocesan bishop, the pastor in individual cases can dispense from the obligation to observe a feast day or a day of penance; or he can commute it to other pious works; the superior of a religious institute or a society of apostolic life of pontifical right if they are clerical can also do the same for his own subjects and others staying in his house day and night.

These two introductory canons repeat canons 1244 and 1245 of the 1917 Code. Canon 87, to which canon 1245 refers, is based on Vatican II's *Decree on the Pastoral Office of Bishops in the Church* (CD 8b).

The legislation on sacred time should not be understood apart from *The Constitution on the Sacred Liturgy*, chapter V, "The Liturgical Year." It is the celebration of the annual cycle of the mysteries of our redemption in the liturgical year which gives meaning to both feasting and fasting.

CHAPTER I
FEAST DAYS
[cc. 1246–1248]

Holy Days of Obligation

Canon 1246 — §1. Sunday is the day on which the paschal mystery is celebrated in light of the apostolic tradition and is to be observed as the foremost holy day of obligation in the universal Church. Also to be observed are Christmas, the Epiphany, the Ascension and Corpus Christi, Holy Mary Mother of God and her Immaculate Conception and Assumption, Saint Joseph, the Apostles Saints Peter and Paul, and finally, All Saints.

§2. However, the conference of bishops can abolish certain holy days of obligation or transfer them to a Sunday with prior approval of the Apostolic See.

The celebrations of the liturgical year are best understood in the light of chapter V of *The Constitution on the Sacred Liturgy,* "The Liturgical Year," and the Sacred Congregation of Rites' *Roman Calendar: Text and Commentary,* March 21, 1969.

This canon rightly places the emphasis on *Sunday; The Constitution on the Sacred Liturgy* states:

By a tradition handed down from the apostles, which took its origin from the very day of Christ's resurrection, the Church celebrates the paschal mystery every seventh day, which day is appropriately called the Lord's Day or Sunday. For on this day Christ's faithful are bound to come together into one place. They should listen to the word of God and take part in the Eucharist, thus calling to mind the passion, resurrection, and glory of the Lord Jesus, and giving thanks to God who "has begotten them again, through the resurrection of Christ from the dead, unto a living hope" (1 Pt 1:3). The Lord's Day is the original feast day, and it should be proposed to the faithful and taught to them so that it may become in fact a day of joy and of freedom from work (*SC* 106).

In addition to Sunday the canon lists ten other solemnities which are to be observed as feast days of obligation. This list is the same as in the 1917 Code, with the omission of the Circumcision (now the Solemnity of Mary, Mother of God, January 1).

In 1983 the bishops of the United States studied the question of which holy days to abolish and which to transfer to Sunday. The question of transferring holy days to Sunday raised difficulties because one of the most important principles of the Second Vatican Council's reform of the liturgical year was the restoration of the Sunday. "Other celebrations, unless they be truly of the greatest importance, shall not have precedence over Sunday, which is the foundation and kernel of the whole liturgical year" (*SC* 106). Subsequently, the bishops did vote to remove the obligation from both the feast of St. Joseph and that of Sts. Peter and Paul. In addition, they agreed to transfer the feast of the Most Holy Body and Blood of Christ (Corpus Christi) and the Epiphany to the nearest Sunday each year.

Rev. John Gurrieri, director of the Secretariat of the Bishops' Committee on the Liturgy, prepared and published the background material used by the bishops in their deliberation: *Holy Days in the United States* (see the bibliography following c. 1253).

When all is said and done, the basic problem is finding a way to make certain moments of the liturgical year true religious holidays on which we can recall with joy the events of our salvation, rather than merely stressing the obligation of assembling to celebrate the Eucharist on days which are often workdays in the United States, and thus by a common effort to do something difficult, establish a Catholic identity which distinguishes us from other Christians.

Observance of Holy Day

Canon 1247 — On Sundays and other holy days of obligation the faithful are bound to participate in the Mass; they are also to abstain from those labors and business concerns which impede the worship to be rendered to God, the joy which is proper to the Lord's Day, or the proper relaxation of mind and body.

The phrase "obligation to hear Holy Mass" of the 1917 Code (*CIC* 1248) has become "bound to participate in the Mass." Also the emphasis of this canon concerning work is very different from the corresponding canon of the 1917 Code. Formerly the focus was on the *work* and the kinds of work that were forbidden. Now the attention is directed to the *purpose* of the celebration of the day and the joy and leisure necessary for that celebration.

Fulfillment of Holy Day Obligation

Canon 1248 — §1. The precept of participating in the Mass is satisfied by assistance at a Mass which is celebrated anywhere in a Catholic rite either on the holy day or on the evening of the preceding day.
§2. If because of lack of a sacred minister or for other grave cause participation in the celebration of the Eucharist is impossible, it is specially recommended that the faithful take part in the liturgy of the word if it is celebrated in the parish church or in another sacred place according to the prescriptions of the diocesan bishop, or engage in prayer for an appropriate amount of time personally or in a family or, as occasion offers, in groups of families.

By the removal of the word "legitimately" from the draft of this canon (. . . assistance at a Mass which is legitimately celebrated . . .), the burden of determining which Mass is legitimately celebrated and which is not is now lifted from the faithful. Participation in any Eucharistic celebration fulfills the obligation. It is the responsibility of the priest presiding to know where and when he can legitimately celebrate.

The second paragraph of this canon is new and was added immediately before the publication of the Code. It reflects a new and contemporary situation in certain parts of the Church—a situation which will become more acute in the years ahead.

CHAPTER II
DAYS OF PENANCE
[cc. 1249–1253]

Purpose and Observance of Penitential Days

Canon 1249 — All members of the Christian faithful in their own way are bound to do penance in virtue of divine law; in order that all may be joined in a common observance of penance, penitential days are prescribed in which the Christian faithful in a special way pray, exercise works of piety and charity, and deny themselves by fulfilling their responsibilities more faithfully and especially by observing fast and abstinence according to the norm of the following canons.

This entire section of the 1917 Code had been reformed by Paul VI on February 17, 1966 with the apostolic constitution *Poenitemini* (see bibliography following c. 1253). The five canons in this chapter of the Code are a summary of part of this document and must not be understood apart from it, especially the very rich discursive section of the document treating the history of penance and its role in the life of every Christian.

Penitential Days

Canon 1250 — All Fridays through the year and the time of Lent are penitential days and times throughout the universal Church.

This canon is taken from *Poenitemini,* part III, II-1.

Days of Abstinence and Fasting

Canon 1251 — Abstinence from eating meat or another food according to the prescriptions of the conference of bishops is to be observed on Fridays throughout the year unless they are solemnities; abstinence and fast are to be observed on Ash Wednesday and on the Friday of the Passion and Death of Our Lord Jesus Christ.

This canon is taken from *Poenitemini,* part III, II-2. *Poenitemini* exempted holy days of obligation from Friday abstinence; this canon extends that exemption to all solemnities whether they are of obligation or not. The Code also gives the conference of bishops the power to substitute another penance to be observed on Fridays in place of abstinence from meat.

Neither *Poenitemini* nor the Code mentions fasting on Holy Saturday whereas *The Constitution on the Sacred Liturgy* (*SC* 109) states:

The paschal fast must be kept sacred. It should be celebrated everywhere on Good Friday, and where possible should be prolonged throughout Holy Saturday so that the faithful may attain the joys of the Sunday of the resurrection with uplifted and responsive minds.

Poenitemini adds the following explanation of abstinence and fast:

The law of abstinence forbids the use of meat, but not of eggs, the products of milk or condiments made of animal fat. The law of fasting allows only one full meal a day, but does not prohibit taking some food in the morning and evening, observing—as far as quantity and quality are concerned—approved local custom (III-1 & 2).

Obligation to Abstain/Fast

Canon 1252 — All persons who have completed their fourteenth year are bound by the law of abstinence; all adults are bound by the law of fast up to the beginning of their sixtieth year. Nevertheless, pastors and parents are to see to it that minors who are not bound by the law of fast and abstinence are educated in an authentic sense of penance.

The completion of the fourteenth year means the day after one's fourteenth birthday. The beginning of the sixtieth year means the obligation ceases at midnight between the fifty-ninth birthday and the next day.

Poenitemini stated that the law of fast bound those who have completed their twenty-first year; the Code uses the term "adults," i.e., those who have completed their eighteenth year (c. 97, §1).

The admonition to pastors and parents to educate those of a lesser age in a true sense of penance is taken from *Poenitemini* and is new to the Code.

Discretion of Conference of Bishops

Canon 1253 — It is for the conference of bishops to determine more precisely the observance of fast and abstinence and to substitute in whole or in part for fast and abstinence other forms of penance, especially works of charity and exercises of piety.

The National Conference of Catholic Bishops in their pastoral statement of November 18, 1966 determined the following:

Catholics in the United States are obliged to abstain from the eating of meat on Ash Wednesday and on all Fridays during the season of Lent. They are also obliged to fast on Ash Wednesday and on Good Friday. Self-imposed observance of fasting on all weekdays of Lent is strongly recommended. Abstinence from flesh meat on all Fridays of the year is especially recommended to individuals and to the Catholic community as a whole.

The entire statement can be found in *Canon Law Digest* (*CLD* 6, 679–684).

BIBLIOGRAPHY

Calabuig, I. *The Dedication of a Church and an Altar: A Theological Commentary.* Washington: USCC, 1980.

ComCICRec. *Comm* 4 (1972): 160–168; 12 (1980): 319–367.

Crichton, J. *The Dedication of a Church: A Commentary.* Dublin: Veritas, 1980.

Gurrieri, J. "Holy Days in America." *W* 54 (1980), 417–446.

National Catholic Cemetery Conference. "Christian Burial Guidelines." *CLD* Supp. through 1979, c. 1203.

Paul VI. *Poenitemini: Apostolic Constitution on Fast and Abstinence.* Feb. 17, 1966. Washington: NCWC, 1966. Original text in *AAS* 58 (1966): 177–198.

SCSDW. *The Roman Pontifical. Dedication of a Church and an Altar.* May 29, 1977. English trans. by ICEL. Washington: USCC, 1978 (cited as *Dedication*).

Secretariat, Bishops' Committee on the Liturgy. *Holy Days in the United States: History, Theology, Celebration.* Washington: USCC, 1984.

BOOK V

THE TEMPORAL GOODS OF THE CHURCH

[cc. 1254–1310]

John J. Myers

No society can function without the means sufficient to attain its purposes and goals. Although the Church's ultimate purpose transcends both this material world and its history, still it is very much part of them. Personnel and resources are necessary for the gospel to be proclaimed and the sacraments to be celebrated. Among these resources are possessions, including income and often property, and the freedom to employ these properly for the purposes of the Church. Its legal discipline reflects this fact.[1]

In various historical situations the particular needs for material resources and the attitudes toward them have varied;[2] so too have the legal systems governing property. Certainly in the twentieth century the emergence of modern capitalism and a large number of independent nations, a process often accompanied by social upheaval and economic instability, has generated new attitudes toward temporal goods in their various forms and shaped new contexts within which they must be administered.

The revision of canon law, then, necessarily had to address those canons by which the Church regulated the possession of property and other material resources and assured their proper integration into its mission. Within the Pontifical Commission for the Reform of the Code of Canon Law a special *coetus,* or committee, was formed to consider the Church's patrimonial law. This committee met on nine occasions from January 1967 until April 1970. From these meetings emerged a draft of fifty-seven canons. These canons were circulated in the Church for comments in 1977.[3]

The committee received eighty responses. In June and November 1979 it examined the responses and made some significant changes while reworking the canons.[4] The results of its efforts were presented as canons 1205–1262 of the 1980 draft of the Code and they are incorporated with a few changes as canons 1254–1310 of the 1983 Code.

The committee declared its intent to follow the teaching and directions of the Second Vatican Council[5] and to adhere to the principles adopted for the revision of the Code of Canon Law,[6] especially the principle of subsidiarity—which it saw as being of particular importance in ordering the relationship between the Church and temporal goods because local conditions vary so widely.[7]

Many basic questions in the matter of property, wealth, and other possessions had to be addressed in the final text regarding patrimonial law. What goods are being considered? To which persons in the Church do they pertain? What is ownership and what are its effects? How are goods acquired, administered, and disposed of? Are there some special matters for the Church to discipline?

The canons on the temporal goods of the Church address these and other questions in five general sections:

- General Canons: cc. 1254–1258

- The Acquisition of Goods: cc. 1259–1272 (title I)

- The Administration of Goods: cc. 1273–1289 (title II)

- Contracts and Alienation in Particular: cc. 1290–1298 (title III)

- Pious Wills in General and Pious Foundations: cc. 1299–1310 (title IV)

Unlike the 1977 draft, the title of part VI of Book III of the 1917 Code is retained for Book V of the revised Code because it is more traditional and because the term *patrimony* may suggest vast wealth[8] in the minds of some. "Temporal goods" as employed in Book V may be understood as all those non-spiritual things which possess an economic value. They may include real property as well as intangible rights and assets.[9]

---

[1]See *CIC* 1409–1494 on benefices and *CIC* 1495–1511 on the temporal goods of the Church.

[2]See, for example, P. Hughes, *A History of the Church*, 5 vols. (London: Sheed and Ward, 1934).

[3]*Comm* 5 (1973), 94–103. See ComCICRec, *Schema Canonum Libri V de iure Patrimoniali Ecclesiae* (Typis Polyglottis Vaticanis, 1977).

[4]*Comm* 12 (1980), 388–435.

[5]*Comm* 5 (1973), 94; *LG* 13, 23; *CD* 6; *PO* 17, 20–21; *GS* 40–42, 63, 71–72, 76, 88; *AA* 10; *AG* 8–9; *DH* 13.

[6]1967 Synod of Bishops, *Comm* 1 (1969), 99.

[7]*Comm* 9 (1977), 269.

[8]*Comm* 12 (1980), 394.

[9]T. Bouscaren, A. Ellis, and F. Korth, *Canon Law: A Text and Commentary,* 4th rev. ed. (Milwaukee: The Bruce Publishing Co., 1966), 805.

General Canons

The introductory canons contain provisions similar to many of those in the 1917 Code. The Church's right to own and use temporal goods for its proper ends is asserted. Account is taken of both the new term "juridic person" as well as the distinction between public and private juridic persons. The concept of ownership of church goods is introduced.

The canons expose an underlying tension. The general canonical legal system as expressed in the Code of Canon Law views itself as the paramount point of reference for various legal matters, including matters of property and other assets. Simultaneously, in most instances, a distinct civil law also claims the right to regulate temporal matters. The same property is thus subject to two different legal systems that sometimes might be either in conflict or, at least, not in perfect accord.

Right to Property

Canon 1254 — §1. The Catholic Church has an innate right to acquire, retain, administer and alienate temporal goods in pursuit of its proper ends independently of civil power.

Paragraph one enunciates a broad general principle by which the Code seeks to ensure the Church's freedom to carry out its mission by possessing temporal goods in a way that is not subject to undue interference from civil governments.

The Church has, in fact, owned and administered property from the earliest times. The New Testament gives evidence of common funds used for the poor.[10] Even before Constantine's Edict of Milan (313), the Church owned and administered some properties. Certainly since then church officials have consistently asserted its right to own and administer material goods in support of its mission.[11]

This is not to say that the right has been universally acknowledged. From time to time reform movements have claimed that the Church, in order to remain pure and incorrupt, should own no prop-

erty.[12] Civil powers, too, have sought to enhance and protect their own power and wealth by a great variety of actions, including confiscation, taxation, restrictions on the Church's right to benefit from bequests, and other similar limitations.[13]

Against this background, it is understandable that the Church would reaffirm its right to acquire, hold, administer, and alienate goods.[14] Clearly affirmed is the conviction that the Church's right to property and goods is not dependent upon recognition by or a grant from any government or legal system. The term "Catholic Church" is employed comprehensively in this first canon of Book V; it is further specified in the following canon.[15]

There have been many theories grounding this right. Some would ground it in the natural law right of any human society to acquire and dispose of property in pursuit of its legitimate ends.[16] Others assert that the Church is governed by divine law in this regard since it was founded by Christ for supernatural purposes and cannot be limited by mere natural considerations.[17]

Often in the past, Catholic theorists have considered both the Church and the State as "perfect societies." This means that both are sovereign in their own spheres and possess all means to achieve their particular purposes. Among these theorists, some went so far as to claim complete ultimate supremacy for the Church since its purpose was nobler. More moderate thinkers have acknowledged areas of autonomy with a need for collaboration when matters were of material interest.[18]

The expression "innate right" in the canon is neutral with reference to those theories, but the phrase "independently of any civil power" contained in the 1917 Code was omitted in canon 1 of the 1977 draft because it was considered to be "somewhat polemic."[19] When the canon was redrafted in 1979, however, the committee discussed objections to omitting the 1917 phrase. Some con-

---

[10]Mk 6:37, Lk 9:13; Jn 4:8, 12:6, 13:29; Acts 2:44, 4:34–37, 5:4.

[11]J. Goodwine, *The Right of the Church to Acquire Temporal Goods*, CanLawStud 131 (Washington, D.C.: Catholic University of America, 1941), 56–98. See also J. McGovern, "The Rise of the New Economic Attitudes in Canon and Civil Law, A.D. 1200–1550," *J* 32 (1972), 39–50 and F. Pototschnig, "Christliche Eigentumsordnung in rechtschistorischer Sicht," *OAKR* (1976), 276–309, a study of Church ownership. V. Rovera discusses property issues in "De structuris oeconomicis in Ecclesia renovandis," *P* 60 (1971), 197–208.

[12]Goodwine, 73–76. Such religious sects would include the Waldenses, Albigenses, Fraticelli, Wycliffites and Lombards as well as political philosophers such as John of Jandem and Marsilius of Padua.

[13]Goodwine, 80–98.

[14]See discussion of *dominium/ownership* in commentary on cc. 1255–1256.

[15]*Comm* 12 (1980), 395.

[16]Goodwine, 6–27.

[17]Ibid.

[18]H. Rommen, *The State in Catholic Thought* (St. Louis: B. Herder Book Co., 1945), 248–268; 507–606 (cited as Rommen).

[19]*Comm* 5 (1973). It was reported that the first draft was intended to eliminate traces of conflict between Church and State. *Comm* 12 (1980), 396.

sultors favored the first draft because it corresponded more clearly to a new ecclesiology that views the Church as subject to the civil power in the administration of goods.[20] The committee voted to restore the phrase "independently of civil power" to avoid giving occasion for doctrinal interpretations that the committee neither foresaw nor intended.

Surely there are significant theological and philosophical problems involved. The perfect society model is compatible with a more institutional ecclesiology and more clearly preserves the freedom of the Church—even in matters involving property and other forms of wealth.[21] The Second Vatican Council recognized the relative autonomy of the secular sphere,[22] and some contemporary thinking interprets this to include the right to govern the administration of all goods, including church goods.[23]

In the practical realm the canon establishes a policy whereby the Church does not recognize the right of the State to confiscate church property, to refuse to grant civil juridic personality (incorporation) to appropriate church bodies, or otherwise to interfere with the possession and administration of church properties. Furthermore, the Church does not recognize the State's right to invalidate bequests made within a certain period of a person's death, limit the amount of an estate left to a religion or charity, or limit the amount of property a church may hold. At the same time, it is understood that, in practice, the church in each locale must reach an accommodation with the civil power which allows for an orderly and peaceful life. The provisions of concordats and other de facto accommodations make it clear that the Church does not always insist on these theoretical rights so long as a workable relationship is permitted.

Purpose of Church Possessions

§2. The following ends are especially proper to the Church: to order divine worship; to provide decent support for the clergy and other ministers; to

perform the works of the sacred apostolate and of charity, especially towards the needy.

The purposes for which the Church holds temporal goods are presented in a general way in paragraph two. Traditional terminology is chosen, using wording from the conciliar *Decree on the Ministry and Life of Priests.*[24] The purposes stated in canon 1496 of the 1917 Code are expanded somewhat with the addition of "works of the sacred apostolate and of charity, especially towards the needy." It was not judged necessary to articulate other ends such as aid to missionaries or the promotion of culture because all such purposes are included in those already stated, e.g., "works of the sacred apostolate and of charity."[25] The final purposes mentioned are much in accord with the insistence of the Second Vatican Council and Pope Paul VI that the Church must neither amass nor even appear to amass goods for their own sake. Excess wealth should be shared, and in a special way with the poor.[26] The Church should live simply, encourage voluntary poverty, and view any of its resources as held in stewardship for the work of the gospel and especially for the poor. The Church must "not only *be* sparing in its use of goods, it must *appear* to be sparing."[27]

Ownership

Canon 1255 — The universal Church and the Apostolic See, the particular churches as well as any other juridic person, whether public or private, are capable of acquiring, retaining, administering and alienating temporal goods in accord with the norm of law.

Canon 1255 specifies that all juridic persons in the Church are capable of acquiring, holding, and administering property. This is true whether they are public or private.

In canon 113, §2 juridic persons are distinguished from physical persons (individual human persons). They are the subject of obligations and rights compatible with their nature. A juridic person in canon law is roughly equivalent to a corporation in civil law.

Juridic persons are established either by the law itself or else by a special decree of the proper ecclesiastical authority (see c. 114). They are communities of persons or complexes of things given a single

[20]*Comm* 12 (1980), 396.
[21]See traditional commentators such as F. Wernz and P. Vidal, *Ius Canonicum*, Tomus IV (Romae: Apud Aedes Universitatis Gregorianae, 1935); M. Conte a Coronata, *Institutiones Iuris Canonici*, vol. II (Romae: Domus Editorialis Marietti, 1948), 441–445; F.M. Cappello, *Summa Iuris Canonici*, vol. II (Romae: Apud Aedes Universitatis Gregorianae, 1951), 549–550.
[22]See *LG* 13; *GS* 40–42, 63, 71–72, 76, 88; *DH* 13.
[23]H. Schmitz, "Das kirchliche Vermogensrecht als Aufgabe der Gesamtkirche und der Teilkirchen" *AkK* (1977), 3–35. For further consideration, see R. McBrien, *Catholicism*, vol. II, 657–691, 1043–1056. The issue is not specifically addressed herein, but the independence of the secular sphere is stressed. Further discussion about the direct or indirect jurisdiction of the Church over temporal goods may be found in P. Bellini, "Potestas Ecclesiae circa temporalia: concezione tradizionale e nuove prospettive," *EIC* (1968), 68–154 and Rommen, 586–605.

[24]*PO* 17.
[25]*Comm* 12 (1980), 396–397.
[26]*CD* 6; *GS* 72, 88. *Populorum progressio* nos. 18–19; *Comm* 12 (1980), 390. See also X. Ochoa, "Acquisitio, distributio et destinatio bonorum temporalium Ecclesiae institutorumque perfectionis ad mentem Concilii Vaticani II," *ComRelMiss* (1970), 20–26.
[27]J.B. Hehir, "The Church in Mission: Canonical Implications," *CLSAP* (1975), 10. For further information about juridic persons, see the commentary on cc. 113–123.

juridic personality that transcends and is distinct from that of the individuals involved. A public juridic person is one that the establishing authority designates to function "in the name of the Church" within its own assigned purpose. All other juridic persons are private (c. 116).

The universal Church and the Apostolic See are moral persons. Juridic persons include the diocese and archdiocese, dicasteries of the Roman Curia, parishes, religious communities, seminaries, universities, colleges, hospitals, orphanages, and other groups established by competent church authorities. Some of these, e.g., colleges, hospitals, and orphanages, may not have a distinct juridic personality in canon law, but may function as part of a superior juridic personality such as a province of a religious community. Juridic status may be given to such groups as St. Vincent de Paul Societies and other pious associations of the faithful, but this would take a specific action of the proper ecclesiastical authority.

It is important that this point be understood, for misunderstandings in this area lead to a great deal of confusion. In the canonical system, by the operation of the law itself or by the action of competent church authority, juridic persons are created which are the subjects of obligations and of rights. In many countries, including the United States of America, a separate civil corporation is required to obtain civil effects, since the canonical action does not have clear civil effect. By the principle established in canon 1255, canon law claims that the juridic person, including all of its properties and other holdings, is to function according to canon law, unless otherwise specified. In fact, the civil corporation and the civil law are usually perceived as having much more urgent claims on the attention of administrators who feel it necessary to protect church holdings in the public forum. Two distinct legal systems are claiming to order the affairs of the church bodies—at least in many instances. This has led to considerable confusion, with some canonists tending to favor canon law and some tending to favor the civil law.[28] Whatever may be said of these complicated interrelationships, the general policy of the 1983 Code clearly continues to favor the canonical disposition of matters except where it is otherwise stated. At the same time, it clearly encourages participation by lay persons in the administration of church temporalities. A healthy balance is to be sought between the legitimate concerns of both legal systems.

Practically, this makes it urgent for church authorities to ensure that the articles of incorporation and the bylaws of the civil law instruments of canonical juridic persons be carefully drawn so that the canonical regulations are properly respected and can have their proper effect in the civil arena while operating through the civil corporation.

Canon 1256 — The right of ownership over goods under the supreme authority of the Roman Pontiff belongs to that juridic person which has lawfully acquired them.

Canon 1256 states, with apparent simplicity, that ownership of goods pertains to the specific juridic persons which acquired them. Some consultors wished to eliminate the phrase "under the supreme authority of the Roman Pontiff" because it was superfluous in this context. The majority, however, judged that the phrase clarified the nature of the Pope's authority over church goods, demonstrating that it is not dominion or ownership.[29]

Similarly, it was proposed that another canon be added which would make it clear that higher ecclesiastical authority could in no way attempt to usurp the ownership which a juridic person enjoyed over its own goods. Such a canon was deemed unnecessary because the principle is clearly derived from canon 1256.[30] Ecclesiastical authorities can dispose of the goods of juridic persons subject to their jurisdiction only according to canonical regulations.

A more complex issue raised by this canon can easily be overlooked. Ownership *dominium* does not have an identical meaning or even the same legal consequences in different legal systems.[31] Canon law and other systems relying more directly on the ancient Roman law speak of *dominium*. *Dominium* in the Roman legal system was close to being absolute, i.e., the owner was clearly identifiable over against all other persons and his or her interest was undivided and complete. No other person was entitled to regard the things as his or hers and no other person could have taken possession of or made use of the thing without the consent of the person having *dominium*.

Three rights are usually included in the concept of *dominium:* the right to make physical use of a

[28]See A. Maida, *Ownership, Control and Sponsorship of Catholic Institutions: A Practical Guide* (Harrisburg, Pa.: Pennsylvania Catholic Conference, 1975) and J. McGrath, *Catholic Institutions in the United States: Civil and Canonical Implications* (Washington, D.C.: Catholic University of America, 1968) (cited as *Catholic Institutions*). This discussion is briefly reviewed by J. Coriden and F. McManus in "The Present State of Roman Catholic Canon Law Regarding Colleges and Sponsoring Religious Bodies," in *Church and Campus*, P. Moots and E. Gaffney, Jr., eds. (Notre Dame, Indiana: University of Notre Dame, 1979), 140–153. Coriden and McManus, while acknowledging that Maida is essentially correct in a technical sense, point out that control need not be overly centralized in the diocesan bishop or church administrator. The expertise and experience of lay boards should be welcomed. See also H. Black, *Black's Law Dictionary*, 3rd ed. (St. Paul, Minnesota: West, 1933), 1312–1313.

[29]*Comm* 12 (1980), 398.
[30]Ibid.
[31]This discussion relies on F. Lawson, *Introduction to the Law of Property* (Oxford: Clarendon Press, 1958), especially 6–14, 87–89. See also F. Schulz, *Classical Roman Law* (Oxford: Clarendon Press, 1961), 334–380.

thing and to possess it (*utendi*); the right to income gained from it in money, kind, or services (*fruendi*); and the right to manage it—well or badly—including conveying it to someone else (*abutendi*). The social policy was to keep these three rights as closely associated as possible—although some exceptions were made—particularly regarding the right to income.

In countries where the civil law tradition is followed, there are fewer difficulties in applying canon law. On the other hand, where the common law system prevails, complications seem inevitable because there is no precise equivalent for *dominium* in the common law. In the common law, there is no fundamental objection to ownership being fragmented, and various aspects of ownership often are separated in varying combinations. One person can hold a legal estate and have possession of something; another can have an equitable interest or have a right to income—a right which can be conveyed. Other burdens such as easements or other servitudes can be attached.

The point of the discussion is this: ecclesiastical juridic persons, especially in a common law country, can come into possession of property or funds and not have *dominium* in any full sense. They might have an equitable interest or a right to income. They might be trustees or legal owners, but they may be required to distribute any income or other proceeds. They might possess property which is otherwise encumbered. Since the Code of Canon Law presumes *dominium,* it neither takes into account nor makes adequate provision for the very complex relationships that can exist between juridic persons and their temporal goods in common law countries.

In practice, with regard to the relationship between the juridic person and property, there appears to be little alternative but to respect the operation of the law under which the property comes. These are, in effect, conditions of accepting ownership and should be respected. Perhaps they should be considered as intended by the donor. Provisions of the Code of Canon Law cannot be disregarded, however, even though such provisions might sometimes be only approximated. Again, a healthy balancing of the concerns of both legal systems is desirable.

Ecclesiastical Goods

Canon 1257 — §1. All temporal goods which belong to the universal Church, the Apostolic See, or other public juridic persons within the Church are ecclesiastical goods and are regulated by the following canons as well as by their own statutes.

§2. The temporal goods of a private juridic person are regulated by their own statutes, but not by the following canons unless express provision is made to the contrary.

Canon 1257 changes the provisions of the 1917 Code in the light of the new distinction between public and private juridic persons in the Church. Formerly, all temporal goods belonging to a moral person in the Church were designated as ecclesiastical goods and were subject to the consequences of that designation (*CIC* 1497, §1). In the 1983 Code only the temporal goods of a public juridic person are considered to be ecclesiastical goods and subject to the provisions of canons 1254–1310.

A certain hesitance about this change in discipline was apparent in the reported committee discussions. As a result of the change, some goods belonging to moral persons (and therefore being ecclesiastical goods) before the 1983 Code became effective might afterward belong to private juridic persons and no longer be considered ecclesiastical goods. To most, this reduced supervision seemed appropriate because these persons do not act in the name of the Church. It is sufficient to ensure that such goods are employed for the approved purposes of the organization to which they belong.[32]

Some consultors worried that the goods of certain lay associations might not be properly supervised. The laity, however, have their own proper freedom and autonomy in apostolic works. The decision was in favor of letting the approved statutes of each association make provision for any needed supervision.[33]

Distinctions among the various kinds of temporal goods contained in the 1917 Code and in the works of its commentators may prove useful. They are not formally contained in this revised Code, but they are compatible with its legal tradition: *corporeal* goods are physical whereas *incorporeal* goods (such as obligations and rights) are intangible; *immovable* goods actually cannot be moved whereas *movable* goods can; *fungible* goods can be consumed in one use whereas *non-fungible* goods can be used repeatedly; *precious* goods have intrinsic, artistic, or historical value whereas *non-precious* goods lack such value; and *sacred* goods are all church property blessed or consecrated for divine worship whereas *profane* goods are not.[34]

Meaning of "Church"

Canon 1258 — In the following canons the term Church signifies not only the universal Church or the Apostolic See, but also any public juridic person within the Church unless it is otherwise apparent from the context of what is written or from the nature of the matter.

For purposes of legal clarity, the precise meaning of "Church" in the following canons is spelled out.

[32]*Comm* 12 (1980), 398–399. See ibid., 6 (1974), 98–101.
[33]*Comm* 12 (1980), 399.
[34]*CIC* 1497. Wernz-Vidal 4, 184–185; Conte a Coronata, 439–440; Cappello, 548–549.

Canon 1498 of the 1917 Code is restated verbatim, with only the minor change required by restricting ecclesiastical property to public juridic persons. This alteration is necessary for accuracy since the term "Church" which is not ordinarily used for all public juridic persons is intended in the canons that follow to include them.

TITLE I
THE ACQUISITION OF GOODS
[cc. 1259–1272]

The goods of the Church come primarily from the faithful who may employ various means in giving their support. The Church has a right to seek the support of the faithful and the faithful have both a right and a duty to offer their assistance (c. 222). The pursuit of the Church's mission in a diocese may be supported by ordinary or extraordinary taxes or by fees for certain executive acts. The *cathedraticum* is no longer mentioned. Collections for special needs may be sought occasionally. In most instances, permission from the local ordinary is necessary to solicit funds in a diocese.

Prescription, which governs special instances of ownership and possession, is here applied to temporal goods. The financial responsibility of the local church to the Apostolic See and the ancient system of church benefices are subject to special treatment in this title.

Means of Acquiring Goods

Canon 1259 — The Church can acquire temporal goods by every just means of natural or positive law permitted to others.

The fundamental right to acquire goods is reaffirmed and specified more clearly by canon 1259. The Church (any public juridic person) may employ any legitimate means of acquiring goods. These might include, among others: purchase and contract; receiving contributions, gifts, and bequests from members and non-members; and seeking special forms of support by labor or donations-in-kind, by prescription (long-standing possession in good faith), by court order, or by fees for certain services. A natural law right is affirmed; the positive law referred to is canon law in the first instance and civil law secondarily.

The act of acquiring goods must be just. The price paid by the Church should be just unless there is some aspect of giving. It would be unjust, for example, to deprive a family of needed support by influencing the last will and testament of someone either very sick or very old. In addition, social justice should be considered in the acquisition of goods. A land-rich Church could not justly continue to acquire more land in the face of widespread poverty unless there were a clear commitment to sharing the wealth.

Civil laws which deny or restrict the right of the Church to receive donations and gifts, to purchase and hold property, to solicit funds from church members and others are clearly rejected by this canon. The 1983 Code, just as the 1917 Code, does not acknowledge the right of the State to legislate in such a manner (see cc. 1299–1302 below).

Seeking Support from the Faithful

Canon 1260 — The Church has an innate right to require from the Christian faithful whatever is necessary for the ends proper to it.

The Church may seek necessary support from the faithful—independently of the State's recognition of this right. Some consultors wanted to reword this canon from the 1977 draft (c. 3) so that it spoke of the duty of the faithful to help meet the needs of the Church. The discussion also brought to the surface the feeling that the proposed phrase "require from the Christian faithful" gave the impression of coercion and the hint of possible sanctions.[35] The committee preferred to keep the version which stated the Church's right to require such support.

Canon 1261 — §1. The Christian faithful may freely give temporal goods to the Church.

§2. The diocesan bishop is bound to admonish the faithful concerning the obligation mentioned in can. 222, §1 and to urge its observance in an appropriate manner.

Not only does the Church have the right to require whatever is necessary for support of its mission from the Christian faithful, but also the faithful may offer temporal goods freely. This right is affirmed over against any potential interference by the State or by anyone else, e.g., family. The duty of the faithful is rooted in their significant share in the mission of the Church. Their share in the Church's mission is emphasized throughout the 1983 Code, but special attention is called to it in canons 208–223. The diocesan bishop is to keep before the people their obligation of sharing their goods with the Church (c. 222). Good leadership and policy would suggest that the obligation regularly and explicitly be related to the Church's mission as well as to the various roles which lay persons have in it.

---

[35] *Comm* 12 (1980), 400. In fact, former commentators, working from the perfect society model, discussed the matter from this perspective. See Wernz-Vidal 4, 202–204 and W.J. Doheny, *Church Property: Modes of Acquisition,* CanLawStud 41 (Washington, D.C.: Catholic University of America, 1927).

Collections and Taxation

Canon 1262 — The faithful are to contribute to the support of the Church by collections and according to the norms laid down by the conference of bishops.

Canon 1263 — The diocesan bishop has the right to impose a moderate tax on public juridic persons subject to his authority; this tax, which should be proportionate to their income, is for diocesan needs and may be imposed only after hearing the diocesan finance council and the presbyteral council; he can impose an extraordinary and moderate tax on other physical and juridic persons only in cases of grave necessity and under the same conditions with due regard for particular laws and customs attributing even more significant rights to him.

It is not sufficient to speak of the right and duty of supporting the mission of the Church in broad terms only. Ultimately, specific means and mechanisms must be provided. Whereas the 1917 Code presumed that much, perhaps most, church support would arise from endowment income,[36] such is not the case in this revised Code.

In canon 5 of the 1977 draft, canon 1263 preceded what is now canon 1262. A significant rewording of canon 1263 occurred in the course of the drafting process.[37] The major issue discussed was what constituted the ordinary means of support for a diocese and for diocesan programs. A diocese might benefit from bequests or from endowment income, of course. Beyond these, collections in one form or another and mandatory assessments or taxes within the diocese are seen as the primary options.[38]

In canon 5, §1 of the 1977 draft the taxing right of the local ordinary was broadly stated. He could impose a tax insofar as it was necessary for the good of the diocese. Many of the consultors objected to such an almost unlimited, unqualified right to tax.[39] The canon as revised and presented in the 1980 draft greatly circumscribed this taxing authority and spoke of the diocesan bishop rather than of the local ordinary. Reflecting canon 1505 of the 1917 Code, the tax permitted in this draft was extraordinary, moderate, and leviable in the face of grave necessity. (This had been customarily referred to as the *subsidium caritativum* by commentators on the former Code.)

The continuation of severe restrictions on a diocesan bishop's ability to tax was opposed strongly in the October 1981 final consultation. In fact, the Secretariat of the Code Commission and the *plenarium* itself appeared to have been in opposition.[40] The Secretariat opted to place the canon on collections first since they constitute the ordinary manner of diocesan support.[41] A right of taxation was maintained, although more limited than in the 1977 draft.

The plenary commission, however, after considerable discussion, voted heavily in favor of the wording which appears as canon 1263 in the 1983 Code. The diocesan bishop may impose a moderate tax—proportionate to their income—on public juridic persons subject to himself. The tax is for the needs of the diocese; it is termed neither ordinary nor extraordinary. Although various arguments may be advanced, the lack of restrictions plus the designation of a secondary and extraordinary tax later in the canon favor the interpretation that this tax may be an ordinary means of diocesan support. From this point of view an annual tax or parish assessment and some form of an annual diocesan fund-raising drive would be considered ordinary means of support. Both the presbyteral council and the finance council are to be consulted before such a tax is levied. Frugé properly points out that this expanded taxing authority represents a significant departure from the canonical tradition.[42]

Throughout the discussions, some questioned the very notion of the Church "taxing." It is rooted in the notion of the Church as a perfect society over and against the State.[43] Even in the face of such contemporary aversion to taxation, especially in a religious context, the Commission determined to continue and even expand the diocesan bishop's right to tax.

The *subsidium caritativum* mentioned earlier is essentially continued in the second half of canon 1263. The tax is not, as formerly, restricted to those possessing a benefice, but it may be directed toward both physical and juridic persons. Both individuals and private and public juridic persons not subject to the diocesan bishop, therefore, could be burdened with this extraordinary tax.

As with the tax for diocesan needs, both the finance council and the presbyteral council must be consulted. An interesting final qualification, however, may weaken the force of the stricter phrases. "With due regard for particular laws and customs attributing even more significant rights to him" appears to permit a diocesan bishop in some instances to tax individuals and other juridic persons moder-

---

[36]*CIC* 1355–1356 and 1505–1506.

[37]See D.J. Frugé, "Taxes in the Proposed Law," *CLSAP* (1982), 274–288 (cited as Frugé).

[38]Various words can be used such as *tributum, exactio,* and *taxa.* The essential element appears to be that one is speaking of a mandatory levy. "Taxa" is also used for the equivalent of "fee" as in c. 1264 below.

[39]*Comm* 12 (1980), 402.

[40]Frugé, 283–287.

[41]*Rel*, 282.

[42]Frugé, 287.

[43]See, for example, Wernz-Vidal 4, 203–204.

ately in circumstances other than in extraordinary cases of grave necessity.

The term "extraordinary" indicates that this exaction is not regularly imposed for diocesan operations but is intended for a specified need or during a specific set of circumstances. "Moderate" is not so easily determined. Canon 1356 of the 1917 Code used a maximum amount of five percent in reference to the seminary tax, but the base for figuring that is open to interpretation. Moreover, that is a tax for a very specific purpose as opposed to the more general purpose specified in the first part of canon 1263. One suspects that specific traditions and the degrees of centralization of certain functions and services in each diocese will help provide the context in which "moderate" will be interpreted.

One should note that an ancient practice of the Church has disappeared from this Code. For centuries, a modest financial tribute called the *cathedraticum* was paid to the diocesan bishop by benefices, churches, and lay confraternities in his diocese as a sign of their subjection to his episcopal authority. The *cathedraticum* as such was not normally part of the life of the Church in the United States, although diocesan assessments have been sometimes designated improperly as such. The final qualification stated in canon 1263 would seem to permit particular law or custom to continue the canonical institute of the *cathedraticum*.

The possibility of a tax for support of the diocesan seminary is continued in canon 264. The tax in canon 1506 of the 1917 Code which the ordinary could have imposed on churches, benefices, and other ecclesiastical institutions subject to himself at the time of their foundation or consecration is not mentioned in this revised Code. Early drafts of this canon made an exception for Mass stipends in all instances, but the 1983 Code does not mention this exception. Such a significant omission leaves open the possibility that a diocesan bishop could tax the income which priests serving in his diocese receive from Mass stipends.

Canon 1262 is broader in its application than merely diocesan finances. Not only does the Church have the right to require support from the faithful, but also the faithful have the obligation to contribute in response to specific appeals by church authorities. It does not suffice for people to give only at a time and in a manner of their own choosing—the common ministry and the common good call for their response to church leadership.

While many instances of authoritative determinations by the conference of bishops mentioned in earlier drafts were eliminated, this one was not: the conference may establish norms to govern collections or any type of aid sought by church administrators. Recourse to or approval by the Apostolic See is not mentioned. The canon speaks not only of dioceses but also implicitly—as indicated by canon

1258—of any public juridic person in the Church. Perhaps the legislator did not intend to give the conference of bishops authority to regulate all collections in its territory—whether those of dioceses, parishes, religious communities, or other public juridic persons—but this canon appears to empower the conference to set down regulations on form, style, accountability, and other such matters. Whether or not collections or other solicitations are to occur is a judgment reserved to the proper ordinary (see c. 1265).

Some such guidelines have already been published for the United States as a result of collaboration between the National Conference of Catholic Bishops and the Leadership Conference of Women Religious and the Conference of Major Superiors of Men. These guidelines recognized the principle of subsidiarity when speaking of the appropriate church authority from whom explicit and clear authorization for fund-raising must be sought. The guidelines address the issues of stewardship, authority, accountability, and techniques of fund-raising. Laudably, they relate the solicitation of funds directly to the mission of the Church and the Christian's share in it.

> Christian stewardship is the practical realization that every thing we have is a gift from God. Stewardship expresses itself as an integral force in Christian life by motivating us to share our goods with others. We are absolute owners of nothing; rather, we are stewards of all we receive and we must use such resources responsibly in our lifelong work of building up the kingdom of God.[44]

The guidelines for fund-raising are important to maintain the explicit relationship between fund-raising and the mission of the Church. They can also help protect the good name and the long-term credibility of the various church bodies which seek contributions and support from the faithful and from the public at large. In addition, when followed, they will also help people to be generous with the secure knowledge that their gifts will be well used and preserved from potential abuse.

Canon 1264 — **Unless the law has provided otherwise, it is the responsibility of a meeting of the bishops of a province:**

1° to fix the amounts of the tax for acts of executive power granting a favor or for the execution of rescripts of the Apostolic See, to be approved by the Apostolic See;

2° to set a limit on the offerings given on the occasion of administering the sacraments and sacramentals.

---

[44]NCCB, *Principles and Guidelines for Fund Raising in the United States by Arch/Dioceses, Arch/Diocesan Agencies and Religious Institutes, CLD* 8 (1977), 415–421.

For centuries support of the Church has come in part from fees associated with juridic actions taken by figures of authority and addressed through proper documents to petitions or requests from those under their jurisdiction as well as from offerings made by the faithful in connection with the sacraments and sacramentals. In the first instance the fees are directed to meeting office expenses and supporting the officials. Such fees are not readily acceptable to much of the contemporary world since a common notion is that those in public service offer their services free of charge and, in turn, are supported from the common treasury. It is especially difficult for some to understand such fees in a religious context, but it might be useful to consider them as being more in the nature of a user's fee. The consultors themselves acknowledged that the connotations of a formal tax were not desirable, yet such fees do exist because they are an important source of income for priests in some parts of the world.[45] In any event, canon 1264, 1° continues this practice for acts of executive power in a diocese and for the execution of rescripts of the Holy See. The determinations are for instances in which the Code does not provide otherwise. The fees established by the bishops of a province "for the execution of rescripts of the Apostolic See" require the approval of the same Apostolic See. Presumably, the approval of the Apostolic See would be required to eliminate these taxes as well.

The 1971 World Synod of Bishops had hoped that the support of the clergy would be separated from ministerial occasions, especially the celebration of the sacraments or the blessing of sacramentals. The consultors knew of this concern, but they also knew that in many countries the offerings of the faithful at the time of ministry are a primary source of clergy support. Since they did not wish to consider this sacramentally related income to be a "tax," the canon speaks of the "offerings" of the faithful on such occasions. Nothing here apparently prevents the bishops of an individual province—or even a region—from determining that offerings on the occasions of sacramental ministrations are either unnecessary or pastorally inappropriate in the particular circumstances of their dioceses.[46] Unlike the prior part of this canon or canon 1507 of the former Code, the approval of the Holy See does not appear to be required for these latter determinations. Canon 455, §2, however, would be applicable if the conference of bishops wished to take action.

Canon 1265 — **§1. With due regard for the right of religious mendicants private persons whether physical or juridic are forbidden to raise funds for any pious or ecclesiastical institution or purpose without the written permission of their own ordinary and that of the local ordinary.**

§2. The conference of bishops can determine norms on fund-raising, which must be observed by everyone including those who are called and really are mendicants by their foundation.

The complex organization of many Church-related organizations today results in a situation in which many individuals may be seeking to raise funds. Some control mechanism is essential, especially when private persons undertake fund-raising. Canon 1265 incorporates the basic controls of canon 1503 of the 1917 Code. Religious mendicants in the strict sense, i.e., those who rely on gifts for their sustenance (e.g., the Capuchins), are the only private persons for whom a right to seek donations without certain written permission is affirmed. All other individuals and private juridic persons need the written permission of their own ordinary and the ordinary of the place where the funds will be raised. Traditional commentators understood this restriction to apply to verbal solicitation of funds but not to the seeking of funds by mail or advertising.[47] Constitutions and statutes of communities of consecrated and apostolic life should clearly delineate the permissions required. The Code thus makes provision for authenticating both the private person seeking support and the cause for which funds are sought as well as enables the local ordinary to keep order within his own jurisdiction.

Today when many persons serve on finance committees and advisory boards of various church bodies, very confusing situations may arise and even misleading fund-raising may occur. Private persons need proper permission to engage in fund-raising. While persons who undertake church fund-raising, by virtue of their public responsibility as the administrators of public juridic persons may well be subject to other regulations, they are not subject to the regulations of canon 1265, §1.[48]

Conferences of bishops may regulate the public solicitation of funds in their territories (see commentary on c. 1263, above). This law does not interfere with the right of persons to receive and hold offerings or bequests which had not been publicly solicited.

Canon 1266 — **The local ordinary may prescribe the taking up of a special collection for specific parochial, diocesan, national or universal projects in all the churches and oratories which are, in fact, habitually open to the Christian faithful, including those belonging to religious institutes; this collection is to be diligently transmitted afterwards to the diocesan curia.**

[45]*Comm* 12 (1980), 403. The Latin "taxa" as used in this canon has a meaning close to a "users' fee" such as one would pay for a driver's license or for certain civil permissions. In some instances, it is similar to "court costs."
[46]Ibid.

[47]See, for example, Cappello, 553.
[48]*Comm* 12 (1980), 404.

It has been an ancient tradition of the Church to take up special collections for particular causes, especially to help the poor, sister churches, or other charitable endeavors. Paul directed collections for special needs, e.g., the Jerusalem Church (Rom 15:26–27; 2 Cor 8). Canon 1266 recognizes the right of the local ordinary to order such collections even in churches and oratories belonging to religious institutes—if they are regularly frequented by the faithful. Since the special collection is directed to an extraordinary need, the local ordinary should make moderate use of his authority in this regard.[49]

Canon 1267 — §1. **Unless the contrary is established, the offerings given to the superiors or administrators of any ecclesiastical juridic person, even to a private one, are presumed to be given to that juridic person.**

§2. The offerings mentioned in §1 may not be refused without a just cause and, in matters of greater importance, without the permission of the ordinary if it is a question of a public juridic person; with due regard for the prescription of can. 1295, the permission of the same ordinary is required to accept those gifts to which are attached a condition or a modal obligation.

§3. The offerings given by the faithful for a definite purpose can be applied only for that same purpose.

The relationship of trust which encourages people to be generous to the Church and her works of religion and charity must be preserved. When the faithful give offerings to church authorities, they must know that their gifts will not be privately used and that they will be used according to their intentions. Canon 1267 enshrines the necessary regulations to protect this trust relationship. The principle stated in canon 1536 of the 1917 Code is clearly reaffirmed: when an administrator of a juridic person receives a donation, it is presumed to be for that juridic person, public or private, unless it is clearly intended otherwise. Paragraph three affirms that the intention of the donor must be honored.

Paragraph two addresses a different aspect of the donor-donee relationship. Sometimes the latter may not wish to receive a gift. An administrator may make such a conclusion for many reasons: perhaps the gift comes from funds or wealth improperly acquired; perhaps the donor hopes for undue influence over church policy or decisions; perhaps public association with certain persons would not be in the best interests of the Church. When a public juridic person is involved, the reason for the refusal of a gift must be just in all instances. Unlike the 1917 Code (*CIC* 1536, §2), the refusal of a gift

in lesser matters is left to the discretion of the administrators. Matters of greater importance, however, require permission of the ordinary. This latter permission is also required if gifts with conditions or other obligations are accepted in the name of public juridic persons—since these burdens can last long after the current administrator is no longer in charge. Permission is also required when accepting foundation Masses or sums which entail an obligation to offer Masses or other prayers for either a definite or indefinite period.[50]

Canon 1267 does not declare the canonical invalidity of the action of refusing gifts, which refusal is presumably reversible by the ordinary. Of greater importance is the fact that, unlike the 1917 Code, canon 1267 does not mention the obligation of restitution on the part of an administrator who improperly declines an offering, or of other legal consequences designed to maintain the Church's right to receive the gift in question.[51]

Prescription Applied to Temporal Goods

Canon 1268 — **Prescription as a means of acquiring property and freeing oneself from an obligation is admitted by the Church in regard to temporal goods according to the norm of cann. 197-199.**

Prescription is a legal means whereby, when certain conditions are satisfied, a subjective right to something is either acquired or lost. It is a legal institute through which a person who has possessed a thing or exercised a right in good faith over the required period of time acquires legal title to the property or vests the right in question. Canon 1268 concerns the prescription of temporal goods.

Unresolved issues of ownership or of the existence and exercise of certain rights could eventually lead to confusion and public disorder. Prescription is the means chosen by legal systems to clarify such situations and maintain order in a society. It is related to the statute of limitations in other systems, which laws also intend to clarify the relationship between possession and ownership. After a certain period, an original owner has no right of recourse against an adverse possessor and eventually can lose title altogether.

Canons 197–199 contain the fundamental principles regarding prescription. It is significant that the civil law of the respective nation is recognized as having binding canonical significance where the Code does not provide otherwise. It is "canonized," so to speak, so as to avoid conflict between canonical and civil law. In the United States, the laws of

---

[49]Ibid., 405.

[50]Cc. 945–958 govern Mass stipends. They are consistent with the principle established in these canons.
[51]*CIC* 1536, §3.

each individual state which normally govern such matters will have to be consulted. These civil laws apply even to prescription between two ecclesiastical juridic persons.

Certain items are not subject to prescription, as outlined in canon 199; Mass stipends and obligations are among the temporal goods so listed.

Canon 1269 — **If sacred objects are privately owned, they may be acquired even by private persons by means of prescription; but it is not lawful to employ them for profane uses unless they have lost their dedication or blessing; if, however, they belong to a public ecclesiastical juridic person, they can be acquired only by another public ecclesiastical juridic person.**

Concern for the proper possession of sacred objects prompts the Code to place some limitations on the use of prescription in their regard. A sacred object is traditionally understood as one dedicated to divine worship or blessed to that end. Prescription cannot transfer ownership of sacred objects from a public juridic person to either a private juridic person or a physical person. Thus, sacred objects belonging to a parish, diocese, or other public juridic person could not be prescribed by an individual no matter how long the possession—even if the requirements of civil law were otherwise met. A sacred object such as a chalice or a rosary which had belonged to a private individual could be transferred to another private individual if all the requirements had been fulfilled.

Canon 1270 — **Immovable properties, precious movable objects, and the personal or real rights and claims which belong to the Apostolic See are subject to a prescription period of one hundred years; those which belong to another public ecclesiastical juridic person are subject to a prescription period of thirty years.**

So as to achieve some degree of uniformity throughout the Church in the matter of prescription, the duration of time required for some objects and rights is spelled out. These time periods are intended to replace whatever time spans the civil law would recognize in these circumstances.

Personal rights or actions are those which govern one's relationship to other persons, whether physical or juridic. Real rights or actions are those which pertain to real property. These and immovable property or movable precious objects which belong to the Apostolic See require one hundred years for prescription and then can only be prescribed by a public ecclesiastical juridic person. The duration required for like properties or objects of other public juridic persons is thirty years. The consultors rejected proposals which would have exempted all

goods of the Apostolic See from prescription and which would have shortened both the one hundred-year and the thirty-year periods.[52]

Other movable objects, even those belonging to the Apostolic See and public juridic persons, are prescribed or not prescribed depending on the operative civil law in various regions. If there is a conflict of civil jurisdictions, the civil method of resolving such conflicts should prevail.

Support of the Apostolic See

Canon 1271 — **In view of their bond of unity and charity and in accord with the resources of their dioceses, bishops are to assist in procuring those means whereby the Apostolic See can properly provide for its service of the universal Church according to the conditions of the times.**

The Second Vatican Council articulated the principle of collegiality whereby all bishops share in responsibility for the entire Church.[53] This principle was given concrete application by Pope Paul VI in his *motu proprio Ecclesiae sanctae* which authorized patriarchal synods and conferences of bishops to assess dioceses for the needs of other dioceses or the support of special programs.[54]

Canon 1271 is much narrower in focus than this broader conciliar concern. It recognizes the bond between the Apostolic See and individual bishops and requires that bishops be responsive to the needs of the Apostolic See in light of the resources available in their dioceses. It does not call for taxation of dioceses or others by the Holy See. Rather the support system appears to be voluntary.

Clearly it is a valid expression of collegiality for bishops to support the universal mission of the bishop of the Church of Rome. This expression of collegiality is complemented by the provisions of canon 1274, §3 which encourages richer dioceses to aid those without sufficient means.

Benefices

Canon 1272 — **In regions where benefices in the strict sense still exist, it is the responsibility of the conference of bishops to supervise the management of such benefices through appropriate norms which are agreeable to and approved by the Apostolic See; this is to be accomplished in such a way that the income from and to the extent that it is possible even the original endowment of these benefices are gradually bestowed upon the institute mentioned in can. 1274, §1.**

---

[52]*Comm* 12 (1980), 407.
[53]*CD* 3.
[54]*ES* 5.

A benefice was defined in the 1917 Code as a "juridic entity perpetually constituted or erected by the competent ecclesiastical authority, consisting of a sacred office and the right to receive the income from the endowment connected with the office."[55] The former Code legislated extensively regarding benefices (*CIC* 1409–1488).[56]

Previous commentators have traced the origin of benefices to the pension granted Roman soldiers worthy of merit or to the Germanic feudal system of rewarding special service by granting a life-income.[57] A contemporary institution analogous to a benefice would be an endowed chair at a university, especially when the professor held tenure.

A benefice was intended to provide permanently for someone holding a sacred office so that he would not need to worry about support while ministering to those assigned to him. It could provide the freedom and independence to proclaim the word of God fearlessly and to serve his people generously.

Nonetheless, because of the danger of the stress on income and principal becoming dominant and because more equitable remuneration for all clergy was deemed desirable, the Second Vatican Council directed that the "so-called system of benefices" be abandoned or reformed so that the right to revenues would be viewed as clearly secondary, and the ecclesiastical office itself would receive primary emphasis.[58] Subsequent church legislation essentially deferred this change to the revision of the Code of Canon Law.[59]

The 1977 draft also contained only one canon on benefices (c. 17). As is true in the 1983 Code, their regulation was remanded to the conference of bishops because there would likely be special issues to be dealt with in each territory. However, the approval of the Apostolic See is required for such conference determinations.

The consultation, however, revealed that many people felt that the draft canon did not clearly enough reflect the fundamental change desired by Vatican II. The draft spoke of moderating or regulating benefices whereas the Council had envisioned their suppression or a more fundamental change.[60]

With these facts in mind, the consultors agreed to alter the final form of the canon to indicate that the goal was suppression of benefices and the transfer of income and the principal, insofar as possible, to the new common fund established in canon 1274,

§1. Thus, working through the conferences of bishops, the 1983 Code makes provision for virtually eliminating the ancient system of benefices in the Church.

Whatever might be said of the previous arrangement, parishes are clearly not considered to be benefices in the 1983 Code.[61] Although there has been some indication that parishes in the United States were canonically to be considered benefices,[62] they have not been operated as such in fact. Canon 1272 will not, therefore, have a major effect in the United States.

TITLE II
THE ADMINISTRATION OF GOODS
[cc. 1273–1289]

Title II of Book V addresses the administration of goods. Administration is not intended here to include personnel administration, pastoral planning, management by objectives, or any of the other potential forms of administration—although these obviously may have some relationship to the administration of property and other resources.

Administration in this context refers to those actions or sets of actions which are directed to preserving church property; improving property or resources; managing the collection and distribution of income from a variety of sources, including offerings of the faithful and return on investments. It also includes keeping accurate records and properly reporting income and expenses.

Administrative Role of Roman Pontiff

Canon 1273 — By virtue of his primacy in governance the Roman Pontiff is the supreme administrator and steward of all ecclesiastical goods.

Canon 332 recognizes the "full and supreme" authority of the Roman Pontiff in the Church. Canon 1273, referring to his governing power, declares him to be the supreme administrator and manager of all ecclesiastical goods. Clearly this neither declares that the pope has dominion or ownership over all ecclesiastical goods[63]—for this is proper to the juridic person to which they belong—nor contradicts the obvious fact that he does not personally administer the goods of all juridic persons in the Church. The Roman Pontiff ordinarily administers

[55]*CIC* 1409.

[56]For a more extensive treatment of benefices, see Cappello, 513–542; Wernz-Vidal 4, 235–252; Conte a Coronata, 358–430. A study of the recent changes is available in "Dal beneficio feudale all' officio ecclesiastico ed ecclesiale," F. Romita, E. Colagiovanni, R. Baccari, and M.J. Carrion-Pinero, *ME* 96 (1971), 367–463.

[57]See, for example, Conte a Coronata, 366–367.

[58]*PO* 20.

[59]*ES* I, 8.

[60]*Comm* 12 (1980), 412.

[61]See c. 515.

[62]*CLD* 2, 698.

[63]*Comm* 12 (1980), 413. See also J.J. Comyns, *Papal and Episcopal Administration of Church Property*, CanLawStud 147 (Washington, D.C.: Catholic University of America, 1942) and W.P. Wolfe, "The Mind of Gratian Regarding the Ownership and Administration of Church Property" (J.C.L. diss., Catholic University of America, 1978).

even the goods of the Apostolic See through various agencies of the Curia. Canon 1273, however, does make it clear that the Supreme Pontiff could personally direct the administration of the goods of juridic persons in the Church should the well-being of the Church so dictate. He might be called upon to correct abuses or to require sacrifice on the part of some for the greater good.

Support of the Clergy

Canon 1274 — §1. Unless other provisions have been made for the support of the clergy, each diocese is to have a special institute which collects goods and offerings and whose purpose is to provide, according to the norm of can. 281, for the support of the clergy who offer their services for the benefit of the diocese.

§2. The conference of bishops is to see to it that an institute exists which sufficiently provides for the social security of the clergy wherever social insurance has not yet been suitably arranged for the benefit of the clergy.

§3. Insofar as it is necessary, each diocese is to establish a common fund through which the bishops can satisfy obligations toward other persons who serve the Church and meet the various needs of the diocese and through which the richer dioceses can also aid poorer ones.

§4. In accord with different local circumstances, the purposes mentioned in §§2 and 3 may be more appropriately obtained through a federation of such diocesan institutes, through some cooperative venture or even through some suitable association established for various dioceses or even for the entire territory of a conference of bishops.

§5. If it is possible, these institutes are to be so established that they are also recognized as effective under the civil law.

Canon 1275 — An aggregate of goods which come from different dioceses is administered according to the norms appropriately agreed upon by the bishops concerned.

Even though the Second Vatican Council decreed a major revision or even elimination of the system of benefices, the Council Fathers did not abandon concern for the support of the clergy and others who serve the Church.[64] Canon 281 expresses the Church's obligation to care for clerics both when they are serving and when they are unable to serve; it also makes some provision for the support of married deacons who serve the Church on a full-time basis. Canon 1286, moreover, insists that all who work for the Church receive a just wage and other social benefits.

Canon 1274 makes provision for this obligation

of supporting the clergy and others who serve the Church. Support of the clergy and others is seen as fundamentally a diocesan obligation. It is not automatically assumed that parishes or other centers of ministry will generate all funds for the support of the assigned clergy; neither is this seen primarily as an obligation of the conference of bishops. The 1977 draft spoke of the faculty of the conference to oversee dioceses in this matter (c. 16). The consultors, however, felt that this draft represented poor theology which would do violence to the proper relationship between the bishops and the conference of bishops.[65] Moreover, the intention of the earlier draft that all clergy have fundamentally equal support (c. 16, §1) was abandoned in the Code since Vatican II apparently allowed for distinctions based on the particular work and the circumstances of time and place.[66]

With the benefice system gone, the Council suggested and canon 1274, §1 continues to suggest that offerings of the faithful and other gifts be collected by a diocesan agency which will see to the adequate support of the clergy as mandated by canon 281. Such a system would mean a major change for most dioceses in the United States where clerics are usually supported by and receive remuneration from the parish or institution to which they are assigned. The phrase "unless other provisions have been made" makes it clear that the new system is not mandatory if the obligations of canon 281 are fulfilled adequately in another manner. In those nations where the clergy are supported by the State in some way, this system would seem superfluous, except for clerics not entitled to support by the State.[67]

The clergy also need social security. *Ecclesiae sanctae* required that this include adequate provision for medical insurance, sickness, and old age. Canon 1274, §2 points out that each conference of bishops should coordinate benefits with those offered by the civil government. Moreover, another agency or institute is called for, apparently on a national level, which would ensure such benefits for the clergy if they are not otherwise available. The canon does not state that the agency would necessarily collect or distribute the required funds. Apparently the institute would establish norms or guidelines for adequate social security for the clergy.[68]

It was suggested that the common fund for the support of the clergy and other persons serving the Church be combined into a single fund. The committee rejected such a proposal both because it did not correspond exactly with Vatican II and because some dioceses already have a fund for the clergy

---

[64] CD 16; PO 20–21; ES I, 8.

[65] *Comm* 12 (1980), 409.
[66] Ibid. See *PO* 20.
[67] See D. Faltin, "De recto usu bonorum ecclesiasticorum ad mentem Concilii Vaticani II," *Apol* (1967), 424–434.
[68] *Comm* 12 (1980), 410.

and would thus need only to establish one for other persons.[69] To the degree it is necessary, therefore, each diocese should have a fund to meet its obligations toward those religious and lay persons who serve there (§3). These obligations are not spelled out. They surely include just remuneration. They might also include health insurance and disability and retirement benefits. Again, it would appear necessary to coordinate such benefits with those provided by the civil government. Once again, any suggestion that the conference of bishops would supervise or otherwise make determinations for individual dioceses was rejected as contrary to sound theology.

The fund discussed in paragraph three is not only for the support of ministerial personnel; it may be used for other diocesan needs. Moreover, richer dioceses may also use these funds to come to the aid of poorer dioceses in the spirit of collegiality discussed earlier.

It is recognized that the Church might benefit if the funds of various dioceses were pooled. Evidently, such an arrangement would be voluntary according to norms approved by the bishops of participating dioceses (c. 1275). No mention is made of the required approval of a higher authority, either the Apostolic See or the conference of bishops. However, one can foresee problems after the establishment of such an association if a new bishop of a participating diocese wished to dissociate it from such an arrangement. Any agreement of this kind should make careful provision for all such possibilities.

Within a diocese, can funds be transferred from one fund to another, e.g., from the fund for the clergy to that for other persons or needs? The consultors felt that no special provision need be made for such a possibility so long as other provisions of the law were followed. The intention of the donor would surely have to be respected as would regulations regarding any alienation.

In such matters, civil law can be extremely important. Any such funds, trusts, or other arrangements should be provided for in a form that has civil effect and protects both the Church and the individuals in the civil forum also. The extent of this requirement is not completely evident. Clearly, all of the funds mentioned in canon 1274 should be civilly protected. Apparently persons who acquire rights or benefits relative to these funds should be able to vindicate them in the civil forum. It does not seem intended, however, that when these various church funds have been established, they would be required to conform voluntarily to every provision of the civil statutes—even when those statutes themselves allow for exemption. One would misinterpret this canon, for example, to assert that every church retirement fund had to meet the require-

ments of the Employment Retirement Income Security Act when that law itself would not so require.

Ordinaries Entrusted with Overseeing Administration

Canon 1276 — §1. It is the responsibility of the ordinary to supervise carefully the administration of all the goods which belong to the public juridic persons subject to him with due regard for legitimate titles attributing even more significant rights to the same ordinary.

§2. Ordinaries are to see to the organization of the entire administration of ecclesiastical goods by issuing special instructions within the limits of universal and particular law with due regard for rights, legitimate customs and circumstances.

Ordinaries here include all those so designated by the law. The term is not limited to local ordinaries or to diocesan bishops, but it also includes pontifical right major superiors both of clerical religious institutes and clerical societies of apostolic life, (see c. 134).

An ordinary is clearly the administrator of those goods belonging to the public juridic person of which he is immediately in charge. He is not the administrator of those juridic persons subject to him, but he does have the duty of supervising their administration. This duty gives him the right of visitation and inspection as well as the right of receiving a full accounting for the administration on a regular basis.

Ordinaries not only may but should provide more detailed directives for the orderly administration of ecclesiastical goods under their supervision. The provisions of universal and particular law must be respected as must subjective rights which might come from a concordat, some other privilege, or legitimate custom.

Role of Finance Council, College of Consultors, and Finance Officer

Canon 1277 — The diocesan bishop must hear the finance council and the college of consultors in order to perform the more important acts of administration in light of the economic situation of the diocese; he needs the consent of this council and that of the college of consultors in order to perform acts of extraordinary administration besides cases specifically mentioned in universal law or in the charter of a foundation. It is for the conference of bishops to define what is meant by acts of extraordinary administration.

Canon 1278 — In addition to the functions mentioned in can. 494, §§3 and 4, the diocesan bishop

---

[69]Ibid., 408–409.

can assign to the finance officer the duties mentioned in cann. 1276, §1 and 1279, §2.

According to canon 492, a finance council should be established in each diocese. The diocesan bishop or his delegate presides over this council which is composed of at least three of the faithful appointed by the bishop for five year terms. Moreover, with the advice of the finance council and of the college of consultors, the diocesan bishop is to appoint a finance officer who will administer the goods of the diocese according to the directives of the finance council and under the authority of the bishop (c. 494). The college of consultors is composed of six to twelve members of the presbyteral council appointed by the bishop for five year terms.

Canons 1277 and 1278 pertain to diocesan administration and to the bishop's role as the administrator of the goods belonging to the diocese as a public juridic person. The value of economic and legal expertise accounts for the requirement of consultation with the finance council. Consultation with the college of consultors provides advice from the viewpoint of diocesan policy and pastoral or other considerations. This consultation is called for in significant matters, deemed as such in light of the economic conditions of the diocese in question. In a large, wealthy diocese, this limit will be considerably different than that in a smaller diocese or one with special problems.[70]

The requirement of consultation in significant matters becomes a requirement for the consent of both bodies when this is called for in the universal law or the founding documents or when the action is one of extraordinary administration.

An action of extraordinary administration is discussed in the commentary on canon 1281. The requirements of consent and consultation are spelled out in canons 127 and 166. The bodies to be consulted should ordinarily be called together.

The revised Code makes it possible for the diocesan bishop to delegate a great deal of financial administration to the finance officer, presumably so that the former can give higher priority to his more important sacramental, pastoral, and teaching responsibilities. In addition to the general administrative duties for the diocese mentioned in canon 494, §3, the diocesan bishop can ask the finance officer to help supervise other public juridic persons (c. 1276, §1) and to name supplemental administrators when they are needed (c. 1279, §2). Certainly, ultimate responsibility and authority remain with the diocesan bishop.

In the 1977 draft it would have been the duty of each diocesan bishop to determine—presumably in

conjunction with the finance council and the college of consultors—what constitutes an act of extraordinary administration for the diocesan public juridic person (c. 25, §2). At the final consultation several bishops urged that the conference of bishops be charged with spelling out what constitutes extraordinary administration for the diocese.[71] The present canon does provide for this, thereby encouraging more uniformity in administrative regulations in each region and, one would hope, more objectivity as well.

Administrators of Juridic Persons

Canon 1279 — §1. The administration of ecclesiastical goods is the responsibility of the individual who immediately governs the person to whom the goods belong unless particular law, statutes or lawful custom provide otherwise and with due regard for the right of the ordinary to intervene in case of negligence by an adminstrator.

§2. As regards the administration of the goods of a public juridic person which does not have its own administrators in virtue of law or the charter of the foundation or its own statutes, the ordinary to whom such a person is subject is to appoint suitable persons as administrators for three year terms, and they may be reappointed by the ordinary.

Canon 1280 — Each juridic person is to have its own finance council or at least two advisors, who according to the norm of its statutes assist the administrator in carrying out his or her function.

A simple general principle replaces the complex prescriptions of canons 1182–1184 of the 1917 Code. The actual administration of ecclesiastical goods is the primary responsiblity of the person who is immediately in charge of the public juridic person which owns the goods. From the very definition of ecclesiastical goods, canon 1279 makes provision for all such goods. The principle is not so absolute, however, that other provisions cannot be made by law or by legitimate custom.

Some members of the consultation committee wanted to declare the right of the ordinary to intervene and act instead of the immediate administrator if the administrator refuses to act or neglects something which the ordinary judges to be good for the juridic person or for the common good. Other consultors disagreed, maintaining that the canons of *De processibus* allow the ordinary to intervene in cases of neglect and that such a provision would in effect make the ordinary the administrator of all the ecclesiastical goods in the diocese.

Canon 1279, §1 is a compromise. In case of the administrator's negligence, the ordinary may inter-

---

[70]The committee did not wish to make further determinations. *Comm* 12 (1980), 414. See also R. Metz, "Les responsables des biens des eglises dans la perspective de Vatican II camparee 'a celle du Code de 1917." *Prawo Kanoniczne* 20 (1977), 53–65.

[71]*Rel*, 285–286.

vene since the public good may be affected. If it is a matter merely of a difference of opinion between the ordinary and the immediate administrator about how opportune a certain course of action is, the consultors judged it to be more prudent for the ordinary to have recourse to the Apostolic See.[72] The principle of subsidiarity is respected because actual administration is kept at the lowest appropriate level. Higher levels function primarily for supervision and coordination.

Conceivably a public juridic person, a non-collegiate person, e.g., an endowment, might lack an administrator. If this were so, the proper ordinary may assign an administrator, man or woman, for three year terms.[73] Should the lack of an administrator be only temporary, the ordinary may also make provision to safeguard the church goods.

The difficult question of who precisely is the ordinary for lay institutes of pontifical right arises once again here. Their major superiors are not ordinaries (see c. 134). Superiors are surely to conduct the internal business of their communities according to canons 613 and 617–620. Pontifical right institutes are immediately and exclusively subject to the Apostolic See in matters of internal governance and discipline (c. 593); however, the Apostolic See could subject them to another authority (c. 591). Is the Sacred Congregation for Religious and Secular Institutes the only ordinary for lay institutes of pontifical right? Or is the local ordinary where the public juridic person in question is situated the ordinary in some instances? The Code is not completely clear. It would be ideal if constitutions and statutes clarified this matter when it might be a problem. Barring that, church practice will have to develop before this area of the law is completely clear. This difficulty of interpretation occurs several times in the canons of Book V.

The 1983 Code, moreover, is consistent in encouraging the use of the expertise of lay men and women in the administration of ecclesiastical goods. Canon 1280 extends the policy of bringing expert advice into the administration of church properties. All juridic persons are to have either a finance council, or at least, two suitable persons to advise the administrator. For parishes, a finance council itself is mandatory (c. 537). By analogy with the diocesan finance council, the members of the council or the counselors are to be experts in legal or financial matters. Presumably, the administrator presides over the council much as the bishop presides over the diocesan finance council. The form and size of parish councils and other juridic persons are not specified.

[72]*Comm* 12 (1980), 415.
[73]The consultors explicitly changed the prior draft to allow women to be administrators. *Comm* 12 (1980), 416. A policy of encouraging lay participation in church administration is certainly consistent with the *Directory*, 133–138.

Acts of Extraordinary Administration

Canon 1281 — §1. **With due regard for the prescriptions of their statutes, administrators invalidly posit acts which go beyond the limits and procedures of ordinary administration unless they first obtain written authority from the ordinary.**

§2. The acts which go beyond the limits and procedures of ordinary administration are to be defined in the statutes; if, however, the statutes do not mention such acts, it is within the competence of the diocesan bishop to determine such acts for persons subject to him after he has heard the finance council.

§3. Unless and to the extent that it is to its own advantage, a juridic person is not held to answer for acts invalidly posited by its administrators. A juridic person, however, is responsible for acts illegitimately but validly posited by its administrators with due regard for the right to sue or to have recourse against administrators who have damaged it.

Canon 1527 of the 1917 Code supposed a distinction between ordinary and extraordinary administrative actions, but at no point did it actually determine this distinction. In general, the commentators on the former Code considered ordinary actions to be those which occurred regularly. Commentators, basing their position on various curial decrees,[74] developed lists of actions considered to be in one category or the other.

Extraordinary actions traditionally included all acts of alienation, the acceptance or refusal of major bequests, land purchases, construction of new buildings or extensive repairs on old buildings, leasing or renting property for longer than nine years, the opening of a cemetery, long-term investment of any kind of capital, the establishment of a school or institution, and taking up special collections. Ordinary administration included the collection of debts, rents, interest, or dividends; ordinary maintenance of the church buildings or support of personnel; opening of regular checking accounts; the acceptance of ordinary donations; and leasing or renting the church property for less than nine years.[75]

The 1983 Code continues this distinction, but it seeks to make provision for even more specific determination by church authority. Canon 1281, §2 states that these limits and the manner of administration should be determined by statute. Clearly they are not to be determined by universal law, but

[74]S. C. Propagandae Fidei, July 21, 1856, *CICFontes*, 7 N. 4841; S. Cong. Consistoriali, July 13, 1963, *CLD* 6, 822–832.
[75]See W.J. Doheny, *Practical Problems in Church Finance* (Milwaukee: Bruce Publishing Co., 1941), 25–27. Also J. Abbo and J. Hannan, *The Sacred Canons*, 2nd ed. (St. Louis: B. Herder Book Co., 1960) 730–731; Conte a Coronata 482; Cappello, 577; Wernz-Vidal, *Tomus* 4, vol. 2, 220–221.

by particular law. The ecclesiastical authority which establishes public juridic persons and approves their statutes or bylaws should ensure that these limits are made clear in them. If the statutes do not so determine them, the bishop of the diocese, after consulting the finance council, will clarify these distinctions for persons subject to him. The principles used in the 1917 Code may be helpful in preparing these regulations.

Canon 1281, §1 echoes the discipline of the former Code. Administrators act invalidly if they perform actions of extraordinary administration without the prior written permission of the ordinary. The term "ordinary" is used in a broad sense, which is not restricted to the diocesan bishop. For institutes of consecrated life or societies of apostolic life, the proper official to grant permissions should be specified in the statutes.

Actions exceeding the limits of ordinary administration are invalid. What is the effect of this invalidity? It is first of all pertinent in the Church's legal system. Before the Church, the action is null and void. Even more, the interrelationship of canon law and civil law becomes important. If corporate charters, bylaws, and other legal documents in the civil arena are properly constructed, they will require that all canons and regulations of the Roman Catholic Church must be followed. If this is the case, church authorities could urge invalidity in the civil forum also. If not, the interests of the Church must be protected as well as possible. In addition, canon 1377 provides for the possibility of ecclesiastical penalties for those who alienate ecclesiastical goods without the proper permission.

Invalid actions can be validated canonically by the authority whose responsibility it was to set the limits or, in some instances, to give written permission in the first place. As the following canons point out, this authority might be the diocesan bishop, a religious superior, or the Apostolic See. The validation might take the form of a decision to renegotiate the transaction with a new effective date or it might simply be a decision to allow the matter to stand as enacted.[76]

When an administrator invalidly performs an administrative action, the juridic person is held to account in this Code only to the degree that it benefited from the invalid transaction. If the action was illegitimate but not invalid, the juridic person will be accountable. Local statutes should make clear this distinction between invalid and illegitimate actions. In both instances the administrator is liable personally for any losses or other injuries to the juridic person. One can foresee the possibility of civil suits based on this liability. Redress may be

sought canonically either by action before a church tribunal or by recourse to a higher ecclesiastical authority.

Duties of Administrators

Canon 1282 — All clerics or lay persons who through a legitimate title take part in the administration of ecclesiastical goods are bound to fulfill their duties in the name of the Church and in accord with the norm of law.

Canon 1283 — Before administrators take office:

1° they must take an oath before the ordinary or his delegate that they will be efficient and faithful administrators;

2° they are to prepare, sign and subsequently renew an accurate and detailed inventory of immovable goods, movable goods, either precious or of significant cultural value, or other goods along with a description and appraisal of them;

3° one copy of this inventory is to be kept in the archives of the administration; the other, in the curial archives; any change whatever which the patrimony may undergo is to be noted on each copy.

Canon 1284 — §1. All administrators are bound to fulfill their office with the diligence of a good householder.

§2. For this reason they must:

1° take care that none of the goods entrusted to their care is in any way lost or damaged and take out insurance policies for this purpose, insofar as such is necessary;

2° take care that the ownership of ecclesiastical goods is safeguarded through civilly valid methods;

3° observe the prescriptions of both canon and civil law or those imposed by the founder, donor or legitimate authority; they must especially be on guard lest the Church be harmed through the nonobservance of civil laws;

4° accurately collect the revenues and income of goods when they are legally due, safeguard them once collected and apply them according to the intention of the founder or according to legitimate norms;

5° pay the interest on a loan or mortgage when it is due and take care that the capital debt itself is repaid in due time;

6° with the consent of the ordinary invest the money which is left over after expenses and which can be profitably allocated for the goals of the juridic person;

7° keep well ordered books of receipts and expenditures;

8° draw up a report on their administration at the end of each year;

9° duly arrange and keep in a suitable and safe

---

[76]The 1917 Code was interpreted otherwise. See *AAS* 11 (1919), 385–386. This decision limited sanation of invalid alienation to the Apostolic See.

archive the documents and deeds upon which are based the rights of the Church or the institution to its goods; deposit authentic copies of them in the archive of the curia when it can be done conveniently.

§3. It is strongly recommended that administrators prepare annual budgets of receipts and expenditures; however, it is left to particular law to issue regulations concerning such budgets and to determine more precisely how they are to be presented.

All persons who share in the administration of ecclesiastical goods thereby assume a position of trust. Their duties are to be carried out for the Church in a manner which will bring credit to it and which is in accord with the purposes of its holding assets (c. 1254, §2). Canon 1521, §2 of the 1917 Code is broadened to include all administrators. The standards and procedures of business or government are not to be uncritically utilized in the name of the Church. All requirements of ecclesiastical administration are to be followed, even by those who may not clearly know them. The administrators must take time to familiarize themselves with the regulations.

Although there was some discussion among the consultors, it was determined to continue the requirement that administrators take an oath of faithful service before the ordinary or his delegate[77] (c. 1283, 1°) rather than simply a promise.

The previous requirement of an inventory, an element of good administration, continues. It should account for all immovable, movable, or other goods as well as a description of them. The administrator should sign it, of course, thereby affirming its contents and taking responsibility. It should be compared with the previous inventory. Insurance records and evaluations may be of great service for both the inventory and the required estimates of value. Copies in both the local archives and the curial archives should be kept up to date as changes occur in the property or other goods.

The provisions of the former Code about administration are largely continued in canon 1284. The administrator should care for church property and goods as if they were his or her own. Other requirements are self-explanatory. The value of insurance in protecting the assets of the Church is underscored (§2, 1°). Strongly emphasized is the need to safeguard the standing of church holdings before the civil law (§2, 2°–3°). Another feature is added: the universal law recommends that an annual budget of anticipated revenues and expenses be prepared. Regulations on the local level are to determine whether or not it is required, what precise form it is to take, and how it is to be reported (§3). (Many agencies—through the various aids and ongoing studies which they provide—help

church administrators faithfully and effectively fulfill their responsibilities.)[78]

Charitable Contributions by Administrators

Canon 1285 — Within the limits of ordinary administration only, it is permissible for administrators to make donations for purposes of piety or Christian charity from movable goods which do not pertain to the stable patrimony.

Apostolic works and works of charity, especially toward the needy, are declared as primary purposes of church possessions (c. 1254, §2). The right and duty of administrators to meet these goals are hereby recognized, within certain limits. The requirements of ordinary administration are to be respected. This amount is to be determined in the bylaws or by the ordinary. In addition, alienation or the invasion of fixed capital is not permitted (these terms will be more fully explained in the commentary on c. 1291); however, ordinary income and savings not designated as fixed capital may be donated. Particular law might well make more detailed provisions in this area of church life.

Social Justice in Labor Relations

Canon 1286 — Administrators of goods:
1° are to observe meticulously the civil laws pertaining to labor and social policy according to Church principles in the employment of workers;
2° are to pay employees a just and decent wage so that they may provide appropriately for their needs and those of their family.

Once again, this time with regard to employees of the Church, the 1983 Code makes it clear that there is no necessary opposition between church law and the various civil laws. Canon 1286, 1° requires church administrators to follow civil laws which govern labor and the social order. In various countries this might include unemployment insurance, workmen's compensation, health insurance, social security, or other retirement provisions. It might also refer to work days, work hours, vacations, working conditions, and other specifications in a particular society or for specific types of work which the civil law directly includes.

Potential problems of interpretation present

---

[77]Comm 5 (1973), 98; 12 (1980), 418.

[78]Some pertinent addresses are the following: National Conference of Catholic Bishops, 1312 Massachusetts Avenue, N.W., Washington, D.C. 20005; National Catholic Stewardship Council, Inc., 1234 Massachusetts Avenue, N.W., Washington, D.C. 20005. The National Association of Church Personnel Administrators might also provide useful information on administrative issues: 100 E. Eighth Street, Cincinnati, Ohio 45202. Consult also the Leadership Conference of Women Religious, 1302 18th Street, N.W., Suite 701, Washington, D.C. 20036; Conference of Major Superiors of Men, 1302 18th Street, N.W., Suite 201, Washington, D.C. 20036.

themselves. Are Church groups hereby required to observe laws which the State itself does not apply to them? Would Catholic schools, for example, be required to follow all the policies of the National Labor Relations Board which the civil system does not deem binding on the Church? In the opinion of the author, canon 1286 does not say this. The Code "canonizes" civil law in various ways and to various degrees; yet, this canon does not appear to intend such a sweeping result.[79] It does appear to require, however, that Church employers not violate civil laws which clearly apply to their situation.

"According to Church principles" (1°) also sets limits to the canon. If the State required health insurance, for example, which was to pay for the expense of abortions, canon law would surely not oblige Catholic groups to follow this requirement.

In a straightforward, non-paternalistic manner, the right of church employees to a just and decent wage is simply recognized as an obligation of administrators. The long and developing tradition of Catholic Church teaching on social justice is hereby applied to those who work for the Church itself. The 1971 World Synod of Bishops declared that "while the Church is bound to give witness to justice, she recognizes that anyone who ventures to speak to people about justice must first be just in their eyes."[80]

One of the rights of workers recognized by the social teaching of the Church is the right of association or organization. Such societies "must be considered the indispensable means to safeguard the dignity and freedom of the human person while leaving intact a sense of responsibility."[81] This canon coupled with the social teaching of the Church would direct that administrators not impede the legitimate efforts of church personnel to form unions or otherwise to organize themselves to promote their own interests within the church family.

Accountability for Administration

Canon 1287 — **§1. Both clerical and lay administrators of any ecclesiastical goods whatsoever which have not been legitimately exempted from** the governing power of the diocesan bishop are bound by their office to present the local ordinary with an annual report, which in turn he is to present to the finance council for its consideration; any contrary custom is reprobated.

§2. Administrators are to render an account to the faithful concerning the goods offered by the faithful to the Church, according to norms to be determined by particular law.

Administrators are accountable for their administration. Canon 1287, §1 requires that administrators of ecclesiastical goods (those belonging to public juridic persons) present an annual account of their administration first of all to their ordinary. The ordinary is to submit the reports to the finance council for its examination. Exempt institutes of consecrated life do not report to the local ordinary. This provision is not a major change from the 1917 Code (*CIC* 1525).

The contemporary climate which understands public administrators, even those in churches and charities, as accountable also to the public finds expression in the revised Code. Following the stipulations of particular law, administrators should—not simply may—give an accounting to the faithful of the funds they contribute. Canon 1287 does not require a complete accounting, unfortunately, for not all income used by the Church comes from the faithful. Investment income, money from the sale of assets, and other sources are not included. This does not change the fact, however, that good policy might well suggest such complete reporting.

The bishop of a diocese would determine the reporting form for those subject to him. He too is to decide in what form and in what detail the diocese itself will make a public report. The accountability for religious is determined by their own particular law. Discussions among the consultors revealed their feeling that sometimes a public attitude of skepticism toward the Church or a lack of understanding of the Church's need for temporal goods might caution against such a public reporting.[82] On the other hand, in many circumstances it is precisely this public accountability and reporting which help to build understanding and trust.

Civil Suits of Administrators

Canon 1288 — **Administrators are neither to initiate nor to contest a lawsuit on behalf of a public juridic person in civil court unless they obtain the written permission of their own ordinary.**

Special problems arise if the Church itself enters the civil courts through a juridic person. Ordinaries of dioceses and religious ordinaries have a special

[79] *Comm* 12 (1980), 419. See L. De Lucca, *La Transazione nel Diritto canonico* (Romae: Edizioni Universitarie, 1942). While the civil form for contracts, for example, is adopted for the most part with canonical effects in c. 1290, cc. 1274, §5 and 1299, §2 do not declare such an unqualified acceptance of the civil laws.

[80] "Justice in the World, Part III." See also *Rerum Novarum* of Leo XIII, *Quadragesimo Anno* 64–71 of Pius XI, *Pacem in Terris* 11 and 20 of John XXIII, *Populorum Progressio* of Paul VI, *Redemptor Hominis* 16 and 17 of John Paul II and *Gaudium et Spes* of the Second Vatican Council.

[81] *Pacem in Terris* 24. See A. Maida, ed., *Issues in the Labor-Management Dialogue: Church Perspectives* (St. Louis: The Catholic Health Association of the United States, 1982).

[82] *Comm* 12 (1980), 421.

responsibility to oversee such matters. Furthermore, they are in a position to consult other superiors, coordinate policies on a broader scale, and bring other legal expertise to bear on a problem. Even when it is a relatively simple matter, e.g., a breach of contract, the administrator requires the written permission of the proper ordinary to begin litigation. This is also required to respond to a court action in the name of the juridic person. For lay institutes of pontifical right the proper ordinary is not altogether clear (see commentary on c. 1279).

Administrators Not Designated As Such

Canon 1289 — Even if they are not bound to administration by the title of an ecclesiastical office, administrators cannot relinquish their responsibilities on their own initiative; if, however, the Church is harmed by such an arbitrary abandonment of duty they are bound to restitution.

Often a person may in fact be an administrator even though the title of the ecclesiastical office does not declare explicitly his or her administrative function. The office of chancellor in many dioceses in the United States is a good example. Moreover, the church benefits greatly from the work of volunteers. People give their time and skills for many purposes, some of which are administrative in character. People help count collections and deposit the money. They help with the maintenance of buildings and grounds. Some may supervise a cemetery for the formal administrator. For both good order and the protection of the Church, it is essential that such persons not simply abandon the responsibilities that they have assumed. Money could be lost, property could deteriorate, or other detrimental consequences might occur. Canon 1289 requires that anyone even in an informal administrative role consult the proper authority in seeking to relinquish their responsibilities. Moreover, if an irresponsible action causes loss to the Church, the person responsible is held to full restitution.

TITLE III
CONTRACTS AND ALIENATION
IN PARTICULAR
[cc. 1290-1298]

The language of commerce is to a great degree the language of contracts. The Code recognizes the language of the marketplace as so dominant in a country and so intertwined with daily life that most requirements of local civil law are recognized also as requirements of canon law.

Long-standing policy leads the Church to protect holdings and assets for both future generations and

effective use in the apostolate.[83] Alienating real estate or related rights is subject to strict control as are other actions which might result in damage to the interests of ecclesiastical persons.

Contracts

Canon 1290 — Whatever general and specific regulations on contracts and payments are determined in civil law for a given territory are to be observed in canon law with the same effects in a matter which is subject to the governing power of the Church, unless the civil regulations are contrary to divine law or canon law makes some other provision, with due regard for the prescription of can. 1547.

The revised Code states with little change one of the more enlightened provisions of the former Code. Prior to 1917 the Church formally had required that the Roman Law regarding contracts be observed when ecclesiastical moral persons entered contracts. Canon 1529 of the former Code made a distinct change as regards the form and manner of contracts. The law of a particular territory in effect at the time the contract was entered was recognized as canonically binding, with some qualifications which will be discussed below. The contractual capacity of physical and juridic persons flows from church law itself, however, and not from civil law.

A contract is variously defined. Briefly, it is a promise enforceable by law. More technically, "a contract is a promise or a set of promises for the breach of which the law gives a remedy, or the performance of which the law in some way recognizes as a duty."[84]

Contracts may be of many kinds and may concern almost anything. In the common law system, there must be a manifestation of mutual assent, some actual consideration, i.e., exchange of some kind; the object of the contract must be legal; and the contracting parties must have legal capacity.[85] All of these matters, of course, are technical and are treated extensively in civil jurisprudence. It cannot be overemphasized that civil lawyers should always be consulted when administrators are entering into major contractual agreements in the name of ecclesiastical juridic persons.

Canon law, therefore, does not have a universal form for contracts. Even when two ecclesiastical juridic persons contract, the proper form for both the civil and canonical realms is the civil form for that

[83] See Wolfe, "Gratian," 30–52.

[84] L. Smith and G. Roberson, *Business Law* (St. Paul: West, 1971), 46 (cited as Smith-Roberson). This is an excellent summary of pertinent law and related matters for the non-lawyer. A good but brief summary of basic elements of contractual law in the common law tradition may be found in Abbo-Hannan, 732–735.

[85] Smith-Roberson, 50, 113–189.

territory or the proper international form, should that be the case. The civil law, therefore, legislates regarding the object and formalities of contracts, about related clauses and conditions, and about their effects. It may set general contractual requirements and special rules for various kinds, such as employment agreements, sale or purchase of land, and the like. It may regulate performance under a contract, such as the amount, time, and place of monetary exchange. It determines obligations which exist and the proper form of judicial action when disputes arise.[86]

This is true unless in some instances the Code provides otherwise. The Code sets invalidating limits on ordinary administration (c. 1281) and invalidating requirements for alienation (cc. 1291–1298). Canon 1290 makes an explicit reference to canon 1547 in order to settle an old argument. The provision of canon 1547 which allows the proof by witnesses is affirmed for contractual law, even if the civil law does not so permit.

The canon states further limits when it says "unless the civil regulations are contrary to divine law or canon law makes some other provision." Any provisions contrary to natural law or to divine positive law are not recognized. Even if civil law allowed the purchase of stolen goods, for example, the Church could not do so. If the formalities have been omitted from a will and the good of the Church is involved, the heirs are to be reminded of their continuing obligation to honor the bequest.[87]

Alienation of Ecclesiastical Goods

Canon 1291 — **The permission of the competent authority according to the norm of law is required in order validly to alienate the goods which through lawful designation constitute the stable patrimony of a public juridic person and whose value exceeds the sum determined in law.**

"Alienation" is a term with a technical meaning in canon law. Simply defined it is the transfer of property or of rights over property from one person to another. The person from whom the transfer proceeds is said to alienate the property or rights involved.

In the strict sense, alienation applies to real property and to invested funds which are similar to immovable property. These latter funds are termed *stable capital* or *fixed capital* and consist of funds invested for a specified purpose.[88] They may be-

come stable capital either by formal designation as such by the proper ecclesiastical authority or by the intention of the donor who gives the funds for a specific purpose.[89]

Money or its equivalent such as stocks, bonds, certificates of deposit, or other securities often comprise a great percentage of the assets of ecclesiastical juridic persons today. Canon law considers money to be a medium of exchange. It is considered *working capital* or *free* or *unstable capital* if it has not formally become stable capital. It is cash-on-hand or money temporarily invested. An administrator might even temporarily designate such funds as part of an endowment for seminarian education, for example, reserving the right to change the designation at a later time. Such funds would not be considered stable capital.[90]

Most real property of public juridic persons is subject to the canons on alienation. Land and buildings generally fall under these regulations. So also do objects of special worth for artistic or historical reasons, objects blessed or consecrated for use in worship, and anything given to the Church as a votive offering. On the other hand, if a juridic person received a donation or bequest of land or buildings to be sold with the proceeds to be used either for general or specific purposes, the sale of those properties is not alienation in this canonical sense. The funds then acquired, however, might be restricted and thereby become stable capital as previously explained.

Sale is not the only transaction which alienates property rights, for many actions limit *dominium* by transferring part of the rights of the Church. Among them are mortgage, lien, easement, option, compromise, settlement, renting, and leasing.

The concept of alienation, rooted as it is in a society in which real property was the primary asset, has caused many complicated discussions of its applicability to situations which church administrators face today. Many consider it too cumbersome. At the October 1981 *plenarium*, Archbishop Joseph Bernardin asked that the concept of *"stable patrimony"* be changed so that a flexible notion of alienation more appropriate for today be adopted. The Secretariate responded that the change was unnecessary because canon 1295 applies the requisites for alienation to any transaction by which the patrimonial condition of the Church might become worse.[91]

---

[86]Cappello, 581–582. See Conte a Coronata, 483–484.
[87]See c. 1299.
[88]See F.G. Morrisey, "The Conveyance of Ecclesiastical Goods," *CLSAP* (1976), 123–137. Although the author does not agree with this article in all particulars, this commentary is indebted to Morrisey's presentation. Doheny, *Practical Problems*, 21–22; Cappello, 582–583; Conte a Coronata, 484–485; Wernz-Vidal, *Tomus* 4, vol. 2, 222–223; A. Vermeersch and J. Creusen, *Epitome Iuris Canonici*, vol. 2 (Mechliniae-Romae:

H. Dessain, 1934), 527. Letter of Apostolic Delegate, November 13, 1936, P.M. 173/358. In *mp PM*, 32, Paul VI granted to residential bishops and certain others the authority "to alienate, pledge, mortgage, rent or perpetually lease," and to "contract debts to the sum of money determined by the national or regional conference of bishops and approved by the Apostolic See."
[89]Doheny, *Practical Problems*, 43–44. See the Letter of the SCProp April 16, 1922 (*AAS* 14 [1922], 281, 307, and Appendix #49).
[90]Morrisey, "Conveyance," 126.
[91]*Rel*, 228.

If this statement is taken seriously, then, alienation cannot be seen simply as those matters traditionally considered as alienation in the strict sense. The term should have a broader meaning. Yet, the law itself does not spell out that meaning.

One might rely on commentators and on official interpretations for insight as had been done in the past, but that is far from ideal. It would be better if the conference of bishops in exercising its responsibility of defining extraordinary administration (c. 1277) and establishing the minimum and maximum limits in alienating goods (c. 1292, §1) would actually set down guidelines and definitions which would, in effect, create the flexible, workable notions which are badly needed.

The conference could establish what kinds of transactions, even within the realm of stable capital, are really only ordinary management activities. It could also clarify the limits to borrowing on an extended line-of-credit beyond which higher consultation is needed. The diocesan bishop or other proper superior, then, could apply these even further to a specific situation through particular legislation. Canon 1293, §2 permits the proper authority to set down further requirements for alienation besides those specified in the Code.

This suggestion implies a great deal of work; but, once it is done it could save a great deal of time and effort. (An excellent beginning may be found in a recent publication of the National Conference of Catholic Bishops entitled *Accounting Principles and Reporting Practices for Churches and Church-Related Organizations.*)[92] Should the conference itself fail to follow this suggestion, other authorities could accomplish much of the task through particular legislation.

Canon 1292 — §1. With due regard for the prescription of can. 638, §3, when the value of the goods whose alienation is proposed is within the range of the minimum and maximum amounts which are to be determined by the conference of bishops for its region, the competent authority is determined in the group's own statutes when it is a question of juridic persons who are not subject to the diocesan bishop; otherwise, the competent authority is the diocesan bishop with the consent of the finance council, the college of consultors and the parties concerned. The diocesan bishop also needs their consent to alienate the goods of the diocese.

§2. The permission of the Holy See is also required for valid alienation when it is a case of goods whose value exceeds the maximum amount, goods donated to the Church through a vow or goods

which are especially valuable due to their artistic or historical value.

§3. If the object to be alienated is divisible, the parts which have previously been alienated must be mentioned in seeking the permission for alienation; otherwise the permission is invalid.

§4. The persons who must take part in alienating goods through their advice or consent are not to give their advice or consent unless they have first been thoroughly informed concerning the economic situation of the juridic person whose goods are proposed for alienation and concerning previous alienations.

In determining the proper authorities and in setting the limits of alienation, the consultors intended to recognize the principle of subsidiarity.[93] Religious institutes are governed by their own duly approved constitutions and statutes and by canon 638, §3 in this matter. The Holy See, not the conference of bishops, will establish a maximum amount for juridic persons of religious institutes in each region beyond which its approval is required for alienation.[94]

The 1977 draft of the canons on alienation envisioned a more extensive role for the conference of bishops.[95] Again most consultors did not favor this potentially active role of the conference in influencing the government of individual dioceses. Hence the consultors deleted the provision for a special conference commission to monitor the activity of diocesan bishops in permitting alienation in certain instances.[96]

The conference of bishops for each region is to establish both minimum and maximum sums regarding alienation when the stable or permanent patrimony is involved. The minimum sum is determined both to recognize subsidiarity and forestall the proper authority from being consulted when inconsequential amounts are involved, while the maximum is established to trigger the additional recourse to the Apostolic See. No mention is made of confirmation or approval of these limits by the Apostolic See, but canon 455, §2 requires such approval in all instances of action of the conference. The action of the conference in this matter, therefore, will have juridical effect for diocesan juridic persons after review by the Apostolic See.

An additional concern of the consultors was for supra-diocesan public juridic persons,[97] e.g., a national university or a regional seminary. Paragraph one states that the statutes of such juridic persons

---

[92]USCC, 1983. (The glossary on pp. 22–25 could be usefully employed in clarifying matters of ordinary and extraordinary administration.) See also C. Ritty, "Changing Economy and the New Code of Canon Law," *J* 26 (1966), 469–484.

[93]*Comm* 5 (1973), 100.
[94]For the U.S., the maximum limit was set at $1,000,000 in 1981. See the letter of the SCC of July 3, 1983 (Prot. N. 165967/III).
[95]See c. 37 of the 1977 draft.
[96]*Comm* 12 (1980), 424.
[97]Ibid.

should make provision for alienation within the established limits.

Within these same limits, the diocesan bishop is designated as the competent authority for those juridic persons subject to himself. Of considerable importance, however, is the requirement of the consent of the diocesan finance council and of the parties concerned. The term "parties concerned" should be interpreted as "interested parties" was in canon 1532, §2 of the 1917 Code. Primarily it means the beneficiaries. The administrator would speak for any juridic persons which are beneficiaries. Several persons might need to be consulted if a collegial juridic person were the beneficiary. A patron or his or her family might be consulted, but this does not seem to be required always and necessarily.[98]

Paragraph two delineates certain circumstances or objects which require the additional approval of the Holy See for valid alienation. Objects which are in the Church's possession because of a vow (votive offerings, e.g., at a shrine) or which are of special historical or artistic value require this additional permission regardless of their monetary value.[99] For juridic persons subject to a diocesan bishop and for supra-diocesan juridic persons, the additional permission of the Apostolic See is required when the value of the transaction exceeds the amount established by the conference of bishops. Canon 1190, moreover, reaffirms the discipline which requires the approval of the Apostolic See if relics or images of notable importance for the faithful are to be alienated. These objects may never be sold. Administrators should recall that blessed or especially dedicated objects or places must not be converted to profane use (c. 1171).

Sometimes an object is divisible, i.e., part of it may be alienated. With money this is easily understood. But, in addition, one must understand that additional mortgages or liens, easements, leases, or the like could be added to property already encumbered. Part of a valuable set of vestments or set of sacred vessels may already have been sold or donated. In this event, the prior action must be brought to the attention of the proper authority for the alienation to be valid (§3).

Counsel or consent (the requirements of which are clarified in c. 127) must be informed. The basic obligations of those exercising this responsibility are stated in paragraph four. Lack of this information for the consent or counsel is not, however, declared invalidating for the alienation in question.

Canon 1293 — §1. To alienate goods whose value exceeds the minimum amount which has been determined, also required are:

1° *a just cause such as urgent necessity, evident*

usefulness, piety, charity or some other serious pastoral reason;

2° *a written estimate from experts concerning the value of the object to be alienated.*

§2. *Other safeguards prescribed by legitimate authority are also to be observed to prevent harm to the Church.*

A serious reason is required to undertake an alienation which could have serious long-term consequences for the Church. The prescriptions of the former Code are largely reaffirmed in this regard. A just cause for alienation must be present and canon 1293, §1, 1° includes a non-exhaustive list of possible reasons. The phrase "some other serious pastoral reason" permits the legitimate authority to enjoy various options as long as the alienation is of significant pastoral importance. Reasons external to the Church may also dictate certain decisions. A situation of economic crisis or collapse in a country or an especially advantageous offer to purchase an asset may indicate a course of action of "evident usefulness" for the Church.

Once again the interests of objectivity and professionalism call for expert consultation. The number of experts is not specified, but their opinion should be in writing so that everyone involved may be both accountable for the action and protected from charges of irresponsibility. Prior commentators interpreted the plural "experts" as requiring at least two experts.[100] It is often advisable for the estimates to be stated as a range of values, indicating a minimum acceptable and the most hopeful value for an object. These stipulations are not required for validity.

The general law cannot foresee all particular circumstances. Particular statutes may, therefore, regulate alienation further; consequently, such requirements of the legitimate authority are not to be ignored.

Canon 1294 — §1. Ordinarily an object must not be alienated for a price which is less than that indicated in the estimate.

§2. *The money realized from the alienation is either to be invested carefully for the advantage of the Church or wisely expended in accord with the purposes of the alienation.*

As a matter of policy, the appraised price of an object should be sought, but the former Code's requirement (*CIC* 1531, §1) is moderated by inserting the qualification "ordinarily" to allow room to adjust to special conditions. Moreover, the requirement of public auction or, at least, public advertising and the acceptance of the highest bid (*CIC* 1531, §2) is not included, again so as to allow the competent authority maximum discretion.[101]

[98]Cappello, 585. See also Conte a Coronata, 489.
[99]See SCC, instr *Opera Artis, AAS,* April 11, 1971, 315–317.

[100]Conte a Coronata, 484.
[101]See Cappello, 487. *Comm* 5 (1973), 100.

The money derived from any alienation is to be used for the benefit of the Church. It is not automatically, however, to be considered as remaining part of the stable patrimony of the juridic person. It may be added to invested funds, either as working capital or as fixed capital. The administrator should make the decision clear. The consultors recognized that an alienation may have been made with a specific pastoral objective or activity in mind, for which purpose the proceeds of a transaction should certainly be used.[102]

Canon 1295 — **The requirements mentioned in cann. 1291-1294, with which the statutes of juridic persons are to be in conformity, must be observed not only in an alienation but also in any transaction through which the patrimonial condition of a juridic person can be worsened.**

Canon 1296 — **Whenever ecclesiastical goods have been alienated without the required canonical formalities but the alienation is civilly valid, it is the responsibility of the competent authority, after a thorough consideration of the situation, to decide whether and what type of action, that is, a personal or real action, is to be initiated to vindicate the rights of the Church as well as by whom and against whom such an action is to be initiated.**

The latter part of canon 1295 was discussed in the commentary on canon 1291. According to the earlier part of this canon the statutes of juridic persons are to conform to all the provisions of canons 1291–1294. This is to ensure orderly administration. It is also important that canonical regulations be clearly set down for those instances when they become important in matters involving the civil law.[103] Statutes and bylaws of civil entities corresponding to public juridic persons should incorporate the canonical norms, especially those regarding alienation and extraordinary administration.

Provision must nonetheless be made for a situation in which an act of alienation or a comparable legal transaction which is canonically invalid or at least irregular is recognized as valid by the civil law in a territory. The 1983 Code provides more generally than did canon 1534 of the former Code. The competent authority whose permission is required for the alienation will determine the nature of the redress to be sought. He or she will decide if there will be an attempted repossession of an object sold or if damages will be sought from the responsible party. The forum, civil or canonical, will be set. If the conflict is between canonical persons, an ecclesiastical procedure may be appropriate. The juridic person to act will be designated. The action in question may, in some instances, simply be allowed to stand.

Canon 1377 establishes that one who alienates ecclesiastical goods without proper permission will be justly punished. No special reference to this penalty is affixed to canon 1296.

Canon 1297 — **After considering local circumstances, it is the responsibility of the conference of bishops to establish norms concerning the leasing of church goods, especially the permission to be obtained from competent ecclesiastical authority.**

Renting or leasing property is generally regulated in some detail by civil law. While the 1917 Code made some detailed provisions for rental of church property (*CIC* 1541–1542), the revised Code recognizes the practical impossibility of general church legislation covering the various situations all over the world. Each conference of bishops, therefore, will establish statutes for its territory regarding the rental or leasing of properties. Such statutes may designate the proper authority for permission, the conditions for entering a contract for lease, as well as the other appropriate canonical formalities. The legal form in this instance is the same as the civil legal form required by canon 1290.[104]

Canon 1298 — **Unless it is an object of little importance, ecclesiastical goods are not to be sold or leased out to their own administrators or to their relatives up to the fourth degree of consanguinity or affinity without the special written permission of the competent authority.**

Self-aggrandizement or favoritism toward family can present a temptation to an administrator. This requirement of the written permission of the competent authority assures objectivity and accountability. Matters of small importance do not require permission, but good policy suggests that such actions would rarely be undertaken.

Practical Considerations

The practical application of the canons on alienation can become exceedingly complex. A dynamic economic system is regularly changing, and the principles established in church law have to be carefully brought to bear on the transaction in question. Some of the more common transactions are discussed in this section with the understanding that the details of individual actions may result in conclusions differing from these.

Alienation Involving Several Public Juridic Persons

The 1983 Code considers the interests of the public juridic person as the overriding consideration

---

[102]*Comm* 5 (1973), 100.
[103]*Comm* 12 (1980), 426.

[104]See Ibid., 427.

when alienation is contemplated. The former Code spoke of the good of the Church as the paramount interest. The regulations governing alienation also apply to transactions between public juridic persons.[105] The diocesan bishop, for example, may not simply transfer the stable assets of a parish to the diocese or to another parish without observing the canonical requirements. The same is true for major religious superiors in regard to their houses or other subordinate juridic persons.

Civil Incorporation

Transferring the assets of a juridic person held by one civil corporation to another civil corporation effectively owned and controlled by the same juridic person is not an act of alienation. If the receiving corporation, however, is not effectively owned and controlled by the same juridic person, alienation is involved and the canonical formalities should be observed.

When colleges or universities or hospitals, for example, are transferred to secularized civil corporations in which the religious community or other juridic person no longer has effective ownership and control, alienation in a real sense occurs and the above-mentioned formalities of law are required.[106] The Code, however, does not indicate a preferred style of civil organization. Groups and communities may well wish—for various reasons—to operate through civil structures not identified with the religious group. It is then important that proper procedures be followed when they are called for.

Exchange

If property, including stocks and bonds, is exchanged for property of approximately equal value, no alienation occurs. Transfer of title in exchange for something in a different category, however, is alienation. Some hold that if property were to be sold with the proceeds to be designated as part of the stable patrimony, alienation would not occur.[107] The Code, however, seems to consider any sale of real estate as alienation and subject to the regulations.

Assuming a Mortgage

Public juridic persons may accept gifts, donations, or property encumbered by a mortgage or other obligation without observing the formalities of alienation, for the condition of the juridic person is actually being improved and not endangered.

Bonds and Collateral for Loans

Financing for construction or remodeling of facilities by a juridic person may involve the issuance of bonds or the placing of some property as collateral. In new construction, if the building or buildings to be built are the only security standing behind the bonds or loan, then alienation has not occurred. On the other hand, if other properties might be endangered by the bonds or loan, then alienation is clearly involved and the legal formalities must be observed.

Stocks, Bonds, Loans, Certificates of Deposit

Stocks, bonds, certificates of deposit, or money involved in prudent loans may belong to a juridic person as part of its stable patrimony if they belong to certain special funds or endowments. Such matters should be regulated by statutes issued by the competent ecclesiastical authority. Changing investments from one safe form into another for an adequate reason is not usually alienation. Should stocks, bonds, or other investments be sold at a significant loss below the purchase price, however, the condition of the juridic person may be worsened and the ordinary regulations apply in view of canon 1295.

When investing the funds of a juridic person, it is important that its investment goals and philosophy relative to those particular funds be communicated clearly to the person who manages the funds.

TITLE IV
PIOUS WILLS IN GENERAL AND PIOUS FOUNDATIONS
[cc. 1299–1310]

As people contemplate their own death and make provision for the disposition of their goods, or consider gifts from their assets during their lifetime, many are willing and able to assist the mission of the Church. Such bequests and gifts are an important means for the Church to acquire resources for its mission. It is important for the faithful to know that their wishes will be respected. It is also important to arrange for the orderly administration of any endowments which are established to aid the Church's mission on an ongoing basis. Title IV of Book V addresses these concerns.

Pious Wills

Canon 1299 — §1. Those who in virtue of natural and canon law are free to dispose of their own

---

[105]Doheny, *Practical Problems*, p. 39. Vermeersch-Creusen 2, 527.

[106]See Maida, *Ownership* and McGrath, *Catholic Institutions*. Maida and McGrath differ with one another on this complex matter. Maida tends to favor canonical provisions and to opt for tight ecclesiastical control. McGrath tends to favor civil law provisions and to accept the de facto loss of ecclesiastical control.

[107]Morrisey, "Conveyance," 130.

goods can leave goods for pious causes through an act which becomes effective during life or at death.

§2. If it is possible, the formalities of civil law are to be observed in the dispositions made for the good of the Church on the occasion of death; if such formalities have been neglected, the heirs must be advised of the obligation by which they are bound to fulfill the will of the testator.

Among the primary ways of transferring one's property to the Church is the last will and testament. Major gifts are also possible, however, during one's lifetime. Paragraph one specifies that the right of the faithful to give to the Church includes the right to do so by bequest. Elsewhere, the Church has taught the person's right to dispose of his or her goods by bequest.[108] This canon is directed against civil law limitations on bequests or donations to the Church or other charities. Some governments, for example, require special formalities for real estate to be transferred when a person is near death or hold as invalid a will or other gifts made within a specified time of death.

A person freely controls his or her goods by natural law if he or she is not an infant, insane, or lacking the use of reason for some other reason. Canon law itself sets limits on some persons in religious institutes from freely disposing of their goods.

The term "pious causes," retained because it is traditional, refers to any good works done for motives flowing from faith in and commitment to Jesus Christ. Paragraph two now reads, "for the good of the Church," as did the 1917 Code (CIC 1513, §2), but it should be interpreted broadly as applying to all good works or causes.[109]

Prior commentators discussed the precise meaning of "actum mortis causa," some of them equating this with "donatio mortis causa," which is used in some civil codes. It refers to a gift made now to the Church, but which becomes effective only at death. A more accurate reading, however, understands that this means any testamentary disposition.[110] This is confirmed by its repetition in both paragraphs of this canon. The 1917 Code made confusion possible by using "ultimis voluntatibus" (CIC 1513, §2), thereby raising the question of whether or not "actum inter mortuos" (CIC 1513, §1) included wills.

The formalities of civil law are to be observed insofar as possible for last wills and testaments. Among other things, these can include the requirements for signatures and witnesses, the regulations on handwritten wills, special regulations about the dispositions of certain kinds of property, and the

dispositions regarding former wills superseded by a new one.[111]

Unlike the forms for contracts, however, the Code does not simply baptize the provisons of civil law. While gifts given during one's lifetime and based on a contractual relationship must be in civilly valid form to have canonical validity (c. 1290), the Church insists that a person may freely bequeath his or her goods to the Church in any humanly valid form. Civil law restrictions may make it impossible to take action in the civil courts to assure that the intention of the testator is fulfilled, but the heirs are to be informed of the true will of the testator and urged to meet their obligation to respect this intention. The ordinary, in virtue of being executor of all pious wills (c. 1301, §1), has the primary responsibility of advising the heirs, but anyone may inform them. The principal consideration must be that the actual and demonstrable intention of the testator to benefit the Church be carried out by anyone with the authority and responsibility for seeing that this is done.

The nature of the obligation of the heirs has been discussed in the past. Some commentators insisted that the obligation of canon 1513 of the 1917 Code bound one in justice.[112] The Pontifical Commission for Authentic Interpretation of the Code of Canon Law seemed to side with the more rigorous position that the obligation was one of conscience, which could be urged even in the internal forum.[113] The 1977 draft of this canon included the phrase "ex iustitia" (c. 45, §2), but the 1983 Code omits it because the consultors felt that it was "too rigid."[114] The consultation committee, therefore, did not take a formal position on the matter, but chose a less rigid stance.

This stance should not be surprising since in such matters the concrete circumstances can vary so widely that ascertaining the true intention of a donor could be quite difficult, if not impossible. A person might have been considering, even discussing, a bequest to the Church. But if a decision were not reached and set in a form binding in civil law, one might easily argue that such a decision was not, in fact, effectively made. In some rare instances, however, the dichotomy between the actual intention of a testator and the civil disposition might exist. At this point, the prescriptions of canon 1299, §2 would be pertinent.

Canon 1300 — **The legitimately accepted wills of the faithful who give or leave their resources to pious causes, whether through an act which becomes effective during life or at death, are to be fulfilled**

[108]Pius XI, *Quadragesimo Anno* 49.

[109]See J. Hannan, *The Canon Law of Wills, CanLawStud* 86 (Washington, D.C.: Catholic University of America, 1934), 282–289.

[110]See Hannan, 47–50.

[111]Ibid., 232–301.

[112]Cappello, 568–569; Conte a Coronata, 467–469.

[113]Pontifical Commission for Authentically Interpreting the Canons of the Code, February 17, 1930, *AAS* 22 (1930), 196.

[114]*Comm* 12 (1980), 429.

with the greatest diligence even as regards the manner of the administration and distribution of the goods, with due regard for the prescription of can. 1301, §3.

The Church, having insisted upon the importance of the intention and will of the donor or testator, must show due regard itself for this intention. Conditions or other qualifications included with a gift or a bequest must be observed. Included could be provisions about time, place, persons, or various other circumstances. The obligation to observe such provisions is not only a moral but also a canonical one as a result of this canon.

Canon 1514 of the 1917 Code is modified by the new phrase once they are "legitimately accepted." Canons 1267, §2 and 1304, §1 require the permission of the ordinary for one to accept certain gifts and bequests. The Church is thus protected from being burdened by bizarre or impossible conditions which might be connected with certain gifts or bequests. It is not left at the mercy of anyone who would wish to control policy or ministry by using gifts or bequests.

Duties of the Ordinary

Canon 1301 — §1. The ordinary is the executor of all pious wills whether they be made during life or on the occasion of death.

§2. In virtue of this right the ordinary can and must exercise vigilance, even through visitation, so that pious wills are fulfilled; other executors must render him an account concerning the performance of their duty.

§3. Stipulations added to last wills and contrary to this right of the ordinary are to be considered non-existent.

The persons responsible for seeing to the proper and complete administration of gifts and bequests must be specified by law. All ordinaries mentioned in canon 134, §1 have this responsibility. Included are the diocesan bishop or whoever takes his place and major superiors of clerical religious institutes and of clerical apostolic societies of pontifical right.

Some consultors wished to make this obligation less burdensome for ordinaries since the term executor seemed to imply personally fulfilling this mandate. The majority felt, however, that the canon merely stated a general principle from which flowed the ordinary's power of overseeing the fulfillment of gifts and bequests. When the responsibility is not clear in the gift or bequest, he must execute it himself. Generally, he need only supervise the implementation of the responsibility.[115] The ordinary's obligation encompasses the right of on-

site inspection. Moreover, other executors must render an account to him.[116]

Clearly the ordinary need not be the civil executor of each civil will in which the Church is named.[117] The term as employed here refers to his canonical responsibility of ensuring the proper execution of the intention of the donor or testator together with any attendant conditions.

The ordinary has this role independently of the will of the testator; it is from the law itself. Once again, the Church claims the primacy of canon law over civil law by holding as null and void any provisions attached to bequests which contradict this right and duty of the ordinary to supervise their proper execution. A provision that the ordinary not even be informed of a bequest, for example, should be ignored as not existing according to this canon.

Canon 1302 — §1. A person who accepts the role of trustee for goods bequeathed for pious causes either through an act made during life or through a last will and testament must inform the ordinary of this trust and also indicate all such goods, whether immovable or movable, along with the obligations attached to them; if, however, the donor expressly and completely prohibits this, the person is not to accept the trust.

§2. The ordinary must demand that the goods held in trust be safeguarded and must exercise vigilance on behalf of the execution of the pious will in accord with the norm of can. 1301.

§3. When goods committed in trust to some member of a religious institute or a society of apostolic life have been designated for the assistance of a place or diocese or their inhabitants or pious causes, the ordinary mentioned in §§1 and 2 is the local ordinary; otherwise, it is the major superior in a clerical institute of pontifical right and in a clerical society of apostolic life of pontifical right or the proper ordinary of a member in other religious institutes.

Canon 1516 of the 1917 Code spoke only of clerics and religious to whom goods were committed for pious causes. Anyone, lay persons included, who accepts goods intended for pious causes is governed by paragraph one of this canon. All goods are covered, whether real estate, precious objects, securities, or other funds. The ordinary should receive an inventory and an accounting of their dispersal. If the dispersal occurs over time, regular accounting is appropriate. Special conditions or obligations should be noted. If the donor attempts to frustrate this obligation of the ordinary, the commission should not be accepted.

---

[115]Ibid.

[116]The term "delegated" qualifying other executors and contained in the 1917 Code (*CIC* 1515, §2) is omitted here.
[117]See Hannan, 467.

Paragraph two expands slightly on canon 1301 by directing the ordinary to ensure that goods destined for pious causes be safely kept.

When members of institutes of consecrated life are engaged in the apostolate in a diocese, they may receive gifts or bequests for a specific work. If it is for a particular school, hospital, nursing home, or a good work in a particular area, the ordinary to be notified is the local ordinary. If the donation is for the institute itself or for its general works, the ordinary in question is the proper ordinary of the member of the institute. Such would be the case if the gift were for the educational efforts of the institute or for its migrant worker ministry. The issue of the ordinary for lay institutes of pontifical right is again present (see commentary on c. 1279).

The donor's intention may not always be clear; a donation entrusted to a member of an institute of consecrated life may be for "Catholic education" or "to aid the poor." As far as possible the intention should be ascertained and followed. Otherwise, it is presumed that the donor left the matter to the wisdom and good judgment of the religious.

Pious Foundations

Canon 1303 — §1. In the law under the title of pious foundations are included:

1° *autonomous pious foundations*, that is, aggregates of things destined for all the purposes mentioned in can. 114, §2 and erected as a juridic person by competent ecclesiastical authority;

2° *non-autonomous pious foundations*, that is, temporal goods given in some manner to a public juridic person with the obligation for a long time, to be determined by particular law, to arrange from the annual income for the celebration of Masses or other specified ecclesiastical functions or otherwise to pursue the purposes mentioned in can. 114, §2.

§2. If the goods of a non-autonomous pious foundation are entrusted to a juridic person subject to a diocesan bishop, they are to be remanded to the institute mentioned in can. 1274, §1 when the specified period of time is completed unless another intention of the founder was expressly manifest; otherwise they belong to the juridic person itself.

Canon 114, §2 states that a juridic person may be established for works of piety, of the apostolate, or of charity—either of a spiritual or temporal nature. The proper ecclesiastical authority may establish a juridic person, or church corporation, as a trust in service of these purposes. Donations or bequests can be received on behalf of these autonomous trusts or pious foundations by their administrators if other provisions of the law are observed.

Often, however, no distinct juridic person will be involved in a trust. Goods are committed, rather, to an already existing public juridic person, the income to be used for specified purposes including the celebration of Masses. Such gifts or bequests are *non-autonomous pious foundations*. A gift or bequest given with the intention of the entire principal being used rather quickly is not a foundation as such.

Canon 1303 does not speak of public juridic persons being burdened by these non-autonomous foundations *in perpetuum*. The consultors felt that modern economic conditions do not warrant such an arrangement.[118] The canon speaks of "a long time." Prior commentators settled for periods of from ten to fifty years as constituting this period.[119] Particular law, either diocesan or regional, should establish regulations, including the length of time. It must be noted, however, that a will probated in the civil courts may contain provisions conflicting with this new policy. Particular law should take this into account and give direction.

When the specified period of time has passed, the principal will go to the common fund established to promote the diocesan apostolate if the public juridic person to which it pertained is the diocese itself or one of its subordinate juridic persons (see c. 1274, §1). The intention of the donor or testator will prevail over this presumption if it is expressly stated. Religious institutes do not benefit directly from the diocesan fund. Funds entrusted to public juridic persons subject to religious institutes for their own purposes, therefore, will be disposed of according to their constitutions or their particular law.

Prior to this revised Code, there was a presumption that the donor or testator always intended to give the goods of a pious foundation to the canonical person to which the foundation pertained. Some consultors objected to paragraph two on these grounds. The consultors reached the conclusion, however, that such would no longer be the presumption when this revised law is in effect.[120] It is imperative, therefore, that those making gifts or bequests to pious foundations and wishing the principal to remain with the public juridic person clearly specify this intention.

Canon 1304 — §1. In order for a foundation to be validly accepted by a juridic person the written permission of the ordinary is required; and he is not to grant that permission until he legitimately determines that the juridic person can fulfill the new obligation as well as those already accepted; he should most specially take care that the income entirely corresponds to the attached obligations in accord with the customs of the place or region.

§2. Further conditions for constituting and accepting foundations are to be defined in particular law.

[118]*Comm* 5 (1973), 102; 12 (1980), 432.
[119]See Hannan, 453–454.
[120]*Comm* 12 (1980), 431–432.

The ordinary's permission must be in writing for the juridic person to accept a foundation validly. Otherwise, canonically, the juridic person cannot be held to the obligations. Once the donation or bequest is accepted civilly, however, one must always be cognizant of civil ramifications.

The ordinary in question is as specified in canon 1302, §3. This ordinary is required to determine if the obligation can be assumed by the juridic person in light of already existing commitments and obligations. Moreover, he is to ensure that the resources involved in the foundation are commensurate with the obligations to be assumed. He is to judge whether or not accepting the foundation is in the best interests of the juridic person and of its ecclesial mission. To make such a judgment he has a right to all requisite information. Circumstances may color the picture. An income sufficient for the task in a rural area, for example, may not be so in an urban area.

Paragraph two is a new provision which seeks to preserve the principle of subsidiarity. Particular law may be diocesan or that which is particular to a religious institute. If the proper conditions were fulfilled, it might be regional. The present canon is broader in this regard than canon 1545 of the former Code which spoke only of the local ordinary. The legislation can be comprehensive, establishing the terms under which pious foundations may be accepted. It clearly encompasses more than the 1917 Code's provision that mentioned only setting an amount below which a foundation could not be established.[121]

Details of Administering Foundations

Canon 1305 — **Money and movable goods assigned to an endowment are immediately to be deposited in a safe place to be approved by the ordinary so that the money or the value of the movable goods will be safeguarded; as soon as possible, these goods are to be invested cautiously and profitably for the benefit of the foundation with express and specific mention made of the burdens attached to the endowment; this investment is to be made in accord with the prudent judgment of the ordinary who is to consult the interested parties as well as his finance council on this matter.**

Canon 1306 — **§1. Foundations, even if made orally, are to be put into writing.**

§2. A copy of the terms of the foundation is to be securely filed in the curial archive and another copy is to be securely filed in the archive of the juridic person to whom the foundation pertains.

Canon 1307 — **§1. With due regard for the prescriptions of cann. 1300-1302 and can. 1287, a list**

of obligations arising from pious foundations is to be drawn up and retained in an obvious place lest the obligations to be fulfilled be neglected.

§2. Besides the book referred to in can. 958, §1, another book is to be kept by the pastor or rector in which the individual obligations, their fulfillment and the offerings are noted.

Administrative procedures are necessary to ensure that obligations accepted are properly recorded and consistently fulfilled. The initial depository need not be designated by the ordinary, but merely approved by him. He must approve any investments in consultation with his finance council and any interested parties. The interested parties will primarily be the juridic persons involved (see the commentary on c. 1292).

Since the administrative personnel involved change but the obligation continues, it is necessary that written records be kept. The terms of the foundation should be recorded. Any civilly binding agreements and the documents which are the source of them should be carefully noted.

Canon 1307 refers to the rectors of churches or institutes. It calls for a general book listing all obligations and a special book for each foundation listing all pertinent information. This latter book should include both anything required to demonstrate that the obligation of a specific foundation was fulfilled as well as details about the distribution of the offering involved. It is distinct from the regular book for Mass intentions and Mass stipends.

These canons do not provide for an annual accounting to the ordinary. This may or may not be important in individual instances. The particular law governing foundations should provide for such details.

Canon 1308 — **§1. The reduction of Mass obligations, to be done only for a just and necessary reason, is reserved to the Apostolic See with due regard for the following prescriptions.**

§2. If it is expressly provided for in the articles of the foundation, the ordinary is empowered to reduce Mass obligations because of diminished income.

§3. The diocesan bishop has the power, when income diminishes, of reducing Masses from independent legacies or foundations of any kind to conform to the level of the offering legitimately established in the diocese for as long as the reason for this reduction continues, provided that there is no one who is bound by the obligation of increasing the offering and can be successfully induced to do so.

§4. The same authority has the power of reducing the obligations or legacies for Masses which bind ecclesiastical institutes if the income proves insufficient to pursue successfully the proper goal of the ecclesiastical institute.

§5. These same powers mentioned in §§3 and 4

---

[121]*Comm* 5 (1973), 102.

are also enjoyed by the supreme moderator of clerical institutes of pontifical right.

Canon 1309 — **The same authorities mentioned in can. 1308 also enjoy the power of transferring for a suitable reason Mass obligations to days, churches or altars different from those determined in the foundation.**

The law takes special precautions regarding Mass stipends, the offerings attached to celebrating a Mass for particular intentions (e.g., see c. 199, 5°). Often, foundations are established to ensure that Mass is offered regularly for a particular intention and for an indefinite period of time. When this is the case, the income from the foundation may diminish or in some other way become inappropriate for the obligation attached to it.

The Apostolic See is empowered to make the necessary adjustments of the canonical obligations involved. The extension of faculties contained in the *motu proprio Pastorale Munus,* numbers 11 and 12, is affirmed in the revised Code. Any reduction of Mass obligations, even that done by the Apostolic See, is to be done for a necessary and just reason; mere inconvenience will not suffice. One may not simply presume that the faculty extends to the obligations arising from a trust established in civil law. In many cases, the intervention of a civil court will be required to resolve civil obligations properly.

A reduction in this instance signifies decreasing the number of Masses to be offered for the stated intentions. The person who establishes the foundation may expressly permit the ordinary to reduce the number of Masses if its income decreases. This must be done equitably and only if necessary.

Even when the foundation articles do not provide for the contingency, a diocesan bishop and the supreme moderator of clerical institutes of consecrated life of pontifical right have the faculty from the law itself of reducing Masses provided for in a foundation established by a will when the income decreases. The faculty is restricted to the instance of diminished income; it is not a general faculty. The reduction may continue as long as the income is diminished, but it would cease if the income resumes at the anticipated level. The reduction, however, is not to result in a Mass stipend greater than that already established in the diocese in question (see c. 952). The faculty of the diocesan bishop, in this instance, extends to foundation-supported Masses of religious communities.

A relative or the civil executor may be charged with seeing to the offering of the Masses. When such is the case, this person should be encouraged to supplement the income of the foundation so that the founder's intentions may be exactly fulfilled.

Perhaps a school, hospital, diocese, parish, or other church institute is obliged to ensure that Masses are offered for certain intentions on an ongoing basis. If the foundation income is not sufficient both to support the ministry of the juridic person and to provide for the Mass offerings, the diocesan bishop and the major superior mentioned above may also reduce the number of Masses to which the institute is obliged.

Canon 1309 also provides that further specifications attached to the Mass obligations regarding the celebrant and the time or place may be changed by the Holy See or the ordinary for suitable reasons. These reasons need not be as weighty as those required in the previous canon.

Canon 1310 — **§1. The ordinary, only for a just and necessary reason, may reduce, moderate or commute the wills of the faithful for pious causes provided such power has been expressly granted him by the founder.**
§2. If, through no fault of the administrator, the fulfillment of the obligations becomes impossible due to diminished income or some other reason, the ordinary can diminish them equitably after consulting the interested parties and his finance council, with due regard for the will of the founder as much as possible; this is not true for Mass obligations, whose reduction is governed by the prescriptions of can. 1308.
§3. In other cases recourse is to be made to the Apostolic See.

Not all foundations need be directed to the offering of Masses. A foundation may provide that a certain number of students be educated, that a specified number of hospital beds be maintained, or that the poor be served in a particular building or in a specified manner. Other works of charity or religion may be required.

For a just and necessary reason the ordinary may reduce or moderate the obligation or commute it to another related one. Increased costs, diminished income, or other substantial changes of circumstance may justify this action. Again, the Code speaks of the canonical obligation. Special civil actions may be required if a civil trust or endowment is involved.

The change of circumstances must have occurred through no fault of the administrator. In addition to the finance council, the ordinary should consult interested parties such as officials of the institute and likely beneficiaries before taking action. He might also consult the family of the founder.

All other cases are reserved to the Apostolic See. Practically speaking, most cases could apparently be handled at a lower level. The effect of paragraph three is to ensure that very special cases are referred to the proper Roman Congregation.

Pontificia Commissio Codicis Iuris Canonici. *Schema Canonum Libri V de iure Patrimoniali Ecclesiae.* Romae: Typis Polyglottis Vaticanis, 1977 (cited as 1977 draft).

Sacred Congregation for Bishops. *Directory on the Pastoral Ministry of Bishops.* Ottawa: Publications Service of the Canadian Catholic Conference, 1974 (cited as *Directory*).

Reference Works

Abbo, J., and Hannan, J. *The Sacred Canons.* 2nd ed. St. Louis: B. Herder Book Co., 1960 (cited as Abbo-Hannan).

Bouscaren, T.L.; Ellis, A.; and Korth, F. *Canon Law.* 4th ed. Milwaukee: The Bruce Publishing Co., 1963.

Bouscaren, T.L., and O'Connor, J.I., eds. *Canon Law Digest.* 6 vols. Milwaukee: The Bruce Publishing Co., 1919–1969. Vol. 7 and supplement edited by J.I. O'Connor. Chicago, 1975.

Cappello, F.M. *Summa Iuris Canonici.* Vol. II. Romae: Apud Aedes Pontificae Universitatis Gregorianae, 1951 (cited as Cappello).

Conte a Coronata, M. *Institutiones Iuris Canonici.* 3rd ed. Vol. II. Romae: Marietti, 1948 (cited as Conte a Coronata).

De Lucca, L. *La Transazione nel diritto canonico.* Romae: Edizioni Universitarie, 1942.

Vermeersch, A., and Creusen, J. *Epitome Iuris Canonici.* 3 vols. Mechliniae-Romae: H. Dessain; vol. I, 8 ed., 1963; vol. II, 5ª ed., 1934; vol. III, 5ª ed., 1936 (cited as Vermeersch-Creusen and volume).

Vorgrimler, H., ed. *Commentary on the Documents of Vatican II.* Translated by L. Adolphus et al. 6 vols. New York: Herder and Herder, 1967–1969.

Wernz, F., and Vidal, P. *Ius Canonicum.* 7 vols. Romae: Universitatis Gregorianae Tomus. IV, Vol. II, 1935 (cited as Wernz-Vidal and volume).

Woywod, S. *A Practical Commentary on the Code of Canon Law.* Rev. ed. New York: J. Wagner, Inc., 1963.

Articles/Studies

Bellini, P. "Potestas Ecclesiae circa temporalia: concezione tradizionale e nuove prospettive" *EIC* (1968): 68–154.

Broussard, G.L. "Ecclesiastical Taxation: An Historical Synopsis." J.C.L. dissertation, Catholic University of America, 1966.

Cleary, J.F. *Canonical Limitations on the Alienation of Church Property: An Historical Synopsis and Commentary.* CanLawStud 100. Washington, D.C.: Catholic University of America, 1936.

Comyns, J.J. *Papal and Episcopal Administration of Church Property: An Historical Synopsis and Commentary.* CanLawStud 142. Washington, D.C.: Catholic University of America, 1942.

Coriden, J., and McManus, F. "The Present State of Roman Catholic Canon Law Regarding Colleges and Sponsoring Religious Bodies," in Moots, P.R., and Gaffney, E.M., Jr., *Church and Campus,* 141–153. Notre Dame, Indiana: University of Notre Dame Press, 1979.

Doheny, W.J. *Church Property: Modes of Acquisition.* CanLawStud 41. Washington, D.C.: Catholic University of America, 1927.

————. *Practical Problems in Church Finance.* Milwaukee: The Bruce Publishing Co., 1943 (cited as *Practical Problems*).

Donovan, T.F. "The Development of the Institute of the Cathedraticum: An Historical Synopsis." J.C.L. dissertation, Catholic University of America, 1964.

Faltin, D. "De recto uso bonorum ecclesiasticorum ad mentem Concilii Vaticani II." *Apol* (1967): 409–441.

Gass, S.F. *Ecclesiastical Pensions,* CanLawStud 157. Washington, D.C.: Catholic University of America, 1942.

Golden, H. *Parochial Benefices in the New Code.* CanLawStud 10. Washington, D.C.: Catholic University of America, 1925.

Goodwine, J.A. *The Right of the Church to Acquire Temporal Goods.* CanLawStud 131. Washington, D.C.: Catholic University of America, 1941 (cited as Goodwine).

Hannan, J.D. *The Canon Law of Wills.* CanLawStud 86. Washington, D.C.: Catholic University of America, 1934 (cited as Hannan).

Hogue, A.R. *Origins of the Common Law.* Bloomington, Indiana: Indiana University Press, 1966.

Maida, A.J. *Ownership, Control and Sponsorship of Catholic Institutions: A Practical Guide.* Harrisburg, Pa.: Pennsylvania Catholic Conference, 1975 (cited as *Ownership*).

————, ed. *Issues in the Labor-Management Dialogue: Church Perspectives.* St. Louis: The Catholic Health Association of the United States, 1982.

Morrisey, F.G., O.M.I. "Conveyance of Ecclesiastical Goods." *CLSAP* (1976): 123–137 (cited as "Conveyance").

Ochoa, X. "Ratio BONORUM TEMPORALIUM IN Ecclesia et Institutis Perfectionis post Concilium Vaticanum Secundum." *ComRelMiss* (1969): 339–348.

————. "Aquisitio, distributio et destinatio bonorum temporalium Ecclesiae institutorumque perfectionis ad mentem Concilii Vaticani II." *ComRelMiss* (1970): 20–33.

Pettinato, S. "La personalita giuridica del fondo per il culto e la questione della proprieta ecclesiastica." *Il Diritto Ecclesiastico* (1976): 173–215.

Pototschnig, F. "Christliche Eigentumsordnung in rechtshistorischer Sicht." *OAKR* (1976): 276–309.

Ritty, C. "Changing Economy and the New Code of Canon Law." *J* 26 (1966): 469–484.

Romita, F.; Colagiovanni, E.; Baccari, R.; Carrion-Pinero, M.J. "Dal beneficio feudale all' officio ecclesiasico ed ecclesiale." *ME* 96 (1971): 367–463.

Rovera, V. "De structuris oeconomicis in Ecclesia renovandis." *P* 60 (1971): 197–250.

Schmitz, H. "Das kirchliche Vermogensrecht als Aufgabe der Gesamtkirche und der Teilkirchen." *AkK* (1977): 3–35.

Schulz, F. *Classical Roman Law.* Oxford: Clarendon Press, 1961.

Stenger, J.B. *The Mortgaging of Church Property.* *CanLawStud* 169. Washington, D.C.: Catholic University of America, 1942.

Thomas, R.R. "Taxation of Church Property." J.C.L. dissertation, Catholic University of America, 1977.

Wolfe, W.P. "The Mind of Gratian Regarding the Ownership and Administration of Church Property." J.C.L. dissertation, Catholic University of America, 1978 (cited as "Gratian").

BOOK VI
SANCTIONS IN THE CHURCH
[cc. 1311–1399]

This Book can hardly be understood without some general reflections on ecclesiastical penal law and on Book V of the 1917 Code of Canon Law which it revises. Accordingly the following introductory observations treat of the phenomena of offenses against the Church's faith or order and of the community's reaction against them in the form of penalties. They are followed by brief comments on the structure of Book V of the 1917 Code.

While the Church is indeed a graced community empowered by the Spirit, its members are sinners reflecting the weaknesses and limitations of the human condition.[1] Occasionally their attitudes are contrary to the faith or their behavior is contrary to the Christian way of life. This provokes a disturbance within the faith community and brings them into conflict especially with those in authority who have a special responsibility to protect the integrity of the community's faith, communion, and service.

Regrettable as this is, it is also understandable. It likewise makes it imperative that there be some kind of framework to restore peace and order and to reintegrate the offending party within the life of the community. This challenge to resolve conflicts arising from breaches of public order is common to Church and State; hence there are certain similarities between ecclesiastical and civil penal law. However, the Church's salvific finality gives to its penal order a distinct character that should not be lost sight of. Historically, various tensions have arisen in the Church because of a failure to recognize the uniqueness of its penal discipline at all times.

Offenses against the Community

The Church's penal order does not relate primarily to an individual's relationship with the Lord in conscience, which is largely inaccessible to the community and public authority and hence beyond its competence. Rather what is principally envisioned is a public act or omission known to the community, which is adversely affected by it. However, ecclesiastical penal law has also dealt with certain occult or non-public offenses that may be known only to a few individuals, e.g., solicitation in confession. It is disputed whether church law should enact penal measures against such relatively private acts; however, there is apparently an understanding that such acts may significantly harm the community and hence are properly matters of penal discipline.

Not every sin is technically an ecclesiastical offense warranting a penalty; yet for any act or omission to be an ecclesiastical offense, it must be seriously sinful. Historically, canonists and moralists have reflected on the phenomenon of anti-ecclesial attitudes or behavior and have refined certain categories of factors that may diminish or even completely preclude imputability or accountability for one's apparently criminal behavior.

Furthermore, not every violation of Church law technically is an ecclesiastical offense warranting a penalty; in fact, it is the exceptional law in the 1917 Code whose violation constitutes an ecclesiastical offense. Throughout the ages there have been noteworthy differences in the Church's understanding of what patterns of thought or behavior were so destructive of its spiritual-moral integrity as to call for an ecclesiastical penalty or deprivation of some good within the control of the Church. In other words, the determination of ecclesiastical offenses reflects at least an implicit hierarchy of values that is operative. The types of penalties appropriate to deal with various offenses have been historically conditioned and have varied given different customs, mores, and styles of living the Christian life.[2] Throughout the ages there has been a continuing effort to clarify the boundaries of ecclesial communion and to refine the understanding of those breaches of ecclesial values which cannot be tolerated.

A significant historical factor affecting the Church's penal discipline has been the status of Church-State relationships. Frequently the Church had recourse to the secular arm to enforce its own discipline, and at times Church authorities implemented distinctly secular or civil penal discipline. Such close Church-State relationships are largely a thing of the past today. There is now a clearer sense of the distinction of ecclesiastical and civil penal orders. This has facilitated structuring the Church's penal discipline in accord with primarily theological considerations; yet there are still significant vestiges of a perfect-society ecclesiology influencing contemporary Church penal law. Such an approach, however valid, does not do justice to the uniqueness of the Church and its implications for penal law.[3]

---

[1] The author is grateful to Rev. Ladislas Orsy, S.J., whose unpublished reflections entitled "Breach of Law and Punishment" were helpful in preparing these introductory observations.

[2] For a brief overview of the evolution of offenses and penalties in the Church, see Michiels I, 30–40.

[3] For a brief overview of contemporary discussions regarding a proper theological rationale for penal law and related issues, see Green, "Future of Penal Law," 215–235.

The Reaction of the Community

If the peace of the community disturbed by the offense is to be restored in a responsible rather than capricious fashion, those in leadership positions, rather than private individuals, should take action against those violating community faith or order. To those questioning the need for penalties in a community of love, one might respond that the community can ill afford to be mute and inactive in the face of significant breaches of its faith or order; otherwise its identity as a sign of God's kingdom would be seriously jeopardized. While a certain type of diversity clearly enriches the Church, it simply cannot tolerate certain divergent patterns of thought or activity if it is to be fair to its own members who joined a reasonably well-defined community and have definite expectations from it. It is also not fair to those outside the community who wish to understand its purposes and the means it uses to realize them. Obviously clarifying the tolerable limits of ecclesial diversity is an ongoing task, especially in an age when the boundaries between various communions are increasingly fluid.

And yet if the Church's penal activity is to reflect its redeeming, healing character, its primary focus must be to affirm ecclesial unity through faith and charity rather than to condemn an individual expounding a heterodox position or engaging in anti-ecclesial conduct. Much more so than in secular society, church authorities should reflect gentleness, patience, and pastoral charity in dealing with those violating the ideals of the community.[4]

Actually the disciplinary action taken by church authorities is not done precisely on their own initiative; it is rather the consequence of an action(s) of an individual who breaks or seriously disturbs his or her unity with the community. The community simply cannot afford to take no notice of those who reject sharing in the Church's mission or refuse the call to Christian witness in a significant way.

This official taking note of and reacting against violations of church faith or order has assumed numerous forms historically. Suffice it to remark here that two noteworthy divisions of ecclesiastical penalties are censures, or so-called medicinal penalties, and so-called vindictive penalties. The Church's penal order has various purposes; however, one way of differentiating these penalties has been in terms of their somewhat different orientations. Censures have strongly emphasized the reconciliation of the offender with the community; their operative force has been directly related to the dispositions of the offender vis-à-vis the community. In other words once the offender repents of the violation of ecclesial order, the penalty must be remitted. On the other hand, so-called vindictive penalties focus much more on restoring community order, repairing

scandal, and deterring would-be violators of ecclesiastical discipline. The continuing force of such penalties is much less directly related to the subjective dispositions of the offender than in the case of censures. In fact the penalties may still be in effect even after the offender has fully repented.

The issue of penalties is complex and can hardly be explored adequately here. Throughout history, questions have been raised about the efficacy of various penalties. In fact it has been questioned whether at times a non-penal pastoral approach would be more appropriate than inflicting a penalty in leading an individual to a fuller life in Christ. This ultimately has to be the rationale for disciplinary measures in a salvific community such as the Church. Similar questions were posed at the time of the 1917 Code; but they are even more urgent today in a world significantly different from that of the 1917 Code.

Book V of the 1917 Code

Book V of the 1917 Code (*CIC* 2195–2414) was the first serious effort to systematize universal penal discipline. It was a complex of norms regulating the establishment, application, and remission of penalties. The purposes of these norms were to foster the good order of the Christian community and to facilitate the observance of the substantive law contained especially in Books I–III.

Book V was structured largely in terms of two interrelated realities: the offense against the community (*CIC* part I, 2195–2213) and the community's penal reaction against the offense (*CIC* part II, 2214–2313). It offered general principles on offenses and penalties and also treated of specific penalties such as censures and so-called vindictive penalties as well as quasi-penal measures such as penal remedies and penances.

A concluding section of Book V dealt specifically with the appropriate penalties for individual offenses according to several categories based on fundamental ecclesial values (*CIC* part III, 2314–2414). In addition to this material a few penal laws were contained in other sections of the 1917 Code.

The Church's universal penal discipline was fundamentally unchanged from the promulgation of the 1917 Code until after Vatican II. While individual penalties were changed, the basic presuppositions of the system were generally unchallenged despite certain legal-pastoral problems it occasioned.[5] The system was rethought in earnest only during the conciliar and post-conciliar period.

---

[4]See *CIC* 2214, §2.

[5]For post-1917 Code changes in penal law, see various editions of *CLD* under headings of cc. 2195–2414. Also A. Bride, "L'evolution du droit pénal depuis le Code," *AC* 2 (1953), 303–321; J. O'Connor, "Trends in Canon Law: the Question of Penalties," *Stud Can* 3 (1969), 209–237.

Contemporary Penal Law Revision

Code Commission Penal Law Committee

After Vatican II a special *coetus,* or committee, of the Code Commission was established to revise penal law. The first meeting of the committee in November 1966 discussed general principles on ecclesiastical offenses and penalties. A preliminary draft of fifty-one canons was formulated in January 1967. Subsequently, in July 1967, the committee prepared a preliminary draft of fifty-one canons on specific penalties, e.g., excommunication, suspension, etc. After further discussion the first noteworthy stage in penal law revision was reached in November 1967: the completion of a draft of seventy-seven canons on offenses and penalties in general. Up to this point no significant work had been done on penalties for specific offenses.

The First Synod of Bishops took place in September–October 1967. Among its accomplishments was the approval of certain principles to guide the Code revision process prepared by the Code Commission. Principle nine dealt with the revision of penal law, whose continued ecclesial viability was reaffirmed since a certain coercive power is necessary for proper order in every society. Nevertheless, the number of penalties was to be reduced and the focus of penal law discipline was to be the so-called external forum (public arena of church life). *Ferendae sententiae,* or inflicted penalties, calling for official ecclesiastical intervention were to be the rule. *Latae sententiae,* or automatic penalties (incurred without formal ecclesiastical intervention through the commission of an offense by one who is accountable for his or her actions), were to be limited to the most serious ecclesiastical offenses.

Further discussion by the committee in late 1967 and early 1968 led to the formulation of another draft of seventy canons on offenses and penalties in general (May 1968). The committee spent the rest of its time dealing with penalties for specific offenses. Finally, in January 1970, it approved a draft of ninety canons. A somewhat shortened version of this document (seventy-three canons) was sent for evaluation to the bishops of the world and other consultative organs in December 1973.[6]

One hundred thirty-four responses were received from the bishops and others involved in the consultative process. Book VI of the revised Code largely reflects the efforts of the penal law committee to rework the original schema in light of those comments.

The Basic Structure and Sources of Book VI

Book VI is organized basically the same as the original 1973 schema, which differed somewhat from the organization of the 1917 Code. While not-

ing certain similarities to the 1917 Code, the following reflections will generally highlight some principal differences between the revised Code and the former document. First some basic organizational differences are presented. Then some noteworthy changes from the 1917 Code are briefly indicated. This will help to put in perspective subsequent comments on individual canons.

First of all the revised Code (eighty-nine canons) is much shorter than the 1917 Code (two hundred twenty canons). While the basic structure of the 1917 Code is largely kept intact, the revised Code notably simplifies the treatment of certain institutes. For example, the former's lengthy section on various types of penalties (*CIC* 2241–2313) is sharply reduced in the latter text (cc. 1331–1340). This shortening has been achieved by dropping definitions, focusing briefly on the effects of the various penalties, and sharply curtailing the detailed treatment of censures in the 1917 Code. This last development is related to the practical elimination of the institute of reservation of censures and the de-emphasizing of the role of the confessor in the remission of penalties. Even more noteworthy is the reduction of the number of penalties for specific offenses from one hundred one in the 1917 Code (*CIC* 2314–2414) to thirty-five in the 1983 text (cc. 1364–1398). Finally title V of part I on the application of penalties (cc. 1341–1353) succinctly integrates materials found in various titles of the 1917 Code, e.g., imputability (title II), the competent legal authority (title V), and those subject to coercive power (title VI).

The sources of the 1983 text are largely the canons of the 1917 Code, occasionally modified in light of subsequent legal developments. Unlike other areas of the revised law, such as sacramental discipline or ecclesiastical organization, there seems to be relatively little direct influence of conciliar sources in the revised penal law. However, certain conciliar themes have indirectly influenced its revision since fidelity to Vatican II is said to be the principal guiding criterion for the committee's work. Among such themes are the following: a renewed awareness of the legal-pastoral implications of human dignity and freedom, an enhanced respect for the ecclesial implications of the principle of subsidiarity, and broader discretion for local ordinaries in shaping the life of the particular churches. The penal law implications of these themes will be seen shortly.

Noteworthy Changes from 1917 Code

Without going into detail here, some noteworthy changes from the 1917 Code might be included. They are particularly significant indicators of the committee's effort to reflect the pastoral thrust of Vatican II and adapt penal discipline to contemporary legal-pastoral realities. The following comments are generally expository in character, clarifying key features of the revised law. They do

---

[6] For critical reflections on the original schema, see Green, "Future of Penal Law," 248–274.

not critically evaluate the adequacy of the text in light of certain theological-legal criteria.

While certain universal norms are deemed necessary for a proper application of penal law throughout the Latin Church, the principle of subsidiarity calls for increased legislative competence for church authorities, such as bishops, below the level of the Holy See. This should facilitate the adaptation of penal discipline to the concrete circumstances of different persons and places. Accordingly universal penal laws are significantly reduced in number. Only those fundamental principles that are necessary to create a basic framework of penal discipline are maintained in part I of the revised text. Only those specific offenses which are so incompatible with the Christian life as to require relatively uniform treatment throughout the Church are presumably incorporated in part II of the 1983 text. However, lest increased infra-universal penal discretion be arbitrary and ecclesially counterproductive, penal law uniformity in the various churches of a given region is strongly encouraged.

A renewed recognition of the salvific character of church law and of the dignity of the human person leads to a stress on penalties as a last resort after all other legal-pastoral measures have proven fruitless. The judicial or administrative discretion of ecclesiastical authorities in confronting various problems is notably enhanced. The somewhat restrictive approach of the 1917 Code in a significant area, such as censures, is notably mitigated. For example, a censure ceases if a subsequent law rescinds a prior law or penalty even if the censure has already been incurred (contrary to *CIC* 2226, §3). Recourse or appeal to higher authority against a decree or sentence imposing a censure has a suspensive effect. In other words, contrary to the 1917 Code, it does not take effect until higher authority upholds the decree or sentence.

Certain penalties are abolished because they seem excessively harsh and minimally effective, e.g., infamy, denial of church burial, and privation of sacramentals. Furthermore, penal discipline is simplified in several respects. For example, the complex 1917 Code restrictions on remitting penalties are largely dropped, e.g., reservation of remission of penalties to the Holy See simply (*simpliciter*), specially (*speciali modo*), and most specially (*specialissimo modo*). Likewise there are broadened possibilities for bishops to remit penalties and thereby minister more effectively to their fellow believers. This is a specific example of the more general tendency in the revised law to enhance the pastoral discretion of bishops.

The committee also wished to preclude undue conflicts between the arena of conscience (internal forum) and the arena of the Church's public order (external forum). In other words there was a desire to avoid situations in which a person might be forgiven his or her sins and thereby be healed in his or her relationship in conscience to the Lord while simultaneously still being subject to an ecclesiastical penalty and thereby remaining in an irregular legal situation in the Church's public order.

This complex issue cannot be explored here. Suffice it to note that penal discipline is largely confined to the external forum and is nearly always within the exclusive competence of bishops and other significant church authorities. In the 1917 Code the confessor played a significant penal role in certain theoretically extraordinary situations (*CIC* 2252–2254; 2290), which practically speaking became increasingly ordinary. On the contrary the revised law ordinarily limits his involvement to remitting non-declared *latae sententiae* penalties in extraordinary circumstances. A non-declared *latae sententiae* penalty is one which has been incurred ipso facto by the commission of an ecclesiastical offense as specified in law. Nevertheless, no ecclesiastical authority has formally confirmed that such a penalty has been incurred. This confirmation can be done judicially or administratively.

Another noteworthy change in the revised law is its theoretical preference for judicial rather than administrative procedure in the infliction of penalties. This question of proper penal procedure was a disputed one in the 1917 Code, but, in practice, administrative procedure was fairly common. Questions have been raised about such administrative procedure because of a fear that the rights of alleged offenders might not be as adequately protected in such circumstances as in judicial procedure. This issue likewise cannot be explored here. Suffice it to note that even in the revised law the competent authority may also impose penalties administratively if there are adequate reasons for doing so. Given the contemporary demands on church tribunals because of the sharp increase in marriage nullity cases, in practice, penalties may continue to be imposed administratively except where judicial procedure is strictly required.

Finally a concern to ensure the personal involvement of church authorities in dealing with potential offenses seems to account for the revised law's noteworthy emphasis on *ferendae sententiae* penalties as a general rule. Accordingly, contrary to the large number of *latae sententiae* penalties in the 1917 Code, the 1983 law contains only seventeen of them (four interdicts, six suspensions, and seven excommunications [only five of which are reserved to the Holy See]). These are incurred apparently only for the most serious offenses as described in part II of the law.[7]

For further reference, a number of tables which give complete lists of various penalties and offenses in the revised Code are included at the end of this commentary on Book VI (prior to the bibliographical material).

---

[7]See Table 10 at the end of this commentary on Book VI.

Part I
OFFENSES AND PENALTIES IN GENERAL
[cc. 1311–1363]

TITLE I
THE PUNISHMENT OF OFFENSES IN GENERAL
[cc. 1311–1312]

Church Penal Rights

Canon 1311 — **The Church has an innate and proper right to coerce offending members of the Christian faithful by means of penal sanctions.**

Several critiques of the original schema suggested that the canons express the rationale for penal law. It was felt that every effort should be made to clarify the foundations of the Church's penal authority, especially in a time of notable resistance or indifference to law.

However, the revised law, like the 1917 Code, simply affirms the Church's innate and proper right to penalize those who violate its laws. Apparently it is judged that developing a rationale for penal authority pertains more to canonical theory than to a legal text. This approach is not surprising since a general reluctance to deal with foundational theological-legal issues has characterized much of the work of the Code Commission.

The Church is said to possess an innate penal right, i.e., a right based on the nature of the Church itself and not derivative from any human power such as the State.[8] This formulation seems to reflect a perfect-society ecclesiology which views the Church as an entity comparable to the State and thereby possessing all the institutional means necessary to achieve its purposes.

Contrary to the initial canon of the 1917 Code (*CIC* 2195), the revised law does not define an ecclesiastical offense. Hence a clarification of who precisely are Christian "offenders" must await an examination of canon 1321 on imputability.

Generally speaking the revised law does not define terms since this is presumably the work of scholars and not of the legislator. This will raise problems in the following examination of the canons since at times it is not entirely clear what is meant by frequently used terms as "scandal," "just penalty," etc.

The "Christian faithful" mentioned here are Roman Catholics, who alone are directly bound by ecclesiastical law (c. 11). This modifies the 1917 Code, which held that all baptized non-Catholics were bound by church law unless explicitly exempt and no exemption was provided for in penal law.

Types of Penalties

Canon 1312 — **§1. The following penal sanctions exist in the Church:**
1° medicinal penalties or censures enumerated in cann. 1331-1333;
2° expiatory penalties enumerated in can. 1336.
§2. The law can establish other expiatory penalties which deprive a believer of some spiritual or temporal good and are consistent with the supernatural end of the Church.
§3. Penal remedies and penances are likewise employed; the former especially in order to prevent offenses, the latter rather to substitute for or to increase a penalty.

The revised law's avoidance of definitions is clear also in this canon on different types of penalties and comparable measures. Contrary to the 1917 Code, which defines medicinal penalties, or censures (*CIC* 2241, §1), and vindictive (now expiatory) penalties (*CIC* 2286), paragraph one simply notes their existence and refers to title IV where their effects are specified.

The term "medicinal" indicates the primary finality of this type of penalty—the correction of the offending party and reintegration within the life of the community. On the contrary the principal thrust of the expiatory penalty is to repair the damage done to the ecclesial order by the offender. Its remission does not depend primarily on the offender's change of heart as in the censure but rather on church authority's determination that the damage done to the ecclesial order has been duly compensated for.

Paragraph two notes the possibility of expiatory penalties other than those enumerated in canon 1336. It also describes such penalties as deprivations of a spiritual or temporal good in accord with the supernatural finalities of the Church. Although this canon deals explicitly only with expiatory penalties, the description actually applies to all penalties (*CIC* 2215). Not every deprivation of some good is a penalty but only that which is directly related to the commission of an ecclesiastical offense.

The reference to a correspondence between penalties and the Church's supernatural purposes seems particularly crucial in judging the genuinely

---

[8]One sees comparable formulations of ecclesiastical rights vis-à-vis the state in cc. 800, §1 (establishment of schools); 807 (establishment of universities); and 1254, §1 (acquisition, retention, administration, and alienation of temporal goods).

pastoral character of the former. In the past, at times, questions have been raised about whether ecclesiastical penal discipline has been too strongly influenced by secular analogates and inadequately sensitive to the uniqueness of the Church.

Paragraph three briefly refers to certain measures such as penal remedies or penances (*CIC* 2306–2313) that may be employed in a somewhat ancillary fashion vis-à-vis penalties. The legislator's concern that penalties be employed only as a last resort is well expressed in the institute of penal remedies, which are geared especially to preventing ecclesiastical offenses. The penal discretion enjoyed by church authorities is evident in the institute of penances, which substitute for or increase a penalty—the latter in instances of heightened imputability.

TITLE II
PENAL LAW AND PENAL PRECEPTS
[cc. 1313–1320]

Change of Law Situation

Canon 1313 — §1. If a law is changed after an offense has been committed the law which is more favorable to the accused is to be applied.

§2. But if the second law abolishes the first law or at least its penalty, the penalty immediately ceases.

A basic principle of legal interpretation states that in penal law a benign approach is to be followed (*CIC* 2219, §1).[9] In other words if the meaning of a text is doubtful, that understanding of the law which favors the alleged offender is preferred. The pastoral thrust of this approach is rather clear. Furthermore, since penal law is always burdensome, a strict interpretation of a law expressing a penalty or defining an offense is always called for (c. 18; *CIC* 19). A strict interpretation means that the law is to be interpreted narrowly; in other words one should restrict rather than enlarge its application. This is particularly true in part II of Book VI dealing with penalties for specific offenses.

The present canon exemplifies the benign approach mentioned earlier. If the law changes after the offense is committed but before the penalty is inflicted, the law more favorable to the alleged offender is to be applied (§1; *CIC* 2226, §2). This moderate approach is most clearly seen in situations in which the law itself or at least the penal sanction is repealed after the offense is committed; in this case the alleged offender is subject to no penalty. Unlike the 1917 Code (*CIC* 2226, §3), which exempted censures from this benign provision, the revised law covers censures as well as expiatory penalties (§2).

Ferendae Sentential *Orientation of Law*

Canon 1314 — Ordinarily a penalty is to be inflicted by a sentence (*ferendae sententiae*) so that it does not bind the guilty party until after it has been imposed; however, a penalty is incurred automatically by the very commission of the offense (*latae sententiae*) if the law or precept expressly determines this.

A principal concern of principle nine guiding the revision is expressed here: a renewed emphasis on *ferendae sententiae* penalties as normative. A significant post-conciliar discussion has concerned the continuing viability of *latae sententiae,* or automatic, penalties.[10] The revised law reflects the view that a service-oriented exercise of authority requires that those in authority normally be brought into direct contact with the concrete circumstances of every alleged breach of law. Hence before a penalty is inflicted, there must normally be an intervention by those in authority, be it judicial or administrative, and an effort at some kind of contact with the alleged offender. Although the 1917 Code stated that penalties were normally *ferendae sententiae* (*CIC* 2217, §2), it contained numerous *latae sententiae* penalties which were fairly common in practice. The revised law does not eliminate these latter penalties but it restricts them to the most serious ecclesiastical offenses (c. 1318). Apparently it is felt that without such *latae sententiae* penalties the public good of the Church would be jeopardized since certain occult or non-public offenses, such as absolution of an accomplice (c. 1378, §1), might otherwise not be penalized. In view of greater legal precision, *latae sententiae* penalties must be expressly stated as such, contrary to the 1917 Code which employed various formulations to indicate such penalties (*CIC* 2217, §2).

Competence To Establish Penal Law

Canon 1315 — §1. Those who have legislative power can also issue penal laws; within the existing limits of their competence by reason of territory or persons, they can by means of their own laws safeguard with an appropriate penalty any divine law or an ecclesiastical law made by a higher authority.

§2. The law itself can determine a penalty or its determination can be left to the prudent assessment of a judge.

§3. Particular law can also add other penalties to the penalties established in universal law for some offense, but this is not to be done except for the most serious necessity. If the universal law threatens a penalty which is indeterminate or facul-

---

[9]Reg. 49 R.I. in VI°.

[10]Green, "Future of Penal Law," 224–228; V. de Paolis, "De legitimate et opportunitate poenarum latae sententiae in iure poenali canonico," *P* 63 (1974), 37–67.

tative, however, particular law can establish in its place a determinate or obligatory penalty.

The other canons in this title seem to refer primarily to church authorities below the universal level. They deal with such matters as penal law competence, uniformity in penal law, and moderation in establishing penalties, especially *latae sententiae* penalties and censures. A significant feature of the revised law is enhanced legislative discretion for infra-universal church authorities. The supreme legislator seems concerned here to set down general guidelines for such legislative activity.

First of all paragraph one states that only those enjoying legislative authority can establish penal laws or penalize the violation of divine law or higher-level ecclesiastical laws which do not carry a particular sanction. Such authority would be enjoyed by bishops and major superiors of clerical religious institutes of pontifical right. Other significant ecclesiastical authorities, such as vicars general, may not establish penalties since their authority is administrative rather than legislative in character (c. 479, §1). This is also true for the officialis or vicar judicial who can only apply penalties already established in law since his authority is judicial rather than legislative in character (c. 1420, §1). To preclude possible abuses in this delicate area, such authority is to be exercised within the territorial (bishop) or personal (religious superior) limits of the authority figure's competence.

Paragraph two differentiates penal laws in virtue of their determinate or indeterminate character (*CIC* 2217, §1, 1°). Frequently, a particular penalty is specified in the law or precept establishing it, e.g., the subjection of the person attacking the pope physically to a *latae sententiae* excommunication reserved to the Holy See (c. 1370, §1). Occasionally the law requires a penalty but leaves its determination up to the discretion of the judge or superior inflicting it after the appropriate judicial or administrative procedure, e.g., the specification of a just penalty for violations of the law on *communicatio in sacris* (c. 1365).

The preceding examples involve perceptive, or obligatory, penalties. However, in other situations the law does not require a penalty but leaves the disposition of the issue entirely up to the judge or superior (so-called *facultative* penalties), e.g., the provision for a possible censure and required retraction if another's reputation is damaged (c. 1390, §2–3).

Paragraph three cautions infra-universal legislators not to add to those penalties specified in the revised Code unless it is an extremely grave necessity. If penalties are too easily multiplied, this may have detrimental pastoral consequences. However, if the revised Code does not specify a particular penalty for an offense or indicates that it is facultative, infra-universal legislators may impose a definite pen-

alty or at least require some type of penalty. This would undoubtedly be due to particularly problematic legal-pastoral circumstances in a given area, e.g., frequent violation of clerical obligations.

Desirable Penal Law Uniformity

Canon 1316 — Diocesan bishops are to see to it that penal laws if they are to be enacted are uniform in the same city or region to the extent that this is possible.

The increased penal latitude for infra-universal legislators might be viewed as a mixed blessing. The conciliar stress on enhancing the governmental power of bishops suggests that they have a certain penal latitude. The penal law committee, in fact, rejected the criticism of certain persons who wished to restrict infra-universal penal law initiative to the episcopal conferences. However, such episcopal discretion could lead to situations in which there might be sharp discrepancies in neighboring dioceses in dealing with certain violations. The same offense might be penalized in notably different ways or certain phenomena might be ecclesiastical offenses in one diocese but not in another. This could be ecclesially counterproductive and might subvert the penal system. Hence neighboring bishops are advised to strive as much as possible for a uniform approach to breaches of church order. Consultations among neighboring particular churches could possibly check arbitrary episcopal discretion that would violate human and Christian dignity and freedom.

Cautious Establishment of Penal Law

Canon 1317 — Penalties should be established to the extent to which they are truly necessary to provide more suitably for ecclesiastical discipline. Dismissal from the clerical state, however, cannot be established by particular law.

The current emphasis on penalties as a last resort in coping with pastoral problems is evident in this admonition to infra-universal legislators to establish penalties only in instances in which it is absolutely necessary to provide appropriately for the exigencies of ecclesiastical discipline. There is a concern to mitigate possibly excessive episcopal penal initiatives here. This same theme is also expressed in the first canon of title V on applying penalties, which deals with the infliction of penalties already established in law (c. 1341). This is a wise caution inasmuch as the sharp reduction in penalties for specific offenses in the revised Code might tempt other legislators to multiply such penalties in particular law.

A concern to protect clerics and respect their distinct ecclesiastical status accounts for the fact that particular law may not determine additional grounds for the serious expiatory penalty of dismissal from the clerical state. Such a penalty is warranted only in those cases explicitly stated in the revised Code. This matter will be dealt with later (in connection with c. 1336, §1, 5°). This provision seems to reflect a fear that possibly arbitrary episcopal discretion may do irrevocable harm to a cleric, even one who has violated the law. The serious effects of dismissal call for special care in determining violations warranting it and a solemn procedure in inflicting it.

Caution Regarding Latae Sententiae *Penalties*

Canon 1318 — A legislator is not to threaten automatic penalties (*latae sententiae*) unless perhaps against certain particularly treacherous offenses which either can result in more serious scandal or cannot be effectively punished by means of inflicted penalties (*ferendae sententiae*); a legislator is not to establish censures, especially excommunication, except with the greatest moderation and only for more serious offenses.

The stress on penal moderation (characteristic of this title) is also evident in the caution regarding the establishment of *latae sententiae* penalties as well as censures, especially excommunication. There is a kind of implicit penal hierarchy of values operative here.

The seriousness of the penalty should be proportionate to the seriousness of the offense (*CIC* 2218, §1). Only if a given offense cannot be dealt with adequately through a *ferendae sententiae* penalty or if it involves serious scandal is there room for a particular law *latae sententiae* penalty. It is not clear precisely what is meant by serious scandal, but it apparently refers to a situation in which a given Christian value(s) would be in serious danger of being taken lightly or violated by members of the Christian community. While the 1917 Code explicitly called for moderation in the use of censures, especially excommunication (*CIC* 2241, §2), the explicit reference to moderation in employing *latae sententiae* penalties is new. The restraint of the revised Code in determining *latae sententiae* penalties (seventeen in present law) and such censures as excommunication (seven in present law) should guide lower-level legislators.

Issuing of Penal Precepts

Canon 1319 — §1. To the extent that one can impose precepts in the external forum by virtue of the power of governance, to that same extent one can also threaten determinate penalties through a precept with the exception of perpetual expiatory penalties.

§2. A penal precept is not to be issued without a mature consideration of the matter and without observing what is stated in cann. 1317 and 1318 concerning particular laws.

This canon reflects some of the above-mentioned concepts, specifically in relationship to so-called penal precepts. Here the revised Code refers to a more particularized situation than is envisioned by the more generalized focus of the law. In other words one who exercises legislative authority, such as a bishop, issues a particular order affecting an individual (particular precept) or a community (general precept) under threat of a penalty. For example, a bishop might threaten a priest with suspension if he does not attend continuing education sessions or if he does not withdraw from certain partisan political activities. Generally speaking, but not always, a precept differs from a law in its focus on the private rather than the public good and in its being personal rather than territorial in orientation. The precept much more than the law takes cognizance of the particular circumstances of the offender.

The revised Code reaffirms the right of such a legislative authority to impose penal precepts (§1). However, it advises moderation in using them (§2) and forbids precepts that threaten perpetual or irrevocable expiatory penalties (§1). The serious implications of such penalties make it imperative that they not be employed lightly but rather that they be implemented only through the strict procedures of law. Whereas only the perpetual expiatory penalty of dismissal from the clerical state cannot be established by particular law, other perpetual expiatory penalties cannot even be threatened by precept, e.g., prohibiting a cleric from ever living in a certain area or permanently depriving him of a particular office. Finally the general cautions of canons 1317 and 1318 on infra-universal legislative activity are equally relevant to penal precepts.

Penalties for Religious

Canon 1320 — Religious can be coerced by penalties by the local ordinary in all matters in which they are subject to him.

This canon on the coercive power of the local ordinary relative to religious in his diocese was a relatively late addition during the consultative process. While the principle it articulates is clear, the need for its explicit affirmation here is not entirely evident.

Certain canons are particularly significant in this connection, e.g., canon 678 on the subjection of religious to the bishop as regards pastoral care, the exercise of divine worship, and other works of the apostolate. However, to appreciate fully the implications of the present canon, it is necessary to consult the commentary on the canons on institutes of consecrated life and on societies of apostolic life (cc. 573–746).

TITLE III
THOSE SUBJECT TO PENAL SANCTIONS
[cc. 1321–1330]

This significant title incorporates various provisions from the first three titles of the 1917 Code on offenses (*CIC* 2195–2213). It is an interesting example of the revised law's effort to streamline the 1917 Code. It should be read in connection with title V (of Part I) on the application of penalties (cc. 1341–1353) since it offers certain basic principles to aid church authorities in determining whether an ecclesiastical offense has been committed and what might be an appropriate penalty.

Notion of Imputability

Canon 1321 — §1. No one is punished unless the external violation of a law or a precept committed by the person is seriously imputable to that person by reason of malice or culpability.

§2. A person who has deliberately violated a law or a precept is bound by the penalty stated in that law or that precept; unless a law or a precept provides otherwise, a person who has violated that law or that precept through a lack of necessary diligence is not punished.

§3. Unless it is otherwise evident, imputability is presumed whenever an external violation has occurred.

Contrary to the 1917 Code (*CIC* 2195), the revised law does not define an ecclesiastical offense. However, this initial canon can facilitate a working understanding of an ecclesiastical offense. Three elements are implied: (1) an external violation of a law or precept (§1); (2) grave imputability rooted primarily in a deliberate intent to violate the law or precept or secondarily in culpable negligence; and finally (3) a legal determination of a penalty (§2). This title deals largely with the second factor—the crucial issue of imputability. At times, perhaps, there is a popular misconception that the mere fact that one breaks a law means that a penalty is necessarily incurred, e.g., remarriage after divorce without an ecclesiastical annulment or dissolution. Yet of the essence of an ecclesiastical offense is serious moral imputability, and the legislator provides detailed guidelines to assist ecclesiastical judges and superiors in making prudent judgments in this area after weighing all the relevant factors.[11]

The significant notions here are *dolus* and *culpa*.

The 1917 Code stated that either could be the basis of imputability (*CIC* 2199). However, the present canon states that normally *dolus,* or deliberate intent to violate the law, is necessary for penal imputability. Negligence is usually not a basis for such imputability (§2). The text does not explicitly state that *dolus,* or malice, is deliberate intent to violate the law or that *culpa,* or culpability, is negligence. However, these inferences seem warranted from the meaning of such terms in the 1917 Code, from the structure of this canon, and from the discussions of the committee leading to its formulation. Furthermore, a study of the committee's discussion of this canon makes it clear that *culpa* also means a false judgment that mitigating circumstances are verified in connection with an alleged offense as well as culpable ignorance of the fact that a law or precept has been violated.

Does the legislator offer any guidelines in assessing imputability in particular cases since many complex factors may be operative in any given violation of law? The 1917 Code stated a rebuttable presumption that if an external offense were committed, *dolus,* or intent to violate the law, was verified (*CIC* 2200, §2). The revised law is somewhat more ambiguous. If there is an external violation of a law, imputability is presumed (§3). This would seem to involve *dolus,* or malice; yet since *culpa,* or culpability, at times grounds imputability, this would also have to be taken into consideration. This seems especially true in light of the importance of interpreting penal law in a benign fashion. The judge or superior should, therefore, be cautious in attributing intent to violate the law too easily to an offending party.

In brief the law places a certain burden on the alleged offender to demonstrate that imputability, or at least grave imputability, is not verified in the case in question. Anglo-American commentators have questioned the retention of such a presumption of imputability even if it is less obnoxious than the prior presumption of *dolus,* or malice. The traditional Anglo-American presumption of innocence until one is proven guilty seems more appropriate. This would place an additional burden on church authorities. However, church law should be no less a guardian of freedom, justice, and equity than civil law—and a corollary of this guardianship function is a presumption of purity of intent even on the part of alleged lawbreakers.

Insanity and Imputability

Canon 1322 — Persons who habitually lack the use of reason are considered incapable of an offense

[11]For an examination of the various factors to be weighed in determining penal imputability in the divorce-remarriage situation, see A. McDevitt et al., "Report of Committee on Alternatives to Tribunal Procedures," *CLSAP* 35 (1975), 162–178 especially 165–173. The excommunication for remar-

riage after a civil divorce which had been decreed by the Third Council of Baltimore was rescinded by the NCCB on May 4, 1977 and confirmed by Pope Paul VI through an October 22, 1977 decree of the SCB. See *CLD* 8, 1213–1214.

even if they have violated a law or a precept while appearing to be sane.

This and the next five canons address various dimensions of individual imputability in the commission of an ecclesiastical offense. Originally it had been proposed to articulate only one succinct canon on factors affecting imputability. However, the present text is almost as detailed as the 1917 Code (*CIC* 2201–2208) in response to requests from various individuals who had evaluated the original schema and apparently had found it wanting as regards practical guidance for judges and superiors in inflicting penalties.

The revised Code systematically improves the 1917 Code by placing in separate canons the various factors eliminating, diminishing, increasing, or having no real effect on imputability. The 1917 Code, on the contrary, had frequently dealt in the same canon with factors which had different effects on imputability. Hence canonical commentators had to systematize the imputability-affecting factors under various rubrics.

Limitations of space permit only brief comments on these factors. This is an area in which the standard commentaries on the 1917 Code might profitably be consulted.[12] Of the essence of imputability is a free, deliberate human act. Hence whatever factors in the human psyche impair one's ability to function freely and deliberately and destroy the integrity of one's decisional process will thereby affect imputability, or one's being held accountable for certain actions or omissions.

Canon 1322 deals with the most radical situation—the insane person or one habitually deprived of the use of reason. Such a one is presumed incapable of an offense even if his or her behavior may have seemed normal when the law or precept was violated. Such an individual is presumably not in possession of his or her faculties and hence is comparable to a child and thereby absolved of responsibility before the community.

Factors Removing Imputability

Canon 1323 — **The following are not subject to penalties when they have violated a law or precept:**

1° a person who has not yet completed the sixteenth year of age;

2° a person who without any fault was unaware of violating a law or precept; however, inadvertence and error are equivalent to ignorance;

3° a person who acted out of physical force or in virtue of a mere accident which could neither be foreseen nor prevented when foreseen;

4° a person who acted out of grave fear, even if only relatively grave, or out of necessity or out of

serious inconvenience unless the act is intrinsically evil or verges on harm to souls;

5° a person who for the sake of legitimate self-defense or defense of another acted against an unjust aggressor with due moderation;

6° a person who lacked the use of reason with due regard for the prescriptions of cann. 1324, §1, n. 2 and 1325;

7° a person who without any fault felt that the circumstances in nn. 4 or 5 were verified.

Contrary to the preceding canon involving the radically impaired individual, the legislator here deals with various violators of a law or precept who are normally in possession of their faculties. Yet such persons are still not subject to a penalty since there is a significant diminishing of their freedom or awareness of the implications of their activity; hence there is no real imputability.

Most of the factors enumerated are comparable to the 1917 Code, e.g., inculpable ignorance of the law or precept, to which error or inadvertence are equivalent (2°; *CIC* 2202, §1). Ignorance means a lack of knowledge about an issue, error refers to a false judgment about the matter at hand, and inadvertence implies a lack of attention to an issue. Likewise exempt from all imputability is one who violates the law in the circumstances of a purely unforeseeable accident. This exemption also applies if it could have been foreseen, but it could not have been prevented (3°; *CIC* 2203, §2). The same is true if one's actions are prompted by external physical force which totally precluded any real freedom (3°; *CIC* 2205, §1). A comparable pressure situation is one in which a person violates the law out of necessity or because of serious inconvenience in observing it. Likewise impaired in his or her decisional process is the person who acts out of grave fear, even if it is only relative, i.e., sufficient to intimidate the alleged offender even if not all persons (4°; *CIC* 2205, §2). However, if the legal violation is an intrinsically evil act (not an easy concept to clarify)[13] or if it will cause pastoral damage, then such factors do not entirely exempt an offender from all imputability. This seems to be true because certain higher values are at stake which the legislator cannot neglect. A person who violated the law or precept while engaged in legitimate self-defense or in defense of another is likewise exempt from a penalty if such resistance were carried out with due modera-

---

[12]See Bouscaren, 866–869; Vermeersch-Creusen, 227–233.

[13]For a challenge to the validity of the concept of intrinsically evil acts, see T. O'Connell, *Principles for a Catholic Morality* (New York: Seabury, 1978), 165–169. For a defense of the validity of such a concept, see G. Grisez and R. Shaw, *Beyond the New Morality: the Responsibilities of Freedom* (Notre Dame, Indiana: University of Notre Dame, 1974). For various positions in the contemporary Catholic discussion of this issue, see C. Curran and R. McCormick (eds.), *Readings in Moral Theology, No. 1: Moral Norms and Catholic Tradition* (New York: Paulist Press, 1979).

tion, i.e., using only that amount of force necessary to repel the unjust aggressor (5°; *CIC* 2205, §4). The legislator also deals here with the situation of the individual temporarily losing control of his or her faculties without any personal fault. This seems to refer to involuntary drunkenness or uncontrollable passion as specified in the 1917 Code (6°; *CIC* 2201, §3; 2206).

While the preceding factors which eliminate all imputability basically restate the 1917 Code, two new considerations are noteworthy. Those under sixteen years of age are entirely exempt from penal imputability—somewhat of a reflection of the civil law tendency to treat juvenile offenders more leniently than other lawbreakers (1°).[14] The revised law is somewhat more benign than the 1917 Code, which stated that being a minor did not eliminate but only mitigated imputability; yet the earlier Code also affirmed that those below puberty were exempt from *latae sententiae* penalties (*CIC* 2204; 2230). Finally the legislator views as non-liable to a penalty the individual erroneously yet inculpably believing that his or her behavior was attributable to grave fear, serious inconvenience, necessity, or legitimate self-defense (7°).

Factors Diminishing Imputability

Canon 1324 — §1. One who violates a law or precept is not exempt from a penalty but the penalty set by law or precept must be tempered or a penance substituted in its place if the offense was committed:

1° by a person with only the imperfect use of reason;

2° by a person who lacked the use of reason due to drunkenness or another similar mental disturbance which was culpable;

3° in the serious heat of passion which did not precede and impede all deliberation of mind and consent of will as long as the passion itself had not been voluntarily stirred up or fostered;

4° by a minor who has completed the age of sixteen years;

5° by a person who was forced through grave fear, even if only relatively grave, or through necessity or serious inconvenience, if the offense was intrinsically evil or verged on harm to souls;

6° by a person who for the sake of legitimate self-defense or defense of another acted against an unjust aggressor but without due moderation;

7° against one gravely and unjustly provoking it;

8° by one who erroneously yet culpably thought one of the circumstances in can. 1323, nn. 4 and 5 was verified;

9° by one who without any fault was unaware that a penalty was attached to the law or precept;

10° by one who acted without full imputability provided there was grave imputability.

§2. A judge can act in the same manner if any other circumstance exists which would lessen the seriousness of the offense.

§3. An accused is not bound by an automatic penalty (*latae sententiae*) in the presence of any of the circumstances enumerated in §1.

This canon systematically lists the different factors that do not remove but diminish imputability. They call for the tempering of the penalty specified in law or the substitution of a lesser measure such as a penance (§1). This canon largely restates the factors noted in the preceding canon. However, the difference is precisely this: instead of the integrity of the offender's decisional process being totally vitiated, it is only partially impaired. Hence the person functions with some freedom and deliberation and, accordingly, is somewhat accountable for the violation of a given law or precept.

The canon provides ample latitude for judicial or administrative discretion in dealing with an offender, and it reflects an awareness of the difficulty in providing an exhaustive catalogue of factors that diminish imputability (§2). Since most of the factors noted here have previously been considered, a few brief comments on paragraph one seem sufficient. The 1917 Code is basically restated, even if not necessarily verbatim. This is true in the following cases: those who have an imperfect use of reason or who are without the full use of their faculties, e.g., senile (1°; *CIC* 2201, §4); those culpably lacking the use of reason due to voluntary drunkenness or another mental disturbance such as might be caused by the use of mind-altering drugs (2°; *CIC* 2201, §3); those caught up in passion which did not totally deprive them of the use of their faculties (3°; *CIC* 2206); the minor who is sixteen or over (4°; *CIC* 2204); the person acting out of fear or other related factors if the legal violation is an intrinsically evil or pastorally detrimental act (5°; *CIC* 2205, §3); the person using excessive force in self-defense or in defense of another against an unjust attack (6°; *CIC* 2205, §4); the person committing an ecclesiastical offense against another who seriously and unjustly provokes such an attack (7°; *CIC* 2205, §4); and finally the person aware of the law or percept but inculpably unaware that a penalty is attached to its violation (9°; *CIC* 2202, §2).

A couple of points in paragraph one are somewhat new in comparison with the 1917 Code, at least in their present formulation. Also subject to a lesser penalty is the person who erroneously but culpably thinks that the excusing causes of grave fear or legitimate self-defense were verified in a given situation (8°). This is actually similar to the fac-

---

[14]Realistically speaking, few ecclesiastical penalties, if any, seem applicable to minors.

tor of culpable ignorance of the penalty mentioned earlier. Furthermore, in light of the traditional principle that penalties are proportionate to grave imputability (*CIC* 2218, §2), the law states generically that if there were no full imputability, for whatever reason, but at least grave imputability, a diminished penalty is warranted (10°).

Paragraph two permits the judge or superior to temper a penalty if any circumstance would lessen the seriousness of the offense. This is another example of a principle of penal proportionality: the graver the offense and the imputability, the graver the penalty, and the less serious the offense and the imputability, the less serious the penalty.

Finally paragraph three notably simplifies the somewhat complex canons 2229–2230 of the 1917 Code on the influence of various mitigating factors on the incurring of *latae sententiae* penalties. It states simply that if any of the factors mentioned in paragraph one are operative, a *latae sententiae* penalty is not incurred. This is another example of legislative caution relative to such penalties. It embodies a concern that normally there be some kind of official intervention to weigh the penal significance of the factors mentioned in paragraph one.

Factors Not Affecting Imputability

Canon 1325 — **Crass, supine or affected ignorance can never be considered in applying the prescriptions of cann. 1323 and 1324; the same is true for drunkenness and other mental disturbances if they are deliberately induced to commit or excuse the offense; this is also true for passion which is deliberately aroused or fostered.**

This canon precludes certain offenders from deliberately taking advantage of some of the previously mentioned mitigating factors. It states that imputability is not affected by cultivated ignorance, deliberately induced drunkenness or other mental disorder such as a drug-induced stupor, or deliberately aroused passion. Hence the offender is to be dealt with as if these ordinarily mitigating factors were not operative (*CIC* 2229; 2201, §3; 2206). Interestingly enough, in the 1917 Code, deliberately aroused passion actually heightened imputability and permitted the imposition of a more stringent penalty than the law provided.

Factors Increasing Imputability

Canon 1326 — **§1. A judge can punish more severely than a law or a precept has stated:**
1° a person who after condemnation or after a declaration of a penalty still commits an offense so as to be prudently presumed to be in continuing bad will in light of the circumstances;
2° a person who has been given some dignified position or who has abused authority or office in order to commit the offense;
3° an accused who although a penalty has been established against a culpable offense, foresaw what was to happen yet nonetheless did not take the precautions which any diligent person would have employed to avoid it.
§2. If the penalty established is an automatic one (*latae sententiae*), another penalty or a penance can be added in those cases mentioned in §1.

The immediately preceding reflections easily lead into a discussion of this canon on various factors which indicate heightened imputability and hence may make the offender liable to a more severe penalty than stated in law. The violation of the ecclesial order is viewed as especially serious if, after being condemned for an offense, the offender breaks the law again in such a way that continuing bad faith can reasonably be presumed (§1, 1°). Traditionally this notion of bad faith, or contumacy, has been viewed as a significant penal factor, especially in the case of censures, whose primary purpose is largely to break the offender's contumacious attitude and foster reconciliation with the community (*CIC* 2208; 2241–2242). This situation of repeated ecclesiastical offenses has been classified technically as legal recidivism.

Imputability is also accentuated if one who has an established rank violates the law (§1, 2°; *CIC* 2207, 1°). The precise meaning of the term *dignitas* is not entirely clear. However, it seems to refer to clerics, and an examination of part II of this Book seems to confirm this. Frequently, special penalties are established for clerics, above and beyond those determined for the laity, e.g., a suspension as well as an interdict for the cleric falsely accusing a confessor of solicitation in confession (c. 1390, §1). There seems to be operative an implicit presumption that the breaking of the law by a cleric is an especially serious breach of ecclesial order. Despite a renewed consciousness of the fundamental equality of all believers, this canon seems to reflect the clericalism of earlier law which viewed the clergy as enjoying a superior status in the Church.

Yet not only clerics may be punished more severely than others in the Church. This canon also views the use of one's authority or office to break the law as heightening imputablity. This would apply to both clerics and the laity in official ecclesiastical positions (§1, 2°; *CIC* 2207, 2°). A key consideration here is the violation of institutional trust in such situations, e.g., reservation to the Holy See of remission of penalty for unauthorized episcopal ordinations (c. 1382).

As noted earlier, imputability is generally based on malice and not culpability unless the law or precept provides otherwise. In fact in part II of this Book, only one offense is specifically related to negligence, i.e., damage caused another by negligent positing or omission of an act of ecclesiastical power, ministry, or duty (c. 1389, §2). In this instance or in a situation in which particular law penalizes some type of negligence, the imputability of the offender is heightened if the conditions noted in this canon (§1, 3°) are verified. This would be true if the offense resulted from the omission of due diligence when an offender foresaw the detrimental consequences of such negligence yet took no reasonable precautions to preclude them. The 1917 Code considered this to be serious negligence almost equivalent to deliberate intent to violate the law (*CIC* 2203, §1); however, it involved ordinary and not increased imputability. The presumably obstinate defiance of the law in such a case must probably be the reason for the heightened imputability in the revised law.

The legislator's desire to deal severely with such heightened imputability is also evident in paragraph two, which permits the addition of a *ferendae sententiae* penalty or penance in instances where the law speaks only of a *latae sententiae* penalty.

Particular Law on Imputability

Canon 1327 — Particular law can determine other exempting, mitigating or aggravating circumstances besides the cases in cann. 1323-1326 either by general norm or for individual offenses. Furthermore, circumstances can be determined in a precept which exempt or mitigate or increase the penalty determined in a precept.

The renewed emphasis on fostering particular law penal initiative accounts for this canon's provision for particular law discretion in determining other factors affecting imputability—either as a general rule or as regards specific offenses. This should facilitate adaptation of the revised Code to particular legal-pastoral circumstances, e.g., heightened violence against church ministers struggling for human rights. Such discretion is operative not simply in the case of laws, universal or particular, but also in the case of precepts.

Attempted Offense

Canon 1328 — §1. A person who has done or omitted something in order to commit an offense but, unwittingly, has not completed it, is not bound by the penalty stated for a completed delict unless the law or precept provides otherwise.

§2. But if such acts or omissions are of their nature conducive to the execution of an offense, their author can be subjected to a penance or a penal remedy unless the author spontaneously ceased from the execution of the offense which had been begun. If, however, scandal or some serious injury or danger has occurred, the author can be punished with a just penalty even if he or she had ceased

spontaneously; but it is to be lighter than that which is established for a completed offense.

This canon attempts to simplify the somewhat complex 1917 Code treatment of so-called attempted and frustrated offenses—situations in which a given offense as specified in law is not actually committed although it has been initiated (*CIC* 2212-2213).

Paragraph one basically drops the 1917 Code differentiation of a simple attempted offense from a frustrated offense. It speaks simply of a frustrated offense in which the effort of the agent's action is not achieved because of circumstances beyond his or her control or intent (*praeter suam voluntatem*). Normally a penalty is not warranted if an offense has not been completed, largely because the community or an individual has not been harmed. In fact there is no penalty for an attempted offense in the revised Code. However, a law or precept could theoretically penalize even an attempted offense, e.g., *CIC* 2350, §2 on attempted suicide.

Paragraph two seems to envision not only the frustrated offense for which a lesser measure such as a penal remedy or a penance, might be imposed, but also it apparently includes the simple attempted offense in which there is a change of heart on the part of the offender after the initial steps to commit the offense have been taken. Such a person would normally be free of all imputability unless even the attempted offense caused great scandal or damage. Here the key issues are the anti-ecclesial intent of the offender and the societal harm resulting from even a halfhearted attempt to violate church law. In any event the penalty to be imposed is lighter than that for the completed offense.

Collaboration in Offense

Canon 1329 — §1. If the penalties established against the principal author are inflicted ones (*ferendae sententiae*), then those who collaborate to commit an offense through a common conspiracy but who are not expressly named in a law or a precept are subject to the same penalties or to other penalties of the same or lesser severity.

§2. Accomplices who are not named in a law or in a precept incur an automatic penalty (*latae sententiae*) attached to an offense if it would not have been committed without their efforts and the penalty is of such a nature that it can punish them; otherwise, they can be punished by inflicted penalties (*ferendae sententiae*).

Thus far the discussion of imputability has focused largely on individual violators of church law. Yet at times a law may be broken by several people acting together, e.g., conspiracy to restrict legitimate church freedom or the use of church goods or to intimidate various church personnel (c. 1375).

This canon is a streamlined version of canon 2209 of the 1917 Code, which differentiated between so-called necessary (*CIC* 2209, §1–3) and secondary (*CIC* 2209, §4–7) collaborators, depending on whether or not the offense could have been committed without their involvement. Necessary collaborators were normally punished as severely as the principal offender, while secondary collaborators were punished less severely given their lesser degree of involvement.

Paragraph one on *ferendae sententiae* penalties generically indicates the different levels of imputability of the various collaborators without going into the detail of the 1917 Code. One may assume that those subject to the same or similar penalties as the principal offender are necessary collaborators, and those subject to lesser penalties are secondary collaborators. However, even so-called necessary collaborators may be somewhat exempt from imputability in virtue of the factors mentioned earlier.

Paragraph two on *latae sententiae* penalties apparently restricts its focus to principal or necessary collaborators since it refers only to those collaborators without whose help the offense could not have been committed. This seems to be another example of the law's effort to circumscribe the impact of *latae sententiae* penalties.

Declaration of Mind or Intent

Canon 1330 — An offense which consists of some declaration or of some other manifestation of will, doctrine or knowledge is not to be considered completed if no one perceives such a declaration or manifestation.

The final canon in this title deals with a relatively restricted type of offense, i.e., the situation in which the violation is not precisely the commission of some act or the omission of proper diligence but rather the expression of one's mind or intent presumably in a fashion contrary to ecclesial values. Such an expression of intent must be perceived by someone if it is to be imputable, but the law unfortunately does not clarify precisely what is meant by such a perception. Is it one person in authority receiving a false denunciation of a confessor (c. 1390) or a class listening to a lecturer espousing allegedly heterodox views (c. 1364)? The former distinction among public, occult, and notorious offenses (*CIC* 2197) having been dropped, this canon raises questions which need to be resolved in the practical working out of penal discipline.[15]

---

[15]The following offenses seem to be examples of the declaration or manifestation mentioned in this canon: heresy and other doctrinal violations (c. 1364); perjury (c. 1368); teaching of condemned doctrine (c. 1371, §1); false denunciation of confessor or calumnious damaging of the reputation of another (c. 1390).

TITLE IV
PENALTIES AND OTHER PUNISHMENTS
[cc. 1331–1340]

As noted earlier the revised Code does not describe various penalties in detail but rather simply clarifies their principal effects. This largely accounts for the significant reduction of the number of canons in this title in contrast to the 1917 Code (*CIC* 2241–2313).

CHAPTER I
CENSURES
[cc. 1331–1335]

The first chapter of the title deals with various censures, penalties depriving contumacious offenders of various ecclesiastical goods, such as the sacraments or church offices, until they cease being contumacious and are restored to full ecclesial communion. Such censures include excommunication, interdict, and suspension. The following reflections will not examine in detail differences from the 1917 Code; rather they will simply focus on key features of these penalties. In several respects the revised Code has mitigated the strictness of its 1917 predecessor.

Effects of Excommunication

Canon 1331 — §1. An excommunicated person is forbidden:
1° to have any ministerial participation in celebrating the Eucharistic Sacrifice or in any other ceremonies whatsoever of public worship;
2° to celebrate the sacraments and sacramentals and to receive the sacraments;
3° to discharge any ecclesiastical offices, ministries or functions whatsoever, or to place acts of governance.
§2. If the excommunication has been imposed or declared, the guilty party:
1° wishing to act against the prescriptions of §1, n. 1, is to be prevented from doing so or the liturgical action is to stop unless a serious cause intervenes;
2° invalidly places acts of governance which are only illicit in accord with the norms of §1, n. 3;
3° is forbidden to enjoy privileges formerly granted;
4° cannot validly acquire a dignity, office or other function in the Church;
5° cannot appropriate the revenues from any dignity, office, function or pension in the Church.

Excommunication is a censure excluding one from communion of the faithful and barring one from various aspects of the Church's public life (*CIC* 2257, §1). The 1917 Code's distinction between the excommunicated person to be avoided (*vitandus*) and the one to be tolerated (*toleratus*) (*CIC* 2258, §1) is dropped.

A key feature of the canon is its distinction between the incurring of a *latae sententiae* penalty and the formal declaration that such a penalty has been incurred. Another significant distinction is between the violation of a law to which a *ferendae sententiae* penalty is attached and the formal imposition of such a penalty. The intervention of church authority lends a certain solemnity to the situation and leads to more extensive legal restrictions than were operative before such intervention.

Some effects of excommunication are liturgical in character, e.g., prohibition of active ministerial participation in the Eucharist and other acts of public worship (§1, 1°) and prohibition of celebrating the sacraments or sacramentals or receiving the sacraments (§1, 2°). Presumably if the excommunicated individual challenges this prohibition, he or she is to be ejected from the sacred place, and the liturgical action is to be discontinued unless there is a grave reason for continuing the celebration. This would seem to be true for most liturgical celebrations; hence the realism of this part of the canon (§2, 1°) may be questioned.

The second set of restrictions pertains to the excommunicated person's role in the non-liturgical public life of the Church. Such a one may not hold various ecclesiastical offices, exercise various ministries or functions, or posit acts of governing power (§1, 3°). If a *latae sententiae* penalty has been declared or a *ferendae sententiae* penalty imposed, such acts would be invalid and not simply illicit (§2, 2°).

The third set of restrictions concerns the eligibility of the penalized individual to receive certain ecclesiastical benefits. Declaration of a *latae sententiae* penalty or imposition of a *ferendae sententiae* penalty prohibits one from the following: (a) enjoying privileges already acquired (§2, 3°); (b) validly acquiring any ecclesiastical dignity, office, or function (§2, 4°); and (c) receiving the income from any dignity, office, function, or pension one may have (§2, 5°).

The most significant issue related to excommunication during the Code revision process was whether it should bar the one penalized from all the sacraments as was the case in the 1917 Code (*CIC* 2260, §1). The original schema would have permitted the excommunicated (or interdicted) individual to receive penance and anointing even before remission of the penalty. Presumably this was an effort to differentiate sharply between the external and internal fora. The external forum, or the arena of the Church's public life, was viewed as the main focus of the Church's penal discipline. In certain conflict situations, however, an individual was to be permit-

ted access to sacramental confession for peace of conscience even prior to formal remission of the penalty in the public forum.

There was sharp criticism of the innovation, especially in German circles;[16] and subsequently a special meeting of the Code Commission in May 1977 voted to restore the 1917 Code prohibition on receiving any sacraments. Apparently it was felt that the original schema failed to take adequate cognizance of the interrelationship between excommunication and the sacrament of penance as well as the conciliar teaching on the implications of penance for reconciliation with the Church. It seemed incongruous that a person could be absolved of sins and yet still be subject to a censure indicating lack of full communion with the Church.[17]

Effects of Interdict

Canon 1332 — An interdicted person is bound by the prohibitions of can. 1331, §1, nn. 1 and 2; if, however, the interdict has been imposed or declared, the prescription of can. 1331, §2, n. 1, is to be observed.

The notion of interdict is somewhat simplified when compared to the 1917 Code, which spoke of personal or local interdicts, depending on whether the penalty affected individuals or a group of believers directly or indirectly through their living in a certain territory (*CIC* 2268). In fact, at times, even individuals not technically guilty of an offense might have been deprived of certain ecclesial goods, such as access to various church services. An interdict differed from an excommunication in that it did not deprive the faithful of communion with the Church although many of its effects were similar.

The revised Code drops any reference to local interdict and makes no mention of an interdict inflicted upon a collective body (*CIC* 2274). This reflects a concern that penalties not be inflicted on the guilty and innocent indiscriminately. Some canonists had suggested that interdicts be dropped entirely since only the personal interdict remains and its effects are largely the same as excommunication. Nevertheless, the penal law committee chose to retain this legal institute.

Practically speaking, the difference between excommunication and interdict is that the latter forbids only certain liturgical activities but does not affect any governmental functions or personal prerogatives, such as privileges or eligibility for various offices.

[16]Scheuermann, 17–20; K. Moersdorf, "Zum Problem der Excommunikation. Bemerkungen zum Schema Documenti quo disciplina sanctionum seu poenarum in Ecclesia denuo ordinatur," *AkK* 143 (1974), 64–68.
[17]*Comm* 9 (1977), 80–81.

Effects of Suspension

Canon 1333 — §1. A suspension, which can affect clerics alone, forbids:
 1° either all or some acts of the power of orders;
 2° either all or some acts of the power of governance;
 3° the exercise of either all or some rights or functions which are attached to an office.
 §2. It can be stated in a law or a precept that a suspended cleric cannot validly place acts of governance after a condemnatory or declaratory sentence.
 §3. A prohibition never affects:
 1° the offices or the power of governance which are not subject to the power of the superior who establishes the penalty;
 2° the right to a dwelling place which the accused may have by reason of his office;
 3° the right to administer goods which may pertain to the office of the suspended cleric himself if the penalty is an automatic one (*latae sententiae*).
 §4. A suspension forbidding one to collect revenues, stipends, pensions or any other such thing carries with it an obligation to make restitution for anything illegitimately collected even in good faith.

Contrary to excommunication and interdict, which all believers may incur, suspension is incurred only by clerics and restricts their liturgical and governmental functioning. This penalty also differs from the preceding ones in that its effects are separable. A suspension is to be determined in the law or precept that establishes a *latae sententiae* censure or in the sentence or decree that inflicts a *ferendae sententiae* censure (c. 1334, §1).[18]

This initial canon on suspension simplifies the 1917 Code (*CIC* 2278–2285). It differentiates between prohibitions of the exercise of the power of government, e.g., deciding a marriage case, and of the exercise of various rights or responsibilities related to a given office, e.g., rights and duties of pastors in canons 528–538 (§1).

After some discussion the penal law committee incorporated a separate paragraph providing for the invalidity of governmental acts of the suspended cleric. However, such an invalidating effect presupposes an official ecclesiastical intervention through judicial sentence or administrative decree (§2; *CIC* 2284).

The legislator's effort to circumscribe the effects of suspension is clear in paragraph three, which limits the power of ecclesiastical superiors to penal-

ize clerics. Particular law suspensions, unlike those specified in the revised Code, can affect only those offices or aspects of the power of government which are under the authority of the penalizing superior. Hence if a cleric were to have an office in a diocese other than his own, he could still exercise it even if he were suspended in his own diocese—in virtue of particular law (§3, 1°).

Another protection of the suspended cleric is the provision that he still enjoy the right of residence connected with his office, e.g., the suspended pastor living in a rectory (§3, 2°). If the suspension were *latae sententiae,* he would also enjoy the right of administering the goods pertaining to his office, e.g., parish property (§3, 3°).

Justice requires that if the suspended cleric has profited illegitimately from the income related to his office, he is to make restitution even if he acted in good faith (§4).

Scope of Suspension

Canon 1334 — §1. Within the limits stated in the preceding canon, the extent of the suspension is defined by the law or precept itself or by the sentence or decree by which it is imposed.
 §2. A law but not a precept can establish an automatic suspension (*latae sententiae*) without any further determination or limitation; such a penalty has all the effects enumerated in can. 1333, §1.

The exact scope of the suspension is to be determined in the law or precept or in the infliction of the penalty (§1). The legislator's caution regarding an indiscriminate use of a general suspension seems evident in paragraph two. Only the law (universal or particular)—but not a precept—may establish a general suspension *latae sententiae* with all the effects specified in canon 1333.

Suspension of Prohibition

Canon 1335 — If a censure prohibits the celebration of the sacraments or sacramentals or the placing of an act of governance, the prohibition is suspended whenever it is necessary to take care of the faithful who are in danger of death; and if an automatic censure (*latae sententiae*) is not a declared one, the prohibition is also suspended whenever a member of the faithful requests a sacrament, a sacramental or act of governance; this request can be made for any just cause whatsoever.

The need to protect a penalized cleric's reputation and to provide for the pastoral welfare of the faithful, especially in extreme situations, underlies this provision which suspends the liturgical-governmental prohibitions affecting the censured (not simply suspended) cleric. Once again the degree of formal ecclesiastical involvement in the incurring of

---

[18]An example of a generalized suspension with all the effects specified in c. 1333 is c. 1394, §1, which penalizes clerics attempting even a civil marriage. An example of a more limited suspension is c. 1383, which prohibits a bishop who ordains without proper dimissorials from conferring the order in question for a year.

the penalty is significant as regards the types of situations in which the censured cleric can function.

In a danger-of-death situation, there are no ministerial restrictions on the censured cleric, no matter whether the censure is *latae sententiae* or *ferendae sententiae*. Outside of this extreme situation, the same ministerial options are available only to the cleric who has incurred a *latae sententiae* censure which has not been declared. On the contrary the legislator restricts the cleric who has incurred either a declared *latae sententiae* censure or a *ferendae sententiae* censure. He may not minister to the faithful seeking a sacrament, sacramental, or act of the power of government for a just reason. If he attempts to do so, acts of the power of orders are valid but illicit. Furthermore, acts of the power of government are valid or not, depending on whether or not the declaratory or condemnatory sentence has specifically provided for such an invalidating effect. This is another example of the less stringent legal effects of the non-declared *latae sententiae* penalty as distinct from a declared *latae sententiae* or a *ferendae sententiae* penalty (*CIC* 2261; 2284).

CHAPTER II
EXPIATORY PENALTIES
[cc. 1336–1338]

Despite the criticism that such penalties seem overly punitive and inadequately pastoral in orientation, the revised Code maintains so-called expiatory (formerly vindictive) penalties. While the spiritual well-being of the offender is certainly envisioned by such penalties, there is more of an emphasis here than in censures on remedying the damage done to societal values by the offense and also on deterring other members of the community from similar behavior. Besides these differences in orientation between censures and expiatory penalties, the remission of the latter does not depend merely on the cessation of contumacy by the offender as is true in the case of the former. Hence such penalties may be inflicted forever, indefinitely, or for a definite period of time. Censures, however, can be inflicted only indefinitely, i.e., until the offender has a change of heart and no longer manifests an anti-ecclesial attitude.

Various Expiatory Penalties

Canon 1336 — §1. Besides other penalties which the law may establish, the following are expiatory penalties which can punish an offender in perpetuity, for a prescribed time or for an indeterminate time:

1° a prohibition or an order concerning living in a certain place or territory;

2° deprivation of power, office, function, right, privilege, faculty, favor, title or insignia, even merely honorary;

3° a prohibition against exercising those things mentioned in n. 2 or a prohibition against exercising them in a certain place or outside a certain place; which prohibitions are never under pain of nullity;

4° a penal transfer to another office;

5° dismissal from the clerical state.[19]

§2. The only expiatory penalties which can be automatic (*latae sententiae*) are those enumerated in §1, n. 3.

The list of expiatory penalties in paragraph one of this canon is not exhaustive. They are taken largely from the list of specifically clerical (as distinct from common) vindictive penalties in the 1917 Code (*CIC* 2298). However, in light of post-conciliar developments that permit laity to hold certain ecclesiastical offices not requiring sacred orders (c. 129, §2), such penalties need not be viewed as exclusively clerical in the future. The list is not exhaustive in order to permit infra-universal legislators to determine particular expiatory penalties corresponding to the mores and circumstances of various regions.

The legislator's desire to restrict the scope of *latae sententiae* penalties is evident in paragraph two, which permits only the prohibitions of paragraph one, number three to be used as *latae sententiae* penalties. And even in this case, such prohibitions do not invalidate acts performed in violation of such restrictions. Apparently, if the offense were serious enough, the appropriate course of action would be to deprive the individual of the power, office, function, etc., as in paragraph one, number two.

Territorial Restrictions

Canon 1337 — §1. A prohibition against living in a certain place or territory can affect either clerics or religious; an order to live in a certain place or territory, however, can affect secular clerics and religious within the limits of their constitutions.

§2. An order to live in a certain place or territory requires the consent of the ordinary of that place unless it is a question of a house of penance or correction set aside also for clerics from outside that diocese.

The next two canons specify the implications of certain penalties in canon 1336. The first penalty, which involves a prohibited or prescribed residence, has had a lengthy history, but it has been significantly modified in modern times due to the notable changes in Church-State relationships and the di-

---

[19] See Table 6 at the end of this commentary on Book VI. See also cc. 290–293 on the loss of the clerical state.

minished ability of church authorities to control the movements of clerics and religious. Accordingly it is questionable how realistic this penalty is for clerics and religious today. The canon restates the 1917 Code's requirement that the local ordinary approve a penalty requiring a cleric to live in a certain territory unless it is a house especially established to reintegrate clerics into the active ministry (*CIC* 2301). Interestingly enough the 1917 Code's caution about employing such a penalty only in very serious cases is not restated (*CIC* 2302). Here the 1917 Code seems more adequate than the revised law in protecting the rights of clerics.

Limitations on Prohibitions

Canon 1338 — §1. The deprivations and prohibitions enumerated in can. 1336, §1, nn. 2 and 3, never affect the powers, offices, functions, rights, privileges, faculties, favors, titles or insignia which are not subject to the power of the superior who establishes the penalty.

§2. There is no such penalty as deprivation of the power of orders, but only the prohibition against exercising it or some acts of orders; there is likewise no such penalty as a deprivation of academic degrees.

§3. The prohibitions listed in can. 1336, §1, n. 3, are to be regulated by the norm given in can. 1335 concerning censures.

The legislator's concern to limit the force of certain penalties is clear here. Paragraph one, like canon 1333, §3, 1° on suspension, clearly states that only those powers and offices subject to the authority of the penalizing superior are affected by the penalty.

Paragraph two reaffirms the theological principle that once the radical power of orders has been conferred it cannot be taken away; only its exercise may be limited. Furthermore, there is also a certain irrevocability about the granting of an academic degree—incongruous as it may seem to discuss this in the same canon as sacred orders.

Finally paragraph three reflects the legislator's concern for the spiritual welfare of the faithful and the reputation of a penalized cleric by suspending the expiatory sacramental and governmental prohibitions on such a cleric in various situations of pastoral need—as was also true for censures (c. 1335).

CHAPTER III
PENAL REMEDIES AND PENANCES
[cc. 1339–1340]

Only relatively brief consideration need be given to these quasi-penal institutes, which serve either to preclude possible offenses or to deal with situations in which an ordinary penalty is not warranted (i.e.,

if it is a case of diminished imputability or if an additional corrective measure is called for even after a penalty has been remitted).

Penal Remedies

Canon 1339 — §1. An ordinary can admonish personally or through another person one who is in the proximate occasion of committing an offense or upon whom, after an investigation has been made, there has fallen a serious suspicion of having committed an offense.

§2. An ordinary can likewise rebuke a person from whose behavior there arises scandal or serious disturbance of order in a manner accommodated to the special conditions of the person and the deed.

§3. Proof of admonishment and of rebuke must always be retained, at least by some document which is preserved in the secret archive of the curia.

The revised Code speaks only of warning and rebuke as penal remedies and drops precept and surveillance from the 1917 Code's list (*CIC* 2306). The warning may be appropriate if a person is in the proximate occasion of committing an offense or if an investigation raises grave suspicion about an offense's having been committed (§1). A rebuke may be called for if an individual's behavior causes scandal or gravely disturbs the ecclesial order even though there is technically no offense (§2). The need to prove that these legal-pastoral steps have been taken accounts for the requirement that they be recorded in the secret curial archives (§3).

This is a rather delicate issue. Hence every effort should be made to ensure that a careful investigation is made of an alleged breach of ecclesial order and that the rights of the alleged offender are duly protected, especially the right to a good name in the community. This is true even given the right of the community to protect itself against serious violations of its integrity.

Penances

Canon 1340 — §1. A penance, which can be imposed in the external forum, is some work of religion, piety or charity to be performed.

§2. A public penance is never to be imposed for an occult transgression.

§3. An ordinary can prudently attach penances to the penal remedy of admonishment or of rebuke.

The 1917 Code listed in detail external forum penances (as distinct from the penance imposed by the confessor in the sacrament of reconciliation) (*CIC* 2313, §1). However, this canon speaks simply of a work of religion, piety, or charity without indicating its purpose (§1).

Such external forum penances are presumably

imposed to preclude a penalty's being inflicted or to complete the steps necessary for its remission (*CIC* 2312, §1). There should be a proportion between the penance and the transgression (*CIC* 2312, §3); therefore, no public penance may be imposed for an occult transgression (§2).[20] Where appropriate, penances, such as prayers, fasting, or almsgiving, may be added to the above-mentioned penal remedies (§3).

TITLE V
THE APPLICATION OF PENALTIES
[cc. 1341–1353]

This title is particularly significant since it expresses some fundamental principles regarding a judicious pastoral approach to the declaration or infliction of penalties. It is not enough for the judge or superior to determine only that an offense has been committed before penalizing someone; rather he must weigh carefully the relevant factors that put the offense in perspective, e.g., factors affecting imputability. At times these factors may suggest that a penalty not be inflicted or that a lesser one than that specified in law be imposed. At certain times the damage done to the Church's mission may suggest that a heavier penalty than that specified in law be inflicted.

Penalties as Last Resort

Canon 1341 — Only after he has ascertained that scandal cannot sufficiently be repaired, that justice cannot sufficiently be restored and that the accused cannot sufficiently be reformed by fraternal correction, rebuke and other ways of pastoral care is the ordinary then to provide for a judicial or administrative procedure to impose or to declare penalties.

This canon should be read together with the next one to gain a proper perspective on the appropriate procedure to be used in dealing with various penal situations. The canon reflects a principal concern underlying penal law reform: penalties should be employed only as a last resort after all other pastoral measures have failed to deal with a problematic situation. Hence church authorities should not be too swift to impose penalties; rather they should use all available legal-pastoral options before imposing penalties. This canon indicates briefly how the legislator views the finalities of penal discipline: the restoration of justice, the reparation of scandal, and the reformation of the offender (*CIC* 2214, §2). The first two seem more properly related to expiatory penalties while the last one falls more properly within the purview of censures.

Another noteworthy point in this canon and the following one is the emphasis on the discretion of the ordinary or superior (usually but not always the bishop). He has a certain latitude in determining not only whether or not there will be a penal procedure but also whether an administrative or judicial procedure is to be used. This latter type of discretion is qualified, however, by the next canon's emphasis on judicial procedure.

Procedure To Be Used

Canon 1342 — §1. As often as just causes preclude a judicial process a penalty can be imposed or declared by an extra-judicial decree; penal remedies and penances, however, can be applied by a decree in any case whatsoever.

§2. Perpetual penalties cannot be imposed or declared by a decree; neither can penalties be so applied when the law or the precept which established them forbids their application by a decree.

§3. What is said in a law or a precept concerning a judge's imposing or declaring a penalty in a trial is to be applied to a superior who would impose or declare a penalty by means of an extra-judicial decree, unless the contrary is evident or unless it is a question of prescriptions which deal only with procedural matters.

One of the most perplexing questions in the 1917 Code was determining precisely when one had to proceed judicially and when one could proceed administratively in the declaration and infliction of penalties. Two pertinent texts were canon 1933 at the beginning of the section on the criminal process in Book IV on procedural law and canon 2225 in the section on the competent penal authority in Book V on penal law. Canonists disputed the relationship of canons 1933 and 2225 and disagreed about the freedom of superiors to proceed administratively. This issue is extremely complex, and a detailed discussion of the various canonical opinions would serve no useful purpose here. Suffice it to note that, in practice, penalties have generally been declared or inflicted administratively (or by way of precept) without any special formalities—according to the discretion of the competent penal authority. This was true unless the 1917 Code specified a formal judicial process, e.g., degradation of a cleric (*CIC* 2305, §1; 1576, §1, 2°), or an administrative process requiring certain formalities, e.g., penal action against non-resident clerics (*CIC* 2168–2175).[21]

The revised Code resolves this issue to a certain extent while leaving ample room for the discretion of the competent penal superior.

The legislator's preference for judicial procedure is affirmed implicitly in paragraph one, which requires due cause if judicial procedure is to be

---

[20]On the public-occult distinction regarding offenses in the 1917 Code, see *CIC* 2197.

[21]For a brief discussion of this issue, see Bouscaren, 876–879.

waived. The reasons for not utilizing judicial procedure are not indicated.[22] However, one might envision a need to proceed expeditiously in certain particularly scandalous situations, e.g., especially serious violations of discipline of religious community. Furthermore, at times, the tribunal staff may be unduly burdened with marriage cases and hence ill-equipped to conduct a formal judicial procedure.

It is not indicated explicitly who decides that such reasons exist, but it would probably be the competent penal superior mentioned in the preceding canon. The canon does not expressly require consultation before such a decision is made; however, in such a serious matter, consultation—at least with the officialis or some other significant diocesan official—seems appropriate.

Paragraph one states also that penal remedies or penances may always be applied by decree or administratively. Since they do not have especially weighty consequences, the formalities of judicial procedure need not necessarily be employed.

On the contrary, the most serious penalties, those of a perpetual or irrevocable character, can be declared or imposed only through a formal judicial procedure (§2). There is a proportion between the seriousness of the penalty, e.g., dismissal from the clerical state, and the seriousness of the procedure declaring or inflicting it. When the consequences of a penalty are so weighty, every effort should be made to provide maximal legal protection for the accused, e.g., services of advocate, access to all relevant documentation for self-defense purposes, possible appeal of adverse decision to higher court. Furthermore, a law or precept which establishes a penalty may state that it must be declared or inflicted judicially.

Paragraph three states a general principle of equivalence between a judge and a superior (ordinary)[23] relative to the subsequent canons on the declaration or infliction of penalties. The judge is the key decisional figure in judicial procedure, and the Ordinary is the key person in administrative procedure. This principle of equivalence is particularly relevant to the broad discretion enjoyed by the one presiding over the penal procedure. Generally speaking, when the canons refer to the judge, they can be applied to the ordinary as well—unless strictly judicial procedure is clearly envisioned.

Facultative Penalties

Canon 1343 — **If a law or a precept gives the judge the power to apply or not to apply a penalty, the judge can also temper the penalty or impose a**

penance in its place in accord with his own conscience and prudence.

Numerous canons in this title stress the prudent discretion of the judge or ordinary in the declaration or infliction of penalties. Apparently this discretion is viewed as a particularly appropriate way of realizing the law's pastoral finalities and dealing sensitively with the specifics of each case.

This canon states that if a given penalty is facultative, or discretionary, e.g., canon 1391 on falsification of ecclesiastical documents, the judge or ordinary may lighten the penalty if one is indicated in law, or he may also substitute a penance. Generally speaking, these are instances of relatively less significant offenses. Normally more serious offenses, such as teaching a condemned doctrine, imply a preceptive, or obligatory, penalty (just penalty—c. 1371, §1). In those instances the judge or ordinary must impose some penalty if the offense is clearly imputable.

Preceptive Penalties

Canon 1344 — **Although a law may employ preceptive words, the judge in accord with his own conscience and prudence can:**

1° postpone to a more opportune time the infliction of a penalty if it is foreseen that greater evils will occur from an overly prompt punishment of the accused;

2° refrain from imposing a penalty, or impose a lighter penalty, or employ a penance if the accused has reformed and scandal has been repaired, or if the accused has been or, it is foreseen, will be sufficiently punished by civil authority;

3° suspend the obligation to observe an expiatory penalty if it was the person's first offense after having led a praiseworthy life and if the need to repair scandal is not pressing; in such a situation, however, if the accused should again commit an offense within the time period set by the judge, the person is to pay the penalty required for both offenses unless, in the interim, time had run out for initiating a penal action for the first offense.

Even if a penalty must be imposed for a stated offense, there is still ample room for judicial or administrative discretion. The infliction of the specified penalty may be deferred if its prompt imposition would cause more problems than a prudent delay, e.g., notable scandal of faithful if their pastor were penalized (1°).

Another option is comparable to the preceding canon: a penalty may be tempered (e.g., a suspension from preaching in a given church instead of a total suspension), or perhaps no penalty at all need be imposed (2°). Here the twin values of reforming

---

[22]For a discussion of this issue by the penal law committee, see *Comm* 9 (1977), 161–162.

[23]Henceforth the author will use only the term "ordinary" to describe the key figure in administrative penal procedure.

the offender and dealing forcefully with any potential scandal must be weighed carefully.

The possible civil law implications of an ecclesiastical offense must be considered as well, however unlikely it would be today that church offenses would have civil law ramifications.[24] Has the individual been punished by civil law in view of repairing the damage done to the larger society by the offense? If such a person has been duly punished, it may be inappropriate for the Church to add its own distinctive penalty even given the different penal finalities of Church and State. In brief the legislator attempts to prevent the penal system from being overly vindictive and overwhelming the offender rather than fostering reconciliation with the Church.

Finally the canon deals with the effects of expiatory penalties on first offenders (3°). The authority figure in question may suspend the obligation of observing such a penalty, provided there is no serious scandal. A concern for the well-being of the offender outweighs the institutional interest in repairing damage done to the public order (*CIC* 2288). However, this section of the canon is provisional in character since it provides for penalizing the offender should another offense be committed during a probationary period specified by church authority. The offender is liable to be penalized for both offenses unless the statute of limitations has run out as regards the first offense.

Waiving of Penalty

Canon 1345 — As often as the offender had only an imperfect use of reason or committed the offense from fear or necessity or in the heat of passion or in drunkenness or another similar mental disturbance, the judge can also abstain from inflicting any penalty if he judges that reform can be better provided for otherwise.

This canon on judicial or administrative discretion in dealing with offenders whose imputability is notably diminished is similar to canons 1323–1324 in title III on those subject to penal sanctions. However, it views the issue from the standpoint of the judge or ordinary rather than that of the offender. The judge or ordinary may abstain from imposing a penalty if the offender's rehabilitation could better be provided for otherwise. In other words, in some instances pastoral counseling and help might be more in accord with the Church's reconciling nature than legal privations and disabilities.

Multiple Offenses

Canon 1346 — Whenever the accused has committed several offenses, it is left to the prudent determination of the judge to moderate the penalties within equitable limits if the cumulative burden of the inflicted (*ferendae sententiae*) penalties appears excessive.

It normally makes little sense pastorally to overwhelm the penalized individual with various penalties even though they may be warranted according to the strict letter of the law when numerous offenses have been committed. In other words, a benign interpretation of penal law calls for an equitable infliction of penalties transcending a purely mathematical yet insufficiently pastoral approach to this issue.

Conditions for a Censure

Canon 1347 — §1. A censure cannot be imposed validly unless the accused has been warned at least once in advance that he or she should withdraw from contumacy and be given a suitable time for repentance.

§2. The guilty party is to be said to have withdrawn from contumacy when he or she has truly repented the offense and furthermore has made suitable reparation for damages and scandal or at least has seriously promised to do so.

This canon on the conditions for inflicting censures should be read in conjunction with canons 1331–1335 on specific censures. It illustrates a key feature of this type of penalty: the requirement that the offender be warned to cease from his or her contumacy within a certain period of time.[25] Only when such contumacy, or contempt of church authority, is clear can such a penalty be validly inflicted. On the contrary no such warning need be given for expiatory penalties to be inflicted. The canon also indicates the criteria for determining when such contumacy has ceased: genuine repentance for the offense and an effort, or at least a serious promise, to repair the damage or scandal caused by the offense, e.g., making a public retraction in cases in which another's reputation has been damaged (c. 1390, §2), or an effort to cope with severe financial losses experienced by a community due to illegal alienation of church property (c. 1377).

The determination whether contumacy has ceased is left to the ordinary who is competent to decide whether there should be a penal procedure at all (c. 1341).

---

[24] Among the ecclesiastical offenses which might have civil ramifications are the following: violence against ecclesiastical figures (c. 1370); sexual offenses of clerics (c. 1395); homicide, abduction, mutilation, or bodily assault (c. 1397); abortion in situations in which it is civilly prohibited (c. 1398).

[25] This requirement of a warning applies only to *ferendae sententiae* censures. In *latae sententiae* censures the warning is presumably contained in the law itself which threatens the penalty.

Other Penal Options

Canon 1348 — When the accused is acquitted of the charge or when no penalty is otherwise imposed on the accused, the ordinary can provide for the public good and for the person's own good by means of appropriate admonitions and other ways of pastoral care or even through penal remedies, if circumstances warrant it.

The issue of administrative discretion surfaces again here. There may be situations in which the penal procedure ends with the judgment that the charges against an individual are unfounded. At other times no penalty may be imposed because of diminished imputability. However, institutional or personal pastoral considerations may suggest warning the individual or imposing some corrective measure. In other words the fact that no penalty technically is incurred does not necessarily mean that all is in order ecclesially or personally. Such measures, however, should be taken by the ordinary (not the judge) only with special caution lest the rights of the alleged offender be violated.

Judicious Application of Penalties

Canon 1349 — If the penalty is indeterminate and the law does not provide otherwise, the judge is not to impose heavier penalties, especially censures, unless the seriousness of the case clearly demands it; he cannot, however, impose perpetual penalties.

While judicial or administrative discretion is stressed throughout this title, this canon introduces a helpful caution as well as a restriction on such discretion. When the law specifies a possible penalty in indeterminate terms, e.g., a just penalty is to be imposed for illegal *communicatio in sacris* (c. 1365), the judge or ordinary is to refrain from imposing heavy penalties, such as censures, unless it is a really serious matter. Normally the legislator does not view a given breach of law quite as seriously as other violations if the corresponding penalty is formulated in indeterminate terms. Furthermore, in such a situation perpetual penalties may not be inflicted. Given their irrevocable implications, they must be specified precisely by the legislator as an appropriate way for the community to respond to the most serious breaches of its order.

Support of Penalized Cleric

Canon 1350 — §1. Unless it is a question of dismissal from the clerical state, when penalties are imposed upon a cleric provision must always be made that he does not lack those things which are necessary for his decent support.
§2. In the best manner possible the ordinary is to see to the care of a person dismissed from the clerical state who is truly in need due to the penalty.

The institutional responsibility to support the penalized yet non-dismissed cleric is reaffirmed, even if it is done in somewhat negative terms (§1). While the original schema had referred only to those clerics subject to expiatory penalties and not to those under censure, the law here makes no such distinction. Even though the cleric has seriously violated the law, his basic right to appropriate support can apparently still be exercised (c. 281). Only formal dismissal from the clerical state technically extinguishes such a right. However, contrary to the 1917 Code (*CIC* 2304, §2), even the dismissed cleric is not viewed as totally beyond the ordinary's pastoral care. The latter is encouraged to provide as best he can for the dismissed cleric who is truly needy as a result of the penalty (§2).

Territorial Scope of Penalty

Canon 1351 — Unless express provision is made otherwise, a penalty binds the guilty party everywhere, even when the authority of the one who established or imposed the penalty has lapsed.

The comprehensive territorial scope of a penalty is clear from this canon, which notes the universally binding force of a penalty even if the ecclesiastical authority that established or inflicted it has ceased functioning in that capacity (*CIC* 2226, §4). This is the general rule; however, the law or precept might provide otherwise, e.g., cessation of penalty at death of ordinary who inflicted it, or limitation of suspension of cleric to a certain area where there might be legitimate scandal if he performed ministerial functions.

Observance of Penalty Suspended

Canon 1352 — §1. If a penalty prohibits the reception of the sacraments or sacramentals, the prohibition is suspended as long as the guilty party is in danger of death.
§2. The obligation to observe an automatic penalty (*latae sententiae*) which has not been declared and which is not notorious in the place where the offender is living is totally or partially suspended to the extent that the person cannot observe it without danger of serious scandal or infamy.

Like its predecessors this canon deals with the practical impact of a penalty on the penalized individual; yet it specifically addresses two particularly urgent situations in which the observance of a penalty might significantly harm an individual. The canon does not deal with the remission of a penalty; rather it concerns only the observance of the full force of the penalty in two critical situations: danger of death or danger of infamy or scandal.

Under certain conditions the personal spiritual needs of the individual offender prevail over considerations of good public order. As noted earlier certain penalties such as excommunication (c. 1331, §1, 2°) and interdict (c. 1332) forbid the reception of the sacraments. Paragraph one provides for reception of the sacraments by the excommunicated or interdicted person by suspending the prohibition in a danger-of-death situation (see *CIC* 2252). However, this does not change the irregular legal status of the penalized person, who still must have the penalty remitted if he or she survives the life-threatening situation. The only exception to this rule would be the confessor's prerogative to remit non-declared *latae sententiae* penalties in urgent cases (c. 1357).

Paragraph two deals with the problems that an individual or a community might experience if certain penalties were observed, e.g., personal infamy or grave scandal for the community. This might happen in a situation in which the original offense of a cleric was an occult one known only to a few persons, e.g., violation of the seal of confession (c. 1388, §1). Observance of the penalty would prevent him from performing certain spiritual functions for a particular community, such as a parish. This could possibly cause him unwarranted personal pain and unduly scandalize the community. Although the original formulation of this canon was fairly broad in the kinds of penalties it envisioned, criticism from various sources led to a reworking of the text, which limits such non-observance of penalties by offenders to non-declared *latae sententiae* penalties. Presumably in the case of both declared *latae sententiae* and *ferendae sententiae* penalties, the appropriate penal authority would have taken cognizance of the offender's existential situation so that recourse to this extraordinary measure of non-observance would be unnecessary.

Recourse against Penalty

Canon 1353 — **An appeal or recourse from judicial sentences or from decrees which impose or declare any penalty whatsoever has a suspensive effect.**

The final canon in this title notably modifies the 1917 Code in its broad provisions for the suspensive effect of recourse or appeal against all penalties. In the 1917 Code recourse against decrees that inflicted censures or appeals from sentences that inflicted them were without suspensive effect (*in devolutivo*). Hence the penalty had to be observed immediately pending the outcome of the recourse or appeal (*CIC* 2243). On the contrary, decrees or sentences that inflicted vindictive penalties admitted of recourse or appeal with suspensive effect (*in suspen-*

sivo). Hence they did not have to be observed pending the outcome of the recourse or appeal (*CIC* 2287).

This canon, however, states that such a suspensive effect is henceforth operative for both censures and expiatory penalties. This change reflects more adequately than the 1917 Code that benign interpretation of law that is a key principle of interpretation in the penal order. It embodies the legislator's emphasis on fostering the pastoral finalities of penal law and on respecting the dignity and basic rights of the offender. One of those basic rights is taking recourse against an adverse administrative decision or appealing an adverse penal sentence. Furthermore, the alleged offender's status in the community should normally not be jeopardized until the original decree or sentence has been confirmed by higher authority.

TITLE VI
THE CESSATION OF PENALTIES
[cc. 1354–1363]

Initially a terminological change might be noted. The 1917 Code spoke of the "absolution" of a censure and of the "dispensation" from a vindictive penalty (*CIC* 2236, §1). This was an example of the lack of terminological uniformity in the 1917 Code where "absolution" also designated the forgiveness of sins in sacramental confession, e.g., *CIC* 872, and "dispensation" also meant the relaxation of the law in a particular case (*CIC* 80). The revised law uses only the generic term "remission" for all types of penalties.

Power of Remitting Penalties

Canon 1354 — **§1. Besides the persons enumerated in cann. 1355-1356, all who can dispense from a law which includes a penalty and all who can exempt one from a precept which threatens a penalty can also remit that penalty.**

§2. Furthermore, a law or a precept which establishes a penalty can also give the power of remission to other persons.

§3. If the Apostolic See reserves to itself or to another the remission of a penalty, such a reservation is to be interpreted strictly.

This title should be read in conjunction with title II on the penal law or precept since there is a close connection between the one who can establish a penalty and the one who can remit it. This is because the penalty is viewed as an integral part of the law itself (§1). Furthermore, the 1983 law speaks of a parity between those who can dispense from a law or precept that threatens a penalty and those who can remit a penalty. Remission of a penalty is viewed as an act of executive power like a dispensation (c. 85).

Paragraph two indicates that a penal law or precept may permit broader remission options than specified in the prior paragraph. However, a broad delegation of remission power has not been fairly common in the past—given the seriousness of penal discipline.

Contrary to the 1917 Code (*CIC* 2236, §3), nothing is stated explicitly about the impossibility of judges' remitting penalties. However, the penal authority of those who are simply judges, e.g., officialis, and not ordinaries, e.g., diocesan bishop, is rather limited. The former who exercise only judicial authority may only apply an established penal law or precept. Once they have applied the law, their office ceases. This is another example of the fairly strict judicial-administrative authority differentiation in canon law.

One of the most perplexing institutes in the 1917 Code was the reservation of the remission of certain censures to the Holy See, the bishop, or some other authority (*CIC* 2245). This meant that only the Holy See, a bishop, or a duly authorized cleric could remit a given censure. The reservation emphasized the gravity of certain offenses, somewhat comparable to the institute of reserved sins (*CIC* 893–900), which is dropped in the revised Code. Unfortunately, the institute of reserved censures tended to make penal discipline overly complex and burdensome, especially for confessors.

Paragraph three of the canon reaffirms the Holy See's right to reserve the remission of certain penalties to itself or to another authority. However, this institute is significantly restricted in the revised law. No penalties are reserved to the bishop, and only five penalties are reserved to the Holy See: canon 1367 (violation of sacred species); canon 1370, §1 (physical attack on pope); canon 1378, §1 (absolution of accomplice); canon 1382 (unauthorized episcopal consecration); and canon 1388, §1 (direct violation of confessional seal by confessor). Hence the concerns of those seeking penal law simplification have largely been responded to.

Remitting Penalties Established by Law

Canon 1355 — §1. Unless it is reserved to the Apostolic See, the following can remit an imposed or declared penalty established by law:

1° the ordinary who set in motion the trial in order to impose or declare the penalty or who imposed or declared it by decree personally or through another;

2° the ordinary of the place where the offender lives, after consulting with the ordinary mentioned in n. 1, unless this is impossible due to extraordinary circumstances.

§2. Unless it is reserved to the Apostolic See an ordinary can remit an automatic (*latae sententiae*) penalty established by law but not declared for his own subjects and those who are living in his terri-tory or who committed an offense there; any bishop, however, can also do this in the act of sacramental confession.

This canon and the next one reflect the enhanced post-conciliar legal-pastoral authority of bishops. Contrary to the limitations on episcopal remitting of penalties in the 1917 Code (*CIC* 2237), the revised law provides fairly broad options, especially for the ordinary where the offender lives as distinct from the ordinary who declared or inflicted the penalty originally. These broader penalty-remitting options presumably take cognizance of increased societal mobility; however, the canon also refers generically to situations in which penalties may be reserved to the Holy See.

Paragraph one of the canon deals with declared *latae sententiae* and *ferendae sententiae* penalties. The penalty-remitting options are somewhat more restricted in scope than in paragraph two. Both the penalizing ordinary and the offender's ordinary of residence may remit penalties. Yet the latter should contact the former before remitting the penalty; only extraordinary circumstances would exempt one from this obligation. Presumably the ordinary who declared or inflicted the penalty can inform the other ordinary of the circumstances surrounding its declaration or infliction. A knowledgeable remission of a penalty normally presupposes access to such information.

Paragraph two of the canon deals with the non-declared, non-reserved *latae sententiae* penalty. Remitting options are broader here than in paragraph one, presumably since no authority figure has been directly involved in the case, prescinding from the legislator's establishing the penalty. The focus is on the power of the ordinary vis-à-vis his subjects, those who happen to be in his territory, and those who committed an offense in that territory.

Futhermore, any bishop (not ordinary) may remit such penalties, yet only in sacramental confession. The rationale for introducing an exceptional internal forum dimension in the otherwise external forum penalty-remitting process is not entirely clear, although it parallels the penalty-remitting power of confessors in canon 1357.

Remitting Penalties Established by Precept

Canon 1356 — §1. The following can remit an inflicted (*ferendae sententiae*) or automatic (*latae sententiae*) penalty established by a precept not issued by the Holy See:

1° the ordinary of the place where the offender lives;

2° if the penalty has been imposed or declared, the ordinary who set in motion the trial in order to impose or declare the penalty or who imposed or declared it by decree personally or through another.

§2. Before such a remission occurs, the author of the precept is to be consulted unless this is impossible due to extraordinary circumstances.

Contrary to the more generalized situation of a penal law in canon 1355, this text deals with the more individualized penal precept issued by an ecclesiastical superior other than the Holy See. The provisions for remitting such a penalty are not quite as broad as in the preceding canon. No reference is made to internal forum remissions, and the canon does not differentiate between the declared and non-declared *latae sententiae* penalty.

Both the ordinary of the place where the offender is living and the ordinary who imposed or declared the penalty can remit it (§1). However, the need to be cognizant of the circumstances surrounding the issuing of the penal precept underlies the requirement that its author be consulted before remission of the penalty, unless for some extraordinary reason this is impossible (§2). As in canon 1355, a heavy burden of consultation is placed on the one remitting a penalty if he had not inflicted or declared the penalty specified in the precept or issued the penal precept. This is in accord with the exigencies of good ecclesial order.

Power of Confessors

Canon 1357 — §1. With due regard for the prescriptions of cann. 508 and 976, any confessor can remit in the internal sacramental forum an automatic (*latae sententiae*) censure of excommunication or interdict which has not been declared if it would be hard on the penitent to remain in a state of serious sin during the time necessary for the competent superior to provide.

§2. In granting a remission, the confessor is to impose on the penitent the burden of having recourse within a month to a superior or a priest endowed with faculties and obeying his mandates under pain of reincidence of the penalty; in the meantime he should impose an appropriate penance and the reparation of any scandal or damage to the extent that it is imperative; recourse can also be made by the confessor without mentioning any names.

§3. After they have recovered, those absolved in accord with can. 976 from an imposed or declared censure or one reserved to the Holy See are bound by the same obligation of recourse.

A noteworthy controversy during the revision of penal law concerned whether those who are excommunicated or interdicted should be able to receive penance and anointing of the sick prior to the remission of the penalty. The original schema permitted such an option; yet the May 1977 plenary meeting of the Code Commission voted to drop it. It was asked then whether any provision should be made for those seeking the sacraments prior to re-mission of a penalty. Some members of the penal law committee wanted to restate the fairly broad provisions of the 1917 Code for confessors to absolve from censures in urgent cases (*CIC* 2254). However, the majority wished to maintain the strongly external forum thrust of penal discipline. Hence the confessor's power to remit penalties was limited to non-declared *latae sententiae* censures of excommunication or interdict. Accordingly he may not remit imposed censures, non-declared *latae sententiae* censures of suspension, or any expiatory penalties.

The present canon reflects that decision. Paragraph one reflects canon 2254 of the 1917 Code by referring to the situation in which it would be hard for a penitent to remain in a state of serious sin for the time necessary to approach one who could remit the penalty. The revised law drops any reference to the penitent's being unable to observe the penalty externally without the danger of grave scandal or infamy. According to the traditional commentators, if a penitent found it burdensome to remain in mortal sin for only one day, the options afforded by this canon could be utilized. The competent superior here refers to those authorized to remit penalties in the prior three canons. Theoretically, at least, the canon is more restrictive than the 1917 Code since the confessor may remit only non-declared *latae sententiae* censures. However, in practice, there may still be significant options for confessors since numerous *latae sententiae* censures may never be declared, especially those affecting the laity.

Reference is made to the special penalty-remitting faculties enjoyed by the canon penitentiary (c. 508, §1)—not too relevant to the American experience but operative in dioceses with chapters of canons. Technically a comparable official will now have to be appointed even by American bishops (c. 508, §2). There is also an allusion to the broad powers of remitting sins and censures enjoyed by any priest in a danger-of-death situation—even if he is laicized or otherwise unauthorized to hear confessions (c. 976; *CIC* 882).

In the 1917 Code the special penalty-remitting powers of confessors were not unqualified since they were viewed as extraordinary measures. The same is true of the revised law, which requires the confessor to impose on the penitent the burden of making recourse within a month to the competent superior or to an authorized priest and observing his mandates or instructions (§2). Should such recourse not be made, the penalty technically is incurred again (reincidence), presumably because of the obstinacy of the offender evidenced in his or her refusal to follow the confessor's directions.[26]

---

[26]For a discussion of the absolution of censures in the 1917 Code, including the issue of reincidence, see Bouscaren, 892–898; Vermeersch-Creusen, 270–279.

A point disputed by authors after the 1917 Code was promulgated still seems unresolved by the 1983 law. What if the penitent makes recourse to the competent superior within a month yet does not observe the superior's mandates? Is the censure incurred again? The phrase "under pain of reincidence" qualifies "having recourse" directly and not "obeying mandates." The position affirming the reincidence of the censure seems more likely; yet the view denying such reincidence seems probable also because of the structure of the canon. Furthermore, in light of the necessarily strict interpretation of penal law, the reincidence of the censure must be proven conclusively.

The confessor also must impose an appropriate penance and require the repairing of any damage or scandal as an integral part of the remission of the penalty. The offender's willingness to accept such a penance and repair any damage caused by the offense is a significant sign of the cessation of contumacy that is a *sine qua non* condition for the remission of a censure.

At times it may be difficult for the penitent to have recourse to the above-mentioned competent superior. In such instances the confessor may fulfill this duty of the penitent, without mentioning any names to protect the penitent's reputation.

Paragraph three of the canon, like the 1917 Code (*CIC* 2252), places a comparable burden of making recourse on those for whom various serious penalties are remitted in a danger-of-death situation (c. 976). The urgency of the situation warrants the granting of broader faculties to confessors than is normally the case (§1).

One other change from the 1917 Code might be noted in conclusion. Recourse to a competent penal authority is theoretically always required even if the confessor fulfills this obligation. The 1917 Code had permitted the confessor himself to provide for the theoretically extraordinary case in which such recourse was morally impossible (*CIC* 2254, §3).

Remission of Censure

Canon 1358 — §1. A remission of a censure cannot be granted unless an offender has withdrawn from contumacy in accord with the norm of can. 1347, §2; remission cannot be denied, however, to a person who withdraws from contumacy.

§2. A person who remits a censure can act in accord with the norm of can. 1348 or even impose a penance.

This canon emphasizes that the cessation of contumacy is a *sine qua non* condition for the remission of a censure and that once such a disposition is verified (c. 1347, §2) the censure is to be remitted (§1). This differentiates the censure from the expiatory penalty, whose remission is not technically related to the cessation of contumacy.

The remission of the censure does not necessarily preclude other legal-pastoral measures. According to canon 1348 the offender may be subject to certain penal measures at the discretion of the competent superior (§2). There may be some detrimental ecclesial effects of the offense that require compensation even after the offender has ceased being contumacious, e.g., notable divisions in a parish occasioned by the abuse of office by a cleric or other parish leadership figure.

Remission of Multiple Penalties

Canon 1359 — If a person is bound by many penalties, the remission has force only for those penalties expressly mentioned in the remission; a general remission, however, takes away all penalties with the exception of those about which the guilty party kept silent in the petition in bad faith.

As implied in canon 1346, an offender committing several offenses may be liable to multiple penalties although a sense of equity might suggest moderation in their application. This canon adapts canon 2249 of the 1917 Code on the remission of censures. One must examine the decree of remission to see which penalties are remitted. Obviously this depends partly on the openness of the offender in acknowledging honestly whatever penalties have been incurred. A general remission covers all penalties except those concealed in bad faith. This provision reflects the law's general approach to censures, which requires proper dispositions of the offender if the penalty is to be remitted.

Coerced Remission of Penalty

Canon 1360 — If the remission of a penalty was extorted through grave fear, it is invalid.

This provision for the invalidity of a coerced remission of a penalty is a specific example of an exception to the general principle of canon 125, §2: legal acts posited through grave fear unjustly induced or through deceit are valid unless the law provides otherwise. Here the law provides otherwise because of the serious threat to church order posed by a failure to prevent such coerced remissions of penalties. Although the canon does not explicitly qualify the fear as unjust, its legal history (*CIC* 2238) and its interpretation by commentators seem to confirm the fact that a fear that is unjust in itself or in the manner of its application is understood here. The use of *extorta* seems to corroborate this opinion.

Format of Remission

Canon 1361 — §1. A remission can be granted even to a person who is not present or even under a condition.

§2. A remission in the external forum is to be given in writing unless a serious cause persuades otherwise.

§3. Care should be taken that a petition for remission or the remission itself not be made public, except to the extent that it would be advantageous to protect the reputation of the guilty party or necessary to repair scandal.

The format of the remission of the penalty is considered here. Since the act of remission is an act of the power of government not per se sacramental, it can be expedited conditionally and without the offender being present (§1). Obviously the internal forum remissions of penalties spoken of in canon 1355, §2 (bishop) and in canon 1357 (confessor) presuppose the presence of the penitent, but these are exceptions to the rule. However, in the latter instance one notices the conditional factor previously mentioned in the requirement of recourse to a competent superior under penalty of reincidence of the censure.

An external forum remission should normally be put in writing so that it can be proved easily unless there is a serious reason for not doing so. The remission should be publicized only if necessary to protect the reputation of the offender or to repair the damage caused in the community. This would seem especially true if the offender occupied a position of public trust in the community, e.g., diocesan official, pastor, director of religious education, etc.

Prescription of Criminal Action

Canon 1362 — §1. A criminal action is extinguished by prescription in three years unless it is a question of:

1° offenses reserved to the Sacred Congregation for the Doctrine of the Faith;

2° an action due to offenses mentioned in cann. 1394, 1395, 1397 and 1398, which have a prescription of five years;

3° offenses which are not punished in common law if particular law has stated another term of prescription.

§2. Prescription starts on the day the offense was committed or on the day when it ceased if the offense is continuous or habitual.

The next two canons on prescription are not placed in the procedural law corpus as in the 1917 Code (*CIC* 1703). Rather it is felt that they are best put in the particular section of the law dealing with the matter subject to prescription. Prescription here means a statute of limitations or a prohibition of pursuing a criminal action after a certain period of time. Generally speaking, criminal actions are subject to prescription three years after the commission of the offense or after the cessation of a so-called continuing or habitual offense, e.g., membership in a forbidden society plotting against the Church (c. 1374). However, provision is also made for a different period of time for certain offenses, e.g., those offenses reserved to the Sacred Congregation for the Doctrine of the Faith, which follows its own special rules; offenses determined in particular law, which might prescribe a longer or shorter period of time; certain serious moral offenses of clerics; and finally abduction, mutilation, homicide, and abortion (five years).

The specification of a longer period of time for a criminal action indicates that certain offenses are more serious than others. Hence it is another confirmation of an implicit hierarchy of values operative in the penal order.

Prescription of Penal Action

Canon 1363 — §1. An action to execute a penalty is extinguished by prescription if the guilty party has not been notified of the judge's executive decree mentioned in can. 1651 within the time limits indicated in can. 1362 which are to be computed from the day on which the condemnatory sentence became a finally judged matter (res iudicata).

§2. All other things being observed that are to be observed, the same holds true if the penalty was imposed through an extra-judicial decree.

This final canon deals with a complex canonical point that need only briefly be noted here. The canon reflects a distinction between (a) a criminal action leading to a sentence condemning an offender and (b) a penal action to ensure that the penalty determined in the criminal action is actually enforced.

Even though an offender might be condemned for committing an offense, the judge or ordinary may defer enforcing a penalty if certain pastoral goals could better be achieved otherwise. Furthermore, the observance of an expiatory penalty for a first offender might be suspended for the same reason(s).

In these situations the institute of prescription is also operative from the time the penal sentence is technically a definitively adjudged matter (c. 1641). The same holds true mutatis mutandis for an administrative procedure. If the statute of limitations runs out, then no one can institute a further action to enforce the observance of the penalty. This whole discussion is relevant only to *ferendae sententiae* penalties since there is no executory decree for latae sententiae penalties, which take effect upon commission of the offense.

Part II
PENALTIES FOR SPECIFIC OFFENSES
[cc. 1364–1399]

This second part of Book VI lists various offenses deemed serious enough to require similar treatment throughout the Church. It significantly simplifies the 1917 Code.

Generally speaking, popular commentaries such as Bouscaren[27] and Abbo-Hannan[28] devote little space to this section of the law. Frequently they simply paraphrase the 1917 Code and provide the reader with various charts to facilitate a study of the law.

This part of the commentary will be relatively brief in contrast to part I, which seems more significant than the present section for most readers. This section briefly introduces the seven titles of part II of Book VI, offers some pertinent reflections on the canons, and indicates references to corresponding canons elsewhere in the revised Code or in the 1917 Code.[29]

TITLE I
OFFENSES AGAINST RELIGION AND THE UNITY OF THE CHURCH
[cc. 1364–1369][30]

This title integrates provisions from two titles in the 1917 Code (title XI on offenses against faith and church unity [*CIC* 2314–2319] and title XII on offenses against religion [*CIC* 2320–2329]). Most of the provisions correspond to similar canons in the 1917 Code, which is notably simplified.

Apostasy, Heresy, and Schism

Canon 1364 — **§1. With due regard for can. 194, §1, n. 2, an apostate from the faith, a heretic or a schismatic incurs automatic (*latae sententiae*) excommunication and if a cleric, he can also be punished by the penalties mentioned in can. 1336, §1, nn. 1, 2 and 3.**

§2. If long lasting contumacy or the seriousness of scandal warrants it, other penalties can be added including dismissal from the clerical state.

The present law does not define apostasy, heresy, or schism[31] but simply specifies that they warrant a *latae sententiae* excommunication comparable to the 1917 Code (*CIC* 2314, §1, 1°). This represents a relatively late change during the consultative process, during most of which a *ferendae sententiae* penalty had been envisioned for these offenses. In maintaining that a *latae sententiae* penalty be incurred in these instances, church authorities need to be sensitive to the complex issues raised by these offenses. It is difficult to determine precisely when an individual or group is guilty of apostasy, heresy, or schism according to law. This is especially true given increased theological pluralism and ecumenical contacts and confessional boundaries that are not as sharply defined as formerly. Furthermore, jurisdictional measures may be inappropriate in dealing with persons who place themselves outside of the Church. It might be better simply to declare formally an incompatibility between their faith and that of the Church. In any event juridical certainty about the existence and imputability of such offenses presupposes a careful inquiry into the pertinent facts.

The determination of doctrinal orthodoxy is a delicate enterprise which has been publicized in recent years due to formal investigations of various theologians. The relevant issues can be dealt with constructively and various ecclesial values preserved only if there are developed workable procedures for dialogue between the magisterium and scholars in various ecclesiastical disciplines.[32]

As is true for various canons, special penalties for clerics are indicated at the end of paragraph one. Clerics are apparently viewed as having special institutional responsibilities, hence their violation of the law is an especially serious breach of church order.

Paragraph two states that long-standing contumacy, or contempt for the law, or serious scandal may justify further penalties—including dismissal from the clerical state. The seriousness of the penalty is proportionate to the obstinacy of the offender and the seriousness of the damage done to the ecclesial order.

Finally another special characteristic of the penalty might be noted. Although excommunication does not necessarily involve the loss of ecclesiastical office, canon 194, §1, 2° specifically provides for this as an administrative consequence of abandoning the Catholic communion.

---

[27]See Bouscaren, 924–975. Only pages 924–950 comment on specific offenses; the other pages contain various study guides.

[28]See Abbo-Hannan II, 864–872. In contrast, a work like Vermeersch-Creusen, geared to a more specialized canonical audience, devotes much more space to an analysis of penalties for specific offenses. See 316–400.

[29]See Tables 1–12 at the end of this commentary on Book VI for a comprehensive listing of various penalties.

[30]For a discussion of these canons by the penal law committee, see *Comm* 9 (1977), 304–306; 319; 321. Also Green, "Penal Law Revisited," 173–178. For the corresponding canons of the 1917 Code, see Bouscaren, 924–927; 930; 932 and Vermeersch-Creusen, 318–322; 326–327.

[31]For such definitions, see c. 751.

[32]This complex issue can hardly be dealt with here. See two 1980 CTSA reports: "Report of the CTSA Committee on Cooperation between Theologians and the Church's Teaching Authority" and "Report of the CTSA Committee on Ecclesiastical Legislation," *J* 40 (1980), 435–452. Also L. O'Donovan (ed.), *Cooperation between Theologians and the Ecclesiastical Magisterium:* a Report of the Joint Committee of the Canon Law Society of America and the Catholic Theological Society of America (Washington, D.C.: CLSA, 1982).

Prohibited Communicatio in Sacris[33]

Canon 1365 — **A person guilty of prohibited participation in sacred rites (***communicatio in sacris***) is to be punished with a just penalty.**

A noteworthy post-conciliar phenomenon has been the development of closer contacts between Catholics and members of other religious traditions. Catholic ecumenical involvement, including participation in sacred rites, is subject to the direction of the whole college of bishops, the Holy See, the episcopal conference, and individual bishops (c. 755). Given diverse ecumenical situations throughout the Church, the universal law understandably specifies only generic guidelines while leaving ample room for such determinations at other levels.

The revised law was apparently felt necessary to cope with serious abuses in sacramental sharing. Like the preceding norm, it should be interpreted strictly lest appropriate ecumenical initiatives be unduly jeopardized.

Non-Catholic Baptism or Education of Children

Canon 1366 — **Parents or those who substitute for parents are to be punished with a censure or another just penalty if they hand their children over to be baptized or educated in a non-Catholic religion.**

Parents or their surrogates have certain profound responsibilities for the religious initiation and formation of their children.[34] This canon punishes the deliberate handing over of one's children to be baptized or educated in a non-Catholic religious tradition.[35] It would probably be relevant only in ecumenical marriages. Furthermore, intensive evangelization or catechesis might preserve legitimate ecclesial values more effectively than penalties.[36]

Violation of Sacred Species

Canon 1367 — **A person who throws away the consecrated species or who takes them or retains them for a sacrilegious purpose incurs an automatic (***latae sententiae***) excommunication reserved to the Apostolic See; if a cleric, he can be punished with another penalty including dismissal from the clerical state.**

This somewhat simplified version of the 1917 Code (*CIC* 2320) reflects the preeminent ecclesial value of reverence for the Eucharist (c. 898). The provision for a *latae sententiae* excommunication, the fact that its remission is reserved to the Holy See, and the fact of possible dismissal from the clerical state indicate the seriousness of the violation.

Perjury

Canon 1368 — **A person who commits perjury while asserting something or promising something before an ecclesiastical authority is to be punished with a just penalty.**

This slightly modified version of the 1917 Code (*CIC* 2323) attempts to ensure the authenticity of ecclesial commitments and processes. Besides possible perjury in ecclesiastical processes such as marriage cases, such an offense might occur in other situations, e.g., candidate for orders falsifying his declaration of free and perpetual ministerial commitment (c. 1036).

Abuse of Church/Religion

Canon 1369 — **A person who uses a public show or speech, published writings, or other media of social communication to blaspheme, seriously damage good morals, express wrongs against religion or against the Church or stir up hatred or contempt against religion or the Church is to be punished with a just penalty.**

The penal law committee felt that the law should address certain contemporary evils, particularly those directly affecting church order. This generically formulated canon embodies such a concern, somewhat comparable to canons 2323 and 2344 of the 1917 Code. The practical relevance of this canon is somewhat questionable because of its lack of precision. Such precision is crucial if the law is to be implemented responsibly. Furthermore, one may wonder whether those normally guilty of such an offense would be Catholics, on whom such a norm might have a beneficial effect.

---

[33]See c. 844 on sacramental sharing and c. 908, which prohibits concelebration with priests or ministers not in full communion with the Catholic Church. See also *CIC* 2316 and 2338, §2.

[34]On the parental responsibility for the baptism of their children, see c. 867. On the parental right and duty to educate their children in the faith, see cc. 226, §2; 774, §2; 1136.

[35]See *CIC* 2319, 3°–4°.

[36]On the responsibility of pastors to aid those in ecumenical marriages, see c. 1128.

TITLE II
OFFENSES AGAINST
ECCLESIASTICAL AUTHORITIES AND
THE FREEDOM OF THE CHURCH
[cc. 1370–1377][37]

Physical Attacks on Religious Figures

Canon 1370 — §1. One who uses physical force against the Roman Pontiff incurs an automatic (*latae sententiae*) excommunication reserved to the Apostolic See; if he is a cleric, another penalty including dismissal from the clerical state can be added in accord with the seriousness of the offense.

§2. One who does this against a person possessing the episcopal character incurs an automatic (*latae sententiae*) interdict; and, if a cleric, he also incurs an automatic (*latae sententiae*) suspension.

§3. One who uses physical force against a cleric or religious out of contempt for the faith, or the Church, or ecclesiastical power, or ministry is to be punished with a just penalty.

This canon reaffirms the 1917 Code[38] despite the reservations of certain critics about its necessity in light of civil law provisions, its efficacy in deterring potential offenders, and its fidelity to conciliar teaching on the fundamental equality of all believers. There is a descending scale of penalties proportionate to one's official ecclesial status. The Church's public good is presumably harmed more or less seriously depending on the institutional dignity of the person who suffers violence. Accordingly one of the few reserved excommunications punishes those doing violence to the pope, whereas somewhat less serious penalties are in order for those attacking bishops or finally clerics or religious.

Doctrinal Violations/Disobedience

Canon 1371 — The following are to be punished with a just penalty:

1° besides the situation mentioned in can. 1364, §1, a person who teaches a doctrine condemned by the Roman Pontiff or by an ecumenical council or who pertinaciously rejects the doctrine mentioned in can. 752 and who does not make a retraction after having been admonished by the Apostolic See or by the ordinary;

2° a person who wrongly does not otherwise comply with the legitimate precepts or prohibitions of the Apostolic See, the ordinary or the superior and who persists in disobedience, after a warning.

This text in part integrates two canons of the 1917 Code: canon 2317 on the teaching of condemned doctrines and canon 2331, §1 on disobedience of legitimate ecclesiastical authority. Like canon 1364, it requires careful interpretation given its fairly broad formulation.

Number one has been expanded during the last stages of the consultative process. It originally referred only to a doctrine clearly condemned by the pope or an ecumenical council even if the doctrine were not technically heretical.[39] However, the revised law refers also to the pertinacious rejection of a doctrine which calls not for an assent of faith since it is not proclaimed as such through a definitive act but rather for religious adherence of mind and will (c. 752). The commentary on the relevant canons in Book III should be consulted for a further clarification of these issues.

The "just penalty" presumably should correspond to the seriousness of the ecclesial damage done and the obstinacy of the offending party even after a warning. This also holds true for the following offense, which involves another area in which regular magisterium-scholar dialogue seems particularly important.

Number two specifies the penal implications of disobedience of legitimate ecclesiastical superiors functioning according to law, including the constitutions of religious communities. This second point is somewhat vaguely formulated and could occasion abuses. Hence it should be stressed that the law envisions a serious breach of discipline here.

Recourse against Pope

Canon 1372 — One who takes recourse against an act of a Roman Pontiff to an ecumenical council or to the college of bishops is to be punished with a censure.

This canon is somewhat perplexing since it apparently reflects the intra-ecclesial conflict of the conciliarist period rather than the very productive contemporary collaboration of the pope and his brother bishops despite certain tensions in that relationship. The revised law speaks in mitigated terms of a censure rather than a specially reserved excommunication as in the 1917 Code (*CIC* 2332).

Opposition to Church Authority

Canon 1373 — One who publicly either stirs up hostilities or hatred among subjects against the Ap-

---

[37]For a discussion of these canons by the penal law committee, see *Comm* 9 (1977), 306–309; 320. Also Green, "Penal Law Revisited," 178–183. For the corresponding canons of the 1917 Code, see Bouscaren, 925–926; 929–930; 932–933; 944 and Vermeersch-Creusen, 322–323; 333–339; 345–350; 384–385.

[38]See *CIC* 2343; 2207, 1°.

[39]For a discussion of the original schema, see Green, "Penal Law Revisited," 181–182. See cc. 750; 752–754 on the proper religious stance of believers relative to various types of magisterial teachings. For examples of condemned doctrines that are not precisely heretical, see Vermeersch-Creusen, 323.

ostolic See or against an ordinary on account of some act of ecclesiastical power or ministry or incites subjects to disobey them is to be punished by an interdict or by other just penalties.

As distinct from the simple disobedience penalized in canon 1371, 2°, this broadly formulated text envisions a conspiracy against church authority which does not necessarily involve any doctrinal violations. Two canons of the 1917 Code are incorporated in the revised law: canon 2331, §2 on conspiracy against lawful authority and canon 2344 on offenses against significant hierarchical figures. One can appreciate the concern to protect the integral exercise of church authority, which is essential to the healthy functioning of the community. However, this canon must be interpreted judiciously lest legitimate criticism of ecclesiastical institutions be arbitrarily curtailed. Such criticism is indispensable if the Church is to fulfill its mission adequately amid changing circumstances.[40]

Membership in Forbidden Societies

Canon 1374 — One who joins an association which plots against the Church is to be punished with a just penalty; one who promotes or moderates such an association, however, is to be punished with an interdict.

This canon notably simplifies the 1917 Code, which had expicitly condemned the Masons, mentioned plotting against the Church or civil governments, and imposed an excommunication simply reserved to the Holy See for membership in various forbidden societies (*CIC* 2335). Furthermore, the revised law neither specifies special penalties for clerics or religious nor requires that such persons be denounced to the Holy Office (*CIC* 2336). The 1983 law differentiates, however, between simple membership (just penalty) and the promoting of or holding office in such a society (interdict). These developments reflect changing historical circumstances and diverse conditions around the world, especially but not exclusively regarding the antiecclesial nature of the Masons. Where, however, the Masons or other groups are actively plotting against the Church, this canon is clearly relevant.

In this latter connection a relatively recent official development should be duly noted. During the revision process a number of bishops, especially the German bishops, argued that the anti-ecclesial stance of the Masons was still a relevant consider-

ation even though for the National Conference of Catholic Bishops and other conferences this was not a major issue. The former argued for an explicit condemnation of the Masons in the revised Code; however, both the Secretariat of the Code Commission and the October 1981 plenarium refused to incorporate such a provision in the revised Code since apparently the problem was not perceived to be a universal one warranting such a provision. Somewhat surprisingly, on the eve of the revised Code's taking effect, the Sacred Congregation for the Doctrine of the Faith published a declaration indicating that Catholics joining the Masons are involved in serious sin and are to be barred from the Eucharist. This judgment was presumably based on the irreconcilability of Masonic principles and Catholic doctrine. The declaration also precludes a contrary judgment by local ecclesiastical authorities that would mitigate the force of the Congregation's judgment. This posture seems somewhat contrary to earlier 1974 and 1981 Congregation pronouncements that seemed to be open to a recognition of the differences in various Masonic associations even if they opposed formal pronouncements of the conferences of bishops on the general nature of such associations.

It is still a bit too soon to clarify fully the implications of this issue. However, in dealing with practical questions that may arise, it seems prudent to recall the traditional principles regarding a strict interpretation of penal law (cc. 18; 1321–1330). Such prudence seems appropriate as well regarding the practical judgment of the serious sinfulness of Masonic affiliation in a given set of circumstances; the traditional principles of moral theology seem pertinent in this context. Furthermore, it seems wise to make every effort to clarify the precise nature of the Masonic associations in different parts of the world in order to assist church authorities in making prudent determinations on membership in such groups.[41]

Violations of Church Freedom

Canon 1375 — Those who impede the freedom of ecclesiastical ministry or election or power, or the legitimate use of sacred goods or other ecclesiastical goods, or who grossly intimidate an elector, or the elected, or the one who exercises ecclesiastical ministry or power, can be punished with a just penalty.

---

[40]On the need for an ongoing critique of the law as a part of church reform, see J. Provost, "Canon Law: True or False Reform in the Church," *J* 38 (1978), 257–267; J. Coriden, "Law in Service to the People of God," ibid. 41 (1981), 1–20.

[41]For the text of the most recent declaration of the SCDF on the Masons dated November 26, 1983, see *Origins* 13/27 (Nov. 15, 1983), 450. For the text of an earlier declaration of the SCDF dated February 17, 1981, see *CLD* 9, 1003–1004. For the text of a July 18, 1974 letter of the SCDF to the NCCB on the Masons, see *CLD* 8, 1211.

This generically formulated canon attempts to ensure the free exercise of various ecclesiastical functions, e.g., the exercise of ecclesiastical office and the use of ecclesiastical goods. The canon is somewhat difficult to interpret because it lacks the specificity of the 1917 Code.[42] The concern to enhance the Church's freedom in the exercise of its mission is commendable. However, the implementation of the law would be facilitated if those violations subject to a sanction were more precisely delineated.

Profanation of Sacred Things

Canon 1376 — One who profanes a movable or immovable sacred thing is to be punished with a just penalty.

A concern for reverence of sacred objects accounts for this provision that should be read in conjunction with canon 1171. Sacred things are those destined for divine worship through their dedication or consecration, be they immovable, e.g., church, or movable, e.g., chalice. The seriousness of the "just penalty" obviously corresponds to the seriousness of the offense, i.e., putting such objects to profane or common use contrary to their cultic orientation.

Unlawful Alienation of Church Property

Canon 1377 — One who alienates ecclesiastical goods without the prescribed permission is to be punished with a just penalty.

A concern for fiscal accountability in the stewardship of church resources accounts for this canon which penalizes those violating the norms on alienating church property.[43] It significantly simplifies the 1917 Code which dealt with different forms of illegal alienation and provided for increasingly more severe penalties proportionate to the seriousness of the offense (*CIC* 2347). The revised law leaves such a determination up to the appropriate ordinary or judge.

TITLE III
USURPATION OF ECCLESIASTICAL FUNCTIONS AND OFFENSES IN THEIR EXERCISE
[cc. 1378–1389][44]

Absolution of Accomplice/Sacramental Simulation

Canon 1378 — §1. A priest who acts against the prescription of can. 977 incurs an automatic (*latae sententiae*) excommunication reserved to the Apostolic See.

§2. The following incur an automatic (*latae sententiae*) penalty of interdict or if a cleric, an automatic (*latae sententiae*) suspension:

1° one who has not been promoted to the priestly order and who attempts to enact the liturgical action of the Eucharistic Sacrifice;

2° outside the case mentioned in §1, a person who attempts to impart sacramental absolution or a person who hears a sacramental confession when one cannot validly give sacramental absolution.

§3. In the case mentioned in §2 other penalties including excommunication can be added in accord with the seriousness of the offense.

This canon addresses particularly serious Eucharistic and penitential abuses.[45] The most serious offense meriting excommunication involves a priest attempting to absolve his accomplice of either sex in a sexual sin (§1). Such an act is invalid except in danger of death.[46] The reason for these provisions is the impropriety of the confessor's absolving one in whose sin he has shared. This sinful complicity impedes the normal priest-penitent relationship. One may wonder, however, why such provisions are limited to the sexual arena.

The revised law simplifies the 1917 Code, which differentiated between the actual attempt to absolve the accomplice and the situation in which the priest's accomplice did not confess the sexual sin due to his influence. The 1983 law also does not refer to another priest's availability in the danger-of-death situation, which formerly affected the incurring of the penalty. However, the seriousness of the offense is clear from the fact that it is one of the very few penalties reserved to the Holy See.

Paragraph two treats of two violations of the

---

[42]The sources of this canon are not entirely clear. However, they probably reflect the following canons of the 1917 Code: 2333, on impeding the exercise of the power of the Holy See; 2334, on injury to the liberty, rights, and jurisdiction of the Church; 2337, on inciting people to impede ecclesiastical jurisdiction; 2345, on usurping the rights or property of the Roman Church; 2346, on the confiscation and appropriation of church property; and 2390, on interference with the freedom of canonical elections.

[43]For the general rules on alienation of church property, see cc. 1290–1296. For alienation of the property of religious, see c. 638, §3–4.

[44]For a discussion of these canons by the penal law committee, see *Comm* 9 (1977), 309–313; 320. Also Green, "Penal Law Revisited," 183–186. For the corresponding canons of the 1917 Code, see Bouscaren, 927; 938–940; 944–947 and Vermeersch-Creusen, 328–329; 367–371; 371–373; 387–388; 390–391; 393.

[45]See *CIC* 2367, on absolution of an accomplice; *CIC* 2322, 1°, on simulation of the Eucharist; and *CIC* 2366, on simulation of sacramental absolution.

[46]For the meaning of such complicity and of changes from *CIC* 884, see the commentary on c. 977.

rules on the proper differentiation of sacramental functions. Number one penalizes those not priests who violate canon 900, §1 on the valid minister of the Eucharistic celebration.[47] Such a person would have to behave around the altar in such a way that others would conclude erroneously that the Eucharist was being celebrated.

Number two penalizes those violating canons 965–975, who attempt to impart sacramental absolution or simply pretend to hear confessions even without such an attempt. In other words an erroneous impression is created that the sacrament of reconciliation is being celebrated. This will probably not be a real issue, especially given the broad penitential options of priests (c. 967, §2). Furthermore, two other canons providing for valid absolution in emergencies are noteworthy here, i.e., canon 144, §2 on positive and probable doubt about such penitential options and canon 976 on danger-of-death situations. In neither situation would this canon be applicable. The penalty is proportionate to the seriousness of the offense; in addition, a special penalty is in order for clerics.

Other Sacramental Simulations

Canon 1379 — Outside the cases mentioned in can. 1378, one who simulates the administration of a sacrament is to be punished with a just penalty.

A similar concern for sacramental integrity underlies this canon which penalizes simulated celebration of the sacraments other than penance and the Eucharist.[48] The "just penalty" provision indicates that such violations are not viewed as seriously as the preceding breaches of Eucharistic and penitential discipline.

Simony and Sacraments

Canon 1380 — One who celebrates or receives a sacrament through simony is to be punished with an interdict or a suspension.

Unlike the 1917 Code which contained several canons on simony (*CIC* 727–730), the revised law contains nothing comparable. While the 1917 Code penalized the simoniacal conferral and reception of church office in various ways (*CIC* 2392), the revised Code simply invalidates such an arrangement (c. 149, §3). Some brief comments on the meaning of simony seem sufficient here.[49] It means an explicit or implicit and externally manifest agreement

whereby one party agrees to confer a sacrament on another in exchange for some temporal good, e.g., money, property, etc. The heart of this offense is the deliberate intent to equalize the spiritual and the temporal, i.e., to deal commercially in sacred things. An effort to preclude irreverence toward the Church's saving mysteries underlies this canon.[50]

Violations of Ecclesiastical Office

Canon 1381 — §1. Whoever usurps an ecclesiastical office is to be punished with a just penalty.
§2. Illegitimate retention after deprivation or cessation of office is equivalent to usurpation.

The realization of the Church's mission presupposes a certain order in the assignment and exercise of various offices. Such order is seriously jeopardized by violations of the rules on appointment to church office.[51] This is especially true for attempts to assume an office on one's own initiative without the appropriate intervention by the competent authority (§1). This text notably simplifies the 1917 Code, which specified in detail the penalties for those illegitimately occupying church office and authority figures collaborating in such a violation. The present canon speaks only of a "just penalty," whereas a June 29, 1950 decree of the Sacred Congregation of the Council[52] specified a *latae sententiae* excommunication specially reserved to the Holy See.

The orderly transfer of ecclesiastical authority is also impeded by individuals who refuse to leave an office after ceasing to function legitimately in it for a reason provided in law (§2).[53] Unlike the 1917 Code which specified various penalties for such an offense (*CIC* 2401), this canon simply provides for a "just penalty."

Unauthorized Episcopal Consecration

Canon 1382 — A bishop who consecrates someone a bishop and the person who receives such a consecration from a bishop without a pontifical mandate incur an automatic (*latae sententiae*) excommunication reserved to the Apostolic See.

The seriousness of this violation is evident from the fact that it warrants one of only five excommunications reserved to the Holy See. The present canon reflects the ecclesial significance of the episcopal office and the importance of close papal-

---

[47]See c. 907, which prohibits deacons and laity from saying prayers and performing actions proper to the priest celebrant.
[48]See *CIC* 2322, 2⁰.
[49]For a discussion of different aspects of simony, see Abbo-Hannan I, 723–733. See *CIC* 2371.

[50]See also c. 1385, on trafficking in the Mass stipends.
[51]See cc. 146–183.
[52]*AAS* 42 (1950), 601. See also *CIC* 2394.
[53]See cc. 184–196.

episcopal relationships for orderly church government.[54]

Unauthorized Sacred Ordination

Canon 1383 — A bishop who violates the prescription of can. 1015 and ordains a person who is not his subject without legitimate dimissorial letters is prohibited for a year from conferring the order; a person who has received ordination in such circumstances is automatically (*ipso facto*) suspended from the order received.

A bishop other than a candidate's proper ordinary presumably does not know the candidate as well as the latter. Accordingly dimissorial letters testifying to the candidate's suitability are to be forwarded by the proper ordinary to another bishop. If the latter ordains the candidate without such dimissorials (c. 1015), he is prohibited from conferring the order for a year (*CIC* 2373, 1°) while the candidate is suspended from exercising it (*CIC* 2374).

Other Instances of Illegitimate Ministry

Canon 1384 — Outside the cases mentioned in cann. 1378-1383, one who illegitimately carries out a priestly function or another sacred ministry can be punished with a just penalty.

Despite criticism of the sweeping character of this canon and canon 1389, they are restated unchanged in the revised law. There is no corresponding canon in the 1917 Code which can help one interpret canon 1384 judiciously.

Two significant values need to be considered here and later in interpreting canon 1389. First of all, the community of believers has a right to expect a certain measure of ministerial accountability from those clerics or laity occupying positions of public trust. Secondly, such officeholders deserve a clear description of their responsibilities lest they be uncertain about what the community expects from them. They also have a right not to be subject to arbitrary penal discretion, which may lead to their removal from office. Accordingly, precise norms on ministerial accountability should be articulated as far as possible, reflecting both the revised Code and more detailed particular law provisions.[55]

Trafficking in Stipends

Canon 1385 — One who illegitimately makes a profit from a Mass stipend is to be punished with a censure or another just penalty.

A need to foster reverence for the Eucharist and to preclude the commercializing of sacred realities accounts for this generically formulated canon which penalizes trafficking in Mass stipends. The revised law corresponds to canon 2324 of the 1917 Code, which explicitly referred to canons 827, 828, and 840, §1 and specified certain penalties for their violation by clerics or laity.[56] Hence the revised law apparently penalizes violations of the following canons: canon 947 which prohibits any semblance of buying or selling regarding Mass stipends; canon 948 which requires that as many Masses be celebrated as stipends are accepted; and canon 955, §1 which determines that in the transfer of stipends the entire sum received is to be forwarded unless any excess over the diocesan stipend scale was clearly intended to benefit the priest to whom the stipends were originally given. The penalty for various violations is proportionate to their seriousness.

Bribery of Church Official

Canon 1386 — One who gives or promises something so that someone who exercises a function in the Church would illegitimately do or omit something is to be punished with a just penalty; likewise, the person who accepts such gifts or promises.

An understandable concern for integrity in the exercise of ecclesiastical office accounts for this canon which penalizes efforts that influence ecclesiastical officials to act illegally. The present canon is more generically formulated than the 1917 Code (*CIC* 2407), but it is similarly concerned with efforts to subvert the faithful fulfillment of ecclesiastical responsibilities. The penalty is incurred even if the officeholder refuses to break the law, e.g., by violating the secrecy of certain ecclesiastical processes. Although the present canon provides only for a "just penalty," other canons indicate more specific penalties for violations of office even without bribery.[57]

Solicitation in Confession

Canon 1387 — Whether in the act or on the occasion or under the pretext of confession, a priest who solicits a penitent to sin against the sixth commandment of the Decalogue is to be punished with suspension, prohibitions and deprivations in accord with the seriousness of the offense; and in more serious cases, he is to be dismissed from the clerical state.

---

[54]For the requirement of a papal mandate prior to an episcopal consecration, see c. 1013.

[55]See Green, "Penal Law Revisited," 197–198.

[56]For a commentary on the 1917 Code, see Abbo-Hannan I, 822–841; Vermeersch-Creusen II, 64–73.

[57]See cc. 1456–1457, on judges and other tribunal officials and 1488–1489, on advocates and procurators.

A concern to preserve the integrity of the priest-penitent relationship accounts for this canon on solicitation and the following one on the seal of confession.

There are some noteworthy differences between the revised law and the 1917 Code which obliged the solicited penitent to denounce the offending confessor (*CIC* 904) and penalized both the soliciting confessor as well as the penitent who knowingly failed to denounce the former (*CIC* 2368). First of all, the revised law on penance neither explicitly obliges the solicited penitent to denounce the soliciting confessor nor requires another confessor to advise the one solicited of the obligation to denounce the offending confessor. Rather, it binds one making a false denunciation to retract it formally and repair any damage done before absolution is granted (c. 982). As will be seen shortly, canon 1390, §1 subjects the false denunciator to the *latae sententiae* penalties of interdict and suspension if a cleric is involved. Both canons are primarily concerned with protecting the reputation of the innocent confessor whose ministerial effectiveness could be seriously jeopardized in such a delicate matter.[58]

Secondly, the present canon describes the meaning of solicitation. It is an invitation to commit a serious sin against the sixth commandment, which is expressed precisely within the penitential context broadly conceived. One may question the restriction of the law to sexual sins, but it clearly involves them alone.

Thirdly, the present canon does not refer to the penitent who knowingly fails to denounce an offending confessor, presumably because the canons on penance do not require such a denunciation. The canon penalizes only the allegedly soliciting confessor, with due latitude for the competent penal authority to act according to the seriousness of the offense. One should proceed very cautiously here, particularly because of the delicate situation of the confessor, who is bound by the seal of confession and hence is somewhat impaired in defending his integrity. Should a confessor be denounced, the instructions of the Holy See are to be followed.[59]

Violation of Confessional Seal

Canon 1388 — §1. A confessor who directly violates the seal of confession incurs an automatic (latae sententiae) excommunication reserved to the Apsotolic See; if he does so only indirectly, he is to be punished in accord with the seriousness of the offense.

§2. An interpreter and other persons mentioned in can. 983, §2, who violate this secrecy are to be punished with a just penalty, not excluding excommunication.

Traditionally one of the most severely penalized offenses has been the violation of the seal of confession because of the serious breach of confidentiality of the priest-penitent relationship. The sacramental seal is the strict and inviolable obligation of keeping secret all matters that have been related to the confessor for the purpose of obtaining absolution, the revelation of which would render the sacrament odious and onerous.[60] If the penitent and his/her sin are easily known from the confessor's behavior, there is a direct violation of the seal, punishable by a *latae ententiae* excommunication. The seriousness of the offense is clear from the fact that it is one of only five excommunications reserved to the Holy See.

If, on the contrary, there is only a danger that the penitent and the sin will be revealed, there is an indirect violation of the seal, punishable according to the seriousness of the confessor's indiscretion (§1). The canon primarily concerns the confessor, yet occasionally others, such as interpreters (cc. 983, §2; 990), may know of the confession. If they violate the seal, they are also subject to a proportionate penalty (§2).

Abuse of Authority/Negligence

Canon 1389 — §1. One who abuses ecclesiastical power or function is to be punished in accord with the seriousness of the act or omission not excluding deprivation from office unless a penalty for such abuse has already been established by a law or a precept.

§2. One who through culpable negligence illegitimately places or omits an act of ecclesiastical power, ministry or function which damages another person is to be punished with a just penalty.

The comments made earlier in connection with canon 1384 seem relevant here as well. Paragraph one apparently corresponds to the rather vaguely formulated canon 2404 of the 1917 Code, which presumably provided the basis for penal action against church authorities when the law did not explicitly penalize abuse of office.

The comments relating to canon 1384 seem likewise relevant to canon 1389, §2 on culpable negligence in the exercise of office, which at times may be as detrimental to the people of God as positive actions contrary to its well-being.

---

[58] The seriousness of this false accusation in the 1917 Code is clear from the fact that it was the only sin whose absolution was reserved to the Holy See (*CIC* 894). Furthermore, remission of the excommunication was likewise especially reserved to the Holy See.

[59] For further information on this issue in the 1917 Code, see Abbo-Hannan II, 30–33.

[60] Ibid., 17. See c. 983; *CIC* 889; 2369.

TITLE IV
THE CRIME OF FALSEHOOD
[cc. 1390–1391][61]

Violations of Reputation

Canon 1390 — §1. **One who falsely accuses a confessor before an ecclesiastical superior of the offense mentioned in can. 1387 incurs an automatic (*latae sententiae*) interdict; and if a cleric, also a suspension.**

§2. One who furnishes an ecclesiastical superior with any other calumnious denunciation of an offense or who otherwise injures the good reputation of another person can be punished with a just penalty, even including a censure.

§3. A calumniator can be coerced also to make suitable reparation.

The first paragraph of this canon has been discussed earlier in connection with canon 1387 on solicitation. The second paragraph deals with other violations of the right to a good reputation. Such violations warrant a "just penalty" and possibly a censure, depending on their seriousness. The third paragraph authorizes the possible requiring of restitution for the damage done to the victim.[62]

Falsification of Documents

Canon 1391 — **The following can be punished with a just penalty in accord with the seriousness of the offense:**

1° one who fabricates a false public ecclesiastical document, or changes, destroys or conceals an authentic document, or uses a false or changed document;

2° one who uses another false or changed document in an ecclesiastical matter;

3° one who states a falsehood in a public ecclesiastical document.

This canon attempts to protect the integrity of the Church's public life by penalizing the offense of tampering with documents and using them in various ecclesiastical procedures. The penalty is incurred even if one does not achieve the purpose(s) of such deception. The revised law simplifies the 1917 Code, which explicitly referred to rescripts of the Holy See or ordinaries, specified particular penalties for clerics and religious, and dealt not only with lying (*obreptio*) but also with concealing part of the truth (*subreptio*) in seeking rescripts (*CIC* 2360–2362). The revised law refers to public docu-

ments in paragraphs one and three, e.g., testimony in a marriage case, and it deals with private documents in paragraph two, e.g., premarital letter of spouse indicating marital intent.[63]

TITLE V
OFFENSES AGAINST PARTICULAR OBLIGATIONS
[cc. 1392–1396][64]

Prohibited Business Activities

Canon 1392 — **Clerics or religious who practice trade or business against the prescriptions of the canons are to be punished in accord with the seriousness of the offense.**

The following canons deal largely with certain serious violations of clerical or religious obligations. This canon penalizes violators of canon 286[65] which prohibits unauthorized clerics from conducting business (*negotiatio*) or trade (*mercatura*). Given the difficulty of clarifying precisely what constitutes such prohibited commercial activities, the canon understandably restates the 1917 Code (*CIC* 2380). It mitigates a March 22, 1950 decree of the Sacred Congregation of the Council,[66] which subjected an offender to an excommunication especially reserved to the Holy See; furthermore, a cleric might even have been liable to dismissal from the clerical state.

Violation of Penal Obligations

Canon 1393 — **One who violates the obligations imposed by a penalty can be punished by a just penalty.**

This provision seems somewhat out of place in this title on violations of clerical and religious obligations. It attempts to reinforce the efficacy of the penal system by indicating that one who disregards the obligations imposed by a penalty, e.g., not exercising an office, may be liable to another penalty for such intransigence.

Violation of Celibacy

Canon 1394 — §1. **With due regard for the prescription of can. 194, §1, n. 3, a cleric who attempts**

[61]For a discussion of these canons by the penal law committee, see *Comm* 9 (1977), 313–314. Also Green, "Penal Law Revisited," 127. For the corresponding canons of the 1917 Code, see Bouscaren, 935–937; Vermeersch-Creusen, 357–358; 361–364.
[62]See *CIC* 2355.
[63]On the meaning of documents, see c. 1540.
[64]For a discussion of these canons by the penal law committee, see *Comm* 9 (1977), 314–316; 320. Also Green, "Penal Law Revisited," 187–189. For the corresponding canons of the 1917 Code, see Bouscaren, 936–937; 941–943 and Vermeersch-Creusen, 359–360; 377–379; 382–384.
[65]Religious are bound by this canon according to c. 672. See also *CIC* 142.
[66]*AAS* 42 (1950), 330.

even a civil marriage incurs an automatic (*latae sententiae*) suspension; but if he is given a warning and he does not have a change of heart and continues to give scandal, he can be punished gradually with various deprivations, even to the point of dismissal from the clerical state.

§2. A religious in perpetual vows who is not a cleric and who attempts even a civil marriage incurs an automatic (*latae sententiae*) interdict, with due regard for the prescription of can. 694.

One of the most serious obligations of most clerics (c. 277)[67] and all religious (c. 599) is observing perfect and perpetual chastity as well as celibacy, which prevents them from marrying. Furthermore, canons 1087–1088 invalidate the attempted marriages of clerics other than married deacons as well as members of religious institutes in perpetual (not temporary) vows. Furthermore, married deacons are prevented from remarrying after the death of their spouses. If a cleric violates the law, he incurs a *latae sententiae* suspension. However, if after a formal warning he contumaciously and scandalously persists in the new relationship, he is liable to increasingly severe *ferendae sententiae* penalties—including dismissal from the clerical state (§1).[68] The non-clerical religious incurs a *latae sententiae* interdict and is automatically dismissed from the religious institute (c. 694, §1, 2°). Both the cleric and the religious automatically lose any ecclesiastical offices they hold (c. 194, §1, 3°). While nothing is stated explicitly about the spouse of the above-mentioned cleric or religious, canon 1329, §2 on complicity in an offense punished by a *latae sententiae* penalty is relevant here.

Various Violations of Clerical Chastity

Canon 1395 — §1. Outside the case mentioned in can. 1394, a cleric who lives in concubinage or a cleric who remains in another external sin against the sixth commandment of the Decalogue which produces scandal is to be punished with a suspension; and if such a cleric persists in such an offense after having been admonished, other penalties can be added gradually including dismissal from the clerical state.

§2. If a cleric has otherwise committed an offense against the sixth commandment of the Decalogue with force or threats or publicly or with a minor below the age of sixteen, the cleric is to be

punished with just penalties, including dismissal from the clerical state if the case warrants it.

A similar concern for an authentic living of clerical chastity prompts this canon on other violations of that virtue[69] besides the one penalized in the preceding canon. Paragraph one treats of concubinage, or an ongoing non-marital sexual relationship between a cleric and a woman. It also encompasses other *habitual* sexual offenses by a cleric that involve scandal yet not the exclusivity of the concubinary relationship. A *ferendae sententiae* suspension is warranted initially, with subsequent increasingly severe penalties which are dependent on the cleric's obstinacy in refusing to heed official warnings.

Paragraph two deals with certain *non-habitual* clerical sexual offenses, which are especially serious if they are perpetrated publicly, or with force or threats, or with a person of either sex under sixteen years of age. Initially such an offense is not viewed as seriously as the preceding ones since only "just penalties" are imposed. Yet if the remedial measures are unsuccessful, even such a cleric may ultimately be dismissed from the clerical state.

Great care should be exercised by church authorities in this delicate area. Frequently the most beneficial approach is a therapeutic rather than a penal one, especially if there is diminished imputability on the part of the cleric. However, while the well-being and future ministry of the offending cleric are key considerations, due cognizance also has to be taken of the damage done to the community and individuals within it.

Violation of Residence Obligation

Canon 1396 — One who seriously violates the obligation of residence to which he is bound by reason of an ecclesiastical office is to be punished with a just penalty including even deprivation of office after a warning.

This provision penalizes those gravely violating the residence obligation attached to certain offices, e.g., bishop,[70] pastor,[71] or parochial vicar.[72] The canon permits a certain discretion in applying penalties depending on the gravity of the offense. Yet if the cleric obstinately refuses to be duly present to

---

[67]An exception to the general rule for clerics is the married deacon (c. 1042, 1°).

[68]See *CIC* 2388. Post-Code developments further reinforced the severity of the excommunication for married priests who sought absolution from the censure yet were unable to separate from their wives. See Bouscaren, 893–896.

[69]See c. 277. Also *CIC* 133; 2358–2359. See also *CIC* 2176–2181 for a special administrative process dealing with clerics living in concubinage, which is not incorporated in the revised law.

[70]See c. 395 for the residence obligation of residential bishops and c. 410 for that of coadjutor and auxiliary bishops.

[71]See c. 533 for the residence obligation of individual pastors and c. 543, §2, 1° for those involved in a team ministry.

[72]See c. 550 for the residence obligation of parochial vicars (formerly assistant pastors or curates).

the community he is serving, he may be deprived of his office.[73]

TITLE VI
OFFENSES AGAINST HUMAN LIFE AND FREEDOM
[cc. 1397–1398][74]

The two canons in this section are preeminent examples of laws dealing with ecclesiastical offenses with civil law implications—although there is probably more statutory diversity regarding abortion (c. 1398) than about the other violations of human life,[75] integrity, and freedom (c. 1397).

Physical Violations of Persons

Canon 1397 — One who commits homicide or who fraudulently or forcibly kidnaps, detains, mutilates or seriously wounds a person is to be punished with the deprivations and prohibitions mentioned in can. 1336 in accord with the seriousness of the offense; however, homicide against the persons mentioned in can. 1370 is punished by the penalties specified there.

The revised law notably simplifies the 1917 Code (*CIC* 2253–2254). Canon 2353 spoke of the abduction of a woman for various reasons whereas the 1983 law speaks generically of the abduction or detention of anyone. Canon 2354 differentiated between laity and clerics regarding various significant offenses comparable to those in the revised law. Lay offenses were viewed as so-called mixed forum violations customarily punished by civil authority. In fact, the distinctly ecclesiastical penalties presupposed a civil law condemnation. On the contrary such clerical offenses were viewed theoretically as distinctly ecclesiastical offenses presumably because of the privilege of the forum (*CIC* 120). The revised law, however, neither differentiates between clergy and laity nor refers to a civil law condemnation. Hence the issue is apparently viewed as an exclusively ecclesiastical matter which involves various expiatory penalties—including dismissal from the clerical state—according to the gravity of the of-

fense. Despite there being no reference to the civil arena, these offenses will probably also be dealt with by civil authorities, given their societal impact. Accordingly there should be as much collaboration as possible between ecclesiastical and civil authorities, given their mutual concerns in the matter.

Abortion

Canon 1398 — A person who procures a completed abortion incurs an automatic (latae sententiae) excommunication.

During the revision process, the following issues were discussed in connection with this offense: the practical efficacy of the penalty, the disparity between the penalty for abortion and for homicide, and the risk of weakening popular support for the Church's position on abortion.

In any event the 1917 Code is largely restated (*CIC* 2350, §1). All involved in the deliberate and successful effort to eject a non-viable fetus from the mother's womb incur a *latae sententiae* excommunication. The 1917 Code is modified in two respects: the penalty is not reserved to the ordinary, and there is no separate penalty for clerics (deposition).

TITLE VII
GENERAL NORM
[c. 1399][76]

Canon 1399 — Besides the cases stated here or in other laws, an external violation of a divine or an ecclesiastical law can be punished by a just penalty only when the particular seriousness of the violation demands punishment and there is an urgent need to preclude or repair scandal.

Book VI closes with a general norm providing for a penalty even if it is not explicitly determined in any statute. The canon raises the issue of the application of the so-called "principle of legality" (*nulla poena sine lege*: "no penalty without a law") in the ecclesiastical arena. The issue is too complex to be dealt with here, hence the reader should consult the following bibliographical references. In any event there was a dispute among those evaluating the original schema (c. 73). Some favored the canon because of the impossibility of exhaustively listing all ecclesiastical offenses. Others opposed it because of a fear of arbitrary action by church authorities which might possibly violate the basic rights of believers. A particularly significant factor influencing the revised law was the approval in principle of this

[73]The residential bishop would take the penal initiative in the case of pastors and parochial vicars. In the case of the residential bishop, the metropolitan reports the problem to the Holy See, which is to take appropriate action (c. 395, §4). Nothing is said explicitly about the coadjutor or auxiliary bishop who seriously violates the obligation of residence; presumably the residential bishop would report the matter to the Holy See for appropriate action.

[74]For a discussion of these canons by the penal law committee, see *Comm* 9 (1977), 317. Also Green, "Penal Law Revisited," 189–190. For the corresponding canons in the 1917 Code, see Bouscaren, 934–935 and Vermeersch-Creusen, 352–353; 356–357.

[75]If the homicide, however, is perpetrated against various hierarchical figures, clerics, and religious, c. 1370 is operative.

[76]For a discussion of this canon by the penal law committee, see *Comm* 9 (1977), 318; 321. See also Green, "Penal Law Revisited," 138–139; 191–192. Id., "Future of Penal Law," 228–232. For the corresponding canon of the 1917 Code (*CIC* 2222, §1), see Bouscaren, 876; Vermeersch-Creusen, 248.

canon by the May 1977 plenary session of the Code Commission.

Great caution should be employed in applying this canon, which speaks of the "particular seriousness of the violation" and the "urgent need to preclude or repair scandal." The just penalty or penance envisioned should normally be less severe than for violations specified in the preceding canons since the alleged offender, however culpable, could neither have anticipated the penalty nor adequately defended himself or herself. Finally, the penalty is clearly expiatory since no warning is necessary and the primary focus is not the reform of the offender but the restoration of the violated ecclesial order.

TABLE 1
EXCOMMUNICATIONS (9)

LS = *latae sententiae* (7)   F = facultative (2)
FS = *ferendae sententiae* (2)

Canon	Brief Designation of Offense	Nature of Penalty
1. 1364, §1	Apostasy, heresy, or schism	*LS*
2. 1367	Violation of sacred species	*LS* (reserved to Holy See)
3. 1370, §1	Physical attack on pope	*LS* (reserved to Holy See)
4. 1378, §1	Absolution of an accomplice	*LS* (reserved to Holy See)
5. 1378, §3	Pretended celebration of Eucharist or conferral of sacramental absolution by one not a priest	*FS*/F (dependent on gravity of offense)
6. 1382	Unauthorized episcopal consecration	*LS* (reserved to Holy See)
7. 1388, §1	Direct violation of confessional seal by confessor	*LS* (reserved to Holy See)
8. 1388, §2	Violation of confessional seal by interpreter and others	*FS*/F
9. 1398	Procuring of abortion	*LS*

TABLE 2
INTERDICTS (7)

LS = *latae sententiae* (4)   P = preceptive (3)
FS = *ferendae sententiae* (3)

Canon	Brief Designation of Offense	Nature of Penalty
1. 1370, §2	Physical attack on bishop	*LS*
2. 1373	Stirring up opposition to Holy See or ordinary	*FS*/P (possibility of other just penalties)
3. 1374	Promoting or governing forbidden society contrary to the Church	*FS*/P
4. 1378, §2	Pretended celebration of Eucharist or conferral of sacramental absolution by one not a priest	*LS*
5. 1380	Simoniacal reception of sacrament	*FS*/P
6. 1390, §1	False accusation of a confessor of solicitation	*LS*
7. 1394, §2	Religious (non-cleric) in perpetual vows attempting civil marriage	*LS*

TABLE 3
Suspensions (9)

LS = *latae sententiae* (6)   P = preceptive (3)
FS = *ferendae sententiae* (3)

Canon	Brief Description of Offense	Nature of Penalty
1. 1370, §2	Cleric physically attacking bishop	*LS*
2. 1378, §2	Cleric not a priest pretending to offer Eucharist or confer sacramental absolution	*LS*
3. 1380	Simoniacal celebration of sacrament	*FS*/P
4. 1383	Bishop ordaining without proper dimissorials	*LS* (no conferral of order for year)
5. 1383	One ordained without proper dimissorials	*LS* (no exercise of order received)
6. 1387	Solicitation in confession by confessor	*FS*/P
7. 1390, §1	Cleric falsely accusing a confessor of solicitation	*LS*
8. 1394, §1	Attempted marriage of cleric	*LS*
9. 1395, §1	Cleric living in concubinage or persisting in other sexual sins	*FS*/P

TABLE 4
References to a Censure Being Imposed without Further Specification (4)
(all *ferendae sententiae*)

F = facultative (1)   P = preceptive (3)

Canon	Brief Description of Offense	Nature of Penalty
1. 1366	Parents/surrogates handing over children for non-Catholic baptism or education	P (other just penalty possible)
2. 1372	Recourse to ecumenical council or college of bishops against papal act	P
3. 1385	Trafficking in Mass stipends	P (other just penalty possible)
4. 1390, §§2–3	Calumnious denunciations of offenses other than solicitation by confessor or damaging of reputation	F (required restitution also possible)

TABLE 5
Generic References to Expiatory Penalties in Canon 1336 (4)
(all *ferendae sententiae*)

F = facultative (2)   P = preceptive (2)

Canon	Brief Description of Offense	Nature of Penalty
1. 1364, §1	Apostasy, heresy, or schism involving cleric	F
2. 1387	Solicitation in confession by confessor	P (dependent on gravity of offense)
3. 1394, §1	Persistence of cleric in attempted marriage after warning	F
4. 1397	Homicide, abduction, and mutilation (except for c. 1370)	P (dependent on gravity of offense)

TABLE 6
Offenses Warranting Dismissal from the Clerical State (7)
(all *ferendae sententiae*)

F = facultative (6)   P = preceptive (1)

Canon	Brief Description of Offense	Nature of Penalty
1. 1364, §2	Contumacy or serious scandal given by cleric in apostasy, heresy, or schism	F (other penalties possible)
2. 1367	Violation of sacred species by cleric	F (other penalty possible)
3. 1370, §1	Physical attack on pope by cleric	F (other penalty possible)
4. 1387	Serious cases of solicitation in confession by confessor	P
5. 1394, §1	Persistence of cleric in attempted marriage after warning	F
6. 1395, §1	Persistence of cleric in concubinage or other sexual offenses after warning	F (other penalties possible)
7. 1395, §2	Clerical commission of other sexual sins through force, threats, done publicly, or with minor under sixteen	F (other just penalties possible)

TABLE 7
Offenses Warranting Deprivation of Office (2)
(both *ferendae sententiae*)

F = facultative (2)

Canon	Brief Description of Offense	Nature of Penalty
1. 1389, §1	Abuse of ecclesiastical office or authority	F
2. 1396	Grave violation of residence after a warning	F

TABLE 8
REFERENCES TO A PENALTY/JUST PENALTY WITHOUT FURTHER SPECIFICATION (18)

(all *ferendae sententiae*)

F = facultative (4)   P = preceptive (14)

Canon	Brief Description of Offense	Nature of Penalty
1. 1365	Prohibited *communicatio in sacris*	P
2. 1368	Perjury before an ecclesiastical authority	P
3. 1369	Abuse of the Church or religious values in media	P
4. 1370, §3	Physical attack on cleric other than pope or bishop or religious in contempt of Church, its authority and ministry	P
5. 1371	Persistent teaching of condemned doctrine or rejection of authentic teaching after warning or persistent disobedience to Holy See, ordinary, or religious superior after warning	P
6. 1374	Membership in forbidden society plotting against Church	P
7. 1375	Various violations of church freedom	F
8. 1376	Profanation of sacred goods	P
9. 1377	Illegal alienation of church property	P
10. 1379	Simulated administration of sacraments other than Eucharist or sacramental absolution	P
11. 1381	Usurpation or illegal retention of ecclesiastical office	P
12. 1384	Instances of illegitimate exercise of priestly office or other ecclesiastical office besides those specified in canons 1378–1383	F
13. 1386	Bribery of church official or acceptance of such a bribe	P
14. 1388, §1	Indirect violation of confessional seal by confessor	P (dependent on gravity of offense)
15. 1389, §2	Culpable negligence in office causing damage	P
16. 1391	Falsification of ecclesiastical documents, making of false assertions in such, or use of them	F (dependent on gravity of offense)
17. 1392	Clerics or religious engaged in illegal speculation	P (dependent on gravity of offense)
18. 1393	Violation of obligations imposed on one by ecclesiastical penalty	F

TABLE 9
REFERENCES TO A JUST PENALTY ALONG WITH A REFERENCE TO OTHER PENALTIES IN THE SAME CANON; REFERENCES ALSO TO OTHER PENALTIES IN CERTAIN CANONS ABOVE AND BEYOND SPECIFIC REFERENCES TO A PARTICULAR PENALTY (13)
(all *ferendae sententiae*)

F = facultative (6)   P = preceptive (7)

Canon	Brief Description of Offense	Nature of Penalty
1. 1364, §2	Protracted contumacy or grave scandal in connection with apostasy, heresy, or schism	F (dismissal from clerical state possible)
2. 1366	Parents/surrogates handing over children for non-Catholic baptism or education	P (censure possible)
3. 1367	Violation of sacred species by cleric	F (dismissal from clerical state possible)
4. 1370, §1	Cleric physically attacking pope	F (dismissal from clerical state possible)
5. 1373	Stirring up opposition to Holy See, ordinary, or religious superior	P (interdict also possible)
6. 1378, §3	Pretended celebration of Eucharist or conferral of sacramental absolution by one not a priest	F (excommunication also possible; dependent on gravity of offense)
7. 1385	Trafficking in Mass stipends	P (censure also possible)
8. 1388, §2	Violation of confessional seal by interpreter or others	P (excommunication possible)
9. 1389, §1	Abuse of ecclesiastical office or authority	P (dependent on gravity of offense; deprivation of office possible)
10. 1390, §2	Calumnious denunciations of offenses other than solicitation by confessor or damaging of reputation	F (censure possible)
11. 1395, §1	Cleric living in concubinage or persisting in other sexual sins even after warning	F (dismissal from clerical state also possible)
12. 1395, §2	Clerical commission of other sexual sins through force, threats, done publicly, or with minor under sixteen	P (dismissal from clerical state also possible)
13. 1396	Grave violation of residence	P (dismissal from clerical state also possible)

TABLE 10
LATAE SENTENTIAE PENALTIES (17)

Excommunications – 7   Interdicts – 4
(5 reserved to Holy See)   Suspensions – 6

Canon	Brief Description of Offense	Nature of Penalty
1. 1364, §1	Apostasy, heresy, or schism	Excommunication
2. 1367	Violation of sacred species	Excommunication (reserved to Holy See)
3. 1370, §1	Physical attack on pope	Excommunication (reserved to Holy See)
4. 1370, §2	Physical attack on bishop	Interdict Suspension (cleric)
5. 1378, §1	Absolution of an accomplice	Excommunication (reserved to Holy See)
6. 1378, §2	Pretended celebration of Eucharist or conferral of sacramental absolution by one not a priest	Interdict Suspension (cleric)
7. 1382	Unauthorized episcopal consecration	Excommunication (reserved to Holy See)
8. 1383	Bishop ordaining without proper dimissorials	Suspension from conferring order for a year
9. 1383	One ordained without proper dimissorials	Suspension from exercise of order
10. 1388, §1	Direct violation of confessional seal by confessor	Excommunication (reserved to Holy See)
11. 1390, §1	False accusation of a confessor of solicitation	Interdict Suspension (cleric)
12. 1394, §1	Attempted marriage of cleric	Suspension
13. 1394, §2	Religious (non-cleric) in perpetual vows attempting civil marriage	Interdict
14. 1398	Procuring of abortion	Excommunication

TABLE 11
PRECEPTIVE PENALTIES (36)
(all *ferendae sententiae*)

Excommunication – 1   Penalty – 3
Interdict – 3   Expiatory penalty – 2
Suspension – 3   Dismissal from clerical state – 2
Censure – 2   Deprivation of office – 2
Just penalty – 18

Canon	Brief Description of Offense	Nature of Penalty
1. 1365	Prohibited *communicatio in sacris*	just penalty
2. 1366	Parents/surrogates handing over children for non-Catholic baptism or education	just penalty
3. 1368	Perjury before an ecclesiastical authority	just penalty
4. 1369	Abuse of the Church or religious values in media	just penalty
5. 1370, §3	Physical attack on cleric other than pope or bishop or religious in contempt of Church, its authority, and ministry	just penalty
6. 1371	Persistent teaching of condemned doctrine or rejection of authentic teaching after warning or persistent disobedience to Holy See, ordinary, or religious superior after warning	just penalty
7. 1372	Recourse to ecumenical council or college of bishops against papal act	censure
8. 1373	Stirring up opposition to Holy See, ordinary, or religious superior	just penalty or interdict
9. 1374	Membership in forbidden society plotting against Church	just penalty
10. 1374	Promoting or governing forbidden society contrary to the Church	interdict
11. 1376	Profanation of sacred goods	just penalty
12. 1377	Illegal alienation of church property	just penalty
13. 1379	Simulated administration of sacraments other than Eucharist or sacramental absolution	just penalty
14. 1380	Simoniacal celebration or reception of sacrament	interdict suspension (cleric)
15. 1381	Usurpation or illegal retention of ecclesiastical office	just penalty
16. 1385	Trafficking in Mass stipends	just penalty (censure possible)
17. 1386	Bribery of church official or acceptance of such a bribe	just penalty
18. 1387	Solicitation in confession by confessor	suspension, expiatory penalties, dismissal from clerical state dependent on gravity of offense
19. 1388, §1	Indirect violation of confessional seal by confessor	penalty dependent on gravity of offense
20. 1388, §2	Violation of confessional seal by interpreter or others	just penalty (excommunciation possible)

TABLE 11   *(continued)*

Canon	Brief Description of Offense	Nature of Penalty
21. 1389, §1	Abuse of ecclesiastical office or authority	penalty (dependent on gravity of offense; deprivation of office possible)
22. 1389, §2	Culpable negligence in office causing damage	just penalty
23. 1392	Clerics or religious engaged in illegal speculation	penalty (dependent on gravity of offense)
24. 1395, §1	Cleric living in concubinage or persisting in other sexual sins	suspension
25. 1395, §2	Clerical commission of other sexual sins through force, threats, done publicly, or with minor under sixteen	just penalties (dismissal from clerical state possible)
26. 1396	Grave violation of residence	just penalty (deprivation of office possible)
27. 1397	Homicide, abduction, and mutilation (except for c. 1370)	various expiatory penalties (dependent on gravity of offense)

TABLE 12
FACULTATIVE PENALTIES (17)
JUDGE OR SUPERIOR MAY BUT NEED NOT INFLICT PENALTY
(all *ferendae sententiae*)

Excommunication – 1	Other penalty – 4
Censure – 1	Expiatory penalty – 2
Just penalty – 5	Dismissal from clerical state – 4

Canon	Brief Description of Offense	Nature of Penalty
1. 1364, §1	Apostasy, heresy, or schism involving cleric	various expiatory penalties
2. 1364, §2	Protracted contumacy or grave scandal in connection with apostasy, heresy, or schism	other penalties (dismissal for cleric possible)
3. 1367	Violation of sacred species by cleric	other penalty including possible dismissal
4. 1370, §1	Cleric physically attacking pope	other penalty including possible dismissal
5. 1375	Various violations of church freedom	just penalty
6. 1378, §3	Pretended celebration of Eucharist or conferral of sacramental absolution by one not a priest	additional penalties including possible excommunication
7. 1384	Instances of illegitimate exercise of priestly office or other ecclesiastical office besides those specified in canons 1378–1383	just penalty
8. 1390, §§2–3	Calumnious denunciations of offenses other than solicitation by confessor or damaging of reputation	just penalty including possible censure and possible requirement of restitution
9. 1391	Falsification of ecclesiastical documents, making false assertions in such, or use of them	just penalty (depending on gravity of offense)
10. 1393	Violation of obligations imposed on one by an ecclesiastical penalty	just penalty
11. 1394, §1	Persistence of cleric in attempted marriage after warning	expiatory penalties including possible dismissal

BIBLIOGRAPHY

Commentaries on the 1917 Code

Abbo, J., and Hannan, J. *The Sacred Canons.* 2 vols. Vol. II, 779–871. St. Louis: B. Herder Book Co., 1952 (cited as Abbo-Hannan and volume).

Bouscaren, T.L.; Ellis, A.; and Korth, F. *Canon Law.* 4th ed., 863–975. Milwaukee: The Bruce Publishing Co., 1962 (cited as Bouscaren).

Michiels, G. *De Delictis et Poenis.* 3 vols., ed. 2a. Parisiis: Desclée, 1961 (cited as Michiels and volume).

Vermeersch, A., and Creusen, I. *Epitome Iuris Canonici.* 3 vols., editio septima. Vol. III, 219–400. Mechliniae-Romae: H. Dessain, 1956 (cited as Vermeersch-Creusen).

Official Code Commission Reports on the Revision of Penal Law

Comm 2 (1970): 99–107 (report on formulation of original 1973 schema).

Comm 7 (1975): 93–97 (report on observations of bishops and others consulted on original schema).

Comm 8 (1976): 166–183 (reworking of original cc. 1–15).

Comm 9 (1977): 147–174 (reworking of original cc. 16–47).

Comm 9 (1977): 304–322 (reworking of original cc. 48–73).

Commentaries on Original 1973 Schema

Green, T., et al. "Report of the Special Committee of the Task Force of the Canon Law Society of America on the Proposed Schema *De delictis et poenis.*" *CLSAP* (1974): 130–140.

Green, T. "The Future of Penal Law in the Church." *J* 35 (1975): 212–275 (bibliography on post-conciliar penal law reform literature on 274–275) (cited as "Future of Penal Law").

de Paolis, V. "Animadversiones ad schema documenti quo disciplina sanctionum seu poenarum in Ecclesia Latina denuo ordinatur." *P* 63 (1974): 489–507.

Provost, J. "Revision of Book V of the Code of Canon Law." *Stud Can* 9 (1975): 135–152.

Scheuermann, A. "Das Schema 1973 für das kommende kirchliche Strafrecht." *AkK* 143 (1974): 3–63.

Commentary on the Revision of the Original 1973 Schema (largely the same as the present Book VI)

Green, T. "Penal Law Revisited: the Revision of the Penal Law Schema." *Stud Can* 15 (1981): 135–198 (cited as "Penal Law Revisited").

BOOK VII
PROCESSES
[cc. 1400–1752]

Lawrence G. Wrenn

1. Ecclesiastical Judgments before Constantine

The Church, it may be said, is one, holy, catholic, apostolic, and adjudicative. Courts and trials have been part of our community life from the very beginning.

According to Matthew, the Evangelist, it was Jesus himself who drafted the first procedural canon of the Church's law:

> If your brother should commit some wrong against you, go and point out his fault, but keep it between the two of you. If he listens to you, you have won your brother over. If he does not listen, summon another, so that every case may stand on the word of two or three witnesses. If he ignores them, refer it to the church. If he ignores even the church, then treat him as you would a Gentile or a tax collector. I assure you, whatever you declare bound on earth shall be held bound in heaven, and whatever you declare loosed on earth shall be held loosed in heaven.[1]

St. Paul obviously approved of the notion of having every case "stand on the word of two or three witnesses" because he twice reiterated that advice, once in his Second Letter to the Corinthians[2] and again in his First Letter to Timothy.[3]

Paul regretted that there should ever be litigations among the followers of Jesus, but he nevertheless accepted them as necessary and inevitable in a sinful Church. In his First Letter to the Corinthians, Paul urged that the incestuous man among them be driven from the community:

> What business is it of mine to judge outsiders? Is it not those inside the community you must judge? God will judge the others. "Expel the wicked man from your midst."[4]

In the next (sixth) chapter of that letter, Paul, amplifying the notion of Christians judging insiders, suggests, in effect, that the Church establish a kind of court system of its own in order to settle its problems internally:

> How can anyone with a case against another dare bring it for judgment to the wicked and not to God's holy people? Do you not know that the be-

lievers will judge the world? If the judgment of the world is to be yours, are you to be thought unworthy of judging in minor matters? Do you not know that we are to judge angels? Surely, then, we are up to deciding everyday affairs. If you have such matters to decide, do you accept as judges those who have no standing in the church? I say this in an attempt to shame you. Can it be that there is no one among you wise enough to settle a case between one member of the church and another? Must brother drag brother into court, and before unbelievers at that?[5]

By the year 197, when Tertullian wrote his *Apology* in an effort to convince the provincial governors of the Roman Empire that Christians were good, decent people, undeserving of the persecutions directed against them, he cited as one example of the uprightness of Christians their laudable court system. In the beautiful thirty-ninth chapter of the *Apology*, Tertullian reminded the Roman rulers that

> family possessions, which generally destroy brotherhood among you, create fraternal bonds among us. One in mind and soul, we do not hesitate to share our earthly goods with one another. All things are common among us but our wives. . . . But it is mainly the deeds of a love so noble that lead many to put a brand upon us. 'See,' they say, 'how they love one another.' . . . We are a body knit together by a common religious profession, by unity of discipline, and by the bond of a common hope. . . . We assemble to read our sacred writing . . . . In the same place also exhortations are made, rebukes and sacred censures are administered. *For with a great gravity is the work of judging carried on among us, as befits those who feel assured that they are in the sight of God; and you have the most notable example of judgment to come when anyone has sinned so grievously as to require his severance from us in prayer, in the congregation and in all sacred intercourse. The tried men of our elders preside over us, obtaining that honor not by purchase, but by established character.*[6]

It is clear from this text that the Matthaean exhortation about bringing one's brother before the community for judgment was still in practice, and,

---

[1] Mt 18: 15–18.
[2] 2 Cor 13: 1.
[3] 1 Tm 5: 19.
[4] 1 Cor 5:12–13.

[5] 1 Cor 6: 1–6
[6] *The Ante Nicene Fathers* III, 46–47. Order of sentences slightly altered; italics the author's.

indeed, of some import at the time of Tertullian. The *Didascalia*, however, probably written within a few decades of the *Apology*, spells out even more clearly what immense importance was attached to the role of judging in the early Church. Page after page of the *Didascalia* is devoted to the Church's court system, with detailed instructions on such matters as how the bishop-judge ought to handle the case of a falsely accused person, how the judge ought not to accept bribes, how both sides should be given a hearing, how the judge ought not to be a respecter of persons, and even how the judicatures of Christians ought to be held on the second day of the week, so that the matter might be settled before the next Sabbath.[7]

The "earliest Church historian," Eusebius, who was the bishop of Caesarea early in the fourth century, tells us that in the year 268, the then bishop of Antioch, because of his heretical beliefs and certain misdemeanors, had to be deposed. Among the specific complaints against the bishop were several that referred to his role as judge. It was alleged, and eventually proved, according to Eusebius that

> he extorts from the brethren, depriving the injured of their rights and promising to assist them for reward, yet deceiving them, and plundering those who in their trouble are ready to give that they may obtain reconciliation with their oppressors . . . and . . . that he practices chicanery in ecclesiastical assemblies, contrives to glorify himself, and deceive with appearances, and astonish the minds of the simple, preparing for himself a Tribunal and lofty throne, not like a disciple of Christ, and possessing a 'secretum,' like the rulers of the world, and so calling it, and strike his thigh with his hand and stamping on the Tribunal with his feet; or in that he rebukes and insults those who do not applaud, and shake their handkerchiefs as in theatres, and shout and leap about like the men and women that are stationed around him.[8]

It seems, therefore, that ecclesiastical courts, both good and bad, grew up along with the Church itself as part of the family. They were used and abused, admired and detested; but, above all, they were a fixture.

2. Ecclesiastical Judgments after Constantine

Once Constantine, the Roman emperor, became a Christian and, in particular, once he granted to bishops the same authority as civil judges in cases brought before them by the mutual consent of the parties,[9] it was inevitable that the procedural law of the Roman civil courts would influence and change the procedures of the Church courts. And so it did.

Perhaps the clearest single illustration of that influence of Roman law on church law is found in Gregory the Great's letter to John the Defender, the letter listed as number 45 in Book XIII of his collected letters.[10] Gregory was born in Rome somewhere around 540 to a distinguished patrician family. Before his ordination, Gregory was himself a judge in the civil system, prefect of the city of Rome, and president of the Roman Senate. When, therefore, he became pope in 590, he was a true expert in law and government. At a point in his pontificate, news came to Gregory of a couple of particularly delicate matters in Spain that had already come to the attention of the local church courts. Gregory sent John the Defender to Spain and, in Letter 45, Gregory instructed John, who had in effect been designated as Gregory's judicial vicar for these particular cases, how to proceed. The pope told John that he wanted him to review and evaluate the procedures, testimony, and merits of the first instance hearing; and time and time again, Gregory quoted chapter and verse for John from Justinian's *Code* and *Novels*. Gregory was saying, in other words, that the rules and directives of Roman civil law (the *Code* and *Novels*, along with two other works called the *Institutes* and *Digest*, were a systematic collection of several centuries of imperial legislation ordered by and published under Emperor Justinian shortly before Gregory was born) could and should be utilized in church courts.

The influence of Roman law on ecclesiastical court procedures still endures. The following chapter headings, for example, which are immediately familiar to anyone conversant with the Codes of Canon Law, are in fact lifted verbatim from the *Corpus Iuris Civilis* (as Justinian's four collections came to be known): *De ordine iudiciorum, De foro competenti, De litis contestatione, De dilationibus, De procuratoribus, De actionibus et exceptionibus, De praescriptionibus, De re iudicata, De effectu sententiarum,* and *De restitutionibus in integrum.*[11]

3. The Decretals of Pope Gregory IX

Although a complete history of procedural law in the Church is far beyond the scope of these few introductory remarks, still there is one essential link between the early Church and the contemporary Church which is altogether too important to go unmentioned: the *Decretals* of Pope Gregory IX. In the year 1234, Gregory IX collected several centu-

---

[7] *Constitutions of the Holy Apostles*, Book II, Sections III–VI, *The Ante Nicene Fathers* VII, 398–421.

[8] *The Church History of Eusebius*, VII, 30, *The Nicene and Post Nicene Fathers*, Second Series, I (New York: The Christian Literature Co., 1890), 314.

[9] *Codex Theodosianus*, I 27, 1: Mommson-Meyers (Berlin, 1905), 62.

[10] *PL* 77, 1294–1300.

[11] *Institutiones* IV 6, 13; *Digesta* IV 1, XLII 1, XLIV 1, 2; *Codex* II 13, III 8, 9, 11, 13.

ries' worth of ecclesiastical laws and arranged them (following the order utilized by Bernard of Pavia in his *Collectio Prima* of some forty years earlier) into five books: *Iudex, Iudicium, Clerus, Connubia,* and *Crimen.*

Book II of the *Decretals* was divided into thirty titles and a mere listing of them, at least for one acquainted with the titles of the two modern Codes, is a dramatic illustration of the continuity of procedural law in the Church over the centuries:

> *De iudiciis*
> *De foro competenti*
> *De libelli oblatione*
> *De mutuis petitionibus*
> *De litis contestatione*
> *Ut lite non contestata non procedatur ad testium receptionem vel ad sententiam definitivam*
> *De iuramento calumniae*
> *De dilationibus*
> *De feriis*
> *De ordine cognitionum*
> *De plus petitionibus*
> *De causa possessionis et proprietatis*
> *De restitutione spoliatorum*
> *De dolo et contumacia*
> *De eo, qui mittitur in possessionem causa rei servandae*
> *Ut lite pendente nihil innovetur*
> *De sequestratione possessionum et fructuum*
> *De confessis*
> *De probationibus*
> *De testibus et attestationibus*
> *De testibus cogendis vel non*
> *De fide instrumentorum*
> *De praesumptionibus*
> *De iureiurando*
> *De exceptionibus*
> *De praescriptionibus*
> *De sententia et re iudicata*
> *De appellationibus, recusationibus, et relationibus*
> *De clericis peregrinantibus*
> *De confirmatione utili vel inutili*[12]

4. An Outline of Book VII

The procedural law of the 1983 Code, which bears an amazingly strong likeness to its ancient ancestor, the *Decretals,* consists of three hundred fifty-three canons (1400–1752) and is divided into five parts: I "Trials in General"; II "The Contentious Trial"; III "Certain Special Procedures"; IV "Penal Procedure"; and V "On the Manner of Procedure in Administrative Recourse and the Removal and Transfer of Pastors."

The specific subjects (called titles) treated in this Book VII are almost exactly the same as those in Book IV of the 1917 Code, but the distribution of

the titles into sections and parts is quite different. Part I of the 1917 Code, as a matter of fact, included all of the titles treated in parts I, II, III, and IV of the revised Code.

The outline following par. 260 provides an overview of how the material is treated in both Codes. There, the author has used the English translation of all headings and occasionally abbreviated them, but, as already pointed out, the original Latin titles are often identical with those found in both Justinian (ca. 535) and Gregory IX (1234).

5. Some General Observations

a. The principal subject of the 1917 Code that is not repeated in the 1983 Code is 1917's part II on beatification and canonization procedures. Canon 1403 of the 1983 Code notes that henceforth investigations regarding canonizations will follow special pontifical norms which will not be included in the general Code of law for the Church.

b. It is also apparent that the 1983 Code introduces two new types of procedure, namely, "The Oral Contentious Process" (part II, section II) and "Recourse against Administrative Decrees" (part V, section I). These will both be discussed in place.

c. The matter of "Methods of Avoiding a Trial" (part III, title III) seems rather oddly placed in both the 1917 and the 1983 Codes, though interestingly, it was assigned the same relative position in the third century *Didascalia*'s own rather lengthy treatment of ecclesiastical judicatories.[13]

d. The first seventeen titles, all treated in the 1917 Code as part I, section I, are better and more clearly distributed in the 1983 Code which treats only the first five titles, all general in nature, under part I, and then devotes part II, section I to a chronological explanation of a specific trial, beginning with "The Introduction of the Case" (title I) and ending with "Execution of the Sentence" (title XI).

e. Although "Matrimonial Procedures" (title I) and "Cases for Declaring Nullity of Sacred Ordination" (title II) are not listed under "The Contentious Trial" (part II), but are, instead, considered "Certain Special Procedures" (part III), it should nevertheless be noted that the canons regarding "Trials in General" (part I) and "The Ordinary Contentious Trial" (part II, section I) *also apply to* canonization cases (c. 1403), the oral contentious trial (c. 1670), marriage nullity cases (c. 1691), marriage separation cases (c. 1693), ordination nullity cases (c. 1710), and penal cases (c. 1728, §1) whenever the specific directives for these types of cases are wanting.

f. It should be noted further that, although marriage cases (which constitute practically the entire work load of our tribunals) have their own special norms and are thus treated under "Certain Special

---

[12] *CorpusIC* II, 239–448.

[13] See also par. 29, a.

Procedures," they are nevertheless considered as falling under the general category of *contentious* cases (c. 1425, §1, 1°).

That marriage cases should automatically be considered contentious is itself a contentious matter. Of course every trial, by its very nature, does involve a legal controversy. A legal controversy, however, may be either *contentious* (where one of the parties, e.g., the defender of the bond, contends the matter) or *non-contentious* (where none of the parties but only a presumption of law disputes the allegation). Many American and other canonists have contended for years that those marriage cases in which neither the respondent nor the defender opposes an annulment should be considered not as contentious, but simply as declarative of a person's official status in the Catholic community.

This is not merely a semantic problem but rather an important question of taxonomy. If, on the one hand, the point of a marriage case is to determine whether a person is married or single "in the eyes of the Church" (and therefore whether that person is or is not free to remarry in the Church and receive the sacraments), then the trial can be conducted with a minimum of formalities, a maximum of privacy and confidentiality, and a suitable, discretionary defense of the marriage bond. But, if on the other hand, a marriage case is automatically considered a contentious matter (even where both parties and even the defender of the bond agree that the marriage was certainly and clearly invalid), then legal formalities and publicity, i.e., publicness, will be increased and the defense of the bond will tend to be artificial.

It is this taxonomical dispute that is at the heart of the procedural differences between the two canonical camps in the Church today.

6. Chronology of the 1983 Revision

The early years of this revision were marked by four significant dates:

• *January 25, 1959* – when Pope John XXIII issued the initial call for a revision of the Code;

• *March 28, 1963* – when the Pontifical Commission for the Revision of the Code was established;

• *November 12, 1963* – when it was decided to postpone the work of revision until the end of the Second Vatican Council;

• *November 20, 1965* – when Pope Paul VI inaugurated the work of the Commission.

Following Pope Paul's inauguration, the consultors comprising the various study groups began their meetings. The *De processibus* group had its first meeting in May 1966 and for the next several years met, for a week or so at a time, two or three times a year.[14]

Finally, after ten years of work, the Commission issued, on November 3, 1976, the *Schema Canonum De Modo Procedendi Pro Tutela Iurium seu de Processibus,* which was distributed to the various bishops of the world and consultative organs. It was accompanied by a request that they return to the Commission any observations they might have on the schema by September 1977.

Using these observations, the consultors then met:

• in April and May of 1978 – to revise the present canons 1400–1490;[15]

• in October, November, and December of 1978 – to revise canons 1491–1649;[16]

• in March and May of 1979 – to revise canons 1650–1752.[17]

The final draft was then incorporated into the 1980 draft of the revised Code and from there, with some few more revisions, into the final text.

The revision of the procedural law for marriage annulment cases has its own history and will be discussed in place.[18]

7. Some Basic Definitions

A *process* (*processus*) is a complexus of acts or solemnities, prescribed by law and to be observed by public authority, for solving questions or settling business.

A *procedure* (*procedura*) is simply a way of proceeding (*modus procedendi*); it can be either judicial or extra-judicial.

A *trial* (*iudicium*) is a hearing, discussion, and settlement by a judge of a legal controversy which arises between a plaintiff and a respondent.

An *ecclesiastical trial* is a discussion and settlement by an ecclesiastical tribunal of a controversy in a matter in which the Church enjoys competence.

8. Basic Elements of a Trial

There are five basic elements to a trial: the material object, the formal object, the active subject, the passive subject, and the form. These five elements comprise the subject matter of part I of this Book

---

[14]These meetings are described in *Comm* 6 (1974), 37–43; 216–219.

[15]These meetings are described in *Comm* 10 (1978), 209–272.

[16]These meetings are described in *Comm* 11 (1979), 67–162.

[17]These meetings are described in *Comm* 11 (1979), 243–296.

[18]See par. 206.

on procedural law. These elements are discussed according to the following order:

c. 1400 – *the material object,* i.e., the matters that can, in general, be addressed by a court.

c. 1401 – *the active subject,* i.e., the judge or tribunal before whom the case is tried. Canon 1401 states the general principle that the Catholic Church does indeed have the right to hear certain cases. Canons 1404–1475 (titles I–III) treat this matter more in detail.

c. 1402 – *the form,* i.e., the procedures or solemnities that are followed in the adjudication of certain matters. This canon states the general rule.

c. 1476 – *the passive subject,* i.e., the petitioner or respondent whose case is being heard. This matter, along with the procurators and advocates for the parties, is treated in canons 1476–1490 (title IV).

c. 1491 – *the formal object,* i.e., the precise claim or counter-claim made by the parties in a particular hearing. This matter is treated in canons 1491–1500 (title V).

CANONS AND COMMENTARY

Part I
TRIALS IN GENERAL
[cc. 1400–1500]

Canon 1400 — **§1. The object of a trial is:**
1° to prosecute or to vindicate the rights of physical or juridic persons, or to declare juridic facts;
2° to impose or declare the penalty for offenses.
§2. However, controversies which have arisen from an act of administrative power can be brought only before the superior or an administrative tribunal.

9. Material Object of a Trial

Paragraph one of this canon states the general principle, while paragraph two states a specification.

The general principle is that the matters that may be addressed by a tribunal are rights to be attained or vindicated or juridic facts to be declared (§1, 1°)—in which case the trial is called *contentious,* and crimes to be examined with a view toward imposing or declaring a penalty (§1, 2°)—in which case the trial is called *penal.* Although the terms *contentious* and *penal* (formerly *criminal*) are not actually contained in this canon (as they had been in *CIC* 1552), it is clear from canon 1425, §1 that the terms are still, in fact, operative and complementary. In other words, the possible division of non-penal cases, mentioned in par. 5, f, into contentious and non-contentious, is not recognized in this Code.

The specification in paragraph two is to the effect that, when such matters are the result of some administrative act (when, for example, one is aggrieved by a decision or decree of a bishop),[19] then, if the dispute cannot be settled informally (c. 1733, §1), the case goes not to an *ordinary* tribunal but either to an *administrative* tribunal or to the hierarchic superior.

The option of going either to the hierarchic superior or to an administrative tribunal was not offered in the 1917 Code. Canon 1601 of that Code, which was concerned with decrees of an ordinary, spoke only of the hierarchic superior. It read, "Against decrees of the Ordinary there is no appeal or recourse to the Sacred Rota; it is rather the Sacred Congregations which enjoy exclusive competence regarding recourses of this kind."

On August 15, 1967, however, as part of the Apostolic Constitution *Regimini Ecclesiae universae,* a second section was established within the Signatura to serve as an administrative tribunal empowered to decide on "contentions which have arisen from the exercise of administrative ecclesiastical power."[20] The supreme administrative tribunal of the Church has now been incorporated into the Code both here and in canon 1445, §2.

---

[19] This does not apply, of course, in what is obviously quite a different matter, namely, when the rights or temporal goods of a juridic person represented by a bishop are at issue. Such cases are heard by the court of appeal (cf. c. 1419, §2). Neither does it apply to penal or contentious cases involving the person of the bishop. Such cases are heard either by the Holy Father or by the Rota (cf. 1405, §1, 3°; §3, 1°).

[20] See paragraph 106 of that constitution in *CLD* 6, 351. For a discussion of the nature of an administrative tribunal, i.e., whether it is judicial, extra-judicial or quasi-judicial, see Gordon, "De iustitia administrativa ecclesiastica tum transacto tempore tum hodierno," *P* 61 (1972), 251–378; idem, "De objecto primario competentiae 'Sectionis Alterius' Supremi Tribunalis Signaturae Apostolicae," *P* 58 (1979), 505–542. See also *Comm* 10 (1978), 217–218.

For a time, indeed, it was envisioned that there would not only be a supreme administrative tribunal in the Church but local administrative tribunals as well. In the 1980 draft of this Code, part V of this Book VII was not entitled "On the Manner of Procedure in Administrative Recourses and the Removal and Transfer of Pastors" as it is now, but simply "The Administrative Procedure," and that part V in the 1980 draft contained twenty canons (cc. 1689–1692, 1697–1698, and 1702–1715) which explained in considerable detail how administrative courts could be constituted at the episcopal conference level (they were envisioned as optional) and how they would function.

In preparation for the October 1981 meeting of the Commission, three members of the Commission recommended that these administrative courts be made obligatory rather than facultative for each conference. The Secretariate responded,

Although it is devoutly to be wished that administrative tribunals be regularly established in the Conference of Bishops, for the safeguarding of subjective rights and for the better ordering of administrative justice, it does not seem opportune to impose such a burden by universal law. Just to establish ordinary tribunals has been replete with difficulties since oftentimes qualified, experienced personnel are lacking; this would be all the more true in setting up administrative courts since the work of such courts is extremely sensitive and important and demands a profound grasp of the law and of justice. Besides, such courts constitute a major innovation in church law and it therefore seems appropriate to move somewhat gradually and voluntarily in a way that is tailored to local resources. Nor should we forget, finally, that hierarchic recourse is always available with the possibility of approaching the Signatura for a final decision.

Nevertheless, let the matter be referred to the Plenary Commission.[21]

In October 1981 the matter was referred to the Plenary Commission and the vote was fifty-three to six in favor of retaining administrative courts as optional rather than mandatory.

Nevertheless, when the Code finally appeared in 1983, all twenty canons dealing with local administrative courts had been deleted, and we are now left with the second section of the Signatura as the sole administrative tribunal in the Church.

10. Active Subject of a Trial

Canon 1401 — **By proper and exclusive right the Church adjudicates:**

1° cases concerning spiritual matters or connected with the spiritual;

2° the violation of ecclesiastical laws and all those cases in which there is a question of sin in respect to the determination of culpability and the imposition of ecclesiastical penalties.

The corresponding canon in the 1917 Code was much more complicated than this, concerning itself with the privilege of the forum (the right of clerics and religious to have been tried before an ecclesiastical rather than a civil court) and also with the problem of the mixed forum (where both the civil and ecclesiastical courts enjoyed competence).

The present canon 1401 makes the simple claim that the Church is exclusively competent (a) in spiritual matters (e.g., faith and morals, the sacraments, liturgy), (b) in those matters connected with the spiritual (e.g., the rights of a pastor to serve in a particular parish), (c) in cases involving a violation of a church law, and (d) in all those matters in which there is present the "ratio peccati," and the consequent possibility of imposing a church penalty. This phrase, the "ratio peccati," according to Charles Augustine, "is an allusion to a famous decretal of Innocent III, *Novit*, in which this great Pontiff assures the King of France and John Lackland of England that he has 'no intention to judge feuds, but to decide concerning sin, which undoubtedly belongs to him.' "[22]

Civil law generally recognizes this right of the Church to judge church matters, at least to the extent that it does not impinge on any civil right. *American Jurisprudence*, for example, the standard and authoritative encyclopedia on American civil law, notes the following:

If civil rights, as contradistinguished from ecclesiastical questions, are passed upon by a church tribunal, the secular courts will usually decide the merits of the case for themselves. But, according to the rule broadly stated by some courts, when a civil right depends upon some matter pertaining to ecclesiastical affairs, the civil tribunal tries the right and nothing more, taking the ecclesiastical decisions out of which the civil right has arisen as it finds them, and accepting such decisions as matters adjudicated by another legally constituted tribunal. Thus the decisions of the church tribunals as to questions of discipline, faith or ecclesiastical rules, customs or law affecting the members of the church must be accepted by legal tribunals as final and binding upon them in their application to a case before them.[23]

[21]*Rel,* 340–341.

[22]Augustine, 6. See also *CorpusIC* II, 242–244. As regards marriage cases, see cc. 1671–1672.
[23]*Am Jur,* 784, 32.

11. Form or Procedures of a Trial

Canon 1402 — With due regard for the norms established for the tribunals of the Apostolic See, all the tribunals of the Church are regulated by the following canons.

Canon 1403 — §1. The causes of the canonization of the servants of God are regulated by special pontifical law.

§2. The prescriptions of this Code, however, are applicable to the aforementioned causes whenever the pontifical law refers to the universal law or when it is a question of norms which affect those causes from the very nature of the matter.

Canon 1402 notes that the tribunals of the Holy See follow their own special procedural norms.[24]

Canon 1403 is discussed briefly in par. 5, a and e.[25]

TITLE I
THE COMPETENT FORUM
[cc. 1404–1416]

12. Extraordinary Forum

Canon 1404 — The First See is judged by no one.

Canon 1405 — §1. It is the right of the Roman Pontiff himself alone to judge in cases mentioned in can. 1401:

1° those who hold the highest civil office in a state;

2° cardinals;

3° legates of the Apostolic See and, in penal cases, bishops;

4° other cases which he has called to his own judgment.

§2. A judge cannot review an act or instrument explicitly (*in forma specifica*) confirmed by the Roman Pontiff without his prior mandate.

§3. Judgment of the following is reserved to the Roman Rota:

1° bishops in contentious cases, with due regard for the prescription of can. 1419, §2;

2° an abbot primate or an abbot superior of a monastic congregation and the supreme moderator of religious institutes of pontifical right;

3° dioceses or other ecclesiastical persons,

whether physical or juridic, which do not have a superior below the Roman Pontiff.

Canon 1406 — §1. Acts and decisions made in violation of the prescription of can. 1404 are considered invalid.

§2. The incompetence of other judges is absolute in the cases mentioned in can. 1405.

a. Canon 1404 is not a statement about the personal impeccability or inerrancy of the Holy Father. Should, indeed, the pope fall into heresy, it is understood that he would lose his office. To fall from Peter's faith is to fall from his chair.[26] The question, however, of who or what body (probably a general council) would determine whether, in fact, the pope had fallen into heresy is unclear historically and is obviously not settled by this canon.

While not a statement about impeccability or inerrancy, canon 1404 *is* a statement about the judicial immunity of the First See. It says that the Holy Father cannot be tried by a secular or religious court and, perhaps particularly, given the history of the question, by a general council. The *Constitution on the Church of Christ* of the First Vatican Council, for example, said,

> We also teach and declare that he [the Roman Pontiff] is the supreme judge of all the faithful, to whose judgment appeal can be made in all matters which come under ecclesiastical examination. But the verdict of the Apostolic See may be rejected by no one, since there is no higher authority, and no one may pass judgment on its judgment. Hence they stray from the right path of truth who affirm that it is permissible to appeal to a General Council against the judgments of the Roman Pontiffs, as if the General Council were a higher authority than the Roman Pontiff.[27]

b. As regards canon 1405, §1, 1°, the purpose of reserving such cases to the Holy See is not to provide a privilege to the governmental head but rather to remove the possibility of a local judge being pressured to give a favorable decision.

c. Canon 1405, §2 appeared in slightly different form as canon 1683 in the 1917 Code in a chapter on "Actions Relating to Invalid Acts" which is now deleted. The sense of the present paragraph is that, once an act has been ratified or sanated (explicitly confirmed) by the pope, then it can no long-

[24]For the norms followed by the Signatura, see the 1968 revision as found in *CLD* 7, 246–272. For those followed by the Rota, see the 1969 revision as found in *CLD* 8, 1055–1079. The SCDF issued norms in 1971 for doctrinal examinations (*CLD* 7, 181–184), in 1973 for privilege of the faith cases (*CLD* 8, 1177–1184), and in 1980 for dispensations from clerical celibacy (*CLD* 9, 92–101).

[25]For a copy of the 1969 revision of the canonization process, see *CLD* 7, 1015–1019.

[26]See T. Izbicki, "Infallibility and the Erring Pope" in *Law, Church and Society*, Pennington and Somerville, eds. (Philadelphia: University of Pennsylvania Press, 1977); M. Schmaus, "Pope" in *Readings, Cases, Materials in Canon Law*, J. Hite, G. Sesto, and D. Ward, eds. (Collegeville: Liturgical Press, 1980); S. Ozment, *The Age of Reform 1250–1550* (New Haven: Yale University Press, 1980), 160–164.

[27]*Ench*, 1830.

er be challenged or adjudicated by an inferior judge without a special mandate. In effect, in other words, it becomes a fifth type of case (added to the four in §1) that is reserved to the pope himself.

d. Canon 1406 introduces the matter of incompetence. A tribunal which would dare to try the pope was regarded by the 1917 Code as *absolutely* incompetent. To be absolutely incompetent might seem like the ultimate in incompetence, but the 1983 Code actually takes this apparent extreme one step further; it regards the acts and decisions of such a tribunal "pro infectis," i.e., as though they never existed. Some people, understandably, regard this kind of canonical overkill, which is satisfied with nothing short of annihilation, as an excessive and triumphalistic legal fiction.

e. Incompetence can be either relative or absolute. (1) Relative incompetence stems from a territorial defect, while absolute incompetence stems from the grade of the tribunal, the dignity of the parties, or the quality of the issue;[28] (2) relative incompetence results in the judge acting illicitly, while absolute incompetence results in his acting invalidly;[29] (3) relative incompetence need not be declared by the judge after the *contestatio litis*, while absolute incompetence should be declared at any stage;[30] (4) relative incompetence may be challenged as an exception only before the *contestatio litis*, while absolute incompetence may be challenged at any time;[31] (5) relative incompetence can be prorogated or extended while absolute incompetence cannot;[32] and (6) relative incompetence does not result in the nullity of the sentence, whereas absolute incompetence results in a sentence that is incurably null.[33]

13. Ordinary Forum (cc. 1407–1416)

a. General Principles

Canon 1407 — §1. No one can be brought into a court of first instance unless before an ecclesiastical judge who is competent in virtue of one of the titles determined in cann. 1408-1414.

§2. The incompetence of a judge who possesses none of these titles is termed relative.

§3. The petitioner follows the forum of the respondent; but if the respondent has a number of fora, the choice of one among them is granted to the petitioner.

---

[28]Goyeneche I, 40.
[29]Regatillo, par. 350.
[30]C. 1461; *Comm* 10 (1978), 257.
[31]C. 1459, §§1, 2.
[32]C. 1405 (where other tribunals are absolutely incompetent) admits of no exceptions, whereas cc. 1411 and 1414 (where other tribunals are relatively incompetent) admit of an extension either by the parties or by the law itself.
[33]C. 1620, 1°.

For the special titles of competence in marriage cases, one should see canon 1673 and par. 209.

b. The Tribunal of Domicile or Quasi-Domicile

Canon 1408 — Anyone can be brought into court before the tribunal of one's own domicile or quasi-domicile.

For the acquisition and loss of domicile and quasi-domicile, one should see canons 102–106. This present canon clearly refers to the domicile or quasi-domicile of the respondent. In a case accepted on this basis, should the respondent relocate after the citation, the hearing is completed in the court in which it was initiated (c. 1512, 2°).

c. The Tribunals of the Transient and of the Unlocatable

Canon 1409 — §1. A transient has the forum of the place of actual residence.
§2. A person whose domicile, quasi-domicile or place of residence is not known can be brought into court in the forum of the petitioner provided no other legitimate forum is available.

The unlocatable person, a rarer phenomenon in 1917 than at present, went unmentioned in the 1917 Code. In our own day, however, there are hundreds of thousands of "missing persons" around the world so it was important for the 1983 Code to reflect that sociological reality.

It bears noting that, in the case of an unlocatable person, the forum of the petitioner acquires competence only if no other legitimate forum is available. To illustrate: a woman petitioner approaches her own United States diocese, e.g., New York, requesting an annulment. The marriage took place in San Juan, Puerto Rico. The husband is certainly somewhere in Puerto Rico but is unlocatable. Since San Juan is a legitimate forum, New York does not enjoy competence by reason of canon 1409, §2, though it might by reason of canon 1673, 4°.

d. The Tribunal of the Disputed Object

Canon 1410 — By reason of the location of a disputed item, a party can be brought into court before the tribunal of the place where the litigated thing is located whenever the action is directed against the thing or whenever it is a question of damages.

The *actio de spolio*, i.e., a suit to recover property of which one has been deprived (despoiled) was, in the 1917 Code, *necessarily* heard in the tribunal of the disputed object. The petitioner could approach only that tribunal to file such a suit. In the present Code that tribunal is merely an *optional* one. The plaintiff is free, in other words, to file his petition either with that tribunal or with one of the other competent tribunals listed in this group under the ordinary forum (c. 1407, §1).

e. The Tribunals of Contract, of Fulfillment and of Election

Canon 1411 — §1. By reason of contract a party can be brought into court before the tribunal of the place in which the contract was entered or must be fulfilled, unless the parties agree to choose another tribunal.

§2. If the case revolves around obligations which arise from another title, the party can be brought into court before the tribunal of the place in which the obligation either originated or is to be fulfilled.

Paragraph two of this canon, not included in the 1917 Code, notes that in what might be called quasi-contracts, i.e., other agreements and business arrangements, the tribunals where the agreement was made and where it is to be implemented are competent. In such cases, however, it would seem that the tribunal of election is not available to the parties.

f. The Tribunal of the Crime

Canon 1412 — In penal cases the accused, even if absent, can be cited before the tribunal of the place where the offense was perpetrated.

g. The Tribunals of Administration and for Bequests

Canon 1413 — A party can be brought into court:
1° in cases which concern administration before the tribunal of the place where the administration was conducted;
2° in cases which concern inheritances or pious legacies before the tribunal of the last domicile, quasi-domicile or place of residence of the person whose inheritance or pious legacy is the object of the action, in accord with the norm of cann. 1408-1409 unless it is a question of the mere execution of a legacy, which is to be examined according to the ordinary norms of competence.

h. The Tribunal of Connection

Canon 1414 — Unless a prescription of the law blocks this, by reason of connection cases which are interrelated are to be tried by one and the same tribunal and in the same procedure.

One should also see par. 60, b.

i. The Tribunal of First Citation

Canon 1415 — By reason of prevention, if two or several tribunals are equally competent, the tribunal which has first legitimately cited the respondent has the right to judge the case.

One should also see par. 48, a and canon 1482, §2.

j. The Settlement of Disputed Competence

Canon 1416 — Conflicts of competence between tribunals subject to the same appellate tribunal are resolved by that tribunal; if the tribunals are not subject to the same appellate tribunal, conflicts of competence are resolved by the Apostolic Signatura.

In the 1917 Code this canon appeared under title III (*CIC* 1612) rather than under title I. Since the canon deals with the determination of the competent forum, its present position seems more logical.

TITLE II
VARIOUS GRADES AND KINDS OF TRIBUNALS
[cc. 1417–1445]

14. General Principles (cc. 1417–1418)

a. Grades and Kinds (Species)

The *grade* of a tribunal is the place it holds in the judicial hierarchy. There are four grades of church tribunals: the first is the diocesan, the second is the metropolitan, the third is the regional, and the fourth is the tribunals of the Holy See.[34] It should be noted that the grade of tribunal does not always coincide with the grade of hearing or instance (*gradus iudicii*). A tribunal of the fourth grade, for example, may hear a case in the first instance (c. 1417).

The *kind (species)* of a tribunal is the particular type or class to which it belongs, depending on a variety of factors, even within the same grade. A tribunal may, for example, be a one-judge, three-judge, or five-judge tribunal; an ordinary or administrative tribunal; a diocesan or religious tribunal; etc.

b. Subordination of Tribunals

Tribunals follow the rules of subordination of canon 1438 when competence is not disputed, and the rules of canon 1416 when competence is disputed.

---

[34]Sipos, 713.

c. Petitioning a Roman Tribunal

Canon 1417 — §1. In virtue of the primacy of the Roman Pontiff, anyone of the faithful is free to bring to or introduce before the Holy See a case either contentious or penal in any grade of judgment and at any stage of litigation.

§2. A recourse made to the Apostolic See, however, does not suspend the exercise of jurisdiction by a judge who has already begun to adjudicate the case except in the case of an appeal; for this reason, the judge can pursue judgment up to the definitive sentence unless the Apostolic See has informed the judge that it has called the case to itself.

One should also see canon 1442.

d. Cooperation between Tribunals

Canon 1418 — Every tribunal has the right to call upon the assistance of another tribunal to instruct a case or to communicate acts.

When one court requests another to receive the testimony of someone residing within the territory of that second court, this request is made by a rogatorial letter,[35] and it is called a rogatorial commission.[36]

For an alternative procedure, one should see canon 1469, §2. As regards the precise place for receiving testimony, one should see canon 1558.

CHAPTER I
THE TRIBUNAL OF FIRST INSTANCE
[cc. 1419–1437]

ARTICLE 1: THE JUDGE
[cc. 1419–1427]

15. Diocesan Judge (cc. 1419–1422)

a. The Diocesan Bishop

Canon 1419 — §1. The diocesan bishop is the judge of first instance in each diocese and for all cases not expressly excepted by law; he can exercise his judicial power personally or through others in accord with the following canons.

§2. But if the action concerns the rights or the temporal goods of a juridic person represented by the bishop, the appellate tribunal judges in first instance.

The principal exceptions mentioned in paragraph one are found in canons 1400, §2; 1404; 1405; 1427, §§1 and 2; and paragraph two of this canon.

[35]Lega-Bartocetti I, 103.
[36]M. Reinhardt, *The Rogatory Commission, CanLawStud* 288 (Washington: Catholic University of America, 1949).

For a comparison of the case mentioned in paragraph two with similar cases, one should see par. 9, note 19.

b. The Judicial Vicar

Canon 1420 — §1. Each diocesan bishop is bound to appoint a judicial vicar or officialis with ordinary power to judge, distinct from the vicar general unless the smallness of the diocese or the small number of cases suggests otherwise.

§2. The judicial vicar constitutes one tribunal with the bishop but he cannot judge cases which the bishop reserves to himself.

§3. The judicial vicar can be given assistants whose title is adjutant judicial vicars or vice-officiales.

§4. Both the judicial vicar and the adjutant judicial vicars must be priests of unimpaired reputations, holding doctorates or at least licentiates in canon law and not less than thirty years of age.

§5. When the see is vacant, they do not cease from their office and they cannot be removed by the diocesan administrator; when the new bishop arrives, however, they need confirmation.

The officialis, or judicial vicar, sometimes referred to as the chief judge, is a priest chosen by the bishop to judge cases with ordinary power.

Although his jurisdiction is ordinary, not delegated; and vicarious, not proper (c. 131), the judicial vicar is distinct from the episcopal vicars discussed in canons 476–481. This is clear from the following: (1) canons 463, §1, 2° and 833, 5° both speak of the episcopal vicars *and* the judicial vicar, clearly indicating that the judicial vicar is not included among the episcopal vicars; (2) canon 472 says that those who exercise judicial power follow different norms from those who exercise administrative power; (3) canon 479 says that episcopal vicars have executive (rather than judicial) power to place administrative (rather than judicial) acts; and (4) canon 481, §1 says that episcopal vicars lose their power when the see is vacant (see also c. 418, §2, 1°) whereas the judicial vicar does not (c. 1420, §5).

The officialis, therefore, though he enjoys ordinary power, is not included when the law speaks about the "ordinary" (c. 134). Neither is he included in the episcopal council (c. 473, §4).

Like the episcopal vicar, however (c. 477, §1), the judicial vicar should be appointed for a definite but unspecified time (c. 1422). The 1917 Code did not suggest that the officialis should have a definite term of office. It did, however, indicate that the officialis was removable "ad nutum episcopi," whereas the 1983 Code (c. 1422) requires the bishop to have a legitimate and serious reason for removing the judicial vicar before his term expires.

c. The Diocesan Judges

Canon 1421 — §1. The bishop is to appoint diocesan judges in the diocese who are clerics.

§2. The conference of bishops can permit lay persons to be appointed judges; when it is necessary, one of them can be employed to form a collegiate tribunal.

§3. The judges are to be of unimpaired reputation and possess doctorates, or at least licentiates, in canon law.

Canon 1422 — The judicial vicar, the adjutant judicial vicars and the other judges are to be appointed for a definite period of time with due regard for the prescription of can. 1420, §5; they cannot be removed except for legitimate and serious cause.

(1) The 1917 Code (*CIC* 1574) did not permit lay persons to serve as judges. This was at least partly based on the common assumption that jurisdiction could be exercised only by those in holy orders.

After the Second Vatican Council, however, interest spread in permitting lay persons as well as clerics to function as judges.[37] In 1971, *Causas matrimoniales*[38] permitted the lay man but not the lay woman to serve as a judge (V, 1) and this regulation was incorporated into the 1976 and 1980 drafts of procedural law. Finally, this 1983 Code, in accord with the October 1981 vote of the members of the Commission to eliminate the discriminatory restriction, allowed that a qualified lay person of either sex may be appointed a judge.

For a discussion of the exercise of jurisdiction by lay persons, one should see the commentary on canon 129.

(2) Canon 1574 of the 1917 Code noted that diocesan judges exercised *delegated* power. The present canon has deleted that observation and, in accord with the definitions found in canon 131, §1, a diocesan judge would now seem to be exercising *ordinary* power.

(3) The law's interest in having key court personnel equipped with academic degrees is particularly apparent in canon 1421, §3. In the 1917 Code (*CIC* 1573, §5; 1574, §1; 1589) it was sufficient if the officialis, judges, and defender of the bond were expert in canon law. The 1983 Code, however (cc. 1420, §4; 1421, §3; 1435), requires that they have their licentiate in the law.

16. Interdiocesan Tribunal

Canon 1423 — §1. With the approval of the Apostolic See, several diocesan bishops may agree to establish for their dioceses a single tribunal of first instance in place of the diocesan tribunals mentioned in cann. 1419-1421; in this case the group of bishops or a bishop designated by them has all the powers which a diocesan bishop has over his own tribunal.

§2. The tribunals mentioned in §1 can be established either for any case whatsoever or only for some types of cases.

Although the 1917 Code does not specifically mention interdiocesan or regional tribunals, they were adverted to in *Regimini Ecclesiae universae* of 1967,[39] and the Signatura issued special norms to govern them in 1970.[40] They have, in fact, been functioning for several years now in various countries.

17. Singular and Collegiate Tribunal

Canon 1424 — In any trial a single judge can make use of two assessors, who are clerics or lay persons of upright life, to serve as his consultors.

Canon 1425 — §1. Every contrary custom being reprobated, the following cases are reserved to a collegiate tribunal of three judges:

1° contentious cases: a) concerning the bond of sacred ordination; b) concerning the bond of marriage with due regard for the prescriptions of cann. 1686 and 1688;

2° penal cases: a) concerning offenses which can entail the penalty of dismissal from the clerical state; b) concerning the imposition or declaration of excommunication.

§2. The bishop can entrust more difficult cases or cases of greater importance to the judgment of three or five judges.

§3. Unless the bishop has determined otherwise for individual cases, the judicial vicar is to assign the judges in order by turn to adjudicate the individual cases.

§4. If it happens that a collegiate tribunal cannot be established for a trial of first instance, the conference of bishops can permit the bishop to entrust cases to a single clerical judge as long as the impossibility of establishing a college perdures; he is to be a cleric and is to employ an assessor and an auditor where possible.

§5. The judicial vicar is not to appoint substitutes for judges once they are assigned unless for a most serious reason, expressed in a decree.

Canon 1426 — §1. A collegiate tribunal must proceed as a collegial body and pass its sentences by majority vote.

§2. The judicial vicar or the adjutant judicial

---

[37]See, for example, P. Frattin, "Lay Judges in Ecclesiastical Tribunals," *J* 28 (1968), 177–184.
[38]See par. 206.

[39]*CLD* 6, 351.
[40]*CLD* 7, 920–926.

vicar must preside over a collegiate tribunal insofar as this is possible.

a. For a discussion on the propriety of automatically considering all marriage cases as contentious, one should consult par. 5, f.

b. For remarks on the use of one judge in marriage cases, one should see par. 206.

c. Canon 1622, 1° notes that a sentence given by fewer judges than here required is null but curable. The 1917 Code (*CIC* 1892, 1°) regarded such a sentence as incurably null.

18. Religious Tribunal

Canon 1427 — §1. If there is a controversy between religious or houses of the same clerical religious institute of pontifical right, the judge of first instance is the provincial superior unless the constitutions provide otherwise; if it is an autonomous monastery, it is the local abbot.

§2. With due regard for the different prescriptions of the constitutions, if it is a contentious case between two provinces, the supreme moderator himself personally or through a delegate shall be the judge in first instance; if the contention is between two monasteries, it shall be the abbot superior of the monastic congregation.

§3. If the controversy arises between religious persons, physical or juridic, of different religious institutes or even of the same clerical or lay institute of diocesan right, or between a religious person and a secular cleric, or a lay person, or a non-religious juridic person, the diocesan tribunal judges in first instance.

ARTICLE 2: AUDITORS AND *RELATORS*
[cc. 1428–1429]

19. Auditor

Canon 1428 — §1. A judge or the president of a collegiate tribunal can designate an auditor to carry out the instruction of a case, selecting one either from among the judges of the tribunal or from among the persons approved for this function by the bishop.

§2. The bishop can approve for the function of auditor clerics or lay persons who are outstanding for their good character, prudence and learning.

§3. The only task of the auditor is to collect the proofs according to the mandate of the judge and to present them to the judge; unless the mandate of the judge states otherwise, the auditor can in the meantime decide which proofs are to be collected and how they are to be collected if such a question perhaps arises while the auditor is exercising his or her function.

a. The question of whether or not it is wise to involve auditors (or judge instructors, as they have been called)[41] in the judicial process, has long been hotly disputed. Cardinal Roberti, one of the more prestigious of the commentators on the procedural law of the 1917 Code, was of the opinion that judge instructors did more harm than good, since their involvement necessarily resulted in the principal judge losing that immediate contact with the parties and witnesses that is so important in deciding a case.[42] The same argument was made in an attempt to suppress the office of auditor in the 1983 Code at the April 8, 1978 meeting of the consultors of the Commission.[43]

The office has, however, been retained in the 1983 Code, and it has indeed been found immensely useful in some courts for many years now. Some American tribunals employ a great many instructors who are responsible for collecting and presenting all the evidence to the defender of the bond and the judge, thus enabling the court to be of assistance to far more people than would ever be possible if the judge had to do all the auditing personally. Roberti's point is, of course, a valid one but must be weighed against the demands being made on tribunals today to serve such large numbers of petitioners.

b. In its treatment of the auditor, the 1917 Code (*CIC* 1580–1583) completely neglected any mention of the qualities to be found in the auditor, except to say that if possible he should be selected from among the synodal judges. This may have been a lacuna but, more likely, it is just another indication that the 1917 Code viewed the auditor as a true, if subsidiary, judge and assumed, therefore, that he should possess the same qualities as the judge. The post-*CIC* commentators, furthermore, were in general agreement that since the auditor exercised judicial power, it would be necessary for him to be a cleric.[44] The present canon 1428, §2, however, explicitly permits the lay person (*Causas matrimoniales* permitted the lay *man*) to serve as auditor.[45]

[41]*CIC* 1614, §1 juxtaposed the auditor with the "principal judge" as though to imply that the auditor was the "subsidiary judge." *CIC* 1580 referred to the auditor as "instructor of the acts" and several commentators used the term "judge instructor." See also par. 89, a. The term "auditor" goes back to the early days of the Rota when the pope judged the case but employed others to audit (in an auditorium) the witnesses and collect and prepare the evidence. As a matter of fact, the men who even now serve as judges on the Rota are still referred to as auditors.

[42]Roberti I, 295.

[43]*Comm* 10 (1978), 232.

[44]Dugan, quoting D'Angelo, disagreed. H. Dugan, *The Judiciary Department of the Diocesan Curia* (Washington, D.C.: Catholic University of America, 1925), 52.

[45]See also par. 15, c.

20. Ponens

Canon 1429 — **The president of a collegiate tribunal must assign one of the collegiate judges as *ponens* or *relator* who reports on the case at the meeting of the judges and puts the sentence into writing; for a just cause the president may substitute another in place of the original *relator*.**

The *ponens,* or *relator,* has also been called the referee,[46] or commissioner (because it is he who "commits" the final sentence to writing).

ARTICLE 3: THE PROMOTER OF JUSTICE,
THE DEFENDER OF THE BOND AND
THE NOTARY
[cc. 1430–1437]

21. Promoter and Defender (cc. 1430–1436)

a. The Appointment of the Promoter

Canon 1430 — **A promoter of justice is to be appointed in a diocese for contentious cases in which the public good could be at stake and for penal cases; the promoter of justice is bound by office to provide for the public good.**

Canon 1431 — **§1. In contentious cases it is the task of the diocesan bishop to judge whether or not the public good could be at stake unless the intervention of the promoter of justice is prescribed by law or it is clearly necessary from the nature of the matter.**
§2. If the promoter of justice has intervened in a preceding instance, such intervention is presumed to be necessary in a further instance.

The promoter of justice, or prosecuting attorney, is involved in all penal cases and in those contentious cases in which the public welfare is involved. The public welfare is involved either (1) when the bishop decides it is (as, for example, when a quarrel between two priests over the possession of an office is judged to have become sufficiently public as to have scandalized the whole diocese), or (2) when the law says it is (as, for example, when c. 1691 indicates that the public good is involved in all marriage nullity cases and when c. 1696 declares that any separation case involves the commonweal), or (3) when the matter is obviously public (as, for example, when it is a highly publicized matter involving well-known people).
A particular promoter may be appointed, as canon 1436, §2 notes, either permanently or on an ad hoc basis, but canon 1430 indicates that there should be a promoter in every diocese.

b. The Appointment of the Defender

Canon 1432 — **A defender of the bond is to be appointed in a diocese for cases concerning the nullity of sacred ordination or the nullity or dissolution of marriage; the defender of the bond is bound by office to propose and clarify everything which can be reasonably adduced against nullity or dissolution.**

The office of defender postdates that of the promoter,[47] and some authors regard the defender as a species of promoter.[48] Like the promoter, a particular defender may be appointed either permanently or on an ad hoc basis (c. 1436, §2), but this canon indicates that there should be a defender in every diocese.

c. The Necessity of the Promoter and the Defender

Canon 1433 — **In cases which require the presence of the promoter of justice or the defender of the bond, the acts are invalid if they were not cited, unless, although not cited, they were actually present, or, at least before the sentence, could have fulfilled their office by inspecting the acts.**

d. The Rights of the Promoter and the Defender

Canon 1434 — **Unless express provision is made to the contrary:**
1° as often as the law requires the judge to hear the parties or one or other of them, the promoter of justice and the defender of the bond are also to be heard if they are present in court;
2° as often as the judge is required to decide something at the request of a party, the request of the promoter of justice or the defender of the bond has the same force when they are present in the court.

e. The Nomination, Qualities, Separateness, and Removal of the Promoter and Defender

Canon 1435 — **It is the task of the bishop to name the promoter of justice and the defender of the bond who are to be clerics or lay persons of unimpaired reputation who hold doctorates or licentiates in canon law and are proven in prudence and in zeal for justice.**

Canon 1436 — **§1. The same person can hold the office of promoter of justice and of defender of the bond but not in the same case.**

---

[46]Augustine, 40; Doheny I, 81.

[47]The promoter served as prosecutor during the Inquisition whereas the office of defender was not instituted until 1741 by Benedict XIV in the Constitution *Dei miseratione.*
[48]Coronata, 45.

§2. The promoter and defender can be appointed for all cases or for particular cases; they can, however, be removed by the bishop for a just cause.

Whereas the 1917 Code (*CIC* 1589) required the promoter and the defender to be priests, lay people may now serve in this capacity. The 1917 Code, however, did not require a licentiate in canon law for the holder of these offices but was satisfied with expertise.

22. Notary

Canon 1437 — §1. A notary is to be present during each procedure so that the acts are considered null if they have not been signed by the notary.
§2. Acts which notaries draw up warrant public trust.

CHAPTER II
THE TRIBUNAL OF SECOND INSTANCE
[cc. 1438–1441]

23. Designation of the Second Instance Court (cc. 1438–1439)

a. For the Diocesan Court

Canon 1438 — With due regard for the prescription of can. 1444, §1, n. 1:
1° from the tribunal of a suffragan bishop appeal is made to the metropolitan tribunal but the prescription of can. 1439 is to be observed;

b. For the Metropolitan Court

2° in cases in first instance tried before the metropolitan, appeal is made to the tribunal which he has permanently designated with the approval of the Apostolic See;

The 1917 Code (*CIC* 1594, §2) said that the court designated as the appeal court for an archdiocese would be named "semel pro semper," i.e., once and for all, but in practice the Holy See was quite prepared to change a metropolitan's court of appeal for a just reason. One American archdiocese, for example, had three different courts of appeal in the twenty-five years between 1953 and 1978. The 1983 Code is more realistic than the 1917 Code in expecting only that the designation be a stable one.

c. For a Religious Court

3° for cases tried before a provincial superior, the tribunal of second instance is before the supreme moderator; for cases tried before the local abbot, the tribunal of second instance is before the abbot superior of the monastic congregation.

d. For the Interdiocesan Court

Canon 1439 — §1. If a single tribunal of first instance has been established for several dioceses in accord with the norm of can. 1423, the conference of bishops must establish a tribunal of second instance with the approval of the Apostolic See unless these dioceses are all suffragans of the same archdiocese.
§2. The conference of bishops can establish one or several tribunals of second instance with the approval of the Apostolic See even beyond the cases mentioned in §1.
§3. The conference of bishops or a bishop designated by it has all the powers over the tribunals of second instance mentioned in §§1 and 2 which the diocesan bishop has over his own tribunal.

The appellate courts mentioned in paragraph two of this canon have become extremely popular in the United States since the promulgation of the 1983 Code.

24. Use of Non-Designated Second Instance Court

Canon 1440 — If competence by reason of grade in accord with cann. 1438 and 1439 is not observed, the incompetence of the judge is absolute.

For some observations regarding absolute incompetence, one should see par. 12, e.

25. Constitution of the Second Instance Court

Canon 1441 — A tribunal of second instance must be constituted in the same way as a tribunal of first instance; nevertheless if a single judge passed sentence in a first instance court in accord with can. 1425, §4, the tribunal of second instance is to proceed in a collegial manner.

a. This canon is included here rather than with canon 1640 because it refers not so much to the way the appeal court *functions* as to the way it is *constituted*. In other words, the same officers mentioned in chapter I regarding the first instance court should also be found in the second instance court.

b. The canon does not say that *every* trial settled by a single judge in first instance must be heard by a college in second, but only those trials which were settled by a single judge in virtue of *canon 1425, §4*. If, therefore, the case is a minor one and not consequently reserved to a college, it may be heard by a single judge in both instances.

c. It is clear that this canon does not regard a simple confirmation or ratification by a college as equivalent to a full hearing by a single judge, since the former is permitted in the law (c. 1682, §2) whereas the latter is not.

CHAPTER III
THE TRIBUNALS OF THE APOSTOLIC SEE
[cc. 1442–1445]

26. General Principle

Canon 1442 — The Roman Pontiff is the supreme judge for the entire Catholic world; he tries cases either personally or through the ordinary tribunals of the Apostolic See or through judges delegated by himself.

One should also see canon 1417.

27. Roman Rota (cc. 1443–1444)

a. As Ordinary Appeal Court

Canon 1443 — The ordinary tribunal established by the Roman Pontiff to receive appeals is the Roman Rota.

Canon 1444 — §1. The Roman Rota tries:
1° in second instance, cases which have been adjudicated by the ordinary tribunals of first instance and brought before the Holy See by means of legitimate appeal;
2° in third and further instance, cases already tried by the Roman Rota itself or by any other tribunals whatsoever, unless the case is considered *res iudicata.*

(1) Although an appeal from a first instance decision is usually lodged with the domestic court of appeal in accord with canon 1438, appellants are also free, in accord with canon 1444, §1, 1°, to appeal directly to the Roman Rota for the second instance hearing.
(2) In accordance with canon 1444, §1, 2°, a case generally goes to the Roman Rota for the third instance when the two lower courts are not in agreement. In Spain, by way of exception and by special indult, a third instance hearing may be conducted by the Spanish Rota. Other conferences of bishops have periodically shown an interest in obtaining an indult to establish a third instance court in their own countries, but Rome has generally taken a dim view of such efforts—partly perhaps because of a concern that a proliferation of third instance courts might give rise to national inbreeding and so result in a loss of jurisprudential catholicity, and partly because of a concern that the individual conferences would not be able to staff these courts with

the kind of Solomonic judges that would be necessary at that level.[49]

b. As Delegated Court

§2. This tribunal also tries in first instance the cases mentioned in can. 1405, §3 and other cases which the Roman Pontiff has summoned to his own tribunal and has entrusted to the Roman Rota of his own accord or at the request of the parties; unless other provisions are made in the rescript of commission, the Rota tries these cases in second and further instance as well.

It is clear from such phrases as "the rescript of commission" that the Rota is here functioning with delegated power.
This matter has been touched upon here, under "Various Grades and Kinds of Tribunals" (title II) but treated *ex professo* under "The Competent Forum" (title I) since it primarily concerns first instance competence.

c. Procedures

The 1917 Code (*CIC* 1598) discussed briefly the constitution and internal procedures of the Roman Rota. The present Code, in accord with canon 1402, treats such matters in extracodal legislation.[50]

28. Signatura

a. In Judicial Matters

Canon 1445 — §1. The Supreme Tribunal of the Apostolic Signatura adjudicates:
1° complaints of nullity, petitions for *restitutio in integrum*, and other recourses against rotal sentences;
2° recourses in cases involving the status of persons which the Roman Rota refuses to admit to a new examination;
3° exceptions of suspicion and other cases against the auditors of the Roman Rota because of acts in the exercise of their function;
4° conflicts of competence mentioned in can. 1416.

b. In Contentious Administrative Matters

§2. This same tribunal deals with contentions legitimately referred to it which arise from an act of ecclesiastical administrative power, with other administrative controversies which are referred to it by the Roman Pontiff or by the dicasteries of the Roman Curia, and with a conflict of competence among these dicasteries.

[49]Regatillo, 253–259. See also E. Egan, "Appeal in Marriage Nullity Cases," *CLSAP* (1981), 135–138.
[50]See par. 11. See also L. Wrenn, *Annulments,* 4th ed. (Washington: CLSA, 1983), 3–7 (henceforth cited as Wrenn, *Annulments,* 4th ed.).

As regards controversies arising from an act of administration, canon 1400, §2 notes that the matter is to be settled either by the superior or by an administrative tribunal. At present the only administrative tribunal in the Church is the *Sectio altera,* the second section of the Signatura.[51]

c. In Non-Contentious Administrative Matters

§3. Furthermore it is the task of this Supreme Tribunal:

1° to exercise its vigilance over the correct administration of justice and to discipline advocates or procurators, if necessary;

2° to extend the competence of tribunals;

3° to promote and approve the erection of the tribunals mentioned in cann. 1423 and 1439.

d. Procedures

The 1917 Code (*CIC* 1602, 1604, 1605) discussed briefly the constitution and internal procedures of the Signatura. The 1983 Code, in accord with canon 1402, treats such matters as extracodal legislation.[52]

TITLE III
THE DISCIPLINE TO BE OBSERVED IN TRIBUNALS
[cc. 1446–1475]

CHAPTER I
THE OFFICE OF JUDGES AND OFFICERS OF THE TRIBUNAL
[cc. 1446–1457]

29. Duties (cc. 1446–1456)

a. To Urge an Out-of-Court Settlement

Canon 1446 — §1. With due regard for justice, all the Christian faithful especially bishops are to strive earnestly to avoid lawsuits among the people of God as much as possible and to resolve them peacefully as soon as possible.

§2. At the very start or even at any point during the litigation, whenever some hope of a happy outcome is perceived, the judge is not to neglect to encourage and assist the parties to collaborate in working out an equitable solution to the controversy as well as indicating suitable ways of reaching such a solution, perhaps even employing the services of reputable persons for mediation.

§3. If the litigation concerns the private good of the parties, the judge should find out whether it can

[51]See par. 9.
[52]See par. 11.

profitably be resolved through a negotiated settlement or through arbitration in accord with the norms of cann. 1713-1716.

This is a generic statement about encouraging a peaceful solution to the problem. It is repeated in more specific form in canons 1659, §1 (regarding the oral contentious process), 1676 (on receiving a petition for a marriage annulment), 1695 (on receiving a petition for separation of spouses), 1713–1716 (regarding contentious matters), 1720 (regarding penal matters), 1733 (when one considers himself or herself aggrieved by a decree), and 1742 and 1748 (regarding the removal or transfer of a pastor).

b. To Avoid Serving in Another Instance on the Same Case

Canon 1447 — A person who has taken part in a case as a judge, promoter of justice, defender of the bond, procurator, advocate, witness or expert cannot afterwards in another instance validly resolve the same case as a judge or act as an assessor in another instance.

This canon appeared in slightly different form in the 1917 Code (*CIC* 1571), under title II on grades and species.

c. To Abstain when Suspect
(1) The Duty of the Official

Canon 1448 — §1. A judge is not to undertake the adjudication of a case in which the judge may have some interest due to consanguinity or affinity in any degree of the direct line and up to the fourth degree of the collateral line, due to functioning as a guardian or trustee, due to close friendship, due to great animosity, or due to a desire to make some profit or avoid some loss.

§2. In the same circumstances the promoter of justice, the defender of the bond, the assessor, and the auditor must disqualify themselves from their office.

(2) The Recusancy of the Party
(a) The Right of the Party

Canon 1449 — §1. If, in the cases mentioned in can. 1448, the judge does not withdraw, the party can lodge an objection against the judge.

(b) The Judge of the Recusancy

§2. The judicial vicar deals with the issue of such an objection; if the judicial vicar is the one objected against, the bishop who is in charge of the tribunal deals with the issue.

§3. If the bishop himself is the judge and an objection is lodged against him, he is to disqualify himself from judging.

§4. If the objection is lodged against the promoter of justice, the defender of the bond or other officers of the tribunal, the president of the collegiate tribunal or the single judge deals with this exception.

(c) The Instance Unchanged

Canon 1450 — **If the objection is accepted, the persons must be changed, but the grade of the court does not change.**

(d) The Procedure

Canon 1451 — **§1. The issue of an objection is to be solved without delay after having heard the parties, the promoter of justice or defender of the bond if they are present and an objection has not been lodged against them.**

For the significance of the phrase "without delay," or "expeditissime," one should see canon 1629, 5°.

(3) The Validity of the Acts

§2. The acts posited by a judge prior to an objection are valid; but those acts posited after the objection has been moved must be rescinded if the party petitions within ten days from the acceptance of the objection.

d. To Proceed Properly in Private and Public Cases

Canon 1452 — **§1. In a matter which concerns private individuals only, a judge can proceed only at the request of a party; once a case has been legitimately introduced, however, a judge can and must proceed, even ex officio, in penal cases and in other cases which involve the public good of the Church or the salvation of souls.**

§2. Furthermore, a judge can supply for the negligence of parties in furnishing proofs or in placing exceptions as often as it is judged necessary in order to avoid a seriously unjust sentence, with due regard for the prescriptions of can. 1600.

(1) Cases Affecting Only Private Individuals

The 1917 Code (*CIC* 1618–1619) noted that the judge should act only at the prompting of the parties and that he should not supply proofs which the parties neglected to offer. This, however, was a general principle. In fact, the law itself explicitly permitted the judge to offer certain proofs on his own

(e.g., *CIC* 1792, 1829, 1832). Besides, several of the commentators recommended that the judge not interpret the general principle too rigorously, since oftentimes the simplicity, ignorance, or inexperience of the parties would deprive the court of important information. Even under the 1917 law, therefore, interest in the whole truth and the principle of equity would have recommended that the judge should arrange, on his own initiative, for the missing evidence to be supplied. Canon 1452, §2 now turns the 1917 canon almost completely around and positively permits the judge to supply for the neglect of the parties.

(2) Cases Affecting the Public Good

Both the 1917 and 1983 Codes instruct the judge to proceed ex officio, i.e., on his own initiative. This does not mean, however, that the judge should, on his own, *initiate* a case but only that once initiated by a petitioner, perhaps the promoter of justice, then the judge should pursue the evidence ex officio.[53]

e. To Bring All Cases to an Expeditious Conclusion

Canon 1453 — **Judges and tribunals are to see to it that, with due regard for justice, all cases are concluded as soon as possible so that in a tribunal of first instance they are not prolonged beyond a year and in a tribunal of second instance beyond six months.**

The stipulated time limits halve those of the 1917 Code.

f. To Take the Oath

Canon 1454 — **All persons who constitute a tribunal or assist it must take an oath that they will fulfill their function properly and faithfully.**

g. To Maintain Confidentiality

Canon 1455 — **§1. Judges and tribunal personnel are always bound to secrecy of office in a penal case; they are also thus bound in a contentious case if the parties may be harmed by the revelation of some procedural act.**

§2. They are also always bound to observe secrecy concerning the discussion among the judges in a collegiate tribunal before passing the sentence and concerning the various votes and opinions offered during the discussion with due regard for the prescription of can. 1609, §4.

§3. Moreover, as often as the nature of a case or the proofs is such that the reputation of others is endangered by divulging the acts or proofs, or an

---

[53]See also c. 1530.

opportunity for discord is provided or scandal or some other similar disadvantage might arise, the judge can bind the witnesses, the experts, the parties and their advocates or proxies by oath to observe secrecy.

This canon is to be understood in the context of canon 1598 which permits the parties and their advocates to inspect the acts prior to the conclusion and discussion. The sense of the present canon is that the officers of the court may not discuss the case with any *third* party, i.e., any party not having legitimate access to the acts.[54]

h. Not To Accept Gifts

Canon 1456 — **The judge and all tribunal officers are forbidden to accept any gifts whatsoever on the occasion of their functioning in a trial.**

30. Penalties for Failure of Duty

Canon 1457 — **§1. Judges who refuse to try a case when they are certainly and obviously competent, who declare themselves competent without any legal basis and hear and decide cases, who violate the law of secrecy or who inflict some damage on litigants out of malice or serious negligence can be punished by the competent authority with fitting penalties, including deprivation of office.**

§2. Officers and personnel of the tribunal are subject to the same sanctions if they do not fulfill their function as above; the judge can also punish all of them.

CHAPTER II
THE ORDER OF ADJUDICATION
[cc. 1458–1464]

31. Distinct Cases

Canon 1458 — **Cases are to be tried in the order in which they are presented and put on the docket unless some of them demand speedier treatment than others, which fact is to be determined in a special decree which states the reasons.**

32. Connected Cases (cc. 1459–1464)

a. Upon receiving a petition, a court does not always move uninterruptedly toward the settlement of the principal issue. Occasionally it gets sidetracked in the settlement of subordinate issues. This section explains at what stage of the proceedings such subordinate issues should be handled.

These issues are of four types: exceptions, judicial acknowledgments, counter-claims, and questions.

b. *An exception* is a claim or complaint made by the defendant which either modifies the court procedures in some way (dilatory exceptions) or quashes the suit altogether (peremptory exceptions).

(1) *Dilatory* exceptions can be either major or minor. Major dilatory exceptions (c. 1459, §1) are those which point out some procedural defect, including the absolute incompetence of the judge, which will result in the nullity of the sentence. These major exceptions may be made at any point in the proceedings. Minor dilatory exceptions. (cc. 1459, §2; 1460), on the other hand, are those which refer either to some procedural point, like the fact that an expert was not used in a case where one was required, or to some matter that refers either to the parties in the case or the court personnel, including the relative incompetence of the judge.[55] These minor exceptions should generally be lodged prior to the joinder of issues, discussed under canons 1513–1516.

(2) *Peremptory* exceptions can be either *closed case* exceptions or *open case* exceptions. Closed case exceptions (c. 1462, §1) claim, in effect, that the case has already been settled by another court. Such exceptions should be lodged before the joinder of issues. Open case exceptions (c. 1462, §2), on the other hand, do not claim that the case was settled by another court but do claim that, for some reason, the matter should not be heard. For example: the plaintiff sues the defendant, stating that the defendant never paid him or her the agreed upon $50,000 for the purchase of a piece of property. The defendant then lodges a peremptory exception, claiming either that he or she already paid the $50,000 or, perhaps, that the original contract was invalid. Such exceptions are treated according to the rules on incidental questions as found in canons 1587–1597.

c. The *judicial acknowledgment* (c. 1461) discussed here is the judge's ex officio recognition (not made by way of exception) that he is absolutely incompetent as noted in canon 1406, §2.[56]

d. The *counter-claim* (c. 1463) is known in Latin as *actio reconventialis,* or *reconventio,* i.e., a reconvening of the plaintiff by the defendant. It is also referred to as a second convening, or reciprocal petition. It may be defined as a petition made by the defendant in order to offset the original petition of the plaintiff. A man, for example, sues his wife for a legal separation; she then countersues him for a divorce.

---

[55]The concluding sentence of c. 1460, §2 notes that, in a case of relative incompetence, a complaint of nullity and reinstatement are not forbidden. Since, however, relative incompetence does not, in itself, result in either invalidity or injustice, the phrase presumably means that, should invalidity or injustice result from some other source in a case in which the judge was relatively incompetent, then a complaint or reinstatement would not be forbidden. See pars. 12, 160–167, 180–185, and *CIC* 1610, §2.

[56]See par. 12, e.

[54]See c. 1470 §1.

e. The *question* (c. 1464) discussed here is the one about the plaintiff's ability to pay for the court expenses.

f. Other aspects of these subordinate issues are discussed elsewhere and more at length under canons 1491–1500 and under canons 1587–1597. The present section concerns itself primarily with the question: at what stage of the proceedings should such matters be settled by the court? With this in mind, a simple listing of the canons (with c. 1461 following rather than preceding c. 1462) should be sufficient:

(1) Exceptions
  (a) Major Dilatory

Canon 1459 — §1. Defects which can render a sentence invalid can be introduced as an exception during any stage or grade of a trial; a judge can likewise declare them ex officio.

(b) Minor Dilatory

§2. Besides the cases mentioned in §1, dilatory exceptions, especially those which concern the persons and the manner of the trial, are to be proposed before the joinder of issues (*contestatio litis*), unless they first emerged only after it; and they are to be settled as soon as possible.

Canon 1460 — §1. If an exception is proposed against the competence of the judge, the same judge must deal with the matter.

§2. In the case of an exception of relative incompetence, if the judge finds for competence, the decision does not admit of appeal; however, a complaint of nullity and *restitutio in integrum* are not forbidden.

§3. But if the judge finds for incompetence, the person who feels injured can appeal to the appellate tribunal within fifteen available days (*dies utiles*).

(c) Closed Case Peremptory

Canon 1462 — §1. The exceptions that the matter has become *res iudicata* and that an agreement had been already reached (*transactio*), as well as other peremptory exceptions which are called *litis finitae* must be proposed and adjudicated before the joinder of issues (*contestatio litis*); a person who proposes them later is not to be rejected but is liable for the court costs unless there is proof that presentation was not maliciously delayed.

(d) Open Case Peremptory

§2. Other peremptory exceptions are to be lodged during the joinder of issues (*contestatio litis*) and are to be treated at their proper time in accord with the regulations which deal with incidental questions.

(2) Judicial Acknowledgment

Canon 1461 — Judges who become aware of their absolute incompetence during any stage of a case must declare that incompetence.

(3) Counter-Claim

Canon 1463 — §1. Counter-claim actions cannot be lodged validly except within thirty days from the joinder of issues (*contestatio litis*).

§2. However, they are to be adjudicated at the same time as the original action, that is, on the same grade with it unless it is necessary to try them separately or the judge deems it more appropriate to try them separately.

(4) Question

Canon 1464 — Questions concerning a deposit for judicial expenses or the granting of gratuitous legal assistance which has been requested from the beginning and other such questions are to be dealt with before the joinder of issues (*contestatio litis*) as a general rule.

CHAPTER III
TIME LIMITS AND DELAYS
[cc. 1465–1467]

33. Non-Prorogability and Non-Restrictability of Peremptory Legal Deadlines

Canon 1465 — §1. *Fatalia legis* or the time limits set by law for extinguishing the right to act cannot be extended nor validly shortened unless the parties request it.

a. Deadlines are of three kinds: legal (when they are defined by the law), judicial (when they are defined by the judge), and conventional (when they are defined by the parties). Legal deadlines can be either peremptory or non-peremptory. Peremptory legal deadlines, called *"fatalia legis,"* are those which extinguish the right in question if the deadline is not met. Non-peremptory deadlines, if unmet, do not extinguish the right. The rule of thumb is that legal deadlines that refer to the parties are peremptory, whereas those which refer to the court are non-peremptory. An example of the *former* is canon 1505, §4 which gives the petitioner ten days to appeal a rejection of a petition. After those ten days the right is considered extinguished. See also canons 1460, §3; 1623; 1630, §1; 1633; and 1646. An example of the *latter* is canon 1453 which says that a court should complete a first instance hearing in a year and a second instance hearing in six months. If, however, the court has not, in fact, completed the instances in the allotted time, no right is extinguished. One should also see canon 1609, §5. For an exception to the rule of thumb, namely, for an example of a legal deadline that refers to the court but is peremptory, one should see canon 1506.

b. For an exception to the prorogation aspect of canon 1465, §1, i.e., for an example of a legal deadline that is peremptory but can be prorogated, one should see canons 1633 and 1635.

c. Although the canon says nothing about the legal, non-peremptory deadline, it would seem that it would follow the rules of canon 1465, §2.

34. Prorogability and Restrictability of Judicial and Conventional Deadlines

§2. Before they have lapsed, however, judicial time limits and agreed upon time limits can be extended by the judge for a just cause after hearing the parties or if they request it; such time limits, however, may never validly be shortened unless the parties agree.

35. Judicial Prorogation (cc. 1465, §3–1466)

a. Moderate

§3. But the judge is to see to it that the litigation is not overly prolonged by such extensions.

b. Tailored

Canon 1466 — When the law does not establish time limits for positing of procedural acts, the judge must define them taking into consideration the nature of each act.[57]

36. A Daylong Legal Prorogation

Canon 1467 — If the tribunal is closed on the day scheduled for a judicial act the time limit is extended to the first day following which is not a holiday.[58]

CHAPTER IV
THE PLACE OF THE TRIAL
[cc. 1468–1469]

37. Judge within His Territory

Canon 1468 — To the extent that it is possible, each tribunal is to be in a permanent place which is open during specified hours.

38. Judge outside His Territory

Canon 1469 — §1. Judges who have been forcibly expelled from their own territory or have been impeded in the exercise of jurisdiction there can exercise jurisdiction and render a sentence outside that territory; however, the diocesan bishop should be informed of this fact by the judge.

§2. Besides the case mentioned in §1, for a just cause and after hearing the parties, judges can travel outside their own territory in order to acquire proofs with the permission of the diocesan bishop of the place they enter and at a site designated by the bishop.

It has always been recognized, both in Roman and in canon law, that as a general rule, a judge cannot exercise his jurisdiction outside of his own territory. This principle was stated explicitly in canon 201, §2 of the 1917 Code. The corresponding canon in the 1983 Code, canon 135, §3, simply says, however, that judicial power should be exercised "*in the manner prescribed by law*" (italics author's). This obvious softening of the principle of territoriality does not, of course, negate the principle entirely, but it does leave room for broader exceptions.

The exception mentioned in paragraph one of this canon, about the judge who has been expelled from his own territory, is a traditional one that was recognized both in medieval law and in the 1917 Code.[59] The exception mentioned in paragraph two, however, is new to this Code.[60] For an alternative procedure to this second paragraph, one should see canon 1418 and par. 14, d.

CHAPTER V
PERSONS TO BE ADMITTED TO THE TRIAL
AND THE MANNER OF ASSEMBLING AND
PRESERVING THE ACTS
[cc. 1470–1475]

39. Persons To Be Admitted (cc. 1470–1471)

a. Necessary Persons

Canon 1470 — §1. Unless particular law provides otherwise, while cases are being tried before a tribunal only those persons are to be present in court whom the law or the judge decides are necessary to expedite the process.

This paragraph, like canon 1455 (par. 29, g), refers to the publicity of the trial in terms of a third

---

[57]See c. 1655, §2.
[58]For details regarding computation, see c. 203.

[59]*Clem* II, 2; *CorpusIC* II, 1144; *CIC* 1637.
[60]See *CIC* 1770, §2, 3°.

party, whereas canon 1598 (par. 145) discusses the publicity of the trial in terms of the two parties.

Clearly, an ecclesiastical trial is much more private regarding third parties than are most civil trials to which private citizens and the press, and sometimes even television cameras, have access.

The necessary people at the hearing of a witness are, besides the judges or auditor, the notary, the defender, and the promoter when they are involved in the case, and, in accord with canon 1559, ordinarily the procurators and advocates and sometimes the parties.

b. Respectful Persons

§2. With appropriate penalties a judge can demand compliance on the part of all who assist at the trial and who are seriously lacking in the respect and obedience owed the tribunal; the judge can also suspend advocates and procurators from exercising their function before ecclesiastical tribunals.

As regards the penalties mentioned in this canon, one should see canon 1336.[61]

c. Interpreters

Canon 1471 — **If a person to be interrogated speaks a language which is not known by the judge or the parties, a sworn interpreter designated by the judge is to be employed. Their statements, however, are to be put into writing in the original language and a translation is to be added. An interpreter is also to be employed if a deaf or mute person must be interrogated unless the judge perhaps prefers that the person respond to questions in writing.**

40. The Acts (cc. 1472–1475)

a. Drafting the Acts

Canon 1472 — **§1. Judicial acts, both the acts of the case, that is, those acts which concern the merits of the question, and the acts of the process, that is, those which pertain to the formal procedure, must be put into writing.**

§2. The individual pages of the acts are to be numbered and authenticated with a seal.

Canon 1473 — **Whenever the signature of the parties or witnesses is required for judicial acts and a party or a witness cannot or will not sign, this is to be noted in the acts; both the judge and the notary are to attest that the act has been read to the**

party or witness verbatim and that the party or witness either could not or would not sign.

Canon 1472 introduces the distinction between the "acta causae" and the "acta processus." The "acta causae" are all those materials which pertain to the merits of the case, like the proofs and the sentence, whereas the "acta processus" are those materials which pertain to the formalities of the case, like the constitution of the tribunal and the acceptance of the petition. All of the acts must be committed to writing since "quod non est in actis non est in mundo"[62] and because, at the conclusion of the instance, the judge must base his decision "ex actis et probatis," that is to say, on the acts and what is proved therein (c. 1608, §2).

Should the instance be terminated by peremption (c. 1522), as mentioned in par. 82, d, the "acta processus" are extinguished but not the "acta causae."

b. Transmitting the Acts

Canon 1474 — **§1. In case of appeal, a copy of the acts authenticated by the attestation of a notary is to be sent to a higher tribunal.**

§2. If the acts as drawn up are in a language unknown to the higher tribunal, they are to be translated into a language known to that tribunal, with due precautions being taken that it be a faithful translation.

This canon deals with *what* is to be transmitted to the appeal court, and is therefore appropriately included in the chapter. Later canons (c. 1633ff.) will deal with such questions as when, how, and to whom the acts will be transmitted.

c. Conserving the Acts

Canon 1475 — **§1. At the completion of the trial documents which belong to private individuals must be returned but a copy of them is to be retained.**

§2. Notaries and the chancellor are forbidden to furnish a copy of judicial acts and of documents which have been acquired for the process without a mandate from the judge.

Canon 469 indicates that the tribunal is part of the diocesan curia. Canon 1475, §2, however, since it establishes a special rule regarding the conservation of judicial acts that is different from the rules that apply to other diocesan documents (cc. 486–491), suggests that the tribunal should have its own special archive.

---

[61]See also cc. 1487–1489.

[62]Loosely translated, this reads, "whatever is not included in the acts is considered non-existent."

TITLE IV
THE PARTIES IN A CASE
[cc. 1476–1490]

CHAPTER I
THE PETITIONER AND THE RESPONDENT
[cc. 1476–1480]

41. General Principles

Canon 1476 — Anyone, whether baptized or not, can act in a trial; however, the respondent who has been legitimately cited must answer.

Canon 1477 — Although a petitioner or respondent has appointed a procurator or an advocate, they themselves are nevertheless bound to be present in person at the trial when the law or the judge prescribes it.

a. The Latin terms for petitioner and respondent are "actor" (the one who institutes the action) and "pars conventa" (the convened party). They are sometimes referred to, especially in penal cases, as the plaintiff and the defendant.

b. It was understood under the 1917 Code, particularly on the basis of *CIC* 87, that a non-baptized person did not have the right to act as petitioner in a case. In 1970, however, Norm 8 of the *American Procedural Norms* (par. 206) permitted "any spouse without qualification" to petition for marriage nullity, and on January 8, 1973, the Pontifical Commission for the Interpretation of the Decrees of Vatican Council II declared that, even outside of the United States, unbaptized people needed no special permission to act as petitioners in marriage cases.[63] This right of the unbaptized is now extended to all types of cases.

c. A similar situation existed under the 1917 Code for baptized non-Catholics. Because they were baptized, it was granted that they enjoyed "judicial capacity," but because they were not Catholic, they were considered to lack the "procedural capacity" to petition in a Catholic tribunal. This was specifically spelled out in Article 35, §3 of *Provida mater* (par. 206),[64] but it was reversed by the American Procedural Norms and the interpretation of January 8, 1973 as indicated above. In those cases in which a non-Catholic did wish a Catholic tribunal to declare his or her marriage null (so that he or she would be free to remarry a Catholic), the procedure was for the non-Catholic to "denounce" the marriage and then for the promoter to petition for annulment.

d. For further remarks on procedural capacity, one should see par. 71, a, (1).

[63]*CLD* 8, 1092.
[64]Doheny I, 116.

42. Minors and Those Lacking Use of Reason

Canon 1478 — §1. Minors and those who lack the use of reason can stand trial only through their parents or guardians or curators, with due regard for the prescription of §3.

§2. If the judge decides that the rights of minors are in conflict with the rights of the parents, guardians or curators, or that the latter cannot satisfactorily safeguard the rights of the former, then they are to be represented in the trial by a guardian or curator appointed by the judge.

§3. But in spiritual cases and in cases connected with spiritual matters, if minors have attained the use of reason, they can act and respond without the consent of parents or guardian; if they have completed their fourteenth year of age, they can do so on their own; if not, through a curator appointed by the judge.

a. Minors are those under eighteen years of age.[65]

b. A *guardian* is assigned to a person because of his or her age; a *curator* because of his or her mental debility.

c. As regards the cases mentioned in paragraph three (which states an exception to the general principle of §1), one should see canon 1401, 1°.

43. Squanderers and Weak-Minded Persons

§4. Those deprived of the administration of their goods and those who are of diminished mental capacity can stand trial personally only to answer for their own offenses or at the prescription of the judge; in all other cases they must act and respond through their curators.

The question might arise here: does the phrase "those who are of diminished mental capacity" include all those who are listed in canon 1095, namely, those who lack the due reason, discretion, or competence for marriage? The answer seems clearly to be *no*. A respondent, for example, whose severe personality disorder deprived him or her of the capacity to enter a marital covenant is not necessarily deprived, by that disorder, of the capacity to enter a non-marital type of contract, or to conduct his or her own legal or judicial affairs. Few people who suffer from personality disorders are appropriately referred to as "those who are of diminished mental capacity," i.e., "ii qui minus firmae mentis sunt." Therefore, not all those respondents in marriage cases, whose marital incompetence is alleged, need have guardians appointed for them, but only those who either lack the use of reason altogether or are weak minded.

[65]See cc. 97–99.

44. Appointment of Guardian and Curator

Canon 1479 — **Whenever a guardian or curator appointed by civil authority is present, this person can be admitted by an ecclesiastical judge after having heard the diocesan bishop of the person to whom the guardian or curator has been given, if this can be done; but if a guardian or curator is not present or does not appear admissible, the judge shall designate a guardian or curator for the case.**

a. The corresponding canon in the 1917 Code (*CIC* 1651) had the *ordinary* either accept the civil law guardian or appoint a new one. A dispute arose, however, regarding the proper procedure when an insane respondent in a marriage case lived in a diocese different from the one hearing the case. Some held, mostly on the basis of *CIC* 1648, §2, that the trial judge could, on his own, appoint a guardian *ad litem*. Others held that the trial judge would have to request the ward's ordinary to appoint a guardian.[66] The present wording, in conjunction with canon 1478, §2, solves the difficulty by clearly permitting the judge to appoint a guardian *pro causa*.

b. The appointment should, of course, be made promptly since at the very beginning of the case it is the guardian, not the respondent, who is cited (c. 1508, §3) in all those cases in which a guardian is required.

45. Juridic Persons

Canon 1480 — **§1. Juridic persons stand trial through their legitimate representatives.**
§2. In a case where the representative is lacking or is negligent, the ordinary himself can stand trial personally or through another in the name of juridic persons which are subject to his power.

CHAPTER II
PROCURATORS FOR THE TRIAL AND ADVOCATES
[cc. 1481–1490]

46. Definitions of Procurator and Advocate

A *procurator* (*ad lites*) is one who, by legitimate mandate, performs judicial business for someone else.

An (ecclesiastical) *advocate* is someone approved by ecclesiastical authority who safeguards the rights of a party in a canonical process by arguments regarding the law and the facts.

47. Constitution of Procurator and Advocate

a. Free Constitution

Canon 1481 — **§1. A party can freely appoint a personal advocate and a procurator; however, except for the cases stated in §§2 and 3, the party can petition and respond personally unless the judge has decided that the services of a procurator or an advocate are necessary.**

b. Necessary Constitution

§2. The accused in a penal trial must always have an advocate either appointed by the accused or given by the judge.
§3. In a contentious trial which involves minors or the public good except for marriage cases, the judge is to appoint ex officio a defender for a party who lacks one.

48. Number of Procurators and Advocates

a. Procurator

Canon 1482 — **§1. A person can appoint only a single procurator who cannot substitute another unless an expressed faculty has been granted the procurator to do this.**
§2. But if several procurators are appointed by the same party for some just cause, they are to be so designated that prevention is operative among them.

The term "prevention" mentioned in paragraph two has the same basic meaning here that it had in canon 1415. In that canon the first judge (among those competent) to cite the respondent thereby acquired competence over the case "ratione praeventionis." According to the present canon, the first procurator to undertake the judicial business becomes the active procurator—by prevention.

The notion of prevention is also expressed in canon law by the term "in solidum" (as opposed to "collegialiter").[67]

b. Advocate

§3. However, several advocates can be appointed to act together.

49. Qualities of Procurator and Advocate

Canon 1483 — **The procurator and the advocate must have at least attained majority and be of good reputation; furthermore, the advocate must be a Catholic unless the diocesan bishop permits other-**

---

[66]G. Sesto, *Guardians of the Mentally Ill in Ecclesiastical Trials* (Washington, D.C.: Catholic University of America, 1956), 97–101; F. Donnelly, "Tribunal Matters," *J* 21 (1961), 108.

[67]See c. 140.

wise, must have a doctorate in canon law or be otherwise truly expert and must be approved by the same bishop.

50. Ordinary Mandate

Canon 1484 — §1. Before a procurator and advocate undertake their function, they must present an authentic mandate to the tribunal.

§2. To prevent the extinction of a right, however, the judge can admit a procurator without the presentation of the mandate provided that some suitable security is furnished if necessary; the procurator's acts, however, lack all force unless the mandate is correctly presented within the peremptory time limits set by the judge.

a. Should one act in the name of another without that mandate, the sentence would be incurably null.[68]

b. As regards extending the judicial deadline, one should see canon 1465, §2.

51. Special Mandate

Canon 1485 — Without a special mandate the procurator cannot validly renounce an action, instance or judicial acts, make a settlement, strike a bargain, enter into arbitration and in general do those things for which the law requires a special mandate.

52. Revocation by Mandator of Procurator and Advocate

Canon 1486 — §1. For the removal of a procurator or advocate to take effect, it is necessary that they be informed and that the judge and the opposing party be notified of the removal if the joinder of issues (*contestatio litis*) has already taken place.

§2. After a definitive sentence has been issued, the procurator retains the right and duty to appeal unless the mandating party has renounced this.

53. Suspension by Judge of Procurator and Advocate

Canon 1487 — For serious cause both the procurator and the advocate can be expelled from the trial by the judge by means of a decree either ex officio or at the request of a party.

The 1917 Code required only a *just* cause for a judge to suspend a procurator or advocate. The present Code requires a *grave* cause. Examples may be found in canons 1470, §2; 1488; and 1489. Procurators and advocates may also be suspended if they lack the qualities mentioned in canon 1483.

[68] See c. 1620, 6°.

54. Sanctions for Illicit Actions

Canon 1488 — §1. Both the procurator and the advocate are forbidden to win the suit through bribery or to strike a bargain for excessive profit or for a claim upon a share of the litigated thing. If they do such things, the agreement is null and the judge can fine them. Furthermore, an advocate can be suspended from office and also stricken from the list of advocates by the bishop in charge of the tribunal if it happens again and again.

§2. Advocates and procurators are liable to the same penalties if they withdraw cases from competent tribunals and submit them to other more favorable tribunals for adjudication in deceit of the law.

Canon 1489 — Advocates and procurators who have betrayed their office for the sake of gifts, promises or any other reason are to be suspended from the exercise of office and fined or punished with other suitable penalties.

Regarding these penalties, one should see canons 1312, §2 and 1336.

55. Permanent Staff

Canon 1490 — Insofar as it is possible, permanent advocates are to be appointed in every tribunal and paid a stipend by that tribunal to exercise the function of advocate or procurator on behalf of parties who wish to choose them especially for marriage cases.

TITLE V
ACTIONS AND EXCEPTIONS
[cc. 1491–1500]

CHAPTER I
ACTIONS AND EXCEPTIONS IN GENERAL
[cc. 1491–1495]

56. Some Observations

a. Exceptions and a certain type of action (the reconvening action or counter-claim) are also discussed in canons 1458–1464 in chapter II of title III ("The Order of Adjudication") (par. 32). That treatment, however, confines itself to the question of the particular stage of the trial at which such matters should be introduced. The present treatment is more general.

b. The 1917 Code, in a rather detailed and involved treatment of actions and exceptions, devoted thirty-nine canons to this title. These were reduced to thirty-five in the 1976 schema and are now down to ten. The present legislator obviously recognized that much of the old law on actions and exceptions had become obsolete.

c. An *action* is a request made by a plaintiff (Latin: *acto*r) for a judicial decision on some matter. An *exception* is a claim or complaint made by the defendant which either modifies the court procedure in some way (these are called dilatory exceptions) or quashes the suit altogether (these are called peremptory exceptions).[69]

d. As noted in par. 8, this title deals with the formal object of the trial.

57. Availability in Law of Actions and Exceptions

Canon 1491 — Every right whatsoever is safeguarded not only by an action but also by an exception unless something to the contrary is expressly stated.

a. This is a simple statement to the effect that in general whenever a right is disputed, some adjudicative process must be available to the parties. St. James' Parish, for example, sells a piece of property to St. Robert's Parish. A bill of sale exists as proof of the transaction, but St. James' continues to occupy and use the property. St. Robert's is entitled to bring an *action* against St. James' in order to obtain possession of the property. But St. James' can then bring an *exception* against St. Robert's, claiming that the contract was, for a stated reason, null and void.

b. Although, in general, every right is sustained by an action, that action, as noted in canon 1400, §2, is not always in an ordinary tribunal.

c. The canon contains an exceptive clause. An example of an exception is found in canon 1062, §2 which states that from the promise of marriage no action is given in law to seek marriage itself.

58. Extinction of Actions and Exceptions

Canon 1492 — §1. Every action is terminated through prescription in accord with the norm of law or by another legitimate method except actions concerning the status of persons which are never terminated.

§2. An exception is always available and is of its very nature perpetual, with due regard for the prescription of can. 1462.

a. It is axiomatic that actions are temporary while exceptions are perpetual. This principle, which seems to the advantage of the respondent, is, in fact, meant to correct the respondent's previous disadvantage in that the petitioner comes to court freely, whereas the respondent is convened and is obliged to appear. If, therefore, a right of a respondent is imperiled by his or her having been summoned and sued, his or her right then to lodge an exception is in no way limited by time.

b. To this general principle, however, there are exceptions on both sides. Some *actions*, namely, those regarding the status of persons, like marriage cases (cc. 1643, 1675), are perpetual; while some *exceptions*, like the peremptory exceptions mentioned in canon 1462,[70] are temporary and are extinguished if unused due to negligence.

c. Concerning the prescription that extinguishes actions, one should see canons 197–199.

59. Multiple Actions

Canon 1493 — A petitioner can bring a respondent to court by several actions at the same time provided they do not conflict among themselves, whether on the same or different matters, and if they do not exceed the competence of the tribunal approached.

A man, for example, may petition both for a separation from his spouse and for the custody of their children.

60. Counter-Claim (cc. 1494–1495)

a. The Right

Canon 1494 — §1. A respondent can file a counter-claim action against the petitioner before the same judge in the same trial either due to a connection of a case with the principal action or to remove or to lessen the charge of the petitioner.

§2. A counter-claim to the counter-claim is not admissible.

Although the counter-claim is, strictly speaking, an action (a reconvening action), it is very similar to an exception.

b. The Judge

Canon 1495 — The counter-claim action is to be presented to the judge before whom the first action was filed even if he were delegated for only one case or were otherwise relatively incompetent.

Even though the judge is acting on delegated power and the terms of delegation empowered him to judge only the one issue, nevertheless his jurisdiction is, by this canon, extended to include the counter-claim. Equity in fact dictates that the counter-claim, like any connected case, not only *may* be but indeed *should* be proposed before the original judge. Canon 1414 reads "cognoscendae sunt," and this canon "proponenda est."[71]

---

[69]See par. 32, b.

[70]See par. 32.
[71]See also c. 1588.

CHAPTER II
ACTIONS AND EXCEPTIONS
SPECIFICALLY
[cc. 1496–1500]

61. Right of Sequestration and Inhibition

Canon 1496 — §1. A person who through at least probable arguments, has demonstrated a right to something retained by another and the threat of damage if that thing is not placed in safekeeping, has the right to obtain its sequestration from the judge.

§2. In similar circumstances a person can obtain an order restraining another from exercising a right.

a. *Sequestration* refers to a person or thing; *inhibition* (or injunction) to the exercise of a right.

b. *Sequestration* is the entrusting of a disputed person or object to a third party (called the sequester agent). *Inhibition* is the temporary prohibition of exercising a disputed right because of probable infringement on the prevailing right of someone else.

c. It is clear from the rubric that both sequestration and inhibition may be entered either as an action or as an exception.

62. Extension of the Right of Sequestration

Canon 1497 — §1. Sequestration of the object is also admitted as security for credit provided the right of the creditor is sufficiently evident.

§2. Sequestration can also be extended to the goods of the debtor which are discovered in the possession of others under any title and to the credit of the debtor.

a. The previous canon referred to (1) sequestration of the *disputed* subject, the "res ipsa" and (2) when the petitioner could show *probable* right to it. This canon refers to (1) sequestration of *other* objects owned by the debtor and (2) when the petitioner can show *certain* right to the disputed object.

b. Some canonists prefer to define sequestration broadly to include the sequestering of any object, and then divide it into two types: *conservatory* sequestration (as described in c. 1496), and *security* sequestration (as described in c. 1497).

63. Condition for Invoking Sequestration and Inhibition

Canon 1498 — Sequestration of a thing and an order to restrain the exercise of a right can in no way be decreed if the harm that is feared can otherwise be repaired and suitable security for its repair can be furnished.

64. Surety Bond

Canon 1499 — The judge, in granting sequestration of a thing or an order restraining the exercise of a right, can impose on the person a prior obligation to compensate for damages if the right is not proven.

65. The Civil Law

Canon 1500 — In regard to the nature and force of a possessory action the prescriptions of the civil law of the place where the thing, the possession of which is in question, is located, are to be observed.

Part II
THE CONTENTIOUS TRIAL
[cc. 1501–1670]

Section I: THE ORDINARY
CONTENTIOUS TRIAL
[cc. 1501–1655]

TITLE I
THE INTRODUCTION OF THE CASE
[cc. 1501–1512]

CHAPTER I
THE INTRODUCTORY PETITION OF THE SUIT
[cc. 1501–1506]

66. Stages of a Trial

A trial may be viewed as consisting of four stages:

• the *introductory* stage (cc. 1501–1525) which includes the petition made to the judge, its acceptance, the citation of the respondent, and the establishment of grounds;

• the *evidentiary, or probatory,* stage (cc. 1526–1600) which includes the collection of all proofs plus any exceptions, counter-claims, or incidental questions introduced by the parties. This stage also includes the publication of the acts and the conclusion "in causa," i.e., the conclusion of the probatory stage of the proceedings;

• the *discussion* stage (cc. 1601–1606) which includes the briefs, animadversions, and whatever oral argument is made;

• the *decisionary* stage (cc. 1607–1655) which includes the sentence, the impugning of the sentence, etc., through the execution of the sentence.

67. Definition of Terms

The Latin word *libellus* means "a little book" or "something in writing." When that something in writing was a slanderous calumny, it was known as a *libellus famosus* and was, precisely because it was in writing, considered a more serious crime than oral slander. In English law, it came to be known simply as *libel*. When, on the other hand, the something in writing was a request made of a judge to hear a case, it was known as a *libellus litis introductorius* or, as we might say in English, the introductory bill of complaint. It is in this latter sense that the term *libellus* is used here.

The *libellus* is commonly referred to simply as the petition, though strictly speaking, canon law still regards the judicial petition as a generic term which includes two types: the written type called the *libellus*, and the oral type called the oral petition.

68. Necessity of a Petition

Canon 1501 — A judge cannot adjudicate any case unless the party concerned or the promoter of justice has presented a petition in accord with the norm of the canons.

This canon says that a judge must, in order to proceed, have some kind of judicial petition, either written or oral. Canon 1620, 4° says that, without that, the sentence will be incurably null. As regards the promoter of justice, one should see par. 21 and par. 41, c.

69. Form of a Petition (cc. 1502–1503)

a. The Rule

Canon 1502 — A person who wishes to bring another to court must present a *libellus* to a competent judge, which explains the object of the controversy and requests the services of the judge.

b. The Exception

Canon 1503 — §1. The judge may accept an oral petition if either the petitioner is impeded from presenting a *libellus* or the case can be easily investigated and is of lesser importance.

§2. But in either situation the judge is to require the notary to put the act into writing, which is to be read to and approved by the petitioner; this then takes the place of and has all the legal effects of a *libellus* written by the petitioner.

70. Contents of a Petition

Canon 1504 — A *libellus* which introduces a suit must:

1° express before which judge the case is being introduced, what is being petitioned and by whom the petition is being made;

2° indicate the basis for the petitioner's right and at least in general the facts and proofs which will be used to prove what has been alleged;

3° be signed by the petitioner or procurator, adding the day, month and year, as well as the address of the petitioner or procurator or the place where they say they reside for the purpose of receiving the acts;

4° indicate the domicile or quasi-domicile of the respondent.

Number two of this canon notes that the petitioner should indicate in general terms both the law and the facts on which the claim is based.

As regards the *law*, only an obscure or unusual law requires explanation. Otherwise, in accord with the axiom *Iura novit Curia*, a simple reference suffices.

As regards the *facts*, enough information should be included to assure the court that the petition is not rash, that a *fumus boni iuris*, i.e., the semblance of a well-founded right, or what we might call "probable cause," is present. The presentation of actual proofs is not in order, but the *via argumentationis*, assuring the court that the allegation can indeed be proved, should be outlined. In a marriage case based on force and fear, for example, the significant circumstances should be mentioned and the names of the witnesses listed.

71. Acceptance or Rejection of a Petition
   (cc. 1505–1506)

a. By Decision

Canon 1505 — §1. After the single judge or the president of a collegiate tribunal has recognized both that the matter is within his competence and that the petitioner does not lack legitimate personal standing in court, he must accept or reject the *libellus* as soon as possible through a decree.

§2. A *libellus* can be rejected only:

1° if the judge or the tribunal is incompetent;

2° if it is undoubtedly clear that the petitioner lacks legitimate personal standing in court;

3° if the prescriptions of can. 1504, nn. 1-3 have not been observed;

4° if from the *libellus* itself it is certainly obvious that it lacks any basis whatsoever and that it is impossible that any such basis would appear through a process.

§3. If the *libellus* has been rejected due to defects which can be corrected, the petitioner can properly draw up a new *libellus* and again present it to the same judge.

§4. A party is always free within ten available days (*tempus utile*) to lodge a reasoned recourse against the rejection of the *libellus* before the appellate tribunal or the college if it had been rejected by its president; the question of the rejection is to be resolved as quickly as possible.

(1) The "ius [vel persona] standi in iudicio" mentioned in paragraph one and paragraph two, number two is also referred to as "procedural capacity" (par. 41). Under the 1917 Code it was understood that an unbaptized person lacked not only procedural capacity but the more profound and basic capacity called "judicial capacity." That concept, however, has now been dropped (c. 1476).

Considered to lack procedural capacity under the 1917 Code were minors, etc. (*CIC* 1648, 1650), baptized non-Catholics (par. 41, c), religious without the consent of their superiors (*CIC* 1652), certain excommunicated persons (*CIC* 1654), and, in marriage cases, those who had been the direct and malevolent cause of the nullity (*CIC* 1971, §1, 1°). Under the 1983 law, the only category of people regarded as lacking the right to stand in judgment are minors, etc. (c. 1478).

It is understood, however, that people who have no direct involvement in a case likewise lack the procedural capacity in regard to that case. Only the marriage partners, for example, or the promoter of justice, can impugn the marriage. The bride's brother would lack the procedural capacity to petition that his sister's marriage be declared null (c. 1674).

(2) When a petition is rejected, the reasons for the rejection must, in accord with canon 1617, be expressed in the decree.

(3) Should the petitioner, in accord with paragraph four, have recourse to the appellate tribunal and that tribunal finds the rejection unwarranted, the procedure then is for the appellate tribunal not to hear the case, but rather to remand the case to the lower tribunal for acceptance of petition and hearing. There is no appeal against the decree by the higher court.[72]

b. By Default

Canon 1506 — If within a month from the presentation of the *libellus* the judge has not issued a decree by which he accepts or rejects the *libellus* in accord with the norm of can. 1505, the interested party can insist that the judge fulfill his duty; but if the judge, nevertheless, remains silent for ten days

after the petitioner's insistence, the petition is considered as having been accepted.

As noted in par. 33, a, this law constitutes an exception to the rule of thumb that says that a legal deadline that refers to the court is non-peremptory. This deadline on the tribunal's activity is peremptory.

CHAPTER II
THE CITATION AND NOTIFICATION OF JUDICIAL ACTS
[cc. 1507–1512]

72. *Decree of Citation*

Canon 1507 — §1. In the decree which accepts the *libellus* of the petitioner the judge or president must either call into court or cite the other parties for the joinder of issues (*contestatio litis*), determining whether they must respond in writing or present themselves personally before the judge in order to join the issues. But if from the written responses the judge perceives that it is necessary to call the parties together for a session, that can be determined in a new decree.

§2. If the *libellus* is considered as having been accepted in virtue of the norm of can. 1506, the decree of citation must be made in court within twenty days from the party's insistence on action as mentioned in that canon.

§3. But if the litigating parties de facto present themselves before the judge in order to proceed with the case, there is no need for a citation; the notary, however, is to note in the acts that the parties were present for the trial.

A citation, in the strict sense, is the judicial summons apprising the respondent of the petition and calling either for a written response to the allegation or an actual appearance at the *concordatio dubii* (par. 75, a). In the broader sense, it also refers to the notification of the defender and the promoter in those cases in which their presence is required.[73] As regards citing the witnesses, one should see canons 1556–1557.

73. *Transmittal of Citation (cc. 1508–1512)*

a. The Persons to Whom the Citation Is Transmitted
(1) The Respondent, etc.

Canon 1508 — §1. The decree of citation to the trial must be forwarded immediately to the respondent and at the same time to others who are to appear.

---

[72]See c. 1629, 4°–5°.

[73]See c. 1433.

§2. The introductory *libellus* is to be joined to the citation unless for serious reasons the judge determines that the *libellus* is not to be made known to the respondent before the latter makes a deposition during the trial.

(2) The Guardian, etc.

§3. If the suit is filed against a person who does not have the free exercise of personal rights or the free administration of the controverted items, the citation is to be made known to the guardian, curator or special procurator, as the case may be, or to the person who is bound to enter the trial in the respondent's name according to the norm of law.

b. The Method of Transmittal

Canon 1509 — §1. Notification of citations, decrees, sentences and other judicial acts are to be made in accordance with the norms determined in particular law through the public postal services or through another method which is the safest.

c. The Recording of the Transmittal

§2. The fact and method of notification must be clear in the acts.

d. The Refusal of the Transmitted Citation

Canon 1510 — A respondent who refuses to accept the document of citation or who prevents its arrival is considered as having been legitimately cited.

e. The Necessity of the Transmittal

Canon 1511 — If the citation has not been legitimately communicated, the acts of the process are null, with due regard for the prescription of can. 1507, §3.

One should also see canon 1622, 5°.

f. The Effects of the Transmittal

Canon 1512 — Once the citation has been legitimately communicated or the parties have appeared before the judge to pursue the case:
1° the issue ceases to be *res integra*;
2° the case becomes proper to that judge or tribunal before whom the action was begun and is competent in other respects;
3° the jurisdiction of a delegated judge is firmly established so that it does not expire when the right of the one delegating ceases;
4° prescription is interrupted unless otherwise provided;

5° the litigation begins to be pending and therefore the principle becomes operative: *while a suit is pending, nothing new is to be introduced.*

When the summons is legitimately sent to the respondent, or when, in accord with canon 1510, the respondent either refuses the summons or blocks its delivery, or when, in accord with canon 1507, §3, the parties appear before the judge without a summons, the five listed effects occur. A word about each:

1° – This means that the trial is officially opened, that the instance is officially begun (c. 1517), and that the matter is then considered litigious.

2° – This refers to the judge who obtains competence by reason of prevention (c. 1415).

3° – This follows the general rule of canon 142, §1.

4° – Prescription is interrupted when the trial officially opens, either because the apprising of the respondent about the claim of the petitioner dissipates the respondent's good faith (good faith is lost at least by the time of *contestatio litis*—c. 1515), which is always required for prescription (c. 198), or simply because the law considers it fair that prescription be interrupted during a trial, especially in order to avoid the possibility of the full term of prescription reaching maturity during the course of the trial.

5° – The 1917 Code (*CIC* 1854–1857) ruled that all *attempts* were invalid. An attempt was anything that, while the trial was pending, one party would innovate against the other or the judge would innovate against one or both parties, while the party whose rights were being prejudiced by the innovation was in dissent. That section on attempts is not included in this Code, but the principle remains: *"lite pendente, nihil innovetur."* Once a trial begins, therefore, the disputed object cannot be transferred from one party to the other or altered in such a way as to depreciate it. Nor, for example, would a person, the validity of whose marriage was judicially under investigation, be permitted to approach the pope to request a dissolution.

TITLE II
THE JOINDER OF ISSUES
(*CONTESTATIO LITIS*)
[cc. 1513–1516]

74. Description of Contestatio Litis

Canon 1513 — §1. The joinder of issues (*contestatio litis*) occurs when the terms of the controversy based on the petitions and responses of the parties are specified by the decree of the judge.

The 1917 Code (*CIC* 1726) used to define the *contestatio litis* as the formal contradiction of the petition by the respondent, made with the intention of litigating before a judge. The 1983 Code, however, defines the *contestatio* quite differently. The *contestatio*, it says, is the defining of the terms of the controversy (based on the petitions and responses of the parties) by the decree of the judge. Under the 1917 law, in other words, the agent of the *contestatio* was the parties; whereas under the 1983 law, the agent is the judge. It should also be noted, perhaps, that, whereas the *contestatio litis* is no longer a true contestation or contradiction, it does remain a true joining of the issues.

75. *Methods of Effecting* Contestatio Litis

§2. The petitions and responses of the parties, besides those in the *libellus* introducing the suit, can be expressed either in response to the citation or in a declaration made orally before the judge; in more difficult cases, however, the parties are to be called together by the judge to specify the question or questions to be answered in the sentence.

a. *Proximately* the *contestatio litis* is always effected, as paragraph one points out, by the decree of the judge. Somewhat more *remotely*, however, there are two methods of effecting the *contestatio*: the simple method and the solemn method. The simple method is for the judge to base the decree on the written or oral petitions and responses of the parties. The solemn method is for the judge to call the two parties together so that they can, in discussion, come to an agreement on the precise terms of the controversy. This is called the *concordatio dubii*, the agreement on the issue (or doubt).

b. The decree of the judge usually states the issue in the form of a question (or doubt). This is called the *formulatio dubii*. In a marriage case, for example, the issue is traditionally formulated as follows: *An constet de nullitate matrimonii Jones-Smith ob caput* _____ or, in English, whether the Jones-Smith marriage has been proved null on the grounds of _____ .

c. The various terms, therefore, have slightly different meanings. The *contestatio litis* is the defining of the issue by the judge. The *formulatio dubii* is the precise formulation of that definition by the judge. And the *concordatio dubii* is the agreement by the parties on the issue.

d. The final phrase of paragraph two notes that the sentence should always speak to the issue. Canon 1611, 1° restates this requirement and canon 1620, 8° notes that, if a sentence completely fails to do that, it is incurably null.

76. *Notification of Parties*

§3. The decree of the judge is to be made known to the parties; unless they have already reached an agreement, they can within ten days make recourse to that judge that it be changed; however, the issue is to be resolved as quickly as possible by a decree of that judge.

When the solemn method for effecting the *contestatio* is followed and both parties cooperate in defining the points at issue, then no further notification would seem to be necessary. When, however, the simple method is followed, then the parties should be apprised of the formulation and be allowed to request a change. In regard to notifying the absent respondent, one should see par. 140, a. For the significance of the phrase "as quickly as possible" *(expeditissime)*, one should see canon 1629, 5°.

77. *Changing the* Contestatio Litis

Canon 1514 — **Once the terms of the controversy have been determined, they cannot validly be changed except for a serious reason through a new decree at the request of one party and after hearing the other parties and considering their reasons.**

It is clear from this canon that the *contestatio* cannot be changed by the judge ex officio but only at the request of one of the parties. The same is true of the original definition of the issue, as is clear from canons 1507, §1 and 1513, §1. Even though it is the judge who defines the issue, it is always done on the basis of the petitions and responses of the parties.

78. *Effects of* Contestatio Litis *(cc. 1515–1516)*

a. *As Regards Prescription*

Canon 1515 — **Once the joinder of issues (*contestatio litis*) has occurred, the possessor of another's property ceases to be in good faith; if therefore, the possessor is sentenced to make restitution, the profits made from the day of the joinder of issues (*contestatio litis*) must also be returned and any damages compensated.**

One should also see canon 1512, 4° and par. 73, f.

b. *As Regards Proofs*

Canon 1516 — **Once the joinder of issues (*contestatio litis*) has occurred, the judge is to furnish the parties suitable time to present and complete proofs.**

TITLE III
THE PROSECUTION OF THE SUIT
[cc. 1517–1525]

79. *Notion of an Instance*

An instance is a *gradus iudicii,* or a certain level of adjudication.[74]

80. *General Principle*

Canon 1517 — **The prosecution of a suit begins with the citation; it ends not only with the pronouncement of a definitive sentence but also through the other methods defined by law.**

a. Under the 1917 law (*CIC* 1725, 1732) the litigation began with the citation, whereas the instance began with the *contestatio litis.* The 1983 law, more simply and logically, recognizes the citation as the beginning both of the litigation (c. 1512) and of the instance (c. 1517).

b. An instance is interrupted by suspension (cc. 1518–1519).

c. An instance is ended by peremption (cc. 1520–1523), by renunciation (cc. 1524–1525), by a sentence (which is the usual way an instance is closed), and by reconciliation or arbitration, should the parties decide, even after the trial has begun, to settle out of court (c. 1713).

81. *Suspension (cc. 1518–1519)*

a. *Description*

A suspension of an instance is the interruption of judicial activity due to some factor relating either to the parties or their representatives.

b. *The Parties*

Canon 1518 — **If the litigating party dies, or changes status, or ceases from the office on behalf of which the suit was initiated:**

1° if the case is not concluded, its prosecution is suspended until the heir of the deceased, the successor or an interested party resumes the suit;

2° if the case is concluded, the judge must proceed to the final acts after having cited the procurator if present or otherwise the heir or the successor of the deceased.

(1) When the canon speaks of a change of status, it refers, of course, only to those changes that would affect one's procedural capacity, such as the loss of the use of reason during the court proceedings (c. 1478, §1).

(2) Although most of the manualists agree that the phrase "causa conclusa" refers to the *conclusio in causa* (cc. 1599 and 1600), an argument could certainly be made that the *conclusion* of the case mentioned in this canon is not something different from the *end* of the case or instance mentioned in the previous canon. The *conclusio in causa* is surely not the same as the "conclusio causae." The *conclusio in causa* refers to the conclusion of only one stage, namely, the probatory stage of the case.

This interpretation, i.e., equating the conclusion of the case with the end of the instance, would avoid the judge's having to pronounce the sentence after one of the parties has died. The obligation to pronounce the sentence after the death of one of the parties would, perhaps, be particularly unseemly in a marriage case, and yet this canon does apply to a marriage case.[75]

c. *Their Representatives*

Canon 1519 — **§1. If a guardian, curator or procurator who is necessary in accord with the norms of can. 1481, §§1 and 3, ceases from office, the prosecution of the suit is suspended in the interim.**

§2. However, the judge is to appoint another guardian or curator as soon as possible; the judge can appoint a procurator for the suit if the party has neglected to do so within the brief time period stated by the judge.

d. *Effects*

The principal effects of suspension are (1) judicial acts placed during the period of suspension are null and (2) the suspension period is not computed relative to peremption.

82. *Peremption or Abatement (cc. 1520–1523)*

a. *Description*

Peremption is the extinction of an instance because of the negligence of the parties.

b. *The Time*

Canon 1520 — **Barring some impediment, if no procedural act is proposed by the parties for six months, the prosecution of the suit is abated. Particular law can state other time limits for abatement.**

The assumption underlying this canon is that, when an unimpeded party takes no interest whatsoever in the trial for a period of six months, such negligence amounts to a tacit renunciation of the instance.

---

[74]See par. 14, a.

[75]See c. 1675, §2.

Although the canon indicates that peremption occurs automatically, nevertheless, in practice, a judge who had been unable to elicit a response or effect involvement by a party would be expected to give notice to the party of the impending decree of peremption in order to determine in fact whether the party was or was not impeded.[76]

c. The Force of Peremption

Canon 1521 — **Abatement takes effect by the law itself against all persons, including minors and those equivalent to minors, and it must also be declared ex officio with due regard for the right of petitioning for indemnity against tutors, guardians, administrators or procurators who have not proved that they were not at fault.**

d. The Effects of Peremption

Canon 1522 — **Abatement extinguishes the acts of the process, but not the acts of the case, which in fact may be operative in another instance provided that the case involves the same persons and the same issue; as regards outsiders the acts of the case have no other value than that of documents.**

One should also see canon 1641, 3°.

e. The Expenses

Canon 1523 — **When a trial is abated, each of the litigants is to bear the expenses which he or she has incurred.**

83. Renunciation (cc. 1524–1525)

a. By the Parties

Canon 1524 — **§1. A petitioner can renounce the instance at any stage or grade of trial; both petitioner and respondent can likewise renounce either all or some of the acts of the process.**

(1) A petitioner might renounce an *instance* because he or she realizes that the evidence needed to prove his or her allegation is not available at the time. Since, however, the renouncing of an instance does not necessarily involve the renouncing of the *action,* the petitioner would be free, should the needed evidence become available at a later time, to reopen the suit by starting a new instance.[77]

(2) Either party may renounce a *procedural* act. If, for example, the respondent had requested that a certain witness be called, he or she could later ask that that person's name be dropped from the list of witnesses.[78]

b. By Their Representatives

§2. In order for them to renounce an instance, the guardians and administrators of juridic persons need to consult with or obtain the consent of those whose involvement is required to place acts which go beyond the limits of ordinary administration.

c. Form and Requisites

§3. In order for a renunciation to be valid it is to be made in writing and also signed by the party or by the party's procurator with a special mandate to do so; it must be communicated to the other party, accepted, or at least not attacked, by that party, and admitted by the judge.

d. Effects and Expenses

Canon 1525 — **A renunciation admitted by the judge has the same effects concerning the renounced acts as an abatement of an instance and it obliges the renouncing party to pay the expenses for the renounced acts.**

TITLE IV
PROOFS
[cc. 1526–1586]

84. Notion of Proof

A judicial proof is a demonstration of a dubious or contested fact through legitimate arguments made to a judge.

85. Kinds of Proof

Although proofs can be divided in many ways (e.g., direct and indirect, judicial and extra-judicial, etc.), the most important division is into full and semi-full. *Full* proof can be gained from a judicial confession in a private matter (c. 1536, §1), from public documents (c. 1541), from witnesses under certain conditions (c. 1573), and from legal presumptions (c. 1585). *Semi-full* proof, on the other hand, is gained from a judicial confession in a public matter (c. 1536, §2), from an extra-judicial confession (c. 1537), from private documents (c. 1542), from witnesses (c. 1573), from experts (c. 1579), and from judicial presumptions (c. 1586).

Semi-full, it should be noted, does not necessarily mean half full, as though two semi-full proofs necessarily add up to one full proof. Proofs, as it is said, should not be numbered but weighed by the judge.[79]

---

[76]Wernz-Vidal, n. 413.
[77]See also c. 1594.
[78]See c. 1551.

[79]*Argumenta non numeranda sed ponderanda sunt* (*SRRDec* 49, 153; 62, 658).

86. Subject (or Burden) of Proof

Canon 1526 — §1. The burden of proof rests upon the person who makes the allegations.

a. Although the burden of proof rests primarily on the claimant, the judge may also, when appropriate, offer proofs on his own.[80]

b. The Latin original of the canon, "Onus probandi incumbit ei qui asserit" is a canonical axiom. In the 1917 Code, paragraph two of the corresponding canon (*CIC* 1748) was another axiom: "actore non probante, reus absolvitur." The term "reus," meaning the accused, or defendant, is now used only in penal cases (elsewhere it has been replaced by the term "pars conventa"), but the sentiment expressed in the axiom remains true, if somewhat obvious, namely, if the petitioner does not prove his or her claim, the respondent's status remains intact. For completeness, however, still another axiom should be mentioned: "reus excipiens fit actor." It might happen, for example, that the petitioner originally sued for an agreed upon but never paid fee for the purchase of real estate. If the respondent then lodges an exception (par. 32, b) claiming that the agreement was invalid, then the burden of proving the invalidity belongs, of course, to the respondent.

87. Object of Proof

The object of judicial proof is uncertain, litigated facts which are relevant to the decision in a case. Therefore:

§2. The following do not need proof:
1° matters which are presumed by the law itself;
2° facts alleged by one of the contending parties and admitted by the other unless proof is nonetheless demanded by the law or by the judge.

a. As regards number one, the following are some examples of things presumed by law: the validity of marriage (c. 1060), the consummation of marriage once the couple has cohabited (c. 1061, §2), and the conformity of internal consent with external expression in entering marriage (c. 1101, §1).

b. As regards number two, it should be noted that, in marriage cases and in other matters of the public good, the law (cc. 1536, 1679) does not consider the mere assertion by one party and admission by the other as constituting full proof.

88. Admissible Proofs

Canon 1527 — §1. Proofs of any type whatever which seem useful for deciding the case and which are licit can be adduced.

§2. If a party insists that a proof rejected by the judge be admitted, the judge is to determine the matter most expeditiously.

For the significance of the phrase "most expeditiously" or "expeditissime," one should see canon 1629, 5°.

89. Designated Receiver

Canon 1528 — If a party or a witness refuses to appear before the judge to testify, it is permitted to hear the person through a lay person assigned by the judge or to seek the person's declaration before a notary public or in any other legitimate manner.

a. When this canon speaks of a person refusing to testify before the *judge,* this clearly includes the *judge instructor,* or auditor, mentioned in canon 1428 (par. 19).

b. The role of the designated receiver, it should be noted, is more limited than that of the auditor. The auditor truly instructs the case, not only collecting the proofs but determining which proofs are to be included; the designated receiver can only audit testimony, etc., as directed by the judge.[81]

c. The clear sense of this canon is that the tribunal should attempt to elicit actual *testimony* both from the principals (in accord with c. 1530) and from those people officially listed as witnesses. The court is allowed to settle for *affidavits* (pars. 99, 100) from those people only when they refuse to testify before the judge. If, in other words, the principals provide the court with the names of people and specifically request that the people be called to testify in court, then the tribunal must comply. If, however, the deponents are listed not as witnesses but only as affiants, i.e., people who would be willing to prepare and swear to an affidavit, then it suffices if the tribunal requests an affidavit from these people, even though they would also be willing to appear in court and give testimony.

90. Commencement of the Probatory Stage

Canon 1529 — Except for a serious cause, the judge is not to proceed to gather proofs before the joinder of issues (contestatio litis).

This canon, which was included (in somewhat different form) in the 1917 Code (*CIC* 1730) under the title dealing with the *contestatio litis* rather than under the title dealing with proofs, was also found (again in different form) in the sixth title of the second book of the *Decretals* of Gregory IX.[82]

---

[80]See cc. 1452 (par. 29, d), 1530, 1574.

[81]See also par. 114, b.
[82]See par. 3.

CHAPTER I
THE DECLARATIONS OF THE PARTIES
[cc. 1530–1538]

91. Judge

Canon 1530 — **The judge can always interrogate the parties so as to reveal the truth more effectively; in fact the judge must do so at the request of a party or to prove a fact which is to be established beyond doubt for the sake of the public interest.**

For the general principle behind this canon, one should see canon 1452.

92. Response

Canon 1531 — **§1. A party legitimately interrogated must answer and tell the whole truth.**
§2. But if a party has refused to answer, it is for the judge to evaluate what can be drawn from that refusal concerning the proof of the facts.

Two observations should be made regarding paragraph one of this canon:
a. A person who commits perjury while testifying before a tribunal is subject to a just penalty (c. 1368).
b. In penal cases the accused is *not* bound to confess the crime and should not be put under oath regarding it (c. 1728, §2).

93. Oath

Canon 1532 — **Unless a serious cause persuades otherwise, the judge is to administer an oath to the parties to tell the truth or at least to confirm the truth of their testimony in cases where the public good is at stake; the judge, in accord with prudential judgment, can do the same in other cases.**

a. Over the years there has been a variety of opinions with regard to oath taking in contentious cases having a bearing on the common good. The 1917 Code (*CIC* 1744) *required* the judge to put the party under oath. The 1976 draft of procedural law (c. 174) said that the judge should *urge the person to take an oath.* At the November 1978 meeting of the consultors there were various opinions: some consultors thought that the judge should *urge the person to tell the truth,* without any oath; some thought it should be left to the *discretion* of the judge; and others thought that the person should be *required* to take an oath, as in the 1917 Code.[83] The present canon is a compromise position, requiring the judge to put the party under oath, "unless a serious cause persuades otherwise."
b. The Latin phrases "de veritate dicenda" (for

the oath "to tell the truth") and "de veritate dictorum" (for the oath "to confirm the truth") are still in common use.

94. Questionnaires

Canon 1533 — **The parties, the promoter of justice and the defender of the bond can present to the judge items on which a party is to be interrogated.**

95. Rules for Interrogation

Canon 1534 — **To the extent it is possible the regulations of cann. 1548, §2, n. 1, 1552 and 1558-1565 on witnesses are to be observed in the interrogation of the parties.**

96. Judicial Confession (cc. 1535–1536)

a. Definition

Canon 1535 — **A judicial confession is a written or oral assertion against oneself made by any party regarding the matter under trial and made before a competent judge, whether spontaneously or upon interrogation by the judge.**

b. Probative Force
(1) In Private Matters

Canon 1536 — **§1. If it is a question of some private matter and the public good is not at stake the judicial confession of one party relieves the other parties from the burden of proof.**

It is in this context that a confession has been called the *regina probationum* or the *probatio probatissima* or the *probatio optima.*

(2) In Public Matters

§2. In cases which concern the public good, however, a judicial confession and the declarations of the parties which are not confessions can have a probative force to be evaluated by the judge along with the other circumstances of the case; but complete probative force cannot be attributed to them unless other elements are present which thoroughly corroborate them.

97. Extra-Judicial Confession

Canon 1537 — **Having weighed all the circumstances, it is for the judge to evaluate the worth of an extra-judicial confession which has been introduced into the trial.**

The extra-judicial confession in a marriage case is somewhat different from one made in a penal

---

[83]See *Comm* 11 (1979), 101–102.

case, because in a marriage case it is often not a confession in the true or strict sense since it is not really *contra se*. Nevertheless, should a party, before or shortly after marriage, mention, for example, that he or she did not intend to have children, that clearly is a significant remark. Article 116 of *Provida* (par. 206) therefore allowed that when an extra-judicial confession was made in "tempore non suspecto," then it could be estimated by the judge as an adminicular support of proof. And Pinna, in a Rotal decision of June 14, 1960,[84] said that when credible witnesses attest to an admission of simulation seriously made by a party at a non-suspect time, then the judge may consider that to be tantamount to an extra-judicial confession.

98. *Invalid Confession*

Canon 1538 — A confession or any other declaration of a party lacks all probative force if it is proved that it was made through an error of fact or it was extorted by force or grave fear.

CHAPTER II
PROOF BY DOCUMENTS
[cc. 1539–1546]

99. *Admissibility of Documents*

Canon 1539 — In every type of trial, proof by means of both public and private documents is admitted.

a. This chapter heading has been rather pointedly changed from "instruments" in the 1917 Code to "documents" in the 1983 Code in order to exclude tape recordings and the like whose authenticity cannot be certified.[85] It should be noted, though, that the 1917 Code's use of the term "instrument" in the chapter and article headings was more a historical nicety than anything else, as a kind of reminder that the term "instrument" had been used in the *Decretals* of Gregory IX. The canons themselves in the 1917 Code always used the word "document."

b. The traditional placement of this material on documents (in *Decretals, CIC*, etc.) was *following* the law on witnesses. The 1983 Code situates it instead *before* the law on witnesses, perhaps in order to enhance its importance. It is, at any rate, true that in the United States, the affidavit (a notarized statement that would be classified as a public document) is now being used extensively, either to supplement the testimony of the witnesses or, if the

affidavits are sufficiently complete, to replace the testimony altogether.[86]

ARTICLE 1: THE NATURE AND
TRUSTWORTHINESS OF DOCUMENTS
[cc. 1540–1543]

100. *Kinds of Documents*

Canon 1540 — §1. Public ecclesiastical documents are those which official persons have drawn up in the exercise of their function in the Church, after having observed the formalities prescribed by law.

§2. Public civil documents are those which are considered to be such in law in accord with the laws of the individual place.

§3. Other documents are private ones.

Public ecclesiastical documents would include acts of the Holy Father, Roman Curia, and ordinaries; judicial acts; official parish books; and authentic copies or attestations regarding records contained in those books. It would also include affidavits used in marriage cases, which had been notarized by an ecclesiastical notary.[87]

Public civil documents would include affidavits used in marriage cases, which had been notarized by a notary public.

Private documents would include receipts, letters, contracts, and wills.

101. *Probative Force (cc. 1541–1543)*

a. *Of Public Documents*

Canon 1541 — Unless contrary and evident arguments show otherwise, public documents are to be trusted concerning everything which is directly and principally affirmed in them.

(1) A public document proves only what is directly and principally affirmed in it. It does not, therefore, prove what is only indirectly or incidentally affirmed. For example:

> directly – a marriage record proves only that the ceremony took place, because this is all that it affirms directly—it does not prove that the marriage was valid;

> principally – a marriage record which includes mention of the baptismal status of the parties

---

[84]*SRRDec* 52, 318.
[85]*Comm* 11 (1979), 105.

[86]See par. 89, c.
[87]Sometimes the signature of the pastor may substitute for that of an ecclesiastical notary (or for that of the ordinary). See, for example, c. 1105, §2, where the mandate for one serving as a proxy in a marriage is regarded as an official document if it is signed either by the pastor or by the ordinary. See also Wernz-Vidal, 469 n. 15.

does not prove that status since it is only an incidental part of the marriage record.

(2) As regards the value of affidavits in marriage cases, however, the following observation of Doheny merits attention:

In English-speaking countries affidavits are frequently resorted to as a means of documentary proof or evidence. These affidavits are written declarations or statements confirmed by oath or solemn affirmation. Since they are oftentimes presented in marriage cases, judges and other officers of the court should be warned not to ascribe to them more probative force than they purport to carry. An affidavit merely certifies that a specific person made a solemn affirmation confirmed by oath before a duly qualified notary public at a certain time. Obviously, such a statement, in itself, even though under oath does not constitute full proof in matrimonial cases. The inherent truth of the statement and the facts attested must be further investigated.[88]

b. Of Private Documents

Canon 1542 — A private document whether acknowledged by a party or recognized by the judge has the same probative force against its author or signer and those deriving a case from them as does an extra-judicial confession; against outsiders it has the same force as the declarations of the parties which are not confessions, in accord with the norm of can. 1536, §2.

c. Of Defective Documents

Canon 1543 — If the documents are shown to have been erased, corrected, interpolated, or affected by another such defect, it is for the judge to assess whether such documents have value and how much.

ARTICLE 2: THE PRESENTATION OF DOCUMENTS
[cc. 1544–1546]

102. Admissible Documents

Canon 1544 — Documents do not have probative force in a trial unless they are originals or presented in authentic copy and are deposited with the chancery of the tribunal so that they may be examined by the judge and the opposing party.

[88]Doheny I, 400.

103. Role of the Judge

Canon 1545 — The judge can order that a document which is common to both parties be exhibited in the process.

The 1917 Code included a title on the *actio ad exhibendum* which recognized the right of a party to institute an action (par. 56), i.e., request the court to include a document in the acts of the case. This procedure has now been deformalized. A party still, of course, has the right, by reason of canons 1526, §1 and 1527, §1, to bring certain documents to the attention of the judge or to list certain people as potential affiants, but such a request need no longer be posited as a formal action. The request is now made informally, and it is for the judge then to decide for or against admission of the document. It should be noted, however, that admission of a document by the judge entitles all parties to inspect it, at least at the time of the publication of the acts (c. 1598). In general, in other words, documents, including affidavits, do not enjoy any sort of confidentiality.

104. Exempt Documents

Canon 1546 — §1. Even if documents are common, no one is obliged to exhibit those which cannot be communicated without risk of harm in accordance with the norm of can. 1548, §2, n. 2, or without risk of violating the obligation to observe secrecy.
§2. Nonetheless, if some excerpt, at least, of a document can be transcribed and can be presented in copy form without the above-mentioned hazards the judge can decree that it be produced.

a. It would seem that a possible reading of this and related canons, as they apply to the affidavit, would be as follows: should a potential affiant determine that his or her affidavit, if seen by the parties, would result in grave evils, he or she has three choices:

(1) decline to issue the affidavits in accord with paragraph one, which deprives the court of that evidence;

(2) present the affidavit to the judge and, in accord with paragraph two, request that certain sections, including perhaps the name of the affiant, be deleted or held confidential;

(3) obtain an assurance from the judge that the affidavit will never be published "in order to avoid very serious dangers" (c. 1598). Some American civil lawyers are of the opinion that Americans enjoy, as a civil right stemming from

their citizenship, the privilege of conveying an affidavit to a priest as a privileged communication, thereby binding him to retain it as confidential material. According to this opinion, the ecclesiastical judge would be bound by American civil law[89] to abide by the wishes of the affiant, even though canon law and specifically canon 1546, §2 leaves to his discretion the determination of which sections of a document can go unpublished.

b. Unlike chapter III on witnesses, which requires that the names of all witnesses be communicated to the parties (c. 1554), this chapter II on documents does not specifically require that the names of affiants be communicated to the parties.

CHAPTER III
WITNESSES AND TESTIMONIES
[cc. 1547–1573]

105. Etymology of Terms

The English word *wit/ness* is a compound word (like gover/ness or high/ness) which means a person having wit or knowledge—not just speculative knowledge but knowledge that comes from one or more of the five senses, or five wits, as they have been called. The German word *wissen* is also a member of this family.

The English word *testimony* (and the Latin word *testis* which means both "testicle" and "witness") derives, no doubt, from the Abrahamic oath ritual in which the patriarch instructed the swearer "place your hand under my thigh" as recorded in Genesis 24:2 and 47:29.[90]

106. Kinds of Witnesses

The canons of this chapter refer to various types of witnesses. These same categories would, of course, also apply to the affiants discussed in chapter II.

a. There are, for example, witnesses *de scientia* (who testify to a fact known from personal observation); *de credulitate,* or *de opinione* (who have reasoned to or deduced something); *de fama* (who report public rumor); and *de auditu ab aliis* or *de auditu ab auditu* (who report something heard from another) (c. 1572, 2°).

b. Witnesses *de scientia* can be either *de visu* (eye witnesses, or ocular witnesses) or *de auditu* (ear witnesses, or auricular witnesses) (c. 1572, 2°).

c. A witness can be *sworn* or *unsworn* (c. 1562).

d. A witness can be *certain* or *vacillating* (c. 1572, 3°).

e. Witnesses can be *qualified* if they testify about something which was done as part of their office (c. 1573) or simply *legitimate,* sometimes referred to as *omni, exceptione maior,* if they are persons of ordinary honesty and perception (c. 1572, 1°; 876).

f. Witnesses are *unsuited* if they lack perfect knowledge (c. 1550, §1), *incapable* if, for reasons stated in the law, they are excluded from testifying (c. 1550, §2), and *suspect* if, for a just reason, e.g., because of bitter public enmity toward one of the parties, they are subject to exclusion by the judge (c. 1555).

g. Witnesses can be either *singular* if they do not agree with each other (c. 1560, §2) or *concordant,* called *testes contestes,* if they do agree with each other (c. 1572, 4°).

h. Singular witnesses are said to be *adversative* if their testimonies are repugnant; *diversative* if their testimonies refer to different matters altogether; and *cumulative,* or adminicular, if they are generally in agreement even though specifically different.

107. Admissibility of Witnesses

Canon 1547 — **Proof by means of witnesses is admitted in every kind of case under the supervision of the judge.**

Although this canon might seem so obvious as to be superfluous, it is included here to emphasize the fact that in canon law, proof by witnesses is *always* admissible, even in the area of contractual law where the Church has agreed to recognize civil procedures (c. 1290) and even where those civil procedures in a particular country do not recognize testimony as admissible evidence.[91]

108. Obligation of Witnesses

a. The Principle

Canon 1548 — **§1. When the judge legitimately interrogates witnesses they must tell the truth.**

b. The Exceptions

§2. With due regard for the prescription of can. 1550, §2, n. 2, the following are exempted from the obligation to answer:
1° clerics in regard to whatever was made known to them in connection with their sacred ministry; civil officials, doctors, midwives, advocates, notaries and others who are bound to professional se-

---

[89]See par. 10.
[90]In ch. 24: *"subter femur meum"*; in ch. 47: *"sub femore meo"*; *The Jerome Biblical Commentary* (24) notes, "Swearing by the genital organs, considered the transmitters of life, added solemnity to the oath."

[91]Coronata, n. 1281; *Comm* 11 (1979), 108.

crecy, even by reason of advice rendered, as regards matters subject to this secrecy;

2° persons who fear that infamy, dangerous vexations or other serious evils will happen to themselves, or their spouse, or persons related to them by consanguinity or affinity, as a result of their testimony.

ARTICLE 1: THOSE WHO CAN BE WITNESSES
[cc. 1549–1550]

109. The Principle

Canon 1549 — All persons can be witnesses unless they are expressly excluded by law, either completely or partially.

110. The Exceptions

a. The Unsuited

Canon 1550 — §1. Minors below the fourteenth year of age and those who are feebleminded are not allowed to give testimony; however, they may be heard by reason of a decree of the judge which declares such a hearing expedient.

b. The Incapable

§2. The following are considered incapable:
1° those who are parties in the case, or who represent the parties in the trial; the judge and assistants, the advocate and others who are assisting or have assisted the parties in the same case;
2° priests as regards everything which has become known to them by reason of sacramental confession, even if the penitent requests their manifestation; moreover, whatever has been heard by anyone or in any way on the occasion of confession cannot be accepted as even an indication of the truth.

ARTICLE 2: THE INTRODUCTION AND
EXCLUSION OF WITNESSES
[cc. 1551–1557]

111. Introduction of Witnesses (cc. 1551–1554)

a. Who Can Introduce (and Renounce) Witnesses

Canon 1551 — The party who has introduced a witness can forego the examination of the witness; but the opposing party can demand that the witness be examined notwithstanding that action.

(1) The right of a party to retract the name of a witness he or she previously suggested is a specifi-

cation of the general principle enunciated in canon 1524, §1 about the right of a party to renounce any act.

(2) The judge, by reason of canon 1452; the defender, by reason of canon 1432; and the promoter of justice, by reason of canons 1430–1434, are also empowered to introduce witnesses.

b. How Witnesses Are Introduced

Canon 1552 — §1. When proof by means of witnesses is demanded, their names and domicile are to be made known to the tribunal.
§2. The items of discussion upon which interrogation of the witnesses is sought are to be presented within the time limit set by the judge; otherwise the petition is to be considered as abandoned.

c. How Many Witnesses May Be Introduced

Canon 1553 — It is the judge's responsibility to curb an excessive number of witnesses.

d. Notification of Witnesses' Names to Parties

Canon 1554 — Before witnesses are examined, their names are to be made known to the parties; however, if in the prudent assessment of the judge, that cannot be done without serious difficulty, it is to be done at least before the publication of the testimony.

The 1936 Instruction, *Provida mater,* on the procedural law to be followed in marriage cases, recognizing the fact that such cases involve special considerations, explicitly permitted witnesses to testify, with the understanding that their names not be revealed to the parties (Art. 131, §2). In such cases, according to the instruction, the judge was to assure himself of the credibility of those witnesses by obtaining testimonials regarding them, but the testimonials were, of course, also exempt from the need for publication (Art. 138, §2). The 1983 law recognizes no such confidentiality, either in this canon or in canons 1678–1680 which deal with the special procedures for marriage cases.

112. Exclusion of Witnesses

Canon 1555 — With due regard for the prescription of can. 1550, a party can request that a witness be excluded if a just cause for exclusion is demonstrated before the interrogation of the witness.

a. Although the exclusion of a witness would primarily be done at the instance of a party, the reference to canon 1550 indicates that the judge can exclude unsuited and incapable people ex officio.
b. In the 1917 Code the party who introduced

the witness was not then free to reprove the witness;[92] only the adversary could do that (*CIC* 1764, §2). This canon, however, allows either party to reprove a witness.

c. The 1917 Code (*CIC* 1764, §4) permitted reproval of the witness even after the testimony was given, providing the adversary could show that the reason for requesting the reproval was unknown to him at the time the testimony was given. The present canon requires that all requests for exclusion be lodged beforehand.

113. Citation of Witnesses

Canon 1556 — **The citation of a witness is done by a decree of the judge made known to the witness according to law.**

Canon 1557 — **A witness who has been duly cited is to appear or inform the judge of the reason for the absence.**

ARTICLE 3: THE EXAMINATION OF WITNESSES
[cc. 1558–1571]

114. Place of Examination

Canon 1558 — **§1. Witnesses must be examined at the tribunal unless it appears otherwise appropriate to the judge.**

§2. Cardinals, patriarchs, bishops and those who, by the law of their state, enjoy a similar right, are to be heard in a place which they themselves select.

§3. The judge is to decide where those are to be heard for whom it is impossible or difficult to come to the tribunal because of distance, illness or other impediment with due regard for the prescriptions of cann. 1418 and 1469, §2.

a. As regards paragraph three, canon 1418 notes that if a witness lives outside the judge's territory, the testimony of that witness may be received by a rogatory commission.[93] Canon 1469, §2 offers an alternative solution by allowing the judge to cross diocesan lines, with the permission of the local bishop, and to receive the testimony himself. In either case, however, it is the local bishop or tribunal who determines the place of examination.

b. When the testimony of a witness is taken away from the tribunal itself, the services of a designated receiver (c. 1528) are often used. He is then the *locum tenens* of the judge (see c. 1561).

115. Manner of Examination (cc. 1559–1565)

a. Those Present

Canon 1559 — **The parties may not assist at the examination of witnesses unless the judge believes that they must be admitted, especially when the matter concerns the private good. On the other hand, their advocates or their procurators may assist unless the judge believes that the process must be carried on in secret because of the circumstances of things or persons.**

Although the present canon allows the judge, when he considers it important, to permit the parties to be present at the questioning of a witness, canon 1678, §2 disallows this in a marriage nullity hearing. In accord, therefore, with the axiom "Generi per speciem derogatur,"[94] the judge in a marriage case may not permit a party to be present during the questioning of a witness.[95]

b. The Witnesses Themselves

Canon 1560 — **§1. Each of the witnesses must be examined individually.**

§2. If the witnesses disagree among themselves or with a party in a serious matter the judge can bring them together or have them come to an agreement with one another, precluding disputes and scandal insofar as it is possible.

The 1917 Code permitted a confrontation only if three conditions concurred: (1) the disagreement was in a substantial matter; (2) there was no better way to discover the truth; and (3) there was no danger either of scandal or of quarrels stemming from the confrontation. Coronata noted that since those three conditions would, in fact, hardly ever be met, an actual confrontation was almost inconceivable in a church court.[96] The present canon makes the institute more practical.

c. The Judge as Questioner

Canon 1561 — **The examination of a witness is conducted by the judge, a delegate or an auditor, who is to be assisted by a notary; as a result, if the parties, or the promoter of justice, or the defender of the bond, or the advocates who are present at the examination have further questions to be put to the witness, they are to propose these questions not to the witness but to the judge or the person taking the judge's place who is to ask them, unless particular law provides otherwise.**

---

[92]This is in accord with the *Regula Iuris*, n. 21 in Boniface VIII's *Liber Sextus*, which reads, "*Quod semel placuit amplius displicere non potest.*" *CorpusIC* II, 1122.
[93]See par. 14, d.

[94]*Regula Iuris*, n. 34, *CorpusIC* II, 1123.
[95]See also *Comm* 11 (1979), 114.
[96]Coronata, 249.

(1) The principal difference between this canon and the corresponding canon in the 1917 Code (*CIC* 1773) is the addition of the final phrase about honoring a local law that prescribes another method of interrogation.

(2) In the 1917 Code, the procedure in a marriage case was for the defender to prepare the questionnaires for all parties and witnesses, and, at the beginning of each session, to present the questionnaires to the judge in a sealed envelope (*CIC* 1968). This procedure is not included in the 1983 Code.

d. The Judge as Promoter of Truth

Canon 1562 — §1. The judge is to call to the attention of the witness the serious obligation to tell the whole truth and only the truth.

§2. The judge is to administer the oath to the witness in accord with can. 1532; but the witness who refuses to take it is to be heard without the oath.

e. The Matter of Questioning

Canon 1563 — The judge, first of all, is to establish the identity of the witness; the judge should seek out what is the relationship of the witness with the parties, and, when addressing specific questions to the witness regarding the case, the judge is also to inquire about the sources of the witness' knowledge and the precise time the witness learned what is asserted.

The judge poses to the witness both *general* questions by which the witness' identity and general relationship to the case are ascertained and *special* questions by which the witness' knowledge of all pertinent facts is explored.

f. The Form of Questioning

Canon 1564 — The questions are to be brief, accommodated to the intelligence of the person being interrogated, not comprising several points at the same time, not captious, nor crafty, nor suggestive of the answer, free from every kind of offense and pertinent to the case being tried.

Canon 1565 — §1. The questions must not be communicated to the witnesses ahead of time.

§2. However, if the matters which are to be testified to are so removed from memory that unless they are recalled earlier they cannot be affirmed with certainty, the judge may advise the witness of some matters if it is thought that this can be done without danger.

116. Responses of the Witness

Canon 1566 — Witnesses are to give testimony orally; they are not to read from written memoranda, unless there is question of calculation and accounts; in such a case they may consult the notes which they brought with them.

The reason for this canon, notes Coronata, is that oral testimony allows the judge to look into the mind of the *witness,* whereas written testimony might reveal only the mind of the *suborner.*[97]

117. Work of the Notary (cc. 1567–1569)

a. Taking the Testimony

Canon 1567 — §1. The answer is to be put in writing at once by the notary who must report the exact words of the testimony given, at least as regards those points which touch directly upon the matter of the trial.

§2. Use of a tape recorder is allowed provided that, afterwards, the answers are transcribed and are signed by those making the depositions, if possible.

b. Recording Other Matters

Canon 1568 — The notary is to make mention in the acts whether the oath was taken, omitted, or refused, also of the presence of the parties and of other persons, the questions added ex officio and, in general, everything noteworthy which may have occurred while the witnesses were being examined.

c. Rereading the Testimony, etc.

Canon 1569 — §1. At the conclusion of the examination what the notary has put in writing from the deposition must be read to the witness or the witness must be given an opportunity to listen to the tape recording of the deposition with the option of adding to, suppressing, correcting or changing it.

§2. Finally the acts must be signed by the witness, the judge and the notary.

118. Rehearing of a Witness

Canon 1570 — Although witnesses have already been examined, they can be recalled for another examination at the request of a party or ex officio but before the acts or the testimony have been published; this is true if the judge believes such a reexamination necessary or useful, provided, however, that there is no danger of collusion or corruption.

[97]Ibid., 252.

a. Collusion, as here understood, is the covert and fraudulent agreement between the witness and one of the parties with a view to distorting the truth.

Corruption or bribery is any influence exercised by a party on the witness for the purpose of having the witness testify to something other than the *tota et sola veritas* (c. 1562, §1).

b. In the revised law the testimony of the witnesses becomes *publici juris* at the time of the publication of the acts (c. 1598).

In the 1917 law the testimony became *publici iuris* immediately after the last witness had testified, at which time there was a special publication of the testimony (*CIC* 1782) which was separate from the publication of the acts (*CIC* 1858) that would take place later.

The 1917 Code contained a separate article, consisting of five canons, on the publication of the testimony (*CIC* 1782–1786). This article was retained in the 1976 schema but was suppressed before the 1980 draft as being superfluous.[98]

119. Expenses of the Witness

Canon 1571 — **In accord with an equitable assessment of the judge, witnesses must be compensated both for the expenses they have incurred and for the income they have lost by rendering testimony.**

ARTICLE 4: THE TRUSTWORTHINESS OF
TESTIMONIES
[cc. 1572–1573]

120. General Criteria

Canon 1572 — **In evaluating testimony, after having obtained testimonial letters if need be, the judge should consider:**

1° the condition and good reputation of the person;

2° whether the witness testifies in virtue of personal knowledge, especially what has been seen and heard personally, or whether the testimony is the witness' opinion, or a rumor or hearsay from others;

3° whether the witness is reliable and firmly consistent or rather inconsistent, uncertain or vacillating;

4° whether the witness has supporting witnesses or whether there is support from other sources of proof.

a. The four numbers of this canon have traditionally been seen by the authors to refer to four different general criteria, namely: (1) the *moral* criteria (the person's honesty, etc.); (2) the *mental* criteria (whether he or she is an eyewitness, etc.); (3) the *material* criteria (whether he or she is consistent, coherent, etc.); and (4) the *numerical* criteria (whether the witnesses agree, etc.).

b. In general, the judge should, in accord with canon 1608, §3, evaluate the evidence "ex sua conscientia."

c. Although the judge should be alert to all of these criteria and their shades of actual presence in witnesses, perhaps a special word is in order regarding the numerical criteria. Most witnesses in marriage cases seem to be a combination of concordant and singular, i.e., part of their testimony tells of events related by other witnesses in substantially the same way, and part of their testimony refers to events apparently unknown by the other witnesses or related differently. The rule of thumb for evaluating such testimony is as follows: concordant testimony is probative;[99] cumulative testimony is corroborative; diversative testimony is neutral; adversative testimony is vitiating.

121. Special Criteria

Canon 1573 — **The deposition of a single witness cannot constitute full proof unless a witness acting in an official capacity makes a deposition regarding duties performed ex officio or unless circumstances of things and persons suggest otherwise.**

a. The general rule about the testimony of one witness not resulting in full proof is a reflection of the axioms "Vox unius vox nullius," and "Testis unus testis nullus."

b. The law states two exceptions to the rule: (1) where the witness is qualified, e.g., the statement of a pastor attesting to his having given delegation; and (2) where circumstances suggest otherwise, e.g., where the marriage lasted only a few weeks and was for the obvious purpose of gaining legal entry to a country of desire.

A third exception, mentioned in the 1980 draft (c. 1525) but not in the 1983 Code, is one in which the law indicates otherwise, as, for example, in canon 876.

CHAPTER IV
EXPERTS
[cc. 1574–1581]

122. Notion of an Expert

An expert is a specialist who is learned, experienced, and skilled in his or her science or profession

---

[98]*Comm* 11 (1979), 118.

[99]This is in accord with Mt 18: 16. See par. 1. See also *CIC* 1791, §2.

and whose scientific report is required either to prove some fact or to diagnose the true nature of something.

The term "expert" refers most often to psychiatrists, psychologists, and others in the mental health fields but applies also to gynecologists, urologists, and even handwriting analysts.

123. Necessity of an Expert

Canon 1574 — The services of experts must be used whenever their examination and opinion, based on the laws of art or science, are required in order to establish some fact or to clarify the true nature of something by reason of a prescription of the law or a judge.

The services of an expert may be prescribed either by the judge or by the law. The only universal law that prescribes the use of an expert is canon 1680 which calls for perite involvement in marriage cases of impotence and defect of consent due to a mental disorder.

124. Nomination of an Expert

Canon 1575 — It is the responsibility of the judge either to name experts after listening to the parties and the names they propose, or to make use of reports, if warranted, already drawn up by other experts.

a. Contrary to canons 1978 and 1982 of the 1917 Code and Article 143 of *Provida,* which did not recognize as potential experts those who examined a party prior to the trial (but did want them called as witnesses), this canon permits the judge to recognize the pretrial physician as an extra-judicial expert.

b. Contrary to canon 1793, §2 of the 1917 Code, the present canon allows the party to propose the name of an expert even in a case involving the public good.

125. Exclusion or Recusal of an Expert

Canon 1576 — Experts can be excluded or rejected for the same reasons that witnesses can be.

The reasons why a *witness* may be excluded are not spelled out in the law (c. 1555) but are understood to be more restrictive than the reasons stated in canon 1448, §1 which render a *judge* suspect and subject to recusancy. Nevertheless, in individual cases, some of the reasons mentioned in canon 1448, §1, e.g., a close blood relationship, would warrant the person's exclusion from the case in the role of expert.

126. The Examination

Canon 1577 — §1. After paying attention to those points which may have been brought forward by the litigants, the judge is to specify by a decree the individual points on which the expert's services must focus.

§2. The acts of the case and other documents and aids which the expert may need in order to function properly and faithfully must be turned over to the expert.

§3. After listening to the expert, the judge should fix the time within which the examination is to be carried out and the report presented.

127. The Report

a. Individual Reports

Canon 1578 — §1. Each of the experts should draw up a report distinct from the others unless the judge orders that one report be made and signed by the experts individually; if this latter is done, differences of opinion, if any, are to be carefully noted.

b. Points To Be Covered

§2. The experts must indicate clearly by what documents or other apt means they have been informed about the identity of persons, things or places, by what path and method they proceeded in discharging the function given to them and on what grounds, for the most part, their conclusions are based.

c. Later Clarifications

§3. An expert can be summoned by the judge to supply further explanations which may seem necessary.

128. Probative Force

Canon 1579 — §1. The judge is to weigh attentively not only the conclusions of the experts, even when they are concordant, but also the other circumstances of the case.

§2. In giving the reasons for the decision, the judge must express what considerations prompted him or her to admit or reject the conclusions of the experts.

a. Although this canon and the others in this section convey the impression that multiple experts are generally used, this is contrary to fact. Except for the more difficult cases, the common practice is for only one expert to be used in those cases where perite involvement is required.[100]

---

[100]See c. 1680.

b. Paragraph one of this canon is a reminder that the judge is the *peritus peritorum* and that, besides the report of the expert, the judge must also be concerned with such questions as whether the data on which the conclusions of the expert are based are truly proved by the evidence. It is in this sense that the *dicta peritorum cribanda sunt,* i.e., that the report of the expert should be "sifted." At the same time, however, *peritis in arte credendum est* and, as Parisella noted, "When it comes to evaluating the weight and importance of the expert's report, the Rota has many times (see the decisions of 10/21/59 coram Lamas, of 8/5/54 coram Pinna, of 11/6/56 coram Mattioli, of 2/26/52 and 4/6/54 coram Felici) taught that it is wrong for the judge to depart from the conclusions of the experts except for very weighty contrary arguments."[101]

129. Expenses of the Expert

Canon 1580 — Both the expenses and the stipends which must be paid to the experts are to be determined justly and equitably by the judge with due regard for particular law.

130. Private Experts

Canon 1581 — §1. The parties may designate private experts who must be approved by the judge.
§2. If the judge admits them, they may inspect the acts of the case if necessary and be present at the discharging of the court experts' function; moreover they can always present their own report.

a. Although the expert has his or her own unique role in tribunal proceedings, the commentators have always observed that the expert shares partly in the nature of a witness and partly in the nature of a judge. They have agreed, furthermore, that, of the two, the witnesslike qualities of the expert tend to predominate over the judgelike qualities. This is reflected, for example, in canon 1576, in which an expert can be rejected not for the same reasons as a judge but for the same reasons as a witness. It is also reflected in canon 1579, in which it is made clear that it is the judge, not the expert, who renders the decision.

b. This new canon on private experts reinforces this philosophy. Under the 1917 law (*CIC* 1793, §2) private experts were not permitted in public, e.g., matrimonial, cases. Now, however, private experts can be proposed by the parties in much the same way that witnesses are proposed. Generally, however, in those cases in which private experts are, in fact, used, it will also be necessary, in order to insure genuine objectivity, for the court to appoint its own expert. The evaluation of their various reports would then be made, perhaps with canon 1572, 1° particularly in mind.

c. The character of the Church's proceedings in matrimonial cases is not adversarial but collaborative in nature. All involved in the proceedings must have as their common aim the ascertainment of the objective truth. All should work together "pro rei veritate." As Pope Pius XII said in his famous allocution of October 2, 1944:

> From this it is clear what must be thought of the principle unfortunately sometimes affirmed or actually followed: "The Advocate," it is said, "has the right and the duty to effect all that benefits his thesis, just as the Defender of the Bond does in respect to the opposing thesis; for neither of the two does the norm 'Pro rei veritate' hold! The evaluation of the truth is exclusively the Judge's competency; to burden the Advocate with that task would signify thwarting or even paralyzing all his activity."

> Such an assertion is based on a theoretical and practical error. It does not recognize the intimate nature and the essential final purpose of the juridical controversy. In matrimonial processes, the juridical controversy cannot be compared to a contest or a tournament in which the two contenders do not have a common final purpose, but in which each one pursues his own particular, absolute aim without respect to, and in fact, in opposition to that of his rival. In other words, each aims to defeat his adversary and carry off the victory.

> The juridical contest of a matrimonial process is entirely different, ...

> From what we have set forth, it appears manifest how in the instruction of marriage cases in the Ecclesiastical Courts, Judge, Defender of the Bond, Promoter of Justice, and Advocate must, as it were, plead a common cause and collaborate, not merging their particular offices, but in conscious deliberate union and subordination to the same end.[102]

To some people this new institute of the private expert (new, that is, to the marriage case) will seem more compatible with an adversarial proceeding than it does with a collaborative proceeding. But this much, at least, should be said: when the private expert *is* used in a marriage case, it must be clear that the expert, in union with everyone else involved in the proceedings, must work "pro rei veritate."

---

[101]*SRRDec* 60, 564–565. The decision is of July 13, 1968.

[102]For an English translation of the entire allocution, see Doheny I, 1097–1107.

CHAPTER V
ACCESS AND JUDICIAL RECOGNIZANCE
[cc. 1582–1583]

131. Usefulness

Canon 1582 — If in order to settle a case the judge considers it opportune to have access to a given place or to inspect something, this should be specified in a decree which describes in summary fashion those elements which must be exhibited at the access, after hearing the parties.

An example of an occasion when inspection by the judge might be useful would be the case of disputed parish boundaries. Another, perhaps, would be when one party, claiming potential injury, seeks to enjoin another from constructing a building.

132. Recording of the Act

Canon 1583 — When the recognizance has been completed, a report of it is to be drawn up.

CHAPTER VI
PRESUMPTIONS
[cc. 1584–1586]

133. Definition and Division

Canon 1584 — A presumption is a probable conjecture about an uncertain matter; one is a presumption of law, which is established by the law itself; another is human, which is formulated by a judge.

a. A legal presumption (*praesumptio iuris*) is one stated in the *positive* law (*ab ipsa lege*). There are several examples of such presumptions in the Code (cc. 15, §2; 76, §2; 1061, §2; 1096, §2; 1101, §1; 1107; 1138, §2).
Presumptions of the *natural* law, not stated in the positive law, would not constitute a legal presumption.[103]
b. A judicial presumption (*praesumptio hominis*) is one that is not stated in the positive law but is conjectured to by the judge. Examples of such presumptions recognized by jurisprudence are (1) in a force and fear case—the presence of an aversion to marry gives rise to the presumption that the person is being forced and (2) in a case involving an intention against children—if a person tenaciously refuses in marriage to be open to children, the

presumption is that the right to children was excluded.[104]
Sometimes the judge uses as the basis for a judicial presumption a presumption of the natural law, particularly when those natural law presumptions have been incorporated into the "Rules of Law." The following are examples of some of those natural law presumptions: *Illud praesumitur factum quod est de iure faciendum* (that is presumed done which the law requires to be done); *Factum praesumitur rite factum* (which is the queen of presumptions); *Nemo malus nisi probetur; Semel malus praesumitur semper malus.*

134. Probative Force (cc. 1585–1586)

a. Of a Legal Presumption

Canon 1585 — A person who has a favorable legal presumption is freed from the burden of proof which then devolves upon the other party.

If the other party proves that the legal presumption is not, in fact, applicable or verified in the case at bar, then the court will, of course, find against the presumption. *Praesumptio cedit veritati.*

b. Of a Judicial Presumption

Canon 1586 — The judge is not to formulate presumptions which are not determined by law unless they arise from a certain and determined fact which is directly connected with the subject matter of the controversy.

(1) Although the phrasing of this canon is negative, it is agreed by the authors that, if the presumption is a genuine one, i.e., a probable (not a rash) conjecture, it should result in semi-full proof.

(2) The negative phrasing, however, is not altogether unwarranted. A judge must always be careful, when accepting a judicial presumption as a proof, that the presumption itself be founded in a demonstrated fact and not in another presumption. *Praesumptio praesumptionis admitti non potest.* For example: Peter sues Paul, claiming injury. As partial proof that it was Paul who inflicted the injury, Peter claims that he was Paul's sworn enemy. Given the right circumstances, the judge may wish to recognize the enmity as partial, presumptive proof of the deed, but, before doing so, the judge should be assured that the enmity was a proven fact and not just another probable conjecture. Otherwise the judge's conclusion would be planted firmly in mid-air.

---

[103]The 1917 Code subdivided legal presumptions into relative (*iuris simpliciter*) and absolute (*iuris et de iure*). This distinction has now been dropped.

[104]Wrenn, *Annulments*, 4th ed., 92–93, 112, 122–127; idem, "Notes But Mostly Footnotes on Presumptions," *J* 30 (1970), 206–215.

TITLE V
INCIDENTAL CASES
[cc. 1587–1597]

135. The Notion

Canon 1587 — **An incidental case is had whenever, after the trial has begun by the citation, a question is proposed which is so pertinent to the case that it very often must be resolved before the principal question, although it is not expressly contained in the *libellus* introducing the suit.**

a. Some examples of an incidental case, at least in the broad sense, are the recusancy or rejection of a judge (c. 1449), the suspension of an advocate (c. 1487), sequestration and inhibition (c. 1496), the rejection of a *libellus* (c. 1505), the admissibility of a certain type of evidence (c. 1527), the exclusion of a witness (c. 1555), and the exclusion of an expert (c. 1576).

The present canon, however, viewing the incidental case in a somewhat more restricted way, defines it as one that occurs after the citation. It would not, therefore, include the rejection of the *libellus* which, accordingly, would follow its own rules.

b. Title V begins with general rules that apply to all incidental cases. It then includes specific rules that apply to two special kinds of incidental cases which are not treated elsewhere in the Code. The first deals with the absence or tardiness of the *two parties* (chapter I), the second with the involvement of a *third party* (chapter II).

136. The Proposal

Canon 1588 — **An incidental case is proposed in writing or orally before the judge who is competent to settle the principal case with an indication of the connection between it and the principal case.**

One should also see pars. 32 and 60, b.

137. Admission or Rejection

Canon 1589 — **§1. The judge, having received the petition and heard the parties, is to decide very promptly whether the proposed incidental question seems to have a basis and a connection with the principal issue, or whether it must be rejected from the outset; and, if it is admitted, whether it is of such seriousness that it must be resolved by an interlocutory sentence or by a decree.**

§2. On the other hand, if the judge decides that the incidental question is not to be resolved before the definitive sentence, the judge is to decree that it will be considered when the principal case is settled.

a. The fact that the acceptance or rejection of the incidental case is one that should be decided "expeditissime" means that the decision of the judge does not admit of appeal (c. 1629, 5°).

b. The acceptance or rejection of an incidental case is always done by decree. Once accepted, however, the case itself may be decided either by decree (in less serious cases) or by sentence (in more serious cases). When an incidental case is settled by sentence, the sentence is called "interlocutory" (see c. 1607; pars. 148, 149).

138. Procedures

Canon 1590 — **§1. If the incidental question must be resolved by sentence, the norms of the oral contentious process are to be observed, unless the judge decides otherwise given the seriousness of the matter.**

§2. But if it must be resolved by decree, the tribunal may turn the matter over to the auditor or to the presiding officer.

a. As regards the oral contentious process, one should see canons 1656–1670.

b. As regards the decree, it should be noted that the reasons in support of the decision should be given in at least summary form (cc. 51, 1617).

139. Revocation or Correction of Decree or Sentence

Canon 1591 — **Before the principal case is closed, if there is just cause, the judge or the tribunal can revoke or reform the decree or the interlocutory sentence either at the request of a party or ex officio after hearing the parties.**

One should see par. 158.

CHAPTER I
PARTIES WHO DO NOT APPEAR IN COURT
[cc. 1592–1595]

140. The Respondent (cc. 1592–1593)

a. Absent

Canon 1592 — **§1. If the respondent, after having been cited, has neither appeared nor offered a suitable excuse for being absent, nor responded in accord with can. 1507, §1, the judge is to declare the respondent absent from the trial and is to decree that the case should proceed to the definitive sentence and its execution, while observing all the formalities which are to be observed.**

§2. Before issuing the decree mentioned in §1, the judge must have proof that the citation drawn

up by law reached the respondent within available time even by issuing a new citation if necessary.

Paragraph one makes it clear that the principal effect of the declaration of absence is that it frees the judge to proceed with the case as usual, omitting, of course, all those parts (and only those parts) which the respondent would play if he or she were present. By his or her absence the respondent is presumed to have ceded rights to all future notifications from the court except perhaps about the sentence itself.[105]

b. Tardy
(1) Before the Decision

Canon 1593 — §1. If the respondent is present in court later or responds before the settlement of the case, the respondent can adduce conclusions and proofs, with due regard for the prescription of can. 1600; however the judge is to take care that the trial is not intentionally prolonged through rather long and unnecessary delays.

(2) After the Decision

§2. Even if the respondent has not appeared or responded before the settlement of the case, the respondent can use challenges against the sentence; if the respondent proves that there was a legitimate impediment for being detained which without personal fault was unable to be made known earlier, the respondent can use a complaint of nullity.

(a) Contrary to the 1917 Code (*CIC* 1880, 8°), this canon awards to the absent respondent the right to appeal the decision. This departure from the tenor of the 1917 law seems to play into the hand of the vindictive respondent whose only wish is to delay the case. Experience has shown that in marriage cases (which constitute nearly all the cases heard in the Church courts),[106] some respondents, although totally disinterested in the outcome of the case as such, nevertheless wish, out of spite, to prevent the petitioner from marrying in the Church or returning to the sacraments. During the trial, therefore, they steadfastly refuse to cooperate in the hope that their silence will frustrate an affirmative decision. The present canon grants to such respondents, even though their declared absenteeism has not been purged, i.e., shown to have been inculpable, the right to appeal, which in practice will often delay the case further by involving the court in full appellate procedures rather than simple ratification. The bona fide rights of respondents should of course be scrupulously guarded by the law, but this particular ruling seems (to this author at least) to be a case of misplaced concern.

(b) The complaint of nullity which would be permitted if the respondent could show that his or her absence was inculpable would be based on canon 1622, 6°.

141. The Petitioner

Canon 1594 — If the petitioner has not appeared on the day and at the hour set for the joinder of issues (*contestatio litis*) and has not offered a suitable excuse:
1° the judge is to cite the petitioner again;
2° a petitioner who does not obey the new citation, is presumed to have renounced the suit in accord with cann. 1524-1525;
3° but if the petitioner later wishes to intervene in the process, can. 1593 is to be observed.

As regards number two, it should be noted that in order for the renunciation to be effective, all the requirements of canons 1524–1525, including acceptance by the respondent and admission by the judge, must be met.

142. Expenses

Canon 1595 — §1. A party who is absent from the trial, whether the petitioner or the respondent, and who has not given proof of a just impediment, is obliged both to pay the expenses of the lawsuit which were incurred because of the absence and also to provide indemnity to the other party, if necessary.
§2. If both the petitioner and the respondent were absent from the trial, they are jointly obliged to pay the expenses of the lawsuit.

According to Augustine, the term "jointly," or "in solidum," here means that if one party is insolvent or beyond reach, the other party is bound to defray the whole expense.[107]

CHAPTER II
INTERVENTION OF A THIRD PARTY
IN A CASE
[cc. 1596–1597]

143. Voluntary Third Party

Canon 1596 — §1. An interested party can be admitted to intervene in a case at any stage of the suit, either as a party defending one's own right or as an accessory to help a given litigant.
§2. However, in order to be admitted, such an interested party before the conclusion of the case

---

[105]See c. 1593, §2; Coronata, par. 1377, b.
[106]*Comm* 10 (1978), 211; 11 (1979), 152, 302; *Statistical Yearbook of the Church, 1975,* published by the Vatican Secretariat of State, 207. This situation existed even in 1950, long before the explosion of marriage cases in the 1970s. See also Bartocetti, 1.

[107]Augustine, 294. For other uses of the term, see par. 48, a.

must present to the judge a *libellus* briefly demonstrating the right to intervene.

§3. The person who intervenes in a case must be admitted at that stage which the case has reached with a brief and peremptory period of time assigned to present proofs if the case has reached the probatory stage.

Paragraph one notes that a third party may intervene either as a principal (to defend one's own right) or as an accessory (to aid another litigant).

A *principal* third party would be illustrated in the following scenario: Peter and Paul are litigating over the ownership of a certain piece of land. James enters the proceedings, claiming that the land belongs to neither Peter nor Paul, but to him.

An *accessory* third party is seen in this example: Peter sues Paul, claiming that he owes him money. James intervenes to prove that Paul already repaid the debt.

144. Necessary Third Party

Canon 1597 — After hearing the parties, the judge must summon to the trial a third party whose intervention seems necessary.

TITLE VI
PUBLICATION OF THE ACTS,
CONCLUSION OF THE CASE AND
DISCUSSION OF THE CASE
[cc. 1598–1606]

145. Publication of Acts

Canon 1598 — §1. After the proofs have been collected the judge by a decree must, under pain of nullity, permit the parties and their advocates to inspect at the tribunal chancery the acts which are not yet known to them; a copy of the acts can also be given to advocates upon request; however, in cases concerned with the public good, in order to avoid very serious dangers, the judge can decree that a given act is not to be shown to anyone, with due concern, however, that the right of defense always remains intact.

§2. In order to complete the proofs the parties may propose additional proofs to the judge; when these have been collected there is an occasion for repeating the decree mentioned in §1 if the judge thinks it necessary.

a. Canons 1455 and 1470, §1 (pars. 29, g and 39, a) dealt with the publicity of a trial as it applies to a third party. This present canon deals with the publicity of a trial as it pertains to the two parties. The question here is whether the two parties have a prevailing right to know what everyone else has said.

b. The publication of the acts has always been viewed by the law as an extremely sensitive stage of the proceedings, precisely because of the tension

that exists between the right of the two parties to know what others have said and the right of those others to have their remarks protected by confidentiality.

A delicate balance must always be maintained between these two sets of rights, but in order to do so, different adjustments must be made in different types of cases. In *penal* cases, in which some crime is being imputed, naturally the defendant's right to know should be emphasized, whereas in a *marriage* case, in which the only issue is the bond of marriage and never the *fault* or *blame* of a party, then perhaps the confidentiality rights should be emphasized.

Recognizing confidentiality rights in marriage cases has special application, at least in the United States, both to experts and to witnesses. Were the reports of *experts* published, i.e., made available to the parties, it would not only be regarded as professionally unethical but would also subject the psychiatrist or other expert to being sued in civil court. In the case of experts, therefore, were confidentiality not recognized in church law, experts would have no choice but to discontinue all affiliation with ecclesiastical tribunals. As regards *witnesses,* it should be noted that some American civil lawyers are of the opinion that, at least in some States of the Union, the citizens enjoy, as a basic civil right protected by civil law,[108] the right to convey certain information to a priest with the understanding that that information will be kept confidential. This right would include information contained in an affidavit (or in testimony) given to a priest for use in a church trial. Such information would be regarded as a privileged communication. Should the Church, therefore, attempt to deprive a citizen of that civil right by ordering the judge to publicize that information which the citizen had given (and had a civil right to give) in confidence, then the offended citizen could sue the ecclesiastical judge in a civil court and impose an injunction on him requiring him to honor the confidentiality privilege of the citizen. Even apart from this possible conflict with civil law, however, the fact is that many potential witnesses in marriage cases would either decline to testify altogether or, in giving testimony, would be inhibited from total frankness if they were not assured that their remarks would be kept confidential.

c. Generally speaking, the Church has, over the years (before the 1917 Code, in the 1917 Code, and in the Instruction, *Provida mater*), followed procedures that were sufficiently nuanced so as to permit the balance of rights—the balance, that is, between the right to know and the right to confidentiality.

(1) *Prior to the 1917 Code* the practice in non-criminal cases was for the acts to be published only if the parties requested it, and even then the judge

[108]See par. 10.

could decline to publish for a legitimate reason, like, for example, maintaining confidentiality. It was understood that publication was not required for validity and did not pertain to the substance of the judgment. From the point of view of the court, the purpose of publication was to establish the credibility of the parties and thereby to assure the judge that he was basing his judgment on solid information. From the point of view of the party, the purpose in petitioning a publication would be to exercise a proper defense.[109]

(2) *The 1917 Code* required that the acts be published (*CIC* 1858) and the authors generally agreed that publication of the acts did pertain to the substance of the case, providing one of the parties requested it,[110] with the purpose again being the right of defense.[111] At the same time, however, the 1917 Code recognized that at least in non-consummation cases, if not all marriage cases, a publication was not necessary (*CIC* 1985).[112]

(3) The Instruction, *Provida mater,* of 1936 (see par. 206), recognizing that marriage cases involved special considerations, explicitly permitted witnesses to testify with the understanding that their names would never be revealed to the parties (Art. 130, §2). In such cases the judge was to assure himself of the credibility of the parties by obtaining testimonials, but it was, of course, permitted for the testimonials to go unpublished as well (Art. 138, §2). This procedure, as noted in par. 111, d, has been discontinued in the 1983 Code.

d. This canon 1598 of the 1983 Code expresses rather successfully[113] the balance of rights in question.

(1) Paragraph one of the canon is in two parts. The first part states the general rule that the judge should permit the parties to inspect the acts and the advocates to be given a copy of them. The second part states an exception to the general rule, noting that in marriage cases (actually in all cases involving the public good),[114] the judge can, under certain circumstances, declare certain acts to be completely confidential.

(2) The phrase "aliquod actum," i.e., "a given act," suggests that, when the judge makes an exception to the general rule, a decision should be made on each individual act to be excepted. At the same time, however, it is clear that a judge may, as a general policy, decide to exclude certain categories of evidence, e.g., the reports of experts, from publication.

(3) The canon notes that a judge may except certain acts from publication "ad gravissima pericula evitanda"—in order to avoid very serious dangers. In attempting to determine more specifically what those dangers might be, one might look to canon 1455, §3 which permits a judge to bind all parties to secrecy for the following reasons: to avoid dissension, scandal, or the endangerment of a person's reputation.

(4) The canon notes finally that, even when a party's right to know is restricted, the "right of defense" must "always" remain intact. Two things are noteworthy here: first, the right of defense, which has historically always been regarded as one of the essential reasons for publication, is now mentioned explicitly in the canon; secondly, the canon recognizes that, at least in certain cases, the right of defense and the right of the parties to know are separable rights—the first can be observed without the second. This is particularly true in a marriage case in which the issue is not the good name of either party but the validity of the marriage bond. From the time of Benedict XIV, and more specifically from the promulgation in 1741 of his *Dei miseratione,* in which the "defensor matrimonii" was called for in every diocese,[115] it has been understood that, in a marriage case, the "ius defensionis" belongs principally and primarily not to the respondent but to the defender of the bond. This point was made explicitly in a rotal decision of November 27, 1958 coram Brennan.[116] The Code does well, therefore, to recognize that under certain conditions, some acts may be withheld from the parties but must, nevertheless, be shown to the defender (the tenor and extent of this canon would not seem to include the defender when it says that the judge may decide that a certain act not be shown to "anyone"—"nemini")[117] so that the right of defense remains intact.[118]

e. Even in those cases in which the judge decides to withhold certain evidence from publication, the parties have a right to know the names of all the witnesses, though not those of the affiants.[119]

f. When a party has been declared absent in accord with canon 1592, he or she need not be afforded the right to inspect the acts at this time.[120]

146. Conclusion "in Causa" (cc. 1599–1600)

a. The Notion

Canon 1599 — §1. When everything pertinent to the production of proofs has been completed, it is time for the conclusion of the case.

---

[109]Wernz V, 467–468; Lega I, 433–434.

[110]Augustine, however, contrary to some, did not regard the publication as necessary for the validity of the trial (302).

[111]See, for example, Coronata, n. 1387.

[112]The non-consummation case is recognized as an exception in the 1983 Code as well. See c. 1703.

[113]It does so much more successfully than either the 1976 draft (c. 257) or the 1980 draft (c. 1550).

[114]See par. 21.

[115]See par. 206.

[116]*SRRDec* 50, 661–662.

[117]See also cc. 1433, 1601, 1602.

[118]See also par. 164, a, (1), (b).

[119]See c. 1554, par. 104.

[120]See par. 140, a; Wernz-Vidal, par. 554; Coronata, par. 1377, b.

The conclusion "in causa" is the closing of the evidentiary, or probatory, stage of the trial (par. 66). It is not the closing of the case or instance, which does not take place until the pronouncement of the sentence (c. 1517).[121]

b. The Methods of Closing

§2. The conclusion takes place whenever the parties declare that they have nothing more to add, or the time set by the judge for proposing proofs has expired, or the judge declares that the case is sufficiently instructed.

c. The Decree

§3. The judge is to issue a decree that the conclusion of the case has been completed, in whatever manner it took place.

d. The Effects

Canon 1600 — **§1. After the conclusion of the case, the judge can still call the same or other witnesses, or arrange for other proofs which had not been previously asked for, only:**
1° in cases in which it is a question solely of the private good of the parties and if all the parties give consent;
2° in other cases, after hearing the parties and provided that there exists a serious reason and all danger of fraud or subornation is removed;
3° in all cases, whenever it is likely that the future sentence may turn out to be unjust because of the reasons listed in can. 1645, §2, nn. 1-3, if new proof is not admitted.
§2. However, the judge can order or allow that a document be exhibited which, perhaps, could not have been exhibited earlier, through no fault of the interested party.
§3. The new proofs are to be published with due regard for can. 1598, §1.

(1) It may even happen that the need for further evidence is not realized until the day scheduled for the deliberation and session by the college of judges. In that event the prescripts of this canon are followed (c. 1609, §5).

(2) Although the principal effect of the conclusion "in causa" refers to the admission of further evidence as described in the canon, another effect is that a third party may no longer intervene in the case (c. 1596, §2).

147. Discussion of the Case (cc. 1601–1606)

a. Stage Three

Here begins the third stage of a trial, the discussion stage (par. 66). It is unfortunate that the Code does not begin a new title here in order to highlight this fact.

b. The Written Discussion
(1) The Briefs and Animadversions

Canon 1601 — **After the conclusion of the case, the judge is to determine an appropriate period of time for the presentation of defense briefs or observations.**

Canon 1602 — **§1. The defense briefs and observations are to be in writing unless the judge with the consent of the parties decides that an oral debate before the tribunal is sufficient.**
§2. If the defense briefs together with the principal documents are to be printed, the prior authorization of the judge is required but with the obligation of secrecy if it exists.
§3. The regulations of the tribunal are to be observed as regards the length of the defense briefs, the number of copies and other additional matters of this kind.

Canon 1602, §1 notes that in the *ordinary* process the briefs and animadversions are, as a rule, in writing; only exceptionally are they made orally. In the *oral* process, as one might expect, they are made orally (c. 1667).

(2) The Rebuttals

Canon 1603 — **§1. After the defense briefs and observations have been communicated to each one, both parties are permitted to present rejoinders within a short period of time set by the judge.**
§2. This right is granted to the parties only once unless it seems to the judge that it must be granted a second time for a serious reason; however, in that case, the grant made to one party is considered made also to the other party.

Although the canon speaks of the "party" issuing the rebuttal, this means party in the broad sense.[122] Generally, of course, the advocate and defender of the bond prepare all the discussion papers.

(3) The Counter-Reply

§3. The promoter of justice and the defender of the bond have the right to reply again to the rejoinders of the parties.

c. The Oral Discussion

Canon 1604 — **§1. It is absolutely forbidden that information given to the judge by the parties or the advocates or other persons remain outside the acts of the case.**

---

[121]See also par. 81, b, (2).

[122]*Comm* 11 (1979), 128.

§2. If the discussion of the case has been done in writing, the judge can determine that moderate oral debate take place before the tribunal to elucidate certain questions.

Canon 1605 — **A notary is to be present at the oral debate mentioned in cann. 1602, §1 and 1604, §2, so that, if the judge orders it or if a party requests it and the judge consents, the notary can immediately record in writing the points discussed and the conclusions.**

(1) Since the judge must base his decision only on the acts (c. 1608, §2), canon 1604, §1 points out that any sort of informal briefings or persuasions are out of order.[123]

(2) Canon 1604, §2 speaks of what might be termed *ancillary* oral discussions. Canon 1602, §1 noted that, by way of exception, the oral discussion could entirely replace the written argument, in which case it might be termed the *principal* oral discussion.

d. The Neglect or Waiver of Defense

Canon 1606 — **If the parties neglect to prepare a defense brief within the time available to them, or if they entrust themselves to the knowledge and the conscience of the judge, the judge can pronounce sentence at once after requesting the observations of the promoter of justice and of the defender of the bond when they are involved in the trial, if the issue is plainly and fully known from the acts and proofs.**

TITLE VII
THE PRONOUNCEMENTS OF
THE JUDGE
[cc. 1607–1618]

148. General Notions

A judicial *pronouncement* is either a sentence or a decree (c. 1617).

A *sentence* is a legitimate pronouncement by which a judge settles either a principal case that was proposed by litigants and was tried judicially or a major incidental case.

A *decree,* as used here, is a legitimate pronouncement by which a judge either settles a minor incidental case (a substantive decree) or simply orders a procedure to be followed (a procedural decree).[124]

149. Kinds of Sentences

Canon 1607 — **After the case has been tried in a judicial manner, if it is the principal case, it is settled by the judge by a definitive sentence; if it is an**

incidental case, it is settled by an interlocutory sentence, with due regard for the prescription of can. 1589, §1.

The reference to canon 1589, §1 simply indicates that a minor incidental case may be settled by a decree rather than by an interlocutory sentence.

150. Moral Certitude

a. The Need

Canon 1608 — **§1. For the pronouncement of any kind of sentence, there must be in the mind of the judge moral certitude regarding the matter to be settled by the sentence.**

Pius XII, in his allocution to the Rota on October 1, 1942, noted that moral certainty exists between the two extremes of absolute certainty on the one hand and quasi-certainty or probability on the other. It is, he said

> characterized on the positive side by the exclusion of well-founded or reasonable doubt, and in this respect it is essentially distinguished from the quasi-certainty which has been mentioned; on the negative side, it does admit the absolute possibility of the contrary, and in this it differs from absolute certainty. The certainty of which We are now speaking is necessary and sufficient for the rendering of a judgment, even though in the particular case it would be possible either directly or indirectly to reach absolute certainty. Only thus is it possible to have a regular and orderly administration of justice, going forward without useless delays and without laying excessive burdens on the tribunal as well as on the parties.[125]

b. The External Source

§2. The judge must derive this certitude from the acts and the proofs.

John Paul II, in his allocution to the Rota on February 4, 1980, observed:

> The judge must draw this certainty "ex actis et probatis." First and foremost "ex actis" since it must be presumed that the documents are a source of truth. Then "ex probatis," because the judge cannot limit himself to giving credence to affirmations alone; on the contrary, he must keep in mind the possibility that, during the preliminary investigation, the objective truth may have been obscured by shadows brought about by different causes, such as the forgetting of some

---

[123]See par. 40, a.
[124]See c. 1617, par. 158, a.

[125]For the entire allocution in English, see Wrenn, *Annulments,* 4th ed., 135–138.

facts, their subjective interpretation, carelessness and sometimes false representation and fraud. The judge must act with a critical sense. A difficult task, because there may be many errors, while truth, on the contrary, is one only.[126]

c. The Internal Source

§3. However, the judge must evaluate the proofs conscientiously with due regard for the prescriptions of the law concerning the efficacy of certain proofs.

The judge is not a legislator. He does not create law but rather, for the most part, applies it or utilizes it. Nevertheless, in a particular case, in accord with canons 16, §3 and 19, he may both interpret a dubious law and supply for a missing law.[127]

d. The Absence of Moral Certitude

§4. A judge who cannot arrive at this certitude, is to pronounce that the right of the petitioner is not established, and is to dismiss the respondent as absolved, unless there is question of a case which enjoys the favor of the law, in which case the decision must be in favor of it.

The rule stated in this canon is an application of the axiom "Actore non probante, reus absolvitur." The exception stated in this paragraph is more interesting. In effect, it says that when a judge is in doubt he must give a *non constat* UNLESS there is a question of a case enjoying the favor of law, in which case the judge "must" give ("pronuntiandum est") a *constat pro ipsa,* i.e., an affirmative decision for the favor.

In a marriage case, for example, when the time arrives for sentencing, the judge is not morally certain about the nullity of the marriage. In accord with this canon, he must give a *non constat.* If, at the same time, however, one of the parties is doubtfully baptized,[128] then, since a doubtful privilege of the faith is one of those cases which "enjoys the favor of the law" (c. 1150), the judge must (or so it appears to this author) give a *constat pro ipsa,* i.e., the person's freedom to marry must be recognized.

Canon 1608, §4 is not substantially different from the corresponding canon in the 1917 Code (*CIC* 1869, §4), which was similarly interpreted (given the fact that only the Pauline Privilege was known at that time) by Lega-Bartocetti.[129]

[126]*OssRomEng,* March 3, 1980, 6.
[127]For more on the interpretative and suppletive role of the judge, see Wrenn, *Annulments,* 4th ed., 1–7.
[128]If the person is certainly unbaptized, a Petrine Privilege should be processed.
[129]Lega-Bartocetti II, 942–944. For a sample sentence in such a case, see Wrenn, *Decisions,* 2nd ed. (Washington: CLSA, 1983), 189–193 (henceforth cited as Wrenn, *Decisions,* 2nd ed.).

151. Procedure in Collegiate Tribunal

Canon 1609 — §1. **If the tribunal is collegiate, the presiding judge of the college is to determine on what day and at what hour the judges are to convene for their deliberation; and the meeting is to be held at the tribunal unless a special reason suggests otherwise.**

§2. On the day assigned for the meeting, the judges shall individually submit in writing their conclusions on the merits of the case and the reasons, both in law and in fact, for arriving at these conclusions, which are to be appended to the acts of the case and are to be kept secret.

§3. After the invocation of the Divine Name, the conclusions of the individual judge are to be made known in the order of precedence, but beginning always with the *ponens* or the *relator* of the case, and there is to be a discussion under the leadership of the presiding judge, especially in order to decide what is to be determined in the dispositive part of the sentence.

§4. In the discussion, however, each judge has the right to retract his or her original conclusions; on the other hand, a judge who does not wish to accede to the decision of the others, can demand that his or her conclusions be transmitted to the higher tribunal if there is an appeal.

§5. But if the judges are unwilling or unable to arrive at a sentence in the first discussion, the decision can be deferred to another meeting but not beyond one week unless the instruction of the case must be completed in accord with the norm of can. 1600.

Regarding this canon, the following observations might be made:

a. The individual opinions or "conclusions" of the judges are, in accord with paragraph two, kept secret. If, however, a dissenting judge exercises the right afforded him in paragraph four (not included in the 1917 Code) of forwarding his opinion to the court of appeal, then to that extent, of course, the secrecy is forfeited.

b. The "*ponens*" or "*relator*" mentioned in paragraph three is sometimes called the commissioner, since it is he who commits the final sentence to writing.

c. The *dispositive* part of the sentence mentioned in paragraph three refers to the actual decision or judgment, usually stated in a sentence or two. The law and the argument which precede this part (along with the facts) are called the *expositive* part of the sentence (c. 1612, §3).

152. Drafting of Sentence

Canon 1610 — §1. **If there is only one judge, he himself will write the sentence.**

§2. In a collegiate tribunal it is the duty of the

ponens or *relator* to write the sentence, drawing the reasons from those which the individual judges brought out in the discussion, unless it has been previously decided by the majority of the judges which reasons are to be preferred; then the sentence is to be submitted for the approval of the individual judges.

§3. The sentence must be issued not beyond one month from the day on which the case was settled, unless, in a collegiate tribunal, the judges set a longer period of time for a serious reason.

a. Basically this canon discusses who drafts the sentence and how and when he or she drafts it.

b. Paragraph two awards the individual judge the right (not recognized in previous law) to approve the sentence drafted by the commissioner. It is obvious that this does not mean that all the judges who sign the sentence necessarily voted in favor of the final dispositive part of the sentence. Presumably, however, it does mean that, given the dispositive part of the sentence, a judge-signatory, though perhaps in basic dissent, is at least not offended by the expositive part of the sentence.

153. Object of Sentence

Canon 1611 — A sentence must:
1° settle the controversy discussed before the tribunal with an appropriate response given to each one of the questions;
2° determine what obligations of the parties arise from the trial and how they must be fulfilled;
3° set forth the reasons, that is, the motives both in law and in fact on which the dispositive section of the sentence is based;
4° make a determination about the expenses of the suit.

The *contestatio litis* determines *the terms of the controversy* (c. 1513, §1). The sentence settles the *controversy itself.* If the sentence fails to do this even partially, then it is incurably null (c. 1620, 8°). If a sentence does not contain the reasons or motives for the decision, then it is curably null (c. 1622, 2°).

154. External Solemnities

Canon 1612 — §1. After the invocation of the Divine Name, the sentence must express in sequence who is the judge or the tribunal; who is the petitioner, the respondent, the procurator, with the names and domiciles correctly indicated; the promoter of justice and the defender of the bond, if they took part in the trial.

§2. Next, it must briefly report the facts together with the conclusions of the parties and the formulation of the doubts.

§3. Following these points is the dispositive section of the sentence preceded by the reasons on which it is based.

§4. It is to close with an indication of the day and place where it was rendered and with the signature of the judge or, if it is a collegiate tribunal, with the signatures of all the judges and the notary.

One might consider a sentence to be composed of an *introduction* (§1); a *corpus,* consisting of the facts; the law and the argument (§§2, 3), and a *conclusion* (§4). The canon itself, however, divides the sentence somewhat differently, as follows:

§1 – the *introduction;*

§2 – the *facts,* that part which includes mention of the grounds both as requested by the parties (these are referred to as "conclusions" in this canon and as "petitions" in c. 1616, §1) and as officially designated by the judge (c. 1513);

§3 – the *law* and the *argument* (necessary for validity—c. 1622, 2°) followed by the decision itself, which decision is called the dispositive part of the sentence;

§4 – the *conclusion* (the date, place and signatures are required for validity—c. 1622, 3°, 4°).

155. Application to Interlocutory Sentence

Canon 1613 — The regulations mentioned above concerning a definitive sentence are to be adapted to an interlocutory sentence.

The legislator apparently wishes to point out that the following canons on publication and correction (cc. 1614–1616) need not be followed in the interlocutory sentence.

156. Publication of Sentence (cc. 1614–1615)

a. The Time

Canon 1614 — The sentence is to be published as soon as possible with an indication of the ways in which it can be challenged; it has no force before publication even if the dispositive section has been made known to the parties with the permission of the judge.

Canon 1593, §2 seems to imply that even the absent respondent should be notified of the sentence and allowed to appeal.[130]

b. The Methods

Canon 1615 — The publication or announcement of the sentence can be made either by giving a copy

---

[130]See Coronata, par. 1377, b.

of the sentence to the parties or their procurators or by sending a copy to them in accord with the norm of can. 1509.

(1) The 1917 Code recognized three methods of publication:

• citing the parties to appear at the tribunal for a reading of the sentence;

• advising the parties that the sentence is available at the tribunal for them (which is different from this canon's first method);

• mailing the sentence to the parties.

(2) The publication of the sentence should not be seen as entirely divorced from the publication of the acts (c. 1598). If, for example, the judge withheld certain acts from being published, and classified them as secret in order to avoid serious dangers, then that evidence should still be considered secret at the time of the publication of the sentence. This could, therefore, involve either deleting certain passages from the sentence for publication purposes, even if published to a procurator, or perhaps even publishing only the dispositive part of the sentence.

157. Correction of Sentence

Canon 1616 — §1. If in the text of the sentence either an error in calculations has crept in, or a material error has occurred in transcribing the dispositive section, or reporting the facts or the petitions of the parties, or if the points required by can. 1612, §4 were omitted, the sentence must be corrected or completed at the request of the parties or ex officio by the tribunal which issued the sentence; the parties, moreover, must always be heard and a decree appended at the bottom of the sentence.

§2. If any party objects, the incidental question is to be settled by decree.

In the 1917 Code this canon (*CIC* 1878) was considered, not under this title regarding the sentence, but under the next title on legal remedies against the sentence. Several of the manualists,[131] however, treated the matter under this title since it referred clearly to the mere correction of a material error and was not, therefore, a genuine remedy against or impugning of the sentence. Their position has prevailed in the 1983 Code.

158. The Decree

Canon 1617 — The other pronouncements of a judge, over and above the sentence, are decrees

which, if they are not merely procedural, have no force unless they express the reasons at least in a summary fashion, or refer to reasons expressed in some other act.

a. An example of a procedural decree (*decretum mere ordinatorium*) is the decree of the conclusion "in causa" mentioned in canon 1599, §3.[132]

b. The requirement that substantial decrees convey, at least summarily or referentially, the reasoning process is an application of the general principle contained in canon 51.

159. Equivalents of Definitive Sentence

Canon 1618 — An interlocutory sentence or a decree has the force of a definitive sentence if it stops the trial, or if it puts an end to the trial or to some grade of the trial as regards at least some party in the case.

Examples of interlocutory sentences or decrees that would be equivalent to a definitive sentence are the decree of absence regarding a petitioner, which results in the presumed renunciation of the instance (c. 1594, 2°), a decree admitting a peremptory exception [c. 1462; par. 32, b, (2)], and especially a decree of confirmation by the appellate court in a marriage case (c. 1682, §2).

Such equivalents of a definitive sentence admit of appeal (c. 1629, 4°). Other interlocutory sentences and decrees do not generally admit of appeal but may be revoked or corrected in accordance with canon 1591.

TITLE VIII
CHALLENGE OF THE SENTENCE
[cc. 1619–1640]

160. Division of Material

This title and the next concern legal redress. This title speaks of two ways of impugning *the sentence itself*: the complaint of nullity (*querela nullitatis*) and appeal. The next title speaks of a way of impugning *the closed judgment* (*res iudicata*),[133] namely, reinstatement (*restitutio in integrum*).

161. Division of Impugnments

By reason of the *judge,* impugnments can be either devolutive or non-devolutive, depending on whether they are or are not deferred to another judge. An appeal, for example, is always devolutive (c. 1628); a complaint of nullity is usually non-devolutive (c. 1624), but is devolutive if lodged along

---

[131]See, for example, Wernz-Vidal, par. 597; Goyeneche II, par. 118; Della Rocca, 286.

[132]See par. 148.

[133]A *res iudicata* is itself a sentence but a kind of sentence plus. See par. 177ff.

with an appeal (c. 1625); reinstatement can be either devolutive or not (c. 1646).

By reason of the *effect,* an impugnment can be either suspensive or non-suspensive, depending on whether or not it suspends execution of the sentence. An appeal is suspensive (c. 1638); reinstatement is generally suspensive if the execution has not yet begun, but admits of exception (c. 1647); a complaint is generally regarded as suspensive but is not specifically designated as such in the Code.

CHAPTER I
COMPLAINT OF NULLITY AGAINST
THE SENTENCE
[cc. 1619–1627]

162. Definition and Division

a. Definition

A complaint of nullity (*querela nullitatis*) is the impugning of a judicial sentence by which one claims that the sentence suffers from some substantial defect and is therefore null.

b. Division

The complaint can claim either curable or incurable nullity. The distinction is based on the purely practical question of whether it can or cannot be cured. *Curable* nullity is automatically healed after three months if no complaint is lodged against it (c. 1623 with c. 1465, §l). It can also be healed, generally speaking, simply by correcting the error or omission that caused the nullity.[134] *Incurable* nullity, on the other hand, is open to perpetual challenge and can never really be healed. On the contrary, for the trial to be valid, it must be repeated in its entirety.

163. Nullity of Acts

Canon 1619 — With due regard for cann. 1622 and 1623, nullities of acts which are established by positive law and which, although they were known to the party proposing the complaint, have not been denounced to the judge before the sentence, are sanated by the sentence itself if it is a case involving the private good.

a. This canon refers only to those acts which are null by reason of the positive law. Acts which are

null by reason of the natural law are not sanatable.[135]

b. The purpose of this canon is to dissuade parties from delaying to denounce invalid acts until after the sentence, with a view toward undermining the entire proceedings.

164. Nullity of Sentence (cc. 1620–1623)

a. Incurable Nullity
(1) The Notion

Canon 1620 — A sentence is vitiated by irremediable nullity if:
1° it was rendered by a judge who is absolutely incompetent;
2° it was rendered by a person who lacks the power of judging in the tribunal in which the case was settled;
3° the judge passed the sentence under duress from force or grave fear;
4° the trial was instituted without the judicial petition mentioned in can. 1501, or was not instituted against some respondent;
5° it was rendered between parties one of whom at least did not have standing in court;
6° one person acted in the name of another without a legitimate mandate;
7° the right of defense was denied to one or other party;
8° it did not settle the controversy even partially.

(a) The 1917 Code listed only three sources of incurable nullity, namely, those now numbered above as one, five, and six. The 1976 draft dropped all of those, or transferred them to curable nullity, and listed four new ones, namely, those numbered above as two, three, four, and eight. The revised Code, therefore, incorporates the three from 1917, the four from 1976, and then adds one more: number seven.

(b) The sense of the eight sources of nullity is clear, generally speaking, but perhaps the following comments are in order:

As regards number one, one should see canons 1406, §2 and 1440 regarding absolute incompetence.

Regarding number five, this would refer to minors or people lacking the use of reason who were either petitioner or respondent in a case without their being represented either by parent or guardian.[136]

In reference to number six, one should see canons 1484–1485 for the law on mandates.

---

[134]If, however, the nullity was caused by the failure to cite a party, which nullifies all the procedural acts (c. 1511) or by the fact that the respondent, though declared absent, was legitimately impeded (c. 1593, §2), then practically the whole trial must be repeated.

[135]See c. 1645, §2, 4°.
[136]See par. 71, a, (1).

Concerning number seven, it should be noted that in a marriage case the term "party" should be understood in the broad sense to include the defender of the bond.[137] The principal issue in a marriage case is not a party's virtue or lack thereof; the principal issue in every marriage case is the bond. Therefore, only when the defender of the bond has been deprived of his or her right to defend the bond has the "right of defense" been denied. It cannot be said that the right of defense has been denied if, for example, the respondent is not allowed to see every document in its entirety (c. 1598, §1). In a rotal decision coram Brennan of November 27, 1958, it was made clear (1) that "in a contentious case properly so called," the petitioner and respondent must indeed be given the total right of defending themselves—otherwise the entire process would be null by reason of the natural law in that an element that would be essentially constitutive of a trial would be lacking,[138] but (2) that in a marriage case the right of defense is sufficiently honored if the defender of the bond is afforded the right.[139] This is not to say, of course, that the parties need not be cited or that the acts need not be published, but only that essentially the right of defense is protected in a marriage case as long as the defender is afforded the right.

Canon 1622, 6° also seems to favor this position. The Code, by including this canon as separate from canon 1620, 7°, seems to take the position that the right of defense is not necessarily denied simply because the respondent never received any notices from the court after the original citation. To put it another way, an absent respondent who, after the sentence, demonstrates that his or her absenteeism was inculpable, then has an automatic right to lodge a complaint of *curable* nullity by reason of canon 1622, 6°; he or she does not necessarily, however, have the automatic right to claim *incurable* nullity by reason of canon 1620, 7°. If he or she did, canon 1622, 6° would be superfluous.[140]

As regards number eight, one should see canons 1513, §2 and 1611, 1°.

(2) The Effect

Canon 1621 — **The complaint of nullity mentioned in can. 1620 can always be proposed by way of exception in perpetuity and by way of action before the judge who pronounced the sentence within ten years from the date of publication of the sentence.**

A complaint of nullity would be proposed as an *action* by petitioning the judge to declare his own sentence null; when proposed as an *exception* it amounts to calling for an injunction (c. 1496, §2) against the implementation of the sentence on the grounds that the sentence itself was null.

b. Curable Nullity
(1) The Notion

Canon 1622 — **A sentence is vitiated by remediable nullity only, if:**
1° it was rendered by an illegitimate number of judges contrary to the prescription of can. 1425, §1;
2° it does not contain the motives, that is, the reasons for the decision;
3° it lacks the signatures prescribed by law;
4° it does not contain reference to the year, month, day and place in which it was pronounced;
5° it is based on a judicial act which is null and whose nullity was not sanated according to the norm of can. 1619;
6° it was rendered against a party who was legitimately absent as provided for in can. 1593, §2.

a. The 1917 Code listed four sources of curable nullity. Three of them corresponded to those numbered two, three, and four above. The fourth was the lack of legitimate citation which has been expanded into the present number five. As regards number one, that was included in the 1917 Code under incurable nullity. Number six was not included at all in the 1917 Code.

The 1976 draft listed seven sources of curable nullity. Five of them corresponded to those numbered one, two, three, five, and six above. The 1976 draft did not consider number four to be a source of nullity at all and it included three that are now listed as constituting incurable nullity, namely, those listed as numbers one, five, and six in the present canon 1620.

b. As regards number two, one should see canon 1611, 3°.

Regarding numbers three and four, one should see canon 1612, §4.

Concerning number five, one should see, for example, canon 1656, §2.

(2) The Effect

Canon 1623 — **The complaint of nullity in the cases mentioned in can. 1622 can be proposed within three months from the notification of publication of the sentence.**

If no complaint is lodged within the allotted time (c. 1465, §1), a source of curable nullity is automatically sanated.

---

[137]*Comm* 11 (1979), 128.
[138]See *CIC* 1680, a canon that has no counterpart in the 1983 Code.
[139]*SRRDec* 50, 660–663.
[140]See also par. 145, d, (4).

165. The Judge

Canon 1624 — **The judge who pronounced the sentence examines the complaint of nullity; but if the party fears that the judge who pronounced the sentence which is being challenged by the complaint of nullity, may be prejudiced and, as a result, regards him or her as suspect, the party can demand that another judge be substituted according to the norm of can. 1450.**

Canon 1625 — **A complaint of nullity can be proposed together with an appeal within the time determined for an appeal.**

Canon 1624 states the general rule that the judge of the complaint is the judge who gave the sentence (non-devolutive). Canon 1625 notes that by way of exception to this rule, the complaint is heard by the appellate judge (devolutive) when it is proposed along with the appeal. Should the appellate judge uphold the complaint, the case is then remanded to the court of previous instance for the regular hearing.

166. Complainant or Retractor

Canon 1626 — **§1. Not only the parties who feel themselves aggrieved can file a complaint of nullity but also the promoter of justice or the defender of the bond whenever they have the right to intervene.**
§2. A judge himself can ex officio retract or amend an invalid sentence which he has pronounced, within the time period for acting set by can. 1623 unless meanwhile an appeal together with a complaint of nullity has been filed, or unless the nullity has been sanated during the course of the time mentioned in can. 1623.

An example of the second exception mentioned in paragraph two would be the following: a sentence is null because the notary neglected to sign it (cc. 1612, §4; 1622, 3°). For the next three months the judge is free to retract the sentence. Should, however, the notary supply the missing signature sometime during that three-month period, then the sentence can no longer be retracted.

167. The Process

Canon 1627 — **Cases involving a complaint of nullity can be treated according to the norms for the oral contentious process.**

One should see canons 1656–1670.

CHAPTER II
THE APPEAL
[cc. 1628–1640]

168. The Notion

An appeal may be defined as recourse to a higher court against a sentence given by a lower court, by one who considers himself or herself aggrieved by the sentence.

This includes the new presentation (*nova propositio*) of a case after a double conforming sentence mentioned in canon 1644. The *nova propositio*, however, follows, in some ways, its own peculiar rules.

169. Subject of Appeal

Canon 1628 — **The party who feels aggrieved by a given sentence and likewise the promoter of justice and the defender of the bond in cases in which their presence is required, have the right to appeal from a sentence to a higher judge, with due regard for the prescription of can. 1629.**

Several commentators on the 1917 Code noted that the word "party" in the corresponding canon of the 1917 law included those people who would succeed the petitioner or respondent in their juridic relationship, such as an heir; and also such people as proxies, guardians, and curators.[141]

170. Object of Appeal

Canon 1629 — **There is no room for appeal:**
1° from a sentence of the Supreme Pontiff himself or of the Apostolic Signatura;
2° from a sentence vitiated by nullity unless it is joined with a complaint of nullity according to the norm of can. 1625;
3° from a sentence which has become *res iudicata;*
4° from the decree of a judge or an interlocutory sentence which does not have the force of a definitive sentence, unless it is joined with an appeal from a definitive sentence;
5° from a sentence or from a decree in a case in which the law provides for a settlement of the matter as quickly as possible.

As regards number one, one should see canons 1442 and 1445.

Regarding number two, the law does not permit appeal only because a more specific type of redress, namely, the complaint of nullity, is designed to remedy this situation.

---

[141]See, for example, Goyeneche II, par. 121; Wernz-Vidal, par. 602. See also c. 1486, §2; *CIC* 1885, §1.

Concerning number three, one should see canons 1641–1644.

With regard to number four, one should see canon 1618 and par. 158.

As regards number five, one should see, as examples of this phrase, canons 1451, §1; 1505, §4; 1513, §3; 1589, §1; and 1631.

171. Introduction of Appeal (cc. 1630–1631)

a. The Tribunal A Quo and the Time

Canon 1630 — §1. An appeal must be filed before the judge who pronounced the sentence within the peremptory time limit of fifteen available days (*tempus utile*) from notification of the publication of the sentence.

b. The Method

§2. If it is made orally, the notary is to put it in writing in the presence of the appellant.

c. The Right of Appeal as Incidental Question

Canon 1631 — If a question arises regarding the right of appeal, the appellate tribunal should examine it as quickly as possible according to the norms of the oral contentious process.

(1) The initial decision whether to accept or reject every incidental case must be made "expeditissime" (c. 1589, §1). The right of appeal, however, is a matter in which the merits of the case itself must also be settled "expeditissime."

(2) The matter is judged, it should be noted, by the tribunal *ad quem*.

(3) The fact that the process to be followed is the oral contentious process indicates that it is considered a *major* incidental question.[142]

172. Transmission of Appeal (cc. 1632–1634)

a. The Tribunal Ad Quem

Canon 1632 — §1. If in the appeal there is no indication of the tribunal to which it is directed, it is presumed to be made to the tribunal mentioned in cann. 1438 and 1439.

§2. If the other party has recourse to another appellate tribunal, the tribunal of higher grade examines the case, with due regard for can. 1415.

Although an appeal from a first instance decision is generally directed to the conventional court of immediate appeal, a party always has the right to appeal instead directly to the Rota (c. 1444, §1, 1°).

[142]See c. 1590, §1; par. 148.

b. The Time

Canon 1633 — An appeal must be prosecuted within a month of its being filed before the judge to whom it is directed, unless the judge from whom appeal is made has set a longer period of time for the party to prosecute it.

One should see canon 1682, §1, however, for the unique process that applies to marriage cases.

c. The Method

Canon 1634 — §1. In order to prosecute an appeal, it is required and suffices that the party call upon the services of the higher judge for the emendation of the challenged sentence, append a copy of this sentence, and indicate the reasons for the appeal.

§2. If the party is unable to obtain a copy of the challenged sentence from the tribunal from which the appeal is being made within the available time, the time limits do not run out in the interval; and the impediment must be indicated to the appellate judge who is to bind the judge from whom the appeal is made with a precept to perform his duty as soon as possible.

§3. Meanwhile the judge from whom the appeal is being made must transmit the acts to the appellate judge according to the norm of can. 1474.

173. Desertion of Appeal

Canon 1635 — If the deadline for appeal either before the judge from whom the appeal is being made or before the judge to whom the appeal is directed has passed without result, the appeal is considered abandoned.

One should see canon 201, §2 for an explanation of "tempus utile," or "available time."

174. Renunciation of Appeal

Canon 1636 — §1. The appellant can renounce the appeal with the effects mentioned in can. 1525.

§2. If the appeal was proposed by the defender of the bond or the promoter of justice, it can be renounced by the defender of the bond or the promoter of justice of the appellate tribunal unless the law provides otherwise.

One should see canon 1682, §2, however, for the unique process that applies to marriage cases.

175. Effects of Appeal (cc. 1637–1638)

a. On the Parties

Canon 1637 — §1. An appeal lodged by the petitioner also benefits the respondent and vice versa.

§2. If there are several respondents or petitioners, and if the sentence is challenged by only one or against only one of them, the challenge is considered made by all of them and against all of them whenever the matter sought is indivisible or it is a joint obligation.

§3. If an appeal is filed by one party regarding one part of the sentence, the other party can place an incidental appeal regarding the other parts within a peremptory time period of fifteen days from the date of being notified of the principal appeal even though the deadline for an appeal has expired.

§4. Unless there is evidence to the contrary, it is presumed that an appeal is made against all parts of a sentence.

Paragraph one of this canon is based on Rule 32 of the "Rules of Law": "Non licet actori quod reo licitum non existet."[143] It does not mean, of course, that when the petitioner appeals a decision, it *benefits* the respondent, but rather that both petitioner and respondent have equal rights in the matter of appeal and are equally affected by appeal.

Paragraph two states an exception to the general rule that when one individual appeals a sentence to the extent that it affects another individual, the appeal affects only those individuals. This canon is saying that that general rule does not hold when the contested matter or obligation is indivisible. Rather, in such cases, the appeal is considered "ab omnibus et contra omnes." Peter, for example, sues Paul, claiming that the house Paul is occupying actually belongs to him. John then intervenes as a third party, claiming that, in fact, he owns the house and that it belongs neither to Peter nor Paul. The court finds in favor of Paul. Peter appeals. The appeal is considered in law both to be made by John as well, and to be against John's claim to the house.

Paragraph three speaks of what is called an "incidental appeal."

Paragraph four is a shortened form of the 1917 Code's canon 1887, §3 which stated the other half of the proposition as well, namely, that if a party specifically appeals only one part of the sentence, then the other parts are regarded as excluded.

b. On the Sentence

Canon 1638 — An appeal suspends the execution of a sentence.

An appeal, therefore, is both devolutive and suspensive.[144]

For an exception to this rule, one should see canon 1644, §2.

---

[143]*CorpusIC* II, 1123.
[144]See par. 161.

176. Procedure within Appeal Court
(cc. 1639–1640)

a. Admission of New Grounds

Canon 1639 — **§1.** With due regard for the prescription of can. 1683, a new basis for petitioning may not be admitted at the appellate level not even by way of helpful cumulation; consequently, the joinder of issues (*contestatio litis*) can focus only on whether the prior sentence is to be confirmed or revised, either totally or partially.

b. Admission of New Proofs

§2. Moreover, new proofs are admitted only in accord with the norm of can. 1600.

c. The Process Itself

Canon 1640 — At the appellate level the procedure is the same as in first instance insofar as it is applicable; however, immediately after the joinder of issues has taken place in accord with the norm of cann. 1513, §1 and 1639, §1, the case is to be discussed and the sentence rendered unless perhaps the proofs must be completed.

Although, in general, the second instance follows the same procedure as the first, it should be noted, as regards the constitution of the tribunal that, even though the case was heard by one judge in first instance, it must, in accord with canon 1441, be heard by a college in second instance, under pain of curable nullity (c. 1622, 1°).

TITLE IX
RES IUDICATA AND
RESTITUTIO IN INTEGRUM
[cc. 1641–1648]

CHAPTER I
RES IUDICATA
[cc. 1641–1644]

177. The Notion

a. Definition

A closed judgment (*res iudicata*) is a definitive judicial sentence which is so firm and final that it no longer admits either of appeal or complaint (*querela*) but only of reinstatement (*restitutio in integrum*).[145]

---

[145]See par. 160.

b. The Four Irreversible Sentences

Canon 1641 — With due regard for the prescription of can. 1643, a *res iudicata* results:

1° if two concordant sentences have been issued between the same persons regarding the same petition and arising out of the same basis for petitioning;

2° if an appeal against the sentence has not been filed within the available time;

3° if, at the appellate level, the prosecution of the suit has been estopped or renounced;

4° if a definitive sentence has been rendered from which no appeal is granted according to the norm of can. 1629.

As regards number one, it is to be noted that both the matter and the grounds must be confirmed in the second instance. If, therefore, both courts declare a contract invalid but the first court does it on the grounds that one of the parties was a minor and the second court on the grounds that the contract was not signed, then there is not really a double conforming sentence.

Regarding number two, one should see canon 1635.

Concerning number three, one should see canons 1520 and 1524.

With regard to number four, this would apply to a sentence given by the pope or Signatura. The other categories mentioned in canon 1629 would, for one reason or another, not seem to apply.

178. *Effect of a* Res Iudicata

Canon 1642 — §1. A *res iudicata* enjoys the stability of law and cannot be directly challenged except in accord with the norm of can. 1645, §1.

§2. It settles an issue between the parties and gives rise to an action for execution and an exception of *res iudicata* which the judge can declare ex officio to prevent a new introduction of the same case.

Paragraph one of this canon states the principal effect of a *res iudicata,* namely, that it is impugnable neither by complaint nor by appeal but only by reinstatement. The sentence, in other words, is considered valid and irreversible but not irrescindable. Paragraph two notes that a *res iudicata* can give rise both to an "action" (by which a party has the right to demand that the sentence be executed) and to an "exception" (by which a party, should he or she be sued later on the same matter, can claim that the matter has already been definitely settled). The judge, as the canon observes, may do the same ex officio.

179. Cases Concerning Status of Persons (cc. 1643–1644)

a. Not Completely Irreversible (the double conforming sentence)

Canon 1643 — Cases concerning the status of persons, especially those concerning the separation of spouses, never become a *res iudicata.*

The principle that underlies the institute of the *res iudicata* is that the tranquility and good order of society require that litigations not be interminable. Appeals cannot go on indefinitely. If limiting the number of appeals results in occasional mistakes or misjudgments, so be it. Cicero, in his "Speech in Defense of Sulla," admitted that the institute of the *res iudicata,* even though it did not happen to benefit his client, Sulla, was nevertheless essential to the common good and should therefore prevail; and eventually there arose the axiom "magis expedit res iudicatas esse firmas quam esse iustas."[146]

It has always been understood, however, that, while such a principle may be valid in respect to real actions, it cannot be applied to personal actions. In cases dealing with the status of persons, the law wishes to remain perpetually open to any reasonable appeal.

b. But Only Extraordinarily Appealable
(1) The Process of Appeal

Canon 1644 — §1. If two concordant sentences have been pronounced in a case concerning the status of persons, it can be appealed at any time to an appellate tribunal if new and serious proofs or arguments are brought forward within the peremptory time period of thirty days from the proposed challenge. However, within a month from the presentation of the new proofs and arguments, the appellate tribunal must settle by decree whether a new presentation of the case must be admitted or not.

(2) The Effect of Appeal

§2. An appeal to a higher tribunal to obtain a new presentation of the case does not suspend the execution of the sentence, unless either the law provides otherwise or the appellate tribunal orders its suspension, in accord with the norm of can. 1650, §3.

This paragraph states an exception to the general principle enunciated in canon 1638.[147]

---

[146] *Oratio pro Sulla* 22; *SRRDec* 14, 192.
[147] See par. 168.

CHAPTER II
RESTITUTIO IN INTEGRUM
[cc. 1645–1648]

180. The Notion

Reinstatement[148] (*restitutio in integrum*) is a legal remedy by which a person who has been seriously injured by a judicial sentence that was manifestly unjust can, for reasons of natural equity, be restored by a competent judge to the status quo *ante,* i.e., before the injurious sentence.

181. Usage of Reinstatement

Canon 1645 — §1. *Restitutio in integrum* is granted against a sentence which has become a *res iudicata* provided that there is clear proof of its injustice.

The 1917 Code (*CIC* 1687, 1905) referred to appeal and complaint as the *ordinary* remedies, and to reinstatement as the *extraordinary* remedy against a sentence. It awarded to minors, as an acknowledgment of their position of disadvantage before the complexities of the law, the right to choose either type of remedy. A minor, in other words, was free to choose either an ordinary remedy or an extraordinary remedy, whichever was more convenient. An adult, however, was not given this choice. An adult was expected first to use the ordinary remedies available; the *extraordinary* remedy of reinstatement was available to the adult only when he or she could show that the state of injury was not the result of his or her having neglected to take advantage of the *ordinary* remedies.

As a result of these canons, canonists and jurists were in general agreement that the *extraordinary* remedy of reinstatement was not available in marriage cases since, in such cases, the *ordinary* remedy of appeal (or *nova propositio*) was always at hand.

In the 1983 Code, however, three points are noteworthy: (1) the distinction between ordinary and extraordinary remedies has been dropped; (2) except in relation to time limits (c. 1646, §3) the distinction between minors and adults (in terms of remedies available to them) has been dropped; and (3) the canon itself is phrased affirmatively (*restitutio in integrum may* be utilized against a *res iudicata*) rather than restrictively (it may *not* be used against other sentences). It seems, therefore (at least to this author), that the remedy of reinstatement may now be utilized in a marriage case, and that a party has a right to choose that remedy over

others whenever the requirement of manifest injustice is verified.

The advantages are obvious. If a marriage case has received a double conforming sentence in first and second instance, a *nova propositio* may be lodged only with a *third* instance court, whereas reinstatement, at least in certain cases, is not devolutive and may be lodged with the court of *first* instance.

Reinstatement remains, of course, the *only* redress against a closed judgment (and their coupling in this title is not therefore illogical). It would seem, however, that, although this particular *illness* (the manifestly unjust *res iudicata*) is *selective* in that it has only one remedy, the remedy itself is *versatile* in that it can be applied to other *illnesses* as well.

182. The Five Manifest Injustices

§2. However, clear proof of injustice is verified only if:
1° the sentence is so based on proofs which are later discovered to be false so that without those proofs the dispositive section of the sentence would not be sustained;
2° afterwards documents have been found which undoubtedly prove new facts which demand a contrary decision;
3° the sentence was pronounced because of the fraud of one party which harmed the other;
4° a prescription of the law which is not merely procedural has been evidently neglected;
5° the sentence is contrary to a preceding sentence which has become a *res iudicata*.

183. Competent Judge and Time Limits

a. Non-Devolutive

Canon 1646 — §1. *Restitutio in integrum* for the reasons mentioned in can. 1645, §2, nn. 1-3 must be sought from the judge who issued the sentence, within three months to be computed from the date of one's becoming aware of the reasons.

b. Devolutive

§2. *Restitutio in integrum* for the reasons mentioned in can. 1645, §2, nn. 4 and 5 must be sought from the appellate tribunal within three months from notification of the publication of the sentence; but if, in the case mentioned in can. 1645, §2, n. 5, notification of the preceding decision is had later, the time limit runs from this notification.

c. Time Limits for Minors

§3. The time limits mentioned above do not expire as long as the injured person is a minor.

---

[148]The English term "restitution" has been avoided because it tends to connote, though it certainly does not denote, restoration of property rather than status.

184. *Effects of Reinstatement*

a. Suspensive

Canon 1647 — **§1. A petition of *restitutio in integrum* suspends the execution of a sentence if the execution has not yet begun.**

b. Non-Suspensive

§2. If, however, from probable indications there is a suspicion that the petition has been made in order to delay the execution of the sentence, the judge can decree that the sentence be executed but with due caution being taken to indemnify the person seeking *restitutio in integrum* if it is granted.

185. *Judgment on Merit*

Canon 1648 — **If *restitutio in integrum* is granted, the judge must pronounce on the merits of the case.**

This is a new canon which serves as a reminder that the granting of reinstatement does not complete a case but rather returns it to its starting point. The double conforming sentence would then be required once again before the matter would be considered adjudged.

TITLE X
COURT COSTS AND
GRATUITOUS LEGAL ASSISTANCE
[c. 1649]

186. *General Norms*

Canon 1649 — **§1. The bishop whose responsibility it is to supervise the tribunal, is to determine norms regarding:**

1° the parties to be liable for paying or compensating for judicial expenses;

2° the honoraria for procurators, advocates, experts and interpreters and the indemnification of witnesses.

3° the granting of gratuitous legal assistance or a diminution of expenses;

4° the recovery of damages which are owed by the one who not only lost the case but also engaged in litigation rashly;

5° the depositing of money or the guarantees to be made concerning the expenses to be paid and the damages to be recovered.

187. *Specific Cases*

§2. From a pronouncement relating to expenses, honoraria and recovery of damages, there is no separate appeal; but the party can have recourse with-

in fifteen days to the same judge who can adjust the assessment.

One should also see canon 1464 as regards this paragraph.

TITLE XI
EXECUTION OF THE SENTENCE
[cc. 1650–1655]

188. *The Notion*

The execution of the sentence is a judicial act by which the vindicated party in the trial is actually provided what was awarded in the sentence.

189. *Conditions for Execution (cc. 1650–1651)*

a. First Condition—
That There Be a Closed Judgment
(1) The Rule

Canon 1650 — **§1. A sentence which has become a *res iudicata* can be executed with due regard for the prescription of can. 1647.**

(2) The Exception

§2. The judge who rendered the sentence and also the appellate judge if an appeal has been filed, can ex officio or at the request of a party order a provisional execution of a sentence which has not yet become a *res iudicata* after having arranged, if the case warrants, for the rendering of appropriate guarantees if there is question of provisions or payments for necessary sustenance or if some other just cause is pressing.

§3. On the other hand if the sentence mentioned in §2 is challenged and if the judge who must take cognizance of the challenge sees that it is probably well-founded and irreparable harm could arise from the execution of the sentence, the judge can suspend its execution or subject it to a safeguard.

(a) In paragraph two, two reasons are given which justify a provisional execution even when there has not been a closed judgment: when execution is necessary to provide support and when there is a just cause. It is clear that the second reason includes the first, but the legislator chose to retain the first reason as a kind of model for granting provisory execution.[149]

Although a marriage nullity case never becomes

---

[149]*Comm* 11 (1979), 244.

a *"res iudicata,"* it does, nevertheless, receive a regular execution in accord with canons 1684 and 1685.

b. Second Condition—That There Be a Decree

Canon 1651 — There can be no execution of a sentence prior to an executory decree of the judge in which it is stated that the sentence must be executed; this decree is to be included in the text of the sentence or issued separately, according to the different types of cases.

190. Rendering of Accounts as Incidental Question

Canon 1652 — If the execution of the sentence demands a prior rendering of accounts, it is an incidental question which must be decided by the judge who passed the sentence ordering the execution.

If, for example, the legitimate representative of a juridic person (c. 1480) is adjudged by the sentence to have squandered an amount, but an undetermined amount, of the juridic person's funds, then, before the sentence can be executed, there must be a rendering of accounts. That rendering is handled as an incidental question in accord with canons 1587–1591.

191. The Executor

a. In a Diocesan Court

Canon 1653 — §1. Unless particular law determines otherwise, the bishop of the diocese in which the first instance sentence was rendered, must execute the sentence personally or through another.

§2. If he refuses or neglects to do so, the execution belongs to the authority to which the appellate tribunal is subject in accord with the provision of can. 1439, §3, at the request of an interested party or ex officio.

It is clear from these paragraphs that only by exception should the judge ever act as executor.

b. In a Religious Court

§3. Among religious the execution of a sentence belongs to the superior who passed the sentence to be executed or who delegated the judge.

192. Exercise of Executive Power

Canon 1654 — §1. Unless something is left to the discretion of the executor in the text of the sentence, the executor must execute the sentence according to the obvious meaning of the words.

§2. The executor may consider exceptions regarding the manner and force of the execution but not regarding the merits of the case; but if it has been discovered from other sources that the sentence is invalid or manifestly unjust according to the norm of cann. 1620, 1622 and 1645 the executor is to refrain from executing it, refer the matter to the tribunal which issued the sentence, and inform the parties.

It is clear from this canon that the role of the executor is not a completely mechanical one but one, rather, that involves a degree of discretion.

193. Time for Execution

Canon 1655 — §1. As regards real actions, wherever a given thing has been adjudicated as belonging to the petitioner, it must be handed over to the petitioner as soon as there is a *res iudicata.*

§2. However, as regards personal actions, when the respondent is condemned to furnish something mobile, to pay money, or to give or to do something else, the judge in the text of the sentence, or the executor with personal discretion and prudence is to set a time limit for fulfilling the obligation, which, however, is not to be less than fifteen days nor more than six months.

Section II: THE ORAL CONTENTIOUS PROCESS
[cc. 1656–1670]

194. Introductory Remarks

a. The Place of the Process in the Judicial Framework

The oral contentious process is special, not by reason of its *matter* (which is basically the same as in all processes: the judge, the petition, the formulation of the doubt, proofs, etc.), but by reason of its *form* (which is designed for speed).

The *oral* contentious process is one of the two species in the genus *contentious process;* the other species being the *ordinary* contentious process.

The oral contentious process has its *remote* roots in the decretal *Saepe contingit*[150] of Pope Clement V (1305–1314) in which he outlined a kind of summary procedure; its *proximate* roots are in a section of the procedural law for the Oriental Churches which was promulgated in 1950.[151]

b. The Nature and Name of the Process

The oral contentious process contains all the essentials of a judicial process: a contradiction, an ac-

---

[150]*Clem* V, 11, 2; *CorpusIC* II, 1200.
[151]"De iudicio contentioso coram unico iudice" (cc. 453–467) in *Sollicitudinem nostram. AAS* 42 (1950), 5–120. See also *CLD* 3, 585–587.

tion, the possibility of an exception, proofs, publication, discussion, and a reasoned sentence. It is, however, simplified with a view toward an expeditious hearing and, as a consequence, certain solemnities, unnecessary time intervals, and much writing are omitted.

The fulcrum of the process is the hearing which is utilized both for the collection and the publication of the proofs, as well as for the discussion.

The name *oral contentious process* demonstrates that its principal difference from the ordinary contentious process is that that process is basically a *written* one whereas this is basically an *oral* one.

195. Applicability of Process

Canon 1656 — §1. All cases which are not excluded by law can be tried in the oral contentious process dealt with in this section, unless a party requests the ordinary contentious process.

§2. If the oral process is used outside of cases permitted by law, the judicial acts are null.

a. By reason of canon 1690, a marriage nullity case may not be handled according to the oral contentious process.

b. The Code, with some qualifications, indicates that the process should or could be followed for major incidental cases (c. 1590, §1), for complaints of nullity (c. 1627), and for separation cases (c. 1693, §1), but this list, as the canon points out, is by no means taxative.

c. In accord with paragraph two, should the process be used where it is not permitted, the judicial acts and consequently the sentence based on those acts are null, the sentence being curably so.[152]

196. The Judge

Canon 1657 — The oral contentious process takes place in first instance before a single judge according to the norm of can. 1424.

Given the type of case for which this process is designed, a single judge would ordinarily be acceptable in second instance as well as in first.[153]

197. The Petition

Canon 1658 — §1. In addition to the points mentioned in can. 1504, the *libellus* by which the suit is introduced must:

1° set forth briefly, completely and clearly the facts on which the requests of the petitioner are based;

2° so indicate the proofs by which the petitioner

intends to demonstrate the facts, but which cannot be produced at once, so that they can be gathered at once by the judge.

§2. The documents on which the petition is based must be attached to the *libellus*, at least in an authentic copy.

a. The petition in the oral process is expected to be more complete than the petition in the ordinary process. This clearly indicates that some of the investigation that would be carried on *during* the course of an ordinary trial is, for the oral trial, carried on *before* the official process begins.

b. An oral petition may be admitted in accord with canon 1503.

198. Notification of Respondent

Canon 1659 — §1. If an attempt at reconciliation according to the norm of can. 1446, §2, has been fruitless, the judge, if he believes that the *libellus* has some foundation, is to order within three days by a decree appended to the bottom of the *libellus* that a copy of the petition be communicated to the respondent, granting the latter the right to send a written response to the chancery of the tribunal within fifteen days.

§2. This notification has the effects of the judicial citation mentioned in can. 1512.

For general remarks on the citation, one should see par. 72.

199. Exceptions Lodged by Respondent

Canon 1660 — If the exceptions of the respondent demand it, the judge is to set a time limit for the petitioner to respond so as to clarify the object of the controversy from the points raised by each of them.

200. Formulation of Doubt

Canon 1661 — §1. When the time limits mentioned in cann. 1659 and 1660 have expired, the judge, after having examined the acts, is to determine the formulation of the doubt; next, the judge is to cite to a hearing, to be held within thirty days, all who must be present at it; the judge is to attach the formula of the doubt to the citation for the parties.

§2. In the citation the parties are to be informed that they can present to the tribunal a brief written statement in support of their allegations at least three days prior to the hearing.

For a general explanation of the formulation of the doubt, one should see pars. 74–75.

[152]See cc. 1622, 5°; 1669.
[153]See c. 1441; par. 25, b.

201. First Hearing (cc. 1662–1665)

a. Subordinate Issues

Canon 1662 — At the hearing the questions mentioned in cann. 1459-1464 are to be treated first.

The questions referred to here include exceptions, judicial acknowledgments, counter-claims, and incidental questions, as discussed in par. 32.

b. Indicated Proofs

Canon 1663 — §1. The proofs are collected at the hearing with due regard for the prescription of can. 1418.

Canon 1418 refers to the so-called rogatory commissions.[154]

c. Presence of the Parties

§2. The party and his or her advocate can be present at the examination of the other parties, of the witnesses, and the experts.

Paragraph two is contrary to the general rule in the ordinary contentious process as explained in canons 1534 and 1559.

d. Taking the Testimony

Canon 1664 — The responses of the parties, witnesses, and the experts, and the petitions and exceptions of the advocates must be put in writing by the notary but in a summary fashion and only as regards those matters which pertain to the substance of the controverted matter, and they must be signed by those making depositions.

Contrary to the practice in the ordinary process, where the testimony should be taken down verbatim (c. 1567, §1), the testimony for the oral process may be recorded in summary fashion. The requirement that the deponent sign the testimony is seen as adequate protection against the inaccuracy of the summary.

e. Added Proofs

Canon 1665 — Only in accord with the norm of can. 1452 can the judge admit proofs which have not been presented or asked for in the petition or the response; however, after even a single witness has been heard, the judge can decree new proofs only in accord with the norm of can. 1600.

The reference to canon 1452 alludes to the judge's instructing the case either at the request of the party or ex officio (par. 29, d). The reference to canon 1600 is to the conditions under which new evidence may be admitted after the conclusion "in causa" (par. 146, d).

202. Second Hearing (cc. 1666–1667)

a. Remaining Proofs

Canon 1666 — If all the proofs cannot be collected at the hearing, a second hearing is to be scheduled.

b. The Oral Discussion

Canon 1667 — When the proofs have been collected, the oral discussion takes place at the same hearing.

Even in the ordinary process, an ancillary oral discussion is always permitted (c. 1604, §2) and sometimes even a principal oral discussion (c. 1602, §1).[155]

203. Sentence

Canon 1668 — §1. Unless from the discussion it is discovered that something must be supplied in the instruction of the case or something else turns up which prevents the due pronouncement of the sentence, the judge immediately decides the case privately when the hearing has been completed; the dispositive part of the sentence is to be read at once in the presence of the parties.
§2. However, the tribunal can defer the decision until the fifth available day because of the difficulty of the matter or for another just cause.
§3. The complete text of the sentence with the reasons expressed is to be made known to the parties as soon as possible, ordinarily not beyond fifteen days.

204. Nullity of Sentence

Canon 1669 — If the appellate tribunal should discover that in a lower grade of the trial the oral contentious process was used in cases excluded by the law, it is to declare the nullity of the sentence and remand the case to the tribunal which passed it.

One should see par. 195, c.

205. Other Procedures

Canon 1670 — In other matters which pertain to the mode of procedure, the prescriptions of the can-

ons concerning the ordinary contentious trial are to be observed. However, the tribunal by a decree giving the reasons, can derogate from procedural norms which have not been determined for validity, in order to expedite matters with due regard for justice.

Part III
CERTAIN SPECIAL PROCEDURES
[cc. 1671–1716]

TITLE I
MATRIMONIAL PROCEDURES
[cc. 1671–1707]

206. *A Brief History*

Paragraph one of this commentary noted that the Church has, virtually from its inception, been an adjudicative community. The early Church was, it seems, involved in the settlement of various sorts of disputes, but one of the earliest cases mentioned in the New Testament was a marriage case, the one in which Paul told the Christians in Corinth that they should sit in judgment of the incestuous man among them and expel him from their midst.[156]

This, as it turned out, was but the first of many such marriage cases in which the Christian community would act as arbiter. In the year 314, the Council of Ancyra imposed a stiff penance on a man who had been involved in a similarly scandalous marital situation.[157] Gratian, particularly in Causes 27–32 of his decree,[158] also tells of many decisions that were made by the popes and fathers on marriage cases and questions over the years. Many other cases were, no doubt, handled at the local level and in administrative fashion, but by the twelfth century at least, marriage cases were generally heard according to the regular judicial process. In 1198, however, Pope Innocent III noted that the ordinary judicial process was not always and everywhere being observed for marriage cases,[159] and, in 1311, Pope Clement V, in his decretal *Dispendiosam*, explicitly permitted marriage cases to be heard by a kind of summary process, a process that would be carried out, as he said "simpliciter et de plano, ac sine strepitu iudicii et figura."[160]

By the sixteenth century, the Council of Trent apparently felt it necessary to crack down a bit and it ordered that marriage cases should no longer be heard by deans or archdeacons; only the local ordinary was empowered to hear such cases, and the judicial process was to be followed.[161]

Abuses, however, persisted and, in an effort to curb them, Pope Benedict XIV issued, on November 3, 1741, his famous constitution *Dei miseratione*.[162] Benedict was particularly upset by the facility with which annulments were being granted in his day. Oftentimes the respondent would not appear at the trial at all, so there would be no one to defend the marriage (there was, in those days, no one designated as a defender of the bond). Sometimes both parties would appear, but either the respondent would be in collusion with the petitioner, or he or she would simply not be interested in appealing higher—the marriage would then be declared null after a single hearing (there was, in those days, no mandatory appeal). As a result, according to Benedict, men and women alike were having their first, second, and even third marriages declared null and were, with the blessing of the Church, blithely entering still another.

Dei miseratione attempted to put an end to all this. *First* it required that every diocese appoint a defender of marriage whose presence in every trial would be absolutely mandatory and whose duty it would be to defend the bond. *Secondly,* it required the defender to appeal every first instance affirmative decision.

The modern era for the adjudication of marriage cases had begun.

A century later, on August 22, 1840, the Congregation of the Council issued a new Instruction[163] designed to reinforce, clarify and amplify *Dei miseratione*. The United States, however, was still mission territory and, until late in the nineteenth century (and, if the truth be known, until much, much later in some dioceses), marriage cases were still being heard quite informally. Father S.B. Smith, for example, in the Preface to his book, *The Marriage Process in the United States*, published in 1893, wrote:

The subject of these pages—the marriage process—is comparatively new in this country. Down to the year 1884, marriage disputes, even those involving the validity of marriages already contracted, were, as a rule, decided, with us, by the bishop, or also by rectors of parishes, and sometimes even by assistant priests, without any judicial formalities whatever.

This mode of procedure was naturally open to serious inconveniences, and was calculated to imperil, in many cases, the stability and indissolubility of marriages.

---

[156]1 Cor 5: 1–13.

[157]See c. 25 of the Council in *Nicene and Post Nicene Fathers*, Second Series, XIV (New York: Scribners, 1900), 75.

[158]*CorpusIC* I, 1046–1148.

[159]C. 1, X, II, 6—*CorpusIC* II, 258–259.

[160]*Clem* II, 1, 2—*CorpusIC* II, 1143. The Latin phrase might be translated "simply and easily and without the pomp and circumstance of a judicial proceeding."

[161]Sess. XXIV, ch. 20.

[162]*CICFontes* I, n. 318, 695–701.

[163]*CICFontes* VI, n. 4069, 345–350.

To obviate these disadvantages, the S.C. de Prop. Fide, in 1884, issued the Instruction *Causae matrimoniales* for this country. This Instruction or law substantially lays down and makes obligatory here, in matrimonial contentions involving the validity of a marriage contracted, the manner of proceeding which is prescribed by the general law of the Church and obtains throughout the entire Church. This mode of deciding marriage disputes is judicial and is to be conducted by the bishop's court for marriage causes.[164]

The Instruction *Causae matrimoniales,*[165] mentioned by Father Smith, required that henceforth all marriage cases heard in the United States follow a strictly judicial process, including involvement by the defender of marriage (7) and mandatory appeal of an affirmative decision (30). *Causae matrimoniales* was the last significant document pertinent to marriage trials prior to the codification, in 1917, of the Church's law.

In their pre-Code manuals, Lega and Wernz both devoted brief sections to the special procedures followed in marriage cases. Lega was satisfied with simply reprinting *Causae matrimoniales,* noting that it was practically the same as previous instructions issued for the Oriental Churches and for Austria.[166] Wernz, on the other hand, wrote his own treatment on the procedures to be followed in marriage cases, in which he commented on such matters as the right to petition for an annulment, the competent judge (marriage cases were heard by a *single* judge), suitable proofs, the involvement of the defender and the mandatory appeal of an affirmative decision.[167]

The 1917 Code, in its section on trials in general, namely, in canon 1576, §1, required that all marriage nullity cases be heard by a college of three judges "with every contrary custom being reprobated and every contrary custom revoked." But, like the pre-Code authors, it also devoted a separate section, namely, canons 1960–1992, to marriage trials in particular, in which it treated briefly the predictable issues of competence, court personnel, the right to petition, proofs, publication, the conclusion *in causa,* the sentence, the appeal, and, finally, certain clear cases, like prior bond, that could be proved by document and could therefore be handled informally.

By 1936 the Holy See, realizing that around the world very few marriage cases were being handled judicially by local tribunals, concluded that the thirty-three canons of the 1917 Code (*CIC* 1960–1992) devoted specifically to marriage cases,

were not sufficient to aid the local judge in applying the canons on trials in general (*CIC* 1552–1924) to marriage cases. Accordingly, on August 15, 1936, the Holy See issued a new Instruction, *Provida mater,*[168] which consisted of two hundred forty articles that attempted, in effect, to rewrite general procedure as it might apply to marriage cases. *Provida mater* was a valiant and, no doubt, well-intentioned effort to assist local judges, but the rigidity and complexity of the Instruction seemed to discourage judges even more, and thousands of bona fide marriage cases continued to go unheard. In the United States, for example, where, by the late 1960s, there were an estimated five million divorced Catholics, only a few hundred first instance affirmative decisions were being given each year.[169]

In an effort to correct this situation, the Canon Law Society of America endorsed, at its annual meeting in 1968, a simple set of norms, called the *American Procedural Norms,* with the request that the National Conference of Catholic Bishops propose them to Rome for approval. Approval was given, effective July 1, 1970, first for a three-year experimental period, then in 1973 for one more year, and finally in 1974, until the new procedural law for the Church universal would be promulgated.[170] The aim of the *American Procedural Norms* was, on the one hand, to provide adequate defense of the marriage bond and thus avoid the scandalous sort of annulment that existed before *Dei miseratione,* but, on the other hand, to provide to tribunals a procedure that could be carried out "simpliciter et de plano, ac sine strepitu iudicii et figura," and could thus enable them to give a hearing to the many thousands of people with legitimate grounds of annulment. The principal features of the *American Procedural Norms* were the recognition of the petitioner's residence as a source of competence, trial by a single judge, discretionary publication by the judge, and discretionary appeal by the defender. The *American Procedural Norms* were dramatically successful. By the late 1970s, thirty thousand annulments a year were being granted, judicially and judiciously, by United States tribunals. Although that figure was still only one-half of one percent of the number of divorced Catholics in the country (six million by that time), the *American Procedural Norms* were, nevertheless, of benefit to a great many people.

Americans were not the only ones interested in simplified procedures. There was considerable interest around the world in providing for a more expeditious handling of marriage cases, and on March 28, 1971, Pope Paul VI issued, for the universal

[164]S.B. Smith, *The Marriage Process in the United States* (New York: Benziger, 1893), 5.
[165]*CICFontes* VII, n. 4901, 479–492.
[166]Lega IV, 592–608.
[167]Wernz IV, 1087–1120.

[168]*AAS* 28 (1936), 313–361; *CLD* 2, 471–529.
[169]*CLSAP* (1969), 155.
[170]For a brief history and evaluation of the *APN,* see T. Green, "The American Procedural Norms: An Assessment," *Stud Can* 8 (1974), 317–347.

Church, the Apostolic Letter *Causas matrimoniales*[171] which was not as liberal in its provisions as the *American Procedural Norms,* but which did modify the prescriptions of the 1917 Code in the areas of competence, the number of judges, the use of lay people, and the appellate procedures.

By this time, of course, the work of revising the 1917 Code, specifically its procedural law, was well under way (par. 6) and when the 1976 schema on procedural law appeared, it contained, as was expected, the modifications introduced by *Causas matrimoniales.* Most of these have, in turn, been incorporated into the 1983 Code.

CHAPTER I
CASES DECLARING NULLITY OF MARRIAGE
[cc. 1671–1691]

ARTICLE 1: THE COMPETENT FORUM
[cc. 1671-1673]

207. Right of Church

Canon 1671 — Marriage cases of the baptized belong to the ecclesiastical judge by proper right.

a. The corresponding canon of the 1917 Code (*CIC* 1960) said that "marriage cases of the baptized belong to the ecclesiastical judge by proper *and exclusive* right." *Causas matrimoniales* I dropped the phrase "and exclusive" in recognition of the rights of other churches and also perhaps in recognition of civil divorce as a fact of life.[172]

b. The term "marriage cases" includes judgment on validity and dissolutions and on the essential rights and obligations of marriage.

c. Although the Church claims the right, by this canon, to hear the cases of two Protestants, that right is in fact never exercised unless one of the parties wishes to marry a Catholic. By the same token, even though the Church, per se, has no right to hear the marriage cases of two unbaptized people, it will, in fact, hear such cases when petitioned by one of those unbaptized spouses (cc. 1476 and 1674, 1° do not require that the spouse be baptized) who wishes to marry a Catholic.

208. Right of State

Canon 1672 — Cases involving the merely civil effects of marriage belong to the civil magistrate unless particular law determines that these cases can be tried and decided by the ecclesiastical judge when they arise as incidental and accessory.

209. Competent Forum

Canon 1673 — In cases regarding the nullity of marriage which are not reserved to the Apostolic See the following are competent:
1° the tribunal of the place in which the marriage was celebrated;
2° the tribunal of the place in which the respondent has a domicile or quasi-domicile;
3° the tribunal of the place in which the petitioner has a domicile, provided that both parties live in the territory of the same conference of bishops and the judicial vicar of the domicile of the respondent agrees, after hearing the respondent;
4° the tribunal of the place in which de facto most of the proofs are to be collected provided that the judicial vicar of the domicile of the respondent gives consent who, before he does so, is to ask if the respondent has any exceptions.

a. The cases reserved to the Holy See include non-consummation cases (c. 1698), Petrine cases (not mentioned in the Code), and cases involving heads of governments (c. 1405, §1, 1°).

b. As regards the various sources of competence or jurisdiction:

1° – a traditional source of competence and may be viewed as a specification of canon 1411, the place of contract.

2° – also a traditional source and an application of the general principle "actor sequitur forum partis conventae" (c. 1407, §3).

3° – a new and sensible source of competence. The *American Procedural Norms* introduced the residency of the petitioner as a source of competence but *Causas matrimoniales* did not include this source in any way. Experience, indeed, showed that the "residency of the petitioner" was too broad a source, first because the term "residency" lent itself to abuses—with some people assuming legal residency in dioceses where favorable decisions might be anticipated, without ever actually establishing themselves in that diocese; and secondly because, when the parties live in different countries, the respondent would often be severely and unjustly disadvantaged if the trial were conducted in a foreign country. The present canon has succeeded in retaining the merits of the basic concept while purifying it of its weakness: the petitioner's *domicile* is now recognized as a source of competence *providing* the respondent lives in the same conference of bishops (c. 10) and *providing* the respondent has been heard and the consent of the respondent's officialis was sought and not declined (c. 127, §2, 1°).

The question arises: what if the whereabouts of

---

[171]The English text of the *APN* and *CM* are found in L. Wrenn, *Annulments,* 3rd ed. (Toledo: CLSA, 1978), 115–123. The Latin texts are found in Gordon-Grocholewski, 248–252; 209–213.

[172]O. Di Iorio, "De potestate iudiciaria Ecclesiae in M.P. *"Causas matrimoniales,"* P 63 (1974), 317–340.

the respondent are unknown? Must canon 1409, §2 be followed, which indicates that, in such a case, the forum of the petitioner may be used only when there is no functioning tribunal in the diocese where the marriage was contracted? Or does the forum of the petitioner enjoy some sort of special legitimacy in a marriage case?

It would seem that a distinction should be made. According to the ordinary rules of competence (cc. 1407–1415), only the forum of the respondent is recognized as a source of competence; the forum of the petitioner is not. In marriage cases, however, this canon 1673, 3° recognizes the forum of the petitioner as well, but only when the respondent resides within the same conference of bishops. When, therefore, the unlocatable respondent probably resides OUTSIDE the conference, then this canon 1673, 3° does *not* apply and canon 1409, §2 must be followed. When, however, the unlocatable respondent certainly resides somewhere WITHIN the conference, then canon 1673, 3° *does* apply and the domicile of the petitioner is then recognized as a legitimate forum. The court is then obliged to fulfill the requirements of this canon, but only insofar as possible. To the impossible no one is held.

4° – a source of competence introduced in the *American Procedural Norms* by the phrase "the decree of the judge to whom the petition is presented that his tribunal is better able to judge the case than any other tribunal." This notion was modified in *Causas matrimoniales* to read "the tribunal of the place in which in fact most of the depositions or proofs have to be collected." This wording of *Causas matrimoniales* has been only slightly changed in the present canon.

c. The 1917 Code had special rules regarding competence when either a non-Catholic or a woman not legally separated from her husband was involved. Both sets of rules, which would be regarded today as clearly discriminatory, have been suppressed.

ARTICLE 2: THE RIGHT TO
CHALLENGE A MARRIAGE
[cc. 1674–1675]

210. Before Death

Canon 1674 — The following are capable of challenging a marriage:
1° the spouses;
2° the promoter of justice when the nullity has become public, if the marriage cannot be convalidated or this is not expedient.

a. As regards the right of the non-Catholic or of the person who was the direct and malevolent cause of nullity, one should see par. 41.

b. It is understood that the promoter would petition for nullity only in exceptional and extraordinary cases.

211. After Death

Canon 1675 — §1. A marriage which has not been impugned during the lifetime of both spouses cannot be impugned after the death of either one or both spouses unless the question of validity is prejudicial to the resolution of another controversy either in the canonical forum or in the civil forum.

§2. However, if a spouse dies while a case is pending, can. 1518 is to be observed.

ARTICLE: 3 THE OFFICE OF THE JUDGES
[cc. 1676–1677]

212. Judge as Minister of Reconciliation

Canon 1676 — Before accepting a case and whenever there seems to be hope of a successful outcome, the judge is to use pastoral means to induce the spouses, if at all possible, to convalidate the marriage and to restore conjugal living.

This is a specific application of the principle stated in canon 1446 about settling matters out of court whenever possible.[173]

213. Notification of Respondent

Canon 1677 — §1. When the *libellus* has been accepted, the presiding judge or the *ponens* is to proceed to the communication of the decree of citation according to the norms of can. 1508.

214. Contestatio Litis *and Notification of Parties*

§2. Unless either party has petitioned for a session on the joinder of the issues (*contestatio litis*), when fifteen days have passed after such a communication, the presiding judge or the *ponens* is to determine the formulation of the doubt or doubts within ten days by a decree ex officio and notify the parties.

§3. The formulation of the doubt not only is to ask whether there is proof of nullity of marriage in the case, but it also must determine on what ground or grounds the validity of the marriage is to be challenged.

For general comments on these matters, one should see pars. 74–76.

_____
[173]See par. 29, a.

215. Decree of Instruction

§4. Ten days after the communication of the decree, the presiding judge or the *ponens* is to arrange for the instruction of the case by a new decree if the parties were not opposed.

Paragraph four of this canon is a specification of canon 1516.

ARTICLE 4: PROOFS
[cc. 1678–1680]

216. Rights of Defender, Advocate, and Promoter

Canon 1678 — §1. The defender of the bond, the advocates of the parties and the promoter of justice, if intervening in the suit, have the right:
1° to be present at the examination of the parties, the witnesses and the experts, with due regard for the prescription of can. 1559;
2° to inspect the judicial acts even though not published and to review the documents produced by the parties.
§2. The parties cannot assist at the examination mentioned in §1, n. 1.

a. The corresponding canons of the 1917 Code (*CIC* 1968–1969) were more detailed and referred only to the defender, not the advocate.

b. As regards paragraph two, one should see par. 115, a.

217. Character Witnesses

Canon 1679 — Unless full proofs are present from other sources, in evaluating the depositions of the parties in accord with can. 1536, the judge is to use witnesses regarding the credibility of the parties, if possible, as well as other indications and aids.

218. Experts

Canon 1680 — In cases of impotence or defect of consent due to mental illness, the judge is to use the services of one or more experts unless it is obvious from the circumstances that this would be useless; in other cases the prescription of can. 1574 is to be observed.

a. For a general discussion of the expert, one should see pars. 122–130.

b. The corresponding canon of the 1917 Code (*CIC* 1976), referring only to impotence and non-consummation cases, required the services of an expert *unless* such services would obviously be useless. The 1976 draft of procedural law (c. 345), referring to impotence and defect of consent cases due to a mental disorder, dropped the "unless"

clause (perhaps because *CIC* 1982 on "amentia" had not contained such a clause), but it was reinstated in the 1980 draft (c. 1632) "either because experts are not always necessary or because they are not available in some places."[174]

c. It should be noted, finally, that lack of due reason, lack of due discretion, and lack of due competence are all regarded as involving a "defect of consent." In general, therefore, whenever a marriage case on one of those grounds seems to involve a psychopathology or mental disorder (*mentis morbus*), the services of an expert are in order.

ARTICLE 5: THE SENTENCE AND THE APPEAL
[cc. 1681–1685]

219. Transmission of Acts to Superior
(cc. 1681–1682, §1)

a. To the Holy See

Canon 1681 — During the instruction of a case, whenever a very probable doubt emerges that the marriage was not consummated, after suspending the nullity case with the consent of the parties, the tribunal can complete the instruction of the case for a dispensation *super rato* and then submit the acts to the Apostolic See together with a petition from either one or from both spouses for a dispensation and with the opinion of the tribunal and the bishop.

The old rule of thumb regarding cases which potentially could be cases either of annulment or dissolution was that first an annulment should be pursued and, if that proved unsuccessful, then a dissolution could be requested. The reason for this was that one should not ask an authority to dissolve a marriage which was already null.

This rule was implicitly incorporated into the 1923 rules for the processing of non-consummation cases[175] and was repeated in *Provida mater.*[176] In those days a local ordinary enjoyed no general faculty to instruct a non-consummation case. The usual procedure for initiating a case, therefore, involved a preliminary step or stage during which the local ordinary would transmit the petition, along with some basic documents and assurances, to the Holy See with a request for delegation to instruct the case. However, both the 1923 rules (rule 3) and *Provida mater* (Art. 206) indicated that if a local court had already initiated a nullity case on the grounds of impotence, but discovered during the course of the trial that although impotence *could not* be proved, non-consummation probably *could*, all the acts could simply be transferred to the Holy

---

[174]*Comm* 11 (1979), 264.
[175]*AAS* 15 (1923), 392; *CLD* 1, 766, Rule 3.
[176]*AAS* 28 (1936), 353–354; *CLD* 2, 520, Art. 206.

See with a petition for dissolution, without the local ordinary having sought advance delegation to audit the case as a non-consummation procedure. Implicit in this procedure, as is evident, was the rule of thumb that dissolution should not be sought unless annulment was unavailable.

In an instruction of March 7, 1972, however,[177] diocesan bishops were given the *general* faculty of instructing non-consummation hearings for transmission to the Holy See. The request for delegation in *individual* cases would no longer be necessary. As part of that instruction, bishops were assured that the traditional transfer from impotence case to non-consummation case was still allowed, but the 1972 instruction also permitted a kind of reversal of the procedure: if, in other words, the original petition was for *dissolution* but, during the course of the investigation a doubt also arose about the *validity* of the marriage, then, according to the instruction (I, e), the petitioner was free to opt for either procedure. That option seemed to disregard the old rule of thumb.

This present canon 1681 reflects that relatively new option even though it does so within the traditional framework of a transfer from nullity to dissolution. This canon does not suggest, in other words, that the impossibility of annulling a marriage be a condition to petitioning for dissolution. It seems, therefore, that the old rule of thumb no longer holds. According to the 1983 law, a case which is potentially either an annulment or a dissolution case can now be pursued as either.

b. To the Appellate Court

Canon 1682 — §1. The sentence which first declared the nullity of the marriage together with the appeals if there are any and the other acts of the trial, are to be sent ex officio to the appellate tribunal within twenty days from the publication of the sentence.

(1) The history of the appeal of a first instance affirmative decision in a marriage case may now be summarized as follows: (a) before 1741 the case was appealed at the discretion of the respondent (par. 206); (b) after 1741 (in this country 1884) the defender of marriage was required to appeal; (c) the *American Procedural Norms* allowed the defender and the respondent to appeal at their discretion; (d) *Causas matrimoniales* required the defender to appeal; (e) the 1976 draft (c. 347) also required the defender to appeal; (f) the present canon allows the defender to appeal at his or her discretion, but by an altogether new provision, it requires the court ex officio to transmit the case to the appellate court, with the actual appellant being the law itself or the legislator.

[177]*AAS* 64 (1972), 244–252; *CLD* 7; 988–997.

(2) If the defender of the bond in first instance does appeal, it seems that that appeal, in accord with canon 1636, §2, may be renounced by the defender of second instance. This renunciation does not, however, absolve the court of second instance of its obligation *either* of confirming the first instance decision by decree *or* admitting the case to a new hearing.

220. Confirmation or New Hearing

§2. If the sentence rendered in favor of the nullity of marriage was in the first grade of trial, the appellate tribunal by its own decree is to confirm the decision without delay or admit the case to an ordinary examination of a new grade of trial, after considering the observations of the defender of the bond and those of the parties if there are any.

a. The defender mentioned in this paragraph is the defender in second instance.

b. This canon, in accord with the general tenor of *Causas matrimoniales* (VIII) and the 1976 draft (c. 347), permits the ratification only of an affirmative sentence.

221. New Ground of Nullity

Canon 1683 — If at the appellate level a new ground of nullity of the marriage is offered, the tribunal can admit it and judge it as if in first instance.

a. This canon states an exception to canon 1639.

b. For the procedure involved in adding a ground, one should see canon 1514.

222. Effect of Judicial Pronouncement

Canon 1684 — §1. After the sentence which first declared the nullity of marriage has been confirmed at the appellate level either by decree or by another sentence, those persons whose marriage was declared null can contract new marriages immediately after the decree or the second sentence has been made known to them unless a prohibition is attached to this sentence or decree, or it is prohibited by a determination of the local ordinary.

a. Since a *nova propositio* is not suspensive (c. 1644, §2), the parties have an immediate right to remarry.

b. The corresponding canon of the 1917 Code (*CIC* 1987) granted the right to remarry only after a ten-day waiting period.

223. Nova Propositio

§2. The prescriptions of can. 1644 must be observed, even if the sentence which declared the nul-

lity of marriage was not confirmed by another
sentence but by a decree.

224. Recording the Annulment

Canon 1685 — Immediately after the sentence
has been executed, the judicial vicar must notify
the ordinary of the place in which the marriage was
celebrated about this. He must take care that notation be made quickly in the matrimonial and baptismal registers concerning the nullity of the marriage
and any prohibitions which may have been determined.

ARTICLE 6: THE DOCUMENTARY PROCESS
[cc. 1686–1688]

225. First Instance Hearing

Canon 1686 — When a petition has been received in accord with can. 1677, the judicial vicar
or a judge designated by him, omitting the formalities of the ordinary process but having cited the
parties and with the intervention of the defender of
the bond, can declare the nullity of a marriage by a
sentence, if from a document which is subject to no
contradiction or exception there is certain proof of
the existence of a diriment impediment or a defect
of legitimate form, provided that it is clear with
equal certitude that a dispensation was not granted;
this can also be done if there is certain proof of the
defect of a valid mandate of procurator.

a. Canon 1990 of the 1917 Code empowered the
local *ordinary* to declare the marriage null and
Causas matrimoniales (X) reiterated that it was the
ordinary alone who had the power. In practice,
however, the ordinary almost always delegated the
officialis to handle such matters and this canon now
empowers the *officialis or judicial vicar* to proceed
in this way.

b. Canon 1990 of the 1917 Code allowed this
documentary procedure in the case of certain selected diriment impediments. *Causas matrimoniales*
extended the process to all diriment impediments
and also to lack of canonical form ("ex defectu formae canonicae") and to the lack of a valid mandate
on the part of the proxy. The 1976 schema (c. 351)
virtually repeated *Causas matrimoniales* but
changed the phrase regarding lack of form to "de
defectu formae." The present canon has now
changed the phrase again to "de defectu legitimae
formae" in order to clarify the fact that this documentary process (involving the citation of the parties and intervention of the defender) need only be
followed in those cases in which the form was followed but invalidly, e.g., where the priest-witness
did not enjoy jurisdiction or where only one witness
was present. Where the form was not followed at
all, i.e., where the parties, at least one of whom was
bound to the form, married before a civil magistrate

or non-Catholic clergyman without a dispensation,
then the nullity of the marriage may be declared administratively. No judicial process, even a documentary one, is required in such cases.[178]

c. Notable among the impediments not included
in canon 1990 of the 1917 Code but now amenable
to the documentary process are impotence and non-
age.

226. The Appeal

Canon 1687 — §1. If the defender of the bond
prudently thinks that either the flaws mentioned in
can. 1686 or the lack of a dispensation are not certain, the defender of the bond must appeal against
this declaration to the judge of second instance, to
whom the acts must be sent and who must be advised in writing that it is a question of a documentary process.

§2. The party who feels aggrieved retains the
right to appeal.

The 1917 Code did not recognize the right of the
petitioner and respondent to appeal, as paragraph
two of this canon does.

227. Second Instance Hearing

Canon 1688 — The judge in second instance with
the intervention of the defender of the bond, having
heard the parties, shall decree in the same way as in
can. 1686 whether the sentence is to be confirmed
or whether the case must rather be handled according to the ordinary process of law; and in that case
the judge remands it to the tribunal of first instance.

In accord with canon 1447, it would seem that if
the case is remanded, the person who had served as
a judge in the documentary process should not
serve again as judge in the ordinary process.

ARTICLE 7: GENERAL NORMS
[cc. 1689–1691]

228. Moral and Civil Obligations
Stemming from Marriage

Canon 1689 — In the sentence the parties are to
be advised of the moral and even civil obligations
which they may have to each other and to their
children as regards the support and education of
the latter.

229. Process in Marriage Nullity Cases
(cc. 1690–1691)

Apart from the prescripts included in this chapter (cc. 1671–1688), the following two canons

[178]*Comm* 11 (1979), 269–270.

should also be observed. The first deals with a process that is *not* applicable to the marriage nullity case, while the second deals with procedures that *are* applicable.

a. Not Applicable

Canon 1690 — Cases declaring the nullity of marriage cannot be treated in an oral contentious process.

This is the process contained in canons 1656–1670.

b. Applicable

Canon 1691 — In other procedural matters, the canons on trials in general and on the ordinary contentious trial are to be applied unless the nature of the matter precludes it; however, the special norms on cases involving the status of persons and affecting the public good are to be observed.

(1) For other types of cases to which these procedures apply, one should see par. 5, e.

(2) The norms for cases involving the status of persons are canons 1643 and 1644.

(3) As regards cases involving the public good, one should see par. 21, a.

CHAPTER II
CASES OF SEPARATION OF SPOUSES
[cc. 1692–1696]

230. History of This Chapter

The 1917 Code contained no such chapter; it contained no canons regulating procedures for separation cases; these canons were first introduced in the 1976 schema. When the consultors met in 1979 to discuss this section, it was proposed that the section should be suppressed because, worldwide, spouses hardly ever bring such matters to a church court; therefore, in those few localities where such cases do come to the attention of a church court, local legislation would suffice. It was finally decided, however, to retain the chapter as a kind of restatement of canon 1671.[179]

231. Ecclesiastical Forum

Canon 1692 — §1. Personal separation of baptized spouses, unless otherwise legally provided for in particular places, can be decided by a decree of a diocesan bishop, or by a sentence of a judge in accord with the following canons.

232. Civil Forum

§2. Where an ecclesiastical decision has no civil effects, or if it is foreseen that a civil sentence is

[179]Ibid., 272–273.

not contrary to divine law, the bishop of the diocese of residence of the spouses can give them permission to approach the civil forum, having considered the particular circumstances.

§3. Also, if a case is concerned only with the merely civil effects of marriage, the judge can determine it is sufficient that the case be deferred to the civil forum from the start, with due regard for the prescription of §2.

233. Process

Canon 1693 — §1. Unless one party or the promoter of justice seeks an ordinary contentious process, an oral contentious process is to be used.

§2. If the ordinary contentious process has been used and an appeal is proposed, the appellate tribunal is to proceed in accord with the norm of can. 1682, §2 while observing everything that is to be observed.

234. Competent Forum

Canon 1694 — The prescriptions of can. 1673 are to be observed in regard to the competence of the tribunal.

235. Judge as Minister of Reconciliation

Canon 1695 — Before accepting the case and whenever it is perceived that there is hope of a successful outcome, the judge is to use pastoral means to reconcile the spouses and induce them to restore conjugal living.

One should see canons 1676 and 1446 and par. 29, a.

236. Promoter of Justice

Canon 1696 — Cases involving the separation of spouses also pertain to the public good; therefore, the promoter of justice must always intervene at them in accord with the norm of can. 1433.

CHAPTER III
PROCEDURE FOR DISPENSATION
OF RATIFIED AND NON-CONSUMMATED
MARRIAGE
[cc. 1697–1706]

237. Brief History of the Procedure

a. The first papal dispensations from non-consummated marriages seem to have occurred in the fifteenth century. Although the Council of Trent (1563) made no pronouncement one way or the other on whether the pope enjoyed such a power, several theologians and canonists over the next couple of centuries claimed that he did and, in fact, there would periodically be reports that the pope had, on this or that occasion, actually exercised the power. It was not, however, until 1741 and *Dei miseratione* that a pope went on record as claiming that the power to dispense from an unconsummated marriage did indeed belong to the papacy.[180]

b. In issuing *Dei miseratione,* Benedict XIV not only formally acknowledged the papal power to dispense, he also outlined a brief process to be followed in seeking the dispensation, which consisted basically in a detailed petition sent to the pope for his study and decision.[181]

The 1917 Code did not devote a separate chapter to non-consummation procedures, as does the 1983 Code, but it chose, instead, to incorporate certain directives regarding such cases into the section on procedures for general marriage cases (*CIC* 1960–1989).

Since the 1917 Code, however, the Holy See has published two major instructions on the procedures to be followed in non-consummation cases, one published on May 7, 1923,[182] and the second published on March 7, 1972.[183] The first contained one hundred six rules describing, in detail, the entire procedure. The second was a fairly brief, eight-page document listing important emendations to the process.

The 1976 schema included a separate section containing eleven canons that briefly describe the process to be followed, and these canons have, for the most part, been incorporated into the 1983 Code.

c. In the decade between 1969 and 1979, Americans seem to have lost interest in the procedure. In 1969, three hundred twenty-five non-consummation cases were sent to Rome from the United States,[184] whereas in 1979, only fifteen cases were sent.[185]

238. *Various Rights (cc. 1697–1699)*

a. *The Right To Petition*

Canon 1697 — Only the spouses or either one, even if the other is not willing, have the right to petition for the favor of a dispensation from a ratified and not consummated marriage.

b. *The Right To Decide*

Canon 1698 — §1. The Apostolic See alone adjudicates the fact of the non-consummation of marriage and of the existence of a just cause for granting the dispensation.

c. *The Right To Grant*

§2. The dispensation, however, is granted by the Roman Pontiff alone.

(1) Although the suggestion was made at the 1979 meeting of the consultors that the faculty to grant the dispensation should be given to bishops, the consultors did not consider this to be opportune.[186]

(2) Although this canon, as well as the rubric, speaks of a dispensation, canon 1142 speaks of a dissolution.

d. *The Right To Instruct*

Canon 1699 — §1. The person competent to accept the *libellus* seeking a dispensation is the diocesan bishop of the domicile or quasi-domicile of the petitioner, who must arrange for the instruction of the process if he is sure of the basis of the pleas.

One should see par. 219, a as regards paragraph one of this canon.

e. *The Right To Consult*

§2. But if the proposed case has special difficulties of the juridical or moral order the diocesan bishop is to consult the Apostolic See.

f. *The Right To Have Recourse*

§3. Recourse is open to the Apostolic See against a decree by which a bishop rejects a *libellus.*

239. *Tribunal or Priest Instructor*

Canon 1700 — §1. With due regard for the prescription of can. 1681, the bishop is to commit the instruction of these processes, either permanently or in individual cases, to his own tribunal, the tribunal of another diocese, or a suitable priest.

§2. But if a judicial petition has been introduced to declare the nullity of this same marriage the instruction is to be committed to the same tribunal.

240. *Defender and Advisor*

Canon 1701 — §1. The defender of the bond must always intervene in these procedures.

---

[180]Noonan, 129–136.
[181]*CICFontes* I, 700. In the constitution *Si datam* issued seven years later, Benedict claimed that the generally restrictive procedures of *Dei miseratione* had, between 1741 and 1748, resulted in a reduction in the number of petitions for dispensations on the grounds of non-consummation. *CICFontes* II, 132.
[182]*AAS* 15 (1923), 392–413; *CLD* 1, 764–792.
[183]*AAS* 64 (1972), 244–252; *CLD* 7, 988–997.
[184]*CLSAP* (1970), 100.
[185]*CLSAP* (1980), 222–230.

[186]*Comm* 11 (1979), 275.

§2. An advocate is not admitted but, because of the difficulties of a case, the bishop can permit that the petitioner or the respondent have the aid of a legal expert.

241. Proofs

Canon 1702 — Insofar as it is possible, each spouse is to be heard during the instruction of the case; and the canons on the collection of proofs in ordinary contentious trials and in cases of marital nullity are to be observed provided they can be reconciled with the distinctive character of these processes.

242. Publication

Canon 1703 — **§1.** There is no publication of the acts; however, when the judge sees that from the proofs introduced a grave obstacle has arisen to the petition of the plaintiff or an exception of the respondent, he is to reveal this prudently to the interested party.

§2. The judge can show to the interested party seeking it a document introduced or testimony received and set a time within which to offer observations.

This canon is a restatement of rule 97 of the 1923 instruction, which likewise permitted the judge instructor to show selected responses or documents to one or both parties in order to prevent non-publication from being injurious.[187]

243. Opinion, or **Votum**, of Bishop

Canon 1704 — **§1.** Having finished the instruction, the judge instructor is to hand over all the acts with an appropriate report to the bishop, who is to prepare his opinion on the truth of the matter both concerning the fact of non-consummation, and the just cause for a dispensation and the opportuneness of the favor.

§2. If the instruction of the process has been committed to another tribunal in accord with can. 1700, the observations in favor of the bond are to be made in the same forum, but the opinion mentioned in §1 pertains to the bishop committing it, to whom the instructor is to forward the acts with an appropriate report.

244. Transmission of Acts

Canon 1705 — **§1.** The bishop is to send to the Apostolic See all the acts with his opinion and the observations of the defender of the bond.

245. Supplemental Instruction

§2. If, in the judgment of the Apostolic See, a supplement to the instruction is required, the bishop will be informed about the points on which the instruction must be completed.

246. Second Presentation

§3. But, if the Apostolic See responds that non-consummation has not been established from the proofs, then the legal expert mentioned in can. 1701, §2 can review the acts of the process but not the opinion of the bishop, at the tribunal, to see whether any serious reasons warrant resubmitting the petition.

247. Rescript, Notification, and Recording

Canon 1706 — The rescript of dispensation is sent to the bishop by the Apostolic See; he shall notify the parties about the rescript and also as soon as possible order the pastor of the place where the marriage was contracted and the pastor of the place of baptism to note the granted dispensation in the registers of marriage and of baptism.

CHAPTER IV
PROCEDURE IN PRESUMED DEATH OF
A SPOUSE
[c. 1707]

248. The Rubric

Although the chapter heading, as well as canon 1707, §1 speak of *presumed* death, it is clear from paragraph two that this is not a presumption in the usual sense of the word, namely, "a probable conjecture about an uncertain matter" (c. 1584). Paragraph two requires moral certitude about the death. The certitude, however, is acquired not through a death certificate but through other means, not excluding certain presumptions.

249. History of Institute

The problem of proving death with less than absolutely certain evidence is an old one. Clement III (1187–1191), to cite but one example, once ruled that a woman whose husband had been missing for many years, was not free to remarry unless she received some certain news of her husband's death.[188]

Two instructions regarding this matter are of particular note: the first *Cum alias* of 1670,[189] the other *Matrimonii vinculo* of 1868.[190]

---

[187]See par. 145 for observations regarding the publication of the acts in ordinary contentious trials.

[188]X, IV, 1, 19; *CorpusIC* II, 668.
[189]*CICFontes* IV, n. 742, 22–25.
[190]*CICFontes* IV, n. 1002, 306–309.

Cum alias (11) noted that if a person died in a hospital, testimony of death should be obtained from the hospital administrator; if buried in a church, from the pastor of the church; or, if a man was killed on the field of battle, from the company commander, but, said the instruction, "if such evidence is not available, the Sacred Congregation does not intend to exclude other proofs which are commonly admitted in law, providing they are legitimate and sufficient."

Matrimonii vinculo was devoted entirely to the question of proving undocumented death, and it provided, from 1868 to the 1983 Code (*CIC* contained no corresponding chapter) the chief guidelines to be used in the solution of these cases. That document discussed the value of various types of evidence: one or two witnesses who testify from their own knowledge, hearsay witnesses, conjectures, presumptions, indications, circumstantial evidence, and even rumors.[191]

250. The Declaration

Canon 1707 — §1. Whenever the death of a spouse cannot be proven by an authentic ecclesiastical or civil document, the other spouse is not considered free from the bond of marriage until after a declaration of presumed death is made by the diocesan bishop.

251. Proofs and Moral Certitude

§2. The diocesan bishop can make the declaration mentioned in §1 only after appropriate investigations have enabled him to attain moral certitude of the death of a spouse from the depositions of witnesses, from rumor, or from indications. The mere absence of a spouse, even for a long time, is insufficient.

252. Uncertain Cases

§3. The bishop is to consult the Apostolic See about uncertain and complex cases.

TITLE II
CASES FOR DECLARING NULLITY OF SACRED ORDINATION
[cc. 1708–1712]

253. The Rubric

The corresponding rubric in the 1917 Code, under which were included canons 1993–1998, referred not merely to ordination *nullity* cases but to *all* "cases against sacred ordination." When those canons were read in conjunction with *CIC*

211–214, which appeared under the rubric "On the Reduction of Clerics to the Lay State,"[192] it was understood that two types of cases could be processed: (1) those which impugned the *validity of the ordination,* either because of a defect in the rite or for some other reason, like lack of capacity or intention on the part of the ordained, and (2) those which impugned the *validity of the obligations* stemming from ordination because of the presence of force at the time of ordination.

On June 9, 1931, the Holy See issued an instruction, very similar to the 1923 instruction for the processing of non-consummation cases (par. 237, b), which provided a detailed explanation of the procedure to be followed in ordination cases.[193] It was still understood, however, that although subdeacons and deacons could be *dispensed* from the obligation of celibacy, a priest was relieved of the obligation only if he could prove the *invalidity* either of the ordination itself or of the obligations.

Besides the fact that the distinction between invalidity of ordination and invalidity of obligations became, over the years, increasingly obscure, the Holy See, in 1964, began *dispensing* priests as well as deacons, from the obligation of celibacy, so the need to prove the *invalidity* of obligations was further reduced.

Beginning in 1964 and over the next several years, the Holy See issued three separate instructions regarding the procedures to be followed in processing requests for dispensations from the obligations of the priesthood. The first was an unpublished circular letter dated February 2, 1964; the second was dated January 13, 1971;[194] and the third was issued on October 14, 1980.[195] Since 1964, thousands of such dispensations have been granted.[196]

The present title, however, deals not with these requests for dispensation but rather with claims of nullity. Such claims are, as one might expect, quite rare.

254. Right To Petition

Canon 1708 — The cleric himself, the ordinary to whom he is subject, or the ordinary in whose diocese he was ordained have the right to impugn the validity of sacred ordination.

The right is awarded to the ordinary insofar as ordination and holy orders affect the common good.

---

[191]For a digest of the 1868 instruction, see Doheny II, 593–596. For a sample decree, see Wrenn, *Decisions,* 2nd ed., 197.

[192]The corresponding rubric in the 1983 Code is entitled "Loss of the Clerical State" and comprises cc. 290–293. See the commentary on those canons.

[193]*AAS* 23 (1931), 457–473; *CLD* 1, 812–832.

[194]*AAS* 63 (1971), 303–312; *CLD* 7, 110–121.

[195]*AAS* 72 (1980), 1132–1137; *J* 41 (1981), 222–227.

[196]J. Keating, "Laicization," *NCE* 16, 243–244; V. Mallon, "Easy Exit for Priests," *HPR* (May 1978), 14–26.

255. Transmittal of Petition to Rome

Canon 1709 — **§1. The *libellus* must be sent to the competent congregation, which shall decide whether the case is to be handled by the congregation of the Roman Curia or by a tribunal designated by it.**

§2. Once the *libellus* is sent, the cleric is forbidden to exercise orders by the law itself.

256. The Judicial Process (cc. 1710–1712)

a. The Process

Canon 1710 — **If the congregation remands the case to a tribunal, the canons on trials in general and on the ordinary contentious trial are to be observed unless the nature of the matter precludes this, with due regard for the prescriptions of this title.**

b. The Defender

Canon 1711 — **In these cases the defender of the bond enjoys the same rights and is bound by the same duties as the defender of the marriage bond.**

c. The Double Conforming Affirmative Sentence

Canon 1712 — **After the second sentence which has confirmed the nullity of sacred ordination the cleric loses all rights proper to the clerical state and is free of all obligations.**

TITLE III
METHODS OF AVOIDING A TRIAL
[cc. 1713–1716]

257. Ways Themselves

Canon 1713 — **To avoid judicial contentions a settlement or reconciliation is usefully employed or the controversy can be entrusted to the judgment of one or more arbiters.**

As noted in pars. 5, c and 29, a, this is a specific application of the general principle that wherever possible, a peaceful, out-of-court solution should be reached.

258. Procedure To Be Followed

Canon 1714 — **The norms chosen by the parties are to be observed in a settlement, a compromise or a trial by arbiters; or, if the parties choose no norms, the law enacted by the conference of bishops is to be observed if there is such, or the civil law in force in the place where the agreement is entered into.**

259. Matters Not Subject to Private Settlement

Canon 1715 — **§1. A settlement or compromise cannot be made validly concerning matters which pertain to the public good and other matters about which the parties cannot freely dispose.**

§2. If it is a question of temporal ecclesiastical goods, whenever the matter requires this, the formalities specified by law for the alienation of ecclesiastical goods are to be observed.

260. Civil Law

a. Judicial Confirmation

Canon 1716 — **§1. If the civil law does not recognize the force of a sentence by arbiters unless it is confirmed by a judge, a sentence by arbiters in an ecclesiastical controversy needs confirmation by an ecclesiastical judge of the place where the sentence was rendered in order to have force in the canonical forum.**

b. Judicial Impugnment

§2. However, if the civil law admits the challenging of a sentence by arbiters before a civil judge, the same challenge can be proposed before an ecclesiastical judge who is competent to judge the controversy in the first instance.

COMPARATIVE OVERVIEW

1917 Code			1983 Code	
Part	Section	Title	Section	Part
		The Competent Forum		
		Grades of Tribunals		I
		Rules to be Observed		Trials in
		The Parties		General
		Actions and Exceptions		
		Introduction of a Case		
		The Joinder of Issues		
		The Instance		
		Interrogation of Parties (1917 only)		
	I	Proofs		
	Trials in	Incidental Cases		
	General	Publication of the Acts, etc.	I	
		The Sentence or Pronouncement	The Ordinary	II
		Challenge of the Sentence	Contentious	The Conten-
		Res Iudicata and *Restitutio*	Trial	tious Trial
		Expenses		
I		Gratuitous Hearings		
Trials		Execution of the Sentence		
			II	
			The Oral	
			Contentious	
			Trial	
				III
	II	Marriage Cases		Special
	Special	Ordination Cases		Procedures
	Trials	Avoiding Trials		IV
		Criminal/Penal Cases	....	Penal Procedure
II				
Beatification and Canon- ization Pro- cedures				
			I	
			Recourse against Adminis- trative Decrees	V
III				Adminis- trative
Various		Removal or Transfer	II	Recourse
Procedures		of Pastors	Removal and	and Pastors
Regarding		Other procedures	Transfer of	
Clerics		(1917 only)	Pastors	

BIBLIOGRAPHY _____

Books

Augustine, C. *A Commentary on the New Code of Canon Law.* Vol. VII, *Ecclesiastical Trials* St. Louis: B. Herder Book Co., 1923 (cited as Augustine).

Bartocetti, V. *De causis matrimonialibus.* Rome, 1950 (cited as Bartocetti).

Bassett, W. and Huizing, P., ed. *Judgment in the Church.* New York: Seabury Press, 1977.

Coronata, M. *Institutiones iuris canonici.* Vol. III, *De processibus.* Rome: Marietti, 1956 (cited as Coronata).

Della Rocca, F. *Canonical Procedure.* Milwaukee: The Bruce Publishing Co., 1961 (cited as Della Rocca).

Doheny, W. *Canonical Procedure in Matrimonial Cases.* 2 vols. Vol. I. Milwaukee: The Bruce Publishing Co., 1944 (cited as Doheny I).

———. *Canonical Procedure in Matrimonial Cases.* 2 vols. Vol. II. Milwaukee: The Bruce Publishing Co., 1948 (cited as Doheny II).

Gordon, I., and Grocholewski, Z., eds. *Documenta Recentiora circa Rem Matrimonialem et Processualem.* 2 vols. Vol. I. Romae: Pontificia Universitas Gregoriana, 1977 (cited as Gordon-Grocholewski).

Goyeneche, S. *De processibus.* 2 parts. Messina, 1958 (cited as Goyeneche and part).

Grocholewski, Z., ed. *Documenta Recentiora circa Rem Matrimonialem et Processualem.* 2 vols. Vol. II. Romae: Pontificia Universitas Gregoriana, 1980).

Lega, M., *Praelectiones de iudiciis ecclesiasticis.* 4 vols. Romae: Typis Vaticanis, 1905 (cited as Lega and volume).

Lega, M., and Bartocetti, V. *Commentarius in iudicia ecclesiastica.* 3 vols. but continuous pagination. Rome: Anonima Libraria Cattolica Italiana, 1938 (cited as Lega-Bartocetti and volume).

Noonan, J. *Power to Dissolve.* Cambridge: The Belknap Press, 1972 (cited as Noonan).

Regatillo, E. *Institutiones iuris canonici.* Vol. II. Santander: Sal Terrae, 1956 (cited as Regatillo).

Roberti, F. *De processibus.* 2 vols. Romae: Libraria Pontificii Instituti Utriusque Iuris, 1941 (cited as Roberti and volume).

Sipos, S. *Enchiridion Iuris Canonici.* Romae: B. Herder Book Co., 1954 (cited as Sipos).

Smith, S. *The Marriage Process in the United States.* New York: Benziger Brothers, 1893.

———. *Elements of Ecclesiastical Law.* Vol. II, *Ecclesiastical Trials.* New York: Benziger Brothers, 1887.

Wernz, F. *Ius Decretalium.* 6 vols. Romae: Typis Vaticanis, 1898 (cited as Wernz and volume).

Wernz, F., and Vidal, P. *Ius Canonicum. Tomus VI, De processibus.* Romae: Universitas Gregoriana, 1949 (cited as Wernz-Vidal).

Woywod, S., and Smith, C. *A Practical Commentary on the Code of Canon Law.* Vol. II. London: B. Herder Book Co., 1948.

Articles

Colagiovanni, A. "M.P. 'Causas matrimoniales.' " *ME* 98 (1973): 3–76.

Di Iorio, O. "Adnotationes in M.P. 'Causas matrimoniales.' " *P* 63 (1974): 559–610; *P* 64 (1975): 147–185; *P* 65 (1976): 347–383.

Egan, E. "Appeal in Marriage Nullity Cases: Two Centuries of Experiment and Reform." *CLSAP* (1981): 132–144.

Felici, P. "Juridical Formalities and Evaluations of Evidence in the Canonical Process." *J* 38 (1978): 153–157.

Frattin, P. "Lay Judges in Ecclesiastical Tribunals." *J* 28 (1968): 177–184.

Green, T. "The Revision of the Code: The First Decade." *J* 36 (1976): 353–441.

———. "Marriage Nullity Procedures in the Schema *De processibus.*" *J* 38 (1978): 311–414.

———. "The Revision of the Procedural Law Schema: Implications for Tribunal Practice." *J* 40 (1980): 349–383.

Morrisey, F. "The Procedural and Administrative Reforms of the Post-Conciliar Church." *Con,* 107 (1977): 77–87 (Amer. ed.).

———. "The Current Status of Procedural Law." *CLSAP* (1978): 49–59.

Ruzick, K. "Competence, Nullity of the Acts, and the Appeal Process: A Look at the Procedural Law of the New Code." *CLSAP* (1982): 105–120.

Part IV
PENAL PROCEDURE
[cc. 1717–1731]

After the significant section on marriage cases, the legislator deals with the less well-known area of the penal process. Such processes may be used only rarely. However, given human frailty and sinfulness, the law must deal with noteworthy breaches of church faith or order. These procedural canons should be read in conjunction with canons 1341–1353 of Book VI on the application of penalties. The following outline of these related canons may be helpful:

• prior investigation regarding appropriateness of penal process: canons 1717 and 1719.

• decision whether to initiate penal process: canons 1342 and 1720–1721.

• special features of penal process prior to sentence or administrative decree: canons 1343–1350.

• appeal or recourse against sentence or decree: canons 1353 and 1727.

• situation of one subject to a penalty after a sentence or decree: canons 1351–1352.

• related issue of an action for damages distinct from the penal action: canons 1729–1731.

The canons on the penal process can be treated briefly since the basic principles on judicial process have been articulated already.

The commentary focuses briefly on some key features of the ecclesiastical penal process. First the 1983 Code is compared with canons 1933–1959 of the 1917 Code.[1] Secondly, some significant aspects

of the preliminary investigation and the evolution of the penal process are considered. Finally, there will be a brief reflection on a separate action for damages resulting from an alleged ecclesiastical offense.

The revised law somewhat modifies the 1917 Code. First of all, the latter document is simplified. Its initial canon 1933 on using the criminal process is dropped. The revised law emphasizes judicial process, yet the ordinary has significant discretion in using judicial or administrative process (cc. 1341; 1718). Also dropped is the section on the accusation and denunciation of an offense (*CIC* 1934–1938). Canon 1721 deals with the formal accusation of an ecclesiastical offense by the promoter of justice. The denunciation of an offense is treated implicitly in the generic reference of canon 1717 to the ordinary's awareness of the possible commission of an offense. Likewise omitted are canons 1947–1953 of the 1917 Code on an official ecclesiastical rebuke: presumably canon 1339, §2 discusses such a rebuke. The 1917 Code on the preliminary investigation (*CIC* 1939–1946) is simplified. Three new canons treat of the investigator, the ordinary's decision after the investigation, and the custody of the acts (cc. 1717–1719).

Secondly, the evolution of the process is treated more fully (cc. 1720–1728) than in the 1917 Code (*CIC* 1954–1959). Unlike the latter document the initial canon deals with administrative penal process. Certain procedural principles are explicitly included, e.g., requirement of advocate for accused (c. 1723) and possible renunciation of the process (c. 1724). Furthermore, several canons explicitate certain rights of the accused, e.g., the right to have the last word in the process before the decision (c. 1725) and the judge's obligation to declare the innocence of the accused as soon as this is clear (c. 1726). The accused may appeal a decision even if it is favorable since at times the law permits the imposition of some penal measure even in such instances (c. 1727, §1).

Thirdly, a new section provides for an action for damages by one adversely affected by an ecclesiastical offense, e.g., religious community suffering because of illegal alienation of its patrimony (c. 1377). Such an action is available even after the penal action to punish the offender has been terminated or prescribed.

---

[1] One difficulty in clarifying the rationale for changes from the 1917 Code is the absence of a report of the Code Commission committee which prepared the original schema. For a report on the revision of the original schema, see *Comm* 12 (1980): 188–200. For a helpful commentary on the 1917 Code, see A. Vermeersch and J. Creusen, *Epitome Iuris Canonici* (Mechliniae-Romae; H. Dessain, 1956), III, 132–144.

CHAPTER I
THE PRIOR INVESTIGATION
[cc. 1717–1719]

Initiation of the Investigation

Canon 1717 — §1. Whenever the ordinary receives information which at least seems to be true of an offense, he shall cautiously inquire personally or through another suitable person about the facts and circumstances and about imputability unless this investigation appears to be entirely superfluous.

§2. Care must be taken lest anyone's good name be endangered by this investigation.

§3. The one who conducts the investigation has the same powers and obligations as an auditor in the process; this person cannot act as a judge in the matter, if a judicial process is set in motion later.

The criminal process is not to be undertaken lightly. Before it can be initiated, there must be a strong probability that an ecclesiastical offense has been committed. Furthermore, the formal initiative for such a process rests with ecclesiastical authority (bishop or religious superior) and not with private individuals (§1).

Despite the importance of protecting the good of the community, the law is particularly concerned about safeguarding the reputation of the person(s) accused of an ecclesiastical offense (§2; c. 220). This is a key value to be kept in mind, especially by the person conducting the preliminary investigation if the ordinary chooses not to do this himself. Most ordinaries would probably not conduct such an inquiry any more than they would be significantly involved in marriage cases. Such an investigator would function in a fashion comparable to the auditor in a regular process.[2] In the interest of objectivity, the preliminary investigator may not be a judge if a formal process is initiated subsequently (§3). The preliminary investigation is geared to ascertaining whether there are solid grounds for judging that an ecclesiastical offense[3] has been committed. The inquiry should focus on the facts of the case, any relevant circumstances, and those factors which may affect the imputability[4] of the alleged of-

[2]See commentary on c. 1428.
[3]See cc. 1364–1398.
[4]See commentary on cc. 1321–1330.

fender. In other words, there should be an effort to clarify an initial profile of the alleged offense. If the ordinary, however, judges that such a profile is already reasonably clear without such an investigation, the next stage of the process may be initiated. At this stage of the process, it is not necessary that the alleged offense be certain; it suffices that there is a strong probability that it has been committed. The determination of the offense, with moral certainty, is to be done through the subsequent process.

Decree of Ordinary Regarding the Penal Process

Canon 1718 — §1. When sufficient evidence appears to have been collected, the ordinary shall decide:

1° whether the process for inflicting or declaring a penalty can be set in motion;

2° whether this is expedient in light of can. 1341;

3° whether a judicial process must be used or unless the law forbids it whether he must proceed by a decree without a trial.

§2. The ordinary is to revoke or change the decree mentioned in §1 whenever it appears to him from new evidence that a different decision is called for.

§3. In issuing the decrees mentioned in §§1 and 2, the ordinary is to hear two or more judges or other experts in the law, if he prudently sees fit to do so.

§4. In order to avoid useless trials, before he makes a decision in accord with §1, the ordinary is to consider whether it is expedient that either he or the investigator equitably solve the question of damages with the consent of the parties.

This canon deals with the situation after the above-mentioned investigation has been completed or if it has not been deemed necessary. It reflects the preeminent role of the ordinary regarding the criminal process. While it is not explicitly stated as such, the investigator presumably reports to the ordinary on the probability of the offense and its imputability.

Number one of paragraph one, deals with the most basic issue: do the facts warrant a penal process? Perhaps the original complaint that generated such an investigation lacks any real foundation or perhaps there are indications but no solid evidence of an ecclesiastical offense. In such instances a process might not be warranted.

In other instances, however, although a process may be warranted and although there is evidence of an ecclesiastical offense, such a process may not be expedient. The well-being of the ecclesial society and especially of the offender might better be ensured by some other legal-pastoral measure rather than a penal process (§1, 2°). As canon 1341 states, penalties are to be imposed only as a last resort when all other legal-pastoral measures have failed.

While the law favors a judicial process (c. 1342), the ordinary may utilize administrative process unless the law specifically requires the former (§1, 3°). This is true in cases involving possible dismissal from the clerical state or in cases involving the imposition or declaration of an excommunication (c. 1425, §1, 2°).

The personal and ecclesial significance of this issue makes it imperative that the ordinary be open to new evidence which might alter his initial decision (§2). It also suggests the wisdom of his consulting with a couple of judges or other legal experts (§3).

Finally, the value of avoiding needless processes underlies paragraph four, which enables the ordinary to resolve a claim for damages equitably—either personally or through the above-mentioned investigator. In other words, there may be no need for a penal process if the only issue is the reparation of certain damages.

Custody of the Acts

Canon 1719 — The acts of the investigation, the decrees of the ordinary by which the investigation was opened and closed, and all that preceded it are to be kept in the secret archive of the curia if they are not necessary for the penal process.

CHAPTER II
THE DEVELOPMENT OF THE PROCESS
[cc. 1720–1728]

This chapter deals largely with those relatively few provisions specific to the judicial penal process. Canon 1728, §1 states that, generally speaking, the rules on trials in general and on ordinary contentious trials are operative here, with special reference to norms which govern cases affecting the public good. Some noteworthy considerations in this section are a concern to vindicate the procedural rights of the alleged offender and to protect the well-being of the community during such a process.[5] By way of

exception, the initial canon treats of *administrative* process in penal cases.

Administrative Penal Process

Canon 1720 — If the ordinary decides that he is to proceed by a decree without a trial:
1° he is to inform the accused about the accusation and the proofs, giving the person the opportunity of self-defense unless the accused neglects to be in court after having been duly summoned;
2° he is to consider carefully the proofs and arguments with two assessors;
3° if the offense is certainly proved and the criminal action has not been terminated, he is to issue the decree in accord with cann. 1342-1350, explaining the reasons in law and in fact, at least briefly.

The general norms on administrative acts in Book I[6] were deemed insufficient to deal with the specifics of the penal process. Accordingly, this canon was formulated to guarantee the alleged offender's right of self-defense, to provide for official consultation before the ordinary's decision, and to specify the exigencies of a reasoned decision.

The involvement of the alleged offender here is required by the basic right to be informed of proposed actions which might prejudicially affect one's rights and the right to be heard in defense of one's rights (1°).

One of the few explicit references to assessors (c. 1424) is indicated here (2°). Presumably by their counsel they can preclude arbitrary action by the ordinary, who, however, is not bound by their advice.[7]

Finally, if there is moral certitude (c. 1608, §1) about the offense and the statute of limitations has not run out on the criminal action (c. 1362), the ordinary is to issue an appropriate decree according to the canons on the application of penalties (cc. 1341–1353). The decree should succinctly clarify the relevant procedural and penal canons as well as the pertinent facts to which the law is to be applied.[8]

The other canons in this section concern the judicial penal process, yet some of the above considerations are relevant here mutatis mutandis.

Role of the Promoter of Justice

Canon 1721 — §1. If the ordinary decrees that a judicial penal process is to be begun, he is to give the acts of the investigation to the promoter of justice who is to present a *libellus* of accusation to the

---

[5]The following brief quotation seems pertinent here by way of correctly interpreting the following canons and conducting proper penal processes: "The dignity of the human person, the principles of fundamental fairness, and the universally applicable presumption of freedom require that no member of the Church arbitrarily be deprived of the exercise of any right or office" (NCCB, *On Due Process*, rev. ed. [Washington: NCCB, 1972], 5) (cited as *Due Process*).

[6]See especially cc. 35–58.
[7]For comparable provisions for consultation before the removal or transfer of pastors, see cc. 1742, §1; 1745, 2°; 1750.
[8]On the importance of reasoned decisions in the administrative arena, see *Due Process*, 33.

judge in accord with the norms of cann. 1502 and 1504.

§2. The promoter of justice constituted as such by the higher court acts as the petitioner before that tribunal.

As in the 1917 Code, the initiation of the judicial process is entrusted to the promoter of justice who acts at the request of the ordinary. The promoter of justice (c. 1430) is institutionally responsible for fostering the public good, whose protection at times requires a penal process. The promoter functions like a petitioner in a marriage case, generally enjoys the same rights, and is bound by the same obligations as the latter (c. 1434). The promoter of justice at this point is to prepare a *libellus,* or petition of accusation, according to law (cc. 1502; 1504). The petition should briefly indicate the goal of the promoter's activity, i.e., the declaration or infliction of a penalty and a succinct presentation of the evidence that an offense has been committed and that the alleged offender is imputable.

Paragraph two notes that if the penal process is also conducted at the appellate level, the second instance promoter functions in the same way as the promoter in first instance.

Restrictions on the Accused

Canon 1722 — To preclude scandals, to protect the freedom of witnesses and to safeguard the course of justice, having heard the promoter of justice and having cited the accused, the ordinary at any stage of the process can remove the accused from the sacred ministry or from any ecclesiastical office or function, can impose or prohibit residence in a given place or territory, or even prohibit public participation in the Most Holy Eucharist; all these measures must be revoked once the reason for them ceases; they also end by the law itself when the penal process ceases.

Most of the concerns noted thus far have related to the alleged offender. This canon, however, focuses on the protection of the community against the potentially disruptive activities of the former. It combines three canons from the 1917 Code (*CIC* 1956–1958) and empowers the ordinary (not the judge) to restrict the alleged offender's exercise of ecclesiastical office or public participation in the Eucharist. Theoretically the alleged offender may also be prevented from living or ordered to live in a given place. Such measures are prompted in part by a concern for the integrity of the process, e.g., protecting the freedom of witnesses and expediting the course of justice. In addition there is a concern about the potential scandal caused by the alleged offender.

That such action is not to be taken lightly and that the rights of the alleged offender are to be pro-

tected are evident from both the required consultation of the ordinary with the promoter of justice and the required citation of the defendant. Obviously if such a party does not appear in court, the measures envisioned here can still be implemented.[9] Furthermore, such measures are to be rescinded once the reason for imposing them is no longer operative, and they automatically cease at the end of the process.

The explicit provision of the 1917 Code which precludes recourse against such a measure (*CIC* 1959) is absent from the 1983 law. Apparently, therefore, recourse is possible according to the usual rules.[10]

Counsel for the Defendant

Canon 1723 — §1. When citing the accused, the judge must invite the accused to appoint an advocate in accord with the norm of can. 1481, §1, within a period of time set by the judge.

§2. But if the accused does not provide for this the judge is to name an advocate before the joinder of issues (*contestatio litis*) who will remain in this function as long as the accused has not personally appointed an advocate.

This canon reflects the insight that the defendant should enjoy the services of counsel in protecting his or her interests. If the defendant does not choose an advocate, the judge is to appoint one before the joinder of the issue so that the defendant's interests are duly protected throughout the process. The court-appointed advocate functions as long as the defendant neglects to choose someone else.[11]

---

[9] See commentary on cc. 1592–1595.

[10] See commentary on cc. 1732–1739.

[11] In connection with this, it might be noted that the committee rejected a suggestion that the law require the name of the accuser to be revealed to the alleged offender. Such a requirement presumably would be inappropriate and possibly destructive. If, however, a given accusation were used as a proof in the process, the accuser would technically be a witness and his or her name would then be revealed to the alleged offender (*Comm* 12 [1980], 194).

Ordinarily the canons on the penal process do not explicitly provide for the revelation of the name of the accuser; however, canon 1561 expresses the legislator's openness to particular law modifications in the examination of witnesses. Accordingly, one might interpret the present canons in light of the following value of the Anglo-American common law tradition: ". . . the right, in the face of accusation which would result in the imposition of a penalty, to confront one's accusers, and those who testify in support of the accusation" (*Due Process,* 5–6). Another passage from the same report also seems pertinent here: "It is a mandate of fundamental fairness that information concerning a person is not to be used as a basis for administrative action adversely affecting that person without disclosing to that person that the information is to be used, and without affording opportunity for explanation, rebuttal or denial of the information in question. Exceptions to this principle of fundamental fairness should be extremely rare and only in the interest of protecting confidentiality deemed essential to the good order of the ecclesial community" (ibid., 34).

Renouncement of the Penal Process

Canon 1724 — §1. In any grade of the trial, renunciation of the instance can be made by the promoter of justice either at the order of or with the consent of the ordinary in light of whose deliberation the process was set in motion.

§2. For validity, the renunciation must be accepted by the accused unless such a one is declared to be absent from the trial.

This is a specific example in the penal process of the general rules stated in canons 1524–1525. The preeminent role of the ordinary is evident from the fact that the promoter of justice cannot renounce the process without the approval of the former, who may himself seek to drop the case.

Last Word for the Defendant

Canon 1725 — In the discussion of the case, whether it be done in writing or orally, the accused always has the right to write or speak last either personally or through an advocate or procurator.

The law's concern to protect the defendant is evident here in this new provision which accords him or her the right to have the last word before the resolution of the case. Formerly, the defender of the bond enjoyed a similar prerogative in marriage cases (*Provida,* Art. 183, §1).

Absolution of the Accused

Canon 1726 — In any grade or stage of the penal trial, if it becomes clearly proven that the offense was not perpetrated by the accused, the judge must declare this in a sentence and absolve the accused, even if it is also proven that the criminal action is terminated.

The basic legal interest in protecting the reputation of an alleged offender accounts for this provision that the alleged offender's innocence be declared as soon as it is clear. This is true even if the statute of limitations for a penal process has run out—without such a declaration there might be a cloud over the reputation of a person accused of an ecclesiastical offense (c. 220).

Appeal by Accused/Promoter

Canon 1727 — §1. The accused can propose an appeal even though dismissed in a sentence solely because the penalty was facultative or because the judge used the power mentioned in cann. 1344 and 1345.

§2. The promoter of justice can appeal whenever it appears that the reparation of scandal or the res

titution of justice has not been provided sufficiently.

Generally speaking, the usual rules on the appeal (cc. 1628–1640) apply in penal cases. This canon, however, contains a couple of points specifically pertinent to these cases.

Paragraph one provides for the situation in which the accused has not been penalized in light of judicial discretion even though he or she was found guilty of committing an ecclesiastical offense. The accused may appeal such a decision in order to obtain a declaration of innocence by a higher court.

Paragraph two indicates that the promoter of justice may appeal a decision that does not seem to protect adequately the interests of the community, e.g., reparation of scandal or restitution of justice. This does not refer simply to a declaration of innocence. It may be a situation in which the guilt of the offender has been established but no penalty has been imposed in accord with judicial discretion.

Pertinent Canons/Self-Incrimination Privilege

Canon 1728 — §1. With due regard for the prescriptions of the canons of this title, unless the nature of the matter is opposed, the canons on trials in general and on ordinary contentious trials must be applied in the penal trial, observing the special norms for cases which refer to the public good.

§2. The accused is not bound to confess the offense and cannot be constrained to take an oath.

The first paragraph has been commented on earlier (see introductory comments to chapter II). Systematically it would probably have been better had paragraph one been placed immediately after canon 1720 since it affects the remaining canons in this part of Book VII.

The right of being protected against self-incrimination accounts for the provision that the alleged offender not be put in the position of having to take an oath or confess the alleged offense (§2).

CHAPTER III
ACTION FOR REPARATION OF DAMAGES
[cc. 1729–1731]

Conditions for the Action for Damages

Canon 1729 — §1. In accord with the norm of can. 1596, an injured party can exercise in the penal trial itself a contentious action for the repairing of damages sustained due to the offense.

§2. The intervention of an injured party, mentioned in §1, is not admitted afterwards if it was not made in the first grade of the penal trial.

§3. The appeal in a case for damages is made in accord with cann. 1628-1640 even if an appeal in the penal trial cannot be made; but if both appeals are proposed, though by different parties, there is to be a single appellate trial with due regard for the prescription of can. 1730.

Deferral of the Action

Canon 1730 — §1. To avoid excessive delays in a penal trial, the judge can postpone a trial for damages until he has rendered a definitive sentence in the penal trial.

§2. The judge who does this must take cognizance of damages after rendering the sentence in a penal trial even if the penal trial is still pending due to a proposed challenge or if the accused has been acquitted for a reason which does not take away the obligation of repairing damage.

Effect of Penal Sentence on the Action

Canon 1731 — Even if the sentence rendered in the penal trial has become a *res iudicata*, in no way

does it establish the right of the injured party unless this party has intervened in accord with can. 1729.

The following brief reflections sufficiently clarify canons 1729–1731. There is a possible separate action for damages suffered as a result of a given offense, prescinding from the penal process already discussed. The general rules on the contentious process are pertinent. While the contentious and penal processes are usually handled simultaneously, the action for damages may be deferred in view of expediting the penal process (c. 1730). The two processes, however, are separate entities, and a decision in the penal process does not exempt the first instance court from its responsibility to deal with the action for damages (cc. 1730, §2; 1731). Furthermore, even if there is no appeal from the decision in the penal process, the allegedly aggrieved party can appeal the decision in the action for damages (c. 1729, §3).

BIBLIOGRAPHY

The bibliographical material provided at the end of Book VI and at the end of Lawrence Wrenn's commentary gives a thorough list of significant references regarding this area of canon law.

Part V
ON THE MANNER OF PROCEDURE IN ADMINISTRATIVE RECOURSE AND THE REMOVAL AND TRANSFER OF PASTORS
[cc. 1732–1752]

Contrary to the rest of Book VII, which deals with the exercise of judicial authority, the last part deals with the exercise of administrative authority in the Church. Before proceeding further, some brief comments on administrative authority are in order.

Administrative authority is that aspect of the power of government which, within the limits of the law, promotes the public good by executing the laws and to some extent interpreting them, if necessary, by supplying for the law and completing it through various decrees and dispositions, by resolving controversies in a disciplinary as distinct from strictly judicial fashion, and by imposing certain penalties.

Perhaps the largest amount of ecclesial decision-making concerns the administrative arena as distinct from the legislative, or lawmaking, sphere or the judicial conflict-resolution sphere. Except for Book VII, most of the revised Code deals with various forms of administrative decision-making in the Church's exercise of its sanctifying, teaching, and pastoral government functions, e.g., the various canons on appointment to office, administration of church property, or the structuring of catechetical ministry.

Since all believers are affected by the decisions of church administrators, it is understandable that this is an area of potentially significant conflict. In other words, the acts of a given administrator may seem to violate someone's rights, e.g., the removal of a pastor, the dismissal of a religious, the suppression of a parish, the imposition of a diocesan tax on a parish. In fact, perhaps the most destructive conflicts within the Church arise precisely because of the exercise of administrative discretion. And to make matters worse, the mechanisms available in the Church to deal with such conflicts have appeared to be quite unsatisfactory.

While canon 1667 of the 1917 Code stated that every right is safeguarded by possible court action to vindicate it, there was also a noteworthy exception to the basic rule. Canon 1601 prohibited complaints against the decrees of ordinaries from being taken to regular tribunals. On the contrary, only the congregations of the Roman Curia were compe-

tent to deal with such administrative recourse. In other words, the 1917 Code's system of hierarchical recourse made it necessary to approach the hierarchical superior of the person against whom the complaint was being made if one wished to challenge some act of administrative discretion, e.g., the bishop if a complaint were against a pastor, the Holy See if a complaint were against a bishop.

This system posed significant difficulties even before Vatican II. It seemed to put ecclesiastical authorities in a favored position, which made it difficult to question their decisions, however unfair, arbitrary, or illegal they might be. The difficulties of access to the Roman congregations for many, if not most, believers further accentuated the perceived inequity of the system. Increasing numbers of canonists felt that if administrators could be made accountable for their actions in open court, not only would the subject be able to vindicate his or her rights, but the superior would be more careful not to violate those rights in the first place.

Official documents, such as the Encyclical *Pacem in Terris* of Pope John XXIII and *Dignitatis Humanae,* (*Declaration on Religious Liberty*) of Vatican II, reflected the increasingly acute contemporary sensitivity to human dignity and the protection of rights.[1] Furthermore, the 1967 Synod of Bishops, in approving principles for the revision of the Code, called for new administrative procedures designed to afford greater protection for the rights of persons affected by administrative action.[2]

Subsequently, the best insights of the American civil law tradition and our canonical heritage were brought to bear upon this issue by a special com-

---

[1] For some thoughtful interdisciplinary reflections on rights in the Church, see J. Coriden, ed., *The Case for Freedom: Human Rights in the Church* (Washington and Cleveland: Corpus, 1969).

[2] *Comm* 1 (1969), 63. English translation by R. Schoenbechler entitled "Principles Which Govern the Revision of the Code of Canon Law" in J. Hite et al., eds., *Readings, Cases, Materials in Canon Law* (Collegeville: Liturgical Press, 1980), 76: "Although it is generally thought that recourses and judicial appeals are sufficiently provided for in the Code of Canon Law according to the demands of justice, it is nevertheless the common opinion of canonists that administrative recourses are still lacking considerably in Church practice and in the administration of justice. Hence the need is everywhere strongly felt to set up in the Church administrative tribunals of various degrees and kinds, so that the defense of one's rights can be taken up in these tribunals according to proper canonical procedure before authorized officials of different ranks. Having accepted this principle, that the rights of the faithful must be safeguarded, then the various functions of ecclesiastical power can be clearly distinguished—namely, the legislative, the administrative and the judicial. Then, too, we can also properly determine what special functions are to be exercised by each arm of the law."

mittee of the Canon Law Society of America (CLSA), which formulated a set of conciliation and arbitration procedures approved by the National Conference of Catholic Bishops (NCCB) in 1969 and ratified by the Holy See in 1971.[3] While conciliation is the preferred and most Christian way of resolving disputes, at times one party to a dispute will neither engage in conciliation nor voluntarily be bound by the decision of an arbitrator. This can pose continuing difficulties which disturb the ecclesial communion and impair the effectiveness of its mission. Hence, the guidelines articulated in the NCCB's *On Due Process* called for a third stage in the resolution of disputes, i.e., the creation of administrative tribunals. Such administrative tribunals were primarily intended to provide binding decisions in disputes. These decisions would not depend on voluntary agreements by the disputing parties that they be bound by arbitrators' decisions.

The development of such administrative tribunals was a major concern of Code Commission efforts to structure administrative recourse in the revised Code. Regrettably, however, during the last stage of the revision process the option of such tribunals was eliminated from the revised Code; there remains only a notably reduced section on administrative recourse, which slightly improves the 1917 Code. Before commenting briefly on this section, some comments on the above-mentioned Commission efforts seem in order.

Initially, there was no separate *coetus* on administrative procedure. In October 1969, however, the *coetus de processibus* voted to establish a special subcommittee to formulate some canons on administrative procedure.[4] Subsequently, Pope Paul VI set up a special papal commission separate from the *coetus*. This papal commission in turn prepared a schema of twenty-six canons, which was submitted to the bishops for their appraisal in April 1972.[5]

After receiving various comments on the 1972 schema, the papal commission worked through 1973 to redraft it accordingly. Nothing further was indicated officially about the progress of the schema for several years. In fact, when the original *De processibus* schema was sent to the bishops for comments in November 1976, the section on adminis-

trative procedure was not included; however, space was left for thirty-nine canons on general norms for administrative procedure (397–435) prior to the last section on the removal and transfer of pastors (436–449). Presumably it was thought unnecessary to send these canons on administrative procedure to the bishops since the earlier schema had been commented upon. Yet that earlier schema had been significantly expanded from twenty-six to thirty-nine canons.

Later, in the summer of 1980, the penultimate version of the revised Code contained twenty-eight canons (1688–1715) on administrative procedure in general. These canons, among others, were to be discussed at the October 1981 plenary session of the Commission. Furthermore, one of the special questions addressed at the plenarium was whether national administrative tribunals should be optional as in the 1980 schema or mandatory as in earlier schemata. The twenty-eight canons were basically endorsed by the Commission, which voted fifty-three to six to leave it up to the discretion of the conferences of bishops whether to establish national administrative tribunals. Unfortunately, during the 1982 papal consultative process, it was apparently decided to drop the detailed references to administrative tribunals contained in the 1980 schema.[6] Since there has been no official report on this process, the reasons for this noteworthy development are unclear.[7] Accordingly, the last part of Book VII contains only a slightly expanded set of canons regarding the traditional hierarchical recourse[8] (cc. 1732–1739) as well as some provisions on the removal and transfer of pastors (cc. 1740–1752). The following reflections deal only with the prior eight canons.

[3]See NCCB, *On Due Process*, rev. ed. (Washington: NCCB, 1972). It might also be noted that the last part of this work discusses at some length the structuring of administrative discretion.

[4]See P. Ciprotti, "De procedura administrativa," *Comm* 2 (1970), 191–195; 4 (1972), 35–38; 5 (1973), 235–243.

[5]See R. Kennedy, "Administrative Law: New Proposed Roman Norms," *CLSAP* 33 (1972), 98–103. See also F. McManus, "Administrative Procedure," *J* 32 (1972), 417–418.

[6]In noting the changes affecting administrative tribunals during the revision process, the author does not want to imply that there are no administrative tribunals in the Church. On the contrary, since 1967 the second section of the Apostolic Signatura has functioned to receive and try complaints against decrees issued by the Roman congregations in answer to complaints made to them. See cc. 1445, §2; 1400, §2.

[7]Although the revised Code does not mention national administrative tribunals, there is no reason why such institutions could not be developed as particular law in the United States or elsewhere. There is no reason to believe that the same kind of legal creativity and bishop-canonist collaboration that led to the development of the aforementioned due process procedures could not be operative once again in structuring appropriate administrative tribunals that might be models for the rest of the Church. The aforementioned procedures certainly influenced the formulation of c. 1733 on conciliation efforts.

[8]The revised Code speaks of "administrative recourse" in this section; that is the term that will be subsequently used in the commentary, although *hierarchical recourse* seems to be a more precise term to describe the thrust of this part of the law.

Section I: RECOURSE AGAINST ADMINISTRATIVE DECREES
[cc. 1732–1739]

Scope of Administrative Recourse

Canon 1732 — What is determined concerning decrees in the canons of this section is also to be applied to all particular administrative acts which are posited in the external forum outside a trial with the exception of those issued by the Roman Pontiff or an ecumenical council.

Before specifying the details of administrative recourse, the legislator indicates what kind of official act is subject to challenge. It is an individual administrative act or an action by a church administrator that affects individual persons or groups and is imposed on them or granted to them in virtue of administrative or executive authority in the external forum. The only exceptions would be an administrative act of the Roman Pontiff or of an ecumenical council; even the acts of their delegates are liable to challenge unless specific papal or conciliar approval of such acts gives them an authority they would not otherwise enjoy.

Although it is not explicitly stated as such, administrative recourse is available in regard to all decrees, rescripts, precepts, dispensations, permissions, and, in general, all administrative acts posited outside of judicial trials.[9]

One cannot challenge a given law as such or its equivalent, but one can challenge its application in a particular case by an administrative decree or its equivalent. For example, one may not challenge the law that permits the bishop to impose a tax on public juridic persons in certain circumstances (c. 1263); however, one may at times challenge the imposition of diocesan assessments on parishes in certain circumstances.

While earlier schemata had contained norms on the issuing of administrative decrees, such norms are not included in this section of the revised Code. One must examine in detail canons 35–58 of Book I to clarify these issues. Any superior examining a recourse petition is bound by the various norms in Book I on the issuing of administrative decrees.[10]

[9]See Book I, title IV on various types of administrative acts (cc. 35–93).

[10]Among the canons in Book I that seem particularly pertinent to the issuance of administrative decrees are the following: cc. 36 and 38 on the interpretation of administrative decrees; c. 50 on consultation of interested parties and the gathering of pertinent data before the issuance of a decree; c. 51 on the expression of written reasons for a decree as a general rule; cc. 54–56 on notification of an administrative decree; and c. 57 on time limits for the issuance of administrative decrees.

Preference for Conciliation

Canon 1733 — §1. It is very desirable that whenever someone feels injured by a decree, there not be a contention between this person and the author of the decree but that care be taken by common counsel to find an equitable solution between them, perhaps through the use of wise persons in mediation and study so that the controversy may be avoided or solved by some suitable means.

§2. The conference of bishops can determine that in every diocese some office or council be permanently established whose function is to find and suggest equitable solutions in accord with norms determined by the same conference; but if the conference has not done this, a bishop can establish a council or office of this kind.

§3. The office or council mentioned in §2 is to be of assistance especially at the time when revocation of a decree has been petitioned in accord with the norm of can. 1734 and the time for recourse has not elapsed; but if recourse has been taken against the decree, the superior who examines the recourse is to urge the one making the recourse and the author of the decree to seek a solution of this type whenever the superior sees hope of a successful outcome.

In the ordinary judicial arena the legislator seeks to avoid formal processes, if possible, since believers should be able to resolve their problems without recourse to such processes (cc. 1446; 1713–1716). A similar concern to minimize instances of formal administrative recourse underlies this canon. It articulates a concern that a fair solution be worked out so as to reconcile parties in conflict without a formal process. It suggests a vehicle for pursuing such conflict-resolution efforts, and it indicates the time when such measures might profitably be employed. The value of fostering informal conciliation procedures is evident also in canon 1734, which requires an aggrieved party normally to request a withdrawal or modification of a problematic administrative decree before pursuing formal administrative recourse.

Through appropriate conciliation efforts, conflicts may be avoided or resolved in some suitable way. Perhaps the superior may voluntarily modify the decree, e.g., changing of a bishop's decision to deny excardination. Perhaps the aggrieved parties may be appropriately compensated, e.g., a more satisfactory arrangement worked out for parishioners whose parish is being suppressed. Perhaps the administrator will be vindicated against an unwarranted charge of arbitrariness in alienating property.

While the canon speaks technically of mediation and the seeking of and suggesting of equitable solutions, the NCCB due process procedures seem appropriate in this context even though they provide for binding arbitration as well as simple mediation in some instances. The present NCCB procedures are optional in dioceses; however, paragraph two of the canon indicates that the NCCB could require the establishment of a conciliation office or council in each diocese to help resolve conflicts. Such an office or council might function in accord with the above-mentioned procedures. Even if the conference of bishops were not to act in this matter, individual bishops would still have a weighty responsibility to provide for fitting conciliation measures since the law views them as principally responsible for seeing to it that conflicts within the Christian community are resolved equitably and justly (c. 1446).

Generally, such an office or council staffed by responsible persons would operate principally in the period between the first move of the one making recourse, i.e., to ask the author of the decree to withdraw or modify it, and the expiration of the time allowed for making administrative recourse (§3). This latter point is somewhat complex and will be clarified in the subsequent discussion of canons 1735 and 1737.

Petition to Withdraw/Modify Decree

Canon 1734 — §1. Before proposing recourse, a person must seek the revocation or emendation of the decree in writing from its author; when such a petition is proposed it is understood that the suspension of the execution of the decree is also being petitioned.

§2. The petition must be made within a peremptory period of ten available days from legal notice of the decree.

§3. The norms of §§1 and 2 are not valid:

1° concerning recourse proposed to the bishop against decrees issued by authorities subject to him;

2° concerning recourse proposed against a decree by which hierarchic recourse is decided unless the decision has been made by the bishop;

3° concerning recourses to be proposed in accord with cann. 57 and 1735.

To preclude precipitous recourse to higher authority, the law normally requires one making recourse first to forward a written request to the author of a challenged decree that it be withdrawn or modified, depending on the seriousness of the complaint. Such a request should not be unduly delayed, lest the efficient functioning of the community be jeopardized. Within ten court days from the notification of the decree, the one making

recourse must make such a request, which also entails a request for the suspension of the decree (§§1–2).

In some circumstances, however, it is not necessary to make such a petition. First of all, it is deemed more expedient to approach the bishop directly if challenging a decree of one of his subordinates. Secondly, unless the bishop himself has ruled on such a challenge, there is no need to approach the authority that has already ruled by decree on one's recourse, e.g., one of the Roman congregations; rather, one may take further recourse against the decree directly to the Signatura. For example, the Sacred Congregation for the Clergy may sustain a bishop's removal of a pastor; if the latter still feels aggrieved, he does not have to ask the Congregation first to change its decision before he approaches the Signatura. Finally, there is no need to seek the withdrawal or modification of a decree in two cases in which it would apparently be superfluous to do so. Canon 57 refers to a superior's failure to act which is tantamount to a rejection of one's petition. Canon 1735 refers to a superior's refusal to withdraw his decree or modify it satisfactorily since this could involve a fruitless multiplication of such petitions (§3).

Time Limits for Recourse

Canon 1735 — If, within thirty days from the time when the petition mentioned in can. 1734 has come to him, the author of the decree communicates a new decree by which he corrects the prior one or decrees that the petition must be rejected, the period for recourse runs from the notice of the new decree; but if within the thirty days he decrees nothing the period runs from the thirtieth day.

This canon specifies the beginning of the time for recourse proper in cases in which there is a petition for withdrawal or modification of a decree. The end of the time for such recourse is clarified in canon 1737, §2, which also specifies when the time for recourse begins if there is no such petition.

In brief, the authority to whom one makes the petition has thirty days to respond. If such a response does not satisfy the one making recourse, then such a one is to make formal administrative recourse within fifteen days from the reception of the response. If the authority fails to respond to the petition within thirty days, the one making recourse likewise has fifteen court days to pursue formal administrative recourse. The law attempts to give the authority in question ample time to reflect on the issues while doing justice to the legitimate claim of the one making recourse for a reasonably expeditious resolution of the matter.

Suspensive Effect of Recourse

Canon 1736 — §1. In those matters in which hierarchic recourse suspends the execution of the decree, the petition also has the same effect as that mentioned in can. 1734.

§2. In other cases, unless within ten days from the time when the petition mentioned in can. 1734 has come to him, the author of the decree decrees that its execution is to be suspended, a suspension can meanwhile be petitioned from his hierarchic superior who can decree it only for grave reasons and always cautiously lest the salvation of souls be injured in some way.

§3. When the execution of the decree has been suspended in accord with §2, if recourse is proposed later, the one who must deal with the recourse in accord with can. 1737, §3 is to determine whether the suspension is to be confirmed or revoked.

§4. If no recourse is proposed against the decree within the stated period, the suspension of the execution effected in the interim in accord with §§1 or 2 ceases by that very fact.

This canon deals with the suspensive effect of recourse against a given decree. In other words, it specifies those situations in which the decree does not take effect until after the recourse is settled.

First of all, there is no taxative listing of instances in which recourse suspends the force of a decree; therefore, one needs to consult the pertinent sections of the revised Code to clarify the implications of paragraph one. For example, canon 1353 indicates that any recourse against a penal decree has suspensive effect; hence, the penalty cannot be enforced until its infliction or declaration is sustained by higher authority. On the contrary, recourse against the removal of a pastor does not have suspensive effect, although a new pastor cannot be named until the bishop's action has been sustained by higher authority (c. 1747, §3).

If a given recourse does not have suspensive effect, the author of the decree may voluntarily suspend it while considering the petition for its withdrawal or modification. The law's concern for the recurrent is evident from the fact that even if the author of the decree refuses to suspend it, the hierarchical superior of the former may be asked to do so. However, the hierarchical superior may suspend the decree on an interim basis only, if serious reasons warrant it and no pastoral harm ensues (§2). If subsequent recourse is pursued, such a suspension needs to be reconfirmed by the hierarchical superior; however, if further recourse is not pursued after the initial request for a withdrawal or modification of the decree, the latter takes effect immediately (§§3–4).

Formalities of Administrative Recourse

Canon 1737 — §1. One who claims to have been injured by a decree can make recourse for any just reason to the hierarchic superior of the one who issued the decree; the recourse can be proposed before the author of the decree, who must immediately transmit it to the competent hierarchic superior.

§2. Recourse must be proposed within a peremptory period of fifteen available days which run from the day on which the decree was published in cases mentioned in can. 1734, §3, but in other cases they run in accord with the norm of can. 1735.

§3. Also in cases in which recourse does not suspend execution of the decree by the law itself, and the suspension was not decreed in accord with can. 1736, §2, nevertheless, the superior can order that the execution be suspended for a grave cause yet cautiously lest the salvation of souls suffer any harm.

The wide options for such recourse are clear from paragraph one; it may be pursued for any just motive. Efforts to restrict such options were rejected during the revision process. As will be seen subsequently, the options for action on the part of the hierarchical superior are equally broad. Although the recourse is directed to the hierarchical superior of the author of the decree, it may be lodged with the latter, who is bound to transmit it immediately to the former. This is somewhat comparable to the appeal process in ordinary trials (cc. 1630–1634).

As noted earlier, the time limit for proposing administrative recourse is fifteen court days from the termination of the initial efforts made to have the decree withdrawn or modified. This time limit is a peremptory one, comparable to the ten-day limit on making the initial petition. In short, if either time limit passes and the aggrieved party fails to act, then such a petition or recourse is technically barred (§2). However, even if the one making recourse has no right to a hearing, the superior may grant one if it is deemed appropriate.

Finally, even if the decree has not been suspended prior to the making of formal recourse, the hierarchical superior may still suspend it for a grave reason while considering the merits of the recourse. This is another indication of the law's concern to balance the legitimate interests of the one making recourse and the broader community (§3).

Right to Counsel

Canon 1738 — The one taking recourse always has a right to use an advocate or a procurator, avoiding useless delays; and indeed an advocate ex officio is to be constituted, if the one taking recourse lacks an advocate and the superior thinks one necessary; but the superior can always command that the one taking recourse be present to be questioned.

A concern to protect the legitimate interests of the one making recourse underlies this provision for an advocate or procurator as the case might be; presumably this is to assist him or her to articulate the nature of the grievance as knowledgeably as possible. This is somewhat comparable to provisions for advocates or procurators in ordinary judicial processes.[11] In fact, if necessary, an advocate may be appointed ex officio to aid the one making recourse, who nevertheless must appear personally during the process if asked to do so. Finally, a concern to expedite the recourse underlies the canon's reference to the avoidance of needless delays that might perhaps result from the appointment of counsel.

Power of Hierarchical Superior

Canon 1739 — **The superior who examines the recourse has the power, as the case requires, not only to confirm the decree or to declare it null but also to rescind, to revoke, or, if it appears to the superior to be more expedient, to amend, subrogate or obrogate the decree.**

The hierarchical superior has the widest possible range of options in deciding the recourse, since such a one has greater administrative authority than the one whose decision is being challenged. Hence, although the hierarchical superior may be significantly distant from the milieu of the original decision, his intervention is apparently not deemed unwarranted by the legislator. Accordingly, the hierarchical superior may confirm the decree or declare it invalid. Furthermore, it may be rescinded, which means it is valid, yet the recurrent has a right to have it withdrawn. The hierarchical superior also may withdraw the challenged decree. Finally, if it seems expedient, the hierarchical superior may amend or change the decree, subrogate it, or substitute another decree in its place, or abrogate it by issuing a decree different from the challenged one.

This canon terminates the first section of part V of Book VII on administrative recourse in general. The following thirteen canons focus on two specialized administrative processes that deal with the removal and transfer of pastors.

[11]See c. 1481 on advocates and procurators in such processes; c. 1701, §2 on the use of a so-called jurisprudent in non-consummation cases; and c. 221, §1 on the basic right to defend and vindicate one's rights in the competent ecclesiastical forum.

BIBLIOGRAPHY

Books

Gordon, I., and Grocholewski, Z., eds. *Documenta Recentiora circa Rem Matrimonialem et Processualem.* 2 vols. Vol. I. Romae: Pontificia Universitas Gregoriana, 1977. 329–331, nn. 2113–2115 (exceptionally fine bibliography).

Grocholewski, Z., ed. *Documenta Recentiora circa Rem Matrimonialem et Processualem.* 2 vols. Vol. II. Romae: Pontificia Universitas Gregoriana, 1980. 303–306, nn. 6389–6390 (exceptionally fine bibliography).

NCCB. *On Due Process.* Rev. ed. (Washington: NCCB, 1972).

Articles

Ciprotti, P. "De procedura administrativa." *Comm* 2 (1970), 191–195; 4 (1972), 35–38; 5 (1973), 235–243.

Dooley, H. "Administrative Procedure." *CLSGBIN* (June 1980), 15–32 (highly recommended).

———."Report on the Schema Canonum de Procedura Administrativa" (unpublished).

Gordon, I. "De iustitia administrativa Ecclesiastica." *P* 61 (1972), 251–378.

Kennedy, R. "Administrative Law: New Proposed Roman Norms." *CLSAP* 33 (1972), 98–103.

McManus, F. "Administrative Procedure." *J* 32 (1972), 417–418.

Mahony, R. "Due Process Within the National Conference of Catholic Bishops." *CLSAP* 41 (1979), 19–23.

Malloy, T. "The Theological Foundation of Due Process." Ibid., 60–67.

———."Administrative Recourse in the Proposed Code of Canon Law." *CLSAP* 44 (1982), 263–273.

Section II: PROCEDURE IN REMOVAL AND TRANSFER OF PASTORS
[cc. 1740–1752]

An ecclesiastical office may be lost in six ways according to canon 184, §1. Two of these ways are by the removal and transfer of pastors. In two chapters, the final thirteen canons of Book VII outline two distinct administrative procedures for the removal and transfer of pastors. Historically the difference between the two is that *removal* results from the inability of the pastor to minister, whereas *transfer* implies that a pastor ministering well in one place is needed elsewhere. While maintaining this distinction, the present discipline has evolved, with significant refinements, from the first attempt at universal legislation for administrative removal procedures which was enacted by the decree *Maxima cura* of 1910.[1]

Pastoral Stability Reviewed

Through several centuries prior to 1910, the notion of pastoral stability had gained favor and had become a time-honored ecclesiastical concept. Within what was formerly known as the benefice system, every permanently established office had a stable source of revenue. The officeholder had a right to the income for his adequate support in return for his fulfillment of pastoral duties. Gradually the notion of the irremovability of the source of income from the office was applied to the officeholder. Thus the *irremovable* pastor enjoyed stability in office. To remove a pastor from his benefice, a bishop normally was required to initiate a judicial process.[2]

By the time of Vatican Council I (1869–1870), some bishops were requesting administrative procedures to expedite the removal and transfer of pastors. Forty years later, responding to what it stated was an urgent need, *Maxima cura* somewhat mitigated the notion of pastoral stability. Emphasizing that stability in the pastoral office was subservient to the principle of *salus animarum* ("the salvation of souls"), the decree allowed bishops to remove pastors administratively for certain verified reasons. The prescriptions of the decree were largely subsumed into the 1917 Code with few modifications.

In its provisions for administrative removal, *Maxima cura* made no distinction between irremovable and removable pastors. Neither did the decree provide norms for administrative transfer. The 1917 Code, however, did both. Canon 454, §2 of the 1917 Code distinguished between irremovable and removable pastors, and this distinction was reflected in the administrative processes contained in titles XXVII–XXVIII of Book IV. While both classes of pastors could be removed, it was more difficult to remove an irremovable pastor. Furthermore, for the first time in universal legislation, norms on the purely administrative transfer of removable pastors were provided in title XXIX. Reflecting the greater stability enjoyed by an irremovable pastor, canon 2163, §1 of the former Code stated that a special faculty was needed from the Holy See to transfer an unwilling irremovable pastor. Thus the 1917 Code provided these three administrative procedures: removal of irremovable pastors; removal of removable pastors; and transfer of removable pastors.

Legal Changes Introduced by Vatican II

Several principles affirmed by Vatican II led to legal changes in these administrative procedures. Two of these principles concerned pastoral stability and episcopal freedom in appointing pastors.[3] The conciliar decree *Christus Dominus* taught that the pastoral office is essentially a spiritual ministry to people, thereby departing somewhat from the former conception of a pastor as a titular of a benefice which was permanently held for his security and material sustenance. While stability in office was still normative, *Christus Dominus* 31 nuanced this principle by stating that each pastor should enjoy that degree of stability which the good of souls requires. In other words, the exercise of the pastoral office should be stable but not permanent.

Another conciliar principle, arising from the Council's effort to enhance the episcopal office, indicated that the diocesan bishop must have the requisite freedom to make the best possible appointments of pastors. Furthermore, the bishop should be enabled to provide more easily for the re-

---

[1]Sacred Consistorial Congregation, *Maxima cura*, Aug. 20, 1910, *AAS* 2 (1910), 636–648. For a commentary on the decree, see J. Parizek, "Canonical Changes of Procedures in the Administrative Removal and Transfer of Pastors since Maxima cura" (J.C.L. thesis, Catholic University of America, 1978) 12–28.

[2]M. Connor, *Administrative Removal of Pastors* (Washington, D.C.: *CanLawStud*, 1937), 9, 16.

[3]W. Onclin, "Commentary" in *The Decree on the Pastoral Office of Bishops in the Church* (New York: Paulist Press, 1967), 66.

placing or removing of pastors.[4] To implement this principle, *Christus Dominus* 31 abrogated the distinction between irremovable and removable pastors. With all pastors thereby rendered movable, the procedures for their removal and transfer were simplified appropriately. The document implementing these simplified legal procedures was the *motu proprio Ecclesiae sanctae,* which was to be employed in conjunction with the 1917 Code until the latter's definitive revision.

The principal source of this section of the revised law on removal of pastors is the 1917 Code, which subsumed many of the provisions of *Maxima cura.* The 1983 Code, however, reflects the emendations of *Ecclesiae sanctae* I, 20, and further refinements in the procedures. The revised text reveals some no-

[4]Some authors find the canonical terms *removal* and *transfer* too negative. One writer suggests a concept of "rotation," whereby the bishop freely rotates his priests according to the needs of the local church. This notion of "rotation" emphasizes the essential equality of offices; see F. Romita, "De parochorum amotione, translatione, et renuntiatione juxta Vaticanum II," *ME* 94 (1969), 441. Limited terms of office would facilitate the concept of "rotation"; see J. Janicki, "Limited Term of Office and Retirement," *CLSAP* (1979), 47.

table developments over the 1917 Code. In general, the 1983 Code implements the principle of subsidiarity by facilitating the bishop's exercise of his pastoral office, and it also provides appropriate administrative measures to protect subjective rights against the non-accountable exercise of authority. Specifically, the 1983 Code favors a stability in the pastoral office which is neither determined by some right of the pastor nor dependent upon the arbitrary will of the bishop. Thus the text allows greater episcopal discretion in discerning due cause for removal and transfer. Yet it seeks to prevent arbitrary action by its procedural safeguards to insure the protection of the rights of all concerned: the bishop, the pastor, and the parishioners. As in the past, hierarchical recourse can be lodged against the administrative decree of removal or transfer.

The following discussion of the revised legislation notes these developments. Basically the exposition of the text proceeds canon by canon and includes the following topics: reasons for removal; procedure for the removal of pastors; procedure for the transfer of pastors; and recourse against decrees of removal and transfer.

CANONS AND COMMENTARY

CHAPTER I
THE MANNER OF PROCEDURE IN REMOVING PASTORS
[cc. 1740–1747]

General Reason for Removal of Pastors

Canon 1740 — **When the ministry of any pastor has become detrimental or at least ineffective for any reason, even through no grave fault of his own, he can be removed from the parish by the diocesan bishop.**

In general terms, for a grave reason a pastor can be removed from office, whether conferred for a definite or indefinite term, by a legitimate decree issued by the competent authority (cf. cc. 192–193). The competent authority for removal is the diocesan bishop and all those equivalent to him in law except the vicar general and episcopal vicar, unless specially mandated (cf. c. 134, §3). In the canons which follow, the focus is on the office of pastor and the subject of the removal action is limited to a pastor, since other canons govern the removal of a parochial vicar (c. 552), a rector (c. 563), and a chaplain (c. 572). The removal procedure succinctly described in canons 1740–1752 is the same for all pastors except those who are members of a religious

institute or of a society of apostolic life, who are removed from office in accord with canon 682, §2 (c. 1742, §2).

Although the law enhances episcopal discretion in determining that the pastor's ministry has become harmful or ineffective, the bishop will find basic criteria for such decisions in the law on pastors, particularly those canons which cite their essential qualities and main duties (e.g., cc. 519, 521, 528–530). In light of these criteria a prudential judgment on pastoral ineffectiveness may be formed. Pastoral competence, however, is relative to the circumstances of the parish: the characteristics of its parishioners, its size and types of programs, and its location. The unique circumstances of different parishes suggest that specific expectations of ministry be mutually understood by the bishop, pastor, and parishioners.[5]

While there is a certain negative connotation to removal, the conciliar principle underlying this procedure is expressed positively: that the bishop may provide more suitably for the care of souls. Thus canon 1740 allows for a pastor's removal even when

[5]In dioceses where the local church has defined diocesan purposes and translated those purposes into concrete and measurable parish goals, such goals may be helpful in determining pastoral effectiveness; see Janicki, "Limited Term," 47.

he is not at fault for his harmful or ineffective ministry.

Examples of Reasons for Removal

Canon 1741 — The reasons for which a pastor can be legitimately removed from his parish are especially the following:

1° a way of acting which is gravely detrimental or disturbing to the ecclesial community;

2° incompetence or a permanent infirmity of mind or body which renders a pastor incapable of performing his duties in a useful way;

3° loss of good reputation among upright and good parishoners or aversion to the pastor which are foreseen as not ceasing in a short time;

4° grave neglect or violation of parochial duties which persist after a warning;

5° poor administration of temporal affairs with grave damage to the Church whenever this problem cannot be remedied in any other way.

In continuity with the former law, canon 1741 indicates generically five reasons for which a pastor may be removed. This list of reasons considerably reworks the five listed in the 1917 Code, namely: (1) "imperitia" (incompetence) and infirmity; (2) "odium" (hostility) toward the pastor; (3) loss of reputation; (4) probable occult crime; and (5) poor administration (*CIC* 2147, §2). The 1983 text retains four of the former examples, adds two new examples, and omits one. Of the two added, disruption of ecclesial communion is entirely new. The other, grave neglect of pastoral duties, was drawn from canons 2182–2185 of the 1917 Code, which provided a distinct procedure for this problem. The factor of a probable occult crime was omitted since all reasons for removal must be manifestly provable.[6]

Like canon 2147, §2 of the former Code, the five reasons stated here form an illustrative, not an extensive list. It is noteworthy, however, that canon 1741 omits a phrase contained in *Ecclesiae sanctae* I, 20, 1, whereby the bishop could remove a pastor "for any of the reasons recognized by law, or for any other similar reason according to the judgment of the bishop." A reason other than those listed[7]

---

[6]Pontificia Commissio Codici Iuris Canonici Recognoscendo, *Schema Canonum de Modo Procedendi pro Tutela Iurium seu De Processibus* (Typis Polyglottis Vaticanis, 1976), *Praenotanda*, n. 73, p. xix.

[7]An example of an insufficient reason for removal is that of a pastor's simply attaining the age of seventy-five. Although c. 538, §3 exhorts a pastor to resign voluntarily at age seventy-five, the 1981 *Relatio* of the Code Commission indicates that the failure to resign at age seventy-five in itself is not sufficient reason for removal; see G. Lobina, "Procedura per la remozione dei parroci," *ME* 105 (1980), 152–153. An example of "other similar reasons" for a pastor's removal may be his resistance to conciliar reforms in the liturgy or to the need for parishes to be united; see Romita, "De parochorum," 441.

may be cited by the bishop, but it should be similarly grave and provable and ultimately lead to a harmful or ineffective ministry.

The bishop is to act only after discerning a serious problem affecting the pastoral ministry. Thus canon 1740 presupposes a prior investigation by the bishop about the existence of the reason for removal (c. 1742, §1). Prior to invoking the canonical process, however, the bishop, in charity but with firmness, is to notify the pastor of his deficiencies. Indeed, the episcopal responsibility to foresee potential problems and provide remedial assistance should be emphasized. To this end, the assistance of the dean (vicar forane) (c. 555) is valuable in preventing problems before a pastor's ministry becomes harmful.

Disruption of Ecclesial Communion

This first cause, an innovation not found in canon 2147, §2 of the 1917 Code, recalls a frequent conciliar emphasis on the Church as a communion. Ecclesial communion exists between the bishop and his priests and between pastors and their parishioners. The bishop strives to appoint a suitable pastor to further the mission of the Church and promote the communion which exists. When ecclesial communion is gravely harmed by the pastor's actions, the mission of the Church which he is ordained to serve is likewise hindered, thereby rendering his ministry harmful. Ecclesial communion may be harmed not only by the pastor's actions, but also by his failure to act, such as not exercising necessary leadership. Failure to achieve and sustain ecclesial communion, however, more likely is included in the fourth reason discussed later.

Incompetence or Permanent Infirmity

"Imperitia" (literally, ignorance or inexperience)[8] and permanent infirmity are repeated as reasons for removal (*CIC* 2147, §2). A pastor's pervasive ignorance in several aspects of ministry would seldom occur; more likely a pastor may be knowledgeable but inept in applying his knowledge practically. Chronic inexperience is likewise possible, even if infrequent. Thus "imperitia" may be better termed "incompetence," which may be evident in one or more of the threefold aspects of the pastoral office: teaching, sanctifying, and governing. Prevalent ineffectiveness in these areas would constitute "imperitia" by today's standards.

Incompetence may be relative or absolute. Relative incompetence means that the pastor's aptitude is inadequate when measured in light of those quali-

---

[8]A correct understanding of "imperitia" is facilitated by reference to commentators on *CIC* 2147, §2. Generally these commentators argued that the term "imperitia" encompasses both ignorance and inexperience; see Parizek, "Canonical Changes," 45, who cites Connor and other authors.

ties requisite for a particular parish. A pastor who is incompetent in one parish may be competent in a different parish. When the incompetence is relative, a transfer would better respect the pastor's human and priestly dignity. In cases in which incompetence is evident, it is the bishop's responsibility to provide remedial assistance. However, if the incompetence perdures and seems absolute, the bishop may remove the pastor, who may still be eligible for an office other than a pastorate.

Another condition which may render a pastor incapable of performing his duties is a permanent infirmity of mind or body. Since this can involve many different types of illnesses and disabilities, it is not useful to attempt a listing. The assessment of the degree of infirmity and the incurability of illness properly belongs to experts, although the law does not require expert diagnosis or prognosis. These judgments pertain to the bishop and his counselors. Commentators on the 1917 Code suggested that an infirmity of a year's duration would be considered permanent. Their suggestion, however, was made in the context of irremovable pastors, who no longer exist. Since the canon does not specify any length of time, the bishop may decide what constitutes a permanent infirmity.

The 1917 Code explicitly permitted the bishop to assign a parochial assistant when the pastor was incompetent or infirm (*CIC* 2147, §2). While canon 1741 makes no such reference, canon 539 calls for the bishop to assign a parochial administrator to provide for the care of the parish when the pastor is incapacitated.[9] Any seriously debilitating condition of mind or body which is irremediable necessitates removal of the pastor. A bishop can responsibly initiate a removal action when the pastor has failed to resign voluntarily.

Loss of Reputation and Aversion to the Pastor

Like *imperitia,* loss of good reputation and aversion to the pastor are relative to the values and temperament of the parishioners. Canon 2147, §2 of the 1917 Code exemplified three ways in which the pastor could lose his reputation; a lifestyle incompatible with the exigencies of the pastoral office; a recent detection of an earlier crime; and scandalous behavior by members of the pastor's household. While these serious problems are indicative of ways in which a good reputation may be ruined, a comprehensive list of such problems is impossible. The issue is one of a true loss of reputation in the opinion of a significant number of sincere and good parishioners. Since each reason for removal is connected with a serious dysfunction in a pastor's

ministry, the bishop is carefully to assess the fruits of his ministry and not simply consider what is rumored about a pastor.

Whereas the 1917 Code listed "odium," or hatred, of the pastor as a reason for removal, the 1983 text cites "aversion." While both terms mean an intense dislike, aversion further connotes a turning away from the object disliked. However, this textual change does not seem significant. Again, the law neither defines the term nor specifies its necessary duration. The concern, as always, is the effect of the aversion on the pastor's ministry. The existence of aversion may be manifested in various ways, e.g., the parishioners' avoidance of the pastor's multifaceted ministry, frequent protests against him, and significant declines in moral and financial support of the parish.

Whether the issue is the pastor's loss of his good reputation or the people's aversion to him, the bishop will consider the catholicity of the critics. Complaints from parishioners who sincerely appreciate the nature of the Church's mission carry more weight than those of persons not so attuned. In these times of hotly contested issues with both moral and political overtones, such as abortion, divorce, nuclear armaments, and social justice, some parishioners may oppose a pastor's stances. They may lessen their esteem for him when in fact he is promoting the teachings and practices of the Church. In any case, it is left to the bishop's discretion to verify both the loss of a good reputation and aversion as well as to determine how long either can be tolerated. The text indicates that if either the loss of a good reputation or aversion to the pastor would dissipate within a short time, there is no reason for removal. Commentators on the former law generally held that if either perdured for the greater part of a year, there is reason for removal. Ultimately, the bishop determines when to act in these cases.

Grave Neglect or Violation of Parish Duties

This fourth reason was not contained in the illustrative list of canon 2147 of the 1917 Code; rather, it was treated separately in canons 2182–2185 of title XXXII. Commentators on the 1917 Code were divided in their opinions whether title XXXII was of a penal or merely administrative nature. The 1983 text makes grave neglect of pastoral duties a reason for administrative removal.

Canon 2182 of the 1917 Code expressly referred to other canons which indicated the chief duties of a pastor. By referring to these canons, the bishop had some basic criteria for judging whether or not there was a reason for removal. Since canon 1741 makes no such reference, one must consider the many duties of pastors which are stated throughout the 1983 Code. Some basic obligations are given in

---

[9]In instances of recourse against a decree of removal due to incompetence or infirmity, the jurisprudence of the Signatura takes into account whether any attempt was made to assist the pastor by assigning an assistant; see Lobina, "Procedura," 152.

canons 528–530 and 535, but others appear, for example, in Books III and IV, which treat the teaching and sanctifying ministries of the Church. The bishop is to determine when a pastor is gravely negligent in fulfilling these duties.[10]

Title XXXII of the 1917 Code directed the bishop to act in progressively more vigorous steps. Initially the bishop would admonish the negligent pastor, reminding him of his duties and informing him of what penalties might befall him. If the pastor did not correct his behavior, the bishop next could inflict a penalty. Finally, if he continued to be negligent, the pastor would be removed. Incorporating grave pastoral negligence as a reason for removal in the revised text, the 1983 Code retains the first step, that of warning the pastor. This is the only reason of the five listed in canon 1741 that explicitly makes mention of admonishing the pastor; however, when other reasons are present, a warning prior to initiating a removal process is certainly appropriate. Above and beyond giving cause for removal, serious violations and neglect of pastoral duties which persist after a warning may also render the pastor subject to penalties.[11]

Poor Administration of Temporal Affairs

Historically, church legislators have shown great concern for the rightful administration of temporalities. Like the 1917 Code, the revised text requires that the pastor's poor administration had to have caused grave damage to the Church before it can constitute a reason for removal. Assuming no crime had been committed, the 1917 Code explicitly offered as a possible remedy the withdrawal of temporal administration from the pastor. However, if neither that nor any other remedy was possible, removal was indicated despite the pastor's effectiveness in exercising the more spiritual aspects of his ministry. Remedial action today might take the form of studies in administration or, as in earlier times, withdrawing the administration of temporal affairs from the pastor. It is noteworthy that canon 537 states that each parish should have a finance council to assist the pastor in the administration of parish goods. With this assistance available, this reason for removal seemingly would occur only rarely. Removal is possible, however, when no remedy is available for the inept administration of temporalities.

Procedure for the Removal of Pastors

Preliminary Remarks

Having examined the illustrative listing of reasons for the removal of pastors, consideration now is given to the procedure for such removal. Certain preliminaries should be noted, however. In the 1917 Code five canons immediately preceded the administrative procedures for removal and transfer. Canons 2142–2146 contained preliminary instructions to be observed to insure the validity of the process undertaken. These five canons indicated that a notary was to keep a written record, that admonitions were to precede any decree, that an oath of secrecy was to be observed by the bishop and his counselors, that witnesses could be admitted, and that recourse could be lodged against the final decree. In keeping with the legislator's desire to avoid repetition, these preliminary instructions do not appear immediately prior to the text now being considered. Reference must be made, therefore, to the norms on issuing administrative decrees, which are contained in Book I of the 1983 law, canons 35–58. These preliminary instructions reflect concretely what is the paramount rubric: the principles of canonical equity and *salus animarum* ("the salvation of souls") govern these administrative procedures. Thus due care will be taken in every phase to respect the legal rights of all.

Prior to examining the revised law, a brief comparison of the steps of the process outlined in the 1983 Code with those of the 1917 text may be helpful. Earlier it was stated that the 1917 Code provided a procedure for removing irremovable pastors which was somewhat lengthier than the process for removable pastors. This greater complexity was due to the irremovable pastor's right to lodge recourse with his bishop against a first decree of removal (*CIC* 2153), requiring the bishop to deliberate further. Since there is no longer this distinction of pastors, the 1983 Code specifies only one procedure, which essentially is a revision of the simpler process of the 1917 Code for removable pastors. There the steps consisted of the bishop's discerning a reason for the pastor's removal; communicating this reason to him and inviting his resignation; receiving the pastor's rebuttal, if any; discussing the matter with two examiners; renewing his invitation to the pastor to resign; decreeing his removal and making provision for the removed pastor. Canons 1740–1747 of the revised law indicate the following steps: the bishop's discussing the reason for removal with two pastors prior to his persuading the pastor to resign; either repeating the invitation to resign when the pastor has not responded, or decreeing his removal when the pastor offers no rebuttal; inviting the pastor to submit his response, while affording him the right to inspect the acts;

[10] For a brief discussion of pastoral obligations, see B. Griffin, "The Pastor's Role and Its Implications for Seminaries," in *Code, Community, Ministry,* J. Provost, ed. (Washington: CLSA, 1983), 75–80.

[11] For example, penalties may be inflicted on one who incites the faithful to disobedience toward the bishop (c. 1373), alienates ecclesiastical goods without the required permission (c. 1377), or abuses an ecclesiastical office (c. 1389).

discussing the issue with the same two pastors as before; decreeing the pastor's removal and making a suitable provision for him. While the simpler procedure of the 1917 Code and the procedure of the 1983 Code are similar, the 1983 legislation requires the bishop to seek counsel twice—prior to seeking the pastor's resignation and after the pastor has offered his rebuttal, if any. The revised procedure allows the pastor to inspect the acts, which is a noteworthy innovation. Like the former law, for good cause the pastor may have recourse against a decree of removal to the Holy See.

Discussion Before Request for Resignation

Canon 1742 — §1. If after an inquiry has been conducted, it is proven that a cause mentioned in can. 1740 is present, the bishop is to discuss the matter with two pastors from the group permanently selected for this by the presbyteral council after their being proposed by the bishop; but if subsequently he decides that the removal must take place, he is paternally to persuade the pastor to resign the pastorate within a period of fifteen days, after he has explained, for validity, the reason and the arguments for removal.

§2. The prescription of can. 682, §2 is to be observed concerning pastors who are members of a religious institute or a society of apostolic life.

As indicated earlier, the bishop makes a preliminary judgment that a reason for removal is present, whether it be one of those in the illustrative listing of canon 1741 or some other similar reason. In doing so and before invoking the canonical process, the bishop may consult with the appropriate dean (vicar forane), who is to be solicitous that priests in his district fulfill their duties.[12] To initiate the removal process, however, the bishop must discuss the matter with two pastors drawn from the committee indicated. The formation and duties of this committee are not mentioned, however, in the law on presbyteral councils (cc. 495–502). Under the former law it was argued by commentators that this consultation was necessary for the validity of the process. Appealing to *Maxima cura,* which required the consent of the counselors for valid action, they cited canon 105 of the 1917 Code, which is substantially repeated in canon 127. Canon 127, §2, 2°, states that if counsel is required, the act of the superior is invalid if the superior did not hear the designated counselors. While canon 1742 specifies for validity only that the bishop explain the reason and the arguments when inviting the pastor to resign, more explicit prescriptions for valid action are given in canon 1745, including a discussion of

the matter with the same two pastors. The bishop will prudently insure the validity of the entire process by consulting with the two pastors in the initial stages of the removal procedure. Although the exact content of the discussion is not indicated in the canon, they are to verify the reason for removal and its seriousness (*CIC* 2148).

Following this discussion, the bishop explains the reasons for removal and reveals the evidence to the pastor concerned. Whereas the former canon (*CIC* 2148, §1) allowed the ordinary to invite the pastor to resign either orally or in writing, the revised canon does not specify a particular approach. Prudently the bishop will preserve a record of both the consultation and the invitation to resign with its underlying reasons, especially in light of the pastor's right to inspect the acts of the case (c. 1745, 1°) and the possibility of his taking recourse against a decree of removal. Moreover, any forthcoming decree must indicate, at least summarily, the motives for the removal according to canon 51.

Like the former law, only those "sui compos" can legitimately resign from office for a serious reason (c. 187). Canon 2148, §1 of the 1917 Code permitted the omission of the invitation when the pastor was suffering from a mental infirmity; under the revised law, the bishop is to exercise great care in persuading a mentally infirm pastor to resign.

When the bishop initially persuades the pastor to resign, he advises the pastor to respond within fifteen days. The specification of the number of days for this response is an improvement over the former law, which simply left the determination of "a certain time" to the bishop.

Resignation: One Possible Response

Canon 1743 — A resignation by a pastor can be submitted not only purely and simply but also conditionally provided that this can be legitimately accepted by the bishop and is actually accepted.

This canon addresses the first of several possible stances a pastor can take, namely, the resignation of his office. Other stances, to be treated later, are the pastor's lack of response, his refusal to resign without giving any reasons, and his refusal accompanied by his refutations of the bishop's argument. The law specifies the different responses that a bishop can make if he wishes to pursue the removal.

Canon 189 states how a resignation is made without, however, mentioning conditional resignation. Canon 1743 allows a conditional resignation, but it provides no indication of what constitutes a legitimate condition. Some indications of possible conditions may be clarified from the former law. Canon 2150, §2 of the 1917 Code allowed the pastor to give another less odious or less serious reason for resigning, provided it was true and honest. The example given was that of "complying with the wish-

---

[12]The law does not mention the previous hearing of the dean as did *mp ES,* I, 19, 2; but in light of the duties of the deans this may be appropriate (c. 555).

es of the ordinary." This may be one example of a legitimate condition as stated in canon 1743. Another condition may be the pastor's receiving another office, provided he has the requisite health and ability (c. 1746). It should be noted, however, that the promise of an office has no juridical effect (c. 153, §3). Other conditions may be allowing an infirm pastor to continue occupying the parochial residence (c. 1747, §2) or giving the resigning pastor a certain pension (c. 1746).

The former law recommended more favorable consideration for the pastor who promptly resigned following the bishop's invitation (*CIC* 2154). Although this recommendation is omitted in the revised law, the bishop may still extend such consideration in similar circumstances.

No Response: A Second Option

Canon 1744 — §1. If the pastor has not answered within the aforementioned time period the bishop is to repeat the invitation extending the available time for response.

§2. If the bishop has the proof that the pastor has received the second invitation but has not responded although not hindered by any impediment or if the pastor refuses to resign giving no reasons, the bishop is to issue the decree of removal.

If the pastor does not respond, either he may not have received the invitation or he was impeded from responding to it within the fifteen days prescribed. Canon 1744, §1 provides for both situations, and in either case the pastor has fifteen days to respond—starting from the day when he receives his letter or when he is able to read it. When an invitation to resign is made orally, it is important that a legal document be filed, indicating that the pastor has been notified. The problem of a pastor's evading the invitation to resign is not mentioned. In the former law, a pastor who evaded an admonition was regarded as warned (*CIC* 2143, §3). Similarly, the Holy See ruled that a pastor who evaded his invitation to resign was to be considered as notified.[13] In continuity with the former law, then, any pastor who evades the invitation to resign should be considered as legitimately invited.

When a pastor could have responded, but did not, or when he refuses to resign without offering his reasons, the bishop issues the decree of removal, observing the appropriate norms of canons 35–58.

Opposition to Removal: A Third Option

Canon 1745 — But if the pastor opposes the cause alleged for removal and its reasons, alleging reasons which appear insufficient to the bishop, in order for the latter to act validly, he is to:

[13]CodCom, Nov. 24, 1920, *AAS* 12 (1920); 577; see also c. 1510.

1° invite the pastor to organize his challenges to removal in a written report, having inspected the acts, and also to offer proofs to the contrary, if he has any;

2° consider the matter with the same pastors mentioned in can. 1742, §1 unless others must be designated due to their inability, after he has completed the instruction if necessary;

3° finally determine whether or not the pastor must be removed and promptly issue a decree on the matter.

Of all canons in this section, canon 1745 shows how a bishop can act much more expeditiously in the removal process than in the former law. It is a substantial reworking and simplification of the former law, due especially to the elimination of any distinction between irremovable and removable pastors. Yet the bishop is legally bound to observe canon 1745 or else he acts invalidly.

A pastor may oppose his removal for the reason indicated and offer his rebuttal. Certainly the bishop must indicate specific motives for removal, since vague allegations would render the pastor's defense virtually impossible. If the pastor's opposition seems sufficient to nullify the alleged reason for removal, the bishop may relent and cease the proceedings, preserving a record of his action. But if the pastor's reasons seem insufficient, the bishop is bound to follow the provisions of canon 1745 for valid action.

In the first of the three steps indicated, there is an innovation of merit: the right of the pastor to inspect the acts of the case. This affords a greater measure of due process and guards against any arbitrary action by the bishop, both of which are particularly important values in light of the more expeditious process in the revised law. It also underscores the necessity of preserving written records of the earlier stages of the process: the paternal invitation to resign, including the bishop's reasons for such action; the nature of the discussion with the two pastors; and any evidence supporting the reason for removal.

Next, the bishop must allow sufficient time for the pastor to prepare his written rebuttal, including the proofs of his case. No time frame is indicated, but the bishop is to proceed expeditiously in accord with his mandate to provide for the care of souls. Some of the reasons listed in canon 1741 yield to contrary proof more easily than others. For example, it may be easier to disprove a permanent infirmity by expert testimony than to disprove the loss of a good reputation. Whatever the indicated reason, the pastor may produce proofs to the contrary. Among his proofs may be witnesses introduced in his defense. The 1917 Code specifically allowed for the admission of witnesses unless the bishop judged that such an action was solely a delaying tactic (*CIC* 2145). When a pastor produces witnesses, their statements are to be committed to writing since the canon refers to a pastor's written rebuttal.

In the second step of canon 1745, the bishop may investigate the matter further, in light of the pastor's opposition and proofs. After the examination has been completed, the bishop consults with the same two pastors involved in the preliminary discussion. Finally, he decides whether or not to remove the pastor and issues an appropriate decree.

Provision Following Removal

Canon 1746 — **When the pastor has been removed, the bishop is to provide for him through an assignment to another office, if he is suitable for this, or through a pension, as the case requires and circumstances permit.**

Formerly, the bishop was obliged to decide on the provision he would make for the removed pastor in consultation with two examiners or consultors. Canon 1746 neither urges nor prevents this further discussion. Based upon the facts and circumstances clarified during the removal proceedings, the bishop decides whether to assign the removed pastor to another office or to give him a pension. Whatever provision the bishop intends may be communicated to the pastor earlier in the process, e.g., when persuading the pastor to resign. A pastor's opposition to removal may be due more to his anxiety regarding his uncertain future rather than to the inadequacy of the reason for removal.

As explained earlier, ineffective or harmful ministry in one parochial office does not preclude the pastor's effectiveness in another office, even another parochial one, provided that he has the proper qualifications. Indeed, the former law allowed the ordinary to transfer a removed pastor to another parish, an option still made possible in canon 1746. If it is not possible or prudent to assign the removed pastor to another office, canon 195 obliges the bishop to provide for his subsistence by means of a pension. This would seem to be a matter of justice, not charity (c. 281). Whether the priest is assigned a new office or is pensioned after his removal, the bishop is to settle the provision as soon as possible, as had been prescribed in canon 2155 of the 1917 Code.

Effects of the Removal

Canon 1747 — **§1. The removed pastor must abstain from exercising the office of pastor, vacate the rectory immediately, and hand over all that pertains to the parish to the one to whom the bishop shall entrust the parish.**

§2. If there is question of a sick pastor who cannot be transferred elsewhere from the rectory without inconvenience, the bishop is to leave the rectory even to his exclusive use while this need lasts.

§3. While recourse is pending against the decree of removal, the bishop cannot name a new pastor but meanwhile is to provide a parish administrator.

When no recourse is taken against the decree of removal, it has several effects. When it has been made known to the pastor, the ecclesiastical office is lost (c. 184, §1), and the removed pastor's ordinary power ceases (c. 143, §1). Hence the removed pastor must refrain from the exercise of his pastoral office to prevent any confusion regarding the validity of any of his actions subsequent to his removal. The vacant office should be filled in timely fashion, since the provision of an office for the care of souls may not be deferred without a serious reason (c. 151). Although unable to exercise the duties and responsibilities of his office validly, a removed pastor might attempt illegitimately to continue possessing it. The office, however, may be conferred on another priest as long as the letter of appointment contains the bishop's declaration that the possession by the former pastor is illegitimate (c. 154).

The removed pastor is to hand over all that pertains to the parish and relinquish the parochial residence as soon as possible. The bishop however, may allow an infirm pastor continued occupancy of the parochial residence. Canon 1747, §2 speaks of the possibility of his exclusive use of the residence if necessary, but otherwise the bishop might allow only those portions of the residence required for the infirm priest's needs; the new pastor could occupy the remainder of the residence.

Canon 1747, §3 repeats canon 2146, §3 of the 1917 Code, yet does so more clearly. The bishop is reminded of his obligation to provide for the care of the parish while avoiding invalid action. If the pastor has taken recourse against his removal within the prescribed fifteen days, the office is not vacant while his recourse is pending. If the bishop attempts to confer the office of pastor on another priest during the recourse, the provision is invalid (c. 153, §1). If recourse is pending, a parochial administrator is to be named, but no new pastor is to be appointed until the recourse is resolved.

CHAPTER II
THE MANNER OF PROCEDURE IN
TRANSFERRING PASTORS
[cc. 1748–1752]

Historically, pastors were transferred for reasons different from those for removing them. Whereas removal followed the judgment that a pastor's ministry was ineffective or harmful, a transfer meant that a pastor was serving his parish well but that his service was needed elsewhere. Canon 1748, in continuity with the corresponding canon of the 1917 Code (*CIC* 2162), recognizes the useful ministry of the pastor. While the latter spoke only of the good of souls as a motive for transfer, canon 1748 also refers to the necessity or utility of the Church. This innovation provides the bishop with a broader basis on which to discern a transfer. This is in accord with the conciliar principle that the bishop have the freedom to assign offices more expeditiously. There is also another innovation of merit in canon 1748: the transfer may be either to another parish or to some other office. The former law provided only for a transfer from one parish to another.

Another notable legal change in the matter of transferring pastors was necessitated by the dissociation of a pastoral office from the notion of a benefice. Formerly, the beneficed cleric had a right to the income of the benefice. Accordingly, the former law required that the parish to which the pastor was being transferred not be significantly inferior to the parish he was leaving (*CIC* 2163, §2). Commentators generally agreed that what constituted an inferior or superior parish was relative to the income of the former benefice. Other considerations, however, could be taken into account, e.g., the location of the parish, the state of repair of parish buildings, the characteristics of the parishioners, and the extensiveness of parish programs. In accord with the conciliar emphasis upon ecclesial office as a service exercised for a spiritual purpose without consideration of material gain, canon 1748 makes no reference to inferior or superior offices.

One administrative procedure for the transfer of pastors is given because there is no longer the former distinction between removable and irremovable pastors. Under the 1917 Code a special faculty from the Holy See was necessary for the ordinary to transfer an unwilling irremovable pastor (*CIC* 2163, §1).

The procedure for transfer of pastors is succinctly outlined in five canons, thereby specifying the threefold directive of canon 190. This canon first prescribes that only that person can effect a transfer who has the right to provide for the office lost and the office to be filled. Secondly, when an officeholder is unwilling to be transferred, a grave reason is then required for such a transfer and also lawful procedures must be observed in effecting it (cc. 1748–1752). Third, for the effectiveness of a transfer, it must be made known in writing. The bishop is the one who judges that a transfer is necessary or useful according to his prudent estimation. Just as a pastor whose office had been conferred for a determined period of time may be removed before this time has elapsed (c. 193, §2), so may he also be urged to transfer for good reason prior to the expiration of his term of office.

Reasons for Transfer

Canon 1748 — If the good of souls or the need or advantage of the Church requires that a pastor be transferred from his parish which he is governing usefully to another parish or to another office, the bishop is to propose the transfer to him in writing and persuade him to consent to it for the love of God and of souls.

Unlike the removal process, there is no listing of possible legal reasons for a transfer. Although the reasons for a transfer are expressed very generically, a bishop would not use the simpler transfer procedure when a removal is indicated. A transfer of a pastor recognizes his fruitful ministry in one place and presupposes his pastoral skills are needed elsewhere for the good of souls or the need or utility of the Church.

In many cases a transfer is made from one pastorate to another. This canon, however, permits a transferral to another office, such as parochial vicar or administrator, curial official, or teacher. When the proposed transfer is not to another pastorate, care should be taken that the transfer in no way implies a deficiency in pastoral ministry, which would be contrary to the notion of a transfer.[14] Whereas in the removal procedure the bishop may persuade the pastor either orally or in writing, in the transfer process the proposal is to be made in writing. Certainly, in persuading the pastor to consent, the bishop may cite reasons which are more specific than the general reason, i.e., the love of God and souls. If the bishop were to refer to the pastor's qualifications for assuming the intended office, the pastor might then perceive more easily the necessity or utility of his transfer.

Opposition to Transfer

Canon 1749 — If the pastor does not intend to yield to the counsel and persuasion of the bishop, he is to explain his reasons in writing.

Following the bishop's proposal, the pastor basically has two options: either to accept the transfer or to oppose it. If the pastor accepts, the bishop enacts the decree of transfer. If the pastor is unwilling to transfer, he has the right to explain his reasons in writing (c. 190, §2). It is useful for the pastor to prepare such a written response in case he would eventually lodge a recourse against a decree of transfer. At that time the acts of the case would be forwarded to the hierarchical superior considering the recourse.

Canon 1748 does not indicate how much time the pastor has to accept or oppose the transfer, nor does canon 1749 specify how much time a pastor has to respond. For the sake of clarity the bishop is first to insure that his proposal actually has been re-

---

[14]Lobina notes the diffidence with which some pastors regard a transfer, influenced as they may be by the proverb, "promoveatur ut amoveatur" ("Procedura," 161).

ceived. Likewise, he is to determine an appropriate time for the pastor's response and make sure that the pastor has not been impeded from responding (cc. 1742, §1; 1744).

The law does not treat the situation in which a pastor neither consents to the bishop's request nor offers a rebuttal. In this event the bishop may simply proceed to the next step.

Discussion Preceding a Second Transfer Proposal

Canon 1750 — Notwithstanding the reasons alleged, if the bishop judges that he is not going to change his plans, he is to discuss the reasons which favor or oppose the transfer with the two pastors chosen in accord with can. 1742, §1; if he then decides to implement the transfer, he is to repeat the paternal exhortations to the pastor.

The bishop may accept the pastor's rebuttal and drop his initial proposal, or he may determine that the reasons favoring a transfer prevail over the pastor's objections. In this case the bishop discusses the reasons with two pastors selected according to canon 1742, §1. Canon 2165 of the 1917 Code explicitly stated that this consultation was necessary "for valid action." Although canon 1750 omits this phrase, the bishop is to consult the two pastors and take their advice seriously even though he is not bound by it (c. 127). This discussion requires little effort, preserves a greater measure of equity, and eliminates one possible complaint of arbitrariness in a possible recourse petition. Following this consultation the bishop is to repeat his exhortation to the pastor to accept the transfer.

Decree of Transfer and Its Effects

Canon 1751 — §1. When this has been done, if the pastor still refuses and the bishop thinks the transfer must be made, he is to issue a decree of transfer stating that the parish shall be vacant after the lapse of a pre-determined time.

§2. If this period of time has passed in vain, he is to declare the parish vacant.

Canon 1752 — In cases of transfer, the prescriptions of can. 1747 are to be applied, with due regard for canonical equity and having before one's eyes the salvation of souls, which is always the supreme law of the Church.

The Decree of Transfer

Following his consultation with the two pastors and his repeated but unsuccessful effort to persuade the pastor in question to accept the transfer, the bishop effects a decree of transfer. The office becomes vacant in either of two ways: the pastor takes

possession of his new office (c. 191, §1); or the bishop declares the parish vacant following the lapse of time determined in the decree. In either case the former parish becomes vacant unless the transferred pastor takes recourse against the decree.

The Effects of the Decree

When the pastor accepts his transfer, the observance of canon 1747 will pose no difficulty. To provide for the transferring pastor, canon 191, §2 prescribes that he is to receive the remuneration which is attached to the prior office until he has canonically obtained possession of the new one. Canon 1747, §2 allows the pastor's continued use of the parochial residence if he is infirm. Most likely a temporary infirmity is implied, since a more permanent infirmity would give reason for removal.

Although this chapter does not explicitly mention possible recourse against the decree of transfer, such recourse may be lodged as indicated by canon 1747, §3 mutatis mutandis. Thus while recourse is pending, the parish may not be considered vacant.

Nothing in canon 1747, §3 or canon 1752 indicates any possible reasons for lodging recourse against the decree of transfer, since it is the bishop's freedom to assign offices for the good of the local church. If the pastor involved has been serving usefully the parish in which he has been holding office, understandably he may be reluctant to transfer. From a pastoral standpoint, a forced transfer will rarely redound to the good of souls. Thus it is desirable that the bishop convince the pastor to accept the transfer willingly rather than insist on it and simply decree it. If, however, a pastor persists in refusing a transfer, this is tantamount to his denying the propriety of episcopal discernment regarding the needs of the Church. If the bishop continues to insist on the transfer, the process takes on the semblance of a removal action, which is inappropriate; such a deadlock may lead to a disruption of ecclesial communion. Perhaps this is the reason why *Ecclesiae sanctae* stated that if a pastor refused a transfer, the bishop would have to observe the removal procedure for a valid decree of transfer (I, 20, 2). This mingling of processes has been clarified by canon 1751, §1, which permits the bishop to issue a decree of transfer in these cases after he has insured that all the prescribed steps have been completed.

Recourse against Removal/Transfer Decrees

Under the 1917 Code, a legal remedy known as recourse was provided for opposing the final decree of removal or transfer. Canon 2146 stated that recourse could be lodged with the Apostolic See within ten days. The pastor was to inform his bishop of his action, and all of the acts of the process were to be forwarded to the appropriate congregation. While the recourse was pending, canon 2146 prescribed that the ordinary could not validly assign another priest permanently to the parish which was to be vacated. The bishop, however, could meanwhile appoint an administrator. The main purpose of such hierarchical recourse was to determine whether a substantial defect vitiated the process.

Earlier drafts of the revised Code had referred to a second possible way of lodging recourse, namely, to an administrative tribunal, wherever such might be established by the conference of bishops. Since the 1983 Code does not provide for the establishment of such administrative tribunals, presently the only recourse available to the removed or transferred pastor is of a hierarchical nature. Canons 1732–1739 provide norms on administrative recourse, known also as hierarchical recourse, against decrees.

Recourse may be lodged by an aggrieved pastor who has a just motive. He might contend, for example, that the decree of removal or transfer resulted from an irregular procedure, or he might impugn the process for its failure to observe canonical equity. The removed or transferred pastor has a peremptory limit of fifteen days to lodge his recourse, beginning from the day on which he was informed of the decree (c. 1737, §2). Recourse by pastors of territories under the common law is directed to the Sacred Congregation for the Clergy; by pastors of territories under missionary law, to the Sacred Congregation for the Evangelization of Peoples.[15] Recourses to the appropriate congregation are *in devolutivo* only; that is, they do not suspend the execution of the administrative decree. However, for a grave reason the congregation can order a suspen-

sion, provided that the spiritual good of persons is not jeopardized (c. 1737, §3).

When recourse is taken to it, the congregation will appraise the merits of the case, the bishop's observance of procedural norms—especially whether the pastor was able to exercise his right of defense—and the application of the principles of canonical equity and the spiritual good of persons. These two principles are the paramount rubrics for the entire process of transfer or removal.[16] The congregation can confirm the decree, modify it, or reject it. It notifies the bishop, who in turn informs the interested party.[17] If the pastor's recourse is rejected by the congregation, he may have yet a further option: a possible recourse to the Apostolic Signatura (c. 1445, §2), whose own rules govern its deliberations.[18]

In any event, while recourse is pending with a dicastery, the bishop may not name a new pastor for the parish from which he removed or transferred the one taking recourse. The pastor, however, may submit to the bishop's proposal and obey the decree of removal or transfer, even in the advanced stages of recourse.

---

[15]Romita, "De parochorum," 443–444.

[16]*Rel,* 346.

[17]Lobina, "Procedura," 162.

[18]According to a reply by the Pontifical Commission for the Interpretation of the Decrees of the Second Vatican Council, July 1, 1971, a recourse interposed from a decision of a congregation to the Signatura, in accord with *RE,* n. 106, is suspensive; *AAS* 63 (1971); 860, as reported in *CLD* 7 (1974), 1023–1024. P. Pinto, however, who has served as secretary of the second section of the Signatura, states that the Signatura's policies are not yet fully delineated to cover all the cases presented; see P. Pinto, *La giustizia amministrativa della Chiesa* (Milan: Giuffre, 1977), reviewed by F. Morrisey, *SC* (1977), 420–421. From 1968 to 1973, ninety-four cases of removal of pastors arrived at the congregations—of these seventeen reached the second section of the Signatura; see I. Gordon, *De Recursibus Administrativis* (Romae: Pontificia Universitas Gregoriana, 1977).

BIBLIOGRAPHY

References

Augustine, C. *A Commentary on the New Code of Canon Law.* 8 vols. Vol. 7. *Ecclesiastical Procedure.* (St. Louis: B. Herder Book Co., 1921).

Cappello, F. *Summa Iuris Canonici.* 3 vols. Vol. 3. *De Processibus.* (Romae: Pontificia Universitas Gregoriana, 1940).

Parizek, J. "Canonical Changes of Procedures in the Administrative Removal and Transfer of Pastors since Maxima cura." (J.C.L. thesis, Catholic University of America, 1978).

Woywod, S. *A Practical Commentary on the Code of Canon Law.* Rev. ed. by C. Smith. (New York: Joseph F. Wagner, Inc., 1952).

Articles

DDC, s.v. "Amotion," by A. Amanieu.

Dooley, M. "The Proposed Law on Administrative Procedure." *CLS-GBIN* 45 (1980): 15–50.

Lobina, G. "De processibus administrativae indolis in dimissione religiosorum et in amotione parochorum." *P* 67 (1978): 679–688.

———. "Procedura per la remozione dei parroci." *ME* 105 (1980): 147–164.

Molloy, T. "Administrative Recourse in the Proposed Code of Canon Law." *CLSAP* (1982): 263–273.

Romita, F. "De parochorum amotione, translatione, et renuntiatione juxta Vaticanum II." *ME* 94 (1969): 430–450.

TABLE OF CORRESPONDING CANONS: 1983 CODE WITH 1917 CODE

Editors' Note: At times there is a literal correspondence between the canons of the 1983 Code and those of the 1917 Code. At other times there is a substantial correspondence between them even though there are notable differences terminologically. At still other times there is only a partial correspondence between the canons of the two Codes. Finally at times there is no correspondence between the canons of the revised Code and those of the former Code, and this is indicated by an "X" in the right-hand column.

1983	1917	1983	1917
	Book I		
1	1	35	X
2	2	36, §1	49; 50
3	3	36, §2	49
4	4	37	56
5	5	38	46
6	6	39	39
7	8, §1	40	53
8, §1	9	41	54, §1
8, §2	X	42	55
9	10	43	57
10	11	44	58
11	12	45	59, §1
12	13	46	73
13, §1	8, §2	47	60, §1
13, §2	14, §1	48	X
13, §3	14, §2	49	X
14	15	50	X
15	16	51	X
16	17	52	X
17	18	53	48, §1–§2
18	19	54, §1	X
19	20	54, §2	24
20	22	55	X
21	23	56	1718
22	X	57	X
23	25	58, §1	X
24	27	58, §2	24
25	26	59	X
26	27; 28	60	36, §1
27	29	61	37
28	30	62	38
29	X	63, §1	42, §1; 45
30	X	63, §2	42, §2
31	X	63, §3	41
32	X	64	43
33	X	65, §1	44, §1
34	X	65, §2	X

1983	1917	1983	1917
65, §3	44, §2	112, §1, 1°	98, §3
66	47	112, §1, 2°	98, §4
67	48	112, §1, 3°	X
68	51	112, §2	98, §5
69	52	113, §1	100, §1
70	54, §2	113, §2	99
71	69	114, §1	100, §1
72	X	114, §2	X
73	60, §2	114, §3	X
74	79	115, §1	X
75	62	115, §2	100, §2
76, §1	X	115, §3	X
76, §2	63, §2	116	X
77	67–68	117	X
78, §1	70	118	X
78, §2	74	119	101
78, §3	75	120	102
79	71	121	X
80	72	122	1500
81	73	123	1501
82	76	124, §1	1680, §1
83	77	124, §2	X
84	78	125	103
85	80	126	104
86	X	127	105
87	81	128	1681
88	82	129	196; 118
89	83	130	196
90	84	131, §1–§2	197
91	201, §3	131, §3	200, §2
92	85	132	66
93	86	133	203
94	X	134, §1–§2	198
95	X	134, §3	X
96	87	135	X
97, §1	88, §1	136	201, §1, §3
97, §2	88, §3	137	199
98, §1–§2	89	138	200, §1
99	88, §3	139	204
100	91	140	205
101	90	141	206
102	92	142	207, §1–§2
103	X	143	208
104	93, §1–§2	144, §1	209
105	93	144, §2	X
106	95	145, §1	145, §1
107	94	145, §2	X
108	96	146	147, §1
109, §1	97, §1–§2	147	148, §1
109, §2	97, §3	148	X
110	X	149	153; 729
111, §1	98, §1; 756, §1–§2	150	154
111, §2	X	151	155

1983	1917	1983	1917
152	156, §1–§2	191	194
153, §1	150, §1	192	192, §1
153, §2	X	193, §1–§3	192, §2–§3
153, §3	150, §2	193, §4	X
154	151	194, §1	188
155	158	194, §2	X
156	159	195	2299, 3°
157	152	196, §1	2298, 6°
158, §1	1457	196, §2	X
158, §2	1460, §1	197	1508
159	X	198	1512
160, §1	1460, §4	199	1509
160, §2	1461	200	31
161, §1	1465, §1	201	35
161, §2	1468	202, §1	32
162	1458, §1; 1465, §1	202, §2	34, §1–§2
163	1466, §1, §3	203, §1	34, §3, 2°–3°
164	160	203, §2	34, §3, 3°–4°
165	161		
166	162, §1–§4	*Book II*	
167, §1	163		
167, §2	168	204–206	X
168	164	207	107
169	165	208–212	X
170	166	213	682
171	167	214–231	X
172	169	232	1352
173	171	233	1353
174	172	234, §1	1354, §1
175	173	234, §2	1364, 3°
176	174	235	972; 1370
177, §1	175	236	X
177, §2	176, §1	237, §1	1354, §2–§3
178	176, §2	237, §2	1354, §3
179, §1–§3	177, §1–§3	238, §1	99
179, §4	176, §3	238, §2	X
179, §5	177, §4	239, §1–§2	1358
180	179	239, §3	X
181	180	240	1361
182	181	241	1363
183	182	242	X
184, §1–§2	183	243	1357, §3
184, §3	X	244	X
185	X	245	X
186	X	246	1367
187	184	247	X
188	185	248	X
189, §1	186; 187, §1	249	1364, 2°
189, §2	189, §1	250	1365, §1–§2
189, §3	189, §2	251	X
189, §4	191, §1	252, §1–§2	X
190, §1–§2	193	252, §3	1365, §2
190, §3	X	253, §1	1366, §1

1983	1917	1983	1917
253, §2	1366, §3	285, §1	138
253, §3	X	285, §2	139, §1
254	X	285, §3	139, §2
255	X	285, §4	139, §3; 137
256, §1	1365, §3	286	142
256, §2	X	287, §1	141
257	X	287, §2	X
258	X	288	X
259	1357, §1–§2	289, §1	141, §1; 121
260	1360, §2	289, §2	72, §3
261, §1	1369, §1	290, 1°	214
261, §2	1369, §3	290, 2°	211, §1
262	1368	290, 3°	211, §1
263	X	291	213, §2
264, §1	1355, 1°–2°	292	213, §1
264, §2	1356	293	212, §2
265	111, §1	294–297	X
266, §1	111, §2	298, §1	685
266, §2	115; 585	298, §2	684
266, §3	X	299, §1–§2	X
267, §1	112	299, §3	686, §1
267, §2	116	300	X
268, §1	X	301	X
268, §2	115	302	X
269	117	303	702, §1
270	X	304, §1	689, §1
271, §1	X	304, §2	688
271, §2	X	305, §1	690, §1
271, §3	144	305, §2	X
272	113	306	692
273	127	307, §1	694, §1
274, §1	118	307, §2	693, §2
274, §2	128	307, §3	693, §4
275	X	308	696
276, §1	124	309	697, §1–§2
276, §2, 1°	X	310	X
276, §2, 2°	X	311	X
276, §2, 3°	135	312, §1	686, §2
276, §2, 4°	126	312, §2	686, §3
276, §2, 5°	125, §2	313	687
277, §1	132	314	689, §1
277, §2	133, §1	315	X
277, §3	133, §3	316, §1	693, §1
278	X	316, §2	696, §2
279, §1	129	317, §1–§2	698, §1
279, §2	131, §1	317, §3	698, §4
279, §3	X	317, §4	X
280	134	318, §1–§2	698, §3
281	980	319, §1	691, §1
282	1473	319, §2	691, §5
283, §1	143	320, §1	699, §2
283, §2	X	320, §2	699, §1
284	136	320, §3	X

1983	1917	1983	1917
321–329	X	371, §1	293, §1
330	X	371, §2	312
331	218, §1	372	X
332, §1	219	373	215, §1
332, §2	221	374, §1	216, §1–§3
333, §1	218, §2	374, §2	217, §1
333, §2	X	375, §1	329, §1
333, §3	228, §2	375, §2	X
334–337	X	376	X
338, §1	222, §1–§2	377, §1	329, §2
338, §2	222, §2; 226	377, §2–§5	X
339, §1–§2	223, §1–§3	378, §1, 1°	331, §1, 4°
340	229	378, §1, 2°	X
341, §1	227	378, §1, 3°	331, §1, 2°
341, §2	X	378, §1, 4°	331, §1, 3°
342–348	X	378, §1, 5°	331, §1, 5°
349	230	378, §2	331, §3
350, §1–§2	231, §1–§2	379	333
350, §3	X	380	332, §2
350, §4	236, §4	381, §1	334, §1
350, §5	236, §1	381, §2	215, §2
350, §6	236, §2	382, §1	334, §2
351, §1	232, §1	382, §2	333
351, §2	233, §1	382, §3	334, §3
351, §3	233, §2	382, §4	X
352, §1	237, §1	383	X
352, §2	237, §2	384	X
352, §3	X	385	X
352, §4	X	386	X
353	X	387	X
354	X	388, §1	339, §1
355, §1–§2	239, §2–§3	388, §2	339, §4
356	238, §1, §3	388, §3	339, §5
357, §1	240, §1	388, §4	339, §6
357, §2	X	389	X
358	266	390	337, §1
359	241	391, §1	335, §1
360	242	391, §2	X
361	7	392	336
362	265	393	X
363	X	394	X
364, 1°	267, §1, 2°	395	338
364, 2°	269, §1	396	343, §1–§2
364, 3°–7°	X	397	344
364, 8°	267, §1, 3°	398	346
365, §1, 1°	267, §1, 1°	399, §1	340, §1
365, §1, 2°	X	399, §2	340, §3
365, §2	X	400, §1	341, §1
366	X	400, §2	342
367	268, §1–§2	400, §3	299
368	215, §2	401	X
369	X	402	X
370	X	403	350

1983	1917	1983	1917
404	353	442, §1, 2°	284, 1°
405, §1	351, §1	442, §1, 3°	288
405, §2	351, §2	442, §2	284, 1°
406	X	443	282; 286
407	X	444, §1	X
408, §1	351, §4	444, §2	287, §1–§2
408, §2	351, §3	445	290
409, §1–§2	355, §1–§3	446	291, §1
410	354	447–459	X
411	X	460	356, §1
412	429, §1	461	356
413, §1	429, §1–§2	462	357, §1
413, §2	429, §3	463	358
413, §3	429, §4	464	359
414	X	465	361
415	429, §5	466	362
416	430, §1	467	X
417	430, §2	468	X
418	430, §3	469	363, §1
419	431, §1–§2	470	364, §1
420	309, §1–§2	471	364, §2
421, §1	432, §1	472	365
421, §2	432, §2	473	X
422	432, §4	474	X
423, §1	433, §1	475, §1	366, §1
423, §2	433, §3	475, §2	366, §3
424	433, §2	476	X
425	434	477, §1	366, §2
426	435, §1	477, §2	366, §3
427, §1	435, §1	478, §1	367, §1
427, §2	438	478, §2	367, §3
428, §1	436	479, §1	368, §1
428, §2	435, §3	479, §2	X
429	440	479, §3	368, §2
430, §1	443, §2	480	369
430, §2	443, §1	481	371
431–434	X	482	372
435	272	483, §1	373, §1–§2
436, §1, 1°	274, 4°	483, §2	373, §3–§4
436, §1, 2°	274, 5°	484	374, §1
436, §1, 3°	274, 3°	485	373, §5
436, §2	X	486, §1–§2	375, §1
436, §3	274, 6°	486, §3	375, §2
437, §1	275	487, §1	377
437, §2	277	487, §2	384, §1
437, §3	278	488	378, §1
438	271	489	379, §1
439, §1	281	490, §1	379, §3
439, §2	X	490, §2	382, §1
440, §1	283	490, §3	379, §4
440, §2	X	491, §1	383, §1
441	X	491, §2	X
442, §1, 1°	284, 2°	491, §3	383, §2; 384, §2

1983	1917	1983	1917
492, §1	1520, §1	531	463
492, §2	X	532	X
492, §3	1520, §2	533, §1	465, §1
493	X	533, §2	465, §2–§4
494	X	533, §3	X
495	X	534, §1	466, §1
496	X	534, §2	466, §2
497	X	534, §3	466, §4
498	X	535, §1	470, §1
499	X	535, §2	470, §2
500	X	535, §3	470, §5
501	X	535, §4	470, §4
502, §1	427	535, §5	X
502, §2–§3	X	536	X
502, §4	302	537	X
503	391, §1	538, §1	2157–2161; 2162–2167
504	392	538, §2	454, §5
505	410, §1–§2	538, §3	X
506	X	539	472; 475
507, §1	393, §1	540, §1–§2	473, §1
507, §2	X	540, §3	473, §2
508, §1	401, §1	541	X
508, §2	X	542	X
509, §1	403	543	X
509, §2	404	544	X
510	402; 415	545, §1	476, §1
511–514	X	545, §2	476, §2
515, §1	216, §1	546	X
515, §2	216, §4	547	477, §1
515, §3	X	548, §1	476, §6
516, §1	216, §2–§3; 451, §2, 1°	548, §2	476, §6
516, §2	X	548, §3	X
517	X	549	X
518	216, §4	550, §1	476, §5
519	451, §1	550, §2	476, §5
520, §1	452, §1	550, §3	X
520, §2	X	551	X
521, §1	453, §1	552	477, §2
521, §2	453, §2; 459, §2	553, §1	445
521, §3	459, §3	553, §2	446, §1
522	454	554, §1	X
523	455, §1	554, §2	X
524	459, §1	554, §3	446, §2
525	455, §2–§3	555, §1	447
526	460	555, §2	448, §1
527, §1	461; 1443	555, §3	447
527, §2	1444, §1	555, §4	447
527, §3	1444, §2	556	479, §1
528, §1	469	557	480
528, §2	467, §1	558	481
529, §1	468, §1–§2	559	482
529, §2	X	560	483
530	562	561	484, §1

1983	1917	1983	1917
562	485	613, §1	X
563	486	613, §2	488, 8°
564	X	614	500, §2
565	X	615	X
566	X	616, §1	498
567	X	616, §2	493
568	X	616, §3	X
569	X	616, §4	X
570	X	617	501; 502
571	X	618	X
572	X	619	509
573	487; 488, 1°	620	488, 8°; 501, §3; 502
574–578	X	621	488, 6°
579	492, §1	622	501; 502
580	494, §1	623	504
581	494, §1	624	505
582	494, §1	625, §1	X
583	495, §2; 618, §2, 1°	625, §2	506, §2, §4
584	493	625, §3	505
585	494, §2	626	507
586	618, §2, 2°	627, §1	516, §1
587	489	627, §2	516, §2
588	488, 4°	628, §1	511
589	488, 3°	628, §2	512
590, §1	X	628, §3	513
590, §2	499, §1	629	508
591	488, 2°; 500, §1; 615	630, §1	X
592, §1	510	630, §2	X
592, §2	509, §1	630, §3	520; 521; 528
593	488, 3°; 494, §1	630, §4	518, §2–§3
594	492, §2	630, §5	530
595	495; 500, §1; 512, §1, 2°	631, §1	501, §1
		631, §2	X
596	501	631, §3	X
597	538	632	X
598, §1	487	633	X
598, §2	593	634, §1	531; 534, §1
599	132; 592	634, §2	X
600	594	635, §1	532, §1
601	501	635, §2	532, §1
602	594, §1	636, §1	516, §2, §4
603–605	X	636, §2	X
606	490	637	535, §1, §3
607, §1	X	638, §1	532, §2
607, §2	488, §1	638, §2	532, §2
607, §3	X	638, §3	534, §1–§2
608	488, 5°; 501, §1	638, §4	534, §1
609, §1	495; 497, §1	639	536
609, §2	497, §1	640	537
610, §1	X	641	543
610, §2	496	642	538; 542, 1°; 555, §1, 1°
611	497, §2–§3	643, §1, 1°	542, 1°; 555, §1, 1°
612	497, §4	643, §1, 2°	542, 1°

1983	1917	1983	1917
643, §1, 3°	542, 1°	663, §3	610
643, §1, 4°	542, 1°	663, §4	595
643, §1, 5°	542, 1°	663, §5	595
643, §2	542	664	595, §1, 3°
644	542, 1°–2°; 544, §4	665, §1	607
645, §1	544, §1	665, §2	X
645, §2	544, §3	666	X
645, §3	X	667	597–606
645, §4	544, §6	668, §1	569
646	X	668, §2	580, §3; 583
647, §1	554, §1	668, §3	580, §1–§2; 594, §2
647, §2	555, §1, 3°	668, §4	581
647, §3	X	668, §5	582
648, §1	555, §1, 2°	669, §1	596
648, §2	555, §2	669, §2	592
648, §3	555, §2; 571, §2	670	X
649, §1	556, §1–§2	671	626
649, §2	X	672	592
650, §1	559, §1; 561, §1	673	X
650, §2	561, §1	674	X
651, §1	559, §1; 560	675	608
651, §2	559, §2; 560	676	X
651, §3	559, §3	677, §1	X
652, §1	562	677, §2	702–703
652, §2	565, §1	678, §1	612
652, §3	561, §1	678, §2	619
652, §4	561, §1	678, §3	X
652, §5	565, §3	679	617; 618, §2
653, §1	571, §1	680	X
653, §2	571, §2	681, §1	631, §1
654	X	681, §2	X
655	574, §1	682, §1	X
656, 1°	573; 572, §1, 1°	682, §2	631, §3
656, 2°	572, §1, 3°	683, §1	512, §2
656, 3°	543; 572, §1, 2°; 575, §2	683, §2	617, §2
		684, §1	632
656, 4°	572, §1, 4°–5°	684, §2	633, §1
656, 5°	572, §1, 6°	684, §3	632
657, §1	577, §1	684, §4	634
657, §2	574, §2	684, §5	X
657, §3	X	685, §1	633, §1
658, 1°	543; 575, §2; 572, §2; 573	685, §2	635, 1°
		686, §1	638
658, 2°	572, §2; 574, §1	686, §2	638
659, §1	593	686, §3	X
659, §2	X	687	639
659, §3	587–591	688, §1	637
660, §1	589, §1	688, §2	X
660, §2	589, §2	689, §1	637
661	591; 593	689, §2	637
662	593	689, §3	X
663, §1	595	690	640, §2
663, §2	595	691	638

1983	1917	1983	1917
692	640, §1, 1°–2°	750	1323, §1
693	640, §1, 2°; 641, §1–§2; 642, §1–§2	751	1325, §2
		752	X
694, §1, 1°	646, §1, 1°	753	1326
694, §1, 2°	646, §1, 3°	754	1324
694, §2	646, §2; 670	755	1325, §3
695, §1	646, §1, 2°	756	1327
695, §2	X	757	1327
696, §1	658	758	1327; 1328
696, §2	647, §1	759	1328
697, 1°	659	760	1347
697, 2°	649; 651; 659–661	761	X
697, 3°	662; 663	762	X
698	647, §2, 3°; 650, §3; 651; 665	763	1327; 349, §1, 1°
		764	1337
699, §1	650, §1–§2; 651; 652, §1, 3°; 663; 666	765	1338
		766	1327; 1342
699, §2	652, §2	767	1344; 1345
700	650, §2; 652, §2–§3; 666	768	1347
		769	1347, §2
701	669–672	770	1349
702	643	771, §1	X
703	653; 668	771, §2	1350
704	510	772	X
705	627, §1, 2°	773	1329
706	628	774	1335
707	629	775	1336
708	X	776	1333; 1334
709	X	777	1330; 1331
710–730	X	778	1334
731	673, §1	779–781	X
732	673, §2; 674	782	1350; 252
733	674	783–786	X
734	675	787, §1	X
735	677; 678	787, §2	1351
736	678	788–792	X
737	679	793	1372
738	675; 679, §1	794	1375
739	679, §1	795–797	X
740	673, §1	798	1372; 1374
741	676	799	X
742	681	800	1375; 1379, §3
743	681	801	X
744	681	802	1379, §1
745	681	803	1381
746	681	804	1381; 1373, §2
		805	1381, §3
Book III		806	1381; 1382
		807	1375
747	1322	808	X
748	1351	809	1379, §2
749, §1–§2	X	810	1381, §2
749, §3	1323, §3	811–815	X

1983	1917	1983	1917
816	1376	853	757, §1
817	1377	854	758
818	X	855	761
819	1380	856	772
820–822	X	857, §1	773
823	1384, §1	857, §2	738
824, §1	1385, §2	858	774
824, §2	1384, §2	859	775
825, §1	1385, §1; 1391	860, §1	776
825, §2	X	860, §2	X
826	1390; 1385, §1, 2°	861, §1	738
827	1385, §1, 1°–2°	861, §2	741–743
828	1389	862	739
829	1392, §1	863	744
830	1393–1394	864	745, §1
831	1386	865, §1	752, §1
832	1385, §3	865, §2	752, §2
833	1406–1407	866	753, §2
		867, §1	770
Book IV		867, §2	770
		868, §1, 1°	750, §2
834, §1	X	868, §1, 2°	750, §2
834, §2	1256	868, §2	750, §1; 751
835	X	869	X
836	X	870	749
837	X	871	747
838, §1	1257	872	762; 769
838, §2	1257	873	764
838, §3	X	874, §1	765; 766
838, §4	1261	874, §2	X
839, §1	X	875	X
839, §2	1259, §1	876	779
840	731, §1	877, §1	777, §1
841	X	877, §2	777, §2
842	X	877, §3	X
843, §1	682	878	778
843, §2	X	879	X
844, §1	731, §2; 1258	880, §1	780
844, §2	1258	880, §2	781, §1
844, §3	731, §2	881	790; 791
844, §4	731, §2	882	782, §1–§2
844, §5	731, §2	883, 1°	782, §1
845	732	883, 2°	X
846	733	883, 3°	X
847, §1	734, §1	884, §1	X
847, §2	735	884, §2	X
848	736	885, §1	785, §1
849	737, §1	885, §2	785, §2
850	X	886, §1	783, §1
851, 1°	752, §1	886, §2	783, §2
851, 2°	X	887	784
852, §1	745, §2, 2°	888	792
852, §2	745, §2, 1°; 754	889, §1	786

1983	1917	1983	1917
889, §2	786	936	1267
890	787	937	1266
891	788	938, §1–§2	1268, §1–§2, §4
892	793; 797	938, §3	1269, §1–§2
893, §1	795; 796	938, §4	1269, §3
893, §2	X	938, §5	1269, §4
894	800	939	1270; 1272
895	798	940	1271
896	799	941	1274, §1
897	801	942	1275
898	801; 1273	943	1274, §2
899	801	944, §1	1291, §1; 1295
900, §1	802	944, §2	1295
900, §2	X	945, §1	824
901	809	945, §2	X
902	803	946	X
903	804, §1–§2	947	827
904	805	948	828
905	806	949	829
906	813	950	830
907	X	951	824, §2
908	X	952	831; 832
909	810	953	835
910	845	954	836
911	850; 514	955, §1	837–839; 840, §1
912	853	955, §2	837
913	854, §1–§2	955, §3	844, §1
914	854, §3–§4	955, §4	844, §2
915	855	956	841
916	807; 856	957	842
917	857	958	843
918	867, §4	959	870
919, §1	858, §1	960	X
919, §2	808	961	X
919, §3	858, §2	962	X
920	859, §1–§2, §4	963	X
921	864	964, §1	908
922	865	964, §2	909
923	866, §1	964, §3	910
924, §1	814	965	871
924, §2	815, §1	966, §1	872
924, §3	815, §2	966, §2	872
925	852	967, §1	873, §1
926	816; 851, §1	967, §2	X
927	817	967, §3	X
928	819	968, §1	873, §1, 2°
929	811, §1	968, §2	873, §2
930	X	969, §1	874
931	820; 821; 867	969, §2	875
932	822	970	877, §1
933	823, §1	971	X
934	1265, §1	972	878, §1
935	1265, §3	973	879, §1

1983	1917	1983	1917
974, §1	880, §1	1016	956
974, §2	X	1017	1008
974, §3	X	1018	958
974, §4	X	1019	964
975	X	1020	960, §1
976	882	1021	961
977	884	1022	962
978, §1	888, §1	1023	963
978, §2	X	1024	968, §1
979	888, §2	1025, §1	968, §1–§2
980	886	1025, §2	969, §2
981	887	1025, §3	969, §3
982	894; 2363	1026	971
983	889	1027	X
984	890	1028	996
985	891	1029	974, §1
986	892	1030	970
987	X	1031, §1	975
988, §1	901	1031, §2–§4	X
988, §2	902	1032, §1	976, §2
989	906	1032, §2–§3	X
990	903	1033	974, §1, 1°
991	905	1034	X
992	911	1035	X
993	X	1036	992
994	911; 930	1037	X
995, §1	912	1038	973, §2
995, §2	913	1039	1001
996	925	1040	983
997	X	1041, 1°	984, 3°
998	937	1041, 2°	985, 1°
999	945	1041, 3°	985, 3°
1000, §1	947, §1	1041, 4°	985, 4°
1000, §2	947, §4	1041, 5°	985, 5°
1001	944	1041, 6°	985, 7°
1002	X	1042, 1°	987, 2°
1003, §1	938, §1	1042, 2°	987, 3°
1003, §2	938, §2	1042, 3°	987, 6°
1003, §3	735	1043	999
1004	940	1044, §1, 1°	X
1005	941	1044, §1, 2°	X
1006	943	1044, §1, 3°	X
1007	942	1044, §2, 1°	X
1008	948	1044, §2, 2°	X
1009, §1	949	1045	988
1009, §2	1002	1046	989
1010	1006, §1–§3	1047	990, §1
1011	1009, §1–§2	1048	990, §2
1012	951	1049	991, §1–§3
1013	953	1050, 1°	993, 2°
1014	954	1050, 2°	993, 1°
1015, §1–§2	955	1050, 3°	993, 1°
1015, §3	959	1051, 1°	993, 3°, 5°

1983	1917	1983	1917
1051, 2°	X	1091	1076
1052	995; 997	1092	1077, §1
1053	1010	1093	1078
1054	1011	1094	1080
1055	1012	1095	X
1056	1013	1096	1082
1057	1081	1097	1083
1058	1035	1098	X
1059	1016	1099	1084
1060	1014	1100	1085
1061	1015	1101	1086
1062	1017	1102, §1	1092, §3
1063, 1°	1018	1102, §2	1092, §4
1063, 2°–4°	X	1102, §3	X
1064	X	1103	1087
1065	1021, §2	1104	1088
1066	1019, §1	1105, §1	1089, §1
1067	1020, §1	1105, §2	1089, §1
1068	1019, §2	1105, §3	1089, §2
1069	1027	1105, §4	1089, §3
1070	1029	1106	1090
1071, §1, 1°	1032	1107	1093
1071, §1, 2°	X	1108, §1	1094
1071, §1, 3°	X	1108, §2	X
1071, §1, 4°	1065, §1	1109	1095, §1, 1°
1071, §1, 5°	1066	1110	1095, §1, 2°
1071, §1, 6°	1034	1111, §1	1095, §2
1071, §1, 7°	1091	1111, §2	1096, §1
1071, §2	1065, §2	1112	X
1072	1067, §2	1113	1096, §2
1073	1036, §2	1114	1097, §1, 1°
1074	1037	1115	1097, §2
1075	1038	1116	1098
1076	1041	1117	1099, §1, 1°–2°
1077	1039	1118	1109
1078, §1–§2	1040	1119	1100
1078, §3	1076, §3	1120	X
1079, §1	1043	1121, §1	1103, §1
1079, §2–§3	1044	1121, §2	1103, §3
1079, §4	X	1121, §3	X
1080, §1–§2	1045, §1–§3	1122	1103, §2
1081	1046	1123	X
1082	1047	1124	1060
1083, §1	1067, §1	1125	1061
1083, §2	X	1126	X
1084	1068	1127, §1	1099, §1, 2°
1085	1069	1127, §2	X
1086	1070	1127, §3	1063, §1
1087	1072	1128	X
1088	1073	1129	1071
1089	1074, §1–§3	1130	1104
1090, §1	1075, 2°	1131	1105
1090, §2	1075, 3°	1132	1106

1983	1917		1983	1917
1133	1107		1176, §2	X
1134	1110		1176, §3	1203, §1
1135	1111		1177, §1	1216, §1
1136	1113		1177, §2	1216, §1
1137	1114		1177, §3	1218, §1
1138	1115		1178	1219, §2
1139	1116		1179	1221, §1
1140	1117		1180, §1	1228, §1
1141	1118		1180, §2	1223, §1
1142	1119		1181	1234, §1; 1235, §2
1143, §1	1120, §1		1182	1238
1143, §2	X		1183, §1	1239, §2
1144	1121		1183, §2	X
1145, §1–§3	1122, §1–§2		1183, §3	X
1146	1123		1184, §1	1240, §1
1147	X		1184, §1, 1°	1240, §1, 1°
1148	1125		1184, §1, 2°	1240, §1, 5°
1149	1125		1184, §1, 3°	1240, §1, 6°
1150	1127		1184, §2	1240, §2
1151	1128		1185	1241
1152, §1	1129, §1		1186	1276
1152, §2	1129, §2		1187	1277, §1
1152, §3	1130		1188	1279, §1–§3
1153	1131		1189	1280
1154	1132		1190, §1	1289, §1
1155	1130		1190, §2	1281, §1
1156	1133		1190, §3	1281, §1
1157	1134		1191	1307
1158	1135		1192, §1	1308, §1
1159	1136		1192, §2	1308, §2
1160	1137		1192, §3	1308, §4
1161, §1–§2	1138, §1–§2		1193	1310, §1
1161, §3	X		1194	1311
1162	1140		1195	1312, §2
1163	1139		1196	1313
1164	1138, §3		1197	1314
1165, §1	1141		1198	1315
1165, §2	X		1199	1316
1166	1144		1200, §1	1317, §1
1167, §1	1145		1200, §2	1317, §2
1167, §2	1148, §1		1201	1318
1168	1146		1202	1319
1169, §1	1147, §1		1203	1320
1169, §2	1147, §2		1204	1321
1169, §3	1147, §4		1205	1154
1170	1149		1206	1155, §1–§2
1171	1150		1207	1156
1172	1151		1208	1158
1173	X		1209	1159, §1
1174	X		1210	X
1175	X		1211	1172, §1; 1173, §1; 1174, §1
1176, §1	1215; 1203, §1; 1239, §1		1212	1170

1983	1917	1983	1917
1213	1160	1252	1254
1214	1161	1253	X
1215, §1	1162, §1		
1215, §2	1162, §2–§3		*Book V*
1215, §3	1162, §4		
1216	1164, §1	1254, §1	1495, §1
1217, §1	1165, §1	1254, §2	X
1217, §2	1165, §3	1255	1495, §2
1218	1168, §1	1256	1499, §2
1219	1171	1257, §1	1497, §1
1220, §1	1178	1257, §2	X
1220, §2	X	1258	1498
1221	1181	1259	1499, §1
1222, §1	1187	1260	1496
1222, §2	X	1261–1262	X
1223	1188, §1	1263	1505; 1506
1224, §1	1192, §1–§2	1264	1507
1224, §2	1193, §3	1265	1503
1225	1193	1266	X
1226	X	1267	1236
1227	1189	1268	1508
1228	1194–1195	1269	1510
1229	1196, §1–§2	1270	1511
1230	X	1271	X
1231	X	1272	X
1232	X	1273	1518
1233	X	1274	X
1234	X	1275	X
1235	1197	1276	1519
1236, §1	1198, §1–§2	1277	1520, §3
1236, §2	X	1278	X
1237, §1	1199, §1	1279, §1	X
1237, §2	1198, §4	1279, §2	1521, §1
1238, §1	1170; 1187; 1200, §1–§2	1280	X
		1281	1527
1238, §2	X	1282	1521, §2
1239	1202	1283	1522
1240, §1	1205, §1–§2	1284	1523
1240, §2	1206, §3	1285	1535
1241, §1	1208, §1–§2	1286	1524
1241, §2	1208, §3	1287	1525
1242	1205, §2	1288	1526
1243	X	1289	1528
1244	1244	1290	1529
1245	1245, §1–§3	1291	1530
1246, §1	1247, §1	1292	1530
1246, §2	X	1293	1530
1247	1248	1294	1531
1248, §1	1249	1295	1533
1248, §2	X	1296	1534
1249	X	1297	1541
1250	X	1298	1540
1251	1252	1299	1513

1983	1917	1983	1917
1300	1514	1326, §1, 2°	2207, 1°
1301	1515	1326, §1, 3°	2203, §1
1302	1516	1326, §2	X
1303	1544	1327	X
1304, §1	1546	1328	2212–2213; 2235
1304, §2	1545	1329, §1–§2	2209, §1–§7
1305	1547	1330	X
1306	1548	1331	2259–2267
1307	1549	1332	2275
1308	1517	1333	2278–2279;
1309	X		2282–2284
1310	X	1334	X
		1335	2261, §1–§2; 2284
Book VI		1336, §1, 1°	2298, 7°–8°
		1336, §1, 2°	2298, 4°, 6°
1311	2214, §1	1336, §1, 3°	2298, 1°
1312, §1, 1°	2216, 1°	1336, §1, 4°	2298, 3°
1312, §1, 2°	2216, 2°	1336, §1, 5°	2298, 12°
1312, §2	X	1336, §2	X
1312, §3	2216, 3°	1337, §1	X
1313	2226, §2–§3	1337, §2	2301
1314	2217, §2; 2217, §1, 2°	1338	X
1315, §1	2221	1339, §1	2307
1315, §2	2217, §1, 1°	1339, §2	2308
1315, §3	X	1339, §3	2309, 5°
1316	X	1340, §1	X
1317	X	1340, §2	2310, §2
1318	2241, §2	1340, §3	2313, §2
1319	X	1341	X
1320	619	1342	X
1321	2195; 2199	1343	2223, §2
1322	2201, §2	1344, 1°	2223, §3, 1°
1323, 1°	2204; 2230	1344, 2°	2223, §3, 2°
1323, 2°	2202, §1, §3	1344, 3°	2288
1323, 3°	2205; 2203, §2	1345	2223, §3, 3°
1323, 4°	2205, §2–§3	1346	2224, §2
1323, 5°	2205, §4	1347, §1	2233, §2
1323, 6°	2201, §1	1347, §2	2242, §3
1323, 7°	X	1348	2223, §3, 3°
1324, §1, 1°	2201, §4	1349	2223, §1
1324, §1, 2°	2201, §3	1350, §1	2299, §3
1324, §1, 3°	2206	1350, §2	2303, §2
1324, §1, 4°	X	1351	2226, §4
1324, §1, 5°	2205, §3	1352, §1	2252
1324, §1, 6°	2205, §4	1352, §2	2232, §1; 2290, §1
1324, §1, 7°	2205, §4	1353	2243; 2287
1324, §1, 8°	X	1354, §1	2236, §1–§2
1324, §1, 9°	2202, §2	1354, §2	X
1324, §1, 10°	X	1354, §3	2246, §2
1324, §2–§3	X	1355	2237; 2253; 2236, §1
1325	2209, §1; 2209, §3, 1°;	1356	2236, §1; 2237
	2201, §3; 2206	1357, §1–§2	2254, §1
1326, §1, 1°	2208, §1	1357, §3	2252

1983	1917	1983	1917
1358, §1	2241, §1; 2242, §3; 2248, §2	1395	2359
		1396	2381
1358, §2	2248, §2	1397	2353–2354
1359	2249, §2	1398	2350, §1
1360	2238	1399	2222, §1
1361, §1–§2	2239, §1–§2		
1361, §3	X		*Book VII*
1362, §1, 1°	1703		
1362, §1, 2°	1703, 2°–3°	1400, §1	1552, §2
1362, §1, 3°	X	1400, §2	1601
1362, §2	1705	1401	1553, §1, 1°–2°
1363	X	1402	1555, §2
1364	2314, §1, 1°–2°	1403	1999–2141
1365	2316	1404	1556
1366	2319, §1, 3°–4°	1405, §1	1557, §1, §3
1367	2320	1405, §2	1683
1368	2323	1405, §3	1557, §2
1369	2323; 2344	1406, §1	X
1370, §1	2343, §1, 1°, 3°	1406, §2	1558
1370, §2	2343, §3	1407	1559
1370, §3	2343, §4	1408	1561, §1
1371, 1°	2317	1409, §1	1563
1371, 2°	2331, §1	1409, §2	X
1372	2332	1410	1564
1373	2331, §2; 2344	1411, §1	1565, §1–§2
1374	2335	1411, §2	X
1375	2333–2334; 2337; 2345–2346; 2390	1412	1566, §1–§2
		1413, 1°–2°	1560, §3–§4
1376	2346	1414	1567
1377	2347	1415	1568
1378, §1	2367, §1	1416	1612, §1–§2
1378, §2, 1°	2322, 1°	1417	1569, §1–§2
1378, §2, 2°	2322, 1°	1418	1570, §2
1378, §3	2322, 1°	1419	1572
1379	2322, 2°	1420, §1–§5	1573, §1–§5
1380	2371	1421, §1	1574, §1
1381, §1	2394	1421, §2	X
1381, §2	2401	1421, §3	1574, §2
1382	2370	1422	1573, §5; 1574, §2
1383	2373, §1; 2374	1423	X
1384	X	1424	1575
1385	2324	1425, §1–§3	1576, §1–§3
1386	2407	1425, §4–§5	X
1387	2368, §1	1426	1577
1388	2369	1427	1579
1389, §1	2404	1428, §1	1580, §1
1389, §2	X	1428, §2	1581
1390, §1	2363	1428, §3	1582
1390, §2–§3	2355	1429	1584
1391	2360–2362; 2406	1430	1586
1392	2380	1431	X
1393	X	1432	1586
1394	2388	1433	1587

1983	1917	1983	1917
1434	X	1475, §1	1645, §1
1435	1589, §1	1475, §2	1645, §3
1436, §1	1588, §1	1476	1646
1436, §2	1588, §2; 1590, §2	1477	1647
1437, §1	1585, §1	1478, §1–§3	1648
1437, §2	X	1478, §4	1650
1438, 1°–3°	1594, §1–§4	1479	1651, §1–§2
1439	X	1480, §1	1649
1440	X	1480, §2	1653, §5
1441	1595–1596	1481, §1	1655, §3
1442	1597	1481, §2	1655, §1
1443	1598, §1	1481, §3	1655, §2
1444	1599	1482, §1–§3	1656, §1–§3
1445, §1, 1°	1603, §1, 3°	1482, §4	X
1445, §1, 2°	1603, §1, 5°	1483	1657, §1–§2
1445, §1, 3°	1603, §1, 2°	1484, §1	1659, §1
1445, §1, 4°	1603, §1, 6°	1484, §2	X
1445, §2–§3	X	1485	1662
1446, §1–§2	1925, §1–§2	1486	1664
1446, §3	1927	1487	1663
1447	1571	1488, §1	1665, §1–§2
1448	1613	1488, §2	X
1449, §1–§4	1614, §1–§3	1489	1666
1450	1615, §1	1490	X
1451, §1	1616	1491	1667
1451, §2	X	1492, §1	1701
1452, §1	1618	1492, §2	1667
1452, §2	1619	1493	1669, §1
1453	1620	1494	1690
1454	1621, §1–§2	1495	1692
1455	1623	1496, §1–§2	1672, §1–§2
1456	1624	1497	1673
1457, §1–§2	1625, §1–§3	1498	1674
1458	1627	1499	X
1459, §1	X	1500	X
1459, §2	1628, §2	1501	X
1460	1610	1502	1706
1461	1611	1503, §1	1707, §1–§2
1462	1629	1503, §2	1707, §3
1463	1630	1504, 1°–2°	1708, 1°–2°
1464	1631	1504, 3°–4°	1708, 3°
1465	1634	1505, §1	1709, §1
1466	X	1505, §2	X
1467	1635	1505, §3–§4	1709, §2–§3
1468	1636; 1638, §1	1506	1710
1469, §1	1637	1507, §1	1711, §1
1469, §2	X	1507, §2	X
1470	1640	1507, §3	1711, §2
1471	1641	1508, §1	1712, §2–§3
1472, §1	1642, §1	1508, §2	1712, §1
1472, §2	1643, §1	1508, §3	1713
1473	1643, §3	1509, §1	1715; 1719; 1724
1474, §1–§2	1644, §1–§2	1509, §2	1722, §1–§2

1983	1917	1983	1917
1510	1718	1555	1764, §1–§2
1511	1723	1556	1765
1512	1725	1557	1766, §1
1513, §1	1726	1558, §1	1770, §1
1513, §2	1727–1728	1558, §2	1770, §2, 1°
1513, §3	X	1558, §3	1770, §2, 2°–4°
1514	1729, §4; 1731, 1°	1559	1771
1515	1731, 3°	1560, §1	1772, §1
1516	1731, 2°	1560, §2	1772, §2–§3
1517	1732	1561	1773, §1–§2
1518	1733	1562, §1	1767, §1, §4
1519, §1–§2	1735	1562, §2	X
1520	1736	1563	1774
1521	1737	1564	1775
1522	1738	1565	1776
1523	1739	1566	1777
1524, §1	1740, §1	1567, §1	1778
1524, §2	X	1567, §2	X
1524, §3	1740, §2	1568	1779
1525	1741	1569	1780
1526, §1	1748, §1	1570	1781
1526, §2, 1°	1747, 2°	1571	1787, §1–§2
1526, §2, 2°	1747, 3°	1572	1789
1527	X	1573	1791, §1–§2
1528	X	1574	1792
1529	1730	1575	1793, §1
1530	1742, §1–§2	1576	1796, §1
1531	1743, §1–§2	1577, §1	1799, §1
1532	1744	1577, §2	X
1533	1745, §1	1577, §3	1799, §2
1534	1745, §2	1578, §1	1802
1535	1750	1578, §2	1801, §3
1536, §1	1751	1578, §3	1801, §2
1536, §2	X	1579	1804
1537	1753	1580	1805
1538	1752	1581	X
1539	1812	1582	1806
1540	1813	1583	1811
1541	1814; 1816	1584	1825, §1–§2
1542	1817	1585	1827
1543	1818	1586	1828
1544	1819–1820	1587	1837
1545	X	1588	1838
1546	1823	1589, §1–§2	1839; 1840, §1
1547	1754	1590, §1	1840, §2
1548, §1–§2	1755, §1–§2	1590, §2	X
1549	1756	1591	1841
1550, §1	1757, §1	1592, §1	1842; 1844, §1
1550, §2, 1°–2°	1757, §3, 1°–2°	1592, §2	1843, §1–§2
1551	1759, §4	1593, §1	1846
1552	1761	1593, §2	1847
1553	1762	1594, 1°	1849
1554	1763	1594, 2°	1850, §1

1983	1917	1983	1917
1594, 3°	X	1635	1886
1595	1851	1636	X
1596	1852	1637	1887–1888
1597	1853	1638	1889, §2
1598, §1	1858–1859	1639	1891
1598, §2	X	1640	X
1599	1860	1641, 1°–4°	1902, 1°–3°
1600, §1–§3	1861, §1–§2	1642	1904
1601	1862, §1	1643	1903
1602, §1	1863, §1	1644, §1	1903
1602, §2	1863, §3–§4	1644, §2	X
1602, §3	1864	1645, §1	1905, §1
1603, §1	1865, §1	1645, §2, 1°–5°	1905, §2, 1°–4°
1603, §2	1865, §2	1646, §1–§2	1906
1603, §3	X	1646, §3	X
1604, §1	1866, §1	1647	1907
1604, §2	1866, §2	1648	X
1605	1866, §4	1649	X
1606	1867	1650, §1–§2	1917, §1–§2
1607	1868, §1	1650, §3	X
1608	1869	1651	1918
1609	1871	1652	1919
1610, §1	1872	1653	1920
1610, §2	1873, §2	1654	1921
1610, §3	X	1655, §1	1922, §1
1611	1873, §1	1655, §2	1922, §2
1612, §1	1874, §1–§2	1656–1670	X
1612, §2–§4	1874, §3–§5	1671	1960
1613	1875	1672	1961
1614	1876	1673, 1°–2°	1964
1615	1877	1673, 3°–4°	X
1616, §1	1878, §1	1674, 1°–2°	1971, §1, 1°–2°
1616, §2	1878, §2–§3	1675, §1	1972
1617	1868, §2	1675, §2	X
1618	X	1676	1965
1619	X	1677	X
1620, 1°–8°	1892, 1°–3°	1678, §1	1968, 1°–2°; 1969, 1°–2°
1621	1893	1678, §2	X
1622, 1°–6°	1894, 1°–4°	1679	X
1623	1895	1680	1976; 1982
1624	1895; 1896	1681	1963, §2
1625	1895	1682, §1–§2	1986
1626	1897	1683	X
1627	X	1684, §1	1987
1628	1879	1684, §2	X
1629, 1°–5°	1880, 1°–8°	1685	1988
1630, §1	1881	1686	1990
1630, §2	1882	1687, §1	1991
1631	X	1687, §2	X
1632	X	1688	1992
1633	1883	1689–1696	X
1634, §1–§2	1884, §1–§2	1697	1973
1634, §3	X	1698, §1	1962

1983	1917	1983	1917
1698, §2	X	1718, §2–§4	X
1699, §1	1963, §1	1719	1946, §2, 1°
1699, §2–§3	X	1720	X
1700, §1	1966	1721, §1	1954
1700, §2	X	1721, §2	X
1701, §1	1967	1722	1956–1958
1701, §2	X	1723–1727	X
1702	X	1728, §1	1959
1703, §1	1985	1728, §2	1744
1703, §2	X	1729–1731	X
1704, §1	1985	1732–1739	X
1704, §2	X	1740	2147, §1; 2157, §1
1705, §1	1985	1741	2147, §2
1705, §2–§3	X	1742, §1	2148, §1–§2; 2158
1706	X	1742, §2	2157, §2
1707	X	1743	2150, §3
1708	1994, §1	1744, §1	2149, §2; 2159
1709, §1	1993 §1	1744, §2	2149, §1; 2159
1709, §2	1997	1745, 1°–2°	2153, §1; 2159
1710	1995	1745, 3°	2153, §3; 2161, §1
1711	1996	1746	2154, §1; 2161, §2
1712	1998, §1	1747, §1	2156, §1
1713	1925, §1; 1929	1747, §2	2156, §2
1714	1926; 1930	1747, §3	2146, §3
1715	1927; 1930	1748	2162
1716	X	1749	2164
1717, §1	1939, §1	1750	2165; 2166
1717, §2	1943	1751	2167
1717, §3	1941, §2–§3; 1944	1752	2156, §1–2; 2146, §3
1718, §1	1946, §2		

TABLE OF CORRESPONDING CANONS: 1917 CODE WITH 1983 CODE

Editors' Note: At times there is a literal correspondence between the canons of the 1983 Code and those of the 1917 Code. At other times there is a substantial correspondence between them even though there are notable differences terminologically. At still other times there is only a partial correspondence between the canons of the two Codes. Finally at times there is no correspondence between the canons of the revised Code and those of the former Code, and this is indicated by an "X" in the right-hand column.

1917	1983	1917	1983
	Book I		
1	1	35	201
2	2	36, §1	60
3	3	36, §2	X
4	4	37	61
5	5	38	62
6	6	39	39
7	361	40	X
8, §1	7	41	63, §3
8, §2	13, §1	42, §1	63, §1
9	8, §1	42, §2	63, §2
10	9	42, §3	X
11	10	43	64
12	11	44, §1	65, §1
13	12	44, §2	X
14	13, §2	45	63, §1–§2
15	14	46	38
16	15	47	66
17	16	48	53; 67
18	17	49	36, §1–§2
19	18	50	36, §1
20	19	51	68
21	X	52	69
22	20	53	40
23	21	54, §1	41
24	54, §2; 58, §2	54, §2	70
25	23	55	42
26	25	56	37
27	26	57	43
28	26	58	44
29	27	59, §1	45
30	28	59, §2	X
31	200	60, §1	47
32	202, §1	60, §2	73
33	X	61	X
34, §1–§2	202, §2	62	75
34, §3, 2°–3°	203, §1	63, §1	X
34, §3, 3°–4°	203, §2	63, §2	76, §2

1917	1983	1917	1983
64	X	105	127
65	X	106	X
66	132	107	207, §1–§2
67	77	108, §1	266, §1
68	77	108, §2–§3	X
69	71	109–110	X
70	78, §1	111, §1	265
71	79	111, §2	266, §1
72	80	112	267, §1
73	81	113	272
74	78, §2	114	X
75	78, §3	115	268, §2
76	82	116	267, §2
77	83	117	269
78	84	118	274, §1
79	74	119	1370, §3
80	85	120	X
81	87	121	289, §1
82	88	122	X
83	89	123	X
84	90	124	276, §1
85	92	125, §1	X
86	93	125, §2	276, §2, 5°
		126	276, §4
Book II		127	273
		128	274, §1
87	96	129	279, §1
88, §1	97, §1	130	X
88, §2	X	131	279, §2
88, §3	97, §2; 99	132	277, §1
89	98, §1–§2	133, §1	277, §2
90	101	133, §2	X
91	100	133, §3	277, §3
92	102	134	280
93	104; 105	135	276, §3
94	107	136, §1	284
95	106	136, §2	X
96	108	136, §3	X
97, §1–§2	109	137	285, §4
97, §3	109, §2	138	285, §1
98, §1	111, §1	139, §1	285, §2
98, §2	X	139, §2	285, §3
98, §3	112, §1, 1°	139, §3	285, §4
98, §4	112, §1, 2°	139, §4	X
98, §5	112, §2	140	X
99	113, §2	141	289, §1
100, §1	113, §1; 114, §1	142	286
100, §2	115, §2	143	283, §1
100, §3	X	144	271, §3
101	119	145, §1	145, §1
102	120	145, §2	X
103	125	146	X
104	126	147, §1	146

1917	1983		1917	1983
147, §2	X		187, §2	X
148, §1	147		188, 1°–3°	X
148, §2	X		188, 4°	194, §1, 2°
149	15		188, 5°	194, §1, 3°
150, §1	153, §1		188, 6°–8°	X
150, §2	153, §3		189, §1	189, §2
151	154		189, §2	189, §3
152	157		190	X
153, §1	149, §1		191, §1	189, §4
153, §2	X		191, §2	X
153, §3	149, §2		192, §1	196, §1
154	150		192, §2–§3	193, §1–§3
155	151		193, §1	190, §1
156, §1–§2	152		193, §2	190, §2
156, §3	X		194	191
157	X		195	X
158	155		196	129–130
159	156		197	131, §1–§2
160	164		198	134, §1–§2
161	165		199	137
162, §1–§4	166		200, §1	138
162, §5	X		200, §2	131, §3
163	167, §1		201, §1	91; 136
164	168		201, §2	X
165	169		201, §3	91; 136
166	170		202	X
167	171		203	133
168	167, §2		204	139
169	172		205	140
170	X		206	141
171, §1–§3	173, §1–§3		207, §1–§2	142
171, §4	X		207, §3	X
171, §5	173, §4		208	143
172, §1–§3	174, §1–§3		209	144, §1
172, §4	X		210	X
173	175		211, §1	290
174	176		211, §2	X
175	177, §1		212, §1	X
176, §1	177, §2		212, §2	293
176, §2	178		213, §1	292
176, §3	179, §4		213, §2	291
177, §1–§3	179, §1–§3		214, §1	290, 1°
177, §4	179, §5		214, §2	1708–1712
178	X		215, §1	373
179	180		215, §2	368; 381, §2
180	181		216, §1–§3	374, §1
181	182		216, §4	X
182	183		217, §1	374, §2
183	184, §1–§2		217, §2	X
184	187		218, §1	331
185	188		218, §2	333, §1
186	189, §1		219	332, §1
187, §1	189, §1		220	X

1917	1983	1917	1983
221	332, §2	274, 6°	436, §3
222, §1	338, §1	275	437, §1
222, §2	338, §1–§2	276	X
223, §1–§2	339, §1	277	437, §2
223, §3	339, §2	278	437, §3
224–225	X	279	X
226	338, §2	280	X
227	341, §1	281	439, §1
228, §1	X	282, §1–§3	443, §1–§6
228, §2	333, §3	283	440, §1
229	340	284, 1°	442, §1, 2°
230	349	284, 2°	442, §1, 1°
231, §1–§2	350, §1–§2	285	X
232, §1	351, §1	286, §1–§3	443, §1–§6
232, §2	X	287, §1–§2	444, §2
233, §1	351, §2	288	442, §1, 3°
233, §2	351, §3	289	X
234	X	290	445
235	X	291, §1	446
236, §1	350, §5	291, §2	X
236, §2	350, §6	292	X
236, §3	X	293, §1	371, §1
236, §4	350, §4	293, §2	X
237, §1	352, §1	294, §1	381, §2
237, §2	352, §2	294, §2	X
238, §1	356	295–298	X
238, §2	X	299	400, §3
238, §3	356	300–301	X
239, §1	X	302	495, §2; 502, §4
239, §2–§3	355, §1–§2	303–308	X
240, §1	357, §2	309, §1	420
240, §2–§3	X	309, §2–§4	X
241	359	310, §1	420
242	360	310, §2	X
243–264	X	311	X
265	362	312	371, §2
266	358	313–318	X
267, §1, 1°	365, §1, 1°	319, §1	370
267, §1, 2°	364, 1°	319, §2–328	X
267, §1, 3°	364, 8°	329, §1	375, §1
267, §2	X	329, §2	377, §1
268, §1–§2	367	329, §3	X
269, §1	364, 2°	330	X
269, §2	X	331, §1, 1°	X
269, §3	X	331, §1, 2°	378, §1, 3°
270	X	331, §1, 3°	378, §1, 4°
271	438	331, §1, 4°	378, §1, 1°
272	435	331, §1, 5°	378, §1, 5°
273	X	331, §2	X
274, 1°–2°	X	331, §3	378, §2
274, 3°	436, §1, 3°	332, §1	X
274, 4°	436, §1, 1°	332, §2	380
274, 5°	436, §1, 5°	333	379; 382, §2

1917	1983	1917	1983
334, §1	381, §1	367, §1	478, §1
334, §2	382, §1	367, §2	X
334, §3	382, §3	367, §3	478, §2
335, §1	391, §1	368, §1	479, §1
335, §2	X	368, §2	479, §3
336	392	369	480
337, §1	390	370	X
337, §2–§3	X	371	481
338	395	372	482
339, §1	388, §1	373, §1–§2	483, §1
339, §2–§3	X	373, §3–§4	483, §2
339, §4	388, §2	373, §5	485
339, §5	388, §3	374, §1	484
339, §6	388, §4	374, §2	X
340, §1	399, §1	375, §1	486, §1–§2
340, §2	X	375, §2	486, §3
340, §3	399, §2	376	X
341, §1	400, §1	377	487, §1
341, §2	X	378, §1	488
342	400, §2	378, §2	X
343, §1–§2	396	379, §1	489
343, §3	X	379, §2	X
344	397	379, §3	490, §1
345	X	379, §4	490, §3
346	398	380	X
347	X	381	X
348	X	382, §1	490, §2
349	X	382, §2	X
350	403	383, §1	491, §1
351, §1	405, §1	383, §2	491, §3
351, §2	405, §2	384, §1	487, §2
351, §3	408, §2	384, §2	491, §3
351, §4	408, §1	385–390	X
352	X	391, §1	503
353	404	391, §2	X
354	410	392	504
355, §1–§3	409, §1–§2	393, §1	507, §1
356	460; 461	393, §2–§3	X
357, §1	462	394–400	X
357, §2	X	401, §1	508, §1
358	463	401, §2	X
359	464	402	510, §1
360	X	403	509, §1
361	465	404	509, §2
362	466	405–409	X
363, §1	469	410, §1–§2	505
363, §2	X	410, §3	X
364, §1	470	411–414	X
364, §2	471	415	510
365	472	416–422	X
366, §1	475, §1	423	502, §1
366, §2	477, §1	424	502, §1
366, §3	475, §1; 477, §2	425, §1	502, §1

1917	1983	1917	1983
425, §2	X	456	X
426, §1–§2	502, §1	457	X
426, §3–§5	X	458	X
427	502, §1	459, §1	524
428	X	459, §2	521, §2
429, §1	412; 413, §1	459, §3	521, §3
429, §2	413, §1	459, §4	X
429, §3	413, §2	460, §1	526, §1
429, §4	413, §3	460, §2	526, §2
429, §5	415	461	527, §1
430, §1	416	462	530
430, §2	417	463	531
430, §3	418	464	X
431, §1–§2	419	465, §1	533, §1
432, §1	421, §1	465, §2–§5	533, §2
432, §2	421, §2	465, §6	X
432, §3	X	466, §1	534, §1
432, §4	422	466, §2	534, §2
433, §1	423, §1	466, §3–§5	X
433, §2	424	467, §1	528, §2
433, §3	423, §2	467, §2	X
434	425	468	529, §1
435, §1	426; 427, §1	469	528, §1
435, §2	X	470, §1	535, §1
435, §3	428, §2	470, §2	535, §2
436	428, §1	470, §3	X
437	X	470, §4	535, §3–§4
438	427, §2	471	X
439	X	472	539
440	429	473	540
441	X	474	X
442	X	475	X
443, §1	430, §2	476, §1–§2	545, §1–§2
443, §2	430, §1	476, §3–§4	547
444	X	476, §5	550, §1
445	553, §1	476, §6	548, §1–§2
446, §1	553, §2	476, §7–§8	X
446, §2	554, §3	477, §1	552
447	555, §1, §3–§4	477, §2	X
448, §1	555, §2	478	X
448, §2	X	479, §1	556
449	X	479, §2	X
450	X	480	557
451, §1	519	481	558
451, §2, 1°	516, §1–§2	482	559
451, §2, 2°	X	483	560
451, §2, 3°	569	484, §1	561
452, §1	520, §1	484, §2	X
452, §2	X	485	562
453	521	486	563
454	522; 538, §2	487	573; 598, §1; 607; 710; 731
455, §1	523		
455, §2–§3	525	488, 1°	573

1917	1983	1917	1983
488, 2°	591	516, §1	627, §1
488, 3°	589; 593	516, §2	627, §2; 636, §1
488, 4°	588	516, §3	X
488, 5°	608	516, §4	636, §1
488, 6°	621	517	X
488, 7°	607, §2	518, §1	X
488, 8°	613, §2; 620	518, §2	630, §4
489	587	518, §3	630, §4
490	606	519	X
491	X	520–528	630
492, §1	579	529	567
492, §2	594	530, §1	630, §5
492, §3	X	530, §2	630, §5
493	584	531	634, §1
494, §1	580; 581; 582	532, §1	635, §1–§2
494, §2	585; 593	532, §2	638, §1–§2
495, §1	583; 594; 595	533, §1–§4	638
495, §2	X	534, §1	638, §3–§4
496	610, §2	534, §2	638, §3
497, §1	609, §1–§2	535, §1–§3	637
497, §2	611	536, §1	639, §1
497, §3	611	536, §2	639, §2
497, §4	612	536, §3	639, §3
498	616, §1	536, §4	639, §4
499, §1	590, §2	536, §5	639, §5
499, §2	X	537	640
500, §1	595	538	597, §1
500, §2	614	539, §1	597, §2
500, §3	X	539, §2	X
501, §1	596; 601; 608; 631, §1	540, §1–§3	X
501, §2	X	541	X
501, §3	620	542, 1°	597, §1; 642; 643, §1, 1°–4°
502	617		
503	X	542, 2°	644; 645, §1
504	623	543	641; 656, 3°; 658
505	624	544, §1	645, §1
506, §1	626	544, §2	X
506, §2	625, §2	544, §3	645, §2
506, §3	X	544, §4	645, §2
506, §4	625, §2	544, §5	684, §1
507, §1	626	544, §6	645, §4
507, §2	626	544, §7	645, §2
507, §3	X	545–553	X
508	629	554, §1	647, §1
509, §1	592, §2	554, §2	X
509, §2	X	554, §3	651, §3
510	592, §1	555, §1, 1°	643, §1, 1°
511	628, §1	555, §1, 2°	648, §1
512, §1	595; 628, §2	555, §1, 3°	648, §1
512, §2	628, §2	555, §2	648, §2
513	628, §3	556, §1	649, §1
514, §1–§4	X	556, §2	649, §1
515	X	556, §3	647, §2

1917	1983	1917	1983
556, §4	647, §1	609	X
557	X	610	663, §3
558	X	611	X
559, §1	650, §1–§2; 651, §1	612	678, §1
559, §2	651, §2	613	X
559, §3	651, §3	614	X
560	651, §1–§3	615	591
561, §1	650, §1–§2; 652, §4	616	X
562, §2	652, §3	617	679; 683, §2
562	652, §1	618, §1	X
563	652, §1	618, §2	583; 586
564, §1	652, §4	619	698, §2
564, §2	X	620–625	X
565, §1	652, §2	626	671
565, §2	X	627	705
565, §3	652, §5	628, 1°	706, 1°
566–570	X	628, 2°	706, 2°
571, §1	653, §1	628, 3°	706, 3°
571, §2	653, §2	629, §1	707, §1
571, §3	X	629, §2	707, §2
572, §1, 1°	656, 1°	630	X
572, §1, 2°	656, 3°	631, §1	681, §1
572, §1, 3°	656, 2°	631, §2	X
572, §1, 4°	656, 4°	631, §3	682, §2
572, §1, 5°	656, 4°	632	684, §1
572, §1, 6°	656, 5°	633, §1	685, §1; 684, §2
572, §2	658, 1°–2°	633, §2	684, §2
573	656, 1°; 658, 1°	633, §3	684, §3
574, §1	655	634	684, §2, §4
574, §2	657, §2	635, 1°	684, §3
575, §1	657, §1; 688, §2	635, 2°	X
575, §2	656, 3°; 658	636	685, §2
576	X	637	688, §1; 689, §1–§2
577, §1	657, §1	638	686, §1–§2; 691, §1–§2
577, §2	657, §3	639	687
578	X	640, §1, 1°	693
579	1088	640, §1, 2°	692; 693
580–586	X	640, §2	690, §1–§2
587–591	659, §3	641	693
592	699, §2; 672	642	X
593	662	643, §1	702, §1
594, §1	X	643, §2	702, §2
594, §2	668, §3	644	X
594, §3	X	645, §1	X
595, §1	663, §1, §3	645, §2	665, §2
595, §2	663, §2	646, §1, 1°	694, §1, 1°
595, §3	X	646, §1, 2°	695, §1; 1395, §1
595, §4	X	646, §1, 3°	694, §1, 2°
596	669, §1	646, §2	694, §2
597–605	667	647, §1	696, §1–§2
606	X	647, §2, 1°	696, §2
607	665, §1	647, §2, 2°	696, §1–§2
608	675	647, §2, 3°	698

1917	1983	1917	1983
647, §2, 4°	700	686, §3	312, §2
647, §2, 5°	702, §2	686, §4–§5	X
648	701; 693	687	313
649	696, §1; 697	688	300
650, §1	699, §1	689, §1	304, §1; 314
650, §2, 1°	700	689, §2	X
650, §2, 2°	700	690, §1	305, §1
650, §3	698	690, §2	X
651, §1	696, §1	691, §1	319, §1
651, §2	698	691, §2–§4	X
652, §1	699, §1; 700	691, §5	319, §2
652, §2	699, §2	692	306
652, §3	699, §1; 700	693, §1	316, §1
653	703	693, §2	307, §2
654	X	693, §3–§5	X
655, §1	699, §1	694, §1	307, §1
655, §2	X	694, §2	X
656	X	695	X
657	X	696, §1	308
658	X	696, §2	316, §2
659	697, 1°–2°	696, §3	X
660	697, 2°	697	309
661, §1	X	698, §1	317, §1–§2
661, §2	X	698, §2	X
661, §3	697, 2°	698, §3	318, §1–§2
662	697, 3°	698, §4	317, §3
663	697, 3°	699, §1	320, §2
664	X	699, §2	320, §1
665	X	700–725	X
666	700		
667	X	*Book III*	
668	703		
669, §1	701	726–730	X
669, §2	X	731, §1	840
670	X	731, §2	844
671	X	732	845
672, §1	X	733	845
672, §2	701	734, §1	847, §1
673, §1	731; 740	734, §2	X
673, §2	588; 732	735	847, §2; 1003, §3
674	579; 584; 585; 732; 733	736	848
675	734; 738	737, §1	849
676	741	737, §2	X
677	735, §1–§2	738	857, §2; 861, §1
678	735, §3; 736	739	862
679, §1	737; 739	740	X
681	742; 743; 744; 745; 746	741	861, §2
682	213	742	861, §2
683	X	743	861, §2
684	298, §2	744	863
685	298, §1	745, §1	864
686, §1	299, §3	745, §2, 1°	852, 2°
686, §2	312, §1	745, §2, 2°	852, 1°

1917	1983	1917	1983
746	X	788	891
747	871	789	X
748	X	790	881
749	870	791	881
750, §1	868, §2	792	888
750, §2	868, §1, 1°–2°	793	892
751	868, §2	794	X
752, §1	851, 1°; 865, §1	795	893, §1
752, §2	865, §2	796	893, §1
753, §1	X	797	892
753, §2	866	798	895
754	852, §2	799	896
755	X	800	894
756, §1–§2	111, §1	801	897–899
756, §3	X	802	900
757, §1	853	803	902
757, §2–§3	X	804, §1–§2	903
758	854	804, §3	X
759	X	805	904
760	X	806	905
761	855	807	916
762	872	808	919, §1–§3
763	X	809	901
764	873	810	909
765	874, §1	811, §1	929
766	874, §1	811, §2	X
767	X	812	X
768	X	813, §1	906
769	872	813, §2	X
770	867	814	924, §1
771	X	815	924, §2–§3
772	856	816	926
773	857, §1	817	927
774	858	818	846, §1
775	859	819	928
776, §1	860, §1	820	931
776, §2	X	821	931
777, §1	877, §1	822	932
777, §2	877, §2	823, §1	933
778	878	823, §2–§3	X
779	876	824, §1	945, §1
780	880, §1	824, §2	951
781, §1	880, §2	825	X
781, §2	X	826	X
782, §1	882; 883, 1°	827	947
782, §2	882	828	948
783	886	829	949
784	887	830	950
785, §1	885, §1	831	952
785, §2	885, §2	832	952
785, §3–§4	X	833	X
786	889	834	X
787	890	835	953

1917	1983	1917	1983
836	954	881	X
837	955, §1–§2	882	976
838	955, §1	883	X
839	955, §1	884	977
840, §1	955, §1	885	X
840, §2	X	886	980
841	956	887	981
842	957	888, §1	978, §1
843	958	888, §2	979
844, §1	955, §3	889	983
844, §2	955, §4	890	984
845	910	891	985
846–849	X	892	986
850	911	893	X
851, §1	926	894	982
851, §2	X	895–900	X
852	925	901	988, §1
853	912	902	988, §2
854, §1–§2	913	903	990
854, §3–§5	914	904	X
855	915	905	991
856	916	906	989
857	917	907	X
858, §1–§2	919, §1–§3	908	964, §1
859, §1–§2	920	909	964, §2
859, §3	X	910	964, §3
859, §4	920	911	992; 994
860–863	X	912	995, §1
864	921	913	995, §2
865	922	914–924	X
866, §1	923	925	996
866, §2–§3	X	926–929	X
867, §1–§3	931	930	994
867, §4	918	931–936	X
867, §5	931	937	998
868	932	938	1003, §1–§2
869	932	939	X
870	959	940	1004
871	965	941	1005
872	966	942	1007
873, §1	967, §1; 968, §1	943	1006
873, §2	968, §1–§2	944	1001
874	969, §1	945	999
875	969, §2	946	X
876	X	947, §1	1000, §1
877, §1	970	947, §2	X
877, §2	X	947, §3	X
878, §1	972	947, §4	1000, §2
878, §2	X	948	1008
879, §1	973	949	1009, §1
879, §2	X	950	X
880, §1	974, §1	951	1012
880, §2–§3	X	952	X

1917	1983	1917	1983
953	1013	987, 7°	X
954	1014	988	1045
955	1015, §1–§2	989	1046
956	1016	990, §1	1047
957	X	990, §2	1048
958	1018	991, §1–§3	1049
959	1015, §3	991, §4	X
960, §1	1020	992	1036, §1
960, §2–§3	X	993, 1°	1050, 2°–3°
961	1021	993, 2°	1050, 1°
962	1022	993, 3°	1051, 1°
963	1023	993, 4°	X
964	1019	993, 5°	1051, 1°
965	X	994	X
966	X	995	1052
967	X	996	1028
968, §1	1024	997	1052
969	1025	998	X
970	1030	999	1043
971	1026	1000	X
972	235	1001	1039
973, §1	X	1002	1009, §2
973, §2	1038	1003	X
973, §3	X	1004	X
974, §1	1029; 1033	1005	X
974, §2	X	1006, §1–§3	1010
975	1031, §1	1006, §4–§5	X
976, §1	X	1007	X
976, §2	1032, §1	1008	1017
976, §3	X	1009, §1–§2	1011
977–982	X	1009, §3	X
983	1040	1010	1053
984, 1°	X	1011	1054
984, 2°	X	1012	1055
984, 3°	1041, 1°	1013	1056
984, 4°	X	1014	1060
984, 5°	X	1015	1061
984, 6°	X	1016	1059
984, 7°	X	1017	1062
985, 1°	1041, 2°	1018	1063, 1°
985, 2°	X	1019, §1	1066
985, 3°	1041, 3°	1019, §2	1068
985, 4°	1041, 4°	1020, §1	1067
985, 5°	1041, 5°	1020, §3	1064
985, 6°	X	1021, §1	X
985, 7°	1041, 6°	1021, §2	1065
986	X	1022	X
987, 1°	1042, 1°	1023–1026	1067
987, 2°	X	1027	1069
987, 3°	1042, 2°	1028	1067
987, 4°	X	1029	1070
987, 5°	X	1030–1031	X
987, 6°	1042, 3°	1032	1071, §1, 1°

1917	1983	1917	1983
1033	1063, 2°	1088	1104
1034	1072	1089, §1	1105, §1–§2
1035	1058	1089, §2	1105, §3
1036, §1	X	1089, §3	1105, §4
1036, §2	1073	1089, §4	X
1036, §3	X	1090	1106
1037	1074	1091	1071, §1, 7°
1038	1075	1092, 1°–2°	X
1039	1077	1092, 3°	1102, §1
1040	1078	1092, 4°	1102, §2
1041	1076	1093	1107
1042	X	1094	1108, §1
1043	1079, §1	1095, §1, 1°	1109
1044	1079, §2–§3	1095, §1, 2°	1110
1045, §1–§3	1080, §1–§2	1095, §1, 3°	X
1046	1081	1095, §2	1111, §1
1047	1082	1096, §1	1111, §2
1048–1059	X	1096, §2	1113
1060	1124	1097, §1, 1°	1114
1061	1125	1097, §1, 2°–3°	X
1062	1127, §3	1097, §2	1115
1063, §1	1127, §3	1098	1116
1063, §2–§3	X	1099, §1, 1°–3°	1117; 1127, §1
1064	X	1099, §2	X
1065, §1	1071, §1, 4°	1100	1119
1065, §2	1071, §2	1101	X
1066	1071, §1, 5°	1102	X
1067, §1	1083, §1	1103, §1	1121, §1
1067, §2	1072	1103, §2	1122
1068	1084	1103, §3	1121, §2
1069	1085	1104	1130
1070	1086	1105	1131
1071	1129	1106	1132
1072	1087	1107	1133
1073	1088	1108	X
1074	1089	1109	1118
1075, 1°	X	1110	1134
1075, 2°	1090, §1	1111	1135
1075, 3°	1090, §2	1112	X
1076	1091	1113	1136
1077, §1	1092	1114	1137
1077, §2	X	1115	1138
1078, §1–§2	1040	1116	1139
1078, §3	1076, §3	1117	1140
1079	X	1118	1141
1080	1094	1119	1142
1081	1057	1120, §1	1143, §1
1082	1096	1120, §2	X
1083	1097	1121	1144
1084	1099	1122, §1–§2	1145, §1–§3
1085	1100	1123	1146
1086	1101	1124	X
1087	1103	1125	1148; 1149

1917	1983	1917	1983
1126	X	1165, §4	X
1127	1150	1165, §5	X
1128	1151	1166	X
1129, §1	1152, §1	1167	X
1129, §2	1152, §2	1168, §1	1218
1130	1152, §3	1168, §2–§3	X
1131	1153	1169	X
1132	1154	1170	1212
1133	1156	1171	1219
1134	1157	1172, §1	1211
1135	1158	1172, §2	X
1136	1159	1173, §1	1211
1137	1160	1173, §2	X
1138, §1–§2	1161, §1–§2	1174	X
1138, §3	1164	1175	X
1139	1163	1176	X
1140	1162	1177	X
1141	1165, §1	1178	1220, §1
1142	X	1179	X
1143	X	1180	X
1144	1166	1181	1221
1145	1167, §1	1182–1186	X
1146	1168	1187	1222, §1; 1238, §1
1147, §1	1169, §1	1188, §1	1223
1147, §2	1169, §2	1188, §2	X
1147, §3	X	1189	1227
1147, §4	1169, §3	1190	X
1148, §1	1167, §2	1191	X
1148, §2	X	1192, §1–§2	1224, §1
1149	1170	1192, §3	1224, §2
1150	1171	1193	1225
1151	1172	1194	1228
1152	X	1195	1228
1153	X	1196, §1–§2	1229
1154	1205	1197	1235
1155, §1–§2	1206	1198, §1–§2	1236, §1
1156	1207	1198, §3	X
1157	X	1198, §4	1237, §2
1158	1208	1199, §1	1237, §1
1159, §1	1209	1199, §2–§3	X
1159, §2	X	1200, §1–§2	1238, §1
1160	1213	1200, §3–§4	X
1161	1214	1201	X
1162, §1	1215, §1	1202	1239
1162, §2	1215, §2	1203, §1	1176, §1, §3
1162, §3	1215, §2	1203, §2	X
1162, §4	1215, §3	1204	X
1163	X	1205, §1	1176, §1
1164, §1	1216	1205, §2	1242
1164, §2	X	1206, §1	1240, §1
1165, §1	1217, §1	1206, §2	1240, §1
1165, §2	X	1206, §3	1240, §2
1165, §3	1217, §2	1207	X

1917	1983	1917	1983
1208, §1	1241, §1	1251	X
1208, §2	1241, §1	1252	1251
1208, §3	1241, §2	1253	X
1209	X	1254	1252
1210–1214	X	1255	X
1215	X	1256	834, §2
1216, §1	1177, §1–§2	1257	838, §1–§2
1216, §2	X	1258	844, §1–§2
1217	1177, §3	1259, §1	839, §2
1218	X	1259, §2	X
1219, §1	1178	1260	X
1219, §2	X	1261	838, §4
1220	1179	1262	X
1221	X	1263	X
1222	X	1264	X
1223, §1	1180, §2	1265, §1	934
1223, §2	X	1265, §2	X
1224	X	1265, §3	935
1225	X	1266	937
1226	X	1267	936
1227	X	1268, §1	938, §1
1228, §1	1180, §1	1268, §2	938, §2
1228, §2	X	1268, §3	X
1229–1233	X	1268, §4	938, §2
1234, §1	1181	1269, §1–§2	938, §3
1234, §2	X	1269, §3	938, §4
1235, §1	X	1269, §4	938, §5
1235, §2	1181	1270	939
1236	X	1271	940
1237	X	1272	939
1238	1182	1273	898
1239, §1	X	1274, §1	941
1239, §2	1183, §1	1274, §2	943
1239, §3	1176, §1	1275	942
1240, §1	1184, §1	1276	1186
1240, §1, 1°	1184, §1, 1°	1277, §1	1187
1240, §1, 2°	X	1277, §2	X
1240, §1, 3°	X	1278	X
1240, §1, 4°	X	1279, §1	1188
1240, §1, 5°	1184, §1, 2°	1279, §2	1188
1240, §1, 6°	1184, §1, 3°	1279, §3	1188
1240, §2	1184, §2	1279, §4	X
1241	1185	1280	1189
1242	X	1281, §1	1190, §2–§3
1243	X	1281, §2	X
1244	1044	1282–1288	X
1245	1245	1289, §1	1190, §1
1246	X	1289, §2	X
1247, §1	1246, §1	1290	X
1247, §2–§3	X	1291, §1	944, §1
1248	1247	1291, §2	X
1249	1248, §1	1292	944
1250	X	1293	X

1917	1983	1917	1983
1294	X	1346	767
1295	944, §2	1347	768
1296–1306	X	1348	X
1307	1191	1349	770
1308, §1	1192, §1	1350, §1	771, §2
1308, §2	1192, §2	1351	748, §2
1308, §3	X	1352	232
1308, §4	1192, §3	1353	233
1309	X	1354, §1	234, §1
1310, §1	1193	1354, §2	237, §1
1310, §2	X	1354, §3	237, §1–§2
1311	1194	1355, 1°–2°	264, §1
1312, §1	X	1355, 3°	X
1312, §2	1195	1356	264, §2
1313	1196	1357, §1–§2	259
1314	1197	1357, §3	243
1315	1198	1358	239, §1–§2
1316	1199	1359	X
1317, §1	1200, §1	1360, §1	X
1317, §2	1200, §2	1360, §2	260
1317, §3	X	1361	240
1318	1201	1362	X
1319	1202	1363	241
1320	1203	1364, 1°	X
1321	1204	1364, 2°	249
1322	747	1364, 3°	234, §2
1323, §1	750	1365, §1–§2	250
1323, §2	749, §1, §2	1365, §2	252, §3
1323, §3	749, §3	1365, §3	256, §1
1324	754	1366, §1	253, §1
1325, §1	X	1366, §2	X
1325, §2	751	1366, §3	253, §2
1325, §3	755	1367	246
1326	753	1368	262
1327	756; 757	1369, §1	261, §1
1328	757–759; 764–766	1369, §2	X
1329	773	1369, §3	261, §2
1330	777	1370	235
1331	777	1371	X
1332	777	1372	793
1333	776	1373	804, §2
1334	776; 778	1374	793; 797; 798
1335	774	1375	800
1336	775	1376	816
1337	764	1377	817
1338	765	1378	X
1339	764	1379	800; 802; 809
1340	764	1380	819
1341	764	1381	803; 805–806; 810
1342	764; 766	1382	806
1343	763	1383	985
1344	767	1384, §1	823
1345	767	1384, §2	824, §2

1917	1983	1917	1983
1385	824–825; 827	1527	1281
1386	831	1528	1289
1387	X	1529	1290
1388	X	1530	1291–1293
1389	828	1531	1294
1390	826	1532	1293
1391	825; 827	1533	1295
1392	829	1534	1296
1393	830	1535	1285
1394	830	1536	1267
1395–1405	X	1537	1171
1406	833	1538	X
1407	833	1539	X
1408	X	1540	1298
1409–1494	X	1541	1297
1495	1255	1542	X
1496	1260	1543	X
1497, §1	1257, §1	1544	1303
1497, §2	X	1545	1304, §2
1498	1258	1546	1304, §1
1499, §1	1259	1547	1305
1499, §2	1256	1548	1306
1500	122	1549	1307
1501	X	1550	X
1502	X	1551	1308
1503	1265		
1504	X		*Book IV*
1505	1263		
1506	1263	1552, §1	X
1507	1264	1552, §2	1400
1508	1268	1553, §1, 1°–2°	1401
1509	199	1553, §1, 3°	X
1510	1269	1553, §2	X
1511	1270	1554	X
1512	198	1555, §1	X
1513	1299	1555, §2	1402
1514	1300	1556	1404
1515	1301	1557, §1	1405, §1, 1°–3°
1516	1302	1557, §2	1405, §3
1517	1308	1557, §3	1405, §1, §4
1518	1273	1558	1406, §2
1519	1276	1559	1407
1520, §1	492, §1	1560, 1°–2°	X
1520, §2	492, §3	1560, 3°–4°	1413, 1°–2°
1520, §3	1277	1561, §1	1408
1520, §4	X	1561, §2	X
1521, §1	1279, §2	1562	X
1521, §2	1282	1563	1409, §1
1522	1283	1564	1410
1523	1284	1565, §1–§2	1411, §1
1524	1286	1566, §1–§2	1412
1525	1207	1567	1414
1526	1288	1568	1415

1917	1983	1917	1983
1569	1417	1613	1448
1570, §1	X	1614, §1–§3	1449, §1–§4
1570, §2	1418	1615, §1	1450
1571	1447	1615, §2–§3	X
1572	1419	1616	1451
1573, §1–§5	1420, §1–§5	1617	X
1573, §6–§7	X	1618	1452, §1
1574, §1–§2	1421, §1–§3	1619	1452, §2
1574, §3	X	1620	1453
1575	1424	1621, §1–§2	1454
1576, §1–§3	1425, §1–§3	1622	X
1577	1426	1623	1455
1578	X	1624	1456
1579	1427	1625, §1–§3	1457, §1–§2
1580, §1	1428, §1	1626	X
1580, §2	X	1627	1458
1581	1428, §2	1628, §1	X
1582	1428, §3	1628, §2	1459, §2
1583	X	1629	1462
1584	1429	1630	1463
1585, §1	1437, §1	1631	1464
1585, §2	X	1632	X
1586	1430; 1432	1633	X
1587	1433	1634	1465
1588	1436, §1–§2	1635	1467
1589, §1	1435	1636	1468
1589, §2	X	1637	1469, §1
1590, §1	X	1638, §1	1468
1590, §2	1436, §2	1638, §2	X
1591	X	1639	X
1592	X	1640	1470
1593	X	1641	1471
1594, §1–§4	1438, 1°–3°	1642, §1	1472, §1
1595	1441	1642, §2	X
1596	1441	1643, §1	1472, §2
1597	1442	1643, §2	X
1598, §1	1443	1643, §3	1473
1598, §2–§4	X	1644, §1–§2	1474, §1–§2
1599	1444	1644, §3	X
1600	X	1645, §1	1475, §1
1601	1400, §2	1645, §2	X
1602	X	1645, §3	1475, §2
1603, §1, 1°	X	1645, §4	X
1603, §1, 2°	1445, §1, 3°	1646	1476
1603, §1, 3°	1445, §1, 1°	1647	1477
1603, §1, 4°	X	1648	1478, §1–§3
1603, §1, 5°	1445, §1, 2°	1649	1480
1603, §1, 6°	1445, §1, 4°	1650	1478, §4
1603, §2	X	1651, §1–§2	1479
1604–1609	X	1652	X
1610	1460	1653, §1–§4	X
1611	1461	1653, §5	1480, §2
1612, §1–§2	1416	1654	X

1917	1983	1917	1983
1655, §1	1481, §2	1715	1509, §1
1655, §2	1481, §3; 1723	1716	X
1655, §3	1481, §1	1717	X
1655, §4	X	1718	1510
1656, §1–§3	1482, §1–§2	1719	1509, §1
1657, §1–§2	1483	1720	X
1657, §3	X	1721	X
1658	1483	1722, §1–§2	1509, §2
1659	1484	1723	1511
1660	X	1724	1509, §1
1661	X	1725	1512
1662	1485	1726	1513, §1
1663	1487	1727	1513, §2
1664	1486	1728	1513, §2
1665, §1–§2	1488, §1	1729, §1–§3	X
1666	1489	1729, §4	1514
1667	1491; 1492, §2	1730	1529
1668	X	1731, 1°	1514
1669, §1	1493	1731, 2°	1516
1669, §2	X	1731, 3°	1515
1670	X	1732	1517
1671	X	1733	1518
1672, §1–§2	1496, §1–§2	1734	X
1672, §3	X	1735	1519, §1–§2
1673	1497	1736	1520
1674	1498	1737	1521
1675–1679	X	1738	1522
1680, §1	124, §1	1739	1523
1680, §2	X	1740, §1	1524, §1
1681	128	1740, §2	1524, §3
1682	X	1741	1525
1683	1405, §2	1742, §1–§2	1530
1684–1689	X	1742, §3	X
1690	1494	1743, §1–§2	1531
1691	X	1743, §3	X
1692	1495	1744	1532; 1728, §2
1693–1700	X	1745, §1	1533
1701	1492, §1	1745, §2	1534
1702–1705	X	1746	X
1706	1502	1747, 1°	X
1707, §1–§2	1503, §1	1747, 2°–3°	1526, §2, 1°–2°
1707, §3	1503, §2	1748, §1	1526, §1
1708, 1°–2°	1504, 1°–2°	1748, §2	X
1708, 3°	1504, 3°–4°	1749	X
1709, §1	1505, §1	1750	1535
1709, §2–§3	1505, §3–§4	1751	1536, §1
1710	1506	1752	1538
1711, §1	1507, §1	1753	1537
1711, §2	1507, §3	1754	1547
1712, §1	1508, §2	1755, §1–§2	1548, §1–§2
1712, §2–§3	1508, §1	1755, §3	X
1713	1508, §3	1756	1549
1714	X	1757, §1	1550, §1

1917	1983	1917	1983
1757, §2	X	1801, §1	X
1757, §3, 1°–2°	1550, §2, 1°–2°	1801, §2	1578, §3
1757, §3, 3°	X	1801, §3	1578, §2
1758	X	1802	1578, §1
1759, §1–§3	X	1803	X
1759, §4	1551	1804	1579
1760	X	1805	1580
1761	1552	1806	1582
1762	1553	1807–1810	X
1763	1554	1811	1583
1764, §1–§2	1555	1812	1539
1764, §3–§5	X	1813	1540
1765	1556	1814	1541
1766, §1	1557	1815	X
1766, §2	X	1816	1541
1767, §1	1562	1817	1542
1767, §2–§3	X	1818	1543
1767, §4	1562	1819	1544
1768	X	1820	1544
1769	X	1821	X
1770, §1	1558, §1	1822	X
1770, §2, 1°	1558, §2	1823	1546
1770, §2, 2°–4°	1558, §3	1824	X
1771	1559	1825, §1–§2	1584
1772, §1	1560, §1	1826	X
1772, §2–§3	1560, §2	1827	1585
1773, §1–§2	1561	1828	1586
1774	1563	1829–1836	X
1775	1564	1837	1587
1776	1565	1838	1588
1777	1566	1839	1589, §1–§2
1778	1567	1840, §1	1589
1779	1568	1840, §2	1590, §1
1780	1569	1840, §3	X
1781	1570	1841	1591
1782–1786	X	1842	1592
1787, §1–§2	1571	1843	1592, §2
1788	X	1844, §1	1592, §1
1789	1572	1844, §2	X
1790	X	1845	X
1791, §1–§2	1573	1846	1593, §1
1792	1574	1847	1593, §2
1793, §1	1575	1848	X
1793, §2–§3	X	1849	1594, 1°
1794	X	1850, §1–§3	X
1795	X	1851	1595
1796, §1	1576	1852	1596
1796, §2–§3	X	1853	1597
1797	X	1854–1857	X
1798	X	1858	1598, §1
1799, §1	1577, §1	1859	1598, §1
1799, §2	1577, §3	1860	1599
1800	X	1861, §1–§2	1600, §1–§3

1917	1983	1917	1983
1862, §1	1601	1907	1647
1862, §2	X	1908–1916	X
1863, §1	1602, §1	1917, §1–§2	1650, §1–§2
1863, §2	X	1918	1651
1863, §3–§4	1602, §2	1919	1652
1864	1602, §3	1920	1653
1865, §1–§2	1603, §1–§2	1921	1654
1866, §1–§2	1604	1922, §1	1655, §1
1866, §3	X	1922, §2–§3	1655, §2
1866, §4	1605	1923	X
1867	1606	1924	X
1868, §1	1607	1925, §1	1446; 1713
1868, §2	1617	1925, §2–§3	X
1869	1608	1926	1714
1870	X	1927	1715
1871	1609	1928	X
1872	1610, §1	1929	1713
1873, §1	1611	1930	1714; 1715
1873, §2	1610, §2	1931–1938	X
1874, §1–§2	1612, §1	1939, §1	1717, §1
1874, §3–§5	1612, §2–§4	1939, §2	X
1875	1613	1940	X
1876	1614	1941, §1	X
1877	1615	1941, §2–§3	1717, §3
1878, §1	1616, §1	1942	X
1878, §2–§3	1616, §2	1943	1717, §2
1879	1628	1944	1717, §3
1880, 1°–8°	1626, 1°–5°	1945	X
1881	1630, §1	1946, §1	X
1882	1630, §2	1946, §2	1718, §1
1883	1663	1946, §2, 1°	1719
1884, §1–§2	1634, §1–§2	1947	X
1885	X	1948–1953	X
1886	1635	1954	1721, §1
1887	1637	1955	X
1888	1637	1956	1722
1889, §1	X	1957	1722
1889, §2	1638	1958	1722
1890	1633	1959	1928, §1
1891	1639	1960	1671
1892, 1°–3°	1620, 1°–8°	1961	1672
1893	1621	1962	1698, §1
1894, 1°–4°	1622, 1°–6°	1963, §1	1699, §1
1895	1623–1625	1963, §2	1681
1896	1624	1964	1673, 1°–2°
1897	1626	1965	1676; 1695
1898–1901	X	1966	1700, §1
1902, 1°–3°	1641, 1°–4°	1967	1701, §1
1903	1643–1644	1968, 1°–2°	1678
1904	1642	1968, 3°	1432
1905, §1	1645, §1	1969, 1°–2°	1678
1905, §2, 1°–4°	1645, §2, 1°–5°	1969, 3°–4°	X
1906	1646	1970	X

1917	1983	1917	1983
1971, §1, 1°–2°	1674, 1°–2°	2161, §2	1746
1971, §2	X	2162	1748
1972	1675, §1	2163	X
1973	1697	2164	1749
1974	X	2165	1750
1975	X	2166	1750
1976	1680	2167	1751
1977–1981	X	2168–2194	X
1982	1680		
1983	X		*Book V*
1984	X		
1985	1703, §1; 1704, §1;	2195	1321, §1
	1705, §1	2196	X
1986	1682, §1–§2	2197	X
1987	1684, §1	2198	X
1988	1685	2199	1321, §1–§2
1989	X	2200, §1	1321, §2
1990	1686	2200, §2	1321, §2
1991	1687	2201, §1	1323, 6°
1992	1688	2201, §2	1322
1993, §1	1709, §1	2201, §3	1324, §1, 2°; 1325
1994, §1	1708	2201, §4	1324, §1, 1°
1994, §2	X	2202, §1	1323, 2°
1995	1710	2202, §2	1324, §1, 9°
1996	1711	2202, §3	1323, 2°
1997	1709, §2	2203, §1	1326, §1, 3°
1998, §1	1712	2203, §2	1323, 3°
1998, §2	X	2204	1323, 1°
1999–2145	X	2205, §1	1323, 3°
2146, §1–§2	X	2205, §2	1323, 4°
2146, §3	1747, §3; 1752	2205, §3	1323, 4°; 1324, §1, 5°
2147, §1	1740	2205, §4	1323, 5°; 1324, §1,
2147, §2	1741		6°–7°
2148	1742, §1	2206	1324, §1, 3°
2149, §1	1744, §2	2207	1326, §1, 2°
2149, §2	1744, §1	2208, §1	1326, §1, 1°
2150, §1–§2	X	2208, §2	X
2150, §3	1743	2209, §1–§7	1329, §1–§2
2151	X	2210	X
2152	X	2211	X
2153, §1	1745, 1°–2°	2212	1328
2153, §2	X	2213	1328
2153, §3	1745, 3°	2214, §1	1311
2154, §1	1746	2214, §2	X
2154, §2	X	2215	X
2155	X	2216, 1°	1312, §1, 1°
2156	1747, §1–§2; 1752	2216, 2°	1312, §1, 2°
2157, §1	1740	2216, 3°	1312, §3
2157, §2	1742, §2	2217, §1, 1°	1315
2158	1742, §1	2217, §1, 2°	1314
2159	1744; 1745, 1°–2°	2217, §2	1314
2160	X	2218	X
2161, §1	1745, 3°	2219	X

1917	1983	1917	1983
2220	X	2253	1355
2221	1315	2254, §1	1357, §1–§2
2222, §1	1399	2254, §2–§3	X
2222, §2	X	2255–2258	X
2223, §1	1349	2259–2267	1331; 1335
2223, §2	1343	2268–2274	X
2223, §3, 1°	1344, 1°	2275	1332
2223, §3, 2°	1344, 2°	2276–2277	X
2223, §3, 3°	1345; 1348	2278–2279	1333
2223, §4	X	2280	X
2224, §1	X	2281	X
2224, §2	1346	2282	1333, §3, 1°
2225	X	2283	X
2226, §1	X	2284	1335
2226, §2–§3	1313	2285	X
2226, §4	1351	2286	X
2227	X	2287	1353
2228	X	2288	1344, 3°
2229	X	2289	X
2230	1323, 1°	2290, §1	1352, §2
2231	X	2290, §2	X
2232, §1	1352, 2°	2291–2297	X
2232, §2	X	2298, 1°	1336, §1, 3°
2233, §1	X	2298, 2°	X
2233, §2	1347, 1°	2298, 3°	1336, §1, 4°
2234	X	2298, 4°	1336, §1, 2°
2235	1328	2298, 5°	X
2236, §1	1354, §1; 1355–1356	2298, 6°	1336, §1, 2°
2236, §2	1354, §1	2298, 7°	1336, §1, 1°
2236, §3	X	2298, 8°	1336, §1, 1°
2237	1355–1356	2298, 9°–11°	X
2238	1360	2298, 12°	1336, §1, 5°
2239	1361, §1–§2	2299, §1–§2	X
2240	1362	2299, §3	1350, §1
2241, §1	1358, §1	2300	X
2241, §2	1318	2301	1337, §2
2242, §1	X	2302	X
2242, §2	X	2303, §1	X
2242, §3	1347, §2; 1358	2303, §2	1350, §2
2243	1353	2304–2306	X
2244	X	2307	1339, §1
2245	X	2308	1339, §2
2246, §1	X	2309, 1°–4°	X
2246, §2	1354, §3	2309, 5°	1339, §3
2246, §3	X	2310–2311	X
2247	X	2312, §1	X
2248, §1	X	2312, §2	1340, §2
2248, §2	1358, §1–§2	2312, §3	X
2248, §3	X	2313, §1	X
2249, §1	X	2313, §2	1340, §3
2249, §2	1359	2314, §1, 1°–2°	1364
2250–2251	X	2314, §1, 3°	X
2252	1357, §3	2314, §2	X

1917	1983	1917	1983
2315	X	2353–2354	1397
2316	1365	2355	1390, §2–§3
2317	1371, 1°	2356–2358	X
2318	X	2359	1395
2319, §1, 1°–2°	X	2360–2362	1391
2319, §1, 3°–4°	1366	2363	1390, §1
2319, §2	X	2363–2365	X
2320	1367	2366	1378, §2, 2°
2321	X	2367, §1	1378, §1
2322, 1°	1378, §2–§3	2367, §2	X
2322, 2°	1379	2368, §1	1387
2323	1368; 1369	2368, §2	X
2324	1385	2369	1388
2325–2330	X	2370	1382
2331, §1	1371, 2°	2371	1380
2331, §2	1373	2372	X
2332	1372	2373, §1	1383
2333–2334	1375	2373, §2–§4	X
2335	1374	2374	1383
2336	X	2375–2379	X
2337	1375	2380	1392
2338–2342	X	2381	1396
2343, §1, 1°	1370, §1	2382–2387	X
2343, §1, 2°	X	2388	1394
2343, §1, 3°	1370, §1	2389	X
2343, §2	X	2390	1375
2343, §3	1370, §2	2391–2393	X
2343, §4	1370, §3	2394	1381, §1
2344	1369; 1373	2395–2400	X
2345	1375	2401	1381, §2
2346	1375–1376	2402–2403	X
2347	1377	2404	1389
2348–2349	X	2405	X
2350, §1	1398	2406	1391
2350, §2	X	2407	1386
2351–2352	X	2408–2414	X

PROFESSION OF FAITH ————————————————————

I, ———————————————————————————— , with firm faith, believe and profess all and everything that is contained in the Symbol of Faith that is:

We believe in one God,
  the Father, the Almighty,
  maker of heaven and earth,
  of all that is seen and unseen.
We believe in one Lord, Jesus Christ,
  the only Son of God,
  eternally begotten of the Father,
  God from God, Light from Light,
  true God from true God
  begotten, not made, one in Being with the Father.
  Through him all things were made.
For us men and for our salvation
    he came down from heaven:
  by the power of the Holy Spirit
    he was born of the Virgin Mary, and became man.
For our sake he was crucified under Pontius Pilate;
    he suffered, died, and was buried.
    On the third day he rose again
      in fulfillment of the Scriptures;
    he ascended into heaven
      and is seated at the right hand of the Father.
He will come again in glory to judge the living and the dead,
    and his kingdom will have no end.
We believe in the Holy Spirit, the Lord and Giver of Life,
  who proceeds from the Father and the Son.
  With the Father and the Son, he is worshipped and glorified.
  He has spoken through the Prophets.
  We believe in one, holy, catholic, and apostolic Church.
  We acknowledge one baptism for the forgiveness of sins.
  We look for the resurrection of the dead,
    and the life of the world to come. Amen.

I firmly embrace and accept
all and everything which has been either defined by the Church's solemn deliberations
or affirmed and declared by its ordinary magisterium concerning the doctrine of faith and morals,
according as they are proposed by it,
especially those things dealing with the mystery of the Holy Church of Christ,
its sacraments and the sacrifice of the Mass,
and the primacy of the Roman Pontiff.

JAMES A. CORIDEN is the Academic Dean at the Washington Theological Union. He earned an S.T.L. and a J.C.D. at the Gregorian and a J.D. at the Catholic University of America. After serving in the tribunal and chancery of the Diocese of Gary, he taught canon law for fifteen years and continues to do so. He has published many articles on canon law and ministry and has edited several studies sponsored by the Canon Law Society of America. He was born in Hammond, Indiana, in 1932.

THOMAS J. GREEN is Associate Professor of canon law at the Catholic University of America. He received an S.T.L. and a J.C.D. from the Gregorian. He has taught at various centers in the country, has lectured widely, and has published articles on canon law in various scholarly periodicals. He is a member of the Canon Law Society of America's editorial board for the commentary on the revised Code and serves as a consultant to the National Conference of Catholic Bishops' Committee on Canonical Affairs.

DONALD E. HEINTSCHEL is a priest of the Diocese of Toledo, Ohio, where he was born in 1924. He is presently the Associate General Secretary of the United States Catholic Conference-National Conference of Catholic Bishops. He holds a doctorate in canon law from the Catholic University of America and has served as Pastor, Tribunal Judge, Justice on the diocesan Court of Equity, and Vicar for Religious in Toledo. He served two terms as President of the Canon Law Society of America, is the founding President of the National Conference of Vicars for Religious, and served for six years as Executive Coordinator of the Canon Law Society of America. He has published articles in *The Jurist* and elsewhere, and served as Editor and Publisher for the Canon Law Society of America from 1975 to 1981.

JOHN A. ALESANDRO is Chancellor of the Diocese of Rockville Centre, New York. He earned an S.T.L. and a J.C.D. at the Gregorian and has served in parish, tribunal, and chancery positions. He is a past President of the Canon Law Society of America and served as *peritus* to the National Conference of Catholic Bishops' delegation to the 1981 meeting of the Commission for the revision of the Code of Canon Law. He has

published widely on canon law and related topics and has spoken frequently on the revised Code.

THOMAS P. DOYLE, O.P. has been Secretary at the Apostolic Delegation in Washington since September 1981. He completed his theological studies at Aquinas Institute in Dubuque, Iowa, has a master's in political science from the University of Wisconsin (Madison), and received a J.C.D. from the Catholic University of America. He has published in scholarly and pastoral journals on canonical and related questions and edits the series *Marriage Studies* for the Canon Law Society of America. He was born in Sheboygan, Wisconsin, in 1944.

EDWARD J. GILBERT, C.Ss.R. is President-Rector of Mount St. Alphonsus Seminary, Esopus, New York. He earned masters degrees at the seminary and a J.C.D. at the Catholic University of America. He chairs an international commission studying the Academia Alfonsiana in Rome, is a member of the provincial council of the Baltimore Province of Redemptorists, and has contributed articles to Redemptorist publications and to encyclopedias. He assists in the training of permanent deacons in the Archdiocese of New York and is an area representative for the metropolitan tribunal.

PAUL L. GOLDEN, C.M. is President of St. Thomas Seminary in Denver, Colorado, and Associate Professor of canon law there. He earned a J.C.D. at the University of St. Thomas in Rome. He has served as Secretary and member of the Board of Governors of the Canon Law Society of America and has taught in St. Louis as well as in Denver. He was born in San Francisco in 1939.

RICHARD A. HILL, S.J. is Associate Professor of canon law at the Jesuit School of Theology at Berkeley. He has served as President of the school for two different periods. He received an S.T.L. from Alma College in Los Gatos, California, and a J.C.D. from the Gregorian. He has served as President of the Canon Law Society of America and as a member of a number of its committees and boards. He has lectured widely on canon law and has written in various publications on the topic. He was born in Los Angeles in 1928.

JORDAN HITE, T.O.R. is Director of Personnel and Lecturer in religion and law at Saint Francis College, Loretto, Pennsylvania. He earned a J.D. at Georgetown University, an LL.M. at George Washington University, and a J.C.L. at Saint Paul University, Ottawa. He serves as chairperson for the Canon Law Society of America's Committee on Religious.

SHARON HOLLAND, I.H.M. is Canonical Consultant to the Delegate for Religious of the Archdiocese of Detroit. She is also an Auditor on the Archdiocesan Tribunal and an adjunct faculty member of St. John's Provincial Seminary. She earned an M.A. from the University of Detroit and a J.C.D. from the Gregorian. She has lectured widely and is a consultant to various religious communities.

JOHN M. HUELS, O.S.M. is Assistant Professor of canon law at the Catholic Theological Union in Chicago. He earned masters degrees at the Union and a J.C.D. at the Catholic University of America. He has written on various topics in liturgical law. He was born in St. Louis in 1950.

JOSEPH A. JANICKI is Vicar for Priest Personnel in the Archdiocese of Milwaukee. He earned a J.C.L. at the Catholic University of America. He has been involved in personnel work for the archdiocese and has made presentations at canon law meetings on the topic. He was born in Waukesha, Wisconsin, in 1938.

ELLSWORTH KNEAL is Directing Judge of the St. Paul Tribunal. He earned a J.C.D. at the Angelicum. He served as Professor of canon law at St. Paul Seminary for twenty-two years. He was born in St. Louis in 1917.

JOHN E. LYNCH, C.S.P. is Chairman of the Department of Canon Law at the Catholic University of America. He earned an M.S.L. at the Pontifical Institute of Mediaeval Studies and a Ph.D. at the University of Toronto. He is a full Professor of medieval history and the history of canon law at the Catholic University of America. He has authored several articles as well as a book dealing with history and canon law. He served as Vice-President of the Canon Law Society of America and as a member of the board and committees of the Society.

ROSE M. McDERMOTT, S.S.J. is Assistant to the Vicar for Religious in the Archdiocese of Philadelphia. She earned a master's degree from Providence College and a J.C.D. at the Catholic University of America. She has served on the board and committees of the Canon Law Society of America and is a consultant to several religious communities.

FREDERICK R. McMANUS is the Vice-President for Academic Affairs at the Catholic University of America and formerly served as the Vice-Provost and Dean of Graduate Studies at the University. He earned a J.C.D. at Catholic University and holds two honorary LL.D. degrees. After serving in pastoral, canonical, and educational positions in the Archdiocese of Boston, he became Professor of canon law at the Catholic University of America in 1958 and has served as Dean of the School of Canon Law, Editor of *The Jurist, peritus* during the Second Vatican Council, and in various ecumenical, liturgical, and canonical organizations. He has published and lectured widely, and he received the Canon Law Society of America's Role of Law Award in 1973.

JOHN J. MYERS is Vicar General and Chancellor of the Diocese of Peoria. He earned an S.T.L. at the Gregorian and a J.C.D. at the Catholic University of America. He has been active on several committees of the Canon Law Society of America and has lectured on the revised Code of Canon Law. He was born in Ottawa, Illinois, in 1941.

LADISLAS ORSY, S.J. is Professor of canon law at the Catholic University of America. He earned a J.C.D. at the Gregorian and is a graduate of the "Honors School of Law" at Oxford. He has taught at the Gregorian, Fordham University and Catholic University and has been Visiting Professor at Georgetown University and Fribourg, Switzerland. He has published and lectured widely. He was born in Hungary in 1921.

JAMES F. PARIZEK is Officialis and Vice-Chancellor of the Diocese of Davenport. He earned an S.T.B. and an M.A. at the Catholic University of Louvain and a J.C.L. at the Catholic University of America. He has held various pastoral and diocesan offices and has served as Secretary of the Canon Law Society of America. He was born in Iowa City, Iowa, in 1946.

JAMES H. PROVOST is Associate Professor of canon law at the Catholic University of America. He also serves as Executive Coordinator of the Canon Law Society of America. He earned an S.T.B. and an M.A. at the Catholic University of Louvain and a J.C.D. at the Lateran. He served as Chancellor and Officialis for twelve years in the Diocese of Helena, Montana. He is Managing

Editor of *The Jurist*, has written in various periodicals on canon law and ministry topics, and has lectured on the revised Code. He was born in Washington, D.C., in 1939.

THOMAS RICHSTATTER, O.F.M. is a member of the faculty of Washington Theological Union. He earned an M.A. at the University of Notre Dame and a D.Th.S. at the Institut Catholique in Paris. He has served as the Executive Secretary for the Federation of Diocesan Liturgical Commissions, conducts workshops around the country, and has produced several popular series of talks on cassette tapes for St. Anthony Messenger Press.

JAMES E. RISK, S.J. is a Synodal Judge for the Diocese of Bridgeport. He earned an S.T.L. at Weston College and a J.C.D. at the Gregorian. He has served as Professor of canon law at the Gregorian and in various capacities in the Tribunal of the Diocese of Bridgeport, including eight years as Officialis. He was born in Central Falls, Rhode Island, in 1903.

ROYCE R. THOMAS is Chancellor, Vice-Officialis, and Vicar for Clergy Personnel for the Diocese of Little Rock. He earned an S.T.L. at the Gregorian and a J.C.L. at the Catholic University of America. He is Rector of the Cathedral of St. Andrew the Apostle and a member of the Board of Governors of the Canon Law Society of America. He was born in Laredo, Texas, in 1944.

LAWRENCE G. WRENN is Officialis of the Archdiocese of Hartford. He earned a J.C.D. at the Lateran. He is author of several books on canon law, received the Role of Law Award from the Canon Law Society of America in 1976, and has published various articles on canonical issues. He was born in New Haven, Connecticut, in 1928.